HALSBURY'S
Laws of England

FOURTH EDITION
2007 REISSUE

LORD MACKAY OF CLASHFERN
Lord High Chancellor of Great Britain
1987–97

Volume 13

2007

LexisNexis®
Butterworths

Members of the LexisNexis Group worldwide

United Kingdom	LexisNexis Butterworths, a Division of Reed Elsevier (UK) Ltd, Halsbury House, 35 Chancery Lane, LONDON, WC2A 1EL, and London House, 20–22 East London Street, EDINBURGH, EH7 4BQ
Argentina	LexisNexis Argentina, Buenos Aires
Australia	LexisNexis Butterworths, Chatswood, New South Wales
Austria	LexisNexis Verlag ARD Orac GmbH & Co KG, Vienna
Benelux	LexisNexis Benelux, Amsterdam
Canada	LexisNexis Canada, Markham, Ontario
Chile	LexisNexis Chile Ltda, Santiago
China	LexisNexis China, Beijing and Shanghai
France	LexisNexis SA, Paris
Germany	LexisNexis Deutschland GmbH Munster
Hong Kong	LexisNexis Hong Kong, Hong Kong
India	LexisNexis India, New Delhi
Italy	Giuffrè Editore, Milan
Japan	LexisNexis Japan, Tokyo
Malaysia	Malayan Law Journal Sdn Bhd, Kuala Lumpur
Mexico	LexisNexis Mexico, Mexico
New Zealand	LexisNexis NZ ltd, Wellington
Poland	Wydawnictwo Prawnicze LexisNexis Sp, Warsaw
Singapore	LexisNexis Singapore, Singapore
South Africa	LexisNexis Butterworths, Durban
USA	LexisNexis, Dayton, Ohio

FIRST EDITION	*Published in 31 volumes between 1907 and 1917*
SECOND EDITION	*Published in 37 volumes between 1931 and 1942*
THIRD EDITION	*Published in 43 volumes between 1952 and 1964*
FOURTH EDITION	*Published in 56 volumes between 1973 and 1987, with reissues between 1988 and 2007*

A CIP Catalogue record for this book is available from the British Library.

ISBN 13 (complete set, standard binding): 9780406047762

ISBN 13: 9781405718462

ISBN 978-1-4057-1846-2

9 781405 718462

Typeset by Letterpart Ltd, Reigate, Surrey

Printed and bound in Great Britain by William Clowes Limited, Beccles, Suffolk

Visit LexisNexis Butterworths at www.lexisnexis.co.uk

HALSBURY'S
Laws of England

FOURTH EDITION
2007 REISSUE

Volume 13

The 2007 Reissue of Volume 13 contains the titles DEEDS AND OTHER INSTRUMENTS, DISCRIMINATION, and DISTRESS. This volume replaces the 4th Edn (Reissue) Volume 13, which may now be archived.

With the publication of Volume 13 (2007 Reissue) a complete set of Halsbury's Laws of England now contains the following volumes (bold figures represent reissue volumes):

1(1) (2001 Reissue), **1(2)**, **2(1)**, **2(2)**, **2(3)**, **3(1)** (2005 Reissue), **3(2)** (2002 Reissue), **4(1)** (2002 Reissue), **4(2)** (2002 Reissue), **4(3)**, **5(1)** (2004 Reissue), **5(2)** (2001 Reissue), **5(3)**, **6** (2003 Reissue), **7(1)** (2004 Reissue), **7(2)** (2004 Reissue), **7(3)** (2004 Reissue), **7(4)** (2004 Reissue), **8(1)** (2003 Reissue), **8(2)**, **8(3)**, **9(1)**, **9(2)** (2006 Reissue), **10**, **11(1)** (2006 Reissue), **11(2)** (2006 Reissue), **11(3)** (2006 Reissue), **11(4)** (2006 Reissue), **12(1)**, **12(2)** (2007 Reissue), **12(3)** (2007 Reissue), **13** (2007 Reissue), **14**, **15(1)** (2006 Reissue), **15(2)** (2006 Reissue), **15(3)** (2007 Reissue), **15(4)** (2007 Reissue), **16(1A)**, **16(1B)**, **16(2)**, **17(1)**, **17(2)**, **18**, **18(1)**, **18(2)**, **19(1)**, **19(2)**, **20(1)**, **20(2)**, **21** (2004 Reissue), **22** (2006 Reissue), **23(1)**, **23(2)**, **24**, **25** (2003 Reissue), **26** (2004 Reissue), **27(1)** (2006 Reissue), **27(2)** (2006 Reissue), **27(3)** (2006 Reissue), **28**, **29(1)**, **29(2)**, **29(3)**, **30(1)**, **30(2)**, **31** (2003 Reissue), **32** (2005 Reissue), **33**, **34**, **35**, **36(1)**, **36(2)**, **37**, **38** (2006 Reissue), **39(1)**, **39(2)**, **40(1)**, **40(2)**, **41** (2005 Reissue), **42**, **43(1)**, **43(2)**, **44(1)**, **44(2)**, **45(1)** (2005 Reissue), **45(2)**, **46(1)**, **46(2)**, **46(3)**, **47** (2001 Reissue), **48** (2000 Reissue), **49(1)** (2005 Reissue), **49(2)** (2004 Reissue), **49(3)** (2004 Reissue), **50** (2005 Reissue), **51**, **52**, **53(1)** (2007 Consolidated Table of Statutes), **53(2)** (2007 Consolidated Table of Statutory Instruments, etc), **54(1)** (2007 Consolidated Table of Cases A–L), **54(2)** (2007 Consolidated Table of Cases M–Z, ECJ Cases), **55** (2006 Consolidated Index A–E), **56** (2006 Consolidated Index F–O), **57** (2006 Consolidated Index P–Z).

May 2007

Editor in Chief

THE RIGHT HONOURABLE

LORD MACKAY OF CLASHFERN

LORD HIGH CHANCELLOR OF GREAT BRITAIN

1987–97

Editors of this Volume

HELEN HALVEY, LLB

RICHARD DEY, BA, LLB, LLM

Sub-editors

TOM MACDONALD, BA

KATE PAMPHILON, MA

Indexer

PAULA BOUWER, BA, LLB

Managing Editor

CLARE BLANCHARD, BA

Publisher

SIMON HETHERINGTON, LLB

DEEDS AND OTHER INSTRUMENTS

Consultant Editor

MARK P THOMPSON LLB, LLM

Professor of Law and Pro-Vice-Chancellor, University of Leicester

DISCRIMINATION

Consultant Editor

IAN SMITH LLB, MA

of Gray's Inn, Barrister;
Clifford Chance Professor of Employment Law, School of Law,
University of East Anglia;
member of the ACAS panel of Industrial Arbitrators

DISTRESS

Consultant Editor

JONATHAN KARAS MA

of Middle Temple;
one of Her Majesty's Counsel

The law stated in this volume is in general that in force on 31 March 2007, although
subsequent changes have been included wherever possible.

Any future updating material will be found in the Current Service and annual
Cumulative Supplement to Halsbury's Laws of England.

TABLE OF CONTENTS

DISTRESS

REFERENCES AND ABBREVIATIONS

ACT	Australian Capital Territory
A–G	Attorney General
Admin	Administrative Court
Admlty	Admiralty Court
Adv–Gen	Advocate General
affd	affirmed
affg	affirming
Alta	Alberta
App	Appendix
art	article
Aust	Australia
B	Baron
BC	British Columbia
C	Command Paper (of a series published before 1900)
c	chapter number of an Act
CA	Court of Appeal
CAC	Central Arbitration Committee
CA in Ch	Court of Appeal in Chancery
CB	Chief Baron
CCA	Court of Criminal Appeal
CCR	County Court Rules 1981 (SI 1981/1687) as subsequently amended
CCR	Court for Crown Cases Reserved
C–MAC	Courts-Martial Appeal Court
CO	Crown Office
COD	Crown Office Digest
CPR	Civil Procedure Rules 1998 (SI 1998/3132) as subsequently amended (see the Civil Court Practice)
Can	Canada
Cd	Command Paper (of the series published 1900–18)
Cf	compare
Ch	Chancery Division
ch	chapter
cl	clause
Cm	Command Paper (of the series published 1986 to date)
Cmd	Command Paper (of the series published 1919–56)

Cmnd..	Command Paper (of the series published 1956–86)
Comm	Commercial Court
Comr..	Commissioner
Court Forms (2nd Edn)	Atkin's Encyclopaedia of Court Forms in Civil Proceedings, 2nd Edn. See note 2 post.
Court Funds Rules 1987............	Court Funds Rules 1987 (SI 1987/821) as subsequently amended
DC..	Divisional Court
DPP..	Director of Public Prosecutions
EAT	Employment Appeal Tribunal
EC	European Community
ECJ..	Court of Justice of the European Community
EComHR..................................	European Commission of Human Rights
ECSC..	European Coal and Steel Community
ECtHR Rules of Court.............	Rules of Court of the European Court of Human Rights
EEC..	European Economic Community
EFTA..	European Free Trade Association
EWCA Civ.................................	Official neutral citation for judgments of the Court of Appeal (Civil Division)
EWCA Crim	Official neutral citation for judgments of the Court of Appeal (Criminal Division)
EWHC	Official neutral citation for judgments of the High Court
Edn	Edition
Euratom....................................	European Atomic Energy Community
Ex Ch.......................................	Court of Exchequer Chamber
ex p..	ex parte
Fam...	Family Division
Fed...	Federal
Forms & Precedents (5th Edn)...	Encyclopaedia of Forms and Precedents other than Court Forms, 5th Edn. See note 2 post.
GLC..	Greater London Council
HC	High Court
HC	House of Commons
HK..	Hong Kong
HL	House of Lords
IAT	Immigration Appeal Tribunal
ILM	International Legal Materials
INLR...	Immigration and Nationality Law Reports
IRC	Inland Revenue Commissioners
Ind	India
Int Rels....................................	International Relations
Ir..	Ireland
J..	Justice
JA...	Judge of Appeal
Kan	Kansas

LA..	Lord Advocate
LC	Lord Chancellor
LCC......................................	London County Council
LCJ	Lord Chief Justice
LJ	Lord Justice of Appeal
LoN	League of Nations
MR.......................................	Master of the Rolls
Man	Manitoba
n	note
NB..	New Brunswick
NI...	Northern Ireland
NS	Nova Scotia
NSW	New South Wales
NY	New York
NZ..	New Zealand
OJ..	The Official Journal of the European Community published by the Office for Official Publications of the European Community
Ont......................................	Ontario
P..	President
PC	Judicial Committee of the Privy Council
PEI.......................................	Prince Edward Island
Pat.......................................	Patents Court
q	question
QB..	Queen's Bench Division
QBD......................................	Queen's Bench Division of the High Court
Qld	Queensland
Que	Quebec
r	rule
RDC	Rural District Council
RPC	Restrictive Practices Court
RSC......................................	Rules of the Supreme Court 1965 (SI 1965/1776) as subsequently amended
reg.......................................	regulation
Res	Resolution
revsd....................................	reversed
Rly	Railway
s	section
SA..	South Africa
S Aust...................................	South Australia
SC..	Supreme Court
SI	Statutory Instruments published by authority
SR & O	Statutory Rules and Orders published by authority
SR & O Rev 1904	Revised Edition comprising all Public and General Statutory Rules and Orders in force on 31 December 1903
SR & O Rev 1948	Revised Edition comprising all Public and General

	Statutory Rules and Orders and Statutory Instruments in force on 31 December 1948
SRNI	Statutory Rules of Northern Ireland
STI	Simon's Tax Intelligence (1973–1995); Simon's Weekly Tax Intelligence (1996-current)
Sask	Saskatchewan
Sch	Schedule
Sess	Session
Sing	Singapore
TCC	Technology and Construction Court
TS	Treaty Series
Tanz	Tanzania
Tas	Tasmania
UDC	Urban District Council
UKHL	Official neutral citation for judgments of the House of Lords
UKPC	Official neutral citation for judgments of the Privy Council
UN	United Nations
V-C	Vice-Chancellor
Vict	Victoria
W Aust	Western Australia
Zimb	Zimbabwe

NOTE 1. A general list of the abbreviations of law reports and other sources used in this work can be found at the beginning of vol 54 (Reissue) Consolidated Table of Cases.

NOTE 2. Where references are made to other publications, the volume number precedes and the page number follows the name of the publication; eg the reference '12 Forms & Precedents (5th Edn) 44' refers to volume 12 of the Encyclopaedia of Forms and Precedents, page 44.

NOTE 3. An English statute is cited by short title or, where there is no short title, by regnal year and chapter number together with the name by which it is commonly known or a description of its subject matter and date. In the case of a foreign statute, the mode of citation generally follows the style of citation in use in the country concerned with the addition, where necessary, of the name of the country in parentheses.

NOTE 4. A statutory instrument is cited by short title, if any, followed by the year and number, or, if unnumbered, the date.

TABLE OF STATUTES

TABLE OF STATUTORY INSTRUMENTS

TABLE OF CIVIL PROCEDURE

Civil Procedure Rules 1998, SI 1998/3132 (CPR)

Practice Directions supplementing CPR

TABLE OF EUROPEAN
COMMUNITY LEGISLATION

TABLE OF CONVENTIONS

TABLE OF CASES

PARA

B

PARA

PARA

C

PARA

PARA

PARA

N

PARA

O

PARA

PARA

PARA

PARA

DEEDS AND OTHER INSTRUMENTS

For	agent.....................................*see*	AGENCY
	bills of sale.............................	BILLS OF SALE
	building agreements...................................	BUILDING CONTRACTS, ARCHITECTS, ENGINEERS, VALUERS AND SURVEYORS
	charitable trusts, construction......................	CHARITIES
	contracts..	CONTRACT
	contracts, law governing place of performance......................................	CONFLICT OF LAWS
	contracts, usages affecting..........................	CUSTOM AND USAGE
	covenants for title...................................	SALE OF LAND
	deeds of arrangement...............................	BANKRUPTCY AND INDIVIDUAL INSOLVENCY
	documentary evidence..............................	EVIDENCE
	electronic conveyancing.............................	LAND REGISTRATION
	execution of documents, proof.....................	EVIDENCE
	family arrangements.................................	SETTLEMENTS
	forgery...	CRIMINAL LAW, EVIDENCE AND PROCEDURE; BILLS OF EXCHANGE AND OTHER NEGOTIABLE INSTRUMENTS
	guarantee, interpretation of.........................	GUARANTEE AND INDEMNITY
	lost documents, evidence.............................	EVIDENCE
	mistake...	MISTAKE
	mortgages, receipt for purchase money............	MORTGAGE; BUILDING SOCIETIES
	negotiable instruments...............................	BILLS OF EXCHANGE AND OTHER NEGOTIABLE INSTRUMENTS
	powers of attorney...................................	AGENCY; EXECUTORS AND ADMINISTRATORS
	rectification...	MISTAKE
	registration of deeds.................................	COMPANIES; LAND CHARGES; LAND REGISTRATION
	rescission..	MISREPRESENTATION AND FRAUD
	restrictive covenants.................................	EQUITY; LANDLORD AND TENANT; REAL PROPERTY
	shipping documents..................................	SHIPPING AND NAVIGATION
	stamp duty..	STAMP DUTIES AND STAMP DUTY RESERVE TAX
	testamentary documents.............................	WILLS

1. DEEDS

(1) DEFINITION AND NATURE OF A DEED

(i) At Common Law

1. Common law definition of a deed. At common law, for an instrument to be a deed it must comply with the following requirements[1]. First, it must be written on parchment or paper[2]. Secondly, it must be executed in the manner specified below by some person or corporation named in the instrument. Thirdly, as to subject matter, it must express that the person or corporation so named makes, confirms, concurs in or consents to some assurance (otherwise than by way of testamentary disposition) of some interest in property or of some legal or equitable right, title, or claim, or undertakes or enters into some obligation, duty or agreement enforceable at law or in equity, or does or concurs in some other act affecting the legal relations or position of a party to the instrument or of some other person or corporation[3].

To be executed by a party as his deed, the instrument must be sealed with a seal which is, or can be regarded as, his seal[4], and must be delivered as his act and deed[5]. An individual, that is a party not a corporation, executing a deed after 1925 must also either sign or place his mark on it; sealing and delivery alone are insufficient execution by such a party[6]. Delivery by a party is constituted by any words or conduct expressly or impliedly acknowledging that he intends to be bound immediately and unconditionally by the provisions of the deed[7].

Several classes of instrument under seal do not comply with all these requirements and are not therefore deeds. These classes include testamentary instruments executed, unusually, under seal; instruments certifying or recording a pre-existing legal status, relationship or position but not confirming some specific assurance; and instruments which are binding and effective before sealing or before delivery so that delivery, in the technical sense defined above, is superfluous and cannot meaningfully be accomplished as a separate or distinct step (and sealing also may have been superfluous). Thus the following documents, although sealed, are not deeds: a will[8], an award[9], a certificate of admission to a learned society[10], a certificate of shares or stock or a share warrant to bearer[11], an agreement signed by directors and sealed with the company's seal[12], a licence to use a patented article[13], letters of ordination[14].

A power of attorney under seal is a deed[15], and so is a transfer of land to which title is registered[16].

Any document which does not comply with all the requirements for a deed may nevertheless, if it complies with the relevant requisites for an instrument under hand, be effective as such an instrument, even though it was intended to be a deed[17].

---

1   As to the modification of the common law rules by the Law of Property (Miscellaneous Provisions) Act 1989 see para 7 post. As to the statutory requirements for instruments executed as deeds after 31 July 1990 see para 8 post.

2   As from 31 July 1990, any rule of law which restricts the substances on which a deed may be written is abolished: see the Law of Property (Miscellaneous Provisions) Act 1989 s 1(1)(a); and paras 2, 7 post.

3   *Goddard's Case* (1584) 2 Co Rep 4b at 5a; Co Litt 35b, 171b; Spelman's Glossary sv Factum; Termes de la Ley sv Fait; Shep Touch 50–51; 2 Bl Com (14th Edn) 295–343; *R v Fauntleroy* (1824) 2 Bing 413 at 423–424, 428; *Hall v Bainbridge* (1848) 12 QB 699; *R v Morton* (1873) LR 2 CCR 22 at 27; *IRC v Angus* (1889) 23 QBD 579 at 582, CA.

4   As from 31 July 1990, any rule of law which requires a seal for the valid execution of an instrument as a deed by an individual is abolished: see the Law of Property (Miscellaneous Provisions) Act 1989 s 1(1)(b); and paras 7, 27, 32 post. As to the application of s 1(1)(b) see s 1(9); and para 7 text and note 4 post.

5   See para 31 post. As to delivery under the Law of Property (Miscellaneous Provisions) Act 1989 see para 34 post.

6　See para 30 post.

7　See para 31 post.

8　*R v Morton* (1873) LR 2 CCR 22 at 27. If an instrument under seal is so expressed as to take effect only in case of death it may be exclusively a testamentary instrument and thus not a deed: see eg *Hawksby v Kane* (1913) 47 ILT 96.

9　*Dod and Herbert* (1655) Sty 459; *Brown v Vawser* (1804) 4 East 584; *R v Morton* (1873) LR 2 CCR 22.

10　*R v Morton* (1873) LR 2 CCR 22.

11　*R v Morton* (1873) LR 2 CCR 22; *Hibblewhite v M'Morine* (1840) 6 M & W 200 at 214; *South London Greyhound Racecourses Ltd v Wake* [1931] 1 Ch 496 at 503.

12　*Solvency Mutual Guarantee Co v Froane* (1861) 7 H & N 5.

13　*Chanter v Johnson* (1845) 14 M & W 408.

14　*R v Morton* (1873) LR 2 CCR 22.

15　*R v Lyon* (1813) Russ & Ry 255; *R v Fauntleroy* (1824) 2 Bing 413; *R v Morton* (1873) LR 2 CCR 22; and see AGENCY vol 2(1) (Reissue) paras 30–31.

16　*Chelsea and Walham Green Building Society v Armstrong* [1951] Ch 853 at 857, [1951] 2 All ER 250 at 252 per Vaisey J.

17　See *Windsor Refrigerator Co Ltd v Branch Nominees Ltd* [1961] Ch 375, [1961] 1 All ER 277, CA; *Byblos Bank SAL v Al Khudhairy* [1987] 1 FTLR 35, [1987] BCLC 232, CA.

2.　Material, language and writing. At common law, a deed is required to be written on paper or on parchment or vellum, and not on any other substance[1]. A sealed writing inscribed on any other substance, as on wood, stone, slate, linen, cloth, leather, or steel, cannot take effect as a deed[2]. A deed may be written in a book[3]. It may be written in any language and in any character[4]; and it is not necessary that the writing be done with pen and ink; it may be executed in pencil or with paint, in print, by engraving, lithography or photography, or in any other mode of representing or reproducing visible words[5].

1　*Goddard's Case* (1584) 2 Co Rep 4b at 5a; Co Litt 35b, 229a; 2 Co Inst 672; Shep Touch 50, 52, 54; 2 Bl Com (14th Edn) 297. As from 31 July 1990, any rule of law which restricts the substances on which a deed may be written is abolished: see the Law of Property (Miscellaneous Provisions) Act 1989 s 1(1)(a); and para 7 post.

2　YB 25 Edw 4, 83, pl 9; YB 44 Edw 3, 21, pl 23; YB 12 Hen 4, 23, pl 3; YB 27 Hen 6, 9, pl 1; Fitzherbert's Grand Abridgement, Fines, 116; Fitz Nat Brev 122, I; Co Litt 35b, 229a.

3　*Fox v Wright* (1598) Cro Eliz 613.

4　Shep Touch 54–55; 2 Bl Com (14th Edn) 297.

5　See *Geary v Physic* (1826) 5 B & C 234 at 237; and cf the meaning of 'writing' in the Interpretation Act 1978 s 5, Sch 1 (see SALE OF LAND vol 42 (Reissue) para 39). For the authorities as to mode of signature see SALE OF LAND vol 42 (Reissue) para 40.

3.　Kinds of deed. Deeds are either deeds poll or indentures[1]. A deed poll is a deed made by and expressing the active intention of one party only, or made by two or more persons joining together in expressing a common active intention of them all. A deed poll is so called because the parchment required for such deeds has usually been shaved even or polled at the top. An indenture is a deed to which two or more persons are parties, and which evidences some act or agreement between them other than the mere consent to join in expressing the same active intention on the part of all. An indenture derives its name from the fact that the parchment on which such a deed was written was indented or cut with a waving or indented line at the top[2].

A deed executed after 1 October 1845, and purporting to be an indenture, has the effect of an indenture, though not actually indented or expressed to be an indenture[3]. A deed, whether or not it is an indenture, may now be described (at its commencement or otherwise) as a deed simply or by a name, such as conveyance, settlement, or mortgage, indicating the nature of the transaction intended to be effected[4]. Hence the terms 'indenture' and, except in certain instances, 'deed poll' have passed out of use[5].

Deeds are also divided into two classes by the distinction, drawn for instance for purposes of enforcement[6], between a deed inter partes and a deed not inter partes. A deed inter partes is a deed which expressly states that it is made between two or more named persons. All deeds inter partes now have the effect of indentures, whether or not indented or expressed to be indentures[7].

1   Littleton's Tenures ss 218, 370–377; Co Litt 35b; Shep Touch 50.
2   Co Litt 229a and n (1); Shep Touch 50; 2 Bl Com (14th Edn) 295–296. The practice of indenting originated in early times, when deeds were short and two or more copies were written on one piece of parchment with some words in between, and each part was cut off in a waving or uneven line, which might afterwards show that it tallied with the other part or parts.
3   Law of Property Act 1925 s 56(2) (replacing the Real Property Act 1845 s 5 (repealed)).
4   Law of Property Act 1925 s 57.
5   It is the same with 'these presents', which was formerly used in any reference to the deed in the body of the deed itself, but the expression is now in practice replaced by 'this deed'.
6   See paras 61, 66 post.
7   Law of Property Act 1925 ss 56(2), 57.

4.   Execution in duplicate.   Where a deed inter partes is executed in duplicate, or in more parts than one, so that each party entitled under it may possess an example of the deed, all the parts are regarded as one deed in law and each part is as efficacious as the other or others[1]. Where one part is executed by the grantor, or assuror, or person undertaking some obligation under the deed, and the other by the grantee, alienee, or person taking the benefit of that obligation, the former part is called the principal deed and the other the counterpart, and in case of inconsistency the counterpart must in general give way[2]; but where all parties execute each part, each part is equally the principal deed[3].

1   YB 38 Hen 6, 25, pl 1; Littleton's Tenures s 370; Co Litt 229a; Shep Touch 52–53; *Pearse v Morrice* (1832) 3 B & Ad 396; *Burchell v Clark* (1876) 2 CPD 88 at 96, CA; and see para 3 note 2 ante.
2   Shep Touch 53; *Burchell v Clark* (1876) 2 CPD 88 at 93–94, 97, CA; *Matthews v Smallwood* [1910] 1 Ch 777 at 784; and see *Trusthouse Forte Albany Hotels Ltd v Daejan Investments Ltd (No 2)* [1989] 2 EGLR 113, [1989] 30 EG 87, CA. Where, however, there is a patent ambiguity in the principal instrument, eg a lease, it may be explained by reference to the counterpart: *Burchell v Clark* supra; *Matthews v Smallwood* supra at 785. Each part is primary evidence of the contents of the deed against the party executing it and his privies; it is secondary evidence only against the non-executing party and his privies (except where used only to prove an ancient act of possession): *Barber v Rowe* [1948] 2 All ER 1050, CA; and see EVIDENCE. As to leases and counterparts of leases see LANDLORD AND TENANT vol 27(1) (2006 Reissue) para 111 et seq.
3   2 Bl Com (14th Edn) 296.

5.   Formal parts of a deed.   In modern conveyancing practice the chief formal parts of a deed are: the words describing the instrument (whether conveyance, settlement, mortgage, or otherwise); the date; the parties' names; the recitals stating the facts on which the act to be evidenced by the deed is grounded; the testatum or witnessing part containing the operative words which express the parties' intention; and the testimonium stating that the parties have sealed the deed in witness of what is written therein.

Further, in assurances of property, the testatum usually contains the following subsidiary formal parts: the parcels or description of the property to be conveyed; the habendum defining the estate or interest to be taken by the alienee; the trusts, if any, imposed on the person taking the legal estate under the deed; and the covenants, if any, entered into by the alienor or alienee. In an assurance of land all that part which precedes the habendum, including the parties' names, the recitals, if any, and the operative words, is called the premises[1]. There are also several formal clauses appropriate to deeds of particular kinds. Thus mortgage deeds contain a proviso for cesser of the mortgage term or for redemption[2], leases at a rent contain a reddendum specifying the rent reserved, and a proviso or condition or re-entry, and settlements contain a variety of trusts and powers always expressed in well-drawn deeds in formal language. In a settlement of land under the Settled Land Act 1925 two deeds were required, the vesting deed and the trust instrument, and the vesting deed had to conform to certain statutory requirements[3]. As from 1 January 1997[4] it is no longer possible to create a new settlement under the Settled Land Act 1925[5].

1　Co Litt 6a, 229b; Shep Touch 75; 2 Bl Com (14th Edn) 298.
2　A legal mortgage can now be created only by demise (in a leasehold mortgage by sub-demise) subject to a proviso for cesser of the mortgage term, or by a charge by deed expressed to be by way of legal mortgage: see the Law of Property Act 1925 ss 85–87 (as amended); and MORTGAGE vol 32 (2005 Reissue) paras 387–388, 390–391.
3　See the Settled Land Act 1925 ss 4(1), 5(1); and SETTLEMENTS vol 42 (Reissue) paras 688–690.
4　Ie the date on which the Trusts of Land and Appointment of Trustees Act 1996 came into force: see s 27(2).
5　See ibid s 2; and SETTLEMENTS vol 42 (Reissue) para 676. As to the limited exceptions see s 2(2), (3); and SETTLEMENTS vol 42 (Reissue) para 676.

6. Method of framing deeds. Conveyancers adhere by common consent to the traditional method of framing deeds, construct them with the usual formal parts and use the established common forms. Provided, however, that the language used in the deed expresses the parties' intention with reasonable certainty[1], the deed will take effect at law, notwithstanding that it is not drawn with the usual formal parts or in accordance with the established conveyancing practice[2]. On the other hand, where any rule of law requires the use of any particular or technical words to carry out the parties' intention, as in the case of the limitation of an estate of inheritance in fee tail in any lands or hereditaments[3], the necessary words must of course be employed[4]. Deeds, whether deeds poll or indentures, may be expressed either in the first or in the third person[5].

All instruments delivered as deeds after 31 July 1990 must comply with the provisions of the Law of Property (Miscellaneous Provisions) Act 1989 in order to be valid deeds[6].

1　*Re Arden, Short v Camm* [1935] Ch 326 at 333 per Clauson J; and see para 172 note 3 post.
2　Co Litt 7a; 2 Bl Com (14th Edn) 297–298; *R v Wooldale Inhabitants* (1844) 6 QB 549.
3　Littleton's Tenures s 1; and see the Law of Property Act 1925 s 130 (amended by the Trusts of Land and Appointment of Trustees Act 1996 s 25(2), Sch 4); REAL PROPERTY vol 39(2) (Reissue) paras 118–119. The amendments and repeals made by the Trusts of Land and Appointment of Trustees Act 1996 do not affect any entailed interest created before 1 January 1997 (ie the date on which the Trusts of Land and Appointment of Trustees Act 1996 came into force: see s 27(2)): s 25(4). As from 1 January 1997 it is no longer possible to grant an entailed interest see s 2, Sch 1 para 5; and SETTLEMENTS vol 42 (Reissue) para 677. An estate in tail is an equitable interest only: see the Law of Property Act 1925 s 1(1), (3). Words of limitation of an estate in fee simple were formerly required, but are not now necessary: see s 60 (as amended); and REAL PROPERTY vol 39(2) (Reissue) para 93.
4　*Re Whiston's Settlement, Lovatt v Williamson* [1894] 1 Ch 661; *Re Ethel and Mitchells and Butlers' Contract* [1901] 1 Ch 945; *Re Irwin, Irwin v Parkes* [1904] 2 Ch 752; *Re Bostock's Settlement, Norrish v Bostock* [1921] 2 Ch 469, CA. Words of limitation were held not to be essential in an appointment of real and personal estate in *Re Nutt's Settlement, McLaughlin v McLaughlin* [1915] 2 Ch 431.
5　Littleton's Tenures ss 371–373; Shep Touch 50–51. As to deeds poll and indentures see para 3 ante.
6　See the Law of Property (Miscellaneous Provisions) Act 1989 s 1(2) (as amended); and para 7 post. As to the application of s 1(2) (as amended) see s 1(9); and para 7 text and note 4 post.

(ii) The Law of Property (Miscellaneous Provisions) Act 1989

7. Deeds and their execution. The common law rules relating to deeds[1] have been considerably modified by the Law of Property (Miscellaneous Provisions) Act 1989[2]. However, nothing in this provision relating to deeds and their execution[3] applies in relation to instruments delivered as deeds before 31 July 1990[4]. The Act abolishes any rule of law which: (1) restricts the substances on which a deed may be written[5]; or (2) requires a seal for the valid execution of an instrument as a deed by an individual[6]; or (3) requires authority by one person to another to deliver an instrument as a deed on his behalf to be given by deed[7].

1 See para 1 et seq ante.
2 See the Law of Property (Miscellaneous Provisions) Act 1989 s 1 (as amended); the text and notes 3–7 infra; and para 8 post.
3 Ie ibid s 1 (as amended): see s 1(11).
4 Ibid s 1(11). This is the date on which s 1 (as originally enacted) came into force: Law of Property (Miscellaneous Provisions) Act 1989 (Commencement) Order 1990, SI 1990/1175. Nothing in the Law of Property (Miscellaneous Provisions) Act 1989 s 1(1)(b), (2), (3), (7) or (8) (s 1(2), (3) as amended) applies in relation to deeds required or authorised to be made under: (1) the seal of the county palatine of Lancaster; (2) the seal of the Duchy of Lancaster; or (3) the seal of the Duchy of Cornwall: s 1(9). The references in s 1 (as amended) to the execution of a deed by an individual do not include execution by a corporation sole: see s 1(10); and para 32 text to note 3 post. As to corporations sole see CORPORATIONS.
5 Ibid s 1(1)(a). The common law rule was that a deed must be written on paper, parchment or vellum and not on any other substance: see para 2 ante.
6 Ibid s 1(1)(b). See paras 27, 32 post.
7 Ibid s 1(1)(c). See para 34 post.

8.   Statutory definition of a deed.   From 31 July 1990[1] an instrument may not be a deed unless: (1) it makes it clear on its face that it is intended to be a deed by the person making it or, as the case may be, by the parties to it (whether by describing itself as a deed or expressing itself to be executed or signed[2] as a deed or otherwise)[3]; and (2) it is validly executed as a deed by that person or a person authorised to execute it in the name or on behalf of that person, or by one or more of those parties or a person authorised to execute it in the name or on behalf of one or more of those parties[4].

1 Ie the date on which the Law of Property (Miscellaneous Provisions) Act 1989 s 1 (as originally enacted) came into force: see s 1(11); and para 7 text and note 4 ante.
2 'Sign' in relation to an instrument includes an individual signing the name of the person or party on whose behalf he executes the instrument, and making one's mark on the instrument; and 'signature' is to be construed accordingly: ibid s 1(4) (amended by the Regulatory Reform (Execution of Deeds and Documents) Order 2005, SI 2005/1906, s 10(1), Sch 1 paras 13, 14).
3 Law of Property (Miscellaneous Provisions) Act 1989 s 1(2)(a). For the purposes of s 1(2)(a), an instrument is not to be taken to make it clear on its face that it is intended to be a deed merely because it is executed under seal: s 1(2A) (added by the Regulatory Reform (Execution of Deeds and Documents) Order 2005, SI 2005/1906, art 8). As to the application of the Law of Property (Miscellaneous Provisions) Act 1989 s 1(2) (as amended) see s 1(9); and para 7 text and note 4 ante.
4 Ibid s 1(2)(b) (substituted by the Regulatory Reform (Execution of Deeds and Documents) Order 2005, SI 2005/1906, art 7(3)). See note 3 supra.

(iii)   Electronic Conveyancing

9.   Electronic dispositions.   The Land Registration Act 2002 contains provisions enabling electronic conveyancing, and when all the necessary implementing subordinate legislation has been made it will be compulsory for registered land conveyancing (including all land contracts and transfers) to be conducted electronically[1]. In the context of dispositions required by the Act to be conducted electronically[2], there are a number of conditions, requirements and other formalities, which apply equally to deeds under seal and to agreements made under hand[3].

A document to which the relevant provisions apply[4] will be regarded as in writing and signed by each individual and sealed by each corporation whose electronic signature it has[5]. Such a document is to be regarded for the purposes of any enactment as a deed[6].

1 See the Land Registration Act 2002 Pt 8 (ss 91–95) (as amended); and LAND REGISTRATION vol 26 (2004 Reissue) para 1049 et seq.
2 See ibid s 91 (as amended); and LAND REGISTRATION vol 26 (2004 Reissue) para 1051.
3 See LAND REGISTRATION vol 26 (2004 Reissue) para 1051.

4   Ie ibid s 91 (as amended): see LAND REGISTRATION vol 26 (2004 Reissue) para 1051.
5   See ibid s 91(4); and LAND REGISTRATION vol 26 (2004 Reissue) para 1051.
6   See ibid s 91(5); and LAND REGISTRATION vol 26 (2004 Reissue) para 1051.

(2) WHEN A DEED IS NECESSARY

(i) At Common Law

10.   Conveyance of incorporeal hereditaments.   A deed is necessary for every transaction which the common law requires to be evidenced by writing[1].

Hence at common law a deed is necessary to make a grant or any other conveyance taking effect between living persons of any incorporeal hereditament[2], or any estate or interest therein, including a chattel interest such as a lease for years of an incorporeal hereditament[3]. This is equally the case whether the grant enures by way of the original creation of some incorporeal hereditament which did not exist before, as in the case of the grant de novo of an easement[4], a profit à prendre (such as the right of killing and taking away game or fish[5]) or a rent[6], or whether the grant takes effect as a transfer of some existing incorporeal hereditament or any estate or interest therein, as where an assignment is made of a rentcharge in fee previously created[7] or where a lease for years of some incorporeal hereditament already existing is made, assigned, or surrendered[8].

1   Littleton's Tenures ss 183, 217, 250, 252, 358–367, 541–542, 551, 618, 628; Co Litt 9b, 49a, 85a, 121b, 143a, 169a, 172a, 307a, 338a. The reason for this is that by the common law a man's writing was required to be authenticated by his seal: see para 59 note 1 post.
2   See e g *Bryan v Whistler* (1828) 8 B & C 288, where it was considered that an exclusive right of burial was a grant of an incorporeal hereditament which to be effectual would need to be granted by deed.
3   Littleton's Tenures ss 183, 551–569, 618, 627–628; Co Litt 9a, b, 42a, 85a, 121a, b, 172a, 307a, 332a, 335b; Shep Touch 227–230; 2 Bl Com (14th Edn) 317. As to the purposes for which a deed is required by statute see para 14 post. As to the effect of an agreement specifically enforceable to grant some incorporeal hereditament see para 26 post. See further LANDLORD AND TENANT vol 27(1) (2006 Reissue) para 73 et seq; REAL PROPERTY vol 39(2) (Reissue) para 232 et seq.
4   *Hewlins v Shippam* (1826) 5 B & C 221; *Bryan v Whistler* (1828) 8 B & C 288; *Cocker v Cowper* (1834) 1 Cr M & R 418; *Durham and Sunderland Rly Co v Walker* (1842) 2 QB 940 at 967, Ex Ch; *Proud v Bates* (1865) 34 LJ Ch 406 at 411; *Armstrong v Sheppard and Short Ltd* [1959] 2 QB 384, [1959] 2 All ER 651, CA; and see *May v Belleville* [1905] 2 Ch 605 at 612. As to easements see EASEMENTS AND PROFITS À PRENDRE.
5   *Wickham v Hawker* (1840) 7 M & W 63 at 76–79; *Ewart v Graham* (1859) 7 HL Cas 331 at 334–335; *Hooper v Clark* (1867) LR 2 QB 200; *Adams v Clutterbuck* (1883) 10 QBD 403 at 405. See also *Lowe v Adams* [1901] 2 Ch 598. As to profits à prendre see EASEMENTS AND PROFITS À PRENDRE.
6   Littleton's Tenures s 218; Co Litt 144a, 160a. See RENTCHARGES AND ANNUITIES vol 39(2) (Reissue) para 777 et seq.
7   Littleton's Tenures ss 556, 616, 618, 627; Co Litt 9a, b, 172a. At common law an existing rentcharge could not be granted over without the attornment of the terre tenant (Littleton's Tenures s 556), but by the Administration of Justice Act 1705 s 9 (now replaced by the Law of Property Act 1925 s 151(1)), the necessity of attornment was abolished.
8   *Lincoln College Case* (1595) 3 Co Rep 53a at 58b, 62b, 63a; Co Litt 85a, n (2), 338a; *Hewlins v Shippam* (1826) 5 B & C 221 at 228–233; *Duke of Somerset v Fogwell* (1826) 5 B & C 875 at 886; *Bird v Higginson* (1835) 2 Ad & El 696 at 704 (affd (1837) 6 Ad & El 824, Ex Ch); *Wood v Leadbitter* (1845) 13 M & W 838 at 842–843; *Thomas v Fredricks* (1847) 10 QB 775 at 783.
      A deed was equally necessary for the conveyance of such incorporeal hereditaments as a reversion or remainder expectant on an estate tail, for life or for years, in land as for the assurance of purely incorporeal hereditaments (Littleton's Tenures ss 515 et seq, 553, 567–573, 578, 618, 627; Co Litt 49a, 172a, 315b, 332a; Shep Touch 230; 2 Bl Com (14th Edn) 310; *Doe d Were v Cole* (1827) 7 B & C 243 at 248; and see *Haggerston v Hanbury* (1826) 5 B & C 101; and the Real Property Act 1845 s 6 (repealed)); but now a reversion or remainder expectant on an estate tail or for life is an equitable interest only, though there can still be a legal reversion on a term of years (see the Law of Property Act 1925 s 1(1), (3)). As to conveyances of legal estates see paras 14–15 post; and as to dispositions of equitable interests see paras 24–25 post.

A deed was also in general necessary at common law to attach to an inter vivos assurance of a freehold estate any condition operating in defeasance of the estate: see Littleton's Tenures ss 365–369; Co Litt 225a, b, 226b, 228a, b; Shep Touch 119–120. Except as provided by the Law of Property Act 1925 s 7(1), (2) (s 7(1) as amended), defeasible freehold estates can no longer exist as legal estates, and any such condition will create equitable interests and may be imposed by any means by which an equitable interest in land may be created: see s 1(1), (3); and para 24 post.

11.   Right to enter on land.   At common law the right to enter upon land and to remain there for a certain time can only be effectually given by deed, unless the grant of that right is coupled with a grant, which is valid without deed, of something on the land[1]. Thus a grant made without deed, although for valuable consideration, of the right to enter upon certain land belonging to the grantor on specified days and to remain there during certain hours of each day (during which races are to be held), since it purports to exceed the privilege given by a mere licence and to confer an interest in the land, is ineffective to do so at common law[2]. If, however, a man has a flock of sheep in his field, and without deed sells to another all the wool on the sheep, together with the right to go into the field and to shear the sheep there, the buyer would have a valid legal right to enter upon the field and to stay there until he had finished the shearing[3].

In equity, and consequently now in any court having jurisdiction to grant equitable remedies, a licence to go upon land granted by contract for valuable consideration may, as a matter of construction of the contract, be irrevocable, and in such a case the licensor (even if the contract was not under seal) will be restrained by injunction from revoking the licence in breach of contract or from acting on such a revocation if made[4]. Moreover, if the licensor revokes the licence, he nevertheless cannot obtain equitable assistance to evict the licensee in aid of his breach of contract[5]. Further, under the doctrine of proprietary estoppel[6], if an equity is made out in appropriate cases it may be satisfied by conferring a licence to enter land. The terms of the licence will vary according to the circumstances[7].

1   *Wood v Leadbitter* (1845) 13 M & W 838 at 845, 853. See also *Armstrong v Sheppard and Short Ltd* [1959] 2 QB 384 at 402, [1959] 2 All ER 651 at 659, CA, per Lord Evershed MR (a right to pass effluent through another's land is a proprietary right which is not capable of grant other than by deed).
2   *Wood v Leadbitter* (1845) 13 M & W 838. At law such a grant amounts to a mere licence to go on the land, and is revocable accordingly. A contract for the sale or other disposition of an interest in land is to be made in writing: see the Law of Property (Miscellaneous Provisions) Act 1989 s 2 (as amended); para 145 post; and SALE OF LAND vol 42 (Reissue) paras 29–40. As regards licences, whether coupled with an interest or not, and the distinction between a licence and a leasehold interest see LANDLORD AND TENANT.
3   *Wood v Manley* (1839) 11 Ad & El 34; *Wood v Leadbitter* (1845) 13 M & W 838. It appears that if there were a mere gift of the wool, coupled with such right of entry as mentioned in the text, no valid legal right of entry and remaining on the land would be conferred, but only a revocable licence, since gifts of chattels cannot be well made, where there is no delivery of possession, without deed: see para 13 post.
4   *Millennium Productions Ltd v Winter Garden Theatre (London) Ltd* [1946] 1 All ER 678, CA; revsd on other grounds sub nom *Winter Garden Theatre (London) Ltd v Millennium Productions Ltd* [1948] AC 173, [1947] 2 All ER 331, HL. In appropriate cases, the licensee may obtain specific performance of a contractual licence: *Verrall v Great Yarmouth Borough Council* [1981] QB 202, [1980] 1 All ER 839, CA. See further CONTRACT vol 9(1) (Reissue) para 981.
5   *Hounslow London Borough Council v Twickenham Garden Developments Ltd* [1971] Ch 233, [1970] 3 All ER 326.
6   See ESTOPPEL vol 16(2) (Reissue) paras 1089–1094.
7   See *Inwards v Baker* [1965] 2 QB 29, [1965] 1 All ER 446, CA (licence for as long as the plaintiff desires); *Greasley v Cooke* [1980] 3 All ER 710, [1980] 1 WLR 1306, CA (licence for as long as the defendant wished); *Re Sharpe (a bankrupt), ex p the trustee of the bankrupt v Sharpe* [1980] 1 All ER 198, [1980] 1 WLR 219 (licence until the loan was repaid).

12.   Release.   An express release, whether of a right in any lands, tenements or hereditaments, goods or chattels[1], or of any real or personal action, claim or demand, can only be made at common law by deed[2]. Thus an express discharge given without valuable consideration of any obligation arising from a breach of contract (such as a debt[3]), or from a wrong[4], must always be made by deed[5]. As a rule an obligation arising (before breach) under a contract executed by the other party to the contract, such as a promise to pay on a future day for goods delivered or money lent in consideration of that promise, can only be discharged, without valuable consideration, by deed[6].

1   It appears that normally an express release of right in goods or chattels must be made by deed: *Jennor and Hardie's Case* (1587) 1 Leon 283 per Anderson CJ; 3 Preston's Abstracts of Title (2nd Edn) 118; and see note 2 infra. In modern law, however, where goods are in the possession of a bailee, the owner may well make a gift of them to the bailee by word of mouth only even though such a gift may appear to be in the nature of a release of right. This is because the change, which takes place in the bailee's possession when he ceases to hold the goods as bailee and begins to keep them as owner, is equivalent to actual delivery of the possession of the goods at the time of the gift: see *Winter v Winter* (1861) 9 WR 747; *Kilpin v Ratley* [1892] 1 QB 582; *Cain v Moon* [1896] 2 QB 283. On this ground it appears that a similar gift may be made to a finder or taker of goods who is in possession of them: Shep Touch 240–241.

2   Littleton's Tenures ss 444 et seq; Co Litt 264b; Shep Touch 320–321, 323; and see *Lampet's Case* (1612) 10 Co Rep 46b at 48a, b; *Jennor and Hardie's Case* (1587) 1 Leon 283; 3 Chitty on Pleading (7th Edn) 112–113, 313. See also *Bank of Credit and Commerce International SA (in liquidation) v Ali* [1999] 2 All ER 1005.

3   *Pinnel's Case* (1602) 5 Co Rep 117a, b; *Edwards v Weeks* (1677) 2 Mod Rep 259; *May v King* (1701) 12 Mod Rep 537; *Reeves v Brymer* (1801) 6 Ves 516; *Cross v Sprigg* (1849) 6 Hare 552; *Edwards v Walters* [1896] 2 Ch 157 at 168, CA.

4   See note 3 supra.

5   An express release of a debt or of the liability to pay damages is of no effect in equity, if not made by deed, unless it is given for valuable consideration (*Edwards v Walters* [1896] 2 Ch 157, CA) or can take effect under the doctrine of promissory estoppel (*Central London Property Trust Ltd v High Trees House Ltd* [1947] KB 130, [1956] 1 All ER 256n; *Tool Metal Manufacturing Co Ltd v Tungsten Electric Co Ltd* [1955] 2 All ER 657, [1955] 1 WLR 761, HL). See further CONTRACT vol 9(1) (Reissue) paras 1030–1035, 1052.

6   *Blackhead v Cock* (1614) 1 Roll Rep 43 at 44; *Foster v Dawber* (1851) 6 Exch 839 at 851; *Edwards v Walters* [1896] 2 Ch 157, CA. The only exception is that a bill of exchange or promissory note is discharged if the holder, at or after the maturity, absolutely and unconditionally renounces his rights against the acceptor or maker, provided that the renunciation is in writing, or the bill or note is delivered up to the acceptor or maker: see BILLS OF EXCHANGE AND OTHER NEGOTIABLE INSTRUMENTS vol 4(1) (2002 Reissue) para 456.

13.   Further instances in which a deed is required. At common law, a deed was required for any power of attorney authorising the attorney to execute a deed or to deliver seisin on the principal's behalf[1]. There are now statutory provisions in relation to the execution of powers of attorney[2], and any rule of law which requires authority by one person to another to deliver an instrument as a deed on his behalf to be given by deed has been abolished[3].

Formerly a corporation aggregate could, as a general rule, only bind itself by deed, which would have been executed under its corporate seal[4]. But, in consequence of the Corporate Bodies' Contracts Act 1960, a deed is no longer required for the making, variation or discharge on or after the 29 July 1960 of a contract by a body corporate, other than a company within the Companies Act 1985[5], whether the body corporate gave its authority before or after that date[6].

Gifts or gratuitous assignments of choses or things in possession (that is, of tangible goods) must, if not accompanied by delivery of possession, be made by deed[7].

It appears that by the common law a deed is required for the assignment of the benefit of letters patent conferring the privilege of the exclusive use of an invention[8].

1   Co Litt 52a; Shep Touch 217; 1 Preston's Abstracts of Title (2nd Edn) 293; *Steiglitz v Egginton* (1815) Holt NP 141; *Berkeley v Hardy* (1826) 5 B & C 355. The rule is also recognised in equity: see *Powell v London and Provincial Bank* [1893] 2 Ch 555 at 563, 566, CA; *Re Seymour, Fielding v Seymour* [1913] 1 Ch 475 at 481, CA, per Joyce J. Where an intended deed has already been signed and sealed, an authority to deliver it and so complete its execution needs a deed: *Windsor Refrigerator Co Ltd v Branch Nominees Ltd* [1961] Ch 88, [1960] 2 All ER 568; revsd on another point [1961] Ch 375, [1961] 1 All ER 277, CA. See

further para 27 note 11 post. It does not appear that an authority to do any other act than the execution of a deed or the delivery of seisin is required to be given by deed. Thus a power for the assignee of a chose or thing in action to sue at law in the assignor's name was not required to be given by deed: *Howell v MacIvers* (1792) 4 Term Rep 690; *Pickford v Ewington* (1835) 4 Dowl 453; *Mangles v Dixon* (1852) 3 HL Cas 702 at 726. An authority to enter on the principal's behalf into any contract not requiring a deed may well be given without deed (see Sugden, Vendors and Purchasers (14th Edn) 145; *Rosenbaum v Belson* [1900] 2 Ch 267); and an authority to sign any document other than a deed on the principal's behalf need not be given by deed (*R v Kent Justices* (1873) LR 8 QB 305 at 307; *Re Whitley Partners Ltd* (1886) 32 ChD 337, CA; *Sims v Landray* [1894] 2 Ch 318). See further para 47 post.

2 See the Powers of Attorney Act 1971 s 1 (as amended); and see AGENCY vol 2(1) (Reissue) para 31. As to deeds executed by attorney see para 47 post. As to the abolition of the procedure for filing instruments creating a power of attorney in the Central Office of the Supreme Court or at the Land Registry see AGENCY vol 2(1) (Reissue) para 32.

3 See the Law of Property (Miscellaneous Provisions) Act 1989 s 1(1)(c). This provision does not apply to instruments delivered as deeds before 31 July 1990 (i e the date on which s 1 came into force): see s 1(11); and para 7 text and note 4 ante.

4 As to execution by corporations see paras 40–41 post. Certificates of shares and share warrants issued under the Companies Act 1985 ss 186, 188 (both as substituted and amended), under seal, are not deeds: see *R v Morton* (1873) LR 2 CCR 22 at 27; para 1 ante; and COMPANIES vol 7(1) (2004 Reissue) para 589.

5 Similar provision was made for these companies by the Companies Acts: see the Companies Act 1985 s 36 (as substituted); and COMPANIES vol 7(2) (2004 Reissue) para 457 et seq.

6 See CORPORATIONS vol 9(2) (2006 Reissue) paras 1122, 1261, 1272, 1274.

7 *Irons v Smallpiece* (1819) 2 B & Ald 551 at 552, 554; *Cochrane v Moore* (1890) 25 QBD 57 at 61, 67, 73, 75, CA. As to avoidance of assignment if unregistered and not followed by delivery of goods assigned within seven days see BILLS OF SALE vol 4(1) (2002 Reissue) para 831. See also *Tuck v Southern Counties Deposit Bank* (1889) 42 ChD 471 at 481, 483, CA; *Antoniadi v Smith* [1901] 2 KB 589, CA; *Casson v Churchley* (1884) 53 LJQB 335 at 338. As to goods in possession of the bailee see para 12 note 1 ante. As regards the need for a deed where the transaction is contractual but gratuitous see para 59 post.

8 *Re Casey's Patents, Stewart v Casey* [1892] 1 Ch 104 at 111, 113, CA (in which case it was, however, decided that an equitable assignment of a patent may well be made without deed, and that such an assignment may be registered as affecting the proprietorship of the patent). Registration of assignments is governed by the Patents Act 1977 ss 30, 32 (as substituted and amended): see PATENTS AND REGISTERED DESIGNS vol 35 (Reissue) paras 400 et seq, 671 et seq.

(ii) By Statute

14. Under the Law of Property Act 1925. Under the Law of Property Act 1925, a deed is required in the following cases: (1) conveyances[1] of land[2] or of any interest in land, with certain exceptions[3], for the purpose of conveying or creating a legal estate[4]; (2) mortgages of any property in order to incorporate therein the powers of sale, of insurance, of appointing a receiver, and of cutting timber conferred by the Act[5]; (3) conveyances by mortgagees exercising the power of sale conferred by the Act[6]; (4) mortgages in the statutory form authorised by the Act of freehold or leasehold land[7]; (5) a release of or a contract not to exercise any power (whether coupled with an interest or not) in exercise of the power to do so conferred by the Act[8]; (6) a disclaimer of a power in exercise of the power to disclaim so conferred[9]; and (7) enlargements under the Act of long terms of years[10].

1 'Conveyance' includes a mortgage, charge, lease, assent, vesting declaration, vesting instrument, disclaimer, release and every other assurance of property or of an interest therein by any instrument, except a will; and 'convey' has a corresponding meaning: Law of Property Act 1925 s 205(1)(ii); but see para 15 post.

2 'Land' includes land of any tenure, and mines and minerals, whether or not held apart from the surface, buildings or parts of buildings (whether the division is horizontal, vertical or made in any other way) and other corporeal hereditaments; also a manor, an advowson, and a rent or other incorporeal hereditaments; and an easement, right, privilege or benefit in, over or derived from land: ibid s 205(1)(ix) (definition amended by the Trusts of Land and Appointment of Trustees Act 1996 s 25(2), Sch 4).

3 As to the exceptions see para 15 post.

4   Law of Property Act 1925 s 52(1). As to the estates, interests and charges in or over land (including certain rights of entry) which can subsist at law and which are, in the Law of Property Act 1925, referred to as 'legal estates' see ss 1(1), (2), (4), 205(1)(x) (ss 1(2), 205(1)(x) as amended); and REAL PROPERTY vol 39(2) (Reissue) paras 45, 47. As to rights of entry see also ss 4(2), (3), 141; and REAL PROPERTY vol 39(2) (Reissue) paras 45, 231. See further REAL PROPERTY vol 39(2) (Reissue) para 232 et seq.
5   See ibid s 101(1); and MORTGAGE vol 32 (2005 Reissue) para 637.
6   See ibid s 104(1); and MORTGAGE vol 32 (2005 Reissue) para 645.
7   See ibid s 117(1); and MORTGAGE vol 32 (2005 Reissue) paras 392, 423.
8   See ibid s 155; and POWERS vol 36(2) (Reissue) para 376.
9   See ibid s 156; and POWERS vol 36(2) (Reissue) para 375.
10   See ibid s 153 (as amended); and REAL PROPERTY vol 39(2) (Reissue) para 108 et seq.

15.   Conveyances for which a deed is not required.   The following conveyances are exceptions to the rule[1] that a conveyance of land or an interest in land must be by deed in order to convey or create a legal estate: (1) assents by a personal representative[2]; (2) disclaimers of onerous property by a trustee in bankruptcy or liquidator[3], and disclaimers not required to be in writing[4]; (3) surrenders by operation of law, including surrenders which, by law, may be effected without writing[5]; (4) leases or tenancies or other assurances not required by law to be made in writing[6]; (5) receipts other than those falling within the provision of the Law of Property Act 1925 relating to reconveyances of mortgages by indorsed receipts[7]; (6) vesting orders of the court or other competent authority[8]; (7) conveyances taking effect by operation of law[9]. In these cases, therefore, a deed is not required[10].

1   See para 14 ante.
2   Law of Property Act 1925 s 52(2)(a). An assent is the usual mode of conveying land by a personal representative to the devisee or other person entitled. This exception preserves the rule that an assent may be made by writing under hand only: see the Administration of Estates Act 1925 s 36(4); and EXECUTORS AND ADMINISTRATORS vol 17(2) (Reissue) para 564.
3   Under the Insolvency Act 1986 s 315 (as amended), a trustee in bankruptcy may disclaim any onerous property: see BANKRUPTCY AND INDIVIDUAL INSOLVENCY vol 3(2) (2002 Reissue) para 472 et seq. A similar power is given to the liquidator of a company by the Insolvency Act 1986 s 178: see COMPANY AND PARNERSHIP INSOLVENCY vol 7(4) (2004 Reissue) para 866 et seq.
4   See the Law of Property Act 1925 s 52(2)(b) (amended by the Insolvency Act 1986 s 439(2), Sch 14). No disclaimers, other than those referred to in note 3 supra, have to be in writing: see *Re Paradise Motor Co Ltd* [1968] 2 All ER 625 at 632, [1968] 1 WLR 1125 at 1143, CA, per Danckwerts LJ. A trustee or executor may disclaim the trust or executorship by conduct and with it the legal estate in land subject to it: *Re Birchall, Birchall v Ashton* (1889) 40 ChD 436 at 439, CA; *Re Clout and Frewer's Contract* [1924] 2 Ch 230. As to disclaimers by deed see para 14 ante.
5   Law of Property Act 1925 s 52(2)(c); and cf the Real Property Act 1845 s 3 (repealed). The Statute of Frauds (1677) s 3 (repealed: now replaced by the Law of Property Act 1925 s 53(1)(a)) required all surrenders of leases or freehold estates to be put in writing, except those made by operation of law. It has been held, however, that if, under an agreement made between a tenant of land for life or years and the immediate reversioner or remainderman in fee, the tenant gives up to the other and the other takes possession of the land, that is equivalent to a surrender by operation of law and the transaction may be valid without deed or writing: see e g *Thomas v Cook* (1818) 2 B & Ald 119; and LANDLORD AND TENANT vol 27(1) (2006 Reissue) para 637.
6   Law of Property Act 1925 s 52(2)(d); and cf the Real Property Act 1845 s 3 (repealed), under which leases required to be in writing had to be under seal. Leases not required to be in writing are those which take effect in possession for a term not exceeding three years (whether or not the lessee is given power to extend the term) at the best rent which can reasonably be obtained without taking a fine: Law of Property Act 1925 s 54(2). A lease to commence at a future date is not a lease 'taking effect in possession' within s 54(2) and is void for the purpose of conveying and creating a legal estate unless made by deed: see *Long v Tower Hamlets London Borough Council* [1998] Ch 197, [1996] 2 All ER 683. As to leases exceeding three years see LANDLORD AND TENANT vol 27(1) (2006 Reissue) para 102.
7   Law of Property Act 1925 s 52(2)(e) (amended by the Law of Property (Miscellaneous Provisions) Act 1989 s 1(8), Sch 1 para 2). The text refers to the Law of Property Act 1925 s 115 (as amended) (see MORTGAGE vol 32 (2005 Reissue) para 846 et seq): see s 52(2)(e) (as so amended). Section 52(2)(e) (as amended) does not apply to instruments delivered as deeds before 31 July 1990 (i e the date on which the Law of Property (Miscellaneous Provisions) Act 1989 s 1 came into force): see s 1(11); and para 7 text and

note 4 ante. As to the application of this provision before 31 July 1990 see the Law of Property Act 1925 s 52(2)(e) (as originally enacted). As to the application of the Law of Property (Miscellaneous Provisions) Act 1989 s 1(8) see s 1(9); and para 7 text and note 4 ante. These receipts are excepted because reconveyances of mortgages may be effected by indorsed receipts: see the Law of Property Act 1925 s 115 (as amended); and MORTGAGE vol 32 (2005 Reissue) para 846 et seq.

8   Ibid s 52(2)(f). A vesting order may operate as a conveyance: see s 9(1)(a); and REAL PROPERTY vol 39(2) (Reissue) para 246.
9   Ibid s 52(2)(g). An example is the vesting of a bankrupt's estate in the trustee: see the Insolvency Act 1986 s 306; and BANKRUPTCY AND INDIVIDUAL INSOLVENCY vol 3(2) (2002 Reissue) para 391.
10   See the Law of Property Act 1925 s 52(2).

16.   Dispositions of registered land.   Instruments intended to be registered under the Land Registration Act 2002 (for example, instruments intended to effect a transfer, charge, or exchange of registered land, or the transfer of any registered charge thereon, or to effect any alteration of a registered charge) are, by the combined operation of that Act and the rules and forms issued under that Act, required to be executed as deeds[1].

1   See the Land Registration Act 2002 s 27; the Land Registration Rules 2003, SI 2003/1417 (as amended); and LAND REGISTRATION vol 26 (2004 Reissue) para 911 et seq. A transfer so executed is a deed: see para 1 ante. As to attestation of such instruments see para 44 post. As to electronic dispositions and electronic conveyancing generally see para 9 ante; and LAND REGISTRATION vol 26 (2004 Reissue) para 1049 et seq.

17.   Leases under the Settled Land Act 1925.   Leases authorised by the Settled Land Act 1925 to be made by tenants for life and others of any settled land are required to be made by deed[1]; but leases at the best rent that can be reasonably obtained without fine, and without exempting the lessee from punishment for waste, may be made by any writing under hand where the term does not extend beyond three years from the date of the writing[2]. As from 1 January 1997[3] it is no longer possible to create any new settlements under the Settled Land Act 1925; but any existing settlements continue in being[4], and accordingly leases may be granted under them as previously[5].

1   See the Settled Land Act 1925 s 42; and SETTLEMENTS vol 42 (Reissue) paras 839–840. As to other leasing powers see ss 41, 43–48 (s 44 as amended); and SETTLEMENTS vol 42 (Reissue) para 837 et seq.
2   See ibid s 42(5)(ii); and SETTLEMENTS vol 42 (Reissue) para 839.
3   Ie the date on which the Trusts of Land and Appointment of Trustees Act 1996 came into force: see s 27(2).
4   See ibid s 2; and SETTLEMENTS vol 42 (Reissue) para 676. As to the limited exceptions see s 2(2), (3); and SETTLEMENTS vol 42 (Reissue) para 676. As to the duration of settlements see the Settled Land Act 1925 s 3 (as amended); and SETTLEMENTS vol 42 (Reissue) para 708.
5   There is nothing in the Trusts of Land and Appointment of Trustees Act 1996 to affect the powers of leasing by tenants for life and others under the Settled Land Act 1925 ss 41–43.

18.   Appointment of new trustee.   An appointment of a new trustee under the Trustee Act 1925, must be made in writing[1] and must be made by deed in every case in which it is intended to transfer any of the trust property by a vesting declaration under that Act, or in which, in the absence of such a declaration, it is intended that the appointment is to operate as if it contained one[2]. A declaration by a trustee of his desire to be discharged under that Act must be made by deed[3].

A memorandum evidencing the appointment or discharge of a trustee of charity property by a resolution must be executed as a deed if it is to operate under the Charities Act 1993 as if it contained a vesting declaration[4].

1   See the Trustee Act 1925 s 36(1), (6) (as amended); and TRUSTS vol 48 (2000 Reissue) paras 729–731.
2   See ibid s 40 (as amended); and TRUSTS vol 48 (2000 Reissue) paras 760–761.
3   See ibid s 39(1) (as amended); and TRUSTS vol 48 (2000 Reissue) para 785. The declaration is only effectual if, after the discharge, there will be either a trust corporation or at least two individuals to act as trustees: see s 39(1) (as amended); and TRUSTS vol 48 (2000 Reissue) para 785.
4   See the Charities Act 1993 s 83(1)–(4); and CHARITIES vol 5(2) (2001 Reissue) paras 257–258.

19.   Disentailing assurances.   Dispositions made by way of disentailing assurance under the Fines and Recoveries Act 1833 by a tenant in tail are required to be made or evidenced by deed[1]. The consent of the protector of a settlement to the disposition by way of disentailing assurance under that Act of any hereditaments, or of any money subject to be invested in the purchase of lands of any tenure to be entailed, is required to be given either by the deed by which the disposition is effected or by a distinct deed[2].

Dispositions by way of disentailing assurance under the Fines and Recoveries Act 1833[3] of any lands, tenements, or hereditaments, corporeal or incorporeal, to which any bankrupt is beneficially entitled at law or in equity for an estate tail or a base fee, are required to be made by deed[4].

All the above requirements (and all other statutory provisions relating to estates tail in real property) apply to entailed personal property[5].

As from 1 January 1997 it is no longer possible to create an entailed interest[6], and it is no longer possible to create any new settlements under the Settled Land Act 1925, but any existing settlements under that Act continue in being[7].

1   See the Fines and Recoveries Act 1833 s 40 (as amended); and REAL PROPERTY vol 39(2) (Reissue) para 125.
2   See ibid s 42 (as amended); and REAL PROPERTY vol 39(2) (Reissue) para 128.
3   The trustee in bankruptcy has the power to exercise in relation to any property comprised in the bankrupt's estate any powers the capacity to exercise which is vested in him under the Insolvency Act 1986 Pts VIII–XI (ss 252–385) (as amended) (see BANKRUPTCY AND INDIVIDUAL INSOLVENCY; COMPANY AND PARTNERSHIP INSOLVENCY): Insolvency Act 1986 s 314, Sch 5 para 12.
4   See the Fines and Recoveries Act 1833 s 56 (amended by the Statute Law Revision (No 2) Act 1888).
5   See the Law of Property Act 1925 s 130(1) (repealed except in relation to any entailed interest created before 1 January 1997); and REAL PROPERTY vol 39(2) (Reissue) para 119; SETTLEMENTS vol 42 (Reissue) paras 678, 939.
6   See the Trusts of Land and Appointment of Trustees Act 1996 s 2, Sch 1 para 5; and SETTLEMENTS vol 42 (Reissue) para 677. As to savings in relation to entailed interests created before 1 January 1997 (i e before the commencement of the Trusts of Land and Appointment of Trustees Act 1996), and savings consequential upon the abolition of the doctrine of conversion, see s 25(4), (5).
7   See ibid s 2; and SETTLEMENTS vol 42 (Reissue) para 676. As to the limited exceptions see s 2(2), (3); and SETTLEMENTS vol 42 (Reissue) para 676.

20.   Conveyances of church property etc.   Leases made by ecclesiastical corporations under the powers given by the Ecclesiastical Leasing Act 1842 are required to be made by deed[1].

The relinquishment of holy orders under the Clerical Disabilities Act 1870 can only be effected by deed[2].

1   See the Ecclesiastical Leasing Act 1842 s 1 (as amended); and ECCLESIASTICAL LAW vol 14 para 1155. This provision is repealed in so far as it applies to any body corporate in any cathedral church by the Cathedrals Measure 1963 s 53, Sch 1, and so far as applying to incumbents by the Endowments and Glebe Measure 1976 s 47(3), Sch 7.
2   See the Clerical Disabilities Act 1870 s 3, by which enrolment and other formalities are required. As to the execution and attestation of such deeds see para 45 post. See further ECCLESIASTICAL LAW vol 14 paras 686, 688.

21.   Transfers of shares under the Companies Clauses Consolidation Act 1845.   Transfers of shares in companies which are subject to the relevant provisions of the Companies Clauses Consolidation Act 1845 must, if carried out under those provisions, be effected by deed[1]. Alternative provisions contained in the Stock Transfer Act 1963 now, however, apply to transfers of fully-paid registered shares in all such companies, and permit transfer by a statutory or other form of transfer which is executed under hand and is not a deed[2].

1   See the Companies Clauses Consolidation Act 1845 s 14; *Powell v London and Provincial Bank* [1893] 2 Ch 555, CA; and COMPANIES vol 7(2) (2004 Reissue) para 1901. Shares in companies registered under

the Companies Act 1985 are transferable in manner provided by the articles of association of the company or, if they are fully-paid registered shares and the company is limited by shares, alternatively in the manner provided by the Stock Transfer Act 1963 (which enables securities of certain descriptions to be transferred by a simplified process), or by regulations made under the Companies Act 1989 s 207 (as amended) (which enable title to securities to be evidenced and transferred without a written instrument): see the Companies Act 1985 s 182(1)(b) (as amended); and COMPANIES vol 7(1) (2004 Reissue) para 820. Articles of association may, but do not necessarily, require transfer by deed: see *Re Tahiti Cotton Co, ex p Sargent* (1874) LR 17 Eq 273 at 280; *Société Générale de Paris v Walker* (1885) 11 App Cas 20 at 22, HL; *Ireland v Hart* [1902] 1 Ch 522 at 524, 527–528.

2   See the Stock Transfer Act 1963 s 1 (as amended); and COMPANIES vol 7(1) (2004 Reissue) para 872.

22.   Bills of sale.   Bills of sale of personal chattels made or given by way of security for the payment of money by the grantor are void unless made by deed in statutory form[1].

Any transfer of a registered ship[2], or a share in such a ship, must be effected by a bill of sale satisfying the prescribed requirements[3], unless the transfer will result in the ship ceasing to have a British connection[4]. A mortgage of a registered ship, or a share in a registered ship, must be made in the form prescribed by or approved under registration regulations[5], and likewise a transfer of a registered mortgage[6].

1   Bills of Sale Act (1878) Amendment Act 1882 s 9, Schedule. See further BILLS OF SALE vol 4(1) (2002 Reissue) paras 663, 692.
2   As to the meaning of 'ship' see the Merchant Shipping Act 1995 s 313(1); and SHIPPING AND NAVIGATION vol 43(1) (Reissue) para 102.
3   As to registration regulations see ibid s 10; the Merchant Shipping (Registration of Ships) Regulations 1993, SI 1993/3138 (as amended); and SHIPPING AND NAVIGATION vol 43(1) (Reissue) para 179 et seq. For the meaning of 'prescribed' for these purposes see the Merchant Shipping Act 1995 Sch 1 para 14; and SHIPPING AND NAVIGATION vol 43(1) (Reissue) para 235.
4   See ibid Sch 1 para 2(1); and SHIPPING AND NAVIGATION vol 43(1) (Reissue) paras 235–236.
5   See ibid Sch 1 para 7; and SHIPPING AND NAVIGATION vol 43(1) (Reissue) para 249.
6   See ibid Sch 1 para 11; and SHIPPING AND NAVIGATION vol 43(1) (Reissue) para 254.

(iii)   In Equity

23.   General rule.   Whenever any question is raised (whether for the purpose of asserting some equitable right or otherwise) in any court possessing equitable jurisdiction as to the effect of any assurance, or alleged assurance, of some legal estate or interest in any real or personal property or other legal right, the invariable rule is that the validity of the assurance, as regards its operation to convey any such legal estate, interest, or right, must be tested by the rules of common law or statute required to be observed in order that it may take effect at law. In other words, equity follows the law with respect to the formalities necessary for the conveyance of any legal estate, interest or right[1].

Thus (unless a declaration of trust is made) equity will not interfere to enforce or uphold a voluntary gift, which is incomplete for want of compliance with the formalities required at law, of any legal estate, interest or right[2]; and a voluntary gift made without deed, and without any declaration of trust, of any legal estate of freehold in possession in any land[3], or of any legal term of years in any land[4], is altogether void in equity as well as at law. A voluntary release of a debt owing at law is void, if not made by deed, both at law and in equity[5].

1   See cases cited in notes 2–5 infra; Story's Equity Jurisprudence (3rd English Edn) 34 s 64. As to the relationship of equity to common law see EQUITY vol 16(2) (Reissue) para 401 et seq.
2   See e g *Colman v Sarrel* (1789) 1 Ves 50 at 52, 55 per Lord Eldon LC; *Ellison v Ellison* (1802) 6 Ves 656 at 662; *Antrobus v Smith* (1805) 12 Ves 39.
3   *Warriner v Rogers* (1873) LR 16 Eq 340. See para 14 ante.
4   *Richards v Delbridge* (1874) LR 18 Eq 11; and see para 14 ante.
5   *Edwards v Walters* [1896] 2 Ch 157 at 168, 172, CA; and see para 12 ante.

24.   Trusts and equitable interests.   A deed is not required by the rules of equity either for the creation of any trust or for the assurance of any equitable estate or interest in any real or personal property held on trust or subject to any equity giving rise to an equitable estate or interest[1]. Thus trusts of personal estate (other than chattels real) may be created by word of mouth[2]. It is, however, provided by statute that no interest in land can be created or disposed of except by writing, signed by the person creating or conveying the interest or by his agent lawfully authorised in writing, or by will or by operation of law[3], and that a declaration of trust respecting land or any interest in it must be manifested and proved by some writing signed by a person who is able to declare the trust[4] or by his will[5]. It is also provided by statute that a disposition of an equitable interest or trust, subsisting at the time of the disposition, must be in writing signed by the person disposing of the same, or by his agent lawfully authorised in writing, or by his will[6]. On the other hand it is not in general required that either a declaration of trust of land, or a disposition of an equitable interest or trust, should be made by deed[7].

1 See Perkins, Profitable Book s 62; 1 Plowd 350; Doctor and Student, Dialogue, 2, cc 22, 23; Bacon's Law Tracts 306–307, 355; Shep Touch 517–521; 1 Fonblanque's Treatise of Equity (5th Edn) 176; 2 Fonblanque's Treatise of Equity (5th Edn) 21; 1 Sanders on Uses (5th Edn) 343–344; Lewin on Trusts (16th Edn) 22 et seq; 2 Davidson's Precedents in Conveyancing (4th Edn) Pt I, 449n; and consider the cases cited in notes 2, 7 infra; and para 25 notes 1–2 post.

2 *Nab v Nab* (1718) 10 Mod Rep 404 at 405 per Parker LC; *Fordyce v Willis* (1791) 3 Bro CC 577n at 587 per Lord Thurlow LC; *Bayley v Boulcott* (1828) 4 Russ 345 at 347 per Leach MR; *Benbow v Townsend* (1833) 1 My & K 506; *M'Fadden v Jenkyns* (1842) 1 Hare 458 at 461 per Wigram V-C (on appeal 1 Ph 153 at 157 per Lord Lyndhurst LC); *Vandenberg v Palmer* (1858) 4 K & J 204; *Jones v Lock* (1865) 1 Ch App 25 at 28 per Lord Cranworth LC. See also TRUSTS.

3 Law of Property Act 1925 s 53(1)(a) (replacing the Statute of Frauds (1677) s 3 (repealed)).

4 See *Dye v Dye* (1884) 13 QBD 147, CA (pre-marital agreement before 1883, signed by husband only, renouncing claim to wife's property; ineffective to create trust for her separate use, as not signed by her).

5 Law of Property Act 1925 s 53(1)(b). This reproduces the Statute of Frauds (1677) s 7 (repealed), and like that provision it is confined to land, including chattels real: see *Smith v Matthews* (1861) 3 De GF & J 139; *Re Cozens, Green v Brisley* [1913] 2 Ch 478 (insufficient evidence of trust). Thus it does not alter the rule that trusts of personal estate, other than chattels real, can be created orally (see the text and notes 1–2 supra).

6 Law of Property Act 1925 s 53(1)(c) (replacing the Statute of Frauds (1677) s 9). The Law of Property Act 1925 s 53(1)(c) does not apply (if it would otherwise do so) in relation to a financial collateral arrangement: see the Financial Collateral Arrangements (No 2) Regulations 2003, SI 2003/3226, reg 4(2). It is well established that the Law of Property Act 1925 s 53(1)(c) applies only to subsisting equitable interests: *Kinane v Mackie-Conteh* [2005] EWCA Civ 45, [2005] 06 EG 140 (CS).

   The Law of Property Act 1925 s 53(1)(c) is not confined to trusts respecting land, but applies also to trusts of personal property (see *Jerdein v Bright* (1861) 2 John & H 325 at 330–331), and expressly extends the requirement of writing to equitable interests generally, as well as to trusts, so that an assignment of an equity of redemption (where not clothed with the legal estate) clearly requires to be made in writing, whether it is for value or not, and since in the case of a legal mortgage the mortgagor now retains a legal estate, the assignment must be made by deed (see para 14 ante). In practice no one would be advised to make a voluntary assurance of any equity of redemption, even where it was not clothed with a legal estate, otherwise than by deed (see para 25 note 5 post). A direction to trustees to hold upon new trusts is a 'disposition' within the statutory provision: *Grey v IRC* [1960] AC 1, [1959] 3 All ER 603, HL; cf *Oughtred v IRC* [1960] AC 206, [1959] 3 All ER 623, HL (effect of oral agreement to exchange reversionary interest in settled shares for shares owned by life tenant); *Neville v Wilson* [1997] Ch 144, [1996] 3 All ER 171, CA. The provision does not apply where there is a disposition, not of the equitable interest alone, but of the entire estate: *Vandervell v IRC* [1967] 2 AC 291 at 311, 317, [1967] 1 All ER 1 at 7, 11, HL, per Lord Upjohn. Two or more documents, provided they are sufficiently interconnected, will satisfy the requirement: *Re Danish Bacon Co Ltd Staff Pension Fund, Christensen v Arnett* [1971] 1 All ER 486, [1971] 1 WLR 248.

7 *Shortridge v Lamplough* (1702) 7 Mod Rep 71 at 76 per Holt CJ; and consider *Forster v Hale* (1798) 3 Ves 696 at 707 (affd (1800) 5 Ves 308); *Rochefoucauld v Boustead* [1897] 1 Ch 196 at 205–207, CA. Dispositions of equitable interests under the Fines and Recoveries Act 1833 must be by deed: see para 19 ante.

25.   Voluntary assurances of equitable interest.   There is no doubt that a deed is not necessary to the validity of an assurance of an equitable interest if made for valuable consideration[1] and it is thought that, upon principle and according to the preponderance of authority, a deed is not necessary to effect the gratuitous assurance of any purely equitable estate, interest, or right, in any real or personal property, provided that the intention of actual and immediate assignment (as distinguished from a mere promise of future assignment or gift) is clearly expressed and that the assurance is put in writing and signed by the assuror[2]. It seems to follow that an express release made gratuitously of any purely equitable estate, interest, or right, in any lands or goods, such as the release of an equitable charge thereon, can also be made without a deed[3]. The conclusive and irrevocable effect of a deed as regards any gratuitous assurance contained in the deed[4], is, however, recognised in equity as well as at law; and any gratuitous assignment made by deed of any purely equitable estate, interest, or right, is effective[5].

1   See the authorities cited in para 24 note 1 ante; and *Re Leathes, ex p Leathes* (1833) 3 Deac & Ch 112; *Re Ogbourne, ex p Heathcoate* (1842) 2 Mont D & De G 711; *Dighton v Withers* (1862) 31 Beav 423 at 424; *Neve v Pennell* (1863) 2 Hem & M 170 at 186; *Tebb v Hodge* (1869) LR 5 CP 73, Ex Ch; *Credland v Potter* (1874) 10 Ch App 8 at 12, 14. It is a general rule of equity that an agreement made for valuable consideration to assign any equitable estate or interest in any property may operate as an equitable assignment thereof: see *Row v Dawson* (1749) 1 Ves Sen 331; *Wright v Wright* (1750) 1 Ves Sen 409; *William Brandt's Sons & Co v Dunlop Rubber Co* [1905] AC 454 at 461–462, HL, per Lord Macnaghten.
2   It has been established that a direct assignment may well be made, without valuable consideration, of an equitable chose or thing in action: see *Kekewich v Manning* (1851) 1 De GM & G 176; *Voyle v Hughes* (1854) 2 Sm & G 18; *Donaldson v Donaldson* (1854) Kay 711; *Gilbert v Overton* (1864) 2 Hem & M 110; *Re Way's Trusts* (1864) 2 De GJ & Sm 365; *Re Patrick, Bills v Tatham* [1891] 1 Ch 82, CA, in all of which cases, though the assignment was made by deed, the point decided was that an actual assignment of, as distinguished from a mere promise to assign, an equitable interest is valid, though made gratuitously. See further CHOSES IN ACTION vol 6 (2003 Reissue) paras 35–40. It has been further held that a gratuitous assignment of an equitable chose or thing in action may be made by a signed writing without deed: *Lambe v Orton* (1860) 1 Drew & Sm 125; *Re King, Sewell v King* (1879) 14 ChD 179; *Harding v Harding* (1886) 17 QBD 442; *Re Griffin, Griffin v Griffin* [1899] 1 Ch 408; and see CHOSES IN ACTION vol 6 (2003 Reissue) paras 30, 38.
3   See *Re Hall, Holland v A-G* [1941] 2 All ER 358; affd on another point [1942] Ch 140, [1942] 1 All ER 10, CA. In that case although Morton J, at 370, came with some hesitation to the decision that the writing in question amounted to a release, he appeared not to doubt that such a writing could amount to a release. In *Re Hancock, Hancock v Berrey* (1888) 57 LJ Ch 793, where a debt secured by a mortgage of an equitable reversionary chose (or thing) in action had become barred by the Statute of Limitations and the mortgagee then sent the mortgage deed to the mortgagor with a letter expressing the intention of giving him the deed, it was held that the mere gift of the mortgage deed did not have the effect of releasing the charge, following *Re Richardson, Shillito v Hobson* (1885) 30 ChD 396, CA (see para 148 post), and declining to follow *Richards v Syms* (1740) Barn Ch 90), which had previously been treated as authoritative, even in the House of Lords (see *Byrn v Godfrey* (1798) 4 Ves 6 at 10; *Duffield v Elwes* (1827) 1 Bli NS 497 at 536, 540, HL; *Cross v Sprigg* (1849) 6 Hare 552 at 556). See para 77 note 3 post. It is submitted that the observation in *Re Hancock, Hancock, v Berrey* supra at 795–796 per Kay J, that he had asked for authority that a gratuitous parol release of a debt could be enforced, but none had been given, is not inconsistent with the proposition in the text since the debt under consideration was a legal chose in action.
4   See para 59 post.
5   See the cases cited in note 2 supra; and see also *Petre v Espinasse* (1834) 2 My & K 496; *Bill v Cureton* (1835) 2 My & K 503; *M'Donnell v Hesilrige* (1852) 16 Beav 346; *Pearson v Amicable Assurance Office* (1859) 27 Beav 229. Hence it is the invariable practice of conveyancers, when instructed to draw any voluntary settlement, assignment, release, or other assurance of any equitable estate, interest, or right, to embody the parties' intention in a deed.

26.   Effect in equity of contract specifically enforceable.   The equitable rule is clear that, with respect to the consequences of any act stipulated in a binding agreement to be performed, what ought to be done is to be treated as actually accomplished[1]. By virtue of this rule, to which effect is given in all courts[2], where a contract specifically enforceable is made for the acquisition of some estate or interest in real or personal property, for the assurance of which a deed is required either by common law or statute, any party to the contract who has duly performed his part of the agreement is entitled, as against all persons against whom the contract can be specifically enforced, to enjoy the like advantages as if the contract had been completed by the deed required[3].

1　*Lechmere v Earl of Carlisle* (1735) 3 P Wms 211 at 215; *Guidot v Guidot* (1745) 3 Atk 254 at 256; *Trafford v Boehm* (1746) 3 Atk 440 at 446; *Crabtree v Bramble* (1747) 3 Atk 680 at 687; *Earl of Buckinghamshire v Drury* (1762) 2 Eden 60 at 65, HL; *Stead v Newdigate* (1817) 2 Mer 521 at 530; *Lysaght v Edwards* (1876) 2 ChD 499; *Re Cary-Elwes' Contract* [1906] 2 Ch 143 at 149. See EQUITY vol 16(2) (Reissue) paras 561–562.

2　See the Supreme Court Act 1981 (prospectively renamed the Senior Courts Act 1981) s 49 (concurrent administration of law and equity); COURTS vol 10 (Reissue) para 930; EQUITY vol 16(2) (Reissue) para 496; PRACTICE AND PROCEDURE vol 37 (Reissue) para 930.

3　See e g *Walsh v Lonsdale* (1882) 21 ChD 9, CA; and LANDLORD AND TENANT vol 27(1) (2006 Reissue) para 76 et seq. It should be noted that, while equitable assignments made without deed by way of sale or mortgage of lands, tenements, or hereditaments, or of shares in companies transferable by deed, are governed by the general rules of equity affecting such dispositions, similar assignments of ships or shares in them are subject to special provisions of the Merchant Shipping Act 1894 s 57 (repealed: see now the Merchant Shipping Act 1995 s 16, Sch 1) (see *Black v Williams* [1895] 1 Ch 408; *Barclay & Co Ltd v Poole* [1907] 2 Ch 284; para 21 ante; and SHIPPING AND NAVIGATION vol 43(1) (Reissue) para 235); and equitable assignments of tangible goods, either absolutely or by way of mortgage, are affected by the Bills of Sale Acts (see BILLS OF SALE vol 4(1) (2002 Reissue) para 605 et seq). As to the necessity of satisfying the Law of Property (Miscellaneous Provisions) Act 1989 s 2 (as amended) (see paras 145, 156 post) see *United Bank of Kuwait plc v Sahib* [1997] Ch 107, [1996] 3 All ER 215, CA.

(3)　EXECUTION OF A DEED

(i)　Formalities of Execution at Common Law

27.　Sealing.　In certain circumstances[1], a deed must be sealed, that is it must have a seal fixed or impressed upon or attached to it, and the party professing to be bound by the deed must do some act expressly or impliedly acknowledging the seal to be his[2]. It is not, however, necessary that any particular kind of seal is used, provided that there is affixed or impressed to or on the deed something purporting to be a seal. Thus the seal may be of wax affixed on the deed or attached to it by a ribbon, or it may be a wafer, or it may be simply impressed on the deed[3]. Indeed it may suffice that there is merely a printed circle inscribed within the letters 'L S' if the document was intended to be delivered as a deed of the party executing it[4].

The seal need not bear any indication that it is the particular seal of the person who affixes it. Thus it need not be stamped with his coat-of-arms, crest, or initials, or otherwise specially marked, and it became the practice to use wax or wafer seals with a plain impression. A deed may be sealed with another person's seal[5]. Where several persons are parties to a deed it is not necessary, though it is the usual practice, for there to be as many seals as there are persons; and they may all seal the deed with one and the same seal[6].

The party sealing need not actually affix or impress the seal himself, so long as he delivers the deed in his own person[7], and in such case he need not touch the seal if he expressly or impliedly acknowledges it to be his[8]. Thus it is sufficient if the seal is affixed by some other person in his presence with his consent, and he so assents to the delivery of the deed[9]; or if some other person in his presence and with his consent writes his name opposite a seal previously affixed in token of his acknowledgment that the seal is his[10]; or if, when the seal has been affixed by some other person in his absence on his behalf, he afterwards in person acknowledges the deed to be his[11]. The traditional formal manner of sealing a deed is for the party to place his finger or thumb on the seal (which is generally already attached) at the same time as he utters the words 'I deliver this as my act and deed', which are equivalent to delivery[12], but even this is not essential; if a party signs a document bearing wax or wafer or other indication of a seal with the intention of executing the document as a deed, that is sufficient adoption or recognition of the seal to amount to due execution as a deed[13].

Where a person executes a deed by stating that it has been 'signed, sealed and delivered' but without in fact sealing it, and another person relies on the deed to his detriment, the person executing the deed is estopped from denying that it was sealed[14].

1 Ie (1) instruments delivered as deeds before 31 July 1990 (see para 1 et seq ante); (2) deeds required or authorised to be made under the seal of the county palatine of Lancaster, the seal of the Duchy of Lancaster, or the seal of the Duchy of Cornwall (see the Law of Property (Miscellaneous Provisions) Act 1989 s 1(9); and para 7 note 4 ante); and (3) the execution of deeds by a corporation sole or a body corporate (see s 1(10); and para 32 text to note 3 post).
  As from 31 July 1990, any rule of law which requires a seal for the valid execution of an instrument as a deed by an individual is abolished: see s 1(1)(b); and paras 7 ante, 32 post.

2 Co Litt 6a; Perkins, Profitable Book ss 129–130; Shep Touch 56–57; *National Provincial Bank of England v Jackson* (1886) 33 ChD 1 at 11, 14, CA; *Re Balkis Consolidated Co Ltd* (1888) 58 LT 300; *Re Smith, Oswell v Shepherd* (1892) 67 LT 64, CA; and see *Stromdale and Ball Ltd v Burden* [1952] Ch 223, [1952] 1 All ER 59; the text and note 12 infra; and paras 1 note 2 ante, 59 note 1 post. There is a presumption in the case of deeds 20 years old produced from proper custody that they have been duly signed, sealed, attested and delivered according to their purport: see the Evidence Act 1938 s 4; and EVIDENCE vol 17(1) (Reissue) para 806.

3 Shep Touch 57; 3 Preston's Abstracts of Title (2nd Edn) 61–62; *R v St Paul, Covent Garden Inhabitants* (1845) 7 QB 232 at 238–239; Sugden, Treatise on Powers (8th Edn) 232; *Re Sandilands* (1871) LR 6 CP 411 at 413; *National Provincial Bank of England v Jackson* (1886) 33 ChD 1 at 11, 14, CA; *Re Smith, Oswell v Shepherd* (1892) 67 LT 64, CA.

4 See *First National Securities Ltd v Jones* [1978] Ch 109, [1978] 2 All ER 221, CA (explaining *Re Balkis Consolidated Co Ltd* (1888) 58 LT 300); applied in *Commercial Credit Services v Knowles* [1978] CLY 794. See however *TCB Ltd v Gray* [1986] Ch 621, [1986] 1 All ER 587 (affd on another point [1987] Ch 458n, [1988] 1 All ER 108, CA); and the text to note 14 infra. The letters 'L S' stand for locus sigilli, meaning the place of the seal.

5 Bract fo 38a; YB 11 Edw 4, 4, pl 7; YB 21 Edw 4, 81, pl 30; Perkins, Profitable Book ss 130–134; *Sutton's Hospital Case* (1612) 10 Co Rep 1a at 30b, Ex Ch; Shep Touch 57; Vin Abr, Faits (H); *Ball v Dunsterville* (1791) 4 Term Rep 313; 3 Preston's Abstracts of Title (2nd Edn) 61–62; *National Provincial Bank of England v Jackson* (1886) 33 ChD 1, CA.

6 Perkins, Profitable Book s 134; Shep Touch 57; *Lord Lovelace's Case* (1632) W Jo 268; *Ball v Dunsterville* (1791) 4 Term Rep 313; *Cooch v Goodman* (1842) 2 QB 580 at 598.

7 Perkins, Profitable Book ss 130, 134; Shep Touch 57; 2 Bl Com (14th Edn) 307. As to delivery see para 31 post.

8 *Ball v Dunsterville* (1791) 4 Term Rep 313; *Tupper v Foulkes* (1861) 9 CBNS 797; *Keith v Pratt* (1862) 10 WR 296.

9 *Ball v Dunsterville* (1791) 4 Term Rep 313.

10 *R v Longnor Inhabitants* (1833) 4 B & Ad 647.

11 *Tupper v Foulkes* (1861) 9 CBNS 797. In these cases, where the party delivers the deed in person, authority to affix the seal, or to write his name as an acknowledgment that the seal is his, may well be given by parol: see e g *R v Longnor Inhabitants* (1833) 4 B & Ad 647; *Tupper v Foulkes* supra. But authority to execute (that is to sign, if necessary, seal and deliver) a deed on behalf of another must be given by deed: see paras 13 ante, 30 note 8 post.

12 Williams and Eastwood on Real Property 430. See para 31 post.

13 *Stromdale and Ball Ltd v Burden* [1952] Ch 223 at 230, [1952] 1 All ER 59 at 62 per Danckwerts J.

14 *TCB Ltd v Gray* [1986] Ch 621, [1986] 1 All ER 587; affd on another point [1987] Ch 458n, [1988] 1 All ER 108, CA.

28. Effect of sealing instrument in blank. A deed must be written before it is sealed[1]. If, therefore, a person seals and delivers a writing which is left blank in some material part (as with regard to the name of the grantor or the grantee or the description of the property to be conveyed), it is void for uncertainty and is not his deed and cannot be made his deed merely by filling up the blanks after his execution of it[2], though it may become his deed if he afterwards re-executes it[3]. A deed, however, is not necessarily void for uncertainty by reason of its having been executed with some blank spaces left in it;

its language may be sufficient without filling up the blanks to ascertain the intention of the party who has executed it to do or enter into some act or agreement valid or enforceable in law[4], and if so, the writing is his deed as it stands[5].

1   Perkins, Profitable Book s 118; Com Dig, Fait (A1); Shep Touch 54; and see note 2 infra.
2   *Markham v Gonaston* (1598) Cro Eliz 626 at 627; *Weeks v Maillardet* (1811) 14 East 568; *Powell v Duff* (1812) 3 Camp 181; *West v Steward* (1845) 14 M & W 47 at 48 per Parke B (where a schedule of creditors, parties to the deed, was omitted); *Hibblewhite v M'Morine* (1840) 6 M & W 200 at 215–216; *Enthoven v Hoyle* (1852) 13 CB 373, Ex Ch; *Tayler v Great Indian Peninsula Rly Co* (1859) 4 De G & J 559; *Swan v North British Australasian Co* (1863) 2 H & C 175, Ex Ch; *France v Clark* (1884) 26 ChD 257 at 263, CA; *Société Générale de Paris v Walker* (1885) 11 App Cas 20, HL; *Powell v London and Provincial Bank* [1893] 1 Ch 610 (affd [1893] 2 Ch 555, CA); *Re Queensland Land and Coal Co, Davis v Martin* [1894] 3 Ch 181 at 183 (the last eight cases relate to transfers of shares or debentures executed in blank: see COMPANIES vol 7(1) (2004 Reissue) para 874; and see now the Stock Transfer Act 1963 s 1(2); and COMPANIES vol 7(1) (2004 Reissue) para 872); *Burgis v Constantine* [1908] 2 KB 484 at 491–492, 497, 500–501, CA (printed form of mortgage by deed of a ship with blank spaces for the necessary particulars executed by intending mortgagor and handed to the mortgagee to fill up).
3   *Hudson v Revett* (1829) 5 Bing 368 at 371; *Hibblewhite v M'Morine* (1840) 6 M & W 200 per Williams J. See further para 54 post.
4   See para 57 post.
5   *Doe d Lewis v Bingham* (1821) 4 B & Ald 672; *Hall v Chandless* (1827) 4 Bing 123; *Hudson v Revett* (1829) 5 Bing 368; *Hibblewhite v M'Morine* (1840) 6 M & W 200 per Parke B; *Adsetts v Hives* (1863) 33 Beav 52. Where a deed with blanks left in it is so valid, filling in the blanks after its execution constitutes an alteration of the deed: see paras 82–83 post. As to the validity of an agreement under hand with an immaterial blank see *Storer v Manchester City Council* [1974] 3 All ER 824, [1974] 1 WLR 1403, CA.

29.   Effect of delivery before sealing.   A deed must be sealed before or at the time of its delivery[1], but if it is delivered without being sealed it may subsequently be sealed and redelivered, in which case the sealing and redelivery will be the only effective execution of the deed[2].

1   *Goddard's Case* (1584) 2 Co Rep 4b at 5a; Finch's Law (1678 Edn) Book II c 2, 108; Shep Touch 57; and see *Davidson v Cooper* (1843) 11 M & W 778 (affd (1844) 13 M & W 343 at 353, Ex Ch).
2   *Tupper v Foulkes* (1861) 9 CBNS 797. See para 54 post.

30.   Signing essential.   Since 31 December 1925, when an individual executes a deed, he must either sign it or place his mark upon it; sealing alone is not enough[1]. Formerly it was not essential that a deed should be signed as well as sealed[2], but it was the regular practice for a person executing a deed to sign his name near the place where his seal was affixed as an acknowledgment that the seal was his and as a guarantee of authenticity[3].

A signature in pencil may be equally binding on the party making it as the signature, if written in another manner, would be[4]. A rubber stamp imprinting a facsimile of the party's signature or mark will probably suffice, provided that it is impressed by the person executing, but if there are exceptional circumstances which make it impossible for the executing party to use the stamp, for example physical disability which prevents him from doing so, it may be that the stamp could be impressed by some third person on his behalf[5]. A typed or printed name (not in facsimile of the party's signature) may be insufficient[6].

It has never been decided whether the writing of the name of a party by another (not authorised by a power of attorney) in the presence and by the direction of the party satisfied the statutory requirement[7] that an individual executing a deed must sign it[8].

1   See, in relation to deeds executed after 31 December 1925, the Law of Property Act 1925 s 73 (repealed). See also *Stromdale and Ball Ltd v Burden* [1952] Ch 223 at 230, [1952] 1 All ER 59 at 62 per Danckwerts J.
      As to the requirement of signing in relation to instruments delivered as deeds after 31 July 1990 see para 33 post.

2 Termes de la Ley, sv Fait; Shep Touch 60; *Maby v Shepherd* (1622) Cro Jac 640; *Cromwell v Grunsden* (1698) 2 Salk 462 per Holt CJ; *R v Goddard* (1703) 3 Salk 171; 2 Bl Com (14th Edn) 306; *Elliot v Davis* (1800) 2 Bos & P 338; *Wright v Wakeford* (1811) 17 Ves 454 at 459; *Ex p Hodgkinson* (1815) 19 Ves 291 at 296 per Lord Eldon LC (a bond); *Taunton v Pepler* (1820) 6 Madd 166; 3 Preston's Abstracts of Title (2nd Edn) 61–62; Sugden, Treatise on Powers (8th Edn) 234–235; *Tupper v Foulkes* (1861) 9 CBNS 797.

3 Termes de la Ley, sv Fait; 3 Preston's Abstracts of Title (2nd Edn) 62; Sugden, Treatise on Powers (8th Edn) 235; Williams and Eastwood on Real Property 434. A deed made in exercise of a power, which by its terms required the deed exercising the power to be signed and sealed, had perhaps to be signed as well as sealed: see para 48 note 5 post.

4 *Lucas v James* (1849) 7 Hare 410 at 419. See, however, *Francis v Grover* (1845) 5 Hare 39; *Re Adams Goods* (1872) LR 2 P & D 367 (these two cases refer to pencil writing in a will).

5 See *Goodman v J Eban Ltd* [1954] 1 QB 550, [1954] 1 All ER 763, CA; *LCC v Agricultural Food Products Ltd* [1955] 2 QB 218, [1955] 2 All ER 229, CA.

6 *Goodman v J Eban Ltd* [1954] 1 QB 550 at 559, [1954] 1 All ER 763 at 767, CA, per Lord Evershed MR; *McDonald v John Twiname Ltd* [1953] 2 QB 304, [1953] 2 All ER 589, CA; cf *Firstpost Homes Ltd v Johnson* [1995] 4 All ER 355, [1995] 1 WLR 1567, CA.

7 See the Law of Property Act 1925 s 73 (repealed); and the text and note 1 supra.

8 It is clear that sealing may be accomplished by another in the presence and by the direction of the executing party: *Ball v Dunsterville* (1791) 4 Term Rep 313; *R v Longnor Inhabitants* (1833) 4 B & Ad 647. See also para 27 ante; and AGENCY vol 2(1) (Reissue) para 30. In *LCC v Agricultural Food Products Ltd* [1955] 2 QB 218 at 223–225, [1955] 2 All ER 229 at 232–233, CA, it was held that in general a person's signature, where required to a document, could be written by someone else authorised by him to do so, but that a statute may require personal signature and so not allow of such a signature by an agent or proxy. As to cases where a statutory requirement of signature permits signature by an agent see para 157 note 4 post. The Law of Property Act 1925 s 73 (repealed), read with the Powers of Attorney Act 1971 s 7(1) (as originally enacted) in relation to instruments delivered as deeds before 31 July 1990 (ie the date on which the Law of Property (Miscellaneous Provisions) Act 1989 came into force), authorised signature to be effected by an attorney under a power of attorney, but might.be argued to be so worded as to have required personal signature in other cases. In *Powell v London and Provincial Bank* [1893] 2 Ch 555 at 563, CA, per Bowen LJ, and at 556 per Kay LJ, it was said that a power of attorney is required to enable someone else to do any part of the execution which makes a deed. The cases on sealing cited above can be reconciled with this principle by regarding them as cases where the directions given by the executing parties to the agent acting in their presence amounted to acknowledgements by them of the seal or seals in question as their own. If signing could validly be effected in a similar manner, the statutory requirement of signature would scarcely add any compulsory element of personal authentication to the formalities of execution of a deed beyond those inherent in sealing and delivery. Moreover, the special statutory provision allowing a power of attorney to be signed and sealed by direction and in the presence of the donor of the power (see the Powers of Attorney Act 1971 s 1(1) (as amended); para 47 post; and AGENCY vol 2(1) (Reissue) para 31) appears to have been enacted on the footing that personal signature would otherwise be required and that it remains necessary for any other deed.

31.   Delivery of deed.   In order to be effective a deed must be delivered as the act and deed of the party expressed to be bound by it, as well as sealed[1]. No special form or observance is necessary for the delivery of a deed, and it may be made in words or by conduct[2]. The traditional form of delivering a deed by words was for the executing party to say, while putting his finger on the seal, 'I deliver this as my act and deed'[3]. It was not necessary, however, to follow this form of execution[4], and it fell into disuse; nor is it necessary that the deed should actually be delivered over into the possession or custody either of the person intended to take the benefit of the deed, or to a third person to the use of the party taking the benefit of the deed[5]; though if the party to be bound so hands over the deed, that is sufficient delivery without any words[6].

What is essential to delivery of the document as a deed is that the party whose deed the document is expressed to be (having first sealed it[7]) must by words or conduct expressly or impliedly acknowledge his intention to be immediately and unconditionally bound by the provisions contained in it[8]. Thus where a deed has been executed by an attorney in excess of his power, a subsequent acknowledgment by the principal, whether oral or in writing, that the deed expresses his intentions amounts to a delivery or redelivery of the deed[9].

If the sealing of a deed is proved, its delivery as a deed may be inferred, provided there is nothing to show that it was only delivered as an escrow[10].

1   See para 1 ante; YB 9 Hen 6, 37, pl 12; 1 Plowd 308; *Goddard's Case* (1584) 2 Co Rep 4b; *Clayton's Case* (1585) 5 Co Rep 1a; *Chamberlain v Stanton* (1588) Cro Eliz 122; Co Litt 35b, 171b; *Willis v Jermin* (1590) Cro Eliz 167 per Gawdy J; Termes de la Ley, sv Fait; Shep Touch 50, 57; 2 Bl Com (14th Edn) 306; 3 Preston's Abstracts of Title (2nd Edn) 63; *Styles v Wardle* (1825) 4 B & C 908 at 911 per Bayley J; *Doe d Garnons v Knight* (1826) 5 B & C 671; *Hall v Bainbridge* (1848) 12 QB 699 at 710; *Tupper v Foulkes* (1861) 9 CBNS 797 at 803; *Xenos v Wickham* (1863) 14 CBNS 435 at 473, Ex Ch (revsd (1866) LR 2 HL 296 at 309, 312, 320, 323); *Mowatt v Castle Steel and Iron Works Co* (1886) 34 ChD 58, CA.
    As to delivery in relation to instruments delivered as deeds after 31 July 1990 see para 34 post.
2   *Chamberlain v Stanton* (1588) Cro Eliz 122; *Thoroughgood's Case* (1612) 9 Co Rep 136b; Co Litt 36a, 49b; Shep Touch 57–58; *Hall v Bainbridge* (1848) 12 QB 699; *Tupper v Foulkes* (1861) 9 CBNS 797; *Xenos v Wickham* (1867) LR 2 HL 296.
3   3 Preston's Abstracts of Title (2nd Edn) 63; *Xenos v Wickham* (1866) LR 2 HL 296; Williams and Eastwood on Real Property 430; and see paras 1, 27 ante.
4   *Tupper v Foulkes* (1861) 9 CBNS 797; *Keith v Pratt* (1862) 10 WR 296.
5   *Doe d Garnons v Knight* (1826) 5 B & C 671 at 689–692; *Exton v Scott* (1833) 6 Sim 31; *Grugeon v Gerrard* (1840) 4 Y & C Ex 119 at 130; *Fletcher v Fletcher* (1844) 4 Hare 67 at 79; *Evans v Grey* (1882) 9 LR Ir 539; *Xenos v Wickham* (1866) LR 2 HL 296; *Macedo v Stroud* [1922] 2 AC 330, PC. See also *Alford v Lee* (1587) Cro Eliz 54 (concerning a bond). As to concealment of execution see para 65 post.
6   *Butler and Baker's Case* (1591) 3 Co Rep 25a at 26b, Ex Ch; *Thoroughgood's Case* (1612) 9 Co Rep 136b; *Doe d Garnons v Knight* (1826) 5 B & C 671; *Xenos v Wickham* (1866) LR 2 HL 296 at 312 per Blackburn J.
7   See para 27 ante.
8   See *Vincent v Premo Enterprises (Voucher Sales) Ltd* [1969] 2 QB 609, [1969] 2 All ER 941, CA; and the cases cited in notes 2, 4–5 supra. See also *Taw v Bury* (1558) 2 Dyer 167a; *Parker v Tenant* (1560) 2 Dyer 192b; *Shelton's Case* (1582) Cro Eliz 7; *Hollingworth v Ascue* (1594) Cro Eliz 355 at 356; *R v Longnor Inhabitants* (1833) 4 B & Ad 647 at 649; *London Freehold and Leasehold Property Co v Baron Suffield* [1897] 2 Ch 608, CA. Compare the cases relating to delivery as an escrow, cited in para 37 notes 6–7 post. Acknowledgment of a deed already sealed, but which is in another room, may be sufficient: *Powell v London and Provincial Bank* [1893] 2 Ch 555 at 566, CA.
9   *Re Seymour, Fielding v Seymour* [1913] 1 Ch 475, CA.
10 *Hall v Bainbridge* (1848) 12 QB 699; *Keith v Pratt* (1862) 10 WR 296; *Xenos v Wickham* (1866) LR 2 HL 296. Consider also the cases cited in note 8 supra; and para 37 notes 6–7 post.
    It appears that if several deeds conveying the same land to different persons were delivered to them simultaneously, that might formerly have operated to vest the land in them as tenants in common in equal shares: *Hopgood v Ernest* (1865) 3 De GJ & Sm 116 per Wood V-C. The decision in that case was reversed in the Court of Appeal on other grounds, assuming the vice-chancellor's decision on the above point to be correct, but without expressing any opinion on it. But now that tenancy in common at law is abolished (see the Law of Property Act 1925 s 1(6); and REAL PROPERTY vol 39(2) (Reissue) para 55), that result could not follow. An alternative might be for the grantees to take as joint tenants on trust for the persons interested in the land under s 34(2) (as amended) (see REAL PROPERTY vol 39(2) (Reissue) para 211), but it is doubtful if the case could be brought within the terms of that provision.

(ii)   Formalities of Execution under the Law of Property (Miscellaneous Provisions) Act 1989

32.   Sealing.   Any rule of law which requires a seal for the valid execution of an instrument as a deed by an individual[1] was abolished by the Law of Property (Miscellaneous Provisions) Act 1989 in relation to instruments delivered as deeds on or after 31 July 1990[2]. The reference to the execution of a deed by an individual does not, however, include execution by a corporation sole[3] or a body corporate, to which the common law rule continues to apply[4]. Where an instrument under seal that constitutes a deed is required for the purposes of an Act passed before 31 July 1990, the provisions relating to deeds and their execution[5] have effect as to signing, sealing or delivery of an instrument by an individual[6] in place of any provision of that Act as to signing, sealing or delivery[7].

1   See para 27 ante.

2 Law of Property (Miscellaneous Provisions) Act 1989 s 1(1)(b). See para 7 ante. As to the application of s 1(1)(b) see s 1(9); and para 7 text and note 4 ante. As to the common law position in relation to instruments delivered as deeds before 31 July 1990 see para 27 ante.

3 Ibid s 1(10).

4 As to the execution of deeds by or on behalf of corporations see the Law of Property Act 1925 s 74 (as amended); and paras 40–42 post. As to execution by a corporation aggregate see also s 74A (as added); and CORPORATIONS vol 9(2) (2006 Reissue) para 1265 ante.

5 Ie the Law of Property (Miscellaneous Provisions) Act 1989 s 1 (as amended) (see paras 7–8 ante): see s 1(7).

6 The reference to signing, sealing or delivery by an individual does not include signing, sealing or delivery by a corporation sole: ibid s 1(10).

7 Ibid s 1(7). As to the application of s 1(7) see s 1(9); and para 7 text and note 4 ante.

33. Signing. An instrument is validly executed as a deed by an individual[1] if, and only if[2]: (1) it is signed[3] by him in the presence of a witness who attests the signature[4], or at his direction and in his presence and the presence of two witnesses who each attests the signature[5]; and (2) it is delivered as a deed[6].

This provision does not apply in relation to instruments delivered as deeds before 31 July 1990[7].

1 This does not include execution by a corporation sole: see the Law of Property (Miscellaneous Provisions) Act 1989 s 1(10); and para 32 text to note 3 ante. As to corporations sole see CORPORATIONS.

2 Ibid s 1(3). The requirement of signing contained in the Law of Property Act 1925 s 73(1) (repealed) has been replaced by the Law of Property (Miscellaneous Provisions) Act 1989 s 1(3) (as amended). See also note 6 infra.

3 For the meaning of 'sign' see para 8 note 2 ante. It has been held, in relation to ibid s 2 (as amended) (see SALE OF LAND vol 42 (Reissue) paras 29–40), that a name printed or typed at the head of a document does not constitute a signature: *Firstpost Homes Ltd v Johnson* [1995] 4 All ER 355, [1995] 1 WLR 1567, CA. It is thought that this is equally true in relation to the Law of Property (Miscellaneous Provisions) Act 1989 s 1 (as amended): see paras 7–8, 32 ante.

4 Ibid s 1(3)(a)(i). Cf *Shah v Shah* [2001] EWCA Civ 527, [2002] QB 35, [2001] 3 All ER 138; and para 36 post. See note 6 infra.

5 Law of Property (Miscellaneous Provisions) Act 1989 s 1(3)(a)(ii). See note 6 infra.

6 Ibid s 1(3)(b) (amended by the Regulatory Reform (Execution of Deeds and Documents) Order 2005, SI 2005/1906, art 10(2), Sch 2).

   The Law of Property (Miscellaneous Provisions) Act 1989 s 1(3) (as amended) applies in the case of an instrument executed by an individual in the name or on behalf of another person whether or not that person is also an individual: s 1(4A) (added by the Regulatory Reform (Execution of Deeds and Documents) Order 2005, SI 2005/1906, art 7(4)). As to the application of the Law of Property (Miscellaneous Provisions) Act 1989 s 1(3) (as amended) see also s 1(9); and para 7 text and note 4 ante.

7 Ie the date on which ibid s 1 came into force: see s 1(11); and para 7 text and note 4 ante.

34. Delivery. Any rule of law which required authority by one person to another to deliver an instrument as a deed on his behalf to be given by deed[1] was abolished by the Law of Property (Miscellaneous Provisions) Act 1989[2].

Where a solicitor[3], duly certificated notary public[4] or licensed conveyancer[5], or an agent or employee of a solicitor, duly certificated notary public or licensed conveyancer, in the course of or in connection with a transaction, purports to deliver an instrument as a deed on behalf of a party to the instrument, it is conclusively presumed in favour of a purchaser[6] that he is authorised so to deliver the instrument[7].

This provision does not apply in relation to instruments delivered as deeds before 31 July 1990[8].

1 See paras 29, 31 ante.

2 Law of Property (Miscellaneous Provisions) Act 1989 s 1(1)(c). See para 7 ante.

3 For the meaning of 'solicitor' see SOLICITORS vol 44(1) (Reissue) para 5.

4   For these purposes, 'duly certified notary public' has the same meaning as it has in the Solicitors Act 1974
     s 87 (see NOTARIES vol 33 (Reissue) para 701): Law of Property (Miscellaneous Provisions) Act 1989
     s 1(6) (definition amended by the Regulatory Reform (Execution of Deeds and Documents)
     Order 2005, SI 2005/1906, arts 9, 10(2), Sch 2).
5   For the meaning of 'licensed conveyancer' see the Administration of Justice Act 1985 s 11(2); and
     SOLICITORS vol 44(1) (Reissue) para 550.
6   'Purchaser' means a purchaser in good faith for valuable consideration and includes a lessee, mortgagee or
     other person who for valuable consideration acquires an interest in property except that in the Law of
     Property Act 1925 Pt I (ss 1–40) (as amended) and elsewhere where so expressly provided 'purchaser'
     only means a person who acquires an interest in or charge on property for money or money's worth; and
     in reference to a legal estate includes a chargee by way of legal mortgage; and where the context so
     requires 'purchaser' includes an intending purchaser; 'purchase' has a meaning corresponding with that of
     'purchaser'; and 'valuable consideration' includes marriage, and formation of a civil partnership, but does
     not include a nominal consideration in money: s 205(1)(xxi) (amended by the Civil Partnership Act 2004
     s 261(1), Sch 27 para 7); definition applied by the Law of Property (Miscellaneous Provisions) Act 1989
     s 1(6) (amended by the Regulatory Reform (Execution of Deeds and Documents) Order 2005,
     SI 2005/1906, art 10(1), Sch 1 paras 13, 15).
7   Law of Property (Miscellaneous Provisions) Act 1989 s 1(5) (amended by the Regulatory Reform
     (Execution of Deeds and Documents) Order 2005, SI 2005/1906, arts 9, 10(2), Sch 2).
8   Ie the date on which the Law of Property (Miscellaneous Provisions) Act 1989 s 1 (as originally enacted)
     came into force: see s 1(11); and para 7 text and note 4 ante.

(iii) Reading over and Attestation

35.   Reading over.   Before a party executes a deed, it should be read by him, or
correctly read over or fully and accurately explained to him, and he cannot be required
to execute it until this has been done[1]. If he is content to execute it without so
informing himself of its contents, it will in general be binding on him, even though its
contents are materially different from what he supposed, and even though he is himself
illiterate or blind[2]. However, if the party executing the deed acts with reasonable care
and yet is mistaken or misled (in particular, if he is illiterate or blind and it is falsely read
over or falsely explained to him), and in consequence there is a radical or fundamental
distinction between what it is and what he believed it to be, not attributable to a mistake
of law as to its effect, the plea of non est factum will be available and the deed will be
void[3]. Even though all the requirements for avoiding the deed on this ground may not
be fulfilled, a misled executing party may be able to treat the deed as voidable under the
law relating to misrepresentation, or it may be void as executed under a mutual mistake
of fact[4].

1   *Thoroughgood's Case* (1584) 2 Co Rep 9a at 9b.
2   *Thoroughgood's Case* (1584) 2 Co Rep 9a at 9b; *Maunxel's Case* (1583) Moore KB 182 at 184. See
     paras 69–71 post.
3   *Saunders v Anglia Building Society* [1971] AC 1004, [1970] 3 All ER 961, HL. See paras 69, 71 post.
4   See para 67 et seq post. As to misrepresentation generally see MISREPRESENTATION AND FRAUD. As to
     mistake generally see MISTAKE.

36.   Attestation.   Unless required by statute, it is not necessary to the validity of a
deed that its execution be attested by any witness[1]. It is and has long been the practice to
execute deeds in the presence of a witness or witnesses, and to indorse on or subscribe
to the deed a statement that it has been so signed, sealed, and delivered, and for the
attesting witness to sign his name to the statement and to add his address and
description[2]. Attestation is now required for the valid execution of a deed by an
individual in instruments delivered on or after 31 July 1990[3]. In other cases attestation
by one or more witnesses is required by statute[4]; but, even where a statute requires
attestation, an unattested instrument may be valid between the parties to it though
ineffective against other persons[5].

A witness must actually be present at and witness the execution of the deed; attestation upon the acknowledgment of the party is not sufficient[6].

It appears that there is now no reason under the general law why husbands and wives should not witness one another's signature[7].

1   *Goddard's Case* (1584) 2 Co Rep 4b at 5a; *Garrett v Lister* (1661) 1 Lev 25; *Keith v Pratt* (1862) 10 WR 296; 2 Bl Com (14th Edn) 307–308, 378; 3 Preston's Abstracts of Title (2nd Edn) 71; Williams and Eastwood on Real Property 476. As to the necessity for attestation in certain cases see para 44 et seq post.

2   Co Litt 6a; 2 Bl Com (14th Edn) 307–308; 3 Preston's Abstracts of Title (2nd Edn) 71; Sugden, Treatise on Powers (8th Edn) 234–235; Williams and Eastwood on Real Property 476. It is always advisable that the execution of deeds should be attested according to the usual practice in order to preserve evidence of their execution (3 Preston's Abstracts of Title (2nd Edn) 71; Williams and Eastwood on Real Property 476). An instrument to the validity of which attestation is requisite may, instead of being proved by an attesting witness, be proved in the manner in which it might be proved if no attesting witness were alive: Evidence Act 1938 s 3; and see EVIDENCE vol 17(1) (Reissue) para 803. The witness must be some person who is not a party to the deed; and a statement of its execution in his presence should be written on the deed and signed by him: *Coles v Trecothick* (1804) 9 Ves 234 at 251; *Freshfield v Reed* (1842) 9 M & W 404; *Wickham v Marquis of Bath* (1865) LR 1 Eq 17 at 24–25; *Seal v Claridge* (1881) 7 QBD 516 at 519, CA.

3   Ie the date on which the Law of Property (Miscellaneous Provisions) Act 1989 came into force: see s 1(3), (11) (s 1(3) as amended); and paras 6, 7, 33 ante. This does not include execution by a corporation sole: see s 1(10); and para 32 text to note 3 ante. As to the application of s 1(3) (as amended) see s 1(9); and para 7 text and note 4 ante.

4   See para 44 et seq post.

5   *National and Grindlays Bank Ltd v Dharamshi Vallabhji* [1967] 1 AC 207, [1966] 2 All ER 626, PC.

6   *Shamu Patter v Abdul Kadir Ravathan* (1912) 28 TLR 583, PC. A signature on a transfer of shares cannot, however, be challenged because the witness did not see the deceased transferor sign or hear her acknowledge her signature if such omission was merely an irregularity which the company involved might waive: *Smellie's Trustees v Smellie* 1953 SLT (Notes) 22. Cf *Shah v Shah* [2001] EWCA Civ 527, [2002] QB 35, [2001] 3 All ER 138 (deed valid although signed in absence of witness); and see also ESTOPPEL vol 16(2) (Reissue) paras 960, 1011.

7   See the letters in The Times dated 24 December 1952 and 5 January 1953 from Lord Asquith of Bishopstone and Professor AL Goodhart QC. Documents so witnessed are accepted for registration at HM Land Registry: see the letter in The Times dated 7 January 1953; and 97 Sol Jo 36.

(iv) Delivery as an Escrow

37. Escrow. An intended deed may, after due completion of the formalities required for execution as a deed[1], be delivered as an escrow (or scroll), that is as a simple writing which is not to become the deed of the party expressed to be bound by it until some condition has been performed[2]. Thus a conveyance on sale or a mortgage or a surrender discharging a mortgage may be delivered in escrow so as to be binding on the grantor only if the grantee pays the consideration money or only if the grantee executes a counterpart[3] or some other deed or document as agreed with the grantor[4].

Like delivery as a deed[5], delivery as an escrow may be made in words or by conduct although it need not be made in any special form or accompanied with any particular words, the essential thing in the case of delivery as an escrow being that the party should expressly or impliedly declare his intention to be bound by the provisions inscribed, not immediately, but only in the case of and upon performance of some condition then[6] stated or ascertained[7]. In the absence of direct evidence whether or not a deed of conveyance was delivered as an escrow, the fact that only part of the purchase price has been paid at the time of delivery justifies the inference that the deed was delivered as an escrow pending payment of the balance[8].

1   As to instruments delivered on or after 31 July 1990 see paras 7, 32–34 ante; and as to instruments delivered before that date see paras 27–31 ante.

2   YB 9 Hen 6, 37, pl 12; Keil (1507) 88 pl 2; Perkins, Profitable Book s 138; *Perryman's Case* (1599) 5 Co Rep 84a, b; Shep Touch 58–59; 2 Bl Com (14th Edn) 307; *Xenos v Wickham* (1866) LR 2 HL 296 at 323;

Venetian Glass Gallery Ltd v Next Properties Ltd [1989] 2 EGLR 42, [1989] 30 EG 92; and see the cases cited in note 7 infra. In the absence of express provision, the condition on which an escrow is delivered will depend on inference from the circumstances: *Kingston v Ambrian Investment Co Ltd* [1975] 1 All ER 120, [1975] 1 WLR 161, CA. The condition must not be such that the deed will only become operative on the death of the grantor; in that case it is a testamentary document and cannot take effect as an escrow: *Governors and Guardians of Foundling Hospital v Crane* [1911] 2 KB 367, CA. As to the time limit for the performance of the condition see *Glessing v Green* [1975] 2 All ER 696, [1975] 1 WLR 863, CA. See also *Terrapin International Ltd v IRC* [1976] 2 All ER 461, [1976] 1 WLR 665.

3   As to counterpart deeds see para 4 ante.

4   See cases cited in note 7 infra.

5   See paras 31, 34 ante.

6   See *Doe d Lloyd v Bennett* (1837) 8 C & P 124.

7   *Johnson v Baker* (1821) 4 B & Ald 440; *Murray v Earl of Stair* (1823) 2 B & C 82; *Bowker v Burdekin* (1843) 11 M & W 128 at 147; *Nash v Flyn* (1844) 1 Jo & Lat 162; *Gudgen v Besset* (1856) 6 E & B 986; *Phillips v Edwards* (1864) 33 Beav 440 at 445–447; *Walker v Ware etc Rly Co* (1865) 35 Beav 52 at 58; *Xenos v Wickham* (1866) LR 2 HL 296 at 311, 323; *Watkins v Nash* (1875) LR 20 Eq 262; *Coupe v Collyer* (1890) 62 LT 927; *Lloyds Bank Ltd v Bullock* [1896] 2 Ch 192 at 194; *London Freehold and Leasehold Property Co v Baron Suffield* [1897] 2 Ch 608 at 620–622, CA; *D'Silva v Lister House Development Ltd* [1971] Ch 17, [1970] 1 All ER 858; *Bentray Investments Ltd v Venner Time Switches Ltd* [1985] 1 EGLR 39, 274 Estates Gazette 43. As to the distinction between an agreement which merely suspends and an agreement which destroys the document see *Hitchings and Coulthurst Co v Northern Leather Co of America and Doushkess* [1914] 3 KB 907 at 909. See para 196 note 3 post. See also *Longman v Viscount Chelsea* (1989) 58 P & CR 189, [1989] 2 EGLR 242, CA.

8   *Thompson v McCullough* [1947] KB 447 at 453–454, [1947] 1 All ER 265 at 267–268, CA, per Morton LJ. See also *AIB Group (UK) plc v Hennelly Properties Ltd* [2000] EGCS 63, [2000] All ER (D) 685 (mortgage unlikely to be delivered as escrow).

38.   To whom escrow may be delivered.   For a deed to be executed as an escrow, it need not be actually delivered into the custody of a stranger[1] to the deed to keep until performance of the condition, and then to deliver it over to the party intended to benefit[2]. A deed may well be delivered as an escrow though the party to be bound retains it in his own possession[3]. It may be delivered as an escrow to an attorney acting for all parties thereto[4], and even to the solicitor acting for the party to benefit under the deed, provided it is handed to him as the agent of all parties for the purpose of such delivery[5].

Where several persons are parties to a deed as grantees and one of them is also the solicitor of the other grantees and of the grantor, and the deed is delivered to him, evidence is admissible to prove that it was delivered to him, not as a grantee, but in his capacity of solicitor to the grantor and as an escrow to take effect only upon the performance of some condition[6].

However, a deed cannot be delivered as an escrow to the party intended to benefit under it, as such, because delivery of the document to him is necessarily its delivery as a deed[7], and any stipulation then made by word of mouth and purporting to suspend the operation of the deed until the performance of some condition would be repugnant to such delivery, and the party delivering the deed would be estopped from averring such a stipulation in contradiction of the deed[8]. Previously in equity, if an instrument was delivered as a deed (or a fortiori as an escrow) to a party to benefit under it, upon an agreement that it should not take effect until the performance of some condition, he would be restrained from enforcing it at law until the condition was fulfilled, and if the condition was not observed, the other party would be relieved from liability under the deed[9].

1   Ie a person who is not a party to the deed or the agent of some party to the deed.

2   In this respect the cases cited in notes 3–6 infra have modified the rule laid down in the earlier authorities cited in note 8 infra.

3   *Gudgen v Besset* (1856) 6 E & B 986; *Phillips v Edwards* (1864) 33 Beav 440; *Walker v Ware etc Rly Co* (1865) 35 Beav 52; *Xenos v Wickham* (1866) LR 2 HL 296.

4   *Millership v Brookes* (1860) 5 H & N 797. But if a deed is delivered to the agent of the grantor to hold until further instructions this does not constitute delivery as an escrow: *Governors and Guardians of Foundling Hospital v Crane* [1911] 2 KB 367, CA; and see *Windsor Refrigerator Co Ltd v Branch Nominees Ltd* [1961] Ch 88, [1960] 2 All ER 568 (revsd on another point [1961] Ch 375, [1961] 1 All ER 277, CA); *Beesly v Hallwood Estates Ltd* [1961] Ch 105, [1961] 1 All ER 90, CA.

5   *Watkins v Nash* (1875) LR 20 Eq 262.

6   *London Freehold and Leasehold Property Co v Baron Suffield* [1897] 2 Ch 608, CA, in which case, however, the court found the fact to be that the deed had been delivered unconditionally.

7   See paras 31, 34 ante.

8   *Whyddon's Case* (1596) Cro Eliz 520; *Williams v Green* (1602) Cro Eliz 884; *Thoroughgood's Case* (1612) 9 Co Rep 136b at 137b; *Holford v Parker* (1618) Hob 246; *Bushell v Pasmore* (1704) 6 Mod Rep 217 at 218; *Coare v Giblett* (1803) 4 East 85 at 95 per Lord Ellenborough CJ; Co Litt 36a, n (3); Shep Touch 58–59; 3 Preston's Abstracts of Title (2nd Edn) 64; *Pym v Campbell* (1856) 6 E & B 370 at 374 per Crompton J; and see *Countess of Rutland's Case* (1604) 5 Co Rep 25b at 26a, b. It is considered that the dictum of Hall V-C in *Watkins v Nash* (1875) LR 20 Eq 262 at 266 (which was made with reference to the delivery of a deed by one grantor, not to the grantee, but to a co-grantor to keep as an escrow), and the decision in *London Freehold and Leasehold Property Co v Baron Suffield* [1897] 2 Ch 608, CA, do not go so far as to overrule the authorities here stated. There are, however, some old cases to the contrary effect: see *Wilcock v Hewson* (1597) Moore KB 696; *Hawksland v Gatchel* (1601) Cro Eliz 835; *Anon* (1603) Noy 50.

9   *Sir George Maxwell's Case* (1720) 1 Eq Cas Abr 20 pl 5; *Walker v Walker* (1740) 2 Atk 98 at 99; *England v Codrington* (1758) 1 Eden 169; *Underhill v Horwood* (1804) 10 Ves 209 at 255; *Carew's Case (No 2)* (1855) 7 De GM & G 43 at 52; *Evans v Bremridge* (1855) 2 K & J 174 (on appeal (1856) 8 De GM & G 100); *Griffin v Clowes* (1855) 20 Beav 61 at 65–66; *Douglas v Culverwell* (1862) 4 De GF & J 20 at 26; *Re Smith, Fleming & Co, ex p Harding* (1879) 12 ChD 557 at 564, CA; *Bond v Walford* (1886) 32 ChD 238. The statement by Sir George Jessel MR in *Luke v South Kensington Hotel Co* (1879) 11 ChD 121 at 125, CA, that 'it is well settled that if two persons execute a deed on the faith that a third will do so, and that is known to the other parties to the deed, the deed does not bind in equity if the third refuses to execute', is expressed too widely: *Lady Naas v Westminster Bank Ltd* [1940] AC 366 at 374–377, [1940] 1 All ER 485 at 488–490, HL, per Viscount Maugham LC; and see further para 62 post. Since the Judicature Acts, this equity may be asserted in all courts: see now the Supreme Court Act 1981 (prospectively renamed the Senior Courts Act 1981) s 49; and COURTS vol 10 (Reissue) para 639. It may not be asserted where the deed operates as a conveyance of property, against persons who have, since the delivery of the deed, acquired some legal or equitable estate or interest under it as purchasers for value without notice of the agreement suspending or modifying the operation of the deed: see *Phillips v Phillips* (1862) 4 De GF & J 208 at 218; *Hunter v Walters* (1871) 7 Ch App 75; *National Provincial Bank of England v Jackson* (1886) 33 ChD 1 at 13, CA; *Lloyds Bank Ltd v Bullock* [1896] 2 Ch 192 at 197; and EQUITY. If the deed was a bond or a covenant, the assignees of the benefit thereof would take subject to all equities existing between the parties thereto: *Athenaeum Life Assurance Society v Pooley* (1858) 3 De G & J 294; *Graham v Johnson* (1869) LR 8 Eq 36 at 43; *Re Palmer's Decoration and Furnishing Co* [1904] 2 Ch 743; and see the Law of Property Act 1925 s 136(1). It is submitted that if a person were to deliver a deed, which purported on the face of it to be an immediate and absolute conveyance of property, to the grantee thereunder as an escrow upon an oral agreement that it should not take effect as a deed until the payment by the grantee of some purchase or mortgage money or the performance of some other condition, he would be estopped, not only by his deed, but also by his conduct in entrusting to the grantee the custody of such a title deed (being the sign of ownership), from averring the oral agreement under which the deed was to take effect as an escrow only: see *Rice v Rice* (1854) 2 Drew 73 at 83–85; *King v Smith* [1900] 2 Ch 425; *Rimmer v Webster* [1902] 2 Ch 163 at 173–174.

39.   Effect of delivery as escrow.   When an instrument[1] is delivered as an escrow it cannot take effect as a deed pending the performance of the condition subject to which it was so delivered, and if that condition is not performed the writing remains entirely inoperative[2]. If, therefore, an instrument delivered as an escrow comes, pending the performance of the condition and without the consent, fault, or negligence of the party who so delivered it, into the possession of the party intended to benefit, it has no effect either in his hands or in the hands of any purchaser from him; for until fulfilment of the condition it is not, and never has been, the deed of the party who so delivered it[3]. When an instrument has been delivered as an escrow to await the performance of some condition, it takes effect as a deed (without any further delivery) immediately the condition is fulfilled, and the rule is that its delivery as a deed will relate back to the time of its delivery as an escrow but only for such purposes as are necessary to give efficacy to the transaction[4]; thus the relation back does not have the effect of validating a notice to quit given at a time when the fee simple was not vested in the person giving it[5]. Where time is of the essence and the time for fulfilling the condition of the escrow has elapsed the doctrine of relation back cannot be applied[6].

It follows that, for a deed delivered as an escrow to take effect, the party making it must be fully capable, at the time of its delivery as an escrow, of doing the act evidenced by the deed. Thus if a minor were to deliver a deed of mortgage as an escrow to take effect on his attaining full age, such delivery would be altogether void[7]. On the other hand, where the party to be bound by the deed has in all respects full capacity to do the act to be evidenced by it at the time of its delivery as an escrow, it will be no ground for avoiding the deed if he dies or ceases to be sui juris before the condition is performed[8].

When a deed has been delivered to a third party as an escrow, possession of the deed by the grantee is prima facie evidence of the performance of the condition[9].

1   In the case of an instrument delivered before 31 July 1990 (i e the date on which the Law of Property (Miscellaneous Provisions) Act 1989 s 1 (as originally enacted) came into force: see s 1(11); and para 7 text and note 4 ante), the instrument is a sealed writing: see paras 27, 32 ante. As to other cases where a seal is still required see para 32 ante.

2   *Gudgen v Besset* (1856) 6 E & B 986; *Phillips v Edwards* (1864) 33 Beav 440 at 446–447; *Walker v Ware etc Rly Co* (1865) 35 Beav 52 at 58; *Lloyds Bank Ltd v Bullock* [1896] 2 Ch 192; *Wm Cory & Son Ltd v IRC* [1964] 3 All ER 66 at 74, [1964] 1 WLR 1332 at 1346, CA, per Diplock LJ; *Vincent v Premo Enterprises (Voucher Sales) Ltd* [1969] 2 QB 609, [1969] 2 All ER 941, CA; *Terrapin International Ltd v IRC* [1976] 2 All ER 461, [1976] 1 WLR 665; *Davy Offshore Ltd v Emerald Field Contracting Ltd* [1992] 2 Lloyd's Rep 142, CA; and see the other cases cited in para 37 note 7 ante.

3   YB 9 Hen 6, 37, p 12; Perkins, Profitable Book ss 138, 142; Vin Abr, Faits (M), pl 1, 4; *Lloyds Bank Ltd v Bullock* [1896] 2 Ch 192. Ex hypothesi no case of estoppel by conduct has arisen: see para 38 notes 8–9 ante.

4   *Jennings v Bragg* (1595) Cro Eliz 447; *Butler and Baker's Case* (1591) 3 Co Rep 25a at 35b, 36a, Ex Ch; *Perryman's Case* (1599) 5 Co Rep 84a at 84b; Shep Touch 59–60; *Graham v Graham* (1791) 1 Ves 272 at 274–275 per Lord Ellenborough CJ; *Coare v Giblett* (1803) 4 East 85 at 94–95; *Copeland v Stephens* (1818) 1 B & Ald 593 at 606; *Edmunds v Edmunds* [1904] P 362 at 374; *Security Trust Co v Royal Bank of Canada* [1976] AC 503, [1976] 1 All ER 381, PC; *Alan Estates Ltd v WG Stores Ltd* [1982] Ch 511, [1981] 3 All ER 481, CA (lease and counterpart delivered in escrow: lease took effect from date of delivery).

5   *Thompson v McCullough* [1947] KB 447 at 455, [1947] 1 All ER 265 at 268, CA, per Morton LJ; *Terrapin International Ltd v IRC* [1976] 2 All ER 461, [1976] 1 WLR 665 (when a document originally delivered as an escrow became effective as a deed, stamp duty was held to attach at the rate applicable at that date).

6   *Security Trust Co v Royal Bank of Canada* [1976] AC 503, [1976] 1 All ER 381, PC.

7   *Thurstan v Nottingham Permanent Benefit Building Society* [1902] 1 Ch 1, CA (affd sub nom *Nottingham Permanent Benefit Building Society v Thurstan* [1903] AC 6, HL); and see the cases cited in note 4 supra. It is thought that for this reason (amongst others) a person cannot make a conveyance valid at law of some legal estate or property in lands or goods, which he has not, but merely expects to have, by delivering a deed, purporting to convey such estate or interest, as an escrow to take effect when such estate or interest is assured to him (see 2 Williams on Vendor and Purchaser (3rd Edn) 1184–1185 n (d)). In *Jennings v Bragg* (1595) Cro Eliz 447, what was in effect decided was that the first delivery of the deed to the stranger off the land was null and void, and was not a good delivery as an escrow, and that the only valid delivery of the deed was that made on the land. It seems obvious that the court put a benevolent construction on the facts (compare the rule laid down in *Butler and Baker's Case* (1591) 3 Co Rep 25a, Ex Ch; *Xenos v Wickham* (1866) LR 2 HL 296 at 312 per Blackburn J). But it is equally obvious that the court put this construction on the facts to avoid the effect of the rule of law (which was thus impliedly acknowledged) that a person who has no estate in land (such as a disseisee) cannot make a valid lease thereof except by estoppel: see *Stephens v Eliot* (1596) Cro Eliz 484. In 2 Preston's Abstracts of Title (2nd Edn) 400, it is stated that a lease made by a disseisee of land by way of escrow to take effect as a deed when he should have re-entered would be inoperative in its inception and could not be made good by a second delivery after he had re-entered, and cites *Jennings v Bragg* (1595) Cro Eliz 447, in support of that proposition; but that case does not support the latter part of the statement in Preston, for the gist of the case is that the first delivery was altogether null and void, and therefore the second might take effect as the only delivery. It is submitted that this is so, notwithstanding the statement in Co Litt 48b.

8   See the cases cited in note 4 supra; *Frosett v Walshe* (1616) J Bridg 49 at 51; *Newton v Metropolitan Rly Co* (1861) 10 WR 102.
9   *Hare v Horton* (1833) 5 B & Ad 715 at 728–730.

(v)   Execution in the case of Corporations, Companies etc

40.   Sealing and delivery.   At common law the deed of a corporation must necessarily be under seal and requires to be delivered as well as sealed[1]. There is a rebuttable presumption that sealing by a corporation imports delivery[2].

It is now provided, however, that a company formed and registered under the Companies Act 1985[3] does not need to have a common seal[4].

1   See paras 27, 32 ante; and CORPORATIONS vol 9(2) (2006 Reissue) para 1261 et seq.
2   *Longman v Viscount Chelsea* (1989) 58 P & CR 189, [1989] 2 EGLR 242, CA.
3   For the meanings of 'company' and 'existing company' see COMPANIES vol 7(1) (2004 Reissue) para 221.
4   See the Companies Act 1985 s 36A (as added and amended); para 41 post; and COMPANIES vol 7(1) (2004 Reissue) para 458. As to companies incorporated outside Great Britain see the Foreign Companies (Execution of Documents) Regulations 1994, SI 1994/950 (as amended); and COMPANIES vol 7(2) (2004 Reissue) para 458.

41.   Mode of execution.   Where by the constitution of a corporation any special mode of execution of its deeds is prescribed, or any particular formality is required to be observed in affixing the corporate seal, every deed of the corporation, in order to be completely binding, must be executed in the manner or with every formality so prescribed[1]. In practice most cases are covered by particular statutory provisions.

In relation to a company formed and registered under the Companies Act 1985[2], it is provided that a document is executed by a company by the affixing of its common seal[3]. A company is no longer required to have a common seal[4], however, and there are further provisions which apply whether it does or not[5]. Thus a document signed by a director and the secretary of a company, or by two directors of a company, and expressed (in whatever form of words) to be executed by the company has the same effect as if executed under the common seal of the company[6]. A document is validly executed by a company as a deed[7] if and only if it is duly executed by the company, and it is delivered as a deed[8]. Finally, in favour of a purchaser[9] a document is deemed to have been duly executed by a company if it purports to be signed by a director and the secretary of the company, or by two directors of the company[10]. So also the deeds of building societies incorporated under the Building Societies Act 1986[11], and of societies incorporated under the Industrial and Provident Societies Act 1965[12], must be executed as required by the rules of the society.

In favour of a purchaser[13], however, a deed executed after 1925 is deemed to have been duly executed by a corporation aggregate if a seal purporting to be the seal of the corporation has been affixed to it, in the presence of and attested by persons purporting to hold certain specified offices[14]; and, even apart from this provision, where a document appears on its face to comply with any formalities required by the constitution of the corporation, the corporation may be estopped from setting up any irregularity which is a matter of its internal management, though it will not be estopped in circumstances amounting to forgery[15].

1   See *Clarke v Imperial Gas Light and Coke Co* (1832) 4 B & Ad 315 at 324–326; and CORPORATIONS vol 9(2) (2006 Reissue) para 1261 et seq.
2   For the meanings of 'company' and 'existing company' see COMPANIES vol 7(1) (2004 Reissue) para 221.
3   See the Companies Act 1985 s 36A(2) (as added); and COMPANIES vol 7(1) (2004 Reissue) para 458. As to companies regulated by the Companies Clauses Acts see COMPANIES vol 7(2) (2004 Reissue) para 1357 et seq.
4   See the Companies Act 1985 s 36A(3) (as added); and COMPANIES vol 7(1) (2004 Reissue) para 458.

5   See ibid s 36A(3)–(8) (as added and amended); and COMPANIES vol 7(1) (2004 Reissue) para 458. See note 6 infra.

6   See ibid s 36A(4) (as added); and COMPANIES vol 7(1) (2004 Reissue) para 458. See also s 36A(4A) (as added), which covers the situation where the document is to be signed by a person as a director or the secretary of more than one company, in which case the document is not taken to be duly signed by that person for the purposes of s 36A(4) (as added) unless the person signs it separately in each capacity; and see COMPANIES.

   Section 36A (as added and amended) applies in the case of a document which is (or purports to be) executed by a company in the name or on behalf of another person whether or not that person is also a company; and for the purposes of s 36A (as added and amended), a document is (or purports to be) signed, in the case of a director or the secretary of a company which is not an individual, if it is (or purports to be) signed by an individual authorised by the director or secretary to sign on its behalf: see s 36A(7), (8) (as added); and COMPANIES.

7   Ie for the purposes of the Law of Property (Miscellaneous Provisions) Act 1989 s 1(2)(b) (as amended): see para 8 ante.

8   See the Companies Act 1985 s 36AA(1) (as added); and COMPANIES. A document is presumed to be delivered for these purposes upon its being executed, unless a contrary intention is proved: see s 36AA(2) (as added); and COMPANIES.

9   For the meaning of 'purchaser' see COMPANIES vol 7(1) (2004 Reissue) para 458.

10 See the Companies Act 1985 s 36A(6) (as added and amended); and COMPANIES. See note 6 supra.

11 See the Building Societies Act 1986 s 5 (as amended); and BUILDING SOCIETIES vol 4(3) (Reissue) paras 410, 426.

12 See the Industrial and Provident Societies Act 1965 s 1 (as amended), s 3, Sch 1 para 13 (as substituted); and INDUSTRIAL AND PROVIDENT SOCIETIES vol 24 (Reissue) paras 8, 20, 22, 32.

13 For the meaning of 'purchaser' see para 34 note 6 ante.

14 See the Law of Property Act 1925 s 74(1), (1A), (1B), (5) (s 74(1) as substituted, s 74(1A), (1B) as added); and CORPORATIONS vol 9(2) (2006 Reissue) paras 1264–1265, 1267. Sealing in accordance with s 74(1) (as substituted) does not constitute delivery: *Bolton Metropolitan Borough Council v Torkington* [2003] EWCA Civ 1634, [2004] Ch 66, [2004] 4 All ER 238.

15 See COMPANIES vol 7(1) (2004 Reissue) para 467. The validity of an act done by a company cannot be called into question on the ground of lack of capacity by reason of anything in the company's memorandum: see the Companies Act 1985 s 35(1) (as substituted); and COMPANIES vol 7(1) (2004 Reissue) para 430. In favour of a person dealing with a company in good faith, the power of the board of directors to bind the company, or authorise others to do so, is deemed to be free of any limitation under the companies constitution: see s 35A(1) (as added); and COMPANIES vol 7(1) (2004 Reissue) para 431. A party to a transaction with a company is not bound to inquire as to whether it is permitted by the company's memorandum or as to any limitation on the powers of the board of directors to bind the company or authorise others to do so: see s 35B (as added); and COMPANIES vol 7(1) (2004 Reissue) para 432. See further COMPANIES vol 7(1) (2004 Reissue) paras 416, 431–432.

42.   Seal of company etc.   A company which has a common seal[1] is required to have its name engraved in legible characters on the seal[2], and if an officer of the company or a person on its behalf uses or authorises the use of any seal purporting to be the seal of the company on which its name is not engraved he is liable to a fine[3].

A society registered under the Industrial and Provident Societies Act 1965[4] must have its registered name engraved in legible characters on relevant notices and publications[5], and the society's rules must make provision for the custody and use of the society's seal if it has one[6].

In the absence of any special or legally binding regulations, the seal of a corporation is not required to bear any special emblems[7].

1   A company is no longer required to have a common seal: see the Companies Act 1985 s 36A(3) (as added); para 41 ante; and COMPANIES vol 7(1) (2004 Reissue) para 458.

2   If it fails to comply with this requirement it is liable to a fine: see ibid s 350(1) (as substituted); and COMPANIES vol 7(1) (2004 Reissue) paras 293, 462.

3   Ibid s 350(2). See further COMPANIES vol 7(1) (2004 Reissue) paras 293, 462.

4   See the Industrial and Provident Societies Act 1965 s 2 (as amended); and INDUSTRIAL AND PROVIDENT SOCIETIES vol 24 (Reissue) paras 19–21.

5   See ibid s 5(6) (as amended); and INDUSTRIAL AND PROVIDENT SOCIETIES vol 24 (Reissue) para 45.

6 See ibid s 1(1), Sch 1 para 13 (as substituted); and INDUSTRIAL AND PROVIDENT SOCIETIES vol 24 (Reissue) paras 32, 48.
7 See further CORPORATIONS vol 9(2) (2006 Reissue) para 1122 et seq.

43. Trustees of a charity incorporated as a body corporate. Where the trustees[1] of a charity[2] have become an incorporated body[3] there are special provisions as respects the execution of documents[4] by the incorporated body[5]. If an incorporated body has a common seal, a document may be executed by the body by the affixing of its common seal[6]. Whether or not it has a common seal, a document may be executed by an incorporated body[7]: (1) by being signed by a majority of the trustees of the relevant charity[8] and expressed (in whatever form of words) to be executed by the body[9]; or (2) by being executed in pursuance of an authority duly given by the trustees of the relevant charity[10]. It is provided that such trustees may, subject to the trusts[11] of the charity, confer on any two or more of its number a general authority, or an authority limited in such manner as the trustees think fit, to execute in the name and on behalf of the body documents for giving effect to transactions to which the body is a party[12]. It is further provided that in any such authority to execute a document in the name and on behalf of an incorporated body there is, unless the contrary intention appears, implied authority also to execute it for the body in the name and on behalf of the official custodian for charities[13] or of any other person, in any case in which the trustees could do so[14]. A document duly executed by an incorporated body which makes it clear on its face that it is intended by the person or persons making it to be a deed has effect, upon delivery, as a deed; and it is presumed, unless a contrary intention is proved, to be delivered upon its being so executed[15].

1 For the meaning of 'trustees' see CHARITIES vol 5(2) (2001 Reissue) para 236.
2 For the meaning of 'charity' see CHARITIES vol 5(2) (2001 Reissue) paras 1–2.
3 For the meaning of 'incorporated body' see CHARITIES vol 5(2) (2001 Reissue) para 236.
4 For the meaning of 'document' see CHARITIES vol 5(2) (Reissue) para 447.
5 See the Charities Act 1993 s 60(1). See further CHARITIES vol 5(2) (Reissue) para 234.
6 Ibid s 60(2).
7 Ibid s 60(3).
8 For the meaning of 'the relevant charity' see CHARITIES vol 5(2) (2001 Reissue) para 236.
9 Charities Act 1993 s 60(3)(a).
10 Ibid s 60(3)(b).
11 For the meaning of 'trusts' see CHARITIES vol 5(2) (2001 Reissue) para 210.
12 Charities Act 1993 s 60(4). Such an authority: (1) suffices for any document if it is given in writing or by resolution of a meeting of the trustees of the relevant charity, notwithstanding the want of any formality that would be required in giving an authority apart from s 60(4) (s 60(5)(a)); (2) may be given so as to make the powers conferred exercisable by any of the trustees, or may be restricted to named persons or in any other way (s 60(5)(b)); (3) subject to any such restriction, and until it is revoked, notwithstanding any change in the trustees of the relevant charity, has effect as a continuing authority given by the trustees from time to time of the charity and exercisable by such trustees (s 60(5)(c)).
13 Ibid s 97(1).
14 Ibid s 60(6).
15 Ibid s 60(7). In favour of a purchaser a document is deemed to have been duly executed by such a body if it purports to be signed: (1) by a majority of the trustees of the relevant charity; or (2) by such of the trustees of the relevant charity as are authorised by the trustees of that charity to execute it in the name and on behalf of the body, and, where the document makes it clear on its face that it is intended by the person or persons making it to be a deed, it is deemed to have been delivered upon its being executed: s 60(8). For this purpose, 'purchaser' means a purchaser in good faith for valuable consideration and includes a lessee, mortgagee or other person who for valuable consideration acquires an interest in property: s 60(8).

(vi) Execution in Various Special Cases

44. Dispositions of registered land. Dispositions of registered land must be effected in the prescribed manner[1]. This is dealt with elsewhere in this work[2].

1   See LAND REGISTRATION vol 26 (2004 Reissue) para 914 et seq.
2   See LAND REGISTRATION vol 26 (2004 Reissue) para 906 et seq. As to electronic dispositions and electronic conveyancing generally see para 9 ante; and LAND REGISTRATION vol 26 (2004 Reissue) para 1049 et seq.

45.   Deeds executed by clerics.   A deed of relinquishment of holy orders made in pursuance of the Clerical Disabilities Act 1870 must be executed in the presence of a witness[1].

1   See the Clerical Disabilities Act 1870 s 3(1), Sch 2; and ECCLESIASTICAL LAW vol 14 para 686 et seq.

46.   Mentally disordered persons.   Where a person suffering from mental disorder[1] has a legal estate[2] in land[3] (whether settled[4] or not) vested in him, either solely or jointly with any other person or persons, his receiver[5] or any person authorised must, under an order of the authority having jurisdiction under Part VII of the Mental Health Act 1983[6], or of the court[7], or under any statutory power, make or concur in making all requisite dispositions for conveying[8] or creating a legal estate in his name and on his behalf[9]. Even where this statutory provision does not apply, it is usual for the person authorised to execute a deed on behalf of a mentally disordered person to do so in the latter's name; and a deed settled by the court will normally be drawn for execution in this manner[10].

If land subject to a trust of land[11] is vested, either solely or jointly with any other person or persons, in a person who is incapable, by reason of mental disorder, of exercising his functions as trustee, a new trustee must be appointed in the place of that person, or he must be otherwise discharged from the trust, before the legal estate is dealt with by the trustees[12].

1   For these purposes, 'mental disorder' has the meaning assigned to it by the Mental Health Act 1983 s 1 (see MENTAL HEALTH vol 30 (Reissue) para 402): Law of Property Act 1925 s 205(1)(xiii) (definition substituted by the Mental Health Act 1959 s 149(1), Sch 7 Pt I; and amended by the Mental Health Act 1983 s 148, Sch 4 para 5(b)). This provision is repealed by the Mental Capacity Act 2005 s 67(1), (2), Sch 6 para 4(1), (3), Sch 7 as from a day to be appointed under s 68(1). At the date at which this volume states the law no such day had been appointed.
2   'Legal estates' means the estates, interests and charges, in or over land (subsisting or created at law) which are by the Law of Property Act 1925 authorised to subsist or to be created as legal estates: s 205(1)(x).
3   As to the meaning of 'land' see para 14 note 2 ante.
4   For these purposes, 'settled land' has the same meaning as in the Settled Land Act 1925 ss 2, 117(1)(xxiv) (see SETTLEMENTS vol 42 (Reissue) para 680): Law of Property Act 1925 s 205(1)(xxvi).
5   'Receiver', in relation to a person suffering from mental disorder, means a receiver appointed for that person under the Mental Health Act 1959 Pt VIII (ss 100–121) (repealed) or the Mental Health Act 1983 Pt VII (ss 93–113) (as amended; prospectively amended and repealed) (see MENTAL HEALTH vol 30 (Reissue) para 674 et seq): Law of Property Act 1925 s 205(1)(xiii) (definition as substituted and amended; prospectively repealed (see note 1 supra)).
6   Ie the Mental Health Act 1983 Pt VII (as amended; prospectively repealed): see MENTAL HEALTH vol 30 (Reissue) para 674 et seq.
7   Unless the contrary intention appears, 'the court' means the High Court or the county court, where those courts respectively have jurisdiction: Law of Property Act 1925 s 203(3) (amended by the Courts Act 1971 s 56(4), Sch 11 Pt II).
8   For the meaning of 'conveying' see para 14 note 1 ante.
9   Law of Property Act 1925 s 22(1) (s 22 substituted by the Mental Health Act 1959 s 149(1), Sch 7 Pt I; and the Law of Property Act 1925 s 22(1) amended by the Mental Health Act 1983 s 148, Sch 4 para 5(a)). As from a day to be appointed the Law of Property Act s 22(1) is further amended so as to refer to a person lacking capacity under the Mental Capacity Act 2005 (instead of a person suffering from a mental disorder) and so as to refer to a deputy appointed by the Court of Protection (instead of a receiver): Law of Property Act 1925 s 22(1) (as so substituted and amended; prospectively amended by the Mental Capacity Act 2005 Sch 6 para 4(1), (2)(a), (b)). At the date at which this volume states the law no such day had been appointed.

As to the powers of a judge or court in respect of the property of a mentally disordered person see the Trustee Act 1925 ss 44(ii)(a), 51(1)(ii)(a), 54 (as substituted and amended; prospectively amended); the Mental Health Act 1983 ss 95–100 (as amended; prospectively repealed); and MENTAL HEALTH vol 30 (Reissue) para 681 et seq.

10 Execution by the person authorised in his own name may be sufficient where it is apparent from the deed that he was acting on behalf of the mentally disordered individual as the person so authorised: *Lawrie v Lees* (1881) 7 App Cas 19, HL. See also para 30 note 8 ante.

11 'Trust of land' means any trust of property which consists of or includes land: Trusts of Land and Appointment of Trustees Act 1996 s 1(1)(a); Interpretation Act 1978 s 5, Sch 1 (definition added by the Trusts of Land and Appointment of Trustees Act 1996 s 25(1), Sch 3 para 16); and see REAL PROPERTY vol 39(2) (Reissue) para 66. As to the creation of trusts of land see SETTLEMENTS vol 42 (Reissue) paras 897–899. As to trustees of land see SETTLEMENTS vol 42 (Reissue) para 900 et seq.

12 Law of Property Act 1925 s 22(2) (as substituted (see note 9 supra); and amended by the Trusts of Land and Appointment of Trustees Act 1996 Sch 3 para 4). As from a day to be appointed the Law of Property Act s 22(2) is further amended so as to refer to a person lacking capacity under the Mental Capacity Act 2005 (instead of a person suffering from a mental disorder): Law of Property Act 1925 s 22(2) (as so substituted and amended; prospectively amended by the Mental Capacity Act 2005 Sch 6 para 4(1), (2)(b)). At the date at which this volume states the law no such day had been appointed.

47. Deeds executed by attorney. Where a deed is to be executed by attorney, the instrument creating a power of attorney must be executed as a deed by the donor of the power[1]. The deed executed by attorney must be so expressed that it is apparent that the act evidenced by it is the act of the principal and not of the attorney, and if the deed is between parties the principal, and not the attorney, must be named as a party thereto, in order that the principal may enjoy the advantages given by law only to parties to the deed[2].

A company may, by writing under its common seal[3], empower any person, either generally or in respect of any specified matters, as its attorney, to execute deeds on its behalf in any place elsewhere than in the United Kingdom[4]. A deed executed by such an attorney on behalf of the company has the same effect as if it were executed under the company's common seal[5].

1 Powers of Attorney Act 1971 s 1(1) (amended by the Law of Property (Miscellaneous Provisions) Act 1989 s 1, Sch 1 para 6(a)). As to the formalities of execution see paras 31–33 ante. See also para 13 note 1 ante; and AGENCY vol 2(1) (Reissue) paras 30–32, 44–47, 58, 72.

2 *Frontin v Small* (1726) 2 Ld Raym 1418; *White v Cuyler* (1795) 6 Term Rep 176; *Berkeley v Hardy* (1826) 5 B & C 355. See also para 61 post.

3 Note that companies are no longer required to have a common seal: see the Companies Act 1985 s 36A (as added and amended); para 41 ante; and COMPANIES vol 7(1) (2004 Reissue) para 458.

4 Ibid s 38(1) (amended by the Companies Act 1989 s 130(7), Sch 17 para 1; and the Law Reform (Miscellaneous Provisions) (Scotland) Act 1990 s 74, Sch 8 Pt II para 33, Sch 9). See further COMPANIES vol 7(1) (2004 Reissue) para 444. 'United Kingdom' means Great Britain and Northern Ireland: Interpretation Act 1978 s 5, Sch 1. 'Great Britain' means England, Scotland and Wales: Union with Scotland Act 1706, preamble art I; Interpretation Act 1978 s 22(1), Sch 2 para 5(a). Neither the Channel Islands nor the Isle of Man are within the United Kingdom. See further CONSTITUTIONAL LAW AND HUMAN RIGHTS vol 8(2) (Reissue) para 3.

5 Companies Act 1985 s 38(2) (substituted by the Companies Act 1989 Sch 17 para 1(3)).

48. Deeds exercising powers. Where any instrument conferring a power of appointment provides that the power is exercisable by deed to be executed with some further or other formality than is required by the general law applicable to the execution of deeds[1], a deed exercising the power may be executed either: (1) in strict compliance with all the requirements of the instrument creating the power; or (2) in the presence of and attested by two or more witnesses in the manner in which deeds are ordinarily executed and attested[2]. To operate as a valid execution of the power it must be executed with all the formalities prescribed by one of these two methods of execution[3]. The second method of execution only excuses exact compliance with the terms of the instrument creating the power in so far as that instrument requires the actual execution and attestation of the deed or instrument exercising the power to be accomplished in some other or more formal manner than is required by the general law. It does not operate to defeat any direction in that instrument that the consent of any particular person is to be necessary to a valid execution, or that, in order to give validity to any appointment under the power, any act is to be performed having no relation to the mode of executing and attesting the instrument exercising the power[4].

Thus a deed exercising a power of appointment which was made exercisable by deed to be executed in the presence of and attested by a witness must be so executed and attested, or it will not be a good execution of the power[5]. A deed exercising a power of appointment which was made exercisable by deed to be executed in the presence of and attested by two or by any greater number of witnesses must be executed in the presence of and attested by two witnesses at least, or it will not be a good execution of the power[6].

1   See para 27 et seq ante.
2   See the Law of Property Act 1925 s 159(1), (3), (4); *Holmes v Coghill* (1802) 7 Ves 499 at 506 per Grant MR; *Hawkins v Kemp* (1803) 3 East 410 at 439–440; *Reid v Shergold* (1805) 10 Ves 370 at 380; Sugden, Treatise on Powers (8th Edn) 206 et seq; Williams and Eastwood on Real Property 240. The defective execution of a power will, however, be aided, even against purchasers from those claiming in default of appointment, if the intended appointee was a purchaser from or the wife or a child or a creditor of the person, who purported to exercise the power, or if the appointment purported to be made was for a charitable purpose: Sugden, Treatise on Powers (8th Edn) 533–536, 542. This relief is only granted to remove defects regarded as not being of the essence of the power, such as the absence of a seal or of a witness or witnesses: Sugden, Treatise on Powers (8th Edn) 548 et seq.
3   See note 2 supra.
4   See the Law of Property Act 1925 s 159(2). As to the execution of powers see generally POWERS.
5   *Earl of Mountague v Earl of Bath* (1693) (as reported in 3 Cas in Ch 55 at 65, 70, 72, 86); *Hawkins v Kemp* (1803) 3 East 410; Sugden, Treatise on Powers (8th Edn) 206–207. The deed may be attested by more witnesses than one: Sugden, Treatise on Powers (8th Edn) 247.
6   See notes 2–5 supra.

49.   Attestation clauses of deeds exercising powers.   Where deeds exercising powers are required by the instrument creating the power to be executed with some additional formality to be performed in the presence of a witness or witnesses, and are also required to be attested, then, if it is proposed to execute the deed in strict compliance with the terms of the power[1], the attestation clause should expressly state that every formality required to be performed has been duly gone through in the presence of the proper number of witnesses[2]. In such a case, if the instrument creating the power requires two or more formalities to be observed, and the attestation clause states only that one of them has been complied with, the power is not well executed[3]. If, however, the circumstances are such that it must necessarily be inferred that all the formalities were duly gone through the power is sufficiently executed[4], although the attestation clause expressly mentions the observance of some or one only of the formalities required[5]; and if the terms of the attestation are general, purporting simply to bear witness to the execution of the deed without specifying in particular the manner of such execution or stating any of the formalities then observed, it will be implied that the required formalities were duly performed and the power will be well executed[6]. Where such a deed is executed in reliance on the provisions of the Law of Property Act 1925[7], the power is well executed if the attestation clause is expressed in the form in which deeds are ordinarily attested.

1   See para 48 ante.
2   See Sugden, Treatise on Powers (8th Edn) 234–238, 245, 247; and note 3 infra.
3   *Wright v Wakeford* (1811) 17 Ves 454; *Doe d Mansfield v Peach* (1814) 2 M & S 576; *Wright v Barlow* (1815) 3 M & S 512; *Vincent v Bishop of Sodor and Man* (1851) 4 De G & Sm 294 at 307; and see Sugden, Treatise on Powers (8th Edn) 234–238, 244–247.

4   *Re Wrey's Trust* (1850) 17 Sim 201; *Vincent v Bishop of Sodor and Man* (1851) 4 De G & Sm 294; *Smith v Adkins* (1872) LR 14 Eq 402; and see Farwell, Treatise on Powers (3rd Edn) 156.
5   See note 4 supra.
6   *Burdett v Spilsbury* (1843) 10 Cl & Fin 340, HL; and see Sugden, Treatise on Powers (8th Edn) 240–241; Farwell, Treatise on Powers (3rd Edn) 157.
7   See the Law of Property Act 1925 s 159; and para 48 ante.

50.   Conflict of laws.   The rules of private international law which govern capacity to contract[1] and the essential validity, interpretation and effect of contracts[2] are dealt with elsewhere in this work. The form, as distinct from the essentials, of a contract must in general comply either with the law of the place where the contract is made or the proper law of the contract, that is the law which the parties intended or are presumed to have intended to govern it[3].

In the case of assignment of property, certain special rules apply. For example, in the case of an immovable[4], both the capacity of the parties and the form required for a valid assignment depend upon the law of the country where the immovable is situated[5].

1   See CONFLICT OF LAWS vol 8(3) (Reissue) para 364.
2   See CONFLICT OF LAWS vol 8(3) (Reissue) para 362 et seq. See also para 166 text and note 10 post.
3   See CONFLICT OF LAWS vol 8(3) (Reissue) para 363.
4   For the distinction between immovables and movables see CONFLICT OF LAWS vol 8(3) (Reissue) para 380.
5   See CONFLICT OF LAWS vol 8(3) (Reissue) para 399. As to the law determining the validity of an assignment of movables see CONFLICT OF LAWS vol 8(3) (Reissue) para 405 et seq. For the application of the principle of renvoi or reference back in determining what system of law is to be applied see CONFLICT OF LAWS vol 8(3) (Reissue) para 6 et seq.

51.   Appointment and discharge of charity trustees by a meeting.   Deeds evidencing the appointment, or discharge, of a charity trustee by a meeting and made under the provisions of the Charities Act 1993 relating to the vesting of the charity property on such an appointment or discharge[1] must be executed either at the meeting by the person presiding or in some other manner directed by the meeting and must be attested by two persons present at the meeting[2].

1   See the Charities Act 1993 s 83; and CHARITIES vol 5(2) (2001 Reissue) paras 257–258.
2   See ibid s 83(1), (2); and CHARITIES vol 5(2) (2001 Reissue) paras 257–258.

(vii)   Conditional and Partial Execution and Re-execution

52.   Conditional execution.   Where a deed is executed by some party or parties to the deed on the condition that the other party or parties to it, or some or one of such parties, shall execute it, it is in fact delivered as an escrow and will not take effect completely as a deed until the condition has been performed[1].

1   See paras 37–39 ante, 62 post.

53.   Partial execution.   It is impossible in law to execute a deed as to part only of its provisions; and the attempted execution of a deed with some proviso purporting to qualify the liability of the executing party, or to express his dissent to be bound by some provision contained in it, is not a perfect execution of the deed, and, as against any person entitled to have the deed executed by the party attempting a partial execution, it is no execution of the deed[1]. It appears, however, that, as against the party so executing a deed, a partial execution may be effectual, and the qualifying proviso may be rejected as repugnant and void[2]. If the party attempting a partial execution accepts some benefit under or otherwise confirms the deed, he is bound by its provisions as if he had completely executed it[3].

1   *Wilkinson v Anglo-Californian Gold Mining Co* (1852) 18 QB 728; *Exchange Bank of Yarmouth v Blethen* (1885) 10 App Cas 293 at 298, PC; *Ellesmere Brewery Co v Cooper* [1896] 1 QB 75.

2   *Exchange Bank of Yarmouth v Blethen* (1885) 10 App Cas 293 at 299, PC; and see para 64 note 1 post.

3   *Exchange Bank of Yarmouth v Blethen* (1885) 10 App Cas 293 at 299, PC; and see para 64 note 1 post. As to the effect of execution by one or some parties only see para 62 post.

54. Re-execution of void deed. When a deed has once been effectually executed, either as a deed or as an escrow, and remains unaltered or uncancelled, it cannot well be executed again, and any attempted re-execution of the deed will have no effect. If, however, delivery of a deed is attempted, in such a way that the attempt is altogether null and void, the deed may again be delivered in circumstances sufficient to make it the effective instrument of the delivering party; and in such a case the later delivery, coupled with the acknowledgment of the sealing implied in such delivery where sealing is required[1], completes the only true and valid execution of the deed[2].

A writing which has been delivered with a blank so left in a material part of it that it is altogether void for uncertainty may be re-executed after the blank has been filled up, and will then for the first time become the deed of the party so executing it[3].

1   This provision does not apply in the case of an instrument delivered before 31 July 1990 (i e the date on which the Law of Property (Miscellaneous Provisions) Act 1989 s 1 (as originally enacted) came into force), where a seal was required: see s 1(11); and para 7 ante. As to the application of s 1(1)(b) see s 1(9), (10); and paras 7, 27, 32 ante. See also paras 27, 32, 40 et seq ante.

2   Shep Touch 60; Perkins, Laws of England s 154; *Jennings v Bragg* (1595) Cro Eliz 447; 3 Co Rep 35b, 36a (see para 39 note 7 ante); Vin Abr, Faits (N); *Goodright d Carter v Straphan* (1774) 1 Cowp 201 at 203–204; *Cole v Parkin* (1810) 12 East 471; *Tupper v Foulkes* (1861) 9 CBNS 797; and see *Powell v London and Provincial Bank* [1893] 2 Ch 555 at 561–563, CA; *Re Seymour, Fielding v Seymour* [1913] 1 Ch 475, CA.

3   See paras 28 note 3 ante, 56 post.

55. Re-execution of voidable deed. If a deed, when delivered, was voidable but not altogether void, as for duress or by reason of the minority of the party making it[1], its redelivery alone after the constraint has ceased or he has attained full age will be inoperative[2]. If he should then re-execute, that is, re-sign as well as redeliver the deed, it would be binding[3]; and redelivery after attaining full capacity might, perhaps, be so made as to import an acknowledgment of his signature and the seal already attached as his seal, which would be equivalent to re-execution[4].

1   See para 67 et seq post.

2   See paras 39 note 7, 54 note 2 ante, 68 post.

3   In the case of redelivery before 31 July 1990 (i e the date on which the Law of Property (Miscellaneous Provisions) Act 1989 s 1 (as originally enacted) came into force: see para 7 note 4 ante), resealing was required in every case. It is now unnecessary because, subject to certain exceptions, a seal is no longer required for execution of a deed by an individual: see s 1(1)(b), (9), (10); and paras 7, 27, 32 ante. As to the application of s 1(1)(b) see s 1(9); and paras 7, 27, 32 ante. Strictly speaking, resealing imports taking the old seal off and putting a new one on: see Bro Abr, Faits, 78, 98; Vin Abr, Faits (N), pl 11. This need not actually be done; a new acknowledgment by the party of the existing seal as his will be sufficient (see note 4 infra).

4   See para 27 ante. It is a question of fact, to be determined from the circumstances of the case, whether resealing where required (see para 27 et seq ante) should be implied from the redelivery: see paras 27 text and note 2, 31 note 8 ante.

56. Re-execution after alteration or cancellation. If a deed originally well executed is afterwards made void by reason of some alteration or erasure being made in a material part of it or of its having been cancelled[1], it may be re-executed by conduct amounting to a redelivery, and will then be binding on the party whose deed it is in its altered state[2].

Where a deed which was valid when originally executed has afterwards been cancelled or altered in a material part and is subsequently re-executed, it must be restamped[3].

1   See paras 76–77 post.
2   *Hudson v Revett* (1829) 5 Bing 368 at 371; *Hibblewhite v M'Morine* (1840) 6 M & W 200 at 215; *Tupper v Foulkes* (1861) 9 CBNS 797 at 807–808 per Williams J.
3   See para 84 note 3 post.

(4) EFFECT OF A DEED

57.   General effect. By executing a deed in accordance with all the requirements for such execution[1], the party whose act and deed it is becomes, as a general rule, conclusively bound by what he is stated in the deed to be effecting, undertaking or permitting[2]. He is, in general, so bound even though another party has not executed the deed[3], or he has himself executed it in a false name[4]. He is, as a rule, estopped from averring and proving by extrinsic evidence that the contents of the deed did not in truth express his intentions or did not correctly express them, or that there are reasons why he should not be obliged to give effect to the deed. This is equally the case whether the deed is expressed to operate as a conveyance of property or as a contract or otherwise[5]. In a claim founded on the deed, an executing party is also in general estopped from denying the truth of a precise and unambiguous representation of fact contained in the deed where the representation is material to the transaction effected by the deed and appears clearly enough to have been made or adopted by him with a view to the other party's relying on it[6]. However, to all these general principles there are exceptions, cases where the deed may be a nullity or may be avoided or corrected[7].

1   See paras 1 et seq, 27–34 ante. An instrument intended in a certain event to be an effective deed may be delivered as an escrow, i e so as to become the delivering party's act and deed only if the event occurs: see paras 37–39 ante.
2   See para 65 post.
3   *Lady Naas v Westminster Bank Ltd* [1940] AC 366 at 374–375, [1940] 1 All ER 485 at 489, HL. As to the effect of non-execution by a party see further para 62 post.
4   See para 69 note 1 post. A person whose execution of a deed has been forged is also estopped from denying that he is bound by the deed if, after becoming aware of the forgery, he delays in informing the person ostensibly entitled to the benefit of the deed, so causing detriment to the latter: *Fung Kai Sun v Chan Fui Hing* [1951] AC 489 at 503, 506, PC; and see para 72 post. As to estoppel generally see ESTOPPEL.
5   Littleton's Tenures ss 58, 693; Co Litt 45a, 47b, 352a, 363b; 1 Plowd 308–309; *Whelpdale's Case* (1604) 5 Co Rep 119a; *Style v Hearing* (1605) Cro Jac 73; 2 Bl Com (14th Edn) 295, 446; *Xenos v Wickham* (1866) LR 2 HL 296.
6   See *Greer v Kettle* [1938] AC 156 at 166–167, [1937] 4 All ER 396 at 401, HL; and ESTOPPEL vol 16(2) (Reissue) para 1014 et seq.
7   See paras 60, 62–63, 67, 88 post.

58.   Rule against derogation. It is a well-established rule that a grantor cannot be permitted to derogate from his grant[1]. Though usually applied to sales and leases of land, it is of wider application[2]. The principle is that if one man agrees to confer a particular benefit on another, he must not do anything which substantially deprives the other of the enjoyment of that benefit, because that would be to take away with one hand what is given with the other[3]. Hence, on the grant by the owner of a tenement of part of that tenement there will pass to the grantee all those easements which are necessary in order that the property may be enjoyed reasonably for the purpose for which it was granted[4]. On the other hand, if the grantor intends to reserve any right over the tenement granted, he must do so expressly, though to this rule there are certain exceptions, notably in cases of what are known as ways of necessity[5].

Where a man sells or lets land for a particular purpose, it is always subject to the proviso that it is lawful to carry on that purpose. Neither the buyer nor the tenant can pray in aid the doctrine of derogation from grant so as to enable him to do something which is unlawful[6].

1   *Wheeldon v Burrows* (1879) 12 ChD 31 at 49, CA, per Thesiger LJ; *Browne v Flower* [1911] 1 Ch 219; *Re Webb's Lease, Sandom v Webb* [1951] Ch 808 at 831–832, [1951] 2 All ER 131 at 146, CA, per Morris LJ; *Cable v Bryant* [1908] 1 Ch 259 (right to access of air); *Woodhouse & Co Ltd v Kirkland (Derby) Ltd* [1970] 2 All ER 587 at 593, [1970] 1 WLR 1185 at 1194; *Lyme Valley Squash Club Ltd v Newcastle under Lyme Borough Council* [1985] 2 All ER 405. For examples of the application of the doctrine in relation to the implied grant or reservation of easements see EASEMENTS AND PROFITS À PRENDRE. In relation to tenancies see *Aldin v Latimer Clark, Muirhead & Co* [1894] 2 Ch 437; *Chartered Trust plc v Davies* (1997) 76 P & CR 396, [1997] 2 EGLR 83, CA; and see LANDLORD AND TENANT vol 27(1) (2006 Reissue) paras 276, 520. A quasi easement must also be continuous and apparent: see *Wheeler v JJ Saunders Ltd* [1996] Ch 19, [1995] 2 All ER 697, CA; and EASEMENTS AND PROFITS À PRENDRE vol 16(2) (Reissue) para 71.

2   See *Molton Builders Ltd v City of Westminster London Borough Council* (1975) 30 P & CR 182, 119 Sol Jo 627, CA; *British Leyland Motor Corpn Ltd v Armstrong Patents Co Ltd* [1986] AC 577, [1986] 1 All ER 850, HL (car owners have an inherent right to repair their cars in the most economical way possible and for that purpose to have access to a free market in spare parts for the car; the plaintiffs were not entitled to derogate from that right).

3   See *Harmer v Jumbil (Nigeria) Tin Areas Ltd* [1921] 1 Ch 200 at 225–226, CA, per Younger LJ, who said it was 'a principle which merely embodies in a legal maxim a rule of common honesty'; cited in *Molton Builders Ltd v City of Westminster London Borough Council* (1975) 30 P & CR 182 at 186, CA, per Denning MR. See also *Johnston & Sons Ltd v Holland* [1988] 1 EGLR 264, CA.

4   *Wheeldon v Burrows* (1879) 12 ChD 31 at 49, CA; *North Eastern Rly Co v Elliott* (1860) 1 John & H 145 at 153 (on appeal sub nom *Elliot v North Eastern Rly Co* (1863) 10 HL Cas 333).

5   *Wheeldon v Burrows* (1879) 12 ChD 31 at 49, CA; *Re Webb's Lease, Sandom v Webb* [1951] Ch 808 at 831, [1951] 2 All ER 131 at 146, CA, per Morris LJ; and, in relation to reservation of sporting rights, cf *Mason v Clarke* [1954] 1 QB 460 at 467–468, [1954] 1 All ER 189 at 192, CA, per Denning LJ (revsd, but not on this point, [1955] AC 778, [1955] 1 All ER 914, HL).

6   *Molton Builders Ltd v City of Westminster London Borough Council* (1975) 30 P & CR 182, 119 Sol Jo 627, CA.

59.   Consideration not necessary.   Where a deed makes a gratuitous assurance of any property or right, or expresses in the form of a contractual obligation a gratuitous promise, it is not open to the party who has so made the assurance or promise to aver or prove that he received nothing by way of consideration in return therefor, and the deed will take effect according to its terms notwithstanding the absence of any consideration[1]. Further, a volunteer who is a party to a deed and a direct covenantee is entitled to claim damages for breach of the covenant[2]. This is especially noteworthy in the cases of gratuitous promises expressed in a deed, because a promise made by deed is a specialty[3] and promises which are not specialties are not enforceable unless given for valuable consideration[4]. A party to a deed who has agreed to modify his strict legal rights under it in favour of another party may not be able, if the agreement was intended to be legally binding and has been acted on, to enforce thereafter the strict legal rights in a manner inconsistent with the agreement of modification, even though the agreement was made without consideration and is not in the form of a deed[5].

In one instance a promise made by deed is not enforceable unless it is made for valuable consideration, and that is where the act or forbearance agreed to be done or observed is in restraint of trade, but is not such as would of itself invalidate the promise for being in unreasonable restraint of trade[6].

A gratuitous promise made by deed is not equally enforceable with a promise made for valuable consideration, for the courts will not order the specific performance of a voluntary covenant[7].

Formerly, when land was conveyed without consideration and without a declaration as to whose use the conveyance was made, the use, and with it the estates conveyed, at once resulted to the transferor. Since the repeal of the Statute of Uses[8] in 1925[9], however, a voluntary conveyance of freehold land expressed to be made simply to the grantee operates according to its tenor to vest the property in the grantee in fee simple for his own benefit[10].

1   Fitzherbert's Grand Abridgment, Barre 37; *Anon* (1563) Moore KB 47, pl 142; *Pinnel's Case* (1602) 5 Co Rep 117a at 117b; Co Litt 212b; *Spicer v Hayward* (1700) Prec Ch 114; *Shubrick v Salmond* (1765) 3 Burr 1637 at 1639; *Bunn v Guy* (1803) 4 East 190 at 200; *Irons v Smallpiece* (1819) 2 B & Ald 551 at 554 per Abbott CJ; *Wallis v Day* (1837) 2 M & W 273 at 277 per Parke B; *Clough v Lambert* (1839) 10 Sim 174; *Watson v Parker* (1843) 6 Beav 283; *Dickinson v Burrell* (1866) LR 1 Eq 337 at 343. See also *Turner v Vaughan* (1767) 2 Wils 339; *Hill v Spencer* (1767) Amb 641 at 643; *Gray v Mathias* (1800) 5 Ves 286; *Nye v Moseley* (1826) 6 B & C 133; *Hall v Palmer* (1844) 3 Hare 532; *Re Stewart, ex p Pottinger* (1878) 8 ChD 621, CA; *Re Vallance, Vallance v Blagden* (1884) 26 ChD 353; *Re Whitaker, Whitaker v Palmer* [1901] 1 Ch 9, CA.

     This effect of a deed has been explained by saying that a deed imports a consideration on account of the solemnity with which it is executed, and this saying has been elevated into a rule of law: 1 Plowd 308–309; Bacon's Law Tracts 310; 2 Bl Com (14th Edn) 446; 1 Fonblanque's Treatise of Equity (5th Edn) 342n; 2 Fonblanque's Treatise of Equity (5th Edn) 26. The truth appears to be that the binding effect of a deed is due to the importance attached in early law to writing as a mode of proof of a person's intention though later it was required that the seal of the person intended to be bound should be affixed to the writing as a guarantee of its authenticity: see paras 1, 27 ante. The peculiar effect so attributed by the early common law to a sealed writing has not been affected by the facts that in modern times writing has ceased to be a rare accomplishment, that oral agreements in the way of executory promises have become enforceable at law where valuable consideration has been given in return for the promise, that unsealed writings have been allowed to be produced in evidence of some oral agreement, and that a lease under seal can be varied by an agreement in writing and even by an oral agreement so long as it is evidenced by writing or has been partly performed: *Mitas v Hyams* [1951] 2 TLR 1215 at 1217, CA, per Denning LJ; *Plymouth Corpn v Harvey* [1971] 1 All ER 623, [1971] 1 WLR 549. Nor is the binding effect of a deed affected by the fact that a seal is no longer required in the case of instruments executed by an individual and delivered on or after 31 July 1990 (ie the date on which the Law of Property (Miscellaneous Provisions) Act 1989 s 1 (as originally enacted) came into force): see s 1(1)(b), (11); and para 7 ante. As to the application of s 1(1)(b) see s 1(9); and paras 7, 27, 32 ante. This does not include execution by a corporation sole: see s 1(10); and para 32 ante.

2   *Cannon v Hartley* [1949] Ch 213 at 217, [1949] 1 All ER 50 at 53 per Romer J.

3   Although the word 'specialty' is sometimes used to denote merely a contract contained in a deed, it is more often used (as here) in the sense of meaning a specialty debt or specialty obligation, ie an obligation under a deed or a debt due from or other obligation of the Crown or a debt or other obligation under statute: see *R v Williams* [1942] AC 541 at 555, [1942] 2 All ER 95 at 101, PC; *Royal Trust Co v A-G for Alberta* [1930] AC 144 at 150–151, PC.

4   As to consideration see CONTRACT vol 9(1) (Reissue) paras 727–766.

5   *Combe v Combe* [1951] 2 KB 215, [1951] 1 All ER 767, CA; *Central London Property Trust Ltd v High Trees House Ltd* [1947] KB 130, [1956] 1 All ER 256n; *Lyle-Meller v A Lewis & Co (Westminster) Ltd* [1956] 1 All ER 247, [1956] 1 WLR 29, CA; *Tool Metal Manufacturing Co Ltd v Tungsten Electric Co Ltd* [1955] 2 All ER 657, [1955] 1 WLR 761, HL; and cf CONTRACT vol 9(1) (Reissue) para 1030 et seq.

6   The explanation of this is that, as a general rule, all contracts in restraint of trade are void, but promises in reasonable restraint of trade have been admitted to be valid as an exception to this principle, upon condition that they should be made for valuable consideration: see *Davis v Mason* (1793) 5 Term Rep 118 at 120; *A Schroeder Music Publishing Co Ltd v Macaulay* [1974] 3 All ER 616, [1974] 1 WLR 1308, HL. See also TRADE, INDUSTRY AND INDUSTRIAL RELATIONS vol 47 (2001 Reissue) para 49.

7   *Colman v Sarrel* (1789) 1 Ves 50 at 55; *Ellison v Ellison* (1802) 6 Ves 656 at 662; *Jefferys v Jefferys* (1841) Cr & Ph 138; *Meek v Kettlewell* (1842) 1 Hare 464 (on appeal (1843) 1 Ph 342); *Dening v Ware* (1856) 22 Beav 184 at 189; *Tatham v Vernon* (1861) 29 Beav 604 at 615; *Re Ellenborough, Towry Law v Burne* [1903] 1 Ch 697. See SPECIFIC PERFORMANCE vol 44(1) (Reissue) para 805.

8   Statute of Uses (1535) s 1 (repealed).

9   See the Law of Property Act 1925 s 207 (as amended), Sch 7.

10   See ibid s 60 (as amended); para 241 post; and EQUITY vol 16(2) (Reissue) para 853; REAL PROPERTY vol 39(2) (Reissue) paras 93, 119, 245; TRUSTS vol 48 (2000 Reissue) para 629. See, however, *Hodgson v Marks* [1971] Ch 892, [1971] 2 All ER 684, CA (where a resulting trust of the beneficial interest to the plaintiff arose out of the voluntary transfer); *Tinsley v Milligan* [1994] 1 AC 340, [1993] 3 All ER 65 at 87, HL, per Lord Browne-Wilkinson. See also GIFTS vol 20(1) (Reissue) para 43; REAL PROPERTY vol 39(2) (Reissue) paras 93, 245.

60.   When a deed takes effect.   A deed takes effect from the time of its delivery, and not from the day on which it is therein stated to have been made or executed; and a party to a deed is not estopped by any statement in the deed as to the day or time of its execution from proving that it was delivered at some other time[1]. If, however, the date of a lease is altered after execution the lessor is estopped from showing that the date inserted by himself in the lease is not the date from which the demise operated, so as to prevent anyone claiming under the lease from relying upon the circumstances existing at the date which the lease bears[2]. A deed may be good although it has no date or bears a false or an impossible date[3].

1   See para 192 post; *Ludford v Gretton* (1576) 2 Plowd 490 at 491; *Goddard's Case* (1584) 2 Co Rep 4b; *Clayton's Case* (1585) 5 Co Rep 1a; *Oshey v Hicks* (1610) Cro Jac 263; Co Litt 46b; Shep Touch 72; *Stone v Bale* (1693) 3 Lev 348; *Hall v Cazenove* (1804) 4 East 477; *Steele v Mart* (1825) 4 B & C 272; *Doe d Lewis v Bingham* (1821) 4 B & Ald 672; *Browne v Burton* (1847) 17 LJQB 49; *Jayne v Hughes* (1854) 10 Exch 430; *Taylor v McCalmont* (1855) 4 WR 59; *Clarke v Roche* (1877) 3 QBD 170; *Leschallas v Woolf* [1908] 1 Ch 641 at 651; *Re Maher and Nugent's Contract* [1910] 1 IR 167. In reckoning a term of years from 'the date' of a deed, the day of the date was held to be included in *English v Cliff* [1914] 2 Ch 376; but see *Cornish v Cawsy* (1648) Aleyn 75; Co Litt 46b; and ESTOPPEL vol 16(2) (Reissue) para 1020; TIME vol 45(2) (Reissue) para 229.
2   *Rudd v Bowles* [1912] 2 Ch 60 at 65 per Neville J.
3   *Goddard's Case* (1584) 2 Co Rep 4b; *Cromwell v Grunsden* (1698) 2 Salk 462.

61.   Who may benefit under a deed.   Any person named or sufficiently indicated in a deed poll may sue to enforce any obligation thereby undertaken in his favour, notwithstanding that he has not executed the deed[1]; but he must observe all stipulations made in the deed of which the performance was a condition precedent to the liability of the maker of the deed[2]. An indenture not inter partes is for this purpose a deed poll[3].

A person may also take, under a deed inter partes to which he is not named as a party, an interest in remainder[4], or by way of trust[5]. A power of attorney may be given by a deed made inter partes to a person not named as a party to it[6].

At common law a person could not take an immediate benefit under an indenture inter partes or maintain an action or claim upon any covenant contained in it unless he were named as a party to the deed[7]. This is still the general rule[8], but by statute a person may take an immediate or other interest in land or other property, or the benefit of any condition, right of entry, covenant or agreement over or respecting land or other property, even though he is not named as a party to the conveyance or other instrument[9]. Such covenants, however, cannot be effectually made with persons not in existence at the time of the execution of the deed, as for instance future owners of the land[10].

The covenants to which this statutory provision[11] applies are confined to those of which the benefit runs with the land[12], and also to cases where the person seeking to take advantage of it falls within the scope of the instrument according to its true construction[13] and is someone with whom there purports to be a covenant or agreement[14], as where the instrument purports to confer some interest on him, for example an option to purchase[15]. Where the identity of the covenantee is clear and unambiguous, the statutory provision does not operate to confer the benefit of the covenant on a party who is not within the ambit of the expressly identified covenantee[16]. Moreover it only allows a person to sue on a covenant, where not named as a party to it, if the covenant purported to be made with him; it is not enough merely to show that the covenant is made for his benefit[17].

The benefit of a covenant implied on a disposition of property[18] is annexed and incident to, and goes with, the estate or interest of the person to whom the disposition is made, and is capable of being enforced by every person in whom that estate or interest is (in whole or in part) for the time being vested[19].

These rules have been significantly relaxed in respect of covenants made after May 2000[20]. Subject to the expression of a contrary intention, a person may sue on a contract to which he is not a party, if the contract purports to confer a benefit on him[21]. Provided that the third party is a member of an identifiable class, such as future owners of adjacent land, he need not be in existence at the time when the covenant was made[22].

1   *Scudamore v Vanderstene* (1587) 2 Co Inst 673; *Green v Horne* (1694) 1 Salk 197; *Lowther v Kelly* (1723) 8 Mod Rep 115 at 118. It is not necessary that he should be designated by name: *Sunderland Marine Insurance Co v Kearney* (1851) 16 QB 925 at 938. As to deeds poll see para 3 ante.

2   *Macdonald v Law Union Insurance Co* (1874) LR 9 QB 328.

3   *Chelsea and Waltham Green Building Society v Armstrong* [1951] Ch 853 at 856, [1951] 2 All ER 250 at 253 per Vaisey J (in this case the plaintiffs were held entitled to enforce a covenant, purporting to have been made with them, contained in a registered transfer of land under seal to which they were not parties). See also 2 Co Inst 673; *Cooker v Child* (1673) 2 Lev 74. As to indentures see para 3 ante.

4   Co Litt 231a. Formerly this rule applied to a legal remainder, but now there cannot be a legal estate in remainder, and the corresponding interest is an equitable interest in remainder: see the Law of Property Act 1925 s 1(1), (3); and para 10 note 8 ante.

5   2 Preston on Conveyancing (3rd Edn) 394.

6   *Moyle v Ewer* (1602) Cro Eliz 905; Shep Touch 217; Co Litt 52b, n (4); *Lowther v Kelly* (1723) 8 Mod Rep 115, 118; *Storer v Gordon* (1814) 3 M & S 308 at 322–323; 2 Preston on Conveyancing (3rd Edn) 400.

7   Co Litt 231a; 2 Co Inst 673; *Windsmore v Hobart* (1585) Hob 313; *Greenwood v Tyler* (1620) Hob 314; *Storer v Gordon* (1814) 3 M & S 308 at 322–323; *Metcalfe v Rycroft* (1817) 6 M & S 75; 2 Preston on Conveyancing (3rd Edn) 394 et seq; *Berkeley v Hardy* (1826) 5 B & C 355; *Lord Southampton v Brown* (1827) 6 B & C 718; *Gardner v Lachlan* (1836) 8 Sim 123 at 126 (affd without reference to this point (1838) 4 My & Cr 129); *Beckham v Drake* (1841) 9 M & W 79 at 95 (on appeal on another point (1849) 2 HL Cas 579); *Chesterfield and Midland Silkstone Colliery Co Ltd v Hawkins* (1865) 3 H & C 677 at 692.

8   *Harmer v Armstrong* [1934] Ch 65 at 86, CA, per Lawrence LJ. For examples of the application of the general rule see *Re Sinclair's Life Policy* [1938] Ch 799, [1938] 3 All ER 124; *Re Foster, Hudson v Foster* [1938] 3 All ER 357; *White v Bijou Mansions Ltd* [1938] Ch 351, [1938] 1 All ER 546, CA.

9   Law of Property Act 1925 s 56(1) (replacing the first part of the Real Property Act 1845 s 5 (repealed)). It is, however, not confined to indentures, but applies to any instrument by which a benefit can be conferred. It has been construed as not extending to personal property (other than chattels real): *Beswick v Beswick* [1968] AC 58, [1967] 2 All ER 1197, HL. See also *Re Selwyn's Conveyance, Hayman v Soole* [1967] Ch 674, [1967] 1 All ER 339. As to execution under a power of attorney see the Powers of Attorney Act 1971 s 7 (as amended); and AGENCY vol 2(1) (Reissue) paras 31, 72–74. As to the rights and liabilities in general of strangers to a contract see CONTRACT vol 9(1) (Reissue) para 748 et seq. As to the assignment of rights under a contract see CONTRACT vol 9(1) (Reissue) para 754–758. As to the effect of the creation of a trust see TRUSTS vol 48 (2000 Reissue) paras 501–648.

10   *Kelsey v Dodd* (1881) 52 LJ Ch 34 at 39; *Dyson v Forster* [1909] AC 98, HL; *Westhoughton UDC v Wigan Coal and Iron Co Ltd* [1919] 1 Ch 159, CA.

11   Ie the Law of Property Act 1925 s 56(1): see the text and note 9 supra.

12   In *Forster v Elvet Colliery Co Ltd* [1908] 1 KB 629, CA, the Court of Appeal held that they are so confined, but doubt was expressed as to this in the House of Lords (reported sub nom *Dyson v Forster* [1909] AC 98 at 102, HL). The decision of the Court of Appeal in that case was, however, treated as binding on the point in *Grant v Edmondson* [1931] 1 Ch 1, CA, although criticised at 28 per Romer LJ. See also *Re Ecclesiastical Comrs for England's Conveyance* [1936] Ch 430 at 437–438 per Luxmoore J; *Drive Yourself Hire Co (London) Ltd v Strutt* [1954] 1 QB 250 at 273–274, [1953] 2 All ER 1475 at 1483, CA, per Denning LJ.

13   *White v Bijou Mansions Ltd* [1938] Ch 351 at 365, [1938] 1 All ER 546 at 554, CA, per Greene MR; *Amsprop Trading Ltd v Harris Distribution Ltd* [1997] 2 All ER 990, [1997] 1 WLR 1025.

14   *White v Bijou Mansions Ltd* [1937] 3 All ER 269 at 276–277 per Simonds J (affd [1938] Ch 351, [1938] 1 All ER 546, CA); *Amsprop Trading Ltd v Harris Distribution Ltd* [1997] 2 All ER 990, [1997] 1 WLR 1025.

15   *Stromdale and Ball Ltd v Burden* [1952] Ch 223, [1952] 1 All ER 59.

16   *Amsprop Trading Ltd v Harris Distribution Ltd* [1997] 2 All ER 990, [1997] 1 WLR 1025 (doubting dicta in *Drive Yourself Hire Co (London) Ltd v Strutt* [1954] 1 QB 250 at 272, [1953] 2 All ER 1475 at 1483, CA, per Denning LJ, in the light of *Beswick v Beswick* [1968] AC 58, [1967] 2 All ER 1197, HL).

17   *Amsprop Trading Ltd v Harris Distribution Ltd* [1997] 2 All ER 990, [1997] 1 WLR 1025.

18   Ie by virtue of the Law of Property (Miscellaneous Provisions) Act 1994 Pt I (ss 1–13) (as amended): see s 7.

19   Ibid s 7 (replacing provisions previously contained in the Law of Property Act 1925 s 76(6) (repealed) in
     relation to covenants implied by s 76 (repealed)). As to covenants in leases see the Landlord and Tenant
     (Covenants) Act 1995; and LANDLORD AND TENANT.
20   The date when the Contracts (Rights of Third Parties) Act 1999 came into force: see s 10(2). As to the
     Contracts (Rights of Third Parties) Act 1999 generally see CONTRACT.
21   See ibid s 1(1).
22   See ibid s 1(3).

62.   Effect of non-execution by party.   When a deed is expressed to be made
between several parties or a deed poll to be made by more persons than one[1], and some
or one only of those parties or persons execute the same, it is not the deed of any person
who has not executed it[2]. Unless, however, it was delivered as an escrow to take effect
only in case of and upon its execution by all or some other of the parties[3], or unless an
equity arises, it is the deed of every person who has executed it, and, owing to his being
estopped from averring anything in contradiction thereof[4], it takes effect, as against him,
according to its purport from the time of his execution of it, notwithstanding that the
other party or parties have neither executed it nor expressed assent to its provisions[5].

For example, an equity arises where a deed, executed on the assumption that another
person then absent will execute it too[6], is sought to be enforced against an executing
party and, owing to the non-execution by the absentee, the obligation which is sought
to be enforced is substantially different from what it would have been if the absentee had
in fact executed the deed[7]. In such a case the deed is not binding on the person who has
executed it until the absentee has joined in its execution[8]. This is so notwithstanding that
the absentee is not named as a party to the deed if he is so referred to in it as to make it
plain that the deed was executed on the supposition that he would ultimately concur in
the intended arrangement[9]. Further, where one party enters into a deed with another
on the basis, which was known to and understood by both of them, that a third party
was also to sign and the third party does not do so, the deed does not bind the parties[10].

1   See para 3 ante.
2   Littleton's Tenures s 373; Bro Abr, Dette (38, 80), Obligation (13, 14, 27). As to his ability to enforce
    covenants in his favour therein contained see para 61 ante.
3   See paras 37–39 ante. See also *Underhill v Horwood* (1804) 10 Ves 209 at 226; *Latch v Wedlake* (1840) 11 Ad
    & El 959 at 965–966; *Bonser v Cox* (1841) 4 Beav 379 at 383; *Evans v Bremridge* (1856) 8 De GM & G
    100; *Beckett v Addyman* (1882) 9 QBD 783 at 788–789, CA, per Field J; *Ellesmere Brewery Co v Cooper*
    [1896] 1 QB 75; and c f *Cooper v Evans* (1867) LR 4 Eq 45.
4   See para 57 ante.
5   *Foster v Mapes* (1591) Cro Eliz 212; Co Litt 229a; *Exton v Scott* (1833) 6 Sim 31; *Cooch v Goodman* (1842)
    2 QB 580 at 600; *Fletcher v Fletcher* (1844) 4 Hare 67; *Morgan v Pike* (1854) 14 CB 473 at 484; *Re Way's
    Trusts* (1864) 2 De GJ & Sm 365; *Xenos v Wickham* (1866) LR 2 HL 296; *Whitmore-Searle v
    Whitmore-Searle* [1907] 2 Ch 332; *Chelsea and Walham Green Building Society v Armstrong* [1951] Ch 853,
    [1951] 2 All ER 250; and see para 63 note 1 post. See also *Moody v Condor Insurance Ltd* [2006] EWHC
    100 (Ch), [2006] 1 All ER 934, [2006] 1 WLR 1847.
6   A deed of family arrangement come to by persons who have signed the deed without the knowledge or
    in the absence of one member of the family intended to be affected by it is regarded, in the absence of
    any provision to the contrary express or implied, as having been entered into on the assumption that
    absent members of the family affected by it will in the due time join in the transaction: *Re Morton, Morton
    v Morton* [1932] 1 Ch 505 at 507–508 per Eve J. See further SETTLEMENTS vol 42 (Reissue) para 1009.
7   *Lady Naas v Westminster Bank Ltd* [1940] AC 366 at 391, [1940] 1 All ER 485 at 500, HL, per
    Lord Russell of Killowen, and at 404–406 and 509–510 per Lord Wright.
8   *Peto v Peto* (1849) 16 Sim 590; *Bolitho v Hillyar* (1865) 34 Beav 180; *Re Morton, Morton v Morton* [1932]
    1 Ch 505.
9   *Re Morton, Morton v Morton* [1932] 1 Ch 505 at 508 per Eve J.
10 *Woollam v Barclays Bank plc* [1988] EGCS 22.

63.   Effect of disclaimer.   If the other party or parties to a deed are under no
obligation, independently of the deed, to execute it or abide by its provisions, the deed
is liable to be avoided by his or their disclaimer of the benefit of it[1]. Thus a deed of grant

or other assurance of property takes effect immediately upon its execution by the grantor or assuror, and then at once passes the property expressed to be assured to the grantee or alienee, although the latter has not executed or assented to the deed, subject, however, to the property revesting in the alienor in case the benefit of the assurance is disclaimed[2]. Further, an obligation or duty undertaken by deed is immediately binding on the person on whom it is incumbent from the moment of his execution of the deed, and before the person who is to take the benefit of the liability so assumed has expressed his assent to the transaction[3] although the latter may subsequently disclaim the benefit of the obligation[4].

1 YB 7 Edw 4, 20 (pl 21), 29 (pl 14); Littleton's Tenures ss 684–685; *Butler and Baker's Case* (1591) 3 Co Rep 25a at 26b, 27a, Ex Ch; *Whelpdale's Case* (1604) 5 Co Rep 119a at 119b; Shep Touch 70, 284–285; *Thompson v Leach* (1690) 2 Vent 198 at 202, 208; *Wankford v Wankford* (1699) 1 Salk 299 at 307 per Holt CJ; *Siggers v Evans* (1855) 5 E & B 367 at 380 et seq; *Peacock v Eastland* (1870) LR 10 Eq 17; *Re Deveze, ex p Cote* (1873) 9 Ch App 27 at 32; *Standing v Bowring* (1885) 31 ChD 282 at 286, 288, 290, CA; *Re Birchall, Birchall v Ashton* (1889) 40 ChD 436 at 439, CA; *Mallott v Wilson* [1903] 2 Ch 494 at 500–502. As to disclaimer see paras 74–75 post.
2 See note 1 supra.
3 *Butler and Baker's Case* (1591) 3 Co Rep 25a at 26b, 27a, Ex Ch; and see *Hall v Palmer* (1844) 3 Hare 532; *Xenos v Wickham* (1866) LR 2 HL 296.
4 *Wetherell v Langston* (1847) 1 Exch 634, Ex Ch; and see note 1 supra.

64. Accepting benefit without execution. Where a person named in some deed, whether as a party to it or not, has, without executing the deed, accepted some benefit thereby assured to him, he is obliged to give effect to all the conditions on which the benefit was therein expressed to be conferred; and he must, therefore, perform or observe all covenants or stipulations on his part which are contained in the deed, and on the performance or observance of which the benefit conferred was meant to be conditional[1]. For example, a mortgagee who has made a loan on mortgage, but has not executed the mortgage deed (which has been executed by the mortgagor only), is bound to give effect to a proviso contained in the deed for reduction of the rate of interest on punctual payment, or for allowing the loan to remain on the mortgage for a certain term[2]. If a person enters into land under an assurance made to him by deed (which he has not executed) for a term of years, for his life or in tail, and it subsequently appears that the grantor who made the assurance had no rightful title to the land, the person who has so entered is estopped from asserting, against the remainderman under the deed, a possessory title to the land as derived from his own wrongful entry and the effect of the Limitation Act 1980[3], even though he may be able to set up such a title against the original rightful owner[4]. Where a company takes the benefit of an apprenticeship agreement which it has not executed, it will be taken to have adopted it and will be bound by it[5].

1 YB 38 Edw 3, 8a; YB 45 Edw 3, 11, (pl 7); YB 8 Edw 4, 8b; Littleton's Tenures s 374; Bro Abr, Dette (38, 80), Obligation (13, 14, 27); 1 Dyer 13b, pl 65; Co Litt 230b and n (1); *Brett v Cumberland* (1619) 2 Roll Rep 63; *R v Houghton-le-Spring* (1819) 2 B & Ald 375; *Webb v Spicer* (1849) 13 QB 886 at 893 (on appeal sub nom *Salmon v Webb and Franklin* (1852) 3 HL Cas 510); *Linwood v Squire* (1850) 5 Exch 234 at 236; *Macdonald v Law Union Insurance Co* (1874) LR 9 QB 328 at 330 and 332; *Aspden v Seddon* (1876) 1 Ex D 496 at 503, CA; *Westhoughton UDC v Wigan Coal and Iron Co Ltd* [1919] 1 Ch 159 at 174, CA; *Halsall v Brizell* [1957] Ch 169, [1957] 1 All ER 371. Before 1926, a grantee of land, subject to the reservation of an easement thereover, was bound, if he accepted the grant, to give effect to the reservation, though he did not execute the conveyance (*May v Belleville* [1905] 2 Ch 605); but now the reservation operates to create the legal estate reserved without execution of the conveyance by the grantee (see the Law of Property Act 1925 s 65(1); and para 239 post).
2 See note 1 supra; and *Morgan v Pike* (1854) 14 CB 473 at 483–486.
3 See the Limitation Act 1980 ss 15, 17 (as amended), Sch 1 (as amended); and LIMITATION OF ACTIONS.
4 *Dalton v Fitzgerald* [1897] 2 Ch 86, CA; cf the Limitation Act 1980 Sch 1 (as amended) (see LIMITATION OF ACTIONS); and see Littleton's Tenures s 374.
5 *McDonald v John Twiname Ltd* [1953] 2 QB 304, [1953] 2 All ER 589, CA.

65.   Concealment of fact of execution.   If a deed is duly executed and delivered as such[1], it will take effect according to its purport, notwithstanding that the fact of its execution is concealed from or unknown to the persons or some person intended to benefit under it[2], unless it is avoided, on coming to their or his knowledge, by disclaimer of the benefit of it[3].

1   See paras 1, 37, 60 ante.

2   *Thompson v Leach* (1690) 2 Vent 198; *Barlow v Heneage* (1702) Prec Ch 210; *Clavering v Clavering* (1704) 2 Vern 473 (affd (1705) 7 Bro Parl Cas 410, HL); *Cecil v Butcher* (1821) 2 Jac & W 565; *Doe d Garnons v Knight* (1826) 5 B & C 671; *Exton v Scott* (1833) 6 Sim 31; *Grugeon v Gerrard* (1840) 4 Y & C Ex 119; *Hall v Palmer* (1844) 3 Hare 532; *Fletcher v Fletcher* (1844) 4 Hare 67; *Siggers v Evans* (1855) 5 E & B 367; *Re Way's Trusts* (1864) 2 De GJ & Sm 365; *Jones v Jones* (1874) 31 LT 535; *Standing v Bowring* (1885) 31 ChD 282, CA; *Sharp v Jackson* [1899] AC 419, HL; *Re McCallum, McCallum v McCallum* [1901] 1 Ch 143, CA; *Mallott v Wilson* [1903] 2 Ch 494. As to loss of documents see further EQUITY vol 16(2) (Reissue) paras 446–447; and see also *East India Co v Boddam* (1804) 9 Ves 464.

3   See para 63 ante.

66.   Execution by non-party.   It appears that by executing a deed a person may incur any liability expressed in it to be undertaken by him, notwithstanding that he is not named as a party to the deed[1]; but, except as previously mentioned[2], a person cannot sue at common law upon any covenant contained in a deed inter partes, even though the covenant is expressed or appears to be made for his benefit, if he is not named as a party to the deed[3]; although at equity he may enforce the covenant provided its provisions are such as to constitute him a beneficiary of a trust of the benefit of the covenant[4]. If, however, a person is named as a party to a deed inter partes, he may sue upon any covenant made with him and contained in the deed without having executed it[5], unless the transaction carried out thereby was such that his own execution of the deed was a condition precedent to his enforcement of the covenant[6]. Thus, if by a lease by deed a house is expressed to be demised for a term exceeding three years[7], and the lessee covenants with the lessor to repair the house during the term, and the lessee executes the counterpart but the lessor does not execute the lease, the lessor cannot sue the lessee upon the covenant to repair without first executing the lease, notwithstanding that the lessee has entered into possession of the house; for it is a condition precedent to the lessee's liability to repair that he has a valid demise of the house for the term agreed upon[8].

1   *Salter v Kidley* (1688) 1 Show 58; 2 Preston on Conveyancing (3rd Edn) 418.

2   See para 61 ante.

3   *Dyson v Forster* [1909] AC 98, HL; and see para 61 note 12 ante.

4   *Hook v Kinnear* (circa 1750) 3 Swan 417n; *Gregory v Williams* (1817) 3 Mer 582 at 590; *Page v Cox* (1852) 10 Hare 163; *Touche v Metropolitan Rly Warehousing Co* (1871) 6 Ch App 671 at 677; *Re Empress Engineering Co* (1880) 16 ChD 125 at 129, CA; *Lloyd's v Harper* (1880) 16 ChD 290 at 315, 317, CA; *Re Flavell, Murray v Flavell* (1883) 25 ChD 89, CA; *Gandy v Gandy* (1885) 30 ChD 57 at 67, 69–70, 73–74, CA.

5   *Clement v Henley* (1643) 2 Roll Abr 22 (F 2); *Rose v Poulton* (1831) 2 B & Ad 822 at 830; *Wetherell v Langston* (1847) 1 Exch 634 at 643; *Pitman v Woodbury* (1848) 3 Exch 4; *British Empire Assurance Co v Browne* (1852) 12 CB 723; *Morgan v Pike* (1854) 14 CB 473. See also paras 61–62, 64 ante.

6   See 1 Wms Saund 320 n (4); 2 Wms Saund 352 n (3); *Linwood v Squire* (1850) 5 Exch 234 at 236; *Wilkinson v Anglo-Californian Gold Mining Co* (1852) 18 QB 728.

7   See paras 14, 15 note 6 ante; and LANDLORD AND TENANT vol 27(1) (2006 Reissue) para 102.

8   *Soprani and Barnardi v Skurro* (1602) Yelv 18; *Pitman v Woodbury* (1848) 3 Exch 4; *Wheatley v Boyd* (1851) 7 Exch 20 at 21; *Swatman v Ambler* (1852) 8 Exch 72; *Toler v Slater* (1867) LR 3 QB 42 at 45.

(5) AVOIDANCE, DISCHARGE, ALTERATION AND RECTIFICATION OF DEEDS

(i) Avoidance in general

67. Grounds for avoiding a deed. Apart from the absence of valuable consideration a person is not precluded by the fact that his act in pais[1] is evidenced by deed from averring any ground of avoidance of that act which he might have asserted if the act had been accomplished by word of mouth or an instrument under hand only. Thus any party to a deed may aver and prove by extrinsic evidence that he has not given such true, full, and free consent to the transaction expressed therein as will render it unimpeachable, or that the deed cannot take effect as expressed by reason of some legal incapacity affecting him, or that on account of some rule of law or equity the deed ought not to bind him according to its purport[2].

1   Acts in pais (i e acts out of court, or literally and anciently 'in the country') are opposed to acts in a court of record, and include deeds: see *Beverley's Case.* (1603) 4 Co Rep 123b at 124a.
2   See para 68 post.

68. Examples of grounds for avoidance. A party to a deed is not estopped from proving that it is void because he was induced by the machinations of some other person to execute it under a mistake of a fundamental nature (not due to his own carelessness) as to the substance of the transaction expressed to be effected thereby[1], or because he and the other parties executed the deed under a mutual mistake of fact[2]. A person may aver, in opposition to his own deed, that he was induced to execute it by fraud[3], misrepresentation[4], duress[5], or undue influence[6], and prove that for this reason it is voidable.

It may equally well be alleged that a party to a deed was at the time of its execution under the disability of infancy[7], mental disorder[8] or drunkenness[9], or, in the case of a corporation, that the act purported to be effected by the deed was at the time ultra vires[10]; and it may be shown that the deed is on that account void or voidable, according to the effect of the particular incapacity pleaded.

Where the object of an agreement made by deed is unlawful, because the act to be performed is illegal[11] or contrary to public policy[12], the agreement is no more enforceable than if it had been made by parol[13].

Under certain circumstances a deed may be rectified, or treated as if rectified[14].

A sale carried out by deed is voidable if it is in effect a sale by a trustee for sale to himself[15].

Where an individual has been adjudged bankrupt and has at a relevant time[16] entered into a transaction with any person at an undervalue[17], the trustee of the bankrupt's estate may apply to the court for an order under the Insolvency Act 1986[18]. On such an application, the court may make such order as it thinks fit for restoring the position to what it would have been if that individual had not entered into that transaction[19], including an order requiring any property, transferred as a part of the transaction, to be vested in the trustee of the bankrupt's estate as part of that estate[20]. There are similar provisions in relation to transactions defrauding creditors, which are not restricted to transactions taking place within a relevant time[21].

1   See para 69 post.
2   *Colyer v Clay* (1843) 7 Beav 188; *Scott v Coulson* [1903] 1 Ch 453 (affd [1903] 2 Ch 249, CA); and see para 70 post. As to mistake generally see MISTAKE.
3   *Edwards v M'Leay* (1815) Coop G 308 (affd with slight variation (1818) 2 Swan 287); *Trevelyan v White* (1839) 1 Beav 588; *Charter v Trevelyan* (1844) 11 Cl & Fin 714, HL; *Stump v Gaby* (1852) 2 De GM & G 623 at 630–631; *National Provincial Bank of England v Jackson* (1886) 33 ChD 1 at 13, 15, CA; *Lloyds*

Bank Ltd v Bullock [1896] 2 Ch 192 at 197. See EQUITY vol 16(2) (Reissue) para 412 et seq; MISREPRESENTATION AND FRAUD vol 31 (2003 Reissue) paras 781–783.

4   See *Carter v Boehm* (1766) 3 Burr 1905; *Hemmings v Sceptre Life Association Ltd* [1905] 1 Ch 365 at 369; *Howatson v Webb* [1908] 1 Ch 1, CA; *Angel v Jay* [1911] 1 KB 666; *Doe d Lloyd v Bennett* (1837) 8 C & P 124. See also MISREPRESENTATION AND FRAUD vol 31 (2003 Reissue) para 714.

5   *Whelpdale's Case* (1604) 5 Co Rep 119a. See also CONTRACT vol 9(1) (Reissue) para 710; EQUITY vol 16(2) (Reissue) para 436.

6   *Sturge v Sturge* (1849) 12 Beav 229; *Gresley v Mousley* (1859) 4 De G & J 78. See also EQUITY vol 16(2) (Reissue) para 416 et seq; MISREPRESENTATION AND FRAUD vol 31 (2003 Reissue) para 839 et seq.

7   Littleton's Tenures s 259; Co Litt 171b; *Whelpdale's Case* (1604) 5 Co Rep 119a. See also CHILDREN AND YOUNG PERSONS vol 5(3) (Reissue) para 12 et seq.

8   *Leach v Thompson* (1698) Show Parl Cas 150, HL; *Yates v Boen* (1738) 2 Stra 1104; *Elliot v Ince* (1857) 7 De GM & G 475; *Re Walker* [1905] 1 Ch 160, CA. See also MENTAL HEALTH vol 30(2) (Reissue) paras 608–609.

9   See *Cole v Robins* (1703) Bull NP 172; *Matthews v Baxter* (1873) LR 8 Exch 132; and CONTRACT vol 9(1) (Reissue) para 717.

10   *Baroness Wenlock v River Dee Co* (1885) 10 App Cas 354, HL; and see COMPANIES vol 7(2) (2004 Reissue) para 1520 et seq. As to a company's capacity and formalities for carrying on business see para 41 note 15 ante; and COMPANIES vol 7(2) (2004 Reissue) paras 416, 430–432, 467.

11   *Collins v Blantern* (1767) 2 Wils 341 at 351–352; *Cannan v Bryce* (1819) 3 B & Ald 179 (illegal stock-jobbing transactions); *Gedge v Royal Exchange Assurance Corpn* [1900] 2 QB 214 (marine policy void for insertion of clause illegal by statute); *Lodge v National Union Investment Co Ltd* [1907] 1 Ch 300 (illegal moneylending).

12   *Mitchel v Reynolds* (1711) 1 P Wms 181 at 189 et seq; *Walker v Perkins* (1764) 1 Wm Bl 517 (bond for cohabitation); *Bennett v Bennett* [1952] 1 KB 249, [1952] 1 All ER 413, CA (covenants purporting to oust jurisdiction of court); and cf *Addison v Brown* [1954] 2 All ER 213, [1954] 1 WLR 779 (covenant purporting to oust jurisdiction of foreign court). However, a deed will be valid if, on the face of it, it is not contrary to public policy: *Rosenburg v Rosenburg* (1954) Times, 16 July. Where a man assigns or charges all his property, the question arises whether such an assignment or charge is unenforceable as being too vague or contrary to public policy in that a man should not be allowed to deprive himself of his livelihood. The question was discussed, but not decided in the following cases: *Re Clarke, Coombe v Carter* (1887) 36 ChD 348, CA (assignment to mortgagee of after-acquired property); *Tailby v Official Receiver* (1888) 13 App Cas 523 at 530–531, HL (bill of sale assigning future book debts); *Re Turcan* (1888) 40 ChD 5, CA (covenant to settle after-acquired property); *Re Kelcey, Tyson v Kelcey* [1899] 2 Ch 530 (general charge on all property); *Syrett v Egerton* [1957] 3 All ER 331, [1957] 1 WLR 1130, DC (charge on all income and estate). In each of these cases it was sought to enforce such an assignment, covenant, charge or bill of sale against specific existing property. Since such transactions were divisible (see *Re Clarke, Coombe v Carter* supra; *Re Turcan* supra) this was possible, and to that extent they were unobjectionable, being neither vague nor contrary to public policy.

13   Co Litt 206b; Shep Touch 371–372; Bac Abr, Obligations (E); and see CONTRACT vol 9(1) (Reissue) para 836 et seq.

14   *Re Bird's Trusts* (1876) 3 ChD 214. See further para 188 post. As to rectification see EQUITY vol 16(2) (Reissue) paras 440–443; MISTAKE vol 32 (2005 Reissue) paras 55–66.

15   *Randall v Errington* (1805) 10 Ves 423; *Silkstone and Haigh Moor Coal Co v Edey* [1900] 1 Ch 167. See also *Holder v Holder* [1968] Ch 353 at 398, [1968] 1 All ER 665 at 677, CA, per Danckwerts LJ; and TRUSTS vol 48 (2000 Reissue) para 831 et seq.

16   For the meaning of 'relevant time' see BANKRUPTCY AND INDIVIDUAL INSOLVENCY vol 3(2) (2002 Reissue) para 660.

17   For the meaning of 'transaction at an undervalue' see BANKRUPTCY AND INDIVIDUAL INSOLVENCY vol 3(2) (2002 Reissue) para 654.

18   Insolvency Act 1986 s 339(1). As to transactions at an undervalue see BANKRUPTCY AND INDIVIDUAL INSOLVENCY vol 3(2) (Reissue) paras 653–662; MISREPRESENTATION AND FRAUD vol 31 (2003 Reissue) para 867.

19   Ibid s 339(2).

20   Ibid s 342(1)(a).

21   See ibid ss 423–425; and BANKRUPTCY AND INDIVIDUAL INSOLVENCY vol 3(2) (2002 Reissue) paras 663–667.

(ii) Plea of Non Est Factum

69.   When plea available. The plea of non est factum, or nient son fait, is that by which a man sought to be charged in some claim or proceeding upon a deed alleged to have been delivered by him avers that it is not his deed[1]. This plea is only available where the party sued can show either that there never has been, or that there is not existing at the time of the plea, any valid execution of the deed on his part[2]. If a man taking reasonable care has nevertheless been induced by the machinations of some other person (whether a party or a stranger to the deed) to execute a deed under a substantial mistake (not merely as to the legal effect of known contents of the deed) such that he believed it to be fundamentally different in substance or in kind from what it was[3], so that when he executed it his mind did not accompany his outward act, he may plead that for this reason that the deed is not his deed, and if this plea is established by the evidence, the deed will be altogether void from the beginning[4]. A deed so procured is no more the deed of the person who was thus induced to execute it than is a forged deed[5].

1 Shep Touch 74. A person cannot avoid liability under a deed by executing it in a name which is not in fact his own name: *Fung Ping Shan v Tong Shun* [1918] AC 403, PC.

2 See *Nichols v Haywood* (1545) 1 Dyer 59a; *Whelpdale's Case* (1604) 5 Co Rep 119a at 119b; and note (c) in Fraser's edition of 1826 (77 English Reports 241); *Pigot's Case* (1614) 11 Co Rep 26b; Co Litt 35b, n (7); Com Dig, Pleader (2, W, 18); Shep Touch 74; *Edwards v Brown* (1831) 1 Cr & J 307; 1 Chitty on Pleading (7th Edn) 510–512.

3 The distinction drawn in *Howatson v Webb* [1907] 1 Ch 537 (affd [1908] 1 Ch 1, CA), and subsequent cases, between the character and contents of the documents was rejected as unsatisfactory in *Saunders v Anglia Building Society* [1971] AC 1004, [1970] 3 All ER 961, HL. A fundamental difference between the deed as it is and as it was believed to be may lie: (1) in the kind of transaction given effect to, as where a conveyance on sale is executed in the belief that it is a contract of guarantee; (2) in the property dealt with, as where a conveyance of Blackacre is made under the impression that the assurance is of Whiteacre; (3) in the person in whose favour the deed is made, as where property is conveyed to John in the belief that it is being assured to William; or (4) in any other particular which goes to the substance of the whole consideration or to the root of the matter. The case of *Howatson v Webb* supra is opposed to this last conclusion, and, if read literally, would appear to exclude all kinds of difference other than as head (1) supra, but was in this respect considered and explained or disapproved by the House of Lords in *Saunders v Anglia Building Society* supra at 1017–1018 and 964–965 per Lord Hodson, at 1022 and 968–969 per Viscount Dilhorne, at 1025 and 971 per Lord Wilberforce, and at 1039 and 982–983 per Lord Pearson.

As to head (1) supra see *Thoroughgood's Case* (1584) 2 Co Rep 9a; *Foster v Mackinnon* (1869) LR 4 CP 704; *Bagot v Chapman* [1907] 2 Ch 222.

As to head (2) supra see *Anon* (1506) Keil 70, pl 6; *Altham's Case* (1610) 8 Co Rep 150b at 155; *Miller v Travers* (1832) 8 Bing 244 at 248; *Doe d Gord v Needs* (1836) 2 M & W 129 at 140; *Raffles v Wichelhaus* (1864) 2 H & C 906; *Van Praagh v Everidge* [1902] 2 Ch 266 (revsd, on a point concerning the Statute of Frauds (1677), [1903] 1 Ch 434, CA), where Kekewich J held the defendant to be estopped from averring his error.

As to head (3) supra see *Boulton v Jones* (1857) 2 H & N 564; *Hardman v Booth* (1863) 1 H & C 803; *Hollins v Fowler* (1875) LR 7 HL 757 at 762–763, 794–795; *Cundy v Lindsay* (1878) 3 App Cas 459, HL; *Re Cooper, Cooper v Vesey* (1882) 20 ChD 611, CA; *Said v Butt* [1920] 3 KB 497; *Saunders v Anglia Building Society* supra at 1019 and 965, where Lord Hodson pointed out that error of personality was not necessarily so vital in deeds as in contracts.

As to head (4) supra see YB 30 Edw 3, 31b; YB 47 Edw 3, 3b, pl 5; YB 9 Hen 6, 59, pl 8; 2 Roll Abr, Faits (S), pl 6–8; Com Dig, Fait (B2); *Simons v Great Western Rly Co* (1857) 2 CBNS 620 at 624 per Willes J; *Kennedy v Panama etc Mail Co* (1867) LR 2 QB 580 at 587–588; *Smith v Hughes* (1871) LR 6 QB 597; *Stewart v Kennedy (No 2)* (1890) 15 App Cas 108, HL; *Saunders v Anglia Building Society* supra at 1019 and 965 per Lord Hodson, at 1017 and 964 per Lord Reid, at 1018 and 965 per Lord Hodson, at 1022 and 968–969 per Viscount Dilhorne, at 1025 and 971 per Lord Wilberforce, and at 1039 and 982–983 per Lord Pearson, explaining *Howatson v Webb* supra at 544–545 per Warrington J (seemingly approved [1908] 1 Ch 1, CA) (where the defendant was a solicitor's managing clerk and could not have been misled if he had read the deed, but chose to execute it without reading it). See also *Bell v Lever Bros Ltd* [1932] AC 161, HL.

As to mistake generally see MISTAKE.

4 *Anon* (1506) Keil 70, pl 6; *Thoroughgood's Case* (1584) 2 Co Rep 9a; *Maunxel's Case* (1583) Moore KB 182 at 184; *Pigot's Case* (1614) 11 Co Rep 26b at 27b, 28a; *Shulter's Case* (1611) 12 Co Rep 90; Shep Touch 56; *Foster v Mackinnon* (1869) LR 4 CP 704; *National Provincial Bank of England v Jackson* (1886) 33 ChD 1 at 10, CA, per Cotton LJ; *Lewis v Clay* (1897) 67 LJQB 224; *Bagot v Chapman* [1907] 2 Ch 222 at 227; and see *Howatson v Webb* [1907] 1 Ch 537 (affd [1908] 1 Ch 1, CA); *Chaplin & Co Ltd v Brammall*

[1908] 1 KB 233 at 234–235, CA; *Taylor v Taylor and Barclay's Bank Ltd* (1933) 77 Sol Jo 319; *Saunders v Anglia Building Society* [1971] AC 1004, [1970] 3 All ER 961, HL. See also para 57 ante; and CONTRACT vol 9(1) (Reissue) para 687.

5   See *Foster v Mackinnon* (1869) LR 4 CP 704.

70.   Conditions necessary for avoidance through mistake as to contents.
The plea of non est factum on the ground of mistake as to contents appears originally to have been allowed in favour of those who were unable to read owing to blindness or illiteracy and who therefore had to trust someone to tell them what they were executing[1]. It is also now allowed to those who are permanently or temporarily unable, through no fault of their own, to have any real understanding, without explanation, of the purport of the particular document, whether their inability arises from defective education, illness or innate incapacity[2]. A person raising the plea must have taken such precautions as he reasonably could[3], and must prove that he took reasonable care as well as proving all the other circumstances necessary to found the relief[4]. Normally, a blind or illiterate person must have had the deed read over or fully explained to him before execution[5], and a person of full capacity can only establish the plea in very exceptional circumstances[6], certainly not where his reason for not scrutinising the document before executing it was that he was too busy or too lazy to do so[7], and his reliance on someone whom he trusted will not usually be regarded as a sufficient reason[8]. Where a person was led to believe that the document was not one affecting his legal rights, there may be cases where the plea can properly be applied in favour of a man of full capacity[9], though it seems that the plea will not be available to anyone who was content to execute the document without taking the trouble either to find out at least its general effect by reading it or to inquire as to its general effect[10].

The mistake must have been induced by a misrepresentation made, whether by words or conduct, by some person other than the executing party raising the plea; the other person need not be a party himself, but a self-induced mistake is insufficient[11].

The plea is not available to a person whose mistake was really a mistake as to the legal effect of the document, whether that was his own mistake or that of his adviser[12].

The degree to which the document must be different from that which it was believed to be has been expressed in a variety of ways, all involving fundamental or at least very substantial difference[13], but the requirement of difference in character has been discarded[14] and the difference may therefore now be in the kind of document or in its substance[15].

In some cases where non est factum cannot be successfully pleaded, a deed whose execution was induced by a misrepresentation may be set aside under the equitable remedies of rescission and cancellation or may be corrected under the equitable remedy of rectification[16]. Conversely, owing in particular to equitable defences, none of these remedies may be available and yet the requirements for establishing non est factum may all be present; it is no answer to this plea that the claimant against whom the plea is raised has acquired property in good faith for value without notice under the deed sought to be treated as a nullity, whereas the equitable remedies are not given to the detriment of such a purchaser. The remedy of rectification will also lie in some cases where a mistake has been made in preparing a deed so that it fails to carry out the intentions of the maker or makers of the deed[17].

These principles apply equally to a person who signs a document in blank[18].

1   *Saunders v Anglia Building Society* [1971] AC 1004 at 1015–1016, [1970] 3 All ER 961 at 963, HL, per Lord Reid, and at 1019–1020 and 966 per Lord Hodson. As to mistake generally see MISTAKE.
2   *Saunders v Anglia Building Society* [1971] AC 1004 at 1016, [1970] 3 All ER 961 at 963, HL, per Lord Reid, at 1023 and 969 per Viscount Dilhorne, at 1025 and 971 per Lord Wilberforce, and at 1034 and 979 per Lord Pearson.

3   *Saunders v Anglia Building Society* [1971] AC 1004 at 1016, [1970] 3 All ER 961 at 963, HL, per Lord Reid, at 1019 and 966 per Lord Hodson, at 1023 and 969 per Viscount Dilhorne, at 1027 and 973 per Lord Wilberforce, and at 1034, 1037–1038 and 979, 981–982 per Lord Pearson (overruling *Carlisle and Cumberland Banking Co v Bragg* [1911] 1 KB 489, CA).

4   *Saunders v Anglia Building Society* [1971] AC 1004 at 1016, [1970] 3 All ER 961 at 963, HL, per Lord Reid, at 1019 and 966 per Lord Hodson, at 1027 and 973 per Lord Wilberforce, and at 1038 and 982 per Lord Pearson.

5   *Thoroughgood's Case* (1584) 2 Co Rep 9a; *Maunxel's Case* (1583) Moore KB 182 at 184; and see *Saunders v Anglia Building Society* [1971] AC 1004 at 1027, [1970] 3 All ER 691 at 972, HL, per Lord Wilberforce.

6   *Saunders v Anglia Building Society* [1971] AC 1004 at 1016, [1970] 3 All ER 961 at 963, HL, per Lord Reid, at 1019 and 965 per Lord Hodson, at 1027 and 973 per Lord Wilberforce, and at 1033–1035 and 978–980 per Lord Pearson. See also *Anon* (1684) Skin 159, pl 6; *Duchess of Albemarle v Earl of Bath* (1693) Freem Ch 193 at 194; Shep Touch 56; *Hunter v Walters* (1871) 7 Ch App 75 at 87 per Mellish LJ; *Howatson v Webb* [1907] 1 Ch 537 (affd [1908] 1 Ch 1 at 4, CA, per Farwell LJ); *Chaplin & Co Ltd v Brammall* [1908] 1 KB 233 at 234–235, CA; *Alliance Credit Bank of London v Owen* (1908) Times, 27 May; *Re Leighton's Conveyance* [1936] 1 All ER 667 (on appeal on another point [1937] Ch 149, [1936] 3 All ER 1033, CA); *Muskham Finance Ltd v Howard* [1963] 1 QB 904 at 912, [1963] 1 All ER 81 at 83–84, CA, per Donovan LJ. In view of these authorities, it seems that the fact that execution was induced by a false representation, fraudulently made, as to the contents of the deed will not, unaided by other circumstances, suffice to excuse a failure by a person of full capacity to read the deed and inform himself of its purport and effect unless perhaps it was not apparent on the face of the deed that it was intended to have legal consequences: see the text and note 9 infra. It has, however, been questioned whether a person can be permitted to rely on an estoppel by deed in his own favour when the party against whom the estoppel is being set up was induced to make the representations relied on by the fraud of a third party acting, or pretending to act, on behalf of the person setting up the estoppel as well as on his own behalf, even though the person setting up the estoppel was wholly innocent of any complicity in the fraud: *Balkis Consolidated Co v Tomkinson* [1893] AC 396 at 410–411, HL, per Lord Macnaghten, quoted by Lord Davey in *Ruben v Great Fingall Consolidated* [1906] AC 439 at 446, HL; and cf *Sheffield Corpn v Barclay* [1905] AC 392, HL. See also *Avon Finance Co Ltd v Bridger* [1985] 2 All ER 281, [1984] CCLR 27, CA.

7   *Saunders v Anglia Building Society* [1971] AC 1004 at 1016, [1970] 3 All ER 961 at 963, HL, per Lord Reid, at 1019 and 966 per Lord Hodson, at 1023 and 969 per Viscount Dilhorne, at 1025–1026 and 971–972 per Lord Wilberforce, and at 1036 and 980–981 per Lord Pearson.

8   *Saunders v Anglia Building Society* [1971] AC 1004 at 1016, [1970] 3 All ER 961 at 963, HL, per Lord Reid, at 1019 and 966 per Lord Hodson, at 1023 and 969 per Viscount Dilhorne, and at 1032–1033, 1036 and 977–978, 980–981 per Lord Pearson.

9   *Saunders v Anglia Building Society* [1971] AC 1004 at 1016, [1970] 3 All ER 961 at 963, HL, per Lord Reid, at 1020 and 966 per Lord Hodson, at 1021, 1023 and 967, 969 per Viscount Dilhorne, at 1027 and 973 per Lord Wilberforce, and at 1034–1035 and 979 per Lord Pearson; *Lewis v Clay* (1897) 67 LJQB 224.

10   The essence of the plea is that the person executing believed that the deed had one character or effect whereas its actual character or effect was quite different, and he can have no such belief unless he has taken steps or been given information establishing a belief. The very busy man of business who signs a pile of documents without reading them and without inquiry as to their general effect, relying entirely on a trusted secretary, is disabled from raising the plea on the ground that he intended to sign the documents placed before him whatever they might be, his mind accompanying his outward act: *Saunders v Anglia Building Society* [1971] AC 1004 at 1016, [1970] 3 All ER 961 at 963, HL, per Lord Reid, at 1019 and 966 per Lord Hodson, at 1023 and 969 per Viscount Dilhorne, at 1026 and 972 per Lord Wilberforce, and at 1036 and 980–981 per Lord Pearson. Similarly if a man executes and delivers at his solicitor's instance some writing which he knows to be a document in some way affecting his property or his legal position or relations, and has such confidence in his solicitor that he is willing to execute it without having it explained to him, he is precluded from averring that it is not his deed: *Hunter v Walters* (1871) 7 Ch App 75 at 88 per Mellish LJ; *King v Smith* [1900] 2 Ch 425 at 430. A person who looks through an agreement and signs it, although he says he does not understand it, cannot avoid liability on a plea of non est factum because it does not carry out a prior verbal agreement: *Blay v Pollard and Morris* [1930] 1 KB 628, CA.

11   See *Tamplin v James* (1880) 15 ChD 215, CA; *Van Praagh v Everidge* [1902] 2 Ch 266 (revsd on other grounds [1903] 1 Ch 434, CA); *Mercantile Credit Co Ltd v Hamblin* [1965] 2 QB 242, [1964] 3 All ER 592, CA.

12   *Saunders v Anglia Building Society* [1971] AC 1004 at 1016, [1970] 3 All ER 961 at 963, HL, per Lord Reid; and see *Powell v Smith* (1872) LR 14 Eq 85; *Tamplin v James* (1880) 15 ChD 215, CA; *Stewart v Kennedy (No 2)* (1890) 15 App Cas 108, HL.

13　See the various alternative tests propounded in *Saunders v Anglia Building Society* [1971] AC 1004 at 1017, [1970] 3 All ER 961 at 964, HL, per Lord Reid ('radical', 'fundamental', 'serious', 'very substantial'), at 1019 and 965 per Lord Hodson ('in a particular which goes to the substance of the whole consideration or to the root of the matter'), at 1022 and 969 per Viscount Dilhorne ('entirely', 'fundamentally'), at 1026 and 972 per Lord Wilberforce ('essentially', 'basically', 'radically', 'fundamentally'), and at 1039 and 983 per Lord Pearson ('fundamentally', 'radically', 'totally').

14　*Saunders v Anglia Building Society* [1971] AC 1004, [1970] 3 All ER 961, HL, explaining *Howatson v Webb* [1907] 1 Ch 537 (affd [1908] 1 Ch 1, CA). Cases before *Saunders v Anglia Building Society* supra must now be read with caution.

15　*Saunders v Anglia Building Society* [1971] AC 1004 at 1017, [1970] 3 All ER 961 at 964, HL, per Lord Reid, at 1018 and 965 per Lord Hodson, at 1022 and 969 per Viscount Dilhorne, at 1026 and 972 per Lord Wilberforce, and at 1039 and 983 per Lord Pearson.

16　See *Lee v Angas* (1866) 7 Ch App 79n; the text to note 17 infra; and MISREPRESENTATION AND FRAUD vol 31 (2003 Reissue) para 812 et seq.

17　See *Re Bird's Trusts* (1876) 3 ChD 214; and EQUITY vol 16(2) (Reissue) para 640; MISTAKE vol 32 (2005 Reissue) paras 55–66.

18　*United Dominions Trust Ltd v Western* [1976] QB 513, [1975] 3 All ER 1017, CA.

71.　Deed executed under common mistake.　Where a deed gives effect to or embodies an agreement entered into under a mistake common to both parties as to some material fact relating to the subject matter of the agreement and not merely to its quality[1], for example a contract made in the belief that some person is living, who is in fact dead, or that some property is in existence, which is not, the agreement is altogether void[2] and not merely voidable[3]. It follows that the deed is void and not voidable; and it appears upon principle that, if either party should be sued in a claim founded on some obligation undertaken by the deed, he might plead non est factum[4].

Where there is a mistake, but not of this character, the deed may be rectified, in certain circumstances, under the equitable jurisdiction to correct mistakes[5].

1　*Kennedy v Panama etc Mail Co* (1867) LR 2 QB 580 at 588 per Blackburn J, quoted by Lord Thankerton in *Bell v Lever Bros Ltd* [1932] AC 161 at 235, HL. Although both parties are under a fundamental mistake as to the nature of the subject matter, the contract will not be a nullity if the parties were to all outward appearances in full agreement: *Frederick E Rose (London) Ltd v William H Pim Junior & Co Ltd* [1953] 2 QB 450 at 459–460, [1953] 2 All ER 739 at 746–747, CA, per Denning LJ. When goods are sold under a known trade description without misrepresentation or breach of warranty, the fact that both parties are unaware that the goods lack any particular quality will not nullify the contract: *Harrison and Jones Ltd v Bunten and Lancaster Ltd* [1953] 1 QB 646 at 658, [1953] 1 All ER 903 at 909 per Pilcher J. As to mistake generally see MISTAKE.

2　Ie the agreement has no legal effect. For the meaning of 'void' in relation to contracts see CONTRACT vol 9(1) (Reissue) para 607.

3　*Hitchcock v Giddings* (1817) 4 Price 135 at 141; *Strickland v Turner* (1852) 7 Exch 208; *Couturier v Hastie* (1856) 5 HL Cas 673; *Cochrane v Willis* (1865) 1 Ch App 58; *Huddersfield Banking Co Ltd v Henry Lister & Son Ltd* [1895] 2 Ch 273 at 276, 281–282, 284, CA; *Scott v Coulson* [1903] 2 Ch 249 at 252, CA. For this purpose, a common mistake of the parties as to some matter of private right (for instance, as to their respective interests in some land or goods) is a mistake of fact and not of law: *Bingham v Bingham* (1748) 1 Ves Sen 126; *Broughton v Hutt* (1858) 3 De G & J 501; *Cooper v Phibbs* (1867) LR 2 HL 149; *Jones v Clifford* (1876) 3 ChD 779; *Huddersfield Banking Co Ltd v Henry Lister & Son Ltd* [1895] 2 Ch 273, CA; *Allcard v Walker* [1896] 2 Ch 369; *Bligh v Martin* [1968] 1 All ER 1157, [1968] 1 WLR 804.

4　See para 69 note 2 ante. An agreement entered into under a common mistake of fact appears to be void for the same reason that a contract or conveyance, which one is induced to make under a mistake as to the substance of the transaction, is void (where the party is not estopped from averring his mistake); that is, because there was no true consent of the parties, their minds not accompanying their outward acts: see para 69 notes 3–4 ante. It is considered that an agreement made under a common mistake of fact is void at law, and there is no necessity for any party to have recourse to equity or to take any proceedings in order to have the agreement set aside or its nullity established: see *Huddersfield Banking Co Ltd v Henry Lister & Son Ltd* [1895] 2 Ch 273 at 281, CA, per Lindley LJ; *Scott v Coulson* [1903] 2 Ch 249 at 252, CA, per Vaughan Williams LJ; *Grist v Bailey* [1967] Ch 532, [1966] 2 All ER 875. It is thought that a deed of conveyance executed under a common mistake of fact is equally void. Thus, if A and B, believing Blackacre to be A's and Whiteacre (which in truth is A's also) to be B's, by deed exchange

Blackacre for Whiteacre, A can recover Blackacre from B: see the cases cited in note 3 supra. As to common mistake as to existence of subject matter or its essential element see MISTAKE vol 32 (2005 Reissue) para 17.

5   See para 88 post.

72. Forged deeds. A plea of non est factum may be supported by proving that the deed is a forgery, the signature[1] of the party charged having been counterfeited[2]. A deed, the signature[3] to which is forged, is a nullity[4]; but if a man in whose name a deed is forged admits or represents the deed to be his, or keeps silent after discovery of the forgery, he may be estopped, as against any person who has altered his position on the faith of the admission, representation or silence, from denying the deed to be his[5].

1   In the case of an instrument delivered before the 31 July 1990 (i e the date on which the Law of Property (Miscellaneous Provisions) Act 1989 s 1 (as originally enacted) came into force: see para 7 note 4 ante), this includes a seal: see s 1(11); and paras 7, 27, 32 ante. As to other cases in which a seal is still required see para 32 ante.

2   See *Re De Leeuw, Jakens v Central Advance and Discount Corpn Ltd* [1922] 2 Ch 540; and cf para 69 note 2 ante. See also *Saunders v Anglia Building Society* [1971] AC 1004 at 1025, [1970] 3 All ER 961 at 971, HL, per Lord Wilberforce; *Swan v North British Australasian Co* (1863) 2 H & C 175, Ex Ch.

3   See note 1 supra.

4   *Governor & Co of Bank of Ireland v Evans' Charities Trustees* (1855) 5 HL Cas 389; *Boursot v Savage* (1866) LR 2 Eq 134; *Re Cooper, Cooper v Vesey* (1882) 20 ChD 611, CA; *Mayor etc & Co of Merchants Staple of England v Governor & Co of Bank of England* (1887) 21 QBD 160, CA; *Barton v North Staffordshire Rly Co* (1888) 38 ChD 458; *Brocklesby v Temperance Building Society* [1895] AC 173 at 184, HL; *A-G v Odell* [1906] 2 Ch 47, CA. For the application of this principle to documents purporting to be issued on behalf of a corporation aggregate see *Ruben v Great Fingall Consolidated* [1904] 2 KB 712, CA (affd [1906] AC 439, HL); *Kreditbank Cassel GmbH v Schenkers Ltd* [1927] 1 KB 826, CA; *South London Greyhound Racecourses Ltd v Wake* [1931] 1 Ch 496; and COMPANIES vol 7(1) (2004 Reissue) paras 467, 471, 590; CORPORATIONS vol 9(2) (2006 Reissue) para 1262. The text to this note was cited as representing the law in *Penn v Bristol and West Building Society* [1997] 3 All ER 470, [1997] 1 WLR 1356, HL.

5   See *Leach v Buchanan* (1802) 4 Esp 226; *Ashpitel v Bryan* (1863) 3 B & S 474 at 492–493 (affd (1864) 5 B & S 723, Ex Ch); *McKenzie v British Linen Co* (1881) 6 App Cas 82 at 99–109, HL; *Bank of England v Cutler* [1908] 2 KB 208, CA; *Greenwood v Martins Bank Ltd* [1933] AC 51, HL; *Fung Kai Sung v Chan Fui Hing* [1951] AC 489, PC; and see also BANKING vol 3(1) (2005 Reissue) para 164; ESTOPPEL vol 16(2) (Reissue) para 1059. If, after a document has been executed, an alteration is made in it by a forger, a different rule applies and the document is null and void only if the alteration goes to the whole or to the essence of the instrument: see *Kwei Tek Chao (t/a Zung Fu Co) v British Traders and Shippers Ltd* [1954] 2 QB 459 at 476, sub nom *Chao (t/a Zung Fu Co) v British Traders and Shippers Ltd (VV Handels-Maatschappij J Smits Import-Export, third party)* [1954] 1 All ER 779 at 787 per Devlin J (alteration in bill of lading). As to the effect of alteration of a deed after execution see para 76 et seq post. As to forgery by one co-owner see *First National Securities Ltd v Hegerty* [1985] QB 850, [1984] 1 All ER 139, CA; *Mortgage Corpn Ltd v Shaire* [2001] Ch 743, [2001] 4 All ER 364. See also para 240 post.

73. Other cases in which plea available. The plea of non est factum is available where the writing on which the party is charged was delivered by him as a mere escrow to take effect in some contingency which has not happened[1]. This plea may also be supported by evidence that the execution of the writing, on which it is sought to charge the party, is at the time of the plea null and void, though it may originally have been valid (as where the writing has been altered in a material part since its execution[2], or has been cancelled by tearing off the seal in the case of an instrument delivered before 31 July 1990[3] or otherwise[4], or has been avoided by the disclaimer of the person for whose benefit it was executed[5]).

A person cannot plead non est factum[6], however, where the deed was merely voidable at his option when he executed it, or was void in consequence of the provisions contained in it. He cannot, therefore, plead that a deed is not his which he was induced to execute by fraud, misrepresentation, duress, or undue influence[7], or which was voidable on account of his infancy[8], or which was void or unenforceable for illegality[9].

1   Com Dig, Pleader (2, W, 18). As to escrows see paras 37–39 ante.

2   *Whelpdale's Case* (1604) 5 Co Rep 119a; *Pigot's Case* (1614) 11 Co Rep 26b; Com Dig, Pleader (2, W,
     18); Shep Touch 74; *Cock v Coxwell* (1835) 2 Cr M & R 291 at 292 per Gurney B; *Calvert v Baker* (1838)
     4 M & W 417 at 418 per Parke B; Chitty on Pleading (7th Edn) 511; *Ellesmere Brewery Co v Cooper*
     [1896] 1 QB 75 at 79. As to alteration after execution by the party entitled see para 82 post.
3   Ie the date on which the Law of Property (Miscellaneous Provisions) Act 1989 s 1 (as originally enacted)
     came into force: see s 1(11); and paras 7, 27, 32 ante. As to other cases where a seal is still required see
     para 32 ante.
4   Com Dig, Pleader (2, W, 18); Shep Touch 69, 74; and see para 76 post.
5   *Whelpdale's Case* (1604) 5 Co Rep 119a; Com Dig, Pleader (2, W, 18); Shep Touch 74; and see
     paras 74–75 post.
6   See paras 69 note 2, 70 ante.
7   *Whelpdale's Case* (1604) 5 Co Rep 119a; Com Dig, Pleader (2, W, 18); Shep Touch 74; *Edwards v Brown*
     (1831) 1 Cr & J 307 at 312–314; and see para 68 ante.
8   See para 68 note 7 ante.
9   See para 68 note 11 ante.

(iii) Disclaimer

74.   Right to disclaim.   No person is obliged to accept any assurance made to him
or obligation undertaken in his favour without his consent[1]. If, therefore, any such
assurance or obligation is so made or undertaken by some deed, he may disclaim the
benefit of the deed; and the disclaimer need not be made by matter of record or deed,
but may be made orally or by conduct[2]; it can, however, only be made with knowledge
of the interest alleged to be disclaimed and with an intention to disclaim it[3], although
for this purpose detailed knowledge is not necessary, and a putative donee may, by
sufficiently explicit words, disclaim whatever interest he may have without knowing in
detail of what it consists[4]. Upon disclaimer the deed and the act evidenced thereby will
become void, and if the deed contained an assurance to the person disclaiming of some
estate or interest in property, the same will revest in the party who made the assurance or
his representatives[5]. A disclaimer of an attempt inter vivos to make a gift is irrevocable
and cannot be withdrawn subsequently[6].

Where, however, property is conveyed to a person upon trust he may, if he has not
accepted the trust, disclaim the property and the trust, and thereupon the conveyance is
made void as regards him and the property revests in the settlor, but the settlor will hold
the property upon the trusts declared by the deed[7].

1   See Bract fo 15b, 16; Shep Touch 229, 267, 394; *Lord Wellesley v Withers* (1855) 4 E & B 750; and note 2
     infra.
2   *Townson v Tickell* (1819) 3 B & Ald 31; *Bingham v Lord Clanmorris* (1828) 2 Mol 253; *Stacey v Elph* (1833)
     1 My & K 195 at 199; *Begbie v Crook* (1835) 2 Bing NC 70; *Doe d Chidgey v Harris* (1847) 16 M & W
     517 at 520–521; *Foster v Dawber* (1860) 8 WR 646; *Re Birchall, Birchall v Ashton* (1889) 40 ChD 436 at
     439, CA; *Re Clout and Frewer's Contract* [1924] 2 Ch 230; and see para 62 ante. See also 5 Davidson's
     Precedents in Conveyancing (3rd Edn) Pt II 661n. Acceptance will be presumed until dissent is signified:
     see GIFTS vol 20(1) (Reissue) para 50.
3   *Lady Naas v Westminster Bank Ltd* [1940] AC 366 at 396, [1940] 1 All ER 485 at 504, HL, per
     Lord Russell of Killowen.
4   *Re Paradise Motor Co Ltd* [1968] 2 All ER 625, [1968] 1 WLR 1125, CA.
5   See para 63 note 1 ante. See also *Stacey v Elph* (1833) 1 My & K 195; *Wyman v Carter* (1871) LR 12 Eq
     309.
6   *Re Paradise Motor Co Ltd* [1968] 2 All ER 625, [1968] 1 WLR 1125, CA. Contrast the position where
     there is a gift by will (with therefore, necessarily, no living rebuffed donor): see *Re Young, Fraser v Young*
     [1913] 1 Ch 272; *Re Cranstoun's Will Trusts, Gibbs v Home of Rest for Horses* [1949] Ch 523, [1949]
     1 All ER 871; and WILLS vol 50 (2005 Reissue) para 444.
7   *Jones v Jones* (1874) 31 LT 535; *Mallott v Wilson* [1903] 2 Ch 494. It seems that a release may operate as a
     disclaimer if that is the intention: *Nicloson v Wordsworth* (1818) 2 Swan 365 at 370, 372; and cf *Crewe v
     Dicken* (1798) 4 Ves 97; *Doe d Wyatt v Stagg* (1839) 5 Bing NC 564. As to disclaimer by trustees see
     TRUSTS vol 48 (2000 Reissue) paras 707–710.

75. When no right to disclaim. When a person has unequivocally expressed his assent to some assurance made to him of some estate, interest, or right he cannot afterwards disclaim it[1]. Nor can he lawfully disclaim any estate, interest, or right assured to him without his concurrence if he is under some legal or equitable obligation to accept it. Thus where a person has entered into a binding contract to purchase land and has paid the price, he is bound to accept a conveyance of the legal estate in the land[2]; his assent was given by entering into the contract, and an attempted disclaimer of the benefit of the conveyance would be ineffectual. So trustees who have accepted and are acting in the trusts of a marriage settlement containing an agreement that the wife's after-acquired property is to be conveyed to them, cannot lawfully disclaim a conveyance to them of such property[3].

1   See *Doe d Smyth v Smyth* (1826) 6 B & C 112 at 117; *Doe d Chidgey v Harris* (1847) 16 M & W 517 at 520, 524; *Bence v Gilpin* (1868) LR 3 Exch 76; *Re Lord and Fullerton's Contract* [1896] 1 Ch 228, CA.
2   *Re Cary-Elwes' Contract* [1906] 2 Ch 143.
3   See *Bence v Gilpin* (1868) LR 3 Exch 76.

(iv) Cancellation: Discharge

76. Meaning and effect of cancellation. The cancellation of a deed is accomplished by obliterating[1] or otherwise altering or defacing it with the intent that it shall become void. A deed may lawfully be cancelled either by the person who has it in his possession as being solely entitled under it or by anyone (including the party bound by the deed) to whom that person has delivered it up to be cancelled[2]. The deed may be cancelled by mutual consent[3] or under the terms of an agreement between the parties[4] or by order of the court[5]. The production of a deed in a cancelled state is prima facie evidence that it is void[6].

When a deed is cancelled it becomes void, and no claim can thereafter be maintained on any covenant or promise contained in it[7]. The cancellation has, however, no retrospective operation; it does not make the deed void ab initio; and if the deed operated as a conveyance of any property, its cancellation does not have the effect of revesting or reconveying the estate or interest which was so assured[8].

1   In the case of a deed delivered before 31 July 1990 (i e the date on which the Law of Property (Miscellaneous Provisions) Act 1989 s 1 (as originally enacted) came into force) this includes removing its seal: see s 1(11); and paras 7, 27, 32 ante. As to other cases where a seal is still required see para 32 ante.
2   See Perkins, Profitable Book ss 135–136; Vin Abr, Faits (X), pl 1–3; Shep Touch 68–70; 2 Bl Com (14th Edn) 308–309; *Harrison v Owen* (1738) 1 Atk 520.
3   See e g *Lord Ward v Lumley* (1860) 5 H & N 87.
4   See *Bamberger v Commercial Credit Mutual Assurance Society* (1855) 15 CB 676 at 693–694 (insurance policy cancelled in accordance with rules of society on failure to pay premium); and INSURANCE vol 25 (2003 Reissue) para 155.
5   See EQUITY vol 16(2) (Reissue) para 499.
6   *Knight v Clements* (1838) 8 Ad & El 215 at 220; *Earl of Falmouth v Roberts* (1842) 9 M & W 469 at 471; *Alsagar v Close* (1842) 10 M & W 576 at 583; *Meiklejohn v Campbell* (1940) 56 TLR 663 at 665 (affd 56 TLR 704, CA).
7   *Mathewson's Case* (1597) 5 Co Rep 22b at 23a; *Pigot's Case* (1614) 11 Co Rep 26b; Shep Touch 70; *Davidson v Cooper* (1843) 11 M & W 778 at 800 per Lord Abinger CB (affd (1844) 13 M & W 343, Ex Ch); *Bamberger v Commercial Credit Mutual Assurance Society* (1855) 15 CB 676 at 693–694; *Lord Ward v Lumley* (1860) 5 H & N 656 at 658 per Bramwell B. As to accidental cancellation see para 86 post.
8   *Nelthorpe v Dorrington* (1674) 2 Lev 113; *Lord Leech v Leech* (1674) 2 Rep Ch 100; *Lady Hudson's Case* (1704) 2 Eq Cas Abr 52, pl 5; *Magennis v Mac-Cullogh* (temp 1714–1727) Gilb Ch 235 at 236; *Harrison v Owen* (1738) 1 Atk 520; *Bolton v Bishop of Carlisle* (1793) 2 Hy Bl 259 at 263; *Roe d Earl of Berkeley v Archbishop of York* (1805) 6 East 86; *Doe d Lewis v Bingham* (1821) 4 B & Ald 672 at 677 per Holroyd J; *Doe d Courtail v Thomas* (1829) 9 B & C 288; *Gummer v Adams* (1843) 13 LJ Ex 40; *Davidson v Cooper* (1843) 11 M & W 778 at 800 (affd (1844) 13 M & W 343, Ex Ch); *Lord Ward v Lumley* (1860) 5 H & N 87; *Re Hancock, Hancock v Berrey* (1888) 57 LJ Ch 793; and see 'The Discharge of Debts' 44 Sol Jo 481; c f *Re Way's Trusts* (1864) 2 De GJ & Sm 365.

77.   Mode of cancellation.   In order that a deed may be indubitably cancelled it should be unmistakably defaced[1]. If the person entitled under the deed simply delivers it up undefaced to the party bound by it, and the latter were to lose possession of it, it might afterwards be put in suit against him, and in that case he would not be able to plead that it was not his deed[2]. It appears, however, that if the person entitled under the deed delivers it to be cancelled or as a gift to the party bound thereby, that is equivalent to a release of any right of action arising under the deed[3].

1   Before the 31 July 1990 (i e the date on which the Law of Property (Miscellaneous Provisions) Act 1989 s 1 (as originally enacted) came into force), every deed had to be sealed, and removal of the seal was an appropriate procedure for cancellation: see s 1(11); and paras 7, 27, 32 ante. It is submitted that this will still be effective in other cases where a seal is still required, e g where a company executes a deed by affixing its common seal: see para 32 ante.

2   *Waberley v Cockerel* (1542) Dyer 51a; *Cross v Powel* (1596) Cro Eliz 483; and see para 69 ante.

3   Shep Touch 70; *Harrison v Owen* (1738) 1 Atk 520; *Richards v Syms* (1740) Barn Ch 90 at 94; *Byrn v Godfrey* (1798) 4 Ves 6 at 10–11; *Duffield v Elwes* (1827) 1 Bli NS 497 at 537–540, HL; *Cross v Sprigg* (1849) 6 Hare 552 at 556. It seems that if a creditor by bond or covenant delivers up the deed to the debtor as a gift or with intention to forgive the debt, that amounts to delivering up the deed to be cancelled, as the donee will then be entitled to deface or destroy it if he will: *Barton v Gainer* (1858) 3 H & N 387; *Rummens v Hare* (1876) 1 Ex D 169, CA. See also 'The Discharge of Debts' 44 Sol Jo 481–482; and para 25 note 3 ante.

78.   Removal of seal of one party.   If more than one party is bound by a deed, each in a several obligation or covenant and not jointly, the removal of the seal of one of them with the intention of cancellation will only avoid the deed as against that one and not as against the others[1]. If they are bound jointly, or jointly and severally, the valid removal of the seal of one of them will avoid the deed as against all[2]. These rules have very limited application since any rule of law which requires a seal for the valid execution of an instrument as a deed by an individual was abolished by the Law of Property (Miscellaneous Provisions) Act 1989 in relation to instruments delivered as deeds on or after 31 July 1990[3].

1   *Mathewson's Case* (1597) 5 Co Rep 22b; *Collins v Prosser* (1823) 1 B & C 682.

2   *Mathewson's Case* (1597) 5 Co Rep 22b at 23a; *Bayly v Garford* (1641) March 125 at 129; *Seaton v Henson* (1678) 2 Show 28 at 29.

3   See the Law of Property (Miscellaneous Provisions) Act 1989 s 1(1)(b); and paras 7, 27, 32 ante. As to the application of s 1(1)(b) see s 1(9); and para 7 text and note 4 ante.

79.   Putting cancelled deed in evidence.   A cancelled deed cannot be put in evidence to maintain a claim to enforce any obligation created by it[1], as the party to be bound can plead that it is not his deed[2]. It may, however, be put in evidence to prove that before it was cancelled it operated as a conveyance of some estate or interest in property[3], or to prove any collateral fact, or any fact other than that the person who executed it thereby undertook some obligation which is now sought to be enforced under the cancelled deed[4].

1   See para 76 note 7 ante.

2   See para 73 note 4 ante.

3   See para 76 note 8 ante.

4   *Hutchins v Scott* (1837) 2 M & W 809; *Earl of Falmouth v Roberts* (1842) 9 M & W 469 at 471; *Agricultural Cattle Insurance Co v Fitzgerald* (1851) 16 QB 432 at 440–441; *Enthoven v Hoyle* (1852) 13 CB 373 at 394, Ex Ch; *Pattinson v Luckley* (1875) LR 10 Exch 330 at 335–336.

80.   Discharge of contracts made by deed.   Contracts made by deed may be discharged, either before or after breach, in the same manner in all respects as simple contracts[1].

Where there are two deeds between the same parties, but of different dates, containing a covenant to settle the same property, though on different trusts, there being no reference to the first deed in the second deed and no evidence of the intention of the parties, the mere fact that one deed is dated after the other does not mean that the first is thereby superseded[2].

1   *Steeds v Steeds* (1889) 22 QBD 537. An obligation created by deed can be varied by simple contract in writing: *Berry v Berry* [1929] 2 KB 316. See further CONTRACT vol 9(1) (Reissue) para 920 et seq.
2   *Re Gundry, Mills v Mills* [1898] 2 Ch 504.

(v) Alteration and Erasure: Rectification

81.   Alteration before execution. A writing proposed to be executed as a deed may be altered by erasure or interlineation or in any other way before it is so executed; any alteration so made before execution does not affect the validity of the deed[1]. Any alteration, erasure or interlineation appearing upon the face of a deed is presumed, in the absence of evidence to the contrary, to have been made before the execution of the deed[2].

1   Perkins, Profitable Book s 155; Co Litt 225b; Shep Touch 55; *Cole v Parkin* (1810) 12 East 471; and see *Matson v Booth* (1816) 5 M & S 223 at 226–227; *Doe d Lewis v Bingham* (1821) 4 B & Ald 672; *Hall v Chandless* (1827) 4 Bing 123; *Jones v Jones* (1833) 1 Cr & M 721. The deed must be construed as altered: *Re Duncan and Pryce* [1913] WN 117. When a writing has been so altered it is the practice to note in the attestation clause what alteration has been made, and this practice should always be followed: see Shep Touch 55.
2   *Doctor Leyfield's Case* (1611) 10 Co Rep 88a at 92b; Co Litt 225b, n (1); *Trowel v Castle* (1661) 1 Keb 21 at 22; *Fitzgerald v Lord Fauconberge* (1729) Fitz-G 207 at 214 per Reynolds CB (affd sub nom *Lord Fauconberge v Fitzgerald* (1730) 6 Bro Parl Cas 295, HL); *Doe d Tatum v Catomore* (1851) 16 QB 745; *Simmons v Rudall* (1851) 1 Sim NS 115 at 136 per Lord Cranworth V-C; and see *Hobson v Bell* (1839) 3 Jur 190 at 194 per Lord Langdale MR; *Williams v Ashton* (1860) 1 John & H 115 at 118 per Wood V-C. It is otherwise in the case of a will: see WILLS vol 50 (2005 Reissue) paras 374–378. As to alterations etc in a contract under hand only see para 158 et seq post.

82.   Alteration after execution by party entitled. If an alteration (by erasure, interlineation, or otherwise) is made in a material[1] part of a deed, after its execution, by or with the consent of any party to or person entitled under it, but without the consent of the party or parties liable under it, the deed is made void. The nullifying effect of this rule[2] in modern conditions is confined to cases which fall strictly within its ambit, and is to be interpreted as liberally and reasonably as possible. The would-be avoider should be able to demonstrate that the alteration was one which, assuming the parties acted in accordance with the other terms of the contract, was potentially prejudicial to his legal rights or obligations under the instrument[3].

The avoidance, however, is not ab initio, or so as to nullify any conveyancing effect which the deed has already had, but only operates as from the time of the alteration and so as to prevent the person who has made or authorised the alteration, and those claiming under him, from putting the deed in suit to enforce against any party bound by it, who did not consent to the alteration, any obligation, covenant, or promise thereby undertaken or made[4].

A material alteration is one which varies the rights, liabilities, or legal position of the parties as ascertained by the deed in its original state, or otherwise varies the legal effect of the instrument as originally expressed[5], or reduces to certainty some provision which was originally unascertained and as such void[6], or which may otherwise prejudice the party bound by the deed as originally executed[7].

The effect of making such an alteration without the consent of the party bound is exactly the same as that of cancelling the deed[8]. The avoidance of the deed is not retrospective, and does not revest or reconvey any estate or interest in property which passed by the deed[9]; and the deed may be put in evidence to prove that that estate or interest so passed, or for any purpose other than to maintain a claim to enforce some agreement contained in the deed[10].

1   As to the kinds of alteration which are not material see para 87 post.

2   This is sometimes referred to as the rule in *Pigot's Case* (1614) 11 Co Rep 26b.

3   See *Raiffeisen Zentralbank Osterreich AG v Crossseas Shipping Ltd* [2000] 1 All ER (Comm) 76, [2000] 1 WLR 1135, CA. It is not, however, necessary for him to show that prejudice had in fact occurred.

4   *Anon* (1511) Keil 162, pl 2; *Gilford v Mills* (1511) Keil 164, pl 7; *Markham v Gonaston* (1598) Cro Eliz 626 at 627; *Pigot's Case* (1614) 11 Co Rep 26b; *Master v Miller* (1791) 4 Term Rep 320 at 329–332, 345 (on appeal (1793) 2 Hy Bl 141 at 142–143, Ex Ch); 1 Smith LC (13th Edn) 789; *Weeks v Maillardet* (1811) 14 East 568; *Langhorn v Cologan* (1812) 4 Taunt 330; *Fairlie v Christie* (1817) 7 Taunt 416; *Forshaw v Chabert* (1821) 3 Brod & Bing 158; *Davidson v Cooper* (1844) 13 M & W 343 at 352, Ex Ch; *Fazakerly v McKnight* (1856) 6 E & B 795; *Sellin v Price* (1867) LR 2 Exch 189; *Suffell v Bank of England* (1882) 9 QBD 555 at 559–560, 571, CA; *Lowe v Fox* (1887) 12 App Cas 206 at 214, 216, HL; *Ellesmere Brewery Co v Cooper* [1896] 1 QB 75; and see also *Bank of Hindostan, China and Japan v Smith* (1867) 36 LJCP 241; *Pattinson v Luckley* (1875) LR 10 Exch 330 at 333–334.

5   *Gardner v Walsh* (1855) 5 E & B 83 at 89; and see para 87 post. See also note 4 supra.

6   *Markham v Gonaston* (1598) Cro Eliz 626 at 627; cf para 28 note 5 ante; *Eagleton v Gutteridge* (1843) 11 M & W 465 at 468–469; *Re Barned's Banking Co, ex p Contract Corpn* (1867) 3 Ch App 105 at 115.

7   See *Burchfield v Moore* (1854) 3 E & B 683 at 686; *Gardner v Walsh* (1855) 5 E & B 83; *Aldous v Cornwell* (1868) LR 3 QB 573 at 578; *Suffell v Bank of England* (1882) 9 QBD 555 at 562–568, 572–574, CA; *Bishop of Crediton v Bishop of Exeter* [1905] 2 Ch 455.

8   See para 76 ante.

9   See para 76 note 8 ante.

10 See para 79 note 4 ante.

83.   Alteration after execution by party liable.   Where a deed is altered or defaced by, or by the direction of, a person subject to some liability under the deed, without the consent of the person entitled, the latter may, nevertheless, enforce that liability against him[1].

1   *Brown v Savage* (1674) Cas temp Finch 184. That was a case of relief in equity, but it is submitted that the modern law coincides with the rule of equity in the above respect.

84.   Alteration by consent.   If, after its execution, a deed is altered in a material[1] part with the consent of the person or persons liable under it, that does not of itself alone avoid the deed or preclude the party entitled under it from enforcing against that person or persons any agreement it contains[2]. If, however, after an instrument has been completely executed, it is altered by consent in such a way as to make it in effect a new instrument, it must be restamped; but restamping will not be necessary where the alteration was made whilst the instrument was still in course of execution or merely to correct a mistake[3].

1   As to the kinds of alteration which are not material see para 87 post.

2   *Markham v Gonaston* (1598) Cro Eliz 626, 9 East 354n (blanks filled up); *Zouch v Claye* (1671) 2 Lev 35 (additional obligee added to a bond); *Paget v Paget* (1688) 2 Rep Ch 410 (blanks filled up); *Bates v Grabham* (1703) 3 Salk 444; *French v Patton* (1808) 9 East 351 at 355–357; *Matson v Booth* (1816) 5 M & S 223 at 227; *Eagleton v Gutteridge* (1843) 11 M & W 465; *Adsetts v Hives* (1863) 33 Beav 52 (as to which see para 87 notes 6, 8 post). In a case where the dates of a series of leases had been altered by agreement, the leases were construed, for the purpose of giving an implied right of way, according to the circumstances existing at the dates as altered: *Rudd v Bowles* [1912] 2 Ch 60.

3   See the Stamp Act 1891 s 14(4) (as amended); and STAMP DUTIES AND STAMP DUTY RESERVE TAX vol 44(1) (Reissue) para 1007. See e g *Bowman v Nichol* (1794) 5 Term Rep 537; *Cole v Parkin* (1810) 12 East 471; *Spicer v Burgess* (1834) 1 Cr M & R 129. See STAMP DUTIES AND STAMP DUTY RESERVE TAX vol 44(1) (Reissue) para 1017. As to the terms on which instruments not duly stamped may be received in evidence see generally EVIDENCE.

85. Alteration by stranger after execution. If after the execution of a deed it is intentionally altered in some material[1] part by a stranger (that is, one who is neither a party nor entitled under it), that alteration has the same effect exactly[2], as against a person entitled under and having the custody of the deed, as an alteration made by that person himself, notwithstanding that the alteration was made without his consent[3]. Where a person entitled under a deed has no present right to keep it in his custody and therefore is not in possession of it, for example because he is entitled only on the death of some other person enjoying some interest or right for life under, and so having possession of, the deed, it appears that a material alteration made without the former person's consent while the deed is in possession of that other person will not prevent the former from putting the deed in evidence to enforce his rights under it[4].

1 As to the kinds of alteration which are not material see para 87 post.
2 See para 82 ante.
3 *Pigot's Case* (1614) 11 Co Rep 26b at 27a; *Davidson v Cooper* (1843) 11 M & W 778 at 779, 801–802 (affd (1844) 13 M & W 343 at 352, Ex Ch); *Bank of Hindostan, China and Japan v Smith* (1867) 36 LJCP 241; *Robinson v Mollett* (1875) LR 7 HL 802 at 813 per Blackburn J; *Pattinson v Luckley* (1875) LR 10 Exch 330 at 333–334; *Suffell v Bank of England* (1882) 9 QBD 555 at 559, 562, 571, CA. It appears, however, that the rule so laid down is open to be reviewed in the House of Lords when the alteration is made against the will of the person having the custody: see *Lowe v Fox* (1887) 12 App Cas 206 at 216–217, HL, per Lord Herschell. The reason given for the rule in *Davidson v Cooper* supra was that the person who has the custody of an instrument is bound to preserve it in its original state. This reaffirmed one half of the strict rule of the old law (see para 86 note 2 post), although the principles on which the rule regarding destruction was changed seem to apply in the case of alterations (see the cases cited in para 86 note 2 post; and *Henfree v Bromley* (1805) 6 East 309 at 311–312 per Lord Ellenborough CJ; 1 Preston's Abstracts of Title (2nd Edn) 157; *Hutchins v Scott* (1837) 2 M & W 809 at 814 per Alderson B; Sugden, Treatise on Powers (8th Edn) 603). It seems also that the actual decision in *Davidson v Cooper* supra concerned an alteration made intentionally, although under a mistake of law, by a clerk or servant: see *Robinson v Mollett* (1875) LR 7 HL 802 at 814 per Blackburn J. It may well be that a person entitled under and in possession of a deed ought to be precluded from asserting that an alteration made therein by a clerk, servant, or agent entrusted by him with the custody of the deed was made without his authority (see *Bank of Hindostan, China and Japan v Smith* (1867) 36 LJCP 241), unless, perhaps, the alteration was made for the custodian's own fraudulent purposes (see *Ruben v Great Fingall Consolidated* [1906] AC 439, HL). The case where a stranger, wrongfully and without the knowledge and against the will of the person entitled under and in possession of a deed, obtains access to and materially alters the deed appears to be entirely different; and to hold that the person injured is precluded from asserting his innocence of the alteration appears to be equivalent to ruling that he must keep the deed safe at his peril: see para 86 note 2 post.
4 See *Dalston v Coatsworth* (1721) 1 P Wms 731 at 732–733. That was a case of relief in equity; but it is thought that in this respect the rule of equity will now prevail: see para 86 note 2 post. Further, in the above case the reason given for the rule in *Davidson v Cooper* (1844) 13 M & W 343 at 352, Ex Ch, does not apply: see note 3 supra.

86. Accidental alteration of a deed. If a deed is wholly or partially obliterated or defaced, or, in a case where a seal is still required[1], the seal is detached or destroyed by accident, without the agency of some responsible human being intending so to alter it (as the case of damage done by accidental fire, animals, a child, or a person of unsound mind), this does not now avoid it or preclude its being given in evidence for any purpose[2]; and if a deed is damaged in this manner so that its contents have become wholly or partially illegible, secondary evidence of what was written is admissible[3]. It appears upon principle that, if damage of the kind mentioned is done to a deed by some human being inadvertently and unintentionally, this will not at the present day avoid the deed in any way or preclude its being put in evidence, even though the damage was done by the person entitled under and having the custody of the deed[4].

1 See para 32 ante. As from 31 July 1990, any rule of law which requires a seal for the valid execution of an instrument as a deed by an individual is abolished: see the Law of Property (Miscellaneous Provisions) Act 1989 s 1(1)(b); and paras 7, 27, 32 ante.

2   *Doctor Leyfield's Case* (1611) 10 Co Rep 88a at 92b, 93a; *Lady Argoll v Cheney* (1626) Palm 402 at 403; *Anon* (circa 1627) Lat 226; *Clerke d Prin v Heath* (1669) 1 Mod Rep 11 per Twisden J; *Read v Brookman* (1789) 3 Term Rep 151 at 158 per Ashhurst J; *Master v Miller* (1791) 4 Term Rep 320 at 339 per Buller J; *Bolton v Bishop of Carlisle* (1793) 2 Hy Bl 259 at 263–264; 1 Preston's Abstracts of Title (2nd Edn) 157; 3 Preston's Abstracts of Title (2nd Edn) 103. The old law was that a party entitled under and having the custody of a deed must keep it safe and undefaced at his peril: *Nichols v Haywood* (1545) 1 Dyer 59a; *Michael v Stockwith* (1588) Cro Eliz 120; *Pigot's Case* (1614) 11 Co Rep 26b at 27a. Relief was first given in equity in case of the casual loss or destruction of a deed, the party being allowed, on proof of such loss or destruction, to give secondary evidence of the contents of the deed: *Wilcox v Sturt* (1682) 1 Vern 77 at 78; *Dalston v Coatsworth* (1721) 1 P Wms 731; *Cowper v Earl Cowper* (1734) 2 P Wms 720 at 748–750; *Cookes v Hellier* (1749) 1 Ves Sen 234 at 235 per Lord Hardwicke LC; *Whitfield v Fausset* (1750) 1 Ves Sen 387 at 389–390; *Saltern v Melhuish* (1754) Amb 247. Afterwards a lost deed was allowed to be pleaded at law without a profert (i e a form of pleading which alleged that the deed was brought into court although this was not actually done; profert was abolished by the Common Law Procedure Act 1852 s 55 (repealed)): *Read v Brookman* (1789) 3 Term Rep 151. This did not do away with the jurisdiction of courts of equity to give relief where a deed had been lost or destroyed by accident: *Atkinson v Leonard* (1791) 3 Bro CC 218 at 224; *Ex p Greenway* (1802) 6 Ves 812 at 813 per Lord Eldon LC; *Bromley v Holland* (1802) 7 Ves 3 at 19–20; *East India Co v Boddam* (1804) 9 Ves 464 at 466. It appears, therefore, that this equitable jurisdiction now resides in the High Court of Justice, and that, supposing the old law to have been to some extent reaffirmed by the case of *Davidson v Cooper* (1844) 13 M & W 343 at 352, Ex Ch (see para 85 note 3 ante), the rule of equity in the above respect should now prevail: see the Supreme Court Act 1981 (prospectively renamed the Senior Courts Act 1981) s 49(1); *Steeds v Steeds* (1889) 22 QBD 537; and COURTS. See also generally EVIDENCE.

3   See the cases in equity cited in note 2 supra; and see *Medlicot v Joyner* (1667) 1 Mod Rep 4; Gilbert, Law of Evidence (6th Edn) 84–85; *Doe d Gilbert v Ross* (1840) 7 M & W 102; *Fitzwalter Peerage* (1844) 10 Cl & Fin 946 at 952–953, HL; *Moulton v Edmonds* (1859) 1 De GF & J 246 at 251. See also EVIDENCE.

4   See the authorities cited at the beginning of note 2 supra; and see *Fernandey v Glynn* (1808) 1 Camp 426n; *Raper v Birkbeck* (1812) 15 East 17 at 20; *Wilkinson v Johnson* (1824) 3 B & C 428; *Novelli v Rossi* (1831) 2 B & Ad 757; *Warwick v Rogers* (1843) 5 Man & G 340 at 373; *Bamberger v Commercial Credit Mutual Assurance Society* (1855) 15 CB 676 at 693–694. It is submitted that if, in the above respect, the old law was reaffirmed by the decision in *Davidson v Cooper* (1844) 13 M & W 343 at 352, Ex Ch (see para 85 note 3 ante), the case put falls within the principle on which courts of equity afforded relief, and that, under the present practice, the rule of equity should prevail (see note 2 supra). See also EVIDENCE.

87.   Immaterial alteration.   An alteration made in a deed, after its execution, in some particular which is not material[1] does not in any way affect the validity of the deed; and this is equally the case whether the alteration was made by a stranger[2] or by a party to the deed[3]. Thus the date of a deed may well be filled in after execution[4]; for a deed takes effect from the date of execution, and is quite good though it is undated[5]. So, also, the names of the occupiers of land conveyed may be inserted in a deed after its execution, where the property assured was sufficiently ascertained without them[6]. It appears that an alteration is not material which does not vary the legal effect of the deed in its original state, but merely expresses that which was implied by law in the deed as originally written[7], or which carries out the intention of the parties already apparent on the face of the deed[8], provided that the alteration does not otherwise prejudice the party liable under it[9]. An alteration made in a deed may be material as against some party or parties thereto but immaterial as against the other or others[10]; and where such an alteration has been made in a deed, any agreement contained in it may be enforced against the party or parties as to whom the alteration is immaterial (if originally liable thereunder) in the same manner as if the deed had remained unaltered[11].

In modern conditions it has been held that the critical question is that of prejudice or potential prejudice as a result of the alteration[12].

1   See para 82 notes 5–7 ante.

2   *Pigot's Case* (1614) 11 Co Rep 26b at 27a. See *Raiffeisen Zentralbank Osterreich AG v Crossseas Shipping Ltd* [2000] 1 All ER (Comm) 76, [2000] 1 WLR 1135, CA.

3   *Aldous v Cornwell* (1868) LR 3 QB 573 at 579; *Bishop of Crediton v Bishop of Exeter* [1905] 2 Ch 455 at 459 (overruling *Pigot's Case* (1614) 11 Co Rep 26b on this point).

4   *Keane v Smallbone* (1855) 17 CB 179; *Adsetts v Hives* (1863) 33 Beav 52; *Bishop of Crediton v Bishop of Exeter* [1905] 2 Ch 455.

5   See para 60 notes 1, 3 ante.

6   *Adsetts v Hives* (1863) 33 Beav 52. It is thought that where the description contained in the deed is such that it is essential to have the occupiers' names in order to ascertain what is intended to be conveyed, the addition of such names, after execution, would be a material alteration: see paras 28, 82 et seq ante. The alteration of the Christian names of one party was held not to avoid a deed: *Re Howgate and Osborn's Contract* [1902] 1 Ch 451; and cf *Eagleton v Gutteridge* (1843) 11 M & W 465. Likewise the striking out of the word 'Company' which had wrongly been inserted in the defendant company's name: *Lombard Finance Ltd v Brookplain Trading Ltd* [1991] 2 All ER 762, [1991] 1 WLR 271, CA. See also *Raiffeisen Zentralbank Osterreich AG v Crossseas Shipping Ltd* [2000] 1 All ER (Comm) 76, [2000] 1 WLR 1135, CA, where the bank had inserted the name, address, telephone and fax numbers of the first defendant.

7   *Waugh v Bussell* (1814) 5 Taunt 707 at 711; *Aldous v Cornwell* (1868) LR 3 QB 573 (adding 'on demand' to a promissory note).

8   *Adsetts v Hives* (1863) 33 Beav 52. The decision in that case as to filling up the date for redemption seems to go beyond the principle expressed above and to have been a benevolent judgment. It may be usual, but it is not inevitably necessary that a loan on mortgage shall be made repayable in six months' time. The alterations made in that case were all made with the consent of the mortgagor. It does not appear that the objection was taken that a new stamp was necessary: see *Eagleton v Gutteridge* (1843) 11 M & W 465 at 468–469; and para 84 ante.

9   See para 82 note 7 ante.

10 *Doe d Lewis v Bingham* (1821) 4 B & Ald 672.

11 *Hall v Chandless* (1827) 4 Bing 123.

12 *Raiffeisen Zentralbank Osterreich AG v Crossseas Shipping Ltd* [2000] 1 All ER (Comm) 76, [2000] 1 WLR 1135, CA.

88.   Rectification.   Where, in carrying into effect an antecedent agreement, a deed is prepared which in some particular fails to carry out the common intentions of the parties as expressed in the antecedent agreement, and the deed so prepared is executed by both or all parties without appreciating that its contents are at variance with the previous agreement (or by one or more without so appreciating, the other or others by words or conduct misrepresenting that it carries out the common intentions), the deed may be rectified (or treated as if rectified) under the equitable jurisdiction to correct mistakes of this character[1].

1   See *Re Bird's Trusts* (1876) 3 ChD 214; *A Roberts & Co v Leicestershire County Council* [1961] Ch 555, [1961] 2 All ER 545; *Wilson v Wilson* [1969] 3 All ER 945, [1969] 1 WLR 1470; *Riverlate Properties Ltd v Paul* [1975] Ch 133, [1974] 2 All ER 656, CA; *Re Butlin's Settlement Trust* [1976] Ch 251, [1976] 2 All ER 483; *Thomas Bates & Son Ltd v Wyndham's (Lingerie) Ltd* [1981] 1 All ER 1077, [1981] 1 WLR 505, CA; *Thames Guaranty Ltd v Campbell* [1985] QB 210, [1984] 2 All ER 585, CA; *Racal Group Services Ltd v Ashmore* [1995] STC 1151, 68 TC 86, CA; and EQUITY vol 16(2) (Reissue) para 443; MISTAKE vol 32 (2005 Reissue) paras 55–66.

2. BONDS

(1) NATURE AND USE

(i) Definitions

89.   In general.   At common law a bond is an instrument under seal[1], usually a deed poll[2], whereby one person binds himself to another for the payment of a specified sum of money either immediately or at a fixed future date[3]. The person who so binds himself is called the obligor, and the person to whom he is bound the obligee; and the instrument itself is sometimes called an obligation[4]. Any rule of law which requires a seal for the valid execution of an instrument as a deed by an individual was abolished by the Law of Property (Miscellaneous Provisions) Act 1989 in relation to instruments delivered as deeds on or after 31 July 1990[5].

1   2 Bl Com (14th Edn) 340; *National Telephone Co v IRC* [1900] AC 1, HL; *British India Steam Navigation Co v IRC* (1881) 7 QBD 165 at 173, DC, per Lindley J.
2   As to deeds poll see para 3 ante.
3   For a wider meaning of the term 'bond' in relation to British government and local authority securities see para 94 post. For the use of the term by insurance companies as describing contracts offered by them primarily for investment purposes see para 95 post.
4   Shep Touch 367.
5   See the Law of Property (Miscellaneous Provisions) Act 1989 s 1(1)(b); and paras 7, 27, 32 ante. This does not include execution by a corporation sole: see s 1(10); and para 32 text to note 3 ante. As to the application of s 1(1)(b) see s 1(9); and para 7 text and note 4 ante. As to the requirements of a deed see s 1(2), (3) (as amended); and paras 8, 33 ante. As to the application of s 1(2), (3) (as amended) see s 1(9); and para 7 text and note 4 ante.

90.   Single bond.   A bond merely for the payment of a certain sum of money, without any condition in or annexed to it, is called a simple or single bond[1]. Such instruments became rare, and the term 'single bond' came to be used sometimes to signify a bond given by one obligor as distinguished from one given by two or more[2].

1   2 Bl Com (14th Edn) 340; *Morrant v Gough* (1827) 7 B & C 206.
2   See *Merchant of Venice*, Act I, scene 3, line 146 et seq: 'Go with me to a notary, seal me there Your single bond; and, in a merry sport, If you repay me not on such a day, In such a place, such sum or sums as are Express'd in the condition, let the forfeit Be … '.

91.   Double or conditional bond.   The ordinary form of bond came to be one accompanied by a condition in the nature of a defeasance[1], the performance of the condition generally being secured by a penalty. This form of bond is called a double or conditional bond[2], and consists of two parts: first, the obligation, and secondly, the condition[3]. The condition, which may be contained in the same or another instrument, or may be indorsed on the back[4], specifies the real agreement between the parties, that is to say, the money to be paid or acts or duties to be performed or observed, the payment, performance, or observance of which is intended to be secured by the bond, and it provides that on due performance of the condition the bond is to be void[5]. The obligation, as in the case of a single bond[6], simply binds the obligor to the payment of a certain sum of money, such sum of money being usually, though not necessarily, a penalty[7], and does not in terms refer to the condition. On breach of the condition the bond is said to become forfeited or absolute, though it does not follow that the obligee is entitled to recover the sum mentioned in the obligation[8].

A conditional bond sometimes contains explanatory recitals. When it does so, the recitals follow the obligation and precede the condition.

1   The term 'defeasance' is more properly employed when the condition is contained in a separate instrument: Shep Touch 367, 396.

2   Shep Touch 367.
3   See *Guyana and Trinidad Mutual Fire Insurance Co Ltd v RK Plummer & Associates Ltd* (1992) 8 Const LJ 171, PC.
4   Shep Touch 367; Vin Abr, Faits (G).
5   The omission of words providing that the obligation is void does not affect the validity of the condition: *Mauleverer v Hauxby* (1670) 2 Saund 78.
6   See para 90 ante.
7   See para 128 post.
8   See para 128 post.

(ii) Use of Bonds

92. Use of bonds otherwise than for financial purposes. The use of double bonds[1] has long been discouraged by conveyancers[2], and they now only survive where required by legislation, or taken by an institution or body adhering to traditional forms, or where the form of a double bond genuinely provides a convenient means of limiting a surety's or guarantor's liability. Thus provision is still made by various enactments for giving security by a double bond for the due observance of conditions of a privilege[3]. The taking of a double bond to secure or guarantee the performance of a building contract is also still common[4], notwithstanding judicial criticism[5]. A performance bond in an international commercial transaction, said to be a new creature so far as the Court of Appeal was concerned in 1978, is now commonplace[6].

In addition, in civil proceedings statutory provisions relating to procedure and rules of court permit or require security to be given by a bond for the performance or discharge of a number of obligations or requirements[7]; the form of bond used for this purpose is generally a double bond.

In criminal proceedings, bonds are not taken but the court may require defendants or witnesses to enter into recognisances, for instance to keep the peace or be of good behaviour, or to appear at the trial[8]. Such recognisances may be required to be given with or without sureties[9]. They have the effect of a double bond, but are taken orally before an officer of the court whose record in writing is the recognisance. In proceedings relating to the care of a juvenile, his parent or guardian may be required to enter into a recognisance to take proper care of and exercise proper control over him[10].

1   For the meaning of 'double bond' see para 91 ante.
2   See e g 5 Davidson's Precedents and Forms in Conveyancing (3rd Edn) (1878) Pt II 267. The intervention of equity (see para 126 post) and subsequently of statute (see para 126 notes 1–2 post) took away from a double bond the advantage which it would otherwise have had over an ordinary covenant or contract of penalising breach of the condition whose performance or observance it was intended to secure: a covenant or contract to perform or observe the condition gave rise, on its breach, to a claim for damages measured by the loss actually suffered, whereas the penalty of a bond was normally fixed at an amount substantially greater than this. Without any such advantage, in a period when the law of contract had been fully developed, double bonds declined in use in favour of the more readily comprehensible and straightforward covenant or simple contract. In appropriate cases, these could be enforced by specific performance or injunction as an alternative or in addition to damages, whereas such equitable remedies might not be as clearly available on a double bond: see *National Provincial Bank of England v Marshall* (1888) 40 ChD 112, CA; para 129 post; and INJUNCTIONS; SPECIFIC PERFORMANCE.
3   See e g the Customs and Excise Management Act 1979 ss 131, 157 (as amended) (bonds for the observance of any condition in connection with customs or excise); and CUSTOMS AND EXCISE vol 12(3) (2007 Reissue) paras 1104, 1167.
4   See BUILDING CONTRACTS, ARCHITECTS, ENGINEERS, VALUERS AND SURVEYORS vol 4(2) (Reissue) para 185. Such a bond is called a 'performance bond'. As to performance bonds generally see GUARANTEE AND INDEMNITY vol 20(1) (Reissue) para 359 et seq.
5   See e g *Trafalgar House Construction (Regions) Ltd v General Surety and Guarantee Co Ltd* [1996] AC 199 at 209, [1995] 3 All ER 737 at 745, HL, per Lord Jauncey of Tullichettle, who found 'great difficulty in understanding the desire of commercial men to embody so simple an obligation in a document which is quite unnecessarily lengthy, which obfuscates its true purpose and which is likely to give rise to unnecessary arguments and litigation as to its meaning'.

6   See *Edward Owen Engineering Ltd v Barclays Bank International Ltd* [1978] QB 159, [1978] 1 All ER 976, CA; and para 99 post. However, as late as 1990 performance bonds were referred to as 'strange documents to an English lawyer': *IE Contractors Ltd v Lloyds Bank plc* [1990] 2 Lloyd's Rep 496 at 502, CA, per Staughton LJ.

7   See paras 101–102 post.

8   See further CRIMINAL LAW, EVIDENCE AND PROCEDURE vol 11(4) (2006 Reissue) paras 1680–1681.

9   Where an accused person is released on entering with sureties into recognisances to appear to stand trial, the sureties are 'bail' for the accused. Bail can also mean the amount of the penalty of the recognisances.

10   See further CHILDREN AND YOUNG PERSONS vol 5(3) (Reissue) para 1638.

93.   Use of bonds as securities for company borrowings. In the financial field, the single bond[1], as an acknowledgment of the existence of, or of the liability to repay, a loan, gave way long ago to the double bond, usually in the form of a common money bond, that is, a bond conditioned for repayment of the loan with interest on the redemption date[2]. In its turn the double bond, as a security issued for a loan, was superseded in the middle of the nineteenth century by the modern forms of debenture and debenture stock, and now survives only where required by some of the older but still extant statutes. Thus the Companies Clauses Consolidation Act 1845[3] still regulates the borrowing of money on mortgage or bond by the statutory companies (incorporated by special Act of Parliament) to which it applies. Where the borrowing is secured by a bond, the Act[4] prescribes that the bond should be in the form scheduled to the Act[5] or to the like effect. The form so scheduled is that of a common money bond. However, there are now comparatively few companies to which this Act applies, and they have been authorised alternatively to raise money by the issue of debenture stock[6] and in some individual cases in other ways. The Companies Act 1862, and its successors, which provide for the incorporation of companies by registration, have never attempted to restrict the nature of the securities which could be issued by companies incorporated under them, in order to raise loan capital; and these companies adopted modern forms of debentures and debenture stock trust deeds in place of the older common money bonds. A bond does not have to employ any particular form of words, and the usual form of a debenture, when by deed, is in fact a single bond with a superadded provision for payment of interest on the amount of the bond, and often, in addition, further provisions which may include a charge on all or some of the assets of the company. Indeed, when the modern form of debentures was first used by companies incorporated under the Companies Act 1862, these securities were sometimes called 'bonds' or 'obligations' or 'debenture bonds', but eventually 'debentures' or, sometimes where they contained a charge, 'mortgage debentures' became the usual expressions to describe instruments of this nature issued by English companies[7]. A debenture is not necessarily by deed[8], and the term has therefore a wider meaning than bond. Although modern company debentures, where executed by deed, are single bonds with added provisions, there is now a large body of law[9] relating only to debentures of companies and not to other bonds[10].

1   For the meaning of 'single bond' see para 90 ante.

2   For the meaning of 'double bond' see para 91 ante. As to common money bonds see para 96 post. For a mid-nineteenth century form of double bond taken by a bank to secure a joint stock company's overdraft on current account see *Royal British Bank v Turquand* (1855) 5 E & B 248; on appeal (1856) 6 E & B 327, Ex Ch.

3   See the Companies Clauses Consolidation Act 1845 ss 38–55 (as amended); and COMPANIES vol 7(2) (2004 Reissue) para 1921 et seq.

4   See ibid s 41; and COMPANIES vol 7(2) (2004 Reissue) para 1925.

5   See ibid Sch (D); and COMPANIES vol 7(2) (2004 Reissue) para 1925.

6   The Companies Clauses Act 1863 Pt III (ss 22–35) (as amended) empowered the companies to which it applied to issue debenture stock subject to the regulations contained in that Act; and by the Companies Clauses Act 1869 s 3, every statutory company having the power under the Companies

Clauses Consolidation Act 1845 (see notes 3–5 supra) to raise money on mortgage or bond was given power to issue such debenture stock. See also COMPANIES vol 7(2) (2004 Reissue) paras 1852, 1938.

7   See *Re Natal Investment Co, Claim of the Financial Corpn* (1868) 3 Ch App 355 at 356–360 per Lord Cairns LC; *Re Florence Land and Public Works Co, ex p Moor* (1878) 10 ChD 530, CA; *British India Steam Navigation Co v IRC* (1881) 7 QBD 165 at 168, DC, per Grove J, and at 172–173 per Lindley J. The use of the expression 'bonds' is still prevalent to describe securities issued by companies incorporated in countries other than the United Kingdom: see e g *Feist v Société Intercommunale Belge D'Électricité* [1934] AC 161, HL.

       There is considerable overlap in the legal terminology in this field. No particular words are required to create a covenant (see para 249 post), and a debenture by deed, apart from being a single bond with superadded provisions, can equally well be regarded as a series of covenants. For some purposes, a debenture (or single bond), though by deed, can be treated as a promissory note: *Re General Estates Co, ex p City Bank* (1868) 3 Ch App 758; but contrast, in relation to stamp duty, *British India Steam Navigation Co v IRC* (1881) 7 QBD 165, DC.

8   See *British India Steam Navigation Co v IRC* (1881) 7 QBD 165 at 172–173, DC, per Lindley J.

9   See COMPANIES vol 7(2) (2004 Reissue) para 1533 et seq.

10   For the purposes of the Companies Act 1985, 'debenture' includes debenture stock, bonds and any other securities of a company, whether constituting a charge on the assets of the company or not: see s 744; and COMPANIES vol 7(2) (2004 Reissue) para 1533.

94. Use of bonds as British government and local authority securities. A more marked departure from the traditional form of bonds has occurred in regard to British government and local authority securities, but the expression 'bonds' has been retained in this field. At the present day, it may be used as describing, or as part of the name of, some issues of securities which are authorised by legislation to be effected as issues of bonds but whose documentation, also so authorised, does not involve the execution of any instrument which either resembles a traditional bond or is within the general legal definition of the word[1].

1   Statutory provision has long been made to allow a holder of British government bearer bonds to deliver them up for conversion into registered form and to have instead a certificate of his holding, transfer of which would thereafter require entry in a register, and to allow the converse process of taking a bearer bond in lieu of the whole or part of a registered holding: see the Exchequer Bills and Bonds Act 1866 s 27 (now repealed, but which provided for optional registration); and the Finance Act 1963 s 71(1) (as amended) (which gives to a registered holder of certain issues of government securities an option to have such a bond, and for the bond so issued to be surrendered so as to be replaced by a registered holding: see MONEY vol 32 (2005 Reissue) para 161). In consequence many issues of government securities are held partly in registered form and partly in the form of bearer bonds, even though the whole issue is called by a name describing it as stock or as bonds. The Treasury may make regulations providing for the issue of documents of title relating to stock and bonds and as to the evidence of title to them, as well as providing for the transfer and keeping of registers of stock and bonds, and may also make regulations for regulating the issue of bearer bonds: see the Finance Act 1942 s 47 (as amended); the Bank of England Act 1946`s 1 (as amended), Sch 1 para 6; the Finance Act 1963 s 71(3); the National Loans Act 1968 s 14(3); the Post Office Act 1969 s 108(1) (as amended); the National Debt Act 1972 ss 3, 11 (both as amended); and BANKING vol 3(1) (2005 Reissue) para 117; MONEY vol 32 (2005 Reissue) para 158. An issue of entirely registered bonds (e g Premium Savings Bonds) none of which can be converted into bearer form may be made: (1) by issuing to (among others) the intending bondholder a prospectus containing the terms and conditions of the bonds; (2) by his completing and signing an application form which merely applies for bonds 'in accordance with the terms of the prospectus' to the value of a specified amount; (3) by his handing or sending the completed application form to the government agency together with the subscription for the bonds; and (4) by his being given one or more 'bonds', each stating the name of the issue and the nominal amount of the bond but not necessarily containing all or any of the other terms and conditions of the issue, the issue of the bonds then being registered in due course. In that event a contract is constituted by the issue of the bonds in acceptance of the application; the terms of the contract will be found in the application and the referentially incorporated prospectus. An issue of registered bonds may alternatively be made by prospectus, and application with subscription, as above, followed by entry on the register and issue of a certificate of the holding of bonds by the applicant, in precisely the same manner as an issue of registered government stock. No document can then be identified as a bond, and the expression merely denotes the contractual relationship established by the application and the allotment (in acceptance) of the holding of bonds. British government bonds are not issued under seal.

95.   Bond investment business of insurance companies. Insurance companies formerly issued investment bonds under which, in return for periodical premiums, a fixed sum was payable by the insurance company at a fixed future date unrelated to any life or other contingency. A bond of this kind was drawn in the form of a double bond[1] imposing on the company the obligation of paying the fixed sum at the fixed date but conditioned so that the obligation was defeated if the periodic premiums were not punctually paid[2]. Such a bond was often used for the redemption of a capital outlay on a wasting asset, for instance a lease, and the business of issuing these contracts came to be called capital redemption business[3]. Since the late 1960s it has become apparent that insurance companies, with the tax privileges given to life assurance business and to purchased life annuities, could offer attractive investment contracts to the investing public. In consequence a growing variety of kinds of investment contract has been offered by insurance companies. These are usually called bonds, but in order to obtain more beneficial tax treatment they have as a rule to be written as life assurance policies or contracts for the purchase of immediate and deferred annuities[4]. The policy or contract is normally executed under hand, and is issued in return generally for a single payment but sometimes for periodic premiums. The issuing company may undertake liability to make payments linked in amount to the price from time to time of units of a particular unit trust, or the current value of buildings or other properties held by a particular fund, or the current value or price of some other selection of assets or commodities, or the current level of some share or other index[5]. The law relating to bonds is not applicable to any of these policies or contracts not by deed except in so far as it is the same as the law applicable to instruments under hand[6].

1   See para 91 ante.
2   See the form of bond referred to in *Re British Equitable Bond and Mortgage Corpn Ltd* [1910] 1 Ch 574 at 575.
3   As to the classification of insurance business generally see INSURANCE vol 25 (2003 Reissue) para 9.
4   As to life assurance and annuity contracts see INSURANCE vol 25 (2003 Reissue) para 525 et seq.
5   For a general account of linked investment bonds of the nature described see the *Report of the Committee on Property Bonds and Equity-linked Life Assurance* (Cmnd 5281) (1973).
6   For the law relating to instruments under hand see para 139 et seq post.

(iii)   Particular Kinds of Bond

96.   Common money bonds. A common money bond[1] is one given to secure the payment of money, the condition being that if the obligor pays to the obligee a smaller sum, usually one-half of the sum named in the obligation, with interest, on a specified day, the bond is to be void.

1   See also para 93 ante.

97.   Post obits. A post obit bond[1] is a bond conditioned for the payment of a sum of money after the death of a specified person, and is usually given in respect of a loan and for a sum greater than that advanced. Such bonds are of two kinds: (1) where the payment depends on a contingency, as for instance in the event of the obligor surviving a relative in regard to whom he has expectations; (2) where the payment is certain, but the time of payment uncertain, as in the case of a bond conditioned for payment of a certain sum on the death of the obligor.

1   See also paras 120 text and note 7, 126 post.

98.   Lloyd's bond. A Lloyd's bond[1] is a security issued by a company either in the form of a common money bond[2], with a recital of the company's indebtedness to the obligee[3] or in the form of an acknowledgment of a debt to a particular person, with a covenant to pay it[4]. Though originally devised for the purpose of raising money, such bonds are invalid when so used by a statutory company not incorporated under the Companies Act 1985 (or enactments replaced by or replacing that Act[5]), unless the borrowing powers of the company authorise their issue[6], except to the extent that the money raised by their issue has been legitimately applied for the company's benefit[7]. Where, however, the bonds are given in consideration of an existing liability incurred by the company in good faith, and not ultra vires as in the case of a debt due to a contractor for work done, they are valid[8]. A bond given on or after 1 January 1973 by a company incorporated under the Companies Act 1985 (or enactments replaced by or replacing that Act) cannot now be called into question on the ground of lack of capacity by reason of anything in the company's memorandum[9].

1   So called after the inventor: *Chambers v Manchester and Milford Rly Co* (1864) 5 B & S 588 at 608 per Crompton J.
2   See para 96 ante.
3   For this form of Lloyd's bond see *Re Cork and Youghal Rly Co* (1869) 4 Ch App 748 at 749.
4   For this form of Lloyd's bond see *Chambers v Manchester and Milford Rly Co* (1864) 5 B & S 588 at 591.
5   See COMPANIES vol 7(1) (2004 Reissue) para 204 et seq.
6   *Chambers v Manchester and Milford Rly Co* (1864) 5 B & S 588. As to borrowing by companies see COMPANIES vol 7(2) (2004 Reissue) para 1517 et seq. See also the Transport Act 1962 s 19 (as amended); and RAILWAYS, INLAND WATERWAYS and PIPELINES vol 39(1) (Reissue) para 382.
7   *Re Cork and Youghal Rly Co* (1869) 4 Ch App 748.
8   *Re Cork and Youghal Rly Co* (1869) 4 Ch App 748 at 757 per Lord Hatherley LC (approving *Chambers v Manchester and Milford Rly Co* (1864) 5 B & S 588 at 611 per Blackburn J; *White v Carmarthen etc Rly Co* (1863) 1 Hem & M 786).
9   See the Companies Act 1985 s 35 (as substituted and amended); and COMPANIES vol 7(1) (2004 Reissue) para 430. As to a company's capacity and formalities of carrying on business see para 41 note 15 ante; and COMPANIES vol 7(1) (2004 Reissue) paras 416, 430–432, 467.

99.   Performance bonds in international trade.   In a typical case the contract will provide for the buyer to provide for the payment of the price of goods to be supplied by a confirmed letter of credit[1], and the supplier arranges for a performance bond to be given for a percentage of the contract price guaranteeing performance of its obligations under the contract. A performance bond has many similarities with a letter of credit; accordingly where a bank has given a performance bond it is required to honour it according to its terms and is not concerned whether either party to the contract which underlays it is in default[2]. The sole exception arises in instances of fraud[3]. However, in the absence of clear contractual words to the contrary, it is implicit in the nature of a performance bond that there will be an accounting between the parties after the bond has been called, so that if the amount received under the bond exceeds the true loss, the party who provided the bond is entitled to recover the overpayment[4].

1   As to the nature of letters of credit see BANKING vol 3(1) (2005 Reissue) para 233 et seq.
2   See *Edward Owen Engineering Ltd v Barclays Bank International Ltd* [1978] QB 159, [1978] 1 All ER 976, CA; *United Trading Corpn SA v Allied Arab Bank Ltd* [1985] 2 Lloyd's Rep 554n, CA; *IE Contractors Ltd v Lloyds Bank plc* [1990] 2 Lloyd's Rep 496, CA; and BANKING vol 3(1) (2005 Reissue) para 237; BUILDING CONTRACTS, ARCHITECTS, ENGINEERS, VALUERS AND SURVEYORS vol 4(3) (Reissue) para 185; SALE OF GOODS AND SUPPLY OF SERVICES vol 41 (2005 Reissue) para 380. As to performance bonds generally see GUARANTEE AND INDEMNITY vol 20(1) (Reissue) para 359 et seq.
3   See *Edward Owen Engineering Ltd v Barclays Bank International Ltd* [1978] QB 159, [1978] 1 All ER 976, CA; *United City Merchants (Investments) Ltd v Royal Bank of Canada* [1983] 1 AC 168, [1982] 2 All ER 720, HL; *Bolivinter Oil SA v Chase Manhattan Bank* [1984] 1 All ER 351n, [1984] 1 Lloyd's Rep 251, CA; *United Trading Corpn SA v Allied Arab Bank Ltd* [1985] 2 Lloyd's Rep 554n, CA; *Themehelp Ltd v West* [1996] QB 84, [1995] 4 All ER 215, CA; *Turkiye Is Bankasi AS v Bank of China* [1998] 1 Lloyd's Rep 250, CA; *Czarnikow-Rionda Sugar Trading Inc v Standard Bank London Ltd* [1999] 1 All ER (Comm) 890, [1999] 2 Lloyd's Rep 187.
4   See *Cargill International SA v Bangladesh Sugar and Food Industries Corpn* [1998] 2 All ER 406, [1998] 1 WLR 461, CA.

100. Administration bonds.   At one time, every person who obtained a grant of administration was required to give a bond to the principal probate registrar; such a bond was called an administration bond[1]. Since 1 January 1972, however, administration bonds are no longer required, but any such bond given before that date may be enforced[2]. Now a guarantee given in pursuance of a requirement enures for the benefit of every person interested in the administration of the estate of the deceased as if contained in a deed made by the surety or sureties with every such person and, where there are two or more sureties, as if they had bound themselves jointly and severally[3].

1   See the Supreme Court of Judicature (Consolidation) Act 1925 s 167(1) (repealed by the Supreme Court Act 1981 (prospectively renamed the Senior Courts Act 1981) s 152(4), Sch 7). As to grants of administration see EXECUTORS AND ADMINISTRATORS vol 17(2) (Reissue) para 72 et seq.
2   See ibid s 167(1) (as substituted by the Administration of Estates Act 1971 s 8; now repealed (see note 1 supra)), which provided that as from 1 January 1972 an administrator might be required to produce sureties.
4   See the Supreme Court Act 1981 (prospectively renamed the Senior Courts Act 1981) s 120(2); and EXECUTORS AND ADMINISTRATORS vol 17(2) (Reissue) para 255.

101. Replevin bonds.   A replevin bond is a security which the owner of chattels alleged to have been wrongfully seized is required to enter into before he can obtain redelivery of the chattels; the condition of the security is that he will commence and prosecute a claim of replevin against the seizor and make a return of the goods, if so ordered in the claim[1].

1   See the County Courts Act 1984 s 144, Sch 1 paras 1, 2 (as amended); and DISTRESS para 1084 post; GUARANTEE AND INDEMNITY vol 20(1) (Reissue) paras 185, 315.

102. Bonds given under order of court.   A bond to be given by any person under or for the purposes of any order of the High Court or the civil division of the Court of Appeal must be given in such form and to such officer of the court as may be prescribed[1] and, if the court so requires, with one or more sureties[2]. The prescribed officer has the power to enforce the bond or to assign it, in accordance with the following provisions, to another person[3].

Where by rules of court an officer is at any time substituted for the officer previously prescribed in relation to bonds of any class, such rules may provide that bonds of that class previously given are to have effect as if the name of the officer previously prescribed were references to the substituted officer[4].

Where it appears to the court that the condition of a bond in accordance with the above provisions has been broken, the court may, on an application in that behalf, order that the bond be assigned to such person as may be specified in the order[5]. That person is then entitled to sue on the bond in his own name as if it had been originally given to him and to recover thereon, as trustee for all persons interested, the full amount recoverable in respect of the breach of condition[6].

A bond may be ordered to be given as security for the costs of proceedings[7], or as security for the due performance of his duties by a receiver appointed for a mental patient by the Court of Protection[8].

1   For these purposes, 'prescribed' means: (1) except in relation to fees, prescribed by rules of court: Supreme Court Act 1981 (prospectively renamed the Senior Courts Act 1981) s 151(1) (definition amended by the Courts Act 2003 s 109(1), (3), Sch 8 para 265, Sch 10).
2   Supreme Court Act 1981 (prospectively renamed the Senior Courts Act 1981) s 135(1).
3   Ibid s 135(2).
4   Ibid s 135(3).
5   Ibid s 135(4).
6   Ibid s 135(5).

7   See now CPR 25.12–25.15. The more usual and convenient mode in which to order security for costs, however, is to require a specified sum to be paid into court within a specified period. As to the special circumstances in which security may be required and the mode of security see generally PRACTICE AND PROCEDURE.

8   See the Court of Protection Rules 2001, SI 2001/824, rr 56–60 (as amended); and MENTAL HEALTH vol 30(2) (Reissue) para 710.

(iv) Form and Execution: Capacity of Parties

103.   Essentials of valid bond.   To constitute a valid bond, there must be an obligor and obligee, and a fixed sum of money in which the obligor is bound; and the instrument must be duly executed by the obligor[1]. Consideration is not necessary, the instrument being delivered as a deed[2].

A bond executed with a blank for the name of the obligee is void, and extrinsic evidence is not admissible to supply the defect; but if it appears from the instrument as a whole to whom the obligor is intended to be bound, as where there is a recital of indebtedness to a person named, the bond is not invalid merely because the obligee's name is not mentioned in the obligatory part[3].

A bond is void unless the obligor is bound in a definite sum of money[4], but it is not invalid merely because the sum is improperly expressed, provided the intention is clear[5].

1   Com Dig, Obligation (A); Shep Touch 56; *Dodson v Kayes* (1610) Yelv 193.
2   *Squire v Whitton* (1848) 1 HL Cas 333.
3   *Langdon v Goole* (1681) 3 Lev 21; *Lambert v Branthwaite* (1733) 2 Stra 945.
4   *Loggins v Titheton* (1612) Yelv 225.
5   *Hulbert v Long* (1621) Cro Jac 607; *Cromwell v Grunsden* (1698) 2 Salk 462; *Coles v Hulme* (1828) 8 B & C 568 (where the obligor acknowledged himself bound in 7,700 without mentioning any species of money, and there being a recital of indebtedness in various sums expressed in pounds sterling, the court supplied the word 'pounds' in the obligatory part).

104.   Form.   No particular form of words is necessary to create a bond. If the essentials of a valid bond[1] are present, any mode of expression by which the intention of the parties is made clear will suffice[2].

A bond may be given by two or more obligors either jointly or severally, or jointly and severally[3]; and may be given to two or more obligees jointly or severally, or, since 1925, jointly and severally[4].

The stamp duty formerly levied on bonds has been abolished[5].

The difference between a bond and a covenant is one of form rather than substance. Covenants are generally found in deeds of the type formerly known as indentures, whereas a bond is usually a deed poll[6]; and a covenant expresses the real agreement between the parties, the penalty or sum fixed by way of liquidated damages, if any, being the subject of a further covenant, whereas in a bond the only undertaking of the obligor is to pay a certain sum of money, such sum in a double bond being either a penalty or liquidated damages, and the real obligation being then expressed in the superadded condition, on due performance of which the instrument is avoided.

1   See para 103 ante.
2   Shep Touch 368.
3   See para 117 post.
4   See para 116 post.
5   See the Stamp Act 1891 s 1, Sch 1 (repealed). See further STAMP DUTIES AND STAMP DUTY RESERVE TAX vol 44(1) (Reissue) para 1066 et seq.
6   As to deeds poll and indentures see para 3 ante.

105.   Execution.   The ordinary rules relating to deeds apply to bonds in regard to their method of execution[1], the possibility of execution in escrow[2], and the time from which execution has effect[3].

Where two or more persons are intended to be bound jointly, or jointly and severally, and the bond is executed by one of them only, it will operate at law as his several bond. However, in equity he may be entitled to have it delivered up to be cancelled as being contrary to intention[4].

1   See paras 27–36, 40–56 ante.
2   See paras 37–39 ante.
3   See para 60 ante.
4   See para 62 ante.

106.   Obligor.   The capacity of a person to become an obligor depends, generally speaking, on his capacity to contract[1]. Nevertheless, though a minor[2] may bind himself to pay a reasonable price for necessaries supplied to him, a bond given by him to secure such payment is either voidable or, if penal, void[3].

1   As to capacity to contract see CONTRACT vol 9(1) (Reissue) para 630.
2   A minor is a person who has not attained the age of 18: see the Family Law Reform Act 1969 s 1; and CHILDREN AND YOUNG PERSONS vol 5(3) (Reissue) para 1.
3   *Martin v Gale* (1876) 4 ChD 428; *Fisher v Mowbray* (1807) 8 East 330; *Baylis v Dineley* (1815) 3 M & S 477; *Ayliff v Archdale* (1603) Cro Eliz 920; and see CHILDREN AND YOUNG PERSONS vol 5(3) (Reissue) para 21. It seems that *Russel v Lee* (1663) 1 Lev 86 must now be considered overruled.

107.   Obligee.   Minors[1], persons of unsound mind[2], and others with limited or no capacity to contract[3] may be obligees because, as a bond is a unilateral contract, the person to whom it is given does not thereby incur any liability. A bond given to a corporation sole (for example, to a bishop) enures to his successors in office and, where so given during a vacancy in the office, takes effect on the vacancy being filled as if it had been filled before the bond was given[4].

1   Bac Abr, Obligations (D2); and see para 106 note 2 ante. As to the contractual capacity of such persons see CHILDREN AND YOUNG PERSONS vol 5(3) (Reisssue) para 12 et seq. See also note 3 infra.
2   Bac Abr, Obligations (D2). As to the contractual capacity of such persons see MENTAL HEALTH vol 30(2) (Reissue) para 600 et seq. See also note 3 infra.
3   For capacity to contract see CONTRACT vol 9(1) (Reissue) para 630.
4   See the Law of Property Act 1925 ss 180(1), (3), 205(1)(xx); the Administration of Estates Act 1925 s 3(5); and CORPORATIONS vol 9(2) (2006 Reissue) paras 1248, 1271.

(2)   OPERATION

(i)   In general

108.   Construction of bonds.   The rules as to the interpretation of deeds generally apply to bonds so far as material to them[1].

In applying the rule that, as a last resort, words should be construed more strongly against the grantor or covenantor[2], the obligatory part of a double bond[3], being a covenant by the obligor for the benefit of the obligee, is always construed more strongly against the obligor; but since the condition is not itself a covenant and is for the benefit of the obligor, it apparently falls to be construed more strongly in his favour[4].

1   For interpretation generally see para 164 et seq post. As to uncertainty in the condition of a double bond, or repugnancy between the condition and obligation of such a bond see para 119 post. As to implications where no time is fixed for performance of the condition see para 121 post. See also *Girozentrale und Bank der Osterreichischen Sparkassen Atkiengesellschaft v TOSG Trust Fund Ltd* (1992) Financial Times, 5 February, CA; *TOSG Trust Fund Ltd v Girozentrale und Bank der Oesterreichischen Sparkassen Atkiengesellschaft* (1992) Financial Times, 10 June.

2   As to this rule see paras 178–179 post.
3   For the meaning of 'double bond' see para 91 ante.
4   Shep Touch 375. It should be noted that, in order to avoid the bond, the condition must be strictly performed according to its true construction: see para 121 post.

109. Liability under bonds. The effect of a single bond[1] is simply to create a specialty debt for the amount of the obligation. The effect of a double or conditional bond at common law was to impose a liability on the obligor to perform the condition, or on its breach to pay the sum named in the obligatory part; but where that sum is a penalty the obligee is now only entitled on breach of the condition to recover a sum commensurate with the actual loss sustained by the breach[2].

A bond made under seal after 31 December 1881 but before 31 July 1990[3] or, subsequently, a bond executed as a deed[4] binds the real estate as well as the personal estate of the obligor, subject to the expression of an intention to the contrary[5].

1   For the meaning of 'single bond' see para 90 ante.
2   See para 126 post. For the meaning of 'double bond' see para 91 ante.
3   Ie the date on which the Law of Property (Miscellaneous Provisions) Act 1989 s 1 (as originally enacted) came into force: see s 1(11); and paras 7, 27, 32 ante.
4   Ie in accordance with ibid s 1 (as amended) after its coming into force: see note 3 supra.
5   Law of Property Act 1925 s 80(1) (amended by the Law of Property (Miscellaneous Provisions) Act 1989 s 1(8), Sch 1 paras 1, 4). On the death of the obligor his real and personal estate pass to his personal representative; they are assets for payment of his debts, and may be followed by creditors notwithstanding any assent of the personal representative: see the Administration of Estates Act 1925 ss 1, 32, 38 (as amended); and EXECUTORS AND ADMINISTRATORS vol 17(2) (Reissue) paras 387–388.

110. Priority in administration of assets. Voluntary bonds are not postponed until after the satisfaction of other debts for valuable consideration in the administration of the assets of a deceased obligor; nor do bond debts for valuable consideration have priority over simple contract debts[1].

1   See the Administration of Estates Act 1925 s 32(1); and EXECUTORS AND ADMINISTRATORS vol 17(2) (Reissue) para 387. As to insolvent estates of deceased persons see the Insolvency Act 1986 s 421 (as amended); and BANKRUPTCY AND INDIVIDUAL INSOLVENCY vol 3(2) (2002 Reissue) para 499.

111. Bond by two or more persons. Where a bond is entered into by two or more persons by which they bind themselves and each of them, the liability is normally joint and several[1], but if each binds himself for a distinct sum the liability will be construed as several only[2]. Where there are no words of severance, prima facie the obligation is only joint, but it may be construed as joint and several if that appears to have been the intention having regard to the terms of the instrument as a whole[3].

1   In the following cases the obligation was held to be joint and several: 'Know all men that we are bound ... for payment whereof I bind myself, my heirs, etc ... Sealed with our seals' (*Sayer v Chaytor* (1699) 1 Lut 695); where A and B were expressed to bind themselves jointly and severally, the condition being that if they or either of them duly paid an annuity to C for life in the following manner, namely one moiety by A during his life and the other moiety by B during the life of A, and after the death of A the whole by B, his heirs, etc, during the life of C, the bond was to be void (*Church v King* (1836) 2 My & Cr 220); where three bound themselves jointly and their respective heirs etc to pay etc conditioned to be void if they or either of them paid etc (*Tippins v Coates* (1853) 18 Beav 401).
2   *Collins v Prosser* (1823) 1 B & C 682 (where the bond was for payments of £1,000 each 'for which payment we bind ourselves, and each of us for himself, for the whole and entire sum of £1,000 each'); *Armstrong v Cahill* (1880) 6 LR Ir 440 (where a bond expressed 'We ... are held and firmly bound in the sum of £50 each ... to which payment ... we hereby bind us and each of us, our and each of our heirs, etc,' was held the separate bond of each for £50).
3   See para 117 post. As to joint and several covenants see paras 260, 263 post.

112. When agreement to pay interest implied. When a bond is conditioned for the payment of a lesser sum of money, interest is recoverable though not expressly reserved, an agreement for payment of interest being implied; and if no date for payment is specified, interest runs from the date of the bond[1]. However, this implication only arises in the case of a penalty bond, that is, where the sum named in the obligatory part is in excess of that named in the condition. A bond in a specified sum conditioned for the payment of the same sum, without interest being mentioned, is, in effect, a single bond[2], and the amount recoverable on the bond is the principal sum without interest[3].

1　　*Re Dixon, Heynes v Dixon* [1900] 2 Ch 561, CA; *Farquhar v Morris* (1797) 7 Term Rep 124. As to the limiting of the aggregate amount recoverable to the amount of the penalty see para 128 post.

2　　For the meaning of 'single bond' see para 90 ante.

3　　*Hogan v Page* (1798) 1 Bos & P 337. As to the power of the High Court to award interest on debts and damages see the Supreme Court Act 1981 (prospectively renamed the Senior Courts Act 1981) s 35A (as added); and DAMAGES vol 12(1) (Reissue) para 848; MONEY vol 32 (2005 Reissue) para 131.

113.　Gold clauses. Clauses to secure payment on a gold value basis are binding and payment must be made in accordance with their provisions[1]. However, in stating an amount, a mere reference to gold coin, or to paper currency equivalent to gold coin, without specifying the weight and fineness of the coin, is to be construed prima facie as a statement of the monetary amount of the debt and not as a requirement to make actual payment in gold or payment measured by the current free market or official price of gold[2]. Where the matter is subject to foreign legislation, the purpose of a gold clause may be defeated[3]. Payment of interest on a gold basis will not be enforced unless the terms of the gold clause expressly extend to interest[4].

1　　*Feist v Société Intercommunale Belge D'Électricité* [1934] AC 161, HL. As to the construction of references to gold see MONEY vol 32 (2005 Reissue) para 124.

2　　*Campos v Kentucky and Indiana Terminal Railroad Co* [1962] 2 Lloyd's Rep 459; *Treseder-Griffin v Co-operative Insurance Society Ltd* [1956] 2 QB 127, [1956] 2 All ER 33, CA; and c f *Syndic in Bankruptcy of Salim Nasrallah Khoury v Khayat* [1943] AC 507, [1943] 2 All ER 406, PC.

3　　*R v International Trustee for Protection of Bondholders Aktiengesellschaft* [1937] AC 500, [1937] 2 All ER 164, HL; and contrast *New Brunswick Rly Co v British and French Trust Corpn Ltd* [1939] AC 1, [1938] 4 All ER 747, HL (proceedings commenced before legislation passed). See also *Assicurazioni Generali v Selim Cotran* [1932] AC 268, PC.

4　　*New Brunswick Rly Co v British and French Trust Corpn Ltd* [1939] AC 1, [1938] 4 All ER 747, HL; *Apostolic Throne of St Jacob v Saba Eff Said* [1940] 1 All ER 54, PC (where the conduct of the parties in making payments of interest in the gold equivalent of the original amount was, under Palestinian law, treated as a conclusive admission that a bond was to be construed as so providing but would not necessarily be followed in favour of a plaintiff or claimant where English law applied); and see para 206 post.

114.　Merger of simple contract debt. Where a bond is given to secure the payment of a simple contract debt, the simple contract debt will merge in the specialty[1], provided that the parties are the same, and that the specialty is co-extensive with the simple contract debt[2], and provided that there is no intention to the contrary[3].

　　If the specialty is not co-extensive with the debt secured by it, as where a bond conditioned for the payment of a limited amount was given to secure the payment of a sum then due, and such further sums as might become due, without specifying any limit to such further sums, it will not operate as a merger[4]; and there will be no merger where the bond is only taken by way of collateral or additional security[5].

1　　*Price v Moulton* (1851) 10 CB 561; *Owen v Homan* (1851) 3 Mac & G 378.

2　　*Boaler v Mayor* (1865) 19 CBNS 76.

3　　*Stamps Comr v Hope* [1891] AC 476 at 483, PC; *Barclays Bank Ltd v Beck* [1952] 2 QB 47 at 51, [1952] 1 All ER 549 at 551, CA, per Somervell LJ, and at 53 and 552 per Denning LJ.

4　　*Norfolk Rly Co v M'Namara* (1849) 3 Exch 628; *Holmes v Bell* (1841) 3 Man & G 213.

5　　*Holmes v Bell* (1841) 3 Man & G 213; *Twopenny v Young* (1824) 3 B & C 208.

115.　Estoppel of obligor by recitals.　Where a bond contains recitals, the obligor is estopped from denying the truth of the facts recited, but not so the obligee[1]. Thus if it is recited that the obligor has received certain moneys due to the obligee, the obligor will not be permitted to prove that he never in fact received such moneys[2]. So if a bond is conditioned for the payment of rent of premises recited to be demised by an instrument at a specified rent, the obligor is estopped from showing that the instrument was never executed, or that a lower rent was reserved thereby than that mentioned in the recital, even if such was the fact[3]. Nor where a particular consideration is recited can the obligor show that the consideration was in fact different, except for the purpose of showing that it was unlawful, and that the bond is therefore void[4].

1　*Baker v Dewey* (1823) 1 B & C 704; *Rowntree v Jacob* (1809) 2 Taunt 141.
2　*Shelley v Wright* (1737) Willes 9. See ESTOPPEL vol 16(2) (Reissue) paras 1014–1015.
3　*Hosier v Searle* (1800) 2 Bos & P 299. However, such estoppel will be overridden by the existence of a valid claim to rectification of the bond: see *Greer v Kettle* [1938] AC 156, [1937] 4 All ER 396, HL (commenting on *Lainson v Tremere* (1834) 1 Ad & El 792); and see also *Wilson v Wilson* [1969] 3 All ER 945, [1969] 1 WLR 1470.
4　*Hill v Manchester and Salford Water Works Co* (1831) 2 B & Ad 544.

116.　Two or more obligees.　A bond given, since 1925, to two or more obligees[1] may be given to them jointly and severally, or jointly or severally[2]. The general rule is that, if the interest of the obligees is joint, the bond will be deemed to have been given to them jointly, and if their interests are several, then severally[3]; but express words in the bond clearly demonstrating a contrary intention will prevail[4]. In the case of a bond which is joint only, the right passes to the survivors on the death of one of the obligees, and they alone can enforce the obligation, the representatives of the deceased not being entitled to sue[5]. If the bond is several, the representatives of a deceased obligee may sue or join with the survivors in suing on it[6]. A bond executed after 31 December 1881, with two or more obligees jointly, to pay money or do any other act is deemed, in the absence of the expression of an intention to the contrary, to include an obligation to pay the money or do the act to or for the benefit of the survivor or survivors of them and of any other person to whom the right to sue on the bond devolves, and where executed after 31 December 1925, is to be construed as being also made with each of them[7]. In the case of a bond executed after 31 December 1881, if the money is expressed to be owing to two or more on a joint account, it is, in the absence of the expression of an intention to the contrary, deemed to remain money belonging to them on joint account, as between them and the obligor, so as to entitle the survivor or survivors, or the representatives of the last survivor, to give a good discharge[8].

1　As to claims on joint, and joint and several, bonds see para 131 post.
2　A bond made since 1925 with two or more obligees jointly is to be construed as being also made with each of them (see the Law of Property Act 1925 s 81(1)), unless a contrary intention is expressed (s 81(3)). In its application to instruments made after 31 July 1990 (ie the date on which the Law of Property (Miscellaneous Provisions) Act 1989 s 1 (as originally enacted) came into force (see s 1(11); and paras 7, 27, 32 ante), the Law of Property Act 1925 s 81(1) is modified: see s 81(5) (as added); para 264 post; and CONTRACT vol 9(1) (Reissue) paras 1081–1082. It appears that a bond given before 1926 could not be given jointly and severally: *Bradburne v Botfield* (1845) 14 M & W 559.
3　See *Steeds v Steeds* (1889) 22 QBD 537; *Haddon v Ayers* (1858) 1 E & E 118; *Palmer v Mallet* (1887) 36 ChD 411, CA.
4　See para 265 post.
5　*Martin v Crompe* (1698) 1 Ld Raym 340; *Anderson v Martindale* (1801) 1 East 497.
6　*Withers v Bircham* (1824) 3 B & C 254; *Palmer v Sparshott* (1842) 4 Man & G 137.
7　See the Law of Property Act 1925 s 81(1), (3), (4); and note 2 supra.
8　See ibid s 111; para 137 post; and MORTGAGE vol 32 (2005 Reissue) para 412.

117.　Two or more obligors.　Two or more obligors may be bound jointly, severally, or jointly and severally[1]. If bound severally, each incurs a separate liability according to the terms of the bond, which will bind his estate and personal representatives. If bound jointly only, the obligation devolves upon the survivors on the death of an obligor, and the estate and representatives of a deceased obligor, other than those of the last survivor, are under no liability[2]. However, a bond, though joint in form, may, in the administration of the estate of a deceased obligor, be construed as joint and several, especially in the case of a bond given by partners, or in substitution for a pre-existing joint and several liability[3]. Where the obligors are bound jointly and severally, the personal representatives of a deceased obligor are liable jointly and severally with the survivors[4].

1   See para 111 ante. As to actions on joint, and joint and several, bonds see para 131 post. As to the discharge of such bonds see para 138 post.
2   *White v Tyndall* (1888) 13 App Cas 263, HL.
3   *Beresford v Browning* (1875) 1 ChD 30, CA; *Lane v Williams* (1693) 2 Vern 292; *Devaynes v Noble, Sleech's Case* (1816) 1 Mer 529 at 564; *Primrose v Bromley* (1739) 1 Atk 89; *Levy v Sale* (1877) 37 LT 709; *Summer v Powell* (1816) 2 Mer 30; *Richardson v Horton* (1843) 6 Beav 185.
4   *Burns v Bryan (or Martin)* (1887) 12 App Cas 184, HL; *Tippins v Coates* (1853) 18 Beav 401; *Church v King* (1836) 2 My & Cr 220.

(ii) Conditions

A. VALIDITY AND EFFECT

118.   Validity of condition.   A condition, to be valid, must be for the performance of an act which is possible and lawful[1], and it must not be repugnant to the obligation.

Where a condition underwritten or indorsed is for the performance of an act which is impossible, the condition is void but the obligatory part of the bond valid[2]; but where such a condition is incorporated with the obligatory part, the bond is altogether void[3]. A condition is not invalid merely because it provides for the performance of an act or the happening of an event which, though possible, is extremely improbable[4].

Where a condition is for the performance of two distinct acts, one of which is impossible, the obligor is bound to perform the other[5]; but if both acts were possible at the time of the execution of the bond, and one of them is made impossible by the act of the obligee, the obligor is altogether excused[6].

1   As to unlawful conditions see para 120 post.
2   *Pullerton v Agnew* (1703) 1 Salk 172; *Duvergier v Fellowes* (1832) 1 Cl & Fin 39, HL; *Holmes v Ivy* (1678) 2 Show 15.
3   Com Dig, Condition (D 8).
4   *Campbell v French* (1795) 6 Term Rep 200 at 211, Ex Ch, per Lord Kenyon CJ.
5   *Da Costa v Davis* (1798) 1 Bos & P 242.
6   Com Dig, Condition (K 2); *Duvergier v Fellowes* (1828) 5 Bing 248. As to supervening impossibility see para 123 post.

119.   Uncertainty or repugnancy.   Where the condition of a bond is expressed in such language as to be unintelligible[1], or is so uncertain that its meaning cannot be ascertained, but the obligatory part is clear, the condition is void, and the obligation binding[2].

Where the condition is repugnant to the obligation, the condition is void and the obligation binding[3].

The condition may in certain circumstances be limited or restrained by recitals to the bond or an indorsement on it[4].

1   *Marker v Cross* (1613) 2 Bulst 133.
2   Shep Touch 373; and cf *Mauleverer v Hawxby* (1670) 2 Saund 78; *Vernon v Alsop* (1663) 1 Lev 77. As to uncertainty in documents generally see paras 214–216 post.

3   Shep Touch 373; Com Dig, Condition (D 8); *Roberts v Harnage* (1704) 2 Salk 659; *Wells v Ferguson* (1708) 11 Mod Rep 191 at 199. As to repugnancy in documents see paras 211–212 post.
4   See paras 218, 220 post.

120. Unlawfulness. If the condition of a bond or the consideration for which it is given is unlawful, the bond is wholly void; and extrinsic evidence is admissible to prove the true nature of the transaction where it does not appear on the face of the instrument[1].

Where the condition is entire, and any portion of it is unlawful, the bond is entirely void[2]; but if it consists of several distinct parts, some of which are lawful and others unlawful, or if there are several independent conditions, some lawful and others unlawful, the bond is valid and subject only to such parts of the condition or such of the conditions, as the case may be, as are lawful[3].

The following are instances of bonds given on conditions or for considerations which are unlawful[4]:

(1)   bonds in consideration of future illicit cohabitation[5];
(2)   bonds in unreasonable restraint of trade[6];
(3)   bonds in general restraint of marriage[7];
(4)   marriage brokage bonds[8];
(5)   bonds conditioned for the commission of a crime or tort[9];
(6)   simoniacal resignation bonds[10];
(7)   bonds for money lost at gaming[11];
(8)   bonds tending to affect the due administration of criminal justice[12];
(9)   bonds relating to a prohibited contract for the supply of goods[13].

Post obit bonds, whether absolute or contingent, are not as such invalid[14]. However, where the consideration is inadequate, or the rate of interest exorbitant, relief may be granted in equity, especially in the case of expectant heirs and reversioners[15].

Where a bond or other security has been given or a debt incurred for an unlawful consideration, and a bond is given in lieu thereof or as security therefor, that bond is also void if the obligee has knowledge of the circumstances[16]; but the validity of the subsequent bond is not affected by the unlawfulness of the original consideration if the obligee is unaware of it[17].

1   *Collins v Blantern* (1767) 2 Wils 341; *Paxton v Popham* (1808) 9 East 408; *Greville v Attkins* (1829) 9 B & C 462; *Lound v Grimwade* (1888) 39 ChD 605.
2   *Collins v Blantern* (1767) 2 Wils 341; *Norton v Syms* (1613) Moore KB 856; *Baker v Hedgecock* (1888) 39 ChD 520; *Yale v R* (1721) 6 Bro Parl Cas 27, HL.
3   *Green v Price* (1845) 13 M & W 695; *Re Burdett, ex p Byrne* (1888) 20 QBD 310, CA; *Newman v Newman* (1815) 4 M & S 66; *Collins v Gwynne* (1831) 5 Moo & P 276 at 282; *Yale v R* (1721) 6 Bro Parl Cas 27, HL.
4   As to the condition becoming unlawful see para 123 post; and as to unlawful contracts generally see CONTRACT vol 9(1) (Reissue) para 836 et seq.
5   *Walker v Perkins* (1764) 3 Burr 1568. However, a bond given in consideration of past illicit intercourse on the determination of the connection is valid (*Marchioness of Annandale v Harris* (1727) 2 P Wms 432, HL; *Turner v Vaughan* (1767) 2 Wils 339; *Priest v Parrot* (1751) 2 Ves Sen 160; *Nye v Moseley* (1826) 6 B & C 133), provided there is no intention to continue the connection in the future (*Friend v Harrison* (1827) 2 C & P 584; *Re Vallance, Vallance v Blagden* (1884) 26 ChD 353).
6   *Mitchel v Reynolds* (1711) 1 P Wms 181; *Baker v Hedgecock* (1888) 39 ChD 520; and contrast *Gravely v Barnard* (1874) LR 18 Eq 518. See further TRADE, INDUSTRY AND INDUSTRIAL RELATIONS vol 47 (2001 Reissue) para 13 et seq.
7   *Hartley v Rice* (1808) 10 East 22. See further CONTRACT vol 9(1) (Reissue) para 862.
8   *Roberts v Roberts* (1730) 3 P Wms 66 at 76; *Drury v Hooke* (1686) 1 Vern 412.
9   Shep Touch 371; *Collins v Blantern* (1767) 2 Wils 341.
10   *Fletcher v Lord Sondes* (1827) 3 Bing 501; and see ECCLESIASTICAL LAW vol 14 para 833.
11   See the Gaming Act 1710 s 1 (as amended); and BETTING, GAMING AND LOTTERIES vol 4(1) (2002 Reissue) para 31. This provision is repealed (subject to transitional provisions) by the Gaming Act 2005 ss 334(1)(a), 356(3)(a), (4), Sch 17 as from 1 September 2007.

See also *Sigel v Jebb* (1819) 3 Stark 1. Note that *Bubb v Yelverton* (1870) LR 9 Eq 471 (where a bond given to avoid the consequences of non-payment of a racing debt was held valid) was overruled by *Hill v William Hill (Park Lane) Ltd* [1949] AC 530, [1949] 2 All ER 452, HL.

12 *Lound v Grimwade* (1888) 39 ChD 605 (where one of the considerations for a bond was that criminal proceedings should be so conducted that the name of a certain person should not be mentioned); *Herman v Jeuchner* (1884) 15 QBD 561, CA (indemnifying bail); *Williams v Bayley* (1866) LR 1 HL 200.

13 *Wahda Bank v Arab Bank plc* [1994] 2 Lloyd's Rep 411 (it was unlawful to make a payment under the bond, which related to a contract for the supply of goods prohibited under the Libya (United Nations Sanctions) Order 1992, SI 1992/975 (revoked) (see now the Libya (United Nations Sanctions) Order 1993, SI 1993/2807 (as amended)), even though the company which had contracted to supply the goods was no longer able to perform the contract by reason of insolvency).

14 See *Adames v Hallett* (1868) LR 6 Eq 468, where the rights of an obligee under a voluntary post obit bond are discussed. For the meaning of 'post obit bonds' see para 97 ante.

15 *Earl of Aylesford v Morris* (1873) 8 Ch App 484; *Fry v Lane, Re Fry, Whittet v Bush* (1888) 40 ChD 312; *Nevill v Snelling* (1880) 15 ChD 679; *Cooke v Lamotte* (1851) 15 Beav 234.

16 *Amory v Meryweather* (1824) 2 B & C 573 (bond in lieu of a promissory note given in respect of illegal stock-jobbing transactions); *Fisher v Bridges* (1854) 3 E & B 642, Ex Ch.

17 *Cuthbert v Haley* (1799) 8 Term Rep 390.

B. PERFORMANCE OR BREACH

121.   Condition to be strictly performed: time for performance.   In order to avoid a bond, the condition must be strictly performed, so as to carry out the object and intention of the parties[1]. If a particular day is named either for the payment of money or for the performance of any other act, the payment must be made or the act performed on or before the day mentioned[2]. When the condition is for the payment of money, and no time is mentioned for payment, the money is payable immediately[3]; and when it is for the performance of any other act, the act must be performed within a reasonable time[4].

In neither case is it necessary that there should be any demand for payment or performance[5] in the absence of an express stipulation to that effect[6].

Where the condition requires payment by instalments or the performance of several acts, the bond will become absolute on default in respect of any one instalment, or in performance of any one of such acts[7].

1   2 Wms Saund 48; *Taylor v Bird* (1750) 1 Wils 280; *Bigland v Skelton* (1810) 12 East 436; *Bache v Proctor* (1780) 1 Doug KB 382; *Cutler v Southern* (1667) 1 Saund 116; *Ker v Mitchell* (1786) 2 Chit 487; *Skinners' Co v Jones* (1837) 3 Bing NC 481; *London, Brighton and South Coast Rly Co v Goodwin* (1849) 3 Exch 736; *Goad v Empire Printing and Publishing Co Ltd* (1888) 52 JP 438.

2   *Bigland v Skelton* (1810) 12 East 436; *Hodgson v Bell* (1797) 7 Term Rep 97; Com Dig, Condition (G).

3   *Farquhar v Morris* (1797) 7 Term Rep 124; Shep Touch 369; Vin Abr, Condition (C b); *Gibbs v Southam* (1834) 5 B & Ad 911; and contrast *Carter v Ring* (1813) 3 Camp 459.

4   Co Litt 208a, b.

5   *Gibbs v Southam* (1834) 5 B & Ad 911; Vin Abr, Condition (C b).

6   *Carter v Ring* (1813) 3 Camp 459; *Capp v Lancaster* (1597) Cro Eliz 548; *Fitzhugh v Dennington* (1704) 2 Salk 585.

7   *Grey v Friar* (1850) 15 QB 901 at 910, Ex Ch; *Coates v Hewit* (1744) 1 Wils 80.

122.   Precedent act of obligee.   Where the performance of the condition by the obligor depends on some precedent act on the part of the obligee, the obligation of the obligor does not attach unless and until the precedent act is duly performed[1]. Thus in the case of a bond conditioned for the performance of one of two things within a certain time at the election of the obligee, performance is excused unless the obligee makes his election within the time limited[2]. However, when the precedent act has been duly performed, it is not necessary, as a general rule, that the obligor should have notice of it in order that his liability should attach[3].

1   2 Wms Saund 107b note 3; Vin Abr, Condition (Y c); *Buckland v Barton* (1793) 2 Hy Bl 136; *Campbell v French* (1795) 6 Term Rep 200, Ex Ch.
2   Bac Abr, Condition (P) 3.
3   *Ker v Mitchell* (1786) 2 Chit 487; *Cutler v Southern* (1667) 1 Saund 116.

123.   Supervening impossibility of performance.   Performance of the condition is excused and the obligor discharged from the bond if, though possible at the time of the execution of the bond[1], performance has become impossible by act of God[2], act of the legislature[3], or act of the obligee[4]. So if the condition is in the disjunctive, and gives the obligor the option of performing one or other of two things, the bond will generally be discharged, if, both being possible at the time of the execution of the bond, the performance of either of them becomes impossible by the act of God[5], or the act of the obligee[6]; though, in the case of discharge by the act of God, the question probably depends in each case on the intention of the parties[7]. However, the obligor is not excused by performance becoming impossible where the impossibility is caused by his own act or neglect[8].

1   As to the position where a condition is originally impossible of performance see para 118 ante.
2   Bac Abr, Conditions (N Q); *Thomas v Howell* (1692) 1 Salk 170; Shep Touch 372; Vin Abr, Condition (G c); Co Litt 206a; Com Dig, Condition (D 1); *Brown v London Corpn* (1861) 9 CBNS 726 at 747 per Williams J (affd (1862) 13 CBNS 828); *Earl of Leitrim v Stewart* (1870) IR 5 CL 27.
3   *Davis v Cary* (1850) 15 QB 418; *Brown v London Corpn* (1862) 13 CBNS 828.
4   Co Litt 206b; Vin Abr, Obligation (R) 2–4; Com Dig, Condition (K 2) (L 5); *Duvergier v Fellows* (1828) 5 Bing 248 at 265–266 (affd on other grounds (1830) 10 B & C 826; on appeal (1832) 1 Cl & Fin 39, HL). As to the effect upon a contract of supervening impossibility of performance see CONTRACT vol 9(1) (Reissue) paras 888–893, 897 et seq. As to the effect of an alien becoming an enemy see WAR AND ARMED CONFLICT vol 49(1) (2005 Reissue) para 573.
5   *Laughter's Case* (1595) 5 Co Rep 21b; *Earl of Leitrim v Stewart* (1870) IR 5 CL 27.
6   *Duvergier v Fellows* (1828) 5 Bing 248 at 265–266 (affd on other grounds (1830) 10 B & C 826; on appeal (1832) 1 Cl & Fin 39, HL); Com Dig, Condition (K 2).
7   *Barkworth v Young* (1856) 4 Drew 1 at 25. See further *Anon* (1697) 1 Salk 170.
8   *Bigland v Skelton* (1810) 12 East 436; and cf *Beswick v Swindells* (1835) 5 Nev & MKB 378, Ex Ch.

(3) ASSIGNMENT

124.   Legal or equitable assignment.   The obligation created by a bond is a legal chose or thing in action[1], and hence any absolute assignment of the bond, which does not purport to be by way of charge only, will, if express notice in writing is given to the obligor, be effectual[2], as from the date of the notice, to transfer to the assignee the legal right and remedies under the bond as well as the power to give a good discharge, without the concurrence of the assignor[3].

In equity the benefit of the obligation may be assigned by an oral agreement for valuable consideration, subject to all equities which exist at the time notice of the assignment is given to the obligor[4].

1   As to choses or things in action see CHOSES IN ACTION.
2   Ie subject to all equities which would have been entitled to priority over the right of the assignor: see *Graham v Johnson* (1869) LR 8 Eq 36 (where, the obligor being entitled, as against the obligee, to cancellation of the bond, it was held that an assignee for valuable consideration was in no better position and could not enforce the bond as against the obligor); *Payne v Mortimer* (1859) 4 De G & J 447. See also *Glasse v Marshall* (1845) 15 Sim 71; *Chambers v Manchester and Milford Rly Co* (1864) 5 B & S 588 at 611 per Blackburn J; *Re Cork and Youghal Rly Co* (1869) 4 Ch App 748 at 760 per Lord Hatherley.
3   See the Law of Property Act 1925 s 136(1); and CHOSES IN ACTION vol 6 (2003 Reissue) para 12. As to the transfer of bonds under the Companies Clauses Consolidation Act 1845 s 46 see *Vertue v East Anglian Rlys Co* (1850) 5 Exch 280; and COMPANIES vol 7(2) (2004 Reissue) para 1936. Special provision is made as to the assignment, after breach, of bonds given under or for the purposes of any order of the High Court or Court of Appeal: see para 102 ante.

4   As to assignments generally, including equitable assignments, see CHOSES IN ACTION vol 6 (2003 Reissue) para 9 et seq.

125.   Estoppel as against assignee. Although, as a general rule, the assignee of a bond takes subject to all equities[1], and acquires no better right than the assignor, the obligor may be estopped by his conduct[2] from denying the validity of the bond as against an assignee for value without notice, or from setting up other defences which would have been available against the assignor[3].

1   See CHOSES IN ACTION vol 6 (2003 Reissue) para 61 et seq.
2   As to estoppel by conduct see ESTOPPEL vol 16(2) (Reissue) paras 957, 1052 et seq.
3   *Re South Essex Estuary Co, ex p Chorley* (1870) LR 11 Eq 157; *Re Hercules Insurance Co, Brunton's Claim* (1874) LR 19 Eq 302 (cases where companies were estopped from denying the validity of bonds, given by them, in the hands of assignees for value without notice); *Dickson v Swansea Vale Rly Co* (1868) LR 4 QB 44. See also *Hawker v Hallewell* (1856) 25 LJ Ch 558.

(4) ENFORCEMENT

(i) Remedies

126.   Payment of the amount of the obligation with relief against penalty. Where a bond to secure payment of money provides for the payment of a larger sum on default in payment of the debt, equitable relief will be granted against payment of any penalty that would be involved in paying the larger sum[1]. Equitable relief against the consequences of breaches of conditions of bonds is not confined to common money bonds[2], but will not be granted where the damages exceed the penalty[3] or where the amount claimed is not a penalty[4]. Equitable relief may be granted upon such terms as will secure justice, as for example the replacement by the debtor of a sum of stock which he has borrowed[5]. The equitable doctrine recognised that the true intent of a penal element in a money bond was to secure payment of principal and interest on the day fixed and also of interest thereafter until actual payment[6]. Relief will only be granted, therefore, on such terms as secure the fulfilment of this intention.

Relief will extend to post obit bonds[7].

Where a bond is conditioned for the payment of a sum of money by stated instalments, and it is provided that in default of payment of any one instalment the whole sum remaining unpaid is to become payable, the acceleration of the payment of the remaining instalments is not a penalty, and on default in respect of any instalment the entire sum may be claimed[8].

If a creditor agrees to accept part payment of a debt in full discharge, and takes a bond for payment of the full amount conditioned to be void on part payment, whether in one sum or by instalments, the full amount of the debt can be claimed in the event of a breach of the condition, though only in respect of one instalment, the amount in the obligatory part not being a penalty, but the sum actually due[9].

If a bond is conditioned for the payment of a principal sum at a future day, and interest at stated periods in the meantime, the principal to become payable immediately in default of the regular payment of interest, the acceleration in the time for payment of the principal is not in the nature of a penalty, and on a breach in respect of the payment of interest the whole sum due for principal and interest may be recovered[10].

The doctrine of penalties, which operates by striking down the penalty and enforcing the condition, does not apply to a simple or single bond[11].

1   *Friend v Burgh* (1679) Cas temp Finch 437; *Buckler v Ash* (1735) Lee temp Hard 124; *Forward v Duffield* (1747) 3 Atk 555; *Codd v Wooden* (1790) 3 Bro CC 73. See also *Peachy v Duke of Somerset* (1721) 1 Stra 447; *Preston v Dania* (1872) LR 8 Exch 19 at 21; *Protector Endowment Loan and Annuity Co v Grice* (1880)

5 QBD 592 at 596, CA, per Bramwell LJ. After it had become established that relief would be granted by courts of equity, provision was made by the Administration of Justice Act 1705 for obtaining, in effect, similar relief in the common law courts, without recourse to a court of equity. The Administration of Justice Act 1705 ss 12, 13 (both repealed) followed and confirmed the equitable doctrine and limited accordingly the amount recoverable at common law (see *Re Dixon, Heynes v Dixon* [1900] 2 Ch 561, CA). The provisions had been repealable by rules of court for many years (see the Supreme Court of Judicature (Consolidation) Act 1925 s 99(1)(f), (g), Sch 1 (now repealed)) and their ultimate repeal by a Statute Law Revision Act cannot have been intended to effect any change of the law. At the present time, courts will grant relief by reason of the rules of equity, which prevail over the common law: see the Supreme Court Act 1981 (prospectively renamed the Senior Courts Act 1981) s 49; and EQUITY vol 16(2) (Reissue) paras 498–500; PRACTICE AND PROCEDURE. The effect of the Administration of Justice Act 1705 s 12 (as originally enacted) was that in the case of a money bond with a penalty no sum could be recovered in excess of the principal and interest payable according to the condition (*England v Watson* (1842) 9 M & W 333), but now the obligor can claim relief in equity, and this may be granted to him subject, in a proper case, to any equitable terms that may be imposed.

The Administration of Justice Act 1705 s 13 (as originally enacted) enabled a defendant in an action on a common money bond to bring into court the principal and interest and costs, and thereby to satisfy his obligation. In so far as this enactment related to payment into court, as distinct from relief against a penalty, it was superseded by RSC Ord 22 rr 1–3 (see now CPR Pt 36), before it was repealed.

2   *Sloman v Walter* (1783) 1 Bro CC 418. The Administration of Justice Act 1696 s 8 (repealed) gave similar relief to the equitable doctrine in the common law courts in respect of double bonds other than common money bonds (relief in common law courts in respect of the latter was given under the Administration of Justice Act 1705: see note 1 supra). The Administration of Justice Act 1696 s 8 (as originally enacted) required the plaintiff to assign breaches of the conditions of the bond and the jury to assess not only the damages at common law (without equitable or statutory relief) under the terms of the obligation but also damages for the proved breaches of the condition. It then provided that judgment should be entered for the former damages, i e the amount of the penalty in the obligation of the bond (without relief), but that execution should issue only for the damages assessed for the proved breaches, the judgment for the penalty remaining as security against any further breaches. On the occurrence of a further breach, the plaintiff was, under the provisions of the Act, entitled to have a writ of scire facias, suggesting the further breaches, and calling on the defendant to show cause why execution should not issue for the damages arising from them, such damages to be ascertained by a writ of inquiry: see *Judd v Evans* (1795) 6 Term Rep 399; *Preston v Dania* (1872) LR 8 Exch 19. After the fusion of the administration of law and equity by the Judicature Act 1873, there was no real need for the statutory relief, but the special procedure established by the Administration of Justice Act 1696 was thought to have advantages and s 8 (as originally enacted) was therefore kept in force. It was repealable by rules of court (see the Supreme Court of Judicature (Consolidation) Act 1925 s 99(1)(f), (g), Sch 1 (now repealed)); and the former RSC Ord 53G r 1(1) (added by the Rules of the Supreme Court (No 1) 1957, SI 1957/1178, r 7; but now revoked) provided that the procedure prescribed by the Administration of Justice Act 1696 s 8 (as originally enacted) and the Civil Procedure Act 1833 ss 16, 18 (as originally enacted) should no longer be followed and those provisions were repealed. The former RSC Ord 53G r 1(2) (as so added; but now revoked) provided that, in an action on a bond, the indorsement of the writ and the statement of claim should be framed so as to claim the amount which the plaintiff was entitled to recover, regard being had to the rules of equity relating to penalties, and not the penalty provided for by the bond. In the 1962 revision of the rules, RSC Ord 53G (as added) was wholly revoked and not replaced. The present position is therefore that there is no longer any statutory relief against a penalty in a bond, but the equitable rule as to penalties has effect and prevails over the common law (see the Supreme Court Act 1981 (prospectively renamed the Senior Courts Act 1981) s 49) and will be applied without the need for the defendant to bring separate proceedings for relief. The procedure in claims on bonds is now the same as in other claims based on contractual claims: see further para 130 post.

3   *Davenport v Longuevile* (1661) 1 Rep Ch 196.

4   *Protector Endowment Loan and Annuity Co v Grice* (1880) 5 QBD 592, CA (loan payable by instalments including interest, expenses and life assurance).

5   *Vaughan v Wood* (1833) 1 My & K 403; and c f *Orchard v Ireland* (1704) 2 Ld Raym 1033 (defendant not required to waive defence of statute of limitation to a simple contract claim also made against him by the plaintiff).

6   *Re Dixon, Heynes v Dixon* [1900] 2 Ch 561 at 578, CA, per Rigby LJ.

7   These bonds were within the Administration of Justice Act 1705 s 12 (repealed) (see note 1 supra), when the money became payable: *Smith v Bond* (1833) 10 Bing 125.

8   *Protector Endowment Loan and Annuity Co v Grice* (1880) 5 QBD 592, CA; *Wallingford v Mutual Society* (1880) 5 App Cas 685, HL.

9   *Re Neil, ex p Burden* (1881) 16 ChD 675, CA; *Thompson v Hudson* (1869) LR 4 HL 1.

10 *Goad v Empire Printing and Publishing Co Ltd* (1888) 52 JP 438.

11 *Jervis v Harris* [1996] Ch 195, [1996] 1 All ER 303, CA. For the meaning of 'single bond' see para 90
    ante.

127.   Distinction between penalty and liquidated damages. Where a bond is
conditioned for the performance of an act or acts other than the payment of money, the
question whether the sum named in the obligatory part is to be deemed a penalty or
liquidated damages depends on the circumstances of the particular case and the
presumed intention of the parties[1]. Where it is in the nature of liquidated damages, the
sum named in the obligatory part is recoverable on breach of the condition[2]. No
equitable relief will be granted in such a case[3].

1   See e g *Wallis v Smith* (1882) 21 ChD 243; *Willson v Love* [1896] 1 QB 626, CA; *Dunlop Pneumatic
     Tyre Co Ltd v New Garage and Motor Co Ltd* [1915] AC 79, HL; *Jervis v Harris* [1996] Ch 195, [1996]
     1 All ER 303, CA (bond in a sum conditioned on tenant's keeping premises in repair would constitute a
     penalty); and see further DAMAGES vol 12(1) (Reissue) para 1065 et seq ante.
2   *Strickland v Williams* [1899] 1 QB 382, CA.
3   See para 126 notes 2–3 ante.

128.   Amount recoverable limited to penalty and costs. The amount
recoverable on a bond forfeited by breach of the condition is in all cases limited, both at
law and in equity, to the amount of the penalty fixed by the obligatory part, with costs,
even where the principal and interest payable according to the condition, or the damages
sustained by the breach, exceed that sum[1]. If, however, a judgment is recovered on the
bond, it will carry interest until satisfied, though the amount of the judgment, with
interest, may exceed the amount of the penalty[2]. Where interest has been paid as
interest, and has been applied as such, the amount ultimately payable may exceed the
amount of the penalty, provided the principal and interest payable at any one time never
exceeds that amount[3].

Where the sum named in the obligatory part is not a penalty, as in the case of a bond
for a specified sum, conditioned for payment of the same sum with interest, the rule that
the amount recoverable is limited to the sum named in the obligatory part does not
apply[4].

1   *Hatton v Harris* [1892] AC 547, HL; *Wilde v Clarkson* (1795) 6 Term Rep 303; *Clarke v Seton* (1801) 6 Ves
     411; *Hughes v Wynne* (1832) 1 My & K 20; *Mackworth v Thomas* (1800) 5 Ves 329; *Brangwin v Perrot* (1778)
     2 Wm Bl 1190; *White v Sealy* (1778) 1 Doug KB 49; *Shutt v Proctor* (1816) 2 Marsh 226. The rule that no
     more can be recovered than the penalty and costs is a general rule applicable to all bonds, and annuity
     bonds (*Butcher v Churchill* (1808) 14 Ves 567) and replevin bonds (*Branscombe v Scarborough, Branscombe v
     Heath* (1844) 6 QB 13; and see para 101 ante; and DISTRESS para 1081 et seq post) are no exception to
     the rule. In *Grant v Grant* (1830) 3 Sim 340, a decree was made in equity for the full payment of principal
     and interest although it exceeded the penalty of the bond, on the ground that the obligor had prevented
     the obligee from recovering by vexatious proceedings, but such a case could hardly occur now. See also
     Mathews v Keble (1868) 3 Ch App 691. It seems that *Lord Londsale v Church* (1788) 2 Term Rep 388 must
     now be considered overruled.
2   *M'Clure v Dunkin* (1801) 1 East 436.
3   *Knipe v Blair* [1900] 1 IR 372.
4   *Francis v Wilson* (1824) Ry & M 105.

129.   Injunction when agreement secured by bond. Where there is a covenant
or agreement not to do a certain act, and a bond is given with a penalty conditioned to
be forfeited on doing the act, the court will not refrain by reason of the giving of the
bond from granting an injunction to restrain a breach of the covenant or agreement,
unless it appears to have been the intention of the parties that the obligor should be
entitled to do the act on condition of paying the penalty; prima facie, if a person agrees
not to do a certain thing, and to pay a certain sum if he does do it, there are two
independent agreements and he is not entitled to break one agreement on condition of
his performing the other[1].

1   *French v Macale* (1842) 2 Dr & War 269; *Hardy v Martin* (1783) 1 Cox Eq Cas 26; *Clarkson v Edge* (1863) 33 Beav 227; *Gravely v Barnard* (1874) LR 18 Eq 518; *Bird v Lake* (1863) 1 Hem & M 111; *Jones v Heavens* (1877) 4 ChD 636; *London and Yorkshire Bank Ltd v Pritt* (1887) 56 LJ Ch 987; *National Provincial Bank of England v Marshall* (1888) 40 ChD 112, CA. As to injunctions generally see INJUNCTIONS.

(ii)   Procedure

130.   Procedure for claims.   Claims to enforce bonds follow the ordinary procedural rules[1].

1   See the CPR; and PRACTICE AND PROCEDURE.

131.   Where two or more obligees or obligors.   In a claim on a bond given to two or more jointly, all the obligees should be joined as claimants[1].

Where there are two or more obligors the effect of the Civil Liability (Contribution) Act 1978[2] is that whether the liability of two or more persons is joint or otherwise, the claimant may choose which of them he wishes to sue[3]. He need not join, nor can he be compelled to join, the other persons also liable to him even if their liability is under a joint bond only[4].

1   *Hopkinson v Lee* (1845) 6 QB 964; *Keightley v Watson* (1849) 3 Exch 716; and see CPR 19.1(2), 19.2, 19.3. However, if the interest of the obligees is several, one may sue without the other or others: *Haddon v Ayers* (1858) 1 E & E 118; *Palmer v Mallet* (1887) 36 ChD 411, CA. See also para 116 ante. It should be noted that a bond made after 1925 with two or more jointly is to be construed as being also made with each of them if and so far as a contrary intention is not expressed in the bond and subject to its provisions: see the Law of Property Act 1925 s 81 (amended by the Law of Property (Miscellaneous Provisions) Act 1989 s 1, Sch 1 para 5). In its application to instruments made after 31 July 1990 (i e the date on which the Law of Property (Miscellaneous Provisions) Act 1989 s 1 (as originally enacted) came into force: see s 1(11); and para 7 ante), the Law of Property Act 1925 s 81 (as amended) is modified: see s 81(5) (as added); para 264 post; and CONTRACT vol 9(1) (Reissue) paras 1081–1082.
2   As to proceedings against persons jointly liable for the same debt or damage see the Civil Liability (Contribution) Act 1978 s 3; and DAMAGES vol 12(1) (Reissue) para 838.
3   See ibid s 1(1); and DAMAGES vol 12(1) (Reissue) para 839.
4   See note 2 supra. As to successive actions against persons liable for the same damage see ibid s 4. As to the addition and substitution of parties see CPR 19.1(2), 19.2, 19.3. As to entitlement to contribution see the Civil Liability (Contribution) Act 1978 s 1; and DAMAGES vol 12(1) (Reissue) para 839. If the defendant desires to obtain a contribution from the other joint obligors he may do so by making his claim under the Civil Liability (Contribution) Act 1978, but this is of no concern to the claimant: see DAMAGES vol 12(1) (Reissue) para 837 et seq.

132.   Claim on lost bond.   A claim may be brought on a lost bond, and the obligation enforced, subject to a proper indemnity being given to the defendant to the satisfaction of the court[1].

1   See *Atkinson v Leonard* (1791) 3 Bro CC 218; *East India Co v Boddam* (1804) 9 Ves 464.

(iii)   Limitation of Action

133.   Period of limitation.   The remedy by action on a bond is barred after 12 years from the accrual of the right of action[1]; but the period may be longer in cases where there is or has been disability, or there has been acknowledgment or part payment, fraud or mistake[2].

1   See the Limitation Act 1980 s 8; and LIMITATION OF ACTIONS vol 28 (Reissue) para 881.
2   See LIMITATION OF ACTIONS vol 28 (Reissue) para 1080 et seq.

134.   When time begins to run.   In the case of a conditional bond, time does not begin to run for the purposes of limitation of actions[1] until breach of the condition[2]; and where the condition is for payment of an annuity or of a principal sum by instalments, or interest at stated times, or for the performance of several acts in succession, a new cause of action arises on each successive breach, unless it is provided that the whole sum is to become due on default in payment of interest or of any one instalment, as the case may be; and a claim may be brought in respect of such of the sums as accrued due, or such of the acts as ought to have been performed, within the 12 years preceding the commencement of the proceedings, though more than 12 years may have elapsed since the first or any other breach of the condition[3].

1　See the Limitation Act 1980 s 8; and LIMITATION OF ACTIONS vol 28 (Reissue) para 881.
2　*Sanders v Coward* (1845) 15 M & W 48; *Re Dixon, Heynes v Dixon* [1900] 2 Ch 561, CA.
3　*Amott v Holden* (1852) 18 QB 593; *Blair v Ormond* (1851) 17 QB 423; *Re Dixon, Heynes v Dixon* [1900] 2 Ch 561, CA; *Amos v Smith* (1862) 1 H & C 238.

135.　Conflict of laws.　Where a claim is brought in England on a bond executed abroad, the question whether or not the remedy is barred by lapse of time is governed by the English statute[1], and not the law of the place where the bond was executed[2].

1　Ie the Limitation Act 1980: see LIMITATION OF ACTIONS.
2　*Alliance Bank of Simla v Carey* (1880) 5 CPD 429. See CONFLICT OF LAWS vol 8(3) (Reissue) para 26.

(5) DISCHARGE

136.　Modes of discharge.　The obligation of a bond may be discharged in any one of the following ways:

(1)　By due performance of the condition, or, in certain cases, by its performance becoming impossible[1].

(2)　By accord and satisfaction. Since the Judicature Acts an accord and satisfaction, though by parol, and whether before or after breach, may be pleaded to a claim on a bond[2].

(3)　By release or covenant not to sue[3].

(4)　By cancellation, by or with the consent of the obligee, with the intention to cancel the bond[4]. However, a cancellation by the obligor or a stranger without the consent of the obligee, or a cancellation by mistake or accident, without the intention of cancelling, will not affect the obligation[5]. Production, however, of a bond in a cancelled state is prima facie evidence that it is void through cancellation by or with the consent of the obligee[6].

(5)　By a material alteration by the obligee after execution[7]. An immaterial alteration will not affect the validity of the bond[8]; nor will an alteration by the obligor, because a person is not permitted to take advantage of his own wrong[9]. Alterations made before the bond is completely executed, with the assent of all the parties, do not affect its validity[10]; and blanks may be filled up, even after execution, by consent of all the parties[11]. However, if, after a bond is executed by some only of several obligors, a material alteration is made without their consent, they are discharged[12].

Moreover, since in equity relief will be granted against a penalty, such as the penal payment required by a common money bond on failure to comply with the condition of the bond, the obligation of the bond is in effect discharged by the payment by the obligor of all that the court would require him to pay[13].

1　See para 123 ante.
2　*Steeds v Steeds* (1889) 22 QBD 537. See further CONTRACT vol 9(1) (Reissue) paras 1052–1054.
3　See CONTRACT vol 9(1) (Reissue) paras 1052–1054; GUARANTEE AND INDEMNITY vol 20(1) (Reissue) para 306 et seq. See also *Major v Major* (1852) 1 Drew 165; *Shore v Shore* (1847) 2 Ph 378; *Hodges v Smith* (1598) Cro Eliz 623. However, an intention to release is not sufficient: *Jorden v Money* (1854) 5 HL Cas

185; *Re Holmes' Estate, Woodward v Humpage, Inskip's Case* (1861) 3 Giff 352. As to the effect of appointing the obligor executor of the obligee's will see para 138 post.

4   *Seaton v Henson* (1678) 2 Lev 220. See paras 76–77 ante. See further CONTRACT vol 9(1) (Reissue) paras 1059–1060.

5   *Re Smith, ex p Smith* (1843) 3 Mont D & De G 378; *Raper v Birkbeck* (1812) 15 East 17; *Wilkinson v Johnson* (1824) 3 B & C 428; *Bolton v Bishop of Carlisle* (1793) 2 Hy Bl 259; *Vanhoven v Giesque* (1706) 4 Bro Parl Cas 622.

6   *Alsager v Close* (1842) 10 M & W 576; *Meiklejohn v Campbell* (1940) 56 TLR 663 (affd 56 TLR 704, CA); and cf *Re Dixon, Heynes v Dixon* [1900] 2 Ch 561, CA.

7   *Pigot's Case* (1614) 11 Co Rep 26b. See further *Raiffeisen Zentralbank Osterreich AG v Crossseas Shipping Ltd* [2000] 1 All ER (Comm) 76, [2000] 1 WLR 1135, CA; and para 81 et seq ante.

8   Shep Touch 69; *Waugh v Bussell* (1814) 5 Taunt 707.

9   Shep Touch 69.

10 *Zouch v Clay* (1671) 1 Vent 185; *Matson v Booth* (1816) 5 M & S 223.

11 *Hudson v Revett* (1829) 2 Moo & P 663 at 692; *Texira v Evans* (1788–1794) cited in 1 Anst 228 at 229.

12 In *Ellesmere Brewery Co v Cooper* [1896] 1 QB 75, a bond by the terms of which four sureties jointly and severally bound themselves, the liability of two of them being limited to £50 each, and of the other two to £25 each, was executed by three of them, the fourth, whose liability was limited to £50, then executed it, adding to his signature '£25 only'; and the obligee accepted the bond so executed without objection. It was held that the first three signatories were discharged by the alteration, and that the fourth was also discharged, because he had executed it as a joint and several, and not as a several, bond.

13 See para 126 ante.

137. Where two or more obligees. A bond given to two or more obligees jointly[1] may be discharged by a payment to[2], or accord and satisfaction with[3], any one of them; and, in the absence of fraud[4], a release by one constitutes a good defence against them all[5], though it is otherwise in the case of a covenant not to sue[6]. In the case of fraud, a release given by one of several joint obligees will in equity be ordered to be delivered up to be cancelled[7]. Where the interests of the obligees are several, a bond, though joint in form, will be construed as a several bond[8], in which case an accord and satisfaction with, or release by, one or more, will not affect rights of the others[9]. However, in the case of bonds executed after 31 December 1881, if the money is expressed to be owing to two or more on a joint account, it is deemed to remain money belonging to them on joint account as between them and the obligor, and the receipt in writing of the survivors or last survivor, or of the personal representatives of the last survivor, is, unless a contrary intention is expressed in the bond, a good discharge, notwithstanding notice of severance of the joint account[10].

1   If the bond is made after 1925 it will be construed as being several as well as joint unless a contrary intention is expressed: see the Law of Property Act 1925 s 81(1). In its application to instruments made after 31 July 1990 (ie the date on which the Law of Property (Miscellaneous Provisions) Act 1989 s 1 (as originally enacted) came into force: see s 1(11); and para 7 ante), the Law of Property Act 1925 s 81(1) is modified: see s 81(5) (as added); para 264 post; and CONTRACT vol 9(1) (Reissue) paras 1081–1082. See also para 116 ante.

2   *Powell v Brodhurst* [1901] 2 Ch 160; *Husband v Davis* (1851) 10 CB 645.

3   *Wallace v Kelsall* (1840) 7 M & W 264; and cf *Steeds v Steeds* (1889) 22 QBD 537.

4   *Barker v Richardson* (1827) 1 Y & J 362.

5   *Wallace v Kelsall* (1840) 7 M & W 264; *Wilkinson v Lindo* (1840) 7 M & W 81; *Wild v Williams* (1840) 6 M & W 490; *Jones v Herbert* (1817) 7 Taunt 421.

6   *Walmesley v Cooper* (1839) 11 Ad & El 216.

7   *Barker v Richardson* (1827) 1 Y & J 362.

8   *Haddon v Ayers* (1858) 1 E & E 118; *Withers v Bircham* (1824) 3 B & C 254; *Palmer v Sparshott* (1842) 4 Man & G 137.

9   *Steeds v Steeds* (1889) 22 QBD 537; explained in *Powell v Brodhurst* [1901] 2 Ch 160. As to cancellation see *Re Smith, ex p Smith* (1843) 3 Mont D & De G 378; and para 76 et seq ante. As to discharge see para 80 ante.

10 See the Law of Property Act 1925 s 111; and MORTGAGE vol 32 (2005 Reissue) para 412.

138.   Where two or more obligors.   A release of one of two or more obligors jointly, and not severally, bound, operates as a release of all in equity as well as at law[1]. The same rule applies in the case of a joint and several bond if the release is an absolute and formal release[2]; but if it purports to be a release of the particular obligor only, or expressly reserves the right to sue the others, it will not operate to discharge them, unless their right of contribution is taken away or injuriously affected by the release[3].

The appointment, by the obligee of a joint and several bond, of one of two or more obligors to be the executor of his will operates on the death of the obligee as a release of all the obligors[4].

A covenant not to sue one or some of two or more joint, or joint and several, obligors, does not operate to discharge the other or others[5].

In the case of a bond under seal[6], if the seal of one of two or more obligors bound jointly, or jointly and severally, is torn off, by or with the consent of the obligee, and with the intention to cancel the bond, it is discharged as regards them all[7]; but where they are bound severally only, the destruction of the seal of one or some of them does not affect the liability of the others[8].

1   *North v Wakefield* (1849) 13 QB 536; *Re Hodgson, Beckett v Ramsdale* (1885) 31 ChD 177 at 188, CA.
2   *North v Wakefield* (1849) 13 QB 536; *Re Wolmershausen, Wolmershausen v Wolmershausen* (1890) 62 LT 541; *Bower v Swadlin* (1738) 1 Atk 294.
3   *Ward v National Bank of New Zealand* (1883) 8 App Cas 755, PC. See further para 80 ante.
4   *Cheetham v Ward* (1797) 1 Bos & P 630; and see *Re Bourne, Davey v Bourne* [1906] 1 Ch 697 at 703, CA. At common law the debt is discharged by release at the date of the death of the testator; in equity it is discharged at the date of the probate because the debt is deemed to have been paid by the debtor to himself as executor: *Jenkins v Jenkins* [1928] 2 KB 501. As to the obligation of the executor to account, although the debt is extinguished, see EXECUTORS AND ADMINISTRATORS vol 17(2) (Reissue) para 21.
5   *Hutton v Eyre* (1815) 6 Taunt 289; *Dean v Newhall* (1799) 8 Term Rep 168; *Lacy v Kinnaston* (1701) 12 Mod Rep 548 at 551.
6   As from 31 July 1990, any rule of law which requires a seal for the valid execution of an instrument as a deed by an individual is abolished: see the Law of Property (Miscellaneous Provisions) Act 1989 s 1(1)(b); and paras 7, 27, 32 ante. As to the application of s 1(1)(b) see s 1(9); and para 7 ante. As to where a seal is still required see para 32 ante. See also para 78 ante.
7   *Seaton v Henson* (1678) 2 Lev 220; *Bayly v Garforth* (1641) March 125; *Collins v Prosser* (1823) 1 B & C 682.
8   *Collins v Prosser* (1823) 1 B & C 682. See further para 78 ante.

3. INSTRUMENTS UNDER HAND ONLY

(1) DEFINITION AND EFFECT OF AN INSTRUMENT UNDER HAND

139. Definition of instrument under hand only. An instrument under hand only is a document in writing which either creates or affects legal or equitable rights or liabilities, and which is authenticated by the signature of the author, but is not executed by him as a deed[1]. Such documents are used in a great variety of transactions, including contracts, assignments, acknowledgments of title, and notices. The expression is not limited to documents of a formal character, and it extends to any duly signed document which is intended by the author to be the means of producing a result recognised in law[2].

1   See e g *Chadwick v Clarke* (1845) 1 CB 700 at 707–708. 'Writing' includes printing and other forms of reproducing words: see paras 155–156 post. See also *Trustees Solutions Ltd v Dubery* [2006] EWHC 1426 (Ch), [2006] All ER (D) 233 (Jun), (2006) Times, 7 August (where amendment to a pension scheme to be made 'by any writing effected under hand' was said to require the amendment to have been made in writing and signed).
2   *Powell v Ely* (1980) Times, 22 May, DC (where it was held that a divorce petition and a statement of arrangements were instruments relating to legal proceedings within the Solicitors Act 1974 s 22(1)(b) (see SOLICITORS vol 44(1) (Reissue) para 528)).

140. Meaning of instrument. The word 'instrument' as applied to a writing may have a still wider scope, and may include documents which affect the pecuniary position of parties although they do not create rights or liabilities recognised in law; but usually it applies to a document under which some right or liability, whether legal or equitable, exists[1].

The phrase 'deed, will, or instrument in writing'[2] has been held to include the printed rules of a savings bank[3]. A power to appoint by 'deed, instrument or will' includes a power to appoint by an instrument under hand[4]. In connection with stamp duties, 'instrument' includes every written document[5], and thus includes an agreement in writing not being a deed securing periodical payments[6].

It has been defined for the purposes of particular statutes as including an Act of Parliament, unless the context otherwise requires[7], and also as not including a statute unless the statute creates a settlement[8].

In general the word is not appropriate to describe an order of the court[9].

A letter or a telegram may constitute a forged[10] instrument[11].

1   *Mason v Schuppisser* (1899) 81 LT 147 (construction of the phrase 'deed, will or other written instrument' in RSC Ord 54A r 1 (revoked)); and c f *Taylor v Holt* (1864) 3 H & C 452; *London, Chatham and Dover Rly Co v South Eastern Rly Co* [1893] AC 429, HL (cases under the Civil Procedure Act 1833 s 28 (repealed: see now the Supreme Court Act 1981 (prospectively renamed the Senior Courts Act 1981) s 35A (as added); and DAMAGES vol 12(1) (Reissue) para 848; MONEY vol 32 (Reissue) para 110); construction of words regarding interest on a debt payable 'by virtue of some written instrument').
2   See the Larceny Act 1916 s 46(1) (repealed).
3   *R v Fletcher* (1862) 31 LJMC 206, CCR.
4   *Brodrick v Brown* (1855) 1 K & J 328.
5   Stamp Duties Management Act 1891 s 27; Stamp Act 1891 s 122(1).
6   See *National Telephone Co Ltd v IRC* [1899] 1 QB 250, CA; affd [1900] AC 1, HL ('bond, covenant or instrument of any kind whatsoever').
7   Trustee Act 1925 s 68(1) para 5.
8   Law of Property Act 1925 s 205(1)(viii); Settled Land Act 1925 s 117(1)(viii); Land Registration Act 2002 s 89; and see LAND REGISTRATION vol 26 (2004 Reissue) para 893.
9   *Jodrell v Jodrell* (1869) LR 7 Eq 461. However, see *Re Holt's Settlement, Wilson v Holt* [1969] 1 Ch 100, [1968] 1 All ER 470; *Sun Alliance Insurance Ltd v IRC* [1972] Ch 133, [1971] 1 All ER 135.

10   Ie within the Forgery and Counterfeiting Act 1981 ss 1, 8 (as amended): see CRIMINAL LAW, EVIDENCE
     AND PROCEDURE vol 11(1) (2006 Reissue) para 346 et seq.
11   See *R v Riley* [1896] 1 QB 309, CCR; *R v Howse* (1912) 107 LT 239; *R v Cade* [1914] 2 KB 209, CCA.

141.   Effect.   The effect of an instrument under hand varies according to the
transaction for which it is used. If it is concerned with a contract, it may either contain
the contract itself or be a memorandum or particulars of a contract previously entered
into[1]. In either case the contract is not enforceable unless it is founded on valuable
consideration[2]. If the contract has been reduced into writing it supersedes any prior
verbal negotiations, and binds the parties to the performance of the terms expressed
therein[3]. If the writing does not itself constitute the contract but is only a memorandum,
signed or adopted by all the parties, of a contract previously made, it will in general
supersede the previous contract and so produce the same effect as a written contract, as
regards the enforcement of the written terms to the exclusion of the parol terms, unless
it can be shown that a parol term not included in the written terms was not intended by
the parties to cease to form part of their agreement but was intended to continue in
force with the written terms[4]. Such a memorandum may be made at a time subsequent
to the contract[5]. Where a memorandum signed by the party to be charged or his agent
is required to satisfy the Statute of Frauds[6], it must be made before a claim is brought[7].

1   Under the Statute of Frauds (1677) s 4 (as amended) (replaced as regards contracts for the sale of land by
    the Law of Property (Miscellaneous Provisions) Act 1989 s 2 (as amended): see paras 11 ante, 145, 156
    post (see SALE OF LAND vol 42 (Reissue) paras 29–40); and repealed as to other contracts, except
    promises to answer for the debt etc of another, by the Law Reform (Enforcement of Contracts) Act 1954
    s 1 (repealed)), either the agreement or a memorandum or note of it must be in writing. The
    Employment Rights Act 1996 s 1 provides that where an employee begins employment with an
    employer, the employer must give to the employee a written statement of particulars of employment: see
    s 1(1); and see EMPLOYMENT vol 16(1A) (Reissue) para 92 et seq.
2   See para 59 note 1 ante; and CONTRACT vol 9(1) (Reissue) para 727 et seq.
3   *Leggott v Barrett* (1880) 15 ChD 306 at 311, CA; and see para 185 post.
4   See para 190 post.
5   *Sievewright v Archibald* (1851) 17 QB 103 at 107; *Bailey v Sweeting* (1861) 9 CBNS 843 at 857; and see
    Roberts v Tucker (1849) 3 Exch 632 at 641.
6   See the Statute of Frauds (1677); and note 1 supra.
7   *Lucas v Dixon* (1889) 22 QBD 357, CA.

142.   Assignment.   If the writing purports to be an assignment, and having regard to
its subject matter is capable of operating as such, it will be effectual to pass the property
in the subject matter in accordance with the intention expressed by the assignor,
whether it is made with or without valuable consideration[1]. If the writing purports to
declare a trust with respect to property belonging to the author, either at law and in
equity, or in equity alone, the trust is well created, although there is no consideration[2].

1   Where writing under hand only is effective at law as an assignment, the absence of consideration is
    immaterial (eg in the case of shares which, under the articles of the company or the Stock Transfer
    Act 1963, are transferable by writing not being a deed, though such an assignment may require some
    further formality, such as registration, to give the assignee the full benefit of it: see COMPANIES vol 7(1)
    (2004 Reissue) paras 861, 876). Similarly an equitable interest can be assigned by writing under hand
    without consideration: see paras 24–25 ante. A chose or thing in action may also be so assigned: see
    CHOSES IN ACTION vol 6 (2003 Reissue) paras 35, 37.
2   As to the nature and creation of trusts see TRUSTS vol 48 (2000 Reissue) paras 501–648.

143.   Acknowledgment, notice etc.   If the writing amounts to an
acknowledgment of title to land or to money charged on land, or of a specialty or a
simple contract debt, it operates to give a new starting point for the running of the
Limitation Act 1980[1]. Other instruments under hand, such as demands, notices, and
consents, operate according to their tenor, provided that no further formality is required
in the particular case.

As regards all such instruments, whether purporting to operate by way of contract, assignment, or otherwise, it is open to the party against whom the instrument is set up to show that it ought not to bind him on the ground that he was under some disability which made his effective participation in the transaction impossible, or that there were circumstances of fraud, misrepresentation, duress, or mistake which entitle him to treat the document as either void or voidable[2].

1   See the Limitation Act 1980 ss 29–31; and LIMITATION OF ACTIONS vol 28 (Reissue) para 1080 et seq.
     A balance sheet is capable of containing or amounting to an acknowledgment in writing: *Jones v Bellgrove Properties Ltd* [1949] 2 KB 700 at 704, [1949] 2 All ER 198 at 201, CA, per Lord Goddard CJ; *Re Gee & Co (Woolwich) Ltd* [1975] Ch 52, [1974] 1 All ER 1149.
2   See paras 67 et seq, 87 note 11 ante; and CONTRACT vol 9(1) (Reissue) paras 630, 687, 701 et seq, 895–896; EQUITY vol 16(2) (Reissue) para 412 et seq; MISREPRESENTATION AND FRAUD; MISTAKE.

(2) TRANSACTIONS FOR WHICH AN INSTRUMENT UNDER HAND IS NECESSARY

144.   When necessary. An instrument required by the common law to be in writing must be executed as a deed[1]; hence at law the requirement of writing under hand only must be looked for in the statutes[2], or in the direction or agreement of the parties[3]. Transactions which at law require a deed are, in general, good in equity, although effected only by writing under hand, provided they are founded on valuable consideration[4]. If voluntary, they are in practice always made by deed, though if the transaction is the assignment of an equitable interest, writing under hand only is in general sufficient[5]. Statutory requirements, and such as are imposed by the parties, are recognised in equity as well as at law[6]. The requirement of writing is very general, and, apart from statute, convenience requires that most matters should be put into writing.

1   See para 10 ante.
2   As to contracts which are required by statute to be in writing or evidenced in writing see CONTRACT vol 9(1) (Reissue) paras 623–628.
3   As to where, for instance, an appointment is required to be made, or a consent given, in writing see para 146 post.
4   See para 25 ante.
5   See paras 25 ante, 148 post.
6   Eg where an appointment is required to be made by deed.

145.   Contracts for the sale of land. A contract for the sale or other disposition[1] of an interest in land[2] can only be made in writing and only by incorporating all the terms which the parties have expressly agreed in one document or, where contracts are exchanged, in each document[3]. This includes the variation of a contract within the Law of Property (Miscellaneous Provisions) Act 1989[4], and an agreement made pursuant to the Town and Country Planning Act 1990[5]. The terms may be incorporated in a document either by being set out in it or by reference to some other document[6].

These provisions[7] do not apply in relation to a contract to grant a short lease[8], a contract made in the course of a public auction[9], or a contract regulated under the Financial Services and Markets Act 2000 other than a regulated mortgage contract[10]; nor do they affect the creation or operation of resulting, implied or constructive trusts[11]. Nor are contracts of disposition, as distinct from executory contracts for disposition, caught by these provisions[12].

1   For the meaning of 'disposition' see para 34 note 6 ante; definition applied by the Law of Property (Miscellaneous Provisions) Act 1989 s 2(6).
2   For the meaning of 'interest in land' see para 34 note 7 ante; definition applied by ibid s 2(6) (amended the Trusts of Land and Appointment of Trustees Act 1996 s 25(2), Sch 4).

3   Law of Property (Miscellaneous Provisions) Act 1989 s 2(1). Nothing in s 2 (as amended) applies in relation to contracts made before 27 September 1989: s 2(7). Section 2 (as amended) supersedes the Law of Property Act 1925 s 40 (repealed): see the Law of Property (Miscellaneous Provisions) Act 1989 s 2(8). See further SALE OF LAND vol 42 (Reissue) paras 29–40. As to electronic conveyancing see para 9 ante; and LAND REGISTRATION vol 26 (2004 Reissue) para 1049 et seq.

4   *McCausland v Duncan Lawrie Ltd* [1996] 4 All ER 995, [1997] 1 WLR 38, CA.

5   *Jelson Ltd v Derby City Council* [1999] 3 EGLR 91, [1999] 39 EG 149. However, this case was doubted in *Nweze v Nwoko* [2004] EWCA Civ 379, [2004] 2 P & CR D2.

6   Law of Property (Miscellaneous Provisions) Act 1989 s 2(2); and see SALE OF LAND vol 42 (Reissue) para 29.

7   Ie ibid s 2 (as amended): see SALE OF LAND vol 42 (Reissue) para 29.

8   Ie such a lease as is mentioned in the Law of Property Act 1925 s 54(2): see LANDLORD AND TENANT vol 27(1) (2006 Reissue) paras 101–102.

9   As to public auction see AUCTION vol 2(3) (Reissue) para 201 et seq.

10   As to activities regulated under the Financial Services and Markets Act 2000 see FINANCIAL SERVICES vol 18(1) (Reissue) para 80 et seq. As to regulated mortgage contracts see FINANCIAL SERVICES vol 18(1) (Reissue) para 177 et seq. See also *Yaxley v Gotts* [2000] Ch 162, [2000] 1 All ER 711, CA.

11   Law of Property (Miscellaneous Provisions) Act 1989 s 2(5) (amended by the Financial Services and Markets Act 2000 (Consequential Amendments and Repeals) Order 2001, SI 2001/3649, art 317(1), (2)). See also SALE OF LAND vol 42 (Reissue) para 29. Where a contract for the sale or other disposition of an interest in land satisfies the conditions of the Law of Property (Miscellaneous Provisions) Act 1989 s 2 (as amended) by reason only of the rectification of one or more documents in pursuance of an order of a court, the contract comes into being, or is deemed to have come into being, at such time as may be specified in the order: s 2(4).

12   *Target Holdings Ltd v Priestley* (1999) 79 P & CR 305.

146.   Appointments of property, and to offices.   Appointments are either appointments of property, appointments of persons to offices or other positions, or appointments of trustees or agents. Appointments of property are frequently authorised to be made by instrument under hand, as well as by deed or will[1]. An appointment of a new trustee may usually be made in writing under hand, but must for certain purposes be made by deed[2]. An appointment of an agent need not in general be in writing, but sometimes this is expressly required[3]. The appointment of a proxy in company and bankruptcy matters[4], and an application for the appointment of a proxy to vote at an election[5], must be in writing. There are certain requirements for instruments to be in writing in regard to the registration, certification and transfer of British government stock[6].

1   See para 140 note 4 ante.

2   See para 18 ante.

3   *Coles v Trecothick* (1804) 9 Ves 234 at 250; and see AGENCY vol 2(1) (Reissue) paras 30, 34. An instrument creating a power of attorney must be executed as a deed by the donor of the power: Powers of Attorney Act 1971 s 1(1) (amended by the Law of Property (Miscellaneous Provisions) Act 1989 s 1, Sch 1 para 6); and see paras 13, 34, 47 ante. In certain cases an authority in writing is necessary to enable an agent to sign an instrument: see para 157 post.

4   As to the appointment of a proxy in company insolvency matters see COMPANY AND PARTNERSHIP INSOLVENCY vol 7(4) (2004 Reissue) paras 657–661. As to the appointment of a proxy in bankruptcy matters see BANKRUPTCY AND INDIVIDUAL INSOLVENCY vol 3(2) (2002 Reissue) para 278 et seq.

5   See eg the Representation of the People Act 2000 s 12, Sch 4 (as amended); the Representation of the People (England and Wales) Regulations 2001, SI 2001/341, Pt IV (regs 50–63A) (as amended); and ELECTIONS vol 15(4) (2007 Reissue) para 372 et seq.

6   See the Government Stock Regulations 2004, SI 2004/1611, Pt 3 (regs 7–35); and MONEY vol 32 (2005 Reissue) para 158 et seq.

147.   Declarations of trusts.   All declarations of trust respecting any land[1] or any interest in land must be evidenced by writing[1].

1   As to the meaning of 'land' see para 14 note 2 ante.

2   See the Law of Property Act 1925 s 53(1)(b) (replacing the Statute of Frauds (1677) s 7). A trust may be declared of personal estate without writing: see para 24 ante; and TRUSTS vol 48 (2000 Reissue) para 544.

148. Assignments. Assignments of the following things must be in writing: (1) equitable interests in land whether created by the assignment or previously subsisting[1]; (2) other equitable interests or trusts, subsisting at the time of the assignment[2]; (3) equitable mortgages[3] (except, perhaps, mortgages by deposit of title deeds where assigned for value[4]); (4) shares and debentures (other than bearer securities)[5]; (5) government stock[6]; (6) copyright[7]; (7) a patent[8]; (8) a registered trade mark[9]; (9) statutory legal assignments of policies of life assurance or marine insurance[10]; and (10) legal assignments of legal choses or things in action[11].

Since an assignee of a registered design must apply for registration of his title to it[12], an assignment inter vivos of a registered design should, in practice, be in writing, so that the title of the assignee may readily be proved.

1   See the Law of Property Act 1925 s 53(1)(a); and para 24 ante. Legal estates, legal interests and legal charges in or over land may in general only be conveyed or transferred by deed (so as to give the grantee a legal estate, interest or charge): see ss 1(4), 52(1); and para 14 ante. For exceptions see s 52(2) (as amended); and para 15 ante.

2   See para 24 ante.

3   See the Law of Property Act 1925 s 53(1)(c); and para 24 ante. See also *Re Richardson, Shillito v Hodson* (1885) 30 ChD 396, CA. For the purposes for which a transfer having effect as a deed is necessary see the Law of Property Act 1925 ss 52(1), 114, 115(2); para 14 ante; and MORTGAGE vol 32 (2005 Reissue) paras 565–566, 850. For the equitable principle by which a person who has paid off the mortgage debt is subrogated to the rights of the mortgagee in the absence of a formal transfer see e g *Cracknell v Janson* (1879) 11 ChD 1 at 18, CA.

4   See *Dryden v Frost* (1838) 3 My & Cr 670 at 673; and MORTGAGE vol 32 (2005 Reissue) paras 967–968. However, it has not been possible since the coming into force of the Law of Property (Miscellaneous Provisions) Act 1989 s 2 (as amended) (see SALE OF LAND vol 42 (Reissue) paras 29–40) to create a mortgage by the mere deposit of title deeds: *United Bank of Kuwait plc v Sahib* [1997] Ch 107, [1996] 3 All ER 215, CA. A vendor's or purchaser's lien may, it seems, be transferred by parol: see *Dryden v Frost* supra; and LIEN vol 28 (Reissue) para 768. A pawnee's special property in the thing pledged may be transferred by sub-pledge: see e g *Donald v Suckling* (1866) LR 1 QB 585; and PLEDGES AND PAWNS vol 36(1) (Reissue) paras 103 et seq, 122 et seq.

5   However, the Uncertificated Securities Regulations 2001, SI 2001/3755 (as amended) enable title to units of a security to be evidenced otherwise than by a certificate and transferred otherwise than by a written instrument in accordance with a computer-based system: see reg 2(1); and COMPANIES vol 7(1) (2004 Reissue) para 592 et seq; MONEY vol 32 (2005 Reissue) para 162. See also para 21 ante.

6   See the Government Stock Regulations 2004, SI 2004/1611, reg 15 (as amended); the Stock Transfer Act 1963 s 1(1), (4)(c) (as amended); and MONEY vol 32 (2005 Reissue) para 162.

7   See COPYRIGHT, DESIGN RIGHT AND RELATED RIGHTS vol 9(2) (2006 Reissue) para 160.

8   See the Patents Act 1977 s 30 (as amended); and PATENTS AND REGISTERED DESIGNS vol 35 (Reissue) para 401.

9   See the Trade Marks Act 1994 s 24; and TRADE MARKS AND TRADE NAMES vol 48 (2000 Reissue) para 124.

10   See the Policies of Assurance Act 1867 s 5, Schedule; the Marine Insurance Act 1906 s 50(3); and INSURANCE vol 25 (2003 Reissue) para 389. As to notice of assignment of a policy of life assurance see para 155 note 6 post.

11   See CHOSES IN ACTION vol 6 (2003 Reissue) para 9 et seq.

12   See the Registered Designs Act 1949 s 19 (as amended); and PATENTS AND REGISTERED DESIGNS vol 35 (Reissue) para 770.

149. Assent on death. An assent by the personal representative of a deceased person to the vesting in any person of a legal estate in real property (including leaseholds and other chattels real) must be in writing[1].

1   See the Administration of Estates Act 1925 ss 36(1), (4), 55(1)(xix); and EXECUTORS AND ADMINISTRATORS vol 17(2) (Reissue) paras 3, 563–564. As to implied assents see *Re King's Will Trusts* [1964] Ch 542, [1964] 1 All ER 833; *Re Edwards' Will Trusts, Edwards v Edwards* [1982] Ch 30, [1981] 2 All ER 941, CA; and EXECUTORS AND ADMINISTRATORS vol 17(2) (Reissue) para 564.

150. Acknowledgments of title or of debts. An acknowledgment for the purposes of the Limitation Act 1980, must be in writing, signed by the person by whom it is made or his agent[1].

1 See the Limitation Act 1980 s 30; and LIMITATION OF ACTIONS vol 28 (Reissue) para 1085.

151. Releases and abandonment of rights. A release of a right in general is required to be by deed[1], but a release under hand only will be effectual on equitable principles if made for valuable consideration[2]. A release of a purely equitable estate, interest, or right, in any lands or goods, may also, it seems, be made in writing signed by the releasor, although gratuitous[3].

A renunciation by the holder of a bill of exchange of his rights against the acceptor, or against other parties to the bill, must be in writing, unless, in the case of the acceptor, the bill is delivered up to him[4].

A disclaimer of any onerous property by a trustee in bankruptcy or a liquidator must be in writing signed by the trustee or liquidator as the case may be[5].

1 See para 12 ante.
2 See *Taylor v Manners* (1865) 1 Ch App 48. Even writing is not essential provided that there is valuable consideration: *Steeds v Steeds* (1889) 22 QBD 537; *Yeomans v Williams* (1865) LR 1 Eq 184; and see para 12 ante.
3 See para 25 ante.
4 See the Bills of Exchange Act 1882 s 62; and BILLS OF EXCHANGE AND OTHER NEGOTIABLE INSTRUMENTS vol 4(1) (2002 Reissue) para 456. Delivery to the executors of the acceptor would apparently be sufficient, but not to his legatee: *Edwards v Walters* [1896] 2 Ch 157 at 172, CA.
5 See the Insolvency Act 1986 ss 178, 315 (as amended); the Insolvency Rules 1986, SI 1986/1925, rr 4.187, 6.178; and BANKRUPTCY AND INDIVIDUAL INSOLVENCY vol 3(2) (2002 Reissue) para 475; COMPANY AND PARTNERSHIP INSOLVENCY vol 7(4) (2004 Reissue) para 869.

152. Notices in writing. In numerous cases notices are required to be in writing, for example: (1) notice of an assignment of a debt or other legal thing in action given to the debtor or other person liable[1]; (2) notice of an assignment of a policy of life assurance[2]; (3) notice served[3] of breach of covenant preparatory to re-entry, and other statutory notices[4]; (4) notice by the tenant for life or statutory owner to trustees of intention to sell, lease or mortgage settled land[5]; (5) notice to treat on the purchase of land under compulsory powers[6]; (6) notices under the Landlord and Tenant Acts 1927 and 1954[7]; (7) notice of distress before sale of the goods distrained[8]; (8) notice to make a tenant wilfully holding over liable for double the yearly value of the premises[9]; (9) certain notices given between landlords, tenants and mortgagees of agricultural holdings[10]; and (10) notices under the Reserve and Auxiliary Forces (Protection of Civil Interests) Act 1951 where application is made for the grant of a new tenancy[11].

Any notice required to be served by an instrument affecting property executed or coming into operation after 31 December 1925 is, it seems, required to be in writing, unless a contrary intention appears[12].

Notices given by a company need not be under its common seal provided that they are signed by certain authorised officers[13].

1 See the Law of Property Act 1925 s 136 (as amended); and CHOSES IN ACTION vol 6 (2003 Reissue) para 12 et seq. Notice is only necessary to complete the legal title to the thing in action; it is not necessary to complete the equitable title arising under an assignment for value; and is only necessary to prevent a subsequent assignee from gaining priority, for which purpose it need not, in all cases, be in writing.
2 See the Policies of Assurance Act 1867 s 3; and INSURANCE vol 25 (2003 Reissue) para 549.
3 Ie under the Law of Property Act 1925 s 146 (as amended): see LANDLORD AND TENANT vol 27(1) (2006 Reissue) para 619 et seq.
4 See ibid s 196(1); and LANDLORD AND TENANT vol 27(1) (2006 Reissue) para 621; REAL PROPERTY vol 39(2) (Reissue) para 204.

5   See the Settled Land Act 1925 s 101(1); and SETTLEMENTS vol 42 (Reissue) para 783.

6   See the Lands Clauses Consolidation Act 1845 s 18; the Compulsory Purchase Act 1965 s 5 (as amended); and COMPULSORY ACQUISITION OF LAND vol 8(1) (2003 Reissue) para 100.

7   See the Landlord and Tenant Act 1927 s 23; the Landlord and Tenant Act 1954 s 66; and LANDLORD AND TENANT vol 27(1) (2006 Reissue) para 703.

8   See the Distress for Rent Act 1689 s 1 (repealed with savings); *Wilson v Nightingale* (1846) 8 QB 1034; and DISTRESS paras 1011, 1044, 1056 post.

9   See the Landlord and Tenant Act 1730 s 1 (as amended); and LANDLORD AND TENANT vol 27(1) (2006 Reissue) para 668.

10   As to a tenant's notice of intention to remove fixtures see AGRICULTURE vol 1(2) (Reissue) para 323; as to notice of increase of rent see AGRICULTURE vol 1(2) (Reissue) para 325; as to notice to terminate a tenancy see AGRICULTURE vol 1(2) (Reissue) para 340; as to a tenant's counter-notice after service of a notice to quit see AGRICULTURE vol 1(2) (Reissue) para 341; as to notice of claim on termination of a tenancy see AGRICULTURE vol 1(2) (Reissue) para 428.

11   See the Reserve and Auxiliary Forces (Protection of Civil Interests) Act 1951 s 29(6), applying the Law of Property Act 1925 s 196 (as amended); and see note 4 supra.

12   See ibid s 196(1), (5); and LANDLORD AND TENANT vol 27(1) (2006 Reissue) paras 227, 621; MORTGAGE vol 32 (2005 Reissue) para 655.

13   See the Companies Clauses Consolidation Act 1845 s 139; the Companies Act 1985 s 41 (as amended); and COMPANIES vol 7(1) (2004 Reissue) para 464; COMPANIES vol 7(2) (2004 Reissue) para 1864. A company is no longer required to have a common seal: see s 36A(3) (as added); para 41 ante; and COMPANIES vol 7(1) (2004 Reissue) para 458.

153.   Appointment of guardian. A parent who has parental responsibility[1] for his child may appoint another individual to be the child's guardian in the event of his death[2], and a guardian of a child may appoint another individual to take his place as the child's guardian in the event of his death, as may a special guardian[3].

Such an appointment does not have effect unless it is made in writing, is dated and is signed by the person making the appointment or: (1) in the case of an appointment made by a will which is not signed by the testator, is signed at the direction of the testator in accordance with the statutory requirements[4]; or (2) in any other case, is signed at the direction of the person making the appointment, in his presence and in the presence of two witnesses who each attest the signature[5].

1   For the meaning of 'parental responsibility' see CHILDREN AND YOUNG PERSONS vol 5(3) (Reissue) para 134.

2   Children and Young Persons Act 1989 s 5(3); and see CHILDREN AND YOUNG PERSONS vol 5(3) (Reissue) para 147.

3   Ibid s 5(4) (as amended); and see CHILDREN AND YOUNG PERSONS vol 5(3) (Reissue) para 147.

4   Ie the requirements of the Wills Act 1837 s 9 (as substituted): see WILLS vol 50 (2005 Reissue) paras 351, 353, 360, 362.

5   Children and Young Persons Act 1989 s 5(5); and see CHILDREN AND YOUNG PERSONS vol 5(3) (Reissue) para 147.

154.   Other matters required to be in writing. Matters required to be in writing also include[1] the following[2]: (1) a representation or assurance made or given concerning the character, conduct, credit, ability, trade, or dealings of any person to the intent that he may obtain credit, money, or goods[3]; (2) a declaration of an undertenant or lodger to prevent distress upon his goods[4]; (3) consent of a beneficiary to a breach of trust so as to entitle the trustee to indemnity against him[5]; (4) a consent or agreement so as to prevent the acquisition of easements[6]; (5) a statement, indicating how the amount of a redundancy payment has been calculated, to be given by the employer to the employee on making such a payment otherwise than in pursuance of a decision of a tribunal which specifies the amount of the payment to be made[7]; (6) a consent by the landlord of an agricultural holding to the making of long-term new improvements[8] and to the payment of compensation for improvements by the incoming to the outgoing tenant[9].

Moreover, settlements and other instruments frequently require that a consent should be given in writing, such as a consent by the tenant for life to a sale, to an advance to a child, or to an investment.

1   As to other matters required to be in writing see para 144 et seq ante.
2   This list must not be taken to be exhaustive; the requirement of writing is very general, and, apart from statute, convenience requires that most matters should be put into writing.
3   Statute of Frauds Amendment Act 1828 s 6. The writing must be signed by the party to be charged: s 6. See GUARANTEE AND INDEMNITY vol 20(1) (Reissue) paras 140, 142.
4   See the Law of Distress Amendment Act 1908 s 1 (as amended); and DISTRESS paras 1011, 1044, 1056 post.
5   See the Trustee Act 1925 s 62 (as amended); and TRUSTS vol 48 (2000 Reissue) para 1022. Where the beneficiary instigates or requests the breach of trust, writing is not necessary: *Griffith v Hughes* [1892] 3 Ch 105; *Re Somerset, Somerset v Earl Poulett* [1894] 1 Ch 231, CA.
6   See the Prescription Act 1832 ss 1–3 (as amended); *Bewley v Atkinson* (1879) 13 ChD 283, CA; and EASEMENTS AND PROFITS À PRENDRE vol 16(2) (Reissue) para 241.
7   See the Employment Rights Act 1996 s 165(1); and EMPLOYMENT vol 16(1B) (Reissue) para 755.
8   See the Agricultural Holdings Act 1986 s 67; and AGRICULTURE vol 1(2) (Reissue) para 416.
9   See the Agricultural Holdings Act 1986 ss 69(2), (3), Sch 9 para 5(2); and AGRICULTURE vol 1(2) (Reissue) para 414.

(3) FORM AND EXECUTION

155.   Form and contents.   The term 'instrument in writing' is used to include not only instruments actually written, but all other instruments in which words are permanently represented in visible form whether by printing, lithography, or otherwise, or partly in one way and partly in another[1]. The writing may be in ink or pencil, or otherwise[2]. The form in which the instrument is expressed is in general immaterial, provided that the intention of the author can be collected from it[3], and provided that it contains all statutory particulars required to be inserted[4].

A bill of exchange may be in any words provided it corresponds to the statutory definition[5]. In general, when a contract or other matter is required to be in writing, the form is immaterial provided that the document contains the particulars of the transaction[6].

1   See *Dench v Dench* (1877) 2 PD 60 (will partly lithographed, partly written); and c f the meaning of 'writing' in the Interpretation Act 1889 s 20 (repealed); and the Interpretation Act 1978 s 5, Sch 1; and see SALE OF LAND vol 42 (Reissue) para 39. See also para 2 note 5 ante.
2   *Geary v Physic* (1826) 5 B & C 234 (indorsement of promissory note in pencil). As to pencil alterations to a document in print, type or ink writing see *Co-operative Bank plc v Tipper* [1996] 4 All ER 366; and para 159 post.
3   *Brodrick v Brown* (1855) 1 K & J 328.
4   See the Statute of Frauds (1677) s 4 (as amended); and para 141 note 1 ante.
    An acknowledgment of title to land or money charged on land, or of a specialty debt, may be contained in a letter (*Stansfield v Hobson* (1852) 16 Beav 236, 3 De GM & G 620, CA), a petition for sale admitting an incumbrance (*Re West's Estate* (1879) 3 LR Ir 77), or other informal document. As to the particulars which may be supplied by extrinsic evidence see LIMITATION OF ACTIONS vol 28 (Reissue) para 1085 et seq.
    The Employment Rights Act 1996 s 1 provides that where an employee begins employment with an employer, the employer must give to the employee a written statement of particulars of employment: see s 1(1); and EMPLOYMENT vol 16(1A) (Reissue) para 92 et seq.
5   See *Ellison v Collingridge* (1850) 9 CB 570; and BILLS OF EXCHANGE AND OTHER NEGOTIABLE INSTRUMENTS vol 4(1) (2002 Reissue) para 315.
6   As to memoranda under the Statute of Frauds (1677) see note 4 supra. Occasionally the statute requiring an instrument to be in writing makes a reference to its form or contents; thus e g a notice of assignment under the Policies of Assurance Act 1867 s 3 must give the date and purport of the assignment (see INSURANCE vol 25 (2005 Reissue) para 549); a notice to trustees and their solicitor of the intention of the tenant for life or statutory owner to sell etc under the Settled Land Act 1925 s 101 must be sent by registered letter or recorded delivery letter (see the Settled Land Act 1925 s 101(1); the Recorded

Delivery Service Act 1962 s 1(1); and SETTLEMENTS vol 42 (Reissue) para 783); a notice or other document issued by a company must contain its name in legible characters (see the Companies Act 1985 s 349(1)(b); and COMPANIES vol 7(1) (2004 Reissue) para 462). As to the contents of a policy of marine insurance see the Marine Insurance Act 1906 s 23(1); and INSURANCE vol 25 (2005 Reissue) para 220. As to an instrument of dissolution of a building society see BUILDING SOCIETIES vol 4(3) (Reissue) para 612. In general the form is merely conditioned by the requirement that the instrument must be in writing and signed.

156. Signature. An agreement in writing must be signed either by all the parties, or by the party to be charged therewith, in such a manner as to authenticate it[1]. Under the Statute of Frauds (1677) it is sufficient that the writing is signed by the party to be charged therewith[2], and various statutes which require a contract to be in writing refer only to signature by one party[3]. Other statutes require the writing to be signed by both or all the parties[4]. Thus, in relation to a contract for the sale or other disposition of land, the document incorporating the terms[5] or, where contracts are exchanged, one of the documents incorporating them (but not necessarily the same one) must be signed[6] by or on behalf of each party to the contract[7]. Where a statute simply requires an agreement to be in writing, without expressly referring to signature, it may be sufficient if the agreement is signed by the party to be charged therewith[8]. In other documents the signature must be by the party to whose intention the document gives effect: in an appointment, by the appointor; in the creation of a trust, by the settlor; in an assignment, by the assignor; in an acknowledgment, by the person who makes the acknowledgment; in a notice or demand, by the person giving the notice or making the demand[9].

In general, attestation is not required for an instrument under hand. The place and manner of signature are immaterial, provided that the signature is inserted in such a manner as to authenticate the document[10], and that it can be identified as representing the name of the party[11].

Although a contract has been signed in such a form as to appear unconditional, extrinsic evidence may be adduced to show that it was not intended to take effect until the performance of a condition precedent[12].

1   It was suggested in *Hunter v Parker* (1840) 7 M & W 322 that signature was not necessary in an instrument called for by statute (a bill of sale of a ship under 3 & 4 Will 4c 55 (Registering of British Vessels) (1833) s 31 (repealed)) unless expressly required; but authentication by signature is practically essential to a document in writing, and is usually essential to give it legal effect.

2   See the Statute of Frauds (1677) s 4 (as amended); and paras 141 note 1, 155 note 4 ante. So an agreement for remuneration for non-contentious business under the Solicitors Act 1974 s 57 (as amended) must be signed by the person to be bound thereby or his agent: see further SOLICITORS vol 44(1) (Reissue) paras 178, 180. A consent or agreement in writing under the Prescription Act 1832 s 3 (as amended) is sufficiently signed by the owner of the dominant tenement: *Bewley v Atkinson* (1879) 13 ChD 283, CA; and see EASEMENTS AND PROFITS À PRENDRE vol 16(2) (Reissue) para 241.

3   A marine insurance policy must be signed by or on behalf of the insurer: see the Marine Insurance Act 1906 s 24(1); and INSURANCE vol 25 (2003 Reissue) para 221.

4   A contract to lend money in consideration of the receipt of a share of profits, without incurring partnership liabilities, must be signed by all the parties: see the Partnership Act 1890 s 2(3)(d); and PARTNERSHIP vol 35 (Reissue) para 16. A seaman's agreement must be signed by the seaman and by or on behalf of the persons employing him: see the Merchant Shipping Act 1995 s 25(1); and SHIPPING AND NAVIGATION vol 43(1) (Reissue) para 483. A regulated agreement under the Consumer Credit Act 1974 must be signed by the debtor or hirer and by or on behalf of the creditor or owner: see s 61(1); and CONSUMER CREDIT vol 9(1) (Reissue) para 160.

5   Thus there was no sufficient signature in *Firstpost Homes Ltd v Johnson* [1995] 4 All ER 355, [1995] 1 WLR 1567, CA, where a letter incorporated a plan, and the plan but not the letter was signed, and the signature on the plan alone did not suffice to create a contract.

6   Printing or typing of a name does not constitute a signature for the purposes of the Law of Property (Miscellaneous Provisions) Act 1989 s 2 (as amended): *Firstpost Homes Ltd v Johnson* [1995] 4 All ER 355, [1995] 1 WLR 1567, CA (citing *Goodman v J Eban Ltd* [1954] 1 QB 550 at 561, [1954] 1 All ER 763 at

768, CA, per Denning LJ: 'In modern English usage when a document is required to be 'signed' by someone, that means that he must write his name with his own hand on it').

7 Law of Property (Miscellaneous Provisions) Act 1989 s 2(3); and see SALE OF LAND vol 42 (Reissue) para 29. This provision does not apply in relation to contracts made before 28 September 1989 (i e the date on which s 2 (as originally enacted) came into force): ss 2(7), 5(3), (4)(a). Section 2 (as amended) does not apply in relation to: (1) a contract to grant such a lease as is mentioned in the Law of Property Act 1925 s 54(2) (short leases) (see SALE OF LAND vol 42 (Reissue) para 29); (2) a contract made in the course of a public auction; or (3) a contract regulated under the Financial Services and Markets Act 2000 other than a regulated mortgage contract, and nothing in the Law of Property (Miscellaneous Provisions) Act 1989 s 2 (as amended) affects the creation or operation of resulting, implied or constructive trusts: s 2(5) (amended by the Financial ʻServices and Markets Act 2000 (Consequential Amendments and Repeals) Order 2001, SI 2001/3649, art 317(1), (2)). It does, however, apply to the variation of a contract within the Law of Property (Miscellaneous Provisions) Act 1989: *McCausland v Duncan Lawrie Ltd* [1996] 4 All ER 995, [1997] 1 WLR 38, CA.

As to public auction see AUCTION vol 2(3) (Reissue) para 201 et seq. As to activities regulated under the Financial Services and Markets Act 2000 see FINANCIAL SERVICES vol 18(1) (Reissue) para 80 et seq. As to regulated mortgage contracts see FINANCIAL SERVICES vol 18(1) (Reissue) para 177 et seq.

8 Opinions on this point vary. In cases on the Attorneys' and Solicitors' Act 1870 s 4 (repealed: see now the Solicitors Act 1974 s 59 (as amended)), it has been said that the agreement in writing for special remuneration must be signed by both parties (*Re Lewis, ex p Munro* (1876) 1 QBD 724; *Pontifex v Farnham* (1892) 41 WR 238); but on the analogy of the Statute of Frauds (1677) it has been decided that signature by the client is sufficient (*Re Thompson, ex p Baylis* [1894] 1 QB 462; *Re Jones* [1895] 2 Ch 719 (on appeal [1896] 1 Ch 222, CA); *Bake v French (No 2)* [1907] 2 Ch 215). See also *TA Ruf & Co v Pauwels* [1919] 1 KB 660 at 666, CA. An arbitration agreement must be in writing but need not be signed by the parties: see the Arbitration Act 1996 ss 5, 6; and ARBITRATION vol 2(3) (Reissue) para 12.

9 In some cases the signature is prescribed by statute. For example, an instrument creating a trust of land must be signed by the party entitled to declare the trust (see para 24 ante); an assignment of a thing in action by the assignor (see the Law of Property Act 1925 s 136(1); and CHOSES IN ACTION vol 6 (2003 Reissue) para 12); a disposition of an equitable interest or trust, by the person disposing of the same or his agent (see para 25 ante); and an assignment of copyright is not effective unless it is in writing signed by or on behalf of the assignor (see the Copyright, Designs and Patents Act 1988 s 92; and COPYRIGHT, DESIGN RIGHT AND RELATED RIGHTS vol 9(2) (2006 Reissue) para 176).

10 *Johnson v Dodgson* (1837) 2 M & W 653. Thus where an instrument is in the handwriting of the party to be charged, it is sufficient if his name is inserted at the commencement: *Ogilvie v Foljambe* (1817) 3 Mer 53 at 62; *Propert v Parker* (1830) 1 Russ & M 625; *Lobb v Stanley* (1844) 5 QB 574; *Holmes v Mackrell* (1858) 3 CBNS 789; cf *Godwin v Francis* (1870) LR 5 CP 295 (name at head of telegram); *Schneider v Norris* (1814) 2 M & S 286; *Sarl v Bourdillon* (1856) 1 CBNS 188 (entry of names of sellers and buyers in order book); *Durrell v Evans* (1862) 1 H & C 174, Ex Ch. The name of a person signing as witness may authenticate the instrument if he cannot be a witness: *Coles v Trecothick* (1804) 9 Ves 234 at 251; *Barkworth v Young* (1856) 4 Drew 1 at 13–15; cf *Gosbell v Archer* (1835) 2 Ad & El 500. A signature may authenticate a memorandum added afterwards (*Bluck v Gompertz* (1852) 7 Exch 862); but a signature not introduced so as to authenticate the entire instrument will not suffice (*Caton v Caton* (1867) LR 2 HL 127; *Stokes v Moore* (1786) 1 Cox Eq Cas 219).

11 Signature in pencil or by initials or by a mark is sufficient: see SALE OF LAND vol 42 (Reissue) para 39. The acknowledgment of a person who was too ill to write was held insufficient in *Re Clendinning, ex p Anderson* (1859) 9 I Ch R 284. Where a party holds the pen and another traces his name, it is his signature: *Harrison v Elvin* (1842) 3 QB 117; *Helsham v Langley* (1841) 11 LJ Ch 17. A rubber stamp imprinting a facsimile of the party's signature or mark suffices, provided that (unless there are exceptional circumstances, e g physical disability, preventing him) it is impressed by himself: see *Goodman v J Eban Ltd* [1954] 1 QB 550, [1954] 1 All ER 763, CA; *LCC v Agricultural Food Products* [1955] 2 QB 218, [1955] 2 All ER 229, CA. A typed or printed name (not a facsimile of the party's signature) may be insufficient: *Goodman v J Eban Ltd* [1954] 1 QB 550 at 559, [1954] 1 All ER 763 at 767, CA, per Lord Evershed MR; *R v Cowper* (1890) 24 QBD 533, CA; *McDonald v John Twiname Ltd* [1953] 2 QB 304, [1953] 2 All ER 589, CA. See also para 30 ante.

12 *Wallis v Littell* (1861) 11 CBNS 369 at 375; *Pattle v Hornibrook* [1897] 1 Ch 25; and see *Furness v Meek* (1857) 27 LJ Ex 34. See paras 37–38 ante, 188 post.

157. Signature by agent.

In general, where a contract or other document is required to be in writing, a signature by an agent on behalf of the party to be bound is sufficient[1], and it is not necessary that the agent should be appointed in writing[2].

In some cases, however, a statute requires that the signature should be that of the party himself, and then an agent cannot sign for him[3]; in others, signature by an agent is expressly allowed[4], and occasionally with the requirement that he is to be authorised in writing[5].

An agent can either sign the name of his principal or his own name but in the latter case the fact of the agency should appear on the document, or he will be liable as a principal[6].

1   *Re Whitley Partners Ltd* (1886) 32 ChD 337, CA; *LCC v Agricultural Food Products Ltd* [1955] 2 QB 218 at 223–225, [1955] 2 All ER 229 at 232–233, CA, per Romer LJ.
       A submission to arbitration under the Arbitration Acts must be in writing (see the Arbitration Act 1996 ss 5, 6; and ARBITRATION vol 2(3) (Reissue) para 12); but since there is no need for signature a fortiori it may be signed by agents. It would appear that signature by agents suffices in the case of an instrument of dissolution of a building society, which requires the consent of a special majority of the members testified 'by their signature' (see the Building Societies Act 1986 s 87(1); *Dennison v Jeffs* [1896] 1 Ch 611; and BUILDING SOCIETIES vol 4(3) (Reissue) para 604). See generally AGENCY vol 2(1) (Reissue) para 29 et seq. As to execution on behalf of a company or corporation aggregate see the Law of Property Act 1925 s 74 (as amended); the Powers of Attorney Act 1971 s 7 (as amended); the Companies Act 1985 ss 36, 37 (s 36 as substituted); the Corporate Bodies' Contracts Act 1960 ss 1, 2 (as amended); and AGENCY vol 2(1) (Reissue) para 72.

2   See AGENCY vol 2(1) (Reissue) paras 29–30.

3   Personal signature is necessary when a statute requires that the instrument must be signed by a particular party, without adding 'or his agent'; such as contracts by seamen under the Merchant Shipping Act 1995 s 25(1): see SHIPPING AND NAVIGATION vol 43(1) (Reissue) para 483. A representation as to character must be signed by the 'party to be charged therewith' (see the Statute of Frauds Amendment Act 1828 s 6; and GUARANTEE AND INDEMNITY vol 20(1) (Reissue) para 142), and this requires personal signature (*Swift v Jewsbury and Goddard* (1874) LR 9 QB 301, Ex Ch; *Hirst v West Riding Union Banking Co* [1901] 2 KB 560, CA). A disclaimer by a trustee in bankruptcy under the Bankruptcy Act 1914 s 54 (repealed: see now the Insolvency Act 1986 ss 178, 315 (as amended); and BANKRUPTCY AND INDIVIDUAL INSOLVENCY vol 3(2) (2002 Reissue) para 472 et seq) must be signed by him personally: *Wilson v Wallani* (1880) 5 Ex D 155.

4   Under the Statute of Frauds (1677) s 4 (as amended) (see paras 141 note 1, 155 note 4 ante), the signature may be by an agent 'lawfully authorised'; and an agent may sign under the Partnership Act 1890 s 2(3)(d) (see PARTNERSHIP vol 35 (Reissue) para 16); the Solicitors Act 1974 s 57 (as amended) (see SOLICITORS vol 44(1) (Reissue) paras 178, 180); and the Marine Insurance Act 1906 s 24 (see INSURANCE vol 25 (2005 Reissue) para 221). All acknowledgments under the Limitation Act 1980 s 29 (see LIMITATION OF ACTIONS vol 28 (Reissue) paras 1081–1083) may be made by or to an agent: see s 30(2); and LIMITATION OF ACTIONS vol 28 (Reissue) para 1084.

5   This is so under the Law of Property Act 1925 s 53(1)(a), (c): see para 24 ante.

6   See AGENCY vol 2(1) (Reissue) para 72 et seq. If the donee of a power of attorney is an individual he may, if he thinks fit, execute any instrument with his own signature and do any other thing in his own name, by the authority of the donor of the power, and any instrument so executed or thing so done is as effective as if it had been executed or done by the donee with the signature or, as the case may be, in the name, of the donor of the power: Powers of Attorney Act 1971 s 7(1) (amended by the Law of Property (Miscellaneous Provisions) Act 1989 s 1, Sch 1 para 7; and the Regulatory Reform (Execution of Deeds and Documents) Order 2005, SI 2005/1906, art 10(1), Sch 1 paras 5, 6). However, where an instrument is executed by the donee as a deed, it is as effective as if executed by the donee in a manner which would constitute due execution of it as a deed by the donor only if it is executed in accordance with the Law of Property (Miscellaneous Provisions) Act 1989 s 1(3)(a) (see para 33 ante): Powers of Attorney Act 1971 s 7(1A) (added by the Regulatory Reform (Execution of Deeds and Documents) Order 2005, SI 2005/1906, Sch 1 paras 5, 7). See further para 1 ante. In general, since an agent cannot delegate his authority, his personal signature is required. Hence, an auctioneer's clerk cannot sign on behalf of a purchaser, unless authorised by the purchaser: see AUCTION vol 2(3) (Reissue) para 211. Delegation of the act of signing to a clerk, however, may be permitted by the ordinary course of business: *Johnson v Osenton* (1869) LR 4 Exch 107; and see *Brown v Tombs* [1891] 1 QB 253 (notice of claim to parliamentary vote). See also BILLS OF EXCHANGE AND OTHER NEGOTIABLE INSTRUMENTS vol 4(1) (2002 Reissue) para 374. As to execution on behalf of a company see COMPANIES vol 7(1) (2004 Reissue) para 458.

(4) ALTERATION AND CANCELLATION

158.   Alteration before execution.   A writing which is intended to be under hand only can be altered by erasure, or interlineation, or otherwise, before it is signed, but it lies upon the party who puts the instrument in suit to explain the alteration and show when it was made[1].

1   The presumption that alterations are made before the execution of the instrument, which arises in the case of a deed (see para 81 ante), does not apply to an instrument under hand, although the reason for the presumption, namely, that the instrument cannot be altered, after it is executed, without fraud or wrong, and that the presumption is against fraud or wrong (*Doe d Tatum v Catomore* (1851) 16 QB 745; and see para 81 ante) seems to exist equally in each case. In the case of instruments other than deeds, the principle has prevailed that it lies on the party who seeks to enforce an altered instrument to prove the circumstances under which the alteration took place: *Henman v Dickinson* (1828) 5 Bing 183; *Knight v Clements* (1838) 8 Ad & El 215; *Cariss v Tattersall* (1841) 2 Man & G 890; *Clifford v Parker* (1841) 2 Man & G 909; *Doe d Tatum v Catomore* supra at 746. However, if the obligation to be enforced does not arise under the altered instrument, but the instrument is introduced merely to explain the obligation, and the alteration does not affect its use for this purpose, no explanation of the alteration need be given: *Earl of Falmouth v Roberts* (1842) 9 M & W 469; *Hutchins v Scott* (1837) 2 M & W 809.

159.   Material alteration by one party.   An alteration in a material part of an instrument under hand made by, or with the consent of, one party to it, but without the consent of the other party, makes the instrument void to the extent that the party responsible for the alteration cannot enforce the instrument against a party not so responsible. The latter party can, however, enforce it against the former, if he can prove the original form of the instrument; and where the instrument operates as a conveyance, the alteration will not prejudice it in this respect[1].

Where a document consists of print, type or ink writing, the most natural inference to draw of an amendment in pencil is that it was not, and was not intended to be, an operative and final alteration[2].

1   The effect of an alteration of an instrument in writing is the same as in the case of deeds. The principle established for deeds by *Pigot's Case* (1614) 11 Co Rep 26b was applied to bills of exchange by *Master v Miller* (1791) 4 Term Rep 320 (affd (1793) 2 Hy Bl 141, Ex Ch); 1 Smith LC (13th Edn) 780; and see *Burchfield v Moore* (1854) 3 E & B 683; *Gardner v Walsh* (1855) 5 E & B 83 at 90. The principle has also been extended to other instruments, such as insurance policies (*Laird v Robertson* (1791) 4 Bro Parl Cas 488; *Campbell v Christie* (1817) 2 Stark 64); bought and sold notes (*Powell v Divett* (1812) 15 East 29; *Mollett v Wackerbarth* (1847) 5 CB 181); guarantees (*Davidson v Cooper* (1844) 13 M & W 343, Ex Ch; *Bank of Hindustan, China and Japan v Smith* (1867) 36 LJCP 241); charterparties (*Croockewit v Fletcher* (1857) 1 H & N 893); building contracts (*Pattinson v Luckley* (1875) LR 10 Exch 330); Bank of England notes (*Suffell v Bank of England* (1882) 9 QBD 555, CA); and a reception order in lunacy (*Lowe v Fox* (1887) 12 App Cas 206, HL). The rules on the subject have already been stated (see para 81 et seq ante), and they are repeated here in abbreviated form, with such authorities as are specially applicable to instruments under hand. In modern conditions it has been held that the critical question is that of prejudice or potential prejudice as a result of the alteration: *Raiffeisen Zentralbank Osterreich AG v Crossseas Shipping Ltd* [2000] 1 All ER (Comm) 76, [2000] 1 WLR 1135, CA. The rules with regard to alteration of a bill of exchange are now contained in the Bills of Exchange Act 1882 s 64(1) and the Decimal Currency Act 1969 s 3(2): see BILLS OF EXCHANGE AND OTHER NEGOTIABLE INSTRUMENTS vol 4(1) (2002 Reissue) para 460. As to what alterations in a bill of exchange are material see BILLS OF EXCHANGE AND OTHER NEGOTIABLE INSTRUMENTS vol 4(1) (2002 Reissue) para 461. As to what alterations are material in other instruments see para 82 ante. Stated generally, the principle is that an alteration is material if it alters the legal effect of the instrument, but not if it adds something that would be implied, or supplies an obvious clerical omission (*Aldous v Cornwell* (1868) LR 3 QB 573 ('on demand' inserted in a promissory note which expressed no time for payment)); and it is also material if, without altering the legal effect, it is important in the use of the instrument, such as the alteration of the number of a Bank of England note (*Suffell v Bank of England* supra; and see *Leeds and County Bank v Walker* (1883) 11 QBD 84; cf *Re Howgate and Osborn's Contract* [1902] 1 Ch 451; *Koch v Dicks* [1933] 1 KB 307, CA (alteration of place where bill drawn)). The party who has altered the instrument and thus loses his remedy on it does not lose his remedy on the original consideration, unless he has by the alteration deprived the other party of some remedy: *Sutton v Toomer* (1827) 7 B & C 416; *Atkinson v*

Hawdon (1835) 2 Ad & El 628; and cf *Alderson v Langdale* (1832) 3 B & Ad 660. The innocent party can only enforce the contract subject to any restrictions or conditions originally contained in it: *Pattinson v Luckley* (1875) LR 10 Exch 330.

2   *Co-operative Bank plc v Tipper* [1996] 4 All ER 366.

160.   Material alteration by stranger.   An alteration made while the instrument is in the custody of one party, although not made with his knowledge or consent, has the same effect in avoiding the instrument as if made by him, on the principle that he who has the custody of an instrument made for his benefit is bound to preserve it in its original state[1]. It is, however, doubtful whether this rule applies when the alteration is made against the will and in fraud of the party having the custody[2], and an alteration made by a stranger, when the instrument is in the custody of neither party, does not affect the document, if its original state can be proved[3].

1   *Davidson v Cooper* (1844) 13 M & W 343, Ex Ch; *Bank of Hindustan, China and Japan v Smith* (1867) 36 LJCP 241; and see *Pattinson v Luckley* (1875) LR 10 Exch 330; *Robinson v Mollett* (1875) LR 7 HL 802 at 813 per Blackburn J.
2   *Lowe v Fox* (1887) 12 App Cas 206 at 217, HL, per Lord Herschell.
3   *Henfree v Bromley* (1805) 6 East 309.
      This paragraph was cited as conveniently summarising the law in *Spector v Ageda* [1973] Ch 30 at 49, [1971] 3 All ER 417 at 431 per Megarry J.

161.   Alteration by accident or mistake.   To avoid the instrument the alteration must be intentional; if it is due to accident or to mistake it will not prejudice the party responsible for the custody of the instrument[1]. An intentional alteration, however, made under a mistake as to the legal effect of the instrument avoids it[2].

1   See para 86 ante. As to mistake see also *Raper v Birkbeck* (1812) 15 East 17; *Wilkinson v Johnson* (1824) 3 B & C 428; *Prince v Oriental Bank Corpn* (1878) 3 App Cas 325, PC.
2   *Bank of Hindustan, China and Japan v Smith* (1867) 36 LJCP 241.

162.   Alteration with consent.   An alteration in an instrument under hand made with the consent of all parties does not avoid it, and it takes effect as altered[1], but if the result is to create in effect a fresh instrument, it will require restamping[2]. An alteration which is not material does not affect the operation of the instrument by whomsoever it is made[3].

1   See para 84 ante. This sentence was cited with approval in *Re Danish Bacon Co Ltd Staff Pension Fund, Christensen v Arnett* [1971] 1 All ER 486 at 496, [1971] 1 WLR 248 at 259 per Megarry J, and applied to an alteration in a nomination, although it was a unilateral instrument requiring signature by the nominator in the presence of a witness.
2   See *Hamelin v Bruck and Hirschfield* (1846) 9 QB 306; *Downes v Richardson* (1822) 5 B & Ald 674.
3   See para 87 ante. As to marine insurance policies see *Sanderson v Symonds* (1819) 1 Brod & Bing 426.

163.   Cancellation.   An instrument under hand is cancelled and made void by striking through the signature with the intention that it is to become void; and this may be done by or under the direction of the person who is entitled to the benefit of the instrument[1]; but cancellation by an agent without authority has no effect[2].

1   See para 76 ante. The authorities there cited relate to deeds, but similar principles apply, it seems, to instruments under hand. As to the cancellation of bills of exchange see BILLS OF EXCHANGE AND OTHER NEGOTIABLE INSTRUMENTS vol 4(1) (2002 Reissue) para 457.
2   *Bank of Scotland v Dominion Bank (Toronto)* [1891] AC 592, HL.

4. INTERPRETATION

(1) GENERAL RULES OF INTERPRETATION

164.   The principles of construction.   In 1998 a fundamental change overtook the branch of the law concerned with the principles by which contractual documents are construed[1]. The result has been, subject to one important exception, to assimilate the way in which such documents are interpreted by judges to the common sense principles by which any serious utterance would be interpreted in ordinary life[2]. The principles may be summarised as follows:

(1)   Interpretation is the ascertainment of the meaning which the document would convey to a reasonable person having all the background knowledge which would reasonably have been available to the parties in the situation in which they were at the time of the contract[3].

(2)   The background was famously described as the 'matrix of fact'[4], but this phrase is, if anything, an understated description of what the background may include. Subject to the requirement that it should have been reasonably available to the parties and to the exception mentioned in head (3) below, it includes absolutely anything which would have affected the way in which the language of the document would have been understood by a reasonable man[5]. This proposition should be regarded with some circumspection. It has been observed that no authority was cited for it, and that it may not have been the subject of argument; and suggested that surrounding circumstances should be confined to what the parties had in mind, and what was going on around them at the time when they were making the contract[6].

(3)   The law excludes from the admissible background the previous negotiations of the parties and their declarations of subjective intent. They are admissible only in a claim for rectification. The law makes this distinction for reasons of practical policy and, in this respect only, legal interpretation differs from the way utterances would be interpreted in ordinary life. The boundaries of this exception are in some respects unclear[7].

(4)   The meaning which a document (or any other utterance) would convey to a reasonable man is not the same thing as the meaning of its words. The meaning of words is a matter of dictionaries and grammars; the meaning of the document is what the parties using those words against the relevant background would reasonably have been understood to mean. The background may not merely enable the reasonable man to choose between the possible meanings of words which are ambiguous but even (as occasionally happens in ordinary life) to conclude that the parties must, for whatever reason, have used the wrong words or syntax[8].

(5)   The 'rule' that words should be given their 'natural and ordinary meaning' reflects the common-sense proposition that we do not easily accept that people have made linguistic mistakes, particularly in formal documents. On the other hand, if one would nevertheless conclude from the background that something must have gone wrong with the language, the law does not require judges to attribute to the parties an intention which they plainly could not have had[9].

It has been observed that there are documents in which the need for certainty is paramount and in relation to which admissible background is restricted to avoid the possibility that the same document may have different meanings for different people according to their knowledge of the background[10]. Documents required by bankers' commercial credits fall within this category[11].

1   See *Investors Compensation Scheme Ltd v West Bromwich Building Society* [1998] 1 All ER 98, [1998] 1 WLR
    896, HL. 'Almost all the old intellectual baggage of 'legal' interpretation has been discarded': *Investors
    Compensation Scheme Ltd v West Bromwich Building Society* supra at 114 and 912 per Lord Hoffmann. See
    also *Atari Corpn (UK) Ltd v Electronics Boutique Stores (UK) Ltd* [1998] QB 539, [1998] 1 All ER
    1010, CA; *Cargill International SA v Bangladesh Sugar and Food Industries Corpn* [1998] 2 All ER 406 at
    413, [1998] 1 WLR 461 at 468, CA, per Potter LJ ('modern principles of construction require the court
    to have regard to the commercial background, the context of the contract and the circumstances of the
    parties, and to consider whether, against that background and in that context, to give the words a
    particular or restricted meaning would lead to an apparently unreasonable and unfair result'); *Don King
    Productions Inc v Warren* [1998] 2 All ER 608, [1999] 3 WLR 276 (affd [2000] Ch 291, [1999] 2 All ER
    218, CA); *Kuma v AGF Insurance Ltd* [1998] 4 All ER 788, [1999] 1 WLR 1747; *C Itoh & Co Ltd v
    Companhia de Navegacao Lloyd Brasileiro and Steamship Mutual Underwriting Association (Bermuda) Ltd* [1999]
    1 Lloyd's Rep 115, CA.
2   *Investors Compensation Scheme Ltd v West Bromwich Building Society* [1998] 1 All ER 98 at 114, [1998]
    1 WLR 896 at 912, HL, per Lord Hoffmann.
3   *Investors Compensation Scheme Ltd v West Bromwich Building Society* [1998] 1 All ER 98 at 114, [1998]
    1 WLR 896 at 912, HL, per Lord Hoffmann.
4   See *Prenn v Simmonds* [1971] 3 All ER 237 at 240–242, [1971] 1 WLR 1381 at 1384–1386, HL, per
    Lord Wilberforce. See also *Reardon Smith Line Ltd v Yngvar Hansen-Tangen* [1976] 3 All ER 570, [1976]
    1 WLR 989, HL; *Gilmartin v West Sussex County Council* (1976) 242 Estates Gazette 203, Times,
    11 December, CA; *Charles M Willie & Co (Shipping) Ltd v Ocean Laser Shipping Ltd* [1999] 1 Lloyd's Rep
    225; *Galaxy Energy International Ltd v Assuranceforeningen Skuld (Ejeusidie)* [1999] 1 Lloyd's Rep 249.
5   *Investors Compensation Scheme Ltd v West Bromwich Building Society* [1998] 1 All ER 98 at 114, [1998]
    1 WLR 896 at 912, HL, per Lord Hoffmann.
6   See *Scottish Power plc v Britoil (Exploration) Ltd* [1997] 47 LS Gaz R 30, CA, per Staughton LJ. See also
    National Bank of Sharjah v Dellborg (9 July 1997) Lexis, CA.
7   *Investors Compensation Scheme Ltd v West Bromwich Building Society* [1998] 1 All ER 98 at 115, [1998]
    1 WLR 896 at 913, HL, per Lord Hoffmann.
8   *Investors Compensation Scheme Ltd v West Bromwich Building Society* [1998] 1 All ER 98 at 115, [1998]
    1 WLR 896 at 913, HL, per Lord Hoffmann. See also *Mannai Investment Co Ltd v Eagle Star Life
    Assurance Co Ltd* [1997] AC 749, [1997] 3 All ER 352, HL.
9   *Investors Compensation Scheme Ltd v West Bromwich Building Society* [1998] 1 All ER 98 at 115, [1998]
    1 WLR 896 at 913, HL, per Lord Hoffmann. 'If detailed semantic and syntactical analysis of words in a
    commercial contract is going to lead to a conclusion that flouts business common sense, it must be made
    to yield to business common sense': *Antaios Cia Naviera SA v Salen Rederierna AB, The Antaios* [1985] AC
    191 at 201, [1984] 3 All ER 229 at 233, HL, per Lord Diplock.
10 *Mannai Investment Co Ltd v Eagle Star Life Assurance Co Ltd* [1997] AC 749 at 779, [1997] 3 All ER 352
    at 380, HL, per Lord Hoffmann. In this case, which involved a notice under a break clause in a lease, it
    was held that the old rule as applied for instance in *Hankey v Clavering* [1942] 2 KB 326, [1942] 2 All ER
    311, CA (which stated that if the words of a document were capable of referring unambiguously to a
    person or thing, no extrinsic evidence was admissible to show that the author was using them to refer to
    something or someone else) should no longer be followed: see *Mannai Investment Co Ltd v Eagle Star Life
    Assurance Co Ltd* supra at 779 and 381 per Lord Hoffmann. See also *Garston v Scottish Widows' Fund and
    Life Assurance Society* [1998] 3 All ER 596, [1998] 2 EGLR 73, CA (notice to determine business tenancy
    and application for new tenancy under the Landlord and Tenant Act 1954). However, it could not cure
    the defect where a purported break notice was given by someone claiming to act as agent for an assignee,
    no assignment having taken place: *Lemmerbell Ltd v Britannia LAS Direct Ltd* [1998] 3 EGLR 67, [1998]
    48 EG 188, CA. See also *Clickex Ltd v McCann* (1999) 32 HLR 324, [1999] 2 EGLR 63, CA (notice
    served for the purpose of creating an assured shorthold tenancy under the Housing Act 1988 s 20 (as
    substituted and amended) (see LANDLORD AND TENANT vol 27(2) (2006 Reissue) para 1051) ineffective
    where dates differed from the tenancy agreement so that it was not obvious which was correct).
11 *Mannai Investment Co Ltd v Eagle Star Life Assurance Co Ltd* [1997] AC 749 at 779, [1997] 3 All ER 352
    at 380, HL, per Lord Hoffmann. 'Article 13(a) of the Uniform Customs and Practice for Commercial
    Credits (1993 Revision) says that the documents must 'upon their face' appear to be in accordance with
    the terms and conditions of the credit': *Mannai Investment Co Ltd v Eagle Star Life Assurance Co Ltd* supra
    at 779 and 380 per Lord Hoffmann.

165.   Object of interpretation.   It has been said that the object of all interpretation
of a written instrument is to discover the real intention of the author, the written
declaration of whose mind it is always considered to be[1], and that consequently, the
construction must be as near to the minds and apparent intention of the parties as is

possible, and as the law will permit[2]. However, the law is not concerned with subjective intentions. All that matters is the objective meaning of the words which the author of those words has used. The law is concerned with what the user of the words would objectively have been understood to mean[3]. The same construction is placed on the words of a deed as on those of an instrument under hand only[4], and on mercantile contracts[5], policies of insurance[6] and guarantees[7] as on other instruments, though, exceptionally, there are documents, such as banker's commercial credits, in which the need for certainty is paramount and where the admissible background is restricted[8]. While no special rules of construction apply to pension schemes, they should be construed in a purposive and practical, rather than a literal way[9].

Documents receive the same construction in equity as at law[10], for there is no such thing as equitable, as distinct from legal, construction of an instrument, equity in this respect following the law[11]. When a general principle for the construction of an instrument has once been laid down, and that construction comes to be accepted and people afterwards make contracts and other instruments on that understanding, the court will normally adhere to that recognised construction and make the most accurate application of it to the circumstances of the particular case, notwithstanding that it may have been applied differently in other cases[12]. Were the court not to proceed on these lines it would be construing instruments contrary to the meaning of those who made them[13]. The House of Lords, of course, retains its power to overrule a rule of construction even though it may have been applied for many years[14].

There are a few statutory provisions relating to the interpretation of written instruments[15]. Such a provision prescribing that in all or certain classes of documents particular words are to have particular meanings will override the ordinary principles of construction[16]. An interpreting enactment may be qualified so as to apply unless the contrary intention appears, that is unless the context and such extrinsic evidence as may be admissible indicate that the enacted rule is not to have effect. Some enactments are qualified by a formula referring to the context, such as 'unless the context otherwise requires'; any contrary intention must then, it seems, be found in the text of the instrument, though not necessarily in the immediate context of the word construed[17].

1   *Marquis of Cholmondeley v Lord Clinton* (1820) 2 Jac & W 1 at 91 per Plumer MR (affd (1821) 4 Bli 1, HL); *Evans v Vaughan* (1825) 4 B & C 261 at 266 per Abbott CJ. Where a document on its face a deed, but witnessed as a will, was admitted to probate, it was said to be 'clear that extrinsic evidence is admissible for the purpose of shewing with what intention an ambiguous paper has been executed': *Re Slinn's Goods* (1890) 15 PD 156 at 158.
     As to the construction of contractual documents generally see para 164 ante.

2   Shep Touch 86; *Throckmerton v Tracy* (1555) 1 Plowd 145 at 160 per Staundford J; *Hilbers v Parkinson* (1883) 25 ChD 200 at 203 per Pearson J. 'As far as it may stand with the rule of law, it is honourable for all judges to judge according to the intention of the parties, and so they ought to do': see Co Litt 314b.

3   *Mannai Investment Co Ltd v Eagle Star Life Assurance Co Ltd* [1997] AC 749 at 779, [1997] 3 All ER 352 at 376, HL, per Lord Hoffmann. See also para 164 ante.

4   See *Seddon v Senate* (1810) 13 East 63 at 74 per Lord Ellenborough CJ.

5   *Southwell v Bowditch* (1876) 1 CPD 374 at 376, CA, per Jessel MR.

6   *Robertson v French* (1803) 4 East 130 at 135 per Lord Ellenborough CJ; *Carr v Montefiore* (1864) 5 B & S 408 at 428, Ex Ch, per Erle CJ.

7   *Eshelby v Federated European Bank Ltd* [1932] 1 KB 254 at 266, DC, per Swift J; affd [1932] 1 KB 423, CA. See GUARANTEE AND INDEMNITY vol 20(1) (Reissue) para 171 et seq.

8   *Mannai Investment Co Ltd v Eagle Star Life Assurance Co Ltd* [1997] AC 749, [1997] 3 All ER 352, HL. Dicta in the cases referred to in notes 5–7 supra may require reconsideration: see para 164 ante.

9   *Derby Daily Telegraph Ltd v Pensions Ombudsman* [1999] ICR 1057, [1999] IRLR 476.

10   *Gladstone v Birley* (1817) 2 Mer 401; *Re Terry and White's Contract* (1886) 32 ChD 14 at 21, CA, per Lord Esher MR. See also *Pentland v Stokes* (1812) 2 Ball & B 68 at 73.

11   *Scott v Liverpool Corpn* (1858) 28 LJ Ch 230 at 235; and see *Midland Great Western Rly of Ireland v Johnson* (1858) 6 HL Cas 798. There is no rule that equity will construe a contract in terms joint as joint and several (*Kendall v Hamilton* (1879) 4 App Cas 504 at 521, 537–539, HL); see, however, on this point

CONTRACT vol 9(1) (Reissue) para 1079 et seq; EXECUTORS AND ADMINISTRATORS vol 17(2) (Reissue) para 779; PARTNERSHIP vol 35 (Reissue) para 39.

12 *Browning v Wright* (1799) 2 Bos & P 13 at 24 per Lord Eldon CJ; *Re Kilpatrick's Policies Trusts, Kilpatrick v IRC* [1966] Ch 730, [1966] 2 All ER 149, CA. In construing a commercial document which uses a standard form, previous decisions on the meaning of that form which are likely to have been accepted by those adopting the form will be followed, whether or not they are authorities binding on the court: *The Annefield* [1971] P 168 at 183, [1971] 1 All ER 394 at 405, CA, per Lord Denning MR, at 185 and 406 per Phillimore LJ; *WN Lindsay & Co Ltd v European Grain and Shipping Agency* [1962] 2 Lloyd's Rep 387 at 396 per Megaw J (revsd but not on this point [1963] 1 Lloyd's Rep 437, CA); and see SHIPPING AND NAVIGATION vol 43(1) (Reissue) para 1457 et seq.

13 *Re National Coffee Palace Co, ex p Panmure* (1883) 24 ChD 367 at 370, CA, per Brett MR. As to the effect of usage upon contracts generally see CUSTOM AND USAGE vol 12(1) (Reissue) para 650 et seq.

14 *Mannai Investment Co Ltd v Eagle Star Life Assurance Co Ltd* [1997] AC 749, [1997] 3 All ER 352, HL, where it was held that the rule which had been applied for at least 200 years to the construction of a notice under a break clause in a lease should no longer be followed: it was said to be 'highly artificial and capable of producing results which offend against common sense': *Mannai Investment Co Ltd v Eagle Star Life Assurance Co Ltd* supra at 778 and 378 per Lord Hoffmann.

15 See para 171 post.

16 *Master and Brethren of the Hospital of St Cross v Lord Howard de Walden* (1795) 6 Term Rep 338.

17 *Re Evans, ex p Evans* [1891] 1 QB 143, CA.

166.   How intention is ascertained. The intention must be gathered from the written instrument[1] read in the light of such extrinsic evidence as is admissible for the purpose of construction[2]. Traditionally it has been said that the function of the court is to ascertain what the parties meant by the words which they have used[3]; to declare the meaning of what is written in the instrument, not of what was intended to have been written[4]; to give effect to the intention as expressed[5], the expressed meaning being, for the purpose of interpretation, equivalent to the intention[6]. These traditional statements must now be read in the light of the changed approach to the construction of documents to be found in more recent decisions of the House of Lords[7]. It is not permissible to guess at the intention of the parties and substitute the presumed for the expressed intention[8]. If, however, in any particular respect, the intention is clear on the whole instrument, effect will be given to that intention, even though it is not stated in express words[9]. Various implications and presumptions will also be made where it is necessary or settled by law or usage[10] to do so.

It has traditionally been held that ordinary rules of construction must be applied, although by so doing the real intention of the parties may in some instances be defeated; and it has been said that such a course tends to establish a greater degree of certainty in the administration of the law[11]. This remains the case, though under the changed approach it is less likely that the parties' intentions will be frustrated, and it is not thought that greater uncertainty in the meaning of a document will be created[12].

1 *Shore v Wilson* (1842) 9 Cl & Fin 355 at 526, HL, per Coleridge J, and at 556 per Parke B; *Rickman v Carstairs* (1833) 5 B & Ad 651 at 663 per Denman CJ; *Northland Airliners Ltd v Dennis Ferranti Meters Ltd* (1970) 114 Sol Jo 845, CA (construction of telegrams).

    As to the construction of contractual documents generally see para 164 ante.

2 See paras 185–209 post. An instrument may be one of a series by which a single transaction is carried into effect, or may incorporate another instrument. All such instruments must be read together for the purpose of ascertaining the intention: see para 176 post.

3 See *Thames and Mersey Marine Insurance Co v Hamilton, Fraser & Co* (1887) 12 App Cas 484 at 491, HL, per Lord Halsbury LC; *Barton v Fitzgerald* (1812) 15 East 530 at 541 per Lord Ellenborough CJ.

4 See the cases cited in note 1 supra; and *Marshall v Berridge* (1881) 19 ChD 233, CA.

5 *Hayne v Cummings* (1864) 16 CBNS 421 at 427; *Monypenny v Monypenny* (1861) 9 HL Cas 114 at 146 per Lord Wensleydale; *Fullwood v Akerman* (1862) 11 CBNS 737; *McConnel v Murphy* (1873) LR 5 PC 203 at 219.

6 *Shore v Wilson* (1842) 9 Cl & Fin 355 at 525, HL, per Coleridge J. Though where the nature of the deed and the relation of the parties, as father and child, give a clue to the 'natural intention', the court will

struggle with the language to give effect to it: *Hope v Lord Clifden* (1801) 6 Ves 499 at 509 per Lord Eldon LC; *Clayton v Earl of Glengall* (1841) 1 Dr & War 1 at 17 per Sugden LC.

7   See *Mannai Investment Co Ltd v Eagle Star Life Assurance Co Ltd* [1997] AC 749, [1997] 3 All ER 352, HL; *Investors Compensation Ltd v West Bromwich Building Society* [1998] 1 All ER 98, [1998] 1 WLR 896, HL; and paras 164–165 ante.

8   *Smith v Lucas* (1881) 18 ChD 531 at 542 per Jessel MR; *Monypenny v Monypenny* (1861) 9 HL Cas 114 at 146 per Lord Wensleydale; *Re Meredith, ex p Chick* (1879) 11 ChD 731 at 739, CA, per Brett LJ. See also *Zoan v Rouamba* [2000] 2 All ER 620, [2000] 1 WLR 1509, CA (a document is not to be given the meaning of one party's perceived intention).

9   'I am to consider the whole instrument, and if there appear a plain intention to give interest, then, though there should be no express words to that effect, and this is the case of a deed, yet I am bound to give it that construction': *Clayton v Earl of Glengall* (1841) 1 Dr & War 1 at 14 per Sugden LC.

10 See para 181 post; and CONTRACT vol 9(1) (Reissue) para 780 et seq; CUSTOM AND USAGE vol 12(1) (Reissue) para 650 et seq.

     If no contrary intention is indicated, it will be presumed that, where a contract is to be performed in the country in which it has been made, the law of that country is intended to apply, but if it is to be performed in another country then the law of that other country is intended to apply: *Chatenay v Brazilian Submarine Telegraph Co Ltd* [1891] 1 QB 79, CA.

11 See *Mallan v May* (1844) 13 M & W 511 at 517 per Pollock CB.

12 See *Mannai Investment Co Ltd v Eagle Star Life Assurance Co Ltd* [1997] AC 749, [1997] 3 All ER 352, HL; *Investors Compensation Ltd v West Bromwich Building Society* [1998] 1 All ER 98, [1998] 1 WLR 896, HL; and paras 164–165 ante.

167.   Functions of judge and jury.   The interpretation of a written document is, generally speaking, a matter of law for the court[1]. However, where there is a jury[2] it must ascertain as a fact the meaning of technical or commercial terms[3] used in a written contract and also, in order to enable the court to construe the document, the surrounding circumstances of the particular case[4]; where there is a latent ambiguity in a written instrument, the question of which meaning was intended is a question for the jury[5]; where the contract is oral or is to be inferred from a series of acts and things done, in the course of which letters are written, but the contract does not depend solely upon the letters, it is for the jury to say what is the real contract between the parties[6].

Thus usually it is a question of fact for the jury whether an instrument has been delivered as an escrow, but where facts are proved by evidence in writing which is undisputed, as, for example, where a form of contract is sent enclosed in a letter explaining why and on what terms it is sent, the construction of the letter, and the question whether the contract is delivered as an escrow, is for the judge[7].

1   *Macbeath v Haldimond* (1786) 1 Term Rep 172; *Ashpitel v Sercombe* (1850) 5 Exch 147; *Glaverbel SA v British Coal Corpn* [1995] FSR 254, [1995] RPC 255, CA; and see note 3 infra. As to foreign documents see para 201 post.

     As to the construction of contractual documents generally see para 164 ante.

2   Juries are rarely summoned in civil claims: see JURIES vol 26 (2004 Reissue) para 520.

3   See *Hill v Evans* (1862) 4 De GF & J 288; and para 170 post. As to ordinary words see *Brutus v Cozens* [1973] AC 854 at 861, [1972] 2 All ER 1297 at 1298–1299, HL, per Lord Reid; *Evans v Godber* [1974] 3 All ER 341 at 348, [1974] 1 WLR 1317 at 1325, DC, per Lord Widgery CJ; *Belgravia Navigation Co SA v Cannor Shipping Ltd, The Troll Park* [1988] 2 Lloyd's Rep 423, CA (meaning of an ordinary English word not a question of law but solely one of fact for the determination of the fact finding tribunal).

4   See *Hutchison v Bowker* (1839) 5 M & W 535; *Neilson v Harford* (1841) 8 M & W 806 at 823 per Parke B; *Simpson v Margitson* (1847) 11 QB 23; *Key v Cotesworth* (1852) 7 Exch 595; *Hill v Evans* (1862) 4 De GF & J 288; *Lyle v Richards* (1866) LR 1 HL 222; *Bowes v Shand* (1877) 2 App Cas 455, HL; *Robey v Arnold* (1898) 14 TLR 220, CA; *George D Emery Co v Wells* [1906] AC 515, PC. The rule that the construction of a document is for the court applies equally where the original document is lost and extrinsic evidence is given of its contents: *Berwick v Horsfall* (1858) 4 CBNS 450. It is for the court, and not the jury, to decipher badly written words: *R v Hucks* (1816) 1 Stark 521. Extrinsic evidence may be given of the surrounding circumstances for the purpose of explaining, but not of varying, the words used: *Mumford v Gething* (1859) 7 CBNS 305 at 321; *Macdonald v Longbottom* (1860) 1 E & E 977; *Carr v Montefiore* (1864) 5 B & S 408, Ex Ch.

5   See para 209 post.

6   *Jones v Littledale* (1837) 6 Ad & El 486; *Wilkinson v Stoney* (1838) 1 Jebb & S 509; *Moore v Garwood* (1849) 4 Exch 681 at 685, 690, Ex Ch; *Gurney v Womersley* (1854) 4 E & B 133; *Begg v Forbes* (1855) 3 CLR 336; *Holding v Elliott* (1860) 5 H & N 117; *Stones v Dowler* (1860) 29 LJ Ex 122, Ex Ch; *Williamson v Barton* (1862) 7 H & N 899; *Bolckow v Seymour* (1864) 17 CBNS 107; *Brook v Hook* (1871) LR 6 Exch 89; *Lakeman v Mountstephen* (1874) LR 7 HL 17; *Long v Millar* (1879) 4 CPD 450, CA; *Stollery v Maskelyn* (1898) 15 TLR 79, CA (affd sub nom *Maskelyne v Stollery* (1899) 16 TLR 97, HL).

7   *Furness v Meek* (1857) 27 LJ Ex 34.

168. Nature of contract. Although the nature of a contract does not depend upon the name given to it (whether for example it is 'insurance' or 'guarantee'), but upon its substance[1], nevertheless, where a particular contract is described by the parties to it as a 'policy of insurance', this fact will, in construing it, be treated by the court as affording some indication of an intention not to enter into a 'guarantee'[2].

1   *Seaton v Heath, Seaton v Burnand* [1899] 1 QB 782 at 792, CA, per Romer LJ. The dicta of the Court of Appeal in this case on this subject are unaffected by the reversal of the decision itself by the House of Lords (sub nom *Seaton v Burnand, Burnand v Seaton* [1900] AC 135, HL). See *Re Denton's Estate, Licenses Insurance Corpn and Guarantee Fund Ltd v Denton* [1904] 2 Ch 178 at 188, CA, per Vaughan Williams LJ. See also *Reynolds v Wheeler* (1861) 10 CBNS 561 at 566; *Sudbury Corpn v Empire Electric Light and Power Co Ltd* [1905] 2 Ch 104 at 116 per Warrington J; *Shaw v Royce Ltd* [1911] 1 Ch 138 at 147 per Warrington J; *Adams v Richardson and Starling Ltd* [1969] 2 All ER 1221 at 1230, [1969] 1 WLR 1645 at 1655–1656, CA, per Winn LJ.

      As to the construction of contractual documents generally see para 164 ante.

2   *Dane v Mortgage Insurance Corpn* [1894] 1 QB 54, CA; and see GUARANTEE AND INDEMNITY vol 20(1) (Reissue) para 110.

169. Words to be taken in ordinary sense. The words of a written instrument must in general be taken in their ordinary or natural sense[1] notwithstanding the fact that such a construction may appear not to carry out the purpose which it might otherwise be supposed the parties intended to carry out[2]; but if the provisions and expressions are contradictory, and there are grounds, appearing on the face of the instrument, affording proof of the real intention of the parties, that intention will prevail against the obvious and ordinary meaning of the words[3]; and where the literal (in the sense of ordinary, natural or primary) construction would lead to an absurd result, and the words used are capable of being interpreted so as to avoid this result, the literal construction will be abandoned[4]. So, too, considerations of inconvenience may be admitted when the construction of the document is ambiguous[5]. If, however, the intention is clearly and unequivocally expressed, then, however capricious it may be, the court is bound by it, unless it is plainly controlled by other parts of the instrument[6]. Most expressions have been said to have a natural meaning, in the sense of their primary meaning in ordinary speech[7]. In some cases, however, the notion of words having a natural meaning has been said not to be a very helpful one. Because the meaning of words is so sensitive to syntax and context, the natural meaning of words in one sentence may be quite unnatural in another. Thus a statement that words have a particular natural meaning may mean no more than that in many contexts they will have that meaning. In other contexts their meaning will be different but no less natural[8]. Further, the concept of the natural and ordinary meaning is not very helpful when on any view the words have not been used in a natural and ordinary way[9].

The rule is that in construing all written instruments the grammatical and ordinary sense of the words is to be adhered to, unless that would lead to some absurdity, or some repugnance or inconsistency with the rest of the instrument, in which case the grammatical and ordinary sense of the words may be modified, so as to avoid that absurdity and inconsistency, but no further[10]. The instrument must be construed according to its literal import, unless there is something in the subject or context which shows that this cannot be the meaning of the words[11].

1   Ie in their plain, ordinary, and popular sense: see *Robertson v French* (1803) 4 East 130 at 135 per Lord Ellenborough CJ (see para 174 note 1 post); *Beard v Moira Colliery Co Ltd* [1915] 1 Ch 257 at 268, CA; *Great Western Rly Co and Midland Rly Co v Bristol Corpn* (1918) 87 LJ Ch 414, HL. A stipulation in a contract that it shall be void in a certain event is to be construed according to its natural meaning, subject to the principle of law that a party may not take advantage of his own wrong: *New Zealand Shipping Co v Société des Ateliers et Chantiers de France* [1919] AC 1, HL. See also *Patent Castings Syndicate Ltd v Etherington* [1919] 2 Ch 254, CA; *Watson v Haggitt* [1928] AC 127, PC (meaning of 'net profits'); *Toepfer v Continental Grain Co* [1974] 1 Lloyd's Rep 11, CA (meaning of 'quality' in contract for sale of wheat providing that official certificates should be conclusive as to quality); *Allen v South Eastern Electricity Board* [1988] 1 EGLR 171, [1988] 07 EG 71, CA (meaning of phrase 'cannot take full advantage of the said planning permission'); *Charter Reinsurance Co Ltd v Fagan* [1997] AC 313, [1996] 3 All ER 46, HL (meaning of 'the sum actually paid'); *Spring House Freehold Ltd v Mount Cook Land Ltd* [2001] EWCA Civ 1833, [2002] 2 All ER 822 (clause in a lease had the meaning as reasonably understood by the commercial men who had entered into the agreement for the lease).
    As to the construction of contractual documents generally see para 164 ante.

2   *Mallan v May* (1844) 13 M & W 511 at 517; *Grey v Pearson* (1857) 6 HL Cas 61 at 106 per Lord Wensleydale; *Directors etc of the Great Western Rly Co v Rous* (1870) LR 4 HL 650 at 659 per Lord Westbury; *Taylor v St Helens Corpn* (1877) 6 ChD 264 at 270, CA; *Caledonian Rly Co v North British Rly Co* (1881) 6 App Cas 114 at 131, HL, per Lord Blackburn; *Lee v Alexander* (1883) 8 App Cas 853 at 869–870, HL; *Birrell v Dryer* (1884) 9 App Cas 345, HL; *Smith v Cooke* [1891] AC 297 at 298, HL, per Lord Halsbury LC; *Edwardes' Menu Co Ltd v Chudleigh* (1897) 14 TLR 64, CA (agreement for letting of bars etc of theatre 'so long as it should remain in his hands'); *Denaby and Cadeby Co v Fenton* (1898) 14 TLR 268 (meaning of 'fatal accident' in a mine); *Felix Hadley & Co Ltd v Hadley* [1898] 2 Ch 680 (meaning of 'securities' for debts); *Wheeler v Fradd* (1898) 14 TLR 302, CA (agreement to repay money after company should go to allotment); *Loates v Maple* (1903) 88 LT 288 ('fail to procure a licence'); *Elliott v Crutchley* [1906] AC 7 at 9, HL, per Lord Halsbury LC; *Croydon RDC v Sutton District Water Co* (1908) 72 JP 217, CA ('damage to property caused by or resulting from execution of works'); *James Shoolbred & Co v Wyndham and Albery* (1908) Times, 1 December (work to be done to 'entire satisfaction' of defendants); *London Music Hall Ltd v Austin* (1908) Times, 16 December; *General Asphalt Co v Anglo-Saxon Petroleum Co Ltd* (1932) 48 TLR 276, HL (agreement to use 'rights' to procure third party to deliver oil). See, however, *M'Cowan v Baine and Johnston, The Niobe* [1891] AC 401, HL, where 'ship' was interpreted to include the ship's tug, although for special reasons (see at 407 per Lord Watson). See also *Blore v Giulini* [1903] 1 KB 356, following *Hartshorne v Watson* (1838) 4 Bing NC 178, where a reservation of a landlord's right of action under a lease was implied notwithstanding that the contract provided for avoidance (in certain events which had happened) of every clause in the lease; *Dominion Coal Co Ltd v Dominion Iron and Steel Co Ltd and National Trust Co Ltd* [1909] AC 293, PC; and para 170 note 7 post.

3   *Lloyd v Lloyd* (1837) 2 My & Cr 192 at 202 per Lord Cottenham LC ('If the parties have themselves furnished a key to the meaning of the words used, it is not material by what expression they convey their intention'). So much regard must not be paid to the natural and proper meaning of the words as to pervert the intention of the parties: Shep Touch 87. There is no rule of general application that the same meaning ought to be given to an expression in every part of the document in which it appears; a difficulty or ambiguity may be solved by resorting to such a device, but it is only in such cases that it is necessary, or permissible to do so: *Watson v Haggitt* [1928] AC 127, PC. But see *Re Birks, Kenyon v Birks* [1900] 1 Ch 417 at 418, CA, per Lindley MR ('I do not know whether it is law or a canon of construction but it is good sense to say that whenever in a deed or will or other document you find that a word used in one part of it has some clear and definite meaning, then the presumption is that it is intended to mean the same thing where, when used in another part of the document, its meaning is not clear'). It is also an accepted rule that the construction of an enactment may be approached on the footing that a word will bear the same meaning throughout the statute, though this rule will readily yield to other indications where injustice or absurdity would result: see *Re National Savings Bank Association Ltd* (1866) 1 Ch App 547 at 550; *Madras Electric Supply Corpn Ltd v Boarland* [1955] AC 667 at 685, [1955] 1 All ER 753 at 759, HL, per Lord MacDermott; *Gartside v IRC* [1968] AC 553, [1968] 1 All ER 121, HL; and STATUTES vol 44(1) (Reissue) para 1484.

4   'If a rational exposition can be given consistent with a fair interpretation of the language used, the court would then relinquish its most valuable powers if it did not abandon a construction, which, although more consonant with the literal interpretation of the words written, leads to a capricious and irrational result': *Laird v Tobin* (1830) 1 Mol 543 at 547 per Hart LC. See also *Re Rothermere, Mellors, Basden & Co v Coutts & Co* [1943] 1 All ER 307; and for a further statement of the principle see *Locke v Dunlop* (1888) 39 ChD 387 at 393, CA, per Stirling J, quoting from the judgment of Lord Cranworth LC, in *Abbott v Middleton* (1858) 7 HL Cas 68 at 89 (both cases on wills). The strict and ordinary sense is taken where the words interpreted in this sense are sensible with reference to the context and extrinsic circumstances: *Enlayde Ltd v Roberts* [1917] 1 Ch 109 at 119.

5   *Re Alma Spinning Co, Bottomley's Case* (1880) 16 ChD 681 at 686 per Jessel MR; *Re Rothermere, Mellors, Basden & Co v Coutts & Co* [1943] 1 All ER 307 ('first charge on the estate').

6   *Hume v Rundell* (1824) 2 Sim & St 174 at 177 per Leach V-C; *Abbott v Middleton* (1858) 7 HL Cas 68 at 89 per Lord Cranworth LC; *Bathurst v Errington* (1877) 2 App Cas 698 at 709, HL; *Re Whitmore, Walters v Harrison* [1902] 2 Ch 66 at 70, CA. If the meaning of ordinary words 'is clear and unambiguous, effect must be given to them because that is what the parties are taken to have agreed to by their contract': *Melanesian Mission Trust Board v Australian Mutual Provident Society* [1997] 2 EGLR 128 at 129, PC.

7   *Charter Reinsurance Co Ltd v Fagan* [1997] AC 313 at 384, [1996] 3 All ER 46 at 50, HL, per Lord Mustill.

8   *Charter Reinsurance Co Ltd v Fagan* [1997] AC 313 at 391, [1996] 3 All ER 46 at 57, HL, per Lord Hoffmann.

9   *Investors Compensation Scheme Ltd v West Bromwich Building Society* [1998] 1 All ER 98 at 116, [1998] 1 WLR 896 at 914, HL, per Lord Hoffmann.

10 *Grey v Pearson* (1857) 6 HL Cas 61 at 106 per Lord Wensleydale, and at 78 per Lord Cranworth LC. This rule Lord Wensleydale called the golden rule of construction: see *Caledonian Rly Co v North British Rly Co* (1881) 6 App Cas 114 at 130 per Lord Blackburn, and at 121 per Lord Selborne LC; *Re Levy, ex p Walton* (1881) 17 ChD 746 at 751, CA, per Jessel MR; *Spencer v Metropolitan Board of Works* (1882) 22 ChD 142 at 148, CA, per Chitty J. Lord Wensleydale enunciated the rule on several occasions: see *Roddy v Fitzgerald* (1858) 6 HL Cas 823 at 876; *Abbott v Middleton* (1858) 7 HL Cas 68 at 114; *Thellusson v Lord Rendlesham* (1859) 7 HL Cas 429 at 519. It was adopted by Lord Wensleydale from the judgment of Burton J in *Warburton v Loveland d Ivie* (1828) 1 Hud & B 623, Ex Ch. See also *Bland v Crowley* (1851) 6 Exch 522 at 529 per Parke B; *Rhodes v Rhodes* (1882) 7 App Cas 192 at 205, PC; *Diederichsen v Farquharson Bros* [1898] 1 QB 150 at 159, CA, per Rigby LJ; *Re Sassoon, IRC v Ezra* [1933] Ch 858 at 878, CA (affd sub nom *IRC v Ezra* [1935] AC 96, HL). See also GUARANTEE AND INDEMNITY vol 20(1) (Reissue) para 171 et seq.

11 *Lowther v Bentinck* (1874) LR 19 Eq 166 at 169 per Jessel MR. A departure may be made from the literal meaning of words, if reading the words literally leads to an absurdity: *Wallis v Smith* (1882) 21 ChD 243 at 257, CA. See also *Liberty Mutual Insurance Co (UK) Ltd v HSBC Bank plc* [2002] EWCA Civ 691, [2002] All ER (D) 232 (May) (in regard to construction of surety bonds, clear words (or the necessity of supplying those clear words by implication) were required if subrogation rights were to be removed).

170. Ordinary meaning determined by common usage. The ordinary meaning of a word, usually called its literal or primary meaning, is not necessarily its etymological meaning[1], but that which the ordinary usage of society applies to it[2]. Hence this is the meaning which prima facie is to be given to the word in construing the instrument in which it occurs[3]. The meaning is not to be capriciously interfered with, and when it is interfered with, the interference must be as slight as possible[4]. Thus evidence may not be received to show that the language was intended to be used by the parties with any meaning other than the ordinary and natural meaning[5]. However, there are three main exceptions to the rule[6].

First, where it has been found as a fact (by the jury, if there is one) that certain words, as for example words or phrases employed in art, or commerce, or in a particular locality, or among a particular sect or group of people, have been used in a special technical sense other than their ordinary sense, then the court will construe them in such special technical sense[7]. In certain cases extrinsic evidence may also be given to explain a latent ambiguity, or to show that the contract was made subject to a condition unexpressed in the writing[8].

Secondly, where the context itself shows that words were not intended to be used in their ordinary sense, the words are construed in harmony with the context[9], and greater regard is paid to the intention of the parties as appearing from the instrument when construed as a whole than to any particular words they may have used to express their intention[10].

Thirdly, where the court concludes from the background that something must have gone wrong with the language, the law does not require the judge to attribute to the parties an intention which they plainly could not have had[11]. If detailed semantic and syntactical analysis of words in a commercial contract is going to lead to a conclusion that flouts business common sense, it must be made to yield to business common sense[12].

1   Etymology is a very unsafe guide to meaning: *Hext v Gill* (1872) 7 Ch App 705n per Wickens V-C; on appeal (1872) 7 Ch App 699.
     As to the construction of contractual documents generally see para 164 ante.

2   *Shore v Wilson* (1842) 9 Cl & Fin 355 at 527, HL, per Coleridge J; *Mannai Investment Co Ltd v Eagle Star Life Assurance Co Ltd* [1997] AC 749, [1997] 3 All ER 352, HL; *Investors Compensation Scheme Ltd v West Bromwich Building Society* [1998] 1 All ER 98, [1998] 1 WLR 896, HL; and see paras 164, 169 ante. As to the power of the court to consult dictionaries to ascertain meaning see para 200 post. See also *Tophams Ltd v Earl of Sefton* [1967] 1 AC 50, [1966] 1 All ER 1039, HL.

3   *Holt & Co v Collyer* (1881) 16 ChD 718 at 720 per Fry J (where there is a popular and common word used in an instrument, that word must be construed prima facie in its popular and common sense; if it is a word of a technical or legal character it must be construed according to its technical or legal meaning; but before evidence can be given of the secondary meaning of a word, the court must be satisfied, from the circumstances of the case, that the word ought to be construed not in its popular or primary signification, but according to its secondary intention). See, however, *Bain v Cooper* (1842) 9 M & W 701 at 708 per Lord Abinger CB; *Re Bedson's Trusts* (1885) 28 ChD 523 at 525, CA, per Brett MR. As to latent ambiguities see para 209 post.

4   *Lucena v Lucena* (1876) 7 ChD 255 at 260 per Jessel MR.

5   *Shore v Wilson* (1842) 9 Cl & Fin 355 at 565–566, HL; *Hitchin v Groom* (1848) 5 CB 515; *McClean v Kennard* (1874) 9 Ch App 336 at 345, 349; *Great Western Rly Co and Midland Rly Co v Bristol Corpn* (1918) 87 LJ Ch 414, HL.

6   See *M'Cowan v Baine and Johnston, The Niobe* [1891] AC 401 at 408, HL. There are also less important exceptions to the rule: see paras 171, 174, 198–207 post.

7   *Studdy v Sanders* (1826) 5 B & C 628; *Goblet v Beechey* (1829) 3 Sim 24 (revsd (1831) 2 Russ & My 624); *Bold v Rayner* (1836) 1 M & W 343; *Mallan v May* (1844) 13 M & W 511 at 518; *Shore v Wilson* (1842) 9 Cl & Fin 355 at 555–556, HL; *Robey v Arnold* (1898) 14 TLR 220, CA (meaning of 're-engagement' in theatrical agent's contract). Evidence of such usage of words is analogous to translation: *Shore v Wilson* supra; *Grant v Maddox* (1846) 15 M & W 737 at 746 per Platt B; and see CUSTOM AND USAGE vol 12(1) (Reissue) para 669. As to translations generally see paras 200–203 post. In *Biddlecombe v Bond* (1835) 4 Ad & El 332, and *Parker v Gossage* (1835) 2 Cr M & R 617, the court refused to construe the word 'insolvency' in a technical sense, there being nothing in the context to justify such a construction. Where a person covenanted not to use a house as a beerhouse, but opened a grocer's shop, where he carried on the sale of beer to be drunk off the premises, evidence to show that 'beerhouse' was understood in the trade to include such a shop was rejected: *Holt & Co v Collyer* (1881) 16 ChD 718; and see *Elliott v Turner* (1845) 2 CB 446 at 461, Ex Ch. In *Mowbray, Robinson & Co v Rosser* (1922) 91 LJKB 524, CA, the court refused to construe the word 'shipment' as meaning loading into railway cars, by custom of the trade in the country of origin of the goods, as that construction would be inconsistent with the expressed term, and would not explain, but vary, the contract.

8   As to the admissibility of extrinsic evidence to alter or explain a written agreement see para 185 et seq post.

9   *St John, Hampstead Vestry v Cotton* (1886) 12 App Cas 1 at 6, HL; *M'Cowan v Baine and Johnston, The Niobe* [1891] AC 401 at 408, HL. See *Re Terry's Will* (1854) 19 Beav 580; *Monypenny v Monypenny* (1861) 9 HL Cas 114; *Hext v Gill* (1872) 7 Ch App 699 at 712; *Hill v Crook* (1873) LR 6 HL 265 at 283 ('children'); *Pigg v Clarke* (1876) 3 ChD 672 ('family'); *Tucker v Linger* (1882) 21 ChD 18 at 36, CA ('minerals'); *College Credit Ltd v National Guarantee Corpn Ltd* [2004] EWHC 978 (Comm), [2004] 2 All ER (Comm) 409 ('advance').

10 *Ford v Beech* (1848) 11 QB 852 at 866.

11 *Investors Compensation Scheme Ltd v West Bromwich Building Society* [1998] 1 All ER 98 at 115, [1998] 1 WLR 896 at 913, HL, per Lord Hoffmann.

12 *Antaios Cia Naviera SA v Salen Rederierna AB, The Antaios* [1985] AC 191 at 201, [1984] 3 All ER 229 at 233, HL, per Lord Diplock.

171.   Statutory meanings.   In all deeds, contracts, wills, orders and other instruments executed, made or coming into operation after 31 December 1925, unless the context otherwise requires, 'person' includes a corporation; and the singular includes the plural and the masculine includes the feminine and vice versa[1].

In the absence of a definition or of any indication of a contrary intention, the expressions 'full age', 'infant', 'infancy', 'minor', 'minority' and similar expressions in any deed, will or other instrument of whatever nature (not being a statutory provision[2]) made on or after 1 January 1970 are to be construed by applying the provision in the Family Law Reform Act 1969[3] that a person attains full age on attaining the age of 18 (or on 1 January 1970 if he had then already attained the age of 18 but not the age of 21)[4]. For the purposes of the above provisions of the Family Law Reform Act 1969, notwithstanding any rule of law, a will or codicil executed before 1 January 1970[5] must not be treated as made on or after that date by reason only that the will or codicil is confirmed by a codicil executed on or after that date[6].

In the Family Law Reform Act 1987 and enactments passed and instruments made after 4 April 1988[7], references (however expressed) to any relationship between two persons are, unless the contrary intention appears, to be construed without regard to whether or not the father and mother of either of them, or the father and mother of any person through whom the relationship is deduced, have or had been married to each other at any time[8].

On and after 15 February 1971 any reference in any cheque, bill of exchange, promissory note, money order or postal order (or in certain similar instruments[9]) drawn, made or issued before that date to an amount of money in the currency previously in force (ie pounds, shillings and old pence) is, so far as it refers to an amount in shillings or pence, to be read as referring to the corresponding amount in decimal currency calculated in accordance with the provisions of Schedule 1 to the Decimal Currency Act 1969[10]. Where an amount of money in the old currency payable on or after 15 February 1971 as one of a series of payments of the same amount payable periodically[11] (not being an amount payable to or by a registered friendly society or industrial assurance company under any friendly society or industrial assurance company contract made before that date[12] or payable to an employee or the holder of any office by way of wages, salary or remuneration[13]) is not a whole number of pounds, so much of it as is in shillings or pence may be paid by paying the corresponding amount in the decimal currency calculated as above[14]. In any event, where an amount of money in the old currency which is not a whole number of pounds falls to be paid after the 31 August 1971[15], the amount payable in respect of so much of it as is in shillings or pence is the corresponding amount in decimal currency calculated as above[16].

In a marine insurance policy in the form set out in Schedule 1 to the Marine Insurance Act 1906, or other similar form, the terms and expressions mentioned in that Schedule are to be construed as having the scope and meaning assigned to them in the Schedule unless the context of the policy otherwise requires and subject to the other provisions of that Act[17].

1   Law of Property Act 1925 s 61. See *Re A Solicitors' Arbitration* [1962] 1 All ER 772, [1962] 1 WLR 353 (singular including plural in a partnership expulsion clause). The statutory provision that the masculine includes the feminine and vice versa may more readily be held not to apply to a provision particularly referring to men, or to women, as opposed to an expression, such as a pronoun, importing the masculine or the feminine: *Re Denley's Trust Deed, Holman v H H Martyn & Co Ltd* [1969] 1 Ch 373, [1968] 3 All ER 65 (reference to employees' subscriptions 'at the rate of two pence per week per man'). 'Month' means calendar month: Law of Property Act 1925 s 61; and see para 174 note 5 post. The definition of 'person' is in accordance with *Willmott v London Road Car Co Ltd* [1910] 2 Ch 525, CA. As to statutory definitions generally see para 165 text and notes 15–17 ante.
      As to the construction of contractual documents generally see para 164 ante.
2   Statutory provisions, whenever enacted, are given a similarly adjusted interpretation by the Family Law Reform Act 1969 s 1(1), (2)(a), (3), (4), (6), Sch 2 (as amended), Sch 3 paras 5–9. However, s 1 is not to affect the construction of any statutory provision where it is incorporated in and has effect as part of any deed, will or other instrument the construction of which is not affected by the corresponding adjustment made (to post–1969 non-statutory instruments) by the Act: Sch 3 para 9.
3   See ibid s 1(1); and CHILDREN AND YOUNG PERSONS vol 5(3) (Reissue) para 2. The time of attainment of a specified age expressed in years is to be the commencement of the relevant anniversary of the date of birth: see s 9; and CHILDREN AND YOUNG PERSONS vol 5(2) (Reissue) para 602.
4   See ibid s 1(1), (2); and CHILDREN AND YOUNG PERSONS vol 5(3) (Reissue) para 1.
5   Ie the date on which ibid s 1 came into force: s 28(3).
6   Ibid s 1(7).
7   Ie the date on which the Family Law Reform Act 1987 s 1 came into force: s 34(2).

8   Ibid s 1(1) (replacing the Family Law Reform Act 1969 s 15 (repealed), which applied to dispositions made on or after 1 January 1970).

9   See the Decimal Currency Act 1969 s 3(3) (amended by the Statute Law (Repeals) Act 1989). In addition to those specifically mentioned in the text, the instruments to which this provision applies include: (1) other instruments to which the Cheques Act 1957 s 4 (as amended) applies (the Consumer Credit Act 1974 s 83 does not apply to a non-commercial agreement, or to any loss in so far as it arises from misuse of an instrument to which the Cheques Act 1957 s 4 (as amended) applies: see the Consumer Credit Act 1974 s 83(2)); (2) any warrant issued by or on behalf of the Director of Savings for the payment of a sum of money; (3) any document not mentioned in the list which is intended to enable a person to obtain through a banker payment of any sum mentioned in the document: see the Decimal Currency Act 1969 s 3(3) (as so amended).

10 See ibid s 3(1), (3) (as amended: see note 9 supra).

11 See ibid s 5(1).

12 See ibid ss 5(3), 6(1); and INDUSTRIAL ASSURANCE vol 24 (Reissue) para 209.

13 See ibid s 5(3).

14 See ibid ss 5(2), 16(1).

15 See ibid s 16(1); and the Decimal Currency (End of Transitional Period) Order 1971, SI 1971/1123.

16 See the Decimal Currency Act 1969 ss 9, s 16(1).

17 See the Marine Insurance Act 1906 s 30, Sch 1; and INSURANCE vol 25 (2003 Reissue) para 225.

172.   Technical words construed in technical sense.   Where technical words occur in a document, whether they are technical scientific or technical legal terms, it is assumed that they are used in their technical sense, and prima facie this is the meaning which such words must bear[1]; but paramount regard must be had to the meaning and intention of the maker of the document, in preference to the technical meaning. Hence the technical meaning of legal terms will give way to the popular meaning or one of several popular meanings if an intention to this effect is manifested by a consideration of the text of the entire instrument and such extrinsic evidence as is admissible[2]. Technical words of limitation, however, will have their strict legal effect[3]. A force majeure clause should be construed in every case with a close attention to the words which precede and follow it, and with a due regard to the nature and terms of the contract[4].

1   *Shore v Wilson* (1842) 9 Cl & Fin 355 at 525, HL, per Coleridge J; *Leach v Jay* (1878) 9 ChD 42, CA; *Holt & Co v Collyer* (1881) 16 ChD 718; *Laird v Briggs* (1881) 19 ChD 22 at 34, CA, per Jessel MR; *IDC Group Ltd v Clark* [1992] 1 EGLR 187, [1992] 08 EG 108 ('licence' in professionally drawn document construed as a personal licence, not an easement). See also *Holloway v Holloway* (1800) 5 Ves 399 at 401; and cf *Roddy v Fitzgerald* (1858) 6 HL Cas 823 at 877 (technical words in wills). 'I do not believe that there is a rebuttable presumption that words in a patent specification that can have a technical meaning do have that technical meaning. The court is entitled to hear evidence as to the meaning of technical words and thereafter must decide the meaning from the context in which they are used': *Hoechst Celanese Corpn v BP Chemicals Ltd* [1999] FSR 319 at 326–327, CA, per Aldous LJ. See also WILLS vol 50 (2005 Reissue) paras 536, 577 et seq. As to admitting evidence of technical meaning see para 201 post.
    As to the construction of contractual documents generally see para 164 ante.

2   See *Marquis of Cholmondeley v Lord Clinton* (1820) 2 Jac & W 1 at 92 per Plumer MR; *Leach v Jay* (1878) 9 ChD 42, CA; *Holt & Co v Collyer* (1881) 16 ChD 718; *Sydall v Castings Ltd* [1967] 1 QB 302 at 314, [1966] 3 All ER 770 at 774, CA, per Diplock LJ ('the phrase 'legal jargon', however, does contain a reminder that non-lawyers are unfamiliar with the meanings which lawyers attach to particular 'terms of art', and that where a word or phrase which is a 'term of art' is used by an author who is not a lawyer, particularly in a document which he does not anticipate may have to be construed by a lawyer, he may have meant by it something different from its meaning when used by a lawyer as a term of art'). See further para 174 post; and cf *Re Jackson, Beattie v Murphy* [1933] Ch 237 (as to wills); *Hill v Grange* (1555) 1 Plowd 164 at 170 ('it is the office of judges to take and expound the words which common people use to express their meaning according to their meaning'). See also *Tester v Bisley* (1948) 64 TLR 184 (on appeal [1948] WN 441, CA) (date of end of war 'fixed' by Prime Minister's statement in House of Commons). As to the effect of contracts or leases for the duration of the war see LANDLORD AND TENANT vol 27(1) (2006 Reissue) para 238.

3   See *Marquis of Cholmondeley v Lord Clinton* (1820) 2 Jac & W 1 at 93. Occasionally the legal effect of limitations to trustees has been altered to suit the general intention of the deed. Thus a limitation to trustees and their heirs has been cut down to an estate for the life of another: *Doe d Compere v Hicks* (1797) 7 Term Rep 433; *Curtis v Price* (1805) 12 Ves 89 at 100; *Beaumont v Marquis of Salisbury* (1854) 19

Beav 198. But, in general, legal limitations, and equitable limitations under an executed trust (*Re Whiston's Settlement, Lovatt v Williamson* [1894] 1 Ch 661), are left to their strict effect (*Re Bostock's Settlement, Norrish v Bostock* [1921] 2 Ch 469, CA). Where strict conveyancing language is not employed, it is sufficient that the instrument should disclose a clear intention: *Re Arden, Short v Camm* [1935] Ch 326 at 333 per Clauson J. A conveyance of freehold land without words of limitation now passes to the grantee the whole interest which the grantor had power to convey: see para 242 note 6 post. A deed may itself afford sufficient evidence of the intention of the parties to enable it to be rectified: *Banks v Ripley* [1940] Ch 719, [1940] 3 All ER 49; and see MISTAKE vol 32 (2005 Reissue) para 56. In a will greater latitude is allowed, the testator being assumed to have acted without legal advice: *Colmore v Tyndall* (1828) 2 Y & J 605 at 622, Ex Ch; *Lewis v Rees* (1856) 3 K & J 132. Under the present law the only legal limitations are in fee simple and for a term of years absolute: see the Law of Property Act 1925 s 1(1).

4   *Lebeaupin v R Crispin& Co* [1920] 2 KB 714 at 720. It seems that a contract will be void if the words of the force majeure clause are so vague and uncertain as to be incapable of any precise meaning (*British Electrical and Associated Industries (Cardiff) Ltd v Patley Pressings Ltd* [1953] 1 All ER 94, [1953] 1 WLR 280); but see the remarks of Denning LJ in *Nicolene Ltd v Simmonds* [1953] 1 QB 543 at 552, [1953] 1 All ER 822 at 825–826, CA. See CONTRACT vol 9(1) (Reissue) para 906.

173.   Local or class usage: foreign words. Where it appears that a word or phrase has a special meaning in the district in which the person using it resides, or among the class to which he belongs, so that in using it he probably used it in this special sense, then such special meaning takes the place of the ordinary meaning for the purpose of construing the document, and is the meaning which prima facie the word or phrase must bear[1]. For a special meaning of this nature to be ascribed to language, it must be a well known peculiar idiomatic meaning in the particular country in which the person using the word was dwelling, or in the particular society of which he formed a member[2].

Where a document is in a foreign language, a translation must be obtained[3].

1   *Shore v Wilson* (1842) 9 Cl & Fin 355 at 555, HL, per Parke B; and see *Barksdale v Morgan* (1693) 4 Mod Rep 185 at 186.
       As to the construction of contractual documents generally see para 164 ante.

2   *Shore v Wilson* (1842) 9 Cl & Fin 355 at 567, HL, per Tindal CJ. See also *Rosin and Turpentine Import Co Ltd v Jacob & Sons Ltd* (1909) 101 LT 56 at 59, CA, per Farwell LJ; affd (1910) 102 LT 81, HL. As to evidence of local or class usage see further para 203 post.

3   See para 201 post.

174.   Further examples of exclusion of ordinary meaning. The ordinary meaning or technical meaning of the words of an instrument may be excluded, and a special meaning substituted, where this is necessitated by the subject matter or context of the instrument[1], or by the external circumstances at the date of the instrument in regard to which it was to operate[2]. Thus, as to subject matter, an instrument dealing with mercantile matters or with insurance is construed in accordance with the meaning placed on its words by persons conversant with the business to which it relates[3], and not in accordance with the meaning placed on it by men of science[4]; as to the context, this may show that a particular word, such as 'month', is used, not in its technical legal sense, but in a special sense[5].

A similar effect may be produced by the external circumstances, so that if the words, taken in the ordinary or technical sense, have no reasonable application in relation to those circumstances, another sense may be substituted. Thus 'children', which until the Family Law Reform Act 1969 was treated in instruments disposing of property as a technical legal term meaning legitimate children[6], was construed as meaning illegitimate children if there were no legitimate children to whom the expression could refer[7]. In general, if the surrounding circumstances at the date of the instrument show that the parties intended to use a word, not in its primary or strict sense, but in some secondary meaning, the court may construe it from those circumstances, according to the intention of the parties[8].

1   See *Doe d Freeland v Burt* (1787) 1 Term Rep 701 at 703. An instrument, whatever its nature, is to be construed according to its sense and meaning, as collected in the first place from the terms used in it, which terms are themselves to be understood in their plain, ordinary, and popular sense, unless they have generally in respect to the subject matter, as by the known usage of trade, or the like, acquired a peculiar sense distinct from the popular sense of the same words; or unless the context evidently points out that they must in the particular instance, and in order to effectuate the immediate intention of the parties to that contract, be understood in some special and peculiar sense: *Robertson v French* (1803) 4 East 130 at 135 per Lord Ellenborough CJ, quoted in *Carr v Montefiore* (1864) 5 B & S 408 at 428, Ex Ch, per Erle CJ; *Hart v Standard Marine Insurance Co* (1889) 22 QBD 499 at 501, CA, per Bowen LJ; *Glynn v Margetson & Co* [1893] AC 351 at 357–358, HL, per Lord Halsbury LC; and cf *Mallan v May* (1844) 13 M & W 511 at 517 per Pollock CB; *Bruner v Moore* [1904] 1 Ch 305 at 310 per Farwell J. See also *Butterley Co Ltd v New Hucknall Colliery Co Ltd* [1909] 1 Ch 37, CA (affd [1910] AC 381, HL); *Jones Construction Co v Alliance Assurance Co Ltd* [1961] 1 Lloyd's Rep 121, CA. See further *Earl of Lonsdale v A-G* [1982] 3 All ER 579, [1982] 1 WLR 887 (whether grant of 'mines and minerals' extended to oil and natural gas); and paras 164, 169–170 ante.
    As to the construction of contractual documents generally see para 164 ante.

2   The primary meaning must be taken if that meaning is not excluded by the context, and is sensible with reference to the extrinsic circumstances in which the writer was placed at the time of writing; by 'sensible with reference to the extrinsic circumstances' is not meant that the extrinsic circumstances make it more or less reasonable or probable that the primary meaning is what the writer should have intended; it is enough if these circumstances do not exclude it, that is, deprive the words of all reasonable application according to such primary meaning: see *Shore v Wilson* (1842) 9 Cl & Fin 355 at 525, HL, per Coleridge J; *Smith v Doe d Jersey* (1821) 2 Brod & Bing 473 at 550, 602.

3   'A grant of 'mines and minerals' is a question of fact 'what these words meant in the vernacular of the mining world, and landowners,' at the time when they were used in the instrument': *Glasgow Corpn v Farie* (1888) 13 App Cas 657 at 669, HL, per Lord Halsbury LC. See also *Southland Frozen Meat and Produce Export Co Ltd v Nelson Bros Ltd* [1898] AC 442 at 444, PC. In effect this is the same as the rule set out in para 173 ante, but the fact of the instrument being a mercantile instrument shows at once that the special sense is to be taken, if any such has been affixed to the terms by mercantile usage: see para 203 post.

4   *Moody v Surridge* (1798) 2 Esp 633 (corn held to include malt); *Hart v Standard Marine Insurance Co* (1889) 22 QBD 499, CA (iron held to include steel); *Borys v Canadian Pacific Rly Co* [1953] AC 217 at 223, [1953] 1 All ER 451 at 455, PC (petroleum held to include gas in solution in the liquid). However, the meaning may vary according to the circumstances in which the word is used: *Borys v Canadian Pacific Rly Co* supra at 223 and 455. See also para 239 post; and FUEL AND ENERGY vol 19(1) (Reissue) para 1402.

5   In instruments executed since 1925, unless the context otherwise requires, 'month' prima facie means lunar month, but it may be shown that having regard to the context it means calendar month: *Lang v Gale* (1813) 1 M & S 111; *R v Chawton Inhabitants* (1841) 1 QB 247; and see *Simpson v Margitson* (1847) 11 QB 23; *Bruner v Moore* [1904] 1 Ch 305. 'Minerals' may be restricted by the context to mean certain minerals only: *Hext v Gill* (1872) 7 Ch App 699 at 712; *Tucker v Linger* (1882) 21 ChD 18 at 36, CA. 'Appertaining' to a messuage may be construed in its popular sense of 'usually occupied with', and not in its strict legal sense: see *Hill v Grange* (1555) 1 Plowd 164 at 170. As to modifying the language so as to carry out the general intention appearing from the instrument see generally *St John, Hampstead Vestry v Cotton* (1886) 12 App Cas 1 at 6, HL, per Lord Halsbury LC. A special meaning prima facie assigned to a word is also capable of being varied by the context or external circumstances; but this is unlikely to occur.

6   *Wilkinson v Adam* (1813) 1 Ves & B 422 at 462 per Lord Eldon LC (on appeal (1823) 12 Price 470, HL); *Hill v Crook* (1873) LR 6 HL 265. As to the meaning of 'child', and the effect of adoption, see CHILDREN AND YOUNG PERSONS vol 5(3) (Reissue) paras 3, 129 et seq. As to the former restriction of the meaning of 'descendants' to those tracing descent exclusively through legitimate relationship see *Sydall v Castings Ltd* [1967] 1 QB 302, [1966] 3 All ER 770, CA. As to the construction of words of relationship see the Family Law Reform Act 1987 s 1 (as amended); and see para 171 ante.

7   *Shore v Wilson* (1842) 9 Cl & Fin 355 at 513, HL, per Erskine J; *Hill v Crook* (1873) LR 6 HL 265 at 282; *Monypenny v Monypenny* (1858) 4 K & J 174 at 182 (on appeal (1861) 9 HL Cas 114). In this connection there is no ground for drawing a distinction between a deed and a will: see *Ebbern v Fowler* [1909] 1 Ch 578 at 585, CA, per Cozens-Hardy MR. As regards wills see *Hill v Crook* (1873) LR 6 HL 265 at

282 per Lord Cairns LC; and WILLS vol 50 (2005 Reissue) paras 516, 638–642. 'Family' may be shown to mean relatives other than children: see *Re Terry's Will* (1854) 19 Beav 580; *Pigg v Clarke* (1876) 3 ChD 672.

8   *Simpson v Margitson* (1847) 11 QB 23 at 31. Thus the surrounding circumstances may show that 'your having this day advanced' in a deed does not mean that the advance was prior to the execution of the deed: *Goldshede v Swan* (1847) 1 Exch 154. A direction to the sheriff to withdraw from possession of goods, 'the goods having been claimed', has been held to be confined to part of the goods, on evidence that only that part had been claimed: *Walker v Hunter* (1845) 2 CB 324. As to what is meant by 'London' see *Beckford v Crutwell* (1832) 1 Mood & R 187; and cf *Mallan v May* (1844) 13 M & W 511. For an instance of the ordinary meaning of 'heretofore' being excluded see *Roe v Siddons* (1888) 22 QBD 224, CA.

175.   Instrument construed as whole.   It is a rule of construction applicable to all written instruments[1] that the instrument must be construed as a whole in order to ascertain the true meaning of its several clauses[2], and the words of each clause must be so interpreted as to bring them into harmony with the other provisions of the instrument, if that interpretation does no violence to the meaning of which they are naturally susceptible[3]. The best construction of deeds is to make one part of the deed expound the other, and so to make all the parts agree[4]. Effect must, as far as possible, be given to every word and every clause[5].

However, the argument from redundancy, namely that the parties are presumed not to say anything unnecessarily, is seldom an entirely secure one[6]. More weight should be attached to differences in wording of individual parts of a document where the whole document has been drafted by one hand on one occasion than where the document has been added to piecemeal over a period of years[7]. The evolution of standard forms is often the result of interaction between the draftsmen and the courts and the efforts of the draftsman cannot be properly understood without reference to the meaning which the judges have given to the language used by his predecessors[8].

It has been said that the court in a case of a patent specification (though the dictum may well have a more general application) must adopt 'a purposive construction rather than a purely literal one derived from applying to it the kind of meticulous verbal analysis in which lawyers are so often tempted by their training to indulge'[9]. The fact that a particular construction leads to a very unreasonable result is a relevant consideration. The more unreasonable the result the more unlikely it is that the parties can have intended it[10]. However, this rule of thumb has its limits. The task of the court is to discover what the parties meant from what they have said. To force upon the words a meaning which they cannot fairly bear would be to substitute for the bargain actually made one which the court believes could better have been made. This would be an illegitimate role for the court to adopt[11].

When a contract is to be ascertained from a series of letters or documents the whole of the correspondence must be looked at and, although two letters in the course of that correspondence may appear to contain a completed contract, the court will not hold the contract to be complete where subsequent letters show that certain terms had not been agreed[12]. When, however, a contract has in fact been completed and reduced to writing the court is not entitled to consider antecedent acts or correspondence, or to look at words deleted before the conclusion of the contract, in order to ascertain the meaning of the contract in writing finally agreed upon[13].

1   *Re Jodrell, Jodrell v Seale* (1890) 44 ChD 590 at 605, CA, per Lord Halsbury LC (affd sub nom *Seale-Hayne v Jodrell* [1891] AC 304, HL); *Crumpe v Crumpe* [1900] AC 127 at 131, HL, per Lord Halsbury LC. As to guarantees see eg *Lord Arlington v Merricke* (1672) 2 Saund 403, 411; and GUARANTEE AND INDEMNITY vol 20(1) (Reissue) para 171 et seq.

As to the construction of contractual documents generally see para 164 ante.

2   'The construction must be on the entire deed': Shep Touch 87; *Throckmerton v Tracy* (1555) 1 Plowd 145 at 161; and see *Shore v Wilson* (1842) 9 Cl & Fin 355 at 511, HL, per Erskine J. 'To pronounce on the

meaning of a detached part or extract from an instrument, if relating to the same subject, is contrary to every principle of correct interpretation': *Marquis of Cholmondeley v Lord Clinton* (1820) 2 Jac & W 1 at 89 per Plumer MR; *Hume v Rundell* (1824) 2 Sim & St 174 at 177 per Leach V-C. See also *Barton v Fitzgerald* (1812) 15 East 530; *Sicklemore v Thistleton* (1817) 6 M & S 9; *Elderslie Steamship Co v Borthwick* [1905] AC 93, HL; *National Provincial Bank of England v Marshall* (1888) 40 ChD 112, CA; *Hulbert v Long* (1621) Cro Jac 607; *Cromwell v Grunsden* (1698) 2 Salk 462; *Coles v Hulme* (1828) 8 B & C 568; *Bickmore v Dimmer* [1903] 1 Ch 158, CA; *Maritime et Commerciale of Geneva SA v Anglo-Iranian Oil Co Ltd* [1954] 1 All ER 529 at 531–532, [1954] 1 WLR 492 at 495–496, CA; *Plumrose Ltd v Real and Leasehold Estates Investment Society Ltd* [1969] 3 All ER 1441 at 1444, [1970] 1 WLR 52 at 55 per Foster J; *Charter Reinsurance Co Ltd v Fagan* [1997] AC 313 at 384, [1996] 3 All ER 46 at 51, HL, per Lord Mustill ('the words must be set in the landscape of the instrument as a whole'); and see *Hulbert v Long* (1621) Cro Jac 607 (bonds); *Holmes v Ivy* (1678) 2 Show 15 (where a condition for the delivery of 35,000 tiles, to the value of £144, at 15s 6d per thousand, was held good for £144 although the number of tiles at the price mentioned did not amount to that sum); *Cromwell v Grunsden* (1698) 2 Salk 462; *Bache v Proctor* (1780) 1 Doug KB 382 (where the condition was that the obligor should render a fair and just account in writing of all sums received and it was held that neglect to pay over such sums was a breach of the condition); *Coles v Hulme* (1828) 8 B & C 568; *National Provincial Bank of England v Marshall* (1888) 40 ChD 112, CA.

3   *North Eastern Rly Co v Lord Hastings* [1900] AC 260 at 267, HL, per Lord Davey; *Chamber Colliery Co Ltd v Twyerould* (1893) [1915] 1 Ch 268n at 272, HL, per Lord Watson; *Adamastos Shipping Co Ltd v Anglo-Saxon Petroleum Co Ltd* [1959] AC 133, [1958] 1 All ER 725, HL. 'The sense and meaning of the parties in any particular part of an instrument may be collected ex antecedentibus et consequentibus; every part of it may be brought into action in order to collect from the whole one uniform and consistent sense, if that may be done': *Barton v Fitzgerald* (1812) 15 East 530 at 541 per Lord Ellenborough CJ. See also *Sicklemore v Thistleton* (1817) 6 M & S 9 at 12 per Lord Ellenborough CJ; and cf *Shelley's Case* (1581) 1 Co Rep 93b at 95b. It has been said that where there is an ambiguity a contract should not be construed in such a way as to bar a legitimate claim: *Bunge SA v Deutsche Conti-Handels-Gesellschaft MbH (No 2)* [1980] 1 Lloyd's Rep 352 at 358 per Donaldson J; and see para 208 post.

4   *Nokes' Case* (1599) 4 Co Rep 80b at 81a. 'An instrument must not be construed in such a way that one part will contradict another part': *Re Bedson's Trusts* (1885) 28 ChD 523 at 525, CA, per Brett MR.

5   See *Shelley's Case* (1581) 1 Co Rep 93b at 95b; *Butler v Duncomb* (1718) 1 P Wms 448 at 457 per Parker LC ('it is a rule in law and equity so to construe the whole deed or will, as that every clause should have its effect'). 'One leans towards treating words as adding something, rather than as mere surplusage': *Maritime et Commerciale of Geneva SA v Anglo-Iranian Oil Co Ltd* [1954] 1 All ER 529 at 531, [1954] 1 WLR 492 at 495, CA, per Somervell LJ.

6   *Beaufort Developments (NI) Ltd v Gilbert-Ash NI Ltd* [1999] 1 AC 266 at 274, [1998] 2 All ER 778 at 784, HL, per Lord Hoffmann.

7   *Tom Walkinshaw Racing Ltd v RAC Motorsports Racing Ltd* (1985) Times, 12 October.

8   *Beaufort Developments (NI) Ltd v Gilbert-Ash NI Ltd* [1999] 1 AC 266 at 274, [1998] 2 All ER 778 at 784, HL, per Lord Hoffmann.

9   *Catnic Components Ltd v Hill & Smith Ltd* [1982] RPC 183 at 243, HL, per Lord Diplock, cited in *Glaverbel SA v British Coal Corpn* [1995] FSR 254 at 264, [1995] RPC 255 at 269, CA, per Staughton LJ.

10   *L Schüler AG v Wickman Machine Tool Sales Ltd* [1974] AC 235 at 251, [1973] 2 All ER 39 at 45, HL, per Lord Reid.

11   *Charter Reinsurance Co Ltd v Fagan* [1997] AC 313 at 388, [1996] 3 All ER 46 at 54, HL, per Lord Mustill.

12   *Hussey v Horne-Payne* (1879) 4 App Cas 311, HL. See, however, the explanation of this case in *Bolton Partners v Lambert* (1889) 41 ChD 295 at 306, CA; *Bristol, Cardiff and Swansea Aerated Bread Co v Maggs* (1890) 44 ChD 616. Where two principals enter into a contract on the face of which no intervention by an agent appears, the court will be slow to import into such a contract a condition contained in a covering letter addressed by a principal to the agent of the other party: *Maconchy v Trower* [1894] 2 IR 663 at 668, HL. See also CONTRACT vol 9(1) (Reissue) para 667 et seq.

13   *Inglis v John Buttery& Co* (1878) 3 App Cas 552, HL; *Leggott v Barrett* (1880) 15 ChD 306, CA; *Lee v Alexander* (1883) 8 App Cas 853, HL; *Bromley v Johnson* (1862) 10 WR 303; *Brady v Oastler* (1864) 3 H & C 112; *Emery v Party* (1867) 17 LT 152; *National Bank of Australasia v Falkingham & Sons* [1902] AC 585 at 591, PC; *Re Duncan and Pryce* [1913] WN 117, DC; *Millbourn v Lyons* [1914] 2 Ch 231, CA; *Taylor v John Lewis Ltd* 1927 SC 891, Ct of Sess; *City and Westminster Properties (1934) Ltd v Mudd* [1959] Ch 129 at 140–141, [1958] 2 All ER 733 at 739–740. In commercial contracts, words struck out may perhaps be looked at if what remains is ambiguous and, where a clause is struck out of a printed form, there is a presumption that the meaning of other clauses not struck out was not meant to be altered: *Louis Dreyfus & Cie v Parnaso Cia Naviera SA* [1959] 1 QB 498, [1959] 1 All ER 502 (revsd on other grounds [1960] 2 QB 49, [1960] 1 All ER 759, CA); and see *Baumvoll Manufactur von Scheibler v Gilchrest & Co* [1892] 1 QB 253 at 256, CA; *Caffin v Aldridge* [1895] 2 QB 648 at 650, CA; *Heimdal Akt v Russian Wood*

Agency Ltd (1933) 46 Ll L Rep 1 at 6, CA; but see *Lyderhorn Sailing Ship Co Ltd v Duncan Fox & Co* [1909] 2 KB 929 at 941, CA; *Ambatielos v Anton Jurgens Margarine Works* [1923] AC 175 at 185, HL; *MA Sassoon & Sons Ltd v International Banking Corpn* [1927] AC 711 at 721, PC. Acts done after an agreement may be material as evidence of facts existing at the time of the agreement, and therefore relevant to its interpretation as part of the surrounding circumstances, but are not admissible to construe the agreement itself: *Monro v Taylor* (1848) 8 Hare 51 at 56; affd (1852) 3 Mac & G 713. If, nevertheless, the instrument is ambiguous, evidence of user under it may in some cases be given to show the sense in which the language was used: *Watcham v A-G of East Africa Protectorate* [1919] AC 533, PC, explained in *L Schüler AG v Wickman Machine Tool Sales Ltd* [1974] AC 235, [1973] 2 All ER 39, HL. See also paras 187 note 4, 206–207 post.

176.   Several instruments.   When a single transaction is carried into effect by several instruments, they are treated as one instrument, and they must all be read together for the purpose of ascertaining the intention of the parties; this is so whether the instruments are actually contemporaneous, that is all executed at the same time, or are executed within so short an interval that the court comes to the conclusion that they in fact represent a single transaction[1]. Where one instrument alone is not effectual to accomplish the object contemplated, such as the execution of a power, it may be supplemented by another instrument[2], provided the two instruments are intended to operate together[3]. Where two instruments relating to the same matter are executed on the same day, the court may inquire which was executed first, but if there is anything in the deeds themselves to show an intention, either that they are to take effect simultaneously or even that the later deed is to take effect in priority to the earlier, they will be presumed to have been executed in the order necessary to give effect to the manifest intention of the parties[4].

1   *Smith v Chadwick* (1882) 20 ChD 27 at 62–63, CA, per Jessel MR (affd (1884) 9 App Cas 187, HL); and see *Harman v Richards* (1852) 10 Hare 81; *Hopgood v Ernest* (1865) 3 De GJ & Sm 116. This case frequently occurred under the old law where conveyancing transactions were carried out by agreements followed by fine or recovery: see *Lord Cromwel's Case* (1601) 2 Co Rep 69b at 76a; *Havergil v Hare* (1616) 3 Bulst 250 at 256; *Ferrers v Fermor* (1622) Cro Jac 643 (where a bargain and sale, fine, and recovery, were treated as one assurance, so that a term which was merged by the bargain and sale and fine, in consequence of the conveyance thereby effected to the lessee, was revived upon the lessee suffering a recovery to the use of a third person); and c f *Selwyn v Selwyn* (1761) 2 Burr 1131 at 1134–1135; *Duke of Bolton v Williams* (1793) 2 Ves 138 at 141, 154–155 (where all the instruments securing an annuity were held to make but one assurance); *Harrison v Mexican Rly Co* (1875) LR 19 Eq 358; *Plumrose Ltd v Real and Leasehold Estates Investment Society Ltd* [1969] 3 All ER 1441, [1970] 1 WLR 52 (where, applying the Law of Property Act 1925 s 58 (see para 217 post), a lease described as supplemental to another lease was read together with it). See, however, *White v Taylor (No 2)* [1969] 1 Ch 160 at 180, [1968] 1 All ER 1015 at 1025 per Buckley J; and para 187 post. It appears also that one document, or a part thereof, may be incorporated in another, although the first document has, of itself, no legal effect: see *Akt Ocean v B Harding & Sons* [1928] 2 KB 371 at 393, CA.
    As to the construction of contractual documents generally see para 164 ante.
2   *Earl of Leicester's Case* (1675) 1 Vent 278.
3   *Hawkins v Kemp* (1803) 3 East 410.
4   *Taylor d Atkyns v Horde* (1757) 1 Burr 60 at 106 per Lord Mansfield CJ (affd (1758) 6 Bro Parl Cas 633, HL); *Gartside v Silkstone and Dodworth Coal and Iron Co* (1882) 21 ChD 762 at 767 per Fry J.

177.   Intention to be given effect.   If the intention of the parties can be ascertained from the written instrument, the court will give effect to that intention notwithstanding ambiguities in the words used or defects in the operation of the instrument. This is expressed by the maxim 'verba ita sunt intelligenda ut res magis valeat quam pereat'[1], or by the wholly English paraphrase: 'a deed shall never be void where the words may be applied to any intent to make it good'[2]. Hence, where words are capable of two meanings, the object with which they were inserted may be looked at in order to arrive at the sense in which they were used[3], and where one interpretation is consistent with what appears to have been the intention of the parties and another repugnant to it, the court will give effect to the apparent intention, provided it can do so without violating any of the established rules of construction[4]. Similarly, the court leans to an interpretation which will effectuate rather than one which will invalidate an instrument[5], and, in construing two contemporaneous documents, to a construction which will reconcile them rather than one which will render them inconsistent[6].

Where the deed is incapable of operating in the mode expressed, it will, if possible, be allowed to operate in some other way having a similar result[7]. A deed intended to take effect as a grant may operate as such, although it does not contain appropriate words of conveyance[8].

In order to give effect to a contract according to what appears to have been the intention of the parties, the court will in certain cases imply a term or condition or a qualification of a clause which is not inconsistent with the general tenor of the document[9], but where the intention of the parties is not sufficiently clear the court will not make a contract for them in order to prevent the whole agreement from being void on the ground of uncertainty or otherwise[10].

1   'A rule of common law and common sense': *Langston v Langston* (1834) 2 Cl & Fin 194 at 243, HL, per Lord Brougham LC. 'And yet no well advised man will trust to such deeds, which the law by construction maketh good, *ut res magis valeat*; but when form and substance concur, then is the deed fair and absolutely good': Co Litt 7a. As to supplying necessary words see para 210 note 10 post.
     See generally para 164 ante.

2   *Throckmerton v Tracy* (1855) 1 Plowd 145 at 160. 'In conveyances we are to respect two things, the form and effect of it; and in all cases where the form and effect cannot stand together, the form shall be rejected and the effect shall stand': *Brent's Case* (1583) 2 Leon 14 at 17. 'Such a construction ought to be made of deeds that the end and design of deeds should take effect rather than the contrary': *Smith d Dormer v Packhurst* (1742) 3 Atk 135 at 136, HL, per Willes CJ; and see *Rosin and Turpentine Import Co Ltd v Jacob & Sons Ltd* (1909) 101 LT 56 at 59, CA, per Farwell LJ (affd (1910) 102 LT 81, HL); *Butterley Co Ltd v New Hucknall Colliery Co Ltd* [1909] 1 Ch 37 at 46, CA, per Cozens-Hardy MR, and at 52–53 per Farwell LJ (affd [1910] AC 381, HL); *Re Baden's Deed Trusts, Baden v Smith* [1969] 2 Ch 388 at 399–400, [1969] 1 All ER 1016 at 1021, CA, per Harman LJ, and at 402 and 1024 per Karminski LJ (revsd on another point sub nom *McPhail v Doulton* [1971] AC 424, [1970] 2 All ER 228, HL). See also para 216 text and note 4 post.

3   *Moody v Surridge* (1798) 2 Esp 633 at 634, explained in *Hart v Standard Marine Insurance Co* (1889) 22 QBD 499, CA; *M'Cowan v Baine and Johnston, The Niobe* [1891] AC 401 at 408, HL. The domicile of the parties and place of execution may also become material: *Marquis of Lansdowne v Marchioness of Lansdowne* (1820) 2 Bli 60, HL; and see *Brown v Fletcher* (1876) 35 LT 165. See *College of Credit Ltd v National Guarantee Corpn Ltd* [2004] EWHC 978 (Comm), [2004] 2 All ER (Comm) 409 (intention of parties in use of term 'advance'); and see also para 170 ante.

4   *Solly v Forbes* (1820) 2 Brod & Bing 38 at 48; *Parkhurst v Smith d Dormer* (1742) Willes 327 at 332, HL; *Hayne v Cummings* (1864) 16 CBNS 421; *Cochran & Son v Leckie's Trustee* (1906) 8 F 975, Ct of Sess. See also *Lively Ltd v City of Munich* [1976] 3 All ER 851, [1976] 1 WLR 1004 (foreign bonds construed so as to give effect to commercial objective of the bonds).

5   *Pugh v Duke of Leeds* (1777) 2 Cowp 714 at 717 per Lord Mansfield LJ; and see *Atkinson v Hutchinson* (1734) 3 P Wms 258 at 260 per Talbot LC, quoted in *Thellusson v Woodford* (1798) 4 Ves 227 at 312; *Stratford v Bosworth* (1813) 2 Ves & B 341; *Solly v Forbes* (1820) 4 Moore CP 448 at 463; *Haigh v Brooks* (1839) 10 Ad & El 309 (affd sub nom *Brooks v Haigh* (1840) 10 Ad & El 323, Ex Ch); *Wilkinson v Gaston* (1846) 9 QB 137; *Pollock v Stacy* (1847) 9 QB 1033; *Goldshede v Swan* (1847) 1 Exch 154; *Mills v Dunham* [1891] 1 Ch 576 at 590, CA. Thus if one construction makes a contract lawful and another unlawful, the former is preferred: *Lewis v Davison* (1839) 4 M & W 654. Before the court applies this principle and leans to an interpretation which effectuates rather than invalidates an instrument, it must have been left, after using all allowable means for ascertaining the true intention of the parties, in a state of real and persistent uncertainty of mind: *IRC v Williams* [1969] 3 All ER 614 at 618, [1969] 1 WLR 1197 at 1201 per Megarry J; and see *Re Baden's Deed Trusts, Baden v Smith* [1969] 2 Ch 388, [1969] 1 All ER 1016, CA (revsd on another point sub nom *McPhail v Doulton* [1971] AC 424, [1970] 2 All ER 228, HL).

6   If one of such documents is ambiguous and the other clear, then force is given to the one which is clear to interpret the other: *Re Phoenix Bessemer Steel Co* (1875) 44 LJ Ch 683.

7   Deeds operate according to the intention of the parties, if by law they may; and if they cannot operate in one form they operate in that which by law will effect the intention: *Goodtitle d Edwards v Bailey* (1777) 2 Cowp 597 at 600 per Lord Mansfield CJ. A deed that is intended and made to one purpose may enure

to another, for if it will not take effect in that way it is intended, it may take effect another way, provided it may have that effect consistently with the intention of the parties: Shep Touch 82.

Recourse was frequently had to this rule under the old law with its diverse and highly technical forms of conveyancing; and a conveyance which was void in its primary form was allowed to take effect, if possible, in some other manner. Thus where a grant, or a release following upon a lease, was void as an attempt to create an estate of freehold in futuro (*Roe d Wilkinson v Tranmarr* (1757) Willes 682; *Doe d Starling v Prince* (1851) 20 LJPC 223), or where a bargain and sale, though duly enrolled, was void for want of a pecuniary consideration (*Crossing v Scudamore* (1674) 1 Vent 137; *Doe d Milburn v Salkeld* (1755) Willes 673 at 676), in any such case, if the conveyance was in favour of a relation by blood or marriage, it might operate as a covenant to stand seised: see notes to *Chester v Willan* (1670) 2 Saund 96; *Marshall v Frank* (1717) Prec Ch 480. Although the conveyance was to trustees, the relationship of the beneficiary to the settlor was sufficient to raise the necessary consideration for a covenant to stand seised: *Doe d Lewis v Davies* (1837) 2 M & W 503 at 516–518.

8 *Shove v Pincke* (1793) 5 Term Rep 124; *Haggerston v Hanbury* (1826) 5 B & C 101; *Doe d Were v Cole* (1827) 7 B & C 243; *Doe d Jones v Williams* (1833) 5 B & Ad 783. So the words 'limit and appoint' may operate as a grant: *MacAndrew v Gallagher* (1874) 8 IR Eq 490. As to deeds which operate as leases see LANDLORD AND TENANT vol 27(1) (2006 Reissue) para 198 et seq. As to deeds operating as execution or release of powers see POWERS vol 36(2) (Reissue) para 270. As to voluntary settlements see SETTLEMENTS vol 42 (Reissue) para 615 et seq.

9 See para 181 post.

10 *Mills v Dunham* [1891] 1 Ch 576 at 580, CA. This principle has application chiefly to the case of contracts in restraint of trade, which become entirely void where the restraint is greater than the law allows, unless the agreement itself severs the lawful from unlawful clauses. See also *Lee-Parker v Izzet (No 2)* [1972] 2 All ER 800, [1972] 1 WLR 775. The court is, however, reluctant to hold void for uncertainty any provision that was intended to have legal effect: *Brown v Gould* [1972] Ch 53, [1971] 2 All ER 1505. In the case of a provision in a lease or conveyance see *Sheffield City Council v Jackson* [1998] 3 All ER 260 at 268, [1998] 1 WLR 1591 at 1599, CA, per Nourse LJ.

178.   Construction against grantor or covenantor.   If a doubt arises upon the construction of a grant, and the doubt can be removed by construing the deed adversely to the grantor, this will be done[1]. The words of a deed, executed for valuable consideration, are to be construed, as far as they properly may, in favour of the grantee[2]. Where there is a grant and an exception out of it, the exception is taken as inserted for the benefit of the grantor, and is construed in favour of the grantee[3].

The obligatory part of a bond, being for the benefit of the obligee, is always construed most strongly against the obligor, but the condition[4], being for the benefit of the obligor, is construed most strongly in his favour[5].

Exceptions in a contract are as a general rule to be construed, as in a grant, strictly against the party for whose benefit they are inserted on the ground that those who wish to introduce words in a contract in order to shield themselves ought to do so in clear words[6]. General words in an exception clause do not ordinarily except the party seeking to rely on the exception from liability for his own negligence or that of his employees unless that is substantially the only scope for the operation of the clause[7]. A clause in a contract exempting a party from liability for the negligence of his employees or agents will not as a rule be extended by implication so as to protect those employees or agents from liability[8]. An exception clause may not on the true construction of the contract give a party protection if he has committed a breach of a fundamental term of the contract[9].

Where there is a doubt on the construction of a settlement whether a trustee would be exempted from liability for breach of trust by a trustee exemption clause, such doubt should be resolved against the trustee and the clause construed so as not to protect him[10].

A settlement in which the same person is at once grantor and grantee is construed as if made by a stranger[11]. Similarly, covenants are construed most strongly against the covenantor, and most beneficially in favour of the covenantee[12].

Generally an instrument must be read most strongly against the party who prepares it and offers it for execution by the other, such as a declaration prepared by an insurance company for signature by an intending insured[13].

1   It is a maxim of the law that every man's grant is taken most strongly against himself: Co Litt 183a; and see also Co Litt 264b, 265a. 'All the words of a deed shall be taken most strongly against him that doth speak them, and most in advantage of the other party': Shep Touch 87; *Throckmerton v Tracey* (1555) 1 Plowd 145; *Doe d Davies v Williams* (1788) 1 Hy Bl 25. See also *Williams v James* (1867) LR 2 CP 577 at 581 per Willes J; *Neill v Duke of Devenshire* (1882) 8 App Cas 135 at 149, HL; *Gluckstein v Barnes* [1900] AC 240 at 250, HL, per Lord Macnaghten; *Re Harper (a bankrupt), Harper v O'Reilly* [1998] 3 FCR 475, [1997] 2 FLR 816. It was held by Jessel MR in *Taylor v St Helens Corpn* (1877) 6 ChD 264 at 270, CA, that having regard to the rule laid down by the House of Lords in *Grey v Pearson* (1857) 6 HL Cas 61 (see para 169 text and note 2 ante), the maxim that a grant in which there is any obscurity or difficulty must be construed most strongly against the grantor has no application at the present time; but see *Leech v Schweder* (1874) 9 Ch App 465n at 466n per Jessel MR (revsd on other grounds 9 Ch App 463). The rule operates in favour of a lessee: *Justice Windham's Case* (1589) 5 Co Rep 7a; *Seaman's Case* (1610) Godb 166; *Manchester College v Trafford* (1678) 2 Show 31; *Dann v Spurrier* (1803) 3 Bos & P 399 at 403; *Doe d Webb v Dixon* (1807) 9 East 15 at 16. It has been held, too, that a guarantee should be construed strictly against the party executing it (*Hargreave v Smee* (1829) 6 Bing 244), that conditions of sale should be construed strictly against the vendor (*Seaton v Mapp* (1846) 2 Coll 556), and that, generally speaking, where there are several ways of performing a contract, the mode may be adopted which is least profitable to the person complaining of a breach (*Cockburn v Alexander* (1848) 6 CB 791 at 814 per Maule J; *Lavarack v Woods of Colchester Ltd* [1967] 1 QB 278 at 293, [1966] 3 All ER 683 at 690, CA, per Diplock LJ). A clause in an insurance policy excluding liability will be construed against the insurers: *Houghton v Trafalgar Insurance Co Ltd* [1954] 1 QB 247, [1953] 2 All ER 1409, CA. As to the contrary rule in the case of Crown grants see para 179 post.
    As to the construction of contractual documents generally see para 164 ante.

2   Co Litt 183a; *Willion v Berkley* (1561) 1 Plowd 223 at 243; *Justice Windham's Case* (1589) 5 Co Rep 7a; *Davenport's Case* (1610) 8 Co Rep 144b; *Re Stroud* (1849) 8 CB 502 at 529 per Wilde CJ; *Johnson v Edgware etc Rly Co* (1866) 35 Beav 480 at 484 per Lord Romilly MR; *Neill v Duke of Devonshire* (1882) 8 App Cas 135 at 149, HL, per Lord Selborne LC.

3   Shep Touch 100; *Earl of Cardigan v Armitage* (1823) 2 B & C 197 at 207; *Bullen v Denning* (1826) 5 B & C 842 at 847, 850; *Savill Bros Ltd v Bethell* [1902] 2 Ch 523 at 537, CA; *Gruhn v Balgray Investments Ltd* (1963) 107 Sol Jo 112, CA. Where there was a reservation of a new interest, e g an easement, not issuing out of the property conveyed, in a conveyance made before 1926 (at any rate if the reservation was not effected by a grant to uses under the Conveyancing Act 1881 s 62 (repealed)), the reservation had to be made by a regrant or by a conveyance executed by the grantee and treated in relation to the reservation as a regrant, and any such reservation was construed against the person making the regrant. Although the doctrine of fictitious regrant has been abolished (by the Law of Property Act 1925 s 65(1)) this principle of constructing a reservation against the persons supposed to be making the regrant still applies: see *St Edmundsbury and Ipswich Diocesan Board of Finance v Clark (No 2)* [1975] 1 All ER 772, [1975] 1 WLR 468, CA, following *Johnstone v Holdway* [1963] 1 QB 601, [1963] 1 All ER 432, CA; *South Eastern Rly Co v Associated Portland Cement Manufacturers (1900) Ltd* [1910] 1 Ch 12 at 24, CA; *Durham and Sunderland Rly Co v Walker* (1842) 2 QB 940, Ex Ch.

4   For the meaning of 'obligatory part' and 'condition' of a bond see para 91 ante.

5   Shep Touch 375.

6   *Blackett v Royal Exchange Assurance Co* (1832) 2 Cr & J 244 at 251; *Taylor v Liverpool and Great Western Steam Co* (1874) LR 9 QB 546; *Burton v English* (1883) 12 QBD 218 at 220, 222, CA. See also *Fowkes v Manchester and London Assurance Association* (1863) 3 B & S 917; *Birrell v Dryer* (1884) 9 App Cas 345, HL; *Savill Bros Ltd v Bethell* [1902] 2 Ch 523, CA; *The Pearlmoor* [1904] P 286; *Price & Co v Union Lighterage Co* [1904] 1 KB 412, CA; *Elderslie Steamship Co v Borthwick* [1905] AC 93, HL; *South Eastern Rly Co v Associated Portland Cement Manufacturers (1900) Ltd* [1910] 1 Ch 12, CA; *Joseph Travers & Sons Ltd v Cooper* [1915] 1 KB 73, CA; *Whelan v Leonard* [1917] 2 IR 323, Ir CA; *Williams v Curzon Syndicate Ltd* (1919) 35 TLR 475, CA; *J Gordon Alison & Co v Wallsend Slipway and Engineering Co* (1927) 43 TLR 323, CA; *John Lee & Son (Grantham) Ltd v Rly Executive* [1949] 2 All ER 581, CA; *Compania Naviera Aeolus SA v Union of India* [1964] AC 868, [1962] 3 All ER 670, HL (once a vessel is on demurrage no exception clause prevents demurrage continuing unless it is clearly worded); *John Carter (Fine Worsteds) Ltd v Hanson Haulage (Leeds) Ltd* [1965] 2 QB 495, [1965] 1 All ER 113, CA; *Adams v Richardson and Starling Ltd* [1969] 2 All ER 1221, [1969] 1 WLR 1645, CA; *Mendelssohn v Normand Ltd* [1970] 1 QB 177, [1969] 2 All ER 1215, CA.

7   *White v John Warrick & Co Ltd* [1953] 2 All ER 1021, [1953] 1 WLR 1285, CA; *AE Farr Ltd v Admiralty* [1953] 2 All ER 512 at 513, [1953] 1 WLR 965 at 967; *James Archdale & Co Ltd v Comservices Ltd* [1954]

1 All ER 210 at 211, [1954] 1 WLR 459 at 461, CA, per Somervell LJ; and see BAILMENT vol 3(1) (2005 Reissue) para 40; CARRIERS vol 5(1) (2004 Reissue) paras 625–630; CONTRACT vol 9(1) (Reissue) para 797 et seq. As to negligence clauses in general see NEGLIGENCE; and see SHIPPING AND NAVIGATION vol 43(1) (Reissue) para 1499.

8   *Adler v Dickson* [1955] 1 QB 158, [1954] 3 All ER 397, CA (contract for the carriage of a passenger by sea). One exception which exists is in the case of a contract for the carriage of goods eg a bill of lading; an exemption clause in such a contract will, it appears, enure for the benefit of all engaged in carrying out the contract: see *Elder, Dempster & Co v Paterson, Zochonis & Co* [1924] AC 522, HL, explained and distinguished in *Adler v Dickson* [1955] 1 QB 158 at 181–184, [1954] 3 All ER 397 at 400–402, CA, per Denning LJ, at 189–195 and 405–408 per Jenkins LJ, and at 198–200 and 411–412 per Morris LJ. See also SHIPPING AND NAVIGATION vol 43(1) (Reissue) paras 1499, 1931. In *Murfin v United Steel Companies Ltd* [1957] 1 All ER 23, [1957] 1 WLR 104, CA, the term negligence was not, on the true construction of an indemnity clause, found to include breach of statutory duty.
     As to exclusion clauses and third parties generally see CONTRACT vol 9(1) (Reissue) para 797 et seq.

9   *Atlantic Shipping and Trading Co v Louis Dreyfus & Co* [1922] 2 AC 250 at 260, HL, per Lord Sumner; *Smeaton, Hanscomb & Co Ltd v Sassoon I Setty Son & Co* [1953] 2 All ER 1471 at 1473, [1953] 1 WLR 1468 at 1470 per Devlin J; *Suisse Atlantique Société d' Armement Maritime SA v NV Rotterdamsche Kolen Centrale* [1967] 1 AC 361, [1966] 2 All ER 61, HL. A clause requiring the claim to be brought within a specified period is an exception for this purpose: *Smeaton, Hanscomb & Co Ltd v Sassoon I Setty Son & Co* supra at 1473 and 1470. A fundamental term is something which underlies the whole contract so that, if it is not complied with, the performance becomes something totally different from that which the contract contemplates: *Smeaton, Hanscomb & Co Ltd v Sassoon I Setty Son & Co* supra at 1473 and 1470. See also CARRIERS vol 5(1) (2004 Reissue) para 625 et seq.

10   *Wight v Olswang* (1998) Times, 17 September; revsd on a different point (1999) Times, 18 May, CA.

11   *Vincent v Spicer* (1856) 22 Beav 380 at 383.

12   *Warde v Warde* (1852) 16 Beav 103 at 105 per Romilly MR. Examples are covenants for title (*Barton v Fitzgerald* (1812) 15 East 530 at 546), or covenants in a lease (*Barrett v Duke of Bedford* (1800) 8 Term Rep 602 at 605; *Webb v Plummer* (1819) 2 B & Ald 746 at 751; *Doe d Sir W Abdy v Stevens* (1832) 3 B & Ad 299 at 303).

13   *Fowkes v Manchester and London Assurance Association* (1863) 3 B & S 917 at 925 per Cockburn CJ. As to exceptions in a bill of lading see *Taylor v Liverpool and Great Western Steam Co* (1874) LR 9 QB 546 at 549 per Lush J; and cf *Birrell v Dryer* (1884) 9 App Cas 345, HL.

179.   Qualifications of the rule.

The rule that words are to be interpreted most strongly against him who uses them[1], expressed in the maxim 'verba fortius accipiuntur contra proferentem', is subject to the general principle that the instrument must be construed in accordance with the expressed intention[2]. The rule does not come into operation until a doubt arises upon the construction of the instrument[3]; nor is it applied when the effect would be to make the grantor's deed work a wrong[4]. Moreover, it is to be applied only when all other rules of construction fail[5].

In the case of a grant by the Crown the rule is reversed, and the grant is taken most strongly against the grantee and in favour of the Crown[6], unless the grant is expressed to be made 'of special grace, mere motion, and certain knowledge'[7].

There is no rule that a contract of guarantee is to be construed with special favour to the guarantor; but a surety is bound only by the strict letter of his engagement[8].

1   See para 178 ante. As to the construction of contractual documents generally see para 164 ante.

2   See *Webb v Plummer* (1819) 2 B & Ald 746 at 751 per Holroyd J.

3   See *Rubery v Jervoise* (1786) 1 Term Rep 229 at 234 per Willes J; *Fowle v Welsh* (1822) 1 B & C 29 at 35 per Bayley J; *Williams v James* (1867) LR 2 CP 577 at 581 per Willes J. The rule that, if the words are doubtful, the construction must be most strong against the covenantor is qualified by the rule that effect must be given to every word, and if when this is done the doubt is removed, there is no room for the former rule: *Patching v Dubbins* (1853) Kay 1 at 13–14 per Wood V-C.

4   'It is a general rule that, whensoever the words of a deed, or of the parties without a deed, may have a double intendment, and the one standeth with law and right, and the other is wrongful and against law, the intendment that standeth with law shall be taken': Co Litt 42a, b; Shep Touch 88. This rule is superior to the rule that the deed is to be construed most strongly against the grantor: *Rodger v Comptoir d'Escompte de Paris* (1869) LR 2 PC 393 at 406.

5   *Borradaile v Hunter* (1843) 5 Man & G 639; *Lindus v Melrose* (1858) 3 H & N 177 at 182, Ex Ch, per Coleridge J; *Macey v Qazi* (1987) Times, 13 January, CA; and see *Burton v English* (1883) 12 QBD 218 at

220, CA, per Brett MR. In accordance with the rule, the words of a deed inter partes are construed most strongly against the party who is to be regarded as using them: see the argument in *Browning v Beston* (1555) 1 Plowd 131 at 134.

6   *Willion v Berkley* (1561) 1 Plowd 223 at 243; *Viscountess Rhondda's Claim* [1922] 2 AC 339 at 353, HL. The maxim, however, does not override the ordinary rules for ascertaining what is included in the grant: *A-G v Ewelme Hospital* (1853) 17 Beav 366 at 386; *Lord v Sydney City Comrs* (1859) 12 Moo PCC 473 at 497. As to Crown grants generally see *Alton Woods' Case* (1600) 1 Co Rep 40b; and CONSTITUTIONAL LAW AND HUMAN RIGHTS vol 8(2) (Reissue) para 858 et seq.

7   *Alton Woods' Case* (1600) 1 Co Rep 40b; Com Dig, Grant (G 12); Vin Abr, Prerogative (Ec 3); *Doe d Devine v Wilson* (1855) 10 Moo PCC 502 at 525; contra *R v Capper, Re Bowler* (1817) 5 Price 217 at 260.

8   See *Eshelby v Federated European Bank Ltd* [1932] 1 KB 254 at 266 (affd [1932] 1 KB 423, CA), citing *Blest v Brown* (1862) 4 De GF & J 367 at 376. See also GUARANTEE AND INDEMNITY vol 20(1) (Reissue) para 171 et seq.

180.   Party taking advantage of his own wrong. Where a claim for breach of contract turns on the construction of a particular clause, a party is not debarred from relying on a construction which would allow him to derive an advantage from a previous breach if no disadvantage is suffered by the other party. The presumption that no man can take advantage of his own wrong does not apply in such circumstances[1]. Whether a clause in an agreement is to be defeated because a party was taking advantage of his own wilful default is essentially a question of construction of the agreement[2].

1   See *Thornton v Abbey National plc* (1993) Times, 4 March, CA (defendant entitled to replacement vehicle 'at intervals of no more than 30 months'; the replacement was outside that period; the plaintiff claimed he was entitled to further replacement within 30 months of the date when it should have been provided, but the defendant successfully argued that the intervals referred to times between replacements).
     As to the construction of contractual documents generally see para 164 ante.

2   See *Alghussein Establishment v Eton College* [1991] 1 All ER 267, [1988] 1 WLR 587, HL.

(2) IMPLICATIONS

181.   Implied terms. Provisions may be implied in an instrument, and in particular in a contract[1], on a variety of grounds. With certain exceptions[2], a provision will be so implied only where the instrument is devoid of any express provision dealing with the matter which is the subject of the implied provision, and the latter must not be inconsistent with, and may be moulded by, the express provisions of the instrument[3]. The cases in which provisions may be implied may be put into a number of overlapping categories. First, where the instrument effects a transaction relating to a particular trade, profession, or branch of commercial or mercantile life or to the letting of land, and notorious usages, reasonable and certain in character but not unlawful, exist either generally throughout the kingdom or in a relevant larger or more local area, the parties will be presumed to be intending to follow and be bound by these usages[4]. Secondly, where it is clearly necessary to imply some unexpressed term in order to give to the transaction effected by the instrument that efficacy which all parties must have intended it to have[5], a reasonable term will be implied for that purpose, provided that it is clear what term ought to be so implied[6]. Thirdly, implications of particular well-defined terms are made in certain particular transactions by the law merchant or the common law as developed and determined by judicial decisions[7]; many of these detailed particular implied terms originated as usages or terms implied by necessity but are now regarded as part of the general law. Fourthly, terms may be implied by statute[8]; some of these statutory implications are a codification of terms implied previously by judicial decisions.

1   See CONTRACT vol 9(1) (Reissue) para 778 et seq. As to the construction of contractual documents generally see para 164 ante.

2   See para 184 post. In addition, a statute occasionally inserts an implied term which it declares cannot be overridden by the instrument: see e g the Landlord and Tenant Act 1985 ss 8, 11–16 (as amended); the

Unfair Contract Terms Act 1977 s 6 (as amended), in relation to certain provisions in the Sale of Goods Act 1979; and the Supply of Goods (Implied Terms) Act 1973. It is also sometimes provided by statute that express terms are not to negative a particular statutory implied term unless inconsistent with it: see e g the Sale of Goods Act 1979 s 55(2) (as amended); the Supply of Goods (Implied Terms) Act 1973 s 12 (as substituted); and SALE OF GOODS AND SUPPLY OF SERVICES.

3   See para 182 post.

4   See *Liverpool City Council v Irwin* [1977] AC 239 at 253, [1976] 2 All ER 39 at 43, HL, per Lord Wilberforce; *Baker v Black Sea and Baltic General Insurance Co Ltd* [1998] 2 All ER 833 at 841, [1998] Lloyd's Rep IR 327 at 339, HL, per Lord Lloyd ('it is very common in mercantile contracts, where there is an established market usage, to add a term to an otherwise complete bilateral contract, on the grounds that it is what the parties would unhesitatingly have agreed'). As to the implied term of confidentiality in commercial arbitrations see *Ali Shipping Corpn v Shipyard Trogir* [1998] 2 All ER 136, [1998] 1 Lloyd's Rep 643, CA. See CUSTOM AND USAGE vol 12(1) (Reissue) para 650 et seq. See also AGRICULTURE vol 1(2) (Reissue) para 307 et seq.

5   *M'Intyre v Belcher* (1863) 14 CBNS 654; *Saner v Bilton* (1878) 7 ChD 815; *The Moorcock* (1889) 14 PD 64, CA; *Ogdens Ltd v Nelson* [1904] 2 KB 410, CA (affd on other grounds [1905] AC 109, HL); *Reigate v Union Manufacturing Co (Ramsbottom) Ltd* [1918] 1 KB 592 at 605, CA, per Scrutton LJ ('the first thing is to see what the parties have expressed in the contract; and then an implied term is not to be added because the court thinks it would have been reasonable to have inserted it in the contract. A term can only be implied if it is necessary in the business sense to give efficacy to the contract; that is, if it is such a term that it can confidently be said that if at the time the contract was being negotiated some one had said to the parties, 'What will happen in such a case', they would both have replied, 'Of course, so and so will happen; we did not trouble to say that, it is too clear.' Unless the court comes to some such conclusion as that, it ought not to imply a term which the parties themselves have not expressed.'); *Shirlaw v Southern Foundries (1926) Ltd* [1939] 2 KB 206, [1939] 2 All ER 113, CA; *Kumar v AGF Insurance Ltd* [1998] 4 All ER 788, [1999] Lloyd's Rep IR 147. See further paras 183, 251, 253, 255 post; and CONTRACT vol 9(1) (Reissue) paras 782–783.

6   *Re Cochrane, Shaw v Cochrane* [1955] Ch 309, [1955] 1 All ER 222; *R v Paddington and St Marylebone Rent Tribunal, ex p Bedrock Investments Ltd* [1947] KB 984 at 990, [1947] 2 All ER 15 at 17, DC, per Lord Goddard CJ (affd [1948] 2 KB 413, [1948] 2 All ER 528, CA), cited with approval in *R v Croydon and District Rent Tribunal, ex p Langford Property Co Ltd* [1948] 1 KB 60, DC; *Penn v Gatenex Co Ltd* [1958] 2 QB 210 at 224, [1958] 1 All ER 712 at 718, CA, per Parker LJ. Where it is necessary to imply a contractual warranty, and there is some choice open as to its terms, the obligation least onerous on the party upon whom it is imposed will be implied: *Compagnie Algerienne De Meunerie v Katana Societa Di Navigatone Marittima SPA* [1959] 1 QB 527 at 540, [1959] 1 All ER 272 at 278 per Diplock J; affd on other grounds [1960] 2 QB 115, [1960] 2 All ER 55, CA.

       See also *French v Barclays Bank plc* [1998] IRLR 646, CA (there was implied into a contract of employment a term that the bank would not act so as to destroy the confidence and trust existing as between the bank and its employee; it would be a breach of that term for the bank to insist on a relocation, offer a bridging loan interest free, and then to seek to alter the terms of the loan to the employee's detriment). The court refused, however, to imply a term to keep the structure of a building in repair in *Adami v Lincoln Grange Management Ltd* (1997) 30 HLR 982, [1998] 1 EGLR 58, CA, distinguishing *Barrett v Lounova (1982) Ltd* [1990] 1 QB 348, [1989] 1 All ER 351, CA, as a decision on its special facts.

7   See paras 251–256, 259 post; and CONTRACT vol 9(1) (Reissue) paras 780–781; CUSTOM AND USAGE vol 12(1) (Reissue) para 650 et seq. Many detailed terms are now implied by law in an open contract for sale of land: see *Re Priestley's Contract* [1947] Ch 469, [1947] 1 All ER 716; and SALE OF LAND vol 42 (Reissue) paras 38, 338 et seq. The terms to be implied in a contract of employment (in the absence of and subject to any express provision) have been developed and crystallised by the courts: *Lister v Romford Ice and Cold Storage Co Ltd* [1957] AC 555, [1957] 1 All ER 125, HL; and see EMPLOYMENT vol 16(1A) (Reissue) para 90.

8   Eg, in relation to sale of land, see the Law of Property Act 1925 s 45; and the Statutory Form of Conditions of Sale 1925, SR & O 1925/779; and SALE OF LAND vol 42 (Reissue) paras 132, 150, 172 (but see *Commission for the New Towns v Cooper (Great Britain) Ltd* [1995] Ch 259, [1995] 2 All ER 929, CA, indicating that it is virtually impossible to create a land contract by correspondence). In relation to conveyances and other assurances of property, see the Law of Property Act 1925 ss 62–63, 77 (as amended), Sch 2 (as amended); para 256 post; and MORTGAGE vol 32 (2005 Reissue) para 394. In relation to tenancies of agricultural land, see the Agricultural Holdings Act 1986 s 7; the Agriculture (Maintenance, Repair and Insurance of Fixed Equipment) Regulations 1973, SI 1973/1473 (as amended); and AGRICULTURE vol 1(2) (Reissue) para 319 et seq. In relation to covenants, see the Law of Property Act 1925 ss 78, 80(1) (as amended); and para 256 post. In relation to the powers of trustees, see the Trustee Act 1925; the Trustee Investments Act 1961; and TRUSTS. In relation to the sale of goods, see the Sale of Goods Act 1979 ss 10, 12–15 (as amended), Sch 1; and SALE OF GOODS AND SUPPLY OF

SERVICES vol 41 (2004 Reissue) para 467. In relation to hire-purchase agreements, see the Supply of Goods (Implied Terms) Act 1973 ss 8–15 (as amended); and CONSUMER CREDIT vol 9(1) (Reissue) para 23 et seq. In relation to partnership, see the Partnership Act 1890 ss 19, 24–25; and PARTNERSHIP.

182. Effect of express provision. An express provision in an instrument excludes any stipulation which would otherwise be implied with regard to the same subject matter. The rule is expressed in the maxim 'expressum facit cessare tacitum'[1], and is based upon the presumption that the parties, having expressed some, have expressed all the conditions by which they intend to be bound under the instrument in respect of the particular subject matter[2].

1   See Co Litt 183b, 210a. As to the situation where the express clause is exactly that implied by the law see para 184 post.

     As to the construction of contractual documents generally see para 164 ante.

2   *Aspdin v Austin* (1844) 5 QB 671 at 684 per Lord Denman CJ; and see *Rhodes v Forwood* (1876) 1 App Cas 256 at 265, HL. Thus, upon an advance on mortgage, if the mortgage deed contains no covenant for payment, a personal obligation to repay the money is implied; but if the deed contains a covenant for payment out of particular funds, the implication of a personal contract is excluded: *Mathew v Blackmore* (1857) 1 H & N 762 at 771–772. Similarly, upon a letting, an express covenant for quiet enjoyment excludes the covenant which would be implied from the use of the word 'demise', or, without that word, from the mere letting: *Nokes' Case* (1599) 4 Co Rep 80b; *Merrill v Frame* (1812) 4 Taunt 329; *Stannard v Forbes* (1837) 6 Ad & El 572; *Line v Stephenson* (1838) 5 Bing NC 183, Ex Ch; *Miller v Emcer Products Ltd* [1956] Ch 304, [1956] 1 All ER 237, CA; and see *Markham v Paget* [1908] 1 Ch 697. See also *Birmingham, Dudley and District Banking Co v Ross* (1888) 38 ChD 295 at 308, CA (express grant of appurtenances); and the cases cited in para 251 note 8 post.

183. Effect of express mention of one of several persons or matters. The principle that the express mention in a provision of one only of several related things, persons or matters indicates that the provision is not intended to include the other or others, is expressed in the maxim 'expressio unius est exclusio alterius'[1]. Thus where an instrument authorises a particular mode of selling or otherwise dealing with property, this excludes any other mode of dealing with it for the same purpose[2]; and generally, where authority to do an act is given upon a defined condition, the expression of that condition excludes the doing of the act under other circumstances than those so defined[3].

The maxim, however, must be applied with caution. The failure to make the provision expressed complete may be accidental[4]; and the maxim ought not to be applied when its application, having regard to the subject matter to which it is to be applied, will lead to inconsistency or injustice[5]. It should only be applied when the instrument, on the face of it, apparently contains all the terms which the parties have agreed upon[6].

In some respects the maxim is the converse of the principles upon which words may be supplied in order to correct clearly inadvertent omissions[7] or upon which terms may be implied if necessary and obviously intended to give efficacy to the instrument[8]. These principles override the maxim because the instrument does not, where they have effect, contain on its face all the terms which the parties have intended.

1   See Co Litt 210a. This maxim has been applied also to statutes: see STATUTES vol 44(1) (Reissue) para 1494.

     As to the construction of contractual documents generally see para 164 ante.

2   *Blackburn v Flavelle* (1881) 6 App Cas 628 at 634, PC. So, in a conveyance of two distinct buildings, the express mention of the fixtures in one of them has been held to exclude those in the other: see *Hare v Horton* (1833) 5 B & Ad 715 at 729.

3   *North Stafford Steel etc Co v Ward* (1868) LR 3 Exch 172 at 177, Ex Ch, per Willes J; and cf *R v Palfrey* [1970] 2 All ER 12 at 15–16 [1970] 1 WLR 416 at 421–422, CA, per Winn LJ.

4   *Colquhoum v Brooks* (1887) 19 QBD 400 at 406 per Wills J, suggesting that the omission may arise from the fact that it never struck the draftsman that the thing supposed to be excluded needed specific mention (on appeal (1888) 21 QBD 52 at 65, CA; (1889) 14 App Cas 493, HL).

5   *Colquhoun v Brooks* (1888) 21 QBD 52 at 65, CA, per Lopes LJ; *Lowe v Dorling & Son* [1906] 2 KB 772 at 785, CA, per Farwell LJ; *Sampson v Caldow* [1977] 1 EGLR 100; and see *Dean v Wiesengrund* [1955] 2 QB 120 at 137, [1955] 2 All ER 432 at 443, CA, per Morris LJ.

6   This paragraph was cited with approval in *McClelland v Northern Ireland General Health Services Board* [1957] 2 All ER 129 at 138, [1957] 1 WLR 594 at 607, HL, per Lord Keith. See also *Devonald v Rosser & Sons* [1906] 2 KB 728 at 745, CA, per Farwell LJ. In the construction of a contract the maxim is not applicable when the expression is found only in one and not in the other clauses of the same contract: *Wade & Sons Co Ltd v Cockerline & Co* (1905) 53 WR 420, CA. Nor is the maxim appropriate where that which is expressed is introduced by the phrase 'such as' or any other expression indicating that what is expressed is not exhaustive: *Prestcold (Central) Ltd v Minister of Labour* [1969] 1 All ER 69 at 76, [1969] 1 WLR 89 at 98, CA, per Lord Diplock.

7   See para 210 post.

8   See paras 181 note 5 ante, 251–254 post.

184.   Expression of implied terms has no effect.   The expression of a clause which is exactly that implied by the law as the necessary consequence of the contract between the parties has no legal operation; this rule is expressed in the maxim 'expressio eorum quae tacite insunt nihil operatur'[1]. It merely serves to remove any doubt which might arise in the mind of a person unacquainted with the law[2]. Consequently, the express clause does not vary the legal results of the implied clause[3], nor did it necessitate any additional stamp duty[4].

The same maxim also expresses a second related principle: where a grant of property confers by implication powers which are essential to its enjoyment, these are not cut down by the express conferment in positive terms of restricted powers to the same effect[5]. Save in this case, an express clause which varies from the implied clause excludes it in accordance with the rule 'expressio unius est exclusio alterius'[6].

The present rule only deprives the words, thus needlessly introduced, of effect upon their own clause. Nevertheless, though they are superfluous for the immediate purpose of that clause, they may affect the construction of other clauses in the instrument[7].

1   *Boroughe's Case* (1596) 4 Co Rep 72b at 73b; Co Litt 205a; and see Co Litt 224b. Thus a reservation of rent to a lessor for his life is not varied by the addition of the words 'and his assigns'; which are implied: *Sury v Cole (or Brown)* (1625) Lat 44, 255; and see *Wooton v Edwin* (1607) 12 Co Rep 36.
    As to the construction of contractual documents generally see para 164 ante.

2   It is useful 'to express and declare to laymen which have no knowledge of the law what the law requires in such cases': *Boroughe's Case* (1596) 4 Co Rep 72b at 73b; and see Littleton's Tenures s 331.

3   Eg an express power of distress, provided its terms do not impose requirements other than those of a common law power of distress: *Browne v Dunnery* (1618) Hob 208; and cf *Doe d Scholefield v Alexander* (1814) 2 M & S 525 at 532, where in a proviso for re-entry on default in payment of rent 'being lawfully demanded,' the introduction of these words added nothing to the clause; and see para 182 note 2 ante.

4   Thus where a mortgage deed expressly secured expenses which, in the absence of express provision, could have been added to add to the security, the present maxim rendered it unnecessary to increase the stamp duty (since abolished by the Finance Act 1971) so as to cover these expenses: *Doe d Scruton v Snaith* (1832) 8 Bing 146 at 154. See also *Doe d Merceron v Bragg* (1838) 8 Ad & El 620 (rates and taxes); *Wroughton v Turtle* (1843) 11 M & W 561 at 570 (fines or renewal); *Frith v Rotherham* (1846) 15 LJ Ex 133 (bankers' commission); *Lawrence v Boston* (1851) 7 Exch 28 (premiums on policy of insurance).

5   Thus, upon an absolute grant of trees, an express power to cut and carry them away during five years does not restrict the implied power to cut and carry them away at any time: *Stukeley v Butler* (1614) Hob 168; and see Dyer 19b, pl 115 (1536); *Ellis v Noakes* [1932] 2 Ch 98n. Where, in a grant of land, there was an exception of minerals to the grantor, his heirs, and assigns, an express liberty for the grantor and his heirs to get them was held not to restrict the general right for the assigns to do so which was implied from the exception in their favour: *Earl of Cardigan v Armitage* (1823) 2 B & C 197; and see *Hodgson v Field* (1806) 7 East 613. 'Heirs' is not now ordinarily used as a word of limitation, descent to the heir being abolished (see the Administration of Estates Act 1925 s 45(1)(a); and EXECUTORS AND ADMINISTRATORS vol 17(2) (Reissue) para 663).

6   See para 183 ante.

7   'The rule *expressio eorum* etc is to be understood having respect to itself only, and not having relation to other clauses. Thus, a grant of land carries the underwoods, and a grant of a house carries the shops in it; but the mention of underwoods or shops will save them from being excluded by a subsequent exception': *Stukeley v Butler* (1614) Hob 168 at 170.

(3) ADMISSION OF EXTRINSIC EVIDENCE

(i) To Vary or Add to Document

185. Extrinsic evidence generally excluded. Where the intention of the parties has been reduced to writing it is, in general, not permissible to adduce extrinsic evidence, whether oral[1] or contained in writings such as instructions[2], drafts[3], articles[4], conditions of sale[5] or preliminary agreements[6] or memoranda provided for the 'protector' of a settlement[7], either to show that intention[8] or to contradict, vary, or add to the terms of the document[9]. This principle applies to records[10], arbitrators' awards[11], bills of exchange and promissory notes[12], bills of lading and charterparties[13], bonds[14], descriptions of boundaries[15], guarantees[16], leases[17], contracts for the sale of goods[18], and patents[19]. Verbal statements made by an auctioneer may not be part of the contract of sale[20].

Extrinsic evidence cannot be received in order to prove the object with which a document was executed[21]; or that the intention of the parties was other than that appearing on the face of the instrument[22].

1   *Robinson v Gee* (1749) 1 Ves Sen 251 at 253; *Davis v Symonds* (1787) 1 Cox Eq Cas 402 at 404–405; *Humble v Hunter* (1848) 12 QB 310; *Halhead v Young* (1856) 6 E & B 312; *O'Rourke v Railways Comr* (1890) 15 App Cas 371, PC; *Neale v Neale* (1898) 79 LT 629, CA; *Vezey v Rashleigh* [1904] 1 Ch 634; *Horncastle v Equitable Life Assurance Society of the United States* (1906) 22 TLR 735, CA; *Goldfoot v Welch* [1914] 1 Ch 213; *Re L Sutro & Co and Heilbut, Symons & Co* [1917] 2 KB 348, CA. See further CONTRACT vol 9(1) (Reissue) paras 622, 690–700.

2   See *Guardhouse v Blackburn* (1866) LR 1 P & D 109.

3   *Miller v Travers* (1832) 8 Bing 244; *National Bank of Australasia v Falkingham & Sons* [1902] AC 585, PC; *City and Westminster Properties (1934) Ltd v Mudd* [1959] Ch 129 at 140–141, [1958] 2 All ER 733 at 739–740 per Harman J. A signed draft may be looked at when the final copies differ: see *Ingleby v Slack* (1890) 6 TLR 284. In a case where the terms of a building agreement and a lease granted in connection with it differed, it was held both permissible and relevant to look at the draft lease under the agreement in order to discover the parties' intention in referring to a particular date in the lease as executed: *Ladbroke Group plc v Bristol City Council* [1988] 1 EGLR 126, CA.

4   *Pritchard v Quinchant* (1752) Amb 147.

5   *Gunnis v Erhart* (1789) 1 Hy Bl 289; *Powell v Edmunds* (1810) 12 East 6; *Doe d Norton v Webster* (1840) 12 Ad & El 442.

6   *Leggott v Barrett* (1880) 15 ChD 306 at 309, CA; and cf *Mercantile Bank of Sydney v Taylor* [1893] AC 317 at 321, PC; *Lee v Alexander* (1883) 8 App Cas 853 at 868, 871–872, HL; *Rainbow Estates Ltd v Tokenhold Ltd* [1999] Ch 64, [1998] 2 All ER 860 (where there is a conflict between a lease and a prior agreement, the rights of the parties are governed by the lease). See also *Kinlen v Ennis UDC* [1916] 2 IR 299 at 305, 308–309, HL.

7   See *IRC v Botnar* [1998] STC 38 at 87–88 per Evans-Lombe J.

8   'No extrinsic evidence of the intention of the party to the deed from his declarations, whether at the time of his executing the instrument, or before or after that time, is admissible; the duty of the court being to declare the meaning of what is written in the instrument, not of what was intended to have been written': *Shore v Wilson* (1842) 9 Cl & Fin 355 at 556, HL, per Parke B, and at 565–567 per Tindal CJ; *Earl of Bradford v Earl of Romney* (1862) 30 Beav 431 at 436; *Reliance Marine Insurance Co v Duder* [1913] 1 KB 265 at 273, CA; *Goldfoot v Welch* [1914] 1 Ch 213 at 218; *Re Aynsley, Kyrle v Turner* [1915] 1 Ch 172, CA; *Tsang Chuen v Li Po Kwai* [1932] AC 715 at 727, PC; *Re Atkinson's Will Trusts* [1978] 1 All ER 1275, [1978] 1 WLR 586 (evidence that testator used word in a special sense inadmissible); *Rabin v Gerson Berger Association Ltd* [1986] 1 All ER 374, [1986] 1 WLR 526, CA (evidence of counsel's opinion given before trust deed executed not admissible). As to the admission of extrinsic evidence to avoid a deed on the ground of forgery, mistake, fraud, illegality etc see para 67 et seq ante.

9   'I have never heard the general rule contradicted, that parol or extrinsic evidence cannot be admitted to contradict, vary, or add to the words of a deed': *Smith v Doe d Jersey* (1821) 2 Brod & Bing 473 at 541, HL, per Park B. If there be a contract which has been reduced into writing, verbal evidence is not allowed to be given of what passed between the parties, either before the written instrument was made, or during the time that it was in a state of preparation, so as to add to or subtract from, or in any manner to vary or qualify the written contract: *Goss v Lord Nugent* (1833) 5 B & Ad 58 at 64 per

Lord Denman CJ. 'The court has no right to resort to correspondence and oral evidence for the purpose of striking out an important provision which the parties agreed upon and expressed in the agreement': *O'Connor v Hume* [1954] 2 All ER 301 at 306, CA, per Romer LJ. The principle enunciated in these dicta has been recognised from early times: see e g *Lord Cromwel's Case* (1601) 2 Co Rep 69b at 76a note (G 1); *Countess of Rutland's Case* (1604) 5 Co Rep 25b at 26a; *Meres v Ansell* (1771) 3 Wils 275; *Lord Irnham v Child* (1781) 1 Bro CC 92; *Haynes v Hare* (1791) 1 Hy Bl 659 at 664; *Woollam v Hearn* (1802) 7 Ves 211; *Henson v Coope* (1841) 3 Scott NR 48; *Ford v Yates* (1841) 2 Man & G 549; *Holmes v Mitchell* (1859) 7 CBNS 361; *Burges v Wickham* (1863) 3 B & S 669; *Inglis v John Buttery & Co* (1878) 3 App Cas 552, HL; *Edward Lloyd Ltd v Sturgeon Falls Pulp Co* (1901) 85 LT 162 (oral evidence not admissible to enlarge the scope of a written warranty); *Tsang Chuen v Li Po Kwai* [1932] AC 715, PC (where consideration is stated in the deed, evidence that there was no consideration is not admissible); *Meates v Westpac Banking Corpn Ltd* (1990) Times, 5 July, PC. Where a document is construed as a contract and as containing a true and complete record of the terms agreed between the parties, extrinsic evidence will not be admitted to prove a different antecedent oral agreement: *Hutton v Watling* [1948] Ch 398 at 404, [1948] 1 All ER 803 at 805, CA, per Lord Greene MR; and see *WF Trustees Ltd v Expo Safety Systems Ltd* (1993) Times, 24 May. See also *Rabin v Gerson Berger Association Ltd* [1986] 1 All ER 374 at 377, [1986] 1 WLR 526 at 530, CA, per Fox LJ.

10 *Dickson v Fisher* (1768) 1 Wm Bl 664; *Prentice v Hamilton* (1831) Dra 410; *Keane v O'Brien* (1871) IR 5 CL 531. Extrinsic evidence may be admitted to explain the record: *Preston v Peeke* (1858) EB & E 336.

11 See ARBITRATION.

12 See *Free v Hawkins* (1817) 8 Taunt 92 (agreement not to demand payment until sale of certain estate and to dispense with notice of dishonour); *Abrey v Crux* (1869) LR 5 CP 37 (agreement to sell securities before suing on bill); *New London Credit Syndicate v Neale* [1898] 2 QB 487, CA (evidence of contemporaneous agreement to renew instrument); *Hitchins and Coulthurst Co v Northern Leather Co of America and Doushkess* [1914] 3 KB 907 (agreement in defeasance); and see further BILLS OF EXCHANGE AND OTHER NEGOTIABLE INSTRUMENTS vol 4(1) (2002 Reissue) paras 317, 348.

13 See e g *Leduc & Co v Ward* (1888) 20 QBD 475, CA; and SHIPPING AND NAVIGATION vol 43(1) (Reissue) para 1425.

14 *Buckler v Millerd* (1688) 2 Vent 107; *Mease v Mease* (1774) 1 Cowp 47 (where it was sought to show that the bond was given by way of indemnity against another bond); *Tippins v Coates* (1853) 18 Beav 401.

15 See *Woolls v Powling* [1999] All ER (D) 125, (1999) Times, 9 March, CA; and BOUNDARIES vol 4(1) (2002 Reissue) para 929.

16 See e g *Holmes v Mitchell* (1859) 7 CBNS 361; and GUARANTEE AND INDEMNITY vol 20(1) (Reissue) para 171 et seq.

17 *Preston v Merceau* (1779) 2 Wm Bl 1249 (evidence not admissible to prove an agreement to pay an additional rent to that mentioned in a lease); *Jones v Lavington* [1903] 1 KB 253, CA; *Crawford v White City Rink (Newcastle-on-Tyne) Ltd* (1913) 29 TLR 318 (collateral oral agreements between landlord and tenant relating to the subject matter of the written contract held inadmissible); *Henderson v Arthur* [1907] 1 KB 10, CA (oral agreement that lessor should take a three months' bill for each quarter's rent as it fell due, which, by the terms of the lease, was payable quarterly in advance, held inadmissible); but see *City and Westminster Properties (1934) Ltd v Mudd* [1959] Ch 129, [1958] 2 All ER 733 (collateral oral agreement, permitting the tenant to continue to reside in the demised premises despite covenant in new lease for business user only, upheld as a defence to the landlord's action seeking forfeiture for breach of covenant); and para 196 post.

18 *Smith v Jeffryes* (1846) 15 M & W 561 (evidence inadmissible to show that a written agreement for the sale of ware potatoes was intended to apply to a particular quality of potatoes of that description); c f *Frederick E Rose (London) Ltd v William H Pim, Junior & Co Ltd* [1953] 2 QB 450, [1953] 2 All ER 739, CA; *Harnor v Groves* (1855) 15 CB 667 (evidence inadmissible to prove a verbal representation amounting to a warranty); and see *Chanter v Hopkins* (1838) 4 M & W 399 at 406. If goods are sold by a written agreement which describes their quality, and makes no reference to any sample, evidence is not admissible at the instance of either buyer or seller to prove that a sample was shown at the time of the sale in order to show that it was a sale by sample: *Tye v Fynmore* (1813) 3 Camp 462; *Meyer v Everth* (1814) 4 Camp 22.

19 *Glaverbel SA v British Coal Corpn* [1995] FSR 254, [1995] RPC 255, CA.

20 See *Powell v Edmunds* (1810) 12 East 6; and AUCTION vol 2(3) (Reissue) para 243.

21 *Prison Comrs v Middlesex Clerk of the Peace* (1882) 9 QBD 506, CA; *R v Pembridge Inhabitants* (1841) Car & M 157; *Palmer v Newell* (1855) 20 Beav 32 (affd (1856) 5 De GM & G 74).

22 See CUSTOM AND USAGE vol 12(1) (Reissue) para 667; WILLS vol 50 (2005 Reissue) para 481 et seq. However, where a document on its face a deed, but witnessed as a will, was admitted to probate, it was said to be 'clear that extrinsic evidence is admissible for the purpose of shewing with what intention an ambiguous paper has been executed': *Re Slinn's Goods* (1890) 15 PD 156 at 158; and see *Cocks v Nash* (1832) 9 Bing 341 at 346; *Halhead v Young* (1856) 6 E & B 312; *Cowlishaw v Hardy* (1857) 25 Beav 169 at 175; *Turner v Turner, Hall v Turner* (1880) 14 ChD 829; *Mercantile Bank of Sydney v Taylor* [1893] AC 317,

PC; *Henderson v Arthur* [1907] 1 KB 10, CA. This rule does not, of course, prejudice any rights the parties may have to rectification or rescission: see para 189 post; and MISTAKE vol 32 (2005 Reissue) para 50 et seq. As to evidence of intention to explain a latent ambiguity see para 209 post. As to the admissibility of evidence of authority to sign a memorandum of a contract see SALE OF LAND vol 42 (Reissue) para 40.

186.   Principal and agent. Extrinsic evidence generally cannot be received in order to prove that a person appearing, on the face of the document, to be a principal was in fact an agent, if that evidence is inconsistent either with the express terms of the written agreement[1] or with an oral declaration made contemporaneously[2]. Where, however, it is not inconsistent with the written contract to show that the contracting party was only an agent, as where he gives himself no special description and there is nothing in the instrument to define his character[3], extrinsic evidence is admissible to show who the principal is, for the purpose either of charging him on the contract or of enabling him to enforce it[4]. Where a person contracts professedly as an agent, then, in order to charge him on the contract, it may be shown by extrinsic evidence that he is in fact the principal[5]. If, on the construction of a written contract made by an agent he undertakes personal liability, extrinsic evidence of intention is not admissible to exonerate him from liability[6], except that by way of equitable defence he may set up an express agreement between himself and the other contracting party to that effect[7].

1   *Humble v Hunter* (1848) 12 QB 310 (where an agent was described in a charterparty as the owner of the vessel, and it was held that extrinsic evidence was inadmissible to show that he was not the owner, so as to entitle the real owner to sue on the contract); *Formby Bros v Formby* (1910) 102 LT 116, CA (where one of the parties was referred to throughout as 'proprietor,' and it was held that evidence was not admissible to prove that party was acting as agent for an undisclosed principal, for the purpose of charging the principal); but see *Epps v Rothnie* [1945] KB 562 at 565, [1946] 1 All ER 146 at 147, CA, per Scott LJ (where the opinion was expressed that neither of these cases can any longer be regarded as good law); and c f *Pontifex and Wood Ltd v Hartley & Co* (1893) 62 LJQB 196, CA (no concluded contract in writing; extrinsic evidence admissible).

2   *Lucas v De la Cour* (1813) 1 M & S 249.

3   *Humble v Hunter* (1848) as reported in 17 LJQB 350 at 352. It is inconsistent with an instrument to show that a party who contracts as owner or proprietor is merely an agent: see *Fred Drughorn Ltd v Rederiaktiebolaget Trans-Atlantic* [1919] AC 203 at 207, HL, per Viscount Haldane LC. The word 'tenant' or 'lessee' is not inconsistent with agency; but it is otherwise in the case of the description 'lessor', for this implies an antecedent interest in the property: *Danziger v Thompson* [1944] KB 654, [1944] 2 All ER 151.

4   *Bateman v Phillips* (1812) 15 East 272; *Wilson v Hart* (1817) 1 Moore CP 45; *Trueman v Loder* (1840) 11 Ad & El 589; *Morris v Wilson* (1859) 5 Jur NS 168; *Spurr v Cass* (1870) LR 5 QB 656; *Calder v Dobell* (1871) LR 6 CP 486, Ex Ch; *Weidner v Hoggett* (1876) 1 CPD 533; *Fred Drughorn Ltd v Rederiaktiebolaget Trans-Atlantic* [1919] AC 203, HL; *Danziger v Thompson* [1944] KB 654, [1944] 2 All ER 151. The consideration must move from the principal in order to enable him to enforce the contract: *Dunlop Pneumatic Tyre Co v Selfridge & Co Ltd* [1915] AC 847, HL. See AGENCY vol 2(1) (Reissue) para 152.

5   *Railton v Hodgson* (1804) 4 Taunt 576n; *Jenkins v Hutchinson* (1849) 13 QB 744; *Carr v Jackson* (1852) 7 Exch 382; *Adams v Hall* (1877) 37 LT 70; *Young v Schuler* (1883) 11 QBD 651, CA; *Hutcheson v Eaton* (1884) 13 QBD 861, CA; and see AGENCY vol 2(1) (Reissue) para 183 et seq. As to the right of the ostensible agent to sue on the contract in such a case see *Bickerton v Burrell* (1816) 5 M & S 383; *Rayner v Grote* (1846) 15 M & W 359; *Schmalz v Avery* (1851) 16 QB 655; *Sharman v Brandt* (1871) LR 6 QB 720, Ex Ch; contrast *Newborne v Sensolid (Great Britain) Ltd* [1954] 1 QB 45, [1953] 1 All ER 708, CA (where the purported principal was a non-existent company and the contract was a nullity); and see further COMPANIES vol 7(1) (2004 Reissue) para 261.

6   See AGENCY vol 2(1) (Reissue) para 183 et seq.

7   See *Cowie v Witt* (1874) 23 WR 76; and AGENCY vol 2(1) (Reissue) para 183 et seq.

187.   Evidence of previous negotiations. The construction of a document cannot be controlled by previous negotiations[1]; and when a written agreement is carried into effect by a conveyance, the conveyance becomes the final evidence of the intention of the parties, and is not liable to be varied by reference to the agreement[2]; nor is the construction of a written instrument varied by the subsequent declaration[3] or conduct[4] of the parties. The instrument is to be construed as at the time of its execution[5].

1 'The law is that whatever the negotiations may be that precede the purchase, still the parties to the conveyance are bound by it': *Prison Comrs v Middlesex Clerk of the Peace* (1882) 9 QBD 506 at 511, CA, per Jessel MR. Drafts cannot be looked at: *National Bank of Australasia v Falkingham & Sons* [1902] AC 585 at 591, PC; and see *Attwood v Small* (1838) 6 Cl & Fin 232, HL; *London Corpn v Sandon, London Corpn v Metropolitan Rly Co, Metropolitan Rly Co v London Corpn* (1872) 26 LT 86; *British Equitable Assurance Co Ltd v Baily* [1906] AC 35, HL; *Millbourn v Lyons* [1914] 2 Ch 231, CA; *City and Westminster Properties (1934) Ltd v Mudd* [1959] Ch 129, [1958] 2 All ER 733. As to the rule see generally *Prenn v Simmonds* [1971] 3 All ER 237, [1971] 1 WLR 1381, HL (evidence of prior negotiations not admissible in construction of agreement for sale of shares); *Investors Compensation Scheme Ltd v West Bromwich Building Society* [1998] 1 All ER 98, [1998] 1 WLR 896, HL. See, however, *Willson v Greene* [1971] 1 All ER 1098, [1971] 1 WLR 635 (evidence of boundary as pegged out and accepted before contract admitted where parcels in conveyance vague and plan expressed to be for purposes of identification only).

2 Where an executory contract has been carried out by deed, the contract is merged in the deed, so far as the deed covers the subject matter of the contract, and it cannot be used to vary the deed: see *Leggott v Barrett* (1880) 15 ChD 306 at 311, CA, per Brett LJ, and at 309 per James LJ ('you have no right to look at the contract either for the purpose of enlarging or diminishing or modifying the contract which is to be found in the deed itself'); *Williams v Morgan* (1850) 15 QB 782; *Teebay v Manchester, Sheffield and Lincolnshire Rly Co* (1883) 24 ChD 572; *Palmer v Johnson* (1884) 13 QBD 351 at 359, CA; *Millbourn v Lyons* [1914] 2 Ch 231, CA; *International Press Centre v Norwich Union Insurance Co* (1986) 36 BLR 130, [1986] 2 FTLR 229; cf *Greswolde-Williams v Barneby* (1900) 49 WR 203; and see *Salaman v Glover* (1875) LR 20 Eq 444 (where, upon a lease being granted pursuant to an agreement, and in accordance with a scheduled form, a proviso in the agreement excluding certain rights of light and air was read as if inserted in the lease). Similarly, conditions of sale cannot control the construction of the conveyance: *Doe d Norton v Webster* (1840) 12 Ad & El 442. But where a condition in an agreement for sale is capable of taking effect after completion and relates to a matter not dealt with by the conveyance, it will continue to have full force and effect after completion: *Eagon v Dent* [1965] 3 All ER 334 (where it was conceded that a condition of sale had not merged in the assignment); *Hissett v Reading Roofing Co Ltd* [1970] 1 All ER 122, [1969] 1 WLR 1757; and see *White v Taylor (No 2)* [1969] 1 Ch 160 at 180, [1968] 1 All ER 1015 at 1025 per Buckley J; *Hashman, Riback and Bel-Aire Estates Ltd v Anjulin Farms Ltd* [1973] 2 WWR 361, Can SC. A patent ambiguity in a lease may be explained by reference to the counterpart: *Matthews v Smallwood* [1910] 1 Ch 777. The purchaser, however, immediately after the agreement and before the conveyance, is entitled to have everything which the agreement, strictly interpreted, gives him: *Humphries v Horne* (1844) 3 Hare 276 at 277 per Wigram V-C.

3 It is always legitimate to look at all the co-existing circumstances, in order to apply the language and so to construe the contract; but subsequent declarations, showing what the party supposed to be the effect of the contract, are not admissible to construe it: *Lewis v Nicholson* (1852) 18 QB 503 at 510 per Lord Campbell CJ; and see *Doe d Norton v Webster* (1840) 12 Ad & El 442; *Bruner v Moore* [1904] 1 Ch 305 at 310 per Farwell J; *Houlder Bros & Co Ltd v Public Works Comr, Public Works Comr v Houlder Bros & Co Ltd* [1908] AC 276, PC.

4 'No point of law can, I apprehend, be better settled than this: that, in construing the agreement, no acts of the parties subsequent to the making of it are, as such, admissible for the purpose of determining its meaning': *Monro v Taylor* (1848) 8 Hare 51 at 56 per Wigram V-C (affd (1852) 3 Mac & G 713); and see *Bruner v Moore* [1904] 1 Ch 305; *Belton v Bass, Ratcliffe and Gretton Ltd* [1922] 2 Ch 449. This is so, if the words are plain and unambiguous: *North Eastern Rly Co v Lord Hastings* [1900] AC 260 at 263, HL, per Lord Halsbury LC. Compare the different rule where the terms of an ancient instrument (or, perhaps, any instrument of title to land) are doubtful: see para 206 post.

5 *Balfour v Welland* (1809) 16 Ves 151 at 156; *Lord Hastings v North Eastern Rly Co* [1899] 1 Ch 656 at 664, CA (affd sub nom *North Eastern Rly Co v Lord Hastings* [1900] AC 260, HL).

188. Contracts. As regards contracts the rule as to the exclusion of extrinsic evidence is not confined to contracts which are required by law to be evidenced by writing in order to be enforceable[1], but applies generally in all cases where the agreement between the parties is in fact reduced to writing[2].

Extrinsic evidence is not only excluded as a general rule in reference to matters which are expressly dealt with by the written agreement, but also in reference to terms implied by law with regard to which the document is silent[3].

1 See CONTRACT vol 9(1) (Reissue) para 623 et seq.

2 However, as to proceedings for discretionary remedies such as rectification, rescission or specific performance see para 189 post. Previously (i e before courts were courts of both law and equity, when the distinction between law and equity was important) the rule was of equal force in equity as at law: see

Price v Dyer (1810) 17 Ves 356; *Clowes v Higginson* (1813) 1 Ves & B 524; *Ball v Storie* (1823) 1 Sim & St 210; *Croome v Lediard* (1834) 2 My & K 251; *Martin v Pycroft* (1852) 2 De GM & G 785 at 795.

3   *Rich v Jackson* (1794) 4 Bro CC 514 (lease silent as to payment of taxes; evidence not admissible to prove a verbal agreement that it was to be free of all taxes); *Croome v Lediard* (1834) 2 My & K 251 (agreement by A to buy an estate from B, and B to buy another estate from A; evidence not admissible to show that a mutual exchange was intended, and that the contracts were to be dependent on each other; specific performance of one of the contracts decreed, though the defendant was unable to show a good title to the property sold by him); *Ford v Yates* (1841) 2 Man & G 549 (written contract for sale of hops, nothing being said as to credit; evidence not admissible to show that by the course of dealing between the parties the buyer was entitled to six months' credit); *Burges v Wickham* (1863) 3 B & S 669 at 696–697 per Blackburn J; *Evans v Roe* (1872) LR 7 CP 138 (written agreement for service at a weekly salary, implying a weekly hiring; evidence of conversations showing an intention that the hiring should be a yearly one not admissible). There is a dictum in *McGrory v Alderdale Estate Co* [1918] AC 503 at 508, HL, to the effect that the implied obligation, in an open contract for the sale of land, to make a good title may be rebutted by evidence that the purchaser knew of a particular defect, but the judgments in this case are directed to the consideration of whether there was a waiver and do not, it is submitted, impugn the statement in the text. As to cases where the document does not contain the whole contract see para 190 note 6 post.

189.   Proceedings in which rule not enforced. The rule as to the exclusion of extrinsic evidence is not enforced when the court is asked to grant a discretionary remedy such as rectification or rescission on the ground of mistake[1] or specific performance. In proceedings for specific performance the defendant is allowed to give extrinsic evidence to show that the written instrument does not represent the real contract between the parties[2] or, if the claimant shows by extrinsic evidence that owing to mutual mistake the written instrument does not represent the real contract, he may be granted specific performance of the instrument as rectified[3].

Moreover the rule is strictly applied only when the language of the instrument is clear[4]; if the construction is doubtful, and the doubt cannot be removed in any other way, it is permissible to refer to a preliminary agreement, at any rate if recited in the instrument[5], or to surrounding circumstances at the time that the instrument was made for the purpose of adding words to it[6], or to acts done in pursuance of the instrument[7], though not to mere subsequent declarations.

1   See eg *Baker v Paine* (1750) 1 Ves Sen 456; and MISTAKE vol 32 (2005 Reissue) para 50 et seq.
2   See eg *Ramsbottom v Gosden* (1812) 1 Ves & B 165 (where the plaintiff was put to his election to have the contract performed according to the oral agreement or to have his proceedings dismissed); and see further MISTAKE vol 32 (2005 Reissue) para 43; SPECIFIC PERFORMANCE vol 44(1) (Reissue) para 876.
3   *Craddock Bros Ltd v Hunt* [1923] 2 Ch 136, CA; *United States of America v Motor Trucks Ltd* [1924] AC 196, PC; and see SPECIFIC PERFORMANCE vol 44(1) (Reissue) para 876. Extrinsic evidence can only be admitted where the written agreement is not drawn according to the intention of the parties: *Omerod v Hardman* (1801) 5 Ves 722 at 730.
4   See *Clifton v Walmesley* (1794) 5 Term Rep 564.
5   *Leggott v Barrett* (1880) 15 ChD 306 at 311, CA, per Brett LJ ('if there is any doubt about the construction of the governing words, the recital may be looked at to determine what is the true construction'). See also para 218 post.
6   *Shipley UDC v Bradford Corpn* [1936] Ch 375 at 389–391, CA, per Clauson J ('per annum' added to '£540' and 'per diem' to '450,000 gallons'). See also *Willson v Greene* [1971] 1 All ER 1098, [1971] 1 WLR 635 (evidence of surrounding circumstances existing before the contract admitted where parcels in conveyance vague and plan expressed to be for purposes of identification only); and para 198 post.
7   See para 206 post.

190.   Intention not to make binding contract. It may be proved by extrinsic evidence that a document which purports to be a contract is informal and was not intended to be a binding agreement, although it is signed by the person who refuses to be bound by it[1] or that it was not intended to contain all the terms[2], or that it was signed by mistake[3]. In the case of bought and sold notes, it may be shown by either party that the sale was merely colourable and the price nominal, and that it was not their intention in signing the notes to make a binding contract[4]; and in the case of a document purporting to be a written agreement for the sale of property, evidence has been admitted to show that it was only a pretended sale to avoid execution against the property[5].

It is in all cases a question of fact whether a particular document was intended to express the whole of the terms of the contract between the parties[6], and with what intention it was signed by one or other of the parties[7], and on these points extrinsic evidence is admissible.

1   *Pattle v Hornibrook* [1897] 1 Ch 25 (document signed by both plaintiff and defendant; it was held that the defendant might prove that he did not intend to be bound until satisfied as to the plaintiff's responsibility). See also *Harris v Rickett* (1859) 4 H & N 1 (oral agreement admissible where writing did not contain, and was not intended to contain, entire obligation); *Clever v Kirkman* (1875) 33 LT 672; *Lewis v Brass* (1877) 3 QBD 667, CA; *Hussey v Horne-Payne* (1879) 4 App Cas 311 at 323, HL, per Lord Selborne; *Gillespie Bros & Co v Cheney, Eggar & Co* [1896] 2 QB 59.
2   See *McCollin v Giplin* (1881) 6 QBD 516 at 518, CA; *Pontifex and Wood Ltd v Hartley & Co* (1893) 62 LJQB 196 at 200, CA; *Lindley v Lacey* (1864) 17 CBNS 578. Other examples are *Jeffery v Walton* (1816) 1 Stark 267; *Allan v Sundius* (1862) 1 H & C 123 at 131; *Lockett v Nicklin* (1848) 2 Exch 93.
3   *Pym v Campbell* (1856) 6 E & B 370 at 374 per Crompton J; and see *Gudgen v Besset* (1856) 6 E & B 986; *Furness v Meek* (1857) 27 LJ Ex 34; *Pattle v Hornibrook* [1897] 1 Ch 25 at 30. Such evidence is admissible not to contradict the face of the agreement but to prove a mistake therein which cannot be proved otherwise: *Baker v Paine* (1750) 1 Ves Sen 456 at 457 per Lord Hardwicke LC; and see *Olley v Fisher* (1886) 34 ChD 367 at 369.
4   *Rogers v Hadley* (1863) 2 H & C 227.
5   *Bowes v Foster* (1858) 2 H & N 779.
6   *Jones v Littledale* (1837) 1 Nev & PKB 677 (invoice by brokers as sellers of goods by auction); *Allen v Pink* (1838) 4 M & W 140 (receipt given on the sale of a horse held not to exclude evidence of a verbal warranty, there being no evidence that the buyer had agreed that the receipt should contain a statement of the whole of the terms of the contract); *Lockett v Nicklin* (1848) 2 Exch 93; *Moore v Campbell* (1854) 10 Exch 323 (broker, employed by buyer, sent contract note to seller; seller sent note to broker varying the terms; it was held, in an action by the buyer, to be a question of fact whether the note sent by the seller was intended by both parties to be the contract between them); *Holding v Elliott* (1860) 5 H & N 117 (invoice); *Long v Millar* (1879) 4 CPD 450, CA (receipt for part payment and memorandum of agreement); *Harling v Eddy* [1951] 2 KB 739, [1951] 2 All ER 212, CA (oral warranty at auction sale of heifer held to override printed auction conditions).
7   *Latch v Wedlake* (1840) 11 Ad & El 959 (agreement expressed to be made between the plaintiff and three partners, executed by the plaintiff and two of the partners; it was held to be a question for the jury whether the two partners intended to sign on behalf of all three, the circumstances indicating that the partners did not intend to be bound unless all three signed); *Young v Schuler* (1883) 11 QBD 651, CA (evidence of contemporaneous statements to show that a person contracting as an agent intended to sign, not only as an agent, but also as a surety for the principal).

191.   Condition precedent to binding contract.   Extrinsic evidence is admissible to show that a written agreement which purports to be unconditional was in fact executed with the intention that it should only take effect as a contract on the performance of a condition precedent[1]. For example, in the case of a written agreement for the assignment of a lease, it may be proved that there was a contemporaneous oral agreement that the contract should be null and void if the lessor did not consent to the assignment[2]; a person signing a contract as a surety may prove that he only intended to be bound in the event of a proposed co-surety joining[3]; it may be shown that an instrument was not intended by a party to it to operate as an agreement unless it was signed by the other party[4] or by a third person[5]; a contemporaneous oral agreement that a written contract should not be a bargain unless a third person approved of it may be proved[6]; and a person who has signed an agreement may prove that he did not intend to bind himself until he had satisfied himself of the responsibility of the other contracting party, and that the other party knew that[7]. So, it may be proved that a written agreement was not intended to operate from the time of its execution but from some future and uncertain time[8].

This principle applies to bills of exchange and other negotiable instruments delivered subject to a condition, as between the immediate parties[9].

1   *Murray v Earl of Stair* (1823) 2 B & C 82; *Latch v Wedlake* (1840) 11 Ad & El 959 (evidence of remarks of plaintiff during negotiations); *Moore v Campbell* (1854) 10 Exch 323 (broker sending a sold note may show that it was only intended to operate as a contract if the person to whom it was sent signed and returned a corresponding note); *Lindley v Lacey* (1864) 17 CBNS 578; *Guardhouse v Blackburn* (1866) LR 1 P & D 109; *Clever v Kirkman* (1875) 33 LT 672; and see notes 2–8 infra. As to the delivery of a deed as an escrow see *Furness v Meek* (1857) 27 LJ Ex 34; and paras 37–39 ante.

2   *Wallis v Littell* (1861) 11 CBNS 369.

3   *Evans v Bremridge* (1856) 8 De GM & G 100.

4   *Furness v Meek* (1857) 27 LJ Ex 34; *McClean v Kennard* (1874) 9 Ch App 336.

5   *Boyd v Hind* (1857) 1 H & N 938, Ex Ch.

6   *Pym v Campbell* (1856) 6 E & B 370.

7   *Pattle v Hornibrook* [1897] 1 Ch 25.

8   *Davis v Jones* (1856) 17 CB 625.

9   See BILLS OF EXCHANGE AND OTHER NEGOTIABLE INSTRUMENTS vol 4(1) (2002 Reissue) para 346.

192.   Further examples of admissibility of extrinsic evidence. Extrinsic evidence is also admissible to show that the transaction is affected by fraud[1], immorality or illegality[2], duress[3], mistake[4] or misrepresentation[5]; to show the true consideration[6], or the existence of consideration[7], or of consideration in addition to that stated[8]; and to show the nature of the transaction[9], or the true relationship of the parties[10].

1   *Clowes v Higginson* (1813) 1 Ves & B 524 at 527 per Plumer V-C; *Foster v Mackinnon* (1869) LR 4 CP 704; *Lewis v Clay* (1897) 67 LJQB 224; *Guildford Trust Ltd v Pohl and Maritch* (1928) 72 Sol Jo 171 at 172; and see generally MISREPRESENTATION AND FRAUD.

2   *Collins v Blantern* (1767) 2 Wils 341; *Woods v Wise* [1955] 2 QB 29, [1955] 1 All ER 767, CA (whether sum payable under an underlease constituted an illegal premium); and see CONTRACT vol 9(1) (Reissue) para 838.

3   See CONTRACT vol 9(1) (Reissue) paras 709–711; EQUITY vol 16(2) (Reissue) para 436.

4   *Clowes v Higginson* (1813) 1 Ves & B 524; *Raffles v Wichelhaus* (1864) 2 H & C 906 at 908; and see generally MISTAKE.

5   *Curtis v Chemical Cleaning and Dyeing Co* [1951] 1 KB 805, [1951] 1 All ER 631, CA; and see generally MISREPRESENTATION AND FRAUD.

6   *R v Scammonden Inhabitants* (1789) 3 Term Rep 474; *Townend v Toker* (1866) 1 Ch App 446 at 459–460; and cf *Cochrane v Moore* (1890) 25 QBD 57, CA.

7   *Re Holland, Gregg v Holland* [1902] 2 Ch 360 at 388, CA.

8   *Clifford v Turrell* (1845) 14 LJ Ch 390; *Re Barnstaple Second Annuitant Society* (1884) 50 LT 424; *Frith v Frith* [1906] AC 254, PC; *Turner v Forwood* [1951] 1 All ER 746, CA; and see para 194 post.

9   *Barton v Bank of New South Wales* (1890) 15 App Cas 379, PC (conveyance on its face absolute may be shown to be a mortgage); *Rochefoucauld v Boustead* [1897] 1 Ch 196, CA (conveyance on its face absolute may be shown to be subject to a trust); *Beattie v Jenkinson* [1971] 3 All ER 495, [1971] 1 WLR 1419 (onus not discharged of proving that conveyance on its face absolute was in fact by way of security); and see *Stoneleigh Finance Ltd v Phillips* [1965] 2 QB 537, [1965] 1 All ER 513, CA; *Kingsley v Sterling Industrial Securities Ltd* [1967] 2 QB 747, [1966] 2 All ER 414, CA; *Snook v London and West Riding Investments Ltd* [1967] 2 QB 786, [1967] 1 All ER 518, CA; *United Dominions Trust Ltd v Beech, Savan, Tabner and Thompson* [1972] 1 Lloyd's Rep 546; *United Dominions Trust Ltd v Western* [1976] QB 513 at 522–523, [1975] 3 All ER 1017 at 1023, CA, per Megaw LJ (note that *Campbell Discount Co Ltd v Gall* [1961] 1 QB 431, [1961] 2 All ER 104, CA, is no longer good law); and CONSUMER CREDIT vol 9(1) (Reissue) para 23 et seq. Cf *Re Boyes, Boyes v Carritt* (1884) 26 ChD 531; *Re Duke of Marlborough, Davis v Whitehead* [1894] 2 Ch 133; and see para 198 et seq post; and TRUSTS vol 48 (2000 Reissue) paras 544, 573; WILLS vol 50 (2005 Reissue) para 481 et seq. As to the right of one of several purchasers to show that they are mutually entitled to the benefit of covenants entered into by each of the purchasers of several plots on one estate, although not expressly mentioned in the conveyance, and the distinction between this right and a collateral agreement see *Spicer v Martin* (1888) 14 App Cas 12, HL; para 196 post; and EQUITY vol 16(2) (Reissue) paras 724–725, 750.

10 See para 185 ante. See also *Newell v Radford* (1867) LR 3 CP 52 (to show the trades of the parties to a memorandum of sale as indicating which was seller and which was buyer); *Macdonald v Whitfield* (1883) 8 App Cas 733 at 745, PC (to prove that three successive indorsees of a bill of exchange were sureties inter se for the same debt); *Re Lander and Bagley's Contract* [1892] 3 Ch 41 (to show date of commencement of

a lease); *Bank of Australasia v Palmer* [1897] AC 540, PC (to show that a document signed by one of the parties to an agreement did not form part of the agreement).

193.   Extrinsic evidence to prove date.   Extrinsic evidence is admissible to prove the date of delivery of a deed, or of the execution of any other written instrument. A deed takes effect from delivery, and any other written instrument from the date of execution, and though the date expressed in the instrument is prima facie to be taken as the date of delivery or execution[1], this does not exclude extrinsic evidence of the actual date; and the actual date, when proved, prevails, in case of variance, over the apparent date[2]. A reference in the deed to its date (for example, a covenant to do a thing within a specified time after the date of the deed) is, however, construed as referring to the date expressed in the deed, unless there is no date so expressed, or an impossible date, and then the reference is taken to be to the date of delivery[3].

1   *Malpas v Clements* (1850) 19 LJQB 435; *Morgan v Whitmore* (1851) 6 Exch 716 at 719; and see *Re Shaw, Public Trustee v Little* (1914) 110 LT 924, CA (appointment of Public Trustee); and para 60 ante.
2   *Goddard's Case* (1584) 2 Co Rep 4b; *Clayton's Case* (1585) 5 Co Rep 1a; Shep Touch 72; *Hall v Cazenove* (1804) 4 East 477; *Steele v Mart* (1825) 4 B & C 272. The rule uniformly acted upon from the time of *Clayton's Case* supra to the present date is that a deed or other writing must be taken to speak from the time of the execution, and not from the date apparent on the face of the deed; that date, indeed, is to be taken prima facie as the true time of execution; but as soon as the contrary appears, the apparent date is to be utterly disregarded: *Browne v Burton* (1847) 5 Dow & L 289 at 292 per Patteson J; and cf *Jayne v Hughes* (1854) 10 Exch 430 at 433; *Reffell v Reffell* (1866) LR 1 P & D 139 at 142.
3   Co Litt 46b; *Styles v Wardle* (1825) 4 B & C 908.

194.   Extrinsic evidence to prove consideration.   Where no consideration[1], or a nominal consideration[2], is expressed in the instrument, or the consideration is expressed in general terms[3] or is ambiguously stated[4], extrinsic evidence is admissible to prove the real consideration[5]; and where a substantial consideration is expressed in the instrument, extrinsic evidence is admissible to prove an additional consideration, provided that this is not inconsistent with the terms of the instrument[6]. It is not in contradiction to the instrument to prove a larger consideration than that which is stated[7]. Extrinsic evidence is admissible to prove the illegality of the consideration[8].

Extrinsic evidence may also be admitted to prove payment of consideration[9] and to prove by whom it was paid[10].

1   Shep Touch 510; *Pott v Todhunter* (1845) 2 Coll 76 at 84; *Townend v Toker* (1866) 1 Ch App 446 at 459; *Llanelly Rly and Dock Co v London and North Western Rly Co* (1873) 8 Ch App 942 at 955 (affd (1875) LR 7 HL 550); *Re Holland, Gregg v Holland* [1902] 2 Ch 360 at 388, CA.
2   *Re British and Foreign Cork Co, Leifchild's Case* (1865) LR 1 Eq 231; *Turner v Forwood* [1951] 1 All ER 746, CA.
3   Shep Touch 510; *Mildmay's Case* (1584) 1 Co Rep 175a at 176a, b; *Tull v Parlett* (1829) Mood & M 472 ('divers good considerations'); *Gale v Williamson* (1841) 8 M & W 405 ('natural love and affection').
4   *Booker v Seddon* (1858) 1 F & F 196.
5   As to non-admissibility for the purpose of explaining the promise of guarantee see GUARANTEE AND INDEMNITY vol 20(1) (Reissue) para 171 et seq. See also *Pao On v Lau Yiu Long* [1980] AC 614 at 631, [1979] 3 All ER 65 at 75, PC.
6   *Villers v Beamont* (1556) 2 Dyer 146a; *Vernon's Case* (1572) 4 Co Rep 1a at 3a; *Bedell's Case* (1607) 7 Co Rep 40a; *R v Scammonden Inhabitants* (1789) 3 Term Rep 474; *Nixon v Hamilton* (1838) 2 Dr & Wal 364 at 385; *Clifford v Turrell* (1841) 1 Y & C Ch Cas 138 at 149 (on appeal (1845) 9 Jur 633 at 633–634 per Lord Lyndhurst LC ('the settled rule of law is, that you may go out of the deed to prove a consideration that stands well with that stated on the face of the deed, but you cannot be allowed to prove a consideration inconsistent with it')); *Frail v Ellis* (1852) 16 Beav 350; *Frith v Frith* [1906] AC 254, PC. In *Peacock v Monk* (1748) 1 Ves Sen 127 at 128, Lord Hardwicke LC expressed the view that, unless the deed said 'and for other considerations', a consideration in addition to that expressed would be contrary to the deed, and evidence of it could not be admitted; but this must be taken to be overruled: see *Clifford v Turrell* supra; *Bayspoole v Collins* (1871) 6 Ch App 228; *Stiles v A-G* (1740) 2 Atk 152.
7   *Clifford v Turrell* (1845) 14 LJ Ch 390; *Frith v Frith* [1906] AC 254, PC; *Turner v Forwood* [1951] 1 All ER 746 at 748, CA, per Lord Goddard CJ.

8   See para 68 ante.
9   *Smith v Battams* (1857) 26 LJ Ex 232.
10 *R v Llangunnor Inhabitants* (1831) 2 B & Ad 616.

195.   Evidence of usage.   Evidence of usage is admissible for the purpose of adding to a written contract provisions (which are not inconsistent therewith) in respect of matters upon which it is silent[1].

1   As to a treatment of the subject in detail see CUSTOM AND USAGE vol 12(1) (Reissue) para 677 et seq.
    See also paras 181 ante, 203 post.

196.   Evidence of collateral oral agreements.   Under certain conditions evidence may be given of an oral agreement contemporaneous with and touching the subject matter of a written agreement and as to which the written agreement is wholly silent[1]. The necessary conditions are that the oral agreement must be entirely collateral to the written agreement[2], that it must not contradict the written agreement[3], and that it must be proved strictly[4]. The oral agreement will be more readily enforced if it was an inducement to entering into the written agreement[5]. The oral agreement, moreover, must not be such as is required by the Statute of Frauds[6] or otherwise to be in writing[7].

1   *Mercantile Agency Co v Flitwick Chalybeate Co* (1897) 14 TLR 90, HL; *Edward Lloyd Ltd v Sturgeon Falls Pulp Co Ltd* (1901) 85 LT 162 (verbal warranty respecting matter on which a written contract was silent); and see notes 2–4 infra.
2   The following agreements have been held to be collateral: (1) an oral agreement by a landlord to destroy rabbits, made on the granting of a lease of grassland (*Morgan v Griffith* (1871) LR 6 Exch 70; *Erskine v Adeane* (1873) 8 Ch App 756); and (2) a verbal representation, amounting to warranty, made upon letting a house, that the drains are in good order (*De Lassalle v Guildford* [1901] 2 KB 215, CA). If the vendor assumes to assert a fact of which the buyer is ignorant, this is evidence of an intention to warrant the fact, but it is not conclusive: *Heilbut, Symons & Co v Buckleton* [1913] AC 30 at 50, HL, overruling on this point *De Lassalle v Guildford* supra. See also *Collins v Hopkins* [1923] 2 KB 617. An oral agreement to put the premises into repair has been held to be collateral (*Mann v Nunn* (1874) 43 LJCP 241); although this case has been doubted (*Angell v Duke* (1875) 32 LT 320). On an agreement to let a house and scheduled furniture a previous oral agreement to provide more furniture is not admissible (*Angell v Duke* supra; *Burtsal v Bianchi* (1891) 65 LT 678); but in *Angell v Duke* (1875) LR 10 QB 174 (an earlier stage), such an agreement was held to be collateral. See also *Lindley v Lacey* (1864) 17 CBNS 578; *Spicer v Martin* (1888) 14 App Cas 12, HL; *Crawford v White City Rink (Newcastle-on-Tyne) Ltd* (1913) 29 TLR 318; *Miller v Cannon Hill Estates Ltd* [1931] 2 KB 113; *Jameson v Kinmell Bay Land Co Ltd* (1931) 47 TLR 593, CA (oral promise by the vendor of a building plot that a road giving access to the plot would be constructed); *City and Westminster Properties (1934) Ltd v Mudd* [1959] Ch 129, [1958] 2 All ER 733 (collateral oral agreement enforced permitting the tenant to continue to reside in the demised premises despite covenant in new lease for business user only). See also *J Evans & Son (Portsmouth) Ltd v Andrea Merzario Ltd* [1976] 2 All ER 930, [1976] 1 WLR 1078, CA (oral assurance that goods in containers would be shipped under deck).
3   *Morgan v Griffith* (1871) LR 6 Exch 70 at 73; *Erskine v Adeane* (1873) 8 Ch App 756 at 766; *New London Credit Syndicate Ltd v Neale* [1898] 2 QB 487, CA; *Edward Lloyd Ltd v Sturgeon Falls Pulp Co Ltd* (1901) 85 LT 162; *Henderson v Arthur* [1907] 1 KB 10, CA; *Hitchings and Coulthurst Co v Northern Leather Co of America and Doushkess* [1914] 3 KB 907. See further BILLS OF EXCHANGE AND OTHER NEGOTIABLE INSTRUMENTS vol 4(1) (2002 Reissue) para 348.
4   *Heilbut, Symons & Co v Buckleton* [1913] AC 30 at 47, HL, per Lord Moulton; *Jacobs v Batavia and General Plantations Trust* [1924] 2 Ch 329 at 335–336, CA; *Hodges v Jones* [1935] Ch 657 at 667–668. Formal written documents should only be qualified by reference to oral transactions where the evidence is clear and compelling, particularly when it is sought to affect persons who were not themselves party to the transactions: *Lee-Parker v Izzet (No 2)* [1972] 2 All ER 800, [1972] 1 WLR 775.
5   *Morgan v Griffith* (1871) LR 6 Exch 70; *Erskine v Adeane* (1873) 8 Ch App 756; and cf *Seago v Deane* (1828) 4 Bing 459.
6   See the Statute of Frauds (1677) s 4 (as amended) (replaced and repealed for certain purposes: see para 141 note 1 ante); and para 145 ante.
7   If the contract is really collateral, it is not required to be in writing merely because the principal agreement, which is in writing, relates to an interest in land: *Angell v Duke* (1875) LR 10 QB 174 at 178; *Boston v Boston* [1904] 1 KB 124, CA; and cf *Mechelen v Wallace* (1837) 7 Ad & El 49. See also CONTRACT vol 9(1) (Reissue) para 627.

197. Evidence of explanatory note accompanying form. Where a form, such as a claim form, obviously intended to be read by lawyers, is accompanied by an explanatory note obviously intended to be read by laymen, it seems that, although it is the terms of the claim form which governs the legal relationship, account may be taken of the note in construing the form[1].

1 See *Investors Compensation Scheme Ltd v West Bromwich Building Society* [1998] 1 All ER 98 at 115, [1998] 1 WLR 896 at 913, HL, per Lord Hoffmann.

(ii) To Explain the Meaning and Application of Words

198. Surrounding circumstances. The object of interpretation is, as already stated, to ascertain the intention of the parties to the instrument as expressed by the words they have used, that is what the user of the words would objectively have been understood to mean[1]; and, since the words are the sole guide to the intention[2], extrinsic evidence of that intention is not admissible, save in the case of a latent ambiguity which cannot otherwise be resolved[3].

Extrinsic evidence is, however, admissible both to ascertain where necessary the meaning of the words used[4], and to identify the persons or objects to which they are to be applied[5], for example to connect the language of a deed with the property conveyed[6], and, since the meaning and the application will depend upon the circumstances surrounding the author at the time when the words were used[7], the same principle requires that evidence of such circumstances should be admitted[8]. The court, which has to construe the document, ought to know the surrounding circumstances at the time when it was executed[9], so as to place itself, as nearly as possible, in the position of the parties[10]. In a commercial contract the court should know the commercial purpose of the contract and this in turn presupposes knowledge of the genesis of the transaction, the background, the context, and the market in which the parties are operating[11]. The intention of the parties is expressed in the words, used as they were with regard to the particular circumstances and facts[12]. Moreover, it may appear from the surrounding circumstances that a series of instruments, although not expressly referring to each other, are part of the same transaction, so that they must be construed together[13]; and evidence is admissible for this purpose[14]. However, the surrounding circumstances which are admissible under these principles may not include any evidence directly proving the state of mind of the maker or makers of the document (for instance, their instructions for preparing it, statements as to what he or they intended to do[15], and his or their known or secret views, likes and dislikes, prejudices and opinions[16], or drafts of the document or the past history of negotiations leading up to it[17], or any evidence that the maker or makers of the document habitually used ordinary words in a sense peculiar to himself or themselves, unless he or they shared this usage with a sizeable class of persons[18] or the words can be shown to form a code intended to prevent their being correctly understood by unauthorised persons[19]).

1 See *Mannai Investment Co Ltd v Eagle Star Life Assurance Co Ltd* [1997] AC 749 at 775, [1997] 3 All ER 352 at 376, HL, per Lord Hoffmann; *Investors Compensation Scheme Ltd v West Bromwich Building Society* [1998] 1 All ER 98 at 114–115, [1998] 1 WLR 896 at 912–913, HL, per Lord Hoffmann. See also paras 164–166 ante.

2 See para 165 ante.

3 See para 209 post. Surrounding circumstances, however strong, will not, it seems, prevail over clear language in the instrument: *National Society for the Prevention of Cruelty to Children v Scottish National Society for the Prevention of Cruelty to Children* [1915] AC 207, HL; *Grigsby v Melville* [1973] 3 All ER 455, [1974] 1 WLR 80, CA (evidence of circumstances surrounding transaction not admissible to contradict plain language of conveyance).

4 Ie evidence to enable the court to discover the meaning of the terms of the written document, and to apply them to the facts: *Shore v Wilson* (1842) 9 Cl & Fin 355 at 555, HL, per Parke B. By 'meaning' is

meant either the ordinary or some special meaning; not the particular meaning, varying from such ordinary or special meaning, which the author of the document may have had in view. See *Henry Boot & Sons Ltd v LCC* [1959] 1 All ER 77 at 79–80, [1959] 1 WLR 133 at 137–138, CA; on appeal sub nom *LCC v Henry Boot & Sons Ltd* [1959] 3 All ER 636 at 640–641, [1959] 1 WLR at 1075–1077, HL (on the question whether holiday credits fell within the expression 'rates of wages' in a rise and fall clause in a building contract, previous views expressed by the London County Council to the other party to the contract, either directly or through the builders' trade association, as to the meaning of the expression in the standard form of contract employed held irrelevant); and see para 203 note 3 post.

5   Extrinsic evidence of every material fact which will enable the court to ascertain the nature and qualities of the subject matter of the instrument, or, in other words, to identify the persons and things to which the instrument refers, must of necessity be received: *Inglis v John Buttery & Co* (1878) 3 App Cas 552, HL (surrounding circumstances to be considered, but not the communings of the parties); *Bank of New Zealand v Simpson* [1900] AC 182 at 188, PC; *Cameron v Wiggins* [1901] 1 KB 1, DC (initial letters N M added to invoice as description of the goods at request of the purchaser); *Van Diemen's Land Co v Table Cape Marine Board* [1906] AC 92, PC; *Charrington & Co Ltd v Wooder* [1914] AC 71, HL; *Janson v Poole* (1915) 84 LJKB 1543 (extrinsic evidence admitted to identify insurance policy which had been reinsured); *Watcham v A-G of East Africa Protectorate* [1919] AC 533, PC (acts of user before grant to explain what was granted); *Laprairie Common Corpn v Compagnie de Jésus* [1921] 1 AC 314 at 323, PC (other documents of like date admitted to explain sense in which words were used in an ancient grant); *White v Taylor (No 2)* [1969] 1 Ch 160 at 180, 183, [1968] 1 All ER 1015 at 1025, 1027 per Buckley J. However, where the document is modern, and the meaning can be discovered by construction, extrinsic evidence is inadmissible: *Re Duncan and Pryce* [1913] WN 117 at 118; *Davies v Powell Duffryn Steam Coal Co Ltd* (1920) 36 TLR 358 at 359 (affd (1921) 91 LJ Ch 40, CA). In relation to wills see WILLS vol 50 (2005 Reissue) para 481 et seq.

6   *Doe d Norton v Webster* (1840) 12 Ad & El 442; *Lyle v Richards* (1866) LR 1 HL 222; *Fox v Clarke* (1874) LR 9 QB 565, Ex Ch; *Plant v Bourne* [1897] 2 Ch 281, CA; and see BOUNDARIES vol 4(1) (2002 Reissue) para 929. Previous acts of user by a grantee from the Crown are admissible where the grant is in confirmation of such user: see *Van Diemen's Land Co v Table Cape Marine Board* [1906] AC 92, PC. In *Watcham v A-G of East Africa Protectorate* [1919] AC 533, evidence of user was admitted to explain what was granted, but this is in general not allowed in a modern grant: see para 206 post.

7   *Shore v Wilson* (1842) 9 Cl & Fin 355 at 580, HL, per Lord Cottenham; *River Wear Comrs v Adamson* (1877) 2 App Cas 743 at 763, HL, per Lord Blackburn.

8   *Mason v Cole* (1849) 4 Exch 375 (building scheme); *Mumford v Gething* (1859) 7 CBNS 305; *Stucley v Baily* (1862) 1 H & C 405; *Cave v Hastings* (1881) 7 QBD 125; *Spicer v Martin* (1888) 14 App Cas 12, HL (restrictive covenants in lease; similar covenants in other leases of premises forming part of the same block of buildings); *Oliver v Hunting* (1890) 44 ChD 205; *Olympia Oil and Cake Co Ltd v North-Eastern Rly Co* (1913) 30 TLR 236 (evidence of existing rates considered before making agreement in respect of rates for traffic over railway siding); *Plumrose Ltd v Real and Leasehold Estates Investment Society Ltd* [1969] 3 All ER 1441, [1970] 1 WLR 52 (where certain letters were admitted as part of the surrounding circumstances in order to show the general object of the transaction and hence the precise meaning of a phrase in a lease). The extent of a repairing covenant in a lease must be measured by the age and class of the buildings demised, and evidence of the state of the premises may be given: *Payne v Haine* (1847) 16 M & W 541; *Proudfoot v Hart* (1890) 25 QBD 42, CA; and see *Burges v Wickham* (1863) 3 B & S 669. As to the precise meaning of a covenant in a lease to use the demised premises for business purposes only see *City and Westminster Properties (1934) Ltd v Mudd* [1959] Ch 129, [1958] 2 All ER 733 (held permissible to consider the nature of the premises and, if they had been adapted in part for use as a residence, the operation of the covenant might have been confined to the part in fact used as business premises; but inadmissible to consider the past history of the matter, and hence it was irrelevant that the tenant had, before the grant of the lease in question, habitually slept on the premises to the knowledge of the landlord; and cf *Levermore v Jobey* [1956] 2 All ER 362, [1956] 1 WLR 697, CA. As to proof of surrounding circumstances to show the nature and extent of a guarantee see eg *Heffield v Meadows* (1869) LR 4 CP 595; and GUARANTEE AND INDEMNITY vol 20(1) (Reissue) para 171 et seq. As to proof of such circumstances to explain the meaning of terms in marine policies see eg *Houlder Bros & Co Ltd v Public Works Comr, Public Works Comr v Houlder Bros & Co Ltd* [1908] AC 276, PC; and INSURANCE vol 25 (2003 Reissue) para 228.

9   'In construing all instruments, you must know what the facts were when the agreement was entered into': *Cannon v Villars* (1878) 8 ChD 415 at 419 per Jessel MR; and see *Smith v Doe d Jersey* (1821) 2 Brod & Bing 473 at 550 per Bayley J; *Shore v Wilson* (1842) 9 Cl & Fin 355 at 512, HL, per Erskine J; *Earl of Bradford v Earl of Romney* (1862) 30 Beav 431 at 436; *Sidebotham v Knott* (1872) 20 WR 415; *Bulstrode v Lambert* [1953] 2 All ER 728 at 730–731 per Upjohn J; *Tophams Ltd v Earl of Sefton* [1967] 1 AC 50 at 63, [1966] 1 All ER 1039 at 1041–1042, HL, per Lord Hodson. The evidence of surrounding circumstances of a contract should be restricted to evidence of the factual background known to the parties at or before the date of the contract, including evidence of the 'genesis' and objectively the 'aim' of the transaction:

Prenn v Simmonds [1971] 3 All ER 237, [1971] 1 WLR 1381, HL. For the purpose of ascertaining rights under an employees' insurance scheme established by trust deed, the court looked at a booklet issued by the employers in connection with the scheme: *Bowskill v Dawson* [1955] 1 QB 13 at 28, [1954] 2 All ER 649 at 659, CA, per Romer LJ. See also *Charrington & Co Ltd v Wooder* [1914] AC 71, HL, where evidence of surrounding circumstances was admitted for the purpose of construing the term 'market' with reference to a particular trade in a stipulation for the supply of goods at 'the fair market price'. The court cannot, however, receive evidence for the purpose of contradicting a document which is unambiguous: *Davies v Powell Duffryn Steam Coal Co* (1920) 36 TLR 358; affd (1921) 91 LJ Ch 40, CA.

10   *Hart v Hart* (1881) 18 ChD 670 at 693 per Kay J; and see *Shore v Wilson* (1842) 9 Cl & Fin 355 at 556, HL, per Lord Wensleydale; *A-G v Drummond* (1842) 1 Dr & War 353 at 367 per Sugden LC; *Grey v Pearson* (1857) 6 HL Cas 61 at 106; *Roddy v Fitzgerald* (1858) 6 HL Cas 823 at 876; *Baird v Fortune* (1861) 5 LT 2, HL. See also *Magee v Lavell* (1874) LR 9 CP 107 at 112; and *Roe v Siddons* (1888) 22 QBD 224 at 233, CA, per Lord Esher MR ('the deed must be construed according to the ordinary rules of construction, one of which is that you are entitled to look at the circumstances existing at the date of the deed'); *Butterley Co Ltd v New Hucknall Colliery Co Ltd* [1909] 1 Ch 37 at 46, 52, CA (affd [1910] AC 381, HL).

11   *Reardon Smith Line Ltd v Yngvar Hansen-Tangen* [1976] 3 All ER 570, [1976] 1 WLR 989, HL; *Bunge SA v Kruse* [1977] 1 Lloyd's Rep 492, CA; *Earl of Lonsdale v A-G* [1982] 3 All ER 579, [1982] 1 WLR 887; *State Trading Corpn of India Ltd v M Golodetz Ltd* [1989] 2 Lloyd's Rep 277, CA; *Barclays Bank plc v Weeks Legg & Dean (a firm)* [1999] QB 309, [1998] 3 All ER 213, CA.

12   *Inglis v John Buttery & Co* (1878) 3 App Cas 552 at 577, HL, per Lord Blackburn. Thus, in ascertaining the premises granted by a lease, the parties have a right to prove all the circumstances connected with the state of the property at the time of the demise: *Osborn v Wise* (1837) 7 C & P 761; *Hall v Lund* (1863) 1 H & C 676 at 684. The circumstances, by explaining the relative position of the parties (e g which is buyer and which is seller) may remove an ambiguity in the contract: *Newell v Radford* (1867) LR 3 CP 52.

13   See para 176 ante. As to cases where the question may be complicated by the application of the Statute of Frauds (1677) s 4 (as amended) (replaced and repealed for certain purposes: see para 141 note 1 ante) or the Law of Property (Miscellaneous Provisions) Act 1989 s 2 (as amended) see SALE OF LAND vol 42 (Reissue) paras 29–40. See also *Roar Marine Ltd v Bimeh Iran Insurance Co* [1998] 1 Lloyd's Rep 423.

14   *Harman v Richards* (1852) 10 Hare 81 at 85; *Graham v O'Keeffe* (1864) 16 I Ch R 1; and see generally SALE OF LAND.

15   See para 185 notes 2, 8 ante. However, a second document containing such statements (and complying with any requisites of the law as to form) may fall to be construed together and so as to form in effect one document with that to be interpreted: see para 176 ante.

16   'In no case whatever is it permitted to explain the language of a deed by evidence of the private views, the secret intentions, or the known principles of the party to the instrument whether religious, political or otherwise, any more than by the expressed parol declarations made by the party himself which are universally excluded': *Shore v Wilson* (1842) 9 Cl & Fin 355 at 565, HL, per Tindal CJ.

17   See paras 185 note 3, 187 ante.

18   See paras 170 note 5, 172–173 ante, 202–203 post. It may be shown from internal evidence that the maker or makers of a document is or are using an ordinary word in a sense peculiar to himself or themselves or to the document alone; for instance, the document may contain definitions of words in artificial senses, and a definition may be implied by obvious use of a word throughout the document in a special or peculiar sense: see *Re Davidson, National Provincial Bank Ltd v Davidson* [1949] Ch 670, [1949] 2 All ER 551; paras 170, 174 ante; and WILLS vol 50 (2005 Reissue) para 481 et seq.

19   See para 200 note 4 post.

199.   Other instances where extrinsic evidence admissible. The following are further examples of admissibility of extrinsic evidence: to identify the parties[1] or property[2] named or described in a written agreement; to identify documents referred to therein[3]; to show the circumstances of the parties from which their relative positions in relation to the contract may be inferred[4]; to prove circumstances from which may be inferred the extent of the property intended to pass by a certain description[5], the nature of the employment intended in such a phrase as 'in consideration of my entering your employ'[6], or the construction of the words 'market price' in a covenant for sale of liquor in a brewer's lease[7]; or to prove circumstances tending to show that representations in letters forming the contract which might be construed as warranties were not intended as such[8]. Where the question was whether the purposes of a trust were exclusively charitable or whether they were or included political purposes, it was held that, the trust deed being ambiguous, in determining the question it was proper to look at the surrounding facts, including the activities of the promoters both before and after the execution of the deed[9]. A letter from a landlord to his tenant has been held as a matter of construction, in the light of all the surrounding circumstances, to operate as a consent enabling the tenant to change the use of the premises[10].

Extrinsic evidence is also admissible to rebut a presumption such as that of trust or advancement[11]. This principle does not form an exception to the general rule already stated[12], since the evidence is admitted not to modify the written instrument in any way, but to support the instrument in its natural sense against the artificial construction placed upon it by equity[13].

1　*Shore v Wilson* (1842) 9 Cl & Fin 355 at 556, HL, per Parke B; *Rayner v Grote* (1846) 15 M & W 359; *Newell v Radford* (1867) LR 3 CP 52; *Sale v Lambert* (1874) LR 18 Eq 1; *Rossiter v Miller* (1878) 3 App Cas 1124, HL; *Carr v Lynch* [1900] 1 Ch 613; *Chapman v Smith* [1907] 2 Ch 97; *Fred Drughorn Ltd v Rederiaktiebolaget Trans-Atlantic* [1919] AC 203, HL.

2　*Ogilvie v Foljambe* (1817) 3 Mer 53; *Paddock v Fradley* (1830) 1 Cr & J 90; *Owen v Thomas* (1834) 3 My & K 353; *R v Wickham Inhabitants* (1835) 2 Ad & El 517; *Shore v Wilson* (1842) 9 Cl & Fin 355, HL; *Cowley v Watts* (1853) 17 Jur 172; *Lord Waterpark v Fennell* (1859) 7 HL Cas 650 at 678 per Lord Chelmsford; *Macdonald v Longbottom* (1860) 1 E & E 977 at 987, Ex Ch; *Lyle v Richards* (1866) LR 1 HL 222; *McMurray v Spicer* (1868) LR 5 Eq 527; *Horsey v Graham* (1869) LR 5 CP 9; *Shardlow v Cotterell* (1881) 20 ChD 90, CA; *Plant v Bourne* [1897] 2 Ch 281, CA; *Van Diemen's Land Co v Table Cape Marine Board* [1906] AC 92, PC; *EW Savory Ltd v World of Golf Ltd* [1914] 2 Ch 566, CA; *Auerbach v Nelson* [1919] 2 Ch 383; *Freeguard v Rogers* [1999] 1 WLR 375, (1998) Times, 22 October, CA.

3　*Hodges v Horsfall* (1829) 1 Russ & M 116 (identification of plan referred to); *Morris v Wilson* (1859) 5 Jur NS 168; *Jones v Victoria Graving Dock Co Ltd* (1877) 2 QBD 314, CA (identification of draft agreement as being that referred to in resolution entered in minute book); *Long v Millar* (1879) 4 CPD 450, CA; *Dewar v Mintoft* [1912] 2 KB 373. Extrinsic evidence is also admissible to prove the connection between two documents such as a letter and the envelope inclosing it: *Pearce v Gardner* [1897] 1 QB 688, CA.

4　*Newell v Radford* (1867) LR 3 CP 52.

5　*Doe d Freeland v Burt* (1787) 1 Term Rep 701; *Goodtitle d Radford v Southern* (1813) 1 M & S 299; *Duke of Beaufort v Swansea Corpn* (1849) 3 Exch 413; *Thomas v Owen* (1887) 20 QBD 225, CA; *Willson v Greene* [1971] 1 All ER 1098, [1971] 1 WLR 635; *Spall v Owen* (1981) 44 P & CR 36 at 43 per Gibson J; *Targett v Ferguson* (1996) 72 P & CR 106, CA; *Freeguard v Rogers* [1999] 1 WLR 375, (1998) Times, 22 October, CA.

6　*Mumford v Gething* (1859) 7 CBNS 305 (previously employed by same employer under an oral agreement).

7　*Charrington & Co Ltd v Wooder* [1914] AC 71, HL. For other cases on the admissibility of evidence to explain words and phrases see *Daintree v Hutchinson* (1842) 10 M & W 85 (initial letters); *Grant v Maddox* (1846) 15 M & W 737 (trade terms); *Doe d Mence v Hadley* (1849) 14 LTOS 102 (land 'marked out'); *Hawk v Freund* (1858) 1 F & F 294 ('same or usual terms'); *Mumford v Gething* (1859) 7 CBNS 305 ('the same ground'); *Albert v Grosvenor Investment Co* (1867) LR 3 QB 123 ('default' in payment of money secured by a bill of sale); *Roots v Snelling* (1883) 48 LT 216 ('freehold equities'); *Bank of New Zealand v Simpson* [1900] AC 182, PC ('total cost of works'). As to when a secondary meaning of a word is admissible see para 170 note 3 ante. As to latent ambiguity see para 209 post.

8　*Stucley v Baily* (1862) 1 H & C 405.

9　*Southwood v A-G* [1998] 40 LS Gaz R 37.

10　*Rose v Stavrou* [1999] 25 LS Gaz R 29 (letter construed by reference to documents in other cases, in similar terms and circumstances).

11　See EQUITY vol 16(2) (Reissue) para 750; TRUSTS vol 48 (2000 Reissue) paras 551, 606, 621; WILLS vol 50 (2005 Reissue) para 481 et seq.

12　See para 185 ante.

13　See *Lord Chichester v Coventry* (1867) LR 2 HL 71; *Re Lacon, Lacon v Lacon* [1891] 2 Ch 482, CA; *Pryor v Petre* [1894] 2 Ch 11, CA.

200. Ascertainment of ordinary meanings of words. The rules already laid down as to the meaning to be ascribed to words[1] indicate the nature of the extrinsic evidence which can be adduced to arrive at their meaning. Primarily words are to be taken in their ordinary popular sense[2]. The court takes judicial notice of the ordinary meaning and, where there is any doubt, may have recourse to dictionaries[3] to ascertain the meaning commonly used by the author of the instrument[4], but a mere obscurity of handwriting is for the court to solve[5].

1   See paras 169–174 ante.
2   See para 169 ante.
3   See an early example of recourse to a dictionary in *Matthew v Purchins* (1608) Cro Jac 203.
4   *Kell v Charmer* (1856) 23 Beav 195.
5   *Remon v Hayward* (1835) 2 Ad & El 666.

201.   Construction of foreign documents.   The construction of a foreign document by the application to it of the foreign law, when ascertained, is for the judge, and not for the witness. Where a written contract is made in a foreign country, and in a foreign language, evidence is admissible to show what is the corresponding meaning in English[1]. Accordingly the court, in order to interpret it, must first obtain a translation of the instrument; secondly, an explanation of the terms of art (if it contains any); thirdly, evidence of any foreign law applicable to the case; and fourthly, evidence of any peculiar rules of construction, if any such rules exist, by the foreign law. With this assistance, the court itself must interpret the contract on ordinary principles of construction[2].

1   *Shore v Wilson* (1842) 9 Cl & Fin 355 at 555, HL, per Parke B. Where the language of the instrument is such that the court does not understand, it is competent to receive evidence of the proper meaning of that language, as when it is written in a foreign tongue: see *Shore v Wilson* supra at 511 per Erskine J, and at 566 per Tindal CJ.
2   *Di Sora v Phillipps* (1863) 10 HL Cas 624 at 633 per Lord Cranworth; *Russian Commercial and Industrial Bank v Comptoir D'Escompte De Mulhouse* [1923] 2 KB 630 at 643, CA (on appeal [1925] AC 112, HL); and cf *Stearine Kaarsen Fabrick Gonda Co v Heintzmann* (1864) 17 CBNS 56; *Chatenay v Brazilian Submarine Telegraph Co* [1891] 1 QB 79, CA; *Serra v Famous Lasky Film Service* (1922) 127 LT 109, CA; *Rouyer Guillet et Cie v Rouyer Guillet & Co Ltd* [1949] 1 All ER 244n, CA. As to foreign legislation see *De Beéche v South American Stores Ltd and Chilian Stores Ltd* [1935] AC 148, HL. See also *H Glynn (Covent Garden) Ltd v Wittleder* [1959] 2 Lloyd's Rep 409 (where it was decided, having regard to the course of negotiations for a contract, that the parties were not bound by the untranslated terms in a German form of contract note, of which part only had been translated into English). As to admissible evidence of foreign law in civil proceedings see the Civil Evidence Act 1972 s 4; and EVIDENCE vol 17(1) (Reissue) paras 551, 554.

202.   Terms of science and art.   Technical words are primarily to be taken in their technical sense[1]; and where the words are technical terms of science or art, the evidence of experts, or of books dealing with the subject, is admissible to inform the court of their meaning[2]. If, however, there is no dispute or the matter is simple, the court will take judicial notice of the meaning of technical terms of a scientific or technological nature, using any reliable means for informing itself. Thus the court may act on the explanations of counsel or may refer to technical textbooks or previously reported decisions, or may rely on its own knowledge, particularly where the court is sitting with assessors, who are experts in the technical matters involved[3].

The court requires no evidence as to technical legal terms[4].

1   See para 170 ante.
2   *Shore v Wilson* (1842) 9 Cl & Fin 355 at 511, HL, per Erskine J, and at 566 per Tindal CJ (if the terms are technical terms of art, their meaning must be ascertained by the evidence of persons skilled in the art to which they refer); *Glaverbel SA v British Coal Corpn* [1995] FSR 254, [1995] RPC 255, CA. 'Patent specifications are intended to be read by persons skilled in the relevant art, but their construction is for the [c]ourt. Thus the court must adopt the mantle of the notional skilled addressee and determine, from the language used, what the notional skilled addressee would understand to be the ambit of the claim. To do that it is often necessary for the [c]ourt to be informed as to the meaning of technical words and phrases and what was, at the relevant time, the common general knowledge; the knowledge that the notional skilled man would have': *Lubrizol Corpn v Esso Petroleum Co Ltd (No 5)* [1998] RPC 727 at

738, CA, per Aldous LJ. See also *Goblet v Beechey* (1829) 3 Sim 24; revsd (1831) 2 Russ & M 624 (a case on a will). An expert may, in giving evidence, refer the court to technical textbooks as setting out his expert knowledge.

3   *Baldwin and Francis Ltd v Patents Appeal Tribunal* [1959] AC 663 at 679, [1959] 2 All ER 433 at 438–439, HL, per Lord Morton, at 684–685 and 442 per Lord Reid, and at 691 and 446 per Lord Denning. As to the appointment of assessors and scientific advisers in patent cases see the Supreme Court Act 1981 (prospectively renamed the Senior Courts Act 1981) s 70; and PRACTICE AND PROCEDURE vol 37 (Reissue) paras 1005, 1076.

4   *Shore v Wilson* (1842) 9 Cl & Fin 355 at 512, HL, per Erskine J; *Roddy v Fitzgerald* (1858) 6 HL Cas 823 at 877 per Lord Wensleydale (as to wills); *Biggs v Gordon* (1860) 8 CBNS 638; *Leach v Jay* (1877) 6 ChD 496 at 499 per Jessel MR (affd (1878) 9 ChD 42, CA); *Smith v Butcher* (1878) 10 ChD 113 at 114.

203.   Local or class usage.   Where a word or phrase has a special meaning in a particular district or among a particular class, evidence of the special meaning may be given[1], as may evidence that the person using it resided in such a district or belonged to such a class[2]. The evidence must refer to the general use of the word, and must lead to the conclusion that the author used the term in the particular instrument in the suggested sense; it must not be direct evidence that in the particular instrument he intended to use the word in some sense differing from its ordinary meaning[3]. Moreover, evidence of this kind must not contradict the provisions of the deed; its effect must be limited to explaining them[4].

Evidence of the special meaning of words is frequently admitted in the case of mercantile contracts, where words may bear a meaning attributed to them by local usage or by the custom of the trade[5].

1   Extrinsic evidence is admissible 'where technical words or peculiar terms, or indeed any expressions are used which at the time the instrument was written had acquired an appropriate meaning, either generally or by local usage, or amongst particular classes': see *Smith v Wilson* (1832) 3 B & Ad 728 at 733 per Parke J; *Shore v Wilson* (1842) 9 Cl & Fin 355 at 555, HL; *Grant v Maddox* (1846) 15 M & W 737 at 745 per Alderson B; *Re North Western Rubber Co Ltd and Hüttenbach & Co* [1908] 2 KB 907 at 923, CA, per Buckley LJ; *Lovell and Christmas Ltd v Wall* (1911) 104 LT 85 at 88, CA, per Cozens-Hardy MR. Such evidence is equivalent to translation: *Grant v Maddox* (1846) 15 M & W 737 at 746 per Platt B. As to local meaning of terms of measurement see *Barksdale v Morgan* (1693) 4 Mod Rep 185 at 186 ('acre'). 'One thousand', as applied to rabbits, has been held in a particular district to mean 1,200: *Smith v Wilson* (1832) 3 B & Ad 728. In a mining lease 'level' has been construed in the particular sense in which it was used by miners in the neighbourhood: *Clayton v Gregson* (1836) 5 Ad & El 302. Similarly, terms which have acquired a peculiar sense in a particular trade are to be construed according to that sense: *Robertson v French* (1803) 4 East 130 at 135.

2   In *Shore v Wilson* (1842) 9 Cl & Fin 355 at 528, 530, 550, 580, HL, the question was as to the meaning of the expression 'godly preachers of Christ's Holy Gospel' as used by Lady Hewley in a deed of 1704; evidence was admitted of the existence of a class of Trinitarian Protestant Dissenters by whom this phrase was used to denote their own ministers, and that Lady Hewley was a member of this party; consequently both Unitarians and Church of England clergymen were excluded. As to 'Protestant Dissenters' cf *Drummond v A-G for Ireland* (1849) 2 HL Cas 837.

3   'Evidence of the particular meaning which the party affixed to his words' cannot be set up 'to contradict or vary the plain language of the instrument itself': see *Shore v Wilson* (1842) 9 Cl & Fin 355 at 566, HL, per Tindal CJ, at 514 per Erskine J, and at 525 per Coleridge J; *Drummond v A-G for Ireland* (1849) 2 HL Cas 837 at 863.

4   *A-G v Clapham* (1855) 4 De GM & G 591 at 627.

5   'For there to be any relevance in any custom or practice, whether in a strict or informal sense, it must be possible to identify the particular custom or practice with some certainty': *Roar Marine Ltd v Bimeh Iran Insurance Co* [1998] 1 Lloyd's Rep 423 at 429 per Mance J. As to the admissibility of usage in the interpretation of mercantile contracts see further CUSTOM AND USAGE vol 12(1) (Reissue) para 665 et seq.

204.   Ancient documents.   Where the instrument is of ancient date, then, whether the words are taken in their ordinary popular sense, or are taken in the sense given to them by a particular place, evidence will be admitted of the meaning of the words at the date of the instrument[1], and such evidence may properly be given by reference to historical and other works[2].

1   Ie where by the lapse of time and change of manners, the words have acquired in the present age a different meaning from that which they bore when originally employed: *Shore v Wilson* (1842) 9 Cl & Fin 355 at 566, HL, per Tindal CJ, at 512–513 per Erskine J, at 527–528 per Coleridge J, at 545 per Gurney B, and at 556 per Parke B; *Drummond v A-G for Ireland* (1849) 2 HL Cas 837 at 863 per Lord Campbell. As to evidence of conduct to explain an ancient document see para 206 post.
2   *Shore v Wilson* (1842) 9 Cl & Fin 355 at 501–502, HL, per Maule J.

205.   Identification.   When the meaning of the words of the instrument has been ascertained, whether their ordinary popular meaning or their special meaning (the special meaning being determined by the context or by extrinsic evidence), it is still necessary to ascertain the particular persons or things to which, in accordance with such meaning, they apply, and this involves the admission of such evidence as is necessary to identify the person or thing mentioned in the instrument[1].

1   For the purpose of applying the instrument to the facts, and determining what passes by it, and who takes an interest under it, a second description of evidence is admissible, namely every material fact that will enable the court to identify the person or thing mentioned in the instrument: *Shore v Wilson* (1842) 9 Cl & Fin 355 at 556, HL, per Parke B; *Lord Waterpark v Fennell* (1859) 7 HL Cas 650 at 678 per Lord Chelmsford; and see paras 198–199 ante.

(iii)   Evidence of Conduct and Contemporaneous Usage

206.   Evidence of conduct.   If, after other methods of interpretation have been exhausted, there remains a doubt as to the effect of an ancient instrument[1], it is permissible to give evidence of the acts done under it as a guide to the intention of the parties[2], in particular, of acts done shortly after the date of the instrument[3]. Evidence of the acts done cannot, however, be admitted to contradict the clear meaning of the instrument[4]. An ancient instrument, for the present purpose, appears to be one that dates from beyond the time of living memory[5].

This doctrine probably also applies to descriptions of the property assured in modern instruments of title to land[6], but with this exception acts done under a modern instrument and, in particular, under a modern commercial contract cannot be admitted as a guide to the intention of the parties, even if there remains a doubt after other methods of interpretation have been exhausted[7].

1   As to the interpretation of words in an ancient document see para 204 ante.
2   'In the construction of ancient grants and deeds, there is no better way of construing them than by usage': *A-G v Parker* (1747) 3 Atk 576 at 577 per Lord Hardwicke LC; 9 Co Rep 28a, n (F). 'One of the most settled rules of law for the construction of ambiguities in ancient instruments is that you may resort to contemporaneous usage to ascertain the meaning of the deed; tell me what you have done under such a deed, and I will tell you what that deed means': *A-G v Drummond* (1842) 1 Dr & War 353 at 368 per Sugden LC; and see *Drummond v A-G for Ireland* (1849) 2 HL Cas 837 at 861 per Lord Cottenham, and at 863 per Lord Campbell. 'If the words of the instrument be ambiguous, we may call in aid the acts done under it as a clue to the intention of the parties': *Doe d Pearson v Ries* (1832) 8 Bing 178 at 181 per Tindal CJ; and see *Chapman v Bluck* (1838) 4 Bing NC 187 at 193; *Wadley v Bayliss* (1814) 5 Taunt 752; *A-G v Brazen Nose College* (1834) 2 Cl & Fin 295 at 317; *Sadlier v Biggs* (1853) 4 HL Cas 435 at 458; *Hebbert v Purchas* (1871) LR 3 PC 605 at 650; *Laprairie Common Corpn v Compagnie de Jésus* [1921] 1 AC 314 at 323, PC (where, in construing a feudal grant of 1694 to the inhabitants of a village, notice was taken of agreements of 1705 and 1724 relating to the effect of the grant). As to charities see *A-G v Bristol Corpn* (1820) 2 Jac & W 294 at 321; *A-G v Boston Corpn* (1847) 1 De G & Sm 519 at 527; and CHARITIES vol 5(2) (2001 Reissue) paras 103–105.
3   This principle is expressed in the maxim 'contemporanea expositio est fortissima in lege': 2 Co Inst 136.
4   In the case of a grant no usage, however long, can countervail the clear words of the instrument, for what is done under usurpation cannot constitute a legal usage: *Chad v Tilsed* (1821) 2 Brod & Bing 403 at 406

per Dallas CJ; and see *R v Varlo* (1775) 1 Cowp 248 at 250 per Lord Mansfield CJ. Usage cannot repeal the positive enactment of a statute: *Lord Advocate v Walker Trustees* [1912] AC 95 at 103, HL; cf *Clifton v Walmesley* (1794) 5 Term Rep 564; *Forbes v Watt* (1872) LR 2 Sc & Div 214, HL; *North Eastern Rly Co v Lord Hastings* [1900] AC 260 at 263, 270, HL; and see *Marshall v Berridge* (1881) 19 ChD 233, CA.

In determining whether a covenant in a lease amounted to a covenant for perpetual renewal, the Court of Chancery refused to admit evidence of the conduct of the parties, on the ground that a covenant for perpetual renewal must be perfectly clear: *Baynham v Guy's Hospital* (1796) 3 Ves 295; not following the decision of the King's Bench in *Cooke v Booth* (1778) 2 Cowp 819. The controversy arising out of this incident induced declarations in the Court of Chancery that evidence of conduct was not admissible: *Baynham v Guy's Hospital* supra; *Eaton v Lyon* (1798) 3 Ves 690 at 694; *Iggulden v May* (1804) 9 Ves 325; *Balfour v Welland* (1809) 16 Ves 151 at 156; and see *Douglas v Allen* (1842) 1 Con & Law 367; *Burrowes v Hayes* (1834) Hayes & Jo 597. As to the abolition of perpetually renewable leases as such see the Law of Property Act 1922 s 145, Sch 15 (as amended); and LANDLORD AND TENANT vol 27(1) (2006 Reissue) paras 541–542.

5   See *North Eastern Rly Co v Lord Hastings* [1900] AC 260 at 269, HL, per Lord Davey; and see the same case in the court below, sub nom *Lord Hastings v North Eastern Rly Co* [1899] 1 Ch 656 at 663, CA, per Lindley MR (where 'contemporanea expositio' is relied on upon the ground that the meaning of the words has changed, the instrument must be old enough to permit of this change).

6   *Watcham v A-G of East Africa Protectorate* [1919] AC 533, PC, explained in *L Schüler AG v Wickman Machine Tool Sales Ltd* [1974] AC 235, [1973] 2 All ER 39, HL; *St Edmundsbury and Ipswich Dioceasan Board of Finance v Clark (No 2)* [1973] 3 All ER 902, [1973] 1 WLR 1572; and see *Neilson v Poole* (1969) 20 P & CR 909.

7   In *Watcham v A-G of East Africa Protectorate* [1919] AC 533, PC, it was held by the Judicial Committee that, in cases of ambiguity, whether patent or latent, evidence of user can be given, to show the sense in which the parties used the language employed, in construing a modern as well as an ancient instrument. This view was also advanced in *Van Diemen's Land Co v Table Cape Marine Board* [1906] AC 92 at 98, PC, and in *WT Lamb & Sons v Goring Brick Co Ltd* [1932] 1 KB 710 at 717, 721, CA. The dictum of Tindal CJ in *Doe d Pearson v Ries* (1832) 8 Bing 178 at 181 (cited in note 2 supra), also referred to a modern instrument. This extension of the doctrine has not met with approval: see *Gaisberg v Storr* [1949] 2 All ER 411 at 415, CA; and para 187 note 4 ante. Finally, in *L Schüler AG v Wickman Machine Tool Sales Ltd* [1974] AC 235, [1973] 2 All ER 39, the House of Lords held that the doctrine was not applicable to modern instruments, reserving however the question whether it could exceptionally be applied to a case (such as *Watcham v A-G of East Africa Protectorate* supra) where the instrument concerned was an instrument of title to land. The House of Lords had previously considered the question of admissibility of conduct under a modern instrument (though without reference to *Watcham v A-G of East Africa Protectorate* supra) in *James Miller & Partners Ltd v Whitworth Street Estates (Manchester) Ltd* [1970] AC 583, [1970] 1 All ER 796. See also *St Edmundsbury and Ipswich Diocesan Board of Finance v Clark (No 2)* [1975] 1 All ER 772 [1975] 1 WLR 468, CA.

See, however, *Manitoba Development Corpn v Columbia Forest Products Ltd* (1973) 43 DLR (3d) 107, Man CA (where the English authorities were reviewed but the court decided that in an appropriate case, where there is ambiguity, it is permissible to examine the subsequent conduct of the parties (meaning of the phrase 'all necessary working capital' in issue)); *Boranga v Flintoff* (1997) 19 WAR 1. See also *Maggs (t/a BM Builders) v Marsh* [2006] EWCA Civ 1058, [2006] BLR 395, [2006] All ER (D) 95 (Jul), where it was held that the principle that what the parties had done or said after the contract date could not be considered in construing the terms of a written contract did not apply to an oral contract or the oral aspects of a partially written and partially oral contract (*James Miller & Partners Ltd v Whitworth Street Estates (Manchester) Ltd* was distinguished).

207.   Contemporaneous usage.

Before evidence of contemporaneous usage can be admitted there must be a doubt on the construction of the instrument, either by reason of the occurrence of general words[1] or because, in consequence of lapse of time, the words may have changed their meaning[2], or on account of some other uncertainty or ambiguity[3].

The evidence is not restricted to direct evidence of contemporaneous usage, which it would frequently be impossible to procure. Modern usage, if there is nothing to countervail it, raises a presumption that the usage was the same immediately after the date of the instrument, and consequently evidence of modern usage is admissible to explain an ancient deed[4].

1   When a grant of remote antiquity contains general words, the best exposition of such a grant is long usage under it: *Chad v Tilsed* (1821) 2 Brod & Bing 403 at 406 per Dallas CJ. 'However general the words

of the ancient deeds may be, they are to be construed by evidence of the manner in which the thing has been always possessed and used': *Weld v Hornby* (1806) 7 East 195 at 199 per Lord Ellenborough CJ; *Lord Waterpark v Fennell* (1859) 7 HL Cas 650 at 680 per Lord Cranworth.

2 See *Lord Hastings v North Eastern Rly Co* [1899] 1 Ch 656 at 663, CA, per Lindley MR; affd sub nom *North Eastern Rly Co v Lord Hastings* [1900] AC 260, HL. Thus, in ascertaining the meaning of terms in an ancient trust deed at the time of execution, evidence is admissible of 'the early and contemporaneous application of the funds of the charity itself by the original trustees': *Shore v Wilson* (1842) 9 Cl & Fin 355 at 569, HL, per Tindal CJ.

3 There can be no doubt that contemporaneous usage may be resorted to for the purpose of explaining an uncertainty or ambiguity in an ancient grant; but then there must be 'uncertainty or ambiguity': *Lord Hastings v North Eastern Rly Co* [1899] 1 Ch 656 at 661, CA, per Vaughan Williams LJ (affd sub nom *North Eastern Rly Co v Lord Hastings* [1900] AC 260, HL); *Doe d Kinglake v Beviss* (1849) 7 CB 456 at 504; *Earl De La Warr v Miles* (1881) 17 ChD 535 at 573, CA.

4 *Chad v Tilsed* (1821) 2 Brod & Bing 403; *Duke of Beaufort v Swansea Corpn* (1849) 3 Exch 413 at 425; *Lord Waterpark v Fennell* (1859) 7 HL Cas 650 at 684; *Simpson v Dendy* (1860) 8 CBNS 433 at 473 (affd sub nom *Dendy v Simpson* (1861) 7 Jur NS 1058, Ex Ch); *Hastings Corpn v Ivall* (1874) LR 19 Eq 558 at 581; *Earl De La Warr v Miles* (1881) 17 ChD 535 at 573, CA. Similarly, in a question of prescription, usage continued during living memory, when there is nothing to the contrary, may justify the presumption of a similar usage from time immemorial: *Neill v Duke of Devonshire* (1882) 8 App Cas 135 at 156, HL, per Lord Selborne LC. Modern usage, carried back for a considerable time, may be used to interpret a doubtful statute, if not inconsistent with the express directions of the statute: *Dunbar Magistrates v Duchess of Roxburghe* (1835) 3 Cl & Fin 335 at 354, HL.

(iv) Ambiguity

208. Patent and other ambiguities. When the meaning of the words of the instrument has been ascertained by intrinsic evidence, and by such extrinsic evidence as is admissible for that purpose (other than evidence admissible only to resolve a latent ambiguity[1]), it may be that the instrument as thus interpreted fails to indicate with certainty any specific intention on the part of the author. Where the instrument as so interpreted has two or more possible meanings it is said to be ambiguous. If, before an attempt is made to identify the persons and things referred to in the instrument, it is apparent on the face of the instrument that it is ambiguous, the ambiguity is called a patent ambiguity. Such an ambiguity may, for instance, arise because the author has contradicted himself, or has expressed alternative intentions without deciding in favour of either, or has omitted something necessary completely to define his meaning[2]. It has been said that where there is an ambiguity a contract should not be construed in such a way as to bar a legitimate claim[3].

No direct evidence of intention can be given to resolve an ambiguity other than a latent ambiguity[4]. To allow such evidence would be regarded as infringing the rule that the terms of a written instrument cannot be varied or contradicted by extrinsic evidence[5]. Sometimes a patent ambiguity may be cured by election[6], and where there is a patent ambiguity on the face of a lease, reference may be made to a counterpart to resolve it[7]. A latent ambiguity may be resolved by the further evidence admissible to solve such an ambiguity, but otherwise an ambiguous deed is, either as to the whole of the deed or, where the ambiguity occurs in a severable part of the deed, as to that part, void for uncertainty[8].

1 As to latent ambiguities and the evidence admissible to resolve them see para 209 post.

2 'There be two sorts of ambiguities of words; the one is ambiguitas patens and the other latens. Patens is that which appears to be ambiguous upon the deed or instrument; latens is that which seemeth certain and without ambiguity, for anything that appeareth upon the deed or instrument; but there is some collateral matter out of the deed that breedeth the ambiguity': Bacon's Law Tracts 99. For an instance of a patent ambiguity arising out of contradiction see *Saunderson v Piper* (1839) 5 Bing NC 425, where in a bill of exchange the amounts in words and in figures were different, though for a reason peculiar to that class of instrument the amount in words prevailed; and see BILLS OF EXCHANGE AND OTHER NEGOTIABLE INSTRUMENTS vol 4(1) (2002 Reissue) para 323. For an instance of a patent ambiguity arising out of the writer's failure to make up his own mind see Shep Touch 250–251 (a grant 'to one of

the children of J S'). For an instance of a patent ambiguity arising from omission to state the intention definitely see *Altham's Case* (1610) 8 Co Rep 150b at 155a (a limitation to two 'et heredibus'); *Pearce v Watts* (1875) LR 20 Eq 492 (reservation of the land 'necessary' for making a railway).

3   See *Bunge SA v Deutsche Conti-Handelsgesellschaft MBH (No 2)* [1980] 1 Lloyd's Rep 352 at 358 per Donaldson J.

4   However, a patent ambiguity 'allows evidence to be admitted to give effect to the intentions of the parties': *Rolfe Lubbell & Co v Keith* [1979] 2 Lloyd's Rep 75 at 77 per Kilner-Brown J; and see *Southwood v A-G* [1998] 40 LS Gaz R 37; and para 199 ante.

5   See para 185 ante.

6   See para 214 post.

7   *Matthews v Smallwood* [1910] 1 Ch 777, 785; *Trusthouse Forte Albany Hotels Ltd v Daejean Investments Ltd (No 2)* [1989] 2 EGLR 113, CA; and see para 4 ante.

8   'All ambiguity of words by matter within the deed, and not out of the deed, shall be holpen by construction, or in some cases by election, but never by averment, but rather shall make the deed void for uncertainty': Bacon's Law Tracts 99–100. Where there is a doubt on the face of the instrument, the law admits no extrinsic evidence to explain it: *Saunderson v Piper* (1839) 5 Bing NC 425 at 431 per Tindal CJ. No averment dehors can make that good, which upon consideration of the deed is apparent to be void: *Altham's Case* (1610) 8 Co Rep 150b at 155a; and see *London Clearing Bankers Committee v IRC* [1896] 1 QB 222 at 227 per Wright J (affd [1896] 1 QB 542, CA).

209.   Latent ambiguity.   When the instrument appears on its face to be free from ambiguity but, upon the endeavour being made to apply it to the persons or things indicated, it appears that the words are equally applicable to two or more persons, or to two or more things, either without any inaccuracy or with a common inaccuracy which may be ignored as a slip, there is a latent ambiguity[1]. The ambiguity, in this case also called an equivocation[2], is not discovered until the instrument comes to be applied to external circumstances. Direct evidence of the author's intention may be then given for the purpose of ascertaining which of the several persons or things to whom the words are applicable was intended to be denoted[3], and where there is a jury the question of which of two or more possible meanings was intended is a question of fact for the jury[4].

1   That is to say, an ambiguity in the terms of the instrument, the existence of which is first shown by extrinsic evidence, whether written or verbal, admissible in any event for the purpose of identifying the persons and things referred to in the instrument (see footnote to *Hitchin v Groom* (1848) 5 CB 515), unless the error is so obvious on the face of the document that the court can remedy it as a mere matter of construction: see *Wilson v Wilson* (1854) 5 HL Cas 40 at 66. See also *Charter v Charter* (1874) LR 7 HL 364; and para 208 note 2 ante.

2   *Doe d Hiscocks v Hiscocks* (1839) 5 M & W 363 at 369; *Douglas v Fellows* (1853) Kay 114 at 120.

3   *Altham's Case* (1610) 8 Co Rep 150b at 155a; *Shore v Wilson* (1842) 9 Cl & Fin 355 at 512–513, 517, HL, per Erskine J, and at 557 per Parke B; *Smith v Jeffryes* (1846) 15 M & W 561 at 562; *Hitchin v Groom* (1848) 5 CB 515 at 520; *Lord Waterpark v Fennell* (1859) 7 HL Cas 650 at 685 per Lord Wensleydale; *Roden v London Small Arms Co* (1876) 46 LJQB 213; and cf *Beaumont v Field* (1818) 1 B & Ald 247. In *M'Adam v Scott* (1912) 50 Sc LR 264, oral evidence was admitted to explain doubtful receipts. As to the application of this principle to documents of particular kinds see BOUNDARIES vol 4(1) (2002 Reissue) para 929; CHARITIES vol 5(2) (2001 Reissue) para 101; GUARANTEE AND INDEMNITY vol 20(1) (Reissue) para 171 et seq; WILLS vol 50 (2005 Reissue) paras 483, 487, 504 et seq.

4   *Sweet v Lee* (1841) 3 Man & G 452; *Daintree v Hutchinson* (1842) 10 M & W 85 (evidence as to meaning of initial letters in contract); *Goldshede v Swan* (1847) 1 Exch 154 (evidence that advance was not a past one); *Smith v Thompson* (1849) 8 CB 44; *Robinson v Great Western Rly Co* (1865) 35 LJCP 123 (oral evidence admitted to show which of two stations of the same name was intended); *Macdonald v Longbottom* (1860) 1 E & E 977 at 987, Ex Ch (evidence as to subject matter of sale of goods); *Lyle v Richards* (1866) LR 1 HL 222 (evidence as to boundary line where map incorrectly drawn); *Hordern v Commercial Union Insurance Co* (1887) 56 LJPC 78 (latent ambiguity in policy of insurance); *The Curfew* [1891] P 131; *M'Adam v Scott* (1912) 50 Sc LR 264 (evidence to explain ambiguous receipts); *EW Savory Ltd v World of Golf Ltd* [1914] 2 Ch 566, CA (evidence to identify subject matter of receipt).

(4) CORRECTION OF ERRORS BY INTRINSIC EVIDENCE

210.   Rejection of words etc.   Since an instrument is to be construed according to the intention of the parties as appearing from the whole of its contents, it follows that

that intention must not be defeated by too strict an adherence to the actual words[1], and any corrections may be made which a perusal of the document shows to be necessary. Thus wrong grammar[2] and spelling[3] may be corrected[4]; words that are merely meaningless[5], or that are repugnant[6], or that have obviously been inserted or left in by mistake[7], or that are immaterial and surplusage[8], and even whole provisions[9], may be rejected; words may be supplied, though more sparingly, when it is clear from the instrument itself that they have been omitted by inadvertence[10], and words and clauses may be transposed[11]. Words will only be supplied or transposed so as to give effect to the clear intentions of the parties; it must therefore be clear not only that a mistake of omission or transposition has been made but also what correction is required in order to carry out the intentions of the parties[12]. Abbreviations will be construed so as to give effect to the instrument[13], and stops and parentheses may be inserted when they are missing[14]. The court will, from the general frame of a settlement, collect the intent contrary to the effect of a particular clause[15], but effect should be given to every word which does not appear to have been left in by mistake[16]. Hence comes the rule that when the court can clearly collect from the language within the four corners of a deed, or other instrument in writing, the real intention of the parties, it is bound to give effect to it by supplying anything necessarily to be inferred from the terms used, and by rejecting as superfluous whatever is repugnant to the intention so discerned[17].

1   'Qui haeret in litera haeret in cortice' (this means literally 'he who sticks to the letter sticks in the bark'): Shep Touch 87; and see *Earl of Northumberland v Earl of Egremont* (1759) 1 Eden 435 at 446. See also the third rule reported to have been laid down by Staunford J in *Throckmerton v Tracy* (1555) 1 Plowd 145 at 160 'thirdly, that the words shall be construed according to the intent of the parties and not otherwise; and here he cited what Bracton, saith, carte non est nisi vestimentum donationis; and the intent directs gifts more than the words'). See also *Smith d Dormer v Packhurst* (1742) 3 Atk 135 at 136, HL, per Willes CJ ('such a construction should be made of the words in a deed as is most agreeable to the intention of the grantor; the words are not the principal things in a deed, but the intent and design of the grantor').

2   *Glen's Trustees v Lancashire and Yorkshire Accident Insurance Co* (1906) 8 F 915, Ct of Sess; *Wells v Wright* (1677) 2 Mod Rep 285. In respect of bonds see *Dobson v Keys* (1610) Cro Jac 261.

3   *Hubert v Long* (1621) Cro Jac 607; *Mauleverer v Hauxby* (1670) 2 Saund 78. In respect of bonds see *Sims v Urry* (1676) 2 Cas in Ch 225; *Dennis v Snape* (1687) Comb 60; *Cromwell v Grunsden* (1698) 2 Salk 462.

4   'Falsa grammatica non vitiat concessionem; falsa orthographia non vitiat chartam': Shep Touch 55, 87; and see *Earl of Shrewsbury's Case* (1610) 9 Co Rep 46b at 48a. False grammar includes a case where the writer has stated the reverse of what he obviously meant, as where a bond is conditioned to be void on failure to make the stipulated payment: *Vernon v Alsop* (1663) 1 Lev 77 ('the obligation shall not be of no effect, if by any means it may be made good'). See further *Mauleverer v Hauxby* (1670) 2 Saund 78 (where the concluding words of the condition, 'then the condition to be void', were rejected as surplusage); *Wells v Wright* (1678) 2 Mod Rep 285 (where the condition provided that, if default was made in performance thereof, the obligation should be void); *Anon* (undated), cited in 1 Doug KB at 384 (where the condition provided that the bond should be void if the obligor did not pay). As to bonds see also *Langdon v Goole* (1681) 3 Lev 21. A double negative does not make an affirmative if the contrary intention is clear: Shep Touch 87. Cases of erroneous spelling are numerous in the early reports: Norton on Deeds (2nd Edn) 103. Many of these are on Latin words, as in *Walter v Pigot* (1602) Cro Eliz 896, where 'septuagintis' was read 'septingentis' so as to make the penalty on a bond £750, the bond being for £500; and in *Matthew v Purchins* (1608) Cro Jac 203, where 'nobulis' was corrected to 'nobilis' (6s 8d).

5   *Goodman v Knight* (1614) Cro Jac 358; *Langdon v Goole* (1681) 3 Lev 21 at 22; *Smith d Dormer v Packhurst* (1742) 3 Atk 135 at 136 (the court 'may reject any words that are merely insensible'); *Wilson v Wilson* (1854) 5 HL Cas 40; *Hanbury v Tyrell* (1856) 21 Beav 322 at 327; *Nicolene Ltd v Simmonds* [1953] 1 QB 543 at 551, [1953] 1 All ER 822 at 826, CA, per Denning LJ.

6   *Wilson v Wilson* (1847) 15 Sim 487 (on appeal (1854) 5 HL Cas 40); *Holmes v Ivy* (1678) 2 Show 15, where in a condition to a bond for 'the delivery of 35,000 tiles to the value of £144 at 15s 6d a thousand', the '35,000' (which should have been 185,000) was rejected; c f *Gwyn v Neath Canal Co* (1868) LR 3 Exch 209; and see para 212 note 4 post. As to rejecting words repugnant to words of limitation see para 244 post.

7   Eg where a contract is contained in a printed from which the parties have omitted to strike out words applicable to a larger or different contract: *Dudgeon v Pembroke* (1877) 2 App Cas 284, HL; and see *Butler v Wigge* (1667) 1 Saund 65. See also *Finbow v Air Ministry* [1963] 2 All ER 647, [1963] 1 WLR 697

(where, the enactment under which a licence was stated to be approved having then been repealed and re-enacted, the approval was nevertheless held effective); *Slough Estates Ltd v Slough Borough Council (No 2)* [1969] 2 Ch 305, [1969] 2 All ER 988, CA (where, on an application for planning permission to develop an undeveloped area coloured on an accompanying plan, outline planning permission was granted for development of the undeveloped area uncoloured on the plan).

8   *Waugh v Bussell* (1814) 5 Taunt 707 at 71.

9   *Glynn v Margetson & Co* [1893] AC 351 at 357, HL, per Lord Halsbury LC. See also *Sze Hai Tong Bank Ltd v Rambler Cycle Co Ltd* [1959] AC 576, [1959] 3 All ER 182, PC; *Jones Construction Co v Alliance Assurance Co Ltd* [1961] 1 Lloyd's Rep 121 at 130, CA, per Danckwerts LJ.

10   The court, it has been said, has no power 'to alter the words or to insert words which are not in the deed': *Smith d Dormer v Packhurst* (1742) 3 Atk 135 at 136 per Willes CJ. This, however, goes too far. There are numerous instance where words accidentally omitted have been supplied. 'The law will, as much as it can, assist the frailties and infirmities of men in their employments, who, in drawing long deeds, may easily make a slip': *Lord Say and Seal's Case* (1711) 10 Mod Rep 40 at 47. Thus the name of the grantor has been inserted in the granting part of the deed (*Lord Say and Seal's Case* supra; *Trethewy v Ellesdon* (1690) 2 Vent 141 at 142); although where there were grantors of separate properties, the insertion of the name of the wrong grantor of one property was held not to be curable by construction (*Mill v Hill* (1852) 3 HL Cas 828 at 847–850). The omission of the name of the grantee in the premises has been supplied from the habendum: *Butler v Dodton* (1579) Cary 86; c f *Bustard v Coulter* (1602); Cro Eliz 902 at 917–918; and see *Spyve v Topham* (1802) 3 East 115 (where the trustee's name was substituted in the premises for the name of the cestui que trust, which had been erroneously inserted there); *Wilson v Wilson* (1854) 5 HL Cas 40 (separation agreement by which wife's trustees by mistake agreed to indemnify husband against his own debts instead of debts of wife). The name of the obligee of a bond may be supplied from the context (*Langdon v Goole* (1681) 3 Lev 21, where it was supplied by reference to the recital); and in *Coles v Hulme* (1828) 8 B & C 568, the sum of '7700' in the penalty of a bond was read '£7,700' by reference to the condition. The word 'assigns' may sometimes be supplied, but this will not be done where the result would be to enable the grantors to derogate from their own grant: *Anglo-Newfoundland Development Co v Newfoundland Pine and Pulp Co* (1913) 83 LJPC 50. 'In every deed there must be such a degree of moral certainty as to leave in the mind of a reasonable man no doubt of the intent of the parties': *Coles v Hulme* supra per Lord Tenterden CJ. The supplying of necessary words is an instance of the maxim that it is better for a thing to have effect than to be made void ('ut res magis valeat quam pereat'): *Langston v Langston* (1834) 2 Cl & Fin 194 at 243, HL. However, it can only be done where clearly required to avoid an absurdity, repugnancy, or inconsistency: *Clements v Henry* (1859) 10 I Ch R 79 (where the court refused to insert 'hereinbefore'); *You & Me Fashions Ltd v Royal Insurance Co Ltd* (1983) 133 NLJ 472.

Other instances of supplying words are: 'life' supplied in the memorial of an annuity (*Flight v Lord Lake* (1835) 2 Bing NC 72); 'hereinbefore declared' read as 'hereinbefore recited to have been declared' (*Hanbury v Tyrell* (1856) 21 Beav 322 at 326); 'pounds' inserted in a bill of exchange (*Phipps v Tanner* (1833) 5 C & P 488) and in a bill of sale (*Mourmand v Le Clair* [1903] 2 KB 216); in a bond securing an annuity for support of illegitimate children and their mother during their joint lives, the words 'and during the life of the survivor' added (*James v Tallent* (1822) 5 B & Ald 889); 'one pound' read as 'one hundred pounds' in a bond (*Waugh v Bussell* (1814) 5 Taunt 707); 'shall have attained the age of 21 years of' supplied in settlement (*Re Hargraves' Trusts, Leach v Leach* [1937] 2 All ER 545); 'without issue' supplied in marriage articles so as to make a gift over take effect only on death without issue and so save the interests of children (*Targus v Puget* (1751) 2 Ves Sen 194; *Kentish v Newman* (1713) 1 P Wms 234); all children who 'being sons' should attain 21 read as 'being sons or daughters' (*Re v Daniel's Settlement Trust* (1875) 1 ChD 375, CA; and see *Wight v Dicksons* (1813) 1 Dow 141, HL; and compare, as to a will, *Greenwood v Greenwood* (1877) 5 ChD 954, CA). The court will not, however, supply a word so as to alter the legal effect of limitations as expressed: see *Re Ethel and Mitchells and Butlers' Contract* [1901] 1 Ch 945, where the court refused to read 'in fee' as 'in fee simple'. As to supplying words inadvertently omitted in wills see *Re Follett, Barclays Bank Ltd v Dovell* [1955] 2 All ER 22, [1955] 1 WLR 429, CA; *Re Cory, Cory v Morel* [1955] 2 All ER 630, [1955] 1 WLR 725; *Re Whitrick, Sutcliffe v Sutcliffe* [1957] 2 All ER 467, [1957] 1 WLR 884, CA; *Re Riley's Will Trusts, Riley v Riley* [1962] 1 All ER 513, [1962] 1 WLR 344; *Re Hammersley Foster v Hammersley* [1965] Ch 481, [1964] 2 All ER 24; and WILLS vol 50 (2005 Reissue) paras 544–545.

11   Words shall be transposed and marshalled so as the feoffment or grant may take effect: Co Litt 217b. In *Uvedale v Halfpenny* (1723) 2 P Wms 151, a portion term in a marriage settlement was transposed so as to take precedence of the limitations in tail; and in *Fenton v Fenton* (1837) 1 Dr & Wal 66, a power to make provision for 'such' to refer to both sons and daughters. As to transposing words in wills see *Re Bacharach's Will Trusts, Minden v Bacharach* [1959] Ch 245, [1958] 3 All ER 618; and WILLS vol 50 (2005 Reissue) paras 544–545.

12 *Schnieder v Mills* [1993] 3 All ER 377, [1993] STC 430. As to wills, cf *Re Follett, Barclays Bank Ltd v Dovell* [1955] 2 All ER 22, [1955] 1 WLR 429, CA; *Re Bacharach's Will Trusts, Minden v Bacharach* [1959] Ch 245, [1958] 3 All ER 618; and see WILLS vol 50 (2005 Reissue) paras 544–545.

13 'Ille numerus et sensus abbreviationum accipiendus est ut concessio non sit inanis': thus ' "tot" ill' maner' in an old deed might be read in the singular or plural, according to the context: *Earl of Shrewsbury's Case* (1610) 9 Co Rep 46b at 48a.

14 *Doe d Willis v Martin* (1790) 4 Term Rep 39 at 65–66.

15 *Earl of Northumberland v Earl of Egremont* (1759) 1 Eden 435 at 446 per Henley, Lord Keeper; *Arundell v Arundell* (1833) 1 My & K 316. A term given absolutely has been held to be determinable on death without express words to that effect: *Coryton v Helyar* (1745) 2 Cox Eq Cas 340.

16 *Shelley's Case, Wolf v Shelley* (1581) 1 Co Rep 93b; *Butler v Duncomb* (1718) 1 P Wms 448 at 457 per Parker LC; *Hayne v Cummings* (1864) 16 CBNS 421 at 427; *Doe d Spencer v Godwin* (1815) 4 M & S 265; *Hitchin v Groom* (1848) 5 CB 515; *Tielens v Hooper* (1850) 5 Exch 830.

17 *Gwyn v Neath Canal Co* (1868) LR 3 Exch 209 at 215 per Kelly CB; *Beaumont v Marquis of Salisbury* (1854) 19 Beav 198 at 206 per Romilly MR.

211. Difference between words and figures, writing and printing. In the case of a difference between written words and figures, the written words as a general rule prevail, and in such a case evidence is not admissible to show that there was an omission from the written words[1].

Where an instrument is in a printed form with written additions or alterations, the written words (subject always to be governed in point of construction by the language and terms with which they are accompanied) are entitled, in case of reasonable doubt as to the meaning of the whole, to have a greater effect attributed to them than the printed words, because the written words are taken as being intended to qualify the printed form, and because they are the terms selected by the parties themselves for the expression of their meaning, whereas the printed words are a general formula adapted equally to their case and that of all other contracting parties on similar occasions and subjects[2].

1 *Saunderson v Piper* (1839) 5 Bing NC 425; *Durham City Estates Ltd v Felicetti* [1990] 1 EGLR 143, [1990] 03 EG 71, CA. However, in *Re Hammond, Hammond v Treharne* [1938] 3 All ER 308 (where there was a legacy of 'the sum of one hundred pounds (£500)', Simonds J regarded the rule that the words prevail as a rule confined to commercial documents, and applied the rule of last resort of resolving repugnancies in wills, namely that the later in order prevail over the earlier, hence holding that the legacy was one of £500); and see further WILLS vol 50 (2005 Reissue) para 523. As to discrepancies between the words and figures in a bill of exchange or promissory note see BILLS OF EXCHANGE AND OTHER NEGOTIABLE INSTRUMENTS vol 4(1) (2002 Reissue) para 323.

2 *Robertson v French* (1803) 4 East 130 at 136 per Lord Ellenborough CJ; *Gumm v Tyrie* (1865) 6 B & S 298, Ex Ch; *Joyce v Realm Insurance Co* (1872) LR 7 QB 580 at 583; *Western Assurance Co of Toronto v Poole* [1903] 1 KB 376 at 388; *Re L Sutro & Co and Heilbut, Symons & Co* [1917] 2 KB 348 at 358, 361, 367, CA; *Hadjipateras v S Weigall & Co* (1918) 34 TLR 360. See *Glynn v Margetson & Co* [1893] AC 351 at 354, 358, HL; *Addis v Burrows* [1948] 1 KB 444 at 449, 457, [1948] 1 All ER 177 at 178, 183, CA, per Evershed LJ; *Neuchatel Asphalte Co Ltd v Barnett* [1957] 1 All ER 362 at 365, [1957] 1 WLR 356 at 360, CA, per Denning LJ; *The Brabant* [1967] 1 QB 588, [1966] 1 All ER 961; *Riley (Inspector of Taxes) v Coglan* [1968] 1 All ER 314, [1967] 1 WLR 1300; but see also *Jessel v Bath* (1867) LR 2 Exch 267. As to whether words deleted in a printed form of mercantile contract may still be used to construe words retained or added see para 175 note 13 ante.

212. Repugnant clauses. If there are two clauses or parts of a deed repugnant to each other the first will be received and the latter rejected, unless there is some special reason to the contrary[1]. This is an expedient to which the court very reluctantly has recourse, and never until it has exhausted every other means in its power to reconcile apparent inconsistencies[2]. The rule is subordinate to the general principle that the intention must be ascertained from the entire contents of the deed[3]. Hence, when one clause is in accordance with, and the other is opposed to, the real intention, the former must be received and the latter rejected whatever their relative position[4].

1   'The general rule is that, if there be a repugnancy, the first words in a deed, and the last words in a will
     shall prevail': *Doe d Leicester v Biggs* (1809) 2 Taunt 109 at 113 per Lord Mansfield CJ; and see *Bateson v
     Gosling* (1871) LR 7 CP 9 at 12 per Willes J; Shep Touch 88; *Cole v Sury* (1627) Lat 264; *Cother v Merrick*
     (1657) Hard 89 at 94 per Nicholas B; *Re Webber's Settlement* (1850) 17 Sim 221 at 222; *Bush v Watkins*
     (1851) 14 Beav 425 at 432; *Forbes v Git* [1922] 1 AC 256 at 259, PC. In *Seaman's Case* (1610) Godb 166,
     a lease was made habendum, after an existing term, for 23 years, to be accounted from the date of these
     presents; the latter words were rejected, and the 23 years ran from the end of the existing term. In *Cope
     v Cope* (1846) 15 Sim 118, in the phrase '£1,000 sterling lawful money of Ireland', the words 'of Ireland'
     were rejected. See *Martin v Martin* (1987) 54 P & CR 238 ('beneficial joint tenants in common in equal
     shares'), distinguishing *Joyce v Barker Bros (Builders) Ltd* (1980) 40 P & CR 512 on similar words.
2   *Bush v Watkins* (1851) 14 Beav 425. As to the similar application to a will of the converse rule see *Re
     Gare, Filmer v Carter* [1952] Ch 80 at 83, [1951] 2 All ER 863 at 864 per Harman J. See generally WILLS.
3   See para 175 ante.
4   'There is no doubt that ... effect ought to be given to that part which is calculated to carry into effect
     the real intention, and that part which would defeat it should be rejected': *Walker v Giles* (1848) 6 CB
     662 at 702 per Wide CJ; and see *Parkhurst v Smith d Dormer* (1742) Willes 327 at 332. As to wills cf *Re
     Bywater, Bywater v Clarke* (1881) 18 ChD 17 at 24, CA. See also *Solly v Forbes* (1820) 2 Brod & Bing 38.
     Therefore a proviso in a bill of exchange drawn by a joint stock company purporting to restrict its
     liability is void, as being repugnant to the nature of a bill of exchange: *Re State Fire Insurance Co,
     ex p Meredith's and Conver's Claim* (1863) 32 LJ Ch 300. Similarly, in *Adamastos Shipping Co Ltd v
     Anglo-Saxon Petroleum Co Ltd* [1959] AC 133, [1958] 1 All ER 725, HL, effect was given to a typed
     clause attached to a charterparty notwithstanding that it purported to relate only to a bill of lading.

213.   Repugnant provisos.   A covenant which, taken by itself, is clearly a personal
covenant cannot be qualified by a proviso excluding personal liability; such a proviso is
repugnant and must be rejected[1]. A proviso which is at first sight repugnant to the
principal clause may, however, be reconciled with it by varying the effect of that clause.
Thus a release to one of two partners, with a proviso that the release is not to prejudice
the claims of the releasor against the other partner, operates not as a release, in which
case the proviso would be repugnant, but as a covenant not to sue[2].

1   *Furnivall v Coombes* (1843) 5 Man & G 736 at 751–752; *Watling v Lewis* [1911] 1 Ch 414; *Forbes v Git*
     [1922] 1 AC 256 at 259, PC; and see *Mildmay's Case* (1584) 1 Co Rep 175a; *Cheshire Lines Committe v
     Lewis & Co* (1880) 50 LJQB 121, CA; *Re Holloway's Trusts, Greenwell Ryan* (1909) 26 TLR 62; *Re
     Tewkesbury Gas Co, Tysoe v Tewkesbury Gas Co* [1911] 2 Ch 279 at 285 (affd [1912] 1 Ch 1, CA). As to a
     proviso postponing the immediate operation of a surrender of copyholds cf *Seagood v Hone* (1633) Cro
     Car 366. But a proviso merely limiting the personal liability under the covenant, without destroying it, is
     good: *Williams v Hathaway* (1877) 6 ChD 544 at 549.
2   *Solly v Forbes* (1820) 2 Brod & Bing 38; cf *Bateson v Gosling* (1871) LR 7 CP 9 (where there was a deed
     of arrangement releasing the debtor, with a proviso reserving the rights of creditors against securities);
     GH Renton & Co Ltd v Palmyra Trading Corpn of Panama [1957] AC 149, [1956] 3 All ER 957, HL
     (printed clause in bill of lading relating to strikes held to qualify initial unqualified agreement to deliver
     goods at London or Hull so as to permit delivery at Hamburg).

(5) WHEN AN INSTRUMENT IS VOID FOR UNCERTAINTY

214.   Uncertainty removable by election.   An uncertainty upon a written
instrument which remains after all methods of interpretation have been exhausted may
sometimes be removed by the election of one of the parties; as where there is a grant of
one of certain definite things[1], or of land defined in amount, but indefinite in position[2];
or where a grant of a definite thing may operate in either of two ways[3]. In the former
case, however, there must be a certainty in the nature or amount of the gift, and an
uncertainty only in the specific gift; if the gift is such as to be reducible to certainty, not
by mere election, but by assessment or other means for which no provision is made, the
uncertainty cannot be removed[4]. There is no right of election against the Crown[5].

1   'If I give you one of my horses, although that be uncertain, yet by your election that may be a good gift':
     Mervyn v Lyds (1553) 1 Dyer 90a at 91a; and see Shep Touch 251; Vin Abr, Grants (H 5); Bac Abr, Grants
     (H) 3; *Savill Bros Ltd v Bethell* [1902] 2 Ch 523 at 538, CA.

2   Eg 'the moiety of a yard-land' in a certain waste (*Hungerford's Case* (1585) 1 Leon 30); or a lease of a farm
    containing 437 acres 'except 33 acres thereof' (*Jenkins v Green* (1858) 27 Beav 437).

3   *Heyward's Case* (1595) 2 Co Rep 35a at 35b (instrument operating either as a demise or a bargain and
    sale).

4   Eg a sale of all the tree 'that can be spared' (*Mervyn v Lyds* (1553) 1 Dyer 90a); or a reservation of 'the
    necessary land for making a railway' (*Pearce v Watts* (1875) LR 20 Eq 492). 'If I bargain with you that I
    will give you for your land as much as it is reasonably worth, this is void for default of certainty; but if the
    judging of this be referred to a third person, and he adjudge it, then it is good': *Mervyn v Lyds* (1553) 1
    Dyer 90a. See also *South Easter Rly Co v Associated Portland Cement Manufacturers (1900) Ltd* [1910]
    1 Ch 12 at 19, CA; *Brown v Gould* [1972] Ch 53, [1971] 2 All ER 1505.

5   *Hungerford's Case* (1585) 1 Leon 30; *Brand v Todd* (1618) Noy 29. Any reference in the grant which
    enables the thing granted to be ascertained with certainty will be sufficient to validate the grant: *Doe d
    Devine v Wilson* (1855) 10 Moo PCC 502 at 525.

215.   Who is to elect and when.   Where an uncertainty is curable by election, the
election lies with the party who has to do the first act towards completion of the grant[1].
Thus where the grant has been actually made, though in an uncertain form, the grantee
can complete it by taking one of the various things offered him[2], or by otherwise
selecting the particular gift within the specified limits[3].

Where the plaintiff agreed to lend the defendant £50 for 'nine or six months', the
borrower, being required to do the act in respect of which the alternative periods were
specified (that is, to repay the money), was held entitled to the option of either period[4].
If a lease is granted simply 'to hold for 7, 14, or 21 years' the tenant has the option of
deciding after which period the lease is to determine, on the principle that a grant is
construed most strongly in favour of the grantee[5]; but where a lease was determinable at
a certain date 'if the parties shall so think fit', this was construed as 'if both parties shall
think fit' and the joint assent of lessor and lessee was held to be necessary[6] for, if the
matter lies only in agreement, then the grantor can fulfil his agreement in accordance
with his own election[7]; and where a promise is in the alternative, and one branch of the
alternative cannot be performed, the promisor is bound as a general rule to perform the
other[8].

Where a party issued an instrument in such ambiguous terms that it might be treated
either as a bill of exchange or a promissory note, the holder was allowed to elect, as
against the maker, to treat it as either[9].

If no interest passes until the election, the election must be made in the lifetime of
the parties, as where A gives to B one of his horses. The certainty begins, and the
property passes, when the election is made by B taking a particular horse; and this must
be in the lifetime of the donor and donee. If an interest passes, however, and the only
doubt is as to the title by which it is to be taken, then the continued life of the parties
is not necessary[10].

1   'He who is the first agent, and ought to do the first act, shall have the election': *Heyward's Case* (1595)
    2 Co Rep 35a at 36a, 37a; Co Litt 145a.

2   *Mervyn v Lyds* (1553) 1 Dyer 90a at 91a; Shep Touch 251. 'If A says to B, 'I grant you a horse out of my
    stable', he puts it in the power of B to take which horse he shall think proper'; *Dann v Spurrier* (1803) 3
    Bos & P 399 at 403. See also *Reed v Kilburn Co-operative Society* (1875) LR 10 QB 264.

3   Eg where there is a grant of a specified amount of land in a defined larger area (*Hungerford's Case* (1585)
    1 Leon 30), or a reservation in similar form (*Jenkins v Green* (1858) 27 Beav 437), or a grant of land of
    specified annual value (*Calthrop's Case* (1574) Moore KB 101 at 102). In *Lee's Case* (1578) 1 Leon 268,
    which appears to be contra, the alienation was perhaps not complete.

4   *Reed v Kilburn Co-operative Society* (1875) LR 10 QB 264. See also *Chippendale v Thurston* (1829) 4 C & P
    98 (where the lender was required to do the act, i e give notice, and therefore was entitled to the option);
    Layton v Pearce (1778) 1 Doug KB 15; *Tilling Ltd v James* (1906) 94 LT 823; *Stewart & Co Ltd v Rendall*
    (1899) 1 F 1002, Ct of Sess; *Christie v Wilson* 1915 SC 645, Ct of Sess (where a landlord agreed to
    supplement the water supply so as to make it adequate, or otherwise to lay a pipe from a well and supply
    a pump, it was held that the option lay with the landlord and not with the tenant).

5   *Dann v Spurrier* (1803) 3 Bos & P 399; *Doe d Webb v Dixon* (1807) 9 East 15; *Price v Dyer* (1810) 17 Ves
     356 at 363; *Powell v Smith* (1872) LR 14 Eq 85. Similarly, where goods are bought at six or nine months'
     credit the purchaser has the option: *Price v Nixon* (1814) 5 Taunt 338; *Deverill v Burnell* (1873) LR 8 CP
     475 at 480. See, however, *Ashforth v Redford* (1873) LR 9 CP 20, where 'from six to eight weeks' was
     held to be used in a special mercantile sense.

6   *Fowell v Tranter* (1864) 3 H & C 458.

7   Under an agreement to grant a lease of a farm of 437 acres, reserving 37 acres, the selection is to be made
     by the person granting the lease (*Jenkins v Green* (1858) 27 Beav 437); if a condition be, that the obligor
     shall enfeoff a man of estate D or S upon request, the obligor has his election of which of the two he shall
     enfeoff him (1 Roll Abr, Condition (Y), pl 3, p 446; *Dann v Spurrier* (1803) 3 Bos & P 399 at 403).

8   *Stevens v Webb* (1835) 7 C & P 60; *McIlquham v Taylor* [1895] 1 Ch 53, CA; *Barkworth v Young* (1856) 4
     Drew 1; *Wigley v Blackwal* (1600) Cro Eliz 780; *Anderson v Commercial Union Assurance Co* (1885) 55
     LJQB 146, CA. A promisor who has elected to perform one alternative is not as a general rule excused
     from performance of the other by reason that performance according to his election has become
     impossible: *Brown v Royal Insurance Co* (1859) 1 E & E 853.

9   *Edis v Bury* (1827) 6 B & C 433. Where a person makes a communication to another in ambiguous terms
     he cannot afterwards complain if the recipient of the communication puts upon it a meaning not
     intended by the sender: *Miles v Haslehurst & Co* (1906) 23 TLR 142 at 143 per Channell J. If the vendor
     uses expressions reasonably capable of misconstruction, or if he uses ambiguous words, the purchaser may
     generally construe them in the manner most advantageous to himself: *Seaton v Mapp* (1846) 2 Coll 556 at
     562 per Knight-Bruce V-C.

10   See *Heyward's Case* (1595) 2 Co Rep 35a; *Savill Bros Ltd v Bethell* [1902] 2 Ch 523 at 539, CA (where the
     things are several, nothing passes before election, and the election ought to be precedent; but when one
     and the same thing shall pass, there it passeth presently, and the election of the title may be subsequent).
     If the election related to a particular piece of land which was to be granted or reserved, and the
     conveyance was to operate at common law and not under the Statute of Uses (1535) (now repealed), the
     effect of the conveyance and subsequent election was to create a future freehold, and hence the
     conveyance was void: *Bullock v Burdett* (1568) 3 Dyer 281a; *Savill Bros Ltd v Bethell* supra at 540.

216.   Deed void if finally unintelligible or doubtful. If after every effort has
been made to construe the deed by intrinsic evidence, with the assistance of such
extrinsic evidence as is admissible under the rules (including, in the case of a latent
ambiguity, direct evidence of intention)[1], the deed is unintelligible[2], or there remains an
uncertainty which is not removable by election, either the whole deed or the particular
clause, as the case may require, will be held void for uncertainty[3]. This is only done with
reluctance[4]; and in cases of ambiguity it is a settled canon of construction that a
construction which will make the clause valid is to be preferred to one which will make
it void[5].

1   See paras 185–209 ante.

2   Thus where a lessor of minerals reserves to himself rights of working the non-demised minerals by a
     clause to which no definite meaning can be given, the clause will be rejected: *Mundy v Duke of Rutland*
     (1883) 23 ChD 81, CA.

3   *Mervyn v Lyds* (1553) 1 Dyer 90a (a patent ambiguity not curable by election); *Lord Cheyney's Case* (1591)
     5 Co Rep 68a (a latent ambiguity, where there was no direct evidence of intention to determine it); and
     see Bacon's Law Tracts 99–100; Shep Touch 250–251. An uncertainty as to the commencement of a lease
     cannot be cured by election: *Anon* (1674) 1 Mod Rep 180; but see *Anon* (1591) 1 Leon 227. See also
     Savill Bros Ltd v Bethell [1902] 2 Ch 523, CA; *South Eastern Rly Co v Associated Portland Cement
     Manufacturers (1900) Ltd* [1910] 1 Ch 12, CA.

4   'The books are full of cases where every shift, if I may so speak, has been resorted to, rather than hold the
     gift void for uncertainty': *Doe d Winter v Perratt* (1843) 6 Man & G 314 at 362, HL, per Lord Brougham
     (on a will).

5   *Mills v Dunham* [1891] 1 Ch 576 at 590, CA, per Kay LJ. See also para 177 ante. For the principle that
     the court will not allow an agreement to fail on the ground of uncertainty if to do so would amount to
     sanctioning a fraud see *Pallant v Morgan* [1953] Ch 43, [1952] 2 All ER 951; and SPECIFIC
     PERFORMANCE vol 44(1) (Reissue) para 847.

(6) RECITALS

(i) Variance between Recitals and Operative Part of Instrument

217. Effect of recitals on construction. In the construction of an instrument the recitals are subordinate to the operative part, and consequently, where the operative part is clear, it is treated as expressing the intention of the parties, and prevails over any suggestion of a contrary intention afforded by the recitals[1]. It has sometimes been suggested that a perfectly clear recital may control the operative part[2]; but where the court cannot effect the intention of the parties by giving the operative words a meaning which they will fairly bear, the proper remedy is, it seems, to rectify the deed[3]. Where, however, the operative part is doubtful, the recitals can be used to explain its meaning[4]; and while, for the purpose of construing the operative part, the whole of the instrument may be referred to, the recitals leading up to it are more likely to furnish the key to its true construction than the subsidiary clauses of the deed[5]. Recourse may be had to a recital to determine between two possible meanings of the operative part, although one of the meanings is the more obvious, and would be preferred if no light could be derived from the rest of the deed[6]. A recital may be used to affirm a result which the deed would naturally produce, and which is not expressed in the operative part[7].

A misrecital of an interest which is referred to in the operative part will not affect the construction if the intention is clear. Thus the grant of a reversion upon a lease is good, notwithstanding an error in the recital of the lease[8]. An error in the recital of a lease may, however, be important where it occurs in the grant of a new lease intended to take effect on the determination of the former lease[9]. If the misrecital is such that the new lease purports to take effect on the determination of a lease which is in fact non-existent, the new lease will commence at once, even though it thereby runs out before an existing lease[10], though, if possible, the new lease will be read so as to avoid this result[11].

A recital will only estop that party whose statement, according to the construction of the instrument, it is[12].

The need for a full recital of an earlier instrument in a later one can be avoided by expressing that the later instrument is supplemental to the earlier. The later instrument will then be read and have effect as if it contained a full recital of the earlier instrument[13].

1   *Bailey v Lloyd* (1829) 5 Russ 330 at 344 per Leach MR; and see *Walsh v Trevanion* (1850) 15 QB 733 at 751 per Patteson J; *Young v Smith* (1865) 35 Beav 87 at 90 per Romilly MR; *Re Moon, ex p Dawes* (1886) 17 QBD 275 at 286, CA, per Lord Esher MR; *Orr v Mitchell* [1893] AC 238 at 254, HL, per Lord Macnaghten. See also *Alexander v Crosbie* (1835) L & G temp Sugd 145; *Holliday v Overton* (1852) 14 Beav 467 at 470 (affd (1852) 16 Jur 751); *Leggott v Barrett* (1880) 15 ChD 306 at 311, CA, per Brett LJ; *Dawes v Tredwell* (1881) 18 ChD 354 at 358, CA, per Jessel MR; *Re Sassoon, IRC v Ezra* [1933] Ch 858 at 879, CA (affd sub nom *IRC v Ezra* [1935] AC 96, HL). See further para 218 post.

2   *Boyd v Petrie* (1872) 7 Ch App 385 at 392; *Australian Joint Stock Bank v Bailey* [1899] AC 396 at 400, PC.

3   *Young v Smith* (1865) 35 Beav 87 at 90; *Gwyn v Neath Canal Co* (1868) LR 3 Exch 209. In *Barratt v Wyatt* (1862) 30 Beav 442, Romilly MR seems to have intimated that the court might, in the case of obvious failure of the operative part to carry out a specific recital, read the deed as amended in accordance with the recital. See, however, the principle enunciated by the same judge in *Young v Smith* supra.

4   See *Re Michell's Trusts* (1878) 9 ChD 5 at 9, CA, per Jessel MR ('We may consider it settled by authority, that where the words of a convenant are ambiguous and difficult to deal with, we may resort to the recitals to see whether they throw any light on its meaning'). See also *Earl Mountague v Earl of Bath* (1693) 3 Cas in Ch 55 at 101; *Crouch v Crouch* [1912] 1 KB 378 (convenant in operative part to pay indefinitely controlled by recital that payment was to be for a specified period). See further para 219 post. As to guarantees see e g *Lord Arlington v Merricke* (1672) 2 Saund 403, 411; and GUARANTEE AND INDEMNITY vol 20(1) (Reissue) para 174.

5   *Orr v Mitchell* [1893] AC 238 at 254, HL, per Lord Macnaghten.

6   *Orr v Mitchell* [1893] AC 238, HL. See also *Marquis of Cholmondeley v Lord Clinton* (1820) 2 Jac & W 1 at 99–101 (affd (1821) 4 Bli 1, HL); *Gwyn v Neath Canal Co* (1868) LR 3 Exch 209 at 219 per Channell B; *Re Coghlan, Broughton v Broughton* [1894] 3 Ch 76 at 84.

7   Eg in a mortgage deed the liability to pay interest: *Ashwell v Staunton* (1861) 30 Beav 52.

8   *Withes v Casson* (1615) Hob 128 at 129; cf *Moody v Lewen* (1593) Cro Eliz 127 (where a grant following a misrecital of a fine was adjudged good, 'for there is sufficient certainty of the thing granted, and of the intention of the parties to grant it').

9   *Co Litt* 46b; *Bishop of Bath's Case* (1605) 6 Co Rep 34b, 36a; *Miller v Manwaring.* (1635) Cro Car 397.

10   *Foote v Berkly* (1670) 1 Lev 234.

11   See *Skinner v Gray* (1595) note to *Mount v Hodgkin* (1554) 2 Dyer 116a; *Foote v Berkly* (1670) 1 Lev 234. A lease cannot be granted so as to take effect more than 21 years from the date of the instrument purporting to create it: see the Law of Property Act 1925 s 149(3); and LANDLORD AND TENANT vol 27(1) (2006 Reissue) para 106; REAL PROPERTY vol 39(2) (Reissue) para 102.

      The decision that a misrecital of a sum due under a lease (eg a rent of £170 instead of £140) in a collateral bond for payment of the sum cannot be corrected by reference to the lease itself (*Lainson v Tremere* (1834) 1 Ad & El 792) was disapproved in *Greer v Kettle* [1938] AC 156 at 166, 169, 172, [1937] 4 All ER 396 at 400, 402, 404, HL. As to a misrecital of title see *Moseley v Motteux* (1842) 10 M & W 533; and as to erroneous recital of a draft will in an instrument purporting to carry out the intention of the draft see *Re Carter's Trusts* (1869) 3 IR Eq 495.

12   See *Greer v Kettle* [1938] AC 156 at 170, [1937] 4 All ER 396 at 403, HL; and see further ESTOPPEL vol 16(2) (Reissue) paras 1014, 1020 et seq.

13   See the Law of Property Act 1925 s 58; and SALE OF LAND vol 42 (Reissue) para 284.

218.   Operative part not controlled by recitals.   Recitals have been held not to control the operative part of an instrument, for example where a bond recites the penalty as a sum smaller than the penal sum actually mentioned[1]. Parcels in a deed described with certainty are not cut down by recitals showing that something less was intended to pass[2], nor are they extended by recitals that more was to pass[3]. A covenant in a marriage settlement on the part of both spouses to settle after-acquired property of the wife will bind the wife, although according to the recitals it is the husband only who is to covenant[4]. On the other hand, a covenant by the husband only will not be extended by the recital of an agreement for settlement of after-acquired property so as to be a covenant by the wife also[5].

1   *Ingleby v Swift* (1833) 10 Bing 84 (where the sum in the recital was £500 and in the operative part £1,000; the debt due at the time of action exceeded £500, and the question was whether the liability of the sureties could be restricted by the recital); *Sansom v Bell* (1809) 2 Camp 39; cf *Australian Joint Stock Bank v Bailey* [1899] AC 396, PC; and see *Evans v Earle* (1854) 10 Exch 1. Recitals in a bond may, however, restrict the onerousness of the condition: see para 220 post.

2   Where, in a marriage settlement, there was a recital of the settlor's intention to settle all his estate except the lands of 'B' and its sub-denominations, and there was in the operative part a specific conveyance of 'K', one of the sub-denominations of 'B', it was held that 'K' passed (*Alexander v Crosbie* (1835) L & G temp Sugd 145); cf *Re Gowen and Shanks, ex p Young* (1839) 4 Deac 185 (recitals relating to joint property of partners did not control operative part which extended to separate property); *Re Medley, ex p Glyn* (1840) 1 Mont D & De G 29 (recitals relating to freeholds subject to a charge did not prevent operative part affecting freeholds not so subject and copyholds). See also *Re Owen's Trust* (1855) 1 Jur NS 1069 (interests included in operative part of settlement, but not in recitals); *Youde v Jones* (1845) 14 Sim 131.

3   *Macnamara v Carey* (1866) IR 1 Eq 9 (recital in settlement of agreement to settle five distinct denominations of land; two were omitted from operative part; these did not pass).

4   *Willoughby v Middleton* (1862) 2 John & H 344. So an absolute covenant not to do an act will not be qualified by a recital of an intention that it may be done on payment (see *Bird v Lake* (1863) 1 Hem & M 111); and an absolute covenant for title will be enforced even as regards a defect appearing in a recital (*Page v Midland Rly Co* [1894] 1 Ch 11, CA); though a doubtful covenant may be explained by a recital (*Re Coghlan, Broughton* [1894] 3 Ch 76, where a covenant by a wife to settle property acquired during her life was restricted to property acquired during coverture). A recital as to the settlor's intention will not control clear words in the operative part, although they fail to carry out that intention: *Re Sassoon, IRC v Ezra* [1933] Ch 858 at 879; affd sub nom *IRC v Ezra* [1935] AC 96, HL.

5   *Hammond v Hammond* (1854) 19 Beav 29; *Young v Smith* (1865) 35 Beav 87; *Re Webb's Trusts* (1877) 46 LJ Ch 769; *Dawes v Tredwell* (1881) 18 ChD 354, CA. If the husband, however, covenants that he and his wife shall settle, and she executes the deed, the recital will justify the deed being read as containing a covenant by the wife: *Re De Ros' Trust, Hardwicke v Wilmot* (1885) 31 ChD 81.

219.   Recital explaining operative part.   The following are instances where the recitals assist the construction of the operative part of an instrument: where there is an ambiguity in the operative part as to the property affected[1]; where the operative part contains general words, and the recital shows that only specific property, comprised in the general words, was intended to pass[2]; and where the recital shows that a limitation in point of time must be placed on the operative part[3]. After a recital that the assignor is entitled to a specific share of property under a will or settlement, an assignment of that specific share 'or other the part or share, parts or shares' to which he is entitled will, if the rest of the instrument supports the recital, be restricted to the specific share[4]. An apparent inaccuracy in a covenant may be corrected by restricting it in the manner indicated by a recital[5]; and the omission in the operative part of reference to a person who executes the deed may be supplied from a recital[6].

1   *Walsh v Trevanion* (1850) 15 QB 733.
2   Although words of specific description are not easily dealt with, yet general words are; and though general words may be in themselves large enough, yet if, upon the whole scope of the instrument, as to which special regard is to be had to what are called introductory recitals, it appears it was not the intention of the parties to pass these properties, it will not pass them: *Howard v Earl of Shrewsbury* (1874) LR 17 Eq 378 at 391 per Jessel MR. See also *Moore v Magrath* (1774) 1 Cowp 9; *Doe d Meyrick v Meyrick* (1832) 2 Cr & J 223; *Rooke v Lord Kensington* (1856) 2 K & J 753; *Hopkinson v Lusk* (1864) 34 Beav 215; *Neame v Moorsom* (1866) LR 3 Eq 91 at 97 per Lord Romilly MR; *Jenner v Jenner* (1866) LR 1 Eq 361; *Re Earl of Durham, Earl Grey v Earl of Durham* (1887) 57 LT 164; *Orr v Mitchell* [1893] AC 238, HL. As to the interests comprised in a disentailing deed see *Grattan v Langdale* (1883) 11 LR Ir 473.
3   *Lord Arlington v Merricke* (1672) 2 Saund 411 (fidelity bond restricted to the original six months of office as appearing from a recital); *Liverpool Waterworks Co v Atkinson* (1805) 6 East 507 (similar case). As to recitals assisting the construction of covenants for title see *Barton v Fitzgerald* (1812) 15 East 530 at 541.
4   *Gray v Earl of Limerick* (1848) 2 De G & Sm 370; *Childers v Eardley* (1860) 28 Beav 648.
5   *Re Neal's Trusts* (1857) 4 Jur NS 6; *Crouch v Crouch* [1912] 1 KB 378. Apparently a recital has more effect in controlling the language of a covenant than of a grant: see *McLurcan v Lane* (1858) 7 WR 135.
6   *Dent v Clayton* (1864) 33 LJ Ch 503 (recital that wife, who executed the deed, joined to release dower, but the wife not mentioned in operative part as releasing).

220.   Condition of a bond controlled by recitals or indorsement.   Recitals may operate in restraint of the condition of a bond[1] where the words of the condition import a larger liability than that contemplated by the recitals[2], especially in favour of sureties[3]. Where, however, the condition is for repayment of money to be advanced, the amount being limited by the recitals to a certain sum, an advance in excess of such sum does not avoid the bond in the absence of an express stipulation to that effect. The effect is merely to limit the liability of the obligor to the sum mentioned in the recitals[4].

The condition will not be controlled or limited by recitals which are not clearly consistent with that condition[5], nor will recitals affect the obligatory part of a bond if that part is clear and unambiguous; recitals are not considered to form part of the obligation, but to be incorporated with and form part of the condition[6].

The condition may be restrained by a memorandum indorsed on the bond, if it appears to have been the intention of the parties that the memorandum should form part of the condition and it was indorsed on the bond before execution[7].

1   For the meanings of 'condition' and 'obligation' of a bond see para 91 ante.
2   *Pearsall v Summersett* (1812) 4 Taunt 593; *Payler v Homersham* (1815) 4 M & S 423; *Liverpool Waterworks Co v Atkinson* (1805) 6 East 507.
3   *Lord Arlington v Merricke* (1672) 2 Saund 411; *African Co v Mason* (1714) cited 1 Str 227.
4   *Parker v Wise* (1817) 6 M & S 239; *Gordon v Rae* (1858) 8 E & B 1065 at 1086–1087.
5   *Bird v Lake* (1863) 1 Hem & M 111; *Australian Joint Stock Bank v Bailey* [1899] AC 396, PC.
6   *Ingleby v Swift* (1833) 10 Bing 84; *Sansom v Bell* (1809) 2 Camp 39. See further para 218 note 1 ante.
7   *Broke v Smith* (1602) Moore KB 679; *Burgh v Preston* (1800) 8 Term Rep 483; *Hurst v Jennings* (1826) 5 B & C 650; *Reed v Norris* (1837) 2 My & Cr 361.

221. Releases and powers of attorney. Releases are especially liable to have general words in the operative part of an instrument controlled by the recitals. The general words in a release are limited always to those things which were specially in the contemplation of the parties at the time when the release was given[1]; and since it is the office of recitals to state the particular considerations upon which a deed is founded, they naturally control the operation of the release[2]. Thus, if in a release of debts there are recitals as to the specific debts to be released, the release will operate only as to these debts[3]; and a release to an administrator, founded on a recital of specified assets having been got in, will not extend to other assets[4]. Similarly, a power of attorney is liable to be restricted by the recitals[5]. In a power of attorney, reciting the principal's intended absence abroad and his desire to appoint attorneys to act during his absence, the operative part, though unlimited, was held to be confined to the principal's absence[6].

This rule has been applied to indemnities and guarantees[7].

1 *Directors of London and South Western Rly Co v Blackmore* (1870) LR 4 HL 610 at 623 per Lord Westbury; *Lyall v Edwards* (1861) 6 H & N 337; *Re Joint Stock Trust and Finance Corpn Ltd* (1912) 56 Sol Jo 272; *Richmond v Savill* [1926] 2 KB 530, CA; *Bank of Credit and Commerce International SA (in liquidation) v Ali* [1999] 2 All ER 1005. See also *Skilbeck v Hilton* (1866) LR 2 Eq 587.

2 If a release is given on a particular consideration recited, notwithstanding that the release concludes with general words, yet the law, in order to prevent surprise, will construe it to relate to the particular matter recited, which was under the contemplation of the parties and intended to be released: *Ramsden v Hylton* (1751) 2 Ves Sen 304 at 310 per Lord Hardwicke LC. See also *Lampon v Corke* (1822) 5 B & Ald 606 at 611 per Best J; *Re Perkins, Poyser v Beyfus* [1898] 2 Ch 182 at 190, CA, per Lindley MR; *Thorpe v Thorpe* (1701) 1 Ld Raym 235, 662. So concurrence in a conveyance to obviate a specified objection as to title binds the concurring party only as regards that objection; contra, if he concurs to obviate objections generally: *Lord Braybroke v Inskip* (1803) 8 Ves 417; *Marquis of Cholmondeley v Lord Clinton* (1817) 2 Mer 171, 355. Similarly, a deed of compromise of ascertained specific questions does not extend to rights not then in dispute: *Cloutte v Storey* [1911] 1 Ch 18, CA.

3 *Payler v Homersham* (1815) 4 M & S 423. The same principle applies as to causes of action: *Simons v Johnson* (1832) 3 B & Ad 175. In the absence of such recitals, however, the general words will have effect: see *Lampon v Corke* (1822) 5 B & Ald 606 at 611.

4 *Anon* (1862) 31 Beav 310. See also *Lindo v Lindo* (1839) 1 Beav 496; *Turner v Turner* (1880) 14 ChD 829 (assets got in by the administrator after release not included in release); *Major v Salisbury* (1845) 14 LJQB 118.

5 A general power of attorney conferring the widest authority may be granted by use of the form prescribed by the Powers of Attorney Act 1971 (see Sch 1) or a form to the like effect but expressed to be made under the Act: s 10(1). The statutory form contains no recitals. See further AGENCY vol 2(1) (Reissue) para 58 et seq.

6 *Danby v Coutts & Co* (1885) 29 ChD 500.

7 As to indemnities see *Boyes v Bluck* (1853) 13 CB 652. As to guarantees see *Pearsall v Summersett* (1812) 4 Taunt 593; *Bain v Cooper* (1842) 9 M & W 701; but see *Sansom v Bell* (1809) 2 Camp 39.

(ii) Effect of Recital as a Covenant

222. Recital constituting covenant. No technical language is needed to make a covenant, and any words in a deed which show an intention that the parties or one of them is to be bound to do or not to do a thing will constitute a covenant[1]. Such an intention may appear from a recital, and then, in the absence of any contrary indication in the deed, the recital will operate as a covenant[2]. This will be so where the recital is that one party has agreed to do or not to do a certain thing, as to pull down a mill and build a larger one[3]; to settle property[4]; to pay a composition on his own debts[5], or to pay the debts of another[6]; not to enforce a debt until the security for it has been realised[7]; in a separation deed, that the husband and wife have agreed to live apart[8]; that one party is to have a certain share of profits[9]; or where the recital is that a certain thing is intended to be done[10]. A recital or acknowledgement that a certain sum of money is due may be construed as a covenant to pay it[11]. For a recital to amount to a covenant, however, it must be plain upon the whole deed that it was so intended[12]. The court will be cautious in spelling a covenant out of a recital in a deed, because that is not the part of the deed in which covenants are usually expressed[13].

1   See para 249 post.
2   *Aspdin v Austin* (1844) 5 QB 671 at 683 per Lord Denman CJ; and see *Severn and Clerk's Case* (1588) 1 Leon 122. As to the effect of recitals as estoppels see ESTOPPEL; and as to the effect of a recital as an execution of a power see POWERS.
3   *Sampson v Easterby* (1829) 9 B & C 505; affd sub nom *Easterby v Sampson* (1830) 6 Bing 644, Ex Ch (here the construction was assisted by an express covenant to keep the new mill in repair).
4   *Buckland v Buckland* [1900] 2 Ch 534 at 540; and see *Graves v White* (1680) Freem Ch 57; *Duckett v Gordon* (1860) 11 I Ch R 181 (where, in a marriage settlement, it was recited that the wife's father desired to settle property).
5   *Lay v Mottram* (1865) 19 CBNS 479; *Brooks v Jennings* (1866) LR 1 CP 476.
6   *Saltoun v Houstoun* (1824) 1 Bing 433; *Carr v Roberts* (1833) 5 B & Ad 78.
7   *Farrall v Hilditch* (1859) 5 CBNS 840.
8   *Re Weston, Davies v Tagart* [1900] 2 Ch 164.
9   See *Barfoot v Freswell and Picard* (1675) 3 Keb 465 (where an indenture recited an agreement that the plaintiff should have one-third part of coals dug in a mine and it was said by Hale CJ, 'Were it but a recital, that before the indenture they were agreed, it is a covenant').
10 *Hollis v Carr* (1676) 2 Mod Rep 86.
11 *Brice v Carre and Emerson* (1661) 1 Lev 47; *Saunders v Milsome* (1866) LR 2 Eq 573; *Isaacson v Harwood* (1868) 3 Ch App 225; *Jackson v North Eastern Rly Co* (1877) 7 ChD 573 at 583; c f *Cheslyn v Dalby* (1840) 4 Y & C Ex 238.
12 *Borrowes v Borrowes* (1872) 6 IR Eq 368.
13 *Farrall v Hilditch* (1859) 5 CBNS 840 at 854.

223.   Recital introduced for other purpose.   A recital will not operate as a covenant if it appears on the whole instrument to have been introduced for some other purpose. Thus where a recital that a debt is due is introductory to a charge for the debt given by the operative part, it will not amount to a covenant so as to make the debt a specialty debt[1]. In accordance with the rules that the operative part prevails over the recitals[2], and that expressed terms exclude implied terms[3], a recital will not create a covenant where the operative part contains an express covenant dealing with the same subject matter[4].

1   *Courtney v Taylor* (1843) 6 Man & G 851 at 868; *Ivens v Elwes* (1854) 3 Drew 25; *Stone v Van Heythusen* (1854) Kay 721; *Marryat v Marryat* (1860) 28 Beav 224 at 226; *Isaacson v Harwood* (1868) 3 Ch App 225 at 228; *Jackson v North Eastern Rly Co* (1877) 7 ChD 573. It seems that a recital of a debt will readily be assumed to be for some other purpose than to create a covenant, for it is easy to insert a covenant for payment if this is intended: *Courtney v Taylor* (1843) 6 Man & G 851. A recital that consideration money has been paid, when in fact it has not been paid, does not imply a covenant to pay it: *Morgan's Patent Anchor Co v Morgan* (1876) 35 LT 811.
2   See paras 217–218 ante.
3   See para 182 ante.
4   *Dawes v Tredwell* (1881) 18 ChD 354, CA; c f *Young v Smith* (1865) LR 1 Eq 180.

(7)   RECEIPT CLAUSES

224.   Conclusiveness of receipt.   A receipt for money though contained in a deed, is not conclusive that the money has been in fact paid and evidence can be given of the non-payment of the whole or part of it[1]. Where, however, a purchaser in good faith for valuable consideration[2] derives title under a deed executed after 31 December 1881 containing in its body, or having indorsed upon it, a receipt for consideration money or other consideration, and that person has no notice that the consideration was not in fact paid or given, either wholly or in part, then in his favour the receipt is sufficient evidence of the payment or giving of the whole amount of the receipt[3].

1　　*Burchell v Thompson* [1920] 2 KB 80 at 86, DC, per Lush J; and see *Greer v Kettle* [1938] AC 156 at 171, [1937] 4 All ER 396 at 404, HL, per Lord Maugham. A receipt in a deed (provided that it was not merely indorsed on the deed and under hand: see *Lampon v Corke* (1822) 5 B & Ald 606 at 612) formerly operated at law to estop the person who had given it from saying that the money had not been paid (*Baker v Dewey* (1823) 1 B & C 704 at 707; and see *Rowntree v Jacob* (1809) 2 Taunt 141 at 143); but this was not so in equity (*Hawkins v Gardiner* (1854) 2 Sm & G 441; *Wilson v Keating* (1859) 27 Beav 121 at 126; and see *Coppin v Coppin* (1725) 2 P Wms 291 at 295; *Gresley v Mousley* (1862) 3 De GF & J 433). At law, also, the fact of non-payment might in some cases be proved, as where a cheque was dishonoured (*Deverell v Whitmarsh* (1841) 5 Jur 963), but not where the receipt was founded on a miscalculation (*Harding v Ambler* (1838) 3 M & W 279). The receipt was not an estoppel where it was not an absolute acknowledgment of payment, but referred to and was qualified by a recital of an agreement to pay (*Bottrell v Summers* (1828) 2 Y & J 407; *Lampon v Corke* supra); and since the Supreme Court of Judicature Act 1873 (see now the Supreme Court Act 1981 (prospectively renamed the Senior Courts Act 1981) s 49(1); and EQUITY vol 16(2) (Reissue) paras 401, 496 et seq), the rule in equity has prevailed. It follows that the unpaid purchase money will be secured by the usual vendor's lien: *Winter v Lord Anson* (1827) 3 Russ 488. The fact that a mortgage contains a recital of an amount as due for costs does not preclude a party to the mortgage from taking out a summons for delivery of a bill of costs, or for taxation of a bill that has been delivered: *Re Foster, Barnato v Foster* [1920] 3 KB 306, CA (disapproving *Re Forsyth* (1865) 34 Beav 140; *Re Gold* (1871) 24 LT 9). An acknowledgement of receipt of premium in a marine insurance policy effected by a broker is conclusive between insurer and assured, but not between insurer and broker: see the Marine Insurance Act 1906 s 54; and INSURANCE vol 25 (Reissue) para 90.

2　　That expression is used to include a lessee, mortgagee or other person who for valuable consideration acquires an interest in property and, in reference to a legal estate, includes a chargee by way of legal mortgage: see the Law of Property Act 1925 s 205(1)(xxi) (amended by the Civil Partnership Act 2004 s 261(1), Sch 27 para 7). As to the position of a transferee of a mortgage see generally MORTGAGE.

3　　Law of Property Act 1925 s 68; and see *Rice v Rice* (1854) 2 Drew 73 at 83; *Bickerton v Walker* (1885) 31 ChD 151, CA; *Lloyds Bank Ltd v Bullock* [1896] 2 Ch 192; *Rimmer v Webster* [1902] 2 Ch 163 at 173–174, where Farwell J distinguished *Carritt v Real and Personal Advance Co* (1889) 42 ChD 263, and said that *Rice v Rice* supra was a case of pure estoppel; *Bateman v Hunt* [1904] 2 KB 530, CA; *Powell v Browne* (1907) 97 LT 854, CA; *Capell v Winter* [1907] 2 Ch 376 at 381, where, however, Parker J observed at 382 that *Rice v Rice* supra and *Lloyds Bank Ltd v Bullock* supra did not really depend on estoppel; *De Lisle v Union Bank of Scotland* [1914] 1 Ch 22, CA; *Re King's Settlement, King v King* [1931] 2 Ch 294; *Tsang Chuen v Li Po Kwai* [1932] AC 715, PC. Although the transaction is between a solicitor and his client, a subsequent purchaser who has knowledge of the fact is not, it seems, normally thereby put upon inquiry: see e g *Powell v Browne* (1907) 97 LT 854, CA. See further, as to receipts SALE OF LAND.

225.　Receipt clause as authority for solicitor to receive money. Where the solicitor[1] for the vendor or for the mortgagor produces a deed having in its body or indorsed thereon a receipt executed or signed by the vendor or mortgagor and in reliance on the statutory authority in that behalf[2] the consideration money is paid to the solicitor, the vendor or the mortgagor is estopped from denying the authority of the solicitor to receive it[3].

1　　The reference to a solicitor includes a licensed conveyancer under the Administration of Justice Act 1985 ss 11(2), 34 (as amended) (see SOLICITORS vol 44(1) (Reissue) paras 550 et seq, 623): s 34(1) (amended by the Land Registration Act 2002 s 135, Sch 13).

2　　See the Law of Property Act 1925 s 69; and SALE OF LAND vol 42 (Reissue) para 315; SOLICITORS vol 44(1) (Reissue) para 123.

3　　*King v Smith* [1900] 2 Ch 425.

(8)　THE PROPERTY CONVEYED

(i)　The Parcels: Inaccurate Descriptions

226.　Description of property. The property comprised in a deed, or the 'parcels', is described by terms having either a general or specific meaning, and usually by two or more such terms. Where possible, full effect will be given to all the terms of description. Thus a grant of all the grantor's freehold land in the county of Hampshire contains a general and also a specific term, and effect is given to both by treating the specific term as restricting the general term. Consequently, of all the grantor's freehold land, only that situate in the county of Hampshire will pass[1]. In such a case both the descriptions are required in order to define the particular property which is being dealt with. It is always a question of fact whether a particular parcel of land is or is not contained in the description of the land conveyed[2].

It may be, however, that, of the various terms used, some are sufficient to define the property with certainty, and the rest add a description which is not true; for example, if there is a grant of a specified house, with words sufficient to ascertain it with certainty, and then there is added 'now in the occupation of A', when the house is in fact in the occupation of B. In this case the additional words cannot be treated as words restricting the previous description. They are simply untrue: they are an inaccurate additional description[3]. Since, however, the rest of the description defines the property intended to be disposed of and the deed must, if possible, be supported, the error is not allowed to prejudice the grant and the erroneous addition is rejected[4].

1   See *Miller v Travers* (1832) 8 Bing 244 (a case of a devise).
2   In order to find the true meaning of any relevant document reference may be made to the recitals: *Doe d White v Osborne* (1840) 4 Jur 941; and see para 219 ante. Evidence outside the deed is admissible to identify the particular lands denoted by the words of the deed (*Dublin and Kingstown Rly Co v Bradford* (1857) 7 ICLR 57, 624; *Lyle v Richards* (1866) LR 1 HL 222 at 239) but not so as to contradict plain language of description in the deed (*Grigsby v Melville* [1973] 3 All ER 455, [1974] 1 WLR 80, CA; *Woolls v Powling* [1999] All ER (D) 125, (1999) Times, 9 March, CA). Words in an instrument of grant, as elsewhere, are to be taken in the sense which the common usage of mankind has applied to them in reference to the context in which they are found, and to the circumstances in which they are used (*Lord v Sydney City Comrs* (1859) 12 Moo PCC 473 at 497) and, where the instrument is an ancient instrument and, probably, even where it is a modern instrument, they may be explained by subsequent possession (*Booth v Ratté* (1890) 15 App Cas 188 at 192, PC; *L Schüler AG v Wickman Machine Tool Sales Ltd* [1974] AC 235, [1973] 2 All ER 39, HL; *St Edmundsbury and Ipswich Diocesan Board of Finance v Clark (No 2)* [1975] 1 All ER 772 [1975] 1 WLR 468, CA; and see paras 205–206 ante). The express mention of certain property, e g 'quarries', may show that other property, such as 'mines', was not intended to pass, on the principle 'expressio unius est exclusio alterius' (see paras 182–183 ante), especially where assisted by the recitals: *Denison v Holliday* (1857) 1 H & N 631 at 648–649; affd (1858) 3 H & N 670. See *Francis v Hayward* (1882) 22 ChD 177, CA (fascia passing as part of a house); *Grigsby v Melville* [1973] 3 All ER 455, [1974] 1 WLR 80, CA (cellar under house passing as part of house although only current access from neighbouring house); *Alan Wibberley Building Ltd v Insley* [1999] 2 All ER 897, [1999] 1 WLR 894, HL (hedge and ditch presumption applied). See also BOUNDARIES vol 4(1) (2002 Reissue) para 927 et seq.
3   'The characteristic of cases within the rule is, that the description, so far as it is false, applies to no subject at all, and, so far as it is true, applies to one only': *Morrell v Fisher* (1849) 4 Exch 591 at 604 per Alderson B. See also *Cowen v Truefitt Ltd* [1899] 2 Ch 309 at 311, CA, per Lindley MR, quoting from Jarman on Wills (5th Edn) 742 (see now 2 Jarman on Wills (8th Edn) 1246–1247); but see para 228 post.
4   See BOUNDARIES vol 4(1) (2002 Reissue) para 928; and c f *Adamastos Shipping Co Ltd v Anglo-Saxon Petroleum Co Ltd* [1959] AC 133, [1958] 1 All ER 725, HL.

227. Effect of false description. That an erroneous description will be rejected is expressed by the rule 'falsa demonstratio non nocet cum de corpore constat'[1]; but this rule is subject to another rule, namely that in general the additional words are not rejected as importing a false description, if they can be read as words of restriction[2]. These two rules govern the construction of parcels. When the premises are sufficiently described, as by giving the particular name of a close or otherwise, an erroneous additional description will be rejected as a 'falsa demonstratio'[3]; but if there is not this certainty in the first description (for example, if it is expressed in general terms) and a particular description is added, the latter controls the former and limits the generality of the earlier description[4], for where words are inserted which thus form an essential part of the description of the subject matter they cannot be rejected[5]. In case of doubt whether words are a 'falsa demonstratio' or words of restriction they must be taken as words of restriction, for the law will not assume that the description is erroneous or false[6]. Of course the additional words may be neither words of restriction nor of false description, but simply an alternative description which exactly fits the premises already described[7]. Here the further description is redundant.

1   Ie a false description does not vitiate when there is no doubt as to who is the person meant. See *Travers v Blundell* (1877) 6 ChD 436 at 442, 444, CA.

2   Ie 'non accipi debent verba in demonstrationem falsam quae competunt in limitationem veram': *Morrell v Fisher* (1849) 4 Exch 591 at 604. But see para 228 post.

3   *Llewellyn v Earl of Jersey* (1843) 11 M & W 183; *Barton v Dawes* (1850) 19 LJCP 302; *Cowen v Truefitt Ltd* [1899] 2 Ch 309, CA; *Watcham v A-G of East Africa Protectorate* [1919] AC 533, PC. Many cases of 'falsa demonstratio' have reference to the construction of wills: see WILLS vol 50 (2005 Reissue) para 561.

4   *Doe d Smith v Galloway* (1833) 5 B & Ad 43 at 51 per Parke J; *Roe d Conolly v Vernon and Vyse* (1804) 5 East 51 (on a will); *Morrell v Fisher* (1849) 4 Exch 591 at 604 per Alderson B. See further para 231 post. Where there are several descriptions which, when evidence of surrounding facts is admitted, are not consistent with one another, there is no general rule by which the court can decide which description ought to prevail; but other things being equal it would seem that the more detailed and precise the description, the more likely it is to accord with the real intention of the parties; the order in which the conflicting descriptions occur is not at all conclusive: *Eastwood v Ashton* [1915] AC 900 at 912, HL, per Lord Parker.

5   *Magee v Lavell* (1874) LR 9 CP 107; and see *Early v Rathbone* (1888) 57 LJ Ch 652.

6   Bacon's Law Tracts 76; *Doe d Harris v Greathed* (1806) 8 East 91 at 104; *Morrell v Fisher* (1849) 4 Exch 591; and see *Doddington's Case, Hall v Peart* (1594) 2 Co Rep 32b at 33a, n(A).

7   Eg 'No 73, Oxford Street, now in the occupation of John Smith', where such is the actual occupation.

228. Descriptions rejected. It follows from the rule 'falsa demonstratio non nocet cum de corpore constat'[1] that, where the particular land is ascertained with certainty by part of the description, an erroneous statement as to the mode in which title to the land is derived[2], or as to tenure[3] or area[4], or mode of user[5] or name[6] or parish[7] or boundary[8] or occupation[9], will be rejected. The description which is rejected as false need not follow the true description. The whole description must be looked at fairly to see which are the leading words of description and which is the subordinate matter[10].

The words of a positive covenant by a vendor in a deed conveying part of his property cannot be relied on to qualify the effect of a clear and unambiguous parcels clause identifying the part of the property that is being conveyed[11].

1   See para 227 ante.

2   Eg 'All my manor of Sale in Dale which I had by descent'. If had by purchase and not by descent, yet the manor, being sufficiently described, passes; but contra if the first description is not specific, as 'all my lands in Dale which I had by descent': Shep Touch 247; *Wrotesley v Adams* (1559) 1 Plowd 187 at 191; *Windham v Windham* (1581) 3 Dyer 376b. The rest of the instrument may show that the words as to title are restrictive: *Clay and Barnet's Case* (1613) Godb 236.

3   Devise of 'my freehold farm and lands situate at Edgware, and now in the occupation of James Bray', held to pass a part of the farm which was copyhold: *Re Bright-Smith, Bright-Smith v Bright-Smith* (1886) 31 ChD 314.

4   Where a piece of land was described by reference to a plan drawn to scale, and was stated to contain 34 perches, whereas the plan showed it to contain 27 perches only, the description '34 perches' was rejected: *Llewellyn v Earl of Jersey* (1843) 11 M & W 183; Shep Touch 247; *Lord Willoughby v Foster* (1553) 1 Dyer 80b; *Jack v McIntyre* (1845) 12 Cl & Fin 151, HL; *Manning v Fitzgerald* (1859) 29 LJ Ex 24. Where a farm sufficiently described was stated to contain 213 acres, certain woodlands, 56 acres in extent, part of the farm, but not included in the 213 acres, were held to pass: *Portman v Mill* (1839) 8 LJ Ch 161. Where premises are sold by name and what was intended to be included under the name cannot be determined on the face of the deed, the evidence of a contemporary survey, made by agreement between the vendor and purchaser for the purpose of determining the boundary between the land sold and land retained by the vendor, may prevail over statements as to the quantity of the land conveyed contained in the deed: *Barnard v De Charleroy* (1899) 81 LT 497, PC; cf *Jervey v Styring* (1874) 29 LT 847; and see BOUNDARIES vol 4(1) (2002 Reissue) paras 937 et seq. Where the dimensions are an essential part of the description and not a mere addition to a description which is in the first place sufficiently certain, they cannot be rejected: *Mellor v Walmesley* [1905] 2 Ch 164 at 175, CA, per Vaughan Williams LJ.

5   Where there was a devise of freehold hereditaments called West Cliff, situate at West Cowes, 'now used as lodging-houses', the whole of the West Cliff estate passed, though only part was used as lodging-houses: *Cunningham v Butler* (1861) 3 Giff 37.

6   *Rorke v Errington* (1859) 7 HL Cas 617 at 626.

7   *Lambe v Reaston* (1813) 5 Taunt 207; cf *Cotterel v Franklin* (1815) 6 Taunt 284; contra *Norris's Case and Campian's Case* (1570) 3 Dyer 292a.

8   *Francis v Hayward* (1882) 22 ChD 177 at 181, CA, per Jessel MR.

9   A demise by lessors of the reversion of all their 'farm in Brosley, in the tenure of Roger Wilcox', passed the farm though not in such tenure: *Wrotesley v Adams* (1559) 1 Plowd 187 at 191. See also *Swyft v Eyres* (1639) Cro Car 546; *Goodtitle d Radford v Southern* (1813) 1 M & S 299; *Wilkinson v Malin* (1832) 2 Cr & J 636; *Doe d Smith v Galloway* (1833) 5 B & Ad 43 (lease of land with in specified abuttals 'now in the occupation of' S); and see *Hardwick v Hardwick* (1873) LR 16 Eq 168 (a devise), where both the situation and occupation were inaccurately described, but the estate, being clearly identified, passed. A reference to occupation will not necessarily limit the premises conveyed, although it is true of only a part of the premises: *Martyr v Lawrence* (1864) 2 De GJ & Sm 261 at 270.

10 *Hardwick v Hardwick* (1873) LR 16 Eq 168 at 175 per Lord Selborne LC; *Re Bright-Smith, Bright-Smith v Bright-Smith* (1886) 31 ChD 314; *Cowen v Truefitt Ltd* [1899] 2 Ch 309, CA. Formerly the earlier words prevailed, and if they were false the grant was void: *Dowtie's Case* (1584) 3 Co Rep 9b; and see *Stukeley v Butler* (1614) Hob 168 at 171.

11 *Rhone v Stephens* (1993) 67 P & CR 9, CA; affd on appeal [1994] 2 AC 310, [1994] 2 All ER 65, HL.

229.   Plans. Frequently when property is conveyed it is described both by words and by reference to a plan[1], and this should be done when practicable so that the plan may be looked at for the purpose of explaining the language of the parcels[2]; but it is imprudent to rely upon a plan alone as the sole description, since slight errors in the drawing may have serious consequences[3]; moreover, a complete and unambiguous description in a deed will prevail over a plan[4]. A description which is sufficient without reference to a plan may be enough[5], but the purchaser, at any rate in simple cases[6], can insist on a plan in order to supplement the general description in the conveyance if the latter is not sufficiently precise. If, however, the description in the contract is sufficient to identify the property, the purchaser cannot require it to be supplemented by a plan at the expense of the vendor[7]. Attaching a plan to a conveyance does not necessarily warrant the accuracy of the plan[8].

1   Where a plan is used, a substantive description of the property should be included in the body of the deed or in a schedule, so that the plan should merely assist the description. It is usual and proper to refer to the plan as being by way of identification, and not as operating to enlarge or restrict the verbal description. Where property is contracted to be bought by a plan, the plan determines the extent of property sold, notwithstanding that particulars subsequently given, purporting to be particulars of the property shown on the plan, are erroneous (*Gordon-Cumming v Houldsworth* [1910] AC 537, HL (a Scottish case)); if the plan shows the lengths of three sides of the plot but not the fourth, the fourth side may, in accordance with the plan, be taken to be a straight line although not readily compatible with the state of the land (see *Hopgood v Brown* [1955] 1 All ER 550, [1955] 1 WLR 213, CA). As to the admissibility of plans and maps generally see EVIDENCE. See also BOUNDARIES vol 4(1) (2002 Reissue) para 939.

2   *Taylor v Parry* (1840) 1 Man & G 604 at 616; *Lyle v Richards* (1866) LR 1 HL 222 at 231; cf *Re Otway's Estate* (1862) 13 I Ch R 222 at 234. If a plan forms part of a conveyance, the fact that it is not referred to in the conveyance does not oblige the court to disregard it: *Leachman v L and K Richardson Ltd* [1969] 3 All ER 20 at 29–30, [1969] 1 WLR 1129 at 1141–1142, distinguishing *Wyse v Leahy* (1875) IR 9 CL 384. A plan on particulars of sale which are referred to in the deed can probably not be looked at: *Barlow v Rhodes* (1833) 1 Cr & M 439.

3   *Llewellyn v Earl of Jersey* (1843) 11 M & W 183; *Barton v Dawes* (1850) 10 CB 261; *Davis v Shepherd* (1866) 1 Ch App 410; *Thompson v Hickman* [1907] 1 Ch 550. See also 1 Dart's Vendors and Purchasers (8th Edn) 479; 1 Williams on Vendor and Purchaser (4th Edn) 653; 1 Davidson's Precedents in Conveyancing (5th Edn) 63–66.

4   *Dublin and Kingstown Rly Co v Bradford* (1857) 7 ICLR 57; *Roe v Lidwell* (1860) 11 ICLR 320, Ex Ch; *Horne v Struben* [1902] AC 454 at 458, PC. This will be so although the words of the deed are general, if sufficiently definite (*Willis v Watney* (1881) 51 LJ Ch 181); but not where the description in the deed is indefinite and requires the plan to explain it; the plan will then prevail (*Eastwood v Ashton* [1915] AC 900, HL; *Wallington v Townsend* [1939] Ch 588, [1939] 2 All ER 225; *Truckell v Stock* [1957] 1 All ER 74, [1957] 1 WLR 161, CA). See also para 228 note 4 ante.

5   *Re Sparrow and James' Contract* (1902) [1910] 2 Ch 60; and see *Eastwood v Ashton* [1915] AC 900, HL (where the plan was required to supplement the verbal description).

6   Ie where the nature of the property does not render the preparation of a plan difficult: see *Re Sansom and Narbeth's Contract* [1910] 1 Ch 741 at 749–750.

7   *Re Sharman and Meade's Contract* [1936] Ch 755, [1936] 2 All ER 1547.

8   *Re Sparrow and James' Contract* (1902) [1910] 2 Ch 60. The representation of a road on a plan does not necessarily amount to an undertaking that the road will be made: *Heriot's Hospital Feoffees v Gibson* (1814) 2 Dow 301; *Squire v Campbell* (1836) 1 My & Cr 459; *Nurse v Lord Seymour* (1851) 13 Beav 254 at 269.

230.   Description in conveyance.   The description of the parcels[1] in the conveyance should correspond with the description of the contract for sale[2]; but, if the language used in the contract does not describe the land with sufficient distinctness, the purchaser is entitled to frame a new description, either by means of a plan or otherwise, so that there can be no doubt as to the effect of the conveyance[3]. The purchaser can insist on an appropriate description of the property as at the date of the conveyance, and on the modern description being connected with the old description[4].

1   As to the meanings of 'lands', 'tenements', and 'hereditaments' see REAL PROPERTY vol 39(2) (Reissue) para 74 et seq. 'Land', in the absence of restrictive expressions, means freehold land (*Hughes v Parker* (1841) 8 M & W 244; Sugden, Vendors and Purchasers (14th Edn) 298), and includes houses and everything permanently affixed. As to the respective rights of a landlord and tenant to trees see FORESTRY vol 19(1) (Reissue) paras 32–33; LANDLORD AND TENANT vol 27(1) (2006 Reissue) para 191 et seq. As to the premises included in a demise see generally LANDLORD AND TENANT vol 27(1) (2006 Reissue) para 159 et seq. As to lands occupied with a house see *Kerford v Seacombe, Hoylake and Deeside Rly Co* (1888) 57 LJ Ch 270. As to the rights of the purchaser in respect of boundary walls see *Baird v Bell* [1898] AC 420, HL; and BOUNDARIES vol 4(1) (2002 Reissue) para 962 et seq. For the principle that a conveyance of land passes mines and minerals unless they are expressly excepted or circumstances exist to rebut the presumption see e g *Harris v Ryding* (1839) 5 M & W 60 at 73; and MINES, MINERALS AND QUARRIES vol 31 (2003 Reissue) para 21. For the wider principle that, unless there is something to the contrary, a conveyance of land includes the surface and all that is supra (houses, trees and the like) and all that is infra (mines, earth, clay etc) see *Mitchell v Mosley* [1914] 1 Ch 438 at 450, CA; *Grigsby v Melville* [1973] 3 All ER 455, [1974] 1 WLR 80, CA (cellar under house). For the effect of exceptions in conveyances see paras 237–239 post. As to the soil of highways bounding the premises see para 232 post.

2   See *Monighetti v Wandsworth London Borough Council* (1908) 73 JP 91.

3   *Re Sansom and Narbeth's Contract* [1910] 1 Ch 741 at 747. As to discrepancy between a plan and detailed description see *Gordon-Cumming v Houldsworth* [1910] AC 537, HL; and para 229 note 1 ante.

4   *Re Sansom and Narbeth's Contract* [1910] 1 Ch 741 at 749. Where the description of the parcels appearing in the last abstracted deed is obsolete, it is generally advisable to frame a new description based on a recent survey, and for identification to incorporate and connect both descriptions in the conveyance.

231.   Restrictive words.   Where the principal words of the description lack the certainty which is necessary for the rejection of the subordinate description as a 'falsa demonstratio'[1], and this subordinate description can be read as limiting the principal description, it will be construed accordingly[2]. This, for example, is done when the first part of the description is expressed in general terms, and the second part is suitable for defining a particular property included in the general terms[3]; and in such a case words describing the occupation of the premises will be construed as words of restriction[4]. However, even if the principal description is in specific form if it does not contain the requisite certainty, it will be restricted by a reference to the occupation[5], or to the situation[6]. Where words of description in the body of a deed refer to a schedule as more particularly describing the property conveyed, the schedule will in general be construed as limiting the description in the deed, and only the premises mentioned in the schedule will pass[7]; but a thing mentioned in the schedule, to which there has been no reference in the body of the deed, will not pass[8].

1   See para 227 ante.

2   See *Slingsby v Grainger* (1859) 7 HL Cas 273 at 283 per Lord Chelmsford LC.

3   In a Crown grant of lands in the city of Wells in the occupation of JB, the words 'in the city of Wells' were held to be restrictive, and lands elsewhere did not pass, although in the occupation of JB

(*Doddington's Case, Hall v Peart* (1594) 2 Co Rep 32b at 33a); a devise of freehold estates in the county of Limerick and in the city of Limerick did not pass estates in the county of Clare (*Miller v Travers* (1832) 8 Bing 244; and see *Doe d Harris v Greathed* (1806) 8 East 91; *Evans v Angell* (1858) 26 Beav 202); but a specific enumeration does not necessarily cut down the effect of previous general words (*Stukeley v Butler* (1614) Hob 168).

4   *Doe d Parkin v Parkin* (1814) 5 Taunt 321 (on a will); *Bartlett v Wright* (1593) Cro Eliz 299 (on a deed); *Ognel's Case* (1587) 4 Co Rep 48b at 50a; *Homer v Homer* (1878) 8 ChD 758, CA (on a will).

5   *Morrell v Fisher* (1849) 4 Exch 591 (devise by a testator of all his leasehold farmhouse, homestead, lands and tenements, at Headington, containing about 170 acres, held under Magdalen College, Oxford, and now in the occupation of B, did not pass land at Headington held by the testator under the college, but not in the occupation of B). See also *Dyne v Nutley* (1853) 14 CB 122; *Magee v Lavell* (1874) LR 9 CP 107 (agreement); *Re Seal, Seal v Taylor* [1894] 1 Ch 316, CA (will).

6   *Webber v Stanley* (1864) 16 CBNS 698 (where a devise of lands referred to as the Tedworth estate, in Hants, was restricted to the part of the estate in that county, though another part was in Wiltshire). See also the principles of construction set out in *Webber v Stanley* supra at 752–753 per Erle CJ; *Pedley v Dodds* (1866) LR 2 Eq 819. As to premises being restricted by reference to a 'will' cf *Gibson v Clark* (1819) 1 Jac & W 159 at 163.

7   *Griffiths v Penson* (1863) 9 Jur NS 385; *Barton v Dawes* (1850) 10 CB 261. The Bills of Sale Act (1878) Amendment Act 1882 s 9 requires the description of the chattels comprised in a bill of sale to be relegated to the schedule: see BILLS OF SALE vol 4(1) (2002 Reissue) para 692. General words assigning things incident to articles specified in the schedule have their due effect: *Cort v Sager* (1858) 3 H & N 370.

8   *Re McManus, ex p Jardine* (1875) 10 Ch App 322.

232.   Land bounded by road or river.   Where a conveyance of land describes the land as bounded by a public road or a river, the conveyance will be construed as passing half the road or half the bed of the river; that is, from the edge of the land to the middle of the road ('ad medium filum viae') or to the middle of the river ('ad medium filum aquae'), unless there is enough in the circumstances, or in the language of the instrument, to show that that is not the intention of the parties[1].

1   *Micklethwait v Newlay Bridge Co* (1886) 33 ChD 133 at 145, CA, per Cotton LJ; *Simpson v Dendy* (1860) 8 CBNS 433 at 472 (affd sub nom *Dendy v Simpson* (1861) 7 Jur NS 1058); *Berridge v Ward* (1861) 10 CBNS 400; *Crossley & Sons Ltd v Lightowler* (1866) LR 3 Eq 274 at 295 (affd with variations (1867) 2 Ch App 478). See also *Central London Rly Co v London City Land Tax Comrs* [1911] 2 Ch 467, CA; affd sub nom *London City Land Tax Comrs v Central London Rly Co* [1913] AC 364, HL. The rule applies to a lease (*Haynes v King* [1893] 3 Ch 439 at 448) and to a Crown grant (*Lord v Sydney City Comrs* (1859) 12 Moo PCC 473), but not in the case of an inclosure award allotting waste lands of a manor bordering on a river, so as to give half the bed of the river with the plots allotted (*Ecroyd v Coulthard* [1897] 2 Ch 554 (affd [1898] 2 Ch 358, CA); cf *Hindson v Ashby* [1896] 2 Ch 1 at 6, 9, CA). The application of the principle of 'ad medium filum aquae' does not depend in any way on the nature and origin of the title of the grantor: *Maclaren v A-G for Quebec* [1914] AC 258 at 276, PC. There is a presumption that the soil of a stream belongs in moieties to the landowners on either side: see *Wishart v Wyllie* (1853) 1 Macq 389, HL. The presumption applies to a private road (*Holmes v Bellingham* (1859) 7 CBNS 329 at 336; *Smith v Howden* (1863) 14 CBNS 398), but apparently not to an inland lake (*Bloomfield v Johnston* (1868) IR 8 CL 68 at 89, 95, 97, Ex Ch). It is immaterial that there are wayside verges separating the highway or private right of way from the adjoining lands: *St Edmundsbury and Ipswich Diocesan Board of Finance v Clark (No 2)* [1973] 3 All ER 902, [1973] 1 WLR 1572; on appeal [1975] 1 All ER 772, [1975] 1 WLR 468, CA (land on either side of accessway expressly included in parcels conveyed to purchaser; accessway also vested in purchaser; the maxim was not discussed in the Court of Appeal). See further on this subject BOUNDARIES vol 4(1) (2002 Reissue) paras 920, 924; HIGHWAYS, STREETS AND BRIDGES vol 21 (2004 Reissue) para 217; WATER vol 49(2) (2004 Reissue) para 58 et seq.

(ii) General Words of Description

233.   Construction of general words.   Where, in the description of property comprised in a conveyance, general words follow an enumeration of specific things or classes of things, then prima facie the general words must be taken in their ordinary meaning, and will receive the extensive construction which that ordinary meaning requires. There may, however, be indications in the language of the instrument that the general words are to have a more limited meaning, and then they will be construed so as to include only things ejusdem generis[1] with those which have been specifically mentioned before[2].

General words in a deed will be construed with reference to the recitals, and may be restrained by a particular recital[3]; general words will also be construed with reference to the subject matter in relation to which they are used and may be limited accordingly[4]; and the court in construing a written contract is entitled to consider the probability that the parties have used words in a sense given to them by well-known judicial construction[5], or that they had certain extrinsic facts appearing from the surrounding circumstances of the particular case in their minds when they entered into the contract[6].

Where a man assigns or charges all his property, the question may arise whether such an assignment or charge is unenforceable as being too vague or contrary to public policy in that no one should be allowed to deprive himself of his livelihood[7].

1   As to the ejusdem generis rule see para 234 post.
2   *Anderson v Anderson* [1895] 1 QB 749 at 753, CA, per Lord Esher MR; *Hadjipateras v S Weigall & Co* (1918) 34 TLR 360; *Parker v Marchant* (1842) 1 Y & C Ch Cas 290 at 300 (on a will). In *Pope v Whitcombe* (1827) 3 Russ 124, a creditor's deed assigning furniture, stock-in-trade, debts, and securities for money, and 'all other the estate and effects' of the assignor, was held not to pass a contingent interest in a testatrix's residuary estate; and, similarly, in *Re Wright's Trusts* (1852) 15 Beav 367; but these decisions would not now be followed: *Ivison v Gassiot* (1853) 3 De GM & G 958. In the last case the specific exception of wearing apparel assisted the general words, and indicated that everything else was to pass; but, apart from this, there is nothing in particular words of this nature to indicate a specific genus and so cut down the general words; moreover, the object of such a deed is to pass everything of value: *Ringer v Cann* (1838) 3 M & W 343; *Doe d Farmer v Howe* (1840) 9 LJQB 352. General words in a commercial document are, like general words in a deed such as a deed of settlement, prima facie to bear their natural and larger meaning and not to be restricted to things ejusdem generis previously enumerated, unless there is something in the document to show an intention so to restrict them: *Chandris v Isbrandtsen-Moller Co Inc* [1951] 1 KB 240 at 244, [1950] 1 All ER 768 at 771–772 per Devlin J. The recitals may show that general words are to be restricted: *Hopkinson v Lusk* (1864) 34 Beav 215; and see para 219 ante. As to the construction of powers of attorney so as to limit them to the specified objects see *Harper v Godsell* (1870) LR 5 QB 422; *Jacobs v Morris* [1902] 1 Ch 816, CA; and para 221 ante. For the principle that general words in an exception clause do not ordinarily except a party from liability for his own negligence see para 178 ante.
3   *Payler v Homersham* (1815) 4 M & S 423; *Danby v Coutts & Co* (1885) 29 ChD 500. Thus where a bill of sale assigned 'all household goods of every kind and description whatsoever in a certain house more particularly mentioned and set forth in an inventory', and the inventory omitted some of the goods, it was held that the operative part of the bill of sale was restricted to the subsequent words: *Wood v Rowcliffe* (1851) 6 Exch 407. In the case of a policy of life assurance this principle extends to reading the policy and declaration together, so that where a policy provided that the policy should be void if any statement in the declaration was untrue, and the declaration declared that the policy should be void if any statement therein was designedly untrue, the declaration was held to explain the clause in the policy, which could accordingly only be avoided by reason of a designedly untrue statement: *Fowkes v Manchester and London Life Assurance and Loan Association* (1863) 3 B & S 917; *Hemmings v Sceptre Life Association Ltd* [1905] 1 Ch 365. As to variations between recitals and operative parts of deeds see para 217 ante.
4   *Thames and Mersey Marine Insurance Co v Hamilton, Fraser & Co* (1887) 12 App Cas 484 at 490, HL, per Lord Halsbury LC; *Gardner v Baillie* (1796) 6 Term Rep 591; *Hay v Goldsmidt* (1804), cited 1 Taunt 349; *Hogg v Snaith* (1808) 1 Taunt 347; *Perry v Holl* (1860) 2 De GF & J 38; *Harper v Godsell* (1870) LR 5 QB 422; *Lewis v Ramsdale* (1886) 55 LT 179; *Metropolitan Rly Co v Postmaster-General* (1916) 85 LJKB 1541.
5   *Thames and Mersey Marine Insurance Co v Hamilton, Fraser & Co* (1887) 12 App Cas 484, HL.
6   *Birrell v Dryer* (1884) 9 App Cas 345 at 353, HL.
7   The question was discussed, but not decided, in the following cases: *Re Clarke, Coombe v Carter* (1887) 36 ChD 348, CA (assignment to mortgagee of after-acquired property); *Tailby v Official Receiver* (1888) 13 App Cas 523 at 530–531, HL (bill of sale assigning future book debts); *Re Turcan* (1888) 40 ChD 5, CA (covenant to settle after-acquired property); *Re Kelcey, Tyson v Kelcey* [1899] 2 Ch 530 (general charge on all property); *Syrett v Egerton* [1957] 3 All ER 331, [1957] 1 WLR 1130, DC (charge on all income and estate). In each of these cases it was sought to enforce such an assignment, covenant, charge or bill of sale against specific existing property. Since these transactions were divisible (see *Re Clarke* supra, *Re Turcan* supra) this was possible, and to the extent of the specific existing property they were unobjectionable, being neither vague nor contrary to public policy. See also para 273 post.

234.   Ejusdem generis rule.   Where the particular things named have some common characteristic which constitutes them a genus, and the general words can be properly regarded as in the nature of a sweeping clause designed to guard against accidental omissions, then the rule of ejusdem generis will apply, and the general words will be restricted to things of the same nature as those which have been already mentioned[1]; but the absence of a common genus between the enumerated words will not necessarily prevent a restricted construction of the general words if justified by the context[2]. The ejusdem generis construction will be assisted if the general scope or language of the deed, or the particular clause, indicates that the general words should receive a limited construction[3] or if an unlimited construction will produce some unforeseen loss to the grantor[4].

A common application of the ejusdem generis rule occurs in the construction of policies of insurance, where special enumerated risks are insured against, followed by a general clause insuring against all risks whatsoever, the last clause being construed as limited to risks of the same nature as those previously mentioned[5].

1   *Moore v Magrath* (1774) 1 Cowp 9 at 12 per Lord Mansfield; *Lambourn v McLellan* [1903] 2 Ch 268, CA. Such cases have given rise to the common enunciation of the ejusdem generis rule as the rule to be prima facie applied 'where a particular class is spoken of, and general words follow': *Lyndon v Standbridge* (1857) 2 H & N 45 at 51 per Pollock CB; *Clifford v Arundell* (1860) 1 De GF & J 307 at 311 per Lord Campbell LC; *Harrison v Blackburn* (1864) 17 CBNS 678 at 690 per Erle CJ; and see *Johnson v Edgware etc Rly Co* (1866) 35 Beav 480 (where in a power to resume possession of any part of demised land 'for the purpose of building, planting, accommodation, or otherwise', 'otherwise' was read ejusdem generis, and did not authorise the resumption of land required by a railway company). If the particular words exhaust a whole genus, however, the general words must refer to some larger genus: *Fenwick v Schmalz* (1868) LR 3 CP 313 at 315 per Willes J.

2   *Johnson v Edgware etc Rly Co* (1866) 35 Beav 480; *Coates v Diment* [1951] 1 All ER 890 at 898 per Streatfield J; *Chandris v Isbrandtsen-Moller Co Ltd* [1951] 1 KB 240 at 246–247, [1950] 1 All ER 768 at 773 per Devlin J.

3   Where, for instance, in a covenant to yield up fixtures at the end of a term, the fixtures particularly enumerated are all 'landlord's fixtures', the general words will be restricted to the same class: *Lambourn v McLellan* [1903] 2 Ch 268, CA. Where an annuity is charged on 'rents or profits or any other moneys' in the hands of trustees, the frame of the deed may readily show that 'other moneys' are to be restricted to moneys in the nature of income (*Chifford v Arundell* (1860) 1 De GF & J 307); where a specific description of leasehold property is followed by general words referring to leaseholds only, freehold property will not pass (*Doungworth v Blair* (1837) 1 Keen 795). The words 'any other cause' following certain specified causes were construed ejusdem generis with the specified causes in *Tillmanns & Co v SS Knutsford Ltd* [1908] 2 KB 385, CA; *Mudie & Co v Strick* (1909) 100 LT 701; *Herman v Morris* (1919) 35 TLR 574, CA. See also *Bolivia Republic v Indemnity Mutual Marine Assurance Co Ltd* [1909] 1 KB 785, CA; *Thorman v Dowgate Steamship Co Ltd* [1910] 1 KB 410; *Ambatielos v Anton Jurgens Margarine Works* [1923] AC 175, HL; and for a discussion of the rule see *Owners of Magnhild v McIntyre Bros & Co* [1920] 3 KB 321.

4   Eg if it will lead to a forfeiture of the property which it is contended is included in the general words: *Re Waley's Trusts* (1855) 3 Drew 165.

5   *Cullen v Butler* (1816) 5 M & S 461; *Lee v Alexander* (1883) 8 App Cas 853, HL; *Thames and Mersey Marine Insurance Co v Hamilton Fraser & Co* (1887) 12 App Cas 484, HL; and see *Crompton v Jarratt* (1885) 30 ChD 298, CA; *Early v Rathbone* (1888) 57 LJ Ch 652; *Lambourn v McLellan* [1903] 2 Ch 268, CA; *Tillmanns & Co v SS Knutsford Ltd* [1908] 2 KB 385; *Larsen v Sylvester & Co* [1908] AC 295, HL; *Mudie & Co v Strick* (1909) 100 LT 701; *Thorman v Dowgate Steamship Co Ltd* [1910] 1 KB 410; *Hadjipateras v s Weigall & Co* (1918) 34 TLR 360; *Herman v Morris* (1919) 35 TLR 574, CA; *Owners of Magnhild v McIntyre Bros & Co* [1920] 3 KB 321. See also INSURANCE vol 25 (2003 Reissue) para 231; SHIPPING AND NAVIGATION vol 43(2) (Reissue) para 1458; STATUTES vol 44(1) (Reissue) para 1491.

(iii)   General Words Conveying Appurtenances, and Conveying or Creating Easements

235.   Use of general words.   In addition to general words of description which either supply defects in the enumeration of things of a specific class (in accordance with the rule of ejusdem generis[1]) or add other land or things not included in the previous enumeration[2], there may be general words intended to bring in various rights incidental to the enjoyment of the property conveyed, for though by statute an appurtenant easement passes without the necessity of express mention or the use of general words[3], nevertheless such mention or general words may still appear in conveyances.

A grant of an easement by general words in a conveyance will be construed as being referable only to the interest which the grantor had in the servient tenement at the time of the grant, and will not bind any larger interest which he may afterwards acquire[4].

The use of general words was always unnecessary in respect of many rights incident to the enjoyment of land, since the mere grant of the property described in the parcels carried the rights as a matter of course, unless expressly excepted[5].

1   See para 234 ante.
2   See para 233 ante.
3   See para 236 post.
4   *Booth v Alcock* (1873) 8 Ch App 663 at 667 per Mellish LJ. See also *Beddington v Atlee* (1887) 35 ChD 317 at 327.
5   This was expressed by the maxim 'cuicunque aliquid conceditur, etiam id sine quo res ipsa non esse potuit'.
        'When anything is granted, all the means to attain it, and all the fruits and effects of it are granted also; and shall pass inclusive, together with the thing, by the grant of the thing itself, without the words 'cum pertinentiis', or other like words': Shep Touch 89; *Earl of Cardigan v Armitage* (1823) 2 B & C 197 at 207; *Rowbotham v Wilson* (1860) 8 HL Cas 348 at 360; *Ramsay v Blair* (1876) 1 App Cas 701 at 703, HL. See also COMMONS vol 6 (2003 Reissue) para 483.

236.   Conveyance under the Law of Property Act 1925.   In order to shorten the length of conveyances of land it is provided by statute[1] that as regards conveyances made since 31 December 1881, a conveyance[2] of land[3] is deemed to include and is to operate to convey with the land, all buildings, erections, fixtures, commons, hedges, ditches, fences, ways, waters, watercourses, liberties, privileges, easements, rights, and advantages whatsoever, appertaining[4] or reputed to appertain to the land, or any part thereof, or at the time of conveyance[5] demised, occupied, or enjoyed with or reputed or known as part or parcel of or appurtenant to the land or any part of it[6]. A conveyance since 31 December 1881 of land, having houses or other buildings on it, is deemed to include and operates to convey with the land, houses or other buildings, all outhouses, erections, fixtures, cellars, areas, courts, courtyards, cisterns, sewers, gutters, drains, ways, passages, lights, watercourses, liberties, privileges, easements, rights and advantages whatsoever, appertaining or reputed to appertain to the land, houses or other buildings conveyed, or any of them, or any part thereof, or at the time of conveyance[7], demised, occupied or enjoyed with, or reputed or known as part or parcel of or appurtenant to, the land, houses or other buildings, conveyed, or any of them, or any part thereof[8]. Corresponding provision is made as to the appurtenances and rights which are deemed to be included in a conveyance of a manor[9].

These statutory provisions apply only if and so far as a contrary intention is not expressed in the conveyance, and they are subject to the terms and provisions of the instrument[10]. Correspondence leading up to the conveyance may be material as showing that a right which was permissive only had been terminated by withdrawal of permission before the conveyance[11].

The statutory provisions are not to be construed as giving to any person a better title to any property, right or thing mentioned in the statutory provisions than the title which the conveyance gives to him to the land or manor expressed to be conveyed, or as conveying to him such property, right or thing, further or otherwise than as the same could have been conveyed to him by the conveying parties[12]. Their object is to show what general words are to be taken as included in a conveyance of land where the conveyance is otherwise silent[13]. They do not affect the contract, so that neither party to the contract is entitled to have these general words included in the conveyance, unless they are justified by the contract and appropriate to the circumstances of the case[14].

1   See the Law of Property Act 1925 s 62 (replacing the Conveyancing Act 1881 s 6); and EASEMENTS AND PROFITS À PRENDRE vol 16(2) (Reissue) para 57. Any conveyance executed for the purpose of the Leasehold Reform, Housing and Urban Development Act 1993 Pt I Ch I (ss 1–38) (as amended), and a lease granted back to the former freeholder in accordance with s 36 (as amended; prospectively amended), must not exclude or restrict the general words implied in conveyances under the Law of Property Act 1925 s 62, or the all-estate clause implied under s 63 (see para 240 post), unless the exclusion or restriction is made for the purpose of preserving or recognising any existing interest of the freeholder in tenant's incumbrances or any existing right or interest of any other person, or the nominee purchaser consents to the exclusion or restriction: see the Leasehold Reform, Housing and Urban Development Act 1993 s 34(1) (as amended; prospectively amended), s 36(4), Sch 7 para 2(1) (prospectively amended), Sch 9 Pt IV para 9; and LANDLORD AND TENANT. As to the effect of this provision on the severance of a holding in creating rights and burdens as between the severed parts see further EASEMENTS AND PROFITS À PRENDRE.

2   For the meaning of 'conveyance' see para 14 note 1 ante. For this purpose, a tenancy agreement for a term not exceeding three years, though under hand only and though expressed as an agreement, has been held to be a conveyance: *Wright v Macadam* [1949] 2 KB 744, [1949] 2 All ER 565, CA.

3   As to the meaning of 'land' see para 14 note 2 ante.

4   Formerly the words 'with the appurtenances' were frequently used (see *Thorpe v Brumfitt* (1873) 8 Ch App 650 (right of way)); but they were in general superfluous, for they referred only to rights strictly appurtenant to the property conveyed (*Bolton v Bolton* (1879) 11 ChD 968 at 971), and such rights passed by the conveyance without these words (Co Litt 121b; Shep Touch 89; *Skull v Glenister* (1864) 16 CBNS 81 at 91); hence the words did not pass an easement formerly existing which had been extinguished by unity of possession (*Plant v James* (1833) 5 B & Ad 791 at 794 (on appeal sub nom *James v Plant* (1836) 4 Ad & El 749, Ex Ch); *Worthington v Gimson* (1860) 2 E & E 618; and see *Baring v Abingdon* [1892] 2 Ch 374 at 394, CA). The words 'with all ways thereunto appertaining' were similarly restricted to ways legally appurtenant to the conveyed premises: *Harding v Wilson* (1823) 2 B & C 96 at 100; *Barlow v Rhodes* (1833) 1 Cr & M 439 at 448; *Brett v Clowser* (1880) 5 CPD 376 at 383. But such words received a wider construction if there was apparent an intention to pass rights not strictly appurtenant; where, for example, there was no way strictly appurtenant to which the words could apply (*Morris v Edgington* (1810) 3 Taunt 24), or where such an intention appeared from the conveyance itself (*Barlow v Rhodes* supra; *James v Plant* (1836) 4 Ad & El 749, Ex Ch; *Dobbyn v Somers* (1860) 13 ICLR 293). In such cases the word 'appurtenant' might be taken in a secondary sense as equivalent to 'used and enjoyed' with the premises conveyed: *Hill v Grange* (1555) 1 Plowd 164 at 170; *Thomas v Owen* (1887) 20 QBD 225 at 232, CA; and see *Hinchcliffe v Earl of Kinnoul* (1838) 5 Bing NC 1 at 25. Under the words 'with the appurtenances' there will pass, as appurtenant to a house (Co Litt 121b), a right of turbary (*Solme v Bullock* (1684) 3 Lev 165; *Dobbyn v Somers* supra; and where a right would not by itself pass without a deed the words may show that the right is treated as appurtenant so as to pass by the conveyance, although not by deed (see *Hurleston v Woodroffe* (1619) Cro Jac 519 (a sheep walk)); and probably a right of common can pass as appurtenant without a deed; but see *Beaudley v Brook* (1607) Cro Jac 189 at 190. Moreover, rights necessary for the enjoyment of the property conveyed, which the grantor can confer, will pass without express mention (see para 235 note 5 ante); but a lease of land and buildings with a pond and the streams leading thereto does not entitle the lessee to water which would percolate to the pond through other land of the lessor (*M'Nab v Robertson* [1897] AC 129, HL).

5   See note 7 infra.

6   See the Law of Property Act 1925 s 62(1), (6); and note 1 supra. Something which by sufferance no one is prevented from doing or enjoying will not pass as a right under s 62, for the words of the provision connote something which is the subject of individual or class enjoyment as opposed to general enjoyment and must therefore be enjoyed in connection with the subject matter of the conveyance: *Le Strange v Pettefar* (1939) 161 LT 300 at 301. The enjoyment must not be merely an enjoyment based on ownership of the quasi-servient tenement by a common owner of both quasi-servient and quasi-dominant tenement: *Long v Gowlett* [1923] 2 Ch 177; and cf *Ward v Kirkland* [1967] Ch 194, [1966] 1 All ER 609. Easements which are reputed to be enjoyed with the land conveyed will pass under the statute although not subsisting at law: see *Lewis v Meredith* [1913] 1 Ch 571; *Hansford v Jago* [1921] 1 Ch 322. See EASEMENTS AND PROFITS À PRENDRE. In *Crow v Wood* [1971] 1 QB 77, [1970] 3 All ER 425, CA, the right to have the fences of neighbouring farmers kept up was held to be a right in the nature of an easement passing under the statute. To pass under it, the right or advantage must be one which is known to the law in the sense that it must be capable of being granted at law so as to be binding on all successors in the title even those who take without notice: *Phipps v Pears* [1965] 1 QB 76, [1964]

2 All ER 35, CA. Cf *Chelsea Yacht and Boat Co Ltd v Pope* [2001] 2 All ER 409, [2000] 1 WLR 1941, CA (moored, but moveable, houseboat neither land not a fixture).

7   In the case of a lease the 'time of the conveyance' is the date of execution, not the date of the commencement of the term: *Goldberg v Edwards* [1950] Ch 247, CA.

8   See the Law of Property Act 1925 s 62(2), (6). In *HE Dibble Ltd (t/as Mill Lane Nurseries) v Moore (West, third party)* [1970] 2 QB 181, [1969] 3 All ER 1465, CA, greenhouses resting on concrete were held not to be part of the land and therefore not 'erections'. See also *Deen v Andrews* (1986) 52 P & CR 17, [1986] 1 EGLR 262 (greenhouse not a 'building' under a contract for the sale of land 'together with the farmhouses and other buildings'); *Elitestone Ltd v Morris* [1997] 2 All ER 513, [1997] 1 WLR 687, HL (bungalow resting on concrete foundations by its own weight not a fixture but part and parcel of the land).

9   See the Law of Property Act 1925 s 62(3), (6).

10   See ibid s 62(4). Such a contrary intention is not indicated by the express grant of a limited easement when the habendum refers to a wider right (*Gregg v Richards* [1926] Ch 521, CA), nor by the fact that a conveyance expressly conveys such easements as were included in an earlier conveyance which did not include the easement in question (*Hapgood v JH Martin & Son Ltd* (1934) 152 LT 72), nor by the use of the words 'with the appurtenances' (*Beddington v Atlee* (1887) 35 ChD 317 at 331; *Hansford v Jago* [1921] 1 Ch 322 at 332; but see *Birmingham, Dudley and District Banking Co v Ross* (1888) 38 ChD 295 at 308, CA), though the use of such words in a contract may limit the conveyance to one of rights strictly appurtenant and exclude the operation of the Law of Property Act 1925 s 62(1) (*Re Peck and London School Board's Contract* [1893] 2 Ch 315). The mere marking of adjacent land as 'building land' on a plan will not show an intention to exclude a right of light over it: *Broomfield v Williams* [1897] 1 Ch 602, CA; *Pollard v Gare* [1901] 1 Ch 834. Further, in considering whether the statutory words apply, regard must be had to the title to the quasi-servient tenement and to the surrounding circumstances at the time of the conveyance, and the statute will not pass rights de facto enjoyed with the demised premises if, as a matter of title, the grantor cannot lawfully convey these rights (*Beddington v Atlee* supra; *Godwin v Schweppes Ltd* [1902] 1 Ch 926 at 932; *Quicke v Chapman* [1903] 1 Ch 659, CA; *Financial Times Ltd v Bell* (1903) 19 TLR 433); nor rights which are merely temporary (*Burrows v Lang* [1901] 2 Ch 502) or which could not reasonably be expected to continue (*Godwin v Schweppes Ltd* supra); but a conveyance may, by virtue of the statute, pass rights which at its date are permissive only (*International Tea Stores Co v Hobbs* [1903] 2 Ch 165) provided that these are sufficiently precise in extent to be the subject of a grant (*Green v Ashco Horticulturist Ltd* [1966] 2 All ER 232, [1966] 1 WLR 889). Cf *Bolton v Bolton* (1879) 11 ChD 968; *Bayley v Great Western Rly Co* (1884) 26 ChD 434 at 457, CA; *Barkshire v Grubb* (1881) 18 ChD 616.

11   *Le Strange v Pettefar* (1939) 161 LT 300 at 302.

12   See the Law of Property Act 1925 s 62(5); and see e g *Quicke v Chapman* [1903] 1 Ch 659, CA. A tenant's right under an earlier lease to receive a supply of hot water and central heating, being essentially a matter of a contract for personal services, will not pass under the general words implied by the Law of Property Act 1925 s 62 in a new lease: *Regis Property Co Ltd v Redman* [1956] 2 QB 612, [1956] 2 All ER 335, CA.

13   *Re Peck and London School Board's Contract* [1893] 2 Ch 315.

14   *Re Hughes and Ashley's Contract* [1900] 2 Ch 595 at 603, CA; *Re Peck and London School Board's Contract* [1893] 2 Ch 315 at 318 per Chitty J; *Re Walmesley and Shaw's Contract* [1917] 1 Ch 93; *Clark v Barnes* [1929] 2 Ch 368.

(iv)   Exceptions and Reservations

237.   Distinction between exception and reservation.   An exception is always of part of the thing granted, and only a thing which exists can be excepted; a reservation is of a thing not in existence, but newly created or reserved out of land or a tenement upon a grant thereof[1].

1   Co Litt 47a; Shep Touch 80. As to exceptions see para 238 post; and as to reservations see para 239 post.

238.   Exceptions.   Upon the grant of land there may be an exception of a specified part, and then this is not included in the grant at all[1], and where the amount to be excepted is specified, but not its position, the uncertainty can be determined by election[2]. The rule for construing exceptions is that what will pass by words in a grant will be excepted by the same or like words in an exception[3]. A vendor who wishes to except some part of the property from parcels which are clearly described and admittedly included in the conveyance must use language which is apt for the purpose[4].

Trees or minerals may be excepted[5]. An exception of trees is held not to extend to fruit trees[6], but it carries so much of the soil as is necessary for the growth of the trees[7]. An exception of 'mines', or of any mineral occupying a continuous space, is an exception also of the space occupied[8]; but a reservation of a right to get minerals does not operate as an exception of the minerals themselves, unless an intention to that effect is clearly shown[9]. An exception of trees[10] or of minerals[11] carries with it the right to do all things necessary[12] for getting and disposing of them. A reservation may in substance be an exception, as where there is a reservation of part of the thing granted[13]; but the reservation will be void if it is repugnant to the grant as a reservation of part of the profits of what is granted[14].

1   *Doe Douglas v Lock* (1835) 2 Ad & El 705 at 744.
2   *Jenkins v Green* (1858) 27 Beav 437; and see para 213 ante.
3   Shep Touch 100. If the exception covers the whole of anything specifically granted as an exception of 'shops' out of a grant of a messuage 'with all the chambers, cellars, and shops', it is repugnant and therefore void: *Horneby v Clifton* (1567) 3 Dyer 264b; *Cochrane v M'Cleary* (1869) IR 4 CL 165, Ex Ch; and see *Cooper v Stuart* (1889) 14 App Cas 286 at 289, PC. As to construing an exception in favour of the grantee see para 178 ante.
4   *Grigsby v Melville* [1973] 3 All ER 455, [1974] 1 WLR 80, CA (cellar of house conveyed not excepted although accessible only from other property of the vendor).
5   *Earl of Cardigan v Armitage* (1823) 2 B & C 197 at 207.
6   *Wyndham v Way* (1812) 4 Taunt 316 at 318n (a); and see *London· v Chapter of Southwell Collegiate Church* (1618) Hob 303; *Bullen v Denning* (1826) 5 B & C 842. See also FORESTRY vol 19(1) (Reissue) paras 32–33; LANDLORD AND TENANT vol 27(1) (2006 Reissue) para 191.
7   *Ive's Case* (1597) 5 Co Rep 11a; Cro Eliz 521; *Liford's Case* (1614) 11 Co Rep 46b. An exception of 'all wood and underwood' perhaps carries the exception of soil further: *Legh v Heald* (1830) 1 B & Ad 622 at 626.
8   *Proud v Bates* (1865) 34 LJ Ch 406; *Duke of Hamilton v Graham* (1871) LR 2 Sc & Div 166, HL.
9   *Duke of Sutherland v Heathcote* [1892] 1 Ch 475 at 483, CA; cf *Duke of Hamilton v Dunlop* (1885) 10 App Cas 813, HL. As to exceptions of minerals see MINES, MINERALS AND QUARRIES vol 31 (2003 Reissue) para 309.
10   Shep Touch 100; *Liford's Case* (1614) 11 Co Rep 46b at 52a; *Hewitt v Isham* (1851) 7 Exch 77.
11   *Earl of Cardigan v Armitage* (1823) 2 B & C 197; *Dand v Kingscote* (1840) 6 M & W 174 at 196; *Rowbotham v Wilson* (1860) 8 HL Cas 348 at 360; *Ramsay v Blair* (1876) 1 App Cas 701 at 703, HL.
12   Consequently rights which are merely convenient for, but not necessarily incident to, the getting of the thing excepted are not implied by the exception: see *Lord Darcy v Askwith* (1618) Hob 234; *Earl of Cardigan v Armitage* (1823) 2 B & C 197 at 211. See also para 184 note 5 ante.
13   Co Litt 143a; *Anon* (1536) 1 Dyer 19a, pl 110; *Fancy v Scott* (1828) 2 Man & Ry KB 335; and see *Doe d Douglas v Lock* (1835) 2 Ad & El 705 at 745.
14   Co Litt 142a.

239. Reservations. Strictly the term 'reservation', implies a right of the nature of rent reserved to a landlord or lord of a manor; thus rent, heriots, suit of mill, and suit of court are reservations, and have been described as the only things, which, according to the legal meaning of the word, are reservations[1]. It is essential to a reservation that it should issue out of the thing granted[2]. The term is frequently used, however, to denote some incorporeal right over a thing granted of which the grantor intends to have the benefit, such as a fishing right or sporting right[3] or a right of way[4]. In this case the reservation formerly operated as a regrant of the right of the grantee to the grantor, and it was not effectual unless the deed in which it was contained was executed by the grantee[5].

In instruments executed after 1925, a reservation of a legal estate[6] operates at law without any execution of the conveyance by the grantee of the legal estate out of which the reservation is made, or any regrant by him, so as to create the legal estate reserved, and so as to vest the same in possession in the person, whether that person is the grantor or not, for whose benefit the reservation is made[7]. A conveyance of a legal estate expressed to be made subject to a legal estate not yet in existence immediately before the date of the conveyance, operates as a reservation unless a contrary intention appears[8].

The reservation of a substance out of the land granted necessarily implies the existence of a right of working and of recovering that substance, for without it the reservation would be meaningless[9]; and where a reservation makes a direct grant of a substance to the vendor, leaving to the purchaser merely such residual rights as remain in him subject to the vendor, and the recovery of the reserved substance by the usual methods involves the egress of another substance which has not been reserved, the vendors are not under an obligation to conserve that other substance, with the consequent denial of their right to recover the reserved substance in the usual way[10].

1   *Doe d Douglas v Lock* (1835) 2 Ad & El 705 at 743. 'Heriot' means the best beast or other chattel of a tenant, seized on his death by the lord. 'Suit of court' means the attendance which tenants owed to the court of their lord.
2   *Durham and Sunderland Rly Co v Walker* (1842) 2 QB 940 at 967, Ex Ch.
3   *Doe d Douglas v Lock* (1835) 2 Ad & El 705; *Wickham v Hawker* (1840) 7 M & W 63; and see further ANIMALS vol 2(1) (Reissue) para 548 et seq.
4   *Durham and Sunderland Rly Co v Walker* (1842) 2 QB 940, Ex Ch.
5   *Doe d Douglas v Lock* (1835) 2 Ad & El 705; *Durham and Sunderland Rly Co v Walker* (1842) 2 QB 940; and see *Thellusson v Liddard* [1900] 2 Ch 635 at 645. As to construing a reservation in favour of the grantee of the property out of which the reservation is made see para 178 ante.
6   The term 'legal estate' includes an easement or right for an interest equivalent to a fee simple or term of years: see the Law of Property Act 1925 s 1(2)(a), (4).
7   Ibid s 65(1), (3); and see *Wickham v Hawker* (1840) 7 M & W 63. This statutory provision does not affect the substance of the obligations: see *Mason v Clarke* [1954] 1 QB 460 at 467, [1954] 1 All ER 189 at 192, CA, per Denning LJ (revsd but not on this point [1955] AC 778, [1955] 1 All ER 914, HL); *St Edmundsbury and Ipswich Diocesan Board of Finance v Clark (No 2)* [1975] 1 All ER 772, [1975] 1 WLR 468, CA.
8   Law of Property Act 1925 s 65(2). See *Wiles v Banks* (1984) 50 P & CR 80, CA.
9   Shep Touch 89; *Rowbotham v Wilson* (1860) 8 HL Cas 348 at 360 per Lord Wensleydale; *Ramsay v Blair* (1876) 1 App Cas 701 at 704, HL, per Lord Hatherley; *Borys v Canadian Pacific Rly Co* [1953] AC 217 at 227–228, 232, [1953] 1 All ER 451 at 457–458, 460, PC.
10 *Borys v Canadian Pacific Rly Co* [1953] AC 217 at 229–230, [1953] 1 All ER 451 at 459, PC.

(v) 'All Estate' Clauses

240.   Effect of all estate clause.   Formerly, it was usual to add to the parcels general words, known as the 'all estate' clause, expressing that the grantor conveyed all his 'estate, interest, right, title[1], claim[2], and demand' in, to, or upon the property conveyed. Now every conveyance made after 31 December 1881 passes all the estate, right, title, interest, claim, and demand which the conveying parties respectively have, or have power to convey, in the property. This rule applies only if and so far as a contrary intention is not expressed in the conveyance, and has effect subject to the terms and provisions of the conveyance[3].

The ordinary effect of a conveyance containing these general words, or operating under the above statutory rule, is to convey every estate or interest vested in the grantor, although not vested in him in the character in which he became a party to the conveyance[4]. If he purports to convey the fee simple, but has in fact only an equitable title to a term, that equitable title will pass[5].

1   As to the distinction between these words see Co Litt 345a, b. According to the old nomenclature, 'estates' are the interests created in land by legal and equitable limitations; 'right' is properly where an estate is turned to a right of entry, as by dissuasion; 'title' is either a lawful cause of entry to defeat an existing estate, as title of condition, or, more generally, it includes 'right'; 'interest' is the widest term, and includes estates, rights and titles. For the purposes of the Law of Property Act 1925, however, 'legal estate' means the estates, interests, and charges, which under s 1 (as amended) are authorised to subsist or to be conveyed or created at law (see ss 1(4), 205(1)(x)), and all other estates, interests, and charges in or

over land take effect as equitable interests (see ss 1(3), s 205(1)(x) (as amended)): see SETTLEMENTS vol 42 (Reissue) para 677. For the meaning of 'equitable interests' see MORTGAGE vol 32 (2005 Reissue) para 305.

2 'Claim' will cover a contingent interest, notwithstanding that it would properly be called a possibility: *Wright v Wright* (1750) 1 Ves Sen 409.

3 See the Law of Property Act 1925 s 63 (reproducing the Conveyancing Act 1881 s 63 (repealed)). Any conveyance executed for the purpose of the Leasehold Reform, Housing and Urban Development Act 1993 Pt I Ch I (ss 1–38) (as amended) must not exclude or restrict the general words implied in conveyances under the Law of Property Act 1925 s 62 (see para 236 ante) or the all-estate clause implied under s 63, unless the exclusion or restriction is made for the purpose of preserving or recognising any existing interest of the freeholder in tenant's incumbrances or any existing right or interest of any other person, or the nominee purchaser consents to the exclusion or restriction: see the Leasehold Reform, Housing and Urban Development Act 1993 s 34(1) (as amended; prospectively amended), Sch 7 para 2(1) (prospectively amended); and LANDLORD AND TENANT vol 27(3) (2006 Reissue) para 1648.

   In *Re Stirrup's Contract* [1961] 1 All ER 805, [1961] 1 WLR 449, the Law of Property Act 1925 s 63, read with the definition of a conveyance in s 205(1)(ii) (see para 14 note 1 ante) and having regard to the broad framework of the Act, was held to produce the result that an instrument in the form of an assent, but happening to be under seal and so complying with s 52(1) (see para 14 ante), was effective to pass whatever estate the conveying party had. Tithe rentcharge (extinguished, with certain exceptions, by the Tithe Act 1936 s 47(1): see ECCLESIASTICAL LAW vol 14 para 1213) is, like tithe, a hereditament separate from the land; and express words are necessary to pass it: *Public Trustee v Duchy of Lancaster* [1927] 1 KB 516, CA.

4 *Drew v Earl Norbury* (1846) 3 Jo & Lat 267 at 284 per Lord St Leonards LC; *Taylor v London and County Banking Co* [1901] 2 Ch 231 at 256, CA, per Stirling LJ; Co Litt 345a; Shep Touch 98; *Johnson v Webster* (1854) 4 De GM & G 474 at 488. Thus a conveyance will carry both the fee and a term of years vested in the grantor, but not merged: *Burton v Barclay* (1831) 7 Bing 745 at 761.

5 *Thellusson v Liddard* [1900] 2 Ch 635. See also the forgery cases at para 72 ante.

241. Construction of estate clause. The words of the estate clause or of the statutory rule, being general words, are subject to the same elasticity of construction as general words in the parcels. They are liable to be controlled by recitals[1], by the scope of the deed read as a whole, and by the surrounding circumstances[2]. A disentailing deed will be restricted to the estate tail which appears to be intended to be barred, and will not extend to another contingent estate tail[3].

1 See para 219 ante.
2 *Re Cooke and Bletcher's Contract* (1895) 13 R 264; *Williams v Pinckney* (1897) 67 LJ Ch 34 at 39, CA. Thus it may appear that a reversion was not intended to pass: *Mullineaux v Ellison* (1863) 8 LT 236. A mortgage deed intended to pass the freehold of certain property, when acquired by the mortgagor under an option to purchase it, was construed, the purchase never having been made, as not comprising a leasehold estate in the property belonging throughout to the mortgagor, although the deed thus became inoperative: *Goodwin v Noble* (1857) 8 E & B 587. A purported conveyance of certain property in fee in the most general words was held, on the construction of the deed as a whole, to pass only the moiety of the property of which the grantor was actually seised in fee and not a moiety of which he was only the lessee: *Francis v Minton* (1867) LR 2 CP 543 (for the abolition of tenancies in common at law see REAL PROPERTY vol 39(2) (Reissue) para 55). See also *Grieveson v Kirsopp* (1842) 5 Beav 283, where, although expressly referring to a moiety, a deed was held to comprise a fifth part only having regard to its general intention. On the other hand, an interest omitted by mistake in the recitals, and in the express operative part, may pass under the general words: *Knapping v Tomlinson* (1870) 18 WR 684.
3 *Grattan v Langdale* (1883) 11 LR Ir 473, 478. See further para 226 et seq ante. As from 1 January 1997 (ie the date on which the Trusts of Land and Appointment of Trustees Act 1996 came into force: see s 27(2)), it is no longer possible to create a new settlement under the Settled Land Act 1925: see s 2; and SETTLEMENTS vol 42 (Reissue) para 676. As to the limited exceptions see s 2(2), (3); and SETTLEMENTS vol 42 (Reissue) para 676.

(9) THE PREMISES AND THE HABENDUM

242. Purposes of premises and habendum. The parts of a deed before the habendum are called the premises of the deed. Their purpose is to name the grantor and grantee, and to define the thing which is granted. In addition, the circumstances preliminary to and leading up to the transaction are stated in the recitals. The office of the habendum is to limit the estate granted, and in doing this the grantee is mentioned again[1], and any liabilities or incidents subject to which the property is conveyed are mentioned[2]. The habendum is not essential, and if the premises, in addition to defining the grantor, the grantee, and the parcels, define also the estate to be taken by the grantee, or leave that to construction of law[3], the deed is effectual[4].

Since a fee simple is the only estate of freehold at law and can now be transferred without words of limitation,[5] words of limitation are only required in the conveyance of an equitable interest, such as an interest for life, though it is usual to insert the words 'in fee simple' in a conveyance of the legal estate[6]. On the sale of land subject to a specified incumbrance or lease, the vendor is entitled to have the conveyance framed accordingly[7]; but he cannot insist on property being conveyed subject to covenants, conditions, and restrictions not mentioned in the abstract[8], or which, though mentioned in the abstract, were not referred to in the particulars or conditions[9].

1　　*Buckler's Case* (1597) 2 Co Rep 55a; *Throchmerton v Tracy* (1555) 1 Plowd 145 at 152; Co Litt 6a; Shep Touch 74.

2　　The statement in the habendum that the property is subject to certain restrictions does not, however, by itself impose any contractual obligation on the purchase: *Re Rutherford's Conveyance, Goadby v Bartlett* [1938] Ch 396, [1938] 1 All ER 495.

3　　A conveyance of freehold land without words of limitation now passes to the grantee the fee simple if the grantor has power to convey it: see note 6 infra.

4　　*Goodtitle d Dodwell v Gibbs* (1826) 5 B & C 709 at 717; Shep Touch 75; *Kerr v Kerr* (1854) 4 I Ch R 493 at 497.

5　　See the Law of Property Act 1925 s 1(1); and REAL PROPERTY vol 39(2) (Reissue) para 36.

6　　Formerly, words of limitation were necessary in a deed in order to confer on the grantee the fee simple. In the absence of the appropriate words ('heirs', 'heirs and assigns', or 'in fee simple'), the grantee took only an estate for life, and this applied also to equitable limitations: *Re Bostock's Settlement, Norrish v Bostock* [1921] 2 Ch 469, CA. In a conveyance of freehold land executed after 1925 without words of limitation, the fee simple or other whole interest which the grantor had power to convey in such land passes to the grantee, unless a contrary intention appears in the conveyance: Law of Property Act 1925 s 60(1), (4). Until 1882 the word 'heirs' was essential to pass the fee simple; after 1881 the words 'in fee simple' were sufficient: see s 60(4)(a) (replacing the Conveyancing Act 1881 s 51 (repealed)). Since the rules of descent have been abolished, 'heirs' is not now appropriate as a word of limitation, though the heir may still take an equitable interest by purchase: see the Law of Property Act 1925 s 132(1); and REAL PROPERTY vol 39(2) (Reissue) paras 89, 1415. As to conveyance to a corporation sole without using the word 'successors' see the Law of Property Act 1925 s 60(2); and CORPORATIONS vol 9(2) (2006 Reissue) para 1248; REAL PROPERTY vol 39(2) (Reissue) para 93.

7　　See *David v Sabin* [1893] 1 Ch 523, CA; *Page v Midland Rly Co* [1894] 1 Ch 11, CA; *May v Platt* [1900] 1 Ch 616.

8　　*Re Monckton and Gilzean* (1884) 27 ChD 555.

9　　*Hardman v Child* (1885) 28 ChD 712; *Re Wallis and Barnard's Contract* [1899] 2 Ch 515.

243. Effect of limitation in premises.

In the premises the grant should be to the grantee simply without words of limitation, and if the estate is expressly limited[1], this should be done in the habendum. Formerly a grant without words of limitation gave only an estate for life[2], and if there was a simple grant to the grantee in the premises and no habendum at all, the grantee would take an estate for life; but if the habendum contained the limitation of the estate, this excluded any implication of a life estate in the premises, and the grantee took the estate limited in the habendum[3]; or if the estate so limited was contrary to the rules of law, the deed was void[4].

1　　See para 242 note 3 ante. For the meaning of 'premises' see para 242 ante.

2　　See para 242 note 6 ante.

3　　*Goodtitle d Dodwell v Gibbs* (1826) 5 B & C 709. Upon a grant to A and B, habendum to A for life, remainder to B for life, the limitation in the habendum excluded the joint tenancy for life which would have been implied from the premises, and gave estates to A and B for life in succession: *Buckler's Case* (1597) 2 Co Rep 55a at 55b; Co Litt 183b; and see also *Scovel v Cabell* (1588) Cro Eliz 89 at 107; *Anon* (1562) Moore KB 43 pl 133.

4   Thus, on a grant by A to C, habendum to B in tail after the death of A, the express limitation in the habendum was void as attempting to create a future freehold, and, since no limitation could be implied in the premises, the grant was void: *Hogg v Cross* (1591) Cro Eliz 254; *Buckler's Case* (1597) 2 Co Rep 55a; *Stukeley v Butler* (1614) Hob 168 at 171.

244.   Habendum cannot cut down estate.   Where an estate has been limited in the premises, this has been treated as indicating the intention of the grantor, and it was formerly generally accepted that the subsequent limitation in the habendum, although it might enlarge the limitation in the premises[1], or might qualify or explain it[2], could not directly abridge it[3], and, so far as repugnant to it or contrary to the rules of law, was to be disregarded[4].

The possibility of contradictions between an estate limited in the premises and the estate limited in the habendum has been removed in the case of grants of legal estates of freehold by the rule that the only estate of freehold which can be conveyed is the fee simple absolute[5], although contradictions may still occur in limitations of equitable interests.

1   See *Kendal v Micfield* (1740) Barn Ch 46 at 47–48, where a grant to A and the heirs of his body, habendum to A and his heirs, gave a fee simple. Sometimes this was said to give an estate tail, and a fee simple expectant: *Altham's Case* (1610) 8 Co Rep 150b at 154b.
2   Thus, in a grant to A and his heirs, habendum to A and the heirs of his body, the habendum explained 'heirs' in the premises, and A took only an estate tail (*Altham's Case* (1610) 8 Co Rep 150b); unless on the whole deed the fee was held to pass (*Turnman v Cooper* (1619) Cro Jac 476). Similarly, upon a grant to A, his heirs and assigns, habendum to A and his assigns during the life of B, the estate for the life of another in the habendum showed that heirs in the premises was used to denote the heir as special occupant, and not as a word of limitation: *Doe d Timmis v Steele* (1843) 4 QB 663; and see also *Pilsworth v Pyet* (1671) T Jo 4; *Pigot v Salisbury* (1674) Poll 146 at 151; *Kerr v Kerr* (1854) 4 1 Ch R 493. The habendum, though void, might, with other parts of the deed, be looked at for the purpose of qualifying the estate granted by the premises: *Throckmerton v Tracy* (1555) 1 Plowd 145 at 153, 160; *Hagarty v Nally* (1862) 13 ICLR 532.
3   See *Throckmerton v Tracy* (1555) 1 Plowd 145; *Kendal v Micfield* (1740) Barn Ch 46; Co Litt 299a. As to ships see *Reid v Fairbanks* (1853) 13 CB 692.
4   See *Carter v Madgwick* (1692) 3 Lev 339; *Goodtitle d Dodwell v Gibbs* (1826) 5 B & C 709 at 717 (where an immediate estate of freehold limited in the premises took effect, and a limitation of a future freehold in the habendum was rejected); *Doe d Timmis v Steele* (1843) 4 QB 663 at 667; *Boddington v Robinson* (1875) LR 10 Exch 270 at 273. In this last case a grant by a tenant for life to J, his executors, administrators, and assigns, was held to be an express limitation for the life of another, but as to this see Challis *Real Property* (3rd Edn) 104, 109, and it prevailed over the limitation of a future freehold in the habendum. See also *Underhay v Underhay* (1592) Cro Eliz 269; and c f *Goshawke v Chiggell* (1629) Cro Car 154; *Bernard v Bonner* (1648) Aleyn 58 at 59; *Germain v Orchard* (1691) 1 Salk 346.
5   See the Law of Property Act 1925 s 1(1); and REAL PROPERTY vol 39(2) (Reissue) para 36.

245.   Grantee different in premises and habendum.   Although the premises ought to contain the name of the grantee, if his name is omitted there, it is sufficient that it is mentioned in the habendum[1]. Under the former law, if a grantee was named in the premises, and the habendum was to him and another, then only the grantee named in the premises could take an immediate estate[2], though the other might take by way of remainder if the limitation in the habendum could be construed as giving him such an estate[3]. If the grant in the premises was to A, habendum to B, the effect was similar; A took an immediate estate and the habendum was void[4], unless it gave to B an estate in remainder after A's estate[5].

As the only legal estate of freehold which may now be conveyed is an estate in fee simple absolute in possession[6], the construction giving the co-grantee in the habendum an estate by way of remainder could only apply to limitations of an equitable interest, and the possibility of successive leases is restricted by the rule that a term limited to take effect more than 21 years from the date of the instrument purporting to create it is void[7].

1　*Spyve v Topham* (1802) 3 East 115; Co Litt 7a; Shep Touch 75. As to leases see *Butler v Dodton* (1579) Cary 86; *Eeles v Lambert* (1648) Aleyn 38 at 41. The contrary opinion in *Bustard v Coulter* (1602) Cro Eliz 902, was not accepted, and in that case, at 917, the omission of the grantee in the premises was held to be cured by the pleadings.

2　*Sammes's Case* (1609) 13 Co Rep 54; *Kirkman and Reignold's Case* (1588) 2 Leon 1. This rule did not formerly affect the limitation of the use, which in such a case might be to A and B (*Sammes's Case* supra); but conveyances to uses were abolished by the repeal of the Statute of Uses (1535) by the Law of Property Act 1925 s 207, Sch 7 (repealed).

3　Co Litt 231a. A lease to A, habendum to A, B and C in succession was void for the uncertainty as to who should begin; but if the habendum was to A, B and C, in the order in which they were written, this was good and they took in succession (*Windsmore v Hobart* (1585) Hob 313; *Grubham's Case* (1613) 4 Leon 246); and similarly in the case of a grant to A, habendum to A and his wife for their lives in succession (*Wheadon v Sugg* (1615) Cro Jac 372; cf *Greenwood v Tyber* (1620) Cro Jac 563; and see *Cochin v Heathcote* (1773) Lofft 190).

4　See *Anon* (1573) 3 Leon 32.

5　See note 3 supra.

6　See the Law of Property Act 1925 s 1(1); and REAL PROPERTY vol 39(2) (Reissue) para 36.

7　Ibid s 149(3); and see LANDLORD AND TENANT vol 27(1) (2006 Reissue) paras 106, 541–542.

246.　Effect of specifying parcels in habendum.　It has been laid down that the parcels must be defined in the premises, and that the mention of lands in the habendum, which have not been expressly or impliedly mentioned in the premises, is of no effect[1]; but any such rule is subject to the general principle that the deed must be construed as a whole, and it is believed that at the present day the mention of lands in the habendum instead of in the premises would not invalidate the grant[2]. Where the parcels have been defined in the premises, it is wrong to repeat them specifically in the habendum, unless for the purpose of expressing different limitations as to different parcels[3].

1　'Nothing shall pass in the habendum if it be not spoken of in the grant, except it be a thing appendant or appurtenant: *Abbess Sion's Case* (1460), cited in *Throckmerton v Tracy* (1555) 1 Plowd 145 at 152; Shep Touch 75–76; and see also *Gregg v Richards* [1926] Ch 521, CA.

2　That is, where no property is mentioned in the premises. If the premises and the habendum are at variance, however, the case is different, and prima facie only the property mentioned in the premises would pass. This is the case put in Shep Touch 76: 'If a man grant Blackacre only in the premises of a deed, habendum Blackacre and Whiteacre, Whiteacre will not pass by this deed'. A right may pass under 'appurtenances' in the habendum, although not named in the premises: *Renwick v Daly* (1877) IR 11 CL 126.

3　Eg habendum, part for 20 years and other part for ten years: *Carew's Case* (1586) Moore KB 222 at 223.

(10)　COVENANTS

(i)　What Constitutes a Covenant

247.　Definition and construction of covenant.　A covenant is an agreement contained in a deed[1] whereby the parties, or some or one of them, are or is bound to do or not to do a specified thing, as covenants in a lease by deed to pay rent or not to carry on certain trades; or whereby they undertake that a certain state of affairs exists, as a covenant in a conveyance that the grantor is entitled or that he has not incumbered[2]. The word will, however, be construed to cover stipulations in an agreement under hand if otherwise it would have no effect, as where a document refers to the 'covenants' contained in a lease which is not by deed[3]. The words of a covenant are to be taken most strongly against the covenantor; but this must be qualified by the observation that due regard must be paid to the intentions of the parties as collected from the whole context of the instrument[4].

1　Much of the matter contained in these paragraphs applies also to agreements under hand. As to illegal covenants see CONTRACT vol 9(1) (Reissue) para 836 et seq. As to covenants to pay amounts in, or including, shillings and old pence see para 171 ante.

2   See *Randall v Lynch* (1810) 12 East 179 at 182; *Russell v Watts* (1885) 10 App Cas 590 at 611, HL. Where in a deed the parties agreed 'by way of declaration and not of covenant', these words were rejected as 'nonsense': *Ellison v Bignold* (1821) 2 Jac & W 503 at 510.

3   See *Hayne v Cummings* (1864) 16 CBNS 421 at 426; *Brookes v Drysdale* (1877) 3 CPD 52. See also *Bashir v Lands Comr* [1960] AC 44, [1960] 1 All ER 117, PC, where special conditions in a Crown grant were construed as covenants.

4   *Browning v Wright* (1799) 2 Bos & P 13 at 22 per Lord Eldon CJ; and see para 175 et seq ante.

248.   Person bound by covenant.   Where a deed, purporting to bind various parties, provides that some one of the parties is to do an act or make a payment, this stipulation is a covenant by that party with the others[1]; and similarly, an agreement of all parties that property is to be dealt with in a particular way is a covenant by those parties whose concurrence is required to give effect to the provisions in favour of those who are to take the benefit of the conveyance[2].

1   *Dawes v Tredwell* (1881) 18 ChD 354 at 359, CA, per Jessel MR; and see *Ramsden v Smith* (1854) 2 Drew 298 at 307–308.

2   *Willoughby v Middleton* (1862) 2 John & H 344 at 354 per Wood V-C.

249.   How a covenant is made.   No particular technical words are necessary for the making of a covenant[1]. Any words which, when properly construed with the aid of all that is legitimately admissible to aid in the construction of a written document, indicate an agreement constitute, when contained in an instrument executed as a deed, a covenant[2]. It must, however, be clear that the words are intended to operate as an agreement[3], and not merely as words of condition or qualification[4]. Express words of agreement, such as 'covenant', 'agree'[5], or 'engage'[6], may be used; but, without such words, an agreement may be collected from the entire instrument, and a covenant when so made out by construction, sometimes called an implied covenant, is for all purposes an express covenant, and is as effectual as if the word 'covenant' had been used[7]. A specific covenant as to one matter may, however, prevent a covenant being implied as to a cognate matter[8].

1   *Lant v Norris* (1757) 1 Burr 287 at 290 per Lord Mansfield CJ; Shep Touch 162; *Sampson v Easterby* (1829) 9 B & C 505 at 512 (affd (1830) 6 Bing 644 Ex Ch); *Wolveridge v Steward* (1833) 1 Cr & M 644 at 657, Ex Ch; *Rigby v Great Western Rly Co* (1845) 14 M & W 811 at 815 per Parke B; *Rashleigh v South Eastern Rly Co* (1851) 10 CB 612 at 632 per Maule J; *Russell v Watts* (1885) 10 App Cas 590 at 611, HL, per Lord Blackburn; *Re Cadogan and Hans Place Estate Ltd, ex p Willis* (1895) 73 LT 387, CA.

2   See *Russell v Watts* (1885) 10 App Cas 590, HL; *Rashleigh v South Eastern Rly Co* (1851) 10 CB 612 at 632; *James v Cochrane* (1852) 7 Exch 170 at 177 per Parke B (on appeal (1853) 8 Exch 556); *Knight v Gravesend and Milton Waterworks Co* (1857) 2 H & N 6 at 11. See *Hill v Carr* (1676) 1 Cas in Ch 294 ('wherever the intent of the parties can be collected out of a deed for the doing or not doing a thing, covenant will lie'); and see also *Brice v Carre and Emerson* (1661) 1 Lev 47.

3   *Courtney v Taylor* (1843) 6 Man & G 851 at 867 per Tindal CJ; *Iven v Elwes* (1854) 3 Drew 25 at 34 per Kindersley V-C. A statement in a deed of a binding intention to create restrictive covenants on the part of vendors who execute the deed, made as an inducement to purchasers, is as effective as a formal covenant: *Mackenzie v Childer* (1889) 43 ChD 265 at 275.

4   *Wolveridge v Steward* (1833) 1 Cr & M 644 at 657, Ex Ch, per Lord Denman CJ; Com Dig, Covenant (A 3); and see paras 252, 257 post.

5   The word 'covenant' is not more powerful than the word 'agree': *Monypenny v Monypenny* (1861) 9 HL Cas 114 at 137 per Lord St Leonards. To create a covenant in a deed the word 'covenant' need not be specifically used: *Saltoun v Houstoun* (1824) 1 Bing 433.

6   *Rigby v Great Western Rly Co* (1845) 14 M & W 811 at 816 per Parke B.

7   Shep Touch 162; *Williams v Burrell* (1845) 1 CB 402 at 431 per Tindal CJ ('the legal effect and operation of the covenant, whether framed in express terms, that is whether it be an express covenant, or whether the covenant be matter of inference and argument, is precisely the same; and an implied covenant in this sense of the term differs nothing in its operation and legal consequences from an express covenant'); see also *Duke of St Albans v Ellis* (1812) 16 East 352 at 355 per Lord Ellenborough CJ; *Brookes v Drysdale* (1877) 3 CPD 52 at 57–58 per Grove J.

8   *Sharp v Waterhouse* (1857) 7 E & B 816 at 827.

(ii) Covenants arising by Construction

250. In what circumstances covenant is implied. A covenant will arise by construction where the instrument shows an intention that the party is to be bound, although it contains no express words of obligation, for it is a general rule of construction that terms of a written instrument which import that the parties have agreed upon certain things being done have the same effect as express promises, or, in the case of a deed, covenants by the respective parties to do all such things as are necessary to carry out the agreement according to the expressed or manifest intention[1]. However, a covenant will not be implied unless the implication is so necessary that the court can have no doubt what covenant or undertaking to write into the agreement[2].

It is immaterial whether the words importing the covenant are contained in the recitals or in the operative part of the instrument[3] and it is sufficient if the intention of the parties mutually to contract appears from the instrument as a whole[4]. A recital of agreement will not, however, import a covenant where there is an express covenant relating to the same subject matter[5], unless the express covenant is so ambiguous as to justify a reference to the recitals in order to explain it[6]. Whether a recital or acknowledgment operates as a covenant is a question of construction in each particular case, and depends on what appears to have been the intention of the parties having regard to the terms of the instrument as a whole and the surrounding circumstances[7].

1 See *Wood v Copper Miners' in England Co* (1849) 7 CB 906 at 936 per Wilde CJ (an agreement between A and B that A shall buy certain property from B imports an undertaking by B to sell the property to A); *Duke of St Albans v Ellis* (1812) 16 East 352 (covenant in lease to plough and cultivate all the premises, except the rabbit warren and sheep walk in a due course of husbandry, imports a covenant not to plough the rabbit warren or sheep walk); *Williams v Burrell* (1845) 1 CB 402 (provision in a lease that the lessor should during the term warrant and defend the lessee against all persons lawfully claiming the premises held equivalent to an express covenant for quiet enjoyment); *Payne v Haine* (1847) 16 M & W 541 (a covenant by a lessee to keep premises in good repair during the term imports a covenant to put them in good repair if they are in bad repair at the commencement of the term); *M'Intyre v Belcher* (1863) 14 CBNS 654 (a promise by the purchaser of the goodwill of a business in consideration of the transfer to pay a certain proportion of the earnings for a specified period imports a promise to carry on the business during such period and not by any wilful act or default to prevent the receipt of earnings); *Telegraph Dispatch and Intelligence Co v McLean* (1873) 8 Ch App 658 (similar case); *Saner v Bilton* (1878) 7 ChD 815 (the same rule applies where the covenant is by the lessor); *Turner v Goldsmith* [1891] 1 QB 544, CA (agreement to employ a person as agent for a specified term for the sale of goods to be submitted to him by samples from time to time, held to import an obligation to submit samples so as to enable the agent to earn his commission); *Ogdens Ltd v Nelson* [1905] AC 109, HL (agreement to give bonus to customers for a certain period varying with the profits of a business imports a promise to continue the business so that the amount of the bonus can be ascertained). See also *Emmens v Elderton* (1853) 4 HL Cas 624; *Devonald v Rosser & Sons* [1906] 2 KB 728, CA; *Lazarus v Cairn Line of Steamships Ltd* (1912) 106 LT 378; *Reigate v Union Manufacturing Co (Ramsbottom) Ltd* [1918] 1 KB 592, CA; and c f *Webb v Plummer* (1819) 2 B & Ald 746 (a provision in a lease that the tenant should during the term fold his flock of sheep which he should keep on the premises held to import a covenant to keep a flock of sheep on the premises); *Earl of Shrewsbury v Gould* (1819) 2 B & Ald 487 (covenant by lessee at all times and seasons of burning lime to supply the lessor and his tenants with lime at a stipulated price for the improvement of his and their lands, etc, held to import a covenant to burn lime at all such seasons); *Rhodes v Forwood* (1876) 1 App Cas 256, HL; *Hamlyn & Co v Wood & Co* [1891] 2 QB 488, CA; *Morell v New London Discount Co Ltd* (1902) 18 TLR 507; *Moon v Camberwell Borough Council* (1903) 68 JP 57, CA; *Bovine Ltd v Dent and Wilkinson* (1904) 21 TLR 82; *A-G v City of Dublin Steam Packet Co* (1909) 25 TLR 696, HL (contract for the carriage of mails held to import an obligation on the Crown to allow such facilities as were reasonably necessary to enable the contractors to perform their obligations under the contract).

2 *R v Paddington and St Marylebone Rent Tribunal, ex p Bedrock Investments Ltd* [1947] KB 984 at 990, [1947] 2 All ER 15 at 17, DC, per Lord Goddard CJ (affd on other grounds [1948] 2 KB 413, [1948] 2 All ER 528, CA); *R v Croydon and District Rent Tribunal, ex p Langford Property Co Ltd* [1948] 1 KB 60, DC; *Penn v Gatenex Co Ltd* [1958] 2 QB 210 at 224, [1958] 1 All ER 712 at 718, CA, per Parker LJ. As to the general law relating to implications see paras 181–184 ante.

3   *Farrall v Hilditch* (1859) 5 CBNS 840; *Lay v Mottram* (1865) 19 CBNS 479; *Brooks v Jennings* (1866) LR 1 CP 476 (a recital in a composition deed that the debtor has agreed to pay a certain composition on his debts was held equivalent to a covenant with each of the creditors to pay such composition).

4   *Wood v Copper Miners' in England Co* (1849) 7 CB 906.

5   *Dawes v Tredwell* (1881) 18 ChD 354, CA (recital in marriage settlement of agreement to settle after-acquired property of either husband or wife; covenant by husband alone that if property should be acquired by either he would settle; it was held that no covenant by the wife was implied to settle property acquired by her for her separate use).

6   *Re De Ros' Trust, Hardwicke v Wilmot* (1885) 31 ChD 81 (marriage settlement containing recital of agreement to settle after-acquired property of either spouse; covenant by husband, that he and the wife would settle, executed by both; held sufficiently ambiguous to justify a reference to the recitals, and that the wife's property was bound by the covenant).

7   *Courtney v Taylor* (1843) 6 Man & G 851; *Farrall v Hilditch* (1859) 5 CBNS 840.

251. Specific cases of implication of covenants. If in an instrument executed as a deed by two persons one agrees to pay a specified sum for the other's land, this implies a covenant[1] by the latter to convey[2]; an agreement in a charterparty that 40 days are to be allowed for unloading and reloading implies a covenant not to detain the ship for a longer period[3]. An agreement by deed to execute a deed which would contain a covenant to pay money creates a specialty debt[4]. An assignment of property, such as an interest in a medicine, may raise an implied covenant by the vendor not to prepare and sell the medicine, on the principle that he must not derogate from his grant[5]; and a conveyance with a restriction against carrying on certain trades will imply a corresponding covenant[6]. On the other hand a clause in a settlement indemnifying trustees in respect of moneys which they do not receive does not imply a covenant by them to account for moneys which they do receive[7]; and an express covenant of indemnity against a mortgage debt given on the purchase of an equity of redemption will exclude the covenant which would otherwise be implied[8]. Where there is a covenant to build specifying the time and mode of building, no further covenant to build can be implied from a covenant to repair[9]; but where it is known that a building has been extensively damaged before a licence to assign the lease is granted and one of the covenants in the licence is to make good and repair within a certain time, a proviso that the covenant is only operative if planning permission can be obtained will be implied[10]. A grant of an exclusive right of burial in a cemetery plot does not imply an obligation to maintain the safety of a tree on the plot[11].

Where an instrument creating a trust contains a declaration of trust, and the trustee executes it, this operates as a covenant by him[12]; though it will not be so if the trustee does not execute the deed, but only acts under it[13], or where the deed, though executed by the trustee, contains only an acceptance by him of the trust[14].

The implication of terms in contracts where it is clear that the parties must have intended the term to be implied or where implication is necessary to give efficacy to the transaction is discussed elsewhere in this work[15].

1   See the cases cited in para 250 notes 1, 3 ante; and see also paras 252–254 post.

2   *Pordage v Cole* (1669) 1 Wms Saund 319 1; and cf *Wood v Copper Miners' in England Co* (1849) 7 CB 906 (where, upon a covenant by a lessee to take coals, there was implied a covenant by the lessor to supply them); *Great Northern Rly Co v Harrison* (1852) 12 CB 576, Ex Ch (contract by one party to supply and by other party to take sleepers as the engineer should call for them).

3   *Randall v Lynch* (1810) 12 East 179.

4   See *Saunders v Milsome* (1866) LR 2 Eq 573; *Kidd v Boone* (1871) LR 12 Eq 89.

5   *Seddon v Senate* (1810) 13 East 63; and cf *Gerard v Lewis* (1867) LR 2 CP 305; *Trego v Hunt* [1896] AC 7, HL. Where partners have assigned all their partnership property, a partner in whom any such property is solely vested impliedly covenants to do what is necessary to transfer it to the assignee but not to pay to the assignee money which he owes to the partnership: *Aulton v Atkins* (1856) 18 CB 249. As to assignments operating by way of covenant see *Deering v Farrington* (1674) 1 Mod Rep 113; *Caister Parish v Eccles Parish* (1701) 1 Ld Raym 683 per Holt CJ.

6   *Hodson v Coppard* (1860) 29 Beav 4.

7   *Bartlett v Hodgson* (1785) 1 Term Rep 42.

8   *Mills v United Counties Bank Ltd* [1912] 1 Ch 231, CA; and cf *Ellis v Glover and Hobson Ltd* [1908] 1 KB 388, CA.

9   *Stephens v Junior Army and Navy Stores Ltd* [1914] 2 Ch 516, CA, disapproving dictum of Stirling J in *Jacob v Down* [1900] 2 Ch 156. For the application of the maxim 'expressum facit cessare tacitum' see para 182 ante. See also *Morell v New London Discount Co* (1902) 18 TLR 507 (agreement that plaintiffs should contribute towards cost of theatre intended to be built by defendants and should become managing directors; no implied obligation on defendants to build theatre).

10 *Sturcke v SW Edwards Ltd* (1971) 23 P & CR 185.

11 *London Cemetery Co v Cundey* [1953] 2 All ER 257, [1953] 1 WLR 786.

12 *Benson v Benson* (1710) 1 P Wms 130; *Mavor v Davenport* (1828) 2 Sim 227; *Turner v Wardle* (1834) 7 Sim 80; *Wood v Hardisty* (1846) 2 Coll 542. A breach of trust constitutes in general only a simple contract debt: *Vernon v Vawdry* (1740) 2 Atk 119.

13 *Richardson v Jenkins* (1853) 1 Drew 477.

14 *Adey v Arnold* (1852) 2 De GM & G 432; *Holland v Holland* (1869) 4 Ch App 449; and cf *Isaacson v Harwood* (1868) 3 Ch App 225.

15 See CONTRACT vol 9(1) (Reissue) para 778 et seq.

252.   Provisos and participial phrases. A grant or a covenant may be followed by words contemplating that one of the parties is to do or abstain from doing some act. Such words are commonly introduced by 'provided that', or 'to be', or they are contained in a participial clause[1]; and they may operate as a condition for, or qualification of, the preceding covenant, or as a separate covenant. For them to operate as a covenant it must appear that the act or abstention is intended to be obligatory. The words 'provided' or 'on condition' may have this effect[2], and when a covenant by a lessee to repair is followed by 'provided always and it is agreed' that the lessor shall find timber or other materials, these words create a covenant by the lessor[3]. On the other hand if a lessee's covenant to repair is followed by a proviso that the lessor shall find timber, without 'agreed', or by such words as 'the lessor first allowing timber', or 'the premises being previously put in repair by the lessor', there will in general be only a qualification of the lessee's covenant[4].

Where, however, the words express the consideration for the previous covenant or grant, or the condition upon which permission or liberty to do an act is conferred, they will usually be obligatory and will make a covenant, as where one person covenants to pay money to another, the latter 'making him an estate' in certain lands[5]; or where a lease is made, the lessee 'yielding and paying' rent[6], or 'rendering' rent clear of taxes[7], or 'doing suit' to the lessor's mill[8]; or, where in a lease trees are reserved to the lessor with liberty to fell them, 'repairing the hedges where they grow'[9]. By similar words a negative covenant may be created. Thus permission to a person to cut down wood for repairs 'without making waste' implies a covenant by him not to commit waste[10]; and a covenant by a lessee to plough and cultivate the demised premises 'except the rabbit warren and sheep walk' implies a covenant not to plough up the excepted part[11].

1   *Westacott v Hahn* [1918] 1 KB 495 at 505, 513, CA.

2   Com Dig, Covenant (A 2); Shep Touch 162; *Brookes v Drysdale* (1877) 3 CPD 52 at 58; and see *Ashton v Stock* (1877) 6 ChD 719.

3   *Brookes v Drysdale* (1877) 3 CPD 52; and see *Ashton v Stock* (1877) 6 ChD 719.

4   *Holder v Tayloe* (1615) 1 Roll Abr 518; *Lord Cromwell's Case* (1601) 2 Co Rep 69b at 72a, n (1); Bac Abr, Covenant (A) note; *Thomas v Cadwallader* (1744) Willes 496; and see Shep Touch 122; Co Litt 203b. However, in *Mucklestone v Thomas* (1739) Willes 146, 'slates being found, allowed, and delivered on the premises' by the lessor implied a covenant by him; and similarly in *Cannock v Jones* (1849) 3 Exch 233, where a lessee covenanted to repair windows and hedges, the premises 'being previously put in repair and kept in repair by' the lessor, the latter words were held to amount to an absolute and independent covenant by the lessor to put the premises in repair. As to such words being a condition precedent see *Neale v Ratcliff* (1850) 15 QB 916; and see para 269 post.

5   *Large v Cheshire* (1671) 1 Vent 147; and cf *Boone v Eyre* (1779) 2 Wm Bl 1312.

6   *Porter v Swetnam* (1654) Sty 406 at 407; *Hellier v Casbard* (1665) 1 Sid 240 at 266; *Webb v Russell* (1789)
     3 Term Rep 393 at 402; *Iggulden v May* (1804) 9 Ves 325 at 330; *Vyvyan v Arthur* (1823) 1 B & C 410; and
     see Platt on Covenants 50.
7   *Giles v Hooper* (1690) Carth 135.
8   *Vyvyan v Arthur* (1823) 1 B & C 410.
9   This is a covenant by the lessor: *Warren v Arthur* (1682) 2 Mod Rep 317.
10   *Stevinson's Case* (1589) 1 Leon 324.
11   *Duke of St Albans v Ellis* (1812) 16 East 352.

253.   Implied covenant to do preliminary act.   Where the terms of an agreement show that the parties contemplated that a certain thing would be done, as to which there is no express covenant, before another thing is done, as to which there is an express covenant, it must be considered whether the agreement can be read as comprising a covenant to do the former. If the two things are so involved that the parties cannot be supposed to have intended to impose an obligation to do one without imposing also an obligation to do the other, then there is, by construction, a covenant to do the first thing[1]; but otherwise it is not to be assumed that the parties intended to bind themselves to do the first thing because they entered into the contract in the expectation that it would be done, treating it as a thing certain to take place and providing only for the event of its taking place. In such a case there will usually be no covenant implied to do the first thing, but if it is not done, then the express covenant to do the other thing does not become operative[2].

1   Thus a covenant by a lessee to fold a flock of sheep in the usual places involves a covenant to keep a flock
     (*Webb v Plummer* (1819) 2 B & Ald 746); and a covenant by a lessee to supply lime to the lessor at all times
     of burning implies a covenant to burn lime (*Earl of Shrewsbury v Gould* (1819) 2 B & Ald 487).
2   See *Rashleigh v South Eastern Rly Co* (1851) 10 CB 612 (on appeal (1852) 16 Jur 567n, Ex Ch); but as to
     this case see *Knight v Gravesend and Milton Waterworks Co* (1857) 2 H & N 6. See, in a mining lease, as to
     sinking pits *James v Cochrane* (1852) 7 Exch 170 (on appeal (1853) 8 Exch 556, Ex Ch). As to obtaining
     a necessary consent see *Smith v Harwich Corpn* (1857) 2 CBNS 651.

254.   Implied covenant for continuance of business etc.   Where an arrangement is entered into which can only take effect by the continuance of a certain existing state of circumstances, there is an implied engagement on the part of the party upon whom this continuance depends that he will do nothing of his own motion to put an end to the state of circumstances in question[1]. Thus where a business is sold in consideration of the vendor receiving a share of the profits for a specified time, there is an implied agreement by the purchaser to carry it on for that time[2]. In general, however, although the effective operation of an agreement may depend upon the continuance of a business (as in the case of a contract to supply all of certain goods produced in a specified period[3]) or of other existing circumstances (as in the keeping up of a patent[4]), there is no obligation to maintain the existing state[5].

A contract to employ and pay specified wages for a fixed period does not bind the employer to carry on the business[6], or to provide work[7], but only to pay the wages if the employee is willing to work[8]. The special circumstances of the engagement may, however, imply a covenant that the employee is to be actually employed[9].

However, an employee is entitled to a minimum period of notice[10] and to be provided with a written statement of reasons for dismissal[11]. An employer may in appropriate circumstances be required to make a redundancy payment[12].

1   *Stirling v Maitland* (1864) 5 B & S 840 at 852 per Cockburn CJ.
2   *M'Intyre v Belcher* (1863) 14 CBNS 654; *Telegraph Dispatch and Intelligence Co v McLean* (1873) 8 Ch App
     658; *Hope v Gibbs* (1877) 47 LJ Ch 82; and see *Ogdens Ltd v Nelson* [1905] AC 109, HL.
3   *Hamlyn & Co v Wood & Co* [1891] 2 QB 488, CA.
4   'The safest rule to follow in such cases, when there is any reasonable doubt whether the parties did
     intend to enter into a covenant such as is sought to be implied here, is to look at the deed and at the

circumstances under which the deed was made; and if you find that there is no such covenant in the deed, and that there has been no bad faith on the part of those against whom it is sought to imply such a covenant, the court ought to be extremely careful how it implies such a covenant in a well considered deed, where there are no words whatever which express that covenant in any way': *Re Railway and Electric Appliances Co* (1888) 38 ChD 597 at 608 per Kay J. A deed is to be more carefully construed than a preliminary agreement: see *Re Railway and Electric Appliances Co* supra at 605 per Kay J; and *Churchward v R* (1865) LR 1 QB 173 at 195 per Cockburn CJ.

5   Thus, on an employment of an agent at a commission for a fixed time, there is no implied agreement that the business is to continue to be carried on (*Re English and Scottish Marine Insurance Co, ex p Maclure* (1870) 5 Ch App 737, CA; *Rhodes v Forwood* (1876) 1 App Cas 256, HL; *Northey v Trevillion* (1902) 18 TLR 648; *Lazarus v Cairn Line of Steamships Ltd* (1912) 106 LT 378), unless there is an express contract to employ the agent as well as to pay the commission (*Turner v Goldsmith* [1891] 1 QB 544, CA). Cf *Beswick v Swindells* (1835) 3 Ad & El 868, Ex Ch, where there was a contract to make a payment if the business was then carried on; and see *Reigate v Union Manufacturing Co (Ramsbottom) Ltd* [1918] 1 KB 592, CA. See also AGENCY vol 2(1) (Reissue) para 209; CONTRACT vol 9(1) (Reissue) para 778 et seq.

6   *Aspdin v Austin* (1844) 5 QB 671; *Dunn v Sayles* (1844) 5 QB 685.

7   *Turner v Sawdon & Co* [1901] 2 KB 653, CA.

8   *Turner v Sawdon & Co* [1901] 2 KB 653, CA; and see *Churchward v R* (1865) LR 1 QB 173. See also *King v Accumulative Life Fund and General Assurance Co* (1857) 3 CBNS 151; *Emmens v Elderton* (1853) 4 HL Cas 624.

9   Thus, if there is an agreement that a musical director of a theatre is to be advertised as such, he must actually fill the post in order to make the advertisements true, and consequently he is entitled to be employed: *Bunning v Lyric Theatre Ltd* (1894) 71 LT 396.

10   See the Employment Rights Act 1996 s 86 (as amended); and EMPLOYMENT vol 16(1B) (Reissue) paras 609–610.

11   See ibid s 92 (as amended); and EMPLOYMENT vol 16(1B) (Reissue) para 629.

12   See ibid s 135; and EMPLOYMENT vol 16(1B) (Reissue) para 707 et seq.

(iii)   Covenants in Law

255.   Covenants implied from word demise.   A covenant in law is an agreement which the law implies from the use of certain words having a known legal operation in the creation of an estate; so that, after they have had their primary operation in creating the estate, the law gives them a secondary force by implying an agreement on the part of the grantor to protect and preserve the estate which by those words has been already created[1].

Thus, upon a lease by deed using the word 'demise' there are implied covenants for title[2] and for quiet enjoyment[3]. The latter covenant is limited in duration to the interest of the lessor[4], but extends to the acts of persons claiming by title paramount to him[5]. The covenant is implied only against the person actually demising, not against one who joins to confirm[6]. Where several demise jointly, the covenant for title is joint but the covenant for quiet enjoyment is several, so that any lessor can be sued alone for disturbance caused by himself[7]. The implication of these covenants will be prevented by the existence of express covenants[8].

1   *Williams v Burrell* (1845) 1 CB 402 at 429.

2   That is, that the lessor has power to let (*Holder v Taylor* (1614) Hob 12; *Burnett v Lynch* (1826) 5 B & C 589 at 609; cf *Kean v Strong* (1845) 9 ILR 74 at 82 (on appeal sub nom *Strong v Kean* (1847) 10 ILR 137)); but this need not be power to grant the term mentioned in the lease; it is sufficient that the lessor is entitled to put the lessee into possession, otherwise this covenant would go beyond the implied covenant for quiet enjoyment, which is restricted to the interest of the lessor (*Adams v Gibney* (1830) 6 Bing 656; *Baynes & Co v Lloyd & Sons* [1895] 2 QB 610, CA; and see *Bragg v Wiseman* (1614) 1 Brownl 22, put upon the ground that a covenant in law must not be extended to make a man do more than he can). It is perhaps more correct to say that only one covenant is implied of which either want of title or an eviction would be a breach: *Line v Stephenson* (1838) 5 Bing NC 183 at 184, Ex Ch, per Alderson B; *Baynes & Co v Lloyd & Sons* [1895] 2 QB 610, CA. See LANDLORD AND TENANT vol 27(1) (2006 Reissue) para 511.

3   *Line v Stephenson* (1838) 5 Bing NC 183, Ex Ch; *Baynes & Co v Lloyd & Sons* [1895] 2 QB 610, CA. An implied contract for quiet enjoyment arises also upon an agreement for letting, out of the mere relation

of landlord and tenant, without any use of the word 'demise' (*Hart v Windsor* (1844) 12 M & W 68 at 85; *Bandy v Cartwright* (1853) 8 Exch 913; *Hall v City of London Brewery Co* (1862) 2 B & S 737; *Mostyn v West Mostyn Coal and Iron Co* (1876) 1 CPD 145; *Robinson v Kilvert* (1889) 41 ChD 88 at 96, CA; *Budd-Scott v Daniell* [1902] 2 KB 351; *Markham v Paget* [1908] 1 Ch 697); although the contract so implied from a mere letting is restricted to the acts of the lessor and those claiming under him (*Jones v Lavington* [1903] 1 KB 253, CA), and is limited to the interest of the lessor (*Penfold v Abbott* (1862) 32 LJQB 67; *Baynes & Co v Lloyd & Sons* supra).

4   See note 2 supra.
5   *Line v Stephenson* (1838) 5 Bing NC 183 at 184–185, Ex Ch.
6   *Smith v Pocklington* (1831) 1 Cr & J 445.
7   *Coleman v Sherwin* (1689) 1 Salk 137.
8   *Stannard v Forbes* (1837) 6 Ad & El 572; *Line v Stephenson* (1838) 5 Bing NC 183, Ex Ch; *Miller v Emcer Products Ltd* [1956] Ch 304, [1956] 1 All ER 237, CA.

256.   Conveyancing: covenants and words implied.   In deeds executed after 1 October 1845, the words 'give' or 'grant' do not imply any covenant in law, save where otherwise provided by statute[1].

Certain covenants are implied by the Law of Property (Miscellaneous Provisions) Act 1994[2] in an instrument[3] effecting or purporting to effect a disposition of property[4], whether or not the disposition is for valuable consideration[5]. A distinction is made between the case where a disposition is expressed to be made with full title guarantee[6], and the case where it is made with limited title guarantee[7]. Liability under certain covenants is excluded in certain cases[8], and the operation of any covenant implied in an instrument by virtue of the provisions relating to implied covenants for title[9] may be limited or extended by a term of that instrument[10].

A covenant relating to land of the covenantee, made after 1925[11], is deemed to be made with the covenantee and his successors in title as if those successors were mentioned[12]; and a covenant[13] relating to land of a covenantor or capable of being bound by him is, if made after 1925 and unless a contrary intention is expressed[14], deemed to be made by a covenantor on behalf of himself and his successors in title and the persons deriving title under him or them as if those successors and other persons were mentioned[15].

A covenant and a bond and an obligation or contract made under seal after 31 December 1881 but before 31 July 1990[16], or executed as a deed[17], binds the real estate as well as the personal estate of the person making the same if and so far as a contrary intention is not expressed in the covenant, bond, obligation or contract[18]. This applies to a covenant implied by virtue of the Law of Property Act 1925[19].

In the construction of a covenant or proviso or other provision implied in a deed or assent by virtue of that Act, words importing the singular or plural number or the masculine gender are read as also importing the plural or singular number or extending to females as the case may require[20].

1   Law of Property Act 1925 s 59(2) (reproducing the Real Property Act 1845 s 4 (repealed)); and see 1 Dart's Vendors and Purchases (8th Edn) 508. Formerly the words 'give' or 'grant' in a deed did operate as a warranty of title: see *Williams v Burrell* (1845) 1 CB 402; Co Litt 384a, n (1). For an instance where covenants are imported from the word 'grant' see the Lands Clauses Consolidation Act 1845 s 132; and COMPULSORY ACQUISITION OF LAND vol 8(1) (2003 Reissue) para 384. In this instance the terms of the covenants to be implied are set out in the statute.
2   See generally the Law of Property (Miscellaneous Provisions) Act 1994 Pt I (ss 1–13) (as amended); and SALE OF LAND vol 42 (Reissue) paras 337, 350–351. As to covenants implied in conveyances made before 1 July 1995 (i e the date on which the Law of Property (Miscellaneous Provisions) Act 1994 Pt I (as originally enacted) came into force) see the Law of Property Act 1925 Sch 2 Pts I–VI (Pts II–III as amended, Pt VI repealed). As to conveyance subject to rents see s 77 (as amended), Sch 2 Pts VII–VIII. See MORTGAGE vol 32 (2005 Reissue) para 423; SALE OF LAND vol 42 (Reissue) para 338 et seq.
3   For the meaning of 'instrument' see SALE OF LAND vol 42 (Reissue) para 350.
4   For the meaning of 'property' see SALE OF LAND vol 42 (Reissue) para 350.
5   See the Law of Property (Miscellaneous Provisions) Act 1994 s 1(1).

6   Ie in this case ibid ss 2, 3(1), (2), 4, 5 (as amended) apply: see s 1(2)(a).
7   Ie in this case ibid ss 2, 3(3), 4, 5 (as amended) apply: see s 1(2)(b).
8   See ibid s 6 (as amended); and SALE OF LAND vol 42 (Reissue) para 350.
9   Ie ibid Pt I (as amended): see s 8(1).
10 Ibid s 8(1); and see SALE OF LAND vol 42 (Reissue) paras 350–351.
11 The Conveyancing Act 1881 s 58 (repealed), however, applies substantially the same law to covenants
    made after 1881, and its effect is saved as regards covenants made before 1926.
12 Law of Property Act 1925 s 78. As to the possible far-reaching effects of the change in wording of s 78
    when compared with the preceding enactment (ie the Conveyancing Act 1881 s 58 (repealed): see note
    11 supra) see *Smith and Snipes Hall Farm Ltd v River Douglas Catchment Board* [1949] 2 KB 500, [1949]
    2 All ER 179, CA; *Williams v Unit Construction Co Ltd* (1955) 19 Conv (NS) 262, CA. As regards
    restrictive covenants see EQUITY vol 16(2) (Reissue) para 613 et seq.
13 This includes a covenant to do an act relating to the land, although the subject matter may not be in
    existence when the covenant is made: see the Law of Property Act 1925 s 79(1). For the second rule in
    Spencer's Case (1583) 5 Co Rep 16a, whereby a covenant concerning land but relating to a thing in
    futuro, eg a covenant to erect new buildings, did not bind assigns unless assigns were expressly mentioned
    see LANDLORD AND TENANT vol 27(1) (2006 Reissue) para 559.
14 Compare *Re Robert Stephenson & Co Ltd, Poole v Robert Stephenson & Co Ltd* [1915] 1 Ch 802 (assigns of
    lessees not expressed but covenant binding on lessees' assigns); and see also *Re Royal Victoria Pavilion,
    Ramsgate, Whelan v FTS (Great Britain) Ltd* [1961] Ch 581, [1961] 3 All ER 83.
15 See the Law of Property Act 1925 s 79. As regards restrictive covenants see EQUITY vol 16(2) (Reissue)
    para 613 et seq. As to further provisions relating to covenants running with land see the Law of Property
    Act 1925 ss 80(2), (4), 141, 142; and LANDLORD AND TENANT vol 27(1) (2006 Reissue) paras 567, 571
    et seq.
16 Ie the date on which the Law of Property (Miscellaneous Provisions) Act 1989 s 1 (as originally enacted)
    came into force: see s 1(11); and para 7 text and note 4 ante. As from 31 July 1990, any rule of law which
    requires a seal for the valid execution of an instrument as a deed by an individual is abolished: see
    s 1(1)(b); and paras 7, 27, 32 ante. As to the application of s 1(1)(b) see s 1(9); and para 7 text and note
    4 ante.
17 Ie in accordance with ibid s 1 (as amended) after its coming into force (see the text to note 16 supra): see
    the Law of Property Act 1925 s 80(1) (as amended: see note 18 infra).
18 Ibid s 80(1) (amended by the Law of Property (Miscellaneous Provisions) Act 1989 s 1, Sch 1 paras 1, 4);
    and see *Kirk v Eustace* [1937] AC 491, [1937] 2 All ER 715, HL; *Langstone v Hayes* [1946] KB 109, [1946]
    1 All ER 114, CA; and para 109 ante.
19 Law of Property Act 1925 s 80(1).
20 Ibid s 83; and cf para 171 ante.

(iv) Qualified Covenants

257.   Conditional covenants.   A covenant may be absolute or qualified, and in the
latter case the qualification may be introduced either by way of condition or by way of
limitation. A qualification by way of condition is introduced by such words as 'on
condition that' or 'provided that', or is expressed in a participial clause[1], and it may take
effect by way of condition precedent or condition subsequent. If it is a condition
precedent, it must be satisfied before the liability on the covenant can arise[2]; if it is a
condition subsequent, then, upon performance of the condition, the liability under the
covenant ceases[3]. A qualification which is repugnant to the rest of the covenant will be
rejected[4].

1   See para 252 ante. As to the qualification implied in 'provided always' see *Martelli v Holloway* (1872) LR
    5 HL 532.
2   Thus in a covenant by a lessee to repair provided that the lessor finds timber, the proviso is a condition
    precedent (see the cases referred to in para 252 note 4 ante). Such a condition may also be a
    cross-covenant (Bac Abr, Covenant (A) 340n). The performance by a lessee of his covenants is, in general,
    a condition precedent to the lessor's liability under a covenant to renew: see *Bastin v Bidwell* (1881) 18
    ChD 238; and Bac Abr, Conditions. As to covenants which are also conditions see para 266 post.
3   A clause providing for cesser of an agent's liability under a charter party on the goods being shipped
    operates as a condition subsequent: *Bannister v Breslauer* (1867) LR 2 CP 497. The condition of a bond is
    technically a condition subsequent, though in substance the liability on the bond is conditional on breach
    of the condition: see para 91 ante. In a covenant not to assign without consent, with a proviso that

consent is not to be unreasonably withheld, the proviso is a qualification of the covenant and operates by way of condition subsequent. Such a proviso is now implied by statute, notwithstanding any express provision to the contrary: see the Landlord and Tenant Act 1927 s 19(1)(a), (1A)–(1E) (as added); and LANDLORD AND TENANT vol 27(1) (2006 Reissue) para 486. If, upon request for consent, it is unreasonably withheld, then the liability under the covenant for that occasion ceases, and the lessee can assign without consent: *Treloar v Bigge* (1874) LR 9 Exch 151; *Sear v House Property and Investment Society* (1880) 16 ChD 387; *Young v Ashley Gardens Properties Ltd* [1903] 2 Ch 112, CA; and see LANDLORD AND TENANT vol 27(1) (2006 Reissue) paras 471, 487, 493. As to conditional promises see also CONTRACT vol 9(1) (Reissue) para 670.

4   *Belcher v Sikes* (1828) 8 B & C 185.

258. Limited covenants. A covenant is qualified by way of limitation when words are introduced into it which limit in some respect the liability of the covenantor, and this is the more usual use of the term 'qualified covenant'[1]. The limitation will be effectual though not introduced into the covenant itself but placed in some other part of the deed, if its application to the particular covenant is clear[2]; and it may arise by construction although not expressly stated[3]. A covenant in form absolute may be qualified by another covenant providing for an alternative event[4].

Where a group of covenants, such as covenants for title, occur in a deed and some of the covenants are expressly qualified and others are in form absolute, the qualifying words may on the construction of the deed be held to apply to the covenants which are absolute in form[5].

1   Thus a covenant for quiet enjoyment may be either absolute, so that the covenantor covenants against lawful disturbance by any person whomsoever, or it may be qualified by a limitation to disturbance by the covenantor or persons rightfully claiming under him: see *Sanderson v Berwick-upon-Tweed Corpn* (1884) 13 QBD 547, CA; *Harrison, Ainslie & Co v Muncaster* [1891] 2 QB 680, CA.
2   See *Brown v Brown* (1661) 1 Lev 57, where covenants for title were qualified by a 'remote agreement at the end of the deed'.
3   See *Sicklemore v Thistleton* (1817) 6 M & S 9 (where a surety for a lessee was not chargeable until after 40 days' default by the lessee and demand made on the surety). In *Hesse v Albert* (1828) 3 Man & Ry KB 406, a covenant to pay an annuity was qualified by a recital so as to be a covenant only to pay out of a particular source. On the other hand a recital in a conveyance which shows a defect in the grantor's title does not qualify his covenants for title, which must be construed with reference to the title expressed to be conveyed in the operative part, and he is liable for a breach arising through this defect (*Page v Midland Rly Co* [1894] 1 Ch 11, CA); nor is a covenant for title qualified by a reference to the instrument under which the title is derived, unless the interest expressed to be conveyed is in the operative part restricted to whatever was thereby acquired (*Cooke v Founds* (1661) 1 Lev 40; *May v Platt* [1900] 1 Ch 616 at 620; and cf *Delmer v M'Cabe* (1863) 14 ICLR 377 at 384).
4   *Hemans v Picciotto* (1857) 1 CBNS 646 (agreement to pay sum by instalments for specified work, with agreement, if work not proceeded with, to refer remuneration to arbitration); and cf *Molyneux v Richard* [1906] 1 Ch 34 (absolute covenant to build house not restricted by power to use land for spoil banks).
5   See e g *Browning v Wright* (1799) 2 Bos & P 13; and SALE OF LAND.

259. Qualification implied from circumstances. Covenants may also be qualified by the circumstances of the particular case. Thus a covenant in terms absolute may be restricted to events which, having regard to the circumstances, both parties, at the time when the covenant was entered into, contemplated, or ought to have contemplated if they had thought properly about the matter[1]. It is not sufficient that one of the parties did in fact contemplate a wider interpretation[2].

1   *Harrison, Ainslie & Co v Muncaster* [1891] 2 QB 680 at 686, CA, per Lord Esher MR. The purchaser of a defective title has a right to a conveyance without any words limiting the implied covenants for title therein: *Re Geraghty and Lyons' Contract* (1919) 53 ILT 57.
2   *Harrison, Ainslie & Co v Muncaster* [1891] 2 QB 680, CA.

(v) Joint and Several Covenants

260. Several covenantors or covenantees. Where there are several covenantors or covenantees the covenant may, as regards the liability of the covenantors, be either joint or several, or at once joint and several; and it may, as regards the benefit to the covenantees, be either joint or several, or now, it seems[1], both joint and several. The effect of the covenant depends upon the ordinary rules of construction, assisted, especially as regards the benefit of the covenant, by the nature of the interests of the parties in its subject matter[2].

1   See para 264 post.
2   See paras 111 ante, 265 post; and CONTRACT vol 9(1) (Reissue) para 1079 et seq.

261. Where liability under covenant is joint. A covenant is joint, as regards the liability of the covenantors, where two or more persons, without any words of severance, covenant for themselves that they will do something, or that they or one of them will do something; that is, where the obligation is imposed upon the covenantors simply[1]. The effect is that, while the covenantors are all living, anyone who is sued alone can insist on the others being joined[2], and upon the death of one the entire liability devolves upon the survivors or survivor[3].

The effect of a covenant which, as regards the liability of the covenantors, is in form clearly joint depends on the words themselves, and it is not controlled by the circumstance that the covenantors have separate interests in the subject matter of the covenant. If, however, it is doubtful whether the covenant is joint or several, this is one of the points to be taken into consideration. In such a case it is permissible to look at the other parts of the deed, the interests of the covenantors, and any other circumstances appearing on the face of the instrument which will aid in the determination of the intention of the parties[4].

There is no principle of equity requiring joint covenants to be treated as joint and several[5]. A joint covenant by partners will be considered as several, at any rate in a mercantile partnership, if it simply represents a pre-existing partnership liability, but not if the obligation arises solely under the covenant. The extent of the covenant is then measured only by its language[6].

1   Eg: We, A and B, bind ourselves, our heirs, executors, and administrators to pay £4,000 (*Simpson v Vaughan*) (1739) 2 Atk 31); A and B do hereby for themselves, their executors, administrators, and assigns, covenant with C that they, A and B or one of them, their executors, administrators, or assigns, will pay the rent reserved by a lease and keep the premises in repair (*Clarke v Bickers* (1845) 14 Sim 639; *White v Tyndall*) (1888) 13 App Cas 263, HL); L and R (R being a surety) covenant with C that they will pay rent, and further that L will repair; the covenant to repair, as well as the covenant to pay the rent, is joint (*Copland v Laporte*) (1835) 3 Ad & El 517). Words purporting to make not only an original obligor, but also his executors, jointly liable with the other obligors, however, have no effect. The liability of executors under a joint and several covenant is necessarily several only: *Read v Price* [1909] 1 KB 577; affd [1909] 2 KB 724, CA.
2   See *King v Hoare* (1844) 13 M & W 494; *Kendall v Hamilton* (1879) 4 App Cas 504 at 515, HL.
3   *White v Tyndall* (1888) 13 App Cas 263, HL.
4   *White v Tyndall* (1888) 13 App Cas 263 at 276, HL, per Lord Herschell.
5   *Sumner v Powell* (1816) 2 Mer 30; and c f *Primrose v Bromley* (1739) 1 Atk 89 at 90.
6   *Sumner v Powell* (1816) 2 Mer 30; *Beresford v Browning* (1875) LR 20 Eq 564 (affd (1875) 1 ChD 30, CA). A covenant for payment off of a partner's share is in general an arrangement for discharging a pre-existing joint and several liability, and will be treated as joint and several: *Beresford v Browning* supra. Where, however, the covenant was the joint covenant of continuing partners to pay sums to an outgoing partner as the purchase price of his share, it was held to be not merely a security but different from the pre-existing liability, and was not several in equity (*Wilmer v Currey* (1848) 2 De G & Sm 347); and joint covenants in a lease taken by partners for partnership purposes have been construed as joint only (*Clarke v Bickers* (1845) 14 Sim 639; *Levy v Sale* (1877) 37 LT 709). In *Sumner v Powell* supra a joint covenant to indemnify the executors of a deceased partner was held to be joint only. The distinction between the circumstances in *Wilmer v Currey* supra and *Beresford v Browning* supra is slight, and the authority of *Wilmer v Currey* supra seems to be doubtful. A joint covenant by partners, although treated in equity as only joint during the lives of the partners, is in effect made several on the death of one, and the covenantee can prove against his estate (*Kendall v Hamilton* (1879) 4 App Cas 504 at 517, HL; *Re Hodgson, Beckett v Ramsdale* (1885) 31 ChD 177, CA), although he cannot maintain an action for administration of

that estate (*Re McRae, Forster v Davis, Norden v McRae* (1883) 25 ChD 16, CA). As to proof in bankruptcy see BANKRUPTCY AND INDIVIDUAL INSOLVENCY vol 3(2) (2002 Reissue) para 490 et seq. As to joint and several liability on a guarantee given by a firm and also by the several partners see *Re Smith, Fleming & Co, ex p Harding* (1879) 12 ChD 557, CA; and CONTRACT vol 9(1) (Reissue) para 1080 et seq; PARTNERSHIP vol 35 (Reissue) para 65.

262. Where liability is several. Where there are several covenantors and each undertakes only as regards his own acts or defaults, the covenant is said to be several, and the effect is the same as if several deeds were written upon the same piece of parchment[1]. This form of covenant is employed when an aggregate sum is to be secured, but each covenantor is to be liable for only a part of it; as where a number of people covenant 'severally' to pay, one person £3, another £3 etc[2], or where, without the word 'severally', they covenant to pay £50 each[3].

1   *Mathewson's Case* (1597) 5 Co Rep 22b.
2   *Mathewson's Case* (1597) 5 Co Rep 22b.
3   *Armstrong v Cahill* (1880) 6 LR Ir 440. So, in *Collins v Prosser* (1823) 1 B & C 682, A and B were bound in £1,000 each; this was several, and was not avoided as to A by the seal of B being removed. See para 111 ante.

263. Where liability is joint and several. In general a covenant is framed so as to be at once joint and several, and then it is at the election of the covenantee in which form he shall sue upon it; whether to charge all the covenantors together or the survivor alone on the joint covenant, or to charge one alone, or the executor of a deceased covenantor, with the entire liability on the several covenant[1]. A joint and several covenant is now usually made by the words 'jointly and severally' but it will arise from any other words which have the same effect, such as we and each of us covenant[2], or A and B covenant for themselves and each of them[3].

1   *May v Woodward* (1677) Freem KB 248.
2   *Robinson v Walker* (1703) 1 Salk 393; *Duke of Northumberland v Errington* (1794) 5 Term Rep 522.
3   *Bolton v Lee* (1672) 2 Lev 56; *Robinson v Walker* (1703) 1 Salk 393. Such a covenant has also been held to arise from the words 'for themselves and either of them' (*Enys v Donnithorne* (1761) 2 Burr 1190; and see *Church v King* (1836) 2 My & Cr 220); and from 'for themselves and every of them' (*May v Woodward* (1677) Freem KB 248). See also *Tippins v Coates* (1853) 18 Beav 401; and paras 110, 116 ante. On the construction of an agreement by joint owners to assign a patent, it was held that they should enter into joint and several covenants of title: *National Society for Distribution of Electricity by Secondary Generators v Gibbs* [1900] 2 Ch 280, CA.

264. Benefit of joint covenant. As regards the benefit of a covenant, the covenant may be made with the covenantees jointly, or with each of them severally. Apparently, apart from statutory provision, a single covenant could not be made with the covenantees jointly and severally, so as to leave it to the election of the covenantees whether to sue together or separately on the same covenant[1].

However, now a covenant made or implied after 31 December 1881 with two or more jointly to pay money or to make a conveyance or to do any other act, to them or for their benefit, is deemed to include and by statute implies an obligation to do the act to, or for the benefit of, the survivor or survivors of them and to, or for the benefit of, any other person to whom the right to sue on the covenant devolves, and where made after 31 December 1925 is construed as being also made with each of them[2].

If the covenant is joint only, then, so long as all the covenantees are living, all must sue together[3]; upon the death of any one of them, the action must be brought by the survivors, whether the breach of covenant occurred before the death[4] or after[5]. If the covenant is joint and several by virtue of the Law of Property Act 1925[6], it can presumably be enforced either as a joint covenant or (as several) by any covenantee or his personal representatives.

A covenant, whether express or implied, or agreement entered into by a person with himself and one or more other persons is construed and capable of being enforced in like manner as if it had been entered into with the other person or persons alone[7]. This provision applies to covenants and agreements whenever entered into[8]. A covenant is, however, enforceable by virtue of this provision only so far as it would have been enforceable if originally entered into with the covenantees other than the covenantor[9].

1   *Slingsby's Case* (1587) 5 Co Rep 18b at 19a, Ex Ch (a man cannot bind himself to three and to each of them to make it joint and several at the election of several persons for one and the same cause).

2   See the Law of Property Act 1925 s 81(1); and see *Josselson v Borst and Gilksten* [1938] 1 KB 723, [1937] 3 All ER 722, CA. In its application to instruments made after 31 July 1990 (i e the date on which the Law of Property (Miscellaneous Provisions) Act 1989 s 1 (as originally enacted) came into force: see s 1(11); and para 7 text and note 4 ante), the Law of Property Act 1925 s 81(1) is modified: see s 81(5) (as added); and CONTRACT vol 9(1) (Reissue) paras 1081–1082. See further para 256 ante. Section 81 (as amended) extends to a covenant implied by the Act: see s 81(2); and para 256 ante. It applies only if and so far as a contrary intention is not expressed in the covenant and has effect subject to the provisions contained in the covenant: s 81(3). The provision also extends to covenants implied under the Law of Property (Miscellaneous Provisions) Act 1994 Pt I (ss 1–13) (as amended): s 8(2).

3   *Sorsbie v Park* (1843) 12 M & W 146 at 157–158; *Lane v Drinkwater* (1834) 1 Cr M & R 599 at 613.

4   *Eccleston v Clipsham* (1668) 1 Saund 153.

5   *Foley v Addenbrooke* (1843) 4 QB 197. As to payment to one of two joint obligees of a bond see *Steeds v Steeds* (1889) 22 QBD 537; *Powell v Brodhurst* [1901] 2 Ch 160 at 164; para 137 ante; and CONTRACT vol 9(1) (Reissue) para 1086.

6   See the Law of Property Act 1925 s 81(1); and note 2 supra.

7   Ibid s 82(1). Formerly the covenant could not be sued on: *Boyce v Edbrooke* [1903] 1 Ch 836; *Ellis v Kerr* [1910] 1 Ch 529 (explaining *Rose v Poulton* (1831) 2 B & Ad 822); *Napier v Williams* [1911] 1 Ch 361. The Law of Property Act 1925 s 82(1) has been held to have no application to the contract constituted by the rules of a trade union viewed as a contract between each member and the other members of the union: *Bonsor v Musicians' Union* [1954] Ch 479 at 493, [1954] 1 All ER 822 at 827–828, CA, per Sir R Evershed MR, and at 521–522 and 844–845 per Jenkins LJ; revsd on other grounds [1956] AC 104, [1955] 3 All ER 518, HL.

8   Law of Property Act 1925 s 82(2). It extends to covenants implied by statute (see para 256 ante) in the case of a person who conveys or is expressed to convey to himself and one or more other persons, but without prejudice to any order of the court made before 1 January 1926: s 82(2).

9   Where on a sale of land before 1926 by owners in common to one of themselves, the purchaser in accordance with an intended building scheme entered into restrictive covenants with the vendors which were unenforceable because the purchaser was also one of the vendors, the defect in the covenants was not cured by ibid s 82 (see the text to notes 7–8 supra), so far as to render them enforceable by a successor in title to other land of the vendors intended to be subject to the scheme; for, if the covenants had in the first instance been entered into with the vendors other than the covenantor, they would not have enured for the benefit of the whole of the interests in the land retained and would not have created the mutuality of obligation which is an essential ingredient for the enforcement of a building scheme: *Ridley v Lee* [1935] Ch 591 at 603–604. As to covenants entered into as part of building schemes see EQUITY vol 16(2) (Reissue) paras 624–625.

265.   Construction affected by interests of covenantees.   The construction of a covenant with several covenantees depends, as regards its being joint or several, very largely on the interests of the covenantees in the subject matter of the covenant. Here, as in other cases, the intention of the parties, as expressed by their words, prevails, and by clear words a covenant may be made with covenantees jointly, although their interests are several, and vice versa. The court leans, however, against this separation between the nature of the covenant and the nature of the interest, and where the interest is joint the covenant will be joint if the words are capable of that construction; where the interests are several, the covenant will in the same manner be construed, if possible, as several[1]. The express language must not be contradicted, but it will be moulded to suit the interests according as they are joint or several[2].

With regard to covenants made on or after 1 January 1926 with two or more persons jointly, the above principles of construction have to be applied while bearing in mind the enactment[3] that, unless a contrary intention is expressed in the covenant and subject to the provisions contained in it, such a covenant is to be construed as being also made with each of the covenantees. Any such joint covenant is therefore, in the absence of an express contrary intention, also several. Apart from the direct effect of this enactment on the construction of a joint covenant, the draftsman of a post-1925 covenant is assumed to be choosing its words so as to operate against background law including the enactment. It can therefore have an indirect effect on the construction of any covenant. The older decided cases where covenants were construed as joint[4] or as several[5] must in relation to post-1925 covenants be applied subject to this qualification and to the direct effect of the enactment.

1   *Sorsbie v Park* (1843) 12 M & W 146; *Bradburne v Botfield* (1845) 14 M & W 559 at 572 per Parke B; *Beer v Beer* (1852) 12 CB 60 at 78; and see *Haddon v Ayers* (1858) 1 E & E 118. It was formerly supposed to be a rule of law that a covenant was, as regards the covenantees, joint when their interests were joint, and vice versa, notwithstanding that the words of the covenant were to the contrary: *Justice Windham's Case* (1589) 5 Co Rep 7a at 8a; *Eccleston v Clipsham* (1668) 1 Saund 153; *James v Emery* (1818) 8 Taunt 245 at 248, Ex Ch; *Withers v Bircham* (1824) 3 B & C 254. This was upon the ground that to allow separate actions when the interest was the same would charge the covenantor twice over: *Slingsby's Case* (1587) 5 Co Rep 18b at 19a, Ex Ch; *Lilly v Hodges* (1723) 8 Mod Rep 166. But in Preston's edition of Sheppard's Touchstone it was suggested (at 166) that the rule was only applicable when the words were ambiguous. In *Sorsbie v Park* (1843) 12 M & W 146 at 157 per Lord Abinger CB, this gloss on the old rule was accepted, and since then the rule has been treated as one of construction only. See further CONTRACT vol 9(1) (Reissue) para 1083.

2   *White v Tyndall* (1888) 13 App Cas 263 at 277, HL, per Lord Herschell. This seems to represent the judgments in *Sorsbie v Park* (1843) 12 M & W 146 and *Bradburne v Botfield* (1845) 14 M & W 559. To enable the test of joint or several interests to be applied, the language of the covenant must not be ambiguous in the ordinary sense; it is sufficient that it is capable of being construed several, though in form joint, and vice versa. This will not be so, however, if it is expressly 'joint' or expressly 'several': see *Bradburne v Botfield* supra at 563 per Parke B.

3   See the Law of Property Act 1925 s 81 (as amended); and para 264 ante. In its application to instruments made after 31 July 1990 (ie the date on which the Law of Property (Miscellaneous Provisions) Act 1989 s 1 (as originally enacted) came into force: see s 1(11); and para 7 text and note 4 ante), the Law of Property Act 1925 s 81(1) is modified: see s 81(5) (as added); para 264 ante; and CONTRACT vol 9(1) (Reissue) paras 1081–1082.

4   The following are instances of covenants which were treated as joint: (1) covenant for title entered into with joint grantees and each of them; in this case the covenant was at first joint, and, since this suited the joint interest, the words 'each of them' were rejected (*Slingsby's Case* (1587) 5 Co Rep 18b, Ex Ch); (2) covenant between co-adventurers by each with the other and others of them; all had the same interest in the covenant and it was joint (*Eccleston v Clipsham* (1668) 1 Saund 153); (3) covenant whereby musicians bound themselves in £20, each to the other jointly and severally, not to play asunder; the interest being joint, 'severally' was repugnant (*Spencer v Durant* (1688) Comb 115 (the actual words were 'omnibus et cuilibet eorum'); and see 1 Show 8; cf *Saunders v Johnson* (1693) Skin 401); (4) covenant with L and B to pay to L and B an annuity of £30, namely, £15 to L and £15 to B, with joint powers for securing the annuity (*Lane v Drinkwater* (1834) 1 Cr M & R 599); (5) covenant between subscribers to a new corn market to pay sums set opposite their names, the covenant being by the subscribers to and with each other, and to and with trustees; the trustees sued alone; held, that the covenant was prima facie joint with the subscribers and the trustees, and that the trustees had no separate interest by which the covenant could be made several (*Sorsbie v Park* (1843) 12 M & W 146; and see *Pugh v Stringfield* (1857) 3 CBNS 2, where, upon a guarantee for the completion of buildings given to three mortgagees of separate properties, it was held that the interest, and also the benefit of the covenant, was joint).

A covenant with two jointly for payment of a sum of money confers a joint legal interest, and the covenant was construed as joint notwithstanding that only one was interested: *Rolls v Yate* (1610) Yelv 177; *Anderson v Martindale* (1801) 1 East 497; *Hopkinson v Lee* (1845) 6 QB 964. Where in a lease by several lessors the lessee entered into a covenant to repair which was capable of being treated as joint it was so treated, notwithstanding that one or more of lessors had no interest in the land (*Southcote v Hoare* (1810) 3 Taunt 87; *Wakefield v Brown* (1846) 9 QB 209 at 223), or that the lessors were tenants in common, although their interests in the land were separate, they had a joint interest in the repairs (*Foley v Addenbrooke* (1843) 4 QB 197; *Bradburne v Botfield* (1845) 14 M & W 559). This was so although the lessors demised 'according to their several estates', and the lessees covenanted with them 'and their respective heirs and assigns': *Thompson v Hakewill* (1865) 19 CBNS 713 at 726. Upon a demise of a reversion on a lease to tenants in common, each could sue on the covenants in the lease without joining the others: *Roberts v Holland* [1893] 1 QB 665. Tenancy in common, however, cannot exist at law (Law of Property Act 1925 s 1(6)), and it can only exist in equity behind a trust of land (see s 34(1); the Settled Land Act 1925 s 36(4) (as amended); and SETTLEMENTS vol 42 (Reissue) para 713). Hence covenants at law can only be with or by the trustees in whom the legal estate is vested and will be joint, and (by the effect of the Law of Property Act 1925 s 81 (as amended): see para 264 ante) also several.

5   The following are instances of covenants treated as several: where grants of different estates were made to A, B, and C respectively, and covenants for title entered into with them and each of them (*Slingsby's Case* (1587) 5 Co Rep 18b, Ex Ch); and similarly, where property was sold to purchasers in specified shares, and the vendor covenanted for title with each of them (*Mills v Ladbroke* (1844) 7 Man & G 218); where collectors of rents for A and B covenanted with A and B to pay a moiety to each of them (*Lilly v Hodges* (1723) 8 Mod Rep 166); where vendors were entitled in specified shares, a covenant with them and each of them to pay the purchase money (*James v Emery* (1818) 8 Taunt 245, Ex Ch); where there were vendors of different lands at separate prices to one purchaser, and the purchaser by the same deed covenanted with each to complete the purchase (*Poole v Hill* (1840) 6 M & W 835); where purchase money, or interest on purchase money, was to be paid to one vendor only (*Tippet v Hawkey* (1689) 3 Mod Rep 263; *Keightley v Watson* (1849) 3 Exch 716); where separate annuities had been granted, and a surety covenanted with the annuitants that, on default by the grantor, he would pay to them the annuities (*Withers v Bircham* (1824) 3 B & C 254); covenant by a ship's captain with part owners to pay moneys to them, 'and to their and every of their several and respective heirs, etc', in specified shares (*Servante v James* (1829) 10 B & C 410). A covenant entered into with partners jointly for the protection of the partnership business may have been enforceable by them severally after dissolution of the partnership: see *Palmer v Mallet* (1887) 36 ChD 411, CA.

(vi) Dependent and Independent Covenants

266.   Three types of covenant.   Where an agreement contains covenants on the part of each party towards the other the question arises whether one party can sue on the covenants in his own favour without alleging and proving either that he has performed, or that he has offered to perform, those on his part. In this respect covenants are classified as follows:

(1)   such as are mutual and independent, and here either party may recover damages from the other for a breach of the covenants in his favour, and it is no defence that he has not performed, or even that he has committed a breach of, those on his part;

(2)   such as are conditional and dependent, in which the performance of one depends on the prior performance of the other; consequently, until the one which is the condition has been performed, no action will lie on the other which is dependent[1];

(3)   such as are mutually conditional (that is covenants which are to be performed at the same time) and here, if one party was ready and offered to perform his own part, and the other has neglected or refused to perform his, the former may maintain an action against the latter, though it is not certain that either was obliged to perform the first act[2].

While these three cases are distinguishable, the second and third are frequently placed together, and the question is treated as being whether the covenants are independent, or whether they or one of them are or is dependent.

1   See *Ughtred's Case* (1591) 7 Co Rep 9b at 10b. The covenant, however, which is a condition as regards the other is itself independent: see para 269 post.
2   See the classification by Lord Mansfield in *Kingston v Preston* (1773), cited in 2 Doug KB at 689; *Jones v Barkley* (1781) 2 Dough KB 684.

267.   Whether covenants dependent or independent.   Whether covenants are to be taken as dependent or independent is to be decided in accordance with the intention of the parties as appearing in the instrument. For this purpose no technical words are necessary[1]; and, indeed, to such intention, when once discovered, all technical forms of expression must give way[2]; the intention is to be collected from the instrument, and from the circumstances, legally admissible in evidence, with reference to which it is to be construed[3]. When the parties have expressly provided that one covenant is to be treated as a condition, effect will be given to this provision[4], unless it has to be rejected as being clearly repugnant to the intention appearing on the whole instrument[5]; or, perhaps, unless a stipulation, though expressed to be conditional, is not in its nature a condition precedent to performance on the other side[6].

1   *Hotham v East India Co* (1787) 1 Term Rep 638 at 645.
2   *Porter v Shephard* (1796) 6 Term Rep 665 at 668 per Lord Kenyon CJ; *Stavers v Curling* (1836) 3 Bing NC 355 at 368 per Tindal CJ; *Roberts v Brett* (1865) 11 HL Cas 337 at 354.
3   *Graves v Legg* (1854) 9 Exch 709 at 716 per Parke B; *Bettini v Gye* (1876) 1 QBD 183 at 187; see *Kingston v Preston* (1773), cited in 2 Doug KB at 689; *Kidner v Stimpson* (1918) 35 TLR 63, CA (where mutual covenants with respect to drainage of land were held to be dependent).
4   *London Guarantee Co v Fearnley* (1880) 5 App Cas 911 at 919, HL.
5   The clearest words of condition must yield to the prominent intention of the parties as gathered from the whole instrument: *London Gas-Light Co v Chelsea Vestry* (1860) 8 CBNS 215 at 239 per Byles J.
6   See *London Guarantee Co v Fearnley* (1880) 5 App Cas 911 at 920, HL, per Lord Selborne LC (dissenting).

268.   Rules of construction. The question whether covenants are dependent or independent does not depend upon the order in which they occur in the deed, but usually either upon the order of time in which the intent of the transaction requires their performance[1], or upon the nature of the contract and the acts to be performed by the contracting parties[2]; and with regard to these two considerations, order of performance in point of time and the nature of the contract, certain rules have been recognised[3]. The rules, however, do not determine absolutely the dependence or independence of covenants in all cases; they merely furnish a guide to the discovery of the intention of the parties[4]; and in general covenants are to be treated as independent rather than as conditions precedent, especially where some benefit has been derived by the covenantor[5].

1   *Kingston v Preston* (1773), cited 2 Doug KB at 689.
2   *Hotham v East India Co* (1787) 1 Term Rep 638 at 645.
3   See paras 269–270 post.
4   *Roberts v Brett* (1865) 11 HL Cas 337 at 354.
5   *Newson v Smythies* (1858) 3 H & N 840 at 843 per Pollock CB.

269.   Rules regarding order of performance. As regards order of performance of covenants in point of time, the following five rules apply[1]:

(1)   If there are mutual covenants between A and B, and A's covenant has to be performed on a specified day, while B's covenant has to be performed on a later day, A's covenant is independent of B's covenant. A must perform it at the fixed date, and the consideration for the performance of it is not the performance of B's covenant, but B's promise to perform it. Consequently A must rely on his remedy against B, and cannot excuse his own non-performance on the ground of B's failure to perform his covenant[2].

(2)   In the same circumstances A's covenant is a condition precedent to the performance of B's, and the latter covenant is dependent[3]. The liability on B's covenant does not arise unless A's covenant is performed. In general, where one covenant is to be performed before the other it is a condition precedent[4]; and conversely, if the time of performance for one covenant is not fixed, but it is stated to be a condition precedent, this prima facie limits the time of its performance to the period antecedent to the date of the other covenant[5], since a later performance cannot be a condition precedent to an earlier[6].

(3)   If while the date of performance of A's covenant is fixed, that of B's covenant is not fixed, but B's covenant may have to be performed after A's covenant, A's covenant is still independent[7].

(4) In the circumstances referred to in head (3) above, B's covenant is also independent. Since neither covenant is necessarily earlier in date, neither is a condition precedent. The two covenants are mutual and independent; and either party relies not on performance by, but on his remedy against, the other[8].

(5) Where the covenants are to be performed at the same time, and each is the consideration for the other, they are mutually dependant; each is a condition precedent to the performance of the other, and neither party can maintain an action without alleging and proving that he has performed, or was ready and willing to perform, his own covenant[9]. Here the consideration moving to each party is the performance by, not the promise of, the other.

1   Heads (1) and (2) in the text correspond to the first two rules in the notes to *Pordage v Cole* (1669) 1 Wms Saund 319 at 320b, c, except that the parts of the first of those rules enclosed in brackets are reserved to be the subject of head (3) in the text: '1. If a day be appointed for payment of money ... or for doing any other act, and the day is to happen, [or may happen] before the thing which is the consideration of the money, or other act, is to be performed, an action may be brought for the money, or for not doing such other act, before performance; for it appears that the party relied upon his remedy, and did not intend to make the performance a condition precedent: [and so it is where no time is fixed for the performance of that which is the consideration of the money or other act] ... But, 2. When a day is appointed for the payment of money etc, and the day is to happen after the thing which is the consideration of the money etc, is to be performed, no action can be maintained for the money etc, before performance'. The rules are taken from the judgment of Holt CJ in *Thorpe v Thorpe* (1701) 1 Salk 171, but when the parts in brackets of the first rule are removed, the second is seen to be merely supplementary to the first, and they are both included in the statement that, when the performances are to take place at successive dates, the earlier covenant is independent as regards the later, but is itself a condition, and the later covenant is dependent upon it. See also notes 7–9 infra.

2   Instances where the performance of one covenant was fixed definitely before that of the other, and was therefore independent of that other, are: *Tolcelser's Case* (1374) stated in 12 Mod Rep 461 (covenant by Pool to serve Tolcelser with three esquires in the French wars, and covenant by Tolcelser to pay him 20 marks before they went to France; Pool could sue for the 20 marks, although the service had not been rendered); *Russen v Coleby* (1736) 7 Mod Rep 236 (covenant by A to pay seamen their wages yearly, and by B in consideration thereof to pay A £42 every month; A was allowed to sue for the £42 without alleging payment of the wages); *Walker v Harris* (1793) 1 Anst 245 (covenant by A to take B as partner from and after 29 September; by B to pay £300 on or before that day); *Terry v Duntze* (1795) 2 Hy Bl 389 (A covenants to build a house by a certain day, and B to pay by instalments as the building proceeds); *Dicker v Jackson* (1848) 6 CB 103; *Yates v Gardiner* (1851) 20 LJ Ex 327; *Weston v Collins* (1865) 34 LJ Ch 353 (all cases where date for payment of purchase-money was fixed, but not for completion otherwise); *Workman, Clark & Co v Lloyd Brazileno* [1908] 1 KB 968, CA (agreement to build steamer, price to be paid in instalments as work proceeded). See also *Judson v Bowden* (1847) 1 Exch 162, where one covenant was to be performed partly before and partly after the other, and was therefore not a condition precedent.

    Instances where performance of the earlier covenant was a condition precedent to suing on the later are: where work is to be done, and then payment is to be made (see cases cited in *Morton v Lamb* (1797) 7 Term Rep 125 at 130); *Earl Feversham v Watson* (1680) Cas temp Finch 445 (covenant in marriage settlement by husband to be performed before covenant by wife's father); cf *Roberts v Brett* (1865) 11 HL Cas 337 (where the performance of an agreement was to be secured by each party's bond, and the giving of the bond was a condition precedent to suing on the contract). See also CONTRACT vol 9(1) (Reissue) para 966 et seq.

3   See note 1 supra.

4   *Neale v Ratcliff* (1850) 15 QB 916; *Henman v Berliner* [1918] 2 KB 236 (lessee's covenant to repair a house, 'the same being first put in repair' by the lessor; the latter is a condition precedent); and see *Peeters v Opie* (1671) 2 Wms Saund 346 at 350 (payment to be made for work done).

5   *London Guarantee Co v Fearnley* (1880) 5 App Cas 911 at 920, HL, per Lord Watson.

6   *London Guarantee Co v Fearnley* (1880) 5 App Cas 911 at 916, HL, per Lord Blackburn.

7   This represents the effect of the first rule in the notes to *Pordage v Cole* (1669) 1 Wms Saund 319, so far as not stated in head (1) in the text. The separate statement of this part of the rule makes the relation of the first two rules in *Pordage v Cole* supra clearer, and leads up to head (4) in the text.

    Instances where the date of one covenant only was fixed, and the other, since it might be performed later, was not a condition precedent, so that the former was independent, are: *Pordage v Cole* supra (agreement between A and B that B pays A a sum of money); *Campbell v Jones* (1796) 6 Term Rep 570 (covenant by A to teach B with all possible expedition a specified art, and by B to pay £250 on a fixed date); *Mattock v Kinglake* (1839) 10 Ad & El 50 (covenant by A on a purchase to pay the purchase money on a fixed day, no day being fixed for conveyance; and see to the same effect *Wilks v Smith* (1842) 10 M & W 355 at 360 and *Sibthorp v Brunel* (1849) 3 Exch 826); *Thames Haven Dock Co v Brymer* (1850) 5 Exch 696, Ex Ch (covenant to deduce title held to be a condition precedent to preparation of conveyance); *Christie v Borelly* (1860) 7 CBNS 561 (guarantee of payment of bills at maturity in consideration of guarantee of payment not fixed as to date; and see *Seeger v Duthie* (1860) 8 CBNS 45).

8   This is not stated in the rules in the notes to *Pordage v Cole* (1669) 1 Wms Saund 319, but is necessary in order to show completely the relation of the two covenants: see *Campbell v Jones* (1796) 6 Term Rep 570; *Jeston v Key* (1871) 6 Ch App 610.

9   This is the fifth rule in the notes to *Pordage v Cole* (1669) 1 Wms Saund 319 at 320e: '5. Where two acts are to be done at the same time, as where A covenants to convey an estate to B on such a day, and in consideration thereof B covenants to pay A a sum of money on the same day, neither can maintain an action without showing a performance of, or an offer to perform, his part though it is not certain which of them is obliged to do the first act; and this particularly applies to all cases of sale'. See *Glazebrook v Woodrow* (1799) 8 Term Rep 366 at 374.

The following cases illustrate the rule: *Kingston v Preston* (1773), cited in 2 Doug KB 689 (covenant by A to give up his business to B, and by B to procure security for the price 'at or before delivery of the deeds'); *Large v Cheshire* (1671) 1 Vent 147 (C covenants to pay L a sum of money, L 'making him' a sufficient estate in certain lands); *Callonel v Briggs* (1703) 1 Salk 112 (A agreed to pay B so much money for stock six months after the bargain, B transferring the stock); and see *Stapleton v Lord Shelburne* (1725) 1 Bro Parl Cas 215, HL; *Goodisson v Nunn* (1792) 4 Term Rep 761; *Morton v Lamb* (1797) 7 Term Rep 125 (agreement by A in consideration that B had bought corn at a certain price, to deliver it within one month); *Glazebrook v Woodrow* (1799) 8 Term Rep 366 (covenant by A to sell a schoolhouse to B, and convey on or before 1 August, and by B to pay £120 on or before 1 August; conveyance and payment were mutual conditions, notwithstanding that possession had been given by A, the conveyance being the material part); *Marsden v Moore and Day* (1859) 4 H & N 500 (covenant for payment of £250 for purchase of share in mining sett). See also *Heard v Wadham* (1801) 1 East 619, where payment and conveyance were to be simultaneous; and as to sale where goods passed on both sides see *Atkinson v Smith* (1845) 14 M & W 695.

It is in general sufficient that the party suing alleges readiness to perform his own covenant (*Turner v Goodwin* (1714) 10 Mod Rep 153, 189, 222); and a vendor of land need not, in an action against the purchaser, aver tender of a conveyance; it is sufficient to allege that he has always been ready and willing to execute a conveyance, it being the purchaser's duty to prepare and tender the conveyance (*Poole v Hill* (1840) 6 M & W 835; *Laird v Pim* (1841) 7 M & W 474). As to other contracts see *Giles v Giles* (1846) 9 QB 164; *Doogood v Rose* (1850) 9 CB 132.

270. Rules regarding nature of contract. As regards the nature of the contract, the following rules apply:

(1)   If the covenants on either side form the entire consideration for each other, they are mutually dependent; each is a condition precedent, and neither party can sue without alleging that he has performed his covenant, or that he is ready and willing to perform it[1].

(2)   If, however, the covenant by A is part only of the consideration for the other covenant by B, and the remainder of that consideration has been performed by A (such remainder being a substantial part of the entire consideration[2]), then A's covenant, although originally a condition precedent, ceases to be so, and B's covenant is treated as an independent covenant. Consequently, A can then sue for a breach of B's covenant without alleging performance of his own covenant[3]. The application of this rule in favour of A, who has performed the substantial part of his consideration, will be facilitated if one of his covenants is to be performed after B's covenant[4]. If, however, the partial performance on one side is exactly compensated by partial performance on the other, the rule does not apply[5].

(3)   Where the opposite covenants are not given by way of mutual consideration, or where they have no relation to each other, they are independent. The damages sustained by breach of one may be no measure of the damages sustained by breach of the other[6], and the parties are left to their remedies by action. Thus covenants on either side to give security for performing an agreement are

independent as regards each other, although as regards the actual obligations of
the agreement on either side they may be conditions precedent[7].

1　This is the fourth rule in the notes to *Pordage v Cole* (1669) 1 Wms Saund 319 at 320e: '4. Where the
mutual covenants go to the whole consideration on both sides, they are mutual conditions and
performance must be averred'. See *Oxford v Provand* (1868) LR 2 PC 135 at 156. Accordingly, where a
vendor had so changed the property by cutting down timber that he could not properly perform his
covenant, he could not sue for the purchase money (*Duke of St Albans v Shore* (1789) 1 Hy Bl 270); and
where a master had disabled himself from fulfilling his duty to teach his apprentice, he could not sue for
desertion (*Ellen v Topp* (1851) 6 Exch 424). Where mutual considerations are indivisible, each side must
perform the whole of his obligations to enable him to sue: *Chanter v Leese* (1838) 4 M & W 295 (affd
(1839) 5 M & W 698, Ex Ch); *Neale v Ratcliff* (1850) 15 QB 916. Where a company agrees to employ a
person as managing director for a fixed period, and he enters into a covenant not to carry on the same
business, the agreements are interdependent, and if the employment is determined in consequence of the
winding up of the company, the restriction on carrying on business cannot be enforced: *Measures Bros Ltd
v Measures* [1910] 2 Ch 248, CA. See also CONTRACT vol 9(1) (Reissue) para 966 et seq.

　　Where a stipulation is introduced as a condition, and not as a covenant, it will be a condition
precedent if it is of great importance to, or goes to the root of, the contract: see *Grafton v Eastern Counties
Rly Co* (1853) 8 Exch 699; *Graves v Legg* (1854) 9 Exch 709; *Bradford v Williams* (1872) LR 7 Exch 259;
Poussard v Spiers and Pond (1876) 1 QBD 410 (opera singer disabled at commencement of engagement);
Bank of China, Japan and The Straits Ltd v American Trading Co [1894] AC 266, PC. However, see *Bettini v
Gye* (1876) 1 QBD 183. As to arbitration being a condition precedent see INSURANCE vol 25 (2003
Reissue) para 188; as to conditions in charterparties see SHIPPING AND NAVIGATION vol 43(1) (Reissue)
para 1460 et seq; and as to covenants in leases see generally LANDLORD AND TENANT.

2　*Ellen v Topp* (1851) 6 Exch 424.

3　See the third rule in the notes to *Pordage v Cole* (1669) 1 Wms Saund 319 at 320c: '3. Where a covenant
goes only to part of the consideration on both sides, and a breach of such covenant may be paid for in
damages, it is an independent covenant, and an action may be maintained for a breach of the covenant on
the part of the defendant, without averring performance in the declaration'. It is only when the rest of
the consideration has been paid that A's covenant ceases to be a condition precedent. It is then no longer
competent for B to insist on the non-performance of that which was originally a condition precedent,
and his covenant becomes independent. This is more correct than to say that A's covenant was never a
condition precedent at all: *Graves v Legg* (1854) 9 Exch 709 at 717; *White v Beeton* (1861) 7 H & N 42 at
50. The reason is that since B has had part of the consideration for which he entered into the agreement,
it would be unjust that, because he has not had the whole, he should therefore be permitted to enjoy that
part without either paying or doing anything for it: *Campbell v Jones* (1796) 6 Term Rep 570. 'Therefore
the law obliges him to perform the agreement on his part, and leaves him to his remedy to recover any
damage he may have sustained in not having received the whole consideration': notes to *Pordage v Cole*
(1669) 1 Wms Saund 319 at 320e; and see *Carter v Scargill* (1875) LR 10 QB 564.

　　The rule was established by *Boone v Eyre* (1779) 1 Hy Bl 273n (a), where A conveyed to B the equity
of redemption of an estate in the West Indies, with the workers upon it, in consideration of £500 and a
life annuity of £160; A covenanted for title, and B covenanted that, A well and truly performing all and
everything therein contained on his part, he would pay the annuity. A having executed part of the
consideration on his side by conveying the land, his want of title to the workers was not a bar to his
action for the annuity. See *Ritchie v Atkinson* (1808) 10 East 295 at 306 per Lord Ellenborough CJ;
Havelock v Geddes (1809) 10 East 555 at 564; *Fothergill v Walton* (1818) 8 Taunt 576 at 582 per Dallas CJ;
Stavers v Curling (1836) 3 Bing NC 355 at 368; *Seeger v Duthie* (1860) 8 CBNS 45 at 71. Examples of the
rule are furnished by *Campbell v Jones* (1796) 6 Term Rep 570; *Carpenter v Cresswell* (1827) 4 Bing 409.
Where mutual covenants are entered into in a marriage settlement and the marriage takes place they are
independent: *Lloyd v Lloyd* (1837) 2 My & Cr 192. Where one party is to supply goods, and the other to
pay an agreed price, the supply of all the goods is not a condition precedent: *Macintosh v Midland Counties
Rly Co* (1845) 14 M & W 548; *Eastern Counties Rly Co v Philipson* (1855) 16 CB 2; *London Gas-Light Co
v Chelsea Vestry* (1860) 8 CBNS 215. See also *Wilkinson v Clements* (1872) 8 Ch App 96; *Huntoon Co v
Kolynos (Inc)* [1930] 1 Ch 528.

　　To the same principle may be referred the rule that in apprenticeship deeds the covenants are
independent, and misconduct on the part of the apprentice does not bar his action against the master for
breach of covenant (*Winstone v Linn* (1823) 1 B & C 460; *Phillips v Clift* (1859) 4 H & N 168); but
desertion by the apprentice (*Hughes v Humphreys* (1827) 6 B & C 680; and see *Branch v Ewington* (1780)
2 Doug KB 518), or serious misconduct (*Westwick v Theodor* (1875) LR 10 QB 224; *Learoyd v Brook*
[1891] 1 QB 431), or refusal to be taught (*Raymond v Minton* (1866) LR 1 Exch 244), excuses the master;
and he need not return any part of the premium, even though the apprentice was willing to return and
the master refused to take him back (*Cuff v Brown* (1818) 5 Price 297).

4   *Newson v Smythies* (1858) 3 H & N 840 at 843 per Bramwell B. The case is also within the first rule
     regarding order of performance (see para 269 ante), and none of A's covenants is a condition precedent.
5   *General Billposting Co Ltd v Atkinson* [1909] AC 118, HL (engagement of employee at a salary, with a
     covenant in restraint of trading after the termination of the engagement; the salary and the service are
     equivalent to each other; this leaves the employment and the restriction mutually conditional, and a
     wrongful dismissal releases from the restriction). See also *Measures Bros Ltd v Measures* [1910]
     2 Ch 248, CA.
6   *Thomas v Cadwallader* (1744) Willes 496 at 499; and see *Warren v Arthur* (1682) 2 Mod Rep 317 (covenant
     by lessee that lessor may fell trees, and by lessor to repair the hedges where they grow); *Cannock v Jones*
     (1849) 3 Exch 233 (covenants by lessor and lessee to repair separate parts of the premises); *Gibson v
     Goldsmid* (1854) 5 De GM & G 757 (covenants as to transfer of property and indemnity in a deed of
     dissolution of partnership); *Chitty v Bray* (1883) 48 LT 860 (restrictive covenants affecting adjoining plots
     of land, but differing as to object and importance, treated as independent); *Fearon v Earl of Aylesford* (1884)
     14 QBD 792, CA (covenants between the husband and the trustee for the wife in a separation deed).
7   *Roberts v Brett* (1865) 11 HL Cas 337.

(vii)   Covenants with a Penalty

271.   Liquidated damages and penalties.   A contract may specify a sum as being
payable upon breach, and, if it contains several stipulations, the sum may be expressed to
be payable on breach either of one or more specified stipulations, or of any of the
stipulations; it is usual to describe such a sum as either a penalty or liquidated damages[1].
Although regard must be had to the description in the contract[2], it is not conclusive; and
if upon the whole instrument it appears that the sum is a penal sum, it will be so treated
and vice versa[3].

1   See *Lowe v Peers* (1768) 4 Burr 2225 at 2228. As to contracts by local authorities specifying a penalty see
     Soothill Upper Urban Council v Wakefield RDC [1905] 2 Ch 516, CA.
2   *Willson v Love* [1896] 1 QB 626 at 630, CA, per Lord Esher MR ('no case, I think, decides that the term
     used by the parties themselves is to be altogether disregarded … where the parties themselves call the sum
     made payable a 'penalty', the onus lies on those who seek to show that it is to be payable as liquidated
     damages'). However, much reliance is not to be placed on the description: *Law v Redditch Local Board*
     [1892] 1 QB 127 at 131, CA; *Clydebank Engineering and Shipbuilding Co Ltd v Don Jose Ramos Yzquierdo y
     Castaneda* [1905] AC 6 at 9, HL. See DAMAGES vol 12(1) (Reissue) para 1065 et seq.
3   *Betts v Burch* (1859) 4 H & N 506 at 511 per Bramwell B (see this case as to the origin of the above rule
     of construction); *Sainter v Ferguson* (1849) 7 CB 716 at 727. See *Robert Stewart & Sons Ltd v Carapanayoti
     & Co Ltd* [1962] 1 All ER 418, [1962] 1 WLR 34; *Robophone Facilities Ltd v Blank* [1966] 3 All ER 128,
     [1966] 1 WLR 1428, CA. See also *Bridge v Campbell Discount Co Ltd* [1962] AC 600, [1962] 1 All ER
     385, HL; and CONSUMER CREDIT vol 9(1) (Reissue) para 23 et seq.

272.   Whether covenantor can elect to break covenant.   When there is a
covenant to do or not to do a specified thing and a sum, whether a penalty or liquidated
damages, is fixed to be paid on breach of the covenant, in general the covenantor has not
the option of breaking the covenant upon payment of the fixed sum[1]. He is bound by
the covenant, and, if positive, it will be enforced in an action for specific performance
(where this is the appropriate remedy)[2], and, if negative, it will be enforced by
injunction[3]. The covenantee cannot, however, get both damages and an injunction; he
must elect which of the two remedies he will take[4]. The question, however, is one of
construction[5], and if the intention of the covenant is that the covenantor is to be at
liberty to do the prohibited act on payment of the penalty or stipulated sum, effect will
be given to it accordingly[6]; and this will usually be the case where the penalty is in the
nature of a recurring remuneration to the covenantee, as in the case of an increased rent
reserved for breach of a covenant not to plough up pasture land[7].

1   See *French v Macale* (1842) 2 Dr & War 269 at 274–275 per Sugden LC ('the general rule of equity is, that
     if a thing be agreed to be done, though there is a penalty annexed to secure its performance, yet the very
     thing itself must be done … So if a man covenant to abstain from doing a certain act, and agree that, if
     he do it, he will pay a sum of money, it would seem that he will be compelled to abstain from doing that

    act, and just as in the converse case, he cannot elect to break his engagement by paying for his violation of the contract'); *Chilliner v Chilliner* (1754) 2 Ves Sen 528; and see also *Prebble v Boghurst* (1818) 1 Swan 309 at 412 n (3); Fry on Specific Performance (6th Edn) 65–74.

2   Eg in cases of bonds to secure an agreement for settlement of property on marriage (*Nandike v Wilkes* (1716) Gilb Ch 114; *Chilliner v Chilliner* (1754) 2 Ves Sen 528; *Prebble v Boghurst* (1818) 1 Swan 309; *Roper v Bartholmew* (1823) 12 Price 797); bond in consideration of marriage to leave property by will (*Logan v Wienholt* (1833) 1 Cl & Fin 611, HL); bond to secure an agreement to grant a lease (*Butler v Powis* (1845) 2 Coll 156); penalty in a contract for purchase of land (*Howard v Hopkyns* (1742) 2 Atk 371). As to specific performance generally see SPECIFIC PERFORMANCE.

3   Eg where a covenant in restraint of trade is secured by a penalty or liquidated damages: *Hardy v Martin* (1783) 1 Cox Eq Cas 26; *Fox v Scard* (1863) 33 Beav 327; *National Provincial Bank of England v Marshall* (1888) 40 ChD 112, CA; and see *Barret v Blagrave* (1800) 5 Ves 555; *Bird v Lake* (1863) 1 Hem & M 111; *Howard v Woodward* (1864) 34 LJ Ch 47; *Jones v Heavens* (1877) 4 ChD 636. Similarly, as to restrictive covenants affecting land, see *Coles v Sims* (1854) 5 De GM & G 1.

4   *Sainter v Ferguson* (1849) 1 Mac & G 286; *Carnes v Nesbitt* (1862) 7 H & N 778; *Fox v Scard* (1863) 33 Beav 327; *Howard v Woodward* (1864) 34 LJ Ch 47; *Young v Chalkley* (1867) 16 LT 286; *General Accident Assurance Corpn v Noel* [1902] 1 KB 377. As to damages generally see DAMAGES.

5   See *Roper v Bartholomew* (1823) 12 Price 797 at 821.

6   *French v Macale* (1842) 2 Dr & War 269 at 284.

7   *Woodward v Gyles* (1690) 2 Vern 119; *Legh v Lillie* (1860) 6 H & N 165. See also *Rolfe v Peterson* (1772) 2 Bro Parl Cas 436; and cf *French v Macale* (1842) 2 Dr & War 269 (where only a single sum per acre was reserved for breach of a covenant not to burn). It is now provided that under such a provision the landlord cannot recover more than a sum representing the damage he has actually suffered by reason of the breach: see the Agricultural Holdings Act 1986 s 24; and AGRICULTURE vol 1(2) (Reissue) paras 317, 338. On the other hand, where an increased rent was reserved upon breach of covenant against offensive trades, with a clause of re-entry on breach of covenant, this did not give the lessee the right to commit a breach, and the lessor had the option of re-entering or requiring payment of the increased rent (*Weston v Metropolitan Asylum District Managers* (1882) 9 QBD 404, CA); cf *Hanbury v Cundy* (1887) 58 LT 155 (lease of tied house with proviso for reduction of rent so long as the tie was observed; the lessee had not the option of breaking the tie and paying the full rent). Cf *Magrane v Archbold* (1813) 1 Dow 107, HL (covenant for perpetual renewal of a lease, subject to a penalty). As to the reservation of penal rents see AGRICULTURE vol 1(2) (Reissue) para 317; LANDLORD AND TENANT vol 27(1) (2006 Reissue) para 251.

(viii)   Covenants operating by way of Assignment or Release

273.   Assignment of after-acquired property. A contract for valuable consideration, by which it is agreed to make a present transfer of property, if it is one of which a court will decree specific performance, passes the beneficial interest at once; or if the property does not then belong to the covenantor, the beneficial interest passes as soon as he acquires the property[1]. Similarly, a covenant to charge property when acquired operates as a charge on the property so soon as acquired[2]. An assignment for valuable consideration of property to be afterwards acquired by the assignor operates as a covenant by the assignor to assign it when acquired, and on acquisition the beneficial interest passes accordingly[3]. Provided that the property is ascertainable with certainty, it is no objection that it is described in general terms[4]. A clause in a building agreement that building materials brought on to the land are to become the property of the landowner does not, however, operate merely as an assignment. On the materials being brought on to the land the legal interest in them passes by virtue of the contract[5].

1   *Holroyd v Marshall* (1862) 10 HL Cas 191; and see *Re Lind, Industrials Finance Syndicate Ltd v Lind* [1915] 2 Ch 345, CA; *Re Dent, ex p Trustee* [1923] 1 Ch 113; and cf Shep Touch 162. As to specific performance generally see SPECIFIC PERFORMANCE.

2   *Metcalfe v Archbishop of York* (1836) 1 My & Cr 547. It does not, however, so operate in favour of a volunteer, since the contract will not be specifically enforced: *Re Earl Lucan, Hardinge v Cobden* (1890) 45 ChD 470. A covenant which amounts only to a licence to seize or creates a mere right in contract must be distinguished from a covenant which creates an equitable charge: see *Collyer v Isaacs* (1881) 19 ChD 342, CA; and BANKRUPTCY AND INDIVIDUAL INSOLVENCY vol 3(2) (2002 Reissue) para 445.

3   *Re Lind, Industrials Finance Syndicate Ltd v Lind* [1915] 2 Ch 345, CA; *Re Gillott's Settlement, Chattock v Reid* [1934] Ch 97; *Re Warren, ex p Wheeler v Trustee in Bankruptcy* [1938] Ch 725, [1938] 2 All ER 331, DC; *Re Haynes Will Trusts, Pitt v Haynes* [1949] Ch 5, [1948] 2 All ER 423.

4   *Tailby v Official Receiver* (1888) 13 App Cas 523, HL (assignment of all book debts acquired during the continuance of the security), approving *Re Clarke, Coombe v Carter* (1887) 36 ChD 348, CA, and overruling *Belding v Read* (1865) 3 H & C 955 (personal effects to be thereafter upon a house) and *Re Count D'Epineuil (No 2) Tadman v D'Epineuil* (1882) 20 ChD 758 (charge on all 'present and future personalty'). See also *Re Kelcey, Tyson v Kelcey* [1899] 2 Ch 530; *Imperial Paper Mills of Canada v Quebec Bank* (1913) 83 LJPC 67. As to covenants in marriage settlements for assignments of after-acquired property see *Lewis v Madocks* (1803) 8 Ves 150; *Hardey v Green* (1849) 12 Beav 182; *Re Reis, ex p Clough* [1904] 2 KB 769 at 777, CA; and SETTLEMENTS vol 42 (Reissue) para 636, 644 et seq. If the general words are too vague for the contract to be enforced, then it is divisible, and can be enforced as to the property sufficiently described: *Clements v Matthews* (1883) 11 QBD 808, CA; *Re Clarke, Coombe v Carter* supra; *Re Turcan* (1888) 40 ChD 5, CA. See also *Syrett v Egerton* [1957] 3 All ER 331, [1957] 1 WLR 1130, DC (income and estate charged, charge on income certain and effective); and see para 233 ante.

5   *Reeves v Barlow* (1884) 12 QBD 436, CA; *Hart v Porthgain Harbour Co Ltd* [1903] 1 Ch 690; cf *Morris v Delobbel-Flipo* [1892] 2 Ch 352 (charge in favour of an agent on stock in his hands); *Re Keen and Keen, ex p Collins* [1902] 1 KB 555; *Re Weibking, ex p Ward* [1902] 1 KB 713. See BILLS OF SALE vol 4(1) (Reissue) para 624; BUILDING CONTRACTS, ARCHITECTS, ENGINEERS, VALUERS AND SURVEYORS vol 4(3) (Reissue) para 86.

274–300.   Covenant not to sue.   A general covenant by a creditor with his debtor not to sue at any time will operate as a release of the debt. This is in order to avoid circuity of action, since the damages in an action on the covenant would be equal to the debt[1]. On the other hand, a covenant not to sue before a stated time does not operate as a release; it only gives the debtor a remedy on the covenant if he is sued before the time[2]. Moreover, a general covenant not to sue does not release the debt for all purposes, and the debt may be kept alive as between persons claiming under the debtor[3]; and where the parties to the covenant are different from the persons interested as debtors or creditors in the debt, then the principle of avoiding circuity of action does not apply, and the covenant does not operate as a release[4].

1   *Ford v Beech* (1848) 11 QB 852 at 511, Ex Ch; *Smith v Mapleback* (1786) 1 Term Rep 441 at 446 per Buller J; and see the notes to *Fowell v Forrest* (1670) 2 Saund 47.

2   *Deux v Jefferies* (1594) Cro Eliz 352; *Thimbleby v Barron* (1838) 3 M & W 210; and see *Morley v Frear* (1830) 6 Bing 547.

3   *Ledger v Stanton* (1861) 2 John & H 687.

4   Thus a covenant with one of two joint debtors (*Hutton v Eyre* (1815) 6 Taunt 289), or joint and several debtors (*Lacy v Kinnaston* (1701) 1 Ld Raym 688 at 690; *Dean v Newhall* (1799) 8 Term Rep 168), not to sue him does not prevent an action being brought for the debt against the other debtor (cf *Salmon v Webb and Franklin* (1852) 3 HL Cas 510). With an actual release it is different, and a release to one of two joint, or joint and several, debtors releases both (Co Litt 232a; *Cheetham v Ward* (1797) 1 Bos & P 630; *Nicholson v Revill* (1836) 4 Ad & El 675 at 683); but not a release to one of two several debtors (*Collins v Prosser* (1823) 1 B & C 682). Where the release is accompanied by a reservation of rights against the co-debtor, its effect as a release is avoided by treating it as a covenant not to sue (*Solly v Forbes* (1820) 2 Brod & Bing 38; and see *Bateson v Gosling* (1871) LR 7 CP 9; *Keyes v Elkins* (1864) 5 B & S 240). See CONTRACT vol 9(1) (Reissue) paras 1052–1053. A covenant by one of several joint creditors not to sue the debtor does not discharge the debt due to the creditors jointly: *Walmesley v Cooper* (1839) 11 Ad & El 216.

DISCRIMINATION

1. INTRODUCTION

(1) SCOPE OF THE TITLE AND LEGISLATIVE FRAMEWORK

301.   The scope of the title.   The law of discrimination can broadly be divided into six main categories: (1) sex, which is governed by the Sex Discrimination Act 1975[1]; (2) race, which is governed by the Race Relations Act 1976[2]; (3) disability, which is governed by the Disability Discrimination Act 1995[3]; (4) religion or belief, which is governed by the Equality Act 2006 and the Employment Equality (Religion or Belief) Regulations 2003[4]; (5) sexual orientation, which is governed by the Employment Equality (Sexual Orientation) Regulations 2003[5] and the Equality Act (Sexual Orientation) Regulations 2007[6]; and (6) age, which is governed by the Employment Equality (Age) Regulations 2006[7]. Each of these categories is dealt with separately in this title, although there are many common concepts[8]. Legislation regarding human rights is relevant to all aspects of discrimination[9].

There are a number of issues related to discrimination that are dealt with elsewhere in this work, particularly offences of incitement to racial hatred and racially aggravated offences and offences of incitement to religious hatred and religiously aggravated offences[10]. Sexual offences[11] and maternity and paternity rights[12] are also dealt with elsewhere in this work.

A new Commission for Equality and Human Rights has been established[13]. In due course, it is to take on the work of the existing Commissions (namely, the Equal Opportunities Commission ('EOC')[14], the Commission for Racial Equality ('CRE')[15], and the Disability Rights Commission ('DRC'))[16], which are to be dissolved[17]. The Commission for Equality and Human Rights is also to assume responsibility for promoting equality and combating unlawful discrimination based on religion or belief, sexual orientation and age; and it is to have responsibility for the promotion of human rights[18].

1   See para 337 et seq post. As to the issue of equal pay see para 419 et seq post.
2   See para 436 et seq post.
3   See para 507 et seq post.
4   Ie the Employment Equality (Religion or Belief) Regulations 2003, SI 2003/1660 (as amended): see para 660 et seq post. In relation to matters outside the employment area, the Equality Act 2006 Pt 2 (ss 44–80) sets out provisions prohibiting discrimination on grounds of religion or belief in the provision of goods, facilities and services, in education, in the use and disposal of premises and in the exercise of public functions: see para 691 et seq post.
5   Ie the Employment Equality (Sexual Orientation) Regulations 2003, SI 2003/1661 (as amended): see para 722 et seq post.
6   Ie the Equality Act (Sexual Orientation) Regulations 2007, SI 2007/1263: see para 753 post.
7   Ie the Employment Equality (Age) Regulations 2006, SI 2006/1031: see para 754 et seq post.
8   As a result of the sharing of common concepts by the different categories of discrimination, case law relating to the interpretation of the statutory provisions governing one form of discrimination may be relevant to the others. Thus, for example, cases decided under legislation relating to race relations may be relevant in interpreting sex discrimination legislation (but see para 438 note 23 post); but note that the provisions of the Disability Discrimination Act 1995 are less similar than those of the Race Relations Act 1976 and the Sex Discrimination Act 1975. Particularly in the last three categories (see heads (4), (5) and (6) in the text), where there was little specific case law at the date at which this volume states the law, cases under the earlier categories (see heads (1), (2) and (3) in the text) may be relevant. This interconnection between the categories is especially important in the following areas: direct and indirect discrimination (with the exception of disability discrimination; and note that direct age discrimination can be justified); harassment; victimisation; liability of employers; enforcement (especially relating to the burden of proof and compensation); and time limits.
9   See paras 303–304 post.
10   As to these offences see CRIMINAL LAW, EVIDENCE AND PROCEDURE vol 11(1) (2006 Reissue) para 562 et seq. See also paras 505–506, 720–721 post.

11 See CRIMINAL LAW, EVIDENCE AND PROCEDURE vol 11(1) (2006 Reissue) para 162 et seq.
12 See EMPLOYMENT vol 16(1A) (Reissue) para 322 et seq.
13 See the Equality Act 1996 Pt 1 (ss 1–43) (as amended); and para 305 et seq post.
14 See para 404 et seq post.
15 See para 488 et seq post.
16 See para 646 et seq post.
17 As to the dissolution of the Equal Opportunities Commission, the Commission for Racial Equality and the Disability Rights Commission see para 306 post.
18 See the Equality Act 2006 s 9; and para 317 post.

302. The Secretary of State and the National Assembly for Wales. Modern statutes generally refer simply to the Secretary of State. In any enactment, 'Secretary of State' means one of Her Majesty's principal Secretaries of State[1]. For the most part the functions of the Secretary of State in regard to discrimination legislation have been carried out in England by the Secretary of State for Trade and Industry[2]. However, all rights and liabilities to which the Secretary of State for Trade and Industry is entitled or subject in connection with the equality functions[3] have now been transferred to the Secretary of State for Communities and Local Government[4].

Many statutory functions vested in Ministers of the Crown are now exercisable in relation to Wales by, or in conjunction with, the National Assembly for Wales[5]. These include certain functions under the Sex Discrimination Act 1975[6], the Race Relations Act 1976[7] and the Disability Rights Commission Act 1999[8].

1   See the Interpretation Act 1978 s 5, Sch 1. As to the office of Secretary of State see CONSTITUTIONAL LAW AND HUMAN RIGHTS vol 8(2) (Reissue) paras 463–465.
2   As to the Secretary of State for Trade and Industry see CONSTITUTIONAL LAW AND HUMAN RIGHTS vol 8(2) (Reissue) para 506; TRADE, INDUSTRY AND INDUSTRIAL RELATIONS vol 47 (2001 Reissue) para 2. As to the Department of Trade and Industry see CONSTITUTIONAL LAW AND HUMAN RIGHTS vol 8(2) (Reissue) paras 505–508.
3   'Equality functions' means the functions under the enactments listed below that were immediately before 5 May 2006 entrusted to the Secretary of State for Trade and Industry and that have been entrusted to the Secretary of State for Communities and Local Government before the making of the Secretary of State for Communities and Local Government Order 2006, SI 2006/1926: art 7(2). The enactments are: (1) the Equal Pay Act 1970 (see para 424 et seq post); (2) the Sex Discrimination Act 1975 (see para 342 et seq post); (3) the Equality Act 2006 Pt 1 (ss 1–43) (as amended) (see para 305 et seq post): Secretary of State for Communities and Local Government Order 2006, SI 2006/1926, art 7(3). As to the Secretary of State for Communities and Local Government see CONSTITUTIONAL LAW AND HUMAN RIGHTS.
4   See ibid art 7(1). Article 7 has effect from 21 August 2006: see art 1(2).
5   See the National Assembly for Wales (Transfer of Functions) Order 1999, SI 1999/672, art 2, Sch 1 (as amended); and the National Assembly for Wales (Transfer of Functions) Order 2000/253, art 2, Sch 1. These instruments were made in pursuance of, inter alia, the Government of Wales Act 1998 s 22 (prospectively repealed by the Government of Wales Act 2006 s 163, Sch 12). As to the National Assembly for Wales see CONSTITUTIONAL LAW AND HUMAN RIGHTS.
    The Government of Wales Act 2006, the majority of whose provisions are to come into force immediately after the ordinary election under the Government of Wales Act 1998 s 3 (prospectively repealed) held in 2007 (see the Government of Wales Act 2006 s 161(1)), provides for the formal separation of the legislative and executive branches of the devolved government in Wales. Part 1 (ss 1–44) makes provision about the legislature (which will continue to be called the National Assembly for Wales) and Pt 2 (ss 45–92) makes provision about the executive, to be known as the Welsh Assembly Government, which will consist of the First Minister or Prif Weinidog (see ss 46, 47), the Welsh Ministers or Gweinidogion Cymru (see s 48), the Counsel General to the Welsh Assembly Government or Cwnsler Cyffredinol i Lywodraeth Cynulliad Cymru ('the Counsel General') (see s 49), and the Deputy Welsh Ministers or Dirprwy Weinidogion Cymru (see s 50): s 45(1). In the Government of Wales Act 2006 and in any other enactment or instrument, the First Minister and the Welsh Ministers appointed under s 48 are referred to collectively as the Welsh Ministers: s 45(2). Subject to s 162(1), Sch 11 para 31, the relevant Assembly functions are transferred to the Welsh Ministers immediately after the end of the initial period: Sch 11 para 30(1). 'The initial period' means the period beginning with the day of the poll at the 2007 election and ending with the day on which the first appointment is made under s 46: s 161(5). 'The relevant Assembly functions' means functions exercisable by the Assembly constituted by the Government of Wales Act 1998: (1) immediately before the end of the initial period,

by virtue of an Order in Council under s 22 (prospectively repealed); (2) immediately before the end of that period, as a result of a designation made under the European Communities Act 1972 s 2(2) by virtue of the Government of Wales Act 1998 s 29(1) (prospectively repealed); (3) immediately before the end of that period, as a result of having been conferred or imposed on it by an enactment contained in an Act, other than an enactment contained in the Government of Wales Act 1998, or by a prerogative instrument; or (4) immediately before the end of that period, as a result of having been conferred or imposed on it by subordinate legislation (including subordinate legislation made under the Government of Wales Act 1998); and for these purposes a function is 'exercisable' at any time even if the enactment transferring, conferring or imposing it has not come into force at that time: Government of Wales Act 2006 Sch 11 para 30(2). Schedule 11 came into force on 25 July 2006: see s 161(2). Her Majesty may by Order in Council: (a) provide for (i) the transfer of any of the relevant Assembly functions to the First Minister or the Counsel General; (ii) the transfer of any of the relevant Assembly functions, other than functions of making, confirming or approving subordinate legislation, to the Assembly Commission; (iii) any of the relevant Assembly functions, other than functions of making, confirming or approving subordinate legislation, to be functions of the Assembly; (iv) any relevant Assembly function that is a function of making, confirming or approving subordinate legislation in relation to any matter not to be transferred to the Welsh Ministers and, unless the Assembly already has power to pass Assembly Measures in relation to that matter, the amendment of Sch 5 Pt 1 to enable the Assembly to have instead power to pass Assembly Measures in relation to that matter either in the same terms as the relevant Assembly function, or in terms differing from those terms to such extent as appears appropriate (see Sch 11 para 31(1), (2)); (b) direct that any function transferred by Sch 11 para 30 is to be exercisable by any one or more of the First Minister, the Counsel General, the Assembly Commission and the Assembly concurrently with the Welsh Ministers (Sch 11 para 31(3)(a)); (c) direct that any function in relation to which provision is made by Sch 11 para 31(1) (see heads (i)–(iii) supra) for it to be transferred to, or continue to be a function of, any person or body is to be exercisable by any other person or body specified in Sch 11 para 31(1) concurrently with that person or body (Sch 11 para 31(3)(b)); or (d) direct that any function transferred by Sch 11 para 30, or transferred to the First Minister or the Counsel General by virtue of Sch 11 para 31(1), is to be exercisable by the Welsh Ministers, the First Minister or the Counsel General only with the agreement of, or after consultation with, the Assembly Commission (Sch 11 para 31(3)(c)). As to the exercise of these powers see further Sch 11 para 31(4)–(8); and CONSTITUTIONAL LAW AND HUMAN RIGHTS. As to the Assembly Commission see s 27. Any provision of an Order in Council under the Government of Wales Act 1998 s 22 (e g the National Assembly for Wales (Transfer of Functions) Order 1999, SI 1999/672 (as amended)), whether included by virtue of the Government of Wales Act 1998 s 22 or any other enactment apart from s 155(2), which is in force immediately before the commencement of the repeal of s 22 by the Government of Wales Act 2006 continues to have effect after the commencement of that repeal as if it were a provision of an Order in Council under s 58: Sch 11 para 26(1).

6   See the National Assembly for Wales (Transfer of Functions) Order 1999, SI 1999/672, Sch 1. Functions transferred are those under the Sex Discrimination Act 1975 s 25 (as amended) (see paras 378–379 post), s 66(5) (as amended) (see para 415 post), s 78 (see para 381 post) and Sch 2 (as amended; prospectively amended) (see para 381 post). The function of the Secretary of State under s 53(1) (as amended; prospectively repealed) (see para 404 post) of making appointments to the Equal Opportunities Commission is exercisable only with the agreement of the Assembly so far as necessary to ensure that there is at all times one Commissioner who has been appointed with the agreement of the Assembly: see the National Assembly for Wales (Transfer of Functions) Order 1999, SI 1999/672, art 5, Sch 2. See note 5 supra.

7   See ibid Sch 1. Functions transferred are those under the Race Relations Act 1976 s 19(2) (repealed), s 19A(2) (as added and amended) (see para 468 post), s 57(5) (as amended) (see para 460 post) and s 58(6) (repealed). The certification function under s 69 (as amended) (see paras 487, 498 post) is exercisable by the Assembly concurrently with any Minister of the Crown by whom it is exercisable; and the references in s 41 (as amended) (see para 486 post) to a Minister of the Crown are to be construed as including reference to the Assembly: see the National Assembly for Wales (Transfer of Functions) Order 1999, SI 1999/672, Sch 1. The function of the Secretary of State under the Race Relations Act 1976 s 43(1) (as amended; prospectively repealed) (see para 488 post) of making appointments to the Commission for Racial Equality is exercisable only with the agreement of the Assembly so far as necessary to ensure that there is at all times one Commissioner who has been appointed with the agreement of the Assembly: see the National Assembly for Wales (Transfer of Functions) Order 1999, SI 1999/672, Sch 2. See note 5 supra.

8   The function of the Secretary of State under the Disability Rights Commission Act 1999 Sch 1 para 2 (as amended; prospectively repealed) (see para 646 post) of making appointments to the Disability Rights Commission is exercisable only with the agreement of the Assembly so far as necessary to ensure that

there is at all times one Commissioner who has been appointed with the agreement of the Assembly: see the National Assembly for Wales (Transfer of Functions) Order 2000, SI 2000/253, Sch 2. See note 5 supra.

303.   The Human Rights Act 1998.   The Human Rights Act 1998[1] was enacted to give further effect to the rights and freedoms guaranteed under the Convention for the Protection of Human Rights and Fundamental Freedoms[2]. Certain provisions of the Convention, known as 'Convention rights', are to have effect for the purposes of the Human Rights Act 1998[3]. The Act has two fundamental purposes: (1) to ensure that domestic legislation is read and given effect in a way which is compatible with the Convention rights, or, if this is not possible, to enable a superior court to make a declaration of incompatibility[4]; and (2) to provide individuals with a right to pursue and rely upon Convention rights in domestic courts, and to provide a remedy for breach of such rights[5].

The Human Rights Act 1998 enables a person to rely on Convention rights, where appropriate, in ordinary civil litigation between individuals. Accordingly, for example, the Convention right to freedom from discrimination on grounds of race[6] might be prayed in aid of a particular construction of the Race Relations Act 1976.

There has been some limited development of discrimination law with the introduction of the Human Rights Act 1998[7].

1   The Human Rights Act 1998 received Royal Assent on 9 November 1998, and ss 18, 20 came into force on the same date, whilst s 19 came into force on 24 November 1998, and the remaining provisions came into force on 2 October 2000. The provisions of the Human Rights Act 1998 are dealt with elsewhere in this work: see CONSTITUTIONAL LAW AND HUMAN RIGHTS.

2   Ie the Convention for the Protection of Human Rights and Fundamental Freedoms (Rome, 4 November 1950; TS 71 (1953); Cmd 8969).

3   See the Human Rights Act 1998 s 1(2). The Convention rights mentioned are those contained in the Convention for the Protection of Human Rights and Fundamental Freedoms arts 2–12, 14, the First Protocol arts 1–3, and the Thirteenth Protocol art 1 (all as read with the Convention arts 16–18): see the Human Rights Act 1998 s 1(1) (amended by the Human Rights Act 1998 (Amendment) Order 2004, SI 2004/1574, art 2(1)). As to the provisions of the Convention for the Protection of Human Rights and Fundamental Freedoms see para 304 post; and CONSTITUTIONAL LAW AND HUMAN RIGHTS vol 8(2) (Reissue) para 122 et seq.

4   See the Human Rights Act 1998 ss 3, 4 (s 4 prospectively amended by the Constitutional Reform Act 2005 s 40(4), Sch 9 para 66(1), (2); the Mental Capacity Act 2005 s 67(1), Sch 6 para 43; and the Armed Forces Act 2006 s 378(1), Sch 16 para 156).

5   See the Human Rights Act 1998 ss 7, 8 (s 7 amended by the Secretary of State for Constitutional Affairs Order 2003, SI 2003/1887, art 9, Sch 2 para 10(2); and the Transfer of Functions (Lord Chancellor and Secretary of State) Order 2005, SI 2005/3429, art 8, Schedule para 3).

6   See para 304 post.

7   See further para 304 post.

304.   The Convention for the Protection of Human Rights and Fundamental Freedoms.   Article 14 of the Convention for the Protection of Human Rights and Fundamental Freedoms provides that the enjoyment of the rights and freedoms set forth in the Convention must be secured without discrimination on any ground such as sex, race, colour, language, religion, political or other opinion, national or social origin, association with a national minority, property, birth or other status[1]. This provision does not create a free standing right to freedom from discrimination on the grounds set out. Rather, it is a parasitic provision which requires states to ensure that the rights and freedoms protected by the Convention are secured, without such discrimination. Therefore, where a right falls outside the Convention, a state has no obligation to avoid discrimination. In practice, this is likely to represent a significant restriction since rights to employment, pay, working conditions, and other social benefits including housing, are not Convention rights[2]. However, the grounds upon which the prohibition against discrimination is prescribed are extensive, and the grounds identified are by way of example only, and not exhaustive. This may give scope for extending the sphere of anti-discrimination legislation.

In order to invoke Article 14, the complainant must establish that the impugned act of a state or public authority comes within the scope of Article 14 and falls within the ambit of a Convention right and that there has been discrimination in the treatment afforded to him. Even if these elements are established, the question of justification arises before the discrimination can be considered unlawful. If a discrimination claim is admissible as being within the ambit of a Convention right, it is not necessary to establish a breach of the substantive Convention right, or even that particular injury has been suffered in relation to the substantive right. It is necessary, however, to establish differential treatment, and usually that the basis for that differential treatment was a prohibited ground such as race, religion or colour[3]. Some grounds of discrimination are recognised as being very serious, and requiring a higher degree of justification than others, such as race[4], religion[5], nationality[6], illegitimacy[7] and sex[8].

Once differential treatment within the ambit of a Convention right has been established (and the grounds for the difference are accepted or established as infringing Article 14), the state must justify the different treatment to avoid a finding of illegality[9]. Justification is not defined by Article 14[10].

The state has a margin of appreciation in relation to its actions[11]. This margin of appreciation is recognised by the court in determining whether the balance has been fairly struck. Where the nature of the discrimination falls into a recognised serious category, such as race discrimination, the margin of appreciation will be more restricted. Another relevant factor is the possibility of an alternative (non-discriminatory) means for achieving the same objective, which may suggest that the means employed by the state to achieve its aim are disproportionate[12].

The following are possible Convention rights which may give rise to discrimination issues:

(1)   the right to a fair trial[13];
(2)   the right to respect for private and family life[14];
(3)   the right to freedom of thought, conscience and religion[15];
(4)   the right to freedom of expression[16];
(5)   the right to freedom of assembly and association[17];
(6)   the right to property[18]; and
(7)   the right to education[19].

1   See the Convention for the Protection of Human Rights and Fundamental Freedoms (Rome, 4 November 1950; TS 71 (1953); Cmd 8969) art 14; and CONSTITUTIONAL LAW AND HUMAN RIGHTS vol 8(2) (Reissue) para 164. As to the incorporation of articles of the Convention into the Human Rights Act 1998 see para 303 ante.
2   As to Convention rights see para 303 note 3 ante.
3   See CONSTITUTIONAL LAW AND HUMAN RIGHTS vol 8(2) (Reissue) para 164.
4   *East African Asians Cases* (1973) 3 EHRR 76, EComHR; Application 4403/70 *Patel v United Kingdom* (East African Asians Case) 36 Collection HR 92.
5   *Hoffmann v Austria* A 255-C (1993) 17 EHRR 293, ECtHR.
6   *Gaygusuz v Austria* (1997) 23 EHRR 364, ECtHR (court indicated that it would require very weighty reasons to justify differential treatment based exclusively on nationality so as to be compatible with the Convention).
7   *Marckx v Belgium* A 31 (1979) 2 EHRR 330, ECtHR; but cf *McMichael v United Kingdom* A 307-B (1995) 20 EHRR 205, ECtHR.
8   *Abdulaziz, Cabales and Balkandali v United Kingdom* A 94 (1985) 7 EHRR 471, ECtHR (where the question was whether a concession allowing resident alien men to be joined by their wives, even though the women lacked any immigration status, was also required to be provided to resident alien women if sex discrimination was to be avoided; the issue fell within the ambit of protection of family life and there was a question as to whether the differential treatment was discriminatory); *Schuler-Zgraggen v Switzerland*

A 263 (1993) 16 EHRR 405, ECtHR; *Burghartz v Switzerland* A 280-B (1994) 18 EHRR 101, ECtHR; *Schmidt v Germany* A 291-B (1994), 18 EHRR 513, ECtHR; Application 20060/92 *Van Raalte v Netherlands* A 732 (1997) 24 EHRR 503, ECtHR.

9   See CONSTITUTIONAL LAW AND HUMAN RIGHTS vol 8(2) (Reissue) para 164.

10   The European Court of Human Rights has stated that justification must be reasonable and objective, and that the existence of such justification must be assessed in relation to the aims and effects of the measure under consideration, regard being had to the principles which normally prevail in democratic societies: see *Belgian Linguistics Case (No 2)* A 6 (1968) 1 EHRR 252, ECtHR (access to language-based state education; the court found that there was no obligation on the state to provide any system of education, but if it did so, access to the system could not be restricted on a discriminatory basis). Thus the means used (which have a discriminatory effect) must be necessary to achieve the aims identified, and strike a fair balance between the protection of the interests of the community and respect for the rights and freedoms safeguarded by the Convention for the Protection of Human Rights and Fundamental Freedoms. Examples of justification advanced by states for discriminatory treatment are the support and encouragement of the traditional family (see *Marckx v Belgium* A 31 (1979) 2 EHRR 330, ECtHR); the protection of the labour market and public order (*Abdulaziz, Cabales and Balkandali v United Kingdom* A 94 (1985) 7 EHRR 471, ECtHR); and the development of linguistic unity in the two language regions in Belgium (*Belgian Linguistics Case* supra).

11   See CONSTITUTIONAL LAW AND HUMAN RIGHTS vol 8(2) (Reissue) para 164.

12   However, the court has stated that the margin of appreciation extends to choosing between two alternatives, and has been reluctant to substitute its own decision for that of the national decision-maker: see *Rasmussen v Denmark* A 87 (1984) 7 EHRR 371, ECtHR (discrimination in relation to time limits for paternity proceedings between husband and wife were held to come within the ambit of the Convention for the Protection of Human Rights and Fundamental Freedoms arts 6 and 8).

13   See the Convention for the Protection of Human Rights and Fundamental Freedoms art 6; and CONSTITUTIONAL LAW AND HUMAN RIGHTS vol 8(2) (Reissue) para 134 et seq. See *Sander v United Kingdom* Application 34129/96 (2000) 31 EHRR 44, (2000) Times, 12 May, ECtHR.

14   See the Convention for the Protection of Human Rights and Fundamental Freedoms art 8; and CONSTITUTIONAL LAW AND HUMAN RIGHTS vol 8(2) (Reissue) para 149 et seq.

15   See ibid art 9; and CONSTITUTIONAL LAW AND HUMAN RIGHTS vol 8(2) (Reissue) para 156 et seq. See *R (on the application of Begum) v Headteacher and Governors of Denbigh High School* [2006] UKHL 15, [2006] 2 All ER 487, [2006] 2 FCR 613 (dispute relating to a school pupil's dress; balancing act between an individual's right to cultural and religious expression and a school's ability to make practical decisions for itself without legal intervention); *Copsey v WWB Devon Clays Ltd* [2005] EWCA Civ 932, [2005] ICR 1789, [2005] IRLR 811 (where a Christian employee who refused to work on Sundays lost a claim for unfair dismissal, the court suggesting that there had been no breach of the Convention for the Protection of Human Rights and Fundamental Freedoms art 9). The latter case was brought under the Convention for the Protection of Human Rights and Fundamental Freedoms art 9 rather than the Employment Equality (Religion or Belief) Regulations 2003, SI 2003/1660 (as amended) (see para 660 et seq post), which had not then come into force. For the first prominent case under those regulations (although the case was also brought under the Convention for the Protection of Human Rights and Fundamental Freedoms art 9) see *Azmi v Kirklees Metropolitan Council* [2007] All ER (D) 528 (Mar), EAT (suspension of a Muslim support worker in a school for her refusal to teach children without wearing a veil when male colleagues were present; it was found by the original tribunal that the Convention for the Protection of Human Rights and Fundamental Freedoms art 9 did not give an absolute right to employees to wear the veil; employee's appeal to EAT dismissed). See also para 660 note 1 post.

16   See the Convention for the Protection of Human Rights and Fundamental Freedoms art 10; and CONSTITUTIONAL LAW AND HUMAN RIGHTS vol 8(2) (Reissue) para 158 et seq.

17   See ibid art 11; and CONSTITUTIONAL LAW AND HUMAN RIGHTS vol 8(2) (Reissue) para 160 et seq.

18   See ibid First Protocol (1952) art 1; and CONSTITUTIONAL LAW AND HUMAN RIGHTS vol 8(2) (Reissue) para 165.

19   See ibid First Protocol (1952) art 2; and CONSTITUTIONAL LAW AND HUMAN RIGHTS vol 8(2) (Reissue) para 166.

(2)   THE COMMISSION FOR EQUALITY AND HUMAN RIGHTS

(i)   The Commission

305.   Establishment and constitution.   A body corporate known as the Commission for Equality and Human Rights has been established[1]. The Secretary of

State must appoint not less than ten or more than 15 individuals as members of the Commission (to be known as 'Commissioners')[2]. The chief executive of the Commission[3] is a Commissioner ex officio[4].

In appointing Commissioners the Secretary of State must appoint an individual only if he thinks that the individual has experience or knowledge relating to a relevant matter[5] or is suitable for appointment for some other special reason[6], and must have regard to the desirability of the Commissioners together having experience and knowledge relating to the relevant matters[7].

The Secretary of State must ensure that the Commission includes: (1) a Commissioner so appointed[8] who is (or has been) a disabled person[9]; (2) a Commissioner so appointed with the consent of the Scottish Ministers, who knows about conditions in Scotland[10]; and (3) a Commissioner so appointed with the consent of the National Assembly for Wales, who knows about conditions in Wales[11]. A person may not be appointed for the purpose of satisfying more than one of heads (1) to (3) above[12].

A Commissioner holds and vacates office in accordance with the terms of his appointment[13]. The appointment of a Commissioner must be expressed to be for a specified period of not less than two years or more than five years[14]. A Commissioner whose period of membership has expired may be re-appointed[15]. A Commissioner may resign by notice in writing to the Secretary of State[16]. The Secretary of State may dismiss a Commissioner who is, in the opinion of the Secretary of State, unable, unfit or unwilling to perform his functions[17].

The Secretary of State must appoint a Commissioner as Chairman, and one or more Commissioners as deputy Chairman[18].

The Chairman must: (a) preside over meetings of the Commission[19]; (b) perform such functions as may be specified in the terms of his appointment[20]; and (c) perform such other functions as may be assigned to him by the Commission[21].

A deputy Chairman: (i) may act for the Chairman when he is unavailable[22]; and (ii) must perform such functions as may be specified in the terms of his appointment, and such other functions as the Chairman may delegate or assign to him[23].

The Chairman or a deputy Chairman: (A) must vacate office if he ceases to be a Commissioner[24]; (B) may resign by notice in writing to the Secretary of State[25]; and (C) otherwise, must hold and vacate office in accordance with the terms of his appointment (and may be re-appointed)[26]. If the Chairman resigns, he ceases to be a Commissioner (although he may be re-appointed as a Commissioner)[27].

The chief executive may not be appointed as Chairman or deputy Chairman[28].

1   Equality Act 2006 s 1. As to the dissolution of the Equal Opportunities Commission, the Commission for Racial Equality and the Disability Rights Commission see para 306 post.

2   Ibid s 2, Sch 1 para 1(1). As to the Secretary of State and the National Assembly for Wales see para 302 ante.

      If an order under s 93 provides for any of ss 1–3 and Sch 1 to come into force (to any extent) at a time before any of ss 8–32 (as amended) come into force (to any extent): (1) the period between that time and the commencement of any of ss 8–32 (as amended) (to any extent) is the 'transitional period' for the purposes of s 41; and (2) the following provisions of s 41 have effect: s 41(1). During the transitional period the minimum number of Commissioners is five (and not as provided by Sch 1 para 1): s 41(2). The Secretary of State must, as soon as is reasonably practicable after making the first appointments under Sch 1 para 1, appoint as additional members of the Commission (known as 'Transition Commissioners'): (a) a commissioner of the Equal Opportunities Commission (see para 404 et seq post) nominated by its chairman; (b) a commissioner of the Commission for Racial Equality (see para 488 et seq post) nominated by its chairman; and (c) a commissioner of the Disability Rights Commission (see para 646 et seq post) nominated by its chairman: s 41(3). A person may nominate himself as a Transition Commissioner: s 41(4). If a Transition Commissioner ceases to be a commissioner of the Commission whose chairman nominated him: (i) he ceases to be a Transition Commissioner; (ii) the chairman of that Commission must nominate a replacement; and (iii) the Secretary of State must appoint the nominated replacement: s 41(5). A person holds appointment as a Transition Commissioner until a time specified by order of the Secretary of State (subject to s 41(5)); and the Secretary of State must specify a time which in his opinion is not more than two years after the time when, by virtue of s 36 (see para 306 post), the Commission whose chairman nominated the Transition Commissioner ceases to exist, or loses its principal functions: s 41(6). In all other respects the provisions of Pt 1 (ss 1–43) (as amended) apply in relation to a Transition Commissioner as in relation to another Commissioner: s 41(7).

    An order of a Minister of the Crown under Pt 1 (as amended) and regulations under Pt 1 (as amended) must be made by statutory instrument: s 39(1). An order of a Minister of the Crown under Pt 1 (as amended) and regulations under Pt 1 (as amended): (A) may make provision generally or only for specified purposes; (B) may make different provision for different purposes; and (C) may include transitional, incidental or consequential provision: s 39(2). An order or regulations under any of the following provisions is subject to annulment in pursuance of a resolution of either House of Parliament: s 15(3) (see para 321 post), s 28 (see para 334 post), s 29 (see para 334 post), s 36 (see para 306 post), and Sch 1 Pt 5 (see para 312 post): s 39(3). An order under s 10(6) (see para 318 post), s 15(6) (see para 321 post), s 27(10) (see para 333 post) or s 33(3) (see para 316 post) may, in particular, make consequential amendment of an enactment (including the Equality Act 2006 and including an enactment in or under an Act of the Scottish Parliament); and may not be made unless a draft has been laid before and approved by resolution of each House of Parliament: s 39(4). Scottish matters generally are beyond the scope of this work. An incidental provision included in an order or in regulations by virtue of head (C) supra may, in particular, impose a requirement for consent to action under or by virtue of the order or regulations: s 39(5).

3   Ie appointed under ibid Sch 1 para 7 (see para 307 post).

4   Ibid Sch 1 para 1(2).

5   Ibid Sch 1 para 2(1)(a)(i). For these purposes, the relevant matters are those matters in respect of which the Commission has functions including, in particular: (1) discrimination (whether on grounds of age, disability, gender, gender reassignment, race, religion or belief, sexual orientation or otherwise); and (2) human rights: Sch 1 para 2(2). 'Race' includes colour, nationality, ethnic origin and national origin; 'religion or belief' has the same meaning as in Pt 2 (ss 44–80) (see para 691 post); and 'sexual orientation' means an individual's sexual orientation towards persons of the same sex as him or her, persons of the opposite sex, or both: s 35.

6   Ibid Sch 1 para 2(1)(a)(ii).

7   Ibid Sch 1 para 2(1)(b).

8   Ie appointed under ibid Sch 1 para 1(1) (see the text and note 2 supra).

9   Ibid Sch 1 para 2(3)(a). 'Disabled person' means a person who: (1) is a disabled person within the meaning of the Disability Discrimination Act 1995 (see para 511 post); or (2) has been a disabled person within that meaning (whether or not at a time when that Act had effect): Equality Act 2006 ss 8(4), 35 (s 8(4) not yet in force).

10   Ibid Sch 1 para 2(3)(b).

11   Ibid Sch 1 para 2(3)(c).

12   See ibid Sch 1 para 2(4).

13   Ibid Sch 1 para 3(1). This is subject to the other provisions of Sch 1: see Sch 1 para 3(1). Schedule 1 para 3 does not apply to the chief executive (see the text to note 4 supra): Sch 1 para 3(6).

14   Ibid Sch 1 para 3(2). See note 13 supra.

15   Ibid Sch 1 para 3(3). See note 13 supra.

16   Ibid Sch 1 para 3(4). See note 13 supra.

17   Ibid Sch 1 para 3(5). See note 13 supra.

18   Ibid Sch 1 para 4(1).

19   Ibid Sch 1 para 4(2)(a).

20   Ibid Sch 1 para 4(2)(b).

21   Ibid Sch 1 para 4(2)(c).

22   Ibid Sch 1 para 4(3)(a).

23   Ibid Sch 1 para 4(3)(b).

24   Ibid Sch 1 para 4(4)(a).

25   Ibid Sch 1 para 4(4)(b).

26   Ibid Sch 1 para 4(4)(c).

27   Ibid Sch 1 para 4(5).

28   Ibid Sch 1 para 4(6).

306.   Dissolution of former Commissions. The Secretary of State[1] may by order provide for any of the former Commissions[2] to cease to exist[3], or for the removal from any of the former Commissions of a specified function[4].

Such an order[5] in respect of any of the former Commissions may provide for the transfer to the Commission for Equality and Human Rights[6] of specified property, rights and liabilities of the former Commission[7].

The Secretary of State may give a former Commission any direction that he thinks appropriate in connection with the dissolution of the former Commission or the establishment of the Commission for Equality and Human Rights; and a direction may, in particular, require the former Commission: (1) to provide information in connection with property, rights or liabilities[8]; (2) to provide information in connection with the exercise of functions[9]; (3) to transfer specified property, rights and liabilities to a specified person[10]; (4) to make property, staff or facilities available, on such terms or conditions as may be specified in the direction, to the Commission for Equality and Human Rights[11]; (5) not to take action of a specified kind or in specified circumstances[12]. The Secretary of State may direct a former Commission to prepare a scheme for the transfer of specified property, rights and liabilities to the Commission for Equality and Human Rights, or another person specified in the direction[13].

An order[14], direction[15] or scheme[16] under or by virtue of the above provisions[17] may, in particular: (a) specify property, rights or liabilities[18]; (b) specify a class or description of property, rights or liabilities[19]; (c) specify property, rights or liabilities to a specified extent[20].

In so far as is appropriate as a consequence of such a transfer of property[21]: (i) anything done by or in relation to any of the former Commissions which has effect immediately before the transfer continues to have effect as if done by or in relation to the Commission for Equality and Human Rights[22]; and (ii) anything (including any legal proceedings) which immediately before the transfer is in the process of being done by or in relation to any of the former Commissions may be continued by or in relation to the Commission for Equality and Human Rights[23]. In so far as is appropriate in consequence of such a transfer, a reference to any of the former Commissions in an agreement, instrument or other document is treated as a reference to the Commission for Equality and Human Rights[24].

The above transfer provisions[25], and a direction, scheme or order under or by virtue of those provisions, operates in relation to property, rights or liabilities: (A) whether or not they would otherwise be capable of being transferred[26]; (B) without any instrument or other formality being required[27]; and (C) irrespective of any requirement for consent that would otherwise apply[28].

1   As to the Secretary of State and the National Assembly for Wales see para 302 ante.
2   'Former Commissions' means: (1) the Equal Opportunities Commission (see para 404 et seq post); (2) the Commission for Racial Equality (see para 488 et seq post); and (3) the Disability Rights Commission (see para 646 et seq post): Equality Act 2006 s 36(2).
3   Ibid s 36(1)(a). The Secretary of State must by exercising the power under s 36(1) ensure that each of the former Commissions ceases to exist not later than the end of 31 March 2009: s 36(3).
    Where a former Commission ceases to exist by virtue of s 36(1)(a), its property, rights and liabilities vest in the Commission for Equality and Human Rights (see note 6 infra); and s 37(5) operates in addition to any transfer provided for by virtue of s 36(1): s 37(5).
    An order under s 36(1)(a) or (b) may: (1) provide for a former Commission to continue to exercise a function in respect of a transitional case of a kind specified; (2) provide for the Commission for Equality and Human Rights to exercise a function of a former Commission in respect of a transitional case of a kind specified: s 42(1). An order under s 93 commencing a provision of Sch 3 (consequential amendments) or Sch 4 (repeals) may include a saving or a consequential or incidental provision for the purpose of the operation of provision made by virtue of s 42(1); and the saving, consequential or incidental provision may, in particular, include provision applying, disapplying or modifying the application of a provision of the Equality Act 2006 or of another enactment (including an enactment in or under an Act of the Scottish Parliament): s 42(2). Scottish matters generally are beyond the scope of this work. A code of practice issued by a Commission dissolved by virtue of s 36, or which relates to a function of a Commission removed by virtue of s 36(1)(b) (see the text and note 4 infra): (a) continues to have effect until revoked by the Secretary of State, at the request of the Commission for Equality and

Human Rights, by order made by statutory instrument; and (b) may be revised by the Commission for Equality and Human Rights as if it had been issued under s 14 (as amended) (see para 321 post): s 42(3). Consultation undertaken by a former Commission in relation to the issue or revision of a code of practice may be relied upon by the Commission for Equality and Human Rights for a purpose of s 14 (as amended) (see para 321 post): s 42(4). An order under head (a) supra is subject to annulment in pursuance of a resolution of either House of Parliament: s 42(5). As to orders and regulations under Pt 1 (ss 1–43) (as amended) generally see para 305 note 2 ante.

4   Ibid s 36(1)(b). See note 3 supra.
5   Ie an order under ibid s 36(1).
6   As to the Commission for Equality and Human Rights, its establishment and constitution see para 305 ante.
7   Equality Act 2006 s 37(1).
8   Ibid s 37(2)(a).
9   Ibid s 37(2)(b).
10 Ibid s 37(2)(c).
11 Ibid s 37(2)(d).
12 Ibid s 37(2)(e).
13 Ibid s 37(3). If the Secretary of State gives a direction under s 37(3): (1) the former Commission must prepare a scheme in accordance with the direction, having consulted either the Commission for Equality and Human Rights or the person specified under s 37(3); and (2) the scheme has effect: (a) when approved by the Secretary of State; and (b) subject to any modifications made by him, having consulted the former Commission and either the Commission for Equality and Human Rights or the person specified: s 37(4).
14 A scheme or order under or by virtue of ibid s 37 which relates to rights or liabilities under a contract of employment: (1) must provide for the application of the Transfer of Undertakings (Protection of Employment) Regulations 1981, SI 1981/1794 (revoked: see now the Transfer of Undertakings (Protection of Employment) Regulations 2006, SI 2006/246) (see EMPLOYMENT vol 16(1A) (Reissue) para 110 et seq); and (2) must provide that for any purpose relating to an employee of a former Commission who becomes an employee of the Commission for Equality and Human Rights by virtue of the scheme or order: (a) a period of employment with the former Commission is treated as a period of employment with the Commission for Equality and Human Rights; and (b) the transfer to that Commission is not treated as a break in service: see the Equality Act 2006 s 38(5).
15 A direction under ibid s 37: (1) must be in writing; (2) may be given only following consultation with the former Commission to which the direction relates and, where the Secretary of State thinks it appropriate, the Commission for Equality and Human Rights; and (3) may be varied or revoked by a further direction: s 38(1).
16 See note 14 supra.
17 Ie under or by virtue of the Equality Act 2006 s 37.
18 Ibid s 37(6)(a).
19 Ibid s 37(6)(b).
20 Ibid s 37(6)(c).
21 Ie a transfer effected by or by virtue of ibid s 37.
22 Ibid s 38(2)(a).
23 Ibid s 38(2)(b).
24 Ibid s 38(3).
25 Ie ibid s 37.
26 Ibid s 38(4)(a).
27 Ibid s 38(4)(b).
28 Ibid s 38(4)(c).

307. Procedure; meetings; staff. The Commission for Equality and Human Rights[1] may regulate its own proceedings[2]. The Commission must determine a quorum for its meetings[3], and at least five Commissioners must participate in the process by which such a determination is made[4].

The Commission: (1) must appoint a chief executive[5]; and (2) may appoint other staff[6]. A person may be appointed under head (1) above only with the consent of the Secretary of State[7]. An appointment may be made under head (2) above only if consistent with arrangements determined by the Commission and approved by the Secretary of State as to numbers and terms and conditions of appointment[8].

The Commission may appoint one or more Investigating Commissioners[9]. An Investigating Commissioner may be appointed only: (a) for the purpose of having delegated to him by the Commission the function of taking certain actions[10]; and (b) with the consent of the Secretary of State[11]. An Investigating Commissioner is not a Commissioner; but certain provisions apply to him as if he were[12].

The Commission may delegate a function to a Commissioner, to staff, or[13] to an Investigating Commissioner[14].

1 As to the Commission for Equality and Human Rights, its establishment and constitution see para 305 ante.
2 Equality Act 2006 s 2, Sch 1 para 5. This is subject to the other provisions of Sch 1: see Sch 1 para 5.
   The validity of proceedings of the Commission is not affected by: (1) a vacancy (whether for Commissioner, Chairman, deputy Chairman or chief executive); or (2) a defect in relation to an appointment: Sch 1 para 33. As to the Commissioners, Chairman, deputy Chairman and the chief executive see para 305 ante.
3 Ibid Sch 1 para 6(1).
4 Ibid Sch 1 para 6(2).
5 Ibid Sch 1 para 7(1)(a).
6 Ibid Sch 1 para 7(1)(b).
7 Ibid Sch 1 para 7(2). As to the Secretary of State and the National Assembly for Wales see para 302 ante.
8 Ibid Sch 1 para 7(3).
9 Ibid Sch 1 para 9(1).
10 Ibid Sch 1 para 9(2)(a). The actions are those of a kind as follows: (1) carrying out an inquiry under s 16 (see para 322 post); (2) carrying out an investigation under s 20 (see para 327 post); (3) giving an unlawful act notice under s 21 (see para 328 post); and (4) entering into an agreement under s 23 (see para 330 post): Sch 1 para 9(3).
11 Ibid Sch 1 para 9(2)(b).
12 Ibid Sch 1 para 9(4). The provisions are those of Sch 1 para 3(1), (4), (5) (see para 305 ante) and Sch 1 para 33 (see note 2 supra); and such provisions apply with the substitution of references to the Commission for references to the Secretary of State: see Sch 1 para 9(4).
13 Ie in accordance with ibid Sch 1 para 9 (see the text and notes 9–12 supra).
14 Ibid Sch 1 para 10(1). Schedule 1 paras 15, 21, 22, 29, 30 (see para 308 post) and Sch 1 para 52 (see para 312 post) make provision about delegation to committees: Sch 1 para 10(2).

308.   Committees.   The Commission for Equality and Human Rights[1] may establish one or more committees[2] (known as 'advisory committees') to advise the Commission or an Investigating Commissioner[3].

The Commission may establish one or more committees to whom the Commission may delegate functions (known as 'decision-making committees')[4]. The Commission must ensure that the Chairman of each decision-making committee is a Commissioner[5]. In allocating its resources the Commission must ensure that each decision-making committee receives a share sufficient to enable it to exercise its functions[6].

A member of a committee holds and vacates office in accordance with the terms of his appointment by the Commission (which may include provision for dismissal)[7].

The Commission may: (1) to any extent, regulate the proceedings of a committee (and may, in particular, determine a quorum for meetings)[8]; (2) to any extent, permit a committee to regulate its own proceedings (and may, in particular, enable a committee to determine a quorum for meetings)[9]; and (3) dissolve a committee[10].

The Commission must establish a decision-making committee to be known as the 'Wales Committee'[11]. The Commission must appoint a Commissioner[12] as the Chairman of the Wales Committee[13]. It must also appoint each member of the Wales Committee for a period of not less than two years or more than five years, subject to the possibilities of re-appointment, and dismissal in accordance with the terms of appointment[14]. The Wales Committee must advise the Commission about the exercise of its functions in so far as they affect Wales[15]; and, before exercising a function in a manner which in the opinion of the Commission is likely to affect persons in Wales, the

Commission must consult the Wales Committee[16]. The Commission's general power of information and advice[17] is to be treated as delegated by the Commission to the Wales Committee in so far as its exercise, in the opinion of the Commission, affects Wales; and to that extent the power is not exercisable by the Commission[18]. Similarly the Commission's powers to advise the government about the effect of an enactment or the likely effect of a proposed change of law[19] are to be treated as having been delegated by the Commission to the Wales Committee in so far as they concern the giving of advice to devolved government about enactments and proposed changes in the law which, in the opinion of the Commission, affect only Wales; and to that extent the powers are not exercisable by the Commission[20]. In allocating its resources the Commission must ensure that the Wales Committee receives a share sufficient to enable it to exercise its functions[21].

1 As to the Commission for Equality and Human Rights, its establishment and constitution see para 305 ante.
2 The validity of proceedings of a committee of the Commission is not affected by: (1) a vacancy (including a vacancy in the office of Chairman); or (2) a defect in relation to an appointment (including a defect in relation to the office of Chairman): Equality Act 2006 s 2, Sch 1 para 34.
3 Ibid Sch 1 para 11(1). As to Investigating Commissioners see para 307 ante.
    An advisory committee may include any of the following: (1) Commissioners; (2) staff; (3) other non-Commissioners: s 2, Sch 1 para 11(2). As to the Commissioners see para 305 ante; and as to staff see para 307 ante.
4 Ibid Sch 1 paras 12(1), 15(1). A decision-making committee may include any of the following: (1) Commissioners; (2) staff; (3) other non-Commissioners: Sch 1 para 12(2). The power under Sch 1 para 15(1) to delegate functions to a decision-making committee is subject to Sch 1 paras 21, 22 (see note 11 infra), Sch 1 paras 29, 30 (see the text and notes 18–20 infra) and Sch 1 para 52 (see para 312 post): Sch 1 para 15(2). As to the Disability Committee see para 312 post.
5 Ibid Sch 1 para 12(3).
6 Ibid Sch 1 para 12(4).
7 Ibid Sch 1 para 13.
8 Ibid Sch 1 para 14(a).
9 Ibid Sch 1 para 14(b).
10 Ibid Sch 1 para 14(c).
11 Ibid Sch 1 para 24(1). The Commission must ensure that the Wales Committee is established before any of ss 8–12 come into force to any extent (see paras 316–319 post): Sch 1 para 24(2).
    The Commission must also establish a decision-making committee to be known as the 'Scotland Committee' and there are provisions corresponding to those of Sch 1 paras 24–31 in regard to such committee: see Sch 1 paras 16–23. Scottish matters generally are beyond the scope of this work.
12 Ie appointed for the purpose of satisfying ibid Sch 1 para 2(3)(c): see para 305 ante.
13 Ibid Sch 1 para 25.
14 Ibid Sch 1 para 26.
15 Ibid Sch 1 para 27.
16 Ibid Sch 1 para 28.
17 Ie the power under ibid s 13: see para 320 post.
18 Ibid Sch 1 para 29(1). Schedule 1 para 29(1) does not apply to the power under s 13 (see para 320 post) in so far as it is treated as delegated to the Disability Committee in accordance with Sch 1 para 52 (see para 312 post): Sch 1 para 29(2). Schedule 1 para 29(1) does not prevent the Commission from making arrangements under s 13(1)(d) or (e) (see para 320 post) for the provision of advice or guidance to persons anywhere in Great Britain: Sch 1 para 29(3). For the meaning of 'Great Britain' see para 325 note 6 post.
19 Ie the powers under ibid s 11(2)(c), (d): see para 319 post.
20 Ibid Sch 1 para 30(1), (2). The provisions of Sch 1 paras 30(1), (2) do not apply to the powers under s 11(2)(c), (d) (see para 319 post) in so far as they are treated as delegated to the Disability Committee in accordance with Sch 1 para 52 (see para 312 post): Sch 1 para 30(3).
21 Ibid Sch 1 para 31.

309. Annual report. The Commission for Equality and Human Rights[1] must prepare a report on the performance of its functions in that year for each financial year (known as its 'annual report')[2].

An annual report must, in particular, indicate in what manner and to what extent the Commission's performance of its functions has accorded to the strategic plan[3]; and the matters addressed by an annual report must, in particular, include the Commission's activities in relation to Scotland and Wales[4].

The Commission must send each annual report to the Secretary of State[5] within such period, beginning with the end of the financial year to which the report relates, as he may specify[6]. The Secretary of State must lay before Parliament a copy of each annual report so received[7]. The Commission must also send a copy of each annual report to the Scottish Parliament and the National Assembly for Wales[8].

1   As to the Commission for Equality and Human Rights, its establishment and constitution see para 305 ante.
2   Equality Act 2006 s 2, Sch 1 para 32(1). For the meaning of 'financial year' in relation to the Commission see para 310 note 15 post.
3   Ibid Sch 1 para 32(2). The strategic plan is the plan required under s 4: see para 314 post.
4   Ibid Sch 1 para 32(3). Scottish matters generally are beyond the scope of this work.
5   As to the Secretary of State see para 302 ante.
6   Equality Act 2006 Sch 1 para 32(4).
7   Ibid Sch 1 para 32(5).
8   Ibid Sch 1 para 32(6). As to the National Assembly for Wales see para 302 ante. Scottish matters generally are beyond the scope of this work.

310.   Financial matters.   The Commission for Equality and Human Rights[1] may pay to the Chairman, a deputy Chairman or another Commissioner[2]: (1) such remuneration as the Secretary of State[3] may determine[4]; and (2) such travelling and other allowances as the Secretary of State may determine[5]. The Commission may pay to or in respect of the Chairman, a deputy Chairman or another Commissioner such sums as the Secretary of State may determine by way of, or in respect of, pensions, allowances or gratuities[6]. If the Secretary of State thinks that there are special circumstances that make it right for a person ceasing to hold office as Chairman, deputy Chairman or Commissioner to receive compensation, the Commission may pay to him such compensation as the Secretary of State may determine[7].

The Commission may pay sums to or in respect of a member or former member of staff by way of or in respect of remuneration, allowances, pensions, gratuities, or compensation for loss of employment[8].

The Commission may, with the approval[9] of the Secretary of State, pay sums to or in respect of a member or former member of an advisory or decision-making committee[10] by way of or in respect of remuneration, allowances, or gratuities[11].

The Secretary of State must pay to the Commission such sums as appear to him reasonably sufficient for the purpose of enabling the Commission to perform its functions[12].

The Commission may make a charge for certain services provided by it[13].

The Commission must: (a) keep proper accounting records[14]; and (b) prepare a statement of accounts in respect of each financial year[15] in such form as the Secretary of State may direct[16]. The Commission must send a copy of a statement under head (b) above to the Secretary of State and to the Comptroller and Auditor General[17]. The Comptroller and Auditor General must: (i) examine, certify and report on a statement so received[18]; and (ii) lay a copy of the statement and his report before Parliament[19].

1   As to the Commission for Equality and Human Rights, its establishment and constitution see para 305 ante.
2   As to the Chairman, deputy Chairman and the Commissioners see para 305 ante.
3   As to the Secretary of State and the National Assembly for Wales see para 302 ante.
4   Equality Act 2006 s 2, Sch 1 para 35(1)(a). Schedule 1 para 35 does not apply to the chief executive: Sch 1 para 35(4).

5   Ibid Sch 1 para 35(1)(b). See note 4 supra.
6   Ibid Sch 1 para 35(2). See note 4 supra.
7   Ibid Sch 1 para 35(3) See note 4 supra.
8   Ibid Sch 1 para 36(1). The Commission must pay to the Minister for the Civil Service such sums as he may determine in respect of any increase attributable to the amendment of the Superannuation Act 1972 Sch 1 (as amended) (see CONSTITUTIONAL LAW AND HUMAN RIGHTS vol 8(2) (Reissue) para 567 et seq) by the Equality Act 2006 Sch 1 para 36(2) (ie the addition of the Commission for Equality and Human Rights to the bodies there listed) in the sums payable out of money provided by Parliament under the Superannuation Act 1972: Equality Act 2006 Sch 1 para 36(3). As to the Minister for the Civil Service see CONSTITUTIONAL LAW AND HUMAN RIGHTS vol 8(2) (Reissue) paras 395, 427.
9   Approval for these purposes may be general or specific: ibid Sch 1 para 37(3).
10 As to advisory and decision-making committees see para 308 ante.
11 Equality Act 2006 Sch 1 para 37(1). Schedule 1 para 37 does not apply in relation to a person who is a member of staff of the Commission: Sch 1 para 37(2).
12 Ibid Sch 1 para 38.
13 Ibid Sch 1 para 39. The services referred to in the text are those provided under s 13 (see para 320 post) or s 27 (as amended) (see para 333 post).
14 Ibid Sch 1 para 40(1)(a).
15 The 'financial year' of the Commission is the period of 12 months ending with 31 March: ibid Sch 1 para 41(1). However, Sch 1 para 41(2) provides that the first financial year of the Commission is the period: (1) beginning with the coming into force of s 1 (see para 305 ante); and (2) ending with the following 31 March, if that provision comes into force on 1 April, and the second following 31 March, in any other case. Section 1 came into force on 18 April 2006: see the Equality Act 2006 (Commencement No 1) Order 2006, SI 2006/1082, art 2(a).
16 Equality Act 2006 Sch 1 para 40(1)(b). The Secretary of State may make a direction under Sch 1 para 40(1)(b) only with the consent of the Treasury: Sch 1 para 40(5). As to the Treasury see CONSTITUTIONAL LAW AND HUMAN RIGHTS vol 8(2) (Reissue) paras 512–517.
17 Ibid Sch 1 para 40(2). A copy of a statement must be so sent within such period, beginning with the end of the financial year to which the statement relates, as the Secretary of State may direct: Sch 1 para 40(3). As to the Comptroller and Auditor General see CONSTITUTIONAL LAW AND HUMAN RIGHTS vol 8(2) (Reissue) paras 724–726.
18 Ibid Sch 1 para 40(4)(a).
19 Ibid Sch 1 para 40(4)(b).

311.   Status and disqualification.   The Commission for Equality and Human Rights[1] is not regarded as the servant or agent of the Crown, nor does it enjoy any status, immunity or privilege of the Crown[2]. Service as Commissioner, Investigating Commissioner[3] or employee of the Commission is not employment in the civil service of the state[4].

The Secretary of State[5] must have regard to the desirability of ensuring that the Commission is under as few constraints as reasonably possible in determining its activities, its timetables and its priorities[6].

The Commission is included in the departments subject to investigation under the Parliamentary Commissioner Act 1967[7].

The legislation covering disqualification from the House of Commons applies to members of the Commission[8], and to Investigating Commissioners and members of decision-making committees[9] of the Commission[10]. A Commissioner or Investigating Commissioner, or a member of a decision-making committee of the Commission, is also disqualified from being a member of the National Assembly for Wales[11].

The legislation on public records[12] and freedom of information[13] applies to the Commission.

1   As to the Commission for Equality and Human Rights, its establishment and constitution see para 305 ante.
2   Equality Act 2006 s 2, Sch 1 para 42(1). As to the status, immunity and privilege of the Crown see generally CONSTITUTIONAL LAW AND HUMAN RIGHTS; CROWN AND ROYAL FAMILY; CROWN PROCEEDINGS AND CROWN PRACTICE; CROWN PROPERTY.
3   As to the Commissioners see para 305 ante. As to Investigating Commissioners see para 307 ante.

4   Equality Act 2006 Sch 1 para 42(2). As to the civil service generally see CONSTITUTIONAL LAW AND HUMAN RIGHTS vol 8(2) (Reissue) para 549 et seq.

5   As to the Secretary of State and the National Assembly for Wales see para 302 ante.

6   Equality Act 2006 Sch 1 para 42(3).

7   See the Parliamentary Commissioner Act 1967 Sch 2 (substituted by the Parliamentary Commissioner (No 2) Order 2005, SI 2005/3430, art 2, Schedule; and amended by the Equality Act 2006 Sch 1 para 43); and ADMINISTRATIVE LAW vol 1(1) (2001 Reissue) para 43.

8   See the House of Commons Disqualification Act 1975 Sch 1 Pt II (amended by the Equality Act 2006 Sch 1 para 44(1)); and PARLIAMENT vol 34 (Reissue) para 610.

9   As to decision-making committees see para 308 ante.

10 See the House of Commons Disqualification Act 1975 Sch 1 Pt III (amended by the Equality Act 2006 Sch 1 para 44(2)); and PARLIAMENT vol 34 (Reissue) para 610.

11 See the Equality Act 2006 Sch 1 para 46.

12 See the Public Records Act 1958 Sch 1 para 3 Table Pt II (amended by the Equality Act 2006 Sch 1 para 47); and CONSTITUTIONAL LAW AND HUMAN RIGHTS vol 8(2) (Reissue) para 835.

13 See the Freedom of Information Act 2000 Sch 1 Pt VI (amended by the Equality Act 2006 Sch 1 para 48); and CONFIDENCE AND DATA PROTECTION vol 8(1) (2003 Reissue) para 583.

312.   Disability Committee.   The Commission for Equality and Human Rights[1] must establish a decision-making committee[2] known as the 'Disability Committee'[3].

The Commission must ensure that: (1) there are not less than seven or more than nine members of the Disability Committee[4]; (2) at least one half of the members are (or have been) disabled persons[5]; and (3) the Chairman is (or has been) a disabled person[6]. The appointment of each member of the Disability Committee is for a period of not less than two years or more than five years, subject to the possibilities of re-appointment, dismissal in accordance with the terms of appointment, and the lapsing of the appointment upon the dissolution of the Committee[7].

The Commission is treated[8] as having delegated[9] to the Disability Committee: (a) the Commission's duty in regard to equality and diversity[10] in so far as it relates to disability matters and may be fulfilled by the exercise of certain specific powers[11]; (b) the Commission's duty in regard to groups[12] in so far as it relates to disability and may be fulfilled by the exercise of those powers[13]; and (c) those powers in so far as they are or may be exercised for the purpose of disability matters[14].

Before exercising a power or fulfilling a duty wholly or partly in relation to a matter affecting disabled persons[15], the Commission must consult the Disability Committee[16]. The Disability Committee must advise the Commission about the exercise of the Commission's functions[17] in so far as they affect disabled persons[18].

In allocating its resources the Commission must ensure that the Disability Committee receives a share sufficient to enable it to exercise its functions[19].

The Disability Committee must for each financial year[20] of the Commission submit to the Commission a report on the Disability Committee's activities in that year[21].

The Commission must arrange for a review[22] of the activities of the Disability Committee to be conducted as soon as is reasonably practicable after the end of the period of five years beginning with the date of the commencement for all purposes of the provisions on equality and diversity[23] and the provisions relating to groups[24] in so far as they relate to disability[25]. The Commission must ensure: (i) that those conducting the above review consult disabled persons and other persons whom they think likely to have an interest[26]; (ii) that those conducting the review submit a report to the Commission which, in particular, recommends for how long the Disability Committee should continue in existence[27]; and (iii) that the report is published[28]. As soon as is reasonably practicable after receiving a report under head (ii) above the Commission must recommend to the Secretary of State[29] for how long the Disability Committee should continue in existence[30]. As soon as is reasonably practicable after receiving such a recommendation the Secretary of State must by order[31] dissolve the Disability Committee with effect from such time as specified in the order[32].

1   As to the Commission for Equality and Human Rights, its establishment and constitution see para 305 ante.

2   As to decision-making committees see para 308 ante.

3   Equality Act 2006 s 2, Sch 1 para 49(1). The Commission must ensure that the Disability Committee is established before either s 8 (see para 317 post) or s 10 (see para 318 post), in so far as they relate to disability, comes into force to any extent: Sch 1 para 49(2).

    The Transition Commissioner nominated by the chairman of the Disability Rights Commission may not be a member of the Disability Committee: Sch 1 para 50(2). As to Transition Commissioners see para 305 ante. As to the Disability Rights Commission see para 646 et seq post.

4   Ibid Sch 1 para 50(1)(a).

5   Ibid Sch 1 para 50(1)(b).

6   Ibid Sch 1 para 50(1)(c).

7   Ibid Sch 1 para 51.

8   Ie by virtue of ibid Sch 1 para 52.

9   Delegation under ibid Sch 1 para 52 does not prevent the exercise by the Commission of a power, or the fulfilment by the Commission of a duty, by action which relates partly to disability matters and partly to other matters: Sch 1 para 52(2).

10 Ie its duty under ibid s 8: see para 317 post.

11 Ibid Sch 1 para 52(1)(a). The powers mentioned in the text are those conferred by or referred to in: s 11 (see para 319 post); s 13(1)(a), (c) or (d) (or s 13(1) (e) or (f) in so far as it relates to s 13(1)(a), (c) or (d)) (see para 320 post); s 14 (as amended) (see para 321 post); s 15 (see para 321 post); s 19 (see para 326 post), in so far as it relates to disability; s 27 (as amended) (see para 333 post); s 28 (see para 334 post); or s 30 (see para 335 post): see Sch 1 para 52(1)(a)(i)–(vii).

12 Ie its duty under ibid s 10: see para 318 post.

13 Ibid Sch 1 para 52(1)(b).

14 Ibid Sch 1 para 52(1)(c). For these purposes, 'disability matters' means: (1) matters provided for in the Disability Discrimination Act 1995 Pt I (ss 1–3) (as amended) (see paras 511–512, 522 post), Pt III (ss 19–28) (as amended; prospectively amended) (see para 583 et seq post), Pt IV (ss 28A–31C) (as amended; prospectively amended) (see para 561 et seq post), Pt V (ss 32–49) (as amended) (see para 627 et seq post), and Pt VB (ss 49G–49I) (as added; prospectively amended) (see para 507 et seq post); (2) the Equality Act s 8 (see para 316 post) and s 10 (see para 318 post), in so far as they relate to disability; and (3) matters addressed in s 14(3), (4) (see para 321 post), s 27(2), (3) (see para 333 post) and s 28(2), (3) (see para 334 post): Sch 1 para 52(3).

    Before exercising powers to which Sch 1 para 21(2) or 22(3) applies (see para 308 note 11 ante), the Disability Committee must consult the Scotland Committee; and before exercising powers to which Sch 1 para 29(2) or 30(3) applies (see para 308 ante), the Disability Committee must consult the Wales Committee: Sch 1 para 52(4), (5). As to the Wales Committee and the Scotland Committee see para 308 ante. Scottish matters generally are beyond the scope of this work.

15 Ie including, in particular, any matter provided for in the Disability Discrimination Act 1995 Pt II (ss 3A–18E) (as amended; prospectively amended) (see para 529 et seq post): see the Equality Act 2006 Sch 1 para 53.

16 Ibid Sch 1 para 53.

17 Ie including, in particular, in so far as they relate to any matter provided for in the Disability Discrimination Act 1995 Pt II (as amended; prospectively amended) (see para 529 et seq post): see the Equality Act 2006 Sch 1 para 54.

18 Ibid Sch 1 para 54.

19 Ibid Sch 1 para 55.

20 For the meaning of 'financial year' in relation to the Commission see para 310 note 15 ante.

21 Equality Act 2006 Sch 1 para 56(1). The Commission must incorporate each such report of the Disability Committee into the relevant annual report of the Commission: Sch 1 para 56(2). As to the annual report of the Commission see para 309 ante.

22 The following may not participate in the review (although those conducting the review may seek views from any of them): (1) a Commissioner or former Commissioner; (2) staff or former staff of the Commission; (3) a person who is or has been an Investigating Commissioner; and (d) a person who is or has been a member of a committee established by the Commission: ibid Sch 1 para 58. As to the Commissioners see para 305 ante. As to Investigating Commissioners and staff of the Commission see para 307 ante. As to committees established by the Commission see para 308 ante.

23 Ie ibid s 8: see para 316 post.

24 Ie ibid s 10: see para 318 post.

25 Ibid Sch 1 para 57.
26 Ibid Sch 1 para 59(a).
27 Ibid Sch 1 para 59(b).
28 Ibid Sch 1 para 59(c).
29 As to the Secretary of State and the National Assembly for Wales see para 302 ante.
30 Equality Act 2006 Sch 1 para 60.
31 An order under ibid Sch 1 para 61 may include provision about: (1) the conduct of the business of the Disability Committee before its dissolution; (2) the conduct of the Commission after the dissolution of the Disability Committee in relation to functions formerly delegated to that committee: Sch 1 para 62. As to orders and regulations under Pt 1 (ss 1–43) (as amended) generally see para 305 note 2 ante.
32 Ibid Sch 1 para 61(a). The Secretary of State must also repeal Sch 1 Pt 5 paras 49–64 from that time: Sch 1 para 61(b).
      The dissolution of the Disability Committee is without prejudice to any power of the Commission under Sch 1 to establish a committee or to delegate to a committee: Sch 1 para 63.
      The Disability Committee may not be dissolved under Sch 1 para 14(c) (see para 308 ante): Sch 1 para 64.

313.   Commission's general duty.   The Commission for Equality and Human Rights[1] must exercise its functions[2] with a view to encouraging and supporting the development of a society in which: (1) people's ability to achieve their potential is not limited by prejudice or discrimination[3]; (2) there is respect for and protection of each individual's human rights[4]; (3) there is respect for the dignity and worth of each individual[5]; (4) each individual has an equal opportunity to participate in society[6]; and (5) there is mutual respect between groups[7] based on understanding and valuing of diversity and on shared respect for equality and human rights[8].

1   As to the Commission for Equality and Human Rights, its establishment and constitution see para 305 ante.
2   Ie its functions under the Equality Act 2006 Pt 1 (ss 1–43) (as amended).
3   Ibid s 3(a).
4   Ibid s 3(b). As to human rights see para 317 post.
5   Ibid s 3(c).
6   Ibid s 3(d).
7   As to groups see para 318 post.
8   Equality Act 2006 s 3(e).

314.   Strategic plan.   The Commission for Equality and Human Rights[1] must prepare a plan showing: (1) activities or classes of activity to be undertaken by the Commission in pursuance of its functions[2]; (2) an expected timetable for each activity or class[3]; and (3) priorities for different activities or classes, or principles to be applied in determining priorities[4].

The Commission must review the plan: (a) at least once during the period of three years beginning with its completion[5]; (b) at least once during each period of three years beginning with the completion of a review[6]; and (c) at such other times as the Commission thinks appropriate[7]. If the Commission thinks it appropriate as a result of a review, the Commission must revise the plan[8].

The Commission must send the plan and each revision to the Secretary of State[9], who must lay a copy before Parliament[10]. The Commission must publish the plan and each revision[11].

Before preparing or reviewing such a plan[12] the Commission must: (i) consult such persons having knowledge or experience relevant to the Commission's functions as the Commission thinks appropriate[13]; (ii) consult such other persons as the Commission thinks appropriate[14]; (iii) issue a general invitation to make representations, in a manner likely in the Commission's opinion to bring the invitation to the attention of as large a class of persons who may wish to make representations as is reasonably practicable[15]; and (iv) take account of any representations made[16].

1   As to the Commission for Equality and Human Rights, its establishment and constitution see para 305 ante.
2   Equality Act 2006 s 4(1)(a). The reference in the text is to the Commission's functions under the Equality Act 2006.
3   Ibid s 4(1)(b).
4   Ibid s 4(1)(c).
5   Ibid s 4(2)(a).
6   Ibid s 4(2)(b).
7   Ibid s 4(2)(c).
8   Ibid s 4(3).
9   As to the Secretary of State and the National Assembly for Wales see para 302 ante.
10 Equality Act 2006 s 4(4).
11 Ibid s 4(5).
12 Ie a plan in accordance with ibid s 4.
13 Ibid s 5(a).
14 Ibid s 5(b).
15 Ibid s 5(c).
16 Ibid s 5(d).

315.   Disclosure. As from a day to be appointed, the following provisions have effect[1]. A person who is or was a Commissioner[2], an Investigating Commissioner[3], an employee of the Commission for Equality and Human Rights[4] or a member of a committee established by the Commission[5] commits an offence if he discloses relevant information[6] unless such disclosure is authorised[7].

A disclosure is authorised if: (1) made for the purpose of the exercise of any of certain functions of the Commission[8]; (2) made in a report of an inquiry, investigation or assessment published by the Commission[9]; (3) made in pursuance of an order of a court or tribunal[10]; (4) made with the consent of each person to whom the disclosed information relates[11]; (5) made in a manner that ensures that no person to whom the disclosed information relates can be identified[12]; (6) made for the purpose of civil or criminal proceedings to which the Commission is party[13]; or (7) the information was acquired by the Commission more than 70 years before the date of the disclosure[14].

A person guilty of such an offence is liable on summary conviction to a fine[15].

1   The Equality Act 2006 s 6 is to be brought into force as from a day to be appointed by order made by the Secretary of State under s 93. At the date at which this volume states the law no such day had been appointed. As to the Secretary of State and the National Assembly for Wales see para 302 ante.
2   As to the Commissioners see para 305 ante.
3   As to Investigating Commissioners see para 307 ante.
4   As to the Commission for Equality and Human Rights, its establishment and constitution see para 305 ante.
5   As to committees established by the Commission see para 308 ante.
6   The Equality Act 2006 s 6 (not yet in force) applies to information acquired by the Commission: (1) by way of representations made in relation to, or otherwise in the course of, an inquiry under s 16 (not yet in force) (see para 322 post); (2) by way of representations made in relation to, or otherwise in the course of, an investigation under s 20 (not yet in force) (see para 327 post); (3) by way of representations made in relation to, or otherwise in the course of, an assessment under s 31 (not yet in force) (see para 336 post); (4) by way of representations made in relation to, or otherwise in connection with, a notice under s 32 (not yet in force) (see para 336 post); or (5) from a person with whom the Commission enters into, or considers entering into, an agreement under s 23 (not yet in force) (see para 330 post): s 6(2) (not yet in force: see note 1 supra).
7   Ibid s 6(1) (not yet in force: see note 1 supra).
8   Ibid s 6(3)(a) (not yet in force: see note 1 supra). The functions are those under s 16 (not yet in force) (see para 322 post), s 20 (not yet in force) (see para 327 post), s 21 (not yet in force) (see para 328 post), s 24 (not yet in force) (see para 331 post), s 25 (as amended; not yet in force) (see para 332 post), s 31 (not yet in force) (see para 336 post) and s 32 (not yet in force) (see para 336 post).
    However, s 6(3) (not yet in force) does not authorise, nor may the Commission make, a disclosure of information provided by or relating to an intelligence service unless the service has authorised the disclosure: s 6(4) (not yet in force: see note 1 supra). For these purposes, 'intelligence service' means: (1) the Security Service; (2) the Secret Intelligence Service; and (3) the Government Communications

Headquarters: s 6(5) (not yet in force: see note 1 supra). As to the security and intelligence services generally see CONSTITUTIONAL LAW AND HUMAN RIGHTS vol 8(2) (Reissue) para 473 et seq.

9   Ibid s 6(3)(b) (not yet in force: see note 1 supra). See note 8 supra.
10   Ibid s 6(3)(c) (not yet in force: see note 1 supra). See note 8 supra.
11   Ibid s 6(3)(d) (not yet in force: see note 1 supra). See note 8 supra.
12   Ibid s 6(3)(e) (not yet in force: see note 1 supra). See note 8 supra.
13   Ibid s 6(3)(f) (not yet in force: see note 1 supra). See note 8 supra.
14   Ibid s 6(3)(g) (not yet in force: see note 1 supra). See note 8 supra.
15   Ibid s 6(6) (not yet in force: see note 1 supra). The fine must not exceed level 5 on the standard scale: see s 6(6). 'Standard scale' means the standard scale of maximum fines for summary offences as set out in the Criminal Justice Act 1982 s 37 (as amended): see the Interpretation Act 1978 s 5, Sch 1 (definition added by the Criminal Justice Act 1988 s 170(1), Sch 15 para 58); and CRIMINAL LAW, EVIDENCE AND PROCEDURE vol 11(4) (2006 Reissue) para 1676; MAGISTRATES vol 29(2) (Reissue) para 804. At the date at which this volume states the law, the standard scale is as follows: level 1, £200; level 2, £500; level 3, £1,000; level 4, £2,500; level 5, £5,000: Criminal Justice Act 1982 s 37(2) (substituted by the Criminal Justice Act 1991 s 17(1)). As to the determination of the amount of the fine actually imposed, as distinct from the level on the standard scale which it may not exceed, see the Criminal Justice Act 2003 s 164; and CRIMINAL LAW, EVIDENCE AND PROCEDURE vol 11(4) (2006 Reissue) para 1678; MAGISTRATES vol 29(2) (Reissue) para 807.

(ii) The Commission's Duties

316.   Equality and diversity. As from a day to be appointed, the following provisions have effect[1]. The Commission for Equality and Human Rights[2] must, by exercising the relevant powers[3]: (1) promote understanding of the importance of equality[4] and diversity[5]; (2) encourage good practice in relation to equality and diversity[6]; (3) promote equality of opportunity[7]; (4) promote awareness and understanding of rights under the equality enactments[8]; (5) enforce the equality enactments[9]; (6) work towards the elimination of unlawful[10] discrimination[11]; and (6) work towards the elimination of unlawful harassment[12].

In promoting equality of opportunity between disabled persons[13] and others, the Commission may, in particular, promote the favourable treatment of disabled persons[14].

1   The Equality Act 2006 s 8 is to be brought into force as from a day to be appointed by order made by the Secretary of State under s 93. At the date at which this volume states the law no such day had been appointed. As to the Secretary of State and the National Assembly for Wales see para 302 ante.
2   As to the Commission for Equality and Human Rights, its establishment and constitution see para 305 ante.
3   Ie the powers under the Equality Act 2006 Pt 1 (ss 1–43) (as amended).
4   For these purposes, 'equality' means equality between individuals: ibid s 8(2) (not yet in force: see note 1 supra).
5   Ibid s 8(1)(a) (not yet in force: see note 1 supra). For these purposes, 'diversity' means the fact that individuals are different: s 8(2) (not yet in force: see note 1 supra).
6   Ibid s 8(1)(b) (not yet in force: see note 1 supra).
7   Ibid s 8(1)(c) (not yet in force: see note 1 supra).
8   Ibid s 8(1)(d) (not yet in force: see note 1 supra). The 'equality enactments' means: (1) the Equal Pay Act 1970 (see para 419 et seq post); (2) the Sex Discrimination Act 1975 (see para 337 et seq post); (3) the Race Relations Act 1976 (see para 436 et seq post); (4) the Disability Discrimination Act 1995 (see para 507 et seq post); (5) the Equality Act 2006 Pt 2 (ss 44–80) (see para 691 et seq post); (6) regulations under Pt 3 (ss 81–82) (see para 753 post); (7) the Employment Equality (Sexual Orientation) Regulations 2003, SI 2003/1661 (as amended) (see para 722 et seq post); (8) the Employment Equality (Religion or Belief) Regulations 2003, SI 2003/1660 (as amended) (see para 660 et seq post); and (9) the Employment Equality (Age) Regulations 2006, SI 2006/1031 (see para 754 et seq post): Equality Act 2006 s 33(1) (amended by the Employment Equality (Age) Regulations 2006, SI 2006/1031, reg 49(1), Sch 8 paras 37, 40). The Secretary of State may by order amend the list in the Equality Act s 33(1) (as amended) so as to add an entry, remove an entry, or vary an entry: s 33(3). At the date at which this volume states the law no such order has been made. As to orders and regulations under Pt 1 (as amended) generally see para 305 note 2 ante.
9   Ibid s 8(1)(e) (not yet in force: see note 1 supra).

10   Except in ibid s 30(3) (not yet in force) (see para 335 post), 'unlawful' means contrary to a provision of
     the equality enactments: ss 8(2), 34(1) (s 8(2) not yet in force: see note 1 supra). However action is not
     unlawful for these purposes by reason only of the fact that it contravenes a duty under or by virtue of: (1)
     the Sex Discrimination Act 1975 s 76A (as added) or s 76B (as added) (public authorities: duty to
     eliminate discrimination, etc) (see paras 343 post); (2) the Race Relations Act 1976 s 71 (as substituted)
     (public authorities: duty to eliminate discrimination, etc) (see para 469 post); or (3) any of the Disability
     Discrimination Act 1995 Pt V (ss 32–49) (as amended; prospectively amended) (public transport) (see
     para 627 et seq post), s 49A (as added), s 49D (as added; prospectively amended) (public authorities) (see
     para 591 post), and s 49G (as added) (consent to tenant's improvements) (see para 611 post): Equality
     Act 2006 ss 8(2), 34(2) (s 8(2) not yet in force: see note 1 supra).
11   Ibid s 8(1)(f) (not yet in force: see note 1 supra).
12   Ibid s 8(1)(g) (not yet in force: see note 1 supra).
13   For the meaning of 'disabled person' see para 305 note 9 ante.
14   Equality Act 2006 s 8(3) (not yet in force: see note 1 supra).

317. Human rights. As from a day to be appointed, the following provisions have
effect[1]. The Commission for Equality and Human Rights[2] must, by exercising the
relevant powers[3]: (1) promote understanding of the importance of human rights[4]; (2)
encourage good practice in relation to human rights[5]; (3) promote awareness,
understanding and protection of human rights[6]; and (4) encourage public authorities to
comply with Convention rights[7].

   In determining what action to take[8] the Commission must have particular regard to
the importance of exercising the relevant powers[9] in relation to the Convention rights[10].
In fulfilling a duty under the provisions relating to equality and diversity[11] and to
groups[12] the Commission must take account of any relevant human rights[13].

1   The Equality Act 2006 ss 7, 9 are to be brought into force as from a day to be appointed by order made
    by the Secretary of State under s 93. At the date at which this volume states the law no such day had been
    appointed. As to the Secretary of State and the National Assembly for Wales see para 302 ante.
2   As to the Commission for Equality and Human Rights, its establishment and constitution see para 305
    ante.
3   Ie the powers conferred by the Equality Act 2006 Pt 1 (ss 1–43) (as amended).
4   Ibid s 9(1)(a) (not yet in force: see note 1 supra). 'Human rights' means: (1) the Convention rights within
    the meaning given by the Human Rights Act 1998 s 1 (as amended) (see para 303 ante); and (2) other
    human rights: Equality Act 2006 ss 9(2), 35 (s 9(2) not yet in force: see note 1 supra).
5   Ibid s 9(1)(b) (not yet in force: see note 1 supra).
6   Ibid s 9(1)(c) (not yet in force: see note 1 supra).
7   Ibid s 9(1)(d) (not yet in force: see note 1 supra). The reference in the text is to compliance with the
    Human Rights Act 1998 s 6 (prospectively amended): see CONSTITUTIONAL LAW AND HUMAN
    RIGHTS.
8   Ie in pursuance of the Equality Act 2006 s 9 (not yet in force).
9   See note 3 supra.
10 Equality Act 2006 s 9(3) (not yet in force: see note 1 supra). See note 13 infra.
11 Ie under ibid s 8 (not yet in force): see para 316 ante.
12 Ie under ibid s 10 (not yet in force): see para 318 post.
13 Ibid s 9(4) (not yet in force: see note 1 supra). A reference in Pt 1 (including s 9 (not yet in force)) to
    human rights does not exclude any matter by reason only of its being a matter to which s 8 (not yet in
    force) (see para 316 ante) or s 10 (not yet in force) (see para 318 post) relates: s 9(5) (not yet in force: see
    note 1 supra).
        The Commission must not take human rights action in relation to a matter if the Scottish Parliament
    has legislative competence to enable a person to take action of that kind in relation to that matter: s 7(1)
    (not yet in force: see note 1 supra). For these purposes, 'human rights action' means action taken: (1) in
    accordance with s 9(1) (not yet in force); and (2) under, by virtue of or in pursuance of s 11(1) (not yet
    in force) (see para 319 post) in so far as it relates to the Human Rights Act 1998, the Equality Act 2006
    s 11(2)(c) or (d) (not yet in force) (see para 319 post), s 12 (not yet in force) (see para 319 post), s 13 (not
    yet in force) (see para 320 post), s 16 (not yet in force) (see para 322 post), s 17 (not yet in force) (see
    para 324 post), or s 30 (not yet in force) (see para 335 post): s 7(2) (not yet in force: see note 1 supra).
    Despite s 9(4) (not yet in force), the Commission must not, in the course of fulfilling a duty under s 8
    (not yet in force) or s 10 (not yet in force), consider the question whether a person's human rights have
    been contravened if the Scottish Parliament has legislative competence to enable a person to consider that
    question: s 7(3) (not yet in force: see note 1 supra). Section 7(1), (3) (not yet in force) does not prevent

the Commission from taking action with the consent (whether general or specific) of a person if: (a) the person is established by Act of the Scottish Parliament; and (b) the person's principal duties relate to human rights and are similar to any of the Commission's duties under s 9 (not yet in force): s 7(4) (not yet in force: see note 1 supra). Section 7(1), (3) (not yet in force) does not prevent the Commission from relying on s 13(1)(f) (not yet in force) (see para 320 post) so as to act jointly or co-operate (but not assist) for a purpose relating to human rights and connected with Scotland: s 7(5) (not yet in force: see note 1 supra). Scottish matters generally are beyond the scope of this work.

318.   Groups.   As from a day to be appointed, the following provisions have effect[1]. The Commission for Equality and Human Rights[2] must, by exercising the relevant powers[3]: (1) promote understanding of the importance of good relations between members of different groups[4], and between members of groups and others[5]; (2) encourage good practice in relation to relations between members of different groups, and between members of groups and others[6]; (3) work towards the elimination of prejudice against, hatred of and hostility towards members of groups[7]; and (4) work towards enabling members of groups to participate in society[8].

In determining what action to take[9] the Commission must have particular regard to the importance of exercising the relevant powers[10] in relation to groups defined by reference to race, religion or belief[11].

The Commission may, in taking action[12] in respect of groups defined by reference to disability and others, promote or encourage the favourable treatment of disabled persons[13].

1   The Equality Act 2006 s 10 is to be brought into force as from a day to be appointed by order made by the Secretary of State under s 93. At the date at which this volume states the law no such day had been appointed. As to the Secretary of State and the National Assembly for Wales see para 302 ante.
2   As to the Commission for Equality and Human Rights, its establishment and constitution see para 305 ante.
3   Ie the powers conferred by the Equality Act 2006 Pt 1 (ss 1–43) (as amended).
4   'Group' means a group or class of persons who share a common attribute in respect of any of the following matters: (1) age; (2) disability; (3) gender; (4) proposed, commenced or completed reassignment of gender (within the meaning given by the Sex Discrimination Act 1975 s 82(1) (definition as substituted): see para 348 note 9 post); (5) race; (6) religion or belief; and (7) sexual orientation: Equality Act 2006 ss 10(2), 35 (s 10(2) not yet in force: see note 1 supra). For the purposes of Pt 1 (as amended), a reference to a group (as defined in s 10(2) (not yet in force)) includes a reference to a smaller group or smaller class, within a group, of persons who share a common attribute (in addition to the attribute by reference to which the group is defined) in respect of any of the matters specified in heads (1)–(7) supra: s 10(3) (not yet in force: see note 1 supra). The Secretary of State may by order amend the list in s 10(2) (not yet in force) so as to: (a) add an entry; or (b) vary an entry: s 10(6) (not yet in force: see note 1 supra). Section 10 (not yet in force) is without prejudice to the generality of s 8 (not yet in force) (see para 316 ante): s 10(7) (not yet in force: see note 1 supra). As to orders and regulations under Pt 1 (as amended) generally see para 305 note 2 ante.
5   Ibid s 10(1)(a) (not yet in force: see note 1 supra).
6   Ibid s 10(1)(b) (not yet in force: see note 1 supra).
7   Ibid s 10(1)(c) (not yet in force: see note 1 supra).
8   Ibid s 10(1)(d) (not yet in force: see note 1 supra).
9   Ie in pursuance of ibid s 10 (not yet in force).
10   Ie the powers conferred by Pt 1 (as amended).
11   Ibid s 10(4) (not yet in force: see note 1 supra).
12   Ie action in pursuance of ibid s 10(1) (not yet in force): see the text and notes 1–8 supra.
13   Ibid s 10(5) (not yet in force: see note 1 supra). For the meaning of 'disabled person' see para 305 note 9 ante.

319.   Monitoring the law and other matters.   As from a day to be appointed, the following provisions have effect[1]. The Commission for Equality and Human Rights[2] must monitor the effectiveness of the equality and human rights enactments[3].

The Commission may: (1) advise central government[4] about the effectiveness of any of the equality and human rights enactments[5]; (2) recommend to central government the amendment, repeal, consolidation (with or without amendments) or replication (with or without amendments) of any of the equality and human rights enactments[6]; (3) advise central or devolved government[7] about the effect of an enactment (including an enactment in or under an Act of the Scottish Parliament)[8]; (4) advise central or devolved government about the likely effect of a proposed change of law[9].

The Commission must from time to time identify: (a) changes in society that have occurred or are expected to occur and are relevant to the aim specified in the Commission's general duty[10]; (b) results at which to aim for the purpose of encouraging and supporting the development of the society as described in that general duty ('outcomes')[11]; and (c) factors by reference to which progress towards those results may be measured ('indicators')[12]. In identifying outcomes and indicators the Commission must: (i) consult such persons having knowledge or experience relevant to the Commission's functions as the Commission thinks appropriate[13]; (ii) consult such other persons as the Commission thinks appropriate[14]; (iii) issue a general invitation to make representations, in a manner likely in the Commission's opinion to bring the invitation to the attention of as large a class of persons who may wish to make representations as is reasonably practicable[15]; and (iv) take account of any representations made[16].

The Commission must from time to time monitor progress towards each identified outcome by reference to any relevant identified indicator[17]. The Commission must publish a report on such progress towards the identified outcomes by reference to the identified indicators: (A) within a period of three years[18]; and (B) within each period of three years beginning with the date on which a report is so published[19]. The Commission must send each report to the Secretary of State, who must lay a copy before Parliament[20].

1　The Equality Act 2006 ss 11, 12 are to be brought into force by order made by the Secretary of State under s 93 as from a day to be appointed. At the date at which this volume states the law no such day had been appointed. As to the Secretary of State and the National Assembly for Wales see para 302 ante.

2　As to the Commission for Equality and Human Rights, its establishment and constitution see para 305 ante.

3　Equality Act 2006 s 11(1) (not yet in force: see note 1 supra). 'Equality and human rights enactments' means the equality enactments (see para 316 note 8 ante) and the Human Rights Act 1998 (see para 303 ante): Equality Act 2006 s 33(2). A reference to the equality enactments includes a reference to any provision of the Equality Act 2006: s 11(3)(c) (not yet in force: see note 1 supra).

4　For these purposes, 'central government' means Her Majesty's government: ibid s 11(3)(a) (not yet in force: see note 1 supra).

5　Ibid s 11(2)(a) (not yet in force: see note 1 supra).

6　Ibid s 11(2)(b) (not yet in force: see note 1 supra).

7　For these purposes, 'devolved government' means the Scottish Ministers, and the National Assembly for Wales: ibid s 11(3)(b) (not yet in force: see note 1 supra). Scottish matters generally are beyond the scope of this work.

8　Ibid s 11(2)(c) (not yet in force: see note 1 supra). See note 7 supra.

9　Ibid s 11(2)(d) (not yet in force: see note 1 supra).

10　Ibid s 12(1)(a) (not yet in force: see note 1 supra). As to the Commission's general duty see s 3; and para 313 ante.

11　Ibid s 12(1)(b) (not yet in force: see note 1 supra).

12　Ibid s 12(1)(c) (not yet in force: see note 1 supra).

13　Ibid s 12(2)(a) (not yet in force: see note 1 supra).

14　Ibid s 12(2)(b) (not yet in force: see note 1 supra).

15　Ibid s 12(2)(c) (not yet in force: see note 1 supra).

16　Ibid s 12(2)(d) (not yet in force: see note 1 supra).

17　Ibid s 12(3) (not yet in force: see note 1 supra).

18　Ibid s 12(4)(a) (not yet in force: see note 1 supra). The period of three years begins with the date on which s 12 comes into force.

19　Ibid s 12(4)(b) (not yet in force: see note 1 supra).

20　Ibid s 12(5) (not yet in force: see note 1 supra).

(iii) The Commission's General Powers

320. Information, advice etc. As from a day to be appointed, the following provisions have effect[1]. In pursuance of its duties in regard to equality and diversity, to human rights and to groups[2], the Commission for Equality and Human Rights[3] may: (1) publish or otherwise disseminate ideas or information[4]; (2) undertake research[5]; (3) provide education or training[6]; (4) give advice or guidance (whether about the effect or operation of an enactment or otherwise)[7]; (5) arrange for a person to do anything within heads (1) to (4) above[8]; (6) act jointly with, co-operate with or assist a person doing anything within heads (1) to (4) above[9].

1 The Equality Act 2006 s 13 is to be brought into force as from a day to be appointed by order made by the Secretary of State under s 93. At the date at which this volume states the law no such day had been appointed. As to the Secretary of State and the National Assembly for Wales see para 302 ante.
2 Ie its duties under ibid ss 8–10 (not yet in force): see paras 316–318 ante.
3 As to the Commission for Equality and Human Rights, its establishment and constitution see para 305 ante.
4 Equality Act 2006 s 13(1)(a) (not yet in force: see note 1 supra).
5 Ibid s 13(1)(b) (not yet in force: see note 1 supra).
6 Ibid s 13(1)(c) (not yet in force: see note 1 supra).
7 Ibid s 13(1)(d) (not yet in force: see note 1 supra). This reference to giving advice does not include a reference to preparing, or assisting in the preparation of, a document to be used for the purpose of legal proceedings: s 13(2) (not yet in force: see note 1 supra).
8 Ibid s 13(1)(e) (not yet in force: see note 1 supra).
9 Ibid s 13(1)(f) (not yet in force: see note 1 supra).

321. Codes of practice. As from a day to be appointed, the following provisions have effect[1]. The Commission for Equality and Human Rights[2] may issue a code of practice in connection with a matter addressed by any of certain listed pieces of legislation[3]. Such a code of practice must contain provision designed to ensure or facilitate compliance with a provision or enactment listed, or to promote equality of opportunity[4].

The Commission may issue a code of practice giving practical guidance to landlords and tenants[5] about: (1) circumstances in which a tenant requires the consent of his landlord to make a relevant improvement[6] to a dwelling house[7]; (2) reasonableness in relation to that consent[8]; and (3) the application in relation to relevant improvements to dwelling houses of certain statutory provisions[9].

The Commission must comply with a direction of the Secretary of State to issue a code[10] in connection with a specified matter if the matter is not listed[11], but the Secretary of State expects to add it by order[12].

Before issuing a code of practice as above the Commission must publish proposals, and consult such persons as it thinks appropriate[13]. Before issuing such a code the Commission must also submit a draft to the Secretary of State, who must: (a) if he approves the draft, notify the Commission, and lay a copy before Parliament[14]; or (b) otherwise, give the Commission written reasons why he does not approve the draft[15].

The Commission may revise a code of practice[16], and a code may be revoked by the Secretary of State, at the request of the Commission, by order[17].

A failure to comply with a provision of a code does not of itself make a person liable to criminal or civil proceedings, but a code: (i) is admissible in evidence in criminal or civil proceedings[18]; and (ii) is taken into account by a court or tribunal in any case in which it appears to the court or tribunal to be relevant[19].

1 The Equality Act 2006 ss 14, 15 (s 14 as amended) are to be brought into force by order made by the Secretary of State under s 93 as from a day to be appointed. At the date at which this volume states the law no such day had been appointed. As to the Secretary of State and the National Assembly for Wales see para 302 ante.

2   As to the Commission for Equality and Human Rights, its establishment and constitution see para 305 ante.

3   Equality Act 2006 s 14(1) (not yet in force: see note 1 supra).
     The legislation referred to in the text is as follows: (1) the Equal Pay Act 1970 (see para 419 et seq post); (2) the Sex Discrimination Act 1975 Pts II–IV (ss 6A–42) (as amended) (see para 361 et seq post), s 76A (as added) or an order under s 76B (as added) (see para 343 post); (3) the Race Relations Act 1976 Pts II–IV (ss 4A–33) (as amended) (see para 446 et seq post), s 71 (as substituted) (see para 469 post); (4) the Disability Discrimination Act 1995 Pts II–IV (ss 3A–31C) (as amended) (see para 525 et seq post), Pt VA (ss 49A–49F) (as amended; prospectively amended) (see paras 591–592 post) except for ss 28D–28E (as added and amended) (see para 564 post); (5) the Equality Act 2006 Pt 2 (ss 44–80) (see para 691 et seq post); (6) regulations under Pt 3 (ss 81–82) (see para 753 post); (7) the Employment Equality (Sexual Orientation) Regulations 2003, SI 2003/1661, Pts II–III (regs 6–23) (as amended) (see para 725 et seq post); (8) the Employment Equality (Religion or Belief) Regulations 2003, SI 2003/1660, Pts II–III (regs 6–23) (as amended) (see para 663 et seq post); and (9) the Employment Equality (Age) Regulations 2006, SI 2006/1031, Pts 2–3 (regs 7–24) (see para 758 et seq post): see the Equality Act 2006 s 14(1) (amended by the Employment Equality (Age) Regulations 2006, SI 2006/1031, reg 49(1), Sch 8 paras 37, 38) (not yet in force: see note 1 supra).

4   Equality Act 2006 s 14(2) (not yet in force: see note 1 supra).

5   Ibid s 14(3) (not yet in force) applies in relation to landlords in England and Wales. For the meanings of 'England' and 'Wales' see para 325 note 6 post. There are also corresponding provisions under which the Commission may issue a code of practice giving practical guidance to landlords and tenants of houses in Scotland about similar matters: see s 14(4) (not yet in force: see note 1 supra). Scottish matters generally are beyond the scope of this work.

6   Ie within the meaning of the Disability Discrimination Act 1995 s 49G(7) (as added): see para 611 post.

7   Equality Act 2006 s 14(3)(a) (not yet in force: see note 1 supra).

8   Ibid s 14(3)(b) (not yet in force: see note 1 supra).

9   Ibid s 14(3)(c) (not yet in force: see note 1 supra). The statutory provisions referred to in the text are: (1) the Landlord and Tenant Act 1927 s 19(2) (consent to improvements) (see LANDLORD AND TENANT vol 27(1) (2006 Reissue) para 470); (2) the Housing Act 1980 ss 81–85 (as amended) (tenant's improvements) (see LANDLORD AND TENANT vol 27(2) (2006 Reissue) para 838); (3) the Housing Act 1985 ss 97–99 (tenant's improvements) (see LANDLORD AND TENANT vol 27(2) (2006 Reissue) para 1330); and (4) the Disability Discrimination Act 1995 s 49G (as added) (see para 611 post): see the Equality Act 2006 s 14(3)(c) (not yet in force: see note 1 supra).

10   Ie under ibid s 14 (as amended).

11   Ibid s 14(5)(a) (not yet in force: see note 1 supra). The text refers to being listed under s 14(1) (not yet in force): see the text and note 3 supra.

12   Ibid s 14(5)(b) (not yet in force: see note 1 supra). The Secretary of State may by order amend s 14 (as amended; not yet in force) so as to vary the range of matters that codes of practice under s 14 (as amended; not yet in force) may address: s 15(6). As to orders and regulations under Pt 1 (ss 1–43) (as amended) generally see para 305 note 2 ante.

13   Ibid s 14(6) (not yet in force: see note 1 supra). See also s 42(4); and para 306 note 3 ante.

14   Ibid s 14(7)(a) (not yet in force: see note 1 supra). Where a draft is laid before Parliament under head (a) in the text, if neither House passes a resolution disapproving the draft within 40 days: (1) the Commission may issue the code in the form of the draft; and (2) it will come into force in accordance with provision made by the Secretary of State by order: s 14(8) (not yet in force: see note 1 supra). The 40-day period specified in s 14(8) (not yet in force): (a) begins with the date on which the draft is laid before both Houses (or, if laid before each House on a different date, with the later date); and (b) is taken not to include a period during which Parliament is prorogued or dissolved, or both Houses are adjourned for more than four days: s 15(2) (not yet in force: see note 1 supra).
     If, or in so far as, a code relates to a duty imposed by or under the Sex Discrimination Act 1975 s 76A (as added) or s 76B (as added) (see para 343 post), the Race Relations Act 1976 s 71 (as substituted) (see para 469 post) or the Disability Discrimination Act 1995 s 49A (as added) or s 49B (as added) (see para 591 post) (public authorities: general anti-discrimination duties), the Secretary of State must consult the Scottish Ministers and the National Assembly for Wales before: (i) approving a draft under the Equality Act 2006 s 14(7)(a) (not yet in force) (see head (a) in the text); or (ii) making an order under s 14(8)(b) (not yet in force) (see head (2) supra): s 14(9) (not yet in force: see note 1 supra). In relation to a code of practice under s 14(4) (not yet in force) (see note 5 supra), the Secretary of State must also consult the Scottish Ministers before: (A) approving a draft under s 14(7)(a) (not yet in force) (see head (a) in the text); or (B) making an order under s 14(8)(b) (not yet in force) (see head (2) supra): s 14(10) (not yet in force: see note 1 supra). See note 5 supra.

15   Ibid s 14(7)(b) (not yet in force: see note 1 supra).

16 Ibid s 15(1) (not yet in force: see note 1 supra). A reference in s 14 (as amended; not yet in force) or s 15 (not yet in force) to the issue of a code is treated as including a reference to the revision of a code: see s 15(1) (not yet in force: see note 1 supra).

17 Ibid s 15(3) (not yet in force: see note 1 supra).

18 Ibid s 15(4)(a) (not yet in force: see note 1 supra).

19 Ibid s 15(4)(b) (not yet in force: see note 1 supra). Section 15(4)(b) (not yet in force) does not apply in relation to a code issued under s 14(4) (not yet in force) (see note 5 supra): s 15(5) (not yet in force: see note 1 supra).

322. Inquiries. As from a day to be appointed, the following provisions have effect[1]. The Commission for Equality and Human Rights[2] may conduct an inquiry into a matter relating to any of the Commission's duties in regard to equality and diversity[3], to human rights[4] and to groups[5].

If in the course of an inquiry the Commission begins to suspect that a person may have committed an unlawful[6] act: (1) in continuing the inquiry the Commission must, so far as possible, avoid further consideration of whether or not the person has committed an unlawful act[7]; (2) the Commission may commence an investigation into that question[8]; (3) the Commission may use information or evidence acquired in the course of the inquiry for the purpose of the investigation[9]; and (4) the Commission must so far as possible ensure (whether by aborting or suspending the inquiry or otherwise) that any aspects of the inquiry which concern the person investigated, or may require his involvement, are not pursued while the investigation is in progress[10].

The report of an inquiry: (a) may not state (whether expressly or by necessary implication) that a specified or identifiable person has committed an unlawful act[11]; and (b) must not otherwise refer to the activities of a specified or identifiable person unless the Commission thinks that the reference will not harm the person, or is necessary in order for the report adequately to reflect the results of the inquiry[12].

Before settling a report of an inquiry which records findings which in the Commission's opinion are of an adverse nature and relate (whether expressly or by necessary implication) to a specified or identifiable person the Commission must: (i) send a draft of the report to the person[13]; (ii) specify a period of at least 28 days during which he may make written representations about the draft[14]; and (iii) consider any representations made[15].

1   The Equality Act 2006 s 16 is to be brought into force as from a day to be appointed by order made by the Secretary of State under s 93. At the date at which this volume states the law no such day had been appointed. As to the Secretary of State and the National Assembly for Wales see para 302 ante.

2   As to the Commission for Equality and Human Rights, its establishment and constitution see para 305 ante.

3   Ie the Commission's duty under the Equality Act 2006 s 8 (not yet in force): see para 316 ante.

4   Ie the Commission's duty under ibid s 9 (not yet in force): see para 317 ante.

5   Ibid s 16(1) (not yet in force: see note 1 supra). The reference to the Commission's duty in regard to groups is to its duty under s 10 (not yet in force): see para 318 ante.
    As to general provisions about inquiries see s 16(6), Sch 2 (not yet in force); and para 323 post.

6   For the meaning of 'unlawful' see para 316 note 10 ante.

7   Equality Act 2006 s 16(2)(a) (not yet in force: see note 1 supra).
    Section 16(2), (3) (not yet in force) does not prevent an inquiry from considering or reporting a matter relating to human rights (whether or not a necessary implication arises in relation to the equality enactments): s 16(4) (not yet in force: see note 1 supra). For the meaning of 'human rights' see para 317 note 4 ante. For the meaning of 'equality enactments' see para 316 note 8 ante.

8   Ibid s 16(2)(b) (not yet in force: see note 1 supra). The investigation is under s 20 (not yet in force): see para 327 post. See note 7 supra.

9   Ibid s 16(2)(c) (not yet in force: see note 1 supra). See note 7 supra.

10 Ibid s 16(2)(d) (not yet in force: see note 1 supra). See note 7 supra.

11 Ibid s 16(3)(a) (not yet in force: see note 1 supra). See note 7 supra.

12 Ibid s 16(3)(b) (not yet in force: see note 1 supra). See note 7 supra.

13 Ibid s 16(5)(a) (not yet in force: see note 1 supra).

14   Ibid s 16(5)(b) (not yet in force: see note 1 supra).

15   Ibid s 16(5)(c) (not yet in force: see note 1 supra).

323.   General provisions on inquiries, investigations and assessments.   As
from a day to be appointed, the following provisions have effect[1]. They apply to
inquiries[2], investigations[3] and assessments[4].

Before conducting an inquiry the Commission for Equality and Human Rights[5]
must: (1) publish the terms of reference of the inquiry in a manner that the Commission
thinks is likely to bring the inquiry to the attention of persons whom it concerns or
who are likely to be interested in it[6]; and (2) in particular, give notice of the terms of
reference to any persons specified in them[7]. Before conducting an investigation the
Commission must: (a) prepare terms of reference specifying the person to be investigated
and the nature of the unlawful act which the Commission suspects[8]; (b) give the person
to be investigated notice of the proposed terms of reference[9]; (c) give the person to be
investigated an opportunity to make representations about the proposed terms of
reference[10]; (d) consider any representations made[11]; and (e) publish the terms of
reference once settled[12]. Before conducting an assessment of a person's compliance with
a duty the Commission must: (i) prepare terms of reference[13]; (ii) give the person notice
of the proposed terms of reference[14]; (iii) give the person an opportunity to make
representations about the proposed terms of reference[15]; (iv) consider any representations
made[16]; and (v) publish the terms of reference once settled[17].

The Commission must make arrangements for giving persons an opportunity to
make representations in relation to inquiries, investigations and assessments[18]. The
Commission must consider representations made in relation to an inquiry, investigation
or assessment[19]. However the Commission may, where it thinks it appropriate, refuse to
consider representations made neither by nor on behalf of a person specified in the terms
of reference, or made on behalf of a person specified in the terms of reference by a
person who is neither a barrister, nor an advocate, nor a solicitor[20].

In the course of an inquiry, investigation or assessment the Commission may give a
notice to any person[21]. The recipient of such a notice may apply to a county court to
have the notice cancelled on the grounds that the requirement imposed by the notice is
unnecessary having regard to the purpose of the inquiry, investigation or assessment to
which the notice relates, or is otherwise unreasonable[22]. Where the Commission thinks
that a person has failed without reasonable excuse to comply with such a notice or is
likely to fail without reasonable excuse to comply with such a notice[23], it may apply to
a county court for an order requiring a person to take such steps as may be specified in
the order to comply with the notice[24].

A person commits an offence and is liable on summary conviction to a fine[25] if
without reasonable excuse he fails to comply with such a notice[26] or such an order[27],
falsifies anything provided or produced in accordance with such a notice or such an
order[28], or makes a false statement in giving oral evidence in accordance with such a
notice[29].

Where a person is given such a notice he must disregard it, and notify the
Commission that he is disregarding it, in so far as he thinks it would require him to
make certain specific intelligence-related disclosures[30]. Where in response to such a
notice[31] a person notifies the Commission as above[32] there are certain consequences[33].
Where the Commission receives information or documents from or relating to an
intelligence service[34] in response to such a notice, the Commission must store and use
the information or documents in accordance with any arrangements specified by the
Secretary of State[35]. The recipient of such a notice may apply to the High Court to have

the notice cancelled on the grounds that the requirement imposed by the notice is undesirable for reasons of national security, other than for the reason that it would require an intelligence-related disclosure[36].

The Commission must publish a report of its findings on an inquiry, investigation or assessment[37].

The Commission may make recommendations as part of a report[38] of an inquiry, investigation, or in respect of a matter arising in the course of an inquiry, investigation or assessment[39]. Such a recommendation may be addressed to any class of person[40]. A person to whom a recommendation in the report of an inquiry, investigation or assessment is addressed must have regard to it[41].

A court or tribunal may have regard to a finding of the report of an inquiry, investigation or assessment, but must not treat it as conclusive[42]. An inquiry, investigation or assessment may not question (whether expressly or by necessary implication) the findings of a court or tribunal[43].

An inquiry may not consider: (A) whether an intelligence service[44] has acted (or is acting) in a way which is incompatible with a person's human rights[45]; or (B) other matters concerning human rights in relation to an intelligence service[46].

1   The Equality Act 2006 ss 16(6), 20(5), 31(2), Sch 2 are to be brought into force by order made by the
    Secretary of State under s 93 as from a day to be appointed. At the date at which this volume states the
    law no such day had been appointed. As to the Secretary of State and the National Assembly for Wales see
    para 302 ante.
2   Ie inquiries under ibid s 16 (not yet in force): see para 322 ante.
3   Ie investigations under ibid s 20 (not yet in force): see para 327 post.
4   See ibid Sch 2 para 1 (not yet in force: see note 1 supra). The reference to assessments is to assessments
    under ibid s 31 (not yet in force): see para 336 post.
5   As to the Commission for Equality and Human Rights, its establishment and constitution see para 305
    ante.
6   Ibid Sch 2 para 2(a) (not yet in force: see note 1 supra). Schedule 2 paras 2–4 (not yet in force) apply in
    relation to revised terms of reference as they apply in relation to original terms of reference: Sch 2 para 5
    (not yet in force: see note 1 supra).
7   Ibid Sch 2 para 2(b) (not yet in force: see note 1 supra). See note 6 supra.
8   Ibid Sch 2 para 3(a) (not yet in force: see note 1 supra). See note 6 supra.
9   Ibid Sch 2 para 3(b) (not yet in force: see note 1 supra). See note 6 supra.
10 Ibid Sch 2 para 3(c) (not yet in force: see note 1 supra). See note 6 supra.
11 Ibid Sch 2 para 3(d) (not yet in force: see note 1 supra). See note 6 supra.
12 Ibid Sch 2 para 3(e) (not yet in force: see note 1 supra). See note 6 supra.
13 Ibid Sch 2 para 4(a) (not yet in force: see note 1 supra). See note 6 supra.
14 Ibid Sch 2 para 4(b) (not yet in force: see note 1 supra). See note 6 supra.
15 Ibid Sch 2 para 4(c) (not yet in force: see note 1 supra). See note 6 supra.
16 Ibid Sch 2 para 4(d) (not yet in force: see note 1 supra). See note 6 supra.
17 Ibid Sch 2 para 4(e) (not yet in force: see note 1 supra). See note 6 supra.
18 Ibid Sch 2 para 6(1) (not yet in force: see note 1 supra). In particular, in the course of an investigation,
    inquiry or assessment the Commission must give any person specified in the terms of reference an
    opportunity to make representations: Sch 2 para 6(2) (not yet in force: see note 1 supra). Arrangements
    under Sch 1 para 6 (not yet in force) may (but need not) include arrangements for oral representations:
    Sch 1 para 7 (not yet in force: see note 1 supra).
19 Ibid Sch 2 para 8(1) (not yet in force: see note 1 supra).
20 Ibid Sch 2 para 8(2) (not yet in force: see note 1 supra). If the Commission refuses to consider
    representations in reliance on Sch 2 para 8(2) (not yet in force) it must give the person who makes them
    written notice of the Commission's decision and the reasons for it: Sch 2 para 8(3) (not yet in force: see
    note 1 supra).
21 Ibid Sch 2 para 9 (not yet in force: see note 1 supra). A notice given to a person under Sch 2 para 9 (not
    yet in force) may require him: (1) to provide information in his possession; (2) to produce documents in
    his possession; or (3) to give oral evidence: Sch 2 para 10(1) (not yet in force: see note 1 supra). Such a
    notice may include provision about: (a) the form of information, documents or evidence; (b) timing:
    Sch 2 para 10(2) (not yet in force: see note 1 supra). Such a notice: (i) may not require a person to
    provide information that he is prohibited from disclosing by virtue of an enactment; (ii) may not require
    a person to do anything that he could not be compelled to do in proceedings before the High Court; and

(iii) may not require a person to attend at a place unless the Commission undertakes to pay the expenses of his journey: Sch 2 para 10(3) (not yet in force: see note 1 supra).

22 Ibid Sch 2 para 11 (not yet in force: see note 1 supra).

23 Ibid Sch 2 para 12(1) (not yet in force: see note 1 supra).

24 Ibid Sch 2 para 12(2) (not yet in force: see note 1 supra).

25 Ie a fine not exceeding level 5 on the standard scale: see ibid Sch 2 para 13(2) (not yet in force: see note 1 supra). As to the standard scale see para 315 note 15 ante.

26 Ie a notice under ibid Sch 2 para 9 (not yet in force) (see the text and note 21 supra).

27 Ibid Sch 2 para 13(1)(a) (not yet in force: see note 1 supra). The text refers to an order under Sch 2 para 12(2) (not yet in force) (see the text and note 24 supra).

28 Ibid Sch 2 para 13(1)(b) (not yet in force: see note 1 supra).

29 Ibid Sch 2 para 13(1)(c) (not yet in force: see note 1 supra).

30 Ibid Sch 2 para 14(1) (not yet in force: see note 1 supra).
    The disclosures referred to in the text are as follows: (1) disclosure of sensitive information within the meaning of the Intelligence Services Act 1994 Sch 3 para 4 (Intelligence and Security Committee) (see CONSTITUTIONAL LAW AND HUMAN RIGHTS vol 8(2) (Reissue) para 475); (2) disclosure of information which might lead to the identification of an employee or agent of an intelligence service (other than one whose identity is already known to the Commission); (3) disclosure of information which might provide details of processes used in recruiting, selecting or training employees or agents of an intelligence service; (4) disclosure of information which might provide details of, or cannot practicably be separated from, information falling within any of heads (1)–(3) supra; or (5) disclosure of information relating to an intelligence service which would prejudice the interests of national security: Equality Act Sch 2 para 14(1) (not yet in force: see note 1 supra). For these purposes, 'intelligence service' means: (a) the Security Service; (b) the Secret Intelligence Service; and (c) the Government Communications Headquarters: Sch 2 para 14(2) (not yet in force: see note 1 supra). As to the security and intelligence services generally see CONSTITUTIONAL LAW AND HUMAN RIGHTS vol 8(2) (Reissue) para 473 et seq.

31 Ie a notice under Sch 1 para 9 (not yet in force) (see the text and note 24 supra).

32 Ie where a person gives a notice under ibid Sch 2 para 14(1) (not yet in force) (see the text and note 30 supra).

33 Ibid Sch 2 para 14(3) (not yet in force: see note 1 supra).
    The consequences are as follows: (1) Sch 1 paras 12, 13 (not in force) do not apply in relation to that part of the notice under Sch 1 para 9 (not yet in force) to which the notice under Sch 2 para 14(1) (not yet in force) relates; (2) the Commission may apply to the tribunal established by the Regulation of Investigatory Powers Act 2000 s 65 (as amended) (see CONSTITUTIONAL LAW AND HUMAN RIGHTS) for an order requiring the person to take such steps as may be specified in the order to comply with the notice; (3) the Regulation of Investigatory Powers Act 2000 s 67(7), (8), (10)–(12) (determination), s 68 (as amended) (procedure), and s 69 (rules) (see CONSTITUTIONAL LAW AND HUMAN RIGHTS) apply in relation to proceedings under the Equality Act 2006 Sch 2 para 14 (not yet in force) as they apply in relation to proceedings under the Regulation of Investigatory Powers Act 2000 (with any necessary modifications); and (4) the tribunal must determine proceedings under the Equality Act 2006 Sch 2 para 14 (not yet in force) by considering the opinion of the person who gave the notice under Sch 2 para 14(1) (not yet in force) in accordance with the principles that would be applied by a court on an application for judicial review of the giving of the notice: Sch 2 para 14(3) (not yet in force: see note 1 supra).

34 For the meaning of 'intelligence service' in ibid Sch 2 para 14(1) (not yet in force) see note 30 supra.

35 Ibid Sch 2 para 14(4) (not yet in force: see note 1 supra).

36 Ibid Sch 2 para 14(5) (not yet in force: see note 1 supra). The disclosure referred to in the text is a disclosure of a kind to which Sch 2 para 14(1) (not yet in force) (see note 30 supra) applies.

37 Ibid Sch 2 para 15 (not yet in force: see note 1 supra).

38 Ie a report under ibid Sch 2 para 15 (not yet in force).

39 Ibid Sch 2 para 16(1) (not yet in force: see note 1 supra).

40 Ibid Sch 2 para 16(2) (not yet in force: see note 1 supra).

41 Ibid Sch 2 para 18 (not yet in force: see note 1 supra).

42 Ibid Sch 2 para 17(1) (not yet in force: see note 1 supra).

43 Ibid Sch 2 para 19 (not yet in force: see note 1 supra).

44 For these purposes, 'intelligence service' has the same meaning as in ibid Sch 1 para 14 (not yet in force) (see note 30 supra): Sch 2 para 20(2) (not yet in force: see note 1 supra).

45 Ibid Sch 2 para 20(1)(a) (not yet in force: see note 1 supra).

46 Ibid Sch 2 para 20(1)(b) (not yet in force: see note 1 supra). For the meaning of 'human rights' see para 317 note 4 ante.

324.   Grants.   As from a day to be appointed, the following provisions have effect[1]. In pursuance of any of its duties in regard to equality and diversity[2], to human rights[3] and to groups[4], the Commission for Equality and Human Rights[5] may make grants to another person[6]. Such a grant may be made subject to conditions (which may, in particular, include conditions as to repayment)[7].

A power[8] to co-operate with or assist a person may not be exercised by the provision of financial assistance otherwise than in accordance with these provisions[9].

1   The Equality Act 2006 s 17 is to be brought into force as from a day to be appointed by order made by the Secretary of State under s 93. At the date at which this volume states the law no such day had been appointed. As to the Secretary of State and the National Assembly for Wales see para 302 ante.
2   Ie its duty under ibid s 8 (not yet in force): see para 316 ante.
3   Ie its duty under ibid s 9 (not yet in force): see para 317 ante.
4   Ie its duty under ibid s 10 (not yet in force): see para 318 ante.
5   As to the Commission for Equality and Human Rights, its establishment and constitution see para 305 ante.
6   Equality Act 2006 s 17(1) (not yet in force: see note 1 supra).
7   Ibid s 17(2) (not yet in force: see note 1 supra).
8   Ie a power under ibid Pt 1 (ss 1–43) (as amended).
9   Ibid s 17(3) (not yet in force: see note 1 supra).

325.   Human rights.   As from a day to be appointed, the following provisions have effect[1]. In pursuance of its duties in regard to human rights[2] the Commission for Equality and Human Rights Commission[3] may[4] co-operate with persons interested in human rights[5] within the United Kingdom[6] or elsewhere[7].

1   The Equality Act 2006 s 18 is to be brought into force as from a day to be appointed by order made by the Secretary of State under s 93. At the date at which this volume states the law no such day had been appointed. As to the Secretary of State and the National Assembly for Wales see para 302 ante.
2   Ie its duties under ibid s 9 (not yet in force): see para 317 ante.
3   As to the Commission for Equality and Human Rights, its establishment and constitution see para 305 ante.
4   Ie without prejudice to the generality of ibid s 13 (not yet in force): see para 320 ante.
5   For the meaning of 'human rights' see para 317 note 4 ante.
6   'United Kingdom' means Great Britain and Northern Ireland: Interpretation Act 1978 s 5, Sch 1. 'Great Britain' means England, Scotland and Wales: Union with Scotland Act 1706, preamble art I; Interpretation Act 1978 s 22(1), Sch 2 para 5(a). Neither the Channel Islands nor the Isle of Man are within the United Kingdom. See further CONSTITUTIONAL LAW AND HUMAN RIGHTS vol 8(2) (Reissue) para 3. 'England' means, subject to any alteration of boundaries of local government areas, the area consisting of the counties established by the Local Government Act 1972 s 1 (see LOCAL GOVERNMENT vol 29(1) (Reissue) paras 5, 25), Greater London and the Isles of Scilly: Interpretation Act 1978 s 5, Sch 1. 'Wales' means the combined area of the counties which were created by the Local Government Act 1972 s 20 (as originally enacted) (see LOCAL GOVERNMENT vol 29(1) (Reissue) paras 5, 41), but subject to any alteration made under s 73 (as amended) (consequential alteration of boundary following alteration of watercourse) (see LOCAL GOVERNMENT vol 29(1) (Reissue) para 93): Interpretation Act 1978 Sch 1 (definition substituted by the Local Government (Wales) Act 1994 s 1(3), Sch 2 para 9). As to local government areas see LOCAL GOVERNMENT vol 29(1) (Reissue) para 23 et seq; and as to boundary changes see LOCAL GOVERNMENT vol 29(1) (Reissue) para 62 et seq. As to Greater London see LONDON GOVERNMENT vol 29(2) (Reissue) para 29.
7   Equality Act s 18 (not yet in force: see note 1 supra).

326.   Groups.   As from a day to be appointed, the following provisions have effect[1]. In pursuance of its duties in regard to groups[2] the Commission for Equality and Human Rights Commission[3] may do anything[4] specified below[5].

The Commission may make, co-operate with or assist in arrangements: (1) for the monitoring of kinds of crime affecting certain groups[6]; (2) designed to prevent or reduce crime within or affecting certain groups[7]; (3) for activities (whether social, recreational, sporting, civic, educational or otherwise) designed to involve members of groups[8].

1   The Equality Act 2006 s 19 is to be brought into force as from a day to be appointed by order made by the Secretary of State under s 93. At the date at which this volume states the law no such day had been appointed. As to the Secretary of State and the National Assembly for Wales see para 302 ante.
2   Ie its duties under ibid s 10 (not yet in force): see para 318 ante.
3   As to the Commission for Equality and Human Rights, its establishment and constitution see para 305 ante.
4   Ie without prejudice to the generality of ibid s 13 (not yet in force): see para 320 ante.
5   Ibid s 19(1) (not yet in force: see note 1 supra).
6   Ibid s 19(2)(a) (not yet in force: see note 1 supra). For the meaning of 'group' see para 318 note 4 ante.
7   Ibid s 19(2)(b) (not yet in force: see note 1 supra).
8   Ibid s 19(2)(c) (not yet in force: see note 1 supra).

(iv) The Commission's Enforcement Powers

327.   Investigations. As from a day to be appointed, the following provisions have effect[1]. The Commission for Equality and Human Rights[2] may investigate whether or not a person: (1) has committed an unlawful[3] act[4]; (2) has complied with a requirement imposed by an unlawful act notice[5]; or (3) has complied with an undertaking[6].

Before settling a report of an investigation recording a finding that a person has committed an unlawful act or has failed to comply with a requirement or undertaking the Commission must: (a) send a draft of the report to the person[7]; (b) specify a period of at least 28 days during which he may make written representations about the draft[8]; and (c) consider any representations made[9].

1   The Equality Act 2006 s 20 is to be brought into force as from a day to be appointed by order made by the Secretary of State under s 93. At the date at which this volume states the law no such day had been appointed. As to the Secretary of State and the National Assembly for Wales see para 302 ante.
2   As to the Commission for Equality and Human Rights, its establishment and constitution see para 305 ante.
3   For the meaning of 'unlawful' see para 316 note 10 ante.
4   Equality Act 2006 s 20(1)(a) (not yet in force: see note 1 supra). The Commission may conduct an investigation under s 20(1)(a) (not yet in force) only if it suspects that the person concerned may have committed an unlawful act: s 20(2) (not yet in force: see note 1 supra). A suspicion for these purposes may (but need not) be based on the results of, or a matter arising during the course of, an inquiry under s 16 (not yet in force) (see para 322 ante): s 20(3) (not yet in force: see note 1 supra).
    As to general provisions about investigations see s 20(5), Sch 2 (not yet in force); and para 323 ante.
5   Ibid s 20(1)(b) (not yet in force: see note 1 supra). The reference in the text is to an unlawful act notice under s 21 (not yet in force): see para 328 post.
6   Ibid s 20(1)(c) (not yet in force: see note 1 supra). The reference in the text is to an undertaking given under s 23 (not yet in force): see para 330 post.
7   Ibid s 20(4)(a) (not yet in force: see note 1 supra).
8   Ibid s 20(4)(b) (not yet in force: see note 1 supra).
9   Ibid s 20(4)(c) (not yet in force: see note 1 supra).

328.   Unlawful act notice. As from a day to be appointed, the following provisions have effect[1]. The Commission for Equality and Human Rights[2] may give a person a notice (an 'unlawful act notice') if: (1) he is or has been the subject of an investigation[3]; and (2) the Commission is satisfied that he has committed an unlawful[4] act[5].

Such a notice must specify the unlawful act[6], and the provision of the equality enactments[7] by virtue of which the act is unlawful[8]. A notice must also inform the recipient of the effect of certain statutory provisions[9]. A notice may: (a) require the person to whom the notice is given to prepare an action plan[10] for the purpose of avoiding repetition or continuation of the unlawful act[11]; (b) recommend action to be taken by the person for that purpose[12].

A person who is given a notice may, within the period of six weeks beginning with the day on which the notice is given, appeal to the appropriate court or tribunal[13] on the grounds: (i) that he has not committed the unlawful act specified in the notice[14]; or (ii) that a requirement for the preparation of an action plan imposed under head (a) above is unreasonable[15].

On such an appeal the court or tribunal may: (A) affirm a notice[16]; (B) annul a notice[17]; (C) vary a notice[18]; (D) affirm a requirement[19]; (E) annul a requirement[20]; (F) vary a requirement[21]; (G) make an order for costs or expenses[22].

1   The Equality Act 2006 s 21 is to be brought into force as from a day to be appointed by order made by the Secretary of State under s 93. At the date at which this volume states the law no such day had been appointed. As to the Secretary of State and the National Assembly for Wales see para 302 ante.
2   As to the Commission for Equality and Human Rights, its establishment and constitution see para 305 ante.
3   Equality Act 2006 s 21(1)(a) (not yet in force: see note 1 supra). The text refers to an investigation under s 20(1)(a) (not yet in force): see para 327 ante.
4   For the meaning of 'unlawful' see para 316 note 10 ante.
5   Equality Act 2006 s 21(1)(b) (not yet in force: see note 1 supra).
6   Ibid s 21(2)(a) (not yet in force: see note 1 supra).
7   For the meaning of 'equality enactments' see para 316 note 8 ante.
8   Equality Act 2006 s 21(2)(b) (not yet in force: see note 1 supra).
9   Ibid s 21(3) (not yet in force: see note 1 supra). The statutory provisions referred to in the text are s 21(5)–(7) (not yet in force) (see the text and notes 13–15 infra), s 20(1)(b) (not yet in force) (see para 327 ante), and s 24(1) (not yet in force) (see para 331 post): see s 21(3)(a)–(c) (not yet in force: see note 1 supra).
10   As to action plans see ibid s 22 (not yet in force); and para 329 post.
11   Ibid s 21(4)(a) (not yet in force: see note 1 supra).
12   Ibid s 21(4)(b) (not yet in force: see note 1 supra).
13   For these purposes, 'appropriate court or tribunal' means: (1) an employment tribunal, if a claim in respect of the alleged unlawful act could be made to it; or (2) a county court, if a claim in respect of the alleged unlawful act could be made to it: ibid s 21(7) (not yet in force: see note 1 supra).
14   Ibid s 21(5)(a) (not yet in force: see note 1 supra).
15   Ibid s 21(5)(b) (not yet in force: see note 1 supra).
16   Ibid s 21(6)(a) (not yet in force: see note 1 supra).
17   Ibid s 21(6)(b) (not yet in force: see note 1 supra).
18   Ibid s 21(6)(c) (not yet in force: see note 1 supra).
19   Ibid s 21(6)(d) (not yet in force: see note 1 supra).
20   Ibid s 21(6)(e) (not yet in force: see note 1 supra).
21   Ibid s 21(6)(f) (not yet in force: see note 1 supra).
22   Ibid s 21(6)(g) (not yet in force: see note 1 supra).

329.   Action plans.   As from a day to be appointed, the following provisions have effect[1]. Where a person has been given an unlawful act notice[2] which requires him[3] to prepare an action plan[4], the notice must specify a time by which the person must give the Commission for Equality and Human Rights[5] a first draft plan[6].

After receiving a first draft plan from a person the Commission must: (1) approve it[7]; or (2) give the person a notice which states that the draft is not adequate[8] and requires the person to give the Commission a revised draft by a specified time[9], and which may make recommendations about the content of the revised draft[10].

An action plan comes into force: (a) if the period of six weeks beginning with the date on which a first draft or revised draft is given to the Commission expires without the Commission giving a notice under head (2) above, or applying for an order under head (ii) below[11]; or (b) upon a court's declining to make an order under head (ii) below in relation to a revised draft of the plan[12].

The Commission may apply to a county court: (i) for an order requiring a person to give the Commission a first draft plan by a time specified in the order[13]; (ii) for an order requiring a person who has given the Commission a revised draft plan to prepare and give to the Commission a further revised draft plan by a time specified in the order, and in accordance with any directions about the plan's content specified in the order[14]; or

(iii) during the period of five years beginning with the date on which an action plan prepared by a person comes into force, for an order requiring the person to act in accordance with the action plan, or to take specified action for a similar purpose[15].

An action plan may be varied by agreement between the Commission and the person who prepared it[16].

A person commits an offence if without reasonable excuse he fails to comply with an order under heads (i) to (iii) above; and a person guilty of such an offence is liable on summary conviction to a fine[17].

1　The Equality Act 2006 s 22 is to be brought into force as from a day to be appointed by order made by the Secretary of State under s 93. At the date at which this volume states the law no such day had been appointed. As to the Secretary of State and the National Assembly for Wales see para 302 ante.
2　Ie a notice under ibid s 21 (not yet in force): see para 328 ante.
3　Ie under ibid s 21(4)(a) (not yet in force): see para 328 head (a) ante.
4　Ibid s 22(1) (not yet in force: see note 1 supra).
5　As to the Commission for Equality and Human Rights, its establishment and constitution see para 305 ante.
6　Equality Act 2006 s 22(2) (not yet in force: see note 1 supra).
7　Ibid s 22(3)(a) (not yet in force: see note 1 supra). Section 22(3) (not yet in force) applies in relation to a revised draft plan as it applies in relation to a first draft plan: s 22(4) (not yet in force: see note 1 supra).
　　Schedule 2 paras 10–14 (not yet in force) (see para 323 ante) apply (but omitting references to oral evidence) in relation to consideration by the Commission of the adequacy of a draft action plan as they apply in relation to the conduct of an inquiry: s 22(8) (not yet in force: see note 1 supra).
8　Ibid s 22(3)(b)(i) (not yet in force: see note 1 supra). See note 7 supra.
9　Ibid s 22(3)(b)(ii) (not yet in force: see note 1 supra). See note 7 supra.
10　Ibid s 22(3)(b)(iii) (not yet in force: see note 1 supra). See note 7 supra.
11　Ibid s 22(5)(a) (not yet in force: see note 1 supra).
12　Ibid s 22(5)(b) (not yet in force: see note 1 supra).
13　Ibid s 22(6)(a) (not yet in force: see note 1 supra).
14　Ibid s 22(6)(b) (not yet in force: see note 1 supra).
15　Ibid s 22(6)(c) (not yet in force: see note 1 supra).
16　Ibid s 22(7) (not yet in force: see note 1 supra).
17　Ibid s 22(8) (not yet in force: see note 1 supra). The fine is one not exceeding level 5 on the standard scale: see s 22(8) (not yet in force: see note 1 supra). As to the standard scale see para 315 note 15 ante.

330.　Agreements. As from a day to be appointed, the following provisions have effect[1]. The Commission for Equality and Human Rights[2] may enter into an agreement with a person under which: (1) the person undertakes not to commit an unlawful[3] act of a specified kind, and to take, or refrain from taking, other specified action (which may include the preparation of a plan for the purpose of avoiding an unlawful act)[4]; and (2) the Commission undertakes not to proceed against the person under the provisions on investigations[5] and unlawful act notices[6] in respect of any unlawful act of the kind specified under head (1) above[7].

The Commission may enter into such an agreement with a person only if it thinks that the person has committed an unlawful act[8]. However, a person is not to be taken to admit to the commission of an unlawful act by reason only of entering into such an agreement[9].

Such an agreement: (a) may be entered into whether or not the person is or has been the subject of an investigation[10]; (b) may include incidental or supplemental provision (which may include provision for termination in specified circumstances)[11]; and (c) may be varied or terminated by agreement of the parties[12].

1　The Equality Act 2006 s 23 is to be brought into force as from a day to be appointed by order made by the Secretary of State under s 93. At the date at which this volume states the law no such day had been appointed. As to the Secretary of State and the National Assembly for Wales see para 302 ante.
2　As to the Commission for Equality and Human Rights, its establishment and constitution see para 305 ante.

3   For the meaning of 'unlawful' see para 316 note 10 ante.

4   Equality Act 2006 s 23(1)(a) (not yet in force: see note 1 supra).
        Section 23 (not yet in force) applies in relation to the breach of a duty specified in s 34(2) (not yet in
     force) (see para 316 note 10 ante) as it applies in relation to the commission of an unlawful act; and for
     that purpose the reference in s 23(1)(b) (not yet in force) (see head (2) in the text) to s 20 (not yet in
     force) (see para 328 ante) or s 21 (not yet in force) (see para 329 ante) are to be taken as a reference to
     s 32 (not yet in force) (see para 336 post): s 23(5) (not yet in force: see note 1 supra).

5   Ie under ibid s 20 (not yet in force): see para 328 ante.

6   Ie under ibid s 21 (not yet in force): see para 329 ante.

7   Ibid s 23(1)(b) (not yet in force: see note 1 supra).

8   Ibid s 23(2) (not yet in force: see note 1 supra).

9   Ibid s 23(3) (not yet in force: see note 1 supra).

10   Ibid s 23(4)(a) (not yet in force: see note 1 supra). The investigation is under s 20 (not yet in force): see
     para 328 ante.

11   Ibid s 23(4)(b) (not yet in force: see note 1 supra).

12   Ibid s 23(4)(c) (not yet in force: see note 1 supra).

331.   Applications to court. As from a day to be appointed, the following
provisions have effect[1]. If the Commission for Equality and Human Rights[2] thinks that
a person is likely to commit an unlawful[3] act, it may apply to a county court for an
injunction restraining the person from committing the act[4].

If the Commission thinks that a party to an agreement[5] has failed to comply, or is
likely not to comply, with an undertaking under the agreement[6], the Commission may
apply to a county court for an order requiring the person: (1) to comply with his
undertaking[7]; and (2) to take such other action as the court may specify[8].

1   The Equality Act 2006 s 24 is to be brought into force as from a day to be appointed by order made by
     the Secretary of State under s 93. At the date at which this volume states the law no such day had been
     appointed. As to the Secretary of State and the National Assembly for Wales see para 302 ante.

2   As to the Commission for Equality and Human Rights, its establishment and constitution see para 305
     ante.

3   For the meaning of 'unlawful' see para 316 note 10 ante.

4   Equality Act 2006 s 24(1)(a) (not yet in force: see note 1 supra). As to applications in Scotland see
     s 24(1)(b) (not yet in force: see note 1 supra). Scottish matters generally are beyond the scope of this
     work.

5   Ie an agreement under ibid s 23 (not yet in force): see para 330 ante.

6   Ibid s 24(2) (not yet in force: see note 1 supra).

7   Ibid s 24(3)(a) (not yet in force: see note 1 supra).

8   Ibid s 24(3)(b) (not yet in force: see note 1 supra).

332.   Application to restrain unlawful advertising, pressure, etc. As from a day
to be appointed, the following provisions have effect[1]. In regard to an act which is
unlawful[2] under statutory provisions relating to discriminatory advertising[3], legal
proceedings may be brought[4] by the Commission for Equality and Human Rights[5]; and
may not be brought by anyone else[6].

Where the Commission thinks that a person has done such an unlawful act[7] the
Commission may: (1) present a complaint to an employment tribunal, where the act is
alleged to be unlawful by reference to certain statutory provisions[8]; or (2) in any other
case, apply to a county court[9]. On such a complaint or application, the tribunal or court
must determine whether the allegation is correct[10].

The Commission may apply to a county court[11] for an injunction restraining a
person from doing such an act[12] where: (a) either a tribunal or a court has determined[13]
that the person has done such an act, or the Commission thinks that the person has done
such an act[14]; and (b) the Commission thinks that if unrestrained the person is likely to
do another such act[15].

1   The Equality Act 2006 ss 25, 26 (s 25 as amended) are to be brought into force by order made by the Secretary of State under s 93 as from a day to be appointed. At the date at which this volume states the law no such day had been appointed. As to the Secretary of State and the National Assembly for Wales see para 302 ante.

2   For the meaning of 'unlawful' see para 316 note 10 ante.

3   Ie any of the following: the Sex Discrimination Act 1975 ss 38–40 (as amended) (see paras 388–390 post); the Race Relations Act 1976 ss 29–31 (as amended) (see paras 473–475 post); the Disability Discrimination Act 1995 ss 16B–16C (as added and amended) (see paras 537–538 post) and ss 28UB, 28UC (both as added and amended) (see para 569 post); the Equality Act 2005 ss 54–55 (see paras 699–700 post); and the Equality Act (Sexual Orientation) Regulations 2007, SI 2007/1263, regs 10, 11 (see para 753 post): s 25(1) (amended by the Disability Discrimination Act 1995 (Amendment) (Further and Higher Education) Regulations 2006, SI 2006/1721, regs 4(1), 22; and the Equality Act (Sexual Orientation) Regulations 2007, SI 2007/1263, reg 32) (not yet in force: see note 1 supra). The Equality Act 2006 s 25(1) (as amended; not yet in force) does not apply to an act which constitutes an offence: s 25(7) (not yet in force: see note 1 supra).

4   Ie in accordance with the Equality Act 2006 s 25 (as amended; not yet in force).

5   Ibid s 25(2)(a) (not yet in force: see note 1 supra). As to the Commission for Equality and Human Rights, its establishment and constitution see para 305 ante.

6   Ibid s 25(2)(b) (not yet in force: see note 1 supra).

7   Ie an unlawful act to which ibid s 25 (as amended; not yet in force) applies.

8   Ibid s 25(3)(a) (not yet in force: see note 1 supra). The statutory provisions referred to in the text are: (1) the Sex Discrimination Act 1975 Pt II (ss 6A–20A) (as amended) (see para 360 et seq post); (2) the Race Relations Act 1976 Pt II (ss 3A–15) (as amended) (see para 441 et seq post); (3) the Disability Discrimination Act 1995 Pt II (ss 3A–18E) (as amended; prospectively amended) (see para 529 et seq post); (4) Pt III (ss 19–28) (as amended; prospectively amended) (see para 582 et seq post) in so far as it relates to employment services; or (5) the Equality Act Pt 2 (ss 44–80) (see para 691 et seq post): see s 25(3)(a) (not yet in force: see note 1 supra).

    A complaint or application under s 25(3) (not yet in force) may be presented or made only: (a) within the period of six months beginning with the date (or last date) on which the alleged unlawful act occurred; or (b) with the permission of the tribunal, court or sheriff: s 26(1) (not yet in force: see note 1 supra).

9   Ibid s 25(3)(b) (not yet in force: see note 1 supra). See note 8 supra.

10 Ibid s 25(4) (not yet in force: see note 1 supra).

    A determination under s 25(4) (not yet in force) must not be relied upon by a county court or the sheriff in proceedings under s 25(5) or (6) (not yet in force) (see the text and notes 11–15 infra) while an appeal against the determination: (1) is pending; or (2) may be brought (disregarding the possibility of an appeal out of time with permission): s 26(2) (not yet in force: see note 1 supra).

11 As to applications in Scotland see ibid s 25(6) (not yet in force: see note 1 supra). Scottish matters generally are beyond the scope of this work.

12 Ie an act to which ibid s 25 (as amended; not yet in force) applies.

13 Ie under ibid s 25(4).

14 Ibid s 25(5)(a) (not yet in force: see note 1 supra). As to injunctions generally see INJUNCTIONS.

    An application under s 25(5) (not yet in force) or s 25(6) (not yet in force) (see note 11 supra) may be made only: (1) within the period of five years beginning with the date (or last date) on which the unlawful act referred to occurred; or (2) with the permission of the court: s 26(3) (not yet in force: see note 1 supra).

15 Ibid s 25(5)(b) (not yet in force: see note 1 supra). See note 14 supra.

333.   Conciliation. As from a day to be appointed, the following provisions have effect[1]. The Commission for Equality and Human Rights[2] may make arrangements for the provision of conciliation services[3] for disputes in respect of which proceedings have been or could be brought under or by virtue of certain statutory provisions[4].

The Commission may make arrangements for the provision of conciliation services for disputes about a landlord's reasonableness in relation to consent to the making of an improvement to a dwelling in England or Wales where the improvement would be likely to facilitate the enjoyment of the premises by the tenant or another lawful occupier having regard to a disability[5].

The Commission must aim to exercise the above powers[6] so as to ensure that, so far as is reasonably practicable, conciliation services are available to parties who want them[7]. Information communicated to a person providing conciliation services in accordance with the above arrangements[8] may not be adduced in legal proceedings without the consent of the person who communicated the information[9].

None of the following may participate in the provision of conciliation services[10]: (1) a Commissioner[11]; (2) a member of the Commission's staff[12]; (3) a member of a committee established by the Commission[13]; and (4) an Investigating Commissioner[14]. The Commission must make administrative arrangements designed to secure that information in connection with conciliation services provided in accordance with arrangements under these provisions[15] is not disclosed to a Commissioner, or a member of the Commission's staff[16].

1 The Equality Act 2006 s 27 (as amended) is to be brought into force as from a day to be appointed by order made by the Secretary of State under s 93. At the date at which this volume states the law no such day had been appointed. As to the Secretary of State and the National Assembly for Wales see para 302 ante.

2 As to the Commission for Equality and Human Rights, its establishment and constitution see para 305 ante.

3 For these purposes, 'conciliation services' means a service which is provided: (1) by a person who is not party to a dispute; (2) to the parties to the dispute; and (3) with the aim of enabling the dispute to be settled by agreement and without legal proceedings: Equality Act 2006 s 27(9) (not yet in force: see note 1 supra).

4 Ibid s 27(1) (not yet in force: see note 1 supra). The statutory provisions referred to in the text are as follows: (1) the Sex Discrimination Act 1975 s 66 (as amended) (see para 415 post); (2) the Race Relations Act 1976 s 57 (as amended) (see para 500 post); (3) the Disability Discrimination Act 1995 s 25 (as amended), ss 28I, 28V (both as added and amended) or s 31AE(1) (as added) (see paras 566, 575, 581, 644 post); (4) the Equality Act 2006 s 66 (see para 711 post); (5) a provision of regulations under Pt 3 (ss 81–82) (see para 753 post) corresponding to s 66; (6) the Employment Equality (Religion or Belief) Regulations 2003, SI 2003/1660, reg 31 (see para 685 post); (7) the Employment Equality (Sexual Orientation) Regulations 2003, SI 2003/1661, reg 31 (see para 747 post); or (8) the Employment Equality (Age) Regulations 2006, SI 2006/1031, reg 39 (as amended) (see para 809 post): Equality Act 2006 s 27(1) (amended by the Employment Equality (Age) Regulations 2006, SI 2006/1031, reg 49(1), Sch 8 paras 37, 39) (not yet in force: see note 1 supra).

   The Secretary of State may by order amend the Equality Act 2006 s 27 (as amended; not yet in force) so as to vary the range of disputes in respect of which the Commission may make arrangements for the provision of conciliation services: s 27(10) (not yet in force: see note 1 supra). As to orders and regulations under Pt 1 (ss 1–43) (as amended) generally see para 305 note 2 ante.

5 Ibid s 27(2) (not yet in force: see note 1 supra). See LANDLORD AND TENANT.

   As to conciliation services for such disputes in Scotland see s 27(3) (not yet in force: see note 1 supra). Scottish matters generally are beyond the scope of this work.

6 Ie the powers in ibid s 27(1)–(3) (as amended; not yet in force).

7 Ibid s 27(4) (not yet in force: see note 1 supra).

8 Ie arrangements under ibid s 27 (as amended; not yet in force).

9 Ibid s 27(5) (not yet in force: see note 1 supra).

10 Ie conciliation services for which arrangements are made under ibid s 27 (as amended; not yet in force).

11 Ibid s 27(6)(a) (not yet in force: see note 1 supra). As to the Commissioners see para 305 ante.

12 Ibid s 27(6)(b) (not yet in force: see note 1 supra). As to the Commission's staff see para 307 ante.

13 Ibid s 27(6)(c) (not yet in force: see note 1 supra). As to committees established by the Commission see para 308 ante.

14 Ibid s 27(6)(d) (not yet in force: see note 1 supra). As to Investigating Commissioners see para 307 ante.

15 Ie provided in accordance with arrangements made under ibid s 27 (as amended; not yet in force).

16 Ibid s 27(7) (not yet in force: see note 1 supra). However, s 27(7) (not yet in force) does not apply to a disclosure: (1) made with the consent of the parties to the dispute to which it relates; (2) which does not identify individuals or enable them to be identified; or (3) of information without which arrangements under s 27 (as amended) cannot be made: s 27(8) (not yet in force: see note 1 supra).

334. Legal assistance. As from a day to be appointed, the following provisions have effect[1]. The Commission for Equality and Human Rights[2] may assist an individual who is or may become party to legal proceedings[3] if: (1) the proceedings relate or may relate (wholly or partly) to a provision of the equality enactments[4]; and (2) the individual alleges that he has been the victim of behaviour contrary to a provision of the equality enactments[5]. The Commission may also assist an individual who is or may become party to legal proceedings if and in so far as the proceedings concern or may concern the question of a landlord's reasonableness in relation to consent to the making of an improvement to a dwelling where the improvement would be likely to facilitate the enjoyment of the premises by the tenant or another lawful occupier having regard to a disability[6].

In giving such assistance the Commission may provide or arrange for the provision of legal advice[7], legal representation[8], facilities for the settlement of a dispute[9], and any other form of assistance[10].

The above provisions[11] are without prejudice to the effect of any restriction imposed in respect of representation: (a) by virtue of an enactment[12]; or (b) in accordance with the practice of a court[13]. A legislative provision which requires insurance or an indemnity in respect of advice given in connection with a compromise contract or agreement does not apply to advice provided by the Commission under the above provisions[14].

Where the Commission has assisted an individual[15] in relation to proceedings[16] and the individual becomes entitled to some or all of his costs in the proceedings (whether by virtue of an award or by virtue of an agreement)[17], the Commission's expenses in providing the assistance: (i) must be charged on sums paid to the individual by way of costs[18]; and (ii) may be enforced as a debt due to the Commission[19].

1   The Equality Act 2006 ss 28, 29 are to be brought into force by order made by the Secretary of State under s 93 as from a day to be appointed. At the date at which this volume states the law no such day had been appointed. As to the Secretary of State and the National Assembly for Wales see para 302 ante.

2   As to the Commission for Equality and Human Rights, its establishment and constitution see para 305 ante.

3   As to legal proceedings see para 335 post.

4   Equality Act 2006 s 28(1)(a) (not yet in force: see note 1 supra). For the meaning of 'equality enactments' see para 316 note 8 ante.

    A reference in s 28 (not yet in force) to a provision of the equality enactments includes a reference to a provision of Community law which relates to discrimination on grounds of sex (including reassignment of gender), racial origin, ethnic origin, religion, belief, disability, age or sexual orientation, and confers rights on individuals: s 28(12) (not yet in force: see note 1 supra). In its application by virtue of s 28(12) (not yet in force), s 28(1)(b) (not yet in force) (see note 5 infra) has effect as if it referred to an allegation by an individual that he is disadvantaged by an enactment (including an enactment in or under an Act of the Scottish Parliament) which is contrary to a provision of Community law, or by a failure by the United Kingdom to implement a right as required by Community law: s 28(13) (not yet in force: see note 1 supra). For the meaning of 'United Kingdom' see para 325 note 6 ante. Scottish matters generally are beyond the scope of this work.

    Assistance may not be given under s 28(1) (not yet in force) in relation to alleged behaviour contrary to a provision of the Disability Discrimination Act 1995 Pt V (ss 32–49) (as amended) (public transport) (see para 617 et seq post): s 28(5) (not yet in force: see note 1 supra).

    Where proceedings relate or may relate partly to a provision of the equality enactments and partly to other matters: (1) assistance may be given under s 28(1) (not yet in force) in respect of any aspect of the proceedings while they relate to a provision of the equality enactments; but (2) if the proceedings cease to relate to a provision of the equality enactments, assistance may not be continued under s 28(1) (not yet in force) in respect of the proceedings (except in so far as it is permitted by virtue of s 28(7) or (8) (not yet in force)): s 28(6) (not yet in force: see note 1 supra). The Lord Chancellor may by order disapply head (2) supra, and enable the Commission to give assistance under s 28(1) (not yet in force), in respect of legal proceedings which: (a) when instituted, related (wholly or partly) to a provision of the equality enactments; (b) have ceased to relate to the provision of the equality enactments; and (c) relate (wholly or partly) to any of the Convention rights within the meaning given by the Human Rights Act 1998 s 1 (as amended) (see para 303 note 3 ante): Equality Act 2006 s 28(7) (not yet in force: see note 1 supra). The Secretary of State may by order enable the Commission to give assistance under s 28 (not yet in force) in respect of legal proceedings in the course of which an individual who is or has been a disabled person relies or proposes to rely on a matter relating to his disability; but such an order may not permit assistance in relation to alleged behaviour contrary to a provision of the Disability Discrimination Act 1995 Pt V (as amended): s 28(8) (not yet in force: see note 1 supra). An order under the Equality Act 2006 s 28(7) or (8) (not yet in force) may make provision generally or only in relation to proceedings of a specified kind or description (which in the case of an order under s 28(7) (not yet in force) may, in particular, refer to specified provisions of the equality enactments) or in relation to specified circumstances: s 28(9) (not yet in force: see note 1 supra). As to the Lord Chancellor see CONSTITUTIONAL LAW AND HUMAN RIGHTS vol 8(2) (Reissue) para 477 et seq. For the meaning of 'disabled person' see para 305 note 9 ante. As to orders and regulations under Pt 1 (ss 1–43) (as amended) generally see para 305 note 2 ante.

5   Ibid s 28(1)(b) (not yet in force: see note 1 supra). See note 4 supra.
6   Ibid s 28(2) (not yet in force: see note 1 supra). See LANDLORD AND TENANT.
        As to such assistance in Scotland see s 28(3) (not yet in force: see note 1 supra). Scottish matters generally are beyond the scope of this work.
7   Ibid s 28(4)(a) (not yet in force: see note 1 supra).
8   Ibid s 28(4)(b) (not yet in force: see note 1 supra).
9   Ibid s 28(4)(c) (not yet in force: see note 1 supra).
10   Ibid s 28(4)(d) (not yet in force: see note 1 supra).
11   Ie ibid s 28 (not yet in force).
12   Ibid s 28(10)(a) (not yet in force: see note 1 supra). The reference in the text to an enactment includes an enactment in or under an Act of the Scottish Parliament.
13   Ibid s 28(10)(b) (not yet in force: see note 1 supra).
14   Ibid s 28(11) (not yet in force: see note 1 supra).
15   Ie under ibid s 28 (not yet in force).
16   Ibid s 29(1)(a) (not yet in force: see note 1 supra). As to the application of s 29 (not yet in force) to Scotland see s 29(6) (not yet in force: see note 1 supra).
17   Ibid s 29(1)(b) (not yet in force: see note 1 supra).
18   Ibid s 29(2)(a) (not yet in force: see note 1 supra).
        A requirement to pay money to the Commission under s 29(2) (not yet in force) ranks after a requirement imposed by virtue of the Access to Justice Act 1999 s 11(4)(f) (recovery of costs in funded cases) (see COSTS vol 10 (Reissue) para 211): Equality Act 2006 s 29(3) (not yet in force: see note 1 supra). As to Scotland see s 29(4) (not yet in force: see note 1 supra).
        For the purposes of s 29(2) (not yet in force), the Commission's expenses are calculated in accordance with such provision (if any) as the Secretary of State makes for the purpose by regulations; and regulations may, in particular, provide for the apportionment of expenditure incurred by the Commission: (1) partly for one purpose and partly for another; or (2) for general purposes: s 29(5) (not yet in force: see note 1 supra).
19   Ibid s 29(2)(b) (not yet in force: see note 1 supra). See note 18 supra.

335.   Judicial review and other legal proceedings.   As from a day to be appointed, the following provisions have effect[1]. The Commission for Equality and Human Rights[2] has capacity to institute or intervene in legal proceedings, whether for judicial review[3] or otherwise, if it appears to the Commission that the proceedings are relevant to a matter in connection with which the Commission has a function[4].

1   The Equality Act 2006 s 30 is to be brought into force as from a day to be appointed by order made by the Secretary of State under s 93. At the date at which this volume states the law no such day had been appointed. As to the Secretary of State and the National Assembly for Wales see para 302 ante.
2   As to the Commission for Equality and Human Rights, its establishment and constitution see para 305 ante.
3   As to judicial review generally see ADMINISTRATIVE LAW vol 1(1) (2001 Reissue) para 58 et seq; PRACTICE AND PROCEDURE vol 37 (Reissue) para 1368.
4   Equality Act 2006 s 30(1) (not yet in force: see note 1 supra). The Commission is taken to have title and interest in relation to the subject matter of any legal proceedings in Scotland which it has capacity to institute, or in which it has capacity to intervene, by virtue of s 30(1) (not yet in force): s 30(2) (not yet in force: see note 1 supra). Scottish matters generally are beyond the scope of this work.
        The Commission may, in the course of legal proceedings for judicial review which it institutes (or in which it intervenes), rely on of the Human Rights Act 1998 s 7(1)(b) (breach of Convention rights) (see para 303 ante); and for that purpose: (1) the Commission need not be a victim or potential victim of the unlawful act to which the proceedings relate; (2) the Commission may act only if there is or would be one or more victims of the unlawful act; (3) s 7(3), (4) do not apply; and (4) no award of damages may be made to the Commission (whether or not the exception in s 8(3) applies); and an expression used in the Equality Act 2006 s 30(3) (not yet in force) and in the Human Rights Act 1998 s 7 (as amended) has the same meaning in the former as in the latter: see the Equality Act 2006 s 30(3) (not yet in force: see note 1 supra).
        The provisions of s 30(1), (2) (not yet in force): (a) do not create a cause of action; and (b) are, except as provided by s 30(3) (not yet in force), subject to any limitation or restriction imposed by virtue of an

enactment (including an enactment in or under an Act of the Scottish Parliament) or in accordance with the practice of a court: s 30(4) (not yet in force: see note 1 supra).

336. Public sector duties: assessment, compliance notices. As from a day to be appointed, the following provisions have effect[1]. The Commission for Equality and Human Rights[2] may assess the extent to which or the manner in which a person has complied with a duty under or by virtue of statutory provisions relating to the duty of public authorities to eliminate discrimination[3].

Where the Commission thinks that a person has failed to comply with a duty under or by virtue of those statutory provisions[4], the Commission may give the person a notice requiring him: (1) to comply with the duty[5]; and (2) to give the Commission, within the period of 28 days beginning with the date on which he receives the notice, written information of steps taken or proposed for the purpose of complying with the duty[6].

Such a compliance notice may require a person to give the Commission information required by the Commission for the purposes of assessing compliance with the duty, in which case the notice must specify: (a) the period within which the information is to be given (which must begin with the date on which the notice is received and must not exceed three months)[7]; and (b) the manner and form in which the information is to be given[8].

A person who receives a compliance notice must comply with it[9]. However, such a notice may not oblige a person to give information: (i) that he is prohibited from disclosing by virtue of an enactment[10]; or (ii) that he could not be compelled to give in proceedings before the High Court[11].

If the Commission thinks that a person, to whom a compliance notice has been given, has failed to comply with a requirement of the notice, the Commission may apply to the court[12] for an order requiring the person to comply[13]. A compliance notice must specify a time before which the Commission may not make such an application in respect of the notice[14].

1   The Equality Act 2006 ss 31, 32 are to be brought into force by order made by the Secretary of State under s 93 as from a day to be appointed. At the date at which this volume states the law no such day had been appointed. As to the Secretary of State and the National Assembly for Wales see para 302 ante.
2   As to the Commission for Equality and Human Rights, its establishment and constitution see para 305 ante.
3   Equality Act 2006 s 31(1) (not yet in force: see note 1 supra). The statutory provisions are as follows: (1) the Sex Discrimination Act 1975 s 76A (as added) or s 76B (as added) (see para 343 post); (2) the Race Relations Act 1976 s 71 (as substituted) (see para 469 post); or (3) the Disability Discrimination Act 1995 s 49A (as added) or s 49D (as added; prospectively amended) (see para 591 post): see the Equality Act 2006 s 31(1) (not yet in force: see note 1 supra).
        Section 31 (not yet in force) is without prejudice to the generality of s 16 (not yet in force) (see para 322 ante) and s 20 (not yet in force) (see para 327 ante): s 31(3) (not yet in force: see note 1 supra). As to general provisions about assessments see s 31(2), Sch 2 (not yet in force); and para 323 ante.
4   Ibid s 32(1) (not yet in force: see note 1 supra). As to the statutory provisions see note 3 supra.
        The Commission may not give a notice under s 32 (not yet in force) in respect of a duty under the Sex Discrimination Act 1975 s 76A (as added) (see para 343 post), the Race Relations Act 1976 s 71(1) (as substituted) (see para 469 post) or the Disability Discrimination Act 1995 s 49A (as added) (see para 591 post) unless: (1) the Commission has carried out an assessment under the Equality Act 2006 s 31 (not yet in force) (see the text and notes 1–3 supra); and (2) the notice relates to the results of the assessment: s 32(4) (not yet in force: see note 1 supra).
5   Ibid s 32(2)(a) (not yet in force: see note 1 supra).
        Schedule 2 paras 11, 14 (not yet in force) (see para 323 ante) have effect (with any necessary modifications) in relation to a requirement imposed by a notice under s 32 (not yet in force) as they have effect in relation to a requirement imposed by a notice under Sch 2 para 9 (not yet in force): s 32(7) (not yet in force: see note 1 supra).
6   Ibid s 32(2)(b) (not yet in force: see note 1 supra). See note 5 supra.
7   Ibid s 32(3)(a) (not yet in force: see note 1 supra). See note 5 supra.
8   Ibid s 32(3)(b) (not yet in force: see note 1 supra). See note 5 supra.

9   Ibid s 32(5) (not yet in force: see note 1 supra). See note 5 supra.
10   Ibid s 32(6)(a) (not yet in force: see note 1 supra). See note 5 supra.
11   Ibid s 32(6)(b) (not yet in force: see note 1 supra). See note 5 supra.
12   For these purposes, 'court' means: (1) where the notice related to a duty under the Sex Discrimination
     Act 1975 s 76A (as added) (see para 343 post), the Race Relations Act 1976 s 71(1) (as substituted) (see
     para 469 ante) or the Disability Discrimination Act 1995 s 49A (as added) (see para 591 post), the High
     Court; and (2) in any other case, a county court: see the Equality Act 2006 s 32(9) (not yet in force: see
     note 1 supra).
13   Ibid s 32(8) (not yet in force: see note 1 supra). See note 5 supra.
        Legal proceedings in relation to a duty by virtue of the Sex Discrimination Act 1975 s 76B (as added)
     (see para 343 post), the Race Relations Act 1976 s 71(2) (as substituted) (see para 469 post) or the
     Disability Discrimination Act 1995 s 49D (as added) (see para 591 post): (1) may be brought by the
     Commission in accordance with the Equality Act 2006 s 32(8) (not yet in force); and (2) may not be
     brought in any other way: s 32(11) (not yet in force: see note 1 supra).
14   Ibid s 32(10) (not yet in force: see note 1 supra). See note 5 supra.

2. SEX DISCRIMINATION

(1) INTRODUCTION

(i) General Overview

337. The scope of the law. The main body of domestic sex discrimination law is contained in the Sex Discrimination Act 1975[1]. Complementary provisions are also contained in the Equal Pay Act 1970[2], although these, unlike the provisions of the Sex Discrimination Act 1975, are restricted to the field of employment and deal specifically with discrimination relating to terms and conditions of employment.

The provisions of domestic sex discrimination law are to be interpreted in the light of relevant European Community legislation[3], in particular the provisions of the Equal Treatment Directive[4]. Article 141 of the EC Treaty[5] and the Equal Pay Directive[6] are also of relevance to consideration of issues relating to equal pay[7]. Furthermore, the Human Rights Act 1998 provides that domestic legislation, including the Sex Discrimination Act 1975, is to be interpreted in accordance with certain provisions of the Convention for the Protection of Human Rights and Fundamental Freedoms[8].

1 See para 342 et seq post.
2 For the provisions of the Equal Pay Act 1970 see para 419 et seq post.
3 Any domestic provision must be interpreted to give effect to a European Community obligation unless it is impossible to do so: *Webb v EMO Air Cargo (UK) Ltd* [1993] ICR 175, [1993] IRLR 27, HL. If necessary, compatibility may be achieved by reading words into the domestic provision: *Litster v Forth Dry Dock & Engineering Co Ltd (in receivership)* [1989] ICR 341, [1989] IRLR 161, HL.
4 Ie EC Council Directive 76/207 (OJ L39, 14.2.76, p 40) on the implementation of the principle of equal treatment for men and women as regards access to employment, vocational training and promotion, and working conditions (as amended): see para 338 post.
   Other relevant European legislation includes EC Council Directive 2000/78 (OJ L303, 2.12.2000, p 16) on establishing a general framework for equal treatment in employment and occupation (see para 508 post); EC Directive 79/7 (OJ L6, 10.1.79, p 24) on the progressive implementation of the principle of equal treatment for men and women in matters of social security (see para 339 post); EC Directive 86/378 (OJ L225, 12.8.86, p 40) on the implementation of the principle of equal treatment for men and women in occupational social security schemes (as amended) (see para 340 post); and EC Directive 86/613 (OJ L359, 19.12.86, p 56) on the application of the principle of equal treatment between men and women engaged in an activity, including agriculture, in a self-employed capacity, and on the protection of self-employed women during pregnancy and motherhood (see para 341 post). As to European Parliament and EC Council Directive 2006/54 (OJ L204, 26.7.2006, p 23) on the implementation of the principle of equal opportunities and equal treatment of men and women in matters of employment and occupation, which from 15 August 2009 repeals and replaces EC Council Directive 76/207 (OJ L39, 14.2.76, p 40) (as amended), EC Directive 86/378 (OJ L225, 12.8.86, p 40) (as amended) and certain other Directives (see paras 340, 418–419 post) see para 338 note 1 post.
5 Ie the Treaty Establishing the European Community (Rome, 25 March 1957; TS 1 (1973); Cmnd 5179). The EC Treaty art 141 (formerly art 119; renumbered by virtue of the Treaty of Amsterdam: see *Treaty Citation (No 2) (Note)* [1999] All ER (EC) 646, ECJ) provides for equal pay for male and female workers for equal work or work of equal value: see para 419 post.
6 Ie EC Directive 75/117 (OJ L45, 19.2.75, p 19) on the approximation of the laws of the member states relating to the application of the principle of equal pay for men and women: see para 419 post.
7 For further discussion of the principle of equal pay in the context of European law see para 419 et seq post.
8 Ie the Convention for the Protection of Human Rights and Fundamental Freedoms (Rome, 4 November 1950; TS 71 (1953); Cmd 8969): see paras 303–304 ante. For the provisions of the Human Rights Act 1998 see CONSTITUTIONAL LAW AND HUMAN RIGHTS.

(ii) European Legislation

338. The Equal Treatment Directive. The Equal Treatment Directive[1] puts into effect in the member states the principle of equal treatment for men and women as regards access to employment, including promotion, and to vocational training and as regards working conditions and, on certain conditions, social security[2]. The principle of equal treatment means that there must be no discrimination whatsoever on grounds of sex either directly or indirectly by reference in particular to marital or family status[3].

Application of the principle of equal treatment means that there must be no direct or indirect discrimination on the grounds of sex in the public or private sectors, including public bodies, in relation to a number of specific matters[4]. To that end, member states must take the necessary measures to ensure that: (1) any laws, regulations and administrative provisions contrary to the principle of equal treatment are abolished[5]; and (2) any provisions contrary to the principle of equal treatment which are included in contracts or collective agreements, internal rules of undertakings or in rules governing the independent occupations and professions and workers' and employers' organisations are or may be declared, null and void or may be amended[6].

Member states must ensure that judicial and/or administrative procedures, including where they deem it appropriate conciliation procedures, for the enforcement of obligations under the Equal Treatment Directive are available to all persons who consider themselves wronged by failure to apply the principle of equal treatment to them, even after the relationship in which the discrimination is alleged to have occurred has ended[7]. Member states must introduce into their national legal systems such measures as are necessary to ensure real and effective compensation or reparation as the member states so determine for the loss and damage sustained by a person injured as a result of discrimination[8] in a way which is dissuasive and proportionate to the damage suffered[9]. Member states must ensure that associations, organisations or other legal entities which have, in accordance with the criteria laid down by their national law, a legitimate interest in ensuring that the provisions of the Directive are complied with, may engage, either on behalf or in support of the complainants, with their approval, in any judicial and/or administrative procedure provided for the enforcement of obligations under the Directive[10].

Member states must introduce into their national legal systems such measures as are necessary to protect employees, including those who are employees' representatives provided for by national laws and/or practices, against dismissal or other adverse treatment by the employer as a reaction to a complaint within the undertaking or to any legal proceedings aimed at enforcing compliance with the principle of equal treatment[11].

The member states were required by the Directive to take care that the provisions adopted pursuant to the Directive, together with the relevant provisions already in force, were brought to the attention of employees by all appropriate means, for example at their place of employment[12]. There are also a number of additional measures that member states are required to take in relation to the promotion of equal treatment and sanctions for infringement of national provisions[13]. Member states may introduce or maintain provisions which are more favourable to the protection of the principle of equal treatment than those laid down in the Directive[14].

The Directive required the member states to put into force the laws, regulations and administrative provisions necessary in order to comply with the Directive[15], and the texts of laws, regulations and administrative provisions adopted in the field covered by the Directive had to be communicated to the EC Commission[16].

---

1   Ie EC Council Directive 76/207 (OJ L39, 14.2.76, p 40) on the implementation of the principle of equal treatment for men and women as regards access to employment, vocational training and promotion, and working conditions (amended by European Parliament and EC Council Directive 2002/73 (OJ L269, 5.10.2002, p 15)).

      As from 15 August 2009, EC Council Directive 76/207 (OJ L39, 14.2.76, p 40) (as amended) and certain other Directives (see paras 340, 418–419 post) are repealed and replaced by European Parliament and EC Council Directive 2006/54 (OJ L204, 26.7.2006, p 23) on the implementation of the principle of equal opportunities and equal treatment of men and women in matters of employment and occupation. This effectively is a consolidation of the relevant Directives and from 15 August 2009 references to the repealed Directives are to be construed as references to EC Council Directive 2006/54 (OJ L204, 26.7.2006, p 23): see art 34.

EC Council Directive 76/207 (OJ L39, 14.2.76, p 40) (as amended) also applies to transsexuals, and it is therefore contrary to the Directive to dismiss a person because he or she has undergone, or intends to undergo, gender reassignment: *Case C-13/94 P v S* [1996] ICR 795, [1996] IRLR 347, ECJ. See also paras 346, 348 post.

See also EC Council Decision 2000/750 (OJ L303, 2.12.2000, p 23) establishing a Community action programme to combat discrimination (2001–2006); EC Council Decision 2001/51 (OJ L17, 19.1.2001, p 22) establishing a programme relating to the Community framework strategy on gender equality (2001–2005) (amended by European Parliament and EC Council Decision 1554/2005 (OJ L255, 30.9.2005, p 9)); EC Council Decision 2003/578 (OJ L197, 5.8.2003, p 13) on guidelines for the employment policies of the EU member states; EC Council Recommendation 2003/579 (OJ L197, 5.8.2003, p 22) on the implementation of EU member states' employment policies; and EC Council Directive 2003/109 (OJ L16, 23.1.2004, p 44) on the status of third-country nationals who are long-term residents of the EU member states.

2   See EC Council Directive 76/207 (OJ L39, 14.2.76, p 40) art 1(1). Member states must actively take into account the objective of equality between men and women when formulating and implementing laws, regulations, administrative provisions, policies and activities in the areas referred to in art 1: art 1(1a) (added by European Parliament and EC Council Directive 2002/73 (OJ L269, 5.10.2002, p 15) art 1).

With a view to ensuring the progressive implementation of the principle of equal treatment in matters of social security, EC Council Directive 76/207 (OJ L39, 14.2.76, p 40) (as amended) provided that the EC Council, acting on a proposal from the EC Commission, would adopt provisions defining its substance, its scope and the arrangements for its application: art 1(2). As to provisions adopted pursuant to art 1(2) see EC Directive 79/7 (OJ L6, 10.1.79, p 24) on the progressive implementation of the principle of equal treatment for men and women in matters of social security) (see para 339 post); and EC Directive 86/378 (OJ L225, 12.8.86, p 40) on the implementation of the principle of equal treatment for men and women in occupational social security schemes (see para 340 post).

EC Council Directive 76/207 (OJ L39, 14.2.76, p 40) (as amended) is subject to no general, as opposed to special, reservations as regards measures taken to protect public safety: *Case 222/84 Johnston v Chief Constable of the Royal Ulster Constabulary* [1987] QB 129, [1986] 3 All ER 135, ECJ. See also Case C-1/95 *Gerster v Freistaat Bayern* [1998] ICR 327, [1997] IRLR 699, ECJ (national rules which provide that part-time employees accrue length of service more slowly than full-time employees, and so gain access to promotion later, must in principle be regarded as contrary to EC Council Directive 76/207 (OJ L39, 14.2.76, p 40) (as amended)); Case C-100/95 *Kording v Senator für Finanzen* [1997] ECR I-5289, [1997] IRLR 710, ECJ (national rules in principle contrary to EC Council Directive 76/207 (OJ L39, 14.2.76, p 40) (as amended) may be justified by objective factors unrelated to any discrimination on the grounds of sex, and if so the mere fact that the rules affect more women than men cannot be regarded as an infringement of the Directive).

EC Council Directive 76/207 (OJ L39, 14.2.76, p 40) (as amended) requires the introduction of measures to protect ex-employees from the retaliatory acts of employers carried out in reaction to equal treatment proceedings: Case C-185/97 *Coote v Granada Hospitality Ltd* [1998] All ER (EC) 865, [1999] ICR 100, ECJ. See also para 358 note 10 post.

3   EC Council Directive 76/207 (OJ L39, 14.2.76, p 40) art 2(1) (art 2 substituted by European Parliament and EC Council Directive 2002/73 (OJ L269, 5.10.2002, p 15) art 2).

'Direct discrimination' means where one person is treated less favourably on grounds of sex than another is, has been or would be treated in a comparable situation; 'indirect discrimination' means where an apparently neutral provision, criterion or practice would put persons of one sex at a particular disadvantage compared with persons of the other sex, unless that provision, criterion or practice is objectively justified by a legitimate aim, and the means of achieving that aim are appropriate and necessary: EC Council Directive 76/207 (OJ L39, 14.2.76, p 40) art 2(2) (as so substituted).

Harassment and sexual harassment are deemed to be discrimination on the grounds of sex and therefore prohibited: art 2(3) (as so substituted). 'Harassment' means where an unwanted conduct related to the sex of a person occurs with the purpose or effect of violating the dignity of a person, and of creating an intimidating, hostile, degrading, humiliating or offensive environment; 'sexual harassment' means where any form of unwanted verbal, non-verbal or physical conduct of a sexual nature occurs, with the purpose or effect of violating the dignity of a person, in particular when creating an intimidating, hostile, degrading, humiliating or offensive environment: art 2(2) (as so substituted). A person's rejection of, or submission to, such conduct may not be used as a basis for a decision affecting that person: art 2(3) (as so substituted).

An instruction to discriminate against persons on grounds of sex is deemed to be discrimination within the meaning of the Directive: art 2(4) (as so substituted). Member states must encourage, in accordance with national law, collective agreements or practice, employers and those responsible for access to vocational training to take measures to prevent all forms of discrimination on grounds of sex, in particular harassment and sexual harassment at the workplace: art 2(5) (as so substituted). Member states may provide, as regards access to employment including the training leading thereto, that a difference of treatment which is based on a characteristic related to sex will not constitute discrimination where, by reason of the nature of the particular occupational activities concerned or of the context in which they are carried out, such a characteristic constitutes a genuine and determining occupational requirement, provided that the objective is legitimate and the requirement is proportionate: art 2(6) (as so substituted).

The Directive is without prejudice to provisions concerning the protection of women, particularly as regards pregnancy and maternity: art 2(7) (as so substituted). As to discrimination on grounds of pregnancy see para 361 post. A woman on maternity leave is entitled, after the end of her period of maternity leave, to return to her job or to an equivalent post on terms and conditions which are no less favourable to her and to benefit from any improvement in working conditions to which she would be entitled during her absence: art 2(7) (as so substituted). Less favourable treatment of a woman related to pregnancy or maternity leave within the meaning of EC Council Directive 92/85 (OJ L348, 28.11.92, p 1) (see HEALTH AND SAFETY AT WORK vol 20(1) (Reissue) paras 638, 660) constitutes discrimination within the meaning of EC Council Directive 76/207 (OJ L39, 14.2.76, p 40): art 2(7) (as so substituted). The Directive is further without prejudice to the provisions of EC Council Directive 96/34 (OJ L145, 19.6.96, p 4) on the framework agreement on parental leave concluded by UNICE, CEEP and the ETUC (as amended) (see EMPLOYMENT vol 16(1A) (Reissue) para 321) and of EC Council Directive 92/85 (OJ L348, 28.11.92, p 1) on the introduction of measures to encourage improvements in the safety and health at work of pregnant workers and workers who have recently given birth or are breastfeeding (see HEALTH AND SAFETY AT WORK vol 20(1) (Reissue) para 542): EC Council Directive 76/207 (OJ L39, 14.2.76, p 40) art 2(7) (as so substituted). It is also without prejudice to the right of member states to recognise distinct rights to paternity and/or adoption leave: art 2(7) (as so substituted). Those member states which recognise such rights must take the necessary measures to protect working men and women against dismissal due to exercising those rights and ensure that, at the end of such leave, they are entitled to return to their jobs or to equivalent posts on terms and conditions which are no less favourable to them, and to benefit from any improvement in working conditions to which they would have been entitled during their absence: art 2(7) (as so substituted). Member states may maintain or adopt measures within the meaning of the Treaty Establishing the European Community (Rome, 25 March 1957; TS 1 (1973); Cmnd 5179) art 141(4) (formerly art 119; renumbered by virtue of the Treaty of Amsterdam: see *Treaty Citation (No 2) (Note)* [1999] All ER (EC) 646, ECJ) with a view to ensuring full equality in practice between men and women: EC Council Directive 76/207 (OJ L39, 14.2.76, p 40) art 2(8) (as so substituted).

The member states must periodically assess the occupational activities referred to in art 2(2) (as substituted) in order to decide, in the light of social developments, whether there is justification for maintaining the exclusions concerned; and they must notify the EC Commission of the results of this assessment: art 9(2). As to discrimination on grounds of sexual orientation see paras 346 note 6, 722 et seq post.

National laws which guarantee women absolute and unconditional prorate for appointments or promotion in sectors in which they are under-represented go beyond the limits of the exception provided by art 2(4): Case C-450/93 *Kalanke v Freie Hansestadt Bremen* [1996] All ER (EC) 66, [1995] IRLR 660, ECJ. But see also Case C-409/95 *Marschall v Land Nordrhein-Westfalen* [1997] All ER(EC) 865, [1998] IRLR 39, ECJ; Case C-158/97 *Re Badeck* [2000] All ER(EC) 289, [2000] IRLR 432, ECJ.

As to the exceptions provided by EC Council Directive 76/207 (OJ L39, 14.2.76, p 40) art 2 (as substituted) see Case 222/84 *Johnston v Chief Constable of the Royal Ulster Constabulary* [1987] QB 129, [1986] 3 All ER 135, ECJ. See also Case 318/86 *EC Commission v France* [1988] ECR 3559, [1989] 3 CMLR 663, ECJ. See further C-273/97 *Sirdar v Army Board* [1999] All ER (EC) 928, [2000] ICR 130, ECJ (female chef excluded from Royal Marines on basis of policy of 'interoperability', i e the need for every marine to be capable of fighting in a commando unit; ECJ held that the principle of equal treatment for men and women is not subject to any general reservation as regards measures for the organisation of the armed forces taken on grounds of the protection of public security but that the United Kingdom government may be entitled under EC Council Directive 76/207 (OJ L39, 14.2.76, p 40) art 2 (as substituted) to exclude women from service in special combat units such as the Royal Marines). See, however, Case C-285/98 *Kreil v Bundesrepublik Deutschland* [2000] ECR I-69, [2002] 1 CMLR 1047, (2000) Times, 22 February, ECJ (female applicant, who had trained in electronics, applied for voluntary service in the Bundeswehr, requesting duties in weapon electronics maintenance; her application was refused on the ground that women were barred by German basic law from serving in military positions involving the use of arms; under German law, women were entitled to enlist as volunteers in the military only in the medical and musical services; ECJ held that this was contrary to EC Council Directive 76/207 (OJ L39, 14.2.76, p 40) (as amended)). See Case C-407/98 *Abrahamsson v Fogelqvist* [2000] ECR I-5539, [2002] ICR 932, ECJ (legislation giving preference to candidate who was a member of under-represented sex with qualifications inferior to those of candidate of the opposite sex contravened EC Council Directive 76/207 (OJ L39, 14.2.76, p 40) art 2 (as substituted)). See also E-1/02 *EFTA Surveillance Authority v Kingdom of Norway* [2003] 1 CMLR 725, [2003] IRLR 318, EFTA Ct (national legislation automatically allocating positions to under-represented class in contravention of EC Council Directive 76/207 (OJ L39, 14.2.76, p 40) (as amended)). As to the test for determining whether indirect discrimination is justified see Case C-226/98 *Jørgensen v Foreningen AF Speciallaeger* [2000] ECR I-2447, [2000] IRLR 726, ECJ. See also Case C-476/99 *Lommers v Minister Van Landbouw, Natuurbeheer en Visserij* [2002] ECR I-2891, [2004] 2 CMLR 1141, ECJ (provision of nursery facilities for female employees but only for male employees in an emergency was not discriminatory). Where a woman is pregnant when she returns to work, she does not have to give her employer advance notice of her pregnancy and she is entitled to return to work for the purpose of qualifying for preferable maternity benefits: Case C-320/01 *Busch v Klinikum Neustadt GmbH & Co Betriebs-KG* [2003] All ER (EC) 985, [2003] IRLR 625, ECJ.

While EC Council Directive 76/207 (OJ L39, 14.2.76, p 40) (as amended) recognises the legitimacy of protecting women in connection with pregnancy and maternity, it does not allow women to be excluded from a certain type of employment solely on the ground that they should be given greater protection than men against risks which affect men and women in the same way and which are distinct from women's specific needs of protection, nor might women be excluded from a certain type of employment solely because they are on average smaller and less strong than average men, while men with similar physical features are accepted for that employment: Case C-203/03 *EC Commission v Austria* [2005] All ER (D) 05 (Feb), ECJ.

4   EC Council Directive 76/207 (OJ L39, 14.2.76, p 40) art 3(1) (art 3 substituted by European Parliament and EC Council Directive 2002/73 (OJ L269, 5.10.2002, p 15) art 3). The specific matters referred to in the text are: (1) conditions for access to employment, to self-employment or to occupation, including selection criteria and recruitment conditions, whatever the branch of activity and at all levels of the professional hierarchy, including promotion; (2) access to all types and to all levels of vocational guidance, vocational training, advanced vocational training and retraining, including practical work experience; (3) employment and working conditions, including dismissals, as well as pay as provided for in EC Council Directive 75/117 (OJ L45, 19.2.75, p 19) (see para 419 post); (4) membership of, and involvement in, an organisation of workers or employers, or any organisation whose members carry on a particular profession, including the benefits provided for by such organisations: EC Council Directive 76/207 (OJ L39, 14.2.76, p 40) art 3(1) (as so substituted).

5   Ibid art 3(2)(a) (as substituted: see note 4 supra).

6   Ibid art 3(2)(b) (as substituted: see note 4 supra).

7   Ibid art 6(1) (art 6 substituted by European Parliament and EC Council Directive 2002/73 (OJ L269, 5.10.2002, p 15) art 5). These provisions are without prejudice to national rules relating to time limits for bringing actions as regards the principle of equal treatment: art 6(4) (as so substituted).

8   Ie contrary to ibid art 3 (as substituted): see the text and notes 4–6 supra.

9   Ibid art 6(2) (as substituted: see note 7 supra). Such compensation or reparation may not be restricted by the fixing of a prior upper limit, except in cases where the employer can prove that the only damage suffered by an applicant as a result of discrimination within the meaning of the Directive is the refusal to take his or her job application into consideration: art 6(2) (as so substituted).

The original version of this provision required substantial revision of the Equal Pay Act 1970: see the Equal Pay (Amendment) Regulations 1983, SI 1983/1794 (as amended); and the Sex Discrimination and Equal Pay (Remedies) Regulations 1993, SI 1993/2798 (revoked). As to the provisions of the Equal Pay Act 1970 see para 419 et seq post.

It is contrary to EC Council Directive 76/207 (OJ L39, 14.2.76, p 40) art 6 (as substituted) to lay down an upper limit on the amount of compensation recoverable by a victim of discrimination in respect of the loss and damage sustained: Case C-271/91 *Marshall v Southampton and South West Hampshire Area Health Authority (Teaching) (No 2)* [1994] QB 126, [1993] 4 All ER 586, ECJ; Case C-180/95 *Draehmpaehl v Urania Immobilienservice ohG* [1997] All ER (EC) 719, [1998] ICR 164, ECJ. It is also contrary to the provision for national legislation to require a finding of fault on the part of the employer before compensation can be awarded for discrimination: Case C-180/95 *Draehmpaehl v Urania Immobilienservice ohG* supra.

10   EC Council Directive 76/207 (OJ L39, 14.2.76, p 40) art 6(3) (as substituted: see note 7 supra). The provisions of art 6(3) (as substituted) are without prejudice to national rules relating to time limits for bringing actions as regards the principle of equal treatment: art 6(4) (as so substituted).

11   Ibid art 7 (substituted by European Parliament and EC Council Directive 2002/73 (OJ L269, 5.10.2002, p 15) art 6).

12   EC Council Directive 76/207 (OJ L39, 14.2.76, p 40) art 8.

13   These measures are as follows. Member states must designate and make the necessary arrangements for a body or bodies for the promotion, analysis, monitoring and support of equal treatment of all persons without discrimination on the grounds of sex; these bodies may form part of agencies charged at national

level with the defence of human rights or the safeguard of individuals' rights ibid art 8a(1) (arts 8a–8d added by European Parliament and EC Council Directive 2002/73 (OJ L269, 5.10.2002, p 15) art 7). Member states must ensure that the competences of these bodies include: (1) without prejudice to the right of victims and of associations, organisations or other legal entities referred to in EC Council Directive 76/207 (OJ L39, 14.2.76, p 40) art 6(3) (as substituted) (see the text and note 10 supra) providing independent assistance to victims of discrimination in pursuing their complaints about discrimination; (2) conducting independent surveys concerning discrimination; (3) publishing independent reports and making recommendations on any issue relating to such discrimination: art 8a(2) (as so added). Member states must, in accordance with national traditions and practice, take adequate measures to promote social dialogue between the social partners with a view to fostering equal treatment, including through the monitoring of workplace practices, collective agreements, codes of conduct, research or exchange of experiences and good practices: art 8b(1) (as so added). Where consistent with national traditions and practice, member states must encourage the social partners, without prejudice to their autonomy, to promote equality between women and men and to conclude, at the appropriate level, agreements laying down anti-discrimination rules in the fields referred to in art 1 (as amended) (see the text and notes 1, 2 supra) which fall within the scope of collective bargaining; these agreements must respect the minimum requirements laid down by the Directive and the relevant national implementing measures: art 8b(2) (as so added). Member states must, in accordance with national law, collective agreements or practice, encourage employers to promote equal treatment for men and women in the workplace in a planned and systematic way: art 8b(3) (as so added). To this end, employers should be encouraged to provide at appropriate regular intervals employees and/or their representatives with appropriate information on equal treatment for men and women in the undertaking; such information may include statistics on proportions of men and women at different levels of the organisation and possible measures to improve the situation in co-operation with employees' representatives: art 8b(4) (as so added). Member states must encourage dialogue with appropriate non-governmental organisations which have, in accordance with their national law and practice, a legitimate interest in contributing to the fight against discrimination on grounds of sex with a view to promoting the principle of equal treatment: art 8c (as so added). Member states must lay down the rules on sanctions applicable to infringements of the national provisions adopted pursuant to the Directive, and must take all measures necessary to ensure that they are applied: art 8d (as so added). The sanctions, which may comprise the payment of compensation to the victim, must be effective, proportionate and dissuasive: art 8d (as so added). The member states must notify those provisions to the EC Commission by 5 October 2005 at the latest and must notify it without delay of any subsequent amendment affecting them: art 8d (as so added).

14   Ibid art 8e(1) (as added: see note 13 supra). The implementation of the Directive must under no circumstances constitute grounds for a reduction in the level of protection against discrimination already afforded by member states in the fields covered by the Directive: art 8(2) (as so added).

15   Ibid art 9(1). The Directive had to be implemented within 30 months of its notification and the member state immediately had to inform the EC Commission of the implementation: see art 9(1). However, as regards the first part of the original version of art 3(2)(c) and the first part of art 5(2)(c) (now repealed), member states were required to carry out a first examination and if necessary a first revision of the laws, regulations and administrative provisions referred to in those provisions within four years of notification of the Directive: art 9(1). Within two years following expiry of the 30-month period laid down in the art 9(1), the member states had to forward all necessary information to the EC Commission to enable it to draw up a report on the application of the Directive for submission to the EC Council: see art 10.

16   Ibid art 9(3).

339. Equal treatment in matters of social security. An EC Directive was passed to implement progressively, in the field of social security and other elements of social protection, the principle of equal treatment for men and women in matters of social security[1]. The Directive applies to the working population (including self-employed persons, workers and self-employed persons whose activity is interrupted by illness, accident or involuntary unemployment, and persons seeking employment) and to retired or invalided workers and self-employed persons[2]. The Directive applies to statutory schemes which provide protection against certain risks[3] and social assistance, in so far as it is intended to supplement or replace the statutory schemes[4].

The Directive states that the principle of equal treatment means that there must be no discrimination whatsoever on ground of sex either directly, or indirectly by reference in particular to marital or family status, in particular as concerns: (1) the scope of the schemes and the conditions of access to them; (2) the obligation to contribute and the calculation of contributions; and (3) the calculation of benefits including increases due in respect of a spouse and for dependants and the conditions governing the duration and retention of entitlement to benefits[5]. The principle of equal treatment is without prejudice to the provisions relating to the protection of women on the grounds of maternity[6].

The Directive required the member states to take the measures necessary to ensure that any laws, regulations and administrative provisions contrary to the principle of equal treatment were abolished[7]. The member states had to introduce into their national legal systems such measures as necessary to enable all persons who consider themselves wronged by failure to apply the principle of equal treatment to pursue their claims by judicial process, possibly after recourse to other competent authorities[8].

The Directive was expressed to be without prejudice to the right of member states to exclude from its scope: (a) the determination of pensionable age for the purposes of granting old-age and retirement pensions and the possible consequences for other benefits[9]; (b) advantages in respect of old-age pension schemes granted to persons who have brought up children, and the acquisition of benefit entitlements following periods of interruption of employment due to the bringing up of children[10]; (c) the granting of old-age or invalidity benefit entitlements by virtue of the derived entitlements of a wife[11]; and (d) the granting of increases of long-term invalidity, old-age, accidents at work and occupational disease benefits for a dependent wife[12]. The member states must periodically examine matters excluded under heads (a) to (d) above in order to ascertain, in the light of social developments in the matter concerned, whether there is justification for maintaining the exclusions concerned[13].

1   See EC Directive 79/7 (OJ L6, 10.1.79, p 24) on the progressive implementation of the principle of equal treatment for men and women in matters of social security, art 1.

2   Ibid art 2. 'Working population' does not apply to people who are not working or seeking work, or to persons whose occupation or efforts to find work were not interrupted by one of the risks referred to in art 3 (see the text and note 3 infra); and 'activity' means an economic activity: Case C-77/95 *Züchner v Handelskrankenkasse (Ersatzkasse) Bremen* [1997] All ER (EC) 359, [1996] ECR I- 5689, ECJ. See also Case 150/85 *Drake v Chief Adjudication Officer* [1987] QB 166, [1986] 3 All ER 65, ECJ; Cases 48/88, 106–107/88 *Achterberg-Te Riele v Sociale Verzekeringsbank* [1989] ECR 1963, [1990] 3 CMLR 323, ECJ.

3   EC Directive 79/7 (OJ L6, 10.1.79, p 24) art 3(1)(a). The risks referred to in the text are sickness, invalidity, old age, accidents at work and occupational diseases, and unemployment: see art 3(1)(a). The Directive does not apply to the provisions concerning survivors' benefits nor to those concerning family benefits, except in the case of family benefits granted by way of increases of benefits due in respect of the risks referred to in art 3(1)(a): art 3(2). With a view to ensuring implementation of the principle of equal treatment in occupational schemes, the EC Council, acting on a proposal from the EC Commission, was required to adopt provisions defining its substance, its scope and the arrangements for its application: art 3(3). In accordance with this provision, the EC Council passed EC Directive 86/378 (OJ L225, 12.8.86, p 40) on the implementation of the principle of equal treatment for men and women in occupational social security schemes (as amended): see para 340 post.

4   EC Directive 79/7 (OJ L6, 10.1.79, p 24) art 3(1)(b). The operation of the Directive is not excluded where the benefit which forms part of a statutory scheme is not paid to the disabled person himself but to a third party: see Case 150/85 *Drake v Chief Adjudication Officer* [1987] QB 166, [1986] 3 All ER 65, ECJ. A non-contributory pension scheme set up by agreement between employer and employees to supplement the benefits available under a social security scheme is not itself a social security scheme, even if adopted in accordance with legislation, and it is therefore within the scope of the Treaty Establishing the European Community (Rome, 25 March 1957; TS 1 (1973); Cmnd 5179) art 141 (formerly art 119; renumbered by virtue of the Treaty of Amsterdam: see *Treaty Citation (No 2) (Note)* [1999] All ER (EC) 646, ECJ): Case 170/84 *Bilka-Kaufhaus GmbH v Weber von Hartz* [1987] ICR 110, [1986] IRLR 317, ECJ. In order to fall within the scope of EC Directive 79/7 (OJ L6, 10.1.79, p 24) a social security benefit must constitute the whole or part of a statutory scheme providing protection against one of the specified risks or a form of social assistance with the same objective: Cases C-63/91, 64/91 *Jackson v Chief Adjudication Officer* [1993] QB 367, [1993] 3 All ER 265, ECJ.

5   EC Directive 79/7 (OJ L6, 10.1.79, p 24) art 4(1). Article 4(1) precludes legislation refusing a pension to a person who has undergone male to female gender reassignment and is aged 60, on the ground that she

has not attained the pensionable age for men of 65: Case C-423/04 *Richards v Secretary of State for Work and Pensions* [2006] ICR 1181, [2006] All ER (EC) 895, ECJ.

6   EC Directive 79/7 (OJ L6, 10.1.79, p 24) art 4(2). See *Walter v Secretary of State for Social Security* [2001] EWCA Civ 1913, [2002] ICR 540.

7   EC Directive 79/7 (OJ L6, 10.1.79, p 24) art 5. The member states were required to bring into force the laws, regulations and administrative provisions necessary to comply with the Directive within six years of its notification, and to immediately inform the EC Commission: see art 8. Within seven years of notification of the Directive, the member states had to forward all information necessary to the EC Commission to enable it to draw up a report on the application of the Directive for submission to the EC Council and to propose such further measures as might be required for the implementation of the principle of equal treatment: art 9.

8   Ibid art 6.

9   Ibid art 7(1)(a). This provision authorises the determination of a statutory pensionable age that differs according to sex and any forms of discrimination necessarily linked to that difference: Case C-9/91 *R v Secretary of State for Social Security, ex p Equal Opportunities Commission* [1992] 3 All ER 577, [1992] ICR 782, ECJ. See also *Thomas v Chief Adjudication Officer* [1991] 2 QB 164, [1991] 3 All ER 315, CA (the application of different age limits when determining applications for disability allowances was not a necessary consequence of fixing different pensionable ages for men and women, and was therefore contrary to EC Directive 79/7 (OJ L6, 10.1.79, p 24)). See further Case C-262/88 *Barber v Guardian Royal Exchange Assurance Group* [1991] 1 QB 344, [1990] 2 All ER 660, ECJ; Case C-382/98 *R v Secretary of State for Social Security, ex p Taylor* [2000] All ER(EC) 80, [1999] ECR I-8955, ECJ; *Trustee Solutions Ltd v Dubery* [2006] EWHC 1426 (Ch), [2007] 1 All ER 308, [2006] All ER (D) 233 (Jun). A member state may use different methods of calculating men's and women's retirement pensions when it maintains different pensionable ages according to sex: Case C-154/96 *Wolfs v Office National Des Pensions* [1998] ECR I-6173, [2000] 3 CMLR 1414, ECJ. See also Application 42735/02 *Barrow v United Kingdom* [2006] All ER (D) 104 (Aug), (2006) Times, 11 September; Application 8374/03 *Pearson v United Kingdom* [2006] All ER (D) 106 (Aug), (2006) Times, 11 September; Application 7212/02 *Walker v United Kingdom*, ECtHR [2006] All ER (D) 102 (Aug), (2006) Times, 11 September.

10   EC Directive 79/7 (OJ L6, 10.1.79, p 24) art 7(1)(b).

11   Ibid art 7(1)(c).

12   Ibid art 7(1)(d). There was also excepted the consequences of the exercise, before the adoption of the Directive, of a right of option not to acquire rights or incur obligations under a statutory scheme: see art 7(1)(e). The member states are required to inform the EC Commission of their reasons for maintaining any existing provisions on the matters referred to in art 7(1) and of the possibilities for reviewing them at a later date: art 8(2).

13   Ibid art 7(2). The text of laws, regulations and administrative provisions adopted in the field covered by the Directive, including measures adopted pursuant to art 7(2) had to be communicated to the EC Commission: see art 8(2).

340.   Equal treatment in occupational social security schemes. An EC Directive[1] was passed to implement, in occupational social security schemes[2], the principle of equal treatment for men and women[3]. The Directive applies to members of the working population (including self-employed persons, persons whose activity is interrupted by illness, maternity, accident or involuntary unemployment and persons seeking employment), to retired and disabled workers and to those claiming under them, in accordance with national law or practice[4]. The Directive applies to occupational schemes which provide protection against specified risks[5], and occupational schemes which provide for other social benefits in cash or in kind, and in particular survivors' benefits and family allowances, if such benefits are accorded to employed persons and thus constitute a consideration paid by the employer to the worker by reason of the latter's employment[6].

The principle of equal treatment implies that there must be no discrimination on the basis of sex, either directly or indirectly, by reference in particular to marital or family status, especially as regards: (1) the scope of the schemes and the conditions of access to them; (2) the obligation to contribute and the calculation of contributions; and (3) the calculation of benefits, including supplementary benefits due in respect of a spouse or dependants, and the conditions governing the duration and retention of entitlement to benefits[7]. The principle of equal treatment does not prejudice the provisions relating to the protection of women by reason of maternity[8].

Provisions contrary to the principle of equal treatment include those based on sex, either directly or indirectly, in particular by reference to marital or family status, for[9]:

(a) determining the persons who may participate in an occupational scheme[10];

(b) fixing the compulsory or optional nature of participation in an occupational scheme[11];

(c) laying down different rules as regards the age of entry into the scheme or the minimum period of employment or membership of the scheme required to obtain the benefits of the scheme[12];

(d) laying down different rules, except as provided for in heads (h) and (i) below, for the reimbursement of contributions when a worker leaves a scheme without having fulfilled the conditions guaranteeing a deferred right to long-term benefits[13];

(e) setting different conditions for the granting of benefits or restricting such benefits to workers of one or other of the sexes[14];

(f) fixing different retirement ages[15];

(g) suspending the retention or acquisition of rights during periods of maternity leave or leave for family reasons which are granted by law or agreement and are paid by the employer[16];

(h) setting different levels of benefit, except in so far as may be necessary to take account of actuarial calculation factors which differ according to sex in the case of defined-contribution schemes (note that, in the case of funded defined-benefit schemes, certain elements[17] may be unequal where the inequality of the amounts results from the effects of the use of actuarial factors differing according to sex at the time when the scheme's funding is implemented)[18];

(i) setting different levels for workers' contributions; or setting different levels for employers' contributions, except in the case of defined-contribution schemes if the aim is to equalise the amount of the final benefits or to make them more nearly equal for both sexes, or in the case of funded defined-benefit schemes where the employer's contributions are intended to ensure the adequacy of the funds necessary to cover the cost of the benefits defined[19]; and

(j) laying down different standards or standards applicable only to workers of a specified sex, except as provided for in heads (h) and (i) above, as regards the guarantee or retention of entitlement to deferred benefits when a worker leaves a scheme[20].

Where the granting of benefits within the scope of the Directive is left to the discretion of the scheme's management bodies, the latter must comply with the principle of equal treatment[21].

The Directive required the member states to take all necessary steps to ensure that provisions contrary to the principle of equal treatment in legally compulsory collective agreements, staff rules of undertakings or any other arrangements relating to occupational schemes were null and void, or may be declared null and void or amended[22], and that schemes containing such provisions could not be approved or extended by administrative measures[23]. All necessary steps to ensure that the provisions of occupational schemes for self-employed workers contrary to the principle of equal treatment were revised had to have effect by 1 January 1993 at the latest[24].

As regards schemes for self-employed workers, the Directive permits the member states to defer compulsory application of the principle of equal treatment with regard to: (i) determination of pensionable age for the purposes of granting old-age or retirement pensions, and the possible implications for other benefits either until the date on which such equality is achieved in statutory schemes, or, at the latest, until such equality is prescribed by a Directive[25]; (ii) survivors' pensions until Community law establishes the principle of equal treatment in statutory social security schemes in that regard[26]; (iii) the setting of different levels of worker contribution[27] to take account of the different actuarial calculation factors[28]. Where men and women may claim a flexible pensionable age under the same conditions, this is not deemed to be incompatible with the Directive[29].

The member states were required to introduce into their national legal systems such measures as necessary to enable all persons who consider themselves injured by failure to apply the principle of equal treatment to pursue their claims before the courts, possibly after bringing the matters before other competent authorities[30]. The member states were also required to take all the necessary steps to protect workers against dismissal where this constitutes a response on the part of the employer to a complaint made at undertaking level or to the institution of legal proceedings aimed at enforcing compliance with the principle of equal treatment[31].

1   Ie EC Directive 86/378 (OJ L225, 12.8.86, p 40) on the implementation of the principle of equal treatment for men and women in occupational social security schemes. Following the judgment in Case C-262/88 *Barber v Guardian Royal Exchange Assurance Group* [1991] 1 QB 344, [1990] 2 All ER 660, ECJ, EC Directive 86/378 (OJ L225, 12.8.86, p 40) was amended by EC Directive 96/97 (OJ L46, 17.2.97, p 20). In regard to a requirement for a deed of trust for changing the retirement age in an occupational pension scheme see *Trustee Solutions Ltd v Dubery* [2006] EWHC 1426 (Ch), [2007] 1 All ER 308, [2006] All ER (D) 233 (Jun).
        As from 15 August 2009, EC Directive 86/378 (OJ L225, 12.8.86, p 40) (as amended) and certain other Directives (see paras 338 ante, 418–419 post) are repealed and replaced by European Parliament and EC Council Directive 2006/54 (OJ L204, 26.7.2006, p 23) on the implementation of the principle of equal opportunities and equal treatment of men and women in matters of employment and occupation. This effectively is a consolidation of the relevant Directives and from 15 August 2009 references to the repealed Directives are to be construed as references to EC Council Directive 2006/54 (OJ L204, 26.7.2006, p 23): see art 34.
        Any measure implementing EC Directive 96/97 (OJ L46, 17.2.97, p 20), as regards paid workers, must cover all benefits derived from periods of employment subsequent to 17 May 1990 and apply retroactively to that date, without prejudice to workers or those claiming under them who have, before that date, initiated legal proceedings or raised an equivalent claim under national law; in that event, the implementation measures must apply retroactively to 8 April 1976 and must cover all the benefits derived from periods of employment after that date: art 2(1). This does not prevent national rules relating to time limits for bringing actions under national law from being relied on against workers or those claiming under them who initiated legal proceedings or raise an equivalent claim under national law before 17 May 1990, provided that they are not less favourable for that type of action than for similar actions of a domestic nature and that they do not render the exercise of Community law impossible in practice: art 2(2).
        The member states were required to bring into force the laws, regulations and administrative provisions necessary to comply with EC Directive 96/97 (OJ L46, 17.2.97, p 20) by 1 July 1997, and were required to inform the Commission immediately they had done so: art 3(1). When member states adopted these provisions, they had to contain a reference to the Directive or be accompanied by such reference on the occasion of their official publication; the methods of making such a reference were to be laid down by the member states: art 3(1). The member states were also required to communicate to the EC Commission, at the latest two years after the entry into force of the Directive (ie 9 March 1997), all information necessary to enable the EC Commission to draw up a report on the application of the Directive: see arts 3(2), 4.
2   'Occupational social security schemes' means schemes not governed by EC Directive 79/7 (OJ L6, 10.1.79, p 24) (see para 339 ante) whose purpose is to provide workers, whether employees or self-employed, in an undertaking or group of undertakings, area of economic activity, occupational sector or group of sectors with benefits intended to supplement the benefits provided by statutory social security schemes or to replace them, whether membership of such schemes is compulsory or optional: EC Directive 86/378 (OJ L225, 12.8.86, p 40) art 2(1) (art 2(1), (2) substituted by EC Directive 96/97 (OJ L46, 17.2.97, p 20)). EC Directive 86/378 (OJ L225, 12.8.86, p 40) (as amended) does not apply to: (1) individual contracts for self-employed workers; (2) schemes for self-employed workers having only one member; (3) insurance contracts to which the employer is not a party, in the case of salaried workers;

(4) optional provisions of occupational schemes offered to participants individually to guarantee them either additional benefits, or a choice of date on which the normal benefits for self-employed workers will start, or a choice between several benefits; and (5) occupational schemes in so far as benefits are financed by contributions paid by workers on a voluntary basis: art 2(2) (as so substituted). The Directive does not preclude an employer granting to persons who have already reached the retirement age for the purposes of granting a pension by virtue of an occupational scheme, but who have not yet reached the retirement age for the purposes of granting a statutory retirement pension, a pension supplement, the aim of which is to make equal or more nearly equal the overall amount of benefit paid to these persons in relation to the amount paid to persons of the other sex in the same situation who have already reached the statutory retirement age, until the persons benefiting from the supplement reach the statutory retirement age: art 2(3) (added by EC Directive 96/97 (OJ L46, 17.2.97, p 20)).

3   EC Directive 86/378 (OJ L225, 12.8.86, p 40) art 1. As to the principle of equal treatment see also para 338 ante.
4   Ibid art 3 (substituted by EC Directive 96/97 (OJ L46, 17.2.97, p 20)).
5   EC Directive 86/378 (OJ L225, 12.8.86, p 40) art 4(a). The risks referred to in the text are: (1) sickness; (2) invalidity; (3) old age, including early retirement; (4) industrial accidents and occupational diseases; and (5) unemployment: see art 4(a).
6   Ibid art 4(b).
7   Ibid art 5(1).
8   Ibid art 5(2).
9   Ibid art 6(1) (art 6 substituted by EC Directive 96/97 (OJ L46, 17.2.97, p 20)).
10 EC Directive 86/378 (OJ L225, 12.8.86, p 40) art 6(1)(a) (as substituted: see note 9 supra).
11 Ibid art 6(1)(b) (as substituted: see note 9 supra).
12 Ibid art 6(1)(c) (as substituted: see note 9 supra).
13 Ibid art 6(1)(d) (as substituted: see note 9 supra).
14 Ibid art 6(1)(e) (as substituted: see note 9 supra).
15 Ibid art 6(1)(f) (as substituted: see note 9 supra).
16 Ibid art 6(1)(g) (as substituted: see note 9 supra).
17 Examples of elements which may be unequal, in respect of funded defined-benefit schemes, as referred to in ibid art 6(1)(h) (as substituted) are: (1) conversion into a capital sum of part of a periodic pension; (2) transfer of pension rights; (3) a reversionary pension payable to a dependant in return for the surrender of part of a pension; and (4) a reduced pension where the worker opts to take early retirement: art 6(1)(h), Annex (art 6(1)(h) as substituted (see note 9 supra); Annex added by EC Directive 96/97 (OJ L46, 17.2.97, p 20)).
18 EC Directive 86/378 (OJ L225, 12.8.86, p 40) art 6(1)(h) (as substituted: see note 9 supra).
19 Ibid art 6(1)(i) (as substituted: see note 9 supra).
20 Ibid art 6(1)(j) (as substituted: see note 9 supra).
21 Ibid art 6(2) (as substituted: see note 9 supra).
22 Ibid art 7(a). The member states were required to bring into force such laws, regulations and administrative provisions as necessary in order to comply with the Directive at the latest three years after notification of the Directive, and immediately to inform the EC Commission that they had done so: see art 12(1). The Directive was notified to the member states on 30 July 1986. The member states were also required to communicate to the EC Commission at the latest five years after notification of the Directive all information necessary to enable the EC Commission to draw up a report on the application of the Directive for submission to the EC Council: see art 12(2).
23 Ibid art 7(b).
24 Ibid art 8(1) (art 8 substituted by EC Directive 96/97 (OJ L46, 17.2.97, p 20)). EC Directive 86/378 (OJ L225, 12.8.86, p 40) (as amended) does not preclude rights and obligations relating to a period of membership of an occupational scheme for self-employed workers prior to revision of that scheme from remaining subject to the provisions of the scheme in force during that period: art 8(2) (as so substituted).
25 Ibid art 9(a) (art 9 substituted by EC Directive 96/97 (OJ L46, 17.2.97, p 20)).
26 EC Directive 86/378 (OJ L225, 12.8.86, p 40) art 9(b) (as substituted: see note 25 supra).
27 Ie under ibid art 6(1)(i) (as substituted) (see head (i) in the text): see art 9(c) (as substituted: see note 25 supra).
28 Ibid art 9(c) (as substituted: see note 25 supra). This provision applied at the latest until 1 January 1999: see art 9(c) (as so substituted).
29 Ibid art 9a (added by EC Directive 96/97 (OJ L46, 17.2.97, p 20)).
30 EC Directive 86/378 (OJ L225, 12.8.86, p 40) art 10.
31 Ibid art 11.

341.   Equal treatment for self-employed men and women.   An EC Directive[1] was passed to ensure application in the member states of the principle of equal treatment as between men and women engaged in an activity in a self-employed capacity, or contributing to the pursuit of such an activity[2].

The Directive covers: (1) self-employed workers[3]; and (2) their spouses where the spouse in question is not an employee or partner and habitually, under the conditions laid down by national law, participates in the activities of the self-employed worker and performs the same tasks or ancillary tasks[4].

The principle of equal treatment implies that there must be no discrimination on grounds of sex, either directly or indirectly, by reference in particular to marital or family status[5].

The Directive required the member states to take all necessary measures, as regards self-employed persons, to ensure the elimination of all provisions which are contrary to the principle of equal treatment[6], especially in respect of the establishment, equipment or extension of a business or the launching or extension of any other form of self-employed activity including financial facilities[7].

The Directive also required the member states, without prejudice to the specific conditions for access to certain activities which apply equally to both sexes, to take all measures necessary to ensure that the conditions for the formation of a company between spouses are not more restrictive than the conditions for the formation of a company between unmarried persons[8].

Where a contributory social security system for self-employed workers existed in a member state, the Directive required that member state to take all necessary measures to enable the spouses of self-employed workers[9] who are not protected under the self-employed workers' social security scheme to join a contributory social security scheme voluntarily[10].

The Directive required member states to undertake to examine under what conditions recognition of the work of the spouses of self-employed workers[11] may be encouraged and, in the light of such examination, to consider any appropriate steps for encouraging such recognition[12].

Member states were also required to undertake to examine whether, and under what conditions, female self-employed workers and the wives of self-employed workers may, during interruptions in their occupational activity owing to pregnancy or motherhood: (a) have access to services supplying temporary replacements or existing national social services; or (b) be entitled to cash benefits under a social security scheme or under any other public social protection system[13].

The member states had to introduce into their national legal systems such measures as necessary to enable all persons who consider themselves wronged by failure to apply the principle of equal treatment in self-employed activities to pursue their claims by judicial process, possibly after recourse to other competent authorities[14].

The Directive required the member states to ensure that the measures adopted pursuant to the Directive, together with any relevant provisions already in force, are brought to the attention of bodies representing self-employed workers and vocational training centres[15].

The Directive also required the member states to bring into force the laws, regulations and administrative provisions necessary to comply with the Directive[16], and to inform the EC Commission immediately of the measures taken to comply with the Directive[17].

1   Ie EC Directive 86/613 (OJ L359, 19.12.86, p 56) on the application of the principle of equal treatment between men and women engaged in an activity, including agriculture, in a self-employed capacity, and on the protection of self-employed women during pregnancy and motherhood. The purpose of the Directive is to cover those aspects that are not already covered by EC Council Directive 76/207 (OJ L39, 14.2.76, p 40) on the implementation of the principle of equal treatment for men and women as regards access to employment, vocational training and promotion, and working conditions (as amended) (see

para 338 ante) and EC Directive 79/7 (OJ L6, 10.1.79, p 24) on the progressive implementation of the principle of equal treatment for men and women in matters of social security (see para 339 ante): EC Directive 86/613 (OJ L359, 19.12.86, p 56) art 1.
2   Ibid art 1.
3   Ibid art 2(a). 'Self-employed workers' are all persons pursuing a gainful activity for their own account under the conditions laid down by national law, and includes farmers and members of the liberal professions: art 2(a).
4   Ibid art 2(b).
5   Ibid art 3.
6   Ie as defined in EC Directive 76/207 (OJ L39, 14.2.76, p 40) (as amended) (see para 338 ante): EC Directive 86/613 (OJ L359, 19.12.86 p 56) art 4.
7   Ibid art 4.
8   Ibid art 5.
9   Ie the spouses referred to in ibid art 2(b): see the text to note 4 supra.
10 Ibid art 6.
11 See note 9 supra.
12 EC Directive 86/613 (OJ L359, 19.12.86 p 56) art 7.
13 Ibid art 8.
14 Ibid art 9.
15 Ibid art 10.
16 Ibid art 12(1). The Directive had to be implemented by 30 June 1989: art 12(1). However, if a member state, in order to comply with art 5 (see the text to note 8 supra), had to amend its legislation on matrimonial rights and obligations then the date on which that member state had to comply with art 5 was 30 June 1991: art 12(1).
17 Ibid art 12(2). Not later than 30 June 1991, the member states had to forward all the necessary information to the EC Commission to enable it to draw up a report on the application of the Directive for submission to the EC Council: art 13.

(iii) Domestic Legislation

342.   The Sex Discrimination Act 1975.   The Sex Discrimination Act 1975 renders unlawful sex discrimination[1] and certain victimisation and harassment[2] in the fields of employment[3] and education[4] and in the provision of goods, facilities, services and premises[5]. The Sex Discrimination Act 1975 also renders unlawful certain discrimination on grounds of gender reassignment[6] and discrimination against married persons and civil partners[7]. Discriminatory practices and advertisements, and instructions and pressure to discriminate are also rendered unlawful[8].

Liability is imposed upon employers and principals in respect of acts done by their employees and agents and on persons knowingly aiding unlawful acts[9].

There are certain general exceptions[10].

The Sex Discrimination Act 1975 established the Equal Opportunities Commission[11] which is obliged to work towards the elimination of discrimination and to promote equality of opportunity between men and women generally[12]. The Act also empowers the Equal Opportunities Commission to assist individuals in relation to certain research and educational activities[13] and in relation to proceedings or prospective proceedings under the Act[14], to conduct formal investigations[15], and to bring proceedings in respect of certain contraventions of the Act[16].

The Act applies, subject to certain limitations, to acts done by the Crown[17]. The Secretary of State may by an order[18], the draft of which has been approved by each House of Parliament, amend certain provisions of the Act[19].

The wording and structure of the Race Relations Act 1976[20] were modelled on the Sex Discrimination Act 1975 and consequently case law relating to the interpretation of the Sex Discrimination Act 1975 is relevant to the interpretation of the Race Relations Act 1976 and vice versa[21].

1   See the Sex Discrimination Act 1975 ss 1, 2 (s 1 as substituted and amended); and para 344 et seq post. Any provision of an Act passed before the Sex Discrimination Act 1975 or an instrument approved or

made by or under such an Act (including one approved or made after the passing of the Sex Discrimination Act 1975) is of no effect in so far as it imposes a requirement to do an act which would be rendered unlawful by Pt II (ss 6–20A) (as amended) (discrimination as respects employment), Pt III (ss 21A–36) (as amended) (discrimination as respects education etc) so far as it applies to vocational training, or Pt IV (ss 37–42) (as amended) (other unlawful acts) so far as it has effect in relation to Pt II (as amended) and Pt III (as amended): Employment Act 1989 s 1(1), (2). Where an Act passed at any time after the Sex Discrimination Act 1975 re-enacts (with or without modification) a provision of an Act passed before the Sex Discrimination Act 1975, that provision as re-enacted is to be treated for the purposes of the Employment Act 1989 s 1(1) as if it continued to be contained in an Act passed before the Sex Discrimination Act 1975: Employment Act 1989 s 1(4). Where in any legal proceedings (of whatever nature) there falls to be determined the question whether s 1(1) operates to negative the effect of any provision in so far as it requires the application by any person of a provision, criterion or practice falling within the Sex Discrimination Act 1975 s 1(2)(b)(i) (as substituted) (see para 355 post) or s 3(1)(b)(i) (as substituted) (see para 349 post) (indirect discrimination on grounds of sex or marital status): (1) it is for any party to the proceedings who claims that the Employment Act 1989 s 1(1) does not so operate in relation to that provision to show the provision, criterion or practice in question to be justifiable as mentioned in the Sex Discrimination Act 1975 s 1(2)(b)(ii) (as substituted) (see para 355 post) or s 3(1)(b)(ii) (as substituted) (see para 351 post); and (2) s 1(2)(b)(ii) (as substituted) or s 3(1)(b)(ii) (as substituted) accordingly has effect in relation to the requirement or condition as if the reference to the person applying it were a reference to any such party to the proceedings: Employment Act 1989 s 1(3) (amended by the Sex Discrimination (Indirect Discrimination and Burden of Proof) Regulations 2001, SI 2001/2660, reg 9). The Secretary of State or, in relation to Wales, the National Assembly for Wales has power to repeal statutory provisions requiring discrimination as respects employment or training: see the Employment Act 1989 s 2(1); and the National Assembly for Wales (Transfer of Functions) Order 1999, SI 1999/672, art 2, Sch 1. As to the Secretary of State and the National Assembly for Wales see para 302 ante.

The Secretary of State or, in relation to Wales, the National Assembly for Wales, may by order make such provision as he or it considers appropriate: (a) for disapplying the Employment Act 1989 s 1(1) in the case of any provision to which it appears to him or it that s 1(1) would otherwise apply; or (b) for rendering lawful under any of the provisions of the Sex Discrimination Act 1975 falling within the Employment Act 1989 s 1(2) acts done in order to comply with any requirement of a provision whose effect is preserved by virtue of head (a) supra, or of an instrument approved or made by or under an Act passed after the Sex Discrimination Act 1975 but before the Employment Act 1989, including one approved or made after the passing of that Act (ie 16 November 1989): see s 6; and the National Assembly for Wales (Transfer of Functions) Order 1999, SI 1999/672, art 2, Sch 1.

2   As to victimisation see the Sex Discrimination Act 1975 s 4 (as amended); and para 358 post. As to harassment see s 4A (as added); and para 347 post.

3   See ibid Pt II (as amended); and para 360 et seq post.

4   See ibid ss 22–28 (as amended); and paras 378–381 post.

5   See ibid ss 29–36 (as amended); and para 382 et seq post.

6   See ibid s 2A (as added); and para 348 post.

7   See ibid s 3 (as substituted); and para 349 post. As to discrimination on the grounds of pregnancy or maternal leave see s 3A (as added); and para 350 post.

8   See ibid ss 37–40 (as amended); and para 386 et seq post.

9   See ibid ss 41, 42 (s 42 as amended); and paras 391–392 post.

10 See ibid Pt V (ss 42A–52A) (as amended); and para 395 et seq post.

11 See ibid Pt VI (ss 53–61) (as amended; prospectively repealed); and para 404 et seq post. As to the Commission for Equality and Human Rights, which is to replace the Equal Opportunities Commission, see para 305 et seq ante.

12 See ibid s 53 (as amended; prospectively repealed); and para 404 post. See note 11 supra.

13 See ibid s 54 (prospectively repealed); and para 405 post. See note 11 supra.

14 See ibid s 75 (as amended; prospectively repealed); and para 411 post. See note 11 supra.

15 See ibid ss 57–61 (as amended; prospectively repealed); and paras 407–410 post. See note 11 supra.

16 See ibid Pt VII (ss 62–76) (as amended; prospectively amended); and para 409 et seq post. See note 11 supra.

17 See ibid s 85 (as amended); and para 375 post.

18 Any power of the Secretary of State to make orders under the provisions of the Sex Discrimination Act 1975 (except s 27 (as amended) (see para 381 post) and s 59(2) (as amended; prospectively repealed) (see para 409 post)) is exercisable by statutory instrument: s 81(1) (amended by the Sex Discrimination Act 1986 s 9(2), Schedule Pt I; and the Employment Act 1989 s 29(4), Sch 7 Pt II). As from a day to be appointed, the Sex Discrimination Act 1975 s 81(1) is further amended by the removal of the reference

to s 59(2) (as amended): s 81(1) (as so amended; prospectively amended by the Equality Act 2006 ss 40, 91, Sch 3 paras 6, 17(a), Sch 4). At the date at which this volume states the law no such day had been appointed.

An order made by the Secretary of State under the Sex Discrimination Act 1975 ss 1–80 (as amended) (except s 21A (as added) (see para 394 post), s 27 (as amended), s 59(2) (as amended; prospectively repealed) and s 80(1) (as amended)) is subject to annulment in pursuance of a resolution of either House of Parliament: s 81(2) (amended by the Sex Discrimination Act 1986 Schedule Pt I; the Employment Act 1989 Sch 7 Pt II; and the Equality Act 2006 s 83(3)(a)).

The provisions of the Sex Discrimination Act 1975 s 81(1), (2) (as amended) do not apply to an order under s 78 (see para 381 post), but an order under s 78 which modifies an enactment must be made by statutory instrument subject to annulment in pursuance of a resolution of either House of Parliament: s 81(3).

An order under s 21A(5) (as added) (see para 394 post) may not be made unless: (1) the Secretary of State has consulted the Commission; and (2) a draft has been laid before and approved by resolution of each House of Parliament: s 81(2A) (added by the Equality Act 2006 s 83(3)(b)). An order under the Sex Discrimination Act 1975 s 76A(3)(i) (as added) or s 76A(4)(e) (as added) (see para 343 post) may not be made unless the Secretary of State has consulted the Commission: s 81(2B) (added by the Equality Act 2006 s 84(2)).

An order under the Sex Discrimination Act 1975 may make different provision in relation to different cases or classes of case, may exclude certain cases or classes of case, and may contain transitional provisions and savings: s 81(4). Any power conferred by the Sex Discrimination Act 1975 to make orders includes power (exercisable in the like manner and subject to the like conditions) to vary or revoke any order so made: s 81(5).

19 See ibid s 80(1). The Secretary of State may amend s 7 (see para 364 post), s 19 (see para 373 post), s 20(1), (2), (3) (see para 361 post), s 31(2) (see para 384 post), s 32 (see para 385 post), ss 34, 35 (see para 383 post) and ss 43–48 (as amended) (see para 395 et seq post) (including any such provision as amended by a previous order under this provision): see s 80(1)(a). The Secretary of State may amend or repeal s 11(4) (see para 366 post), s 12(4) (see para 367 post), s 33 (see para 383 post) and s 49 (as amended) (see para 400 post) (including any such provision as amended by a previous order under this provision): see s 80(1)(b). The Secretary of State may also amend Pt II (as amended), Pt III (as amended) or Pt IV (as amended) so as to render lawful an act which, apart from the amendment, would be unlawful by reason of s 6(1) or (2) (see paras 361–362 post), s 29(1) (see para 382 post), s 30 or s 31 (see para 384 post): see s 80(1)(c). An order under s 80(1)(c) may make such amendments to the list of provisions given in s 80(1)(a) as in the opinion of the Secretary of State are expedient having regard to the contents of the order: s 80(3).

The Secretary of State may not lay before Parliament the draft of an order under s 80(1) unless he has consulted the Equal Opportunities Commission about the contents of the draft: s 80(2).

20 For the provisions of the Race Relations Act 1976 see para 436 et seq post.
21 There are, however, some differences in the scope of the Race Relations Act 1976 and the Sex Discrimination Act 1975: see para 438 note 23 post.

(iv) Statutory Duty of Public Authorities

343. Public authorities: general statutory duty. A public authority[1] must in carrying out its functions[2] have due regard to the need: (1) to eliminate unlawful discrimination[3] and harassment[4]; and (2) to promote equality of opportunity between men and women[5].

The Secretary of State may by order impose on a person to whom the above duty[6] applies, or in so far as that duty applies to a person, a duty which the Secretary of State thinks will ensure better performance of the above duty[7].

Where the Equal Opportunities Commission thinks that a person has failed to comply with the above duty[8], the Commission may give the person a notice requiring him to comply with the duty, and to give the Commission, within the period of 28 days beginning with the date on which he receives the notice, written information of steps taken for the purpose of complying with the duty[9].

The Commission is given the power to issue a code of practice about performance of the above duties[10].

1　For these purposes, 'public authority' includes any person who has functions of a public nature (subject to the Sex Discrimination Act 1975 s 76A(3), (4) (as added): see note 4 infra): s 76A(2)(a) (s 76A added by the Equality Act 2006 s 84(1)).

2　For these purposes, 'functions' means functions of a public nature: Sex Discrimination Act 1975 s 76A(2)(b) (as added: see note 1 supra).

3　For these purposes, the reference to unlawful discrimination must be treated as including a reference to contravention of terms of contracts having effect in accordance with an equality clause within the meaning of the Equal Pay Act 1970 s 1 (as amended) (see para 424 post): Sex Discrimination Act 1975 s 76A(2)(c) (as added: see note 1 supra).

4　Ibid s 76A(1)(a) (as added: see note 1 supra). The duty in s 76A(1) (as added) does not apply to: (1) the House of Commons; (2) the House of Lords; (3) the Scottish Parliament; (4) the General Synod of the Church of England; (5) the Security Service; (6) the Secret Intelligence Service; (7) the Government Communications Headquarters; (8) a part of the armed forces of the Crown which is, in accordance with a requirement of the Secretary of State, assisting the Government Communications Headquarters; or (9) a person specified (either generally or in respect of specified functions only) for the purpose of this provision by order of the Secretary of State: s 76A(3) (as so added). The duty in s 76A(1) (as added) does not apply to the exercise of: (a) a function in connection with proceedings in the House of Commons or the House of Lords; (b) a function in connection with proceedings in the Scottish Parliament (other than a function of the Scottish parliamentary corporate body); (c) a judicial function (whether in connection with a court or a tribunal); (d) a function exercised on behalf of or on the instructions of a person exercising a judicial function (whether in connection with a court or a tribunal); or (e) a function specified for the purpose of this provision by order of the Secretary of State: s 76A(4) (as so added). Head (2) in the text is without prejudice to the effect of any exception to or limitation of the law about sex discrimination: s 76A(5) (as so added). A failure in respect of performance of the duty under s 76A(1) (as added) does not confer a cause of action at private law: s 76A(6) (as so added). As to the Secretary of State and the National Assembly for Wales see para 302 ante. As to orders under s 76A (as added) see para 342 note 18 ante. As to the security and intelligence services generally see CONSTITUTIONAL LAW AND HUMAN RIGHTS vol 8(2) (Reissue) para 473 et seq. As to the armed forces generally see ARMED FORCES. Scottish matters generally are beyond the scope of this work.

　　Section 76A (as added) binds the Crown: s 85(3B) (added by the Equality Act 2006 s 84(3)).

5　Sex Discrimination Act 1975 s 76A(1)(b) (as added: see note 1 supra). See also s 76A(5) (as added); and note 4 supra.

6　Ie the duty in ibid s 76A(1) (as added): see the text and notes 1–5 supra.

7　Ibid s 76B(1) (s 76B added by the Equality Act 2006 s 85(1)). Before making an order under the Sex Discrimination Act 1975 s 76B(1) (as added) the Secretary of State must consult the Equal Opportunities Commission: s 76B(2) (as so added). The Secretary of State: (1) must consult the National Assembly for Wales before making an order under s 76B(1) (as added) in respect of a person exercising functions in relation to Wales; and (2) may not, without the consent of the National Assembly for Wales, make an order under s 76B(1) (as added) in respect of a person all of whose functions are public functions in relation to Wales: s 76B(3) (as so added). A failure in respect of performance of a duty imposed under s 76B(1) (as added) does not confer a cause of action at private law: s 76B(4) (as so added). As to the order that has been made under s 76B(1) (as added) see the Sex Discrimination Act 1975 (Public Authorities) (Statutory Duties) Order 2006, SI 2006/2930. As to the Equal Opportunities Commission see para 404 et seq post. As to the Commission for Equality and Human Rights, which is to replace the Equal Opportunities Commission, see para 305 et seq ante.

8　Ie the duty imposed under the Sex Discrimination Act 1975 s 76B (as added). See note 7 supra.

9　Ibid s 76D(1), (2) (s 76D added by the Equality Act 2006 s 85(1)). The Sex Discrimination Act 1975 s 76D (as added) is repealed by the Equality Act 2006 ss 40, 91, Sch 3 para 15, Sch 4 as from a day to be appointed. At the date at which this volume states the law no such day had been appointed.

　　A notice under the Sex Discrimination Act 1975 s 76D (as added) may require a person to give the Commission information required by the Commission for the purposes of assessing compliance with the duty; in which case the notice must specify: (1) the period within which the information is to be given (which must begin with the date on which the notice is received and must not exceed three months); and (2) the manner and form in which the information is to be given: s 76D(3) (as so added). A person who receives a notice under s 76D (as added) must comply with it: s 76D(4) (as so added). However, a notice under s 76D (as added) does not oblige a person to give information that he could not be compelled to give in proceedings before the High Court: s 76D(5) (as so added). If the Commission thinks that a person, to whom a notice under s 76D (as added) has been given, has failed to comply with a requirement of the notice, the Commission may apply to a county court for an order requiring the person to comply: s 76D(6) (as so added). See the Gender Equality Duty Code of Practice (England and Wales) (April 2007) made under the Sex Discrimination Act 1975 s 76E(1) (as added; prospectively repealed); and note 10 infra. As to codes of practice generally see para 406 post.

10 Ie the duty under ibid s 76A(1) (as added) or a duty imposed under s 76B (as added): see s 76E(1) (s 76E
    added by the Equality Act 2006 s 86); and the Sex Discrimination Code of Practice (Public Authorities)
    (Duty to Promote Equality) (Appointed Day) Order 2007, SI 2007/741. The Sex Discrimination
    Act 1975 s 76E (as added) is repealed by the Equality Act 2006 Sch 3 para 16, Sch 4 as from a day to be
    appointed. At the date at which this volume states the law no such day had been appointed.
        Section 56A(2)–(11) (as added and amended) (see para 406 post) applies to a code under s 76E (as
    added) as to a code under s 56A (as added and amended) (see para 406 post) (for which purpose a
    reference in s 56A(10) (as added) to specified proceedings before an employment tribunal is treated as a
    reference to criminal or civil proceedings before any court or tribunal): s 76E(2) (as so added). The
    Secretary of State must consult the National Assembly for Wales before approving a draft under
    s 56A(4)(a) (as added) (see para 406 post) as applied by s 76E(2) (as added), or making an order under
    s 56A(7) (as added) (see para 406 post) as applied by s 76E(2) (as added): s 76E(3) (as so added).

(2) PROHIBITION OF DISCRIMINATION

(i) Meaning of Discrimination

344.   Direct discrimination defined. The scheme of the Sex Discrimination
Act 1975 is first to declare what constitutes 'discrimination' for the purposes of the Act
and then to indicate in what instances such discrimination is unlawful[1].

The phrase 'direct discrimination' does not appear in the Sex Discrimination
Act 1975 itself but it is a well–established and recognised shorthand for the primary type
of discrimination with which the Act is concerned[2].

A person[3] directly discriminates[4] against a woman[5] in any circumstances relevant for
the purposes of any provision of the Sex Discrimination Act 1975[6] if on the ground of
her sex[7] he treats her less favourably[8] than he treats or would treat[9] a man[10].

1   The two issues are separate and should be kept so: *Peake v Automotive Products Ltd* [1977] QB 780, [1977]
    ICR 480, EAT; revsd on different grounds [1978] QB 233, [1978] 1 All ER 106, CA.
        As to legislation prohibiting discrimination or harassment on grounds of sexual orientation see the
    Employment Equality (Sexual Orientation) Regulations 2003, SI 2003/1661 (as amended); and para 722
    et seq post.
2   Similarly, the phrase 'indirect discrimination' (see paras 351, 355 post) does not appear in the Sex
    Discrimination Act 1975 but is a convenient shorthand for the secondary, and arguably more
    sophisticated, area of protection afforded by the Act.
3   'Person' includes a body of persons, corporate or unincorporate: Interpretation Act 1978 s 5, Sch 1. As to
    the liability of principals and employers for the acts of their agents and employees see the Sex
    Discrimination Act 1975 s 41; and para 391 post. As to the liability of those who knowingly aid unlawful
    acts see s 42 (as amended); and para 392 post.
4   References to discrimination refer to any discrimination falling within ibid ss 1–4 (as amended) (see the
    text to note 10 infra; and paras 351–358 post); references to sex discrimination refer to any
    discrimination falling with s 1 (as substituted and amended), s 2 or s 3A (as added); and related
    expressions are to be construed accordingly: ss 5(1), 82(1) (s 5(1) amended by the Employment Equality
    (Sex Discrimination) Regulations 2005, SI 2005/2467, reg 6). See *Cornelius v University College of
    Swansea* [1987] IRLR 141, CA ('discrimination' in the Sex Discrimination Act 1975 Pts II, Pt III (as
    amended) means sex discrimination as in s 1 (as substituted and amended) and victimisation as in s 4 (as
    amended)). Discrimination is only unlawful in the specific instances referred to in the Sex Discrimination
    Act 1975: *Kassam v Immigration Appeal Tribunal* [1980] 2 All ER 330, sub nom *R v Immigration Appeal
    Tribunal, ex p Kassam* [1980] 1 WLR 1037, CA (exercise of powers in Immigration Act 1971 and rules
    under that Act not covered by the Sex Discrimination Act 1975); approved in *Re Amin* [1983] 2 AC 818,
    sub nom *Amin v Entry Clearance Officer, Bombay* [1983] 2 All ER 864, HL.
5   'Woman' includes a female of any age: Sex Discrimination Act 1975 ss 5(2), 82(1). See note 10 infra.
6   There is an exception for provisions to which ibid s 1(2) (as substituted and amended) applies (see
    para 351 post), specifically any provision of Pt II (ss 6–20A) (as amended) (see para 360 et seq post), s 35A
    (as added and amended) (see para 374 post), and any other provision of Pt III (ss 21A–36) (as amended),
    so far as it applies to vocational training: s 1(3) (s 1 substituted by the Sex Discrimination (Indirect
    Discrimination and Burden of Proof) Regulations 2001, SI 2001/2660, reg 3). 'Vocational training'
    means all types, and all levels, of vocational training, advanced vocational training and retraining, and
    vocational guidance, and includes practical work experience undertaken for a limited period for the

purposes of a person's vocational training as so defined: Sex Discrimination Act 1975 s 82(1) (definition added by the Employment Equality (Sex Discrimination) Regulations 2005, SI 2005/2467, reg 33(1), (4)).

7 As to what constitutes 'on the ground of her sex' see para 346 post.
8 As to what constitutes 'less favourable treatment' see para 345 post.
9 As to the nature of the comparison to be made see para 356 post.
10 Sex Discrimination Act 1975 s 1(1)(a) (as substituted: see note 6 supra). Section 1 (as substituted) applies equally to the treatment of men, with the requisite modifications: see s 2(1); and para 357 post. 'Man' includes a male of any age: ss 5(2), 82(1). As to sex discrimination against men see para 357 post. As to discrimination on the grounds of gender reassignment see para 348 post.

345.   Less favourable treatment.   Direct sex discrimination[1] can only be established if the complainant was treated less favourably than a person of the opposite gender was or would have been treated[2]. Both acts and omissions amount to 'treatment'[3]. The treatment need not be specifically directed at the complainant for it to amount to discrimination[4]. However, there does need to be some relationship between the complainant and the alleged discriminator[5].

The question of whether treatment is less favourable is to be determined on a mixed subjective and objective basis. The complainant must show more than a mere genuine belief that the treatment is less favourable[6]. However, there is no need for the complainant to prove that the treatment is objectively less favourable: it is sufficient to show that an option is given or withheld on the basis of success without showing that a person is actually better off who exercises the option[7].

Sexual harassment[8] is also capable of amounting to less favourable treatment for the purposes of a claim of direct sex discrimination[9].

If the difference in treatment is de minimis then it may not be sufficient to amount to less favourable treatment for the purposes of a claim of direct sex discrimination[10].

1 See para 344 ante.
2 Sex Discrimination Act 1975 s 1(1)(a) (substituted by the Sex Discrimination (Indirect Discrimination and Burden of Proof) Regulations 2001, SI 2001/2660, reg 3). As to the scope of the Sex Discrimination Act 1975 s 1 (as substituted and amended) see para 344 ante. See also para 351 post. See *Department for Work and Pensions v Thompson* [2004] IRLR 348, EAT (requirement that men wear a suit and tie, when women only required to 'dress appropriately and to a similar standard', not less favourable treatment).
3 Less favourable treatment can take many different forms including words, acts and failures to provide opportunities.
4 See e g *Weathersfield Ltd (t/a Van & Truck Rentals) v Sargent* [1998] ICR 198, [1998] IRLR 14, EAT. Cf *Stewart v Cleveland Guest (Engineering) Ltd* [1994] ICR 535, [1994] IRLR 440, EAT; *Smith v Gardner Merchant Ltd* [1998] 3 All ER 852, [1998] IRLR 510, CA.
5 Thus where the alleged discriminator neither intends nor could reasonably anticipate that the complainant would become aware of acts or words complained of, this cannot constitute less favourable treatment of the complainant: *De Souza v Automobile Association* [1986] ICR 514, [1986] IRLR 103, CA.
6 See *Burrett v West Birmingham Health Authority* [1994] IRLR 7, EAT.
7 Thus in *Birmingham City Council v Equal Opportunities Commission* [1989] AC 1155, sub nom *Equal Opportunities Commission v Birmingham City Council* [1989] 1 All ER 769, HL, the loss of the chance of selective education which was reasonably thought to be of better value than non-selective education was sufficient to amount to less favourable treatment without proof that selective education was objectively better. See also *Gill v El Vino Co Ltd* [1983] QB 425, [1983] 1 All ER 398, CA.
8 Sexual harassment was previously not specifically referred to in the Sex Discrimination Act 1975, but s 4A (as added) now takes over from and supersedes the previous case law on the subject: see para 347 post.
9 See para 347 post.
10 It has been held that trivial differences of treatment may not be sufficient to amount to 'less favourable treatment' (see *Peake v Automotive Products Ltd* [1978] QB 233, sub nom *Automotive Products Ltd v Peake* [1977] IRLR 365, CA; explained in *Ministry of Defence v Jeremiah* [1980] QB 87, [1979] 3 All ER 833, CA), but no later cases have affirmed this approach.

346.   On the ground of sex.   Less favourable treatment[1] must be on the ground of the complainant's sex if it is to amount to sex discrimination[2]. The test is on a mixed subjective and objective basis[3]. There is no need to establish a discriminatory motive on the part of the alleged discriminator. Indeed the question of any conscious motivation or intention on the part of the alleged discriminator is irrelevant[4]. The sexual ground need not be the sole cause of the discriminatory treatment or even the main cause but must be an operative or effective cause[5].

Less favourable treatment on the ground of the sexual orientation rather than the sex of the complainant does not amount to sex discrimination for the purposes of the Sex Discrimination Act 1975[6].

1   See para 345 ante.
2   See the Sex Discrimination Act 1975 s 1(1)(a) (substituted by the Sex Discrimination (Indirect Discrimination and Burden of Proof) Regulations 2001, SI 2001/2660, reg 3). As to the scope of the Sex Discrimination Act 1975 s 1 (as substituted and amended) see para 344 ante. See also para 351 post.
    As to discrimination on grounds of pregnancy see para 361 post.
    Discrimination on grounds of gender reassignment has been held to fall within the provisions of EC Council Directive 76/207 (OJ L39, 14.2.76, p 40) on the implementation of the principle of equal treatment for men and women as regards access to employment, vocational training and promotion, and working conditions (the 'Equal Treatment Directive') (as amended) (see para 338 ante) (C-13/94 *P v S* [1996] ICR 795, [1996] IRLR 347, ECJ) and it has also been held to fall within the provisions of the Sex Discrimination Act 1975 s 1(1)(a) (as substituted) (*Chessington World of Adventures Ltd v Reed* [1998] ICR 97, [1997] IRLR 556, EAT). However, the addition of the Sex Discrimination Act 1975 s 2A(1)(a) (added by the Sex Discrimination (Gender Reassignment) Regulations 1999, SI 1999/1102, reg 2) has brought such cases expressly within the protection of the Sex Discrimination Act 1975: see para 348 post.
    See also C-313/02 *Wippel v Peek & Cloppenburg GmbH & Co KG* [2004] ECR I-9483, [2005] ICR 1604, ECJ; *Williams v Ministry of Defence* [2003] All ER (D) 142 (Oct), EAT.
    As to legislation prohibiting discrimination or harassment on grounds of sexual orientation see the Employment Equality (Sexual Orientation) Regulations 2003, SI 2003/1661 (as amended); and para 722 et seq post.
3   See *Birmingham City Council v Equal Opportunities Commission* [1989] AC 1155, sub nom *Equal Opportunities Commission v Birmingham City Council* [1989] 1 All ER 769, HL; *James v Eastleigh Borough Council* [1990] 2 AC 751, [1990] ICR 554, HL; *Grieg v Community Industry* [1979] ICR 356, [1979] IRLR 158, EAT. See also *Skyrail Oceanic Ltd v Coleman* [1981] ICR 864, sub nom *Coleman v Skyrail Oceanic Ltd (t/a Goodmos Tours)* [1981] IRLR 398, CA; *Ministry of Defence v Jeremiah* [1980] QB 87, [1979] 3 All ER 833, CA; *Gill v El Vino Co Ltd* [1983] QB 425, [1983] 1 All ER 398, CA; *Porcelli v Strathclyde Regional Council* [1986] ICR 564, sub nom *Strathclyde Regional Council v Porcelli* [1986] IRLR 134, Ct of Sess; *P & O European Ferries (Dover) Ltd v Iverson* [1999] ICR 1088, EAT; *Hobson v Hackney London Borough Council* [2002] EWCA Civ 1237, [2002] All ER (D) 47 (Sep). See also para 345 ante.
4   The intention of the alleged discriminator may be non-discriminatory or even laudable, but this is still irrelevant: see *Ministry of Defence v Jeremiah* [1980] QB 87, [1979] 3 All ER 833, CA; *R v Commission for Racial Equality, ex p Westminster City Council* [1984] ICR 770, [1984] IRLR 230; *Birmingham City Council v Equal Opportunities Commission* [1989] AC 1155, sub nom *Equal Opportunities Commission v Birmingham City Council* [1989] 1 All ER 769, HL; *O'Neill v Governors of St Thomas More Roman Catholic Voluntary Aided Upper School* [1997] ICR 33, [1996] IRLR 372, EAT.
5   See *O'Neill v Governors of St Thomas More Roman Catholic Voluntary Aided Upper School* [1997] ICR 33, [1996] IRLR 372, EAT; approved in *Smith v Gardner Merchant Ltd* [1998] 3 All ER 852, [1998] IRLR 510, CA.
6   See *Smith v Gardner Merchant Ltd* [1998] 3 All ER 852, [1998] IRLR 510, CA. See also *Pearce v Governing Body of Mayfield School* [2003] UKHL 34, [2003] ELR 655; *Macdonald v Advocate General for Scotland* [2003] UKHL 34, [2004] 1 All ER 339. Nor does less favourable treatment on this ground amount to actionable discrimination under European Union law: see Case C-249/96 *Grant v South-West Trains Ltd* [1998] All ER (EC) 193, [1998] ICR 449, ECJ; *R v Secretary of State for Defence, ex p Perkins (No 2)* [1998] IRLR 508, [1998] Fam Law 730. However, discrimination on grounds of sexual orientation has been held by the European Court of Human Rights to amount to a breach of the Convention for the Protection of Human Rights and Fundamental Freedoms (Rome, 4 November 1950; TS 71 (1953); Cmd 8969): see *Lustig-Prean and Beckett v United Kingdom* Application Nos 31417/96 and 32377/96 (1999) 29 EHRR 548, (1999) Times, 11 October; *Smith and Grady v United Kingdom* [1999] IRLR 734, ECtHR. See now the Employment Equality (Sexual Orientation) Regulations 2003, SI 2003/1661 (as amended), which implement the provisions of EC Council Directive 2000/78 (OJ L303, 2.12.2000, p 16) (see para 508 post) in so far as it relates to discrimination on the grounds of sexual orientation; and para 722 et seq post. See also *R (on the application of Amicus — MSF Section) v Secretary of State for Trade and*

Industry [2004] EWHC 860 (Admin), [2004] IRLR 430, in which the vires of certain of the provisions of the Employment Equality (Sexual Orientation) Regulations 2003, SI 2003/1661 (as amended) were unsuccessfully challenged.

347. Harassment, including sexual harassment. A person[1] subjects a woman[2] to harassment if: (1) on the ground of her sex[3], he engages in unwanted conduct that has the purpose or effect of violating her dignity or of creating an intimidating, hostile, degrading, humiliating or offensive environment for her[4]; (2) he engages in any form of unwanted verbal, non-verbal or physical conduct of a sexual nature that has the purpose or effect of violating her dignity or of creating an intimidating, hostile, degrading, humiliating or offensive environment for her[5]; or (3) on the ground of her rejection of or submission to unwanted conduct of a kind mentioned in head (1) or head (2) above he treats her less favourably than he would treat her had she not rejected or submitted to the conduct[6].

A person ('A') subjects another person ('B') to harassment if: (a) A, on the ground that B intends to undergo, is undergoing or has undergone gender reassignment, engages in unwanted conduct that has the purpose or effect of violating B's dignity or of creating an intimidating, hostile, degrading, humiliating or offensive environment for B[7]; or (b) A, on the ground of B's rejection of or submission to unwanted conduct of a kind mentioned in head (a) above, treats B less favourably than A would treat B had B not rejected, or submitted to, the conduct[8].

For these purposes, a relevant provision[9] framed with reference to harassment of women is to be treated as applying equally to the harassment of men, and for that purpose has effect with such modifications as are requisite[10].

1   As to the meaning of 'person' see para 344 note 3 ante.

2   As to the meaning of 'woman' see para 344 note 5 ante.

3   As to what constitutes 'on the ground of her sex' see para 346 ante.

4   Sex Discrimination Act 1975 s 4A(1)(a) (s 4A added by the Employment Equality (Sex Discrimination) Regulations 2005, SI 2005/2467, reg 5). Conduct is only to be regarded as having any of the effects mentioned in heads (1) and (2) in the text if, having regard to all the circumstances, including in particular the perception of the woman, it should reasonably be considered as having such an effect: Sex Discrimination Act 1975 s 4A(2) (as so added).

    Section 4A(1) (as added) is to be read as applying equally to the harassment of men, and for that purpose has effect with such modifications as are requisite: s 4A(5) (as so added).

    As to legislation prohibiting discrimination or harassment on grounds of sexual orientation see the Employment Equality (Sexual Orientation) Regulations 2003, SI 2003/1661 (as amended); and para 722 et seq post.

    The provisions of the Sex Discrimination Act 1975 s 4A (as added) take over from and supersede the previous case law: see also para 345 ante. Sexual harassment may give rise to a tort at common law although the legal basis for this in English law is somewhat uncertain: see *Khorasandjian v Bush* [1993] QB 727, [1993] 3 All ER 669, CA; *Hunter v Canary Wharf Ltd* [1997] AC 655, [1997] 2 All ER 426, HL. However, the enactment of the Sex Discrimination Act 1975 s 4A (as added) and of the Protection from Harassment Act 1997 (see CRIMINAL LAW, EVIDENCE AND PROCEDURE; TORT) has rendered the scope and nature of common law liability much less important. Further, within the employment field, sexual harassment may amount to a breach of contract on the part of the employer, for example where a relevant harassment policy or code of conduct has been incorporated into the contract of employment or where the employer's conduct is such as to be in breach of the implied duty to maintain trust and confidence. As to discrimination in the employment field see para 360 et seq post.

    As to whether the Sex Discrimination Act 1975 s 4A(1)(a) (as added) correctly complies with EC Council Directive 76/207 (OJ L39, 14.2.76, p 40) on the implementation of the principle of equal treatment for men and women as regards access to employment, vocational training and promotion, and working conditions (as amended) (see para 338 ante), which it purports to implement, see *R (on the application of the Equal Opportunities Commission) v Secretary of State for Trade and Industry* [2007] EWHC 483 (Admin), [2007] All ER (D) 183 (Mar).

5   Sex Discrimination Act 1975 s 4A(1)(b) (as added: see note 4 supra). See note 4 supra.

6   Ibid s 4A(1)(c) (as added: see note 4 supra). See note 4 supra.

7   Ibid s 4A(3)(a) (as added: see note 4 supra). Conduct is only to be regarded as having any of the effects
     mentioned in head (a) in the text if, having regard to all the circumstances, including in particular the
     perception of B, it should reasonably be considered as having such an effect: s 4A(4) (as so added).
8   Ibid s 4A(3)(b) (as added: see note 4 supra).
9   Ie a provision of ibid Pt II (ss 6–20A) (as amended) or Pt III (ss 21A–36) (as amended).
10   Ibid s 4A(6) (as added: see note 4 supra).

348.   Discrimination on the grounds of gender reassignment. A person[1] ('A')
discriminates[2] against another person ('B') in any circumstances relevant for the purposes
of: (1) the provisions relating to discrimination in the employment field[3]; (2) the
provisions relating to discrimination by or in relation to barristers[4]; and (3) any provision
relating to education[5] or goods, facilities, services and premises[6], so far as it applies to
vocational training[7], if he treats B less favourably than he treats or would treat[8] other
persons, and does so on the ground that B intends to undergo, is undergoing or has
undergone gender reassignment[9].

For these purposes, B is treated less favourably than others under arrangements[10]
made by any person in relation to another's absence from work or from vocational
training[11] if, in the application of the arrangements to any absence due to B undergoing
gender reassignment[12]: (a) he is treated less favourably than he would be if the absence
was due to sickness or injury[13]; or (b) he is treated less favourably than he would be if
the absence was due to some other cause and, having regard to the circumstances of the
case, it is reasonable for him to be treated no less favourably[14].

1   As to the meaning of 'person' see para 344 note 3 ante.
2   For the meaning of 'discrimination' see para 344 note 4 ante.
3   Sex Discrimination Act 1975 s 2A(1)(a) (added by the Sex Discrimination (Gender Reassignment)
     Regulations 1999, SI 1999/1102, reg 2). The provisions relating to employment are those contained in
     the Sex Discrimination Act 1975 Pt II (ss 6–20A) (as amended) (see para 360 post): see s 2A(1)(a) (as so
     added).
4   Ibid s 2A(1)(b) (as added: see note 3 supra). The provisions relating to barristers are those of s 35A (as
     added and amended): see para 374 post.
5   'Education' includes any form of training or instruction: ibid s 82(1). 'Training' includes any form of
     education or instruction: s 82(1).
6   Ie any provision of ibid Pt III (ss 21A–36) (as amended) other than s 35A (as added and amended): see
     s 2A(1)(c) (as added: see note 3 supra).
7   Ibid s 2A(1)(c) (as added: see note 3 supra).
8   As to the nature of the comparison to be made see para 356 post.
9   Sex Discrimination Act 1975 s 2A(1) (as added: see note 3 supra). 'Gender reassignment' means a process
     which is undertaken under medical supervision for the purpose of reassigning a person's sex by changing
     physiological or other characteristics of sex, and includes any part of such a process: s 82(1) (definition
     added by the Sex Discrimination (Gender Reassignment) Regulations 1999, SI 1999/1102, reg 2(3)). A
     provision mentioned in the Sex Discrimination Act 1975 s 2A(1) (as added) framed with reference to
     discrimination against women is to be treated as applying equally to the treatment of men with such
     modifications as are requisite: see s 2A(5) (as so added). See *Bavin v NHS Trust Pensions Agency* [1999]
     ICR 1192, EAT. See also *Ashton v Chief Constable of West Mercia Constabulary* [2001] ICR 67, [2000] All
     ER (D) 1091, EAT (no discrimination where employee dismissed on grounds of poor work performance
     linked to side effects of treatment prescribed during gender reassignment); *Croft v Royal Mail Group plc
     (formerly Consignia plc)* [2003] EWCA Civ 1045, [2003] ICR 1425, [2003] IRLR 592 (no discrimination
     where employer refused request of employee to use female facilities prior to employee's surgery for
     gender reassignment).
        The Gender Recognition Act 2004 makes provision for and in connection with change of gender:
     see CONSTITUTIONAL LAW AND HUMAN RIGHTS.
        As to legislation prohibiting discrimination or harassment on grounds of sexual orientation see the
     Employment Equality (Sexual Orientation) Regulations 2003, SI 2003/1661 (as amended); and para 722
     et seq post.
10   'Arrangements' includes terms, conditions or arrangements on which employment, a pupillage or
     tenancy or vocational training is offered: Sex Discrimination Act 1975 s 2A(4) (as added: see note 3
     supra).
11   See ibid s 2A(2) (as added: see note 3 supra).

12   Ibid s 2A(3) (as added: see note 3 supra).
13   Ibid s 2A(3)(a) (as added: see note 3 supra).
14   Ibid s 2A(3)(b) (as added: see note 3 supra).

349.   Discrimination against married persons and civil partners in the employment field.   A person[1] discriminates[2] against a person ('A') who is married[3] or a civil partner[4] in any circumstances relevant for the purposes of any of the provisions relating to employment[5] if: (1) on the ground of being so married or a civil partner he treats A less favourably than he treats or would treat[6] a person who was not married or a civil partner[7]; or (2) he applies to A a provision, criterion or practice which he applies or would apply equally to a person who is not married nor a civil partner, but (a) which puts or would put persons who are married or civil partners at a particular disadvantage when compared with persons who are not married or civil partners; and (b) which puts A at that disadvantage; and (c) which he cannot show to be a proportionate means of achieving a legitimate aim[8].

The Secretary of State or, in relation to Wales, the National Assembly for Wales has power to exempt discrimination in favour of lone parents in connection with training[9].

1   As to the meaning of 'person' see para 344 note 3 ante.
2   For the meaning of 'discrimination' see para 344 note 4 ante.
3   It was held that the predecessor of this provision did not apply to a single person even where the action was taken because of impending marriage: *Bick v Royal West of England Residential School for the Deaf* [1976] IRLR 326, IT. However, if it can be shown that a woman in such circumstances was treated less favourably than a man would have been in similar circumstances then this may amount to direct sex discrimination under the Sex Discrimination Act 1975 s 1 (as substituted and amended) (see para 344 ante): *McLean v Paris Travel Service Ltd* [1976] IRLR 202, IT.
4   As to civil partnerships generally see MATRIMONIAL LAW. As to legislation prohibiting discrimination or harassment on grounds of sexual orientation see the Employment Equality (Sexual Orientation) Regulations 2003, SI 2003/1661 (as amended); and para 722 et seq post.
5   Sex Discrimination Act 1975 s 3(1), (2) (s 3 substituted by the Civil Partnership Act 2004 s 251(1), (2)). The provisions relating to employment are those in the Sex Discrimination Act 1975 Pt II (ss 6–20A) (as amended): see para 360 et seq post. For these purposes, a provision of Pt II (as amended) framed with reference to discrimination against women is to be treated as applying equally to the treatment of men, and for that purpose has effect with such modifications as are requisite: s 3(3) (as so substituted). As to the meaning of 'woman' see para 344 note 5 ante; and as to the meaning of 'man' see para 344 note 10 ante. As to sex discrimination against men see para 357 post.
6   As to the nature of the comparison to be made see para 356 post.
7   Sex Discrimination Act 1975 s 3(1)(a) (as substituted: see note 5 supra). Further, if an employer makes unsupported assumptions as to the role and behaviour of a married woman then this may be discrimination on the ground of marital status but may also be direct sex discrimination under s 1 (as substituted and amended) (see para 344 ante): *Skyrail Oceanic Ltd v Coleman* [1981] ICR 864, sub nom *Coleman v Skyrail Oceanic Ltd* [1981] IRLR 398, CA; *Horsey v Dyfed County Council* [1982] ICR 755, [1982] IRLR 395, EAT.
8   Sex Discrimination Act 1975 s 3(1)(b) (as substituted: see note 5 supra). See *Hurley v Mustoe* [1981] ICR 490, [1981] IRLR 208, EAT (policy of employer not to employ women with small children; capable of being both sex discrimination under the predecessor of the Sex Discrimination Act 1975 s 1 (as substituted and amended) and indirect discrimination against married persons under the predecessor of s 3(1)(b) (as substituted) since married persons are less likely to be able to comply with a 'no children' rule); *Kidd v DRG (UK) Ltd* [1985] ICR 405, [1985] IRLR 190, EAT (part-time employees selected for redundancy before full-time employees; claim of indirect discrimination on ground that due to child care responsibilities fewer married women are able to comply with requirement as to full-time employment than men or single women; claim rejected because it could no longer be assumed that a greater proportion of married women than men or single women undertook child care so as to be unavailable for full-time employment); *Chief Constable of the Bedfordshire Constabulary v Graham* [2002] IRLR 239, [2001] All ER (D) 89 (Sep), EAT (police force policy of preventing spouses from working in same division not justified). See also note 7 supra. Provision has been made in relation to discrimination of the ground of pregnancy or maternity leave: see the Sex Discrimination Act 1975 s 3A (as added); and para 350 post.

9   See the Employment Act 1989 s 8 (as amended); and the National Assembly for Wales (Transfer of Functions) Order 1999, SI 1999/672, art 2, Sch 1. As to the Secretary of State and the National Assembly for Wales see para 302 ante. The Secretary of State or the National Assembly for Wales may by order provide with respect to:

  (1)   any specified arrangements made under the Employment and Training Act 1973 s 2 (as substituted and amended) (see EMPLOYMENT vol 16(1B) (Reissue) para 765); or

  (2)   any specified class or description of training for employment provided otherwise than in pursuance of that provision,

that the Employment Act 1989 s 8 (as amended) is to apply to such special treatment afforded to or in respect of lone parents in connection with their participation in those arrangements, or in that training or scheme, as is specified or referred to in the order: s 8(1) (amended by the Statute Law (Repeals) Act 2004). 'Employment' and 'training' have the same meanings as in the Employment and Training Act 1973 (see EMPLOYMENT vol 16(1B) (Reissue) para 765); and 'lone parent' has the same meaning as it has for the purposes of any regulations made in pursuance of the Social Security Act 1986 s 20(1)(a) (repealed) (income support: see SOCIAL SECURITY AND PENSIONS): Employment Act 1989 s 8(4).

   Where s 8 (as amended) applies to any treatment afforded to or in respect of lone parents, neither the treatment so afforded nor any act done in the implementation of any such treatment is to be regarded for the purposes of the Sex Discrimination Act 1975 as giving rise to any discrimination falling within s 3 (as substituted) (see the text and notes 1–8 supra): Employment Act 1989 s 8(2). An order under s 8(1) (as amended) may specify or refer to special treatment afforded as mentioned in s 8(1) (as amended), whether it is afforded by the making of any payment or by the fixing of special conditions for participation in the arrangements, training or scheme in question, or otherwise, and whether it is afforded by the Secretary of State, the National Assembly for Wales, or by some other person; and, without prejudice to the generality of head (2) supra, any class or description of training for employment specified in such an order by virtue of head (2) supra may be framed by reference to the person, or the class or description of persons, by whom the training is provided: s 8(3).

350.   Discrimination on the ground of pregnancy or maternity leave. In any relevant circumstances[1], a person[2] discriminates[3] against a woman[4] if: (1) at a time in a protected period[5], and on the ground of the woman's pregnancy[6], he treats her less favourably[7] than he would treat her had she not become pregnant[8]; (2) on the ground that the woman is exercising or seeking to exercise, or has exercised or sought to exercise, a statutory right to maternity leave[9], the person treats her less favourably than he would treat her if she were neither exercising nor seeking to exercise, and had neither exercised nor sought to exercise, such a right[10]; or (3) on the ground that the relevant provision relating to compulsory maternity leave[11] has to be complied with in respect of the woman, he treats her less favourably than he would treat her if that provision did not have to be complied with in respect of her[12].

1   Ie circumstances which are relevant for the purposes of any provision of the Sex Discrimination Act 1975 Pt II (ss 6–20A) (as amended), s 35A (as added and amended), and any other provision of Pt III (ss 21A–36) (as amended) so far as Pt III (as amended) applies to vocational training: s 3A(5) (s 3A added by the Employment Equality (Sex Discrimination) Regulations 2005, SI 2005/2467, reg 4).
    As to whether the Sex Discrimination Act 1975 s 3A (as added) correctly complies with EC Council Directive 76/207 (OJ L39, 14.2.76, p 40) on the implementation of the principle of equal treatment for men and women as regards access to employment, vocational training and promotion, and working conditions (as amended) (see para 338 ante), which it purports to implement, see *R (on the application of the Equal Opportunities Commission) v Secretary of State for Trade and Industry* [2007] EWHC 483 (Admin), [2007] All ER (D) 183 (Mar).

2   As to the meaning of 'person' see para 344 note 3 ante.

3   For the meaning of 'discrimination' see para 344 note 4 ante.

4   As to the meaning of 'woman' see para 344 note 5 ante.

5   In relation to a woman, a protected period begins each time she becomes pregnant, and the protected period associated with any particular pregnancy of hers ends: (1) if she is entitled to ordinary but not additional maternity leave in connection with the pregnancy, at the end of her period of ordinary maternity leave connected with the pregnancy or, if earlier, when she returns to work after the end of her pregnancy; (2) if she is entitled to ordinary and additional maternity leave in connection with the pregnancy, at the end of her period of additional maternity leave connected with the pregnancy or, if earlier, when she returns to work after the end of her pregnancy; or (3) if she is not entitled to ordinary maternity leave in respect of the pregnancy, at the end of the two weeks beginning with the end of the

pregnancy: Sex Discrimination Act 1975 s 3A(3)(a) (as added: see note 1 supra). 'Ordinary maternity leave' and 'additional maternity leave' are to be construed in accordance with the Employment Rights Act 1996 ss 71, 73 (as substituted and amended) (see EMPLOYMENT vol 16(1A) (Reissue) para 322): Sex Discrimination Act 1975 s 3A(4) (as so added).

6   Where a person's treatment of a woman is on grounds of illness suffered by the woman as a consequence of a pregnancy of hers, that treatment is to be taken to be on the ground of the pregnancy: ibid s 3A(3)(b) (as added: see note 1 supra).

7   As to what constitutes less favourable treatment see para 345 ante.

8   Sex Discrimination Act 1975 s 3A(1)(a) (as added: see note 1 supra).

9   'Statutory right to maternity leave' means a right conferred by the Employment Rights Act 1996 s 71(1) or (3) (as substituted) (see EMPLOYMENT vol 16(1A) (Reissue) para 322): Sex Discrimination Act 1975 s 3A(3)(c) (as added: see note 1 supra).

10 Ibid s 3A(1)(b) (as added: see note 1 supra).

11 Ie the Employment Rights Act 1996 s 72(1) (as substituted): see EMPLOYMENT vol 16(1A) (Reissue) para 322.

12 Sex Discrimination Act 1975 s 3A(2) (as added: see note 1 supra).

351.   Indirect discrimination in non–employment–related cases. A person[1] indirectly discriminates[2] against a woman[3] if he applies to her a requirement or condition[4] which he applies or would apply equally to a man[5] but which: (1) is such that the proportion of women who can comply with it is considerably smaller than the proportion of men who can comply with it[6]; and (2) he cannot show to be justifiable irrespective of the sex of the person to whom it is applied[7]; and (3) is to her detriment because she cannot comply with it[8].

1   As to the meaning of 'person' see para 344 note 3 ante.

2   For the meaning of 'discrimination' see para 344 note 4 ante. See also para 344 note 2 ante.
    As to indirect discrimination in employment-related cases see the Sex Discrimination Act 1975 s 1(2), (3) (as substituted); and para 355 post.

3   For the meaning of 'woman' see para 344 note 5 ante. These provisions apply equally to the treatment of men, with requisite modifications: see ibid s 2(1); and para 357 ante.

4   The leading cases on the interpretation of 'requirement or condition' have been decided under the equivalent provisions in the Race Relations Act 1976: see para 342 text to note 21 ante. For the equivalent provisions in the Race Relations Act 1976 see para 440 post. The general approach has been to construe the words 'requirement or condition' so that failure to comply must be an absolute bar: see *Perera v Civil Service Commission (No 2)* [1983] ICR 428, [1983] IRLR 166, CA (applicant born in Sri Lanka applied for job as legal assistant; he could comply with the absolute requirement that he must be a solicitor or barrister but other criteria, including experience in the United Kingdom, command of English language and British nationality, were taken into account; the Court of Appeal held that none of those criteria amounted to an absolute bar and so the applicant could not establish that a requirement or condition had been applied). See also *Meer v Tower Hamlets London Borough Council* [1988] IRLR 399, CA; *Brook v Haringey London Borough Council* [1992] IRLR 478, EAT.
    However, the Employment Appeal Tribunal, when considering the meaning of 'requirement or condition' in claims brought under the sex discrimination legislation, has tended to take a rather broader approach: see *Clarke v Eley (IMI) Kynock Ltd* [1983] ICR 165, [1982] IRLR 482, EAT (but cf the contrary decision on its facts in *Kidd v DRG (UK) Ltd* [1985] ICR 405, [1985] IRLR 190, EAT); *Watches of Switzerland Ltd v Savell* [1983] IRLR 141, EAT; *Home Office v Holmes* [1984] ICR 678, [1984] IRLR 299, EAT. See also *Meade-Hill v British Council* [1995] ICR 847, [1995] IRLR 478, CA; *Falkirk Council v Whyte* [1997] IRLR 560, EAT.
    The European Court of Justice adopts a broader approach to the concept of indirect discrimination when considering claims under the Treaty Establishing the European Community (the 'EC Treaty') (Rome, 25 March 1957; TS 1 (1973); Cmnd 5179) art 141 (formerly art 119; renumbered by virtue of the Treaty of Amsterdam: see *Treaty Citation (No 2) (Note)* [1999] All ER (EC) 646, ECJ): see Case C-127/92 *Enderby v Frenchay Health Authority and Secretary of State for Health* [1994] ICR 112, [1993] IRLR 591, ECJ. See also *British Road Services Ltd v Loughran* [1997] IRLR 92, NI CA. The Employment Appeal Tribunal has rejected arguments that the indirect discrimination provisions under the Sex Discrimination Act 1975 should be interpreted so as to be consistent with the approach of the European Court of Justice to claims under the EC Treaty art 141 (formerly art 119): see *Bhudi v IMI Refiners Ltd* [1994] ICR 307, [1994] IRLR 204, EAT; but cf *Staffordshire County Council v Black* [1995] IRLR 234, EAT; *Falkirk Council v Whyte* [1997] IRLR 560, EAT.

There must be a requirement or condition for the Sex Discrimination Act 1975 s 1(1)(b) (as substituted) (see the text and notes 5–8 infra) to operate and generally unfavourable conditions are not of themselves enough: *Francis v British Airways Engineering Overhaul Ltd* [1982] IRLR 10, EAT. The distinction between a requirement or condition as opposed to a feature of the job in question has been considered in a number of other cases: see *Home Office v Holmes* [1984] ICR 678, [1984] IRLR 299, EAT (refusal of request to change from full-time to part-time work on return from maternity leave held to be application of a condition that applicant had to work full-time in order to be able to remain in employment); *Clymo v Wandsworth London Borough Council* [1989] ICR 250, [1989] IRLR 241, EAT (applicant and husband employed as librarians; on her return from maternity leave she asked to job share with her husband so they could jointly look after the child but her request was refused; the Employment Appeal Tribunal held that full-time working was not a requirement or condition but was simply part of the job); *Briggs v North Eastern Education and Library Board* [1990] IRLR 181, NI CA (an instruction to supervise badminton after school which a teacher was unable to comply with due to childcare commitments was a 'requirement'). See also *British Telecommunications plc v Roberts* [1996] ICR 625, [1996] IRLR 601, EAT; *Barry v Midland Bank plc* [1999] 3 All ER 974, [1999] IRLR 581, HL.

Where the requirement or condition itself discriminates then this will constitute direct rather than indirect discrimination: *James v Eastleigh Borough Council* [1990] 2 AC 751, [1990] ICR 554, HL.

See also *Whiffen v Milham Ford Girls' School* [2001] EWCA Civ 385, [2001] ICR 1023, [2001] IRLR 468 (employer failed to justify a condition that only permanent employees were eligible for a redundancy selection procedure (but note that this case was decided before the Fixed-term Employees (Prevention of Less Favourable Treatment) Regulations 2002, SI 2002/2034 (see EMPLOYMENT vol 16(1A) (Reissue) para 75) came into force)); *Allonby v Accrington and Rossendale College* [2001] EWCA Civ 529, [2001] 2 CMLR 559 (tribunal had to demonstrate that it had objectively weighed the justification for imposing a condition against its discriminatory effect).

5   Sex Discrimination Act 1975 s 1(1)(b) (s 1 substituted by the Sex Discrimination (Indirect Discrimination and Burden of Proof) Regulations 2001, SI 2001/2660, reg 3). See note 4 supra. As to the meaning of 'man' see para 344 note 10 ante. See also para 344 ante.

6   Sex Discrimination Act 1975 s 1(1)(b)(i) (as substituted: see note 5 supra). See note 4 supra. See also para 352 post.

7   Ibid s 1(1)(b)(ii) (as substituted: see note 5 supra). See note 4 supra. See also para 354 post.

8   Ibid s 1(1)(b)(iii) (as substituted: see note 5 supra). See note 4 supra. See para 353 post.

352.   Disparate impact.   Once it has been shown that a condition or requirement has been applied[1] it is then necessary, in order to show discrimination, to show that the proportion of women[2] that can comply with it is considerably smaller than the proportion of men[3]. The starting point is generally to determine the correct pool for comparison[4]. Next it is necessary to consider the proportion of men and women that can comply[5]. Finally, it must be decided whether the proportion of women that can comply is considerably smaller than the proportion of men[6].

1   See the Sex Discrimination Act 1975 s 1(1)(b) (as substituted); and para 351 ante.

2   As to the meaning of 'woman' see para 344 note 5 ante. These provisions apply equally to the treatment of men, with requisite modifications: see ibid s 2(1); and para 357 ante.

3   See ibid s 1(1)(b)(i) (as substituted); and para 351 ante. As to the meaning of 'man' see para 344 note 10 ante.

    For guidance on the approach a tribunal should adopt to the analysis of such statistics see *Harvest Town Circle Ltd v Rutherford* [2001] 3 CMLR 691, [2002] ICR 123, EAT. See also *Coker v Lord Chancellor* [2001] EWCA Civ 1756, [2002] ICR 321(no breach of the Sex Discrimination Act 1975 s 1(1)(b)(i) (as substituted) where the Lord Chancellor appointed a person, well known to him, as special adviser without advertising the post).

4   It is important to consider the wording of the Sex Discrimination Act 1975 s 1(1)(b)(i) (as substituted) when determining the correct pool for comparison. First, it is the proportion of men to women that is specified rather than the actual numbers. Secondly, s 5(3) (as substituted) requires that the relevant circumstances of the comparison are the same or not materially different: see para 356 post. See *Jones v University of Manchester* [1993] ICR 474, [1993] IRLR 218, CA (appropriate pool for comparison when dealing with job applicants is those who have the required qualifications for the post save for the requirement complained of as being discriminatory). See also para 353 post.

    The identification of the pool for comparison will determine the statistical evidence to be put forward. Choosing the correct pool is ultimately a question of fact for the employment tribunal and will only be overturned if the selection is so irrationally inappropriate as to put it outside the range of selection for any reasonable tribunal: *Kidd v DRG (UK) Ltd* [1985] ICR 405, [1985] IRLR 190, EAT.

There may be a number of potential pools for comparison and an applicant will often be wise to prepare evidence in respect of a number of potential pools. However, this need not always involve production of elaborate statistical evidence (see e g *Perera v Civil Service Commission (No 2)* [1983] ICR 428, [1983] IRLR 166, CA; *Greater Manchester Police Authority v Lea* [1990] IRLR 372, EAT) but some evidence will be required if the applicant is to discharge the burden of proof (see *Barry v Midland Bank plc* [1999] 3 All ER 974, [1999] IRLR 581, HL).

Where a party is put at a disadvantage by the tribunal's decision as to the appropriate pool in that it had no means of knowing in advance of the hearing what that decision was to be and precisely what statistical evidence would be required, then the tribunal should be prepared to adjourn the case to enable that party to compile relevant evidence: *Kidd v DRG (UK) Ltd* supra.

However, in many cases anticipation of the wrong pool by a party will create significant difficulties: see *Pearse v City of Bradford Metropolitan Council* [1988] IRLR 379, EAT; *London Underground Ltd v Edwards* [1995] ICR 574, [1995] IRLR 355, EAT.

It is important to ensure that the pool is not itself discriminatory: see *R v Secretary of State for Education, ex p Schaffter* [1987] IRLR 53. This case concerned the provision of hardship grants to students. Students with children who had once been married but whose spouse had died received a grant whereas those who had never married did not. The proportion of lone parents that had never been married was about 20% for both men and women. It was argued on this basis that there was no discrimination. However, this was rejected since about 80% of lone parents were female and the correct pool for comparison was not single lone parents but all students with dependent children claiming grants. The High Court stressed the need to avoid the risk of incorporating an act of discrimination when selecting the pool.

5   The court should first consider the proportion of men that can comply with the requirement or condition, then the proportion of women, and then compare those proportions: *R v Secretary of State for Education, ex p Schaffter* [1987] IRLR 53.

The test for 'can comply' is not one of 'can physically or theoretically comply' but rather 'can comply in practice'; the current usual behaviour of women in practice is therefore to be taken into account: see *Price v Civil Service Commission* [1978] 1 All ER 1228, [1978] ICR 27, EAT (requirement that job applicants be aged between 17 and 28; no significant difference in numbers of men and women between those ages; however, since many women face childcare commitments, in practice there would be fewer women than men able to comply with the age requirement). This approach has been approved by the House of Lords in the context of race discrimination: see *Mandla v Powell Lee* [1983] 2 AC 548, [1983] ICR 385, HL. As to the application of the test see *Price v Civil Service Commission and Civil Service National Whitley Council (Staff Side) (No 2)* [1978] IRLR 3, IT; *Hurley v Mustoe* [1981] ICR 490, [1981] IRLR 208, EAT; *Home Office v Holmes* [1984] ICR 678, [1984] IRLR 299, EAT; *Clarke v Eley (IMI) Kynock Ltd* [1983] ICR 165, [1982] IRLR 482, EAT.

Although a practical approach is required, that approach must be realistic. On the one hand stereotypes of traditional women's roles should be avoided; for example it would be wrong to assume that childcare is necessarily a female role in every instance since attitudes have changed and are continuing to change and some men share partly or fully in looking after their children. On the other hand it would be unrealistic to suggest that women do not in general terms play the major role in terms of childcare. See *Price v Civil Service Commission* supra; *Briggs v North Eastern Education and Library Board* [1990] IRLR 181, NI CA. But c f *Kidd v DRG (UK) Ltd* [1985] ICR 405, [1985] IRLR 190, EAT (a case decided before *Briggs v North Eastern Education and Library Board* supra which is explicable by the failure of the applicant to put forward statistical evidence dealing with the proportions of men and women with primary childcare commitments).

6   Whether the proportion of women that can comply with a requirement or condition is considerably smaller than the proportion of men is a matter of fact for the employment tribunal and is to be interpreted in accordance with the ordinary meaning of the words 'considerably smaller' in common usage (see *Staffordshire County Council v Black* [1995] IRLR 234, EAT); and a tribunal is entitled to take into account its own knowledge and experience (see *Price v Civil Service Commission* [1978] 1 All ER 1228, [1978] ICR 27, EAT; *Briggs v North Eastern Education and Library Board* [1990] IRLR 181, NI CA).

The relevant test relates to the proportion of women that can comply and not merely the number of women: *Perera v Civil Service Commission (No 2)* [1982] ICR 350, sub nom *Perera v Civil Service Commission and the Department of Customs and Excise* [1982] ICR 350, [1982] IRLR 147, EAT; affd [1983] ICR 428, [1983] IRLR 166, CA.

Views are likely to vary as to whether a difference in proportions is sufficient to be 'considerable': see *Kidd v DRG (UK) Ltd* [1985] ICR 405, [1985] IRLR 190, EAT. The Employment Appeal Tribunal has refused to find perverse a finding by a tribunal that 95.3% was a considerably smaller proportion than 99.4%: see *Greater Manchester Police Authority v Lea* [1990] IRLR 372, EAT. Elaborate statistical arguments may not be appropriate in all cases (see *Perera v Civil Service Commission (No 2)* supra) but where statistics are used it is important to ensure that the right statistical comparison is made (see *McCausland v Dungannon District Council* [1993] IRLR 583, NI CA). Further, where the number of women employed is so low as to be statistically insignificant a strict statistical approach may not be appropriate and the tribunal may consider whether the effect on female employees would have been disproportionate if there had been a greater number of women employed: see *London Underground Ltd v Edwards (No 2)* [1999] ICR 494, [1998] IRLR 364, CA (only one woman out of 21 was unable to comply with the condition whereas all 2,023 men could comply; held sufficient to justify a finding that a considerably smaller proportion of women could comply). If no women at all can comply with a condition then this would be such as to satisfy the test for a 'considerably smaller' proportion for the purposes of the comparison: see *Greencroft Social Club and Institute v Mullen* [1985] ICR 796, EAT.

See also *R v Secretary of State for Trade and Industry, ex p Unison* [1996] ICR 1003, [1996] IRLR 438, DC (where the court indicated that it would be likely to view a 4% disparity between the proportions of men and women who could comply with a two-year qualifying period of employment as coming within the de minimis exception).

In Case C-167/97 *R v Secretary of State for Employment, ex p Seymour-Smith* [1999] 2 AC 554, [1999] ICR 447, ECJ, it was held that it is for the national court to verify whether statistics available indicate that a considerably smaller percentage of women than men is able to fulfil a condition or requirement; the European Court of Justice indicated that the disparity of 8.5% between the proportions of men and women who could comply with a two-year qualifying period of employment (there being 77.4% of men and 68.9% of women who could comply) 'did not appear, on the face of it, to show that a considerably smaller percentage of women than men was able to fulfil the requirement imposed by the disputed rule'. The House of Lords has held (by a majority of 3 to 2) that this disparity does satisfy the 'considerably smaller' test but that it could be objectively justified: *R v Secretary of State, ex p Seymour-Smith (No 2)* [2000] 1 All ER 857, [2000] 1 WLR 435, HL.

See also *Secretary of State for Trade and Industry v Rutherford (No 2); Secretary of State for Trade and Industry v Bentley* [2004] EWCA Civ 1186, [2005] ICR 119, [2004] 3 CMLR 1158; affd *Rutherford v Secretary of State for Trade and Industry* [2006] UKHL 19, [2006] IRLR 551, [2006] All ER (D) 30 (May) (difference between number of men and women who could comply with upper age limit to bring unfair dismissal claim was very small, not considerable).

353. Detriment. Once it has been established that a condition or requirement has been applied[1] to a woman[2] and that the proportion of women that can comply with that condition or requirement is considerably smaller than the proportion of men[3], it is then necessary, to show discrimination, to show that it is to the detriment[4] of the woman because she cannot comply with it[5].

1   See the Sex Discrimination Act 1975 s 1(1)(b) (as substituted); and para 351 ante.
2   As to the meaning of 'woman' see para 344 note 5 ante. These provisions apply equally to the treatment of men, with requisite modifications: see ibid s 2(1); and para 357 ante.
3   See ibid s 1(1)(b)(i) (as substituted); and para 351 ante. As to the meaning of 'man' see para 344 note 10 ante.
4   References in ibid Pt II (ss 6–20A) (as amended) and Pt III (ss 21A–36) (as amended) to subjecting a person to detriment do not include subjecting a person to harassment: s 82(1) (definition added by the Employment Equality) (Sex Discrimination) Regulations 2005, SI 2005/2467, reg 33). As to harassment, including sexual harassment, see the Sex Discrimination Act 1975 s 4A (as added); and para 347 ante.
    The determination of whether a requirement or condition is to the detriment of an applicant is a question of fact for the employment tribunal: see *Raval v Department of Health and Social Security and the Civil Service Commission* [1985] ICR 685, [1985] IRLR 370, EAT.
    The test as to whether a person has suffered a detriment is whether his treatment is of such a kind that a reasonable worker would or might take the view that in all the circumstances it is to his detriment: *Moyhing v Barts and London NHS Trust* [2006] IRLR 860, [2006] All ER (D) 64 (Jun), EAT (not unreasonable for male nurse to feel it was demeaning and irritating to be chaperoned while treating female patients).
    Some authorities have indicated that a narrow definition of 'detriment' is appropriate: see *Clymo v Wandsworth London Borough Council* [1989] ICR 250, [1989] IRLR 241, EAT. However, a broader and more purposive approach is seen in other authorities (see e g *Briggs v North Eastern Education and Library Board* [1990] IRLR 181, NI CA), and this seems to accord better with the purpose of the legislation.
5   See the Sex Discrimination Act 1975 s 1(1)(b)(iii) (as substituted); and para 351 ante. The determination of whether a woman 'cannot comply' has in certain authorities been given a narrow interpretation: see *Turner v Labour Party* [1987] IRLR 101, CA (benefits under a superannuation scheme were provided to survivors of married parents but not to those of parents, such as the applicant, who had been divorced; the requirement could not be said to be to her detriment because 'she cannot comply with it' since the benefit would not be determined until a later date by which time she could have married if she so wished). Other authorities give a broader meaning: see *Clarke v Eley (IMI) Kynock Ltd* [1983] ICR 165,

[1982] IRLR 482, EAT; *Commission for Racial Equality v Dutton* [1989] QB 783, [1989] 1 All ER 306, CA; *Briggs v North Eastern Education and Library Board* [1990] IRLR 181, NI CA. See also *Zurich Insurance Co v Gulson* [1998] IRLR 118, EAT (employee claimed that she could not comply with new working hours due to childcare commitments; tribunal entitled to refuse cross-examination as to her family's ability to pay for full-time nanny).

354. Justification. Even where a prima facie case of indirect discrimination is made out[1], there will be no finding of discrimination if it is shown that the requirement or condition that was applied was justifiable irrespective of the sex of the person to whom it was applied[2].

1   See para 351 ante.

2   The onus is on the alleged discriminator to prove on the balance of probabilities that the condition or requirement is justifiable: *Singh v Rowntree MacKintosh Ltd* [1979] ICR 554, [1979] IRLR 199, EAT.
     A variety of different formulations of the test for justification are found in early authorities ranging from a strict test of necessity (see eg *Steel v Union of Post Office Workers* [1978] 2 All ER 504, [1978] 1 WLR 64, EAT (was the requirement necessary, and could other non-discriminatory methods be found for achieving the alleged discriminator's objective?); *Hurley v Mustoe* [1981] ICR 490, [1981] IRLR 208, EAT) to a rather broader definition (see eg *Singh v Rowntree Mackintosh Ltd* supra; *Panesar v Nestlé Co Ltd* [1980] ICR 144n, [1980] IRLR 64, CA; *Ojutiku and Oburoni v Manpower Services Commission* [1982] ICR 661, [1982] IRLR 418, CA (where it was held that it was sufficient to establish a reason which is acceptable to right thinking people as sound and tolerable) (cases decided in the context of the Race Relations Act 1976)). See also *Kidd v DRG (UK) Ltd* [1985] ICR 405, [1985] IRLR 190, EAT; *Clymo v Wandsworth London Borough Council* [1989] ICR 250, [1989] IRLR 241, EAT.
     However, it is now established that justification requires an objective balance to be struck between the discriminatory effect of the requirement or condition and the reasonable needs of the person who applies it: *Hampson v Department of Education and Science* [1989] ICR 179, [1989] IRLR 69, CA (revsd on other grounds [1991] 1 AC 171, [1990] 2 All ER 513, HL); *Webb v EMO Air Cargo (UK) Ltd* [1993] ICR 175, [1993] IRLR 27, HL. There should be no significant difference between the approach to justification in indirect discrimination claims and that in equal pay claims: *Hampson v Department of Education and Science* supra. As to equal pay claims see Case 170/84 *Bilka-Kaufhaus GmbH v Weber von Hartz* [1986] ECR 1607, [1989] 2 CMLR 701, ECJ; *Rainey v Greater Glasgow Health Board* [1987] AC 224, [1987] 1 All ER 65, HL. See also *Greater Glasgow Health Board v Carey* [1987] IRLR 484, EAT; *Secretary of State for Employment v Chandler* [1986] ICR 436, EAT; *Greater Manchester Police Authority v Lea* [1990] IRLR 372, EAT.
     It is for the employment tribunal to decide as a matter of fact whether a claim of justification is made out: *Raval v Department of Health and Social Security* [1985] ICR 685, [1985] IRLR 370, EAT; *Mandla v Dowell Lee* [1983] 2 AC 548, [1983] 1 All ER 1062, HL; *Home Office v Holmes* [1984] ICR 678, [1984] IRLR 299, EAT; *Cobb v Secretary of State for Employment* [1989] ICR 506, [1989] IRLR 464, EAT. It may therefore be difficult to predict with any degree of certainty the outcome of justification arguments relating to any given set of facts: see *Greater Glasgow Health Board v Carey* supra; cf *Home Office v Holmes* supra.
     However, certain factors will generally be relevant for consideration by the tribunal. The number of employees that will be affected by a policy and the extent of the detriment that they will suffer should be considered: *Jones v University of Manchester* [1993] ICR 474, [1993] IRLR 218, CA. The reason for the application of the requirement or condition and whether the objective could be achieved without discrimination will also be considered and if an alternative is available then its cost will be relevant: *London Underground Ltd v Edwards (No 2)* [1997] IRLR 157, EAT. Redundancy selection on the basis of 'last in first out' will normally be justified: *Clarke v Eley (IMI) Kynock Ltd* [1983] ICR 165, [1982] IRLR 482; *Brook v Haringey London Borough Council* [1992] IRLR 478, EAT.
     For further consideration of the test see also *Steel v Union of Post Office Workers* [1978] 2 All ER 504, [1978] 1 WLR 64, EAT (discrimination against postwomen as a result of the operation of a seniority rule; discrimination not justifiable); *Cobb v Secretary of State for Employment* supra (conditions of entry to a community programme, although discriminatory, may be justified for economic and administrative reasons); *Bullock v Alice Ottley School* [1993] ICR 138, [1992] IRLR 564, CA (objective justification for differing retirement dates may be on economic grounds alone, but can include administrative efficiency); *Page v Freight Hire (Tank Haulage) Ltd* [1981] 1 All ER 394, [1981] ICR 299, EAT (employer cannot justify discrimination simply by relying on risk to safety; all circumstances of risk and measures necessary to eliminate it must be considered). See also *Barry v Midland Bank plc* [1999] 3 All ER 974, [1999] IRLR 581, HL.

For an important statement of principle on justification see also *Hardy & Hansons plc v Lax* [2005] EWCA Civ 846, [2005] ICR 1565, [2005] IRLR 726 (employer's justification had to be reasonably necessary; employer did not have a margin of discretion).

355.   Indirect discrimination in employment-related cases.   The definition in the Sex Discrimination Act 1975 of indirect discrimination[1] now applies to any circumstances relevant for the purposes of any provision of the Act, other than specified provisions related to employment[2]. In any circumstances relevant to any of those specified provisions[3], a person[4] indirectly discriminates[5] against a woman[6] if he applies to her a provision[7], criterion or practice which he applies or would apply equally to a man[8], but which: (1) puts or would put women at a particular disadvantage when compared with men[9]; (2) puts her at that disadvantage[10]; and (3) he cannot show to be a proportionate means of achieving a legitimate aim[11].

1   Ie the Sex Discrimination Act 1975 s 1(1)(b) (as substituted): see para 351 ante. See also para 344 note 2 ante.
2   The provisions referred to in the text are any provision of the Sex Discrimination Act 1975 Pt II (ss 6–20A) (as amended) (see para 360 et seq post), s 35A (as added and amended) (see para 374 post), and any other provision of Pt III (ss 21A–36) (as amended) so far as Pt III (as amended) applies to vocational training: see s 1(3) (as substituted); and para 351 ante. For the meaning of 'vocational training' see para 344 note 6 ante.
3   See note 2 supra.
4   As to the meaning of 'person' see para 344 note 3 ante.
5   For the meaning of 'discrimination' see para 344 note 4 ante.
6   For the meaning of 'woman' see para 344 note 5 ante. These provisions apply equally to the treatment of men, with requisite modifications: see the Sex Discrimination Act 1975 s 2(1); and para 357 ante.
7   A 'provision' could be a discretionary management decision not applying to others; the question is whether the provision would also be applied to others: *British Airways plc v Starmer* [2005] IRLR 862, [2005] All ER (D) 323 (Jul), EAT.
8   Sex Discrimination Act 1975 s 1(2)(b) (substituted by the Employment Equality (Sex Discrimination) Regulations 2005, SI 2005/2467, reg 3(1)). As to the meaning of 'man' see para 344 note 10 ante.
9   Sex Discrimination Act 1975 s 1(2)(b)(i) (as substituted: see note 8 supra).
10 Ibid s 1(2)(b)(ii) (as substituted: see note 8 supra).
11 Ibid s 1(2)(b)(iii) (as substituted: see note 8 supra).

356.   Nature of the comparison.   Where the case of a person is to be compared with that of a person of different sex[1], a comparison is to be made in relation to gender reassignment[2], or a comparison is made between people who are married or civil partners and those that are not[3], for the purposes of deciding whether there has been discrimination[4], the comparison must be such that the relevant circumstances in the one case are the same, or not materially different, in the other[5].

1   Ie under the Sex Discrimination Act 1975 s 1(1), (2) (as substituted and amended): see paras 344–355 ante.
2   Ie a comparison for the purposes of ibid s 2A (as added): see para 348 ante. For the meaning of 'gender reassignment' see para 348 note 9 ante.
3   Ie a comparison for the purposes of ibid s 3 (as substituted): see para 349 ante.
4   For the meaning of 'discrimination' see para 344 note 4 ante.
5   Sex Discrimination Act 1975 s 5(3) (substituted by the Civil Partnerships Act 2004 s 251(1), (3)).
    The comparison may be made with an actual or hypothetical comparator but in any case all of the relevant characteristics must be materially the same: see *Shomer v B & R Residential Lettings Ltd* [1992] IRLR 317, CA. Thus, where the complainant is a homosexual man, sexuality is a relevant characteristic and the appropriate female comparator must therefore also be homosexual: see *Smith v Gardner Merchant Ltd* [1998] 3 All ER 852, [1998] IRLR 510, CA. As to legislation prohibiting discrimination or harassment on grounds of sexual orientation see the Employment Equality (Sexual Orientation) Regulations 2003, SI 2003/1661 (as amended); and para 722 et seq post.
    See also *Greig v Community Industry* [1979] ICR 356, [1979] IRLR 158, EAT (a female applying to work with an otherwise all-male work team should be compared with a male applying to work with the same team rather than a male applying to work with an otherwise all-female work team; taking a

'mirror-image' approach is not appropriate); *Pearce v Governing Body of Mayfield School, MacDonald v Advocate General for Scotland* [2003] UKHL 34, [2004] 1 All ER 339.

Care must be taken to ensure that the relevant characteristics taken into account for the purposes of comparison do not include characteristics which are themselves discriminatory: see *James v Eastleigh Borough Council* [1990] 2 AC 751, [1990] ICR 554, HL (pensionable age could not be included as a relevant characteristic since that age was different for men and women).

Where an employer behaves in an unreasonable manner towards the complainant he may also behave unreasonably towards the relevant comparator; the relevant circumstances in such a case may include the unreasonableness of the employer towards all of his employees: *Glasgow City Council v Zafar* [1998] ICR 120, sub nom *Zafar v Glasgow City Council* [1998] IRLR 36, HL.

A medical condition resulting from gender reassignment is not comparable with pregnancy-related illness because it is not gender specific: *Ashton v Chief Constable of West Mercia Constabulary* [2001] ICR 67, [2000] All ER (D) 1091, EAT; and see para 348 ante.

Where no exact actual comparator can be found, the tribunal must construct a picture of how a hypothetical comparator would have been treated in comparable surrounding circumstances: *Vento v Chief Constable of West Yorkshire Police* [2002] EWCA Civ 1871, [2003] ICR 318, [2003] IRLR 102, [2002] All ER (D) 363 (Dec).

See *Shamoon v Chief Constable of the Royal Ulster Constabulary (Northern Ireland)* [2003] UKHL 11, [2003] 2 All ER 26, [2003] ICR 337 (female police chief inspector removed from role as assessor of staff appraisals; relevant circumstances included complaints and representations about her handling of such appraisals, as well as consideration of how other chief inspectors would have been treated in same role).

See also *Saunders v Home Office* [2006] ICR 318, (2005) Times, 2 December, EAT (female prison officer transferred to women's prison for refusing to carry out rub-down searches of male inmates).

357.   Sex discrimination against men.   The provisions relating to direct and indirect discrimination against women[1], and the provisions relating to sex discrimination[2] against women in the employment field[3] and in relation to education and goods, facilities, services and premises[4], are to be read as applying equally to the treatment of men[5], with the requisite modifications[6]. In the application of this provision no account is to be taken of special treatment afforded to women in connection with pregnancy or childbirth[7].

1   Ie the Sex Discrimination Act 1975 s 1 (as substituted and amended): see para 344 et seq ante. As to the meaning of 'woman' see para 344 note 5 ante.
2   For the meaning of 'discrimination' see para 344 note 4 ante.
3   Ie the Sex Discrimination Act 1975 Pt II (ss 6–20) (as amended): see para 360 et seq post.
4   Ie ibid Pt III (ss 21A–36) (as amended): see para 378 et seq post.
5   As to the meaning of 'man' see para 344 note 10 ante.
6   See the Sex Discrimination Act 1975 s 2(1). See *Assoukou v Select Service Partners Ltd* [2006] EWCA Civ 1442, [2006] All ER (D) 122 (Oct).
7   Sex Discrimination Act 1975 s 2(2). As to discrimination on the grounds of pregnancy or maternity leave see para 350 ante; and as to maternity rights see EMPLOYMENT vol 16(1A) (Reissue) para 322 et seq.

358.   Discrimination by way of victimisation.   A person[1] discriminates[2] against another person in any circumstances relevant for the purposes of the Sex Discrimination Act 1975 if he treats the person victimised less favourably than in those circumstances he treats or would treat other persons, and does so by reason that[3] the person victimised[4] has: (1) brought proceedings under any of the specified provisions against the discriminator or any other person[5]; (2) given evidence or information in connection with such proceedings brought by any person against the discriminator or any other person[6]; (3) otherwise done anything under or in relation to any of the specified provisions[7] in relation to the discriminator or any other person[8]; (4) alleged that the discriminator or any other person has committed an act which (whether or not the allegation so states) would amount to a contravention of the Sex Discrimination Act 1975 or give rise to a relevant claim[9]. The prohibition of victimisation extends to circumstances in which the discriminator treats the person victimised less favourably because he knows the person victimised intends to do any of the specified protected acts, or suspects the person victimised has done, or intends to do, any of them[10].

This provision does not apply to treatment of a person by reason of any allegation made by him if the allegation was false and not made in good faith[11].

1　As to the meaning of 'person' see para 344 note 3 ante.

2　For the meaning of 'discrimination' see para 344 note 4 ante.

3　It is now established that there is no need to show that the alleged victimiser was consciously motivated by the protected act: *Nagarajan v London Regional Transport* [2000] 1 AC 501, [1999] 4 All ER 65, HL. The test is therefore the same as for direct discrimination: see para 346 ante.

4　Sex Discrimination Act 1975 s 4(1). For the purposes of s 4(1) (as amended), a provision of Pt II (ss 6–20A) (as amended) (see para 360 et seq post) or Pt III (ss 21A–36) (as amended) (see para 378 et seq post) framed with reference to discrimination against women is to be treated as applying equally to the treatment of men and for that purpose has effect with such modifications as are requisite: s 4(3). As to sex discrimination against men see para 357 ante. As to the meaning of 'woman' see para 344 note 5 ante; and as to the meaning of 'man' see para 344 note 10 ante.

　　An employer does not infringe the provisions of s 4 (as amended) by the honest and reasonable conduct of its defence to the protected proceedings: *St Helens Metropolitan Borough Council v Derbyshire* [2005] EWCA Civ 977, [2006] ICR 90, [2005] IRLR 801, [2005] All ER (D) 468 (Jul) (employer's attempt to compromise proceedings by sending letters to employees did not amount to victimisation). See *Khan v Chief Constable of West Yorkshire Police* [2001] UKHL 48, [2001] 4 All ER 834, [2001] IRLR 830 (a race discrimination case); and para 442 post. See also *Arthurton v Chief Constable of Norfolk* [2007] All ER (D) 143 (Jan), EAT (where *St Helens Metropolitan Borough Council v Derbyshire* supra and *Khan v Chief Constable of West Yorkshire Police* supra were applied).

5　Sex Discrimination Act 1975 s 4(1)(a) (s 4(1)(a)–(d) amended by the Pensions Act 1995 s 66(2)). The text refers to proceedings under the Sex Discrimination Act 1975, the Equal Pay Act 1970 (see para 419 et seq post) and the Pensions Act 1995 ss 62–65 (as amended) (equal treatment) (see SOCIAL SECURITY AND PENSIONS vol 44(2) (Reissue) para 782 et seq): see the Sex Discrimination Act 1975 s 4(1)(a) (as so amended).

　　A narrow interpretation of the protected acts has been adopted in some cases: see *Cornelius v University College of Swansea* [1987] IRLR 141, 131 Sol Jo 358, CA (whilst sexual harassment proceedings against the employer were unresolved, the employer refused to allow the employee to transfer or invoke the grievance procedure; the Court of Appeal accepted that the employee suffered detriment but concluded that the treatment resulted from the fact that proceedings had been brought rather than that they had specifically been brought under the Sex Discrimination Act 1975).

6　Sex Discrimination Act 1975 s 4(1)(b) (as amended: see note 5 supra).

7　Ie the provisions mentioned in ibid s 4(1)(a) (as amended): see note 5 supra.

8　Ibid s 4(1)(c) (as amended: see note 5 supra).

9　Ibid s 4(1)(d) (as amended: see note 5 supra). A relevant claim is one brought under the Equal Pay Act 1970 (see para 419 et seq post) or the Pensions Act 1995 ss 62–65 (as amended) (see SOCIAL SECURITY AND PENSIONS vol 44(2) (Reissue) para 782 et seq): see the Sex Discrimination Act 1975 s 4(1)(d) (as so amended).

　　A narrow approach to the interpretation of the protected acts may be adopted: see *British Airways Engine Overhaul Ltd v Francis* [1981] ICR 278, [1981] IRLR 9, EAT.

　　The act complained of must, if proven, amount to a breach of the relevant provision: see *Waters v Metropolitan Police Comr* [1997] ICR 1073, [1997] IRLR 589, CA; revsd in part [2000] 4 All ER 934, [2000] ICR 1064, HL.

10　Sex Discrimination Act 1975 s 4(1). In the employment field, in order to comply with EC Council Directive 76/207 (OJ L39, 14.2.76, p 40) on the implementation of the principle of equal treatment for men and women as regards access to employment, vocational training and promotion, and working conditions, art 6 (as substituted) (see para 338 ante), the Sex Discrimination Act 1975 s 4 (as amended) must be interpreted to provide protection against detrimental treatment by an ex-employer as a reaction to protected acts: Case C-185/97 *Coote v Granada Hospitality Ltd* [1998] All ER (EC) 865, [1999] ICR 100, ECJ; *Coote v Granada Hospitality Ltd (No 2)* [1999] ICR 942, [1999] IRLR 452, EAT.

11　Sex Discrimination Act 1975 s 4(2).

359. Application of the Sex Discrimination Act 1975 to the Crown. The Sex Discrimination Act 1975 applies to an act[1] done by or for the purposes of a Minister of the Crown[2] or a government department, or to an act done on behalf of the Crown by a statutory body, or a person holding a statutory office[3], as it applies to an act done by a private person[4]. However, the Crown's liability under the Act is limited by exceptions concerning acts done under statutory authority[5] and acts safeguarding national security[6].

1　'Act' includes a deliberate omission: Sex Discrimination Act 1975 s 82(1).

2 As to Ministers of the Crown see CONSTITUTIONAL LAW AND HUMAN RIGHTS vol 8(2) (Reissue) para 394 et seq.
3 'Statutory body' means a body set up by or in pursuance of an enactment; and 'statutory office' means an office so set up: Sex Discrimination Act 1975 s 85(10).
4 Ibid s 85(1). For provisions relating to the Crown in its capacity as employer see s 85(2)–(9E) (as amended); and para 375 post. As to the application of the Crown Proceedings Act 1947 in relation to proceedings under the Sex Discrimination Act 1975 see s 85(8) (as amended); and CROWN PROCEEDINGS AND CROWN PRACTICE vol 12(1) (Reissue) para 113. As to the meaning of 'person' see para 344 note 3 ante.
5 See the Sex Discrimination Act 1975 s 51A (as added); and para 402 post.
6 See ibid s 52 (as amended); and para 403 post.

(ii) Discrimination in Particular Circumstances

A. DISCRIMINATION IN THE EMPLOYMENT FIELD

(A) In general

360. Discrimination by employers. The Sex Discrimination Act 1975 prohibits[1] discrimination[2] by an employer[3] only in relation to employment[4] of a person by him at an establishment[5] in Great Britain[6]. The Act covers both recruitment[7] and the treatment of existing employees[8].

1 As to the enforcement of individual rights in the employment field see para 414 et seq post. As to provisions relating to discrimination against office-holders see the Sex Discrimination Act 1975 ss 10A, 10B (as added); and para 377 post. As to selection of candidates by registered political parties see s 42A (as added); and para 367 note 4 post.
2 For the meaning of 'discrimination' see para 344 note 4 ante.
3 Any reference to an employer (however expressed) includes a reference to the governing body at a school acting in the exercise of its employment powers: see the Education (Modification of Enactments Relating to Employment) (England) Order 2003, SI 2003/1964, art 3(1)(a), (b), Schedule; and the Education (Modification of Enactments Relating to Employment) (Wales) Order 2006, SI 2006/1073, art 3, Schedule.
    As to the liability of employers and principals for acts done by persons in the course of employment see para 391 post.
4 'Employment' means employment under a contract of service or of apprenticeship or a contract personally to execute any work or labour, and related expressions (including 'employer') are to be construed accordingly: Sex Discrimination Act 1975 s 82(1). For the purposes of the Sex Discrimination Act 1975, two employers are to be treated as associated if one is a company of which the other (directly or indirectly) has control or if both are companies of which a third person (directly or indirectly) has control: s 82(1), (2). If the contracting party is able to delegate work, the contract is not one personally to execute work; the work or labour must be the dominant purpose of the contract: *Gunning v Mirror Group Newspapers Ltd* [1986] 1 All ER 385, sub nom *Mirror Group Newspapers Ltd v Gunning* [1986] 1 WLR 546, CA. The office of justice of the peace is not 'employment' within the meaning of the Sex Discrimination Act 1975; neither does it fall under the protection provided by s 85(2) (as amended) (see para 375 post) or s 86(2) (repealed): see *Knight v A-G* [1979] ICR 194, (1978) 123 Sol Jo 32, EAT. See also *Oliver v JP Malnick & Co (a firm)* [1983] 3 All ER 795, [1983] ICR 708, EAT (solicitor's articled clerk in 'employment' of firm); *Gunning v Mirror Group Newspapers Ltd* supra (agency for wholesale distribution of newspapers held not to be employment); *Hugh-Jones v St John's College, Cambridge* [1979] ICR 848, 123 Sol Jo 603, EAT (research fellowship at Cambridge college held to be employment); *Tanna v Post Office* [1981] ICR 374, EAT (sub-postmaster not employee for the purposes of the parallel provisions of the Race Relations Act 1976). It appears that a claim may be brought under the Sex Discrimination Act 1975 if a family practitioner committee discriminates against a general practitioner: *Roy v Kensington and Chelsea and Westminster Family Practitioner Committee* [1992] 1 AC 624, [1992] 1 All ER 705, HL.
    The definition can include self-employed persons provided they satisfy the criteria in the Sex Discrimination Act 1975 s 82(1): *Quinnen v Hovells* [1984] ICR 525, [1984] IRLR 227, EAT. An employee may bring a claim under the Sex Discrimination Act 1975 even if her contract of employment is illegal, as protection under the Act does not involve enforcing, relying on, or founding a claim on the employment contract: *Leighton v Michael* [1995] ICR 1091, [1996] IRLR 67, EAT. A 'contract personally

to execute work' may cover work done by an independent contractor: *Kelly v Northern Ireland Housing Executive* [1999] 1 AC 428, [1998] 3 WLR 735, HL (a case under the Fair Employment (Northern Ireland) Act 1976).

A 'volunteer' successfully brought a claim where there was a legally binding contract between a charitable organisation and the worker, the dominant purpose of which was the provision of labour by the volunteer: Application No 43538/94 *Armitage v Relate* (1994, unreported), ET. However, it is clear that there must be a contract between the party doing the work and the party for whom the work is being done in order for there to be an employment relationship: *BP Chemicals Ltd v Gillick and Roevin Management Services* [1995] IRLR 128, EAT. As to contract workers see para 365 post.

In *Percy v Church of Scotland Board of National Mission* [2005] UKHL 73, [2006] 2 AC 28, [2006] 4 All ER 1354 (see para 373 post), it was accepted that the claimant could not claim unfair dismissal as she was not an employee under the Employment Rights Act 1996 s 230 (as amended) although she was one under the extended definition under the Sex Discrimination Act 1975 s 82(1).

As to ministers of religion see para 373 post. As to barristers and barristers' clerks see para 374 post. As to the application of the Sex Discrimination Act 1975 to service in the police force see para 371 post; and as to prison officers see para 372 post. Other Crown employees are generally treated as if they were employed by a private person: see para 375 post.

Members of the armed forces were brought within the protection of the Sex Discrimination Act 1975 by the Sex Discrimination Act 1975 (Application to Armed Forces etc) Regulations 1994, SI 1994/3276, which removed the exclusion previously set out in the Sex Discrimination Act 1975 s 85(4) (as originally enacted): see para 375 post. EC Council Directive 76/207 (OJ L39, 14.2.76, p 40) on the implementation of the principle of equal treatment for men and women as regards access to employment, vocational training and promotion, and working conditions (as amended) (see para 338 ante) has direct effect against the state without the need for domestic legislation. The Directive also requires that member states introduce measures to protect ex-employees from the retaliatory acts of employers carried out in reaction to equal treatment proceedings: Case C-185/97 *Coote v Granada Hospitality Ltd* [1998] All ER (EC) 865, [1999] ICR 100, ECJ; applied in *Coote v Granada Hospitality Ltd (No 2)* [1999] ICR 942, [1999] IRLR 452, EAT (where the Sex Discrimination Act 1975 s 6(2) (see para 361 post) was construed so as to apply to retaliatory acts carried out by employers against ex-employees).

5 Where work is not done at an establishment it is to be treated as done at the establishment with which it has the closest connection: see the Sex Discrimination Act 1975 s 10(4). In the case of employment on board a ship registered at a port of registry in Great Britain (except where the employee does his work wholly outside Great Britain, and s 10(1A) (as added) (see note 6 infra) does not apply), the ship is deemed to be an establishment: s 10(3) (amended by the Employment Equality (Sex Discrimination) Regulations 2005, SI 2005/2467, reg 11(1), (5)). For the meaning of 'Great Britain' see para 325 note 6 ante.

6 The equivalent territorial limitation under the Race Relations Act 1976 (see para 446 post) was challenged in *Bossa v Nordstress Ltd* [1998] ICR 694, [1998] IRLR 284, EAT. In this case, an Italian applicant for a job with Alitalia in Italy was refused an interview by reason of his Italian nationality. The tribunal declined jurisdiction in respect of his complaint. The Employment Appeal Tribunal reversed this decision holding that the Treaty Establishing the European Community (the 'EC Treaty') (Rome, 25 March 1957; TS 1 (1973); Cmnd 5179) art 39 (formerly art 48; renumbered by virtue of the Treaty of Amsterdam: see *Treaty Citation (No 2) (Note)* [1999] All ER (EC) 646, ECJ) conferred enforceable rights on European Union workers to work anywhere in the European Union. Thus the Race Relations Act 1976 s 8 was disapplied by virtue of its conflict with the EC Treaty art 39 (formerly art 48).

Employment is to be regarded as being at an establishment in Great Britain if the employee does his work wholly or partly in Great Britain or if the employee does his work wholly outside Great Britain and: (1) the employer has a place of business at an establishment in Great Britain; (2) the work is for the purposes of the business carried on at that establishment; and (3) the employee is ordinarily resident in Great Britain at the time when he applies for or is offered the employment, or at any time during the course of the employment: Sex Discrimination Act 1975 s 10(1), (1A) (s 10(1) substituted, and s 10(1A) added by the Employment Equality (Sex Discrimination) Regulations 2005, SI 2005/2467, reg 11(1), (2)). In relation to the Sex Discrimination Act 1975 s 10(1) (as originally enacted), it was considered that it was not a contractual test but a factual test, looking at where the employee 'wholly or mainly' worked at the time of the alleged discrimination: *Carver v Saudi Arabian Airlines* [1999] IRLR 370, [1999] 3 All ER 61, CA.

The reference to 'employment' in the Sex Discrimination Act 1975 s 10(1) (as amended) includes: (a) employment on board a ship, but only if the ship is registered at a port of registry in Great Britain; and (b) employment on aircraft or hovercraft, but only if the aircraft or hovercraft is registered in the United Kingdom and operated by a person who has his principal place of business, or is ordinarily resident, in Great Britain: s 10(2) (substituted by the Equal Opportunities (Employment Legislation) (Territorial Limits) Regulations 1999, SI 1999/3163, reg 2(3); and amended by the Employment Equality (Sex

Discrimination) Regulations 2005, SI 2005/2467, reg 11(1), (3), (4)). For the meaning of 'United Kingdom' see para 325 note 6 ante. Employment on a ship, aircraft or hovercraft the property of Her Majesty in right of the government of the United Kingdom is regarded as employment at an establishment in Great Britain: see the Sex Discrimination Act 1975 s 85(7). Work carried out mainly outside British territorial waters on a German-registered ship does not come within the jurisdiction even where the employer is based in Britain: *Haughton v Olau Line (UK) Ltd* [1986] 2 All ER 47, [1986] 1 WLR 504, CA.

The Sex Discrimination Act 1975 s 10(1)–(4) (as modified, where an Order in Council is in force under s 10(5) (see FUEL AND ENERGY vol 19(2) (Reissue) para 1598)) applies, with specified modifications, for the purposes of determining whether contract work, within the meaning of s 9 (as amended) (see para 365 post), is at an establishment in Great Britain: see s 10(8) (added by the Employment Equality (Sex Discrimination) Regulations 2005, SI 2005/2467, reg 11(1), (7)).

As to the application of the Sex Discrimination Act 1975 s 10 (as amended) to employment concerned with exploration of the sea bed or subsoil or the exploitation of their natural resources see s 10(5)–(7) (s 10(5) amended by the Employment Equality (Sex Discrimination) Regulations 2005, SI 2005/2467, reg 11(1), (6); prospectively amended by the Petroleum Act 1998 s 50, Sch 4 para 8); and FUEL AND ENERGY vol 19(2) (Reissue) para 1598. See also the Sex Discrimination and Equal Pay (Offshore Employment) Order 1987, SI 1987/930.

7   See the Sex Discrimination Act 1975 s 6(1); and para 361 post.
8   See ibid s 6(2); and para 361 post. As to the application of s 6 (as amended) to governing bodies of schools and institutions of higher or further education where such bodies have delegated budgets see the Education (Modification of Enactments Relating to Employment) (England) Order 2003, SI 2003/1964, art 3, Schedule; and the Education (Modification of Enactments Relating to Employment) (Wales) Order 2006, SI 2006/1073, art 3, Schedule.

361.   Types of discrimination in employment.   It is unlawful for a person[1], in relation to employment[2] by him at an establishment in Great Britain[3] to discriminate against a woman[4] in the arrangements he makes for the purpose of determining who should be offered that employment[5], in the terms on which he offers her that employment[6], or by refusing or deliberately omitting to offer her that employment[7].

It is unlawful for an employer to discriminate against a woman[8] in the way he affords her access to opportunities for promotion[9], transfer or training[10], or to any other benefits, facilities or services[11], or by refusing or deliberately omitting to afford her access to them[12], or by dismissing[13] her, or subjecting her to any other detriment[14].

There has been detailed discussion as to the meaning of 'detriment' for these purposes[15]. An obligation to work full-time has been held to be more discriminatory towards women and therefore unlawful[16]. Sexual harassment is of itself a detriment[17], and there is now also a specific statutory provison making it unlawful for an employer, in relation to employment by him at an establishment in Great Britain, to subject to harassment a woman whom he employs or a woman who has applied to him for employment[18]. It is unclear whether the test for detriment is objective or subjective[19]. An employer who allows staff to be harassed by a third party may be liable[20]. The failure to allow an employee to share her full-time job with another following a period of maternity leave does not amount to a detriment[21]. However, a failure to carry out a risk assessment under health and safety regulations can amount to a detriment as long as some disadvantage was suffered as a consequence[22]. Originally it was thought that the dismissal of, or other act causing a detriment to, a pregnant woman on grounds of her pregnancy could not amount to sex discrimination because no meaningful comparison could be made with the position of a man[23]. However, it has been held that refusal of employment on the grounds of pregnancy amounts to discrimination on the grounds of sex and it is inappropriate to compare the pregnant woman with a sick man for these purposes[24]. It is now clear that action taken against a woman will be unlawful sex discrimination whenever there is a pregnancy-related reason for the action[25]. Grooming and uniform rules, whilst they may give rise to detriment in particular cases, have frequently been held not to constitute less favourable treatment[26].

1   As to the meaning of 'person' see para 344 note 3 ante.

2   For the meaning of 'employment' see para 360 note 4 ante. As to the liability of employers and principals for acts done by persons in the course of employment see para 391 post.

As to provisions relating to discrimination against office-holders see the Sex Discrimination Act 1975 ss 10A, 10B (as added); and para 377 post. As to selection of candidates by registered political parties see s 42A (as added); and para 367 note 4 post.

3   For the meaning of 'Great Britain' see para 325 note 6 ante.

4   See the Sex Discrimination Act 1975 s 6(1). As to the meaning of 'woman' see para 344 note 5 ante. These provisions apply equally to the treatment of men, with requisite modifications: see s 2(1); and para 357 ante. Section 6 (as amended) applies to discrimination on the grounds of gender reassignment with the omission of s 6(4)–(6) (as amended): s 6(8) (added by the Sex Discrimination (Gender Reassignment) Regulations 1999, SI 1999/1102, reg 3(1)). As to discrimination on the grounds of gender reassignment see para 348 ante.

Until 1 September 1983, the Sex Discrimination Act 1975 s 6(1) did not apply to employment as a midwife: see s 20(1) (amended by the Sex Discrimination Act 1975 (Amendment of Section 20) Order 1983, SI 1983/1202, art 2). See *Saunders v Richmond-upon-Thames London Borough Council* [1978] ICR 75, [1977] IRLR 362, EAT; *Department of the Environment v Fox* [1980] 1 All ER 58, [1979] ICR 736, EAT; *Hurley v Mustoe* [1981] ICR 490, [1981] IRLR 208, EAT; *Timex Corpn v Hodgson* [1982] ICR 63, [1981] IRLR 530, EAT; *Brennan v JH Dewhurst Ltd* [1984] ICR 52, [1983] IRLR 357, EAT. See, however, Case 165/82 *EC Commission v United Kingdom* [1984] 1 All ER 353, [1983] ECR 3431, ECJ (justification of temporary restrictions concerning male midwives). As to midwives see MEDICAL PROFESSIONS vol 30(1) (Reissue) para 691 et seq.

5   Sex Discrimination Act 1975 s 6(1)(a). The word 'arrangements' is wide and covers aspects of the selection process such as shortlisting (*Saunders v Richmond-upon-Thames London Borough Council* [1978] ICR 75, [1977] IRLR 362, EAT) but it does not cover the placing of discriminatory advertisements (*Cardiff Women's Aid v Hartup* [1994] IRLR 390, EAT (decided under the equivalent provisions of the Race Relations Act 1976)).

The Equal Opportunities Commission's Code of Practice on Sex Discrimination: Equal Opportunity Policies, Procedures and Practices in Employment (30 April 1995) contains the following recommendations for good practice in the area of recruitment: (1) each individual should be assessed according to his or her personal capability to carry out a given job, it should not be assumed that men only or women only will be able to carry out certain kinds of work; (2) any qualifications or requirements applied to a job which effectively inhibit applications from one sex or from married people should be retained only if they are justifiable in terms of the job to be done; (3) any age limits should be retained only if they are necessary for the job (an unjustifiable age limit could constitute unlawful indirect discrimination, for example, against women who have taken time out of employment for child-rearing); and (4) where trade unions uphold such qualifications as union policy, they should amend policy in the light of any potentially unlawful effect: see para 13. As to codes of practice generally see para 406 post. As to the Equal Opportunities Commission see para 404 et seq post. As to the Commission for Equality and Human Rights, which is to replace the Equal Opportunities Commission, see para 305 et seq ante.

See also *Brennan v JH Dewhurst Ltd* [1984] ICR 52, [1983] IRLR 357, EAT (the question is not whether the employer deliberately discriminates in the arrangements made but whether the arrangements in fact have a discriminatory effect). Discriminatory arrangements will be unlawful even if the post is not ultimately filled: *Roadburg v Lothian Regional Council* [1976] IRLR 283. Where it is alleged that arrangements which limit eligible applicants to a specified category have a discriminatory effect, the correct comparison is between men and women qualified for the employment in question and not between those eligible or not eligible to apply: *Pearse v City of Bradford Metropolitan Council* [1988] IRLR 379, EAT.

Asking a person a question in interview which would not be asked of a person of the opposite sex is not necessarily unlawful discrimination; there must be less favourable treatment, which will depend on the circumstances and purpose of the questions: *Saunders v Richmond upon Thames Borough Council* [1978] ICR 75, [1977] IRLR 362, EAT. It is sufficient to show that a person conducting the interview behaved in a discriminatory fashion; it is not necessary to show that someone actually set up the interview arrangements in a discriminatory fashion: *Nagarajan v London Regional Transport* [2000] 1 AC 501, [1999] 4 All ER 65, HL (decided under the equivalent provisions in the Race Relations Act 1976). A finding that one or more of those interviewing an applicant for a job showed bias is insufficient of itself to justify an inference of discrimination: *Marks & Spencer plc v Martins* [1998] ICR 1005, sub nom *Martins v Marks & Spencer plc* [1998] IRLR 326, CA (race discrimination case). Selection from amongst friends or acquaintances without advertisement of the post may give rise to indirect discrimination: *Coker and Osamor v Lord Chancellor and Lord Chancellor's Department* [1999] IRLR 396, ET.

6   Sex Discrimination Act 1975 s 6(1)(b). Subject to s 8(3), s 6(1)(b) does not apply to any provision for the payment of money which, if the woman in question were given the employment, would be included (directly or otherwise) in the contract under which she was employed: s 6(5) (amended by the Sex Discrimination Act 1986 s 9(2), Schedule Pt II).

The Equal Pay Act 1970 s 1(1) (as substituted) (see para 424 post) does not apply in determining, for the purposes of the Sex Discrimination Act 1975 s 6(1)(b), the terms on which employment is offered: s 8(2). Where a person offers a woman employment on certain terms, and if she accepted the offer then, by virtue of an equality clause, any of those terms would fall to be modified, or any additional term would fall to be included, the offer is to be taken to contravene s 6(1)(b): s 8(3). Where a person offers a woman employment on certain terms, and s 8(3) would apply but for the fact that, on her acceptance of the offer, the Equal Pay Act 1970 s 1(3) (as substituted and amended) (see para 424 post) would prevent the equality clause from operating, the offer is to be taken not to contravene the Sex Discrimination Act 1975 s 6(1)(b): s 8(4). For the meaning of 'equality clause' see para 424 post; definition applied by s 82(1). Where a woman was offered less pay than a comparator after accepting employment s 6(1) did not apply; the claim should have been made under the Equal Pay Act 1970: see *Oliver v JP Malnick & Co (No 2)* [1984] ICR 458.

In its application to any discrimination on the grounds of gender reassignment, the Sex Discrimination Act 1975 s 8 (as amended) has effect with the omission of s 8(3), (4) and of s 8(5)(b) (see note 14 head (2) infra): s 8(7) (added by the Sex Discrimination (Gender Reassignment) Regulations 1999, SI 1999/1102, reg 3(2)).

The provisions of the Sex Discrimination Act 1975 s 6(1)(b) and s 6(2) (see the text and notes 8–14 infra) do not make it unlawful to deprive a woman who is on ordinary maternity leave of any benefit from the terms and conditions of her employment relating to remuneration, but this does not apply to: (1) benefit by way of maternity-related remuneration; (2) benefit by way of remuneration in respect of times when the woman is neither on ordinary maternity leave nor on additional maternity leave, including increase-related remuneration in respect of such times; or (3) benefit by way of maternity-related remuneration that is increase-related: s 6A(1), (2), (5) (s 6A added by the Employment Equality (Sex Discrimination) Regulations 2005, SI 2005/2467, reg 8). 'On ordinary maternity leave' means absent from work in exercise of the right conferred by the Employment Rights Act 1996 s 73(1) (as substituted) (see EMPLOYMENT vol 16(1A) (Reissue) para 322); 'remuneration' means benefits that consist of the payment of money to an employee by way of wages or salary and that are not benefits whose provision is regulated by the employee's contract of employment; 'maternity-related remuneration', in relation to a woman, means remuneration to which she is entitled as a result of being pregnant or being on ordinary or additional maternity leave; and 'on additional maternity leave' means absent from work in exercise of the right conferred by s 71(1) (as substituted) (see EMPLOYMENT vol 16(1A) (Reissue) para 322) or in consequence of the prohibition in s 72(1) (as substituted) (see EMPLOYMENT vol 16(1A) (Reissue) para 322): Sex Discrimination Act 1975 s 6A(7) (as so added). Remuneration is increase-related so far as it falls to be calculated by reference to increases in remuneration that the woman would have received had she not been on ordinary or additional maternity leave: s 6A(6) (as so added).

Nor do the provisions of s 6(1)(b), (2) make it unlawful to deprive a woman who is on additional maternity leave of any benefit from the terms and conditions of her employment, but this does not apply to: (a) benefit by way of maternity-related remuneration; (b) the benefit of her employer's implied obligation to her of trust and confidence; (c) any benefit of terms and conditions in respect of notice of the termination by her employer of her contract of employment, compensation in the event of redundancy, disciplinary or grievance procedures, or membership of a pension scheme; (d) benefit by way of remuneration in respect of times when the woman is neither on ordinary maternity leave nor on additional maternity leave, including increase-related remuneration in respect of such times; or (e) benefit by way of maternity-related remuneration that is increase-related: s 6A(3)–(5) (as so added).

As to whether the provisions of s 6A(1), (4), (7) (as added) correctly comply with EC Council Directive 76/207 (OJ L39, 14.2.76, p 40) on the implementation of the principle of equal treatment for men and women as regards access to employment, vocational training and promotion, and working conditions (as amended) (see para 338 ante), which they purport to implement, see *R (on the application of the Equal Opportunities Commission) v Secretary of State for Trade and Industry* [2007] EWHC 483 (Admin), [2007] All ER (D) 183 (Mar). See also note 24 infra.

The impact of a contractual term (for the purposes of an indirect discrimination claim (see paras 351, 355 ante)) is to be judged at the moment when that term becomes incorporated into the contract, not at some later stage, e g when the applicant finds herself unable to comply with the term: *Meade-Hill v British Council* [1996] 1 All ER 79, [1995] ICR 847, CA.

An employee who is already in a post cannot claim under the Sex Discrimination Act 1975 s 6(1)(b) but must claim instead under s 6(2) (see the text and notes 8–14 infra): *Clymo v Wandsworth London Borough Council* [1989] ICR 250, [1989] IRLR 241, EAT.

7   Sex Discrimination Act 1975 s 6(1)(c). As the relevant act is the appointment itself and not the state of affairs resulting from it, the appointment must have been made after the statute came into force: *Amies v Inner London Education Authority* [1977] 2 All ER 100, [1977] ICR 308, EAT. Where a better qualified female candidate for a job is rejected in favour of a male candidate, there is a prima facie case for the employers to answer: *Humphreys v Board of Managers of St George's Church of England (Aided) Primary School*

[1978] ICR 546, 13 ITR 13, EAT. An employer will not be able to justify refusing to employ women with children on the basis of a generalisation that they are unreliable: *Hurley v Mustoe* [1981] ICR 490, [1981] IRLR 208, EAT. It appears that the Sex Discrimination Act 1975 s 6(1)(c) also applies to selection for revised jobs amongst employees facing redundancy (*Timex Corpn v Hodgson* [1982] ICR 63, [1981] IRLR 530, EAT), although this is contrary to what was said in *Clymo v Wandsworth London Borough Council* [1989] ICR 250, [1989] IRLR 241, EAT (where Wood J held that the Sex Discrimination Act 1975 s 6(1) applied to situations arising before a contract of employment was entered into).

8 See the Sex Discrimination Act 1975 s 6(2). See also notes 2, 6 supra.

A claim under s 6(2) can be brought after employment has ended: *Relaxion Group plc v Rhys-Harper, D'Souza v Lambert London Borough Council, Jones v 3M Healthcare Ltd, Kirker v British Sugar plc, Angel v New Possibilities NHS Trust, Bond v Hackney Citizens Advice Bureau* [2003] UKHL 33, [2003] 4 All ER 1113, [2003] IRLR 484.

9 A factor used by an employer as a criterion for selection for a managerial post may amount to a 'requirement or condition' within the meaning of the Sex Discrimination Act 1975 s 1(1)(b) (as substituted) (see para 351 ante) even where it is said to be a desirable qualification rather than an absolute bar if it is clear that it operated as the decisive factor in the selection process: *Falkirk Council v Whyte* [1997] IRLR 560, EAT. However, where a particular category of workers did not have any promotion opportunities, no discriminatory requirement or condition had been applied, although the position may be different if an applicant is able to compare herself with other similar categories of employee with greater promotion opportunities: *Francis v British Airways Engineering Overhaul Ltd* [1982] IRLR 10, EAT. A refusal to offer a woman a secondment based on an assumption that married women will follow their husbands' jobs is discriminatory: *Horsey v Dyfed County Council* [1982] ICR 755, [1982] IRLR 395, EAT.

10 For the meaning of 'training' see para 348 note 5 ante. The Equal Opportunities Commission's Code of Practice on Sex Discrimination: Equal Opportunity Policies, Procedures and Practices in Employment (30 April 1995) contains the following specific recommendations in respect of promotion, transfer and training: (1) where an appraisal system is in operation, the assessment criteria should be examined to ensure that they are not unlawfully discriminatory and the scheme monitored to assess how it is working in practice; (2) when a group of workers predominantly of one sex is excluded from an appraisal scheme, access to promotion, transfer and training and to other benefits should be reviewed, to ensure that there is no unlawful direct discrimination; (3) promotion and career development patterns should be reviewed to ensure that the traditional qualifications are justifiable requirements for the job to be done (in some circumstances, for example, promotion on the basis of length of service could amount to unlawful indirect discrimination, as it may unjustifiably affect more women than men); (4) when general ability and personal qualities are the main requirements for promotion to a post, care should be taken to consider favourably candidates of both sexes with differing career patterns and general experience; (5) rules which restrict or preclude transfer between certain jobs should be questioned and changed if they are found to be unlawfully discriminatory (employees of one sex may be concentrated in sections from which transfers are traditionally restricted without real justification); (6) policies and practices regarding selection for training, day release and personal development should be examined for unlawful direct and indirect discrimination, and, where there is found to be an imbalance in training as between sexes, the cause should be identified to ensure that it is not discriminatory; and (7) age limits for access to training and promotion should be questioned: see para 25.

11 The terms 'benefits, facilities or services' are not defined in the Sex Discrimination Act 1975. References in the Sex Discrimination Act 1975 to the affording by any persons of access to benefits, facilities or services are not limited to benefits, facilities or services provided by that person himself, but include any means by which it is in that person's power to facilitate access to benefits, facilities or services provided by any other person (the 'actual provider'): s 50(1). Where by any provision of the Sex Discrimination Act 1975 the affording by any person of access to benefits, facilities or services in a discriminatory way is in certain circumstances prevented from being unlawful, the effect of the provision extends also to the liability under the Act of any actual provider: s 50(2).

Section 6(2) does not apply to benefits, facilities or services of any description if the employer is concerned with the provision (for payment or not) of benefits, facilities or services of that description to the public, or to a section of the public comprising the woman in question, unless: (1) that provision differs in a material respect from the provision of the benefits, facilities or services by the employer to his employees; (2) the provision of the benefits, facilities or services to the woman in question is regulated by her contract of employment; or (3) the benefits, facilities or services relate to training: s 6(7).

Section 6(2)(a) (see the text to note 12 infra) is concerned with the employer's acts or omissions in affording access to opportunities, benefits, facilities or services which already exist: *Clymo v Wandsworth London Borough Council* [1989] ICR 250, [1989] IRLR 241, EAT; and see *British Telecommunications plc v Roberts* [1996] ICR 625, [1996] IRLR 601, EAT (refusal to allow women returning to work after maternity leave to jobshare prevented from may amount to indirect discrimination).

Arrangements made to ensure safety or good administration are not unlawful: *Peake v Automotive Products Ltd* [1978] QB 233, [1978] 1 All ER 106, CA (no unlawful discrimination against male employees where women employees were allowed to leave factory five minutes before them). See, however, *Page v Freight Hire (Tank Haulage) Ltd* [1981] 1 All ER 394, [1981] ICR 299, EAT (employer cannot justify discrimination simply by relying on risk to safety; all circumstances of risk and measures necessary to eliminate it must be considered). See also *Steel v Union of Post Office Workers* [1978] 2 All ER 504, [1978] 1 WLR 64, EAT (way in which employer allocated postal walks was manner of affording workers access to opportunity for transfer, or other benefits or facilities).

The principle contained in the Sex Discrimination Act 1975 s 50(1) applies to opportunities for promotion, transfer or training: see *Iske v P & O European Ferries (Dover) Ltd* [1997] IRLR 401, EAT. See also *Barry v Midland Bank plc* [1998] 1 All ER 805, [1998] IRLR 138, CA (plaintiff worked part-time after birth of her child; severance pay calculated on part-time salary; no discrimination because rules of scheme not discriminatory; any variation between plaintiff's contract and that of male comparator was due to material factor not based on sex).

12   Sex Discrimination Act 1975 s 6(2)(a). See also notes 6 supra, 13 infra. Until 1 September 1983, s 6(2)(a) did not apply to promotion, transfer or training as a midwife: see s 20(2) (amended by the Sex Discrimination Act 1975 (Amendment of Section 20) Order 1983, SI 1983/1202, art 2).

13   References to the dismissal of a person from employment or to the expulsion of a person from a position as partner (see para 366 post) include references: (1) to the termination of that person's employment or partnership by the expiration of any period (including a period expiring by reference to an event or circumstance), not being a termination immediately after which the employment or partnership is renewed on the same terms; and (2) to the termination of that person's employment or partnership by any act of his (including the giving of notice) in circumstances such that he is entitled to terminate it without notice by reason of the conduct of the employer or, as the case may be, the conduct of the other partners: Sex Discrimination Act 1975 s 82(1A) (added by the Sex Discrimination Act 1986 s 2(3)). As to the application of the Sex Discrimination Act 1975 s 82(1A) (as added) to governing bodies of schools and institutions of higher or further education where such bodies have delegated budgets see the Education (Modification of Enactments Relating to Employment) (England) Order 2003, SI 2003/1964, art 3, Schedule; and the Education (Modification of Enactments Relating to Employment) (Wales) Order 2006, SI 2006/1073, art 3, Schedule.

The dismissal of female employees on marriage followed by the offer of alternative employment is discriminatory: *North East Midlands Co-operative Society Ltd v KM Allen* [1977] IRLR 212, EAT. The dismissal of a female employee on marriage to an employee in a rival firm was also discriminatory where the woman's employer assumed the husband would be the breadwinner: *Skyrail Oceanic Ltd v Coleman* [1981] ICR 864, sub nom *Coleman v Skyrail Oceanic Ltd* [1981] IRLR 398, CA.

14   Sex Discrimination Act 1975 s 6(2)(b). Section 6(2) does not apply to benefits consisting of the payment of money when the provision of those benefits is regulated by the woman's contract of employment: s 6(6). An act does not contravene s 6(2) if: (1) it contravenes a term modified or included by virtue of an equality clause (see para 424 post); or (2) it would contravene such a term but for the fact that the equality clause is prevented from operating by the Equal Pay Act 1970 s 1(3) (as substituted) (see para 424 post): Sex Discrimination Act 1975 s 8(5). See also notes 6, 13 supra.

It is right to accept jurisdiction in respect of post-employment victimisation claims where there is a substantial connection with the employment relationship, or a sufficiently close connection with the employment: *Shoebridge v Metropolitan Police Service* [2004] ICR 1690, [2004] All ER (D) 87 (Jul), EAT. A bonus payment which is paid as of right to all qualifying employees but which varies in amount each year at the discretion of the employer is a benefit regulated by the contract of employment within the meaning of the Sex Discrimination Act 1975 s 6(6): *Hoyland v Asda Stores Ltd* [2006] IRLR 468. See also *Watson v National Union of Teachers* [2006] All ER (D) 84 (Aug), EAT.

15   Subjection to a detriment means 'putting him under a disadvantage': *Ministry of Defence v Jeremiah* [1980] QB 87 at 99, [1979] 3 All ER 833 at 837, CA, per Brandon LJ. 'Since "subjecting him to any other detriment" ... is to be given its broad ordinary meaning ... it is plain that almost any discriminatory conduct by employer against employee in relation to the latter's employment will be rendered unlawful': *Barclays Bank plc v Kapur* [1989] ICR 753, CA, at 767 per Bingham LJ; affd [1991] 2 AC 355, [1991] 1 All ER 646, HL (a case where the equivalent provisions of the Race Relations Act 1976). See also *Coutts and Co plc v Cure* [2005] ICR 1098, (2004) Times, 25 October, EAT. See also para 345 ante.

16   *Home Office v Holmes* [1984] 3 All ER 549, [1985] 1 WLR 71, EAT. See also *Ministry of Defence v Jeremiah* [1980] QB 87, [1979] 3 All ER 833, CA (requirement that only male examiners should work overtime in area of factory where there were unpleasant conditions was held to be a detriment to male employees). See also para 345 ante.

17   See *Porcelli v Strathclyde Regional Council* [1985] ICR 177, sub nom *Strathclyde Regional Council v Porcelli* [1984] IRLR 467, EAT; and para 347 ante.

18   See the Sex Discrimination Act 1975 s 6(2A) (added by the Employment Equality (Sex Discrimination) Regulations 2005, SI 2005/2467, reg 7(2), (4)). As to harassment, including sexual harassment, see the Sex Discrimination Act 1975 s 4A (as added); and para 347 ante.

19 *Wileman v Minilec Engineering Ltd* [1988] ICR 318, [1988] IRLR 144, EAT, suggests a subjective test but the Employment Appeal Tribunal in Scotland has suggested an objective test (*Scott v Combined Property Services Ltd* (2 December 1996) Lexis, EAT). In *Reed v Bull Information Systems Ltd v Steadman* [1999] IRLR 299, EAT, it was stated that the test is a subjective one; however, where there is conduct which only a very sensitive person would object to, the tribunal should consider whether the individual has made it clear that she finds the conduct unacceptable, and if the objection would be clear to a reasonable person, repetition of the conduct will generally constitute harassment. An applicant who makes a complaint of sexual harassment may expose herself to cross-examination about her attitude to sexual matters generally: *Snowball v Gardner Merchant Ltd* [1987] ICR 719, [1987] IRLR 397, EAT. See also para 347 ante.

20 *Burton v De Vere Hotels* [1997] ICR 1, [1996] IRLR 596, EAT (decided under the equivalent provisions of the Race Relations Act 1976). A manager can be held jointly and severally liable where he consciously fosters and encourages a discriminatory culture against a pregnant woman by behaviour and example: *Gilbank v Miles* [2006] EWCA Civ 543, [2006] ICR 1297, [2006] IRLR 538, [2006] All ER (D) 160 (May).

21 *Clymo v Wandsworth London Borough Council* [1989] ICR 250, [1989] IRLR 241, EAT.

22 *Day v T Pickles Farms Ltd* [1999] IRLR 217, EAT. See also *Hardman v Mallon (t/a Orchard Lodge Nursing Home)* [2002] 2 CMLR 1467, [2002] IRLR 516, [2002] All ER (D) 439 (May), EAT (failure to carry out risk assessment in respect of pregnant woman was sex discrimination even though employer would not have carried out assessment for comparable male employee or non-pregnant female employee).

23 *Turley v Allders Department Stores Ltd* [1980] ICR 66, [1980] IRLR 4, EAT; and see also *Hayes v Malleable Working Men's Club and Institute* [1985] ICR 703, [1985] IRLR 367, EAT.

24 Case C-177/88 *Dekker v Stichting Vormingscentrum voor Jong Volwassenen (VJV-Centrum) Plus* [1990] ECR I–3941, [1992] ICR 325, ECJ. The European Court of Justice has also ruled that dismissal of a woman because of pregnancy will be in breach of EC Council Directive 76/207 (OJ L39, 14.2.76, p 40) (as amended) (see para 349 ante): Case 179/88 *Handels-og Kontorfunktionaerernes Forbund I Danmark v Dansk Arbejdsgiverforening* [1992] ICR 332, [1991] IRLR 31, ECJ. Case C-177/88 *Dekker v Stichtiing Vormingscentrum voor Jong Volwassenen (VJV-Centrum) Plus* supra was applied in Case C-32/93 *Webb v EMO Air Cargo (UK) Ltd* [1994] QB 718, [1994] 4 All ER 115, ECJ, which confirmed that where a woman's contract of employment is for an indefinite period, it is an act of sex discrimination to dismiss her on the grounds that her pregnancy will prevent her from performing her work on a temporary basis. This principle was reaffirmed by the European Court of Justice in Case C-207/98 *Mahlburg v Land Mecklenburg-Vorpommern* [2001] ICR 1032, [2000] IRLR 276, ECJ. In *Webb v EMO Air Cargo (UK) Ltd (No 2)* [1995] 4 All ER 577, [1995] 1 WLR 1454, HL, it was found that the provisions of the Sex Discrimination Act 1975 were consistent with the ruling of the European Court of Justice but it was said that there might be no sex discrimination where the contract of employment was for a fixed period and the woman who was dismissed or refused employment would be unavailable during that period because of her pregnancy. See also *R (on the application of the Equal Opportunities Commission) v Secretary of State for Trade and Industry* [2007] EWHC 483 (Admin), [2007] All ER (D) 183 (Mar); and note 6 supra.

As to the question of absences from work caused by pregnancy-related illness see Case C-394/96 *Brown v Rentokil Ltd* [1998] All ER (EC) 791, [1998] IRLR 445, ECJ, (action taken against a woman on the grounds of pregnancy-related illness, whether occurring during pregnancy or maternity leave, is unlawful discrimination; however, where the illness arises after the end of maternity leave, the woman's treatment may be compared with that of a sick man (an otherwise impermissible comparison)).

EC Council Directive 76/207 (OJ L39, 14.2.76, p 40) art 5(1) precludes a worker recruited for a fixed period from being dismissed on the ground of pregnancy, even if she fails to inform the employer that she is pregnant: Case C-109/00 *Tele Danmark A/S v Handels-OG Kontorfunktionaerernes Forbund I Danmark (HK) (acting on behalf of Brandt-Nielsen)* [2001] All ER (EC) 941, [2001] ECR I-6993, ECJ.

25 *Abbey National plc v Formoso* [1999] IRLR 222, EAT (woman who was unable to attend a disciplinary hearing for pregnancy-related reasons and who was then dismissed was discriminated against on the grounds of her sex). Similarly, a woman not consulted when a redundancy selection exercise is taking place in part because she is absent on maternity leave suffers unlawful discrimination: *McGuigan v TG Baynes & Sons* (24 November 1998) Lexis, EAT.

A woman who was a self-employed contractor successfully claimed sex discrimination when her fixed-term contract was not renewed because of her pregnancy: *Caruana v Manchester Airport plc* [1996] IRLR 378, EAT. As to contract workers see para 365 post.

There is some uncertainty as to whether sex discrimination related to pregnancy is properly regarded as direct or indirect discrimination: see C-177/88 *Dekker v Stichting Vormingscentrum voor Jong Volwassenen (VJV-Centrum) Plus* [1990] ECR-I 3941, [1992] ICR 325, ECJ (where the European Court of Justice's view was that it is direct discrimination); but cf *Webb v EMO Air Cargo (UK) Ltd (No 2)* [1995] 4 All ER 577, [1995] 1 WLR 1454, HL (which seems to allow for the possibility of justification).

Pregnancy need not be the only or even the main cause of the dismissal, although where there are other factors the tribunal may exercise its discretion not to award full compensation: *O'Neill v Governors* of St Thomas More Roman Catholic Voluntary Aided Upper School [1997] ICR 33, [1996] IRLR 372, EAT (unmarried teacher pregnant by Roman Catholic priest); cf *Berrisford v Woodward Schools (Midlands Division) Ltd* [1991] ICR 564, [1991] IRLR 247, EAT (no unlawful discrimination where pregnant matron with no plans to marry was felt to convey an adverse example to pupils at the school).

There was unlawful discrimination when an employee on maternity leave missed out on an assessment necessary for her to qualify for annual pay rises and promotion: Case C-136/95 *Caisse Nationale d'Assurance Vieillesse Des Travailleurs Salariés v Thibault Casse* [1998] All ER (EC) 385, [1998] IRLR 399, ECJ. As to terms in a maternity leave scheme which were held not to be discriminatory although they were less favourable than certain terms of the employer's sickness absence provisions see Case C-411/96 *Boyle v Equal Opportunities Commission* [1998] All ER (EC) 879, [1998] IRLR 717, ECJ (comparison with a sick man was inappropriate). However, the European Court of Justice has decided that it is discriminatory not to pay a pregnant woman absent due to pregnancy-related illness (but not on maternity leave) the same pay as an employee absent due to illness of some other type; the crucial point appears to be whether the maternity leave period has started or not; a woman on maternity leave is not comparable to a sick man but a pre- or post-maternity leave sick woman may be comparable: Case C-66/96 *Handsels-og Kontorfunktionaerernes Forbund I Danmark (acting on behalf of Pedersen) v Faellesforeningen for Danmarks Brugsforeninger (acting on behalf of Kvickly Skive)* [1999] All ER (EC) 138, [1999] IRLR 55, ECJ.

See *Gus Home Shopping Ltd v Green, Gus Home Shopping Ltd v McLaughlin* [2001] IRLR 75, EAT (woman who was not paid discretionary loyalty bonus because of absence on maternity leave was unlawfully discriminated against). Refusal to re-employ a woman, employed on a fixed-term contract, on account of her pregnancy constitutes direct discrimination on the grounds of sex contrary to EC Council Directive 76/207 (OJ L39, 14.2.76, p 40) (as amended) (see para 338 ante): Case C-438/99 *Jiménez Melgar v Ayuntamiento de Los Barrios* [2001] ECR I-6915, [2003] 3 CMLR 67, ECJ. A rule of a sick leave scheme providing for the reduction of sick pay after a specified duration which applies to pregnancy-related illness as it does to any other illness does not constitute discrimination, provided that the amount of payment made is not so low as to undermine the objective of protecting pregnant workers: Case C-191/03 *North Western Health Board v McKenna* [2006] All ER (EC) 455, [2006] ICR 477, ECJ. Where a woman is promoted while she is on maternity leave, her seniority must be calculated from the date of her appointment rather than the date on which she returns to work: Case C-294/04 *Herrero v Instituto Madrileño de la Salud* [2006] 2 CMLR 816, [2006] IRLR 296, [2006] All ER (D) 220 (Feb), ECJ.

Dismissal for a pregnancy related reason is automatically unfair under the Employment Rights Act 1996 s 99 (as substituted and amended): see EMPLOYMENT vol 16(1B) (Reissue) para 659.

26   *Smith v Safeway plc* [1996] ICR 868, [1996] IRLR 456, CA (differences in grooming and uniform requirements may not be considered less favourable treatment where they reflect conventions about appearance for the particular gender). A requirement that women wear overalls has been held not to be serious enough to amount to a detriment (see *Schmidt v Austicks Bookshops Ltd* [1978] ICR 85, [1977] IRLR 360, EAT), and the requirement that female nurses wear a cap as part of their uniform has been held not to be discriminatory (see *Burrett v West Birmingham Health Authority* [1994] IRLR 7, EAT).

362. Discrimination in relation to occupational pension schemes. The above provisions[1] do not render it unlawful for a person[2] to discriminate[3] against a woman[4] in relation to her membership of, or rights under, an occupational pension scheme[5] in such a way that, were any term of the scheme to provide for discrimination in that way, then, by reason only of any provision relating to equal treatment[6], an equal treatment rule[7] would not operate in relation to that term[8].

1   Ie the Sex Discrimination Act 1975 s 6(1)(b), (2): see paras 360–361 ante. The European Court of Justice has held that the Treaty Establishing the European Community (Rome, 25 March 1957; TS 1 (1973); Cmnd 5179) (the 'EC Treaty') art 141 (formerly art 119; renumbered by virtue of the Treaty of Amsterdam: see *Treaty Citation (No 2) (Note)* [1999] All ER (EC) 646, ECJ) applied to all pension schemes and such schemes must give equality in relation to access, contributions and benefits; employers, whether public or private, may not discriminate in relation to retirement ages: Case C-262/88 *Barber v Guardian Royal Exchange Assurance Group* [1991] 1 QB 344, [1990] 2 All ER 660, ECJ (applies only to pension benefits accruing after the date of the decision (i e 17 May 1990) unless there was discrimination in relation to access to the scheme). In regard to a requirement for a deed of trust for changing the retirement age in an occupational pension scheme see *Trustee Solutions Ltd v Dubery* [2006] EWHC 1426 (Ch), [2007] 1 All ER 308, [2006] All ER (D) 233 (Jun). Where there was discrimination in relation to access to the scheme, EC Treaty art 141 (formerly art 119) can be relied upon so as to claim benefits linked to access back to 1976: Case C-57/93 *Vroege v NCIV Instituut voor Volkshuisvesting BV* [1995] All ER (EC) 193, [1995] ICR 635, ECJ. See also Case C-200/91 *Coloroll Pension Trustees Ltd v Russell* [1995]

All ER (EC) 23, [1995] ICR 179, ECJ; Case C-408/92 *Smith v Avdel Systems Ltd* [1995] All ER (EC) 132, [1995] ICR 596, ECJ; C-128/93 *Fisscher v Voorhuis Hengelo BV* [1995] All ER (EC) 193, [1995] ICR 635, ECJ; Case C-7/93 *Bestuur van het Algemeen Burgerlijk Pensioenfonds v Beune* [1995] All ER (EC) 97, [1995] IRLR 103, ECJ; Case C-28/93 *Van den Akker v Stichting Shell Pensioenfonds* [1995] All ER (EC) 156, [1995] ICR 596, ECJ.

See also *Quirk v Burton Hospitals NHS Trust* [2002] EWCA Civ 149, [2002] ICR 602, [2002] IRLR 353 (disparity arising as a result of calculating male worker's benefits in relation to pensionable service on or after 17 May 1990 not unlawfully discriminatory). Unless it is objectively justifiable, a requirement of being employed under a contract of employment as a precondition for membership of an occupational pension scheme is contrary to the EC Treaty art 141 and must not be applied where, among the persons who are workers within the meaning of that provision, there is a much higher percentage of women than of men who fulfil all of the other conditions for membership: Case C-256/01 *Allonby v Accrington and Rossendale College* [2005] All ER (EC) 289, [2004] ECR I-873, ECJ. See also Case C-379/99 *Pensionskasse für die Angestellten der Barmer Ersatzkasse VVAG v Menauer* [2003] All ER (EC) 193, [2001] ECR I-7275, ECJ (rule in occupational pension fund that widow would receive pension, but that widower would not necessarily receive pension, contravened EC Treaty art 141).

As to equal treatment in matters of social security see para 339 ante; and as to equal treatment in occupational social security schemes 340 ante. As to equal pay see para 419 et seq post.

2   As to the meaning of 'person' see para 344 note 3 ante.

3   For the meaning of 'discrimination' see para 344 note 4 ante.

4   As to the meaning of 'woman' see para 344 note 5 ante. These provisions apply equally to the treatment of men, with requisite modifications: see the Sex Discrimination Act 1975 s 2(1); and para 357 ante.

5   'Occupational pension scheme' has the same meaning as in the Pension Schemes Act 1993 (see SOCIAL SECURITY AND PENSIONS vol 44(2) (Reissue) para 853): Sex Discrimination Act 1975 s 6(4A) (added by the Pensions Act 1995 s 66(3)).

6   Ie made by or under the Pensions Act 1995 ss 62–64 (s 63 as amended): see SOCIAL SECURITY AND PENSIONS vol 44(2) (Reissue) para 782 et seq.

7   'Equal treatment rule' has the meaning given by ibid s 62 (see SOCIAL SECURITY AND PENSIONS vol 44(2) (Reissue) para 782): Sex Discrimination Act 1975 s 6(4A) (as added: see note 5 supra).

8   Ibid s 6(4) (substituted by the Pensions Act 1995 s 66(3)).

As to provisions relating to discrimination against office-holders see the Sex Discrimination Act 1975 ss 10A, 10B (as added); and para 377 post. As to selection of candidates by registered political parties see s 42A (as added); and para 367 note 4 post.

363.   Exceptions where sex is a genuine occupational qualification. The prohibitions in the Sex Discrimination Act 1975 against sex discrimination[1] (but not discrimination by way of victimisation[2]) relating to employment[3] or opportunities for promotion, transfer or training[4] do not apply to any employment where being a man[5] is a genuine occupational qualification[6] for the job[7].

Being a man is a genuine occupational qualification for a job only where[8]:

(1)   the essential nature of the job calls for a man for reasons of physiology (excluding physical strength or stamina) or, in dramatic performances or other entertainment, for reasons of authenticity, so that the essential nature of the job would be materially different if carried out by a woman[9];

(2)   the job needs to be held by a man to preserve decency or privacy because it is likely to involve physical contact with men in circumstances where they might reasonably object to its being carried out by a woman, or the holder of the job is likely to do his work in circumstances where men might reasonably object to the presence of a woman because they are in a state of undress or are using sanitary facilities[10];

(3)   the job is likely to involve the holder of the job doing his work, or living, in a private home and needs to be held by a man because objection might reasonably be taken to allowing to a woman the degree of physical or social contact with a person living in the home, or the knowledge of intimate details of such a person's life, which is likely, because of the nature or circumstances of the job or of the home, to be allowed to, or available to, the holder of the job[11];

(4)   the nature or location of the establishment makes it impracticable for the holder

of the job to live elsewhere than in premises provided by the employer, and the only such premises which are available for persons holding that kind of job are lived in, or normally lived in, by men and are not equipped with separate sleeping accommodation for women and sanitary facilities which could be used by women in privacy from men, and it is not reasonable to expect the employer either to equip those premises with such accommodation and facilities or to provide other premises for women[12];

(5)   the nature of the establishment, or of the part of it within which the work is done, requires the job to be held by a man because it is, or is part of, a hospital, prison or other establishment for persons requiring special care, supervision or attention, and those persons are all men (disregarding any woman whose presence is exceptional), and it is reasonable, having regard to the essential character of the establishment or that part, that the job should not be held by a woman[13];

(6)   the holder of the job provides individuals with personal services promoting their welfare or education[14], or similar personal services, and those services can most effectively be provided by a man[15];

(7)   the job needs to be held by a man because it is likely to involve the performance of duties outside the United Kingdom[16] in a country whose laws or customs are such that the duties could not, or could not effectively, be performed by a woman[17]; or

(8)   the job is one of two to be held: (a) by a married couple; (b) by a couple who are civil partners of each other; or (c) by a married couple or a couple who are civil partners of each other[18].

The above exception applies where some only of the duties of the job fall within heads (1) to (7) above as well as where all of them do[19]. However, head (1), (2), (4), (5), (6) or (7) above do not apply in relation to the filling of a vacancy at a time when the employer already has male employees[20] who are capable of carrying out the duties falling within that head[21], whom it would be reasonable to employ on those duties[22] and whose numbers are sufficient to meet the employer's likely requirements in respect of those duties without undue inconvenience[23].

1   For the meaning of 'discrimination' see para 344 note 4 ante.
2   As to discrimination by way of victimisation see para 358 ante.
3   Ie the Sex Discrimination Act 1975 s 6(1)(a), (c): see para 361 ante. For the meaning of 'employment' see para 360 note 4 ante.
4   Ie ibid s 6(2)(a): see para 361 ante. As to the meaning of 'training' see para 348 note 5 ante.
5   As to the meaning of 'man' see para 344 note 10 ante.
6   'Genuine occupational qualification' is to be construed in accordance with the Sex Discrimination Act 1975 s 7(2) (as amended) (see heads (1)–(8) in the text), except in the expression 'supplementary genuine occupational qualification': s 82(1) (definition amended by the Sex Discrimination (Gender Reassignment) Regulations 1999, SI 1999/1102, reg 4(6)). For the meaning of 'supplementary genuine occupational qualification' see para 364 note 12 post.
7   See the Sex Discrimination Act 1975 s 7(1). As to the application of s 7 (as amended) to governing bodies of schools and institutions of higher or further education where such bodies have delegated budgets see the Education (Modification of Enactments Relating to Employment) (England) Order 2003, SI 2003/1964, art 3, Schedule; and the Education (Modification of Enactments Relating to Employment) (Wales) Order 2006, SI 2006/1073, art 3, Schedule.
        As to provisions relating to discrimination against office-holders see the Sex Discrimination Act 1975 ss 10A, 10B (as added); and para 377 post. As to selection of candidates by registered political parties see s 42A (as added); and para 367 note 4 post.
8   Ibid s 7(2). An employer can only excuse itself on the grounds that sex is a genuine occupational qualification on one of the listed grounds: *Greig v Community Industry* [1979] ICR 356, [1979] IRLR 158, EAT.
9   Sex Discrimination Act 1975 s 7(2)(a). As to the meaning of 'woman' see para 344 note 5 ante.

10 Ibid s 7(2)(b). See *Wylie v Dee & Co (Menswear) Ltd* [1978] IRLR 103 (employer's plea of genuine occupational qualification failed in circumstances where it was found that it would not really be necessary for a woman to undertake inside leg measurement). This approach was followed in *Etam plc v Rowan* [1989] IRLR 150, EAT (held that it would be easy for the fitting and measurement tasks to be carried out by female sales assistants and the male applicant could perform the bulk of the other duties required). See also *Sisley v Britannia Security Systems Ltd* [1983] ICR 628, [1983] IRLR 404, EAT.

11 Sex Discrimination Act 1975 s 7(2)(ba) (added by the Sex Discrimination Act 1986 s 1(2)).

12 Sex Discrimination Act 1975 s 7(2)(c). Residence is a question of fact and does not include cases where the employee is obliged to remain on the premises for a limited period of time: *Sisley v Britannia Security Systems Ltd* [1983] ICR 628, [1983] IRLR 404, EAT.

13 Sex Discrimination Act 1975 s 7(2)(d).

14 As to the meaning of 'education' see para 348 note 5 ante. The Court of Appeal has emphasised the need for a postholder to be involved in the provision of personal services, meaning services that are individual and private, and involving direct contact between giver and recipient: *Lambeth London Borough Council v Commission for Racial Equality* [1990] ICR 768, [1990] IRLR 231, CA (decided under the similar provision in the Race Relations Act 1976).

15 Sex Discrimination Act 1975 s 7(2)(e). The phrase 'can most effectively be provided' assumes that the services could be provided by others; the tribunal must consider whether as a matter of fact they would be less effectively provided by those others: see *Tottenham Green Under Fives' Centre v Marshall* [1989] ICR 214, [1989] IRLR 147, EAT (decided under the similar provision in the Race Relations Act 1976).

16 For the meaning of 'United Kingdom' see para 325 note 6 ante.

17 Sex Discrimination Act 1975 s 7(2)(g).

18 Ibid s 7(2)(h) (amended by the Civil Partnership Act 2004 s 251(1), (4)). As to civil partners generally see MATRIMONIAL LAW.

19 Sex Discrimination Act 1975 s 7(3).

20 Ibid s 7(4) (amended by the Employment Act 1989 ss 3, 29(4), (6), Sch 7 Pt II, Sch 9).

21 Sex Discrimination Act 1975 s 7(4)(a). See also *Lasertop Ltd v Webster* [1997] ICR 828, [1997] IRLR 498, EAT (health club had not yet opened, so at the time when the vacancy was filled, the employer did not have sufficient female employees capable of carrying out the prohibited duties and whom it would be reasonable to employ on those duties without undue inconvenience).

22 Sex Discrimination Act 1975 s 7(4)(b).

23 Ibid s 7(4)(c).

364. Exception relating to gender reassignment. In their application to discrimination[1] on the grounds of gender reassignment[2], the provisions relating to employment discrimination[3] do not make unlawful an employer's treatment of another person[4] if: (1) in relation to the employment in question[5], being a man[6] is a genuine occupational qualification for the job[7] or being a woman[8] is a genuine occupational qualification for the job[9]; and (2) the employer can show that the treatment is reasonable[10].

In relation to discrimination on the grounds of gender reassignment, the provisions relating to recruitment[11] do not apply to any employment where there is a supplementary genuine occupational qualification[12] for the job[13], the provision relating to access to opportunities for promotion or training[14] does not apply to a refusal or deliberate omission to afford access to such opportunities[15], and the provision relating to dismissal or subjection to detriment[16] does not apply to dismissing an employee from, or otherwise not allowing him to continue in, such employment[17].

There is a supplementary genuine occupational qualification for a job only if[18]:

(a) the job involves the holder of the job being liable to be called upon to perform intimate physical searches pursuant to statutory powers[19];

(b) the job is likely to involve the holder of the job doing his work, or living, in a private home and needs to be held otherwise than by a person who is undergoing or has undergone gender reassignment, because objection might reasonably be taken to allowing to such a person: (i) the degree of physical or social contact with a person living in the home; or (ii) the knowledge of intimate details of such a person's life, which is likely, because of the nature or circumstances of the job or of the home, to be allowed to, or available to, the holder of the job[20];

(c) the nature or location of the establishment makes it impracticable for the holder of the job to live elsewhere than in premises provided by the employer, and: (i) the only such premises which are available for persons holding that kind of job are such that reasonable objection could be taken, for the purpose of preserving decency and privacy, to the holder of the job sharing accommodation and facilities with either sex whilst undergoing gender reassignment; and (ii) it is not reasonable to expect the employer either to equip those premises with suitable accommodation or to make alternative arrangements[21]; or

(d) the holder of the job provides vulnerable individuals with personal services promoting their welfare, or similar personal services, and in the reasonable view of the employer those services cannot be effectively provided by a person whilst that person is undergoing gender reassignment[22].

1 For the meaning of 'discrimination' see para 344 note 4 ante.

2 Ie discrimination falling within the Sex Discrimination Act 1975 2A (as added): see para 348 ante. For the meaning of 'gender reassignment' see para 348 note 9 ante.

   A transsexual person who has undergone gender reassignment surgery and lives as a member of the reassigned gender is, for the purposes of employment, entitled to be treated equally with non-transsexual members of the reassigned gender: *A v Chief Constable of West Yorkshire Police* [2004] UKHL 21, [2005] 1 AC 51, [2004] 3 All ER 145.

3 Ie the Sex Discrimination Act 1975 s 6(1), (2): see para 361 ante. For the meaning of 'employment' see para 360 note 4 ante.

4 Ibid s 7A(1) (ss 7A, 7B added by the Sex Discrimination (Gender Reassignment) Regulations 1999, SI 1999/1102, reg 4(1)).

   The Sex Discrimination Act 1975 s 7A(1) (as added) does not apply in relation to discrimination against a person whose gender has become the acquired gender under the Gender Recognition Act 2004: Sex Discrimination Act 1975 s 7A(4) (added by the Gender Recognition Act 2004 s 14, Sch 6 para 2). See further CONSTITUTIONAL LAW AND HUMAN RIGHTS.

   As to provisions relating to discrimination against office-holders see the Sex Discrimination Act 1975 ss 10A, 10B (as added); and para 377 post. As to selection of candidates by registered political parties see s 42A (as added); and para 367 note 4 post.

5 The reference to the employment in question is a reference: (1) in relation to any of ibid s 6(1)(a), (b) or (c) (see para 361 ante), to the employment mentioned in that provision; (2) in relation to s 6(2) (see para 361 ante): (a) in its application to opportunities for promotion or transfer to any employment or for training for any employment, to that employment; (b) otherwise, to the employment in which the person discriminated against is employed or from which that person is dismissed: s 7A(2) (as added: see note 4 supra). As to the meaning of 'training' see para 348 note 5 ante.

6 As to the meaning of 'man' see para 344 note 10 ante.

7 In determining for these purposes whether being a man or being a woman is a genuine occupational qualification for a job, the Sex Discrimination Act 1975 s 7(4) (as amended) (see para 363 ante) applies in relation to dismissal from employment as it applies in relation to the filling of a vacancy: s 7A(3) (as added: see note 4 supra).

8 As to the meaning of 'woman' see para 344 note 5 ante.

9 Sex Discrimination Act 1975 s 7A(1)(a) (as added: see note 4 supra). See notes 4, 7 supra.

10 Ibid s 7A(1)(b) (as added: see note 4 supra). The treatment must be reasonable in view of the circumstances described in the relevant paragraph of s 7(2) (as amended) (see para 363 ante) and any other relevant circumstances: s 7A(1)(b) (as so added). See note 4 supra.

11 Ie ibid s 6(1)(a) or (c): see para 361 ante.

12 'Supplementary genuine occupational qualification' is to be construed in accordance with ibid s 7B(2) (as added): s 82(1) (definition amended by the Sex Discrimination (Gender Reassignment) Regulations 1999, SI 1999/1102, reg 4(5)). For the meaning of 'genuine occupational qualification' see para 363 note 6 ante.

13 Sex Discrimination Act 1975 s 7B(1)(a) (as added: see note 4 supra).

14 Ie ibid s 6(2)(a): see para 361 ante.

15 Ibid s 7B(1)(b) (as added: see note 4 supra).

16 Ie ibid s 6(2)(b): see para 361 ante.

17 Ibid s 7B(1)(c) (as added: see note 4 supra).

18 Ibid s 7B(2) (as added: see note 4 supra). This is expressed to be subject to s 7B(3) (as added): see note 21 infra. Section 7B(2) (as added) does not apply in relation to discrimination against a person whose gender has become the acquired gender under the Gender Recognition Act 2004: Sex Discrimination Act 1975 s 7B(3) (substituted by the Gender Recognition Act 2004 Sch 6 para 3). See further CONSTITUTIONAL LAW AND HUMAN RIGHTS.

19 Sex Discrimination Act 1975 s 7B(2)(a) (as added: see note 4 supra). Section 7B(2)(a) (as added) does not apply in relation to the filling of a vacancy at a time when the employer already has employees: (1) who do not intend to undergo and are not undergoing gender reassignment and either have not undergone gender reassignment or whose genders have become acquired genders under the Gender Recognition Act 2004; (2) who are capable of carrying out the duties falling within Sex Discrimination Act 1975 s 7B(2)(a) (as added); (3) whom it would be reasonable to employ on those duties; and (4) whose numbers are sufficient to meet the employer's likely requirements in respect of those duties without undue inconvenience: s 7B(4), (5) (added by the Employment Equality (Sex Discrimination) Regulations 2005, SI 2005/2467, reg 9). See note 18 supra.

As to intimate physical searches pursuant to statutory powers see eg the Police and Criminal Evidence Act 1984 s 55 (as amended) (see CRIMINAL LAW EVIDENCE AND PROCEDURE vol 11(2) (2006 Reissue) para 1007); and the Prison Rules 1999, SI 1999/728, r 41 (see PRISONS vol 36(2) (Reissue) para 590).

20 Sex Discrimination Act 1975 s 7B(2)(b) (as added: see note 4 supra). See note 18 supra.

21 Ibid s 7B(2)(c) (as added: see note 4 supra). Section 7B(2)(c), (d) (as added) (see heads (c), (d) in the text) apply only in relation to discrimination against a person who intends to undergo gender reassignment, or is undergoing gender reassignment: s 7B(3) (as so added). See note 18 supra.

22 Ibid s 7B(2)(d) (as added: see note 4 supra). See notes 18, 21 supra.

(B) Particular Forms of Employment

365.   Contract workers.   The Sex Discrimination Act 1975 makes special provision to protect employees who are contracted out by their employers to work for other people, and who may suffer discrimination from a person who is not their employer[1].

It is unlawful for a principal[2], in relation to such work, to discriminate against a woman[3] who is a contract worker[4]: (1) in the terms on which he allows her to do that work[5]; (2) by not allowing her to do it or continue to do it[6]; (3) in the way he affords her access to any benefits, facilities or services[7] or by refusing or deliberately omitting to afford her access to them[8]; or (4) by subjecting her to any other detriment[9]. It is also unlawful for a principal, in relation to contract work at an establishment in Great Britain, to subject a contract worker to harassment[10].

In relation to discrimination on the grounds of gender reassignment, the principal does not contravene head (1), (2), (3) or (4) above by doing any act in relation to a woman if[11]: (a) he does it at a time when, if the work were to be done by a person taken into his employment, being a man would be a genuine occupational qualification for the job or being a woman would be a genuine occupational qualification for the job[12]; and (b) he can show that the act is reasonable in view of the circumstances relevant for the purposes of head (a) above and any other relevant circumstances[13].

1 See the Sex Discrimination Act 1975 s 9 (as amended); and the text and notes 2–13 infra. For the meaning of 'employment' see para 360 note 4 ante. See also *Rice v Fon-A-Car* [1980] ICR 133, EAT. As to the application of the Sex Discrimination Act 1975 s 9 (as amended) to governing bodies of schools and institutions of higher or further education where such bodies have delegated budgets see the Education (Modification of Enactments Relating to Employment) (England) Order 2003, SI 2003/1964, art 3, Schedule; and the Education (Modification of Enactments Relating to Employment) (Wales) Order 2006, SI 2006/1073, art 3, Schedule.

As to provisions relating to discrimination against office-holders see the Sex Discrimination Act 1975 ss 10A, 10B (as added); and para 377 post. As to selection of candidates by registered political parties see s 42A (as added); and para 367 note 4 post.

2 Ie a person who has work at an establishment in Great Britain available for contract workers (see note 4 infra): see ibid s 9(1) (amended by the Employment Equality (Sex Discrimination) Regulations 2005, SI 2005/2467, reg 10(1), (2)). As to the meaning of 'person' see para 344 note 3 ante. For the meaning of 'Great Britain' see para 325 note 6 ante. The work must be done for the principal and the workers must be to some extent in the control of the principal. There is no requirement that the supply of

workers should be the dominant purpose of the contract between the employer and the principal: see *Harrods Ltd v Remick* [1998] 1 All ER 52, [1997] IRLR 583, CA (a race discrimination case). See also *CJ O'Shea Construction Ltd v Bassi* [1998] ICR 1130, EAT. Youth Opportunities Programme trainees, and, presumably, comparable trainees on government schemes, are not contract workers, because, if they are employed under a contract at all, it is a training contract, and not a contract to execute work: *Daley v Allied Suppliers Ltd* [1983] ICR 90, [1983] IRLR 14, EAT.

3   As to the meaning of 'woman' see para 344 note 5 ante. These provisions apply equally to the treatment of men, with requisite modifications: see the Sex Discrimination Act 1975 s 2(1); and para 357 ante. As to discrimination on the grounds of gender reassignment see para 348 ante; and for the meaning of 'gender reassignment' see para 348 note 9 ante.

4   Ibid s 9(2). A contract worker is an individual who is employed not by the principal himself but by another person, who supplies workers under a contract made with the principal: see s 9(1) (as amended: see note 2 supra). See *Allonby v Accrington and Rossendale College* [2001] EWCA Civ 529, [2001] 2 CMLR 559, [2001] ICR 1189.

5   Sex Discrimination Act 1975 s 9(2)(a).

6   Ibid s 9(2)(b). See *BP Chemicals Ltd v Gillick* [1995] IRLR 128, EAT (worker who stopped work due to pregnancy and was not allowed to return to her previous position was entitled to rely on the Sex Discrimination Act 1975 s 9 (as amended)). Subject to the Sex Discrimination Act 1975 s 9(3A) (as added), the principal does not contravene s 9(2)(b) by doing any act in relation to a woman at a time when, if the work were to be done by a person taken into his employment, being a man would be a genuine occupational qualification for the job: s 9(3) (amended by the Sex Discrimination (Gender Reassignment) Regulations 1999, SI 1999/1102, reg 4(2)). For the meaning of 'genuine occupational qualification' see para 363 note 6 ante. The Sex Discrimination Act 1975 s 9(3) (as amended) does not apply in relation to discrimination on the grounds of gender reassignment: see s 9(3A) (s 9(3A), (3B), (3C) added by the Sex Discrimination (Gender Reassignment) Regulations 1999, SI 1999/1102, reg 4(3)). In relation to discrimination on the grounds of gender reassignment, the principal does not contravene the Sex Discrimination Act 1975 s 9(2)(b) by doing any act in relation to a woman at a time when, if the work were to be done by a person taken into his employment, there would be a supplementary genuine occupational qualification for the job: s 9(3C) (as so added). For the meaning of 'supplementary genuine occupational qualification' see para 364 note 12 ante.

Section 9(3B), (3C) (as added) does not apply in relation to discrimination against a person whose gender has become the acquired gender under the Gender Recognition Act 2004: Sex Discrimination Act 1975 s 9(3D) (added by Gender Recognition Act 2004 s 14, Sch 6 paras 1, 4). See further CONSTITUTIONAL LAW AND HUMAN RIGHTS.

7   As to the affording of access to benefits, facilities or services see para 361 note 11 ante.

8   Sex Discrimination Act 1975 s 9(2)(c). Section 9(2)(c) does not apply to benefits, facilities or services of any description if the principal is concerned with the provision (for payment or not) of benefits, facilities or services of that description to the public, or to a section of the public to which the woman belongs, unless that provision differs in a material respect from the provision of the benefits, facilities or services by the principal to his contract workers: s 9(4).

9   Ibid s 9(2)(d).

10   Ibid s 9(2A) (added by the Employment Equality (Sex Discrimination) Regulations 2005, SI 2005/2467, reg 10(1), (4)). As to harassment, including sexual harassment, see the Sex Discrimination Act 1975 s 4A (as added); and para 347 ante.

11   Ibid s 9(3B) (as added: see note 6 supra). See note 6 supra.

12   Ibid s 9(3B)(a) (as added: see note 6 supra). See note 6 supra.

13   Ibid s 9(3B)(b) (as added: see note 6 supra). See note 6 supra.

366.   Discrimination in partnerships.   It is unlawful for a firm[1], in relation to a position as partner[2] in the firm, to discriminate[3] against a woman[4]: (1) in the arrangements it makes for the purpose of determining who should be offered that position[5]; (2) in the terms on which it offers her that position[6]; or (3) by refusing or deliberately omitting to offer her that position[7].

In a case where the woman already holds that position it is unlawful for the firm to discriminate against her in the way it affords her access to any benefits, facilities or services[8], or by refusing or deliberately omitting to afford her access to them[9], or by expelling[10] her from that position, or subjecting her to any other detriment[11]. It is also unlawful for a firm, in relation to a position as partner in the firm, to subject to harassment a woman who holds or has applied for that position[12].

In relation to discrimination on the grounds of gender reassignment, the above provisions[13] do not make unlawful a firm's treatment of a person in relation to a position as partner where[14]: (a) if it were employment[15], being a man would be a genuine occupational qualification for the job[16] or being a woman would be a genuine occupational qualification for the job[17]; and (b) the firm can show that the treatment is reasonable in view of the circumstances relevant for the purposes of head (a) above and any other relevant circumstances[18]. In addition, heads (1) and (3) above and the prohibition on expulsion[19] do not apply to a position as partner where, if it were employment, there would be a supplementary genuine occupational qualification[20] for the job[21].

1   'Firm' has the meaning given by the Partnership Act 1890 s 4 (see PARTNERSHIP vol 35 (Reissue) para 1): Sex Discrimination Act 1975 s 82(1). The prohibitions against discrimination by firms apply in relation to persons proposing to form themselves into a partnership as they apply in relation to a firm: s 11(2). As to discrimination in partnerships generally see PARTNERSHIP vol 35 (Reissue) para 100.

2   In the case of a limited partnership, references to a partner are to be construed as references to a general partner as defined in the Limited Partnerships Act 1907 s 3 (see PARTNERSHIP vol 35 (Reissue) para 207): Sex Discrimination Act 1975 s 11(5). Section 11 (as amended) applies to a limited liability partnership as it applies to a firm; and, in its application to a limited liability partnership, references to a partner in a firm are references to a member of the limited liability partnership: s 11(6) (added by the Limited Liability Partnerships Regulations 2001, SI 2001/1090, reg 9(1), Sch 5 para 6). As to limited liability partnerships see PARTNERSHIP.

3   For the meaning of 'discrimination' see para 344 note 4 ante.

4   Sex Discrimination Act 1975 s 11(1) (amended by the Sex Discrimination Act 1986 ss 1(3), 9(2), Schedule Pt II). As to the meaning of 'woman' see para 344 note 5 ante. These provisions apply equally to the treatment of men, with requisite modifications: see the Sex Discrimination Act 1975 s 2(1); and para 357 ante. As to the meaning of 'man' see para 344 note 10 ante. As to discrimination on the grounds of gender reassignment see para 348 ante; and for the meaning of 'gender reassignment' see para 348 note 9 ante.
    As to provisions relating to discrimination against office-holders see ss 10A, 10B (as added); and para 377 post. As to selection of candidates by registered political parties see s 42A (as added); and para 367 note 4 post.

5   Ibid s 11(1)(a). See also note 7 infra. For the similar provision relating to employers see s 6(1)(a); and para 361 ante.

6   Ibid s 11(1)(b). For the similar provision relating to employers see s 6(1)(b); and para 361 ante.

7   Ibid s 11(1)(c). For the similar provision relating to employers see s 6(1)(c); and para 361 ante. Subject to s 11(3A) (as added), the provisions in s 11(1)(a), (c) do not apply to a position as partner where, if it were employment, being a man would be a genuine occupational qualification for the job: s 11(3) (amended by the Sex Discrimination (Gender Reassignment) Regulations 1999, SI 1999/1102, reg 4(4)). For the meaning of 'genuine occupational qualification' see para 363 note 6 ante. The Sex Discrimination Act 1975 s 11(3) (as amended) does not apply in relation to discrimination on the grounds of gender reassignment: s 11(3A) (s 11(3A), (3B), (3C) added by the Sex Discrimination (Gender Reassignment) Regulations 1999, SI 1999/1102, reg 4(5)).

8   As to the affording of access to benefits, facilities or services see para 361 note 11 ante.

9   Sex Discrimination Act 1975 s 11(1)(d)(i).

10   As to the expulsion of a person from a position as partner see para 361 note 13 ante.

11   Sex Discrimination Act 1975 s 11(1)(d)(ii).

12   Ibid s 11(2A)(added by the Employment Equality (Sex Discrimination) Regulations 2005, SI 2005/2467, reg 14(1), (2)). As to harassment, including sexual harassment, see the Sex Discrimination Act 1975 s 4A (as added); and para 347 ante.

13   Ie ibid s 11(1) (as amended): see the text to notes 1–11 supra.

14   Ibid s 11(3B) (as added: see note 7 supra).
    The provisions of s 11(3B), (3C) (as added) do not apply in relation to discrimination against a person whose gender has become the acquired gender under the Gender Recognition Act 2004: Sex Discrimination Act 1975 s 11(3D) (added by the Gender Recognition Act 2004 s 14, Sch 6 paras 1, 5). See further CONSTITUTIONAL LAW AND HUMAN RIGHTS.

15   For the meaning of 'employment' see para 360 note 4 ante.

16   Sex Discrimination Act 1975 s 11(3B)(a)(i) (as added: see note 7 supra). See note 14 supra.

17   Ibid s 11(3B)(a)(ii) (as added: see note 7 supra). See note 14 supra.

18   Ibid s 11(3B)(b) (as added: see note 7 supra). See note 14 supra.

19   Ie s 11(1)(d)(ii): see the text to note 11 supra.

20   For the meaning of 'supplementary genuine occupational qualification' see para 364 note 12 ante.
21   Sex Discrimination Act 1975 s 11(3C) (as added: see note 7 supra). See note 14 supra.

367.   Discrimination by trade unions and employers' associations. It is unlawful for an organisation of workers, an organisation of employers[1], or any other organisation whose members carry on a particular profession[2] or trade[3] for the purposes of which the organisation exists[4], in the case of a woman[5] who is not a member of the organisation, to discriminate[6] against her[7] in the terms on which it is prepared to admit her to membership[8], or by refusing, or deliberately omitting to accept, her application for membership[9].

It is unlawful for such an organisation, in the case of a woman who is a member of the organisation, to discriminate against her[10] in the way it affords her access to any benefits, facilities or services[11], or by refusing or deliberately omitting to afford her access to them[12], by depriving her of membership, or varying the terms on which she is a member[13], or by subjecting her to any other detriment[14].

It is also unlawful for such an organisation, in relation to membership of that organisation, to subject to harassment a woman who is a member of the organisation or has applied for membership of the organisation[15].

1   For the meaning of 'employer' see para 360 note 4 ante.
2   'Profession' includes any vocation or occupation: Sex Discrimination Act 1975 s 82(1).
3   'Trade' includes any business: ibid s 82(1).
4   Ibid s 12(1). An individual chapel of a national trade union may be an 'organisation of workers' for the purposes of s 12 (as amended), and may consequently be proceeded against for discrimination separately from the national union: *Record Production Chapel of the Daily Record and Sunday Mail Ltd, West Branch of the Scottish Graphical Division of SOGAT '82 v Turnbull* (16 April 1984) Lexis, EAT. The provisions may apply although the membership includes self-employed people as well as employees: *National Federation of Self-Employed and Small Businesses Ltd v Philpott* [1997] ICR 518, [1997] IRLR 340, EAT.

        The Labour Party's policy of having all-women shortlists for the selection of parliamentary candidates in some constituencies was held to be unlawful under the Sex Discrimination Act 1975 s 12 (as amended): *Jepson v Labour Party* [1996] IRLR 116, IT. As to *Jepson v Labour Party* supra see now the Sex Discrimination Act 1975 s 42A (added by the Sex Discrimination (Election Candidates) Act 2002 s 1). Nothing in the Sex Discrimination Act 1975 Pt II (ss 6–20A) (as amended), Pt III (ss 21A–36) (as amended) or Pt IV (ss 37–42) (as amended) is to be construed as affecting certain arrangements, or renders unlawful anything done in accordance with such arrangements: s 42A(1) (as so added). The arrangements are those made by a registered political party which regulate the selection of the party's candidates in a relevant election, and are adopted for the purpose of reducing inequality in the numbers of men and women elected, as candidates of the party, to be members of the body concerned: s 42A(2) (as so added). The following elections are relevant elections for these purposes: parliamentary elections, elections to the European Parliament, elections to the Scottish Parliament, elections to the National Assembly for Wales, local government elections within the meaning of the Representation of the People Act 1983 s 191, s 203 or s 204 (as amended) (excluding any election of the Mayor of London) (see ELECTIONS): Sex Discrimination Act 1975 s 42A(3) (as so added). 'Registered political party' means a party registered in the Great Britain register under the Political Parties, Elections and Referendums Act 2000 Pt II (ss 22–40) (as amended) (see ELECTIONS vol 15(3) (2007 Reissue) para 260): Sex Discrimination Act 1975 s 42A(4) (as so added). The Sex Discrimination (Election Candidates) Act 2002 expires at the end of 2015 unless an order is made under s 3: s 3(1). At any time before the Act expires the Secretary of State may by order provide that s 3(1) has effect with the substitution of a later time for the time specified there (whether originally or by virtue of a previous order): s 3(2). An order under s 3 must be made by statutory instrument, but no order may be made unless a draft has been laid before, and approved by resolution of, each House of Parliament: s 3(3). At the date at which this volumes states the law no order has been made under s 3.

        As to provisions relating to discrimination against office-holders see the Sex Discrimination Act 1975 ss 10A, 10B (as added); and para 377 post.
5   As to the meaning of 'woman' see para 344 note 5 ante. These provisions apply equally to the treatment of men, with requisite modifications: see ibid s 2(1); and para 357 ante. As to the meaning of 'man' see para 344 note 10 ante. As to discrimination on the grounds of gender reassignment see para 348 ante; and for the meaning of 'gender reassignment' see para 348 note 9 ante.
6   For the meaning of 'discrimination' see para 344 note 4 ante.
7   Sex Discrimination Act 1975 s 12(2).

8   Ibid s 12(2)(a).
9   Ibid s 12(2)(b). For a successful action brought against a chapel which excluded women see *Record
     Production Chapel of the Daily Record and Sunday Mail Ltd, West Branch of the Scottish Graphical Division of
     SOGAT '82 v Turnbull* (16 April 1984) Lexis, EAT.
10   Sex Discrimination Act 1975 s 12(3).
11   As to the affording of access to benefits, facilities or services see para 361 note 11 ante. See *Fire Brigades
     Union v Fraser* [1998] IRLR 697, Ct of Sess (Inner House of the Court of Session reversed a decision of
     the Employment Appeal Tribunal that a refusal by a union to provide legal support to a male union
     member accused of harassing a female union member amounted to unlawful discrimination; less
     favourable treatment of the accused than of the victim did not give rise to an inference of sex
     discrimination; the correct inference was that the difference in treatment was related to conduct).
12   Sex Discrimination Act 1975 s 12(3)(a).
13   Ibid s 12(3)(b).
14   Ibid s 12(3)(c). As to the responsibilities of trade unions see the Equal Opportunities Commission's Code
     of Practice on Sex Discrimination: Equal Opportunity Policies, Procedures and Practices in Employment
     (30 April 1995) paras 6–8. As to codes of practice generally see para 406 post. As to the Equal
     Opportunities Commission see para 404 et seq post. As to the Commission for Equality and Human
     Rights, which is to replace the Equal Opportunities Commission, see para 305 et seq ante.
15   Sex Discrimination Act 1975 s 12(3A) (added by the Employment Equality (Sex Discrimination)
     Regulations 2005, SI 2005/2467, reg 15(1), (2)). As to harassment, including sexual harassment, see the
     Sex Discrimination Act 1975 s 4A (as added); and para 347 ante. See also *Shepherd v North Yorkshire
     County Council* [2006] IRLR 190, [2005] All ER (D) 354 (Dec), EAT.

368.   Discrimination by qualifying bodies.   It is unlawful for an authority or
body which can confer an authorisation or qualification which is needed for, or
facilitates, engagement in a particular profession[1] or trade[2] to discriminate[3] against a
woman[4] in the terms on which it is prepared to confer[5] on her that authorisation or
qualification[6], by refusing or deliberately omitting to grant her application for it[7], or by
withdrawing it from her or varying the terms on which she holds it[8]. It is also unlawful
for such a body to subject to harassment a woman who holds or applies for such an
authorisation or qualification[9].

Where an authority or body is required by law to satisfy itself as to a person's good
character before conferring on him an authorisation or qualification which is needed
for, or facilitates, his engagement in any profession or trade then, without prejudice to
any other duty to which it is subject, that requirement is to be taken to impose on the
authority or body a duty to have regard to any evidence tending to show that he, or any
of his employees[10] or agents (whether past or present), has practised unlawful
discrimination in, or in connection with, the carrying on of any profession or trade[11].
The test as to whether this provision applies is whether the qualification, authorisation
or certification objectively and as a matter of fact facilitates engagement in a particular
profession or trade, not whether it is intended to do so[12].

1   As to the meaning of 'profession' see para 367 note 2 ante.
2   As to the meaning of 'trade' see para 367 note 3 ante. A body which does not have the power to confer
     an authorisation or qualification which is needed for, or facilitates, engagement in a particular profession
     or trade, but which merely stipulates for its commercial agreements that a particular qualification is
     required is not an authority or body within the meaning of the equivalent provision of the Race
     Relations Act 1976: *Tattari v Private Patients Plan Ltd* [1998] ICR 106, 38 BMLR 24, CA. See also *Arthur
     v A-G* [1999] ICR 631, EAT (where leave was given to appeal to the Court of Appeal). See further
     Sawyer v Ahsan [1999] IRLR 609, EAT (Labour Party was treated as a qualifying body in relation to a
     Labour councillor's unsuccessful application for re-selection). In *Hampson v Department of Education and
     Science* [1990] 2 All ER 25, [1989] ICR 179, CA (revsd on other grounds [1991] 1 AC 171, [1990]
     2 All ER 513, HL), the respondents conceded that the Secretary of State for Education was a qualifying
     body for the purposes of the equivalent provision of the Race Relations Act 1976 when exercising his
     statutory function of notifying applicants that they were qualified teachers, without which notification
     teachers could not be employed as teachers in schools (see EDUCATION vol 15(2) (2006 Reissue)
     para 769). It was conceded in *R v Department of Health, ex p Gandhi* [1991] 4 All ER 547, [1991] 1 WLR
     1053, DC, that the Medical Practices Committee (now abolished: see the Health and Social Care
     Act 2001 s 14; and NATIONAL HEALTH SERVICE vol 33 (Reissue) para 183 et seq) was a qualifying body.

3   For the meaning of 'discrimination' see para 344 note 4 ante.
4   Sex Discrimination Act 1975 s 13(1). As to the meaning of 'woman' see para 344 note 5 ante. These
     provisions apply equally to the treatment of men, with requisite modifications: see s 2(1); and para 357
     ante. As to the meaning of 'man' see para 344 note 9 ante. As to discrimination on the grounds of gender
     reassignment see para 348 ante; and for the meaning of 'gender reassignment' see para 348 note 9 ante.
         Section 13(1) does not apply to discrimination which is rendered unlawful by s 22 (as amended)
     (bodies in charge of educational establishments) (see para 378 post) or s 23 (as amended) (other
     discrimination by local education authorities) (see para 378 post): s 13(4). Section 13(1) must be read in
     accordance with s 19 (as substituted): see para 373 post.
         As to provisions relating to discrimination against office-holders see ss 10A, 10B (as added); and
     para 377 post. As to selection of candidates by registered political parties see s 42A (as added); and
     para 367 note 4 ante.
5   'Confer' includes renew or extend: ibid s 13(3)(b).
6   Ibid s 13(1)(a). 'Authorisation or qualification' includes recognition, registration, enrolment, approval and
     certification: s 13(3)(a). See note 4 supra.
7   Ibid s 13(1)(b). See note 4 supra.
8   Ibid s 13(1)(c). See note 4 supra.
9   Ibid s 13(1A) (added by the Employment Equality (Sex Discrimination) Regulations 2005,
     SI 2005/2467, reg 16(1), (2)). The Sex Discrimination Act 1975 s 13(1A) (as added) does not apply to
     harassment which is rendered unlawful by s 22 (as amended) or s 23 (as amended) (see para 378 post):
     s 13(5) (added by the Employment Equality (Sex Discrimination) Regulations 2005, SI 2005/2467,
     reg 16(1), (3)). As to harassment, including sexual harassment, see the Sex Discrimination Act 1975 s 4A
     (as added); and para 347 ante.
10   For the meaning of 'employee' see para 360 note 4 ante.
11   Sex Discrimination Act 1975 s 13(2).
12   *British Judo Association v Petty* [1981] ICR 660, [1981] IRLR 484, EAT.

369.   Discrimination in the provision of vocational training. It is unlawful, in
the case of a woman[1] seeking or receiving vocational training[2], for any person[4] who
provides, or makes arrangements for the provision of, facilities[5] for vocational training to
discriminate[6] against her[7] in the arrangements that person makes for the purposes of
selecting people to receive vocational training[8], in the terms on which that person
affords her access to any vocational training or facilities concerned with vocational
training[9], by refusing or deliberately omitting to afford her such access[10], by terminating
her training[11], or by subjecting her to any detriment during the course of her training[12].
It is also unlawful for a provider of vocational training, in relation to such training, to
subject to harassment a woman to whom he is providing such training or who has asked
him to provide such training[13].

     It is unlawful for the Secretary of State[14] to discriminate, or subject a woman to
harassment, in the provision of facilities or services[15] for the purpose of assisting persons
to select, train for, obtain and retain employment suitable for their ages and capacities or
of assisting persons to obtain suitable employees[16].

1   As to the meaning of 'woman' see para 344 note 5 ante. These provisions apply equally to the treatment
     of men, with requisite modifications: see the Sex Discrimination Act 1975 s 2(1); and para 357 ante. As
     to the meaning of 'man' see para 344 note 10 ante. As to discrimination on the grounds of gender
     reassignment see para 348 ante; and for the meaning of 'gender reassignment' see para 348 note 9 ante.
2   For these purposes, 'vocational training' includes (if it would not otherwise do so) any training which
     would help fit her for any employment: ibid s 14(1B) (added by the Employment Equality (Sex
     Discrimination) Regulations 2005, SI 2005/2467, reg 17(1)). For the meaning of 'employment' see
     para 360 note 4 ante. See also para 344 note 6 ante.
4   As to the meaning of 'person' see para 344 note 3 ante.
5   As to access to facilities see para 361 note 11 ante.
6   For the meaning of 'discriminate' see para 344 note 4 ante.
7   Sex Discrimination Act 1975 s 14(1) (s 14 substituted by the Employment Act 1989 s 7(1); and the Sex
     Discrimination Act 1975 s 14(1) substituted by the Employment Equality (Sex Discrimination)
     Regulations 2005, SI 2005/2467, reg 17(1)). The Sex Discrimination Act 1975 s 14(1) (as substituted)
     does not apply to discrimination which is rendered unlawful by s 6(1) or (2) (discrimination against
     employees (see para 361 ante) or s 22 (as amended) (bodies in charge of educational establishments) (see

para 378 post) or s 23 (as amended) (other discrimination by local education authorities) (see para 378 post), or discrimination which would be rendered unlawful by any of those provisions but for the operation of any other provision of the Sex Discrimination Act 1975: s 14(2) (as so substituted). Until 1 September 1983, the Sex Discrimination Act 1975 s 14 did not apply to training as a midwife: see s 20(3) (amended by the Sex Discrimination Act 1975 (Amendment of section 20) Order 1983, SI 1983/1202, art 2). As to midwives see MEDICAL PROFESSIONS vol 30(1) (Reissue) para 691 et seq.

As to provisions relating to discrimination against office-holders see the Sex Discrimination Act 1975 ss 10A, 10B (as added); and para 377 post. As to selection of candidates by registered political parties see s 42A (as added); and para 367 note 4 ante.

8 Ibid s 14(1)(a) (as substituted: see note 7 supra).
9 Ibid s 14(1)(b) (as substituted: see note 7 supra).
10 Ibid s 14(1)(c) (as substituted: see note 7 supra).
11 Ibid s 14(1)(d) (as substituted: see note 7 supra). See *Lana v Positive Action Training in Housing (London) Ltd* [2001] IRLR 501, [2001] All ER (D) 23 (Jun), EAT; and para 391 post.
12 Sex Discrimination Act 1975 s 14(1)(e) (as substituted: see note 7 supra). See *Fletcher v NHS Pensions Agency* [2005] ICR 1458, [2005] IRLR 689, EAT (withdrawal of financial support for vocational trainees who became pregnant was discriminatory notwithstanding blanket policy of removing support for all long-term absentees).
13 Sex Discrimination Act 1975 s 14(1A) (added by the Employment Equality (Sex Discrimination) Regulations 2005, SI 2005/2467, reg 17(1)). As to harassment, including sexual harassment, see the Sex Discrimination Act 1975 s 4A (as added); and para 347 ante.
14 As to the Secretary of State and the National Assembly for Wales see para 302 ante.
15 Ie under the Employment and Training Act 1973 s 2 (as substituted and amended): see EMPLOYMENT vol 16(1B) (Reissue) para 765.
16 See the Sex Discrimination Act 1975 s 16(1) (substituted by the Employment and Training Act 1981 s 9, Sch 2 para 18; and amended by the Employment Act 1988 s 33(1), Sch 3 para 11(2); the Employment Act 1989 s 29(4), Sch 7 Pt I; and the Employment Equality (Sex Discrimination) Regulations 2005, SI 2005/2467, reg 19(1), (2)). The Sex Discrimination Act 1975 s 16 (as amended) does not apply where s 14 (as substituted and amended) applies, or where the Secretary of State is acting as an employment agency: s 16(2) (amended by the Employment Act 1989 s 29(3), Sch 6 para 12). As to employment agencies see para 370 post.

Discriminatory training programmes are purported to be allowed by the Sex Discrimination Act 1975 s 47 (as amended): see para 399 post. However, it may well be that positive discrimination in training programmes would be held to be unlawful by the European Court of Justice: see Case C-450/93 *Kalanke v Freie Hansestadt Bremen* [1996] All ER(EC) 66, [1995] IRLR 660, ECJ. See, however, Case C-158/97 *Re Badeck* [2000] All ER (EC) 289, [2000] ECR I-1875, ECJ.

370. Discrimination by employment agencies. It is unlawful for an employment agency[1] to discriminate[2] against a woman[3] in the terms on which the agency offers to provide any of its services[4], or by refusing or deliberately omitting to provide any of its services[5], or in the way it provides any of its services[6]. It is also unlawful for an employment agency, in relation to the provision of its services, to subject to harassment a woman to whom it provides such services or who has requested the provision of such services[7].

It is unlawful for a local education authority or an education authority or any other person to do any act[8] in providing services in pursuance of arrangements made, or a direction given, in the performance of its statutory functions of providing a careers service[9] which constitutes discrimination[10].

These provisions[11] do not apply if the discrimination only concerns employment which the employer could lawfully refuse to offer the woman[12]. An employment agency or local education authority, education authority or other person is not subject to any liability if it proves: (1) that it acted in reliance on a statement made to it by the employer to the effect that, by reason of the operation of this provision, its action would not be unlawful; and (2) that it was reasonable for it to rely on the statement[13].

1 'Employment agency' means a person who, for profit or not, provides services for the purpose of finding employment for workers or supplying employers with workers: Sex Discrimination Act 1975 s 82(1). As to the meaning of 'person' see para 344 note 1 ante. For the meaning of 'employment' see para 360 note 4 ante. See *Rice v Fon-A-Car* [1980] ICR 133, EAT (taxi-cab firm not an employment agency for taxi

drivers). It was held under the equivalent provision of the Race Relations Act 1976 that the head of careers at a school, when asked by an employer to supply a school leaver for a vacancy, is acting as an employment agency: *Commission for Racial Equality v Imperial Society of Teachers of Dancing* [1983] ICR 473, [1983] IRLR 315, EAT.

2   For the meaning of 'discrimination' see para 344 note 4 ante.
3   Sex Discrimination Act 1975 s 15(1). As to the meaning of 'woman' see para 344 note 5 ante. These provisions apply equally to the treatment of men, with requisite modifications: see s 2(1); and para 357 ante. As to the meaning of 'man' see para 344 note 10 ante. As to discrimination on the grounds of gender reassignment see para 348 ante; and for the meaning of 'gender reassignment' see para 348 note 9 ante.
       As to provisions relating to discrimination against office-holders see ss 10A, 10B (as added); and para 377 post. As to selection of candidates by registered political parties see s 42A (as added); and para 367 note 4 ante.
4   Ibid s 15(1)(a). References to the services of an employment agency include guidance on careers and any other services related to employment: s 15(3).
5   Ibid s 15(1)(b). See note 4 supra.
6   Ibid s 15(1)(c). See note 4 supra.
7   Ibid s 15(1A) (added by the Employment Equality (Sex Discrimination) Regulations 2005, SI 2005/2467, reg 18). As to harassment, including sexual harassment, see the Sex Discrimination Act 1975 s 4A (as added); and para 347 ante.
8   As to the meaning of 'act' see para 359 note 1 ante.
9   Ie under the Employment and Training Act 1973 s 10 (as substituted): see EMPLOYMENT vol 16(1B) (Reissue) para 771. As to local education authorities and education authorities see EDUCATION vol 15(1) (2006 Reissue) para 20 et seq.
10   Sex Discrimination Act 1975 s 15(2) (substituted by the Trade Union Reform and Employment Rights Act 1993 s 49(2), Sch 8 para 8).
11   Ie the Sex Discrimination Act 1975 s 15 (as amended).
12   Ibid s 15(4). See further para 363 ante.
13   Ibid s 15(5) (amended by the Trade Union Reform and Employment Rights Act 1993 s 49(2), Sch 8 para 8).
       A person who knowingly or recklessly makes such a statement which in a material respect is false or misleading commits an offence, and is liable on summary conviction to a fine not exceeding level 5 on the standard scale: Sex Discrimination Act 1975 s 15(6) (amended by virtue of the Criminal Justice Act 1982 ss 38, 46). As to the standard scale see para 315 note 15 ante.

371.   Discrimination in the police. The holding of the office of police constable[1] or appointment as a police cadet[2] is treated as employment[3] by the chief officer of police[4] as respects any act[5] done by him in relation to a constable or the office of constable, and employment by the police authority[6] as respects any act done by it in relation to a constable or the office of constable[7].

Regulations made in relation to police[8] must not treat men[9] and women[10] differently except[11]: (1) as to requirements relating to height, uniform or equipment, or allowances in lieu of uniform or equipment[12]; (2) so far as special treatment is accorded to women in connection with pregnancy or childbirth[13]; or (3) in relation to pensions to or in respect of special constables or police cadets[14].

Any compensation, costs or expenses awarded against a chief officer of police in any proceedings brought against him under the Sex Discrimination Act 1975, and any costs or expenses incurred by him in any such proceedings so far as not recovered by him in the proceedings are to be paid out of the police fund[15]. The police fund is also to pay any sum required by a chief officer of police for the settlement of any claim made against him under the Sex Discrimination Act 1975 if the settlement is approved by the police authority[16].

1   As to the office of police constable see POLICE vol 36(1) (Reissue) para 201 et seq. A special constable holds the office of constable and is entitled to protection in the same way as a regular constable: *Sheikh v Chief Constable of Greater Manchester Police* [1990] 1 QB 637, [1989] 2 All ER 684, CA.

2 'Police cadet' means any person appointed to undergo training with a view to becoming a constable: Sex Discrimination Act 1975 s 17(7). As to the meaning of 'training' see para 348 note 5 ante. As to police cadets see POLICE vol 36(1) (Reissue) para 213 et seq.

3 Ibid s 17(1). For the meaning of 'employment' see para 360 note 4 ante.

As to provisions relating to discrimination against office-holders see ss 10A, 10B (as added); and para 377 post. As to selection of candidates by registered political parties see s 42A (as added); and para 367 note 4 ante.

4 'Chief officer of police': (1) in relation to a person appointed, or an appointment falling to be made, under the Metropolitan Police Act 1829, the City of London Police Act 1839 or the Police Act 1996, has the same meaning as in the Police Act 1996 (see POLICE vol 36(1) (Reissue) para 205); and (2) in relation to any other person or appointment means the officer who has the direction and control of the body of constables or cadets in question: Sex Discrimination Act 1975 s 17(7) (definition amended by the Police Act 1996 s 103(1), Sch 7 para 27; the Police Act 1997 s 134(1), Sch 9 para 31; and the Serious Organised Crime and Police Act 2005 ss 59, 174(2), Sch 4 para 28(a), Sch 17 Pt 2).

Any proceedings under the Sex Discrimination Act 1975 which, by virtue of s 17(1) (as amended) or s 17(1A) (as added) (see the text and note 7 infra), would lie against a chief officer of police must be brought against the chief officer of police for the time being or, in the case of a vacancy in that office, against the person for the time being performing the functions of that office: see s 17(5) (amended by the Equality Act 2006 s 83(2)).

In relation to a constable of a force who is not under the direction and control of the chief officer of police for that force, references in the Sex Discrimination Act 1975 s 17 (as amended) to the chief officer of police are references to the chief officer for the force under whose direction and control he is: s 17(9) (added by the Sex Discrimination Act 1975 (Amendment) Regulations 2003, SI 2003/1657, reg 2(1), (9)).

5 As to the meaning of 'act' see para 359 note 1 ante.

6 'Police authority', in relation to a person appointed, or an appointment falling to be made, under the Metropolitan Police Act 1829, the City of London Police Act 1839 or the Police Act 1996, has the same meaning as in the Police Act 1996 (see POLICE vol 36(1) (Reissue) para 202); and in relation to any other person or appointment, means the authority by whom the person in question is or on appointment would be paid: Sex Discrimination Act 1975 s 17(7) (definition amended by the Police Act 1996 Sch 7 para 27; and the Serious Organised Crime and Police Act 2005 Sch 4 para 28(b), Sch 17 Pt 2). As to police authorities see POLICE vol 36(1) (Reissue) para 316 et seq.

In relation to a constable of a force who is not under the direction and control of the chief officer of police for that force, references in the Sex Discrimination Act 1975 s 17 (as amended) to the police authority are references to the relevant police authority for the force under whose direction and control he is: see s 17(9) (added by the Sex Discrimination Act 1975 (Amendment) Regulations 2003, SI 2003/1657, reg 2(1), (9)).

The Sex Discrimination Act 1975 s 17 (as amended) does not prevent individual officers also being liable for sex discrimination: *AM v WC and SPV* [1999] ICR 1218, [1999] IRLR 410, EAT.

7 Sex Discrimination Act 1975 s 17(1), (6) (s 17(6) amended by the Sex Discrimination Act 1975 (Amendment) Regulations 2003, SI 2003/1657, reg 2(1), (5)).

For the purposes of the Sex Discrimination Act 1975 s 41 (see para 391 ante), the holding of the office of constable is to be treated as employment by the chief officer of police, and as not being employment by any other person, and anything done by a person holding such an office in the performance, or purported performance, of his functions is to be treated as done in the course of that employment: s 17(1A) (added by the Sex Discrimination Act 1975 (Amendment) Regulations 2003, SI 2003/1657, reg 2(1), (3)).

Management acts such as the posting of police officers are acts in respect of which discrimination proceedings may be brought: *Chief Constable of Cumbria v McGlennon* [2002] ICR 1156, [2002] All ER (D) 231 (Jul), EAT.

8 Ie under the Police Act 1996 s 50, s 51 or s 52 (as amended): see POLICE vol 36(1) (Reissue) paras 210, 375.

9 As to the meaning of 'man' see para 344 note 10 ante. As to sex discrimination against men see para 357 ante. For the meaning of 'discrimination' see para 344 note 4 ante. As to discrimination on the grounds of gender reassignment see para 348 ante; and for the meaning of 'gender reassignment' see para 348 note 9 ante.

10 As to the meaning of 'woman' see para 344 note 5 ante.

11 Sex Discrimination Act 1975 s 17(2) (amended by the Police Act 1996 Sch 7 para 27).

12 Sex Discrimination Act 1975 s 17(2)(a). Nothing in Pt II (ss 6–20A) (as amended) renders unlawful any discrimination between male and female constables or police cadets as to matters such as are mentioned in s 17(2)(a): s 17(3), (6).

13 Ibid s 17(2)(b).

14 Ibid s 17(2)(c). As to special constables see POLICE vol 36(1) (Reissue) paras 208–212.

15   Ibid s 17(4)(a). 'Police fund' in relation to a chief officer of police within note 4 head (1) supra has the same meaning as in the Police Act 1996 (see POLICE vol 36(1) (Reissue) para 205), and in any other case means money provided by the police authority: Sex Discrimination Act 1975 s 17(7) (definition amended by the Police Act 1996 Sch 7 para 27; the Police Act 1997 Sch 9 para 31; and the Serious Organised Crime and Police Act 2005 Sch 4 para 28(c), Sch 17 Pt 2).

     A police authority may, in such cases and to such extent as appear to it to be appropriate, pay out of the police fund: (1) any compensation, costs or expenses awarded in proceedings under this Act against a person under the direction and control of the chief officer of police; (2) any costs or expenses incurred and not recovered by such a person in such proceedings; and (3) any sum required in connection with the settlement of a claim that has or might have given rise to such proceedings: Sex Discrimination Act 1975 s 17(5A) (added by the Sex Discrimination Act 1975 (Amendment) Regulations 2003, SI 2003/1657, reg 2(1), (4)).

16   Sex Discrimination Act 1975 s 17(4)(b). See note 15 supra.

372. Discrimination in relation to prison officers. The provisions relating to discrimination in the employment field[1] do not render unlawful any discrimination between male and female prison officers as to requirements relating to height[2].

1   Ie the Sex Discrimination Act 1975 Pt II (ss 6–20A) (as amended): see para 360 et seq ante. For the meaning of 'discrimination' see para 344 note 4 ante. For the meaning of 'employment' see para 360 note 4 ante.

2   Ibid s 18(1). See also PRISONS vol 36(2) (Reissue) para 515.

     As to provisions relating to discrimination against office-holders see ss 10A, 10B (as added); and para 377 post.

373. Discrimination in relation to ministers of religion. Nothing in the provisions relating to discrimination in the employment field[1] makes it unlawful to apply a requirement in relation to employment where: (1) the employment is for purposes of an organised religion; (2) the requirement is to be of a particular sex, not to be undergoing or to have undergone gender reassignment[2], relates to not being married or not being a civil partner[3] or which, applied in relation to a person who is married or is a civil partner, relates to the person, or the person's spouse or civil partner, not having a living former spouse or a living former civil partner, or to how the person, or the person's spouse or civil partner, has at any time ceased to be married or ceased to be a civil partner; and (3) the requirement is applied so as to comply with the doctrines of the religion or (because of the nature of the employment and the context in which it is carried out) so as to avoid conflicting with the strongly-held religious convictions of a significant number of the religion's followers[4].

     Nothing in the provisions relating to qualifying bodies[5] makes it unlawful to apply a requirement in relation to an authorisation or qualification[6] where the authorisation or qualification is for purposes of an organised religion, the requirement is a requirement specified in head (2) above, and the requirement is applied so as to comply with the doctrines of the religion or by the authority or body concerned (or by the person by whom the authority or body acts in a particular case) so as to avoid conflicting with the strongly-held religious convictions of a significant number of the religion's followers[7].

1   Ie the Sex Discrimination Act 1975 Pt II (ss 6–20A) (as amended): see para 360 et seq ante. For the meaning of 'discrimination' see para 344 note 4 ante. For the meaning of 'employment' see para 360 note 4 ante.

     See *Percy v Church of Scotland Board of National Mission* [2005] UKHL 73, [2006] 2 AC 28, [2006] 4 All ER 1354 (holding of ecclesiastical office under agreement conferring contractual obligation was employment for purposes of the Sex Discrimination Act 1975).

2   For the meaning of 'gender reassignment' see para 348 note 9 ante. As to discrimination on the grounds of gender reassignment see para 348 ante.

3   As to civil partnerships generally see MATRIMONIAL LAW.

4   See the Sex Discrimination Act 1975 s 19(1), (3) (s 19 substituted by the Employment Equality (Sex Discrimination) Regulations 2005, SI 2005/2467, reg 20(1)).

     As to provisions relating to discrimination against office-holders see the Sex Discrimination Act 1975 ss 10A, 10B (as added); and para 377 post.

5 Ie ibid s 13 (as amended) (see para 368 ante): see s 19(2) (as substituted: see note 4 supra).
6 For the meaning of 'authorisation or qualification' see para 368 note 6 ante; definition applied by ibid
   s 19(2) (as substituted: see note 4 supra).
7 Ibid s 19(2), (3) (as substituted: see note 4 supra).

374. Discrimination by and in relation to barristers and their clerks. It is unlawful for a barrister or barrister's clerk[1], in relation to any offer of a pupillage or tenancy[2], to discriminate[3] against a woman[4] in the arrangements which are made[5] for the purpose of determining to whom it should be offered[6], in respect of any terms on which it is offered[7], or by refusing, or deliberately omitting, to offer it to her[8].

It is unlawful for a barrister or barrister's clerk, in relation to a woman who is a pupil or tenant in the chambers in question, to discriminate against her[9]: (1) in respect of any terms applicable to her as a pupil or tenant[10]; (2) in the opportunities for training[11], or gaining experience[12], which are afforded or denied to her[13]; (3) in the benefits, facilities or services which are afforded or denied to her[14]; or (4) by terminating her pupillage or by subjecting her to any pressure to leave the chambers or other detriment[15].

It is also unlawful for a barrister or barrister's clerk, in relation to a pupillage or tenancy, to subject to harassment a person who is, or who has applied to be, a pupil or tenant in the set of chambers concerned[16].

It is unlawful for any person[17], in relation to the giving, withholding or acceptance of instructions to a barrister, to discriminate against a woman by subjecting her to a detriment, or to subject a woman to harassment[18].

Where there has been a relevant relationship between a woman and another person ('the relevant person')[19], and the relationship has come to an end[20], it is unlawful for a relevant person to discriminate against the woman by subjecting her to a detriment where the discrimination arises out of and is closely connected to the relevant relationship[21]. It is unlawful for the relevant person to subject a woman to harassment where that treatment arises out of or is closely connected to the relevant relationship[22].

1 'Barrister's clerk' includes any person carrying out any of the functions of a barrister's clerk: Sex
   Discrimination Act 1975 s 35A(4) (s 35A added by the Courts and Legal Services Act 1990 s 64(1)).
2 'Pupil', 'pupillage', 'tenancy' and 'tenant' have the meanings commonly associated with their use in the
   context of a set of barristers' chambers, but 'tenant' also includes any barrister permitted to work in a set
   of chambers who is not a tenant (and 'tenancy' is to be construed accordingly): Sex Discrimination
   Act 1975 s 35A(4) (as added (see note 1 supra); and definition amended by the Employment Equality
   (Sex Discrimination) Regulations 2005, SI 2005/2467, reg 24(1), (5)). See BARRISTERS vol 3(1) (2005
   Reissue) para 471 et seq.
3 For the meaning of 'discrimination' see para 344 note 4 ante.
4 Sex Discrimination Act 1975 s 35A(1) (as added: see note 1 supra). These provisions apply equally to the
   treatment of men, with requisite modifications: see s 2(1); and para 357 ante. The prohibition on
   discrimination by barristers or barristers' clerks is contained in Pt III (ss 21A–36) (as amended), and
   consequently should be enforced through a county court, rather than an employment tribunal: see
   para 415 post. As to the meaning of 'woman' see para 344 note 5 ante; and as to the meaning of 'man' see
   para 344 note 10 ante. As to discrimination on the grounds of gender reassignment see para 348 ante; and
   for the meaning of 'gender reassignment' see para 348 note 9 ante.
      As to provisions relating to discrimination against office-holders see ss 10A, 10B (as added); and
   para 377 post.
5 The scope of this provision is presumably similar to that of ibid s 6(1)(a) (discrimination in arrangements
   made for the purpose of determining who should be offered employment: see para 361 ante). In the
   context of barristers' chambers, indirect discrimination by reliance upon word of mouth
   recommendations or social or family contacts for the recruitment of pupils may be particularly relevant;
   as may discrimination by concentration on certain universities as sources of recruitment.
6 Ibid s 35A(1)(a) (as added: see note 1 supra).
7 Ibid s 35A(1)(b) (as added: see note 1 supra).
8 Ibid s 35A(1)(c) (as added: see note 1 supra).
9 Ibid s 35A(2) (as added: see note 1 supra).
10 Ibid s 35A(2)(a) (as added: see note 1 supra).
11 As to the meaning of 'training' see para 348 note 5 ante.

12 This provision would presumably cover discrimination by a barrister's clerk in the allocation of work to tenants or pupils.

13 Sex Discrimination Act 1975 s 35A(2)(b) (as added: see note 1 supra).

14 Ibid s 35A(2)(c) (as added: see note 1 supra). As to the affording of access to benefits, facilities or services see para 361 note 11 ante.

15 Ibid s 35A(2)(d) (as added: see note 1 supra).

16 Ibid s 35A(2A) (added by the Employment Equality (Sex Discrimination) Regulations 2005, SI 2005/2467, reg 24(1), (3)). As to harassment, including sexual harassment, see the Sex Discrimination Act 1975 s 4A (as added); and para 347 ante.

17 As to the meaning of 'person' see para 344 note 3 ante.

18 Sex Discrimination Act 1975 s 35A(3) (as added (see note 1 supra); and amended by the Employment Equality (Sex Discrimination) Regulations 2005, SI 2005/2467, reg 24(1), (4)). This provision would cover discrimination by a solicitor, or anyone instructing a barrister, and discrimination by a barrister's clerk, either against a barrister, or against the solicitor or lay client. It would cover e g the withholding of certain work from a barrister, or the refusal to accept a set of instructions, if as a result of sex discrimination.

The Sex Discrimination Act 1975 s 3 (as substituted) (discrimination against married persons and civil partners in the employment field) (see para 349 ante) applies for the purposes of this provision as it applies for the purposes of any provision of Pt II (ss 6–20A) (as amended): s 35A(5) (as so added).

19 A 'relevant relationship' is a relationship during the course of which an act of discrimination by one party to the relationship against the other party to it is unlawful under ibid s 35A (as added and amended), or any other provision of ss 22–35 (as amended), so far as the provision applies to vocational training: s 35C(2) (s 35C(1)–(3) added by the Sex Discrimination Act 1975 (Amendment) Regulations 2003, SI 2003/1657, reg 4). For the meaning of 'vocational training' see para 344 note 6 ante.

20 Ie whether before or after the commencement of the Sex Discrimination Act 1975 s 35C (as added): see s 35C(1) (as added: see note 19 supra).

21 Ibid s 35C(1), (3) (as added: see note 19 supra).

22 Ibid s 35C(4) (added by the Employment Equality (Sex Discrimination) Regulations 2005, SI 2005/2467, reg 26).

375. Crown servants. In general, those in the service of the Crown[1] are treated under the Sex Discrimination Act 1975[2] as if they were employed by a private person, and as if references to a contract of employment included references to their terms of service[3]. However, nothing in the Act renders unlawful an act[4] done for the purpose of ensuring the combat effectiveness of the armed forces[5].

The provisions of the Act prohibiting discrimination in employment and other discriminatory acts apply to service in the armed forces, if at the time when the act complained of was done the complainant was serving in the armed forces and the discrimination in question relates to his service in those forces[8]. Certain procedures must be followed[9].

1 Ie those engaged in service for purposes of a Minister of the Crown or government department, or service on behalf of the Crown for the purposes of a person holding a statutory office or the purposes of a statutory body, or service in the armed forces: see the Sex Discrimination Act 1975 s 85(2) (amended by the Armed Forces Act 1996 s 21(2)). 'Service for purposes of a Minister of the Crown or government department' does not include service in any office in the House of Commons Disqualification Act 1975 s 2, Sch 2 (as amended) (ministerial offices) (see PARLIAMENT vol 34 (Reissue) para 611) as for the time being in force: Sex Discrimination Act 1975 s 85(10) (substituted by the Armed Forces Act 1996 s 21(5)). 'Armed forces' means any of the naval, military or air forces of the Crown: Sex Discrimination Act 1975 s 85(10) (as so substituted). See further ARMED FORCES.

As to provisions relating to discrimination against office-holders see ss 10A, 10B (as added); and para 377 post.

2 Ie under ibid Pt II (ss 6–20A) (as amended), Pt IV (ss 37–42) (as amended) (prohibiting discrimination in employment and other discriminatory acts).

3 See ibid s 85(2). Section 85(1), (2) (as amended) has effect subject to s 17 (as amended) (police) (see para 371 ante): s 85(3). Both s 21A (as added) (see para 394 post) and s 76A (as added) (see para 343 ante) bind the Crown: see s 85(3A), (3B) (added by the Equality Act 2006 ss 83(4), 84(3)).

4 As to the meaning of 'act' see para 359 note 1 ante.

5 Sex Discrimination Act 1975 s 85(4) (substituted by the Sex Discrimination Act 1975 (Application to Armed Forces etc) Regulations 1994, SI 1994/3276, reg 2(a); and amended by the Armed Forces Act 1996 s 21(3)). It has been held that EC Council Directive 76/207 (OJ L39, 14.2.76, p 40) on the

implementation of the principle of equal treatment for men and women as regards access to employment, vocational training and promotion, and working conditions (as amended) (see para 338 ante) does apply in general to the organisation of the armed forces but that the United Kingdom government may be entitled under art 2(2) to exclude women from special combat units such as the Royal Marines: see Case C-273/97 *Sirdar v Army Board and Secretary of State for Defence* [1999] All ER (EC) 928, [2000] IRLR 47, ECJ. See also ARMED FORCES.

8　　See the Sex Discrimination Act 1975 s 85(9A) (s 85(9A)–(9E) added by the Armed Forces Act 1996 s 21(4)).

9　　No complaint to which the Sex Discrimination Act 1975 s 85(9A) (as added) applies may be presented to an employment tribunal under s 63 (as amended) (see para 414 post) unless: (1) the complainant has made a complaint to an officer under the service redress procedures applicable to him and has submitted that complaint to the Defence Council under those procedures; and (2) the Defence Council has made a determination with respect to the complaint: s 85(9B) (as added: see note 8 supra). 'The service redress procedures' means the procedures, excluding those which relate to the making of a report on a complaint to Her Majesty, referred to in the Army Act 1955 s 180 (as substituted and amended), the Air Force Act 1955 s 180 (as substituted and amended) and the Naval Discipline Act 1957 s 130 (as substituted and amended) (see ARMED FORCES vol 2(2) (Reissue) para 314): Sex Discrimination Act 1975 s 85(10) (as substituted (see note 1 supra); prospectively repealed by the Armed Forces Act 2006 s 378(1), Sch 16 para 71). As to the Defence Council see ARMED FORCES vol 2(2) (Reissue) para 2; CONSTITUTIONAL LAW AND HUMAN RIGHTS vol 8(2) (Reissue) para 443 et seq.

　　Regulations may make provision enabling a complaint to be presented to an employment tribunal under the Sex Discrimination Act 1975 s 63 (as amended) (see para 414 post) in such circumstances as may be specified by the regulations, notwithstanding that s 85(9B) (as added) would otherwise preclude the presentation of the complaint to an employment tribunal: s 85(9C) (as added (see note 8 supra); and amended by virtue of the Employment Rights (Dispute Resolution) Act 1998 s 1(2)(a)). Where a complaint is so presented to an employment tribunal, the service redress procedures may continue after the complaint is so presented: Sex Discrimination Act 1975 s 85(9D) (as added (see note 8 supra); and amended by virtue of the Employment Rights (Dispute Resolution) Act 1998 s 1(2)(a)). Regulations under the Sex Discrimination Act 1975 s 85(9C) (as added and amended) must be made by the Secretary of State by statutory instrument and are subject to annulment in pursuance of a resolution of either House of Parliament: s 85(9E) (as added: see note 8 supra). As to the Secretary of State and National Assembly for Wales see para 302 ante. In exercise of this power, the Sex Discrimination (Complaints to Employment Tribunals) (Armed Forces) Regulations 1997, SI 1997/2163 (as amended) have been made. A person may present a complaint to an employment tribunal under the Sex Discrimination Act 1975 s 63 (as amended) (see para 414 post), notwithstanding that s 85(9B) (as added) would otherwise preclude the presentation of such a complaint, where: (a) he has made a complaint in respect of the same matter to an officer under the service redress procedures; and (b) that complaint has not been withdrawn: Sex Discrimination (Complaints to Employment Tribunals) (Armed Forces) Regulations 1997, SI 1997/2163, reg 2(1) (amended by virtue of the Employment Rights (Dispute Resolution) Act 1998 s 1(2)). A person is to be treated as having withdrawn his complaint if, having made a complaint to an officer under the service redress procedures, he fails to submit that complaint to the Defence Council under those procedures: Sex Discrimination (Complaints to Employment Tribunals) (Armed Forces) Regulations 1997, SI 1997/2163, reg 2(2).

376.　House of Commons and House of Lords staff. The provisions of the Sex Discrimination Act 1975 prohibiting discrimination in employment and other discriminatory acts[1] apply:

(1)　to an act[2] done by an employer[3] of a relevant member of the House of Commons staff[4], and to service as such a member, as they apply to an act done by and to service for the purposes of a Minister of the Crown or government department, and accordingly apply as if references to a contract of employment included references to the terms of service of such a member[5]; and

(2)　in relation to employment as a relevant member of the House of Lords staff[6] as they apply in relation to other employment[7].

1　Ie the Sex Discrimination Act 1975 Pt II (ss 6–20A) (as amended) and Pt IV (ss 37–42) (as amended).
2　As to the meaning of 'act' see para 359 note 1 ante.
3　For the meaning of 'employer' see para 360 note 4 ante.
4　'Relevant member of the House of Commons staff' means any person who was appointed by the House of Commons Commission or is employed in the refreshment department, or who is a member of the Speaker's personal staff: Employment Rights Act 1996 s 195(5); definition applied by the Sex

Discrimination Act 1975 s 85A(2) (s 85A added by the Trade Union and Labour Relations (Consolidation) Act 1992 s 300(2), Sch 2 para 6; and the Sex Discrimination Act 1975 s 85A(2) amended by the Employment Rights Act 1996 s 240, Sch 1 para 6(1), (2)). The provisions of the Employment Rights Act 1996 s 195(6)–(12) (as amended) (person to be treated as employer of House of Commons staff) (see EMPLOYMENT vol 16(1A) (Reissue) para 136) apply, with any necessary modifications, for the purposes of the Sex Discrimination Act 1975 Pts II, IV (as amended) as they apply by virtue of s 85A (as added and amended): s 85A(2) (as so added and amended). See further EMPLOYMENT vol 16(1A) (Reissue) para 134–136; PARLIAMENT vol 34 (Reissue) para 652.

5   Ibid s 85A(1) (as added: see note 4 supra).
     As to provisions relating to discrimination against office-holders see ss 10A, 10B (as added); and para 377 post.

6   'Relevant member of the House of Lords staff' means any person who is employed under a contract of employment with the Corporate Officer of the House of Lords: Employment Rights Act 1996 s 194(6); definition applied by the Sex Discrimination Act 1975 s 85B(2) (s 85B added by the Trade Union Reform and Employment Rights Act 1993 s 49(1), Sch 7 para 9; and the Sex Discrimination Act 1975 s 85B(2) amended by the Employment Rights Act 1996 Sch 1 para 6(1), (3)). The Employment Rights Act 1996 s 194(7) applies for these purposes: see the Sex Discrimination Act 1975 s 85B(2) (as so added and amended). See further EMPLOYMENT vol 16(1A) (Reissue) para 1359; PARLIAMENT vol 34 (Reissue) para 652.

7   Ibid s 85B(1) (as added: see note 6 supra).

377. Office-holders. It is unlawful for a relevant person[1], in relation to an appointment[2] to a relevant office or post[3], to discriminate against a woman[4] in the arrangements which he makes for the purpose of determining to whom the appointment should be offered, in the terms on which he offers her the appointment, or by refusing[5] to offer her the appointment[6].

It is unlawful, in relation to an appointment to a relevant office or post which is one to which appointments are made on the recommendation of, or subject to the approval of, a specified person[7], for a relevant person on whose recommendation, or subject to whose approval, appointments to the office or post are made, to discriminate against a woman in the arrangements which he makes for the purpose of determining who should be recommended or approved in relation to the appointment, or in making or refusing to make a recommendation, or giving or refusing to give an approval, in relation to the appointment[8].

It is unlawful for a relevant person, in relation to a woman who has been appointed to a relevant office or post, to discriminate against her in the terms of the appointment, in the opportunities which he affords her for promotion, transfer, training or receiving any other benefit, or by refusing to afford her any such opportunity, by terminating the appointment[9], or by subjecting her to any other detriment in relation to the appointment[10].

It is unlawful for a relevant person, in relation to a relevant office or post, to subject to harassment a woman who has been appointed to the office or post, who is seeking or being considered for appointment to the office or post, or who, in relation to appointment to the office or post, is seeking or being considered for a recommendation or approval[11].

1   For these purposes, 'relevant person', in relation to an office or post, means: (1) in a case relating to an appointment to an office or post, the person with power to make that appointment; (2) in a case relating to the making of a recommendation or the giving of an approval in relation to an appointment, a person or body referred to in the Sex Discrimination Act 1975 s 10A(1)(b) (as added) (see note 3 head (2) infra) with power to make that recommendation or, as the case may be, to give that approval; (3) in a case relating to a term of an appointment, the person with power to determine that term; (4) in a case relating to a working condition afforded in relation to an appointment, the person with power to determine that working condition or, where there is no such person, the person with power to make the appointment; (5) in a case relating to the termination of an appointment, the person with power to terminate the appointment; and (6) in a case relating to the subjection of a person to any other detriment or to harassment, any person or body falling within one or more of heads (1)–(5) supra in relation to such cases as are there mentioned: s 10B(9) (ss 10A, 10B added by the Employment Equality (Sex Discrimination)

Regulations 2005, SI 2005/2467, reg 13(1)). References to making a recommendation include references to making a negative recommendation: Sex Discrimination Act 1975 s 10B(11)(a) (as so added). 'Working condition' includes any opportunity for promotion, transfer, training or receiving any other benefit: s 10B(10) (as so added). As to harassment, including sexual harassment, see s 4A (as added); and para 347 ante.

2   Appointment to an office or post does not include election to an office or post: ibid s 10A(5) (as added: see note 1 supra).

3   An office or post is a relevant office or post if it is one: (1) to which persons are appointed to discharge functions personally under the direction of another person and in respect of which they are entitled to remuneration; (2) to which appointments are made by a Minister of the Crown, a government department or the National Assembly for Wales; or (3) to which appointments are made on the recommendation of, or subject to the approval of, a person referred to in head (2) supra: ibid s 10A(1) (as added: see note 1 supra). For the purposes of head (1) supra, the holder of an office or post is to be regarded as discharging her functions under the direction of another person if that other person is entitled to direct her as to when and where she discharges those functions, and is not to be regarded as entitled to remuneration merely because she is entitled to payments in respect of expenses incurred by her in carrying out the functions of the office or post, or by way of compensation for the loss of income or benefits she would or might have received from any person had she not been carrying out the functions of the office or post: s 10A(4) (as so added).

An office or post is not a relevant office or post if any of s 6 (as amended) (see para 361 ante), s 9 (as amended) (see para 365 ante), s 11 (as amended) (see para 366 ante), or s 35A (as added and amended) (see para 374 ante) apply in relation to an appointment to the office or post or would so apply but for the operation of any other provision of the Sex Discrimination Act 1975: s 10A(2) (as so added).

The following are not relevant offices or posts: (a) any office of the House of Commons held by a member of it; (b) a life peerage within the meaning of the Life Peerages Act 1958 (see CONSTITUTIONAL LAW AND HUMAN RIGHTS vol 8(2) (Reissue) para 212; PARLIAMENT vol 34 (Reissue) para 540; PEERAGES AND DIGNITIES), or any office of the House of Lords held by a member of it; (c) any office mentioned in the House of Commons Disqualification Act 1975 Sch 2 (as amended) (see PARLIAMENT vol 34 (Reissue) para 611); (d) the offices of Leader of the Opposition, Chief Opposition Whip or Assistant Opposition Whip within the meaning of the Ministerial and other Salaries Act 1975 (see CONSTITUTIONAL LAW AND HUMAN RIGHTS vol 8(2) (Reissue) para 219); (e) any office of the National Assembly for Wales held by a member of it; (f) in England, any office of a county council, a London borough council, a district council or a parish council held by a member of it; (g) in Wales, any office of a county council, a county borough council or a community council held by a member of it; (h) any office of the Greater London Authority held by a member of it; (i) any office of the Common Council of the City of London held by a member of it; (j) any office of the Council of the Isles of Scilly held by a member of it; and (k) any office of a political party: Sex Discrimination Act 1975 s 10A(3) (as so added). This provision also refers to various Scottish offices, but Scottish matters generally are beyond the scope of this work. As to the National Assembly for Wales see para 302 ante. As to local government authorities in England and Wales see LOCAL GOVERNMENT vol 29(1) (Reissue) para 23 et seq; as to London borough councils see LONDON GOVERNMENT vol 29(2) (Reissue) para 35 et seq; as to the Greater London Authority see LONDON GOVERNMENT vol 29(2) (Reissue) para 70 et seq; as to the Common Council of the City of London see LONDON GOVERNMENT vol 29(2) (Reissue) para 51 et seq; and as to the Council of the Isles of Scilly see LOCAL GOVERNMENT vol 29(1) (Reissue) para 40.

4   As to the meaning of 'woman' see para 344 note 5 ante. These provisions apply equally to the treatment of men, with requisite modifications: see ibid s 2(1); and para 357 ante.

5   References to refusal include references to deliberate omission: ibid s 10B(11)(b) (as added: see note 1 supra).

6   Ibid s 10B(1) (as added: see note 1 supra). This does not apply to any act in relation to an office or post where, if holding the office or post constituted employment, that act would be lawful by virtue of s 7 (as amended) (see para 364 ante) ss 7A, 7B (as added and amended) (see para 364 ante) or s 19 (as substituted) (see para 373 ante): s 10B(5) (as so added).

As to selection of candidates by registered political parties see s 42A (as added); and para 367 note 4 ante.

7   Ie a person specified in ibid s 10A(1)(b) (as added): see note 3 head (2) supra.

8   Ibid s 10B(2) (as added: see note 1 supra). This does not apply to any act in relation to an office or post where, if holding the office or post constituted employment, it would be lawful by virtue of s 7 (as amended) (see para 364 ante) ss 7A, 7B (as added and amended) (see para 364 ante) or s 19 (as substituted) (see para 373 ante) to refuse to offer the person such employment: s 10B(6) (as so added).

9   The reference to the termination of the appointment includes a reference: (1) to the termination of the appointment by the expiration of any period, including a period expiring by reference to an event or circumstance, not being a termination immediately after which the appointment is renewed on the same terms and conditions; and (2) to the termination of the appointment by any act of the person appointed,

including the giving of notice, in circumstances such that she is entitled to terminate the appointment without notice by reason of the conduct of the relevant person: ibid s 10B(8) (as added: see note 1 supra).

10 Ibid s 10B(3) (as added: see note 1 supra). This does not apply to any act in relation to an office or post where, if holding the office or post constituted employment, that act would be lawful by virtue of s 7 (as amended) (see para 364 ante) ss 7A, 7B (as added and amended) (see para 364 ante) or s 19 (as substituted) (see para 373 ante): s 10B(5) (as so added). Nor does it apply to benefits of any description if the relevant person is concerned with the provision, for payment or not, of benefits of that description to the public, or a section of the public to which the person appointed belongs, unless: (1) that provision differs in a material respect from the provision of the benefits to persons appointed to offices or posts which are the same as, or not materially different from, that which the person appointed holds; (2) the provision of the benefits to the person appointed is regulated by the terms and conditions of her appointment; or (3) the benefits relate to training: s 10B(7) (as so added). 'Benefits' includes facilities and services: s 10B(11)(c) (as so added).

11 Ibid s 10B(4) (as added: see note 1 supra). The recommendation or approval mentioned in the text is one that is referred to in s 10A(1)(c) (as added): see note 3 head (3) supra.

B. DISCRIMINATION IN EDUCATION

378. Discrimination by bodies in charge of schools, universities and other educational establishments. The Sex Discrimination Act 1975 in general terms protects potential and actual pupils[1] of educational establishments from discrimination on the part of the individuals or bodies who are responsible for those establishments[2].

It is unlawful for a responsible body to discriminate[3] against a woman[4] in the terms on which it offers to admit her to the establishment as a pupil[5], or by refusing or deliberately omitting to accept an application for her admission to the establishment as a pupil[6].

It is unlawful for a responsible body to discriminate against a woman where she is a pupil of the establishment in the way it affords her access to any benefits, facilities or services, or by refusing or deliberately omitting to afford her access to them[7], or by excluding her from the establishment or subjecting her to any other detriment[8].

It is also unlawful for the governing body of an institution of further or higher education[9]: (1) to discriminate against a woman in the arrangements it makes for the purpose of selecting people for admission to the institution[10]; and (2) to subject a woman to harassment if that woman is a student at the institution or has applied for admission to the institution[11].

It is also unlawful for the following bodies to do any act[12] which constitutes sex discrimination[13]:

(a) a local education authority in carrying out any of its other functions under the Education Acts[14];

(b) the Learning and Skills Council for England, the Higher Education Funding Council for England or the Higher Education Funding Council for Wales in carrying out their functions under the Education Acts and the Learning and Skills Act 2000 and the National Assembly for Wales in carrying out its functions under Part II of the Learning and Skills Act 2000[15]; and

(c) the Training and Development Agency for Schools in carrying out its functions under any enactment[16].

1 'Pupil' includes any person who receives education at a school or institution to which the Sex Discrimination Act 1975 s 22 (as amended) applies: s 22A (added by the Further and Higher Education Act 1992 s 93(1), Sch 8 paras 75, 77). 'School' has the meaning given by the Education Act 1996 s 4 (as amended) (see EDUCATION vol 15(1) (2006 Reissue) para 96): Sex Discrimination Act 1975 s 82(1) (definition amended by the Education Act 1996 s 582(1), Sch 37 para 36).

2 As to the establishments within the ambit of the Sex Discrimination Act 1975, and their respective 'responsible bodies' see s 22(1) (as amended); and EDUCATION vol 15(1) (2006 Reissue) para 6.

3 For the meaning of 'discrimination' see para 344 note 4 ante.

4   These provisions apply equally to the treatment of men, with requisite modifications: see the Sex Discrimination Act 1975 s 2(1); and para 357 ante. As to exceptions for single-sex establishments see para 381 post. As to the meaning of 'woman' see para 344 note 5 ante; and as to the meaning of 'man' see para 344 note 10 ante. As to discrimination on the grounds of gender reassignment see para 348 ante; and for the meaning of 'gender reassignment' see para 348 note 9 ante.

5   Ibid s 22(1)(a) (s 22 renumbered as s 22(1) by the Employment Equality (Sex Discrimination) Regulations 2005, SI 2005/2467, reg 1(1)).

6   Sex Discrimination Act 1975 s 22(1)(b) (as renumbered: see note 5 supra).

7   As to the affording of access to benefits, facilities or services see para 361 note 11 ante. Ibid ss 22, 23 and 25 (all as amended) do not apply to benefits, facilities or services outside Great Britain, except travel on a ship registered at a port of registry in Great Britain, and benefits, facilities or services provided on such a ship: s 36(5). For the meaning of 'Great Britain' see para 325 note 6 ante.

        Cases decided under EC Council Directive 76/207 (OJ L39, 14.2.76, p 40) (as amended) (see para 338 ante) in the context of employment do not apply equally to exclusion from an educational establishment: *R v South Bank University, ex p Coggeran* [2000] ICR 1342, [2000] All ER (D) 1173, CA.

8   Sex Discrimination Act 1975 s 22(1)(c) (as renumbered: see note 5 supra). See *R v South Bank University, ex p Coggeran* [2000] ICR 1342, [2000] All ER (D) 1173, CA; and note 7 supra.

        The Secretary of State or, in relation to Wales, the National Assembly for Wales has special powers of enforcement in relation to the duties imposed on local education authorities and educational establishments in the public sector. As to the Secretary of State and the National Assembly for Wales see para 302 ante. Under the Education Act 1996 s 496 (as amended) they have the power to require duties under that Act to be exercised reasonably, and under s 497 (as amended) they have additional powers where the bodies in question are in default: see EDUCATION vol 15(1) (2006 Reissue) paras 57–58. The Sex Discrimination Act 1975 applies these powers to the performance by a local education authority or an educational establishment of the duties imposed upon it by ss 22, 23 (both as amended), ss 23A, 23D (both as added and amended), and s 25(1): see s 25(2) (amended by the Education Act 1993 s 307(1), Sch 19 para 59; the Education Act 1994 s 24, Sch 2 para 5(1), (4); the Education Act 1996 Sch 37 para 35; and the School Standards and Framework Act 1998 s 140(3), Sch 31). They are the only sanctions for a breach by a relevant body of its duties under the Sex Discrimination Act 1975 s 25(1), but without prejudice to the enforcement of ss 22, 23 (both as amended) and ss 23A, 23D (both as added and amended) under s 66 (as amended) (see para 415 post) or otherwise (where the breach is also a contravention of any of those provisions): s 25(4) (amended by the Education Act 1993 Sch 19 para 59; the Education Act 1994 Sch 2 para 5(1), (4); the Education Act 1996 Sch 37 para 35; and the School Standards and Framework Act 1998 Sch 31). The bodies to which these powers apply are specified in the Sex Discrimination Act 1975 s 25(6) (as amended) and are as follows:

    (1)   local education authorities in England and Wales (s 25(6)(a));

    (2)   the governing body of an educational establishment maintained by a local education authority in so far as that governing body is the responsible body for the purposes of s 22 (as amended) (s 22, Table para 1, s 25(6)(c)(i) (s 22, Table para 1 amended by the Education Act 1980 s 1(3), Sch 1 para 27; and the School Standards and Framework Act 1998 s 140(1), Sch 30 para 5));

    (3)   the proprietor of a special school not maintained by a local education authority (Sex Discrimination Act 1975 s 22, Table para 3, s 25(6)(c)(i));

    (4)   the governing body of an institution within the further education sector (within the meaning of the Further and Higher Education Act 1992 s 91(3): see EDUCATION vol 15(1) (2006 Reissue) para 579) (Sex Discrimination Act 1975 s 22, Table para 3B, s 25(6)(c)(i) (s 22, Table para 3B added, and s 25(6)(c)(i) amended, by the Further and Higher Education Act 1992 s 93, Sch 8 paras 75, 76, 79(1)));

    (5)   an establishment assisted by a local education authority for the purposes of the Education Act 1996 (ie an establishment designated under the Sex Discrimination Act 1975 s 24(1)) (s 25(6)(c)(ii) (amended by the Education Reform Act 1988 s 237, Sch 13 Pt II));

    (6)   an establishment in respect of which grants are payable out of money provided by Parliament under the Education Act 1996 s 485 (ie an establishment designated under the Sex Discrimination Act 1975 s 24(1)) (s 25(6)(c)(iii) (amended by the Education Act 1996 s 582(1), Sch 37 para 35)); and

    (7)   the Training and Development Agency for Schools (Sex Discrimination Act 1975 s 25(6)(f) (added by the Education Act 1994 Sch 2 para 5(1), (4); and substituted by the Education Act 2005 s 98, Sch 14 para 6)).

    'Proprietor' in relation to a school has the meaning given by the Education Act 1996 s 579 (as amended) (see EDUCATION vol 15(1) (2006 Reissue) para 60): Sex Discrimination Act 1975 s 82(1) (definition amended by the Education Act 1996 Sch 37 para 36(d)). Any power conferred by the Sex Discrimination Act 1975 to designate establishments or persons may be exercised either by naming them or by identifying them by reference to a class or other description: s 82(1), (3). 'Further education' has the meaning given by the Education Act 1996 s 2 (as amended) (see EDUCATION vol 15(1) (2006 Reissue) para 18): Sex Discrimination Act 1975 s 82(1).

Civil proceedings under s 22 (as amended) or s 23 (as amended) in respect of a claim of discrimination or harassment by any body in the public sector (to which s 25 (as amended) applies) must not be instituted unless the claimant has given notice to the Secretary of State or, in relation to Wales, to the National Assembly for Wales, and either the Secretary of State or the Assembly has by notice informed the claimant that he or it does not require further time to consider the matter, or the period of two months has elapsed since the complainant gave notice, but this does not apply to a counterclaim: see s 66(5) (amended by the Employment Equality (Sex Discrimination) Regulations 2005, SI 2005/2467, reg 30(1), (5)); and the National Assembly for Wales (Transfer of Functions) Order 1999, SI 1999/672, art 2, Sch 1. 'Notice' means a notice in writing: Sex Discrimination Act 1975 s 82(1).

Proceedings brought by way of judicial review are not affected by these special provisions: see *R v Bradford Metropolitan Borough Council, ex p Sikander Ali* [1994] ELR 299 at 315–316 obiter per Jowitt J.

9 'Institution of further or higher education' means an establishment falling within the Sex Discrimination Act 1975 s 22(1), Table para 3B, 4 or 4A (Table para 3B, 4A as added): s 22(4) (s 22(2)–(4) added by Employment Equality (Sex Discrimination) Regulations 2005, SI 2005/2467, reg 22(3)).

10 Sex Discrimination Act 1975 s 22(2) (as added: see note 9 supra).

11 Ibid s 22(3) (as added: see note 9 supra). As to harassment, including sexual harassment, see s 4A (as added); and para 347 ante.

12 As to the meaning of 'act' see para 359 note 1 ante.

13 See the Sex Discrimination Act 1975 s 23(1) (as amended), s 23A (as added and amended), s 23D (as added and amended); and the text and notes 14–16 infra. For the meaning of 'discrimination' see para 344 note 4 ante.

14 See ibid s 23(1) (amended by the Education Act 1996 Sch 37 para 31). This provision covers functions apart from those which fall under the Sex Discrimination Act 1975 s 22 (as amended) (see the text and notes 3–11 supra): see s 23(1) (as so amended). See also the Education Act 1996 ss 13–15B (as amended and added); and EDUCATION vol 15(1) (2006 Reissue) para 20 et seq. Such functions include contributing to the spiritual, moral, mental and physical development of the community by securing the efficient provision of educational facilities. This would include, for example, the provision of school meals and transport, educational welfare, and the teaching of English as a second language. More specifically this would include the provision of sufficient schools within the authority's area. For the meaning of 'area' see *R v Secretary of State, ex p Connon* (26 April 1996) Lexis.

The closing of a single-sex boys' school whilst retaining single sex girls' schools in the same area constitutes less favourable treatment for boys and is unlawful: see *R v Secretary of State for Education and Science, ex p Keating* (1985) 84 LGR 469, (1985) Times, 3 December.

It is unlawful to require girls to repeat a year's school in the same class when the reason for the requirement is not connected with their aptitude, ability or individual qualities but solely because of their sex: see *Debell, Sevket and Teh v Bromley London Borough Council* (12 November 1984, unreported).

A local education authority is in breach of the Sex Discrimination Act 1975 s 23(1) (as amended) if its system of selective education is such that fewer places are provided for girls than for boys at selective schools so that girls have to achieve a higher mark than boys to gain entry: *Birmingham City Council v Equal Opportunities Commission* [1989] AC 1155, sub nom *Equal Opportunities Commission v Birmingham City Council* [1989] 1 All ER 769, HL. See also *R v Birmingham City Council, ex p Equal Opportunities Commission (No 2)* (1992) 90 LGR 492, [1992] 2 FCR 746, DC; affd *Equal Opportunities Commission v Birmingham City Council* [1993] 1 FCR 753, sub nom *R v Birmingham City Council, ex p Equal Opportunities Commission (No 2)* [1994] ELR 282, CA.

The Education Act 1996 ss 496, 497 (both as amended) apply to the performance by a local education authority of its functions: see note 8 supra. As to the territorial extent of these functions see note 7 supra.

'The Education Acts' has the meaning given by the Education Act 1996 s 578 (as amended) (see EDUCATION vol 15(1) (2006 Reissue) para 1): Sex Discrimination Act 1975 s 82(1) (definition added by the Education Act 1996 Sch 37 para 36(a)).

15 See the Sex Discrimination Act 1975 s 23A (added by the Further and Higher Education Act 1992 Sch 8 paras 75, 78; and amended by the Education Act 1996 Sch 37 para 32; the Learning and Skills Act 2000 s 149, Sch 9 paras 1, 5; and the National Council for Education and Training for Wales (Transfer of Functions to the National Assembly for Wales and Abolition) Order 2005, SI 2005/3238, art 9(1), Sch 1 paras 3, 4). See further EDUCATION. See also note 14 supra. As to the Learning and Skills Act 2000 Pt II (ss 31–41) (as amended) see EDUCATION vol 15(2) (2006 Reissue) para 1129 et seq.

16 See the Sex Discrimination Act 1975 s 23D (added by the Education Act 1994 Sch 2 para 5(1), (3); and amended by the Education Act 2005 Sch 14 para 5). As to the Training and Development Agency for Schools see EDUCATION vol 15(2) (2006 Reissue) para 784 et seq.

379.   General duty in the public sector.   The Sex Discrimination Act 1975 imposes a general duty on local education authorities and other educational bodies in the public sector[1] to secure that the facilities for education[2] provided by them, and any ancillary benefits or services, are provided without sex discrimination[3].

1   See the Sex Discrimination Act 1975 s 25(1). As to the bodies on which this duty is imposed and the sanctions for breach of it see para 378 note 8 ante. See also para 398 post.
2   As to the meaning of 'education' see para 348 note 5 ante.
3   Sex Discrimination Act 1975 s 25(1). For the meaning of 'discrimination' see para 344 note 4 ante.

380.   General duty in relation to post–16 education and training.   The Learning and Skills Council for England[1] and the National Assembly for Wales[2] are under a general duty to secure that certain facilities[3] and any ancillary benefits or services[4] are provided without sex discrimination[5]. Those facilities are facilities for education[6], training[7], and organised leisure-time occupation connected with such education or training, the provision of which is secured by the Learning and Skills Council for England or the National Assembly for Wales by virtue of its functions under Part II of the Learning and Skills Act 2000[8].

1   As to the Learning and Skills Council for England see EDUCATION vol 15(2) (2006 Reissue) para 1072 et seq.
2   As to the National Assembly for Wales see para 302 ante.
3   Ie facilities falling within the Sex Discrimination Act 1975 s 25A(2) (as added and amended): see the text and notes 6–8 infra.
4   As to the affording of access to benefits, facilities or services see para 361 note 11 ante.
5   Sex Discrimination Act 1975 s 25A(1) (s 25A added by the Learning and Skills Act 2000 s 149, Sch 9 paras 1, 6; and the Sex Discrimination Act 1975 s 25A(1) amended by the National Council for Education and Training for Wales (Transfer of Functions to the National Assembly for Wales and Abolition) Order 2005, SI 2005/3238, art 9(1), Sch 1 paras 3, 5(a)).
      The provisions of the Learning and Skills Act 2000 s 25 (see EDUCATION vol 15(2) (2006 Reissue) para 1103) are the only sanction for breach of the general duty in the Sex Discrimination Act 1975 s 25A(1) (as added and amended) by the Learning and Skills Council for England: s 25A(3) (s 25A as so added; and s 25A(3) substituted, and s 25A(4), (5) added, by the National Council for Education and Training for Wales (Transfer of Functions to the National Assembly for Wales and Abolition) Order 2005, SI 2005/3238, Sch 1 paras 3, 5(c)). There is no sanction for breach of the general duty in the Sex Discrimination Act 1975 s 25A(1) (as added and amended) by the National Assembly for Wales: s 25A(4) (as so added). The provisions of s 25A(3), (4) (as added) are without prejudice to the enforcement of s 23A (as added and amended) (see para 378 ante) under s 66 (as amended) (see para 415 post) or otherwise (where the breach is also a contravention of that provision): s 25A(5) (as so added).
6   As to the meaning of 'education' see para 348 note 5 ante.
7   As to the meaning of 'training' see para 348 note 5 ante.
8   Sex Discrimination Act 1975 s 25A(2) (as added (see note 5 supra); and amended by the National Council for Education and Training for Wales (Transfer of Functions to the National Assembly for Wales and Abolition) Order 2005, SI 2005/3238, Sch 1 paras 3, 5(b)). As to the Learning and Skills Act 2000 Pt II (ss 31–41) (as amended) see EDUCATION vol 15(2) (2006 Reissue) para 1129 et seq.

381.   Exceptions to discrimination in education.   The provisions relating to sex discrimination[1] by an educational establishment[2] in the terms on which admission to the establishment is offered, or by refusal or deliberate omission to accept an application for admission or in the provision of educational facilities or in regard to related general duties[3] do not apply to the admission of pupils[4] to any single-sex establishment[5], that is to say one which admits pupils of one sex only, or which would be taken to admit pupils of one sex only if there were disregarded pupils of the opposite sex whose admission is exceptional[6], or whose numbers are comparatively small and whose admission is confined to particular courses of instruction or teaching classes[7].

Where a school[8] which is not a single-sex establishment has some pupils as boarders and others as non-boarders, and admits as boarders pupils of one sex only (or would be taken to admit as boarders pupils of one sex only if there were disregarded boarders of the opposite sex whose numbers are comparatively small), certain provisions relating to sex discrimination in education do not apply[9].

Where at any time: (1) the responsible body for a single-sex establishment[10] determines to alter its admissions arrangements so that the establishment will cease to be a single-sex establishment[11]; or (2) a school is not a single-sex establishment but the provision relating to the admission of single-sex boarders[12] applies to that school[13] and the responsible body for that school determines to alter its admissions arrangements so that the provision relating to boarders ceases so to apply[14], the responsible body may apply[15] for a transitional exemption order authorising discriminatory admissions during the transitional period specified in the order[16]. Where, during the transitional period specified in a transitional exemption order applying to an establishment, the responsible body refuses or deliberately omits to accept an application for the admission of a person to the establishment as a pupil, the refusal or omission is not to be taken to contravene any provision of the Sex Discrimination Act 1975[17], unless the refusal or omission contravenes any condition of the transitional exemption order[18]. Where, during the period between the making of an application for a transitional exemption order in relation to an establishment and the determination of the application, the responsible body refuses or deliberately omits to accept an application for the admission of a person to the establishment as a pupil that refusal or omission is also not to be taken to contravene any provision of the Act[19].

The provisions relating to sex discrimination in education[20] do not apply outside Great Britain[21].

There is an exemption for discrimination in connection with certain educational appointments[22]. There is also an exception in relation to educational charities[23].

1   For the meaning of 'discrimination' see para 344 note 4 ante. These provisions apply not only in relation to women but equally to the treatment of men, with requisite modifications: see the Sex Discrimination Act 1975 s 2(1); and para 357 ante. As to the meaning of 'woman' see para 344 note 5 ante; and as to the meaning of 'man' see para 344 note 10 ante. As to discrimination on the grounds of gender reassignment see para 348 ante; and for the meaning of 'gender reassignment' see para 348 note 9 ante.

2   As to discrimination by bodies in charge of educational establishments see para 378 ante. As to the meaning of 'education' see para 348 note 5 ante.

3   Ie the Sex Discrimination Act 1975 s 22(1)(a), (b), s 25 (as amended), s 25A (as added and amended) (see paras 378– 380 ante).

4   For these purposes, 'pupil' includes any person who receives education at that establishment: see ibid ss 26(4), 27(6) (both added by the Further and Higher Education Act 1992 s 93(1), Sch 8 paras 75, 80, 81).

5   Sex Discrimination Act 1975 s 26(1) (amended by the Learning and Skills Act 2000 s 149, Sch 9 paras 1, 7(1), (2); and the Employment Equality (Sex Discrimination) Regulations 2005, SI 2005/2467, reg 22(4)(a)).

6   Sex Discrimination Act 1975 s 26(1)(a).

7   Ibid s 26(1)(b). Where an establishment is a single-sex establishment by reason of its inclusion in s 26(1)(b), the fact that pupils of one sex are confined to particular courses of instruction or teaching classes is not to be taken to contravene s 22(c)(i) (access to benefits, facilities or services) (see para 378 ante) or the general duties in s 25 (as amended) (see paras 378–379 ante) or s 25A (as added and amended) (see para 380 ante): s 26(3) (amended by the Learning and Skills Act 2000 Sch 9 paras 1, 7(1), (3)).

8   For the meaning of 'school' see para 378 note 1 ante.

9   Sex Discrimination Act 1975 s 26(2) (amended by the Learning and Skills Act 2000 Sch 9 paras 1, 7(2); and the Employment Equality (Sex Discrimination) Regulations 2005, SI 2005/2467, reg 24(4)(b)). The provisions that are disapplied are: (1) the Sex Discrimination Act 1975 s 22(1)(a), (b) (as amended), s 25 (as amended), s 25A (as added and amended) (see paras 378–380 ante), which are disapplied in relation to the admission of boarders to a school falling within s 26(2) (as amended); and (2) s 22(1)(c)(i), s 25 (as amended) and s 25A (as added and amended), which are disapplied in relation to boarding facilities at such a school: see s 26(2) (as so amended).

10   Ie an establishment falling within ibid s 22(1), Table column 1 (as amended): see para 378 ante.

11   Ibid s 27(1)(a) (amended by the Employment Equality (Sex Discrimination) Regulations 2005, SI 2005/2467, reg 22(5)).

12 Ie the Sex Discrimination Act 1975 s 26(2) (as amended): see the text to note 9 supra.

13 Ie a school falling within ibid s 22(1), Table column 1 (as amended): see para 378 ante.

14 Ibid s 27(1)(b).

15 Ie in accordance with ibid s 27, Sch 2 (both as amended): see EDUCATION vol 15(1) (2006 Reissue) paras 148, 174.

16 Ibid s 27(1). Without prejudice to s 27(1), a transitional exemption order may be made in accordance with the School Standards and Framework Act 1998 Sch 6 para 21 or 22 or Sch 7 para 17 (as amended) (transitional exemption orders for purposes of the Sex Discrimination Act 1975) (see EDUCATION vol 15(1) (2006 Reissue) paras 148, 192, 201): Sex Discrimination Act 1975 s 27(1A) (added by the School Standards and Framework Act 1998 s 140(1), Sch 30 para 6).

17 Sex Discrimination Act 1975 s 27(2). Except as mentioned in s 27(2), a transitional exemption order does not afford any exemption from liability under the Sex Discrimination Act 1975: s 27(4).

18 See ibid s 27(3).

19 Ibid s 27(5).

20 Ie ibid ss 22, 23, 25 (all as amended): see para 378 ante.

21 See ibid s 36(5). An exception is made for: (1) travel on a ship registered at a port of registry in Great Britain; and (2) benefits, facilities or services provided on a ship so registered: s 36(5). For the meaning of 'Great Britain' see para 325 note 6 ante. There is a further more general exception in relation to sporting events under s 44: see para 396 post.

22 Nothing in ibid Pts II–IV (ss 6–42) (as amended) renders unlawful any act done by a person in connection with the employment of another person as the head teacher or principal of any educational establishment if it was necessary for that person to do that act in order to comply with any requirement of any instrument relating to the establishment that its head teacher or principal should be a member of a particular religious order: Employment Act 1989 s 5(1). Nothing in the Sex Discrimination Act 1975 Pt II (ss 6–20A) (as amended), or Pt IV (ss 37–42) (as amended) so far as it has effect in relation to Pt II (as amended), renders unlawful any act done by a person in connection with the employment of another person as a professor in any university if the professorship in question is, in accordance with any Act or instrument relating to the university, either a canon professorship or one to which a canonry is annexed: Employment Act 1989 s 5(2). Nothing in the Sex Discrimination Act 1975 Pt II (as amended), or Pt IV (as amended) so far as it has effect in relation to Pt II (as amended), renders unlawful any act done by a person in connection with the employment of another person as the head, a fellow or any other member of the academic staff of any college, or institution in the nature of a college, in a university if it was necessary for that person to do that act in order to comply with any requirement of any instrument relating to the college or institution that the holder of the position in question should be a woman: Employment Act 1989 s 5(3). Section 5(3) does not apply in relation to instruments taking effect after 16 November 1989; and the Interpretation Act 1978 s 6(b) (words importing the feminine gender to include the masculine) does not apply to that provision: Employment Act 1989 s 5(4).

The Secretary of State may provide that the provisions of s 5(1)–(3) do not have effect in relation to specified educational establishments or universities: see s 5(5), (6) (amended by the Further and Higher Education Act 1992 Sch 8 para 93). As to the Secretary of State and the National Assembly for Wales see para 302 ante.

Nothing in the Employment Act 1989 s 5 (as amended) is to be construed as prejudicing the operation of the Sex Discrimination Act 1975 s 19 (as substituted) (see para 373 ante) (exemption for discrimination in relation to employment of ministers of religion): Employment Act 1989 s 5(7).

23 See the Sex Discrimination Act 1975 s 78. The exception applies to any trust deed or other instrument: (1) which concerns property applicable for or in connection with the provision of education in any establishment in s 22(1), Table paras 1–5 (as amended) (see para 378 ante); and (2) which in any way restricts the benefits available under the instrument to persons of one sex: s 78(1). If on the application of the trustees, or of the responsible body (see para 378 ante), the Secretary of State is satisfied that the removal or modification of the restriction would conduce to the advancement of education without sex discrimination, he may by order make such modifications of the instrument as appear to him expedient for removing or modifying the restriction, and for any supplemental or incidental purposes: s 78(2). If the trust was created by gift or bequest, no order may be made until 25 years after the date on which the gift or bequest took effect, unless the donor or his personal representatives, or the personal representatives of the testator, have consented in writing to the making of the application for the order: s 78(3). The Secretary of State must require the applicant to publish notice: (1) containing particulars of the proposed order; and (2) stating that representations may be made to the Secretary of State within a period specified in the notice: s 78(4). The period specified in the notice must not be less than one month from the date of the notice: s 78(5). The applicant must publish the notice in such manner as may be specified by the Secretary of State, and the cost of any publication of the notice may be defrayed out of the property of the trust: s 78(6). Before making the order the Secretary of State must take into account any representations duly made in accordance with the notice: s 78(7). In relation to Wales, the functions of

the Secretary of State under s 78 are carried out by the National Assembly for Wales: National Assembly for Wales (Transfer of Functions) Order 1999, SI 1999/672, art 2, Sch 1; and see para 302 ante.

C. GOODS, FACILITIES, SERVICES AND PREMISES

382. Discrimination in the provision of goods, facilities and services. It is unlawful for any person[1] concerned with the provision (for payment or not) of goods, facilities or services[2] to the public or a section of the public[3] to discriminate[4] against a woman[5] who seeks to obtain or use those goods, facilities or services[6] by refusing or deliberately omitting to provide her with any of them[7], or by refusing or deliberately omitting to provide her with goods, facilities or services of the like quality, in the like manner and on the like terms as are normal[8] in his case in relation to male members of the public or (where she belongs to a section of the public) to male members of that section[9].

The Sex Discrimination Act 1975 does not apply to the provision of banking or insurance facilities, or grants, loans, credit or finance where the facilities are for a purpose to be carried out, or in connection with risks wholly or mainly arising outside Great Britain[10]. Generally, the Sex Discrimination Act 1975 does not apply to the provision of other goods, facilities or services outside Great Britain[11]. However, the Act's protection extends to the provision of facilities for travel outside Great Britain where the refusal or omission occurs in Great Britain or on certain ships, aircraft or hovercraft[12]. Protection is also extended to the provision of other goods, facilities or services on and in relation to any ship registered at a port of registry in Great Britain, or any aircraft or hovercraft registered in the United Kingdom and operated by a person with a principal place of business or ordinary residence in Great Britain[13]. These provisions do not render unlawful an act done in or over a country outside the United Kingdom, or in or over that country's territorial waters, for the purpose of complying with the laws of that country[14].

1   As to the meaning of 'person' see para 344 note 3 ante.
2   The following are examples of facilities and services: (1) access to and use of any place which members of the public or a section of the public are permitted to enter; (2) accommodation in a hotel, boarding house or other similar establishment; (3) facilities by way of banking or insurance or for grants, loans, credit or finance; (4) facilities for education; (5) facilities for entertainment, recreation or refreshment; (6) facilities for transport or travel; (7) the services of any profession or trade, or any local or other public authority: Sex Discrimination Act 1975 s 29(2). As to the meaning of 'education' see para 348 note 5 ante. As to the meaning of 'profession' see para 367 note 2 ante. For a further definition of the term 'profession' see *Carr v IRC* [1944] 2 All ER 163, CA (a special skill, ability or qualifications derived from training or experience). As to the meaning of 'trade' see para 367 note 3 ante.
     The list is not intended to be exhaustive: see *Applin v Race Relations Board* [1975] AC 259 at 291, [1974] 2 All ER 73 at 93, HL, per Lord Simon of Glaisdale. Other more specific examples include assistance by a police office (held to be a service: see *Farah v Metropolitan Police Comr* [1998] QB 65, [1997] 1 All ER 289, CA (case under the Race Relations Act 1976)); tax advice from a tax officer (held to be a service or facility: see *Savjani v IRC* [1981] QB 458, [1981] 1 All ER 1121, CA (case under the Race Relations Act 1976)); the registration of births, deaths and marriages (held to be a facility or service: see *Tejani v Superintendent Registrar for the District of Peterborough* [1986] IRLR 502, CA (case under the Race Relations Act 1976)); the ability to stand for election to the governing body of a friendly society (held to be a facility: see *Jones v Royal Liver Friendly Society* (1982) Times, 2 December, CA); the provision of a hire purchase credit scheme (held to be a facility or service: see *Quinn v Williams Furniture Ltd* [1981] ICR 328, CA); surgical treatment (see *R v North West Lancashire Health Authority, ex p A* (21 December 1998, unreported) (affd [2000] 1 WLR 977, [2000] 2 FCR 525, CA); and the provision of advertising space (see *Bain v Bowles* [1991] IRLR 356, CA). See also *Conwell v Newham London Borough Council* [2000] 1 All ER 696, [2000] ICR 42, EAT.
     Further, for the purposes of head (1) supra, members of the public can be allowed entrance into private places: see *Race Relations Board v Bradmore Working Men's Club* (1970) Times, 10 April (a case under the parallel provisions of the Race Relations Act 1976; private club hired for work party; tickets sold to employees who were allowed to bring guests; refusal to admit employee and guests on grounds of race held to be unlawful).

A facility should, however, arguably be contrasted with a mere permission to use. This distinction was drawn in *Re Amin* [1983] 2 AC 818, sub nom *Amin v Entry Clearance Officer, Bombay* [1983] 2 All ER 864, HL (where the Sex Discrimination Act 1975 s 29 (as amended) was held only to apply to 'the direct provision of facilities or services, and not the mere grant of permission to use the facilities': see at 834 and 872 per Lord Fraser of Tullybelton). See also *Kassam v Immigration Appeal Tribunal* [1980] 2 All ER 330, sub nom *R v Immigration Appeal Tribunal, ex p Kassam* [1980] 1 WLR 1037, CA; *Savjani v IRC* [1981] QB 458, [1981] 1 All ER 1121, CA.

A further distinction has been drawn by the House of Lords between public and private acts: see *Re Amin* supra (where the Sex Discrimination Act 1975 s 29 (as amended) was held only to render unlawful acts on behalf of the public authorities 'which are of a kind similar to acts that might be done by a private person': see at 835 and 873 per Lord Fraser of Tullybelton). See also *R v Secretary of State for Social Security, ex p Nessa* (1995) 7 Admin LR 402; *Savjani v IRC* supra.

3   Examples of cases in which goods, facilities or services were not held to be provided to the public or a section of it include: *Charter v Race Relations Board* [1973] AC 868, [1973] 1 All ER 512, HL (a Conservative club was held not to be offering its facilities or services to the public or a section of it); *Dockers' Labour Club and Institute Ltd v Race Relations Board* [1976] AC 285, [1974] 3 All ER 592, HL (a working men's club, which belonged to a union of clubs, did not unlawfully discriminate against a member of another club in the union by refusing him membership since members of the other clubs in the union were not considered to be a section of the public).

Examples of cases in which goods, facilities or services have been held to be provided to the public or a section of it include: *Gill v El Vino Co Ltd* [1983] QB 425, [1983] 1 All ER 398, CA (wine bars); *McConomy v Croft Inns Ltd* [1992] IRLR 561, NI HC; *Hector v Smethwick Labour Club and Institute* (29 November 1988) Lexis, CA (private clubs which admit non-members on payment of a fee); *Applin v Race Relations Board* [1975] AC 259, [1974] 2 All ER 73, HL (a case under the Race Relations Act 1968; foster parents providing homes for children in the care of a local authority; the Race Relations Act 1976 s 23(2) (see para 462 post) now provides an exemption for foster parents); *Bateson v YMCA* [1980] NI 135 (a case involving the Sex Discrimination (Northern Ireland) Order 1976, SI 1976/1042; snooker rooms available to 'well-behaved' members of the public); *Alexander v Home Office* [1988] 2 All ER 118, [1988] 1 WLR 968, CA (prisons).

See also *James v Eastleigh Borough Council* [1990] 2 AC 751, [1990] ICR 554, HL (unlawful for a section of the public to be defined in a way that incorporates discrimination; a special rate was available to pensioners but pensionable age was different for men and women; the fee structure was therefore discriminatory and fell foul of the Sex Discrimination Act 1975 s 29 (as amended)). A similar conclusion has been reached by the European Court of Justice in the context of EC Directive 79/7 (OJ L6, 10.1.79, p 24) on the progressive implementation of the principle of equal treatment for men and women in matters of social security (see para 339 ante): see Case C-137/94 *R v Secretary of State for Health, ex p Richardson* [1995] All ER (EC) 865, [1996] ICR 471, ECJ.

4   For the meaning of 'discrimination' see para 344 note 4 ante.

5   As to the meaning of 'woman' see para 344 note 5 ante. These provisions apply equally to the treatment of men, with requisite modifications: see the Sex Discrimination Act 1975 s 2(1); and para 357 ante. As to the meaning of 'man' see para 344 note 10 ante. As to discrimination on the grounds of gender reassignment see para 348 ante; and for the meaning of 'gender reassignment' see para 348 note 9 ante. See also note 9 infra.

6   Ibid s 29(1). For the avoidance of doubt it is declared in the Sex Discrimination Act 1975 that where a particular skill is commonly exercised in a different way for men and for women it does not contravene s 29(1) for a person who does not normally exercise it for women to insist on exercising it for a woman only in accordance with his normal practice or, if he reasonably considers it impracticable to do that in her case, to refuse or deliberately omit to exercise it: s 29(3).

7   Ibid s 29(1)(a).

8   The use of the word 'normal' suggests that a person who provides goods, facilities or services on a one-off basis is not covered by this provision. There must be some regular or recurrent provision: see *Dockers' Labour Club and Institute Ltd v Race Relations Board* [1976] AC 285, [1974] 3 All ER 592, HL.

9   Sex Discrimination Act 1975 s 29(1)(b). In its application in relation to vocational training to discrimination on the grounds of gender reassignment s 29(1)(b) has effect as if references to male members of the public, or of a section of the public, were references to members of the public, or of a section of the public, who do not intend to undergo, are not undergoing and have not undergone gender reassignment: s 29(4) (added by the Sex Discrimination (Gender Reassignment) Regulations 1999, SI 1999/1102, reg 6).

10   See the Sex Discrimination Act 1975 s 36(1)(b).

11   See ibid s 36(1(a). For the meaning of 'Great Britain' see para 325 note 6 ante.

12   See ibid s 36(2). The provision also applies where the refusal or omission occurs on a British registered ship, or an aircraft or hovercraft registered in the United Kingdom and operated by a person who has his

principal place of business, or is ordinarily resident, in Great Britain, even if the ship, aircraft or hovercraft is outside the United Kingdom: see s 36(2), (3). For the meaning of 'United Kingdom' see para 325 note 6 ante.

13   See ibid s 36(3).

14   Ibid s 36(4).

383. Exceptions to discrimination in the provision of goods, facilities and services. A person[1] who provides at any place facilities or services restricted to men[2] does not for that reason contravene the statutory provision relating to the provision of goods, facilities and services[3] if:

(1)   the place is, or is part of, a hospital, resettlement unit[4] or other establishment for persons requiring special care, supervision or attention[5]; or

(2)   the place is (permanently or for the time being) occupied or used for the purposes of an organised religion, and the facilities or service are restricted to men so as to comply with the doctrines of that religion or avoid offending the religious susceptibilities of a significant number of its followers[6]; or

(3)   the facilities or services are provided for, or are likely to be used by, two or more persons at the same time[7], and: (a) the facilities or services are such, or those persons are such, that male users are likely to suffer serious embarrassment at the presence of a woman[8]; or (b) the facilities or services are such that a user is likely to be in a state of undress and a male user might reasonably object to the presence of a female user[9].

A person who provides facilities or services restricted to men does not for that reason commit a contravention[10] if the services or facilities are such that physical contact between the user and any other person is likely, and that other person might reasonably object if the user were a woman[11].

The statutory provision relating to the provision of goods, facilities and services[12] does not apply to discrimination[13] which is rendered unlawful by the employment or education provisions of the Sex Discrimination Act 1975[14], or which would be rendered unlawful by them if not covered by one of the specified exceptions to the Act[15] or to discrimination which contravenes a term modified or included by virtue of an equality clause[16].

Nothing in the statutory provision relating to the provision of goods, facilities and services[17] is to be construed as affecting any special provision for persons of one sex only in the constitution, organisation or administration of a political party[18], nor does it render unlawful an act[19] done in order to give effect to such a special provision[20].

There is also an exception for a voluntary body, the activities of which are carried on otherwise than for profit, and which was not set up by any enactment[21]. The statutory provision relating to the provision of goods, facilities and services[22] is not to be construed as rendering unlawful: (i) the restriction of membership of any such body to persons of one sex (disregarding any minor exceptions)[23]; or (ii) the provision of benefits, facilities or services to members of any such body where the membership is so restricted[24], even though membership of the body is open to the public, or to a section of the public[25]. Where the main object of such a voluntary body is the conferring of benefits on persons of one sex only (disregarding any benefits to persons to the opposite sex which are exceptional or are relatively insignificant), nothing in that statutory provision affects this or renders unlawful an act which is done to give effect to this[26].

1   As to the meaning of 'person' see para 344 note 3 ante.

2   As to the meaning of 'man' see para 344 note 10 ante.

3   Sex Discrimination Act 1975 s 35(1). The provision referred to in the text is s 29 (as amended): see para 382 ante.

4   The Sex Discrimination Act 1975 refers to a resettlement unit provided under the Supplementary
     Benefits Act 1976 Sch 5, but this has been repealed. As to resettlement under the Jobseekers Act 1995 see
     SOCIAL SERVICES AND COMMUNITY CARE vol 44(2) (Reissue) para 1081.
5   Sex Discrimination Act 1975 s 35(1)(a) (amended by the Social Security Act 1980 s 20, Sch 4 para 11).
6   Sex Discrimination Act 1975 s 35(1)(b).
7   Ibid s 35(1)(c). See also para 398 note 3 post.
8   Ibid s 35(1)(c)(i). As to the meaning of 'woman' see para 344 note 5 ante. These provisions apply equally
     to the treatment of men, with requisite modifications: see s 2(1); and para 357 ante. As to discrimination
     on the grounds of gender reassignment see para 348 ante; and for the meaning of 'gender reassignment'
     see para 348 note 9 ante.
9   Ibid s 35(1)(c)(ii).
10   Ie contravention of ibid s 29(1): see para 382 ante.
11   Ibid s 35(2).
12   Ie ibid s 29(1): see para 382 ante. This provision also applies to discrimination in the provision of premises
     and housing (see para 385 post): see s 35(3).
13   For the meaning of 'discrimination' see para 344 note 4 ante.
14   See the Sex Discrimination Act 1975 s 35(3)(a). The employment or education provisions of the Act are
     those contained in Pt II (ss 6–20A) (as amended) and in s 22 (as amended) or s 23 (as amended) (see
     para 360 et seq ante): see s 35(3), Table.
15   See ibid s 35(3)(b). The exceptions mentioned in the text are those contained in s 7(1)(b) (see para 364
     ante), s 15(4) (see para 370 ante), s 19 (as substituted) (see para 373 ante), s 20 (as amended) (see para 361
     ante), ss 26, 27 (as amended) (see para 381 ante), Sch 4 paras 1, 2, 4 (transitional provisions): see s 35(3),
     Table (amended by the Employment Equality (Sex Discrimination) Regulations 2005, SI 2005/2467,
     reg 23(1)(b)).
16   Sex Discrimination Act 1975 s 35(3)(c). For the meaning of 'equality clause' see para 424 note 10 post.
17   Ie ibid s 29 (as amended): see para 382 ante.
18   Ibid s 33(2). Section 33 applies to a political party if: (1) it has as its main object, or one of its main
     objects, the promotion of parliamentary candidatures for the Parliament of the United Kingdom; or (2)
     it is an affiliate of, or has an affiliate, or has similar formal links with, a political party within head (1)
     supra: s 33(1). For the meaning of 'United Kingdom' see para 325 note 6 ante.
          As to selection of candidates by registered political parties see s 42A (as added); and para 367 note 4
     ante.
19   As to the meaning of 'act' see para 359 note 1 ante.
20   Sex Discrimination Act 1975 s 33(3).
21   See ibid s 34(1). 'Enactment' is not defined by the Sex Discrimination Act 1975 but has been given a
     broad meaning: see *Rathbone v Bundock* [1962] 2 QB 260, [1962] 2 All ER 257, DC. A company which
     is a voluntary body should therefore be covered by the exception since it was set up 'under' an enactment
     (ie the relevant Companies Act) rather than 'by' one.
22   Ie the Sex Discrimination Act 1975 s 29 (as amended): see para 382 ante.
23   Ibid s 34(2)(a).
24   Ibid s 34(2)(b).
25   Ibid s 34(2). This provision also applies to discrimination in the provision of premises and housing (see
     para 385 post): see s 34(2).
26   See ibid s 34(3), (4).

384.   Premises and housing.   It is unlawful for a person[1], in relation to premises[2] in
Great Britain[3] of which he has power to dispose[4], to discriminate[5] against a woman[6] in
the terms on which he offers her those premises[7], by refusing her application for those
premises[8], or in his treatment of her in relation to any list of persons in need of premises
of that description[9].

It is also unlawful for a person, in relation to premises managed by him, to
discriminate against a woman occupying the premises[10] in the way he affords her access
to any benefits or facilities, or by refusing or deliberately omitting to afford her access to
them[11], or by evicting her, or subjecting her to any other detriment[12].

Where the licence or consent of the landlord or of any other person is required for
the disposal to any person of premises in Great Britain comprised in a tenancy[13], it is
unlawful for the landlord or other person to discriminate against a woman by
withholding the licence or consent for disposal[14] of the premises to her[15].

1   As to the meaning of 'person' see para 344 note 3 ante. In this context person includes a local authority. The allocation of council housing falls within the scope of the protection of the Sex Discrimination Act 1975 s 30: see *Ealing London Borough Council v Race Relations Board* [1972] AC 342, [1972] 1 All ER 105, HL.

2   'Premises' is not defined in the Sex Discrimination Act 1975. It is submitted that 'premises' should include land, houses, flats and business premises. Note that accommodation in a hotel is dealt with separately under s 29 (as amended): see para 382 ante.

3   For the meaning of 'Great Britain' see para 325 note 6 ante.

4   'Dispose', in relation to premises, includes granting a right to occupy the premises; and any reference to acquiring premises is to be construed accordingly: Sex Discrimination Act 1975 s 82(1).

     It is not necessary for the premises to have been completed in order for the power to dispose of them to exist: see *Race Relations Board v Geo H Haigh and Co* (1969) 119 NLJ 858.

5   For the meaning of 'discrimination' see para 344 note 4 ante.

6   Sex Discrimination Act 1975 s 30(1). As to the meaning of 'woman' see para 344 note 5 ante. These provisions apply equally to the treatment of men, with requisite modifications: see s 2(1); and para 357 ante. As to the meaning of 'man' see para 344 note 10 ante. As to discrimination on the grounds of gender reassignment see para 348 ante; and for the meaning of 'gender reassignment' see para 348 note 9 ante.

7   Ibid s 30(1)(a). See note 9 infra.

8   Ibid s 30(1)(b). See note 9 infra.

9   Ibid s 30(1)(c).

     It has been conceded that a list of persons in need of accommodation included a local authority housing list: see *Ealing London Borough Council v Race Relations Board* [1972] AC 342, [1972] 1 All ER 105, HL. However, people such as estate agents who fail to provide lists of premises available would fall within the Sex Discrimination Act 1975 s 29 (as amended) (see para 382 ante) rather than s 30: see *Race Relations Board v London Accommodation Bureau* (unreported, but cited in Report of Race Relations Board 1973 p 44).

     The Sex Discrimination Act 1975 s 30(1) does not apply to a person who owns an estate or interest in the premises and wholly occupies them unless he uses the services of an estate agent for the purposes of the disposal of the premises, or publishes or causes to be published an advertisement in connection with the disposal: s 30(3). 'Estate agent' means a person who, by way of profession or trade, provides services for the purpose of finding premises for persons seeking to acquire them or assisting in the disposal of premises: s 82(1). As to the meaning of 'profession' see para 367 note 2 ante; and as to the meaning of 'trade' see para 367 note 3 ante. As to discriminatory advertisements generally see para 388 post.

10   Ibid s 30(2).

11   Ibid s 30(2)(a). As to the affording of access to benefits, facilities or services see para 361 note 11 ante.

12   Ibid s 30(2)(b).

13   'Tenancy' means a tenancy, whenever made, created by a lease or sub-lease, by an agreement for a lease or sub-lease, by a tenancy agreement, or in pursuance of any enactment: ibid s 31(3), (4).

14   'Disposal', in relation to premises comprised in a tenancy, includes assignment or assignation of the tenancy and sub-letting or parting with possession of the premises or any part of the premises: ibid s 31(3).

15   Ibid s 31(1). Section 31(1) does not apply if: (1) the person withholding a licence or consent, or a near relative of his (called 'the relevant occupier') resides, and intends to continue to reside, on the premises; and (2) there is on the premises, in addition to the accommodation occupied by the relevant occupier, accommodation (not being storage accommodation or means of access) shared by the relevant occupier with other persons residing on the premises who are not members of his household; and (3) the premises are small premises as defined in s 32(2) (see para 385 post): s 31(2). A person is a 'near relative' of another if that person is the wife or husband or civil partner, parent or child, grandparent or grandchild, or brother or sister of the other (whether of full blood or half blood or by marriage or civil partnership); and 'child' includes an illegitimate child and the wife or husband or civil partner of an illegitimate child: s 82(1), (5) (s 82(5) amended by the Civil Partnership Act s 261(1), Sch 27 para 54). As to civil partnerships generally see MATRIMONIAL LAW.

385. Exceptions to discrimination in the provision of premises and housing.

The most important exception to the statutory provisions concerning the disposal and management of premises[1] is the exception for small premises[2]. The statutory provisions do not apply to the provision by a person[3] of accommodation in any premises, or the disposal[4] of premises by him[5], if: (1) that person or a near relative[6] of his (called 'the relevant occupier') resides, and intends to continue to reside, on the premises[7]; and (2) there is on the premises, in addition to the accommodation occupied by the relevant occupier, accommodation (not being storage accommodation or means of access) shared by the relevant occupier with other persons residing on the premises who are not members of his household[8]; and (3) the premises are small premises[9]. A similar exception applies where the relevant occupier is the person withholding a licence or consent to the assignment or sub-letting of a tenancy[10].

Other exceptions prevent overlap between the provisions concerning goods, facilities, services and premises and the employment and education provisions of the Sex Discrimination Act 1975[11].

There is also an exception for voluntary bodies[12].

1 Ie the Sex Discrimination Act 1975 s 30: see para 384 ante.
2 'Premises' is not defined in the Sex Discrimination Act 1975. Premises are to be treated as small premises if: (1) in the case of premises comprising residential accommodation for one or more households (under separate letting or similar agreements) in addition to the accommodation occupied by the relevant occupier, there is not normally residential accommodation for more than two such households and only the relevant occupier and any member of his household reside in the accommodation occupied by him; or (2) in the case of premises not falling within head (1) supra, there is not normally residential accommodation on the premises for more than six persons in addition to the relevant occupier and any members of his household: s 32(2).
3 As to the meaning of 'person' see para 344 note 3 ante.
4 As to the meaning of 'dispose' see para 384 note 4 ante.
5 Sex Discrimination Act 1975 s 32(1).
6 For the meaning of 'near relative' see para 384 note 15 ante.
7 Sex Discrimination Act 1975 s 32(1)(a).
8 Ibid s 32(1)(b).
9 Ibid s 32(1)(c).
10 See ibid s 31(2); and para 384 ante.
11 See ibid s 35(3) (as amended); and para 383 ante. The employment and education provisions referred to in the text are those of Pt II (ss 6–20A) (as amended) and ss 22, 23 (both as amended).
12 See ibid s 34; and para 383 ante.

D. OTHER UNLAWFUL ACTS

386. Discriminatory practices. Proceedings may be brought by the Equal Opportunities Commission alone[1] against a person[2] who applies a discriminatory practice[3], or operates practices or other arrangements which in any circumstances would call for the application by him of a discriminatory practice[4].

1 See the Sex Discrimination Act 1975 s 37(3). Such proceedings are brought in accordance with ss 67–71 (as amended; prospectively repealed) (see para 413 post): see s 37(3). As from a date to be appointed, s 37(3) is amended so as to refer to the Equality Act ss 20–24 (see para 327 et seq ante) rather than the Sex Discrimination Act 1975 ss 67–71 (as amended; prospectively repealed): s 37(3) (prospectively amended by the Equality Act 2006 s 40, Sch 3 paras 6, 7). At the date at which this volume states the law no such day had been appointed.
   As to the Equal Opportunities Commission see para 404 et seq post. As to the Commission for Equality and Human Rights, which is to replace the Equal Opportunities Commission, see para 305 et seq ante.
2 As to the meaning of 'person' see para 344 note 3 ante.
3 'Discriminatory practice' means: (1) the application of a provision, criterion or practice which results in an act of discrimination which is unlawful by virtue of any provision of the Sex Discrimination Act 1975 Pt II (ss 6–20A) (as amended) or Pt III (ss 21A–36) (as amended) taken with s 1(1)(b) (as substituted) (see para 351 ante) or s 3(1)(b) (as substituted) (see para 349 ante) or which would be likely to result in such an act of discrimination if the persons to whom it is applied were not all of one sex; or (2) the application of a requirement or condition which results in an act of discrimination which is unlawful by virtue of any provision of Pt III (as amended) taken with s 1(1)(b) (as substituted) (see para 351 ante) or which would be likely to result in such an act of discrimination if the persons to whom it is applied were not all of one sex: s 37(1) (substituted by the Sex Discrimination (Indirect Discrimination and Burden of Proof) Regulations 2001, SI 2001/2660, reg 8(2)). As to the meaning of 'act' see para 359 note 3 ante. For the

meaning of 'discrimination' see para 344 note 4 ante. See also *McConomy v Croft Inns Ltd* [1992] IRLR
561, NI HC (refusing to provide a male with refreshment facilities because he is wearing an earring is
unlawful discrimination on the grounds of sex).
4   Sex Discrimination Act 1975 s 37(2).

387.   Relationships which have come to an end.   Where there has been a
relevant relationship[1] between a woman[2] and another person ('the relevant person'), and
the relationship has come to an end[3], it is unlawful for a relevant person to discriminate
against the woman by subjecting her to a detriment where the discrimination arises out
of and is closely connected to the relevant relationship[4].

It is also unlawful for the relevant person to subject a woman to harassment[5] where
that treatment arises out of or is closely connected to the relevant relationship[6].

1   A 'relevant relationship' is a relationship during the course of which an act of discrimination by one party
     to the relationship against the other party to it is unlawful under the Sex Discrimination Act 1975 ss 6–20
     (as amended): s 20A(2) (s 20A added by the Sex Discrimination Act 1975 (Amendment)
     Regulations 2003, SI 2003/1657, reg 3).
2   As to the meaning of 'woman' see para 344 note 5 ante. These provisions apply equally to the treatment
     of men, with requisite modifications: see the Sex Discrimination Act 1975 s 2(1); and para 357 ante.
3   Ibid s 20A(1) (as added: see note 1 supra).
4   Ibid s 20A(3) (as added: see note 1 supra). These provisions apply whether the relationship has come to an
     end before or after the commencement of s 20A (as added): s 20A(1) (as so added).
5   As to harassment, including sexual harassment, see ibid s 4A (as added); and para 347 ante.
6   Ibid s 20A(4) (added by the Employment Equality (Sex Discrimination) Regulations 2005,
     SI 2005/2467, reg 21).

388.   Discriminatory advertisements.   It is unlawful to publish or cause to be
published an advertisement[1] which indicates, or might reasonably be understood as
indicating, an intention[2] by a person[3] to do any act[4] which is or might be unlawful[5]. The
publisher of an advertisement has a defence to proceedings under this provision if he
proves[6]: (1) that the advertisement was published in reliance on a statement made to him
by the person who caused it to be published to the effect that the publication would not
be unlawful[7]; and (2) that it was reasonable for him to rely on the statement[8]. It is an
offence knowingly or recklessly to make such a statement which in a material respect is
false or misleading[9].

1   'Advertisement' includes every form of advertisement, whether to the public or not, and whether in a
     newspaper or other publication, by television or radio, by display of notices, signs, labels, showcards or
     goods, by distribution of samples, circulars, catalogues, price lists or other material, by exhibition of
     pictures, models or films, or in any other way; and references to the publishing of advertisements are to
     be construed accordingly: Sex Discrimination Act 1975 s 82(1).
         A notice in a public house has been held to constitute an advertisement: see *Commission for Racial
     Equality v Dutton* [1989] QB 783, [1989] 1 All ER 306, CA.
2   Use of a job description with a sexual connotation (such as 'waiter', 'salesgirl', 'postman' or 'stewardess')
     are to be taken to indicate an intention to discriminate, unless the advertisement contains an indication to
     the contrary: Sex Discrimination Act 1975 s 82(3). For the meaning of 'discrimination' see para 344 note
     4 ante.
         The test is partly objective and is satisfied if an ordinary person without special knowledge would
     understand the advertisement to be discriminatory; the actual intention of the advertiser is irrelevant: see
     Race Relations Board v Associated Newspapers Group Ltd [1978] 3 All ER 419, sub nom *Racial Equality
     Commission v Associated Newspapers Group Ltd* [1978] 1 WLR 905, CA.
3   As to the meaning of 'person' see para 344 note 3 ante.
4   As to the meaning of 'act' see para 359 note 1 ante.
5   Sex Discrimination Act 1975 s 38(1). An act may be unlawful by virtue of Pt II (ss 6–20A) (as amended)
     or Pt III (ss 21A–36) (as amended): see s 38(1). Section 38(1) does not apply to an advertisement if the
     intended act would not in fact be unlawful: s 38(2).
         As from a day to be appointed, a new provision is added to s 38 (as amended) stating that proceedings
     in respect of a contravention of s 38(1) may be brought only by the Commission for Equality and Human
     Rights, and in accordance with the Equality Act 2006 s 25 (as amended; not yet in force) (see para 332

ante): Sex Discrimination Act 1975 s 38(6) (prospectively added by the Equality Act 2006 s 40, Sch 3 paras 6, 8). At the date at which this volume states the law no such day had been appointed. As to the Commission for Equality and Human Rights, which is to replace the Equal Opportunities Commission, see para 305 et seq ante.

6. See the Sex Discrimination Act 1975 s 38(4).

7 Ie that it would not be unlawful by reason of the operation of ibid s 38(2): see note 5 supra.

8 Ibid s 38(4)(b).

9 See ibid s 38(5). The penalty on summary conviction of such an offence is a fine not exceeding level 5 on the standard scale: see s 38(5) (amended by virtue of the Criminal Justice Act 1982 ss 38, 46). As to the standard scale see para 315 note 15 ante.

389. Instructions to discriminate. It is unlawful for a person[1] who has authority over another person[2], or in accordance with whose wishes that other person is accustomed to act[3], to instruct him to do any act[4] of unlawful discrimination[5], or procure or attempt to procure the doing by him of any such act[6].

1 As to the meaning of 'person' see para 344 note 3 ante.

2 Sex Discrimination Act 1975 s 39(a). See note 6 infra.

3 Ibid s 39(b). See note 6 infra. There must be some relationship between the two persons and it is not sufficient merely to show that the other person was accustomed to act in accordance with the wishes of anyone in the same position as the person giving the instruction: see *Commission for Racial Equality v Imperial Society of Teachers of Dancing* [1983] ICR 473, [1983] IRLR 315, EAT.

4 As to the meaning of 'act' see para 359 note 1 ante.

5 Ie any act which is unlawful by virtue of the Sex Discrimination Act 1975 Pt II (ss 6–20A) (as amended) or Pt III (ss 21A–36) (as amended): see s 39. See note 6 infra.

6 Ibid s 39. It is irrelevant for the purposes of s 39 whether or not the act of unlawful discrimination actually takes place.

As from a day to be appointed, s 39 is renumbered as s 39(1), and a new provision is added stating that proceedings in respect of a contravention of s 39(1) (as renumbered) may be brought only by the Commission for Equality and Human Rights, and in accordance with the Equality Act 2006 s 25 (as amended; not yet in force) (see para 332 ante): Sex Discrimination Act 1975 s 39(1), (2) (s 39(1) prospectively renumbered, and s 39(2) prospectively added, by the Equality Act 2006 s 40, Sch 3 paras 6, 9). At the date at which this volume states the law no such day had been appointed. As to the Commission for Equality and Human Rights, which is to replace the Equal Opportunities Commission, see para 305 et seq ante.

390. Pressure to discriminate. It is unlawful to induce, or attempt to induce, a person[1] to do any act[2] of unlawful discrimination[3] by providing or offering to provide him with any benefit[4], or subjecting or threatening to subject him to any detriment[5]. An offer or threat is not prevented from falling within this provision because it is not made directly to the person in question, if it is made in such a way that he is likely to hear of it[6].

1 As to the meaning of 'person' see para 344 note 3 ante.

2 As to the meaning of 'act' see para 359 note 1 ante.

3 See the Sex Discrimination Act 1975 s 40(1). An unlawful act is one which contravenes Pt II (ss 6–20A) (as amended) or Pt III (ss 21A–36) (as amended): see s 40(1).

As from a day to be appointed, a new provision is added stating that proceedings in respect of a contravention of s 40(1) may be brought only by the Commission for Equality and Human Rights, and in accordance with the Equality Act 2006 s 25 (as amended; not yet in force) (see para 332 ante): Sex Discrimination Act 1975 s 40(3) (prospectively added by the Equality Act 2006 s 40, Sch 3 paras 6, 10). At the date at which this volume states the law no such day had been appointed. As to the Commission for Equality and Human Rights, which is to replace the Equal Opportunities Commission, see para 305 et seq ante.

As to selection of candidates by registered political parties see the Sex Discrimination Act 1975 s 42A (as added); and para 367 note 4 ante.

4 Ibid s 40(1)(a). See note 3 supra.

5 Ibid s 40(1)(b). See note 3 supra.

6 Ibid s 40(2). It is irrelevant for the purposes of s 40 whether or not the act of unlawful discrimination actually takes place.

391.　Liability of employers and principals.　Anything done by a person in the course of his employment[1] is to be treated for the purposes of the Sex Discrimination Act 1975 as done by his employer[2] as well as by him, whether or not it was done with the employer's knowledge or approval[3].

Anything done by a person as agent for another person with the authority (whether express or implied, and whether precedent or subsequent) of that other person is to be treated for the purposes of the Act as done by that other person as well as by him[4].

In proceedings brought under the Act against any person in respect of an act[5] alleged to have been done by an employee[6] of his it is a defence for that person to prove that he took such steps as were reasonably practicable[7] to prevent the employee from doing that act, or from doing in the course of his employment acts of that description[8].

1　For the meaning of 'employment' see para 360 note 4 ante. 'In the course of his employment' is more liberally defined in the context of discrimination than at common law. The provisions must be interpreted in accordance with their purpose (see *Jones v Tower Boot Co Ltd* [1997] 2 All ER 406, [1997] IRLR 168, CA) and in accordance with common sense. Otherwise, the more serious the act, the more easily the employer will avoid liability. See also *ST v North Yorkshire County Council* [1999] IRLR 98, CA; *Heasmans v Clarity Cleaning Co Ltd* [1987] IRLR 286, CA; *Irving v Post Office* [1987] ICR 949, [1987] IRLR 289, CA; *Bracebridge Engineering Ltd v Darby* [1990] IRLR 3, EAT.

　　In relation to acts outside the workplace see *Waters v Metropolitan Police Comr* [1997] ICR 1073, [1997] IRLR 589, CA; revsd in part [2000] 4 All ER 934, [2000] ICR 1064, HL (where, albeit the alleged act took place in a section house, the person alleged to have committed the discriminatory act and the person allegedly discriminated against were both off duty and the former was a visitor to the latter's room at a time and in circumstances which placed them in no different position from that which would have applied if they had been social acquaintances only, with no working connection, the alleged act of discrimination could not be said to have been committed in the course of employment); *Chief Constable of Lincolnshire Police v Stubbs* [1999] ICR 547, [1999] IRLR 81, EAT (alleged sexual harassment in a public bar where a number of officers had retired after their shifts, and at a party organised as a 'leaving do'; held to be within the course of employment on the basis that each occurred in what amounted to an 'extension of the workplace'). See also *Kingston v British Railways Board* [1984] ICR 781, [1984] IRLR 146, CA.

2　For the meaning of 'employer' see para 360 note 4 ante.

3　Sex Discrimination Act 1975 s 41(1). See also para 392 post. The seniority of the employee is also irrelevant: see *De Souza v Automobile Association* [1986] ICR 514, [1986] IRLR 103, CA. As to the application of the Sex Discrimination Act 1975 s 41 to governing bodies of schools and institutions of higher or further education where such bodies have delegated budgets see the Education (Modification of Enactments Relating to Employment) (England) Order 2003, SI 2003/1964, art 3, Schedule; and the Education (Modification of Enactments Relating to Employment) (Wales) Order 2006, SI 2006/1073, art 3, Schedule.

4　Sex Discrimination Act 1975 s 41(2). See also para 392 post.

　　See *Lana v Positive Action Training in Housing (London) Ltd* [2001] IRLR 501, [2001] All ER (D) 23 (Jun), EAT (company placed trainee with third party which was to provide training; third party acted as agent for company; company liable for discrimination by agent when placement terminated on discovery of trainee's pregnancy).

　　In a claim by a police officer, the decision whether the alleged discriminatory acts are to be considered as being done with the authority of the chief constable is a matter to be decided by the employment tribunal: *Chief Constable of Kent County Constabulary v Baskerville* [2003] EWCA Civ 1354, [2003] ICR 1463, [2003] All ER (D) 27 (Sep).

5　As to the meaning of 'act' see para 359 note 1 ante.

6　For the meaning of 'employee' see para 360 note 4 ante.

7　As to the meaning of 'reasonably practicable' see *Palmer v Southend-on-Sea Borough Council* [1984] ICR 372, [1984] IRLR 119, CA. See also EMPLOYMENT vol 16(1B) (Reissue) para 852.

8　Sex Discrimination Act 1975 s 41(3). See *Balgobin v Tower Hamlets London Borough Council* [1987] ICR 829, [1987] IRLR 401, EAT; *Enterprise Glass Co Ltd v Miles* [1990] ICR 787, EAT.

392.　Aiding discrimination.　A person[1] who knowingly aids[2] another person to do an act[3] made unlawful by the Sex Discrimination Act 1975 is to be treated for the purposes of the Act as himself doing an unlawful act of the like description[4].

A person does not knowingly aid another to do an unlawful act[5] if he acts in reliance on a statement made to him by that other person that the act which he aids would not be unlawful[6], and it is reasonable for him to rely on the statement[7]. It is an offence knowingly or recklessly to make such a statement which in a material respect is false or misleading[8].

1   As to the meaning of 'person' see para 344 note 3 ante.
2   See *Anyanwu v South Bank Students' Union* [2001] UKHL 14, [2001] 2 All ER 353, [2001] IRLR 305 ('aid' must be given its familiar meaning, that is assisting or helping, the degree to which it contributed to the discrimination being irrelevant, unless not so slight as to be negligible). Cf *Hallam v Avery* [2000] 1 WLR 966, [2000] ICR 583, CA.
3   As to the meaning of 'act' see para 359 note 1 ante.
4   Sex Discrimination Act 1975 s 42(1). For the purposes of s 42(1), an employee or agent for whose act the employer or principal is liable under s 41 (see para 391 ante) (or would be so liable but for s 41(3)) is to be deemed to aid the doing of the act by the employer or principal: s 42(2). For the meanings of 'employee' and 'employer' see para 360 note 4 ante. See also *AM v WC and SPV* [1999] ICR 1218, [1999] IRLR 410, EAT. The commission of unlawful sex discrimination can only be 'aided' through a conscious act: *Sinclair Roche and Temperley v Heard* [2004] IRLR 763, EAT. See also *Gilbank v Miles* [2006] EWCA Civ 543, [2006] ICR 1297, [2006] IRLR 538, [2006] All ER (D) 160 (May); *Shepherd v North Yorkshire County Council* [2006] IRLR 190, [2005] All ER (D) 354 (Dec), EAT.
5   Sex Discrimination Act 1975 s 42(3).
6   Ie that it would not be unlawful by reason of any provision of the Sex Discrimination Act 1975: see s 42(3)(a).
7   Ibid s 42(3)(a), (b).
8   See ibid s 42(4). The penalty on summary conviction of such an offence is a fine not exceeding level 5 on the standard scale: s 42(4) (amended by virtue of the Criminal Justice Act 1982 ss 38, 46). As to the standard scale see para 315 note 15 ante.

393. Discriminatory contracts. A term of a contract is void where its inclusion renders the making of the contract unlawful by virtue of the Sex Discrimination Act 1975[1], or it is included in furtherance of an act rendered unlawful by the Act[2], or it provides for the doing of an act[3] which would be rendered unlawful by the Act[4]. A term, the inclusion of which constitutes, or is in furtherance of, or provides for, unlawful discrimination[5] against a party to the contract, is not void, but is unenforceable against that party[6]. Any person interested in such a contract may apply to a county court for such order as the court thinks just for removing or modifying any unenforceable term[7].

A term in a contract which purports to exclude or limit any provision of the Sex Discrimination Act 1975 or the Equal Pay Act 1970[8] is unenforceable by any person in whose favour the term would otherwise operate[9]. This provision[10] does not apply to: (1) a contract settling a complaint in the employment field[11] where the contract is made with the assistance of a conciliation officer[12]; (2) a contract settling such a complaint if the conditions regulating compromise contracts under the Sex Discrimination Act 1975[13] are satisfied in relation to the contract[14]; or (3) a contract settling a complaint of discrimination outside the employment field[15].

The provisions[16] set out above apply, as they apply to the term of a contract[17], to:

(a) any term of a collective agreement[18], including an agreement which was not intended, or is presumed not to have been intended, to be a legally enforceable contract[19];

(b) any rule made by an employer for application to all or any of the persons who are employed by him or who apply to be, or are, considered by him for employment[20]; and

(c) any rule made by an organisation, authority or body[21] for application to all or any of its members or prospective members or to all or any of the persons on whom it has conferred authorisations or qualifications or who are seeking the authorisations or qualifications which it has power to confer[22].

A person[23] may present a complaint to an employment tribunal that a term or rule is void[24] if he has reason to believe[25]: (i) that the term or rule may at some future time have effect in relation to him[26]; and (ii) where he alleges that it is void[27], that an act for the doing of which it provides may at some such time be done in relation to him, and the act would be, or be deemed to be[28], rendered unlawful by the Sex Discrimination Act 1975 if done in relation to him in present circumstances[29]. When an employment tribunal finds that a complaint presented to it is well-founded, the tribunal must make an order declaring that the term or rule is void[30].

The avoidance of any term or rule[31] which provides for any person to be discriminated against is without prejudice to the following rights (except in so far as they enable any person to require another person to be treated less favourably than himself), namely, such of the rights of the person to be discriminated against, and such of the rights of any person who will be treated more favourably in direct or indirect consequence of the discrimination, as are conferred by or in respect of a contract made or modified wholly or partly in pursuance of, or by reference to, that term or rule[32].

1   Sex Discrimination Act 1975 s 77(1)(a).
2   Ibid s 77(1)(b).
3   As to the meaning of 'act' see para 359 note 1 ante.
4   Sex Discrimination Act 1975 s 77(1)(c).
5   For the meaning of 'discrimination' see para 344 note 4 ante.
6   See the Sex Discrimination Act 1975 s 77(2). As to void and voidable contracts see CONTRACT vol 9(1) (Reissue) para 836 et seq.
7   See ibid s 77(5). Such an order must not be made unless all persons affected have been given notice of the application (except where, under rules of court, notice may be dispensed with) and have been afforded an opportunity to make representations to the court: s 77(5). For the meaning of 'notice' see para 378 note 8 ante. Such an order may include provision as respects any period before the making of the order: s 77(6). However, any such provision included in an order must be confined to provisions which are ancillary or consequential on the main part of the order and may not therefore include an order for repayment of a sum overpaid in consequence of unlawful discrimination: see *Orphanos v Queen Mary College* [1985] AC 761, [1985] 2 All ER 233, HL.
8   As to the Equal Pay Act 1970 see para 424 et seq post.
9   Sex Discrimination Act 1975 s 77(3). See *Clarke v Redcar and Cleveland Borough Council, Wilson v Stockton-on-Tees Borough Council* [2006] ICR 897, [2006] IRLR 324, EAT.
10 Ie the Sex Discrimination Act 1975 s 77(3): see the text to note 9 supra.
11 Ie a complaint to which ibid s 63(1) (as amended) (see para 414 post) or the Equal Pay Act 1970 s 2 (as amended) (see para 435 post) applies.
12 Sex Discrimination Act 1975 s 77(4)(a). See also note 15 infra. As to conciliation officers see EMPLOYMENT vol 16(1A) (Reissue) para 122. See *Clarke v Redcar and Cleveland Borough Council, Wilson v Stockton-on-Tees Borough Council* [2006] ICR 897, [2006] IRLR 324, EAT.
13 The conditions regulating compromise contracts under the Sex Discrimination Act 1975 are that: (1) the contract must be in writing; (2) the contract must relate to the particular complaint; (3) the complainant must have received advice from a relevant independent adviser as to the terms and effect of the proposed contract and in particular its effect on his ability to pursue his complaint before an employment tribunal; (4) there must be in force, when the adviser gives the advice, a contract of insurance, or an indemnity provided for members of a profession or professional body, covering the risk of a claim by the complainant in respect of loss arising in consequence of the advice; (5) the contract must identify the adviser; and (6) the contract must state that the conditions regulating compromise contracts under the Act are satisfied: s 77(4A) (added by the Trade Union Reform and Employment Rights Act 1993 s 39(2), Sch 6 para 1; and amended by the Employment Rights (Dispute Resolution) Act 1998 ss 1(2)(a), 9(1), (2)(a), 10(1), (2)(a)). In relation to head (2) supra see *Lunt v Merseyside TEC Ltd* [1999] ICR 17, [1999] IRLR 458, EAT.
    A person is a relevant independent adviser for the purposes of head (3) supra if: (a) he is a qualified lawyer; (b) he is an officer, official, employee or member of an independent trade union who has been certified in writing by the trade union as competent to give advice and as authorised to do so on behalf of the trade union; (c) he works at an advice centre (whether as an employee or a volunteer) and has been certified in writing by the centre as competent to give advice and as authorised to do so on behalf of the centre; or (d) he is a person of a description specified in an order made by the Secretary of State: Sex Discrimination Act 1975 s 77(4B) (added by the Trade Union Reform and Employment Rights Act 1993 s 39(2), Sch 6 para 1; and substituted by the Employment Rights (Dispute Resolution) Act 1998 s 15, Sch 1 para 2). For the purposes of head (d) supra, a Fellow of the Institute of Legal Executives employed by a solicitors' practice has been specified: see the Compromise Agreements (Description of Person) Order 2004, SI 2004/754 (amended by SI 2004/2515). As to the Secretary of State and the National

Assembly for Wales see para 302 ante. For the meaning of 'employment' see para 360 note 4 ante. 'Qualified lawyer' means a barrister (whether in practice as such or employed to give legal advice), a solicitor who holds a practising certificate, or a person other than a barrister or solicitor who is an authorised advocate or authorised litigator (within the meaning of the Courts and Legal Services Act 1990: see BARRISTERS vol 3(1) (2005 Reissue) para 501; SOLICITORS vol 44(1) (Reissue) paras 78–79): Sex Discrimination Act 1975 s 77(4BB) (added by the Employment Rights (Dispute Resolution) Act 1998 Sch 1 para 2). 'Independent trade union' has the same meaning as in the Trade Union and Labour Relations (Consolidation) Act 1992 (see TRADE, INDUSTRY AND INDUSTRIAL RELATIONS vol 47 (2001 Reissue) para 1014): Sex Discrimination Act 1975 s 77(4BC) (added by the Employment Rights (Dispute Resolution) Act 1998 Sch 1 para 2).

However, a person is not a relevant independent adviser for the purposes of head (3) supra in relation to the complainant: (i) if he is, or is employed by, or is acting in the matter for, the other party or a person who is connected with the other party; (ii) in the case of a person within head (b) or head (c) supra, if the trade union or advice centre is the other party or a person who is connected with the other party; (iii) in the case of a person within head (c) supra, if the complainant makes a payment for the advice received from him; or (iv) in the case of a person of a description specified in an order under head (d) supra, if any condition specified in the order in relation to the giving of advice by persons of that description is not satisfied: Sex Discrimination Act 1975 s 77(4BA) (added by the Employment Rights (Dispute Resolution) Act 1998 Sch 1 para 2). For these purposes, any two persons are to be treated as connected if one is a company of which the other (directly or indirectly) has control, or if both are companies of which a third person (directly or indirectly) has control: Sex Discrimination Act 1975 s 77(4C) (added by the Trade Union Reform and Employment Rights Act 1993 Sch 6 para 1; and substituted by the Employment Rights (Dispute Resolution) Act 1998 Sch 1 para 2). See also note 15 infra.

14 Sex Discrimination Act 1975 s 77(4)(aa) (added by the Trade Union Reform and Employment Rights Act 1993 Sch 6 para 1). See also note 15 infra.

15 Sex Discrimination Act 1975 s 77(4)(b). Section 77 (as amended) applies to claims to which s 66 (as amended) applies (see para 415 post): see s 77(4)(b).

An agreement entered into on or after 1 August 1998 under which the parties agree to submit a dispute to arbitration: (1) is to be regarded for the purposes of s 77(4)(a), (aa) (as added) as being a contract settling a complaint if the dispute is covered by a scheme having effect by virtue of an order under the Trade Union and Labour Relations (Consolidation) Act 1992 s 212A (as added and amended) (see TRADE, INDUSTRY AND INDUSTRIAL RELATIONS), and the agreement is to submit it to arbitration in accordance with the scheme; but (2) is to be regarded for those purposes as neither being nor including such a contract in any other case: Sex Discrimination Act 1975 s 77(4D) (added by the Employment Rights (Dispute Resolution) Act 1998 s 8(1)); Employment Rights (Dispute Resolution) Act 1998 (Commencement No 1 and Transitional and Saving Provisions) Order 1998, SI 1998/1658, art 3(4).

16 Ie the Sex Discrimination Act 1975 s 77 (as amended): see the text and notes 1–15 supra.

17 Sex Discrimination Act 1986 s 6(1). This is expressed to be without prejudice to the generality of the Sex Discrimination Act 1975 s 77 (as amended). Section 77 (as amended) applies for these purposes whenever the agreement or rule in question was made: see the Sex Discrimination Act 1986 s 6(1). For the purposes of the Sex Discrimination Act 1975 s 77 (as amended), a term or rule is deemed to provide for the doing of an act which would be rendered unlawful by the Sex Discrimination Act 1975 if: (1) it provides for the inclusion in any contract of employment of any term which by virtue of an equality clause would fall either to be modified or to be supplemented by an additional term; and (2) that clause would not be prevented from operating in relation to that contract by the Equal Pay Act 1970 s 1(3) (as substituted and amended) (material factors justifying discrimination) (see para 430 post): Sex Discrimination Act 1986 s 6(3). Nothing in the Sex Discrimination Act 1975 s 77 (as amended) affects the operation of any term or rule in so far as it provides for the doing of a particular act in circumstances where the doing of that act would not be, or be deemed by virtue of the Sex Discrimination Act 1986 s 6(3) to be, rendered unlawful by the Sex Discrimination Act 1975: Sex Discrimination Act 1986 s 6(4).

Section 6 (as amended) has effect as if the terms of any service to which the Sex Discrimination Act 1975 Pt II (ss 6–20A) (as amended) and Pt IV (ss 37–42) (as amended) apply by virtue of s 85(2) (as amended) (Crown application) (see para 375 ante) were terms of a contract of employment and, in relation to the terms of any such service, as if service for the purposes of any person mentioned in s 85(2) (as amended) were employment by that person: Sex Discrimination Act 1986 s 6(7).

18 'Collective agreement' means any agreement relating to one or more of the matters mentioned in the Trade Union and Labour Relations (Consolidation) Act 1992 s 178(2) (meaning of trade dispute) (see TRADE, INDUSTRY AND INDUSTRIAL RELATIONS vol 47 (2001 Reissue) para 1301), being an agreement made by or on behalf of one or more employers or one or more organisations of employers or

associations of such organisations with one or more organisations of workers or associations of such organisations: Sex Discrimination Act 1986 s 6(6) (amended by the Trade Union and Labour Relations (Consolidation) Act 1992 s 300(2), Sch 2 para 36).

19   Sex Discrimination Act 1986 s 6(1)(a).

20   Ibid s 6(1)(b).

21   Ie (1) any organisation of workers; (2) any organisation of employers; (3) any organisation whose members carry on a particular profession or trade for the purposes of which the organisation exists; and (4) any authority or body which can confer an authorisation or qualification which is needed for, or facilitates, engagement in a particular profession or trade: ibid s 6(2).

22   Ibid s 6(1)(c).

23   In the case of a complaint about: (1) a term of a collective agreement made by or on behalf of an employer, an organisation of employers of which an employer is a member, or an association of such organisations of one of which an employer is a member; or (2) a rule made by an employer, the person who may present a complaint is any person who is, or is genuinely and actively seeking to become, one of his employees: ibid s 6(4B) (s 6(4A)–(4D) added by the Trade Union Reform and Employment Rights Act 1993 s 32). In the case of a complaint about a rule made by an organisation, authority or body (see note 21 supra), a complaint can be presented by any person: (a) who is, or is genuinely and actively seeking to become, a member of the organisation, authority or body; (b) on whom the organisation, authority or body has conferred an authorisation or qualification; or (c) who is genuinely and actively seeking an authorisation or qualification which the organisation, authority or body has power to confer: Sex Discrimination Act 1986 s 6(4C) (as so added).

24   Ie by virtue of the Sex Discrimination Act 1975 s 77(1): see the text to notes 1–4 supra.

25   Sex Discrimination Act 1986 s 6(4A) (as added (see note 23 supra); and amended by virtue of the Employment Rights (Dispute Resolution) Act 1998 s 1(2)(a)).

26   Sex Discrimination Act 1986 s 6(4A)(a) (as added: see note 23 supra).

27   Ie by virtue of the Sex Discrimination Act 1975 s 77(1)(c): see the text to note 4 supra.

28   Ie by virtue of the Sex Discrimination Act 1986 s 6(3): see note 17 supra.

29   Ibid s 6(4A)(b) (as added: see note 23 supra).

30   Ibid s 6(4D) (as added (see note 23 supra); and amended by virtue of the Employment Rights (Dispute Resolution) Act 1998 s 1(2)(a)).

31   Ie by virtue of the Sex Discrimination Act 1975 s 77 (as amended): see the text and notes 1–15 supra.

32   Sex Discrimination Act 1986 s 6(5).

394.   Public authorities. It is unlawful for a public authority[1] exercising a function[2] to do any act which constitutes discrimination or harassment[3]. The above prohibition[4] does not apply to: (1) the House of Commons; (2) the House of Lords; (3) the Security Service; (4) the Secret Intelligence Service; (5) the Government Communications Headquarters; or (6) a part of the armed forces of the Crown which is, in accordance with a requirement of the Secretary of State, assisting the Government Communications Headquarters[5]. The above prohibition does not apply to certain specific functions and actions[6].

The above provisions bind the Crown[7].

1   For these purposes, 'public authority' includes any person who has functions of a public nature (subject to the Sex Discrimination Act 1975 s 21A(3) (as added) and s 21A(4) (as added): see the text and notes 4–6 infra): s 21A(2)(a) (s 21A added by the Equality Act 2006 s 83(1)).

2   For these purposes, 'function' means a function of a public nature: Sex Discrimination Act 1975 s 21A(2)(b) (as added: see note 1 supra).

3   Ibid s 21A(1) (as added: see note 1 supra). For the meaning of 'discrimination' see para 344 note 4 ante. The reference to harassment is to harassment within the meaning of s 4A(1), (2), (5), (6) (as added) (see para 347 ante): see s 21A(1) (as so added). See also the Gender Equality Duty Code of Practice (England and Wales) (April 2007); and para 343 ante. As to codes of practice generally see para 406 post.

4   Ie the prohibition in the Sex Discrimination Act 1975 s 21A(1) (as added): see the text and notes 1–3 supra.

5   Ibid s 21A(3) (as added: see note 1 supra). As to the security and intelligence services generally see CONSTITUTIONAL LAW AND HUMAN RIGHTS vol 8(2) (Reissue) para 473 et seq. As to the armed forces generally see ARMED FORCES.

6   Ibid s 21A(4) (as added: see note 1 supra). The functions and actions referred to in the text are those listed in the Table of Exceptions: see s 21A(9) (as so added). The Secretary of State may by order amend the Table of Exceptions: s 21A(5) (as so added). As to the Secretary of State and National Assembly for Wales see para 302 ante. The functions and actions listed in the Table of Exceptions are as follows:

(1) preparing, making, or considering: (a) an Act of Parliament; (b) a Bill for an Act of Parliament; (c) an Act of the Scottish Parliament; or (d) a Bill for an Act of the Scottish Parliament;

(2) preparing, making, confirming, approving, or considering legislation made or to be made: (a) by a Minister of the Crown; (b) by Order in Council; (c) by the Scottish Ministers or any member of the Scottish Executive; (d) by the National Assembly for Wales; or (e) by or by virtue of a Measure of the General Synod of the Church of England;

(3) action which is necessary, or in so far as it is necessary, for the purpose of complying with: (a) an Act of Parliament; (b) an Act of the Scottish Parliament; or (c) legislation of a kind described in head (2) supra;

(4) a judicial function (whether in connection with a court or a tribunal);

(5) anything done on behalf of or on the instructions of a person exercising a judicial function (whether in connection with a court or a tribunal);

(6) a decision not to institute or continue criminal proceedings;

(7) anything done for the purpose of reaching, or in pursuance of, a decision not to institute or continue criminal proceedings;

(8) the provision of a service for one sex only where only persons of that sex require the service;

(9) the provision of separate services for each sex where a joint service would or might be less effective;

(10) the provision of a service for one sex only where: (a) the service is also provided jointly for both sexes; and (b) if the service were provided only jointly it would or might be insufficiently effective;

(11) the provision of a service for one sex only where: (a) if the service were provided for both sexes jointly it would or might be less effective; and (b) the extent to which the service is required by the other sex makes it not reasonably practicable to provide separate services for that sex;

(12) the provision of separate services for each sex in different ways or to different extents where: (a) if the service were provided for both sexes jointly it would or might be less effective; and (b) the extent to which the service is required by one sex makes it not reasonably practicable to provide the service for that sex in the same way or to the same extent as for the other sex;

(13) action taken for the purpose of assisting one sex to overcome: (a) a disadvantage (as compared with the other sex); or (b) the effects of discrimination;

(14) the exercise of a function of the Charity Commissioners for England and Wales or the holder of the Office of the Scottish Charity Regulator in relation to an instrument in relation to which s 43 (as amended) (see para 395 post) applies;

(15) action which is unlawful by virtue of another provision of the Sex Discrimination Act 1975;

(16) action which would be unlawful by virtue of another provision of the Sex Discrimination Act 1975 but for an express exception.

In an action under s 66 (as amended) (see para 415 post) in respect of a contravention of s 21A (as added), the court must not grant an injunction unless satisfied that it will not prejudice criminal proceedings or a criminal investigation, and the court must grant any application to stay the proceedings under s 66 (as amended) on the grounds of prejudice to criminal proceedings or to a criminal investigation, unless satisfied that the proceedings or investigation will not be prejudiced: s 21A(6) (as so added). In s 21A (as added), 'criminal investigation' means: (i) an investigation into the commission of an alleged offence; and (ii) a decision whether to institute criminal proceedings: s 21A(8) (as so added).

Section 74(2)(b) (as amended) (see para 417 post) does not apply in relation to a respondent's reply, or a failure to reply, to a question in connection with an alleged contravention of s 21A (as added): (A) if the respondent reasonably asserts that to have replied differently or at all might have prejudiced criminal proceedings or a criminal investigation; (B) if the respondent reasonably asserts that to have replied differently or at all would have revealed the reason for not instituting or not continuing criminal proceedings; (C) where the reply is of a kind specified for the purposes of this provision by order of the Secretary of State; (D) where the reply is given in circumstances specified for the purposes of this provision by order of the Secretary of State; or (E) where the failure occurs in circumstances specified for the purposes of this provision by order of the Secretary of State: s 21A(7) (as so added). At the date at which this volume states the law no order had been made for these purposes.

7 Ibid s 85(3A) (added by the Equality Act 2006 s 83(4)).

(iii) General Exceptions

395. Charities. The Sex Discrimination Act 1975 makes special provision for charities[1]. Any provision which is contained in a charitable instrument[2] and which provides for conferring benefits on persons of one sex only (disregarding any benefits to persons of the opposite sex which are exceptional or are relatively insignificant)[3] is not rendered unlawful by the Sex Discrimination Act 1975[4] and nor is any act[5] which is done to give effect to such a provision[6].

1   See the Sex Discrimination Act 1975 s 43 (as amended); and the text and notes 2–6 infra. See also *Hugh-Jones v St John's College, Cambridge* [1979] ICR 848, 123 Sol Jo 603, EAT. There is a specific exception in relation to educational charities: see para 381 note 23 ante.
2   'Charitable instrument' means an enactment or other instrument so far as it relates to charitable purposes; and 'charitable purposes' means purposes which are exclusively charitable according to the law of England and Wales: Sex Discrimination Act 1975 s 43(3) (substituted by the Sex Discrimination Act 1975 (Amendment of Section 43) Order 1977, SI 1977/528, art 2). See further CHARITIES vol 5(2) (2001 Reissue) para 4 et seq.
3   See the Sex Discrimination Act 1975 s 43(2).
4   Ie ibid Pts II–IV (ss 6–42) (as amended).
5   As to the meaning of 'act' see para 359 note 1 ante.
6   See the Sex Discrimination Act 1975 s 43(1).

396.   Sporting events.   Nothing in Parts II to IV of the Sex Discrimination Act 1975[1], in relation to any sport, game or other activity of a competitive nature where the physical strength, stamina or physique of the average woman[2] puts her at a disadvantage to the average man[3], renders unlawful any act[4] related to the participation of a person as a competitor in events involving that activity which are confined to competitors of one sex[5].

1   Ie the Sex Discrimination Act 1975 Pts II–IV (ss 6–42) (as amended).
2   As to the meaning of 'woman' see para 344 note 5 ante.
3   As to the meaning of 'man' see para 344 note 10 ante.
4   As to the meaning of 'act' see para 359 note 1 ante.
5   Sex Discrimination Act 1975 s 44. See *Greater London Council v Farrar* [1980] 1 WLR 608, [1980] ICR 266, EAT; *British Judo Association v Petty* [1981] ICR 660, [1981] IRLR 484, EAT; *Bennett v Football Association Ltd* (28 July 1988, unreported), CA. For an exception in relation to sport in the context of education see para 381 ante.

397.   Insurance.   Nothing in Parts II to IV of the Sex Discrimination Act 1975[1] renders unlawful the treatment of a person in relation to an annuity, life assurance policy, accident insurance policy, or similar matter involving the assessment of risk[2], where the treatment: (1) was effected by reference to actuarial or other data from a source on which it was reasonable to rely[3]; and (2) was reasonable having regard to the data and any other relevant factors[4].

1   Ie the Sex Discrimination Act 1975 Pts II–IV (ss 6–42) (as amended).
2   Ibid s 45. See generally INSURANCE. See also *Pinder v Friends Provident* (1985) Times, 16 December.
3   Sex Discrimination Act 1975 s 45(a).
4   Ibid s 45(b).

398.   Communal accommodation.   Nothing in Part II or Part III of the Sex Discrimination Act 1975[1] renders unlawful sex discrimination[2] in the admission of persons to communal accommodation[3] if the accommodation is managed in a way which, given the exigencies of the situation, comes as near as may be to fair and equitable treatment of men and women[4]. In applying this provision account must be taken of: (1) whether and how far it is reasonable to expect that the accommodation should be altered or extended, or that further alternative accommodation should be provided[5]; and (2) the frequency of the demand or need for use of the accommodation by men as compared with women[6].

In addition, nothing in Part II or Part III of the Sex Discrimination Act 1975 renders unlawful sex discrimination against a woman, or against a man, as respects the provision of any benefit, facility or service[7] if: (a) the benefit, facility or service cannot properly and effectively be provided except for those using communal accommodation[8]; and (b) in the relevant circumstances the woman or, as the case may be, the man could lawfully be refused the use of the accommodation[9].

Neither of the above provisions is a defence to an act[10] of sex discrimination in the field of employment[11] unless such arrangements as are reasonably practicable are made to compensate for the detriment caused by the discrimination[12].

1   Ie the Sex Discrimination Act 1975 Pt II (ss 6–20A) (as amended) or Pt III (ss 21A–36) (as amended).

2   For the meaning of 'discrimination' see para 344 note 4 ante.

3   'Communal accommodation' means residential accommodation which includes dormitories or other shared sleeping accommodation which for reasons of privacy or decency should be used by men only, or by women only (but which may include some shared sleeping accommodation for men, and some for women, or some ordinary sleeping accommodation): Sex Discrimination Act 1975 s 46(1). 'Communal accommodation' also includes residential accommodation all or part of which should be used by men only, or by women only, because of the nature of the sanitary facilities serving the accommodation: s 46(2). As to the meaning of 'man' see para 344 note 10 ante; and as to the meaning of 'woman' see para 344 note 5 ante.

4   Ibid s 46(3). Section 25 (as amended) (general duty in public sector of education) (see para 379 ante) does not apply to sex discrimination within s 46(3) or s 46(5) (see the text and note 7 infra): s 46(7).

     Section 46 is without prejudice to the generality of s 35(1)(c) (see para 383 ante): s 46(8).

5   Ibid s 46(4)(a).

6   Ibid s 46(4)(b).

7   Ibid s 46(5). See also note 4 supra.

8   Ibid s 46(5)(a).

9   Ibid s 46(5)(b). A woman or man could lawfully be refused the use of accommodation by virtue of s 46(3) (see the text and notes 1–4 supra): see s 46(5)(b).

10   As to the meaning of 'act' see para 359 note 1 ante.

11   Ie under the Sex Discrimination Act 1975 Pt II (as amended).

12   Ibid s 46(6). In considering whether the use of communal accommodation could lawfully be refused (in a case based on Pt II (as amended) (employment)), it is to be assumed that the requirements of s 46(6) have been complied with as respects s 46(3) (see the text and notes 1–4 supra): s 46(6).

399. Positive action. Nothing in Parts II to IV of the Sex Discrimination Act 1975[1] renders unlawful any act[2] done in relation to particular work by any person[3] in, or in connection with: (1) affording women[4] only, or men[5] only, access to facilities for training[6] which would help to fit them for that work[7]; or (2) encouraging women only, or men only, to take advantage of opportunities for doing that work[8], where it reasonably appears to that person that at any time within the 12 months[9] immediately preceding the doing of the act there were no persons of the sex in question doing that work in Great Britain[10], or the number of persons of that sex doing the work in Great Britain was comparatively small[11].

Where in relation to particular work it reasonably appears to any person that although the above condition is not met for the whole of Great Britain it is met for an area within Great Britain, nothing in Parts II to IV of the Sex Discrimination Act 1975[12] renders unlawful any act done by that person in, or in connection with[13]: (a) affording persons who are of the sex in question, and who appear likely to take up that work in that area, access to facilities for training which would help to fit them for that work[14]; or (b) encouraging persons of that sex to take advantage of opportunities in the area for doing that work[15].

In addition, nothing in Parts II to IV of the Sex Discrimination Act 1975[16] renders unlawful any act done by any person in, or in connection with, affording persons access to facilities for training which would help to fit them for employment, where it reasonably appears to that person that those persons are in special need of training by reason of the period for which they have been discharging domestic or family responsibilities to the exclusion of regular full-time employment[17]. The discrimination in relation to which this provision applies may result from confining the training to persons who have been discharging domestic or family responsibilities, or from the way persons are selected for training, or both[18].

The above provisions[19] do not apply in relation to any unlawful discrimination relating to discrimination against applicants and employees[20].

Parts II to IV of the Sex Discrimination Act 1975[21] do not render unlawful any act done by an employer[22] in relation to particular work in his employment, being an act done in, or in connection with: (i) affording his female employees only, or his male employees only, access to facilities for training which would help to fit them for that work[23]; or (ii) encouraging women only, or men only, to take advantage of opportunities for doing that work[24], where at any time within the 12 months immediately preceding the doing of the act there were no persons of the sex in question among those doing that work or the number of persons of that sex doing the work was comparatively small[25].

The provision relating to discrimination by trade unions and other relevant organisations[26] does not render unlawful any act done by an organisation to which that provision applies in, or in connection with: (A) affording female members of the organisation only, or male members of the organisation only, access to facilities for training which would help to fit them for holding a post of any kind in the organisation[27]; or (B) encouraging female members only, or male members only, to take advantage of opportunities for holding such posts in the organisation[28], where at any time within the 12 months immediately preceding the doing of the act there were no persons of the sex in question among persons holding such posts in the organisation or the number of persons of that sex holding such posts was comparatively small[29]. In addition, it is not unlawful for such an organisation to do any act in, or in connection with, encouraging women only, or men only, to become members of the organisation where at any time within the 12 months immediately preceding the doing of the act there were no persons of the sex in question among those members or the number of persons of that sex among the members was comparatively small[30].

1   Ie the Sex Discrimination Act 1975 Pts II–IV (ss 6–42) (as amended).
2   As to the meaning of 'act' see para 359 note 1 ante.
3   As to the meaning of 'person' see para 344 note 3 ante. In this context 'person' includes any provider of training for employment including training bodies.
4   As to the meaning of 'woman' see para 344 note 5 ante.
5   As to the meaning of 'man' see para 344 note 10 ante.
6   As to the meaning of 'training' see para 348 note 5 ante. As to the affording of access to facilities see para 361 note 11 ante.
7   Sex Discrimination Act 1975 s 47(1)(a).
8   Ibid s 47(1)(b).
9   'Month' means calendar month: Interpretation Act 1978 s 5, Sch 1.
10 For the meaning of 'Great Britain' see para 325 note 6 ante.
11 Sex Discrimination Act 1975 s 47(1) (amended by the Sex Discrimination Act 1986 s 4).
12 Ie in the Sex Discrimination Act 1975 Pts II–IV (as amended).
13 Ibid s 47(2) (amended by the Sex Discrimination Act 1986 s 4).
14 Sex Discrimination Act 1975 s 47(2)(a).
15 Ibid s 47(2)(b).
16 Ie in ibid Pts II–IV (as amended).
17 Ibid s 47(3) (amended by the Sex Discrimination Act 1986 s 4).
18 Sex Discrimination Act 1975 s 47(3) (as amended: see note 17 supra).
19 Ie ibid s 47(1)–(3) (as amended): see the text and notes 1–18 supra.
20 See ibid s 47(4) (substituted by the Sex Discrimination Act 1986 s 4). As to discrimination against applicants and employees see the Sex Discrimination Act 1975 s 6 (as amended); and paras 361–362 ante.
21 Ie ibid Pts II–IV (as amended).
22 For the meaning of 'employer' and related expressions see para 360 note 4 ante.
23 Sex Discrimination Act 1975 s 48(1)(a).

24 Ibid s 48(1)(b).
25 Ibid s 48(1).
26 Ie ibid s 12 (as amended): see para 367 ante.
27 Ibid s 48(2)(a).
28 Ibid s 48(2)(b).
29 Ibid s 48(2).
30 Ibid s 48(3).

400.   Trade union elective bodies. If a trade union or other relevant organisation[1] comprises a body the membership of which is wholly or mainly elected, the provision relating to discrimination by trade unions and other relevant organisations[2] does not render unlawful provision which ensures that a minimum number of persons of one sex are members of the body[3]: (1) by reserving seats on the body for persons of that sex[4]; or (2) by making extra seats on the body available (by election or co-option or otherwise) for persons of that sex on occasions when the number of persons of that sex in the other seats is below the minimum[5], where in the opinion of the organisation the provision is in the circumstances needed to secure a reasonable lower limit to the number of members of that sex serving on the body, and nothing in Parts II to IV of the Sex Discrimination Act 1975[6] renders unlawful any act[7] done in order to give effect to such a provision[8].

This provision is not to be taken as making lawful: (a) discrimination[9] in the arrangements for determining the persons entitled to vote in an election of members of the body, or otherwise to choose the persons to serve on the body[10]; or (b) discrimination in any arrangements concerning membership of the organisation itself[11].

1   Ie an organisation to which the Sex Discrimination Act 1975 s 12 (as amended) applies: see para 367 ante.
2   Ie ibid s 12 (as amended): see para 367 ante.
3   Ibid s 49(1).
4   Ibid s 49(1)(a).
5   Ibid s 49(1)(b).
6   Ie ibid Pts II–IV (ss 6–42) (as amended).
7   As to the meaning of 'act' see para 359 note 1 ante.
8   Sex Discrimination Act 1975 s 49(1).
9   For the meaning of 'discrimination' see para 344 note 4 ante.
10 Sex Discrimination Act 1975 s 49(2)(a).
11 Ibid s 49(2)(b).

401.   Acts done for the purposes of protection of women. Any act[1] done by a person[2] in relation to a woman[3] is not unlawful[4] if: (1) it was necessary for that person to do it in order to comply with a requirement of an existing statutory provision[5] concerning the protection of women[6]; or (2) it was necessary for that person to do it in order to comply with a requirement of a relevant statutory provision[7] and it was done by that person for the purpose of the protection of the woman in question (or of any class of women that included that woman)[8].

1   As to the meaning of 'act' see para 359 note 1 ante.
2   As to the meaning of 'person' see para 344 note 3 ante.
3   As to the meaning of 'woman' see para 344 note 5 ante.
4   Ie under the Sex Discrimination Act 1975 Pt II (ss 6–20A) (as amended), Pt III (ss 21A–36) (as amended) so far as it applies to vocational training, or Pt IV (ss 37–42) (as amended) so far as it has effect in relation to the provisions mentioned in heads (1) and (2) in the text: see s 51(1) (s 51 substituted by the Employment Act 1989 s 3(1), (3)). In the provisions of any Order in Council modifying the effect of the Sex Discrimination Act 1975 s 52 (see para 403 post), 'vocational training' includes advanced vocational training and retraining; and any reference to vocational training in those provisions is to be construed as including a reference to vocational guidance: s 52A (added by the Employment Act 1989 s 3(1), (4); and amended by the Employment Equality (Sex Discrimination) Regulations 2005, SI 2005/2467, reg 17(2)). As to the meaning of 'training' see para 348 note 5 ante.

5　'Existing statutory provision' means any provision of: (1) an Act passed before the Sex Discrimination Act 1975; or (2) an instrument approved or made by or under such an Act (including one approved or made after the passing of the Sex Discrimination Act 1975): s 51(3) (as substituted: see note 4 supra). Where an Act passed after the Sex Discrimination Act 1975 re-enacts (with or without modification) a provision of an Act passed before the Sex Discrimination Act 1975, that provision as re-enacted is to be treated for the purposes of s 51(3) (as substituted) as if it continued to be contained in an Act passed before the Sex Discrimination Act 1975: s 51(4) (as so substituted). 'Instruments' covers not only statutory instruments. For instance, in cases concerning s 51 (as originally enacted) the statutes of an Oxford college (see *Hugh-Jones v St John's College, Cambridge* [1979] ICR 848, 123 Sol Jo 603, EAT) and a local authority wrestling licence (see *Greater London Council v Farrar* [1980] 1 WLR 608, [1980] ICR 266, EAT) were both held to be 'instruments'.

6　Sex Discrimination Act 1975 s 51(1)(i) (as substituted: see note 4 supra). The reference to an existing statutory provision concerning the protection of women is a reference to: (1) any such provision having effect for the purpose of protecting women as regards pregnancy or maternity; or (2) other circumstances giving rise to risks specifically affecting women, whether the provision relates only to such protection or to the protection of any other class of persons as well: s 51(2)(a) (as so substituted).

7　Ie within the meaning of the Health and Safety at Work etc Act 1974 Pt I (ss 1–54) (as amended): see HEALTH AND SAFETY AT WORK vol 20(1) (Reissue) para 502. See *Page v Freight Hire (Tank Haulage) Ltd* [1981] 1 All ER 394, [1981] ICR 299, EAT.

8　Sex Discrimination Act 1975 s 51(1)(ii) (as substituted: see note 4 supra). The reference to the protection of a particular woman or class of women is a reference to the protection of that woman or those women as regards any circumstances falling within head (1) or head (2) in note 6 supra: s 51(2)(b) (as so substituted).
　　　Without prejudice to the operation of s 51 (as substituted), nothing in Pt II (as amended), Pt III (as amended) so far as it applies to vocational training, or Pt IV so far as it has effect in relation to Pt II (as amended) or Pt III (as amended), renders unlawful any act done by a person in relation to a woman (i e a female person of any age) if it was necessary for that person to do that act in order to comply with any requirement of any of the specified provisions concerned with the protection of women at work: see the Employment Act 1989 s 4. As to the specified provisions see s 4, Sch 1.

402.　Acts done under statutory authority.　An act[1] done by a person[2] is not rendered unlawful by the relevant provisions of the Sex Discrimination Act 1975[3] if it was necessary for that person to do it in order to comply with a requirement of an existing statutory provision[4].

1　As to the meaning of 'act' see para 359 note 1 ante.
2　As to the meaning of 'person' see para 344 note 3 ante.
3　Ie the relevant provisions of the Sex Discrimination Act 1975 Pt III (ss 21A–36) (as amended), or Pt IV (ss 37–42) (as amended) so far as it has effect in relation to those provisions: s 51A(a), (b) (s 51A added by the Employment Act 1989 s 3(1), (3)). 'The relevant provisions of Pt III' means the provisions of the Sex Discrimination Act 1975 Pt III (as amended) except so far as they apply to vocational training: see s 51A(2) (as so added). As to the meaning of 'vocational training' see para 401 note 4 ante.
4　Ibid s 51A(1) (as added: see note 3 supra). For the meaning of 'existing statutory provision' see para 401 note 5 ante; definition applied by s 51A(1) (as so added).

403.　Acts safeguarding national security.　Nothing in Parts II to IV of the Sex Discrimination Act 1975[1] renders unlawful an act[2] done for the purpose of safeguarding national security[3]. A certificate purporting to be signed by or on behalf of a Minister of the Crown and certifying that an act specified in the certificate was done for the purpose of safeguarding national security is conclusive evidence that it was done for that purpose[4].

1　Ie the Sex Discrimination Act 1975 Pts II–IV (ss 6–42) (as amended): see s 52(1).
2　As to the meaning of 'act' see para 359 note 1 ante.
3　Sex Discrimination Act 1975 s 52(1).
4　Ibid s 52(2). A document purporting to be such a certificate must be received in evidence and, unless the contrary is proved, is deemed to be such a certificate: s 52(3). The provisions in s 52(2), (3) no longer have effect in relation to the determination of the question as to whether any act is rendered unlawful by Pt II (ss 6–20A) (as amended), by Pt III (ss 21A–36) (as amended) so far as it applies to vocational training, or by Pt IV (ss 37–42) (as amended) taken with Pt II (as amended) or with Pt III (as amended) so far as it so applies: Sex Discrimination (Amendment) Order 1988, SI 1988/249, art 2. In effect the

court may now determine the applicability of this defence in cases relating to employment and vocational training. See Case 222/84 *Johnston v Chief Constable of the Royal Ulster Constabulary* [1987] QB 129, [1986] 3 All ER 135, ECJ.

(3) THE EQUAL OPPORTUNITIES COMMISSION

(i) Establishment, Duties and Powers

404. Establishment, incorporation and status. The Sex Discrimination Act 1975 established the Equal Opportunities Commission ('EOC')[1] which is a body of commissioners[2] consisting of at least eight but not more than fifteen individuals[3] each appointed by the Secretary of State on a full-time or part-time basis[4]. The Secretary of State is obliged to appoint one of the commissioners to be chairman of the EOC, and either one or two of the commissioners, as the Secretary of State thinks fit, to be deputy chairman or deputy chairmen of the EOC[5].

The EOC is a body corporate with perpetual succession and a common seal[6]. It is not an emanation of the Crown, and is not to act or be treated as the servant or agent of the Crown[7].

The EOC may, after consultation with the Secretary of State, appoint such officers and servants as it thinks fit, subject to the approval of the Minister for the Civil Service as to numbers and as to remuneration and other terms and conditions of service[8].

The EOC is to be replaced by the Commission for Equality and Human Rights[9].

1 See the Sex Discrimination Act 1975 s 53 (as amended). Part VI (ss 53–61) (as amended) and Sch 3 (as amended) are repealed by the Equality Act 2006 ss 40, 91, Sch 3 paras 6, 11, 20, Sch 4 as from a day to be appointed under s 93. At the date at which this volume states the law no such day had been appointed. As to the Commission for Equality and Human Rights, which is to replace the EOC, see para 305 et seq ante.

2 For these purposes, 'commissioner' means a member of the EOC: Sex Discrimination Act 1975 s 82(1).

3 The Secretary of State may by order amend ibid s 53(1) (as amended) so far as it regulates the number of commissioners: s 53(3). So far as exercisable in relation to Wales, the function of the Secretary of State under s 53(1) (as amended) of making appointments to the EOC is exercisable only with the agreement of the National Assembly for Wales so far as necessary to ensure that there is at all times one commissioner who has been appointed with the agreement of the Assembly: National Assembly for Wales (Transfer of Functions) Order 1999, SI 1999/672, art 5(1), Sch 2. As to the Secretary of State and the National Assembly for Wales see para 302 ante.

   The validity of any proceedings of the EOC are not affected by any vacancy among its members or by any defect in the appointment of any commissioner or additional commissioner: Sex Discrimination Act 1975 s 53(4), Sch 3 para 12. As to additional commissioners see para 407 post. As to the quorum for meetings see Sch 3 para 13.

4 See ibid s 53(1). A commissioner must hold and vacate his office in accordance with the terms of his appointment: Sch 3 para 3(1). A person may not be appointed a commissioner for more than five years: Sch 3 para 3(2). With the consent of the commissioner concerned, the Secretary of State may alter the terms of an appointment so as to make a full-time commissioner into a part-time commissioner or vice versa, or for any other purpose: Sch 3 para 3(3). A commissioner may resign by notice to the Secretary of State: Sch 3 para 3(4). The Secretary of State may terminate the appointment of a commissioner if satisfied that: (1) without the consent of the EOC, he failed to attend the meetings of the EOC during a continuous period of six months beginning not earlier than nine months before the termination; (2) he is an undischarged bankrupt, or has made an arrangement with his creditors; or (3) he is by reason of physical or mental illness, or for any other reason, incapable of carrying out his duties: Sch 3 para 3(5). Past service as a commissioner is no bar to re-appointment: Sch 3 para 3(6). The Secretary of State may pay, or make such payments towards the provision of, such remuneration, pensions, allowances or gratuities to or in respect of the commissioners or any of them as, with the consent of the Minister for the Civil Service, he may determine: Sch 3 para 5. Where a person ceases to be a commissioner otherwise than on the expiry of his term of office, and it appears to the Secretary of State that there are special circumstances which make it right for that person to receive compensation, the Secretary of State may with the consent of the Minister for the Civil Service direct the EOC to make to that person a

payment of such amount as, with the consent of that Minister, the Secretary of State may determine: Sch 3 para 6. As to the Minister for the Civil Service see CONSTITUTIONAL LAW AND HUMAN RIGHTS vol 8(2) (Reissue) para 427 et seq.

The Secretary of State must pay to the EOC expenses incurred or to be incurred by it under Sch 3 paras 6, 7 and 8 (see para 407 post), and, with the consent of the Minister for the Civil Service and the Treasury, must pay to the EOC such sums as the Secretary of State thinks fit for enabling the EOC to meet other expenses: Sch 3 para 14. As to the Treasury see CONSTITUTIONAL LAW AND HUMAN RIGHTS vol 8(2) (Reissue) paras 512–517.

There is to be defrayed out of money provided by Parliament sums required by the Secretary of State for making payments under Sch 3 para 5 or Sch 3 para 14, and for defraying any other expenditure falling to be made by him under or by virtue of the Sex Discrimination Act 1975: s 84(a).

5   Ibid s 53(2)(a), (b). The chairman and each deputy chairman must hold and vacate his office in accordance with the terms of his appointment, and may resign by notice to the Secretary of State: Sch 3 para 4(1). The office of the chairman or a deputy chairman is vacated if he ceases to be a commissioner: Sch 3 para 4(2). Past service as chairman or a deputy chairman is no bar to re-appointment: Sch 3 para 4(3).

6   See ibid Sch 3 para 1. As to bodies corporate see generally CORPORATIONS.

7   See ibid Sch 3 para 2(1). Accordingly, neither the EOC nor a commissioner or member of its staff as such is entitled to any status, immunity, privilege or exemption enjoyed by the Crown (Sch 3 para 2(2)(a)); the commissioners and members of the staff of the EOC as such are not civil servants (Sch 3 para 2(2)(b)); and the EOC's property is not property of, or held on behalf of, the Crown (Sch 3 para 2(2)(c)). As to Crown privilege see CROWN AND ROYAL FAMILY vol 12(1) (Reissue) para 52 et seq; and see also CONSTITUTIONAL LAW AND HUMAN RIGHTS; CROWN PROCEEDINGS AND CROWN PRACTICE; CROWN PROPERTY. Due to its independence from the Crown, the EOC is able to take legal action against government departments: see e g *R v Secretary of State for Employment, ex p Equal Opportunities Commission* [1995] 1 AC 1, sub nom *Equal Opportunities Commission v Secretary of State for Employment* [1994] 1 All ER 910, HL; and c f *Home Office v Commission for Racial Equality* [1982] QB 385, [1981] 1 All ER 1042.

8   Sex Discrimination Act 1975 Sch 3 para 8. Employment with the EOC is included among the kinds of employment to which a superannuation scheme under the Superannuation Act 1972 s 1 (as amended) can apply: see the Sex Discrimination Act 1975 Sch 3 para 9(1). See also the Superannuation Act 1972 s 1, Sch 1 (both as amended); and CONSTITUTIONAL LAW AND HUMAN RIGHTS vol 8(2) (Reissue) para 567 et seq. Where a person who is employed by the EOC and who is, by reference to that employment, a participant in such a scheme becomes a commissioner or an additional commissioner, the Minister for the Civil Service may determine that his service as a commissioner or additional commissioner is to be treated for the purposes of the scheme as service as an employee of the EOC; and his rights under the scheme are not affected by the Sex Discrimination Act 1975 Sch 3 para 5 or Sch 3 para 7(2): Sch 3 para 9(2).

The Employers' Liability (Compulsory Insurance) Act 1969 (see EMPLOYMENT vol 16(1A) (Reissue) para 40 et seq) does not require insurance to be effected by the EOC: Sex Discrimination Act 1975 Sch 3 para 10.

9   See note 1 supra.

405.   General duties and powers. The duties of the Equal Opportunities Commission ('EOC') are as follows: (1) to work towards the elimination of discrimination[1]; (2) to work towards the elimination of harassment that is contrary to any of the provisions of the Sex Discrimination Act 1975[2]; (3) to promote equality of opportunity between men[3] and women[4] generally[5]; (4) to promote equality of opportunity, in the field of employment[6] and of vocational training, for persons who intend to undergo, are undergoing or have undergone gender reassignment[7]; and (5) to keep under review the working of the Sex Discrimination Act 1975 and the Equal Pay Act 1970[8] and, when it is so required by the Secretary of State[9] or otherwise thinks it necessary, to draw up and submit to the Secretary of State proposals for amending them[10]. The EOC may undertake or assist, financially or otherwise, the undertaking by other persons of any research, and any educational activities, which appear to the EOC necessary or expedient for these purposes[11].

Without prejudice to the generality of heads (1) to (5) above, the EOC, in pursuance of the duties imposed by heads (1) and (2) above[12]: (a) must keep under review the relevant statutory provisions[13] in so far as they require men and women to be treated differently[14]; and (b) if so required by the Secretary of State, make to him a report on any matter specified by him which is connected with those duties and concerns the relevant statutory provisions[15]. Any such report must be made within the time specified by the Secretary of State, and the Secretary of State must cause the report to be published[16]. Whenever the EOC thinks it necessary, it must draw up and submit to the Secretary of State proposals for amending the relevant statutory provisions[17]. The EOC must carry out its duties in relation to the relevant statutory provisions in consultation with the Health and Safety Commission[18].

The EOC may make arrangements for the regulation of its proceedings and business and may vary or revoke those arrangements[19].

The EOC must make an annual report as soon as practicable after the end of each calendar year to the Secretary of State on its activities during the year[20]. It is also the duty of the EOC: (i) to keep proper accounts and proper records in relation to the accounts; (ii) to prepare in respect of each accounting year a statement of accounts in such form as the Secretary of State may direct with the approval of the Treasury; and (iii) to send copies of the statement to the Secretary of State and the Comptroller and Auditor General before the end of the month of November next following the accounting year to which the statement relates[21].

1   Sex Discrimination Act 1975 s 53(1)(a). Part VI (ss 53–61) (as amended) and Sch 3 (as amended) are repealed by the Equality Act 2006 ss 40, 91, Sch 3 paras 6, 11, 20, Sch 4 as from a day to be appointed under s 93. At the date at which this volume states the law no such day had been appointed. As to the Commission for Equality and Human Rights, which is to replace the EOC, see para 305 et seq ante.
    For the meaning of 'discrimination' see para 310 note 4 ante.
    See *R v Secretary of State for Employment, ex p Equal Opportunities Commission* [1995] 1 AC 1, sub nom *Equal Opportunities Commission v Secretary of State for Employment* [1994] 1 All ER 910, HL (EOC held to have locus standi in bringing proceedings against the Secretary of State for the purpose of challenging as incompatible with European Community law certain provisions of the Employment Protection (Consolidation) Act 1978 (now repealed) limiting the rights of employees to compensation for unfair dismissal and receipt of statutory redundancy pay). See also *Home Office v Commission for Racial Equality* [1982] QB 385, [1981] 1 All ER 1042 (a case involving the parallel provisions under the Race Relations Act 1976).
2   Sex Discrimination Act 1975 s 53(1)(aa) (added by the Employment Equality (Sex Discrimination) Regulations 2005, SI 2005/2467, reg 27(1)). As to harassment, including sexual harassment, see the Sex Discrimination Act 1975 s 4A (as added); and para 347 ante.
3   As to the meaning of 'man' see para 344 note 10 ante.
4   As to the meaning of 'woman' see para 344 note 5 ante.
5   Sex Discrimination Act 1975 s 53(1)(b).
6   For the meaning of 'employment' see para 360 note 4 ante.
7   Sex Discrimination Act 1975 s 53(1)(ba) (added by the Sex Discrimination (Gender Reassignment) Regulations 1999, SI 1999/1102, reg 7(1)). For the meaning of 'gender reassignment' see para 348 note 9 ante. As to discrimination on the grounds of gender reassignment see para 348 ante.
8   As to the Equal Pay Act 1970 see para 424 et seq post.
9   As to the Secretary of State and the National Assembly for Wales see para 302 ante.
10 Sex Discrimination Act 1975 s 53(1)(c).
11 Ibid s 54(1). The EOC may make charges for educational or other facilities or services made available by it: s 54(2).
12 See ibid s 55(1).
13 'The relevant statutory provisions' has the meaning given by the Health and Safety at Work etc Act 1974 s 53 (as amended) (see HEALTH AND SAFETY AT WORK vol 20(1) (Reissue) para 502): Sex Discrimination Act 1975 s 55(4).
14 Ibid s 55(1)(a).
15 Ibid s 55(1)(b).
16 Ibid s 55(1).
17 Ibid s 55(2).
18 Ibid s 55(3). As to the Health and Safety Commission see HEALTH AND SAFETY AT WORK vol 20(1) (Reissue) para 562 et seq.
19 Ibid s 53(4), Sch 3 para 11(1). The arrangements may, with the approval of the Secretary of State, provide for the discharge under the general direction of the EOC of any of the EOC's functions by a committee

of the EOC, or by two or more commissioners: Sch 3 para 11(2). Anything done by or in relation to a committee, or commissioners, in the discharge of the EOC's functions has the same effect as if done by or in relation to the EOC: Sch 3 para 11(3).

20 See ibid s 56(1). Each annual report must include a general survey of developments, during the period to which it relates, in respect of matters falling within the scope of the EOC's duties: s 56(2). The Secretary of State must lay a copy of every annual report before each House of Parliament, and cause the report to be published: s 56(3).

21 Ibid Sch 3 para 15(2) (Sch 3 para 15 substituted by the Race Relations Act 1976 s 79(4), Sch 4 para 9). The accounting year of the EOC is the 12 months ending on 31 March: Sex Discrimination Act 1975 Sch 3 para 15(1) (as so substituted). The Comptroller and Auditor General must examine, certify and report on each such statement received by him and must lay copies of each statement and of his report before each House of Parliament: Sch 3 para 15(3) (as so substituted). As to the Comptroller and Auditor General see CONSTITUTIONAL LAW AND HUMAN RIGHTS vol 8(2) (Reissue) paras 724–726. As to the Treasury see CONSTITUTIONAL LAW AND HUMAN RIGHTS vol 8(2) (Reissue) paras 512–517.

(ii) Specific Functions

406.   Power to issue codes of practice.   The Equal Opportunities Commission ('EOC') may issue codes of practice containing such practical guidance as it thinks fit for the elimination of discrimination[1] in the field of employment[2], the elimination in that field of harassment that is contrary to the provisions of the Sex Discrimination Act 1975[3], the promotion of equality of opportunity in that field between men[4] and women[5], and the promotion of equality of opportunity in that field for persons who intend to undergo, are undergoing or have undergone gender reassignment[6].

When the EOC proposes to issue a code of practice, it must prepare and publish a draft of that code, and consider any representations made to it about the draft, and may modify the draft accordingly[7].

In the course of preparing any draft code of practice for eventual publication, the EOC must consult with such organisations or associations of organisations representative of employers or of workers, and such other organisations or bodies, as appear to the EOC to be appropriate[8]. If the EOC determines to proceed with any draft code of practice, the draft must be approved by the Secretary of State who, if he approves it, must lay it before both Houses of Parliament[9].

The EOC may from time to time revise the whole or any part of a code of practice and issue a revised code[10].

A failure on the part of any person[11] to observe any provision of a code of practice does not of itself render him liable to any proceedings, but in any proceedings under the Sex Discrimination Act 1975 or the Equal Pay Act 1970 before an employment tribunal any code of practice issued[12] is admissible in evidence, and if any provision of such a code appears to the tribunal to be relevant to any question arising in the proceedings it must be taken into account in determining that question[13].

The EOC has issued a code of practice on equal opportunity policies, procedures and practices in employment[4], and a code of practice on equal pay[15]. The EOC has also issued the gender equality duty code of practice[16].

Employment tribunals considering cases of alleged sexual harassment can receive assistance from the code of practice[17]. However, a code of practice does not impose legal obligations of itself[18].

1 For the meaning of 'discrimination' see para 344 note 4 ante.

2 See the Sex Discrimination Act 1975 s 56A(1)(a) (s 56A added by the Race Relations Act 1976 s 76, Sch 4 para 1). The Sex Discrimination Act 1975 Pt VI (ss 53–61) (as amended) is repealed by the Equality Act 2006 ss 40, 91, Sch 3 paras 6, 11, Sch 4 as from a day to be appointed under s 93. At the date at which this volume states the law no such day had been appointed. As to the Commission for Equality and Human Rights, which is to replace the EOC, see para 305 et seq ante.

For the meaning of 'employment' see para 360 note 4 ante.

Without prejudice to the Sex Discrimination Act 1975 s 56A(1) (as added and amended), a code of practice issued under this provision may include such practical guidance as the EOC thinks fit as to what steps it is reasonably practicable for employers to take for the purpose of preventing their employees from doing in the course of their employment acts made unlawful by the Sex Discrimination Act 1975: s 56A(11) (as so added). See also para 343 notes 9, 10 ante.

3   Ibid s 56A(1)(aa) (added by the Employment Equality (Sex Discrimination) Regulations 2005, SI 2005/2467, reg 27(2)). As to harassment, including sexual harassment, see the Sex Discrimination Act 1975 s 4A (as added); and para 347 ante.

4   As to the meaning of 'man' see para 344 note 10 ante.

5   Sex Discrimination Act 1975 s 56A(1)(b) (as added: see note 2 supra). As to the meaning of 'woman' see para 344 note 5 ante.

6   Ibid s 56A(1)(ba) (added by the Sex Discrimination (Gender Reassignment) Regulations 1999, SI 1999/1102, reg 7(2)). For the meaning of 'gender reassignment' see para 348 note 9 ante. As to discrimination on the grounds of gender reassignment see para 348 ante.

7   Sex Discrimination Act 1975 s 56A(2) (as added: see note 2 supra).

8   Ibid s 56A(3) (as added: see note 2 supra).

9   See ibid s 56A(4) (as added: see note 2 supra). If the EOC determines to proceed with the draft, it must transmit the draft to the Secretary of State who must, if he approves of it, lay it before both Houses of Parliament, and, if he does not approve of it, publish details of his reasons for withholding approval: s 56A(4) (as so added). If, within the period of 40 days beginning with the day on which a copy of a draft code of practice is laid before each House of Parliament, or, if such copies are laid on different days, with the later of the two days, either House so resolves, no further proceedings may be taken on that draft, but without prejudice to the laying before Parliament of a new draft: s 56A(5) (as so added). In reckoning the period of 40 days, no account is to be taken of any period during which Parliament is dissolved or prorogued or during which both Houses are adjourned for more than four days: s 56A(6) (as so added). If no such resolution is passed, the EOC may issue the code in the form of the draft and the code will come into effect on such day as the Secretary of State may by order appoint, and such order may contain transitional provisions and savings: see s 56A(7), (8) (as so added).

10 Ibid s 56A(9) (as added: see note 2 supra). Section 56A(2)–(8) (as added) applies to the revised code as it applies to the first issue of a code: see s 56A(9) (as so added).

11 As to the meaning of 'person' see para 344 note 3 ante.

12 Ie issued under the Sex Discrimination Act 1975 s 56A (as added and amended).

13 Ibid s 56A(10) (as added (see note 2 supra); and amended by the Trade Union Reform and Employment Rights Act 1993 s 49(1), Sch 7 para 15; and by virtue of the Employment Rights (Dispute Resolution) Act 1998 s 1(2)(a)). As to the Equal Pay Act 1970 see para 424 et seq post.

14 See the Equal Opportunities Commission's Code of Practice: Equal Opportunity Policies, Procedures and Practices in Employment (30 April 1985); and the Sex Discrimination Code of Practice Order 1985, SI 1985/387.

15 See the Equal Opportunities Commission's Code of Practice on Equal Pay, which came into effect on 1 December 2003 (revising the version dated 26 March 1997); and the Code of Practice on Equal Pay Order 2003, SI 2003/2865.

16 See the Equal Opportunities Commission's Gender Equality Duty Code of Practice (England and Wales) (April 2007); and para 343 ante. The new duty referred to in that code is said to challenge public bodies to provide services and adopt policies that promote equality for men and women, rather than leaving it to individuals to challenge poor practice. As to the statutory duties see the Sex Discrimination Act 1975 s 21A (as added and amended) (see para 394 ante) and s 76A (as added) (see para 343 ante).

17 *Wadman v Carpenter Farrer Partnership* [1993] IRLR 374, EAT.

18 See *West Midlands Passenger Executive v Singh* [1988] 2 All ER 873, [1988] 1 WLR 730, CA; *Carrington v Helix Lighting Ltd* [1990] ICR 125, [1990] IRLR 6, EAT.

407.   Power to conduct formal investigations.   The Equal Opportunities Commission ('EOC') may if it thinks fit, and must if required by the Secretary of State[1], conduct a formal investigation for any purpose connected with the carrying out of its general duties[2].

The EOC may, with the approval of the Secretary of State, appoint, on a full-time or part-time basis, one or more individuals as additional commissioners[3] for the purposes of a formal investigation[4]. The EOC may nominate one or more commissioners, with or without one or more additional commissioners, to conduct a formal investigation on its behalf, and may delegate any of its functions in relation to the investigation to the persons so nominated[5]. The Secretary of State, or the EOC acting with his approval, may terminate the appointment of an additional commissioner in certain circumstances[6].

1   As to the Secretary of State and the National Assembly for Wales see para 302 ante.

2   See the Sex Discrimination Act 1975 s 57(1). This power is without prejudice to the EOC's general power to do anything requisite for the performance of its duties under s 53(1) (as amended) (see para 405 ante): s 57(1). Part VI (ss 53–61) (as amended) and Sch 3 (as amended) are repealed by the Equality Act 2006 ss 40, 91, Sch 3 paras 6, 11, 20, Sch 4 as from a day to be appointed under s 93. At the date at which this volume states the law no such day had been appointed. As to the Commission for Equality and Human Rights, which is to replace the EOC, see para 305 et seq ante.

3   The EOC may pay, or make such payments towards the provision of, such remuneration, pensions, allowances or gratuities to or in respect of an additional commissioner as the Secretary of State, with the consent of the Minister for the Civil Service, may determine: Sex Discrimination Act 1975 s 53(4), Sch 3 para 7(2). For the meaning of 'commissioner' see para 404 note 2 ante. As to the Minister for the Civil Service see CONSTITUTIONAL LAW AND HUMAN RIGHTS vol 8(2) (Reissue) para 427 et seq. With the approval of the Secretary of State and the consent of the additional commissioner concerned, the EOC may alter the terms of an appointment of an additional commissioner so as to make a full-time additional commissioner into a part-time additional commissioner or vice versa, or for any other purpose: Sch 3 para 7(3). An additional commissioner may resign by notice to the EOC: Sch 3 para 7(4). The appointment of an additional commissioner terminates at the conclusion of the investigation for which he was appointed, if not sooner: Sch 3 para 7(6). Schedule 3 paras 2(2), 3(1), (6), 6 (see para 404 ante) apply to additional commissioners appointed under s 57(2) as they apply to commissioners: Sch 3 para 7(1).

4   Ibid s 57(2).

5   Ibid s 57(3). In practice the commissioners will inevitably rely upon the EOC employees to collect evidence during any investigation. They are entitled to do so: cf *R v Commission for Racial Equality, ex p Cottrell and Rothon* [1980] 1 WLR 1580, [1980] IRLR 279.

6   The Secretary of State, or the EOC acting with the approval of the Secretary of State, may terminate the appointment of an additional commissioner if satisfied that: (1) without reasonable excuse he failed to carry out the duties for which he was appointed during a continuous period of three months beginning not earlier than six months before the termination; (2) he is an undischarged bankrupt or has made an arrangement with his creditors; or (3) he is by reason of physical or mental illness, or for any other reason, incapable of carrying out his duties: see the Sex Discrimination Act 1975 Sch 3 para 7(5).

408. Conduct of formal investigations. The Equal Opportunities Commission ('EOC') must not embark on a formal investigation[1] unless the following requirements have been complied with[2]. Terms of reference for the investigation must be drawn up by the EOC or, if the EOC was required by the Secretary of State[3] to conduct the investigation, by the Secretary of State after consulting the EOC[4]. The EOC must give general notice[5] of the holding of the investigation unless the terms of reference confine it to activities of persons[6] named in them, but in such a case the EOC must in the prescribed[7] manner give those persons notice of the holding of the investigation[8]. Where the terms of reference of the investigation confine it to activities of persons named in them and the EOC in the course of it proposes to investigate any act[9] made unlawful by the Sex Discrimination Act 1975 which it believes that a person so named may have done[10], the EOC must inform that person of its belief and of its proposal to investigate the act in question[11] and offer him an opportunity of making oral or written representations or both with regard to it[12]. A person so named who avails himself of the opportunity of making oral representations may be represented by counsel or a solicitor[13] or by some other person of his choice, not being a person to whom the EOC objects on the ground that he is unsuitable[14].

1   'Formal investigation' means an investigation under the Sex Discrimination Act 1975 s 57 (see para 407 ante): s 82(1). That definition is repealed by the Equality Act 2006 ss 40, 91, Sch 3 paras 6, 18(a)(ii), Sch 4 as from a day to be appointed under s 93. At the date at which this volume states the law no such day had been appointed. See also note 2 infra.

2   See the Sex Discrimination Act 1975 s 58(1). Part VI (ss 53–61) (as amended) is repealed by the Equality Act 2006 ss 40, 91, Sch 3 paras 6, 11, Sch 4 as from a day to be appointed under s 93. At the date at

which this volume states the law no such day had been appointed. As to the Commission for Equality and Human Rights, which is to replace the EOC, see para 305 et seq ante.

3 As to the Secretary of State and the National Assembly for Wales see para 302 ante.

4 Sex Discrimination Act 1975 s 58(2). The EOC or, if the EOC was required by the Secretary of State to conduct the investigation, the Secretary of State after consulting the EOC may from time to time revise the terms of reference; and the provisions of s 58(1), (3), (3A) (as added) apply to the revised investigation and terms of reference as they applied to the original: s 58(4) (amended by the Race Relations Act 1976 s 79(4), Sch 4 para 2).

5 'General notice', in relation to any person, means a notice published by him at a time and in a manner appearing to him suitable for securing that the notice is seen within a reasonable time by persons likely to be affected by it: Sex Discrimination Act 1975 s 82(1). For the meaning of 'notice' see para 378 note 8 ante.

6 As to the meaning of 'person' see para 344 note 3 ante.

7 'Prescribed' means prescribed by regulations made by the Secretary of State by statutory instrument: ibid s 82(1). See note 8 infra.

8 Ibid s 58(3). As to the prescribed manner of giving notice see the Sex Discrimination (Formal Investigations) Regulations 1975, SI 1975/1993 (amended by SI 1977/843). Where, in pursuance of the Sex Discrimination Act 1975 s 58 (as amended), notice of the holding of a formal investigation falls to be given by the EOC to a person named in the terms of reference for the investigation, that person must be served with a notice setting out the terms of reference: Sex Discrimination (Formal Investigations) Regulations 1975, SI 1975/1993, reg 4(1). Where the terms of reference for a formal investigation are revised, reg 4(1) applies in relation to the revised investigation and terms of reference as it applied to the original: reg 4(2). Any reference to a person being served with a notice, in regs 4, 5 and 6, is a reference to service of the notice on him being effected: (1) by delivering it to him; (2) by sending it by post to him at his usual or last-known residence or place of business; (3) where the person is a body corporate or is a trade union or employers' association (see TRADE, INDUSTRY AND INDUSTRIAL RELATIONS vol 47 (2001 Reissue) paras 1001, 1201), by delivering it to the secretary or clerk of the body, union or association at its registered or principal office or by sending it by post to that secretary or clerk at that office; or (4) where the person is acting by a solicitor, by delivering it at, or by sending it by post to, the solicitor's address for service: reg 3.

9 As to the meaning of 'act' see para 359 note 1 ante.

10 Sex Discrimination Act 1975 s 58(3A) (added by the Race Relations Act 1976 s 79(4), Sch 4 para 2). There can be no investigation into a named person unless and until the EOC has sufficient evidence to believe that relevant acts may have occurred; if there is no such belief any investigation will constitute an error of law: see *Re Prestige Group plc* [1984] 1 WLR 335, [1984] ICR 473, HL. See also *Hillingdon London Borough Council v Commission for Racial Equality* [1982] AC 779, [1982] 3 WLR 159, HL. The High Court has jurisdiction to conduct a judicial review of the conduct of an investigation where the EOC has exceeded its powers or acted unfairly: see *R v Commssion for Racial Equality, ex p Cottrell and Rothon* [1980] 1 WLR 1580, [1980] IRLR 279; *R v Commssion for Racial Equality, ex p Westminster City Council* [1985] ICR 827, [1985] IRLR 426, CA.

11 Sex Discrimination Act 1975 s 58(3A)(a) (as added: see note 10 supra).

12 Ibid s 58(3A)(b) (as added: see note 10 supra).

13 Ibid s 58(3A)(i) (as added: see note 10 supra).

14 Ibid s 58(3A)(ii) (as added: see note 10 supra).

409. Power to obtain information. For the purposes of a formal investigation[1] the Equal Opportunities Commission ('EOC') may by notice[2] require any person[3] to furnish such written information as may be described in the notice, and may specify the time at which, and the manner and form in which, the information is to be furnished[4]; and it may also require him to attend at such time and place as is specified in the notice and give oral information about, and produce all documents in his possession or control relating to, any matter specified in the notice[5].

Except where the investigation is as to compliance with a non-discrimination notice[6], a notice may be served only where it has been authorised by an order made by or on behalf of the Secretary of State[7], or the terms of reference of the investigation state that the EOC believes that a person named in them may have done or may be doing unlawful acts of discrimination or harassment[8], or may have contravened the provisions of the Sex Discrimination Act 1975 relating to discriminatory practices[9], or advertisements, or instructions or pressure to discriminate[10], or may be doing acts in breach of a term modified or included by virtue of an equality clause[11], and confine the investigation to those acts[12].

1   For the meaning of 'formal investigation' see para 408 note 1 ante.
2   Sex Discrimination Act 1975 s 59(1). The notice must be in the prescribed form and served in the prescribed manner: see s 59(1). Part VI (ss 53–61) (as amended) is repealed by the Equality Act 2006 ss 40, 91, Sch 3 paras 6, 11, Sch 4 as from a day to be appointed under s 93. At the date at which this volume states the law no such day had been appointed. As to the Commission for Equality and Human Rights, which is to replace the EOC, see para 305 et seq ante.
    For the meaning of 'notice' see para 378 note 8 ante; and for the meaning of 'prescribed' see para 408 note 7 ante. For the prescribed form see the Sex Discrimination (Formal Investigations) Regulations 1975, SI 1975/1993, reg 5, Sch 1. As to the service of notices see para 408 note 8 ante.
3   As to the meaning of 'person' see para 344 note 3 ante.
4   Sex Discrimination Act 1975 s 59(1)(a). See also note 5 infra.
5   Ibid s 59(1)(b). A notice may not require a person: (1) to give information, or produce any documents, which he could not be compelled to give in evidence, or produce, in civil proceedings before the High Court; or (2) to attend at any place unless the necessary expenses of his journey to and from that place are paid or tendered to him: s 59(3).
    If a person fails to comply with a notice served on him or the EOC has reasonable cause to believe that he intends not to comply with it, the EOC may apply to a county court for an order requiring him to comply with it or with such directions for the like purpose as may be contained in the order: s 59(4). A person who fails to comply with such an order made by a county court is liable to a fine: see s 59(4) (amended by the County Courts Act 1984 s 148(1), Sch 2 para 54). See also the County Courts Act 1984 s 55 (as amended); and PRACTICE AND PROCEDURE vol 37 (Reissue) para 985.
    A person commits an offence punishable on summary conviction by a fine not exceeding level 5 on the standard scale if he: (a) wilfully alters, suppresses, conceals or destroys a document which he has been required by a notice or order to produce; or (b) in complying with such a notice or order, knowingly or recklessly makes any statement which is false in a material particular: Sex Discrimination Act 1975 s 59(6) (amended by virtue of the Criminal Justice Act 1982 ss 38, 46). As to the standard scale see para 315 note 15 ante. Proceedings for an offence under the Sex Discrimination Act 1975 s 59(6) (as amended) may (without prejudice to any jurisdiction exercisable apart from this provision) be instituted against any person at any place at which he has an office or other place of business or against an individual at any place where he resides, or at which he is for the time being: s 59(7).
6   Ie under ibid s 69. If the terms of reference of a formal investigation state that its purpose is to determine whether any requirements of a non-discrimination notice are being or have been carried out, but s 59(2)(b) (as amended) does not apply, and s 58(3) (see para 408 ante) is complied with in relation to the investigation on a date ('the commencement date') not later than the expiration of the period of five years beginning when the non-discrimination notice became final, the EOC may within a specified period serve notices under s 59(1) for the purposes of the investigation without needing to obtain the consent of the Secretary of State: s 69(1). The specified period begins on the commencement date and ends on the later of either the date on which the period of five years beginning when the non-discrimination notice became final expires or the date two years after the commencement date: s 69(2). As to the terms of reference see para 408 ante. As to the Secretary of State and the National Assembly for Wales see para 302 ante. Section 69 is repealed by the Equality Act 2006 ss 40, 91, Sch 3 paras 6, 12, Sch 4 as from a day to be appointed under s 93. At the date at which this volume states the law no such day had been appointed. See also note 2 supra.
7   Sex Discrimination Act 1975 s 59(2)(a).
8   See ibid s 59(2)(b)(i) (amended by the Employment Equality (Sex Discrimination) Regulations 2005, SI 2005/2467, reg 27(3)). As to the meaning of 'act' see para 359 note 1 ante. For the meaning of 'discrimination' see para 344 note 4 ante. As to harassment, including sexual harassment, see the Sex Discrimination Act 1975 s 4A (as added); and para 347 ante.
9   Ie the Sex Discrimination Act 1975 s 37 (as amended) (see para 386 ante): see s 59(2)(b)(ii).
10 Ie ibid s 38 (as amended), s 39 (as amended), or s 40 (prospectively amended) (see paras 388–390 ante): see s 59(2)(b)(iii).
11 Ibid s 59(2)(b)(iv). For the meaning of 'equality clause' see para 361 note 6 ante.
12 Ibid s 59(2)(b).

410.   Restrictions on disclosure of information.   No information given to the Equal Opportunities Commission ('EOC') by any person[1] ('the informant') in connection with a formal investigation[2] may be disclosed by the EOC, or by any person who is or has been a commissioner[3], additional commissioner[4] or employee[5] of the EOC, except in specified circumstances[6]. Those circumstances are: (1) on the order of any court[7]; (2) with the informant's consent[8]; (3) in the form of a summary or other general statement published by the EOC which does not identify the informant or any other person to whom the information relates[9]; (4) in a report of the investigation published by the EOC or made available for inspection[10]; (5) to the commissioners, additional commissioners or employees of the EOC, or, so far as may be necessary for the proper performance of the functions of the EOC, to other persons[11]; or (6) for the purpose of any civil proceedings under the Sex Discrimination Act 1975 to which the EOC is a party, or any criminal proceedings[12]. In preparing any report for publication or for inspection the EOC must exclude, so far as is consistent with its duties and the object of the report, any matter which relates to the private affairs of any individual or business interests of any person where the publication of that matter might, in the opinion of the EOC, prejudicially affect that individual or person[13].

1　As to the meaning of 'person' see para 344 note 3 ante.
2　For the meaning of 'formal investigation' see para 408 note 1 ante.
3　For the meaning of 'commissioner' see para 404 note 2 ante.
4　As to additional commissioners see para 407 ante.
5　For the meaning of 'employee' see para 360 note 4 ante.
6　Sex Discrimination Act 1975 s 61(1). Any person who discloses information in contravention of this provision commits an offence and is liable on summary conviction to a fine not exceeding level 5 on the standard scale: s 61(2) (amended by virtue of the Criminal Justice Act 1982 ss 38, 46). As to the standard scale see para 315 note 15 ante. The Sex Discrimination Act 1975 Pt VI (ss 53–61) (as amended) is repealed by the Equality Act 2006 ss 40, 91, Sch 3 paras 6, 11, Sch 4 as from a day to be appointed under s 93. At the date at which this volume states the law no such day had been appointed. As to the Commission for Equality and Human Rights, which is to replace the EOC, see para 305 et seq ante.
7　Sex Discrimination Act 1975 s 61(1)(a).
8　Ibid s 61(1)(b).
9　Ibid s 61(1)(c).
10　Ibid s 61(1)(d). A report may be available for inspection under s 60(5) (see para 411 post): see s 61(1)(d).
11　Ibid s 61(1)(e).
12　Ibid s 61(1)(f).
13　Ibid s 61(3).

411.　Recommendations and reports on formal investigations. The Equal Opportunities Commission ('EOC') must make recommendations if, in the light of any of its findings in a formal investigation[1], it appears to the EOC necessary or expedient, whether during the course of the investigation or after its conclusion[2]. The EOC may make recommendations: (1) to any person[3] for changes in his policies or procedures, or as to any other matters, with a view to promoting equality of opportunity between men[4] and women[5] who are affected by any of that person's activities[6]; or (2) to the Secretary of State[7], whether for changes in the law or otherwise[8].

The EOC must prepare a report of its findings in any formal investigations conducted by it[9].

1　For the meaning of 'formal investigation' see para 408 note 1 ante.
2　Sex Discrimination Act 1975 s 60(1). Part VI (ss 53–61) (as amended) is repealed by the Equality Act 2006 ss 40, 91, Sch 3 paras 6, 11, Sch 4 as from a day to be appointed under s 93. At the date at which this volume states the law no such day had been appointed. As to the Commission for Equality and Human Rights, which is to replace the EOC, see para 305 et seq ante.
3　As to the meaning of 'person' see para 344 note 3 ante.
4　As to the meaning of 'man' see para 344 note 10 ante.
5　As to the meaning of 'woman' see para 344 note 5 ante.
6　Sex Discrimination Act 1975 s 60(1)(a).
7　As to the Secretary of State and the National Assembly for Wales see para 302 ante.
8　Sex Discrimination Act 1975 s 60(1)(b).

9   Ibid s 60(2). If the formal investigation is one required by the Secretary of State (see para 407 ante), the EOC must deliver the report to the Secretary of State to be published by him, and must not publish the report itself, unless required by the Secretary of State to do so: see s 60(3). If the formal investigation is not one required by the Secretary of State, the EOC must either publish the report, or make it, or a copy of it, available for inspection: see s 60(4), (6). Where a report is to be made available for inspection, any person is entitled, on payment of such fee (if any) as may be determined by the EOC, to inspect the report during ordinary office hours and take copies of all or any part of the report, or to obtain from the EOC a copy, certified by the EOC to be correct, of the report: s 60(5). The EOC must give general notice of the place or places where, and the times when, reports may be inspected: s 60(7). For the meaning of 'general notice' see para 408 note 5 ante.

412.   Assistance to individuals. The Equal Opportunities Commission ('EOC') may give assistance[1] to an individual who is an actual or prospective complainant or claimant in relation to proceedings or prospective proceedings either under the Sex Discrimination Act 1975 or in respect of an equality clause[2].

Where such an individual applies to the EOC for assistance, the EOC must consider the application and may grant it if it thinks fit to do so on the ground that the case raises a question of principle[3], or it is unreasonable, having regard to the complexity of the case or the applicant's position in relation to the respondent[4] or another person involved or any other matter, to expect the applicant to deal with the case unaided[5], or by reason of any other special consideration[6].

In so far as expenses are incurred by the EOC in providing the applicant with assistance, the recovery of those expenses[7] constitutes a first charge for the benefit of the EOC[8] on any costs or expenses which are payable to the applicant[9] by any other person in respect of the matter in connection with which the assistance is given[10], and so far as relates to any costs or expenses, on his rights under any compromise or settlement arrived at in connection with that matter to avoid or bring to an end any proceedings[11].

1   Assistance by the EOC may include:
    (1)   giving advice (Sex Discrimination Act 1975 s 75(2)(a));
    (2)   procuring or attempting to procure the settlement of any matter in dispute (s 75(2)(b));
    (3)   arranging for the giving of advice or assistance by a solicitor or counsel (s 75(2)(c));
    (4)   arranging for representation by any person including all such assistance as is usually given by a solicitor or counsel in the steps preliminary or incidental to any proceedings, or in arriving at or giving effect to a compromise to avoid or bring to an end any proceedings (s 75(2)(d)); or
    (5)   any other form of assistance which the EOC may consider appropriate (s 75(2)(e) (added by the Race Relations Act 1976 s 79(4), Sch 4 para 7)).
    The Sex Discrimination Act 1975 s 75(2)(d) (see head (4) supra) does not affect the law and practice regulating the descriptions of persons who may appear in, conduct, defend and address the court in, any proceedings: s 75(2). Section 75 is repealed by the Equality Act 2006 ss 40, 91, Sch 3 paras 6, 13, Sch 4 as from a day to be appointed under s 93. At the date at which this volume states the law no such day had been appointed. As to the Commission for Equality and Human Rights, which is to replace the EOC, see para 305 et seq ante.
2   See the Sex Discrimination Act 1975 s 75(1).
3   Ibid s 75(1)(a).
4   'Respondent' includes a prospective respondent: ibid s 75(5). As to possible assistance to respondents in sex discrimination cases see *Krengel v GN Taylor Builders Ltd* (1977) Times, 11 November, EAT.
5   Sex Discrimination Act 1975 s 75(1)(b).
6   Ibid s 75(1).
7   Ie expenses as taxed or assessed in such manner as may be prescribed by rules or regulations: see ibid s 75(3). 'Rules or regulations': (1) in relation to county court proceedings, means county court rules; and (2) in relation to employment tribunal proceedings, means employment tribunal procedure regulations under the Employment Tribunals Act 1996 Pt I (ss 1–19) (as amended) (see EMPLOYMENT vol 16(1B) (Reissue) para 816 et seq): Sex Discrimination Act 1975 s 75(5) (amended by the Employment Tribunals Act 1996 s 43, Sch 1 para 3; and by virtue of the Employment Rights (Dispute Resolution) Act 1998 s 1(2)(a), (c)).
8   Sex Discrimination Act 1975 s 75(3). This charge is subject to any charge imposed by the Access to Justice Act 1999 s 10(7) (see LEGAL AID vol 27(3) (2006 Reissue) para 2099), and to any provision in or made under that Act for payment of any sum to the Legal Services Commission: Sex Discrimination

Act 1975 s 75(4) (amended by the Legal Aid 1988 s 45, Sch 5 para 6; and by the Access to Justice Act 1999 s 24, Sch 4 para 13). See further LEGAL AID. As to the Legal Services Commission see LEGAL AID vol 27(3) (2006 Reissue) para 2014 et seq.

9   Ie whether by virtue of a judgment or order of a court or tribunal or an agreement or otherwise: see the Sex Discrimination Act 1975 s 75(3)(a). Note that if assistance is given on terms that the individual will not personally incur any cost then the EOC, not being a party, will be unable to recover costs through that individual: see *Walsall Metropolitan Borough Council v Sidhu* [1980] ICR 519, EAT.

10   Sex Discrimination Act 1975 s 75(3)(a).

11   Ibid s 75(3)(b).

(4) ENFORCEMENT

(i) Enforcement by the Equal Opportunities Commission

413.   Non-discrimination notices, injunctions and other enforcement proceedings.   If in the course of a formal investigation[1] the Equal Opportunities Commission ('EOC') becomes satisfied that a person[2] is committing, or has committed, an unlawful discriminatory act[3], or has applied a discriminatory practice[4], published a discriminatory advertisement or instructed or put pressure on a person to discriminate[5], or has acted in breach of a term modified or included by virtue of an equality clause[6], the EOC may, in the prescribed[7] manner, serve on him a non-discrimination notice[8] in the prescribed form[9]. Such a notice requires the person not to commit any such acts[10] and, where compliance involves changes in any of his practices or other arrangements, to inform the EOC that he has effected those changes and what those changes are, and to take such steps as may be reasonably required by the notice for the purpose of affording that information to other persons concerned[11].

Before serving a non-discrimination notice, the EOC must: (1) give the person concerned notice that it is minded to issue a non-discrimination notice in his case, specifying the grounds on which it contemplates doing so[12]; (2) offer him an opportunity of making oral or written representations or both in the matter within a period of not less than 28 days specified in the notice[13]; and (3) take account of any representations so made by him[14].

A person on whom a non-discrimination notice has been served may appeal against any requirement contained in the notice within six weeks of service[15]. Appeal is to an employment tribunal, so far as the requirement relates to acts which are within the jurisdiction of the tribunal[16] and to a county court so far as the requirement relates to acts which are within the jurisdiction of the court and are not within the jurisdiction of an employment tribunal[17]. Where the court or tribunal considers a requirement in respect of which an appeal is brought to be unreasonable because it is based on an incorrect finding of fact or for any other reason, the court or tribunal must quash the requirement[18].

The EOC must establish and maintain a register of non-discrimination notices which have become final[19].

The EOC may apply to a county court for an injunction if, within five years after the date on which a non-discrimination notice became final or a finding was made by a court or tribunal[20] that a person had done an unlawful discriminatory act or an act in breach of a term modified or included by virtue of an equality clause, it appears to the EOC that unless restrained he is likely to commit one or more unlawful discriminatory acts or acts in breach of a term modified or included by virtue of an equality clause or acts constituting the application of a discriminatory practice[21]. If the court is satisfied that the application is well-founded, it may grant the injunction in the terms applied for or in more limited terms[22].

Proceedings in relation to the provisions of the Sex Discrimination Act 1975 which prohibit discriminatory advertisements, instructions to discriminate and pressure to discriminate[23] may be brought only by the EOC[24]. Where the case is based on the employment provisions of the Sex Discrimination Act 1975[25], the EOC's application should be made to an employment tribunal[26], and in any other case to a county court[27]. The proceedings brought by the EOC may be: (a) an application for a decision whether the alleged contravention occurred[28]; or (b) where it appears to the EOC that a person has done an act which by virtue of the relevant provisions[29] was unlawful and that unless restrained he is likely to do further unlawful acts, an application to a county court for an injunction restraining him from doing such acts[30].

The EOC also has the power to present a complaint to an employment tribunal that a person has done an act within the jurisdiction of an employment tribunal[31], with a view to taking future proceedings against that person in a county court for an injunction[32], and if the tribunal considers that the complaint is well-founded it must make a finding to that effect[33].

1   For the meaning of 'formal investigation' see para 408 note 1 ante.
2   As to the meaning of 'person' see para 344 note 3 ante.
3   Sex Discrimination Act 1975 s 67(1)(a). For the meaning of 'discrimination' see para 344 note 4 ante; and as to the meaning of 'act' see para 359 note 1 ante. Sections 67–73 (as amended) are repealed by the Equality Act 2006 ss 40, 91, Sch 3 paras 6, 12, Sch 4 as from a day to be appointed under s 93. At the date at which this volume states the law no such day had been appointed. As to the Commission for Equality and Human Rights, which is to replace the EOC, see para 305 et seq ante.
4   See the Sex Discrimination Act 1975 s 67(1)(b). A discriminatory practice is one in contravention of s 37 (as amended) (see para 386 ante): see s 67(1)(b).
5   See ibid s 67(1)(c). Such offences are those in contravention of s 38 (as amended), s 39 (as amended) or s 40 (as amended) (see paras 388–390 ante): see s 67(1)(c).
6   See ibid s 67(1)(d). For the meaning of 'equality clause' see para 361 note 6 ante.
7   For the meaning of 'prescribed' see para 408 note 7 ante.
8   For the meaning of 'notice' see para 378 note 8 ante.
9   Sex Discrimination Act 1975 s 67(2). Section 67 applies whether or not proceedings have been brought in respect of the act: s 67(1). Section 67(2) does not apply to any acts in respect of which the Secretary of State could exercise the powers conferred on him by s 25(2) (as amended) (see para 378 ante), but if the EOC becomes aware of any such acts it must give notice of them to the Secretary of State or, in relation to Wales, to the National Assembly for Wales: s 67(6); National Assembly for Wales (Transfer of Functions) Order 1999, SI 1999/672, art 2, Sch 1. As to the Secretary of State and the National Assembly for Wales see para 302 ante. For the prescribed form see the Sex Discrimination (Formal Investigations) Regulations 1975, SI 1975/1993, reg 6, Sch 2 (Sch 2 substituted by SI 1977/843). As to the service of notices see para 408 note 8 ante.
10   Sex Discrimination Act 1975 s 67(2)(a).
11   Ibid s 67(2)(b). A non-discrimination notice may also require the person on whom it is served to furnish the EOC with such other information as may be reasonably required by the notice in order to verify that the notice has been complied with: s 67(3). The notice may specify the time at which, and the manner and form in which, any information is to be furnished to the EOC, but the time at which any information is to be furnished in compliance with the notice must not be later than five years after the notice has become final: s 67(4).

     For the purposes of the Sex Discrimination Act 1975, a non-discrimination notice or a finding by a court or tribunal becomes final when an appeal against the notice or finding is dismissed, withdrawn or abandoned or when the time for appealing expires without an appeal having been brought; and for this purpose an appeal against a non-discrimination notice is to be taken to be dismissed if, notwithstanding that a requirement of the notice is quashed on appeal, a direction is given in respect of it under s 68(3) (see note 18 infra): s 82(1), (4). As from a day to be appointed under the Equality Act 2006 s 93, the definition of a 'non-discrimination notice' in the Sex Discrimination Act 1975 s 82(1) (i e a notice under s 67) is repealed by the Equality Act 2006 Sch 3 paras 6, 18(a)(ii), Sch 4; and the Sex Discrimination Act 1975 s 82(4) is amended by the removal of reference to a non-discrimination notice and to appeals against such a notice (see s 82(4) (prospectively amended by the Equality Act 2006 Sch 3 paras 6, 18(b), Sch 4)). At the date at which this volume states the law no such day had been appointed.

     If a person fails to comply with a non-discrimination notice which has become final, or the EOC has reasonable grounds to believe that he intends not to comply with it, the EOC may apply to a county court for an order requiring him to comply with it or with such directions for the like purpose as may be contained in the order: see the Sex Discrimination Act 1975 s 67(7) (applying s 59(4) (as amended) (see para 409 note 5 ante)).

12 Ibid s 67(5)(a).

13 Ibid s 67(5)(b).

14 Ibid s 67(5)(c).

15 See ibid s 68(1). For an example of a case dealing with such an appeal see *Commission for Racial Equality v Amari Plastics Ltd* [1982] QB 1194, [1982] 2 All ER 499, CA.

As to the procedure on such an appeal see the Employment Tribunals (Constitution and Rules of Procedure) Regulations 2004, SI 2004/1861 (as amended); and EMPLOYMENT vol 16(1B) (Reissue) para 816 et seq.

16 Sex Discrimination Act 1975 s 68(1)(a) (s 68(1)(a), (b) amended by virtue of the Employment Rights (Dispute Resolution) Act 1998 s 1(2)(a)). See note 15 supra.

As well as this specific statutory appeal procedure it may be possible in certain circumstances to apply for judicial review in relation to the non-discrimination notice: see *R v Commission for Racial Equality, ex p Westminster City Council* [1985] ICR 827, [1985] IRLR 426, CA.

17 Sex Discrimination Act 1975 s 68(1)(b) (as amended: see note 16 supra). See note 15 supra.

18 Ibid s 68(2). On quashing a requirement the court or tribunal may direct that the non-discrimination notice is to be treated as if, in place of the requirement quashed, it had contained a requirement in terms specified in the direction: s 68(3). There is no right of appeal under s 68(1) (as amended) against a requirement treated as included in a notice by virtue of such a direction: see s 68(4).

19 Ibid s 70(1). Any person is entitled, on payment of such fee (if any) as may be determined by the EOC, to inspect the register or a copy of it during ordinary office hours and take copies of any entry, or to obtain from the EOC a copy, certified by the EOC to be correct, of any entry in the register: see s 70(2), (3). The EOC must give general notice of the place or places where and the times when, the register or a copy of it may be inspected: s 70(4). For the meaning of 'general notice' see para 408 note 5 ante.

20 Ie a finding under ibid s 63 (as amended) or s 66 (as amended) (see paras 414–415 post), or the Equal Pay Act 1970 s 2 (as amended) (see para 435 post): see the Sex Discrimination Act 1975 s 71(1).

21 Ibid s 71(1). As to discriminatory practices see note 4 supra. In proceedings under this provision the EOC may not allege that the person to whom the proceedings relate has done an act which is within the jurisdiction of an employment tribunal (see note 31 infra) unless a finding by an employment tribunal that he did that act has become final: s 71(2) (amended by virtue of the Employment Rights (Dispute Resolution) Act 1998 s 1(2)(a)).

22 Sex Discrimination Act 1975 s 71(1).

23 Ie ibid s 38 (as amended), s 39 (as amended), or s 40 (as amended): see paras 388–390 ante.

24 Ibid s 72(1).

25 Ie ibid Pt II (ss 6–20A) (as amended): see para 360 et seq ante.

26 Ibid s 72(3)(a) (amended by virtue of the Employment Rights (Dispute Resolution) Act 1998 s 1(2)(a)).

27 Sex Discrimination Act 1975 s 72(3)(b).

28 Ibid s 72(2)(a).

29 Ie by virtue of ibid s 38 (as amended), s 39 (as amended), or s 40 (as amended): see paras 388–390 ante.

30 Ibid s 72(2)(b), (4) (s 72(4) amended by the Race Relations Act 1976 s 79(4), (5), Sch 4 para 6, Sch 5). The court, if satisfied that the application is well-founded, may grant the injunction in the terms applied for or more limited terms: Sex Discrimination Act 1975 s 72(4) (as so amended). In proceedings under s 72(4) (as amended) the EOC may not allege that the person to whom the proceedings relate has done an act which is unlawful under the Sex Discrimination Act 1975 and within the jurisdiction of an employment tribunal (see note 31 infra) unless a finding by an employment tribunal that he did that act has become final: s 72(5) (amended by virtue of the Employment Rights (Dispute Resolution) Act 1998 s 1(2)(a)).

31 Acts 'within the jurisdiction of an employment tribunal' are those in respect of which such jurisdiction is conferred by the Sex Discrimination Act 1975 s 63 (as amended) (see para 414 post) and s 72 (as amended) and by the Equal Pay Act 1970 s 2 (as amended) (see para 435 post): see the Sex Discrimination Act 1975 s 73(4) (amended by virtue of the Employment Rights (Dispute Resolution) Act 1998 s 1(2)(a)).

32 Ie under the Sex Discrimination Act 1975 s 71(1) (see the text and note 21 supra) or s 72(4) (as amended): see s 73(1) (amended by virtue of the Employment Rights (Dispute Resolution) Act 1998 s 1(2)(a)).

33 Sex Discrimination Act 1975 s 73(1) (as amended: see note 32 supra). The tribunal, if it thinks it just and equitable to do so in the case of an act contravening any provision of Pt II (as amended), may also (as if the complaint had been presented by the person discriminated against) make an order declaring the rights of the complainant and the respondent in relation to the act to which the complaint relates, or a recommendation that the respondent take within a specified period action appearing to the tribunal to be

practicable for the purpose of obviating or reducing the effect on the person discriminated against of any act of discrimination to which the complaint relates, or both: see ss 65(1), 73(1) (as so amended). Section 73(1) (as amended) is without prejudice to the jurisdiction conferred by s 72(2) (see the text and notes 28–30 ante): s 73(2).

Any finding of an employment tribunal under the Sex Discrimination Act 1975 or the Equal Pay Act 1970 in respect of any act is, if it has become final, to be treated as conclusive: (1) by the county court on an application under the Sex Discrimination Act 1975 s 71(1) (see the text and note 21 supra) or s 72(4) (as amended) (see the text and note 30 supra) or in proceedings on an equality clause; and (2) by an employment tribunal on a complaint made by the person affected by the act under s 63 (as amended) (see para 414 post) or in relation to an equality clause: see s 73(3) (amended by virtue of the Employment Rights (Dispute Resolution) Act 1998 s 1(2)(a)).

(ii) Enforcement by Individuals

414. Enforcement in the employment field. A complaint by any person ('the complainant') that another person[1] ('the respondent') has committed an act of discrimination[2] or harassment[3] against the complainant which is unlawful by virtue of the provisions prohibiting discrimination in employment[4] may be presented to an employment tribunal[5].

Where an employment tribunal finds that a complaint presented to it is well-founded the tribunal must make such of the following as it considers just and equitable[6]: (1) an order declaring the rights of the complainant and the respondent in relation to the act to which the complaint relates[7]; (2) an order requiring the respondent to pay to the complainant compensation[8]; or (3) a recommendation that the respondent take within a specified period action appearing to the tribunal to be practicable for the purpose of obviating or reducing the adverse effect on the complainant of any act of discrimination to which the complaint relates[9].

As respects an unlawful act of indirect discrimination[10], if the respondent proves that the provision, criterion or practice in question was not applied with the intention of treating the complainant unfavourably on the ground of his sex or (as the case may be) that the complainant is married or a civil partner[11], an order for compensation may be made under head (2) above only in certain circumstances[12].

1   As to the meaning of 'person' see para 344 note 3 ante.
2   As to the meaning of 'act' see para 359 note 1 ante; and for the meaning of 'discrimination' see para 344 note 4 ante.
3   As to harassment, including sexual harassment, see the Sex Discrimination Act 1975 s 4A (as added); and para 347 ante.
4   Ie ibid Pt II (ss 6–20A) (as amended) or s 35A (as added and amended): see para 360 et seq ante.
5   Ibid s 63(1) (amended by virtue of the Employment Rights (Dispute Resolution) Act 1998 s 1(2)(a); and by the Employment Equality (Sex Discrimination) Regulations 2005, SI 2005/2467, reg 28(1)–(3)). See *Housing Corpn v Bryant* [1999] ICR 123, CA. As to the procedure on application to an employment tribunal see EMPLOYMENT vol 16(1B) (Reissue) para 852 et seq. A complaint may also be presented against an employer or principal or person aiding an unlawful act who is to be treated (by virtue of the Sex Discrimination Act 1975 s 41 or s 42 (as amended) (see paras 391–392 ante) as having committed an act of discrimination or harassment against the complainant: see s 63(1) (as so amended).

    Section 63(1) (as amended) does not apply to a complaint against a qualifying body (ie under s 13 (as amended): see para 368 ante) of an act in respect of which an appeal, or proceedings in the nature of an appeal, may be brought under any enactment: s 63(2).

    As to the burden of proof in relation to any complaint presented under s 63 (as amended) see s 63A (as added and amended); and para 418 post.
6   Ibid s 65(1) (amended by virtue of the Employment Rights (Dispute Resolution) Act 1998 s 1(2)(a)).
7   Sex Discrimination Act 1975 s 65(1)(a). The discriminating party's motive may be relevant to the question of whether to award a remedy under s 65 (as amended): *Chief Constable of Greater Manchester Police v Hope* [1999] ICR 338, EAT.
8   See the Sex Discrimination Act 1975 s 65(1)(b). There is now no limit on the amount of compensation a tribunal may award: see Case C-271/91 *Marshall v Southampton and South West Hampshire Health Authority (No 2)* [1994] QB 126, [1993] ICR 893, ECJ (the limit on compensation did not comply with

the requirement in EC Council Directive 76/207 (OJ L39, 14.2.76, p 40) on the implementation of the principle of equal treatment for men and women as regards access to employment, vocational training and promotion, and working conditions, art 6 that compensation for sex discrimination should be adequate). The removal of the limits was effected by the Sex Discrimination and Equal Pay (Remedies) Regulations 1993, SI 1993/2798 (revoked). The removal of the compensation limits has retrospective effect: *Harvey v Institute of the Motor Industry (No 2)* [1996] ICR 981, [1995] IRLR 416. Where an award of compensation was made in a race discrimination case prior to the removal of the limits, there was no power to reopen the question of compensation for race discrimination later when a reinstatement order made under the unfair dismissal jurisdiction was not complied with: *Lambeth London Borough Council v D'Souza* [1999] IRLR 240, CA.

Compensation must be of an amount corresponding to any damages which the respondent could have been ordered by a county court to pay to the complainant if the complaint had fallen to be dealt with under the Sex Discrimination Act 1975 s 66 (as amended) (see para 415 post): see s 65(1)(b). Compensation must be awarded on a county court basis and there is no power to award what is 'just and equitable': *Hurley v Mustoe (No 2)* [1983] ICR 422, EAT; cf *Wileman v Minilec Engineering Ltd* [1988] ICR 318, [1988] IRLR 144, EAT.

In applying the Sex Discrimination Act 1975 s 66 (as amended) (see para 415 post) for the purposes of s 65(1)(b), no account is to be taken of s 66(3) (as amended): s 65(1A) (s 65(1A), (1B) added by the Sex Discrimination and Equal Pay (Miscellaneous Amendments) Regulations 1996, SI 1996/438, reg 2). This means that damages may be awarded for unintentional indirect sex discrimination in the employment field (see para 355 ante), although there are still restrictions in respect of non-employment related sex discrimination (see para 351 ante) and all types of race discrimination. An award of compensation may include compensation for injury to feelings: see the Sex Discrimination Act 1975 s 66(4) (as amended); and para 415 post. The injury must arise directly from the act of sex discrimination in question: *Skyrail Oceanic Ltd v Coleman* [1981] ICR 864, sub nom *Coleman v Skyrail Oceanic Ltd (t/a Goodmos Tours)* [1981] IRLR 398, CA. However, tribunals should need little persuading that a discriminatory act has injured feelings: *Murray v Powertech (Scotland) Ltd* [1992] IRLR 257; *Ministry of Defence v Cannock* [1995] 2 All ER 449, [1994] ICR 918. Principles to be applied when considering what sum to award for injury to feelings are set out in *HM Prison Service v Johnson* [1997] ICR 275, sub nom *Armitage, Marsden and HM Prison Service v Johnson* [1997] IRLR 162, EAT. The sum of £500 is probably the least which should be awarded under this head: *Ministry of Defence v Hunt* [1996] ICR 554, [1996] IRLR 139, EAT; and see also *Sharifi v Strathclyde Regional Council* [1992] IRLR 259, EAT; *Orlando v Didcot Power Station Sports and Social Club* [1996] IRLR 262, EAT. If there is a loss of congenial employment, this should be reflected in the injury to feelings award and not treated as a separate head of damages: *Ministry of Defence v Cannock* supra. Tribunals also have power to award damages for personal injury sustained as a result of discrimination: *Sheriff v Klyne Tugs (Lowestoft) Ltd* [1999] ICR 1170, [1999] IRLR 481, CA. See also *HM Prison Service v Salmon* [2001] IRLR 425, [2001] All ER (D) 154 (Apr), EAT (an award of compensation for injury to feelings in addition to an award of damages for psychiatric injury did not amount to double recovery as combined total was not excessive). Guidance has been given on the proper level of damages to be awarded in discrimination cases for injury to feelings and other forms of non-pecuniary damage: *Vento v Chief Constable of West Yorkshire Police* [2002] EWCA Civ 1871, [2003] ICR 318, [2003] IRLR 102, [2002] All ER (D) 363 (Dec). In that case there were set out three broad bands of compensation for injury to feelings, as distinct from compensation for psychiatric or similar personal injury, as follows: (1) a top band of between £15,000 and £25,000, such sums to be awarded in the most serious cases such as where there had been a lengthy campaign of discriminatory harassment on the ground of race or sex; (2) a middle band of between £5,000 and £15,000 which would be used for serious cases which did not merit an award in the highest band; and (3) a bottom band of between £500 and £5,000 which would be appropriate for less serious cases, such as where the act of discrimination was an isolated occurrence. In general, awards of less than £500 are to be avoided altogether, as they risk being regarded as so low as not to be a proper recognition of injury to feelings. See also *Ministry of Defence v Hunt* supra. See further *Scott v IRC* [2004] EWCA Civ 400, [2004] ICR 1410, [2004] IRLR 713 (award of £15,000 in respect of psychiatric damage required revision in the light of a correct appraisal of the medical evidence); *Assoukou v Select Service Partners Ltd* [2006] EWCA Civ 1442, [2006] All ER (D) 122 (Oct) (man in sex discrimination case awarded £500 compensation for anger and frustration). A tribunal has jurisdiction to make a joint and several award of compensation, but should: (a) state its reasons for doing so; (b) not, in general, make an award for the full amount of damage against each respondent; and (c) refrain from making a joint and several award on the basis of the relative financial resources of the respondent: *Way v Crouch* [2005] ICR 1362, [2005] IRLR 603, EAT.

Aggravated damages are available where a respondent has behaved 'in a high-handed, malicious, insulting or oppressive manner in committing the act of discrimination': *Alexander v Home Office* [1988] 2 All ER 118 at 122, [1988] ICR 685 at 692, CA, per May LJ; following *Cassell & Co v Broome* [1972] AC 1027, [1972] 1 All ER 801, HL. There must be a causal connection between the conduct or motive which constitutes the aggravating feature and the loss or injury sustained by the complainant: *Ministry of*

Defence v Meredith [1995] IRLR 539, EAT. Although an award for aggravated damages separate from the award for injury to feelings has been made in many cases, the Court of Appeal has indicated that one global figure should be awarded: *McConnell v Police Authority for Northern Ireland* [1997] IRLR 625, NI CA. If a respondent apologises, this may reduce the level of aggravation: *HM Prison Service v Johnson* supra. An honest if misguided attempt to defend a discrimination case should not generally be regarded as an aggravating element, nor should the fact that the employer is a public body which should be setting an example be treated as an aggravating feature: *McConnell v Police Authority for Northern Ireland* supra. Any claim for aggravated damages should be pleaded, setting out the allegedly aggravating features: *Ministry of Defence v Meredith* supra. As to aggravated damages see DAMAGES vol 12(1) (Reissue) para 1111 et seq.

Exemplary damages are not available in discrimination claims: *Deane v Ealing London Borough Council* [1993] ICR 329, [1993] IRLR 209, EAT (applying *AB v South West Water Services Ltd* [1993] QB 507, [1993] 1 All ER 609, CA; and contrary to *Bradford City Metropolitan Council v Arora* [1991] 2 QB 507, [1991] 3 All ER 545, CA). As to exemplary damages see DAMAGES vol 12(1) (Reissue) para 1115 et seq.

In assessing loss of earnings resulting from an act of discrimination, it is appropriate to assess percentages which reflect the chance that, for example, an applicant in a pregnancy dismissal case would have returned to work after maternity leave, would have remained in work for a particular period and would have been promoted at some stage, and to reduce the award accordingly. The fact that a chance is less than 50% does not prevent an applicant from recovering compensation for loss of that chance: *Ministry of Defence v Cannock* supra. Where there are multiple different percentage chances, the tribunal should make a cumulative calculation based on a percentage of a percentage: *Ministry of Defence v Hunt* supra; *Ministry of Defence v Wheeler* [1998] 1 All ER 790, [1998] ICR 242, CA. An applicant should show that she has taken reasonable steps to mitigate her loss: *Ministry of Defence v Cannock* supra.

Some social security and other benefits will have to be set off against damages: *Chan v Hackney London Borough Council* [1997] ICR 1014 (a race discrimination case, where it was held to be appropriate to set off the applicant's invalidity benefits against his compensation for loss of earnings). Pensions payable on retirement or earlier disablement should not be set off against loss of earnings. Guidance as to which benefits should be set off against which heads of loss can be derived from personal injury cases: see e g *Parry v Cleaver* [1970] AC 1, [1969] 1 All ER 555, HL; *Smoker v London Fire and Civil Defence Authority* [1991] 2 AC 502, [1991] 2 All ER 449, HL; *Longden v British Coal Corpn* [1998] AC 653, [1998] 1 All ER 289, HL; *Hodgson v Trapp* [1989] AC 807, [1988] 3 All ER 870, HL; *Palfrey v Greater London Council* [1985] ICR 437; *Metropolitan Police Receiver v Croydon Corpn* [1957] 2 QB 154, [1957] 1 All ER 78, CA; *Sully v Doggett* (5 December 1984) Lexis, CA.

Notional expenses which would have been incurred in earning the money, for example the costs of childcare, are also deductible: *Ministry of Defence v Cannock* supra.

Sums which were or should have been earned by way of mitigation should be deducted prior to the deduction of the percentage which reflects the possibility that the applicant might not have remained in the job: *Ministry of Defence v Wheeler* [1998] 1 All ER 790, [1998] ICR 242, CA. Sums paid by the employer should also be deducted prior to the percentage reduction: see *Digital Equipment Co Ltd v Clements (No 2)* [1997] ICR 237, [1997] IRLR 140, EAT (an unfair dismissal case).

Pension loss may be calculated using the guidelines drawn up to assist Industrial Tribunals and published in the HMSO booklet *Industrial tribunals: Compensation for loss of pension rights* (1990). These have no statutory force, however, and tribunals are not obliged to use them: *Bingham v Hobourn Engineering Ltd* [1992] IRLR 298, EAT. Alternatively, parties may call actuarial evidence or use the method often adopted in personal injury cases and based on guidance in *Auty v National Coal Board* [1985] 1 All ER 930, [1985] 1 WLR 784, CA.

Interest is payable on past losses in accordance with the Employment Tribunals (Interest on Awards in Discrimination Cases) Regulations 1996, SI 1996/2803 (amended by virtue of the Employment Rights (Dispute Resolution) Act 1998 s 1(2)). Interest is also payable on the award itself once made under the Employment Tribunals (Interest) Order 1990, SI 1990/479 (amended by virtue of the Employment Rights (Dispute Resolution) Act 1998 s 1(2)).

An appellate court may interfere with an award of compensation made by a tribunal if the tribunal has acted on a wrong principle of law or has misapprehended the facts or for other reasons has made a wholly erroneous estimate of the damages suffered: *Skyrail Oceanic Ltd v Coleman* supra.

9   Sex Discrimination Act 1975 s 65(1)(c). A recommendation under s 65(1)(c) should not include matters relating to wages: *Prestcold Ltd v Irvine* [1981] ICR 777, [1981] IRLR 281, CA. The tribunal does not have power to make general recommendations about a respondent's employment practices; the recommendation must be aimed at obviating or reducing the effect of the discrimination on the complainant: *Bayoomi v British Railways Board* [1981] IRLR 431, IT. Nor can a tribunal recommend that a candidate discriminated against in respect of a particular post should be given priority in respect of future posts because there may be better qualified candidates: *North West Thames Regional Health Authority v Noone* [1988] ICR 813, sub nom *Noone v North West Thames Regional Health Authority (No 2)* [1988] ICR 865, [1988] IRLR 530, CA (decided under the equivalent provisions of the Race Relations Act 1976). In *British Gas plc v Sharma* [1991] ICR 19 [1991] IRLR 101, EAT (decided under the Race

Relations Act 1976) it was held that a tribunal cannot recommend that an applicant should be promoted to the next available post as this would amount to unlawful positive discrimination and also such a recommendation would not be susceptible to the imposition of a time limit for implementation. See, however, Case C-158/97 *Re Badeck* [2000] All ER (EC) 289, [2000] ECR I-1875, ECJ.

If without reasonable justification the respondent to a complaint fails to comply with a recommendation made by an employment tribunal under the Sex Discrimination Act 1975 s 65(1)(c), then, if it thinks it just and equitable to do so: (1) the tribunal may increase the amount of compensation required to be paid to the complainant in respect of the complaint by an order made under s 65(1)(b); or (2) if an order under s 65(1)(b) was not made, the tribunal may make such an order: s 65(3) (amended by the Race Relations Act 1976 s 79(4), Sch 4 para 4; the Sex Discrimination and Equal Pay (Remedies) Regulations 1993, SI 1993/2798, regs 1(3), 2, Schedule para 1; the Sex Discrimination and Equal Pay (Miscellaneous Amendments) Regulations 1996, SI 1996/438, reg 2; and by virtue of the Employment Rights (Dispute Resolution) Act 1998 s 1(2)(a)). For a rare example of a case in which justification was shown see *Nelson v Tyne and Wear Passenger Transport Executive* [1978] ICR 1183, EAT.

See also *Vento v Chief Constable of West Yorkshire Police* [2002] EWCA Civ 1871, [2003] ICR 318, [2003] IRLR 102, [2002] All ER (D) 363 (Dec) (recommendation that interviews be conducted to discuss findings of tribunal was appropriate). See note 8 supra.

10   Ie an act falling within the Sex Discrimination Act 1975 s 1(2)(b) (as substituted) (see para 355 ante) or s 3(1)(b) (as substituted) (see para 349 ante).

11   Ie on the ground of fulfilment of the condition in ibid s 3(2) (as substituted): see para 349 ante. As to civil partnerships generally see MATRIMONIAL LAW.

12   Ibid s 65(1B) (as added (see note 8 supra); and amended by the Employment Rights (Dispute Resolution) Act 1998 s 1(2)(a); the Civil Partnership Act 2004 s 251(1), (5); and the Sex Discrimination (Indirect Discrimination and Burden of Proof) Regulations 2001, SI 2001/2660, reg 8(3)). In such circumstances, an order may be made under head (2) in the text only if the employment tribunal: (1) makes such order under head (1) in the text and such recommendation under head (3) in the text (if any) as it would have made if it had no power to make an order under head (2) in the text; and (2) where it makes an order under head (1) in the text or a recommendation under head (3) in the text or both, considers that it is just and equitable to make an order under head (2) in the text as well: Sex Discrimination Act 1975 s 65(1B) (as so added).

415.   Enforcement outside the employment field.

A claim by any person[1] ('the claimant') that another person ('the respondent') has committed an act of discrimination[2] or harassment[3] against the claimant which is unlawful by virtue of the provisions prohibiting discrimination in fields other than employment[4], or is to be treated as having committed such an act of discrimination or harassment against the claimant[5], may be made the subject of civil proceedings in like manner as any other claim in tort[6].

Except as provided by the Sex Discrimination Act 1975, no proceedings, whether civil or criminal, lie against any person in respect of an act by reason that the act is unlawful by virtue of a provision of that Act[7].

Proceedings must be brought in a county court[8] but all such remedies are obtainable in such proceedings as would otherwise[9] be obtainable in the High Court[10].

No award of damages may be made as respects indirect discrimination[11] if the respondent proves that the requirement or condition in question was not applied with the intention of treating the claimant unfavourably on the ground of his sex[12].

Damages in respect of an unlawful act of discrimination or harassment may include compensation for injury to feelings whether or not they include compensation under any other head[13].

Proceedings relating to discrimination by certain educational authorities must not be instituted unless the claimant has given notice of the claim to the Secretary of State[14].

1   As to the meaning of 'person' see para 344 note 3 ante.

2   As to the meaning of 'act' see para 359 note 1 ante; and for the meaning of 'discrimination' see para 344 note 4 ante.

3   As to harassment, including sexual harassment, see the Sex Discrimination Act 1975 s 4A (as added); and para 347 ante.

4   See ibid s 66(1)(a) (amended by the Employment Equality (Sex Discrimination) Regulations 2005,
    SI 2005/2467, regs 1(1), 30(1), (2)). The provisions referred to are those in the Sex Discrimination
    Act 1975 Pt III (ss 21A–36) (as amended) other than s 35A (as added and amended) (see para 378 et seq
    ante): see s 66(1)(a) (as so amended).
5   Ibid s 66(1)(b) (amended by the Employment Equality (Sex Discrimination) Regulations 2005,
    SI 2005/2467, regs 1(1)). A person is treated as having committed such an act by virtue of the Sex
    Discrimination Act 1975 s 41 or s 42 (as amended) (see paras 391–392 ante): see s 66(1)(b) (as so
    amended).
6   Ibid s 66(1). As to claims in tort see TORT.
        As to the burden of proof in relation to any claim brought under s 66 (as amended) see s 66A (as
    added and amended); and para 418 post.
        Rules of court may make provision for enabling a county court in which a claim is brought under
    s 66(1), where the court considers it expedient in the interests of national security: (1) to exclude from all
    or part of the proceedings: (a) the claimant; (b) the claimant's representatives; (c) any assessors; (2) to
    permit a claimant or representative who has been excluded to make a statement to the court before the
    commencement of the proceedings, or the part of the proceedings, from which he is excluded; (3) to
    take steps to keep secret all or part of the reasons for the court's decision in the proceedings: s 66B(1)
    (s 66B added by the Equality Act 2006 s 87). The Attorney General may appoint a person to represent the
    interests of a claimant in, or in any part of, proceedings from which the claimant or his representatives are
    excluded by virtue of the Sex Discrimination Act 1975 s 66B(1) (as added): s 66B(2) (as so added). A
    person may be appointed under s 66B(2) (as added) only if he has a general qualification (within the
    meaning of the Courts and Legal Services Act 1990 s 71 (as amended; prospectively amended): see
    SOLICITORS vol 44(1) (Reissue) para 91): Sex Discrimination Act 1975 s 66B(3) (as so added). A person
    appointed under s 66B(2) (as added) is not responsible to the person whose interests he is appointed to
    represent: s 66B(4) (as so added). As to the Attorney General see CONSTITUTIONAL LAW AND HUMAN
    RIGHTS vol 8(2) (Reissue) para 529.
7   Ibid s 62(1) (s 62 substituted by the Race Relations Act 1976 s 79(4), Sch 4 para 3). The Sex
    Discrimination Act 1975 s 62(1) (as substituted) does not preclude the making of a quashing order
    (formerly certiorari), a mandatory order (formerly mandamus) or a prohibiting order (formerly
    prohibition): see s 62(2) (as so substituted). As to such orders see ADMINISTRATIVE LAW vol 1(1) (2001
    Reissue) para 117 et seq.
8   Ibid s 66(2)(a). A county court has jurisdiction to entertain proceedings with respect to an act done on a
    ship, aircraft or hovercraft outside its district, including such an act done outside Great Britain: see
    s 66(8). For the meaning of 'Great Britain' see para 325 note 6 ante.
9   Ie apart from ibid s 66 (as amended) and s 62(1) (as substituted).
10 Ibid s 66(2) (amended by the Race Relations Act 1976 Sch 4 para 5). For the purposes of such
    proceedings: (1) the County Courts Act 1984 s 63(1) (as amended; prospectively substituted) (assessors)
    (see COURTS) applies with the omission of the words 'on the application of any party'; and (2) the
    remuneration of assessors appointed under that provision is to be at such rate as may be determined by
    the Lord Chancellor with the approval of the Minister for the Civil Service: Sex Discrimination Act 1975
    s 66(6) (amended by the County Courts Act 1984 s 148(1), Sch 2 Pt V para 55). As to the
    Lord Chancellor see CONSTITUTIONAL LAW AND HUMAN RIGHTS vol 8(2) (Reissue) para 477 et seq;
    and as to the Minister for the Civil Service see CONSTITUTIONAL LAW AND HUMAN RIGHTS vol 8(2)
    (Reissue) para 427 et seq.
        There is to be defrayed out of money provided by Parliament payments falling to be made under the
    Sex Discrimination Act 1975 s 66(6) (as amended) in respect of the remuneration of assessors: s 84(b).
    Any increase attributable to the provisions of the Sex Discrimination Act 1975 in the sums payable out of
    money provided by Parliament under any other Act is also to be defrayed out of money provided by
    Parliament: see s 84(c).
11 Ie an unlawful act of discrimination falling within ibid s 1(1)(b) (as substituted): see para 351 ante.
12 Ibid s 66(3) (amended by the Sex Discrimination and Equal Pay (Miscellaneous Amendments)
    Regulations 1996, SI 1996/438, reg 2). The Sex Discrimination Act 1975 s 66(3) (as amended) does not
    affect the award of damages in respect of an unlawful act of discrimination falling within s 1(2)(b) (as
    substituted) (see para 355 ante): s 66(3A) (added by the Sex Discrimination (Indirect Discrimination and
    Burden of Proof) Regulations 2001, SI 2001/2660, reg 7).
13 Sex Discrimination Act 1975 s 66(4) (amended by the Employment Equality (Sex Discrimination)
    Regulations 2005, SI 2005/2467, reg 30(1), (4)). Important guidance has been given on the proper level
    of damages to be awarded in discrimination cases for injury to feelings and other forms of non-pecuniary
    damage: see *Vento v Chief Constable of West Yorkshire Police* [2002] EWCA Civ 1871, [2003] ICR 318,
    [2003] IRLR 102, [2002] All ER (D) 363 (Dec); and para 414 note 8 ante. See also DAMAGES.
14 See the Sex Discrimination Act 1975 s 66(5) (as amended); and para 378 ante. See further EDUCATION.
    As to the Secretary of State and the National Assembly for Wales see para 302 ante.

416.   Time limits. An employment tribunal must not consider a complaint of discrimination in the employment field[1] unless it is presented to the tribunal[2] before the end of the period of three months beginning when the act[3] complained of was done[4], or in a case relating to discrimination within the armed forces[5], the period of six months so beginning[6].

Proceedings before the county court in respect of discrimination in other fields[7] must be instituted[8] before the end of the period of six months beginning when the act complained of was done[9], or, in respect of discrimination by certain educational establishments[10], the period of eight months so beginning[11].

Where proceedings or prospective proceedings[12] relate to the act or omission of a qualifying institution[13], and the dispute concerned is referred as a complaint under the student complaints scheme[14] before the end of the period of six months mentioned above[15], that period[16] is extended by two months[17].

Applications to an employment tribunal or county court by the Equal Opportunities Commission ('EOC') in respect of discriminatory advertisements, instructions to discriminate or pressure to discriminate[18], or in respect of preliminary action in employment cases[19] must be made before the end of the period of six months beginning when the act to which it relates was done[20]. Applications brought by the EOC for an injunction relating to discriminatory advertisements, instructions to discriminate or pressure to discriminate[21] must be made before the end of the period of five years beginning when the act to which the application relates was done[22].

A court or tribunal may nevertheless consider any such complaint, claim or application which is out of time if, in all the circumstances of the case[23], it considers that it is just and equitable to do so[24]. The question whether it is 'equitable' to consider complaints out of time is one of fact and degree for a tribunal to consider in each case. However, a tribunal which takes a wrong view of how to exercise its discretion may commit an error of law which can be corrected on appeal[25]. In claims brought directly on the basis of a directly effective European Directive where the domestic law has failed to implement the Directive, the time limit only begins to run when there is full and proper implementation of the Directive; the appropriate time limit is that appropriate to claims under similar actions of a domestic nature[26]. It may be relevant to the discretion to extend time that the claim is additional to and overlaps with an existing timely complaint which has not yet been heard[27]. The fact that an applicant relied on incorrect legal advice may also be a reason for extending time[28].

Special provision is made for acts which cannot be easily identified as occurring at a specific moment. Where the inclusion of any term in a contract renders the making of the contract an unlawful act that act is to be treated as extending throughout the duration of the contract[29]. Any act extending over a period is to be treated as done at the end of that period[30]. A deliberate omission is to be treated as done when the person in question decided upon it[31].

1   Ie under the Sex Discrimination Act 1975 s 63 (as amended) (see para 414 ante): see s 76(1) (as amended: see note 2 infra). For the meaning of 'discrimination' see para 344 note 4 ante; and for the meaning of 'employment' see para 360 note 4 ante.

2   Ibid s 76(1) (amended by virtue of the Employment Rights (Dispute Resolution) Act 1996 s 1(2)(a)).

3   As to the meaning of 'act' see para 359 note 1 ante.

4   Sex Discrimination Act 1975 s 76(1)(a) (added by the Armed Forces Act 1996 s 21(6)). The rules on 'effective date of termination' for unfair dismissal purposes (see EMPLOYMENT vol 16(1B) (Reissue) para 639) do not apply so, where the act of discrimination is dismissal, the tribunal may take a broader view as to when the act takes place: see *Gloucester Working Men's Club and Institute v James* [1986] ICR 603, EAT (the 'act complained of' did not occur on the date written notice of dismissal was received but when dismissal took effect); *Lupetti v Wrens Old House Ltd* [1984] ICR 348, 81 LS Gaz 279, EAT (a decision under the Race Relations Act 1976). It was held in *Adekeye v Post Office* [1993] ICR 464, [1993] IRLR 324, EAT, that, if an applicant unsuccessfully appeals against a dismissal, the three-month time

period may run from the date of the appeal rather than from the date of the original act; but this decision was overruled in *Relaxion Group plc v Rhys-Harper, D'Souza v Lambert London Borough Council, Jones v 3M Healthcare Ltd, Kirker v British Sugar plc, Angel v New Possibilities NHS Trust, Bond v Hackney Citizens Advice Bureau* [2003] UKHL 33, [2003] 4 All ER 1113, [2002] IRLR 484, where it was decided that sex and disability discrimination claims incident to employment could be brought after the end of employment. See para 361 ante. See also *Cure v Coutts & Co plc* [2005] ICR 1098, (2004) Times, 25 October, EAT.

5   Ie a case to which the Sex Discrimination Act 1975 s 85(9A) (as added) (see para 375 ante) applies: see s 76(1)(b) (added by the Armed Forces Act 1996 s 21(6)).

6   Sex Discrimination Act 1975 s 76(1)(b) (as added: see note 5 supra).

7   Ie under ibid s 66 (as amended): see para 415 ante.

8   See ibid s 76(2).

9   Ibid s 76(2)(a) (added by the Race Relations Act 1976 s 79(4), Sch 4 para 8).

      As from a day to be appointed, a new provision is added providing that the period allowed by s 76(2)(a) or (b) (as added) is extended by three months in the case of a dispute which is referred for conciliation in pursuance of arrangements under the Equality Act 2006 s 27 (as amended; not yet in force) (see para 333 ante) (unless the period is extended under the Sex Discrimination Act 1975 s 76(2A) (as added) (see the text to notes 12–17 infra): s 76(2C) (prospectively added by the Equality Act 2006 s 40, Sch 3 paras 6, 14(1), (3)). At the date at which this volume states the law no such day had been appointed.

10   Ie cases to which the Sex Discrimination Act 1975 s 66(5) (as amended) (see paras 378, 415 ante) applies: see s 76(2)(b) (added by the Race Relations Act 1976 Sch 4 para 8).

11   Sex Discrimination Act 1975 s 76(2)(b) (as added: see note 10 supra). See note 9 supra.

12   Ie under ibid s 66 (as amended): see para 415 ante.

13   Ibid s 76(2A)(a) (s 76(2A), (2B) added by the Higher Education Act 2004 s 19(1)). For the meaning of 'qualifying institution' see EDUCATION vol 15(2) (2006 Reissue) para 1040; definition applied by the Sex Discrimination Act 1975 s 76(2B) (as so added).

14   'The students complaints scheme' means a scheme for the review of qualifying complaints, as defined by the Higher Education Act 2004 s 12 (see EDUCATION vol 15(2) (2006 Reissue) para 1040), that is provided by the designated provider, as defined by s 13(5)(b) (see EDUCATION vol 15(2) (2006 Reissue) para 1040): Sex Discrimination Act 1975 s 76(2B) (as added: see note 13 supra).

15   Ibid s 76(2A)(b) (as added: see note 13 supra). The period referred to in the text is that mentioned in s 76(2)(a) (as added): see the text to note 9 supra.

16   Ie the period allowed by ibid s 76(2)(a) (as added): see the text to note 9 supra.

17   Ibid s 76(2A) (as added: see note 13 supra). As from a day to be appointed, the reference to 'two months' is replaced by a reference to 'three months': s 76(2A) (prospectively amended by the Equality Act 2006 Sch 3 paras 6, 14(1), (2)). At the date at which this volume states the law no such day had been appointed.

18   Ie under the Sex Discrimination Act 1975 s 72(2)(a): see para 413 ante.

19   Ie under ibid s 73(1) (as amended): see para 413 ante.

20   See ibid s 76(3), (4) (s 76(3) substituted by the Race Relations Act 1976 Sch 4 para 8; and s 76(3), (4) amended by virtue of the Employment Rights (Dispute Resolution) Act 1996 s 1(2)(a)). The Sex Discrimination Act 1975 s 76(3), (4) (as substituted and amended) is repealed by the Equality Act 2006 s 91, Sch 3 paras 6, 14(1), (4), Sch 4 as from a day to be appointed under s 93. At the date at which this volume states the law no such day had been appointed. As to the Commission for Equality and Human Rights, which is to replace the EOC, see para 305 et seq ante.

21   Ie under the Sex Discrimination Act 1975 s 72(4) (as amended): see para 413 ante.

22   See ibid s 76(3) (as substituted and amended: see note 20 supra). See note 20 supra.

23   The words 'in all the circumstances of the case' refer to the facts of the case so far as they are relevant to the consideration of whether to extend the time limit; the words do not require a tribunal to try the case on its merits: *Hutchison v Westward Television Ltd* [1977] ICR 279, [1977] IRLR 69, EAT.

24   Sex Discrimination Act 1975 s 76(5). As from a day to be appointed, the reference to 'complaint, claim or application' is replaced by a reference to 'complaint or claim': s 76(5) (prospectively amended by the Equality Act 2006 Sch 3 paras 6, 14(1), (5)). At the date at which this volume states the law no such day had been appointed.

      The exercise by a court or a tribunal of its discretion to hear a discrimination claim out of time may be challenged only on the basis that it took into account irrelevant considerations, failed to take into account relevant considerations, or reached a decision that no reasonable tribunal could have reached: see *Eke v Customs and Excise Comrs* [1981] IRLR 334, EAT. A tribunal's exercise of its discretion was in breach of natural justice where the tribunal took into account the merits of the claim without any argument being presented to it on the merits, and without inviting counsel to make submissions on the subject: *Lupetti v Wrens Old House Ltd* [1984] ICR 348, 81 LS Gaz 279, EAT.

      In *Aniagwu v Hackney London Borough Council and Owens* [1999] IRLR 303, EAT, it was held just and equitable to extend time where the delay was caused by the fact that the applicant was attempting to resolve the grievance through the employer's internal procedures. It has been held that the discretion to extend time is as wide as that given to the civil courts by the Limitation Act 1980 s 33 (as amended) to determine whether time should be extended in personal injury actions (see LIMITATION OF ACTIONS vol 28 (Reissue) para 907 et seq): *British Coal Corpn v Keeble* [1997] IRLR 336, EAT. See also *Berry v Ravensbourne NHS Trust* [1993] ICR 871, EAT.

There is no positive duty on a tribunal chairman to raise the question of whether an applicant wishes to apply for an extension of time: *Dimtsu v Westminster City Council* [1991] IRLR 450, EAT.

Where it is sought to introduce a claim of discrimination by means of amendment of an existing originating application, if the tribunal does not find that it would be just and equitable to extend time, the complaint will be barred just as it would have been had it been brought in a new originating application, although the existence of the original proceedings may feature largely in the question of whether it is just and equitable to extend time: *Harvey v Port of Tilbury (London) Ltd* [1999] ICR 1030, [1999] IRLR 693, EAT. However a claim of 'discrimination' is apt to include both direct and indirect discrimination and victimisation: *Quarcoopome v Sock Shop Holdings Ltd* [1995] IRLR 353, EAT.

25 *Foster v South Glamorgan Health Authority* [1988] ICR 526, [1988] IRLR 277, EAT (claimant did not present claim within time limit because she did not think she had a claim; subsequent decision of European Court of Justice in Case 152/84 *Marshall v Southampton and South West Hampshire Area Health Authority (Teaching)* [1986] QB 401, [1986] 2 All ER 584, ECJ, changed the position; complaint out of time should be allowed). In *British Coal Corpn v Keeble* [1997] IRLR 336, EAT, an extension of time was allowed in respect of a complaint of sex discrimination made out of time because the applicants' legal advisers had failed to appreciate the significance of the decision in Case C-262/88 *Barber v Guardian Royal Exchange Assurance Group Ltd* [1991] 1 QB 344, [1990] IRLR 240, ECJ. The Employment Appeal Tribunal also held that dicta of the Court of Appeal in *Biggs v Somerset County Council* [1996] 2 All ER 734, [1996] IRLR 203, CA, to the effect that it was contrary to the principle of legal certainty to allow back-dated claims to be heard because the law had not yet been explained or fully understood were restricted to cases such as unfair dismissal cases, where the test is whether it was reasonably practicable for the claim to be presented in time: see *British Coal Corpn v Keeble* supra. See also *DPP v Marshall* [1998] ICR 518, EAT (complaint out of time allowed when made within three months of European Court of Justice decision providing ground for complaint).

26 Case C-208/90 *Emmott v Minister for Social Welfare and A-G* [1993] ICR 8, [1991] IRLR 387, ECJ. Such claims can only be brought by public sector employees.

27 *Berry v Ravensbourne National Health Service Trust* [1993] ICR 871, EAT.

28 *Hawkins v Ball and Barclays Bank plc* [1996] IRLR 258, EAT.

29 Sex Discrimination Act 1975 s 76(6)(a). See *Hendricks v Metropolitan Police Comr* [2002] EWCA Civ 1686, [2003] 1 All ER 654, [2003] ICR 530; and note 30 infra.

30 Sex Discrimination Act 1975 s 76(6)(b). The act itself and not merely the consequences must be continuing, e g an appointment to a particular post is not a continuing act: *Amies v Inner London Education Authority* [1977] 2 All ER 100, [1977] ICR 308, EAT. See also *Sougrin v Haringey Health Authority* [1991] ICR 791, [1991] IRLR 447, EAT (receipt of lower pay as a result of a grading decision was a consequence of the disputed decision and not a continuing act); *Owusu v London Fire and Civil Defence Authority* [1995] IRLR 574, EAT (an act extends over a period of time if it takes the form of a policy, rule or practice in accordance with which decisions are taken from time to time and a succession of specific instances can indicate the existence of a practice; individual failures to promote were not continuing acts, but a denial of opportunities might be). Where a respondent operates a continuous regime or policy which it is open to him to alter at any time, it should be regarded as an act extending over a period, not as a deliberate omission to provide an equally favourable regime. Therefore, the provision of less favourable pension rights to Asian employees constituted an act extending over the whole period of the employees' employment. An employee could complain of racial discrimination in his pension entitlement until three months after his employment had terminated, although the original decision with regard to his pension had been made before the Race Relations Act 1976 had been enacted: *Barclays Bank plc v Kapur* [1991] 2 AC 355, [1991] 1 All ER 646, HL. See also *Calder v James Finlay Corpn Ltd* [1989] ICR 157n, [1989] IRLR 55, EAT (a rule of a mortgage subsidy scheme denying the benefit of a scheme to females was a discriminatory act extending over the period of employment); *Cast v Croydon College* [1998] ICR 500, [1998] IRLR 318, CA (in the case of a discriminatory policy, the discriminatory act extended over the period of employment and was to be treated as having been done at the end of the complainant's employment; in any case, a decision might be an act of discrimination whether or not it was made on the same facts as a previous decision, provided that it resulted from a further consideration of the matter). Cf *Rovenska v General Medical Council* [1998] ICR 85, [1997] IRLR 367, CA, in which the Court of Appeal found that a repeated refusal constituted a new act but did not hold that the policy was a continuing act. A failure fully to act on a promise to remedy alleged racial abuse is capable of being a continuing act: *Littlewoods Organisation plc v Traynor* [1993] IRLR 154, EAT. In determining whether an act is a continuing one, extending over a period of time, it is necessary to distinguish between one full act and a succession of unrelated acts for which time runs from

the date when each act is committed: *Hendricks v Metropolitan Police Comr* [2002] EWCA Civ 1686, [2003] 1 All ER 654, [2003] ICR 530. See also *Mates v Ministry of Defence* [2006] All ER (D) 358 (Nov), EAT. Failure to promote is a continuing act of discrimination extending to the end of the complainant's employment: *Kells v Pilkington plc* [2002] IRLR 693, [2002] All ER (D) 33 (May), EAT.

31　Sex Discrimination Act 1975 s 76(6)(c). In the absence of evidence establishing the contrary a person is to be taken for these purposes to decide upon an omission when he does an act inconsistent with doing the omitted act or, if he has done no such inconsistent act, when the period expires within which he might reasonably have been expected to do the omitted act if it was to be done: s 76(6). 'Decided' in s 76(6)(c) means 'decided at a time and in circumstances when he was in a position to implement that decision': *Swithland Motors plc v Clarke* [1994] ICR 231 at 236, [1994] IRLR 275 at 277, EAT, per Judge Hull QC.

417.　Help for complainants. With a view to helping a person ('the person aggrieved') who considers he may have been discriminated[1] against or subjected to harassment[2] to decide whether to institute proceedings and, if he does so, to formulate and present his case in the most effective manner, the Secretary of State[3] has prescribed forms[4] by which the person aggrieved may question the respondent[5] on his reasons for doing any relevant act[6], or on any other matter which is or may be relevant and by which the respondent may if he so wishes reply[7]. This procedure is called the 'questionnaire procedure'.

Any such questions and replies[8] are admissible as evidence in the proceedings[9]. If it appears to the court or tribunal that the respondent deliberately, and without reasonable excuse, omitted to reply within the applicable period[10] or that his reply is evasive or equivocal, the court or tribunal may draw any inference from that fact that it considers it just and equitable to draw, including an inference that he committed an unlawful act[11].

The Secretary of State has prescribed by order the period within which questions must be served in order to be admissible[12] and the manner in which a question, and any reply by the respondent, may be served[13].

A court has the power to order the disclosure of documents in another party's possession[14].

A court may order any party to clarify any matter which is in dispute in the proceedings or give additional information in relation to any such matter[15]. In the context of case management a chairman of an employment tribunal may at any time either on the application of a party or on his own initiative make an order in relation to a number of matters including the provision of additional information, the disclosure of documents or information to a party to allow a party to inspect such material as might be ordered by a county court, or the provision of written answers to questions put by the tribunal or the chairman[16].

1　For the meaning of 'discrimination' see para 344 note 4 ante.
2　As to harassment, including sexual harassment, see the Sex Discrimination Act 1975 s 4A (as added); and para 347 ante.
3　As to the Secretary of State and the National Assembly for Wales see para 302 ante.
4　See the Sex Discrimination (Questions and Replies) Order 1975, SI 1975/2048, art 3, Schs 1, 2.
5　'Respondent' includes a prospective respondent: Sex Discrimination Act 1975 s 74(6).
6　As to the meaning of 'act' see para 359 note 1 ante.
7　See the Sex Discrimination Act 1975 s 74(1) (amended by the Employment Equality (Sex Discrimination) Regulations 2005, SI 2005/2467, reg 32(1), (2)). In answer to questions by an unsuccessful applicant for a job, the respondent need not disclose the name and address of a successful applicant but if requested should disclose the qualifications of a successful applicant: *Oxford v Department of Health and Social Security* [1977] ICR 884, [1977] IRLR 225, EAT. See also *Williams v Dyfed County Council* [1986] ICR 449, [1986] NLJ Rep 893, EAT.
8　Ie whether they are made in accordance with the prescribed forms or not: see the Sex Discrimination Act 1975 s 74(2).
9　See ibid s 74(2)(a). The admissibility of questions and replies is subject to any enactment or rule of law regulating the admissibility of evidence in interim and preliminary matters in proceedings before a county court or employment tribunal: s 74(5) (amended by virtue of the Employment Rights (Dispute

Resolution) Act 1998 s 1(2)(a)). County court rules may enable the court entertaining a claim under the Sex Discrimination Act 1975 s 66 (as amended) (see para 415 ante) to determine, before the date fixed for the hearing of the claim, whether a question or reply is admissible or not: s 74(4), (6)(a).

10 Ie within the period applicable under ibid s 74(2A) (as added): see s 74(2)(b) (as amended: see the text and note 11 infra). This period is eight weeks beginning with the day when the question was served on the respondent, if the question relates to discrimination under any provision of Pt II (ss 6–20A) (as amended), s 35A (as added and amended) (see para 360 et seq ante) or any other provision of Pt III (ss 21A–36) (as amended) (see para 378 et seq ante) so far as it applies to vocational training, or within a reasonable period as regards any other question: s 74(2)(2A) (added by the Employment Equality (Sex Discrimination) Regulations 2005, SI 2005/2467, reg 32(1), (4)).

11 Sex Discrimination Act 1975 s 74(2)(b) (amended by the Employment Equality (Sex Discrimination) Regulations 2005, SI 2005/2467, reg 32(1), (3)).

12 Ie under the Sex Discrimination Act 1975 s 74(2)(a): see s 74(3).

In proceedings before a court, a question is only admissible as evidence where: (1) it was served before those proceedings had been instituted, if it was so served during the period of six months beginning when the act complained of was done, or in a case to which s 66(5) (as amended) (see para 378 ante) applies, the period of eight months so beginning; or (2) where it was served when those proceedings had been instituted, if it was served with the leave of, and within a period specified by, the court: Sex Discrimination (Questions and Replies) Order 1975, SI 1975/2048, art 4 (amended by SI 1977/844).

In proceedings before a tribunal, a question is only admissible as evidence: (a) where it was served before a complaint had been presented to a tribunal, if it was so served within the period of three months beginning when the act complained of was done, or where the period under the Sex Discrimination Act 1975 s 76 (as amended) (see para 416 ante) within which proceedings must be brought is extended by the Employment Act 2002 (Dispute Resolution) Regulations 2004, SI 2004/752, reg 15 (see EMPLOYMENT vol 16(1B) (Reissue) para 594), within that extended period; or (b) where it was served when a complaint had been presented to a tribunal, either if it was so served within the period of 21 days beginning with the day on which the complaint was presented or if it was so served later with leave given, and within a period specified, by a direction of a tribunal: Sex Discrimination (Questions and Replies) Order 1975, SI 1975/2048, art 5 (amended by the Employment Act 2002 (Dispute Resolution) Regulations 2004, SI 2004/752, reg 17(a)).

13 Sex Discrimination Act 1975 s 74(3). A question and any reply to it may be served on the respondent or, as the case may be, on the person aggrieved: (1) by delivering it to him; (2) by sending it by post to him at his usual or last-known residence or place of business; (3) where the person to be served is a body corporate or is a trade union or employers' association (see TRADE, INDUSTRY AND INDUSTRIAL RELATIONS vol 47 (2001 Reissue) paras 1001, 1201), by delivering it to the secretary or clerk of the body, union or association at its registered or principal office or by sending it by post to the secretary or clerk at that office; (4) where the person to be served is acting by a solicitor, by delivering it at, or by sending it by post to, the solicitor's address for service; or (5) where the person to be served is the person aggrieved, by delivering the reply, or sending it by post, to him at his address for reply as stated by him in the document containing the questions: Sex Discrimination (Questions and Replies) Order 1975, SI 1975/2048, art 6.

14 As to disclosure and inspection of documents see CPR Pt 31. Disclosure is limited to standard disclosure unless the court orders otherwise: see CPR 31.5. Standard disclosure generally means disclosure of all documents upon which the disclosing party relies, all documents which adversely affect his own or another party's case, and all documents which support another party's case: see CPR 31.6. The court may order specific disclosure or specific inspection of any document (CPR 31.12) but will take into account all of the circumstances of the case and in particular the overriding objective set out in CPR Pt 1 and the concept of proportionality before making any such order: see *Practice Direction—Disclosure and Inspection* (1999) PD 31 para 5.4. See also PRACTICE AND PROCEDURE. As to rules of procedure in employment tribunals see generally the Employment Tribunals (Constitution and Rules of Procedure) Regulations 2004, SI 2004/1861 (as amended); and EMPLOYMENT vol 16(1B) (Reissue) para 816 et seq.

Disclosure may be granted against either the applicant or the respondent, but in practice it is most likely to be used by the applicant, since most relevant information is usually in the possession of the respondent. The disclosure and inspection of documents, like the questionnaire procedure (see the text to notes 1–13 supra), is a method by which Parliament offsets the applicant's disadvantage in having the burden of proving his case notwithstanding that the bulk of the relevant evidence is likely to be in the possession of the respondent: see *British Library v Palyza* [1984] ICR 504, [1984] IRLR 306, EAT. The questionnaire procedure is not intended to be a substitute for, but an addition to, the complainant's rights of disclosure and inspection of documents: *Science Research Council v Nassé, Leyland Cars v Vyas* [1980] AC 1028 at 1069, [1979] 3 All ER 673 at 683, HL, per Lord Salmon. Disclosure may include documents relating to incidents prior to the act complained of by the applicant: see *Selvarajan v Inner London*

Education Authority [1980] IRLR 313, EAT (applicant obtained disclosure of documents relating to the respondent's procedures for recruitment to various jobs for which the applicant had applied between 1961 and 1976).

The principles upon which the disclosure of confidential documents should be ordered in a case under the Race Relations Act 1976 or the Sex Discrimination Act 1975 were considered by the House of Lords in *Science Research Council v Nassé, Leyland Cars v Vyas* supra. The applicants, who had applied unsuccessfully for promotion or transfer, sought the disclosure of confidential reports relating to other applicants for the jobs in question. The House of Lords held that confidential employment documents were not immune from disclosure. However, a court or tribunal ought not to grant disclosure of documents automatically because they are relevant to the proceedings. Disclosure should only be ordered if the documents are necessary for disposing fairly of the proceedings. Where documents are confidential, the court or tribunal should consider carefully whether the necessary information could be obtained by other means, not involving a breach of confidence, and should inspect the documents. It should consider whether justice could be done by covering up parts of the documents, or substituting anonymous references for specific names, or, rarely, by hearing the case in camera. It is a matter of convenience in each case whether the documents should be examined at an interim stage or as the matter arises in the hearing: *British Railways Board v Natarajan* [1979] 2 All ER 794, [1979] ICR 326, EAT.

Disclosure must not be granted if it would be oppressive. It may be oppressive if it requires the provision of material not readily to hand which can only be made available with difficulty and at great expense, or if it requires the party ordered to make disclosure to embark on a course which will add unreasonably to the length and cost of the hearing: *West Midlands Passenger Executive v Singh* [1988] 2 All ER 873, [1988] 1 WLR 730, CA.

Disclosure may be obtained of statistics in the possession of the respondent which help to demonstrate a pattern in the respondent's treatment of a particular group. Although the authorities all concern the Race Relations Act 1976, there is no reason why similar disclosure should not be obtained to illustrate treatment of different genders. In *West Midlands Passenger Executive v Singh* supra the applicant had applied unsuccessfully for promotion to the post of senior inspector, and alleged racial discrimination on the part of his employers; the Court of Appeal upheld the tribunal's decision to grant disclosure of the details of the ethnic origins of applicants for, and appointees to, comparable posts between October 1984 and December 1985. The evidence requested was relevant: since direct discrimination involved the less favourable treatment of a person because of his membership of a group, statistical evidence of the respondent's treatment of other members of that group might establish a discernible pattern of treatment. If the pattern showed a regular failure by members of the group to obtain promotion to particular jobs, and demonstrated the under-representation of members of the group in those jobs, it could give rise to an inference of discrimination. For the probative importance of statistical evidence in discrimination cases see also *Chattopadhyay v Headmaster of Holloway School* [1982] ICR 132, [1981] IRLR 487, EAT; *Carrington v Helix Lighting Ltd* [1990] ICR 125, [1990] IRLR 6, EAT.

An order for disclosure may only be made in relation to documents which exist and which are in the possession of the party from whom disclosure is requested. It is not appropriate to order disclosure where it would amount to an order to collect the information sought and create a new document: *Carrington v Helix Lighting Ltd* supra. In this case the applicant sought a schedule of evidence showing the ethnic composition of the respondent's workforce. The Employment Appeal Tribunal held that a tribunal had no power to order the production of the schedule, at least where it did not simply record the contents of existing documents. A court might be able to order the production of such a schedule pursuant to its power to order further information, but a tribunal had no equivalent power. However, where a respondent employer does not keep records of the ethnic composition of his workforce, his failure to abide by the recommendation of ethnic monitoring in the Commission for Racial Equality's Statutory Code of Practice on Racial Equality in Employment (April 2006) (see para 491 post) could be taken into account by a tribunal.

The decision whether to order disclosure is to be made at the discretion of the tribunal or court, but is reviewable by the Employment Appeal Tribunal or Court of Appeal which may exercise its own discretion and is not limited to intervening only when the tribunal or court has exercised its discretion on the wrong principles, at least when the decision was made before the substantive hearing, so that the tribunal or court could not have been influenced by evidence: *British Library v Palyza* [1984] ICR 504, [1984] IRLR 306, EAT.

15   See CPR 18.1. See also PRACTICE AND PROCEDURE.
16   See the Employment Tribunals (Constitution and Rules of Procedure) Regulations 2004, SI 2004/1861, reg 16, Sch 1 r 10 (as amended); and EMPLOYMENT vol 16(1B) (Reissue) para 867.

418.   Proving discrimination; statutory reversal of the burden of proof.
Provisions[1] were introduced into the Sex Discrimination Act 1975 in 2001 to replace the previous law on proof. Where, on the hearing of a complaint presented to an

employment tribunal[2], the complainant proves facts from which the tribunal could otherwise conclude in the absence of an adequate explanation that the respondent has committed an act of discrimination[3] or harassment[4] against the complainant which is unlawful[5], or is[6] to be treated as having committed such an act of discrimination or harassment against the complainant, the tribunal must uphold the complaint unless the respondent proves that he did not commit, or, as the case may be, is not to be treated as having committed, that act[7].

Previously it was for the applicant to prove on the balance of probabilities that he has been discriminated against on the grounds of sex[8], or by way of victimisation[9], in circumstances in which such discrimination was unlawful under the provisions of the Sex Discrimination Act 1975[10]. Where the allegation was of indirect discrimination[11], and the respondent wished to rely upon justifiability[12] as a defence, it was for the respondent to prove on the balance of probabilities that the condition or requirement at issue was justifiable[13].

There may be limited situations where the previous law is still relevant[14].

1 Ie the Sex Discrimination Act 1975 ss 63A, 66A (as added and amended): see the text to notes 2–7 infra.

2 Ie under ibid s 63 (as amended): see para 414 ante.

3 For the meaning of 'discrimination' see para 344 note 4 ante.

4 As to harassment, including sexual harassment, see the Sex Discrimination Act 1975 s 4A (as added); and para 347 ante.

5 Ie by virtue of ibid Pt II (ss 6–20A) (as amended) (see para 360 et seq ante) or s 35A (as added and amended) (see para 374 ante).

6 Ie by virtue of ibid s 41 (see para 391 ante) or s 42 (as amended) (see para 392 ante).

7 Ibid s 63A (added by the Sex Discrimination (Indirect Discrimination and Burden of Proof) Regulations 2001, SI 2001/2660, reg 5; and amended by the Employment Equality (Sex Discrimination) Regulations 2005, SI 2005/2467, reg 29(1)–(3)). This provision applies in regard to employment tribunals, but there is a similar provision in regard to county courts. Where, on the hearing of a claim brought under the Sex Discrimination Act 1975 s 66(1) (as amended) (see para 415 ante), the claimant proves facts from which the court could otherwise conclude in the absence of an adequate explanation that the respondent has committed an act of discrimination or harassment against the claimant which is unlawful by virtue of any provision of Pt III (ss 21A–36) (see para 378 et seq ante) so far as it applies to vocational training, or is by virtue of s 41 (see para 391 ante) or s 42 (as amended) (see para 392 ante) to be treated as having committed such an act of discrimination or harassment against the claimant, the court must uphold the claim unless the respondent proves that he did not commit, or, as the case may be, is not to be treated as having committed, that act: s 66A (added by the Sex Discrimination (Indirect Discrimination and Burden of Proof) Regulations 2001, SI 2001/2660, reg 6; and amended by the Employment Equality (Sex Discrimination) Regulations 2005, SI 2005/2467, reg 29(1)–(3)). These provisions are in implementation of EC Directive 97/80 (OJ L14, 20.1.98, p 6) on the burden of proof in cases of discrimination based on sex, which is applied to the United Kingdom by EC Directive 98/52 (OJ L205, 22.7.98, p 66) on the extension of EC Directive 97/80 on the burden of proof in cases of discrimination based on sex to the United Kingdom of Great Britain and Northern Ireland. As from 15 August 2009, EC Council Directive 97/80 (OJ L14, 20.1.98, p 6) and certain other Directives (see paras 338, 340 ante, 419 post) are repealed and replaced by European Parliament and EC Council Directive 2006/54 (OJ L204, 26.7.2006, p 23) on the implementation of the principle of equal opportunities and equal treatment of men and women in matters of employment and occupation. This effectively is a consolidation of the relevant Directives and from 15 August 2009 references to the repealed Directives are to be construed as references to EC Council Directive 2006/54 (OJ L204, 26.7.2006, p 23): see art 34.

The respondent would usually be expected to produce cogent evidence to discharge his burden of proof, since he would normally be in possession of the facts necessary to prove that he did not commit an act of discrimination: *Barton v Investec Henderson Crosthwaite Securities Ltd* [2003] ICR 1205, [2003] IRLR 332, EAT; applied in *Wong v Igen Ltd (Equal Opportunities Commission and others intervening), Emokpae v Chamberlin Solicitors (Equal Opportunities Commission and others intervening), Webster v Brunel University (Equal Opportunities Commission and others intervening)* [2005] EWCA Civ 142, [2005] 3 All ER 812, [2005] ICR 931. See also *Hundal v Initial Security Ltd* [2006] All ER (D) 74 (Aug), EAT. Guidance from *Barton v Investec Henderson Crosthwaite Securities Ltd* supra is amended and set out as an Annex to the judgement in *Wong v Igen Ltd (Equal Opportunities Commission and others intervening), Emokpae v Chamberlin Solicitors (Equal Opportunities Commission and others intervening), Webster v Brunel University (Equal*

Opportunities Commission and others intervening) supra (a case involving race and sex discrimination with implications for all categories of discrimination). At the date at which this volume states the law this guidance is used as a checklist by tribunals.

It may be that the burden on the employee to show a prima facie case of discrimination is particularly relevant in a case of indirect discrimination (with the requirement of a provision, criterion or practice to the detriment of a considerably larger proportion of women than of men): *Nelson v Carillion Services Ltd* [2003] EWCA Civ 544, [2003] ICR 1256, [2003] IRLR 428. However, the approach in that case was based at least in part on the view that the statutory reversal of the burden of proof had merely codified the existing law, a view that was dissented from in *Wong v Igen Ltd (Equal Opportunities Commission and others intervening), Emokpae v Chamberlin Solicitors (Equal Opportunities Commission and others intervening), Webster v Brunel University (Equal Opportunities Commission and others intervening)* supra. Even with the statutory reversal, the initial burden on the employee means that there is no reversal merely on the employee's accusation; the requirement to show a prima facie case of less favourable treatment on the grounds of sex means that it is insufficient to show less favourable treatment and a difference of gender: *University of Huddersfield v Wolff* [2004] ICR 828, [2004] IRLR 534, EAT; *Sinclair Roche & Temperley v Howard* [2004] IRLR 763, EAT. See also *Martin v Lancehawk Ltd (t/a European Telecom Solutions)* [2004] All ER (D) 400 (Mar), EAT; *EB v BA* [2006] EWCA Civ 132, [2006] IRLR 471; *Thomatheram v Leicester City Council* [2006] All ER (D) 88 (Aug), EAT; *Laing v Manchester City Council* [2006] ICR 1519, [2006] IRLR 748, EAT; *Network Rail Infrastructure Ltd v Griffiths-Henry* [2006] IRLR 865, [2006] All ER (D) 15 (Jul), EAT; *Fox v Rangecroft* [2006] EWCA Civ 1112; *A v B* [2007] All ER (D) 18 (Jan), EAT; *Madarassy v Nomura International plc* [2007] EWCA Civ 33, [2007] All ER (D) 226 (Jan). In *Laing v Manchester City Council* supra it was suggested that the guidelines in *Wong v Igen Ltd (Equal Opportunities Commission and others intervening), Emokpae v Chamberlin Solicitors (Equal Opportunities Commission and others intervening), Webster v Brunel University (Equal Opportunities Commission and others intervening)* supra should not be interpreted and applied too literally, in a way that would require the tribunal to go through 'mental gymnastics'.

See also *Bahl v Law Society* [2004] EWCA Civ 1070, [2004] IRLR 799, [2004] All ER (D) 563 (Jul); and note 10 infra.

8   See para 344 et seq ante.

9   As to victimisation see para 358 ante.

10   In practice, applicants in cases of discrimination have always faced special difficulties in proving their cases, as has been acknowledged by the courts, particularly in race discrimination cases: see *Baker v Cornwall County Council* [1990] ICR 452, [1990] IRLR 194, CA; *North West Thames Regional Health Authority v Noone* [1988] ICR 813, sub nom *Noone v North West Thames Regional Health Authority (No 2)* [1998] IRLR 530, CA; *Khanna v Ministry of Defence* [1981] ICR 653, [1981] IRLR 331, EAT; *Oxford v Department of Health and Social Security* [1977] ICR 884, [1977] IRLR 225, EAT; *Wallace v South Eastern Education and Library Board* [1980] IRLR 193, NI CA; *Chattopadhyay v Headmaster of Holloway School* [1982] ICR 132, [1981] IRLR 487, EAT; *Barking and Dagenham London Borough Council v Camara* [1988] ICR 865, [1988] IRLR 373, EAT. Direct evidence of discrimination is only rarely available, and applicants have had to rely on the questionnaire procedure (see para 417 ante), the inspection and disclosure of documents (see para 417 ante), and statistical evidence which may establish a discernible pattern of treatment of a particular group: *Barking and Dagenham London Borough Council v Camara* supra. The affirmative evidence of discrimination normally consists of inferences to be drawn by the court or tribunal from the primary facts: *Khanna v Ministry of Defence* supra. A finding of 'no case to answer' so that the applicant's case is dismissed at the end of his evidence, will be exceptional, and will be confined to cases which are wholly without merit: *British Gas plc v Sharma* [1991] ICR 19, [1991] IRLR 101, EAT; *Oxford v Department of Health and Social Security* supra.

Early cases concerning the proof of discrimination suggested that, where the applicant had succeeded in establishing that he had been less favourably treated than another person who was of a different racial group or gender, the evidential burden of proof would shift to the respondent. In other words, unless the respondent could provide a satisfactory explanation for the less favourable treatment of the applicant, the tribunal must draw the inference that it was on the ground of race or sex: see *Moberly v Commonwealth Hall (University of London)* [1977] ICR 791, [1977] IRLR 176, EAT; *Oxford v Department of Health and Social Security* supra; *Wallace v South Eastern Educational and Library Board* supra; *Chattopadhyay v Headmaster of Holloway School* supra. Later cases, at least in England and Wales, disapproved of the use of the notion of a shifting burden of proof, as more likely to obscure than to illuminate the right answer: see *British Gas plc v Sharma* supra; *Khanna v Ministry of Defence* supra; *Barking and Dagenham London Borough Council v Camara* supra. See the approach set out authoritatively in the context of racial discrimination in *King v Great Britain-China Centre* [1992] ICR 516 at 528–529, [1991] IRLR 513 at 518, CA, per Neill LJ; approved in *Glasgow City Council v Zafar* [1998] ICR 120, sub nom *Zafar v Glasgow City Council* [1998] IRLR 36, HL. Employment tribunals must be careful to judge the facts objectively and not substitute their own views: see *Marks & Spencer plc v Martin* [1998] ICR 1005, sub nom *Martins v Marks & Spencer plc* [1998] IRLR 326, CA (employment tribunal erroneously drew an inference of race discrimination after substituting its own view of the applicant for those of an interview panel which had considered her for a post). A failure by an employer to follow its own equal opportunities procedure in respect of an applicant is evidence from which an inference of discrimination may be drawn, but such an inference will not always be appropriate: *Qureshi v Newham London Borough Council* [1991] IRLR 264, CA.

Although discrimination may be inferred if there is no explanation for unreasonable treatment, that is not an inference from the unreasonable treatment itself but from the absence of any explanation for it; the inference may be rebutted by a respondent leading evidence of a genuine reason which was not discriminatory: *Bahl v Law Society* [2004] EWCA Civ 1070, [2004] IRLR 799, [2004] All ER (D) 563 (Jul) (a case involving both sex and racial discrimination). This case was decided since the new provisions of the Sex Discrimination Act 1975 ss 63A, 66A (both as added and amended) (see the text and notes 1–7 supra) and the Race Relations Act 1976 ss 54A, 57ZA (as added) (see para 504 post) but the previous law may still be relevant because: (a) that case confirms the point that bad treatment is not per se discrimination (which requires worse treatment that that given to a comparator); (b) there is an argument that the previous law had almost reached the new position introduced with the statutory provisions anyway via the ability of a tribunal to draw inferences. The difference, however, is that under the new provisions this is not an ability but an obligation on the tribunal or court. In this context see *Wong v Igen Ltd (Equal Opportunities Commission and others intervening), Emokpae v Chamberlin Solicitors (Equal Opportunities Commission and others intervening), Webster v Brunel University (Equal Opportunities Commission and others intervening)* [2005] EWCA Civ 142, [2005] 3 All ER 812, [2005] ICR 931 (a case involving sex and racial discrimination but with implications across all categories of discrimination), which shows that the burden of proof does not shift simply on accusation. See note 7 supra.

11 Ie contrary to the Sex Discrimination Act 1975 s 1(1)(b) (as substituted): see para 351 ante.
12 See ibid s 1(1)(b)(ii) (as substituted); and para 351 ante.
13 As to the meaning of 'justifiable' see para 354 note 2 ante.
14 See note 10 supra. See also note 7 supra.

3. EQUAL PAY

(1) IN GENERAL

419. The principle of equal pay. Article 141 of the EC Treaty[1] requires that men and women should receive equal pay for equal work and work of equal value[2]. Article 141 is supplemented by the Equal Pay Directive[3] and the European Commission Code of Practice[4].

The principle of equal pay forms part of the foundations of the European Union[5]. Any provision of national law must be interpreted, so far as possible, to accord with Article 141. If it is not possible to construe the provision in a compatible manner it must be set aside[6]. Article 141 prohibits any breach of the principle of equal pay whatever system gives rise to the inequality[7].

Courts are not required to carry out an overall assessment of a package of benefits. The principle of equal pay applies to each element of remuneration[8]. Once discrimination in pay is established, the only proper way of complying with Article 141 is to grant the disadvantaged person the benefits paid to the advantaged class[9]. Where inequality could be removed by a procedural measure, such as adoption of a common retirement age, a woman will be able to rely on the principle of equal pay to receive equal remuneration up to the date the measure is adopted.

Article 141 is of direct effect and may be relied upon in national courts[10]. However, it does not provide a free-standing right of action in the employment tribunal[11].

1   See the Treaty Establishing the European Community (Rome, 25 March 1957; TS 1 (1973); Cmnd 5179) art 141(2) (formerly art 119; renumbered by virtue of the Treaty of Amsterdam: see *Treaty Citation (No 2) (Note)* [1999] All ER (EC) 646, ECJ).

    As to reasonable time limits for bringing a claim under this article see *Rankin v British Coal Corpn* [1995] ICR 774, [1993] IRLR 69, EAT.

2   The predecessor of the EC Treaty art 141 (as renumbered) (i e art 119) did not expressly require equal pay for work of equal value, although it had been interpreted by the European Court of Justice to incorporate this concept: Case 69/80 *Worringham v Lloyds Bank Ltd* [1981] ICR 558, [1981] IRLR 178, ECJ. See Case C-381/99 *Brunnhofer v Bank der Österreichischen Postsparkasse AG* [2001] All ER (EC) 693, [2001] ECR I-4961, ECJ.

3   Ie EC Directive 75/117 (OJ L45, 19.2.75, p 19) on the approximation of the laws of the member states relating to the application of the principle of equal pay for men and women, which introduced the concept of equal pay for work of equal value and provides for the implementation of the principle of equal pay. For the history of its introduction see Case 43/74 *Defrenne v Sabena (No 2)* [1981] 1 All ER 122, [1976] ICR 547, ECJ. As from 15 August 2009, EC Directive 75/117 (OJ L45, 19.2.75, p 19) and certain other Directives (see paras 338, 340, 418 ante) are repealed and replaced by European Parliament and EC Council Directive 2006/54 (OJ L204, 26.7.2006, p 23) on the implementation of the principle of equal opportunities and equal treatment of men and women in matters of employment and occupation. This effectively is a consolidation of the relevant Directives and from 15 August 2009 references to the repealed Directives are to be construed as references to EC Council Directive 2006/54 (OJ L204, 26.7.2006, p 23): see art 34.

4   Ie the EC Commission's Code of Practice on the implementation of equal pay for work of equal value for women and men (17 July 1996) (COM(94) 6). Courts and tribunals may consider the Code of Practice when interpreting and applying the European Union measures and United Kingdom implementing legislation.

5   Case 43/74 *Defrenne v Sabena (No 2)* [1981] 1 All ER 122, [1976] ICR 547, ECJ.

6   Case 106/77 *Amministrazione delle Finanze dello Stato v Simmenthal SpA* [1978] ECR 629, ECJ.

7   Case C-262/88 *Barber v Guardian Royal Exchange Assurance Group* [1991] 1 QB 344, [1990] ICR 616, ECJ.

8   Case C-262/88 *Barber v Guardian Royal Exchange Assurance Group* [1991] 1 QB 344, [1990] ICR 616, ECJ. See Case C-381/99 *Brunnhofer v Bank der Österreichischen Postsparkasse AG* [2001] All ER (EC) 693, [2001] ECR I-4961, ECJ. As to overtime payments for full-time and part-time workers see Case C-285/02 *Elsner-Lakeberg v Land Nordrhein-Westfalen* [2004] 2 CMLR 874, [2005] IRLR 209, ECJ.

9   Case C-408/92 *Smith v Avdel Systems Ltd* [1995] ICR 596, [1994] IRLR 602, ECJ.

10   Case 43/74 *Defrenne v Sabena (No 2)* [1981] 1 All ER 122, [1976] ICR 547, ECJ. The European Court
      of Justice drew a distinction between 'direct and overt' discrimination, which may be identified solely
      with the aid of criteria based on equal work and equal pay referred to in the EC Treaty art 141 (as
      renumbered), and 'indirect and disguised' discrimination, which can only be identified by reference to
      more explicit implementing provisions of a community or national character in relation to which art 141
      (as renumbered) is not of direct effect. However, it is now clear that art 141 (as renumbered) is of direct
      effect where inequality of pay arises as a result of indirect discrimination in the form of disparate impact:
      Case 170/84 *Bilka-Kaufhaus GmbH v Weber Von Hartz* [1987] ICR 110, [1986] IRLR 317, ECJ. See also
      para 422 post. As to the meaning of 'direct effect' see 26/62 *NV Algemene Transport en Expeditie
      Onderneming van Gend & Loos v Nederlandse Administratie der Belastingen* [1963] ECR 1, ECJ.

11   *Biggs v Somerset County Council* [1996] 2 All ER 734, [1995] ICR 811, EAT. Reliance must be placed on
      the statutory authority, modified, if necessary, by striking out any provisions incompatible with the EC
      Treaty art 141 (as renumbered).

420.   The meaning of 'pay' in European law.   'Pay' is defined as the ordinary
basic or minimum wage or salary and any other consideration, whether in cash or in
kind, which the worker receives directly or indirectly, in respect of his employment,
from his employer[1]. The European Court of Justice has adopted an extremely broad
definition of pay[2].

The term 'pay' includes salary, overtime rates where men and women work the same
hours[3], automatic pay increases[4], bonus payments that amount to retroactive pay for
work carried out during the course of the year[5], allowances for periods carrying out
duties away from work[6], sick pay (provided it is paid by the employer rather than a social
security body)[7] and certain non-monetary benefits[8].

Maternity pay constitutes pay for the purpose of Article 141 of the EC Treaty[9].
However, where maternity pay is lower than normal contractual remuneration[10] or sick
pay[11] there is no breach of the principle of equal pay. This is because discrimination
involves the application of different rules to comparable situations or the application of
the same rule to different situations. The position of a woman absent on maternity leave
is unique and is not comparable to that of a man at work or a man who is absent due to
ill-health[12]. However, where a woman is absent from work for a pregnancy-related
illness prior to the period of maternity leave there will be a breach of the principle of
equal pay if she is not paid at the same rate as a man absent through ill-health[13]. Once
she returns to work, a woman is entitled to the benefit of any pay rise that was
implemented while she was absent on maternity leave[14].

Various payments made on or after the termination of employment constitute pay.
These include notice monies[15], statutory and contractual redundancy payments[16], and
unfair dismissal compensation[17].

1   Treaty Establishing the European Community (EC Treaty) (Rome, 25 March 1957; TS 1 (1973);
     Cmnd 5179) (the 'EC Treaty') art 141(2) (formerly art 119; renumbered by virtue of the Treaty of
     Amsterdam: see *Treaty Citation (No 2) (Note)* [1999] All ER (EC) 646, ECJ). As to the EC Treaty art 141
     (as renumbered) see para 419 ante.

2   See Case C-167/97 *R v Secretary of State for Employment, ex p Seymour-Smith* [1999] 2 AC 554, [1999]
     ICR 447, ECJ. See also Case C-381/99 *Brunnhofer v Bank der Österreichischen Postsparkasse AG* [2001] All
     ER (EC) 693, [2001] ECR I-4961, ECJ.

3   Where men and women work the same hours they are entitled to the same overtime rate; however, the
     principle of equal pay does not require that women who work part-time are paid overtime rates for work
     beyond their normal hours: Case C-399/92 *Stadt Lengerich v Helmig* [1996] ICR 35, [1995] IRLR 216,
     ECJ. See also Case C-236/98 *Jämställdhetsombudsmannen v Örebro Läns Landsting* [2000] ECR I-2189,
     [2001] ICR 249, [2000] 2 CMLR 708, ECJ.

4   Case C-184/89 *Nimz v Freie und Hansestadt Hamburg* [1991] ECR I-297, [1991] IRLR 222, ECJ; Case
     C-243/95 *Hill and Stapleton v IRC and Department of Finance* [1998] All ER (EC) 722, [1998] IRLR 466,
     ECJ; cf Case C-1/95 *Gerster v Freistaat Bayern* [1998] ICR 327, [1997] IRLR 699, ECJ.

5   Case C-333/97 *Lewen v Denda* [2000] All ER (EC) 261, [2000] IRLR 67, ECJ; Case C-281/97 *Krüger
     v Kreiskrankenhaus Ebersberg* [1999] ECR I-5127, [1999] IRLR 808, ECJ.

6   Case C-360/90 *Arbeiterwohlfahrt der Stadt Berlin eV v Bötel* [1992] ECR I-3589, [1992] IRLR 423, ECJ; Case C-457/93 *Kuratorium für Dialyse Und Nierentransplantation eV v Lewark* [1996] ECR I-243, [1996] IRLR 637, ECJ. Cf *Manor Bakeries Ltd v Nazir* [1996] IRLR 604, EAT.

7   Case 171/88 *Rinner-Kühn v FWW Spezial-Gebäudereinigung GmbH & Co KG* [1989] ECR 2743, [1989] IRLR 493, ECJ.

8   Case 12/81 *Garland v British Rail Engineering Ltd* [1982] ECR 359, [1982] IRLR 111, ECJ.

9   Case C-342/93 *Gillespie v Northern Health and Social Services Board* [1996] ICR 498, [1996] IRLR 214, ECJ. As to maternity rights see EMPLOYMENT vol 16(1A) (Reissue) para 132 et seq.

10   Case C-342/93 *Gillespie v Northern Health and Social Services Board* [1996] ICR 498, [1996] IRLR 214, ECJ.

11   *Todd v Eastern Health and Social Services Board, Gillespie v Northern Health and Social Services Board (No 2)* [1997] IRLR 410, NI CA.

12   *Gillespie v Northern Health and Social Services Board (No 2)* [1997] IRLR 410, NI CA. See also Case C-411/96 *Boyle v Equal Opportunities Commission* [1998] All ER (EC) 879, [1998] IRLR 717, ECJ; Case C-218/98 *Abdoulaye v Régie Nationale des Usines Renault SA* [1999) ECR I-5723, [1999] IRLR 811, ECJ; Case C-249/97 *Gruber v Silhouette International Schmeid GmbH & Co KG* [1999] ECR I-5295, ECJ. Employers can continue to pay higher wages in recognition of experience and length of service even if it is detrimental to women who have maternity leave but have no automatic right to the same pay as male colleagues who are doing the same job but have not had time off: see Case C-17/05 *Cadman v Health and Safety Executive* [2007] All ER (EC) 1, [2006] ICR 1623, ECJ.

13   Case C-66/96 *Pedersen* [1999 All ER (EC) 138, [1999] IRLR 55, ECJ.

14   Case C-342/93 *Gillespie v Northern Health and Social Services Board* [1996] ICR 498, [1996] IRLR 214, ECJ.

15   The European Court of Justice has not been called upon to decide whether payments in lieu of notice amount to pay for the purpose of the EC Treaty art 141 (as renumbered). However, the Court of Appeal's provisional view was that the concept of pay could include statutory notice payments made by the Secretary of State in the event of an employer's insolvency: *Clark v Secretary of State for Employment* [1997] ICR 64, [1996] IRLR 578, CA.

16   Case C-262/88 *Barber v Guardian Royal Exchange Assurance Group* [1991] 1 QB 344, [1990] ICR 616, ECJ. See also *Hammersmith and Queen Charlotte's Special Hospital Authority v Cato* [1988] 1 CMLR 3, [1988] ICR 132, EAT.

17   Case C-167/97 *R v Secretary of State for Employment, ex p Seymour-Smith* [1999] 2 AC 554, [1999] ICR 447, ECJ. See also *Mediguard Services Ltd v Thame* [1994] ICR 751, [1994] IRLR 504, EAT; followed in *Methilhill Bowling Club v Hunter* [1995] ICR 793, [1995] IRLR 32, EAT.

421.   Equal pay and pensions. Article 141 of the EC Treaty[1] does not apply to social security pension schemes[2]. However, benefits paid under the majority of European Union occupational pension schemes are pay for the purposes of Article 141[3]. United Kingdom occupational pension schemes are covered by the principle of equal pay, whether contracted out[4] or not[5]. Article 141 is likely to apply to the majority of public sector pension schemes[6].

The principle of equal pay extends to the right to join a pension scheme[7] and to the payment of benefits under the scheme[8]. Specific time limits apply to such claims[9]. Men and women are entitled to receive the same benefits at the same age[10]. Payments made to the dependants of pension scheme members also constitute pay[11].

Compulsory employees' contributions constitute pay. Men and women are entitled to equal gross pay before the deduction of such contributions[12]. However, in a final salary pension scheme it is lawful for employers' contributions to vary between men and women to take account of actuarial factors[13].

Where an element of a pension derives from additional voluntary contributions, it does not amount to pay for the purpose of Article 141, as the pension scheme does no more than provide the members with the arrangements for management of their contributions[14].

Article 141 may be relied upon to mount a claim against the trustees of an occupational pension fund, who may be required to exercise their powers under the scheme in accordance with the principle of equal pay and, if necessary, apply to the court for a variation of the trust deed[15].

1	Ie the Treaty Establishing the European Community (Rome, 25 March 1957; TS 1 (1973); Cmnd 5179) art 141 (formerly art 119; renumbered by virtue of the Treaty of Amsterdam: see *Treaty Citation (No 2) (Note)* [1999] All ER (EC) 646, ECJ). See para 419 ante.

2	Case 80/70 *Defrenne v Belgium* [1971] ECR 445, ECJ (the European Court of Justice drew a distinction between state benefits, determined by considerations of social policy, and schemes that provide benefits determined by the employment relationship). As to state retirement pensions see SOCIAL SECURITY AND PENSIONS vol 44(2) (Reissue) para 561 et seq.

3	Case 170/84 *Bilka-Kaufhaus GmbH v Weber Von Hartz* [1987] ICR 110, [1986] IRLR 317, ECJ (the European Court of Justice held that it was contrary to the EC Treaty art 141 (as renumbered: see note 1 supra) to exclude part-time employees from the benefits of an occupational pension scheme, where the exclusion affects a far greater number of women than men, unless the exclusion is based on objectively justified factors unrelated to any discrimination on grounds of sex); followed in Case C-50/96 *Deutsche Telekom v Schröder* [2000] ECR I743, [2002] 2 CMLR 583, ECJ. As to occupational pension schemes see SOCIAL SECURITY AND PENSIONS vol 44(2) (Reissue) para 741 et seq.

4	Case C-262/88 *Barber v Guardian Royal Exchange Assurance Group* [1991] 1 QB 344, [1990] ICR 616, ECJ. As to contracting out see SOCIAL SECURITY AND PENSIONS vol 44(2) (Reissue) para 877 et seq.

5	Case C-200/91 *Coloroll Pension Trustees Ltd v Russell* [1995] All ER (EC) 23, [1995] ICR 179, ECJ.

6	Case C-7/93 *Bestuur Van het Algemeen Burgerlijk Pensioenfonds v Beune* [1995] All ER (EC) 97, [1995] IRLR 103, ECJ. See, however, indications to the contrary in Case 192/85 *Newstead v Department of Transport* [1988] 1 All ER 129, [1988] 1 WLR 612, ECJ; *Griffin v London Pension Fund Authority* [1993] ICR 564, [1993] IRLR 248, EAT. As to public service pension schemes see SOCIAL SECURITY AND PENSIONS vol 44(2) (Reissue) para 874 et seq.

7	Case C-170/84 *Bilka-Kauhaus GmbH v Weber Von Hartz* [1987] ICR 110, [1986] IRLR 317, ECJ (which strictly speaking did not concern the right to join a pension scheme but has been repeatedly quoted as authority for the proposition in subsequent cases); Case C-57/93 *Vroege v NCIV Instituut Voor Volkshuisvesting BV* [1995] All ER (EC) 193, [1995] ICR 635, ECJ; Case C-128/93 *Fisscher v Voorhuis Hengelo BV* [1995] All ER (EC) 193, [1995] ICR 635, ECJ; Case C-246/96 *Magorrian v Eastern Health and Social Services Board* [1998] All ER (EC) 38, [1998] ICR 979, ECJ.

8	Case C-262/88 *Barber v Guardian Royal Exchange Assurance Group* [1991] 1 QB 344, [1990] ICR 616, ECJ.

9	As a matter of European Union law, claims in respect of benefits payable under pension schemes can be brought only in relation to periods of service subsequent to the date of the judgment in Case C-262/88 *Barber v Guardian Royal Exchange Assurance Group* [1991] 1 QB 344, [1990] ICR 616, ECJ, save where the employee had brought proceedings before that date: Case C-200/91 *Coloroll Pension Trustees Ltd v Russell* [1995] 1 All ER (EC) 23, [1995] ICR 179, [1994] IRLR 586, ECJ. Claims for membership of a pension scheme may be brought in respect of any period of service from 8 April 1976, when the European Court of Justice gave its decision in Case 43/74 *Defrenne v Sabena (No 2)* [1981] 1 All ER 122, [1976] ICR 547, ECJ: see Case C-57/93 *Vroege v NCIV Instituut Voor Volkshuisvesting BV* [1995] All ER (EC) 193, [1995] ICR 635, ECJ. Employers and pension fund trustees may rely on limitations provided for in national legislation provided they are not less favourable than for similar actions of a domestic nature and do not render the exercise of rights conferred by European law impossible in practice: Case C-128/93 *Fisscher v Voorhuis Hengelo BV* [1995] All ER (EC) 193, [1995] ICR 635, ECJ. In Case C-246/96 *Magorrian v Eastern Health and Social Services Board* [1998] All ER (EC) 38, [1998] IRLR 86, ECJ, it was held that the provisions of the Occupational Pension Schemes (Equal Access to Membership) Regulations (Northern Ireland) 1976, SI 1976/238, which limit the right to claim membership of a scheme to the period of two years prior to a claim being instigated, were incompatible with European Union law, as they made the claim in respect of access to the scheme impossible in practice.

This approach was followed in Case C-78/98 *Preston v Wolverhampton Healthcare NHS Trust, Fletcher v Midland Bank plc* [2001] 2 AC 415, [2000] All ER (EC) 714, ECJ, in which it was held that the two-year limitation under the Equal Pay Act 1970 s 2(5) (as then in force) (see para 435 post) was in breach of the principle of effectiveness in that it rendered any action by individuals relying on European law impossible in practice. This decision allows claims to be brought in relation to the exclusion of part-time workers from occupational pension schemes covering periods after the date of the judgment in Case 43/74 *Defrenne v Sabena (No 2)* supra (i e 8 April 1976). The European Court of Justice also held in Case C-78/98 *Preston v Wolverhampton Healthcare NHS Trust, Fletcher v Midland Bank plc* supra that the six-month time limit provided by the Equal Pay Act 1970 s 2(4) (as then in force) (see para 435 post) was not contrary to the principle of effectiveness as it did not render impossible or excessively difficult the exercise of rights conferred by European law; it was for the national court to determine whether the provision complied with the principle of equivalence in that it was not less favourable than other procedural rules applicable to similar proceedings of a domestic nature considering both the purpose and essential characteristics of allegedly similar domestic actions. A subsidiary issue concerned the position of teachers employed on consecutive short-term contracts concluded at regular intervals; it was held that where such short-term contracts are part of a stable employment relationship, it is unlawful for a procedural rule to require that a claim be brought within six months of the end of each contract of employment, as had been held to be the case by the Court of Appeal. See also the House of Lords decision at [2001] UKHL 5, [2001] 2 AC 455, [2001] ICR 217. See further *Preston v Wolverhampton Healthcare NHS Trust (No 3), Fletcher v Midland Bank plc (No 3)* [2006] UKHL 13, [2006] 3 All ER 193 (in relation to claims against the transferor, the six-month limitation period was held to run from the date of transfer of employment).

10 Case C-262/88 *Barber v Guardian Royal Exchange Assurance Group* [1991] 1 QB 344, [1990] ICR 616, ECJ. See also Case C-110/91 *Moroni v Collo GmbH* [1995] ICR 137, [1994] IRLR 130, ECJ; Case C-408/92 *Smith v Avdel Systems Ltd* [1995] All ER (EC) 132, [1995] ICR 596, ECJ; Case C-28/93 *Van den Akker v Stichting Shell Pensioenfonds* [1995] All ER (EC) 156, [1995] ICR 596, ECJ; cf Case C-132/92 *Roberts v Birds Eye Walls Ltd* [1994] ICR 338, [1994] IRLR 29, ECJ.

11 Case C-109/91 *Ten Oever v Stichting Bedrijfspensioenfonds Voor Het Glazenwassers-en Schoonmaakbedrijf* [1995] ICR 74, [1993] IRLR 601, ECJ. See also Case C-117/01 *KB v National Health Service Pensions Agency* [2004] All ER (EC) 1089, [2004] ICR 781, ECJ.

12 Case C-69/80 *Worringham v Lloyd's Bank Ltd* [1981] ICR 558, [1981] IRLR 178, ECJ; Case 192/85 *Newstead v Department of Transport* [1988] 1 All ER 129, [1988] 1 WLR 612, ECJ.

13 Case C-152/91 *Neath v Hugh Steeper Ltd* [1995] ICR 158, [1994] IRLR 91, ECJ; Case C-200/91 *Coloroll Pension Trustees Ltd v Russell* [1995] All ER (EC) 23, [1995] ICR 179, [1994] IRLR 586, ECJ.

14 Case C-200/91 *Coloroll Pension Trustees Ltd v Russell* [1995] All ER (EC) 23, [1995] ICR 179, [1994] IRLR 586, ECJ.

15 Case C-200/91 *Coloroll Pension Trustees Ltd v Russell* [1995] All ER (EC) 23, [1995] ICR 179, [1994] IRLR 586, ECJ.

422.   Establishing a breach of the principle of equal pay.   The principle of equal pay[1] has been described as a particular expression of the general principle of non-discrimination[2]. In the majority of the cases before the European Court of Justice there has been no suggestion that the applicant and her comparator were not engaged in equal work or work of equal value. However, if this is not the case, the principle of equal pay cannot apply[3]. The situation of a woman and her comparator must be properly comparable[4].

The principle of equal pay is breached where there is either direct or indirect discrimination[5].

Where a provision affects a considerably greater number[6] of women than men, it is contrary to Article 141 of the EC Treaty[7] unless it is established that the exclusion is based on objectively justified factors unrelated to any discrimination on grounds of sex. The objective must correspond to a real need on the part of the undertaking, and the means chosen must be appropriate with a view to achieving the objective in question and be necessary to that end[8]. Where a legitimate objective could be achieved without discrimination this should be done.

Although it is for the national court to determine whether a provision is objectively justified, the European Court of Justice has been prepared to give some guidance[9]. Where a pay structure disproportionately affects a group of employees that is predominantly made up of women it is for the employer to establish that the structure is objectively justified[10], particularly if the pay structure is lacking in transparency[11]. Mere generalisations about particular categories of workers do not provide objective justification[12].

The European Court of Justice has adopted a less restrictive approach where discrimination is alleged to result from the application of a legislative provision[13]. Social policy is a matter for the member states who are entitled to introduce legislative provisions provided they reasonably consider that the legislation in question is necessary in order to achieve a social policy aim unrelated to any discrimination on grounds of sex.

1   See para 419 ante.

2   Case C-342/93 *Gillespie v Northern Health and Social Services Board* [1996] All ER (EC) 284, [1996] ICR 498, ECJ.

See Case C-381/99 *Brunnhofer v Bank der Österreichischen Postsparkasse AG* [2001] All ER (EC) 693, [2001] ECR I-4961, ECJ (difference in pay received from commencement of employment cannot be justified by factors which can only be assessed after commencement of employment); applied in *Sharp v Caledonia Group Services Ltd* [2006] ICR 218, [2006] IRLR 4, EAT. See also note 9 infra.

3 Case C-309/97 *Angestelltenbetriebsrat der Wiener Gebietskrankenkasse v Wiener Gebietskrankenkasse* [1999] ECR I-2865, [1999] IRLR 804, ECJ. In this case, psychotherapists were paid differently depending on whether they had been trained as psychologists or doctors. The European Court of Justice held that the two groups could not be treated as carrying out like work. The court noted that the two groups were recruited on the basis of their different training and drew upon knowledge and skills acquired in very different disciplines. The court held that as a result of their different professional training, which resulted in them being called on to perform different tasks or duties, their situations could not be regarded as being comparable.

4 For example, in the context of maternity pay see Case C-342/93 *Gillespie v Northern Health and Social Services Board* [1996] All ER (EC) 284, [1996] ICR 498, ECJ; Case C-411/96 *Boyle v Equal Opportunities Commission* [1998] All ER (EC) 879, [1998] IRLR 717, ECJ; Case C-218/98 *Abdoulaye v Régie Nationale des Usines Renault SA* [1999] ECR I-5723, [1999] IRLR 811; Case C-249/97 *Gruber v Silhouette International Schmeid GmbH & Co KG* [1999] ECR I-5295, ECJ. See also *Barry v Midland Bank plc* [1999] 3 All ER 974, [1999] ICR 859, HL.

5 Provisions (i e statutory rules, contractual terms, policies, practices or pay structures) may discriminate in one of two main ways. First, a provision may entirely exclude men or women from access to a particular benefit. For instance, the rules of a pension scheme may entitle a woman to a pension at 60 whereas a man would have to wait until the age of 65; at the age of 60 all men are excluded from a benefit that is available to all women. Such a rule gives rise to direct discrimination. Alternatively, a rule may appear neutral, applying to both men and women, but have a much greater effect on women than men. The most obvious example is a provision that prevents part-time workers obtaining a benefit. If it can be established that a substantial majority of part-time workers are women, the rule will have disparate impact and give rise to indirect discrimination. As to direct and indirect discrimination in the context of sex discrimination see paras 344, 351, 355 ante.

6 The general approach was set out in Case 170/84 *Bilka-Kaufhaus GmbH v Weber Von Hartz* [1987] ICR 110, [1986] IRLR 317, ECJ. The European Court of Justice referred to exclusion of part-time workers from the pension scheme in question as affecting a 'far greater proportion' of women than men. The court has adopted a number of differing formulations for the relevant proportion. However, in more recent cases the court has settled on the test of whether the provision affects a considerably greater number of women than men: see e g Case C-167/97 *R v Secretary of State for Employment, ex p Seymour-Smith* [1999] 2 AC 554, [1999] ICR 447, ECJ. The European Court of Justice suggested that a smaller difference may be sufficient where the difference persists over a long period. This is because the shorter the time frame over which statistics are analysed, the greater the risk that they may have been affected by purely fortuitous or short-term factors. It is for the national court to assess the validity of the statistical material: Case C-127/92 *Enderby v Frenchay Health Authority* [1994] ICR 112, [1993] IRLR 591, ECJ. See also *R v Secretary of State for Employment, ex p Seymour-Smith* [2000] ICR 244, [2000] IRLR 263, HL.

7 Ie the Treaty Establishing the European Community (EC Treaty) (Rome, 25 March 1957; TS 1 (1973); Cmnd 5179) art 141 (formerly art 119; renumbered by virtue of the Treaty of Amsterdam: see *Treaty Citation (No 2) (Note)* [1999] All ER (EC) 646, ECJ). See para 419 ante.

8 Case 170/84 *Bilka-Kaufhaus GmbH v Weber Von Hartz* [1987] ICR 110, [1986] IRLR 317, ECJ.

9 For a consideration of specific factors see Case 170/84 *Bilka-Kaufhaus GmbH v Weber Von Hartz* [1987] ICR 110, [1986] IRLR 317, ECJ. See, however, Case 171/88 *Rinner-Kühn v FWW Spezial-Gebäudereinigung GmbH & Co KG* [1989] ECR 2743, [1989] IRLR 493, ECJ; Case 109/88 *Handels-og Kontorfunktionaerernes Forbund i Danmark v Dansk Arbejdsgiverforening* [1991] ICR 74, [1989] IRLR 532, ECJ; Case C-184/89 *Nimz v Freie und Hansestadt Hamburg* [1991] ECR I-297, [1991] IRLR 222, ECJ; Case C-127/92 *Enderby v Frenchay Health Authority* [1994] ICR 112, [1993] IRLR 591, ECJ; Case C-243/95 *Hill v IRC* [1998] All ER (EC) 722, [1998] IRLR 466, ECJ; Case C-167/97 *R v Secretary of State for Employment, ex p Seymour-Smith* [1999] 2 AC 554, [1999] ICR 447, ECJ. As a general rule, recourse to the criterion of length of service was appropriate to attain the legitimate objective of rewarding experience acquired which enabled a worker better to perform his duties; the employer did not have to justify recourse to this criterion unless the worker provided evidence capable of raising serious doubts: see Case C-17/05 *Cadman v Health and Safety Executive* [2006] All ER (EC) 1, [2006] ICR 1623, ECJ.

As to the question of what the employer has to justify see also Case C-381/99 *Brunnhofer v Bank der Österreichischen Postsparkasse AG* [2001] All ER (EC) 693, [2001] ECR I-4961, ECJ; *Sharp v Caledonia Group Services Ltd* [2006] ICR 218, [2006] IRLR 4, EAT; and note 2 supra. One reading of Case C-381/99 *Brunnhofer v Bank der Österreichischen Postsparkasse AG* supra is that any proved inequality of treatment needs to be justified while generally the approach in the United Kingdom cases (at least until

Sharp v Caledonia Group Services Ltd supra) has been that there has to be a sexually discriminatory practice (producing the unequal pay) before there is a burden on the employer to show objective justification; if not it is enough just to show a non-generic reason (eg different history of collective bargaining) without having to justify it: see *Tyldesley v TML Plastics Ltd* [1996] ICR 356, [1996] IRLR 395, EAT. See *Villalba v Merill Lynch & Co Inc* [2006] IRLR 437, EAT (where the Employment Appeal Tribunal took the line that objective justification is only necessary once a prima facie case of indirect sex discrimination has been made out); and see *Parliamentary Comr for Administration v Fernandez* [2004] 2 CMLR 59, [2004] ICR 123, EAT. See also *Best v Tyne and Wear Passenger and Transport Executive (t/a Nexus)* [2006] All ER (D) 362 (Dec), EAT, where *Villalba v Merill Lynch & Co Inc* supra was applied.

10 Case C-127/92 *Enderby v Frenchay Health Authority* [1994] ICR 112, [1993] IRLR 591, ECJ. Where one group of employees is disadvantaged in comparison to another group which is predominantly male, the employer is required objectively to justify the difference irrespective of whether the disadvantaged group contains a significant number of men: *Home Office v Bailey* [2005] EWCA Civ 327, [2005] ICR 1057, [2005] IRLR 369. See also note 9 supra.

11 Case 109/88 *Handels-og Kontorfunktionaerernes Forbund i Danmark v Dansk Arbejdsgiverforening (acting for Danfoss)* [1991] ICR 74, [1989] IRLR 532.

12 Case 171/88 *Rinner-Kühn v FWW Spezial-Gebäudereinigung GmbH & Co KG* [1989] ECR 2743, [1989] IRLR 493, ECJ.

13 Case C-317/93 *Nolte v Landesversicherungsanstalt Hannover* [1996] All ER (EC) 212, [1996] IRLR 225, ECJ. See also Case C-167/97 *R v Secretary of State for Employment, ex p Seymour-Smith* [1999] 2 AC 554, [1999] ICR 447, ECJ. Cf Case C-281/99 *Kruger v Kreiskrankenhaus Ebersberg* [1999] ECR I-5127, ECJ.

423.   United Kingdom statutory provisions. A claim that there has been a breach of the principle of equal pay[1] must be brought in the United Kingdom under the provisions of either the Equal Pay Act 1970 or the Sex Discrimination Act 1975[2].

The Equal Pay Act 1970 operates by deeming that the woman's contract of employment includes an equality clause[3]. The Equal Pay Act 1970 is framed with reference to women, and their treatment in relation to men, but applies equally where a man does not receive equal pay[4]. The Equal Pay Act 1970 covers all contractual provisions, and it is of wider scope than the principle of equal pay. However, it does not apply to non-contractual remuneration. In such a case a claim must be brought under the Sex Discrimination Act 1975. The inter-relation of the two Acts is complex[5].

The Equal Pay Act 1970 received Royal Assent on 29 May 1970. However, it did not come into force until 29 December 1975[6]. The delay was designed to give employers an opportunity to eradicate discrimination from their pay practices voluntarily. The Equal Pay Act 1970 was brought into force on the same day as the Sex Discrimination Act 1975, and the fact that both Acts came into force on the same date emphasises that they are to be treated as a single code[7].

However, the Equal Pay Act 1970 and the Sex Discrimination Act 1975 are mutually exclusive; a claim must lie under one or the other, although proceedings may be brought claiming under both in the alternative.

1   See para 419 ante.

2   As to claims under the Equal Pay Act 1970 see para 424 et seq post. As to claims under the Sex Discrimination Act 1975 see para 342 et seq ante. See also *Biggs v Somerset County Council* [1996] 2 All ER 734, [1996] ICR 364, CA. For the meaning of 'United Kingdom' see para 325 note 6 ante.

3   See the Equal Pay Act 1970 s 1(1) (as substituted); and para 424 post.

4   See ibid s 1(13) (added by the Sex Discrimination Act 1975 s 8(6), Sch 1 Pt I; and amended by the Equal Pay (Amendment) Regulations 1983, SI 1983/1794, reg 3(2); and the Equal Pay Act 1970 (Amendment) Regulations 2003, SI 2003/1656, reg 10).

5   As to the inter-relationship between the Equal Pay Act 1970 and the Sex Discrimination Act 1975 see ss 6, 8 (both as amended); and para 360 et seq ante. See also *Peake v Automotive Products Ltd* [1977] QB 780, [1977] ICR 480, EAT; revsd on other grounds [1978] QB 233, [1977] IRLR 365, CA.

6   See the Equal Pay Act 1970 s 9 (amended by the Sex Discrimination Act 1975 Sch 1 Pt I).

7   See *Strathclyde Regional Council v Wallace* [1998] 1 All ER 394, [1998] IRLR 146, HL.

(2) EQUAL PAY ACT 1970

424. Operation of the Equal Pay Act 1970. The Equal Pay Act 1970 applies where a woman[1] is employed[2] at an establishment[3] in Great Britain[4]. The woman must be employed on like work[5], work rated as equivalent[6] or work of equal value[7] with a man in the same employment[8]. In other words, the woman must be able to point to a male comparator[9]. In such circumstances an equality clause is implied into the woman's contract of employment which will entitle her to contractual benefits equal to those of her male comparator[10]. However, the equality clause does not operate in respect of a variation between the woman's and the man's contract of employment if the employer proves that the variation is genuinely due to a material factor which is not the difference of sex[11].

For the purposes of the Equal Pay Act 1970 it is immaterial whether the law which is the law applicable to the contract of employment is the law of any part of the United Kingdom or not[12].

A provision in a collective agreement that is in breach of the principle of equal pay is unlawful[13].

The Equal Pay Act 1970 contains provisions to help a complainant decide whether to institute proceedings under the Act and to present her case in the most effective manner[14].

1 These provisions apply equally to men: see the Equal Pay Act 1970 s 1(13) (as added and amended); and para 423 ante. 'Man' and 'woman' are to be read as applying to persons of whatever age: s 11(2). A woman is under a disability if she is a minor or of unsound mind: s 11(2A) (added by the Equal Pay Act 1970 (Amendment) Regulations 2003, SI 2003/1656, reg 9).

2 'Employed' means employed under a contract of service or of apprenticeship or a contract personally to execute any work or labour; and related expressions are to be construed accordingly: Equal Pay Act 1970 s 1(6)(a). On the face of it, where a contract is tainted with illegality an employee will not be able to make a claim under the Equal Pay Act 1970 as such a claim is founded on the contract of employment. Cf the position under the Sex Discrimination Act 1975: see *Leighton v Michael* [1995] ICR 1091, [1996] IRLR 67, EAT. The Equal Pay Act 1970 applies to a self employed person if he or she agrees to provide services personally: see e g *Quinnen v Hovells* [1984] ICR 525, 1984 IRLR 227, EAT. As to the similar definition in the Sex Discrimination Act 1975 see s 82(1); and para 360 note 4 ante.

3 The term 'establishment' is not defined in the Equal Pay Act 1970. Some assistance may be obtained where the term is used in other employment law statutes without being defined: see e g *Secretary of State for Employment and Productivity v Vic Hallam Ltd* (1969) 5 ITR 108, 114 Sol Jo 31, DC; *Barley v Amey Roadstone Corpn Ltd (No 2)* [1978] ICR 190, EAT. However, the principle of equal pay should not be circumvented by applying a narrow definition of 'establishment'. For the purposes of the Sex Discrimination Act 1975, where work is not carried out at an establishment it is treated as being done at the establishment from which it is done or the establishment with which it has the closest connection: see s 10(4); and para 360 note 5 ante.

4 See the Equal Pay Act 1970 s 1(1) (substituted by the Sex Discrimination Act 1975 s 8(1)). For the meaning of 'Great Britain' see para 325 note 6 ante. For the purposes of the Equal Pay Act 1970, 'Great Britain' includes such of the territorial waters of the United Kingdom as are adjacent to Great Britain: s 1(12) (added by the Sex Discrimination Act 1975 s 8(6), Sch 1 Pt I). For the meaning of 'United Kingdom' see para 325 note 6 ante. As to work conducted on the Continental Shelf see the Sex Discrimination Act 1975 s 10(5) (as amended; prospectively amended); and para 360 note 6 ante. As to the meaning of employment at an establishment in Great Britain for the purposes of the Sex Discrimination Act 1975 see s 10 (as amended; prospectively amended); and para 360 note 6 ante. The limitation to employment in establishments in Great Britain has been placed in doubt by the Employment Appeal Tribunal: see *Bossa v Nordstress Ltd* [1998] ICR 694, [1998] IRLR 284, EAT.

See also *Wild v Serco Group plc* [2007] All ER (D) 92 (Feb), EAT, where it was held that a letter in which the employee had complained about the lack of pay reviews and her low rate of pay generally compared to other (male) members of the team was sufficient to constitute a grievance for the purposes of her subsequent claim based on the Equal Pay Act 1970, given the context of previous complaints about sex discrimination in relation to pay.

5 See para 427 post. See also note 10 infra.

6 See para 428 post. See also note 10 infra.

7   See para 429 post. See also note 10 infra.
8   See para 426 post. See also note 10 infra.
9   See para 425 post. A female employee making a complaint of discrimination in relation to the payment
     of maternity pay is not required to prove there is a male comparator: *Alabaster v Barclays Bank plc* [2005]
     EWCA Civ 508, [2005] ICR 1246, [2005] All ER (D) 02 (May).
10   See the Equal Pay Act 1970 s 1(1) (s 1(1), (2) substituted by the Sex Discrimination Act 1975 s 8(1)).
         An equality clause is a provision which relates to terms (whether concerned with pay or not) of a
     contract under which a woman is employed (the 'woman's contract'), and has the effect that:
     (1)   where the woman is employed on like work with a man in the same employment, if (apart from
           the equality clause) any term of the woman's contract is or becomes less favourable to the woman
           than a term of a similar kind in the contract under which that man is employed, that term of the
           woman's contract is treated as so modified as not to be less favourable; and if (apart from the
           equality clause) at any time the woman's contract does not include a term corresponding to a
           term benefiting that man included in the contract under which he is employed, the woman's
           contract is treated as including such a term (Equal Pay Act 1970 s 1(2)(a) (as so substituted));
     (2)   where the woman is employed on work rated as equivalent with that of a man in the same
           employment, if (apart from the equality clause) any term of the woman's contract determined by
           the rating of the work is or becomes less favourable to the woman than a term of a similar kind
           in the contract under which that man is employed, that term of the woman's contract is treated as
           so modified as not to be less favourable; and if (apart from the equality clause) at any time the
           woman's contract does not include a term corresponding to a term benefiting that man included
           in the contract under which he is employed and determined by the rating of the work, the
           woman's contract is treated as including such a term (s 1(2)(b) (as so substituted));
     (3)   where a woman is employed on work which, not being work in relation to which head (1) or
           head (2) supra applies, is, in terms of the demands made on her (for instance, under such headings
           as effort, skill and decision), of equal value to that of a man in the same employment, if (apart
           from the equality clause) any term of the woman's contract is or becomes less favourable to the
           woman than a term of a similar kind in the contract under which that man is employed, that term
           of the woman's contract is treated as so modified as not to be less favourable; and if (apart from
           the equality clause) at any time the woman's contract does not include a term corresponding to a
           term benefiting that man included in the contract under which he is employed, the woman's
           contract is treated as including such a term (s 1(2)(c) (added by the Equal Pay (Amendment)
           Regulations 1983, SI 1983/1794, reg 2(1)));
     (4)   where (a) any term of the woman's contract regulating maternity-related pay provides for any of
           her maternity-related pay to be calculated by reference to her pay at a particular time; (b) after
           that time (but before the end of the statutory maternity leave period) her pay is increased, or
           would have increased had she not been on statutory maternity leave; and (c) the maternity-related
           pay is neither what her pay would have been had she not been on statutory maternity leave nor
           the difference between what her pay would have been had she not been on statutory maternity
           leave and any statutory maternity pay to which she is entitled, if (apart from the equality clause)
           the terms of the woman's contract do not provide for the increase to be taken into account for
           the purpose of calculating the maternity-related pay, the term mentioned in head (a) supra is be
           treated as so modified as to provide for the increase to be taken into account for that purpose
           (Equal Pay Act s 1(2)(d) (s 1(2)(d)–(f) added by the Employment Equality (Sex Discrimination)
           Regulations 2005, SI 2005/2467, reg 36(1), (2)));
     (5)   if (apart from the equality clause) the terms of the woman's contract as to: (a) pay (including pay
           by way of bonus) in respect of times before she begins to be on statutory maternity leave; (b) pay
           by way of bonus in respect of times when she is absent from work in consequence of the
           prohibition in the Employment Rights Act 1996 s 72(1) (as substituted) (compulsory maternity
           leave) (see EMPLOYMENT vol 16(1A) (Reissue) para 322); or (c) pay by way of bonus in respect of
           times after she returns to work following her having been on statutory maternity leave, do not
           provide for such pay to be paid when it would be paid but for her having time off on statutory
           maternity leave, the woman's contract is treated as including a term providing for such pay to be
           paid when ordinarily it would be paid (Equal Pay Act 1970 s 1(2)(e) (as so added));
     (6)   if (apart from the equality clause) the terms of the woman's contract regulating her pay after
           returning to work following her having been on statutory maternity leave provide for any of that
           pay to be calculated without taking into account any amount by which her pay would have
           increased had she not been on statutory maternity leave, the woman's contract is treated as
           including a term providing for the increase to be taken into account in calculating that pay
           (s 1(2)(f) (as so added)).
         For the purposes of s 1(2)(d)–(f) (as added) (see heads (4)–(6) supra), 'maternity-related pay', in
     relation to a woman, means pay (including pay by way of bonus) to which she is entitled as a result of
     being pregnant or in respect of times when she is on statutory maternity leave, except that it does not

include any statutory maternity pay to which she is entitled; 'statutory maternity leave period', in relation to a woman, means the period during which she is on statutory maternity leave; an increase in an amount is taken into account in a calculation if in the calculation the amount as increased is substituted for the unincreased amount: s 1(5A) (s 1(5A), (5B) added by the Employment Equality (Sex Discrimination) Regulations 2005, SI 2005/2467, reg 36(1), (4)). For the purposes of the Equal Pay Act 1970 s 1(2)(d)–(f) (as added) (see heads (4)–(6) supra) and s 1(5A) (as added), 'on statutory maternity leave' means absent from work: (i) in exercise of the right conferred by the Employment Rights Act 1996 s 71(1) (as substituted) or s 73(1) (as substituted) (ordinary or additional maternity leave) (see EMPLOYMENT vol 16(1A) (Reissue) para 322); or (ii) in consequence of the prohibition in s 72(1) (as substituted) (compulsory maternity leave) (see EMPLOYMENT vol 16(1A) (Reissue) para 322): Equal Pay Act 1970 s 1(5B) (as so added).

11 See para 430 post.

12 Equal Pay Act 1970 s 1(11) (added by the Sex Discrimination Act 1975 Sch 1 Pt I; and amended by the Contracts (Applicable Law) Act 1990 s 5, Sch 4 para 1).

13 Where the terms of a collective agreement breach the principle of equal pay, they should be disapplied and the employees in the disadvantaged group should be awarded the benefits provided to those in the advantaged group: see Case C-184/89 *Nimz v Freie und Hansestadt Hamburg* [1991] ECR I–297, [1991] IRLR 222, ECJ; Case C-33/89 *Kowalska v Freie und Hansestadt Hamburg* [1992] ICR 29, [1990] IRLR 447, ECJ. EC Directive 75/117 (OJ L45, 19.2.75, p 19) on the approximation of the laws of the member states relating to the application of the principle of equal pay for men and women (the 'Equal Pay Directive'), art 4 provides that member states must take the necessary measures to ensure that provisions appearing in collective agreements, wage scales, wage agreements or individual contracts of employment which are contrary to the principle of equal pay must be, or may be declared, null and void or may be amended.

Collective agreements were originally dealt with by the Equal Pay Act 1970 s 3, but this provision has been repealed, save in respect of agricultural wages orders. See now the Sex Discrimination Act 1975 s 77 (as amended); the Sex Discrimination Act 1986 s 6 (as amended); and para 393 ante.

14 With a view to helping a complainant to decide whether to institute proceedings and, if she does so, to formulate and present her case in the most effective manner, the Secretary of State must by order prescribe forms by which the complainant may question the respondent on any matter which is or may be relevant, and forms by which the respondent may if he so wishes reply to any questions: Equal Pay Act 1970 s 7B(2) (s 7B added by the Employment Act 2002 s 42). As to the order that has been made see the Equal Pay (Questions and Replies) Order 2003, SI 2003/722. For the purposes of the Equal Pay Act 1970 s 7B (as added), a person who considers that she may have a claim under s 1 (as amended) is referred to as 'the complainant', and a person against whom the complainant may decide to make, or has made, a complaint under s 2(1) (as substituted and amended) (see para 435 post) or s 7A(3) (as added and amended) (see para 432 post) is referred to as 'the respondent': s 7B(1) (as so added). As to the Secretary of State and the National Assembly for Wales see para 302 ante.

Where the complainant questions the respondent (whether in accordance with an order under s 7B(2) (as added) or not), the question and any reply by the respondent (whether in accordance with such an order or not) are, subject to the following provisions of s 7B (as added), admissible as evidence in any proceedings under s 2(1) (as substituted and amended) or s 7A(3) (as added and amended): s 7B(3) (as so added). If in any such proceedings it appears to the employment tribunal that the complainant has questioned the respondent (whether in accordance with an order under s 7B(2) (as added) or not) and that: (1) the respondent deliberately and without reasonable excuse omitted to reply within such period as the Secretary of State may by order prescribe; or (2) the respondent's reply is evasive or equivocal, it may draw any inference which it considers it just and equitable to draw, including an inference that the respondent has contravened a term modified or included by virtue of the complainant's equality clause or corresponding term of service: s 7B(4) (as so added).

Where the Secretary of State questions an employer in relation to whom he may decide to make, or has made a reference under s 2(2) (as amended) (see para 435 post), the question and any reply by the employer are, subject to the following provisions of s 7B (as added), admissible as evidence in any proceedings under that provision: s 7B(5) (as so added). If in any proceedings on such a reference under s 2(2) (as amended) it appears to the employment tribunal that the Secretary of State has questioned the employer to whom the reference relates and that: (a) the employer deliberately and without reasonable excuse omitted to reply within such period as the Secretary of State may by order prescribe; or (b) the employer's reply is evasive or equivocal, it may draw any inference which it considers it just and equitable to draw, including an inference that the employer has contravened a term modified or included by virtue of the equality clause of the woman, or women, as respects whom the reference is made: s 7B(6) (as so added).

The Secretary of State may by order: (i) prescribe the period within which questions must be duly served in order to be admissible under s 7B(3) 9as added) or s 7B(5) (as added); and (ii) prescribe the manner in which a question, and any reply, may be duly served: s 7B(7) (as so added).

Power to make orders under s 7B (as added) is exercisable by statutory instrument subject to annulment in pursuance of a resolution of either House of Parliament: s 7B(9) (as so added). An order under s 7B (as added) may make different provision for different cases: s 7B(10) (as so added).

Section 7B (as added) is without prejudice to any other enactment or rule of law regulating interim and preliminary matters in proceedings before an employment tribunal, and has effect subject to any enactment or rule of law regulating the admissibility of evidence in such proceedings: s 7B(8) (as so added).

425. Choice of comparator. A woman[1] who brings an equal pay claim must first choose her comparator or comparators[2]. This is an important step. If it turns out that she is not employed in like work[3], work rated as equivalent[4] or work of equal value[5] with her comparator the claim will fail. It does not matter that a claim against other men would have succeeded[6]. It is for the woman to pick her comparator[7].

During the course of litigation it may become apparent that the wrong comparator has been chosen. In such circumstances an application may be made to amend the proceedings by the introduction of a new comparator[8].

A woman need not limit herself to one comparator; a number may be chosen to limit the risk that a particular man will be found to be in an anomalous situation, such that no comparison can be made or so that there is a genuine material factor defence available to the employer[9]. However, an applicant should not cast her net over too wide a choice of comparators[10].

The Equal Pay Act 1970 does not specifically require a comparator to be chosen who is representative of his group of employees. However, if the comparator is in an unusual position this may provide the employer with a material factor defence[11]. The situation of the applicant and her comparator must be genuinely comparable[12].

The fact that one or more women is employed in the group which includes the comparator does not preclude a claim being brought[13]. However, where there is broad equality of men and women employed in a particular group, it may suggest that any inequality in pay does not arise from sex discrimination. Unless a significantly greater proportion of a particular group are women than men, it will not be possible to establish disparate impact and it will be easier for an employer to establish that there is a genuine material factor other than the difference in sex that explains the pay differential. In such circumstances it will not be necessary for the employer to establish that the difference is objectively justified[14].

A comparison may be made with a male predecessor[15] or successor[16]. However, a change of relevant circumstances will often provide a material factor defence[17].

Once a woman has made out a prima facie claim she is entitled to disclosure of documents that will help her establish the appropriate comparator[18].

1 These provisions apply equally to men: see the Equal Pay Act 1970 s 1(13) (as added and amended); and para 423 ante. For the meanings of 'woman' and 'man' see para 424 note 1 ante.

2 A comparison for the purposes of the Equal Pay Act 1970 and the Treaty Establishing the European Community (Rome, 25 March 1957; TS 1 (1973); Cmnd 5179) (the 'EC Treaty') art 141 (formerly art 119; renumbered by virtue of the Treaty of Amsterdam: see *Treaty Citation (No 2) (Note)* [1999] All ER (EC) 646, ECJ) must be between a man and a woman. An unusual situation arose in *Collins v Wilkin Chapman Ltd* (14 March 1994) Lexis, EAT (a comparator who appeared to be a man was, in fact, a woman suffering from gender dysphoria syndrome; held that the Equal Pay Act 1970 requires a comparison with a person who is biologically of the opposite sex). See *Degnan v Redcar and Cleveland Borough Council* [2005] EWCA Civ 726, [2005] IRLR 615; *Cheshire and Wirral Partnership NHS Trust v Abbott* [2006] EWCA Civ 523, [2006] ICR 1267. See also *Best v Tyne and Wear Passenger and Transport Executive (t/a Nexus)* [2006] All ER (D) 362 (Dec), EAT, where it was held that it was settled law that where a female employee sought to demonstrate that pay disparities between two groups performing like work were tainted by sex, the burden was on that party to demonstrate that at least a bare majority of the disadvantaged group was female. See also *Wild v Serco Group plc* [2007] All ER (D) 92 (Feb), EAT; and para 424 ante.

3 See para 427 post.

4　See para 428 post.

5　See para 429 post.

6　*Dance v Dorothy Perkins Ltd* [1978] ICR 760, sub nom *Dorothy Perkins Ltd v Dance* [1977] IRLR 226, EAT.

7　*Ainsworth v Glass Tubes & Components Ltd* [1977] ICR 347, [1977] IRLR 74, EAT. For an example of the type of problems that can arise see *Evesham v North Hertfordshire Health Authority and Secretary of State for Health* [1999] IRLR 155, EAT.

8　*Smith v Gwent District Health Authority* [1996] ICR 1044, EAT. The employment tribunal chairman has a discretion to allow such an application bearing in mind the extent to which the applicant may be prejudiced if the application is refused as against any prejudice that will be suffered by the respondent if it is allowed. Where a comparator has brought separate proceedings against the employer, the claimant relying on that comparator can apply for a stay of proceedings pending the decision in the comparator's claim: *South Ayrshire Council v Milligan* [2003] IRLR 153, IH.

9　See para 430 post.

10　See *Leverton v Clwyd County Council* [1989] ICR 33 at 65, [1989] IRLR 28 at 33–34, HL, obiter per Lord Bridge of Harwich.

11　*Thomas v National Coal Board* [1987] ICR 757, [1987] IRLR 451, EAT.

12　*Barry v Midland* Bank plc [1999] 3 All ER 974, [1999] ICR 859, HL. See also para 422 note 4 ante.

13　*Pickstone v Freemans plc* [1989] AC 66, [1988] 2 All ER 803, HL.

14　Case 129/79 *Macarthys Ltd v Smith* [1981] QB 180, [1980] ICR 672, ECJ (woman was entitled to claim equal pay with her male predecessor as the EC Treaty art 119 (now renumbered as art 141) provided a freestanding right). That reasoning cannot stand in the light of the more recent decision in *Barber v Staffordshire County Council* [1996] 2 All ER 748, sub nom *Staffordshire County Council v Barber* [1996] ICR 379, CA. However, the same result can be achieved by adopting a broad and purposive construction of the Equal Pay Act 1970 s 1 (as amended), as was suggested as a possibility in *Albion Shipping Agency v Arnold* [1982] ICR 22, [1981] IRLR 525, EAT.

15　*Strathclyde Regional Council v Wallace* [1998] 1 All ER 394, [1998] IRLR 146, HL.

16　*Diocese of Hallam Trustee v Connaughton* [1996] ICR 860, [1996] IRLR 505, EAT. See para 430 post.

17　See e g *Albion Shipping Agency v Arnold* [1982] ICR 22, [1981] IRLR 525, EAT.

18　*Leverton v Clwyd County Council* [1987] ICR 158, sub nom *Clwyd County Council v Leverton* [1985] IRLR 197, EAT; affd [1989] ICR 33, [1989] IRLR 28, HL.

426.　In the same employment.　A woman[1] who brings an equal pay claim and her comparator must be in the same employment[2]. There are two possible situations: (1) where the woman and her comparator are employed at the same establishment[3] either by the same employer or by associated employers[4]; and (2) where the woman and her comparator are employed by the same or associated employers at different establishments at which common terms and conditions of employment are observed. There is no requirement that common terms and conditions of employment are observed where the applicant and her comparator are employed at the same establishment[5].

An example of where employees who work at different establishments are to be treated as employed on common terms and conditions is where their employment is governed by the same collective agreement[6]. However, the Equal Pay Act 1970 covers more than cases where the applicant and her comparator have terms and conditions of employment governed by the same collective agreement. The comparison is made between the terms and conditions upon which the comparator is employed, as against the terms and conditions upon which a man in the same employment is or would be employed, at the applicant's place of work[7].

1　These provisions apply equally to men: see the Equal Pay Act 1970 s 1(13) (as added and amended); and para 423 ante. For the meanings of 'man' and 'woman' see para 424 note 1 ante.

2　Men are to be treated as in the same employment with a woman if they are men employed by her employer or any associated employer at the same establishment or at establishments in Great Britain which include that one and at which common terms and conditions of employment are observed either generally or for employees of the relevant classes: ibid s 1(6) (amended by the Sex Discrimination Act 1975 s 8(6), Sch 1 Pt I). For the meaning of 'Great Britain' see para 325 note 6 ante.

3　See para 424 note 3 ante.

4　Two employers are to be treated as associated if one is a company of which the other (directly or indirectly) has control or if both are companies of which a third person (directly or indirectly) has control: Equal Pay Act 1970 s 1(6)(c). On a direct reading of this provision there must be a company which is controlled by a body that either may or may not be a company, or there must be two companies which are controlled by such a body. On this basis the Northern Ireland Court of Appeal held that the Equal Opportunities Commission for Northern Ireland and the Fair Employment Agency could not be treated as associate employers for the purposes of a similar provision of the Equal Pay Act (Northern Ireland) 1970: see *Hasley v Fair Employment Agency* [1989] IRLR 106, NI CA. However, this decision must be in some doubt in the light of the broader interpretation that has to be given to the term 'associated employers' to give effect to the principle of equal pay in European Union law: see para 419 ante. In Case 43/74 *Defrenne v Sabena (No 2)* [1981] 1 All ER 122, [1976] ICR 547, ECJ, it was held that the principle of equal pay applies in cases in which men and women receive unequal pay for equal work, which is carried out in the same establishment or service, whether private or public. To the extent that this includes a wider class of comparators than that contained in the Equal Pay Act 1970 s 1(6) (as amended), s 1(6) (as amended) is displaced by the requirements of the Treaty Establishing the European Community (Rome, 25 March 1957; TS 1 (1973); Cmnd 5179) (the 'EC Treaty') art 141 (formerly art 119; renumbered by virtue of the Treaty of Amsterdam: see *Treaty Citation (No 2) (Note)* [1999] All ER (EC) 646, ECJ), which is directly effective: see *Scullard v Knowles* [1996] ICR 399, [1996] IRLR 344, EAT. See also *Lawrence v Regent Office Care Ltd* [1999] ICR 654, [1999] IRLR 148, EAT.

　　See further *South Ayrshire Council v Morton* [2002] ICR 956, [2002] IRLR 256, IH (teacher entitled to rely on the EC Treaty art 141 (as renumbered) to compare herself with teacher employed by different education authority in Scotland). Where a difference in pay between workers performing equal work cannot be attributed to a single source, there is no body responsible for restoring equal treatment and the EC Treaty art 141 (as renumbered) does not apply: Case C-320/00 *Lawrence v Regent Office Care Ltd* [2002] 3 CMLR 761, [2003] ICR 1092, ECJ; Case C-256/01 *Allonby v Accrington and Rossendale College* [2005] All ER (EC) 289, [2004] ECR I-873, ECJ; and see *Robertson v Department for Environment Food and Rural Affairs* [2005] EWCA Civ 138, [2005] ICR 750, [2005] IRLR 363; *Armstrong v Newcastle upon Tyne NHS Hospital Trust* [2005] EWCA Civ 1608, [2006] IRLR 124. See also *Dolphin v Hartlepool Borough Council; Middleton v South Tyneside Metropolitan Borough Council* [2006] All ER (D) 54 (Aug), EAT.

5　*Lawson v British Ltd* [1987] ICR 726, [1988] IRLR 53, EAT.
6　*Leverton v Clywd County Council* [1989] AC 706, [1989] ICR 33, HL.
7　*British Coal Corpn v Smith* [1996] ICR 515, [1996] IRLR 404, HL.

427.　Meaning of 'like work'.　A woman can claim equal pay on the basis that she is employed on like work[1]. A woman is to be regarded as employed on like work with men[2] if, but only if, her work and theirs is of the same or a broadly similar nature, and the differences (if any) between the things she does and the things they do are not of practical importance in relation to terms and conditions of employment; and accordingly in comparing her work with theirs regard must be had to the frequency or otherwise with which any such differences occur in practice as well as to the nature and extent of the differences[3].

The test is in two parts which must be considered separately. The first question is whether the work of the woman and her comparator are the same or broadly similar in nature. The second question is whether, if there are any differences, they are of practical importance in relation to terms and conditions of employment[4]. The entirety of the woman's and the man's jobs should be considered, and it is not legitimate to hive off certain of the activities undertaken by one or the other[5]. The only exception will be where it can genuinely be said that certain functions are to be treated as an entirely separate job[6].

The burden of proof rests on the applicant to establish that she is engaged in the same work, or work of a broadly similar nature to that of her comparator. However, once this has been established, the burden shifts to the employer to show that any differences are of practical importance[7].

The tribunal should consider the work that is actually done, rather than what may be required under the contract of employment, in determining whether it is the same or broadly similar[8].

The next stage is to consider whether any differences between the things done by the woman and her comparator are of practical importance in relation to the terms and conditions of employment. Again, the emphasis is on what is actually done rather than what may be required under the contract of employment[9]. A practical guide is whether the differences are such as would put the two posts into different categories of a job evaluation study[10]. The Equal Pay Act 1970 specifically requires the tribunal to have regard to the frequency or otherwise with which any differences occur in practice as well as the nature and extent of the differences[11].

The issue of whether a woman and her comparator are engaged in like work is a question of fact[12].

1 See para 424 ante. These provisions apply equally to men: see the Equal Pay Act 1970 s 1(13) (as added and amended); and para 423 ante. For the meaning of 'woman' see para 424 note 1 ante.

2 For the meaning of 'man' see para 424 note 1 ante.

3 Equal Pay Act 1970 s 1(4). The concept of 'like work' is not restricted by a requirement of contemporaneous employment: *Kells v Pilkington plc* [2002] IRLR 693, [2002] 2 CMLR 1529, EAT.

4 *Waddington v Leicester Council for Voluntary Services* [1977] 1 WLR 544, [1977] ICR 266, EAT.

5 *Maidment v Cooper & Co (Birmingham) Ltd* [1978] ICR 1094, [1978] IRLR 462, EAT.

6 An example is that of two cleaners, one male and one female, who do identical work during the week; if the man was also paid for coming into work on Saturdays to cut the grass it might be appropriate to ignore these duties for the purposes of the comparison: see *Maidment v Cooper & Co (Birmingham) Ltd* [1978] ICR 1094, [1978] IRLR 462, EAT. See also *Doncaster Education Authority v Gill* (24 March 1992) Lexis, EAT. Such cases will be rare in practice.

7 *Shields v E Coombes (Holdings) Ltd* [1978] ICR 1159, sub nom *E Coombes (Holdings) Ltd v Shields* [1978] IRLR 263, CA.

8 *Redland Roof Tiles Ltd v Harper* [1977] ICR 349, EAT; *Capper Pass Ltd v Lawton* [1977] QB 852, [1977] ICR 83, EAT. It is only necessary to consider whether the jobs are broadly similar at the first stage. A pedantic approach should not be adopted: *Capper Pass Ltd v Lawton* supra.

9 *Shields v E Coombes (Holdings) Ltd* [1978] ICR 1159, sub nom *E Coombes (Holdings) Ltd v Shields* [1978] IRLR 263, CA; *Redland Roof Tiles Ltd v Harper* [1977] ICR 349, EAT.

10 *British Leyland (UK) Ltd v Powell* [1978] IRLR 57, EAT (decided before the Equal Pay Act 1970 had been amended to permit claims for work of equal value: see para 429 post). It is a defence to an equal value claim to establish that the applicant and her comparator have been placed in different categories in a job evaluation study: see para 428 post.

11 See the Equal Pay Act 1970 s 1(4).

12 Each case will be determined on its own facts. For examples of the factors that have been considered by the appellate courts see *Dugdale v Kraft Foods Ltd* [1977] ICR 48, [1976] IRLR 368, EAT (the fact that men and women work at different times of day is to be ignored in determining like work, this may be reflected in night work premium); *Electrolux Ltd v Hutchinson* [1977] ICR 252, [1976] IRLR 410, EAT (mere fact of a contractual entitlement to require men to work shifts did not amount to a difference of practical importance); *Capper Pass Ltd v Lawton* [1977] QB 852, [1977] ICR 83, EAT (difference in duties of a cook working from a kitchen that served directors and their guests did not amount to a difference of practical importance preventing her being engaged on like work with men employed in the factory canteen); *Waddington v Leicester Council for Voluntary Services* [1977] 1 WLR 544, [1977] ICR 266, EAT (additional responsibility could amount to a difference of practical importance); *Redland Roof Tiles Ltd v Harper* [1977] ICR 349, EAT (industrial tribunal entitled to consider that minor additional role of a male employee as trainee manager did not amount to a difference of practical importance); *Shields v E Coombes (Holdings) Ltd* [1978] ICR 1159, sub nom *E Coombes (Holdings) Ltd v Shields* [1978] IRLR 263, CA (theoretical role of bookmakers' male counter hand in dealing with unruly customers did not amount to a difference of practical importance as he was not called upon to carry out those duties in practice); *British Leyland (UK) Ltd v Powell* [1978] IRLR 57, EAT (occasional requirement of a van driver to drive on public highway did not amount to a difference of practical importance); *De Brito v Standard Chartered Bank Ltd* [1978] ICR 650, EAT (experienced women employees in trustee department of bank, who had trained applicant, had different duties of practical importance); *National Coal Board v Sherwin* [1978] ICR 700, [1978] IRLR 122, EAT (mere fact duties carried out at a different time irrelevant); *Noble v David Gold & Sons (Holdings) Ltd* [1980] ICR 543, [1980] IRLR 252, CA (male employees who carried out heavier work that involved experience of organisation not engaged on like work); *Capper Pass Ltd v Allan* [1980] ICR 194, [1980] IRLR 236, EAT (additional duties of male canteen staff employed at higher grade were differences of practical importance); *Thomas v National Coal Board* [1987] ICR 757, [1987] IRLR 451, EAT (male canteen assistant worked at night alone and there was an element of personal risk and additional responsibility; this amounted to a difference of practical importance, being more than a mere difference in the time at which the activities were carried out). Differences in the duties conducted by male and female employees may also amount to genuine material factors unrelated to sex discrimination for the purposes of the Equal Pay Act 1970 s 1(3) (as substituted

and amended): see para 430 post. Although these cases give some idea of the factors that courts have considered of importance, careful consideration must be given to the facts of any individual case. A number of the authorities were decided in the first few years of operation of the Equal Pay Act 1970. In the intervening years the courts have become more accustomed to discrimination claims and more astute to uphold the principle of equal pay.

428.   Work rated as equivalent.   A woman can claim equal pay on the basis that her work has been rated as equivalent under a job evaluation study[1]. Job evaluation studies have a double importance in that the study may entitle a woman to claim equal pay but may also provide a defence in an equal value claim where the jobs have been rated differently[2].

As a matter of European Union law, where a job classification system is used for determining pay, it must be based on the same criteria for both men and women and so drawn up as to exclude any discrimination on grounds of sex[3]. It must exclude both direct and indirect discrimination[4]. The evaluation study should be carried out objectively, the criteria should be applied equally to men and women, particular attributes more commonly found in men than women may be taken into account provided the job is objectively analysed and, where possible, factors that tend to favour men should be counter-balanced by factors that tend to favour women[5].

Under the Equal Pay Act 1970, a woman is to be regarded as employed on work rated as equivalent with that of any men if, but only if, her job and their job have been given an equal value, in terms of the demand made on a worker under various headings (such as effort, skill and decision), on a study undertaken with a view to evaluating in those terms the jobs to be done by all or any of the employees in an undertaking or group of undertakings, or would have been given an equal value but for the evaluation being made on a system setting different values for men and women on the same demand under any heading[6].

The job evaluation study must be analytical[7].

Before the woman and her comparator can be compared the scheme must have been completed[8]. However, a job evaluation study will be effective once it has been completed even if terms and conditions of employment have not been amended as a result[9].

To obtain the benefit of a job evaluation study a woman must be within a group of employees that have been evaluated[10].

1   See para 424 ante. These provisions apply equally to men: see the Equal Pay Act 1970 s 1(13) (as added and amended); and para 423 ante. For the meanings of 'man' and 'woman' see para 424 note 1 ante.

2   See ibid s 2A(2), (2A) (as substituted and added); and para 429 post.

3   See EC Directive 75/117 (OJ L45, 19.2.75, p 19) on the approximation of the laws of the member states relating to the application of the principle of equal pay for men and women, art 1. See also para 419 ante.
    See C-220/02 *Österreichischer Gewerkshatsbund, Gewerkschaft Der Privatangestellten v Wirtschaftskammer Österreich* [2004] 3 CMLR 784, [2004] All ER (D) 03 (Jun), ECJ.

4   In *Greene v Broxtowe District Council* [1977] ICR 241, [1977] IRLR 34, EAT, the Employment Appeal Tribunal concluded that a job evaluation study can only be challenged if it is shown that there is some fundamental error in the study or that there was a plain error on the face of the record. The wording of the Equal Pay Act 1970 appears to support a relatively narrow approach to the challenges that can be made to a job evaluation study. However, in order to give effect to the United Kingdom's obligations under the Treaty Establishing the European Community (Rome, 25 March 1957; TS 1 (1973); Cmnd 5179) (the 'EC Treaty') art 141 (formerly art 119; renumbered by virtue of the Treaty of Amsterdam: see *Treaty Citation (No 2) (Note)* [1999] All ER (EC) 646, ECJ) the courts must be able to invalidate any job evaluation study which incorporates direct or indirect discrimination. See C-220/02 *Österreichischer Gewerkshatsbund, Gewerkschaft Der Privatangestellten v Wirtschaftskammer Österreich* [2004] 3 CMLR 784, [2004] All ER (D) 03 (Jun), ECJ.

5   Case 237/85 *Rummer v Dato-Druck GmbH* [1987] ICR 774, [1987] IRLR 32, ECJ.

6   Equal Pay Act 1970 s 1(5). See also the guidance given by the Equal Opportunities Commission in 'Good Practice Guide—Job Evaluation Schemes Free of Sex Bias'; and the EC Commission's Code of Practice on the implementation of equal pay for work of equal value for women and men (17 July 1996) (COM(94) 6).

7   *Bromley v H & J Quick Ltd* [1988] ICR 623, [1988] IRLR 249, CA. The major types of job evaluation study were set out as an appendix to *Eaton Ltd v Nuttall* [1977] ICR 272, [1977] IRLR 71, EAT. The evaluation of the employee's and the comparator's jobs have to be carried out under the same study: *Douglas v Islington London Borough Council* (2004) Times, 27 May, [2004] All ER (D) 233 (Apr), EAT.

8   *Springboard Sunderland Trust v Robson* [1992] ICR 554, [1992] IRLR 261, EAT (study not concluded until scores converted into grades). In *Arnold v Beecham Group Ltd* [1982] ICR 744, [1982] IRLR 307, EAT, the Employment Appeal Tribunal held that there is no complete job evaluation study falling within the Equal Pay Act 1970 s 1(5) unless and until it has been accepted or adopted by employers and employees as regulating their relationship. See, however, *Dibro Ltd v Hore* [1990] ICR 370, [1990] IRLR 129, EAT, which provides some support for a wider approach (an employee was allowed to bring evidence to support a defence under the Equal Pay Act 1970 s 2A(2)(a) (as then in force) (see para 429 post) in relation to a job evaluation study which had been commenced after an originating application had been made to the tribunal; the Employment Appeal Tribunal did not suggest that the applicant would be able to render the exercise ineffective by refusing to accept its results).

9   *O'Brien v Sim-Chem Ltd* [1980] ICR 573, [1980] IRLR 373, HL.

10   *McAuley v Eastern Health and Social Services Board* [1991] IRLR 467, NI CA.

429.   Equal value. A woman can claim equal pay on the basis that she is employed on work of equal value[1]. A woman can claim on this basis where she is employed on work which, in terms of demands made on her (for instance, under such headings as effort, skill and decision), is of equal value to that of a man in the same employment[2].

The procedure for equal value claims is set out in the complementary rules of procedure[3]. If a claim of like work or work rated as equivalent is included, it should be determined first[4].

Where, on a complaint or reference made to an employment tribunal, a dispute arises as to whether any work is of equal value[5] the tribunal may either proceed to determine that question, or require a member of the panel of independent experts[6] to prepare a report with respect to that question[7]. Where a tribunal is required to determine whether any work is of equal value[8] and the work of the woman and the work of the man in question have been given different values on an evaluation study[9], the tribunal must determine that the work of the woman and that of the man are not of equal value unless the tribunal has reasonable grounds for suspecting that the evaluation contained in the study: (1) was[10] made on a system which discriminates on grounds of sex; or (2) is otherwise unsuitable to be relied upon[11]. The employer may put forward its material factor defence at the initial hearing[12].

The tribunal has a number of general powers to manage proceedings[13]. When in an equal value claim there is a dispute as to whether any work is of equal value[14], the tribunal must conduct a 'stage 1 equal value hearing'[15]. At such a hearing the tribunal has a number of obligations[16]. Wherever the tribunal has decided to require an independent expert to prepare a report on certain matters there are a number of rules applicable to the expert's involvement in fact finding[17].

Where the tribunal has decided to require an independent expert to prepare a report on the question it must conduct a 'stage 2 equal value hearing'[18]. At this hearing the tribunal has a number of further obligations[19].

In proceedings in relation to which an independent expert has prepared a report, unless the tribunal determines that the report is not based on the facts relating to the question, the report of the independent expert must be admitted in evidence in those proceedings[20]. If the tribunal does not so admit the report of an independent expert, it may determine the question itself or require another independent expert to prepare a report on the question[21]. The tribunal may refuse to admit evidence of facts or hear argument as to issues which have not been disclosed to the other party as required[22], unless it was not reasonably practicable for the party to have so complied[23].

When a tribunal requires an independent expert to prepare a report with respect to the question or an appropriate order is made[24], that independent expert must be informed of the duties and powers he has[25]. Expert evidence must be restricted to that which, in the opinion of the tribunal, is reasonably required to resolve the proceedings[26]. There are a number of further rules in regard to·the use of expert evidence[27]. When any expert (including an independent expert) has prepared a report, a party or any other expert (including an independent expert) involved in the proceedings may put written questions about the report to the expert who has prepared the report[28]. Finally there are rules on general procedural matters involving independent experts[29] and about equal value cases that are also national security proceedings[30].

1   See para 424 ante. These provisions apply equally to men: see the Equal Pay Act 1970 s 1(13) (as added and amended); and para 423 ante. For the meanings of 'man' and 'woman' see para 424 note 1 ante.
2   See ibid s 1(2)(c) (as added); and para 424 note 10 ante. This provision was added as a result of the decision in Case 61/81 *EC Commission v United Kingdom* [1982] ICR 578, [1982] IRLR 333, ECJ, in which the limitation of the Equal Pay Act 1970 to claims for like work and work rated as equivalent was held to be in breach of European Community law.
3   See the Employment Tribunals (Constitution and Rules of Procedure) Regulations 2004, SI 2004/1861, reg 16(4), Sch 6 (reg 16(4), Sch 6 added by SI 2004/2351; and the Employment Tribunals (Constitution and Rules of Procedure) Regulations 2004, SI 2004/1861, Sch 6 amended by SI 2005/1865). See also EMPLOYMENT vol 16(1B) (Reissue) para 911. In relation to an earlier version of the regulations, the courts have commented on the excessive complexity of the rules of procedure and the delay that this causes: *Sheffield Metropolitan District Council v Siberry* [1989] ICR 208, EAT; *Tennants Textile Colours Ltd v Todd* [1989] IRLR 3, EAT.
4   This follows from the wording of the Equal Pay Act 1970 s 1(2)(c) (as added), which limits an equal value claim to one where s 1(2)(a) (as substituted) (like work) (see paras 424, 427 ante) and s 1(2)(b) (as substituted) (work rated as equivalent) (see paras 424, 428 ante) do not apply.
5   Ie as mentioned in ibid s 1(2)(c) (as added): see para 424 note 10 ante.
6   A reference to a member of the panel of independent experts is a reference to a person who is for the time being designated by the Advisory, Conciliation and Arbitration Service ('ACAS') for the purposes of ibid s 2A(1) (as added and amended) as such a member, being neither a member of the Council of that Service nor one of its officers or servants: s 2A(4) (s 2A added by the Equal Pay (Amendment) Regulations 1983, SI 1983/1794, reg 3(1); and the Equal Pay Act 1970 s 2A(4) amended by the Equal Pay Act 1970 (Amendment) Regulations 2004, SI 2004/2352, reg 2(1), (6)).
7   Equal Pay Act 1970 s 2A(1) (as added (see note 6 supra); and amended by the Sex Discrimination and Equal Pay (Miscellaneous Amendments) Regulations 1996, SI 1996/438, reg 3(2); the Equal Pay Act 1970 (Amendment) Regulations 2004, SI 2004/2352, reg 2(1), (2); and by virtue of the Employment Rights (Dispute Resolution) Act 1998 s 1(2)(a)).
    Where the tribunal has required a member of the panel of independent experts to prepare a report under the Equal Pay Act 1970 s 2A(1) (as added and amended), the tribunal may: (1) withdraw the requirement; and (2) request the member of the panel of independent experts to provide it with any documentation specified by it or make any other request to him connected with the withdrawal of the requirement: s 2A(1A), (1B) (s 2A(1A)–(1C) added by the Equal Pay Act 1970 (Amendment) Regulations 2004, SI 2004/2352, reg 2(1), (2)). If the requirement has not been withdrawn under head (1) supra, the tribunal may not make any determination under the Equal Pay Act 1970 s 2A(1) (as added and amended) unless it has received the report: s 2A(1C) (as so added).
8   Ie as mentioned in ibid s 1(2)(c): see para 424 note 10 ante.
9   Ibid s 2A(2) (as added (see note 6 supra); and substituted by the Equal Pay Act 1970 (Amendment) Regulations 2004, SI 2004/2352, reg 2(1), (4)). The study is such as is mentioned in the Equal Pay Act 1970 s 1(5): see para 428 ante.
10 Ie within the meaning of ibid s 2A(3) (as added). An evaluation contained in a study such as is mentioned in s 1(5) (see para 428 ante) is made on a system which discriminates on grounds of sex where a difference, or coincidence, between values set by that system on different demands under the same or different headings is not justifiable irrespective of the sex of the person on whom those demands are made: s 2A(3) (as added: see note 6 supra). It seems that a job evaluation study may be valid for the purposes of s 2A (as added and amended) even if it is commissioned by the employer after proceedings have been commenced: *Dibro Ltd v Hore* [1990] ICR 370, [1990] IRLR 129, EAT (decided under an earlier version of the provision). However, the mere fact that an employer is carrying out a wide ranging

job evaluation study will generally not entitle him to a stay of proceedings to allow the exercise to be completed: see *Avon County Council v Foxall* [1989] ICR 407, [1989] IRLR 435, EAT. It appears from the express wording of the Equal Pay Act 1970 s 2A(2) (as added and amended) that all an applicant is required to do is to show that there are reasonable grounds for believing that the evaluation study discriminates on grounds of sex. However, there is no presumption of discrimination and the burden of proof lies upon the applicant to show reasonable grounds: *Neil v Ford Motor Co Ltd* [1984] IRLR 339, IT.

11 Equal Pay Act 1970 s 2A(2A) (added by the Equal Pay Act 1970 (Amendment) Regulations 2004, SI 2004/2352, reg 2(1), (5)).

12 Under the Employment Tribunals (Constitution and Rules of Procedure) Regulations 2004, SI 2004/1861 (as amended) that initial hearing is the 'stage 1 equal value hearing': see the text and note 15 infra. The tribunal may, on the application of a party, hear evidence upon and permit the parties to address it upon the issue of the defence of a genuine material factor (see para 430 post) before determining whether to require an independent expert to prepare a report: see Sch 6 r 4(5) (as added: see note 3 supra). Generally this will be permitted as the proceedings will be dismissed without the requirement for an expert's report where the defence is successful: see *Reed Packaging Ltd v Boozer* [1988] ICR 391, [1988] IRLR 333, EAT (decided under an earlier version of the regulations).

13 See the Employment Tribunals (Constitution and Rules of Procedure) Regulations 2004, SI 2004/1861, Sch 6 r 3 (as added: see note 3 supra).
In addition to the power to make orders described in Sch 1 r 10 (see EMPLOYMENT vol 16(1B) (Reissue) para 867), the tribunal or chairman has power (subject to Sch 6 rr 4(3), 7(4) (as added and amended) (see notes 16, 19 infra)) to make the following orders: (1) the standard orders set out in Sch 6 r 5 (as added) or Sch 6 r 8 (as added) (see notes 16, 19 infra), with such addition to, omission or variation of those orders (including specifically variations as to the periods within which actions are to be taken by the parties) as the chairman or tribunal considers is appropriate; (2) an order that no new facts be admitted in evidence by the tribunal unless they have been disclosed to all other parties in writing before a date specified by the tribunal (unless it was not reasonably practicable for a party to have done so); (3) an order that the parties may be required to send copies of documents or provide information to the other parties and to the independent expert; (4) an order that the respondent be required to grant the independent expert access to his premises during a period specified by the tribunal or chairman in order for the independent expert to conduct interviews with persons identified as relevant by the independent expert; (5) when more than one expert is to give evidence in the proceedings, an order that those experts present to the tribunal a joint statement of matters which are agreed between them and those matters on which they disagree; (6) where proceedings have been joined, an order that lead claimants be identified: Sch 6 r 3(1) (as so added). Any reference in Sch 1 (as amended) or Sch 2 to an order made under Sch 1 r 10 includes reference to an order made in accordance with Sch 6 (as added and amended): Sch 6 r 3(2) (as so added).

14 Ie as mentioned in the Equal Pay Act 1970 s 1(2)(c) (as added): see para 424 note 10 ante.

15 Employment Tribunals (Constitution and Rules of Procedure) Regulations 2004, SI 2004/1861, Sch 6 r 4(1) (as added: see note 3 supra). Such a hearing is conducted in accordance with both Sch 6 r 4 (as added) and the rules applicable to pre-hearing reviews in Sch 1 (as amended): see EMPLOYMENT vol 16(1B) (Reissue) para 854 et seq.

16 These obligations are as follows: (1) where the Equal Pay Act s 2A(2) (as added and substituted) (see the text to note 9 supra) applies, the tribunal must strike out the claim (or the relevant part of it) if, in accordance with s 2A(2A) (as added) (see heads (1) and (2) in the text), the tribunal must determine that the work of the claimant and the comparator are not of equal value; (2) it must decide, in accordance with the Equal Pay Act s 2A(1) (as added and amended) (see the text to note 7 ante), either that: (a) it will determine the question; or (b) it requires a member of the panel of independent experts to prepare a report with respect to the question; (3) it must make the standard orders for the stage 1 equal value hearing as set out in the Employment Tribunals (Constitution and Rules of Procedure) Regulations 2004, SI 2004/1861, Sch 6 r 5 (as added); (4) if it has decided to require an independent expert to prepare a report on the question, it must require the parties to copy to the independent expert all information which they are required by an order to disclose or agree between each other; (5) if it has decided to require an independent expert to prepare a report on the question, it must fix a date for the stage 2 equal value hearing (see the text to note 18 infra), having regard to the indicative timetable; (6) if it has not decided to require an independent expert to prepare a report on the question, it must fix a date for the hearing, having regard to the indicative timetable; (7) it must consider whether any further orders are appropriate: Sch 6 r 4(3) (as added: see note 3 supra). As to the indicative timetable see Sch 6 Annex.
Before a claim or part of one is struck out under head (1) supra, a notice must be sent to the claimant giving him the opportunity to make representations to the tribunal as to whether the evaluation contained in the study in question falls within either head (1) or head (2) in the text; no such notice need be sent if the claimant has been given an opportunity to make such representations orally to the tribunal as to why such a judgment should not be issued: see Sch 6 r 4(4) (as so added). When notice is given to the parties of the stage 1 equal value hearing, notice must also be given to the parties of the matters

which the tribunal may and must consider at that hearing which are described in Sch 6 r 4(3) (as added) and Sch 6 r 4(5) (as added) (see note 12 supra) and notice must be given of the standard orders in Sch 6 r 5 (as added): see Sch 6 r 4(6) (as so added).

At a stage 1 equal value hearing a tribunal must, unless it considers it inappropriate to do so, order that: (a) before the end of the period of 14 days after the date of the stage 1 equal value hearing the claimant: (i) must disclose in writing to the respondent the name of any comparator, or, if the claimant is not able to name the comparator he must instead disclose such information as enables the comparator to be identified by the respondent; and (ii) must identify to the respondent in writing the period in relation to which he considers that the claimant's work and that of the comparator are to be compared; (b) before the end of the period of 28 days after the date of the stage 1 equal value hearing: (i) where the claimant has not disclosed the name of the comparator to the respondent under head (a) supra, if the respondent has been provided with sufficient detail to be able to identify the comparator, he must disclose in writing the name of the comparator to the claimant; (ii) the parties must provide each other with written job descriptions for the claimant and any comparator; (iii) the parties must identify to each other in writing the facts which they consider to be relevant to the question; (c) the respondent must grant access to the claimant and his representative (if any) to his premises during a period specified by the tribunal or chairman in order for him or them to interview any comparator; (d) the parties before the end of the period of 56 days after the date of the stage 1 equal value hearing must present to the tribunal a joint agreed statement in writing of the following matters: (i) job descriptions for the claimant and any comparator; (ii) facts which both parties consider are relevant to the question; (iii) facts on which the parties disagree (as to the fact or as to the relevance to the question) and a summary of their reasons for disagreeing; (e) the parties, at least 56 days prior to the hearing (see the text to note 20 infra), must disclose to each other, to any independent or other expert and to the tribunal written statements of any facts on which they intend to rely in evidence at the hearing; and (f) the parties, at least 28 days prior to the hearing, must present to the tribunal a statement of facts and issues on which the parties are in agreement, a statement of facts and issues on which the parties disagree and a summary of their reasons for disagreeing: Sch 6 r 5(1) (as so added). Any of these standard orders for the stage 1 equal value hearing may be added to, varied or omitted as the tribunal considers appropriate: Sch 6 r 5(2) (as so added).

17   In such proceedings a tribunal or chairman may if it or he considers it appropriate at any stage of the proceedings order an independent expert to assist the tribunal in establishing the facts on which the independent expert may rely in preparing his report: ibid Sch 6 r 6(1), (2) (as added: see note 3 supra). Examples of the circumstances in which the tribunal or chairman may make such an order may include: (1) where a party is not legally represented; (2) where the parties are unable to reach agreement as required by an order of the tribunal or chairman; (3) where the tribunal or chairman considers that insufficient information may have been disclosed by a party and this may impair the ability of the independent expert to prepare a report on the question; (4) where the tribunal or chairman considers that the involvement of the independent expert may promote fuller compliance with orders made by the tribunal or a chairman: Sch 6 r 6(3) (as so added). A party to such proceedings may make an application for an order under Sch 6 r 6(2) (as added): see Sch 6 r 6(4) (as so added).

18   See ibid Sch 6 para 7(1), (2) (as added (see note 3 supra); and Sch 6 r 7(2) amended by SI 2005/1865). Such a hearing is conducted in accordance with both the Employment Tribunals (Constitution and Rules of Procedure) Regulations 2004, SI 2004/1861, Sch 6 r 7 (as added and amended) and the rules applicable to pre-hearing reviews in Sch 1 (as amended) (see EMPLOYMENT vol 16(1B) (Reissue) para 854 et seq.

19   At the stage 2 equal value hearing the tribunal must make a determination of facts on which the parties cannot agree which relate to the question and must require the independent expert to prepare his report on the basis of facts which have (at any stage of the proceedings) either been agreed between the parties or determined by the tribunal (referred to as 'the facts relating to the question'): Sch 6 r 7(3) (as added: see note 3 supra). At the stage 2 equal value hearing the tribunal must: (1) subject to Sch 6 r 8 (as added) and having regard to the indicative timetable, make the standard orders for the stage 2 equal value hearing; (2) make any orders which it considers appropriate; (3) fix a date for the hearing, having regard to the indicative timetable: Sch 6 r 7(4) (as so added; and amended by SI 2005/1865). The facts relating to the question must, in relation to the question, be the only facts on which the tribunal relies at the hearing: Employment Tribunals (Constitution and Rules of Procedure) Regulations 2004, SI 2004/1861, Sch 6 r 7(4) (as so added). At any stage of the proceedings the independent expert may make an application to the tribunal for some or all of the facts relating to the question to be amended, supplemented or omitted: Sch 6 r 7(5) (as so added; and amended by SI 2005/1865). When notice is given to the parties and to the independent expert of the stage 2 equal value hearing, there must also be given notice of the standard orders in the Employment Tribunals (Constitution and Rules of Procedure) Regulations 2004, SI 2004/1861, Sch 6 r 8 (as added) and the attention of the parties must be drawn to Sch 6 r 7(4), (5) (as added and amended): Sch 6 r 7(7) (as so added).

At a stage 2 equal value hearing a tribunal must, unless it considers it inappropriate to do so and subject to Sch 6 r 8(2) (as added), order that: (a) by a date specified by the tribunal (with regard to the indicative timetable) the independent expert must prepare his report on the question and (subject to Sch 6 r 14 (as added) as to national security proceedings: see note 30 infra) send copies of it to the parties and to the tribunal; and (b) the independent expert must prepare his report on the question on the basis of the facts relating to the question and no other facts which may or may not relate to the question: Sch 6 r 8(1) (as so added). Any of these standard orders for the stage 2 equal value hearing may be added to, varied or omitted as the tribunal considers appropriate: Sch 6 r 8(2) (as so added).

20 Ibid Sch 6 r 9(1) (as added: see note 3 supra).

21 Ibid Sch 6 r 9(2) (as added: see note 3 supra).

22 Ie as required by the Employment Tribunals (Constitution and Rules of Procedure) Regulations 2004, SI 2004/1861 (as amended) or any order under those regulations.

23 Ibid Sch 6 r 9(3) (as added: see note 3 supra).

24 Ie an order under ibid Sch 6 r 6(2) (as added): see note 17 supra.

25 Ibid Sch 6 r 10(1) (as added: see note 3 supra). The text refers to duties and powers under Sch 6 r 10 (as added). The independent expert is informed by the secretary of employment tribunals (see EMPLOYMENT vol 16(1B) (Reissue) para 855).

The independent expert has a duty to the tribunal to: (1) assist it in furthering the overriding objective to deal with cases justly (see reg 3 (as substituted and amended); and EMPLOYMENT vol 16(1B) (Reissue) para 854); (2) comply with the requirements of the Employment Tribunals (Constitution and Rules of Procedure) Regulations 2004, SI 2004/1861 (as amended) and any orders made by the tribunal or a chairman in relation to the proceedings; (3) keep the tribunal informed of any delay in complying with any order in the proceedings with the exception of minor or insignificant delays in compliance; (4) comply with any timetable imposed by the tribunal or chairman in so far as this is reasonably practicable; (5) inform the tribunal or a chairman on request of progress in the preparation of the independent expert's report; (6) prepare a report on the question based on the facts relating to the question and (subject to Sch 6 r 14 (as added) as to national security proceedings: see note 30 infra) send it to the tribunal and the parties; (7) make himself available to attend hearings in the proceedings: Sch 6 r 10(2) (as so added).

The independent expert may make an application for any order or for a hearing to be held as if he were a party to the proceedings: Sch 6 r 10(3) (as so added). At any stage of the proceedings the tribunal may, after giving the independent expert the opportunity to make representations, withdraw the requirement for the independent expert to prepare a report; if it does so, the tribunal may itself determine the question, or it may determine that a different independent expert should be required to prepare the report: Sch 6 r 10(4) (as so added). When Sch 6 r 10(4) (as added) applies, the independent expert who is no longer required to prepare the report must provide the tribunal with all documentation and work in progress relating to the proceedings by a date specified by the tribunal; and such documentation and work in progress must be in a form which the tribunal is able to use; such documentation and work in progress may be used in relation to those proceedings by the tribunal or by another independent expert: Sch 6 r 10(5) (as so added). When an independent expert has been required to prepare a report in proceedings, the secretary of employment tribunals must give the independent expert notice of all hearings, orders or judgments in those proceedings as if the independent expert were a party to those proceedings and when the Employment Tribunals (Constitution and Rules of Procedure) Regulations 2004, SI 2004/1861 (as amended) require a party to provide information to another party, such information must also be provided to the independent expert: Sch 6 r 10(6) (as so added).

26 Ibid Sch 6 r 11(1) (as added: see note 3 supra).

27 An expert has a duty to assist the tribunal on matters within his expertise; this duty overrides any obligation to the person from whom he has received instructions or by whom he is paid: ibid Sch 6 r 11(2) (as added: see note 3 supra). No party may call an expert or put in evidence an expert's report without the permission of the tribunal; nor may any expert report be put in evidence unless it has been disclosed to all other parties and any independent expert at least 28 days prior to the hearing: Sch 6 r 11(3) (as so added). In proceedings in which an independent expert has been required to prepare a report on the question, the tribunal may not admit evidence of another expert on the question unless such evidence is based on the facts relating to the question: Sch 6 r 11(4) (as so added). Unless the tribunal considers it inappropriate to do so, any such expert report must be disclosed to all parties and to the tribunal on the same date on which the independent expert is required to send his report to the parties and to the tribunal: Sch 6 r 11(4) (as so added). If an expert (other than an independent expert) does not comply with the Employment Tribunals (Constitution and Rules of Procedure) Regulations 2004, SI 2004/1861 (as amended) or an order made by the tribunal or a chairman, the tribunal may order that the evidence of that expert is not to be admitted: Sch 6 r 11(5) (as so added). Where two or more parties wish to submit expert evidence on a particular issue, the tribunal may order that the evidence on that issue is to be given by one joint expert only; when such an order has been made, if the parties wishing to instruct the joint expert cannot agree who should be the expert, the tribunal may select the expert: Sch 6 r 11(6) (as so added).

28 Ibid Sch 6 r 12(1) (as added: see note 3 supra).

Unless the tribunal or chairman agrees otherwise, written questions under Sch 6 r 12(1) (as added): (1) may be put once only; (2) must be put within 28 days of the date on which the parties were sent the report; (3) must be for the purpose only of clarifying the factual basis of the report; (4) must be copied to all other parties and experts involved in the proceedings at the same time as they are sent to the expert who prepared the report: Sch 6 r 12(2) (as so added). When written questions have been put to an expert in accordance with Sch 6 r 12(2) (as added) he must answer those questions within 28 days of receiving them: Sch 6 r 12(3) (as so added). An'expert's answers to questions put in accordance with Sch 6 r 12(2) (as added) are treated as part of the expert's report: Sch 6 r 12(4) (as so added). Where a party has put a written question in accordance with Sch 6 r 12 (as added) to an expert instructed by another party and the expert does not answer that question, or does not do so within 28 days, the tribunal may order that the party instructing the expert may not rely on the evidence of that expert: Sch 6 r 12(5) (as so added).

29   In proceedings in which an independent expert has been required to prepare a report, the secretary of employment tribunals must send him notices and inform him of any hearing, application, order or judgment in those proceedings as if he were a party to those proceedings: Sch 6 r 13(1) (as added: see note 3 supra). For the avoidance of doubt, any requirement in Sch 6 (as added and amended) to hold a stage 1 or a stage 2 equal value hearing does not preclude holding more than one of each of those types of hearing or other hearings from being held in accordance with Sch 1 (as amended) (see EMPLOYMENT vol 16(1B) (Reissue) para 854; Sch 6 r 13(2) (as so added). Any power conferred on a chairman in Sch 1 (as amended) may (subject to the provisions of Sch 6 (as added and amended)) be carried out by a tribunal or a chairman in relation to proceedings to which Sch 6 (as added and amended) applies: Sch 6 r 13(3) (as so added).

30   In equal value cases which are also national security proceedings (see EMPLOYMENT vol 16(1B) (Reissue) para 855), if a tribunal has required an independent expert to prepare a report on the question, the independent expert must send a copy of the report to the tribunal and must not send it to the parties; in such proceedings if written questions have been put to the independent expert under ibid Sch 6 r 12 (as added) (see the text and note 28 supra), the independent expert must send any answers to those questions to the tribunal and not to the parties: Sch 6 r 14(1) (as added: see note 3 supra). Before the secretary of employment tribunals sends to the parties a copy of a report or answers which have been sent to him by the independent expert under Sch 6 r 14(1) (as added), he must follow the procedure set out in Sch 2 r 10 (see EMPLOYMENT vol 16(1B) (Reissue) para 886) as if that rule referred to the independent expert's report or answers (as the case may be) instead of written reasons, except that the independent expert's report or answers must not be entered on the register: Sch 6 r 14(2) (as so added). If the minister does not give a direction under Sch 2 r 10(3) (see EMPLOYMENT vol 16(1B) (Reissue) para 886) within the period of 28 days from the date on which the minister was sent the report or answers to written questions the secretary of employment tribunals must send a copy of the independent expert's report or answers to written questions (as the case may be) to the parties: Sch 6 r 14(3) (as so added).

430.   Material factor defence.   Where an applicant has established that she[1] is employed in like work[2], work rated as equivalent[3] or work of equal value[4] to a man in the same employment, the employer will, nonetheless, have a defence if he can prove that the variation is genuinely due to a material factor which is not the difference of sex of the applicant and her comparator[5]. The burden of proof rests on the employer to establish a material factor defence[6].

There is a three stage test[7]. The employer must establish: (1) that the variation is genuinely due to that factor[8]; (2) that the factor is material[9]; and (3) that the factor is not the difference of sex between the applicant and her comparator[10]. Over the years the courts have considered a wide range of factors[11].

1   These provisions apply equally to men: see the Equal Pay Act 1970 s 1(13) (as added and amended); and para 423 ante. For the meanings of 'man' and 'woman' see para 424 note 1 ante.

2   See ibid s 1(2)(a); and paras 424, 427 ante.

3   See ibid s 1(2)(b); and paras 424, 428 ante.

4   See ibid s 1(2)(c) (as added); and paras 424, 429 ante.

5   Ibid s 1(3) (substituted by the Equal Pay (Amendment) Regulations 1983, SI 1983/1794, reg 2(2); and amended by the Employment Equality (Sex Discrimination) Regulations 2005, SI 2005/2467, reg 36(1), (3)). In relation to claims of like work or work rated as equivalent the factor must be a material difference between the woman's case and the man's (Equal Pay Act 1970 s 1(3)(a) (as so substituted)), whereas in relation to a claim of equal value, the factor may be a material difference (s 1(3)(b) (as so substituted)). The difference relates to the history of the provision. The Equal Pay Act 1970 was originally limited to claims of like work or work rated as equivalent. At the stage that the Act was amended to include claims of equal value, there was authority to the effect that a material factor must be limited to

what was described as the 'personal equation' of the woman as compared to the man; factors such as market forces, which did not relate to the personal equation, could not provide a material factor defence: *Clay Cross (Quarry Services) Ltd v Fletcher* [1979] ICR 1, sub nom *Fletcher v Clay Cross (Quarry Services) Ltd* [1978] IRLR 361, CA. It seems likely that the substituted Equal Pay Act 1970 s 1(3) was worded so that it was clear that in equal value claims, at least, factors outside the personal equation could be taken into account in determining whether there was a material factor defence. Subsequently, it has been held in *Rainey v Greater Glasgow Health Board* [1987] AC 224, [1987] 1 All ER 65, HL, that the material factor defence was not limited to the personal equation. Thus it appears that the difference in wording is no longer of any significance.

Whether an employer has satisfied the requirements of the Equal Pay Act 1970 s 1(3) (as substituted and amended) is not susceptible to being taken as a preliminary point: *R v Secretary of State for Social Services, ex p Clarke* [1988] 1 CMLR 279, [1988] IRLR 22, DC. See also *Douglas v Islington London Borough Council* (2004) Times, 27 May, [2004] All ER (D) 233 (Apr), EAT; Case C-17/05 *Cadman v Health and Safety Executive* [2006] All ER (EC) 1, [2006] ICR 1623, ECJ; *Bainbridge v Redcar and Cleveland Borough Council* [2006] All ER (D) 197 (Nov), EAT.

6   The standard of proof is the balance of probabilities: *National Vulcan Engineering Insurance Group Ltd v Wade* [1979] QB 132, [1978] ICR 800, CA. The burden of establishing a case of indirect discrimination is on the applicant: *Nelson v Carillion Services Ltd* [2003] EWCA Civ 544, [2003] ICR 1256, [2003] IRLR 428; and see para 418 note 7 ante.

7   *Strathclyde Regional Council v Wallace* [1998] 1 All ER 394, [1998] IRLR 146, HL.

8   The difference in pay will be treated as genuinely due to the factor if it is not a sham or pretence: *Strathclyde Regional Council v Wallace* [1998] 1 All ER 394, [1998] IRLR 146, HL.

9   Material is used in the sense of 'significant and relevant': *Rainey v Greater Glasgow Health Board* [1987] AC 224, [1987] 1 All ER 65, HL. Where there is no direct or indirect discrimination there is no need for the factor to be objectively justified: *Strathclyde Regional Council v Wallace* [1998] 1 All ER 394, [1998] IRLR 146, HL; *Glasgow City Council v Marshall* 1998 SLT 799 (affd [2000] 1 All ER 641, [2000] ICR 196, HL). See *Parliamentary Comr for Administration v Fernandez* [2004] 2 CMLR 59, [2004] ICR 123, EAT. See also *Anderson v South Tyneside Metropolitan Borough Council* [2007] All ER (D) 410 (Mar), EAT (where *Glasgow City Council v Marshall* supra was applied).

10   A factor may be challenged on the basis that it is directly discriminatory in that all women are treated less favourably than all men, or that it is indirectly discriminatory in that it has a disparate impact between men and women although it appears to be gender neutral. If the factor results in disparate impact it is necessary for the factor to be objectively justified in the sense that it corresponds to a real need on the part of the undertaking, is appropriate with a view to achieving that objective and is necessary to that end: Case 170/84 *Bilka-Kaufhaus GmbH v Weber Von Hartz* [1987] ICR 110, [1986] IRLR 317, ECJ. Where there is no direct or indirect discrimination there is no need for the factor to be objectively justified: see note 9 supra. See also *Anderson v South Tyneside Metropolitan Borough Council* [2007] All ER (D) 410 (Mar), EAT (where Case 170/84 *Bilka-Kaufhaus GmbH v Weber Von Hartz* supra was applied). The genuine material factor defence must be approached on an objective rather than a subjective view; and European Court of Justice decisions that have provided clear guidelines in equal pay cases as to the need for objective justification in all cases should be followed in so far as there is a conflict between those decisions and earlier United Kingdom decisions: see *Sharp v Caledonia Group Services Ltd* [2006] ICR 218, [2006] IRLR 4, EAT; but see also para 422 ante.

11   However, the cases must be treated with caution. In many of the cases the courts did not draw a clear distinction between the issues of whether the difference in treatment is genuinely due to the factor, whether the factor is material and whether the factor is not the difference of sex. What is more, many of the cases were decided before a distinction was drawn between those factors that gave rise to disparate impact, in relation to which objective justification must be shown, and those that are non-discriminatory and so do not require objective justification. Accordingly, when considering a defence under the Equal Pay Act 1970 s 1(3) (as substituted and amended) the starting point must be to consider whether the factor is potentially either directly or indirectly discriminatory. If it is, consideration must be given as to whether it can be objectively justified. As to objective justification see para 422 ante. If there is no question of discrimination, and it can be shown that the difference in treatment is genuinely due to the factor put forward by the employer, it is likely that the court will consider the factor as material. The list of factors that have been considered by the courts must be approached in this context. The factors that have been considered by the courts include: market forces (see *Rainey v Greater Glasgow Health Board* [1987] AC 224, [1987] 1 All ER 65, HL; Case C-127/92 *Enderby v Frenchay Health Authority* [1994] ICR 112, [1993] IRLR 591, ECJ; c f *Ratcliffe v North Yorkshire County Council* [1995] 3 All ER 597, [1995] IRLR 439, HL; *Clay Cross (Quarry Services) Ltd v Fletcher* [1979] ICR 1, sub nom *Fletcher v Clay Cross (Quarry Services) Ltd* [1978] IRLR 361, CA); collective bargaining (see *Enderby v Frenchay Health Authority* supra; c f *Strathclyde Regional Council v Wallace* [1998] 1 All ER 394, [1998] IRLR 146, HL; *Glasgow City Council v Marshall* 1998 SLT 799 (affd [2000] 1 All ER 641, [2000] ICR 196, HL)); red circle (see *Benveniste v University of Southampton* [1989] ICR 617, [1989] IRLR 122, CA; *Outlook Supplies Ltd v*

Parry [1978] 2 All ER 707, [1978] ICR 388, EAT; *Snoxall v Vauxhall Motors Ltd* [1978] QB 11, [1977] ICR 700, EAT; *United Biscuits Ltd v Young* [1978] IRLR 15, EAT; *Methven v Cow Industrial Polymers Ltd* [1980] ICR 463, [1980] IRLR 289, EAT; *Sun Alliance and London Insurance Ltd v Dudman* [1978] ICR 551, [1978] IRLR 169, EAT; *Charles Early and Marriott (Whitney) Ltd v Smith* [1978] QB 11, [1977] ICR 700, EAT; *Avon and Somerset Police Authority v Emery* [1981] ICR 229, EAT; *Ministry of Defence v Farthing* [1980] ICR 705, sub nom *Farthing v Ministry of Defence* [1980] IRLR 402, EAT; *Trico Folberth Ltd v Groves and Aiston* [1976] IRLR 327, IT); special duties (*Shields v E Coombes (Holdings) Ltd* [1978] ICR 1159, sub nom *E Coombes (Holdings) Ltd v Shields* [1978] IRLR 263, CA); responsibility (*Edmonds v Computer Services (South West) Ltd* [1977] IRLR 359, EAT); experience (*de Brito v Standard Chartered Bank Ltd* [1978] ICR 650, EAT; *Tyldesley v TML Plastics Ltd* [1996] ICR 356, [1996] IRLR 395, EAT); length of service (*ARW Transformers Ltd v Cupples* [1977] IRLR 228, 12 ITR 355, EAT; *Boyle v Tennent Caledonian Breweries Ltd* [1978] IRLR 321, EAT); time at which work undertaken (*National Coal Board v Sherwin* [1978] ICR 700, [1978] IRLR 122, EAT; cf *Thomas v National Coal Board* [1987] ICR 757, [1987] IRLR 451, EAT; *Kerr v Lister & Co Ltd* [1977] IRLR 259, EAT); number of hours worked (*Leverton v Clwyd County Council* [1989] AC 706, [1989] ICR 33, HL; and see also Case 170/84 *Bilka-Kaufhaus GmbH v Weber Von Hartz* [1987] ICR 110, [1986] IRLR 317, ECJ (disparate impact)); place of work (*Navy Army and Airforce Institute v Varley* [1977] ICR 11, [1976] IRLR 408, EAT); and mistake (*Yorkshire Blood Transfusion Service v Plaskitt* [1994] ICR 74, EAT; and see also *Tyldesley v TML Plastics Ltd* supra).

431. Application of the Equal Pay Act 1970 to specific groups. The requirement of equal treatment applies to: (1) service for purposes of a Minister of the Crown or government department[1], other than service of a person holding a statutory office; or (2) service on behalf of the Crown for purposes of a person holding a statutory office or purposes of a statutory body, as it applies to employment by a private person, and so applies as if references to a contract of employment included references to the terms of service[2]. The requirement also applies in relation to service as a relevant member of the House of Commons staff[3] as in relation to service for the purposes of a Minister of the Crown or government department, and accordingly applies as if references to a contract of employment included references to the terms of service of such a member[4]. It also applies in relation to employment as a relevant member of the House of Lords staff[5] as in relation to other employment[6].

The requirement of equal treatment also applies to: (a) the holding of an office or post to which persons are appointed to discharge functions personally under the direction of another person, and in respect of which they are entitled to remuneration; and (b) any office or post to which appointments are made by, or on the recommendation of or subject to the approval of, a Minister of the Crown, a government department, or the National Assembly for Wales, as it applies to employment by a private person, and so applies as if references to a contract of employment included references to the terms of appointment, and as if references to the employer included references to the person responsible for paying any remuneration that a holder of the office or post is entitled to in respect of the office or post[7].

1 Service 'for purposes of' a Minister of the Crown or government department does not include service in any office in the House of Commons Disqualification Act 1975 s 2, Sch 2 (as amended) (ministerial offices) (see CONSTITUTIONAL LAW AND HUMAN RIGHTS vol 8(2) (Reissue) para 400; PARLIAMENT vol 34 (Reissue) para 611) as for the time being in force: Equal Pay Act 1970 s 1(10) (added by the Sex Discrimination Act 1975 s 8(6), Sch 1 Pt I).

2 Equal Pay Act 1970 s 1(8) (substituted by the Sex Discrimination Act 1975 Sch 1 Pt I). 'Statutory body' means a body set up by or in pursuance of an enactment (including an enactment comprised in, or in an instrument made under an Act of the Scottish Parliament); and 'statutory office' means an office so set up: Equal Pay Act 1970 s 1(10) (as added (see note 1 supra); and amended by the Scotland Act 1998 (Consequential Modifications) Order 2006, SI 2000/2040, art 2(1), Schedule para 4). Scottish matters generally are beyond the scope of this work.

3 'Relevant member of the House of Commons staff' has the same meaning as in the Employment Rights Act 1996 s 195 (as amended) (see EMPLOYMENT vol 16(1A) (Reissue) para 136); and s 195(6)–(12) (as amended) (person to be treated as employer of House of Commons staff), applies, with any necessary modifications, for the purposes of the Equal Pay Act 1970 s 1 (as amended): s 1(10A) (added by the Trade

Union and Labour Relations (Consolidation) Act 1992 s 300(2), Sch 2 para 3; and amended by the Employment Rights Act 1996 s 240, Sch 1 para 1(1), (2)).

4 Equal Pay Act 1970 s 1(10A) (as added and amended: see note 3 supra).

5 'Relevant member of the House of Lords staff' has the same meaning as in the Employment Rights Act 1996 s 194 (as amended) (see EMPLOYMENT vol 16(1A) (Reissue) para 135); and s 194(7) applies for the purposes of the Equal Pay Act 1970 s 1 (as amended): s 1(10B) (added by the Trade Union Reform and Employment Rights Act 1993 s 49(1), Sch 7 para 8; and amended by the Employment Rights Act 1996 Sch 1 para 1(1), (3)).

6 Equal Pay Act 1970 s 1(10B) (as added and amended: see note 5 supra).

7 Ibid s 1(6A) (s 1(6A)–(6C) added by the Employment Equality (Sex Discrimination) Regulations 2005, SI 2005/2467, reg 35(1), (2)). For these purposes, the holder of an office or post: (1) is to be regarded as discharging her functions under the direction of another person if that other person is entitled to direct her as to when and where she discharges those functions; and (2) is not to be regarded as entitled to remuneration merely because she is entitled to payments in respect of expenses incurred by her in carrying out the functions of the office or post, or by way of compensation for the loss of income or benefits she would or might have received from any person had she not been carrying out the functions of the office or post: s 1(6B) (as so added). For these purposes, 'office or post' does not include a political office (see heads (a)–(k) infra) and appointment to an office or post does not include election to an office or post: s 1(6C) (as so added). For the purposes of s 1(6C) (as added), the following are political offices: (a) any office of the House of Commons held by a member of it; (b) a life peerage within the meaning of the Life Peerages Act 1958 (see CONSTITUTIONAL LAW AND HUMAN RIGHTS vol 8(2) (Reissue) para 212; PARLIAMENT vol 34 (Reissue) para 540; PEERAGES AND DIGNITIES), or any office of the House of Lords held by a member of it; (c) any office mentioned in the House of Commons Disqualification Act 1975 Sch 2 (as amended) (see PARLIAMENT vol 34 (Reissue) para 611); (d) the offices of Leader of the Opposition, Chief Opposition Whip or Assistant Opposition Whip within the meaning of the Ministerial and other Salaries Act 1975 (see CONSTITUTIONAL LAW AND HUMAN RIGHTS vol 8(2) (Reissue) para 219); (e) any office of the National Assembly for Wales held by a member of it; (f) in England, any office of a county council, a London borough council, a district council or a parish council held by a member of it; (g) in Wales, any office of a county council, a county borough council or a community council held by a member of it; (h) any office of the Greater London Authority held by a member of it; (i) any office of the Common Council of the City of London held by a member of it; (j) any office of the Council of the Isles of Scilly held by a member of it; and (k) any office of a political party: see the Equal Pay Act 1970 s 1A (added by the Employment Equality (Sex Discrimination) Regulations 2005, SI 2005/2467, reg 35(1), (3)). As to the National Assembly for Wales see para 302 ante. This provision also refers to various Scottish offices, but Scottish matters generally are beyond the scope of this work. As to local government authorities in England and Wales see LOCAL GOVERNMENT vol 29(1) (Reissue) para 23 et seq; as to London borough councils see LONDON GOVERNMENT vol 29(2) (Reissue) para 35 et seq; as to the Greater London Authority see LONDON GOVERNMENT vol 29(2) (Reissue) para 70 et seq; as to the Common Council of the City of London see LONDON GOVERNMENT vol 29(2) (Reissue) para 51 et seq; and as to the Council of the Isles of Scilly see LOCAL GOVERNMENT vol 29(1) (Reissue) para 40.

432. Service pay and conditions. The provisions relating to equal pay[1] apply, with modifications[2], to service by a woman[3] in any of the armed forces[4] as they apply to employment by a private person[5].

Any claim in respect of the contravention of a term of service modified or included, in relation to a woman's service in any of the armed forces, by a term corresponding to an equality clause in a contract of employment (including a claim for arrears of pay or damages in respect of the contravention) may be presented by way of complaint to an employment tribunal, and any such contravention is to be regarded for the purposes of a claim as if it were a breach of contract[6].

Where any claim is brought by a woman claimant arising from such a contravention of a term of service[7], no complaint in respect of the claim may be presented to an employment tribunal unless: (1) the claimant has made a complaint to an officer under the service redress procedures[8] applicable to her and has submitted that complaint to the Defence Council under those procedures[9]; and (2) the Defence Council has made a determination with respect to the complaint[10]. Regulations may make provision enabling a complaint in respect of the claim to be presented to an employment tribunal in such circumstances as may be specified by the regulations[11]. Where a complaint is presented to an employment tribunal by virtue of such regulations, the service redress procedures may continue after the complaint is presented[12].

No determination may be made by an employment tribunal in proceedings on a complaint in respect of the claim unless the complaint is presented on or before the qualifying date[13]. A specific time limit is provided for[14].

1   Ie the Equal Pay Act 1970 ss 1, 6 (both as amended).
2   Ie the modifications mentioned in ibid s 7A(2) (as added and amended) and any other necessary modifications. In the application of ss 1, 6 (both as amended) to service by a woman in any of the armed forces: (1) references to a contract of employment are to be regarded as references to the terms of service; (2) in s 1, s 1(6)(c) and the words 'or any associated employer' and s 1(6A)–(11) (as amended) and s 1(13) (as added and amended) are to be omitted; and (3) references to an equality clause are to be regarded as referring to a corresponding term of service capable of requiring the terms of service applicable in her case to be treated as modified or as including other terms: s 7A(2) (s 7A added by the Armed Forces Act 1996 s 24(2); and the Equal Pay Act 1970 s 7A(2) amended by the Equal Pay Act 1970 (Amendment) Regulations 2003, SI 2003/1656, reg 6(1), (2); and the Employment Equality (Sex Discrimination) Regulations 2005, SI 2005/2467, reg 35(1), (5)).
3   These provisions apply equally to men: see the Equal Pay Act 1970 s 1(13) (as added and amended); and para 423 ante. For the meaning of 'woman' see para 424 note 1 ante.
4   'Armed forces' means the naval, military or air forces of the Crown: Equal Pay Act 1970 s 7A(12) (as added (see note 2 supra); and amended by the Equal Pay Act 1970 (Amendment) Regulations 2003, SI 2003/1656, reg 6(1), (5)).
5   Equal Pay Act 1970 s 7A(1) (as added: see note 2 supra).
6   Ibid s 7A(3) (as added (see note 2 supra); and amended by virtue of the Employment Rights (Dispute Resolution) Act 1998 s 1(2)(a)).
7   See the Equal Pay Act 1970 s 7A(4) (as added: see note 2 supra).
8   'The service redress procedures' means the procedures, excluding those which relate to the making of a report on a complaint to Her Majesty, referred to in the Army Act 1955 s 180 (as substituted an amended), the Air Force Act 1955 s 180 (as substituted and amended) and the Naval Discipline Act 1957 s 130 (as substituted and amended) (see ARMED FORCES vol 2(2) (Reissue) para 314): Equal Pay Act 1970 s 7A(12) (as added and amended: see notes 2, 4 supra).
9   Ibid s 7A(5)(a) (as added: see note 2 supra). As to the Defence Council see ARMED FORCES vol 2(2) (Reissue) para 2; CONSTITUTIONAL LAW AND HUMAN RIGHTS vol 8(2) (Reissue) para 443 et seq.
10 Ibid s 7A(5)(b) (as added: see note 2 supra). ·
11 Ibid s 7A(6) (as added (see note 2 supra); and amended by virtue of the Employment Rights (Dispute Resolution) Act 1998 s 1(2)(a)). This is notwithstanding that the Equal Pay Act 1970 s 7A(5) (as added) (see the text and notes 9, 10 supra) would otherwise preclude its presentation: see s 7A(6) (as so added and amended). Such regulations must be made by statutory instrument which is subject to annulment in pursuance of a resolution of either House of Parliament: s 7A(11) (as so added: see note 2 supra). In exercise of this power, the Equal Pay (Complaints to Employment Tribunals (Armed Forces) Regulations 1997, SI 1997/2162 (as amended) have been made.
        A person may present a complaint to an employment tribunal under the Equal Pay Act 1970 s 7A (as added and amended), notwithstanding that s 7A(5) (as added and amended) (see the text and notes 9, 10 supra) would otherwise preclude the presentation of such a complaint, where: (1) the person has made a complaint in respect of the same matter to an officer under the service redress procedures; and (2) that complaint has not been withdrawn: Equal Pay (Complaints to Employment Tribunals (Armed Forces) Regulations 1997, SI 1997/2162, reg 2(1), (2) (reg 2(1) amended by virtue of the Employment Rights (Dispute Resolution) Act 1998 s 1(2)(a)). A person is treated as having withdrawn a complaint if, having made a complaint to an officer under the service redress procedures, that person fails to submit that complaint to the Defence Council under those procedures: Equal Pay (Complaints to Employment Tribunals (Armed Forces) Regulations 1997, SI 1997/2162, reg 2(3). This provision applies where the complaint concerns a claim in respect of the contravention of a term of service relating to membership of, or rights under, any relevant scheme: reg 2(4). 'Relevant scheme' means: (a) any occupational pension scheme (ie within the meaning of the Pensions Schemes Act 1993 s 1 (see SOCIAL SECURITY AND PENSIONS vol 44(2) (Reissue) para 741) made under the Naval and Marine Pay and Pensions Act 1865 s 3 (as amended); (b) the Army Pensions Warrant 1977; or (c) any occupational pension scheme made under the Air Force (Constitution) Act 1917 s 2 (see ARMED FORCES vol 2(2) (Reissue) paras 162, 263 et seq): Equal Pay (Complaints to Employment Tribunals (Armed Forces) Regulations 1997, SI 1997/2162, reg 2(5).
12 Equal Pay Act 1970 s 7A(7) (as added (see note 2 supra); and amended by virtue of the Employment Rights (Dispute Resolution) Act 1998 s 1(2)(a)).

13 Equal Pay Act 1970 s 7A(8) (as added (see note 2 supra); and substituted by the Equal Pay Act 1970 (Amendment) Regulations 2003, SI 2003/1656, reg 6(1), (3)). As to the compatibility of an earlier version of this provision with the European Union principle of equivalence see Case C-78/98 *Preston v Wolverhampton Healthcare NHS Trust, Fletcher v Midland Bank plc* [2001] 2 AC 415, [2000] All ER (EC) 714, ECJ; and see para 421 ante. See also *Preston v Wolverhampton Healthcare NHS Trust (No 2)* [2001] UKHL 5, [2001] 2 AC 455, [2001] ICR 217.

The reference in the Equal Pay Act 1970 s 7A(8) (as added and substituted) to the qualifying date is a reference to such date as determined in accordance with s 7AA (as added): see s 7AA(1) (added by the Equal Pay Act 1970 (Amendment) Regulations 2003, SI 2003/1656, reg 7; and modified by the Occupational Pension Schemes (Equal Treatment) (Amendment) Regulations 2005, SI 2005/1923, regs 7, 9). In a standard case, the qualifying date is the date falling nine months after the last day of the period of service during which the claim arose: Equal Pay Act 1970 s 7AA(3) (as so added). In a case which is a concealment case (but not also a disability case), the qualifying date is the date falling nine months after the day on which the woman discovered the qualifying fact in question (or could with reasonable diligence have discovered it): s 7AA(4) (as so added). In a case which is a disability case (but not also a concealment case), the qualifying date is the date falling nine months after the day on which the woman ceased to be under a disability: s 7AA(5) (as so added). In a case which is both a concealment and a disability case, the qualifying date is the later of the dates referred to in s 7AA(4), (5) (as added): s 7AA(6) (as so added). For these purposes, 'concealment case' means a case where: (1) the employer deliberately concealed from the woman any fact (a 'qualifying fact') which is relevant to the contravention to which the complaint relates, and without knowledge of which the woman could not reasonably have been expected to present the complaint; and (2) the woman did not discover the qualifying fact (or could not with reasonable diligence have discovered it) until after the last day of the period of service during which the claim arose; 'disability case' means a case where the woman was under a disability at any time during the nine months after: (a) the last day of the period of service during which the claim arose; or (b) the day on which she discovered (or could with reasonable diligence have discovered) the qualifying fact deliberately concealed from her by the employer (if that day falls after the day referred to in head (a) supra), as the case may be; and 'standard case' means a case which is not: (i) a concealment case; (ii) a disability case; or (iii) both: s 7AA(2) (as so added).

14 See ibid s 7A(9) (as added (see note 2 supra); and amended by the Equal Pay Act 1970 (Amendment) Regulations 2003, SI 2003/1656, reg 6(1), (4)). A woman is not entitled to be awarded any payment by way of arrears of pay or damages in respect of a time earlier than the arrears date determined in accordance with the Equal Pay Act 1970 s 7AB (as added): see s 7AB(1) (added by the Equal Pay Act 1970 (Amendment) Regulations 2003, SI 2003/1656, reg 8; and modified by the Occupational Pension Schemes (Equal Treatment) (Amendment) Regulations 2005, SI 2005/1923, regs 7, 11(1), (3)). In a standard case, the arrears date is the date falling six years before the day on which the complaint under the service redress procedures was made: Equal Pay Act 1970 s 7AB(3) (as so added). In a case which is a concealment or a disability case or both, the arrears date is the date of the contravention: s 7AB(4) (as so added). Where, in accordance with regulations made under s 7A(6) (as added and amended) (see the text and note 11 supra), proceedings are instituted without a complaint having been made under the service redress procedures, references to the making of a complaint under the service redress procedures are to be read as references to the institution of proceedings: s 7AB(5), (6) (as so added). For these purposes, 'concealment case' means a case where: (1) the employer deliberately concealed from the woman any fact which is relevant to the contravention to which the proceedings relate, and without knowledge of which the woman could not reasonably have been expected to institute the proceedings; and (2) the woman made a complaint under the service redress procedures within six years of the day on which she discovered the fact (or could with reasonable diligence have discovered it); 'disability case' means a case where: (a) the woman was under a disability at the time of the contravention to which the proceedings relate; and (b) the woman made a complaint under the service redress procedures within six years of the day on which she ceased to be under a disability; and 'standard case' means a case which is not: (i) a concealment case; (ii) a disability case; or (iii) both: s 7AB(2) (as so added).

433. Agricultural wages orders. Where an agricultural wages order[1] contains any provision applying specifically to men[2] only or to women[3] only, the order may be referred by the Secretary of State[4] to the Central Arbitration Committee[5] to declare what amendments need to be made in the order[6], so as to remove that discrimination between men and women; and when the Central Arbitration Committee has declared the amendments needing to be so made, it is the duty of the Agricultural Wages Board, by a further agricultural wages order coming into operation not later than five months after the date of the Central Arbitration Committee's decision, either to make those amendments in the order referred to the Central Arbitration Committee or otherwise to replace or amend that order so as to remove the discrimination[7].

An agricultural wages order must be referred to the Central Arbitration Committee if in any case it appears to the Secretary of State that the order may be amendable or if the Secretary of State is requested so to refer it[8]: (1) by a body for the time being entitled to nominate for membership of the Agricultural Wages Board persons representing employers (or, if provision is made for any of the persons representing employers to be elected instead of nominated, then by a member or members representing employers)[9]; or (2) by a body for the time being entitled to nominate for membership of the Agricultural Wages Board persons representing workers (or, if provision is made for any of the persons representing workers to be elected instead of nominated, then by a member or members representing workers)[10].

1   'Agricultural wages order' means an order of the Agricultural Wages Board under the Agricultural Wages Act 1948; and 'the Agricultural Wages Board' means the Agricultural Wages Board for England and Wales: Equal Pay Act 1970 s 5(4). See AGRICULTURE vol 1(2) (Reissue) para 929 et seq.

2   For the meaning of 'man' see para 424 note 1 ante.

3   For the meaning of 'woman' see para 424 note 1 ante.

4   As to the Secretary of State and the National Assembly for Wales see para 302 ante.

5   As to the Central Arbitration Committee see TRADE, INDUSTRY AND INDUSTRIAL RELATIONS vol 47 (2001 Reissue) paras 1352–1354.

6   Ie in accordance with the like rules as apply under the Equal Pay Act 1970 s 3(4) (repealed with savings) to the amendment under that provision of a collective agreement: see s 5(1) (as amended: see note 7 infra).

7   Ibid s 5(1) (amended by the Employment Protection Act 1975 s 125(1), Sch 16 Pt IV). Where the Agricultural Wages Board certifies that the effect of an agricultural wages order is only to make such amendments of a previous order as have been declared by the Central Arbitration Committee to be needed, or to make such amendments with minor modifications or modifications of limited application, or is only to revoke and reproduce with such amendments a previous order, then the Agricultural Wages Board may instead of complying with the Agricultural Wages Act 1948 Sch 4 paras 1, 2 (see AGRICULTURE vol 1(2) (Reissue) para 942) give notice of the proposed order in such manner as appears to the Agricultural Wages Board expedient in the circumstances, and may make the order at any time after the expiration of seven days from the giving of the notice: Equal Pay Act 1970 s 5(2) (s 5(2), (3) amended by the Employment Protection Act 1975 Sch 16 Pt IV; and the Sex Discrimination Act 1975 s 8(6), Sch 1 para 6(2)).

8   Equal Pay Act 1970 s 5(3) (as amended: see note 7 supra).

9   Ibid s 5(3)(a). See also AGRICULTURE vol 1(2) (Reissue) para 941.

10   Ibid s 5(3)(b). See also AGRICULTURE vol 1(2) (Reissue) para 941.

434. Exclusion of requirement for equal treatment. An equality clause[1] does not operate in relation to terms affected by compliance with the laws regulating the employment of women[2], or affording special treatment to women in connection with pregnancy or childbirth[3].

An equality clause does not operate in relation to terms relating to a person's membership of, or rights under, an occupational pension scheme[4], being terms in relation to which, by reason only of any provisions made[5], an equal treatment rule[6] would not operate if the terms were included in the scheme[7].

1   As to equality clauses see paras 423–424 ante. See also para 419 ante.

2   Equal Pay Act 1970 s 6(1)(a) (s 6(1) substituted by the Sex Discrimination Act 1975 s 8(6), Sch 1 para 3; and amended by the Sex Discrimination Act 1986 s 9(1), (3)).

3   Equal Pay Act 1970 s 6(1)(b) (as substituted and amended: see note 2 supra). For provision relating to pregnancy and maternity leave see s 1(2)(d)–(f), (5A), (5B) (as added); and para 424 note 10 ante. Section s 6(1)(b) (as substituted and amended) does not affect the operation of an equality clause falling within s 1(2)(d), (e) or (f) (as added) (see para 424 note 10 ante): s 6(1AA) (added by the Employment Equality (Sex Discrimination) Regulations 2005, SI 2005/2467, reg 36(1), (5)).

4   'Occupational pension scheme' has the same meaning as in the Pension Schemes Act 1993 (see SOCIAL
    SECURITY AND PENSIONS vol 44(2) (Reissue) para 853): Equal Pay Act 1970 s 6(1C) (added by the
    Pensions Act 1995 s 66(1)). As to occupational pension schemes see SOCIAL SECURITY AND PENSIONS
    vol 44(2) (Reissue) para 741 et seq.

5   Ie by or under the Pensions Act 1995 ss 62–64 (as amended) (equal treatment): see SOCIAL SECURITY
    AND PENSIONS vol 44(2) (Reissue) para 782 et seq.

6   'Equal treatment rule' has the meaning given by ibid s 62 (see SOCIAL SECURITY AND PENSIONS
    vol 44(2) (Reissue) para 782): Equal Pay Act 1970 s 6(1C) (as added: see note 4 supra).

7   Ibid s 6(1B) (added by the Pensions Act 1995 s 66(1)).

435.   Enforcement.   The underlying right to equal pay derives from Article 141 of
the EC Treaty[1]. Accordingly, any procedural provision must comply with the principle
of equivalence, in that it must not be less favourable than other national procedural rules
governing similar domestic actions, and the principle of effectiveness, in that the
procedural rule must not render making a claim impossible in practice or excessively
difficult[2].

Any claim in respect of the contravention of a term modified or included by virtue of
an equality clause, including a claim for arrears of remuneration or damages in respect of
the contravention, may be presented by way of a complaint to an employment tribunal[3].
As the Equal Pay Act 1970 operates by implying the equality clause into the applicant's
contract of employment[4], its breach can give rise to a claim of breach of contract that
can be brought before the employment tribunal[5], in the county court or in the High
Court. However, where any real issue arises as to whether there has been a breach of the
principle of equal pay, the employment tribunal is the appropriate venue for the matter
to be litigated. Where it appears to the court in which any proceedings are pending that
a claim or counter-claim in respect of the operation of an equality clause could more
conveniently be disposed of separately by an employment tribunal, the court may direct
that the claim or counter-claim is to be struck out[6]. Without prejudice to this, where in
proceedings before any court a question arises as to the operation of an equality clause,
the court may on the application of any party to the proceedings or otherwise refer that
question, or direct it to be referred by a party to the proceedings, to an employment
tribunal for determination by the tribunal, and may stay the proceedings in the
meantime[7].

Where a dispute arises in relation to the effect of an equality clause, the employer
may apply to an employment tribunal for an order declaring the rights of the employer
and the employee in relation to the matter in question[8].

Where it appears to the Secretary of State[9] that there may be a question whether the
employer of any women[10] is or has been contravening a term modified or included by
virtue of their equality clauses, but that it is not reasonable to expect them to take steps
to have the question determined, the question may be referred by him as respects all or
any of them to an employment tribunal and must be dealt with as if the reference were
of a claim by the women or a woman against the employer[11].

Conciliation is available for complaints under the Equal Pay Act 1970[12].

It is unlawful to victimise a person for bringing a claim under the Equal Pay
Act 1970[13].

No determination may be made by an employment tribunal on a relevant
complaint[14], application[15] or reference[16], unless the proceedings are instituted on or
before the qualifying date[17].

A claim may be brought for arrears of remuneration or damages[18]. The arrears may be
claimed in standard cases over a six year period[19], except in relation to claims for
exclusion from membership of pension schemes, to which special rules apply[20]. It is not

possible to claim an entitlement to a higher rate of pay than the comparator[21]; the right under the Equal Pay Act 1970 is to receive the same basic rate of pay as the male comparator[22].

As the Equal Pay Act 1970 operates by implying an equality clause into the applicant's contract of employment, the variation to the applicant's contract will remain in force until it is terminated or there is a valid variation[23].

The Equal Opportunities Commission ('EOC') also has a role to play in dealing with equal pay claims[24]. In brief, it may provide financial or other assistance to an applicant[25], issue a non-discrimination notice[26], seek a preliminary finding as to whether there have been infringements of the Equal Pay Act 1970[27] and apply for an injunction to restrain persistent discrimination[28].

1   Ie the Treaty Establishing the European Community (Rome, 25 March 1957; TS 1 (1973); Cmnd 5179) art 141 (formerly art 119; renumbered by virtue of the Treaty of Amsterdam: see *Treaty Citation (No 2) (Note)* [1999] All ER (EC) 646, ECJ).

2   Case C-271/91 *Marshall v Southampton and South West Hampshire Health Authority (Teaching) (No 2)* [1994] QB 126, [1993] 4 All ER 586, ECJ; Case C-128/93 *Fisscher v Voorhuis Hengelo BV* [1995] All ER (EC) 193, [1995] ICR 635, ECJ.

3   Equal Pay Act 1970 s 2(1) (substituted by the Sex Discrimination Act 1975 s 8(6), Sch 1 Pt I; and amended by virtue of the Employment Rights (Dispute Resolution) Act 1998 s 1(2)(a)).

       As to the questioning by the complainant of the respondent, including the admissibility of the questions and replies as evidence in proceedings, see the Equal Pay Act 1970 s 7B (as added); and para 424 note 14 ante.

4   See ibid s 1(1) (as substituted); and para 424 ante.

5   See the Employment Tribunals Extension of Jurisdiction (England and Wales) Order 1994, SI 1994/1623 (as amended); and EMPLOYMENT vol 16(1B) (Reissue) paras 825–826.

6   Equal Pay Act 1970 s 2(3) (amended by the Sex Discrimination Act 1975 Sch 1 Pt I; and amended by virtue of the Employment Rights (Dispute Resolution) Act 1998 s 1(2)(a)).

7   Equal Pay Act 1970 s 2(3) (as amended: see note 6 supra).

8   Ibid s 2(1A) (added by the Sex Discrimination Act 1975 Sch 1 Pt I; and amended by virtue of the Employment Rights (Dispute Resolution) Act 1998 s 1(2)(a)).

       In the Equal Pay Act 1970 s 2 (as amended), 'employer', in relation to the holder of an office or post to which s 1 (as amended) applies by virtue of s 1(6A) (as added) (see para 431 ante), is to be construed in accordance with s 1(6A) (as added): s 2(5A) (added by the Employment Equality (Sex Discrimination) Regulations 2005, SI 2005/2467, reg 35(1), (4)).

9   As to the Secretary of State and the National Assembly for Wales see para 302 ante.

10   For the meaning of 'woman' see para 424 note 1 ante. These provisions apply equally to men: see the Equal Pay Act 1970 s 1(13) (as added and amended); and para 423 ante.

11   Ibid s 2(2) (amended by the Sex Discrimination Act 1975 Sch 1 Pt I; and amended by virtue of the Employment Rights (Dispute Resolution) Act 1998 s 1(2)(a)).

12   See the Employment Tribunals Act 1996 s 18(1) (as amended); and EMPLOYMENT vol 16(1A) (Reissue) para 123.

13   See the Sex Discrimination Act 1975 s 4 (as amended); and para 358 ante.

14   Ie a complaint under the Equal Pay Act 1970 s 2(1) (as substituted and amended): see the text to note 3 supra.

15   Ie an application under ibid s 2(1A) (as added and amended): see the text to note 8 supra.

16   Ie a reference under ibid s 2(2) (as amended): see the text to note 11 supra.

17   Ibid s 2(4) (substituted by the Equal Pay Act 1970 (Amendment) Regulations 2003, SI 2003/1656, reg 3(1), (2)). The reference to the qualifying date is a reference to the qualifying date determined in accordance with the Equal Pay Act 1970 s 2ZA (as added): see s 2ZA(1) (added by the Equal Pay Act 1970 (Amendment) Regulations 2003, SI 2003/1656, reg 4). In a standard case, the qualifying date is the date falling six months after the last day on which the woman was employed in the employment: Equal Pay Act 1970 s 2ZA(3) (as so added). In a case which is a stable employment case (but not also a concealment or a disability case or both), the qualifying date is the date falling six months after the day on which the stable employment relationship ended: s 2ZA(4) (as so added). In a case which is a concealment case (but not also a disability case), the qualifying date is the date falling six months after the day on which the woman discovered the qualifying fact in question (or could with reasonable diligence have discovered it): s 2ZA(5) (as so added). In a case which is a disability case (but not also a concealment case), the qualifying date is the date falling six months after the day on which the woman ceased to be under a disability: s 2ZA(6) (as so added). In a case which is both a concealment and a disability case, the

qualifying date is the later of the dates referred to in s 2ZA(5), (6) (as added): s 2ZA(7) (as so added). For these purposes, 'concealment case' means a case where: (1) the employer deliberately concealed from the woman any fact (a 'qualifying fact') which is relevant to the contravention to which the proceedings relate, and without knowledge of which the woman could not reasonably have been expected to institute the proceedings; and (2) the woman did not discover the qualifying fact (or could not with reasonable diligence have discovered it) until after the last day on which she was employed in the employment, or the day on which the stable employment relationship between her and the employer ended, as the case may be; 'disability case' means a case where the woman was under a disability at any time during the six months after: (a) the last day on which she was employed in the employment; (b) the day on which the stable employment relationship between her and the employer ended; or (c) the day on which she discovered (or could with reasonable diligence have discovered) the qualifying fact deliberately concealed from her by the employer (if that day falls after the day referred to in head (a) or (b) supra, as the case may be), as the case may be; 'stable employment case' means a case where the proceedings relate to a period during which a stable employment relationship subsists between the woman and the employer, notwithstanding that the period includes any time after the ending of a contract of employment when no further contract of employment is in force; and 'standard case' means a case which is not: (i) a stable employment case; (ii) a concealment case; (iii) a disability case; or (iv) both a concealment and a disability case: s 2ZA(2) (as so added).

Where an employee works under a series of contracts the claim must be brought within six months of the termination of the contract in relation to which the claim is made: *Preston v Wolverhampton Health Care NHS Trust* [1998] ICR 227, [1998] IRLR 197, HL (the House of Lords referred to the European Court of Justice the question whether the six-month time limit is compatible with European Union law). In *Young v National Power plc* [2001] 2 All ER 339, [2001] ICR 328, CA (distinguishing *Preston v Wolverhampton Health Care NHS Trust* supra), it was held that a claim must be brought within six months of termination of the employment contract as opposed to termination of the actual job on which the claim is based. See also *Allan v Newcastle upon Tyne City Council, Degnan v Redcar and Cleveland Borough Council* [2005] ICR 1170, [2005] IRLR 504, EAT (unlike sex and race discrimination, the Equal Pay Act 1970 does not allow the successful claimant to claim compensation for non-economic loss, e g injury to feelings or aggravated/exemplary damages). The six-month limitation period imposed by the Equal Pay Act 1970 s 2(4) (as then in force) for an EC Treaty claim was held to be not less favourable than the six-year limitation period imposed for a domestic contractual claim, which is a suitable comparator in *Preston v Wolverhampton Healthcare NHS Trust (No 2)* [2001] UKHL 5, [2001] 2 AC 455, [2001] ICR 217. See also *Preston v Wolverhampton Healthcare NHS Trust (No 3)*, *Fletcher v Midland Bank plc (No 3)* [2006] UKHL 13, [2006] 3 All ER 193. Where an employee is employed on a permanent basis consequent to working under a series of temporary contracts, a claim relating to the series of temporary contracts must be brought within six months of the termination of the last contract in that series: *Jeffery v Secretary of State for Education* [2006] ICR 1062, [2006] All ER (D) 99 (Jun), EAT.

18 See the Equal Pay Act 1970 s 2(1) (as substituted: see note 3 supra).
19 The Equal Pay Act 1970 provides that a woman is not entitled, in proceedings brought in respect of a failure to comply with an equality clause (including proceedings before an employment tribunal), to be awarded any payment by way of arrears of remuneration or damages in respect of a time earlier than the arrears date: s 2(5) (substituted by the Equal Pay Act 1970 (Amendment) Regulations 2003, SI 2003/1656, reg 3(1), (3)). The reference to the arrears date is a reference to the arrears date determined in accordance with the Equal Pay Act 1970 s 2ZB (as added): see s 2ZB(1) (added by the Equal Pay Act 1970 (Amendment) Regulations 2003, SI 2003/1656, reg 5). In a standard case, the arrears date is the date falling six years before the day on which the proceedings were instituted: Equal Pay Act 1970 s 2ZB(3) (as so added). In a case which is a concealment or a disability case or both, the arrears date is the date of the contravention: s 2ZB(4) (as so added). For these purposes, 'concealment case' means a case where: (1) the employer deliberately concealed from the woman any fact which is relevant to the contravention to which the proceedings relate, and without knowledge of which the woman could not reasonably have been expected to institute the proceedings; and (2) the woman instituted the proceedings within six years of the day on which she discovered the fact (or could with reasonable diligence have discovered it); 'disability case' means a case where: (a) the woman was under a disability at the time of the contravention to which the proceedings relate; and (b) the woman instituted the proceedings within six years of the day on which she ceased to be under a disability; and 'standard case' means a case which is not: (i) a concealment case; (ii) a disability case; or (iii) both: s 2ZB(2) (as so added).

The two-year limitation on recovery of payment provided for in s 2(5) (as then in force) breached the principle of equivalence and was unlawful and claims may be made over a six-year period: *Levez v TH Jennings (Harlow Pools) Ltd (No 2)* [2000] ICR 58, [1999] IRLR 764, EAT; and see Case C-326/96 *Levez v TH Jennings (Harlow Pools) Ltd* [1999] All ER (EC) 1, [1999] IRLR 36, ECJ.

20 See para 421 note 9 ante.
21 *Evesham v North Hertfordshire Health Authority and Secretary of State for Health* [1999] IRLR 155, EAT.

22 An additional payment made for shift work or night work should not be taken into account provided it is not a mere sham set up to provide male employees with a higher rate of pay: *Dugdale v Kraft Foods Ltd* [1977] 1 All ER 454, [1977] ICR 48, EAT. A material factor may be put forward that objectively justifies a part, but not all, of the difference in pay between the applicant and her comparator; in such circumstances the applicant should be awarded that proportion of the difference of pay that is not objectively justified: Case C-127/97 *Enderby v Frenchay Health Authority* [1994] ICR 112, [1993] IRLR 591, ECJ.

23 *Sorbie v Trust House Forte Hotels Ltd* [1977] QB 931, [1977] 2 All ER 155, EAT.

24 The involvement of the Equal Opportunities Commission is the same as in relation to claims under the Sex Discrimination Act 1975: see para 404 et seq ante. As to the Equal Opportunities Commission see para 404 et seq ante. As to the Commission for Equality and Human Rights, which is to replace the Equal Opportunities Commission, see para 305 et seq ante.

25 See ibid s 75(1) (prospectively repealed); and para 412 ante.

26 See ibid s 67(1)(d) (prospectively repealed); and para 413 ante.

27 See ibid s 73 (as amended; prospectively repealed); and para 413 ante.

28 See ibid s 71 (as amended; prospectively repealed); and para 413 ante.

4. RACE RELATIONS

(1) INTRODUCTION

436. Scope of the law. The main body of race relations law is contained in the Race Relations Act 1976[1]. Relevant provisions are also contained in the Public Order Act 1986 which deals with criminal offences relating to incitement to racial hatred[2], in the Crime and Disorder Act 1998 in regard to racially aggravated offences[3], and in the Local Government Act 1988[4]. Provisions relating to genocide are dealt with elsewhere in this work[5].

The provisions of the Race Relations Act 1976 do not affect the right to bring any proceedings, whether civil[6] or criminal[7], which might have been brought if the Race Relations Act 1976 had not been passed.

1   The Race Relations Act 1976 supersedes the Race Relations Acts 1965 and 1968. As a matter of international law, the United Kingdom is bound by the provisions of the International Convention on the Elimination of all forms of Racial Discrimination (New York, 7 March 1966; TS 77 (1966); Cmnd 4108). Certain types of racial discrimination may be contrary to the common law: see note 6 infra.

2   See para 505 post; and CRIMINAL LAW, EVIDENCE AND PROCEDURE vol 11(1) (2006 Reissue) para 562 et seq.

3   See para 506 post; and CRIMINAL LAW, EVIDENCE AND PROCEDURE vol 11(1) (2006 Reissue) paras 154–156.

4   See para 469 post.

5   The Genocide Act 1969, which made it an offence to commit any act falling within the definition of 'genocide' in the Convention on the Prevention and Punishment of the Crime of Genocide (Paris, 9 December 1948; TS 58; Cmnd 4421), has been repealed: see now the International Criminal Court Act 2001 ss 50–52, Sch 8; and FOREIGN RELATIONS LAW.

6   At common law, innkeepers (see INNS AND INNKEEPERS vol 24 (Reissue) para 1113 et seq) and common carriers (see CARRIERS vol 5(1) (2004 Reissue) para 541 et seq) are under a duty to serve all comers without arbitrary discrimination, including racial discrimination: *Constantine v Imperial Hotels Ltd* [1944] 1 KB 693, [1944] 2 All ER 171; c f *Rothfield v Northern British Rly Co* 1920 SC 805, 57 SLR 661. It seems that a person may not be excluded from his 'right to work' arbitrarily or with unfair discrimination by those controlling his profession or trade: *Edwards v Society of Graphical and Allied Trades* [1971] Ch 354 at 376, [1970] 3 All ER 689 at 695–696, CA, per Lord Denning MR. See also *Nagle v Feilden* [1966] 2 QB 633 at 655, [1966] 1 All ER 689 at 700, CA, obiter per Salmon LJ; but see *Weinberger v Inglis (No 2)* [1919] AC 606, HL. An agreement by two or more persons to act together to prevent someone on racial grounds from obtaining residential accommodation or employment might constitute a civil conspiracy: *Mogul Steamship Co v McGregor Gow & Co* [1892] AC 25, HL; *Quinn v Leathem* [1901] AC 495, HL; *Crofter Hand Woven Harris Tweed Co Ltd v Veitch* [1942] AC 435, [1942] 1 All ER 142, HL; *Huntley v Thornton* [1957] 1 All ER 234, [1957] 1 WLR 321. The courts will refuse to recognise foreign slavery laws on grounds of public policy: *Regazzoni v KC Sethia (1944) Ltd* [1956] 2 QB 490 at 524, [1956] 2 All ER 487 at 496, CA, obiter per Parker LJ (affd [1968] AC 301, [1957] 3 All ER 286, HL) (a contract would not be enforced in England as a matter of public policy because its performance would have involved the violation of a law (not revenue or penal) of another country). It is a well-established principle that the courts, as regards assets within their jurisdiction, will not give effect to a foreign law which is penal, or confiscatory, at any rate if it is of a discriminatory or oppressive character (*Frankfurther v WL Exner Ltd* [1947] Ch 629; *Novello & Co Ltd v Hinrichsen Edition Ltd* [1951] Ch 595, [1951] 1 All ER 779 (affd on appeal on another point [1951] Ch 1026, [1951] 2 All ER 457, CA)), but the principle does not, it seems, extend to a law in so far as it simply deprives a person of citizenship (*Oppenheimer v Cattermole (Inspector of Taxes)* [1973] Ch 264, [1972] 3 All ER 1106, CA; affd on different grounds [1976] AC 249, [1975] 1 All ER 538, HL). In Canada covenants restricting the alienation of land by reference to the race of the alienee have been held to be void for uncertainty (*Noble and Wolf v Alley* [1951] SCR 64, [1951] 1 DLR 321, Can SC (where it was also held that the burden of such a covenant could not run with the land), or void as contrary to public policy (*Re Drummond Wren* [1945] OR 778, [1945] 4 DLR 674 (Ont)).

7   Eg an offence contrary to the International Criminal Court Act 2001 s 51 (as amended): see note 5 supra.

437.   European law.   There is a European Directive prohibiting racial
discrimination[1]. The provisions of the EC Treaty[2] relating to the free movement of
labour also have effect in the United Kingdom[3]. Discrimination based on nationality
between workers of member states as regards employment, remuneration and other
working conditions is rendered unlawful as a result.

1   See EC Council Directive 2000/43 (OJ L180, 19.07.2000, p 22) implementing the principle of equal
     treatment between persons irrespective of racial or ethnic origin. This Directive was introduced pursuant
     to the Treaty of Amsterdam art 13 (see para 337 ante), which provides that the EC Council, acting
     unanimously on a proposal from the EC Commission and after consulting the European Parliament, may
     take appropriate action to combat discrimination based on sex, racial or ethnic origin, religion or belief,
     disability, age or sexual orientation. As to directives in regard to sex discrimination see para 338 et seq
     ante, and in regard to equal pay see para 420 et seq ante).
2   Ie the Treaty Establishing the European Community (Rome, 25 March 1957; TS 1 (1973); Cmnd 5179).
3   See the EC Treaty Title III Ch 1 (arts 39–42) (renumbered by virtue of the Treaty of Amsterdam: see
     Treaty Citation (No 2) (Note) [1999] All ER (EC) 646, ECJ). In particular, the EC Treaty art 39 (as
     renumbered) (dealing with free movement of workers within the European Union) has direct effect and
     can be relied upon by an individual: see Case C-41/74 *Van Duyn v Home Office* [1975] Ch 358, [1975]
     3 All ER 190, ECJ. The EC Treaty art 39 provides for freedom of movement without discrimination
     based on nationality between workers of the member states as regards employment, remuneration and
     other conditions of work and employment. Accordingly, it is capable of being relied upon in race
     discrimination proceedings where this enhances rights conferred by the Race Relations Act 1976, but
     only in circumstances where the complainant is a European Union national: see *Bossa v Nordstress Ltd*
     [1998] ICR 694, [1998] IRLR 284, EAT. Under the rules relating to the freedom of movement of
     workers, a measure may still be discriminatory on grounds of nationality notwithstanding that it may put
     at a disadvantage some of the nationals of the member state in question as well as nationals of other
     member states: Case C-281/98 *Angonese v Cassa di Risparmio di Bolzano SpA* [2000] All ER (EC) 577,
     [2000] ECR I-4139, ECJ. As to discrimination on grounds of nationality see Case C-346/04 *Conijn v
     Finanzamt Hamburg-Nord* [2006] 3 CMLR 1000, [2006] All ER (D) 58 (Jul), ECJ, where it was held that
     certain national legislation (which did not allow a person with restricted tax liability to deduct from his
     taxable income as special expenditure the costs incurred in obtaining tax advice for preparing his tax
     return in the same way as a person with unrestricted tax liability) constituted a restriction on freedom of
     establishment prohibited by the EC Treaty).

438.   The Race Relations Act 1976.   The Race Relations Act 1976 renders
unlawful racial discrimination[1] and certain victimisation[2] in the fields of employment[3]
and education[4], in the provision of goods, facilities, services and premises[5] and in the
exercise of planning functions by a planning authority[6]. Certain harassment in a racial
context is made unlawful[7].

Discriminatory practices and advertisements, and instructions and pressure to
discriminate are also rendered unlawful[8]. Liability is imposed upon employers and
principals in respect of acts done by their employees and agents and on persons
knowingly aiding unlawful acts[9].

There are certain general exceptions[10].

Local authorities are required by the Act to make appropriate arrangements to secure
that their various functions are carried out with due regard to the need to eliminate
unlawful racial discrimination and to promote equality of opportunity and good
relations between people of different racial groups[11].

The Act established the Commission for Racial Equality ('CRE')[12] to replace both
the Race Relations Board and the Community Relations Commission. The Act obliges
the CRE to work towards the elimination of discrimination and to promote equality of
opportunity and good race relations[13]. The Act also empowers the CRE to assist
organisations[14] and individuals[15], to conduct formal investigations[16], and to bring
proceedings in respect of certain contraventions of the Act[17].

The Act applies, subject to certain limitations, to acts done by the Crown[18].

The Secretary of State[19] may by an order[20] (the draft of which has been approved by
each House of Parliament) amend certain provisions of the Race Relations Act 1976[21].

The wording and structure of the Act are modelled upon the Sex Discrimination Act 1975[22] (which was itself developed from the Race Relations Acts of 1965 and 1968), and many provisions are almost identical in the two Acts[23]. Consequently, case law relating to the interpretation of the Sex Discrimination Act 1975 (and to the interpretation of the linked Equal Pay Act 1970) is relevant to the interpretation of the Race Relations Act 1976.

1　See the Race Relations Act 1976 s 1 (as amended); and para 439 et seq post.
2　See ibid s 2; and para 442 post.
3　See ibid Pt II (ss 4–15) (as amended); and para 446 et seq post. A claim under the Race Relations Act 1976 Pt II (as amended) survives the death of the claimant: *Harris (Andrews' Personal Representative) v Lewisham and Guys Mental Health NHS Trust* [2000] IRLR 320, CA.
4　See the Race Relations Act 1976 ss 17–18D (as amended); and para 460 post. See also note 11 infra.
5　See ibid ss 20–26 (as amended); and para 461 et seq post.
6　See ibid s 19A (as added and amended); and para 468 post.
7　See s 3A (as added); and para 444 post.
8　See ibid ss 28–31 (as amended); and paras 471–475 post.
9　See ibid ss 32, 33 (s 33 as amended); and paras 476–477 post.
10　See ibid Pt VI (ss 35–42) (as amended); and paras 482–487 post.
11　See ss 71–7E (as amended; ss 71C–71E prospectively repealed); and paras 469–470 post.
12　See ibid Pt VII (ss 43–52) (as amended; prospectively repealed); and para 488 et seq post. As to the Commission for Equality and Human Rights, which is to replace the CRE, see para 305 et seq ante.
13　See ibid s 43 (as amended; prospectively repealed); and para 489 post.
14　See ibid s 44 (prospectively repealed); and para 490 post.
15　See ibid s 45 (prospectively repealed); and para 497 post.
16　See ibid ss 48–52 (as amended; prospectively repealed); and para 492 post.
17　See ibid Pt VIII (ss 53–69) (as amended; ss 58–64, 66 prospectively repealed); see para 498 post.
18　See ibid s 75 (as amended); and para 443 post.
19　As to the Secretary of State and the National Assembly for Wales see para 302 ante.
20　As to orders and regulations see para 468 post.
21　The Secretary of State may: (1) amend or repeal the Race Relations Act 1976 s 9 (as amended) (including that provision as amended by a previous order) (see paras 446–449 post); (2) amend Pt II (as amended), Pt III (as amended) or Pt IV (as amended) so as to render lawful an act which, apart from the amendment, would be unlawful by reason of s 4(1) or (2), s 19B (as added and amended), s 20(1), s 21 (as amended), s 24 (as amended) or s 25 (see para 446 et seq post); or (3) amend s 10(1) or s 25(1)(a) (see paras 450, 465 post) so as to alter the number of partners or members specified in that provision: s 73(1) (amended by the Race Relations (Amendment) Act 2000 s 9(1), Sch 2 para 16). The Secretary of State may not lay before Parliament the draft of such an order unless he has consulted the CRE about the contents of the draft: Race Relations Act 1976 s 73(2).

　　Racial discrimination claims often arise in the context of procedure: e g see *Teinaz v London Borough of Wandsworth* [2002] EWCA Civ 1040, [2002] ICR 1471, [2002] IRLR 1471, which was applied in *Deman v Coates* [2006] All ER (D) 231 (Jul), EAT (liability proceedings progressing in absence of respondent); *Barracks v Coles* [2006] EWCA Civ 1041, [2006] All ER (D) 310 (Jul) (failure of police to disclose reason for not passing vetting procedure and allegation of racial discrimination); and *Aziz v Crown Prosecution Service* [2006] EWCA Civ 1136, [2006] All ER (D) 468 (Jul) (failure by employer to follow its own disciplinary code amounted to racial discrimination).
22　As to the provisions of the Sex Discrimination Act 1975 see para 342 et seq ante.
23　However, one important difference is that the Race Relations Act 1976 covers discrimination in the contract of employment which, in the law relating to sex discrimination, is dealt with by the Equal Pay Act 1970 rather than the Sex Discrimination Act 1975: see para 424 et seq ante. Another difference is that the Race Relations Act 1976 makes it unlawful to segregate a person from other persons on forbidden grounds (see para 439 post), while the Sex Discrimination Act 1975 has no similar provision.

(2) PROHIBITION OF DISCRIMINATION

(i) Meaning of Discrimination

439. Direct discrimination. Racial discrimination is commonly described as either direct or indirect discrimination[1], although these terms do not appear in the Race Relations Act 1976 itself.

A person[2] discriminates directly against another in any circumstances relevant for the purposes of any provision of the Race Relations Act 1976 if on racial grounds[3] he treats that other less favourably than he treats or would treat other persons[4].

Discrimination 'on racial grounds' does not require an intention to discriminate on the part of the alleged discriminator, and does not depend on the discriminator's subjective reasons for his conduct[5]. The test is an objective one. It is sufficient if a person is treated less favourably than others because of his race, or, in other words, if the complainant would have received the same treatment as others 'but for' his race[6]. It is no defence for an alleged discriminator to show that he discriminated against the complainant to prevent industrial unrest by other prejudiced employees[7], objectively in the best interests of his business[8], in the interests of safety and good administration, or from chivalry and courtesy[9], or because of customer preference, or to save money, or to avoid controversy[10]. Although the alleged discriminator's motives are not necessary to establish a claim, they may be relevant as evidence of why action was taken, and therefore as evidence of the grounds on which it was taken[11]. Race need not be the only ground for the acts complained of. It is sufficient if a breach of the Race Relations Act 1976 is a substantial and effective cause of the defendant's actions[12]. It is not sufficient to consider whether race is any part of the background or is a causa sine qua non of what happens. The question to be answered is whether race is the activating cause of the relevant treatment[13].

'Treatment' involves some relationship between the person treating and the person treated. If the alleged discriminator did not intend the complainant to find out about the words or acts complained of, and did not know and should not reasonably have anticipated that the complainant would become aware of them, then the complainant cannot properly be said to have been 'treated' less favourably[14]. The motive of the person responsible for the treatment is irrelevant[15]. Words or acts of discouragement may amount to discriminatory treatment[16]. In order for treatment to be less favourable, it must be different from the treatment afforded to others in the absence of the relevant racial grounds[17]. 'Less favourable treatment' includes depriving a person of a choice which is valued by him and reasonably valued by others[18]. It may consist of treatment of a particular type to which a person would not have been vulnerable but for his race, colour, nationality, or ethnic or national origins, such as racial harassment or abuse. This is so even where the abuse or harassment is motivated by dislike, and a person of a different race would have been treated equally unpleasantly, although in a different way[19]. Less favourable treatment may be based on assumptions about the characteristics of particular racial groups which have the effect that a person is treated not as an individual, but as a racial stereotype[20].

For the purposes of the Race Relations Act 1976, segregating a person from other persons on racial grounds is treating him less favourably than those others are treated[21].

1　As to indirect discrimination see para 440 post.
　　In appropriate circumstances, a claim in respect of both direct and indirect discrimination may be brought on the same facts: *Jaffrey v Department of Environment, Transport and Regions* [2002] IRLR 688, [2002] All ER (D) 111 (Jul), EAT.

2　As to the meaning of 'person' see para 344 note 3 ante. As to the liability of principals and employers for the acts of their agents and employees see the Race Relations Act 1976 s 32; and para 476 post. As to the liability of those who knowingly aid unlawful acts see s 33 (as amended); and para 476 post.

3　Ie any of the following grounds, namely colour, race, nationality, or ethnic or national origin: see ibid s 3(1); and para 441 post. Discrimination 'on racial grounds' includes discrimination against a person because of the race of a third party, as where an employee is dismissed for refusing to carry out his employer's instructions to discriminate: *Showboat Entertainment Centre Ltd v Owens* [1984] 1 All ER 836, [1984] 1 WLR 384, EAT; *Zarczynska v Levy* [1979] 1 All ER 814, [1979] 1 WLR 125, EAT; *Race Relations Board v Applin* [1973] QB 815 at 828, [1973] 2 All ER 1190 at 1196, CA, per Lord Denning MR, and at 831 and 1199 per Stephenson LJ. See also *Weathersfield Ltd (t/a Van & Truck*

Rentals) v Sargent [1999] ICR 425, [1999] IRLR 94, CA (an employee is less favourably treated on racial grounds where he is required to carry out a racially discriminatory policy even though the instruction relates to people of a different racial group than the employee).

4 Race Relations Act 1976 s 1(1)(a). This provision contemplates a comparison between the treatment afforded to the complainant and the treatment of other actual or hypothetical persons. Pursuant to s 3(4) (as amended) the comparison between the complainant and a person not of his racial group must be such that the relevant circumstances in the one case are the same or not materially different in the other: see para 443 post. The conduct of a hypothetical reasonable employer is irrelevant in deciding whether the claimant has been treated less favourably by the person against whom discrimination is alleged: *Glasgow City Council v Zafar* [1998] 2 All ER 953, sub nom *Zafar v Glasgow City Council* [1998] IRLR 36, HL. Where an employer dismisses an employee for his retaliation to racial abuse, a complaint of direct racial discrimination is not assisted by the fact that the dismissal is unfair: *Sidhu v Aerospace Composite Technology Ltd* [2001] ICR 167, [2000] IRLR 602, CA. See also *Aziz v Crown Prosection Service* [2006] EWCA Civ 1136, [2006] All ER (D) 468 (Jul), in which a finding of racial discrimination was reinstated where the employer had knowingly failed to comply with its own code of practice in regard to both preliminary inquiries on allegations of serious misconduct and the right of representation at any hearing on formal disciplinary action. See also *Nassir-Deen v North East London Strategic Health Authority* [2006] All ER (D) 272 (Dec), EAT (an unreasonable but non-discriminatory explanation for the detriment, providing it was found to be genuine, could not lead to an inference of discrimination); *Ismail v Metropolitan Police Commissioner* [2007] All ER (D) 229 (Jan), EAT (tribunal decision to dismiss employee's race discrimination claim as unfounded and no error of law or perversity found).

5 See note 15 infra.

6 See, on the similar wording 'on the grounds of her sex' in the Sex Discrimination Act 1975 s 1(1)(a) (as substituted) (see para 346 ante), *Birmingham City Council v Equal Opportunities Commission* [1989] AC 1155 at 1193–1194, sub nom *Equal Opportunities Commission v Birmingham City Council* [1989] 1 All ER 769 at 774, HL, per Lord Goff of Chieveley (fewer grammar school places for girls than boys); *James v Eastleigh Borough Council* [1990] 2 AC 751 at 764–766, [1990] 2 All ER 607 at 611–612, HL, per Lord Bridge of Harwich, and at 773 and 618 per Lord Goff of Chieveley (concessions given by local authority to people of 'pensionable age'); *Grieg v Community Industry* [1979] ICR 356, [1979] IRLR 158, EAT (woman refused job on all-male painting team). As to the Race Relations Act 1976 see *R v Commission for Racial Equality, ex p Westminster City Council* [1984] ICR 770, [1984] IRLR 230 (affd [1985] ICR 827, [1985] IRLR 426, CA) (well-intentioned employer dismissed black refuse collector because of threat of industrial action by prejudiced employees); *Din v Carrington Viyella Ltd* [1982] ICR 256 at 259, EAT (employee not re-employed following allegedly racially-motivated dispute with manager which had caused explosive industrial situation). See also *Barclays Bank plc v Kapur (No 2)* [1995] IRLR 87, CA (no discrimination where employer refused to take account of employee's service in East Africa for pension purposes even though that had been done for European comparators, as employees were otherwise compensated for loss of pension rights); *Chief Constable of Greater Manchester Police v Hope* [1999] ICR 338, EAT (application of the 'but-for' test without regard to motive where a police sergeant who was disciplined for a sexual relationship with a 17-year old civilian trainee complained of sex and race discrimination when told that the offence was more serious because he was white and the girl Asian, and this would be particularly disapproved of within her community).

7 *R v Commission for Racial Equality, ex p Westminster City Council* [1984] ICR 770; affd [1985] ICR 827, CA.

8 *Grieg v Community Industry* [1979] ICR 356, [1979] IRLR 158, EAT.

9 *Ministry of Defence v Jeremiah* [1980] QB 87, [1979] 3 All ER 833, CA (overruling in part *Peake v Automotive Products Ltd* [1978] QB 233, [1978] 1 All ER 106, CA).

10 *Birmingham City Council v Equal Opportunities Commission* [1989] AC 1155, sub nom *Equal Opportnities Commission v Birmingham City Council* [1989] 1 All ER 769, HL. See also *Porcelli v Strathclyde Regional Council* [1986] ICR 564, Ct of Sess.

11 *R v Commission for Racial Equality, ex p Westminster City Council* [1984] ICR 770, [1984] IRLR 230; affd [1985] ICR 827, [1985] IRLR 426, CA.

12 *O'Neill v Governors of St Thomas More Catholic Voluntary Aided Upper School* [1997] ICR 33, [1996] IRLR 372, EAT (sex discrimination case); *R v Commission for Racial Equality, ex p Westminster City Council* [1984] ICR 770, [1984] IRLR 230 (affd [1985] ICR 827, [1985] IRLR 426, CA); *Owen and Briggs v James* [1982] ICR 618 at 623–624, CA, per Sir David Cairns.

13 See *Seide v Gillette Industries Ltd* [1980] IRLR 427 at 430–431, EAT; *Din v Carrington Viyella Ltd* [1982] ICR 256, EAT; *Balgobin v Tower Hamlets London Borough Council* [1987] ICR 829, [1987] IRLR 401, EAT; *R v Cleveland County Council, ex p Commission for Racial Equality* (1991) Times, 28 October, 135 Sol Jo LB 205, DC. See also *Redfearn v Serco Ltd (t/a West Yorkshire Transport Service)* [2006] EWCA Civ 659, [2006] IRLR 623, [2006] All ER (D) 366 (May) (decision to dismiss employee for belonging to political party with racist agenda, where most customers Asian, not discrimination on racial grounds).

14 *De Souza v Automobile Association* [1986] ICR 514, [1986] IRLR 103, CA (no discriminatory treatment where a racial remark was not intended to be overheard by the employee).

15 The Race Relations Act 1976 s 1(1)(a) is concerned with 'treatment' and not with the motive or objective of the person responsible for it: *Porcelli v Strathclyde Regional Council* [1986] ICR 564, Ct of Sess. See also note 3 supra.

16 *Simon v Brimham Associates* [1987] ICR 596, [1987] IRLR 307, CA; *Tower Hamlets London Borough Council v Rabin* [1989] ICR 693, EAT.

17 See *Simon v Brimham Associates* [1987] ICR 596, [1987] IRLR 307, CA (no discrimination against a Jewish job applicant where all applicants were asked about their religion).

18 See *Birmingham City Council v Equal Opportunities Commission* [1989] AC 1155, sub nom *Equal Opportunities Commission v Birmingham City Council* [1989] 1 All ER 769, HL (girls deprived of the choice of a grammar school education on the same terms as boys). See also *Gill v El Vino Co Ltd* [1983] QB 425, [1983] 1 All ER 398, CA (refusal to serve women at the bar of a wine bar).

19 See *Porcelli v Strathclyde Regional Council* [1986] ICR 564, Ct of Sess (a sex discrimination case, concerning the sexual harassment of a laboratory technician).

20 See *Alexander v Home Office* [1988] 2 All ER 118, [1988] 1 WLR 968, CA (prisoner described as showing 'the anti-authoritarian arrogance that seems to be common in most coloured inmates'); and see (for examples of sex stereotyping) *Hurley v Mustoe* [1981] ICR 490, [1981] IRLR 208, EAT; *Skyrail Oceanic Ltd v Coleman* [1981] ICR 864, sub nom *Coleman v Skyrail Oceanic Ltd* [1981] IRLR 398, CA; *Horsey v Dyfed County Council* [1982] ICR 755, [1982] IRLR 395, EAT.

21 Race Relations Act 1976 s 1(2). This provision recognises the proposition accepted by the United States Supreme Court in *Brown v Topeka Board of Education* 347 US 483 (1954), that separate facilities for different racial groups are inherently unequal. The prohibition of segregation applies only where a person acts to keep people apart from other people on racial grounds: *Furniture, Timber and Allied Trades Union v Modgill, Pel Ltd v Modgill* [1980] IRLR 142, EAT; *R v Cleveland County Council, ex p Commission for Racial Equality* (1991) Times, 28 October, 135 Sol Jo LB 205, DC.

440.   Indirect discrimination.   A person[1] discriminates against another indirectly[2] if he applies to that other a requirement or condition[3] which he applies or would apply equally[4] to persons not of the same racial group[5] as that other[6], but: (1) which is such that the proportion of persons of the same racial group as that other who can comply[7] with it is considerably smaller[8] than the proportion of persons not of that racial group who can comply with it[9]; (2) which he cannot show to be justifiable[10] irrespective of the colour, race, nationality, or ethnic or national origins of the person to whom it is applied[11]; and (3) which is to the detriment[12] of that other because he cannot comply with it[13].

In employment-related cases[14] a person discriminates against another if he applies to that other a provision, criterion or practice which he applies or would apply equally to persons not of the same race or ethnic or national origins as that other[15], but: (a) which puts or would put persons of the same race or ethnic or national origins as that other at a particular disadvantage when compared with other persons[16]; (b) which puts that other at that disadvantage[17]; and (c) which he cannot show to be a proportionate means of achieving a legitimate aim[18].

A criterion for selection for employment is not a 'requirement or condition' unless failure to comply with it is an absolute bar to employment[19]. Selection procedures for employment or promotion which have a discriminatory impact are lawful, as long as the discriminatory factors in the procedures are merely preferences, and not 'musts', even though the result of such procedures is likely to be the exclusion of members of a particular racial group[20]. In the context of sex discrimination[21], it has been held that the requirement to work full-time could in the case of some jobs be regarded as a condition or requirement. In some earlier cases, the obligation to work full-time was regarded as part and parcel of the job itself, and therefore outside the ambit of this provision, although this line of authority has not been followed more recently[22].

Examples of requirements and conditions that are prima facie discriminatory are: a requirement imposed by a furniture company that its employees should not live in the centre of Liverpool (where a far larger proportion of the city's black population than the white population lived)[23]; a requirement that an employee must have an English Language 'O' level (although on the facts the requirement was justified)[24]; a condition, which adversely affected Sikhs, that employees must not wear beards (justifiable on hygienic grounds in a sweet factory)[25]; a requirement that overseas graduates with non-law degrees should take a two year diploma course in order to qualify for admission to the Bar finals course, while United Kingdom graduates were only required to take a one year course[26]; and a 'No travellers' sign in a public house which had a disproportionate impact on gipsies[27].

In order to decide whether a considerably smaller proportion of people of the complainant's racial group than of people not of his racial group can comply with a condition, a court or tribunal must choose the appropriate pool of people amongst whom the comparison is to be made. The choice may be crucial to a finding of a disproportionate impact. The choice of the pool of comparison is a question of fact[28]. In an employment case, the ideal comparison should be made amongst people who are otherwise qualified for the job, apart from the condition or requirement under challenge[29]. However, the pool taken does not have to be shown to be statistically a perfect match of the persons who would be capable of filling and interested in a job[30]. If the pool is criticised as being too wide or too narrow, a court or tribunal may still accept it as a proper basis for comparison in the absence of rebutting statistics from the respondent showing the true position, or evidence showing that the complainant's statistics distort the picture in a relevant way[31]. The pool of comparison that is selected must not itself involve any element of racial discrimination[32].

1   As to the meaning of 'person' see para 344 note 3 ante.

2   For guidance to employment tribunals regarding the proper approach to allegations of indirect discrimination see *Raval v Department of Health and Social Security* [1985] ICR 685, [1985] IRLR 370, EAT.

      In appropriate circumstances, a claim in respect of both direct and indirect discrimination may be brought on the same facts: *Jaffrey v Department of Environment, Transport and Regions* [2002] IRLR 688, [2002] All ER (D) 111 (Jul), EAT. See also *R (on the application of Elias) v Secretary of State for Defence* [2006] EWCA Civ 1293, [2006] 1 WLR 3213, [2006] IRLR 934, [2006] All ER (D) 104 (Oct), where it was held that the eligibility criteria for a prisoner of war compensation scheme, although not directly discriminating against the claimant on racial grounds, did indirectly discriminate against her.

3   The words 'requirement or condition' should be given their natural meaning, and not any narrower meaning which would exclude cases falling within the mischief with which the Race Relations Act 1976 was meant to deal: *Clarke v Eley (IMI) Kynoch Ltd* [1983] ICR 165 at 170–171, EAT, per Browne-Wilkinson J. See also *Home Office v Holmes* [1984] 3 All ER 549 at 553, [1985] 1 WLR 71 at 75, EAT.

4   Indirect discrimination concerns equal treatment which has unequal effect or a disparate impact. Treatment which is itself discriminatory cannot amount to indirect discrimination, only direct discrimination: see para 439 ante. Therefore, if a condition is applied to different racial groups which requires them to be treated differently (ie one group less favourably than the other), the complaint should be of direct, not indirect discrimination. See the example of the discriminatory condition of 'pensionable age', meaning men over 65 and women over 60: *James v Eastleigh Borough Council* [1990] 2 AC 751, [1990] 2 All ER 607, HL.

5   Ie a group of persons defined by reference to colour, race, nationality or ethnic or national origins: see the Race Relations Act 1976 s 3(1); and para 441 post.

6   Ibid s 1(1)(b). Note that since the addition of s 1(1A) (as added) (see heads (a)–(c) in the text), the definition in s 1(1)(b) only applies outside employment-related cases.

7   The words 'can comply' do not mean 'can physically comply', but 'can comply in practice', or 'can comply consistently with the customs and cultural conditions of the racial group' to which the complainant belongs: *Price v Civil Service Commission* [1978] 1 All ER 1228, [1977] 1 WLR 1417, EAT; *Mandla v Dowell Lee* [1983] 2 AC 548, [1983] 1 All ER 1062, HL; *Commission for Racial Equality v Dutton* [1989] QB 783, [1989] 1 All ER 306, CA. If a person is reasonably able to comply with a requirement or condition, but prefers not to, a tribunal is justified in taking the view that he can comply with it: *Clymo v Wandsworth London Borough Council* [1989] 2 CMLR 577, [1989] ICR 250, EAT.

      The complainant's ability to comply with a condition or requirement is to be judged at the date of the alleged detriment suffered by the complainant. The fact that the complainant has had past

.opportunities to comply or might be able to comply with the condition in the future is immaterial: *Commission for Racial Equality v Dutton* supra (a nomadic gipsy could not comply with a 'No Travellers' condition at the moment he entered a pub, irrespective of the fact that he could cease to be a nomad in the future without abandoning the customs of gipsies); *Clarke v Eley (IMI) Kynoch Ltd* [1983] ICR 165, EAT (a part-time worker could not comply with a condition giving preference in selection for redundancy to full-time workers; it was immaterial that she had been given the opportunity to work full-time in the past); *Raval v Department of Health and Social Security* [1985] ICR 685, [1985] IRLR 370, EAT (an Asian could not comply with a condition requiring job applicants to have English 'O' level, unless the qualification was already obtained when she applied for the job, notwithstanding her ability to obtain the qualification in the future).

In *Enderby v Frenchay Health Authority* [1994] ICR 112, [1992] IRLR 15, CA, the Court of Appeal suggested that a speech therapist can comply with a condition requiring her to be a pharmacist in order to receive higher pay for work of equal value, because she could have qualified as a pharmacist if she had chosen to do so, but referred the case to the European Court of Justice. The European Court of Justice considered that a prima facie case of indirect discrimination was made out (even though there was no requirement or condition applied to the complainant preventing her from qualifying as a pharmacist) because women were proportionately affected by the pay policy or practice to a much greater extent than men: Case C-127/92 *Enderby v Frenchay Health Authority and Secretary of State for Health* [1994] ICR 112, [1993] IRLR 591, ECJ. The European Court of Justice's approach to indirect discrimination is much broader than that adopted by the United Kingdom courts in this respect.

Where a condition or requirement will only come into effect, to the detriment of a complainant, at a future date, the complainant's present inability to comply with the condition will not be sufficient if he could comply with it before suffering detriment: *Turner v Labour Party and Labour Party Superannuation Society* [1987] IRLR 101, CA.

In the context of a claim for equal pay for work of equal value, under the Equal Pay Act 1970 (see para 424 et seq ante), the European Court of Justice held that indirect discrimination is constituted by the imposition of a condition or requirement 'which has a disproportionate effect on women because they are women': *Enderby v Frenchay Health Authority and Secretary of State for Health* supra. In other words, women or members of a particular racial group must be unable to comply with the condition because of a reason related to their gender or race: the factor causing the disparate impact must be tainted by gender or race. However, *Enderby v Frenchay Health Authority and Secretary of State for Health* supra was considered to be restricted to equal pay claims under the Treaty Establishing the European Community (Rome, 25 March 1957; TS 1 (1973); Cmnd 5179) (the 'EC Treaty') art 141 (formerly art 119; renumbered by virtue of the Treaty of Amsterdam: see *Treaty Citation (No 2) (Note)* [1999] All ER (EC) 646, ECJ): see *Bhudi v IMI Refiners Ltd* [1994] ICR 307, [1994] IRLR 204, EAT.

8   'The question how large a proportion must be before it can properly be called 'considerable' is very much a matter of personal opinion on which views are liable to vary over a wide field': *Kidd v DRG (UK) Ltd* [1985] ICR 405 at 409, EAT, per Waite J. The Employment Appeal Tribunal has refused to find perverse a finding by a tribunal that 95.3% was a considerably smaller proportion than 99.4%: *Greater Manchester Police Authority v Lea* [1990] IRLR 372, EAT.

If no members of the complainant's racial group can comply with a condition, the proportion of nil may be regarded as a considerably smaller proportion for the purposes of the Race Relations Act 1976: *Greencroft Social Club and Institute v Mullen* [1985] ICR 796, EAT.

In Case C-167/97 *R v Secretary of State for Employment, ex p Seymour-Smith* [1999] 2 AC 554, [1999] ICR 447, ECJ (a sex discrimination case), the European Court of Justice ruled that it is for the national court to verify whether statistics available indicate that a considerably smaller percentage of women than men is able to fulfil the requirement; the statistics must be valid and significant; this is a pure question of fact to be decided on a case by case basis. On remission to the House of Lords, dealing with the question whether the statistical evidence established disparate impact at the date of dismissal in 1991, the House of Lords ruled that in the light of the European Court of Justice's judgment and looking at the figures for 1985–1991, a proportion of 10 to 9 of men to women who could qualify was sufficient, because of the persistent and constant nature of the disparity, to establish disparate impact: *R v Secretary of State for Employment, ex p Seymour-Smith* [2000] ICR 244, [2000] IRLR 263, HL. See also *London Underground Ltd v Edwards (No 2)* [1999] ICR 494, [1998] IRLR 364, CA.

A tribunal is entitled to use its own knowledge and experience in deciding whether a considerably smaller proportion of the complainant's racial group can comply with a condition or requirement: *Price v Civil Service Commission* [1978] 1 All ER 1228, [1977] 1 WLR 1417, EAT; *Briggs v North Eastern Education and Library Board* [1990] IRLR 181, NI CA. It is undesirable that, in cases of indirect discrimination, elaborate statistical evidence should be required before the case can be found proved: *Perera v Civil Service Commission (No 2)* [1982] ICR 350, [1982] IRLR 147, EAT (affd [1983] ICR 428, [1983] IRLR 166, CA); *Briggs v North Eastern Education and Library Board* supra.

9 Race Relations Act 1976 s 1(1)(b)(i). See *Coker v Lord Chancellor* [2001] EWCA Civ 1756, [2002] ICR 321, [2002] IRLR 80 (no breach of the Race Relations Act 1976 s 1(1)(b)(i) when Lord Chancellor appointed a person who was well known to him as special adviser without advertising the post).

10 The onus is on the alleged discriminator to prove on the balance of probabilities that the condition or requirement is justifiable: *Singh v Rowntree MacKintosh Ltd* [1979] ICR 554 at 557, EAT. It is a question of fact whether a requirement or condition is justifiable: *Raval v Department of Health and Social Security* [1985] ICR 685, [1985] IRLR 370, EAT; *Mandla v Dowell Lee* [1983] 2 AC 548, [1983] 1 All ER 1062, HL. The widely differing decisions and the extent of the discretion left to employment tribunals deciding justifiability have been criticised: *Clarke v Eley (IMI) Kynoch Ltd* [1983] ICR 165 at 174, EAT.

A variety of tests have been formulated by the courts in an attempt to define the requirements of justifiability: see *Steel v Union of Post Office Workers* [1978] 2 All ER 504, [1978] 1 WLR 64, EAT (was the requirement necessary, and could other non-discriminatory methods be found of achieving the alleged discriminator's objective?); *Ojutiku v Manpower Services Commission* [1982] ICR 661, CA (was the requirement 'reasonably necessary' to the party applying it, balancing its discriminatory effect against the discriminator's need for it? (per Stephenson LJ at 674); has the alleged discriminator produced reasons which would be 'acceptable to right thinking people as sound and tolerable reasons'? (per Eveleigh LJ at 668)). See also *Panesar v Nestlé Co Ltd* [1980] ICR 144n, [1980 IRLR 64, CA; *Kidd v DRG (UK) Ltd* [1985] ICR 405, [1985] IRLR 190, EAT; *Clymo v Wandsworth London Borough Council* [1989] 2 CMLR 577, [1989] ICR 250, EAT.

The authoritative test is that formulated by the Court of Appeal in *Hampson v Department of Education and Science* [1990] 2 All ER 25, [1989] ICR 179 (revsd on other grounds [1991] 1 AC 171, [1990] 2 All ER 513, HL). The Court of Appeal adopted Stephenson LJ's test from *Ojutiku v Manpower Services Commission* supra, but emphasised the necessity for an objective justification of the requirement or condition: 'justifiability' requires an objective balance between the discriminatory effect of the condition and the reasonable needs of the person who applies the condition. The court held that there was no significant difference between this test and the objective test adopted in sex discrimination and equal pay cases, derived from European Community case law. See Case 170/84 *Bilka-Kaufhaus GmbH v Weber von Hartz* [1986] 2 CMLR 701, [1987] ICR 110, ECJ; *Rainey v Greater Glasgow Health Board* [1987] AC 224, [1987] 1 All ER 65, HL. This test requires that the condition or requirement should correspond to a real need on the part of the undertaking concerned, should be appropriate with a view to achieving the objectives pursued, and should be necessary to that end. The test in *Hampson v Department of Education and Science* supra was applied in *Board of Governors of St Mathias Church of England School v Crizzle* [1993] ICR 401, [1993] IRLR 472, EAT. See further *Cobb v Secretary of State for Employment* [1989] ICR 506, [1989] IRLR 464, EAT. When striking the balance, a court or tribunal should consider the discriminatory effect of the requirement or condition upon people in the complainant's circumstances generally, and not its particular effect having regard to the complainant's own circumstances: *University of Manchester v Jones* [1992] ICR 52, EAT.

It is vital in claims for indirect race or sex discrimination that an employer obeys a tribunal's order to set out fully any objective justification defence: *Spicer v Government of Spain* [2004] EWCA Civ 1046, [2005] ICR 213.

11 Race Relations Act 1976 s 1(1)(b)(ii). A requirement will not be justifiable where it is closely bound up with the racial group of the complainant: *Orphanos v Queen Mary College* [1985] AC 761, [1985] 2 All ER 233, HL (college discriminated against Cypriot student by charging higher fees to non-European Community nationals).

12 The complainant must be able to show that he has suffered some detriment, in order to have standing to bring a complaint. Detriment means 'putting under a disadvantage': see *Ministry of Defence v Jeremiah* [1980] QB 87, [1979] 3 All ER 833, CA; *De Souza v Automobile Association* [1986] ICR 514, [1986] IRLR 103, CA; *Clymo v Wandsworth London Borough Council* [1989] 2 CMLR 577, [1989] ICR 250, EAT; *Briggs v North Eastern Education and Library Board* [1990] IRLR 181, NI CA. See also *Barclays Bank plc v Kapur (No 2)* [1995] IRLR 87, CA. See further para 446 post.

A complainant who cannot comply with a requirement or condition may nevertheless have suffered no detriment if he could comply with it easily in the future, and could have complied with it easily in the past, eg by sitting an examination which he could pass with ease: *Raval v Department of Health and Social Security* [1985] ICR 685, [1985] IRLR 370, EAT.

13 Race Relations Act 1976 s 1(1)(b)(iii). As to the origins of the concept of indirect discrimination see *Griggs v Duke Power Co* 401 US 424 (1971). See also the International Convention on the Elimination of all Forms of Racial Discrimination (New York, 7 March 1966; TS (1969) 77; Cmnd 4108).

14 Ie in any circumstances relevant for the purposes of the following provisions of the Race Relations Act 1976: (1) Pt II (ss 4–15) (as amended) (see para 446 et seq post); (2) ss 17–18D (as amended) (see para 460 post); (3) s 19B (as added and amended) (see para 470 post), so far as relating to: (a) any form of social security; (b) health care; (c) any other form of social protection; and (d) any form of social advantage, which does not fall within s 20 (as amended) (see para 461 et seq post); (4) ss 20–24 (as amended) (see para 461 et seq post); (5) s 26A (as added and amended) (see para 456 post); (6) s 76 (as amended) (see para 457 post) and

s 76ZA (as added) (see para 459 post); and (7) Pt IV (ss 27A–33) (as amended) (see para 472 et seq post), in its application to the provisions referred to in heads (1)–(6) supra: s 1(1B) (s 1(1A)–(1C) added by the Race Relations Act 1976 (Amendment) Regulations 2003, SI 2003/1626, reg 3). 'Social protection' and 'social advantage' have the same meanings as in EC Council Directive 2000/43 (OJ L180, 19.07.2000, p 22) implementing the principle of equal treatment between persons irrespective of racial or ethnic origin, art 3: Race Relations Act 1976 s 78(1) (definition added by the Race Relations Act 1976 (Amendment) Regulations 2003, SI 2003/1626, reg 52).

15 Race Relations Act 1976 s 1(1A) (as added: see note 14 supra). Where, by virtue of s 1(1A) (as added), a person discriminates against another, s 1(1)(b) (see the text to notes 1–13 supra) does not apply to him: s 1(1C) (as so added).

16 Ibid s 1(1A)(a) (as added: see note 14 supra). See note 15 supra.

17 Ibid s 1(1A)(b) (as added: see note 14 supra). See note 15 supra.

18 Ibid s 1(1A)(c) (as added: see note 14 supra). See note 15 supra.

19 *Perera v Civil Service Commission* [1983] ICR 428, [1983] IRLR 166, CA; *Meer v Tower Hamlets London Borough Council* [1988] IRLR 399, CA (although Balcombe LJ pointed out that there are strong arguments that the absolute bar construction of the phrase 'requirement or condition' may be inconsistent with the object of the Race Relations Act 1976, and that the law as stated by *Perera v Civil Service Commission* supra requires reform). Further disapproval of *Perera v Civil Service Commission* supra in this respect has been voiced, suggesting that a requirement that was desirable rather than essential should be sufficient in the context of eliminating unlawful race discrimination: see *Falkirk Ltd v Whyte* [1997] IRLR 560 at 562, Scottish EAT, per Lord Johnston.

20 Contrast the more liberal approach of the Employment Appeal Tribunal in the context of the similar wording of the Sex Discrimination Act 1975 s 1(1)(b) (as then in force) (see para 351 ante), in *Watches of Switzerland Ltd v Savell* [1983] IRLR 141, EAT (held that it was a 'requirement or condition' of promotion that an employee could satisfy or comply with the promotion procedure as a whole).

21 Ie the Sex Discrimination Act 1975 s 1(1)(b) (as substituted): see para 351 ante.

22 *Clymo v Wandsworth London Borough Council* [1989] 2 CMLR 577, [1989] ICR 250, EAT. This decision was doubted in *Briggs v North Eastern Education and Library Board* [1990] IRLR 181, NI CA, in which the court preferred the broader construction of the Sex Discrimination Act 1975 s 1(1)(b) (as then in force) adopted in *Home Office v Holmes* [1984] 3 All ER 549, [1984] 1 WLR 71, EAT, and *Clarke v Eley (IMI) Kynoch Ltd* [1983] ICR 165, EAT, to the Employment Appeal Tribunal's approach in *Clymo v Wandsworth London Borough Council* supra. It is submitted that the Northern Ireland Court of Appeal's approach is to be preferred, as giving effect to the objects and policy of the legislation.

23 *Hussein v Saints Complete House Furnishers* [1979] IRLR 337.

24 *Raval v Department of Health and Social Security* [1985] ICR 685, [1985] IRLR 370, EAT.

25 *Singh v Rowntree MacKintosh Ltd* [1979] ICR 554, [1979] IRLR 199, EAT; *Panesar v Nestlé Co Ltd* [1980] ICR 144n, [1980] IRLR 64, CA.

26 *Bohon-Mitchell v Common Professional Examination Board and Council of Legal Education* [1978] IRLR 525.

27 *Commission for Racial Equality v Dutton* [1989] QB 783, [1989] 1 All ER 306, CA.

28 *Kidd v DRG (UK) Ltd* [1985] ICR 405 at 415, EAT, per Waite J. See also *Pearse v City of Bradford Metropolitan Council* [1988] IRLR 379, EAT; *Greater Manchester Police Authority v Lea* [1990] IRLR 372 at 374, EAT. An appeal court will only interfere if the tribunal has chosen to make the proportionate comparison within an area of society so irrationally inappropriate as to put it outside the range of selection for any reasonable tribunal. See *University of Manchester v Jones* [1992] ICR 52, EAT.

29 *Pearse v City of Bradford Metropolitan Council* [1988] IRLR 379, EAT.

30 See *Greater Manchester Police Authority v Lea* [1990] IRLR 372 at 375, EAT, in which the choice of the economically active population of the United Kingdom as a pool of comparison was upheld.

31 *Perera v Civil Service Commission (No 2)* [1982] ICR 350, [1982] IRLR 47, EAT (affd [1983] ICR 428, [1983] IRLR 166, CA); *Greater Manchester Police Authority v Lea* [1990] IRLR 372, EAT. In *Perera v Civil Service Commission (No 2)* supra, the tribunal stated that it considered it 'most undesirable that, in all cases of indirect discrimination, elaborate statistical evidence should be required before the case can be found proved. The time and expense involved in preparing and proving statistical evidence can be enormous, as experience in the United States has demonstrated. It is not good policy to require such evidence to be put forward'. In *Price v Civil Service Commission (No 2)* [1978] IRLR 3, the tribunal indicated that it should not be made too difficult to establish a prima facie case of indirect discrimination, since compliance with the Race Relations Act 1976 s 1(1)(b)(i) (see head (1) in the text) was only a preliminary step which did not lead to a finding that an act was one of discrimination unless the person acting failed to show that it was justifiable.

An applicant may be in difficulties if he anticipates that a particular pool of comparison is appropriate, and compiles relevant statistical evidence, and the court or tribunal then chooses another pool: see *Pearse v Bradford Metropolitan Council* [1988] IRLR 379, EAT. In such circumstances, the tribunal should grant an adjournment to enable the applicant to compile evidence: *Kidd v DRG (UK) Ltd* [1985] ICR 405 at 417, EAT, per Waite J.

32 *R v Secretary of State for Education, ex p Schaffter* [1987] IRLR 53. See also *James v Eastleigh Borough Council* [1990] 2 AC 751 at 766, [1990] 2 All ER 607 at 613, HL.

441. 'Racial grounds' and 'racial group'. In the Race Relations Act 1976, unless the context otherwise requires, 'racial grounds'[1] means any of the following grounds, namely colour, race, nationality[2] or ethnic[3] or national origins[4].

'Racial group' means a group of persons defined by reference to colour, race, nationality, or ethnic[5] or national origins, and references to a person's racial group refer to any racial group into which he falls[6].

1 The Fair Employment (Northern Ireland) Act 1989 applies to the appointment of a partnership to carry out work: *Kelly v Northern Ireland Housing Executive* [1999] 1 AC 428, [1998] 3 WLR 735, HL. Discrimination against Jews as an ethnic group (see note 5 infra) is unlawful, but discrimination against Jews on purely religious grounds may be outside the ambit of the Race Relations Act 1976: *Tower Hamlets London Borough Council v Rabin* [1989] ICR 693, EAT. As to religious discrimination see para 660 et seq post.

2 'Nationality' includes citizenship: Race Relations Act 1976 s 78.

3 'Ethnic origin' is not strictly a racial concept, but includes other characteristics which might commonly be thought of as being associated with common racial origin: *Mandla v Dowell Lee* [1983] 2 AC 548, [1983] 1 All ER 1062, HL (Sikhs a racial group). See also *Commission for Racial Equality v Dutton* [1989] QB 783, [1989] 1 All ER 306, CA (gipsies a racial group). See further note 5 infra. A tribunal has held that a Scottish person is neither of a different nationality nor of a different ethnic origin from a person from any other part of the United Kingdom: *McGregor v Proctor Paper and Board Ltd* (24 January 1992, unreported).

4 Race Relations Act 1976 ss 3(1), 78(1). 'National origin' refers to racial origin, as opposed to nationality: *Ealing London Borough Council v Race Relations Board* [1972] AC 342, [1972] 1 All ER 105, HL (a decision in the context of the Race Relations Act 1968, which resulted in the addition of 'nationality' in the Race Relations Act 1976). Discrimination against a British national born abroad is accordingly not within the scope of the Race Relations Act 1976: *Tejani v Superintendent Registrar for the District of Peterborough* [1986] IRLR 502, CA. See also *Northern Joint Police Board v Power* [1997] IRLR 610, EAT (where it was held that 'national origins' refers to identifiable historical and geographical elements pointing to the existence of a nation at some point in time; the Scots and the English are 'racial groups' defined by reference to 'national origins'). See also *BBC Scotland v Souster* [2001] IRLR 150, IH.

5 The meaning of 'a group defined by reference to ethnic origins' was considered in *Mandla v Dowell Lee* [1983] 2 AC 548, [1983] 1 All ER 1062, HL. Such a group must regard itself and be regarded by others as a distinct community by virtue of certain characteristics. Some are essential, others are not. The two essential characteristics are: (1) a long shared history, of which the group is conscious as distinguishing it from other groups, and the memory of which it keeps alive; and (2) a cultural tradition of its own, including family and social occasions and manners, often, but not necessarily associated with religious observance. The non-essential relevant characteristics were identified as: (a) a common geographical origin, or descent from a small number of common ancestors; (b) a common language, not necessarily peculiar to the group; (c) a common literature peculiar to the group; (d) a common religion different from neighbouring groups or the general community; and (e) being a minority, or an oppressed or dominant group within a larger community. The definition may include converts and exclude apostates. Provided a person who joins the group feels himself to be a member of it and is accepted by other members, then he is, for the purposes of the Race Relations Act 1976, a member. By this definition, the Sikhs constituted a racial group. Gipsies are a racial group (*Commission for Racial Equality v Dutton* [1989] QB 783, [1989] 1 All ER 306, CA); as are Jews (*King-Ansell v Police* [1979] 2 NZLR 531, NZ CA; *Seide v Gillette Industries Ltd* [1980] IRLR 427, EAT). English-speaking inhabitants of Wales do not constitute a racial group; the difference in language alone is not sufficient to distinguish them from the Welsh-speaking inhabitants: *Gwynedd County Council v Jones* [1986] ICR 833, EAT. Muslims are not a racial group, but a group defined by religion: *Nyazi v Rymans Ltd* (10 May 1988, unreported) EAT/6/88 (Transcript). Rastafarians lack a sufficiently long shared history to be a racial group; and the Employment Appeal Tribunal also doubted whether they had a sufficient cultural tradition: *Crown Suppliers (Property Services Agency) v Dawkins* [1991] ICR 583, EAT; affd [1993] ICR 517, CA.

6 Race Relations Act 1976 ss 3(1), 78(1). A person may be a member of several racial groups, e g West Indian by national or racial origins, black by colour, and British by nationality. The fact that a racial group comprises two or more distinct racial groups does not prevent it from constituting a particular racial group for the purposes of the Act: s 3(2). Where a complainant is a member of a number of racial groups, he should be aware that not all of those groups may be disproportionately affected by the application of a particular condition. He must state which of his racial groups has suffered disparate impact: see *Orphanos v Queen Mary College* [1985] AC 761, [1985] 2 All ER 233, HL, in which the

respondents conceded that the proportion of Cypriots who could comply with a requirement of three years' residence in the European Community was considerably smaller than the proportion of people not of that racial group who could comply with the condition. Lord Fraser of Tullybelton considered that the concession was wrongly made: the applicant belonged to three racial groups: non-British, non-EC national, and Cypriot. Only the first two were disproportionately affected by the condition. There was no reason to suspect that any more non-Cypriots (including all other nationalities) than Cypriots could comply with the condition.

442. Discrimination by way of victimisation. The Race Relations Act 1976 contains provisions for the protection of people who are victimised as a result of complaining of racial discrimination or assisting another person's complaint. The Act's definition of discrimination includes discrimination by way of victimisation[1].

A person[2] discriminates against another person in any circumstances relevant for the purposes of the Race Relations Act 1976 if he treats him less favourably than in those circumstances he treats or would treat other persons and does so by reason that the person victimised[3] has: (1) brought proceedings under the Act against the discriminator or any other person[4]; (2) given evidence or information in connection with proceedings brought by any person against the discriminator or any other person under the Act[5]; (3) otherwise done anything under or by reference to the Act in relation to the discriminator or any other person[6]; or (4) alleged that the discriminator or any other person has committed an act[7] which would amount to a contravention of the Act[8].

The prohibition of victimisation extends to circumstances in which the discriminator treats the person victimised less favourably because he knows that the person victimised intends to do any of the above acts, or suspects that he has done or intends to do them[9].

The provision does not apply where a person is treated less favourably by reason of any allegation made by him which was false and not made in good faith[10].

1 See the Race Relations Act 1976 s 2.

2 As to the meaning of 'person' see para 344 note 3 ante. As to the liability of principals and employers for the acts of their agents and employees see ibid s 32; and para 476 post. As to the liability of those who knowingly aid unlawful acts see s 33 (as amended); and para 477 post.

3 See ibid s 2(1). See also note 8 infra.

   An employer's refusal to provide an employee with a reference to preserve its legal position in pending discrimination proceedings is not treating the employee less favourably by reason that the employee has brought proceedings: *Khan v Chief Constable of West Yorkshire Police* [2001] UKHL 48, [2001] 4 All ER 834, sub nom *Chief Constable of West Yorkshire Police v Khan* [2001] IRLR 830.

4 Race Relations Act 1976 s 2(1)(a). See also note 8 infra. See *Khan v Chief Constable of West Yorkshire Police* [2001] UKHL 48, [2001] 4 All ER 834, sub nom *Chief Constable of West Yorkshire Police v Khan* [2001] IRLR 830; and note 3 supra.

5 Race Relations Act 1976 s 2(1)(b). See also note 8 infra.

6 Ibid s 2(1)(c). See also note 8 infra.

7 'Act' includes a deliberate omission: ibid s 78(1).

8 Ibid s 2(1)(d). A complainant under s 2(1) must show: (1) that he has done 'a protected act' (i e one of the four acts set out in s 2(1): see heads (1)–(4) in the text); (2) that he has been treated less favourably than others whose circumstances are the same as or not materially different from his own, but who have not done a protected act; and (3) that the less favourable treatment of him is by reason that he did a protected act: see *Nagarajan v London Regional Transport* [2000] 1 AC 501, [1999] 4 All ER 65, HL; *Aziz v Trinity Street Taxis Ltd* [1989] QB 463, [1988] 2 All ER 860, CA; *Kirby v Manpower Services Commission* [1980] 3 All ER 334, [1980] 1 WLR 725, EAT; *British Airways Engine Overhaul Ltd v Francis* [1981] ICR 278, EAT. See also *Cornelius v University College Swansea* [1987] IRLR 141, CA (refusal by employer to initiate grievance procedure, because applicant had brought legal proceedings, was not victimisation, where employer would have acted the same way whether the proceedings were under the Sex Discrimination Act 1975 or any other legislation); *Brown v TNT Express Worldwide (UK) Ltd* [2001] ICR 182, CA. See also *Khan v Chief Constable of West Yorkshire Police* [2001] UKHL 48, [2001] 4 All ER 834, sub nom *Chief Constable of West Yorkshire Police v Khan* [2001] IRLR 830; *Lindsay v Alliance & Leiciester plc* [2000] ICR 1234, [2000] All ER (D) 282, EAT. See *IRC v Morgan* [2002] IRLR 776, [2002] All ER (D) 67 (Feb), EAT (circulation of memorandum concerning employee amounted to victimisation since it was clear that other employees would not have received same treatment).

9 Race Relations Act 1976 s 2(1). See note 8 supra. There is no requirement that the discriminator must have been consciously motivated in treating the person victimised less favourably: *Nagarajan v London Regional Transport* [2000] 1 AC 501, [1999] 4 All ER 65, HL. See also *Khan v Chief Constable of West Yorkshire Police* [2001] UKHL 48, [2001] 4 All ER 834, sub nom *Chief Constable of West Yorkshire Police v Khan* [2001] IRLR 830.

10 See the Race Relations Act 1976 s 2(2).

443. Nature of the comparison. Where the case of a person of a particular racial group[1] is compared with that of a person not of that group for the purpose of deciding whether there has been discrimination, the comparison must be such that the relevant circumstances in the one case are the same, or not materially different, in the other[2]. It is a question of fact what circumstances are relevant for the purposes of the comparison, but the comparison must be made without taking matters of race into account[3]. The relevant circumstances must not themselves involve direct or indirect discrimination[4].

1 For the meaning of 'racial group' see para 441 ante.

2 See the Race Relations Act 1976 s 3(4) (amended by the Race Relations Act 1976 (Amendment) Regulations 2003, SI 2006/1626, reg 4). The provision is not an exception to the operation of the Act, but merely an interpretation provision directed to ensuring that like is compared with like: see *Bain v Bowles* [1991] IRLR 356, CA (magazine refused to accept advertisements for female domestic staff placed by single men living abroad, because of past difficulties with sexual harassment; held to be unlawful discrimination under the Sex Discrimination Act 1975). See also *Marks & Spencer plc v Martins* [1998] ICR 1005, sub nom *Martins v Marks & Spencer plc* [1988] IRLR 326, CA (a finding of bias on the part of interviewers interviewing the complainant for a post is not a relevant or meaningful finding for the purposes of the Race Relations Act 1976); *Wakeman v Quick Corpn* [1999] IRLR 424, CA (discrimination in pay rates as between United Kingdom recruited managers in a Japanese firm in the United Kingdom, and their Japanese colleagues on secondment from Japan, was due to the fact of being on secondment so that there was no 'like for like' comparison within the Race Relations Act 1976 s 3(4) (as then in force) and the causal link with any racial factor was not therefore established). Where an employment tribunal chairman rejects a comparator named by an applicant, he should construct a hypothetical comparator against whom to test the applicant's case: *Balamoody v United Kingdom Central Council for Nursing, Midwifery and Health Visiting* [2001] EWCA Civ 2097, [2002] ICR 646, [2002] IRLR 288. See also *Spicer v Government of Spain* [2004] EWCA Civ 1046, [2005] ICR 213 (Spanish civil servants working in Spanish state school in London on secondment paid relocation allowances; British and Spanish workers were the same for purposes of the Race Relations Act 1976 s 3(4) (as then in force).

3 'Although one has to compare like with like, in judging whether there has been discrimination you have to compare the treatment actually meted out with the treatment which would have been afforded to a man having all the same characteristics as the complainant except his race or his attitude to race; only by excluding matters of race can you discover whether the differential treatment was on racial grounds': *Showboat Entertainment Centre Ltd v Owens* [1984] 1 All ER 836 at 842, [1984] 1 WLR 384 at 391, EAT, per Browne-Wilkinson J. See also *Grieg v Community Industry* [1979] ICR 356 at 360–361, EAT, per Slynn J; *Horsey v Dyfed County Council* [1982] ICR 755 at 760–761, EAT; *Mecca Leisure Group plc v Chatprachong* [1993] ICR 688, EAT.

4 *James v Eastleigh Borough Council* [1990] 2 AC 751 at 766, [1990] 2 All ER 607 at 613, HL, per Lord Bridge of Harwich. In *Dhatt v McDonalds Hamburgers Ltd* [1991] 3 All ER 692, [1991] 1 WLR 527, CA, an Indian national with indefinite leave to remain in the United Kingdom (who consequently did not require a work permit to work in the United Kingdom) was held not to have been discriminated against on racial grounds by being required to produce evidence of his right to work in the United Kingdom in order to obtain employment with the respondents, which evidence would not have been required from a British or EC national: the relevant comparison, for the purposes of the Race Relations Act 1976 s 3(4) (as then in force), was not to be made between two young men seeking work, in which case the requirement based upon the applicant's nationality would have been discriminatory on racial grounds, but was to be made between those who did not require work permits (ie British and EC nationals) and those who required work permits or indefinite leave to remain (ie non-EC nationals). The Court of Appeal distinguished *James v Eastleigh Borough Council* supra on the grounds that Parliament had restricted the right of non-EC nationals to work in the United Kingdom, whereas it had not required local authorities to restrict free entry to swimming pools to those of pensionable age. It is submitted that this decision is not only inconsistent with the House of Lords decision in *James v Eastleigh Borough Council* supra, but also with the policy and objects of the legislation. Conditions which are themselves based upon race, colour, nationality or ethnic or national origins should not be relevant circumstances for the purposes of the Race Relations Act 1976 s 3(4) (as amended).

444. Harassment. A person subjects another to harassment in any circumstances relevant for specified purposes[1] where, on grounds of race or ethnic or national origins[2], he engages in unwanted conduct which has the purpose or effect of violating that other person's dignity[3], or creating an intimidating, hostile, degrading, humiliating or offensive environment for him[4]. Conduct is to be regarded as having the effect specified above only if, having regard to all the circumstances, including in particular the perception of that other person, it should reasonably be considered as having that effect[5].

1   Ie for the purposes of the Race Relations Act 1976 Pt II (ss 4–15) (as amended) (see para 446 et seq post); ss 17–18D (as amended) (see para 460 et seq post); s 19B (as added and amended) (see para 470 post), so far as relating to any form of social security, health care, any other form of social protection, and any form of social advantage, which does not fall within s 20 (as amended) (see para 461 post); ss 20–24 (as amended) (see para 461 et seq post); s 26A (as added and amended) (see para 456 post); s 76 (as amended) (see para 457 post) and s 76ZA (as added) (see para 459 post); and Pt IV (ss 27A–33) (as amended) (see para 471 et seq post), in its application to the provisions referred to above. For the meanings of 'social protection' and 'social advantage' see para 440 note 14 ante.
2   As to the meaning of 'race or ethnic or national origins' see para 441 ante.
3   Race Relations Act 1976 s 3A(1)(a) (s 3A added by the Race Relations Act 1976 (Amendment) Regulations 2003, SI 2003/1626, reg 5). This provision supersedes the previous case law on the subject. See *Nyateka v Queenscourt Ltd* [2007] All ER (D) 246 (Jan), EAT (conduct of officer amounted to harassment but employer had erred in not inviting employee to participate in grievance investigations following an incident of racial abuse at the workplace).
4   Race Relations Act 1976 s 3A(1)(b) (as added: see note 3 supra).
5   Ibid s 3A(2) (as added: see note 3 supra).

445. Application of the Race Relations Act 1976 to the Crown. The Race Relations Act 1976 applies to an act done by or for the purposes of a Minister of the Crown[1] or a government department, or to an act done on behalf of the Crown by a statutory body, or a person holding a statutory office[2], as it applies to an act done by a private person[3]. However, the Crown's liability under the Act is limited by exceptions concerning acts done under statutory authority[4] and acts safeguarding national security[5].

1   'Minister of the Crown' includes the Treasury and the Defence Council: Race Relations Act 1976 s 78(1). As to the Treasury see CONSTITUTIONAL LAW AND HUMAN RIGHTS vol 8(2) (Reissue) paras 512–517. As to the Defence Council see ARMED FORCES vol 2(2) (Reissue) para 2; CONSTITUTIONAL LAW AND HUMAN RIGHTS vol 8(2) (Reissue) para 443 et seq.
2   'Statutory body' means a body set up by or in pursuance of an enactment; and 'statutory office' means an office so set up: ibid s 75(10)(b).
3   Ibid s 75(1). For provisions relating to the Crown in its capacity as employer see s 75(2)–(9) (as amended); and para 457 post. As to the application of the Crown Proceedings Act 1947 in relation to proceedings under the Race Relations Act 1976 see s 75(6) (as amended); and CROWN PROCEEDINGS AND CROWN PRACTICE vol 12(1) (Reissue) para 113. As to the meaning of 'person' see para 344 note 3 ante. Section 75(1) has effect subject to ss 76A, 76B (both as added and amended) (see para 455 post): s 75(3) (amended by the Race Relations (Amendment) Act 2000 s 9(1), Sch 2 para 18(a)).
4   See the Race Relations Act 1976 s 41 (as amended); and para 486 post.
5   See ibid s 42 (as amended); and para 487 post.

(ii) Discrimination in Particular Circumstances

A. DISCRIMINATION IN THE EMPLOYMENT FIELD

(A) In general

446. Discrimination and harassment by employers. The Race Relations Act 1976 prohibits[1] discrimination by an employer[2] only in relation to employment[3] of a person by him at an establishment[4] in Great Britain[5]. The Act covers both recruitment[6] and the treatment of existing employees[7].

It is unlawful for a person[8] to discriminate against another in the arrangements he makes for the purpose of determining who should be offered employment[9], in the terms on which he offers him employment[10], or by refusing or deliberately omitting to offer him employment[11].

It is unlawful for an employer to discriminate against an employee in the terms of employment which he affords him[12], in the way he affords him access to opportunities for promotion, transfer or training[13], or to any other benefits, facilities or services[14], or by refusing or deliberately omitting to afford him access to them[15], or by dismissing[16] him, or subjecting him to any other detriment[17].

It is unlawful for an employer, in relation to employment by him at an establishment in Great Britain, to subject to harassment a person whom he employs or who has applied to him for employment[18].

1   As to the enforcement of individual rights in the employment field see para 499 et seq post.

2   The meaning of 'employer' has been modified by the Education (Modification of Enactments Relating to Employment) (England) Order 2003, SI 2003/1964, art 3, Schedule, which provides that any references to an employer (however expressed) include references to the governing body of a school exercising employment powers. See also the Education (Modification of Enactments Relating to Employment) (Wales) Order 2006, SI 2006/1073, art 3, Schedule.

3   'Employment' means employment under a contract of service or of apprenticeship or a contract personally to execute any work or labour and related expressions (eg including 'employer') are to be construed accordingly: Race Relations Act 1976 s 78(1). The correct test for determining whether there is a contract 'personally to execute any work or labour' is whether the sole or dominant purpose of the contract was the execution of any work or labour by the contracting party personally. A contract between a newspaper publisher and a distributor is not such a contract as there was no obligation on the distributor personally to execute the work: *Gunning v Mirror Group Newspapers Ltd* [1986] 1 All ER 385, sub nom *Mirror Group Newspapers Ltd v Gunning* [1986] 1 WLR 546, CA. See also *Quinnen v Hovells* [1984] ICR 525, [1984] IRLR 227, EAT (definition of employment extends to all self-employed people supplying personal services); *Tanna v Post Office* [1981] ICR 374, EAT (sub-postmaster not employed as he was not obliged personally to execute any work); *Hugh-Jones v St John's College, Cambridge* [1979] ICR 848, EAT (research fellow employed). A general practitioner is not employed by the Family Practitioner Committee, the Medical Committee or the Secretary of State for Health: *Wadi v Cornwall and Isles of Scilly Family Practitioner Committee* [1985] ICR 492, EAT; followed in *David-John v North Essex Health Authority* [2004] ICR 112, [2003] All ER (D) 84 (Aug), EAT. In considering whether a contract involves an obligation personally to execute any work or labour, a tribunal should consider the substance and not the form of the contract in question: *Mankoo v British School of Motoring Ltd* (4 March 1983, unreported), EAT/657/82 (Transcript). See also *Mingeley v Pennock and Ivory (t/a Amber Cars)* [2004] EWCA Civ 328, [2004] ICR 727, [2004] IRLR 373 (taxi driver not employed where dominant purpose of contract was provision of access to taxi firm's radio and computer booking system for fee).

      See also *Sheikh v Chief Constable of Greater Manchester Police* [1990] 1 QB 637, [1989] 2 All ER 684, CA (special police constable not employed). As to the application of the Race Relations Act 1976 to service in the police force see para 455 post; and see *Knight v A-G* [1979] ICR 194, EAT (justice of the peace not employed, but holder of a public office). As to the Crown's duty not to discriminate in relation to appointments to public offices see para 457 post. As to Crown service generally, including service in the armed forces see para 457 post.

      A trainee under the Youth Opportunities Programme (and presumably under subsequent comparable government schemes) is not an employee as there are no mutually binding obligations between trainee and employer; if a contract did exist, it would be a contract for training, not employment: *Daley v Allied Suppliers Ltd* [1983] ICR 90, [1983] IRLR 14, EAT. Trainees are now protected by the Race Relations Act 1976 s 13 (as substituted and amended): see para 453 post. Contrast *Mankoo v British School of Motoring Ltd* supra, in which it was held that the dismissal of a driving instructor while he was on a training course for the training of franchisees of the British School of Motoring was within the employment provisions of the Race Relations Act 1976. The franchise involved an obligation to perform personal services, and the training course was a part of the arrangements for determining who should be offered employment as a franchisee. Discrimination in the operation of the training course would contravene s 4(1)(a): see the text and note 9 infra.

4   Where work is not done at an establishment it is to be treated as done at the establishment from which it is done or with which it has the closest connection: see ibid s 8(4). In the case of employment on board a ship registered at a port of registry in Great Britain (except where the employee does his work wholly outside Great Britain) the ship is deemed to be an establishment: s 8(3). For the meaning of 'Great Britain' see para 325 note 6 ante.

5   See ibid s 4 (amended by the Race Relations Act 1976 (Amendment) Regulations 2003, SI 2003/1626, reg 6). This territorial limitation was challenged in *Bossa v Nordstress Ltd* [1998] ICR 694, [1998] IRLR 284, EAT, where an Italian applicant for a job with Alitalia in Italy was refused an interview by reason of his Italian nationality. The tribunal declined jurisdiction in respect of his complaint. The Employment Appeal Tribunal reversed this decision holding that the Treaty Establishing the European Community (Rome, 25 March 1957; TS 1 (1973); Cmnd 5179) (the 'EC Treaty') art 39 (formerly art 48; renumbered by virtue of the Treaty of Amsterdam: see *Treaty Citation (No 2) (Note)* [1999] All ER (EC) 646, ECJ) conferred enforceable rights on European Union workers to work anywhere in the Community; accordingly the Race Relations Act 1976 s 8 (as amended) was disapplied by virtue of its conflict with the EC Treaty art 39 (as renumbered).

      In general, employment is to be regarded as being at an establishment in Great Britain if the employee does his work wholly or partly in Great Britain, or does his work wholly outside Great Britain and the Race Relations Act 1976 s 8(1A) (as added) applies: s 8(1) (amended by the Race Relations Act 1976 (Amendment) Regulations 2003, SI 2003/1626, reg 11(1)). The Race Relations Act 1976 s 8(1A) (as added) applies if, in a case involving discrimination on grounds of race or ethnic or national origins, or harassment: (1) the employer has a place of business at an establishment in Great Britain; (2) the work is for the purposes of the business carried on at that establishment; and (3) the employee is ordinarily resident in Great Britain: (a) at the time when he applies for or is offered the employment; or (b) at any time during the course of the employment: s 8(1A) (added by the Race Relations Act 1976 (Amendment) Regulations 2003, SI 2003/1626, reg 11(2)). For the meaning of 'harassment' see para 444 ante. The entire length of the employment relationship is relevant to whether a person was employed at an establishment in Great Britain, not simply the period during which the alleged acts of discrimination took place: *Saggar v Ministry of Defence* [2005] EWCA Civ 413, [2005] ICR 1073, [2005] All ER (D) 382 (Apr). Employment on a ship, aircraft or hovercraft the property of Her Majesty in right of the government of the United Kingdom is regarded as employment at an establishment in Great Britain: see the Race Relations Act 1976 s 75(4). As to the application of s 8 (as amended) to employment concerned with exploration of the sea bed or subsoil or the exploitation of their natural resources see s 8(5)–(7) (s 8(5) prospectively amended by the Petroleum Act 1998 s 50, Sch 4 para 11); and FUEL AND ENERGY vol 19(2) (Reissue) para 1598. See also the Race Relations (Offshore Employment) Order 1987, SI 1987/929.

      An employee is to be regarded as doing his work wholly outside Great Britain if it was contemplated that he would do so at the time of the act of discrimination: *Deria v General Council of British Shipping* [1986] 1 WLR 1207, [1986] ICR 172, CA (Somali sailor from Cardiff refused employment on ship which was intended to sail to Gibraltar, but which in fact sailed to Southampton: held to be outside ambit of Race Relations Act 1976). See also *Wood v Cunard Line Ltd* [1989] ICR 398, [1989] IRLR 431, EAT.

      The exemption in the Race Relations Act 1976 s 9(1) (as amended) applies to the extent that the discrimination relates to the pay the person receives in respect of his employment, and amounts to discrimination against the person on the basis of his nationality: s 9(1) (amended by the Race Relations Act 1976 (Seamen Recruited Abroad) Order 2003, SI 2003/1651, reg 2(1), (2)). 'Pay' includes retirement or death benefit; and 'retirement or death benefit' means a pension, annuity, lump sum, gratuity or other similar benefit which will be paid or given to the employee or contract worker or a member of his family or household in the event of his retirement or death: Race Relations Act 1976 s 9(5) (added by the Race Relations Act 1976 (Seamen Recruited Abroad) Order 2003, SI 2003/1651, reg 2(1), (4)).

6   See the Race Relations Act 1976 s 4(1); and the text and notes 8–11 infra. This provision deals only with situations arising before a contract of employment has been entered into, and does not cover acts done to an existing employee: *Clymo v Wandsworth London Borough Council* [1989] 2 CMLR 577, [1989] ICR 250, EAT.

7   See the Race Relations Act 1976 s 4(2); and the text to notes 12–17 infra. An employer may be liable to an employee for unlawful race discrimination committed by a third party where the employer had sufficient control over the circumstances in which the discrimination occurred to have allowed him to prevent it: *Burton v De Vere Hotels* [1997] ICR 1, [1996] IRLR 596, EAT (hotel manager responsible for comedian in hotel subjecting waitresses to offensive remarks). Where less favourable treatment has been shown, the burden of proof rests on the employer to demonstrate that it was not on racial grounds: *Dhesi v Glasgow City Council* 2006 SLT 128. See also *Abergaze v South East Essex College* [2006] ICR 468, [2005] All ER (D) 49 (Nov), EAT. See also para 504 post.

      A claim under the Race Relations Act 1976 s 4(2) can be brought after employment has ended: *Relaxion Group plc v Rhys-Harper, D'Souza v Lambert London Borough Council, Jones v 3M Healthcare Ltd, Kirker v British Sugar plc, Angel v New Possibilities NHS Trust, Bond v Hackney Citizens Advice Bureau* [2003] UKHL 33, [2003] 4 All ER 1113, [2003] IRLR 484.

8   As to the meaning of 'person' see para 344 note 3 ante.

9   See the Race Relations Act 1976 s 4(1)(a). This provision covers the range of recruitment methods used by employers. The Commission for Racial Equality ('CRE'), in its Statutory Code of Practice on Racial

Equality in Employment (April 2006), recommends methods by which employers can eliminate racial discrimination from recruitment arrangements. As to the CRE see para 488 et seq post. As to the Commission for Equality and Human Rights, which is to replace the CRE, see para 305 et seq ante. As to the status of the Statutory Code of Practice on Racial Equality in Employment (April 2006), and its admissibility as evidence, see para 491 post.

Arrangements for the purpose of determining who should be offered employment are unlawful if they operate so as to discriminate, even if they were not made with the purpose of discriminating: *Brennan v JH Dewhurst Ltd* [1984] ICR 52, [1983] IRLR 357, EAT. See also *Tyagi v BBC World Service* [2001] EWCA Civ 549, [2001] IRLR 465. The following are examples of 'arrangements' within the ambit of the Race Relations Act 1976 s 4(1)(a):

(1) Advertising. Proceedings in respect of the publication of discriminatory advertisements may be brought only by the CRE: see the Race Relations Act 1976 ss 29, 63 (both as amended); and paras 473, 498 post. However, individuals may complain of discriminatory advertisements where they form part of an employer's recruitment arrangements: *Brindley v Tayside Health Board* [1976] IRLR 364, IT. This decision was not followed in *Cardiff Women's Aid v Hartup* [1994] IRLR 390, EAT, where the Employment Appeal Tribunal held that the CRE had exclusive jurisdiction to police discriminatory advertising under the Race Relations Act 1976 s 63 (as amended). The CRE recommends that employers should not confine advertisements unjustifiably to those areas or publications which would exclude or disproportionately reduce the numbers of applicants of a particular racial group. Employers should also avoid prescribing requirements such as length of residence or experience in the United Kingdom, and where a particular qualification is required, it should be made clear that a fully comparable overseas qualification is as acceptable as a United-Kingdom qualification; the CRE recommends that employers should include the statement that they are equal opportunities employers on literature they send to applicants: see the Statutory Code of Practice on Racial Equality in Employment (April 2006) para 4.11.

(2) Sources of recruitment. The CRE recommends that employers should not unjustifiably confine their recruitment to those agencies, job centres, careers offices and schools which provide only or mainly applicants of a particular racial group. Employers should not recruit solely or in the first instance through the recommendations of existing employees where the workforce is wholly or predominantly white or black and the labour market is multi-racial; or through trade unions where this means that only members of a particular racial group, or a disproportionately high number of them, come forward: see the Statutory Code of Practice on Racial Equality in Employment (April 2006) para 4.11.

(3) Criteria for recruitment. Selection criteria and tests may be unlawful if they have an unjustifiable disparate adverse impact upon particular racial groups, such as a requirement of a standard of English higher than that needed for the job (see *Raval v Department of Health and Social Security* [1985] ICR 685, [1985] IRLR 370, EAT, in which, on the facts, a requirement of English 'O' level was justified). The CRE recommends that overseas qualifications which are comparable with United Kingdom qualifications should be accepted as equivalents: see the Statutory Code of Practice on Racial Equality in Employment (April 2006) para 4.11. See also *Bohon-Mitchell v Common Professional Examination Board and Council of Legal Education* [1978] IRLR 525.

(4) Interviews. It is not automatically discriminatory to ask a member of one racial group a question at a job interview which would not be asked of an applicant of another racial group; whether such questions are discriminatory is an issue of fact, depending on the circumstances and purpose of the question: *Saunders v Richmond-upon-Thames London Borough Council* [1978] ICR 75, [1977] IRLR 362, EAT (concerned with the equivalent provision of the Sex Discrimination Act 1975). See also *Virdee v ECC Quarries Ltd* [1978] IRLR 295 (Sikh applicant for job asked questions about working with white staff). Words or acts of discouragement at an interview may amount to less favourable treatment, but if the same questions are asked of applicants of all racial groups, there is no direct discrimination: *Simon v Brimham Associates* [1987] ICR 596, [1987] IRLR 307, CA. The CRE recommends that staff responsible for shortlisting, interviewing and selecting candidates should be clearly informed of selection criteria and of the need for their consistent application, be given guidance or training on the effects which generalised assumptions and prejudices about race can have on selection decisions, and be made aware of the possible misunderstandings that can occur in interviews between persons of different cultural background: see the Statutory Code of Practice on Racial Equality in Employment (April 2006) para 4.11.

In relation to discrimination on grounds of race or ethnic or national origins, neither the Race Relations Act 1976 s 4(1)(a) nor s 4(1)(c) (see the text and note 11 infra) apply to any employment where s 4A(2) (as added) applies: s 4A(1)(a) (s 4A added by the Race Relations Act 1976 (Amendment) Regulations 2003, SI 2003/1626, reg 7). The Race Relations Act 1976 s 4A(2) (as added) applies where, having regard to the nature of the employment or the context in which it is carried out: (a) being of a particular race or of particular ethnic or national origins is a genuine and determining occupational requirement; (b) it is proportionate to apply that requirement in the particular case; and (c) either (i) the person to whom that requirement is applied does not meet it; or (ii) the employer is not satisfied, and in all the circumstances it is reasonable for him not to be satisfied, that that person meets it: s 4A(2) (s 4A as so added).

A complainant may succeed under s 4(1)(a) even if he cannot show that he would have been appointed to the job but for his race, and may be awarded damages for injury to his feelings (see para 499 post) or for the loss of the chance of appointment (see para 499 post).

10 Ibid s 4(1)(b). Employers will be liable for unlawful discrimination under this provision if they impose unjustifiable contractual conditions upon their workforce which have a disparate impact on particular racial groups. An example is the refusal to allow employees to wear beards or turbans, which adversely affects Sikhs: see *Singh v Rowntree Mackintosh Ltd* [1979] ICR 554, [1979] IRLR 199, EAT; *Panesar v Nestlé Co Ltd* [1980] ICR 144n, [1980] IRLR 64, CA, in which a condition that employees must not wear beards in a sweet factory was justifiable on hygienic grounds. As to the special protection of Sikhs from race discrimination in connection with requirements as to wearing of safety helmets see para 480 post. As to protection of Sikhs from religious discrimination in this context see para 681 post.

11 See the Race Relations Act 1976 s 4(1)(c). As to where s 4(1)(c) does not apply see note 9 supra. Discrimination in selection for redundancy, where the job content of the remaining jobs is to be altered, should be regarded as discrimination in deliberately omitting to offer the complainant the revised job, not discrimination by dismissing the complainant (which would be prohibited by s 4(2)(c): see the text to note 17 infra): *Timex Corpn v Hodgson* [1982] ICR 63, [1981] IRLR 530, EAT. Discriminatory selection for redundancy in these circumstances may thus be defended on the grounds that race is a genuine occupational qualification for the revised job: see the Race Relations Act 1976 s 5 (as amended); and para 447 post. The defence under s 5 (as amended) is not available for discriminatory dismissals. A dismissed employee seeking reinstatement was previously not considered an employee for the purposes of s 4(1)(c) as his employment was thought to end on the day of dismissal unless there was an express provision in his contract of employment that the contract was to continue pending an appeal: see *Post Office v Adekeye* [1997] ICR 110, sub nom *Adekeye v Post Office* [1997] IRLR 105, CA; but this has now been overruled by *Relaxion Group plc v Rhys-Harper, D'Souza v Lambert London Borough Council, Jones v 3M Healthcare Ltd, Kirker v British Sugar plc, Angel v New Possibilities NHS Trust, Bond v Hackney Citizens Advice Bureau* [2003] UKHL 33, [2003] 4 All ER 1113, [2003] IRLR 484. See note 7 supra. See, also, the approach adopted in relation to this question in respect of the equivalent sex discrimination legislation: see Case C-185/97 *Coote v Granada Hospitality Ltd* [1998] All ER (EC) 865, [1999] ICR 100, ECJ; *Coote v Granada Hospitality Ltd (No 2)* [1999] ICR 942, [1999] IRLR 452, EAT.

12 Race Relations Act 1976 s 4(2)(a).

13 'Training' includes any form of education or instruction: ibid s 78(1). 'Education' includes any form of training or instruction: s 78(1). The criteria for selection for promotion, transfer or training must not be directly or indirectly discriminatory: see *Watches of Switzerland Ltd v Savell* [1983] IRLR 141, EAT. However, criteria for selection for promotion, transfer or training which have a disproportionate adverse impact on a particular racial group will not be unlawful unless they operate as an 'absolute bar' to selection: *Perera v Civil Service Commission (No 2)* [1983] ICR 428, [1983] IRLR 166, CA; *Meer v London Borough of Tower Hamlets* [1988] IRLR 399, CA. See also *Afolabi v Southwark London Borough Council* [2003] EWCA Civ 15, [2003] ICR 800, [2003] All ER (D) 217 (Jan). An annual placement scheme operated by the Government Legal Service has been considered within the broad definition of 'training' in the context of a claim under the Race Relations Act 1976 s 13 (as substituted) (see para 453 post): *Chenge v Treasury Solicitors Department* [2007] All ER (D) 203 (Feb), EAT.

The suitability of candidates can rarely be measured objectively; and subjective judgments will be made. If there is evidence of a high percentage rate of failure to achieve promotion at particular levels by members of a particular racial group, this may indicate that the real reason for refusal is a conscious or unconscious racial attitude which involves stereotyped assumptions about that group: *West Midlands Passenger Transport Executive v Jaquant Singh* [1988] 2 All ER 873 at 877, [1988] 1 WLR 730 at 736, CA, per Balcombe LJ. As to the use of statistical evidence see para 503 post.

The CRE recommends that staff responsible for selecting employees for transfer to other jobs should be instructed to apply selection criteria without unlawful discrimination; and that industry or company agreements and arrangements of custom and practice on job transfers should be examined and amended if they are found to contain requirements or conditions which appear to be indirectly discriminatory: see the Statutory Code of Practice on Racial Equality in Employment (April 2006) para 3.16. The CRE further recommends that employers should regularly monitor the effects of selection decisions and personnel practices and procedures, in order to assess whether equal opportunity is being achieved.

14 The terms 'benefits, facilities or services' are not specifically defined in the Race Relations Act 1976. For the meaning of 'facilities' in the context of the acts of government officials see para 461 post. References to the affording by any person of access to benefits, facilities or services are not limited to benefits, facilities or services provided by that person himself, but include any means by which it is in that person's power to facilitate access to benefits, facilities or services provided by any other person ('the actual provider'): s 40(1). Where by any provision of the Race Relations Act 1976 the affording by any person

of access to benefits, facilities or services in a discriminatory way is in certain circumstances prevented from being unlawful, the effect of the provision extends also to the liability of any actual provider: s 40(2).

15 Ibid s 4(2)(b). In relation to discrimination on grounds of race or ethnic or national origins, s 4(2)(b) does not apply to promotion or transfer to, or training for, any employment where s 4A(2) (as added) applies (see note 9 supra): s 4A(1)(a) (s 4A as added: see note 9 supra).

Section 4(2) is very widely phrased. It is apt to cover discrimination in the way an employer affords access to any contractual or non-contractual benefits related to the employee's employment, or a refusal or omission to provide access to such benefits. A refusal by an employer to investigate an employee's complaint of unfair treatment, whether or not the treatment complained of was related to race, may be a refusal of access to benefits, facilities or services. To be unlawful, the refusal to investigate must be on racial grounds: *Eke v Customs and Excise Comrs* [1981] IRLR 334, EAT. An employee need not show that he has suffered a detriment to succeed under this provision, but simply that he has been directly or indirectly discriminated against.

The Race Relations Act 1976 s 4(2)(b) does not apply to benefits, facilities or services of any description if the employer is concerned with the provision (for payment or not) of benefits, facilities or services of that description to the public, or to a section of the public comprising the employee in question: s 4(4). However, it does apply where the employer's provision of benefits, facilities or services to the public differs in a material respect from the provision of the benefits, facilities or services by the employer to his employee, or where the provision to the employee in question is regulated by his contract of employment, or where the benefits, facilities or services relate to training: s 4(4). The purpose of this exception was to prevent an overlap with s 20 (as amended), which deals with the provision of goods, facilities and services to the public, or a section of the public: see para 461 post. Cases exempt from s 4 (as amended) under s 4(4) should be brought under s 20 (as amended): see para 461 post. As to the meaning of 'section of the public' see para 461 note 3 post.

The 'benefits, facilities or services' in question must be already in existence; the provisions of s 4(2)(b) do not cover a refusal or omission by an employer to provide new facilities for an employee: *Clymo v Wandsworth London Borough Council* [1989] 2 CMLR 577, [1989] ICR 250, EAT.

16 'Dismissal' includes dismissal by a local education authority following notification of a determination by the governing body of a school: see the Education (Modification of Enactments Relating to Employment) (England) Order 2003, SI 2003/1964, art 3(1), Schedule, and the Education (Modification of Enactments Relating to Employment) (Wales) Order 2006, SI 2006/1073, art 3, Schedule.

There is an overlap between this provision and the remedies for unfair dismissal provided under the Employment Rights Act 1996: see EMPLOYMENT vol 16(1B) (Reissue) para 682 et seq. There are differences in the calculation of compensation (see para 499 post) and in the qualifying periods under the two Acts. A discriminatory dismissal will not necessarily be unfair (e g because it may be caused by unintentional indirect discrimination): *Clarke v Eley (IMI) Kynoch Ltd* [1983] ICR 165, [1982] IRLR 482, EAT. The CRE recommends that staff responsible for selecting employees for dismissal, including redundancy, should be instructed not to discriminate on racial grounds; and that selection criteria for redundancies should be examined to ensure that they are not indirectly discriminatory: Statutory Code of Practice on Racial Equality in Employment (April 2006) para 1.17.

17 Race Relations Act 1976 s 4(2)(c). The reference to the dismissal of a person from employment includes, where the discrimination is on grounds of race or ethnic or national origins, reference to the termination of that person's employment by the expiration of any period, including a period expiring by reference to an event or circumstance, not being a termination immediately after which the employment is renewed on the same terms, and to the termination of that person's employment by any act of his, including the giving of notice, in circumstances such that he is entitled to terminate it without notice by reason of the conduct of the employer: s 4(4A) (added by the Race Relations Act 1976 (Amendment) Regulations 2003, SI 2003/1626, reg 6(2)(c)). In relation to discrimination on grounds of race or ethnic or national origins, the Race Relations Act 1976 s 4(2)(c) does not apply to dismissal from any employment where s 4A(2) (as added) applies (see note 9 supra): s 4A(1)(a) (as added: see note 9 supra).

'Detriment' does not include conduct of a nature such as to constitute harassment under s 3A (as added) (see para 444 ante): s 78(1) (definition added by the Race Relations Act 1976 (Amendment) Regulations 2003, SI 2003/1626, reg 52). 'Subjecting him to any other detriment' means no more than 'putting him under a disadvantage': *Ministry of Defence v Jeremiah* [1980] QB 87, [1979] 3 All ER 833, CA; *BL Cars Ltd v Brown* [1983] ICR 143, [1983] IRLR 193, EAT. The question is whether a reasonable worker would or might take the view that he had been disadvantaged in the circumstances in which he had to work after that time: *De Souza v Automobile Association* [1986] ICR 514, [1986] IRLR 103, CA (no detriment where racial remark was not intended to be heard by black employee, and it was unclear whether she did hear it). In *Barclays Bank plc v Kapur* [1989] ICR 753, [1989] IRLR 387, CA (affd [1991] 2 AC 355, [1991] 1 All ER 646, HL), Bingham LJ commented that 'since 'subjecting him to any other detriment' is to be given its broad, ordinary meaning … it is plain that almost any discriminatory conduct by employer against employee in relation to the latter's employment will be rendered unlawful by [the Race Relations Act 1976] s 4(2)'. A mere failure to provide an advantage which is not offered to others in the same employment cannot amount to a detriment: *Clymo v Wandsworth London Borough Council* [1989] 2 CMLR 577, [1989] ICR 250, EAT. See also *Weathersfield Ltd (t/a Van & Truck Rentals) v Sargent* [1999] ICR 425, [1999] IRLR 94, CA (unfavourable treatment of an employee, who refused to go along with employer's policy of refusing customers from ethnic minorities, was detrimental treatment on racial grounds). See *Governing Body of Addey and Stanhope School v Vakante* [2003] ICR 290, [2002] All ER (D) 79 (Oct), EAT (dismissed asylum-seeker, whose contract of employment was illegal under immigration legislation, could bring claim under the Race Relations Act 1976 s 4(2)(c)). Enduring psychological injury can be capable of constituting a detriment: *Jiad v Byford* [2003] EWCA Civ 135, [2003] IRLR 232. See also *Aziz v Crown Prosecution Service* [2006] EWCA Civ 1136, [2006] All ER (D) 468 (Jul), in which a finding of racial discrimination was reinstated where the employee had suffered from a detriment due to the employer knowingly failing to comply with its own code of practice in regard to both preliminary inquiries on allegations of serious misconduct and the right of representation at any hearing on formal disciplinary action.

18 Race Relations Act 1976 s 4(2A) (added by the Race Relations Act 1976 (Amendment) Regulations 2003, SI 2003/1626, reg 6(2)(a)).

447. Exceptions to employment discrimination. The prohibitions[1] in the Race Relations Act 1976 against employment discrimination[2] do not apply to employment for the purposes of a private household[3].

The prohibitions in the Act against racial discrimination[4] (but not discrimination by way of victimisation[5]) do not apply to employment or opportunities for promotion, or transfer to, or training[6] for employment, where being of a particular racial group[7] is a genuine occupational qualification for the job[8].

The circumstances in which being of a particular racial group is a genuine occupational qualification for the job are set out in the Act[9]. They are where:

(1) the job involves participation in a dramatic performance or other entertainment in a capacity for which a person of that racial group is required for reasons of authenticity[10];

(2) the job involves participation as an artist's or photographic model in the production of a work of art, visual image or sequence of visual images for which a person of that racial group is required for reasons of authenticity[11];

(3) the job involves working in a place where food or drink is (for payment or not) provided to and consumed by members of the public or a section of the public in a particular setting for which, in that job, a person of that racial group is required for reasons of authenticity[12]; or

(4) the holder of the job provides persons of that racial group with personal services promoting their welfare, and those services can most effectively be provided by a person of that racial group[13].

In relation to head (4) above, the courts have said that[14]:

(a) the racial group must be clearly and, if necessary, narrowly defined, because it will have to be the racial group of the holder of the post and of the recipient of the personal services[15];

(b) the post holder must be directly involved in the provision of services, and it is insufficient if the holder of the post directs others, as the services must be personal; the services need not be provided on a one-to-one basis[16];

(c) if the post holder provides several personal services to the recipient, the defence is established provided that one of those services genuinely falls within head (4) above[17];

(d) 'promoting their welfare' is a very wide expression, and should not be narrowed[18];

(e) the question is not whether the services could only be provided by a member of that racial group, but whether they could most effectively be provided by such a person[19].

The Act does not render unlawful any act[20] done by an employer, on grounds other than those of race or ethnic or national origins, for the benefit of a person not ordinarily resident in Great Britain in or in connection with employing him at an establishment in Great Britain, where the purpose of that employment is to provide him with training in skills which he appears to the employer to intend to exercise wholly outside Great Britain[21].

The exceptions apply to the extent that the act relates to the pay[22] the person receives in respect of his employment, and amounts to discrimination against the person on the basis of his nationality[23].

1   For general exceptions to the operation of the Race Relations Act 1976 see para 481 et seq post. As to action that may be lawfully be taken by an employer, in relation to the special needs of particular racial groups see s 35; and para 482 post. As to positive action that may be taken by an employer where a disproportionately small number of employees of a particular racial group is employed by him on particular work see s 37 (as amended), s 38; and para 484 post.

2   Ie ibid s 4(1), (2): see para 446 ante. For the meaning of 'employment' see para 446 note 3 ante.

3   See ibid s 4(3).

4   Ie ibid s 4(1)(a), (c), (2) (in cases where s 4A (as added) does not apply): see para 446 ante. References to discrimination refer to any discrimination falling within s 1 (as amended) or s 2 (see paras 439–442 ante) (s 3(3)(a)); references to racial discrimination refer to any discrimination falling within s 1 (as amended) (see paras 439–440 ante) (s 3(3)(b)); and related expressions are to be construed accordingly: ss 3(3), 78(1).

5   As to discrimination by way of victimisation see para 442 ante.

6   As to the meaning of 'training' see para 446 note 13 ante.

7   For the meaning of 'racial group' see para 441 ante.

8   Race Relations Act 1976 ss 5(1), 78(1) (s 5(1) amended by the Race Relations Act 1976 (Amendment) Regulations 2003, SI 2003/1626, reg 8). The Race Relations Act 1976 s 5 (as amended), as an exception to s 4 (as amended), should be strictly construed: *Lambeth London Borough Council v Commission for Racial Equality* [1989] ICR 641, [1989] IRLR 379, EAT; affd [1990] ICR 768, [1990] IRLR 231, CA.

9   See the Race Relations Act 1976 s 5(2); and heads (1)–(4) in the text. The provision applies where some only of the duties of the job fall within heads (1)–(4) in the text as well as where all of them do: s 5(3). These provisions do not apply in relation to the filling of a vacancy at a time when an employer already has employees of the racial group in question who are capable of carrying out the duties falling within heads (1)–(4) in the text, whom it would be reasonable to employ on those duties, and whose numbers are sufficient to meet the employer's likely requirements in respect of those duties without undue inconvenience: s 5(4). As to the application of s 5 (as amended) to governing bodies of schools and institutions of higher or further education where such bodies have delegated budgets see the Education (Modification of Enactments Relating to Employment) (England) Order 2003, SI 2003/1964, art 3, Schedule; and the Education (Modification of Enactments Relating to Employment) (Wales) Order 2006, SI 2006/1073, art 3, Schedule.

10   Race Relations Act 1976 s 5(2)(a).

11   Ibid s 5(2)(b).

12   Ibid s 5(2)(c).

13   Ibid s 5(2)(d). See note 14 infra.

14   The scope of this provision has been considered by the courts, particularly in the context of local authorities seeking to recruit employees belonging to particular ethnic minorities: see *Tottenham Green Under Fives' Centre v Marshall* [1989] ICR 214, [1989] IRLR 147, EAT (the respondent centre advertised for an Afro-Caribbean worker with a personal awareness of Caribbean culture to work at a nursery where an ethnic balance was maintained among the children). The Court of Appeal in *Lambeth London Borough Council v Commission for Racial Equality* [1990] ICR 768, [1990] IRLR 231, CA, indorsed the Employment Appeal Tribunal's approach in *Tottenham Green Under Fives' Centre v Marshall* supra (see heads (a)–(e) in the text). The court emphasised the need for the post-holder to be involved in the provision of personal services, meaning services that are individual and private, and involving direct contact between giver and recipient. The tribunal's decision that two managerial posts in the respondent's housing benefit department did not involve the provision of personal services was upheld.

        The Race Relations Act 1976 s 5(2)(d) should not be regarded as concerned with the promotion of positive action to meet the special needs of particular racial groups, akin to ss 35, 37, 38 (s 37 as amended) (see paras 482, 484 post): *Lambeth London Borough Council v Commission for Racial Equality* supra.

        When *Tottenham Green Under Fives' Centre v Marshall* supra was remitted to a tribunal for rehearing, the tribunal found that one of the services to be provided by the nursery worker, that of reading and talking to the children in patois, could be more effectively provided by an Afro-Caribbean. However, the tribunal took the view that this service was merely a 'desirable extra' for the post-holder, and that the defence under the Race Relations Act 1976 s 5 was not made out. The case returned to the Employment Appeal Tribunal as *Tottenham Green Under Fives' Centre v Marshall (No 2)* [1991] ICR 320, [1991] IRLR 162, EAT, and this approach was rejected. With the exception of duties which are so trivial as to be de minimis, or which are a sham, included to circumvent the Race Relations Act 1976, a tribunal may not disregard any duty performed by the post-holder.

15   *Tottenham Green Under Fives' Centre v Marshall* [1989] ICR 214, EAT, at 218 per Wood J. The racial group may, however, be defined by colour: *Lambeth London Borough Council v Commission for Racial Equality* [1990] ICR 768, [1990] IRLR 231, CA.

16   *Tottenham Green Under Fives' Centre v Marshall* [1989] ICR 214, EAT, at 218 per Wood J.

17   *Tottenham Green Under Fives' Centre v Marshall* [1989] ICR 214, EAT, at 218 per Wood J. For a similar conclusion reached in the context of the Sex Discrimination Act 1975 see *Timex Corpn v Hodgson* [1982] ICR 63, [1981] IRLR 530, EAT.

18   *Tottenham Green Under Fives' Centre v Marshall* [1989] ICR 214, EAT, at 219 per Wood J.

19   *Tottenham Green Under Fives' Centre v Marshall* [1989] ICR 214, EAT, at 219 per Wood J. This is a matter of fact to be decided by a tribunal, balancing the need to guard against discrimination and the need to promote racial integration. The tribunal should give considerable weight to the conscious decision of a responsible employer to commit an act of discrimination and rely on the exception in the Race Relations Act 1976 s 5: see *Tottenham Green Under Fives' Centre v Marshall* supra at 219 per Wood J.

20   As to the meaning of 'act' see para 442 note 7 ante.

21   Race Relations Act 1976 s 6 (amended by the amended by the Race Relations Act 1976 (Amendment) Regulations 2003, SI 2003/1626, reg 9). For the meaning of 'Great Britain' see para 325 note 6 ante.

22   As to the meaning of 'pay' in this context see para 446 note 5 ante.

23   Race Relations Act 1976 s 9(1) (amended by the Race Relations Act 1976 (Seamen Recruited Abroad) Order 2003, SI 2003/1651, art 2(1), (2)). For the purposes of this provision, a person brought to Great Britain with a view to his entering into an agreement in Great Britain to be employed on any ship is to be treated as having applied for the employment outside Great Britain: Race Relations Act 1976 s 9(4). This exception does not apply to employment or work concerned with exploration of the sea bed or subsoil or the exploitation of their natural resources in any area for the time being designated under the Continental Shelf Act 1964 s 1(7) (as amended: see FUEL AND ENERGY vol 19(2) (Reissue) para 1411), not being an area or part of an area in which the law of Northern Ireland applies: Race Relations Act 1976 s 9(3). This provision is prospectively amended by the Petroleum Act 1998 s 50, Sch 4 para 11 as from a day to be appointed by order made under s 52. At the date at which this volume states the law, no such day had been appointed.

(B) Particular Forms of Employment

448.   Contract workers.   The Race Relations Act 1976 makes special provision to protect employees who are contracted out by their employers to work for other people, and who may suffer discrimination from a person who is not their employer[1].

It is unlawful for a principal[2], in relation to such work, to discriminate[3] against a contract worker[4] in the terms on which he allows him to do the work[5], or by not allowing him to do it or to continue to do it[6], or in the way he affords him access to any benefits, facilities or services[7] or by refusing or deliberately omitting to afford him access to them[8], or by subjecting him to any other detriment[9].

It is unlawful for the principal, in relation to such work to subject a contract worker to harassment[10].

These provisions are modified in their application to governing bodies of schools and institutions of higher education where such bodies have delegated budgets[11].

1   See the Race Relations Act 1976 s 7 (as amended); the text and notes 2–11 infra; and para 449 post.

2   Ie a person who has work available for contract workers (see note 4 infra): see ibid s 7(1). As to the meaning of 'person' see para 344 note 3 ante.

3   For the meaning of 'discrimination' see para 447 note 4 ante.

4   Ie an individual who is employed not by the principal himself but by another person who supplies him under a contract made with the principal: see the Race Relations Act 1976 s 7(1). The definition of 'employment' in s 78(1) as employment under a contract of service or of apprenticeship or a contract personally to execute any work or labour is wide enough to include as contract workers those who are self-employed: see para 446 ante. However, the work done by the contract worker must be supplied by

the employer as a contractual obligation to the principal. Where the employer has no obligation to the principal to supply the worker, s 7 (as amended) does not apply: see *Rice v Fon-A-Car* [1980] ICR 133, EAT (in the context of the comparable provisions of the Sex Discrimination Act 1975 s 9 (as then in force) (see para 365 ante)). It is not necessary that the principal exercises managerial power or control over those doing the work, nor that the supply of workers is the primary or dominant purpose of the contract between the principal and the employer: *Harrods Ltd v Remick* [1998] 1 All ER 52, [1997] IRLR 583, CA. See also *CJ O'Shea Construction Ltd v Bassi* [1998] ICR 1130, EAT. Youth Opportunities Programme trainees, and, presumably, comparable trainees on government schemes, are not contract workers, because, if they are employed under a contract at all, it is a training contract, and not a contract to execute work: *Daley v Allied Suppliers Ltd* [1983] ICR 90, [1983] IRLR 14, EAT. As to the application of the Race Relations Act 1976 to such trainees see s 13 (as substituted and amended); and para 453 post.

5 Ibid s 7(2)(a).
6 Ibid s 7(2)(b). As to the similar provisions relating to employers see s 4(1)(b), (c); and para 446 ante.
7 As to benefits, facilities or services see para 446 ante.
8 Race Relations Act 1976 s 7(2)(c). For the similar provision relating to employers see s 4(2)(b); and para 446 ante. This provision does not apply to benefits, facilities or services of any description if the principal is concerned with the provision (for payment or not) of benefits, facilities or services of that description to the public, or to a section of the public to which the contract worker in question belongs, unless that provision differs in a material respect from the provision of the benefits, facilities or services by the principal to his contract workers: s 7(5). Discrimination in the provision of the benefits, facilities or services to the public is rendered unlawful by s 20 (as amended): see para 461 post.
9 Ibid s 7(2)(d). For the similar provision relating to employers see s 4(2)(c); and para 446 ante. As to the meaning of 'detriment' see paras 440 note 12, 446 note 17 ante.
10 Ibid s 7(3A) (added by the Race Relations Act 1976 (Amendment) Regulations 2003, SI 2003/1626, reg 10(2)(b)). For the meaning of 'harassment' see para 444 ante.
11 See the Education (Modification of Enactments Relating to Employment) (England) Order 2003, SI 2003/1964, art 3(1), Schedule; and the Education (Modification of Enactments Relating to Employment) (Wales) Order 2006, SI 2006/1073, art 3, Schedule.

449. Exceptions to contract work discrimination. There are a number of particular exceptions[1] to the operation of the Race Relations Act 1976 as regards contract workers and their principals, which are analogous to the exceptions covering the acts of employers[2].

The Act is not contravened if a principal[3] does any act[4] in relation to a person not of a particular racial group[5], or not of a particular race or particular ethnic or national origins, at a time when, if the work were to be done by a person taken into the principal's employment, being of that racial group or of that race or those origins would be a genuine occupational qualification or, as the case may be, that act would be lawful[6], for the job[7].

The Act does not render unlawful any act done by a principal on grounds other than those of race or ethnic or national origins, for the benefit of a contract worker[8] not ordinarily resident in Great Britain[9] in or in connection with allowing him to do work, where the purpose of his being allowed to do that work is to provide him with training skills which he appears to the principal to intend to exercise wholly outside Great Britain[10].

The exception applies to the extent that the act relates to the pay[11] the person receives in respect of his work, and amounts to discrimination against the person on the basis of his nationality[12].

1 For general exceptions to the Race Relations Act 1976 see paras 481–487 post.
2 See para 447 ante.
3 For the meaning of 'principal' see para 448 note 2 ante.
4 As to the meaning of 'act' see para 442 note 7 ante.
5 For the meaning of 'racial group' see para 441 ante. As to the meanings of 'ethnic origins' and 'national origins' see para 441 ante.
6 Ie lawful by virtue of the Race Relations Act 1976 s 4A (as added): see para 446 ante.
7 Ibid s 7(3) (amended by the Race Relations Act 1976 (Amendment) Regulations 2003, SI 2003/1626, reg 10(2)(a)). As to the scope of the exception where race is a genuine occupational qualification for the job see the Race Relations Act 1976 s 5 (as amended); and para 447 ante.

8   For the meaning of 'contract worker' see para 448 note 4 ante.

9   For the meaning of 'Great Britain' see para 325 note 6 ante.

10   Race Relations Act 1976 s 7(4) (amended by the Race Relations Act 1976 (Amendment) Regulations 2003, SI 2003/1626, reg 10(2)(c)).

11   As to the meaning of 'pay' in this context see para 446 note 5 ante.

12   Race Relations Act 1976 s 9(2) (amended by the Race Relations Act 1976 (Seamen Recruited Abroad) Order 2003, SI 2003/1651, art 2(1), (3)). This exception does not apply to employment or work concerned with the exploration of the sea bed or subsoil or the exploitation of their natural resources in any area for the time being designated under the Continental Shelf Act 1964 s 1(7) (as amended: see FUEL AND ENERGY vol 19(2) (Reissue) para 1411), not being an area or part of an area to which the law of Northern Ireland applies: Race Relations Act 1976 s 9(3). This provision is prospectively amended by the Petroleum Act 1998 s 50, Sch 4 para 11 as from a day to be appointed by order made under s 52. At the date at which this volume states the law, no such day had been appointed.

450.   Discrimination and harassment in partnerships. It is unlawful for a firm[1] consisting of six or more partners[2], in relation to a position as partner in the firm, to discriminate[3] against a person[4]: (1) in the arrangements it makes for the purpose of determining who should be offered that position[5]; (2) in the terms on which it offers him that position[6]; or (3) by refusing or deliberately omitting to offer him that position[7].

In the case of an existing partner, it is unlawful for the firm to discriminate against him in the way it affords him access to any benefits, facilities or services[8], or by refusing or deliberately omitting to afford him access to them[9], or by expelling him from his position as a partner, or subjecting him to any other detriment[10].

It is also unlawful for a firm, in relation to a position as a partner in the firm, to subject to harassment[11] a person who holds or has applied for that position[12].

1   'Firm' has the meaning given by the Partnership Act 1890 s 4 (see PARTNERSHIP vol 35 (Reissue) para 1): Race Relations Act 1976 s 78(1). The provisions of the Race Relations Act 1976 s 10(1), (1A), (1B) (as added) apply in relation to persons proposing to form themselves into a partnership as they apply in relation to a firm: s 10(2) (amended by the Race Relations Act 1976 (Amendment) Regulations 2003, SI 2003/1626, reg 12(b)). As to discrimination in partnerships generally see PARTNERSHIP vol 35 (Reissue) para 100. See note 2 infra.

2   In the case of a limited partnership, references to a partner are to be construed as references to a general partner as defined in the Limited Partnerships Act 1907 s 3 (as amended) (see PARTNERSHIP vol 35 (Reissue) para 207): Race Relations Act 1976 s 10(4). Section 10 (as amended) applies to a limited liability partnership as it applies to a firm; and, in its application to a limited liability partnership, references to a partner in a firm are references to a member of the limited liability partnership: s 10(5) (added by the Limited Liability Partnership Regulations 2001, SI 2001/1090, reg 9(1), Sch 5 para 7).

The limitation of the Race Relations Act 1976 s 10(1) (as amended) to six or more partners does not apply in relation to discrimination on grounds of race or ethnic or national origins: s 10(1A) (added by the Race Relations Act 1976 (Amendment) Regulations 2003, SI 2003/1626, reg 12(a)). For the meaning of 'discrimination' see para 447 note 4 ante. As to the meanings of 'ethnic origins' and 'national origins' see para 441 ante. See note 1 supra.

3   See note 2 supra.

4   Race Relations Act 1976 s 10(1). As to the meaning of 'person' see para 344 note 3 ante.

5   Ibid s 10(1)(a). For the similar provision relating to employers see s 4(1)(a); and para 446 ante. Heads (1) and (3) in the text do not apply to a position as partner where, if it were employment, s 4A (as added) (see para 446 ante) or s 5 (as amended) (see para 447 ante) would apply to such employment: s 10(3) (amended by the Race Relations Act 1976 (Amendment) Regulations 2003, SI 2003/1626, reg 12(c)). For the meaning of 'employment' see para 446 note 3 ante.

6   Race Relations Act 1976 s 10(1)(b). For the similar provision relating to employers see s 4(1)(b); and para 446 ante.

7   Ibid s 10(1)(c). For the similar provision relating to employers see s 4(1)(c); and para 446 ante. Heads (1) and (3) in the text do not apply to a position as partner where, if it were employment, s 4A (as added) (see para 446 ante) or s 5 (as amended) (see para 447 ante) would apply to such employment: s 10(3) (as amended: see note 5 supra). As to genuine occupational qualifications see s 5 (as amended); and para 447 ante.

8   As to the affording of access to benefits, facilities or services see para 446 note 14 ante.

9   For the similar provision relating to employers see the Race Relations Act 1976 s 4(2)(b); and para 446 ante.

10   Ibid s 10(1)(d). For the similar provision relating to employers see s 4(2)(c); and para 446 ante. As to the
     meaning of 'detriment' see paras 440 note 12, 446 note 17 ante. In relation to their employees,
     partnerships are subject to the Race Relations Act 1976 s 4 (as amended): see para 446 ante. A trainee
     solicitor should be regarded as employed by the firm, rather than by an individual partner: *Oliver v JP
     Malnick & Co* [1983] 3 All ER 795, [1983] ICR 708, EAT.
         The reference in the Race Relations Act 1976 s 10(1)(d) to the expulsion of a person from a position
     as partner includes, where the discrimination is on grounds of race or ethnic or national origins,
     reference: (1) to the termination of that person's partnership by the expiration of any period, including a
     period expiring by reference to an event or circumstance, not being a termination immediately after
     which the partnership is renewed on the same terms; and (2) to the termination of that person's
     partnership by any act of his, including the giving of notice, in circumstances such that he is entitled to
     terminate it without notice by reason of the conduct of the other partners: s 10(6) (added by the Race
     Relations Act 1976 (Amendment) Regulations 2003, SI 2003/1626, reg 12(d)).
11   For the meaning of 'harassment' see para 444 ante.
12   Race Relations Act 1976 s 10(1B) (added by the Race Relations Act 1976 (Amendment)
     Regulations 2003, SI 2003/1626, reg 12(a)). See note 1 supra.

**451. Discrimination and harassment by trade unions and employers'
associations.** It is unlawful for an organisation of workers, an organisation of
employers, or any other organisation whose members carry on a particular profession[1]
or trade[2] for the purposes of which the organisation exists[3] to discriminate[4] against a
person who is not a member of the organisation[5] in the terms on which it is prepared to
admit him to membership[6], or by refusing, or deliberately omitting to accept, his
application for membership[7].

It is unlawful for such an organisation to discriminate against a person who is a
member of the organisation[8] in the way it affords him access to any benefits, facilities or
services[9], or by refusing or deliberately omitting to afford him access to them[10], or by
depriving him of membership, or varying the terms on which he is a member[11], or by
subjecting him to any other detriment[12].

It is also unlawful for an organisation of workers, an organisation of employers, or any
other organisation whose members carry on a particular profession or trade for the
purposes of which the organisation exists, in relation to a person's membership or
application for membership of that organisation, to subject him to harassment[13].

1   'Profession' includes any vocation or occupation: Race Relations Act 1976 s 78(1). A professional society
    is an 'organisation of workers': *Sadek v Medical Protection Society* [2004] EWCA Civ 865, [2004] 4 All ER
    118.
2   'Trade' includes any business: Race Relations Act 1976 s 78(1).
3   See ibid s 11(1). An individual chapel of a national trade union may be an 'organisation of workers'
    within the meaning of s 11 (as amended), and may consequently be proceeded against for discrimination
    separately from the national union: *Record Production Chapel of the Daily Record and Sunday Mail Ltd, West
    Branch of the Scottish Graphical Division of SOGAT '82 v Turnbull* (16 April 1984), Lexis. As to other
    associations and clubs see the Race Relations Act 1976 s 25; and para 465 post.
        Trade unions have an important role to play in the promotion of equality of opportunity in the
    workplace (and may also be instrumental in retarding the progress of equality: see *R v Commission for
    Racial Equality, ex p Westminster City Council* [1985] ICR 827, [1985] IRLR 426, CA (where the threat of
    industrial action by white workers, including union shop stewards, motivated the employers to
    discriminate against a black employee). The Race Relations Act 1976 s 31 (as amended), which prohibits
    pressure to commit unlawful acts (see para 475 post), and s 33 (as amended), which imposes liability upon
    persons who knowingly aid another to do an unlawful act of discrimination (see para 477 post), may be
    particularly relevant to acts by trade unions. For example, a trade union must not pressure or aid an
    employer to maintain practices involving the restriction of the numbers of a particular racial group in a
    section, grade or department, or to maintain indirectly discriminatory practices in recruitment or
    transfer, training and promotion.
        Trade unions may take positive action to encourage and provide training for members of a particular
    racial group which is under-represented in trade union membership or activities: see s 38; and para 484
    post.

Part 5 of the Statutory Code of Practice on Racial Equality in Employment (April 2006) concerns the responsibilities of trade unions and other employers' associations. As to the admissibility of the Statutory Code of Practice on Racial Equality in Employment (April 2006) as evidence see para 491 post.

4 For the meaning of 'discrimination' see para 447 note 4 ante.
5 Race Relations Act 1976 s 11(2).
6 Ibid s 11(2)(a).
7 Ibid s 11(2)(b). For a successful action brought under the comparable provisions of the Sex Discrimination Act 1975 against a chapel of SOGAT '82 which excluded women see *Record Production Chapel of the Daily Record and Sunday Mail Ltd, West Branch of the Scottish Graphical Division of SOGAT '82 v Turnbull* (16 April 1984, unreported), EAT/955/83 (Transcript).
8 Race Relations Act 1976 s 11(3).
9 As to the affording of access to benefits, facilities and services see para 446 note 14 ante.
10 Race Relations Act 1976 s 11(3)(a). For the similar provision relating to employers see s 4(2)(b); and para 446 ante. In *Weaver v National Association of Teachers in Further and Higher Education* [1988] ICR 599, EAT, a trade union refused to support a member in bringing a complaint of racial discrimination against a fellow member, on the grounds that it was union policy not to support a member of the union where the tenure of another member was at risk, and that the complaint was without merit; the tribunal, in a decision upheld by the Employment Appeal Tribunal, held that the union had an obligation to provide legal advice and assistance to its members, and that its refusal was potentially a refusal of a service under the Race Relations Act 1976 s 11(3)(a); however, on the facts, there was no discrimination. In *Furniture, Timber and Allied Trades Union v Modgill, Pel Ltd v Modgill* [1980] IRLR 142, EAT, it was held that the tribunal was wrong to find that the union had discriminated against Asian members by giving them insufficient support or information, when there was no evidence that union members of other racial groups were treated any more favourably by the union.
11 Race Relations Act 1976 s 11(3)(b).
12 Ibid s 11(3)(c). For the similar provision relating to employers see s 4(2)(c); and para 446 ante. As to the meaning of 'detriment' see paras 440 note 12, 446 note 17 ante.
13 Ibid s 11(4) (added by the Race Relations Act 1976 (Amendment) Regulations 2003, SI 2003/1626, reg 13). For the meaning of 'harassment' see para 444 ante.

452. Discrimination and harassment by qualifying bodies. It is unlawful for an authority or body which can confer an authorisation or qualification[1] which is needed for, or facilitates, engagement in a particular profession or trade[2] to discriminate[3] against a person[4] in the terms on which it is prepared to confer[5] on him an authorisation or qualification[6], or by refusing or deliberately omitting to grant his application for it[7], or by withdrawing it from him or varying the terms on which he holds it[8].

It is also unlawful for an authority or body which can confer an authorisation or qualification which is needed for, or facilitates, engagement in a particular profession or trade, in relation to an authorisation or qualification conferred by it, to subject to harassment[9] a person who holds or applies for such an authorisation or qualification[10].

1 'Authorisation or qualification' includes recognition, registration, enrolment, approval and certification: Race Relations Act 1976 s 12(2)(a).
2 Ibid s 12(1). As to the meaning of 'profession' see para 451 note 1 ante; and as to the meaning of 'trade' see para 451 note 2 ante. The test of whether a body is within the ambit of this provision is whether the qualification conferred by it in fact facilitates engagement, not whether it is intended to do so: *British Judo Association v Petty* [1981] ICR 660, [1981] IRLR 484, EAT (British Judo Association held to be the qualifying body for judo referees). In *Hampson v Department of Education and Science* [1990] 2 All ER 25, [1989] ICR 179, CA (revsd on other grounds [1991] 1 AC 171, [1990] 2 All ER 513, HL), the respondents conceded that the Secretary of State for Education was a qualifying body for the purposes of the Race Relations Act 1976 s 12(1), when exercising his statutory function of notifying applicants that they were qualified teachers, without which notification teachers could not be employed as teachers in schools (see EDUCATION vol 15(2) (2006 Reissue) para 776); but Russell LJ doubted whether the concession was rightly made. It was conceded in *R v Department of Health, ex p Gandhi* [1991] 4 All ER 547, [1991] 1 WLR 1053, DC, that the Medical Practices Committee was a qualifying body (see MEDICAL PROFESSIONS vol 30(1) (Reissue) para 25). Note that the Medical Practices Committee has been abolished and its property, rights and liabilities transferred to the Secretary of State: see the Health and Social Care Act 2001 s 14(1), (2); and NATIONAL HEALTH SERVICE vol 33 (Reissue) para 183 et seq. A body which does not have the power to confer an authorisation or qualification which is needed for, or facilitates, engagement in a particular profession or trade, but which merely stipulates for its

commercial agreements that a particular qualification is required is not an authority or body within the meaning of the Race Relations Act 1976 s 12: *Tattari v Private Patients Plan Ltd* [1998] ICR 106, [1997] IRLR 586, CA. See also *Arthur v A-G* [1999] ICR 631, EAT (leave to appeal to Court of Appeal was given). See further *Sawyer v Ahsan* [2000] ICR 1, [1999] IRLR 609, EAT (Labour Party was treated as a qualifying body in relation to a Labour councillor's unsuccessful application for re-adoption; the Employment Appeal Tribunal also held that the Race Relations Act 1976 s 12 could apply to non-employment relationships). A political party, in conferring an approval on a member seeking selection as a party candidate, is not a 'qualifying body' for the purposes of s 12(1): *McDonagh v Ali* [2002] EWCA Civ 93, [2002] ICR 1026, [2002] All ER (D) 87 (Feb).

3   For the meaning of 'discrimination' see para 447 note 4 ante.

4   Race Relations Act 1976 s 12(1).

5   'Confer' includes renew or extend: ibid s 12(2)(b).

6   Ibid s 12(1)(a). See *Patterson v Legal Services Commission* [2003] EWCA Civ 1558, [2004] ICR 312, [2004] IRLR 153.

7   Race Relations Act 1976 s 12(1)(b). See *Patterson v Legal Services Commission* [2003] EWCA Civ 1558, [2004] ICR 312, [2004] IRLR 153.

8   Race Relations Act 1976 s 12(1)(c). Section 12 (as amended) does not apply to discrimination rendered unlawful by s 17 (as amended) or s 18 (as amended) (see para 460 post): s 12(3) (substituted by the Race Relations Act 1976 (Amendment) Regulations 2003, SI 2003/1626, reg 14(b)).

A complainant may not present to an employment tribunal a complaint of an act in breach of the Race Relations Act 1976 s 12(1) in respect of which an appeal, or proceedings in the nature of an appeal, may be brought under any enactment: see s 54(2) (amended by the Armed Forces Act 1996 s 35(2), Sch 7 Pt III). As to the meaning of 'act' see para 442 note 7 ante. In such cases, the complainant's redress is through the statutory appeal procedure: *Wadi v Cornwall and Isles of Scilly Family Practitioner Committee* [1985] ICR 492, EAT. Where a complainant alleges racial discrimination against a qualifying body in breach of the Race Relations Act 1976 s 12 (as amended), and pursues his statutory right to appeal, the body determining the appeal is not obliged to pronounce separately on the complaint of discrimination, or to grant any specific redress in relation to it, but it is required to consider the provisions of the Act in its determination of the appeal. If, for example the complainant was denied authorisation by a qualifying body solely on racial grounds, his appeal should be allowed. An oral hearing of the appeal is not obligatory, but should be held where in all the circumstances the issue cannot be fairly resolved otherwise. The complainant is entitled to disclosure of all documents necessary to present his appeal. See *R v Department of Health, ex p Gandhi* [1991] 4 All ER 547, [1991] 1 WLR 1053, DC (appeal by a doctor in relation to a decision of the Medical Practices Committee (now abolished: see note 2 supra)). An employment tribunal has no jurisdiction to consider a doctor's complaint of discrimination in relation to a decision of the General Medical Council Review Board for Overseas Practitioners, as the review board procedure under the Medical Act 1983 amounts to proceedings in the nature of an appeal: *Khan v General Medical Council* [1996] ICR 1032, [1994] IRLR 646, CA. See also *Pathak v Secretary of State for Health, Chaudhary v Specialist Training Authority Appeal Panel* (2004) 80 BMLR 151, [2004] All ER (D) 29 (Jan); *Chaudhary v Specialist Training Authority Appeal Panel (No 2)* [2005] EWCA Civ 282, [2005] ICR 1086, [2005] All ER (D) 256 (Mar).

9   For the meaning of 'harassment' see para 444 ante.

10   Race Relations Act 1976 s 12(1A) (added by the Race Relations Act 1976 (Amendment) Regulations 2003, SI 2003/1626, reg 14(a)).

453.   Discrimination and harassment in the context of vocational training.
It is unlawful, in the case of an individual seeking or undergoing training[1] which would help fit him for any employment[2], for any person[3] who provides, or makes arrangements for the provision of, facilities for such training to discriminate against him[4] in the terms on which that person affords him access to any training course or other facilities concerned with such training[5], or by refusing or deliberately omitting to afford him such access[6], or by terminating his training[7], or by subjecting him to any detriment during the course of his training[8].

It is unlawful for any person who provides, or makes arrangements for the provision of, facilities for training as above[9], in relation to such facilities or training, to subject to harassment[10] a person to whom he provides such training or who is seeking to undergo such training[11].

It is unlawful for the Secretary of State[12] to discriminate or subject a person to harassment in the provision of facilities or services[13] for the purpose of assisting persons to select, train for, obtain and retain employment suitable for their ages and capacities or of assisting persons to obtain suitable employees[14].

1   As to the meaning of 'training' see para 446 note 13 ante.
2   As to the meaning of 'employment' see para 446 note 3 ante.
3   As to the meaning of 'person' see para 344 note 3 ante. As to the liability of principals and employers for the acts of their servants or agents see the Race Relations Act 1976 s 32; and para 476 post. As to the liability of those who knowingly aid unlawful acts see s 33 (as amended); and para 477 post.
4   Ibid s 13(1) (s 13 substituted by the Employment Act 1989 s 7(2)). For the meaning of 'discrimination' see para 447 note 4 ante. The Race Relations Act 1976 s 13 (as substituted) does not apply to discrimination which would be rendered unlawful by s 4(1) or (2) (discrimination against employees) (see para 446 ante) or by s 17 (as amended) or s 18 (as amended) (see para 460 post), or which would be rendered unlawful by any of those provisions but for the operation of any other provision of the Act: s 13(2) (as so substituted).
    Formerly, section 13 (as amended) applied only to specified government agencies. The new provisions protect trainees from discrimination inflicted by private employers with whom they are undergoing training. Such arrangements are not covered by the employment provisions of s 4 (as amended) or s 7 (as amended) (see paras 446–449 ante): *Daley v Allied Suppliers Ltd* [1983] ICR 90, [1983] IRLR 14, EAT. See also *Chenge v Treasury Solicitors Department* [2007] All ER (D) 203 (Feb), EAT (in regard to what was included within 'training' in the context of a claim under the Race Relations Act 1976 s 13 (as substituted)); and para 446 ante.
5   Race Relations Act 1976 s 13(1)(a) (as substituted: see note 4 supra).
6   Ibid s 13(1)(b) (as substituted: see note 4 supra). As to the affording of access to facilities see para 446 note 14 ante.
7   Ibid s 13(1)(c) (as substituted: see note 4 supra).
8   Ibid s 13(1)(d) (as substituted: see note 4 supra). As to the meaning of 'detriment' see paras 440 note 12, 446 note 17 ante.
9   Ie to which ibid s 13(1) (as substituted) applies.
10 For the meaning of 'harassment' see para 444 ante.
11 Race Relations Act 1976 s 13(3) (s 13(3), (4) added by the Race Relations Act 1976 (Amendment) Regulations 2003, SI 2003/1626, reg 15). The Race Relations Act 1976 s 13(3) (as added) does not apply to harassment which is rendered unlawful by s 4(2A) (as added) (see para 446 ante) or by s 17 (as amended) or s 18 (as amended) (see para 460 post): s 13(4) (as so added).
12 As to the Secretary of State and the National Assembly for Wales see para 302 ante.
13 Ie under the Employment and Training Act 1973 s 2 (as substituted and amended): see EMPLOYMENT vol 16(1B) (Reissue) para 765.
14 See the Race Relations Act 1976 s 15(1) (substituted by the Employment and Training Act 1981 s 9, Sch 2 para 20; and amended by the Employment Act 1988 s 33(1), Sch 3 para 12(2); the Employment Act 1989 s 29(4), Sch 7 Pt I; and the Race Relations Act 1976 (Amendment) Regulations 2003, SI 2003/1626, reg 17). This provision does not apply where the Race Relations Act 1976 s 13 (as amended) applies, or where the Secretary of State is acting as an employment agency: s 15(2) (amended by the Employment Act 1989 s 29(3), Sch 6 para 15). As to employment agencies see para 454 post.

454. Discrimination and harassment by employment agencies. It is unlawful for an employment agency[1] to discriminate[2] against a person in the terms on which the agency offers to provide any of its services[3], or by refusing or deliberately omitting to provide any of its services, or in the way it provides any of its services[4].

It is unlawful for an employment agency, in relation to the provision of its services, to subject to harassment[5] a person to whom it provides such services or who requests the provision of such services[6].

It is unlawful for a local education authority or an education authority or any other person to do any act in the performance of its statutory functions of providing a careers service[7] which constitutes discrimination or harassment[8].

These provisions do not apply if the discrimination only concerns employment which the employer could lawfully refuse to offer the person in question[9].

1   'Employment agency' means a person who, for profit or not, provides services for the purpose of finding employment for workers or supplying employers with workers: Race Relations Act 1976 s 78(1). As to the meaning of 'person' see para 344 note 3 ante. See *Rice v Fon-A-Car* [1980] ICR 133, EAT, for an inconclusive discussion of the parallel provision under the Sex Discrimination Act 1975. The head of

careers at a school, when asked by an employer to supply a school leaver for a vacancy, is acting as an employment agency: *Commission for Racial Equality v Imperial Society of Teachers of Dancing* [1983] ICR 473, [1983] IRLR 315, EAT.

2   For the meaning of 'discrimination' see para 447 note 4 ante.

3   References in the Race Relations Act 1976 s 14(1) and s 14(1A) (as added) to the services of an employment agency include guidance on careers and any other services related to employment: s 14(3) (amended by the Race Relations Act 1976 (Amendment) Regulations 2003, SI 2003/1626, reg 16(c)). For the meaning of 'employment' see para 446 note 3 ante.

4   Race Relations Act 1976 s 14(1).

5   For the meaning of 'harassment' see para 444 ante.

6   Race Relations Act 1976 s 14(1A) (added by the Race Relations Act 1976 (Amendment) Regulations 2003, SI 2003/1626, reg 16(a)).

7   Ie under the Employment and Training Act 1973 s 10 (as substituted): see EMPLOYMENT vol 16(1B) (Reissue) para 771. As to local education authorities and education authorities see EDUCATION vol 15(1) (2006 Reissue) para 20 et seq.

8   Race Relations Act 1976 s 14(2) (substituted by the Trade Union Reform and Employment Rights Act 1993 s 49(2), Sch 8 para 9; and amended by the Race Relations Act 1976 (Amendment) Regulations 2003, SI 2003/1626, reg 16(b)).

9   Race Relations Act 1976 s 14(4). An employment agency, local education authority, education authority or other person is not subject to any liability under s 14 (as amended) if it proves: (1) that it acted in reliance on a statement made to it by the employer to the effect that the employment is employment which the employer could lawfully refuse to offer the person in question, so that the agency's or authority's actions would not be unlawful; and (2) that it was reasonable for it to rely on the employer's statement: see s 14(5) (amended by the Trade Union Reform and Employment Rights Act 1993 Sch 8 para 9).

  A person who knowingly or recklessly makes such a statement which in a material respect is false or misleading commits an offence, and is liable on summary conviction to a fine not exceeding level 5 on the standard scale: Race Relations Act 1976 s 14(6) (amended by virtue of the Criminal Justice Act 1982 ss 38, 46). As to the standard scale see para 315 note 15 ante.

455.   Discrimination in the police. For the purposes of the provisions on discrimination in the employment field[1], the holding of a relevant police office[2] is treated as employment[3]: (1) by the chief officer of police[4] as respects any act done by him in relation to that office or a holder of it[5]; (2) by the police authority as respects any act done by it in relation to that office or a holder of it[6]. For the purposes of the provisions on the liability of employers and principals[7]: (a) the holding of a relevant police office is be treated as employment by the chief officer of police (and as not being employment by any other person)[8]; and (b) anything done by a person holding such an office in the performance, or purported performance, of his functions is treated as done in the course of that employment[9].

There is be paid out of the police fund: (i) any compensation, costs or expenses awarded against a chief officer of police in any proceedings brought against him under the Race Relations Act 1976, and any costs or expenses incurred by him in any such proceedings so far as not recovered by him in the proceedings[10]; and (ii) any sum required by a chief officer of police for the settlement of any claim made against him under the Act if the settlement is approved by the police authority[11]. A police authority may, in such cases and to such extent as appear to it to be appropriate, pay out of the police fund: (A) any damages or costs awarded in proceedings under the Race Relations Act 1976 against a person under the direction and control of the chief officer of police[12]; (B) any costs incurred and not recovered by such a person in such proceedings[13]; and (C) any sum required in connection with the settlement of a claim that has or might have given rise to such proceedings[14].

1   Ie the Race Relations Act 1976 Pt II (ss 4–15) (as amended): see paras 446–454 ante.

2   For these purposes, 'relevant police office' means: (1) the office of constable held as a member of a police force, or on appointment as a special constable for a police area; or (2) an appointment as police cadet to undergo training with a view to becoming a member of a police force: ibid s 76A(1) (ss 76A, 76B added

by the Race Relations (Amendment) Act 2000 s 4). As to the office of constable generally see POLICE vol 36(1) (Reissue) para 201 et seq. As to cadets generally see POLICE vol 36(1) (Reissue) para 213 et seq.
3   For the meaning of 'employment' see para 446 note 3 ante.
4   For the meaning of 'chief officer of police' see POLICE vol 36(1) (Reissue) para 205 note 6.
5   Race Relations Act 1976 s 76A(2)(a) (as added: see note 2 supra).
      Section 76A (as added) replaces s 16 (as amended), which is repealed: one of the aims of the new provisions is to impose vicarious liability on a chief constable e g in a case where an officer alleges discrimination or harassment by a fellow officer. It seems that this was not the situation under the former provisions: *Chief Constable of Bedfordshire Police v Liversidge* [2002] EWCA Civ 894, [2002] ICR 1135, [2002] IRLR 651.
      The Race Relations Act 1976 s 76A (as added) applies in relation to any other body of constables or cadets as it applies in relation to a police force, but as if any reference: (1) to the chief officer of police were to the officer or other person who has the direction and control of the body in question; (2) to the police authority were to the authority by whom the members of the body are paid; (3) to the police fund were to money provided by that authority: s 76B(2) (as added (see note 2 supra); and amended by the Serious Organised Crime and Police Act 2005 ss 59, 174(2), Sch 4 paras 33, 34(1), (3), Sch 17 Pt 2). Constables serving with the Serious Organised Crime Agency do not constitute a body of constables for the purposes of the Race Relations Act 1976 s 76B(2) (as added and amended): s 76B(2A) (s 76B as so added; and s 76B(2A) added by the Serious Organised Crime and Police Act 2005 Sch 4 paras 33, 34(1), (4)). In relation to a member of a police force or a special constable who is not under the direction and control of the chief officer of police for that police force or, as the case may be, for the police area to which he is appointed, references in the Race Relations Act 1976 s 76A (as added) to the chief officer of police are references to the chief officer under whose direction and control he is: s 76B(3) (as so added). For the meanings of 'police authority' and 'police force' see POLICE vol 36(1) (Reissue) para 202. For the meaning of 'police fund' see POLICE vol 36(1) (Reissue) para 205. As to the Serious Organised Crime Agency see POLICE.
6   Ibid s 76A(2)(b) (as added: see note 2 supra). See note 5 supra.
7   Ie ibid s 32: see para 476 post.
8   Ibid s 76A(3)(a) (as added: see note 2 supra). See note 5 supra.
9   Ibid s 76A(3)(b) (as added: see note 2 supra). See note 5 supra.
10 Ibid s 76A(4)(a) (as added: see note 2 supra). See note 5 supra.
      Any proceedings under the Race Relations Act 1976 which, by virtue of s 76A (as added), would lie against a chief officer of police must be brought against:
      (1) the chief officer of police for the time being; or
      (2) in the case of a vacancy in that office, against the person for the time being performing the functions of that office,
      and references in s 76A(4) (as added) to the chief officer of police are to be construed accordingly: s 76A(5) (as so added).
11 Ibid s 76A(4)(b) (as added: see note 2 supra). See note 5 supra.
12 Ibid s 76A(5)(a) (as added: see note 2 supra). See note 5 supra.
13 Ibid s 76A(5)(b) (as added: see note 2 supra). See note 5 supra.
14 Ibid s 76A(5)(c) (as added: see note 2 supra). See notes 5, 10 supra.

456.   Discrimination and harassment by and in relation to barristers and their clerks.   It is unlawful for a barrister or barrister's clerk[1], in relation to any offer of a pupillage or tenancy[2], to discriminate[3] against a person[4] in the arrangements which are made[5] for the purpose of determining to whom it should be offered[6], or in respect of any terms on which it is offered[7], or by refusing or deliberately omitting to offer it to him[8].

It is also unlawful for a barrister or barrister's clerk, in relation to a pupil or tenant in the chambers in question, to discriminate against him[9]: (1) in respect of any terms applicable to him as a pupil or tenant[10]; (2) in the opportunities for training[11], or gaining experience[12], which are afforded or denied to him[13]; (3) in the benefits, facilities or services which are afforded or denied to him[14]; or (4) by terminating his pupillage or by subjecting him to any pressure to leave the chambers or other detriment[15].

It is unlawful for any person[16], in relation to the giving, withholding or acceptance of instructions to a barrister to discriminate against any person or to subject them to harassment[17].

It is also unlawful for a barrister or barrister's clerk, in relation to a pupillage or tenancy in the set of chambers in question, to subject to harassment a person who is, or has applied to be, a pupil or tenant[18].

1 'Barrister's clerk' includes any person carrying out any of the functions of a barrister's clerk: Race Relations Act 1976 s 26A(4) (s 26A added by the Courts and Legal Services Act 1990 s 64(2)). As to barristers' clerks see BARRISTERS.

2 'Pupil', 'pupillage', 'tenancy' and 'tenant' have the meanings commonly associated with their use in the context of a set of barristers' chambers: Race Relations Act 1976 s 26A(4) (as added: see note 1 supra). See BARRISTERS vol 3(1) (2005 Reissue) para 471 et seq.

3 For the meaning of 'discrimination' see para 447 note 4 ante.

4 Race Relations Act 1976 s 26A(1) (as added: see note 1 supra). The provision is unusually drafted, in an attempt to take account of the unique (and often undefined) organisation of barristers' chambers. The provision is contained in the Race Relations Act 1976 Pt III (ss 17–27) (as amended), and consequently should be enforced through a designated county court, rather than an employment tribunal: see para 500 post.

5 The scope of this provision is presumably similar to that of ibid s 4(1)(a) (discrimination in arrangements made for the purpose of determining who should be offered employment: see para 446 ante). In the context of barristers' chambers, indirect discrimination by reliance upon word of mouth recommendations or social or family contacts for the recruitment of pupils may be particularly relevant; as may discrimination by the concentration on certain universities as sources of recruitment.

6 Ibid s 26A(1)(a) (as added: see note 1 supra).

7 Ibid s 26A(1)(b) (as added: see note 1 supra).

8 Ibid s 26A(1)(c) (as added: see note 1 supra).

9 Ibid s 26A(2) (as added: see note 1 supra).

10 Ibid s 26A(2)(a) (as added: see note 1 supra).

11 As to the meaning of 'training' see para 446 note 13 ante.

12 This provision would presumably cover discrimination by a barrister's clerk in the allocation of work to tenants or pupils.

13 Race Relations Act 1976 s 26A(2)(b) (as added: see note 1 supra).

14 Ibid s 26A(2)(c) (as added: see note 1 supra). As to the affording of access to benefits, facilities and services see para 446 note 14 ante.

15 Ibid s 26A(2)(d) (as added: see note 1 supra). As to the meaning of 'detriment' see paras 440 note 12, 446 note 17 ante.

16 As to the meaning of 'person' see para 344 note 3 ante.

17 Race Relations Act 1976 s 26A(3) (as added (see note 1 supra); and amended by the Race Relations Act 1976 (Amendment) Regulations 2003, SI 2003/1626, reg 27(2)(a)). For the meaning of 'harassment' see para 444 ante. This provision would cover discrimination or harassment by a solicitor or anyone instructing a barrister and discrimination or harassment by a barrister's clerk, either against a barrister or against the solicitor or lay client. It would also cover, for example, the withholding of certain work from a barrister on racial grounds, or the refusal to accept a set of instructions on racial grounds.

18 Race Relations Act 1976 s 26A(3A) (s 26A as added (see note 1 supra); and s 26A(3A) added by the Race Relations Act 1976 (Amendment) Regulations 2003, SI 2003/1626, reg 27(2)(b)).

457. Crown servants. In general, those in the service of the Crown[1] are treated under the Race Relations Act 1976[2] as if they were employed by a private person, and as if references to a contract of employment included references to their terms of service[3].

However, the Act does not invalidate any rules (whenever made) restricting employment[4] in the service of the Crown, or employment by any prescribed public body[5], to persons of particular birth, nationality, descent or residence[6].

The provisions of the Act prohibiting discrimination in employment and other discriminatory acts apply to service in the armed forces[7], but no complaint of such discrimination may be made to an employment tribunal[8] unless certain procedures have been followed[9].

Ministers of the Crown and government departments have a statutory duty in relation to any appointment by them to an office or post where the employment provisions of the Act[10] do not apply in relation to the appointment[11]. The Minister of the Crown or government department must not do any act in making the appointment and making the arrangements for determining who should be offered the office or post which would be unlawful under the employment provisions of the Act if the Crown were the employer[12].

Ministers of the Crown and government departments have a statutory duty in relation to: (1) any recommendation (other than a negative recommendation) made by them, in relation to an appointment to an office or post where the employment provisions of the Act[13] do not apply in relation to the appointment, and any approval given by them in relation to any such appointment; (2) any recommendation (other than a negative recommendation) made by them in relation to a conferment by the Crown of a dignity or honour, and any approval given by them in relation to any such appointment[14]. The Minister of the Crown or government department must not do any act in making the recommendation, or giving such approval, and in making such arrangements for determining who should be recommended or approved, which would be unlawful under the employment provisions of the Act if the recommendation or approval were an offer of employment and the Crown were the employer[15].

Ministers of the Crown and government departments have a statutory duty in relation to: (a) any negative recommendation made by them, or any refusal[16] to make a recommendation by them, in relation to an appointment by them to an office or post where the employment provisions of the Race Relations Act 1976 do not apply in relation to the appointment, and any approval refused by them in relation to any such appointment; and (b) any negative recommendation made by them, or any refusal to make a recommendation by them, in relation to a conferment by the Crown of a dignity or honour, and any approval refused by them in relation to any such conferment[17]. The Minister of the Crown or the government department must not do any act in making a negative recommendation, or in refusing to make a recommendation or give an approval, and in making such arrangements for determining whether to make such a recommendation or refusal, which would be unlawful under the Act's employment provisions if the recommendation or refusal were a refusal to offer the person concerned employment and the Crown were the employer[18].

Ministers of the Crown and government departments also have a statutory duty in relation to any appointment to an office or post where the Act's employment provisions do not apply and the appointment is made by either of them, or the office or post is an office or post in relation to which either of them has made a recommendation (other than a negative recommendation) or given an approval[19]. The Minister of the Crown or government department must not do any act in connection with the terms of the appointment, access for the person appointed to opportunities for promotion, transfer or training, or to any other benefits, facilities or services, or the termination of the appointment[20], or subjecting the person appointed to any other detriment[21], which would be unlawful under the Act's employment provisions if the Crown were the employer[22].

On an application for judicial review, the High Court may make a declaration to the effect that a Minister of the Crown or government department has contravened the relevant provisions[23], and may award damages in respect of the contravention[24].

1　　Ie those engaged in service for the purposes of a Minister of the Crown or government department, or service on behalf of the Crown for the purposes of a person holding a statutory office or the purposes of a statutory body: see the Race Relations Act 1976 s 75(2)(a), (b). The provisions of s 75(2)–(2B) (as amended) have effect subject to ss 76A, 76B (both as added and amended) (see para 455 ante): s 75(3) (amended by the Race Relations (Amendment) Act 2000 s 9(1), Sch 2 para 18(a)). Service 'for the purposes of' a Minister of the Crown or government department does not include service in any office in the House of Commons Disqualification Act 1975 s 2, Sch 2 (as amended) (ministerial offices) (see PARLIAMENT vol 34 (Reissue) para 611) as for the time being in force: Race Relations Act 1976 s 75(10)(c). For the meaning of 'Minister of the Crown' see para 445 note 1 ante. The provision does not cover the service of a person holding a statutory office, eg a justice of the peace: *Knight v A-G* [1979] ICR 194, EAT.

2 Ie under the Race Relations Act 1976 Pt II (ss 4–15) (as amended), Pt IV (ss 27A–33) (as amended) (prohibiting discrimination in employment and other discriminatory acts): see s 75(2). See note 1 supra.

3 See ibid s 75(2). Section s 75(2) does not apply in relation to ss 19B–19F (as added and amended) (see para 470 post), s 71 (as substituted) (see para 469 post), ss 71A–71E (as added and amended; ss 71C–71E prospectively repealed) (see para 469 post), s 76 (as amended) or Sch 1A (as added and amended) (see para 469 post), which bind the Crown; and the other provisions of the Race Relations Act 1976, so far as they relate to those provisions, are to be construed accordingly: s 75(2A), (2B) (added by the Race Relations (Amendment) Act 2000 s 9(1), Sch 2 para 17). See note 1 supra.

4 For these purposes, 'employment' includes service of any kind: Race Relations Act 1976 s 75(5).

5 Ie any public body prescribed by regulations made by the Minister for the Civil Service: see ibid s 75(5)(a). 'Public body' means a body of persons, whether corporate or unincorporate, carrying on a service or undertaking of a public nature: s 75(5). As to the prescribed public bodies see the Race Relations (Prescribed Public Bodies) (No 2) Regulations 1994, SI 1994/1986. As to the Minister for the Civil Service see CONSTITUTIONAL LAW AND HUMAN RIGHTS vol 8(2) (Reissue) para 427.

6 Race Relations Act 1976 s 75(5)(a). As to the meaning of 'nationality' see para 441 note 2 ante. Nothing in the Race Relations Act 1976 renders unlawful the publication, display or implementation of any such rules, or the publication of advertisements stating the gist of any such rules: s 75(5)(b). The exception for rules restricting employment in the service of the Crown to persons of particular nationality is subject to European Community law as regards EC nationals.

7 Ibid s 75(2)(c). 'The armed forces' means any of the naval, military or air forces of the Crown: s 75(10)(a) (amended by the Armed Forces Act 1981 s 28(2), Sch 5 Pt I). See generally ARMED FORCES. See note 1 supra.

8 Ie a complaint made under the Race Relations Act 1976 s 54 (as amended): see para 499 post.

9 See ibid s 75(8), (9) (s 75(9) substituted by the Armed Forces Act 1996 s 23(2); and amended by virtue of the Employment Rights (Dispute Resolution) Act 1998 s 1(2)). No complaint may be made to an employment tribunal unless: (1) the complainant has made a complaint to an officer under the service redress procedures applicable to him and has submitted that complaint to the Defence Council under those procedures (Race Relations Act 1976 s 75(9)(a) (as so substituted)); and (2) the Defence Council has made a determination with respect to the complaint (s 75(9)(b) (as so substituted)). As to the Defence Council see ARMED FORCES vol 2(2) (Reissue) para 2; CONSTITUTIONAL LAW AND HUMAN RIGHTS vol 8(2) (Reissue) para 443 et seq.

Regulations may make provision enabling a complaint to be presented to an employment tribunal under s 54 (as amended) (see para 499 post) in such circumstances as may be specified by the regulations, notwithstanding that s 75(9) (as substituted and amended) would otherwise preclude the presentation of the complaint to an employment tribunal: s 75(9A) (added by the Armed Forces Act 1996 s 23(2); and amended by virtue of the Employment Rights (Dispute Resolution) Act 1998 s 1(2)). Where a complaint is presented to an employment tribunal by virtue of such regulations, the service redress procedures may continue after the complaint is so presented: Race Relations Act 1976 s 75(9B) (added by the Armed Forces Act 1996 s 23(2); and amended by virtue of the Employment Rights (Dispute Resolution) Act 1998 s 1(2)). 'Regulations' means regulations made by the Secretary of State: Race Relations Act 1976 s 75(10)(aa) (added by the Armed Forces Act 1996 s 23(3)). As to the Secretary of State and the National Assembly for Wales see para 302 ante. As to the regulations that have been made see the Race Relations (Complaints to Employment Tribunals) (Armed Forces) Regulations 1997, SI 1997/2161 (amended by virtue of the Employment Rights (Dispute Resolution) Act 1998 s 1(2)). 'The service redress procedures' means the procedures, excluding those which relate to the making of a report on a complaint to Her Majesty, referred to in the Army Act 1955 s 180 (as substituted and amended), the Air Force Act 1955 s 180 (as substituted and amended) and the Naval Discipline Act 1957 s 130 (as substituted and amended) (see ARMED FORCES vol 2(2) (Reissue) para 314): Race Relations Act 1976 s 75(10)(ab) (added by the Armed Forces Act 1996 s 23(3)).

A body considering a complaint under these provisions is obliged to give full effect to the substantive provisions of the Race Relations Act 1976, and to make specific findings as to whether there has been unlawful discrimination. It should give proper consideration to the question whether compensation or other redress ought to be granted. It has a duty to act fairly: there must be a proper hearing of the complaint, although it need not necessarily be an oral hearing; the complaint must be investigated; all the material gathered in the investigation must be considered; and the complainant must be given an opportunity to respond to it. All material seen by the body should be disclosed to the complainant (unless covered by public interest immunity): see *R v Army Board of the Defence Council, ex p Anderson* [1992] QB 169, [1991] 3 All ER 375, DC.

10 Ie the Race Relations Act 1976 s 4 (as amended): see paras 446–447 ante.

11   Ibid s 76(1) (amended by the Race Relations (Amendment) Act 2000 s 3(1), (2)). An example of such an office is the office of justice of the peace: *Knight v A-G* [1979] ICR 194, EAT.

      References in the Race Relations Act 1976 s 76 (as amended) to Ministers of the Crown and government departments include references to the National Assembly for Wales and, so far as they relate to the making of a recommendation or a refusal to make a recommendation, or the giving or refusal of an approval, in relation to a conferment of a peerage for life under the Life Peerages Act 1958 s 1 (prospectively amended by the Constitutional Reform Act 2005 ss 145, 146, Sch 17 para 15, Sch 18 Pt 5) (see CONSTITUTIONAL LAW AND HUMAN RIGHTS vol 8(2) (Reissue) para 212; PARLIAMENT vol 34 (Reissue) para 540; PEERAGES AND DIGNITIES), include references to any body established by a Minister of the Crown to make such a recommendation to the Prime Minister or to determine whether to give such an approval: Race Relations Act 1976 s 76(15)(b), (c) (s 76(3)–(15) added by the Race Relations (Amendment) Act 2000 s 3(1), (3)). 'Body' includes an unincorporated association: Race Relations Act 1976 s 78(1) (definition added by the Race Relations (Amendment) Act 2000 s 9(1), Sch 2 para 19).

12   Race Relations Act 1976 s 76(2). There is no statutory duty on the Crown not to discriminate against existing office holders, in the terms upon which it employs them, in the way it affords them access to any benefits, facilities or services, or by refusing to afford them access to benefits, facilities or services, or by dismissing them, or by subjecting them to any other detriment. Cf, in relation to employees, s 4(2); and see para 446 ante.

13   Ie ibid s 4 (as amended): see paras 446–447 ante.

14   Ibid s 76(3), (4), (6) (as added: see note 11 supra).

15   Ibid s 76(5) (as added: see note 11 supra).

16   References to refusal include references to deliberate omission: ibid s 76(15)(a) (as added: see note 11 supra).

17   Ibid s 76(7), (8) (as added: see note 11 supra).

18   Ibid s 76(9) (as added: see note 11 supra).

19   Ibid s 76(10) (as added (see note 11 supra); and amended by the Race Relations Act 1976 (Amendment) Regulations 2003, SI 2003/1626, reg 50(a)).

20   In the Race Relations Act 1976 s 76(11) (as added), reference to the termination of the appointment includes, where the act is committed on the grounds of race or ethnic or national origins, reference to the termination of the appointment by the expiration of any period, including a period expiring by reference to an event or circumstance, not being a termination immediately after which the appointment is renewed on the same terms and conditions, and to the termination of the appointment by any act of the person appointed, including the giving of notice, in circumstances such that he is entitled to terminate the appointment by reason of the conduct of the minister or the department, as the case may be: s 76(11A) (s 76(11A), (11B) added by the Race Relations Act 1976 (Amendment) Regulations 2003, SI 2003/1626, reg 50(b)). It is unlawful for a Minister of the Crown or government department to subject to harassment a person who has been appointed, or who is seeking or being considered for, the appointment: Race Relations Act 1976 s 76(11B) (as so added). As to ethnic or national origins see para 441 ante. For the meaning of 'harassment' see para 444 ante.

21   As to the meaning of 'detriment' see paras 440 note 12, 446 note 17 ante.

22   Race Relations Act 1976 s 76(11) (as added: see note 11 supra).

23   Ie ibid s 76(5), (9) (as added), in relation to an appointment to an office or post in relation to which a Minister of the Crown or government department has made a recommendation (other than a negative recommendation) or given an approval under s 76(10) (as added and amended), s 76(11) (as added), or s 76(11B) (as added).

24   Ibid s 76(12) (as added (see note 11 supra); and amended by the Race Relations Act 1976 (Amendment) Regulations 2003, SI 2003/1626, reg 50(c)). The provision made by the Race Relations Act 1976 s 76(12) (as added and amended) in respect of judicial review does not affect the ability, where an act on grounds of race or ethnic or national origins, or harassment, is alleged, to present a complaint to an employment tribunal under s 54A(1) (as added) (see para 452 ante): s 76(14) (substituted by the Race Relations Act 1976 (Amendment) Regulations 2003, SI 2003/1626, reg 50(d)). As to judicial review see ADMINISTRATIVE LAW vol 1(1) (2001 Reissue) para 58 et seq; PRACTICE AND PROCEDURE vol 37 (Reissue) para 1368.

458.   House of Commons and House of Lords staff. The provisions of the Race Relations Act 1976 prohibiting discrimination in employment and other discriminatory acts[1] apply:

     (1)   to an act[2] done by an employer of a relevant member of the House of Commons staff[3], and to service as such a member, as they apply to an act done by and to service for the purposes of a Minister of the Crown[4] or government

department[5], and accordingly apply as if references to a contract of employment[6] included references to the terms of service of such a member[7]; and

(2) in relation to employment as a relevant member of the House of Lords staff[8] as they apply in relation to other employment[9].

1 Ie the Race Relations Act 1976 Pt II (ss 4–15) (as amended) and Pt IV (ss 27A–33) (as amended).

2 As to the meaning of 'act' see para 442 note 7 ante.

3 'Relevant member of the House of Commons staff' means any person who was appointed by the House of Commons Commission or is employed in the refreshment department, or who is a member of the Speaker's personal staff: Employment Rights Act 1996 s 195(5); definition applied by the Race Relations Act 1976 s 75A(2) (s 75A added by the Trade Union and Labour Relations (Consolidation) Act 1992 s 300(2), Sch 2 para 7; and the Race Relations Act 1976 s 75A(2) amended by the Employment Rights Act 1996 s 240, Sch 1 para 10(1), (2)). The provisions of the Employment Rights Act 1996 s 195(6)–(12) (as amended) (person to be treated as employer of House of Commons staff) (see EMPLOYMENT vol 16(1A) (Reissue) para 136) apply, with any necessary modifications, for the purposes of the Race Relations Act 1976 Pts II, IV (as amended) as they apply by virtue of this provision: s 75A(2) (as so added and amended). See further EMPLOYMENT vol 16(1A) (Reissue) paras 134–136; PARLIAMENT vol 34 (Reissue) para 652.

4 For the meaning of 'Minister of the Crown' see para 445 note 1 ante.

5 See para 457 ante.

6 For the meaning of 'employment' see para 446 note 3 ante.

7 Race Relations Act 1976 s 75A(1) (as added: see note 3 supra).

8 'Relevant member of the House of Lords staff' means any person who is employed under a contract of employment with the Corporate Officer of the House of Lords: Employment Rights Act 1996 s 194(6); definition applied by the Race Relations Act 1976 s 75B(2) (s 75B added by the Trade Union Reform and Employment Rights Act 1993 s 49(1), Sch 7 para 10; and the Race Relations Act 1976 s 75B(2) amended by the Employment Rights Act 1996 Sch 1 para 10(1), (3)). The Employment Rights Act 1996 s 194(7) applies for these purposes: see the Race Relations Act 1976 s 75B(2) (as so added and amended). See further EMPLOYMENT vol 16(1A) (Reissue) para 135; PARLIAMENT vol 34 (Reissue) para 652.

9 Ibid s 75B(1) (as added: see note 8 supra).

459. Other office-holders. It is unlawful for a relevant person[1] to discriminate against a person on the grounds of race or ethnic or national origins in the arrangements which he makes for the purpose of determining to whom the appointment should be offered[2], in the terms on which he offers him the appointment[3], or by refusing or deliberately omitting to offer him the appointment[4].

It is unlawful for a relevant person to discriminate against a person who has been appointed to an office or post[5] on grounds of race or ethnic or national origins in the terms of the appointment[6], in the way he affords him access to opportunities for promotion, transfer, training or to any other benefits, facilities or services, or by refusing or deliberately omitting to afford him access to them[7], by terminating the appointment[8], or by subjecting him to any other detriment[9] in relation to the appointment[10]. It is unlawful for a relevant person to subject to harassment a person who has been appointed to, or is seeking or being considered for appointment to, such an office or post[11].

The above provisions apply to any office or post, other than a political office or post[12], where: (1) certain other provisions[13] do not apply in relation to appointment to that office or post[14]; (2) it is an office or post to which persons are appointed to discharge functions personally under the direction of another person[15]; and (3) it is an office or post in respect of which they are entitled to remuneration[16].

1 'Relevant person' in relation to an office or post, means any person with power to make or terminate appointments to the office or post, or to determine the terms of appointment, and any person with power to determine the working conditions of a person appointed to the office or post in relation to opportunities for promotion, a transfer, training or for receiving any other benefit: Race Relations Act 1976 s 76ZA(9)(c) (s 76ZA added by the Race Relations Act 1976 (Amendment) Regulations 2003, SI 2003/1626, reg 51). As to the meaning of 'person' see para 344 note 3 ante.

2 Race Relations Act 1976 s 76ZA(1)(a) (as added: see note 1 supra).

3 Ibid s 76ZA(1)(b) (as added: see note 1 supra).

4   Ibid s 76ZA(1)(c) (as added: see note 1 supra).

5   Appointment to an office or post does not include election to an office or post: ibid s 76ZA(9)(a) (as added: see note 1 supra).

6   Ibid s 76ZA(2)(a) (as added: see note 1 supra).

7   Ibid s 76ZA(2)(b) (as added: see note 1 supra).

8   Ibid s 76ZA(2)(c) (as added: see note 1 supra). The reference to the termination of the appointment includes reference to the termination of the appointment by the expiration of any period, including a period expiring by reference to an event or circumstance, not being a termination immediately after which the appointment is renewed on the same terms and conditions, and to the termination of the appointment by any act of the person appointed, including the giving of notice, in circumstances such that he is entitled to terminate the appointment by reason of the conduct of the relevant person: s 76ZA(6) (as so added).

9   As to the meaning of 'detriment' see paras 440 note 12, 446 note 17 ante.

10 Race Relations Act 1976 s 76ZA(2)(d) (as added: see note 1 supra). The provisions of s 76ZA(1), (2) (as added) do not apply to any act in relation to an office or post where, if the office or post constituted employment, the act would be lawful by virtue of s 4A (as added) (see para 446 ante): s 76ZA(4) (as so added). Section 76ZA(2) (as added) does not apply to benefits, facilities or services of any description if the relevant person is concerned with the provision, for payment or not, of benefits, facilities or services of that description to the public, or a section of the public to which the person belongs, unless: (1) that provision differs in a material respect from the provision of the benefits, facilities or services to persons appointed to offices or posts which are the same as, or not materially different from, that to which the person has been appointed; (2) the provision of the benefits, facilities or services to the person appointed is regulated by the terms and conditions of his appointment; or (3) the benefits, facilities or services relate to training: s 76ZA(5) (as so added).

11 Ibid s 76ZA(3) (as added: see note 1 supra).

12 'Political office or post' means: (1) any office of the House of Commons held by a member of it; (2) a life peerage within the meaning of the Life Peerages Act 1958 (see CONSTITUTIONAL LAW AND HUMAN RIGHTS vol 8(2) (Reissue) para 212; PARLIAMENT vol 34 (Reissue) para 540; PEERAGES AND DIGNITIES), or any office held in the House of Lords by a member of it; (3) any office mentioned in the House of Commons Disqualification Act 1975 Sch 2 (as amended) (see PARLIAMENT vol 34 (Reissue) para 611); (4) the offices of Leader of the Opposition, Chief Opposition Whip or Assistant Opposition Whip within the meaning of the Ministerial and other Salaries Act 1975 (see CONSTITUTIONAL LAW AND HUMAN RIGHTS vol 8(2) (Reissue) para 219); (5) any office of the National Assembly for Wales held by a member of it; (6) in England, any office of a county council, a London borough council, a district council or a parish council held by a member of it; (7) in Wales, any office of a county council, a county borough council or a community council held by a member of it; (8) any office of the Greater London Authority held by a member of it; (9) any office of the Common Council of the City of London held by a member of it; (10) any office of the Council of the Isles of Scilly held by a member of it; or (11) any office of a political party: Race Relations Act 1976 s 76ZA(9)(b) (as added: see note 1 supra). This provision also refers to various Scottish offices, but Scottish matters generally are beyond the scope of this work. As to the National Assembly for Wales see para 302 ante. As to local government authorities in England and Wales see LOCAL GOVERNMENT vol 29(1) (Reissue) para 23 et seq; as to the Greater London Authority see LONDON GOVERNMENT vol 29(2) (Reissue) para 70 et seq; as to the Common Council of the City of London see LONDON GOVERNMENT vol 29(2) (Reissue) para 51 et seq; and as to the Council of the Isles of Scilly see LOCAL GOVERNMENT vol 29(1) (Reissue) para 40.

13 Ie ibid ss 4 (as amended) (see para 446 ante), s 7 (as amended) (see para 448 ante), s 10 (as amended) (see para 450 ante), s 26A (as added and amended) (see para 456 ante), and s 76 (as amended) (see para 457 ante).

14 Ibid s 76ZA(7)(a) (as added: see note 1 supra).

15 Ibid s 76ZA(7)(b) (as added: see note 1 supra). The holder of an office or post is to be regarded as discharging his functions under the direction of another person if that other person is entitled to direct him as to when and where he discharges those functions, and is not to be regarded as entitled to remuneration merely because he is entitled to payments in respect of expenses incurred by him in carrying out the functions of the office or post, or by way of compensation for the loss of income or benefits he would or might have received from any person had he not been carrying out the functions of the office or post: s 76ZA(8) (as so added).

16 Ibid s 76ZA(7)(c) (as added: see note 1 supra).

B. DISCRIMINATION IN EDUCATION

460. Discrimination and harassment by bodies in charge of schools, universities and other educational establishments. The Race Relations Act 1976 protects potential and actual pupils[1] of educational establishments from discrimination on the part of the individuals or bodies who are responsible for those establishments[2].

It is unlawful for a responsible body to discriminate[3] against a person in the terms on which it offers to admit him to the establishment as a pupil[4], or by refusing or deliberately omitting to accept an application for his admission to the establishment as a pupil[5].

It is unlawful for a responsible body to discriminate against a person where he is a pupil of the establishment in the way it affords him access to any benefits, facilities or services, or by refusing or deliberately omitting to afford him access to them[6], or by excluding him[7] from the establishment or by subjecting him to any other detriment[8].

It is also unlawful for a responsible body to subject to harassment[9]: (1) a person who applies for admission to the establishment as a pupil; or (2) a pupil at the establishment[10].

It is unlawful for the following bodies to do any act[11] which constitutes racial discrimination or harassment[12]:

(1) a local education authority in carrying out any of its other functions under the Education Acts[13];

(2) the Learning and Skills Council for England, the Higher Education Funding Council for England or the Higher Education Funding Council for Wales in carrying out their functions under the Education Acts and the Learning and Skills Act 2000[14]; and

(3) the Training and Development Agency for Schools in carrying out its functions under any enactment[15].

1   'Pupil' includes any person who receives education at a school or institution to which the Race Relations Act 1976 s 17 (as amended) applies (see note 2 infra): s 17A (added by the Further and Higher Education Act 1992 s 93(1), Sch 8 paras 84, 86). For the meaning of 'education' see para 446 note 13 ante. 'School' has the meaning given by the Education Act 1996 s 4 (as substituted) (see EDUCATION vol 15(1) (2006 Reissue) para 81): Race Relations Act 1976 s 78(1) (definition amended by the Education Act 1996 s 582(1), Sch 37 para 43).

2   As to the establishments within the ambit of the Race Relations Act 1976, and their respective 'responsible bodies', see s 17 (as amended); and EDUCATION vol 15(1) (2006 Reissue) para 8.

3   For the meaning of 'discrimination' see para 447 note 4 ante. In the context of education, a condition or requirement which is prima facie indirectly discriminatory, because it has a disparate adverse impact on a particular racial group, can be justified only on objective educational grounds.

4   Race Relations Act 1976 s 17(1)(a) (renumbered by the Race Relations Act 1976 (Amendment) Regulations 2003, SI 2003/1626, reg 18(2)). See also *Mandla v Dowell Lee* [1983] 2 AC 548, [1983] 1 All ER 1062, HL, in which a requirement that school pupils should wear caps was found to be indirectly discriminatory against Sikhs. It is discriminatory for a private school or college to charge higher fees to pupils or students from overseas; higher fees based on nationality would be directly discriminatory, and higher fees based on residence in the United Kingdom would be indirectly discriminatory: see *Orphanos v Queen Mary College* [1985] AC 761, [1985] 2 All ER 233, HL (higher fees charged to non-EC students not justifiable). A claim for damages for discrimination on the grounds of nationality contrary to Community law may not be brought under the Racial Discrimination Act 1976: *Nabadda v Westminster City Council; Gomilsek v Haringey London Borough Council* [2000] ICR 951, [2000] All ER (D) 121, CA. It is lawful for universities, polytechnics, and other further education establishments to charge higher fees to students without sufficient residence in the United Kingdom, by virtue of the Education (Fees and Awards) Act 1983 and the Education (Fees and Awards) Regulations 1997, SI 1997/1972 (as amended): see EDUCATION vol 15(2) (2006 Reissue) para 638.

5   Race Relations Act 1976 s 17(1)(b) (as renumbered: see note 4 supra). Examples of racial discrimination in admissions to schools and other educational establishments are the operation of racial quotas to maintain a racial balance of pupils, and the operation of directly or indirectly discriminatory criteria for admission. See *Birmingham City Council v Equal Opportunities Commission* [1989] AC 1155, sub nom *Equal Opportunities Commission v Birmingham City Council* [1989] 1 All ER 769, HL (a case under the Sex

Discrimination Act 1975, where girls were deprived of a grammar school education on the same terms as boys because the local education authority maintained more boys' grammar school places than girls' places). See also 'Medical School Admissions: Report of a formal investigation into St George's Hospital Medical School', published by the Commission for Racial Equality in 1988 (medical school computer which sorted applications gave adverse weighting to ethnic minority candidates, so that their chances of admission were diminished). The admission of pupils from a particular catchment area might be indirectly discriminatory, if the area contained a disproportionate number of pupils from particular racial groups. Such a criterion might be justifiable, e g if the catchment area was selected for its convenience for travel to the school. Acceding to a parent's request that her child be transferred to a school where the majority of pupils share that child's ethnic group is not discriminatory: *R v Cleveland County Council, ex p Commission for Racial Equality* [1993] 1 FCR 597, [1994] ELR 44, CA.

6 As to the affording of access to benefits, facilities and services see para 446 note 14 ante. The Race Relations Act 1976 ss 17–18D (as amended) do not apply to benefits, facilities or services outside Great Britain, except travel on a ship registered at a port of registry in Great Britain, and benefits, facilities or services provided on such a ship: s 27(1) (amended by the Race Relations (Amendment) Act 2000 s 9(1), Sch 2 para 2). For the meaning of 'Great Britain' see para 325 note 6 ante.

7 Exclusion would include expulsion or suspension: see e g 'Birmingham LEA and Schools: Referral and Suspension of Pupils', published by the Commission for Racial Equality in 1985 (a report of a formal investigation which found that black pupils were more likely to be suspended than white pupils, on average at a younger age, and after shorter periods and fewer incidents of disruption).

8 Race Relations Act 1976 s 17(1)(c) (as renumbered: see note 4 supra). See *Mandla v Dowell Lee* [1983] 2 AC 548, [1983] 1 All ER 1062, HL. As to the meaning of 'detriment' see paras 440 note 12, 446 note 17 ante.

  The Secretary of State or, in relation to Wales, the National Assembly for Wales (see the National Assembly for Wales (Transfer of Functions) Order 1999, SI 1999/672, art 2, Sch 1; and para 302 ante) has special powers of enforcement in relation to the duties imposed on local education authorities and educational establishments in the public sector. Under the Education Act 1996 s 496 (as amended) the Secretary of State or the Assembly has the power to require duties under that Act to be exercised reasonably, and under s 497 (as amended) he or it has additional powers where the bodies in question are in default: see EDUCATION vol 15(1) (2006 Reissue) paras 57–58. As to the Secretary of State and the National Assembly for Wales see para 302 ante.

  Civil proceedings under the Race Relations Act 1976 s 17 (as amended) or s 18 (as amended) in respect of a claim of discrimination by any body to which s 57(5A) (as added) applies must not be instituted unless the claimant has given notice to the Secretary of State: s 57(5) (amended by the Race Relations (Amendment) Act 2000 Sch 2 para 6). As to the meaning of 'body' see para 457 note 11 ante. 'Notice' means a notice in writing: Race Relations Act 1976 s 78(1). The bodies to which s 57(5A) (as added) applies are: (1) local education authorities in England and Wales; and (2) any body which is a responsible body in relation to an establishment falling within s 17(1), Table para 3 or 3B (as renumbered and added), namely the proprietor in regard to a special school not maintained by a local education authority, and a governing body in regard to an institution within the further education sector (within the meaning of the Further and Higher Education Act 1992 s 91(3): see EDUCATION vol 15(2) (2006 Reissue) para 579): Race Relations Act 1976 s 57(5A) (added by the Race Relations (Amendment) Act 2000 Sch 2 para 7). 'Proprietor' in relation to a school has the meaning given by the Education Act 1996 s 579 (see EDUCATION vol 15(1) (2006 Reissue) para 60): Race Relations Act 1976 s 78(1) (definition amended by the Education Act 1996 Sch 37 para 43). Any power conferred by the Race Relations Act 1976 to designate establishments or persons may be exercised either by naming them or by identifying them by reference to a class or other description: s 78(3).

  In exercising his general education powers, the Secretary of State himself has a duty to have regard to the Race Relations Act 1976: see *R v Secretary of State for Education and Science, ex p Keating* (1985) 84 LGR 469.

  The Race Relations Act 1976 s 20 (as amended) prohibits discrimination in the provision of facilities for education: see para 461 post. The prohibition presumably covers all educational establishments outside the ambit of s 17 (as amended) (e g private crammers).

9 For the meaning of 'harassment' see para 444 ante.

10 Race Relations Act 1976 s 17(2) (added by the Race Relations Act 1976 (Amendment) Regulations 2003, SI 2003/1626, reg 18(2)).

11 As to the meaning of 'act' see para 442 note 7 ante.

12 See the Race Relations Act 1976 s 18(1) (as amended), s 18A (as added and amended), s 18D (as added and amended).

13 See ibid s 18(1) (amended by the Education Act 1996 s 582(1), Sch 37 para 39; and the Race Relations Act 1976 (Amendment) Regulations 2003, SI 2003/1626, reg 19(3)). This provision covers functions apart from those which fall under the Race Relations Act 1976 s 17 (as amended): see s 18(1) (as so amended). See the Education Act 1996 ss 13–15B (as amended); and EDUCATION vol 15(1) (2006

Reissue) para 20 et seq. Such functions would include the provision of school meals and transport, educational welfare, and the teaching of English as a second language. In an action under this provision, it is not necessary to show that the local education authority is in breach of its duties under the Education Acts. It is sufficient to show that in carrying out its functions under those Acts the authority did an act (or deliberately omitted to do an act) where such act or omission constituted unlawful discrimination: *Birmingham City Council v Equal Opportunities Commission* [1989] AC 1155, sub nom *Equal Opportunities Commission v Birmingham City Council* [1989] 1 All ER 769, HL. See also *R v Secretary of State for Education and Science, ex p Keating* (1985) 84 LGR 469. The Education Act 1996 ss 496, 497 (both as amended) apply to the performance by a local education authority of these duties: see note 8 supra. As to the territorial extent of this duty see note 6 supra. See also *R v Birmingham City Council, ex p Equal Opportunities Commission* [1992] 2 FCR 746, [1992] 2 FLR 133, DC (concerning local education authority's obligations under the Sex Discrimination Act 1975); *R v Cleveland County Council, ex p Commission for Racial Equality* (1991) 135 Sol Jo LB 205, (1991) Times, 28 October, DC (local education authority not in breach of its duty under the Race Relations Act 1976 s 18 (as amended) when, in accordance with its statutory duty under the Education Act 1980 s 6, it complied with a parent's request to move a white child from a school with a large proportion of Asian pupils to a predominantly white school).

'The Education Acts' has the meaning given by the Education Act 1996 s 578 (as amended) (see EDUCATION vol 15(1) (2006 Reissue) para 1): Race Relations Act 1976 s 78(1) (definition added by the Education Act 1996 s 582(1), Sch 3 para 43(a)).

14 See the Race Relations Act 1976 s 18A (added by the Further and Higher Education Act 1992 Sch 8 paras 84, 87; and amended by the Education Act 1996 Sch 37 para 40; the Learning and Skills Act 2000 s 149, Sch 9 paras 1, 9; the Race Relations Act 1976 (Amendment) Regulations 2003, SI 2003/1626, reg 19(3); and the National Council for Education and Training for Wales (Transfer of Functions of the National Assembly for Wales and Abolition) Order 2005, SI 2005/3238, art 9(1), Sch 1 paras 6, 7). See further EDUCATION vol 15(1) (2006 Reissue) para 8 et seq.

15 See the Race Relations Act 1976 s 18D (added by the Education Act 1994 Sch 2 para 6(1), (3); and amended by the Education Act 2005 s 98, Sch 14 para 7; and the Race Relations Act 1976 (Amendment) Regulations 2003, SI 2003/1626, reg 19(3)). As to the Training and Development Agency for Schools see EDUCATION vol 15(2) (2006 Reissue) para 784 et seq.

C. GOODS, FACILITIES, SERVICES AND PREMISES

461. Discrimination and harassment in the provision of goods, facilities and services. It is unlawful for any person[1] concerned with the provision (for payment or not) of goods, facilities or services[2] to the public[3] or a section of the public[4] to discriminate[5] against a person who seeks to obtain or use those goods, facilities or services[6] by refusing or deliberately omitting to provide him with any of them[7], or by refusing or deliberately omitting to provide him with goods, facilities or services of the like quality, in the like manner and on the like terms as are normal[8] in relation to other members of the public or (where the person so seeking belongs to a section of the public) to other members of that section[9].

It is also unlawful for any person concerned with the provision of goods, facilities or services to the public or a section of the public, in relation to such provision, to subject to harassment[10] a person who seeks to obtain or use those goods, facilities or services, or a person to whom he provides those goods, facilities or services[11].

Generally, the Race Relations Act 1976 does not apply to the provision of goods, facilities or services outside Great Britain[12], or to banking or insurance facilities, or grants, loans, credit or finance where the facilities are for a purpose to be carried out, or in connection with risks wholly or mainly arising, outside Great Britain[13]. However, the Act's protection extends to the provision of goods and services outside Great Britain in the case of facilities for travel outside Great Britain where the refusal or omission occurs in Great Britain[14]. Protection is also extended against discrimination on and in relation to any ship registered at a port of registry in Great Britain, or in relation to any aircraft or hovercraft registered in the United Kingdom and operated by a person with a principal place of business or ordinary residence in the United Kingdom[15]. These provisions do not render unlawful an act done in or over a country outside the United Kingdom, or in or over that country's territorial waters, for the purpose of complying with the laws of that country[16].

1   As to the meaning of 'person' see para 344 note 3 ante. As to the liability of principals and employers for the acts of their agents and employees see the Race Relations Act 1976 s 32; and para 476 post. As to the liability of those who knowingly aid unlawful acts see s 33 (as amended); and para 477 post.

2   The following are examples of facilities and services: (1) access to and use of any place which members of the public are permitted to enter; (2) accommodation in a hotel, boarding house or similar establishment; (3) facilities by way of banking or insurance or for grants, loans, credit or finance; (4) facilities for education; (5) facilities for entertainment, recreation or refreshment; (6) facilities for transport or travel; and (7) the services of any profession or trade or any local or other public authority: ibid s 20(2). For the meaning of 'education' see para 446 note 13 ante; as to the meaning of 'profession' see para 451 note 1 ante; and as to the meaning of 'trade' see para 451 note 2 ante.

The Court of Appeal in *Rodrigues v Conkey* (4 November 1991, unreported), CA, did not conclusively reject the proposition that the provision of religious services, including allowing the complainant to read the scripture and to assist in the service of communion, might be within the ambit of the Race Relations Act 1976 s 20 (as then in force), but was very doubtful that such services were within the ambit of the Act.

In spite of the specific statutory reference to the example of the services of any public authority, the Sex Discrimination Act 1975 s 29 (as amended) (see para 382 ante) (which is the equivalent provision to the Race Relations Act 1976 s 20 (as amended)) has been narrowly construed by the Court of Appeal and by a majority decision of the House of Lords in the context of the actions of government officials and it has been held that the provision applies only to 'marketplace activities' and to the provision of facilities that are akin to goods and services: *Kassam v Immigration Appeal Tribunal* [1980] 2 All ER 330, sub nom *R v Immigration Appeal Tribunal, ex p Kassam* [1980] 1 WLR 1037, CA; *Re Amin* [1983] 2 AC 818, sub nom *Amin v Entry Clearance Officer, Bombay* [1983] 2 All ER 864, HL. Accordingly, an entry clearance officer is not providing a facility or service to would-be immigrants, but is performing his duty to control them.

It was held that the Inland Revenue (now Her Majesty's Commissioners for Customs and Excise) performed a duty of collecting revenue, but also provided a service to members of the public in giving advice about, and enabling members of the public to obtain, tax relief: *Savjani v IRC* [1981] QB 458, [1981] 1 All ER 1121, CA; *Re Amin* supra.

A registrar of births, marriages and deaths provides facilities and services to the public within the meaning of the Race Relations Act 1976 s 20 (as amended): *Tejani v Superintendent Registrar for the District of Peterborough* [1986] IRLR 502, CA.

It was conceded in *Alexander v Home Office* [1988] 2 All ER 118, [1988] 1 WLR 968, CA, that allocation of specific jobs in prison was a facility or service provided to prisoners.

Those parts of a police officer's duties involving assistance to or protection of members of the public are services to the public within the Race Relations Act 1976 s 20 (as amended) and accordingly, it is unlawful for a police officer to discriminate against a person seeking to obtain such services: *Farah v Metropolitan Police Comr* [1998] QB 65, [1997] 1 All ER 289, CA. In *Conwell v Newham London Borough Council* [2000] ICR 42, EAT, it was held that 'facilities and services' cover the activities of a local authority in relation to children 'looked after by the local authority'; this extends beyond the decision to look after a child, to day-to-day decisions made thereafter while the child is looked after by or on behalf of the authority.

The Race Relations Act 1976 s 20 (as amended) applies to the direct provision of goods, facilities and services, and not to the mere grant of permission to use facilities or services: *Re Amin* supra.

Quite apart from any liability under the Race Relations Act 1976 s 20 (as amended), a public authority which acts on irrational racially discriminatory grounds while exercising its powers or performing its duties acts ultra vires, and its decision may be quashed by the Divisional Court: see *Cumings v Birkenhead Corpn* [1972] Ch 12 at 37–38, [1971] 2 All ER 881 at 885, CA, obiter per Lord Denning MR (local education authority policy that children who attended Roman Catholic primary schools would only be considered for Roman Catholic secondary schools, because of a shortage of non-Roman Catholic secondary school places, not ultra vires). The ambit of Lord Denning's dictum is narrow: a policy that was discriminatory, but based on valid educational reasons, such as a policy of educating immigrant children separately because of their special language needs, would be intra vires, but a decision to allocate children to particular schools simply because of the colour of their skin would be ultra vires. As to ultra vires acts see ADMINISTRATIVE LAW vol 1(1) (2001 Reissue) para 74 et seq.

3   The leading cases concerning the meaning of 'public' or 'section of the public' are cases decided in the context of the Race Relations Act 1968 s 2 (repealed). In *Charter v Race Relations Board* [1973] AC 868, [1973] 1 All ER 512, HL, it was held that the words 'a section of the public' are intended to limit the

operation of the Act; the word 'public' is used in contrast to 'private'. A members' club is not within the definition of a section of the public if it has rules which make provision for a genuine selection of persons to be members on grounds of their acceptability, and the rules are in practice complied with. As a result, Parliament extended the law in the Race Relations Act 1976, so that clubs are now covered by s 25: see para 465 post. See also *Dockers' Labour Club and Institute Ltd v Race Relations Board* [1976] AC 285, [1974] 3 All ER 592, HL (members of the Dockers' Labour club were not a section of the public, nor were their guests and associates, although there were approximately one million associates). Foster parents were held to be providing facilities to a section of the public, i e to the children who are in care of the local authority, coming to the foster parents haphazardly from the public at large (see *Applin v Race Relations Board* [1975] AC 259, [1974] 2 All ER 73, HL), but Parliament reversed the effect of this decision in the Race Relations Act 1976 (see s 23(2); and para 462 post). It is doubtful whether a local authority may be considered a member of the public: *Applin v Race Relations Board* supra (held that the services of foster parents were sought by the local authority on behalf of the children, who were a section of the public). A private club which admits persons who are not members (e g a golf club which admits members of the public at certain times on payment of a 'green fee') is concerned with the provision of a service to the public: *Hector v Smethwick Labour Club and Institute* (29 November 1988) Lexis, CA.

4   A section of the public may not be defined in a way which itself involves discrimination: *James v Eastleigh Borough Council* [1990] 2 AC 751, [1990] 2 All ER 607, HL; *Tejani v Superintendent Registrar for the District of Peterborough* [1986] IRLR 502, CA. It was conceded in *Alexander v Home Office* [1988] 2 All ER 118, [1988] 1 WLR 968, CA, that prisoners are a section of the public.

5   For the meaning of 'discrimination' see para 447 note 4 ante.

6   Race Relations Act 1976 s 20(1).

7   Ibid s 20(1)(a).

8   The presence of the word 'normal' indicates that the provision is not intended to deal with a discriminator who provides goods, facilities or services upon an isolated occasion, but is intended to deal with one who holds himself out as engaged regularly, or at least recurrently, in providing such goods, facilities or services to the public: *Dockers' Labour Club and Institute Ltd v Race Relations Board* [1976] AC 285 at 296–297, [1974] 3 All ER 592 at 599, HL, per Lord Diplock. See also *Hector v Smethwick Labour Club and Institute* (29 November 1988) Lexis, CA.

9   Race Relations Act 1976 s 20(1)(b). See also *Gill v El Vino Co Ltd* [1983] QB 425, [1983] 1 All ER 398, CA (refusal to serve women at the bar of a wine bar); *Quinn v Williams Furniture Ltd* [1981] ICR 328, CA (refusal of hire-purchase facilities to woman without husband's guarantee). For exceptions see para 462 post.

10   For the meaning of 'harassment' see para 444 ante.

11   Race Relations Act 1976 s 20(3) (added by the Race Relations Act 1976 (Amendment) Regulations 2003, SI 2003/1626, reg 22(2)).

12   See the Race Relations Act 1976 s 27(2)(a). For the meaning of 'Great Britain' see para 325 note 6 ante.

13   See ibid s 27(2)(b).

14   See ibid s 27(3). The provision also applies where the refusal or omission occurs on a British registered ship, or an aircraft or hovercraft registered in the United Kingdom and operated by a person who has his principal place of business, or is ordinarily resident, in Great Britain, even if the ship, aircraft or hovercraft is outside the United Kingdom: see s 27(3), (4). For the meaning of 'the United Kingdom' see para 325 note 6 ante.

15   Ibid s 27(4).

16   Ibid s 27(5).

462. Exceptions to discrimination and harassment in the provision of goods, facilities and services. The provisions concerning the provision of goods, facilities and services[1] do not apply to discrimination or harassment[2] which is rendered unlawful by the employment or education provisions of the Race Relations Act 1976[3], or which would be rendered unlawful by them if not covered by an exception to the Act[4].

The provisions do not apply to foster parents and those in a similar position[5]. The provisions do not apply to anything done by a person as a participant in arrangements under which he (for reward or not) takes into his home[6], and treats as if they were members of his family, children, elderly persons, or persons requiring a special degree of care and attention[7].

The provisions do not render unlawful any act[8] done in affording persons of a particular racial group access to facilities or services to meet the special needs of persons of that group in regard to their education, training or welfare, or any ancillary benefits[9].

The provisions do not apply to small dwellings[10].

1   Ie the Race Relations Act 1976 ss 20, 21 (as amended): see paras 461 ante, 463 post.
2   For the meaning of 'harassment' see para 444 ante.
3   See the Race Relations Act 1976 s 23(1)(a) (s 23(1) amended by the Race Relations Act 1976
    (Amendment) Regulations 2003, SI 2003/1626, reg 25(2)(a); and the Race Relations Act 1976 s 23(1)(a)
    amended by the Race Relations Act 1976 (Amendment) Regulations 2003, SI 2003/1626, reg 25(2)(b)).
    The employment or education provisions of the Race Relations Act 1976 are those in Pt II (ss 4–15) (as
    amended), and in s 17 (as amended) or s 18 (as amended): see para 446 et seq ante.
4   See ibid s 23(1)(b) (amended by the Race Relations Act 1976 (Amendment) Regulations 2003,
    SI 2003/1626, reg 25(2)(c)). The exceptions mentioned are those in the Race Relations Act 1976 s 4(3)
    (as amended), s 4A(1)(b) (as added), s 5(1)(b), s 6 (as amended), s 7(4) (as amended), s 9 (as amended;
    prospectively amended) and s 14(4) (see para 446 et seq ante): see s 23(1)(b) (as so amended).
5   See ibid s 23(2).
6   The exception covers only those who actually take people into their homes; discrimination by local
    authorities or agencies who place the children and others in need of care would be unlawful since they
    do not fall within this exception.
7   Race Relations Act 1976 s 23(2). There is no specific exception under the Race Relations Act 1976 to
    cover the provision of services and facilities by political parties, in contrast to the Sex Discrimination
    Act 1975, which excludes from the Act special provision for persons of one sex only in the constitution,
    organisation or administration of a political party: see the Sex Discrimination Act 1975 s 33 (as
    amended); and para 383 ante. However, 'black sections' of political parties are justifiable as facilities or
    services to meet the special needs of particular racial groups, under the Race Relations Act 1976 s 35: see
    para 482 post.
8   As to the meaning of 'act' see para 442 note 7 ante.
9   See the Race Relations Act 1976 s 35; and para 482 post.
10 See ibid s 22 (as amended); and para 464 post.

463.   Premises and housing.   The Race Relations Act 1976 provides for the
protection of potential tenants and purchasers of property from discrimination by
landlords and vendors[1].

It is unlawful for a person[2], in relation to premises[3] in Great Britain[4] of which he has
power to dispose[5], to discriminate against another[6] in the terms on which he offers him
those premises[7], or by refusing his application for those premises[8], or in his treatment of
him in relation to any list[9] of persons in need of premises of that description[10].

Existing tenants are also protected, both against landlords and against others such as
managing agents[11]. It is unlawful for a person, in relation to premises managed by him,
to discriminate against a person occupying the premises[12] in the way he affords him
access to any benefits or facilities[13], or by refusing or deliberately omitting to afford him
access to them[14], or by evicting him, or subjecting him to any other detriment[15].

It is also unlawful for a person, in relation to premises in Great Britain of which he
has power to dispose, or in relation to premises managed by him, to subject to
harassment[16] a person who applies for or, as the case may be, occupies such premises[17].

The Act gives further protection to potential sub-tenants in circumstances in which
the licence or consent of the landlord or of any other person is required for the disposal
to any person of premises in Great Britain comprised in a tenancy[18]. It is unlawful for
the landlord or person whose consent is needed, to discriminate against a person by
withholding the licence or consent for disposal[19] of the premises to him, or in relation
to such a licence or consent, to subject to harassment a person who applies for the
licence or consent, or from whom the licence or consent is witheld[20].

1   For the meaning of 'discrimination' see para 447 note 4 ante. The Race Relations Act 1976 s 47 (as
    amended; prospectively repealed) (see para 491 post) gives the Commission for Racial Equality ('CRE')
    the power to issue codes of practice relating to housing. As to the CRE see para 488 et seq post. As to the
    Commission for Equality and Human Rights, which is to replace the CRE, see para 305 et seq ante. The
    CRE has produced a revised Code of Practice on Racial Equality in Housing (replacing earlier codes
    from 1991 and 1992 about rented and non-rented (owner occupied) housing). See para 491 post. See
    also the Race Relations Code of Practice (Housing) Order 2006, SI 2006/2239.

2 As to the meaning of 'person' see para 344 note 3 ante.

3 'Premises', unless the context otherwise requires, includes land of any description: Race Relations Act 1976 s 78(2).

4 For the meaning of 'Great Britain' see para 325 note 6 ante.

5 'Dispose', in relation to premises, includes granting the right to occupy the premises, and any reference to acquiring premises is to be construed accordingly: Race Relations Act 1976 s 78(1). Section 21 (as amended) therefore protects potential tenants as well as purchasers. It should be noted that the provision only covers discrimination and harassment by the lessor or vendor, who has the right to dispose of the property. The provision does not cover estate agents who are covered by s 20 (as amended), as persons who provide a facility or service to the public: see para 461 ante. They are also subject to the Estate Agents Act 1979 s 3 (as amended), under which the Office of Fair Trading may, if it is satisfied that an estate agent has committed discrimination in the course of estate agency work, make an order prohibiting him from doing any estate agency work at all, or from doing estate agency work of a description specified in the order: see AGENCY vol 2(1) (Reissue) para 22. As to the Office of Fair Trading see TRADE, INDUSTRY AND INDUSTRIAL RELATIONS vol 47 (2001 Reissue) paras 504–507.

6 Race Relations Act 1976 s 21(1). This provision does not apply to discrimination, on grounds other than those of race or ethnic or national origins, by a person who owns an estate or interest in the premises and wholly occupies them unless he uses the services of an estate agent for the purposes of the disposal of the premises, or publishes or causes to be published an advertisement in connection with the disposal: s 21(3) (amended by the Race Relations Act 1976 (Amendment) Regulations 2003, SI 2003/1626, reg 23(2)(b)). As to the meanings of 'ethnic origins' and 'national origins' see para 441 ante. 'Estate agent' means a person who, by way of profession or trade, provides services for the purpose of finding premises for persons seeking to acquire them or assisting in the disposal of premises: Race Relations Act 1976 s 78(1). As to the meaning of 'profession' see para 451 note 1 ante; and as to the meaning of 'trade' see para 451 note 2 ante. A vendor is liable for the acts of his estate agent done with his authority: see s 32(2); and para 476 post. As to discriminatory advertisements generally see s 29 (as amended; prospectively amended); and para 473 post.

7 Ibid s 21(1)(a).

8 Ibid s 21(1)(b).

9 This provision is wide enough to cover local authorities who discriminate in the allocation of council property to those on the local authority housing list. See further HOUSING vol 22 (2006 Reissue) para 239 et seq.

10 Race Relations Act 1976 s 21(1)(c).

11 See ibid s 21(2); and the text and notes 12–15 infra.

12 Ibid s 21(2).

13 As to the affording of access to benefits, facilities and services see para 446 note 14 ante.

14 Race Relations Act 1976 s 21(2)(a).

15 Ibid s 21(2)(b). As to the meaning of 'detriment' see paras 440 note 12, 446 note 17 ante.

16 For the meaning of 'harassment' see para 444 ante.

17 Race Relations Act 1976 s 21(2A) (added by the Race Relations Act 1976 (Amendment) Regulations 2003, SI 2003/1626, reg 23(2)(a)).

18 See the Race Relations Act 1976 s 24(1). 'Tenancy' means a tenancy, whenever made, created by a lease or sub-lease, by an agreement for a lease or sub-lease, or by a tenancy agreement or in pursuance of any enactment: see s 24(4), (5).

19 'Disposal', in relation to premises comprised in a tenancy, includes assignment or assignation of the tenancy and sub-letting or parting with possession of the premises or any part of the premises: ibid s 24(4).

20 Ibid s 24(1) (amended by the Race Relations Act 1976 (Amendment) Regulations 2003, SI 2003/1626, reg 26(2)(a)). This provision does not apply to discrimination on grounds other than those of race or ethnic or national origins if the person withholding the licence or consent or a near relative of his (called 'the relevant occupier') resides, and intends to continue to reside, on the premises, and there is on the premises, in addition to the accommodation occupied by the relevant occupier, accommodation (not being storage accommodation or means of access) shared by the relevant occupier with other persons residing on the premises who are not members of his household, and the premises are small premises, as defined by s 22(2) (see para 464 post): s 24(2), (3) (s 24(2) amended by the Race Relations Act 1976 (Amendment) Regulations 2003, SI 2003/1626, reg 26(2)(b)). A person is a 'near relative' of another if that person is the wife or husband or civil partner, parent or child, grandparent or grandchild, or brother or sister of the other (whether of full blood or half blood or by marriage or civil partnership); and 'child' includes an illegitimate child and the wife or husband or civil partner of an illegitimate child: Race Relations Act 1976 s 78(1), (5) (s 78(5) amended by the Civil Partnership Act 2004 s 261(1), Sch 27 para 55(a)). As to civil partnerships generally see MATRIMONIAL LAW.

464. Exceptions to discrimination in the provision of premises and housing. The most important exception to the provisions of the Race Relations Act 1976 concerning the disposal and management of premises[1] is the exception for small premises[2]. The provisions do not apply to discrimination on grounds other than those of race or ethnic or national origins[3] in either the provision by a person[4] of accommodation in any premises or the disposal[5] of premises by him[6] if that person or a near relative of his (called 'the relevant occupier') resides, and intends to continue to reside, on the premises[7], and there is on the premises, in addition to the accommodation occupied by the relevant occupier, accommodation (not being storage accommodation or means of access) shared by the relevant occupier with other persons who are not members of his household[8], and the premises are small premises[9]. A similar exception applies where the relevant occupier is the person withholding a licence or consent to the assignment or sub-letting of a tenancy[10].

Other exceptions prevent overlap between the provisions concerning goods, services and premises and the employment and education provisions of the Act[11].

Acts done to afford access to facilities and services to meet the special housing needs of a particular racial group are lawful[12].

1   Ie the Race Relations Act 1976 s 21 (as amended): see para 463 ante. As to the meaning of 'premises' see para 463 note 3 ante. This exception also applies to s 20(1): see para 461 ante.
2   Premises are to be treated as small premises if: (1) in the case of premises comprising residential accommodation for one or more households (under separate letting or similar agreements) in addition to the accommodation occupied by the relevant occupier (see the text to note 7 infra), there is not normally residential occupation for more than two such households and only the relevant occupier and any member of his household reside in the accommodation occupied by him (ibid s 22(2)(a)); and (2) in the case of premises not falling within head (1) supra, there is not normally residential accommodation for more than six persons in addition to the relevant occupier and any members of his household (s 22(2)(b)).
3   As to the meanings of 'ethnic origins' and 'national origins' see para 441 ante.
4   As to the meaning of 'person' see para 344 note 3 ante.
5   As to the meaning of 'dispose' see para 463 note 5 ante.
6   Race Relations Act 1976 s 22(1) (amended by the Race Relations Act 1976 (Amendment) Regulations 2003, SI 2003/1626, reg 24).
7   Race Relations Act 1976 s 22(1)(a). As to when a person is a near relative see para 463 note 20 ante.
8   Ibid s 22(1)(b).
9   Ibid s 22(1)(c).
10   See ibid s 24(2) (as amended); and para 463 ante.
11   See ibid s 23 (as amended); and para 462 ante.
12   See ibid s 35; and para 482 post.

D. CLUBS AND ASSOCIATIONS

465. Scope of provisions as to clubs and associations. The employment provisions of the Race Relations Act 1976 prohibit discrimination by trade unions and employers' associations[1]. Other clubs and associations are dealt with under other provisions of the Act[2], and there is no overlap between the two sets of provisions[3]. Similarly, the provisions as to clubs and associations do not apply to clubs which provide services or facilities to the public[4]. Subject to the above, any association is within the scope of the Act whether it is corporate or unincorporated, and whether or not its activities are carried on for profit, if it has 25 or more members, and if admission to membership is regulated by its constitution[5].

1   See the Race Relations Act 1976 s 11 (as amended); and para 451 ante.
2   See ibid ss 25, 26; and paras 466–467 post. These provisions are enforced by complaint to a county court (see s 57 (as amended); and paras 499–500 post), whereas the employment provisions are enforced by a complaint to an employment tribunal (see s 54 (as amended); and para 499 post).

3   Ibid s 25 applies only to associations that are not organisations to which s 11 (as amended) applies: s 25(1)(c).

4   See ibid s 25(1)(b). Such clubs are covered by s 20 (as amended): see para 461 ante. As to the test to be applied to determine whether a club is providing services to the public see *Charter v Race Relations Board* [1973] AC 868, [1973] 1 All ER 512, HL. See also para 461 ante. The enactment of the Race Relations Act 1976 s 25 overruled the effect of the actual decision in *Charter v Race Relations Board* supra.

5   See the Race Relations Act 1976 s 25(1). See generally CLUBS vol 6 (2003 Reissue) para 103.

466.   Prohibitions on membership.   It is unlawful for an association to which the Race Relations Act 1976 applies[1] to discriminate[2] against a person who is not a member of the association in the terms on which it is prepared to admit him to membership[3], or by refusing or deliberately omitting to accept his application for membership[4].

It is unlawful for such an association to discriminate against a member[5] or associate[6] of the association[7] in the way it affords him access to any benefits, facilities or services[8], or by refusing or deliberately omitting to afford him access to them[9], or by depriving a member of his membership or by varying the terms on which he is a member[10], or by depriving an associate of his rights as an associate or by varying those rights[11], or by subjecting a member or associate to any other detriment[12].

1   Ie an association to which the Race Relations Act 1976 s 25 applies: see para 465 ante.

2   Ibid s 25(2). For the meaning of 'discrimination' see para 447 note 4 ante.

3   Ibid s 25(2)(a).

4   Ibid s 25(2)(b).

5   A person is a member of an association if he belongs to it by virtue of his admission to any sort of membership provided for by its constitution (and is not merely a person with certain rights under its constitution by virtue of his membership of some other association); and references to membership of an association are to be construed accordingly: ibid s 25(4)(a).

6   A person is an associate of an association if, not being a member of it, he has under its constitution some or all of the rights enjoyed by members (or would have apart from any provision in its constitution authorising the refusal of those rights in particular cases): ibid s 25(4)(b).

7   Ibid s 25(3).

8   As to the affording of access to benefits, facilities and services see para 446 note 14 ante.

9   Race Relations Act 1976 s 25(3)(a).

10   See ibid s 25(3)(b).

11   See ibid s 25(3)(c).

12   See ibid s 25(3)(d). As to the meaning of 'detriment' see paras 440 note 12, 446 note 17 ante.

467.   Exceptions for clubs and associations.   Apart from the general exceptions to the provisions of the Race Relations Act 1976[1], certain associations are subject to a special exception. These are associations of which the main object[2] is to enable the benefits of membership (whatever they may be) to be enjoyed by persons of a particular racial group defined otherwise than by reference to colour[3]. The acts[4] of such associations are not unlawful under the provisions concerning associations unless they involve discrimination[5] on the ground of colour[6].

1   See para 481 et seq post.

2   In determining the main object of an association, regard is to be had to the essential character of the association and to all the relevant circumstances including, in particular, the extent to which the affairs of the association are so conducted that the persons primarily enjoying the benefits of membership are of the racial group in question: Race Relations Act 1976 s 26(1). For the meaning of 'racial group' see para 441 ante.

3   Ibid s 26(1).

4   As to the meaning of 'act' see para 442 note 7 ante.

5   For the meaning of 'discrimination' see para 447 note 4 ante.

6   See the Race Relations Act 1976 s 26(2). For example, the operation of a colour bar by a social club of more than 25 members is unlawful, the operation of a bar against Jews by a social club is unlawful unless the club has as a main object the provision of benefits to Christians, a club for the benefit of Afro-Caribbeans is lawful, and a club which provides access for blacks to facilities and services to meet their special educational, training and welfare needs is lawful: see further s 35; and para 482 post.

E. PLANNING FUNCTIONS

468.   Planning functions.   It is unlawful for a planning authority to discriminate[1]
against a person in carrying out its planning functions[2].

A planning authority is a county, county borough, district or London borough
council, the Broads Authority, a national park authority or a joint planning board[3] and
includes an urban development corporation and a body having functions[4] (whether as an
enterprise zone authority or as a body invited to prepare a scheme) in relation to
enterprise zones[5]. 'Planning functions' means functions under the Town and Country
Planning Act 1990, the Planning (Listed Buildings and Conservation Areas) Act 1990,
and the Planning (Hazardous Substances) Act 1990, and such other functions as may be
prescribed[6], and includes, in relation to an urban development corporation, planning
functions under Part XVI of the Local Government, Planning and Land Act 1980[7] and,
in relation to an enterprise zone authority or body invited to prepare an enterprise zone
scheme, functions under Part XVIII of that Act[8].

1   For the meaning of 'discrimination' see para 447 note 4 ante.
2   Race Relations Act 1976 s 19A(1) (s 19A added by the Housing and Planning Act 1986 s 55).
3   Race Relations Act 1976 s 19A(2)(a) (as added (see note 2 supra); and amended by the Norfolk and
     Suffolk Broads 1988 s 2(5), Sch 3 para 29; the Local Government (Wales) Act 1994 s 66(6), Sch 16
     para 52; and the Environment Act 1995 ss 78, 120(3), Sch 10 para 15(1), Sch 24). As to local government
     authorities in England and Wales see LOCAL GOVERNMENT vol 29(1) (Reissue) para 23 et seq; and as to
     London borough councils see also LONDON GOVERNMENT vol 29(2) (Reissue) para 35 et seq. As to the
     Broads Authority see OPEN SPACES AND ANCIENT MONUMENTS vol 34 (Reissue) para 130; and as to
     national park authorities see OPEN SPACES AND ANCIENT MONUMENTS vol 34 (Reissue) para 157 et
     seq. As to joint planning boards see TOWN AND COUNTRY PLANNING vol 46(1) (Reissue) para 30; as to
     urban development corporations see TOWN AND COUNTRY PLANNING vol 46(3) (Reissue) para 1428 et
     seq; and as to enterprise zones see TOWN AND COUNTRY PLANNING vol 46(3) (Reissue) para 1495.
4   Ie under the Local Government, Planning and Land Act 1980 s 179, Sch 32 (both as amended): see
     TOWN AND COUNTRY PLANNING vol 46(3) (Reissue) para 1491 et seq.
5   Race Relations Act 1976 s 19A(2) (as added: see note 2 supra). See further TOWN AND COUNTRY
     PLANNING vol 46(1) (Reissue) para 28 et seq.
6   Ibid s 19A(3)(a) (as added (see note 2 supra); and amended by the Planning (Consequential Provisions)
     Act 1990 s 4, Sch 2 para 36). See further TOWN AND COUNTRY PLANNING. 'Prescribed' means
     prescribed by regulations made by the Secretary of State: Race Relations Act 1976 s 78(1). At the date at
     which this volume states the law, no regulations had been made for these purposes. As to the Secretary of
     State and the National Assembly for Wales see para 302 ante.
         Any power of a Minister of the Crown to make orders or regulations under the provisions of the
     Race Relations Act 1976 (except s 50(2)(a) (prospectively repealed) (see para 494 post)) is exercisable by
     statutory instrument: s 74(1) (amended by the Employment Act 1989 s 29(3), Sch 6 para 16). An order
     made by a Minister of the Crown under ss 1–73 (as amended) (except s 50(2)(a) (prospectively repealed)
     and s 73(1) (as amended) (see para 438 ante)), and any regulations made under s 56(5), (6) (as added and
     amended) (see para 499 post) or s 75(5)(a), (9A) (as added and amended) (see para 457 ante), are subject
     to annulment in pursuance of a resolution of either House of Parliament: s 74(2) (amended by the
     Employment Act 1989 s 29(4), Sch 7 Pt II; the Race Relations (Remedies) Act 1994 s 2(2); and the
     Armed Forces Act 1996 s 23(5)). An order under the Race Relations Act 1976 may make different
     provision in relation to different cases or classes of case, may exclude certain cases or classes of case, and
     may contain transitional provisions and savings: s 74(3). Any power conferred by the Race Relations
     Act 1976 to make orders includes power (exercisable in the like manner and subject to the like
     conditions) to vary or revoke any order so made: s 74(4). As from a day to be appointed, the words
     '(except s 50(2)(a))' in s 74(1), the words '(except s 50(2)(a) and s 73(1))' in s 74(2), and s 74(5) (see
     para 494 post) are removed: s 74 (prospectively amended by the Equality Act 2006 ss 40, 91, Sch 3
     paras 21, 32, Sch 4). At the date at which this volume states the law no such day had been appointed.
7   Ie the Local Government, Planning and Land Act 1980 Pt XVI (ss 134–172) (as amended): see TOWN
     AND COUNTRY PLANNING vol 46(3) (Reissue) para 1426 et seq.
8   Race Relations Act 1976 s 19A(3) (as added: see note 2 supra). The functions referred to in the text are
     those under the Local Government, Planning and Land Act 1980 Pt XVIII (s 179) (as amended) (see
     TOWN AND COUNTRY PLANNING vol 46(3) (Reissue) para 1491 et seq): see the Race Relations
     Act 1976 s 19A(3) (as so added).

F. LOCAL AUTHORITIES AND OTHER PUBLIC AUTHORITIES

469. Duty of local authorities. Every body[1] or other person[2] specified in the Race Relations Act 1976[3] or of a description falling within the Race Relations Act 1976[4] must, in carrying out its functions, have due regard to the need to eliminate unlawful racial discrimination[5] and to promote equality of opportunity and good relations between persons of different racial groups[6]. In relation to the carrying out of immigration and nationality functions[7], this duty[8] is to have due regard to the need to eliminate unlawful racial discrimination and to promote good relations between persons of different racial groups[9].

The Secretary of State[10] may make an order amending the list of specified bodies and other persons referred to above[11], but no such order may extend the bodies and other persons[12] unless the Secretary of State considers that the extension relates to a person who exercises functions of a public nature[13].

The Secretary of State may, after consulting the Commission for Racial Equality ('CRE')[14], make an order imposing on all such persons[15] as he considers appropriate such duties as he considers appropriate for the purpose of ensuring the better performance by those persons of their duties[16]. The Secretary of State must consult the National Assembly for Wales before making such an order[17] in relation to functions exercisable in relation to Wales by a person who is not a Welsh public authority[18] and must not make an order in relation to functions of a Welsh public authority except with the consent of the National Assembly for Wales[19].

If the CRE is satisfied that a person has failed to comply with, or is failing to comply with, any duty imposed by such an order[20], it may serve on that person a compliance notice[21]. The CRE may issue codes of practice containing such practical guidance as it thinks fit in relation to the performance by persons of certain duties[22]. The CRE may apply to a designated county court for an order requiring a person[23] to furnish any information required by a compliance notice if the person fails to furnish the information to the CRE in accordance with the notice, or the CRE has reasonable cause to believe that the person does not intend to furnish the information[24]. If the CRE considers that a person has not, within three months of the date on which a compliance notice was served on that person, complied with any requirement of the notice for that person to comply with a duty imposed by an appropriate order[25], it may apply to a designated county court for an order requiring the person to comply with the requirement of the notice[26]. If the court is satisfied that the application is well-founded, it may grant the order in the terms applied for or in more limited terms[27].

Local authorities[28] have previously relied on this general duty[29] to justify steps taken by them to ensure that the companies with which such authorities contract for the supply of goods and services are operating equal opportunities policies (a process known as 'contract compliance'). The content and scope of the duty as it relates to contract compliance was transformed by the Local Government Act 1988. The purpose of this Act was to prohibit local authorities from taking political considerations, and other non-commercial matters, into account when awarding contracts[30]. The Act prohibits the operation of contract compliance schemes by public authorities, but makes a limited and closely defined saving for local authorities to allow for their duty under the Race Relations Act 1976[31].

By the Local Government Act 1988, public authorities[32], including local authorities, have a duty, in exercising regulated functions[33] in relation to their public supply or works contracts[34], to exercise any such function without reference to non-commercial matters[35]. However, local authorities and other public authorities may take into account non-commercial matters in accordance with their duty under the Race Relations Act 1976, but only as specifically provided by the Local Government Act 1988[36].

Where it is reasonably necessary to secure compliance with a local or other public authority's duty under the Race Relations Act 1976, the authority may: (1) ask approved questions[37] seeking information or undertakings relating to workforce matters[38] and may consider the responses to them; or (2) may include in a draft contract or draft tender for a contract terms or provisions relating to workforce matters, and may consider the responses to them[39].

An authority's powers under these provisions[40] do not apply to the termination of a subsisting contract, and, in relation to functions as respects approved lists or proposed contracts, do not authorise questions in other than written form[41].

1   As to the meaning of 'body' see para 457 note 11 ante. The bodies and persons subject to the general statutory duty under the Race Relations Act 1976 s 71 (as substituted) are those specified in Sch 1A (as added and amended).

Those bodies and persons specified in Sch 1A Pt I (as added and amended) include Ministers of the Crown and government departments (not including the Security Service, the Intelligence Service or the Government Communications Headquarters), the National Assembly for Wales and Assembly subsidiaries, the armed forces, strategic health authorities, special health authorities, primary care trusts, NHS trusts, NHS foundation trusts, local authorities, the Greater London Authority, the Common Council of the City of London in its capacity as a local authority or port health authority, the Sub-Treasurer of the Inner Temple or the Under-Treasurer of the Middle Temple, in his capacity as a local authority, the Council of the Isles of Scilly, parish meetings, charter trustees, fire and rescue authorities, waste disposal authorities, port health authorities, internal drainage boards, local probation boards established under the Criminal Justice and Court Services Act 2000 s 4, joint authorities established under the Local Government Act 1985 Pt IV (ss 23–42) (as amended) (see LOCAL GOVERNMENT), the London Fire and Emergency Planning Authority, bodies corporate established pursuant to an order under s 67 or the Local Government Act 1992 s 22 (see LOCAL GOVERNMENT), the Broads Authority, specified local authority joint committees and joint boards, joint authorities established under s 21 (as amended) (see LOCAL GOVERNMENT), passenger transport executives, Transport for London, the London Development Agency, regional development agencies, national park authorities, specified joint planning boards in Wales, magistrates' courts committees, governing bodies of educational establishments maintained by local education authorities, governing bodies of institutions within the further and the higher education sectors, the Housing Corporation, housing action trusts, police authorities, the Metropolitan Police Authority, and the Common Council of the City of London in its capacity as a police authority: Race Relations Act 1976 Sch 1A Pt I (added by the Race Relations (Amendment) Act 2000 s 2(2), Sch 1; and amended by the Health and Social Care (Community Health and Standards) Act 2003 Sch 4 para 22; the Fire and Rescue Services Act 2004 Sch 1 para 48; the Serious Organised Crime and Police Act 2005 Sch 4 para 35, Sch 17 Pt 2; the National Health Service (Consequential Provisions) Act 2006 s 2, Sch 1 paras 55, 56; the Race Relations Act 1976 (General Statutory Duty) Order 2001, SI 2001/3457; and the Race Relations Act 1976 (General Statutory Duty) Order 2003, SI 2003/3007).

Those bodies and persons specified in the Race Relations Act 1976 Sch 1A Pt II (as added and amended) include the Royal College of General Practitioners and other royal medical colleges in respect of their public functions, and various other health bodies; various educational bodies; the British Transport Police, specified chief constables, the Civil Nuclear Police Authority, the chief constable of the Civil Nuclear Constabulary, the police commissioners for the Metropolis and the City of London, the Serious Organised Crime Agency, and other specified police bodies; various libraries, museums and other bodies and individuals associated with the arts; in respect of their public functions, the Bank of England and the British Broadcasting Corporation, and other specified public corporations and nationalised industries; various regulatory, audit and inspection bodies, including the Advisory, Conciliation and Arbitration Service, the Financial Services Authority and, in respect of their public functions, the General Council of the Bar of England and Wales, and the Law Society of England and Wales; various research bodies; the British Waterways Board; the Children and Family Court Advisory and Support Service; the Commission for Equality and Human Rights; the Commission for Racial Equality; the Electoral Commission; the Environment Agency; the Equal Opportunities Commission; the Health and Safety Executive; the Law Commission; the Legal Services Commission; the Sentencing Advisory Panel; and the Strategic Rail Authority: Sch 1A Pt II (added by the Race Relations Act 1976 (General Statutory Duty) Order 2001, SI 2001/3457, art 2(d), Schedule; and amended by the Courts Act 2003 Sch 8 para 187(1); the Health and Social Care (Community Health and Standards) Act 2003 Sch 14 Pt IV; the Health Protection Agency Act 2004 Sch 3 para 8; the Energy Act 2004 Sch 14 para 4; the Gambling

Act 2005 Sch 16 para 9; the Serious Organised Crime and Police Act 2005 Sch 4 para 35; the General and Specialist Medical Practice (Education, Training and Qualifications) Order 2003, SI 2003/1250; the Health Professions Order 2001 (Consequential Amendments) Order 2003, SI 2003/1590; the Race Relations Act 1976 (General Statutory Duty) Order 2003, SI 2003/3007; the Health Act 1999 (Consequential Amendments) (Nursing and Midwifery) Order 2004, SI 2004/1771; the Health and Social Care (Community Health and Standards) Act 2003 (Commission for Healthcare Audit and Inspection and Commission for Social Care Inspection) (Consequential Provisions) Order 2004, SI 2004/2987; the Race Relations Act 1976 (General Statutory Duty) Order 2004, SI 2004/3127; the Education Act 2005 Sch 14 para 8; and, in relation to Wales, by the Library Advisory Council for Wales Abolition and Consequential Amendments Order 2004, SI 2004/803; the Welsh Development Agency (Transfer of Functions to the National Assembly for Wales and Abolition) Order 2005, SI 2005/3226; the National Council for Education and Training for Wales (Transfer of Functions to the National Assembly for Wales and Abolition) Order 2005, SI 2005/3238; the Qualifications, Curriculum and Assessment Authority for Wales (Transfer of Functions to the National Assembly for Wales and Abolition) Order 2005, SI 2005/3239; the Historic Buildings Council for Wales (Abolition) Order 2006, SI 2006/63; and the Ancient Monuments Board for Wales (Abolition) Order 2006, SI 2006/64). The references to the Commission for Racial Equality and the Equal Opportunities Commission are prospectively repealed (see the Equality Act 2006 Sch 3 para 35, Sch 4), as is the reference to the Strategic Rail Authority (see the Railways Act 2005 s 60(2)).

Those bodies and persons specified in the Race Relations Act 1976 Sch 1A Pt III (as added and amended) include the Commission for Patient and Public Involvement in Health, the Council for the Regulation of Health Care Professionals, the Health Professions Council, the Nursing and Midwifery Council, the National College for School Leadership, the Independent Police Complaints Commission and other specified police bodies, various regulatory, audit and inspection bodies, the Countryside Agency and, in respect of its public functions, the Royal College of Veterinary Surgeons: Sch 1A Pt III (added by the Race Relations Act 1976 (General Statutory Duty) Order 2003, SI 2003/3007, art 2(c), Schedule; and amended by the Serious Organised Crime and Police Act 2005 Sch 4 para 35; and the Race Relations Act 1976 (General Statutory Duty) Order 2004, SI 2004/3127).

Those bodies specified in the Race Relations Act 1976 Sch 1A Pt IV (as added and amended) include the Commission for Healthcare Audit and Inspection, the Independent Regulator of NHS Foundation Trusts, the Commission for Social Care Inspection, the Office of Communications ('OFCOM'), the Social Fund Commissioner of the Independent Review Service, the National Museum for Science and Industry, Remploy Limited, Royal Parks in England, UK Sport and Women's National Commission: Sch 1A Pt IV (added by the Race Relations Act 1976 (General Statutory Duty) Order 2004, SI 2004/3127, art 2(c), Schedule).

Those bodies and persons specified in the Race Relations Act 1976 Sch 1A Pt V (as added and amended) include the Arts and Humanities Research Council, the Football Licensing Authority, the Gas and Electricity Markets Authority, the Pensions Regulator, Bòrd na Gàidhlig, the Board of the Pension Protection Fund, the British Transport Police Authority, the Office for Fair Access, and the Risk Management Authority: Sch 1A Pt V (added by the Race Relations Act 1976 (General Statutory Duty) Order 2006, SI 2006/2470, art 2(e), Schedule).

2   As to the meaning of 'person' see para 344 note 3 ante.

3   Ie specified in the Race Relations Act 1976 Sch 1A (as added and amended): see note 1 supra.

4   Ie falling within ibid Sch 1A (as added and amended): see note 1 supra.

5   For the meaning of 'discrimination' see para 447 note 4 ante.

6   Race Relations Act 1976 s 71(1) (s 71 substituted, and ss 71A–71D added, by the Race Relations (Amendment) Act 2000 s 2(1)). For the meaning of 'racial group' see para 441 ante.

Where an entry in the Race Relations Act 1976 Sch 1A (as added and amended) (see note 1 supra) is limited to a person in a particular capacity, s 71(1) (as substituted) does not apply to that person in any other capacity: s 71A(2) (as so added). Where an entry in Sch 1A (as added and amended) is limited to particular functions of a person, s 71(1) (as substituted) does not apply to that person in relation to any other functions: s 71A(3) (as so added).

7   'Immigration and nationality functions' means functions exercisable by virtue of the Immigration Acts (excluding certain provisions of the Immigration Act 1971 relating to offences), the British Nationality Act 1981, the British Nationality (Falkland Islands) Act 1983, the British Nationality (Hong Kong) Act 1990, the Hong Kong (War Wives and Widows) Act 1996, the British Nationality (Hong Kong) Act 1997, the Special Immigration Appeals Commission Act 1997, provision made under the European Communities Act 1972 s 2(2) (as amended) which relates to the subject matter of any of the above enactments, or any provision of Community law which relates to the subject matter of any of those enactments: Race Relations Act 1976 s 71A(1A) (s 71A as added (see note 6 supra); and s 71A(1A) added by the Nationality, Immigration and Asylum Act 2000 s 6(5)(b)).

8   Ie the duty under the Race Relations Act 1976 s 71(1) (as substituted): see the text and notes 1–6 supra.

9   Ibid s 71A(1) (s 71A as added (see note 6 supra); and s 71A(1) amended by the Nationality, Immigration and Asylum Act 2000 ss 6(5)(a), 161, Sch 9).
10   As to the Secretary of State and the National Assembly for Wales see para 302 ante.
11   Ie in the Race Relations Act 1976 Sch 1A (as added and amended): see note 1 supra.
12   Ie extend the application of ibid s 71 (as substituted). The provisions of s 71 (as substituted) are without prejudice to the obligation of any person to comply with any other provision of the Race Relations Act 1976: s 71(7) (as substituted: see note 6 supra).
13   Ibid s 71(5) (as substituted: see note 6 supra). Such an order may contain such incidental, supplementary or consequential provision as the Secretary of State considers appropriate, including provision amending or repealing provision made by or under the Race Relations Act 1976 or any other enactment: s 71(6) (as so substituted).
14   As to the CRE see para 488 et seq post. As to the Commission for Equality and Human Rights, which is to replace the CRE, see para 305 et seq ante.
15   Ie such persons falling within the Race Relations Act 1976 Sch 1A (as added and amended): see note 1 supra.
16   Ibid s 71(2)–(4) (as substituted: see note 6 supra). The duties referred to are those under s 71(1) (as substituted): see the text and notes 1–6 supra. As to the orders that have been made see the Race Relations Act 1976 (Statutory Duties) Order 2001, SI 2001/3458 (amended by SI 2002/2469; SI 2003/3006; SI 2004/3125; SI 2005/617; SI 2005/3238; SI 2006/594; SI 2004/3168; SI 2005/2929; SI 2006/63; SI 2006/64); the Race Relations Act 1976 (Statutory Duties) Order 2003, SI 2003/3006; the Race Relations Act 1976 (Statutory Duties) Order 2004, SI 2004/3125; and the Race Relations Act 1976 (Statutory Duties) Order 2006, SI 2006/2471.
17   Ie under the Race Relations Act 1976 s 71(2) (as substituted): see the text and notes 15–16 supra.
18   'Welsh public authority' means any person whose functions are exercisable only in relation to Wales and includes the National Assembly for Wales: ibid s 71B(4) (as added: see note 6 supra).
19   Ibid s 71B(2), (3) (as added: see note 6 supra).
20   Ie an order under ibid s 71(2) (as substituted): see the text and notes 15–16 supra.
21   Ibid s 71D(1) (as added: see note 6 supra). A compliance notice requires the person concerned to comply with the duty concerned and to inform the CRE, within 28 days of the date on which the notice is served, of the steps that the person has taken, or is taking, to comply with the duty; and may also require the person concerned to furnish the CRE with such other written information as may be reasonably required by the notice in order to verify that the duty has been complied with: s 71D(2), (3) (as so added). The notice may specify the time, no later than three months from the date on which the notice is served, at which any information is to be furnished to the CRE, and the manner and form in which any such information is to be so furnished, but may not require a person to furnish information which the person could not be compelled to furnish in evidence in civil proceedings before the High Court: s 71D(4), (5) (as so added). See note 27 infra. Section 71D (as added) is repealed by the Equality Act 2006 ss 40, 91, Sch 3 paras 21, 31, Sch 4 as from a day to be appointed under s 93. At the date at which this volume states the law no such day had been appointed.
22   Race Relations Act 1976 s 71C(1) (as added: see note 6 supra). The duties referred to in the text are those imposed by s 71(1), (2) (as substituted): see the text and notes 1–6, 15–16 supra. As to such codes of practice see further para 491 post. Section 71C (as added) is repealed by the Equality Act 2006 Sch 3 paras 21, 31, Sch 4 as from a day to be appointed under s 93. At the date at which this volume states the law no such day had been appointed.
23   Ie a person falling within the Race Relations Act 1976 Sch 1A (as added and amended): see note 1 supra.
24   Ibid s 71E(1) (as added: see note 6 supra). Section 71E (as added) is repealed by the Equality Act 2006 Sch 3 paras 21, 31, Sch 4 as from a day to be appointed under s 93. At the date at which this volume states the law no such day had been appointed.
25   Ie an order under the Race Relations Act 1976 s 71(2) (as substituted): see the text and notes 15–16 supra.
26   Ibid s 71E(2) (as added: see note 6 supra). See note 24 supra.
27   Ibid s 71E(3) (as added: see note 6 supra). The sanctions in ss 71D, 71E (both as added; prospectively repealed) are the only sanctions for breach of any duty imposed by an order under s 71(2) (as substituted) (see the text and notes 15–16 supra), but without prejudice to the enforcement under s 57 (as amended) (see paras 460 ante, 500 post) or otherwise of any other provision of the Race Relations Act 1976 (where the breach is also a contravention of s 57 (as amended)): s 71E(4) (as so added). See note 24 supra.
28   Local authorities are included amongst the bodies in ibid Sch 1A Pt I (as added and amended): see note 1 supra.
29   Ie the duty under the previous version of ibid s 71 (as substituted), now replaced by the provisions in s 71 (as substituted) and ss 71A–71E (as added; ss 71D, 71E prospectively repealed): see the text and notes 1–27 supra.
30   See the Local Government Act 1988 s 17–20, Sch 2 (as amended); and LOCAL GOVERNMENT vol 29(1) (Reissue) para 419 et seq.

31   See ibid ss 17, 18 (both as amended); and LOCAL GOVERNMENT vol 29(1) (Reissue) paras 419, 422.

32   The public authorities are specified in ibid s 17(2), Sch 2 (as amended): see LOCAL GOVERNMENT vol 29(1) (Reissue) para 419.

33   The functions regulated by ibid s 17 (as amended) are: (1) the inclusion of persons in or the exclusion of persons from any list of persons approved for the purposes of public supply or works contracts (see note 34 infra) with the authority, or any list of persons from whom tenders for such contracts may be invited (s 17(4)(a)); (2) in relation to a proposed public supply or works contract with the authority, the inclusion of persons in or the exclusion of persons from the group of persons from whom tenders are invited, the accepting or not accepting of the submission of tenders for the contract, the selecting of the person with whom to enter into the contract, or the giving or withholding of approval for, or the selecting or nominating of, persons to be sub-contractors for the purposes of the contract (s 17(4)(b)); and (3) in relation to a subsisting public supply or works contract with the authority, the giving or withholding of approval for, or the selecting or nominating of persons to be sub-contractors for the purposes of the contract, or the termination of the contract (s 17(4)(c)).

34   The contracts which are public supply or works contracts are contracts for the supply of goods or materials, for the supply of services or for the execution of works, entered into after 7 April 1988: see ibid ss 17(3), 23.

35   See ibid s 17(1). The following are relevant non-commercial matters in the context of race relations: (1) the terms and conditions of employment by contractors of their workers or the composition of, the arrangements for the promotion, transfer or training of or the other opportunities afforded to, their workforces ('workforce matters') (ss 17(5)(a), s 18(7)); and (2) the country or territory of origin of supplies to, or the location in any country or territory of the business activities or interests of, contractors (s 17(5)(e)). Head (2) supra supersedes the decision in *R v Lewisham London Borough Council, ex p Shell UK Ltd* [1988] 1 All ER 938, DC. See also *R v London Borough of Islington, ex p Building Employers' Confederation* [1989] IRLR 382, DC (clause in council's contracts providing that contractor should at all times comply with the employment provisions of the Sex Discrimination Act 1975 related to a 'non-commercial' matter).

36   See the Local Government Act 1988 s 18 (as amended); and LOCAL GOVERNMENT vol 29(1) (Reissue) para 422. Except to the extent permitted by the Local Government Act 1988 s 18(2) (as amended) (see the text and note 39 infra), the Race Relations Act 1976 s 71 (as substituted) does not require or authorise a public authority to exercise any function regulated by the Local Government Act 1988 s 17 (as amended) (see the text and note 35 supra) by reference to a non-commercial matter: see s 18(1) (amended by the Race Relations (Amendment) Act 2000 s 9(1), Sch 2 paras 20, 21).

37   The Secretary of State may specify in writing questions which are to be approved questions for the purposes of this provision: Local Government Act 1988 s 18(5)(a). See Department of the Environment Circular 8/1988 Annex B.

     Where it is permissible to ask a question, it is also permissible to make, if it is in writing, an approved request for evidence in support of an answer to the question: Local Government Act 1988 s 18(4). The Secretary of State may specify in writing descriptions of evidence which, in relation to approved questions, are to be approved descriptions of evidence: s 18(5)(b). See Department of the Environment Circular 8/1988 Annex B.

38   See note 35 head (1) supra.

39   See the Local Government Act 1988 s 18(2) (amended by the Race Relations (Amendment) Act 2000 Sch 2 para 21(b)).

40   Ie the Local Government Act 1988 s 18(2) (as amended): see the text to note 39 supra.

41   See ibid s 18(3).

470.   Discrimination and harassment by public authorities.   It is unlawful for a public authority[1] in carrying out any of its functions to do any act which constitutes discrimination[2]. Further, it is unlawful for a public authority to subject a person to harassment in the course of carrying out any functions of the authority which consist of the provision of: (1) any form of social security[3]; (2) healthcare[4]; (3) any other form of social protection[5]; or (4) any form of social advantage[6].

The prohibitions[7] do not apply to:

(a)   any judicial act, whether done by a court, tribunal or other person, or any act done on the instructions, or on behalf, of a person acting in a judicial capacity[8];

(b)   any act of, or relating to, making, confirming or approving any enactment or Order in Council or any instrument made by a Minister of the Crown[9] under an enactment[10];

(c)   any act of, or relating to, making or approving arrangements, or imposing requirements or conditions, of certain acts of discrimination[11];

(d)   any act of, or relating to, imposing a requirement, or giving an express authorisation, of a relevant authorisation[12] in relation to the carrying out of immigration functions[13];

(e)   a decision not to institute criminal proceedings and, where such a decision has been made, any act done for the purpose of enabling the decision whether to institute criminal proceedings to be made[14]; and

(f)   where criminal proceedings are not continued as a result of a decision not to continue them, the decision and, where such a decision has been made, any act done for the purpose of enabling the decision whether to continue the proceedings to be made and any act done for the purpose of securing that the proceedings are not continued[15].

The prohibitions[16] do not make it unlawful for a relevant person[17] to discriminate against another person on grounds of nationality or ethnic or national origins in carrying out immigration functions[18].

1   'Public authority' includes any person certain of whose functions are functions of a public nature: Race Relations Act 1976 s 19B(2)(a) (ss 19B–19F added by the Race Relations (Amendment) Act 2000 s 1). The following persons are excluded from the definition of public authority: (1) either House of Parliament; (2) a person exercising functions in connection with proceedings in Parliament; (3) the Security Service; (4) the Secret Intelligence Service; (5) the Government Communications Headquarters; and (6) any unit or part of a unit of any of the naval, military or air forces of the Crown which is for the time being required by the Secretary of State to assist the Government Communications Headquarters in carrying out its functions: Race Relations Act 1976 s 19B(2)(b), (3) (as so added). In relation to a particular act, a person is not a public authority by virtue only of s 19B(2)(a) (as added) if the nature of the act is private: s 19B(4) (as so added). As to the meaning of 'person' see para 344 note 3. As to the security and intelligence services generally see CONSTITUTIONAL LAW AND HUMAN RIGHTS vol 8(2) (Reissue) para 473 et seq. As to the armed forces generally see ARMED FORCES.

2   Ibid s 19B(1) (as added: see note 1 supra). Nothing in s 19B (as added and amended) makes unlawful any act of discrimination or harassment which is made unlawful by virtue of any other provision of the Race Relations Act 1976 or would be made unlawful but for any provision made by or under that Act: s 19B(6) (as so added; and amended by the Race Relations Act 1976 (Amendment) Regulations 2003, SI 2003/1626, reg 20(2)(b)). For the meaning of 'harassment' see para 444 ante. The Race Relations Act 1976 s 19B (as added and amended) is subject to ss 19C–19F (as added and amended) (see the text and notes 7–18 infra): s 19B(5) (as so added). For the meaning of 'discrimination' see para 447 note 4 ante. In its application in relation to granting entry clearance (see BRITISH NATIONALITY, IMMIGRATION AND ASYLUM), s 19B (as added and amended) applies in relation to acts done outside the United Kingdom, as well as those done within Great Britain: s 27(1A) (added by the Race Relations (Amendment) Act 2000 s 9(1), Sch 2 para 3). For the meanings of 'United Kingdom' and 'Great Britain' see para 325 note 6 ante. See *R (on the application of European Roma Rights Centre) v Immigration Officer at Prague Airport (United Nations High Comr for Refugees intervening)* [2004] UKHL 55, [2005] 2 AC 1, [2005] 1 All ER 527 (under an immigration control scheme, operated in the Czech Republic, persons of Romany origin were subjected to more rigorous questioning than others and were more likely to be refused entry: held to be unlawful discrimination).

3   Race Relations Act 1976 s 19B(1A)(a) (s 19B(1A) added by the Race Relations Act 1976 (Amendment) Regulations 2003, SI 2003/1626, reg 20(2)(a)).

4   Race Relations Act 1976 s 19B(1A)(b) (as added: see note 3 supra).

5   Ibid s 19B(1A)(c) (as added: see note 3 supra). For the meaning of 'social protection' see para 440 note 14 ante.

6   Ibid s 19B(1A)(d) (as added: see note 3 supra). For the meaning of 'social advantage' see para 440 note 14 ante.

7   Ie the prohibitions in ibid s 19B (as added and amended): see the text and notes 1–6 supra.

8   Ibid s 19C(1) (as added: see note 1 supra).

9   'Minister of the Crown' includes, for the purposes of ibid s 19C (as added), the National Assembly for Wales, a member of the Scottish Executive, the Treasury and the Defence Council: s 19C(5) (as added: see note 1 supra), s 78(1). As to the National Assembly for Wales see para 302 ante. As to the Treasury see CONSTITUTIONAL LAW AND HUMAN RIGHTS vol 8(2) (Reissue) paras 512–517. As to the Defence

Council see ARMED FORCES vol 2(2) (Reissue) para 2; CONSTITUTIONAL LAW AND HUMAN RIGHTS vol 8(2) (Reissue) para 443 et seq. Scottish matters generally are beyond the scope of this work.

10 Ibid s 19C(2) (as added: see note 1 supra).

11 Ie acts of discrimination of a kind excepted by ibid s 41 (as amended) (see para 486 post): s 19C(3) (as added (see note 1 supra); and amended by the Race Relations Act 1976 (Amendment) Regulations 2003, SI 2003/1626, reg 21).

12 'Relevant authorisation' means a requirement imposed or express authorisation given: (1) with respect to a particular case or class of case, by a Minister of the Crown acting personally; (2) with respect to a particular class of case by any of the enactments mentioned in note 13 heads (1)–(4) infra or any instrument made under or by virtue of any of those enactments: Race Relations Act 1976 s 19D(3) (as added: see note 1 supra).

13 Ibid s 19C(4) (as added (see note 1 supra); and amended by the Nationality, Immigration and Asylum Act 2002 (Consequential and Incidental Provisions) Order 2003, SI 2003/1016, art 3, Schedule para 2). 'Immigration functions' means functions exercisable by virtue of: (1) the Immigration Acts (within the meaning of the Asylum and Immigration (Treatment of Claimants, etc) Act 2004 s 44 (repealed)) excluding the Immigration Act 1971 ss 28A–28K (as added and amended) so far as they relate to offences under Pt III (ss 24–28L) (as amended) and excluding the Asylum and Immigration (Treatment of Claimants, etc) Act 2004 s 14 (as amended); (2) the Special Immigration Appeals Commission Act 1997; (3) provision made under the European Communities Act 1972 s 2(2) (as amended) which relates to immigration or asylum; or (4) any provision of Community law which relates to immigration or asylum: Race Relations Act 1976 s 19C(5) (as so added; and amended by the Nationality, Immigration and Asylum Act 2002 (Consequential and Incidental Provisions) Order 2003, SI 2003/1016, Schedule para 2); Race Relations Act 1976 s 19D(4), (5) (as so added; and substituted by the Nationality, Immigration and Asylum Act 2002 s 6(1), (3); and amended by the Asylum and Immigration (Treatment of Claimants, etc) Act 2004 s 14(4)). See further BRITISH NATIONALITY, IMMIGRATION AND ASYLUM.

14 Race Relations Act 1976 s 19F(a) (as added: see note 1 supra). 'Criminal proceedings' includes proceedings on dealing summarily with a charge under the Army Act 1955 or the Air Force Act 1955 or on summary trial under the Naval Discipline Act 1957, proceedings before a summary appeal court constituted under any of those enactments, proceedings before a court-martial constituted under the Army Act 1955, the Air Force Act 1955 or a disciplinary court constituted under the Naval Discipline Act 1957 s 52G (repealed), proceedings before the Courts-Martial Appeal Court and proceedings before a standing civilian court: Race Relations Act 1976 s 78(1) (definition added by the Race Relations (Amendment) Act 2000 s 9(1), Sch 2 para 19).

15 Race Relations Act 1976 s 19F(b) (as added: see note 1 supra). As to the remedies available for an act done by a person in carrying out public investigator functions or functions as a public prosecutor which is unlawful by virtue of s 19B (as added and amended) see para 500 post.

16 Ie the prohibitions in ibid s 19B (as added and amended): see the text and notes 1–6 supra.

17 'Relevant person' means a Minister of the Crown acting personally or any other person acting in accordance with a relevant authorisation: ibid s 19D(2) (as added: see note 1 supra). For the meaning of 'Minister of the Crown' see para 445 note 1 ante.

18 Ibid s 19D(1) (as added (see note 1 supra); and amended by the Nationality, Immigration and Asylum Act 2002 s 6(1), (2)).

The Secretary of State must, after consulting the Commission for Racial Equality ('CRE'), appoint a person who is not a member of his staff to act as a monitor: Race Relations Act 1976 s 19E(1), (2) (as added: see note 1 supra). The person so appointed must monitor, in such manner as the Secretary of State may determine: (1) the likely effect on the operation of the exception in s 19D (as added and amended) of any relevant authorisation relating to the carrying out of immigration functions which has been given by a Minister of the Crown acting personally; and (2) the operation of that exception in relation to acts which have been done by a person acting in accordance with such an authorisation: s 19E(3) (as so added; and amended by the Nationality, Immigration and Asylum Act 2002 s 6(4)(a)). The monitor must make an annual report on the discharge of his functions to the Secretary of State who must lay a copy of any such report before each House of Parliament: Race Relations Act 1976 s 19E(4), (5) (as so added). The Secretary of State must pay to the monitor such fees and allowances, if any, as he may determine: s 19E(6) (as so added). As to the Secretary of State and National Assembly for Wales see para 302 ante. As to the CRE see para 488 et seq post. As to the Commission for Equality and Human Rights, which is to replace the CRE, see para 305 et seq ante.

G. OTHER UNLAWFUL ACTS

471. Discriminatory practices. Proceedings may be brought by the Commission for Racial Equality ('CRE') alone[1] against a person[2] who applies a discriminatory practice[3], or against a person who operates practices or other arrangements which in any circumstances would call for the application by him of a discriminatory practice[4].

1   See the Race Relations Act 1976 s 28(3). As to enforcement by the CRE see ss 58–62 (as amended; prospectively repealed); and para 498 post. As to the CRE see para 488 et seq post. As to the Commission for Equality and Human Rights, which is to replace the CRE, see para 305 et seq ante.
    As from a day to be appointed, s 28(3) is amended so that the reference to ss 58–62 (as amended; prospectively repealed) is replaced by a reference to the Equality Act 2006 ss 20–24 (see para 327 et seq ante): Race Relations Act 1976 s 28(3) (prospectively amended by the Equality Act 2006 s 40, Sch 3 paras 21, 22). At the date at which this volume states the law no such day had been appointed.
2   As to the meaning of 'person' see para 344 note 3 ante. As to the liability of principals and employers for the acts of their agents or servants see the Race Relations Act 1976 s 32; and para 476 post. As to the liability of a person who knowingly aids an unlawful act see s 33 (as amended); and para 477 post.
3   'Discriminatory practice' means: (1) the application of a requirement or condition which results in an act of discrimination which is unlawful by virtue of any provision of ibid Pt II (ss 4–15) (as amended) or Pt III (ss 17–27) (as amended) read with s 1(1)(b) (see para 440 ante), or which would be likely to result in such an act of discrimination if the persons to whom it is applied included persons of any particular racial group as regards which there has been no occasion for applying it; or (2) the application of a provision, criterion or practice which results in an act of discrimination which is unlawful by virtue of any provision referred to in s 1(1B) (as added), taken with s 1(1A) (as added) (see para 440 ante), or which would be likely to result in such an act of discrimination, if the persons to whom it is applied included persons of any particular race or of any particular ethnic or national origins, as regards which there has been no occasion for applying it: s 28(1) (amended by the Race Relations Act 1976 (Amendment) Regulations 2003, SI 2003/1626, reg 1(1)). For the meaning of 'discrimination' see para 447 note 4 ante; as to the meaning of 'act' see para 442 note 7 ante; and for the meaning of 'racial group' see para 441 ante. As to the meanings of 'ethnic origins' and 'national origins' see para 441 ante.
4   Race Relations Act 1976 s 28(2).

472.   Relationships which have come to an end.   Where a relevant relationship[1] has come to an end it is unlawful for the relevant party[2] to discriminate against another party, on grounds of race or ethnic or national origins[3], by subjecting him to a detriment[4], or to subject another party to harassment[5], where the discrimination or harassment arises out of and is closely connected to that relationship[6].

1   A 'relevant relationship' is a relationship during the course of which an act of discrimination by one party to the relationship ('the relevant party') against another party to the relationship, on grounds of race or ethnic or national origins, or harassment of another party to the relationship by the relevant party, is unlawful: Race Relations Act 1976 s 27A(1)(a), (b) (s 27A added by the Race Relations Act 1976 (Amendment) Regulations 2003, SI 2003/1626, reg 29). For the purposes of the Race Relations Act 1976 s 27A(1) (as added), 'unlawful' includes unlawful by virtue of any provision referred to in s 1(1B) (as added), taken with s 1(1) or s 1(1A) (as added) or, as the case may be, by virtue of s 3A (as added) (see paras 440, 444 ante): s 27A(1) (as so added). A reference to an act of discrimination or harassment which is unlawful includes, in the case of a relationship which has come to an end before the commencement of s 27A (as added), reference to such an act which would, after that date, be unlawful: s 27A(3) (as so added). As to the meaning of 'act' see para 442 note 7 ante. For the meaning of 'discrimination' see para 447 note 4 ante. As to the meanings of 'ethnic origins' and 'national origins' see para 441 ante. For the meaning of 'harassment' see para 444 ante.
2   See note 1 supra.
3   See note 1 supra.
4   Race Relations Act 1976 s 27A(2)(a) (as added: see note 1 supra). As to the meaning of 'detriment' see para 446 note 17 ante.
5   Ibid s 27A(2)(b) (as added: see note 1 supra).
6   Ibid s 27A(2) (as added: see note 1 supra). For the purposes of any proceedings in respect of an unlawful act under s 27A(2) (as added), that act is to be treated as falling within circumstances relevant for the purposes of such of the provisions, or Parts, referred to in s 27A(1) (as added) as determine most closely the nature of the relevant relationship: s 27A(4) (as so added).

473.   Discriminatory advertisements.   It is unlawful to publish or to cause to be published an advertisement[1] which indicates, or might reasonably be understood as indicating, an intention[2] by a person[3] to do an act[4] of discrimination[5], whether the doing of that act by him would be lawful or unlawful[6]. The publisher of an advertisement has a defence to proceedings under this provision if he proves that the advertisement was published in reliance on a statement made to him by the person who caused it to be published to the effect that the publication would not be unlawful[7] and that it was reasonable for him to rely on that statement[8]. It is an offence knowingly or recklessly to make such a statement which in a material respect is false or misleading[9].

1   'Advertisement' includes every form of advertisement or notice, whether to the public or not, and whether in a newspaper or other publication, by television or radio, by display of notices, signs, labels, showcards or goods, by distribution of samples, circulars, catalogues, price lists or other material, by exhibition of pictures, models or films, or in any other way, and references to the publishing of advertisements are to be construed accordingly: Race Relations Act 1976 s 78(1). The breadth of this definition is illustrated by the decision that a hand-written notice in a pub reading 'No Travellers' is an advertisement for the purposes of the Act: *Commission for Racial Equality v Dutton* [1989] QB 783, [1989] 1 All ER 306, CA.

2   These words were considered in the context of the equivalent, similarly worded, provision of the Race Relations Act 1968 s 6(1) (repealed) in *Race Relations Board v Associated Newspapers Group Ltd* [1978] 3 All ER 419, [1978] 1 WLR 905, CA (advertisement for nurses to work in South Africa said 'all white patients'). The Court of Appeal did not interfere with the decision of the county court judge and two assessors that the advertisement did not indicate an intention to discriminate. Lord Denning MR stated at 421 and 988 that the question to be asked, as in a libel case, is: what is the natural and ordinary meaning of the words? No evidence is admissible to show what was intended by the words by the person who inserted or published the advertisement, or what the readers of the advertisement understood by the words; the question is what an ordinary reasonable man or woman without special knowledge would understand by the words. See also *Hough v London Express Newspapers Ltd* [1940] 2 KB 507, [1940] 3 All ER 31; *Cardiff Women's Aid v Hartup* [1994] IRLR 390, EAT.

3   As to the meaning of 'person' see para 344 note 3 ante.

4   As to the meaning of 'act' see para 442 note 7 ante.

5   For the meaning of 'discrimination' see para 447 note 4 ante.

6   See the Race Relations Act 1976 s 29(1). Proceedings in respect of a contravention of this provision may be brought only by the Commission for Racial Equality ('CRE'): see s 63 (as amended; prospectively repealed); and para 498 post. As to the CRE see para 488 et seq post. As to the Commission for Equality and Human Rights, which is to replace the CRE, see para 305 et seq ante. As from a day to be appointed, s 29 (as amended) is further amended so as to provide that proceedings in respect of a contravention of s 29(1) may be brought only by the Commission for Equality and Human Rights, and in accordance with the Equality Act 2006 s 25 (as amended) (see para 332 ante): Race Relations Act 1976 s 29(6) (prospectively added by the Equality Act 2006 s 40, Sch 3 paras 21, 23). At the date at which this volume states the law no such day had been appointed.

      The Race Relations Act 1976 s 29(1) does not apply to an advertisement if the intended act would be lawful by virtue of s 5 (as amended) (genuine occupational qualification: see para 447 ante), s 6 (as amended) (employment for training for work overseas: see para 447 ante), s 7(3), (4) (as amended) (equivalent provisions in relation to contract workers: see para 449 ante), s 10(3) (as amended) (genuine occupational qualification in relation to partnerships: see para 450 ante), s 26 (exception for associations for members of a particular racial group: see para 467 ante)), s 34(2)(b) (exception for charities: see para 481 post), the general exceptions contained in ss 35–39 (as amended) (see paras 482–485 post), or s 41 (as amended) (acts done under statutory authority: see para 486 post): s 29(2)(a). Further, it is not unlawful to publish or cause to be published an advertisement relating to the services of an employment agency which indicates an intention to do a discriminatory act where the intended act only concerns employment which would be exempt from the Act under the genuine occupational qualification exception (ie by virtue of s 5, s 6, or s 7(3), (4) (as amended)): see s 29(2)(b). For the meaning of 'employment agency' see para 454 note 1 ante; and for the meaning of 'employment' see para 446 note 3 ante. Nor is it unlawful to publish or cause to be published an advertisement which indicates that persons of any class defined otherwise than by reference to colour, race or ethnic or national origins are required for employment outside Great Britain: s 29(3). For the meaning of 'Great Britain' see para 325 note 6 ante. Outside the ambit of these exceptions, the publication of any advertisement indicating an intention to discriminate is unlawful: *Lambeth London Borough Council v Commission for Racial Equality* [1990] ICR 768, [1990] IRLR 231, CA.

7   Ie by reason of the exceptions contained in the Race Relations Act 1976 s 29(2) or (3): see s 29(4)(a).

8   Ibid s 29(4)(a), (b).

9   See ibid s 29(5). The offence is punishable on summary conviction by a fine not exceeding level 5 on the standard scale: s 29(5) (amended by virtue of the Criminal Justice Act 1982 ss 38, 46). As to the standard scale see para 315 note 15 ante.

474.   Instructions to discriminate. It is unlawful for a person[1] who has authority over another person[2], or in accordance with whose wishes that other person is accustomed to act[3], to instruct him to do any act[4] of unlawful discrimination[5], or procure or attempt to procure[6] the doing by him of any such act[7].

1   As to the meaning of 'person' see para 344 note 3 ante.
2   Race Relations Act 1976 s 30(a). See note 7 infra.
3   Ibid s 30(b). See note 7 infra.
         Section 30 requires that there should be some relationship between the person giving the instructions or doing the procuring and the other person. It is not sufficient to show that the other person is accustomed to act in accordance with the wishes of persons in the same position as the person giving the instructions; there must have been prior dealings between the person instructed and the person giving the instructions: *Commission for Racial Equality v Imperial Society of Teachers of Dancing* [1983] ICR 473, [1983] IRLR 315, EAT (employee of the respondents telephoned the head of careers at a school and asked her to send applicants for a job, saying that she would prefer the school not to send anyone coloured because they would feel out of place: it was held that there was no contravention of the Race Relations Act 1976 s 30, because there had been no prior contact between the school and the respondents, although the school was used to dealing with employers). However, see para 475 post. In the case of a body corporate, it is sufficient if the person instructed is accustomed to act in accordance with the wishes of the body and there need not have been previous dealings with the employee giving the instructions: *Commission for Racial Equality v Imperial Society of Teachers of Dancing* supra.
4   As to the meaning of 'act' see para 442 note 7 ante.
5   Ie any act which is unlawful by virtue of the Race Relations Act 1976 Pt II (ss 4–15) (as amended) (see para 446 et seq ante), Pt III (ss 17–27) (as amended) (see para 460 et seq ante), s 76ZA (as added) (see para 459 ante) or, where it renders an act unlawful on grounds of race or ethnic or national origins, s 76 (as amended) (see para 457 ante). For the meaning of 'discrimination' see para 447 note 4 ante. As to the meanings of 'ethnic origins' and 'national origins' see para 441 ante.
6   The words 'procure or attempt to procure' have a wide meaning, and are apt to include the use of words, such as the expression of a preference, which bring about or attempt to bring about a certain course of action: *Commission for Racial Equality v Imperial Society of Teachers of Dancing* [1983] ICR 473, [1983] IRLR 315, EAT.
7   Race Relations Act 1976 s 30 (amended by the Race Relations Act 1976 (Amendment) Regulations 2003, SI 2003/1626, reg 31(2)). Proceedings for a contravention of the Race Relations Act 1976 s 30 (as amended) may be brought only by the Commission for Racial Equality ('CRE'): see s 63 (as amended; prospectively repealed); and para 498 post. As to the CRE see para 488 et seq post. As to the Commission for Equality and Human Rights, which is to replace the CRE, see para 305 et seq ante. As from a day to be appointed, s 30 (as amended) is renumbered as s 30(1), and s 30(2) is added so as to provide that proceedings in respect of a contravention of s 30(1) (as renumbered) may be brought only by the Commission for Equality and Human Rights, and in accordance with the Equality Act 2006 s 25 (as amended) (see para 332 ante): Race Relations Act 1976 s 30(1), (2) (s 30(1) prospectively renumbered, and s 30(2) prospectively added, by the Equality Act 2006 s 40, Sch 3 paras 21, 24). At the date at which this volume states the law no such day had been appointed.

475.   Pressure to discriminate. It is unlawful to induce[1], or attempt to induce, a person to do any act[2] of unlawful discrimination[3]. An attempted inducement is not prevented from falling within this provision because it is not made directly to the person in question, if it is made in such a way that he is likely to hear of it[4].

1   The words 'to induce' mean 'to persuade or to prevail upon or to bring about': *Commission for Racial Equality v Imperial Society of Teachers of Dancing* [1983] ICR 473 at 476, EAT.
2   As to the meaning of 'act' see para 442 note 7 ante.
3   Race Relations Act 1976 s 31(1) (amended by the Race Relations Act 1976 (Amendment) Regulations 2003, SI 2003/1626, reg 32(2)). An act of unlawful discrimination is one which contravenes the Race Relations Act 1976 Pt II (ss 4–15) (as amended), Pt III (ss 17–27) (as amended), s 76ZA (as added) (see para 459 ante) or, where it renders an act unlawful on grounds of race or ethnic or national origins, s 76 (as amended) (see para 457 ante): s 31(1) (as so amended). For the meaning of 'discrimination' see para 447 note 4 ante. As to the meanings of 'ethnic origins' and 'national origins' see para 441 ante.
         As from a day to be appointed, s 31 (as amended) is further amended so as to provide that proceedings in respect of a contravention of s 31(1) (as amended) may be brought only by the Commission for Equality and Human Rights, and in accordance with the Equality Act 2006 s 25 (as

amended) (see para 332 ante): Race Relations Act 1976 s 31(3) (prospectively added by the Equality Act 2006 s 40, Sch 3 paras 21, 25). At the date at which this volume states the law no such day had been appointed. As to the Commission for Equality and Human Rights, which is to replace the Commission for Racial Equality, see para 305 et seq ante.

The wording of the Race Relations Act 1976 s 31 (as amended) is wider than that of the equivalent provision of the Sex Discrimination Act 1975 which requires an inducement to be made by a person who provides or offers to provide the other person with a benefit, or subjects or threatens to subject him to a detriment: see the Sex Discrimination Act 1975 s 40 (prospectively amended); and para 390 ante. There is no requirement for the offer of a benefit or threat of a detriment under the Race Relations Act 1976 s 31 (as amended): *Commission for Racial Equality v Imperial Society for Teachers of Dancing* [1983] ICR 473 at 476, EAT.

4   Race Relations Act 1976 s 31(2). See note 3 supra.

476.   Liability of employees, employers, principals and agents.   Anything done by a person in the course of his employment[1] is to be treated for the purposes of the Race Relations Act 1976[2] as done by his employer[3] as well as by him, whether or not it was done with the employer's knowledge or approval[4]. An employer has a defence to proceedings brought against him in respect of an act[5] alleged to have been done by an employee if he proves that he took such steps as were reasonably practicable to prevent the employee from doing that act, or from doing in the course of his employment acts of that description[6].

Anything done by a person as agent for another person with the authority, whether express or implied, and whether precedent or subsequent, of that other person is to be treated for the purposes of the Act[7] as done by that other person as well as by him[8].

The employee or agent for whose act the employer or principal is liable under this provision is subject to a further potential liability, as he is deemed to aid the doing of the act by the employer[9], and so, if he has the requisite knowledge, he may also be liable for knowingly aiding an unlawful act[10].

1   For the meaning of 'employment' see para 446 note 3 ante. In determining whether conduct complained of is done by a person in the course of employment, the phrase is not to be construed restrictively by reference to the case law for establishing an employer's vicarious liability for the torts committed by an employee; rather a purposive construction requires the phrase to be given a broad interpretation in the sense it is used in everyday speech: *Jones v Tower Boot Co Ltd* [1997] 2 All ER 406, [1997] IRLR 168, CA (employer liable for racial harassment by applicant's work colleagues). This is now a question of fact for the court or tribunal concerned. Earlier cases such as *Irving and Irving v Post Office* [1987] IRLR 289, CA (where a postman who wrote a racially offensive message on a letter delivered to the applicants was held not to be acting in the course of his employment with the Post Office, since the writing of the message was not an act authorised by his employers, nor an unauthorised means of doing an authorised act) should be regarded with caution. See also *Chief Constable of Lincolnshire Police v Stubbs* [1999] ICR 547, [1999] IRLR 81, EAT; *ST v North Yorkshire County Council* [1999] IRLR 98, CA (decided in the context of the parallel provisions in the Sex Discrimination Act 1975 s 41).

2   Ie except as regards offences under the Race Relations Act 1976: see s 32(1).

3   For the meaning of 'employer' see para 446 note 3 ante.

4   Race Relations Act 1976 s 32(1). As to the application of this provision to governing bodies of schools and institutions of higher or further education where such bodies have delegated budgets see the Education (Modification of Enactments Relating to Employment) (England) Order 2003, SI 2003/1694, art 3, Schedule; and the Education (Modification of Enactments Relating to Employment) (Wales) Order 2006, SI 2006/1073, art 3, Schedule.

5   As to the meaning of 'act' see para 442 note 7 ante.

6   Race Relations Act 1976 s 32(3). The burden on an employer under this provision is now generally regarded as onerous, although it has not always been treated as such: see *Balgobin v Tower Hamlets London Borough Council* [1987] ICR 829, [1987] IRLR 401, EAT, in which the Employment Appeal Tribunal refused to disturb a finding by a tribunal that the employers had taken all steps that were reasonably practicable to prevent the applicants being sexually harassed, on evidence that the employers were unaware of the acts that were taking place, were exercising adequate supervision over their employees, and had an equal opportunities policy, although nothing had been done to implement the policy.

7   Ie except as regards offences under the Race Relations Act 1976: see s 32(2).

8   Ibid s 32(2). See further AGENCY vol 2(1) (Reissue) para 151.

9   Ibid s 33(2). See *AM v WC and SPV* [1999] ICR 1218, [1999] IRLR 410, EAT (decided in the context of the Sex Discrimination Act 1975), which illustrates the relation between the provisions relating to vicarious liability and liability for aiding and abetting. See also *Anyanwu v South Bank Students' Union* [2000] 1 All ER 1, [2000] IRLR 36, CA.

10   Ie under the Race Relations Act 1976 s 33 (as amended): see para 477 post.

477. Aiding discrimination. A person[1] who knowingly aids another person to do an act[2] made unlawful[3] by the Race Relations Act 1976 is to be treated for the purposes of the Act as himself doing an unlawful act of the like description[4]. A person has a defence to this provision if he acts in reliance on a statement made to him by that other person that the act which he aids would not be unlawful[5], and it was reasonable for him to rely on that statement[6]. It is an offence knowingly or recklessly to make such a statement which in a material respect is false or misleading[7].

1   As to the meaning of 'person' see para 344 note 3 ante.
2   As to the meaning of 'act' see para 442 note 7 ante.
3   Offences are not excepted from this provision: c f the Race Relations Act 1976 s 32 (see para 476 ante).
4   Ibid s 33(1).
5   Ie by reason of any provision of the Race Relations Act 1976: see s 33(3)(a).
6   Ibid s 33(3)(a), (b). By contrast with the similar provision relating to advertisements (see para 473 ante) this provision does not state that the respondent has the burden of proving this defence. It is submitted that it was Parliament's intention that the respondent should be required to prove this defence.
7   See ibid s 33(4). The offence is punishable on summary conviction by a fine not exceeding level 5 on the standard scale: s 33(4) (amended by virtue of the Criminal Justice Act 1982 ss 38, 46). As to the standard scale see para 315 note 15 ante.

478. Discriminatory contracts. A term of a contract is void where its inclusion renders the making of the contract unlawful by virtue of the Race Relations Act 1976[1], or it is included in furtherance of or provides for the doing of an act[2] which is or would be rendered unlawful by the Act[3]. A term the inclusion of which constitutes, or is in furtherance of, or provides for, unlawful discrimination[4] against or harassment[5] of a party to the contract is not void, but is unenforceable against that party[6]. Any person interested in such a contract may apply to a designated county court[7] for such order as the court thinks just for removing or modifying any unenforceable term[8].

A term in a contract which purports to exclude or limit any provision of the Race Relations Act 1976 is unenforceable by any person in whose favour the term would otherwise operate[9]. This provision does not apply to: (1) a contract settling a complaint of discrimination in the employment field[10] where the contract is made with the assistance of a conciliation officer[11]; (2) a contract settling such a complaint if the conditions regulating compromise contracts under the Race Relations Act 1976[12] are satisfied in relation to the contract[13]; or (3) a contract settling a complaint of discrimination outside the employment field[14].

1   Race Relations Act 1976 s 72(1)(a).
2   As to the meaning of 'act' see para 442 note 7 ante.
3   Race Relations Act 1976 s 72(1)(b), (c). Section 72 (as amended) applies only to discriminatory contracts and does not apply to collective agreements or rules of undertakings, unlike the Sex Discrimination Act 1975 s 77 (as amended), which is so applied by the Sex Discrimination Act 1986 s 6 (as amended): see para 393 ante. That provision, necessitated by enforcement proceedings brought by the European Commission against the United Kingdom government, renders void terms which are discriminatory on grounds of sex contained in collective agreements, the great majority of which do not have contractual force. There is no remedy for racially discriminatory collective agreements as such. However, employees affected by them would have claims under the Race Relations Act 1976 ss 4, 11 (as amended), against both the employer and the union: see paras 446, 451 ante. Affected employees could claim for less favourable access to the benefits and facilities of the collective bargaining process afforded to them by both employer and union, and for any detriment suffered by them as a result of the conclusion of a discriminatory collective agreement.
4   For the meaning of 'discrimination' see para 447 note 4 ante.

5   For the meaning of 'harassment' see para 444 ante.

6   Race Relations Act 1976 s 72(2) (amended by the Race Relations Act 1976 (Amendment) Regulations 2003, SI 2003/1626, reg 48). See also *Orphanos v Queen Mary College* [1985] AC 761, [1985] 2 All ER 233, HL. As to void and voidable contracts see CONTRACT vol 9(1) (Reissue) para 836 et seq.

7   As to designated county courts see para 500 note 20 post.

8   See the Race Relations Act 1976 s 72(5). Such an order must not be made unless all persons affected have been given notice of the application (except where under the rules of court notice may be dispensed with) and have been afforded an opportunity to make representations to the court: s 72(5). For the meaning of 'notice' see para 460 note 8 ante. Such an order may include provision as respects any period before the making of the order: s 72(6).

9   See ibid s 72(3).

10   Ie a complaint to which ibid s 54(1) (as amended) applies (see para 499 post): see s 72(4)(a). For the meaning of 'employment' see para 446 note 3 ante.

11   Ibid s 72(4)(a). See also note 12 infra.

12   The conditions regulating compromise contracts under the Race Relations Act 1976 are that: (1) the contract must be in writing; (2) the contract must relate to the particular complaint; (3) the complainant must have received advice from a relevant independent adviser as to the terms and effect of the proposed contract and in particular its effect on his ability to pursue his complaint before an employment tribunal; (4) there must be in force, when the adviser gives the advice, a contract of insurance, or an indemnity provided for members of a profession or professional body, covering the risk of a claim by the complainant in respect of loss arising in consequence of the advice; (5) the contract must identify the adviser; and (6) the contract must state that the conditions regulating compromise contracts under the Act are satisfied: s 72(4A) (added by the Trade Union Reform and Employment Rights Act 1993 s 39(2), Sch 6 para 2; and amended by the Employment Rights (Dispute Resolution) Act 1998 ss 1(2)(a), 9(1), (2)(b), 10(1), (2)(b)).

        A person is a relevant independent adviser for the purposes of head (3) supra if: (a) he is a qualified lawyer; (b) he is an officer, official, employee or member of an independent trade union who has been certified in writing by the trade union as competent to give advice and as authorised to do so on behalf of the trade union; (c) he works at an advice centre (whether as an employee or a volunteer) and has been certified in writing by the centre as competent to give advice and as authorised to do so on behalf of the centre; or (d) he is a person of a description specified in an order made by the Secretary of State: Race Relations Act 1976 s 72(4B) (added by the Trade Union Reform and Employment Rights Act 1993 Sch 6 para 2; and substituted by the Employment Rights (Dispute Resolution) Act 1998 s 15, Sch 1 para 3). For the purposes of head (d) supra, a fellow of the Institute of Legal Executives employed by a solicitors' practice has been specified: see the Compromise Agreements (Description of Person) Order 2004, SI 2004/754 (amended by SI 2004/2515). As to the Secretary of State and the National Assembly for Wales see para 302 ante. 'Qualified lawyer' means a barrister (whether in practice as such or employed to give legal advice), a solicitor who holds a practising certificate, or a person other than a barrister or solicitor who is an authorised advocate or authorised litigator (within the meaning of the Courts and Legal Services Act 1990: see BARRISTERS vol 3(1) (2005 Reissue) para 501; SOLICITORS vol 44(1) (Reissue) paras 78–79): Race Relations Act 1976 s 72(4BB) (added by the Employment Rights (Dispute Resolution) Act 1998 Sch 1 para 3). 'Independent trade union' has the same meaning as in the Trade Union and Labour Relations (Consolidation) Act 1992 (see TRADE, INDUSTRY AND INDUSTRIAL RELATIONS vol 47 (2001 Reissue) para 1014): Race Relations Act 1976 s 72(4BC) (added by the Employment Rights (Dispute Resolution) Act 1998 Sch 1 para 3).

        However, a person is not a relevant independent adviser for the purposes of head (3) supra in relation to the complainant: (i) if he is, or is employed by or is acting in the matter for the other party or a person who is connected with the other party; (ii) in the case of a person within head (b) or head (c) supra, if the trade union or advice centre is the other party or a person who is connected with the other party; (iii) in the case of a person within head (c) supra, if the complainant makes a payment for the advice received from him; or (iv) in the case of a person of a description specified in an order under head (d) supra, if any condition specified in the order in relation to the giving of advice by persons of that description is not satisfied: Race Relations Act 1976 s 72(4BA) (added by the Employment Rights (Dispute Resolution) Act 1998 Sch 1 para 3). For these purposes, any two persons are to be treated as connected if one is a company of which the other (directly or indirectly) has control, or if both are companies of which a third person (directly or indirectly) has control: Race Relations Act 1976 s 72(4C) (added by the Employment Rights (Dispute Resolution) Act 1998 Sch 1 para 3).

13   See the Race Relations Act 1976 s 72(4)(aa) (added by the Trade Union Reform and Employment Rights Act 1993 Sch 6 para 2).

14   Race Relations Act 1976 s 72(4)(b). This provision applies to claims to which s 57 (as amended) applies (see paras 499–500 post): see s 72(4)(b).

        An agreement entered into on or after 1 August 1998 under which the parties agree to submit a dispute to arbitration: (1) is to be regarded for the purposes of s 72(4)(a), (aa) (as added) as being a contract settling a complaint if the dispute is covered by a scheme having effect by virtue of an order under the Trade Union and Labour Relations (Consolidation) Act 1992 s 212A (as added and amended) (see TRADE, INDUSTRY AND INDUSTRIAL RELATIONS), and the agreement is to submit it to arbitration in accordance with the scheme; but (2) is to be regarded for those purposes as neither being nor including such a contract in any other case: Race Relations Act 1976 s 72(4D) (added by the Employment Rights (Dispute Resolution) Act 1998 s 8(2)).

479.   Collective agreements and rules of undertakings.   Any relevant term or rule is void where: (1) the making of the collective agreement[1] is, by reason of the inclusion of the term, unlawful[2] on grounds of race or ethnic or national origins[3]; (2) the term or rule is included or made in furtherance of an act which is unlawful on such grounds by virtue of such a provision[4]; or (3) the term or rule provides for the doing of such an act[5].

The provisions set out above apply to: (a) any term of a collective agreement, including an agreement which was not intended, or is presumed not to have been intended, to be a legally enforceable contract[6]; (b) any rule made by an employer for application to all or any of the persons who are employed by him or who apply to be, or are, considered by him for employment[7]; (c) any rule made by an organisation[8] or a body[9] for application to all or any of its members or prospective members, or all or any of the persons on whom it has conferred authorisations or qualifications or who are seeking the authorisations or qualifications which it has power to confer[10].

A person[11] may present a complaint to an employment tribunal that a term or rule is void[12] if he has reason to believe: (i) that the term or rule may at some future time have effect in relation to him[13]; and (ii) where he alleges that it is void[14], that an act for the doing of which it provides may at some such time be done in relation to him, and the act would be rendered unlawful[15] on grounds of race or ethnic or national origins if done in relation to him in present circumstances[16]. When an employment tribunal finds that a complaint presented to it is well-founded, the tribunal must make an order declaring that the term or rule is void[17].

The avoidance of any term or rule[18] which provides for any person to be discriminated against must be without prejudice to the following rights (except in so far as they enable any person to require another person to be treated less favourably than himself), namely, such of the rights of the person to be discriminated against, and such of the rights of any person who will be treated more favourably in direct or indirect consequence of the discrimination, as are conferred by or in respect of a contract made or modified wholly or partly in pursuance of, or by reference to, that term or rule[19].

1   'Collective agreement' means any agreement relating to one or more of the matters mentioned in the Trade Union and Labour Relations (Consolidation) Act 1992 s 178(2) (see TRADE, INDUSTRY AND INDUSTRIAL RELATIONS vol 47 (2001 Reissue) paras 1301–1302), being an agreement made by or on behalf of one or more employers or one or more organisations of employers or associations of such organisations with one or more organisations of workers or associations of such organisations: Race Relations Act 1976 s 72A(4) (ss 72A, 72B added by the Race Relations Act 1976 (Amendment) Regulations 2003, SI 2003/1626, reg 49).
2   Ie by a provision referred to in the Race Relations Act 1976 s 1(1B) (as added) (see para 440 ante): s 72A(2)(a) (as added: see note 1 supra).
3   Ibid s 72A(2)(a) (as added: see note 1 supra).
4   Ibid s 72A(2)(b) (as added: see note 1 supra).
5   Ibid s 72A(2)(c) (as added: see note 1 supra). Section 72A(2) (as added) applies whether the agreement was entered into, or the rule made, before, on or after the date of the commencement of s 72A (as added); but in the case of an agreement entered into, or a rule made, before that date, s 72A(2) (as added) does not apply in relation to any period before that date: s 72A(3) (as so added).
6   Ibid s 72A(1)(a) (as added: see note 1 supra).
7   Ibid s 72A(1)(b) (as added: see note 1 supra).
8   Ie an organisation to which ibid s 11 (as amended) applies: see para 451 ante.
9   Ie a body to which ibid s 11 (as amended) applies: see para 451 ante.

10 Ibid s 72A(1)(c) (as added: see note 1 supra).
11 In the case of a complaint about: (1) a term of a collective agreement made by or on behalf of an employer, an organisation of employers of which an employer is a member, or an association of such organisations of one of which an employer is a member; or (2) a rule made by an employer, within the meaning of ibid s 72A(1)(b) (see the text to note 7 supra), s 72A(1) (as added) applies to any person who is, or is genuinely and actively seeking to become, one of his employees: s 72B(2) (as added: see note 1 supra). In the case of a complaint about a rule made by an organisation or body to which s 72A(1)(c) (as added) applies (see the text to notes 8–10 supra), s 72A(1) (as added) applies to any person: (a) who is, or is genuinely and actively seeking to become, a member of the organisation or body; (b) on whom the organisation or body has conferred an authorisation or qualification; or (c) who is genuinely and actively seeking an authorisation or qualification which the organisation or body has power to confer: s 72B(1)(c) (as so added).
12 Ie by virtue of ibid s 72A (as added): see the text to notes 1–10 supra.
13 Ibid s 72B(1)(a) (as added: see note 1 supra).
14 Ie by virtue of ibid s 72A(2)(c) (as added): see the text to note 5 supra.
15 Ie by a provision referred to in ibid s 1(1B) (as added): see para 440 ante.
16 Ie under s 72A(1) (as added): see the text to notes 6–10 supra.
17 Ibid s 72B(4) (as added: see note 1 supra). An order under s 72B(4) (as added) may include provision as respects any period before the making of the order (but after the commencement of s 72B (as added) (i e 19 July 2003)): s 72B(5) (as so added).
18 Ie by virtue of ibid s 72A(2) (as added): see the text to notes 1–5 supra.
19 Ibid s 72B(6) (as added: see note 1 supra).

480. Protection of Sikhs from racial discrimination in connection with the wearing of safety helmets. Where: (1) any person[1] applies to a Sikh[2] any requirement or condition relating to the wearing by him of a safety helmet[3] while he is on a construction site[4]; and (2) at the time when he so applies the requirement or condition that person has no reasonable grounds for believing that the Sikh would not wear a turban at all times when on such a site[5], then, for the purpose of determining whether the application of the requirement or condition to the Sikh constitutes an act of indirect discrimination[6], the requirement or condition is to be taken to be one which cannot be shown to be justifiable under the Race Relations Act 1976[7].

Any special treatment afforded to a Sikh in consequence of the provision exempting Sikhs from the requirements as to the wearing of safety helmets on construction sites[8] is not to be regarded for the purposes of the Race Relations Act 1976 as giving rise, in relation to any other person, to any discrimination under that Act[9].

1 As to the meaning of 'person' see para 344 note 3 ante.
2 Any reference to a Sikh is a reference to a follower of the Sikh religion: Employment Act 1989 ss 11(8), 12(3).
3 'Safety helmet' means any form of protective headgear: ibid ss 11(7), 12(3).
4 Ibid s 12(1)(a). 'Construction site' means any place where any building operations or works of engineering construction are being undertaken: ss 11(7), 12(3). Any reference to a Sikh being on a construction site is a reference to his being there whether while at work or otherwise: ss 11(8), 12(3).
      As to the special protection of Sikhs from religious discrimination in connection with requirements as to wearing of safety helmets see para 681 post.
5 Ibid s 12(1)(b).
6 Ie an act falling within the Race Relations Act 1976 s 1(1)(b) (indirect racial discrimination): see para 440 ante.
7 Employment Act 1989 s 12(1). A person discriminates against another if he commits an act which he cannot show to be justifiable irrespective of the colour, race, nationality or ethnic or national origins of the person to whom it is applied: see the Race Relations Act 1976 s 1(1)(b)(ii); and para 440 ante.
8 Ie under the Employment Act 1989 s 11.
9 Ibid s 12(2). The text refers to any discrimination falling within the Race Relations Act 1976 is s 1 (as amended): see para 439 et seq ante.

(iii) General Exceptions

481. Charities. The Race Relations Act 1976 makes special provision for charities[1]. Any provision which is contained in a charitable instrument[2] (whenever that instrument took or takes effect) and which provides for conferring benefits on persons of a class defined otherwise than by reference to colour[3] is not rendered unlawful by the Race Relations Act 1976[4] and nor is any act[5] which is done in order to give effect to such a provision[6]. A provision which is contained in a charitable instrument (whenever that instrument took or takes effect) and which provides for conferring benefits on persons of a class defined by reference to colour has effect for all purposes as if it provided for conferring the like benefits[7] on persons of the class which results if the restriction by reference to colour is disregarded[8], or where the original class is defined by reference to colour only, on persons generally[9].

1   See the Race Relations Act 1976 s 34 (as amended); and the text and notes 2–9 infra.
2   'Charitable instrument' means an enactment or other instrument passed or made for charitable purposes,
     or an enactment or other instrument so far as it relates to charitable purposes; 'charitable purposes' means
     purposes which are exclusively charitable according to the law of England and Wales: ibid s 34(4). See
     further CHARITIES vol 5(2) (2001 Reissue) para 4 et seq.
3   Ie including a class resulting from the operation of ibid s 34(1) (see the text and notes 7–9 infra): see
     s 34(3).
4   Ie ibid Pts II–IV (ss 4–33) (as amended): see para 446 et seq ante.
5   As to the meaning of 'act' see para 442 note 7 ante. The reference to an act does not include an act which
     is unlawful, on grounds of race or ethnic or national origins, by virtue of ibid s 4 (as amended) (see
     para 446 ante) or s 7 (as amended) (see para 448 ante): s 34(3A) (added by the Race Relations Act 1976
     (Amendment) Regulations 2003, SI 2003/1626, reg 33). As to the meanings of 'ethnic origins' and
     'national origins' see para 441 ante.
6   See the Race Relations Act 1976 s 34(2).
7   Ibid s 34(1). For an application of s 34(1) see *Re Harding, Gibbs v Harding* [2007] EWHC 3 (Ch), [2007]
     All ER (D) 28 (Jan) (where the deceased's intended gift to the black community of Hackney, Haringey,
     Islington and Tower Hamlets was held to be a valid charitable gift but without the reference to colour).
     See also CHARITIES vol 5(2) (2001 Reissue) para 14.
8   Race Relations Act 1976 s 34(1)(a). See note 7 supra.
9   Ibid s 34(1)(b). See note 7 supra.

482.   Special needs: education, training or welfare.   Nothing in the provisions of Parts II to IV of the Race Relations Act 1976[1] renders unlawful any act[2] done in affording persons of a particular racial group[3] access to facilities or services[4] to meet the special needs[5] of persons of that group in regard to their education[6], training[7] or welfare, or any ancillary benefits[8].

1   Ie the Race Relations Act 1976 Pts II–IV (ss 4–33) (as amended): see para 446 et seq ante.
2   As to the meaning of 'act' see para 442 note 7 ante.
3   For the meaning of 'racial group' see para 441 ante.
4   As to the affording of access to benefits, facilities and services see para 446 note 14 ante.
5   The Race Relations Act 1976 does not define 'special needs'.
6   As to the meaning of 'education' see para 446 note 13 ante.
7   As to the meaning of 'training' see para 446 note 13 ante.
8   Race Relations Act 1976 s 35.

483.   Education or training for persons not ordinarily resident in Great Britain.   Nothing in the provisions of Parts II to IV of the Race Relations Act 1976[1] renders unlawful any act[2] done by a person[3], on grounds other than race or ethnic or national origins[4], for the benefit of persons not ordinarily resident in Great Britain[5] in affording them access to facilities[6] for education[7] or training[8] or any ancillary benefits, where it appears to him that the persons in question do not intend to remain in Great Britain after their period of education or training there[9].

1   Ie the Race Relations Act 1976 Pts II–IV (ss 4–33) (as amended): see para 446 et seq ante.
2   As to the meaning of 'act' see para 442 note 7 ante.
3   As to the meaning of 'person' see para 344 note 3 ante.
4   As to the meanings of 'ethnic origins' and 'national origins' see para 441 ante.

5   For the meaning of 'Great Britain' see para 325 note 6 ante. As to ordinary residence see BRITISH NATIONALITY, IMMIGRATION AND ASYLUM vol 4(2) (2002 Reissue) para 134; CONFLICT OF LAWS vol 8(3) (Reissue) para 58.

6   As to the affording of access to benefits, facilities and services see para 446 note 14 ante.

7   As to the meaning of 'education' see para 446 note 13 ante.

8   As to the meaning of 'training' see para 446 note 13 ante.

9   Race Relations Act 1976 s 36 (amended by the Race Relations Act 1976 (Amendment) Regulations 2003, SI 2003/1626, reg 34). See also the Race Relations Act 1976 s 6 (as amended) (exception for employment intended to provide training in skills to be exercised outside Great Britain); and para 447 ante.

484.   Positive action. The Race Relations Act 1976 permits certain positive action which would otherwise be unlawful discrimination in the fields of training and employment in areas of work where a particular racial group is under-represented[1]. Nothing in the provisions of Parts II to IV of the Race Relations Act 1976[2] renders unlawful any act[3] done in relation to particular work by any person[4] in or in connection with affording only persons of a particular racial group[5] access to facilities for training[6] which would help fit them for that work[7], or encouraging only persons of a particular racial group to take advantage of opportunities for doing that work[8], provided that at least one of the following conditions is satisfied. The conditions are that it must reasonably appear to that person that at any time within the 12 months immediately preceding the doing of the act either: (1) there were no persons of that group among those doing that work in Great Britain; or (2) the proportion of persons of that group among those doing that work in Great Britain was small in comparison with the proportion of persons of that group among the population of Great Britain[9].

Similar exceptions apply to employers[10]. Nothing in the provisions of Parts II to IV of the Race Relations Act 1976 renders unlawful any act done by an employer in relation to particular work in his employment[11] at a particular establishment in Great Britain[12] being an act done in or in connection with[13] affording only those of his employees working at that establishment who are of a particular racial group access to facilities for training which would help to fit them for that work[14], or encouraging only persons of a particular racial group to take advantage of opportunities for doing that work at that establishment[15], provided that at least one of the following conditions is established at any time within the 12 months immediately preceding the doing of the act in question[16]. The conditions are: (a) that there are no persons of the racial group in question among those doing that work at that establishment[17]; or (b) that the proportion of persons of that group among those doing that work at that establishment is small in comparison with the proportion of persons of that group among all those employed by that employer there, or among the population of the area from which that employer normally recruits persons for work in his employment at that establishment[18].

An organisation of workers, employers' association or similar organisation[19] may take positive action in or in connection with[20] affording only members of the organisation who are of a particular racial group access to facilities for training which would help to fit them for holding a post of any kind in the organisation[21], or encouraging only members of the organisation who are of a particular racial group to take advantage of opportunities for holding such posts in the organisation[22], provided that either of the following conditions was satisfied at any time within the 12 months immediately preceding the doing of the act[23]. The conditions are: (i) that there are no persons of the racial group in question among persons holding such posts in the organisation[24]; or (ii) that the proportion of persons of that group among those holding posts in that organisation is small in comparison with the proportion of persons of that group among the members of the organisation[25].

Such organisations may also lawfully encourage only persons of a particular racial group to become members of the organisation where at any time within the 12 months immediately preceding the doing of the act[26] no persons of that group were members of the organisation[27], or the proportion of persons of that group among members of the organisation was small in comparison with the proportion of persons of that group among those eligible for membership of the organisation[28].

1   See the Race Relations Act 1976 s 37 (as amended), s 38; and the text and notes 2–28 infra. Section 37 (as amended) does not apply to any discrimination which is rendered unlawful by virtue of s 4(1) or (2) (ie discrimination in the recruitment or the treatment of employees) (see para 446 ante): s 37(3) (substituted by the Employment Act 1989 s 7(3)). For the meaning of 'discrimination' see para 447 note 4 ante.
2   Ie the Race Relations Act 1976 Pts II–IV (ss 4–33) (as amended): see para 446 et seq ante.
3   As to the meaning of 'act' see para 442 note 7 ante.
4   Race Relations Act 1976 s 37(1) (amended by the Employment Act 1989 s 7(3)). As to the meaning of 'person' see para 344 note 3 ante.
5   For the meaning of 'racial group' see para 441 ante.
6   As to the affording of access to facilities see para 446 note 14 ante. As to the meaning of 'training' see para 446 note 13 ante.
7   Race Relations Act 1976 s 37(1)(a).
8   Ibid s 37(1)(b).
9   See ibid s 37(1)(i), (ii) (as amended: see note 4 supra). For the meaning of 'Great Britain' see para 325 note 6 ante. Similar protection is given to persons undertaking positive action where the racial imbalance in relation to particular work is local rather than national. Where, in relation to particular work, it reasonably appears to any person that although the condition for the operation of s 37(1) (as amended) is not met for the whole of Great Britain it is met for an area within Great Britain, nothing in Pts II–IV (as amended) renders unlawful any act done by that person in or in connection with: (1) affording persons of the racial group in question, and who appear likely to take up that work in that area, access to facilities for training which would help to fit them for that work; or (2) encouraging persons of that group to take advantage of opportunities in the area for doing that work: s 37(2) (amended by the Employment Act 1989 s 7(3)).
10 See the Race Relations Act 1976 s 38.
11 For the meaning of 'employment' see para 446 note 3 ante.
12 For the meaning of 'employment at an establishment in Great Britain' see para 446 ante; definition applied by the Race Relations Act 1976 s 38(6).
13 Ibid s 38(1).
14 Ibid s 38(1)(a).
15 Ibid s 38(1)(b).
16 Ibid s 38(1). The exception applies only to an employer's acts in relation to his actual employees. An employer may not rely on an ethnic imbalance in his workforce as a justification for recruiting only members of an under-represented racial group.
17 Ibid s 38(2)(a).
18 Ibid s 38(2)(b).
19 Ie an organisation to which ibid s 11 (as amended) applies (see para 451 ante), namely an organisation of workers, an organisation of employers, or any other organisation whose members carry on a particular profession or trade for the purposes of which the organisation exists (see s 11(1)): see s 38(3).
20 See ibid s 38(3).
21 Ibid s 38(3)(a).
22 Ibid s 38(3)(b).
23 See ibid s 38(3).
24 Ibid s 38(4)(a).
25 Ibid s 38(4)(b).
26 Ibid s 38(5).
27 Ibid s 38(5)(a).
28 Ibid s 38(5)(b).

485.   Sports and competitions.   Nothing in the provisions of Parts II to IV of the Race Relations Act 1976[1] renders unlawful any act[2] by which a person[3] discriminates[4] against another on the basis of that other's nationality[5] or place of birth or the length of time for which he has been resident in a particular area or place if the act is done[6]: (1) in selecting persons to represent a country, place or area, or any related association, in any sport or game[7]; or (2) in pursuance of the rules of any competition so far as they relate to eligibility to compete in any sport or game[8].

1 Ie the Race Relations Act 1976 Pts II–IV (ss 4–33) (as amended): see para 446 et seq ante.
2 As to the meaning of 'act' see para 442 note 7 ante.
3 As to the meaning of 'person' see para 344 note 3 ante.
4 For the meaning of 'discrimination' see para 447 note 4 ante.
5 As to the meaning of 'nationality' see para 441 note 2 ante.
6 Race Relations Act 1976 s 39.
7 Ibid s 39(a).
8 Ibid s 39(b).

486. Acts done under statutory authority. An act of discrimination[1] is not rendered unlawful by Parts II to IV of the Race Relations Act 1976[2] if it is done in pursuance of any enactment or Order in Council[3], or in pursuance of any instrument made under any enactment by a Minister of the Crown[4], or in order to comply with any condition or requirement imposed by a Minister of the Crown[5] by virtue of any enactment[6].

The exemption for acts done under statutory authority is broadened in relation to any act of discrimination on the basis of a person's nationality[7] or place of ordinary residence[8], or the length of time for which he has been present or resident in or outside the United Kingdom[9] or an area within the United Kingdom[10]. Such discrimination[11] is lawful if the act in question is done: (1) in pursuance of any enactment or Order in Council[12]; (2) in pursuance of any instrument made under any enactment by a Minister of the Crown[13]; (3) in order to comply with any requirement imposed by a Minister of the Crown, whether before or after the passing of the Race Relations Act 1976, by virtue of any enactment[14]; (4) in pursuance of any arrangements made, whether before or after the passing of the Act, by or with the approval of, or for the time being approved by, a Minister of the Crown[15]; or (5) in order to comply with any condition imposed, whether before or after the passing of the Act, by a Minister of the Crown[16].

1 As to the meaning of 'act' see para 442 note 7 ante; and for the meaning of 'discrimination' see para 447 note 4 ante.
2 Ie by the Race Relations Act 1976 Pts II–IV (ss 4–33) (as amended): see para 446 et seq ante.
3 Ibid s 41(1)(a). References in s 41 (as amended) to an enactment, Order in Council or instrument include an enactment, Order in Council or instrument passed or made after the passing of the Race Relations Act 1976 (ie 22 November 1976): s 41(1) (amended by the Race Relations Act 1976 (Amendment) Regulations 2003, SI 2003/1626, reg 35(a)).
    The Race Relations Act 1976 s 41(1) (as amended) does not apply to an act which is unlawful, on grounds of race or ethnic or national origins, by virtue of a provision referred to in s 1(1B) (as added) (see para 440 ante): s 41(1A) (added by the Race Relations Act 1976 (Amendment) Regulations 2003, SI 2003/1626, reg 35(b)). As to the meanings of 'ethnic origins' and 'national origins' see para 441 ante.
4 Race Relations Act 1976 s 41(1)(b). See notes 3 supra, 6 infra. For the meaning of 'Minister of the Crown' see para 445 note 1 ante. The references in s 41 (as amended) to a Minister of the Crown are to be construed as including a reference to the National Assembly for Wales: National Assembly for Wales (Transfer of Functions) Order 1999, SI 1999/672, art 2, Sch 1. As to the National Assembly for Wales see para 302 ante.
5 Ie whether the condition or requirement in question was imposed before or after the passing of the Race Relations Act 1976: see s 41(1)(c).
6 Ibid s 41(1)(c). The House of Lords considered the ambit of s 41(1) in *Hampson v Department of Education and Science* [1991] 1 AC 171, [1990] 2 All ER 513, HL (Hong Kong teacher claimed that the Department of Education and Science had discriminated against her because the Secretary of State did not approve the teacher training course she had completed in Hong Kong). The House of Lords held that statutory protection under the Race Relations Act 1976 s 41(1)(b) for any act of discrimination done 'in pursuance of any instrument made under any enactment by a Minister of the Crown' extended to acts done in the necessary performance of an express obligation contained in the instrument but not to acts done in the exercise of a power or discretion conferred by the instrument. The words 'in pursuance of' in the

provision bear the same meaning as the words 'necessary ... in order to comply with', which are used in the equivalent provision of the Sex Discrimination Act 1975 (see s 51 (as substituted); and para 401 ante). See also *General Medical Council v Goba* [1988] ICR 885, [1988] IRLR 425, EAT; *Mukoro v European Bank for Reconstruction and Development* [1994] ICR 897, EAT. The Race Relations Act 1976 s 41 (as amended) is not limited to provisions which specify a requirement of discrimination: where a statutory requirement compelled a local education authority to act in compliance with parental preference, it was held that an act of discrimination done by the authority in compliance with parental preference was protected by s 41 (as then in force): *R v Cleveland County Council, ex p Commission for Racial Equality* (1991) 135 Sol Jo LB 205, Times, 28 October, DC. See further EDUCATION vol 15(1) (2006 Reissue) para 396.

7   As to the meaning of 'nationality' see para 441 note 2 ante.
8   As to ordinary residence see BRITISH NATIONALITY, IMMIGRATION AND ASYLUM vol 4(2) (2002 Reissue) para 134; CONFLICT OF LAWS vol 8(3) (Reissue) para 58.
9   For the meaning of 'United Kingdom' see para 325 note 6 ante.
10   See the Race Relations Act 1976 s 41(2).
11   Ie as mentioned in the text and notes 7–10 supra.
12   Race Relations Act 1976 s 41(2)(a) (s 41(2)(a), (b) substituted, and s 41(2)(c)–(e) added, by the Race Relations Act 1976 (Amendment) Regulations 2003, SI 2003/1626, reg 35(c)).
13   Race Relations Act 1976 s 41(2)(b) (as substituted: see note 12 supra).
14   Ibid s 41(2)(c) (as added: see note 12 supra).
15   Ibid s 41(2)(d) (as added: see note 12 supra).
16   Ibid s 41(2)(e) (as added: see note 12 supra).

487.   Acts safeguarding national security.   Nothing in Parts II to IV of the Race Relations Act 1976[1] renders unlawful an act[2] done for the purpose of safeguarding national security if the doing of the act was justified for that purpose[3]. In any proceedings under the Race Relations Act 1976 or certain other enactments[4], a certificate signed by or on behalf of a Minister of the Crown[5], or in relation to Wales by the National Assembly for Wales[6], and certifying that any arrangements or conditions specified in the certificate were made, approved or imposed by a Minister of the Crown and were in operation at a time or throughout a period so specified is conclusive evidence of the matters certified[7]. A document purporting to be such a certificate must be received in evidence and, unless the contrary is proved, is to be deemed to be such a certificate[8].

1   Ie the Race Relations Act 1976 Pts II–IV (ss 4–33) (as amended): see para 446 et seq ante.
2   As to the meaning of 'act' see para 442 note 7 ante.
3   Race Relations Act 1976 s 42 (amended by the Race Relations (Amendment) Act 2000 s 7(1)).
4   Ie any enactment mentioned in the Race Relations Act 1976 s 19D(5) (as added and amended): see para 470 ante.
5   For the meaning of 'Minister of the Crown' see para 445 note 1 ante.
6   The certification function under the Race Relations Act 1976 s 69 (as amended) is exercisable by the National Assembly for Wales concurrently with any Minister of the Crown by whom it is exercisable: National Assembly for Wales (Transfer of Functions) Order 1999, SI 1999/672, art 2, Sch 1. As to the National Assembly for Wales see para 302 ante.
7   Race Relations Act 1976 s 69(2) (amended by the Race Relations (Amendment) Act 2000 ss 7(2), 9(1), (2), Sch 2 para 15, Sch 3).
8   Race Relations Act 1976 s 69(3). In the field of sex discrimination, the equivalent provisions (ie the Sex Discrimination Act 1975 s 52(2), (3)) have been amended so as to exclude their operation in the fields of employment and vocational training, as a result of the United Kingdom's obligations under EC Council Directive 76/207 (OJ L 39, 14.2.76, p 40) on the implementation of the principle of equal treatment for men and women as regards access to employment, vocational training and promotion, and working conditions (the 'Equal Treatment Directive'), and the decision of the European Court of Justice in Case 222/84 *Johnston v Chief Constable of the Royal Ulster Constabulary* [1987] QB 129, [1986] 3 All ER 135, ECJ: see para 338 ante. The provisions of the Race Relations Act 1976 s 69(2), (3) are unaffected by these changes.
     Before the amendments to s 69(2) (see note 7 supra), the Divisional Court was asked, in *R v Secretary of State for Transport, ex p Evans* (2 December 1991, unreported), CO/1390/90, DC, to consider whether the Race Relations Act 1976 ss 42, 69(2) (as originally enacted) were void in so far as they provided: (1) a national security defence to a claim by a worker who is a national of a member state of the European

Union that he is a victim of discrimination on the ground of nationality by his employer; and (2) that in relation to such a claim a certificate that an act was done for the purpose of safeguarding national security is conclusive evidence of the matters certified. The argument was based on the Treaty Establishing the European Community (Rome, 25 March 1957; TS 1 (1973); Cmnd 5179) (the 'EC Treaty') art 48; and EC Council Regulation 1612/68 (OJ L257, 19.10.68, p 2) on freedom of movement for workers within the Community, art 7, prohibiting discrimination in employment on the grounds of nationality. The Divisional Court declined to decide the matter, holding on the facts that there was no discrimination.

(3) THE COMMISSION FOR RACIAL EQUALITY

(i) Establishment, Duties and Powers

488. Establishment, incorporation and status. The Race Relations Act 1976 established the Commission for Racial Equality ('CRE'), to replace the Race Relations Board and the Community Relations Commission, which were both abolished by the Act[1]. The CRE consists of between eight and 15 individuals[2], each appointed by the Secretary of State on a full-time or part-time basis[3]. The Secretary of State is obliged to appoint one of the commissioners to be chairman of the CRE[4], and either one or more of the commissioners, as the Secretary of State thinks fit, to be deputy chairman or chairmen[5].

The CRE is a body corporate[6]. It is not an emanation of the Crown and is not to act or be treated as the servant or agent of the Crown[7].

The CRE may, after consultation with the Secretary of State, appoint such officers and servants as it thinks fit, subject to the approval of the Minister for the Civil Service as to numbers and as to remuneration and other terms and conditions of service[8].

The CRE is to be replaced by the Commission for Equality and Human Rights[9].

1 See the Race Relations Act 1976 s 43(5) (repealed). Part VII (ss 43–52) (as amended) and Sch 1 are repealed by the Equality Act 2006 ss 40, 91, Sch 3 paras 21, 26, 34, Sch 4 as from a day to be appointed under s 93. At the date at which this volume states the law no such day had been appointed. As to the Commission for Equality and Human Rights, which is to replace the CRE, see para 305 et seq ante.

2 The Secretary of State may by order amend the Race Relations Act 1976 s 43(1) (as amended) so far as it regulates the number of commissioners: s 43(3). As to the Secretary of State and the National Assembly for Wales see para 302 ante. 'Commissioner' means a member of the CRE: s 78(1). The validity of any proceedings of the CRE are not affected by any vacancy among the members of the CRE or by any defect in the appointment of any commissioner or additional commissioner: s 43(4), Sch 1 para 14. As to additional commissioners see para 492 post. As to the quorum for meetings see Sch 1 para 15.

3 See ibid s 43(1). The function of the Secretary of State under s 43(1) of making appointments to the CRE is exercisable only with the agreement of the National Assembly for Wales so far as necessary to ensure that there is at all times one commissioner who has been appointed with the agreement of the Assembly: National Assembly for Wales (Transfer of Functions) Order 1999, SI 1999/672, art 5(1), Sch 2.

A commissioner holds and vacates his office in accordance with the terms of his appointment: Race Relations Act 1976 Sch 1 para 3(1). A person may not be appointed a commissioner for more than five years: Sch 1 para 3(2). With the consent of the commissioner concerned, the Secretary of State may alter the terms of an appointment so as to make a full-time commissioner into a part-time commissioner or vice versa, or for any other purpose: Sch 1 para 3(3). A commissioner may resign by notice to the Secretary of State: Sch 1 para 3(4). The Secretary of State may terminate the appointment of a commissioner if satisfied that: (1) without the consent of the CRE, he failed to attend the meetings of the CRE during a continuous period of six months beginning not earlier than nine months before the termination; (2) he is an undischarged bankrupt, or has made an arrangement with his creditors; or (3) he is by reason of physical or mental illness, or for any other reason, incapable of carrying out his duties: Sch 1 para 3(5). Past service as a commissioner is no bar to re-appointment: Sch 1 para 3(6). The Secretary of State may pay, or make such payments towards the provision of, such remuneration, pensions, allowances or gratuities to or in respect of the commissioners or any of them as, with the consent of the Minister for the Civil Service, he may determine: Sch 1 para 5. There is to be defrayed out of money provided by Parliament: (a) sums required by the Secretary of State for making payments under Sch 1 paras 5, 15 and for defraying any other expenditure falling to be made by him under or by virtue of the Race Relations Act 1976; and (b) any increase attributable to the provisions of the Race Relations Act 1976 in the sums payable out of money provided by Parliament under any other Act: s 77(a), (d).

Where a person ceases to be a commissioner otherwise than on the expiry of his term of office, and it appears to the Secretary of State that there are special circumstances which make it right for that person to receive compensation, the Secretary of State may, with the consent of the Minister for the Civil Service, direct the CRE to make to that person a payment of such amount as, with the consent of that Minister, the Secretary of State may determine: Sch 1 para 6. As to the Minister for the Civil Service see CONSTITUTIONAL LAW AND HUMAN RIGHTS vol 8(2) (Reissue) para 427 et seq.

The Secretary of State is to pay to the CRE expenses incurred or to be incurred by it under Sch 1 para 6, 7, 8 or 10 (see note 8 infra; and para 492 post) and, with the consent of the Minister for the Civil Service and the Treasury, is to pay to the CRE such sums as the Secretary of State thinks fit for enabling the CRE to meet other expenses: Sch 1 para 16. As to the Treasury see CONSTITUTIONAL LAW AND HUMAN RIGHTS vol 8(2) (Reissue) paras 512–517.

4   Ibid s 43(2)(a). As to the tenure of office of the chairman see note 5 infra.
5   Ibid s 43(2)(b). The chairman and each deputy chairman holds and vacates his office in accordance with the terms of his appointment, and may resign by notice to the Secretary of State: Sch 1 para 4(1). The office of the chairman or a deputy chairman is vacated if he ceases to be a commissioner: Sch 1 para 4(2). Past service as chairman or a deputy chairman is no bar to re-appointment: Sch 1 para 4(3).
6   See ibid Sch 1 para 1.
7   Ibid Sch 1 para 2(1). Accordingly, neither the CRE nor a commissioner nor a member of its staff as such is entitled to any status, immunity, privilege or exception enjoyed by the Crown (Sch 1 para 2(2)(a)); the commissioners and members of the staff of the CRE as such are not civil servants (Sch 1 para 2(2)(b)); and the CRE's property is not property of, or held on behalf of, the Crown (Sch 1 para 2(2)(c)). The CRE's independence from the Crown has enabled it to take legal action against government departments in the exercise of its law enforcement functions: see e g *Home Office v Commission for Racial Equality* [1982] QB 385, [1981] 1 All ER 1042. As to Crown privilege see CROWN AND ROYAL FAMILY vol 12(1) (Reissue) para 52 et seq; and see also CONSTITUTIONAL LAW AND HUMAN RIGHTS; CROWN PROCEEDINGS AND CROWN PRACTICE; CROWN PROPERTY.
8   Race Relations Act 1976 Sch 1 para 8. Employment with the CRE is included among the kinds of employment to which a superannuation scheme under the Superannuation Act 1972 s 1 (as amended) can apply: see the Race Relations Act 1976 Sch 1 para 9(1); and see also the Superannuation Act 1972 s 1, Sch 1 (as amended); and CONSTITUTIONAL LAW AND HUMAN RIGHTS vol 8(2) (Reissue) para 567 et seq. Where a person who is employed by the CRE and is by reference to that employment a participant in such a scheme becomes a commissioner or an additional commissioner, the Minister for the Civil Service may determine that his service as a commissioner, or additional commissioner is to be treated for the purposes of the scheme as service as an employee of the CRE: Race Relations Act 1976 Sch 1 para 9(2). As to provisions relating to private pension schemes and as to employees who previously worked for the Community Relations Committee see Sch 1 para 10.
9   See note 1 supra.

489.   General duties. The duties of the Commission for Racial Equality ('CRE') are as follows: (1) to work towards the elimination of discrimination and harassment[1]; (2) to promote equality of opportunity, and good relations between persons of different racial groups generally[2]; and (3) to keep under review the working of the Race Relations Act 1976 and, when it is so required by the Secretary of State[3] or otherwise thinks it necessary, to draw up and submit to the Secretary of State proposals for amending it[4].

The CRE must make an annual report as soon as practicable after the end of the calendar year to the Secretary of State on its activities during the year[5]. It is also the duty of the CRE: (a) to keep proper accounts and proper records in relation to the accounts; (b) to prepare in respect of each accounting year a statement of accounts in such form as the Secretary of State may direct with the approval of the Treasury; and (c) to send copies of the statement to the Secretary of State and the Comptroller and Auditor General before the end of the month of November next following the accounting year to which the statement relates[6].

1   Race Relations Act 1976 s 43(1)(a) (amended by the Race Relations Act 1976 (Amendment) Regulations 2003, SI 2003/1626, reg 36). For the meaning of 'discrimination' see para 447 note 4 ante. For the meaning of 'harassment' see para 444 ante. The Race Relations Act 1976 Pt VII (ss 43–52) (as amended) and Sch 1 are repealed by the Equality Act 2006 ss 40, 91, Sch 3 paras 21, 26, 34, Sch 4 as from a day to be appointed under s 93. At the date at which this volume states the law no such day had

been appointed. As to the establishment of the CRE see para 488 ante. As to the Commission for Equality and Human Rights, which is to replace the CRE, see para 305 et seq ante.

2   Race Relations Act 1976 s 43(1)(b). For the meaning of 'racial group' see para 441 ante.

3   As to the Secretary of State and the National Assembly for Wales see para 302 ante.

4   Race Relations Act 1976 s 43(1)(c). See 'Review of the Race Relations Act 1976: Proposals for Change', published by the Commission for Racial Equality in July 1985.

5   See the Race Relations Act 1976 s 46(1). Each annual report must include a general survey of developments during the period to which it relates, in respect of matters falling within the scope of the CRE's functions, and must be laid before Parliament and published by the Secretary of State: see s 46(2), (3).

6   Ibid s 43(4), Sch 1 para 17(2). The accounting year of the CRE is the 12 months ending on 31 March: Sch 1 para 17(1). The Comptroller and Auditor General must examine, certify and report on each statement received and must lay copies of each statement and of his report before each House of Parliament: see Sch 1 para 17(3). As to the Comptroller and Auditor General see CONSTITUTIONAL LAW AND HUMAN RIGHTS vol 8(2) (Reissue) para 724 et seq. As to the Treasury see CONSTITUTIONAL LAW AND HUMAN RIGHTS vol 8(2) (Reissue) paras 512–517.

490.   General powers.   The Commission for Racial Equality ('CRE') may give financial or other assistance to any organisation appearing to the CRE to be concerned with the promotion of equality of opportunity, and good relations, between persons of different racial groups[1].

The CRE may also undertake or assist, financially or otherwise, the undertaking by other persons of any research and educational activities, which appear to the CRE necessary or expedient in connection with the discharge of its duties[2]. The CRE may make charges for educational or other facilities or services made available by it[3].

The CRE may, with the approval of the Secretary of State, appoint advisory committees for the purpose of such of its functions as it thinks fit[4].

The CRE has various powers and functions in relation to the enforcement of the Race Relations Act 1976[5], including the provision of assistance to individual complainants[6].

1   Race Relations Act 1976 s 44(1). For the meaning of 'racial group' see para 441 ante. Part Pt VII (ss 43–52) (as amended) and Sch 1 are repealed by the Equality Act 2006 ss 40, 91, Sch 3 paras 21, 26, 34, Sch 4 as from a day to be appointed under s 93. At the date at which this volume states the law no such day had been appointed.
      The approval of the Secretary of State given with the consent of the Treasury is required for the giving of financial assistance out of money provided by Parliament: see the Race Relations Act 1976 s 44(1). This function and other functions of the CRE in relation to matters connected with the giving of such financial or other assistance as is mentioned within s 44(1) is to be discharged under the general direction of the CRE by a committee of the CRE consisting of at least three but not more than five commissioners, of whom one is to be the deputy chairman of the CRE: see s 44(2). For the meaning of 'commissioner' see para 488 note 2 ante. As to the establishment of the CRE see para 488 ante. As to the Commission for Equality and Human Rights, which is to replace the CRE, see para 305 et seq ante. As to the Secretary of State and the National Assembly for Wales see para 302 ante. As to the Treasury see CONSTITUTIONAL LAW AND HUMAN RIGHTS vol 8(2) (Reissue) paras 512–517.
      Under the power in s 44(1), the CRE funds Community Relations Councils.

2   Ibid s 45(1). As to the duties of the CRE see para 489 ante.

3   Ibid s 45(2).

4   Ibid s 43(4), Sch 1 para 12. Subject to the provisions of the Race Relations Act 1976, the CRE must discharge its functions in accordance with arrangements made by the CRE and approved by the Secretary of State; and arrangements so made and approved may provide for the discharge under the general direction of the CRE of any of the CRE's functions by a committee of the CRE, or by two or more commissioners: Sch 1 para 13(1). Anything done by or in relation to a committee of the CRE or commissioners has the same effect as if done by or in relation to the CRE: Sch 1 para 13(2). There is to be defrayed out of money provided by Parliament any expenses incurred by the Secretary of State with the consent of the Treasury in undertaking, or financially assisting the undertaking by other persons of, research into any matter connected with relations between persons of different racial groups: s 77(b).

5   See ibid ss 58–66 (as amended; s 58–64, 66 prospectively repealed); and para 498 post.

6   See ibid s 66 (as amended; prospectively repealed); and para 497 post.

(ii) Specific Functions

491. Power to issue codes of practice. The Commission for Racial Equality ('CRE') may issue codes of practice containing such practical guidance as the CRE thinks fit for the elimination of discrimination[1] and harassment[2] in the fields of employment[3] and housing, and the promotion of equality of opportunity in those fields between people of different racial groups[4]. The CRE may also issue codes of practice containing such practical guidance as it thinks fit in relation to the performance by specified persons of certain duties[5].

When the CRE proposes to issue a code of practice, it must prepare and publish a draft of the code, and consider any representations made to it about the draft, and may modify the draft accordingly[6].

In the course of preparing any draft code of practice the CRE has a duty to consult with appropriate organisations, associations of organisations, and bodies[7]. The draft code of practice must be approved by the Secretary of State and laid before Parliament[8].

The CRE may from time to time revise the whole or any part of a code of practice and issue a revised code[9].

A failure on the part of any person[10] to observe any provision of a code of practice does not of itself render him liable to any proceedings[11]. However, its provisions are admissible in evidence in any proceedings before an employment tribunal or a county court, and if any provision of such a code appears to the tribunal or the court to be relevant to any question arising in the proceedings it must be taken into account in determining that question[12].

In 2006, the CRE issued codes of practice relating to employment[13] and to housing[14]. The CRE has also, in the education field, issued a code of practice for the elimination of racial discrimination in education, which was published in December 1989[15]. In the area of health care there are two published codes of practice: one for the elimination of racial discrimination and the promotion of equal opportunities in primary health care services, which was published in 1992[16]; and the other dealing with maternity services, which was published in 1994[17].

1   For the meaning of 'discrimination' see para 447 note 4 ante.

2   For the meaning of 'harassment' see para 444 ante

3   Such a code may include such practical guidance as the CRE thinks fit as to what steps it is reasonably practicable for employers to take for the purpose of preventing their employees from doing in the course of their employment acts made unlawful by the Race Relations Act 1976: s 47(11). For the meaning of 'employment' see para 446 note 3 ante; and as to the meaning of 'act' see para 442 note 7 ante. Part VII (ss 43–52) (as amended) is repealed by the Equality Act 2006 ss 40, 91, Sch 3 paras 21, 26, Sch 4 as from a day to be appointed under s 93. At the date at which this volume states the law no such day had been appointed. As to the establishment of the CRE see para 488 ante. As to the Commission for Equality and Human Rights, which is to replace the CRE, see para 305 et seq ante.

4   Race Relations Act 1976 s 47(1) (amended by the Housing Act 1988 s 137(1), (2); the Local Government and Housing Act 1989 ss 180, 194, Sch 12 Pt II; and the Race Relations Act 1976 (Amendment) Regulations 2003, SI 2003/1626, reg 37). For the meaning of 'racial group' see para 441 ante.

5   Race Relations Act 1976 s 71C(1) (s 71C added by the Race Relations (Amendment) Act 2000 s 2(1)). The Race Relations Act 1976 s 71C (as added) is repealed by the Equality Act 2006 Sch 3 paras 21, 30, Sch 4 as from a day to be appointed under s 93. At the date at which this volume states the law no such day had been appointed.

The duties referred to in the text are those imposed by the Race Relations Act 1976 s 71(1), (2) (as substituted) (see para 469 ante).

A code may include such practical guidance as the CRE thinks fit as to what steps it is reasonably practicable for persons to take for the purpose of preventing their staff from doing in the course of their duties acts made unlawful by the Race Relations Act 1976: s 71C(12) (as so added). See the Race Relations Act 1976 (General Statutory Duty: Code of Practice) Order 2002, SI 2002/1435.

6   Race Relations Act 1976 ss 47(2), 71C(2) (s 71C(2) as added: see note 5 supra).

7   See ibid s 47(3), (3A) (s 47(3) amended, and s 47(3A) added, by the Housing Act 1988 s 137(1), (3); and the Race Relations Act 1976 s 47(3A) amended by the Local Government and Housing Act 1989 ss 180, 194, Sch 12 Pt II); and the Race Relations Act 1976 s 71C(3) (as added: see note 5 supra). In relation to codes of practice relating to the field of employment, the CRE is obliged to consult with such organisations or associations of organisations representative of employers or of workers and such other organisations or bodies as appear to it to be appropriate: see the Race Relations Act 1976 s 47(3) (as so amended). In relation to codes of practice relating to housing, the CRE is obliged to consult with such organisations or bodies as appear to it appropriate having regard to the content of the draft code: see s 47(3A) (as so added and amended). In relation to codes of practice under s 71 (as substituted) (see para 469 ante), the CRE is obliged to consult with such organisations or bodies as appear to it to be appropriate having regard to the content of the draft code: see s 71C(3) (as added).

8   If the CRE determines to proceed with a draft code of practice, it must transmit the draft to the Secretary of State who must, if he approves of it, lay it before both Houses of Parliament; and, if he does not approve of it, publish details of his reasons for withholding approval: ibid s 47(4) (amended by the Housing Act 1988 s 137(4)). As to the Secretary of State and the National Assembly for Wales see para 302 ante. If, within the period of 40 days beginning with the day on which a copy of a draft code of practice is laid before each House of Parliament, or, if such copies are laid on different days, with the later of the two days, either House so resolves, no further proceedings may be taken, but without prejudice to the laying before Parliament of a new draft: see the Race Relations Act 1976 s 47(5). In reckoning the period of 40 days, no account is to be taken of any period during which Parliament is dissolved or prorogued or during which both Houses are adjourned for more than four days: s 47(6). If no such resolution is passed, the CRE may issue the code in the form of the draft and the code will come into effect on such day as the Secretary of State may by order appoint, and such order may contain transitional provisions and savings: see s 47(7), (8). The procedure in relation to the CRE's power to issue a code under s 71C(1) (as added) is substantially the same as the procedure under s 47(1) (as amended), except that the Secretary of State must consult the Scottish Ministers and the National Assembly for Wales before deciding whether to approve it: see s 71C(4)–(9) (as added: see note 5 supra). Scottish matters generally are beyond the scope of this work.

9   See ibid ss 47(9), 71C(10) (s 71C as added: see note 5 supra). The provisions of s 47(2)–(8) (as amended) apply to a revised code, with appropriate modifications: see s 47(9). The CRE has power to revoke or revise a code made under s 71C(1) (as added); and where it revises the whole or any part of the code, it must issue the revised code and the provisions of s 71C(2)–(9) (as added) apply with appropriate modifications to such a revised code as they apply to the first issue of a code: see s 71C(10) (as so added).

10 As to the meaning of 'person' see para 344 note 3 ante.

11 See the Race Relations Act 1976 ss 47(10), 71C(11) (s 71C as added: see note 5 supra).

12 Ibid s 47(10) (amended by the Housing Act 1988 s 137(5); and by virtue of the Employment Rights (Dispute Resolution) Act 1998 s 1(2)(a)); Race Relations Act 1976 s 71C(11) (as added: see note 5 supra). See *West Midlands Passenger Transport Executive v Jaquant Singh* [1988] 2 All ER 873, [1988] 1 WLR 730, CA; *Carrington v Helix Lighting Ltd* [1990] ICR 125, [1990] IRLR 6, EAT.

13 See the Statutory Code of Practice on Racial Equality in Employment, which came into effect on 6 April 2006; and the Race Relations Code of Practice relating to Employment (Appointed) Day) Order 2006, SI 2006/630. See para 446 et seq ante.

14 See the Statutory Code of Practice on Racial Equality in Housing, which came into effect on 1 October 2006; and the Race Relations Code of Practice (Housing) (Appointed Day) Order 2006, SI 2006/2239. Previously there were separate codes of practice in regard to rented housing and non-rented (owner occupied) housing. See para 463 ante.

15 See the Race Relations Code of Practice for the elimination of racial discrimination in Education (1984).

16 See the Race Relations Code of Practice in Primary Health Care Services for the elimination of racial discrimination and the promotion of equal opportunities (1992).

17 See the Race Relations Code of Practice in Maternity Services for the elimination of racial discrimination and the promotion of equal opportunities (1994).

492.   Power to conduct formal investigations. ·The Commission for Racial Equality ('CRE') may if it thinks fit, and must if required to do so by the Secretary of State[1], conduct a formal investigation[2] for any purpose connected with the carrying out of its general duties[3].

There are three types of formal investigation which may be conducted by the CRE: (1) a formal investigation at the request of the Secretary of State, in which case responsibility for drawing the terms of reference for the investigation lies upon the Secretary of State; (2) a formal investigation of a general character with terms of reference drawn by the CRE (that is, a 'general investigation'); and (3) a formal investigation into the conduct of a person named in terms of reference drawn by the CRE, who the CRE believes may have done or be doing unlawful discriminatory acts (that is, a 'named person investigation')[4].

1   As to the Secretary of State and the National Assembly for Wales see para 302 ante.
2   In *Commission for Racial Equality v Amari Plastics Ltd* [1982] QB 1194 at 1203, [1982] 2 All ER 499 at 503, CA, Lord Denning MR criticised the elaborate and cumbersome machinery provided by the Race Relations Act 1976 for the conduct of formal investigations. The CRE has criticised the statutory machinery for the conduct of formal investigations in its 'Review of the Race Relations Act 1976: Proposals for Change', published in July 1985.
3   See the Race Relations Act 1976 s 48(1). Part VII (ss 43–52) (as amended) is repealed by the Equality Act 2006 ss 40, 91, Sch 3 paras 21, 26, Sch 4 as from a day to be appointed under s 93. At the date at which this volume states the law no such day had been appointed. As to the establishment of the CRE see para 488 ante. As to the Commission for Equality and Human Rights, which is to replace the CRE, see para 305 et seq ante. For the CRE's general duties see the Race Relations Act 1976 s 43(1) (as amended); and para 489 ante. This power is without prejudice to the CRE's general power to do anything requisite for the performance of its duties under s 43(1) (as amended): s 48(1). The scope of the CRE's power to conduct investigations is broad. It includes the power to investigate the immigration service, since it has an impact on race relations: *Home Office v Commission for Racial Equality* [1982] QB 385, [1981] 1 All ER 1042.
    With the approval of the Secretary of State, the CRE may appoint, on a full-time or part-time basis, one or more individuals as additional commissioners for the purposes of a formal investigation: Race Relations Act 1976 s 48(2). The CRE may also nominate one or more commissioners, with or without one or more additional commissioners, to conduct a formal investigation on its behalf, and may delegate any of its functions in relation to the investigation to the persons so nominated: s 48(3). For the meaning of 'commissioner' see para 488 note 2 ante.
    The CRE may pay, or make such payments towards the provision of, such remuneration, pensions, allowances or gratuities to or in respect of an additional commissioner as the Secretary of State, with the consent of the Minister for the Civil Service, may determine: s 43(4), Sch 1 para 7(2). As to the Minister for the Civil Service see CONSTITUTIONAL LAW AND HUMAN RIGHTS vol 8(2) (Reissue) para 427 et seq. With the approval of the Secretary of State and the consent of the additional commissioner concerned, the CRE may alter the terms of an appointment of an additional commissioner so as to make a full-time additional commissioner into a part-time additional commissioner or vice versa, or for any other purpose: Sch 1 para 7(3). An additional commissioner may resign by notice to the CRE: Sch 1 para 7(4). The Secretary of State, or the CRE acting with the approval of the Secretary of State, may terminate the appointment of an additional commissioner if satisfied that without reasonable excuse he failed to carry out the duties for which he was appointed during a continuous period of three months beginning not earlier than six months before the termination, or that he is an undischarged bankrupt or has made an arrangement with his creditors, or that he is by reason of physical or mental illness, or for any other reason, incapable of carrying out his duties: see Sch 1 para 7(5). Schedule 1 paras 2(2), 3(1), (6), and 6 (see para 488 ante) apply to additional commissioners appointed under s 48(2) as they apply to commissioners: Sch 1 para 7(1). The appointment of an additional commissioner terminates at the conclusion of the investigation for which he was appointed, if not sooner: Sch 1 para 7(6).
4   See *R v Commission for Racial Equality, ex p Hillingdon London Borough Council* [1982] QB 276, [1981] 3 WLR 520, CA, per Griffiths LJ (affd sub nom *Hillingdon London Borough Council v Commision for Racial Equality* [1982] AC 779, [1982] 3 WLR 159, HL). It is a condition precedent to the exercise by the CRE of its power to conduct an investigation which by its terms of reference is confined to the activities of persons named in it (a 'named person investigation') that the CRE should have already formed a suspicion that the persons named may have committed some unlawful act of discrimination and had at any rate some grounds for so suspecting, albeit that the grounds upon which any such suspicion was based might be no more than tenuous because they had not yet been tested: *Re Prestige Group plc* [1984] 1 WLR 335 at 343, [1984] ICR 473 at 481, HL, per Lord Diplock. See also *Hillingdon London Borough Council v Commission for Racial Equality* supra. To be entitled to embark upon a named person investigation, the CRE must have material before it which is sufficient to raise in the minds of reasonable people possessed of the experience of covert racial discrimination that has been acquired by the CRE, a suspicion that there may have been acts by the person named of racial discrimination of the kind that it is proposed to investigate: *Hillingdon London Borough Council v Commission for Racial Equality* supra at 786 and 164 per Lord Diplock.

493.   Conduct of formal investigations. Before the Commission for Racial Equality ('CRE') may embark on a formal investigation[1] the following requirements must be complied with[2]. Terms of reference for the investigation must be drawn up by the CRE or, if the CRE was required by the Secretary of State[3] to conduct the investigation, by the Secretary of State after consulting the CRE[4]. The CRE must give general notice[5] of the holding of the investigation unless the terms of reference confine it to activities of persons named in them, but in such a case the CRE must in the prescribed[6] manner give those persons notice of the holding of the investigation[7]. In a named person investigation in the course of which the CRE proposes to investigate any act[8] made unlawful by the Race Relations Act 1976 which it believes that a named person may have done[9], the CRE must inform that person of its belief and of its proposal to investigate the act in question[10] and offer him an opportunity of making oral or written representations or both with regard to it[11]. A person availing himself of this opportunity to make oral representations may be represented by counsel or a solicitor or by another person of his choice, not being a person to whom the CRE objects on the ground that he is unsuitable[12].

The High Court has jurisdiction to conduct a judicial review of the CRE's conduct of an investigation, including the formulation by the CRE of terms of reference, and its hearing of representations by the persons investigated, in any case where the CRE may have exceeded its powers or acted irrationally or unfairly[13].

1   'Formal investigation' means an investigation under the Race Relations Act 1976 s 48 (see para 492 ante): s 78(1). This definition is repealed by the Equality Act 2006 ss 40, 91, Sch 3 paras 21, 33(a)(ii), Sch 4 as from a day to be appointed under s 93. At the date at which this volume states the law no such day had been appointed.

2   See the Race Relations Act 1976 s 49(1). Part VII (ss 43–52) (as amended) is repealed by the Equality Act 2006 Sch 3 paras 21, 26, Sch 4 as from a day to be appointed under s 93. At the date at which this volume states the law no such day had been appointed. As to the establishment of the CRE see para 488 ante. As to the Commission for Equality and Human Rights, which is to replace the CRE, see para 305 et seq ante.

3   As to the Secretary of State and the National Assembly for Wales see para 302 ante.

4   Race Relations Act 1976 s 49(2). In the case of a named person investigation (see para 492 ante), the terms of reference must be confined to the particular kinds of acts which the CRE genuinely believes the persons named to have done; accordingly, the CRE was not entitled to draw up terms of reference which referred generally to the provision of facilities or services to the homeless by a council, when it believed that the council might have discriminated unlawfully only in relation to homeless immigrants arriving at Heathrow: *Hillingdon London Borough Council v Commission for Racial Equality* [1982] AC 779, [1982] 3 WLR 159, HL. However, the terms of reference may be wider than the material on which the investigation is based if that material allows the drawing of an inference by the CRE that a more general policy of discrimination was being followed: *Hillingdon London Borough Council v Commission for Racial Equality* supra. The terms of reference of a named person investigation must state the nature of the CRE's belief that the named persons have committed unlawful acts, and must particularise with reasonable specificity the kinds of acts to which the proposed investigation is to be directed and confined: *Re Prestige Group plc* [1984] 1 WLR 335, [1984] ICR 473, HL; *Hillingdon London Borough Council v Commission for Racial Equality* supra.

Terms of reference may be revised from time to time by the CRE, or, if the CRE was required by the Secretary of State to conduct the investigation, the Secretary of State after consulting the CRE; and the provisions of the Race Relations Act 1976 s 49(1), (3), (4) (see the text and notes 2 supra, 7–12 infra) apply to the revised investigation and terms of reference as they applied to the original: s 49(5).

5   'General notice', in relation to any person, means a notice published by him at a time and in a manner appearing to him suitable for securing that the notice is seen within a reasonable time by persons likely to be affected by it: ibid s 78(1). For the meaning of 'notice' see para 460 note 8 ante.

6   For the meaning of 'prescribed' see para 468 note 6 ante.

7   Race Relations Act 1976 s 49(3). As to the prescribed manner of giving notice see the Race Relations (Formal Investigations) Regulations 1977, SI 1977/841. Where, in pursuance of the Race Relations Act 1976 s 49, notice of the holding of a formal investigation falls to be given by the CRE to a person named in the terms of reference for the investigation, that person must be served with a notice setting out the terms of reference: Race Relations (Formal Investigations) Regulations 1977, SI 1977/841, reg 4(1). Where the terms of reference for a formal investigation are revised, reg 4(1) applies in relation to the revised investigation and terms of reference as it applied to the original: reg 4(2). Any reference to a person being served with a notice, in regs 4, 5 and 6, is a reference to service of the notice on him

being effected: (1) by delivering it to him; or (2) by sending it by post to him at his usual or last-known residence or place of business; or (3) where the person is a body corporate or is a trade union or employers' association (see TRADE, INDUSTRY AND INDUSTRIAL RELATIONS vol 47 (2001 Reissue) paras 1001, 1201), by delivering it to the secretary or clerk of the body, union or association at its registered or principal office or by sending it by post to that secretary or clerk at that office; or (4) where the person is acting by a solicitor, by delivering it at, or by sending it by post to, the solicitor's address for service: reg 3 (modified by SI 1991/2684).

8   As to the meaning of 'act' see para 442 note 7 ante.
9   See the Race Relations Act 1976 s 49(4).
10   Ibid s 49(4)(a).
11   See ibid s 49(4)(b).
12   See ibid s 49(4)(i), (ii). The CRE has an obligation to act fairly to the named person at this preliminary inquiry stage, and must particularise the acts of which he is suspected: *Hillingdon London Borough Council v Commission for Racial Equality* [1982] AC 779, [1982] 3 WLR 159, HL. The purpose of the preliminary inquiry is to give the named person an opportunity to make representations that the investigation should not be proceeded with, or that it should be proceeded with on narrower terms of reference or in a certain manner; it is not an occasion for adducing evidence to the CRE: *Hillingdon London Borough Council v Commission for Racial Equality* supra. A person who is subject to a formal investigation has a further opportunity to make oral or written representations before a non-discrimination notice is served on him by the CRE: see the Race Relations Act 1976 s 58(5)(b) (prospectively repealed); and para 498 post. The CRE's obligation to act fairly in the conduct of the investigation and in hearing representations does not oblige it to permit the cross-examination of witnesses whose evidence has been relied on by the CRE: *R v Commission for Racial Equality, ex p Cottrell and Rothon* [1980] 3 All ER 265, [1980] 1 WLR 1580, DC.
13   As to the principles upon which judicial review may be granted see *Council of Civil Service Unions v Minister for the Civil Service* [1985] AC 374, [1984] 3 All ER 935, HL; and ADMINISTRATIVE LAW vol 1(1) (2001 Reissue) para 58 et seq. The court's power is not confined to cases where bad faith is alleged: see *Hillingdon London Borough Council v Commission for Racial Equality* [1982] AC 779, [1982] 3 WLR 159, HL. See also *Re Prestige Group plc* [1984] 1 WLR 335, [1984] ICR 473, HL; *Home Office v Commission for Racial Equality* [1982] QB 385, [1981] 1 All ER 1042; *R v Commission for Racial Equality, ex p Cottrell and Rothon* [1980] 3 All ER 265, [1980] 1 WLR 1580, DC; *R v Commission for Racial Equality, ex p Westminster City Council* [1985] ICR 827, [1985] IRLR 426, CA (finding of fact in non-discrimination notice challenged as perverse and unreasonable).

494.   Power to obtain information.   For the purposes of a formal investigation[1] the Commission for Racial Equality ('CRE') may by notice[2] require any person[3]: (1) to furnish such written information as may be described in the notice, and may specify the time at which, and the manner and form in which, the information is to be furnished[4]; and (2) to attend at such time and place as is specified in the notice and give oral information about, and produce all documents in his possession or control relating to, any matter specified in the notice[5].

Except where the investigation is as to compliance with a non-discrimination notice[6], a notice may be served only where it is authorised by an order of the Secretary of State[7], or where the terms of reference of the investigation state that the CRE believes that a person named in them may have done or may be doing unlawful acts of discrimination or harassment[8], or may have contravened the provisions of the Race Relations Act 1976 relating to discriminatory practices[9] or to advertisements or instructions or pressure to discriminate[10], and confine the investigation to those acts[11].

1   For the meaning of 'formal investigation' see para 493 note 1 ante.
2   Race Relations Act 1976 s 50(1). Part VII (ss 43–52) (as amended) is repealed by the Equality Act 2006 Sch 3 paras 21, 26, Sch 4 as from a day to be appointed under s 93. At the date at which this volume states the law no such day had been appointed. As to the establishment of the CRE see para 488 ante. As to the Commission for Equality and Human Rights, which is to replace the CRE, see para 305 et seq ante.
     The notice must be in the prescribed form and served in the prescribed manner: Race Relations Act 1976 s 50(1). For the meaning of 'notice' see para 460 note 8 ante; and for the meaning of 'prescribed' see para 468 note 6 ante. For the prescribed form see the Race Relations (Formal Investigations) Regulations 1977, SI 1977/841, reg 5, Sch 1.

3   As to the meaning of 'person' see para 344 note 3 ante. As to the service of notices see para 493 note 7
     ante.

4   Race Relations Act 1976 s 50(1)(a). See also note 5 infra.

5   Ibid s 50(1)(b). A notice must not require a person to give information or produce documents which he
     could not be compelled to give in evidence or produce in civil proceedings before the High Court, or to
     attend at any place unless the necessary expenses of his journey to and from that place are paid or
     tendered to him: s 50(3).
          If a person fails to comply with a notice served on him under this provision, or the CRE has
     reasonable cause to believe that he intends not to comply with it, the CRE may apply to a county court
     for an order requiring him to comply with it or with such directions for the like purpose as may be
     contained in the order: s 50(4). A person who fails to comply with such an order made by a county court
     is liable to a fine: see s 50(5) (amended by the County Courts Act 1984 s 148(1), Sch 2 Pt V para 61). See
     also the County Courts Act 1984 s 55 (as amended); and EVIDENCE vol 17(1) (Reissue) para 997.
          It is an offence punishable on summary conviction by a fine not exceeding level 5 on the standard
     scale for a person wilfully to alter, suppress, conceal or destroy a document which he has been required
     by a notice or order to produce, or for a person, in complying with such a notice or order, knowingly or
     recklessly to make any statement which is false in a material particular: see the Race Relations Act 1976
     s 50(6) (amended by virtue of the Criminal Justice Act 1982 ss 38, 46). As to the standard scale see
     para 315 note 15 ante. Proceedings for an offence under the Race Relations Act 1976 s 50(6) (as
     amended) may (without prejudice to any jurisdiction exercisable apart from this provision) be instituted
     against any person at any place at which he has an office or other place of business or against an
     individual at any place where he resides or at which he is for the time being: s 50(7).

6   Ie under ibid s 60: see s 50(2). If: (1) the terms of reference of a formal investigation state that its purpose
     is to determine whether any requirements of a non-discrimination notice are being or have been carried
     out, but s 50(2)(b) does not apply (see the text and notes 9–12 infra); and (2) s 49(3) (see para 493 ante)
     is complied with in relation to the investigation on a date ('the commencement date') not later than the
     expiration of the period of five years beginning when the non-discrimination notice became final, the
     CRE may within a specified period serve notices under s 50(1) for the purposes of the investigation
     without needing to obtain the consent of the Secretary of State: s 60(1). The said period begins on the
     commencement date and ends on the later of either the date on which the period of five years
     mentioned in s 50(1)(b) expires or the date two years after the commencement date: s 60(2). As to when
     a notice becomes final see para 498 note 10 post. As to the terms of reference see para 493 ante. As to the
     Secretary of State and the National Assembly for Wales see para 302 ante. Section 60 is repealed by the
     Equality Act 2006 Sch 3 paras 21, 27, Sch 4 as from a day to be appointed under s 93. At the date at
     which this volume states the law no such day had been appointed.

7   Race Relations Act 1976 s 50(2)(a). Any document purporting to be an order made by the Secretary of
     State under this provision and to be signed by him or on his behalf is to be received in evidence, and,
     unless the contrary is proved, is to be deemed to be made by him: s 74(5) (amended by the Employment
     Act 1989 s 29(4), Sch 7 Pt II). The Race Relations Act 1976 s 74(5) (as amended) is repealed by the
     Equality Act 2006 Sch 3 paras 21, 32(c), Sch 4 as from a day to be appointed under s 93. At the date at
     which this volume states the law no such day had been appointed.

8   See the Race Relations Act 1976 s 50(2)(b)(i) (amended by the Race Relations Act 1976 (Amendment)
     Regulations 2003, SI 2003/1626, reg 38). As to the meaning of 'act' see para 442 note 7 ante. For the
     meaning of 'discrimination' see para 447 note 4 ante; and for the meaning of 'harassment' see para 444
     ante.

9   Ie the Race Relations Act 1976 s 28: (see para 471 ante): see s 50(2)(b)(ii).

10   Ie ibid ss 29, 30 or 31 (as amended) (see paras 473–475 ante): see s 50(2)(b)(iii).

11   Ibid s 50(2)(b).

495. Restrictions on disclosure of information. No information given to the
Commission for Racial Equality ('CRE') by any person[1] in connection with a formal
investigation[2] may be disclosed by the CRE, or by any person who is or has been a
commissioner[3], additional commissioner[4] or employee[5] of the CRE, except in specified
circumstances[6]. Those circumstances are: (1) on the order of any court[7]; (2) with the
informant's consent[8]; (3) in the form of a summary or other general statement published
by the CRE which does not identify the informant or any other person to whom the
information relates[9]; (4) in a report of the investigation published by the CRE or made
available for inspection[10]; (5) to the commissioners, additional commissioners or
employees of the CRE or, so far as may be necessary for the proper performance of the

functions of the CRE, to other persons[11]; (6) for the purpose of any civil proceedings under the Race Relations Act 1976 to which the CRE is a party[12] or any criminal proceedings[13].

In preparing any report for publication or for inspection, the CRE must exclude, so far as is consistent with its duties and the object of the report, any matter which relates to the private affairs of any individual, or the business interests of any person, where the publication of that matter might, in the opinion of the CRE, prejudicially affect that individual or person[14].

1   As to the meaning of 'person' see para 344 note 3 ante.
2   For the meaning of 'formal investigation' see para 493 note 1 ante.
3   For the meaning of 'commissioner' see para 488 note 2 ante.
4   As to additional commissioners see para 492 ante.
5   For the meaning of 'employee' see para 446 note 3 ante.
6   Race Relations Act 1976 s 52(1). Part VII (ss 43–52) (as amended) is repealed by the Equality Act 2006 Sch 3 paras 21, 26, Sch 4 as from a day to be appointed under s 93. At the date at which this volume states the law no such day had been appointed. As to the establishment of the CRE see para 488 ante. As to the Commission for Equality and Human Rights, which is to replace the CRE, see para 305 et seq ante.
      The disclosure of information in contravention of this provision is an offence punishable on summary conviction by a fine not exceeding level 5 on the standard scale: Race Relations Act 1976 s 52(2) (amended by virtue of the Criminal Justice Act 1982 ss 38, 46). As to the standard scale see para 315 note 15 ante. As to the extension of the disclosure powers under the Race Relations Act 1976 s 52(1) see the Anti-Terrorism, Crime and Security Act 2001 s 17, Sch 4 para 14 (Sch 4 para 14 prospectively repealed by the Equality Act 2006 ss 40, 91, Sch 3 para 61(a), Sch 4).
7   Race Relations Act 1976 s 52(1)(a).
8   Ibid s 52(1)(b).
9   Ibid s 52(1)(c).
10   Ibid s 52(1)(d). A report may be available for inspection under s 51 (see para 496 post): see s 52(1)(d).
11   Ibid s 52(1)(e). As to the functions of the CRE see para 489 ante.
12   It should be noted that the CRE may not disclose such information if it is giving assistance to an individual who is bringing proceedings under the Race Relations Act 1976 (pursuant to s 66 (as amended; prospectively repealed): see para 497 post) but is not itself a party to those proceedings: s 52(1). There is an exception where the CRE is itself a party to the proceedings: s 52(1)(f).
13   Ibid s 52(1)(f). Note that there is no exception allowing the CRE to disclose information to the Equal Opportunities Commission.
14   Ibid s 52(3).

496. Recommendations and reports on formal investigations.

The Commission for Racial Equality ('CRE') must make recommendations if, in the light of its findings in a formal investigation[1], it appears necessary or expedient whether during the course of the investigation or after its conclusion[2]. The CRE may make recommendations: (1) to any person[3] for changes in his policies or procedures, or as to any other matters, with a view to promoting equality of opportunity between persons of different racial groups[4] who are affected by any of that person's activities[5]; or (2) to the Secretary of State[6], whether for changes in the law or otherwise[7]. The CRE must prepare a report of its findings in any formal investigation conducted by it[8].

1   For the meaning of 'formal investigation' see para 493 note 1 ante.
2   Race Relations Act 1976 s 51(1). Part VII (ss 43–52) (as amended) is repealed by the Equality Act 2006 Sch 3 paras 21, 26, Sch 4 as from a day to be appointed under s 93. At the date at which this volume states the law no such day had been appointed. As to the establishment of the CRE see para 488 ante. As to the Commission for Equality and Human Rights, which is to replace the CRE, see para 305 et seq ante.
3   As to the meaning of 'person' see para 344 note 3 ante.
4   For the meaning of 'racial group' see para 441 ante.
5   Race Relations Act 1976 s 51(1)(a).
6   As to the Secretary of State and the National Assembly for Wales see para 302 ante.
7   Race Relations Act 1976 s 51(1)(b).

8   Ibid s 51(2). If the formal investigation is one required by the Secretary of State (see para 492 ante), the CRE must deliver the report to the Secretary of State to be published by him, and must not publish the report itself, unless required by the Secretary of State: see s 51(3). If the formal investigation is not one required by the Secretary of State, the CRE must either publish the report or make it, or a copy of it, available for inspection: see s 51(4), (6). Where a report is to be made available for inspection, any person is entitled, on payment of a fee (if any) determined by the CRE, to inspect the report during ordinary office hours and take copies of all or any part of the report, or to obtain from the CRE a copy, certified by the CRE to be correct, of the report: s 51(5). The CRE must give general notice of the place or places where, and the times when, reports may be inspected: s 51(7). For the meaning of 'general notice' see para 493 note 5 ante.

The timing of the publication of the CRE's report may lead to difficulties where there is an appeal against the findings of a non-discrimination notice served as a result of a formal investigation: if the report is published before the appeal, the person named in it as acting unlawfully may be damaged, and confidence in the CRE is likely to suffer if the appeal succeeds; however, given the slow speed at which appeals are heard, the subject matter of the investigation is likely to be stale by the time the report appears if it is reserved until after the appeal. See *Commission for Racial Equality v Amari Plastics Ltd* [1982] QB 1194, [1982] 2 All ER 499, CA. As to non-discrimination notices see para 498 post.

497.   Assistance to individuals. The Commission for Racial Equality ('CRE') may give assistance[1] to an individual who is an actual or prospective complainant or claimant in relation to proceedings or prospective proceedings under the Race Relations Act 1976[2].

Where such an individual applies for assistance, the CRE must consider the application[3], and may grant it if it thinks fit to do so on the ground that the case raises a question of principle[4], or on the ground that it is unreasonable[5] to expect the applicant to deal with the case unaided[6], or by reason of any other special consideration[7].

Where an application for assistance is made in writing, the CRE must within the period of two months beginning when the application is received[8]: (1) consider the application after making such inquiries as it thinks fit[9]; (2) decide whether to grant it[10]; and (3) inform the applicant of its decision, stating whether or not assistance is to be provided by the CRE, and, if so, what form it will take[11].

In so far as expenses are incurred by the CRE in providing the applicant with assistance, the recovery of those expenses[12] constitutes a first charge for the benefit of the CRE[13] on any costs or expenses which are payable to the applicant[14] by any other person in respect of the matter in connection with which assistance is given[15], and on his rights under any compromise or settlement arrived at in connection with that matter to avoid or bring to an end any proceedings, so far as relates to any costs or expenses[16].

The above provisions[17] also apply to proceedings or prospective proceedings under the Special Immigration Appeals Commission Act 1997 or Part 5 of the Nationality, Immigration and Asylum Act 2002[18] so far as they relate to acts which may be unlawful by virtue of the Race Relations Act 1976[19] as they apply to proceedings or prospective proceedings under that Act[20].

1   Assistance by the CRE may include: (1) giving advice (Race Relations Act 1976 s 66(2)(a)); (2) procuring or attempting to procure the settlement of any matter in dispute (s 66(2)(b)); (3) arranging for the giving of advice or assistance by a solicitor or counsel (s 66(2)(c)); (4) arranging for representation by any person, including all such assistance as is usually given by a solicitor or counsel in the steps preliminary or incidental to any proceedings, or in arriving at or giving effect to a compromise to avoid or bring to an end any proceedings (s 66(2)(d)); and (5) any other form of assistance which the CRE may consider appropriate (s 66(2)(e)). Section 66(2)(d) (see head (4) supra) does not affect the law and practice regulating the descriptions of persons who may appear in, conduct, defend, and address the court in, any proceedings: s 66(2). Section 66 (as amended) is repealed by the Equality Act 2006 ss 40, 91, Sch 3 paras 21, 28, Sch 4 as from a day to be appointed under s 93. At the date at which this volume states the law no such day had been appointed. As to the establishment of the CRE see para 488 ante. As to the Commission for Equality and Human Rights, which is to replace the CRE, see para 305 et seq ante.
2   See the Race Relations Act 1976 s 66(1).
3   Applications are considered by the CRE's Complaints Committee.
4   Race Relations Act 1976 s 66(1)(a).

5   Ie having regard to the complexity of the case, or to the applicant's position in relation to the respondent
    or another person involved, or to any other matter: see ibid s 66(1)(b). 'Respondent' includes a
    prospective respondent: s 66(7).
6   Ibid s 66(1)(b).
7   Ibid s 66(1)(c).
8   Ibid s 66(3). The CRE may within the period of two months give notice to the applicant that, in relation
    to his application, the period of two months allowed is by virtue of the notice extended to three months,
    and the reference to two months in s 68(3) (as amended; prospectively repealed) (see para 502 post) is by
    virtue of the notice to be read as a reference to three months, and ss 66(3), 68(3) (as amended;
    prospectively repealed) have effect accordingly: s 66(4).
9   Ibid s 66(3)(a).
10 Ibid s 66(3)(b).
11 Ibid s 66(3)(c).
12 Ie as taxed or assessed in such manner as may be prescribed by rules or regulations: see ibid s 66(5). 'Rules
    or regulations' in relation to county court proceedings, means county court rules (see COURTS vol 10
    (Reissue) para 702), and in relation to employment tribunal proceedings means employment tribunal
    procedure regulations under the Employment Tribunals Act 1996 Pt I (ss 1–19) (as amended) (see
    EMPLOYMENT vol 16(1B) (Reissue) para 816 et seq): Race Relations Act 1976 s 66(7) (amended by the
    Employment Tribunals Act 1996 s 43, Sch 1 para 4(1), (3); and by virtue of the Employment Rights
    (Dispute Resolution) Act 1998 s 1(2)(a), (c)).
13 Race Relations Act 1976 s 66(5). This charge is subject to any charge imposed by the Access to Justice
    Act 1999 s 10(7), and to any provision in or made under that Act for payment of any sum to the Legal
    Services Commission: Race Relations Act 1976 s 66(6) (amended by the Legal Aid Act 1988 s 45(1), (3),
    Sch 5 para 7(b); and the Access to Justice Act 1999 s 24, Sch 4 para 14). As to the Legal Services
    Commission see LEGAL AID vol 27(3) (2006 Reissue) para 2014 et seq.
14 Ie whether by virtue of a judgment or order of a court or tribunal or an agreement or otherwise: see the
    Race Relations Act 1976 s 66(5)(a).
15 Ibid s 66(5)(a).
16 Ibid s 66(5)(b).
17 Ie ibid s 66(1)–(3), (5)–(7) (as amended).
18 Ie the Nationality, Immigration and Asylum Act 2002 Pt 5 (ss 81–117) (as amended): see BRITISH
    NATIONALITY, IMMIGRATION AND ASYLUM.
19 Ie unlawful by virtue of the Race Relations Act 1976 s 19B (as added and amended): see para 470 ante.
20 Ibid s 66(8) (s 66(8), (9) added by the Race Relations (Amendment) Act 2000 s 9(1), Sch 2 para 11; and
    amended by the Nationality, Immigration and Asylum Act 2002 s 114(3), Sch 7 para 15). In the Race
    Relations Act 1976 s 66(8) (as added and amended), in relation to proceedings under the Special
    Immigration Appeals Commission Act 1997, 'rules or regulations' means rules under that Act and, in
    relation to proceedings under the Nationality, Immigration and Asylum Act 2002 Pt 5 (as amended),
    'rules or regulations' means rules under that Act: Race Relations Act 1976 s 66(9) (as so added and
    amended).

(4) ENFORCEMENT

(i) Enforcement by the Commission for Racial Equality

**498.   Non-discrimination notices, injunctions and other enforcement
proceedings.**   If in the course of a formal investigation[1] the Commission for Racial
Equality ('CRE')[2] becomes satisfied that a person is committing or has committed an
unlawful act of discrimination or harassment[3], or has applied a discriminatory practice[4],
published a discriminatory advertisement or instructed or put pressure on a person to
discriminate[5], it may in the prescribed[6] manner serve on him a notice[7] in the prescribed
form (a 'non-discrimination notice')[8]. The notice requires the person not to commit any
such acts[9] and, where compliance involves changes in any of his practices or other
arrangements, to inform the CRE that he has effected those changes and what those
changes are and to take such steps as may be reasonably required by the notice to afford
that information to other persons concerned[10].

Before serving a non-discrimination notice the CRE must: (1) give the person
concerned notice that it is minded to issue a non-discrimination notice in his case,

specifying the grounds on which it contemplates doing so[11]; (2) offer him an opportunity of making oral or written representations in the matter, or both oral and written representations if he thinks fit[12]; and (3) take account of any representations made by the person[13].

A person on whom a non-discrimination notice has been served may appeal against any requirement contained in the notice within six weeks of service[14]. An appeal is made to an employment tribunal so far as the requirement relates to acts which are within the jurisdiction of the tribunal[15] or to a designated county court[16] so far as the requirement relates to acts which are within the jurisdiction of the court and are not within the jurisdiction of an employment tribunal[17]. The tribunal or court must quash a requirement if it considers it to be unreasonable because it is based on an incorrect finding of fact or for any other reason[18].

The CRE must establish and maintain a register of non-discrimination notices which have become final[19].

The CRE may apply to a designated county court for an injunction against a person if within five years after the date on which a non-discrimination notice became final or a finding was made by a tribunal or court[20] that he has done an unlawful act of discrimination or harassment, or a finding under the Special Immigration Appeals Commission Act 1997 or Part 5 of the Nationality, Immigration and Asylum Act 2002[21] was made that he has done an unlawful act[22], it appears to the CRE that unless restrained the person is likely to commit an unlawful act of discrimination or harassment or contravene the provisions on discriminatory practices[23]. If the court is satisfied that the application is well-founded, it may grant the injunction in the terms applied for or in more limited terms[24].

Proceedings in relation to the provisions of the Race Relations Act 1976 which prohibit discriminatory advertisements, instructions to discriminate and pressure to discriminate[25] may only be brought by the CRE[26]. Where the case is based on the employment provisions of the Act[27], the CRE's application should be made to an employment tribunal; and in any other case, the application should be made to a designated county court[28]. The proceedings brought by the CRE may be: (a) an application for a decision whether the alleged contravention occurred[29]; or (b) where it appears to the CRE that a person has done an unlawful act and is likely to do further unlawful acts unless restrained, an application to a designated county court for an injunction restraining him from doing such acts[30].

The CRE also has the power to present a complaint to an employment tribunal that a person has done an act within the jurisdiction of an employment tribunal[31], with a view to taking future proceedings against that person in a county court for an injunction[32], and if the tribunal considers that the complaint is well-founded it must make an order to that effect[33].

1   For the meaning of 'formal investigation' see para 493 note 1 ante.
2   As to the CRE see para 488 et seq ante. As to the Commission for Equality and Human Rights, which is to replace the CRE, see para 305 et seq ante.
3   Race Relations Act 1976 s 58(1)(a) (amended by the Race Relations Act 1976 (Amendment)-Regulations 2003, SI 2003/1626, reg 44). As to the meaning of 'person' see para 344 note 3 ante. As to the meaning of 'act' see para 442 note 7 ante. For the meaning of 'discrimination' see para 447 note 4 ante; and for the meaning of 'harassment' see para 444 ante. The Race Relations Act 1976 ss 58–64 (as amended) are repealed by the Equality Act 2006 Sch 3 paras 21, 27, Sch 4 as from a day to be appointed under s 93. At the date at which this volume states the law no such day had been appointed.
4   Ie in contravention of the Race Relations Act 1976 s 28 (as amended; prospectively amended) (see para 471 ante): see s 58(1)(b).
5   Ie in contravention of ibid s 29 (as amended; prospectively amended), s 30 (as amended; prospectively amended) or s 31 (as amended; prospectively amended) (see paras 473–475 ante): see s 58(1)(c).
6   For the meaning of 'prescribed' see para 468 note 6 ante.

7   For the meaning of 'notice' see para 460 note 8 ante.
8   See the Race Relations Act 1976 s 58(1), (2) (s 58(1) as amended: see note 3 supra). For the prescribed
    form see the Race Relations (Formal Investigations) Regulations 1977, SI 1977/841, reg 6, Sch 2. As to
    the service of notices see para 493 note 7 ante.
9   Race Relations Act 1976 s 58(2)(a).
10 Ibid s 58(2)(b). A non-discrimination notice may also require the person on whom it is served to furnish
    the CRE with such other information as may be reasonably required by the notice in order to verify that
    the notice has been complied with: s 58(3). The notice may specify the time at which, and the manner
    and form in which, any information is to be furnished to the CRE, but the time at which any
    information is to be furnished in compliance with the notice must not be later than five years after the
    notice has become final: s 58(4). For the purposes of the Race Relations Act 1976 a non-discrimination
    notice or a finding by a court or tribunal becomes final when an appeal against the notice or finding is
    dismissed, withdrawn or abandoned or when the time for appealing expires without an appeal having
    been brought; and for this purpose an appeal against a non-discrimination notice is to be taken to be
    dismissed if, notwithstanding that a requirement of the notice is quashed on appeal, a direction is given
    in respect of it under s 59(3) (see note 17 infra): s 78(1), (4). As from a day to be appointed, the definition
    in s 78(1) and the reference in s 78(4) to a non-discrimination notice and an appeal against such a notice
    are omitted: s 78(1), (4) (prospectively amended by the Equality Act 2006 Sch 3 paras 21, 33(a)(ii), (b),
    Sch 4). At the date at which this volume states the law no such day had been appointed. Any finding by
    a court or employment tribunal under the Race Relations Act 1976, in respect of any act, if it has
    become final, is to be treated as conclusive in any proceedings under that Act: s 69(1) (amended by virtue
    of the Employment Rights (Dispute Resolution) Act 1998 s 1(2)(a)).
        If a person fails to comply with a non-discrimination notice which has become final, or the CRE has
    reasonable grounds to believe that he intends not to comply with it, the CRE may apply to a county
    court for an order requiring him to comply with it or with such directions for the like purpose as may be
    contained in the order: see the Race Relations Act 1976 s 58(7) (applying s 50(4) (prospectively repealed)
    (see para 494 ante)).
11 Ibid s 58(5)(a).
12 Ibid s 58(5)(b). The representations must be made within a period of not less than 28 days specified in the
    notice: s 58(5)(b). The CRE is obliged to act fairly in hearing any representations, but is not obliged to
    permit the person or his representative to cross-examine the witnesses relied upon by the CRE: *R v
    Commission for Racial Equality, ex p Cottrell and Rothon* [1980] 3 All ER 265, [1980] 1 WLR 1580, DC.
13 Race Relations Act 1976 s 58(5)(c).
14 See ibid s 59(1). As to the procedure on such an appeal see the Employment Tribunals (Constitution and
    Rules of Procedure) Regulations 2004, SI 2004/1861; and EMPLOYMENT vol 16(1B) (Reissue) para 816
    et seq. Guidelines as to the procedure on appeal were also given in *Commission for Racial Equality v Amari
    Plastics Ltd* [1982] QB 265, [1981] 3 WLR 511, EAT; affd [1982] QB 1194, [1982] 2 All ER 499, CA.
    In particular, the notice of appeal should specify each finding of fact in the non-discrimination notice
    which is challenged, each allegation of fact which the employers intend to prove and any other grounds
    on which it is alleged that the requirements of the notice are unreasonable; the hearing of the appeal
    should be opened by the employer who has the burden of showing that the true facts are different from
    those set out in the document accompanying the non-discrimination notice so as to render the
    requirements unreasonable; all findings of fact in a non-discrimination notice may be appealed against;
    and the right of appeal is not limited to requirements in the notice relating to future actions: see
    Commission for Racial Equality v Amari Plastics Ltd supra.
        Where there is no dispute as to the facts and the sole issue is whether, as a matter of law, the notice
    should have been served, it is appropriate to apply for judicial review: *R v Commission for Racial Equality,
    ex p Westminster City Council* [1984] ICR 770, [1984] IRLR 230; affd on a different point [1985] ICR
    827, [1985] IRLR 426, CA. See also *Commission for Racial Equality v Amari Plastics Ltd* supra. As to
    judicial review see ADMINISTRATIVE LAW vol 1(1) (2001 Reissue) para 58 et seq.
15 Race Relations Act 1976 s 59(1)(a) (s 59(1) amended by virtue of the Employment Rights (Dispute
    Resolution) Act 1998 s 1(2)(a)).
16 As to designated county courts see para 500 note 20 post.
17 Race Relations Act 1976 s 59(1)(b) (s 59(1) as amended (see note 15 supra); and s 59(1)(b) amended by
    the Race Relations (Amendment) Act 2000 s 9(1), Sch 2 para 8). In determining whether a county court
    has jurisdiction, no account is to be taken of the Race Relations Act 1976 s 57A (as added and amended)
    (see para 500 post): see s 59(1)(b) (as so amended).
18 Ibid s 59(2). On quashing a requirement the tribunal or court may direct that the non-discrimination
    notice is to be treated as if, in place of the requirement quashed, it had contained a requirement in terms
    specified in the direction: s 59(3). There is no right of appeal under s 59(1) (as amended) to such a
    requirement: see s 59(4).
19 Ibid s 61(1). Any person is entitled, on payment of such fee (if any) as may be determined by the CRE,
    to inspect the register or a copy of it during ordinary office hours and to take copies of any entry, or to

obtain from the CRE a copy, certified by the CRE to be correct, of any entry in the register: s 61(2), (3). The CRE must give general notice of the place or places where, and the times when, the register or a copy of it may be inspected: s 61(4). For the meaning of 'general notice' see para 493 note 5 ante.

20 Ie under ibid s 54 (as amended) or s 57 (as amended) (see paras 499–500 post): see s 62(1)(b) (amended by the Race Relations Act 1976 (Amendment) Regulations 2003, SI 2003/1626, reg 45).

21 Ie the Nationality, Immigration and Asylum Act 2002 Pt 5 (ss 81–117) (as amended): see BRITISH NATIONALITY, IMMIGRATION AND ASYLUM.

22 Ie an act unlawful by virtue of the Race Relations Act 1976 s 19B (as added and amended) (see para 470 ante): see s 62(1)(ba) (added by the Race Relations (Amendment) Act 2000 s 9(1), Sch 2 para 9).

23 See the Race Relations Act 1976 s 62(1). As to the provisions on discriminatory practices see s 28 (as amended; prospectively amended); and para 471 ante. The CRE must not allege that the person to whom the proceedings relate has done an unlawful act of discrimination or harassment or applied a discriminatory practice in contravention of s 28 (as amended; prospectively amended) which is within the jurisdiction of an employment tribunal unless a finding by an employment tribunal that he did that act has become final: s 62(2) (amended by virtue of the Employment Rights (Dispute Resolution) Act 1998 s 1(2)(a)). The CRE may itself apply to an employment tribunal for such a finding: see the Race Relations Act 1976 s 64 (as amended); and the text and notes 31–33 infra.

24 Ibid s 62(1).

25 Ie ibid ss 29–31 (as amended; prospectively amended): see paras 473–475 ante.

26 See ibid s 63(1). See e g *Commission for Racial Equality v Imperial Society of Teachers of Dancing* [1983] ICR 473, [1983] IRLR 315, EAT.

27 Ie the Race Relations Act 1976 Pt II (ss 4–15) (as amended): see para 446 et seq ante.

28 See ibid s 63(3) (amended by virtue of the Employment Rights (Dispute Resolution) Act 1998 s 1(2)(a)).

29 Race Relations Act 1976 s 63(2)(a).

30 See ibid s 63(2)(b), (4). The court, if satisfied that the application is well-founded, may grant the injunction in the terms applied for or more limited terms: s 63(4). In proceedings for an injunction the CRE must not allege that the person to whom the proceedings relate has done an unlawful act within the jurisdiction of an employment tribunal unless a finding by an employment tribunal that he did that act has become final: s 63(5) (amended by virtue of the Employment Rights (Dispute Resolution) Act 1998 s 1(2)(a)). The CRE may itself apply to an employment tribunal for such a finding: see s 64 (as amended); and the text and notes 31–33 infra.

31 Ie an act in respect of which jurisdiction is conferred on an employment tribunal by ibid ss 54, 63 (both as amended) (acts in the employment field): see s 64(3).

32 Ie under ibid s 62(1) (as amended) (see the text and notes 20–24 supra) or s 63(4) (see the text and note 30 supra).

33 Ibid s 64(1) (amended by virtue of the Employment Rights (Dispute Resolution) Act 1998 s 1(2)(a)). The tribunal may also, if it thinks it just and equitable to do so, in the case of an act contravening the employment provisions of the Race Relations Act 1976 Pt II (as amended), make an order declaring the rights of the person concerned and the respondent in relation to the act to which the complaint relates, or make a recommendation that the respondent take within a specified period action appearing to the tribunal to be practicable for the purpose of obviating or reducing the effect on the person discriminated against of any act of discrimination to which the complaint relates, or both: see ss 56(1)(a), (c), 64(1) (s 64(1) amended by the Race Relations Act 1976 (Amendment) Regulations 2003, SI 2003/1626, reg 46). The Race Relations Act 1976 s 64(1) (as amended) is without prejudice to the jurisdiction conferred by s 63(2) (see the text and notes 29–30 supra): s 64(2).

(ii) Enforcement by Individuals

499. Enforcement in the employment field. A complaint by any person ('the complainant') that another person[1] ('the respondent') has committed a relevant unlawful act[2] against the complainant may be presented to an employment tribunal[3].

Where an employment tribunal finds that a complaint presented to it is well-founded, it must make such of the following as it considers just and equitable[4]: (1) an order declaring the rights of the complainant and the respondent in relation to the act to which the complaint relates[5]; (2) an order requiring the respondent to pay to the complainant compensation[6]; or (3) a recommendation that the respondent take within a specified period action appearing to the tribunal to be practicable for the purpose of obviating or reducing the adverse effect on the complainant of any act of discrimination to which the complaint relates[7].

Appeals from any decision of an employment tribunal on a point of law are made to the Employment Appeal Tribunal[8].

The Secretary of State[9] may by regulations make provision for enabling a tribunal, where an amount of compensation falls to be awarded[10], to include in the award interest on that amount[11], and specifying, for cases where a tribunal decides that an award is to include an amount in respect of interest, the manner in which and the periods and rate by reference to which the interest is to be determined[12].

1   As to the meaning of 'person' see para 344 note 1 ante.

2   Ie an act which is unlawful by virtue of the Race Relations Act 1976 Pt II (ss 4–15) (as amended) (see para 446 et seq ante), s 76ZA (as added) (see para 459 ante) or, in relation to discrimination on grounds of race or ethnic or national origins or harassment, s 26A (as added and amended) (see para 456 ante) or s 76 (as amended) (see para 457). As to the meaning of 'act' see para 442 note 7 ante. For the meaning of 'discrimination' see para 447 note 4 ante. As to the meanings of 'ethnic origins' and 'national origins' see para 441 ante. For the meaning of 'harassment' see para 444 ante.

3   Ibid s 54(1)(a) (amended by virtue of the Employment Rights (Dispute Resolution) Act 1998 s 1(2)(a); and by the Race Relations Act 1976 (Amendment) Regulations 2003, SI 2003/1626, reg 40(a), (b)). As to the procedure on application to an employment tribunal see EMPLOYMENT vol 16(1B) (Reissue) para 852 et seq. A complaint may also be presented against an employer or principal or person aiding an unlawful act who is to be treated by virtue of the Race Relations Act 1976 s 32 or s 33 (as amended) (see paras 476–477 ante) as having committed such an unlawful act against the complainant: s 54(1)(b) (amended by the Race Relations Act 1976 (Amendment) Regulations 2003, SI 2003/1626, reg 40(a)).

    The Race Relations Act 1976 s 54(1) (as amended) does not apply to a complaint against a qualifying body (ie under s 12 (as amended): see para 452 ante) of an act in respect of which an appeal, or proceedings in the nature of an appeal, may be brought under any enactment: s 54(2) (amended by the Armed Forces Act 1996 s 35(2), Sch 7 Pt III). See also *Wadi v Cornwall and Isles of Scilly Family Practitioner Committee* [1985] ICR 492, EAT; *R v Department of Health, ex p Gandhi* [1991] 4 All ER 547, [1991] 1 WLR 1053, DC; *Khan v General Medical Council* [1996] ICR 1032, [1994] IRLR 646, CA; *Harris (Andrews' Personal Representative) v Lewisham and Guys Mental Health NHS Trust* [2000] IRLR 320, CA; *British Medical Association v Chaudhary* [2003] EWCA Civ 645, [2003] ICR 1510, [2003] All ER (D) 208 (May).

    If a discriminatory act contravenes the employment provisions of the Race Relations Act 1976, a complaint may be made to an employment tribunal under s 54 (as amended), notwithstanding that the respondent's action might also constitute discriminatory advertising, or pressure or instructions to discriminate, which could only be dealt with by the Commission for Racial Equality ('CRE') under s 63 (as amended; prospectively repealed) (see para 498 ante): *Zarczynska v Levy* [1979] 1 All ER 814, [1979] 1 WLR 125, EAT. As to the CRE see para 488 et seq ante. As to the Commission for Equality and Human Rights, which is to replace the CRE, see para 305 et seq ante.

    As to the burden of proof in relation to any complaint presented under the Race Relations Act 1976 s 54 (as amended) see s 54A (as added and amended); and para 504 post.

4   Ibid s 56(1) (amended by virtue of the Employment Rights (Dispute Resolution) Act 1998 s 1(2)(a)). The words 'just and equitable' refer to the decision whether to make the order in question, not to the contents of the order: *Hurley v Mustoe (No 2)* [1983] ICR 422, EAT.

5   Race Relations Act 1976 s 56(1)(a). Such an order may be the basis for a later application for an injunction by the CRE under s 62 (as amended; prospectively repealed), if the respondent appears likely to do further unlawful acts: see para 498 ante. A complaint by a bankrupt employee will vest in his trustee in bankruptcy unless it is limited to one for a declaration of discriminatory conduct under s 56(1)(a) and/or one for injury to feelings under s 57(4) (see para 500 post): *Khan v Trident Safeguards Ltd* [2004] EWCA Civ 624, [2004] ICR 1591, [2004] IRLR 961.

6   Race Relations Act 1976 s 56(1)(b). Compensation must be of an amount corresponding to any damages which the respondent could have been ordered to pay by the county court if the complaint had related to other fields of discrimination, and had fallen to be dealt with under s 57 (as amended) (see para 500 post): see s 56(1)(b). Consequently, the claim is to be treated like any other claim in tort: see s 57(1) (as amended); and para 500 post. The compensation should be for the reasonably foreseeable loss which the applicant has suffered in consequence of the wrong: *Skyrail Oceanic Ltd v Coleman* [1981] ICR 864, sub nom *Coleman v Skyrail Oceanic Ltd* [1981] IRLR 398, CA; *Stone v Hills of London Ltd* (1983) EAT/12/83 (Transcript).

    Where compensation is awarded under the Employment Rights Act 1996 for unfair dismissal, and under the Race Relations Act 1976, the employment tribunal may not award compensation under one of the Acts in respect of any loss for which an award has been made under the other: see the Employment Rights Act 1996 s 126 (as amended); and EMPLOYMENT vol 16(1B) (Reissue) para 692. The Secretary of

State may by regulations modify the operation of any order made under the Employment Tribunals Act 1996 s 14 (power to make provision as to interest on sums payable in pursuance of employment tribunal decisions) (see EMPLOYMENT vol 16(1B) (Reissue) para 893) to the extent that it relates to an award of compensation under the Race Relations Act 1976 s 56(1)(b): s 56(6) (added by the Race Relations (Remedies) Act 1994 s 2(1); and amended by virtue of the Employment Rights (Dispute Resolution) Act 1998 s 1(2)(a), (c)).

An appellate court may interfere with an award of compensation made by an employment tribunal if the tribunal has acted on a wrong principle of law or has misapprehended the facts or for other reasons has made a wholly erroneous estimate of the damage suffered: *Coleman v Skyrail Oceanic Ltd* supra.

Guidance has been given on the proper level of damages to be awarded in discrimination cases for injury to feelings and other forms of non-pecuniary damage: *Vento v Chief Constable of West Yorkshire Police* [2002] EWCA Civ 1871, [2003] ICR 318, [2003] IRLR 102, [2002] All ER (D) 363 (Dec). This case, which related to sex discrimination, sets out three broad bands of compensation for injury to feelings, as distinct from compensation for psychiatric or similar personal injury, as follows: (1) a top band of between £15,000 and £25,000, such sums being awarded in the most serious cases such as where there had been a lengthy campaign of discriminatory harassment on the ground of race or sex; (2) a middle band of between £5,000 and £15,000, used for serious cases which do not merit an award in the highest band; and (3) a bottom band of between £500 and £5,000, appropriate for less serious cases, such as where the act of discrimination was an isolated or one off occurrence. In general, awards of less than £500 are to be avoided altogether, as they risk being regarded as so low as not to be a proper recognition of injury to feelings. See *Ministry of Defence v Hunt* [1998] 1 All ER 790, [1998] ICR 242, CA. See also para 414 note 8 ante.

An appellate court may interfere with an award even if the tribunal has put it in the correct category: *Doshoki v Draeger Ltd* [2002] IRLR 340, [2002] All ER (D) 139 (Mar), EAT.

7   Race Relations Act 1976 s 56(1)(c). See also *Chief Constable of Greater Manchester Police v Hope* [1999] ICR 338, EAT. If without reasonable justification the respondent fails to comply with a recommendation made by an employment tribunal, the tribunal may, if it thinks it just and equitable to do so, increase the compensation payable to the applicant, or may make an order for compensation if none was previously made: see the Race Relations Act 1976 s 56(4) (amended by the Race Relations (Remedies) Act 1994 s 3(2), Schedule; and by virtue of the Employment Rights (Dispute Resolution) Act 1998 s 1(2)(a)). An employment tribunal's power to make a recommendation is limited; it extends only to measures which will obviate or reduce the effect of discrimination on the applicant, and cannot be used to make general recommendations affecting others; eg, a tribunal has no jurisdiction to recommend that a discriminatory employment practice should be changed, unless the recommendation will benefit the applicant: *Bayoomi v British Railways Board* [1981] IRLR 431.
      A tribunal may not make a recommendation requiring the respondent to offer the applicant the next suitable available job vacancy, at least where the effect of the recommendation would be to nullify the statutory procedure for appointments to the National Health Service: *North West Thames Regional Health Authorityv Noone* [1988] ICR 813, sub nom *Noone v North West Thames Regional Health Authority (No 2)* [1988] IRLR 530, CA.
8   See EMPLOYMENT vol 16(1B) (Reissue) para 843.
9   As to the Secretary of State and the National Assembly for Wales see para 302 ante.
10   Ie under the Race Relations Act 1976 s 56(1)(b): see head (2) in the text.
11   Ibid s 56(5)(a) (s 56(5) added by the Race Relations (Remedies) Act 1994 s 2(1)).
12   Race Relations Act 1976 s 56(5)(b) (as added: see note 11 supra). The regulations may contain such incidental and supplementary provisions as the Secretary of State considers appropriate: s 56(5) (as so added). In exercise of this power the Secretary of State has made the Employment Tribunals (Interest on Awards in Discrimination Cases) Regulations 1996, SI 1996/2803 (as amended): see EMPLOYMENT vol 16(1B) (Reissue) para 894. See *Derby Specialist Fabrication Ltd v Burton* [2001] 2 All ER 840, [2001] IRLR 69, EAT (appropriateness of award of interest on compensation for injury to feelings considered by appeal tribunal).

500.   Enforcement outside the employment field.   A claim by any person ('the claimant') that another person[1] ('the respondent') has committed an act[2] against the claimant which is unlawful by virtue of certain of the provisions prohibiting discrimination in fields other than employment[3] or is to be treated[4] as having committed such an act[5], may be made the subject of civil proceedings in like manner as any other claim in tort[6].

No proceedings may be so brought by a claimant[7] in respect of an immigration claim[8] if: (1) the act to which the claim relates was done in the taking by an immigration authority of a relevant decision and the question whether that act was unlawful[9] has been or could be raised in proceedings on an appeal which is pending[10], or could be brought, under the Special Immigration Appeals Commission Act 1997 or Part 5 of the Nationality, Immigration and Asylum Act 2002[11]; or (2) it has been decided in relevant immigration proceedings[12] that that act was not unlawful[13]. Where it has been decided in relevant immigration proceedings that an act to which an immigration claim relates was unlawful[14], any court hearing that claim[15] must treat that act as an act which is unlawful[16] for the purposes of the proceedings before it[17]. No relevant decision of an immigration authority involving an act to which an immigration claim relates and no relevant decision of an immigration appellate body in relation to such a decision may be subject to challenge or otherwise affected by virtue of a decision of a court hearing the immigration claim[18].

Except as provided by the Race Relations Act 1976 or the Special Immigration Appeals Commission Act 1997 or Part 5 of the Nationality, Immigration and Asylum Act 2002, no proceedings, whether civil or criminal, lie against any person in respect of an act by reason that the act is unlawful by virtue of a provision of the Race Relations Act 1976[19].

Proceedings must be brought only in a designated county court[20], normally within six months of the act complained of[21]. Except as otherwise provided[22], all such remedies are available as would be obtainable in the High Court[23].

No award of damages may be made as regards indirect discrimination[24] if the respondent proves that the requirement or condition in question was not applied with the intention of treating the claimant unfavourably on racial grounds[25].

Damages in respect of an unlawful act of discrimination may include compensation for injury to feelings whether or not they include compensation under any other head[26]. Compensation may also be awarded by way of damages for personal injury, including physical and psychiatric injury, caused by the statutory tort of unlawful discrimination[27].

Proceedings relating to discrimination by certain educational bodies may not be instituted unless the claimant has given notice of the claim to the Secretary of State[28].

1   As to the meaning of 'person' see para 344 note 3 ante.
2   As to the meaning of 'act' see para 442 note 7 ante.
3   Race Relations Act 1976 s 57(1)(a) (amended by the Race Relations Act 1976 (Amendment) Regulations 2003, SI 2003/1626, reg 42(2)(a), (b)). The provisions referred to in the text are those contained in the Race Relations Act 1976 Pt III (ss 17–27) (as amended) other than, in relation to discrimination on grounds of race or ethnic or national origin or harassment, s 26A (as added and amended) (see para 456 ante): see para 460 et seq ante. For the meaning of 'discrimination' see para 447 note 4 ante. As to the meanings of 'ethnic origins' and 'national origins' see para 441 ante. For the meaning of 'harassment' see para 444 ante.
       As to the burden of proof in relation to any claim brought under s 57 (as amended) see s 57ZA (as added); and para 504 post.
4   Ie by virtue of ibid s 32 or s 33 (as amended): see paras 476–477 ante.
5   Ibid s 57(1)(b) (amended by the Race Relations Act 1976 (Amendment) Regulations 2003, SI 2003/1626, reg 42(2)(a)). An employment tribunal which makes an order under this provision for payment of compensation may include interest on the sums awarded: see the Employment Tribunals (Interest on Awards in Discrimination Cases) Regulations 1996, SI 1996/2803, reg 2 (as amended); and EMPLOYMENT vol 16(1B) (Reissue) para 893.
6   Race Relations Act 1976 s 57(1). As to claims in tort generally see TORT; PRACTICE AND PROCEDURE.
       Once a causal link has been established between an act of racial discrimination and a loss, the complainant is entitled to damages for all consequential losses, not only those which are reasonably foreseeable: *Essa v Laing Ltd* [2004] EWCA Civ 2, [2004] ICR 746, [2004] IRLR 313.
7   Ie under the Race Relations Act 1976 s 57(1) (as amended): see the text to notes 1–6 supra. Section 57 (as amended) is subject to s 57A (as added and amended) (see the text and notes 8–18 infra): see s 57(7) (added by the Race Relations (Amendment) Act 2000 s 6(1)).
8   An 'immigration claim' is a claim that a person has committed a relevant act of discrimination against the claimant which is unlawful by virtue of the Race Relations Act 1976 s 19B (as added and amended) (see para 470 ante) or is, by virtue of s 32 or s 33 (as amended) (see paras 476–477 ante), to be treated as having committed such an act of discrimination against the claimant: s 57A(2), (5) (s 57A added by the

Race Relations (Amendment) Act 2000 s 6(2)). 'Relevant act of discrimination' means an act of discrimination done by an immigration authority in taking any relevant decision: Race Relations Act 1976 s 57A(5) (as so added). 'Immigration authority' means the Secretary of State, an immigration officer or a person responsible for the grant or refusal of entry clearance within the meaning of the Immigration Act 1971 s 33(1) (as amended) (see BRITISH NATIONALITY, IMMIGRATION AND ASYLUM vol 4(2) (2002 Reissue) para 96): Race Relations Act 1976 s 57A(5) (definition substituted by the Nationality, Immigration and Asylum Act 2002 s 114(3), Sch 7 para 12(d)). As to the Secretary of State and the National Assembly for Wales see para 302 ante. 'Relevant decision' means: (1) in relation to an immigration authority, any decision under the Immigration Act 1971, the Immigration Act· 1988, the Asylum and Immigration Appeals Act 1993, the Asylum and Immigration Act 1996, the Immigration and Asylum Act 1999, the Nationality, Immigration and Asylum Act 2002 and the Asylum and Immigration (Treatment of Claimants) Act 2004 relating to the entitlement of the claimant to enter or remain in the United Kingdom; and (2) in relation to an immigration appellate body, any decision on an appeal under the Special Immigration Appeals Commission Act 1997 or the Nationality, Immigration and Asylum Act 2002 Pt 5 (ss 81–117) (as amended) in relation to a decision falling within head (1) supra: Race Relations Act 1976 s 57A(5) (as so added; definition amended by the Nationality, Immigration and Asylum Act 2002 Sch 7 para 12(f)). 'Immigration appellate body' means the Asylum and Immigration Tribunal, the Special Immigration Appeals Commission, the Court of Appeal or the House of Lords: Race Relations Act 1976 s 57A(5) (as so added; definition amended by the Immigration, Asylum and Nationality Act 2006 s 14, Sch 1 para 12). As from a day to be appointed, the reference in this definition to the House of Lords is replaced by a reference to the Supreme Court: Race Relations Act 1976 s 57A(5) (as so added and amended; prospectively amended by the Constitutional Reform Act 2005 s 114(3), Sch 7 para 12(d)). At the date at which this volume states the law, no such day had been appointed.

9 Ie unlawful by virtue of the Race Relations Act 1976 s 19B (as added and amended): see para 470 ante.

10 'Pending' has the same meaning as in the Special Immigration Appeals Commission Act 1997 or, as the case may be, the Nationality, Immigration and Asylum Act 2002 Pt 5 (as amended) (see BRITISH NATIONALITY, IMMIGRATION AND ASYLUM): Race Relations Act 1976 s 57A(5) (s 57A as added (see note 8 supra); definition amended by the Nationality, Immigration and Asylum Act 2002 Sch 7 para 12(e)).

11 Race Relations Act 1976 s 57A(1)(a) (s 57A as added (see note 8 supra); s 57A(1)(a) amended by the Nationality, Immigration and Asylum Act 2002 Sch 7 para 12(a)).

12 'Relevant immigration proceedings' means proceedings on an appeal under the Special Immigration Appeals Commission Act 1997 or the Nationality, Immigration and Asylum Act 2002 Pt 5 (as amended): Race Relations Act 1976 s 57A(5) (s 57A as added (see note 8 supra); definition amended by the Nationality, Immigration and Asylum Act 2002 Sch 7 para 12(g)).

13 Race Relations Act 1976 s 57A(1)(b) (as added: see note 8 supra).

14 Ie unlawful by virtue of ibid s 19B (as added and amended): see para 470 ante.

15 Ie under ibid s 57 (as amended).

16 Ie unlawful by virtue of ibid s 19B (as added and amended): see para 470 ante.

17 Ibid s 57A(3) (as added: see note 8 supra).

18 Ibid s 57A(4) (as added: see note 8 supra). The immigration claim is heard under s 57 (as amended).

19 Ibid s 53(1) (amended by the Race Relations (Amendment) Act 2000 Sch 2 para 4; and the Nationality, Immigration and Asylum Act 2002 Sch 7 para 11). The Race Relations Act 1976 s 53(1) (as amended) does not preclude the making of a quashing order (formerly certiorari), a mandatory order (formerly mandamus) or a prohibiting order (formerly prohibition): s 53(2). Section 53(2) does not, except so far as provided by s 76 (as amended) (see para 457 ante), apply to any act which is unlawful by virtue of s 76(5) or (9) (as added) or by virtue of s 76(10)(b), (11), (11B) (as added): s 53(4) (added by the Race Relations (Amendment) Act 2000 Sch 2 para 5; and amended by the Race Relations Act 1976 (Amendment) Regulations 2003, SI 2003/1626, reg 39).

20 Race Relations Act 1976 s 57(2)(a). A 'designated' county court is one designated for the time being for those purposes by an order made by the Lord Chancellor with the concurrence of the Lord Chief Justice: s 67(1) (amended by the Constitutional Reform Act 2005 s 15(1), Sch 4 para 87(1), (2)); Race Relations Act 1976 s 78(1). As to orders under this provision see the Civil Courts Order 1983, SI 1983/713 (as amended); and COURTS vol 10 (Reissue) para 707; PRACTICE AND PROCEDURE vol 37 (Reisssue) para 115. As to the Lord Chancellor see CONSTITUTIONAL LAW AND HUMAN RIGHTS vol 8(2) (Reissue) para 477 et seq. As to the Lord Chief Justice see CONSTITUTIONAL LAW AND HUMAN RIGHTS vol 8(2) (Reissue) para 303; COURTS vol 10 (Reissue) para 515. An order designating any county court for the purposes of the Race Relations Act 1976 must assign to that court as its district for those purposes any county court district or two or more county court districts: s 67(2). A designated county court has jurisdiction to entertain proceedings under the Race Relations Act 1976 with respect to an act done on a ship, aircraft or hovercraft outside its district, including such an act done outside Great Britain: s 67(3). A designated county court has jurisdiction to entertain proceedings under the Race Relations Act 1976

with respect to an act done outside the United Kingdom where s 19B (as added and amended) (see para 470 ante) applies in relation to such an act by virtue of s 27(1A) (as added) (see para 470 ante): s 67(3A) (added by the Race Relations (Amendment) Act 2000 Sch 2 para 12). For the meanings of 'Great Britain' and 'United Kingdom' see para 325 note 6 ante.

In any proceedings under the Race Relations Act 1976 in a designated county court the judge must, unless with the consent of the parties he sits without assessors, be assisted by two assessors appointed from a list of persons prepared and maintained by the Secretary of State, being persons appearing to the Secretary of State to have special knowledge and experience of problems connected with relations between persons of different racial groups: s 67(4). The provisions of CPR 35.15, which regulate the procedure whereby an assessor is summoned on the application of a party, apply with appropriate modifications. The remuneration of assessors appointed is to be at such rate as may, with the approval of the Minister for the Civil Service, be determined by the Lord Chancellor: see the Race Relations Act 1976 s 67(5). As to the Minister for the Civil Service see CONSTITUTIONAL LAW AND HUMAN RIGHTS vol 8(2) (Reissue) para 427 et seq. There is to be defrayed out of money provided by Parliament payments falling to be made under s 67(5) in respect of the remuneration of assessors: s 77(c). For guidance as to the role of assessors in race discrimination claims before a county court see *Ahmed v Governing Body of the University of Oxford* [2002] EWCA Civ 1907, [2003] 1 All ER 915, [2003] ICR 733. Without prejudice to the Race Relations Act 1976 s 74(3) (see para 468 ante), an order for the discontinuance of the jurisdiction of any county court under the Race Relations Act 1976, whether wholly or within a part of the district assigned to it for the purposes of that Act, may include provision with respect to any proceedings under that Act commenced in that court before the order comes into operation: s 67(6).

21 As to time limits see para 502 post.

22 Ie apart from the Race Relations Act 1976 ss 57(2), 53(1) (as amended), the Special Immigration Appeals Commission Act 1997 or the Nationality, Immigration and Asylum Act 2002 Pt 5 (as amended): see the text to note 8 supra.

23 See the Race Relations Act 1976 s 57(2).

24 Ie discrimination falling within ibid s 1(1)(b): see para 440 ante.

25 Ibid s 57(3). See also *Orphanos v Queen Mary College* [1985] AC 761, [1985] 2 All ER 233, HL. An employer applies a requirement or condition with the intention of discriminating if, at the time that the relevant act is done, he wants to bring about the state of affairs constituting the prohibited result of unfavourable treatment on racial grounds and he knows that a prohibited result will follow from such an act: *JH Walker Ltd v Hussain* [1996] ICR 291, [1996] IRLR 11, EAT. This position contrasts with the position under the Sex Discrimination Act 1975 where compensation is generally available in indirect discrimination cases by virtue of the Sex Discrimination and Equal Pay (Miscellaneous Amendments) Regulations 1996, SI 1996/438, reg 2: see the Sex Discrimination Act 1975 s 65(1A), (1B) (as added), s 65(3) (as amended); and para 414 ante.

26 Race Relations Act 1976 s 57(4). Compensation has generally been payable only for injury to feelings resulting from the applicant's knowledge that he has suffered an act of racial discrimination: see *Skyrail Oceanic Ltd v Coleman* [1981] ICR 864, sub nom *Coleman v Skyrail Oceanic Ltd* [1981] IRLR 398, CA (decided in relation to the provisions of the Sex Discrimination Act 1975: see para 414 ante). In *Alexander v Home Office* [1988] 2 All ER 118, [1988] 1 WLR 968, CA, the court commented on the difficulty of assessing awards for injury to feelings, because of the impossibility of determining restitution for the wrong suffered. The amount should not be minimal, since this would trivialise or diminish respect for the public policy to which the Race Relations Act 1976 gives effect. Nor should it be excessive, since injury to feelings is less serious, and more short-lived, than bodily injury. In this case, a prisoner who had been assessed as a racial stereotype was awarded £500 for injury to feelings. The applicant in *North West Thames Regional Health Authority v Noone* [1988] ICR 813, sub nom *Noone v North West Thames Regional Health Authority (No 2)* [1988] IRLR 530, CA, was awarded £5,000 for injury to feelings by the tribunal. The figure was regarded as too high by the Court of Appeal, which reduced it to £3,000, making it clear that this should be regarded as the top end of the bracket. The applicant was a Sri Lankan biologist who was complaining of failure to be appointed to a consultant's post. In fixing the award, the Court of Appeal took into account the overall ceiling on compensation (at that time £7,500), which was to take into account damages for actual loss and increased compensation payable because of a respondent's failure to comply with a recommendation, as well as injury to feelings. There is no longer any upper limit on the amount of compensation that a tribunal can award in respect of unlawful race discrimination by virtue of the Race Relations (Remedies) Act 1994: see s 1(1) (amended by virtue of the Employment Rights (Dispute Resolution) Act 1998 s 1(2)(a)). See also *HM Prison Service v Johnson* [1997] ICR 275, [1997] IRLR 162, EAT (an award of £21,000 compensation for injury to feelings in respect of a campaign of racial harassment, £1,000 of which was to be paid personally by two colleagues of the claimant, was not grossly out of line with the general range of personal injury awards and was not excessive). Guidance has been given on the proper level of damages to be awarded in discrimination cases

for injury to feelings and other forms of non-pecuniary damage: see *Vento v Chief Constable of West Yorkshire Police* [2002] EWCA Civ 1871, [2003] ICR 318, [2003] IRLR 102, [2002] All ER (D) 363 (Dec); and para 499 note 6 ante.

Aggravated damages may be awarded for racial discrimination, where e g the respondent has behaved in a high-handed, malicious, insulting or oppressive manner in committing the act of discrimination: *Alexander v Home Office* supra. Such damages are additional compensation for the injured feelings of the applicant where his sense of injury is justifiably heightened by the manner in which or the motive for which the respondent did it: *Cassell & Co Ltd v Broome* [1972] AC 1027 at 1124, [1972] 1 All ER 801 at 869, HL, per Lord Diplock.

Exemplary damages, which are intended to be punitive rather than compensatory, may not be awarded for unlawful racial discrimination. Previously it was thought that exemplary damages could occasionally be justified in a discrimination complaint in certain circumstances (eg: (1) inappropriate, arbitrary or unconstitutional action by the servants of government; or (2) where the respondent's conduct has been calculated by him to make a profit for himself which may exceed the compensation payable to the applicant): *Rookes v Barnard* [1964] AC 1129, [1964] 1 All ER 367, HL; *Cassell and Co Ltd v Broome* supra. However, in *AB v South West Water Services Ltd* [1993] QB 507, [1993] 1 All ER 609, CA, the Court of Appeal held that exemplary damages could only be awarded for torts already recognised as grounding a claim for exemplary damages at the time of the House of Lords' decision in *Rookes v Barnard* supra. The Employment Appeals Tribunal disallowed an award of exemplary damages in *Deane v Ealing London Borough Council* [1993] ICR 329, [1993] IRLR 209, EAT, on this basis, as the race (and sex) discrimination legislation had not been introduced in 1964. See also *Ministry of Defence v Meredith* [1995] IRLR 539, EAT.

See also *Gbaja-Biamila v DHL International (UK) Ltd* [2000] ICR 730, EAT (appropriateness of award of aggravated damages considered by appeal tribunal). A complaint by a bankrupt employee will vest in his trustee in bankruptcy unless it is limited to one for a declaration of discriminatory conduct under the Race Relations Act 1976 s 56(1)(a) (see para 499 ante) and/or one for injury to feelings under s 57(4): *Khan v Trident Safeguards Ltd* [2004] EWCA Civ 624, [2004] ICR 1591, [2004] IRLR 961.

As respects an act which is done, or by virtue of the Race Relations Act 1976 s 32 or s 33 (as amended) (see paras 476–477 ante) is treated as done, by a person in carrying out public investigator functions or functions as a public prosecutor and which is unlawful by virtue of s 19B (as added and amended) (see para 470 ante), no remedy other than damages or a declaration are obtainable unless the court is satisfied that the remedy concerned would not prejudice a criminal investigation, a decision to institute criminal proceedings or any criminal proceedings: s 57(4A) (s 57(4A)–(4D) added by the Race Relations (Amendment) Act 2000 s 5(1)). Where a party to proceedings under the Race Relations Act 1976 s 57(1) (as amended) which have arisen by virtue of s 19B (as added and amended) (see para 470 ante) has applied for a stay of those proceedings on the grounds of prejudice to particular criminal proceedings, a criminal investigation or a decision to institute criminal proceedings, the court must grant the stay unless it is satisfied that the continuation of those proceedings would not result in the prejudice alleged: s 57(4C), (4D) (as so added). 'Public investigator functions' means functions of conducting criminal investigations or charging offenders: s 57(4B) (as so added). 'Criminal investigation' means any investigation which a person in carrying out functions to which s 19B (as added and amended) applies has a duty to conduct with a view to it being ascertained whether a person should be charged with an offence (including any offence under the Army Act 1955, the Air Force Act 1955 or the Naval Discipline Act 1957: see ARMED FORCES) or whether a person charged with such an offence is guilty of it, or any investigation which is conducted by a person in carrying out functions to which the Race Relations Act 1976 s 19B (as added and amended) (see para 470 ante) applies and which in the circumstances may lead to a decision by that person to institute criminal proceedings which the person has power to conduct: s 57(4B) (as so added). As to the meaning of 'criminal proceedings' see para 470 note 14 ante.

27 *Sheriff v Klyne Tugs (Lowestoft) Ltd* [1999] ICR 1170, [1999] IRLR 481, CA.
28 Ie discrimination in contravention of the Race Relations Act 1976 s 17 (as amended) or s 18 (as amended) by a body to which s 57(5A) (as added) applies: see s 57(5), (5A) (as added); paras 457–460 ante; and EDUCATION vol 15(1) (2006 Reissue) para 8.

501.   National security procedure.   County court rules may make provision for enabling a court in which relevant proceedings[1] have been brought, where it considers it expedient in the interests of national security, to exclude specified persons[2] from all or part of the proceedings[3]; to permit a claimant or representative who has been excluded to make a statement to the court before the commencement of the proceedings, or the part of the proceedings, from which he is excluded[4]; and to take steps to keep secret all or part of the reasons for its decision in the proceedings[5]. Where the claimant or his representatives are so excluded from relevant proceedings, the Attorney General[6] may appoint a person to represent the interests of a claimant in, or in any part of, any such proceedings[7].

1　'Relevant proceedings' means proceedings brought under the Race Relations Act 1976 in a designated county court: s 67A(5) (s 67A added by the Race Relations (Amendment) Act 2000 s 8). See generally COURTS.

2　Ie the claimant, the claimant's representatives or the assessors (if any) appointed by virtue of the Race Relations Act 1976 s 67(4) (see para 500 ante): see s 67A(1)(a)(i)–(iii) (as added: see note 1 supra).

3　Ibid s 67A(1)(a), (5) (as added: see note 1 supra).

4　Ibid s 67A(1)(b), (5) (as added: see note 1 supra).

5　Ibid s 67A(1)(c), (5) (as added: see note 1 supra).

6　As to the Attorney General see CONSTITUTIONAL LAW AND HUMAN RIGHTS vol 8(2) (Reissue) para 529

7　Race Relations Act 1976 s 67A(2) (s 67A as added (see note 1 supra); s 67A(2) amended by the Equality Act 2006 s 90). A person so appointed must have a general qualification (see SOLICITORS vol 44(1) (Reissue) para 91), and is not responsible to the person whose interests he is appointed to represent: Race Relations Act 1976 s 67A(3), (4) (as so added). See also *Practice Direction—Claims Under the Race Relations Act 1976 (National Security)* PD 39C.

502. Time limits. An employment tribunal may not consider a complaint of discrimination[1] in the employment field[2] unless it is presented to the tribunal[3] before the end of three months beginning when the act complained of[4] was done[5], or in a case relating to discrimination within the armed forces[6], the period of six months so beginning[7].

A respondent to a claim must make a response within 28 days of receiving a copy of the claim[8]. The respondent may apply for an extension of the time limit and such application must be presented within 28 days of receiving the claim and the limit will only be extended if the tribunal chairman is satisfied that it is just and equitable to do so[9]. Wasted costs may be ordered against the defaulting respondent[10].

Proceedings before a county court in respect of discrimination in other fields[11] must be instituted within the period of six months beginning when the act complained of was done[12]. If an application for assistance[13] in relation to proceedings or prospective proceedings in the county court is made to the Commission for Racial Equality ('CRE') before the end of the six-month period, the period allowed for instituting proceedings in the county court is extended by two months[14]. Where (1) proceedings or prospective proceedings[15] relate to the act or omission of a qualifying institution[16]; (2) the dispute concerned is referred as a complaint under the students complaints scheme[17] before the end of the period of six months[18]; and (3) the above extension provision[19] does not apply[20], the period allowed[21] for instituting proceedings in respect of the claim is extended by two months[22].

Applications to an employment tribunal or county court by the CRE in respect of discriminatory advertisements, instructions to discriminate or pressure to discriminate[23], or in respect of preliminary action in employment cases[24], must be made within the period of six months beginning when the act to which the application relates was done[25]. Applications brought by the CRE for an injunction relating to discriminatory advertisements, instructions to discriminate or pressure to discriminate[26] must be made within five years beginning when the act to which the application relates was done[27].

A court or tribunal nevertheless may consider any such complaint, claim or application which is out of time if, in all the circumstances of the case, it considers that it is just and equitable to do so[28].

Special provision is made for acts which cannot be easily identified as occurring at a specific moment. When the inclusion of any term in a contract renders the making of the contract an unlawful act, that act is to be treated as extending throughout the duration of the contract[29]. Any act extending over a period is to be treated as done at the end of that period[30]. A deliberate omission is to be treated as done when the person in question decided upon it[31].

1   For the meaning of 'discrimination' see para 447 note 4 ante. In order to amount to a complaint of discrimination, an application must be submitted in writing, and must contain sufficient information to identify the applicant and the respondent and to show what sort of claim it is; it need not be free from defect or contain particulars of the complaint; and it need not specify whether the applicant's complaint is brought under the Sex Discrimination Act 1975 or the Race Relations Act 1976: *Dodd v British Telecommunications plc* [1988] ICR 116, [1988] IRLR 16, EAT. See also *Burns International Security Services (UK) Ltd v Butt* [1983] ICR 547, EAT. As to rules of procedure for employment tribunals see EMPLOYMENT vol 16(1B) (Reissue) para 854.

2   Ie under the Race Relations Act 1976 s 54 (as amended): see para 499 ante.

3   Ibid s 68(1) (amended by virtue of the Employment Rights (Dispute Resolution) Act 1998 s 1(2)(a)). An application is 'presented' to a tribunal when it is received by the tribunal office and there is no need for it to be registered or processed by the tribunal in any way: *Dodd v British Telecommunications plc* [1988] ICR 116, [1988] IRLR 16, EAT.

4   As to the meaning of 'act' see para 442 note 7 ante. 'The act complained of' is 'a plain but flexible phrase likely to have a different significance in different contexts. So we do not think it appropriate for us to deduce, still less to endeavour to propound, any principle applicable in all cases': *Eke v Customs and Excise Comrs* [1981] IRLR 334, EAT, per Waite J. In this case, the Employment Appeal Tribunal held that an internal appeal against the imposition of a disciplinary penalty that was alleged to be discriminatory was not a part of the act complained of. The right to appeal was regarded as a right to appeal against a decision that had already been wholly taken. Where the act complained of is dismissal, it should be regarded as occurring on the date upon which the employment was terminated, not on the date notice of termination was given: *Lupetti v Wrens Old House* [1984] ICR 348, EAT. The decision in *Adekeye v Post Office* [1993] ICR 464, [1993] IRLR 324, EAT, was overruled by *Relaxion Group plc v Rhys-Harper, D'Souza v Lambert London Borough Council, Jones v 3M Healthcare Ltd, Kirker v British Sugar plc, Angel v New Possibilities NHS Trust, Bond v Hackney Citizens Advice Bureau* [2003] UKHL 33, [2003] 4 All ER 1113, [2003] IRLR 484: see para 416 ante.

5   See the Race Relations Act 1976 s 68(1)(a) (s 68(1)(a), (b) added by the Armed Forces Act 1996 s 23(4)). Although acts of discrimination occurring prior to the enactment of the Race Relations Act 1976 or outside the time limits imposed by the Act cannot be relied on to justify any award, they may be taken into account by a court or tribunal in determining whether acts of discrimination have occurred within the time limits: *Din v Carrington Viyella Ltd (Jersey Kapwood Ltd)* [1982] ICR 256, [1982] IRLR 281, EAT; *Eke v Customs and Excise Comrs* [1981] IRLR 334, EAT. See also *Littlewoods Organisation plc v Traynor* [1993] IRLR 154, EAT (as long as agreed remedial measures are not taken, a situation involving racial discrimination continues, and allowing that situation to continue amounts to a continuing act). The time limit will not be extended because the complainant has delayed bringing proceedings while awaiting the outcome of his employer's internal grievance procedure: *Apelogun-Gabriels v Lambeth London Borough Council* [2001] EWCA Civ 1853, [2002] ICR 713, [2002] IRLR 116. The Employment Appeal Tribunal is not entitled to have regard to conduct occurring after an originating complaint when considering whether to extend the time limit: *Robertson v Bexley Community Centre(t/a Leisure Link)* [2003] EWCA Civ 576, [2003] IRLR 434.

6   Ie a case to which the Race Relations Act 1976 s 75(8) applies: see para 457 ante.

7   Ibid s 68(1)(b) (as added: see note 5 supra).

8   See the Employment Tribunals (Constitution and Rules of Procedure) Regulations 2004, SI 2004/1861, reg 16(2), Sch 1 r 4(1).

9   See ibid Sch 1 rr 4(4), 11, 33.

10 *Kwik Save Stores Ltd v Swain* [1997] ICR 49, EAT (a case under an earlier version of the regulations).

11 Ie under the Race Relations Act 1976 s 57 (as amended): see para 500 ante.

12 Ibid s 68(2)(a) (amended by the Race Relations (Amendment) Act 2000 s 9(1), Sch 2 para 13, Sch 3). In relation to an immigration claim within the meaning of the Race Relations Act 1976 s 57A (as added and amended) (see para 500 ante), that six-month time limit begins on the expiry of the period during which, by virtue of s 57A(1)(a) (as added and amended), no proceedings may be brought under s 57(1) (as amended) in respect of the claim (see para 500 ante): s 68(2A) (added by the Race Relations (Amendment) Act 2000 Sch 2 para 14).

As from a day to be appointed, the period allowed by the Race Relations Act 1976 s 68(2)(a) (as amended) is extended by three months in the case of a dispute which is referred for conciliation in pursuance of arrangements under the Equality Act 2006 s 27 (as amended) (see para 333 ante) (unless it is extended under the Race Relations Act 1976 s 68(3A) (as added) (see the text and note 22 infra)):

s 68(3C) (prospectively added by the Equality Act 2006 Sch 3 paras 21, 29(1), (4)). At the date at which this volume states the law no such day had been appointed.

13 Ie under the Race Relations Act 1976 s 66 (as amended): see para 497 ante. As to the circumstances in which the Commission for Racial Equality ('CRE') may offer assistance, and the types of assistance it may provide see para 497 ante. As to the CRE see para 488 et seq ante. As to the Commission for Equality and Human Rights, which is to replace the CRE, see para 305 et seq ante.

14 See ibid s 68(3) (amended by the Race Relations (Amendment) Act 2000 s 9(2), Sch 3). This provision is repealed by the Equality Act 2006 ss 40, 91, Sch 3 paras 21, 29(1), (2), Sch 4 as from a day to be appointed under s 93. At the date at which this volume states the law no such day had been appointed.

15 Ie by way of a claim under the Race Relations Act 1976 s 57 (as amended): see para 500 ante.

16 Ibid s 68(3A)(a) (s 68(3A), (3B) added by the Higher Education Act 2004 s 19(2)). For the meaning of 'qualifying institution' see EDUCATION vol 15(2) (2006 Reissue) para 1040; definition applied by the Race Relations Act 1976 s 68(3B) (as so added).

17 'Students complaints scheme' means a scheme for the review of qualifying complaints, as defined by the Higher Education Act 2004 s 12 (see EDUCATION vol 15(2) (2006 Reissue) para 1040), that is provided by the designated provider, as defined by s 13(5)(b) (see EDUCATION vol 15(2) (2006 Reissue) para 1040): Race Relations Act 1976 s 68(3B) (as added: see note 16 supra).

18 Ibid s 68(3A)(b) (as added: see note 16 supra). The six-month period referred to in the text is that mentioned in s 68(2) (as amended) (see the text and note 12 supra).

19 Ie ibid s 68(3) (as amended) (see the text to note 14 supra).

20 Ibid s 68(3A)(c) (as added: see note 16 supra). This provision is repealed by the Equality Act 2006 Sch 3 paras 21, 29(1), (3)(a), Sch 4 as from a day to be appointed under s 93. At the date at which this volume states the law no such day had been appointed.

21 Ie by the Race Relations Act 1976 s 68(2) (as amended) (see the text and note 12 supra).

22 Ibid s 68(3A) (as added: see note 16 supra). As from a day to be appointed, the reference to 'two months' is replaced by a reference to 'three months': s 68(3A) (as so added; prospectively amended by the Equality Act 2006 Sch 3 paras 21, 29(1), (3)(b)). At the date at which this volume states the law no such day had been appointed.

23 Ie under the Race Relations Act 1976 s 63(2)(a): see para 498 ante.

24 Ie under ibid s 64(1) (as amended; prospectively repealed): see para 498 ante.

25 See ibid s 68(4), (5) (s 68(4), (5) amended by virtue of the Employment Rights (Dispute Resolution) Act 1998 s 1(2)(a)). The provisions of the Race Relations Act 1976 s 68(4), (5) (as amended) are repealed by the Equality Act 2006 Sch 3 paras 21, 29(1), (5), Sch 4 as from a day to be appointed under s 93. At the date at which this volume states the law no such day had been appointed.

26 Ie under the Race Relations Act 1976 s 63(4) (prospectively repealed): see para 498 ante.

27 See ibid s 68(4) (as amended; prospectively repealed); and note 25 supra.

28 Ibid s 68(6). As from a day to be appointed, the reference to 'complaint, claim or application' is replaced by a reference to 'complaint or claim': s 68(6) (prospectively amended by the Equality Act 2006 Sch 3 paras 21, 29(1), (6)). At the date at which this volume states the law no such day had been appointed.

The Race Relations Act 1976 s 68(6) confers a wide discretion upon a court or tribunal, which entitles it to take into account anything which it judges to be relevant, including the merits of the case, which may be gauged by hearing some evidence: see *Hutchison v Westward Television Ltd* [1977] ICR 279, [1977] IRLR 69, EAT (a sex discrimination case).

The exercise by a court or a tribunal of its discretion to hear a discrimination claim out of time may be challenged only on the basis that it took into account irrelevant considerations, failed to take into account relevant considerations, or reached a decision that no reasonable tribunal could have reached: *Eke v Customs and Excise Comrs* [1981] IRLR 334, EAT. A tribunal's exercise of its discretion was in breach of natural justice where the tribunal took into account the merits of the claim without any argument being presented to it on the merits, and without inviting counsel to make submissions on the subject: *Lupetti v Wrens Old House Ltd* [1984] ICR 348, EAT. A tribunal chairman is under no obligation to raise the question of whether the applicant wished to apply for an extension of time under the Race Relations Act 1976 s 68(6) in circumstances in which the applicant's representative had not requested an extension: *Dimtsu v Westminster City Council* [1991] IRLR 450, EAT.

29 Race Relations Act 1976 s 68(7)(a).

30 Ibid s 68(7)(b). Where a respondent operates a continuous regime or policy which it is open to him to alter at any time, it should be regarded as an act extending over a period, not as a deliberate omission to provide an equally favourable regime; therefore, the provision of less favourable pension rights to Asian employees constituted an act extending over the whole period of the employees' employment; and an employee could complain of racial discrimination in his pension entitlement until three months after his employment had terminated, although the original decision with regard to his pension had been made before the Race Relations Act 1976 had been enacted: *Barclays Bank plc v Kapur* [1991] 2 AC 355, [1991] 1 All ER 646, HL. See also *Calder v James Finlay Corpn Ltd* [1989] ICR 157n, [1989] IRLR 55, EAT, in which a continuing policy of providing mortgage subsidies only to male employees was held to be an act

extending over the whole period of a woman's employment, although she had last applied for a mortgage subsidy more than three months before her employment terminated. A distinction must be drawn between an act extending over a period, and a 'one-off' act which has continuing effects. The failure to promote an employee is not an act continuing over a period, although its effects may continue over a period. By contrast, a continuing policy not to appoint women or members of particular racial groups to certain posts would constitute an act extending over a period. Any person discriminated against because of the policy would have three months from the time it was abrogated to bring a complaint: *Amies v Inner London Education Authority* [1977] 2 All ER 100, [1977] ICR 308, EAT. See also *Sougrin v Haringey Health Authority* [1991] ICR 791, [1991] IRLR 447, EAT; affd [1992] ICR 650, [1992] IRLR 416, CA (it was held that an employer's decision to pay a black nurse less than a white colleague following a regrading exercise was not a 'continuing act'; her complaint was that she was not upgraded; the fact that she continued to be paid less than her comparator was a consequence of the decision, and was not of itself a continuing act of discrimination; the relevant contractual term was that the complainant would be paid according to her grade, not that she would be paid less than her comparator). See also *Owusu v London Fire and Civil Defence Authority* [1995] IRLR 574, EAT (an act extends over a period of time if it takes the form of a policy, rule or practice in accordance with which decisions are taken from time to time and a succession of specific instances can indicate the existence of a practice). As to continuing acts of indirect discrimination see *Rovenska v General Medical Council* [1998] ICR 85, [1997] IRLR 367, CA (refusal to give limited registration for doctor first qualified in Czech Republic, whereas doctors first qualified in certain Commonwealth universities were exempt from specified admittance requirements); *Cast v Croydon College* [1998] ICR 500, [1998] IRLR 318, CA. In determining whether an act is a continuing one, extending over a period of time, it is necessary to distinguish between one full act and a succession of unrelated acts for which time runs from the date when each act is committed: *Hendricks v Metropolitan Police Comr* [2002] EWCA Civ 1686, [2003] 1 All ER 654, [2003] ICR 530. See *Lyfar v Brighton and Sussex University Hospitals Trust* [2006] EWCA Civ 1548, [2006] All ER (D) 182 (Nov); and *Qing-Ping Ma v Merck Sharp and Dohme Ltd* [2007] All ER (D) 66 (Feb), EAT where the test in *Hendricks v Metropolitan Police Comr* supra was applied. See also *Barclays Bank plc v Kapur* supra.

31   Race Relations Act 1976 s 68(7)(c). In the absence of evidence establishing the contrary, a person is to be taken for the purposes of this provision to decide upon an omission when he does an act inconsistent with doing the omitted act or, if he has done no inconsistent act, when the period expires within which he might reasonably have been expected to do the omitted act if it was to be done: s 68(7).

503.   Help for complainants. With a view to helping a person who considers he may have been discriminated[1] against or subjected to harassment[2] ('the person aggrieved') to decide whether to institute proceedings and, if he does so, to formulate and present his case in the most effective manner, the Secretary of State[3] has prescribed forms[4] by which the person aggrieved may question the respondent[5] on his reasons for doing any relevant act or on any other matter that may be relevant and by which the respondent may if he so wishes reply[6]. The person aggrieved may question the respondent without using the prescribed form and second or subsequent questionnaires may be administered with the leave of the court or tribunal[7].

Any questions and replies[8] are admissible in evidence in the proceedings[9]. If it appears to the court or the tribunal that the respondent deliberately, and without reasonable excuse, omitted to reply within a reasonable period or, where the question relates to discrimination on grounds of race or ethnic or national origins[10] or to harassment, within the period of eight weeks beginning with the day on which the question was served on him, or that his reply is evasive or equivocal, the court or tribunal may draw any inference from that fact that it considers it just and equitable to draw, including an inference that he committed an unlawful act[11].

The Secretary of State has prescribed by order the period within which questions must be served to be admissible[12] and the manner in which a question and any reply by the respondent may be duly served[13].

An employment tribunal has the power to make an order for disclosure in circumstances where disclosure would be ordered in the county court[14]. A county court has a general discretion to order standard disclosure and inspection of all documents upon which the party relies, all documents which adversely affect his own or another party's case, and documents which support another party's case[15]. A county court may also order a party to be interrogated on matters within his own knowledge[16]. In the context of case management, a chairman of an employment tribunal may at any time either on the application of a party or on his own initiative make an order in relation to various matters[17]. The orders that he may make include an order that a party provide additional information, an order requiring any person in Great Britain to disclose documents or information to a party to allow a party to inspect such material as might be ordered by a county court, or an order that written answers be provided to questions put by the tribunal or the chairman[18].

1　For the meaning of 'discrimination' see para 447 note 4 ante.

2　For the meaning of 'harassment' see para 444 ante.

3　As to the Secretary of State and the National Assembly for Wales see para 302 ante.

4　See the Race Relations (Questions and Replies) Order 1977, SI 1977/842, art 3, Schs 1, 2.

5　'Respondent' includes a prospective respondent: Race Relations Act 1976 s 65(6).

6　See ibid s 65(1) (amended by the Race Relations Act 1976 (Amendment) Regulations 2003, SI 2003/1626, reg 47(a)). The Employment Appeal Tribunal has stressed the importance of the questionnaire procedure. Since direct evidence of discrimination is unlikely to be available, complainants must often rely on disclosure of documents and questionnaires: *Barking and Dagenham London Borough Council v Camara* [1988] ICR 865, [1988] IRLR 373, EAT; *Carrington v Helix Lighting Ltd* [1990] ICR 125, [1990] IRLR 6, EAT.

　　The Race Relations Act 1976 s 65 (as amended) does not apply in relation to any proceedings under the Special Immigration Appeals Commission Act 1997 or the Nationality, Immigration and Asylum Act 2002 Pt 5 (ss 81–117) (as amended) (see BRITISH NATIONALITY, IMMIGRATION AND ASYLUM): Race Relations Act 1976 s 65(7) (added by the Race Relations (Amendment) Act 2000 s 9(1), Sch 2 para 10; and amended by the Nationality, Immigration and Asylum Act 2002 s 114(3), Sch 7 para 14).

7　*Carrington v Helix Lighting Ltd* [1990] ICR 125, [1990] IRLR 6, EAT. An application for leave must be made on notice.

8　Ie whether they are made in accordance with the prescribed forms or not: see the Race Relations Act 1976 s 65(2).

9　Ibid s 65(2)(a). The admissibility of questions and replies is subject to any enactment or rule of law regulating the admissibility of evidence in county court or employment tribunal proceedings: see s 65(5) (amended by virtue of the Employment Rights (Dispute Resolution) Act 1998 s 1(2)(a)). See further EMPLOYMENT vol 16(1B) (Reissue) para 852 et seq; PRACTICE AND PROCEDURE. County court rules may enable a county court determining a claim under the Race Relations Act 1976 s 57 (as amended) (see para 500 ante) to determine the admissibility of questions or replies before the date fixed for the hearing of the claim: see s 65(4).

10　As to the meanings of 'ethnic origins' and 'national origins' see para 441 ante.

11　Race Relations Act 1976 s 65(2)(b) (amended by the Race Relations Act 1976 (Amendment) Regulations 2003, SI 2003/1626, reg 47(b)). Such an inference was drawn by a tribunal in *Virdee v EEC Quarries Ltd* [1978] IRLR 295, in circumstances in which the respondents did not answer most of the questions on the questionnaire, although they were aware of and had looked at the provisions of the Race Relations Act 1976 s 65 (as amended). See also *King v Great Britain-China Centre* [1992] ICR 516, [1991] IRLR 513, CA.

　　The Race Relations Act 1976 s 65(2)(b) (as amended) does not apply in section 19B proceedings in relation to a failure to reply, or a particular reply if, at the time of doing any relevant act, the respondent was carrying out public investigator functions or was a public prosecutor and he reasonably believes that a reply or (as the case may be) a different reply would be likely to prejudice any criminal investigation, any decision to institute criminal proceedings or any criminal proceedings or would reveal the reasons behind a decision not to institute, or a decision not to continue, criminal proceedings: s 65(4A), (4B) (s 65(4A)–(4C) added by the Race Relations (Amendment) Act 2000 s 5(2)). 'Section 19B proceedings' means proceedings in respect of a claim under the Race Relations Act 1976 s 57 (as amended) (see para 500 ante) which has arisen by virtue of s 19B (as added and amended) (see para 470 ante): s 65(4C) (as so added). For the meaning of 'public investigator functions' see para 500 note 26 ante; definition applied by s 65(4C) (as so added). For the meaning of 'criminal investigation' see para 500 note 26 ante; definition applied by s 78(1) (amended by the Race Relations (Amendment) Act 2000 Sch 2 para 19). As to the meaning of 'criminal proceedings' see para 470 note 14 ante.

12　Ie under the Race Relations Act 1976 s 65(2)(a): see s 65(3). In proceedings before a court, a question is only admissible as evidence where: (1) it was served before those proceedings had been instituted, if it was so served during the period of six months beginning when the act complained of was done or, in a case to which s 57(5) (as amended) (see para 460 ante) applies, the period of eight months so beginning;

or (2) it was served when those proceedings had been instituted, if it was served with the leave of, and within a period specified by, the court: Race Relations (Questions and Replies) Order 1977, SI 1977/842, art 4.

In proceedings before a tribunal, a question is only admissible as evidence where: (a) it was served before a complaint had been presented to a tribunal, if it was so served within the period of three months beginning when the act complained of was done or, where the period under the Race Relations Act 1976 s 68 (as amended) within which proceedings must be brought is extended by the Employment Act 2002 (Dispute Resolution) Regulations 2004, SI 2004/752, reg 15 (see EMPLOYMENT vol 16(1B) (Reissue) para 594), within that extended period; (b) it was served when a complaint had been presented to a tribunal, if it was so served within the period of 21 days beginning with the day on which the complaint was presented or if it was so served later with leave given, and within a period specified, by a direction of a tribunal: Race Relations (Questions and Replies) Order 1977, SI 1977/842, art 5 (amended by SI 2004/752).

13 See the Race Relations Act 1976 s 65(3); and the Race Relations (Questions and Replies) Order 1977, SI 1977/842 (as amended). A question and any reply to it may be served on the respondent or, as the case may be, on the person aggrieved: (1) by delivering it to him; (2) by sending it by post to him at his usual or last-known residence or place of business; (3) where the person to be served is a body corporate or is a trade union or employers' association (see TRADE, INDUSTRY AND INDUSTRIAL RELATIONS vol 47 (2001 Reissue) paras 1001, 1201) by delivering it to the secretary or clerk of the body, union or association at its registered or principal office or by sending it by post to the secretary or clerk at that office; (4) where the person to be served is acting by a solicitor, by delivering it at, or by sending it by post to, the solicitor's address for service; or (5) where the person to be served is the person aggrieved, by delivering the reply, or sending it by post, to him at his address for reply as stated by him in the document containing the questions: art 6 (modified by SI 1991/2684).

14 See the Employment Tribunals (Constitution and Rules of Procedure) Regulations 2004, SI 2004/1861, reg 16(2), Sch 1 r 10(2)(d). See also EMPLOYMENT vol 16(1B) (Reissue) para 687; and see COURTS.

15 See CPR Pt 31.

Disclosure may be granted against either the applicant or the respondent, but in practice, it is most likely to be used by the applicant, since most relevant information is usually in the possession of the respondent. The disclosure and inspection of documents, like the questionnaire procedure, is a method by which Parliament offsets the applicant's disadvantage in having the burden of proving his case notwithstanding that the bulk of the relevant evidence is likely to be in the possession of the respondent: see *British Library v Palyza* [1984] ICR 504, [1984] IRLR 306, EAT. The questionnaire procedure is not intended to be a substitute for, but an addition to, the complainant's rights of disclosure and inspection of documents: *Science Research Council v Nassé* [1980] AC 1028, [1979] 3 All ER 673, HL, per Lord Salmon. Disclosure may include documents relating to incidents prior to the act complained of by the applicant: see *Selvarajan v Inner London Education Authority* [1980] IRLR 313, EAT, in which the applicant obtained disclosure of documents relating to the respondent's procedures for recruitment to various jobs for which the applicant had applied between 1961 and 1976.

The principles upon which the disclosure of confidential documents should be ordered in a case under the Race Relations Act 1976 or the Sex Discrimination Act 1975 were considered by the House of Lords in *Science Research Council v Nassé* supra and *Leyland Cars v Vyas* [1980] AC 1028, [1979] 3 All ER 673, HL. In both cases, the applicants, who had applied unsuccessfully for promotion or transfer, sought the disclosure of confidential reports relating to other applicants for the jobs in question. The House of Lords held that confidential employment documents were not immune from disclosure. However, a court or tribunal ought not to grant disclosure of documents automatically because they were relevant to the proceedings. Disclosure should only be ordered if the documents were necessary for disposing fairly of the proceedings. Where documents were confidential, the court or tribunal should consider carefully whether the necessary information could be obtained by other means, not involving a breach of confidence, and should inspect the documents. It should consider whether justice could be done by covering up parts of the documents, or substituting anonymous references for specific names, or, rarely, by hearing the case in private. It is a matter of convenience in each case whether the documents should be examined at the interim stage or as the matter arises in the hearing: *British Railways Board v Natarajan* [1979] 2 All ER 794, [1979] ICR 326, EAT.

Disclosure must not be granted if it would be oppressive. It may be oppressive if it requires the provision of material not readily to hand which can only be made available with difficulty and at great expense, or if it requires the party ordered to make disclosure to embark on a course which will add unreasonably to the length and cost of the hearing: see *West Midlands Passenger Transport Executive v Jaquant Singh* [1988] 2 All ER 873, [1988] 1 WLR 730, CA.

Disclosure may be obtained of statistics in the possession of the respondent which help to demonstrate a pattern to his treatment of other members of the applicant's ethnic group. In *West Midlands Passenger Transport Executive v Jaquant Singh* supra, the applicant had applied unsuccessfully for promotion to the post of senior inspector, and alleged racial discrimination on the part of his employers. Disclosure was requested of the details of the ethnic origins of applicants for, and appointees to, comparable posts between October 1984 and December 1985. The Court of Appeal upheld the tribunal's decision to grant the disclosure. The evidence requested was relevant: since direct discrimination involved the less favourable treatment of a person because of his membership of a group, statistical evidence of the respondent's treatment of other members of that group might establish a discernible pattern of treatment. If the pattern showed a regular failure by members of the group to obtain promotion to particular jobs, and demonstrated the under-representation of members of the group in those jobs, it could give rise to an inference of discrimination. As to the probative importance of statistical evidence in discrimination cases see also *Chattopadhyay v Headmaster of Holloway School* [1982] ICR 132, [1981] IRLR 487, EAT; *Carrington v Helix Lighting Ltd* [1990] ICR 125, [1990] IRLR 6, EAT. See further the Commission for Racial Equality's Statutory Code of Practice on Racial Equality in Employment (April 2006), which recommends ethnic monitoring of the workforce and of applications for promotion and recruitment: see para 491 ante.

An order for disclosure may only be made in relation to documents which exist and which are in the possession of the party from whom disclosure is requested. It is not appropriate where it would amount to an order to collect the information sought and create a new document: *Carrington v Helix Lighting Ltd* supra. In this case the applicant sought a schedule of evidence showing the ethnic composition of the respondent's workforce. The Employment Appeal Tribunal held that a tribunal had no power to order the production of the schedule, at least where it did not simply record the contents of existing documents. A county court might be able to order the production of such a schedule pursuant to its power to order interrogatories, but a tribunal had no equivalent power. However, where a respondent employer does not keep records of the ethnic composition of his workforce, his failure to abide by the recommendation of ethnic monitoring in the Statutory Code of Practice on Racial Equality in Employment (April 2006) could be taken into account by a tribunal.

The decision whether to order disclosure is to be made at the discretion of the court or tribunal, but is reviewable by the Employment Appeal Tribunal or Court of Appeal. The appeal court may exercise its own discretion, and is not limited to intervening only when the court or tribunal has exercised its discretion on the wrong principles, at least when the decision was made before the substantive hearing, so that the court or tribunal could not have been influenced by evidence: see *British Library v Palyza* supra.

16   See CPR 18.1.
17   See the Employment Tribunals (Constitution and Rules of Procedure) Regulations 2004, SI 2004/1861, reg 16, Sch 1 r 10 (as amended); and EMPLOYMENT vol 16(1B) (Reissue) para 867. For the meaning of 'Great Britain' see para 325 note 6 ante.
18   See note 17 supra.

504.   Proving discrimination; statutory reversal of the burden of proof.
Provisions[1] were introduced into the Race Relations Act 1976 in 2003 to replace the previous law on proof. Where a complaint is presented[2] that the respondent:

(1)   has committed an act of discrimination[3], on grounds of race or ethnic or national origins[4], which is unlawful by virtue of provisions relating to indirect discrimination[5]; or

(2)   has committed an act of harassment[6],

and where, on the hearing of the complaint, the complainant proves facts from which the tribunal could conclude in the absence of an adequate explanation that the respondent: (a) has committed such an act of discrimination or harassment against the complainant; or (b) is[7] to be treated as having committed such an act of discrimination or harassment against the complainant, the tribunal must uphold the complaint unless the respondent proves that he did not commit or, as the case may be, is not to be treated as having committed, that act[8].

Previously it was for the applicant to prove on the balance of probabilities that he had been discriminated against racially[9], or by way of victimisation[10], in circumstances in which such discrimination is unlawful under the provisions of the Race Relations Act 1976[11]. Where the allegation was of indirect discrimination[12], and the respondent wished to rely upon justifiability[13] as a defence, it was for the respondent to prove on the balance of probabilities that the condition or requirement at issue was justifiable[14].

There are limited situations where the previous law is still relevant[15].

1 Ie the Race Relations Act 1976 ss 54A, 57ZA (as added): see the text and notes 2–8 infra.

2 Ie under ibid s 54 (as amended): see para 499 ante.

3 As to the meaning of 'act' see para 442 note 7 ante. For the meaning of 'discrimination' see para 447 note 4 ante.

4 As to the meanings of 'ethnic origins' and 'national origins' see para 441 ante.

5 Ie by virtue of any provision referred to in the Race Relations Act 1976 s 1(1B)(a), (e) or (f) (as added) (see para 440 ante), or Pt IV (ss 27A–33) (as amended) in its application to those provisions.

6 Ibid s 54A(1) (s 54A added by the Race Relations Act 1976 (Amendment) Regulations 2003, SI 2003/1626, reg 41). For the meaning of 'harassment' see para 444 ante. See also note 8 infra.

7 Ie by virtue of the Race Relations Act 1976 s 32 or s 33 (as amended): see paras 476–477 ante.

8 Ibid s 54A(2) (as added: see note 6 supra). Section 54A (as added) applies in regard to employment tribunals; there is provision in regard to county courts in similar terms. Where a claim is brought under s 57 (as amended) (see para 500 ante) and the claim is that the respondent:

   (1) has committed an act of discrimination, on grounds of race or ethnic or national origins, which is unlawful by virtue of any provision referred to in s 1(1B)(b)–(d) (as added) (see para 440 ante), or Pt IV (ss 27A–33) (as amended) in its application to those provisions; or

   (2) has committed an act of harassment,

and where, on the hearing of the claim, the claimant proves facts from which the court could conclude in the absence of an adequate explanation that the respondent: (a) has committed such an act of discrimination or harassment against the claimant; or (b) is by virtue of s 32 or s 33 (as amended) (see paras 476–477 ante) to be treated as having committed such an act of discrimination or harassment against the claimant, the court must uphold the claim unless the respondent proves that he did not commit or, as the case may be, is not to be treated as having committed, that act: s 57ZA(1), (2) (added by the Race Relations Act 1976 (Amendment) Regulations 2003, SI 2003/1626, reg 43). These provisions are in accordance with EC Council Directive 2000/43 (OJ L180, 19.07.2000, p 22) implementing the principle of equal treatment between persons irrespective of racial or ethnic origin: see para 437 ante.

   The respondent would usually be expected to produce cogent evidence to discharge his burden of proof, since he would normally be in possession of the facts necessary to prove that he did not commit an act of discrimination: *Barton v Investec Henderson Crosthwaite Securities Ltd* [2003] ICR 1205, [2003] IRLR 332, EAT; applied in *Wong v Igen Ltd (Equal Opportunities Commission and others intervening), Emokpae v Chamberlin Solicitors (Equal Opportunities Commission and others intervening), Webster v Brunel University (Equal Opportunities Commission and others intervening)* [2005] EWCA Civ 142, [2005] 3 All ER 812, [2005] ICR 931. See also *Hundal v Initial Security Ltd* [2006] All ER (D) 74 (Aug), EAT. There is an annex to the judgment in *Wong v Igen Ltd (Equal Opportunities Commission and others intervening), Emokpae v Chamberlin Solicitors (Equal Opportunities Commission and others intervening), Webster v Brunel University (Equal Opportunities Commission and others intervening)* supra (a case involving race and sex discrimination but with implications for all categories of discrimination) containing guidance for tribunals: see para 418 note 7 ante. Other cases have been decided in relation to sex discrimination since the statutory reversal of the burden of proof: see *Nelson v Carillion Services Ltd* [2003] EWCA Civ 544, [2003] ICR 1256, [2003] IRLR 428, CA; *University of Huddersfield v Wolff* [2004] ICR 828, [2004] IRLR 534, EAT; *Sinclair Roche & Temperley v Howard* [2004] IRLR 763, EAT; *EB v BA* [2006] EWCA Civ 132, [2006] IRLR 471; *Madarassy v Nomura International plc* [2007] EWCA Civ 33, [2007] All ER (D) 226 (Jan); and para 418 note 7 ante.

   In relation to race discrimination and the Race Relations Act 1976 s 54A (as added) see *Dattani v Chief Constable of West Mercia Police* [2005] IRLR 327, [2005] All ER (D) 95 (Feb), EAT; *Dresdner Kleinwort Wasserstein Ltd v Adebayo* [2005] IRLR 514, [2005] All ER (D) 371 (Mar), EAT; *Hundal v Initial Security Ltd* [2006] All ER (D) 74 (Aug), EAT; *Laing v Manchester City Council* [2006] ICR 1519, [2006] IRLR 748, [2006] All ER (D) 452 (Jul), EAT. See also *Crofton v Yeboah* [2002] EWCA Civ 794, [2002] IRLR 634; *Williams v Corus Hotels plc* [2006] All ER (D) 09 (Sep), EAT; *Network Rail Infrastructure Ltd v Griffiths-Henry* [2006] IRLR 865, [2006] All ER (D) 15 (Jul), EAT; *Li v Atkins and Gregory Ltd* [2006] All ER (D) 26 (Oct), EAT; *Thomatheram v Leicester City Council* [2006] All ER (D) 88 (Aug), EAT; *Famy v Hilton UK Hotels Ltd* [2006] All ER (D) 112 (Oct), EAT; *Weerasinghe v University of East London* [2006] All ER (D) 251 (Dec), EAT; *Dalley v Levenes Solicitors* [2007] All ER (D) 52 (Jan), EAT; *Brown v Croydon London Borough Council* [2007] EWCA Civ 32, [2007] All ER (D) 239 (Jan); *Appiah v Bishop Douglass Roman Catholic High School* [2007] EWCA Civ 10, [2007] All ER (D) 240 (Jan). As to subconscious discrimination see *Appiah v Bishop Douglass Roman Catholic High School* supra, where it was held that consideration of motive was rarely a useful exercise, except where statute specifically required it: the better course was to focus on whether discrimination was on racial grounds, bearing in mind that racial grounds might be conscious or subconscious on the part of the discriminator. See also *Bahl v Law Society* [2004] EWCA Civ 1070, [2004] IRLR 799, [2004] All ER (D) 563 (Jul); and note 11 infra.

9 See para 446 et seq ante.

10 As to victimisation see para 442 ante.

11   In practice, applicants in cases of racial discrimination have always faced special difficulties in proving their cases, as has been acknowledged by the courts: see *Baker v Cornwall County Council* [1990] ICR 452, [1990] IRLR 194, CA; *North West Thames Regional Health Authority v Noone* [1988] ICR 813, sub nom *Noone v North West Thames Regional Health Authority (No 2)* [1998] IRLR, 530, CA; *Khanna v Ministry of Defence* [1981] ICR 653, [1981] IRLR 331, EAT; *Oxford v Department of Health and Social Security* [1977] ICR 884, [1977] IRLR 225, EAT; *Wallace v South Eastern Education and Library Board* [1980] IRLR 193, NI CA; *Chattopadhyay v Headmaster of Holloway School* [1982] ICR 132, [1981] IRLR 487, EAT; *Barking and Dagenham London Borough Council v Camara* [1988] ICR 865, [1988] IRLR 373, EAT.

Direct evidence of discrimination is only rarely available. Applicants have to rely on the questionnaire procedure (see para 503 ante), the inspection and disclosure of documents (see para 503 ante), and statistical evidence which may establish a discernible pattern of treatment of a particular group: *Barking and Dagenham London Borough Council v Camara* supra. The affirmative evidence of discrimination normally consists of inferences to be drawn by the court or tribunal from the primary facts: *Khanna v Ministry of Defence* supra.

A finding of 'no case to answer', so that the applicant's case is dismissed at the end of his evidence, will be exceptional, and will be confined to cases which are wholly without merit: *British Gas plc v Sharma* [1991] ICR 19, [1991] IRLR 101, EAT; *Oxford v Department of Health and Social Security* supra.

Earlier cases concerning the proof of discrimination suggested that, where the applicant had succeeded in establishing that he had been less favourably treated than another person who was of a different racial group or gender, the evidential burden of proof would shift to the respondent. In other words, unless the respondent could provide a satisfactory explanation for the less favourable treatment of the applicant, the tribunal must draw the inference that it was on the ground of race or sex: see *Oxford v Department of Health and Social Security* supra; *Wallace v South Eastern Educational and Library Board* supra; *Chattopadhyay v Headmaster of Holloway School* supra. Other cases, at least in England and Wales, have disapproved of the use of the notion of a shifting burden of proof, as more likely to obscure than to illuminate the right answer: *British Gas plc v Sharma* supra; *Khanna v Ministry of Defence* supra; *Barking and Dagenham London Borough Council v Camara* supra. See also *Anya v University of Oxford* [2001] EWCA Civ 405, [2001] ICR 847, [2001] IRLR 377. See the authoritative approach in *King v Great Britain-China Centre* [1992] ICR 516, [1991] IRLR 513 at 518, CA, per Neill LJ; approved by the House of Lords in *Glasgow City Council v Zafar* [1998] ICR 120, sub nom *Zafar v Glasgow City Council* [1998] IRLR 36, HL. See also *Nassir-Deen v North East London Strategic Health Authority* [2006] All ER (D) 272 (Dec), EAT (an unreasonable but non-discriminatory explanation for the detriment, providing it was found to be genuine, could not lead to an inference of discrimination), where *Glasgow City Council v Zafar* supra was applied.

Although discrimination may be inferred if there is no explanation for unreasonable treatment, that is not an inference from the unreasonable treatment itself but from the absence of any explanation for it; the inference may be rebutted by a respondent leading evidence of a genuine reason which was not discriminatory: *Bahl v Law Society* [2004] EWCA Civ 1070, [2004] IRLR 799, [2004] All ER (D) 563 (Jul) (a case involving both racial and sex discrimination). This case was decided since the introduction of the Race Relations Act 1976 ss 54A, 57ZA (as added) (see the text and notes 1–8 supra) and of the Sex Discrimination Act 1975 ss 63A, 66A (as added and amended) (see para 418 ante) but the previous law may still be relevant because:

(a)   the case confirms the point that bad treatment is not per se discrimination (which requires worse treatment than that given to a comparator);

(b)   there is an argument that the previous law had almost reached the new position introduced with the statutory provisions anyway via the ability of a tribunal to draw inferences (although under the new provisions the tribunal or court has an obligation rather than an ability to draw inferences).

An important case in the new context is *Wong v Igen Ltd (Equal Opportunities Commission and others intervening), Emokpae v Chamberlin Solicitors (Equal Opportunities Commission and others intervening), Webster v Brunel University (Equal Opportunities Commission and others intervening)* [2005] EWCA Civ 142, [2005] 3 All ER 812, [2005] ICR 931 (a case involving race and sex discrimination but with implications across all categories of discrimination): see note 8 supra. One point arising in that decision is that the burden of proof does not shift simply on accusation, although quite what the claimant has to do remains unclear.

12   Ie contrary to the Race Relations Act 1976 s 1(1)(b): see para 440 ante.

13   See ibid s 1(1)(b)(ii); and para 440 ante.

14   As to the meaning of 'justifiable' see para 440 note 10 ante.

15   See note 11 supra. See also note 8 supra.

(5) INCITEMENT TO RACIAL HATRED AND RACIALLY AGGRAVATED OFFENCES

505. Criminal offences of incitement to racial hatred. Provisions relating to criminal offences of incitement to racial hatred[1] are contained in Part III of the Public Order Act 1986[2]. It is an offence to use threatening, abusive or insulting words or behaviour or to display, publish or distribute any such written material with the intention of stirring up racial hatred, or as a result of which racial hatred is likely to be stirred up[3]. It is also an offence to give a public performance of a play[4], to distribute, show or play a recording[5] or to broadcast a programme[6] which has or is likely to have such an effect. The possession of racially inflammatory material with a view to displaying, publishing, distributing, showing, playing or broadcasting it for the purpose of stirring up racial hatred is also an offence[7]. Any racially inflammatory material may be ordered to be forfeited[8].

1 'Racial hatred' means hatred against a group of persons defined by reference to colour, race, nationality (including citizenship) or ethnic or national origins: see the Public Order Act 1986 s 17 (amended by the Anti-Terrorism, Crime and Security Act 2001 ss 37, 125, Sch 8 Pt 4).
2 See the Public Order Act 1986 Pt III (ss 17–29) (as amended); and CRIMINAL LAW, EVIDENCE AND PROCEDURE vol 11(1) (2006 Reissue) para 562 et seq.
3 See ibid s 18 (as amended), s 19; and CRIMINAL LAW, EVIDENCE AND PROCEDURE vol 11(1) (2006 Reissue) paras 562–563.
4 See ibid s 20 (as amended); and CRIMINAL LAW, EVIDENCE AND PROCEDURE vol 11(1) (2006 Reissue) para 564.
5 See ibid s 21 (as amended); and CRIMINAL LAW, EVIDENCE AND PROCEDURE vol 11(1) (2006 Reissue) para 565.
6 See ibid s 22 (as amended); and CRIMINAL LAW, EVIDENCE AND PROCEDURE vol 11(1) (2006 Reissue) para 566.
7 See ibid s 23 (as amended); and CRIMINAL LAW, EVIDENCE AND PROCEDURE vol 11(1) (2006 Reissue) para 567. Powers of entry and search may be given to a constable if there are reasonable grounds for suspecting that a person has materials in contravention of s 23 (as amended): see s 24; and CRIMINAL LAW, EVIDENCE AND PROCEDURE vol 11(1) (2006 Reissue) para 567.
8 See ibid s 25; and CRIMINAL LAW, EVIDENCE AND PROCEDURE vol 11(1) (2006 Reissue) para 568.

506. Racially aggravated offences. The Crime and Disorder Act 1998 introduced, among other things, a number of racially aggravated offences[1]. In particular, it introduced offences of racially aggravated assaults[2], racially aggravated criminal damage[3], racially aggravated public order offences[4] and racially aggravated harassment[5]. These offences are dealt with elsewhere in this work[6].

1 See the Crime and Disorder Act 1998 ss 28–32 (as amended); and CRIMINAL LAW, EVIDENCE AND PROCEDURE vol 11(1) (2006 Reissue) paras 154–156, 335, 561. These provisions also apply in regard to religiously aggravated offences: see para 721 post.
2 See ibid s 29 (as amended); and CRIMINAL LAW, EVIDENCE AND PROCEDURE vol 11(1) (2006 Reissue) para 155.
3 See ibid s 30 (as amended); and CRIMINAL LAW, EVIDENCE AND PROCEDURE vol 11(1) (2006 Reissue) para 335.
4 See ibid s 31 (as amended); and CRIMINAL LAW, EVIDENCE AND PROCEDURE vol 11(1) (2006 Reissue) para 561.
5 See ibid s 32 (as amended); and CRIMINAL LAW, EVIDENCE AND PROCEDURE vol 11(1) (2006 Reissue) para 156.
6 See CRIMINAL LAW, EVIDENCE AND PROCEDURE vol 11(1) (2006 Reissue) paras 154–156, 335, 561.

5. DISABILITY DISCRIMINATION

(1) INTRODUCTION

507.   Scope of the law.   The law of disability discrimination is largely contained in the Disability Discrimination Act 1995 which provides a statutory framework for disabled persons who have been treated less favourably than others to bring a claim[1]. It also introduces the concept of positive discrimination for the first time, as in certain circumstances there is a duty to take reasonable steps in respect of disabled people where there is no duty to act generally[2]. The duties fall upon employers[3], trade organisations[4], service providers[5] and owners and managers of premises[6], as well as in different respects upon transport providers[7] and the education sector[8].

The Disability Discrimination Act 1995 has been amended and supplemented by the Disability Discrimination Act 2005 and to some extent also by the Equality Act 2006.

The Disability Rights Commission Act 1999 established the Disability Rights Commission ('DRC')[9], but this Act is to be repealed by the Equality Act 2006, which also establishes the Commission for Equality and Human Rights[10].

1   See para 509 et seq post.
2   See para 525 post.
3   See the Disability Discrimination Act 1995 ss 4–7D (as amended); and para 529 et seq post.
4   See ibid ss 13–14D (as amended); and para 540 et seq post.
5   See ibid ss 19–21A (as amended); and para 582 et seq post.
6   See ibid ss 22–24M (as amended); and para 599 et seq post.
7   See ibid Pt V (ss 32–49) (as amended); and para 617 et seq post.
8   As to the prohibition of discrimination against disabled pupils in schools see the Disability Discrimination Act 1995 Pt IV Ch I (ss 28A–28Q) (as added and amended); and para 561 et seq post. As to the prohibition of discrimination against disabled pupils in further and higher education see Pt IV Ch II (ss 28R–31A) (as added and amended); and para 569 et seq post. As to the prohibition of discrimination in connection with general qualifications bodies see Pt IV Ch IIA (ss 31AA–31AF) (as added); and para 578 et seq post.
9   See the Disability Rights Commission Act 1999; and para 646 et seq post. See also the text and note 10 infra.
10 The Disability Rights Commission Act 1999 is repealed by the Equality Act 2006 ss 40, 91, Sch 3 para 59, Sch 4 as from a day to be appointed under s 93. At the date at which this volume states the law no such day had been appointed. The Equality Act 2006 Pt 1 (ss 1–43) provides for the dissolution of the DRC and the transfer of its property, rights and liabilities to the Commission for Equality and Human Rights. As to the Commission for Equality and Human Rights, which is to replace the DRC, see para 305 et seq ante.

508.   Equal treatment in employment and occupation.   European Community legislation sets out a general framework[1] for combating discrimination on the grounds of religion or belief, disability[2], age or sexual orientation as regards employment and occupation, with a view to putting into effect in the member states the principle of equal treatment[3]. This applies to all persons, as regards both the public and private sectors, including public bodies, in relation to: (1) conditions for access to employment, to self-employment or to occupation, including selection criteria and recruitment conditions, whatever the branch of activity and at all levels of the professional hierarchy, including promotion; (2) access to all types and to all levels of vocational guidance, vocational training, advanced vocational training and retraining, including practical work experience; (3) employment and working conditions, including dismissals and pay; and (4) membership of, and involvement in, an organisation of workers or employers, or any organisation whose members carry on a particular profession, including the benefits provided for by such organisations[4]. Member states may impose occupational requirements for the application of these provisions[5].

In order to guarantee compliance with the principle of equal treatment in relation to persons with disabilities, reasonable accommodation must be provided[6]. Member states may provide that differences of treatment on grounds of age do not constitute discrimination, if, within the context of national law, they are objectively and reasonably justified by a legitimate aim, including legitimate employment policy, labour market and vocational training objectives, and if the means of achieving that aim are appropriate and necessary[7]. Member states are not prevented from taking positive action for combating discrimination[8].

Member states must ensure that judicial and/or administrative procedures for the enforcement of obligations under these provisions are available to all persons who consider themselves wronged by failure to apply the principle of equal treatment to them, even after the relationship in which the discrimination is alleged to have occurred has ended[9]. Member states are also required to protect employees against dismissal or other adverse treatment by the employer as a reaction to a complaint within the undertaking or to any legal proceedings aimed at enforcing compliance with the principle of equal treatment[10].

Member states are required to disseminate information about provisions adopted pursuant to the provisions above[11], and to promote dialogue between the social partners with a view to fostering equal treatment[12].

Member states must ensure that any laws, regulations and administrative provisions contrary to the principle of equal treatment are abolished, and any provisions contrary to the principle of equal treatment which are included in contracts or collective agreements, internal rules of undertakings or rules governing the independent occupations and professions and workers' and employers' organisations are, or may be, declared null and void or are amended[13].

1   See EC Council Directive 2000/78 (OJ L303, 2.12.2000, p 16) on establishing a general framework for equal treatment in employment and occupation. This Directive is without prejudice to measures laid down by national law which, in a democratic society, are necessary for public security, for the maintenance of public order and the prevention of criminal offences, for the protection of health and for the protection of the rights and freedoms of others: art 2(5). As to implementation of EC Council Directive 2000/78 (OJ L303, 2.12.2000, p 16) in the United Kingdom in regard to religion or belief see para 660 et seq post; as to its implemention in regard to sexual orientation see para 722 et seq post; and as to its impementation in regard to age see para 754 et seq post. For the meaning of 'United Kingdom' see para 325 note 6 ante.

2   Sickness does not amount to disability: Case C-13/05 *Navas v Eurest Colectividades SA* [2007] All ER (EC) 59, [2006] IRLR 706, ECJ. See also *Coleman v Attridge Law* [2006] All ER (D) 326 (Dec), EAT (a claimant who was not disabled herself sought to bring an unlawful discrimination claim on behalf of her son for whom she was carer; the question arose as to whether such 'associative discrimination' was forbidden by EC Council Directive 2000/78 (OJ L303, 2.12.2000, p 16); preliminary ruling sought from the European Court of Justice).

3   EC Council Directive 2000/78 (OJ L303, 2.12.2000, p 16) art 1. The 'principle of equal treatment' means that there must be no direct or indirect discrimination whatsoever on any of the grounds referred to in art 1: art 2(1). See note 1 supra.

4   Ibid art 3(1). EC Council Directive 2000/78 (OJ L303, 2.12.2000, p 16) does not cover differences of treatment based on nationality or payments of any kind made by state schemes or similar, including state social security or social protection schemes: see art 3(2), (3).

5   Ibid art 4.

6   Ibid art 5. 'Reasonable accommodation for disabled persons' means that employers must take appropriate measures, where needed in a particular case, to enable a person with a disability to have access to, participate in, or advance in employment, or to undergo training, unless such measures would impose a disproportionate burden on the employer: art 5. A burden is not disproportionate when it is sufficiently remedied by measures existing within the framework of the disability policy of the member state concerned: art 5.

7   Ibid art 6(1).

8   Ibid art 7. Member states may introduce or maintain provisions which are more favourable to the protection of the principle of equal treatment than those laid down in EC Council Directive 2000/78 (OJ L303, 2.12.2000, p 16) and may not reduce existing protection against discrimination: art 8.

9   Ibid art 9(1). Subject to certain exceptions, member states must also ensure that, when persons who consider themselves wronged because the principle of equal treatment has not been applied to them establish facts from which it may be presumed that there has been direct or indirect discrimination, it is for the respondent to prove that there has been no breach of the principle of equal treatment: art 10.
10   Ibid art 11.
11   Ibid art 12.
12   Ibid art 13. Member states are also required to encourage dialogue with appropriate non-governmental organisations which have a legitimate interest in contributing to the fight against discrimination with a view to promoting the principle of equal treatment: art 14.
13   Ibid art 16. Member states were required to adopt the laws, regulations and administrative provisions necessary to comply with these provisions by 2 December 2003 at the latest: art 18.
        Member states were also required to lay down the rules on sanctions applicable to infringements of the national provisions adopted pursuant to EC Council Directive 2000/78 (OJ L303, 2.12.2000, p 16) and to notify those provisions to the EC Commission by not later than 2 December 2003: art 17.
        Member states had to communicate to the EC Commission, by 2 December 2005 at the latest, all the information necessary for the EC Commission to draw up a report to the European Parliament and the Council on the application of EC Council Directive 2000/78 (OJ L303, 2.12.2000, p 16), and must communicate such information every five years thereafter: art 19(1).

509.   The Disability Discrimination Act 1995. The Disability Discrimination Act 1995[1] renders unlawful discrimination against persons who have a disability[2]: (1) in relation to employment and membership of locally-electable authorities[3]; (2) in the provision of goods, facilities, services, and by public authorities or private clubs or in relation to premises[4]; and (3) in the provision of public transport[5]. There are certain duties to avoid discrimination in the education sector[6]. There are also certain new duties imposed on public authorities[7], and in regard to improvements to dwelling houses[8].

The Act imposes liability on employers and principals in respect of acts done by their employees and agents and on persons knowingly aiding unlawful acts[9].

The Act also makes provision for codes of practice to give practical guidance[10].

The Act applies with certain limitations to acts done by the Crown and Parliament[11].

Generally, any power under the Act to make regulations or orders is exercisable by statutory instrument[12].

1   The Disability Discrimination Act 1995 has been amended and supplemented by the Disability Discrimination Act 2005, and to some extent also by the Equality Act 2006. This disability discrimination legislation can be seen against the background of EC Council Directive 2000/78 (OJ L303, 2.12.2000, p 16) on establishing a general framework for equal treatment in employment and occupation: see para 508 ante.
2   Sickness does not amount to disability: see Case C-13/05 *Navas v Eurest Colectividades SA* [2007] All ER (EC) 59, [2006] IRLR 706, ECJ. See also *Coleman v Attridge Law* [2006] All ER (D) 326 (Dec), EAT; and para 508 note 2 ante.
3   See the Disability Discrimination Act 1995 Pt II (ss 3A–18E) (as amended; prospectively amended); and para 529 et seq post.
4   See ibid Pt III (ss 19–28) (as amended; prospectively amended); and para 582 et seq post.
5   See ibid Pt V (ss 32–49) (as amended); and para 617 et seq post.
6   See para 507 note 8 ante.
7   See the Disability Discrimination Act 1995 Pt VA (ss 49A–49F) (as added and amended; prospectively amended); and paras 591–592 post.
8   See ibid Pt VB (ss 49G, 49H) (as added; prospectively amended); and paras 611–612 post.
9   See ibid ss 57, 58 (as amended); and paras 527–528 post.
10   As to codes of practice see para 655 post.
11   See the Disability Discrimination Act 1995 ss 64, 65 (as amended); and paras 553–555 post.
12   Ibid s 67(1) (amended by the Disability Discrimination Act 2005 s 19(1), Sch 1 paras 1, 33(1), (2)). 'Regulations' means regulations made by the Secretary of State, except in the Disability Discrimination Act 1995 s 2(3) (as amended) (see para 522 post), s 28D (as added and amended) (see para 564 post), s 28L(6) (as added and amended) (see para 567 post), s 33 (as amended) (see para 628 post), ss 49D–49F (as added and amended; ss 49E, 49F prospectively repealed) (see paras 591–592 post) and s 67 (as amended; prospectively amended) (provisions where the meaning of 'regulations' is apparent): s 68(1) (definition amended by the Disability Discrimination Act 2005 Sch 1 paras 1, 34(1), (6)). As from a day to be appointed, this definition is amended so as to remove the reference to the Disability Discrimination

Act 1995 ss 49E, 49F (as added and amended; prospectively repealed): see the Equality Act 2006 ss 40, 91, Sch 3 paras 41, 54, Sch 4. At the date at which this volume states the law no such day had been appointed. The Disability Discrimination Act 1995 s 67(1) (as amended) does not require an order under s 43 (see para 638 post) which applies only to a specified vehicle, or to vehicles of a specified person, to be made by statutory instrument but such an order is as capable of being amended or revoked as an order which is made by statutory instrument: s 67(6).

Any power to make regulations or orders may be exercised to make different provision for different cases, including different provision for different areas or localities: s 67(2). Any such power includes power: (1) to make such incidental, supplemental, consequential or transitional provision as appears to the person by whom the power is exercisable to be expedient; and (2) to provide for a person to exercise a discretion in dealing with any matter: s 67(3) (amended by the Disability Discrimination Act 2005 Sch 1 paras 1, 33(1), (3)). Nothing in the Disability Discrimination Act 1995 s 34(4) (see para 629 post), s 40(6) (see para 635 post) or s 46(5) (see para 617 post) affects the powers conferred by s 67(2), (3) (as amended): s 67(7).

Where regulations under s 21D(7)(b) (as added) (see para 594 post) provide for the omission of s 21D(5) (as added), the provision that may be made by the regulations in exercise of the power conferred by head (1) supra includes provision amending s 21D (as added) for the purpose of omitting references to s 21D(5) (as added): s 67(3A) (s 67(3A)–(3C) added by the Disability Discrimination Act 2005 Sch 1 paras 1, 33(1), (4)). The provision that may be made by regulations under the Disability Discrimination Act 1995 s 21G(5)(b) (as added) (see para 597 post) in exercise of the power conferred by head (1) supra includes provision amending or repealing s 21G(4) (as added): s 67(3B) (as so added). The provision that may be made by regulations under any of s 49D(1)–(4) (as added) (see para 591 post) in exercise of the power conferred by head (1) supra includes provision amending or repealing an enactment: s 67(3C) (as so added).

In the case of the following regulations, namely:

(a) the first regulations to be made under s 21H(1) (as added (see para 598 post);
(b) the first regulations to be made under each of s 31AE(1), (2) and (4) (as added) (see para 581 post);
(c) regulations under s 31AE(1), (2) or (4) (as added) that amend the Disability Discrimination Act 1995;
(d) regulations under s 31AE(1) (as added) that make provision as to remedies;
(e) regulations under s 47J(3) (as added) (see para 624 post);
(f) regulations under s 49D(1) or (2) (as added) (see para 591 post) that, in exercise of the power under head (1) supra, amend or repeal an enactment contained in an Act or in an Act of the Scottish Parliament;
(g) regulations under s 67A(3) (as added);
(h) regulations under Sch 1 para 6A(2) (as added) (see para 516 post),

no such regulations are to be made unless a draft of the statutory instrument containing the regulations (whether containing the regulations alone or with other provisions) has been laid before, and approved by a resolution of, each House of Parliament: s 67(4), (4A) (s 67(4), (5) substituted, and s 67(4A)–(4D), (5A) added, by the Disability Discrimination Act 2005 Sch 1 paras 1, 33(1), (5)). Scottish matters generally are beyond the scope of this work.

In the case of regulations under the Disability Discrimination Act 1995 s 49D(3) or (4) (as added) (see para 591 post) that, in exercise of the power under head (1) supra, amend or repeal any enactment contained in an Act or in an Act of the Scottish Parliament, no such regulations are to be made unless a draft of the statutory instrument containing the regulations (whether containing the regulations alone or with other provisions) has been laid before, and approved by a resolution of, the Scottish Parliament: s 67(4B), (4C) (as so added). A statutory instrument: (i) that contains regulations under s 49D(3) or (4) (as added), and is not subject to the requirement in s 67(4C) (as added) that a draft of the instrument be laid before, and approved by, the Scottish Parliament; or (ii) that contains regulations or an order made by the Scottish Ministers under s 33 (as amended) (see para 628 post), is subject to annulment in pursuance of a resolution of the Scottish Parliament: s 67(4D) (as so added).

A statutory instrument:

(A) that contains regulations made by the Secretary of State under the Disability Discrimination Act 1995, and is not subject to the requirement in s 64(4A) (as added) that a draft of the instrument be laid before, and approved by a resolution of, each House of Parliament; or
(B) that contains an order made by the Secretary of State under the Disability Discrimination Act 1995 that is not an order under s 3(9) (see para 512 post), s 47(1) (as substituted) (see para 618 post), s 53A(6)(a) (as added; prospectively repealed) (see para 655 post) or s 70(3),

is subject to annulment in pursuance of a resolution of either House of Parliament: s 67(5) (as so substituted). As from a day to be appointed, the reference to s 53A(6)(a) (as added) is omitted: s 67(5) (prospectively amended by the Equality Act 2006 Sch 3 paras 41, 53, Sch 4). At the date at which this volume states the law no such day had been appointed.

A statutory instrument that contains an order under the Disability Discrimination Act 1995 s 47(1) (as substituted) (see para 618 post), if made without a draft having been laid before, and approved by a resolution of, each House of Parliament, is subject to annulment in pursuance of a resolution of either House, but the exercise of the discretion thus conferred is subject to s 67A (as added): s 67(5A) (as so added). Before the Secretary of State decides which of the parliamentary procedures available under s 67(5A) (as added) is to be adopted in connection with the making of any particular order under s 47(1) (as substituted), he must consult the Disabled Persons Transport Advisory Committee (see ROAD TRAFFIC vol 40(1) (Reissue) para 56): s 67A(1) (s 67A added by the Disability Discrimination Act 2005 s 6(4)). An order under the Disability Discrimination Act 1995 s 47(1) (as substituted) may be made without a draft of the instrument that contains it having been laid before, and approved by a resolution of, each House of Parliament only if regulations under s 67A(3) (as added) are in force, and the making of the order without such laying and approval is in accordance with the regulations: s 67A(2) (as so added). Regulations may set out the basis on which the Secretary of State, when he comes to make an order under s 47(1) (as substituted), will decide which of the parliamentary procedures available under s 67(5A) (as added) is to be adopted in connection with the making of the order: s 67A(3) (as so added). Before making regulations under s 67A(3) (as added), the Secretary of State must consult the Disabled Persons Transport Advisory Committee, and such other persons as he considers appropriate: s 67A(4) (as so added).

510. Application of the Disability Discrimination Act 1995 to the Crown. Most provisions of the Disability Discrimination Act 1995[1] apply[2] to an act[3] done by or for purposes of a Minister of the Crown[4] or government department[5], or to an act done on behalf of the Crown by a statutory body[6], or a person holding a statutory office[7], as they apply to an act done by a private person[8].

1 Ie other than the provisions mentioned in heads (1), (2) infra. The following provisions bind the Crown:
   (1) the Disability Discrimination Act 1995 ss 21B–21E (as added) (see paras 593–595 post) and Pt VA (ss 49A–49F) (as added and amended; ss 49E, 49F prospectively repealed) (see paras 591–592 post); and
   (2) the other provisions of the Disability Discrimination Act 1995 so far as applying for the purposes of provisions mentioned in head (1) supra,
   and s 57 (as amended) (see paras 509, 528, 638 post) and s 58 (see para 527 post) apply for purposes of provisions mentioned in head (1) supra as if service as a Crown servant were employment by the Crown: s 64(A1) (added by the Disability Discrimination Act 2005 s 19(1), Sch 1 paras 1, 31(1), (2)). The Disability Discrimination Act 1995 s 64(A1)–(2) (as added and amended) has effect subject to s 64A (as added and amended) (see para 554 post): s 64(2A) (added by the Disability Discrimination Act 1995 (Amendment) Regulations 2003, SI 2003/1673, regs 3(1), 24(b); and amended by the Disability Discrimination Act 2005 Sch 1 paras 1, 31(1), (4)).
2 Disability Discrimination Act 1995 s 64(1) (amended by the Disability Discrimination Act 2005 Sch 1 paras 1, 31(1), (3)). See note 1 supra.
3 'Act' includes a deliberate omission: Disability Discrimination Act 1995 s 68(1).
4 'Minister of the Crown' includes the Treasury and the Defence Council: ibid s 68(1) (definition amended by the Disability Discrimination Act 1995 (Amendment) Regulations 2003, SI 2003/1673, regs 3(1), 27(a)(iv)). As to the Treasury see CONSTITUTIONAL LAW AND HUMAN RIGHTS vol 8(2) (Reissue) paras 512–517. As to the Defence Council see ARMED FORCES vol 2(2) (Reissue) para 2; CONSTITUTIONAL LAW AND HUMAN RIGHTS vol 8(2) (Reissue) para 443 et seq. There is to be paid out of money provided by Parliament: (1) any expenditure incurred by a Minister of the Crown under the Disability Discrimination Act 1995; and (2) any increase attributable to the Disability Discrimination Act 1995 in the sums payable out of money so provided under or by virtue of any other enactment: s 69. 'Enactment' includes subordinate legislation and any Order in Council: s 68(1).
5 Ibid s 64(1)(a). See note 1 supra.
6 'Statutory body' means a body set up by or under an enactment: ibid s 64(8).
7 Ibid s 64(1)(b). 'Statutory office' means an office set up by or under an enactment: s 64(8). See note 1 supra.
8 Ibid s 64(1). See note 1 supra.
   For provisions relating to the Crown in its capacity as employer see the Disability Discrimination Act 1995 s 64(2), (8) (as amended); and para 553 post. As to the application of the Crown Proceedings Act 1947 in relation to proceedings under the Disability Discrimination Act 1995 see s 64(3), (4) (s 64(3) amended by the Civil Procedure (Modification of Crown Proceedings Act 1947) Order 2005,

SI 2005/2712, art 3, Sch 2 para 3). See also CROWN PROCEEDINGS AND CROWN PRACTICE vol 12(1) (Reissue) para 113. As to the meaning of 'person' see para 344 note 3 ante.

(2) MEANING OF DISABILITY

(i) Introduction

511. Disability. 'Disabled person' means a person who has a disability[1]. A person has a disability for the purposes of the Disability Discrimination Act 1995 if he has a physical[2] or mental[3] impairment which has a substantial[4] and long-term[5] adverse effect on his ability to carry out normal day-to-day activities[6]. The elements of the definition fall broadly into two categories: (1) proof of an impairment, which is the diagnosis-based element of the test; and (2) the consequence of the impairment on the person's life, which is the effect-based part of the test[7].

1   Disability Discrimination Act 1995 s 1(2). See *Ginn v Tesco Stores Ltd* [2005] All ER (D) 259 (Oct), EAT.
2   As to physical impairment see para 513 post.
3   As to mental impairment see para 514 post.
4   As to substantial effects see para 515–517 post.
5   As to long-term effects see para 518–519 post.
6   Disability Discrimination Act 1995 s 1(1). As to adverse effect on normal day-to-day activities see para 520 post. The test has been broken down into four parts: (1) the impairment condition, i e the question whether the applicant has an impairment which is either mental or physical; (2) the adverse effect condition, i e whether the impairment affects the applicant's ability to carry out normal day-to-day activities in one of the respects set out in Sch 1 para 4(1) (see para 520 post), and whether it has an adverse effect; (3) the substantial condition, i e whether the adverse condition (upon the applicant's ability) is substantial; and (4) the long-term condition, i e whether the adverse condition (upon the applicant's ability) is long-term: *Goodwin v Patent Office* [1999] ICR 302, [1999] IRLR 4, EAT. See *Millar v Inland Revenue Commissioners* [2006] IRLR 112 (employment tribunal failed to determine whether complainant's condition was a physical or mental impairment); *Beales v Secretary of State for Work and Pensions* [2006] All ER (D) 118 (Sep), EAT (employment tribunal entitled to find insufficient evidence to support claim of mental illness or that the claimant's carpal tunnel syndrome had substantial and long-term effects on her ability to carry out day-to-day activities). See also Case C-13/05 *Navas v Eurest Colectividades* [2007] All ER (EC) 59, [2006] IRLR 706, ECJ (whether dismissal for sickness was disability discrimination); *O'Hanlon v Revenue and Customs Comrs* [2007] EWCA Civ 283, [2007] All ER (D) 516 (Mar) (no discrimination in how employer's sick pay rules followed); *Fowler v Waltham Forest London Borough Council* [2007] All ER (D) 126 (Feb), EAT (no discrimination or duty to make further payments of wages/sick pay by way of a reasonable adjustment).
7   See note 6 supra.

512. Guidance as to disability. The Secretary of State[1] may issue guidance[2] about matters to be taken into account in determining whether a person[3] is a disabled person[4]. Without prejudice to the generality of this power, the Secretary of State may in particular issue guidance about the matters to be taken into account in determining[5] whether an impairment[6] has a substantial adverse effect[7] on a person's ability to carry out normal day-to-day activities[8], or whether such an impairment has a long-term effect[9].

Without prejudice to the generality of the above power[10], the guidance[11] may, among other things, give examples of[12]:

(1)   effects which it would be reasonable, in relation to particular activities, to regard for the purposes of the Disability Discrimination Act 1995 as substantial adverse effects[13];

(2)   effects which it would not be reasonable, in relation to particular activities, to regard for such purposes as substantial adverse effects[14];

(3)   substantial adverse effects which it would be reasonable to regard, for such purposes, as long-term[15];

(4) substantial adverse effects which it would not be reasonable to regard, for such purposes, as long-term[16].

An adjudicating body[17] determining, for any purpose of the Disability Discrimination Act 1995, whether a person is a disabled person must take into account any guidance which appears to it to be relevant[18].

In preparing a draft of any guidance, the Secretary of State must consult such persons as he considers appropriate[19]. Where the Secretary of State proposes to issue any guidance, he must publish a draft of it, consider any representations that are made to him about the draft and, if he thinks it appropriate, modify his proposals in the light of any of those representations[20]. If the Secretary of State decides to proceed with any proposed guidance, he must lay a draft of it before each House of Parliament[21]. If, within a 40-day period[22], either House resolves not to approve the draft, the Secretary of State may take no further steps in relation to the proposed guidance[23]. If no such resolution is made within the 40-day period, the Secretary of State must issue the guidance in the form of his draft[24] and it comes into force on such date as the Secretary of State may appoint by order[25].

The Secretary of State may from time to time revise the whole or part of any guidance and re-issue it[26], or by order revoke any guidance[27].

In pursuance of these powers, the Secretary of State has issued a publication entitled *Guidance on matters to be taken into account in determining questions relating to the definition of disability*[28].

1   As to the Secretary of State and the National Assembly for Wales see para 302 ante.
2   'Guidance' means guidance issued by the Secretary of State under the Disability Discrimination Act 1995 s 3 (as amended) and includes guidance which has been revised and re-issued: s 3(12). As to the guidance that has been issued see the text and note 28 infra. The guidance gives illustrations and examples and is not a checklist: see *Vicary v British Telecommunications plc* [1999] IRLR 680, EAT.
3   As to the meaning of 'person' see para 344 note 3 ante.
4   Disability Discrimination Act 1995 s 3(A1) (added by the Disability Discrimination Act 2005 s 19(1), Sch 1 paras 1, 3(1), (2)). For the meaning of 'disabled person' see para 511 ante.
5   Disability Discrimination Act 1995 s 3(1) (amended by the Disability Discrimination Act 2005 Sch 1 paras 1, 3(1), (3)).
6   As to impairment see paras 513–514 post.
7   As to substantial adverse effects see paras 515–517 post.
8   Disability Discrimination Act 1995 s 3(1)(a). As to normal day-to-day activities see para 520 post.
9   Ibid s 3(1)(b). As to long-term effects see paras 518–519 post.
10 Ie the power in ibid s 3(A1) (as added): see the text and notes 1–4 supra.
11 Ie about the matters mentioned in ibid s 3(1) (as amended): see the text and notes 5–9 supra.
12 Ibid s 3(2) (amended by the Disability Discrimination Act 2005 Sch 1 paras 1, 3(1), (4)).
13 Disability Discrimination Act 1995 s 3(2)(a).
14 Ibid s 3(2)(b).
15 Ibid s 3(2)(c).
16 Ibid s 3(2)(d).
17 'Adjudicating body' means a court, tribunal and any other person who, or body which, may decide a claim under ibid Pt IV (ss 28A–31C) (as amended; prospectively amended) (see para 561 et seq post): s 3(3A) (added by the Special Educational Needs and Disability Act 2001 s 38(1), (4)).
18 Disability Discrimination Act 1995 s 3(3) (amended by the Special Educational Needs and Disability Act 2001 s 38(1), (3); and the Disability Discrimination Act 2005 Sch 1 paras 1, 3(1), (5)).
19 Disability Discrimination Act 1995 s 3(4).
20 Ibid s 3(5).
21 Ibid s 3(6).
22 In relation to the draft of any proposed guidance, '40-day period' means: (1) if the draft is laid before one House of Parliament on a day later than the day on which it is laid before the other House, the period of 40 days beginning with the later of the two days; and (2) in any other case, the period of 40 days beginning with the day on which the draft is laid before each House, no account being taken of any period during which Parliament is dissolved or prorogued or during which both Houses are adjourned for more than four days: ibid s 3(12).

23   Ibid s 3(7). Section 3(7) does not prevent a new draft of the proposed guidance from being laid before Parliament: s 3(10).
24   Ibid s 3(8).
25   See ibid s 3(9).
26   Ibid s 3(11)(a).
27   Ibid s 3(11)(b).
28   *Guidance on matters to be taken into account in determining questions relating to the definition of disability* (issued on 29 March 2006) came into force on 1 May 2006: see the Disability Discrimination (Guidance on the Definition of Disability) Appointed Day Order 2006, SI 2006/1005, art 2. The guidance does not impose any legal obligations in itself, nor is it an authoritative statement of the law. However, the Disability Discrimination Act 1995 s 3(3) (as amended) (see the text to note 18 supra) requires that an adjudicating body, which is determining for any purpose of the Act whether a person is a disabled person, must take into account any of the guidance which appears to it to be relevant.

(ii) Elements of the Statutory Definition

A. IMPAIRMENT

513.   Physical impairment. 'Physical impairment' is not defined in the Disability Discrimination Act 1995 but is likely to encompass any organic or bodily detriment[1]. The guidance issued by the Secretary of State[2] indicates that it includes sensory impairments[3], but some physical impairments are excluded[4].

1   See *McNicol v Balfour Beatty Rail Maintenance Ltd* [2002] EWCA Civ 1074, [2002] ICR 1498, [2002] IRLR 711; and para 514 post. A physical impairment can be something that results from an illness as well as it being the illness: *College of Ripon and York St John v Hobbs* [2002] IRLR 185, EAT.
2   Ie *Guidance on matters to be taken into account in determining questions relating to the definition of disability* (29 March 2006): see para 512 ante. As to the Secretary of State and the National Assembly for Wales see para 302 ante.
3   Eg those affecting sight or hearing (but not expressly smell, taste and touch): see *Guidance on matters to be taken into account in determining questions relating to the definition of disability* (29 March 2006).
4   Regulations have been made as to the conditions to be treated as impairments: see para 523 post.

514.   Mental impairment. 'Mental impairment' previously included an impairment resulting from or consisting of a mental illness only if the illness was a clinically well-recognised illness but this requirement has now been removed[1]. Presumably a mental illness must still go beyond a reaction that could be described as a normal human emotion[2]. Some conditions which can be mental illnesses are expressly excluded from being impairments[3].

1   See the Disability Discrimination Act 1995 s 1(1), Sch 1 para 1(1) (repealed by the Disability Discrimination Act 2005 ss 18(1), (2), 19(1), Sch 2). See also *Goodwin v Patent Office* [1999] ICR 302, [1999] IRLR 4, EAT; *McNicol v Balfour Beatty Rail Maintenance Ltd* [2002] EWCA Civ 1074, [2002] ICR 1498, [2002] IRLR 711 (a decision as to whether an applicant has a physical or mental impairment must be made without substituting for the statutory language a different form of words in an attempt to describe or to define the concept of 'impairment'); *Morgan v Staffordshire University* [2002] ICR 475, [2002] IRLR 190, EAT (guidance on the approach to be taken when considering whether a person is suffering from mental impairment for the purposes of the Disability Discrimination Act 1995). For earlier caselaw see *Bolam v Friern Hospital Management Committee* [1957] 2 All ER 118, [1957] 1 WLR 582 (doctor is not negligent if following a course supported by a responsible body of professional opinion); approved in *Sidaway v Board of Governors of the Bethlem Royal Hospital and the Maudsley Hospital* [1985] AC 871, [1985] 1 All ER 643, HL. See also *McLoughlin v O'Brian* [1983] 1 AC 410, [1982] 2 All ER 298, HL.
     'Mental impairment' does not have the same meaning as in the Mental Health Act 1983 (see MENTAL HEALTH vol 30 (Reissue) para 403) but the fact that an impairment would be a mental impairment for the purposes of that Act does not prevent it from being a mental impairment for the purposes of the Disability Discrimination Act 1995: s 68(1) (definition amended by the Disability Discrimination Act 1995 s 19(1), Sch 1 paras 34(1), (4)).
2   See *McLoughlin v O'Brian* [1983] 1 AC 410 at 431, [1982] 2 All ER 298 at 311–312, HL, per Lord Bridge of Harwich.

3   Regulations have been made as to the conditions to be treated as impairments: see para 523 post. See
     Dunham v Ashford Windows [2005] ICR 1584, [2005] IRLR 608, EAT (evidence of employee's learning
     difficulties; it was not open to the employment tribunal to decline to accept psychologist's report as to
     the employee's condition on the basis that the report was not produced by a doctor).

B. SUBSTANTIAL EFFECT

515.   Meaning of 'substantial'.   A 'substantial' effect is one that is significant or
more than de minimis. The word 'substantial' is not used in the sense of large or
considerable, but something which is more than minor or trivial[1]. The cumulative effect
on the normal day-to-day activities needs to be considered when deciding whether the
impairment has a substantial adverse effect[2]. The way a person who suffers from an
impairment behaves or modifies his behaviour should be taken into account[3], as should
his environment[4]. An impairment which consists of a severe disfigurement is to be
treated as having a substantial adverse effect on the ability of the person concerned to
carry out normal day-to-day activities[5].

1   *Guidance on matters to be taken into account in determining questions relating to the definition of disability*
     (29 March 2006) Pt 2 Section B. As to the guidance see para 512 ante. A disability must be a limitation
     going beyond the normal differences in ability which may exist among people: *Guidance on matters to be
     taken into account in determining questions relating to the definition of disability* (29 March 2006) Pt 2 para B1.
     Factors for assessing what is substantial include the time taken to carry out an activity (ie whether the
     claimant is slower than normal) and the way in which an activity is carried out (ie whether the claimant
     has to utilise a particular or unusual method): see *Guidance on matters to be taken into account in determining
     questions relating to the definition of disability* (29 March 2006) Pt 2 paras B2, B3.
2   A court or tribunal needs to look at the cumulative adverse effect in all the circumstances in deciding
     whether that effect is substantial: see *Guidance on matters to be taken into account in determining questions
     relating to the definition of disability* (29 March 2006) Pt 2 para B4. Thus a person may suffer a number of
     minor effects or impairments which together make a substantial adverse effect.
3   A person can be reasonably expected to mitigate the effects of the impairment: see *Guidance on matters to
     be taken into account in determining questions relating to the definition of disability* (29 March 2006) Pt 2 para B7
     et seq. Some people have 'coping' strategies which cease to work in certain circumstances which should
     be taken into account and looked at cumulatively to see whether they amount to a substantial effect:
     Guidance on matters to be taken into account in determining questions relating to the definition of disability
     (29 March 2006) Pt 2 para B9.
4   Factors such as such as temperature, humidity, the time of day or night, how tired the person is or how
     much stress he is under, and the extent to which such environmental factors are likely to occur and thus
     have an impact on a claimant's life should be considered: *Guidance on matters to be taken into account in
     determining questions relating to the definition of disability* (29 March 2006) Pt 2 para B10.
5   Disability Discrimination Act 1995 s 1(1), Sch 1 para 3(1). Disfigurements can include scars, birthmarks,
     limb or postural deformation (including restricted bodily development), or diseases of the skin: *Guidance
     on matters to be taken into account in determining questions relating to the definition of disability* (29 March 2006)
     Pt 2 para B21. Cf the Judicial Studies Board Guidelines for the Assessment of General Damages in
     Personal Injury Cases (4th Edn) for the assessment of severity, which classifies facial disfigurement
     separately from scarring to other parts of the body, assesses non-facial or not readily visible disfigurements
     as less serious and treats scarring to females and males differently, scarring to females attracting
     considerably higher awards of damages. Regulations may provide that in prescribed circumstances a
     severe disfigurement is not to be treated as having this effect: Disability Discrimination Act 1995 Sch 1
     para 3(2). For the meaning of 'regulations' see para 509 note 12 ante. As to the making of regulations see
     para 523 post. 'Prescribed' generally means prescribed by regulations (except in s 28D (as added), where
     it has the meaning given by s 28D(17) (as added and substituted) (see para 564 post)): s 68(1) (definition
     amended by the Disability Discrimination Act 2005 s 19(1). Sch 1 paras 1, 34(1), (5)). Such regulations
     may, in particular, make provision with respect to deliberately acquired disfigurements: Disability
     Discrimination Act 1995 Sch 1 para 3(3). For the purposes of Sch 1 para 3, a severe disfigurement is not
     to be treated as having a substantial adverse effect on the ability of the person concerned to carry out
     normal day-to-day activities if it consists of: (1) a tattoo (which has not been removed); or (2) a piercing
     of the body for decorative or other non-medical purposes, including any object attached through the
     piercing for such purposes: Disability Discrimination (Meaning of Disability) Regulations 1996,
     SI 1996/1455, reg 5.
         Regulations may make provision for the purposes of the Disability Discrimination Act 1995: (a) for
     an effect of a prescribed kind on the ability of a person to carry out normal day-to-day activities to be

treated as a substantial adverse effect; (b) for an effect of a prescribed kind on the ability of a person to carry out normal day-to-day activities to be treated as not being a substantial adverse effect: Sch 1 para 5. See the Disability Discrimination (Meaning of Disability) Regulations 1996, SI 1996/1455.

516. The effect of medical treatment. A person can be disabled[1] although effective medical treatment may prevent any substantial adverse effect on his activities, since in assessing whether the impairment has a substantial effect, the treatment or corrective measures are to be disregarded[2]. The impairment is to be treated as having the effect it would have without the measures in question[3], which is referred to as the 'deduced effects'[4]. This provision applies even if the measures result in the effects being completely under control or not at all apparent[5].

1   A person who has cancer, HIV infection or multiple sclerosis is to be deemed to have a disability, and hence to be a disabled person: Disability Discrimination Act 1995 s 1(1), Sch 1 para 6A(1) (Sch 1 para 6A added by the Disability Discrimination Act 2005 s 18(1), (3)). 'HIV infection' means infection by a virus capable of causing the acquired immune deficiency syndrome: Sch 1 para 9 (added by the Disability Discrimination Act 2005 s 18(1), (5)). Regulations may provide for the Disability Discrimination Act 1995 Sch 1 para 6A(1) (as added) not to apply in the case of a person who has cancer if he has cancer of a prescribed description: Sch 1 para 6A(2) (as so added). For the meaning of 'regulations' see para 509 note 12 ante. 'Prescribed' generally means prescribed by regulations: see para 515 note 5 ante. A description of cancer prescribed under Sch 1 para 6A(2) (as added) may (in particular) be framed by reference to consequences for a person of his having it: Sch 1 para 6A(3) (as so added). At the date at which this volume states the law no regulations had been made for these purposes.

2   Ibid Sch 1 para 6(1). This provision does not apply: (1) in relation to the impairment of a person's sight, to the extent that the impairment is, in his case, correctable by spectacles or contact lenses or in such other ways as may be prescribed; or (2) in relation to such other impairments as may be prescribed, in such circumstances as may be prescribed: Sch 1 para 6(3). See note 1 supra. 'Measures' includes, in particular, medical treatment and the use of a prosthesis or other aid: Sch 1 para 6(2). See *Woodrup v Southwark London Borough Council* [2002] EWCA Civ 1716, [2003] IRLR 111.

3   See *Guidance on matters to be taken into account in determining questions relating to the definition of disability* (29 March 2006) Pt 2 para B11. As to the guidance see para 512 ante.

4   *Goodwin v Patent Office* [1999] ICR 302, [1999] IRLR 4, EAT (the tribunal should examine how the applicant's abilities had actually been affected at the material time, whilst on medication, and then address the difficult question as to the effects which it thinks there would have been but for the medication, ie the deduced effects; the question is then whether the actual and deduced effects on the applicant's abilities to carry out normal day-to-day activities is clearly more than trivial). As to normal day-to-day activities see para 520 post.

5   *Guidance on matters to be taken into account in determining questions relating to the definition of disability* (29 March 2006) Pt 2 para B12.

517. Progressive conditions. A person who has a progressive condition that is symptomatic and is likely to worsen so as to have a substantial adverse effect in the future is deemed to have a disability[1]. The Disability Discrimination Act 1995 recognises the likely future of the impairment in identifying whether it can presently be classified as a substantial adverse effect[2].

1   See the Disability Discrimination Act 1995 s 1(1), Sch 1 para 8(1) (amended by the Disability Discrimination Act 2005 s 19(1), Sch 1 paras 1, 36), which refers expressly to progressive conditions such as cancer, multiple sclerosis, muscular dystrophy or HIV infection. For the meaning of 'HIV infection' see para 516 note 1 ante. Regulations may make provision, for the purposes of this provision: (1) for conditions of a prescribed description to be treated as being progressive; or (2) for conditions of a prescribed description to be treated as not being progressive: Disability Discrimination Act 1995 Sch 1 para 8(2). For the meaning of 'regulations' see para 509 note 12 ante. 'Prescribed' generally means prescribed by regulations: see para 515 note 5 ante. As to the making of regulations see para 523 post. At the date at which this volume states the law no such regulations had been made. See *Kirton v Tetrosyl Ltd* [2003] EWCA Civ 619, [2003] ICR 1237, [2003] IRLR 353 (symptoms resulting from surgery used to treat a progressive condition could be protected by the Disability Discrimination Act 1995 Sch 1 para 8(1)). In order to fall within the Disability Discrimination Act 1995 Sch 1 para 8(1) (as amended), a person has to establish that it is more likely than not that at some stage in the future he will have an impairment which will have a substantial adverse effect on his ability to carry out normal day-to-day activities: see *Mowat-Brown v University of Surrey* [2002] IRLR 235, [2001] All ER (D) 115 (Dec), EAT.

2   See *Guidance on matters to be taken into account in determining questions relating to the definition of disability*
     (29 March 2006) Pt 2 para B16 et seq. As to the guidance see para 512 ante.

C. LONG TERM

518.   Meaning of 'long term'.   The effect of an impairment[1] is a long-term effect
if: (1) it has lasted at least 12 months; (2) the period for which it lasts is likely to be at
least 12 months; or (3) it is likely to last for the rest of the life of the person affected[2].

For the purpose of deciding whether a person has had a disability in the past, a
long-term effect of an impairment is one which lasted at least 12 months[3]. It is not
necessary for the effect to be the same throughout the relevant period. The effect on
day-to-day activities may vary: activities which are initially very difficult may become
possible, some adverse effects might reduce, while others continue or develop. If the
impairment has, or is likely to have, an adverse effect throughout the period, there is a
long-term effect[4]. In assessing the likelihood of an effect lasting for any period, account
should be taken of the total period for which the effect exists, together with medical
evidence[5].

1   As to physical impairment see para 513 ante; and as to mental impairment see para 514 ante.
2   Disability Discrimination Act 1995 s 1(1), Sch 1 para 2(1). Regulations may prescribe circumstances in
     which, for the purposes of the Disability Discrimination Act 1995: (1) an effect which would not
     otherwise be a long-term effect is to be treated as such an effect; or (2) an effect which would otherwise
     be a long-term effect is to be treated as not being such an effect: Sch 1 para 2(4). For the meaning of
     'regulations' see para 509 note 12 ante. 'Prescribed' generally means prescribed by regulations: see
     para 515 note 5 ante. As to the making of regulations see para 523 post. At the date at which this volume
     states the law no regulations had been made for these purposes.
3   See ibid s 2(2), Sch 2 para 5.
4   *Guidance on matters to be taken into account in determining questions relating to the definition of disability*
     (29 March 2006) Pt 2 Section C. As to the guidance see para 512 ante.
5   See *Guidance on matters to be taken into account in determining questions relating to the definition of disability*
     (29 March 2006) Pt 2 para C3. The total picture should be considered including any time before the
     discriminatory behaviour occurred as well as afterwards; account should also be taken of both the typical
     length of such an effect on an individual and any relevant factors specific to this individual (e g general
     state of health, age, etc): *Guidance on matters to be taken into account in determining questions relating to the
     definition of disability* (29 March 2006) Pt 2 para C3.

519.   Recurring effects.   Where an impairment ceases to have a substantial adverse
effect[1] on a person's ability to carry out normal day-to-day activities, it is to be treated as
continuing to have that effect if that effect is likely to recur[2]. The definition of disability
therefore includes permanent conditions with only sporadic or short-lived effects[3]. If
treatment is likely to cure an impairment, recurrence may be unlikely, but if treatment
only relieves the symptoms so that a recurrence would be likely if the treatment was
stopped, that treatment must be disregarded[4].

1   As to adverse effect see para 520 post.
2   Disability Discrimination Act 1995 s 1(1), Sch 1 para 2(2). For the purposes of Sch 1 para 2(2), the
     likelihood of an effect recurring may be disregarded in prescribed circumstances: Sch 1 para 2(3).
     'Prescribed' generally means prescribed by regulations: see para 515 note 5 ante. See the Disability
     Discrimination (Meaning of Disability) Regulations 1996, SI 1996/1455.
        For it to be established that an illness is likely to recur, it must be shown that it is more probable than
     not that it will: see *Latchman v Reed Business Information Ltd* [2002] ICR 1453, EAT. In the case of a
     clinically well-recognised mental illness, the question for the tribunal is whether the substantial adverse
     effect is likely to recur, not whether the mental illness itself is likely to recur: see *Swift v Chief Constable
     of Wiltshire Constabulary* [2004] ICR 909, [2004] All ER (D) 299 (Feb), [2004] IRLR 540, EAT;
     Crossingham v European Wellcare Lifestyles Ltd [2006] All ER (D) 279 (Oct), EAT. However, see para 514
     ante.
3   *Guidance on matters to be taken into account in determining questions relating to the definition of disability*
     (29 March 2006) Pt 2 para C4. As to the guidance see para 512 ante.
4   See the Disability Discrimination Act 1995 Sch 1 para 6(1); and para 516 ante.

D. ADVERSE EFFECT

520. Normal day-to-day activities. It is necessary to show that the impairment has an adverse effect upon activities that are: (1) normal; and (2) day-to-day[1]. The fact that a person can carry out day-to-day activities does not mean that his ability to carry them out has not been impaired[2]. A normal activity is one which is normal for the majority of people[3]. An impairment is to be taken to affect the ability of the person concerned to carry out normal day-to-day activities only if it affects one of the following[4]: (a) mobility[5]; (b) manual dexterity[6]; (c) physical co-ordination[7]; (d) continence[8]; (e) ability to lift, carry or otherwise move everyday objects[9]; (f) speech, hearing or eyesight[10]; (g) memory or ability to concentrate, learn or understand[11]; or (h) perception of the risk of physical danger[12].

A realistic approach must be taken to determine whether or not activities are affected: it is not only circumstances where the activity is impossible or not feasible, but also where it is not reasonable in practice to expect an activity to be performed[13]. The effect of a disability on a person's ability to conduct his daily life may have a cumulative effect, in the sense that more than one of the capacities have been impaired[14].

1   See the Disability Discrimination Act 1995 s 1(1). It is not for a doctor to express an opinion as to what is a normal day-to-day activity or what is a substantial adverse effect; that is a matter for the tribunal to consider using basic common sense: *Vicary v British Telecommunications plc* [1999] IRLR 680, EAT.

2   *Goodwin v Patent Office* [1999] ICR 302, [1999] IRLR 4, EAT. As to physical impairment see para 513 ante; and as to mental impairment see para 514 ante.

     While an overall assessment must be made of whether the adverse effect of an impairment on an activity or a capacity is substantial, it is necessary to concentrate on what a person cannot do or can only do with difficulty, rather than on the things that he can do: *Leonard v Southern Derbyshire Chamber of Commerce* [2001] IRLR 19, EAT.

3   'Normal' does not include work of any particular form, because no particular form of work is normal for most people: *Guidance on matters to be taken into account in determining questions relating to the definition of disability* (29 March 2006) Pt 2 para D4 et seq. As to the guidance see para 512 ante.

     What is a normal activity is to be addressed without regard to whether it is normal to the person concerned: *Abadeh v British Telecommunications plc* [2001] ICR 156, [2001] IRLR 23, EAT (the question is whether a person's inability to use such normal forms of public transport as the Underground or aeroplanes amounts to an impairment having a substantial and long-term adverse effect). Where the activity in question is a specialised one undertaken in the course of a person's work, it should be considered to be a normal activity: *Cruickshank v Vaw Motorcast Ltd* [2002] ICR 729, [2002] IRLR 24, EAT. Where an activity is limited to one particular social group, it must not be dismissed as not qualifying as a normal activity where it is undertaken by the majority of the group: *Ekpe v Metropolitan Police Comr* [2001] ICR 1084, [2001] IRLR 605, EAT (application of make-up normal activity for the purposes of the Disability Discrimination Act 1995).

4   Disability Discrimination Act 1995 s 1(1), Sch 1 para 4(1). Regulations may prescribe: (1) circumstances in which an impairment which does not have an effect falling within Sch 1 para 4(1) (see heads (a)–(h) in the text) is to be taken to affect the ability of the person concerned to carry out normal day-to-day activities; and (2) circumstances in which an impairment which has such an effect is to be taken not to affect the ability of the person concerned to carry out normal day-to-day activities: Sch 1 para 4(2). For the meaning of 'regulations' see para 509 note 12 ante. 'Prescribe' generally means prescribe by regulations: see para 515 note 5 ante. As to the making of regulations see para 523 post. See the Disability Discrimination (Meaning of Disability) Regulations 1996, SI 1996/1455.

5   Disability Discrimination Act 1995 Sch 1 para 4(1)(a). Mobility is moving or changing position in a wide sense: *Guidance on matters to be taken into account in determining questions relating to the definition of disability* (29 March 2006) Pt 2 para D20.

     An impairment has no substantial adverse effect on mobility if the applicant chooses not to socialise: *Ashton v Chief Constable of West Mercia Constabulary* [2001] ICR 67, EAT.

6   Disability Discrimination Act 1995 Sch 1 para 4(1)(b). Manual dexterity is the ability of a person to use his hands and fingers with precision: *Guidance on matters to be taken into account in determining questions relating to the definition of disability* (29 March 2006) Pt 2 para D21.

7   Disability Discrimination Act 1995 Sch 1 para 4(1)(c). Physical co-ordination includes balanced and effective interaction of body movement, including hand and eye co-ordination: see *Guidance on matters to be taken into account in determining questions relating to the definition of disability* (29 March 2006) Pt 2 para D22.

8   Disability Discrimination Act 1995 Sch 1 para 4(1)(d). Continence is the ability to control urination or defecation: *Guidance on matters to be taken into account in determining questions relating to the definition of disability* (29 March 2006) Pt 2 para D23.

9   Disability Discrimination Act 1995 Sch 1 para 4(1)(e). The ability to lift, carry or otherwise move everyday objects includes the ability to repeat such functions or to bear weights over a reasonable period of time: *Guidance on matters to be taken into account in determining questions relating to the definition of disability* (29 March 2006) Pt 2 para D24.

10 Disability Discrimination Act 1995 Sch 1 para 4(1)(f). Speech, hearing or eyesight includes face to face, telephone and written communication: *Guidance on matters to be taken into account in determining questions relating to the definition of disability* (29 March 2006) Pt 2 para D25. Adverse impacts on the senses of smell or taste are not mentioned in the Disability Discrimination Act 1995 or in the *Guidance on matters to be taken into account in determining questions relating to the definition of disability* (29 March 2006).

11 Disability Discrimination Act 1995 Sch 1 para 4(1)(g). Memory or ability to concentrate, learn or understand is the ability to remember, organise thoughts, plan a course of action and carry it out, take in new knowledge or understand spoken or written instructions: *Guidance on matters to be taken into account in determining questions relating to the definition of disability* (29 March 2006) Pt 2 para D26.

    A person who has difficulty in understanding normal social interaction and/or the subtleties of human non-factual communication can be regarded as having his understanding affected: *Hewett v Motorola Ltd* [2004] IRLR 545, EAT (complainant suffered Asperger's syndrome).

12 Disability Discrimination Act 1995 Sch 1 para 4(1)(h). The perception of the risk of physical danger includes both the underestimation and overestimation of physical danger, including danger to well-being: *Guidance on matters to be taken into account in determining questions relating to the definition of disability* (29 March 2006) Pt 2 para D27.

13 See *Guidance on matters to be taken into account in determining questions relating to the definition of disability* (29 March 2006) Pt 2 paras D4–D6.

14 *Goodwin v Patent Office* [1999] ICR 302 at 309, [1999] IRLR 4 at 7, EAT, per Morison J; *Guidance on matters to be taken into account in determining questions relating to the definition of disability* (29 March 2006) Pt 2 para B4 et seq.

(iii) Other Matters

521.   Deemed disability.   In certain circumstances a person is deemed to be disabled where he was formerly a holder of a green card under the Disabled Persons (Employment) Act 1944[1]. A certificate of registration is conclusive evidence, in relation to the person with respect to whom it was issued, of the matters certified[2].

1   Any person whose name, both on 12 January 1995 and on 2 December 1996 (i e the date when the Disability Discrimination Act 1995 s 1(1), Sch 1 para 7 came into force), is in the register of disabled persons maintained under the Disabled Persons (Employment) Act 1944 s 6 (repealed) (see EMPLOYMENT) is deemed: (1) during the initial period, to have a disability, and hence to be a disabled person; and (2) afterwards, to have had a disability and hence to have been a disabled person during that period: Disability Discrimination Act 1995 Sch 1 para 7(1), (2). 'Initial period' means the period of three years beginning on 2 December 1996: see Sch 1 para 7(7).

2   Ibid Sch 1 para 7(3). 'Certificate of registration' means a certificate issued under regulations made under the Disabled Persons (Employment) Act 1944 s 6 (repealed): Disability Discrimination Act 1995 Sch 1 para 7(7). Unless the contrary is shown, any document purporting to be a certificate of registration is to be taken to be such a certificate and to have been validly issued: Sch 1 para 7(4). Regulations may provide for prescribed descriptions of person to be deemed to have disabilities, and hence to be disabled persons, for the purposes of the Disability Discrimination Act 1995: Sch 1 para 7(5). For the meaning of 'regulations' see para 509 note 12 ante. 'Prescribed' generally means prescribed by regulations: see para 515 note 5 ante. As to the making of regulations see para 523 post. The generality of Sch 1 para 7(5) must not be taken to be prejudiced by the other provisions of Sch 1 (as amended): Sch 1 para 7(5A) (added by the Disability Discrimination Act 2005 s 18(1), (4)). Regulations may also prescribe circumstances in which a person who has been so deemed to be a disabled person is to be treated as no longer being deemed to be such a person: Sch 1 para 7(6). See the Disability Discrimination (Blind and Partially Sighted Persons) Regulations 2003, SI 2003/712. A person is deemed to have a disability, and hence to be a disabled person, for the purposes of the Disability Discrimination Act 1995 where: (1) he is certified as blind or partially sighted by a consultant ophthalmologist in accordance with the relevant guidance; or (2) he is a registered person: Disability Discrimination (Blind and Partially Sighted Persons) Regulations 2003, SI 2003/712, reg 3. In the case of a person mentioned in head (1) supra, a certificate signed by a consultant ophthalmologist is conclusive evidence of the matters certified in relation to the person with respect to whom it was issued; and in the case of a person mentioned in head (2) supra, a

certificate issued by or on behalf of a local authority stating that he is a registered person is conclusive evidence of the matters certified in relation to the person with respect to whom it was issued: reg 4(1). Unless the contrary is shown, any document purporting to be such a certificate is to be taken to have been validly issued: reg 4(2).

522. Past disability. A person who has previously had a disability can bring a claim under the provisions of the Disability Discrimination Act 1995 relating to employment and to goods, facilities, services and premises[1]. The time when the person suffered from the disability may be at a time before the commencement of the Act, but the act of discrimination must itself come after the commencement of the relevant provisions[2]. A claimant must adduce evidence to show that the physical or mental impairment from which he has recovered had, at the time, a substantial and long-term adverse effect on his ability to carry out normal day-to-day activities.

Any regulations or order made under the Act[3] may include provision with respect to persons who have had a disability[4].

1   The provisions of the Disability Discrimination Act 1995 Pt I (ss 1–3) (as amended), Pt II (ss 3A–18E) (as amended; prospectively amended), Pt III (ss 19–28) (as amended; prospectively amended), Pt IV (ss 28A–31C) (as amended; prospectively amended) and Pt VA (ss 49A–49F) (as added and amended; prospectively amended) apply in relation to a person who has had a disability as they apply in relation to a person who has that disability: s 2(1) (amended by the Special Educational Needs and Disability Act 2001 s 38(1), (2)(a); and the Disability Discrimination Act 2005 s 19(1), Sch 1 paras 1, 2(1), (2)). In such cases, those provisions are subject to the following modifications:

   (1) references in the Disability Discrimination Act 1995 Pts II–IV (as amended; prospectively amended) and Pt VA (as added and amended; prospectively amended) to a disabled person are to be read as references to a person who has had a disability (s 2(2), Sch 2 para 2 (amended by the Special Educational Needs and Disability Act 2001 s 38(1), (11); and the Disability Discrimination Act 2005 s 19(1), Sch 1 paras 1, 37(1), (2)));

   (2) amendments are made to the Disability Discrimination Act 1995 s 4A(1), (3)(b) (as added) (see para 532 post), s 4B(4) (as added) and s 4E(1), (3)(b) (as added) (see para 540 post), s 4H(1), (3)(b) (as added) (see para 557 post), s 6B(1), (3)(b) (as added) (see para 545 post), s 7B(1), (4)(b) (as added) (see para 548 post), s 14(1), (3)(b) (as substituted) (see para 542 post), s 14B(1), (3)(b) (as added) (see para 550 post), s 14D(1), (3)(b) (as added) (see para 550 post), s 16A(4), (6) (as added) (see para 536 post), s 21A(4)(a) (as added) (see para 585 post) (see Sch 2 paras 3, 4 (substituted by the Disability Discrimination Act 1995 (Amendment) Regulations 2003, SI 2003/1673, reg 3(1), 29(1)(b), (c); and amended by the Disability Discrimination Act 2005 Sch 1 paras 1, 37(1), (4)(a), (5)(a); and the Disability Discrimination Act 1995 (Pensions) Regulations 2003, SI 2003/2770, regs 2, 4(4)(a), (b), (5)(a)));

   (3) the Disability Discrimination Act 1995 Sch 1 para 2(1)–(3) (see paras 518–519 ante) is substituted so as to provide: (1) the effect of an impairment is a long-term effect if it has lasted for at least 12 months; (2) where an impairment ceases to have a substantial adverse effect on a person's ability to carry out normal day-to-day activities, it is to be treated as continuing to have that effect if that effect recurs; (3) for these purposes the recurrence of an effect is to be disregarded in prescribed circumstances (see Sch 2 para 5);

   (4) references in Pt IV Ch I (ss 28A–28Q) (as added and amended) (see para 561 et seq post) to a disabled pupil are to be read as references to a pupil who has had a disability (Sch 2 para 2A (Sch 2 paras 2A, 2B added by the Special Educational Needs and Disability Act 2001 s 38(1), (12)));

   (5) references in the Disability Discrimination Act 1995 Pt IV Ch II (ss 28R–31A) (as added and amended) (see para 569 et seq post) to a disabled student are to be read as references to a student who has had a disability (Sch 2 para 2B (as so added));

   (6) an amendment is made to s 3A(5) (as added) (see para 531 post) so as to refer to a person not having that particular disability and who has not had that particular disability (Sch 2 para 2C (added by the Disability Discrimination Act 1995 (Amendment) Regulations 2003, SI 2003/1673, regs 3(1), 29(1)(a)));

   (7) amendments are made to the Disability Discrimination Act 1995 s 24(3)(e)(i), (f)(i) (as added) (see para 599 post), s 24D(2)(a) (as added) (see para 605 post), s 24J(3)(b) (as added) (see para 608 post), s 28B(3)(a), (4) (as added) (see paras 562–563 post), s 28C(1)(a), (b) (as added) (see para 563 post), s 28S(3)(a) (as added) and s 28S(6)(a), (10) (as added and substituted) (see para 570 post), s 28T(1) (as added and substituted) and s 28T(1A), (1B), (1C), (1D) (as added) (see para 571 post) (see Sch 2 paras 4ZA–4E (Sch 2 paras 4ZA, ZB added by the Disability Discrimination Act 2005

Sch 1 paras 1, 37(1), (6); and the Disability Discrimination Act 1995 Sch 2 paras 4A–4E added by the Special Educational Needs and Disability Act 2001 s 38(1), (13); and amended by the Disability Discrimination Act 1995 (Amendment) Further and Higher Education) Regulations 2006, SI 2006/1721, regs 4(1), 18)).

As from a day to be appointed, references are added in head (2) supra to the Disability Discrimination Act 1995 s 31AD (1)(d), (2)(c), (3), (4)(b) (prospectively added) (see para 580 post) (see Sch 2 paras 3, 4 (as so substituted and amended; prospectively amended by the Disability Discrimination Act 2005 Sch 1 paras 1, 37(1), (4)(b), (5)(b))); and references are added in head (6) supra to the Disability Discrimination Act 1995 s 31AB(8) (prospectively added) (see para 579 post) (Sch 2 para 2C (as so added; prospectively amended by the Disability Discrimination Act 2005 Sch 1 paras 1, 37(1), (3))). At the date at which this volume states the law no such day had been appointed.

See also *Greenwood v British Airways plc* [1999] ICR 969, [1999] IRLR 600, EAT.

2   In any proceedings under the Disability Discrimination Act 1995 Pt II (as amended; prospectively amended), Pt III (as amended), Pt IV (as amended; prospectively amended) or Pt VA (as added and amended; prospectively amended), the question whether a person had a disability at the relevant time must be determined, for these purposes, as if the provisions of, or made under, the Disability Discrimination Act 1995 in force when the act complained of was done had been in force at the relevant time: s 2(4) (amended by the Special Educational Needs and Disability Act 2001 s 38(11), (2)(b); and the Disability Discrimination Act 2005 Sch 1 paras 1, 2(1), (4)). The relevant time may be a time before the passing of the Disability Discrimination Act 1995 (ie before 8 November 1995): s 2(5). As to the meaning of 'act' see para 510 note 3 ante.

3   Ie by the Secretary of State or the National Assembly for Wales: see para 302 ante. For the meaning of 'regulations' see para 509 note 12 ante. As to the making of regulations see para 523 post.

4   Disability Discrimination Act 1995 s 2(3) (amended by the Disability Discrimination Act 2005 Sch 1 paras 1, 2(1), (3)).

523. Conditions to be treated or not to be treated as impairments.

Regulations[1] may make provision, for the purposes of the Disability Discrimination Act 1995 for conditions of a prescribed[2] description to be treated as amounting to impairments[3] or for conditions of a prescribed description to be treated as not amounting to impairments[4].

Addiction to alcohol, nicotine or any other substance is to be treated as not amounting to an impairment for the purposes of the Disability Discrimination Act 1995[5]. The condition known as seasonal allergic rhinitis (hay fever) is also to be treated as not amounting to an impairment[6].

The following conditions are also to be treated as not amounting to impairments: (1) a tendency to set fires; (2) a tendency to steal; (3) a tendency to physical or sexual abuse of other persons; (4) exhibitionism; and (5) voyeurism[7].

1   For the meaning of 'regulations' see para 509 note 12 ante.

2   'Prescribed' generally means prescribed by regulations: see para 515 note 5 ante.

3   As to physical impairment see para 513 ante; and as to mental impairment see para 514 ante.

4   Disability Discrimination Act 1995 s 1(1), Sch 1 para 1(2). Regulations under Sch 1 para 1(2) may make provision as to the meaning of 'condition' for the purposes of those regulations: Sch 1 para 1(3). As to the regulations made under Sch 1 para 1(2) see the Disability Discrimination (Meaning of Disability) Regulations 1996, SI 1996/1455; and the text and notes 5–7 infra.

     A claimant may have both a legitimate impairment and an excluded condition: the critical question is one of causation (namely, what was the reason for the less favourable treatment?); accordingly if the reason was the legitimate impairment, then that is prima facie discrimination: *Edmund Nuttall Ltd v Butterfield* [2006] ICR 77, [2005] IRLR 751, EAT (disapproving the conclusion in *Murray v Newham Citizens Advice Bureau Ltd (No 2)* [2003] ICR 643, [2003] IRLR 340, EAT, that the conditions which may be prescribed were free-standing conditions, rather than conditions which were the direct consequences of a physical or mental impairment within the meaning of the Disability Discrimination Act 1995 s 1(1)).

5   Disability Discrimination (Meaning of Disability) Regulations 1996, SI 1996/1455, reg 3(1). This does not apply to addiction which was originally the result of administration of medically prescribed drugs or other medical treatment: reg 3(2). 'Addiction' includes a dependency: reg 2. Cf *Guidance on matters to be taken into account in determining questions relating to the definition of disability* (29 March 2006) Pt 1 para A8, which states that liver disease that is as a result of alcohol dependency is an impairment. As to the guidance generally see para 512 ante.

See *Power v Panasonic UK Ltd* [2003] IRLR 151, EAT (instead of focusing on whether the claimant's addiction to alcohol had caused the depression so as to bring the case within the Disability Discrimination (Meaning of Disability) Regulations 1996, SI 1996/1455, reg 3(1), the tribunal should have considered whether the depression had a substantial and long-term adverse effect on the claimant's ability to carry out normal activities).

6   Disability Discrimination (Meaning of Disability) Regulations 1996, SI 1996/1455, reg 4(2). This does not prevent that condition from being taken into account for the purposes of the Disability Discrimination Act 1995 where it aggravates the effect of another condition: Disability Discrimination (Meaning of Disability) Regulations 1996, SI 1996/1455, reg 4(3).   ·

7   Ibid reg 4(1).

524.   Young children.   Where a child under six years of age has an impairment[1] which does not have an adverse effect[2] that impairment is to be taken to have a substantial[3] and long-term[4] adverse effect on the ability of that child to carry out normal day-to-day activities[5] where it would normally have a substantial and long-term adverse effect on the ability of a person aged six years or over to carry out normal day-to-day activities[6].

1   As to physical impairment see para 513 ante; and as to mental impairment see para 514 ante.
2   Ie an effect falling within the Disability Discrimination Act 1995 s 1(1), Sch 1 para 4(1): see para 520 ante.
3   As to the meaning of 'substantial' see para 515 ante.
4   As to the meaning of 'long-term' see para 518 ante.
5   As to normal day-to-day activities see para 520 ante.
6   Disability Discrimination (Meaning of Disability) Regulations 1996, SI 1996/1455, reg 6.

(3)   PROHIBITION OF DISCRIMINATION

(i)   General Provisions

525.   Duty to make adjustments.   Employers[1], trade organisations[2] and service providers[3], persons or bodies responsible for appointing office-holders, firms (in relation to a position of partner), barristers and barrister's clerks, qualification bodies and providers of work experience placements[4], are all under various duties to make such adjustments as it is reasonable to make to prevent disabled persons[5] from being placed at a substantial disadvantage when compared to others. It is no longer possible to justify a failure to make an adjustment[6]. Where any provision, criterion or practice applied by or on behalf of an employer or trade organisation[7], or in regard to office-holders, partners, barristers, qualification bodies or practical work experience[8], or any physical feature of premises[9] occupied by the employer, trade organisation or other relevant body[10], place the disabled person concerned at a substantial disadvantage in comparison with persons who are not disabled[11], it is the duty of the employer, trade organisation or other relevant body to take such steps as it is reasonable, in all the circumstances of the case, for it to have to take in order to prevent the provision, criterion, practice or feature having that effect[12]. Where a service provider offers services to the public, it has a duty to take such steps as it is reasonable for it to take in all the circumstances of the case to change any practice, policy or procedure which makes it impossible or unreasonably difficult for disabled people to make use of services[13]; to provide a reasonable alternative method of making services available to disabled persons where a physical feature makes it impossible or unreasonably difficult for disabled persons to make use of them[14]; and to provide an auxiliary aid or service if it would enable (or make it easier for) disabled persons to make use of services[15].

1   As to employers see para 529 et seq post.
2   As to trade organisations see para 541 et seq post.
3   As to service providers see para 582 et seq post.

4 See paras 543–551 post.
5 For the meaning of 'disabled person' see para 511 ante.
6 It is in certain circumstances possible to justify less favourable treatment: see the Disability Discrimination Act 1995 s 3A(3) (as added); and para 530 post. However, treatment of a disabled person cannot be justified under s 3A(3) (as added) if it amounts to direct discrimination: see s 3A(4), (5) (as added); and para 531 post. In relation to services, there can be justification if the service provider believes that one or more of the relevant conditions are satisfied (see paras 588–589 post) and it is reasonable in all the circumstances of the case for that person to hold that opinion: s 20(3). See also para 535 post.
7 See ibid s 4A(1)(a) (as added), s 14(1)(a) (as substituted); and paras 532, 542 post.
8 See ibid s 4E(1)(a) (as added), s 6B(1)(a) (as added), s 7B(1)(a) (as added), s 14B(1)(a) (as added), s 14D(1)(a) (as added); and paras 543–551 post.
9 'Premises' includes land of any description: ibid s 68(1).
10 See ibid s 4A(1)(b) (as added), s 14(1)(b) (as substituted); and paras 532, 542 post. See also s 4E(1)(b) (as added), s 6B(1)(b) (as added), s 7B(1)(b) (as added), s 14B(1)(b) (as added), s 14D(1)(b) (as added); and paras 543–551 post.
11 In relation to past disabilities, the comparison is to be made with people who are not disabled and have not had a disability: see ibid s 2(2), Sch 2 para 3 (as amended); and para 522 ante.
12 See ibid s 4A(1) (as added), s 14(1) (as substituted); and paras 532, 542 post. See also s 4E(1) (as added), s 6B(1) (as added), s 7B(1) (as added), s 14B(1) (as added), s 14D(1) (as added); and paras 543–551 post.
   See _Fu v Camden London Borough Council_ [2001] IRLR 186, [2001] All ER (D) 222 (Jan), EAT. See also _Farmiloe v Lane Group plc_ [2004] All ER (D) 08 (Mar), EAT (an employer, who attempted to find alternative equipment or employment for a disabled employee who could wear personal protective equipment provided, discharged the duty to make reasonable adjustments).
   As to the matters to be considered in determining whether it is reasonable for an employer, a trade organisation or other body to have to take a particular step in order to comply with these requirements see the Disability Discrimination Act 1995 s 18B(1) (as added); and para 532 post.
13 See ibid s 21(1); and para 587 post. As to transport vehicles see s 21ZA (as added); and para 587 post.
14 See ibid s 21(2); and para 587 post. See note 13 supra.
15 See ibid s 21(4); and para 587 post. See note 13 supra.

526. Discrimination by way of victimisation. For the purposes of the provisions of the Disability Discrimination Act 1995 relating to employment and members of locally-electable authorities[1], the provision of goods, facilities, services and premises[2], and education[3], a person ('A') discriminates against another person ('B')[4] if he treats B less favourably than he treats or would treat other persons whose circumstances are the same as B's[5], and he does so for one of the following reasons[6]:

(1) B has: (a) brought proceedings against A or any other person under the Disability Discrimination Act 1995[7]; (b) given evidence or information in connection with such proceedings brought by any person[8]; (c) otherwise done anything under, or by reference to, that Act in relation to A or any other person[9]; or (d) alleged that A or any other person has (whether or not the allegation so states) contravened that Act[10]; or

(2) A believes or suspects that B has done or intends to do any of those things[11].

In the case of an act[12] which constitutes discrimination by virtue of the provision set out above[13], certain provisions of the Disability Discrimination Act 1995[14] also apply to discrimination against a person who is not disabled[15].

1 Ie the Disability Discrimination Act 1995 Pt II (ss 3A–18E) (as amended; prospectively amended): see para 529 et seq post.
2 Ie ibid Pt III (ss 19–28) (as amended; prospectively amended), other than ss 24A–24L (as added and amended): see para 582 et seq post. As to the meaning of 'premises' see para 525 note 9 ante.
3 Ie ibid Pt IV (ss 28A–31C) (as amended; prospectively amended): see para 561 et seq post.
4 Ibid s 55(1) (amended by the Special Educational Needs and Disability Act 2001 s 38(1), (7); and the Disability Discrimination Act 2005 s 19(1), Sch 1 paras 1, 29(1), (2)).
   As to victimisation under the Sex Discrimination Act 1975 see para 358 ante; and as to victimisation under the Race Relations Act 1976 see para 442 ante.
5 Disability Discrimination Act 1995 s 55(1)(a). Where B is a disabled person, or a person who has had a disability, the disability in question must be disregarded in comparing his circumstances with those of any other person for the purposes of s 55(1)(a): s 55(3). Section 55(1) (as amended) does not apply to

treatment of a person because of an allegation made by him if the allegation was false and not made in good faith: s 55(4). For the meaning of 'disabled person' see para 511 ante. As to when a person has a disability see para 511 ante. Treatment should be compared with the treatment which the employer has meted out or would mete out to persons who have not done the relevant protected act; the relevant circumstances do not include the fact that the complainant has done a protected act: *Aziz v Trinity Street Taxis Ltd* [1989] QB 463, [1988] ICR 534, CA; c f *Kirby v Manpower Services Commission* [1980] 3 All ER 334, [1980] IRLR 229, EAT.

6　　Disability Discrimination Act 1995 s 55(1)(b). See note 5 supra.
7　　Ibid s 55(2)(a)(i). For the purposes of Pt IV Ch I (ss 28A–28Q) (as added and amended) (see para 561 et seq post): (1) references in s 55(2) (as amended) to B include references to: (a) a person who is, for the purposes of Pt IV Ch I (as added and amended), B's parent; and (b) a sibling of B; and (2) references in s 55(2) (as amended) are, as respects a person mentioned head (1)(a) or (1)(b) supra, restricted to Pt IV Ch I (as added and amended): s 55(3A) (added by the Special Educational Needs and Disability Act 2001 s 38(1), (8)).
8　　Disability Discrimination Act 1995 s 55(2)(a)(ii). See note 7 supra.
9　　Ibid s 55(2)(a)(iii) (amended by the Disability Discrimination Act 2005 s 19(1), Sch 1 paras 1, 29(1), (3)). See note 7 supra.
10　Disability Discrimination Act 1995 s 55(2)(a)(iv). See note 7 supra.
11　Ibid s 55(2)(b). See note 7 supra.
12　As to the meaning of 'act' see para 510 note 3 ante.
13　Ie by virtue of the Disability Discrimination Act 1995 s 55 (as amended).
14　Ie ibid s 4 (as substituted) (see para 534 post), s 4B (as added) (see para 540 post), s 4D (as added) (see para 543 post), s 4G (as added) (see para 556 post), s 6A (as added) (see para 545 post), s 7A (as added) (see para 547 post), s 13 (as substituted) (see para 541 post), s 14A (as added) (see para 549 post), s 14C (as added) (see para 551 post), s 15B (as added) (see para 558 post) and s 16A (as added and amended) (see para 536 post).
15　Ibid s 55(5) (added by the Disability Discrimination Act 1995 (Amendment) Regulations 2003, SI 2003/1673, regs 3(1), 21; and amended by the Disability Discrimination Act 1995 (Pensions) Regulations 2003, SI 2003/2770, regs 2, 4(3); and the Disability Discrimination Act 2005 Sch 1 paras 1, 29(1), (4)).

527.　Liability of employers and principals.　Anything done by a person in the course of his employment[1] is to be treated for the purposes of the Disability Discrimination Act 1995 as also done by his employer, whether or not it was done with the employer's knowledge or approval[2].

Anything done by a person as agent for another person[3] with the authority of that other person is to be treated for the purposes of the Disability Discrimination Act 1995 as also done by that other person[4].

In proceedings under the Disability Discrimination Act 1995 against any person in respect of an act alleged to have been done by an employee of his, it is a defence for that person to prove that he took such steps as were reasonably practicable to prevent the employee[5] from doing that act[6], or doing, in the course of his employment, acts of that description[7].

1　　As to discrimination in the employment field see para 529 et seq post. The words 'course of employment' are not to be construed in any sense more limited than their everyday natural meaning and are not confined to the tortious sense: *Jones v Tower Boot Co Ltd* [1997] 2 All ER 406, [1997] ICR 254, CA; *Waters v Metropolitan Police Comr* [1997] ICR 1073, [1997] IRLR 589, CA (revsd in part [2000] 4 All ER 934, [2000] ICR 1064, HL). See also *Irving v Post Office* [1987] IRLR 289, CA. As to vicarious liability generally see TORT vol 45(2) (Reissue) para 801 et seq.
2　　Disability Discrimination Act 1995 s 58(1). The provisions of s 58(1), (2) do not apply in relation to an offence under s 57(4) (see para 528 post): s 58(4).
3　　As to the meaning of 'person' see para 344 note 3 ante.
4　　Disability Discrimination Act 1995 s 58(2). See also note 2 supra. Section 58(2) applies whether the authority was express or implied or given before or after the act in question was done: s 58(3). As to the meaning of 'act' see para 510 note 3 ante.
5　　Ibid s 58(5).
6　　Ibid s 58(5)(a). This provision provides a defence for an employer who has taken, in advance of the alleged discriminatory treatment, all reasonable and practicable steps to prevent discrimination from occurring: *Martins v Marks & Spencer plc* [1998] ICR 1005, [1998] IRLR 326, CA. The burden of proof

is on the alleged discriminator to establish his defence and it will be a question of fact in every case for the court or tribunal whether the employer has taken such steps as were reasonably practicable to prevent the discrimination. In unusual circumstances an employer or principal may be able to discharge the onus of proving the defence is made out if there are no practical steps which it can take: *Balgobin v Tower Hamlets London Borough Council* [1987] ICR 829, [1987] IRLR 401, EAT. As to the burden of proof generally in discrimination legislation see also *Wong v Igen Ltd (Equal Opportunities Commission and others intervening), Emokpae v Chamberlin Solicitors (Equal Opportunities Commission and others intervening), Webster v Brunel University (Equal Opportunities Commission and others intervening)* [2005] EWCA Civ 142, [2005] 3 All ER 812, [2005] ICR 931; and paras 418, 504 ante. See also para 643 post.

The employee remains liable for aiding even if his employer has a good defence that it tried to prevent the discrimination: *Read v Tiverton District Council* [1977] IRLR 202, IT. It is a matter for the discretion of the court or tribunal whether an award ought to be made against an individual as well as his employer: *HM Prison Service v Johnson* [1997] ICR 275, sub nom *Armitage, Marsden and HM Prison Service v Johnson* [1997] IRLR 162, EAT.

7 Disability Discrimination Act 1995 s 58(5)(b).

528. Aiding discrimination. A person who knowingly aids another person[1] to do an unlawful act[2] of unlawful discrimination[3] is to be treated as himself doing the same kind of unlawful act[4].

A person does not knowingly aid another to do an unlawful act[5] if: (1) he acts in reliance on a statement made to him by that other person that, because of any provision of the Disability Discrimination Act 1995, the act would not be unlawful[6]; and (2) it is reasonable for him to rely on the statement[7].

A person who knowingly or recklessly makes such a statement which is false or misleading in a material respect is guilty of an offence[8].

1 As to the meaning of 'person' see para 344 note 3 ante.
2 'Unlawful act' means an act made unlawful by any provision of the Disability Discrimination Act 1995 other than a provision contained in Pt IV Ch I (ss 28A–28Q) (as added and amended) (see para 561 et seq post): s 57(6) (added by the Special Educational Needs and Disability Act 2001 s 38(1), (10)). As to the meaning of 'act' see para 510 note 3 ante.
3 Ie an act made unlawful by the Disability Discrimination Act 1995.
4 Ibid s 57(1) (amended by the Special Educational Needs and Disability Act 2001 s 38(1), (9)). An employee or agent for whose act the employer or principal is liable under the Disability Discrimination Act 1995 s 58 (or would be so liable but for s 58(5)) (see para 527 ante) is to be taken to have aided the employer or principal to do the act: s 57(2).
5 Ibid s 57(3).
6 Ibid s 57(3)(a).
7 Ibid s 57(3)(b).
8 Ibid s 57(4). Any person guilty of such an offence is liable on summary conviction to a fine not exceeding level 5 on the standard scale: s 57(5). As to the standard scale see para 315 note 15 ante. Section 57(4) does not apply to employers and principals: see s 58(4); and para 527 ante.

(ii) Discrimination in Particular Circumstances

A. DISCRIMINATION IN THE EMPLOYMENT FIELD AND IN REGARD TO MEMBERS OF LOCALLY-ELECTABLE AUTHORITIES

(A) In general

529. Employees and applicants for employment. The Disability Discrimination Act 1995 applies to disabled persons[1] who are employed[2] at an establishment in Great Britain[3]. The status of a worker is mainly a question of fact (except where the status depends solely on the construction of contractual documentation) and depends on the context[4]. One necessary element is that the work is done personally[5], but all the factors in each particular case must be weighed up to decide whether a person is an employee[6]. It is also unlawful to discriminate against a disabled person who is an applicant for employment[7]. Employers must not discriminate in the arrangements which they make to choose between candidates for employment, in the terms of the contract of employment on offer or by refusing to offer, or deliberately not offering, employment to the disabled person[8].

1   For the meaning of 'disabled person' see para 511 ante.

2   'Employment' means, subject to any prescribed provision, employment under a contract of service or of apprenticeship or a contract personally to do any work; and related expressions (including 'employee' and 'employer') are to be construed accordingly: Disability Discrimination Act 1995 s 68(1). 'Prescribed' generally means prescribed by regulations: see para 515 note 5 ante. For the purposes of Pt II (ss 3A–18E) (as amended; prospectively amended), 'employer' includes a person who has no employees but is seeking to employ another person: Disability Discrimination Act 1995 s 18D(2) (s 18D added by the Disability Discrimination Act 1995 (Amendment) Regulations 2003, SI 2003/1673, regs 3(1), 18). The Disability Discrimination Act 1995 Pt II (as amended; prospectively amended) now extends to discrimination by persons in the employment field other than employers: see paras 532, 543 et seq post. See also paras 540–542 post.

    The definition includes an independent contractor as long as the work must be done personally by the person concerned: *Sheehan v Post Office Counters Ltd* [1999] ICR 734, EAT (the work which the person is obliged to do personally must be the dominant purpose of the contract). See also *Quinnen v Hovells* [1984] ICR 525, [1984] IRLR 227, EAT; *Gunning v Mirror Group Newspapers* [1986] 1 All ER 385, sub nom *Mirror Group Newspapers Ltd v Gunning* [1986] 1 WLR 546, CA; *Tanna v Post Office* [1981] ICR 374, EAT. The definition of employment is wide enough to cover the provision of services by a professional and may even extend to a company or firm: *Loughran and Kelly v Northern Ireland Housing Executive* [1998] ICR 828, [1998] IRLR 593, HL. A university research fellow is a 'person employed': *Hugh-Jones v St John's College Cambridge* [1979] ICR 848, 123 Sol Jo 603, EAT. A general practitioner is not employed by a health services authority: *Ealing, Hammersmith and Hounslow Family Health Services Authority v Shukla* [1993] ICR 710, EAT; but see *Roy v Kensington and Chelsea and Westminster Family Practitioner Committee* [1992] 1 AC 624, [1992] 1 All ER 705, HL.

    The present tense used in the definition of 'employment' in the Disability Discrimination Act 1995 tended to suggest that, as with the Race Relations Act 1976, an ex-employee cannot claim discrimination: see *Post Office v Adekeye* [1997] ICR 110, sub nom *Adekeye v Post Office (No 2)* [1997] IRLR 105, CA. However, this case has been overruled, and it seems now that an ex-employee can claim discrimination: see *Relaxion Group plc v Rhys-Harper, D'Souza v Lambert London Borough Council, Jones v 3M Healthcare Ltd, Kirker v British Sugar plc, Angel v New Possibilities NHS Trust, Bond v Hackney Citizens Advice Bureau* [2003] UKHL 33, [2003] 4 All ER 1113, [2003] IRLR 484. See *Nagarajan v London Underground Ltd* [1995] ICR 520, sub nom *Nagarajan v Agnew* [1994] IRLR 61, EAT; *J Sainsbury Ltd v Savage* [1981] ICR 1, sub nom *Savage v J Sainsbury Ltd* [1980] IRLR 109, CA. See also *Bull v Harrods* (6 July 1999) Lexis; *Coote v Granada Hospitality Ltd (No 2)* [1999] ICR 942, [1999] IRLR 452, EAT (following Case C-185/97 *Coote v Granada Hospitality Ltd* [1998] All ER (EC) 865, [1999] ICR 100, ECJ). As to the status of a volunteer see *South East Sheffield Citizens Advice Bureau v Grayson* [2004] ICR 1138, [2004] IRLR 353, EAT.

    The meaning of 'employer' has been modified by the Education (Modification of Enactments Relating to Employment) (England) Order 2003, SI 2003/1964, art 3, Schedule, which provides that any references to an employer (however expressed) include references to the governing body of a school exercising employment powers. The modification is the result of the delegation of financial management and powers to appoint staff to governing bodies of grant-maintained schools.

3   Disability Discrimination Act 1995 s 4(6) (s 4 substituted by the Disability Discrimination Act 1995 (Amendment) Regulations 2003, SI 2003/1673, regs 3(1), (5)).

    Employment (including employment on board a ship to which the Disability Discrimination Act 1995 s 68(2B) (as added) applies or on an aircraft or hovercraft to which s 68(2C) (as added) applies) is to be regarded as being employment at an establishment in Great Britain if the employee: (1) does his work wholly or partly in Great Britain; or (2) does his work wholly outside Great Britain and s 68(2A) (as added) applies: s 68(2) (s 68(2) substituted, and s 68(2A)–(2D) added, by the Disability Discrimination Act 1995 (Amendment) Regulations 2003, SI 2003/1673, regs 3(1), 27(b)). The Disability Discrimination Act 1995 s 68(2A) (as added) applies if: (a) the employer has a place of business at an establishment in Great Britain; (b) the work is for the purposes of the business carried on at the establishment; and (c) the employee is ordinarily resident in Great Britain at the time when he applies for or is offered the employment, or at any time during the course of the employment: s 68(2A) (as so added). Section 68(2B) (as added) applies to a ship if: (i) it is registered at a port of registry in Great Britain; or (ii) it belongs to or is possessed by Her Majesty in right of the government of the United Kingdom: s 68(2B) (as so added). Section 68(2C) (as added) applies to an aircraft or hovercraft if: (A) it is registered in the United Kingdom, and operated by a person who has his principal place of business, or is ordinarily resident, in Great Britain; or (B) it belongs to or is possessed by Her Majesty in right of the government of the United Kingdom: s 68(2C) (as so added). The following are not to be regarded as being employment at an establishment in Great Britain: (aa) employment on board a ship to which s 68(2B) (as added) does not apply; (bb) employment on an aircraft or hovercraft to which s 68(2C) (as added) does not apply: s 68(2D) (as so added). For the meanings of 'Great Britain' and 'United Kingdom' see para 325 note 6 ante. For the purposes of determining if employment concerned with the exploration of the sea bed or subsoil or the exploitation of their natural resources is outside Great Britain, the provisions of s 68(2)(a), (b) (as substituted) (see heads (1), (2) supra), s 68(2A), (2C) (as added) each have effect as if 'Great Britain' had the same meaning as that given to the last reference to Great Britain in the Sex Discrimination Act 1975 s 10(1) (as substituted) by s 10(5) (as amended) read with the Sex Discrimination and Equal Pay (Offshore Employment) Order 1987, SI 1987/930 (see para 360 note 6 ante): Disability Discrimination Act 1995 s 68(4A) (added by the Disability Discrimination Act 1995 (Amendment) Regulations 2003, SI 2003/1673, regs 3(1), 27(c)).

An establishment is construed in related contexts as a unit to which employees are assigned in order to carry out their duties, whether or not it is possessed of separate decision-making functions: Case C-449/93 *Rockfon A/S v Specialarbejdforforbundet i Danmark* [1996] ICR 673, [1996] IRLR 168, ECJ. Employment at an establishment is defined in the Disability Discrimination Act 1995 s 68(1) so that where an employee works 'wholly or mainly' outside Great Britain, his employment is not at an establishment in Great Britain even if he does some of his work at such an establishment: see *Wood v Cunard Line Ltd* [1991] ICR 13, [1990] IRLR 281, CA (on the meaning of 'wholly outside Great Britain' in a related provision in the Employment Rights Act 1996); cf *Royle v Globtik Management Ltd* [1977] ICR 552, EAT. This exclusion is arguably contrary to the Treaty Establishing the European Community (Rome, 25 March 1957; TS 1 (1973); Cmnd 5179) (the 'EC Treaty') art 39 (formerly art 48; renumbered by virtue of the Treaty of Amsterdam: see *Treaty Citation (No 2) (Note)* [1999] All ER (EC) 646, ECJ): *Bossa v Nordstress Ltd* [1998] ICR 694, [1998] IRLR 284, EAT. However, see now the Disability Discrimination Act 1995 s 68(2) (as substituted) and s 68(2A)–(2D) (as added).

Employment of a prescribed kind, or in prescribed circumstances, is to be regarded as not being employment at an establishment in Great Britain: s 68(1), (4). At the date at which this volume states the law no regulations had been made under this provision.

4   A worker may be an employee despite the fact that he is self-employed for tax purposes: *Airfix Footwear Ltd v Cope* [1978] ICR 1210, [1978] IRLR 396, EAT.

5   If a worker is entitled to send along a substitute to perform his duties in his place, that will usually take that person outside the protection of the Disability Discrimination Act 1995: *Ready-Mixed Concrete (South East) Ltd v Minister of Pensions and National Insurance* [1968] 2 QB 497, [1968] 1 All ER 433.

6   *Hall (Inspector of Taxes) v Lorimer* [1994] 1 All ER 250, [1994] ICR 218, CA. See also the 'organisational' test (see *Stevenson Jordan and Harrison Ltd v MacDonald and Evans* [1952] 1 TLR 101, 69 RPC 10, CA); and the 'economic reality' test (see *Lee Ting Sang v Chung Chi-Keung* [1990] 2 AC 374, [1990] ICR 409, PC).

7   See the Disability Discrimination Act 1995 s 4(1) (as substituted); and para 534 post. There is no statutory definition of 'applicants for employment' but it is submitted that it must include anyone who has learned that a post or position is available and has in some way communicated to the employer a desire to be considered for the role. The applicant does not strictly have to be someone who has applied for employment so it appears possible for a potential applicant to bring a complaint.

8   See ibid s 4(1) (as substituted); and para 534 post. Section 4(1) (as substituted) adopts the same wording and formulation of discriminatory practices used in the Sex Discrimination Act 1975 s 6(1) (see para 360 ante) and the Race Relations Act 1976 s 4(1) (see para 446 ante). See *Murray v Newham Citizens Advice Bureau* [2001] ICR 708, [2000] All ER (D) 1493, EAT (volunteer training programme capable of being 'arrangement' for purpose of determining to whom employment should be offered).

530.   Discrimination by less favourable treatment.   For the purposes of the provisions of the Disability Discrimination Act 1995 relating to employment and members of locally-electable authorities[1], a person[2] discriminates against a disabled person[3] if: (1) for a reason which relates to the disabled person's disability[4], he treats him less favourably than he treats or would treat other persons to whom that reason[5] does not or would not apply[6]; and (2) he cannot show that the treatment in question is justified[7].

Subject to the duty to make reasonable adjustments[8], nothing in those provisions[9] is to be taken to require a person to treat a disabled person more favourably than he treats or would treat others[10].

1   Ie the Disability Discrimination Act 1995 Pt II (ss 3A–18E) (as amended; prospectively amended).

        Part II (as amended; prospectively amended) does not apply in relation to the provision, otherwise than in the course of a Part II relationship, of premises by the regulated party to the other party: s 18E(1) (s 18E added by the Disability Discrimination Act 2005 s 19(1), Sch 1 paras 1, 12). For these purposes, 'Part II relationship' means a relationship during the course of which an act of discrimination against, or harassment of, one party to the relationship by the other party to it is unlawful under the Disability Discrimination Act 1995 ss 4–15C (as amended) (see paras 529 ante, 532 et seq post); and, in relation to a Part II relationship, 'regulated party' means the party whose acts of discrimination, or harassment, are made unlawful by ss 4–15C (as amended): s 18E(2) (as so added). For the meaning of 'harassment' see para 533 post. As to the meaning of 'premises' see para 525 note 9 ante.

2   As to the meaning of 'person' see para 344 note 3 ante. Note the change from the previous version of this provision (ie ibid s 5 (repealed)), which referred to 'employer'. This is because Pt II (as amended; prospectively amended) now extends to discrimination by persons in the employment field other than employers: see paras 532, 543 et seq post. See also paras 540–542 post.

3   Ibid s 3A(1) (s 3A added by the Disability Discrimination Act 1995 (Amendment) Regulations 2003, SI 2003/1673, regs 3(1), 4(2)). For the meaning of 'disabled person' see para 511 ante. See also para 535 post. As to victimisation generally see the Disability Discrimination Act 1995 s 55 (as amended); and para 526 ante.

4   As to when a person has a disability see para 511 ante. An employer must have some knowledge of the disability or its material features before he can discriminate: *O'Neill v Symm & Co Ltd* [1998] ICR 481, [1998] IRLR 233, EAT; disapproved in *HJ Heinz Co Ltd v Kenrick* [2000] ICR 491, [2000] IRLR 144, EAT (the expression may include a reason deriving from how the disability manifests itself even where there is no knowledge of the disability as such; however, knowledge of the disability or its absence may still be material to the test of justification. See *Hammersmith and Fulham London Borough Council v Farnsworth* [2000] IRLR 691, EAT (agent's actual knowledge of employee's disability imputed to employer).

There is no room for the interpretation that the treatment may relate to another person's disability (cf the Race Relations Act 1976 s 1(1): see para 439 et seq ante): *Showboat Entertainment Centre Ltd v Owens* [1984] 1 All ER 836, [1984] 1 WLR 384, EAT. However, it may be reasonable to draw inferences that the reason relates to disability in the same way as under the Race Relations Act 1976 s 1(1): see *King v Great Britain–China Centre* [1992] ICR 516, [1991] IRLR 513, CA.

5   'That reason' refers only to the facts constituting the reason for the treatment, and does not include the added requirement of a causal link with disability; that is more properly regarded as the cause of the reason for the treatment than as in itself a reason for the treatment: *Clark v TDG Ltd (t/a Novacold)* [1999] ICR 951 at 962, [1999] IRLR 318 at 321, CA, per Mummery LJ (decided in relation to an earlier version of the legislation). See also *British Sugar plc v Kirker* [1998] IRLR 624, EAT. See further *Rowden v Dutton Gregory (a firm)* [2002] ICR 971, EAT (tribunal could infer disability discrimination from employer's unsatisfactory explanation for employee's dismissal); *Murphy v Slough Borough Council* [2005] EWCA Civ 122, [2005] ICR 721, [2005] IRLR 382 (employee who suffered from heart disorder as a result of which pregnancy would endanger her life treated less favourably when denied paid post-natal leave to care for child by surrogate mother). Cf the narrower test under the Race Relations Act 1976 s 1(1) (see paras 439–440 ante) and the Sex Discrimination Act 1975 s 1(1) (as substituted) (see para 344 et seq ante) which is on the grounds of sex or racial grounds and which is an objective test of causal connection: *James v Eastleigh Borough Council* [1990] 2 AC 751, [1990] 2 All ER 607, HL. The basic question is what is the 'effective and predominant cause' or the 'real and efficient cause' of the treatment: *O'Neill v Governors of St Thomas More Roman Catholic Voluntarily Aided Upper School* [1997] ICR 33, [1996] IRLR 372, EAT (citing *Banque Bruxelles Lambert SA v Eagle Star Insurance Co Ltd* [1997] AC 191, HL). See also *Murphy v Sheffield Hallam University* (2000) 635 IRLB 14. It need not be the sole cause: *Owen and Briggs v James* [1982] ICR 618, [1982] IRLR 502, CA.

6   Disability Discrimination Act 1995 s 3A(1)(a) (as added: see note 3 supra). See also s 13 (as substituted) (see para 541 post), s 20(1) (see para 582 post), s 24(1) (as amended) (see para 599 post), s 28B (as added) (see paras 562–563 post), s 28S (as added and amended) (see para 570 post), s 31AB (as added) (see para 579 post). See also note 7 infra.

As to discrimination for failure to comply with a duty to make reasonable adjustments see s 3A(2) (as added); and para 532 post.

7   Ibid s 3A(1)(b) (as added: see note 3 supra). See also s 13 (as substituted) (see para 541 post), s 20(1) (see para 582 post), s 24(1) (as amended) (see para 599 post), s 28B (as added) (see paras 562–563 post), s 28S (as added and amended) (see para 569 post), s 31AB (as added) (see para 579 post). See also note 6 supra.

For these purposes, treatment is justified if, but only if, the reason for it is both material to the circumstances of the particular case and substantial: s 3A(3) (as so added). Treatment of a disabled person cannot be justified under s 3A(3) (as added) if it amounts to direct discrimination: see s 3A(4), (5) (as added); and para 531 post.

If, in a case falling within s 3A(1) (as added), a person is under a duty to make reasonable adjustments in relation to a disabled person but fails to comply with that duty, his treatment of that person cannot be justified under s 3A(3) (as added) unless it would have been justified even if he had complied with that duty: s 3A(6) (as so added). 'Duty to make reasonable adjustments' means a duty imposed by or under s 4A (as added) (see para 532 post), s 4B(5) or (6) (as added) (see para 540 post), s 4E (as added) (see para 544 post), s 4H (as added) (see para 557 post), s 6B (as added) (see para 546 post), s 7B (as added) (see para 548 post), s 14 (as substituted) (see para 542 post), s 14B (as added) (see para 550 post), s 14D (as added) (see para 552 post), s 15C (as added) (see para 559 post) or s 16A(5) (as added) (see para 536 post): s 18D(2) (s 18D added by the Disability Discrimination Act 1995 (Amendment) Regulations 2003, SI 2003/1673, regs 3(1), 18; definition amended by the Disability Discrimination Act 1995 (Pensions) Regulations 2003, SI 2003/1770, regs 2, 4(2)(b); and the Disability Discrimination Act 2005 s 19(1), Sch 1 paras 1, 11(a)).

The question whether treatment has been shown to be justified is a question of fact to be determined on a proper self direction on the relevant law, taking into account any relevant code of practice: *Clark v TDG (t/a Novacold)* [1999] ICR 951, [1999] IRLR 318, CA (decided in relation to an earlier version of the legislation). It is an objective test and the court or tribunal must decide whether the employer's failure to comply with his duty was in fact objectively justified, and whether the reason for failure to comply was in fact material to the circumstances of the particular case and in fact substantial: see *Morse v Wiltshire County Council* [1998] ICR 1023, [1998] IRLR 352, EAT (decided in relation to an earlier version of the provision). If an employer can show a reason for the treatment which relates to the individual circumstances in question and is not just trivial or minor then justification has to be held to exist (at least where there is no duty to make adjustments: see para 532 post): *HJ Heinz Co Ltd v Kenrick* [2000] ICR 491, [2000] IRLR 144, EAT. The relevant circumstances must include the circumstances of both the employer and the employee: *Baynton v Saurus General Engineers Ltd* [2000] ICR 375, [1999] IRLR 604, EAT. See also *Collins v Home Office* [2005] EWCA Civ 598, [2005] All ER (D) 300 (May) (employer had acted reasonably in the circumstances of prolonged absence); *McHugh v NCH Scotland* [2006] All ER (D) 242 (Dec), EAT (tribunal had erred in making no finding on justification) (cases relating to the Disability Discrimination Act 1995 s 5 (repealed)). See further *R (on the application of T) v Governing Body of OL Primary School* [2005] EWHC 753 (Admin), [2005] ELR 522, [2005] All ER (D) 213 (Apr). In relation to services (see the Disability Discrimination Act 1995 s 20(3)(b); and para 588 post), there is a two-stage test: (1) that the service provider believes that one or more of the relevant conditions are satisfied (the subjective test); and (2) that it is reasonable in all the circumstances of the case for that person to hold that opinion (the objective test): *Rose v Bouchet* [1999] IRLR 463, Sh Ct.

8   See note 7 supra.
9   Ie the Disability Discrimination Act 1995 Pt II (as amended; prospectively amended).
10   Ibid s 18D(1) (as added: see note 7 supra).

531.   Direct discrimination.   Treatment of a disabled person[1] cannot be justified under the Disability Discrimination Act 1995[2] if it amounts to direct discrimination[3]. For these purposes, a person[4] directly discriminates against a disabled person if, on the ground of the disabled person's disability[5], he treats the disabled person less favourably than he treats or would treat a person not having that particular disability whose relevant circumstances, including his abilities, are the same as, or not materially different from, those of the disabled person[6].

Subject to the duty to make reasonable adjustments[8], nothing in the provisions of the Disability Discrimination Act 1995 relating to employment and members of locally-electable authorities[9] is to be taken to require a person to treat a disabled person more favourably than he treats or would treat others[10].

1   For the meaning of 'disabled person' see para 511 ante.
2   Ie under the Disability Discrimination Act 1995 s 3A(3) (as added): see para 530 ante. See also para 535 post.
3   Ibid s 3A(4) (s 3A added by the Disability Discrimination Act 1995 (Amendment) Regulations 2003, SI 2003/1673, regs 3(1), 4(2)). The reference is to direct discrimination falling within the Disability Discrimination Act 1995 s 3A(5) (as added): see the text and notes 4–6 infra.
4   As to the meaning of 'person' see para 344 note 3 ante. See also para 530 ante.
5   As to when a person has a disability see para 511 ante. See also para 530 ante.
6   Disability Discrimination Act 1995 s 3A(5) (as added: see note 3 supra). For an attempt at defining the dividing line between direct discrimination under s 3A(5) (as added) (termed 'discrimination on the ground of disability') and indirect discrimination under s 3A(1) (as added) (see para 530 ante) (termed 'disability-related discrimination') see *High Quality Lifestyles Ltd v Watts* [2006] IRLR 850, [2006] All ER (D) 216 (Apr), EAT (where, in a case relating to the dismissal of an HIV-positive employee who had not disclosed his condition when obtaining the job, an appeal on indirect discrimination was upheld and one on direct discrimination was not).

8   For the meaning of 'duty to make reasonable adjustments' see para 530 note 7 ante.

9   Ie the Disability Discrimination Act 1995 Pt II (ss 3A–18E) (as amended; prospectively amended).

10 See ibid s 18D(1) (as added); and para 530 ante.

532. Discrimination by failure to adjust. For the purposes of the provisions of the Disability Discrimination Act 1995 relating to employment and members of locally-electable authorities[1], a person[2] also discriminates against a disabled person[3] if he fails to comply with a duty to make reasonable adjustments[4] imposed on him in relation to the disabled person[5].

Where a provision, criterion or practice[6] applied by or on behalf of an employer[7], or any physical feature of premises[8] occupied by the employer[9], place the disabled person concerned[10] at a substantial disadvantage in comparison with persons who are not disabled[11], it is the duty of the employer to take such steps as it is reasonable, in all the circumstances of the case, for him to have to take in order to prevent the provision, criterion, practice or feature having that effect[12].

The following are examples of steps which a person[13] may have to take in relation to a disabled person in order to comply with a duty to make reasonable adjustments[14]:

(1)   making adjustments to premises[15];

(2)   allocating some of the disabled person's duties to another person[16];

(3)   transferring him to fill an existing vacancy[17];

(4)   altering his hours of working or training[18];

(5)   assigning him to a different place of work or training[19];

(6)   allowing him to be absent during working or training hours for rehabilitation, assessment or treatment[20];

(7)   giving, or arranging for, training or mentoring (whether for the disabled person or any other person)[21];

(8)   acquiring or modifying equipment[22];

(9)   modifying instructions or reference manuals[23];

(10) modifying procedures for testing or assessment[24];

(11) providing a reader or interpreter[25]; and

(12) providing supervision or other support[26].

No duty is imposed on an employer in relation to a disabled person if the employer does not know and could not reasonably be expected to know[27]: (a) in the case of an applicant or potential applicant, that the disabled person concerned is, or may be, an applicant for the employment[28]; or (b) in any case, that that person has a disability and is likely to be placed at a substantial disadvantage[29].

Subject to any duty to make reasonable adjustments, nothing in the provisions of the Disability Discrimination Act 1995 relating to employment and locally-electable authorities[30] is to be taken to require a person to treat a disabled person more favourably than he treats or would treat others[31].

A provision imposing a duty to make reasonable adjustments[32] applies only for the purpose of determining whether a person has discriminated against a disabled person; and accordingly a breach of any such duty is not actionable as such[33].

For the purposes of a duty to make reasonable adjustments, where under any binding obligation[34] a person is required to obtain the consent of any person to any alteration of the premises occupied by him it is always reasonable for him to have to take steps to obtain that consent and it is never reasonable for him to have to make that alteration before that consent is obtained[35]. The steps mentioned above are not to be taken to include an application to a court or tribunal[36].

1   Ie the Disability Discrimination Act 1995 Pt II (ss 3A–18E) (as amended; prospectively amended). Part II (as amended; prospectively amended) now extends to discrimination by persons in the employment field other than employers: see also para 543 et seq post.

2   As to the meaning of 'person' see para 344 note 3 ante. The earlier version of the provision referred to
     'employer': see para 530 ante.
3   For the meaning of 'disabled person' see para 511 ante.
4   For the meaning of 'duty to make reasonable adjustments' see para 530 note 7 ante.
5   Disability Discrimination Act 1995 s 3A(2) (s 3A added by the Disability Discrimination Act 1995
     (Amendment) Regulations 2003, SI 2003/1673, regs 3(1), 4(2)). The previous version of this provision
     (i e the Disability Discrimination Act 1995 s 5 (repealed)) allowed the employer to justify this failure:
     under the new provision such a failure can no longer be justified. As to the determination of whether it
     is reasonable for a person to have to take a particular step in order to comply with a duty to make
     reasonable adjustments, and examples of steps which he may have to take, see s 18B (as added); and the
     text and notes 6–26 infra.
         See *Morse v Wiltshire County Council* [1998] IRLR 352, EAT; *Clark v TDG Ltd (t/a Novacold)* [1999]
     ICR 951, [1999] IRLR 318, CA; *Collins v Royal National Theatre Board Ltd* [2004] EWCA Civ 144,
     [2004] 2 All ER 851, [2004] IRLR 395; *Williams v J Walter Thompson Group Ltd* [2005] EWCA Civ 133,
     [2005] IRLR 376; *R (on the application of T) v Governing Body of OL Primary School* [2005] EWHC 753
     (Admin), [2005] ELR 522. See also *Ferguson v Barnet London Borough Council* [2006] All ER (D) 192
     (Dec), EAT (where the appeal was allowed as the tribunal had not identified the stages to be taken before
     making a finding that there had been a breach of the reasonable adjustment requirement).
6   'Provision, criterion or practice' includes any arrangements: Disability Discrimination Act 1995 s 18D(2)
     (s 18D added by the Disability Discrimination Act 1995 (Amendment) Regulations 2003, SI 2003/1673,
     regs 3(1), 18). See also note 7 infra.
7   Disability Discrimination Act 1995 s 4A(1)(a) (s 4A added by the Disability Discrimination Act 1995
     (Amendment) Regulations 2003, SI 2003/1673, regs 3(1), 5). For the meaning of 'employer' see para 529
     note 2 ante.
         Dismissal is not an employment arrangement, although this may include arrangements leading up to
     dismissal: *Clark v TDG (t/a Novacold)* [1999] ICR 951, [1999] IRLR 318, CA (overruling *Morse v
     Wiltshire County Council* [1998] ICR 1023, [1998] IRLR 352, EAT). Not every arrangement which
     could be made to facilitate a disabled person's employment falls within the statutory definition of
     arrangements: *Kenny v Hampshire Constabulary* [1998] ICR 27, [1999] IRLR 76, EAT. These cases relate
     to the previous provision (i e the Disability Discrimination Act 1995 s 6 (repealed)).
         See also *Paul v National Probation Service* [2004] IRLR 190, [2003] All ER (D) 177 (Nov), EAT
     (assessing the suitability of an applicant for a position by reference to the stressful nature of the job is an
     arrangement made by or on behalf of an employer); *Difalco v NTL Group Ltd* [2006] EWCA Civ 1508,
     [2006] All ER (D) 136 (Oct) (employment tribunal had failed to articulate the 'arrangements' that had
     given rise to the substantial disadvantage to the employee, which had invoked the employer's duty to
     make reasonable adjustments).
8   As to the meaning of 'premises' see para 525 note 9 ante. 'Physical feature', in relation to any premises,
     includes (subject to any provision under the Disability Discrimination Act 1995 s 15C(4)(e) (as added):
     see para 559 post) any of the following (whether permanent or temporary): (1) any feature arising from
     the design or construction of a building on the premises; (2) any feature on the premises of any approach
     to, exit from or access to such a building; (3) any fixtures, fittings, furnishings, furniture, equipment or
     material in or on the premises; (4) any other physical element or quality of any land comprised in the
     premises: s 18D(2) (as added (see note 6 supra); definition amended by the Disability Discrimination
     Act 2005 s 19(1), Sch 1 paras 1, 11(b)).
9   Disability Discrimination Act 1995 s 4A(1)(b) (as added: see note 7 supra).
10   'The disabled person concerned' means: (1) in the case of a provision, criterion or practice for
     determining to whom employment should be offered, any disabled person who is, or has notified the
     employer that he may be, an applicant for that employment; or (2) in any other case, a disabled person
     who is: (a) an applicant for the employment concerned; or (b) an employee of the employer concerned:
     ibid s 4A(2) (as added: see note 7 supra). As to the application of these provisions to past disabilities see
     para 522 ante.
11   A person with photosensitive epilepsy who was interviewed in a room with bright fluorescent lighting
     was not placed at a substantial disadvantage: *Ridout v TC Group* [1998] IRLR 628, EAT.
         In relation to past disabilities, the comparison is to be made with people who are not disabled and
     have not had a disability: see the Disability Discrimination Act 1995 s 2(2), Sch 2 para 3 (as amended);
     and para 522 ante.
12   Ibid s 4A(1) (as added: see note 7 supra). In determining whether it is reasonable for a person to have to
     take a particular step in order to comply with a duty to make reasonable adjustments, regard must be had,
     in particular, to: (1) the extent to which taking the step would prevent the effect in relation to which the
     duty is imposed; (2) the extent to which it is practicable for him to take the step; (3) the financial and
     other costs which would be incurred by him in taking the step and the extent to which taking it would
     disrupt any of his activities; (4) the extent of his financial and other resources; (5) the availability to him
     of financial or other assistance with respect to taking the step; (6) the nature of his activities and the size

of his undertaking; (7) where the step would be taken in relation to a private household, the extent to which taking it would disrupt that household, or disturb any person residing there: s 18B(1)(a)–(f) (s 18B added by the Disability Discrimination Act 1995 (Amendment) Regulations 2003, SI 2003/1673, regs 3(1), 17(2)). As to alterations to premises occupied under leases see para 560 post. It should be noted that the Disability Discrimination Act 1995 s 18B (as added) does not only apply to employers (cf s 4A (as added)), but more generally to 'persons'.

What is reasonably practicable is less strict than determining what is possible in practice, and has been construed in other contexts as a test of 'reasonable feasibility': *Palmer v Southend-on-Sea Borough Council* [1984] 1 All ER 945, [1984] 1 WLR 1129, CA; *Dedman v British Building and Engineering Appliances Ltd* [1974] 1 All ER 520, [1974] 1 WLR 171, CA. A defendant's resources in a negligence action are relevant to precautions as a body with very substantial resources is expected to have undertaken better precautions and a higher standard of care is required: see *British Railways Board v Herrington* [1972] AC 877, [1972] All ER 749, HL. As to negligence generally see NEGLIGENCE.

It does not follow that, because the employee or his medical witness does not suggest a useful adjustment, the employer's duty is satisfied: *Cosgrove v Caesar and Howie* [2001] IRLR 653, [2001] All ER (D) 118 (Jun), EAT. See *Johnson & Johnson Medical Ltd v Filmer* [2002] ICR 292, EAT (decision to combine disciplinary and harassment proceedings in which disabled applicant was involved did not constitute 'reasonable adjustment'). These cases relate to earlier versions of the provisions.

See also *Smith v Churchills Stairlifts plc* [2005] EWCA Civ 1220, [2006] ICR 524, [2006] IRLR 41.

13   Note that the Disability Discrimination Act 1995 s 18B (as added) applies broadly to persons rather than just to the employer: see note 12 supra. See also the text and notes 2, 7, 12 supra.

14   Ibid s 18B(2) (as added: see note 12 supra).

15   Ibid s 18B(2)(a) (as added: see note 12 supra).

16   Ibid s 18B(2)(b) (as added: see note 12 supra).

17   Ibid s 18B(2)(c) (as added: see note 12 supra). Where there are no vacancies at the same or lower grade, the duty may in certain circumstances require an employer to transfer without competition a suitably qualified applicant to a higher grade: *Archibald v Fife Council* [2004] UKHL 32, [2004] 4 All ER 303, [2004] ICR 954. This case was controversial in that it showed that the Disability Discrimination Act 1995 did not involve neutral equality and at times could result in something approaching positive discrimination. See also *Meikle v Nottinghamshire County Council* [2004] EWCA Civ 859, [2004] 4 All ER 97, [2005] ICR 1, which seemed to indicate that there were situations where the ordinary sick pay limitations may be disapplied if the absence was through disability; but see *O'Hanlon v Revenue and Customs Comrs* [2007] EWCA Civ 283, [2007] All ER (D) 516 (Mar), which suggested that this was only the case when the disability absence was actually caused by the prior failure of the employer to make adjustments for the disability. See also *Royal Liverpool Children's NHS Trust v Dunsby* [2006] IRLR 351, [2006] All ER (D) 244 (Jan), EAT, suggesting that there is no rule of law that disability absence must be stripped out when calculating sick pay entitlement. See also *Fowler v Waltham Forest London Borough Council* [2007] All ER (D) 126 (Feb), EAT (no discrimination or duty to make further payments of wages or sick pay by way of a reasonable adjustment).

18   Disability Discrimination Act 1995 s 18B(2)(d) (as added: see note 12 supra).

19   Ibid s 18B(2)(e) (as added: see note 12 supra). See *HM Prison Service v Beart* [2003] EWCA Civ 119, [2003] ICR 1068, [2003] IRLR 238 (employer's failure to relocate employee to different prison constituted breach of duty under an earlier version of the provisions).

20   Disability Discrimination Act 1995 s 18B(2)(f) (as added: see note 12 supra).

21   Ibid s 18B(2)(g) (as added: see note 12 supra).

22   Ibid s 18B(2)(h) (as added: see note 12 supra).

23   Ibid s 18B(2)(i) (as added: see note 12 supra).

24   Ibid s 18B(2)(j) (as added: see note 12 supra).

25   Ibid s 18B(2)(k) (as added: see note 12 supra). Providing a reader or interpreter is an adjustment that will necessarily involve a fairly considerable cost unless a colleague who is already employed can provide the necessary assistance, but employers are not under a statutory duty to provide carers to attend to their employee's personal needs: *Kenny v Hampshire Constabulary* [1998] ICR 27, [1999] IRLR 76, EAT.

26   Disability Discrimination Act 1995 s 18B(2)(l) (as added: see note 12 supra).

27   Ibid s 4A(3) (as added: see note 7 supra). This requires a tribunal to measure the extent of the duty, if any, against the actual or constructive knowledge of the employer both as to the disability and its likelihood of causing the individual a substantial disadvantage in comparison with persons who are not disabled: *Ridout v TC Group* [1998] IRLR 628, EAT (case relating to an earlier version of the provision). See *Tarbuck v Sainsbury's Supermarkets Ltd* [2006] IRLR 664, [2006] All ER (D) 50 (Jun), EAT (although it will always be good practice to consult with the employee about what reasonable adjustments might be made, there is no separate and distinct duty to consult; the single question was whether the employer had complied with his obligations). See also *Ferguson v Barnet London Borough Council* [2006] All ER (D) 192 (Dec), EAT (where the appeal was allowed as the tribunal had not identified the steps to be taken before making a finding that there had been a breach of the reasonable adjustment requirement); *Hay v Surrey*

County Council [2007] EWCA Civ 93, [2007] All ER (D) 199 (Feb) (a separate, formal risk assessment need not be undertaken in every case involving an employee returning to work after injury; and the authority had carefully considered the employee's work in light of professional advice and offered alternative work).

28   Disability Discrimination Act 1995 s 4A(3)(a) (as added: see note 7 supra).

29   See ibid s 4A(3)(b) (as added: see note 7 supra). In relation to past disabilities, this provision applies if that person has or has had a disability: see Sch 2 para 3 (as amended); and para 522 ante.

30   Ie ibid Pt II (as amended; prospectively amended).

31   See ibid s 18D(1) (as added); and para 530 ante.

32   Ie a provision of ibid Pt II (as amended; prospectively amended). See also note 11 supra.

33   Ibid s 18B(6) (as added: see note 12 supra).

34   'Binding obligation' means a legally binding obligation, not contained in a lease in relation to the premises, whether arising from an agreement or otherwise: ibid s 18B(5) (as added: see note 12 supra). For the meaning of 'lease' see para 560 post.

35   Ibid s 18B(3) (as added: see note 12 supra).

36   Ibid s 18B(4) (as added: see note 12 supra).

533.   Harassment.   For the purposes of the provisions relating to the field of employment and members of locally-electable authorities[1], a person subjects a disabled person[2] to harassment where, for a reason which relates to the disabled person's disability, he engages in unwanted conduct which has the purpose or effect of violating the disabled person's dignity[3], or creating an intimidating, hostile, degrading, humiliating or offensive environment for him[4].

1   Ie the Disability Discrimination Act 1995 Pt II (ss 3A–18E) (as amended; prospectively amended).

2   For the meaning of 'disabled person' see para 511 ante.

3   Disability Discrimination Act 1995 s 3B(1)(a) (s 3B added by the Disability Discrimination Act 1995 (Amendment) Regulations 2003, SI 2003/1673, regs 3(1), 4(2)). Cf harassment under the Sex Discrimination Act 1975 (see para 347 ante) and under the Race Relations Act 1976 (see para 444 ante).

4   Disability Discrimination Act 1995 s 3B(1)(b) (as added: see note 3 supra). Conduct is to be regarded as having the effect referred to in s 3B(1)(a) or (b) (as added) only if, having regard to all the circumstances, including in particular the perception of the disabled person, it should reasonably be considered as having that effect: s 3B(2) (as so added).

534.   Discrimination and harassment in regard to applicants and employees.   In relation to employment[1] at an establishment in Great Britain[2], it is unlawful for an employer[3] to discriminate[4] against a disabled person[5]: (1) in the arrangements which he makes for the purpose of determining to whom he should offer employment[6]; (2) in the terms on which he offers that person employment[7]; or (3) by refusing to offer, or deliberately not offering, him employment[8].

It is unlawful for an employer to discriminate against a disabled person whom he employs[9]: (a) in the terms of employment which he affords him[10]; (b) in the opportunities which he affords him for promotion, transfer, training or receiving any other benefit[11]; (c) by refusing to afford him, or deliberately not affording him, any such opportunity[12]; or (d) by dismissing him[13], or subjecting him to any other detriment[14].

It is also unlawful for an employer, in relation to employment by him, to subject to harassment[15] a disabled person whom he employs, or a disabled person who has applied to him for employment[16].

In certain circumstances[17], the above provisions also apply to discrimination against a person who is not disabled[18].

1   For the meaning of 'employment' see para 529 note 2 ante.

2   See the Disability Discrimination Act 1995 s 4(6) (as substituted); and para 529 ante. For the meaning of 'Great Britain' see para 325 note 6 ante. For the meaning of 'employment at an establishment in Great Britain' see para 529 note 3 ante.

3   For the meaning of 'employer' see para 529 note 2 ante. The provisions of ibid Pt II (ss 3A–18E) (as amended; prospectively amended) now extend to discrimination by persons in the employment field other than employers: see paras 532 ante, 543 et seq post. See also paras 540–542 post.

4 As to discrimination by employers see para 529 ante.

5 Disability Discrimination Act 1995 s 4(1) (s 4 substituted by the Disability Discrimination Act 1995 (Amendment) Regulations 2003, SI 2003/1673, regs 3(1), 5). For the meaning of 'disabled person' see para 511 ante. As to the application of these provisions to past disabilities see para 522 ante.

6 Disability Discrimination Act 1995 s 4(1)(a) (as substituted: see note 5 supra). Interview questions can be arrangements: *Saunders v Richmond-upon-Thames Borough Council* [1978] ICR 75, [1977] IRLR 362, EAT. It is not automatically unlawful to ask questions of a disabled person that would not be asked of a non-disabled person as it will often be necessary for an employer to inform himself about the nature and effects of the disability so that proper adjustments can be considered; cf where an applicant may be asked to produce evidence of his right to work in the United Kingdom so the employer may comply with work permit regulations: see *Dhatt v McDonald's Hamburgers Ltd* [1991] 3 All ER 692, [1991] 1 WLR 527, CA. Arrangements may be unlawful not only if they were made in a way that discriminates but also if neutral arrangements are then operated in a way that has a discriminatory effect: *Brennan v JH Dewhurst Ltd* [1984] ICR 52, [1983] IRLR 357, EAT. These cases relate to earlier but similar versions of the relevant provisions.

See also *Paul v National Probation Service* [2004] IRLR 190, [2003] All ER (D) 177 (Nov), EAT (employer unlawfully discriminated by assessing suitability of applicant by reference to stressful nature of job).

7 Disability Discrimination Act 1995 s 4(1)(b) (as substituted: see note 5 supra). Section 4(1)(b) (as substituted) only applies to the offering of terms and conditions at the commencement of employment, as once the applicant has accepted the employment he is an employee and falls under s 4(2) (as substituted) (see the text and notes 9–14 infra): *Clymo v Wandsworth London Borough Council* [1989] ICR 250, [1989] IRLR 241, EAT (case relating to an earlier but similar version of the relevant provisions).

8 Disability Discrimination Act 1995 s 4(1)(c) (as substituted: see note 5 supra). Section 4(1)(c) (as substituted) applies not only where there is an actual refusal by the employer to offer employment to the applicant, but also where there is no refusal but still a deliberate failure to offer the job: *Johnson v Timber Tailors (Midlands) Ltd* [1978] IRLR 146, IT. A refusal to offer employment may come at any stage in the selection process, even at the initial consideration stage (*Owen and Briggs v James* [1982] ICR 618, [1982] IRLR 502, CA), or by refusing to offer an interview (*Panesar v Nestlé Co Ltd* [1980] IRLR 64, EAT; approved [1980] ICR 144n, [1980] IRLR 64, CA), and may even extend to existing employees who are facing redundancy and are applying for new positions (*Timex Corpn v Hodgson* [1982] ICR 63, [1981] IRLR 530, EAT). These cases relate to earlier but similar versions of the relevant provisions.

9 Disability Discrimination Act 1995 s 4(2) (as substituted: see note 5 supra). Section 4(2) (as substituted) does not apply to benefits of any description if the employer is concerned with the provision (whether or not for payment) of benefits of that description to the public, or to a section of the public which includes the employee in question, unless: (1) that provision differs in a material respect from the provision of the benefits by the employer to his employees; (2) the provision of the benefits to the employee in question is regulated by his contract of employment; or (3) the benefits relate to training: s 4(4) (as so substituted). 'Benefits', except in ss 4G–4K (as added) (see paras 556–557 post), includes facilities and services: s 18D(2) (s 18D added by the Disability Discrimination Act 1995 (Amendment) Regulations 2003, SI 2003/1673, regs 3(1), 18; definition amended by the Disability Discrimination Act 1995 (Pensions) Regulations 2003, SI 2003/2770, SI 2003/2770, regs 2, 4(2)(a)).

An employment tribunal has jurisdiction to hear a complaint of discrimination made against an employer under the Disability Discrimination Act 1995 by an employee whose period of employment has terminated: see *Relaxion Group plc v Rhys-Harper, D'Souza v Lambert London Borough Council, Jones v 3M Healthcare Ltd, Kirker v British Sugar plc, Angel v New Possibilities NHS Trust, Bond v Hackney Citizens Advice Bureau* [2003] UKHL 33, [2003] 4 All ER 1113, [2003] IRLR 484.

10 Disability Discrimination Act 1995 s 4(2)(a) (as substituted: see note 5 supra).

11 Ibid s 4(2)(b) (as substituted: see note 5 supra). Where a person applies for promotion, transfer or training, it is unlawful if discrimination plays a part in the selection process: *Khanna v Ministry of Defence* [1981] ICR 653, [1981] IRLR 331, EAT; *Iske v P & O European Ferries (Dover) Ltd* [1997] IRLR 401, EAT. There is no positive obligation to provide training to enable the employee to qualify for promotion: *Mecca Leisure Group plc v Chatprachong* [1993] ICR 688, [1993] IRLR 531. An employer cannot avoid the effect of the Disability Discrimination Act 1995 by contracting out a job to which the employee could be transferred: *Iske v P & O European Ferries (Dover) Ltd* supra. All significant benefits which are available to employees as part of their employment are covered by the Disability Discrimination Act 1995 s 4 (as substituted); a trivial disadvantage in treatment is not to be regarded as the denial of a benefit: *Peake v Automotive Products Ltd* [1978] QB 233, [1978] 1 All ER 106, CA; cf *Ministry of Defence v Jeremiah* [1980] QB 87, [1979] 3 All ER 833, CA. A refusal to investigate complaints of unfair treatment can be a refusal of access to benefits: *Eke v Customs and Excise Comrs* [1981] IRLR 334, EAT. These cases relate to earlier but similar versions of the relevant provisions.

12 Disability Discrimination Act 1995 s 4(2)(c) (as substituted: see note 5 supra).

13   The reference in ibid s 4(2)(d) (as substituted) to the dismissal of a person includes a reference: (1) to the termination of that person's employment by the expiration of any period (including a period expiring by reference to an event or circumstance), not being a termination immediately after which the employment is renewed on the same terms; and (2) to the termination of that person's employment by any act of his (including the giving of notice) in circumstances such that he is entitled to terminate it without notice by reason of the conduct of the employer: s 4(5) (as substituted: see note 5 supra).

A dismissal for discriminatory reasons is not automatically unfair, but will very often be unfair contrary to the Employment Rights Act 1996 s 98 (as amended) (see EMPLOYMENT vol 16(1B) (Reissue) para 640): *Timex Corpn v Hodgson* [1982] ICR 63, [1981] IRLR 530, EAT; *Clarke v Eley (IMI) Kynoch Ltd* [1983] ICR 165, [1982] IRLR 482, EAT. The phrase 'by dismissing him' in a previous version of the Disability Discrimination Act 1995 s 4(2)(d) (as substituted) was held not to include a constructive dismissal: see *Metropolitan Police Comr v Harley* [2001] ICR 927, [2001] IRLR 263, EAT. However, see *Meikle v Nottinghamshire County Council* [2004] EWCA Civ 859, [2004] 4 All ER 97, [2005] ICR 1, where it was held that a constructive dismissal constitutes 'dismissal' within the meaning of the provision. See also *Taylor v OCS Group Ltd* [2006] EWCA Civ 702, [2006] ICR 1602, [2006] IRLR 613 (it was wrong to argue that in order to demonstrate that the employee had been dismissed for a reason related to his disability it was unnecessary to show that the reason relating to the disability was present in the employer's mind).

14   Disability Discrimination Act 1995 s 4(2)(d) (as substituted: see note 5 supra). 'Detriment', except in s 16C(2)(b) (as added) (see para 538 post), does not include conduct of the nature referred to in s 3B (as added) (see para 533 ante): s 18D(2) (as added: see note 9 supra). Subject to this, 'any other detriment' is a wide phrase, which means only that the disabled person has been put at a disadvantage in some way: *Kirby v Manpower Services Commission* [1980] 3 All ER 334, [1980] 1 WLR 725, EAT. See also *BL Cars Ltd v Brown* [1983] ICR 143, [1983] IRLR 193, EAT. However it is not just any disadvantage; it must be something serious or important: *Ministry of Defence v Jeremiah* [1980] QB 87, [1979] 3 All ER 833, CA; *Schmidt v Austicks Bookshops Ltd* [1978] ICR 85, [1977] IRLR 360, EAT, following *Peake v Automotive Products Ltd* [1978] QB 233, [1978] 1 All ER 106, CA. An objectionable discriminatory remark may constitute a detriment even if made to people other than the complainant (*Hereford and Worcester County Council v Clayton* (1996) Times, 8 October, EAT), but there must be circumstances in which the complainant was intended or reasonably expected to hear the remark (*De Souza v Automobile Association* [1986] ICR 514, [1986] IRLR 103, CA). An employer may subject an employee to detriment by exposing him to offensive conduct from others: see *Burton v De Vere Hotels* [1997] ICR 1, [1996] IRLR 596, EAT. An employee can be subjected to a detriment by not being offered an advantage even though there is no statutory or contractual right to it, if others would be or were offered it: *Iske v P & O European Ferries (Dover) Ltd* [1997] IRLR 401, EAT. Discouraging words by management on their own have been found to amount to a detriment: *Simon v Brimham Associates* [1987] ICR 596, [1987] IRLR 307, CA. The detriment needs to be connected with the disabled person's employment: *Tower Hamlets London Borough Council v Rabin* [1989] ICR 693, EAT. These cases relate to earlier but similar versions of the relevant provisions.

15   For the meaning of 'harassment' see para 533 ante.

16   Disability Discrimination Act 1995 s 4(3) (as substituted: see note 5 supra).

17   Ie in the case of an act which constitutes discrimination by way of victimisation by virtue of ibid s 55 (as amended): see para 526 ante. As to the meaning of 'act' see para 510 note 3 ante.

18   See ibid s 55(5) (as added and amended); and para 526 ante.

535.   Justification. Discriminatory treatment[1] is justified[2] if, but only if, the reason for it is both material to the circumstances of the particular case[3] and substantial (and treatment cannot be justified if it amounts to direct discrimination)[4]. This is an objective test[5]. The question whether treatment has been shown to be justified is a question of fact to be determined on a proper self direction on the relevant law[6]. A failure to make adjustments may be unreasonable and it is no longer possible for it to be justified[7].

1   Ie treatment under the Disability Discrimination Act 1995 s 3A(1) (as added): see para 530 ante.

2   Note that it is no longer possible to justify a failure to make reasonable adjustments: see para 532 ante.

3   The Disability Discrimination Act 1995 s 3A(3) (as added) (see para 530 ante) provides a low threshold; if an employer could show a reason for the treatment which relates to the individual circumstances in question and is not just trivial or minor then justification has to be held to exist (at least where there is no duty to make adjustments: see paras 530 note 7, 532 ante): *HJ Heinz Co Ltd v Kenrick* [2000] ICR 491, [2000] IRLR 144, EAT (affg in part *Baynton v Saurus General Engineers Ltd* [2000] ICR 375, [1999] IRLR 604). The relevant circumstances must include the circumstances of both the employer and the employee, but the balancing of interests test must take into account the comparatively limited requirements of the Disability Discrimination Act 1995 s 3A(3) (as added) (see para 530 ante). It does not

require a wider survey of what is reasonable having regard to specific features such as is found in s 4A (as added) (see para 532 ante). The phrase 'if, but only if' suggests that an employer must look exclusively at the individual particular circumstances when considering whether treatment can be justified. A general assumption would not in itself be a material reason. If, in a case falling within s 3A(1) (as added) (see para 530 ante), the person (including an employer) is under a duty to make reasonable adjustments in relation to the disabled person but fails to comply with that duty, his treatment of that person cannot be justified under s 3A(3) (as added) (see para 530 ante) unless it would have been justified even if he had complied with that duty: see s 3A(6) (as added); and para 530 ante.

    See *Royal Liverpool Children's NHS Trust v Dunsby* [2006] IRLR 351, [2006] All ER (D) 244 (Jan), EAT (failure by tribunal to consider question of justification). It is essential for a tribunal to give reasons if it is to conclude that there is no connection between an employee's conduct and his disability: *Edwards v Mid Suffolk District Council* [2001] ICR 616, [2001] IRLR 190, EAT.

    The Disability Discrimination Act 1995 Pt II (ss 3A–18E) (as amended; prospectively amended) now extends to discrimination by persons in the employment field other than employers: see paras 532 ante, 543 et seq post. See also paras 540–542 post.

4   See ibid s 3A(3)–(5) (as added); and paras 530–531 ante. The concept of what is substantial for the purposes of justification should be approached in the same way as what is a substantial adverse effect on day to day activities: see para 520 ante. See note 2 supra.

    A defence of justification cannot be thought up after the event when it has never been considered during the period of employment: *Quinn v Schwarzkopf Ltd* [2001] IRLR 67, EAT.

5   *Morse v Wiltshire County Council* [1998] ICR 1023, [1998] IRLR 352, EAT (the question was whether the employer's failure to comply with his duty was in fact objectively justified, and whether the reason for failure to comply was in fact material to the circumstances of the particular case and in fact substantial). Justification in the context of indirect sex discrimination (see para 351 ante) requires 'an objective balance between the discriminatory effect of the condition and the reasonable needs of the party who applies the condition': see *Webb v Emo Air Cargo (UK) Ltd (No 2)* [1995] 4 All ER 577, [1995] 1 WLR 1454, HL; *Hampson v Department of Education and Science* [1989] ICR 179, [1989] IRLR 69, CA. The tribunal must not substitute its discretion for that of the person who is supposed to exercise it, but should decide whether there are policy reasons to suggest that the treatment was objectively justifiable and could realistically be described as necessary: *Staffordshire County Council v Black* [1995] IRLR 234, EAT.

    An employment tribunal is confined to a consideration of whether the reason given for less favourable treatment of a disabled employee meets the statutory criteria of being both material to the circumstances and substantial, and may not substitute its own appraisal: *Jones v Post Office* [2001] EWCA Civ 558, [2001] ICR 805, [2001] IRLR 384. See also *Callagan v Glasgow City Council* [2001] IRLR 724, EAT (dismissal due to poor attendance record not discriminatory); *Harman v Ministry of Defence* [2006] All ER (D) 86 (Oct), EAT (tribunal should have made reference to reasonable responses of a reasonable employer in the employer's decision to dismiss rather than whether the decision was irrational); *Jenkins v Heathrow Express Operating Co Ltd* [2007] All ER (D) 144 (Feb), EAT (tribunal's role in relation to the employee's fitness to return to work as a customer services representative in a train company was to review the employer's decision, not to assess the medical evidence for itself and substitute its own conclusion for that of the employer).

6   See *Clark v TDG (t/a Novacold)* [1999] ICR 951, [1999] IRLR 318, CA.

7   See note 2 supra. Under the previous provision (i e the Disability Discrimination Act 1995 s 5 (repealed)) it was possible to justify a failure to make adjustments but the current provision (i e s 3A (as added)) only provides scope for justification for discriminatory treatment. See in particular s 3A(6) (as added); and para 530 ante.

536. Relationships that have come to an end. Where there has been a relevant relationship[1] between a disabled person[2] and another person ('the relevant person') and the relationship has come to an end[3] it is unlawful for the relevant person to discriminate against the disabled person by subjecting him to a detriment, or to subject the disabled person to harassment, where the discrimination or harassment arises out of and is closely connected to the relevant relationship[4].

    Where a provision, criterion or practice applied by the relevant person to the disabled person in relation to any matter arising out of the relevant relationship, or a physical feature[5] of premises[6] which are occupied by the relevant person, places the disabled person at a substantial disadvantage in comparison with persons who are not disabled but are in the same position as the disabled person in relation to the relevant person[7], it is the duty of the relevant person to take such steps as it is reasonable[8], in all the circumstances of the case, for him to have to take in order to prevent the provision, practice, criterion or feature having that effect[9].

No duty is imposed on the relevant person if he does not know, and could not reasonably be expected to know, that the disabled person has a disability and is likely to be placed at a substantial disadvantage[10].

1   A 'relevant relationship' is: (1) a relationship during the course of which an act of discrimination against, or harassment of, one party to the relationship by the other party to it is unlawful under the Disability Discrimination Act 1995 ss 3A–14D (as added and amended) (see para 525 et seq ante); or (2) a relationship between a person providing employment services and a person receiving such services: s 16A(2) (s 16A added by the Disability Discrimination Act 1995 (Amendment) Regulations 2003, SI 2003/1673, regs 3(1), 15(1); and the Disability Discrimination Act 1995 s 16A(2) amended by the Disability Discrimination Act 2005 s 19, Sch 1 paras 1, 7, Sch 2). For the meaning of 'harassment' see para 533 ante. For the meaning of 'employment services' see para 585 note 9 post.
    In the case of a relationship which has come to an end before the commencement of the Disability Discrimination Act 1995 s 16A (as added), an act of discrimination or harassment which is unlawful includes such an act which would, after the commencement of s 16A (as added), be unlawful: s 16A(7) (as so added).
2   For the meaning of 'disabled person' see para 511 ante. As to the application of these provisions to past disabilities see para 522 ante.
3   Disability Discrimination Act 1995 s 16A(1) (as added: see note 1 supra).
4   Ibid s 16A(3) (as added: see note 1 supra).
5   As to the meaning of 'physical feature' see para 532 note 8 ante.
6   As to the meaning of 'premises' see para 525 note 9 ante.
7   Disability Discrimination Act 1995 s 16A(4) (as added: see note 1 supra).
8   As to the determination of whether it is reasonable for a relevant person to have to take a particular step, and examples of steps which he may have to take, see para 532 ante.
9   Disability Discrimination Act 1995 s 16A(5) (as added: see note 1 supra).
10 Ibid s 16A(6) (as added: see note 1 supra).

537.   Discriminatory advertisements.   It is unlawful for a person[1] to publish or cause to be published an advertisement[2] which: (1) invites applications for a relevant appointment or benefit[3]; and (2) indicates, or might reasonably be understood to indicate, that an application will or may be determined to any extent by reference to: (a) the applicant not having any disability, or any particular disability[4]; (b) the applicant not having had any disability, or any particular disability[5]; or (c) any reluctance of the person determining the application to comply with a duty to make reasonable adjustments[6] or, in relation to employment services, with the duty to change a practice, policy or procedure which places disabled persons[7] at a substantial disadvantage[8].

A person who publishes an advertisement of the kind described above[9] is not subject to any liability[10] in respect of the publication of the advertisement if he proves: (i) that the advertisement was published in reliance on a statement made to him by the person who caused it to be published to the effect that[11] the publication would not be unlawful[12]; and (ii) that it was reasonable for him to rely on the statement[13].

1   As to the meaning of 'person' see para 344 note 3 ante.
2   'Advertisement' includes every form of advertisement or notice, whether to the public or not: Disability Discrimination Act 1995 s 16B(4) (s 16B added by the Disability Discrimination Act 1995 (Amendment) Regulations 2003, SI 2003/1673, regs 3(1), 15(1)).
3   Disability Discrimination Act 1995 s 16B(1)(a) (s 16B as added (see note 2 supra); and s 16B(1) substituted by the Disability Discrimination Act 2005 s 10(1), (2)). 'Relevant appointment or benefit' means: (1) any employment, promotion or transfer of employment; (2) membership of, or a benefit under, an occupational pension scheme; (3) an appointment to any office or post to which the Disability Discrimination Act 1995 s 4D (as added) applies (see para 543 ante); (4) any partnership in a firm (within the meaning of s 6A (as added) (see para 545 ante)); (5) any tenancy or pupillage (within the meaning of s 7A (as added) (see para 547 ante)); (6) any membership of a trade organisation (within the meaning of s 13 (as substituted) (see para 541 ante)); (7) any professional or trade qualification (within the meaning of s 14A (as added) (see para 549 ante)); (8) any work placement (within the meaning of s 14C (as added

and amended) (see para 551 ante)); (9) any employment services (see para 585 note 9 post)): s 16B(3) (as so added; and amended by the Disability Discrimination Act 2005 ss 10(4), 19, Sch 1 paras 1, 8(1), (3), Sch 2).

The Disability Discrimination Act 1995 16B(1) (as added and substituted) does not apply where it would not in fact be unlawful under Pt II (ss 3A–18E) (as amended; prospectively amended) or, to the extent that it relates to the provision of employment services, Pt III (ss 19–28) (as amended; prospectively amended) for an application to be determined in the manner indicated, or understood to be indicated, in the advertisement: s 16B(2) (as so added). For the meaning of 'employment services' see para 585 note 9 post.

Section 16B(1) (as added and substituted) does not apply in relation to an advertisement so far as it invites persons to apply, in their capacity as members of an authority to which s 15B (as added) (see para 558 ante) and s 15C (as added) (see para 559 ante) apply, for a relevant appointment or benefit which the authority is intending to make or confer: s 16B(2C) (s 16B as so added; and s 16B(2C) added by the Disability Discrimination Act 2005 Sch 1 paras 1, 8(1), (2)).

As from a day to be appointed, proceedings in respect of a contravention of the Disability Discrimination Act 1995 s 16B(1) (as added and substituted) may be brought only: (a) by the Commission for Equality and Human Rights; and (b) in accordance with the Equality Act 2006 s 25 (as amended) (see para 332 ante): Disability Discrimination Act 1995 s 16B(5) (s 16B as so added; and s 16B(5) prospectively added by the Equality Act 2006 s 40, Sch 3 paras 41, 42). At the date at which this volume states the law no such day had been appointed. As to the Commission for Equality and Human Rights, which is to replace the Disability Rights Commission, see para 305 et seq ante.

4　Disability Discrimination Act 1995 s 16B(1)(b)(i) (as added and substituted: see notes 2, 3 supra). See note 3 supra.
5　Ibid s 16B(1)(b)(ii) (as added and substituted: see notes 2, 3 supra). See note 3 supra.
6　For the meaning of 'duty to make reasonable adjustments' see para 530 note 7 ante.
7　For the meaning of 'disabled person' see para 511 ante.
8　Disability Discrimination Act 1995 s 16B(1)(b)(iii) (as added and substituted: see notes 2, 3 supra). The reference to the duty to change a practice, policy or procedure which places disabled persons at a substantial disadvantage is a reference to the duty imposed by s 21(1) as modified by s 21A(6) (as added) (see para 587 ante): s 16B(1)(b)(iii) (as so added and substituted). See note 3 supra.
9　Ie of the kind described in ibid s 16B(1) (as added and substituted): see the text and notes 1–8 supra.
10　Ie any liability under ibid s 16B(1) (as added and substituted): see the text and notes 1–8 supra.
11　Ie by reason of the operation of ibid s 16B(2) (as added): see note 3 supra.
12　Ibid s 16B(2A)(a) (s 16B as added (see note 2 supra); and s 16B(2A), (2B) added by the Disability Discrimination Act 2005 s 10(1), (3)).

A person who knowingly or recklessly makes a statement such as is mentioned in the Disability Discrimination Act 1995 s 16B(2A)(a) (as added) which in a material respect is false or misleading commits an offence, and is liable on summary conviction to a fine not exceeding level 5 on the standard scale: s 16B(2B) (as so added). As to the standard scale see para 315 note 15 ante.
13　Ibid s 16B(2A)(b) (as added: see notes 2, 12 supra).

538.　Instructions and pressures to discriminate. It is unlawful for a person who has authority over another person[1], or in accordance with whose wishes that other person is accustomed to act[2], to instruct him to do any act which is unlawful[3], or to procure or attempt to procure the doing by him of any such act[4]. It is also unlawful to induce, or attempt to induce[5], a person to do any act which contravenes specified disability discrimination and harassment[6] provisions[7] by providing or offering to provide him with any benefit[8], or subjecting or threatening to subject him to any detriment[9].

1　Disability Discrimination Act 1995 s 16C(1)(a) (s 16C added by the Disability Discrimination Act 1995 (Amendment) Regulations 2003, SI 2003/1673, regs 3(1), 15(1)). As to the meaning of 'person' see para 344 note 3 ante.
2　Disability Discrimination Act 1995 s 16C(1)(b) (as added: see note 1 supra).
3　Ie unlawful under ibid Pt II (ss 3A–18E) (as amended; prospectively amended) or, to the extent that it relates to the provision of employment services, Pt III (ss 19–28) (as amended; prospectively amended). For the meaning of 'employment services' see para 585 note 9 post.
4　Ibid s 16C(1) (as added: see note 1 supra).
5　An attempted inducement is not prevented from falling within ibid s 16C(2) (as added) because it is not made directly to the person in question, if it is made in such a way that he is likely to hear of it: s 16C(3) (as added: see note 1 supra).
6　For the meaning of 'harassment' see para 533 ante.

7   Ie the provisions of the Disability Discrimination Act 1995 Pt II (as amended; prospectively amended) or, to the extent that it relates to the provision of employment services, Pt III (as amended; prospectively amended).

8   Ibid s 16C(2)(a) (as added: see note 1 supra).

9   Ibid s 16C(2)(b) (as added: see note 1 supra).

As from a day to be appointed, proceedings in respect of a contravention of s 16C (as added) may be brought only: (1) by the Commission for Equality and Human Rights; and (2) in accordance with the Equality Act 2006 s 25 (as amended) (see para 332 ante): Disability Discrimination Act 1995 s 16C(4) (s 16C as so added; and s 16C(4) prospectively added by the Equality Act 2006 s 40, Sch 3 paras 41, 43). At the date at which this volume states the law no such day had been appointed. As to the Commission for Equality and Human Rights, which is to replace the Disability Rights Commission, see para 305 et seq ante.

539.   Appointment by the Secretary of State of advisors.

The Secretary of State[1] may appoint such persons[2] as he thinks fit to advise or assist him in connection with matters relating to the employment[3] of disabled persons[4] and persons who have had a disability[5]. Persons may be appointed by the Secretary of State to act generally or in relation to a particular area or locality[6]. The Secretary of State may pay to any person so appointed such allowances and compensation for loss of earnings as he considers appropriate[7].

The Secretary of State has by order abolished the national advisory council and district advisory committees[8].

1   As to the Secretary of State and the National Assembly for Wales see para 302 ante.

2   As to the meaning of 'person' see para 344 note 3 ante.

3   For the general meaning of 'employment' see para 529 note 2 ante. However, for these purposes, 'employment' includes self-employment: Disability Discrimination Act 1995 s 60(5).

4   For the meaning of 'disabled person' see para 511 ante.

5   Disability Discrimination Act 1995 s 60(1). As to when a person has a disability see para 511 ante.

6   Ibid s 60(2).

7   Ibid s 60(3). The approval of the Treasury is required for any payment under this provision: s 60(4). As to the Treasury see CONSTITUTIONAL LAW AND HUMAN RIGHTS vol 8(2) (Reissue) paras 512–517.

8   See ibid s 60(6), (7), (8); the Disability Discrimination (Abolition of District Advisory Committees) Order 1997, SI 1997/536; and the Disability Discrimination (Repeal of section 17 of, and Schedule 2 to, the Disabled Persons (Employment) Act 1944) Order 1998, SI 1998/565.

(B)   *Particular Forms of Employment*

(a)   Contract Workers

540.   Discrimination and harassment of contract workers.

It is unlawful for a principal[1], in relation to contract work[2] done at an establishment in Great Britain[3], to discriminate against a disabled person who is a contract worker (a 'disabled contract worker')[4]: (1) in the terms on which he allows him to do that work[5]; (2) by not allowing him to do it or continue to do it[6]; (3) in the way he affords him access to any benefits[7] or by refusing or deliberately omitting to afford him access to them[8]; or (4) by subjecting him to any other detriment[9].

It is also unlawful for a principal, in relation to contract work, to subject a disabled contract worker to harassment[10].

These provisions[11] apply to a disabled contract worker where, by virtue of a provision, criterion or practice[12] applied by or on behalf of all or most of the principals to whom he is or might be supplied, or a physical feature[13] of premises[14] occupied by such persons, he is likely, on each occasion when he is supplied to a principal to do contract work, to be placed at a substantial disadvantage in comparison with persons who are not disabled which is the same or similar in each case[15].

In the case of an act[16] which constitutes discrimination by way of victimisation[17], this provision also applies to discrimination against a person who is not disabled[18].

1 'Principal' means a person ('A') who makes work available for doing by individuals who are employed by another person who supplies them under a contract made with A: Disability Discrimination Act 1995 s 4B(9) (s 4B added by the Disability Discrimination Act 1995 (Amendment) Regulations 2003, SI 2003/1673, regs 3(1), 5). Where there is an unbroken chain of contracts between an individual and an end-user, the end-user is the principal: see *MHC Consulting Services Ltd v Tansell* [2000] ICR 789, [2000] IRLR 387, CA. 'Contract worker' means any individual who is supplied to the principal under such a contract: Disability Discrimination Act 1995 s 4B(9) (as so added). 'Contract work' means work so made available: s 4B(9) (as so added). The definition of 'contract worker' applies to a situation where the principal contracts with another for the supply of labour only, and then uses that contract worker as one of the principal's own workers. However, the definition also seems apt for the situation where a principal contracts with a firm to supply labour, equipment and services: see *Harrods Ltd v Remick* [1998] 1 All ER 52, [1998] ICR 156, CA (staff employed by concessionaires at Harrods were contract workers).

2 See note 1 supra. The absence of a contractual nexus between principal and contract worker means that their relationship is not covered by the definition of 'employment' in the Disability Discrimination Act 1995 s 68(1) (see para 529 note 2 ante): *BP Chemicals Ltd v Gillick* [1995] IRLR 128, EAT.
    The Disability Discrimination Act 1995 s 4A (as added) (see para 532 ante) applies to any principal, in relation to contract work, as if he were, or would be, the employer of the disabled contract worker and as if any contract worker supplied to do work for him were an employee of his: s 4B(6) (as added: see note 1 supra). As to the meaning of 'employer' see para 529 note 2 ante.

3 See ibid s 4B(8) (as added: see note 1 supra). The provisions of s 68 (as amended) relating to the meaning of 'employment at an establishment in Great Britain' (see para 529 note 3 ante) apply for these purposes with the appropriate modifications: see s 4B(8) (as so added). For the meaning of 'Great Britain' see para 325 note 6 ante.

4 Ibid s 4B(1) (as added: see note 1 supra). For the meaning of 'disabled person' see para 511 ante. For the meaning of 'contract worker' see note 1 supra.

5 Ibid s 4B(1)(a) (as added: see note 1 supra).

6 Ibid s 4B(1)(b) (as added: see note 1 supra).

7 As to the meaning of 'benefits' see para 534 note 9 ante.

8 Disability Discrimination Act 1995 s 4B(1)(c) (as added: see note 1 supra). Section 4B(1) (as added) does not apply to benefits of any description if the principal is concerned with the provision (whether or not for payment) of benefits of that description to the public, or to a section of the public which includes the contract worker in question, unless that provision differs in a material respect from the provision of the benefits by the principal to contract workers: s 4B(3) (as so added).

9 Ibid s 4B(1)(d) (as added: see note 1 supra). As to the meaning of 'detriment' see para 534 note 14 ante.

10 Ibid s 4B(2) (as added: see note 1 supra). For the meaning of 'harassment' see para 533 ante.

11 Ie ibid s 4B (as added).

12 As to the meaning of 'provision, criterion or practice' see para 532 note 6 ante.

13 As to the meaning of 'physical feature' see para 532 note 8 ante.

14 As to the meaning of 'premises' see para 525 note 9 ante.

15 Disability Discrimination Act 1995 s 4B(4) (as added: see note 1 supra). Where s 4B(4) (as added) applies to a disabled contract worker, his employer must take such steps as he would have to take under s 4A (as added) (see para 532 ante) if the provision, criterion or practice were applied by him or on his behalf or, as the case may be, if the premises were occupied by him: s 4B(5) (as so substituted). However, for the purposes of s 4A (as added) as applied by s 4B(6) (as added) (see note 2 supra), a principal is not required to take a step in relation to a disabled contract worker if, under s 4B (as added), the disabled contract worker's employer is required to take the step in relation to him: s 4B(7) (as so added).

16 As to the meaning of 'act' see para 510 note 3 ante.

17 Ie by virtue of the Disability Discrimination Act 1995 s 55 (as amended): see para 526 ante.

18 See ibid s 55(5) (as amended); and para 526 ante.

(b) Trade Organisations

541. Discrimination and harassment by trade organisations. It is unlawful for a trade organisation[1] to discriminate against a disabled person[2]: (1) in the arrangements which it makes for the purpose of determining who should be offered membership of the organisation[3]; (2) in the terms on which it is prepared to admit him to membership of the organisation[4]; or (3) by refusing to accept, or deliberately not accepting, his application for membership[5].

It is unlawful for a trade organisation, in the case of a disabled person who is a member of the organisation[6], to discriminate against him: (a) in the way it affords him access to any benefits[7] or by refusing or deliberately omitting to afford him access to them[8]; (b) by depriving him of membership, or varying the terms on which he is a member[9]; or (c) by subjecting him to any other detriment[10].

It is also unlawful for a trade organisation, in relation to membership of that organisation, to subject to harassment[11] a disabled person who: (i) is a member of the organisation[12]; or (ii) has applied for membership of the organisation[13].

Trade organisations are responsible for the actions of their employees in the course of their employment[14]. Trade organisations can also be service providers to the general public and so owe duties under Part III of the Disability Discrimination Act 1995[15].

In the case of an act[16] which constitutes discrimination by way of victimisation[17], this provision also applies to discrimination against a person who is not disabled[18].

1   'Trade organisation' means an organisation of workers, an organisation of employers or any other organisation whose members carry on a particular profession or trade for the purposes of which the organisation exists: Disability Discrimination Act 1995 ss 13(4), 68(1) (s 13 substituted by the Disability Discrimination Act 1995 (Amendment) Regulations 2003, SI 2003/1673, regs 3(1), 13). 'Profession' includes any vocation or occupation: Disability Discrimination Act 1995 s 68(1). 'Trade' includes any business: s 68(1). As to the meaning of 'employer' see para 529 note 2 ante. The definition includes bodies such as trade unions, employers' associations, the Law Society and chartered professional institutions which exist for the purposes of the profession or trade which their members carry on. All trade organisations are subject to the Disability Discrimination Act 1995 regardless of their size or the number of members that they have. The General Medical Council is not a 'trade organisation' for these purposes: *General Medical Council v Cox* (2002) 70 BMLR 31, [2002] All ER (D) 383 (Mar), EAT. Cf *Horton v Higham* [2004] EWCA Civ 941, [2004] 3 All ER 852 (set of barristers' chambers a trade organisation). These cases relate to earlier versions of the Disability Discrimination Act 1995 s 13 (as substituted).

2   For the meaning of 'disabled person' see para 511 ante.

3   Disability Discrimination Act 1995 s 13(1)(a) (as substituted: see note 1 supra).
    A trade organisation also comes within the general prohibition of less favourable treatment of a disabled person unless the treatment in question is justified: see s 3A (as added); and paras 530–532, 535 ante. Section 3A (as added) is broader than its predecessor (i e s 5 (repealed)) as it refers to 'person' rather than 'employer', and the previous provision specifically relating to trade organisations has been removed. See also para 542 post.

4   Ibid s 13(1)(b) (as substituted: see note 1 supra). See note 3 supra. It would be unlawful for a disabled applicant to be offered different (and less favourable) terms than a non-disabled applicant (unless the trade organisation can show objective justification for such a differential). Once the applicant has accepted membership he arguably falls under s 13(2) (as substituted) (see the text and notes 6–10 infra): cf *Clymo v Wandsworth London Borough Council* [1989] ICR 250, [1989] IRLR 241, EAT (decided in relation to the equivalent provisions relating to employment under the Sex Discrimination Act 1975).

5   Disability Discrimination Act 1995 s 13(1)(c) (as substituted: see note 1 supra). See note 3 supra. This includes both an active or passive mechanism to the failure of the disabled person to get membership, i e a refusal or a deliberate failure to admit to membership. See *Horton v Higham* [2004] EWCA Civ 941, [2004] 3 All ER 852 (application for pupillage at set of barristers' chambers not within an earlier version of the provision as not an application for membership of the chambers).

6   Membership of a trade organisation consists of a private contractual relationship between the member and the organisation: see *O'Reilly v Mackman* [1983] 2 AC 237, [1982] 3 All ER 1124, HL; *Cheall v Association of Professional Executive Clerical and Computer Staff* [1983] ICR 398, [1983] IRLR 215, HL. A disabled complainant will have to show that he is a paid up member under the rules or constitution of the trade organisation and thus entitled to bring a claim against it under the Disability Discrimination Act 1995. It was previously thought that former members were likely to be dealt with in the same way as ex-employees due to *Post Office v Adekeye* [1997] ICR 110, sub nom *Adekeye v Post Office (No 2)* [1997] IRLR 105, CA, but this case was overruled by *Relaxion Group plc v Rhys-Harper, D'Souza v Lambert London Borough Council, Jones v 3M Healthcare Ltd* [2003] UKHL 33, [2003] 4 All ER 1113, [2003] IRLR 484. See also *J Sainsbury Ltd v Savage* [1981] ICR 1, sub nom *Savage v J Sainsbury Ltd* [1980] IRLR 109, CA.

7   As to the meaning of 'benefits' see para 534 note 9 ante. Any benefit will include all significant benefits which are available to members as part of their membership, but it is unlikely that a trivial disadvantage in treatment will be regarded as the denial of a benefit: *Peake v Automotive Products Ltd* [1978] QB 233, [1978] 1 All ER 106, CA (women employees permitted to leave factory at the end of a shift five minutes earlier than men). Such treatment is de minimis: see *Ministry of Defence v Jeremiah* [1980] QB 87, [1979] 3 All ER 833, CA.

8   Disability Discrimination Act 1995 s 13(2)(a) (as substituted: see note 1 supra). See note 3 supra.

9   Ibid s 13(2)(b) (as substituted: see note 1 supra). See note 3 supra.

10 Ibid s 13(2)(c) (as substituted: see note 1 supra). See note 3 supra.

11 For the meaning of 'harassment' see para 533 ante.

12 Disability Discrimination Act 1995 s 13(3)(a) (as substituted: see note 1 supra). See note 3 supra.

13 Ibid s 13(3)(b) (as substituted: see note 1 supra). See note 3 supra.

14 See ibid s 58(1); and para 527 ante. It is a defence for the trade organisation to show that it took all reasonably practicable steps to prevent the employee from unlawfully discriminating against disabled people: see s 58(5); and para 527 ante.

15 As to ibid Pt III (ss 19–28) (as amended; prospectively amended) see para 582 et seq post.

16 As to the meaning of 'act' see para 510 note 3 ante.

17 Ie by virtue of the Disability Discrimination Act 1995 s 55 (as amended): see para 526 ante.

18 See ibid s 55(5) (as amended); and para 526 ante.

542.   Duty of trade organisations to make adjustments.   Where a provision, criterion or practice[1] applied by or on behalf of a trade organisation[2], or any physical feature[3] of premises[4] occupied by the organisation[5], places the disabled person concerned[6] at a substantial disadvantage in comparison with persons who are not disabled, it is the duty of the organisation to take such steps as it is reasonable[7], in all the circumstances of the case, for it to have to take in order to prevent the provision, criterion, practice or feature having that effect[8].

Nothing in the above provisions imposes any duty on an organisation in relation to a disabled person if the organisation does not know and could not reasonably be expected to know: (1) in the case of an applicant or potential applicant, that the disabled person concerned is, or may be, an applicant for membership of the organisation[9]; or (2) in any case, that the person has a disability[10] and is likely to be placed at a substantial disadvantage[11].

Subject to any duty to make reasonable adjustments, a trade organisation is not required[12] to treat a disabled person more favourably than it treats or would treat others[13].

1   As to the meaning of 'provision, criterion or practice' see para 532 note 6 ante.

2   Disability Discrimination Act 1995 s 14(1)(a) (s 14 substituted by the Disability Discrimination Act 1995 (Amendment) Regulations 2003, SI 2003/1673, regs 3(1), 13). For the meaning of 'trade organisation' see para 541 note 1 ante.

3   As to the meaning of 'physical feature' see para 532 note 8 ante.

4   As to the meaning of 'premises' see para 525 note 9 ante.

5   Disability Discrimination Act 1995 s 14(1)(b) (as substituted: see note 2 supra).

6   'The disabled person concerned' means: (1) in the case of a provision, criterion or practice for determining to whom membership should be offered, any disabled person who is, or has notified the organisation that he may be, an applicant for membership; and (2) in any other case, a disabled person who is: (a) a member of the organisation; or (b) an applicant for membership of the organisation: ibid s 14(2) (as substituted: see note 1 supra). For the meaning of 'disabled person' see para 511 ante.

7   As to the determination of whether it is reasonable for a trade organisation to have to take a particular step, and examples of steps which it may have to take, see ibid s 18B (as added); and para 532 ante.

8   Ibid s 14(1) (as substituted: see note 2 supra). As to alterations to premises occupied under leases see para 560 post.

9   Ibid s 14(3)(a) (as substituted: see note 2 supra).

10 As to when a person has a disability see para 511 ante.

11 See the Disability Discrimination Act 1995 s 14(3)(b) (as substituted: see note 2 supra).

12 Ie by ibid Pt II (ss 3A–18E) (as amended; prospectively amended).

13 See ibid s 18D(1) (as added); and para 530 ante.

(c)   Office-holders

543.   Discrimination and harassment in relation to office-holders.   In relation to an appointment to an office or post[1], it is unlawful for a relevant person[2] to discriminate against a disabled person[3] in the arrangements which he makes for the purpose of determining who should be offered the appointment[4], in the terms on which he offers him the appointment[5], or by refusing[6] to offer him the appointment[7].

In relation to an appointment to certain government offices or posts[8], it is unlawful for a relevant person to discriminate against a disabled person in the arrangements which he makes for the purpose of determining who should be recommended or approved in relation to the appointment[9], or in making or refusing to make a recommendation[10], or giving or refusing to give an approval, in relation to the appointment[11].

In relation to a disabled person who has been appointed to an office or post[12], it is unlawful for a relevant person to discriminate against him[13]: (1) in the terms of the appointment[14]; (2) in the opportunities which he affords him for promotion, transfer, training or receiving any other benefit, or by refusing to afford him any such opportunity[15]; (3) by terminating the appointment[16]; or (4) by subjecting him to any other detriment[17] in relation to the appointment[18].

It is also unlawful for a relevant person, in relation to an office or post[19], to subject to harassment[20] a disabled person: (a) who has been appointed to the office or post[21]; (b) who is seeking or being considered for appointment to the office or post[22]; or (c) who is seeking or being considered for a recommendation or approval in relation to an appointment to an office or post[23].

In the case of an act[24] which constitutes discrimination by way of victimisation[25], this provision also applies to discrimination against a person who is not disabled[26].

1   Ie an office or post to which the Disability Discrimination Act 1995 s 4D (as added) applies. The Disability Discrimination Act 1995 s 4D (as added) and s 4E (as added) (see para 544 post) apply to an office or post if: (1) none of s 4 (as substituted) (see para 534 ante), s 4B (as added) (see para 540 ante), s 6A (as added) (see para 545 post), s 7A (as added) (see para 547 post), s 14C (as added) (see para 551 post) or s 15B(3)(b) (as added) (see para 558 post) apply in relation to an appointment to the office or post; and (2) one or more of the following conditions is satisfied: (a) the office or post is one to which persons are appointed to discharge functions personally under the direction of another person, and in respect of which they are entitled to remuneration; (b) the office or post is one to which appointments are made by a Minister of the Crown, a government department, or the National Assembly for Wales; (c) the office or post is one to which appointments are made on the recommendation of, or subject to the approval of, a person referred to in head (b) supra: s 4C(1)–(3) (ss 4C–4F added by the Disability Discrimination Act 1995 (Amendment) Regulations 2003, SI 2003/1673, regs 3(1), 5); and the Disability Discrimination Act 1995 s 4C(2) amended by the Disability Discrimination Act 2005 s 19(1), Sch 1 paras 1, 5). For the purposes of head (2)(a) supra, the holder of an office or post: (i) is to be regarded as discharging his functions under the direction of another person if that other person is entitled to direct him as to when and where he discharges those functions; (ii) is not to be regarded as entitled to remuneration merely because he is entitled to payments in respect of expenses incurred by him in carrying out the functions of the office or post, or by way of compensation for the loss of income or benefits he would or might have received from any person had he not been carrying out the functions of the office or post: Disability Discrimination Act 1995 s 4C(4) (as so added). As to the meaning of 'benefits' see para 534 note 9 ante.

Sections 4D, 4E (both as added and amended) do not apply to: (A) any office of the House of Commons held by a member of it; (B) a life peerage within the meaning of the Life Peerages Act 1958 (see CONSTITUTIONAL LAW AND HUMAN RIGHTS vol 8(2) (Reissue) para 212; PARLIAMENT vol 34 (Reissue) para 540; PEERAGES AND DIGNITIES), or any office of the House of Lords held by a member of it: (C) any office mentioned in the House of Commons Disqualification Act 1975 Sch 2 (as amended) (see PARLIAMENT vol 34 (Reissue) para 611); (D) the offices of Leader of the Opposition, Chief Opposition Whip or Assistant Opposition Whip within the meaning of the Ministerial and other Salaries Act 1975 (see CONSTITUTIONAL LAW AND HUMAN RIGHTS vol 8(2) (Reissue) para 219); (E) any office of the National Assembly for Wales held by a member of it; (F) in England, any office of a county council, a London borough council, a district council or a parish council held by a member of it; (G) in Wales, any office of a county council, a county borough council or a community council held by a member of it; (H) any office of the Greater London Authority held by a member of it; (I) any office of the Common Council of the City of London held by a member of it; (J) any office of the Council of the Isles of Scilly held by a member of it; or (K) any office of a political party: Disability Discrimination Act 1995 s 4C(5) (as so added). This provision also refers to various Scottish offices, but Scottish matters generally are beyond the scope of this work. As to the National Assembly for Wales see para 302 ante. As to local government authorities in England and Wales see LOCAL GOVERNMENT vol 29(1) (Reissue) para 23 et seq; as to London borough councils see LONDON GOVERNMENT vol 29(2) (Reissue) para 35 et seq; as to the Greater London Authority see LONDON GOVERNMENT vol 29(2) (Reissue) para 70 et seq; as to the Common Council of the City of London see LONDON GOVERNMENT vol 29(2) (Reissue) para 51 et seq; and as to the Council of the Isles of Scilly see LOCAL GOVERNMENT vol 29(1) (Reissue) para 40.

　　For the purposes of ss 4C–4E (as added and amended), appointment to an office or post does not include election to an office or post: s 4F(1) (as so added).

2　'Relevant person' means: (1) in a case relating to an appointment to an office or post, the person with power to make that appointment; (2) in a case relating to the making of a recommendation or the giving of an approval in relation to an appointment, a person or body referred to in note 1 head (2)(b) supra with power to make that recommendation or (as the case may be) to give that approval; (3) in a case relating to a term of an appointment, the person with power to determine that term; (4) in a case relating to a working condition afforded in relation to an appointment: (a) the person with power to determine that working condition; or (b) where there is no such person, the person with power to make the appointment; (5) in a case relating to the termination of an appointment, the person with power to terminate the appointment; (6) in a case relating to the subjection of a disabled person to any other detriment or to harassment, any person or body falling within one or more of heads (1)–(5) supra in relation to such cases as are there mentioned: ibid s 4F(2) (as added: see note 1 supra). 'Working condition' includes any opportunity for promotion, transfer, training or receiving any other benefit, and any physical feature of premises at or from which the functions of an office or post are performed: s 4F(3) (as so added). As to the meaning of 'physical feature' see para 532 note 8 ante. As to the meaning of 'premises' see para 525 note 9 ante.

3　For the meaning of 'disabled person' see para 511 ante. As to the application of these provisions to past disabilities see para 522 ante.

4　Disability Discrimination Act 1995 s 4D(1)(a) (as added: see note 1 supra).

5　Ibid s 4D(1)(b) (as added: see note 1 supra).

6　For these purposes, 'refusal' includes deliberate omission: ibid s 4D(7)(b) (as added: see note 1 supra).

7　Ibid s 4D(1)(c) (as added: see note 1 supra).

8　Ie to which ibid s 4D (as added) applies and which satisfies the condition set out in note 1 head (2)(c) supra.

9　Ibid s 4D(2)(a) (as added: see note 1 supra).

10　Making a recommendation includes making a negative recommendation: ibid s 4D(7)(a) (as added: see note 1 supra).

11　Ibid s 4D(2)(b) (as added: see note 1 supra).

12　Ie to which ibid s 4D (as added) applies (see note 1 supra).

13　Ibid s 4D(3) (as added: see note 1 supra). Section 4D(3) (as added) does not apply to benefits of any description if the relevant person is concerned with the provision (for payment or not) of benefits of that description to the public, or a section of the public to which the disabled person belongs, unless: (1) that provision differs in a material respect from the provision of the benefits to persons appointed to offices or posts which are the same as, or not materially different from, that to which the disabled person has been appointed; (2) the provision of the benefits to the person appointed is regulated by the terms and conditions of his appointment; or (3) the benefits relate to training: s 4D(5) (as so added).

14　Ibid s 4D(3)(a) (as added: see note 1 supra).

15　Ibid s 4D(3)(b) (as added: see note 1 supra).

16　Ibid s 4D(3)(c) (as added: see note 1 supra). Termination of the appointment includes: (1) termination of the appointment by the expiration of any period, including a period expiring by reference to an event or circumstance, not being a termination immediately after which the appointment is renewed on the same terms and conditions; and (2) termination of the appointment by any act of the person appointed, including the giving of notice, in circumstances such that he is entitled to terminate the appointment by reason of the conduct of the relevant person: s 4D(6) (as so added).

17　As to the meaning of 'detriment' see para 534 note 14 ante.

18　Disability Discrimination Act 1995 s 4D(3)(d) (as added: see note 1 supra).

19　Ie to which ibid s 4D (as added) applies (see note 1 supra).

20　For the meaning of 'harassment' see para 533 ante.

21　Disability Discrimination Act 1995 s 4D(4)(a) (as added: see note 1 supra).

22　Ibid s 4D(4)(b) (as added: see note 1 supra).

23　Ibid s 4D(4)(c) (as added: see note 1 supra). The office or post referred to in the text is an office or post satisfying the condition set out in note 1 head (1)(c) supra.

24　As to the meaning of 'act' see para 510 note 3 ante.

25　Ie by virtue of the Disability Discrimination Act 1995 s 55 (as amended): see para 526 ante.

26　See ibid s 55(5) (as amended); and para 526 ante.

544.   Duty of office-holders to make adjustments.   Where a provision, criterion or practice[1] applied by or on behalf of a relevant person[2], or any physical feature[3] of premises[4] under the control of a relevant person and at or from which the functions of an office or post[5] are performed, places the disabled person concerned[6] at a substantial disadvantage in comparison with persons who are not disabled, it is the duty of the relevant person to take such steps as it is reasonable[7], in all the circumstances of the case, for him to have to take in order to prevent the provision, criterion, practice or feature having that effect[8].

No duty is imposed on the relevant person in relation to a disabled person if the relevant person does not know, and could not reasonably be expected to know: (1) in the case of a person who is being considered for, or is or may be seeking, appointment to, or a recommendation or approval in relation to, an office or post, that the disabled person concerned is, or may be, seeking appointment to or, as the case may be, seeking a recommendation or approval in relation to, that office or post, or is being considered for appointment to or, as the case may be, for a recommendation or approval in relation to, that office or post[9]; or (2) in any case, that that person has a disability and is likely to be placed at a substantial disadvantage[10].

Subject to any duty to make reasonable adjustments[11], a relevant person is not required[12] to treat a disabled person more favourably than he treats or would treat others[13].

1   As to the meaning of 'provision, criterion or practice' see para 532 note 6 ante.
2   Disability Discrimination Act 1995 s 4E(1)(a) (ss 4E, 4F added by the Disability Discrimination Act 1995 (Amendment) Regulations 2003, SI 2003/1673, regs 3(1), 5). For the meaning of 'relevant person' see para 543 note 2 ante.
3   As to the meaning of 'physical feature' see para 532 note 8 ante.
4   As to the meaning of 'premises' see para 525 note 9 ante.
5   Ie an office or post to which the Disability Discrimination Act 1995 s 4E (as added) applies: see para 543 note 1 ante.
6   'The disabled person concerned' means: (1) in the case of a provision, criterion or practice for determining who should be appointed to, or recommended or approved in relation to, an office or post to which ibid s 4E (as added) applies (see note 5 supra), any disabled person who: (a) is, or has notified the relevant person that he may be, seeking appointment to or, as the case may be, a recommendation or approval in relation to, that office or post; or (b) is being considered for appointment to or, as the case may be, a recommendation or approval in relation to, that office or post; or (2) in any other case, a disabled person: (a) who is seeking or being considered for appointment to, or a recommendation or approval in relation to, the office or post concerned; or (b) who has been appointed to the office or post concerned: s 4F(2) (as added: see note 1 supra). For the meaning of 'disabled person' see para 511 ante. As to the application of these provisions to past disabilities see para 522 ante.
7   As to the determination of whether it is reasonable for a relevant person to have to take a particular step, and examples of steps which he may have to take, see ibid s 18B (as added); and para 532 ante.
8   Ibid s 4E(1) (as added: see note 1 supra).
9   Ibid s 4E(3)(a) (as added: see note 1 supra).
10 Ibid s 4E(3)(b) (as added: see note 1 supra).
11 As to the meaning of 'duty to make reasonable adjustments' see para 530 note 7 ante.
12 Ie by the Disability Discrimination Act 1995 Pt II (ss 3A–18E) (as amended; prospectively amended).
13 See ibid s 18D(1) (as added); and para 530 ante.

(d)   Partnerships

545.   Discrimination and harassment by partnerships.   In relation to a position as partner in a firm[1], it is unlawful for the firm to discriminate against a disabled person[2]: (1) in the arrangements which it makes for the purpose of determining who should be offered the position[3]; (2) in the terms on which it offers him the position[4]; (3) by refusing or deliberately omitting to offer him that position[5]; (4) in a case where the person already holds that position: (a) in the way it affords him access to any benefits, or by refusing or deliberately omitting to afford him access to them[6]; or (b) by expelling him from that position[7] or subjecting him to any other detriment[8].

It is also unlawful for a firm, in relation to a position as partner in the firm, to subject to harassment[9] a disabled person who holds or has applied for that position[10].

In the case of an act[11] which constitutes discrimination by way of victimisation[12], this provision also applies to discrimination against a person who is not disabled[13].

1　The Disability Discrimination Act 1995 s 6A(1)(a)–(c) (as added) and s 6B(2) (as added) (see para 546 post) apply in relation to persons proposing to form themselves into a partnership as they apply in relation to a firm: s 6C(1) (ss 6A–6C added by the Disability Discrimination Act 1995 (Amendment) Regulations 2003, SI 2003/1673, regs 3(1), 6). The Disability Discrimination Act 1995 s 6A (as added) and s 6B (as added) (see para 546 post) apply to a limited liability partnership as they apply to a firm; and, in the application of those provisions to a limited liability partnership, references to a partner in a firm are references to a member of the limited liability partnership: s 6C(2) (as so added). In the case of a limited partnership, references in s 6A (as added) and s 6B (as added) to a partner are to be construed as references to a general partner as defined in the Limited Partnerships Act 1907 s 3 (see PARTNERSHIP vol 35 (Reissue) para 207): Disability Discrimination Act 1995 s 6C(3) (as so added). In ss 6A–6C (as added), 'firm' has the meaning given by the Partnership Act 1890 s 4 (as amended) (see PARTNERSHIP vol 35 (Reissue) para 1): Disability Discrimination Act 1995 s 6C(4) (as so added). As to limited liability partnerships see PARTNERSHIP.

2　Ibid s 6A(1) (as added: see note 1 supra). For the meaning of 'disabled person' see para 511 ante. As to the application of these provisions to past disabilities see para 522 ante.

　　Section 6A(1) (as added) does not apply to benefits of any description if the firm is concerned with the provision (whether or not for payment) of benefits of that description to the public, or to a section of the public which includes the partner in question, unless that provision differs in a material respect from the provision of the benefits to other partners: s 6A(3) (as so added). As to the meaning of 'benefits' see para 534 note 9 ante.

3　Ibid s 6A(1)(a) (as added: see note 1 supra).

4　Ibid s 6A(1)(b) (as added: see note 1 supra).

5　Ibid s 6A(1)(c) (as added: see note 1 supra).

6　Ibid s 6A(1)(d)(i) (as added: see note 1 supra).

7　Expulsion of a person from a position as partner includes termination of that person's partnership: (1) by the expiration of any period, including a period expiring by reference to an event or circumstance, not being a termination immediately after which the partnership is renewed on the same terms; and (2) by any act of his, including the giving of notice, in circumstances such that he is entitled to terminate it without notice by reason of the conduct of the other partners: ibid s 6A(4) (as added: see note 1 supra).

8　Ibid s 6A(1)(d)(ii) (as added: see note 1 supra).

9　For the meaning of 'harassment' see para 533 ante.

10　Disability Discrimination Act 1995 s 6A(2) (as added: see note 1 supra).

11　As to the meaning of 'act' see para 510 note 3 ante.

12　Ie by virtue of the Disability Discrimination Act 1995 s 55 (as amended): see para 526 ante.

13　See ibid s 55(5) (as amended); and para 526 ante.

546.　Duty of partnerships to make adjustments.　Where a provision, criterion or practice applied by or on behalf of a firm[1], or any physical feature[2] of premises[3] occupied by the firm, places the disabled person concerned[4] at a substantial disadvantage in comparison with persons who are not disabled, it is the duty of the firm to take such steps as it is reasonable[5], in all the circumstances of the case, for it to have to take in order to prevent the provision, criterion, practice or feature having that effect[6].

No duty is imposed on a firm in relation to a disabled person if the firm does not know, and could not reasonably be expected to know: (1) in the case of a candidate or potential candidate, that the disabled person concerned is, or may be, a candidate for the position of partner[7]; or (2) in any case, that that person has a disability and is likely to be placed at a substantial disadvantage[8].

Subject to any duty to make reasonable adjustments[9], a firm is not required[10] to treat a disabled person more favourably than it treats or would treat others[11].

1　As to the meaning of 'provision, criterion or practice' see para 532 note 6 ante. As to the meaning of 'firm' see para 545 note 1 ante.

2   As to the meaning of 'physical feature' see para 532 note 8 ante.

3   As to the meaning of 'premises' see para 525 note 9 ante.

4   'The disabled person concerned' means: (1) in the case of a provision, criterion or practice for determining to whom the position of partner should be offered, any disabled person who is, or has notified the firm that he may be, a candidate for that position; (2) in any other case, a disabled person who is: (a) a partner; or (b) a candidate for the position of partner: Disability Discrimination Act 1995 s 6B(2) (s 6B added by the Disability Discrimination Act 1995 (Amendment) Regulations 2003, SI 2003/1673, regs 3(1), 6). For the meaning of 'disabled person' see para 511 ante. As to the application of these provisions to past disabilities see para 522 ante.

5   As to the determination of whether it is reasonable for a firm to have to take a particular step, and examples of steps which it may have to take, see the Disability Discrimination Act 1995 s 18B (as added); and para 532 ante.

6   Ibid s 6B(1) (as added: see note 4 supra). Where a firm is required by s 6B (as added) to take any steps in relation to the disabled person concerned, the cost of taking those steps is to be treated as an expense of the firm; and the extent to which such cost should be borne by that person, where he is or becomes a partner in the firm, may not exceed such amount as is reasonable, having regard in particular to the proportion in which he is entitled to share in the firm's profits: s 6B(4) (as so added).

7   Ibid s 6B(3)(a) (as added: see note 4 supra).

8   Ibid s 6B(3)(b) (as added: see note 4 supra).

9   As to the meaning of 'duty to make reasonable adjustments' see para 530 note 7 ante.

10   Ie by the Disability Discrimination Act 1995 Pt II (ss 3A–18E) (as amended; prospectively amended).

11   See ibid s 18D(1) (as added); and para 530 ante.

(e)   Barristers

547.   Discrimination and harassment by or in relation to barristers.   In relation to any offer of a pupillage[1] or tenancy[2], it is unlawful for a barrister or a barrister's clerk[3] to discriminate against a disabled person[4]: (1) in the arrangements which are made for the purpose of determining to whom it should be offered[5]; (2) in respect of any terms on which it is offered[6]; or (3) by refusing, or deliberately omitting, to offer it to him[7].

In relation to a disabled pupil or tenant in the set of chambers[8] in question, it is unlawful for a barrister or a barrister's clerk to discriminate against him: (a) in respect of any terms applicable to him as a pupil or tenant[9]; (b) in the opportunities for training, or gaining experience, which are afforded or denied to him[10]; (c) in the benefits which are afforded or denied to him[11]; (d) by terminating his pupillage or by subjecting him to any pressure to leave the chambers[12]; or (e) by subjecting him to any other detriment[13].

It is unlawful for a barrister or barrister's clerk, in relation to a pupillage or tenancy, to subject to harassment[14] a disabled person who is, or has applied to be, a pupil or tenant in the set of chambers in question[15].

It is also unlawful for any person, in relation to the giving, withholding or acceptance of instructions to a barrister, to discriminate against a disabled person or to subject him to harassment[16].

In the case of an act[17] which constitutes discrimination by way of victimisation[18], this provision also applies to discrimination against a person who is not disabled[19].

1   'Pupillage' and 'pupil' have the meanings commonly associated with their use in the context of barristers practising in independent practice: Disability Discrimination Act 1995 s 7A(5) (s 7A added by the Disability Discrimination Act 1995 (Amendment) Regulations 2003, SI 2003/1673, regs 3(1), 8).

2   'Tenancy' and 'tenant' have the meanings commonly associated with their use in the context of barristers practising in independent practice, but they also include reference to any barrister permitted to practise from a set of chambers: Disability Discrimination Act 1995 s 7A(5) (as added: see note 1 supra).

3   'Barrister's clerk' includes any person carrying out any of the functions of a barrister's clerk: ibid s 7A(5) (as added: see note 1 supra).

4   For the meaning of 'disabled person' see para 511 ante. As to the application of these provisions to past disabilities see para 522 ante.

5   Disability Discrimination Act 1995 s 7A(1)(a) (as added: see note 1 supra).

6   Ibid s 7A(1)(b) (as added: see note 1 supra).

7   Ibid s 7A(1)(c) (as added: see note 1 supra).

8   'Set of chambers' has the meaning commonly associated with its use in the context of barristers practising in independent practice: ibid s 7A(5) (as added: see note 1 supra).

9   Ibid s 7A(3)(a) (as added: see note 1 supra).

10 Ibid s 7A(3)(b) (as added: see note 1 supra).

11 Ibid s 7A(3)(c) (as added: see note 1 supra).

12 Ibid s 7A(3)(d) (as added: see note 1 supra).

13 Ibid s 7A(3)(e) (as added: see note 1 supra).

14 For the meaning of 'harassment' see para 533 ante.

15 Disability Discrimination Act 1995 s 7A(3) (as added: see note 1 supra).

16 Ibid s 7A(4) (as added: see note 1 supra).

17 As to the meaning of 'act' see para 510 note 3 ante.

18 Ie by virtue of the Disability Discrimination Act 1995 s 55 (as amended): see para 526 ante.

19 See ibid s 55(5) (as amended); and para 526 ante.

548.   Duty of barristers to make adjustments.   Where a provision, criterion or practice[1] applied by or on behalf of a barrister or barrister's clerk[2], or any physical feature[3] of premises[4] occupied by a barrister or a barrister's clerk, places the disabled person concerned[5] at a substantial disadvantage in comparison with persons who are not disabled, it is the duty of the barrister or barrister's clerk to take such steps as it is reasonable[6], in all the circumstances of the case, for him to have to take in order to prevent the provision, criterion, practice or feature having that effect[7].

No duty is imposed on a barrister or a barrister's clerk in relation to a disabled person if he does not know, and could not reasonably be expected to know: (1) in the case of a candidate or potential candidate, that the disabled person concerned is, or may be, an applicant or potential applicant for a pupillage or tenancy[8]; or (2) in any case, that that person has a disability and is likely to be placed at a substantial disadvantage[9].

Subject to any duty to make reasonable adjustments[10], a barrister or barrister's clerk is not required[11] to treat a disabled person more favourably than he treats or would treat others[12].

1   As to the meaning of 'provision, criterion or practice' see para 532 note 6 ante.

2   As to the meaning of 'barrister's clerk' see para 547 note 3 ante.

3   As to the meaning of 'physical feature' see para 532 note 8 ante.

4   As to the meaning of 'premises' see para 525 note 9 ante.

5   'The disabled person concerned' means: (1) in the case of a provision, criterion or practice for determining to whom a pupillage or tenancy should be offered, any disabled person who is, or has notified the barrister or the barrister's clerk concerned that he may be, an applicant for a pupillage or tenancy; (2) in any other case, a disabled person who is a tenant, a pupil, or an applicant for a pupillage or tenancy: Disability Discrimination Act 1995 s 7B(3) (s 7B added by the Disability Discrimination Act 1995 (Amendment) Regulations 2003, SI 2003/1673, regs 3(1), 8). For the meaning of 'disabled person' see para 511 ante. As to the application of these provisions to past disabilities see para 522 ante. For the meanings of 'pupillage' and 'pupil see para 547 note 1 ante; and for the meanings of 'tenancy' and 'tenant' see para 547 note 2 ante.

6   As to the determination of whether it is reasonable for a barrister or barrister's clerk to have to take a particular step, and examples of steps which he may have to take, see the Disability Discrimination Act 1995 s 18B (as added); and para 532 ante.

7   Ibid s 7B(1) (as added: see note 5 supra). In a case where s 7B(1) (as added) applies in relation to two or more barristers in a set of chambers, the duty in s 7B(1) (as added) is a duty on each of them to take such steps as it is reasonable, in all of the circumstances of the case, for him to have to take: s 7B(7) (as so added). For the meaning of 'set of chambers' see para 547 note 8 ante.

8   Ibid s 7B(4)(a) (as added: see note 5 supra).

9   Ibid s 7B(4)(b) (as added: see note 5 supra).

10 As to the meaning of 'duty to make reasonable adjustments' see para 530 note 7 ante.

11 Ie by the Disability Discrimination Act 1995 Pt II (ss 3A–18E) (as amended; prospectively amended).

12 See ibid s 18D(1) (as added); and para 530 ante.

(f) Qualifications Bodies

549. Discrimination and harassment by qualifications bodies. It is unlawful for a qualifications body[1] to discriminate against a disabled person[2]: (1) in the arrangements which it makes for the purpose of determining upon whom to confer[3] a professional or trade qualification[4]; (2) in the terms on which it is prepared to confer a professional or trade qualification on him[5]; (3) by refusing or deliberately omitting to grant any application by him for such a qualification[6]; or (4) by withdrawing such a qualification from him or varying the terms on which he holds it[7].

It is also unlawful for a qualifications body, in relation to a professional or trade qualification conferred by it, to subject to harassment[8] a disabled person who holds or has applied for such a qualification[9].

In the case of an act[10] which constitutes discrimination by way of victimisation[11], this provision also applies to discrimination against a person who is not disabled[12].

1   'Qualifications body' means any authority or body which can confer a professional or trade qualification, but it does not include: (1) a responsible body within the meaning of the Disability Discrimination Act 1995 Pt IV Ch I or Ch II (ss 28A–31A) (as added and amended) (see para 561 et seq post); or (2) a local education authority: see s 14A(5) (s 14A added by the Disability Discrimination Act 1995 (Amendment) Regulations 2003, SI 2003/1673, regs 3(1), 13). As to local education authorities see EDUCATION vol 15(1) (2006 Reissue) para 20.

2   For the meaning of 'disabled person' see para 511 ante. As to the application of these provisions to past disabilities see para 522 ante.

      In determining for the purposes of the Disability Discrimination Act 1995 s 14A(1) (as added) whether the application by a qualifications body of a competence standard to a disabled person constitutes discrimination, the application of the standard is justified for the purposes of s 3A(1)(b) (as added) (see paras 530, 532, 535 ante) if, but only if, the qualifications body can show that: (1) the standard is, or would be, applied equally to persons who do not have his particular disability; and (2) its application is a proportionate means of achieving a legitimate aim: s 14A(3) (as so added). 'Competence standard' means an academic, medical or other standard applied by or on behalf of a qualifications body for the purpose of determining whether or not a person has a particular level of competence or ability: s 14A(5) (as so added). For the purposes of s 14A(3) (as added): (a) the provisions of s 3A(2), (6) (as added) (see paras 525, 530 ante) do not apply; and (b) s 3A(4) (as added) (see para 532 ante) has effect as if the reference to s 3A(3) (as added) were a reference to s 14A(3) (as added): s 14A(4) (as so added).

3   'Confer' includes renew or extend: ibid s 14A(5) (as added: see note 1 supra).

4   Ibid s 14A(1)(a) (as added: see note 1 supra). 'Professional or trade qualification' means an authorisation, qualification, recognition, registration, enrolment, approval or certification which is needed for, or facilitates engagement in, a particular profession or trade: s 14A(5) (as so added).

5   Ibid s 14A(1)(b) (as added: see note 1 supra).

6   Ibid s 14A(1)(c) (as added: see note 1 supra).

7   Ibid s 14A(1)(d) (as added: see note 1 supra).

8   For the meaning of 'harassment' see para 533 ante.

9   Disability Discrimination Act 1995 s 14A(2) (as added: see note 1 supra).

10 As to the meaning of 'act' see para 510 note 3 ante.

11 Ie by virtue of the Disability Discrimination Act 1995 s 55 (as amended): see para 526 ante.

12 See ibid s 55(5) (as amended); and para 526 ante.

550. Duty of qualifications bodies to make adjustments. Where a provision, criterion or practice[1] (other than a competence standard[2]) applied by or on behalf of a qualifications body, or any physical feature[3] of premises[4] occupied by a qualifications body, places the disabled person concerned[5] at a substantial disadvantage in comparison with persons who are not disabled, it is the duty of the qualifications body to take such steps as it is reasonable[6], in all the circumstances of the case, for it to have to take in order to prevent the provision, criterion, practice or feature having that effect[7].

No duty is imposed on a qualifications body in relation to a disabled person if the body does not know, and could not reasonably be expected to know: (1) in the case of an applicant or potential applicant, that the disabled person concerned is, or may be, an applicant for the conferment of a professional or trade qualification[8]; or (2) in any case, that that person has a disability and is likely to be placed at a substantial disadvantage[9].

Subject to any duty to make reasonable adjustments[10], a qualifications body is not required[11] to treat a disabled person more favourably than it treats or would treat others[12].

1 As to the meaning of 'provision, criterion or practice' see para 532 note 6 ante.
2 For the meaning of 'competence standard' see para 549 note 2 ante.
3 As to the meaning of 'physical feature' see para 532 note 8 ante.
4 As to the meaning of 'premises' see para 525 note 9 ante.
5 'The disabled person concerned' means: (1) in the case of a provision, criterion or practice for determining on whom a professional or trade qualification is to be conferred, any disabled person who is, or has notified the qualifications body that he may be, an applicant for the conferment of that qualification; (2) in any other case, a disabled person who holds a professional or trade qualification conferred by the qualifications body or who applies for a professional or trade qualification which it confers: Disability Discrimination Act 1995 s 14B(2) (s 14B added by the Disability Discrimination Act 1995 (Amendment) Regulations 2003, SI 2003/1673, regs 3(1), 13). For the meaning of 'disabled person' see para 511 ante. As to the application of these provisions to past disabilities see para 522 ante. For the meaning of 'qualifications body' see para 549 note 1 ante.
6 As to the determination of whether it is reasonable for a qualifications body to have to take a particular step, and examples of steps which it may have to take, see the Disability Discrimination Act 1995 s 18B (as added); and para 532 ante.
7 Ibid s 14B(1) (as added: see note 5 supra).
8 Ibid s 14B(3)(a) (as added: see note 5 supra).
9 Ibid s 14B(3)(b) (as added: see note 5 supra).
10 As to the meaning of 'duty to make reasonable adjustments' see para 530 note 7 ante.
11 Ie by the Disability Discrimination Act 1995 Pt II (ss 3A–18E) (as amended; prospectively amended).
12 See ibid s 18D(1) (as added); and para 530 ante.

(g) Practical Work Experience

551. Discrimination and harassment in regard to work placements. In the case of a disabled person[1] seeking or undertaking a work placement[2], it is unlawful for a placement provider[3] to discriminate against him: (1) in the arrangements which he makes for the purpose of determining who should be offered a work placement[4]; (2) in the terms on which he affords him access to any work placement or any facilities concerned with such a placement[5]; (3) by refusing or deliberately omitting to afford him such access[6]; (4) by terminating the placement[7]; or (5) by subjecting him to any other detriment in relation to the placement[8].

It is also unlawful for a placement provider, in relation to a work placement, to subject to harassment[9] a disabled person to whom he is providing a placement[10], or who has applied to him for a placement[11].

In the case of an act[12] which constitutes discrimination by way of victimisation[13], this provision also applies to discrimination against a person who is not disabled[14].

1 For the meaning of 'disabled person' see para 511 ante. As to the application of these provisions to past disabilities see para 522 ante.
2 'Work placement' means practical work experience undertaken for a limited period for the purposes of a person's vocational training: Disability Discrimination Act 1995 s 14C(4) (added by the Disability Discrimination Act 1995 (Amendment) Regulations 2003, SI 2003/1673, regs 3(1), 13).
3 'Placement provider' means any person who provides a work placement to a person whom he does not employ: Disability Discrimination Act 1995 s 14C(4) (as added: see note 2 supra).
4 Ibid s 14C(1)(a) (as added: see note 2 supra). See note 8 infra.
5 Ibid s 14C(1)(b) (as added: see note 2 supra). See note 8 infra.
6 Ibid s 14C(1)(c) (as added: see note 2 supra). See note 8 infra.
7 Ibid s 14C(1)(d) (as added: see note 2 supra). See note 8 infra.
8 Ibid s 14C(1)(e) (as added: see note 2 supra). Section 14C (as added and amended) and s 14D (as added) (see para 552 post) do not apply to: (1) anything made unlawful by s 4 (as substituted) (see para 534 ante), ss 19–21A (as amended) (see para 582 et seq post), ss 21F–21J (as added) (see para 596 et seq post) or

Pt IV (ss 28A–31C) (as amended; prospectively amended) (see para 561 et seq post); (2) anything which would be unlawful under any such provision but for the operation of any provision in or made under the Disability Discrimination Act 1995; or (3) a work placement undertaken in any of the naval, military and air forces of the Crown: s 14C(3), (5) (s 14C as so added; s 14C(3) substituted by the Disability Discrimination Act 2005 s 19(1), Sch 1 paras 1, 6).

9   For the meaning of 'harassment' see para 533 ante.

10   Disability Discrimination Act 1995 s 14C(2)(a) (as added: see note 2 supra). See note 8 supra.

11   Ibid s 14C(2)(b) (as added: see note 2 supra). See note 8 supra.

12   As to the meaning of 'act' see para 510 note 3 ante.

13   Ie by virtue of the Disability Discrimination Act 1995 s 55 (as amended): see para 526 ante.

14   See ibid s 55(5) (as amended); and para 526 ante.

552. Duty to make adjustments in regard to work placements. Where a provision, criterion or practice[1] applied by or on behalf of a placement provider[2], or any physical feature[3] of premises[4] occupied by the placement provider, places the disabled person concerned[5] at a substantial disadvantage in comparison with persons who are not disabled, it is the duty of the placement provider to take such steps as it is reasonable[6], in all the circumstances of the case, for him to have to take in order to prevent the provision, criterion, practice or feature having that effect[7].

No duty is imposed on a placement provider in relation to a disabled person if he does not know, and could not reasonably be expected to know: (1) in the case of an applicant or potential applicant, that the disabled person concerned is, or may be, an applicant for the work placement[8]; or (2) in any case, that that person has a disability and is likely to be placed at a substantial disadvantage[9].

Subject to any duty to make reasonable adjustments[10], a qualifications body is not required[11] to treat a disabled person more favourably than it treats or would treat others[12].

1   As to the meaning of 'provision, criterion or practice' see para 532 note 6 ante.

2   For the meaning of 'placement provider' see para 551 note 3 ante.

3   As to the meaning of 'physical feature' see para 532 note 8 ante.

4   As to the meaning of 'premises' see para 525 note 9 ante.

5   'The disabled person concerned' means: (1) in the case of a provision, criterion or practice for determining to whom a work placement should be offered, any disabled person who is, or has notified the placement provider that he may be, an applicant for that work placement; (2) in any other case, a disabled person who is an applicant for the work placement concerned or who is undertaking a work placement with the placement provider: Disability Discrimination Act 1995 s 14D(2) (added by the Disability Discrimination Act 1995 (Amendment) Regulations 2003, SI 2003/1673, regs 3(1), 13). For the meaning of 'disabled person' see para 511 ante. As to the application of these provisions to past disabilities see para 522 ante.

6   As to the determination of whether it is reasonable for a placement provider to have to take a particular step, and examples of steps which he may have to take, see the Disability Discrimination Act 1995 s 18B (as added); and para 532 ante.

7   Ibid s 14D(1) (as added: see note 5 supra). As to where s 14D (as added) does not apply see para 551 note 8 ante.

8   Ibid s 14D(3)(a) (as added: see note 5 supra). See note 7 supra.

9   Ibid s 14D(3)(b) (as added: see note 5 supra). See note 7 supra.

10   As to the meaning of 'duty to make reasonable adjustments' see para 530 note 7 ante.

11   Ie by the Disability Discrimination Act 1995 Pt II (ss 3A–18E) (as amended; prospectively amended).

12   See ibid s 18D(1) (as added); and para 530 ante.

(h) Crown Servants

553. Application of provisions to Crown servants. The provisions relating to discrimination in employment and members of locally-electable authorities[1] apply to service for purposes of a Minister of the Crown[2] or government department[3] (other than service of a person holding a statutory office)[4], or to service on behalf of the Crown for purposes of a person holding a statutory office or purposes of a statutory body[5], as they apply to employment by a private person[6]. There is an exemption from the provisions for service in any of the naval, military or air forces of the Crown[7].

1 Disability Discrimination Act 1995 s 64(2) (amended by the Disability Discrimination Act 1995 (Amendment) Regulations 2003, SI 2003/1673, regs 3(1), 24(a)). The provisions referred to in the text are those contained in the Disability Discrimination Act 1995 Pt II (ss 3A–18E) (as amended; prospectively amended): see para 529 et seq ante. For the meaning of 'employment' see para 529 note 2 ante.

 Section 64(2) (as amended) has effect subject to s 64A (as added and amended) (see para 554 post): see s 64(2A) (as added and amended); and para 510 note 1 ante.

2 For the meaning of 'Minister of the Crown' see para 510 note 4 ante.

3 'Service for purposes of a Minister of the Crown or government department' does not include service in any office for the time being mentioned in the House of Commons Disqualification Act 1975 s 2, Sch 2 (as amended) (ministerial offices) (see PARLIAMENT vol 34 (Reissue) para 611): Disability Discrimination Act 1995 s 64(8).

4 Ibid s 64(2)(a). For the meaning of 'statutory office' see para 510 note 7 ante. See note 1 supra.

5 Ibid s 64(2)(b). For the meaning of 'statutory body' see para 510 note 6 ante. See note 1 supra.

6 Ibid s 64(2). See note 1 supra.

7 See ibid s 64(7).

(i) Police

554. Discrimination and harassment in the police. For the purposes of the discrimination and harassment provisions relating to the field of employment and members of locally-electable authorities[1], the holding of the office of constable[2] or appointment as a police cadet[3] is to be treated as employment[4] by the chief officer of police[5] as respects any act[6] done by him in relation to a constable or that office, and by the police authority[7] as respects any act done by it in relation to a constable or that office[8].

 Any compensation, costs or expenses awarded against a chief officer of police in any proceedings[9], and any costs or expenses incurred by him in any such proceedings so far as not recovered by him in the proceedings[10], and any sum required by a chief officer of police for the settlement of any claim made against him[11], if the settlement is approved by the police authority[12], are to be paid out of the police fund[13].

 Further, a police authority may, in such cases and to such extent as appear to it to be appropriate, pay out of the police fund any compensation, any costs or expenses awarded in proceedings[14] against a person under the direction and control of the chief officer of police[15], any costs or expenses or incurred and not recovered by such a person in such proceedings[16], and any sum required in connection with the settlement of a claim that has or might have given rise to such proceedings[17].

1 Ie the Disability Discrimination Act 1995 Pt II (ss 3A–18E) (as amended; prospectively amended): see para 529 et seq ante. For the meaning of 'harassment' see para 533 ante.

2 As to the office of police constable see POLICE vol 36(1) (Reissue) para 201 et seq. For the purposes of ibid s 58 (liability of employers and principals: see para 527 ante), the holding of the office of constable is to be treated as employment by the chief officer of police (and as not being employment by any other person); and anything done by a person holding such an office in the performance, or purported performance, of his functions is to be treated as done in the course of that employment: s 64A(2) (s 64A added by the Disability Discrimination Act 1995 (Amendment) Regulations 2003, SI 2003/1673, regs 3(1), 25). See note 5 infra.

3 'Police cadet' means any person appointed to undergo training with a view to becoming a constable: Disability Discrimination Act 1995 s 64A(7) (as added: see note 2 supra). As to police cadets see POLICE vol 36(1) (Reissue) para 213 et seq.

4 For the meaning of 'employment' see para 529 note 2 ante.

5 'Chief officer of police': (1) in relation to a person appointed, or an appointment falling to be made, under the Metropolitan Police Act 1829, the City of London Police Act 1839 or the Police Act 1996, has the same meaning as in the Police Act 1996 (see POLICE vol 36(1) (Reissue) para 205); and (2) in relation to any other person or appointment, means the officer who has the direction and control of the body of

constables or cadets in question: Disability Discrimination Act 1995 s 64A(7) (as added (see note 2 supra); definition amended by the Serious Organised Crime and Police Act 2005 ss 59, 174(2), Sch 4 para 65(1), (2)(a), Sch 17 Pt 2).

Any proceedings under the Disability Discrimination Act 1995 Pt II (as amended; prospectively amended) (see para 529 et seq ante) or Pt III (ss 19–28) (as amended; prospectively amended) (see para 582 et seq post) which, by virtue of s 64A (as added and amended), would lie against a chief officer of police must be brought against the chief officer of police for the time being or, in the case of a vacancy in that office, against the person for the time being performing the functions of that office: s 64A(4) (as so added; and amended by the Disability Discrimination Act 2005 s 4).

6 As to the meaning of 'act' see para 510 note 3 ante.
7 'Police authority': (1) in relation to a person appointed, or an appointment falling to be made, under the Metropolitan Police Act 1829, the City of London Police Act 1839 or the Police Act 1996, has the same meaning as in the Police Act 1996 (see POLICE vol 36(1) (Reissue) para 202); (2) in relation to any other person or appointment, means the authority by whom the person in question is or on appointment would be paid: Disability Discrimination Act 1995 s 64A(7) (as added (see note 2 supra); definition amended by the Serious Organised Crime and Police Act 2005 Sch 4 para 65(1), (2)(b), Sch 17 Pt 2). As to police authorities see POLICE vol 36(1) (Reissue) para 316 et seq.
8 Disability Discrimination Act 1995 s 64A(1), (6) (as added: see note 2 supra).
9 Ie proceedings brought against him under ibid Pt II (as amended; prospectively amended) or Pt III (as amended; prospectively amended).
10 Ibid s 64A(3)(a) (as added (see note 2 supra); and amended by the Disability Discrimination Act 2005 s 4(1), (2)).
11 Ie a claim under the Disability Discrimination Act 1995 Pt II (as amended; prospectively amended) or Pt III (as amended; prospectively amended).
12 Ibid s 64A(3)(b) (as added (see note 2 supra); and amended by the Disability Discrimination Act 2005 s 4(1), (2)).
13 Disability Discrimination Act 1995 s 64A(3) (as added: see note 2 supra). 'Police fund', in relation to a chief officer of police within note 5 head (1) supra, has the same meaning as in the Police Act 1996 (see POLICE vol 36(1) (Reissue) para 205); and, in any other case, means money provided by the police authority: Disability Discrimination Act 1995 s 64A(7) (as so added; definition amended by the Serious Organised Crime and Police Act 2005 Sch 4 para 65(1), (2)(c), Sch 17 Pt 2).
14 Ie proceedings brought against him under the Disability Discrimination Act 1995 Pt II (as amended; prospectively amended) or Pt III (as amended; prospectively amended).
15 Ibid s 64A(5)(a) (as added (see note 2 supra); and amended by the Disability Discrimination Act 2005 s 4(1), (2)). In relation to a constable of a force who is not under the direction and control of the chief officer of police for that force, references in the Disability Discrimination Act 1995 s 64A (as added and amended) to the chief officer of police are references to the chief officer of the force under whose direction and control he is; and references in s 64A (as added and amended) to the police authority are references to the relevant police authority for that force: s 64A(8) (as so added).
16 Ibid s 64A(5)(b) (as added: see note 2 supra).
17 Ibid s 64A(5)(c) (as added: see note 2 supra).

(j) Parliament

555. Application to Parliament. The Disability Discrimination Act 1995 applies to an act[1] done by or for purposes of the House of Lords or the House of Commons as it applies to an act done by a private person[2].

For the purposes of the application of the provisions relating to employment[3] in relation to the House of Commons, the Corporate Officer of that House[4] is to be treated as the employer of a person who is (or would be) a relevant member of the House of Commons staff[5].

For the purposes of the application of the provisions relating to goods, services and facilities[6], the provider of services is: (1) as respects the House of Lords, the Corporate Officer of that House[7]; and (2) as respects the House of Commons, the Corporate Officer of that House[8]. However, where the service in question is access to and use of any place in the Palace of Westminster which members of the public are permitted to enter, the Corporate Officers of both Houses jointly are the provider of that service[9].

Nothing in any rule of law or the law or practice of Parliament prevents proceedings being instituted before an employment tribunal[10] or before any court[11].

1   As to the meaning of 'act' see para 510 note 3 ante.
2   Disability Discrimination Act 1995 s 65(1).
3   Ie ibid Pt II (ss 3A–18E) (as amended; prospectively amended): see para 529 et seq ante.
4   As to the Corporate Officer of the House of Commons see PARLIAMENT vol 34 (Reissue) para 694.
5   Disability Discrimination Act 1995 s 65(2) (amended by the Employment Rights Act 1996 s 240, Sch 1 para 69). The text refers to a person who is a relevant member of the House of Commons staff for the purposes of the Employment Rights Act 1996 s 195 (see EMPLOYMENT vol 16 (Reissue) para 79): see the Disability Discrimination Act 1995 s 65(2) (as so amended).
6   Ie ibid ss 19–21 (as amended) (see para 582 et seq post): see s 65(3).
7   Ibid s 65(3)(a).
8   Ibid s 65(3)(b).
9   Ibid s 65(4).
10 The text refers to instituting proceedings before an employment tribunal under ibid Pt II (as amended; prospectively amended) (see para 529 et seq ante) or Pt III (ss 19–28) (as amended; prospectively amended) (see para 582 et seq post).
11 Ibid s 65(5) (amended by virtue of the Employment Rights (Dispute Resolution) Act 1998 s 1(2)(a); and by the Disability Discrimination Act 2005 s 19(1), Sch 1 paras 1, 32). The text refers to instituting proceedings before a court under the Disability Discrimination Act 1995 Pt III (as amended) (see para 582 et seq post): see s 65(5) (as so amended).

(k) Occupational Pension Schemes

556. Discrimination and harassment in occupational pension schemes.
Every occupational pension scheme[1] is to be taken to include a provision called 'a non-discrimination rule'[2]: (1) requiring the trustees or managers[3] of the scheme to refrain from discriminating against a relevant disabled person[4] in carrying out any of their functions in relation to the scheme, including in particular their functions relating to the admission of members[5] to the scheme and the treatment of members of the scheme[6]; (2) requiring the trustees or managers of the scheme not to subject a relevant disabled person to harassment[7] in relation to the scheme[8]. The other provisions of the scheme are to have effect subject to the non-discrimination rule[9].

It is unlawful for the trustees or managers of an occupational pension scheme to discriminate against a relevant disabled person contrary to head (1) supra[10], or to subject a relevant disabled person to harassment contrary to head (2) supra[11]. The non-discrimination rule does not apply in relation to rights accrued, or benefits payable, in respect of periods of service prior to the coming into force of these provisions[12], but it does apply to communications[13] with members or prospective members of the scheme in relation to such rights or benefits[14].

The trustees or managers of an occupational pension scheme may by resolution make such alterations to the scheme as may be required to secure conformity with the non-discrimination rule if they do not otherwise have power to make such alterations, or if they have such power but the procedure for doing so is liable to be unduly complex or protracted, or involves the obtaining of consents which cannot be obtained, or can only be obtained with undue delay or difficulty[15]. Such alterations may have effect in relation to a period before the alterations are made, but may not have effect in relation to a period before the coming into force of these provisions[16].

Where[17] a relevant disabled person presents a complaint to an employment tribunal that the trustees or managers of an occupational pension scheme have acted in relation to him in a way which is unlawful[18], the employer[19] in relation to that scheme must, for the purposes of the rules governing procedure, be treated as a party and is entitled to appear and be heard in accordance with those rules[20].

Where (a) a relevant disabled person presents[21] to an employment tribunal a complaint that the trustees or managers of an occupational pension scheme have acted in relation to him in a way which is unlawful[22], or an employer has so acted in relation to him[23]; (b) the complaint relates to the terms on which persons become members of an occupational pension scheme, or the terms on which members of the scheme are treated[24]; (c) the disabled person is not a pensioner member of the scheme[25]; and (d) the tribunal finds that the complaint is well-founded[26], the tribunal may[27] make a declaration that the complainant has a right to be admitted to the scheme in question[28], or to membership of the scheme without discrimination[29].

Such a declaration may be made in respect of such period as the declaration may specify, but may not be made in respect of any period before the coming into force of this provision[30]. Further, such a declaration may make such provision as the tribunal considers appropriate as to the terms on which, or the capacity in which, the disabled person is to enjoy such admission or membership[31]. The tribunal may not award the disabled person any compensation[32], whether in relation to arrears of benefits or otherwise, other than compensation for injury to feelings or certain compensation where a tribunal's recommendation has not been complied with[33].

In their application to communications, these provisions[34] apply in relation to a disabled person who is entitled to the present payment of dependants' or survivors' benefits under an occupational pension scheme, or who is a pension credit member[35] of such a scheme, as they apply in relation to a disabled person who is a pensioner member of the scheme[36].

In the case of an act[37] which constitutes discrimination by way of victimisation[38], these provisions also apply to discrimination against a person who is not disabled[39].

1   'Occupational pension scheme' has the same meaning as in the Pension Schemes Act 1993 (see SOCIAL SECURITY AND PENSIONS vol 44(2) (Reissue) para 853): Disability Discrimination Act 1995 s 68(1).

2   Ibid s 4G(1) (ss 4G, 4I, 4J, 4K added by the Disability Discrimination Act 1995 (Pensions) Regulations 2003, SI 2003/2770, regs 2, 3).

3   'Trustees or managers', in relation to an occupational pension scheme, means in the case of a trust scheme, the trustees of the scheme, and in any other case, the managers of the scheme; and, in relation to an occupational pension scheme other than a trust scheme, 'managers' means the persons responsible for the management of the scheme: Pensions Act 1995 s 4K(2); applied by the Disability Discrimination Act 1995 s 4K(2) (as added: see note 2 supra).

4   'Relevant disabled person', in relation to an occupational pension scheme, means a disabled person who is a member or prospective member of the scheme: ibid s 4K(2) (as added: see note 2 supra). For the meaning of 'disabled person' see para 511 ante. 'Member', in relation to an occupational pension scheme, means any active, deferred or pensioner member: s 4K(2) (as so added). In relation to an occupational pension scheme, 'active member' means a person who is in pensionable service under the scheme; 'deferred member' means a person, other than an active or pensioner member, who has accrued rights under the scheme; and 'pensioner member' means a person who, in respect of his pensionable service under the scheme or by reason of transfer credits, is entitled to the present payment of pension or other benefits and who is not an active member of the scheme: Pensions Act 1995 s 124(1); applied by the Disability Discrimination Act 1995 s 4K(2) (as so added). 'Prospective member' means any person who, under the terms of his contract of employment or the scheme rules or both: (1) is able, at his own option, to become a member of the scheme; (2) will become so able if he continues in the same employment for a sufficiently long period; (3) will be admitted to it automatically unless he makes an election not to become a member; or (4) may be admitted to it subject to the consent of his employer: s 4K(2) (as so added).

5   See note 4 supra.

6   Disability Discrimination Act 1995 s 4G(1)(a) (as added: see note 2 supra).

7   For the meaning of 'harassment' see para 533 ante.

8   Disability Discrimination Act 1995 s 4G(1)(b) (as added: see note 2 supra).

9   Ibid s 4G(2) (as added: see note 2 supra).

10   Ibid s 4G(3)(a) (as added: see note 2 supra).

11   Ibid s 4G(3)(b) (as added: see note 2 supra).

12   Ie ibid s 4G (as added), which came into force on 1 December 2003 for certain purposes and on 1 October 2004 for remaining purposes.

13   'Communications' includes the provision of information and the operation of a dispute resolution procedure: s 4K(2) (as added: see note 2 supra).

14   Ibid s 4G(4) (as added: see note 2 supra).

15   Ibid s 4G(5) (as added: see note 2 supra).

16 Ibid s 4G(6) (as added: see note 2 supra). As to the commencement of s 4G (as added) see note 12 supra.
17 Ie under ibid s 17A (as added and amended): see para 643 post.
18 Ie unlawful under Pt II (ss 3A–18E) (as amended; prospectively amended): see para 529 et seq ante.
19 'Employer', in relation to an occupational pension scheme, means the employer of persons in the description or category of employment to which the scheme in question relates: Pensions Act 1995 s 124(1); applied by the Disability Discrimination Act 1995 s 4I(2) (as added: see note 2 supra). As from a day to be appointed, the words 'or category' are omitted from this definition: see the Pensions Act 1995 s 124(1) (definition prospectively amended by the Pensions Act 2004 s 320, Sch 13 Pt 1). At the date at which this volume states the law no such day had been appointed.
20 Disability Discrimination Act 1995 s 4I(1) (as added: see note 2 supra).
21 Ie under ibid s 17A (as added and amended): see para 643 post.
22 Ie unlawful under ibid Pt II (as amended; prospectively amended): see para 529 et seq ante.
23 Ibid s 4J(1)(a) (as added: see note 2 supra).
24 Ibid s 4J(1)(b) (as added: see note 2 supra).
25 Ibid s 4J(1)(c) (as added: see note 2 supra).
26 Ibid s 4J(1)(d) (as added: see note 2 supra).
27 Ie without prejudice to the generality of its power under ibid s 17A(2)(a) (as added and amended): see para 643 post.
28 Ibid s 4J(2)(a) (as added: see note 2 supra).
29 Ibid s 4J(2)(b) (as added: see note 2 supra).
30 Ibid s 4J(3)(a) (as added: see note 2 supra). The provision referred to in the text is s 4J (as added), which came into force on 1 December 2003 for certain purposes and on 1 October 2004 for remaining purposes.
31 Ibid s 4J(3)(b) (as added: see note 2 supra).
32 Ie compensation under ibid s 17A(2)(b) (as added and amended): see para 643 post.
33 Ibid s 4J(4) (as added: see note 2 supra). The compensation referred to in the text is compensation under s 17A(5) (as added and amended): see para 643 post.
34 Ie ibid ss 4G, 4I, 4J (all as added) (see the text and notes 1–33 supra), and s 4H (as added) (see para 557 post).
35 'Pension credit member', in relation to an occupational pension scheme, means a person who has rights under the scheme which are attributable, directly or indirectly, to a pension credit: Pensions Act 1995 s 124(1); applied by the Disability Discrimination Act 1995 s 4K(2) (as added: see note 2 supra).
36 Ibid s 4K(1) (as added: see note 2 supra).
37 As to the meaning of 'act' see para 510 note 3 ante.
38 Ie by virtue of the Disability Discrimination Act 1995 s 55 (as amended): see para 526 ante.
39 See ibid s 55(5) (as amended); and para 526 ante.

557. Duty to make adjustments in occupational pension schemes. Where a provision, criterion or practice[1] (including a scheme rule) applied by or on behalf of the trustees or managers[2] of an occupational pension scheme, or any physical feature[3] of premises[4] occupied by the trustees or managers, places a relevant disabled person[5] at a substantial disadvantage in comparison with persons who are not disabled, it is the duty of the trustees or managers to take such steps as it is reasonable[6], in all the circumstances of the case, for them to have to take in order to prevent the provision, criterion, practice or feature having that effect[7].

No duty is imposed on trustees or managers in relation to a disabled person if they do not know, and could not reasonably be expected to know: (1) that the disabled person is a relevant disabled person[8]; or (2) that that person has a disability and is likely to be placed at a substantial disadvantage[9].

Subject to any duty to make reasonable adjustments[10], a trustee or manager is not required[11] to treat a disabled person more favourably than he treats or would treat others[12].

1 As to the meaning of 'provision, criterion or practice' see para 532 note 6 ante.
2 For the meaning of 'trustees or managers' see para 556 note 3 ante.
3 As to the meaning of 'physical feature' see para 532 note 8 ante.
4 As to the meaning of 'premises' see para 525 note 9 ante.
5 For the meaning of 'relevant disabled person' see para 556 note 4 ante. As to the application of these provisions to past disabilities see para 522 ante.

6 The making of alterations to scheme rules is an example of a step which trustees or managers may have to take in order to comply with their duty to make adjustments under the Disability Discrimination Act 1995 s 4H(1) (as added): s 4H(2) (s 4H added by the Disability Discrimination Act 1995 (Pensions) Regulations 2003, SI 2003/2770, regs 2, 3). As to the determination of whether it is reasonable for trustees or managers to have to take a particular step, and examples of steps which they may have to take, see further the Disability Discrimination Act 1995 s 18B (as added); and para 532 ante.

7 Ibid s 4H(1) (as added: see note 6 supra).

8 Ibid s 4H(3)(a) (as added: see note 6 supra).

9 Ibid s 4H(3)(b) (as added: see note 6 supra).

10 As to the meaning of 'duty to make reasonable adjustments' see para 530 note 7 ante.

11 Ie by the Disability Discrimination Act 1995 Pt II (ss 3A–18E) (as amended; prospectively amended).

12 See ibid s 18D(1) (as added); and para 530 ante.

(l) Locally-electable Authorities

558. Discrimination and harassment in regard to members of locally-electable authorities. It is unlawful for an authority[1] to discriminate[2] against a disabled person[3] who is a member[4] of the authority: (1) in the opportunities which it affords the disabled person to receive training, or any other facility, for his carrying out of official business[5]; (2) by refusing to afford, or deliberately not affording, the disabled person any such opportunities[6]; or (3) by subjecting the disabled person to any other detriment[7] in connection with his carrying out of official business[8].

It is unlawful for such an authority to subject a disabled person who is a member of the authority to harassment[9] in connection with his carrying out of official business[10].

Regulations[11] may make provision as to the circumstances in which discriminatory treatment is to be taken to be justified, or is to be taken not to be justified[12].

In the case of an act[13] which constitutes discrimination by way of victimisation[14], this provision also applies to discrimination against a person who is not disabled[15].

1 Ie an authority to which the Disability Discrimination Act 1995 s 15B (as added) and s 15C (as added) (see para 559 post) applies. Such authorities are as follows: (1) the Greater London Authority; (2) a county council in England or Wales; (3) a county borough council in Wales; (4) a district council in England; (5) a London borough council; (6) the Common Council of the City of London; (7) the Council of the Isles of Scilly; (8) a parish council in England; and (9) a community council in Wales: see s 15A(1) (ss 15A, 15B added by the Disability Discrimination Act 2005 s 1). This provision also refers to Scottish authorities, but Scottish matters generally are beyond the scope of this work. As to local government authorities in England and Wales see LOCAL GOVERNMENT vol 29(1) (Reissue) para 23 et seq; as to London borough councils see LONDON GOVERNMENT vol 29(2) (Reissue) para 35 et seq; as to the Greater London Authority see LONDON GOVERNMENT vol 29(2) (Reissue) para 70 et seq; as to the Common Council of the City of London see LONDON GOVERNMENT vol 29(2) (Reissue) para 51 et seq; and as to the Council of the Isles of Scilly see LOCAL GOVERNMENT vol 29(1) (Reissue) para 40.

2 If, in a case falling within the Disability Discrimination Act 1995 s 3A(1) (as added) (see paras 530, 532 ante) as it has effect for the interpretation of 'discriminate' in s 15B(1) (as added), an authority to which s 15B (as added) applies (see note 1 supra) is under a duty imposed by s 15C (as added) (see para 559 post) in relation to a disabled person but fails to comply with that duty, its treatment of that person cannot be justified under s 15B(4) (as added) (see the text and note 12 infra) unless it would have been justified even if it had complied with that duty: s 15B(6) (as added: see note 1 supra).

3 For the meaning of 'disabled person' see para 511 ante.

4 For the purposes of the Disability Discrimination Act 1995 ss 15A–15C (as added), 'member', in relation to the Greater London Authority, means the Mayor of London or a member of the London Assembly: s 15A(3) (as added: see note 1 supra). As to the Mayor of London and the London Assembly see LONDON GOVERNMENT vol 29(2) (Reissue) para 81 et seq.

5 Ibid s 15B(1)(a) (as added: see note 1 supra). In relation to a member of an authority to which ss 15B, 15C (both as added) apply (see note 1 supra), a reference to his carrying out of official business is a reference to his doing of anything: (1) as member of the authority; (2) as member of any body to which he is appointed by, or is appointed following nomination by, the authority or a group of bodies that includes the authority; or (3) as member of any other body if it is a public body: s 15A(2) (as added: see note 1 supra).

6 Ibid s 15B(1)(b) (as added: see note 1 supra).

7   As to the meaning of 'detriment' see para 534 note 14 ante. See also note 8 infra.

8   Disability Discrimination Act 1995 s 15B(1)(c) (as added: see note 1 supra). A member of an authority to which s 15B (as added) applies (see note 1 supra) is not subjected to a detriment for the purposes of s 15B(1)(c) (as added) by reason of: (1) his not being appointed or elected to an office of the authority; (2) his not being appointed or elected to, or to an office of, a committee or sub-committee of the authority; or (3) his not being appointed or nominated in exercise of any power of the authority, or of a group of bodies that includes the authority, to appoint or nominate for appointment to any body: s 15B(3) (as so added).

9   For the meaning of 'harassment' see para 533 ante.

10 Disability Discrimination Act 1995 s 15B(2) (as added: see note 1 supra).

11 For the meaning of 'regulations' see para 509 note 12 ante.

12 Disability Discrimination Act 1995 s 15B(4) (as added: see note 1 supra). Regulations may make such provision for the purposes of s 3A(1)(b) (as added) (see paras 530, 535 ante) as it has effect for the interpretation of 'discriminate' in s 15B(1) (as added): see s 15B(4) (as so added). See note 2 supra.

   Regulations under s 15B(4) (as added) may (in particular) provide for s 3A(3) (as added) (see para 530 ante) to apply with prescribed modifications, or not to apply, for those purposes; but treatment of a disabled person cannot be justified under s 15B(4) (as added) if it amounts to direct discrimination falling within s 3A(5) (as added) (see para 531 ante): s 15B(5) (as so added). 'Prescribed' generally means prescribed by regulations: see para 515 note 5 ante. At the date at which this volume states the law, no such regulations had been made.

13 As to the meaning of 'act' see para 510 note 3 ante.

14 Ie by virtue of the Disability Discrimination Act 1995 s 55 (as amended): see para 526 ante.

15 See ibid s 55(5) (as amended); and para 526 ante.

559.   Duty to make adjustments in regard to locally-electable authorities.
Where a provision, criterion or practice[1] applied by or on behalf of an authority[2], or any physical feature[3] of premises[4] occupied by, or under the control of, such an authority, places a disabled person[5] who is a member[6] of the authority at a substantial disadvantage, in comparison with members of the authority who are not disabled persons, in connection with his carrying out of official business[7], it is the duty of the authority to take such steps as it is reasonable[8], in all the circumstances of the case, for it to have to take in order to prevent the provision, criterion, practice or feature having that effect[9]. This does not impose any duty on an authority in relation to a member of the authority who is a disabled person if the authority does not know, and could not reasonably be expected to know, that the member has a disability, and is likely to be affected in that way[10].

Regulations[11] may make provision[12]: (1) as to circumstances in which a provision, criterion or practice, or physical feature, is to be taken to have the effect mentioned above[13]; (2) as to circumstances in which a provision, criterion or practice, or physical feature, is to be taken not to have that effect[14]; (3) as to circumstances in which it is, or as to circumstances in which it is not, reasonable for an authority to have to take steps of a prescribed[15] description[16]; (4) as to steps which it is always, or as to steps which it is never, reasonable for an authority to have to take[17]; (5) as to things which are, or as to things which are not, to be treated as physical features[18].

Subject to any duty to make reasonable adjustments[19], an authority is not required[20] to treat a disabled person more favourably than he treats or would treat others[21].

1   As to the meaning of 'provision, criterion or practice' see para 532 note 6 ante.

2   Ie an authority to which the Disability Discrimination Act 1995 s 15C (as added) applies: see para 558 note 1 ante.

3   As to the meaning of 'physical feature' see para 532 note 8 ante. This meaning is subject to any provision under ibid s 15C(4)(e) (as added): see head (5) in the text.

4   As to the meaning of 'premises' see para 525 note 9 ante.

5   For the meaning of 'disabled person' see para 511 ante.

6   For the meaning of 'member' see para 558 note 4 ante.

7   Disability Discrimination Act 1995 s 15C(1) (s 15C added by the Disability Discrimination Act 2005 s 1). As to references to an authority's carrying out of official business see para 558 note 5 ante.

8   As to the determination of whether it is reasonable for an authority to have to take a particular step, and examples of steps which he may have to take, see the Disability Discrimination Act 1995 s 18B (as added); and para 532 ante. See also heads (1)–(5) in the text.

9   Ibid s 15C(2) (as added: see note 7 supra).

10 Ibid s 15C(3) (as added: see note 7 supra).

11 For the meaning of 'regulations' see para 509 note 12 ante.

12 Ie for the purposes of the Disability Discrimination Act 1995 s 15C (as added).

13 Ibid s 15C(4)(a) (as added: see note 7 supra). The effect referred to in the text is that mentioned in s 15C(1) (as added): see the text and notes 1–7 supra. At the date at which this volume states the law, no regulations had been made under s 15C(4) (as added).

14 Ibid s 15C(4)(b) (as added: see note 7 supra). See note 13 supra.

15 'Prescribed' generally means prescribed by regulations: see para 515 note 5 ante.

16 Disability Discrimination Act 1995 s 15C(4)(c) (as added: see note 7 supra). See note 13 supra.

17 Ibid s 15C(4)(d) (as added: see note 7 supra). See note 13 supra.

18 Ibid s 15C(4)(e) (as added: see note 7 supra). See note 13 supra.

19 As to the meaning of 'duty to make reasonable adjustments' see para 530 note 7 ante.

20 Ie by the Disability Discrimination Act 1995 Pt II (ss 3A–18E) (as amended; prospectively amended): see para 529 et seq ante.

21 See ibid s 18D(1) (as added); and para 530 ante.

(C)   Other Matters

560.   Alterations to premises occupied under leases.   Where (1) a person to whom a duty to make reasonable adjustments[1] applies ('the occupier') occupies premises[2] under a lease[3]; (2) but for this provision, the occupier would not be entitled to make a particular alteration to the premises[4]; and (3) the alteration is one which the occupier proposes to make in order to comply with that duty[5], then certain provisions are implied in the lease[6]. Except to the extent to which it expressly so provides, the lease has effect as if it provided[7]: (a) for the occupier to be entitled to make the alteration with the written consent of the lessor[8]; (b) for the occupier to have to make a written application to the lessor for consent if he wishes to make the alteration[9]; (c) if such an application is made, for the lessor not to withhold his consent unreasonably[10]; and (d) for the lessor to be entitled to make his consent subject to reasonable conditions[11].

In relation to sub-leases or sub-tenancies, except to the extent to which it expressly so provides, any superior lease under which the premises are held has effect in relation to the lessor and lessee who are parties to that lease as if it provided[12]: (i) for the lessee to have to make a written application to the lessor for consent to the alteration[13]; (ii) if such an application is made, for the lessor not to withhold his consent unreasonably[14]; and (iii) for the lessor to be entitled to make his consent subject to reasonable conditions[15].

Regulations may make provision as to circumstances[16] in which a lessor is to be taken to have withheld his consent[17], withheld his consent unreasonably[18], or acted reasonably in withholding his consent[19]. Regulations may also make provision as to when a condition subject to which a lessor has given his consent is to be taken to be reasonable or unreasonable[20].

If any question arises as to whether the occupier has failed to comply with any duty to make reasonable adjustments, by failing to make a particular alteration to the premises, any constraint attributable to the fact that he occupies the premises under a lease is to be ignored unless he has applied to the lessor in writing for consent to the making of the alteration[21].

1   As to the meaning of 'duty to make reasonable adjustments' see para 530 note 7 ante.

2   As to the meaning of 'premises' see para 525 note 9 ante.

3   Disability Discrimination Act 1995 s 18A(1)(a) (s 18A added by virtue of the Disability Discrimination Act 1995 (Amendment) Regulations 2003, SI 2003/1673, regs 3(1), 14(2); and the Disability Discrimination Act 1995 s 18A(1)(a) amended by the Disability Discrimination Act 1995 (Amendment)

Regulations 2003, SI 2003/1673, regs 3(1), 14(3)(a)). 'Lease' includes a tenancy, sub-lease or sub-tenancy and an agreement for a lease, tenancy, sub-lease or sub-tenancy: Disability Discrimination Act 1995 s 18A(3) (as so added). 'Sub-lease' means any sub-term created out of or deriving from a leasehold interest; and 'sub-tenancy' means any tenancy created out of or deriving from a superior tenancy: s 18A(3); Disability Discrimination (Employment Field) (Leasehold Premises) Regulations 2004, SI 2004/153, reg 8.

4   Disability Discrimination Act 1995 s 18A(1)(b) (as added: see note 3 supra). If the terms and conditions of a lease impose conditions which are to apply if the occupier alters the premises, or entitle the lessor to impose conditions when consenting to the occupier's altering the premises, the occupier is to be treated for these purposes as not being entitled to make the alteration: s 18A(4) (as so added).

5   Ibid s 18A(1)(c) (as added (see note 3 supra); and amended by the Disability Discrimination Act 1995 (Amendment) Regulations 2003, SI 2003/1673, regs 3(1), 14(3)(b)).

6   See the Disability Discrimination Act 1995 s 18A(2) (as added); and the text and notes 7–11 infra.

7   Ibid s 18A(2) (as added: see note 3 supra).

8   Ibid s 18A(2)(a) (as added: see note 3 supra). The Secretary of State may by regulations make provision supplementing, or modifying, the provision made by s 18A (as added) or any provision made by or under Sch 4 Pt I (as amended) in relation to cases where the occupier occupies premises under a sub-lease or sub-tenancy: Sch 4 para 4 (amended by the Disability Discrimination Act 1995 (Amendment) Regulations 2003, SI 2003/1673, regs 3(1), 29(3)(g)). As to the Secretary of State and the National Assembly for Wales see para 302 ante. For the meaning of 'regulations' see para 509 note 12 ante. Where the occupier occupies premises under a sub-lease or sub-tenancy, s 18A (as added and amended) and Sch 4 para 1 (as amended) are modified so that for references to 'lessor' there are substituted references to the lessor who is the occupier's immediate landlord; and Sch 4 paras 2, 3 (as amended) are modified for these purposes so that references to 'lessor' include any superior landlord: Disability Discrimination (Employment Field) (Leasehold Premises) Regulations 2004, SI 2004/153, reg 9.

9   Disability Discrimination Act 1995 s 18A(2)(b) (as added: see note 3 supra).

10 Ibid s 18A(2)(c) (as added: see note 3 supra).

11 Ibid s 18A(2)(d) (as added: see note 3 supra).

12 Ibid s 18A(2A) (s 18A as added (see note 3 supra); and s 18A(2A) added by the Disability Discrimination (Employment Field) (Leasehold Premises) Regulations 2004, SI 2004/153, reg 9).

13 Disability Discrimination Act 1995 s 18A(2A)(i) (as added: see notes 3, 12 supra).

14 Ibid s 18A(2A)(ii) (as added: see notes 3, 12 supra).

15 Ibid s 18A(2A)(iii) (as added: see notes 3, 12 supra).

16 Ibid Sch 4 para 3. As to regulations under this provision see the Disability Discrimination (Employment Field) (Leasehold Premises) Regulations 2004, SI 2004/153.

17 Disability Discrimination Act 1995 Sch 4 para 3(a)(i) (Sch 4 para 3(a) amended by the Disability Discrimination Act 1995 (Amendment) Regulations 2002, SI 2003/1673, regs 3(1), 29(3)(g)). A lessor is to be taken to have withheld his consent to an alteration where he has received a written application by or on behalf of the occupier for consent to make the alteration and has failed to meet certain requirements: Disability Discrimination (Employment Field) (Leasehold Premises) Regulations 2004, SI 2004/153, reg 4(1). The requirements are that the lessor, within a period of 21 days (beginning with the day on which he receives the application) or such longer period as is reasonable, replies consenting to or refusing the application, or replies consenting to the application subject to obtaining the consent of another person required under a superior lease or pursuant to a binding obligation, and seeks that consent: reg 4(2). A lessor who fails to meet these requirements but who subsequently meets those requirements (except as to time) is taken to have withheld his consent from the date of such failure, and is taken not to have withheld his consent from the time he met those requirements (except as to time): reg 4(3). For these purposes, a lessor is to be treated as not having sought another person's consent unless he has applied in writing to that person, indicating that the lessor's consent to the alteration has been applied for in order to comply with a duty to make reasonable adjustments, and that he has given his consent conditionally upon obtaining the other person's consent: reg 4(4). 'Binding obligation' means a legally binding obligation (not contained in a lease) in relation to the premises whether arising from an agreement or otherwise: reg 2.

18 Disability Discrimination Act 1995 Sch 4 para 3(a)(ii). A lessor is to be taken to have withheld his consent unreasonably where: (1) the lease provides that consent must or will be given to an alteration of the kind in question; (2) the lease provides that consent must or will be given to an alteration of the kind in question if the consent is sought in a particular way and the consent has been sought in that way; or (3) the lessor is to be taken to have withheld his consent by virtue of reg 4 (see note 17 supra): see the Disability Discrimination (Employment Field) (Leasehold Premises) Regulations 2004, SI 2004/153, reg 5.

19 Disability Discrimination Act 1995 Sch 4 para 3(a)(iii). A lessor is to be taken to have acted reasonably in withholding his consent where: (1) there is a binding obligation requiring the consent of any person to the alteration; (2) he has taken steps to seek that consent; and (3) that consent has not been given or has

been given subject to a condition making it reasonable for him to withhold his consent: Disability Discrimination (Employment Field) (Leasehold Premises) Regulations 2004, SI 2004/153, reg 6(1). A lessor is also to be taken to have acted reasonably in withholding his consent where: (a) he is bound by an agreement which allows him to consent to the alteration in question subject to a condition that he makes a payment; and (b) that condition does not permit the lessor to make his own consent subject to a condition that the occupier reimburse him the payment: reg 6(2).

20 See the Disability Discrimination Act 1995 Sch 4 para 3(b), (c). A condition subject to which a lessor has given his consent is to be taken to be reasonable in all circumstances if it is any of the following (or a condition to similar effect): (1) that the occupier must obtain any necessary planning permission and any other consent or permission required by or under any enactment; (2) that the occupier must submit any plans or specifications for the alteration to the lessor for approval (provided that the condition binds the lessor not to withhold approval unreasonably) and that the work is carried out in accordance with such plans or specifications; (3) that the lessor must be permitted a reasonable opportunity to inspect the work when completed; and (4) that the occupier must repay to the lessor the costs reasonably incurred in connection with the giving of his consent: Disability Discrimination (Employment Field) (Leasehold Premises) Regulations 2004, SI 2004/153, reg 7(1). In a case where it would be reasonable for the lessor to withhold consent, a condition that upon expiry of the lease the occupier (or any assignee or successor) must reinstate any relevant part of the premises which is to be altered to its state before the alteration was made is to be taken as reasonable: reg 6(2).

21 Disability Discrimination Act 1995 Sch 4 para 1 (amended by the Disability Discrimination Act 1995 (Amendment) Regulations 2003, SI 2003/1673, regs 3(1), 29(3)(c)). As to joining lessors in proceedings see para 643 post.

B. DISCRIMINATION IN EDUCATION

(A) Schools

561. Discrimination against disabled pupils and prospective pupils. It is unlawful for the body responsible for a school[1] (the 'responsible body')[2] to discriminate against a disabled person: (1) in the arrangements it makes for determining admission to the school as a pupil[3]; (2) in the terms on which it offers to admit him to the school as a pupil[4]; or (3) by refusing or deliberately omitting to accept an application for his admission to the school as a pupil[5]. It is also unlawful for the responsible body to discriminate against a disabled pupil[6]: (a) in the education or associated services provided for, or offered to, pupils at the school by that body[7]; or (b) by excluding him from the school, whether permanently or temporarily[8]. These provisions[9] also apply to discrimination against a person who is not disabled where the act which constitutes discrimination is victimisation[10].

1 'School' means: (1) a maintained school within the meaning of the School Standards and Framework Act 1998 s 20(7) (see EDUCATION vol 15(1) (2006 Reissue) para 98); (2) a maintained nursery school within the meaning of s 22(9) (see EDUCATION vol 15(1) (2006 Reissue) para 94); (3) an independent school within the meaning of the Education Act 1996 s 463 (as substituted) (see EDUCATION vol 15(1) (2006 Reissue) para 465); (4) a special school which is not a maintained special school but which is approved by the Secretary of State, or by the National Assembly for Wales, under the Education Act 1996 s 342 (as substituted) (see EDUCATION vol 15(1) (2006 Reissue) para 1027); (5) a pupil referral unit within the meaning of the Education Act 1996 s 19(2) (see EDUCATION vol 15(1) (2006 Reissue) para 457): Disability Discrimination Act 1995 s 28Q(4), (5) (s 28Q added by the Special Educational Needs and Disability Act 2001 s 25). See generally EDUCATION.

2 Disability Discrimination Act 1995 s 28A(5) (s 28A added by the Special Educational Needs and Disability Act 2001 s 11). The bodies responsible for schools in England and Wales are set out in the Disability Discrimination Act 1995 Sch 4A para 1 Table (Sch 4A added by the Special Educational Needs and Disability Act 2001 s 11(2), Sch 2; and amended by the Education Act 2002 s 215(1), Sch 21 para 29). The local education authority (within the meaning of the School Standards and Framework Act 1998 s 22(8): see EDUCATION vol 15(1) (2006 Reissue) para 20) is the responsible body in relation to a maintained school, a pupil referral unit, or a maintained nursery school: Disability Discrimination Act 1995 Sch 4A para 1 Table items 1, 2 (as so added; and amended by Education Act 2002 Sch 21 para 29 supra). In the case of a maintained school, the governing body is the responsible body if it has the function in question: Disability Discrimination Act 1995 Sch 4A para 1 Table item 1 (as so added). 'Governing body', in relation to a maintained school, means the body corporate (constituted in

accordance with regulations under the Education Act 2002 s 19) which the school has as a result of s 19: Disability Discrimination Act 1995 s 28Q(7) (as added (see note 1 supra); and amended by the Education Act 2002 Sch 21 para 28). The proprietor (within the meaning of the Education Act 1996 s 579 (as amended): see EDUCATION vol 15(1) (2006 Reissue) para 60) is the responsible body in relation to an independent school, or a special school not maintained by a local education authority: Disability Discrimination Act 1995 Sch 4A para 1 Table items 4, 5 (as so added).

3 Ibid s 28A(1)(a) (as added: see note 2 supra). 'Pupil' has the meaning given the Education Act 1996 s 3(1) (as amended) (see EDUCATION vol 15(1) (2006 Reissue) para 16): Disability Discrimination Act 1995 s 28Q(3) (as added: see note 1 supra).

Part IV (ss 28A–31C) (as amended) applies to the Isles of Scilly as if the Isles were a separate non-metropolitan county (and the Council of the Isles of Scilly were a county council), and with such other modifications as may be specified in an order made by the Secretary of State: s 31C (added by the Special Educational Needs and Disability Act 2001 s 39). At the date at which this volume states the law, no such order had been made. As to county councils see LOCAL GOVERNMENT vol 29(1) (Reissue) para 23 et seq.

4 Disability Discrimination Act 1995 s 28A(1)(b) (as added: see note 2 supra).

5 Ibid s 28A(1)(c) (as added: see note 2 supra).

6 'Disabled pupil' means a pupil who is a disabled person: ibid s 28Q(2) (as added: see note 1 supra). For the meaning of 'disabled person' see para 511 ante.

7 Ibid s 28A(2) (as added: see note 2 supra). See *K v X School* (2007) Times, 11 April, CA (not discrimination to refuse to clean and change incontinent paraplegic pupil after bowel accident). The Secretary of State may by regulations prescribe services which are, or services which are not, to be regarded for the purposes of the Disability Discrimination Act 1995 s 28A(2) (as added) as being either education or an associated service: s 28A(3) (as so added). As to the Secretary of State and the National Assembly for Wales see para 302 ante. For the meaning of 'regulations' see para 509 note 12 ante. 'Prescribe' generally means prescribe by regulations: see para 515 note 5 ante. At the date this volume states the law no regulations had been made for these purposes.

8 Ibid s 28A(4) (as added: see note 2 supra).

9 Ie ibid s 28A (as added).

10 Ibid s 28A(6) (as added: see note 2 supra). As to discrimination by way of victimisation see s 55 (as amended); and para 526 ante.

562. Discrimination by less favourable treatment. A responsible body discriminates against a disabled person[1] if: (1) for a reason which relates to his disability, it treats him less favourably than it treats or would treat others to whom that reason does not or would not apply[2]; and (2) it cannot show that the treatment in question is justified[3]. Less favourable treatment of a person is justified if it is the result of a permitted form of selection[4]. Otherwise, less favourable treatment is justified only if the reason for it is both material to the circumstances of the particular case and substantial[5]. The taking of a particular step by a responsible body in relation to a person does not amount to less favourable treatment if it shows that at the time in question it did not know, and could not reasonably have been expected to know, that he was disabled[6].

In relation to a failure to take a particular step, a responsible body does not discriminate against a person if it shows that: (a) at the time in question, it did not know and could not reasonably have been expected to know, that he was disabled[7]; and (b) its failure to take the step was attributable to that lack of knowledge[8].

1 Ie for the purposes of the Disability Discrimination Act 1995 s 28A (as added): see para 561 ante. As to responsible bodies see para 561 ante.

2 Ibid s 28B(1)(a) (s 28B added by the Special Educational Needs and Disability Act 2001 s 12). See *McAuley Catholic High School v C* [2003] EWHC 3045 (Admin), [2004] 2 All ER 436, [2004] ICR 1563 (in the case of a school, the comparator was the school population as a whole who were not disabled and who had not misbehaved).

3 Disability Discrimination Act 1995 s 28B(1)(b) (as added: see note 2 supra).

4 Ibid s 28B(5), (6) (as added: see note 2 supra). 'Permitted form of selection' means: (1) if the school is a maintained school which is not designated as a grammar school under the School Standards and Framework Act 1998 s 104 (see EDUCATION vol 15(1) (2006 Reissue) para 438), any form of selection mentioned in s 99(2) or (4) (see EDUCATION vol 15(1) (2006 Reissue) para 433); (2) if the school is a maintained school which is so designated, any of its selective admission arrangements; (3) if the school is an independent school, any arrangements which make provision for any or all of its pupils to be selected

by reference to general or special ability or aptitude, with a view to admitting only pupils of high ability or aptitude: Disability Discrimination Act 1995 s 28Q(9) (s 28Q added by the Special Educational Needs and Disability Act 2001 s 25).

5   Disability Discrimination Act 1995 s 28B(5), (7) (as added: see note 2 supra). However, if, in a case falling within s 28B(1)(a) or (b) (as added) (see heads (1), (2) in the text), the responsible body is under a duty imposed by s 28C (as added); prospectively amended) (see para 563 post) in relation to the disabled person, but, it fails without justification to comply with that duty, its treatment of that person cannot be justified under s 28B(7) (as added) unless that treatment would have been justified even if it had complied with that duty: s 28B(5), (8) (as so added). See *Governing Body of O Comprehensive School v E* [2006] EWHC 1468 (Admin), [2006] All ER (D) 247 (Jun) (tribunal had not considered final words of the Disability Discrimination Act 1995 s 28B(8) (as added)).

6   Disability Discrimination Act 1995 s 28B(4) (as added: see note 2 supra).

7   Ibid s 28B(3)(a) (as added: see note 2 supra).

8   Ibid s 28B(3)(b) (as added: see note 2 supra).

563. Discrimination by failure to take reasonable steps. A responsible body discriminates against a disabled person[1] if: (1) it fails, to his detriment, to comply with the following provisions[2]; and (2) it cannot show that its failure to comply is justified[3]. A failure to comply is justified only if the reason for it is both material to the circumstances of the particular case and substantial[4].

The responsible body must take such steps as it is reasonable[5] for it to have to take to ensure that: (a) in relation to the arrangements it makes for determining the admission of pupils to the school, disabled persons are not placed at a substantial disadvantage in comparison with persons who are not disabled[6]; and (b) in relation to education and associated services provided for, or offered to, pupils at the school by it, disabled pupils are not placed at a substantial disadvantage in comparison with pupils who are not disabled[7]. The responsible body is not thereby required to remove or alter a physical feature (for example, one arising from the design or construction of the school premises or the location of resources)[8], or provide auxiliary aids or services[9].

In relation to a failure to take a particular step, a responsible body does not discriminate against a person if it shows that: (i) at the time in question it did not know, and could not reasonably have been expected to know, that he was disabled[10]; and (ii) its failure to take the step was attributable to that lack of knowledge[11].

In determining whether it is reasonable for a responsible body to have to take a particular step in order to comply with its duty under the above provisions[12] in relation to a person with respect to whom a confidentiality request[13] has been made, of which the responsible body is aware, regard must be had to the extent to which taking the step in question is consistent with compliance with the confidentiality request[14].

Duties are imposed under the above provisions[15] only for the purpose of determining whether a responsible body has discriminated against a disabled person; and accordingly a breach of any such duty is not actionable as such[16].

1   Ie for the purposes of the Disability Discrimination Act 1995 s 28A (as added): see para 561 ante. As to responsible bodies see para 561 ante.

2   Ie ibid s 28C (as added).

3   Ibid s 28B(2) (s 28B added by the Special Educational Needs and Disability Act 2001 s 12).

4   Disability Discrimination Act 1995 s 28B(5), (7) (as added: see note 3 supra). However, if, in a case falling within s 28B(1)(a) or (b) (as added) (see para 562 ante), the responsible body is under a duty imposed by s 28C (as added) in relation to the disabled person, but, it fails without justification to comply with that duty, its treatment of that person cannot be justified under s 28B(7) (as added) unless that treatment would have been justified even if it had complied with that duty: s 28B(5), (8) (as so added). See *Governing Body of O Comprehensive School v E* [2006] EWHC 1468 (Admin), [2006] All ER (D) 247 (Jun); and para 562 ante.

5   In considering whether it is reasonable for it to have to take a particular step in order to comply with its duty under the Disability Discrimination Act 1995 s 28C(1) (as added), a responsible body must have regard to any relevant provisions of a code of practice issued under s 53A (as added and amended; prospectively repealed) (see para 655 post): s 28C(4) (s 28C added by the Special Educational Needs and

Disability Act 2001 s 13). As from a day to be appointed the reference to the Disability Discrimination Act 1995 s 53A (as added and amended; prospectively repealed) is replaced by a reference to the Equality Act 2006 s 14 (not yet in force) (see para 321 ante): Disability Discrimination Act 1995 s 28C(4) (prospectively amended by the Equality Act 2006 s 40, Sch 3 paras 41, 46). At the date at which this volume states the law no such day had been appointed.

Regulations may make provision, for the purposes of the Disability Discrimination Act 1995 s 28C (as added), as to: (1) circumstances in which it is reasonable for a responsible body to have to take steps of a prescribed description; (2) steps which it is always reasonable for a responsible body to have to take; (3) circumstances in which it is not reasonable for a responsible body to have to take steps of a prescribed description; (4) steps which it is never reasonable for a responsible body to have to take: s 28C(3) (as so added). For the meaning of 'regulations' see para 509 note 12 ante. 'Prescribe' generally means prescribe by regulations: see para 515 note 5 ante. At the date this volume states the law no regulations had been made for these purposes.

6   Ibid s 28C(1)(a) (as added: see note 5 supra).
7   Ibid s 28C(1)(b) (as added: see note 5 supra). See *K v X School* (2007) Times, 11 April, CA (school had taken reasonable steps to ensure that an incontinent paraplegic pupil was not placed at a substantial disadvantage; not discrimination to refuse to clean and change him after bowel accident).
8   Disability Discrimination Act 1995 s 28C(2)(a) (as added: see note 5 supra).
9   Ibid s 28C(2)(b) (as added: see note 5 supra).
10 Ibid s 28B(3)(a) (as added: see note 3 supra).
11 Ibid s 28B(3)(b) (as added: see note 3 supra).
12 Ie ibid s 28C(1) (as added): see the text and notes 5–7 supra.
13 'Confidentiality request' means a request which asks for the nature, or asks for the existence, of a disabled person's disability to be treated as confidential and which is either made by that person's parent or by the disabled person himself and the responsible body reasonably believes that he has sufficient understanding of the nature of the request and of its effect: ibid s 28C(7) (as added: see note 5 supra). 'Parent' has the meaning given in the Education Act 1996 s 576 (as amended) (see EDUCATION vol 15(1) (2006 Reissue) para 510): Disability Discrimination Act 1995 s 28Q(8) (s 28Q added by the Special Educational Needs and Disability Act 2001 s 25).
14 Disability Discrimination Act 1995 s 28C(5), (6) (as added: see note 5 supra).
15 Ie ibid s 28C (as added).
16 Ibid s 28C(8) (as added: see note 5 supra).

564.   Accessibility strategies and plans.   Each local education authority[1] must prepare, in relation to schools for which it is the responsible body an accessibility strategy[2] for (over a prescribed[3] period): (1) increasing the extent to which disabled pupils[4] can participate in the schools' curriculums[5]; (2) improving the physical environment of the schools for the purpose of increasing the extent to which disabled pupils are able to take advantage of education and associated services[6] provided or offered by the schools[7]; and (3) improving the delivery to disabled pupils, within a reasonable time, and in ways which are determined after taking account of their disabilities and any preferences expressed by them or their parents, of information which is provided in writing for pupils who are not disabled[8]. Further such strategies must be prepared at such times as may be prescribed[9].

Each local education authority must implement its accessibility strategy[10] and keep it under review during the period to which it relates and, if necessary, revise it[11]. In relation to Wales, an inspection[12] of a local education authority may extend to the performance by the authority of its functions in relation to the preparation, review, revision and implementation of its accessibility strategy[13].

Corresponding provision is made[14] for the preparation, review, revision, implementation, and inspection of accessibility plans by the responsible body for: (a) maintained schools[15]; (b) independent schools[16]; and (c) special schools which are not maintained special schools but which are approved[17] by the Secretary of State or by the National Assembly for Wales[18].

In preparing its accessibility strategy, a local education authority must have regard to: (i) the need to allocate adequate resources for implementing the strategy[19]; and (ii) any guidance issued[20]. Copies of accessibility strategies and plans must be given, if requested, to the Secretary of State in England and the National Assembly for Wales in Wales[21], and copies must also be made available for inspection at reasonable times[22].

If the Secretary of State, in relation to England, or the National Assembly for Wales, in relation to Wales, is satisfied[23] (whether on a complaint or otherwise) that a responsible body: (A) has acted, or is proposing to act, unreasonably in the discharge of a duty imposed[24] in relation to accessibility strategies or plans[25]; or (B) has failed to discharge such a duty[26], the Secretary of State or the National Assembly for Wales may give that body such directions as to the discharge of the duty as appear to be expedient[27]. Directions may be given even if the performance of the duty is contingent upon the opinion of the responsible body[28].

1 Ie within the meaning of the Education Act 1996 s 12 (see EDUCATION vol 15(1) (2006 Reissue) para 20): Disability Discrimination Act 1995 s 28D(16) (s 28D added by the Special Educational Needs and Disability Act 2001 s 14(1)). As to responsible bodies see para 561 ante.

2 Disability Discrimination Act 1995 s 28D(1)(a) (as added: see note 1 supra). An accessibility strategy must be in writing: s 28D(3) (as so added).

3 In ibid s 28D (as added and amended), 'prescribed' means prescribed in regulations; and 'regulations' means, in relation to England, regulations made by the Secretary of State, and, in relation to Wales, regulations made by the National Assembly for Wales: s 28D(17) (as added (see note 1 supra); and substituted by the Disability Discrimination Act 2005 s 19(1), Sch 1 para 24(1), (2)). As to the prescribed period in relation to England see the Disability Discrimination (Prescribed Periods for Accessibility Strategies and Plans for Schools) (England) Regulations 2005, SI 2005/3221; and as to the prescribed period in relation to Wales see the Disability Discrimination (Prescribed Periods for Accessibility Strategies and Plans for Schools) (Wales) Regulations 2003, SI 2003/2531. As to the Secretary of State and the National Assembly for Wales see para 302 ante.

4 'Disabled pupil' includes a disabled person who may be admitted to the school as a pupil: Disability Discrimination Act 1995 s 28D(18) (as added: see note 1 supra).

5 Ibid s 28D(2)(a) (as added: see note 1 supra).

6 Regulations may prescribe services which are, or services which are not, to be regarded for these purposes as being education or an associated service: ibid s 28D(15) (as added: see note 1 supra). At the date at which this volume states the law no such regulations had been made.

7 Ibid s 28D(2)(b) (as added: see note 1 supra).

8 Ibid s 28D(2)(c) (as added: see note 1 supra).

9 Ibid s 28D(1)(b) (as added: see note 1 supra).

10 Ibid s 28D(5) (as added: see note 1 supra).

11 Ibid s 28D(4) (as added: see note 1 supra).

12 Ie under the Education Act 1997 s 38: see EDUCATION vol 15(2) (2006 Reissue) para 1350.

13 Disability Discrimination Act 1995 s 28D(6) (as added: see note 1 supra). At the date at which this volume states the law, s 28D(6) (as added) was repealed in relation to England but not in relation to Wales: see the Children Act 2004 s 64, Sch 5 Pt 3; and the Children Act 2004 (Commencement No 1) Order 2005, SI 2005/394, art 2(2)(g).

14 See the Disability Discrimination Act 1995 s 28D(8)–(13) (as added (see note 1 supra); and amended by the Education Act 2005 s 61, Sch 9 para 8). As to the regulations made see note 3 supra.

15 Ie within the meaning of the School Standards and Framework Act 1998 s 20(7) (see EDUCATION vol 15(1) (2006 Reissue) para 94): Disability Discrimination Act 1995 s 28D(19) (as added: see note 1 supra), s 28Q(5) (s 28Q added by the Special Educational Needs and Disability Act 2001 s 25). In relation to Wales, the reference to maintained schools includes a reference to maintained nursery schools: see the Disability Discrimination Act 1995 s 28D(7) (as added and amended: see note 7 infra). For a maintained school or a maintained nursery school, the duties imposed by s 28D(8)–(12) (as added) are duties of the governing body: s 28D(14) (s 28D as added (see note 1 supra); and amended by the Education Act 2002 s 215(1), Sch 21 para 26).

16 Ie within the meaning of the Education Act 1996 s 463 (as substituted) (see EDUCATION vol 15(1) (2006 Reissue) para 465): Disability Discrimination Act 1995 s 28D(19) (as added: see note 1 supra), s 28Q(5) (as added: see note 15 supra).

17 Ie under the Education Act 1996 s 342 (as substituted): see EDUCATION vol 15(1) (2006 Reissue) para 1028.

18 Disability Discrimination Act 1995 s 28D(7) (as added (see note 1 supra); and amended in relation to Wales by the Education Act 2002 (Transitional Provisions and Consequential Amendments) (Wales) Regulations 2005, SI 2005/2913, reg 3).

19 Disability Discrimination Act 1995 s 28E(1)(a) (s 28E added by the Special Educational Needs and Disability Act 2001 s 15). In preparing an accessibility plan, the responsible body must have regard to the need to allocate adequate resources for implementing the plan: Disability Discrimination Act 1995 s 28E(4) (as so added).

20 Guidance may be issued as to an accessibility strategy's content, form, and consultation requirements: ibid s 28E(1)(b) (as added: see note 19 supra). A local education authority must also have regard to any guidance issued as to compliance with the requirements of s 28D(4) (as added) (see the text and note 11 supra): s 28E(2) (as so added). Guidance for England is issued by the Secretary of State and guidance for Wales is issued by the National Assembly for Wales: s 28E(3) (as so added).

21 Ibid s 28E(5), (6) (as added (see note 19 supra); and amended by the Education Act 2002 s 65(3), Sch 7 para 5(2)).

22 Disability Discrimination Act 1995 s 28E(7), (8) (s 28E as added (see note 19 supra); and s 28E(8) amended by the Education Act 2002 Sch 7 para 5(2)).

23 Disability Discrimination Act 1995 s 28M(8) (s 28M added by the Special Educational Needs and Disability Act 2001 s 22).

24 Ie under the Disability Discrimination Act 1995 s 28D (as added and amended) or s 28E (as added and amended): see the text and notes 1–22 supra.

25 Ibid s 28M(1)(a) (as added: see note 23 supra).

26 Ibid s 28M(1)(b) (as added: see note 23 supra).

27 Ibid s 28M(1) (as added: see note 23 supra). Similar provision is made in relation to special schools which are not maintained special schools but which are approved by the Secretary of State or by the National Assembly for Wales under the Education Act 1996 s 342 (as substituted) (see EDUCATION vol 15(2) (2006 Reissue) para 1028) and in relation to city academies, but only in relation to the responsible body's duty to provide copies of its accessibility plan and to make copies available for inspection: see the Disability Discrimination Act 1995 s 28M(2), (3) (as so added). Directions may be varied or revoked by the Secretary of State or the National Assembly for Wales; and may be enforced on the application of the Secretary of State or the National Assembly by Wales by a mandatory order obtained in accordance with the Supreme Court Act 1981 s 31 (as amended): Disability Discrimination Act 1995 s 28M(7), (9) (as so added). The Supreme Court Act 1981 is to be renamed as the Senior Courts Act 1981 and, as from a day to be appointed, the Disability Discrimination Act 1995 s 28M(7) (as added) is amended to reflect this change: see s 28M(7) (as so added; prospectively amended by the Constitutional Reform Act 2005 s 59(5), Sch 11 para 1). At the date at which this volume states the law no such day had been appointed.

28 Disability Discrimination Act 1995 s 28M(4) (as added: see note 23 supra).

565. Residual duty not to discriminate. In discharging a function[1] of a local education authority[2] (but not any prescribed function[3]), it is unlawful for the authority to discriminate against a disabled pupil or a disabled person who may be admitted to a school as a pupil[4]. However, an act done in the discharge of a function to which these provisions[5] apply is unlawful as a result of this residual duty not to discriminate[6] only if no other provision relating to discrimination in schools[7] makes that act unlawful[8]. These provisions also apply to discrimination against a person who is not disabled where the act which constitutes discrimination is victimisation[9].

Each local education authority must take such steps as it is reasonable for it to have to take to ensure that, in discharging any function to which the above provisions[10] apply: (1) disabled persons who may be admitted to a school as pupils are not placed at a substantial disadvantage in comparison with persons who are not disabled; and (2) disabled pupils are not placed at a substantial disadvantage in comparison with pupils who are not disabled[11]. However, this does not require the authority to remove or alter a physical feature or provide auxiliary aids or services[12]. Duties are imposed under these provisions[13] only for the purpose of determining whether an authority has discriminated against a disabled person; and accordingly a breach of any such duty is not actionable as such[14].

1 Ie the functions of a local education authority (see note 2 infra) under the Education Acts: Disability Discrimination Act 1995 s 28F(1)(a) (ss 28F, 28G added by the Special Educational Needs and Disability Act 2001 s 16). For the meaning of 'the Education Acts' see the Education Act 1996 s 578 (as amended); and EDUCATION vol 15(1) (2006 Reissue) para 1 (definition applied by the Disability Discrimination Act 1995 s 28F(7) (as so added)).

2   For the meaning of 'local education authority' see EDUCATION vol 15(1) (2006 Reissue) para 20;
     definition applied by the Disability Discrimination Act 1995 s 28F(6) (as added: see note 1 supra).
3   Ibid s 28F(2) (as added: see note 1 supra). 'Prescribed' generally means prescribed by regulations: see
     para 515 note 5 ante. At the date at which this volume states the law no regulations had been made for
     these purposes.
4   Ibid s 28F(3) (as added: see note 1 supra). Section 28B (as added) (discrimination by less favourable
     treatment: see para 562 ante) applies with modifications for the purposes of s 28F (as added): s 28G(1) (as
     added: see note 1 supra).
5   Ie ibid s 28F (as added).
6   Ie under ibid s 28F(3) (as added): see the text and note 4 supra.
7   Ie under ibid Pt IV Ch I (ss 28A–28Q) (as added and amended).
8   Ibid s 28F(4) (as added: see note 1 supra).
9   Ibid s 28F(5) (as added: see note 1 supra). As to discrimination by way of victimisation see s 55 (as
     amended); and para 526 ante.
10   Ie ibid s 28F (as added).
11   Ibid s 28G(2), (7) (as added: see note 1 supra).
12   Ibid s 28G(3) (as added: see note 1 supra).
13   Ie ibid s 28G (as added).
14   Ibid s 28G(4) (as added: see note 1 supra).

566.   Special Educational Needs and Disability Tribunal.   The Special
Educational Needs Tribunal has changed its name to the Special Educational Needs and
Disability Tribunal[1] and exercises jurisdiction (in addition to its jurisdiction under the
Education Act 1996[2]) in relation to claims of disability discrimination in schools in
England[3].

A claim that a responsible body[4] has discriminated against a person ('A') in a way
which is unlawful[5], or is to be treated[6] as having discriminated against a person ('A') in
such a way, may be made to the Tribunal by A's parent[7]. If the Tribunal considers that a
claim is well founded, it may declare that A has been unlawfully discriminated against[8]
and, if it does so, it may make such order as it considers reasonable in all the
circumstances of the case[9]. If the Secretary of State is satisfied (whether on a complaint
or otherwise) that the responsible body concerned: (1) has acted, or is proposing to act,
unreasonably in complying with an order made by the Tribunal; or (2) has failed to
comply with the order, he may give that body such directions as to compliance with the
order as appear to him to be expedient[10].

Regulations may make provision about the proceedings of the Tribunal on a claim of
unlawful discrimination and the making of a claim[11]. In particular, provision may be
made[12]: (a) as to the manner in which a claim must be made; (b) if the jurisdiction of
the Tribunal is being exercised by more than one tribunal: (i) for determining by which
tribunal any claim is to be heard; and (ii) for the transfer of proceedings from one
tribunal to another; (c) for enabling functions which relate to matters preliminary or
incidental to a claim[13] to be performed by the president, or by the chairman; (d)
enabling hearings to be conducted in the absence of any member other than the
chairman; (e) as to the persons who may appear on behalf of the parties; (f) for granting
any person such disclosure or inspection of documents or right to further particulars as
might be granted by a county court; (g) requiring persons to attend to give evidence and
produce documents[14]; (h) for authorising the administration of oaths to witnesses; (i) for
the determination of claims without a hearing in prescribed circumstances; (j) as to the
withdrawal of claims; (k) for enabling the Tribunal to stay proceedings on a claim; (l) for
the award of costs or expenses; (m) for taxing or otherwise settling costs or expenses
(and, in particular, for enabling costs to be taxed in the county court); (n) for the
registration and proof of decisions and orders; and (o) for enabling prescribed decisions
to be reviewed, or prescribed orders to be varied or revoked, in such circumstances as
may be determined in accordance with the regulations.

A person who without reasonable excuse fails to comply with a requirement in respect of the disclosure or inspection of documents imposed under head (f) above, or a requirement imposed under head (g) above is guilty of an offence[15].

Except as provided above[16], no civil or criminal proceedings may be brought against any person in respect of an act merely because the act is unlawful under the provisions[17] concerning disability discrimination in schools[18]. However, this does not prevent the making of an application for judicial review[19], or the bringing of proceedings in respect of an offence of failing to comply with a requirement in respect of the disclosure or inspection of documents[20].

1   Disability Discrimination Act 1995 s 28H(1) (s 28H added by the Special Educational Needs and Disability Act 2001 s 17).
2   Ie under the Education Act 1996 Pt IV (ss 312–349) (as amended).
3   Disability Discrimination Act 1995 s 28H(3) (as added: see note 1 supra). For the meaning of 'school' see para 561 note 1 ante. The provisions of s 28H(2), (3) are substituted by the Education Act 2002 s 195, Sch 18 paras 7, 8(1) to take account of the Special Educational Needs Tribunal for Wales. As to the Special Educational Needs Tribunal for Wales see the Education Act 1996 s 336ZA (as added); and EDUCATION vol 15(2) (2006 Reissue) para 1032.
4   This reference to a responsible body is to be read as including a reference to a local education authority in relation to a function to which the Disability Discrimination Act 1995 s 28F (as added) (see para 565 ante) applies: s 28G(5) (s 28G added by the Special Educational Needs and Disability Act 2001 s 16). As to responsible bodies see para 561 ante. As to local education authorities see EDUCATION vol 15(1) (2006 Reissue) para 20.
5   Ie which is made unlawful by the Disability Discrimination Act 1995 Pt IV Ch I (ss 28A–28Q) (as added and amended).
6   Ie by virtue of ibid s 58 (employers' liability for acts of employees): see para 527 ante.
7   Ibid s 28I(1) (s 28I added by the Special Educational Needs and Disability Act 2001 s 18). The Disability Discrimination Act 1995 s 28I (as added) is amended by the Education Act 2002 Sch 18 paras 7, 9(1), (2) to take account of the Special Educational Needs Tribunal for Wales. Subject to regulations under the Disability Discrimination Act 1995 s 28J(8) (as added and amended) (see note 11 infra), the appropriate tribunal for a claim is either the Special Educational Needs Tribunal (for a claim against the responsible body of a school in England) or the Special Educational Needs Tribunal for Wales (for a claim against the responsible body of a school in Wales): see s 28I(5) (s 28I as so added; and s 28I(5) added by the Education Act 2002 Sch 18 paras 7, 9). For the meaning of 'parent' see para 563 note 13 ante.
    Separate provisions apply in relation to claims relating to admissions decisions and exclusion decisions (see para 567 post): Disability Discrimination Act 1995 s 28I(2) (as so added).
    Claims must be made within six months from the date of the act complained of: Sch 3 para 10(1) (Sch 3 paras 9–11 added by the Special Educational Needs and Disability Act 2001 s 19(2), Sch 3 para 1). The Disability Discrimination Act 1995 Sch 3 para 10 (as added) is also amended by the Education Act 2002 Sch 18 para 12 to take account of the Special Educational Needs Tribunal for Wales. For the purposes of the Disability Discrimination Act 1995 Sch 3 para 10(1) (as added): (1) if an unlawful act of discrimination is attributable to a term in a contract, that act is to be treated as extending throughout the duration of the contract; (2) any act extending over a period must be treated as done at the end of that period; and (3) a deliberate omission must be treated as done when the person in question decided upon it: Sch 3 para 10(5) (as so added). In the absence of evidence establishing the contrary, a person is to taken for these purposes to decide upon an omission: (a) when he does an act inconsistent with doing the omitted act; or (b) if he has done no such inconsistent act, when the period expires within which he might reasonably have been expected to do the omitted act if it was to be done: Sch 3 para 10(6) (as so added). As to the meaning of 'act' see para 510 note 3 ante.
    If, in relation to proceedings or prospective proceedings under s 28I (as added and amended), the dispute concerned is referred for conciliation in pursuance of arrangements under s 31B (as added and amended; prospectively repealed) (see para 657 post) before the end of the period of six months mentioned in Sch 3 para 10(1) (as added), the period allowed by that provision is extended by two months: Sch 3 para 10(2) (as so added). As from a day to be appointed, Sch 3 para 10 (as added) is amended so that, instead of referring to s 31B (as added and amended; prospectively repealed), it refers to the Equality Act 2006 s 27 (as amended; not yet in force) (see para 333 ante) and so as to refer to three months instead of two: see the Disability Discrimination Act 1995 Sch 3 para 10(2) (as so added; prospectively amended by the Equality Act 2006 s 40, Sch 3 paras 41, 56(2)(a)). At the date at which this volume states the law no such day had been appointed.
    The Tribunal may consider any claim which is out of time if, in all the circumstances of the case, it considers that it is just and equitable to do so; but this does not permit the Special Educational Needs

Tribunal for Wales to decide to consider a claim if a decision not to consider that claim has previously been taken: see the Disability Discrimination Act 1995 Sch 3 para 10(3), (4) (as so added).

8 Ibid s 28I(3)(a) (as added and amended: see note 7 supra).

9 Ibid s 28I(3)(b) (as added and amended: see note 7 supra).This power may, in particular, be exercised with a view to obviating or reducing the adverse effect on the person concerned of any matter to which the claim relates, but does not include power to order the payment of any sum by way of compensation: s 28I(4) (as so added). As to compensation generally see para 643 post.

10 Ibid s 28M(5), (6) (s 28M added by the Special Educational Needs and Disability Act 2001 s 22). The Disability Discrimination Act 1995 s 28M(5) (as added) is amended by the Education Act 2002 Sch 18 paras 7, 11 to take account of the Special Educational Needs Tribunal for Wales. As to variation, revocation, and enforcement of directions given by the Secretary of State see the Disability Discrimination Act 1995 s 28M(7) (as added; prospectively amended); and para 564 note 27 ante. As to the Secretary of State and the National Assembly for Wales see para 302 ante.

11 Ibid s 28J(1) (s 28J added by the Special Educational Needs and Disability Act 2001 s 19). The Disability Discrimination Act 1995 s 28J (as amended) is also amended by the Education Act 2002 Sch 18 paras 7, 10 to take account of the Special Educational Needs Tribunal for Wales. If made with the agreement of the National Assembly for Wales, the regulations apply equally to the Special Educational Needs Tribunal for Wales, subject to such modifications as may be specified in the regulations: see the Disability Discrimination Act 1995 s 28J(2A) (s 28J as so added; and s 28J(2A) added by the Education Act 2002 Sch 18 paras 7, 10). For the meaning of 'regulations' see para 509 note 12 ante. As to regulations made under the Disability Discrimination Act 1995 s 28J(1)–(3), (8) (as added and amended) see the Special Educational Needs and Disability Tribunal (General Provisions and Disability Claims Procedure) Regulations 2002, SI 2002/1985.

Proceedings before the Tribunal are to be held in private, except in prescribed circumstances: Disability Discrimination Act 1995 s 28J(3) (as so added; and amended by the Education Act 2002 Sch 18 paras 7, 10).

The Secretary of State may pay such allowances for the purpose of or in connection with the attendance of persons at the Tribunal as he may, with the consent of the Treasury, determine: Disability Discrimination Act 1995 s 28J(5) (as so added; and amended by the Education Act 2002 Sch 18 paras 7, 10). As to the Treasury see CONSTITUTIONAL LAW AND HUMAN RIGHTS vol 8(2) (Reissue) paras 512–517. In relation to the Special Educational Needs Tribunal for Wales, the power conferred by the Disability Discrimination Act 1995 s 28J(5) (as added and amended) may be exercised only with the agreement of the National Assembly for Wales: s 28J(6) (as so added; and amended by the Education Act 2002 Sch 18 paras 7, 10).

The Arbitration Act 1996 Pt I (ss 1–84) (as amended) (see ARBITRATION) does not apply to proceedings before the Tribunal but regulations may make provision, in relation to such proceedings, corresponding to any provision of Pt I (as amended): Disability Discrimination Act 1995 s 28J(7) (as so added; and amended by the Education Act 2002 Sch 18 paras 7, 10). Regulations may make provision for a claim to be heard, in prescribed circumstances, with an appeal under the Education Act 1996 Pt IV (as amended), including provision for determining the appropriate tribunal for the purposes of s 28I (as added and amended) for such a claim and for the transfer of proceedings between the Tribunal and its Welsh equivalent: Disability Discrimination Act 1995 s 28J(8) (as so added; and amended by the Education Act 2002 Sch 18 paras 7, 10).

12 See the Disability Discrimination Act 1995 s 28J(2)(a)–(o) (as added: see note 11 supra).

13 Ie including, in particular, decisions under ibid Sch 3 para 10(3) (as added): see note 7 supra.

14 As to evidence provided by way of a certificate signed by or on behalf of a Minister of the Crown see ibid Sch 3 para 11 (as added and amended). In any proceedings under s 28I (as added and amended), s 28K (as added and amended) or s 28L (as added and amended) (see para 567 post), a certificate signed by or on behalf of a Minister of the Crown and certifying that any conditions or requirements specified in the certificate: (1) were imposed by a Minister of the Crown; and (2) were in operation at a time or throughout a time so specified, are conclusive evidence of the matters certified: Sch 3 para 11(1) (Sch 3 para 11 as added (see note 7 supra); and Sch 3 para 11(1) amended by the Disability Discrimination Act 2005 s 19(1), Sch 1 paras 1, 38(1), (9)). In any proceedings under the Disability Discrimination Act 1995 s 28I (as added and amended), s 28K (as added and amended) or s 28L (as added and amended), a certificate signed by or on behalf of the National Assembly for Wales and certifying that any conditions or requirements specified in the certificate: (a) were imposed by the Assembly; and (b) were in operation at a time or throughout a time so specified, are conclusive evidence of the matters certified: Sch 3 para 11(1B) (Sch 3 para 11 as so added; and Sch 3 para 11(1B) added by the Disability Discrimination Act 2005 Sch 1 paras 1, 38(1), (10)). A document purporting to be such a certificate as is mentioned above must be received in evidence and, unless the contrary is proved, must be deemed to be such a certificate: Disability Discrimination Act 1995 Sch 3 para 11(2) (Sch 3 para 11 as so added; and Sch 3 para 11(2) amended by the Disability Discrimination Act 2005 Sch 1 paras 1, 38(1), (11)).

15 Disability Discrimination Act 1995 s 28J(9) (as added: see note 11 supra). A person guilty of such an offence is liable on summary conviction to a fine not exceeding level 3 on the standard scale: s 28J(10) (as so added). As to the standard scale see para 315 note 15 ante.

16 Ie by ibid s 28I (as added and amended), s 28K (as added and amended), or s 28L (as added and amended).

17 Ie ibid Pt IV Ch I (ss 28A–28Q) (as added and amended).

18 Ibid Sch 3 para 9(1) (as added (see note 7 supra); and amended by the Disability Discrimination Act 2005 Sch 1 paras 1, 38(1), (7)).

19 Disability Discrimination Act 1995 Sch 3 para 9(2) (as added: see note 7 supra).

20 Ibid Sch 3 para 9(3) (added by the Disability Discrimination Act 2005 Sch 1 paras 1, 38(1), (8)). The text refers to an offence under the Disability Discrimination Act 1995 s 28J(9) (as added) (see the text and note 15 supra).

567.   Admissions and exclusions.   A claim in relation to an admissions decision[1] that a responsible body: (1) has discriminated against a person ('A') in a way which is unlawful[2]; or (2) is to be treated[3] as having discriminated against a person ('A') in such a way, must be made under appeal arrangements[4] where such arrangements have been made enabling an appeal to be made against the decision by A's parent[5].

A claim in relation to an exclusion decision[6] that a responsible body[7]: (a) has discriminated against a person ('A') in a way which is unlawful[8]; or (b) is to be treated[9] as having discriminated against a person ('A') in such a way, must be made under appeal arrangements[10] where such arrangements have been made enabling an appeal to be made against the decision by A or by his parent[11].

1   'Admissions decision' means: (1) a decision of a kind mentioned in the School Standards and Framework Act 1998 s 94(1) or (2) (see EDUCATION vol 15(1) (2006 Reissue) para 415); (2) a decision as to the admission of a person to an Academy taken by the responsible body or on its behalf: Disability Discrimination Act 1995 s 28K(5) (s 28K added by the Special Educational Needs and Disability Act 2001 s 20; and the Disability Discrimination Act 1995 s 28K(5) amended by the Education Act 2002 s 65(3), Sch 7 para 5(1), (3)). As to responsible bodies see para 561 ante. See also note 7 infra.

2   Ie under the Disability Discrimination Act 1995 Pt IV Ch I (ss 28A–28Q) (as added and amended).

3   Ie by virtue of ibid s 58 (employers' liability for acts of employees): see para 527 ante.

4   Ie made under the School Standards and Framework Act 1998 s 94 (see EDUCATION vol 15(1) (2006 Reissue) para 415), or under an agreement entered into between the responsible body for an Academy and the Secretary of State under the Education Act 1996 s 482 (as substituted) (see EDUCATION vol 15(1) (2006 Reissue) para 496).

5   Disability Discrimination Act 1995 s 28K(1)–(3) (as added (see note 1 supra); and s 28K(2) amended by Education Act 2002 Sch 7 para 5(1), (3)). For the meaning of 'parent' see para 563 note 13 ante. The body hearing the claim has the powers which it has in relation to an appeal under the appeal arrangements: Disability Discrimination Act 1995 s 28K(4) (as so added).

6   'Exclusion decision' means: (1) a decision of a kind mentioned in the Education Act 2002 s 52(3)(c) (see EDUCATION vol 15(1) (2006 Reissue) para 562); (2) a decision not to reinstate a pupil who has been permanently excluded from an Academy by its head teacher, taken by the responsible body or on its behalf: Disability Discrimination Act 1995 s 28L(5) (s 28L added by the Special Educational Needs and Disability Act 2001 s 21; and the Disability Discrimination Act 1995 s 28L(5) amended by the Education Act 2002 s 215(1), Sch 7 para 5(1), (4), Sch 21 para 27(1), (2)).

7   For these purposes, 'responsible body', in relation to a maintained school, includes the discipline committee of the governing body if that committee is required to be established as a result of regulations made under the Education Act 2002 s 19 (see EDUCATION vol 15(1) (2006 Reissue) para 457): Disability Discrimination Act 1995 s 28L(6) (as added (see note 6 supra); and amended by the Education Act 2002 Sch 21 para 27(1), (3)). 'Maintained school' has the meaning given in the School Standards and Framework Act 1998 s 20(7) (see EDUCATION vol 15(1) (2006 Reissue) para 98): Disability Discrimination Act 1995 s 28L(7) (as added: see note 6 supra), s 28Q(5) (s 28Q added by the Special Educational Needs and Disability Act 2001 s 25).

8   See note 2 supra.

9   See note 3 supra.

10 Ie made under the Education Act 2002 s 52(3)(c) (see EDUCATION vol 15(1) (2006 Reissue) para 562), or under an agreement entered into between the responsible body for an Academy and the Secretary of State under the Education Act 1996 s 482 (as substituted) (see EDUCATION vol 15(1) (2006 Reissue) para 496).

11 Disability Discrimination Act 1995 s 28L(1)–(3) (as added (see note 6 supra); and s 28L(2) amended by the Education Act 2002 Sch 7 para 5(1), (4), Sch 21 para 27(1), (2)). The body hearing the claim has the powers which it has in relation to an appeal under the appeal arrangements: Disability Discrimination Act 1995 s 28L(4) (as so added).

568. Validity and revision of agreements of responsible bodies. Any term in a contract or other agreement made by or on behalf of a responsible body is void so far as it purports to: (1) require a person to do anything which would contravene any provision of, or made under, the provisions[1] concerning disability discrimination in schools[2]; (2) exclude or limit the operation of any provision of, or made under, those provisions[3]; or (3) prevent any person from making a claim under those provisions[4]. On the application of any person interested in such an agreement, a county court may make such order as it thinks just for modifying the agreement[5].

1 Ie the Disability Discrimination Act 1995 Pt IV Ch I (ss 28A–28Q) (as added and amended).
2 Ibid s 28P(1)(a) (s 28P added by Special Educational Needs and Disability Act 2001 s 24). A reference in the Disability Discrimination Act 1995 s 28P (as added) to a responsible body is to be read as including an educational authority in relation to a function to which s 28F (as added and amended) (see para 565 ante) applies: s 28G(6) (s 28P added by Special Educational Needs and Disability Act 2001 s 16). As to responsible bodies see para 561 ante. As to local education authorities see EDUCATION vol 15(1) (2006 Reissue) para 20.
3 Disability Discrimination Act 1995 s 28P(1)(b) (as added: see note 2 supra). This does not apply to an agreement settling a claim under s 28I (as added and amended) (see para 566 ante) or to which s 28K (as added and amended) or s 28L (as added and amended) (see para 567 ante) applies: s 28P(2) (as so added).
4 Ibid s 28P(1)(c) (as added: see note 2 supra). This does not apply to an agreement settling a claim under s 28I (as added and amended) (see para 566 ante) or to which s 28K (as added and amended) or s 28L (as added and amended) (see para 567 ante) applies: s 28P(2) (as so added).
5 Ibid s 28P(3) (as added: see note 2 supra). No such order may be made unless all persons affected have been given notice of the application and afforded an opportunity to make representations to the court, subject to any rules of court providing for notice to be dispensed with: s 28P(4), (5) (as so added). An order under s 28P(3) (as added) may include provision as respects any period before the making of the order: s 28P(6) (as so added).

(B) Further and Higher Education

569. Discrimination and harassment against disabled students. It is unlawful for the body responsible for an educational institution[1] (the 'responsible body')[2] to discriminate against a disabled person: (1) in the arrangements it makes for determining admissions to the institution[3]; (2) in the terms on which it offers to admit him to the institution[4]; or (3) by refusing or deliberately omitting to accept an application for his admission to the institution[5]. It is also unlawful for the responsible body to discriminate against a disabled student[6]: (a) in the student services it provides, or offers to provide[7]; or (b) by excluding him from the institution, whether permanently or temporarily[8].

It is unlawful for the body responsible for an educational institution to discriminate against a disabled person: (i) in the arrangements which it makes for the purpose of determining upon whom to confer a qualification[9]; (ii) in the terms on which it is prepared to confer a qualification on him[10]; (iii) by refusing or deliberately omitting to grant any application by him for a qualification[11]; or (iv) by withdrawing a qualification from him or varying the terms on which he holds it[12].

It is unlawful for the body responsible for an educational institution to subject to harassment[13] a disabled person who: (A) holds or applies for a qualification conferred by the institution[14]; (B) is a student at the institution[15]; or (C) seeks admission as a student to the institution[16].

These provisions[17] also apply to discrimination against a person who is not disabled where the act which constitutes discrimination is victimisation[18].

The relevant provisions[19] apply with modifications in relation to higher and further education secured by a local education authority[20], and in relation to recreational or training facilities secured by a local education authority[21].

1   'Educational institution' means an institution: (1) within the higher education sector; (2) within the further education sector; or (3) designated in an order made by the Secretary of State: Disability Discrimination Act 1995 ss 28R(6), 31A(4) (ss 28R, 31A added by the Special Educational Needs and Disability Act 2001 ss 26, 33). These provisions are to be read together with the Further and Higher Education Act 1992 s 91 (as amended) (see EDUCATION vol 15(1) (2006 Reissue) para 562): Disability Discrimination Act 1995 s 28R(8) (as so added). The Secretary of State may not make an order under s 28R(6)(c) (as added) (see head (3) supra) unless he is satisfied that the institution concerned is wholly or partly funded from public funds: s 28R(9) (as so added). In exercise of the power, the Secretary of State has made the Disability Discrimination (Designation of Educational Institutions) Order 2002, SI 2002/1459. As to the Secretary of State and the National Assembly for Wales see para 302 ante.

2   Disability Discrimination Act 1995 s 28R(5) (as added: see note 1 supra). As to the responsible bodies see Sch 4B para 1, Table (Sch 4B added by the Special Educational Needs and Disability Act 2001 s 26(2), Sch 4). The governing body is the responsible body in relation to an institution within the further education sector, a university, or an institution (other than a university) within the higher education sector: Disability Discrimination Act 1995 Sch 4B para 1, Table items 1–3 (as so added). In relation to an institution designated under s 28R(6)(c) (as added) (see note 1 head (3) supra), the responsible body is the body specified in the order as the responsible body: Sch 4B para 1, Table item 4 (as so added).

3   Ibid s 28R(1)(a) (as added: see note 1 supra).

4   Ibid s 28R(1)(b) (as added: see note 1 supra).

5   Ibid s 28R(1)(c) (as added: see note 1 supra).

6   'Disabled student' means a student who is a disabled person: ibid s 31A(2) (as added: see note 1 supra). 'Student' means a person who is attending, or undertaking a course of study at, an educational institution: s 31A(3) (as so added). For the meaning of 'disabled person' see para 511 ante.

7   Ibid s 28R(2) (as added: see note 1 supra). 'Student services' means services of any description which are provided wholly or mainly for students: s 28R(11) (as so added). Regulations may make provision as to services which are, or are not, to be regarded for the purposes of s 28R(2) (as added) as student services: s 28R(12) (as so added). For the meaning of 'regulations' see para 509 note 12 ante. At the date at which this volume states the law no such regulations had been made.

8   Ibid s 28R(3) (as added: see note 1 supra).

9   Ibid s 28R(3A)(a) (s 28R as added (see note 1 supra); and s 28R(3A), (3B) added by the Disability Discrimination Act 1995 (Amendment) (Further and Higher Education) Regulations 2006, SI 2006/1721, reg 4(1), (5)). 'Qualification' means any authorisation, qualification, approval or certification conferred by a responsible authority: Disability Discrimination Act 1995 s 31A(6) (s 31A as added (see note 1 supra); and s 31A(6), (9) added by the Disability Discrimination Act 1995 (Amendment) (Further and Higher Education) Regulations 2006, SI 2006/1721, regs 4(1), (7)). References (however expressed) to the conferment of a qualification on a person by a responsible body include: (1) the renewal or extension of a qualification; and (2) the authentication of a qualification awarded to him by another person: Disability Discrimination Act 1995 s 31A(9) (as so added).

10   Ibid s 28R(3A)(b) (as added: see notes 1, 9 supra).

11   Ibid s 28R(3A)(c) (as added: see notes 1, 9 supra).

12   Ibid s 28R(3A)(d) (as added: see notes 1, 9 supra).

13   A responsible body subjects a disabled person to harassment where, for a reason which relates to the disabled person's disability, that body engages in unwanted conduct which has the purpose or effect of: (1) violating the disabled person's dignity; or (2) creating an intimidating, hostile, degrading, humiliating or offensive environment for him: ibid s 28SA(1) (s 28SA added by the Disability Discrimination Act 1995 (Amendment) (Further and Higher Education) Regulations 2006, SI 2006/1721, reg 4(1), (7)). Conduct is regarded as having the effect referred to in the Disability Discrimination Act 1995 s 28SA(1)(a) or (b) (as added) (see heads (1), (2) supra) only if, having regard to all the circumstances, including in particular the perception of the disabled person, it should reasonably be considered as having that effect: s 28SA(2) (as so added). In Pt IV Ch II (ss 28R–31A) (as added and amended), 'harassment' is to be construed in accordance with s 28SA (as added): s 31A(8) (as added: see note 1 supra).

14   Ibid s 28R(3B)(a) (as added: see notes 1, 9 supra).

15   Ibid s 28R(3B)(b) (as added: see notes 1, 9 supra).

16   Ibid s 28R(3B)(c) (as added: see notes 1, 9 supra).

17   Ie ibid s 28R (as added and amended).

18   Ibid s 28R(4) (as added: see note 1 supra). As to discrimination by way of victimisation see s 55 (as amended); and para 526 ante.

19   Ie ibid Pt IV Ch II (ss 28R–31A) (as added and amended).

20 Ibid s 28U(1) (s 28U substituted by the Disability Discrimination Act 1995 (Amendment) (Further and Higher Education) Regulations 2006, SI 2006/1721, regs 4(1), 10). See further the Disability Discrimination Act 1995 Sch 4C Pt I (substituted by the Disability Discrimination Act 1995 (Amendment) (Further and Higher Education) Regulations 2006, SI 2006/1721, regs 4(1), 21).

21 Disability Discrimination Act 1995 s 28U(2) (as substituted: see note 20 supra). See further the Disability Discrimination Act 1995 Sch 4C Pt IA (substituted by the Disability Discrimination Act 1995 (Amendment) (Further and Higher Education) Regulations 2006, SI 2006/1721, regs 4(1), 21).

570. Meaning of 'discrimination'. A responsible body discriminates against a disabled person[1] if[2]: (1) for a reason which relates to his disability, it treats him less favourably than it treats or would treat others to whom that reason does not or would not apply[3]; and (2) it cannot show that the treatment in question is justified[4]. A responsible person also discriminates against a disabled person if it fails to comply with a duty to make adjustments[5] in relation to the disabled person[6].

In relation to a failure to take a particular step, a responsible body does not discriminate against a person if it shows that: (a) at the time in question it did not know, and could not reasonably have been expected to know, that he was disabled[7]; and (b) its failure to take the step was attributable to that lack of knowledge[8].

Treatment, other than the application of a competence standard[9], is justified[10] for the purposes of head (2) above if, but only if, the reason for it is both material to the circumstances of the particular case and substantial[11]. The application by a responsible body of a competence standard to a disabled person is justified[12] for the purposes of head (2) above if, but only if, the body can show that: (i) the standard is, or would be, applied equally to persons who do not have his particular disability[13]; and (ii) its application is a proportionate means of achieving a legitimate aim[14].

A responsible body directly discriminates against a disabled person if, on the ground of the disabled person's disability, it treats the disabled person less favourably than it treats or would treat a person not having that particular disability whose relevant circumstances, including his abilities, are the same as, or not materially different from, those of the disabled person[15].

1 Ie for the purposes of the Disability Discrimination Act 1995 Pt IV Ch II (ss 28R–31A) (as added and amended): see para 569 ante. For the meaning of 'disabled person' see para 511 ante. As to responsible bodies see para 569 ante.

2 Ibid s 28S(1) (s 28S added by the Special Educational Needs and Disability Act 2001 s 27; and the Disability Discrimination Act 1995 s 28S(1) amended by the Disability Discrimination Act 1995 (Amendment) (Further and Higher Education) Regulations 2006, SI 2006/1721, regs 4(1), 6(1)). In the Disability Discrimination Act 1995 Pt IV Ch II (as added and amended), 'discriminate', 'discrimination' and other related expressions are to be construed in accordance with s 28S (as added and amended): s 31A(7) (added by the Disability Discrimination Act 1995 (Amendment) (Further and Higher Education) Regulations 2006, SI 2006/1721, regs 4(1), 17).

3 Disability Discrimination Act 1995 s 28S(1)(a) (as added: see note 2 supra).

4 Ibid s 28S(1)(b) (as added: see note 2 supra).

5 Ie a duty imposed under ibid s 28T (as added and amended) (see para 571 post) or under s 28UA(5) (as added) (see para 572 post).

6 Ibid s 28S(2) (as added (see note 2 supra); and substituted by the Disability Discrimination Act 1995 (Amendment) (Further and Higher Education) Regulations 2006, SI 2006/1721, regs 4(1), 6(2)).

7 Disability Discrimination Act 1995 s 28S(3)(a) (as added: see note 2 supra).

8 Ibid s 28S(3)(b) (as added: see note 2 supra).

9 In ibid ss 28S, 28T (both as added and amended), 'competence standard' means an academic, medical or other standard applied by or on behalf of a responsible body for the purpose of determining whether or not a person has a particular level of competence or ability: s 28S(11) (s 28S as added (see note 2 supra); and s 28S(5)–(9) substituted, and s 28S(10), (11) added, by the Disability Discrimination Act 1995 (Amendment) (Further and Higher Education) Regulations 2006, SI 2006/1721, regs 4(1), 6(4)).

10 Ie subject to the Disability Discrimination Act 1995 s 28S(7)–(9) (as added and substituted). If in a case falling within s 28S(1) (as added and amended) (see heads (1), (2) in the text), other than a case where the treatment is the application of a competence standard, a responsible body is under a duty under s 28T (as added and amended) (see para 571 post) or under s 28UA(5) (as added) (see para 572 post) in relation to

the disabled person, but fails to comply with that duty, its treatment of that person cannot be justified under s 28S(5) (as added and substituted) unless that treatment would have been justified even if it had complied with that duty: s 28S(7) (as added and substituted: see notes 2, 9 supra). Subject to s 28S(9) (as added and substituted), regulations may make provision, for purposes of s 28S (as added and amended), as to circumstances in which treatment is, or as to circumstances in which treatment is not, to be taken to be justified: s 28S(8) (as so added and substituted). Treatment of a disabled person by a responsible body cannot be justified under s 28S(5), (6) or (8) (as added and substituted) if it amounts to direct discrimination falling within s 28S(10) (as added) (see the text and note 15 supra): s 28S(9) (as so added and substituted). For the meaning of 'regulations' see para 509 note 12 ante. At the date at which this volume states the law no such regulations had been made.

11 Ibid s 28S(5) (as added and substituted: see notes 2, 9 supra).

12 Ie subject to ibid s 28S(8), (9) (as added and substituted): see note 10 supra.

13 Ibid s 28S(6)(a) (as added and substituted: see notes 2, 9 supra).

14 Ibid s 28S(6)(b) (as added and substituted: see notes 2, 9 supra).

15 Ibid s 28S(10) (as added: see notes 2, 9 supra).

571. Duty of resonible bodies to make adjustments. Where (1) a provision, criterion or practice[1], other than a competence standard[2], is applied by or on behalf of a responsible body[3]; (2) it is a provision, criterion or practice relating to the arrangements it makes for determining admissions to the institution, or student services[4] provided for, or offered to, students by the responsible body[5]; and (3) that provision, criterion or practice places disabled persons at a substantial disadvantage in comparison with persons who are not disabled[6], it is the duty of the responsible body to take such steps as it is reasonable, in all the circumstances of the case, for it to have to take in order to prevent the provision, criterion or practice having that effect[7].

Where (a) a provision, criterion or practice, other than a competence standard, is applied by or on behalf of a responsible body[8]; (b) it is a provision, criterion or practice for determining on whom a qualification[9] is to be conferred[10]; (c) a disabled person is, or has notified the body that he may be, an applicant for the conferment of that qualification[11]; and (d) the provision, criterion or practice places the disabled person at a substantial disadvantage in comparison with persons who are not disabled[12], it is the duty of the responsible body to take such steps as it is reasonable, in all the circumstances of the case, for it to have to take in order to prevent the provision, criterion or practice having that effect[13].

Where (i) a provision, criterion or practice, other than a competence standard, is applied by or on behalf of a responsible body[14]; (ii) it is a provision, criterion or practice other than one mentioned in head (2) or head (b) above[15]; and (iii) it places a disabled person who holds a qualification conferred by the responsible body, or applies for a qualification which the responsible body confers, at a substantial disadvantage in comparison with persons who are not disabled[16], it is the duty of the responsible body to take such steps as it is reasonable, in all the circumstances of the case, for it to have to take in order to prevent the provision, criterion or practice having that effect[17].

Where any physical feature[18] of premises occupied by a responsible body places disabled persons at a substantial disadvantage in comparison with persons who are not disabled in relation to the arrangements which that body makes for determining admissions to the institution[19], or in relation to student services provided for, or offered to, students by that body[20], it is the duty of the body to take such steps as it is reasonable, in all the circumstances of the case, for it to have to take in order to prevent the feature having that effect[21].

Where any physical feature of premises occupied by a responsible body places a disabled person who applies for a qualification which that body confers[22], or holds a qualification which was conferred by that body[23], at a substantial disadvantage in comparison with persons who are not disabled, it is the duty of the body to take such steps as it is reasonable, in all the circumstances of the case, for it to have to take in order to prevent the feature having that effect[24].

In considering whether it is reasonable for it to have to take a particular step in order to comply with its duty under the above provisions[25], a responsible body must have regard to any relevant provisions of a code of practice[26].   •

In determining whether it is reasonable for a responsible body to have to take a particular step in order to comply with its duty under the above provisions[27] in relation to a person with respect to whom a confidentiality request[28] has been made, of which the responsible body is aware, regard must be had to the extent to which taking the step in question is consistent with compliance with the confidentiality request[29].

Duties are imposed under the above provisions[30] only for the purpose of determining whether a responsible body has discriminated against a disabled person; and accordingly a breach of any such duty is not actionable as such[31].

In relation to a failure to take a particular step, a responsible body does not discriminate against a person if it shows that at the time in question it did not know, and could not reasonably have been expected to know, that he was disabled and its failure to take the step was attributable to that lack of knowledge[32].

1   'Provision, criterion or practice' includes any arrangements: Disability Discrimination Act 1995 s 31A(5) (s 31A added by the Special Educational Needs and Disability Act 2001 s 33; and the Disability Discrimination Act 1995 s 31A(5), (10) added by the Disability Discrimination Act 1995 (Amendment) (Further and Higher Education) Regulations 2006, SI 2006/1721, regs 4(1), 17).
2   For the meaning of 'competence standard' see para 570 note 9 ante.
3   Disability Discrimination Act 1995 s 28T(1)(a) (s 28T added by the Special Educational Needs and Disability Act 2001 s 28; and the Disability Discrimination Act 1995 s 28T(1) substituted, and s 28T(1A)–(1D) added, by the Disability Discrimination Act 1995 (Amendment) (Further and Higher Education) Regulations 2006, SI 2006/1721, regs 4(1), 8). As to responsible bodies see para 569 ante.
4   For the meaning of 'student services' see para 569 note 7 ante.
5   Disability Discrimination Act 1995 s 28T(1)(b) (as added and substituted: see note 3 supra).
6   Ibid s 28T(1)(c) (as added and substituted: see note 3 supra).
7   Ibid s 28T(1) (as added and substituted: see note 3 supra).
8   Ibid s 28T(1A)(a) (as added: see note 3 supra).
9   For the meaning of 'qualification' see para 569 note 9 ante.
10   Disability Discrimination Act 1995 s 28T(1A)(b) (as added: see note 3 supra).
11   Ibid s 28T(1A)(c) (as added: see note 3 supra).
12   Ibid s 28T(1A)(d) (as added: see note 3 supra).
13   Ibid s 28T(1A) (as added: see note 3 supra).
14   Ibid s 28T(1B)(a) (as added: see note 3 supra).
15   Ibid s 28T(1B)(b) (as added: see note 3 supra).
16   Ibid s 28T(1B)(c) (as added: see note 3 supra).
17   Ibid s 28T(1B) (as added: see note 3 supra).
18   'Physical feature', in relation to any premises, includes any of the following (whether permanent or temporary): (1) any feature arising from the design or construction of a building on the premises; (2) any feature on the premises of any approach to, exit from or access to such a building; (3) any fixtures, fittings, furnishings, furniture, equipment or material in or on the premises; and (4) any other physical element or quality of any land comprised in the premises: ibid s 31A(10) (as added: see note 1 supra). As to the meaning of 'premises' see para 525 note 9 ante.
19   Ibid s 28T(1C)(a) (as added: see note 3 supra).
20   Ibid s 28T(1C)(b) (as added: see note 3 supra).
21   Ibid s 28T(1C) (as added: see note 3 supra).
22   Ibid s 28T(1D)(a) (as added: see note 3 supra).
23   Ibid s 28T(1D)(b) (as added: see note 3 supra).
24   Ibid s 28T(1D) (as added: see note 3 supra).
25   Ie under any of ibid s 28T(1) (as added and substituted), s 28T(1A)–(1D) (as added).
26   Ibid s 28T(2) (as added (see note 3 supra); and amended by the Disability Discrimination Act 1995 (Amendment) (Further and Higher Education) Regulations 2006, SI 2006/1721, regs 4(1), 9). The text refers to a code of practice issued under the Disability Discrimination Act 1995 s 53A (as added and amended) (see para 655 post). As from a day to be appointed, the reference to s 53A (as added and

amended) is amended so as to refer to the Equality Act 2006 s 14 (as amended; not yet in force) (see para 321 ante): Disability Discrimination Act 1995 s 28T(2) (prospectively amended by the Equality Act 2006 s 40, Sch 3 paras 41, 46). At the date at which this volume states the law no such day had been appointed.

27 See note 25 supra.
28 'Confidentiality request' means a request made by a disabled person, which asks for the nature, or asks for the existence, of his disability to be treated as confidential: Disability Discrimination Act 1995 s 28T(5) (as added: see note 3 supra).
29 Ibid s 28T(3), (4) (as added: see note 3 supra).
30 Ie ibid s 28T (as added and amended).
31 Ibid s 28T(6) (as added: see note 3 supra).
32 See ibid s 28S(3) (as added); and para 570 ante.

572.   Discrimination in relationships that have come to an end. Where (1) there has been a relevant relationship[1] between a disabled person[2] and a responsible body[3]; and (2) that relationship has come to an end[4], it is unlawful for the responsible body: (a) to discriminate against the disabled person by subjecting him to a detriment[5]; or (b) to subject the disabled person to harassment[6], where the discrimination or harassment arises out of and is closely connected to the relevant relationship[7].

Where (i) a provision, criterion or practice[8] applied by the responsible body to the disabled person in relation to any matter arising out of the relevant relationship[9]; or (ii) a physical feature[10] of premises[11] which are occupied by the responsible body[12], places the disabled person at a substantial disadvantage in comparison with persons who are not disabled but are in the same position as the disabled person in relation to the responsible body[13], it is the duty of the responsible body to take such steps as it is reasonable, in all the circumstances of the case, for it to have to take in order to prevent the provision, criterion, practice or feature having that effect[14]. Such duties[15] are only for the purpose of determining whether a responsible body has discriminated against a disabled person; and accordingly a breach of any such duty is not actionable as such[16]. Furthermore no duty is imposed[17] on the responsible body if it does not know, and could not reasonably be expected to know, that the person has a disability and is likely to be affected in the way mentioned[18].

1   A 'relevant relationship' is a relationship during the course of which an act of discrimination against, or harassment of, one party to the relationship by the other party to it is unlawful under any provisions of the Disability Discrimination Act 1995 Pt IV Ch II (ss 28R–31A) (as added and amended) (see para 569 et seq ante): s 28UA(2) (s 28UA added by the Disability Discrimination Act 1995 (Amendment) (Further and Higher Education) Regulations 2006, SI 2006/1721, regs 4(1), 12). As to the meaning of 'act' see para 510 note 3 ante. As to discrimination see para 570 ante. For the meaning of 'harassment' see para 569 note 13 ante.
        In the Disability Discrimination Act 1995 s 28UA(2) (as added), reference to an act of discrimination or harassment which is unlawful includes, in the case of a relationship which has come to an end before the commencement of the provision, reference to such an act which would, after the commencement, be unlawful: s 28UA(8) (as so added).
2   For the meaning of 'disabled person' see para 511 ante.
3   Disability Discrimination Act 1995 s 28UA(1)(a) (as added: see note 1 supra). As to responsible bodies see para 569 ante.
4   Ibid s 28UA(1)(b) (as added: see note 1 supra).
5   Ibid s 28UA(3)(a) (as added: see note 1 supra).
6   Ibid s 28UA(3)(b) (as added: see note 1 supra).
7   Ibid s 28UA(3) (as added: see note 1 supra).
8   As to the meaning of 'provision, criterion or practice' see para 571 note 1 ante.
9   Disability Discrimination Act 1995 s 28UA(4)(a) (as added: see note 1 supra).
10 As to the meaning of 'physical feature' see para 571 note 18 ante.
11 As to the meaning of 'premises' see para 525 note 9 ante.
12 Disability Discrimination Act 1995 s 28UA(4)(b) (as added: see note 1 supra).
13 Ibid s 28UA(4) (as added: see note 1 supra).
14 Ibid s 28UA(5) (as added: see note 1 supra).
15 Ie imposed by ibid s 28UA(5) (as added): sees the text and note 14 supra.

16 Ibid s 28UA(6) (as added: see note 1 supra).
17 See note 15 supra.
18 Disability Discrimination Act 1995 s 28UA(7) (as added: see note 1 supra).

573. Instructions and pressure to discriminate. It is unlawful for a responsible body[1] to instruct another person[2] to do any act[3] which is unlawful[4] or to procure or attempt to procure the doing of any such unlawful act by that other person[5].

It is also unlawful for a responsible body to induce, or attempt to induce[6], another person to do any act which is unlawful[7] by: (1) providing or offering to provide that person with any benefit[8]; or (2) subjecting or threatening to subject that person to any detriment[9].

1 As to responsible bodies see para 569 ante.
2 As to the meaning of 'person' see para 344 note 3 ante.
3 As to the meaning of 'act' see para 510 note 3 ante.
4 Ie which is unlawful under the Disability Discrimination Act 1995 Pt IV Ch II (ss 28R–31A) (as added and amended).
5 Ibid s 28UB(1) (s 28UB added by the Disability Discrimination Act 1995 (Amendment) (Further and Higher Education) Regulations 2006, SI 2006/1721, regs 4(1), 13).
6 An attempted inducement is not prevented from falling within the Disability Discrimination Act 1995 s 28UB(2) (as added) because it is not made directly to the person in question, if it is made in such a way that he is likely to hear of it: s 28UB(3) (as added: see note 5 supra).
7 See note 4 supra.
8 Disability Discrimination Act 1995 s 28UB(2)(a) (as added: see note 5 supra).
9 Ibid s 28UB(2)(b) (as added: see note 5 supra).

574. Discriminatory advertisements. It is unlawful for a responsible body[1] to publish or cause to be published an advertisement[2] which: (1) invites applications in relation to any course or student service provided or offered by it, or any qualification[3] conferred by it[4]; and (2) indicates, or might reasonably be understood to indicate, that such an application will or may be determined to any extent by reference to the applicant not having any disability[5], or any particular disability, or any reluctance on the part of the person determining the application to comply with a duty to make adjustments[6].

1 As to responsible bodies see para 569 ante.
2 'Advertisement' includes every form of advertisement or notice, whether to the public or not: Disability Discrimination Act 1995 s 28UC(3) (s 28UC added by the Disability Discrimination Act 1995 (Amendment) (Further and Higher Education) Regulations 2006, SI 2006/1721, regs 4(1), 14).
3 For the meaning of 'qualification' see para 569 note 9 ante.
4 Disability Discrimination Act 1995 s 28UC(1)(a) (as added: see note 2 supra).
   Section 28UC(1) (as added) does not apply where it would not in fact be unlawful under Pt IV Ch II (ss 28R–31A) (as added and amended) for an application to be determined in the manner indicated (or understood to be indicated) in the advertisement: s 28UC(2) (as so added).
5 As to having a disability see para 511 ante.
6 Disability Discrimination Act 1995 s 28UC(1)(b) (as added: see note 2 supra). The duty referred to in the text is a duty imposed by s 28T (as added and amended): see para 571 ante. See note 4 supra.

575. Enforcement, remedies and procedures. A claim by a person: (1) that a responsible body[1] has discriminated[2] against him or subjected him to harassment[3] in a way which is unlawful under the provisions concerning disability discrimination in further and higher education[4]; (2) that a responsible body is to be treated[5] as having done so[6]; or (3) that a person is to be treated[7] as having done so[8], may be made the subject of civil proceedings in the same way as any other claim in tort for breach of statutory duty[9].

Where (a) a claim is brought under the above provisions[10]; and (b) the claimant proves facts from which the court could, apart from this provision[11], conclude in the absence of an adequate explanation that the defendant has acted in a way which is unlawful[12], the court must uphold the claim unless the defendant proves that he did not so act[13].

Damages in respect of unlawful discrimination may include compensation for injury to feelings whether or not they include compensation under any other head[14].

Except as provided above[15], no civil or criminal proceedings may be brought against any person in respect of an act merely because the act is unlawful under the relevant provisions[16] concerning disability discrimination in further and higher education[17]. However, this does not prevent the making of an application for judicial review[18].

There are also enforcement measures for the provisions relating to discrimination in relationships that have come to an end[19] and those relating to instructions and pressure to discriminate[20]. Where an act is unlawful under those provisions[21], legal proceedings may be brought by the Disability Rights Commission[22], and where the Commission thinks that a person has done an unlawful act[23] it may apply to a county court[24]. On such an application, the court must determine whether the allegation is correct[25].

The Commission may apply to a county court for an injunction restraining a person from doing such unlawful act where: (i) either a court has determined that the person has done an unlawful act, or the Commission thinks that the person has done such an act[26]; and (ii) the Commission thinks that if unrestrained the person is likely to do another such act[27].

1   As to responsible bodies see para 569 ante.

2   As to discrimination see para 570 ante.

3·   For the meaning of 'harassment' see para 569 note 13 ante.

4   Disability Discrimination Act 1995 s 28V(1)(a) (s 28V added by the Special Educational Needs and Disability Act 2001 s 30(1); and s 28V(1)(a) amended by the Disability Discrimination Act 1995 (Amendment) (Further and Higher Education) Regulations 2006, SI 2006/1721, regs 4(1), 15(1), (2)(a)). The provisions referred to in the text are those in the Disability Discrimination Act 1995 Pt IV Ch II (ss 28R–31A) (as added and amended).

5   Ie by virtue of ibid s 57 (as amended) (see para 528 ante) or s 58 (see para 527 ante).

6   Ibid s 28V(1)(b) (as added (see note 4 supra); and amended by the Disability Discrimination Act 1995 (Amendment) (Further and Higher Education) Regulations 2006, SI 2006/1721, regs 4(1), 15(1), (2)(b)).

7   Ie by virtue of the Disability Discrimination Act 1995 s 57 (as amended): see para 528 ante.

8   Ibid s 28V(1)(c) (as added (see note 4 supra); and amended by the Disability Discrimination Act 1995 (Amendment) (Further and Higher Education) Regulations 2006, SI 2006/1721, regs 4(1), 15(1), (2)(b)).

9   Disability Discrimination Act 1995 s 28V(1) (as added: see note 4 supra). Proceedings may be brought only in a county court but the remedies available are those which are available in the High Court: s 28V(3), (5) (as so added). The fact that a person who brings proceedings under Pt IV (ss 28A–31C) (as amended; prospectively amended) against a responsible body may also be entitled to bring proceedings against that body under Pt II (ss 3A–18E) (as amended; prospectively amended) is not to affect the proceedings under Pt IV (as amended; prospectively amended): s 28V(6) (as so added).

Claims must be made within six months from the date of the act complained of: Sch 3 para 13(1) (Sch 3 paras 12–15 added by the Special Educational Needs and Disability Act 2001 s 30(2), Sch 3 para 2). The six-month limitation period is extended by two months where the dispute is referred to conciliation under the Disability Discrimination Act 1995 s 31B (as added and amended; prospectively repealed) (see para 657 post) or where it relates to a complaint under the student complaints scheme (see EDUCATION vol 15(2) (2006 Reissue) para 1040): see Sch 3 para 13(2) (as so added; and substituted by the Higher Education Act 2004 s 19(3)). As from a day to be appointed, the reference to the Disability Discrimination Act 1995 s 31B (as added and amended; prospectively repealed) is replaced by a reference to the Equality Act 2006 s 27 (as amended; not yet in force) (see para 333 ante) and the reference to an extension of two months is replaced by a reference to one of three months: Disability Discrimination Act 1995 Sch 3 para 13(2) (as so added and substituted; prospectively amended by the Equality Act 2006 s 40, Sch 3 paras 41, 56(2)). At the date at which this volume states the law no such day had been appointed.

In any proceedings under the Disability Discrimination Act 1995 s 28V (as added and amended), a certificate signed by or on behalf of a Minister of the Crown and certifying that any conditions or requirements specified in the certificate were imposed by a Minister of the Crown, and were in operation at a time or throughout a time so specified, is conclusive evidence of the matters certified: Sch 3 para 15(1) (as so added). Similarly in any such proceedings, a certificate signed by or on behalf of the National Assembly for Wales and certifying that any conditions or requirements specified in the certificate were imposed by the Assembly, and were in operation at a time or throughout a time so specified, is conclusive evidence of the matters certified: Sch 3 para 15(1B) (Sch 3 para 15 as so added; and Sch 3 para 15(1B) added by the Disability Discrimination Act 2005 s 19(1), Sch 1 paras 1, 38(1), (12)). A document purporting to be such a certificate is to be received in evidence, and deemed to be such a certificate unless the contrary is proved: Sch 3 para 15(2) (as so added; and amended by the Disability Discrimination Act 2005 Sch 1 paras 1, 38(1), (13)). As to the meaning of 'Minister of the Crown' see para 510 note 4 ante. As to the National Assembly for Wales see para 302 ante.

As to joinder of lessors in a case concerning the occupation of premises by educational institutions see the Disability Discrimination Act 1995 Sch 4 para 12 (Sch 4 paras 10–14 added by the Special Educational Needs and Disability Act 2001 s 31(2), Sch 6). In proceedings on a claim under the Disability Discrimination Act 1995 s 28V (as added and amended), in a case to which Sch 4 Pt III (as added and amended) (see also paras 576–577 post) applies, the claimant or the responsible body concerned may ask the court to direct that the lessor be joined as a party to the proceedings: Sch 4 para 12(1) (as so added). The request must be granted if it is made before the hearing of the claim begins: Sch 4 para 12(2) (as so added). The court may refuse the request if it is made after the hearing of the claim begins: Sch 4 para 12(3) (as so added). The request may not be granted if it is made after the court has determined the claim: Sch 4 para 12(4) (as so added). If a lessor has been so joined as a party to the proceedings, the court may determine: (1) whether the lessor has refused consent to the alteration, or consented subject to one or more conditions; and (2) if so, whether the refusal or any of the conditions was unreasonable: Sch 4 para 12(5) (as so added). If, under Sch 4 para 12(5) (as added), the court determines that the refusal or any of the conditions was unreasonable it may take one or more of the following steps: (a) make such a declaration as it considers appropriate; (b) make an order authorising the responsible body to make the alteration specified in the order; (c) order the lessor to pay compensation to the complainant: Sch 4 para 12(6) (as so added). An order under head (b) supra may require the responsible body to comply with conditions specified in the order: Sch 4 para 12(7) (as so added). If the court orders the lessor to pay compensation, it may not order the responsible body to do so: Sch 4 para 12(8) (as so added).

10 Ibid s 28V(1A)(a) (s 28V(1A) added by the Disability Discrimination Act 1995 (Amendment) (Further and Higher Education) Regulations 2006, SI 2006/1721, regs 4(1), 15(1), (3)). The provisions referred to are those of the Disability Discrimination Act 1995 s 28V(1) (as added and amended).

11 Ie apart from ibid s 28V(1A) (as added).

12 Ibid s 28V(1A)(b) (as added: see note 10 supra). The reference in the text is to being unlawful under Pt IV Ch II (ss 28R–31A) (as added and amended).

13 Ibid s 28V(1A) (as added: see note 10 supra).

14 Ibid s 28V(2) (as added: see note 4 supra). However, the amount of any damages awarded as compensation for injury to feelings must not exceed the prescribed amount: Sch 3 para 14 (as added: see note 9 supra). As to compensation generally see para 643 post.

15 Ie under ibid Pt IV Ch II (as added and amended).

16 See note 4 supra.

17 Disability Discrimination Act 1995 Sch 3 para 12(1) (as added (see note 9 supra); and amended by the Disability Discrimination Act 1995 (Amendment) (Further and Higher Education) Regulations 2006, SI 2006/1721, regs 4(1), 19(1), (2)).

18 Disability Discrimination Act 1995 Sch 3 para 12(2) (as added: see note 9 supra).

19 Ie ibid s 28UA (as added): see para 572 ante.

20 Ie ibid s 28UB (as added): see para 573 ante.

21 Ibid s 28VA(1) (ss 28VA, 28VB added by the Disability Discrimination Act 1995 (Amendment) (Further and Higher Education) Regulations 2006, SI 2006/1721, regs 23(1), (2)(b)). The Disability Discrimination Act 1995 s 28VA(1) (as added) does not apply to an act which constitutes an offence: s 28VA(7) (as so added).

22 Such legal proceedings may only be brought by the Disability Rights Commission in accordance with the Disability Discrimination Act 1995 s 28VA (as added): see s 28V(2) (as added: see note 21 supra). As to the Disability Rights Commission see para 646 et seq post. As to the Commission for Equality and Human Rights, which is to replace the Disability Rights Commission, see para 305 et seq ante.

23 Ie an act to which the Disability Discrimination Act 1995 s 28VA (as added) applies.

24 Ibid s 28VA(3) (as added: see note 21 supra).

An application under s 28VA(3) (as added) may be presented or made only: (1) within the period of six months beginning with the date (or last date) on which the alleged unlawful act occurred; or (2) with the permission of the court: s 28VB(1) (as so added).

25 Ibid s 28VA(4) (as added: see note 21 supra).

A determination under s 28VA(4) (as added) must not be relied upon by a county court in proceedings under s 28VA(5) (as added) (see heads (1) and (2) in the text) while an appeal against the determination is pending, or may be brought (disregarding the possibility of an appeal out of time with permission): s 28VB(2) (as so added).

26   Ibid s 28VA(5)(a) (as added: see note 21 supra). As to injunctions see generally INJUNCTIONS.

An application under s 28VA(5) (as added) may be made only: (1) within the period of five years beginning with the date (or last date) on which the unlawful act referred to occurred; or (2) with the permission of the court: s 28BV(3) (as so added).

27   Ibid s 28VA(5)(b) (as added: see note 21 supra). See note 26 supra.

576.   Alteration to premises occupied by educational institutions under leases. Where (1) premises are occupied by an educational institution[1] under a lease[2]; (2) but for this provision, the responsible body[3] would not be entitled to make a particular alteration to the premises[4]; and (3) the alteration is one which the responsible body proposes to make in order to comply with its duty to take reasonable steps[5], then except to the extent to which it expressly so provides, the lease has effect, as a result of this provision, as if it provided: (a) for the responsible body to be entitled to make the alteration with the written consent of the lessor[6]; (b) for the responsible body to have to make a written application to the lessor for consent if it wishes to make the alteration[7]; (c) if such an application is made, for the lessor not to withhold his consent unreasonably[8]; and (d) for the lessor to be entitled to make his consent subject to reasonable conditions[9].

1   For the meaning of 'educational institution' see para 569 note 1 ante.
2   Disability Discrimination Act 1995 s 28W(1)(a) (s 28W added by the Special Educational Needs and Disability Act 2001 s 31(1)). 'Lease' includes a tenancy, sub-lease or sub-tenancy and an agreement for a lease, tenancy, sub-lease or sub-tenancy; and 'sub-lease' and 'sub-tenancy' have such meaning as may be prescribed: Disability Discrimination Act 1995 s 28W(3) (as so added). Regulations may make provision supplementing, or modifying, s 28W (as added and amended) or any provision made by or under Sch 4 Pt III (as added) in relation to cases where the premises of the educational institution are occupied under a sub-lease or sub-tenancy: Sch 4 para 14 (Sch 4 paras 10–14 added by the Special Educational Needs and Disability Act 2001 s 31(2), Sch 6). 'Prescribed' generally means prescribed by regulations: see para 515 note 5 ante. For the meaning of 'regulations' see para 509 note 12 ante. See the Disability Discrimination (Educational Institutions) (Alteration of Leasehold Premises) Regulations 2005, SI 2005/1070. See also note 6 infra.

      If the terms and conditions of a lease: (1) impose conditions which are to apply if the responsible body alters the premises; or (2) entitle the lessor to impose conditions when consenting to the responsible body's altering the premises, the responsible body is to be treated for the purposes of the Disability Discrimination Act 1995 s 28W(1) (as added and amended) as not being entitled to make the alteration: s 28W(4) (as so added).

3   As to responsible bodies see para 569 ante.
4   Disability Discrimination Act 1995 s 28W(1)(b) (as added: see note 2 supra). As to the meaning of 'premises' see para 525 note 9 ante.
5   Ibid s 28W(1)(c) (as added: see note 2 supra). As to the duty to take reasonable steps see s 28T (as added and amended) (see para 571 ante) or s 28UA(5) (as added) (see para 572 ante). If any question arises as to whether a responsible body has failed to comply with the duty imposed by s 28T (as added and amended) or s 28UA(5) (as added), by failing to make a particular alteration to premises, any constraint attributable to the fact that the premises are occupied by the educational institution under a lease is to be ignored unless the responsible body has applied to the lessor in writing for consent to the making of the alteration: Sch 4 para 10 (as added (see note 2 supra); and amended by the Disability Discrimination Act 1995 (Amendment) (Further and Higher Education) Regulations 2006, SI 2006/1721, regs 4(1), 20). See note 2 supra.
6   Disability Discrimination Act 1995 s 28W(2)(a) (as added: see note 2 supra).

      If the lessor refuses consent or makes his consent subject to one or more conditions, the responsible body, or a disabled person who has an interest in the proposed alteration to the premises being made, may refer the matter to a county court: see Sch 4 para 11(1) (as added: see note 2 supra). On such a reference the court must determine whether the lessor's refusal was unreasonable or (as the case may be) whether the condition is, or any of the conditions are, unreasonable: Sch 4 para 11(2) (as so added). If the court determines that the lessor's refusal was unreasonable, or that the condition is, or any of the conditions are, unreasonable, it may make such declaration as it considers appropriate or an order authorising the responsible body to make the alteration specified in the order: Sch 4 para 11(3) (as so added). Such an order may require the responsible body to comply with conditions specified in the order: Sch 4 para 11(4) (as so added).

Regulations may make provision as to circumstances in which: (1) a lessor is to be taken, for the purposes of s 28W (as added and amended) and Sch 4 Pt III (as added and amended) to have: (a) withheld his consent; (b) withheld his consent unreasonably; (c) acted reasonably in withholding his consent; (2) a condition subject to which a lessor has given his consent is to be taken to be reasonable; (3) a condition subject to which a lessor has given his consent is to be taken to be unreasonable: Sch 4 para 13 (as so added). See the Disability Discrimination (Educational Institutions) (Alteration of Leasehold Premises) Regulations 2005, SI 2005/1070. See also note 2 supra.

7   Disability Discrimination Act 1995 s 28W(2)(b) (as added: see note 2 supra). See also note 6 supra.
8   Ibid s 28W(2)(c) (as added: see note 2 supra). See also note 6 supra.
9   Ibid s 28W(2)(d) (as added: see note 2 supra). See also note 6 supra.

577.   Validity and revision of agreements.   Any term in a contract or other agreement made by or on behalf of a responsible body[1] for an educational institution[2] is void so far as it purports to: (1) require a person to do anything which would contravene any provision of, or made under, the provisions[3] concerning disability discrimination in further and higher education[4]; (2) exclude or limit the operation of any provision of, or made under, those provisions[5]; or (3) prevent any person from making a claim under those provisions[6]. On the application of any person interested in such an agreement, a county court may make such order as it thinks just for modifying the agreement[7].

1   As to responsible bodies see para 569 ante. See also para 568 ante.
2   For the meaning of 'educational institution' see para 569 note 1 ante.
3   Ie the Disability Discrimination Act 1995 Pt IV Ch II (ss 28R–31A) (as added and amended).
4   Ibid s 28P(1)(a) (s 28P added by Special Educational Needs and Disability Act 2001 s 24); applied in relation to responsible bodies for educational institutions by the Disability Discrimination Act 1995 s 28X (added by the Special Educational Needs and Disability Act 2001 s 32).
5   Disability Discrimination Act 1995 s 28P(1)(b) (as added and applied: see note 4 supra). This does not apply to an agreement settling a claim under s 28V (as added and amended) (see para 575 ante): s 28P(2) (as so added and applied).
6   Ibid s 28P(1)(c) (as added and applied: see note 4 supra). This does not apply to an agreement settling a claim under s 28V (as added and amended) (see para 575 ante): s 28P(2) (as so added and applied).
7   Ibid s 28P(3) (as added and applied: see note 4 supra). No such order may be made unless all persons affected have been given notice of the application and have been afforded an opportunity to make representations to the court, subject to any rules of court providing for notice to be dispensed with: s 28P(4), (5) (as so added and applied). An order under s 28P(3) (as added and applied) may include provision as respects any period before the making of the order: s 28P(6) (as so added and applied).

(C)   General Qualifications Bodies

578.   Discrimination and harassment by general qualifications bodies.   As from a day to be appointed, the following provisions have effect[1]. It is unlawful for a general qualifications body[2] to discriminate[3] against a disabled person[4]: (1) in the arrangements which it makes for the purpose of determining upon whom to confer a relevant qualification[5]; (2) in the terms on which it is prepared to confer a relevant qualification on him[6]; (3) by refusing or deliberately omitting to grant any application by him for such a qualification[7]; or (4) by withdrawing such a qualification from him or varying the terms on which he holds it[8].

It is also unlawful for a general qualifications body, in relation to a relevant qualification conferred by it, to subject to harassment[9] a disabled person who holds or applies for such a qualification[10].

In the case of an act which constitutes discrimination by victimisation[11] the above provisions[12] also apply to discrimination against a person who is not disabled[13].

1   The Disability Discrimination Act 1995 Pt IV Ch IIA (ss 31AA–31AF) is added by the Disability Discrimination Act 2005 s 15 as from a day to be appointed by order made by the Secretary of State

under s 20(3). At the date at which this volume states the law no such day had been appointed. As to the Secretary of State and the National Assembly for Wales see para 302 ante.

2   'General qualifications body' means any authority or body which can confer a relevant qualification, but it does not include: (1) a responsible body (within the meaning of the Disability Discrimination Act 1995 Pt IV Ch I or Ch II (ss 28A–31A) (as added and amended): see para 561 et seq ante); (2) a local education authority in England or Wales (see para 561 ante); or (3) an authority or body of a prescribed description or in prescribed circumstances: s 31AA(6)(a) (as added: see note 1 supra).

In ss 31AA, 31AD (as added), 'relevant qualification' means an authorisation, qualification, approval or certification of a prescribed description: s 31AA(4) (as so added). See also note 5 infra. However an authorisation, qualification, approval or certification may not be prescribed under s 31AA(4) (as added) if it is a professional or trade qualification (within the meaning given by s 14A(5) (as added): see para 549 note 4 ante): s 31AA(5) (as so added).

'Prescribed' generally means prescribed by regulations: see para 515 note 5 ante. Before making regulations under Pt IV Ch IIA (as added), the Secretary of State must consult such persons as it appears to him to be appropriate to consult, having regard to the substance and effect of the regulations in question: s 31AF(1) (as so added). Without prejudice to the generality of s 31AF(1) (as added), the Secretary of State must consult the National Assembly for Wales before making such regulations: see s 31AF(2) (as so added). For the meaning of 'regulations' see para 509 note 12 ante. At the date at which this volume states the law no regulations had been made for these purposes.

3   As to discrimination see para 579 post.

4   Disability Discrimination Act 1995 s 31AA(1) (as added: see note 1 supra). For the meaning of 'disabled person' see para 511 ante.

5   Ibid s 31AA(1)(a) (as added: see note 1 supra). References (however expressed) to the conferment of a qualification on a person include: (1) the renewal or extension of a qualification; and (2) the authentication of a qualification awarded to him by another person: s 31AA(6)(b) (as so added).

6   Ibid s 31AA(1)(b) (as added: see note 1 supra).

7   Ibid s 31AA(1)(c) (as added: see note 1 supra).

8   Ibid s 31AA(1)(d) (as added: see note 1 supra).

9   For these purposes, a body subjects a disabled person to 'harassment' where, for a reason which relates to the disabled person's disability, the body engages in unwanted conduct which has the purpose or effect of: (1) violating the disabled person's dignity; or (2) creating an intimidating, hostile, degrading, humiliating or offensive environment for him: s 31AC(1) (as added: see note 1 supra). Conduct is regarded as having the effect referred to in head (1) or head (2) supra only if, having regard to all the circumstances (including in particular the perception of the disabled person), it should reasonably be considered as having that effect: s 31AC(2) (as so added).

10 Ibid s 31AA(2) (as added: see note 1 supra).

11 Ie by virtue of ibid s 55 (as amended): see para 526 ante.

12 Ie ibid s 31AA (as added).

13 Ibid s 31AA(3) (as added: see note 1 supra).

579. Meaning of 'discrimination'. As from a day to be appointed, the following provisions have effect[1]. For the purposes of the general provisions on discrimination[2], a body discriminates against a disabled person[3] if: (1) for a reason which relates to the disabled person's disability, it treats him less favourably than it treats or would treat others to whom that reason does not or would not apply[4]; and (2) it cannot show that the treatment in question is justified[5]. For the purposes of those provisions[6], a body also discriminates against a disabled person if it fails to comply with a duty to make adjustments[7] in relation to the disabled person[8].

Treatment, other than the application of a competence standard[9], is justified[10] for the purposes of head (2) above if, but only if, the reason for it is both material to the circumstances of the particular case and substantial[11].

The application by a body of a competence standard to a disabled person is justified[12] for the purposes of head (2) above if, but only if, the body can show that: (a) the standard is, or would be, applied equally to persons who do not have his particular disability[13]; and (b) its application is a proportionate means of achieving a legitimate aim[14].

A body directly discriminates against a disabled person if, on the ground of the disabled person's disability, it treats the disabled person less favourably than it treats or would treat a person not having that particular disability whose relevant circumstances, including his abilities, are the same as, or not materially different from, those of the disabled person[15].

1 The Disability Discrimination Act 1995 Pt IV Ch IIA (ss 31AA–31AF) is added by the Disability Discrimination Act 2005 s 15 as from a day to be appointed by order made by the Secretary of State under s 20(3). At the date at which this volume states the law no such day had been appointed. As to the Secretary of State and the National Assembly for Wales see para 302 ante.
2 Ie for the purposes of the Disability Discrimination Act 1995 s 31AA (as added): see para 578 ante.
3 For the meaning of 'disabled person' see para 511 ante.
4 Disability Discrimination Act 1995 s 31AB(1)(a) (as added: see note 1 supra).
5 Ibid s 31AB(1)(b) (as added: see note 1 supra).
6 See note 2 supra.
7 Ie a duty imposed on it by the Disability Discrimination Act 1995 s 31AD (as added): see para 580 post.
8 Ibid s 31AB(2) (as added: see note 1 supra).
9 'Competence standard' means an academic, medical or other standard applied by or on behalf of a general qualifications body for the purpose of determining whether or not a person has a particular level of competence or ability: ibid s 31AB(9) (as added: see note 1 supra). For the meaning of 'general qualifications body' see para 578 note 2 ante.
10 Ie subject to ibid s 31AB(5)–(7) (as added). If, in a case falling within s 31AB(1) (as added) other than a case where the treatment is the application of a competence standard, a body is under a duty under s 31AD (as added) (see para 580 post) in relation to the disabled person but fails to comply with that duty, its treatment of that person cannot be justified under s 31AD(3) (as added) unless it would have been justified even if the body had complied with that duty: s 31AB(5) (as added: see note 1 supra). Regulations may make provision, for purposes of s 31AB (as added), as to circumstances in which treatment is, or as to circumstances in which treatment is not, to be taken to be justified: s 31AB(6) (as so added). However, treatment of a disabled person cannot be justified under s 31AB(3), (4) (as added) (see the text to notes 11–14 infra) or s 31AB(6) (as added) if it amounts to direct discrimination falling within s 31AB(8) (as added) (see the text to note 15 infra) s 31AB(7) (as so added). For the meaning of 'regulations' see para 509 note 12 ante. As to the making of regulations see para 578 note 2 ante. At the date at which this volume states the law no regulations had been made for these purposes.
11 Ibid s 31AB(3) (as added: see note 1 supra).
12 Ie subject to ibid s 31AB(6), (7) (as added): see note 10 supra.
13 Ibid s 31AB(4)(a) (as added: see note 1 supra).
14 Ibid s 31AB(4)(b) (as added: see note 1 supra).
15 Ibid s 31AB(8) (as added: see note 1 supra).

580. Duty of general qualifications bodies to make adjustments. As from a day to be appointed, the following provisions have effect[1]. Where: (1) a provision, criterion or practice[2], other than a competence standard[3], is applied by or on behalf of a general qualifications body[4]; (2) it is a provision, criterion or practice for determining on whom a relevant qualification[5] is to be conferred[6]; (3) a disabled person[7] is, or has notified the body that he may be, an applicant for the conferment of that qualification[8]; and (4) the provision, criterion or practice places the disabled person at a substantial disadvantage in comparison with persons who are not disabled[9], it is the duty of the body to take such steps as it is reasonable, in all the circumstances of the case, for it to have to take in order to prevent the provision, criterion or practice having that effect[10].

Where (a) a provision, criterion or practice, other than a competence standard, is applied by or on behalf of a general qualifications body[11]; (b) it is a provision, criterion or practice other than one for determining on whom a relevant qualification is to be conferred[12]; and (c) it places a disabled person, who holds a relevant qualification conferred by the body or who applies for a relevant qualification which the body confers, at a substantial disadvantage in comparison with persons who are not disabled[13], it is the duty of the body to take such steps as it is reasonable, in all the circumstances of the case, for it to have to take in order to prevent the provision, criterion or practice having that effect[14].

Where any physical feature of premises[15] occupied by a general qualifications body places a disabled person, who holds a relevant qualification conferred by the body[16] or who applies for a relevant qualification which the body confers[17], at a substantial disadvantage in comparison with persons who are not disabled, it is the duty of the body to take such steps as it is reasonable, in all the circumstances of the case, for it to have to take in order to prevent the feature having that effect[18].

Nothing in the above provisions[19] imposes a duty on a general qualifications body in relation to a disabled person if the body does not know and could not reasonably be expected to know: (i) in the case of an applicant or potential applicant for the conferment of a relevant qualification, that the disabled person concerned is, or may be, such an applicant[20]; or (ii) in any case, that that person has a disability and is likely to be affected in the way mentioned in those provisions[21].

The above provisions[22] impose duties only for the purpose of determining whether a body has discriminated against a disabled person; and accordingly a breach of any such duty is not actionable as such[23].

1   The Disability Discrimination Act 1995 Pt IV Ch IIA (ss 31AA–31AF) is added by the Disability Discrimination Act 2005 s 15 as from a day to be appointed by order made by the Secretary of State under s 20(3). At the date at which this volume states the law no such day had been appointed. As to the Secretary of State and the National Assembly for Wales see para 302 ante.
2   'Provision, criterion or practice' includes (subject to any provision under the Disability Discrimination Act 1995 s 31AD(6)(e) (as added): (see note 10 head (5) infra) any arrangements: s 31AD(5)(a) (as added: see note 1 supra).
3   For the meaning of 'competence standard' see para 579 note 9 ante; definition applied by ibid s 31AD(5)(b) (as added: see note 1 supra).
4   Ibid s 31AD(1)(a) (as added: see note 1 supra). For the meaning of 'general qualifications body' see para 578 note 2 ante.
5   For the meaning of 'relevant qualification' see para 578 note 2 ante.
6   Disability Discrimination Act 1995 s 31AD(1)(b) (as added: see note 1 supra).
7   For the meaning of 'disabled person' see para 511 ante.
8   Disability Discrimination Act 1995 s 31AD(1)(c) (as added: see note 1 supra).
9   Ibid s 31AD(1)(d) (as added: see note 1 supra). See also note 10 infra.
10   Ibid s 31AD(1) (as added: see note 1 supra). Regulations may make provision, for purposes of s 31AD (as added): (1) as to circumstances in which a provision, criterion or practice is to be taken to have, or as to circumstances in which a provision, criterion or practice is to be taken not to have, the effect mentioned in s 31AD(1)(d) (as added) (see head (4) in the text) or in s 31AD(2)(c) (as added) (see head (c) in the text); (2) as to circumstances in which a physical feature is to be taken to have, or as to circumstances in which a physical feature is to be taken not to have, the effect mentioned in s 31AD(3) (as added) (see the text to notes 15–18 infra); (3) as to circumstances in which it is, or as to circumstances in which it is not, reasonable for a body to have to take steps of a prescribed description; (4) as to steps which it is always, or as to steps which it is never, reasonable for a body to have to take; (5) as to what is, or as to what is not, to be included within the meaning of 'provision, criterion or practice' (see note 2 supra); (6) as to things which are, or as to things which are not, to be treated as physical features: s 31AD(6) (as so added). For the meaning of 'regulations' see para 509 note 12 ante. As to the making of regulations generally see para 578 note 2 ante. At the date at which this volume states the law no regulations had been made for these purposes.
11   Ibid s 31AD(2)(a) (as added: see note 1 supra).
12   Ibid s 31AD(2)(b) (as added: see note 1 supra).
13   Ibid s 31AD(2)(c) (as added: see note 1 supra). See also note 10 supra.
14   Ibid s 31AD(2) (as added: see note 1 supra).
15   As to the meaning of 'premises' see para 525 note 9 ante.
16   Disability Discrimination Act 1995 s 31AD(3)(a) (as added: see note 1 supra). See also note 10 supra.
17   Ibid s 31AD(3)(b) (as added: see note 1 supra). See also note 10 supra.
18   Ibid s 31AD(3) (as added: see note 1 supra). See also note 10 supra.
19   Ie ibid s 31AD(1), (2) or (3) (as added): see the text and notes 1–18 supra.
20   Ibid s 31AD(4)(a) (as added: see note 1 supra).
21   Ibid s 31AD(4)(b) (as added: see note 1 supra).
22   Ie ibid s 31AD (as added).
23   Ibid s 31AD(7) (as added: see note 1 supra).

581.   Claims, leased premises and certain agreements. As from a day to be appointed, the following provisions have effect[1]. Regulations[2] may make provision for, or in connection with, the making of a claim by a person[3]: (1) that a general qualifications body[4] has discriminated[5] against him, or subjected him to harassment[6], in a way which is unlawful[7]; (2) that a general qualifications body is to be treated[8] as having done so[9]; or (3) that a person is to be treated[10] as having done so[11].

Regulations may, in relation to a case where premises[12] are occupied by a general qualifications body under a lease[13], make provision modifying the lease, or make provision for its modification, in connection with the making of alterations to the premises in pursuance of a duty to make adjustments[14]. Such regulations may also make provision in connection with the determination of questions that are about the body's compliance with any such duty and are related to the making of alterations to the premises[15].

Any term in a contract or other agreement made by or on behalf of a general qualifications body is void so far as it purports to: (a) require a person to do anything which would contravene any relevant provision[16]; (b) exclude or limit the operation of any such provision[17]; or (c) prevent any person making a claim of a kind mentioned in heads (1) to (3) above[18]. Regulations may make provision for head (b) or head (c) above not to apply to an agreement settling a claim of a kind mentioned in heads (1) to (3) above[19]. They may also make provision modifying an agreement to which heads (b) and (c) above apply, or make provision for the modification of such an agreement, in order to take account of the effect of those heads[20].

The provision that may be made[21] includes in particular: (i) provision as to the court or tribunal to which a claim, or an application in connection with a modification, may be made[22]; (ii) provision for the determination of claims or matters otherwise than by the bringing of proceedings before a court or tribunal[23]; (iii) provision for a person who is a lessor[24] in relation to a lease under which a general qualifications body occupies premises to be made a party to proceedings[25]; (iv) provision as to remedies[26]; (v) provision as to procedure[27]; (vi) provision as to appeals[28]; (vii) provision as to time limits[29]; (viii) provision as to evidence[30]; (ix) provision as to costs or expenses[31].

Except as provided in regulations under heads (1) to (3) above, no civil or criminal proceedings may be brought against any person in respect of an act[32] merely because the act is unlawful under the Disability Discrimination Act 1995[33]. However, this does not prevent the making of an application for judicial review[34].

1   The Disability Discrimination Act 1995 Pt IV Ch IIA (ss 31AA–31AF) is added by the Disability Discrimination Act 2005 s 15 as from a day to be appointed by order made by the Secretary of State under s 20(3). At the date at which this volume states the law no such day had been appointed. As to the Secretary of State and the National Assembly for Wales see para 302 ante.

2   For the meaning of 'regulations' see para 509 note 12 ante. As to the making of regulations generally see para 578 note 2 ante. At the date at which this volume states the law no regulations had been made under the Disability Discrimination Act 1995 s 31AE (as added).

3   As to the meaning of 'person' see para 344 note 3 ante.

4   For the meaning of 'general qualifications body' see para 578 note 2 ante.

5   As to discrimination generally see paras 578–579 ante.

6   For the meaning of 'harassment' see para 578 note 9 ante.

7   Disability Discrimination Act 1995 s 31AE(1)(a) (as added: see note 1 supra). The text refers to being unlawful under Pt IV Ch IIA (ss 31AA–31AF) (as added).

8   Ie by virtue of ibid s 57 (as amended) (see para 528 ante) or s 58 (see para 527 ante).

9   Ibid s 31AE(1)(b) (as added: see note 1 supra).

10   Ie by virtue of ibid s 57 (as amended): see para 528 ante.

11   Ibid s 31AE(1)(c) (as added: see note 1 supra).

12   As to the meaning of 'premises' see para 525 note 9 ante.

13   Regulations may make provision as to the meaning of 'lease' or 'lessor' in the Disability Discrimination Act 1995 s 31AE (as added): s 31AE(7) (as added: see note 1 supra). See note 2 supra.

14   Ibid s 31AE(2)(a) (as added: see note 1 supra). The reference is to a duty imposed on the body under s 31AD (as added): see para 580 ante.

15   Ibid s 31AE(2)(b) (as added: see note 1 supra).

16 Ibid s 31AE(3)(a) (as added: see note 1 supra). The provisions referred to in the text are any provision of or made under Pt IV Ch IIA (as added).
17 Ibid s 31AE(3)(b) (as added: see note 1 supra).
18 Ibid s 31AE(3)(c) (as added: see note 1 supra).
19 Ibid s 31AE(4)(a) (as added: see note 1 supra).
20 Ibid s 31AE(4)(b) (as added: see note 1 supra).
21 Ie under ibid s 31AE(1), (2) or (4) (as added): see the text and notes 1–15, 19, 20 supra. Such provision may take the form of amendments of the Disability Discrimination Act 1995: s 31AE(6) (as added: see note 1 supra).
22 Ibid s 31AE(5)(a) (as added: see note 1 supra).
23 Ibid s 31AE(5)(b) (as added: see note 1 supra).
24 See note 13 supra.
25 Disability Discrimination Act 1995 s 31AE(5)(c) (as added: see note 1 supra).
26 Ibid s 31AE(5)(d) (as added: see note 1 supra).
27 Ibid s 31AE(5)(e) (as added: see note 1 supra).
28 Ibid s 31AE(5)(f) (as added: see note 1 supra).
29 Ibid s 31AE(5)(g) (as added: see note 1 supra).
30 Ibid s 31AE(5)(h) (as added: see note 1 supra).
31 Ibid s 31AE(5)(i) (as added: see note 1 supra).
32 As to the meaning of 'act' see para 510 note 3 ante.
33 Disability Discrimination Act 1995 s 31AE(8) (as added: see note 1 supra). The reference in the text is to being unlawful under Pt IV Ch IIA (as added).
34 Ibid s 31AE(9) (as added: see note 1 supra). As to judicial review see ADMINISTRATIVE LAW vol 1(1) (2001 Reissue) para 58 et seq; PRACTICE AND PROCEDURE vol 37 (Reissue) para 1368.

C. GOODS, FACILITIES AND SERVICES

(A) Discrimination in relation to Goods, Facilities and Services

582. Discrimination in relation to goods, facilities and services. A provider of services[1] discriminates against a disabled person if[2]: (1) for a reason which relates to the disabled person's disability[3], he treats him less favourably than he treats or would treat others to whom that reason does not or would not apply[4]; and (2) he cannot show that the treatment in question is justified[5]. A provider of services also discriminates against a disabled person if he fails to comply with a duty to make adjustments[6] imposed on him in relation to the disabled person[7], and he cannot show that his failure to comply with that duty is justified[8].

In relation to employment services[9], a provider of services also discriminates against a disabled person if he fails to comply with a duty to make adjustments imposed on him in relation to the disabled person[10]:

1 For the meaning of 'provider of services' see para 584 post.
2 Disability Discrimination Act 1995 s 20(1). For the meaning of 'disabled person' see para 511 ante.
    As to the application of s 20 (as amended) to 'employment services' as defined see para 585 note 9 post.
3 As to when a person has a disability see para 511 ante. Where a charging regime was based on means and was indifferent to the receipt of disability living allowance by an applicant, there was no discrimination: *R v Powys County Council, ex p Hambidge (No 2)* [2000] 2 FCR 69, (2000) Times, 16 March, CA.
4 Disability Discrimination Act 1995 s 20(1)(a).
5 Ibid s 20(1)(b). As to justification see paras 588–589 post.
6 Ie a duty under ibid s 21: see para 586 post. As to the duty to make adjustments see paras 586–587 post. In relation to employment services, the duty referred to is the duty imposed on the provider of services by s 21(2) or (4): s 21A(5)(b) (s 21A added by the Disability Discrimination Act 1995 (Amendment) Regulations 2003, SI 2003/1673, regs 3(1), 19(1)).
7 Disability Discrimination Act 1995 s 20(2)(a).
8 Ibid s 20(2)(b).
9 For the meaning of 'employment services' see para 585 note 9 post.
10 Disability Discrimination Act 1995 s 21A(5)(a) (as added: see note 6 supra).

583. The service. The duty not to discriminate is placed on those providing goods, facilities and services to the public or any section of the public[1]. It is the provision of the service which is important and not the nature of the service or business. 'Goods, facilities and services' is likely to be given a broad definition[2].

1   See the Disability Discrimination Act 1995 s 19(2)(a), (b) (s 19(2) amended by the Disability Discrimination Act 2005 s 19(1), Sch 1 paras 1, 13(1), (2)).
      Nothing in the Disability Discrimination Act 1995 ss 19–21A (as amended) applies to the provision of a service in relation to which discrimination is unlawful under Pt IV (ss 28A–31C) (as amended; prospectively amended) (see para 561 et seq ante): s 19(5A) (added by the Disability Discrimination Act 2005 Sch 1 paras 1, 13(1), (4)).
2   'Goods' is not defined in the Disability Discrimination Act 1995, but see by way of example the Sales of Goods Act 1979 s 61(1) ('all personal chattels other than things in action and money') (see SALE OF GOODS AND SUPPLY OF SERVICES vol 41 (2005 Reissue) para 30). A facility is usually a manner, method or opportunity for the easier performance of anything and may include instances where a person is not providing goods or a service, but access to those goods or services. It is irrelevant whether a service is provided on payment or without payment: Disability Discrimination Act 1995 s 19(2)(c). The following are examples of services to which ss 19–21 (as amended) apply: (1) access to and use of any place which members of the public are permitted to enter; (2) access to and use of means of communication; (3) access to and use of information services; (4) accommodation in a hotel, boarding house or other similar establishment; (5) facilities by way of banking or insurance or for grants, loans, credit or finance; (6) facilities for entertainment, recreation or refreshment; (7) facilities provided by employment agencies or under the Employment and Training Act 1973 s 2 (as substituted and amended) (see EMPLOYMENT vol 16(1B) (Reissue) para 765); and (8) the services of any profession or trade, or any local or other public authority: Disability Discrimination Act 1995 s 19(3).

584. The service provider. A person[1] is 'a provider of services' if he is concerned with the provision, in the United Kingdom[2], of services to the public or to a section of the public[3]. Manufacturers and designers of products are not covered by the provisions of the Disability Discrimination Act 1995 relating to the provision of goods, facilities and services[4] where they distribute to retail outlets, except where they provide services direct to the public[5].

1   As to the meaning of 'person' see para 344 note 3 ante.
2   For the meaning of 'United Kingdom' see para 325 note 6 ante.
3   Disability Discrimination Act 1995 ss 19(2)(b), 68(1). It is irrelevant whether a service is provided on payment or without payment: s 19(2)(c).
4   See para 582 ante.
5   See the Code of Practice on Rights of Access: services to the public, public authority functions, private clubs and premises (December 2006) para 3.30. However, if a manufacturer does provide services direct to the public, then it may have duties under the Disability Discrimination Act 1995 as a service provider: see the Code of Practice on Rights of Access: services to the public, public authority functions, private clubs and premises (December 2006) para 3.31. As to codes of practice see para 655 post.

585. Discrimination by a provider of services. It is unlawful for a provider of services[1] to discriminate[2] against a disabled person[3]: (1) in refusing to provide, or deliberately not providing, to the disabled person any service which he provides, or is prepared to provide, to members of the public[4]; (2) in failing to comply with any duty to make adjustments[5] in circumstances in which the effect of that failure is to make it impossible or unreasonably difficult for the disabled person to make use of any such service[6]; (3) in the standard of service which he provides to the disabled person or the manner in which he provides it to him[7]; or (4) in the terms on which he provides a service to the disabled person[8]; or (5) in relation to employment services[9], in failing to comply with a duty to make adjustments[10] in circumstances in which the effect of that failure is to place the disabled person at a substantial disadvantage in comparison with persons who are not disabled in relation to the provision of the service[11].

In the case of an act which constitutes discrimination by way of victimisation[12], the above provision[13] also applies to discrimination against a person who is not disabled[14].

It is unlawful for a provider of employment services, in relation to such services, to subject to harassment[15] a disabled person to whom he is providing such services, or who has requested him to provide such services[16].

1　For the meaning of 'provider of services' see para 584 ante. For examples of services see para 583 note 2 ante.

2　As to discrimination in relation to goods, services and facilities see para 582 ante.

3　Disability Discrimination Act 1995 s 19(1). For the meaning of 'disabled person' see para 511 ante. Regulations may provide for s 19(1) not to apply, or to apply only to a prescribed extent, in relation to a service of a prescribed description: s 19(5) (substituted by the Disability Discrimination Act 2005 s 19(1), Sch 1 para 13(1), (3)). For the meaning of 'regulations' see para 509 note 12 ante. 'Prescribed' generally means prescribed by regulations: see para 515 note 5 ante. At the date at which this volume states the law no regulations had been made for these purposes.

4　Disability Discrimination Act 1995 s 19(1)(a). There must be evidence of a direct refusal or, where there has been a failure to serve, the deliberate mental element must be shown. Where there is a deliberate element it may be necessary to establish knowledge of the disability by the discriminator: cf *O'Neill v Symm & Co Ltd* [1998] ICR 481, [1998] IRLR 233, EAT; but see *HJ Heinz Co Ltd v Kenrick* [2000] ICR 491, [2000] IRLR 144, EAT. See notes 3 supra, 11 infra.

5　Ie the duty imposed by the Disability Discrimination Act 1995 s 21: see para 586 post. In relation to employment services (see note 9 infra), the duty referred to is the duty imposed on the provider of services by s 21(2) or (4): s 21A(4) (s 21A added by the Disability Discrimination Act 1995 (Amendment) Regulations 2003, SI 2003/1673, regs 3(1), 19(1)).

6　Disability Discrimination Act 1995 s 19(1)(b). See note 3 supra.

7　Ibid s 19(1)(c). A service provider does not have to stock special products or provide a special service: see the Code of Practice on Rights of Access: services to the public, public authority functions, private clubs and premises (December 2006) paras 10.22, 10.23. As to codes of practice see para 655 post. See notes 3 supra, 11 infra.

8　Disability Discrimination Act 1995 s 19(1)(d). This includes unjustified extra charges or deposits: see the Code of Practice on Rights of Access: services to the public, public authority functions, private clubs and premises (December 2006) para 10.24. See notes 3 supra, 11 infra.

9　'Employment services' means vocational guidance, vocational training, or services to assist a person to obtain or retain employment, or to establish himself as self-employed: Disability Discrimination Act 1995 s 21A(1) (as added (see note 5 supra); and amended by the Disability Discrimination Act 2005 s 19(1), Sch 1 paras 15(1), (2)).

　　In their application to employment services, the following provisions have effect as described below: see the Disability Discrimination Act 1995 s 21A(3) (as so added). Section 19 (as amended) has effect as if: (1) after s 19(1)(a), s 19(1)(aa) were added, providing that it is unlawful to discriminate against a disabled person in failing to comply with a duty imposed by s 21(1) in circumstances in which the effect of that failure is to place the disabled person at a substantial disadvantage in comparison with persons who are not disabled in relation to the provision of the service; (2) in s 21(1)(b) (see paras 586–587 post) the reference to s 21 were replaced by a reference to s 21(2) or (4); (3) in s 21(2) (see para 587 post), the reference to ss 20–21ZA (as amended) were replaced by a reference to ss 20–21A (as amended): see s 21A(4) (as so added; and amended by the Disability Discrimination Act 2005 Sch 1 paras 1, 15(1), (3)). The Disability Discrimination Act 1995 s 20 (as amended) (see para 588 post) has effect as if: (a) after s 20(1), s 20(1A) were added, providing that for the purposes of s 19 (as amended), a provider of services also discriminates against a disabled person if he fails to comply with a duty imposed on him by s 21(1) in relation to the disabled person; (b) in s 21(2)(a) (see para 587 post), the reference to 'a s 21 duty imposed' were replaced by a reference to 'a duty imposed by s 21(2) or (4)'; (c) after s 21(3) (see para 587 post), there were added s 21(3A), providing that treatment of a disabled person cannot be justified under s 21(3) if it amounts to direct discrimination falling within s 3A(5) (as added): see s 21A(5) (as so added). Section 21 (see paras 586–587 post) has effect as if: (i) in s 21(1), for the words 'makes it impossible or unreasonably difficult for disabled persons to make use of' there were substituted 'places disabled persons at a substantial disadvantage in comparison with persons who are not disabled in relation to the provision of'; (ii) after s 21(1), there were added s 21(1A), providing that in s 21(1) 'practice, policy or procedure' includes a provision or criterion: see s 21A(6) (as so added).

10　Ie imposed on him by ibid s 21(1): see para 587 post.

11　Ibid s 21A(4) (as added: see note 5 supra). The provisions of s 19(1)(a), (c), (d) do not apply in relation to a case where the service is a transport service and, as provider of that service, the provider of services discriminates against a disabled person: (1) in not providing, or in providing, him with a vehicle; or (2) in not providing, or in providing, him with services when he is travelling in a vehicle provided in the course of the transport service: s 21ZA(1) (s 21ZA added by the Disability Discrimination Act 2005 s 5). In the Disability Discrimination Act 1995 s 21ZA (as added), 'transport service' means a service which (to any extent) involves transport of people by vehicle; and 'vehicle' means a vehicle for transporting people by land, air or water, and includes in particular: (a) a vehicle not having wheels; and (b) a vehicle constructed or adapted to carry passengers on a system using a mode of guided transport: s 21ZA(4) (as so added). For the meaning of 'guided transport' see RAILWAYS, INLAND WATERWAYS AND PIPELINES vol 39(1) (Reissue) para 166; definition applied by virtue of s 21ZA(4) (as so added). Regulations may provide for s 21ZA(1) (as added) not to apply, or to apply only to a prescribed extent, in relation to vehicles of a prescribed description: s 21ZA(3) (as so added). At the date at which this volume states the law no such regulations had been made.

12　Ie by virtue of ibid s 55 (as amended): see para 526 ante.

13　Ie ibid s 19 (as amended).

14　Ibid s 19(4).

15　For the meaning of 'harassment' see para 533 ante.

16　Disability Discrimination Act 1995 s 21A(2) (as added: see note 5 supra).

(B)　Reasonable Adjustments .

586.　Duty of providers of services to make adjustments. It is unlawful for a provider of services[1] to fail to comply with a duty to make reasonable adjustments[2] in relation to a disabled person[3] except where he can show that his failure to comply is justified[4]. A service provider has to take such steps as it is reasonable, in all the circumstances of the case, for him to have to take where it is impossible or unreasonably difficult[5] for a disabled person to take advantage of the service provided to the public[6]. Factors to be taken into account in deciding what is reasonable include: (1) whether taking any particular steps would be effective in overcoming the difficulty that disabled people face in accessing the services in question; (2) the extent to which it is practicable for the service provider to take the steps[7]; (3) the financial and other costs of making the adjustment; (4) the extent of any disruption which taking the steps would cause; (5) the extent of the service provider's financial and other resources[8]; (6) the amount of any resources already spent on adjustments; and (7) the availability of financial or other assistance[9].

1　For the meaning of 'provider of services' see para 584 ante.

2　Ie under the Disability Discrimination Act 1995 s 21: see para 587 post.

3　For the meaning of 'disabled person' see para 511 ante.

4　Disability Discrimination Act 1995 s 20(2).

5　'Unreasonably difficult' is not defined, but is likely to be judged objectively by reference to whether the time, inconvenience, effort or discomfort entailed in using the service would be considered unreasonable by other people if they had to endure similar difficulties: Code of Practice on Rights of Access: services to the public, public authority functions, private clubs and premises (December 2006) para 6.36. As to codes of practice see para 655 post.

6　See the Disability Discrimination Act 1995 s 21(1). As to the application of s 21(1) to 'employment services' as defined see para 585 note 9 ante. Regulations may provide for s 21(1) not to apply, or to apply only to a prescribed extent, in relation to a service of a prescribed description: s 19(5) (substituted by the Disability Discrimination Act 2005 s 19(1), Sch 1 para 13(1), (3)). For the meaning of 'regulations' see para 509 note 12 ante. 'Prescribed' generally means prescribed by regulations: see para 515 note 5 ante. At the date at which this volume states the law no regulations had been made for these purposes. See also para 587 post.

　　The duty is owed to disabled people at large and not just an individual customer of whom the service provider is aware. The need for adjustments must be kept under review. The actual knowledge and experience of the service provider in question will be taken into account in determining whether he has taken reasonable steps: see the Code of Practice on Rights of Access: services to the public, public authority functions, private clubs and premises (December 2006) para 6.14 et seq.

7　The test of reasonable practicability amounts to what is reasonably feasible in assessing the practicability of instituting employment claims: see *Palmer v Southend-on-Sea Borough Council* [1984] 1 All ER 945, [1984] 1 WLR 1129, CA.

8　It is more likely to be reasonable for a service provider with substantial financial resources to have to make an adjustment with a significant cost than for a service provider with fewer resources: Code of Practice on Rights of Access: services to the public, public authority functions, private clubs and premises (December 2006) para 6.25.

9   Code of Practice on Rights of Access: services to the public, public authority functions, private clubs and
     premises (December 2006) para 6.25.

587.   Adjustments that must be made.   Where a provider of services[1] has a
practice, policy or procedure[2] which makes it impossible or unreasonably difficult for
disabled persons[3] to make use of a service which he provides, or is prepared to provide,
to other members of the public, it is his duty to take such steps as it is reasonable, in all
the circumstances of the case, for him to have to take in order to change that practice,
policy or procedure so that it no longer has that effect[4].

In relation to employment services[5], the duty of the provider of services arises where
his practice, policy or procedure (including a provision or criterion) places disabled
persons at a substantial disadvantage in comparison with persons who are not disabled in
relation to the provision of a service which he provides, or is prepared to provide, to
other members of the public[6].

Where a physical feature[7] makes it impossible or unreasonably difficult for disabled
persons to make use of such a service, it is the duty of the provider of that service to take
such steps as it is reasonable, in all the circumstances of the case, for him to have to take[8]
in order to remove the feature[9]; to alter it so that it no longer has that effect[10]; to provide
a reasonable means of avoiding the feature[11]; or to provide a reasonable alternative
method of making the service in question available to disabled persons[12].

Where an auxiliary aid or service (for example, the provision of information on
audio tape or a sign language interpreter) would enable disabled persons to make use of
a service which a provider of services provides, or is prepared to provide, to members of
the public[13], or facilitate the use by disabled persons of such a service[14], it is the duty of
the provider of that service to take such steps as it is reasonable, in all the circumstances
of the case, for him to have to take in order to provide that auxiliary aid or service[15].

For the purposes of the above provisions[16], it is never reasonable for a provider of
services, as a provider of a transport service[17]: (1) to have to take steps which would
involve the alteration or removal of a physical feature of a vehicle[18] used in providing the
service[19]; (2) to have to take steps which would affect whether vehicles are provided in
the course of the service or what vehicles are so provided or, where a vehicle is provided
in the course of the service, affect what happens in the vehicle while someone is
travelling in it[20].

Regulations may be made in relation to the adjustments that may be made[21].

A provider of services is not required to take any steps which would fundamentally
alter the nature of the service in question or the nature of his trade[22], profession[23] or
business[24].

The above provisions impose duties only for the purpose of determining whether a
provider of services has discriminated against a disabled person; and accordingly a breach
of any such duty is not actionable as such[25].

1   For the meaning of 'provider of services' see para 584 ante.
2   This would appear to cover what a service provider actually does (its practice), what a service provider
     intends to do (its policy) and how a service provider plans to go about it (its procedure): see the Code of
     Practice on Rights of Access: services to the public, public authority functions, private clubs and premises
     (December 2006) para 7.7. As to codes of practice see para 655 post.
3   For the meaning of 'disabled person' see para 511 ante.
4   Disability Discrimination Act 1995 s 21(1). As to the application of s 21(1) to 'employment services' as
     defined see para 585 note 9 ante. Regulations may provide for s 21(1), (2), (4) not to apply, or to apply
     only to a prescribed extent, in relation to a service of a prescribed description: s 19(5) (substituted by the
     Disability Discrimination Act 2005 s 19(1), Sch 1 para 13(1), (3)). For the meaning of 'regulations' see
     para 509 note 12 ante. 'Prescribed' generally means prescribed by regulations: see para 515 note 5 ante.
     See note 21 infra.
5   For the meaning of 'employment services' see para 585 note 9 ante.

6   Disability Discrimination Act 1995 s 21A(6) (s 21A added by the Disability Discrimination Act 1995 (Amendment) Regulations 2003, SI 2003/1673, regs 3(1), 19(1)).

7   For example, one arising from the design or construction of a building or the approach or access to premises: see the Disability Discrimination Act 1995 s 21(2). As to the meaning of 'premises' see para 525 note 9 ante. See notes 4 supra, 12, 21 infra.

8   Ibid s 21(2). See notes 4 supra, 12, 21 infra.

9   Ibid s 21(2)(a). See notes 4 supra, 12, 21 infra.

10   Ibid s 21(2)(b). See notes 4 supra, 12, 21 infra.

11   Ibid s 21(2)(c). See notes 4 supra, 12, 21 infra.

12   Ibid s 21(2)(d). Regulations may prescribe: (1) matters which are to be taken into account in determining whether any provision of a kind mentioned in s 21(2)(c) or (d) is reasonable; and (2) categories of providers of services to whom s 21(2) does not apply: s 21(3). See also notes 4 supra, 21 infra.
     The duty is to provide access to a service as close as is reasonably possible to the standard normally offered to the public at large: *Ross v Ryanair Ltd* [2004] EWCA Civ 1751, [2005] 1 WLR 2447, [2004] All ER (D) 333 (Dec).

13   Disability Discrimination Act 1995 s 21(4)(a). See notes 4, 12 supra, 21 infra.

14   Ibid s 21(4)(b). See notes 4, 12 supra, 21 infra.

15   Ibid s 21(4). See notes 4, 12 supra, 21 infra.
     A service provider is not required to provide an auxiliary aid or service to be used for personal purposes unconnected to the services being provided or to be taken away by the disabled person after use: but see the Code of Practice on Rights of Access: services to the public, public authority functions, private clubs and premises (December 2006) para 7.12 et seq.

16   Ie for the purposes of the Disability Discrimination Act 1995 s 21(1), (2), (4).

17   For the meaning of 'transport service' see para 585 note 11 ante.

18   For the meaning of 'vehicle' see para 585 note 11 ante.

19   Disability Discrimination Act 1995 s 21ZA(1)(a) (s 21ZA added by the Disability Discrimination Act 2005 s 5). Regulations may provide for the Disability Discrimination Act 1995 s 21ZA(1) (as added) not to apply, or to apply only to a prescribed extent, in relation to vehicles of a prescribed description: s 21ZA(3) (as so added). At the date at which this volume states the law no such regulations had been made.

20   Ibid s 21ZA(1)(b) (as added: see note 19 supra). See also note 19 supra.

21   Ibid s 21(5). Regulations may be made as to: (1) circumstances in which it is reasonable for a provider of services to have to take steps of a prescribed description; (2) circumstances in which it is not reasonable for a provider of services to have to take steps of a prescribed description; (3) what is to be included within the meaning of 'practice, policy or procedure'; (4) what is not to be included within the meaning of that expression; (5) things which are to be treated as physical features; (6) things which are not to be treated as such features; (7) things which are to be treated as auxiliary aids or services; (8) things which are not to be treated as auxiliary aids or services: see s 21(5).
     As to regulations under this provision see the Disability Discrimination (Providers of Services) (Adjustment of Premises) Regulations 2001, SI 2001/3253 (amended by SI 2004/1429; SI 2005/1121) (made under heads (1), (2) supra); the Disability Discrimination (Service Providers and Public Authorities Carrying Out Functions) Regulations 2005, SI 2005/2901 (made under heads (1), (2), (5) supra); and the Disability Discrimination (Transport Vehicles) Regulations 2005, SI 2005/3190 (made under heads (5), (6), (8) supra).
     For the purposes of the Disability Discrimination Act 1995 s 21(1), (2), (4) (as added), it is never reasonable for a provider of services, as a provider of a transport service: (a) to have to take steps which would involve the alteration or removal of a physical feature of a vehicle used in providing the service; (b) to have to take steps which would affect whether vehicles are provided in the course of the service or what vehicles are so provided, or where a vehicle is provided in the course of the service, affect what happens in the vehicle while someone is travelling in it: s 21ZA(2) (as added: see note 19 supra).

22   As to the meaning of 'trade' see para 541 note 1 ante.

23   As to the meaning of 'profession' see para 541 note 1 ante.

24   Disability Discrimination Act 1995 s 21(6).
     As from a day to be appointed, the following provisions have effect. Nothing in s 21 requires a provider of services to take any steps which would cause him to incur expenditure exceeding the prescribed maximum: s 21(7). Regulations under s 21(7) may provide for the prescribed maximum to be calculated by reference to: (1) aggregate amounts of expenditure incurred in relation to different cases; (2) prescribed periods; (3) services of a prescribed description; (4) premises of a prescribed description; or (5) such other criteria as may be prescribed: s 21(8). Regulations may provide, for the purposes of s 21(7), for expenditure incurred by one provider of services to be treated as incurred by another: s 21(9). At the date at which this volume states the law no such day had been appointed, and no such regulations have been made.

25   Ibid s 21(10).

(C) Justification

588. Objective and subjective justification. Treatment[1] is justified only if in the opinion of the provider of services[2], one or more of the specified conditions are satisfied[3], and it is reasonable, in all the circumstances of the case, for him to hold that opinion[4]. In relation to employment services[5], treatment of a disabled person[6] cannot be justified[7] if it amounts to direct discrimination[8].

The conditions are that:

(1) in any case, the treatment is necessary in order not to endanger the health or safety of any person (which may include that of the disabled person)[9];

(2) in any case, the disabled person is incapable of entering into an enforceable agreement, or of giving an informed consent, and for that reason the treatment is reasonable in that case[10];

(3) if there has been a failure to provide services to a disabled person[11], the treatment is necessary because the provider of services would otherwise be unable to provide the service to members of the public[12];

(4) if there has been discrimination in the standard of service or terms of service provided to a disabled person[13], the treatment is necessary in order for the provider of services to be able to provide the service to the disabled person or to other members of the public[14]; and

(5) if there has been discrimination in the terms of service provided to a disabled person[15], the difference in the terms on which the service is provided to the disabled person and those on which it is provided to other members of the public reflects the greater cost to the provider of services in providing the service to the disabled person[16].

Regulations may make provision as to circumstances in which it is reasonable or not reasonable for a provider of services to hold the opinion that treatment is justified[17]. Regulations may also make provision as to circumstances in which treatment is to be taken to be justified[18].

1 In the Disability Discrimination Act 1995 s 20(3), (4), (8), 'treatment' includes failure to comply with a duty to make adjustments under s 21 (see para 586 ante): s 20(9).

2 For the meaning of 'provider of services' see para 584 ante.

3 Disability Discrimination Act 1995 s 20(3)(a). For the subjective part of the test, what is in issue is the honest opinion of the person carrying out the discriminatory act: *Rose v Bouchet* [1999] IRLR 463, Sh Ct.

As to the application of the Disability Discrimination Act 1995 s 20 (as amended) to 'employment services' as defined see para 585 note 9 ante. See also note 5 infra.

4 Ibid s 20(3)(b). The opinion reached must be a reasonable one on the facts then known: *Rose v Bouchet* [1999] IRLR 463, Sh Ct. The reasonable service provider would not take into account spurious and trivial reasons however genuinely the accused provider held its opinion: See the Code of Practice on Rights of Access: services to the public, public authority functions, private clubs and premises (December 2006) para 10.21. As to codes of practice see para 655 post.

5 For the meaning of 'employment services' see para 585 note 9 ante. See also note 3 supra.

6 For the meaning of 'disabled person' see para 511 ante.

7 Ie under the Disability Discrimination Act 1995 s 20(3): see the text and notes 1–4 supra.

8 Ibid s 21A(5)(c) (s 21A added by the Disability Discrimination Act 1995 (Amendment) Regulations 2003, SI 2003/1673, regs 3(1), 19(1)). The text refers to direct discrimination falling within the Disability Discrimination Act 1995 s 3A(5) (as added): see para 531 ante.

9 Ibid s 20(4)(a). The health risk must be real and arise out of the circumstances of the particular case. It is a matter of fact and degree for the court to consider whether the reasonable service provider would dismiss the health risk as trivial, or consider that it was significant and not worth taking. The reasonableness of such an opinion may depend not only on the magnitude of the risk (i e the likelihood of the problem occurring) but also the potential consequences of the problem (i e the degree of harm caused by the problem if it occurs): c f *Paris v Stepney Borough Council* [1951] AC 367, [1951] 1 All ER 42, HL (cited in the employment context in *London Underground Ltd v Bragg* (23 June 1999) Lexis, EAT).

10   Disability Discrimination Act 1995 s 20(4)(b). The presumption is that a disabled person is perfectly able to enter into any contract: see the Code of Practice on Rights of Access: services to the public, public authority functions, private clubs and premises (December 2006) para 8.11. Regulations may make provision for the Disability Discrimination Act 1995 s 20(4)(b) not to apply in prescribed circumstances where: (1) a person is acting for a disabled person under a power of attorney; or (2) functions conferred by or under the Mental Health Act 1983 Pt VII (ss 93–113) (as amended; prospectively repealed) (see MENTAL HEALTH vol 30(2) (Reissue) para 671 et seq) are exercisable in relation to a disabled person's property or affairs: see the Disability Discrimination Act 1995 s 20(7). As from a day to be appointed, the reference to the Mental Health Act 1983 Pt VII (ss 93–113) (as amended; prospectively repealed) is replaced by a reference to the Mental Capacity Act 2005: Disability Discrimination Act 1995 s 20(7) (prospectively amended by the Mental Capacity Act 2005 s 67(1), Sch 6 para 41). At the date at which this volume states the law no such day had been appointed. For the meaning of 'regulations' see para 509 note 12 ante. 'Prescribed' generally means prescribed by regulations: see para 515 note 5 ante. See the Disability Discrimination (Services Providers and Public Authorities Carrying Out Functions) Regulations 2005, SI 2005/2901; and see para 589 post. It is unjustifiable to rely on this ground if the service provider can make a reasonable adjustment which would solve the problem: see the Code of Practice on Rights of Access: services to the public, public authority functions, private clubs and premises (December 2006) para 8.11 et seq.

11   Ie in a case falling within the Disability Discrimination Act 1995 s 19(1)(a): see para 589 post.

12   See ibid s 20(4)(c). Refusing service to a disabled person is only justifiable if other people would be effectively prevented from using the service at all: Code of Practice on Rights of Access: services to the public, public authority functions, private clubs and premises (December 2006) para 10.43.

13   Ie in a case falling within the Disability Discrimination Act 1995 s 19(1)(c) or (d): see para 589 post.

14   See ibid s 20(4)(d). See also the Code of Practice on Rights of Access: services to the public, public authority functions, private clubs and premises (December 2006) para 10.46 et seq. Objective justification excludes prejudice as the hypothetical reasonable service provider would not be swayed by the prejudices of its clients even if they take their custom elsewhere. A service provider does not have to adjust the service in a way which would so alter the nature of its business that the service provider would effectively be providing a completely different kind of service: see the Disability Discrimination Act 1995 s 21(6); and para 587 ante.

15   Ie in a case falling within ibid s 19(1)(d): see para 589 post.

16   See ibid s 20(4)(e). Any increase in the cost of providing a service to a disabled person which results from compliance by a provider of services with a duty to make adjustments under s 21 (see para 586 ante) is to be disregarded for the purposes of s 20(4)(e): s 20(5). See also the Code of Practice on Rights of Access: services to the public, public authority functions, private clubs and premises (December 2006) para 10.49.

17   See the Disability Discrimination Act 1995 s 20(6).

18   Ibid s 20(8). As to regulations under this provision see the Disability Discrimination (Services Providers and Public Authorities Carrying Out Functions) Regulations 2005, SI 2005/2901; and para 589 post.

589.   Insurance, guarantees and deposits.   Regulations have made provision as to the circumstances in which less favourable treatment is justified in relation to insurance, guarantees and deposits in respect of goods and facilities[1].

Where, for a reason which relates to the disabled person's disability[2], a provider of services[3] treats a disabled person less favourably than he treats or would treat others to whom that reason does not or would not apply, that treatment is taken to be justified[4] if the less favourable treatment is: (1) in connection with insurance business[5] carried on by the provider of services[6]; (2) based upon information (for example, actuarial or statistical data or a medical report) which is relevant to the assessment of the risk to be insured and is from a source on which it is reasonable to rely[7]; and (3) reasonable having regard to the information relied upon and any other relevant factors[8].

In relation to guarantees, discriminatory treatment is taken to be justified[9] in the following circumstances: (a) the provider of services provides a guarantee (whether or not legally enforceable)[10] that the purchase price of services that he has provided will be refunded if the services are not of satisfactory quality[11], or services in the form of goods that he has provided will be replaced or repaired if those goods are not of satisfactory quality[12]; (b) the provider refuses to provide a replacement, repair or refund under the guarantee because damage has occurred for a reason which relates to the disabled person's disability, and the damage is above the level at which the provider would normally provide a replacement, repair or refund under the guarantee[13]; and (c) it is reasonable in all the circumstances of the case for the provider to refuse to provide a replacement, repair or refund under the guarantee[14].

In relation to deposits, discriminatory treatment is taken to be justified in the following circumstances[15]: (i) when goods or facilities are provided, the disabled person is required to provide a deposit which is refundable if the goods or facilities are undamaged[16]; (ii) the provider refuses to refund some or all of the deposit because damage has occurred to the goods or facilities for a reason which relates to the disabled person's disability, and the damage is above the level at which the provider would normally refund the deposit in full[17]; and (iii) it is reasonable in all the circumstances of the case for the provider to refuse to refund the deposit in full[18].

1   See the Disability Discrimination (Services Providers and Public Authorities Carrying Out Functions) Regulations 2005, SI 2005/2901, regs 4, 7, 8; and the text and notes 2–18 infra.
2   For the meaning of 'disabled person' see para 511 ante. As to when a person has a disability see para 511 ante.
3   For the meaning of 'provider of services' see para 584 ante.
4   Disability Discrimination (Services Providers and Public Authorities Carrying Out Functions) Regulations 2005, SI 2005/2901, reg 4(1). The text refers to justification for the purposes of the Disability Discrimination Act 1995 s 20 (as amended; prospectively amended): see para 588 ante.
5   'Insurance business' means business which consists of effecting or carrying out contracts of insurance: Disability Discrimination (Services Providers and Public Authorities Carrying Out Functions) Regulations 2005, SI 2005/2901, reg 2.
6   See ibid reg 4(2)(a). As to transitional provisions relating to existing policies of insurance, cover documents and master policies see regs 5, 6.
7   Ibid reg 4(2)(b). Treatment will not be justified if an insurer makes an assessment based on stereotypes or generalisations in respect of a disabled person: Code of Practice on Rights of Access: services to the public, public authority functions, private clubs and premises (December 2006) paras 9.4, 9.5. Information should generally be specific to the particular case and general data, even actuarial data, is not a reasonable source in all circumstances, although it often will be. As to codes of practice see para 655 post.
8   Disability Discrimination (Services Providers and Public Authorities Carrying Out Functions) Regulations 2005, SI 2005/2901, reg 4(2)(c).
9   See ibid reg 7(1).
10 Ibid reg 7(2)(a). 'Guarantee' includes any document having the effect referred to in reg 7(2)(a) whether or not that document is described as a guarantee by the provider: reg 7(3).
11 Ibid reg 7(2)(a)(i).
12 Ibid reg 7(2)(a)(ii).
13 Ibid reg 7(2)(b).
14 Ibid reg 7(2)(c).
15 See ibid reg 8(1).
16 Ibid reg 8(2)(a).
17 Ibid reg 8(2)(b).
18 Ibid reg 8(2)(c).

(D)   Other Matters

590.   Alterations to premises occupied under leases.   Where (1) a provider of services[1], a public authority[2] or an association[3] is the occupier of premises[4] under a lease[5]; (2) but for this provision, the occupier would not be entitled to make a particular alteration to the premises[6]; and (3) the alteration is one which the occupier proposes to make in order to comply with a duty to make adjustments[7], then certain provisions are implied in the lease. Except to the extent to which it expressly so provides, the lease has effect as if it provided[8]: (a) for the occupier to be entitled to make the alteration with the written consent of the lessor[9]; (b) for the occupier to have to make a written application to the lessor for consent if he wishes to make the alteration[10]; (c) if such an application is made, for the lessor not to withhold his consent unreasonably[11]; and (d) for the lessor to be entitled to make his consent subject to reasonable conditions[12].

1   For the meaning of 'provider of services' see para 584 ante.
2   Ie within the meaning given by the Disability Discrimination Act 1995 s 21B (as added): see para 593 post.
3   Ie to which ibid s 21F (as added) applies: see para 596 post.
4   As to the meaning of 'premises' see para 525 note 9 ante.
5   Disability Discrimination Act 1995 s 27(1)(a) (amended by the Disability Discrimination Act 2005 s 19(1), Sch 1 paras 1, 23(a)). 'Lease' includes a tenancy, sub-lease or sub-tenancy and an agreement for a lease, tenancy, sub-lease or sub-tenancy; and 'sub-lease' and 'sub-tenancy' have such meanings as may be prescribed: Disability Discrimination Act 1995 s 27(3). 'Prescribed' generally means prescribed by regulations: see para 515 note 5 ante. For the meaning of 'regulations' see para 509 note 12 ante. The Secretary of State may by regulations make provision supplementing, or modifying, the provision made by s 27 (as amended) or any provision made by or under s 27(5), Sch 4 Pt II (as amended) in relation to cases where the occupier occupies premises under a sub-lease or sub-tenancy: Sch 4 para 9. As to the Secretary of State and the National Assembly for Wales see para 302 ante. As to the regulations made see the Disability Discrimination (Providers of Services) (Adjustment of Premises) Regulations 2001, SI 2001/3253 (amended by SI 2004/1429; SI 2005/1121; SI 2005/2901); and the Disability Discrimination (Service Providers and Public Authorities Carrying Out Functions) Regulations 2005, SI 2005/2901. For the purposes of the Disability Discrimination Act 1995 s 27 (as amended), 'sub-lease' means any sub-term created out of, or deriving from, a superior leasehold interest; and 'sub-tenancy' means any tenancy created out of, or deriving from, a superior tenancy: Disability Discrimination (Providers of Services) (Adjustment of Premises) Regulations 2001, SI 2001/3253, reg 4.
    The Disability Discrimination (Providers of Services) (Adjustment of Premises) Regulations 2001, SI 2001/3253 (as amended) prescribe particular circumstances in which: (1) a relevant lessor is to be taken, for the purposes of the Disability Discrimination Act 1995 s 27, Sch 4 Pt II (as amended), to have: (a) withheld his consent for alterations to premises (see the Disability Discrimination (Providers of Services) (Adjustment of Premises) Regulations 2001, SI 2001/3253, reg 5); (b) acted unreasonably in withholding his consent for alterations to premises (see reg 6); and (c) acted reasonably in withholding his consent for alterations to premises (see reg 7); and (2) a condition, subject to which a relevant lessor has given his consent to alterations to premises, is to be taken, for the purposes of the Disability Discrimination Act 1995 s 27, Sch 4 Pt II (as amended), to be reasonable (see the Disability Discrimination (Providers of Services) (Adjustment of Premises) Regulations 2001, SI 2001/3253, reg 8). 'Relevant lessor' means a lessor who has received a written application by or on behalf of the occupier for consent to make an alteration to premises for the purposes of the Disability Discrimination Act 1995 s 27, Sch 4 Pt II (as amended): Disability Discrimination (Providers of Services) (Adjustment of Premises) Regulations 2001, SI 2001/3253, reg 2. The Disability Discrimination (Providers of Services) (Adjustment of Premises) Regulations 2001, SI 2001/3253 (as amended) also modify the Disability Discrimination Act 1995 Sch 4 paras 5–7 (as amended) in relation to any case where the occupier occupies premises under a sub-lease or sub-tenancy: see the Disability Discrimination (Providers of Services) (Adjustment of Premises) Regulations 2001, SI 2001/3253, reg 9.
6   Disability Discrimination Act 1995 s 27(1)(b) (amended by the Disability Discrimination Act 2005 Sch 1 paras 1, 23(b)). If the terms and conditions of a lease: (1) impose conditions which are to apply if the occupier alters the premises; or (2) entitle the lessor to impose conditions when consenting to the occupier's altering the premises, the occupier is to be treated for the purposes of the Disability Discrimination Act 1995 s 27(1) (as amended) as not being entitled to make the alteration: s 27(4).
7   Ibid s 27(1)(c) (amended by the Disability Discrimination Act 2005 Sch 1 paras 1, 23(c)). The duty referred to in the text is a section 21 duty (see para 586 ante) or a duty imposed under the Disability Discrimination Act 1995 s 21E (as added) (see para 595 post) or s 21H (as added) (see para 598 post): see s 27(1)(c) (as so amended). 'Section 21 duty' means any duty imposed by or under s 21 (see para 586 ante): s 68(1). If any question arises as to whether the occupier has failed to comply with the section 21 duty or a duty imposed under s 21E (as added) or s 21H (as added), by failing to make a particular alteration to premises, any constraint attributable to the fact that he occupies the premises under a lease is to be ignored unless he has applied to the lessor in writing for consent to the making of the alteration: Sch 4 para 5 (amended by the Disability Discrimination Act 2005 Sch 1 paras 1, 40(1), (4)).
8   See the Disability Discrimination Act 1995 s 27(2).
9   Ibid s 27(2)(a). If the occupier has applied in writing to the lessor for consent to the alteration and: (1) that consent has been refused; or (2) the lessor has made his consent subject to one or more conditions, the occupier, or a disabled person who has an interest in the proposed alteration to the premises being made, may refer the matter to a county court: Sch 4 para 6(1). On such a reference the court must determine whether the lessor's refusal was unreasonable or (as the case may be) whether the condition is,

or any of the conditions are, unreasonable: Sch 4 para 6(3). If the court determines that the lessor's refusal was unreasonable, or that the condition is, or any of the conditions are, unreasonable, it may make such declaration as it considers appropriate or an order authorising the occupier to make the alteration specified in the order: Sch 4 para 6(4). Such an order may require the occupier to comply with conditions specified in the order: Sch 4 para 6(5).

10 Ibid s 27(2)(b).

11 Ibid s 27(2)(c). Regulations may make provision as to circumstances in which: (1) a lessor is to be taken to have withheld his consent, withheld his consent unreasonably, and acted reasonably in withholding his consent; (2) a condition subject to which a lessor has given his consent is to be taken to be reasonable; and (3) a condition subject to which a lessor has given his consent is to be taken to be unreasonable: Sch 4 para 8. As to the regulations made see the Disability Discrimination (Providers of Services) (Adjustment of Premises) Regulations 2001, SI 2001/3253 (as amended); and the Disability Discrimination (Service Providers and Public Authorities Carrying Out Functions) Regulations 2005, SI 2005/2901; and see note 5 supra.

12 Disability Discrimination Act 1995 s 27(2)(d).

D. PUBLIC AUTHORITIES

(A) General Duties of Public Authorities

591. General duty of public authorities. Every public authority[1] must in carrying out its functions have due regard to: (1) the need to eliminate discrimination that is unlawful under the Disability Discrimination Act 1995[2]; (2) the need to eliminate harassment of disabled persons[3] that is related to their disabilities[4]; (3) the need to promote equality of opportunity between disabled persons and other persons[5]; (4) the need to take steps to take account of disabled persons' disabilities, even where that involves treating disabled persons more favourably than other persons[6]; (5) the need to promote positive attitudes towards disabled persons[7]; and (6) the need to encourage participation by disabled persons in public life[8].

The above provision[9] does not apply to: (a) a judicial act (whether done by a court, tribunal or other person)[10]; or (b) an act done on the instructions, or on behalf, of a person acting in a judicial capacity[11]. Nor does it apply to any act[12] of, or relating to, making or approving an Act of Parliament or an Order in Council[13]. Heads (3) and (4) above do not apply to an act done in connection with recruitment to any of the naval, military or air forces of the Crown[14], or an act done in relation to a person[15] in connection with service by him as a member of any of those forces[16]. Regulations may provide for one or more of heads (1) to (6) above[17] not to apply to an act of a prescribed description[18].

The Secretary of State[19] may by regulations impose on a public authority[20] such duties as he considers appropriate for the purpose of ensuring the better performance by that authority of its duty under heads (1) to (6) above[21]. Before making such regulations, the Secretary of State must consult the Disability Rights Commission[22]. Before making such regulations in relation to functions exercisable in relation to Wales by a public authority that is not a relevant Welsh authority[23], the Secretary of State must consult the National Assembly for Wales[24]; and he must not make such regulations in relation to a relevant Welsh authority except with the consent of the National Assembly for Wales[25].

1 For the purposes of the Disability Discrimination Act 1995 Pt VA (ss 49A–49F) (as added), 'public authority': (1) includes any person certain of whose functions are functions of a public nature; but (2) does not include: (a) any person mentioned in s 21B(3) (as added) (see para 593 post); (b) the Scottish Parliament; or (c) a person, other than the Scottish Parliamentary Corporate Body, exercising functions in connection with proceedings in the Scottish Parliament: s 49B(1) (ss 49A–49D added by the Disability Discrimination Act 2005 s 3). Scottish matters generally are beyond the scope of this work. As to the meaning of 'person' see para 301 note 3 ante. In relation to a particular act, a person is not a public authority by virtue only of head (1) supra if the nature of the act is private: Disability Discrimination Act 1995 s 49B(2) (as so added). Regulations may provide for a person of a prescribed description to be

treated as not being a public authority for the purposes of Pt VA (as added): s 49B(3) (as so added). For the meaning of 'regulations' see para 509 note 12 ante. 'Prescribed' generally means prescribed by regulations: see para 515 note 5 ante. At the date at which this volume states the law no regulations had been made for these purposes.

2 Ibid s 49A(1)(a) (as added: see note 1 supra). Section 49A(1) (as added) is without prejudice to any obligation of a public authority to comply with any other provision of the Disability Discrimination Act 1995: s 49A(2) (as so added). As to discrimination by public authorities see para 593–595 post.

3 For the meaning of 'disabled person' see para 511 ante.

4 Disability Discrimination Act 1995 s 49A(1)(b) (as added: see note 1 supra). See note 2 supra.

5 Ibid s 49A(1)(c) (as added: see note 1 supra). See note 2 supra.

6 Ibid s 49A(1)(d) (as added: see note 1 supra). See note 2 supra.

7 Ibid s 49A(1)(e) (as added: see note 1 supra). See note 2 supra.

8 Ibid s 49A(1)(f) (as added: see note 1 supra). See note 2 supra.

9 Ie ibid s 49A(1) (as added).

10 Ibid s 49C(1)(a) (as added: see note 1 supra).

11 Ibid s 49C(1)(b) (as added: see note 1 supra).

12 As to the meaning of 'act' see para 510 note 3 ante.

13 Disability Discrimination Act 1995 s 49C(2) (as added: see note 1 supra). This provision also refers to an Act of the Scottish Parliament. See note 1 supra.

14 Ibid s 49C(3)(a) (as added: see note 1 supra). See ARMED FORCES.

15 See note 1 supra.

16 Disability Discrimination Act 1995 s 49C(3)(b) (as added: see note 1 supra).

17 Ie one or more specified paragraphs of ibid s 49A(1) (as added).

18 Ibid s 49C(4) (as added (see note 1 supra); and amended by the Equality Act 2006 s 88). At the date at which this volume states the law no regulations had been made under the Disability Discrimination Act 1995 s 49C(4) (as added and amended).

19 As to the Secretary of State and the National Assembly for Wales see para 302 ante.

20 Ie other than a relevant Scottish authority or a cross-border authority. As to other provisions affecting Scotland see the Disability Discrimination Act 1995 s 49D(2), (3), (4), (8), (9), (10) (as added: see note 1 supra). See note 1 supra.

21 Ibid s 49D(1) (as added: see note 1 supra). The duties referred to are those under s 49A(1) (as added): see the text and notes 1–8 supra. The Secretary of State may also by regulations impose on a cross-border authority such duties as the Secretary of State considers appropriate for the purpose of ensuring the better performance by that authority of its duty under s 49A(1) (as added) so far as relating to such of its functions as are not Scottish functions: s 49D(2) (as so added). As to the regulations made see the Disability Discrimination (Public Authorities) (Statutory Duties) Regulations 2005, SI 2005/2966 (amended by SI 2007/618).

22 Disability Discrimination Act 1995 s 49D(5) (as added: see note 1 supra). As from a day to be appointed, the reference to the Disability Rights Commission is replaced by a reference to the Commission for Equality and Human Rights: s 49D(5) (prospectively amended by the Equality Act 2006 s 40, Sch 3 paras 41, 48). At the date at which this volume states the law no such day had been appointed. As to the Disability Rights Commission see para 646 et seq post. As to the Commission for Equality and Human Rights, which is to replace the Disability Rights Commission, see para 305 et seq ante. See note 21 supra.

23 'Relevant Welsh authority' means: (1) the National Assembly for Wales; or (2) a public authority whose functions are exercisable only in relation to Wales: Disability Discrimination Act 1995 s 49D(10) (as added: see note 1 supra).

24 Ibid s 49D(6) (as added: see note 1 supra). See note 21 supra.

25 Ibid s 49D(7) (as added: see note 1 supra). See note 21 supra.

592. Compliance notices. Where the Disability Rights Commission ('DRC')[1] is satisfied that a public authority[2] has failed to comply with, or is failing to comply with, a duty imposed on it by the relevant regulations[3], the DRC may serve a notice on it[4].

In regard to a notice so served on an authority[5], it must require the authority: (1) to comply with the duty concerned[6]; and (2) to furnish the DRC, by the end of the period of 28 days beginning with the day on which the notice is served, with details of the steps that it has taken, or is taking, to comply with the duty[7]. The notice may also require the authority to furnish the DRC with other information specified in the notice if the DRC reasonably requires the information in order to verify that the duty has been complied with[8].

The notice must specify the time by which the authority is to furnish information which it is required to furnish[9]. The notice may specify the manner and form in which the authority is to furnish information which the notice requires it to furnish to the DRC[10].

The notice must not require the authority to furnish information which it could not be compelled to furnish in evidence in civil proceedings before the High Court[11].

If (a) a public authority on which a compliance notice[12] has been served fails to furnish the DRC, in accordance with the notice, with any information required by the notice[13]; or (b) the DRC has reasonable cause to believe that a public authority on which a notice has been so served does not intend to furnish the information required by the notice[14], the DRC may apply to a county court for an order requiring the authority to furnish any information required by the notice[15]. If on such an application[16] the court is satisfied that either of the conditions specified in heads (a) and (b) above is met, the court may grant the order in the terms applied for or in more limited terms[17].

If (i) the period of three months beginning with the day on which a compliance notice is served on a public authority[18] has ended[19]; (ii) the notice required the authority to comply with a duty imposed on it by the relevant regulations[20]; and (iii) the DRC considers that the authority has not complied with the duty[21], the DRC may apply to a county court for an order requiring the authority to comply with the duty[22]. If on such an application[23] the court is satisfied: (A) that the conditions specified in heads (i) and (ii) above are met[24]; and (B) that the authority has not complied with the duty[25], the court may grant the order in the terms applied for or in more limited terms[26].

The above sanctions[27] are the only sanctions for breach of any duty imposed by the relevant regulations[28], but without prejudice to the enforcement of any other provision of the Disability Discrimination Act 1995 (where the breach is also a contravention of that provision)[29].

1   As to the DRC see para 646 et seq post. As to the Commission for Equality and Human Rights, which is to replace the DRC, see para 305 et seq ante.
2   As to the meaning of 'public authority' see para 591 note 1 ante.
3   Ie regulations under the Disability Discrimination Act 1995 s 49D (as added; prospectively amended): see para 591 ante.
4   Ibid s 49E(1) (ss 49E, 49F added by the Disability Discrimination Act 2005 s 3). The Disability Discrimination Act 1995 ss 49E, 49F (both as added) are repealed by the Equality Act 2006 ss 40, 91, Sch 3 paras 41, 49, Sch 4 as from a day to be appointed under s 93. At the day at which this volume states the law no such day had been appointed. As to compliance notices under the Equality Act 2006 see para 336 ante.
5   Disability Discrimination Act 1995 s 49E(2) (as added: see note 4 supra).
6   Ibid s 49E(3)(a) (as added: see note 4 supra).
7   Ibid s 49E(3)(b) (as added: see note 4 supra).
8   Ibid s 49E(4) (as added: see note 4 supra).
9   Ibid s 49E(5) (as added: see note 4 supra). A time specified under s 49E(5) (as added) must not be later than the end of the three months beginning with the day on which the notice is served: s 49E(6) (as so added).
10   Ibid s 49E(7) (as added: see note 4 supra).
11   Ibid s 49E(8) (as added: see note 4 supra).
12   Ie a notice under ibid s 49E (as added): see the text and notes 1–11 supra.
13   Ibid s 49F(1)(a) (as added: see note 4 supra).
14   Ibid s 49F(1)(b) (as added: see note 4 supra).
15   Ibid s 49F(1) (as added: see note 4 supra).
16   Ie an application under s 49F(1)(as added): see the text and notes 12–15 supra.
17   Ibid s 49F(2) (as added: see note 4 supra).
18   Ie under ibid s 49E (as added): see the text and notes 1–11 supra.
19   Ibid s 49F(3)(a) (as added: see note 4 supra).
20   Ibid s 49F(3)(b) (as added: see note 4 supra). The regulations referred to are those under s 49D (as added; prospectively amended): see para 591 ante.

21 Ibid s 49F(3)(c) (as added: see note 4 supra).
22 Ibid s 49F(3) (as added: see note 4 supra).
23 Ie an application under ibid s 49F(3) (as added): see the text and notes 18–22 supra.
24 Ibid s 49F(4)(a) (as added: see note 4 supra).
25 Ibid s 49F(4)(b) (as added: see note 4 supra).
26 Ibid s 49F(4) (as added: see note 4 supra).
27 Ie sanctions in ibid ss 49E, 49F (as added).
28 Ie regulations under ibid s 49D (as added; prospectively amended): see para 591 ante.
29 Ibid s 49F(5) (as added: see note 4 supra).

(B) Discrimination by Public Authorities

593. Discrimination by public authorities. It is unlawful for a public authority[1] to discriminate[2] against a disabled person[3] in carrying out its functions[4]. In the case of an act[5] which constitutes discrimination by victimisation[6], this provision also applies to discrimination against a person who is not disabled[7].

The above provision[8] does not apply to anything which is unlawful under any other provision of the Disability Discrimination Act 1995[9] and does not apply[10] to anything which would be unlawful under any such provision but for the operation of any provision in or made under the Disability Discrimination Act 1995[11].

There are a number of exceptions from the application of the above provision[12]. It does not apply to a judicial act (whether done by a court, tribunal or other person) or an act done on the instructions, or on behalf, of a person acting in a judicial capacity[13]. It does not apply to any act of, or relating to, making, confirming or approving an Act or an Order in Council or an instrument made under an Act by a Minister of the Crown[14] or the National Assembly for Wales[15]. It does not apply to any act of, or relating to, imposing certain conditions or requirements of a kind falling within the provision relating to statutory authority and national security[16]. It does not apply to: (1) a decision not to institute criminal proceedings[17]; (2) where such a decision is made, an act done for the purpose of enabling the decision to be made[18]; (3) a decision not to continue criminal proceedings[19]; or (4) where such a decision is made, an act done for the purpose of enabling the decision to be made, or an act done for the purpose of securing that the proceedings are not continued[20]. Finally, it does not apply to an act of a prescribed description[21].

1 In the Disability Discrimination Act 1995 ss 21B, 21D, 21E (all as added) (see also paras 594–595 post), 'public authority': (1) includes any person certain of whose functions are functions of a public nature; but (2) does not include any person mentioned in s 21B(3) (as added): s 21B(2) (ss 21B, 21C added by the Disability Discrimination Act 2005 s 2). In relation to a particular act, a person is not a public authority by virtue only of head (1) supra if the nature of the act is private: s 21B(4) (as so added). The persons referred to in head (2) supra are: (a) either House of Parliament; (b) a person exercising functions in connection with proceedings in Parliament; (c) the Security Service; (d) the Secret Intelligence Service; (e) the Government Communications Headquarters; and (f) a unit, or part of a unit, of any of the naval, military or air forces of the Crown which is for the time being required by the Secretary of State to assist the Government Communications Headquarters in carrying out its functions: s 21B(3) (as so added). As to the security and intelligence services generally see CONSTITUTIONAL LAW AND HUMAN RIGHTS vol 8(2) (Reissue) para 473 et seq.
   Regulations may provide for a person of a prescribed description to be treated as not being a public authority for purposes of ss 21B, 21D, 21E (all as added): s 21B(5) (as so added). For the meaning of 'regulations' see para 509 note 12 ante. 'Prescribed' generally means prescribed by regulations: see para 515 note 5 ante. At the date at which this volume states the law no regulations had been made for these purposes.
   As to the general duties of public authorities see para 591 ante.
2 As to discrimination see also paras 594–595 post.
3 For the meaning of 'disabled person' see para 511 ante.
4 Disability Discrimination Act 1995 s 21B(1) (as added: see note 1 supra).
5 As to the meaning of 'act' see para 510 note 3 ante.
6 Ie by virtue of the Disability Discrimination Act 1995 s 55 (as amended): see para 526 ante.

7 See ibid s 55 (as amended); and para 526 ante.

8 Ie ibid s 21B(1) (as added): see the text and notes 1–4 supra.

9 Ie under any provision of the Disability Discrimination Act 1995 other than s 21B(1) (as added).

10 Ie subject to ibid s 21B(8), (9) (as added). Section 21B(1) (as added) does apply in relation to a public authority's function of appointing a person to, and in relation to a public authority's functions with respect to a person as holder of, an office or post if: (1) none of the conditions specified in s 4C(3) (as added) (see para 543 ante) is satisfied in relation to the office or post; and (2) ss 4D, 4E (both as added) (see paras 543–544 ante) would apply in relation to an appointment to the office or post if any of those conditions was satisfied: s 21B(8) (as so added). Section 21B(1) (as added) also applies in relation to a public authority's functions with respect to a person as candidate or prospective candidate for election to, and in relation to a public authority's functions with respect to a person as elected holder of, an office or post if: (a) the office or post is not membership of a House of Parliament, the Scottish Parliament, the National Assembly for Wales or an authority mentioned in s 15A(1) (as added) (see para 558 ante); (b) none of the conditions specified in s 4C(3) (as added) (see para 543 ante) is satisfied in relation to the office or post; and (c) ss 4D, 4E (both as added) (see paras 543–544 ante) would apply in relation to an appointment to the office or post if any of those conditions was satisfied, and s 4F(1) (as added) (see paras 543–544 ante) (but not s 4C(5) (as added) (see para 543 ante)) was omitted: s 21B(9) (as so added). As to the National Assembly for Wales see para 302 ante. Scottish matters generally are beyond the scope of this work.

Section 21B(8), (9) (as added) is not to be taken to prejudice the generality of s 21B(1) (as added), but is subject to s 21C(5) (as added) (see the text to note 21 infra): s 21B(10) (as so added).

11 Ibid s 21B(7) (as added: see note 1 supra). See the Code of Practice on Rights of Access: services to the public, public authority functions, private clubs and premises (December 2006) paras 3.6–3.8. As to codes of practice see para 655 post.

12 Ie from the application of the Disability Discrimination Act 1995 s 21B(1) (as added) (see the text and notes 1–4 supra): see s 21C (as added); and the text to notes 13–21 infra.

13 Ibid s 21C(1) (as added: see note 1 supra).

14 For the meaning of 'Minister of the Crown' see para 510 note 4 ante.

15 Disability Discrimination Act 1995 s 21C(2) (as added: see note 1 supra).

16 Ibid s 21C(3) (as added: see note 1 supra). The provision referred to in the text is s 59(1)(c) (as substituted): see para 616 post.

17 Ibid s 21C(4)(a) (as added: see note 1 supra). 'Criminal proceedings' includes: (1) proceedings on dealing summarily with a charge under the Army Act 1955 or the Air Force Act 1955 or on summary trial under the Naval Discipline Act 1957; (2) proceedings before a summary appeal court constituted under any of those Acts; (3) proceedings before a court-martial constituted under any of those Acts or a disciplinary court constituted under the Naval Discipline Act 1957 s 52G (repealed); (4) proceedings before the Courts-Martial Appeal Court; and (5) proceedings before a standing civilian court: Disability Discrimination Act 1995 s 68(1) (definition added by the Disability Discrimination Act 2005 s 19(1), Sch 1 paras 1, 34(1), (2)). As to the armed forces generally see ARMED FORCES.

18 Disability Discrimination Act 1995 s 21C(4)(b) (as added: see note 1 supra).

19 Ibid s 21C(4)(c) (as added: see note 1 supra).

20 Ibid s 21C(4)(d) (as added: see note 1 supra).

21 Ibid s 21C(5) (as added: see note 1 supra). At the date at which this volume states the law no regulations had been made in relation to acts of prescribed description.

594. Meaning of 'discrimination'. For the purposes of the general provision on discrimination by such authorities[1], a public authority[2] discriminates against a disabled person[3] if: (1) for a reason which relates to the disabled person's disability, it treats him less favourably than it treats or would treat others to whom that reason does not or would not apply[4]; and (2) it cannot show that the treatment in question is justified[5].

For the same purposes, a public authority also discriminates against a disabled person if: (a) it fails to comply with a duty to make adjustments[6] in circumstances in which the effect of that failure is to make it impossible or unreasonably difficult for the disabled person to receive any benefit that is or may be conferred[7], or unreasonably adverse for the disabled person to experience being subjected to any detriment to which a person is or may be subjected[8], by the carrying out of a function by the authority[9]; and (b) it cannot show that its failure to comply with that duty is justified[10].

Treatment, or a failure to comply with a duty, is justified if: (i) in the opinion of the public authority[11], one or more specified conditions[12] are satisfied[13]; and (ii) it is reasonable, in all the circumstances of the case, for it to hold that opinion[14]. Treatment, or a failure to comply with a duty, is also justified if the acts of the public authority which give rise to the treatment or failure are a proportionate means of achieving a legitimate aim[15].

1   Ie for the purposes of the Disability Discrimination Act 1995 s 21B(1) (as added): see para 593 ante.
2   For the meaning of 'public authority' see para 593 note 1 ante.
3   For the meaning of 'disabled person' see para 511 ante.
4   Disability Discrimination Act 1995 s 21D(1)(a) (s 21D added by the Disability Discrimination Act 2005 s 2).
5   Disability Discrimination Act 1995 s 21D(1)(b) (as added: see note 4 supra). The text refers to justification under s 21D(3), (5) or (7)(c) (as added): see the text to notes 12–15infra; and see note 12 head (c) infra.
6   Ie a duty imposed by ibid s 21E (as added): see para 595 post.
7   Ibid s 21D(2)(a)(i) (as added: see note 4 supra).
8   Ibid s 21D(2)(a)(ii) (as added: see note 4 supra).
9   Ibid s 21D(2)(a) (as added: see note 4 supra).
10   Ibid s 21D(2)(b) (as added: see note 4 supra). The text refers to justification under s 21D(3), (5) or (7)(c) (as added): see the text to notes 12–15 infra; and see note 12 head (c) infra.
11   Regulations may make provision, for purposes of ibid s 21C (as added), as to circumstances in which it is, or as to circumstances in which it is not, reasonable for a public authority to hold the opinion mentioned in s 21C(3)(a) (as added): s 21D(6). For the meaning of 'regulations' see para 509 note 12 ante. At the date at which this volume states the law no such regulations had been made. See also note 12 infra.
12   Ie conditions specified in ibid s 21D(4) (as added). The conditions are as follows: (1) that the treatment, or non-compliance with the duty, is necessary in order not to endanger the health or safety of any person (which may include that of the disabled person); (2) that the disabled person is incapable of entering into an enforceable agreement, or of giving an informed consent, and for that reason the treatment, or non-compliance with the duty, is reasonable in the particular case; (3) that, in the case of treatment mentioned in s 21C(1) (as added), treating the disabled person equally favourably would in the particular case involve substantial extra costs and, having regard to resources, the extra costs in that particular case would be too great; (4) that the treatment, or non-compliance with the duty, is necessary for the protection of rights and freedoms of other persons: s 21D(4) (as added: see note 4 supra).
     Regulations may: (a) amend or omit a condition specified in s 21D(4) (as added) or make provision for it not to apply in prescribed circumstances; (b) amend or omit s 21D(5) (as added) (see the text to note 15 infra) or make provision for it not to apply in prescribed circumstances; (c) make provision for purposes of s 21D (as added) (in addition to any provision for the time being made by s 21D(3)–(5) (as added) (see the text and notes 13–15 infra)) as to circumstances in which treatment, or a failure to comply with a duty, is to be taken to be justified: s 21D(7) (as added: see note 4 supra). 'Prescribed' generally means prescribed by regulations: see para 515 note 5 ante. For regulations made under head (a) supra see the Disability Discrimination (Service Providers and Public Authorities Carrying Out Functions) Regulations 2005, SI 2005/2901.
13   Disability Discrimination Act 1995 s 21D(3)(a) (as added: see note 4 supra).
14   Ibid s 21D(3)(b) (as added: see note 4 supra).
15   Ibid s 21D(5) (as added: see note 4 supra).

595. Duty of public bodies to make adjustments. Where a public authority[1] has a practice, policy or procedure[2] which makes it: (1) impossible or unreasonably difficult for disabled persons[3] to receive any benefit that is or may be conferred[4]; or (2) unreasonably adverse for disabled persons to experience being subjected to any detriment to which a person is or may be subjected[5], by the carrying out of a function by the authority[6], it is the duty of the authority to take such steps as it is reasonable, in all the circumstances of the case, for the authority to have to take in order to change that practice, policy or procedure so that it no longer has that effect[7].

Where a physical feature[8] makes it: (a) impossible or unreasonably difficult for disabled persons to receive any benefit that is or may be conferred[9]; or (b) unreasonably adverse for disabled persons to experience being subjected to any detriment to which a person is or may be subjected[10], by the carrying out of a function by a public authority[11], it is the duty of the authority to take such steps as it is reasonable, in all the circumstances of the case, for the authority to have to take in order to: (i) remove the feature[12]; (ii) alter it so that it no longer has that effect[13]; (iii) provide a reasonable means of avoiding the feature[14]; or (iv) adopt a reasonable alternative method of carrying out the function[15].

Where an auxiliary aid or service[16] would: (A) enable disabled persons to receive, or facilitate the receiving by disabled persons of, any benefit that is or may be conferred[17]; or (B) reduce the extent to which it is adverse for disabled persons to experience being subjected to any detriment to which a person is or may be subjected[18], by the carrying out of a function by a public authority[19], it is the duty of the authority to take such steps as it is reasonable, in all the circumstances of the case, for the authority to have to take in order to provide that auxiliary aid or service[20].

Nothing in the above provisions[21] requires a public authority to take any steps which, apart from the provisions, it has no power to take[22].

The above provisions impose duties only for the purposes of determining whether a public authority has[23] discriminated against a disabled person; and accordingly a breach of any such duty is not actionable as such[24].

1   For the meaning of 'public authority' see para 593 note 1 ante.
2   As to regulations about the meaning of 'practice, policy or procedure' see note 7 infra.
3   For the meaning of 'disabled person' see para 511 ante.
4   Disability Discrimination Act 1995 s 21E(1)(a) (s 21E added by the Disability Discrimination Act 2005 s 2).
5   Disability Discrimination Act 1995 s 21E(1)(b) (as added: see note 4 supra).
6   Ibid s 21E(1) (as added: see note 4 supra).
7   Ibid s 21E(2) (as added: see note 4 supra).
    Regulations may make provision, for the purposes of s 21E (as added): (1) as to circumstances in which it is, or as to circumstances in which it is not, reasonable for a public authority to have to take steps of a prescribed description; (2) as to steps which it is always, or as to steps which it is never, reasonable for a public authority to have to take; (3) as to what is, or as to what is not, to be included within the meaning of 'practice, policy or procedure'; (4) as to things which are, or as to things which are not, to be treated as physical features; (5) as to things which are, or as to things which are not, to be treated as auxiliary aids or services: s 21E(8) (as so added). As to regulations made under heads (1), (4) supra see the Disability Discrimination (Service Providers and Public Authorities Carrying Out Functions) Regulations 2005, SI 2005/2901.
8   As to regulations about physical features see note 7 supra.
9   Disability Discrimination Act 1995 s 21E(3)(1)(a) (as added: see note 4 supra).
10 Ibid s 21E(3)(1)(b) (as added: see note 4 supra).
11 Ibid s 21E(3) (as added: see note 4 supra).
12 Ibid s 21E(4)(a) (as added: see note 4 supra).
    Regulations may prescribe: (1) matters which are to be taken into account in determining whether any provision of a kind mentioned in s 21E(4)(c) or (d) (as added) (see the text to notes 14–16 infra) is reasonable; (2) categories of public authorities to whom s 21E(4) (as added) does not apply: s 21E(5) (as so added). For the meaning of 'regulations' see para 509 note 12 ante. 'Prescribe' generally means prescribe by regulations: see para 515 note 5 ante. See also note 7 supra. At the date at which this volume states the law no regulations had been made for these purposes.
13 Ibid s 21E(4)(b) (as added: see note 4 supra). See note 12 supra. If any question arises as to whether the occupier has failed to comply with a duty imposed under s 21E (as added), by failing to make a particular alteration to premises, any constraint attributable to the fact that he occupies the premises under a lease is to be ignored unless he has applied to the lessor in writing for consent to the making of the alteration: see Sch 4 para 5 (as amended); and para 590 note 7 ante. As to reference to court in relation to such consent see Sch 4 para 6; and para 590 note 9 ante.
14 Ibid s 21E(4)(c) (as added: see note 4 supra). See note 12 supra.
15 Ibid s 21E(4)(d) (as added: see note 4 supra). See note 12 supra.
16 As to regulations about auxiliary aid or service see note 7 supra.
17 Disability Discrimination Act 1995 s 21E(6)(a) (as added: see note 4 supra).
18 Ibid s 21E(6)(b) (as added: see note 4 supra).
19 Ibid s 21E(6) (as added: see note 4 supra).
20 Ibid s 21E(7) (as added: see note 4 supra).
21 Ie in ibid s 21E (as added).

22 Ibid s 21E(9) (as added: see note 4 supra).
23 Ie for the purposes of ibid s 21B(1) (as added): see para 593 ante.
24 Ibid s 21E(10) (as added: see note 4 supra).

E. PRIVATE CLUBS AND ASSOCIATIONS

596. Discrimination by private clubs etc. These provisions[1] apply to any association of persons[2] (however described, whether corporate or unincorporate, and whether or not its activities are carried on for profit) if: (1) it has 25 or more members[3]; (2) admission to membership is regulated by its constitution and is so conducted that the members do not constitute a section of the public[4]; and (3) it is not a trade organisation[5].

It is unlawful for such an association[6], in the case of a disabled person[7] who is not a member of the association, to discriminate[8] against him in the terms on which it is prepared to admit him to membership[9] or by refusing or deliberately omitting to accept his application for membership[10].

It is unlawful for such an association, in the case of a disabled person who is a member or associate[11] of the association, to discriminate against him: (a) in the way it affords him access to a benefit, facility or service[12]; (b) by refusing or deliberately omitting to afford him access to a benefit, facility or service[13]; (c) in the case of a member, by depriving him of membership or by varying the terms on which he is a member[14]; (d) in the case of an associate, by depriving him of his rights as an associate or by varying those rights[15]; or (e) by subjecting him to any other detriment[16].

It is unlawful for such an association to discriminate against a disabled person: (i) in the way it affords him access to a benefit, facility or service[17]; (ii) by refusing or deliberately omitting to afford him access to a benefit, facility or service[18]; or (iii) by subjecting him to any other detriment[19], in his capacity as a guest[20] of the association[21].

It is unlawful for such an association to discriminate against a disabled person: (A) in the terms on which it is prepared to invite him, or permit a member or associate to invite him, to be a guest of the association[22]; (B) by refusing or deliberately omitting to invite him to be a guest of the association[23]; or (C) by not permitting a member or associate to invite him to be a guest of the association[24].

It is unlawful for such an association to discriminate against a disabled person in failing in prescribed circumstances[25] to comply with a duty to make adjustments[26].

In the case of an act which constitutes discrimination by victimisation[27], the above provisions[28] also apply to discrimination against a person who is not disabled[29].

1   Ie the Disability Discrimination Act 1995 s 21F (as added).
2   As to the meaning of 'person' see para 344 note 3 ante.
3   Disability Discrimination Act 1995 s 21F(1)(a) (ss 21F, 21J added by the Disability Discrimination Act 2005 s 12). For the purposes of the Disability Discrimination Act 1995 s 21F–21J (as added), a person is a 'member' of an association to which s 21F (as added) applies if he belongs to it by virtue of his admission to any sort of membership provided for by its constitution (and is not merely a person with certain rights under its constitution by virtue of his membership of some other association); and references to membership of an association are to be construed accordingly: s 21J(1)(a) (as so added). See the Code of Practice on Rights of Access: services to the public, public authority functions, private clubs and premises (December 2006) paras 3.9, 3.10. As to codes of practice see para 655 post.
4   Disability Discrimination Act 1995 s 21F(1)(b) (as added: see note 3 supra). The reference is to a section of the public within the meaning of s 19(2) (as amended): see paras 583–584 ante.
5   Ibid s 21F(1)(c) (as added: see note 3 supra). The reference is to an organisation to which s 13 (as substituted) applies: see para 541 ante.
6   Ie an association to which ibid s 21F (as added) applies.
7   For the meaning of 'disabled person' see para 511 ante.
8   As to discrimination see also paras 594, 595 post.
9   Disability Discrimination Act 1995 s 21F(2)(a) (as added: see note 3 supra).
10 Ibid s 21F(2)(b) (as added: see note 3 supra).

11 For the purposes of ibid ss 21F–21J (as added), a person is an 'associate' of an association to which s 21F (as added) applies if, not being a member of it, he has under its constitution some or all of the rights enjoyed by members (or would have apart from any provision in its constitution authorising the refusal of those rights in particular cases): s 21J(1)(b) (as added: see note 3 supra).
12 Ibid s 21F(3)(a) (as added: see note 3 supra).
13 Ibid s 21F(3)(b) (as added: see note 3 supra).
14 Ibid s 21F(3)(c) (as added: see note 3 supra).
15 Ibid s 21F(3)(d) (as added: see note 3 supra).
16 Ibid s 21F(3)(e) (as added: see note 3 supra).
17 Ibid s 21F(4)(a) (as added: see note 3 supra).
18 Ibid s 21F(4)(b) (as added: see note 3 supra).
19 Ibid s 21F(4)(c) (as added: see note 3 supra).
20 References in ibid ss 21F–21H (as added) to a 'guest' of an association include a person who is a guest of the association by virtue of an invitation issued by a member or associate of the association and permitted by the association: s 21J(2) (as added: see note 3 supra). Regulations may make provision, for purposes of ss 21F–21H (as added), as to circumstances in which a person is to be treated as being, or as to circumstances in which a person is to be treated as not being, a guest of an association: s 21J(3) (as so added). For the meaning of 'regulations' see para 509 note 12 ante. At the date at which this volume states the law no such regulations had been made.
21 Ibid s 21F(4) (as added: see note 3 supra).
22 Ibid s 21F(5)(a) (as added: see note 3 supra).
23 Ibid s 21F(5)(b) (as added: see note 3 supra).
24 Ibid s 21F(5)(c) (as added: see note 3 supra).
25 'Prescribed' generally means prescribed by regulations: see para 515 note 5 ante. See note 26 infra.
26 Disability Discrimination Act 1995 s 21F(6) (as added: see note 3 supra). The reference is to a duty imposed on the association under s 21H (as added): see para 598 post. As to regulations made see the Disability Discrimination (Private Clubs etc) Regulations 2005, SI 2005/3258.
27 Ie discrimination by virtue of the Disability Discrimination Act 1995 s 55 (as amended): see para 526 ante.
28 Ie ibid s 21F (as added).
29 Ibid s 21F(7) (as added: see note 3 supra).

597.   Meaning of 'discrimination'.   For the purposes of the general provision on discrimination by private clubs[1], an association[2] discriminates against a disabled person[3] if: (1) for a reason which relates to the disabled person's disability, the association treats him less favourably than it treats or would treat others to whom that reason does not or would not apply[4]; and (2) it cannot show that the treatment in question is justified[5].

For the above purposes[6], treatment is justified only if: (a) in the opinion of the association, one or more of the specified conditions[7] are satisfied[8]; and (b) it is reasonable, in all the circumstances, for it to hold that opinion[9].

Regulations[10] may: (i) make provision[11] as to circumstances in which it is, or as to circumstances in which it is not, reasonable for an association to hold the opinion mentioned in head (a) above[12]; (ii) amend or omit a specified condition[13] or make provision for it not to apply in prescribed circumstances[14]; (iii) make provision as to circumstances[15] in which treatment is to be taken to be justified[16].

For the purposes of the general provision on discrimination by private clubs[17], an association also discriminates against a disabled person if: (A) it fails to comply with a duty to make adjustments[18] in relation to the disabled person[19]; and (B) it cannot show that its failure to comply with that duty is justified[20].

1   Ie for the purposes of the Disability Discrimination Act 1995 s 21F (as added): see para 596 ante.
2   As to associations see para 596 ante.
3   For the meaning of 'disabled person' see para 511 ante.
4   Disability Discrimination Act 1995 s 21G(1)(a) (s 21G added by the Disability Discrimination Act 2005 s 12).
5   Disability Discrimination Act 1995 s 21G(1)(b) (as added: see note 4 supra).
6   Ie for the purposes of ibid s 21G(1) (as added).
7   Ie the conditions mentioned in ibid s 21G(3) (as added). The conditions are that: (1) the treatment is necessary in order not to endanger the health or safety of any person (which may include that of the

disabled person); (2) the disabled person is incapable of entering into an enforceable agreement, or giving an informed consent, and for that reason the treatment is reasonable in that case; (3) in a case falling within s 21F(2)(a) (as added) (see para 596 text to note 9 ante), s 21F(3)(a) (as added) (see para 596 head (a) ante), s 21F(3)(c)(ii) (as added) (see para 596 head (c) ante), s 21F(3)(d)(ii) (as added) (see para 596 head (d) ante) or s 21F(3)(e) (as added) (see para 596 head (e) ante), s 21F(4)(a) (as added) (see para 596 head (i) ante), s 21F(4)(c) (as added) (see para 596 head (iii) ante) or 21F(5)(a) (as added) (see para 596 head (A) ante), the treatment is necessary in order for the association to be able to afford members, associates or guests of the association, or the disabled person, access to a benefit, facility or service; (4) in a case falling within s 21F(2)(b) (as added) (see para 596 text to note 10 ante), s 21F(3)(b) (as added) (see para 596 head (b) ante), s 21F(3)(c)(i) (as added) (see para 596 head (c) ante), s 21F(3)(d)(i) (as added) (see para 596 head (d) ante), s 21F(4)(b) (as added) (see para 596 head (ii) ante), s 21F(5)(b) (as added) (see para 596 head (B) ante) or s 21F(5)(c) (as added) (see para 596 head (C) ante), the treatment is necessary because the association would otherwise be unable to afford members, associates or guests of the association access to a benefit, facility or service; (5) in a case falling within s 21F(2)(a) (as added) (see para 596 text to note 9 ante), the difference between the terms on which membership is offered to the disabled person and those on which it is offered to other persons reflects the greater cost to the association of affording the disabled person access to a benefit, facility or service; (6) in a case falling within s 21F(3)(a) (as added) (see para 596 head (a) ante), s 21F(3)(c)(ii) (as added) (see para 596 head (c) ante), s 21F(3)(d)(ii) (as added) (see para 596 head (d) ante) or s 21F(4)(a) (as added) (see para 596 head (i) ante), the difference between the association's treatment of the disabled person and its treatment of other members or (as the case may be) other associates or other guests of the association reflects the greater cost to the association of affording the disabled person access to a benefit, facility or service; (7) in a case falling within s 21F(5)(a) (as added) (see para 596 head (A) ante), the difference between the terms on which the disabled person is invited, or permitted to be invited, to be a guest of the association and those on which other persons are invited, or permitted to be invited, to be guests of the association reflects the greater cost to the association of affording the disabled person access to a benefit, facility or service: s 21G(3) (as added: see note 4 supra). For the meaning of 'member' see para 596 note 3 ante. For the meaning of 'associate' see para 596 note 11 ante. For the meaning of 'guest' see para 596 note 20 ante.

Any increase in the cost of affording a disabled person access to a benefit, facility or service which results from compliance with a duty under s 21H (as added) (see para 598 post) must be disregarded for the purposes of s 21G(3)(e), (f) and (g) (as added) (see heads (5), (6), (7) supra): s 21G(4) (as so added).

9 Ibid s 21G(2)(b) (as added: see note 4 supra).
10 For the meaning of 'regulations' see para 509 note 12 ante. See note 12 infra.
11 Ie for the purposes of the Disability Discrimination Act 1995 s 21G (as added).
12 Ibid s 21G(5)(a) (as added: see note 4 supra). As to regulations under s 21G(5) (as added) and s 21G(7) (as added) (see note 19 infra) see the Disability Discrimination (Private Clubs etc) Regulations 2005, SI 2005/3258.
13 Ie a condition specified in the Disability Discrimination Act 1995 s 21G(3) (as added): see note 8 supra.
14 Ibid s 21G(5)(b) (as added: see note 4 supra). 'Prescribed' generally means prescribed by regulations: see para 515 note 5 ante. See also notes 12 supra, 19 infra.
15 Ie other than any for the time being mentioned in ibid s 21G(3) (as added): see note 8 supra.
16 Ibid s 21G(5)(c) (as added: see note 4 supra). The text refers to justification for the purposes of s 21G(1) (as added). See also notes 12 supra, 19 infra.
17 See note 1 supra.
18 Ie a duty imposed on it under the Disability Discrimination Act 1995 s 21H (as added): see para 598 post.
19 Ibid s 21G(6)(a) (as added: see note 4 supra). Regulations may make provision as to circumstances in which failure to comply with a duty under s 21H (as added) (see para 598 post) is to be taken to be justified for the purposes of s 21G(6) (as added): s 21G(7) (as so added). See note 12 supra.
20 Ibid s 21G(6)(b) (as added: see note 4 supra). See notes 12, 19 supra.

598. Duty of associations to make adjustments. Regulations[1] may make provision imposing on an association[2]: (1) a duty to take steps for a purpose relating to a policy, practice or procedure of the association, or a physical feature, which adversely affects disabled persons[3] who are, or might wish to become, members[4] or associates[5] of the association, or are, or are likely to become, guests[6] of the association[7]; (2) a duty to take steps for the purpose of making an auxiliary aid or service available to any such disabled persons[8].

Such regulations may in particular: (a) make provision as to the cases in which a duty is imposed[9]; (b) make provision as to the steps which a duty requires to be taken[10]; (c) make provision as to the purpose for which a duty requires steps to be taken[11].

Any duty imposed under these provisions[12] is imposed only for the purpose of determining whether an association has discriminated[13] against a disabled person; and accordingly a breach of any such duty is not actionable as such[14].

1   For the meaning of 'regulations' see para 509 note 12 ante. See note 7 infra.
2   Ie an association to which the Disability Discrimination Act 1995 s 21F (as added) applies: see para 596 ante.
3   For the meaning of 'disabled person' see para 511 ante.
4   For the meaning of 'member' see para 596 note 3 ante.
5   For the meaning of 'associate' see para 596 note 11 ante.
6   For the meaning of 'guest' see para 596 note 20 ante.
7   Disability Discrimination Act 1995 s 21H(1)(a) (s 21H added by the Disability Discrimination Act 2005 s 12). As to regulations made under the Disability Discrimination Act 1995 s 21H(1), (2) (as added) see the Disability Discrimination (Private Clubs etc) Regulations 2005, SI 2005/3258.
     If any question arises as to whether the occupier has failed to comply with a duty imposed under the Disability Discrimination Act 1995 s 21H (as added), by failing to make a particular alteration to premises, any constraint attributable to the fact that he occupies the premises under a lease is to be ignored unless he has applied to the lessor in writing for consent to the making of the alteration: see Sch 4 para 5 (as amended); and para 590 note 7 ante. As to reference to court in relation to such consent see Sch 4 para 6; and para 590 note 9 ante.
8   Ibid s 21H(1)(b) (as added: see note 7 supra). See head 7 supra.
9   Ibid s 21H(2)(a) (as added: see note 7 supra). See head 7 supra.
10   Ibid s 21H(2)(b) (as added: see note 7 supra). See head 7 supra.
11   Ibid s 21H(2)(c) (as added: see note 7 supra). See head 7 supra.
12   Ie imposed under ibid s 21H (as added).
13   Ie for the purposes of ibid s 21F (as added): see para 596 ante.
14   Ibid s 21H(3) (as added: see note 7 supra).

F. PREMISES AND HOUSING

(A) Discrimination in relation to Premises Generally

599. Discrimination in relation to premises. A person[1] ('A') discriminates against a disabled person[2] if: (1) for a reason which relates to the disabled person's disability[3], he treats him less favourably than he treats or would treat others to whom that reason does not or would not apply[4]; and (2) he cannot show that the treatment in question is justified[5].

Treatment is justified only if in A's opinion one or more of the following conditions are satisfied[6], and it is reasonable, in all the circumstances of the case, for him to hold that opinion[7]. The conditions are that: (a) in any case, the treatment is necessary in order not to endanger the health or safety of any person (which may include that of the disabled person)[8]; (b) in any case, the disabled person is incapable of entering into an enforceable agreement, or of giving an informed consent, and for that reason the treatment is reasonable in that case[9]; (c) in relation to the use of benefits or facilities[10], the treatment is necessary in order for the disabled person or the occupiers of other premises[11] forming part of the building to make use of the benefit or facility[12]; (d) if there has been a refusal or omission to permit a disabled person to use any benefits or facilities[13], the treatment is necessary in order for the occupiers of other premises forming part of the building to make use of the benefit or facility[14]; (e) in relation to the terms offered as to the disposal of any premises[15], the terms are less favourable in order to recover costs which, as a result of the disabled person having a disability, are incurred in connection with the disposal of the premises, and are not costs incurred in connection with taking steps to avoid liability[16]; or (f) in relation to any detriment suffered[17], the disabled person is subjected to the detriment in order to recover costs which, as a result of the disabled person having a disability, are incurred in connection with the management of the premises, and are not costs incurred in connection with taking steps to avoid liability[18].

Regulations may make provision as to additional circumstances in which treatment is to be taken to be justified[19].

1 As to the meaning of 'person' see para 344 note 3 ante.
2 Ie for the purposes of the Disability Discrimination Act 1995 s 22 (as amended) (see para 600 post) and s 22A (as added) (see para 601 post): see s 24(1) (amended by the Disability Discrimination Act 2005 s 19(1), Sch 1 paras 1, 19(1), (2)). For the meaning of 'disabled person' see para 511 ante.
3 As to when a person has a disability see para 511 ante.
4 Disability Discrimination Act 1995 s 24(1)(a). See *Williams v Richmond Court (Swansea) Ltd* [2006] EWCA Civ 1719, [2006] All ER (D) 218 (Dec) (a two-stage process is usually required in determining whether there has been discrimination: identify first the relevant act or omission, and second the relevant act or omission towards the relevant comparators; and managers are not under any positive obligation to make adjustments, in contrast to other provisions of the legislation).
5 Disability Discrimination Act 1995 s 24(1)(b).
6 Ibid s 24(2)(a). For the subjective part of the test, what is in issue is the honest opinion of the person carrying out the discriminatory act: *Rose v Bouchet* [1999] IRLR 463, Sh Ct. As to the application of the test in relation to secure and assured tenancies see *Manchester City Council v Romano, Manchester City Council v Samari* [2004] EWCA Civ 834, [2004] 4 All ER 21, [2005] 1 WLR 2775.
7 Disability Discrimination Act 1995 s 24(2)(b). Regulations may make provision as to circumstances in which it is or is not reasonable for a person to hold this opinion: see s 24(4). For the meaning of 'regulations' see para 509 note 12 ante. At the date at which this volume states the law no such regulations had been made. The opinion reached must be a reasonable one on the facts then known: *Rose v Bouchet* [1999] IRLR 463, Sh Ct. See also the Code of Practice on Rights of Access: services to the public, public authority functions, private clubs and premises (December 2006) paras 13.15, 13.16. As to codes of practice see para 655 post.
8 Disability Discrimination Act 1995 s 24(3)(a).
9 Ibid s 24(3)(b). Regulations may make provision for the condition specified in s 24(3)(b) not to apply in prescribed circumstances: s 24(4A) (added by the Disability Discrimination Act 2005 Sch 1 paras 1, 19(1), (5)). As to the regulations made see the Disability Discrimination (Premises) Regulations 2006, SI 2006/887.
10 Ie in a case falling within the Disability Discrimination Act 1995 s 22(3)(a): see para 600 post.
11 As to the meaning of 'premises' see para 525 note 9 ante.
12 Disability Discrimination Act 1995 s 24(3)(c).
13 Ie in a case falling within ibid s 22(3)(b): see para 600 post.
14 Ibid s 24(3)(d).
15 Ie in a case to which ibid s 24(3A) (as added) applies, i e if: (1) the case falls within s 22(1)(a) (see para 600 post); (2) the premises are to let; (3) the person with power to dispose of the premises is a controller of them; and (4) the proposed disposal of the premises would involve the disabled person becoming a person to whom they are let: s 24(3A) (s 24(3A)–(3C) added by the Disability Discrimination Act 2005 Sch 1 paras 1, 19(1), (4)). The provisions of the Disability Discrimination Act 1995 s 24G(3), (4) (as added) (see para 607 post) apply for the purposes of s 24(3A) (as added) as for those of s 24G (as added); and the provisions of s 24A(3), (4) (see para 604 post) apply for the purposes of s 24(3B) (as added) as for those of s 24A (as added): s 24(3C) (as so added).
16 Ibid s 24(1)(e) (s 24(1)(e), (f) added by the Disability Discrimination Act 2005 Sch 1 paras 1, 19(1), (3)). The text refers to liability under the Disability Discrimination Act 1995 s 24G(1) (as added): see para 607 post.
17 Ie in a case to which ibid s 24(3B) (as added) applies, i e if: (1) the case falls within s 22(3)(c) (see para 600 post); (2) the detriment is not eviction; (3) the premises are let premises; (4) the person managing the premises is a controller of them; and (5) the disabled person is a person to whom the premises are let or, although not a person to whom they are let, is lawfully under the letting an occupier of them: s 24(3B) (as added: see note 15 supra). See note 15 supra.
18 Ibid s 24(1)(f) (as added: see note 16 supra). The text refers to liability under s 24A(1) (as added) (see para 604 post) or s 24G(1) (as added) (see para 607 post).
19 Ibid s 24(5). As to regulations made see the Disability Discrimination (Premises) Regulations 2006, SI 2006/887. Where, for a reason which relates to the disabled person's disability, a person with power to dispose of any premises ('the provider') treats a disabled person less favourably than he treats or would treat others to whom that reason does not or would not apply, that treatment is to be taken to be justified for the purposes of the Disability Discrimination Act 1995 s 24 (as amended) in certain circumstances: Disability Discrimination (Premises) Regulations 2006, SI 2006/887, reg 3(1). The circumstances are

that: (1) the provider grants a disabled person a right to occupy premises (whether by means of a formal tenancy agreement or otherwise); (2) the disabled person is required to provide a deposit which is refundable at the end of the occupation provided that the premises and contents are not damaged; (3) the provider refuses to refund some or all of the deposit because the premises or contents have been damaged for a reason which relates to the disabled person's disability, and the damage is above the level at which the provider would normally refund the deposit in full; and (4) it is reasonable in all the circumstances of the case for the provider to refuse to refund the deposit in full: reg 3(2).

600.   Disposal and management of premises.   It is unlawful for a person[1] with power to dispose of any premises in the United Kingdom[2] to discriminate[3] against a disabled person[4]: (1) in the terms on which he offers to dispose[5] of those premises to the disabled person[6]; (2) by refusing to dispose of those premises to the disabled person[7]; or (3) in his treatment of the disabled person in relation to any list of persons in need of premises of that description[8].

This provision does not apply to a person who owns an estate or interest in the premises and wholly occupies them unless, for the purpose of disposing of the premises[9], he uses the services of an estate agent[10], or publishes an advertisement[11] or causes an advertisement to be published[12].

It is unlawful for a person managing any premises to discriminate against a disabled person occupying those premises[13]: (a) in the way he permits the disabled person to make use of any benefits or facilities[14]; (b) by refusing or deliberately omitting to permit the disabled person to make use of any benefits or facilities[15]; or (c) by evicting the disabled person or subjecting him to any other detriment[16].

It is unlawful for any person whose licence or consent is required for the disposal of any premises comprised in a tenancy, whenever created[17], to discriminate against a disabled person by withholding his licence or consent for the disposal of the premises to the disabled person[18].

In the case of an act[19] which constitutes discrimination by way of victimisation[20], the above provisions also apply to discrimination against a person who is not disabled[21].

1   As to the meaning of 'person' see para 344 note 3 ante.
2   As to the meaning of 'premises' see para 525 note 9 ante. Examples are dwelling-houses, office blocks, flats, bed-sits, factory premises, industrial or commercial sites, and agricultural land: see the Code of Practice on Rights of Access: services to the public, public authority functions, private clubs and premises (December 2006) para 14.10. As to codes of practice see para 655 post. The Disability Discrimination Act 1995 s 22 (as amended) applies only in relation to premises in the United Kingdom: s 22(8). For the meaning of 'United Kingdom' see para 325 note 6 ante.
3   As to discrimination in relation to premises see para 599 ante.
4   Disability Discrimination Act 1995 s 22(1). For the meaning of 'disabled person' see para 511 ante.
5   'Dispose', in relation to premises, includes granting a right to occupy the premises, and, in relation to premises comprised in a tenancy, includes: (1) assigning the tenancy; and (2) sub-letting or parting with possession of the premises or any part of the premises; and 'disposal' is to be construed accordingly: ibid s 22(6). See also the Code of Practice on Rights of Access: services to the public, public authority functions, private clubs and premises (December 2006) para 14.11. 'Tenancy' means a tenancy created: (a) by a lease or sub-lease; (b) by an agreement for a lease or sub-lease; (c) by a tenancy agreement; or (d) in pursuance of any enactment: Disability Discrimination Act 1995 s 22(6). As to the meaning of 'enactment' see para 510 note 4 ante. See *North Devon Homes Ltd v Brazier* [2003] EWHC 574 (QB), [2003] HLR 905.
6   Disability Discrimination Act 1995 s 22(1)(a). See also the Code of Practice on Rights of Access: services to the public, public authority functions, private clubs and premises (December 2006) para 14.14.
7   Disability Discrimination Act 1995 s 22(1)(b). See also the Code of Practice on Rights of Access: services to the public, public authority functions, private clubs and premises (December 2006) para 14.15.
8   Disability Discrimination Act 1995 s 22(1)(c). See also the Code of Practice on Rights of Access: services to the public, public authority functions, private clubs and premises (December 2006) para 14.16.
9   Disability Discrimination Act 1995 s 22(2).
10   Ibid s 22(2)(a). 'Estate agent' means a person who, by way of profession or trade, provides services for the purpose of finding premises for persons seeking to acquire them or assisting in the disposal of premises: s 22(6). This also includes letting agents: see the Code of Practice on Rights of Access: services to the

public, public authority functions, private clubs and premises (December 2006) para 14.13. As to the meanings of 'profession' and 'trade' see para 541 note 1 ante. As to estate agents see AGENCY vol 2(1) (Reissue) para 14 et seq.

11　'Advertisement' includes every form of advertisement or notice, whether to the public or not: Disability Discrimination Act 1995 s 22(6).

12　Ibid s 22(2)(b).

13　Ibid s 22(3). See also the Code of Practice on Rights of Access: services to the public, public authority functions, private clubs and premises (December 2006) para 14.17 et seq.

14　Disability Discrimination Act 1995 s 22(3)(a). See note 16 infra. See also the Code of Practice on Rights of Access: services to the public, public authority functions, private clubs and premises (December 2006) para 14.20. See *Williams v Richmond Court (Swansea) Ltd* [2006] EWCA Civ 1719, [2006] All ER (D) 218 (Dec); and para 599 note 4 ante.

15　Disability Discrimination Act 1995 s 22(3)(b). See note 16 infra. See also the Code of Practice on Rights of Access: services to the public, public authority functions, private clubs and premises (December 2006) para 14.20.

16　Disability Discrimination Act 1995 s 22(3)(c). For purposes of s 22(3), regulations may make provision: (1) as to who is to be treated as being, or as to who is to be treated as not being, a person who manages premises; and (2) as to who is to be treated as being, or as to who is to be treated as not being, a person occupying premises: s 22(3A) (added by the Disability Discrimination Act 2005 s 19(1), Sch 1 paras 1, 16). For the meaning of 'regulations' see para 509 note 12 ante. as to the regulations made see the Disability Discrimination (Premises) Regulations 2006, SI 2006/887.

　　'Any other detriment' means only that the disabled person has been put at a disadvantage in some way: *Kirby v Manpower Services Commission* [1980] 3 All ER 334, [1980] 1 WLR 725, EAT. See also *BL Cars Ltd v Brown* [1983] ICR 143, [1983] IRLR 193, EAT. However, it is not just any disadvantage; it must be something serious or important: *Ministry of Defence v Jeremiah* [1980] QB 87, [1979] 3 All ER 833, CA; *Schmidt v Austicks Bookshops Ltd* [1978] ICR 85, [1977] IRLR 360, EAT (following *Peake v Automotive Products Ltd* [1978] QB 233, [1978] 1 All ER 106, CA). Harassment can constitute a detriment (*Wileman v Minilec Engineering Ltd* [1988] ICR 318, [1988] IRLR 144), and an objectionable discriminatory remark may constitute a detriment even if made to people other than the complainant (*Hereford and Worcester County Council v Clayton* (1996) Times, 8 October, EAT), but there must be circumstances in which the complainant was intended or reasonably expected to hear the remark (*De Souza v Automobile Association* [1986] ICR 514, [1986] IRLR 103, CA).

17　See the Disability Discrimination Act 1995 s 22(5).

18　Ibid s 22(4). See also the Code of Practice on Rights of Access: services to the public, public authority functions, private clubs and premises (December 2006) para 14.23.

19　As to the meaning of 'act' see para 510 note 3 ante.

20　Ie by virtue of the Disability Discrimination Act 1995 s 55 (as amended): see para 526 ante.

21　Ibid s 22(7).

601.　Discrimination in regard to commonholds.　It is unlawful for any person[1] whose licence or consent is required for the disposal[2] of an interest in a commonhold unit[3] by the unit-holder[4] to discriminate[5] against a disabled person[6] by withholding his licence or consent for the disposal of the interest in favour of, or to, the disabled person[7].

Where it is not possible for an interest in a commonhold unit to be disposed of by the unit-holder unless some other person is a party to the disposal of the interest, it is unlawful for that other person to discriminate against a disabled person by deliberately not being a party to the disposal of the interest in favour of, or to, the disabled person[8].

In the case of an act[9] which constitutes discrimination by victimisation[10], the above provisions[11] also apply to discrimination against a person who is not disabled[12].

1　As to the meaning of 'person' see para 344 note 3 ante.

2　Regulations may make provision, for purposes of the Disability Discrimination Act 1995 s 22A (as added): (1) as to what is, or as to what is not, to be included within the meaning of 'dispose' (and 'disposal'); (2) as to what is, or as to what is not, to be included within the meaning of 'interest in a commonhold unit': s 22A(4) (s 22A added by the Disability Discrimination Act 2005 s 19(1), Sch 1 paras 1, 17). For the meaning of 'regulations' see para 509 note 12 ante. See also note 7 infra. As to regulations made under the Disability Discrimination Act 1995 s 22A(4) (as added) see the Disability Discrimination (Premises) Regulations 2006, SI 2006/887. See also the Code of Practice on Rights of

Access: services to the public, public authority functions, private clubs and premises (December 2006) para 16.6 et seq. As to codes of practice see para 655 post.

3 'Commonhold unit', and 'unit-holder' in relation to such a unit, have the same meaning as in the Commonhold and Leasehold Reform Act 2002 Pt 1 (ss 1–70) (see COMMONHOLD vol 7(1) (2004 Reissue) para 1 et seq): Disability Discrimination Act 1995 s 22A(5) (as added: see note 2 supra).

4 See note 3 supra.

5 As to discrimination generally see paras 599–600 ante.

6 For the meaning of 'disabled person' see para 511 ante.

7 Disability Discrimination Act 1995 s 22A(1), (7) (as added: see note 2 supra). Regulations may provide for s 22A(1) or (2) (as added) not to apply, or to apply only, in cases of a prescribed description: s 22A(3) (as so added). 'Prescribed' generally means prescribed by regulations: see para 515 note 5 ante. See note 2 supra.

8 Ibid s 22A(2) (as added: see note 2 supra). See note 2 supra.

9 As to the meaning of 'act' see para 510 note 3 ante.

10 Ie discrimination by virtue of the Disability Discrimination Act 1995 s 55 (as amended): see para 526 ante.

11 Ie ibid s 22A (as added).

12 Ibid s 22A(6) (as added: see note 2 supra).

602. Exceptions to discrimination in the provision of premises. The provisions relating to discrimination in the disposal and management of premises[1] do not apply if the following conditions are satisfied[2]: (1) the relevant occupier[3] resides, and intends to continue to reside, on the premises[4]; (2) the relevant occupier shares accommodation on the premises with persons who reside on the premises and are not members of his household[5]; (3) the shared accommodation is not storage accommodation or a means of access[6]; and (4) the premises are small premises[7].

Premises are small premises if they satisfy the following requirements[8]:

(a) only the relevant occupier and members of his household reside in the accommodation occupied by him[9];

(b) the premises comprise, in addition to the accommodation occupied by the relevant occupier, residential accommodation for at least one other household[10];

(c) the residential accommodation for each other household is let, or available for letting, on a separate tenancy or similar agreement[11]; and

(d) there are not normally more than two such other households[12].

Premises are also small premises if there is not normally residential accommodation on the premises for more than six persons in addition to the relevant occupier and any members of his household[13].

1 Ie the Disability Discrimination Act 1995 s 22(1), (3), (4): see para 600 ante. As to the meaning of 'premises' see para 525 note 9 ante.

2 See ibid s 23(1).

3 'The relevant occupier' means: (1) in a case falling within ibid s 22(1) (see para 600 ante), the person with power to dispose of the premises, or a near relative of his; (2) in a case falling within s 22(3) (see para 600 ante), the person managing the premises, or a near relative of his; and (3) in a case falling within s 22(4) (see para 600 ante), the person whose licence or consent is required for the disposal of the premises, or a near relative of his: s 23(6) (amended by the Disability Discrimination Act 2005 s 19(1), Sch 1 paras 1, 18). 'Near relative' means a person's spouse or civil partner, partner, parent, child, grandparent, grandchild, or brother or sister (whether of full or half blood or by marriage or civil partnership); and 'partner' means the other member of a couple consisting of: (a) a man and a woman who are not married to each other but are living together as husband and wife; or (b) two people of the same sex who are not civil partners of each other but are living together as if they were civil partners: Disability Discrimination Act 1995 s 23(7) (amended by the Civil Partnership Act 2004 s 261(1), Sch 27 para 150). As to civil partnerships generally see MATRIMONIAL LAW.

4 Disability Discrimination Act 1995 s 23(2)(a).

5 Ibid s 23(2)(b).

6 Ibid s 23(2)(c). See the Code of Practice on Rights of Access: services to the public, public authority functions, private clubs and premises (December 2006) para 17.6. As to codes of practice see para 655 post.

7 Disability Discrimination Act 1995 s 23(2)(d). See also the Code of Practice on Rights of Access: services to the public, public authority functions, private clubs and premises (December 2006) para 17.8 et seq.
8 See the Disability Discrimination Act 1995 s 23(3).
9 Ibid s 23(4)(a).
10 Ibid s 23(4)(b).
11 Ibid s 23(4)(c).
12 Ibid s 23(4)(d).
13 Ibid s 23(5).

603. Non-application of provisions relating to premises generally. The provisions relating to premises generally[1] do not apply: (1) in relation to the provision of premises[2] by a provider of services[3] where he provides the premises in providing services[4] to members of the public[5]; (2) in relation to the provision, in the course of a Part II relationship[6], of premises by the regulated party[7] to the other party[8]; (3) in relation to the provision of premises to a student[9] or prospective student by a responsible body[10] or by a local education authority[11]; or (4) to anything which is unlawful under the provision on discrimination by private clubs and related associations[12] or which would be unlawful under that provision but for the operation of any provision in or made under the Disability Discrimination Act 1995[13].

1 Ie the Disability Discrimination Act 1995 ss 22–24L (as amended): see paras 599–602 ante, 604–610 post.
2 As to the meaning of 'premises' see para 525 note 9 ante.
3 For the meaning of 'provider of services' see para 584 ante; definition applied by the Disability Discrimination Act 1995 s 24M(3) (s 24M added by the Disability Discrimination Act 2005 s 19(1), Sch 1 paras 1, 20).
4 See note 3 supra.
5 Disability Discrimination Act 1995 s 24M(1)(a) (as added: see note 3 supra). Section 24M(1)(a) (as added) has effect subject to any prescribed exceptions: s 24M(2) (as so added). 'Prescribed' generally means prescribed by regulations: see para 515 note 5 ante. At the date at which this volume states the law no regulations had been made prescribing exceptions.
6 For the purposes of ibid s 24M(1)(b) (as added): (1) 'Part II relationship' means a relationship during the course of which an act of discrimination against, or harassment of, one party to the relationship by the other party to it is unlawful under ss 4–15C (as amended); and (2) in relation to a Part II relationship, 'regulated party' means the party whose acts of discrimination, or harassment, are made unlawful by ss 4–15C (as amended): s 24M(4) (as added: see note 3 supra). For the meaning of 'harassment' see para 533 ante.
7 See note 6 supra.
8 Disability Discrimination Act 1995 s 24M(1)(b) (as added: see note 3 supra).
9 'Student' includes pupil: ibid s 24M(5) (as added: see note 3 supra).
10 Ie a responsible body within the meaning of ibid Pt IV Ch I (ss 28A–28Q) (as added and amended) (see para 561 et seq ante).
11 Ibid s 24M(1)(c) (as added: see note 3 supra). The reference to a local education authority is a reference to an authority discharging any functions mentioned in s 28F(1) (as added): see para 565 ante.
12 Ie unlawful under ibid s 21F (as added): see para 596 ante.
13 Ibid s 24M(1)(d) (as added: see note 3 supra).

(B) Discrimination in relation to Let Premises and Premises to Let

604. Discrimination in relation to let premises. It is unlawful in the United Kingdom[1] for a controller[2] of let[3] premises to discriminate against a disabled person[4]: (1) who is a person[5] to whom the premises are let[6]; or (2) who, although not a person to whom the premises are let, is lawfully under the letting an occupier of the premises[7]. There are a number of exceptions to the application of this provision[8].

For the above purposes[9], a controller of let premises also discriminates against a disabled person if: (a) he fails to comply with a relevant duty[10] imposed on him by reference to the disabled person[11]; and (b) he cannot show that failure to comply with the duty is justified[12].

1 For the meaning of 'United Kingdom' see para 325 note 6 ante.

2   For the purposes of the Disability Discrimination Act 1995 ss 24A–24F (as added), a person is a controller of let premises if he is: (1) a person by whom the premises are let; or (2) a person who manages the premises: s 24A(3) (ss 24A, 24B added by the Disability Discrimination Act 2005 s 13). For the purposes of the Disability Discrimination Act 1995 ss 24A–24F (as added): (a) 'let' includes sub-let; and (b) premises are treated as let by a person to another where a person has granted another a contractual licence to occupy them: s 24A(4) (as so added). As to the meaning of 'premises' see para 525 note 9 ante.

3   See note 2 supra.

4   Disability Discrimination Act 1995 s 24A(1), (5) (as added: see note 2 supra). For the meaning of 'disabled person' see para 511 ante. See note 8 infra.

5   As to the meaning of 'person' see para 344 note 3 ante.

6   Disability Discrimination Act 1995 s 24A(1)(a) (as added: see note 2 supra). See note 8 infra.

7   Ibid s 24A(1)(b) (as added: see note 2 supra). See note 8 infra.

8   Ibid s 24A(1) (as added) does not apply:
    (1)   if (a) the premises are, or have at any time been, the only or principal home of an individual who is a person by whom they are let; and (b) since entering into the letting the individual has not, and where he is not the sole person by whom the premises are let, no other person by whom they are let has, used for the purpose of managing the premises the services of a person who, by profession or trade, manages let premises (s 24B(1) (as added: see note 2 supra));
    (2)   if the premises are of a prescribed description (s 24B(2) (as so added));
    (3)   where the conditions mentioned in s 23(2) (see para 602 ante) are satisfied (s 24B(3) (as so added)).
    For the purposes of s 23 (as amended), 'the relevant occupier' means, in a case falling within s 24A(1) (as added), a controller of the let premises, or a near relative of his: s 24B(2) (as so added). For the meaning of 'near relative' see para 602 note 3 ante; definition applied by s 24B(4) (as so added). As to the meanings of 'profession' and 'trade' see para 541 note 1 ante. 'Prescribed' generally means prescribed by regulations: see para 515 note 5 ante. At the date at which this volume states the law no regulations had been made under s 24B(2) (as added).

9   Ie for the purposes of ibid s 24A(1) (as added).

10   Ie a duty under ibid s 24C (as added) or s 24D (as added): see para 605 post.

11   Ibid s 24A(2)(a) (as added: see note 2 supra).

12   Ibid s 24A(2)(b) (as added: see note 2 supra). As to justification see s 24K (as added); and para 609 post.

605.   Duties in relation to let premises. Where (1) a controller[1] of let[2] premises[3] receives a request made by or on behalf of a person[4] to whom the premises are let[5]; (2) it is reasonable to regard the request as a request that the controller take steps in order to provide an auxiliary aid or service[6]; and (3) either the first condition[7] or the second condition[8] is satisfied[9], it is the duty of the controller to take such steps as it is reasonable, in all the circumstances of the case, for him to have to take in order to provide the auxiliary aid or service[10].

Where (a) a controller of let premises has a practice, policy or procedure which has the effect of making it impossible, or unreasonably difficult, for a relevant disabled person to enjoy the premises, or to make use of any benefit or facility, which by reason of the letting is one of which he is entitled to make use[11]; or (b) a term of the letting has that effect[12], and (in either case) certain conditions[13] are satisfied[14], it is the duty of the controller to take such steps as it is reasonable, in all the circumstances of the case, for him to have to take in order to change the practice, policy, procedure or term so as to stop it having that effect[15].

The above provisions[16] impose duties only for the purpose of determining whether a person has discriminated[17] against another; and accordingly a breach of any such duty is not actionable as such[18].

1   For the meaning of 'controller of let premises' see para 604 note 2 ante. See also notes 2, 3 infra.

2   For the meaning of 'let' see para 604 note 2 ante.

3   As to the meaning of 'premises' see para 525 note 9 ante.

4   As to the meaning of 'person' see para 344 note 3 ante.

5   Disability Discrimination Act 1995 s 24C(1)(a) (ss 24C–24E added by the Disability Discrimination Act 2005 s 13).

For the purposes of the Disability Discrimination Act 1995 ss 24C, 24D (as added), the terms of a letting of premises include the terms of any agreement which relates to the letting of the premises: s 24E(4) (as so added).

6   Ibid s 24C(1)(b) (as added: see note 5 supra).
7   The first condition is that: (1) the auxiliary aid or service: (a) would enable a relevant disabled person to enjoy, or facilitate such a person's enjoyment of, the premises; but (b) would be of little or no practical use to the relevant disabled person concerned if he were neither a person to whom the premises are let nor an occupier of them; and (2) it would, were the auxiliary aid or service not to be provided, be impossible or unreasonably difficult for the relevant disabled person concerned to enjoy the premises: ibid s 24C(3) (as added: see note 5 supra). In ss 24C, 24D (as added), 'relevant disabled person', in relation to let premises, means a particular disabled person: (i) who is a person to whom the premises are let; or (ii) who, although not a person to whom the premises are let, is lawfully under the letting an occupier of the premises: s 24E(3) (as so added). For the meaning of 'disabled person' see para 511 ante.
8   The second condition is that: (1) the auxiliary aid or service: (a) would enable a relevant disabled person to make use, or facilitate such a person's making use, of any benefit or facility, which by reason of the letting is one of which he is entitled to make use; but (b) would be of little or no practical use to the relevant disabled person concerned if he were neither a person to whom the premises are let nor an occupier of them; and (2) it would, were the auxiliary aid or service not to be provided, be impossible or unreasonably difficult for the relevant disabled person concerned to make use of any benefit, or facility, which by reason of the letting is one of which he is entitled to make use: ibid s 24C(4) (as added: see note 5 supra).
10   Ibid s 24C(2) (as added: see note 5 supra). For the purposes of ss 24C, 24D (as added), it is never reasonable for a controller of let premises to have to take steps consisting of, or including, the removal or alteration of a physical feature: s 24E(1) (as so added).
11   Ibid s 24D(1)(a) (as added: see note 5 supra).
12   Ibid s 24D(1)(b) (as added: see note 5 supra).
13   Ie the conditions specified in ibid s 24D(2) (as added). The conditions are: (1) that the practice, policy, procedure or term would not have that effect if the relevant disabled person concerned did not have a disability; (2) that the controller receives a request made by or on behalf of a person to whom the premises are let; and (3) that it is reasonable to regard the request as a request that the controller take steps in order to change the practice, policy, procedure or term so as to stop it having that effect: s 24D(2) (as added: see note 5 supra).
14   Ibid s 24D(1) (as added: see note 5 supra).
15   Ibid s 24D(3) (as added: see note 5 supra). See also s 24E(1) (as added); and note 10 supra.
16   Ie ibid ss 24C, 24D (as added).
17   Ie for the purposes of ibid s 24A (as added): see para 604 ante.
18   Ibid s 24E(2) (as added: see note 5 supra).

606.   Victimisation of persons to whom premises are let.

Where a relevant duty[1] is imposed on a controller[2] of let[3] premises[4] by reference to a person[5] who, although not a person to whom the premises are let, is lawfully under the letting an occupier of the premises, it is unlawful for a controller of the let premises to discriminate against a person to whom the premises are let[6].

For the above purposes[7], a controller of the let premises discriminates against a person to whom the premises are let if: (1) the controller treats that person ('T') less favourably than he treats or would treat other persons whose circumstances are the same as T's[8]; and (2) he does so because of costs incurred in connection with taking steps to avoid liability[9] for failure to comply with the duty[10].

1   Ie a duty under the Disability Discrimination Act 1995 s 24C (as added) or s 24D (as added): see para 605 ante.
2   For the meaning of 'controller of let premises' see para 604 note 2 ante. See also notes 3, 4 infra.
3   For the meaning of 'let' see para 604 note 2 ante.
4   As to the meaning of 'premises' see para 525 note 9 ante.
5   As to the meaning of 'person' see para 344 note 3 ante.
6   Disability Discrimination Act 1995 s 24F(1) (s 24F added by the Disability Discrimination Act 2005 s 13).
7   Ie for the purposes of ibid s 24F(1) (as added).
8   Ibid s 24F(2)(a) (as added: see note 6 supra). In comparing T's circumstances with those of any other person for the purposes of s 24F(2)(a) (as added), the following (as well as the costs having been incurred) are to be disregarded: (1) the making of the request that gave rise to the imposition of the duty; and (2) the disability of each person who: (a) is a disabled person or a person who has had a disability; and (b) is

a person to whom the premises are let or, although not a person to whom the premises are let, is lawfully under the letting an occupier of the premises: s 24F(3) (as so added).

9 Ie liability under ibid s 24A(1) (as added): see para 604 ante.

10 Ibid s 24F(2)(b) (as added: see note 6 supra).

607. Discrimination in relation to premises that are to let. Where in the United Kingdom[1]: (1) a person[2] has premises[3] to let[4]; and (2) a disabled person[5] is considering taking a letting of the premises[6], it is unlawful for a controller[7] of the premises to discriminate against the disabled person[8]. There are exceptions to the application of this provision[9].

For these purposes[10], a controller of premises that are to let discriminates against a disabled person if: (a) he fails to comply with a relevant duty[11] imposed on him by reference to the disabled person[12]; and (b) he cannot show that failure to comply with the duty is justified[13].

1 For the meaning of 'United Kingdom' see para 325 note 6 ante.

2 As to the meaning of 'person' see para 344 note 3 ante.

3 As to the meaning of 'premises' see para 525 note 9 ante.

4 Disability Discrimination Act 1995 s 24G(1)(a), (5) (ss 24G, 24H added by the Disability Discrimination Act 2005 s 13). For the purposes of the Disability Discrimination Act 1995 ss 24G, 24H, 24J (as added): (1) 'let' includes sub-let; (2) premises are treated as to let by a person to another where a person proposes to grant another a contractual licence to occupy them; and references to a person considering taking a letting of premises are to be construed accordingly: s 24G(4) (as so added). See note 9 infra.

5 For the meaning of 'disabled person' see para 511 ante.

6 Disability Discrimination Act 1995 s 24G(1)(b) (as added: see note 4 supra). See note 9 infra.

7 For the purposes of ibid s 24G, 24H, 24J (as added), a person is a controller of premises that are to let if he is: (1) a person who has the premises to let; or (2) a person who manages the premises: s 24G(3) (as added: see note 4 supra).

8 Ibid s 24G(1) (as added: see note 4 supra). See note 9 infra.

9 Ibid s 24G(1) (as added) does not apply:
   (1) in relation to premises that are to let, if the premises are, or have at any time been, the only or principal home of an individual who is a person who has them to let and: (a) the individual does not use; and (b) where he is not the sole person who has the premises to let, no other person who has the premises to let uses, the services of an estate agent (within the meaning given by s 22(6): see para 600 note 10 ante) for the purposes of letting the premises (s 24H(1) (as added: see note 4 supra));
   (2) if the premises are of a prescribed description (s 24H(2) (as so added));
   (3) where the conditions mentioned in s 23(2) (see para 602 ante) are satisfied (s 24H(3) (as so added)).
   For the purposes of s 23 (as amended), 'the relevant occupier' means, in a case falling within s 24G(1) (as added) (see the text and notes 1–9 supra), a controller of the premises that are to let, or a near relative of his; and 'near relative' has the same meaning as in s 23 (as amended) (see para 602 note 3 ante): s 24H(4) (as so added). 'Prescribed' generally means prescribed by regulations: see para 515 note 5 ante. At the date at which this volume states the law no regulations had been made under s 24H(2) (as added) (see head (2) supra).

10 Ie for the purposes of ibid s 24G(1) (as added): see the text and notes 1–9 supra.

11 Ie a duty under ibid s 24J (as added): see para 608 post.

12 Ibid s 24G(2)(a) (as added: see note 4 supra).

13 Ibid s 24G(2)(b) (as added: see note 4 supra). As to justification see s 24K (as added); and para 609 post.

608. Duties in relation to premises to let. Where (1) a controller[1] of premises[2] that are to let[3] receives a request made by or on behalf of a relevant disabled person[4]; (2) it is reasonable to regard the request as a request that the controller take steps in order to provide an auxiliary aid or service[5]; (3) the auxiliary aid or service would enable the relevant disabled person to become, or facilitate his becoming, a person to whom the premises are let, but would be of little or no practical use to him if he were not considering taking a letting of the premises[6]; and (4) it would, were the auxiliary aid or service not to be provided, be impossible or unreasonably difficult for the relevant disabled person to become a person to whom the premises are let[7], it is the duty of the controller to take such steps as it is reasonable, in all the circumstances of the case, for the controller to have to take in order to provide the auxiliary aid or service[8].

Where (a) a controller of premises that are to let has a practice, policy or procedure which has the effect of making it impossible, or unreasonably difficult, for a relevant disabled person to become a person to whom the premises are let[9]; (b) the practice, policy or procedure would not have that effect if the relevant disabled person did not have a disability[10]; (c) the controller receives a request made by or on behalf of the relevant disabled person[11]; and (d) it is reasonable to regard the request as a request that the controller take steps in order to change the practice, policy or procedure so as to stop it having that effect[12], it is the duty of the controller to take such steps as it is reasonable, in all the circumstances of the case, for him to have to take in order to change the practice, policy or procedure so as to stop it having that effect[13].

The above provisions[14] impose duties only for the purpose of determining whether a person has discriminated[15] against another; and accordingly a breach of any such duty is not actionable as such[16].

1   For the meaning of 'controller of let premises' see para 607 note 7 ante. See notes 2, 3 infra.
2   As to the meaning of 'premises' see para 525 note 9 ante.
3   For the meaning of 'let' see para 607 note 4 ante.
4   Disability Discrimination Act 1995 s 24J(1)(a) (s 24J added by the Disability Discrimination Act 2005 s 13). 'Relevant disabled person', in relation to premises that are to let, means a particular disabled person who is considering taking a letting of the premises: Disability Discrimination Act 1995 s 24J(6) (as so added). For the meaning of 'disabled person' see para 511 ante.
5   Ibid s 24J(1)(b) (as added: see note 4 supra).
6   Ibid s 24J(1)(c) (as added: see note 4 supra).
7   Ibid s 24J(1)(d) (as added: see note 4 supra).
8   Ibid s 24J(2) (as added: see note 4 supra). For the purposes of s 24J (as added), it is never reasonable for a controller of premises that are to let to have to take steps consisting of, or including, the removal or alteration of a physical feature: s 24J(5) (as so added).
9   Ibid s 24J(3)(a) (as added: see note 4 supra).
10   Ibid s 24J(3)(b) (as added: see note 4 supra).
11   Ibid s 24J(3)(c) (as added: see note 4 supra).
12   Ibid s 24J(3)(d) (as added: see note 4 supra).
13   Ibid s 24J(4) (as added: see note 4 supra). See also s 24J(5) (as added); and note 8 supra.
14   Ie ibid s 24J (as added).
15   Ie for the purposes of ibid s 24G (as added): see para 607 ante.
16   Ibid s 24J(7) (as added: see note 4 supra).

609. Justification in regard to let premises and premises to let. For the purposes of the provisions on discrimination in both let premises and premises to let[1], a person's[2] failure to comply with a duty is justified only if: (1) in his opinion, a condition mentioned below is satisfied[3]; and (2) it is reasonable, in all the circumstances of the case, for him to hold that opinion[4].

The conditions referred to above are: (a) that it is necessary to refrain from complying with the duty in order not to endanger the health or safety of any person (which may include that of the disabled person[5] concerned)[6]; (b) that the disabled person concerned is incapable of entering into an enforceable agreement, or of giving informed consent, and for that reason the failure is reasonable[7].

Regulations[8] may: (i) make provision[9] as to circumstances in which it is, or as to circumstances in which it is not, reasonable for a person to hold the opinion mentioned in head (1) above[10]; (ii) amend or omit a condition specified in heads (a) and (b) above or make provision for it not to apply in prescribed[11] circumstances[12]; (iii) make provision[13] as to circumstances (other than any for the time being mentioned in heads (a) and (b) above) in which a failure is to be taken to be justified[14].

1   Ie for the purposes of the Disability Discrimination Act 1995 s 24A(2) (as added) (see para 604 ante) and s 24G(2) (as added) (se para 607 ante).
2   As to the meaning of 'person' see para 344 note 3 ante.
3   Disability Discrimination Act 1995 s 24K(1)(a) (s 24K added by the Disability Discrimination Act 2005 s 13).
4   Disability Discrimination Act 1995 s 24K(1)(b) (as added: see note 3 supra).
5   For the meaning of 'disabled person' see para 511 ante.
6   Disability Discrimination Act 1995 s 24K(2)(a) (as added: see note 3 supra).
7   Ibid s 24K(2)(b) (as added: see note 3 supra).
8   For the meaning of 'regulations' see para 509 note 12 ante. See note 10 infra.
9   Ie for purposes of the Disability Discrimination Act 1995 s 24K (as added).
10 Ibid s 24K(3)(a) (as added: see note 3 supra). As to regulations made under s 24K(3) (as added) see the Disability Discrimination (Premises) Regulations 2006, SI 2006/887.
11 'Prescribed' generally means prescribed by regulations: see para 515 note 5 ante.
12 Disability Discrimination Act 1995 s 24K(3)(b) (as added: see note 3 supra). See note 10 supra.
13 See note 9 supra.
14 Disability Discrimination Act 1995 s 24K(3)(c) (as added: see note 3 supra). See note 10 supra.

610.   Power to make supplementary provision in regard to let premises and premises to let. Regulations[1] may make provision, for purposes of the provisions on discrimination in regard to let premises and premises to let[2]: (1) as to circumstances in which premises[3] are to be treated as let to a person[4]; (2) as to circumstances in which premises are to be treated as not let to a person[5]; (3) as to circumstances in which premises are to be treated as being, or as not being, to let[6]; (4) as to who is to be treated as being, or as to who is to be treated as not being, a person who, although not a person to whom let premises are let, is lawfully under the letting an occupier of the premises[7]; (5) as to who is to be treated as being, or as to who is to be treated as not being, a person by whom premises are let[8]; (6) as to who is to be treated as having, or as to who is to be treated as not having, premises to let[9]; (7) as to who is to be treated as being, or as to who is to be treated as not being, a person who manages premises[10]; (8) as to things which are, or as to things which are not, to be treated as auxiliary aids or services[11]; (9) as to what is, or as to what is not, to be included within the meaning of 'practice, policy or procedure'[12]; (10) as to circumstances in which it is, or as to circumstances in which it is not, reasonable for a person to have to take steps of a prescribed[13] description[14]; (11) as to steps which it is always, or as to steps which it is never, reasonable for a person to have to take[15]; (12) as to circumstances in which it is, or as to circumstances in which it is not, reasonable to regard a request as being of a particular kind[16]; (13) as to things which are, or as to things which are not, to be treated as physical features[17]; (14) as to things which are, or as to things which are not, to be treated as alterations of physical features[18].

1   For the meaning of 'regulations' see para 509 note 12 ante. See note 4 infra.
2   Ie for purposes of the Disability Discrimination Act 1995 s 24(3A), (3B) (as added) (see para 599 ante) and ss 24A–24K (as added) (see paras 604–609 ante).
3   As to the meaning of 'premises' see para 525 note 9 ante.
4   Disability Discrimination Act 1995 s 24L(1)(a) (s 24L added by the Disability Discrimination Act 2005 s 13). As to the meaning of 'person' see para 344 note 3 ante.
    Regulations under the Disability Discrimination Act 1995 s 24L(1)(a) (as added) may (in particular) provide for premises to be treated as let to a person where they are a commonhold unit of which he is a unit-holder; and 'commonhold unit', and 'unit-holder' in relation to such a unit, have the same meaning as in the Commonhold and Leasehold Reform Act 2002 Pt 1 (ss 1–70) (see COMMONHOLD vol 7(1) (2004 Reissue) para 1 et seq): Disability Discrimination Act 1995 s 24L(2) (as so added).
    As to regulations made under s 24L(1), (2) (as added) see the Disability Discrimination (Premises) Regulations 2006, SI 2006/887.
5   Disability Discrimination Act 1995 s 24L(1)(b) (as added: see note 4 supra). See note 4 supra.
6   Ibid s 24L(1)(c) (as added: see note 4 supra). See note 4 supra.
7   Ibid s 24L(1)(d) (as added: see note 4 supra). See note 4 supra.
8   Ibid s 24L(1)(e) (as added: see note 4 supra). See note 4 supra.

9   Ibid s 24L(1)(f) (as added: see note 4 supra). See note 4 supra.
10 Ibid s 24L(1)(g) (as added: see note 4 supra). See note 4 supra.
11 Ibid s 24L(1)(h) (as added: see note 4 supra). See note 4 supra.
12 Ibid s 24L(1)(i) (as added: see note 4 supra). See note 4 supra.
13 'Prescribed' generally means prescribed by regulations: see para 515 note 5 ante. See note 4 supra.
14 Disability Discrimination Act 1995 s 24L(1)(j) (as added: see note 4 supra). See note 4 supra.
      The powers under s 24L(1)(j), (k) (as added) are subject to s 24E(1) (as added) (see para 605 ante) and s 24J(5) (as added) (see para 608 ante): s 24L(3) (as so added).
15 Ibid s 24L(1)(k) (as added: see note 4 supra). See notes 4, 14 supra.
16 Ibid s 24L(1)(l) (as added: see note 4 supra). See note 4 supra.
17 Ibid s 24L(1)(m) (as added: see note 4 supra). See note 4 supra.
18 Ibid s 24L(1)(n) (as added: see note 4 supra). See note 4 supra.

(C) Improvements to Let Dwelling Houses

611. Consent of landlord to improvements. In relation to a lease[1] of a dwelling house, if: (1) the tenancy is not a protected tenancy[2], a statutory tenancy[3] or a secure tenancy[4]; (2) the tenant[5] or any other person[6] who lawfully occupies or is intended lawfully to occupy the premises[7] is a disabled person[8]; (3) the person mentioned in head (2) above occupies or is intended to occupy the premises as his only or principal home[9]; (4) the tenant is entitled under the lease to make improvements[10] to the premises with the consent of the landlord[11]; and (5) the tenant applies to the landlord for his consent to make a relevant improvement[12], then, if the consent of the landlord is unreasonably withheld, it must be taken to have been given[13].

Where the tenant applies in writing for the consent: (a) if the landlord refuses to give consent, he must give the tenant a written statement of the reason why the consent was withheld[14]; (b) if the landlord neither gives nor refuses to give consent within a reasonable time, consent must be taken to have been withheld[15]. If the landlord gives consent to the making of an improvement subject to a condition which is unreasonable, the consent must be taken to have been unreasonably withheld[16]. In any question as to whether: (i) the consent of the landlord was unreasonably withheld[17]; or (ii) a condition imposed by the landlord is unreasonable[18], it is for the landlord to show that it was not[19].

If the tenant fails to comply with a reasonable condition imposed by the landlord on the making of a relevant improvement, the failure is to be treated as a breach by the tenant of an obligation of his tenancy[20].

The above provisions[21] apply to a lease only to the extent that provision of a like nature is not made by the lease itself[22].

1 'Lease' includes a sub-lease or other tenancy; and 'landlord' and 'tenant' must be construed accordingly: Disability Discrimination Act 1995 s 49G(9) (s 49G added by the Disability Discrimination Act 2005 s 16(1)).
2 'Protected tenancy' has the same meaning as in the Rent Act 1977 s 1 (see LANDLORD AND TENANT vol 27(2) (2006 Reissue) para 810): Disability Discrimination Act 1995 s 49G(9) (as added: see note 1 supra).
3 'Statutory tenancy' must be construed in accordance with the Rent Act 1977 s 2 (as amended) (see LANDLORD AND TENANT vol 27(2) (2006 Reissue) para 810): Disability Discrimination Act 1995 s 49G(9) (as added: see note 1 supra).
4 Ibid s 49G(1)(a) (as added: see note 1 supra). 'Secure tenancy' has the same meaning as in the Housing Act 1985 s 79 (see LANDLORD AND TENANT vol 27(2) (2006 Reissue) paras 889, 1300): Disability Discrimination Act 1995 s 49G(9) (as so added).
      See the Code of Practice on Rights of Access: services to the public, public authority functions, private clubs and premises (December 2006) paras 1.5, 18.11 et seq. As to codes of practice see para 655 post.
5 For the meaning of 'tenant' see note 1 supra.
6 As to the meaning of 'person' see para 344 note 3 ante.
7 As to the meaning of 'premises' see para 525 note 9 ante.
8 Disability Discrimination Act 1995 s 49G(1)(b) (as added: see note 1 supra). For the meaning of 'disabled person' see para 511 ante.

9   Ibid s 49G(1)(c) (as added: see note 1 supra).

10 'Improvement' means any alteration in or addition to premises and includes: (1) any addition to or alteration in landlord's fittings and fixtures; (2) any addition or alteration connected with the provision of services to the premises; (3) the erection of a wireless or television aerial; and (4) the carrying out of external decoration: ibid s 49G(9) (as added: see note 1 supra).

11 Ibid s 49G(1)(d) (as added: see note 1 supra). For the meaning of 'landlord' see note 1 supra.

12 Ibid s 49G(1)(e) (as added: see note 1 supra). An improvement to premises is a 'relevant improvement' if, having regard to the disability which the disabled person has (see s 49G(1)(b) (as added); and head (2) in the text), it is likely to facilitate his enjoyment of the premises: s 49G(7) (as so added).

13 Ibid s 49G(2) (as added: see note 1 supra).

14 Ibid s 49G(3)(a) (as added: see note 1 supra).

15 Ibid s 49G(3)(b) (as added: see note 1 supra).

16 Ibid s 49G(4) (as added: see note 1 supra).

17 Ibid s 49G(5)(a) (as added: see note 1 supra).

18 Ibid s 49G(5)(b) (as added: see note 1 supra).

19 Ibid s 49G(5) (as added: see note 1 supra).

20 Ibid s 49G(6) (as added: see note 1 supra).

21 Ie ibid s 49G(2)–(6) (as added): see the text and notes 13–20 supra.

22 Ibid s 49G(8) (as added: see note 1 supra).

612.   Conciliation of disputes about withholding of consent. The Disability Rights Commission[1] may make arrangements with any other person[2] for the provision of conciliation services by, or by persons appointed by, that person in relation to a dispute of any description concerning the question whether it is unreasonable for a landlord to withhold consent to the making of a relevant improvement[3] to a dwelling house[4].

1 As to the Disability Rights Commission see para 646 et seq post. As to the Commission for Equality and Human Rights, which is to replace the Disability Rights Commission, see para 305 et seq ante.

2 As to the meaning of 'person' see para 344 note 3 ante.

3 For the meaning of 'relevant improvement' see para 611 note 12 ante; definition applied by the Disability Discrimination Act 1995 s 49H(3) (s 49H added by the Disability Discrimination Act 2005 s 16(1)). The Disability Discrimination Act 1995 s 49H (as added) is repealed by the Equality Act 2006 ss 40, 91, Sch 3 paras 41, 50, Sch 4 as from a day to be appointed under s 93. At the date at which this volume states the law no such day had been appointed.

4 Disability Discrimination Act 1995 s 49H(1) (as added: see note 3 supra). Section 28(2)–(8) (as substituted; prospectively repealed) (see para 657 post) applies for the purposes of s 49H (as added) as it applies for the purposes of s 28 (as substituted; prospectively repealed); and for that purpose a reference in that provision to a dispute arising under Pt III (ss 19–28) (as amended; prospectively amended) must be construed as a reference to a dispute mentioned in s 49H(1) (as added) and arrangements under that provision must be construed as a reference to arrangements under s 49H (as added): s 49H(2) (as so added). As to the withholding of consent in regard to improvements to dwelling houses see para 611 ante.

G. OTHER UNLAWFUL ACTS

613.   Settlements and other contracts. A term of a contract is void where: (1) the making of the contract is, by reason of the inclusion of the term, unlawful by virtue of the provisions of the Disability Discrimination Act 1995 on employment and members of locally-electable authorities[1] or, to the extent that it relates to the provision of employment services[2] or the provision under group insurance arrangement of facilities by way of insurance[3], the provisions of the Act relating to discrimination in other areas[4]; (2) it is included in furtherance of an act which is thus unlawful[5]; or (3) it provides for the doing of an act which is unlawful[6]. These provisions do not apply to a term the inclusion of which constitutes, or is in furtherance of, or provides for, unlawful discrimination against, or harassment[7] of, a party to the contract, but the term is unenforceable against that party[8]. On the application of a disabled person[9] interested in a contract to which head (1) or head (2) above applies, a county court may make such order as it thinks fit for removing or modifying any term rendered void as above[10], or for removing or modifying any term made unenforceable as above[11]. However, such an order must not be made unless all persons affected have been given notice in writing of the application (except where under rules of court notice may be dispensed with) and have been afforded an opportunity to make representations to the court[12].

A term in a contract which purports to exclude or limit any provision relating to disability discrimination or harassment in the field of employment and locally-electable authorities[13] is unenforceable by any person in whose favour the term would operate[14]. However, a contract is not so unenforceable[15] in the case of a contract settling a complaint[16] where the contract is made with the assistance of a conciliation officer[17], or if the conditions regulating compromise contracts are satisfied[18]. An agreement under which the parties agree to submit a dispute to arbitration is be regarded as being a contract settling a complaint[19] if the dispute is covered by a scheme having effect by virtue of an order under the Trade Union and Labour Relations (Consolidation) Act 1992[20], and the agreement is to submit it to arbitration in accordance with the scheme[21].

The conditions regulating compromise contracts referred to above are that: (a) the contract must be in writing[22]; (b) the contract must relate to the particular complaint[23]; (c) the complainant must have received advice from a relevant independent adviser[24] as to the terms and effect of the proposed contract and in particular its effect on his ability to pursue a complaint before an employment tribunal[25]; (d) there must be in force, when the adviser gives the advice, a contract of insurance, or an indemnity provided for members of a profession or professional body, covering the risk of a claim by the complainant in respect of loss arising in consequence of the advice[26]; (e) the contract must identify the adviser[27]; and (f) the contract must state that the conditions regulating compromise contracts are satisfied[28].

Any term in a contract for the provision of goods, facilities or services[29] or in any other agreement is void so far as it purports to[30]: (i) require a person[31] to do anything which would contravene any provision of, or made under, the provisions of the Disability Discrimination Act 1995 relating to the provision of goods, facilities or services[32]; (ii) exclude or limit the operation of any such provision[33]; or (iii) prevent any person from making a claim under such a provision[34]. On the application of any person interested in an agreement relating to the provision of goods, facilities or services, a county court may make such order as it thinks just for modifying the agreement[35]. No such order may be made unless all persons affected have been given notice of the application[36], and afforded an opportunity to make representations to the court[37].

1   Ie by virtue of the Disability Discrimination Act 1995 Pt II (ss 3A–18E) (as amended; prospectively amended): see para 529 et seq ante.

2   For the meaning of 'employment services' see para 585 note 9 ante.

3   'Group insurance arrangement' means an arrangement between an employer and another for the provision by the other of facilities by way of insurance to the employer's employees or to any class of those employees: Disability Discrimination Act 1995 s 68(1) (definition added by the Disability Discrimination Act 2005 s 11(3)).

4   Ie the Disability Discrimination Act 1995 Pt III (ss 19–28) (as amended; prospectively amended): see para 582 et seq ante.

5   Ie by virtue of ibid Pt II (as amended; prospectively amended) or, to the extent that it relates to the provision of employment services or the provision under a group insurance arrangement of facilities by way of insurance, Pt III (as amended; prospectively amended).

6   Ibid s 17C, Sch 3A para 1(1), 11 (s 17C, Sch 3A added by the Disability Discrimination Act 1995 (Amendment) Regulations 2003, SI 2003/1673, regs 3(1), 16, Schedule; and the Disability Discrimination Act 1995 Sch 3A para 11 substituted by the Disability Discrimination Act 2005 s 19(1), Sch 1 paras 1, 39(1), (3)). Head (3) in the text refers to an act which is unlawful by virtue of the Disability Discrimination Act 1995 Pt II (as amended; prospectively amended) or, to the extent that it relates to the provision of employment services or the provision under a group insurance arrangement of facilities by way of insurance, Pt III (as amended; prospectively amended).

Schedule 3A para 1(1)–(3) (as added) applies whether the contract was entered into before or after the date on which Sch 3A (as added and amended) came into force; but in the case of a contract made before Sch 3A (as added and amended) came into force, it does not apply in relation to any period before that date: Sch 3A para 1(4) (as so added). Schedule 3A (as added and amended) came into force on 3 July 2003 for certain purposes and on 1 October 2004 for remaining purposes: see the Disability Discrimination Act 1995 (Amendment) Regulations 2003, SI 2003/1673, reg 1(2), (3).

7   For the meaning of 'harassment' see para 533 ante.

8   Disability Discrimination Act 1995 Sch 3A para 1(2) (as added: see note 6 supra). See note 6 supra.

9   For the meaning of 'disabled person' see para 511 ante.

10   Ie rendered void by the Disability Discrimination Act 1995 Sch 3A para 1(1) (as added): see the text and notes 1–6 supra.

11   Ibid Sch 3A para 3(1) (as added: see note 6 supra). The text refers to a term made unenforceable by Sch 3A para 1(2) (as added): see the text and note 8 supra.

12   Ibid Sch 3A para 3(1) (as added: see note 6 supra). An order under Sch 3A para 3(1) (as added) may include provision as respects any period before the making of the order (but after the coming into force of Sch 3A (as added)): Sch 3A para 3(2) (as so added).

13   Ie under ibid Pt II (as amended; prospectively amended).

14   Ibid Sch 3A para 1(3) (as added: see note 6 supra). See note 6 supra.

15   Ie under ibid Sch 3A para 1(3) (as added): see the text and notes 13–14 supra.

16   Ie a contract settling a complaint to which ibid s 17A(1) (as added and amended) (see para 643 post) or s 25(8) (as added) (see para 644 post) applies: see Sch 3A para 2(1)(a) (as added: see note 6 supra).

17   'Conciliation officer' means a person designated under the Trade Union and Labour Relations (Consolidation) Act 1992 s 211 (as amended) (see TRADE, INDUSTRY AND INDUSTRIAL RELATIONS vol 47 (2001 Reissue) para 1437): Disability Discrimination Act 1995 s 68(1).

18   Ibid Sch 3A para 2(1) (as added: see note 6 supra).

19   Ie for the purposes of ibid Sch 3A para 2(1) (as added): see the text and notes 15–18 supra.

20   Ie an order under the Trade Union and Labour Relations (Consolidation) Act 1992 s 212A (as added and amended) (see EMPLOYMENT vol 16(1B) (Reissue) para 696).

21   Disability Discrimination Act 1995 Sch 3A para 2(8)(a) (as added: see note 6 supra). However, such an agreement is to be regarded as neither being nor including such a contract in any other case: Sch 3A para 2(8)(b) (as so added).

22   Ibid Sch 3A para 2(2)(a) (as added: see note 6 supra).

23   Ibid Sch 3A para 2(2)(b) (as added: see note 6 supra).

24   A person is a 'relevant independent adviser' for the purposes of ibid Sch 3A para 2(2)(c) (as added) if he: (1) is a qualified lawyer; (2) is an officer, official, employee or member of an independent trade union who has been certified in writing by the trade union as competent to give advice and as authorised to do so on behalf of the trade union; (3) works at an advice centre, whether as an employee or a volunteer, and has been certified in writing by the centre as competent to give advice and as authorised to do so on behalf of the centre; or (4) if he is a person of a description specified in an order made by the Secretary of State: Sch 3A para 2(3) (as added (see note 6 supra); and amended by the Disability Discrimination Act 2005 s 19(2), Sch 1 para 39(1), (2), Sch 2). As to the Secretary of State and the National Assembly for Wales see para 302 ante. For the purposes of head (4) supra, a fellow of the Institute of Legal Executives employed by a solicitors' practice is specified: Compromise Agreements (Description of Person) Order 2005, SI 2005/2364. A person is not a relevant independent adviser for the purposes of the Disability Discrimination Act 1995 Sch 3A para 2(2)(c) (as added) in relation to the complainant: (a) if he is employed by or is acting in the matter for the other party or a person who is connected with the other party; (b) in the case of a person within head (1) or head (2) supra, if the trade union or advice centre is the other party or a person who is connected with the other party; or (c) in the case of a person within head (3) supra, if the complainant makes a payment for the advice received from him: Sch 3A para 2(4) (as so added). In head (1) supra, 'qualified lawyer' means a barrister (whether in practice as such or employed to give legal advice), a solicitor who holds a practising certificate, or a person other than a barrister or solicitor who is an authorised advocate or authorised litigator (within the meaning of the Courts and Legal Services Act 1990: see BARRISTERS vol 3(1) (2005 Reissue) para 501; SOLICITORS vol 44(1) (Reissue) paras 78–79): Disability Discrimination Act 1995 Sch 3A para 2(5) (as so added). In head (2) supra, 'independent trade union' has the same meaning as in the Trade Union and Labour Relations (Consolidation) Act 1992 (see TRADE, INDUSTRY AND INDUSTRIAL RELATIONS vol 47 (2001 Reissue) para 1014): Disability Discrimination Act 1995 Sch 3A para 2(6) (as so added). For the purposes of head (a) supra, any two persons are to be treated as connected if one is a company of which the other (directly or indirectly) has control, or if both are companies of which a third person (directly or indirectly) has control: Sch 3A para 2(7) (as so added).

25   Ibid Sch 3A para 2(2)(c) (as added: see note 6 supra).

26   Ibid Sch 3A para 2(2)(d) (as added: see note 6 supra).

27   Ibid Sch 3A para 2(2)(e) (as added: see note 6 supra).

28 Ibid Sch 3A para 2(2)(f) (as added: see note 6 supra).

29 As to the provision of goods, facilities and services see para 582 et seq ante.

30 Disability Discrimination Act 1995 s 26(1). Section 26(1) does not apply to: (1) any term in a contract for the provision of employment services; (2) any term in a contract which is a group insurance arrangement; or (3) a term which is in an agreement which is not a contract of either of those kinds, and relates to the provision of employment services or the provision under a group insurance arrangement of facilities by way of insurance: s 26(1A) (added by the Disability Discrimination Act 1995 (Amendment) Regulations 2003, SI 2003/1673, regs 3(1), 19(3); and substituted by the Disability Discrimination Act 2005 Sch 1 paras 1, 22). Where a term to which head (3) supra applies is a term in an agreement which is not a contract, the Disability Discrimination Act 1995 Sch 3A paras 1–3 (as added and amended) have effect as if the agreement were a contract: Sch 3A para 12 (added by the Disability Discrimination Act 2005 Sch 1 paras 1, 39(1), (3)).

31 As to the meaning of 'person' see para 344 note 3 ante.

32 Disability Discrimination Act 1995 s 26(1)(a). The provisions of the Disability Discrimination Act 1995 referred to in the text are those in Pt III (as amended; prospectively amended). See note 30 supra.

33 Ibid s 26(1)(b). The provisions of s 26(1)(b), (c) do not apply to an agreement settling a claim to which s 25 (as amended) applies (see para 644 post): see s 26(2). See note 30 supra.

34 Ibid s 26(1)(c). See note 30 supra.

35 Ibid s 26(3). The agreement may be modified to take account of the effect of s 26(1): see s 26(3). An order under s 26(3) may include provision as respects any period before the making of the order: s 26(6).

36 Ibid s 26(4)(a). Section 26(4) applies subject to any rules of court providing for that notice to be dispensed with: s 26(5).

37 Ibid s 26(4)(b).

614.   Collective agreements and rules of undertakings.   Any term of a collective agreement[1], any rule made by an employer[2], or any rule made by a trade organisation[3] or qualifications body[4] is void[5] where: (1) the making of the collective agreement is, by reason of the inclusion of the term, unlawful[6]; (2) the term or rule is included in furtherance of an act which is unlawful[7]; or (3) the term or rule provides for the doing of an act which is unlawful[8].

A disabled person[9]: (a) who is, or is genuinely and actively seeking to become, an employee or a member of an organisation or body[10]; (b) who is a person on whom the organisation or body has conferred an authorisation or qualification[11]; or (c) who is genuinely and actively seeking an authorisation or qualification which the organisation or body has power to confer[12], may present a complaint to an employment tribunal[13]. His complaint may be that a term or rule is void[14] if he has reason to believe: (i) that the term or rule may at some future time have effect in relation to him[15]; and (ii) where he alleges that it is void because it provides for the doing of an act which is unlawful under head (b) above, that an act for the doing of which it provides may at some such time be done in relation to him[16], and the act would be unlawful[17] if done in relation to him in present circumstances[18]. When an employment tribunal finds that such a complaint presented to it is well-founded, it must make an order declaring that the term or rule is void[19].

1 Ie including an agreement which was not intended, or is presumed not to have been intended, to be a legally enforceable contract: Disability Discrimination Act 1995 s 17C, Sch 3A para 4(1)(a) (s 17C, Sch 3A added by the Disability Discrimination Act 1995 (Amendment) Regulations 2003, SI 2003/1673, regs 3(1), 16). 'Collective agreement' means any agreement relating to one or more of the matters mentioned in the Trade Union and Labour Relations (Consolidation) Act 1992 s 178(2) (see TRADE, INDUSTRY AND INDUSTRIAL RELATIONS vol 47 (2001 Reissue) para 1301), being an agreement made by or on behalf of one or more employers or one or more organisations of employers or associations of such organisations with one or more organisations of workers or associations of such organisations: Disability Discrimination Act 1995 Sch 3A para 10 (as so added).

2 Ie a rule for application to all or any of the persons who are employed by him or who apply to be, or are, considered by him for employment: ibid Sch 3A para 4(1)(b) (as added: see note 1 supra).

3 For the meaning of 'trade organisation' see para 541 note 1 ante.

4 Ie a rule for application to: (1) all or any of the body's members or prospective members; or (2) all or any of the persons on whom the body has conferred authorisations or qualifications or who are seeking the

authorisations or qualifications which the body has power to confer: Disability Discrimination Act 1995 Sch 3A para 4(1)(c) (as added: see note 1 supra). For the meaning of 'qualifications body' see para 549 note 1 ante.

5   The avoidance by virtue of ibid Sch 3A para 4(2) (as added) of any term or rule which provides for any person to be discriminated against is without prejudice to the following rights, except in so far as they enable any person to require another person to be treated less favourably than himself: (1) such of the rights of the person to be discriminated against; and (2) such of the rights of any person who will be treated more favourably in direct or indirect consequence of the discrimination, as are conferred by or in respect of a contract made or modified wholly or partly in pursuance of, or by reference to, that term or rule: Sch 3A para 9 (as added: see note 1 supra).

6   Ie by virtue of ibid Pt II (ss 3A–18E) (as amended; prospectively amended) (see para 529 et seq ante) or, to the extent that it relates to the provision of employment services or the provision under a group insurance arrangement of facilities by way of insurance, Pt III (ss 19–28) (as amended; prospectively amended) (see para 582 et seq ante): Sch 3A paras 4(2)(a), 11 (Sch 3A as added (see note 1 supra); and Sch 3A para 11 substituted by the Disability Discrimination Act 2005 s 19(1), Sch 1 paras 1, 39(1), (3)). For the meaning of 'employment services' see para 585 note 9 ante. For the meaning of 'group insurance arrangement' see para 613 note 2 ante. The Disability Discrimination Act 1995 Sch 3A para 4(2) (as added) applies whether the agreement was entered into, or the rule made, before or after the date on which Sch 3A (as added and amended) came into force; but in the case of an agreement entered into, or a rule made, before the date on which Sch 3A (as added and amended) came into force, it does not apply in relation to any period before that date: Sch 3A para 4(3) (as so added).

7   Ie by virtue of ibid Pt II (as amended; prospectively amended) or, to the extent that it relates to the provision of employment services or the provision under a group insurance arrangement of facilities by way of insurance, Pt III (as amended; prospectively amended): Sch 3A paras 4(2)(b), 11 (Sch 3A as added (see note 1 supra); and Sch 3A para 11 as substituted (see note 6 supra)).

8   Ie by virtue of ibid Pt II (as amended; prospectively amended) or, to the extent that it relates to the provision of employment services or the provision under a group insurance arrangement of facilities by way of insurance, Pt III (as amended; prospectively amended): Sch 3A paras 4(2)(c), 11 (Sch 3A as added (see note 1 supra); and Sch 3A para 11 as substituted (see note 6 supra)).

9   For the meaning of 'disabled person' see para 511 ante.

10 See the Disability Discrimination Act 1995 Sch 3A paras 6, 7(a) (as added: see note 1 supra).

11 See ibid Sch 3A para 7(b) (as added: see note 1 supra).

12 See ibid Sch 3A para 7(c) (as added: see note 1 supra).

13 Ibid Sch 3A paras 5–7 (as added: see note 1 supra).

14 Ie by virtue of ibid Sch 3A para 4 (as added).

15 Ibid Sch 3A para 5(a) (as added: see note 1 supra).

16 Ibid Sch 3A para 5(b)(i) (as added: see note 1 supra).

17 Ie by virtue of ibid Pt II (as amended; prospectively amended) or, to the extent that it relates to the provision of employment services or the provision under a group insurance arrangement of facilities by way of insurance, Pt III (as amended; prospectively amended).

18 Ibid Sch 3A paras 5(b)(ii), 11 (Sch 3A as added (see note 1 supra); and Sch 3A para 11 as substituted (see note 6 supra)).

19 Ibid Sch 3A para 8(1) (as added: see note 1 supra). An order under Sch 3A para 8(1) (as added) may include provision as respects any period before the making of the order (but after the coming into force of Sch 3A (as added and amended): Sch 3A para 8(2) (as so added).

H. EXCEPTIONS

615.   Charities. Nothing in the provisions of the Disability Discrimination Act 1995 relating to employment and members of locally-electable authorities[1]: (1) affects any charitable instrument[2] which provides for conferring benefits[3] on one or more categories of person determined by reference to any physical or mental capacity[4]; or (2) makes unlawful any act[5] done by a charity[6] in pursuance of any of its charitable purposes, so far as those purposes are connected with persons so determined[7].

Nothing in the Disability Discrimination Act 1995[8] prevents: (a) a person[9] who provides supported employment[10] from treating members of a particular group of disabled persons[11] more favourably than other persons in providing such employment[12]; or (b) the Secretary of State[13] from agreeing to arrangements for the provision of supported employment which will, or may, have that effect[14].

1 Ie the Disability Discrimination Act 1995 Pt II (ss 3A–18E) (as amended; prospectively amended). For the meaning of 'employment' see para 529 note 2 ante.

2 'Charitable instrument' means an enactment or other instrument (whenever taking effect) so far as it relates to charitable purposes: ibid s 18C(3) (s 18C added by the Disability Discrimination Act 1995 (Amendment) Regulations 2003, SI 2003/1673, regs 3(1), 11). 'Charitable purposes' means purposes which are exclusively charitable according to the law of England and Wales: Disability Discrimination Act 1995 s 18C(4) (as so added). As to charitable purposes see CHARITIES vol 5(2) (2001 Reissue) para 1 et seq. As to the meaning of 'enactment' see para 510 note 2 ante.

3 As to the meaning of 'benefits' see para 534 note 9 ante.

4 Disability Discrimination Act 1995 s 18C(1)(a) (as added: see note 2 supra).

5 As to the meaning of 'act' see para 510 note 3 ante.

6 'Charity' has the same meaning as in the Charities Act 1993 (see CHARITIES vol 5(2) (2001 Reissue) para 1): Disability Discrimination Act 1995 s 18C(3) (as added: see note 2 supra).

7 Ibid s 18C(1)(b) (as added: see note 2 supra).

8 Ie in ibid Pt II (as amended; prospectively amended).

9 As to the meaning of 'person' see para 344 note 3 ante.

10 'Supported employment' means facilities provided, or in respect of which payments are made, under the Disabled Persons (Employment) Act 1944 s 15 (as amended) (see EMPLOYMENT vol 16(1A) (Reissue) para 535): Disability Discrimination Act 1995 s 18C(3) (as added: see note 2 supra).

11 For the meaning of 'disabled person' see para 511 ante.

12 Disability Discrimination Act 1995 s 18C(2)(a) (as added: see note 2 supra).

13 As to the Secretary of State and the National Assembly for Wales see para 302 ante.

14 Disability Discrimination Act 1995 s 18C(2)(b) (as added: see note 2 supra).

616. Acts done under statutory authority and acts safeguarding national security. Nothing in the Disability Discrimination Act 1995 makes unlawful any act done[1]: (1) in pursuance of any enactment[2]; or (2) in pursuance of any instrument[3] made under any enactment by a Minister of the Crown[4] or the National Assembly for Wales[5]; or (3) to comply with any condition or requirement imposed by a Minister of the Crown[6] or by the National Assembly for Wales[7] by virtue of any enactment[8].

Nothing in Part II of the Disability Discrimination Act 1995[9] or, to the extent that it relates to the provision of employment services[10], Part III of the Act[11], makes unlawful any act done for the purpose of safeguarding national security if the doing of the act was justified by that purpose[12]. Nothing in any other provision of the Act makes unlawful any act done for the purpose of safeguarding national security[13].

Rules of court may make provision for enabling a county court in which a claim is brought in respect of alleged discrimination contrary to the Disability Discrimination Act 1995[14], where the court considers it expedient in the interests of national security: (1) to exclude from all or part of the proceedings the claimant, the claimant's representatives, or any assessors[15]; (2) to permit a claimant or representative who has been excluded to make a statement to the court before the commencement of the proceedings, or the part of the proceedings, from which he is excluded[16]; (3) to take steps to keep secret all or part of the reasons for the court's decision in the proceedings[17]. The Attorney General[18] may appoint a person to represent the interests of a claimant in, or in any part of, proceedings from which the claimant or his representatives are excluded by virtue of the above provision[19].

1 Disability Discrimination Act 1995 s 59(1). As to the meaning of 'act' see para 510 note 3 ante.

2 Ibid s 59(1)(a). As to the general meaning of 'enactment' see para 510 note 4 ante. However, for these purposes, 'enactment' includes one passed or made after the date on which the Disability Discrimination Act 1995 was passed (ie 8 November 1995): s 59(2). Section 59 (as amended) represents the 'belt and braces' approach in the statute since the existence of a material statute authorising or requiring what otherwise would be discriminatory suggests readily demonstrable justification: see *Jones v Post Office* [2000] ICR 388, EAT. An act in pursuance of an enactment is confined to actions reasonably necessary in order to comply with a statutory obligation (*Hampson v Department of Education and Science* [1990] 2 All ER 513, [1990] IRLR 302, HL), therefore an act done pursuant to a decision on a matter where a discretion is given by a statute will not be immune from challenge under the Disability Discrimination Act 1995 s 59 (as amended).

3 'Instrument' includes one made after the date on which the Disability Discrimination Act 1995 was passed (see note 2 supra): s 59(2).

4 As to the meaning of 'Minister of the Crown' see para 510 note 4 ante.

5 Disability Discrimination Act 1995 s 59(1)(b) (s 59(1)(b), (c) substituted by the Disability Discrimination Act 2005 s 19(1), Sch 1 paras 1, 30). As to the National Assembly for Wales see para 302 ante. This provision also refers to the Scottish Executive, but Scottish matters generally are beyond the scope of this work.

6 Ie whether before or after the passing of the Disability Discrimination Act 1995 (see note 2 supra).

7 Ie whether before or after the coming into force of the relevant provision (ie 30 June 2005).

8 Disability Discrimination Act 1995 s 59(1)(c) (as substituted: see note 5 supra). See note 5 supra.

9 Ie ibid Pt II (ss 3A–18E) (as amended; prospectively amended): see para 529 et seq ante.

10 For the meaning of 'employment services' see para 585 note 9 ante.

11 Ie the Disability Discrimination Act 1995 Pt III (ss 19–28) (as amended; prospectively amended): see para 582 et seq ante.

12 Ibid s 59(2A) (added by the Disability Discrimination Act 1995 (Amendment) Regulations 2003, SI 2003/1673, regs 3(1), 23(a)).

13 Disability Discrimination Act 1995 s 59(3) (amended by the Disability Discrimination Act 1995 (Amendment) Regulations 2003, SI 2003/1673, regs 3(1), 23(b)).

14 Ie including anything treated by virtue of the Disability Discrimination Act 1995 as amounting to discrimination contrary to that Act.

15 Ibid s 59A(1)(a) (s 59A added by the Equality Act 2006 s 89). At the date at which this volume states the law no such rules of court had been made.

16 Disability Discrimination Act 1995 s 59A(1)(b) (as added: see note 15 supra). See note 15 supra.

17 Ibid s 59A(1)(c) (as added: see note 15 supra). See note 15 supra.

18 As to the Attorney General see CONSTITUTIONAL LAW AND HUMAN RIGHTS vol 8(2) (Reissue) para 529.

19 Disability Discrimination Act 1995 s 59A(2) (as added: see note 15 supra). The provision referred to in the text is s 59A(1) (as added): see the text and notes 14–17 supra. See note 15 supra.

A person may be appointed under s 59A(2) (as added) only if he has a general qualification (within the meaning of the Courts and Legal Services Act 1990 s 71 (as amended; prospectively amended): see SOLICITORS vol 44(1) (Reissue) para 91): Disability Discrimination Act 1995 s 59A(3) (as so added). A person appointed under s 59A(2) (as added) is not responsible to the person whose interests he is appointed to represent: s 59A(4) (as so added).

I. PUBLIC TRANSPORT

(A) Rail Vehicles

617. Rail vehicle accessibility regulations. The Secretary of State[1] may make rail vehicle[2] accessibility regulations[3] for the purpose of securing that it is possible[4] for disabled persons[5] to get on to and off regulated rail vehicles[6] in safety and without unreasonable difficulty[7], and to be carried in such vehicles in safety and in reasonable comfort[8], and for disabled persons in wheelchairs to get on to and off such vehicles in safety and without unreasonable difficulty while remaining in their wheelchairs[9], and to be carried in such vehicles in safety and in reasonable comfort while remaining in their wheelchairs[10].

Rail vehicle accessibility regulations may, in particular, make provision as to the construction, use and maintenance of regulated rail vehicles[11] including provision as to:

(1) the fitting of equipment to vehicles[12];

(2) equipment to be carried by vehicles[13];

(3) the design of equipment to be fitted to, or carried by, vehicles[14];

(4) the use of equipment fitted to, or carried by, vehicles[15];

(5) the toilet facilities to be provided in vehicles[16];

(6) the location and floor area of the wheelchair accommodation[17] to be provided in vehicles[18]; and

(7) assistance to be given to disabled persons[19].

If a regulated rail vehicle which does not conform with any provision of the rail vehicle accessibility regulations with which it is required to conform is used for carriage[20], the operator[21] of the vehicle is guilty of an offence[22].

Different provision may be made in rail vehicle accessibility regulations: (a) as respects different classes or descriptions of rail vehicle[23]; (b) as respects the same class or description of rail vehicle in different circumstances[24]; and (c) as respects different networks[25].

The Rail Vehicle Accessibility Regulations 1998[26], which were made in exercise of this power, apply to rail vehicles used on railways, tramways, monorail systems or magnetic levitation systems[27].

1   As to the Secretary of State and the National Assembly for Wales see para 302 ante.
2   'Rail vehicle' means a vehicle: (1) constructed or adapted to carry passengers on any railway, tramway or
     prescribed system; and (2) first brought into use, or belonging to a class of vehicle first brought into use,
     after 31 December 1998: Disability Discrimination Act 1995 ss 46(6), 68(1). As from a day to be
     appointed, this definition is substituted so as to refer to any rail vehicle constructed or adapted to carry
     passengers on any railway, tramway or prescribed system: s 46(6) (definition prospectively substituted by
     the Disability Discrimination Act 2005 s 6(2)). At the date at which this volume states the law no such
     day had been appointed.
         'Prescribed system' means a system using a prescribed mode of guided transport ('guided transport'
     having the same meaning as in the Transport and Works Act 1992: see RAILWAYS, INLAND WATERWAYS
     AND PIPELINES vol 39(1) (Reissue) para 166); and 'railway' and 'tramway' have the same meanings as in
     that Act (see RAILWAYS, INLAND WATERWAYS AND PIPELINES vol 39(1) (Reissue) para 166): Disability
     Discrimination Act 1995 s 46(7). The Secretary of State may by regulations make provision as to the time
     when a rail vehicle, or a class of rail vehicle, is to be treated, for these purposes, as first brought into use:
     s 46(8). Regulations under s 46(8) may include provision for disregarding periods of testing and other
     prescribed periods of use: s 46(9). The provisions of s 46(8)–(10) are repealed by the Disability
     Discrimination Act 2005 s 19(2), Sch 2 as from a day to be appointed under s 20(3). At the date at which
     this volume states the law no such day had been appointed.
         'Prescribed' generally means prescribed by regulations: see para 515 note 5 ante. For the meaning of
     'regulations' see para 509 note 12 ante. As to regulations made under this power see the Rail Vehicle
     Accessibility Regulations 1998, SI 1998/2456 (as amended); and RAILWAYS, INLAND WATERWAYS AND
     PIPELINES vol 39(1) (Reissue) para 232.
3   'Rail vehicle accessibility regulations' means regulations made under the Disability Discrimination
     Act 1995 s 46(1): s 68(1). See note 2 supra. Before making any regulations under s 46(1) or s 47 (as
     amended) (see para 618 post) the Secretary of State must consult the Disabled Persons Transport Advisory
     Committee and such other representative organisations as he thinks fit: s 46(11). As to the Disabled
     Persons Transport Advisory Committee see ROAD TRAFFIC vol 40(1) (Reissue) para 56.
4   Ibid s 46(1).
5   For the meaning of 'disabled person' see para 511 ante.
6   'Regulated rail vehicle' means any rail vehicle to which the rail vehicle accessibility regulations are
     expressed to apply: Disability Discrimination Act 1995 ss 46(6), 68(1). As from a day to be appointed, this
     definition is amended so as to refer to any such vehicle to which provisions of those regulations are
     expressed to apply: s 46(6) (definition prospectively amended by the Disability Discrimination Act 2005
     s 19(1), Sch 1 paras 1, 27(b)). At the date at which this volume states the law no such day had been
     appointed.
7   Disability Discrimination Act 1995 s 46(1)(a)(i).
8   Ibid s 46(1)(a)(ii).
9   Ibid s 46(1)(b)(i).
10   Ibid s 46(1)(b)(ii).
11   Ibid s 46(2).
12   Ibid s 46(2)(a).
13   Ibid s 46(2)(b).
14   Ibid s 46(2)(c).
15   Ibid s 46(2)(d).
16   Ibid s 46(2)(e).
17   'Wheelchair accommodation' has such meaning as may be prescribed: ibid s 46(6). At the date at which
     this volume states the law no order prescribing the meaning of 'wheelchair accommodation' had been
     made. See, however, the Rail Vehicle Accessibility Regulations 1998, SI 1998/2456 (as amended); and
     RAILWAYS, INLAND WATERWAYS AND PIPELINES vol 39(1) (Reissue) para 232.
18   Disability Discrimination Act 1995 s 46(2)(f).

19 Ibid s 46(2)(g).

20 For the purposes of ibid ss 46, 47 (as amended; prospectively amended), a person uses a vehicle for carriage if he uses it for the carriage of members of the public for hire or reward at separate fares: s 46(10). This provision is prospectively repealed: see note 2 supra. As from a day to be appointed, it is provided that, for the purposes of ss 46–47H (as amended; prospectively amended) (see also para 618 et seq post), a person uses a vehicle for carriage if he uses it for the carriage of passengers: s 47M(2) (prospectively added by the Disability Discrimination Act 2005 s 8(1)). At the date at which this volume states the law no such day had been appointed.

21 'Operator', in relation to any rail vehicle, means the person having the management of that vehicle: Disability Discrimination Act 1995 s 46(6). This definition is repealed by the Disability Discrimination Act 2005 Sch 2 as from a day to be appointed under s 20(3). At the date at which this volume states the law no such day had been appointed.

     As from a day to be appointed, it is provided that for the purposes of the Disability Discrimination Act 1995 ss 46–47H (as amended; prospectively amended) (see also para 618 et seq post) 'operator', in relation to any rail vehicle, means the person having the management of that vehicle: s 47M(1) (prospectively added by the Disability Discrimination Act 2005 s 8(1)). At the date at which this volume states the law no such day had been appointed.

22 Disability Discrimination Act 1995 s 46(3). A person who is guilty of such an offence is liable, on summary conviction, to a fine not exceeding level 4 on the standard scale: s 46(4). As to the standard scale see para 315 note 15 ante. As to offences by bodies corporate see para 641 post. These provisions are repealed by the Disability Discrimination Act 2005 Sch 1 paras 1, 27(a), Sch 2 as from a day to be appointed under s 20(3). At the date at which this volume states the law no such day had been appointed.

     As from a day to be appointed, the Secretary of State may make rail vehicle accessibility regulations so as to secure that on and after 1 January 2020 every rail vehicle is a regulated rail vehicle, although without affecting the powers conferred by 47(5) (see para 618 post) or s 67(2) (see para 509 ante): s 46(4A) (prospectively added by the Disability Discrimination Act 2005 s 6(1)). At the date at which this volume states the law no such day had been appointed.

23 Disability Discrimination Act 1995 s 46(5)(a).

24 Ibid s 46(5)(b).

25 Ibid s 46(5)(c). 'Network' means any permanent way or other means of guiding or supporting rail vehicles or any section of it: s 46(6).

26 Ie the Rail Vehicle Accessibility Regulations 1998, SI 1998/2456 (as amended), which came into force on 1 November 1998 (see reg 1). See further RAILWAYS, INLAND WATERWAYS AND PIPELINES vol 39(1) (Reissue) para 232.

27 See ibid reg 3 (as amended); and RAILWAYS, INLAND WATERWAYS AND PIPELINES vol 39(1) (Reissue) para 232.

618.   Exemptions.   The Secretary of State[1] may by order (an 'exemption order') authorise the use for carriage[2] of any regulated rail vehicle[3] even though the vehicle does not conform with the provisions of the rail vehicle accessibility regulations[4] with which it is required to conform[5]. The Secretary of State may also authorise a regulated rail vehicle to be used for carriage otherwise than in conformity with the provisions of rail vehicle accessibility regulations with which use of the vehicle is required to conform[6]. Such authority[7] may be for any regulated rail vehicle that is specified[8] or is of a specified description[9], or for use in specified circumstances of any regulated rail vehicle or any regulated rail vehicle that is specified or is of a specified description[10].

Regulations[11] may make provision with respect to exemption orders including, in particular, provision as to the persons[12] by whom applications for exemption orders may be made[13], the form in which such applications are to be made[14], information to be supplied in connection with such applications[15], the period for which exemption orders are to continue in force[16], and the revocation of exemption orders[17].

After considering any application for an exemption order and consulting the Disabled Persons Transport Advisory Committee[18] and such other persons as he considers appropriate, the Secretary of State may[19] make an exemption order in the terms of the application[20], make an exemption order in such other terms as he considers appropriate[21], or refuse to make an exemption order[22]. An exemption order may be made subject to such restrictions and conditions as may be specified[23]. There is a requirement for annual reports to be prepared in regard to rail vehicle exemption orders[24].

The Rail Vehicle (Exemption Applications) Regulations 1998[25] specify that every application must be made in writing to the Secretary of State and must contain certain particulars[26].

Many exemption orders have been made, particularly in respect of certain new trains and rail vehicles which fail to meet the accessibility regulations[27].

1   As to the Secretary of State and the National Assembly for Wales see para 302 ante.
2   As to when a person uses a vehicle for carriage see para 617 note 20 ante.
3   For the meaning of 'regulated rail vehicle' see para 617 note 6 ante.
4   For the meaning of 'rail vehicle accessibility regulations' see para 617 note 3 ante.
5   Disability Discrimination Act 1995 s 47(1)(a) (s 47(1) substituted, and s 47(1A) added, by the Disability Discrimination Act 2005 s 6(3)).
6   Disability Discrimination Act 1995 s 47(1)(b) (as substituted: see note 5 supra).
7   Ie under ibid s 47(1)(a) or (b) (as substituted): see the text and notes 1–6 supra.
8   'Specified' means specified in an exemption order: ibid s 47(5).
9   Ibid s 47(1A)(a) (as added: see note 5 supra).
10 Ibid s 47(1A)(b) (as added: see note 5 supra).
11 As to regulations made under this power see the Rail Vehicle (Exemption Applications) Regulations 1998, SI 1998/2457; and RAILWAYS, INLAND WATERWAYS AND PIPELINES vol 39(1) (Reissue) para 232.
12 As to the meaning of 'person' see para 344 note 3 ante.
13 Disability Discrimination Act 1995 s 47(2)(a).
14 Ibid s 47(2)(b).
15 Ibid s 47(2)(c).
16 Ibid s 47(2)(d).
17 Ibid s 47(2)(e).
18 As to the Disabled Persons Transport Advisory Committee see ROAD TRAFFIC vol 40(1) (Reissue) para 56.
19 Disability Discrimination Act 1995 s 47(3).
20 Ibid s 47(3)(a).
21 Ibid s 47(3)(b).
22 Ibid s 47(3)(c).
23 Ibid s 47(4).
24 The Secretary of State must after each 31 December prepare, in respect of the year that ended with that day, a report on: (1) the exercise in that year of the power to make orders under ibid s 47(1) (as substituted) (see the text and notes 1–6 supra); and (2) the exercise in that year of the discretion under s 67(5A) (as added) (see para 509 ante): s 67B(1) (s 67B added by the Disability Discrimination Act 2005 s 6(5)). Such a report must (in particular) contain: (a) details of each order made under the Disability Discrimination Act 1995 s 47(1) (as substituted) in the year in respect of which the report is made; and (b) details of consultation carried out under s 47(3) (see the text and notes 18–22 supra) and s 67A(1) (as amended) (see para 509 ante) in connection with orders made in that year under s 47(1) (as substituted): s 67B(2) (as so added). The Secretary of State must lay before each House of Parliament each report that he prepares under s 67B (as added): s 67B(3) (as so added).
25 Ie the Rail Vehicle (Exemption Applications) Regulations 1998, SI 1998/2457, which came into force on 1 November 1998 (see reg 1). See further RAILWAYS, INLAND WATERWAYS AND PIPELINES vol 39(1) (Reissue) para 233.
26 See ibid reg 3; and RAILWAYS, INLAND WATERWAYS AND PIPELINES vol 39(1) (Reissue) para 233. Exemptions only continue in force for the periods specified and may be revoked by notice by the Secretary of State if the operator requests or if (having consulted the operator) the Secretary of State is satisfied that the operator has failed to comply with any restriction or condition subject to which the exemption was granted: see reg 4; and RAILWAYS, INLAND WATERWAYS AND PIPELINES vol 39(1) (Reissue) para 233.
27 See e g the Rail Vehicle Accessibility (Virgin West Coast Class 390) Exemption Order 2005, SI 2005/329; the Rail Vehicle Accessibility (Croydon Tramlink Class CR4000 Vehicles) Exemption (Amendment) Order 2005, SI 2005/395; the Rail Vehicle Accessibility (Heathrow Express Class 360/2) Exemption (Amendment) Order 2005, SI 2005/1404; and the Rail Vehicle Accessibility (Gatwick Express Class 458 Vehicles) Exemption Order 2006, SI 2006/933.

619. Penalty for using rail vehicle not conforming with accessibility regulations. As from a day to be appointed, the following provisions have effect[1]. Where it appears to the Secretary of State that a regulated rail vehicle[2] does not conform with a provision of rail vehicle accessibility regulations[3] with which the vehicle is required to conform[4], the Secretary of State may give to the operator[5] of the vehicle a notice: (1) identifying the vehicle, the provision and how the vehicle fails to conform with the provision[6]; and (2) specifying the improvement deadline[7].

Where (a) the Secretary of State has given a notice under heads (1) and (2) above[8]; (b) the improvement deadline specified in the notice has passed[9]; and (c) it appears to the Secretary of State that the vehicle still does not conform with the provision identified in the notice[10], the Secretary of State may give to the operator a further notice: (i) identifying the vehicle, the provision and how the vehicle fails to conform to the provision[11]; and (ii) specifying the final deadline[12].

If (A) the Secretary of State has given such further notice[13] to the operator of a regulated rail vehicle[14]; and (B) the vehicle is used for carriage at a time after the final deadline when the vehicle does not conform with the provision identified in the notice[15], the Secretary of State may require the operator to pay a penalty[16].

1   The Disability Discrimination Act 1995 ss 47E, 47M are added by the Disability Discrimination Act 2005 s 8(1) as from a day to be appointed by order made by the Secretary of State under s 20(3). At the date at which this volume states the law no such day had been appointed. As to the Secretary of State and the National Assembly for Wales see para 302 ante.

2   For the meaning of 'regulated rail vehicle' see para 617 note 6 ante. See also para 617 notes 2, 22 ante.

3   For the meaning of 'rail vehicle accessibility regulations' see para 617 note 3 ante.

4   Where an exemption order under the Disability Discrimination Act 1995 s 47 (as amended; prospectively amended) (see para 618 ante) authorises use of a rail vehicle even though the vehicle does not conform with a provision of rail vehicle accessibility regulations, references in ss 47A–47G (as added) (see also para 620 et seq post) to provisions of rail vehicle accessibility regulations with which the vehicle is required to conform do not, in the vehicle's case, include that provision: s 47M(3) (as added: see note 1 supra). For the meaning of 'rail vehicle' see para 617 note 2 ante.

5   For the meaning of 'operator' see para 617 note 21 ante.

6   Disability Discrimination Act 1995 s 47E(1)(a) (as added: see note 1 supra).

7   Ibid s 47E(1)(b) (as added: see note 1 supra). The improvement deadline specified in a notice under s 47E(1) (as added) may not be earlier than the end of the prescribed period beginning with the day when the notice is given to the operator: s 47E(2) (as so added). 'Prescribed' generally means prescribed by regulations: see para 515 note 5 ante. At the date at which this volume states the law no regulations had been made under s 47E (as added).

8   Ibid s 47E(3)(a) (as added: see note 1 supra).

9   Ibid s 47E(3)(b) (as added: see note 1 supra).

10   Ibid s 47E(3)(c) (as added: see note 1 supra).

11   Ibid s 47E(4)(a) (as added: see note 1 supra).

12   Ibid s 47E(4)(b) (as added: see note 1 supra). The final deadline specified in a notice under s 47E(4) (as added) may not be earlier than the end of the prescribed period beginning with the day when the notice is given to the operator: s 47E(5) (as so added). See note 7 supra.

13   Ie a notice under ibid s 47E(4) (as added): see the text and notes 11–12 supra.

14   Ibid s 47E(6)(a) (as added: see note 1 supra).

15   Ibid s 47E(6)(b) (as added: see note 1 supra).

16   Ibid s 47E(6) (as added: see note 1 supra). As to penalties see paras 624–626 post.

620. Penalty for using rail vehicle otherwise than in conformity with accessibility regulations. As from a day to be appointed, the following provisions have effect[1]. Where it appears to the Secretary of State that a regulated rail vehicle[2] has been used for carriage[3] otherwise than in conformity with a provision of rail vehicle accessibility regulations[4] with which use of the vehicle is required to conform[5], the Secretary of State may give to the operator[6] of the vehicle a notice: (1) identifying the provision and how it was breached[7]; (2) identifying which of the regulated rail vehicles operated by the operator is or are covered by the notice[8]; and (3) specifying the improvement deadline[9].

Where (a) the Secretary of State has given a notice under heads (1) to (3) above[10]; (b) the improvement deadline specified in the notice has passed[11]; and (c) it appears to the Secretary of State that a vehicle covered by the notice has after that deadline been used for carriage otherwise than in conformity with the provision identified in the notice[12], the Secretary of State may give to the operator a further notice: (i) identifying the provision and how it was breached[13]; (ii) identifying which of the regulated rail vehicles covered by the notice under heads (1) to (3) above is or are covered by the further notice[14]; and (iii) specifying the final deadline[15].

If (A) the Secretary of State has given such further notice[16]; and (B) a vehicle covered by the notice is at a time after the final deadline used for carriage otherwise than in conformity with the provision identified in the notice[17], the Secretary of State may require the operator of the vehicle to pay a penalty[18].

1 The Disability Discrimination Act 1995 s 47F is added by the Disability Discrimination Act 2005 s 8(1) as from a day to be appointed by order made by the Secretary of State under s 20(3). At the date at which this volume states the law no such day had been appointed. As to the Secretary of State and the National Assembly for Wales see para 302 ante.

2 For the meaning of 'regulated rail vehicle' see para 617 note 6 ante. See also para 617 notes 2, 22 ante.

3 As to use of a vehicle for carriage see para 617 note 20 ante.

4 For the meaning of 'rail vehicle accessibility regulations' see para 617 note 3 ante.

5 As to exemption orders and non-conformity with the rail vehicle accessibility regulations see para 619 note 4 ante.

6 For the meaning of 'operator' see para 617 note 21 ante. For the purposes of the Disability Discrimination Act 1995 s 47F(1) (as added), a vehicle is operated by a person if that person is the operator of the vehicle: s 47F(7) (as added: see note 1 supra).

7 Ibid 47F(1)(a) (as added: see note 1 supra).

8 Ibid s 47F(1)(b) (as added: see note 1 supra).

9 Ibid s 47F(1)(c) (as added: see note 1 supra). The improvement deadline specified in a notice under s 47F(1) (as added) may not be earlier than the end of the prescribed period beginning with the day when the notice is given to the operator: s 47F(2) (as so added). 'Prescribed' generally means prescribed by regulations: see para 515 note 5 ante. At the date at which this volume states the law no regulations had been made under s 47F (as added).

10 Ibid s 47F(3)(a) (as added: see note 1 supra).

11 Ibid s 47F(3)(b) (as added: see note 1 supra).

12 Ibid s 47F(3)(c) (as added: see note 1 supra).

13 Ibid s 47F(4)(a) (as added: see note 1 supra).

14 Ibid s 47F(4)(b) (as added: see note 1 supra).

15 Ibid s 47F(4)(c) (as added: see note 1 supra). The final deadline specified in a notice under s 47F(4) (as added) may not be earlier than the end of the prescribed period beginning with the day when the notice is given to the operator: s 47F(5) (as so added). See note 9 supra.

16 Ibid s 47F(6)(a) (as added: see note 1 supra). The further notice referred to in the text is a notice under s 47F(4) (as added): see the text and notes 13–15 supra.

17 Ibid s 47F(6)(b) (as added: see note 1 supra).

18 Ibid s 47F(6) (as added: see note 1 supra). As to penalties see paras 624–626 et seq post.

621. Inspection of rail vehicles. As from a day to be appointed, the following provisions have effect[1]. Where the Secretary of State has reasonable grounds for suspecting that a regulated rail vehicle[2] may not conform with provisions of rail vehicle accessibility regulations[3] with which it is required to conform[4], a person authorised by the Secretary of State: (1) may inspect[5] the vehicle for conformity with the provisions[6]; (2) for the purpose of exercising his power under head (1) above, may enter premises[7] if he has reasonable grounds for suspecting the vehicle to be at those premises, and may enter the vehicle[8]; and (3) for the purpose of exercising his power under head (1) or head (2) above, may require any person to afford such facilities and assistance with respect to matters under that person's control as are necessary to enable the power to be exercised[9].

Where the Secretary of State has given a notice under the provisions on non-conformity with rail vehicle accessibility regulations[10], a person authorised by the Secretary of State: (a) may inspect the vehicle concerned for conformity with the provision specified in the notice[11]; (b) for the purpose of exercising his power under head (a) above, may enter premises if he has reasonable grounds for suspecting the vehicle to be at those premises, and may enter the vehicle[12]; and (c) for the purpose of exercising his power under head (a) or head (b) above, may require any person to afford such facilities and assistance with respect to matters under that person's control as are necessary to enable the power to be exercised[13].

A person exercising power under heads (1) to (3) or heads (a) to (b) above[14] must, if required to do so, produce evidence of his authority to exercise the power[15].

Where a person obstructs the exercise of power under heads (1) to (3) above, the Secretary of State may[16] draw such inferences from the obstruction as appear proper[17].

Where (i) a person obstructs the exercise of power under heads (a) to (b) above[18]; and (ii) the obstruction occurs before a further notice under the provisions on non-conformity with rail vehicle accessibility regulations[19] is given in respect of the vehicle concerned[20], the Secretary of State may treat the vehicle as not conforming with the provision identified in the notice[21] in the case concerned[22].

Where a person obstructs the exercise of power under heads (a) to (b) above and the obstruction occurs: (A) after a further notice under the provisions on non-conformity with rail vehicle accessibility regulations[23] has been given in respect of the vehicle concerned[24]; and (B) as a result of the operator[25], or a person who acts on his behalf, behaving in a particular way with the intention of obstructing the exercise of the power[26], the Secretary of State may require the operator of the vehicle to pay a penalty[27].

1   The Disability Discrimination Act 1995 s 47G is added by the Disability Discrimination Act 2005 s 8(1) as from a day to be appointed by order made by the Secretary of State under s 20(3). At the date at which this volume states the law no such day had been appointed. As to the Secretary of State and the National Assembly for Wales see para 302 ante.
2   For the meaning of 'regulated rail vehicle' see para 617 note 6 ante. See also para 617 notes 2, 22 ante.
3   For the meaning of 'rail vehicle accessibility regulations' see para 617 note 3 ante.
4   As to exemption orders and non-conformity with the rail vehicle accessibility regulations see para 619 note 4 ante.
5   'Inspect' includes test: Disability Discrimination Act 1995 s 47G(7) (as added: see note 1 supra).
6   Ibid s 47G(1)(a) (as added: see note 1 supra).
7   As to the meaning of 'premises' see para 525 note 9 ante.
8   Disability Discrimination Act 1995 s 47G(1)(b) (as added: see note 1 supra).
9   Ibid s 47G(1)(c) (as added: see note 1 supra).
10 Ie under ibid s 47E(1) or (4) (as added): see para 619 ante.
11 Ibid s 47G(2)(a) (as added: see note 1 supra).
12 Ibid s 47G(2)(b) (as added: see note 1 supra).
13 Ibid s 47G(2)(c) (as added: see note 1 supra).
14 Ie under ibid s 47G(1) or (2) (as added): see the text and notes 1–13 supra.
15 Ibid s 47G(3) (as added: see note 1 supra).
16 Ie for the purposes of ibid s 47E(1) (as added) (see para 619 ante) or s 47F(1) (as added) (see para 620 ante).
17 Ibid s 47G(4) (as added: see note 1 supra).
18 Ibid s 47G(5)(a) (as added: see note 1 supra).
19 Ie a notice under ibid s 47E(4) (as added): see para 619 ante.
20 Ibid s 47G(5)(b) (as added: see note 1 supra).
21 Ie he may treat ibid s 47E(3)(c) (as added) as satisfied: see para 619 ante.
22 Ibid s 47G(5) (as added: see note 1 supra).
23 See note 19 supra.

24 Disability Discrimination Act 1995 s 47G(6)(a) (as added: see note 1 supra).
25 For the meaning of 'operator' see para 617 note 21 ante.
26 Disability Discrimination Act 1995 s 47G(6)(b) (as added: see note 1 supra).
27 Ibid s 47G(6) (as added: see note 1 supra). As to penalties see paras 624–626 post.

622. Supplementary powers in regard to using rail vehicles not in conformity with accessibility regulations. As from a day to be appointed, the following provisions have effect[1]. For the purposes of the provisions on rail vehicle use not conforming with rail vehicle accessibility regulations[2], the Secretary of State may give notice to a person[3] requiring the person to supply the Secretary of State, by a time specified in the notice[4], with a vehicle number or other identifier for a rail vehicle[5]: (1) of which that person is the operator[6]; and (2) which is described in the notice[7]. If a person to whom such a notice is given does not comply with the notice by the time specified in the notice, the Secretary of State may require the person to pay a penalty[8].

Where the Secretary of State has given a notice to a person under the provisions on rail vehicle use not conforming with rail vehicle accessibility regulations[9], the Secretary of State may request that person to supply the Secretary of State, by a time specified in the request, with a statement detailing the steps taken in response to the notice[10]. The time specified in such a request must: (a) if the request relates to an initial notice under those provisions[11], be no earlier than the improvement deadline[12]; and (b) if the request relates to a further notice under those provisions[13], be no earlier than the final deadline[14]. Where such a request: (i) relates to a an initial notice under the provisions[15]; and (ii) is not complied with by the time specified in the request[16], the Secretary of State may treat the vehicle as not conforming with the provision identified in the notice[17] or (as the case may be) may treat the vehicle as having been used otherwise than in conformity with the provision identified in the notice[18] in the case concerned[19].

1 The Disability Discrimination Act 1995 s 47H is added by the Disability Discrimination Act 2005 s 8(1) as from a day to be appointed by order made by the Secretary of State under s 20(3). At the date at which this volume states the law no such day had been appointed. As to the Secretary of State and the National Assembly for Wales see para 302 ante.
2 Ie for the purposes of the Disability Discrimination Act 1995 s 47E (as added): see para 619 ante. For the meaning of 'rail vehicle accessibility regulations' see para 617 note 3 ante.
3 As to the meaning of 'person' see note 344 note 3 ante.
4 The time specified in a notice given to a person under the Disability Discrimination Act 1995 s 47H(1) (as added) may not be earlier than the end of 14 days beginning with the day when the notice is given to the person: s 47H(2) (as added: see note 1 supra).
5 For the meaning of 'rail vehicle' see para 617 note 2 ante. See also para 617 notes 6, 22 ante.
6 Disability Discrimination Act 1995 s 47H(1)(a) (as added: see note 1 supra). For the meaning of 'operator' see para 617 note 21 ante.
7 Ibid s 47H(1)(b) (as added: see note 1 supra).
8 Ibid s 47H(3) (as added: see note 1 supra). As to penalties see paras 624–626 et seq post.
9 Ie under ibid s 47E(1) or (4) (as added) (see para 619 ante) or under s 47F(1) or (4) (as added) (see para 620 ante).
10 Ibid s 47H(4) (as added: see note 1 supra).
11 Ie a notice under ibid s 47E(1) (as added) (see para 619 ante) or s 47F(1) (as added) (see para 620 ante).
12 Ibid s 47H(5)(a) (as added: see note 1 supra).
13 Ie a notice under ibid s 47E(4) (as added) (see para 619 ante) or s 47F(4) (as added) (see para 620 ante).
14 Ibid s 47H(5)(b) (as added: see note 1 supra).
15 Ibid s 47H(6)(a) (as added: see note 1 supra). See also note 11 supra.
16 Ibid s 47H(6)(b) (as added: see note 1 supra).
17 Ie he may treat ibid s 47E(3)(c) (as added) as satisfied: see para 619 ante.
18 Ie he may treat ibid s 47F(3)(c) (as added) as satisfied: see para 620 ante.
19 Ibid s 47H(6)(b) (as added: see note 1 supra).

623. Rail vehicle accessibility certificates. As from a day to be appointed, the following provisions have effect[1]. A regulated rail vehicle[2] if it is prescribed[3] or is of a prescribed class or description[4] must not be used for carriage[5] unless a rail vehicle accessibility compliance certificate is in force for the vehicle[6]. A 'rail vehicle accessibility compliance certificate' is a certificate that the Secretary of State is satisfied that the regulated rail vehicle conforms with those provisions of rail vehicle accessibility regulations[7] with which the vehicle is required to conform[8]. Such a certificate may provide that it is subject to conditions specified in the certificate[9].

Where (1) the Secretary of State refuses an application for the issue of a rail vehicle accessibility compliance certificate for a regulated rail vehicle[10]; and (2) before the end of the prescribed period, the applicant asks the Secretary of State to review the decision and pays any relevant fee[11], the Secretary of State: (a) must review the decision[12]; and (b) in doing so, must consider any representations made to him in writing, before the end of the prescribed period, by the applicant[13].

Regulations may make provision with respect to rail vehicle accessibility compliance certificates[14].

If a regulated rail vehicle[15] is used for carriage at a time when no rail vehicle accessibility compliance certificate is in force for the vehicle, the Secretary of State may require the operator[16] of the vehicle to pay a penalty[17].

1   The Disability Discrimination Act 1995 ss 47A–47C are added by the Disability Discrimination Act 2005 s 7(1), and the Disability Discrimination Act 1995 s 47D is added by the Disability Discrimination Act 2005 s 8(1), as from a day to be appointed by order made by the Secretary of State under s 20(3). At the date at which this volume states the law no such day had been appointed. As to the Secretary of State and the National Assembly for Wales see para 302 ante.

2   For the meaning of 'regulated rail vehicle' see para 617 note 6 ante. See also para 617 notes 2, 22 ante.

3   'Prescribed' generally means prescribed by regulations: see para 515 note 5 ante. For the meaning of 'regulations' see para 509 note 12 ante. See notes 4, 11, 14 infra.

4   Disability Discrimination Act 1995 s 47A(2) (as added: see note 1 supra). At the date at which this volume states the law no regulations had been made under s 47A(2) (as added).

5   As to when a person uses a vehicle for carriage see para 617 note 20 ante.

6   Disability Discrimination Act 1995 s 47A(1) (as added: see note 1 supra).

7   For the meaning of 'rail vehicle accessibility regulations' see para 617 note 3 ante.

8   Disability Discrimination Act 1995 s 47A(3) (as added: see note 1 supra); s 68(1) (definition prospectively added by the Disability Discrimination Act 2005 s 7(3)).

9   Disability Discrimination Act 1995 s 47A(4) (as added: see note 1 supra).

10 Ibid s 47A(5)(a) (as added: see note 1 supra).

11 Ibid s 47A(5)(b) (as added: see note 1 supra). The reference to a fee is a reference to any fee fixed under s 47C (as added). Such fees, payable at such times, as may be prescribed may be charged by the Secretary of State in respect of: (1) applications for, and the issue of, rail vehicle accessibility compliance certificates; (2) copies of such certificates; (3) reviews under s 47A (as added); (4) referrals of disputes under provision that, in accordance with s 47B(6)(d) (as added) (see note 14 head (iv) infra), is contained in regulations under s 47B(1) (as added) (see note 14 infra): s 47C(1) (as so added). Any such fees received by the Secretary of State must be paid by him into the Consolidated Fund: s 47C(2) (as so added). As to the Consolidated Fund see CONSTITUTIONAL LAW AND HUMAN RIGHTS vol 8(2) (Reissue) para 711 et seq; PARLIAMENT vol 34 (Reissue) paras 952–955. Regulations under s 47C(1) (as added) may make provision for the repayment of fees, in whole or in part, in such circumstances as may be prescribed: s 47C(3) (as so added). Before making any regulations under s 47C(1) (as added) the Secretary of State must consult such representative organisations as he thinks fit: s 47C(4) (as so added). At the date at which this volume states the law no regulations had been made under s 47C (as added).

12 Ibid s 47A(6)(a) (as added: see note 1 supra).

13 Ibid s 47A(6)(b) (as added: see note 1 supra).

14 Ibid s 47B(1) (as added: see note 1 supra). At the date at which this volume states the law no regulations had been made under s 47B (as added).

    The provision that may be made under s 47B(1) (as added) includes (in particular): (1) provision for certificates to be issued on application; (2) provision specifying conditions to which certificates are subject; (3) provision as to the period for which certificates are to continue in force or as to circumstances in which certificates are to cease to be in force; (4) provision (other than provision of a kind mentioned in head (3) supra) dealing with failure to comply with a condition to which a certificate is subject; (5) provision for the withdrawal of certificates issued in error; (6) provision for the correction of errors in certificates; (7) provision with respect to the issue of copies of certificates in place of certificates which have been lost or destroyed; (8) provision for the examination of a rail vehicle before a certificate is issued in respect of it: s 47B(2) (as so added).

In making provision of the kind mentioned in head (1) supra, regulations under s 47B(1) (as added) may (in particular): (a) make provision as to the persons by whom applications may be made; (b) make provision as to the form in which applications are to be made; (c) make provision as to information to be supplied in connection with an application, including (in particular) provision requiring the supply of a report of a compliance assessment: s 47B(3) (as so added). For the purposes of s 47B (as added), a 'compliance assessment' is an assessment of a rail vehicle against provisions of rail vehicle accessibility regulations with which the vehicle is required to conform: s 47B(4) (as so added). In requiring a report of a compliance assessment to be supplied in connection with an application, regulations under s 47B(1) (as added) may make provision as to the person who must carry out the assessment, and may (in particular) require that the assessment be one carried out by a person who has been appointed by the Secretary of State to carry out compliance assessments (an 'appointed assessor'): s 47B(5) (as so added).

For the purposes of any provisions in regulations under s 47B(1) (as added) with respect to the supply of reports of compliance assessments carried out by appointed assessors, such regulations: (i) may make provision about appointments of appointed assessors, including in particular: (A) provision for an appointment to be on application or otherwise than on application; (B) provision as to who may be appointed; (C) provision as to the form of applications for appointment; (D) provision as to information to be supplied with applications for appointment; (E) provision as to terms and conditions, or the period or termination, of an appointment; and (F) provision for terms and conditions of an appointment, including any as to its period or termination, to be as agreed by the Secretary of State when making the appointment; (ii) may make provision authorising an appointed assessor to charge fees in connection with, or incidental to, its carrying out of a compliance assessment, including in particular: (A) provision restricting the amount of a fee; (B) provision authorising fees that contain a profit element; and (C) provision for advance payment of fees; (iii) may make provision requiring an appointed assessor to carry out a compliance assessment, and to do so in accordance with any procedures that may be prescribed, if prescribed conditions, which may include conditions as to the payment of fees to the assessor, are satisfied; (iv) must make provision for the referral to the Secretary of State of disputes between: (A) an appointed assessor carrying out a compliance assessment; and (B) the person who requested the assessment, relating to which provisions of rail vehicle accessibility regulations the vehicle is to be assessed against or relating to what amounts to conformity with any of those provisions: s 47B(6) (as so added). In heads (ii)–(iv) supra, 'compliance assessment' includes pre-assessment activities (e g a consideration of how the outcome of a compliance assessment would be affected by the carrying out of particular proposed work): s 47B(7) (as so added).

15　Ie to which ibid s 47A(1) (as added) applies.

16　For the meaning of 'operator' see para 617 note 21 ante.

17　Disability Discrimination Act 1995 s 47D (as added: see note 1 supra). As to penalties see paras 624–626 post.

624.　Penalties generally. As from a day to be appointed, the following provisions have effect[1]. The amount of a penalty[2]: (1) must not exceed the maximum prescribed[3]; and (2) must not exceed ten per cent of the turnover of the person on whom it is imposed[4].

A penalty must be paid to the Secretary of State before the end of the prescribed period[5]. Any sum payable to the Secretary of State as a penalty may be recovered by the Secretary of State as a debt due to him[6]. Any sum paid to the Secretary of State as a penalty must be paid by him into the Consolidated Fund[7].

The Secretary of State must issue a code of practice specifying matters to be considered in determining the amount of a penalty[8]; and he may from time to time revise the whole or any part of the code and issue the code as revised[9]. The Secretary of State must have regard to the code (in addition to any other matters he thinks relevant): (a) when imposing a penalty[10]; and (b) when considering[11] a notice of objection[12].

1　The Disability Discrimination Act 1995 s 47J is added by the Disability Discrimination Act 2005 s 8(1) as from a day to be appointed by order made by the Secretary of State under s 20(3). At the date at which this volume states the law no such day had been appointed. As to the Secretary of State and the National Assembly for Wales see para 302 ante.

2   For these purposes, 'penalty' means a penalty under any of the Disability Discrimination Act 1995
    ss 47D–47H (as added) (see paras 619–623 ante): s 47J(1) (as added: see note 1 supra). As to the
    procedure in relation to penalties see para 625 post. As to appeals against penalties see para 626 post.

3   Ibid s 47J(2)(a) (as added: see note 1 supra). 'Prescribed' generally means prescribed by regulations: see
    para 515 note 5 ante. For the meaning of 'regulations' see para 509 note 12 ante. At the date at which this
    volume states the law no regulations had been made under s 47J (as added).

4   Ibid s 47J(2)(b) (as added: see note 1 supra). For the purposes of s 47J(2)(b) (as added), a person's turnover
    must be determined in accordance with regulations: s 47J(3) (as so added). See note 3 supra.

5   Ibid s 47J(4) (as added: see note 1 supra). See note 3 supra.

6   Ibid s 47J(5) (as added: see note 1 supra). In proceedings under s 47J(5) (as added) for enforcement of a
    penalty, no question may be raised as to: (1) liability to the imposition of the penalty; or (2) its amount:
    s 47J(6) (as so added).

7   Ibid s 47J(7) (as added: see note 1 supra). As to the Consolidated Fund see CONSTITUTIONAL LAW AND
    HUMAN RIGHTS vol 8(2) (Reissue) para 711 et seq; PARLIAMENT vol 34 (Reissue) paras 952–955.

8   Ibid s 47J(8) (as added: see note 1 supra).

9   Ibid s 47J(9) (as added: see note 1 supra). Before issuing the first or a revised version of the code, the
    Secretary of State must lay a draft of that version before Parliament: s 47J(10) (as so added). After laying
    the draft of a version of the code before Parliament, the Secretary of State may bring that version of the
    code into operation by order: s 47J(11) (as so added).

10 Ibid s 47J(12)(a) (as added: see note 1 supra).

11 Ie under ibid s 47K(6) (as added): see para 625 post.

12 Ibid s 47J(12)(b) (as added: see note 1 supra). The reference in the text is to a notice of objection under
    s 47K(4) (as added): see para 625 post.

625.   Procedure as to penalties.   As from a day to be appointed, the following
provisions have effect[1]. If the Secretary of State decides that a person[2] is liable to a
penalty[3], the Secretary of State must notify the person of the decision[4]. Such notification
must: (1) state the Secretary of State's reasons for deciding that the person is liable to the
penalty[5]; (2) state the amount of the penalty[6]; (3) specify the date before which, and the
manner in which, the penalty must be paid[7]; and (4) include an explanation of the steps
that the person may take if he objects to the penalty[8].

Where a person to whom the above notification[9] is issued objects on the ground that:
(a) he is not liable to the imposition of a penalty[10]; or (b) the amount of the penalty is
too high[11], the person may give a notice of objection to the Secretary of State[12].

Where the Secretary of State receives a notice of objection to a penalty[13], he must
consider it and: (i) cancel the penalty[14]; (ii) reduce the penalty[15]; or (iii) determine to do
neither of those things[16]. Where the Secretary of State considers[17] a notice of
objection[18], he must: (A) inform the objector of his decision before the end of the
prescribed period or such longer period as he may agree with the objector[19]; and (B) if
he reduces the penalty, notify the objector of the reduced amount[20].

1   The Disability Discrimination Act 1995 s 47K is added by the Disability Discrimination Act 2005 s 8(1)
    as from a day to be appointed by order made by the Secretary of State under s 20(3). At the date at which
    this volume states the law no such day had been appointed. As to the Secretary of State and the National
    Assembly for Wales see para 302 ante.

2   As to the meaning of 'person' see para 344 note 3 ante.

3   For these purposes, 'penalty' means a penalty under any of the Disability Discrimination Act 1995
    ss 47D–47H (as added) (see paras 619–623 ante): s 47K(1) (as added: see note 1 supra). As to the amount,
    the due date and recovery in relation to penalties see para 624 ante. As to appeals against penalties see
    para 626 post.

4   Ibid s 47K(2) (as added: see note 1 supra).

5   Ibid s 47K(3)(a) (as added: see note 1 supra).

6   Ibid s 47K(3)(b) (as added: see note 1 supra).

7   Ibid s 47K(3)(c) (as added: see note 1 supra).

8   Ibid s 47K(3)(d) (as added: see note 1 supra).

9   Ie a notification under ibid s 47K(2) (as added): see the text and notes 2–4 supra.

10 Ibid s 47K(4)(a) (as added: see note 1 supra).

11 Ibid s 47K(4)(b) (as added: see note 1 supra).

12 Ibid s 47K(4) (as added: see note 1 supra). A notice of objection must: (1) be in writing; (2) give the objector's reasons; and (3) be given before the end of the prescribed period: s 47K(5) (as so added). 'Prescribed' generally means prescribed by regulations: see para 515 note 5 ante. For the meaning of 'regulations' see para 509 note 12 ante. At the date at which this volume states the law no regulations had been made under s 47K (as added).

13 Ie in accordance with ibid s 47K (as added).

14 Ibid s 47K(6)(a) (as added: see note 1 supra).

15 Ibid s 47K(6)(b) (as added: see note 1 supra).

16 Ibid s 47K(6)(c) (as added: see note 1 supra).

17 Ie under ibid s 47K(6) (as added): see the text and notes 13–16 supra.

18 Ie a notice under ibid s 47K(4) (as added): see the text and notes 9–12 supra.

19 Ibid s 47K(7)(a) (as added: see note 1 supra). See note 12 supra.

20 Ibid s 47K(7)(b) (as added: see note 1 supra).

626.   Appeals against penalties. As from a day to be appointed, the following provisions have effect[1]. A person[2] may appeal to the court[3] against a penalty[4] on the ground that: (1) he is not liable to the imposition of a penalty[5]; or (2) the amount of the penalty is too high[6].

On such an appeal[7], the court may: (a) allow the appeal and cancel the penalty[8]; (b) allow the appeal and reduce the penalty[9]; or (c) dismiss the appeal[10].

Such an appeal is a re-hearing of the Secretary of State's decision to impose a penalty, and is determined having regard to: (i) any code of practice[11] which has effect at the time of the appeal[12]; and (ii) any other matters which the court thinks relevant[13].

Such an appeal may be brought by a person against a penalty whether or not he has given notice of objection[14] or the penalty has been reduced[15].

1   The Disability Discrimination Act 1995 s 47L is added by the Disability Discrimination Act 2005 s 8(1) as from a day to be appointed by order made by the Secretary of State under s 20(3). At the date at which this volume states the law no such day had been appointed. As to the Secretary of State and the National Assembly for Wales see para 302 ante.

2   As to the meaning of 'person' see para 344 note 3 ante.

3   Ie a county court: Disability Discrimination Act 1995 s 47L(5) (as added: see note 1 supra).

4   Ie a penalty imposed on him under any of the provisions of ibid ss 47D–47H (as added) (see paras 619–623 ante): see s 47L(1) (as added: see note 1 supra). As to the amount, the due date and recovery in relation to penalties see para 624 ante. As to procedure as to penalties see para 625 ante.

5   Ibid s 47L(1)(a) (as added: see note 1 supra).

6   Ibid s 47L(1)(b) (as added: see note 1 supra).

7   Ie an appeal under ibid s 47L (as added).

8   Ibid s 47L(2)(a) (as added: see note 1 supra).

9   Ibid s 47L(2)(b) (as added: see note 1 supra).

10 Ibid s 47L(2)(c) (as added: see note 1 supra).

11 Ie any code of practice under ibid s 47J (as added): see para 624 ante.

12 Ibid s 47L(3)(a) (as added: see note 1 supra).

13 Ibid s 47L(3)(b) (as added: see note 1 supra). The other matters referred to in the text may include matters of which the Secretary of State was unaware: see s 47L(3)(b) (as so added).

14 Ibid s 47L(4)(a) (as added: see note 1 supra). As to the notice of objection see s 47K(4) (as added); and para 625 ante.

15 Ibid s 47L(4)(b) (as added: see note 1 supra). As to the reduction of a penalty see s 47K(6) (as added); and para 625 ante.

(B) Taxis

627.   Taxi accessibility. As from a day to be appointed[1], the Secretary of State[2] may make taxi[3] accessibility regulations[4] for the purpose of securing that it is possible[5]: (1) for disabled persons[6] to get into and out of taxis in safety[7] and to be carried in taxis in safety and in reasonable comfort[8]; and (2) for disabled persons in wheelchairs to be conveyed in safety into and out of taxis while remaining in their wheelchairs[9], and to be carried in taxis in safety and in reasonable comfort while remaining in their wheelchairs[10].

Taxi accessibility regulations may, in particular:

(a) require any regulated taxi[11] to conform with provisions of the regulations[12] as to the size of any door opening which is for the use of passengers[13], the floor area of the passenger compartment[14], the amount of headroom in the passenger compartment[15], and the fitting of restraining devices designed to ensure the stability of a wheelchair while the taxi is moving[16];

(b) require the driver of any regulated taxi which is plying for hire, or which has been hired, to comply with provisions of the regulations as to the carrying of ramps or other devices designed to facilitate the loading and unloading of wheelchairs[17]; and

(c) require the driver of any regulated taxi in which a disabled person who is in a wheelchair is being carried (while remaining in his wheelchair) to comply with provisions of the regulations as to the position in which the wheelchair is to be secured[18].

If the driver of a regulated taxi which is plying for hire, or which has been hired, fails to comply with any requirement imposed on him by the regulations[19], or if the taxi fails to conform with any provision of the regulations with which it is required to conform[20], the driver is guilty of an offence[21].

1   The Disability Discrimination Act 1995 s 32 is to come into force as from a day to be appointed. At the date at which this volume states the law, no such day had been appointed.
2   As to the Secretary of State and the National Assembly for Wales see para 302 ante.
3   'Taxi' means a vehicle licensed under: (1) the Town Police Clauses Act 1847 s 37 (as amended); or (2) the Metropolitan Public Carriage Act 1869 s 6 (as substituted), but does not include a taxi which is drawn by a horse or other animal: Disability Discrimination Act 1995 ss 32(5), 68(1) (s 32(5) not yet in force: see note 1 supra). As to the licensing of taxis see ROAD TRAFFIC.
4   For the meaning of 'regulations' see para 509 note 12 ante. At the date at which this volume states the law no regulations had been made for these purposes.
5   Disability Discrimination Act 1995 s 32(1) (not yet in force: see note 1 supra).
6   For the meaning of 'disabled person' see para 511 ante.
7   Disability Discrimination Act 1995 s 32(a)(i) (not yet in force: see note 1 supra).
8   Ibid s 32(a)(ii) (not yet in force: see note 1 supra).
9   Ibid s 32(b)(i) (not yet in force: see note 1 supra).
10 Ibid s 32(b)(ii) (not yet in force: see note 1 supra).
11 'Regulated taxi' means any taxi to which the regulations are expressed to apply: ibid ss 32(5), 68(1) (s 32(5) not yet in force: see note 1 supra). See note 4 supra.
12 Ibid s 32(2)(a) (not yet in force: see note 1 supra).
13 Ibid s 32(2)(a)(i) (not yet in force: see note 1 supra).
14 Ibid s 32(2)(a)(ii) (not yet in force: see note 1 supra). 'Passenger compartment' has such meaning as may be prescribed: s 32(5) (not yet in force: see note 1 supra). 'Prescribed' generally means prescribed by regulations: see para 515 note 5 ante. See note 4 supra.
15 Ibid s 32(2)(a)(iii) (not yet in force: see note 1 supra).
16 Ibid s 32(2)(a)(iv) (not yet in force: see note 1 supra).
17 Ibid s 32(2)(b) (not yet in force: see note 1 supra).
18 Ibid s 32(2)(c) (not yet in force: see note 1 supra).
19 Ibid s 32(3)(a) (not yet in force: see note 1 supra).
20 Ibid s 32(3)(b) (not yet in force: see note 1 supra).
21 A person who is guilty of such an offence is liable, on summary conviction, to a fine not exceeding level 3 on the standard scale: ibid s 32(4) (not yet in force: see note 1 supra). As to the standard scale see para 315 note 15 ante.

628.   Designated transport facilities.   As from a day to be appointed[1], the Secretary of State[2] may by regulations[3] provide for the application of any taxi provision[4] in relation to: (1) vehicles used for the provision of services under a franchise agreement[5]; or (2) the drivers of such vehicles[6].

1   The Disability Discrimination Act 1995 s 33 is to come into force as from a day to be appointed. At the date at which this volume states the law, no such day had been appointed.

2   This provision refers to the 'appropriate national authority', which means, in relation to transport facilities in England and Wales, the Secretary of State: see ibid s 33(4) (definition added by the Disability Discrimination Act 2005 s 19(1), Sch 1 paras 1, 26(1), (4); not yet in force (see note 1 supra)). As to the Secretary of State and the National Assembly for Wales see para 302 ante.

3   For the meaning of 'regulations' see para 509 note 12 ante. At the date at which this volume states the law no such regulations had been made.

4   Disability Discrimination Act 1995 s 33(2) (amended by the Disability Discrimination Act 2005 Sch 1 paras 1, 26(1), (2); not yet in force (see note 1 supra)). Any such regulations may apply any taxi provision with such modifications as the authority making the regulations considers appropriate: Disability Discrimination Act 1995 s 33(3) (amended by the Disability Discrimination Act 2005 Sch 1 paras 1, 26(1), (3); not yet in force (see note 1 supra)). 'Taxi provision' means any provision of the Disability Discrimination Act 1995 which applies in relation to taxis or the drivers of taxis: s 33(4) (not yet in force: see note 1 supra). For the meaning of 'taxi' see para 627 note 3 ante. See note 3 supra.

5   Ibid s 33(2)(a) (not yet in force: see note 1 supra). 'A franchise agreement' means a contract entered into by the operator of a designated transport facility for the provision by the other party to the contract of hire car services: (1) for members of the public using any part of the transport facility; and (2) which involve vehicles entering any part of that facility: s 33(1) (not yet in force: see note 1 supra). 'Designated' means designated for these purposes by an order made by the Secretary of State (see note 2 supra); 'hire car' has such meaning as may be specified by regulations made by the Secretary of State (see note 2 supra); 'operator', in relation to a transport facility, means any person who is concerned with the management or operation of the facility; and 'transport facility' means any premises which form part of any port, airport, railway station or bus station: s 33(4) (amended by the Disability Discrimination Act 2005 Sch 1 paras 26(1), (2), (5); not yet in force (see note 1 supra)).

6   Disability Discrimination Act 1995 s 33(2)(b) (not yet in force: see note 1 supra).

629.   New licences.   As from a day to be appointed[1], no licensing authority[2] may grant a licence for a taxi to ply for hire unless the vehicle conforms with those provisions of the taxi accessibility regulations[3] with which it will be required to conform if licensed[4]. This does not apply if such a licence was in force with respect to the vehicle at any time during the period of 28 days immediately before the day on which the licence is granted[5].

1   The Disability Discrimination Act 1995 s 34 is to come into force as from a day to be appointed. At the date at which this volume states the law, no such day had been appointed.

2   'Licensing authority' (except in ibid s 37A (as added): see para 633 post) means: (1) in relation to the area to which the Metropolitan Public Carriage Act 1869 applies (see ROAD TRAFFIC vol 40(2) (Reissue) para 1098 et seq), the Secretary of State or the holder of any office for the time being designated by the Secretary of State; or (2) in relation to any other area in England and Wales, the authority responsible for licensing taxis in that area: Disability Discrimination Act 1995 s 68(1) (definition amended by the Private Hire Vehicles (Carriage of Guide Dogs etc) Act 2002 s 5). As to the Secretary of State and the National Assembly for Wales see para 302 ante. For the meaning of 'taxi' see para 627 note 3 ante.

3   'Taxi accessibility regulations' means regulations made under the Disability Discrimination Act 1995 s 32(1) (not yet in force) (see para 627 ante): s 68(1).

4   Ibid s 34(1) (not yet in force: see note 1 supra).

5   Ibid s 34(2) (not yet in force: see note 1 supra). The Secretary of State may by order provide for s 34(2) (not yet in force) to cease to have effect on such date as may be specified in the order: s 34(3) (not yet in force: see note 1 supra). Separate orders may be made with respect to different areas or localities: s 34(4) (not yet in force: see note 1 supra). At the date at which this volume states the law no such order had been made.

630.   Exemption from taxi accessibility regulations.   As from a day to be appointed[1], the Secretary of State[2] may make exemption regulations[3] for the purpose of enabling any relevant licensing authority[4] to apply to him for an exemption order exempting the authority from the requirements of the provision relating to taxis[5]. Exemption regulations may, in particular, make provision requiring a licensing authority proposing to apply for an exemption order[6] to carry out such consultations as may be prescribed[7], to publish the proposal in the prescribed manner[8], to consider any representations made to it about the proposal, before applying for the order[9], and to make its application in the prescribed form[10].

A licensing authority may apply for an exemption order only if it is satisfied[11] that, having regard to the circumstances prevailing in its area, it would be inappropriate for the requirements relating to taxis[12] to apply[13], and that the application of the requirements would result in an unacceptable reduction in the number of taxis in its area[14].

After considering any application for an exemption order and consulting the Disabled Persons Transport Advisory Committee[15] and such other persons as he considers appropriate[16], the Secretary of State may: (1) make an exemption order in the terms of the application[17]; (2) make an exemption order in such other terms as he considers appropriate[18]; or (3) refuse to make an exemption order[19].

The Secretary of State may by regulations make provision requiring any exempt taxi[20] plying for hire in an area in respect of which an exemption order is in force to conform with provisions of the regulations as to the fitting and use of swivel seats[21].

1   The Disability Discrimination Act 1995 s 35 is to come into force as from a day to be appointed. At the date at which this volume states the law, no such day had been appointed.
2   As to the Secretary of State and the National Assembly for Wales see para 302 ante.
3   For the meaning of 'regulations' see para 509 note 12 ante. At the date at which this volume states the law no regulations had been made for these purposes.
4   'Relevant licensing authority' means a licensing authority responsible for licensing taxis in any area of England and Wales other than the area to which the Metropolitan Public Carriage Act 1869 applies (see ROAD TRAFFIC vol 40(2) (Reissue) para 1098 et seq): Disability Discrimination Act 1995 s 35(7) (not yet in force: see note 1 supra). For the meaning of 'licensing authority' see para 629 note 2 ante. For the meaning of 'taxi' see para 627 note 3 ante.
5   Ibid s 35(1) (not yet in force: see note 1 supra). The provision referred to in the text is s 34 (not yet in force): see para 629 ante.
6   Ibid s 35(2) (not yet in force: see note 1 supra).
7   Ibid s 35(2)(a) (not yet in force: see note 1 supra). 'Prescribed' generally means prescribed by regulations: see para 515 note 5 ante. See note 3 supra.
8   Ibid s 35(2)(b) (not yet in force: see note 1 supra).
9   Ibid s 35(2)(c) (not yet in force: see note 1 supra).
10 Ibid s 35(2)(d) (not yet in force: see note 1 supra).
11 Ibid s 35(3) (not yet in force: see note 1 supra).
12 Ie ibid s 34 (not yet in force): see para 629 ante.
13 Ibid s 35(3)(a) (not yet in force: see note 1 supra).
14 Ibid s 35(3)(b) (not yet in force: see note 1 supra).
15 As to the Disabled Persons Transport Advisory Committee see ROAD TRAFFIC vol 40(1) (Reissue) para 56.
16 Disability Discrimination Act 1995 s 35(4) (not yet in force: see note 1 supra).
17 Ibid s 35(4)(a) (not yet in force: see note 1 supra).
18 Ibid s 35(4)(b) (not yet in force: see note 1 supra).
19 Ibid s 35(4)(c) (not yet in force: see note 1 supra).
20 'Exempt taxi' means a taxi in relation to which ibid s 34(1) (not yet in force) (see para 629 ante) would apply if the exemption order were not in force: s 35(7) (not yet in force: see note 1 supra).
21 Ibid s 35(5) (not yet in force: see note 1 supra). 'Swivel seats' has such meaning as may be prescribed: s 35(7) (not yet in force: see note 1 supra). The Secretary of State may by regulations make provision with respect to swivel seat regulations similar to that made by s 34 (not yet in force) (see para 629 ante) with respect to taxi accessibility regulations: s 35(6) (not yet in force: see note 1 supra). For the meaning of 'taxi accessibility regulations' see para 629 note 3 ante.

631. Carrying of passengers in wheelchairs. As from a day to be appointed[1], certain duties are imposed on the driver of a regulated taxi[2] which has been hired[3] by or for a disabled person[4] who is in a wheelchair[5], or by a person who wishes such a disabled person to accompany him in the taxi[6].

The duties are:

(1)   to carry[7] the passenger[8] while he remains in his wheelchair[9];
(2)   not to make any additional charge for doing so[10];
(3)   if the passenger chooses to sit in a passenger seat, to carry the wheelchair[11];

(4)   to take such steps as are necessary to ensure that the passenger is carried in safety and in reasonable comfort[12]; and

(5)   to give such assistance as may be reasonably required[13]: (a) to enable the passenger to get into or out of the taxi[14]; (b) if the passenger wishes to remain in his wheelchair, to enable him to be conveyed into and out of the taxi while in his wheelchair[15]; (c) to load the passenger's luggage into or out of the taxi[16]; and (d) if the passenger does not wish to remain in his wheelchair, to load the wheelchair into or out of the taxi[17].

The above provisions do not require the driver of any taxi, except in the case of a taxi of a prescribed[18] description, to carry more than one person in a wheelchair, or more than one wheelchair, on any one journey[19], or to carry any person in circumstances in which it would otherwise be lawful for him to refuse to carry that person[20].

A driver of a regulated taxi who fails to comply with any duty imposed on him by the above provisions is guilty of an offence[21]. In any proceedings for such an offence, it is a defence for the accused to show that, even though at the time of the alleged offence the taxi conformed with those provisions of the taxi accessibility regulations[22] with which it was required to conform, it would not have been possible for the wheelchair in question to be carried in safety in the taxi[23].

If the licensing authority[24] is satisfied that it is appropriate to exempt a person from the duties imposed by the above provisions on medical grounds[25], or on the ground that his physical condition makes it impossible or unreasonably difficult for him to comply with the duties imposed on drivers[26], it must issue him with a certificate of exemption[27]. A certificate of exemption is issued for such period as may be specified in the certificate[28]. The driver of a regulated taxi is exempt from the above duties if a certificate of exemption issued to him under this provision is in force[29], and the prescribed notice of his exemption is exhibited on the taxi in the prescribed manner[30].

1   The Disability Discrimination Act 1995 s 36 is to come into force as from a day to be appointed. At the date at which this volume states the law, no such day had been appointed.

2   For the meaning of 'regulated taxi' see para 627 note 11 ante; and for the meaning of 'taxi' see para 627 note 3 ante.

3   Disability Discrimination Act 1995 s 36(1) (not yet in force: see note 1 supra).

4   For the meaning of 'disabled person' see para 511 ante.

5   Disability Discrimination Act 1995 s 36(1)(a) (not yet in force: see note 1 supra).

6   Ibid s 36(1)(b) (not yet in force: see note 1 supra).

7   'Carry' means carry in the taxi concerned: ibid s 36(2) (not yet in force: see note 1 supra).

8   The 'passenger' means the disabled person concerned: ibid s 36(2) (not yet in force: see note 1 supra).

9   Ibid s 36(3)(a) (not yet in force: see note 1 supra).

10   Ibid s 36(3)(b) (not yet in force: see note 1 supra).

11   Ibid s 36(3)(c) (not yet in force: see note 1 supra).

12   Ibid s 36(3)(d) (not yet in force: see note 1 supra).

13   Ibid s 36(3)(e) (not yet in force: see note 1 supra).

14   Ibid s 36(3)(e)(i) (not yet in force: see note 1 supra).

15   Ibid s 36(3)(e)(ii) (not yet in force: see note 1 supra).

16   Ibid s 36(3)(e)(iii) (not yet in force: see note 1 supra).

17   Ibid s 36(3)(e)(iv) (not yet in force: see note 1 supra).

18   'Prescribed' generally means prescribed by regulations: see para 515 note 5 ante. At the date at which this volume states the law no regulations had been made for these purposes.

19   Disability Discrimination Act 1995 s 36(4)(a) (not yet in force: see note 1 supra).

20   Ibid s 36(4)(b) (not yet in force: see note 1 supra).

21   Ibid s 36(5) (not yet in force: see note 1 supra). Such a driver is liable, on summary conviction, to a fine not exceeding level 3 on the standard scale: see s 36(5) (not yet in force: see note 1 supra). As to the standard scale see para 315 note 15 ante.

22   For the meaning of 'taxi accessibility regulations' see para 629 note 3 ante.

23   Disability Discrimination Act 1995 s 36(6) (not yet in force: see note 1 supra).

24   For the meaning of 'licensing authority' see para 629 note 2 ante.

25   Disability Discrimination Act 1995 s 36(7)(a) (not yet in force: see note 1 supra).

26 Ibid s 36(7)(b) (not yet in force: see note 1 supra).
27 Ibid s 36(7) (not yet in force: see note 1 supra). As to appeal against the refusal of an exemption certificate see para 634 post.
28 Ibid s 36(8) (not yet in force: see note 1 supra).
29 Ibid s 36(9)(a) (not yet in force: see note 1 supra).
30 Ibid s 36(9)(b) (not yet in force: see note 1 supra).

632. Carrying of guide dogs, hearing dogs and other assistance dogs in taxis. The driver of a taxi[1] which has been hired[2] by or for a disabled person[3] who is accompanied by his guide dog[4] or hearing dog[5], or by a person who wishes such a disabled person to accompany him in the taxi[6] is under a duty to carry the passenger's dog and allow it to remain with the passenger[7], and not to make any additional charge for doing so[8]. A driver of a taxi who fails to comply with this duty is guilty of an offence[9].

If the licensing authority[10] is satisfied that it is appropriate on medical grounds to exempt a person from this duty, it may issue him with a certificate of exemption[11]. In determining whether to issue a certificate of exemption, the licensing authority must, in particular, have regard to the physical characteristics of the taxi which the applicant drives or those of any kind of taxi in relation to which he requires the certificate[12]. A certificate of exemption must be issued with respect to a specified taxi or a specified kind of taxi[13], and for such period as may be specified in the certificate[14].

The driver of a taxi is exempt from the above duty if a certificate of exemption issued to him is in force with respect to the taxi[15], and the prescribed notice of his exemption is exhibited on the taxi in the prescribed manner[16].

These provisions have been extended so as to apply in relation to certain assistance dogs trained to assist a disabled person who has a disability of a prescribed kind[17].

1 For the meaning of 'taxi' see para 627 note 3 ante.
2 Disability Discrimination Act 1995 s 37(1).
3 For the meaning of 'disabled person' see para 511 ante. The disabled person is referred to in this provision as 'the passenger': ibid s 37(2).
4 'Guide dog' means a dog which has been trained to guide a blind person: ibid s 37(11).
5 Ibid s 37(1)(a). 'Hearing dog' means a dog which has been trained to assist a deaf person: s 37(11).
6 Ibid s 37(1)(b).
7 Ibid s 37(3)(a).
8 Ibid s 37(3)(b). As to the carriage of disabled persons accompanied by guide dogs, hearing dogs or other assistance dogs in private hire vehicles see s 37A (as added); and para 633 post.
9 Ibid s 37(4). He is liable, on summary conviction, to a fine not exceeding level 3 on the standard scale: see s 37(4). As to the standard scale see para 315 note 15 ante.
10 For the meaning of 'licensing authority' see para 629 note 2 ante.
11 Disability Discrimination Act 1995 s 37(5). As to appeal against the refusal of an exemption certificate see para 634 post.
12 Ibid s 37(6).
13 Ibid s 37(7)(a).
14 Ibid s 37(7)(b).
15 Ibid s 37(8)(a).
16 Ibid s 37(8)(b). 'Prescribed' generally means prescribed by regulations: see para 515 note 5 ante. As to the regulations made see the Disability Discrimination Act 1995 (Taxis) (Carrying of Guide Dogs etc) (England and Wales) Regulations 2000, SI 2000/2990 (amended by SI 2006/1616).
17 The Secretary of State has power to prescribe any other category of dog trained to assist a disabled person who has a disability of a prescribed kind, and the Disability Discrimination Act 1995 s 37 applies in relation to any such prescribed category of dog as it applies in relation to guide dogs: see s 37(9), (10). Assistance dogs have been prescribed as a category of dog for these purposes: see the Disability Discrimination Act 1995 (Taxis) (Carrying of Guide Dogs etc) (England and Wales) Regulations 2000, SI 2000/2990, reg 3.

633. Carrying of assistance dogs in private hire vehicles. It is an offence for the operator[1] of a private hire vehicle[2] to: (1) fail or refuse to accept a booking for a private hire vehicle if: (a) the booking is requested by or on behalf of a disabled person[3], or a person who wishes a disabled person to accompany him[4]; and (b) the reason for the failure or refusal is that the disabled person will be accompanied by his assistance dog[5]; (2) make an additional charge for carrying an assistance dog which is accompanying a disabled person[6].

It is an offence for the driver[7] of a private hire vehicle to fail or refuse to carry out a booking for a private hire vehicle if: (i) the booking was made by or on behalf of a disabled person, or a person who wishes a disabled person to accompany him[8]; and (ii) the reason for the failure or refusal is that the disabled person is accompanied by his assistance dog[9].

A person who is guilty of an offence under the provisions above is liable on summary conviction to a fine[10].

If the licensing authority[11] is satisfied that it is appropriate on medical grounds to issue a certificate of exemption to a driver, it must do so[12]. A certificate of exemption must be issued with respect to a specified private hire vehicle or a specified kind of private hire vehicle, and for such period as may be specified in the certificate[13].

No offence is committed by a driver under the provision above[14] if a certificate of exemption issued to him is in force with respect to the private hire vehicle[15] and the prescribed notice[16] is exhibited on the private hire vehicle in the prescribed manner[17].

1   'Operator' means a person who holds a licence granted under: (1) the Private Hire Vehicles (London) Act 1998 s 3 (as amended) (see ROAD TRAFFIC vol 40(2) (Reissue) para 1122); (2) the Local Government (Miscellaneous Provisions) Act 1976 s 55 (see ROAD TRAFFIC vol 40(2) (Reissue) para 1071); or (3) an equivalent provision of a local enactment: Disability Discrimination Act 1995 s 37A(9) (s 37A added by the Private Hire Vehicles (Carriage of Guide Dogs etc) Act 2002 s 1(1)).

2   'Private hire vehicle' means a vehicle licensed under: (1) the Private Hire Vehicles (London) Act 1998 s 6 (see ROAD TRAFFIC vol 40(2) (Reissue) para 1125); (2) the Local Government (Miscellaneous Provisions) Act 1976 s 48 (as amended) (see ROAD TRAFFIC vol 40(2) (Reissue) para 1125); or (3) an equivalent provision of a local enactment: Disability Discrimination Act 1995 s 37A(9) (as added: see note 1 supra).

3   For the meaning of 'disabled person' see para 511 ante.

4   Disability Discrimination Act 1995 s 37A(1)(a) (as added: see note 1 supra).

5   Ibid s 37A(1)(b) (as added: see note 1 supra). For these purposes, 'assistance dog' means a dog which has been trained: (1) to guide a blind person; (2) to assist a deaf person; or (3) by a prescribed charity to assist a disabled person who has a disability which: (a) consists of epilepsy; or (b) otherwise affects his mobility, manual dexterity, physical co-ordination or ability to lift, carry or otherwise move everyday objects: s 37A(9) (as so added). 'Prescribed' generally means prescribed by regulations: see para 515 note 5 ante. As to the prescribed charities see the Disability Discrimination Act 1995 (Private Hire Vehicles) (Carriage of Guide Dogs etc) (England and Wales) Regulations 2003, SI 2003/3122, reg 3.

6   Disability Discrimination Act 1995 s 37A(2) (as added: see note 1 supra).

7   'Driver' means a person who holds a licence granted under: (1) the Private Hire Vehicles (London) Act 1998 s 13 (as amended) (see ROAD TRAFFIC vol 40(2) (Reissue) para 1132); (2) the Local Government (Miscellaneous Provisions) Act 1976 s 51 (as amended) (see ROAD TRAFFIC vol 40(2) (Reissue) para 1070); or (3) an equivalent provision of a local enactment: Disability Discrimination Act 1995 s 37A(9) (as added: see note 1 supra).

8   Ibid s 37A(3)(a) (as added: see note 1 supra).

9   Ibid s 37A(3)(b) (as added: see note 1 supra).

10 Ibid s 37A(4) (as added: see note 1 supra). The fine referred to in the text is a fine not exceeding level 3 on the standard scale: see s 37A(4) (as so added). As to the standard scale see para 315 note 15 ante.

11 'Licensing authority', in relation to any area of England and Wales, means the authority responsible for licensing private hire vehicles in that area: ibid s 37A(9) (as added: see note 1 supra).

12 Ibid s 37A(5) (as added: see note 1 supra). As to appeals against the refusal of exemption certificates see para 634 post.

13 Ibid s 37A(7) (as added: see note 1 supra). In determining whether to issue a certificate of exemption, the licensing authority must, in particular, have regard to the physical characteristics of the private hire vehicle which the applicant drives or those of any kind of private hire vehicle in relation to which he requires the certificate: s 37A(6) (as so added).

14 Ie ibid s 37A(3) (as added): see the text and notes 7–9 supra.

15 Ibid s 37A(8)(a) (as added: see note 1 supra).

16 As to the certificate of exemption issued by a licensing authority in England see the Disability
    Discrimination Act 1995 (Private Hire Vehicles) (Carriage of Guide Dogs etc) (England and Wales)
    Regulations 2003, SI 2003/3122, reg 2(1), Sch 1 (amended by SI 2006/1617); and as to the certificate of
    exemption issued by a licensing authority in Wales see the Disability Discrimination Act 1995 (Private
    Hire Vehicles) (Carriage of Guide Dogs etc) (England and Wales) Regulations 2003, SI 2003/3122, Sch 2
    (amended by SI 2006/1617). The prescribed manner of exhibiting a notice of exemption is: (1) by
    displaying it on the private hire vehicle facing outwards, and in a manner that readily permits its removal;
    (2) so that its front is clearly visible from the outside of the private hire vehicle, and its back is clearly
    visible from the driver's seat of the private hire vehicle: Disability Discrimination Act 1995 (Private Hire
    Vehicles) (Carriage of Guide Dogs etc) (England and Wales) Regulations 2003, SI 2003/3122, reg 2(2)
    (substituted by SI 2006/1617).
17 Disability Discrimination Act 1995 s 37A(8)(b) (as added: see note 1 supra).

634.   Appeal against refusal of exemption certificate. Any person[1] who is
aggrieved by the refusal of a licensing authority[2] to issue an exemption certificate[3] may
appeal to a magistrates' court[4] before the end of the period of 28 days beginning with
the date of the refusal[5]. On an appeal to it, the court may direct the licensing authority
concerned to issue the appropriate certificate of exemption to have effect for such
period as may be specified in the direction[6].

1 As to the meaning of 'person' see para 344 note 3 ante.
2 For the meaning of 'licensing authority' see para 629 note 2 ante.
3 Ie under the Disability Discrimination Act 1995 s 36, s 37 or s 37A (as added): see paras 631–633 ante.
4 See MAGISTRATES.
5 Disability Discrimination Act 1995 s 38(1) (amended by the Private Hire Vehicles (Carriage of Guide
    Dogs etc) Act 2002 s 3; and the Courts Act 2003 s 109(1), Sch 8 para 368(1), (2)).
6 Disability Discrimination Act 1995 s 38(2).

(C) Public Service Vehicles

635.   Public service vehicle accessibility. The Secretary of State[1] may make
public service vehicle[2] ('PSV') accessibility regulations[3] for the purpose of securing that
it is possible for disabled persons[4] to get on to and off regulated public service vehicles[5]
in safety and without unreasonable difficulty (and, in the case of disabled persons in
wheelchairs, to do so while remaining in their wheelchairs)[6], and to be carried in such
vehicles in safety and in reasonable comfort[7].

PSV accessibility regulations may, in particular, make provision as to the construction,
use and maintenance of regulated public service vehicles[8] including provision as to:
  (1)   the fitting of equipment to vehicles[9];
  (2)   equipment to be carried by vehicles[10];
  (3)   the design of equipment to be fitted to, or carried by, vehicles[11];
  (4)   the fitting and use of restraining devices designed to ensure the stability of
        wheelchairs while vehicles are moving[12];
  (5)   the position in which wheelchairs are to be secured while vehicles are moving[13].
Any person who: (a) contravenes or fails to comply with any provision of the PSV
accessibility regulations[14]; (b) uses on a road a regulated public service vehicle which
does not conform with any provision of the regulations with which it is required to
conform[15]; or (c) causes or permits to be used on a road such a regulated public service
vehicle[16], is guilty of an offence[17].

Different provision may be made in regulations as respects different classes or
descriptions of vehicle[18], and as respects the same class or description of vehicle in
different circumstances[19].

1 As to the Secretary of State and the National Assembly for Wales see para 302 ante.
2 'Public service vehicle' means a vehicle which is: (1) adapted to carry more than eight passengers; and (2)
    a public service vehicle for the purposes of the Public Passenger Vehicles Act 1981 (see ROAD TRAFFIC
    vol 40(2) (Reissue) para 818): Disability Discrimination Act 1995 ss 40(5), 68(1).

3   For the meaning of 'regulations' see para 509 note 12 ante. 'PSV accessibility regulations' means regulations made under ibid s 40(1): s 68(1). Before making any regulations under s 40, s 41 (see para 636 post) or s 42 (see para 637 post), the Secretary of State must consult the Disabled Persons Transport Advisory Committee and such other representative organisations as he thinks fit: s 40(7). As to the Disabled Persons Transport Advisory Committee see ROAD TRAFFIC vol 40(1) (Reissue) para 56. As to the regulations made see the Public Service Vehicles Accessibility Regulations 2000, SI 2000/1970 (amended by SI 2000/3318; SI 2002/2981; SI 2003/1818; SI 2005/2988).
4   Disability Discrimination Act 1995 s 40(1). For the meaning of 'disabled person' see para 511 ante.
5   'Regulated public service vehicle' means any public service vehicle to which the PSV accessibility regulations are expressed to apply: ibid ss 40(5), 68(1).
6   Ibid s 40(1)(a).
7   Ibid s 40(1)(b).
8   Ibid s 40(2).
9   Ibid s 40(2)(a).
10   Ibid s 40(2)(b).
11   Ibid s 40(2)(c).
12   Ibid s 40(2)(d).
13   Ibid s 40(2)(e).
14   Ibid s 40(3)(a).
15   Ibid s 40(3)(b).
16   Ibid s 40(3)(c).
17   Ibid s 40(3). A person who is guilty of such an offence is liable, on summary conviction, to a fine not exceeding level 4 on the standard scale: s 40(4). As to the standard scale see para 315 note 15 ante. As to offences by bodies corporate see para 641 post.
18   Ibid s 40(6)(a).
19   Ibid s 40(6)(b).

636.   Accessibility certificates.   A regulated public service vehicle[1] must not be used on a road unless[2]: (1) a vehicle examiner[3] has issued an accessibility certificate that such provisions of the PSV accessibility regulations[4] as may be prescribed[5] are satisfied in respect of the vehicle[6]; or (2) an approval certificate has been issued[7] in respect of the vehicle[8].

The Secretary of State[9] may make regulations with respect to applications for, and the issue of, accessibility certificates[10], providing for the examination of vehicles in respect of which applications have been made[11], and with respect to the issue of copies of accessibility certificates in place of certificates which have been lost or destroyed[12].

If a regulated public service vehicle is used in contravention of this provision, the operator[13] of the vehicle is guilty of an offence[14].

1   For the meaning of 'regulated public service vehicle' see para 635 note 5 ante.
2   Disability Discrimination Act 1995 s 41(1).
3   'Vehicle examiner' means an examiner appointed under the Road Traffic Act 1988 s 66A (as added and amended) (see ROAD TRAFFIC vol 40(1) (Reissue) para 465): Disability Discrimination Act 1995 s 68(1).
4   For the meaning of 'PSV accessibility regulations' see para 635 note 3 ante. As to the regulations made see the Public Service Vehicles Accessibility Regulations 2000, SI 2000/1970 (amended by SI 2000/3318; SI 2002/2981; SI 2003/1818; SI 2005/2988).
5   'Prescribed' generally means prescribed by regulations: see para 515 note 5 ante. For the meaning of 'regulations' see para 509 note 12 ante. See note 4 supra.
6   Disability Discrimination Act 1995 s 41(1)(a).
7   Ie a certificate issued under ibid s 42: see para 637 post.
8   Ibid s 41(1)(b).
9   As to the Secretary of State and the National Assembly for Wales see para 302 ante.
10   Disability Discrimination Act 1995 s 41(2)(a). See note 4 supra.
11   Ibid s 41(2)(b). See note 4 supra.
12   Ibid s 41(2)(c). See note 4 supra.
13   'Operator' has the same meaning as in the Public Passenger Vehicles Act 1981 (see ROAD TRAFFIC vol 40(2) (Reissue) para 818): Disability Discrimination Act 1995 s 41(4).
14   Ibid s 41(3). A person guilty of such an offence is liable on summary conviction to a fine not exceeding level 4 on the standard scale: see s 41(3). As to the standard scale see para 315 note 15 ante.

637. Approval certificates. Where the Secretary of State[1] is satisfied that such provisions of the PSV accessibility regulations[2] as may be prescribed[3] are satisfied in respect of a particular vehicle he may approve the vehicle[4]. A vehicle which has been so approved is a 'type vehicle'[5].

Where a declaration in the prescribed form has been made by an authorised person[6] that a particular vehicle conforms in design, construction and equipment with a type vehicle[7], then a vehicle examiner[8] may, after examining (if he thinks fit) the vehicle to which the declaration applies, issue an approval certificate in the prescribed form stating that it conforms to the type vehicle[9].

The Secretary of State may make regulations[10] with respect to applications for, and grants of, approval[11], with respect to applications for, and the issue of, approval certificates[12], providing for the examination of vehicles in respect of which applications have been made[13], and with respect to the issue of copies of approval certificates in place of certificates which have been lost or destroyed[14]. The Secretary of State may at any time withdraw his approval of a type vehicle[15].

1 As to the Secretary of State and the National Assembly for Wales see para 302 ante.
2 For the meaning of 'PSV accessibility regulations' see para 635 note 3 ante. As to the regulations made see the Public Service Vehicles Accessibility Regulations 2000, SI 2000/1970 (amended by SI 2000/3318; SI 2002/2981; SI 2003/1818; SI 2005/2988).
3 Ie prescribed for the purposes of the Disability Discrimination Act 1995 s 41: see para 636 ante. 'Prescribed' generally means prescribed by regulations: see para 515 note 5 ante. For the meaning of 'regulations' see para 509 note 12 ante. See note 2 supra.
4 Ibid s 42(1).
5 Ibid s 42(2).
6 'Authorised person' means a person authorised by the Secretary of State for these purposes: see ibid s 42(8).
7 Ibid s 42(3).
8 For the meaning of 'vehicle examiner' see para 636 note 3 ante.
9 Disability Discrimination Act 1995 s 42(4).
10 See notes 2, 3 supra.
11 Disability Discrimination Act 1995 s 42(5)(a).
12 Ibid s 42(5)(b).
13 Ibid s 42(5)(c).
14 Ibid s 42(5)(d).
15 Ibid s 42(6). Where an approval is withdrawn: (1) no further approval certificates may be issued by reference to the type vehicle; but (2) any approval certificate issued by reference to the type vehicle before the withdrawal continues to have effect for the purposes of s 41 (see para 636 ante): s 42(7).

638. Special authorisations. The Secretary of State[1] may by order authorise the use on roads of any regulated public service vehicle[2] of a class or description specified by the order[3], or any regulated public service vehicle which is so specified[4], and nothing in the provisions relating to public service vehicles[5] prevents the use of any vehicle in accordance with the order[6]. Any such authorisation may be given subject to such restrictions and conditions as may be specified by or under the order[7].

The Secretary of State may also by order make provision for the purpose of securing that, subject to such restrictions and conditions as may be specified by or under the order, provisions of the PSV accessibility regulations[8] apply to regulated public service vehicles of a description specified by the order subject to such modifications or exceptions as may be specified by the order[9].

1 As to the Secretary of State and the National Assembly for Wales see para 302 ante.
2 For the meaning of 'regulated public service vehicle' see para 635 note 5 ante.
3 Disability Discrimination Act 1995 s 43(1)(a). See note 6 infra.
4 Ibid s 43(1)(b).
5 Ie ibid s 40, s 41 or s 42: see paras 635–637 ante.

6   Ibid s 43(1). At the date at which this volume states the law no such order had been made. Section 67(1)
     (as amended) (see para 509 ante) does not require an order under s 43 which applies only to a specified
     vehicle, or to vehicles of a specified person, to be made by statutory instrument but such an order is as
     capable of being amended or revoked as an order which is made by statutory instrument: s 67(6).
7   Ibid s 43(2).
8   For the meaning of 'PSV accessibility regulations' see para 635 note 3 ante. As to the regulations made see
     the Public Service Vehicles Accessibility Regulations 2000, SI 2000/1970 (amended by SI 2000/3318;
     SI 2002/2981; SI 2003/1818; SI 2005/2988).
9   Disability Discrimination Act 1995 s 43(3).

639.   Reviews and appeals.   Where: (1) the Secretary of State[1] refuses an
application for the approval of a vehicle[2]; and (2) before the end of the prescribed
period[3] the applicant asks the Secretary of State to review the decision and pays any fee[4],
the Secretary of State must review the decision[5], and, in doing so, he must consider any
representations made to him in writing before the end of the prescribed period by the
applicant[6].

A person applying for an accessibility certificate[7] or an approval certificate[8] may
appeal to the Secretary of State against the refusal of a vehicle examiner[9] to issue such a
certificate[10]. An appeal must be made within the prescribed time and in the prescribed
manner[11]. Regulations may make provision as to the procedure to be followed in
connection with appeals[12].

On the determination of an appeal, the Secretary of State may confirm, vary or
reverse the decision appealed against[13], and give such directions as he thinks fit to the
vehicle examiner for giving effect to his decision[14].

1   As to the Secretary of State and the National Assembly for Wales see para 302 ante.
2   Disability Discrimination Act 1995 s 44(1)(a). As to approval of vehicles see s 42(1); and para 637 ante.
3   'Prescribed' generally means prescribed by regulations: see para 515 note 5 ante. For the meaning of
     'regulations' see para 509 note 12 ante. As to the regulations made for these purposes see the Public
     Service Vehicles Accessibility Regulations 2000, SI 2000/1970 (amended by SI 2000/3318;
     SI 2002/2981; SI 2003/1818; SI 2005/2988).
4   Disability Discrimination Act 1995 s 44(1)(b). Fees are payable under s 45: see para 640 post.
5   Ibid s 44(2)(a).
6   Ibid s 44(2)(b).
7   'Accessibility certificate' means a certificate issued under ibid s 41(1)(a) (see para 636 ante): s 68(1).
8   'Approval certificate' means a certificate issued under ibid s 42(4) (see para 637 ante): s 68(1).
9   For the meaning of 'vehicle examiner' see para 636 note 3 ante.
10   Disability Discrimination Act 1995 s 44(3).
11   Ibid s 44(4).
12   Ibid s 44(5). See note 3 supra.
13   Ibid s 44(6)(a).
14   Ibid s 44(6)(b).

640.   Fees.   Such fees, payable at such times, as may be prescribed[1] may be charged
by the Secretary of State[2] in respect of: (1) applications for, and grants of, approval[3]; (2)
applications for, and the issue of, accessibility certificates[4] and approval certificates[5]; (3)
copies of such certificates[6]; and (4) reviews and appeals[7].

Any such fees received by the Secretary of State are to be paid by him into the
Consolidated Fund[8].

Regulations may make provision for the repayment of fees, in whole or in part, in
such circumstances as may be prescribed[9].

1   'Prescribed' generally means prescribed by regulations: see para 515 note 5 ante. For the meaning of
     'regulations' see para 509 note 12 ante. As to the regulations made for these purposes see the Public
     Service Vehicles Accessibility Regulations 2000, SI 2000/1970 (amended by SI 2000/3318;
     SI 2002/2981; SI 2003/1818; SI 2005/2988).
2   As to the Secretary of State and the National Assembly for Wales see para 302 ante.

3   Disability Discrimination Act 1995 s 45(1)(a). Approval is applied for and granted under s 42(1): see para 637 ante.

4   For the meaning of 'accessibility certificate' see para 639 note 7 ante.

5   Disability Discrimination Act 1995 s 45(1)(b). For the meaning of 'approval certificate' see para 639 note 8 ante.

6   Ibid s 45(1)(c).

7   Ibid s 45(1)(d). Reviews and appeals are brought under s 44: see para 639 ante.

8   Ibid s 45(2). As to the Consolidated Fund see CONSTITUTIONAL LAW AND HUMAN RIGHTS vol 8(2) (Reissue) para 711 et seq; PARLIAMENT vol 34 (Reissue) paras 952–955.

9   Ibid s 45(3). Before making any such regulations, the Secretary of State must consult such representative organisations as he thinks fit: s 45(4). See note 1 supra.

(D) Supplementary Provisions

641. Offences by bodies corporate. Where an offence relating to public service vehicles or railways[1] committed by a body corporate is committed with the consent or connivance of, or is attributable to any neglect on the part of, a director[2], manager, secretary or other similar officer of the body, or a person purporting to act in such a capacity, he as well as the body corporate is guilty of the offence[3].

1   Ie an offence under the Disability Discrimination Act 1995 s 40 (see para 635 ante) or s 46 (as amended; prospectively amended) (see para 617 ante). See note 3 infra.

2   'Director', in relation to a body corporate whose affairs are managed by its members, means a member of the body corporate: ibid s 48(2).

3   Ibid s 48(1). As from a day to be appointed, the reference to s 46 (as amended; prospectively amended) (see note 1 supra) is removed: s 48(1) (prospectively amended by the Disability Discrimination Act 2005 s 19(2), Sch 2). At the date at which this volume states the law no such day had been appointed.

642. Forgery and false statements. If a person[1], with intent to deceive[2]: (1) forges, alters or uses a relevant document[3]; (2) lends a relevant document to any other person[4]; (3) allows a relevant document to be used by any other person[5]; or (4) makes or has in his possession any document which closely resembles a relevant document[6], he is guilty of an offence[7].

A person who knowingly makes a false statement for the purpose of obtaining an accessibility certificate or an approval certificate is guilty of an offence[8].

1   As to the meaning of 'person' see para 344 note 3 ante.

2   Disability Discrimination Act 1995 s 49(2).

3   Ibid s 49(2)(a). 'Relevant document' means: (1) a certificate of exemption issued under s 36, s 37 or s 37A (as added) (see paras 631–633 ante); (2) a notice of a kind mentioned in s 36(9)(b), s 37(8)(b) or s 37A(8)(b) (as added) (see paras 631–633 ante); (3) an accessibility certificate; or (4) an approval certificate: s 49(1) (amended by the Private Hire Vehicles (Carriage of Guide Dogs etc) Act 2002 s 4). For the meaning of 'accessibility certificate' see para 639 note 7 ante; and for the meaning of 'approval certificate' see para 639 note 8 ante. As from a day to be appointed, this definition is amended so as to refer also to a rail vehicle accessibility compliance certificate (see para 623 ante): Disability Discrimination Act 1995 s 49(1) (as so amended; prospectively amended by the Disability Discrimination Act 2005 ss 7(2)(a), 19(2), Sch 2). At the date at which this volume states the law no such day had been appointed.

4   Disability Discrimination Act 1995 s 49(2)(b).

5   Ibid s 49(2)(c).

6   Ibid s 49(2)(d).

7   Ibid s 49(2). A person who is guilty of such an offence is liable: (1) on summary conviction, to a fine not exceeding the statutory maximum; and (2) on conviction on indictment, to imprisonment for a term not exceeding two years or to a fine or to both: s 49(3). The 'statutory maximum', with reference to a fine or penalty on summary conviction for an offence, is the prescribed sum within the meaning of the Magistrates' Courts Act 1980 s 32 (as amended): see the Interpretation Act 1978 s 5, Sch 1 (definition added by the Criminal Justice Act 1988 s 170(1), Sch 15 para 58); and CRIMINAL LAW, EVIDENCE AND PROCEDURE vol 11(4) (2006 Reissue) para 1674; MAGISTRATES vol 29(2) (Reissue) para 804. The 'prescribed sum' means £5,000 or such sum as is for the time being substituted in this definition by order under the Magistrates' Courts Act 1980 s 143(1) (as substituted): see s 32(9) (amended by the Criminal

Justice Act 1991 s 17(2)); and CRIMINAL LAW, EVIDENCE AND PROCEDURE vol 11(4) (2006 Reissue) para 1675; MAGISTRATES vol 29(2) (Reissue) para 804.

8   Disability Discrimination Act 1995 s 49(4). A person guilty of such an offence is liable on summary conviction to a fine not exceeding level 4 on the standard scale: see s 49(4). As to the standard scale see para 315 note 15 ante. As from a day to be appointed, s 49(4) is amended so as to refer also to a rail vehicle accessibility compliance certificate: s 49(4) (prospectively amended by the Disability Discrimination Act 2005 s 7(2)(b)). At the date at which this volume states the law no such day had been appointed.

As from a day to be appointed, the Disability Discrimination Act 1995 s 49(5) is added so as to provide that a person who falsely pretends to be a person authorised to exercise power under s 47G (as added) (inspection of rail vehicles: see para 621 ante) is guilty of an offence and liable on summary conviction to a fine not exceeding level 4 on the standard scale: Disability Discrimination Act 1995 s 49(5) (prospectively added by the Disability Discrimination Act 2005 s 8(2)). At the date at which this volume states the law no such day had been appointed.

(4) ENFORCEMENT, REMEDIES AND PROCEDURE

643.   Employment discrimination. A complaint by any person that another person[1] has discriminated against him, or subjected him to harassment[2], in a way which is unlawful under the provisions of the Disability Discrimination Act 1995 relating to employment and members of locally-electable authorities[3], or is to be treated[4] as having done so[5], may be presented to an employment tribunal[6]. The above provisions[7] do not apply to a complaint under the provisions relating to discrimination and harassment by qualifications bodies[8] of an act in respect of which an appeal, or proceedings in the nature of an appeal, may be brought under any enactment[9].

Where, on the hearing of a complaint under the above provisions[10], the complainant proves facts from which the tribunal could, apart from this provision[11], conclude in the absence of an adequate explanation that the respondent has acted in a way which is unlawful[12], the tribunal must uphold the complaint unless the respondent proves that he did not so act[13].

Where an employment tribunal finds that a complaint presented to it is well-founded, it must take such of the following steps as it considers just and equitable[14]. The steps are:

(1)   making a declaration as to the rights of the complainant and the respondent in relation to the matters to which the complaint relates[15];

(2)   ordering the respondent to pay compensation to the complainant[16]; and

(3)   recommending that the respondent take, within a specified period, action appearing to the tribunal to be reasonable, in all the circumstances of the case, for the purpose of obviating or reducing the adverse effect on the complainant of any matter to which the complaint relates[17].

Where necessary, a lessor may be joined in proceedings before an employment tribunal[18].

Except as described above, no civil or criminal proceedings may be brought against any person in respect of an act merely because the act is unlawful under the provisions of the Disability Discrimination Act 1995 on employment and locally-electable authorities[19].

In any proceedings under the above provisions, a certificate signed by or on behalf of a Minister of the Crown[20] and certifying that any conditions or requirements specified in the certificate were imposed by a Minister of the Crown and were in operation at a time or throughout a time so specified is conclusive evidence of the matters certified[21].

Only the Disability Rights Commission[22] may bring proceedings in respect of a contravention of the provisions of the Disability Discrimination Act 1995 relating to discriminatory advertisements[23] or instructions and pressure to discriminate[24]. The Commission may present to an employment tribunal a complaint that a person has done an act which is unlawful under those provisions[25]; and if the tribunal finds that the complaint is well-founded it must make a declaration to that effect[26]. Where a tribunal has made a finding[27] that a person has done an act which is unlawful under those provisions, that finding has become final, and it appears to the Commission that, unless restrained, he is likely to do a further act which is unlawful under the provisions, the Commission may apply to a county court for an injunction restraining him from doing such an act; and the court, if satisfied that the application is well-founded, may grant the injunction in the terms applied for or in more limited terms[28].

1   As to the meaning of 'person' see para 344 note 3 ante.
2   For the meaning of 'harassment' see para 533 ante.
3   Disability Discrimination Act 1995 s 17A(1)(a) (s 17A added by virtue of the Disability Discrimination
    Act 1995 (Amendment) Regulations 2003, SI 2003/1673, regs 3(1), 9(1); and the Disability
    Discrimination Act 1995 s 17A(1)(a) amended by the Disability Discrimination Act 1995 (Amendment)
    Regulations 2003, SI 2003/1673, regs 3(1), 9(2)(a)). The provisions referred to in the text are those in
    the Disability Discrimination Act 1995 Pt II (ss 3A–18E) (as amended; prospectively amended): see
    para 529 et seq ante. For the meaning of 'employment' see para 529 note 2 ante.
4   Ie by virtue of ibid s 57 (as amended) or s 58: see paras 527–528 ante.
5   Ibid s 17A(1)(b) (as added (see note 3 supra); and amended by the Disability Discrimination Act 1995
    (Amendment) Regulations 2003, SI 2003/1673, regs 3(1), 9(2)(b)).
6   Disability Discrimination Act 1995 s 17A(1) (as added (see note 3 supra); and s 17A(1), (2) amended by
    virtue of the Employment Rights (Dispute Resolution) Act 1998 s 1(2)(a)). An employment tribunal may
    not consider a complaint unless it is presented before the end of the period of three months beginning
    when the act complained of was done: Disability Discrimination Act 1995 s 17A(8) (as so added), Sch 3
    para 3(1) (amended by the Employment Rights (Dispute Resolution) Act 1998 s 1(2)(a); and the
    Disability Discrimination Act 1995 (Amendment) Regulations 2003, SI 2003/1673, regs 3(1), 29(2)(c)).
    As to the meaning of 'act' see para 510 note 3 ante. For these purposes: (1) where an unlawful act is
    attributable to a term in a contract, that act is to be treated as extending throughout the duration of the
    contract; (2) any act extending over a period is to be treated as done at the end of that period; and (3) a
    deliberate omission is to be treated as done when the person in question decided upon it: Disability
    Discrimination Act 1995 Sch 3 para 3(3) (amended by the Disability Discrimination Act 1995
    (Amendment) Regulations 2003, SI 2003/1673, regs 3(1), 29(2)(d)). In the absence of evidence
    establishing the contrary, a person is to be taken to decide upon an omission: (a) when he does an act
    inconsistent with doing the omitted act; or (b) if he has done no such inconsistent act, when the period
    expires within which he might reasonably have been expected to do the omitted act if it was to be done:
    Sch 3 para 3(4).
        A tribunal may, however, consider any such complaint which is out of time if, in all the circumstances
    of the case, it considers that it is just and equitable to do so: Sch 3 para 3(2).
        See *Robinson v Post Office* [2000] IRLR 804, EAT (no extension of time limit for complaint presented
    out of time due to employee's pursuit of internal appeal against dismissal); applied in *Apelogun-Gabriels v
    Lambeth London Borough Council* [2001] EWCA Civ 1853, [2002] ICR 713, [2002] IRLR 116.
7   Ie the Disability Discrimination Act 1995 s 17A(1) (as added and amended).
8   Ie ibid s 14A(1) or (2) (as added): see para 549 ante.
9   Ibid s 17A(1A) (s 17A(1A), (1C) added by the Disability Discrimination Act 1995 (Amendment)
    Regulations 2003, SI 2003/1673, regs 3(1), 9(2)(c)).
10 Ie under the Disability Discrimination Act 1995 s 17A(1) (as added and amended).
11 Ie apart from ibid s 17A(1C) (as added).
12 Ie unlawful under ibid Pt II (as amended; prospectively amended).
13 Ibid s 17A(1C) (as added: see note 9 supra).
        As to the burden of proof generally in discrimination legislation see also *Wong v Igen Ltd (Equal
    Opportunities Commission and others intervening), Emokpae v Chamberlin Solicitors (Equal Opportunities
    Commission and others intervening), Webster v Brunel University (Equal Opportunities Commission and others
    intervening)* [2005] EWCA Civ 142, [2005] 3 All ER 812, [2005] ICR 931; and paras 418, 504 ante.
14 Disability Discrimination Act 1995 s 17A(2) (as added and amended: see notes 3, 6 supra).
15 Ibid s 17A(2)(a) (as added: see note 3 supra).
16 Ibid s 17A(2)(b) (as added: see note 3 supra). Where a tribunal orders compensation, the amount of the
    compensation is to be calculated by applying the principles applicable to the calculation of damages in
    claims in tort: see s 17A(3) (as so added). See DAMAGES vol 12(1) (Reissue) para 851 et seq.
    Compensation in respect of discrimination under this provision may include compensation for injury to
    feelings whether or not it includes compensation under any other head: see s 17A(4) (as so added).

Regulations may make provision: (1) for enabling a tribunal, where an amount of compensation falls to be awarded under s 17A(2)(b) (as added), to include in the award interest on that amount; and (2) specifying, for cases where a tribunal decides that an award is to include an amount in respect of interest, the manner in which and the periods and rate by reference to which the interest is to be determined: s 17A(6) (as so added). For the meaning of 'regulations' see para 509 note 12 ante. Regulations may also modify the operation of any order made under the Employment Tribunals Act 1996 s 14 (as amended) (power to make provision as to interest on sums payable in pursuance of employment tribunal decisions: see EMPLOYMENT vol 16(1B) (Reissue) para 893) to the extent that it relates to an award of compensation under the Disability Discrimination Act 1995 s 17A(2)(b) (as added): s 17A(7) (as so added; and amended by the Employment Tribunals Act 1996 s 43, Sch 1 para 12(1), (2); and the Employment Rights (Dispute Resolution) Act 1998 s 1(2)(a), (c)). As to regulations under this provision see the Employment Tribunals (Interest on Awards in Discrimination Cases) Regulations 1996, SI 1996/2803 (amended by the Employment Rights (Dispute Resolution) Act 1998 s 1(2)).

As to guidance on the proper level of damages to be awarded in discrimination cases (of all categories) for injury to feelings and other forms of non-pecuniary damage see *Vento v Chief Constable of West Yorkshire Police* [2002] EWCA Civ 1871, [2003] ICR 318, [2003] IRLR 102, [2002] All ER (D) 363 (Dec); and paras 414, 499 ante.

See also *HM Prison Service v Beart (No 2)* [2005] EWCA Civ 467, [2005] ICR 1206, [2005] IRLR 568.

17 Disability Discrimination Act 1995 s 17A(2)(c) (as added: see note 3 supra). If the respondent to a complaint fails, without reasonable justification, to comply with a recommendation made by an employment tribunal under s 17A(2)(c) (as added), the tribunal may, if it thinks it just and equitable to do so: (1) increase the amount of compensation required to be paid to the complainant in respect of the complaint, where an order was made under s 17A(2)(b) (as added); or (2) make an order under s 17A(2)(b) (as added): s 17A(5) (amended by the Employment Rights (Dispute Resolution) Act 1998 s 1(2)(a)).

18 In any proceedings under the Disability Discrimination Act 1995 s 17A (as added and amended), in a case to which s 18A (as added and amended) applies (alterations to premises occupied under leases: see para 560 ante), the complainant or the occupier may ask the tribunal hearing the complaint to direct that the lessor be joined as a party to the proceedings: s 18A(5) (added by virtue of the Disability Discrimination Act 1995 (Amendment) Regulations 2003, SI 2003/1673, regs 3(1), 14(2)); Disability Discrimination Act 1995 Sch 4 para 2(1) (amended by the Disability Discrimination Act 2005 Sch 1 paras 1, 40(1), (2)(b); and the Disability Discrimination Act 1995 (Amendment) Regulations 2003, SI 2003/1673, regs 3(1), 29(3)(e)). The request must be granted if it is made before the hearing of the complaint begins: Disability Discrimination Act 1995 Sch 4 para 2(2). The tribunal may refuse the request if it is made after the hearing of the complaint begins: Sch 4 para 2(3). The request may not be granted if it is made after the tribunal has determined the complaint: Sch 4 para 2(4).

Where a lessor has been so joined as a party to the proceedings, the tribunal may determine: (1) whether the lessor has refused consent to the alteration, or consented subject to one or more conditions; and (2) if so, whether the refusal or any of the conditions was unreasonable: Sch 4 para 2(5). If the tribunal determines that the refusal or any of the conditions was unreasonable, it may take one or more of the following steps: (a) make such declaration as it considers appropriate; (b) make an order authorising the occupier to make the alteration specified in the order; or (c) order the lessor to pay compensation to the complainant: Sch 4 para 2(6). An order under head (b) supra may require the occupier to comply with conditions specified in the order: Sch 4 para 2(7). Any step taken by the tribunal under Sch 4 para 2(6) may be in substitution for, or in addition to, any step taken by the tribunal under s 17A(2) (as added and amended) (see heads (1)–(3) in the text): Sch 4 para 2(8) (Sch 4 para 2(8), (9) amended by the Disability Discrimination Act 1995 (Amendment) Regulations 2003, SI 2003/1673, regs 3(1), 29(3)(f)).

If the tribunal orders the lessor to pay compensation it may not make an order under the Disability Discrimination Act 1995 s 17A(2) (as added and amended) ordering the occupier to do so: Sch 4 para 2(9) (as so amended).

19 Ibid Sch 3 para 2(1) (substituted by the Disability Discrimination Act 1995 (Amendment) Regulations 2003, SI 2003/1673, regs 3(1), 29(2)(b)). The provisions referred to in the text are those of the Disability Discrimination Act 1995 Pt II (as amended; prospectively amended). Schedule 3 para 2(1) (as substituted) does not prevent the making of an application for judicial review (see ADMINISTRATIVE LAW vol 1(1) (2001 Reissue) para 59 et seq; PRACTICE AND PROCEDURE) or the investigation or determination of any matter in accordance with the Pension Schemes Act 1983 Pt X (ss 145–152) (as amended) by the Pensions Ombudsman (see SOCIAL SECURITY AND PENSIONS): Disability Discrimination Act 1995 Sch 3 para 2(2) (amended by the Disability Discrimination Act 1995 (Pensions) Regulations 2003, SI 2003/2770, regs 2, 4(5)). The Disability Discrimination Act 1995 Sch 3 para 2(1)

(as substituted) does not prevent the bringing of proceedings in respect of an offence under s 16B(2B) (as added) (see para 537 ante): Sch 3 para 2(3) (added by the Disability Discrimination Act 2005 Sch 1 paras 1, 38(1), (2)).

20 As to the meaning of 'Minister of the Crown' see para 510 note 4 ante.

21 Disability Discrimination Act 1995 Sch 3 para 4(1) (amended by the Employment Relations Act 1999 ss 41, 44, Sch 8 para 7, Sch 9 Table 12; and the Disability Discrimination Act 1995 (Amendment) Regulations 2003, SI 2003/1673, regs 3(1), 29(2)(e)). Similarly, in any such proceedings, a certificate signed by or on behalf of the National Assembly for Wales, and certifying that any conditions or requirements specified in the certificate were imposed by the Assembly and were in operation at a time or throughout a time so specified, is to be conclusive evidence of the matters certified: Disability Discrimination Act 1995 Sch 3 para 4(1B) (added by the Disability Discrimination Act 2005 Sch 1 paras 1, 38(1), (3)). A document purporting to be such a certificate as mentioned in the Disability Discrimination Act 1995 Sch 3 para 4(1), (1B) (as amended and added) must be received in evidence and, unless the contrary is proved, must be deemed to be such a certificate: Sch 3 para 4(2) (amended by the Disability Discrimination Act 2005 Sch 1 paras 1, 38(1), (4)).

22 As to the Disability Rights Commission see para 646 et seq post. As to the Commission for Equality and Human Rights, which is to replace the Disability Rights Commission, see para 305 et seq ante.

23 Ie the Disability Discrimination Act 1995 s 16B (as added and amended): see para 537 ante.

24 Ibid s 17B(1) (s 17B added by the Disability Discrimination Act 1995 (Amendment) Regulations 2003, SI 2003/1673, regs 3(1), 16(1); and the Disability Discrimination Act 1995 s 17B(1) amended by the Disability Discrimination Act 2005 Sch 1 paras 1, 10(1), (2)). The Disability Discrimination Act 1995 s 17B (as added and amended) is repealed by the Equality Act 2006 ss 40, 91, Sch 3 paras 41, 44, Sch 4 as from a day to be appointed under s 93. At the date at which this volume states the law no such day had been appointed.

    The reference in the text to the provisions on instructions and pressure to discriminate is a reference to the Disability Discrimination Act 1995 s 16C (as added; prospectively amended): see para 538 ante.

25 Ie under ibid s 16B (as added and amended) (see para 537 ante) or s 16C (as added; prospectively amended) (see para 538 ante).

26 Ibid s 17B(2), (3) (s 17B as added (see note 24 supra); and s 17B(3) amended by the Disability Discrimination Act 2005 Sch 1 paras 1, 10(1), (2)). See note 28 infra.

27 Ie a finding pursuant to the Disability Discrimination Act 1995 s 17B(3) (as added and amended).

28 Ibid s 17B(2), (4) (s 17B as added (see note 24 supra); and s 17B(4) amended by the Disability Discrimination Act 2005 Sch 1 paras 1, 10(1), (2), (3)).

    A finding of a tribunal under the Disability Discrimination Act 1995 s 17B(3) (as added and amended) in respect of any act must, if it has become final, be treated as conclusive by a county court on an application under s 17B(4) (as added and amended): s 17B(5) (as so added). A finding of a tribunal becomes final for the purposes of s 17B (as added and amended) when an appeal against it is dismissed, withdrawn or abandoned or when the time for appealing expires without an appeal having been brought: s 17B(6) (as so added). An employment tribunal must not consider a complaint under s 17B(3) (as added and amended) unless it is presented before the end of the period of six months beginning when the act to which it relates was done; and a county court must not consider an application under s 17B(4) (as added and amended) unless it is made before the end of the period of five years so beginning: s 17B(7) (as so added). However, a court or tribunal may consider any such complaint or application which is out of time if, in all the circumstances of the case, it considers that it is just and equitable to do so: s 17B(8) (as so added). The provisions of Sch 3 para 3(3), (4) (as amended) (see note 6 supra) apply for the purposes of s 17B(7) (as added) as they apply for the purposes of Sch 3 para 3(1) (as amended): s 17B(9) (as so added).

644. Non-employment discrimination.

A claim by any person that another person[1] has committed unlawful discrimination in relation to the provision of goods, facilities, services or premises[2] against him[3], or is to be treated[4] as having discriminated against him in such a way[5], may be made the subject of civil proceedings in the same way as any other claim in tort[6].

The above provisions[7] do not apply in relation to a claim by a person that another person: (1) has discriminated against him in relation to the provision under a group insurance arrangement[8] of facilities by way of insurance[9]; or (2) is to be treated[10] as having discriminated against him in relation to the provision under such an arrangement of such facilities[11]. Nor do the above provisions apply in relation to a claim by a person that another person: (a) has discriminated against him in relation to the provision of employment services[12]; or (b) is to be treated[13] as having discriminated against him in relation to the provision of employment services[14]. Such a claim[15], or a claim by a person that another has subjected him to harassment[16] in a way which is unlawful[17] or is to be treated[18] as having subjected him to harassment in such a way, may be presented as a complaint to an employment tribunal[19].

Damages in respect of such unlawful discrimination[20] may include compensation for injury to feelings whether or not they include compensation under any other head[21]. Proceedings may be brought only in a county court[22] and the remedies available in such proceedings are those which are available in the High Court[23].

In certain circumstances, a lessor may be joined in proceedings[24].

Except as described above, no civil or criminal proceedings may be brought against any person in respect of an act merely because the act is unlawful under the provisions of Part III of the Disability Discrimination Act 1995[25].

In any proceedings under the above provisions, a certificate signed by or on behalf of a Minister of the Crown[26] and certifying that any conditions or requirements specified in the certificate were imposed by a Minister of the Crown and were in operation at a time or throughout a time so specified[27], or that an act specified in the certificate was done for the purpose of safeguarding national security[28], is conclusive evidence of the matters certified[29].

1   As to the meaning of 'person' see para 344 note 3 ante.
2   Ie in contravention of the Disability Discrimination Act 1995 Pt III (ss 19–28) (as amended; prospectively amended): see para 582 et seq ante.
3   Ibid s 25(1)(a).
4   Ie by virtue of ibid s 57 (as amended) or s 58: see paras 527–528 ante.
5   Ibid s 25(1)(b).
6   Ibid s 25(1). See generally TORT.
7   Ie ibid s 25(1): see the text and notes 1–6 supra.
8   For the meaning of 'group insurance arrangement' see para 613 note 2 ante.
9   Disability Discrimination Act 1995 s 25(6A)(a) (s 25(6A) added by the Disability Discrimination Act 2005 s 11(2)).
10   Ie by virtue of the Disability Discrimination Act 1995 s 57 (as amended) or s 58: see paras 527–528 ante.
11   Ibid s 25(6A)(b) (as added: see note 9 supra).
12   Ibid s 25(7)(a) (s 27(7)–(9) added by the Disability Discrimination Act 1995 (Amendment) Regulations 2003, SI 2003/1673, regs 3(1), 19(2); and the Disability Discrimination Act 1995 s 27(7), (8) substituted by the Disability Discrimination Act 2005 s 19(1), Sch 1 paras 1, 21). For the meaning of 'employment services' see para 585 note 9 ante.
13   See note 10 supra.
14   Disability Discrimination Act 1995 s 25(7)(b) (as added and substituted: see note 12 supra).
15   Ie of the kind referred to in ibid s 25(6A) (as added) or s 25(7) (as added and substituted).
16   For the meaning of 'harassment' see para 533 ante.
17   Ie unlawful under the Disability Discrimination Act 1995 s 21A(2) (as added): see para 585 ante.
18   See note 10 supra.
19   Disability Discrimination Act 1995 s 25(8) (as added and substituted: see note 12 supra). Section 17A(1A)–(7) (as added and amended) and Sch 3 paras 3, 4 (as amended) (see para 643 ante) apply in relation to a complaint under s 25(8) (as added and substituted) as if it were a complaint under s 17A(1) (as added and amended) (and Sch 3 paras 6–8 (as amended; prospectively amended) (see notes 21, 22 and the text and notes 26–29 infra) do not apply in relation to such a complaint): s 25(9) (as added: see note 12 supra).
20   Ie unlawful under ibid Pt III (as amended; prospectively amended).
21   Ibid s 25(2). In any proceedings under s 25 (as amended), the amount of any damages awarded as compensation for injury to feelings must not exceed the prescribed amount: s 25(6), Sch 3 para 7. 'Prescribed' generally means prescribed by regulations: see para 515 note 5 ante. At the date at which this volume states the law no regulations had been made under this provision. See note 19 supra.
        As to guidance on the proper level of damages to be awarded in discrimination cases (of all categories) for injury to feelings and other forms of non-pecuniary damage see *Vento v Chief Constable of West Yorkshire Police* [2002] EWCA Civ 1871, [2003] ICR 318, [2003] IRLR 102, [2002] All ER (D) 363 (Dec); and paras 414, 499 ante.
22   Disability Discrimination Act 1995 s 25(3). A county court may not consider a claim under s 25 (as amended) unless proceedings in respect of the claim are instituted before the end of the period of six

months beginning when the act complained of was done: Sch 3 para 6(1). As to the meaning of 'act' see para 510 note 3 ante. Where, in relation to proceedings or prospective proceedings under s 25 (as amended), the dispute concerned is referred for conciliation in pursuance of arrangements under s 28 (as substituted; prospectively repealed) (see para 657 post) before the end of the period of six months mentioned in Sch 3 para 6(1), the period allowed is extended by two months: Sch 3 para 6(2) (amended by the Disability Rights Commission Act 1999 s 14(1), Sch 4 para 3(1), (3)). As from a day to be appointed, the Disability Discrimination Act 1995 Sch 3 para 6(2) (as added and amended) is replaced by a new provision in similar terms but referring to conciliation under the Equality Act 2006 s 27 (as amended) (see para 333 ante) and an extension of three months: Disability Discrimination Act 1995 Sch 3 para 6(2) (prospectively substituted by the Equality Act 2006 s 40, Sch 3 paras 41, 56(1)). At the date at which this volume states the law no such day had been appointed.

For the purposes of the Disability Discrimination Act 1995 Sch 3 para 6(1): (1) where an unlawful act of discrimination is attributable to a term in a contract, that act is to be treated as extending throughout the duration of the contract; (2) any act extending over a period is to be treated as done at the end of that period; (3) a deliberate omission is to be treated as done when the person in question decided upon it: Sch 3 para 6(4). In the absence of evidence establishing the contrary, a person is to be taken to decide upon an omission: (a) when he does an act inconsistent with doing the omitted act; or (b) if he has done no such inconsistent act, when the period expires within which he might reasonably have been expected to do the omitted act if it was to be done: Sch 3 para 6(5).

A court may consider any claim under s 25 (as amended) which is out of time if, in all the circumstances of the case, it considers that it is just and equitable to do so: Sch 3 para 6(3).

Where a party to proceedings under s 25 (as amended) which have arisen by virtue of s 21B(1) (as added) (see para 593 ante) has applied for a stay of those proceedings on the grounds of prejudice to: (i) particular criminal proceedings; (ii) a criminal investigation; or (iii) a decision to institute criminal proceedings, the court must grant the stay unless it is satisfied that the continuance of the proceedings under s 25 (as amended) would not result in the prejudice alleged: Sch 3 para 6A(1), (2) (Sch 3 paras 6A, 6B added by the Disability Discrimination Act 2005 Sch 1 paras 1, 38(1), (5)). 'Criminal investigation' means: (A) any investigation which a person in carrying out functions to which the Disability Discrimination Act 1995 s 21B(1) (as added) (see para 593 ante) applies has a duty to conduct with a view to it being ascertained whether a person should be charged with an offence, or whether a person charged with or prosecuted for an offence is guilty of it; or (B) any investigation which is conducted by a person in carrying out functions to which s 21B(1) (as added) applies and which in the circumstances may lead to a decision by that person to institute criminal proceedings which the person has power to conduct: s 68(1), (1A) (s 68(1) amended, and s 68(1A) added, by the Disability Discrimination Act 2005 Sch 1 paras 34(1), (2), (7)). In the Disability Discrimination Act 1995 s 68(1A), (1B) (as added), 'offence' includes any offence of a kind triable by court-martial under the Army Act 1955, the Air Force Act 1955 or the Naval Discipline Act 1957 (see ARMED FORCES); and 'offender' is to be construed accordingly: Disability Discrimination Act 1995 s 68(1C) (added by the Disability Discrimination Act 2005 Sch 1 paras 1, 34(1), (7)). As to the meaning of 'criminal proceedings' see para 593 note 17 ante.

In the case of a remedy other than damages, or a declaration, in proceedings under the Disability Discrimination Act 1995 s 25 (as amended), the remedy is obtainable in respect of a relevant discriminatory act only if the court is satisfied that no criminal investigation, no decision to institute criminal proceedings, and no criminal proceedings, would be prejudiced by the remedy: Sch 3 para 6B(1), (2) (as so added). For these purposes, 'relevant discriminatory act' means an act which is done, or by virtue of s 57 (as amended) or s 58 (see paras 527–528 ante) is treated as done, by a person in carrying out public investigator functions or in carrying out functions as a public prosecutor, and which is unlawful by virtue of s 21B(1) (as added) (see para 593 ante): Sch 3 para 6B(3) (as so added). 'Public investigator functions' means functions of conducting criminal investigations or charging offenders: s 68(1), (1B) (s 68(1) amended, and s 68(1B) added, by the Disability Discrimination Act 2005 Sch 1 paras 1, 34(1), (2), (7)). See note 19 supra.

23 Disability Discrimination Act 1995 s 25(5). See note 22 supra.

24 In any proceedings on a claim under ibid s 25 (as amended) in a case to which s 27 (as amended) (see para 590 ante) applies, other than a claim presented as a complaint under s 25(8) (as added), the claimant or the occupier concerned may ask the court to direct that the lessor be joined as a party to the proceedings: see s 27(5), Sch 4 para 7(1) (amended by the Disability Discrimination Act 2005 Sch 1 paras 1, 40(1), (5)). The request must be granted if it is made before the hearing of the claim begins: Disability Discrimination Act 1995 Sch 4 para 7(2). The court may refuse the request if it is made after the hearing of the claim begins: Sch 4 para 7(3). The request may not be granted if it is made after the court has determined the claim: Sch 4 para 7(4). Where a lessor has been so joined as a party to the proceedings, the court may determine whether the lessor has refused consent to the alteration, or consented subject to one or more conditions, and if so, whether the refusal or any of the conditions was unreasonable: Sch 4 para 7(5). If the court determines that the refusal or any of the conditions was unreasonable it may take one or more of the following steps: (1) make such declaration as it considers

appropriate; (2) make an order authorising the occupier to make the alteration specified in the order; or (3) order the lessor to pay compensation to the complainant: Sch 4 para 7(6). An order under head (2) supra may require the occupier to comply with conditions specified in the order: Sch 4 para 7(7). If the court orders the lessor to pay compensation it may not order the occupier to do so: Sch 4 para 7(8).

As to joining lessors in proceedings relating to group insurance or employment services see Sch 4 para 7A (as added). In any proceedings on a complaint under s 25(8) (as added) in a case to which s 27 (as amended) (see para 590 ante) applies, the complainant or the occupier may ask the tribunal hearing the complaint to direct that the lessor be joined as a party to the proceedings: Sch 4 para 7A(1) (Sch 4 para 7A added by the Disability Discrimination Act 2005 Sch 1 paras 1, 40(1), (6)). The request must be granted if it is made before the hearing of the complaint begins: Disability Discrimination Act 1995 Sch 4 para 7A(2) (as so added). The tribunal may refuse the request if it is made after the hearing of the complaint begins: Sch 4 para 7A3) (as so added). The request may not be granted if it is made after the tribunal has determined the complaint: Sch 4 para 7A(4) (as so added). Where a lessor has been so joined as a party to the proceedings, the tribunal may determine: (a) whether the lessor has refused consent to the alteration, or consented subject to one or more conditions; and (b) if so, whether the refusal or any of the conditions was unreasonable Sch 4 para 7A(5) (as so added). If the tribunal determines that the refusal or any of the conditions was unreasonable, it may take one or more of the following steps: (i) make such declaration as it considers appropriate; (ii) make an order authorising the occupier to make the alteration specified in the order; (iii) order the lessor to pay compensation to the complainant: Sch 4 para 7A(6) (as so added). An order under head (ii) supra may require the occupier to comply with conditions specified in the order: Sch 4 para 7A(7) (as so added). Any step taken by the tribunal under heads (i)–(iii) supra may be in substitution for, or in addition to, any step taken by the tribunal under s 17A(2) (as added and amended) (see para 643 ante): Sch 4 para 7A(8) (as so added). If the tribunal orders the lessor to pay compensation, it may not make an order under s 17A(2) (as added and amended) (see para 643 ante) ordering the occupier to do so: Sch 4 para 7A(8) (as so added).

25 Ibid Sch 3 para 5(1). As to Pt III (as amended; prospectively amended) see para 582 et seq ante. Schedule 3 para 5(1) does not prevent the making of an application for judicial review: Sch 3 para 5(2). As to judicial review see ADMINISTRATIVE LAW vol 1(1) (2001 Reissue) para 59 et seq; PRACTICE AND PROCEDURE. See also note 22 supra.
26 As to the meaning of 'Minister of the Crown' see para 510 note 4 ante.
27 Disability Discrimination Act 1995 Sch 3 para 8(1)(a). See note 19 supra.
28 Ibid Sch 3 para 8(1)(b). See note 19 supra. As to acts safeguarding national security see para 616 ante.
29 Ibid Sch 3 para 8(1). A document purporting to be such a certificate must be received in evidence and, unless the contrary is proved, must be deemed to be such a certificate: Sch 3 para 8(2). See note 19 supra.
    Similarly, in regard to Wales, in any proceedings under s 25 (as amended), a certificate signed by or on behalf of the National Assembly for Wales and certifying that any conditions or requirements specified in the certificate: (1) were imposed by the Assembly; and (2) were in operation at a time or throughout a time so specified, is conclusive evidence of the matters certified: Sch 3 para 8(4) (Sch 3 para 8(4), (5) added by the Disability Discrimination Act 2005 Sch 1 paras 1, 38(1), (6)). A document purporting to be such a certificate must be received in evidence and, unless the contrary is proved, must be deemed to be such a certificate: Disability Discrimination Act 1995 Sch 3 para 8(5) (as so added). As to the National Assembly for Wales see para 302 ante.

645. Help for aggrieved persons in obtaining information etc.

With a view to helping the person aggrieved[1] decide whether to institute proceedings and, if he does so, to formulate and present his case in the most effective manner, the Secretary of State[2] must by order prescribe forms[3] by which the person aggrieved may question the respondent[4] on his reasons for doing any relevant act[5], or on any other matter which is or may be relevant[6], and forms by which the respondent may if he so wishes reply to any questions[7].

Where the person aggrieved questions the respondent in accordance with such prescribed forms, the question, and any reply by the respondent (whether in accordance with such an order or not), is admissible as evidence in any proceedings[8]. If it appears to the court or tribunal in any such proceedings that the respondent deliberately, and without reasonable excuse, omitted to reply within the period of eight weeks beginning with the day on which the question was served on him[9], or that the respondent's reply is evasive or equivocal[10], it may draw any inference which it considers it just and equitable to draw, including an inference that the respondent has committed an unlawful act[11].

1   A person who considers that he may have been: (1) discriminated against, in contravention of the Disability Discrimination Act 1995 Pt II (ss 3A–18E) (as amended; prospectively amended) (see para 529 et seq ante) or Pt III (ss 19–28) (as amended; prospectively amended) (see para 582 et seq ante); or (2) subjected to harassment in contravention of Pt II (as amended; prospectively amended) or s 21A(2) (as added) (see para 585 ante), is referred to as 'the person aggrieved': s 56(1)(a) (s 56 substituted by the Disability Discrimination Act 2005 s 17). For the meaning of 'harassment' see para 533 ante.

2   As to the Secretary of State and the National Assembly for Wales see para 302 ante.

3   Disability Discrimination Act 1995 s 56(2) (as substituted: see note 1 supra). As to the order that has been made see the Disability Discrimination (Questions and Replies) Order 2005, SI 2005/2703.

4   A person against whom the person aggrieved may decide to institute, or has instituted, proceedings in respect of such discrimination and harassment as is mentioned in the Disability Discrimination Act 1995 s 56(1)(a) (as substituted) (see note 1 supra) is referred to as 'the respondent': s 56(1)(b) (as substituted: see note 1 supra).

5   As to the meaning of 'act' see para 510 note 3 ante.

6   Disability Discrimination Act 1995 s 56(2)(a) (as substituted: see note 1 supra). For the form see the Disability Discrimination (Questions and Replies) Order 2005, SI 2005/2703, art 2(a), Sch 1.

7   Disability Discrimination Act 1995 s 56(2)(b) (as substituted: see note 1 supra). For the form see the Disability Discrimination (Questions and Replies) Order 2005, SI 2005/2703, art 2(b), Sch 2.

8   Disability Discrimination Act 1995 s 56(3)(a) (as substituted: see note 1 supra). The proceedings mentioned in the text are any proceedings under Pt II (as amended; prospectively amended) or Pt III (as amended; prospectively amended): see s 56(3)(a) (as substituted). Section 56 (as substituted) is without prejudice to any other enactment or rule of law regulating interim and preliminary matters before a county court or an employment tribunal, and has effect subject to any enactment or rule of law regulating the admissibility of evidence in such proceedings: s 56(5) (as so substituted).

The Secretary of State may by order prescribe: (1) the period within which questions must be duly served in order to be admissible under s 56(3)(a) (as substituted); and (2) the manner in which a question, and any reply by the respondent, may be duly served: s 56(4) (as so substituted).

In proceedings before a court, a question is, for the purposes of s 56(3) (as substituted), only admissible as evidence in any proceedings under Pt III (as amended; prospectively amended) other than s 21A (as added and amended) (employment services) (see paras 582, 585–587 ante) and ss 19–21 (as amended) (see paras 582–587 ante) in so far as they relate to a group insurance arrangement (see para 613 note 2 ante): (a) where proceedings have not commenced: (i) if it was served within the period of six months beginning on the date of the act complained of; or (ii) where the dispute has been referred by the Disability Rights Commission for conciliation in pursuance of arrangements under s 28 (as substituted; prospectively repealed) (see para 657 post), if it was served within the period of eight months beginning on the date of the act complained of; (b) where proceedings have commenced, only if it is served with leave of the court and within the period specified by it: Disability Discrimination (Questions and Replies) Order 2005, SI 2005/2703, art 3. A question or, as the case may be, a reply may be duly served: (A) where the person to be served is the respondent, by delivering the question to him, or by sending it by post to him at his usual or last known residence or place of business; or (B) where the person to be served is the person aggrieved, by delivering the reply to him, or by sending it by post to him at his address for reply as stated by him in the document containing the questions or, if no address is so stated, at his usual or last known residence; or (C) where the person to be served is a body corporate or is a trade union or employers' association within the meaning of the Trade Union and Labour Relations (Consolidation) Act 1992 (see TRADE, INDUSTRY AND INDUSTRIAL RELATIONS vol 47 (2001 Reissue) para 1201), by delivering it to the secretary or clerk of the body, union or association at its registered or principal office or by sending it by post to the secretary or clerk at that office; or (D) where the person to be served is acting by a solicitor, by delivering it at, or by sending it by post to, the solicitor's address for service: Disability Discrimination (Questions and Replies) Order 2005, SI 2005/2703, art 4.

9   Disability Discrimination Act 1995 s 56(3)(b)(i) (as substituted: see note 1 supra).

10 Ibid s 56(3)(b)(ii) (as substituted: see note 1 supra).

11 Ibid s 56(3)(b) (as substituted: see note 1 supra).

In proceedings in respect of a 'section 21B claim' (ie a claim under s 25 (as amended) (see para 644 post) by virtue of s 21B (as added) (see para 593 ante)), s 56(3)(b) (as substituted) does not apply in relation to a failure to reply, or a particular reply, if the following conditions are met: (1) that, at the time of doing any relevant act, the respondent was carrying out public investigator functions or was a public prosecutor; and (2) that the respondent reasonably believes that a reply or (as the case may be) a different reply would be likely to prejudice any criminal investigation, any decision to institute criminal proceedings or any criminal proceedings or would reveal the reasons behind a decision not to institute, or a decision not to continue, criminal proceedings: s 56(6), (9) (as so substituted). For the meaning of 'public investigator functions see para 644 note 22 ante. As to the meaning of 'criminal proceedings' see para 593 note 17 ante.

Regulations may provide for s 56 (as substituted) not to have effect, or to have effect with prescribed modifications, in relation to section 21B claims of a prescribed description: s 56(7) (as so substituted). For the meaning of 'regulations' see para 509 note 12 ante. 'Prescribed' generally means prescribed by regulations: see para 515 note 5 ante. At the date at which this volume states the law no regulations had been made under s 56(7) (as added).

(5) DISABILITY RIGHTS COMMISSION

646. Constitution and membership. The Disability Rights Commission ('DRC') was established on 25 April 2000 and replaced the National Disability Council[1].

The DRC is a body corporate[2]. It is not the servant or agent of the Crown, it does not enjoy any status, immunity or privilege of the Crown, and its property is not to be regarded as property of or as held on behalf of the Crown[3].

The DRC consists of not less than 10 and not more than 15 commissioners appointed by the Secretary of State[4]. The Secretary of State may appoint as a commissioner a person who is not disabled[5] and has not had a disability[6] only if satisfied that after the appointment more than half of the commissioners will be disabled persons or persons who have had a disability[7]. The Secretary of State must appoint one commissioner as chairman of the DRC and either one or two other commissioners as deputy chairmen[8]. The Secretary of State must exercise his powers of appointment with a view to securing that at least one of the persons holding office as chairman or deputy chairman is a disabled person or a person who has had a disability[9].

The DRC may pay to any commissioner such remuneration or expenses[10], and pay, or make provision for the payment of, such sums by way of pensions, allowances or gratuities to or in respect of any commissioner[11], as the Secretary of State may determine[12].

The DRC has a chief executive appointed by the DRC, subject to the approval of the Secretary of State[13], and such other employees as the DRC may appoint, subject to the approval of the Secretary of State as to numbers and terms and conditions of service[14].

The Secretary of State must pay to the DRC such sums as he thinks fit to enable it to meet its expenses[15].

The DRC may regulate its own procedure, including quorum[16]. The validity of any proceedings of the DRC is not affected by a vacancy among the commissioners or by a defect in the appointment of a commissioner[17].

The DRC is to be replaced by the Commission for Equality and Human Rights[18].

1 Disability Rights Commission Act 1999 s 1(1), (4) (s 1(4) repealed); Disability Rights Commission Act 1999 (Commencement No 2 and Transitional Provision) Order 2000, SI 2000/880.

The Disability Rights Commission Act 1999 is repealed by the Equality Act 2006 ss 40, 91, Sch 3 para 59, Sch 4 as from a day to be appointed under s 93. At the date at which this volume states the law no such day had been appointed. As to the Commission for Equality and Human Rights, which is to replace the DRC, see para 305 et seq ante.

2 Disability Rights Commission Act 1999 s 1(3), Sch 1 para 1(1).

3 Ibid Sch 1 para 1(2). The provisions of the Disability Rights Commission Act 1999 bind the Crown but do not affect Her Majesty in her private capacity or in right of the Duchy of Lancaster or the Duke of Cornwall: s 15.

4 Ibid Sch 1 para 2(1). As to the Secretary of State and the National Assembly for Wales see para 302 ante. One of the commissioners must be a person who appears to the Secretary of State to have special knowledge of Scotland: Sch 1 para 2(1) (added by the Scotland Act 1998 (Modification of Functions) Order 2000, SI 2000/1458, art 2). Scottish matters generally are beyond the scope of this work. The function of the Secretary of State under the Disability Rights Commission Act 1999 Sch 1 para 2 (as amended) of making appointments to the DRC is exercisable only with the agreement of the National

Assembly for Wales so far as necessary to ensure that there is at all times one commissioner who has been appointed with the agreement of the Assembly: National Assembly for Wales (Transfer of Functions) Order 2000, SI 2000/253, art 3, Sch 2.

A commissioner must hold and vacate office in accordance with the terms of his appointment: Disability Rights Commission Act 1999 Sch 1 para 3(1). A person may not be appointed a commissioner for less than two or more than five years, but a person who has served as a commissioner may be re-appointed: Sch 1 para 3(2). A commissioner may resign by notice in writing to the Secretary of State: Sch 1 para 4. The Secretary of State may terminate the appointment of a commissioner if satisfied that: (1) without the consent of the chairman he has failed to attend meetings of the DRC during a continuous period of six months beginning not earlier than nine months before the termination; (2) he has become bankrupt, has had his estate sequestrated or has made a composition or arrangement with, or granted a trust deed for, his creditors; or (c) he is otherwise unable or unfit to carry out his functions as a commissioner: Sch 1 para 5.

5 For the meaning of 'disabled person' see para 511 ante.

6 As to when a person has a disability see para 511 ante.

7 Disability Rights Commission Act 1999 Sch 1 para 2(2). This provision does not apply in respect of the first three appointments of commissioners: Sch 1 para 2(3).

8 Ibid Sch 1 para 6(1). A person appointed as chairman or deputy chairman: (1) must hold and vacate that office in accordance with the terms of his appointment; (2) may resign that office by notice in writing to the Secretary of State; and (3) must cease to hold that office if he ceases to be a commissioner: Sch 1 para 7.

9 Ibid Sch 1 para 6(2).

10 Ibid Sch 1 para 8(a).

11 Ibid Sch 1 para 8(b).

12 Ibid Sch 1 para 8. If the Secretary of State determines that there are special circumstances which make it right that a person who has ceased to be a commissioner should receive compensation, the Secretary of State may direct the DRC to pay that person such sum by way of compensation as the Secretary of State may determine: Sch 1 para 9.

13 Ibid Sch 1 para 10(1)(a). The first appointment of a chief executive was made by the Secretary of State: see Sch 1 para 10(2).

14 Ibid Sch 1 para 10(1)(b). Employment with the DRC is included among the kinds of employment to which a scheme under the Superannuation Act 1972 s 1 (as amended) (see CONSTITUTIONAL LAW AND HUMAN RIGHTS vol 8(2) (Reissue) para 567) may apply: see the Disability Rights Commission Act 1999 Sch 1 para 11.

15 Ibid s 1(2).

16 Ibid Sch 1 para 12(1). The quorum for meetings of the DRC in the first instance is to be determined by a meeting of the DRC attended by at least five commissioners: Sch 1 para 12(2).

17 Ibid Sch 1 para 13.

18 See note 1 supra.

647. General functions and duties. The Disability Rights Commission ('DRC') has the following duties[1]:

(1) to work towards the elimination of discrimination[2] against and harassment[3] of disabled persons[4];

(2) to promote the equalisation of opportunities for disabled persons[5];

(3) to take such steps as it considers appropriate with a view to encouraging good practice in the treatment of disabled persons[6]; and

(4) to keep under review the working of the Disability Discrimination Act 1995 and the Disability Rights Commission Act 1999[7].

The DRC may, for any purpose connected with the performance of its functions: (a) make proposals or give other advice to any Minister of the Crown[8] as to any aspect of the law[9] or a proposed change to the law[10]; (b) make proposals or give other advice to any government agency or other public authority as to the practical application of any law[11]; and (c) undertake, or arrange for or support (whether financially or otherwise), the carrying out of research or the provision of advice or information[12]. The DRC's powers are not limited to heads (a) to (c) above[13]. The DRC may make charges for facilities or services made available by it for any purpose[14].

The DRC may authorise any committee of the DRC or any commissioner to exercise such of its functions (other than functions relating to the conduct of a formal investigation[15]) as it may determine[16].

The DRC is required to keep proper accounts and proper records in relation to the accounts[17]. It must prepare a statement of accounts in respect of each accounting year[18], and it must send copies of the statement to the Secretary of State[19] and the Comptroller and Auditor General[20] not later than the 31 August following the end of the accounting year to which it relates[21].

As soon as practicable after the end of each accounting year the DRC must submit to the Secretary of State a report on its activities during that year[22].

The DRC must maintain a list of the organisations it has consulted generally for the purposes of any of its functions[23] and must make the list available to the public in whatever way it considers appropriate and subject to any charge it may impose[24].

1   As to the establishment of the DRC see para 646 ante. As to the Commission for Equality and Human Rights, which is to replace the DRC, see para 305 et seq ante. See also note 2 infra.
2   'Discrimination' means anything which is discrimination for the purposes of any provision of the Disability Discrimination Act 1995 Pt II (ss 3A–18E) (as amended; prospectively amended) (see para 529 et seq ante), Pt III (ss 19–28) (as amended; prospectively amended) (see para 582 et seq ante) or Pt IV (ss 28A–31C) (as amended; prospectively amended) (see para 561 et seq ante): Disability Rights Commission Act 1999 s 2(5) (definition amended by the Special Educational Needs and Disability Act 2001 s 35, Sch 7 paras 1, 2; and the Disability Discrimination Act 2005 s 19(1), Sch 1 para 50(1), (2)(a)). The Disability Rights Commission Act 1999 is repealed by the Equality Act 2006 ss 40, 91, Sch 3 para 59, Sch 4 as from a day to be appointed under s 93. At the date at which this volume states the law no such day had been appointed. See also note 1 supra.
3   'Harassment' means anything which is harassment for the purposes of any provision of the Disability Discrimination Act 1995 Pt II (as amended; prospectively amended), Pt III (as amended; prospectively amended) or Pt IV (as amended; prospectively amended): Disability Rights Commission Act 1999 s 2(5) (definition added by the Disability Discrimination Act 1995 (Amendment) Regulations 2003, SI 2003/1673, regs 3(2), 30(a)(ii)); and amended by the Disability Discrimination Act 2005 Sch 1 para 50(1), (2)(b)).
4   Disability Rights Commission Act 1999 s 2(1)(a) (amended by the Disability Discrimination Act 1995 (Amendment) Regulations 2003, SI 2003/1673, regs 3(2), 30(a)(i)). For the meaning of 'disabled person' see para 511 ante. For these purposes, 'disabled persons' includes persons who have had a disability: Disability Rights Commission Act 1999 s 2(5). As to when a person has a disability see para 511 ante.
5   Ibid s 2(1)(b).
6   Ibid s 2(1)(c).
7   Ibid s 2(1)(d).
8   As to the meaning of 'Minister of the Crown' see para 510 note 4 ante; definition applied by ibid s 13(2).
9   'The law' includes Community law and the international obligations of the United Kingdom: ibid s 2(5). For the meaning of 'United Kingdom' see para 325 note 6 ante.
10   Ibid s 2(2)(a). The DRC must make proposals or give other advice under this provision on any matter specified in a request from a Minister of the Crown: s 2(3).
11   Ibid s 2(2)(b).
12   Ibid s 2(2)(c).
13   See ibid s 2(3).
14   Ibid s 2(4).
15   As to formal investigations see para 648 post.
16   Disability Rights Commission Act 1999 s 1(3), Sch 1 para 14(1). This provision does not affect any power of the DRC to authorise its employees to do anything on its behalf: Sch 1 para 14(2).
17   Ibid Sch 1 para 15(1)(a).
18   Ibid Sch 1 para 15(1)(b). The DRC's accounting year is the 12 months ending with 31 March: Sch 1 para 15(3). The DRC's first accounting year is to be the period of not more than 12 months beginning with the DRC's establishment and ending with 31 March: Sch 1 para 15(4).
19   As to the Secretary of State and the National Assembly for Wales see para 302 ante.
20   As to the Comptroller and Auditor General see CONSTITUTIONAL LAW AND HUMAN RIGHTS vol 8(2) (Reissue) paras 724–726.
21   Disability Rights Commission Act 1999 Sch 1 para 15(1)(c). The Comptroller and Auditor General must examine, certify and report on the statement of accounts and lay copies of the statement and of his report before each House of Parliament: Sch 1 para 15(2).

22 Ibid Sch 1 para 16(1). The report must include (among other things): (1) a report on anything done by the DRC, in the performance of its functions under s 2(1)(a)–(c), jointly or otherwise in co-operation with any other organisation; (2) a general survey of developments in matters within the scope of the DRC's functions; and (3) proposals for the DRC's activities in the current year: Sch 1 para 16(2). The Secretary of State must lay a copy of the report before Parliament and arrange for such further publication of it as he considers appropriate: Sch 1 para 16(3). See also para 649 text and note 37 post.

23 Ibid Sch 1 para 17(1). An organisation may be removed from the list if it has not been consulted generally in the 12 months preceding its removal: Sch 1 para 17(2). Consultation is general unless it relates only: (1) to an investigation to which s 3(5), Sch 3 para 3 (see para 649 post) applies; (2) to assistance under s 7 (as amended) (see para 656 post); or (3) otherwise to a particular individual or individuals: Sch 1 para 17(3).

24 Ibid Sch 1 para 17(4).

648. Formal investigations. The Disability Rights Commission[1] ('DRC') may decide to conduct a formal investigation for any purpose connected with the performance of its duties[2]. The DRC must conduct a formal investigation if directed to do so by the Secretary of State[3] for any such purpose[4]. The DRC may at any time decide to stop or to suspend the conduct of a formal investigation[5].

The DRC may, as respects any formal investigation which it has decided or been directed to conduct[6], nominate one or more commissioners, with or without one or more additional commissioners[7] appointed for the purposes of the investigation, to conduct the investigation on its behalf[8], and authorise those persons to exercise such of its functions in relation to the investigation (which may include drawing up or revising terms of reference) as it may determine[9].

1 As to the establishment of the DRC see para 646 ante. As to the Commission for Equality and Human Rights, which is to replace the DRC, see para 305 et seq ante. See also note 2 infra.

2 Disability Rights Commission Act 1999 s 3(1). The Disability Rights Commission Act 1999 is repealed by the Equality Act 2006 ss 40, 91, Sch 3 para 59, Sch 4 as from a day to be appointed under s 93. At the date at which this volume states the law no such day had been appointed. See also note 1 supra. As to the duties of the DRC see the Disability Rights Commission Act 1999 s 2(1); and para 647 ante. As to the conduct of formal investigations see para 649 post.

3 As to the Secretary of State and the National Assembly for Wales see para 302 ante.

4 Disability Rights Commission Act 1999 s 3(2).

5 Ibid s 3(3). Any such decision requires the approval of the Secretary of State if the investigation is being conducted in pursuance of a direction under s 3(2): see s 3(3).

6 Ibid s 3(4).

7 The DRC may, with the approval of the Secretary of State, appoint one or more individuals as additional commissioners for the purposes of a formal investigation: ibid s 3(5), Sch 2 para 1(1). An additional commissioner is not the servant or agent of the Crown: Sch 2 para 1(2). An additional commissioner holds and vacates office in accordance with the terms of his appointment and may be re-appointed: Sch 2 para 2(1). The DRC may not alter the terms of appointment of an additional commissioner except with his consent and the approval of the Secretary of State: Sch 2 para 2(2). The DRC may: (1) pay such remuneration or expenses to any additional commissioner as the Secretary of State may determine; and (2) pay, or make provision for the payment of, such sums by way of pensions, allowances or gratuities to or in respect of any additional commissioner as the Secretary of State may determine: Sch 2 para 3. An additional commissioner may resign by notice in writing to the DRC: Sch 2 para 4(1). The DRC may, with the approval of the Secretary of State, terminate the appointment of an additional commissioner if satisfied that: (a) without reasonable excuse he has failed to carry out his duties during a continuous period of three months beginning not earlier than six months before the termination; (b) he has become bankrupt, has had his estate sequestrated or has made a composition or arrangement with, or granted a trust deed for, his creditors; or (c) he is otherwise unable or unfit to carry out his duties: Sch 2 para 4(2). The appointment of an additional commissioner otherwise terminates at the conclusion of the investigation for which he was appointed: Sch 2 para 4(3). If the Secretary of State determines that there are special circumstances which make it right that a person who has ceased to be an additional commissioner should receive compensation, the Secretary of State may direct the DRC to pay that person such sum by way of compensation as the Secretary of State may determine: Sch 2 para 5.

8 Ibid s 3(4)(a).

9 Ibid s 3(4)(b).

649. Conduct of formal investigations. There are procedures to be followed as to formal investigations[1] which the Disability Rights Commission[2] ('DRC') has decided or has been directed to conduct[3].

The DRC may not take any steps in the conduct of a formal investigation until terms of reference for the investigation have been drawn up[4], and notice[5] of the holding of the investigation and the terms of reference has been served or published[6]. The terms of reference for the investigation must be drawn up (and may be revised)[7], if the investigation is held at the direction of the Secretary of State, by the Secretary of State after consulting the DRC[8], and in any other case, by the DRC[9].

Where the DRC proposes to investigate in the course of a formal investigation (whether or not the investigation has already begun) whether: (1) a person[10] has committed or is committing any unlawful act[11]; (2) any requirement imposed by a non-discrimination notice[12] served on a person (including a requirement to take action specified in an action plan) has been or is being complied with[13]; or (3) any undertaking given by a person in an agreement made with the DRC[14] is being or has been complied with[15], then the DRC may not investigate any such matter unless the terms of reference of the investigation confine it to the activities of one or more named persons (and the person concerned is one of those persons)[16].

The DRC may not investigate whether a person has committed or is committing any unlawful act unless it has reason to believe that the person concerned may have committed or may be committing the act in question[17], or that matter is to be investigated in the course of a formal investigation into his compliance with any requirement or undertaking mentioned in head (2) or head (3) above[18].

The DRC must serve a notice on the person concerned offering him the opportunity to make written and oral representations about the matters being investigated[19]. If the DRC is investigating whether the person concerned has committed or is committing any unlawful act (otherwise than in the course of a formal investigation into his compliance with any requirement or undertaking mentioned in head (2) or head (3) above), the DRC must include in the notice a statement informing that person that the DRC has reason to believe that he may have committed or may be committing any unlawful act[20]. The DRC must not make any findings in relation to any matter mentioned in heads (1) to (3) above without giving the person concerned or his representative a reasonable opportunity to make written and oral representations[21].

For the purposes of a formal investigation, the DRC may serve a notice on any person[22] requiring him to give such written information as may be described in the notice[23], or to attend and give oral information about any matter specified in the notice, and to produce all documents in his possession or control relating to any such matter[24].

The DRC may make recommendations in the light of its findings in a formal investigation[25], and it must prepare a report of its findings in any such investigation[26].

Where the DRC has decided to conduct a formal investigation and fails to publish the investigation report[27] before the expiration of the specified period[28], or where the Secretary of State has directed the DRC to conduct a formal investigation and it fails to serve the investigation report on the Secretary of State before the expiration of the specified period[29], then: (a) any requirement contained in a non-discrimination notice served by the DRC in relation to the formal investigation ceases to have effect[30]; (b) any requirement contained in an information notice served in relation to the formal investigation which has not yet been complied with ceases to have effect[31]; and (c) no steps or further steps may be taken by the DRC in the conduct of the formal investigation[32]. The Secretary of State may allow to the DRC: (i) such extended period for the purpose of taking steps or further steps in the conduct of a formal investigation as the Secretary of State may specify[33]; or (ii) where an extended period has already been allowed once or more than once under this provision, such further extended period for that purpose as the Secretary of State may specify[34]. Where the reporting period or any extended period allowed has started to run, it ceases to run during any period beginning with the day specified in an information notice[35] for compliance with the notice and ending with the day on which the notice is fully complied with[36].

The DRC must include in its annual report[37] a statement of any extended period which was allowed[38] during the accounting year to which the annual report relates[39], a statement of any suspension of a period[40] which has occurred during that accounting year[41], and where head (a), (b) or (c) above has applied in relation to any formal investigation during that accounting year, a statement of that fact, and a statement of the reasons for the failure to publish or serve the investigation report[42].

1   'Formal investigation' means an investigation under the Disability Rights Commission Act 1999 s 3 (see para 648 ante): s 13(1). The Disability Rights Commission Act 1999 is repealed by the Equality Act 2006 ss 40, 91, Sch 3 para 59, Sch 4 as from a day to be appointed under s 93. At the date at which this volume states the law no such day had been appointed. See also note 2 infra.

2   As to the establishment of the DRC see para 646 ante. As to the Commission for Equality and Human Rights, which is to replace the DRC, see para 305 et seq ante. See also note 1 supra.

3   See the Disability Rights Commission Act 1999 s 3(5), Sch 3 para 1(1). Any subsequent action required or authorised by Sch 3 Pt I (as amended) (or by Sch 3 Pt IV) to be taken by the DRC in relation to the conduct of a formal investigation may be taken, so far as they are authorised to do so, by persons nominated under s 3(4) (see para 648 ante) for the purposes of the investigation: Sch 3 para 1(2). The Secretary of State may make regulations making provision supplementing Sch 3 Pt I (as amended) in connection with any matter concerned with the conduct of formal investigations: see Sch 3 para 26(a). As to the Secretary of State and the National Assembly for Wales see para 302 ante.

4   Ibid Sch 3 para 2(1)(a).

5   'Notice' means notice in writing: ibid s 13(1). Any notice required or authorised by any provision of Sch 3 (as amended) to be served on a person may be served by delivering it to him, by leaving it at his proper address or by sending it by post to him at that address: Sch 3 para 25(1). Any such notice may: (1) in the case of a body corporate, be served on the secretary or clerk of that body; (2) in the case of a partnership, be served on any partner or a person having control or management of the partnership business; or (3) in the case of an unincorporated association (other than a partnership), may be served on any member of its governing body: Sch 3 para 25(2). For these purposes, the proper address of any person is: (a) in the case of a body corporate, its secretary or clerk, the address of its registered or principal office in the United Kingdom; (b) in the case of an unincorporated association (other than a partnership) or a member of its governing body, its principal office in the United Kingdom; or (c) in any other case, his usual or last-known address (whether of his residence or of a place where he carries on business or is employed): Sch 3 para 25(3). For the meaning of 'United Kingdom' see para 325 note 6 ante.

6   Ibid Sch 3 para 2(1)(b). Where the terms of reference confine the investigation to activities of one or more named persons, notice of the holding of the investigation and the terms of reference must be served on each of those persons: Sch 3 para 2(3). Where the terms of reference do not confine the investigation to activities of one or more named persons, notice of the holding of the investigation and the terms of reference must be published in such manner as appears to the DRC appropriate to bring it to the attention of persons likely to be affected by it: Sch 3 para 2(4).

7   Ibid Sch 3 para 2(2). If the terms of reference are revised, Sch 3 para 2 applies again in relation to the revised investigation and its terms of reference: Sch 3 para 2(5).

8   Ibid Sch 3 para 2(2)(a).

9   Ibid Sch 3 para 2(2)(b).

10   As to the meaning of 'person' see para 344 note 3 ante.

11   Disability Rights Commission Act 1999 Sch 3 para 3(1)(a). 'Unlawful act' means an act which is unlawful for the purposes of any provision of the Disability Discrimination Act 1995 Pt II (ss 3A–18E) (as amended; prospectively amended) (see para 529 et seq ante), Pt III (ss 19–28) (as amended; prospectively amended) (see para 582 et seq ante) or Pt IV (ss 28A–31C) (as amended; prospectively amended) (see para 561 et seq ante) or any other unlawful act of a description prescribed for these purposes: Disability Rights Commission Act 1999 Sch 3 para 3(10) (amended by the Special Educational Needs and Disability Act 2001 s 35, Sch 7 paras 1, 9; the Disability Discrimination Act 2005 s 19(1), Sch 1 para 50(1), (3); and the Disability Discrimination Act 1995 (Amendment) Regulations 2003, SI 2003/1673, regs 3(2), 30(f)). As the meaning of 'act' see para 510 note 3 ante. 'Prescribed' means prescribed in regulations made by the Secretary of State: Disability Rights Commission Act 1999 s 13(1).

At the date at which this volume states the law no such regulations had been made. Any power under the Disability Rights Commission Act 1999 to make regulations is exercisable by statutory instrument: s 12(1). Any such regulations may make: (1) different provision for different cases or areas; (2) provision enabling a person to exercise a discretion in dealing with any matter; and (3) incidental, supplemental, consequential or transitional provision: s 12(2). A statutory instrument containing any such regulations is subject to annulment in pursuance of a resolution of either House of Parliament: s 12(3).

12 As to non-discrimination notices see ibid s 4 (as amended); and para 650 post.

13 Ibid Sch 3 para 3(1)(b).

14 Ie under ibid s 5 (as amended): see para 652 post.

15 Ibid Sch 3 para 3(1)(c).

16 Ibid Sch 3 para 3(2).

17 Ibid Sch 3 para 3(3)(a).

18 Ibid Sch 3 para 3(3)(b).

19 Ibid Sch 3 para 3(4). A notice required by Sch 3 para 3(4) may be included in a notice required by Sch 3 para 2(3) (see note 6 supra): Sch 3 para 3(9).

20 Ibid Sch 3 para 3(5).

21 Ibid Sch 3 para 3(6). The DRC may refuse to receive oral representations made on behalf of the person concerned by a person (not being counsel or a solicitor) to whom the DRC reasonably objects as being unsuitable: Sch 3 para 3(7). If the DRC refuses to receive oral representations from a person, it must give reasons in writing for its objection: Sch 3 para 3(8).

22 Such a notice may only be served on the written authority of the Secretary of State unless the terms of reference confine the investigation to the activities of one or more named persons and the person being served is one of those persons: ibid Sch 3 para 4(2). A person may not be required by such a notice: (1) to give information, or produce a document, which he could not be compelled to give in evidence or produce in civil proceedings before the High Court; or (2) to attend at any place unless the necessary expenses of his journey to and from that place are paid or tendered to him: Sch 3 para 4(3). The DRC may apply to a county court for an order if: (a) a person has been served with such a notice; and (b) he fails to comply with it or the DRC has reasonable cause to believe that he intends not to comply with it: Sch 3 para 5(1). An order under this provision is an order requiring the person concerned to comply with the notice or with such directions for the same purpose as may be contained in the order: Sch 3 para 5(2).

23 Ibid Sch 3 para 4(1)(a).

24 Ibid Sch 3 para 4(1)(b).

25 Ibid Sch 3 para 6(1). The recommendations may be: (1) recommendations to any person for changes in his policies or procedures, or as to any other matter, with a view to promoting the equalisation of opportunities for disabled persons or persons who have had a disability; or (2) recommendations to the Secretary of State, for changes in the law or otherwise: Sch 3 para 6(2). The DRC may make such recommendations before the conclusion of the investigation concerned: Sch 3 para 6(3). For the meaning of 'disabled person' see para 511 ante. As to when a person has a disability see para 511 ante.

26 Ibid Sch 3 para 7(1). The DRC must exclude from such a report any matter which relates to an individual's private affairs or any person's business interests if: (1) publication of that matter might, in the DRC's opinion, prejudicially affect that individual or person; and (2) its exclusion is consistent with the DRC's duties and the object of the report: Sch 3 para 7(2). The report of an investigation carried out at the direction of the Secretary of State must be published by the Secretary of State or, if the Secretary of State so directs, by the DRC: Sch 3 para 7(3). The report of any other investigation must be published by the DRC: Sch 3 para 7(4). Nothing in this provision affects the DRC's power to issue a non-discrimination notice before a report is prepared or published: Sch 3 para 7(5).

27 'Investigation report' means the report which the DRC is required to prepare of its findings in a formal investigation under ibid Sch 3 para 7: Disability Rights Commission (Time Limits) Regulations 2000, SI 2000/879, reg 1(2).

28 Ibid reg 2(1)(a). The period referred to is: (1) the reporting period; or (2) where one or more extended periods are allowed, that extended period or the last of those extended periods, as the case may be: reg 2(2). 'Reporting period' means 18 months beginning with the day on which notice of the holding of the investigation and the terms of reference is first served or published in accordance with the Disability Rights Commission Act 1999 Sch 3 para 2(3) or (4) (see note 6 supra), as the case may be: Disability Rights Commission (Time Limits) Regulations 2000, SI 2000/879, reg 1(2). 'Terms of reference' means the terms of reference for a formal investigation which are required to be drawn up under the Disability Rights Commission Act 1999 Sch 3 para 2: Disability Rights Commission (Time Limits) Regulations 2000, SI 2000/879, reg 1(2).

29 Ibid reg 2(1)(b). As to the specified period see note 28 supra.

30 Ibid reg 2(3)(a).

31 Ibid reg 2(3)(b).

32 Ibid reg 2(3)(c). For the purposes of reg 2(3)(c) and (4), and without prejudice to the generality thereof, 'steps' include the service of a non-discrimination notice, and the preparation, publication or service of an investigation report: reg 2(7).
33 Ibid reg 2(4)(a).
34 Ibid reg 2(4)(b).
35 'Information notice' means a notice served by the DRC under the Disability Rights Commission Act 1999 Sch 3 para 4(1) (power to obtain information for the purposes of a formal investigation: see the text and notes 23, 24 supra): Disability Rights Commission (Time Limits) Regulations 2000, SI 2000/879, reg 1(2).
36 Ibid reg 2(5).
37 'Annual report' means the report submitted by the DRC to the Secretary of State in accordance with the Disability Rights Commission Act 1999 s 1(3), Sch 1 para 16 (see para 647 text and note 22 ante): Disability Rights Commission (Time Limits) Regulations 2000, SI 2000/879, reg 1(2).
38 Ie under ibid reg 2(4): see the text to notes 33, 34 supra.
39 Ibid reg 2(6)(a).
40 Ie by virtue of ibid reg 2(5): see the text to note 36 supra.
41 Ibid reg 2(6)(b).
42 Ibid reg 2(6)(c). The reasons for failure are specified in reg 2(1): see the text and notes 28, 29 supra.

650. Non-discrimination notices. If in the course of a formal investigation[1] the Disability Rights Commission[2] ('DRC') is satisfied that a person[3] has committed or is committing an unlawful act[4], it may serve on him a non-discrimination notice[5] which gives details of the unlawful act which the DRC has found that he has committed or is committing[6], and requires him not to commit any further unlawful acts of the same kind (and, if the finding is that he is committing an unlawful act, to cease doing so)[7]. The notice may include recommendations to the person concerned as to action which the DRC considers he could reasonably be expected to take with a view to ceasing to commit such acts[8]. The notice may also require the person concerned to propose an adequate action plan[9] with a view to ceasing to commit such acts[10], and once an action plan proposed by him has become final, to take any action which is specified in the plan and which he has not already taken, at the time or times specified in the plan[11].

1 For the meaning of 'formal investigation' see para 649 note 1 ante.
2 As to the establishment of the DRC see para 646 ante. As to the Commission for Equality and Human Rights, which is to replace the DRC, see para 305 et seq ante. See also note 4 infra.
3 As to the meaning of 'person' see para 344 note 3 ante.
4 'Unlawful act' means an act which is unlawful for the purposes of any provision of the Disability Discrimination Act 1995 Pt II (ss 3A–18E) (as amended; prospectively amended) (see para 529 et seq ante), Pt III (ss 19–28) (as amended; prospectively amended) (see para 582 et seq ante) or Pt IV (ss 28A–31C) (as amended; prospectively amended) (see para 561 et seq ante) or any other unlawful act of a description prescribed for these purposes: Disability Rights Commission Act 1999 s 4(5) (amended by the Special Educational Needs and Disability Act 2001 s 35, Sch 7 paras 1, 3; the Disability Discrimination Act 2005 s 19(1), Sch 1 para 50(1), (3); and the Disability Discrimination Act 1995 (Amendment) Regulations 2003, SI 2003/1673, regs 3(2), 30(b)). The Disability Rights Commission Act 1999 is repealed by the Equality Act 2006 ss 40, 91, Sch 3 para 59, Sch 4 as from a day to be appointed under s 93. At the date at which this volume states the law no such day had been appointed. See also note 2 supra. As to the meaning of 'act' see para 510 note 3 ante. 'Prescribed' means prescribed in regulations: see para 649 note 11 ante. At the date at which this volume states the law no such unlawful act had been prescribed.
5 Disability Rights Commission Act 1999 s 4(1).
6 Ibid s 4(1)(a).
7 Ibid s 4(1)(b).
8 See ibid s 4(2).
9 Ie subject to and in accordance with ibid s 4(6), Sch 3 Pt III: see para 653 post. An action plan is a document drawn up by the person concerned specifying action (including action he has already taken) intended to change anything in his practices, policies, procedures or other arrangements which: (1) caused or contributed to the commission of the unlawful act concerned; or (2) is liable to cause or contribute to a failure to cease to commit such acts: see s 4(4)(a). An action plan is adequate if the action specified in it would be sufficient to ensure, within a reasonable time, that he is not prevented from

complying with that requirement by anything in his practices, policies, procedures or other arrangements: s 4(4)(b). The action specified in an action plan may include ceasing an activity or taking continuing action over a period: s 4(4).

10   See ibid s 4(3)(a).
11   Ibid s 4(3)(b).

651.   Procedure relating to non-discrimination notices.   The Disability Rights Commission[1] ('DRC') may not issue a non-discrimination notice[2] addressed to any person[3] unless it has complied with certain requirements[4]. The DRC must serve on the person concerned a notice[5] informing him that the DRC is considering issuing a non-discrimination notice and of the grounds for doing so[6], and offering him the opportunity to make written and oral representations[7]. On issuing a non-discrimination notice, the DRC must serve a copy on the person to whom it is addressed[8].

A person on whom a non-discrimination notice is served may, within the period of six weeks beginning on the day after the day on which the notice is served on him, appeal against any requirement imposed by the notice[9].

During the period of five years beginning on the date on which a non-discrimination notice served on a person has become final[10], the DRC may apply to a county court for an order requiring the person concerned to comply with the requirement or with any directions contained in the order[11], if it appears to the DRC that the person concerned has failed to comply with any requirement imposed by a non-discrimination notice[12], or the DRC has reasonable cause to believe that he intends not to comply with any such requirement[13].

The DRC must maintain a register of non-discrimination notices which have become final[14].

1   As to the establishment of the DRC see para 646 ante. As to the Commission for Equality and Human Rights, which is to replace the DRC, see para 305 et seq ante. See also note 2 infra.
2   'Non-discrimination notice' means a notice under the Disability Rights Commission Act 1999 s 4 (as amended) (see para 650 ante): s 13(1). The Disability Rights Commission Act 1999 is repealed by the Equality Act 2006 ss 40, 91, Sch 3 para 59, Sch 4 as from a day to be appointed under s 93. At the date at which this volume states the law no such day had been appointed. See also note 1 supra. For the meaning of 'notice' see para 649 note 5 ante.
3   As to the meaning of 'person' see para 344 note 3 ante.
4   Disability Rights Commission Act 1999 s 4(6), Sch 3 para 8(1). The Secretary of State may make regulations making provision supplementing Sch 3 Pt II in connection with any matter concerned with the procedure for issuing non-discrimination notices: see Sch 3 para 26(a). As to the Secretary of State and the National Assembly for Wales see para 302 ante. As to the making of regulations see para 649 note 11 ante. As to the regulations made see the Disability Rights Commission (Time Limits) Regulations 2000, SI 2000/879.
5   Disability Rights Commission Act 1999 Sch 3 para 8(2).
6   Ibid Sch 3 para 8(2)(a).
7   Ibid Sch 3 para 8(2)(b). The DRC must give the person concerned or his representative the opportunity of making oral and written representations within a period specified in the notice of not less than 28 days: Sch 3 para 8(3). The DRC may refuse to receive oral representations made on behalf of the person concerned by a person (not being counsel or a solicitor) to whom the DRC reasonably objects as being unsuitable: Sch 3 para 8(4). If the DRC refuses to receive oral representations from a person, it must give reasons in writing for its objection: Sch 3 para 8(5).
8   Ibid Sch 3 para 9.
9   Ibid Sch 3 para 10(1). An appeal under this provision lies: (1) to an employment tribunal, so far as the requirement relates to acts within the tribunal's jurisdiction; and (2) to a county court so far as the requirement relates to acts which are not within the jurisdiction of an employment tribunal: Sch 3 para 10(2). The court or tribunal may quash any requirement appealed against: (a) if it considers the requirement to be unreasonable; or (b) in the case of a requirement imposed under head (2) in the text, if it considers that the DRC's finding that the person concerned had committed or is committing the unlawful act in question was based on an incorrect finding of fact: Sch 3 para 10(3). On quashing a requirement, the court or tribunal may direct that the non-discrimination notice has effect with such modifications as it considers appropriate: Sch 3 para 10(4). The modifications which may be included in such a direction include the substitution of a requirement in different terms, and, in the case of a

requirement imposed under head (2) in the text, modifications to the details given under head (1) in the text so far as necessary to describe any unlawful act on which the requirement could properly have been based: Sch 3 para 10(5). The right to appeal does not apply to any modifications contained in such a direction: Sch 3 para 10(6). If the court or tribunal allows an appeal under this provision without quashing or recalling the whole of the non-discrimination notice, the DRC may by notice to the person concerned vary the non-discrimination notice by revoking or altering any recommendation included in pursuance of the DRC's power under s 4(2) (see para 650 ante), or by making new recommendations in pursuance of that power: Sch 3 para 10(7).

10 A non-discrimination notice becomes final when: (1) an appeal is dismissed, withdrawn or abandoned or the time for appealing expires without an appeal having been brought; or (2) an appeal is allowed without the whole notice being quashed: ibid s 13(1), Sch 3 para 11.

11 Ibid Sch 3 para 12(3).

12 See ibid Sch 3 para 12(2)(a).

13 Ibid Sch 3 para 12(2)(b).

14 Ibid Sch 3 para 13(1). In the case of notices which impose a requirement to propose an action plan, the DRC must note on the register the date on which any action plan proposed by the person concerned has become final: Sch 3 para 13(2). The DRC must arrange for the register to be available for inspection at all reasonable times, and for certified copies of any entry to be provided if required by any person: Sch 3 para 13(3). The DRC must publish those arrangements in such manner as it considers appropriate to bring them to the attention of persons likely to be interested: Sch 3 para 13(4).

652. Agreements in lieu of enforcement action. If the Disability Rights Commission[1] ('DRC') has reason to believe that a person[2] has committed or is committing an unlawful act, it may enter into an agreement in writing with that person on the assumption that that belief is well founded (whether or not that person admits that he committed or is committing the act in question)[4].

Under such an agreement: (1) the DRC undertakes not to take any relevant enforcement action[5] in relation to the unlawful act in question[6]; and (2) the person concerned undertakes not to commit any further unlawful acts of the same kind (and, where appropriate, to cease committing the unlawful act in question)[7], and to take such action (which may include ceasing an activity or taking continuing action over any period) as may be specified in the agreement[8]. These undertakings are binding on the parties to the agreement[9].

An agreement may include terms providing for incidental or supplementary matters (including the termination of the agreement, or the right of either party to terminate it, in certain circumstances)[10], and may be varied or revoked by agreement of the parties[11].

The above provisions do not affect the DRC's powers to settle or compromise legal proceedings of any description[12].

1 As to the establishment of the DRC see para 646 ante. As to the Commission for Equality and Human Rights, which is to replace the DRC, see para 305 et seq ante. See also note 3 infra.

2 As to the meaning of 'person' see para 344 note 3 ante.

3 'Unlawful act' means an act which is unlawful for the purposes of the Disability Discrimination Act 1995 Pt II (ss 3A–18E) (as amended; prospectively amended) (see para 529 et seq ante), Pt III (ss 19–28) (as amended; prospectively amended) (see para 582 et seq ante) or Pt IV (ss 28A–31C) (as amended; prospectively amended) (see para 561 et seq ante) or any other unlawful act of a description prescribed for these purposes: Disability Rights Commission Act 1999 s 5(11) (amended by the Special Educational Needs and Disability Act 2001 s 35, Sch 7 paras 1, 4; the Disability Discrimination Act 2005 s 19(1), Sch 1 para 50(1), (3); and the Disability Discrimination Act 1995 (Amendment) Regulations 2003, SI 2003/1673, regs 3(2), 30(c)). The Disability Rights Commission Act 1999 is repealed by the Equality Act 2006 ss 40, 91, Sch 3 para 59, Sch 4 as from a day to be appointed under s 93. At the date at which this volume states the law no such day had been appointed. See also note 1 supra. As the meaning of 'act' see para 510 note 3 ante. 'Prescribed' means prescribed in regulations: see para 649 note 11 ante. At the date at which this volume states the law no such unlawful act had been prescribed.

4 Disability Rights Commission Act 1999 s 5(1). This is expressed to be subject to s 3(3): see para 648 ante.

5 'Relevant enforcement action' means: (1) beginning a formal investigation into the commission by the person concerned of the unlawful act in question; (2) if such an investigation has begun (whether or not the investigation is confined to that matter), taking any further steps in the investigation of that matter; and (3) taking any steps, or further steps, with a view to the issue of a non-discrimination notice based

on the commission of the unlawful act in question: ibid s 5(4). For the meaning of 'formal investigation' see para 649 note 1 ante; and for the meaning of 'non-discrimination notice' see para 651 note 2 ante.

6   Ibid s 5(2)(a).

7   Ibid s 5(2)(b)(i). See also note 9 infra.

8   Ibid s 5(2)(b)(ii). The action specified in such an undertaking must be action intended to change anything in the practices, policies, procedures or other arrangements of the person concerned which: (1) caused or contributed to the commission of the unlawful act in question; or (2) is liable to cause or contribute to a failure to comply with his undertaking under s 5(2)(b)(i): s 5(5). See also note 9 infra.

9   Ibid s 5(3). Undertakings under s 5(2)(b) are enforceable by the DRC only as provided by s 5(8): see s 5(3). The DRC may apply to a county court for an order requiring the other party to comply with the undertaking or with such directions for the same purpose as are contained in the order if: (1) the other party to an agreement under this provision has failed to comply with any undertaking under s 5(2)(b); or (2) the DRC has reasonable cause to believe that he intends not to comply with any such undertaking: s 5(8), (9). The County Courts Act 1984 s 55 (as amended) (see EVIDENCE vol 17(1) (Reissue) para 997) has effect with modifications in relation to a failure to comply with an order made by a county court under the Disability Rights Commission Act 1999: see s 5(12), Sch 3 para 23. If the DRC applies to a county court to enforce an order, the court may modify the order: see Sch 3 para 23.

10   Ibid s 5(6)(a). An agreement may not include any provisions other than terms mentioned in s 5(2), (6)(a) unless their inclusion is authorised by regulations made by the Secretary of State for these purposes, but any provisions so authorised are not enforceable by the DRC under s 5(8) (see note 9 supra): s 5(7). As to the Secretary of State and the National Assembly for Wales see para 302 ante.

11   Ibid s 5(6)(b).

12   Ibid s 5(10).

653.   Action plans. Where a person[1] ('P') has been served with a non-discrimination notice[2] which has become final[3] and includes a requirement for him to propose an action plan[4], then P must serve his proposed action plan on the Disability Rights Commission[5] ('DRC') within such period as may be specified in the non-discrimination notice[6].

If the DRC considers that a proposed action plan served on it is not an adequate action plan[7], the DRC may give notice[8] to P[9] stating its view that the plan is not adequate[10], and inviting him to serve on the DRC a revised action plan which is adequate within such period as may be specified in the notice[11].

If the DRC considers that a proposed action plan served on it is not an adequate action plan it may apply to the county court for an order[12] declaring that the proposed action plan in question is not an adequate action plan[13], requiring P to revise his proposals and serve on the DRC an adequate action plan within such period as the order may specify[14], and containing such directions (if any) as the court considers appropriate as to the action which should be specified in the adequate action plan required by the order[15].

Where an order of the court requires P to serve an adequate action plan on the DRC[16], and, in response to the order, P serves an action plan on the DRC, that action plan becomes final at the end of the prescribed period[17] unless the DRC has applied to a county court to enforce the order on the ground that the plan does not comply with the order and any directions[18].

An action plan which has become final may be varied by agreement in writing between the DRC and P[19].

If, during the period of five years beginning on the date on which an action plan drawn up by P becomes final[20], the DRC considers that P has failed to comply with the requirement[21] to carry out any action specified in the action plan, the DRC may apply to a county court for an order[22] requiring P to comply with that requirement or with such directions for the same purpose as are contained in the order[23].

For the purposes of determining whether an action plan proposed by P is an adequate action plan[24], or whether P has complied or is complying with the requirement to take the action specified in an action plan which has become final[25], the DRC may serve a notice on any person requiring him to give such information in writing, or copies of documents in his possession or control, relating to those matters as may be described in the notice[26].

1 As to the meaning of 'person' see para 344 note 3 ante.

2 For the meaning of 'non-discrimination notice' see para 651 note 2 ante.

3 As to when a non-discrimination notice becomes final see para 651 note 10 ante.

4 Disability Rights Commission Act 1999 s 4(6), Sch 3 para 14(1). The Disability Rights Commission Act 1999 is repealed by the Equality Act 2006 ss 40, 91, Sch 3 para 59, Sch 4 as from a day to be appointed under s 93. At the date at which this volume states the law no such day had been appointed. See also note 5 infra. As to the requirement to propose an action plan see para 650 ante.

5 As to the establishment of the DRC see para 646 ante. As to the Commission for Equality and Human Rights, which is to replace the DRC, see para 305 et seq ante. See also note 4 supra.

6 Disability Rights Commission Act 1999 Sch 3 para 15(1). If P fails to do so, the DRC may apply to a county court for an order directing him to serve his proposed action plan within such period as the order may specify: Sch 3 para 15(2). If P serves a proposed action plan on the DRC in response to the non-discrimination notice, or an order under Sch 3 para 15(2), the action plan becomes final at the end of the prescribed period, unless the DRC has given notice to P under Sch 3 para 16: Sch 3 para 15(3). 'Prescribed' means prescribed in regulations: see para 649 note 11 ante. The period prescribed for the purposes of Sch 3 para 15(3) is 12 weeks beginning with the day on which the proposed action plan is served on the DRC: Disability Rights Commission (Time Limits) Regulations 2000, SI 2000/879, reg 3(1). Any period prescribed for these purposes which has started to run ceases to run during any period beginning with the day on which a notice is served by the DRC under the Disability Rights Commission Act 1999 Sch 3 para 21(1)(a) (power to obtain information for the purposes of determining whether a proposed action plan is adequate: see the text to note 23 infra) and ending with the day on which the notice is fully complied with: Disability Rights Commission (Time Limits) Regulations 2000, SI 2000/879, reg 3(9).

7 'Adequate' in relation to a proposed action plan means adequate (as defined in the Disability Rights Commission Act 1999 s 4(4)(b): see para 650 note 9 ante) for the purposes of the requirement not to commit further unlawful discrimination: see Sch 3 para 14(2).

8 A notice under this provision may include recommendations as to action which the DRC considers might be included in an adequate action plan: ibid Sch 3 para 16(2). For the meaning of 'notice' see para 649 note 5 ante.

9 Ibid Sch 3 para 16(1).

10 Ibid Sch 3 para 16(1)(a).

11 Ibid Sch 3 para 16(1)(b). If P serves a revised proposed action plan on the DRC in response to such a notice, it supersedes the previous proposed action plan and becomes final at the end of the prescribed period, unless the DRC has applied for an order under Sch 3 para 17: Sch 3 para 16(3). The period prescribed for the purposes of Sch 3 para 16(3) is eight weeks beginning with the day on which the revised action plan is served on the DRC: Disability Rights Commission (Time Limits) Regulations 2000, SI 2000/879, reg 3(2). If P does not serve a revised action plan in response to such a notice, the action plan previously served on the DRC becomes final at the end of the prescribed period, unless the DRC has applied for an order under the Disability Rights Commission Act 1999 Sch 3 para 17: Sch 3 para 16(4). The period prescribed for the purposes of Sch 3 para 16(4) is four weeks beginning with the expiration of: (1) the original period specified in the notice served under Sch 3 para 16(1) for service of the revised action plan; or (2) where the DRC has extended the period for such service beyond that originally specified in the notice, that extended period: Disability Rights Commission (Time Limits) Regulations 2000, SI 2000/879, reg 3(3), (4). Any period prescribed for the purposes of the Disability Rights Commission Act 1999 Sch 3 para 16(3), (4) which has started to run ceases to run during any period beginning with the day on which a notice is served by the DRC under Sch 3 para 21(1)(a) (power to obtain information for the purposes of determining whether a proposed action plan is adequate: see the text to note 24 infra) and ending with the day on which the notice is fully complied with: Disability Rights Commission (Time Limits) Regulations 2000, SI 2000/879, reg 3(9).

The Secretary of State may make regulations making provision amending the Disability Rights Commission Act 1999 Sch 3 Pt III in relation to the procedures for finalising action plans: see Sch 3 para 26(b). As to the Secretary of State and the National Assembly for Wales see para 302 ante. At the date at which this volume states the law no such regulations had been made.

12 Ibid Sch 3 para 17(1). The DRC may not make such an application in relation to the first proposed action plan served on it by P (even where it was served in compliance with an order of the court under Sch 3 para 15(2) (see note 6 supra)) unless: (1) a notice under Sch 3 para 16 (see the text and notes 7–11 supra) has been served on P in relation to that proposed action plan; and (2) P has not served a revised action plan on the DRC in response to it within the period specified in the notice under Sch 3

para 16(1)(b) (see the text and note 11 supra): Sch 3 para 17(2). If on an application under this provision the court does not make an order, the proposed action plan in question becomes final at the end of the prescribed period: Sch 3 para 17(4). The period prescribed for the purposes of Sch 3 para 17(4) is: (a) where the court does not make an order because it has decided not to do so, seven days beginning with the day on which the decision has become final; and (b) where the court does not make an order because the DRC withdraws its application for an order, seven days beginning with the day on which the withdrawal is notified to the person who served the action plan on the DRC: Disability Rights Commission (Time Limits) Regulations 2000, SI 2000/879, reg 3(5). A decision of a court becomes final for these purposes when an appeal against it is dismissed, withdrawn or abandoned or when the time for appealing expires without an appeal having been brought: reg 3(10).

13   Disability Rights Commission Act 1999 Sch 3 para 17(3)(a).

14   Ibid Sch 3 para 17(3)(b).

15   Ibid Sch 3 para 17(3)(c).

16   See ibid Sch 3 para 18(1).

17   The period prescribed for these purposes is eight weeks beginning with the day on which the action plan is served on the DRC: Disability Rights Commission (Time Limits) Regulations 2000, SI 2000/879, reg 3(6). Any period prescribed for these purposes which has started to run ceases to run during any period beginning with the day on which a notice is served by the DRC under the Disability Rights Commission Act 1999 Sch 3 para 21(1)(a) (power to obtain information for the purposes of determining whether a proposed action plan is adequate: see the text to note 24 infra) and ending with the day on which the notice is fully complied with: Disability Rights Commission (Time Limits) Regulations 2000, SI 2000/879, reg 3(9).

18   Disability Rights Commission Act 1999 Sch 3 para 18(2). Directions are given under Sch 3 para 17(3)(c) (see the text and note 15 supra): see Sch 3 para 18(2). Where such an application is made: (1) if the DRC withdraws its application, the action plan in question becomes final at the end of the prescribed period (Sch 3 para 18(3)(a)); and (2) if the court considers that the action plan in question complies with the order, that action plan becomes final at the end of the prescribed period (Sch 3 para 18(3)(b)). The period prescribed for the purposes of Sch 3 para 18(3)(a) is seven days beginning with the day on which the withdrawal of the application of the DRC is notified to the person who served the action plan on the DRC: Disability Rights Commission (Time Limits) Regulations 2000, SI 2000/879, reg 3(7). The period prescribed for the purposes of the Disability Rights Commission Act 1999 Sch 3 para 18(3)(b) is seven days beginning with the day on which the decision of the court on the application made as mentioned in Sch 3 para 18(2) has become final: Disability Rights Commission (Time Limits) Regulations 2000, SI 2000/879, reg 3(8). A decision of a court becomes final for these purposes when an appeal against it is dismissed, withdrawn or abandoned or when the time for appealing expires without an appeal having been brought: reg 3(10).

19   Disability Rights Commission Act 1999 Sch 3 para 19.

20   See ibid Sch 3 para 20(1).

21   Ie under ibid s 4(3)(b): see para 650 ante.

22   See ibid Sch 3 para 20(2).

23   See ibid Sch 3 para 20(3).

24   Ibid Sch 3 para 21(1)(a).

25   Ibid Sch 3 para 21(1)(b).

26   Ibid Sch 3 para 21(1). A person may not be required by a notice under this provision to give information, or produce a document, which he could not be compelled to give in evidence or produce in civil proceedings before the High Court: Sch 3 para 21(2). The DRC may apply to a county court for an order requiring the person concerned to comply with the notice or with such directions for the same purpose as may be contained in the order if a person has been served with a notice and fails to comply with it: see Sch 3 para 21(3), (4). As to restrictions on the disclosure of information see para 658 post.

654.   Persistent discrimination. If during the specified period[1] it appears to the Disability Rights Commission[2] ('DRC') that unless restrained the person[3] concerned is likely to do one or more unlawful acts[4], the DRC may apply to a county court for an injunction restraining him from doing so[5]. The court, if satisfied that the application is well-founded, may grant the injunction in the terms applied for or in more limited terms[6].

1   The specified period is the period of five years beginning on the date on which any of the following has become final: (1) a non-discrimination notice served on a person; (2) a finding in proceedings under the Disability Discrimination Act 1995 s 17A (as added and amended) (see para 643 ante), s 25 (as amended) (see para 644 ante), s 28I (as added and amended) (see para 566 ante), s 28K (as added and amended) (see

para 567 ante), s 28L (as added and amended) (see para 567 ante) or s 28V (as added and amended) (see para 575 ante) that a person has committed an act which is unlawful discrimination for the purposes of any provision of Pt II (ss 3A–18E) (as amended; prospectively amended) (see para 529 et seq ante), Pt III (ss 19–28) (as amended; prospectively amended) (see para 582 et seq ante) or Pt IV (ss 28A–31C) (as amended; prospectively amended) (see para 561 et seq ante); or (3) a finding by a court or tribunal in any other proceedings that a person has committed an act of a description prescribed under the Disability Rights Commission Act 1999 s 6(4) (as amended) (see note 4 infra): s 6(1) (amended by the Special Educational Needs and Disability Act 2001 s 35, Sch 7 paras 1, 5; the Disability Discrimination Act 2005 s 19(1), Sch 1 para 50(1), (4)(b); and the Disability Discrimination Act 1995 (Amendment) Regulations 2003, SI 2003/1673, regs 3(2), 30(d)(i)). For the meaning of 'non-discrimination notice' see para 651 note 2 ante. As to the meaning of 'act' see para 510 note 3 ante. As from a day to be appointed, a reference is added in head (2) supra to proceedings under provision made under the Disability Discrimination Act 1995 s 31AE (as added) (see para 581 ante): Disability Rights Commission Act 1999 s 6(1) (as so amended; prospectively amended by the Disability Discrimination Act 2005 Sch 1 para 50(1), (4)(a)). At the date at which this volume states the law no such day had been appointed. A finding becomes final for these purposes when an appeal against it is dismissed, withdrawn or abandoned or when the time for appealing expires without an appeal having been brought: Disability Rights Commission Act 1999 s 6(5) (amended by the Special Educational Needs and Disability Act 2001 s 42(6), Sch 7 paras 1, 7, Sch 9). The Disability Rights Commission Act 1999 is repealed by the Equality Act 2006 ss 40, 91, Sch 3 para 59, Sch 4 as from a day to be appointed under s 93. At the date at which this volume states the law no such day had been appointed. See also note 2 infra.

2   As to the establishment of the DRC see para 646 ante. As to the Commission for Equality and Human Rights, which is to replace the DRC, see para 305 et seq ante. See also note 1 supra.

3   As to the meaning of 'person' see para 344 note 3 ante.

4   'Unlawful act' means an act which is unlawful discrimination or harassment for the purposes of any provision of the Disability Discrimination Act 1995 Pt II (as amended; prospectively amended), Pt III (as amended; prospectively amended) or Pt IV (as amended; prospectively amended) or any other unlawful act of a description prescribed for these purposes: Disability Rights Commission Act 1999 s 6(4) (amended by the Special Educational Needs and Disability Act 2001 Sch 7 paras 1, 6; the Disability Discrimination Act 2005 Sch 1 para 50(1), (3); and the Disability Discrimination Act 1995 (Amendment) Regulations 2003, SI 2003/1673, regs 3(2), 30(d)(ii)). 'Prescribed' means prescribed in regulations: see para 649 note 11 ante. At the date at which this volume states the law no such act had been prescribed.

5   Disability Discrimination Act 1995 s 6(2). As to injunctions generally see INJUNCTIONS.

6   Ibid s 6(3).

655.   Codes of practice. The Disability Rights Commission[1] ('DRC') may prepare and issue codes of practice[2] giving practical guidance on how to avoid acts which are unlawful under the provisions of the Disability Discrimination Act 1995 relating to employment and members of locally-electable authorities, education and certain others areas[3], or on any other matter relating to the operation of any such provision[4], to: (1) employers[5]; (2) service providers[6]; (3) public authorities[7]; (4) certain associations of persons[8]; (5) bodies which are responsible bodies for the purposes of the provisions of the Disability Discrimination Act 1995 on schools and further and higher education[9]; or (4) other persons to whom certain provisions of the Disability Discrimination Act 1995 apply[10]. The Commission may prepare and issue codes of practice giving practical guidance to any persons on any other matter with a view to: (a) promoting the equalisation of opportunities for disabled persons[11] and persons who have had a disability[12]; or (b) encouraging good practice in the way such persons are treated[13], in any field of activity regulated by any provision of the provisions of the Disability Discrimination Act 1995 relating to employment and members of locally-electable authorities, education and certain other areas[14]. The DRC may prepare and issue codes of practice giving practical guidance to persons subject to duties under the provisions on public authorities[15] on how to perform those duties[16]. The DRC may prepare and issue codes of practice giving practical guidance to landlords and tenants as to: (i) circumstances in which a tenant requires the consent of his landlord for making a relevant improvement[17] to a dwelling house[18]; (ii) circumstances in which it is unreasonable to withhold such consent[19]; and (iii) the application of the improvement provisions[20] in relation to relevant improvements to dwelling houses[21].

The DRC, when requested to do so by the Secretary of State, must prepare a code of practice dealing with the matters specified in the request[22].

In preparing a code of practice the DRC must carry out such consultations as it considers appropriate (which must include the publication for public consultation of proposals relating to the code)[23].

The DRC may not issue a code of practice unless a draft of it has been submitted to and approved by the Secretary of State and laid by him before both Houses of Parliament[24], and the 40-day period[25] has elapsed without either House resolving not to approve the draft[26]. If the Secretary of State does not approve a draft code of practice submitted to him he must give the DRC a written statement of his reasons[27].

A code of practice issued by the DRC comes into effect on such day as the Secretary of State may by order appoint[28]. It may be revised in whole or part, and re-issued, by the DRC[29], and it may be revoked by an order made by the Secretary of State at the request of the DRC[30].

Failure to observe any provision of a code of practice does not of itself make a person liable to any proceedings[31]. However if a provision of a code of practice appears to a court, tribunal or other body hearing certain proceedings[32] to be relevant, it must take that provision into account[33].

Nothing in the above provisions affects the DRC's powers to give practical guidance on matters connected with its functions[34].

1   As to the establishment of the DRC see para 646 ante. As to the Commission for Equality and Human Rights, which is to replace the DRC, see para 305 et seq ante. See also note 2 infra.

2   'Code of practice' means a code of practice under the Disability Discrimination Act 1995 s 53A (as added and amended): s 53A(9) (s 53A added by the Disability Rights Commission Act 1999 s 9). The Disability Discrimination Act 1995 s 53A (as added and amended) is repealed by the Equality Act 2006 ss 40, 91, Sch 3 paras 41, 52, Sch 4 as from a day to be appointed under s 93. At the date at which this volume states the law no such day had been appointed. See also note 1 supra. Codes of practice were formerly prepared by the Secretary of State under the Disability Discrimination Act 1995 s 53 (repealed). As to the Secretary of State and the National Assembly for Wales see para 302 ante. As to codes of practice by the Commission for Equality and Human Rights see para 321 ante.

     The Disability Discrimination Act 1995 Code of Practice on the Rights of Access to Goods, Facilities, Services and Premises (February 2002) came into effect on 27 May 2002: see the Disability Discrimination Code of Practice (Goods, Facilities, Services and Premises) (Appointed Day) Order 2002, SI 2002/720 (but was revoked, subject to transitional provisions, with effect from 4 December 2006: see note 30 infra). See now the Disability Discrimination Act 1995 Code of Practice on Rights of Access: services to the public, public authority functions, private clubs and premises (December 2006), which came into effect on 4 December 2006; and the Disability Discrimination Code of Practice (Services, Public Functions, Private Clubs and Premises) (Appointed Day) Order 2006, SI 2006/1967. The Disability Rights Commission Code of Practice for Schools and the Disability Rights Commission Code of Practice for providers of Post-16 education and related services came into effect on 1 September 2002: see the Disability Discrimination Codes of Practice (Education) (Appointed Day) Order 2002, SI 2002/2216. The Disability Discrimination Act 1995 Code of Practice on Employment and Occupation and the Disability Discrimination Act 1995 Code of Practice for Trade Organisations and Qualifications Bodies came into effect on 1 October 2004: see the Disability Discrimination Codes of Practice (Employment and Occupation, and Trade Organisations and Qualification Bodies) Appointed Day Order 2004, SI 2004/2302. The Code of Practice entitled 'The Duty to Promote Disability Equality: Statutory Code of Practice (England and Wales)' came into effect on 5 December 2005: see the Disability Discrimination Code of Practice (Public Authorities) (Duty to Promote Equality) (Appointed Day) Order 2005, SI 2005/3340. The Code of Practice entitled 'Supplement to Part 3 Code of Practice: Provision and Use of Transport Vehicles' came into effect on 18 April 2006: see the Disability Discrimination Code of Practice (Supplement to Part 3 Code of Practice) (Provision and Use of Transport Vehicles) (Appointed Day) Order 2006, SI 2006/1094.

3   Ie under the Disability Discrimination Act 1995 Pt II (ss 3A–18E) (as amended; prospectively amended) (see para 529 et seq ante), Pt III (ss 19–28) (as amended; prospectively amended) (see para 582 et seq ante) or Pt IV (ss 28A–31C) (as amended; prospectively amended) (see para 561 et seq ante).

4   Ibid s 53A(1) (as added (see note 2 supra); substituted by the Special Educational Needs and Disability
      Act 2001 s 36(1), (2); and amended by the Disability Discrimination Act 1995 (Amendment)
      Regulations 2003, SI 2003/1673, regs 3(1), 20(a)). The provisions referred to in the text are any
      provision of the Disability Discrimination Act 1995 Pt II (as amended; prospectively amended), Pt III (as
      amended; prospectively amended) or Pt IV (as amended; prospectively amended). See note 14 infra.
5   Ibid s 53A(1)(a) (as added and substituted: see notes 2, 4 supra). For the meaning of 'employer' see
      para 529 note 2 ante. See note 14 infra.
6   Ibid s 53A(1)(b) (as added and substituted: see notes 2, 4 supra). For the meaning of 'provider of services'
      see para 584 post. See note 14 infra.
7   Ibid s 53A(1)(ba) (s 53A as added (see note 2 supra); and s 53A(ba), (bb) added by the Disability
      Discrimination Act 2005 s 19(1), Sch 1 paras 1, 28(1), (2)(a)). The reference in the text is to public
      authorities within the meaning given by the Disability Discrimination Act 1995 s 21B (as added): see
      para 593 ante. See note 14 infra.
8   Ibid s 53A(1)(bb) (as added: see notes 2, 7 supra). The reference in the text is to associations to which
      s 21F (as added) applies: see para 596 ante. See note 14 infra.
9   Ibid s 53A(1)(c) (as added and substituted: see notes 2, 4 supra). The reference in the text is to bodies
      which are responsible bodies for the purposes of Pt IV Ch I (ss 28A–28Q) (as added and amended) (see
      para 561 ante) or Pt IV Ch II (ss 28R–31A) (as added and amended) (see para 569 ante). See note 14
      infra.
10   Ibid s 53A(1)(d) (as added and substituted (see notes 2, 4 supra); and amended by the Disability
      Discrimination Act 2005 Sch 1 paras 1, 28(1), (2)(b)). The provisions referred to in the text are those of
      the Disability Discrimination Act 1995 Pt II (as amended; prospectively amended), Pt III (as amended;
      prospectively amended), Pt IV Ch II (as added and amended) or Pt IV Ch IIA (ss 31AA–31AF) (as
      added) (see para 578 et seq ante). See note 14 infra.
11   For the meaning of 'disabled person' see para 511 ante.
12   Disability Discrimination Act 1995 s 53A(1A)(a) (s 53A as added (see note 2 supra); and s 53A(1A), (1B)
      added by the Special Educational Needs and Disability Act 2001 s 36(1), (2)). As to when a person has a
      disability see para 511 ante. See note 14 infra.
13   Disability Discrimination Act 1995 s 53A(1A)(b) (as added: see notes 2, 12 supra). See note 14 infra.
14   Ibid s 53A(1A) (as added: see notes 2, 12 supra). The provisions referred to in the text are those of Pt II
      (as amended; prospectively amended), Pt III (as amended; prospectively amended) or Pt IV (as amended;
      prospectively amended). Neither s 53A(1) (as added, substituted and amended) nor s 53A(1A) (as added)
      applies in relation to any duty imposed by or under s 28D (as added and amended) or s 28E (as added and
      amended) (see para 564 ante): s 53A(1B) (as so added).
15   Ie duties under ibid s 49A (as added) or s 49D (as added; prospectively amended): see para 591 ante.
16   Ibid s 53A(1C) (added by the Disability Discrimination Act 2005 Sch 1 paras 1, 28(1), (3)). Where a draft
      of a code of practice that deals with performance of duties under the Disability Discrimination Act 1995
      s 49A (as added) or s 49D (as added; prospectively amended) (see para 591 ante) is submitted to the
      Secretary of State for approval, he must consult the National Assembly for Wales before deciding whether
      to approve it: see s 53A(4A) (added by the Disability Discrimination Act 2005 Sch 1 paras 1, 28(1), (4)).
17   'Relevant improvement' means an improvement (within the meaning of the Disability Discrimination
      Act 1995 s 49G(9) (as added): see para 611 ante) to premises which, having regard to the disability which
      a disabled person who lawfully occupies or is intended lawfully to occupy the premises has, is likely to
      facilitate his enjoyment of the premises: s 53A(9) (definition added by the Disability Discrimination
      Act 2005 Sch 1 paras 1, 28(1), (7)). As to the meaning of 'premises' see para 525 note 9 ante.
18   Disability Discrimination Act 1995 s 53A(1D)(a) (s 53A as added (see note 2 supra); and s 53A(1D), (1E)
      added by the Disability Discrimination Act 2005 s 16(2)).
19   Disability Discrimination Act 1995 s 53A(1D)(b) (as added: see notes 2, 18 supra).
20   For this purpose, the improvement provisions are: (1) the Landlord and Tenant Act 1927 s 19(2) (see
      LANDLORD AND TENANT vol 27(1) (2006 Reissue) para 470); (2) the Housing Act 1980 ss 81–85 (as
      amended) (see LANDLORD AND TENANT vol 27(2) (2006 Reissue) para 838); (3) the Housing Act 1985
      ss 97–99 (see LANDLORD AND TENANT vol 27(2) (2006 Reissue) para 1330 et seq); and (4) the Disability
      Discrimination Act 1995 s 49G (as added) (see para 611 ante): s 53A(1E) (as added: see notes 2, 18 supra).
21   Ibid s 53A(1D)(c) (as added: see notes 2, 18 supra).
22   Ibid s 53A(2) (as added: see note 2 supra).
23   Ibid s 53A(3) (as added: see note 2 supra).
        The DRC may treat any consultation undertaken by the National Disability Council under s 52(2)
      (repealed) as being as effective for the purposes of s 53A(3) (as added and amended) as if it had been
      undertaken by the DRC: Disability Rights Commission Act 1999 s 9(2). This provision is repealed by the
      Equality Act 2006 Sch 3 para 59, Sch 4 as from a day to be appointed under s 93. At the date at which
      this volume states the law no such day had been appointed. See also note 2 supra; and para 646 note 1
      ante.
24   Disability Discrimination Act 1995 s 53A(4)(a) (as added: see note 2 supra).

25 For the meaning of '40-day period' see para 512 note 22 ante; definition applied by ibid s 53A(9) (as added: see note 2 supra).

26 Ibid s 53A(4)(b) (as added: see note 2 supra).

27 Ibid s 53A(5) (as added: see note 2 supra).

28 Ibid s 53A(6)(a) (as added: see note 2 supra). Before appointing a day under s 53A(6)(a) (as added) for the coming into effect of a code of practice that deals with performance of duties under s 49A (as added) or s 49D (as added; prospectively amended), the Secretary of State must consult the National Assembly for Wales: s 53A(6A) (s 53A as so added; and s 53A(6A) added by the Disability Discrimination Act 2005 Sch 1 paras 1, 28(1), (5)).

As to statutory instruments made under the Disability Discrimination Act 1995 s 53A(6)(a) (as added) see the Disability Discrimination Code of Practice (Goods, Facilities, Services and Premises) (Appointed Day) Order 2002, SI 2002/720; the Disability Discrimination Codes of Practice (Education) (Appointed Day) Order 2002, SI 2002/2216; the Disability Discrimination Codes of Practice (Employment and Occupation, and Trade Organisations and Qualifications Bodies) Appointed Day Order 2004, SI 2004/2302; the Disability Discrimination Code of Practice (Public Authorities) (Duty to Promote Equality) (Appointed Day) Order 2005, SI 2005/3340; the Disability Discrimination Code of Practice (Supplement to Part 3 Code of Practice) (Provision and Use of Transport Vehicles) (Appointed Day) Order 2006, SI 2006/1094; and the Disability Discrimination Code of Practice (Services, Public Functions, Private Clubs and Premises) (Appointed Day) Order 2006, SI 2006/1967. See also note 2 supra.

29 Disability Discrimination Act 1995 s 53A(6)(b) (as added: see note 2 supra). Where the DRC proposes to revise a code of practice: (1) it must comply with s 53A(3) (as added and amended) (see the text and note 23 supra) in relation to the revisions; and (2) s 53A (as added and amended) applies to the revised code of practice as it applies to a new code of practice: s 53A(7) (as so added).

30 Ibid s 53A(6)(c) (as added: see note 2 supra). See the Disability Discrimination Code of Practice (Goods, Facilities, Services and Premises) (Revocation) Order 2006, SI 2006/1966. See note 2 supra.

31 Disability Discrimination Act 1995 s 53A(8) (as added (see note 2 supra); and amended by the Special Educational Needs and Disability Act 2001 ss 36(1), (3), 42(6), Sch 9).

32 Ie any proceedings under the Disability Discrimination Act 1995 Pt II (as amended; prospectively amended), Pt III (as amended; prospectively amended), Pt IV (as amended; prospectively amended) or Pt VA (ss 49A–49F) (as added and amended) (see paras 591–592 ante), or any proceedings relating to a relevant improvement (see note 17 supra).

33 Ibid s 53A(8A) (s 53A as added (see note 2 supra); and s 53A(8A) added by the Special Educational Needs and Disability Act 2001 s 36(1), (4); and amended by the Disability Discrimination Act 2005 Sch 1 paras 1, 28(1), (6)).

34 Disability Rights Commission Act 1999 s 9(3). This provision is repealed by the Equality Act 2006 Sch 3 para 59, Sch 4 as from a day to be appointed under s 93. At the date at which this volume states the law no such day had been appointed. As to the functions of the DRC see para 647 ante.

656. Assistance in relation to proceedings. An individual may apply to the Disability Rights Commission[1] ('DRC') for assistance in relation to: (1) proceedings which he has brought or proposes to bring[2] in connection with complaints and claims about unlawful discrimination or harassment[3]; (2) proceedings of any description to the extent that the question whether it is unreasonable for a landlord to withhold consent to the making of a relevant improvement[4] to a dwelling house falls to be considered in the proceedings[5]; and (3) proceedings of a description prescribed[6] for these purposes, being proceedings in which an individual who has or has had a disability[7] relies or proposes to rely on a matter relating to that disability[8]. Where the individual concerned applies to the DRC for assistance in relation to any such proceedings, the DRC may grant the application on any of the following grounds[9]: (a) that the case raises a question of principle[10]; (b) that it is unreasonable to expect the applicant to deal with the case unaided (because of its complexity, because of the applicant's position in relation to another party or for some other reason)[11]; or (c) that there is some other special consideration which makes it appropriate for the DRC to provide assistance[12].

If the DRC grants an application, it may provide or arrange for the provision of legal advice[13], arrange for legal or other representation (which may include any assistance usually given by a solicitor or counsel)[14], seek to procure the settlement of any dispute[15], or provide or arrange for the provision of any other assistance which it thinks appropriate[16].

The DRC may authorise any employee of the DRC to exercise such of its functions under this provision as it may determine[17].

Where the DRC has given an individual assistance in relation to any proceedings[18], and any costs or expenses (however described) have become payable to him by another person in respect of the matter in connection with which the assistance is given[19], a sum equal to any expenses incurred by the DRC in providing the assistance is to be a first charge for the benefit of the DRC on the costs or expenses concerned[20]. It is immaterial for these purposes whether the costs or expenses concerned are payable by virtue of a decision of a court or tribunal, an agreement arrived at to avoid proceedings or to bring them to an end, or otherwise[21].

1 As to the establishment of the DRC see para 646 ante. As to the Commission for Equality and Human Rights, which is to replace the DRC, see para 305 et seq ante. See also note 3 infra.

2 Ie under the Disability Discrimination Act 1995 s 17A (as added and amended) (see para 643 ante), s 25 (as amended) (see para 644 ante), s 28I (as added and amended) (see para 566 ante), s 28K (as added and amended) (see para 567 ante), s 28L (as added and amended) (see para 567 ante) or s 28V (as added and amended) (see para 575 ante). See note 3 supra.

3 Disability Rights Commission Act 1999 s 7(1)(a) (amended by the Special Educational Needs and Disability Act 2001 s 35, Sch 7 paras 1, 8; the Disability Discrimination Act 2005 s 19(1), Sch 1 para 50(1), (5); and the Disability Discrimination Act 1995 (Amendment) Regulations 2003, SI 2003/1673, regs 3(2), 30(e)). Such complaints and claims are those made under the Disability Discrimination Act 1995 Pt II (ss 3A–18E) (as amended; prospectively amended) (see para 529 et seq ante), Pt III (ss 19–28) (as amended; prospectively amended) (see para 582 et seq ante) and Pt IV (ss 28A–31C) (as amended; prospectively amended) (see para 561 et seq ante): see the Disability Rights Commission Act 1999 s 7(1)(a) (as so amended). As from a day to be appointed, this provision also refers to proceedings under provision made under the Disability Discrimination Act 1995 s 31AE (as added) (see para 581 ante) (see note 2 supra): Disability Rights Commission Act 1999 s 7(1)(a) (prospectively amended by the Disability Discrimination Act 2005 Sch 1 para 50(1), (5)). At the date at which this volume states the law no such day had been appointed. The Disability Rights Commission Act 1999 is repealed by the Equality Act 2006 ss 40, 91, Sch 3 para 59, Sch 4 as from a day to be appointed under s 93. At the date at which this volume states the law no such day had been appointed. See also note 1 supra.

4 A relevant improvement is an improvement (within the meaning of the Disability Discrimination Act 1995 s 49G(9) (as added): see para 611 ante) to premises which, having regard to the disability which a disabled person who lawfully occupies or is intended lawfully to occupy the premises has, is likely to facilitate his enjoyment of the premises: Disability Rights Commission Act 1999 s 7(4A) (added by the Disability Discrimination Act 2005 s 16(3)(b)). For the meaning of 'disabled person' see para 511 ante. As to the meaning of 'premises' see para 525 note 9 ante.

5 Disability Rights Commission Act 1999 s 7(1)(aa) (added by the Disability Discrimination Act 2005 s 16(3)(a)).

6 'Prescribed' means prescribed in regulations: see para 649 note 11 ante. As to the making of regulations see para 649 note 11 ante. At the date at which this volume states the law no proceedings had been prescribed for these purposes.

7 As to when a person has a disability see para 511 ante.

8 Disability Rights Commission Act 1999 s 7(1)(b).

9 Ibid s 7(2).

10 Ibid s 7(2)(a).

11 Ibid s 7(2)(b).

12 Ibid s 7(2)(c).

13 Ibid s 7(3)(a).

14 Ibid s 7(3)(b). Section 7(3)(b) does not affect the law and practice as to who may represent a person in relation to any proceedings: s 7(4).

15 Ibid s 7(3)(c).

16 Ibid s 7(3)(d).

17 Ibid s 7(5).

18 Ibid s 8(1)(a).

19 Ibid s 8(1)(b).

20 Ibid s 8(2). The charge created by this provision is subject to any charge imposed by the Access to Justice Act 1999 s 10(7) (see LEGAL AID vol 27(3) (2006 Reissue) para 2099) and any provision in, or made under, Pt I (ss 1–26) for the payment of any sum to the Legal Services Commission: Disability Rights Commission Act 1999 s 8(4)(a) (amended by the Access to Justice Act 1999 s 24, Sch 4 para 56). As to the Legal Services Commission see LEGAL AID vol 27(3) (2006 Reissue) para 2014 et seq. Provision may be made by regulations made by the Secretary of State for the determination of the expenses of the DRC in cases where this provision applies: Disability Rights Commission Act 1999 s 8(5). As to the Secretary of State and the National Assembly for Wales see para 302 ante. At the date at which this volume states the law no such regulations had been made.

21 Ibid s 8(3).

657. Conciliation of disputes. The Disability Rights Commission[1] ('DRC') may make arrangements[2] with any other person[3] for the provision of conciliation services[4] by, or by persons appointed by, that person in relation to disputes arising under the provisions of the Disability Discrimination Act 1995 relating to goods, services, facilities, public authorities, private clubs or premises[5]. In deciding what arrangements (if any) to make, the DRC must have regard to the desirability of securing, so far as reasonably practicable, that conciliation services are available for all such disputes which the parties may wish to refer to conciliation[6]. No member or employee of the DRC may provide conciliation services in relation to such disputes[7]. The DRC must ensure that any arrangements include appropriate safeguards to prevent the disclosure to members or employees of the DRC of information obtained by a person in connection with the provision of conciliation services in pursuance of the arrangements[8]. Anything communicated to a person while providing conciliation services in pursuance of any such arrangements is not admissible in evidence in any proceedings except with the consent of the person who communicated it to that person[9].

The DRC may also make arrangements with any other person for the provision of conciliation services[10] by, or by persons appointed by, that person in connection with disputes arising under provisions of the Disability Discrimination Act 1995 in regard to education[11]. In deciding what arrangements, if any, to make, the DRC must have regard to the desirability of securing, so far as reasonably practicable, that conciliation services are available for all disputes which the parties may wish to refer to conciliation[12]. No member or employee of the DRC may provide conciliation services in connection with disputes[13]. The DRC must ensure that any arrangements include appropriate safeguards to prevent the disclosure to members or employees of the DRC of information obtained by any person in connection with the provision of conciliation services in accordance with the arrangements[14]. Anything communicated to a person providing conciliation services in accordance with any such arrangements is not admissible in evidence in any proceedings except with the consent of the person who communicated it[15].

1   As to the establishment of the DRC see para 646 ante. As to the Commission for Equality and Human Rights, which is to replace the DRC, see para 305 et seq ante. See also notes 4, 10 infra.

2   The Secretary of State was formerly responsible for making arrangements for the provision of advice and assistance under the Disability Discrimination Act 1995 s 28 (as originally enacted). As to the Secretary of State and the National Assembly for Wales see para 302 ante. See note 4 infra.

3   As to the meaning of 'person' see para 344 note 3 ante.

4   'Conciliation services' means advice and assistance provided by a conciliator to the parties to a dispute with a view to promoting its settlement otherwise than through the courts: Disability Discrimination Act 1995 s 28(8) (s 28 substituted by the Disability Rights Commission Act 1999 s 10). The Disability Discrimination Act 1995 s 28 (as substituted) is repealed by the Equality Act 2006 ss 40, 91, Sch 3 paras 41, 45, Sch 4 as from a day to be appointed under s 93. At the date at which this volume states the law no such day had been appointed. See also note 1 supra. As to conciliation under the Equality Act 2006 see para 333 ante.

5   See the Disability Discrimination Act 1995 s 28(1) (as substituted: see note 4 supra). The reference in the text is to provisions under Pt III (ss 19–28) (as amended; prospectively amended): see para 582 et seq ante.

6   Ibid s 28(2) (as substituted: see note 4 supra).

7 Ibid s 28(3) (as substituted: see note 4 supra).
8 Ibid s 28(4) (as substituted: see note 4 supra). This does not apply to information relating to a dispute which is disclosed with the consent of the parties to that dispute: s 28(5) (as so substituted). It also does not apply to information which: (1) is not identifiable with a particular dispute or a particular person; and (2) is reasonably required by the DRC for the purpose of monitoring the operation of the arrangements concerned: s 28(6) (as so substituted).
9 Ibid s 28(7) (as substituted: see note 4 supra).
10 'Conciliation services' means advice and assistance provided to the parties to a dispute, by a conciliator, with a view to promoting its settlement otherwise than through a court, tribunal or other body: ibid s 31B(8) (s 31B added by the Special Educational Needs and Disability Act 2001 s 37). The Disability Discrimination Act 1995 s 31B (as added) is repealed by the Equality Act 2006 ss 40, 91, Sch 3 paras 41, 47, Sch 4 as from a day to be appointed under s 93. At the date at which this volume states the law no such day had been appointed. See also note 1 supra. As to conciliation under the Equality Act 2006 see para 333 ante.
11 Disability Discrimination Act 1995 s 31B(1) (as added: see note 10 supra). 'Dispute' means a dispute arising under Pt IV Ch I (ss 28A–28Q) (as added and amended) (see para 561 et seq ante) or Pt IV Ch II (ss 28R–31A) (as added and amended) (see para 569 et seq ante) concerning an allegation of discrimination: s 31B(9) (as so added). 'Discrimination' means anything which is made unlawful discrimination by a provision of Pt IV Ch I (as added and amended) or Pt IV Ch II (as added and amended): s 31B(10) (as so added). As from a day to be appointed, the provisions of s 31B(9), (10) are substituted so as to provide that 'dispute' means a dispute arising under Pt IV Ch I (as added and amended), Pt IV Ch II (as added and amended) or Pt IV Ch IIA (s 31AA–31AF) (as added) (see para 578 et seq ante) concerning an allegation of discrimination or harassment; 'discrimination' means anything which is made unlawful discrimination by a provision of the chapter concerned; and 'harassment' means anything which is made unlawful harassment by a provision of the chapter concerned: s 31B(9) (as so added; prospectively substituted by the Disability Discrimination Act 2005 s 19(1), Sch 1 paras 1, 25). At the date at which this volume states the law no such day had been appointed.
12 Disability Discrimination Act 1995 s 31B(2) (as added: see note 10 supra).
13 Ibid s 31B(3) (as added: see note 10 supra).
14 Ibid s 31B(4) (as added: see note 10 supra). This does not apply to information which is disclosed with the consent of the parties to the dispute to which it relates: s 31B(5) (as so added). Nor does it apply to information which: (1) does not identify a particular dispute or a particular person; and (2) is reasonably required by the DRC for the purpose of monitoring the operation of the arrangements concerned: s 31B(6) (as so added).
15 Ibid s 31B(7) (as added: see note 10 supra).

658. Restriction on disclosure of information. No information given to the Disability Rights Commission[1] ('DRC') by an informant in connection with a formal investigation[2], or the exercise of any of its functions in relation to non-discrimination notices[3], action plans[4] and agreements in lieu of enforcement action[5], may be disclosed by the DRC or by any person who is or has been a commissioner, an additional commissioner or an employee of the DRC[6]. A person who unlawfully discloses such information is guilty of an offence[7].

The prohibition does not apply to any disclosure made:

(1) on the order of a court[8];

(2) with the informant's consent[9];

(3) in the form of a summary or other general statement published by the DRC which does not identify the informant or any other person[10] to whom the information relates[11];

(4) in a report of the investigation published by the DRC[12];

(5) to a commissioner, an additional commissioner or an employee of the DRC, or, so far as is necessary for the proper performance of the DRC's functions, to other persons[13]; or

(6) for the purpose of any civil proceedings to which the DRC is a party, or of any criminal proceedings[14].

1 As to the establishment of the DRC see para 646 ante. As to the Commission for Equality and Human Rights, which is to replace the DRC, see para 305 et seq ante. See also note 4 infra.
2 For the meaning of 'formal investigation' see para 649 note 1 ante.

3   For the meaning of 'non-discrimination notice' see para 651 note 2 ante.
4   Disability Rights Commission Act 1999 ss 4(6), 5(12), Sch 3 para 22(1)(a). The Disability Rights
    Commission Act 1999 is repealed by the Equality Act 2006 ss 40, 91, Sch 3 para 59, Sch 4 as from a day
    to be appointed under s 93. At the date at which this volume states the law no such day had been
    appointed. See note 1 supra. As to action plans see para 653 ante.
5   Disability Rights Commission Act 1999 Sch 3 para 22(1)(a). As to agreement in lieu of enforcement
    action see s 5 (as amended); and para 652 ante.
6   Ibid Sch 3 para 22(1). As to commissioners, additional commissioners and employees see paras 646, 648
    ante.
7   Ibid Sch 3 para 22(3). A person guilty of such an offence is liable on summary conviction to a fine not
    exceeding level 5 on the standard scale: see Sch 3 para 22(3). As to the standard scale see para 315 note
    15 ante.
8   Ibid Sch 3 para 22(2)(a).
9   Ibid Sch 3 para 22(2)(b).
10 As to the meaning of 'person' see para 344 note 3 ante.
11 Disability Rights Commission Act 1999 Sch 3 para 22(2)(c).
12 Ibid Sch 3 para 22(2)(d).
13 Ibid Sch 3 para 22(2)(e). As to the DRC's functions see para 647 ante.
14 Ibid Sch 3 para 22(2)(f).

659.   Offences.   A person[1] who: (1) deliberately alters, suppresses, conceals or
destroys a document to which a notice[2] or an order[3] relates[4]; or (2) in complying with
a notice[5], a non-discrimination notice[6], an agreement in lieu of enforcement action[7], or
an order of a court[8], makes any statement which he knows to be false or misleading in
a material particular or recklessly makes a statement which is false or misleading in a
material particular[9], is guilty of an offence[10].

Proceedings for an offence under this provision (without prejudice to any jurisdiction
otherwise exercisable) may be instituted against any person at any place at which he has
an office or other place of business[11], or against an individual at any place where he
resides, or at which he is for the time being[12].

1   As to the meaning of 'person' see para 344 note 3 ante.
2   For the meaning of 'notice' see para 649 note 5 ante.
3   Ie a notice or an order under the Disability Rights Commission Act 1999 s 3(5), Sch 3 para 5 or Sch 3
    para 21(3): see paras 649, 653 ante. The Disability Rights Commission Act 1999 is repealed by the
    Equality Act 2006 ss 40, 91, Sch 3 para 59, Sch 4 as from a day to be appointed under s 93. At the date
    at which this volume states the law no such day had been appointed.
4   Disability Rights Commission Act 1999 Sch 3 para 24(1)(a).
5   Ibid Sch 3 para 24(1)(b)(i). The notice referred to in the text is a notice under Sch 3 para 4 or Sch 3
    para 21 (see paras 649, 653 ante): see Sch 3 para 24(1)(b)(i).
6   Ibid Sch 3 para 24(1)(b)(ii). For the meaning of 'non-discrimination notice' see para 651 note 2 ante.
7   Ibid Sch 3 para 24(1)(b)(iii). As to agreements in lieu of enforcement action see s 5 (as amended); and
    para 652 ante.
8   Ibid Sch 3 para 24(1)(b)(iv). An order of the court is made under s 5(8) or under any provision of Sch 3
    (as amended): see Sch 3 para 24(1)(b)(iv).
9   Ibid Sch 3 para 24(1)(b).
10 Ibid Sch 3 para 24(1). Such a person is liable on summary conviction to a fine not exceeding level 5 on
    the standard scale: Sch 3 para 24(1). As to the standard scale see para 315 note 15 ante.
11 Ibid Sch 3 para 24(2)(a).
12 Ibid Sch 3 para 24(2)(b).

6. RELIGIOUS DISCRIMINATION

(1) DISCRIMINATION IN THE EMPLOYMENT FIELD

(i) In general

660. Discrimination on grounds of religion or belief. For the purposes of the Employment Equality (Religion or Belief) Regulations 2003[1], a person[2] ('A') discriminates against another person ('B') if:

(1) on the grounds of the religion or belief[3] of B or of any other person except A (whether or not it is also A's religion or belief), A treats B less favourably than he treats or would treat other persons[4]; or

(2) A applies to B a provision, criterion or practice which he applies or would apply equally to persons not of the same religion or belief as B, but:

    (a) which puts or would put persons of the same religion or belief as B at a particular disadvantage when compared with other persons;

    (b) which puts B at that disadvantage; and

    (c) which A cannot show to be a proportionate means of achieving a legitimate aim[5].

A comparison of B's case with that of another person under the above provisions must be such that the relevant circumstances in the one case are the same, or not materially different, in the other[6].

1   Ie for the purposes of the Employment Equality (Religion or Belief) Regulations 2003, SI 2003/1660 (as amended): see the text and notes 2–6 infra; and para 661 et seq post. The regulations came into force on 2 December 2003 (reg 1(1)); and do not extend to Northern Ireland (reg 1(2)). They are made by the Secretary of State under the European Communities Act 1972 s 2(2) and implement the relevant provisions of EC Council Directive 2000/78 (OJ L303, 2.12.2000, p 16) establishing a general framework for equal treatment in employment and occupation (the 'EC Framework Employment Directive'): see para 508 ante. As to the Secretary of State and the National Assembly for Wales see para 302 ante.

    For a comparison between the rights conferred by the Employment Equality (Religion or Belief) Regulations 2003, SI 2003/1660 (as amended) and the right to freedom of thought, conscience and religion under the Human Rights Act 1998 s 1(3), Sch 1 Pt I art 9 (incorporating into domestic law the Convention for the Protection of Human Rights and Fundamental Freedoms (Rome, 4 November 1950; TS 71 (1953); Cmd 8969) art 9) see *Copsey v WWB Devon Clays Ltd* [2005] EWCA Civ 932 at [8], [2005] ICR 1789 at [8], [2005] IRLR 811 at [8] per Mummery LJ. This case was brought before the commencement of the Employment Equality (Religion or Belief) Regulations 2003, SI 2003/1660 (as amended). See also para 304 note 15 ante. As to the Human Rights Act 1998 and the Convention for the Protection of Human Rights and Fundamental Freedoms see paras 303–304 ante.

    For the first significant case under the Employment Equality (Religion or Belief) Regulations 2003, SI 2003/1660 (as amended) (which was also brought under the Convention for the Protection of Human Rights and Fundamental Freedoms art 9) see *Azmi v Kirklees Metropolitan Council* [2007] All ER (D) 528 (Mar), EAT. This case relates to the suspension of a bilingual Muslim support worker from a school for her refusal to teach children without wearing a veil when male colleagues were present. Before the employment tribunal the claimant was unsuccessful in her claims of direct and indirect discrimination on the basis of religion or belief and harassment (see para 662 post) but successful in her claim for victimisation on the basis of religion or belief; the tribunal also found that the Convention for the Protection of Human Rights and Fundamental Freedoms art 9 did not give an absolute right to employees to wear the veil. As far as the direct discrimination claim was concerned, the comparator was said to be a non-Muslim person who covered their face rather than a Muslim woman who did not do so. The claim for indirect discrimination was also dismissed as the method of achieving the legitimate aim of communication with the children was found to be proportionate. On appeal to the Employment Appeal Tribunal, two principal issues fell to be determined: (1) whether the tribunal had erred in the identification of the appropriate comparator; and (2) whether the tribunal had erred in its approach to the question of proportionality: on both these issues it was held that the employment tribunal had taken the right approach.

For a case in the context of human rights law with a similar balancing act between an individual's right to cultural and religious expression and a school's ability to make practical decisions for itself without legal intervention see *R (on the application of Begum) v Headteacher and Governors of Denbigh High School* [2006] UKHL 15, [2006] 2 All ER 487, [2006] 2 FCR 613. For a similar case, in the context of the Race Relations Act 1976, see *Harrods Ltd v Remick* [1998] 1 All ER 52, [1997] IRLR 583, CA; and para 448 ante.

2   As to the meaning of 'person' see para 344 note 3 ante.

3   For these purposes: (1) 'religion' means any religion, and a reference to religion includes a reference to lack of religion; and (2) 'belief' means any religious or philosophical belief, and a reference to belief includes a reference to lack of belief: Employment Equality (Religion or Belief) Regulations 2003, SI 2003/1660, reg 2(1) (substituted by the Equality Act 2006 s 77(2)).

4   Employment Equality (Religion or Belief) Regulations 2003, SI 2003/1660, reg 3(1)(a) (substituted by the Equality Act 2006 s 77(2)).
     Circumstances where it is agreed that an employee can maintain his beard at one fist's length, in accordance with his religion, provided it is tidy, do not give rise to an inference of less favourable treatment: see *Mohmed v West Coast Trains Ltd* [2006] All ER (D) 224 (Nov), EAT.

5   Employment Equality (Religion or Belief) Regulations 2003, SI 2003/1660, reg 3(1)(b). As to the special protection of Sikhs from discrimination in connection with requirements as to wearing of safety helmets see reg 26; and para 681 post.
     As to direct and indirect discrimination under the Sex Discrimination Act 1975 see paras 344, 351, 355 ante; and as to direct and indirect discrimination under the Race Relations Act 1976 see paras 439–440 ante.

6   Employment Equality (Religion or Belief) Regulations 2003, SI 2003/1660, reg 3(3).

661.   Discrimination by way of victimisation.   For the purposes of the Employment Equality (Religion or Belief) Regulations 2003[1], a person[2] ('A') discriminates against another person ('B') if he treats B less favourably than he treats or would treat other persons in the same circumstances, and does so by reason that B has:

(1)   brought proceedings against A or any other person under those regulations;

(2)   given evidence or information in connection with proceedings brought by any person against A or any other person under those regulations;

(3)   otherwise done anything under or by reference to those regulations in relation to A or any other person; or

(4)   alleged that A or any other person has committed an act[3] which (whether or not the allegation so states) would amount to a contravention of those regulations,

or by reason that A knows that B intends to do any of those things, or suspects that B has done or intends to do any of them[4].

The above provisions do not, however, apply to treatment of B by reason of any allegation made by him, or evidence or information given by him, if the allegation, evidence or information was false and not made or, as the case may be, given in good faith[5].

1   Ie for the purposes of the Employment Equality (Religion or Belief) Regulations 2003, SI 2003/1660 (as amended).

2   As to the meaning of 'person' see para 344 note 3 ante.

3   For these purposes, 'act' includes a deliberate omission: Employment Equality (Religion or Belief) Regulations 2003, SI 2003/1660, reg 2(3).

4   Ibid reg 4(1). See *Azmi v Kirklees Metropolitan Council* [2007] All ER (D) 528 (Mar), EAT; and para 660 note 1 ante.
     As to victimisation under the Sex Discrimination Act 1975 see para 358 ante; and as to victimisation under the Race Relations Act 1976 see para 442 ante.

5   Employment Equality (Religion or Belief) Regulations 2003, SI 2003/1660, reg 4(2).

662.   Harassment on grounds of religion or belief.   For the purposes of the Employment Equality (Religion or Belief) Regulations 2003[1], a person[2] ('A') subjects another person ('B') to harassment where, on grounds of religion or belief[3], A engages in unwanted conduct which has the purpose or effect of:

(1)   violating B's dignity; or

(2) creating an intimidating, hostile, degrading, humiliating or offensive environment for B[4].

Conduct is to be regarded as having the effect specified in head (1) or head (2) above only if, having regard to all the circumstances, including in particular the perception of B, it should reasonably be considered as having that effect[5].

1   Ie for the purposes of the Employment Equality (Religion or Belief) Regulations 2003, SI 2003/1660 (as amended).
2   As to the meaning of 'person' see para 344 note 3 ante.
3   For the meanings of 'religion' and 'belief' see para 660 note 3 ante.
4   Employment Equality (Religion or Belief) Regulations 2003, SI 2003/1660, reg 5(1). Cf harassment under the Sex Discrimination Act 1975 (see para 347 ante) and under the Race Relations Act 1976 (see para 444 ante).
    See *Azmi v Kirklees Metropolitan Council* [2007] All ER (D) 528 (Mar), EAT; and para 660 note 1 ante.
5   Employment Equality (Religion or Belief) Regulations 2003, SI 2003/1660, reg 5(2).

(ii) Discrimination in Employment and Vocational Training

663. Unlawful discrimination against applicants and employees; exception for genuine occupational requirement. It is unlawful for an employer[1]:

(1) in relation to employment[2] by him at an establishment in Great Britain[3], to discriminate[4] against a person:
   (a) in the arrangements he makes for the purpose of determining to whom he should offer employment;
   (b) in the terms on which he offers that person employment; or
   (c) by refusing to offer, or deliberately not offering, him employment[5];

(2) in relation to a person whom he employs at an establishment in Great Britain, to discriminate against that person:
   (a) in the terms of employment which he affords him;
   (b) in the opportunities which he affords him for promotion, a transfer, training, or receiving any other benefit[6];
   (c) by refusing to afford him, or deliberately not affording him, any such opportunity; or
   (d) by dismissing him[7], or subjecting him to any other detriment[8];

(3) in relation to employment by him at an establishment in Great Britain, to subject to harassment[9] a person whom he employs or who has applied to him for employment[10].

Head (2) above does not apply to benefits of any description if the employer is concerned with the provision, for payment or not, of benefits of that description to the public, or to a section of the public which includes the employee in question, unless:
   (i) that provision differs in a material respect from the provision of the benefits by the employer to his employees; or
   (ii) the provision of the benefits to the employee in question is regulated by his contract of employment; or
   (iii) the benefits relate to training[11].

In relation to discrimination on grounds of religion or belief[12]:
   (A) neither head (1)(a) nor head (1)(c) above applies to any employment;
   (B) neither head (2)(b) nor head (2)(c) above applies to promotion or transfer to, or training for, any employment; and
   (C) head (2)(d) above does not apply to dismissal from any employment,

where either of the specified exceptions[13] applies[14]. The first such exception applies where, having regard to the nature of the employment or the context in which it is carried out, being of a particular religion or belief is a genuine and determining occupational requirement, it is proportionate to apply that requirement in the particular case, and either the person to whom that requirement is applied does not meet it or the employer is not satisfied, and in all the circumstances it is reasonable for him not to be satisfied, that that person meets it[15]. This exception applies whether or not the employer has an ethos based on religion or belief[16]. The second such exception applies where an employer has an ethos based on religion or belief and, having regard to that ethos and to the nature of the employment or the context in which it is carried out, being of a particular religion or belief is a genuine occupational requirement for the job, it is proportionate to apply that requirement in the particular case, and either the person to whom that requirement is applied does not meet it or the employer is not satisfied, and in all the circumstances it is reasonable for him not to be satisfied, that that person meets it[17].

1   For these purposes, references to 'employer', in their application to a person at any time seeking to employ another, include a person who has no employees at that time: Employment Equality (Religion or Belief) Regulations 2003, SI 2003/1660, reg 2(3). As to the meaning of 'person' see para 344 note 3 ante.

2   'Employment' means employment under a contract of service or of apprenticeship or a contract personally to do any work; and related expressions are to be construed accordingly: ibid reg 2(3).

3   For the purposes of ibid Pt II (regs 6–21) (as amended) ('the relevant purposes'), employment is to be regarded as being at an establishment in Great Britain if the employee: (1) does his work wholly or partly in Great Britain; or (2) does his work wholly outside Great Britain and reg 9(2) applies: reg 9(1). Regulation 9(2) applies if: (a) the employer has a place of business at an establishment in Great Britain; (b) the work is for the purposes of the business carried on at that establishment; and (c) the employee is ordinarily resident in Great Britain at the time when he applies for or is offered the employment, or at any time during the course of the employment: reg 9(2). The reference to 'employment' in reg 9(1) includes employment on board a ship only if the ship is registered at a port of registry in Great Britain, and employment on an aircraft or hovercraft only if the aircraft or hovercraft is registered in the United Kingdom and operated by a person who has his principal place of business, or is ordinarily resident, in Great Britain: reg 9(3). Subject to reg 9(5), for the purposes of determining if employment concerned with the exploration of the sea bed or subsoil or the exploitation of their natural resources is outside Great Britain, reg 9 has effect as if references to Great Britain included: (i) any area designated under the Continental Shelf Act 1964 s 1(7) (as amended) (see FUEL AND ENERGY vol 19(2) (Reissue) para 1411) except an area or part of an area in which the law of Northern Ireland applies; and (ii) in relation to employment concerned with the exploration or exploitation of the Frigg Gas Field, the part of the Norwegian sector of the Continental Shelf described in the Employment Equality (Religion or Belief) Regulations 2003, SI 2003/1660, Sch 1 (reg 9(4)); but this does not apply to employment which is concerned with the exploration or exploitation of the Frigg Gas Field unless the employer is: (A) a company registered under the Companies Act 1985 (see COMPANIES); (B) an oversea company which has established a place of business within Great Britain from which it directs the exploration or exploitation in question; or (C) any other person who has a place of business within Great Britain from which he directs the exploration or exploitation in question (Employment Equality (Religion or Belief) Regulations 2003, SI 2003/1660, reg 9(5)). For these purposes, 'the Frigg Gas Field' means the naturally occurring gas-bearing sand formations of the lower Eocene age located in the vicinity of the intersection of the line of latitude 59 degrees 53 minutes North and of the dividing line between the sectors of the Continental Shelf of the United Kingdom and the Kingdom of Norway and includes all other gas-bearing strata from which gas at the start of production is capable of flowing into the above-mentioned gas-bearing sand formations; and 'oversea company' has the same meaning as in the Companies Act 1985 s 744 (see COMPANIES vol 7(2) (2004 Reissue) para 1816): Employment Equality (Religion or Belief) Regulations 2003, SI 2003/1660, reg 9(6).

     For the meaning of 'Great Britain' generally see para 325 note 6 ante. For these purposes, 'Great Britain', except where the context otherwise requires in reg 26 (protection of Sikhs from discrimination in connection with requirements as to wearing of safety helmets: see para 681 post), includes such of the territorial waters of the United Kingdom as are adjacent to Great Britain: reg 2(3). As to the territorial waters of the United Kingdom see WATER vol 49(2) (2004 Reissue) para 15. For the meaning of 'United Kingdom' see para 325 note 6 ante.

4   For the purposes of the Employment Equality (Religion or Belief) Regulations 2003, SI 2003/1660 (as amended), references to discrimination are references to any discrimination falling within reg 3 (as amended) (discrimination on grounds of religion or belief: see para 660 ante) or reg 4 (discrimination by way of victimisation: see para 661 ante); and related expressions are to be construed accordingly: reg 2(2).

5   Ibid reg 6(1).

6   'Benefits', except in ibid reg 9A (as added) (trustees and managers of occupational pension schemes: see
     para 665 post), includes facilities and services: reg 2(3) (definition substituted by SI 2003/2828).
7   For the purpose of the Employment Equality (Religion or Belief) Regulations 2003, SI 2003/1660,
     reg 6(2)(d) (see head (2)(d) in the text), reference to the dismissal of a person from employment includes
     reference: (1) to the termination of that person's employment by the expiration of any period (including
     a period expiring by reference to an event or circumstance), not being a termination immediately after
     which the employment is renewed on the same terms; and (2) to the termination of that person's
     employment by any act of his (including the giving of notice) in circumstances such that he is entitled to
     terminate it without notice by reason of the conduct of the employer: reg 6(5). As to the meaning of 'act'
     see para 661 note 3 ante.
8   Ibid reg 6(2). 'Detriment' does not include harassment within the meaning of reg 5 (see para 662 ante):
     reg 2(3).
9   For the purposes of the Employment Equality (Religion or Belief) Regulations 2003, SI 2003/1660 (as
     amended), references to harassment are to be construed in accordance with reg 5 (harassment on grounds
     of religion or belief: see para 662 ante): reg 2(2).
10   Ibid reg 6(3).
11   Ibid reg 6(4).
12   Ie discrimination falling within ibid reg 3 (as amended): see para 660 ante.
13   Ie ibid reg 7(2) or reg 7(3): see the text and notes 15–17 infra.
14   Ibid reg 7(1).
15   Ibid reg 7(2)(a)–(c).
16   Ibid reg 7(2).
17   Ibid reg 7(3).

664.   Contract workers.   It is unlawful for a principal[1], in relation to contract work[2] at an establishment in Great Britain[3], to discriminate[4] against a contract worker[5]:

(1)   in the terms on which he allows him to do that work;

(2)   by not allowing him to do it or continue to do it;

(3)   in the way he affords him access to any benefits[6] or by refusing or deliberately not affording him access to them; or

(4)   by subjecting him to any other detriment[7].

A principal does not, however, contravene head (2) above by doing any act[8] in relation to a contract worker where, if the work were to be done by a person taken into the principal's employment, that act would be lawful by virtue of the statutory exception[9] for a genuine occupational requirement[10]. Furthermore, heads (1) to (4) above do not apply to benefits of any description if the principal is concerned with the provision, for payment or not, of benefits of that description to the public, or to a section of the public to which the contract worker in question belongs, unless that provision differs in a material respect from the provision of the benefits by the principal to his contract workers[11].

It is also unlawful for a principal, in relation to contract work at an establishment in Great Britain, to subject a contract worker to harassment[12].

1   'Principal' means a person ('A') who makes work available for doing by individuals who are employed by
     another person who supplies them under a contract made with A: Employment Equality (Religion or
     Belief) Regulations 2003, SI 2003/1660, reg 8(5). As to the meaning of 'person' see para 344 note 3 ante.
2   'Contract work' means work made available as described in note 1 supra: ibid reg 8(5).
3   Ibid reg 9 (meaning of employment and contract work at establishment in Great Britain: see para 663
     note 3 ante) applies in relation to contract work within the meaning of reg 8 as it applies in relation to
     employment; and, in its application to contract work, references to 'employee', 'employer' and
     'employment' are references to (respectively) 'contract worker', 'principal' and 'contract work' within the
     meaning of reg 8: reg 9(7). As to the meaning of 'Great Britain' see para 663 note 3 ante.
4   For the meaning of references to discrimination see para 663 note 4 ante.
5   'Contract worker' means any individual who is supplied to the principal under such a contract as is
     described in note 1 supra: Employment Equality (Religion or Belief) Regulations 2003, SI 2003/1660,
     reg 8(5).
6   As to the meaning of 'benefits' see para 663 note 6 ante.
7   Employment Equality (Religion or Belief) Regulations 2003, SI 2003/1660, reg 8(1). As to the meaning
     of 'detriment' see para 663 note 8 ante.

8 As to the meaning of 'act' see para 661 note 3 ante.
9 Ie by virtue of the Employment Equality (Religion or Belief) Regulations 2003, SI 2003/1660, reg 7: see para 663 ante.
10 Ibid reg 8(3).
11 Ibid reg 8(4).
12 Ibid reg 8(2). For the meaning of references to harassment see para 663 note 9 ante.

665. Trustees and managers of occupational pension schemes. It is unlawful, except in relation to rights accrued or benefits payable in respect of periods of service prior to 2 December 2003[1], for the trustees or managers[2] of an occupational pension scheme[3] to discriminate[4] against a member[5] or prospective member[6] of the scheme in carrying out any of their functions in relation to it, including in particular their functions relating to the admission of members to the scheme and the treatment of members of it[7]. It is also unlawful for the trustees or managers of an occupational pension scheme, in relation to the scheme, to subject to harassment[8] a member or prospective member of it[9].

Every occupational pension scheme must be treated as including a provision ('the non-discrimination rule') containing a requirement that the trustees or managers of the scheme refrain from doing any act which is unlawful by virtue of the above provisions[10]; and the other provisions of the scheme are to have effect subject to the non-discrimination rule[11]. The trustees or managers of an occupational pension scheme may:

(1) if they do not otherwise have power to make such alterations to the scheme as may be required to secure conformity with the non-discrimination rule; or

(2) if they have such power but the procedure for doing so is liable to be unduly complex or protracted, or involves the obtaining of consents which cannot be obtained, or can only be obtained with undue delay or difficulty,

by resolution make such alterations to the scheme[12]. Alterations made by such a resolution may have effect in relation to a period before the alterations are made, but may not have effect in relation to any time before 2 December 2003[13].

1 Ie prior to the coming into force of the Employment Equality (Religion or Belief) Regulations 2003, SI 2003/1660 (as amended). The regulations came into force on 2 December 2003: see para 660 note 1 ante.

2 For these purposes, 'trustees or managers' has the meaning given by the Pensions Act 1995 s 124(1) (as amended) (see SOCIAL SECURITY AND PENSIONS vol 44(2) (Reissue) para 612): Employment Equality (Religion or Belief) Regulations 2003, SI 2003/1660, reg 9A(3)(a), Sch 1A para 1(1), (3) (reg 9A, Sch 1A added by SI 2003/2828).

3 For these purposes, 'occupational pension scheme' has the same meaning as in the Pension Schemes Act 1993 (see SOCIAL SECURITY AND PENSIONS vol 44(2) (Reissue) para 853): Employment Equality (Religion or Belief) Regulations 2003, SI 2003/1660, Sch 1A para 1(1), (3) (as added (see note 2 supra); definition amended by SI 2006/1031).

4 For the meaning of references to discrimination see para 663 note 4 ante.

5 'Member', in relation to an occupational pension scheme, means any active member, deferred member or pensioner member; and 'active member', 'deferred member' and 'pensioner member' have the meanings given by the Pensions Act 1995 s 124(1) (as amended) (see SOCIAL SECURITY AND PENSIONS vol 44(2) (Reissue) para 612): Employment Equality (Religion or Belief) Regulations 2003, SI 2003/1660, Sch 1A para 1(1), (3) (as added (see note 2 supra); and amended by SI 2006/1031).

6 'Prospective member', in relation to an occupational pension scheme, means any person who, under the terms of his employment or the rules of the scheme or both: (1) is able, at his own option, to become a member of the scheme; (2) is to become so able if he continues in the same employment for a sufficient period of time; (3) is to be admitted to it automatically unless he makes an election not to become a member; or (4) may be admitted to it subject to the consent of his employer: Employment Equality (Religion or Belief) Regulations 2003, SI 2003/1660, Sch 1A para 1(1), (3) (as added: see note 2 supra). For the meaning of 'employment' see para 663 note 2 ante.

7 Ibid reg 9A(1) (as added: see note 2 supra).

8 For the meaning of references to harassment see para 663 note 9 ante.

9   Employment Equality (Religion or Belief) Regulations 2003, SI 2003/1660, reg 9A(2) (as added: see note 2 supra).

10   Ibid reg 9A(3)(b), Sch 1A para 2 (as added: see note 2 supra).

11   Ibid Sch 1A para 3 (as added: see note 2 supra).

12   Ibid reg 9A(3)(c), Sch 1A para 4 (as added: see note 2 supra).

13   Ibid Sch 1A para 5 (as added: see note 2 supra).

666.   Office-holders etc.   The following provisions apply to:

(1)   any office or post to which persons[1] are appointed to discharge functions personally under the direction of another person[2], and in respect of which they are entitled to remuneration[3]; and

(2)   any office or post to which appointments are made by, or on the recommendation of or subject to the approval of, a Minister of the Crown[4], a government department, or the National Assembly for Wales[5] or any part of the Scottish Administration[6],

but not to a political office[7] or a case where the provisions relating to applicants and employees[8], contract workers[9], barristers[10] or partnerships[11] apply, or would apply but for the operation of any other provision of the Employment Equality (Religion or Belief) Regulations 2003[12].

It is unlawful:

(a)   for a relevant person[13], in relation to an appointment to an office or post[14] to which these provisions apply, to discriminate[15] against a person:

(i)   in the arrangements which he makes for the purpose of determining to whom the appointment should be offered;

(ii)   in the terms on which he offers him the appointment; or

(iii)   by refusing[16] to offer him the appointment[17];

(b)   in relation to an appointment to an office or post to which these provisions apply and which is an office or post referred to in head (2) above, for a relevant person on whose recommendation, or subject to whose approval, appointments to the office or post are made, to discriminate against a person:

(i)   in the arrangements which he makes for the purpose of determining who should be recommended or approved in relation to the appointment; or

(ii)   in making or refusing to make a recommendation[18], or giving or refusing to give an approval, in relation to the appointment[19];

(c)   for a relevant person, in relation to a person who has been appointed to an office or post to which these provisions apply, to discriminate against him:

(i)   in the terms of the appointment;

(ii)   in the opportunities which he affords him for promotion, a transfer, training or receiving any other benefit[20], or by refusing to afford him any such opportunity;

(iii)   by terminating the appointment[21]; or

(iv)   by subjecting him to any other detriment[22] in relation to the appointment[23];

(d)   for a relevant person, in relation to an office or post to which these provisions apply, to subject to harassment[24] a person:

(i)   who has been appointed to the office or post;

(ii)   who is seeking or being considered for appointment to the office or post; or

(iii)   who is seeking or being considered for a recommendation or approval in relation to an appointment to an office or post referred to in head (2) above[25].

Heads (a) and (c) above do not, however, apply to any act[26] in relation to an office or post where, if the office or post constituted employment[27], that act would be lawful by virtue of the statutory exception for a genuine occupational requirement[28]; and head (b) above does not apply to any act in relation to an office or post where, if the office or post constituted employment, it would be lawful by virtue of that statutory exception to refuse to offer the person such employment[29]. Nor does head (c) above apply to benefits of any description if the relevant person is concerned with the provision, for payment or not, of benefits of that description to the public, or a section of the public to which the person appointed belongs, unless:

(A)   that provision differs in a material respect from the provision of the benefits by the relevant person to persons appointed to offices or posts which are the same as, or not materially different from, that which the person appointed holds; or

(B)   the provision of the benefits to the person appointed is regulated by the terms and conditions of his appointment; or

(C)   the benefits relate to training[30].

1   As to the meaning of 'person' see para 344 note 3 ante.

2   For these purposes, the holder of an office or post is to be regarded as discharging his functions under the direction of another person if that other person is entitled to direct him as to when and where he discharges those functions: Employment Equality (Religion or Belief) Regulations 2003, SI 2003/1660, reg 10(9)(a).

3   For these purposes, the holder of an office or post is not to be regarded as entitled to remuneration merely because he is entitled to payments: (1) in respect of expenses incurred by him in carrying out the functions of the office or post; or (2) by way of compensation for the loss of income or benefits he would or might have received from any person had he not been carrying out the functions of the office or post: ibid reg 10(9)(b).

4   'Minister of the Crown' includes the Treasury and the Defence Council: ibid reg 2(3). As to the Treasury see CONSTITUTIONAL LAW AND HUMAN RIGHTS vol 8(2) (Reissue) paras 512–517. As to the Defence Council see ARMED FORCES vol 2(2) (Reissue) para 2; CONSTITUTIONAL LAW AND HUMAN RIGHTS vol 8(2) (Reissue) para 443 et seq.

5   As to the National Assembly for Wales see para 302 ante.

6   Matters relating to the composition, procedures and powers of the Scottish Administration fall outside the scope of this work.

7   For these purposes, 'political office' means: (1) any office of the House of Commons held by a member of it; (2) a life peerage within the meaning of the Life Peerages Act 1958 (see CONSTITUTIONAL LAW AND HUMAN RIGHTS vol 8(2) (Reissue) para 212; PARLIAMENT vol 34 (Reissue) para 540; PEERAGES AND DIGNITIES), or any office of the House of Lords held by a member of it; (3) any office mentioned in the House of Commons Disqualification Act 1975 Sch 2 (as amended) (ministerial offices: see PARLIAMENT vol 34 (Reissue) para 611); (4) the offices of Leader of the Opposition, Chief Opposition Whip or Assistant Opposition Whip within the meaning of the Ministerial and other Salaries Act 1975 (see CONSTITUTIONAL LAW AND HUMAN RIGHTS vol 8(2) (Reissue) para 219); (5) any office of the National Assembly for Wales held by a member of it; (6) in England, any office of a county council, a London borough council, a district council, or a parish council held by a member of it; (7) in Wales, any office of a county council, a county borough council, or a community council held by a member of it; (8) any office of the Greater London Authority held by a member of it; (9) any office of the Common Council of the City of London held by a member of it; (10) any office of the Council of the Isles of Scilly held by a member of it; (11) any office of a political party: Employment Equality (Religion or Belief) Regulations 2003, SI 2003/1660, reg 10(10)(b). This provision also refers to various Scottish offices, but see note 6 supra. As to local government authorities in England and Wales see LOCAL GOVERNMENT vol 29(1) (Reissue) para 23 et seq; as to London borough councils see LONDON GOVERNMENT vol 29(2) (Reissue) para 35 et seq; as to the Greater London Authority see LONDON GOVERNMENT vol 29(2) (Reissue) para 70 et seq; as to the Common Council of the City of London see LONDON GOVERNMENT vol 29(2) (Reissue) para 51 et seq; and as to the Council of the Isles of Scilly see LOCAL GOVERNMENT vol 29(1) (Reissue) para 40.

8   Ie ibid reg 6: see para 663 ante.

9   Ie ibid reg 8: see para 664 ante.

10   Ie ibid reg 12: see para 668 post. As to advocates see reg 13 (which only applies in relation to Scotland). See note 6 supra.

11   Ie ibid reg 14: see para 669 post.

12   Ibid reg 10(8).

13 For these purposes, 'relevant person', in relation to an office or post, means: (1) any person with power to make or terminate appointments to the office or post, or to determine the terms of appointment; (2) any person with power to determine the working conditions of a person appointed to the office or post in relation to opportunities for promotion, transfer, training or for receiving any other benefit; and (3) any person or body referred to in ibid reg 10(8)(b) (see head (2) in the text) on whose recommendation or subject to whose approval appointments are made to the office or post: reg 10(10)(c).

14 For these purposes, appointment to an office or post does not include election to an office or post: ibid reg 10(10)(a).

15 For the meaning of references to discrimination see para 663 note 4 ante.

16 For these purposes, references to refusal include references to deliberate omission: Employment Equality (Religion or Belief) Regulations 2003, SI 2003/1660, reg 10(10)(e).

17 Ibid reg 10(1).

18 For these purposes, references to making a recommendation include references to making a negative recommendation: ibid reg 10(10)(d).

19 Ibid reg 10(2).

20 As to the meaning of 'benefits' see para 663 note 6 ante.

21 The reference in head (c)(iii) in the text to the termination of the appointment includes a reference: (1) to the termination of the appointment by the expiration of any period (including a period expiring by reference to an event or circumstance), not being a termination immediately after which the appointment is renewed on the same terms and conditions; and (2) to the termination of the appointment by any act of the person appointed (including the giving of notice) in circumstances such that he is entitled to terminate the appointment without notice by reason of the conduct of the relevant person: Employment Equality (Religion or Belief) Regulations 2003, SI 2003/1660, reg 10(7).

22 As to the meaning of 'detriment' see para 663 note 8 ante.

23 Employment Equality (Religion or Belief) Regulations 2003, SI 2003/1660, reg 10(3).

24 For the meaning of references to 'harassment' see para 663 note 9 ante.

25 Employment Equality (Religion or Belief) Regulations 2003, SI 2003/1660, reg 10(4).

26 As to the meaning of 'act' see para 661 note 3 ante.

27 For the meaning of 'employment' see para 663 note 2 ante.

28 Ie by virtue of the Employment Equality (Religion or Belief) Regulations 2003, SI 2003/1660, reg 7: see para 663 ante.

29 Ibid reg 10(5).

30 Ibid reg 10(6).

667. Police and the Serious Organised Crime Agency. For the purposes of the regulations prohibiting unlawful discrimination in employment and vocational training[1], the holding of the office of constable is to be treated[2] as employment[3]:

(1) by the chief officer of police[4] as respects any act[5] done by him in relation to a constable or that office;

(2) by the police authority[6] as respects any act done by it in relation to a constable or that office[7],

and this applies to a police cadet[8] and appointment as a police cadet as it applies to a constable and the office of constable[9].

There must be paid out of the police fund[10]:

(a) any compensation, costs or expenses awarded against a chief officer of police in any proceedings brought against him[11] under the Employment Equality (Religion or Belief) Regulations 2003[12], and any costs or expenses incurred by him in any such proceedings so far as not recovered by him in the proceedings; and

(b) any sum required by a chief officer of police for the settlement of any claim made against him under those regulations if the settlement is approved by the police authority[13].

A police authority may, in such cases and to such extent as appear to it to be appropriate, pay out of the police fund:

(i) any compensation, costs or expenses awarded in proceedings under the Employment Equality (Religion or Belief) Regulations 2003 against a person under the direction and control of the chief officer of police;

(ii) any costs or expenses incurred and not recovered by such a person in such proceedings; and

(iii) any sum required in connection with the settlement of a claim that has or might have given rise to such proceedings[14].

For the purposes of the Employment Equality (Religion or Belief) Regulations 2003[15], any constable or other person who has been seconded to the Serious Organised Crime Agency ('SOCA') to serve as a member of its staff is to be treated as employed by SOCA[16].

1 Ie for the purposes of the Employment Equality (Religion or Belief) Regulations 2003, SI 2003/1660, Pt II (regs 6–21) (as amended).
2 Ie subject to ibid reg 11A (as added): see the text and notes 15–16 infra.
3 For the meaning of 'employment' see para 663 note 2 ante.
4 For these purposes, and subject to the Employment Equality (Religion or Belief) Regulations 2003, SI 2003/1660, reg 11(8), 'chief officer of police': (1) in relation to a person appointed or an appointment falling to be made under a specified Act, has the same meaning as in the Police Act 1996 (see POLICE vol 36(1) (Reissue) para 205); (2) in relation to any other person or appointment, means the officer or other person who has the direction and control of the body of constables or cadets in question: Employment Equality (Religion or Belief) Regulations 2003, SI 2003/1660, reg 11(7) (definition amended by SI 2006/594). In relation to a constable of a force who is not under the direction and control of the chief officer of police for that force, references in the Employment Equality (Religion or Belief) Regulations 2003, SI 2003/1660, reg 11 (as amended) to the chief officer of police are references to the chief officer of the force under whose direction and control he is: reg 11(8).
    'Specified Act' means the Metropolitan Police Act 1829, the City of London Police Act 1839 or the Police Act 1996: Employment Equality (Religion or Belief) Regulations 2003, SI 2003/1660, reg 11(7).
5 As to the meaning of 'act' see para 661 note 3 ante.
6 For these purposes, and subject to the Employment Equality (Religion or Belief) Regulations 2003, SI 2003/1660, reg 11(8), 'police authority': (1) in relation to a person appointed or an appointment falling to be made under a specified Act (see note 4 supra), has the same meaning as in the Police Act 1996 (see POLICE vol 36(1) (Reissue) para 202); (2) in relation to any other person or appointment, means the authority by whom the person in question is or on appointment would be paid: Employment Equality (Religion or Belief) Regulations 2003, SI 2003/1660, reg 11(7) (definition amended by SI 2006/594). In relation to a constable of a force who is not under the direction and control of the chief officer of police for that force, references to the police authority are references to the relevant police authority for the force under whose direction and control he is: Employment Equality (Religion or Belief) Regulations 2003, SI 2003/1660, reg 11(8). As to the meaning of 'person' see para 344 note 3 ante.
7 Ibid reg 11(1) (amended by SI 2006/594).
8 For these purposes, 'police cadet' means any person appointed to undergo training with a view to becoming a constable: Employment Equality (Religion or Belief) Regulations 2003, SI 2003/1660, reg 11(7).
9 Ibid reg 11(6).
10 For these purposes, and subject to ibid reg 11(8) (see notes 4, 6 supra), 'police fund': (1) in relation to a chief officer of police within the definition of that term set out in note 4 head (1) supra, has the same meaning as in the Police Act 1996 (see POLICE vol 36(1) (Reissue) para 205); (2) in any other case means money provided by the police authority: Employment Equality (Religion or Belief) Regulations 2003, SI 2003/1660, reg 11(7).
11 Any proceedings under the Employment Equality (Religion or Belief) Regulations 2003, SI 2003/1660 (as amended), which, by virtue of reg 11(1) (as amended) (see the text and notes 1–7 supra), would lie against a chief officer of police must be brought against the chief officer of police for the time being or, in the case of a vacancy in that office, against the person for the time being performing the functions of that office; and references in reg 11(3) (see heads (a)–(b) in the text) to the chief officer of police are to be construed accordingly: reg 11(4).
12 Ie under the Employment Equality (Religion or Belief) Regulations 2003, SI 2003/1660 (as amended).
13 Ibid reg 11(3).
14 Ibid reg 11(5).
15 See note 1 supra.
16 Employment Equality (Religion or Belief) Regulations 2003, SI 2003/1660, reg 11A(1), (3) (added by SI 2006/594). As to the Serious Organised Crime Agency see POLICE.

668. Barristers. It is unlawful for a barrister or barrister's clerk[1]:

(1) in relation to any offer of a pupillage[2] or tenancy[3], to discriminate[4] against a person[5]:

    (a) in the arrangements which are made for the purpose of determining to whom the pupillage or tenancy should be offered;

    (b) in respect of any terms on which it is offered; or

    (c) by refusing, or deliberately not offering, it to him[6];

(2) in relation to a pupil[7] or tenant[8] in the set of chambers[9] in question, to discriminate against him:

    (a) in respect of any terms applicable to him as a pupil or tenant;

    (b) in the opportunities for training, or gaining experience, which are afforded or denied to him;

    (c) in the benefits[10] which are afforded or denied to him; or

    (d) by terminating his pupillage, or by subjecting him to any pressure to leave the chambers or other detriment[11];

(3) in relation to a pupillage or tenancy in the set of chambers in question, to subject to harassment[12] a person who is, or has applied to be, a pupil or tenant[13].

It is also unlawful for any person, in relation to the giving, withholding or acceptance of instructions to a barrister, to discriminate against any person by subjecting him to a detriment, or to subject him to harassment[14].

1   'Barrister's clerk' includes any person carrying out any of the functions of a barrister's clerk: Employment Equality (Religion or Belief) Regulations 2003, SI 2003/1660, reg 12(5). Regulation 12 extends to England and Wales only: reg 12(6).

2   For these purposes, 'pupil' and 'pupillage' have the meanings commonly associated with their use in the context of barristers practising in independent practice: ibid reg 12(5).

3   For these purposes, 'tenancy' and 'tenant' have the meanings commonly associated with their use in the context of barristers practising in independent practice, but also include reference to any barrister permitted to work in a set of chambers who is not a tenant: ibid reg 12(5). See also note 9 infra.

4   For the meaning of references to discrimination see para 663 note 4 ante.

5   As to the meaning of 'person' see para 344 note 3 ante.

6   Employment Equality (Religion or Belief) Regulations 2003, SI 2003/1660, reg 12(1).

7   See note 2 supra.

8   See note 3 supra.

9   For these purposes, 'set of chambers' has the meaning commonly associated with its use in the context of barristers practising in independent practice: Employment Equality (Religion or Belief) Regulations 2003, SI 2003/1660, reg 12(5).

10 As to the meaning of 'benefits' see para 663 note 6 ante.

11 Employment Equality (Religion or Belief) Regulations 2003, SI 2003/1660, reg 12(2). As to the meaning of 'detriment' see para 663 note 8 ante.

12 For the meaning of references to harassment see para 663 note 9 ante.

13 Employment Equality (Religion or Belief) Regulations 2003, SI 2003/1660, reg 12(3).

14 Ibid reg 12(4).

669. Partnerships. It is unlawful for a firm[1], in relation to a position as partner[2] in the firm:

(1) to discriminate[3] against a person[4]:

    (a) in the arrangements it makes for the purpose of determining to whom it should offer that position;

    (b) in the terms on which it offers him that position;

    (c) by refusing to offer, or deliberately not offering, him that position; or

    (d) in a case where the person already holds that position, in the way it affords him access to any benefits[5] or by refusing to afford, or deliberately not affording, him access to them, or by expelling him from that position[6], or subjecting him to any other detriment[7];

(2) to subject to harassment[8] a person who holds or has applied for that position[9].

Heads (1)(a) to (1)(c) and head (2) above apply in relation to persons proposing to form themselves into a partnership as they apply in relation to a firm[10]. Head (1) above does not, however, apply to any act[11] in relation to a position as partner where, if the position were employment[12], that act would be lawful by virtue of the statutory exception[13] for a genuine occupational requirement[14].

1 For these purposes, 'firm' has the meaning given by the Partnership Act 1890 s 4 (see PARTNERSHIP vol 35 (Reissue) para 1): Employment Equality (Religion or Belief) Regulations 2003, SI 2003/1660, reg 14(7). Regulation 14 applies to a limited liability partnership as it applies to a firm: reg 14(6).
2 In the case of a limited partnership, references in ibid reg 14 to a partner are to be construed as references to a general partner as defined in the Limited Partnerships Act 1907 s 3 (see PARTNERSHIP vol 35 (Reissue) para 207) (Employment Equality (Religion or Belief) Regulations 2003, SI 2003/1660, reg 14(5)); and, in the application of reg 14 to a limited liability partnership, references to a partner in a firm are references to a member of the limited liability partnership (reg 14(6)).
3 For the meaning of references to discrimination see para 663 note 4 ante.
4 As to the meaning of 'person' see para 344 note 3 ante.
5 As to the meaning of 'benefits' see para 663 note 6 ante.
6 In the Employment Equality (Religion or Belief) Regulations 2003, SI 2003/1660, reg 14(1)(d) (see head (1)(d) in the text), reference to the expulsion of a person from a position as partner includes reference: (1) to the termination of that person's partnership by the expiration of any period (including a period expiring by reference to an event or circumstance), not being a termination immediately after which the partnership is renewed on the same terms; and (2) to the termination of that person's partnership by any act of his (including the giving of notice) in circumstances such that he is entitled to terminate it without notice by reason of the conduct of the other partners: reg 14(8).
7 Ibid reg 14(1). As to the meaning of 'detriment' see para 663 note 8 ante.
8 For the meaning of references to harassment see para 663 note 9 ante.
9 Employment Equality (Religion or Belief) Regulations 2003, SI 2003/1660, reg 14(2).
10 Ibid reg 14(3).
11 As to the meaning of 'act' see para 661 note 3 ante.
12 For the meaning of 'employment' see para 663 note 2 ante.
13 Ie by virtue of the Employment Equality (Religion or Belief) Regulations 2003, SI 2003/1660, reg 7: see para 663 ante.
14 Ibid reg 14(4).

670. Trade organisations. It is unlawful for a trade organisation[1]:

(1) to discriminate[2] against a person[3]:
    (a) in the terms on which it is prepared to admit him to membership of the organisation; or
    (b) by refusing to accept, or deliberately not accepting, his application for membership[4];

(2) in relation to a member of the organisation, to discriminate against him:
    (a) in the way it affords him access to any benefits[5] or by refusing or deliberately omitting to afford him access to them;
    (b) by depriving him of membership, or varying the terms on which he is a member; or
    (c) by subjecting him to any other detriment[6];

(3) in relation to a person's membership or application for membership of that organisation, to subject that person to harassment[7].

1 For these purposes, 'trade organisation' means an organisation of workers, an organisation of employers, or any other organisation whose members carry on a particular profession or trade for the purposes of which the organisation exists; 'profession' includes any vocation or occupation; and 'trade' includes any business: Employment Equality (Religion or Belief) Regulations 2003, SI 2003/1660, reg 15(4).
2 For the meaning of references to discrimination see para 663 note 4 ante.
3 As to the meaning of 'person' see para 344 note 3 ante.
4 Employment Equality (Religion or Belief) Regulations 2003, SI 2003/1660, reg 15(1).
5 As to the meaning of 'benefits' see para 663 note 6 ante.

6   Employment Equality (Religion or Belief) Regulations 2003, SI 2003/1660, reg 15(2). As to the meaning of 'detriment' see para 663 note 8 ante.
7   Ibid reg 15(3). For the meaning of references to harassment see para 663 note 9 ante.

671. Qualifications bodies. It is unlawful for a qualifications body[1]:

(1) to discriminate[2] against a person[3]:

    (a) in the terms on which it is prepared to confer a professional or trade qualification on him;

    (b) by refusing or deliberately not granting any application by him for such a qualification; or

    (c) by withdrawing such a qualification from him or varying the terms on which he holds it[4];

(2) in relation to a professional or trade qualification conferred by it, to subject to harassment[5] a person who holds or applies for such a qualification[6].

1   For these purposes, 'qualifications body' means any authority or body which can confer a professional or trade qualification, but it does not include:
    (1) an educational establishment to which the Employment Equality (Religion or Belief) Regulations 2003, SI 2003/1660, reg 20 (institutions of further and higher education: see para 675 post) applies, or would apply but for the operation of any other provision of the regulations; or
    (2) a school;
'confer' includes renew or extend; 'professional or trade qualification' means any authorisation, qualification, recognition, registration, enrolment, approval or certification which is needed for, or facilitates engagement in, a particular profession or trade; and 'profession' and 'trade' have the same meanings as in reg 15 (see para 670 ante): reg 16(3). 'School' has the meaning given by the Education Act 1996 s 4 (as amended) (see EDUCATION vol 15(1) (2006 Reissue) para 81); and references to a school are to an institution in so far as it is engaged in the provision of education under s 4 (as amended): Employment Equality (Religion or Belief) Regulations 2003, SI 2003/1660, reg 2(3).
2   For the meaning of references to discrimination see para 663 note 4 ante.
3   As to the meaning of 'person' see para 344 note 3 ante.
4   Employment Equality (Religion or Belief) Regulations 2003, SI 2003/1660, reg 16(1).
5   For the meaning of references to harassment see para 663 note 9 ante.
6   Employment Equality (Religion or Belief) Regulations 2003, SI 2003/1660, reg 16(2).

672. Providers of vocational training. It is unlawful, in relation to a person[1] seeking or undergoing training[2] which would help fit him for any employment[3], for any training provider[4] to discriminate[5] against him:

(1) in the terms on which the training provider affords him access to any training;

(2) by refusing or deliberately not affording him such access;

(3) by terminating his training; or

(4) by subjecting him to any other detriment[6] during his training[7];

but this does not apply if the discrimination only concerns training for employment which, by virtue of the statutory exception for a genuine occupational requirement[8], the employer could lawfully refuse to offer the person seeking training[9].

It is also unlawful for a training provider, in relation to a person seeking or undergoing training which would help fit him for any employment, to subject him to harassment[10].

1   As to the meaning of 'person' see para 344 note 3 ante.
2   For these purposes, 'training' includes: (1) facilities for training; and (2) practical work experience provided by an employer to a person whom he does not employ: Employment Equality (Religion or Belief) Regulations 2003, SI 2003/1660, reg 17(4). As to the meaning of 'employer' see para 663 note 1 ante.
3   For the meaning of 'employment' see para 663 note 2 ante.
4   For these purposes, 'training provider' means any person who provides, or makes arrangements for the provision of, training which would help fit another person for any employment, but it does not include: (1) an employer in relation to training for persons employed by him; (2) an educational establishment to

which the Employment Equality (Religion or Belief) Regulations 2003, SI 2003/1660, reg 20 (institutions of further and higher education: see para 675 post) applies, or would apply but for the operation of any other provision of the regulations; or (3) a school: reg 17(4). For the meaning of 'school' see para 671 note 1 ante.

5   For the meaning of references to discrimination see para 663 note 4 ante.
6   As to the meaning of 'detriment' see para 663 note 8 ante.
7   Employment Equality (Religion or Belief) Regulations 2003, SI 2003/1660, reg 17(1).
8   Ie by virtue of ibid reg 7: see para 663 ante.
9   Ibid reg 17(3).
10 Ibid reg 17(2). For the meaning of references to harassment see para 663 note 9 ante.

673.   Employment agencies, careers guidance etc.   It is unlawful for an employment agency[1] to discriminate[2] against a person:

(1)   in the terms on which the agency offers to provide any of its services;
(2)   by refusing or deliberately not providing any of its services; or
(3)   in the way it provides any of its services[3],

but this does not apply to discrimination if it only concerns employment which, by virtue of the statutory exception for a genuine occupational requirement[4], the employer could lawfully refuse to offer the person in question[5].

It is also unlawful for an employment agency, in relation to a person to whom it provides its services or who has requested it to provide its services, to subject that person to harassment[6].

An employment agency is not subject to any liability under the above provisions if it proves that:

(a)   it acted in reliance on a statement made to it by the employer to the effect that, by reason of the operation of the above-mentioned statutory exception[7], its action would not be unlawful; and
(b)   it was reasonable for it to rely on the statement[8].

A person who knowingly or recklessly makes a statement such as is referred to in head (a) above which in a material respect is false or misleading commits an offence, and is liable on summary conviction to a fine[9].

1   For these purposes: (1) 'employment agency' means a person who, for profit or not, provides services for the purpose of finding employment for workers or supplying employers with workers, but it does not include: (a) an educational establishment to which the Employment Equality (Religion or Belief) Regulations 2003, SI 2003/1660, reg 20 (institutions of further and higher education: see para 675 post) applies, or would apply but for the operation of any other provision of the regulations; or (b) a school; and (2) references to the services of an employment agency include guidance on careers and any other services related to employment: reg 18(6). For the meanings of 'employer' and 'employment' see para 663 notes 1, 2 ante; and for the meaning of 'school' see para 671 note 1 ante. As to the meaning of 'person' see para 344 note 3 ante.
2   For the meaning of references to discrimination see para 663 note 4 ante.
3   Employment Equality (Religion or Belief) Regulations 2003, SI 2003/1660, reg 18(1).
4   Ie by virtue of ibid reg 7: see para 663 ante.
5   Ibid reg 18(3).
6   Ibid reg 18(2). For the meaning of references to harassment see para 663 note 9 ante.
7   See note 4 supra.
8   Employment Equality (Religion or Belief) Regulations 2003, SI 2003/1660, reg 18(4).
9   Ibid reg 18(5). The fine referred to in the text is a fine not exceeding level 5 on the standard scale: see reg 18(5). As to the standard scale see para 315 note 15 ante.

674.   Assisting persons to obtain employment etc.   It is unlawful for the Secretary of State[1] to discriminate[2] against any person[3] by subjecting him to a detriment[4], or to subject a person to harassment[5], in the provision of facilities or services under the statutory arrangements[6] for assisting persons to obtain employment[7].

1   As to the Secretary of State and the National Assembly for Wales see para 302 ante.
2   For the meaning of references to discrimination see para 663 note 4 ante.

3   As to the meaning of 'person' see para 344 note 3 ante.

4   As to the meaning of 'detriment' see para 663 note 8 ante.

5   For the meaning of references to harassment see para 663 note 9 ante.

6   Ie under the Employment and Training Act 1973 s 2 (as substituted and amended): see EMPLOYMENT vol 16(1B) (Reissue) para 765.

7   Employment Equality (Religion or Belief) Regulations 2003, SI 2003/1660, reg 19(1). Regulation 19 does not apply in a case where: (1) reg 17 (providers of vocational training: see para 672 ante) applies, or would apply but for the operation of any other provision of the regulations; or (2) the Secretary of State is acting as an employment agency within the meaning of reg 18 (see para 673 ante): reg 19(3).

675.   Institutions of further and higher education.   The provisions set out below apply to the following educational establishments in England and Wales, namely:

(1)   an institution within the further education sector[1];

(2)   a university[2];

(3)   an institution[3], other than a university, within the higher education sector[4].

It is unlawful, in relation to an educational establishment to which these provisions apply, for the governing body of that establishment to discriminate[5] against a person[6]:

(a)   in the terms on which it offers to admit him to the establishment as a student[7];

(b)   by refusing or deliberately not accepting an application for his admission to the establishment as a student; or

(c)   where he is a student of the establishment:

    (i)   in the way it affords him access to any benefits[8];

    (ii)   by refusing or deliberately not affording him access to them; or

    (iii)   by excluding him from the establishment or subjecting him to any other detriment[9],

but this does not apply if the discrimination only concerns training which would help fit a person for employment[10] which, by virtue of the statutory exception for a genuine occupational requirement[11], the employer[12] could lawfully refuse to offer the person in question[13].

It is also unlawful, in relation to an educational establishment to which these provisions apply, for the governing body of that establishment to subject to harassment[14] a person who is a student at the establishment, or who has applied for admission to the establishment as a student[15].

In relation to specified institutions[16], these provisions apply with the modification that head (b) above does not apply in so far as it is necessary for an institution to give preference in its admissions to persons of a particular religion or belief in order to preserve that institution's religious ethos[17]; but that modification does not apply in relation to any admission to a course of vocational training[18].

1   Ie within the meaning of the Further and Higher Education Act 1992 s 91(3): see EDUCATION vol 15(2) (2006 Reissue) para 579.

2   For these purposes, 'university' includes a university college and a college, school or hall of a university: Employment Equality (Religion or Belief) Regulations 2003, SI 2003/1660, reg 20(6).

3   Ie an institution within the higher education sector within the meaning of the Further and Higher Education Act 1992 s 91(5): see EDUCATION vol 15(2) (2006 Reissue) para 646.

4   Employment Equality (Religion or Belief) Regulations 2003, SI 2003/1660, reg 20(4). This is subject to reg 20(4A) (as added) (see the text and notes 16–17 infra): reg 20(4) (amended by SI 2004/437).

5   For the meaning of references to discrimination see para 663 note 4 ante.

6   As to the meaning of 'person' see para 344 note 3 ante.

7   For these purposes, 'student' means any person who receives education at an educational establishment to which the Employment Equality (Religion or Belief) Regulations 2003, SI 2003/1660, reg 20 (as amended) applies: reg 20(6).

8   As to the meaning of 'benefits' see para 663 note 6 ante.

9   Employment Equality (Religion or Belief) Regulations 2003, SI 2003/1660, reg 20(1). As to the meaning of 'detriment' see para 663 note 8 ante.

10   For the meaning of 'employment' see para 663 note 2 ante.

11   Ie the Employment Equality (Religion or Belief) Regulations 2003, SI 2003/1660, reg 7: see para 663 ante.
12   As to the meaning of 'employer' see para 663 note 1 ante.
13   Employment Equality (Religion or Belief) Regulations 2003, SI 2003/1660, reg 20(3).
14   For the meaning of references to harassment see para 663 note 9 ante.
15   Employment Equality (Religion or Belief) Regulations 2003, SI 2003/1660, reg 20(2).
16   The specified institutions are: Aquinas Sixth Form College, Stockport; Cardinal Newman College, Preston; Carmel College, St Helens; Christ The King Sixth Form College, Lewisham; Holy Cross Sixth Form College, Bury; Loreto College, Manchester; Notre Dame Catholic Sixth Form College, Leeds; St Brendan's Sixth Form College, Brislington, Bristol; St Charles Catholic Sixth Form College, London W10; St David's Catholic College/Coleg Catholig Dewi Sant, Cardiff; St Dominic's Sixth Form College, Harrow on the Hill; St Francis Xavier Sixth Form College, Clapham; Saint John Rigby Catholic Sixth Form College, Orrell, Wigan; St Mary's College, Blackburn; St Mary's Sixth Form College, Middlesbrough; and Xaverian Sixth Form College, Manchester: ibid reg 20(4A), Sch 1B para 1 (added by SI 2004/437).
17   Employment Equality (Religion or Belief) Regulations 2003, SI 2003/1660, reg 20(4A), Sch 1B para 2 (as added: see note 16 supra).
18   Ibid Sch 1B para 3 (as added: see note 16 supra).

676. Relevant relationships which have come to an end. A 'relevant relationship' is a relationship during the course of which an act[1] of discrimination[2] against, or harassment[3] of, one party to the relationship ('B') by the other party to it ('A') is unlawful[4] by virtue of provisions of the Employment Equality (Religion or Belief) Regulations 2003[5] regarding discrimination in employment and vocational training[6]. Where a relevant relationship has come to an end, it is unlawful for A:

   (1)   to discriminate against B by subjecting him to a detriment[7]; or
   (2)   to subject B to harassment,

where the discrimination or harassment arises out of and is closely connected to that relationship[8].

1   As to the meaning of 'act' see para 661 note 3 ante.
2   For the meaning of references to discrimination see para 663 note 4 ante.
3   For the meaning of references to harassment see para 663 note 9 ante.
4   For these purposes, reference to an act of discrimination or harassment which is unlawful includes, in the case of a relationship which has come to an end before 2 December 2003 (ie the date of the coming into force of the Employment Equality (Religion or Belief) Regulations 2003, SI 2003/1660 (as amended): see para 660 note 1 ante), reference to an act of discrimination or harassment which would, after that date, be unlawful: reg 21(3).
5   Ie ibid Pt II (regs 6–21) (as amended): see para 663 et seq ante.
6   Ibid reg 21(1).
7   As to the meaning of 'detriment' see para 663 note 8 ante.
8   Employment Equality (Religion or Belief) Regulations 2003, SI 2003/1660, reg 21(2).

(iii) Other Unlawful Acts

677. Liability of employers and principals. Anything done by a person[1] in the course of his employment[2] is to be treated for the purposes of the Employment Equality (Religion or Belief) Regulations 2003[3] as done by his employer[4] as well as by him, whether or not it was done with the employer's knowledge or approval[5].

For these purposes:

   (1)   the holding of the office of constable is to be treated[6] as employment by the chief officer of police[7], and as not being employment by any other person, and anything done by a person holding such an office in the performance, or purported performance, of his functions is be treated as done in the course of that employment[8];
   (2)   the secondment of any constable or other person to the Serious Organised Crime Agency ('SOCA') to serve as a member of its staff is to be treated as

employment by SOCA, and not as being employment by any other person, and anything done by a person so seconded in the performance, or purported performance, of his functions is to be treated as done in the course of that employment[9].

Anything done by a person as agent for another person with the authority, whether express or implied, and whether precedent or subsequent, of that other person is to be treated for the purposes of the Employment Equality (Religion or Belief) Regulations 2003 as done by that other person as well as by him[10].

In proceedings brought under those regulations against any person in respect of an act[11] alleged to have been done by an employee of his, it is, however, a defence for that person to prove that he took such steps as were reasonably practicable to prevent the employee from doing that act or from doing in the course of his employment acts of that description[12].

1   As to the meaning of 'person' see para 344 note 3 ante.
2   For the meaning of 'employment' see para 663 note 2 ante.
3   Ie for the purposes of the Employment Equality (Religion or Belief) Regulations 2003, SI 2003/1660 (as amended).
4   As to the meaning of 'employer' see para 663 note 1 ante.
5   Employment Equality (Religion or Belief) Regulations 2003, SI 2003/1660, reg 22(1). See *Jones v Tower Boot Co Ltd* [1997] 2 All ER 406, [1997] IRLR 168, CA (a case under the Race Relations Act 1976); and para 476 ante.
    As to the liability of employers and principals under the Sex Discrimination Act 1975 see para 391 ante; and as to their liability under the Race Relations Act 1976 see para 476 ante.
6   Ie subject to the Employment Equality (Religion or Belief) Regulations 2003, SI 2003/1660, reg 11A (as added): see head (2) in the text; and para 667 ante.
7   For the meaning of 'chief officer of police' see para 667 note 4 ante.
8   Employment Equality (Religion or Belief) Regulations 2003, SI 2003/1660, reg 11(2) (amended by SI 2006/594). Head (1) in the text applies to a police cadet and appointment as a police cadet as it applies to a constable and the office of constable: Employment Equality (Religion or Belief) Regulations 2003, SI 2003/1660, reg 11(6). For the meaning of 'police cadet' see para 667 note 8 ante.
9   Ibid reg 11A(2), (3) (added by SI 2006/594). As to the Serious Organised Crime Agency see POLICE.
10 Employment Equality (Religion or Belief) Regulations 2003, SI 2003/1660, reg 22(2).
11 As to the meaning of 'act' see para 661 note 3 ante.
12 Employment Equality (Religion or Belief) Regulations 2003, SI 2003/1660, reg 22(3).

678.   Aiding unlawful acts.   A person[1] who knowingly aids another person to do an act[2] made unlawful by the Employment Equality (Religion or Belief) Regulations 2003[3] is to be treated for the purpose of those regulations as himself doing an unlawful act of the like description[4]; and for these purposes an employee or agent for whose act the employer[5] or principal is liable[6], or would be so liable but for the statutory defence that he took reasonably practicable steps to prevent that act[7], is to be deemed to aid the doing of the act by the employer or principal[8]. A person does not, however, knowingly aid another to do an unlawful act under these provisions if:

(1)   he acts in reliance on a statement made to him by that other person that, by reason of any provision of the relevant regulations, the act which he aids would not be unlawful; and

(2)   it is reasonable for him to rely on the statement[9].

A person who knowingly or recklessly makes a statement such as is referred to in head (1) above which in a material respect is false or misleading commits an offence, and is liable on summary conviction to a fine[10].

1   As to the meaning of 'person' see para 344 note 3 ante.
2   As to the meaning of 'act' see para 661 note 3 ante.
3   Ie the Employment Equality (Religion or Belief) Regulations 2003, SI 2003/1660 (as amended).
4   Ibid reg 23(1).
5   As to the meaning of 'employer' see para 663 note 1 ante.

6   Ie under the Employment Equality (Religion or Belief) Regulations 2003, SI 2003/1660, reg 22: see para 677 ante.
7   Ie but for ibid reg 22(3): see para 677 ante.
8   Ibid reg 23(2). As to aiding discrimination under the Sex Discrimination Act 1975 see para 392 ante; and as to aiding discrimination under the Race Relations Act 1976 see para 477 ante.
9   Employment Equality (Religion or Belief) Regulations 2003, reg 23(3).
10   Ibid reg 23(4). The fine referred to in the text is a fine not exceeding level 5 on the standard scale: see reg 23(4). As to the standard scale see para 315 note 15 ante.

(iv) General Exceptions

679. Exception for national security. Nothing in Part II[1] or Part III[2] of the Employment Equality (Religion or Belief) Regulations 2003 renders unlawful an act[3] done for the purpose of safeguarding national security, if the doing of the act was justified by that purpose[4].

1   Ie the Employment Equality (Religion or Belief) Regulations 2003, SI 2003/1660, Pt II (regs 6–21) (as amended): see para 663 et seq ante.
2   Ie ibid Pt III (regs 22–23): see paras 677–678 ante.
3   As to the meaning of 'act' see para 661 note 3 ante.
4   Employment Equality (Religion or Belief) Regulations 2003, SI 2003/1660, reg 24.
      As to national security under the Sex Discrimination Act 1975 see para 403 ante; as to national security under the Race Relations Act 1976 see para 487 ante; and as to national security under the Disability Discrimination Act 1995 see para 616 ante.

680. Exceptions for positive action. Nothing in Part II[1] or Part III[2] of the Employment Equality (Religion or Belief) Regulations 2003 renders unlawful any act[3]:
(1)   done in or in connection with:
     (a)   affording persons[4] of a particular religion or belief[5] access to facilities for training which would help fit them for particular work; or
     (b)   encouraging persons of a particular religion or belief to take advantage of opportunities for doing particular work,
     where it reasonably appears to the person doing the act that it prevents or compensates for disadvantages linked to religion or belief suffered by persons of that religion or belief doing that work or likely to take up that work[6];
(2)   done by a trade organisation[7] in or in connection with:
     (a)   affording only members of the organisation who are of a particular religion or belief access to facilities for training which would help fit them for holding a post of any kind in the organisation; or
     (b)   encouraging only members of the organisation who are of a particular religion or belief to take advantage of opportunities for holding such posts in the organisation,
     where it reasonably appears to the organisation that the act prevents or compensates for disadvantages linked to religion or belief suffered by those of that religion or belief holding such posts or likely to hold such posts[8];
(3)   done by a trade organisation[9] in or in connection with encouraging only persons of a particular religion or belief to become members of the organisation where it reasonably appears to the organisation that the act prevents or compensates for disadvantages linked to religion or belief suffered by persons of that religion or belief who are, or are eligible to become, members[10].

1   Ie the Employment Equality (Religion or Belief) Regulations 2003, SI 2003/1660, Pt II (regs 6–21) (as amended): see para 663 et seq ante.
2   Ie ibid Pt III (regs 22–23): see paras 677–678 ante.
3   As to the meaning of 'act' see para 661 note 3 ante.
4   As to the meaning of 'person' see para 344 note 3 ante.

5 For the meanings of 'religion' and 'belief' see para 660 note 3 ante.
6 Employment Equality (Religion or Belief) Regulations 2003, SI 2003/1660, reg 25(1).
7 Ie within the meaning of ibid reg 15: see para 670 ante.
8 Ibid reg 25(2).
9 See note 7 supra.
10 Employment Equality (Religion or Belief) Regulations 2003, SI 2003/1660, reg 25(3).

681. Protection of Sikhs from discrimination in connection with requirements as to wearing of safety helmets. Where:

(1) any person[1] applies to a Sikh[2] any provision, criterion or practice relating to the wearing by him of a safety helmet[3] while he is on a construction site[4]; and

(2) at the time when he so applies the provision, criterion or practice that person has no reasonable grounds for believing that the Sikh would not wear a turban at all times when on such a site,

then, for the relevant statutory purposes[5], the provision, criterion or practice is to be taken to be one which cannot be shown to be a proportionate means of achieving a legitimate aim[6].

Any special treatment afforded to a Sikh in consequence of the statutory exemption of Sikhs from requirements as to the wearing of safety helmets on construction sites[7] is not to be regarded as giving rise, in relation to any other person, to any discrimination[8] falling within the relevant regulation[9].

1 As to the meaning of 'person' see para 344 note 3 ante.
2 For these purposes, any reference to a Sikh is a reference to a follower of the Sikh religion: Employment Equality (Religion or Belief) Regulations 2003, SI 2003/1660, reg 26(4)(a).
3 For these purposes, 'safety helmet' means any form of protective headgear: ibid reg 26(3).
4 For these purposes: (1) 'construction site' means any place in Great Britain where any building operations or works of engineering construction are being undertaken, but does not include any site within the territorial sea adjacent to Great Britain unless there are being undertaken on that site such operations or works as are activities falling within the Health and Safety at Work etc Act 1974 (Application outside Great Britain) Order 2001, SI 2001/2127, art 8(1)(a) (see HEALTH AND SAFETY AT WORK vol 20(1) (Reissue) para 505) (Employment Equality (Religion or Belief) Regulations 2003, SI 2003/1660, reg 26(3)); and (2) any reference to a Sikh being on a construction site is a reference to his being there whether while at work or otherwise (reg 26(4)(b)). As to the territorial waters of the United Kingdom see WATER vol 49(2) (2004 Reissue) para 15. For the meaning of 'United Kingdom' see para 325 note 6 ante.
5 Ie for the purposes of ibid reg 3(1)(b)(iii): see para 660 head (2)(c) ante.
6 Ibid reg 26(1).
7 Ie in consequence of the Employment Act 1989 s 11(1) or (2): see para 480 ante.
8 Ie any discrimination falling within the Employment Equality (Religion or Belief) Regulations 2003, SI 2003/1660, reg 3 (as amended): see para 660 ante.
9 Ibid reg 26(2).

(v) Enforcement

682. Restriction of proceedings for breach of the regulations. Except as provided by the Employment Equality (Religion or Belief) Regulations 2003[1], no proceedings, whether civil or criminal, lie against any person[2] in respect of an act[3] by reason that the act is unlawful by virtue of a provision of those regulations[4]. This does not, however, prevent the making of an application for judicial review[5] or the investigation or determination of any matter in accordance with Part X of the Pension Schemes Act 1993[6] by the Pensions Ombudsman[7].

1 Ie the Employment Equality (Religion or Belief) Regulations 2003, SI 2003/1660 (as amended).
2 As to the meaning of 'person' see para 344 note 3 ante.
3 As to the meaning of 'act' see para 661 note 3 ante.
4 Employment Equality (Religion or Belief) Regulations 2003, SI 2003/1660, reg 27(1).
5 As to judicial review see generally ADMINISTRATIVE LAW vol 1(1) (2001 Reissue) para 59 et seq.

6 Ie in accordance with the Pension Schemes Act 1993 Pt X (ss 145–152) (as amended) (investigations: the Pensions Ombudsman): see SOCIAL SECURITY AND PENSIONS vol 44(2) (Reissue) para 663 et seq.
7 Employment Equality (Religion or Belief) Regulations 2003, SI 2003/1660, reg 27(2) (amended by SI 2003/2828).

683. Jurisdiction of employment tribunals; time limit and burden of proof.
The following provision applies to any act[1] of discrimination[2] or harassment[3] which is unlawful by virtue of any provision of Part II of the Employment Equality (Religion or Belief) Regulations 2003[4] other than:

(1) where the act is one in respect of which an appeal or proceedings in the nature of an appeal may be brought under any enactment[5], the provision relating to qualifications bodies[6];

(2) the provision relating to institutions of further and higher education[7]; or

(3) where the act arises out of and is closely connected to a relationship between the complainant and the respondent which has come to an end but during the course of which an act of discrimination against, or harassment of, the complainant by the respondent would have been unlawful by virtue of the provision referred to in head (2) above[8], the provision relating to relevant relationships[9] which have come to an end[10].

A complaint by any person[11] ('the complainant') that another person ('the respondent'): (a) has committed against the complainant an act to which this provision applies; or (b) is to be treated[12] as having committed against the complainant such an act, may be presented to an employment tribunal[13].

Where under the above provision a member[14] or prospective member[15] of an occupational pension scheme[16] presents to an employment tribunal a complaint that the trustees or managers[17] of the scheme:

(i) have committed against him an act which is unlawful by virtue of the provision relating to unlawful discrimination by the trustees and managers of occupational pension schemes[18] or of the provision relating to relevant relationships which have come to an end[19]; or

(ii) are to be treated[20] as having committed against him such an act,

the employer[21] in relation to the scheme is, for the purposes of the rules governing procedure, to be treated as a party and to be entitled to appear and be heard in accordance with those rules[22].

An employment tribunal may not consider a complaint under the above provisions[23] unless it is presented to the tribunal before the end of the period of three months beginning when the act complained of was done[24], or, in a case relating to the armed forces[25], the period of six months so beginning[26]. Where, however, the period within which a complaint must so be presented is extended[27], the period within which the complaint must be presented is the extended period rather than the period mentioned above[28]. A tribunal may nevertheless consider any such complaint which is out of time if, in all the circumstances of the case, it considers that it is just and equitable to do so[29].

Where, on the hearing of any complaint presented under the above provisions[30] to an employment tribunal, the complainant proves facts from which the tribunal could otherwise conclude in the absence of an adequate explanation that the respondent:

(A) has committed against the complainant an act to which the above provisions apply; or

(B) is to be treated[31] as having committed against the complainant such an act,

the tribunal must uphold the complaint unless the respondent proves that he did not commit, or, as the case may be, is not to be treated as having committed, that act[32].

1 As to the meaning of 'act' see para 661 note 3 ante.
2 For the meaning of references to discrimination see para 663 note 4 ante.

3 For the meaning of references to harassment see para 663 note 9 ante.

4 Ie any provision of the Employment Equality (Religion or Belief) Regulations 2003, SI 2003/1660, Pt II (regs 6–21) (as amended): see para 663 et seq ante.

5 For these purposes, 'enactment' includes an enactment comprised in, or in an instrument made under, an Act of the Scottish Parliament: ibid reg 28(4). Scottish matters generally are beyond the scope of this work.

6 Ie ibid reg 16: see para 671 ante.

7 Ie ibid reg 20 (as amended): see para 675 ante.

8 Ie by virtue of ibid reg 20 (as amended): see para 675 ante. For the purpose of head (3) in the text, reference to an act of discrimination or harassment which would have been unlawful includes, in the case of a relationship which has come to an end before 2 December 2003 (ie the date of the coming into force of the Employment Equality (Religion or Belief) Regulations 2003, SI 2003/1660 (as amended): see para 660 note 1 ante), reference to an act of discrimination or harassment which would, after that date, have been unlawful: reg 28(3). The regulations do not otherwise have retrospective effect: see *Bari v Hashi* [2004] All ER (D) 496 (Mar), EAT.

9 Ie the Employment Equality (Religion or Belief) Regulations 2003, SI 2003/1660, reg 21: see para 676 ante.

10 Ibid reg 28(2).

11 As to the meaning of 'person' see para 344 note 3 ante.

12 Ie by virtue of the Employment Equality (Religion or Belief) Regulations 2003, SI 2003/1660, reg 22 or reg 23: see paras 677–678 ante.

13 Ibid reg 28(1). As to employment tribunals and the procedure before them see EMPLOYMENT vol 16(1B) (Reissue) para 816 et seq.

14 For the meaning of 'member' see para 665 note 5 ante.

15 For the meaning of 'prospective member' see para 665 note 6 ante.

16 For the meaning of 'occupational pension scheme' see para 665 note 3 ante.

17 For the meaning of 'trustees or managers' see para 665 note 2 ante.

18 Ie by virtue of the Employment Equality (Religion or Belief) Regulations 2003, SI 2003/1660, reg 9A (as added): see para 665 ante.

19 See note 9 supra.

20 See note 12 supra.

21 As to the meaning of 'employer' see para 663 note 1 ante.

22 Employment Equality (Religion or Belief) Regulations 2003, SI 2003/1660, reg 9A(3)(d), Sch 1A para 6 (added by SI 2003/2828).

23 Ie presented under the Employment Equality (Religion or Belief) Regulations 2003, SI 2003/1660, reg 28: see the text and notes 1–13 supra.

24 For these purposes and the purposes of ibid reg 33 (help for persons in obtaining information etc: see para 686 post): (1) when the making of a contract is, by reason of the inclusion of any term, an unlawful act, that act is to be treated as extending throughout the duration of the contract; and (2) any act extending over a period is to be treated as done at the end of that period; and (3) a deliberate omission is to be treated as done when the person in question decided upon it; and in the absence of evidence establishing the contrary a person is to be taken for these purposes to decide upon an omission when he does an act inconsistent with doing the omitted act or, if he has done no such inconsistent act, when the period expires within which he might reasonably have been expected to do the omitted act if it was to be done: reg 34(4).

25 Ie a case to which ibid reg 36(7) (armed forces) applies: see para 689 post.

26 Ibid reg 34(1). As to time limits under the Sex Discrimination Act 1975 see para 416 ante; and as to time limits under the Race Relations Act 1976 see para 502 ante.

27 Ie by the Employment Act 2002 (Dispute Resolution) Regulations 2004, SI 2004/752, reg 15: see EMPLOYMENT vol 16(1B) Reissue) para 594.

28 Employment Equality (Religion or Belief) Regulations 2003, SI 2003/1660, reg 34(1A) (added by SI 2004/752).

29 Employment Equality (Religion or Belief) Regulations 2003, SI 2003/1660, reg 34(3).

30 See note 23 supra.

31 See note 12 supra.

32 Employment Equality (Religion or Belief) Regulations 2003, SI 2003/1660, reg 29(1), (2). See also *Wong v Igen Ltd (Equal Opportunities Commission and others intervening), Emokpae v Chamberlin Solicitors (Equal Opportunities Commission and others intervening), Webster v Brunel University (Equal Opportunities Commission and others intervening)* [2005] EWCA Civ 142, [2005] 3 All ER 812, [2005] ICR 931 (see paras 418, 504 ante); applied in *Mohmed v West Coast Trains Ltd* [2006] All ER (D) 224 (Nov), EAT.

On the true construction of the Employment Equality (Religion or Belief) Regulations 2003, SI 2003/1660, reg 29, a two-stage test is involved. At stage one it is for the employee to prove the facts. He does so only where the 'fact' in question is either admitted or evidence led by the employer is rejected on that point; and those facts have to be viewed in the overall factual matrix as found by the tribunal. The tribunal must disregard any adequate (exculpatory) explanation advanced by the employer at that stage, but it can take into account evidence of an unsatisfactory explanation by the employer to support the employee's case. Once the employee has proved primary facts from which an inference of unlawful discrimination can be drawn, the burden shifts to the employer to provide an explanation untainted by religious belief, failing which the claim will succeed. See *Mohmed v West Coast Trains Ltd* supra (where, on the primary facts found by the tribunal, the Employment Appeal Tribunal held that it was open to the tribunal to conclude that no inference of less favourable treatment could be drawn in circumstances where it was agreed that the employee could maintain his beard at one fist's length, in accordance with his religion, provided it was tidy; no prima facie case of unlawful discrimination had therefore been made out).

684. Remedies on complaints in employment tribunals. Where an employment tribunal finds that a complaint presented to it[1] is well-founded, the tribunal must make such of the following as it considers just and equitable:

(1) an order declaring the rights of the complainant and the respondent in relation to the act[2] to which the complaint relates;

(2) an order requiring the respondent to pay to the complainant compensation[3] of an amount corresponding to any damages he could have been ordered by a county court to pay to the complainant if the complaint had fallen to be dealt with under the provisions relating to the jurisdiction of county courts[4];

(3) a recommendation that the respondent take within a specified period action appearing to the tribunal to be practicable for the purpose of obviating or reducing the adverse effect on the complainant of any act of discrimination[5] or harassment[6] to which the complaint relates[7].

As respects an unlawful act of discrimination consisting of the application of a provision, criterion or practice[8], if the respondent proves that the provision, criterion or practice was not applied with the intention of treating the complainant unfavourably on grounds of religion or belief[9], an order may be made under head (2) above only if the employment tribunal:

(a) makes such order under head (1) above, if any, and such recommendation under head (3) above, if any, as it would have made if it had no power to make an order under head (2) above; and

(b) where it makes an order under head (1) above or a recommendation under head (3) above, or both, considers that it is just and equitable to make an order under head (2) above as well[10].

If without reasonable justification the respondent to a complaint fails to comply with a recommendation made by an employment tribunal under head (3) above, then, if it thinks it just and equitable to do so, the tribunal may increase the amount of compensation required to be paid to the complainant in respect of the complaint by an order made under head (2) above or, if an order under that head was not made, the tribunal may make such an order[11].

The above provisions have effect subject to the following provisions relating to occupational pension schemes[12]. Where:

(i) a member[13] or prospective member[14] of an occupational pension scheme[15] ('the complainant') presents to an employment tribunal[16] a complaint against the trustees or managers[17] of the scheme or an employer[18];

(ii) the complainant is not a pensioner member[19] of the scheme;

(iii) the complaint relates to the terms on which persons[20] become members of the scheme, or the terms on which members of the scheme are treated; and

(iv) the tribunal finds the complaint to be well-founded,

then the employment tribunal may, without prejudice to the generality of its power under head (1) above, make an order declaring that the complainant has a right:

(A)　where the complaint relates to the terms on which persons become members of the scheme, to be admitted to the scheme;

(B)　where the complaint relates to the terms on which members of the scheme are treated, to membership of the scheme without discrimination[21].

Such an order may be made in respect of such period as is specified in the order, but may not be made in respect of any time before 2 December 2003[22]; and it may make such provision as the employment tribunal considers appropriate as to the terms on which, or the capacity in which, the complainant is to enjoy such admission or membership[23]. The employment tribunal may not, however, make an order for compensation under head (2) above, whether in relation to arrears of benefits or otherwise, except for injury to feelings or where without reasonable justification the respondent to a complaint fails to comply with a recommendation[24] made by the tribunal[25].

1　Ie under the Employment Equality (Religion or Belief) Regulations 2003, SI 2003/1660, reg 28: see para 683 ante.
2　As to the meaning of 'act' see para 661 note 3 ante.
3　Where an amount of compensation falls to be awarded under head (2) in the text, the tribunal may include in the award interest on that amount subject to, and in accordance with, the provisions of the Employment Tribunals (Interest on Awards in Discrimination Cases) Regulations 1996, SI 1996/2803 (amended by virtue of the Employment Rights (Dispute Resolution) Act 1998 s 1(2)): Employment Equality (Religion or Belief) Regulations 2003, SI 2003/1660, reg 30(4).
　　As to guidance on the proper level of damages to be awarded in discrimination cases (of all categories) for injury to feelings and other forms of non-pecuniary damage see *Vento v Chief Constable of West Yorkshire Police* [2002] EWCA Civ 1871, [2003] ICR 318, [2003] IRLR 102, [2002] All ER (D) 363 (Dec); and para 414 ante.
4　Ie under the Employment Equality (Religion or Belief) Regulations 2003, SI 2003/1660, reg 31: see para 685 post. An award of compensation under head (2) in the text may be made on a joint and several basis so that each respondent is liable to pay the whole of the award of compensation: see *Way v Crouch* [2005] IRLR 603, EAT; and para 414 note 8 ante.
5　For the meaning of references to discrimination see para 663 note 4 ante.
6　For the meaning of references to harassment see para 663 note 9 ante.
7　Employment Equality (Religion or Belief) Regulations 2003, SI 2003/1660, reg 30(1).
8　Ie an unlawful act of discrimination falling within ibid reg 3(1)(b): see para 660 ante at head (2) in the text.
9　For the meanings of 'religion' and 'belief' see para 660 note 3 ante.
10　Employment Equality (Religion or Belief) Regulations 2003, SI 2003/1660, reg 30(2).
11　Ibid reg 30(3).
12　Ibid reg 30(5) (added by SI 2003/2828).
13　For the meaning of 'member' see para 665 note 5 ante.
14　For the meaning of 'prospective member' see para 665 note 6 ante.
15　For the meaning of 'occupational pension scheme' see para 665 note 3 ante.
16　See note 1 supra.
17　For the meaning of 'trustees or managers' see para 665 note 2 ante.
18　As to the meaning of 'employer' see para 663 note 1 ante.
19　For the meaning of 'pensioner member' see para 665 note 5 ante.
20　As to the meaning of 'person' see para 344 note 3 ante.
21　Employment Equality (Religion or Belief) Regulations 2003, SI 2003/1660, reg 9A(3)(d), Sch 1A para 7(1), (2) (reg 9A, Sch 1A added by SI 2003/2828).
22　Ie the date of the coming into force of the Employment Equality (Religion or Belief) Regulations 2003, SI 2003/1660 (as amended): see para 660 note 1 ante.
23　Ibid Sch 1A para 7(3) (as added: see note 21 supra).
24　Ie by virtue of ibid reg 30(3): see the text and note 11 supra.
25　Ibid Sch 1A para 7(4) (as added: see note 21 supra).

685. Jurisdiction of county courts; time limit, burden of proof and remedies. The following provisions apply to any act[1] of discrimination[2] or harassment[3] which is unlawful by virtue of:

(1)　the provision relating to institutions of further and higher education[4]; or

(2)   where the act arises out of and is closely connected to a relationship between the claimant and the respondent which has come to an end but during the course of which an act of discrimination against, or harassment of, the claimant by the respondent would have been unlawful[5] by virtue of the provision mentioned in head (1) above, the provision relating to relevant relationships[6] which have come to an end[7].

A claim by any person[8] ('the claimant') that another person ('the respondent'):

(a)   has committed against the claimant an act to which this provision applies; or

(b)   is to be treated[9] as having committed against the claimant such an act,

may be made the subject of civil proceedings in like manner as any other claim in tort for breach of statutory duty[10]. Proceedings so brought may be brought only in a county court[11] and must be instituted before the end of the period of six months beginning when the act complained of was done[12]; but a court may nevertheless consider any such claim which is out of time if, in all the circumstances of the case, it considers that it is just and equitable to do so[13]. Damages in respect of an unlawful act to which this provision applies may include compensation for injury to feelings whether or not they include compensation under any other head[14].

Where, on the hearing of the claim, the claimant proves facts from which the court could otherwise conclude in the absence of an adequate explanation that the respondent:

(i)   has committed against the claimant an act to which the above provision applies; or

(ii)   is to be treated[15] as having committed against the claimant such an act,

the court must uphold the claim unless the respondent proves that he did not commit, or, as the case may be, is not to be treated as having committed, that act[16].

1   As to the meaning of 'act' see para 661 note 3 ante.
2   For the meaning of references to discrimination see para 663 note 4 ante.
3   For the meaning of references to harassment see para 663 note 9 ante.
4   Ie the Employment Equality (Religion or Belief) Regulations 2003, SI 2003/1660, reg 20: see para 675 ante.
5   For the purposes of head (2) in the text, reference to an act of discrimination or harassment which would have been unlawful includes, in the case of a relationship which has come to an end before 2 December 2003 (ie the date of the coming into force of the Employment Equality (Religion or Belief) Regulations 2003, SI 2003/1660 (as amended): see para 660 note 1 ante), reference to an act of discrimination or harassment which would, after that date, have been unlawful: reg 31(5).
6   Ie ibid reg 21: see para 676 ante.
7   Ibid reg 31(4).
8   As to the meaning of 'person' see para 344 note 3 ante.
9   Ie by virtue of the Employment Equality (Religion or Belief) Regulations 2003, SI 2003/1660, reg 22 or reg 23: see paras 677–678 ante.
10   Ibid reg 31(1).
11   Ibid reg 31(2)(a).
12   See ibid reg 34(2). As to when the act was done see reg 34(4); and para 683 note 24 ante.
13   Ibid reg 34(3).
14   See ibid reg 31(3). Cf the position under the Employment Rights Act 1996 s 123(1) (as amended) (compensatory award for unfair dismissal: see EMPLOYMENT vol 16(1B) para 690): see *Dunnachie v Kingston upon Hull City Council* [2004] UKHL 36, [2005] 1 AC 226, [2004] 3 All ER 1011, HL.
15   See note 9 supra.
16   Employment Equality (Religion or Belief) Regulations 2003, SI 2003/1660, reg 32(1), (2).

686.   Help for persons in obtaining information etc.   In accordance with the following provisions, a person[1] ('the person aggrieved') who considers he may have been discriminated[2] against, or subjected to harassment[3], in contravention of the Employment Equality (Religion or Belief) Regulations 2003[4], may serve on the respondent[5] to a complaint presented to an employment tribunal[6] or a claim brought in the county court[7] questions in the prescribed form[8] or forms to the like effect with such variation as the circumstances require; and the respondent may if he so wishes reply to such questions by way of the prescribed form[9] or forms to the like effect with such variation as the circumstances require[10].

Where the person aggrieved questions the respondent, whether in accordance with the above provision or not:

(1)   the questions, and any reply by the respondent, whether in accordance with the above provision or not, are, subject to the following provisions, to be admissible as evidence in the proceedings;

(2)   if it appears to the court or tribunal that the respondent deliberately, and without reasonable excuse, omitted to reply within eight weeks of service of the questions or that his reply is evasive or equivocal, the court or tribunal may draw any inference from that fact that it considers it just and equitable to draw, including an inference that he committed an unlawful act[11].

In proceedings before a county court, however, a question is only to be admissible as evidence in pursuance of head (1) above:

(a)   where it was served before those proceedings had been instituted, if it was so served within the period of six months beginning when the act complained of was done[12];

(b)   where it was served when those proceedings had been instituted, if it was served with the leave of, and within a period specified by, the court in question[13],

and in proceedings before an employment tribunal, a question is only to be admissible as evidence in pursuance of head (1) above:

(i)   where it was served before a complaint had been presented to a tribunal, if it was so served within the period of three months beginning when the act complained of was done[14], or, where the period within which a complaint must be presented has been extended[15], within the extended period;

(ii)   where it was served when a complaint had been presented to the tribunal, if it was so served within the period of 21 days beginning with the day on which the complaint was presented, or if it was so served later with leave given, and within a period specified, by a direction of the tribunal[16].

The above provisions are without prejudice to any other enactment or rule of law regulating preliminary matters in proceedings before a county court or employment tribunal, and have effect subject to any enactment or rule of law regulating the admissibility of evidence in such proceedings[17].

Either party may apply to the court to determine whether the question or any reply is admissible under the above provisions[18].

1   As to the meaning of 'person' see para 344 note 3 ante.

2   For the meaning of references to discrimination see para 663 note 4 ante.

3   For the meaning of references to harassment see para 663 note 9 ante.

4   Ie in contravention of the Employment Equality (Religion or Belief) Regulations 2003, SI 2003/1660 (as amended): see para 660 et seq ante.

5   For these purposes, 'respondent' includes a prospective respondent: ibid reg 33(7). A question and any reply to it may be served on the respondent or, as the case may be, on the person aggrieved: (1) by delivering it to him; (2) by sending it by post to him at his usual or last-known residence or place of business; (3) where the person to be served is a body corporate or is a trade union or employers' association within the meaning of the Trade Union and Labour Relations (Consolidation) Act 1992 (see TRADE, INDUSTRY AND INDUSTRIAL RELATIONS vol 47 (2001 Reissue) para 1201), by delivering it to the secretary or clerk of the body, union or association at its registered or principal office or by sending it by post to the secretary or clerk at that office; (4) where the person to be served is acting by a solicitor, by delivering it at, or by sending it by post to, the solicitor's address for service; or (5) where the person to be served is the person aggrieved, by delivering the reply, or by sending it by post, to him at his address for reply as stated by him in the document containing the questions: Employment Equality (Religion or Belief) Regulations 2003, SI 2003/1660, reg 33(5).

6   Ie under ibid reg 28: see para 683 ante.
7   Ie under ibid reg 31: see para 685 ante.
8   For the prescribed form see ibid reg 33(1), Sch 2.
9   For the prescribed form see ibid reg 33(1), Sch 3.
10 Ibid reg 33(1).
11 Ibid reg 33(2). As to the meaning of 'act' see para 661 note 3 ante.
12 As to when the act was done see ibid reg 34(4); and para 683 note 24 ante.
13 Ibid reg 33(3).
14 See note 12 supra.
15 Ie where the Employment Equality (Religion or Belief) Regulations 2003, SI 2003/1660, reg 34(1A) (as added) applies: see para 683 ante.
16 Ibid reg 33(4) (amended by SI 2004/752). See also the Employment Equality (Religion or Belief) Regulations 2003, SI 2003/1660, reg 34(4); and para 683 note 24 ante.
17 Ibid reg 33(6).
18 See *Practice Direction—Proceedings under Enactments relating to Discrimination* paras 4.1(e), 4.2. The provisions of CPR 3.4 (power to strike out a statement of case: see PRACTICE AND PROCEDURE vol 37 (Reissue) para 917) apply to the question and any answer as they apply to a statement of case: *Practice Direction—Proceedings under Enactments relating to Discrimination* para 4.3.

(vi) Supplemental Provisions

687. Validity and revision of contracts. A term of a contract is void where:
(1)   the making of the contract is, by reason of the inclusion of the term, unlawful by virtue of the Employment Equality (Religion or Belief) Regulations 2003[1];
(2)   it is included in furtherance of an act[2] which is unlawful by virtue of those regulations; or
(3)   it provides for the doing of an act which is unlawful by virtue of those regulations[3],
but this does not apply to a term the inclusion of which constitutes, or is in furtherance of, or provides for, unlawful discrimination[4] against, or harassment[5] of, a party to the contract, although the term is unenforceable against that party[6].

A term in a contract which purports to exclude or limit any provision of those regulations is unenforceable by any person[7] in whose favour the term would otherwise operate[8], but this does not apply:
(a)   to a contract settling a complaint[9] falling within the jurisdiction of an employment tribunal[10] where the contract is made with the assistance of a conciliation officer[11];
(b)   to a contract settling such a complaint if the prescribed conditions regulating compromise contracts[12] are satisfied in relation to the contract; or
(c)   to a contract settling a claim falling within the jurisdiction[13] of the county courts[14].

The prescribed conditions regulating compromise contracts are that:
(i)   the contract must be in writing;
(ii)   the contract must relate to the particular complaint;
(iii) the complainant must have received advice from a relevant independent adviser[15] as to the terms and effect of the proposed contract and in particular its effect on his ability to pursue a complaint before an employment tribunal;
(iv)   there must be in force, when the adviser gives the advice, a contract of insurance, or an indemnity provided for members of a profession or professional body, covering the risk of a claim by the complainant in respect of loss arising in consequence of the advice;
(v)   the contract must identify the adviser; and
(vi)   the contract must state that the prescribed conditions regulating compromise contracts are satisfied[16].

On the application of a person interested in a contract which either contains a void term[17] or a term which is unenforceable[18], a county court may make such order as it thinks fit for removing or modifying any term rendered void[19] or removing or modifying any term made unenforceable[20] by the above provisions, but such an order may not be made unless all persons affected have been given notice in writing of the application, except where under rules of court notice may be dispensed with, and those persons have been afforded an opportunity to make representations to the court[21]. Such an order may include provision as respects any period before the making of the order but after 2 December 2003[22]. A person affected by the proposed variation must be made a respondent to the application unless the court orders otherwise[23].

1 Ie the Employment Equality (Religion or Belief) Regulations 2003, SI 2003/1660 (as amended).

2 As to the meaning of 'act' see para 661 note 3 ante.

3 Equality (Religion or Belief) Regulations 2003, SI 2003/1660, reg 35, Sch 4 para 1(1). Schedule 4 para 1(1)–(3) applies whether the contract was entered into before or after 2 December 2003 (i e the date on which the regulations came into force: see para 660 note 1 ante); but, in the case of a contract made before that date, Sch 4 para 1(1)–(3) does not apply in relation to any period before that date: Sch 4 para 1(4).

4 For the meaning of references to discrimination see para 663 note 4 ante.

5 For the meaning of references to harassment see para 663 note 9 ante.

6 Equality (Religion or Belief) Regulations 2003, SI 2003/1660, Sch 4 para 1(2). See also note 3 supra.

7 As to the meaning of 'person' see para 344 note 3 ante.

8 Equality (Religion or Belief) Regulations 2003, SI 2003/1660, Sch 4 para 1(3). See also note 3 supra.

9 An agreement under which the parties agree to submit a dispute to arbitration: (1) is to be regarded for the purposes of ibid Sch 4 para 2(1)(a) and (b) (see heads (a)–(b) in the text) as being a contract settling a complaint if: (a) the dispute is covered by a scheme having effect by virtue of an order under the Trade Union and Labour Relations (Consolidation) Act 1992 s 212A (as added and amended) (see EMPLOYMENT vol 16(1B) (Reissue) para 696); and (b) the agreement is to submit it to arbitration in accordance with the scheme; but (2) is to be regarded as neither being nor including such a contract in any other case: Employment Equality (Religion or Belief) Regulations 2003, SI 2003/1660, Sch 4 para 2(8).

10 Ie a complaint to which ibid reg 28(1) applies: see para 683 ante.

11 Ie within the meaning of the Trade Union and Labour Relations (Consolidation) Act 1992 s 211 (as amended): see TRADE, INDUSTRY AND INDUSTRIAL RELATIONS vol 47 (2001 Reissue) para 1437.

12 Ie the conditions regulating compromise contracts under the Employment Equality (Religion or Belief) Regulations 2003, SI 2003/1660, Sch 4: see heads (i)–(vi) in the text.

13 Ie a claim to which ibid reg 31 applies: see para 685 ante.

14 Ibid Sch 4 para 2(1).

15 A person is a relevant independent adviser for these purposes: (1) if he is a qualified lawyer; (2) if he is an officer, official, employee or member of an independent trade union who has been certified in writing by the trade union as competent to give advice and as authorised to do so on behalf of the trade union; or (3) if he works at an advice centre (whether as an employee or a volunteer) and has been certified in writing by the centre as competent to give advice and as authorised to do so on behalf of the centre (ibid Sch 4 para 2(3)); but a person is not a relevant independent adviser for these purposes in relation to the complainant: (a) if he is, is employed by or is acting in the matter for the other party or a person who is connected with the other party; (b) in the case of a person within head (2) or head (3) supra, if the trade union or advice centre is the other party or a person who is connected with the other party; or (c) in the case of a person within head (3) supra, if the complainant makes a payment for the advice received from him (Sch 4 para 2(4)). In head (1) supra, 'qualified lawyer' means, as respects England and Wales, a barrister (whether in practice as such or employed to give legal advice), a solicitor who holds a practising certificate, or a person other than a barrister or solicitor who is an authorised advocate or authorised litigator (within the meaning of the Courts and Legal Services Act 1990: see BARRISTERS vol 3(1) (2005 Reissue) para 501; SOLICITORS vol 44(1) (Reissue) paras 78–79) (Employment Equality (Religion or Belief) Regulations 2003, SI 2003/1660, Sch 4 para 2(5)(a)); and a person is to be treated as being a qualified lawyer if he is a fellow of the Institute of Legal Executives employed by a solicitors' practice (Sch 4 para 2(5A) (added by SI 2004/2520)). In head (2) supra, 'independent trade union' has the same meaning as in the Trade Union and Labour Relations (Consolidation) Act 1992 (see TRADE, INDUSTRY AND INDUSTRIAL RELATIONS vol 47 (2001 Reissue) para 1014): Employment Equality (Religion or Belief) Regulations 2003, SI 2003/1660, Sch 4 para 2(6). For the purposes of head (a) supra, any two

persons are to be treated as connected if one is a company of which the other (directly or indirectly) has control or if both are companies of which a third person (directly or indirectly) has control: Sch 4 para 2(7).
16 Ibid Sch 4 para 2(2).
17 Ie a contract to which ibid Sch 4 para 1(1) applies: see heads (1)–(3) in the text.
18 Ie a contract to which ibid Sch 4 para 1(2) applies: see the text and notes 4–6 supra.
19 Ie by ibid Sch 4 para 1(1): see the text and notes 1–3 supra.
20 Ie by ibid Sch 4 para 1(2): see the text and notes 4–6 supra.
21 Ibid Sch 4 para 3(1).
22 Ibid Sch 4 para 3(2). As to the significance of 2 December 2003 see note 3 supra.
23 See *Practice Direction—Proceedings under Enactments relating to Discrimination* paras 7.1(f), 7.2.

688. Collective agreements and rules of undertakings. The following provisions apply to:

(1) any term of a collective agreement[1], including an agreement which was not intended, or is presumed not to have been intended, to be a legally enforceable contract;

(2) any rule made by an employer[2] for application to all or any of the persons[3] who are employed by him or who apply to be, or are, considered by him for employment[4];

(3) any rule made by a trade organisation[5] or a qualifications body[6] for application to all or any of its members or prospective members, or all or any of the persons on whom it has conferred professional or trade qualifications[7] or who are seeking the professional or trade qualifications which it has power to confer[8].

Any such term or rule is void where:

(a) the making of the collective agreement is, by reason of the inclusion of the term, unlawful by virtue of the Employment Equality (Religion or Belief) Regulations 2003[9];

(b) the term or rule is included or made in furtherance of an act[10] which is unlawful by virtue of those regulations; or

(c) the term or rule provides for the doing of an act which is unlawful by virtue of those regulations[11],

and this applies whether the agreement was entered into, or the rule made, before or after 2 December 2003[12]; but, in the case of an agreement entered into, or a rule made, before that date, it does not apply in relation to any period before that date[13]. The avoidance by virtue of heads (a) to (c) above of any term or rule which provides for any person to be discriminated[14] against is without prejudice to the following rights, except in so far as they enable any person to require another person to be treated less favourably than himself, namely:

(i) such of the rights of the person to be discriminated against; and

(ii) such of the rights of any person who will be treated more favourably in direct or indirect consequence of the discrimination,

as are conferred by or in respect of a contract made or modified wholly or partly in pursuance of, or by reference to, that term or rule[15].

A person to whom this provision applies[16] may present a complaint to an employment tribunal that a term or rule is void by virtue of the above provisions if he has reason to believe:

(A) that the term or rule may at some future time have effect in relation to him; and

(B) where he alleges that it is void by virtue of head (c) above, that an act for the doing of which it provides may at some such time be done in relation to him, and the act would be unlawful by virtue of the relevant regulations if done in relation to him in present circumstances[17].

When an employment tribunal finds that a complaint so presented to it is well-founded the tribunal must make an order declaring that the term or rule is void[18]; and such an order may include provision as respects any period before the making of the order but after 2 December 2003[19].

1 For these purposes, 'collective agreement' means any agreement relating to one or more of the matters mentioned in the Trade Union and Labour Relations (Consolidation) Act 1992 s 178(2) (meaning of trade dispute: see TRADE, INDUSTRY AND INDUSTRIAL RELATIONS vol 47 (2001 Reissue) para 1301), being an agreement made by or on behalf of one or more employers or one or more organisations of employers or associations of such organisations with one or more organisations of workers or associations of such organisations: Employment Equality (Religion or Belief) Regulations 2003, SI 2003/1660, reg 35, Sch 4 para 10.
2 As to the meaning of 'employer' see para 663 note 1 ante.
3 As to the meaning of 'person' see para 344 note 3 ante.
4 For the meaning of 'employment' see para 663 note 2 ante.
5 Ie within the meaning of the Employment Equality (Religion or Belief) Regulations 2003, SI 2003/1660, reg 15: see para 670 ante.
6 Ie within the meaning of ibid reg 16: see para 671 ante.
7 See note 6 supra.
8 Employment Equality (Religion or Belief) Regulations 2003, SI 2003/1660, Sch 4 para 4(1).
9 Ie by virtue of the Employment Equality (Religion or Belief) Regulations 2003, SI 2003/1660 (as amended).
10 As to the meaning of 'act' see para 661 note 3 ante.
11 Employment Equality (Religion or Belief) Regulations 2003, SI 2003/1660, Sch 4 para 4(2).
12 Ie the date when the Employment Equality (Religion or Belief) Regulations 2003, SI 2003/1660 (as amended) came into force: see para 660 note 1 ante.
13 Ibid Sch 4 para 4(3).
14 For the meaning of references to discrimination see para 663 note 4 ante.
15 Employment Equality (Religion or Belief) Regulations 2003, SI 2003/1660, Sch 4 para 9.
16 In the case of a complaint about: (1) a term of a collective agreement made by or on behalf of an employer, an organisation of employers of which an employer is a member, or an association of such organisations of one of which an employer is a member; or (2) a rule made by an employer within the meaning of ibid Sch 4 para 4(1)(b) (see head (2) in the text), Sch 4 para 5 (see the text and note 17 infra) applies to any person who is, or is genuinely and actively seeking to become, one of his employees: Sch 4 para 6. In the case of a complaint about a rule made by an organisation or body to which Sch 4 para 4(1)(c) applies (see head (3) in the text), Sch 4 para 5 applies to any person: (a) who is, or is genuinely and actively seeking to become, a member of the organisation or body; (b) on whom the organisation or body has conferred a professional or trade qualification (within the meaning of reg 16: see para 671 note 1 ante); or (c) who is genuinely and actively seeking such a professional or trade qualification which the organisation or body has power to confer: Sch 4 para 7.
17 Ibid Sch 4 para 5.
18 Ibid Sch 4 para 8(1).
19 Ibid Sch 4 para 8(2). As to the significance of 2 December 2003 see note 12 supra.

689. Application to the Crown etc. The Employment Equality (Religion or Belief) Regulations 2003[1] apply:

(1) to an act[2] done by or for purposes of a Minister of the Crown[3] or government department; or

(2) to an act done on behalf of the Crown by a statutory body[4], or a person holding a statutory office[5],

as they apply to an act done by a private person[6].

The regulations also apply to:

(a) service for purposes of a Minister of the Crown or government department[7], other than service of a person holding a statutory office;

(b) service on behalf of the Crown for purposes of a person holding a statutory office or purposes of a statutory body; or

(c) service in the armed forces[8],

as they apply to employment[9] by a private person, and so apply as if references to a contract of employment included references to the terms of service[10].

The following provisions apply to any complaint by a person ('the complainant') that another person:

(i) has committed an act of discrimination[11] or harassment[12] against the complainant which is unlawful by virtue of the relevant provisions relating to applicants and employees[13]; or

(ii) is to be treated[14] as having committed such an act of discrimination or harassment against the complainant,

if at the time when the act complained of was done the complainant was serving in the armed forces and the discrimination or harassment in question relates to his service in those forces[15]. A complainant may present such a complaint to an employment tribunal[16] only if:

(A) he has made a complaint in respect of the same matter to an officer under the service redress procedures[17] applicable to him; and

(B) that complaint has not been withdrawn[18],

and for these purposes a complainant is to be treated as having withdrawn his complaint if, having made a complaint to an officer under the service redress procedures applicable to him, he fails to submit that complaint to the Defence Council under those procedures[19]. Where a complaint is so presented to an employment tribunal, the service redress procedures may continue after the complaint is so presented[20].

1   Ie the Employment Equality (Religion or Belief) Regulations 2003, SI 2003/1660 (as amended).

2   As to the meaning of 'act' see para 661 note 3 ante.

3   As to the meaning of 'Minister of the Crown' see para 666 note 4 ante.

4   For these purposes, 'statutory body' means a body set up by or in pursuance of an enactment: Employment Equality (Religion or Belief) Regulations 2003, SI 2003/1660, reg 36(11).

5   For these purposes, 'statutory office' means an office set up by or in pursuance of an enactment: see ibid reg 36(11).

6   Ibid reg 36(1). Regulation 36(1), (2) has effect subject to reg 11 (as amended) (police: see paras 667, 677 ante): reg 36(3).

7   For these purposes, 'service for purposes of a Minister of the Crown or government department' does not include service in any office mentioned in the House of Commons Disqualification Act 1975 Sch 2 (as amended) (ministerial offices: see PARLIAMENT vol 34 (Reissue) para 611): Employment Equality (Religion or Belief) Regulations 2003, SI 2003/1660, reg 36(11).

8   For these purposes, 'armed forces' means any of the naval, military or air forces of the Crown: ibid reg 36(11).

9   For the meaning of 'employment' see para 663 note 2 ante.

10 Employment Equality (Religion or Belief) Regulations 2003, SI 2003/1660, reg 36(2). See also note 6 supra. Regulation 9(3) (meaning of employment and contract work at establishment in Great Britain: see para 663 note 3 ante) has effect in relation to any ship, aircraft or hovercraft belonging to or possessed by Her Majesty in right of the government of the United Kingdom as it has effect in relation to a ship, aircraft or hovercraft specified in reg 9(3)(a) or (b): reg 36(4). For the meaning of 'United Kingdom' see para 325 note 6 ante.

11 For the meaning of references to discrimination see para 663 note 4 ante.

12 For the meaning of references to harassment see para 663 note 9 ante.

13 Ie by virtue of the Employment Equality (Religion or Belief) Regulations 2003, SI 2003/1660, reg 6: see para 663 ante.

14 Ie by virtue of ibid reg 22 or reg 23: see paras 677–678 ante.

15 Ibid reg 36(7). The provisions of the Crown Proceedings Act 1947 Pts II–IV (ss 13–40) (as amended) apply to proceedings against the Crown under the Employment Equality (Religion or Belief) Regulations 2003, SI 2003/1660 (as amended) as they apply to proceedings in England and Wales which by virtue of the Crown Proceedings Act 1947 s 23 (as amended) are treated for the purposes of Pt II (as amended) as civil proceedings by or against the Crown, except that in their application to proceedings under those regulations s 20 (as amended) (removal of proceedings from county court to High Court) does not apply: Employment Equality (Religion or Belief) Regulations 2003, SI 2003/1660, reg 36(6).

16 Ie under ibid reg 28: see para 683 ante.

17 For these purposes, 'the service redress procedures' means the procedures, excluding those which relate to the making of a report on a complaint to Her Majesty, referred to in the Army Act 1955 s 180 (as substituted and amended), the Air Force Act 1955 s 180 (as substituted and amended) and the Naval

Discipline Act 1957 s 130 (as substituted and amended) (see ARMED FORCES vol 2(2) (Reissue) para 314): Employment Equality (Religion or Belief) Regulations 2003, SI 2003/1660, reg 36(11).

18   Ibid reg 36(8).

19   Ibid reg 36(9). As to the Defence Council see ARMED FORCES vol 2(2) (Reissue) para 2; CONSTITUTIONAL LAW AND HUMAN RIGHTS vol 8(2) (Reissue) para 443 et seq.

20   Ibid reg 36(10).

690. Application to House of Commons and House of Lords staff. The Employment Equality (Religion or Belief) Regulations 2003[1] apply:

(1)   to an act[2] done by an employer[3] of a relevant member of the House of Commons staff[4], and to service as such a member, as they apply to an act done by and to service for purposes of a Minister of the Crown[5] or government department, and accordingly apply as if references to a contract of employment[6] included references to the terms of service of such a member[7];

(2)   in relation to employment as a relevant member of the House of Lords staff[8] as they apply in relation to other employment[9].

1   Ie the Employment Equality (Religion or Belief) Regulations 2003, SI 2003/1660 (as amended).

2   As to the meaning of 'act' see para 661 note 3 ante.

3   As to the meaning of 'employer' see para 663 note 1 ante. See also note 4 infra.

4   For these purposes, 'relevant member of the House of Commons staff' means any person:
    (1)   who was appointed by the House of Commons Commission; or
    (2)   who is a member of the Speaker's personal staff,
and the Employment Rights Act 1996 s 195(6)–(12) (as amended) (person to be treated as employer of House of Commons staff: see EMPLOYMENT vol 16(1A) (Reissue) para 136) applies, with any necessary modifications, for the purposes of the Employment Equality (Religion or Belief) Regulations 2003, SI 2003/1660 (as amended): reg 37(2).

5   As to the meaning of 'Minister of the Crown' see para 666 note 4 ante.

6   For the meaning of 'employment' see para 663 note 2 ante.

7   Employment Equality (Religion or Belief) Regulations 2003, SI 2003/1660, reg 37(1).

8   For these purposes, 'relevant member of the House of Lords staff' means any person who is employed under a contract of employment with the Corporate Officer of the House of Lords; and the Employment Rights Act 1996 s 194(7) (continuity of employment: see EMPLOYMENT vol 16(1A) (Reissue) para 135) applies: Employment Equality (Religion or Belief) Regulations 2003, SI 2003/1660, reg 38(2).

9   Ibid reg 38(1).

(2) DISCRIMINATION IN THE PROVISION OF GOODS, FACILITIES, SERVICES AND EDUCATION ETC

(i) In general

691. Introduction. Part 2 of the Equality Act 2006[1] is concerned with unlawful discrimination[2] on the grounds of religion or belief in fields other than that of employment[3]. For these purposes:

(1)   'religion' means any religion;

(2)   'belief' means any religious or philosophical belief;

(3)   a reference to religion includes a reference to lack of religion; and

(4)   a reference to belief includes a reference to lack of belief[4].

Part 2 of the Act applies in relation to anything done in Great Britain[5] and also applies to the provision of:

(a)   facilities for travel on a British ship[6], a British hovercraft[7] or a British aircraft[8]; and

(b)   benefits, facilities or services[9] provided on a British ship, a British hovercraft or a British aircraft[10], but this does not make it unlawful to do anything in or over a country other than the United Kingdom[11], or in or over the territorial waters of a country other than the United Kingdom, for the purpose of complying with a law of the country[12].

1   Ie the Equality Act 2006 Pt 2 (ss 44–80). The provisions of ss 52(6), 70, 71 (see paras 713–714 post) came into force on 18 April 2006: see the Equality Act 2006 (Commencement No 1) Order 2006, SI 2006/1082, art 2(e), (f). The remaining provisions of the Equality Act 2006 Pt 2 came into force on 30 April 2007: see the Equality Act 2006 (Commencement No 2) Order 2007, SI 2007/1092, art 2(b), (c), (d).
2   For the meaning of 'discrimination' see para 692 post.
3   As to discrimination in the employment field see the Employment Equality (Religion or Belief) Regulations 2003, SI 2003/1660 (as amended); and para 660 et seq ante.
4   Equality Act 2006 s 44. Cf the meanings of 'religion' and 'belief' for the purposes of the Employment Equality (Religion or Belief) Regulations 2003, SI 2003/1660 (as amended): see para 660 note 3 ante.
5   Equality Act 2006 s 80(1). For the meaning of 'Great Britain' see para 325 note 6 ante.
6   For these purposes, 'British ship' means a ship which is: (1) registered in Great Britain; or (2) owned by or used for purposes of the Crown: ibid s 80(4).
7   For these purposes, 'British hovercraft' means a hovercraft registered in Great Britain: ibid s 80(4).
8   For these purposes, 'British aircraft' means an aircraft registered in Great Britain: ibid s 80(4).
9   A reference in ibid Pt 2 to providing a service, facility or benefit of any kind includes a reference to facilitating access to the service, facility or benefit (s 76)); but a reference to the provision of facilities or services does not, in so far as it applies to an educational institution, include a reference to educational facilities or educational services provided to students of the institution (s 59(3)).
10 Ibid s 80(2).
11 For the meaning of 'United Kingdom' see para 325 note 6 ante.
12 Equality Act 2006 s 80(5).

692.   Meaning of 'discrimination'.   The Equality Act 2006[1] provides that a person[2] ('A') discriminates against another ('B') for the statutory purposes[3]:

(1)   if on grounds of the religion[4] or belief[5] of B or of any other person[6] except A, whether or not it is also A's religion or belief, A treats B less favourably than he treats or would treat others, in cases where there is no material difference in the relevant circumstances[7];

(2)   if A applies to B a provision, criterion or practice:

   (a)   which he applies or would apply equally to persons not of B's religion or belief;

   (b)   which puts persons of B's religion or belief at a disadvantage compared to some or all others, where there is no material difference in the relevant circumstances;

   (c)   which puts B at a disadvantage compared to some or all persons who are not of his religion or belief, where there is no material difference in the relevant circumstances; and

   (d)   which A cannot reasonably justify by reference to matters other than B's religion or belief[8];

(3)   if A treats B less favourably than he treats or would treat another and does so by reason of the fact that, or by reason of A's knowledge or suspicion that, B:

   (a)   has brought or intended to bring, or intends to bring, proceedings under Part 2 of the Equality Act 2006[9];

   (b)   has given or intended to give, or intends to give, evidence in proceedings under that Part;

   (c)   has provided or intended to provide, or intends to provide, information in connection with proceedings under that Part;

   (d)   has done or intended to do, or intends to do, any other thing under or in connection with that Part; or

   (e)   has alleged or intended to allege, or intends to allege, that a person contravened that Part[10], but head (3) above does not apply where A's treatment of B relates to B's making or intending to make, not in good faith, a false allegation[11].

1 As to the commencement of the Equality Act 2006 Pt 2 (ss 44–80) see para 691 note 1 ante.
2 As to the meaning of 'person' see para 344 note 3 ante.
3 Ie for the purposes of the Equality Act 2006 Pt 2.
4 For the meaning of 'religion' see para 691 ante; and see note 6 infra.
5 For the meaning of 'belief' see para 691 ante; and see note 6 infra.
6 For the purposes of head (1) in the text, a reference to a person's religion or belief includes a reference to a religion or belief to which he is thought to belong or subscribe: Equality Act 2006 s 45(2).
7 Ibid s 45(1).
8 Ibid s 45(3).
9 Ie under ibid Pt 2.
10 Ibid s 45(4).
11 Ibid s 45(5).

693. Goods, facilities and services. The Equality Act 2006[1] provides that it is unlawful for a person[2] ('A') concerned with the provision to the public or a section of the public of goods, facilities or services[3] to discriminate[4] against a person ('B') who seeks to obtain or use those goods, facilities or services:

(1) by refusing[5] to provide B with goods, facilities or services;

(2) by refusing to provide B with goods, facilities or services of a quality which is the same as or similar to the quality of goods, facilities or services that A normally provides to the public, or to a section of the public to which B belongs;

(3) by refusing to provide B with goods, facilities or services in a manner which is the same as or similar to that in which A normally provides goods, facilities or services to the public, or to a section of the public to which B belongs; or

(4) by refusing to provide B with goods, facilities or services on terms which are the same as or similar to the terms on which A normally provides goods, facilities or services to the public, or a section of the public to which B belongs[6].

The above provisions apply, in particular, to:

(a) access to and use of a place which the public are permitted to enter;

(b) accommodation in a hotel, boarding house or similar establishment;

(c) facilities by way of banking or insurance or for grants, loans, credit or finance;

(d) facilities for entertainment, recreation or refreshment;

(e) facilities for transport or travel; and

(f) the services of a profession or trade[7],

but do not apply:

(i) in relation to the provision of goods, facilities or services by a person exercising a public function; and

(ii) to discrimination in relation to the provision of goods, facilities or services if discrimination in relation to that provision:

(A) is unlawful by virtue of another provision of Part 2 of the Equality Act 2006[8] or by virtue of a provision of the Employment Equality (Religion or Belief) Regulations 2003[9]; or

(B) would be unlawful by virtue of another provision of that Part or of those regulations but for an express exception[10].

Where, however, a skill is commonly exercised in different ways in relation to or for the purposes of different religions or beliefs, a person who normally exercises it in relation to or for the purpose of a religion or belief[11] does not contravene the above provisions by insisting on exercising the skill in the way in which he exercises it in relation to or for the purposes of that religion or belief, or, if he reasonably considers it impracticable to exercise the skill in that way in relation to or for the purposes of another religion or belief, by refusing to exercise it in relation to or for the purposes of that other religion or belief[12].

1   As to the commencement of the Equality Act 2006 Pt 2 (ss 44–80) see para 691 note 1 ante.
2   As to the meaning of 'person' see para 344 note 3 ante.
3   For these purposes it is immaterial whether or not a person charges for the provision of goods, facilities or services: Equality Act 2006 s 46(5). For the meaning of references to providing a service, facility or benefit of any kind see para 691 note 9 ante.
4   For the meaning of 'discrimination' see para 692 ante.
5   For the purposes of the Equality Act 2006 Pt 2, a reference to refusal includes a reference to deliberate omission: s 79(2)(b).
6   Ibid s 46(1).
7   Ibid s 46(2).
8   Ie by virtue of another provision of ibid Pt 2.
9   Ie by virtue of a provision of the Employment Equality (Religion or Belief) Regulations 2003, SI 2003/1660 (as amended): see para 660 et seq ante.
10 Equality Act 2006 s 46(4).
11 For the meanings of 'religion' and 'belief' see para 691 ante.
12 Equality Act 2006 s 46(3).

694. Premises. The Equality Act 2006[1] provides that it is unlawful for a person[2]:
(1)   to discriminate[3] against another:
    (a)   in the terms on which he offers to dispose of premises[4] to him;
    (b)   by refusing[5] to dispose of premises to him; or
    (c)   in connection with a list of persons requiring premises[6];
(2)   managing premises to discriminate against an occupier:
    (a)   in the manner in which he provides access to a benefit or facility;
    (b)   by refusing access to a benefit or facility;
    (c)   by evicting him; or
    (d)   by subjecting him to another detriment[7];
(3)   to discriminate against another by refusing permission for the disposal of premises to him[8].

Heads (1) to (3) above do not, however, apply to anything done in relation to the disposal or management of part of premises by a person ('the landlord') if:
(i)   the landlord or a near relative[9] resides, and intends to continue to reside, in another part of the premises;
(ii)   the premises include parts (other than storage areas and means of access) shared by residents of the premises; and
(iii)   the premises are not normally sufficient to accommodate, in the case of premises to be occupied by households, more than two households in addition to that of the landlord or his near relative, or, in the case of premises to be occupied by individuals, more than six individuals in addition to the landlord or his near relative[10],

and heads (1) and (3) above do not apply to the disposal of premises by a person who:
(A)   owns an estate or interest in the premises;
(B)   occupies the whole of the premises;
(C)   does not use the services of an estate agent for the purposes of the disposal; and
(D)   does not arrange for the publication of an advertisement for the purposes of the disposal[11].

1   As to the commencement of the Equality Act 2006 Pt 2 (ss 44–80) see para 691 note 1 ante.
2   As to the meaning of 'person' see para 344 note 3 ante.
3   For the meaning of 'discrimination' see para 692 ante.
4   The Equality Act 2006 s 47 applies only to premises in Great Britain: s 47(4). For the meaning of 'Great Britain' see para 325 note 6 ante.

5   As to the meaning of 'refusal' see para 693 note 5 ante.
6   Equality Act 2006 s 47(1).
7   Ibid s 47(2).
8   Ibid s 47(3).
9   For these purposes, 'near relative' means: (1) spouse or civil partner; (2) parent or grandparent: (3) child or grandchild (whether or not legitimate); (4) the spouse or civil partner of a child or grandchild; (5) brother or sister (whether of full blood or half blood); and (6) any of the relationships listed in heads (1)–(5) supra that arises through marriage, civil partnership or adoption: ibid s 48(2).
10 Ibid s 48(1).
11 Ibid s 48(3).

695. Educational establishments. The Equality Act 2006[1] provides that it is unlawful for the local education authority or governing body of a school maintained by a local education authority, or for the proprietor of an independent school or a special school not maintained by the local education authority[2] to discriminate[3] against a person[4]:

(1)   in the terms on which it offers to admit him as a pupil[5];
(2)   by refusing[6] to accept an application to admit him as a pupil; or
(3)   where he is a pupil of the establishment:
    (a)   in the way in which it affords him access to any benefit, facility or service;
    (b)   by refusing him access to a benefit, facility or service;
    (c)   by excluding him from the establishment; or
    (d)   by subjecting him to any other detriment[7].

Heads (1), (2) and (3)(a) and (3)(b) above do not, however, apply in relation to:

(i)   a foundation or voluntary school with religious character[8]; or
(ii) a school listed in the register of independent schools for England or for Wales if the school's entry in the register records that the school has a religious ethos[9],

nor do head (3)(a), head (3)(b) or head (3)(d) above apply in relation to anything done in connection with the content of the curriculum, or with acts of worship or other religious observance organised by or on behalf of an educational establishment, whether or not forming part of the curriculum[10].

The Secretary of State may by order[11]:

(A)   amend or repeal an exception set out above;
(B)   provide for an additional exception;
(C)   make provision about the construction or application of the statutory provision referring to reasonable justification for a provision, criterion or practice[12] in relation to unlawful discrimination[13] by educational establishments[14].

1   As to the commencement of the Equality Act 2006 Pt 2 (ss 44–80) see para 691 note 1 ante.
2   Ie the responsible body of an educational establishment listed in ibid s 49, Table. In the application of s 49, an expression also used in any of the Education Acts (within the meaning of the Education Act 1996 s 578 (as amended): see EDUCATION vol 15(1) (2006 Reissue) para 1) has the same meaning as in that Act: Equality Act 2006 s 49(2)(a). As to local education authorities see EDUCATION vol 15(1) (2006 Reissue) para 20 et seq. As to maintained schools see EDUCATION vol 15(1) (2006 Reissue) para 94 et seq; as to independent schools see EDUCATION vol 15(1) (2006 Reissue) para 465 et seq; and as to special schools see EDUCATION vol 15(2) (2006 Reissue) para 1027.
3   For the meaning of 'discrimination' see para 692 ante.
4   As to the meaning of 'person' see para 344 note 3 ante.
5   'Pupil' in relation to an establishment includes any person who receives education at the establishment: Equality Act 2006 s 49(2)(b).
6   As to the meaning of 'refusal' see para 693 note 5 ante.
7   Equality Act 2006 s 49(1).
8   Ie a school designated under the School Standards and Framework Act 1998 s 69(3): see EDUCATION vol 15(2) (2006 Reissue) para 951.
9   Equality Act 2006 s 50(1)(a), (b).
10 Ibid s 50(2).

11 Such an order: (1) may include transitional, incidental or consequential provision (including provision amending an enactment); (2) may make provision generally or only in respect of specified cases or circumstances (which may, in particular, be defined by reference to location); (3) may make different provision in respect of different cases or circumstances (which may, in particular, be defined by reference to location); (4) must be made by statutory instrument; (5) may not be made unless the Secretary of State has consulted the National Assembly for Wales and such other persons as he thinks appropriate; and (6) may not be made unless a draft has been laid before and approved by resolution of each House of Parliament: see s 50(4). As to the Secretary of State and the National Assembly for Wales see para 302 ante. At the date at which this volume states the law no such order had been made.

12 Ie the construction or application of ibid s 45(3)(d): see para 692 head (2)(d) ante.

13 Ie in relation to ibid s 49: see the text and notes 1–7 supra.

14 Ibid s 50(3).

696. Local education authorities. The Equality Act 2006[1] provides that it is unlawful for a local education authority in the exercise of its functions to discriminate[2] against a person[3]. This prohibition does not, however, apply to:

(1) the exercise of an authority's statutory functions relating to the provision of schools[4];

(2) the exercise of an authority's functions in relation to transport;

(3) the exercise of an authority's functions under its general statutory responsibility for education[5] in so far as they relate to a matter specified in head (1) or head (2) above; or

(4) the exercise of functions as the responsible body for a specified educational establishment[6].

1 As to the commencement of the Equality Act 2006 Pt 2 (ss 44–80) see para 691 note 1 ante.

2 For the meaning of 'discrimination' see para 692 ante.

3 Equality Act 2006 s 51(1). As to the meaning of 'person' see para 344 note 3 ante.

4 Ie its functions under the Education Act 1996 s 14 (as amended): see EDUCATION vol 15(1) (2006 Reissue) para 26.

5 Ie its functions under ibid s 13 (as amended): see EDUCATION vol 15(1) (2006 Reissue) para 21.

6 Equality Act 2006 s 51(2). The text refers to an establishment listed in the Equality Act 2006 s 49, Table: see para 695 ante.

697. Public authorities generally. The Equality Act 2006[1] provides that it is unlawful for a public authority[2] exercising a function[3] to do any act[4] which constitutes discrimination[5]. This prohibition does not, however, apply to:

(1) the House of Commons;

(2) the House of Lords;

(3) the authorities of either House of Parliament;

(4) the Security Service;

(5) the Secret Intelligence Service;

(6) the Government Communications Headquarters; or

(7) a part of the armed forces of the Crown which is, in accordance with a requirement of the Secretary of State, assisting the Government Communications Headquarters[6].

Nor does it apply to:

(a) the exercise of a judicial function, whether in connection with a court or a tribunal;

(b) anything done on behalf of or on the instructions of a person exercising a judicial function, whether in connection with a court or a tribunal;

(c) preparing, passing or making, confirming, approving or considering an enactment, including legislation made by or by virtue of a Measure of the General Synod of the Church of England;

(d) the making of an instrument by a Minister of the Crown under an enactment;

(e) a decision of any of the following kinds taken in accordance with immigration rules[7] or anything done for the purposes of or in pursuance of a decision of any of those kinds:

    (i) a decision to refuse entry clearance[8] or leave to enter the United Kingdom on the grounds that the exclusion of the person from the United Kingdom is conducive to the public good;

    (ii) a decision to cancel leave to enter or remain in the United Kingdom on the grounds that the exclusion of the person from the United Kingdom is conducive to the public good;

    (iii) a decision to refuse an application to vary leave to enter or remain in the United Kingdom on the grounds that it is undesirable to permit the person to remain in the United Kingdom;

    (iv) a decision to vary leave to enter or remain in the United Kingdom on the grounds that it is undesirable to permit the person to remain in the United Kingdom;

(f) a decision in connection with an application for entry clearance or for leave to enter or remain in the United Kingdom or anything done for the purposes of or in pursuance of a decision of that kind, whether or not the decision is taken in pursuance of a provision of immigration rules, if the decision is taken on the grounds:

    (i) that a person holds an office or position in connection with a religion or belief[9] or provides services in connection with a religion or belief;

    (ii) that a religion or belief is not to be treated in the same way as certain other religions or beliefs; or

    (iii) that the exclusion from the United Kingdom of a person to whom head (i) above applies is conducive to the public good;

(g) a decision taken, or guidance given, by the Secretary of State in connection with a decision of a kind specified in head (e) or head (f) above;

(h) a decision taken in accordance with guidance given by the Secretary of State in connection with a decision of a kind specified in head (e) or head (f) above;

(i) a decision not to institute or continue criminal proceedings, and anything done for the purpose of reaching, or in pursuance of, such a decision;

(j) action in relation to:

    (i) the curriculum of an educational institution;

    (ii) admission to an educational institution which has a religious ethos;

    (iii) acts of worship or other religious observance organised by or on behalf of an educational institution, whether or not forming part of the curriculum;

    (iv) the governing body of an educational institution which has a religious ethos;

    (v) transport to or from an educational institution; or

    (vi) the establishment, alteration or closure of educational institutions;

(k) the exercise of the statutory power to promote well-being[10]; or

(l) action which:

    (i) is unlawful by virtue of another provision of Part 2 of the Equality Act 2006[11] or by virtue of a provision of the Employment Equality (Religion or Belief) Regulations 2003[12]; or

    (ii) would be unlawful by virtue of another provision of Part 2 of the Equality Act 2006 (other than the provision relating to goods, facilities and services[13]), or by virtue of a provision of the Employment Equality (Religion or Belief) Regulations 2003, but for an express exception[14].

In proceedings for a claim for breach of statutory duty where a contravention of these provisions is alleged, there are restrictions on the court's power to grant an injunction; and the court must, in specified circumstances, grant a stay of the proceedings[15]. There are also restrictions on bringing such a claim if the question of the lawfulness of the act could have been raised, and has not been raised, in immigration proceedings[16].

1   As to the commencement of the Equality Act 2006 Pt 2 (ss 44–80) see para 691 note 1 ante.
2   For these purposes, 'public authority' includes any person who has functions of a public nature, subject to ibid s 52(3), (4) (see heads (1)–(7) and (a)–(l) in the text): s 52(2)(a). As to the meaning of 'person' see para 344 note 3 ante.
3   For these purposes, 'function' means function of a public nature: ibid s 52(2)(b).
4   For the purposes of ibid Pt 2, a reference to action includes a reference to deliberate omission: s 79(2)(a).
5   Ibid s 52(1). For the meaning of 'discrimination' see para 692 ante. Section 52 binds the Crown: see para 719 post.
6   Ibid s 52(3). As to the Secretary of State and the National Assembly for Wales see para 302 ante.
7   Ie rules under the Immigration Act 1971 s 3(2): see BRITISH NATIONALITY, IMMIGRATION AND ASYLUM vol 4(2) (2002 Reissue) para 83.
8   The Equality Act 2006 s 52, in so far as it relates to granting entry clearance (within the meaning of the Immigration Acts: see BRITISH NATIONALITY, IMMIGRATION AND ASYLUM vol 4(2) (2002 Reissue) para 96), applies to anything done whether inside or outside the United Kingdom (Equality Act 2006 s 80(3)); but this does not make it unlawful to do anything in or over a country other than the United Kingdom, or in or over the territorial waters of a country other than the United Kingdom, for the purpose of complying with a law of the country (s 80(5)). For the meaning of 'United Kingdom' see para 325 note 6 ante.
9   For the meanings of 'religion' and 'belief' see para 691 ante.
10   Ie the power under the Local Government Act 2000 s 2: see LOCAL GOVERNMENT vol 29(1) (Reissue) para 412.
11   Ie another provision of the Equality Act 2006 Pt 2.
12   Ie a provision of the Employment Equality (Religion or Belief) Regulations 2003, SI 2003/1660 (as amended): see para 660 et seq ante.
13   Ie other than the Equality Act 2006 s 46: see para 693 ante.
14   See ibid s 52(4). This provision makes some reference to Scottish matters, but Scottish matters generally are beyond the scope of this work.
15   See ibid s 52(5); and paras 711–712 post.
16   See ibid s 67; and para 711 post.

(ii) Other Unlawful Acts

698. Discriminatory practices. The Equality Act 2006[1] provides that it is unlawful for a person[2]:

(1)   to operate a practice which would be likely to result in unlawful discrimination[3] if applied to persons of any religion or belief[4];

(2)   to adopt or maintain a practice or arrangement in accordance with which in certain circumstances a practice would be operated in contravention of head (1) above[5].

Proceedings in respect of a contravention of these provisions may be brought only by the Commission for Equality and Human Rights[6] and in accordance with the specified statutory provisions[7].

1   As to the commencement of the Equality Act 2006 Pt 2 (ss 44–80) see para 691 note 1 ante.
2   As to the meaning of 'person' see para 344 note 3 ante.
3   For these purposes, 'unlawful discrimination' means discrimination which is unlawful by virtue of any of the provisions of the Equality Act 2006 ss 46–52 (see para 693 et seq ante): s 53(3). For the meaning of 'discrimination' see para 692 ante.
4   Ibid s 53(1). For the meanings of 'religion' and 'belief' see para 691 ante.
5   Ibid s 53(2).
6   As to the Commission for Equality and Human Rights see para 305 et seq ante.
7   Equality Act 2006 s 53(4). The specified provisions are ss 20–24: see paras 327–331 ante.

699. Discriminatory advertisements. The Equality Act 2006[1] provides that it is unlawful to publish an advertisement, or to cause an advertisement to be published, if it indicates, expressly or impliedly, an intention by any person[2] to discriminate unlawfully[3].

Proceedings in respect of a contravention of this provision may be brought only by the Commission for Equality and Human Rights[4] and in accordance with the specified statutory provision[5]. A person who publishes an advertisement is not, however, to be liable in such proceedings in respect of the publication of the advertisement if he proves that:

(1) he published in reliance on a statement, made by a person causing the advertisement to be published, that the above prohibition would not apply; and

(2) that it was reasonable to rely on that statement[6].

A person commits an offence if he knowingly or recklessly makes a false statement of the kind mentioned in head (1) above, and is liable on summary conviction to a fine[7].

1 As to the commencement of the Equality Act 2006 Pt 2 (ss 44–80) see para 691 note 1 ante.
2 As to the meaning of 'person' see para 344 note 3 ante.
3 Equality Act 2006 s 54(1). The reference in s 54(1) to unlawful discrimination is a reference to discrimination which is unlawful by virtue of any of the provisions of ss 46–52 (see paras 693–697 ante): s 54(2). For the meaning of 'discrimination' see para 692 ante.
4 As to the Commission for Equality and Human Rights see para 305 et seq ante.
5 Equality Act 2006 s 54(3). The specified provision is s 25 (as amended): see para 332 ante.
6 Ibid s 54(4).
7 See ibid s 54(5), (6). The fine referred to in the text is a fine not exceeding level 5 on the standard scale: see s 54(6). As to the standard scale see para 315 note 15 ante.

700. Instructing or causing discrimination. The Equality Act 2006[1] provides that it is unlawful for a person[2]:

(1) to instruct another to unlawfully discriminate[3];

(2) to cause or attempt to cause another to unlawfully discriminate[4];

(3) to induce or attempt to induce[5] another to unlawfully discriminate[6].

Proceedings in respect of a contravention of heads (1) to (3) above may be brought only by the Commission for Equality and Human Rights[7], and in accordance with the specified statutory provision[8].

1 As to the commencement of the Equality Act 2006 Pt 2 (ss 44–80) see para 691 note 1 ante.
2 As to the meaning of 'person' see para 344 note 3 ante.
3 Equality Act 2006 s 55(1). In s 55, a reference to unlawful discrimination is a reference to discrimination which is unlawful by virtue of any of the provisions of ss 46–52 (see paras 693–697 ante): s 55(5). For the meaning of 'discrimination' see para 692 ante.
4 Ibid s 55(2).
5 For these purposes, the inducement may be direct or indirect: ibid s 55(4).
6 Ibid s 55(3).
7 As to the Commission for Equality and Human Rights see para 305 et seq ante.
8 Equality Act 2006 s 55(6). The specified provision is s 25 (prospectively amended): see para 332 ante.

(iii) General Exceptions

701. Complying with statutory requirements. The Equality Act 2006[1] provides that nothing in Part 2 of the Act[2] makes it unlawful to do anything which is necessary, or in so far as it is necessary, for the purpose of complying with:

(1) an Act of Parliament;

(2) legislation made or to be made by a Minister of the Crown, by Order in Council, by the National Assembly for Wales, or by or by virtue of a Measure of the General Synod of the Church of England; or

(3) a condition or requirement imposed by a Minister of the Crown by virtue of anything listed in heads (1) and (2) above[3].

1   As to the commencement of the Equality Act 2006 Pt 2 (ss 44–80) see para 691 note 1 ante.
2   Ie ibid Pt 2.
3   Ibid s 56. As to the National Assembly for Wales see para 302 ante.

702.   Organisations relating to religion or belief.   The following provisions of the Equality Act 2006[1] apply to an organisation the purpose of which is:

(1)   to practice a religion or belief[2];
(2)   to advance a religion or belief;
(3)   to teach the practice or principles of a religion or belief;
(4)   to enable persons of a religion or belief to receive any benefit, or to engage in any activity, within the framework of that religion or belief; or
(5)   to improve relations, or maintain good relations, between persons of different religions or beliefs[3],

but do not apply to an organisation whose sole or main purpose is commercial[4].

Nothing in Part 2 of the Act[5] makes it unlawful:

(a)   for an organisation to which these provisions apply or anyone acting on behalf of or under the auspices of such an organisation:
  (i)   to restrict membership of the organisation;
  (ii)   to restrict participation in activities undertaken by the organisation or on its behalf or under its auspices;
  (iii) to restrict the provision of goods, facilities or services[6] in the course of activities undertaken by the organisation or on its behalf or under its auspices; or
  (iv)   to restrict the use or disposal of premises owned or controlled by the organisation[7];

(b)   for a minister[8]:
  (i)   to restrict participation in activities carried on in the performance of his functions in connection with or in respect of an organisation to which these provisions apply; or
  (ii)   to restrict the provision of goods, facilities or services in the course of activities carried on in the performance of his functions in connection with or in respect of such an organisation[9].

Heads (a) and (b) above, however, permit a restriction only if imposed by reason of or on the grounds of the purpose of the organisation, or in order to avoid causing offence, on grounds of the religion or belief to which the organisation relates, to persons of that religion or belief[10].

1   As to the commencement of the Equality Act 2006 Pt 2 (ss 44–80) see para 691 note 1 ante.
2   For the meanings of 'religion' and 'belief' see para 691 ante.
3   Equality Act 2006 s 57(1).
4   Ibid s 57(2).
5   Ie ibid Pt 2.
6   For the meaning of references to providing a service, facility or benefit of any kind see para 691 note 9 ante.
7   Equality Act 2006 s 57(3).
8   For these purposes, the reference to a minister is a reference to a minister of religion, or other person, who: (1) performs functions in connection with a religion or belief to which an organisation, to which ibid s 57 applies, relates; and (2) holds an office or appointment in, or is accredited, approved or recognised for purposes of, such an organisation: s 57(6).
9   Ibid s 57(4).
10   Ibid s 57(5).

703.   Charities relating to religion or belief.   The Equality Act 2006[1] provides that nothing in Part 2 of the Act[2] makes it unlawful:

(1) for a person[3] to provide benefits[4] only to persons of a particular religion or belief[5], if:

    (a) he acts in pursuance of a charitable instrument[6]; and

    (b) the restriction of benefits to persons of that religion or belief is imposed by reason of or on the grounds of the provisions of the charitable instrument[7];

(2) for the Charity Commission to exercise a function in relation to a charity in a manner which appears to the Commission to be expedient in the interests of the charity, having regard to the provisions of the charitable instrument[8].

1   As to the commencement of the Equality Act 2006 Pt 2 (ss 44–80) see para 691 note 1 ante.
2   Ie ibid Pt 2.
3   As to the meaning of 'person' see para 344 note 3 ante.
4   For the meaning of references to providing a service, facility or benefit of any kind see para 691 note 9 ante.
5   For the meanings of 'religion' and 'belief' see para 691 ante.
6   For these purposes, 'charitable instrument': (1) means an instrument establishing or governing a charity; and (2) includes a charitable instrument made before the commencement of the Equality Act 2006 s 58 (see note 1 supra): s 58(3). 'Charity' has the meaning given by the Charities Act 2006 (see CHARITIES): Equality Act 2006 s 79(1)(a). As from a day to be appointed, the reference to the Charities Act 2006 is amended so as to refer to s 1(1) (see CHARITIES): Equality Act 2006 s 79(1)(a) (prospectively amended by the Charities Act 2006 s 75(1), Sch 8 para 212(1), (3)). At the date at which this volume states the law no such day had been appointed.
7   Equality Act 2006 s 58(1).
8   Ibid s 58(2) (amended by the Charities Act 2006 s 75(1), Sch 8 paras 212(1), (2)).

704. Faith schools. The Equality Act 2006[1] provides that nothing in Part 2 of the Act[2] makes it unlawful for an educational institution, established or conducted for the purpose of providing education relating to, or within the framework of, a specified religion or belief[3], to restrict the provision of goods, facilities or services[4] or to restrict the use or disposal of premises[5]. This provision, however, permits a restriction only if imposed by reason of or on the grounds of the purpose of the institution, or in order to avoid causing offence, on grounds of the religion or belief to which the institution relates, to persons[6] connected with the institution[7].

1   As to the commencement of the Equality Act 2006 Pt 2 (ss 44–80) see para 691 note 1 ante.
2   Ie ibid Pt 2.
3   For the meanings of 'religion' and 'belief' see para 691 ante.
4   For the meaning of references to providing a service, facility or benefit of any kind see para 691 note 9 ante.
5   Equality Act 2006 s 59(1).
6   As to the meaning of 'person' see para 344 note 3 ante.
7   Equality Act 2006 s 59(2).

705. Certain membership requirements for charities. The Equality Act 2006[1] provides that nothing in Part 2 of the Act[2] makes it unlawful for a charity[3] to require members, or persons wishing to become members, to make a statement which asserts or implies membership or acceptance of a religion or belief[4]; but this applies to the imposition of a requirement by a charity only if:

(1) the charity, or an organisation of which the charity is part, first imposed a requirement of that kind before 18 May 2005; and

(2) the charity or organisation has not ceased since that date to impose a requirement of that kind[5].

1   As to the commencement of the Equality Act 2006 Pt 2 (ss 44–80) see para 691 note 1 ante.
2   Ie ibid Pt 2.
3   For the meaning of 'charity' see para 703 note 6 ante.
4   Equality Act 2006 s 60(1). For the meanings of 'religion' and 'belief' see para 691 ante.
5   Ibid s 60(2).

706. Education, training and welfare. The Equality Act 2006[1] provides that nothing in Part 2 of the Act[2] makes it unlawful to do anything by way of:

(1) meeting special needs for education, training or welfare of persons[3] of a religion or belief[4]; or

(2) providing ancillary benefits in connection with meeting the needs mentioned in head (1) above[5].

1 As to the commencement of the Equality Act 2006 Pt 2 (ss 44–80) see para 691 note 1 ante.
2 Ie ibid Pt 2.
3 As to the meaning of 'person' see para 344 note 3 ante.
4 For the meanings of 'religion' and 'belief' see para 691 ante.
5 Equality Act 2006 s 61.

707. Care within the family. The Equality Act 2006[1] provides that nothing in Part 2 of the Act[2] makes it unlawful for a person[3] to take into his home, and treat in the same manner as a member of his family, a person who requires a special degree of care and attention, whether by reason of being a child or an elderly person or otherwise[4].

1 As to the commencement of the Equality Act 2006 Pt 2 (ss 44–80) see para 691 note 1 ante.
2 Ie ibid Pt 2.
3 As to the meaning of 'person' see para 344 note 3 ante.
4 Equality Act 2006 s 62.

708. National security. The Equality Act 2006[1] provides that nothing in Part 2 of the Act[2] makes unlawful anything which is done for, and justified by, the purpose of safeguarding national security[3].

1 As to the commencement of the Equality Act 2006 Pt 2 (ss 44–80) see para 691 note 1 ante.
2 Ie ibid Pt 2 (ss 44–80).
3 Ibid s 63.

709. Secretary of State's power to amend exceptions. The Equality Act 2006[1] provides that the Secretary of State may by order[2] amend Part 2 of the Act[3] so as to:

(1) create an exception to the prohibition of unlawful discrimination by a public authority exercising a public function[4]; or

(2) vary an exception to a prohibition under that Part[5].

Before making such an order the Secretary of State must consult the Commission for Equality and Human Rights[6].

1 As to the commencement of the Equality Act 2006 Pt 2 (ss 44–80) see para 691 note 1 ante.
2 An order under ibid s 64(1): (1) may include transitional, incidental or consequential provision (including provision amending an enactment); (2) may make provision generally or only for specified cases or circumstances; (3) may make different provision for different cases or circumstances; (4) must be made by statutory instrument; and (5) may not be made unless a draft has been laid before and approved by resolution of each House of Parliament: s 64(3). At the date at which this volume states the law no such order had been made. As to the Secretary of State and the National Assembly for Wales see para 302 ante.
3 Ie ibid Pt 2.
4 Ie the prohibition under ibid s 52(1): see para 697 ante.
5 Ibid s 64(1).
6 Ibid s 64(2). As to the Commission for Equality and Human Rights see para 305 et seq ante.

(iv) Enforcement

710. Restriction on proceedings. Except as provided by the Equality Act 2006[1], no proceedings, whether criminal or civil, may be brought against a person[2] on the grounds that an act[3] is unlawful by virtue of Part 2[4] of that Act[5]; but this does not prevent an application for judicial review[6], proceedings under the Immigration Acts[7] or proceedings under the Special Immigration Appeals Commission Act 1997[8].

1   As to the commencement of the Equality Act 2006 Pt 2 (ss 44–80) see para 691 note 1 ante.
2   As to the meaning of 'person' see para 344 note 3 ante.
3   As to the meaning of 'action' see para 697 note 4 ante.
4   Ie the Equality Act 2006 Pt 2.
5   Ibid s 65(1).
6   As to judicial review see ADMINISTRATIVE LAW vol 1(1) (2001 Reissue) para 59 et seq.
7   For the meaning of 'the Immigration Acts' see BRITISH NATIONALITY, IMMIGRATION AND ASYLUM vol 4(2) (2002 Reissue) para 83.
8   Equality Act 2006 s 65(2)(a)–(c). As to proceedings under the Special Immigration Appeals Commission Act 1997 see BRITISH NATIONALITY, IMMIGRATION AND ASYLUM vol 4(2) (2002 Reissue) para 184 et seq.

711.   Claim of unlawful action.   The Equality Act 2006[1] provides that a claim that a person[2] has done anything that is unlawful by virtue of Part 2 of the Act[3] may be brought in a county court by way of proceedings in tort for breach of statutory duty[4]. Proceedings alleging that a local education authority or the responsible body of a specified educational establishment[5] has acted unlawfully by virtue of the relevant statutory provisions[6] may not, however, be brought unless the claimant has given written notice to the Secretary of State[7].

Proceedings under these provisions may be brought only:

(1)   within the period of six months beginning with the date of the act[8], or last act, to which the proceedings relate[9]; or

(2)   with the permission of the court in which the proceedings are brought[10].

In proceedings under these provisions, if the claimant proves facts from which the court could conclude, in the absence of a reasonable alternative explanation, that an act which is unlawful by virtue of Part 2 of the Act has been committed, the court must assume that the act was unlawful unless the respondent proves that it was not[11].

In a claim[12] under these provisions in respect of a contravention of the prohibition of unlawful discrimination by a public authority exercising public functions[13], the court must grant any application to stay the proceedings on the grounds of prejudice to criminal proceedings or to a criminal investigation[14], unless satisfied that the proceedings or investigation will not be prejudiced[15].

Proceedings may not be brought under these provisions alleging that a person has acted unlawfully by virtue of the prohibition of unlawful discrimination by a public authority exercising public functions[16] if the question of the lawfulness of the act could be raised, and has not been raised, in immigration proceedings[17], disregarding the possibility of proceedings brought out of time with permission[18]. If in immigration proceedings a court or tribunal has found that an act was unlawful by virtue of that prohibition, a court hearing proceedings under the above provisions must accept that finding[19].

1   As to the commencement of the Equality Act 2006 Pt 2 (ss 44–80) see para 691 note 1 ante.
2   As to the meaning of 'person' see para 344 note 3 ante.
3   Ie the Equality Act 2006 Pt 2. In s 66(1), the reference to a claim that a person has done an unlawful act includes a reference to a claim that a person is to be treated by virtue of Pt 2 as having done an unlawful act: s 66(4).
4   Ibid s 66(1).
5   Ie the responsible body of an educational establishment listed in ibid s 49, Table: see para 695 ante. As to local education authorities see EDUCATION vol 15(1) (2006 Reissue) para 20 et seq.
6   Ie by virtue of ibid s 49 (see para 695 ante) or s 51 (see para 696 ante).
7   Ibid s 66(2). As to the Secretary of State and the National Assembly for Wales see para 302 ante.
8   As to the meaning of 'action' see para 697 note 4 ante.
9   In relation to immigration proceedings within the meaning of the Equality Act 2006 s 67 (see note 17 infra), the period specified in head (1) in the text begins with the first date on which proceedings under s 66 may be brought: s 69(2).
10   Ibid s 69(1).

11 Ibid s 66(5). See *Wong v Igen Ltd (Equal Opportunities Commission and others intervening), Emokpae v Chamberlin Solicitors (Equal Opportunities Commission and others intervening), Webster v Brunel University (Equal Opportunities Commission and others intervening)* [2005] EWCA Civ 142, [2005] 3 All ER 812, [2005] ICR 931; and paras 418, 504 ante.

12 The statutory wording is 'action'; but see PRACTICE AND PROCEDURE vol 37 (Reissue) para 15.

13 Ie a contravention of the Equality Act 2006 s 52: see para 697 ante.

14 For these purposes, 'criminal investigation' means: (1) an investigation into the commission of an alleged offence; and (2) a decision whether to institute criminal proceedings: ibid s 52(7).

15 Ibid s 52(5)(b).

16 Ie by virtue of ibid s 52: see para 697 ante.

17 For these purposes, 'immigration proceedings' means proceedings under or by virtue of: (1) the Immigration Acts; or (2) the Special Immigration Appeals Commission Act 1997: Equality Act 2006 s 67(3). For the meaning of 'the Immigration Acts' see BRITISH NATIONALITY, IMMIGRATION AND ASYLUM vol 4(2) (2002 Reissue) para 83; and as to proceedings under the Special Immigration Appeals Commission Act 1997 see BRITISH NATIONALITY, IMMIGRATION AND ASYLUM vol 4(2) (2002 Reissue) para 184 et seq.

18 Equality Act 2006 s 67(1).

19 Ibid s 67(2).

712.   Remedies.   The Equality Act 2006[1] provides that where proceedings in tort for breach of statutory duty are brought[2] on a claim that a person[3] has done anything that is unlawful by virtue of Part 2 of the Act[4], a court may, in addition to any remedy available to it in proceedings for tort, grant any remedy that the High Court could grant in proceedings for judicial review[5]. In a claim[6] under the above provisions in respect of a contravention of the prohibition of unlawful discrimination by a public authority exercising public functions[7], the court may not, however, grant an injunction unless satisfied that it will not prejudice criminal proceedings or a criminal investigation[8].

A court may award damages by way of compensation for injury to feelings, whether or not other damages are also awarded[9]. A court may not, however, award damages in proceedings in respect of an act that is unlawful by virtue of the application of a provision, criterion or practice[10] if the respondent proves that there was no intention to treat the claimant unfavourably on grounds of religion or belief[11].

1   As to the commencement of the Equality Act 2006 Pt 2 (ss 44–80) see para 691 note 1 ante.

2   Ie proceedings under ibid s 66: see para 711 ante.

3   As to the meaning of 'person' see para 344 note 3 ante.

4   Ie the Equality Act 2006 Pt 2.

5   See ibid s 68(1), (2).

6   The statutory wording is 'action'; but see PRACTICE AND PROCEDURE vol 37 (Reissue) para 15.

7   Ie a contravention of the Equality Act 2006 s 52: see para 697 ante.

8   Ibid ss 52(5)(a), 68(6). For the meaning of 'criminal investigation' for these purposes see para 711 note 14 ante.

9   Ibid s 68(4). As to guidance on the proper level of damages to be awarded in discrimination cases (of all categories) for injury to feelings and other forms of non-pecuniary damage see *Vento v Chief Constable of West Yorkshire Police* [2002] EWCA Civ 1871, [2003] ICR 318, [2003] IRLR 102, [2002] All ER (D) 363 (Dec); and paras 414, 499 ante.

10 Ie by virtue of the Equality Act 2006 s 45(3): see para 692 ante.

11 Ibid s 68(3). For the meanings of 'religion' and 'belief' see para 691 ante.

713.   Information.   The Equality Act 2006[1] provides that the Secretary of State must by order[2] prescribe:

(1)   forms by which a claimant[3] or potential claimant[4] may question the respondent or a potential respondent[5] about the reasons for an action[6] or about any matter that is or may be relevant; and

(2)   forms by which a respondent or potential respondent may reply, if he wishes[7].

A claimant's or potential claimant's questions, and a respondent or potential respondent's replies, in each case whether or not put by a prescribed form, are to be admissible as evidence in proceedings in respect of the act to which the questions relate if, and only if, the questions are put:

(a) within the period of six months beginning with the date of the act, or last act, to which they relate[8]; and

(b) in such manner as the Secretary of State may prescribe by order[9].

A court may draw an inference from:

(i) a failure to reply to a claimant's or potential claimant's questions, whether or not put by a prescribed form, within the period of eight weeks beginning with the date of receipt; or

(ii) an evasive or equivocal reply to a claimant's or potential claimant's questions, whether or not put by a prescribed form[10],

but this does not apply in relation to a reply, or a failure to reply, to a question in connection with an alleged contravention of the prohibition of unlawful discrimination by a public authority exercising public functions[11]:

(A) if the respondent or potential respondent reasonably asserts that to have replied differently or at all might have prejudiced criminal proceedings or a criminal investigation[12];

(B) if the respondent or potential respondent reasonably asserts that to have replied differently or at all would have revealed the reason for not instituting or not continuing criminal proceedings;

(C) where the reply is of a kind specified for these purposes by order[13] of the Secretary of State;

(D) where the reply is given in circumstances specified for these purposes by order of the Secretary of State; or

(E) where the failure occurs in circumstances specified for these purposes by order of the Secretary of State[14].

1   As to the commencement of the Equality Act 2006 Pt 2 (ss 44–80) see para 691 note 1 ante.

2   See note 7 infra. An order under ibid s 70 must be made by statutory instrument and is subject to annulment in pursuance of a resolution of either House of Parliament: s 70(7). As to the Secretary of State and the National Assembly for Wales see para 302 ante.

3   For these purposes, a reference to a claimant is a reference to a person who has brought proceedings under ibid Pt 2: s 70(1)(a). As to the meaning of 'person' see para 344 note 3 ante.

4   For these purposes, a reference to a potential claimant is a reference to a person who: (1) thinks he may have been the subject of an act that is unlawful by virtue of ibid Pt 2; and (2) wishes to consider whether to bring proceedings under Pt 2: s 70(1)(b).

5   For these purposes, a person questioned by a potential claimant for the purpose of considering whether to bring proceedings is referred to as a potential respondent: ibid s 70(1)(c).

6   As to the meaning of 'action' see para 697 note 4 ante.

7   Equality Act 2006 s 70(2). As to the order that has been made see the Religion or Belief (Questions and Replies) Order 2007, SI 2007/1038.

8   The Secretary of State may by order amend the Equality Act 2006 s 70(3)(a) (see head (a) in the text) so as to substitute a new period for that specified: s 70(5). At the date at which this volume states the law no such order had been made.

9   Ibid s 70(3). At the date at which this volume states the law no such order had been made.

10   Ibid s 70(4).

11   Ie a contravention of ibid s 52: see para 697 ante.

12   For the meaning of 'criminal investigation' for these purposes see para 711 note 14 ante.

13   An order under the Equality Act 2006 s 52(6)(c)–(e) (see heads (C)–(E) in the text): (1) may include transitional or incidental provision; (2) may make provision generally or only for specified cases or circumstances; (3) may make different provision for different cases or circumstances; (4) must be made by statutory instrument; and (5) is subject to annulment in pursuance of a resolution of either House of Parliament: s 52(8).

14   Ibid ss 52(6), 70(8).

714.　National security. The Equality Act 2006[1] provides that rules of court may make provision for enabling a county court in which a claim for breach of statutory duty under the relevant provision of the Act is brought[2], where the court considers it expedient in the interests of national security:

(1)　to exclude from all or part of the proceedings the claimant, the claimant's representatives and any assessors;

(2)　to permit a claimant or representative who has been excluded to make a statement to the court before the commencement of the proceedings, or the part of the proceedings, from which he is excluded;

(3)　to take steps to keep secret all or part of the reasons for the court's decision in the proceedings[3].

The Attorney General may appoint a person to represent the interests of a claimant in, or in any part of, proceedings from which the claimant or his representatives are excluded by virtue of the above provision[4]. A person may be so appointed only if he has a general qualification[5] within the meaning of the Courts and Legal Services Act 1990[6]; and a person so appointed is not to be responsible to the person whose interests he is appointed to represent[7].

1　As to the commencement of the Equality Act 2006 Pt 2 (ss 44–80) see para 691 note 1 ante.
2　Ie in which a claim under ibid s 66 is brought: see para 711 ante.
3　Ibid s 71(1). See further *Practice Direction—Proceedings under Enactments relating to Discrimination* para 5.
4　Equality Act 2006 s 71(2).
5　Ie within the meaning of the Courts and Legal Services Act 1990 s 71 (as amended): see SOLICITORS vol 44(1) (Reissue) para 91.
6　Equality Act 2006 s 71(3).
7　Ibid s 71(4).

715.　Validity and revision of contracts. The Equality Act 2006[1] provides that a term of a contract is void where:

(1)　its inclusion renders the making of the contract unlawful by virtue of Part 2 of the Act[2];

(2)　it is included in furtherance of an act[3] which is unlawful by virtue of that Part; or

(3)　it provides for the doing of an act which would be unlawful by virtue of that Part[4],

but this does not apply to a term the inclusion of which constitutes, or is in furtherance of, or provides for, unlawful discrimination[5] against a party to the contract, although the term is unenforceable against that party[6].

A term in a contract which purports to exclude or limit a provision of Part 2 of the Act is unenforceable by a person[7] in whose favour the term would otherwise operate[8]; but this does not apply to a contract settling a claim[9] for breach of statutory duty[10].

On the application of a person interested in a contract to which heads (1) to (3) above apply, a county court may make an order for removing or modifying a term made unenforceable by those heads; but an order may not be made unless all persons affected have been given notice of the application, except where notice is dispensed with in accordance with rules of court, and those persons have been afforded an opportunity to make representations to the court[11]. Such an order may include provision in respect of a period before the making of the order[12]. A person affected by the proposed variation must be made a respondent to the application unless the court orders otherwise[13].

1　As to the commencement of the Equality Act 2006 Pt 2 (ss 44–80) see para 691 note 1 ante.
2　Ie by virtue of ibid Pt 2.
3　As to the meaning of 'action' see para 697 note 4 ante.
4　Equality Act 2006 s 72(1).

5   For the meaning of 'discrimination' see para 692 ante.

6   Equality Act 2006 s 72(1).

7   As to the meaning of 'person' see para 344 note 3 ante.

8   Equality Act 2006 s 72(3).

9   Ie a claim under ibid s 66: see para 711 ante.

10 Ibid s 72(4).

11 Ibid s 72(5).

12 Ibid s 72(6).

13 See *Practice Direction—Proceedings under Enactments relating to Discrimination* paras 7.1(d), 7.2.

(v) General and Supplemental Matters

716. Aiding unlawful acts. The Equality Act 2006[1] provides that it is unlawful knowingly to help another person[2], whether or not as his employee or agent, to do anything which is unlawful under Part 2[3] of the Act[4]. A person commits an offence if he knowingly or recklessly makes a false statement, in connection with assistance sought from another, that a proposed act[5] is not unlawful under that Part, and such a person is liable on summary conviction to a fine[6].

1   As to the commencement of the Equality Act 2006 Pt 2 (ss 44–80) see para 691 note 1 ante.

2   As to the meaning of 'person' see para 344 note 3 ante.

3   Ie by virtue of the Equality Act 2006 Pt 2.

4   Ibid s 73(1). As to aiding discrimination under the Sex Discrimination Act 1975 see para 392 ante; and as to aiding discrimination under the Race Relations Act 1976 see para 477 ante.

5   As to the meaning of 'action' see para 697 note 4 ante.

6   See the Equality Act 2006 s 73(2), (3). The fine referred to in the text is a fine not exceeding level 5 on the standard scale: see s 73(3). As to the standard scale see para 315 note 15 ante.

717. Employers' and principals' liability. The Equality Act 2006[1] provides that anything done by a person[2]:

(1)   in the course of his employment[3] is to be treated for the purposes of Part 2 of the Act[4] as done by the employer as well as by the person[5];

(2)   as agent for another is to be treated for the purposes of that Part as done by the principal as well as by the agent[6],

and it is immaterial for these purposes whether an employer or principal knows about or approves of an act[7]. These provisions do not, however, apply to the commission of an offence under the statutory provisions[8] prohibiting discriminatory advertisements[9].

In proceedings under Part 2 of the Act against a person in respect of an act alleged to have been done by his employee, it is a defence for the employer to provide that he took such steps as were reasonably practicable to prevent the employee from doing the act, or from doing acts of that kind in the course of his employment[10].

1   As to the commencement of the Equality Act 2006 Pt 2 (ss 44–80) see para 691 note 1 ante.

2   As to the meaning of 'person' see para 344 note 3 ante.

3   As to employment in the police force see para 718 post.

4   Ie by virtue of the Equality Act 2006 Pt 2.

5   Ibid s 74(1). See *Jones v Tower Boot Co Ltd* [1997] 2 All ER 406, [1997] IRLR 168, CA (a case under the Race Relations Act 1976); and para 476 ante. As to the liability of employers and principals under the Sex Discrimination Act 1975 see para 391 ante; and as to their liability under the Race Relations Act 1976 see para 476 ante.

6   Equality Act 2006 s 74(2).

7   Ibid s 74(3).

8   Ie under ibid s 54: see para 699 ante.

9   Ibid s 74(5).

10 Ibid s 74(4).

718. Application to the police. The Equality Act 2006[1] provides that a person[2] who is:

(1)   a constable who is a member of a police force maintained under the Police Act 1996;

(2)   a special constable appointed for a police area in accordance with the Police Act 1996; or

(3)   a person appointed as a police cadet in accordance with thePolice Act 1996[3],

is to be treated for the purposes of Part 2 of the Equality Act 2006[4] as the employee of his chief officer of police; and anything done by the person in the performance or purported performance of his functions is to be treated as done in the course of that employment[5].

There must be paid out of the police fund:

(a)   compensation, costs or expenses awarded against a chief officer of police in proceedings brought against him under Part 2 of the Equality Act 2006;

(b)   costs or expenses incurred by a chief officer of police in proceedings brought against him under that Part so far as not recovered in the proceedings;

(c)   sums required by a chief officer of police for the settlement of a claim made against him under that Part if the settlement is approved by the police authority[6],

and a police authority may pay out of the police fund:

(i)   damages or costs awarded in proceedings under that Part against a person under the direction and control of the chief officer of police;

(ii)   costs incurred and not recovered by such a person in such proceedings;

(iii) sums required in connection with the settlement of a claim that has or might have given rise to such proceedings[7].

1   As to the commencement of the Equality Act 2006 Pt 2 (ss 44–80) see para 691 note 1 ante.
2   As to the meaning of 'person' see para 344 note 3 ante.
3   As to police forces maintained under the Police Act 1996 see POLICE vol 36(1) (Reissue) para 313 et seq; as to constables see POLICE vol 36(1) (Reissue) para 201 et seq; as to special constables see POLICE vol 36(1) (Reissue) para 208 et seq; and as to police cadets see POLICE vol 36(1) (Reissue) para 213 et seq.
4   Ie for the purposes of the Equality Act 2006 Pt 2.
5   See ibid s 75(1), (2).
6   Ibid s 75(3).
7   Ibid s 75(4).

719.   Application to the Crown.   The Equality Act 2006[1] provides that the prohibition on unlawful discrimination by a public authority exercising public functions[2] binds the Crown[3]; and the remainder of Part 2 of the Equality Act 2006[4] applies to an act[5] done on behalf of the Crown as it applies to an act done by a private person[6]. For these purposes an act is done on behalf of the Crown if, and only if, done:

(1)   by or on behalf of a Minister of the Crown;

(2)   by a government department;

(3)   by a body established by an enactment acting on behalf of the Crown;

(4)   by or on behalf of the holder of an office established by an enactment acting on behalf of the Crown[7].

1   As to the commencement of the Equality Act 2006 Pt 2 (ss 44–80) see para 691 note 1 ante.
2   Ie ibid s 52: see para 697 ante.
3   Ibid s 78(1).
4   Ie ibid ss 44–51, 53–80: see para 691 et seq ante.
5   As to the meaning of 'action' see para 697 note 4 ante.
6   Equality Act 2006 s 78(2). As to the meaning of 'person' see para 344 note 3 ante. The provisions of the Crown Proceedings Act 1947 Pts II–IV (ss 13–40) (as amended) apply to proceedings against the Crown under the Equality Act 2006 Pt 2 as they apply to proceedings in England and Wales which by virtue of the Crown Proceedings Act 1947 s 23 (as amended) are treated for the purposes of Pt II of that Act as

civil proceedings by or against the Crown; but s 20 (as amended) (removal of proceedings from county court to High Court) does not apply to proceedings under the Equality Act 2006 Pt 2: s 78(4).

7   Ibid s 78(3)(a), (c)–(e). Section 78(3)(b) refers to Scottish matters, but Scottish matters generally are beyond the scope of this work.

(3) INCITEMENT TO RELIGIOUS HATRED AND RELIGIOUSLY AGGRAVATED OFFENCES

720. Criminal offences of incitement of hatred against persons on religious grounds. As from a day or days to be appointed, the provisions in Part IIIA of the Public Order Act 1986 have effect[1]. They set out criminal offences of incitement to hatred against persons on religious grounds[2]. It will be an offence to use threatening words or behaviour or to publish or distribute any such written material with the intention of stirring up religious hatred[3]. It will also be an offence to give a public performance of a play[4], to distribute, show or play a recording[5] or to broadcast a programme or include a programme in a programme service[6] which has or is likely to have such an effect. The possession of religiously inflammatory material with a view to displaying, publishing, distributing, showing, playing, broadcasting or including it in a programme service for the purpose of stirring up racial hatred will also be an offence[7]. Any religiously inflammatory material may be ordered to be forfeited[8]. These provisions are dealt with elsewhere in this work[9].

1   See the Public Order Act 1986 Pt IIIA (ss 29A–29N) (added by the Racial and Religious Hatred Act 2006 s 1, Schedule); and CRIMINAL LAW, EVIDENCE AND PROCEDURE vol 11(1) (2006 Reissue) para 569 et seq. These provisions are subject to the Public Order Act 1986 s 29J (as added) in regard to freedom of expression: see CRIMINAL LAW, EVIDENCE AND PROCEDURE vol 11(1) (2006 Reissue) para 576. The provisions of the Public Order Act 1986 Pt IIIA (as added) are to be brought into force as from a day to be appointed by order made by the Secretary of State under the Racial and Religious Hatred Act 2006 s 3(2). At the date at which this volume states the law no such day or days had been appointed. As to the Secretary of State and the National Assembly for Wales see para 302 ante.
      As to offences under the Public Order Act 1986 relating to incitement of racial hatred see para 505 ante.
2   'Religious hatred' means hatred against a group of persons defined by reference to religious belief or lack of religious belief: see ibid ss 29A, 29N (both as added: see note 1 supra).
3   See ibid ss 29B, 29C (both as added); and CRIMINAL LAW, EVIDENCE AND PROCEDURE vol 11(1) (2006 Reissue) paras 569–570.
4   See ibid s 29D (as added); and CRIMINAL LAW, EVIDENCE AND PROCEDURE vol 11(1) (2006 Reissue) para 571.
5   See ibid s 29E (as added); and CRIMINAL LAW, EVIDENCE AND PROCEDURE vol 11(1) (2006 Reissue) para 572.
6   See ibid s 29F (as added); and CRIMINAL LAW, EVIDENCE AND PROCEDURE vol 11(1) (2006 Reissue) para 573.
7   See ibid s 29G (as added); and CRIMINAL LAW, EVIDENCE AND PROCEDURE vol 11(1) (2006 Reissue) para 574. Powers of entry and search may be given to a constable if there are reasonable grounds for suspecting that a person has materials in contravention of s 29G (as added): see s 29H (as added); and CRIMINAL LAW, EVIDENCE AND PROCEDURE vol 11(1) (2006 Reissue) para 575.
8   See ibid s 29I (as added); and CRIMINAL LAW, EVIDENCE AND PROCEDURE vol 11(1) (2006 Reissue) para 575.
9   See CRIMINAL LAW, EVIDENCE AND PROCEDURE vol 11(1) (2006 Reissue) para 569 et seq.

721. Religiously aggravated offences. The Crime and Disorder Act 1998 contains, among other things, a number of religiously aggravated offences[1]. In particular, it includes offences of religiously aggravated assaults[2], religiously aggravated criminal damage[3], religiously aggravated public order offences[4] and religiously aggravated harassment[5]. These offences are dealt with elsewhere in this work[6].

1   See the Crime and Disorder Act 1998 ss 28–32 (as amended); and CRIMINAL LAW, EVIDENCE AND PROCEDURE vol 11(1) (2006 Reissue) paras 154–156, 335, 561. These provisions also apply in regard to racially aggravated offences: see para 506 ante.

2   See ibid s 29 (as amended); and CRIMINAL LAW, EVIDENCE AND PROCEDURE vol 11(1) (2006 Reissue) para 155.

3   See ibid s 30 (as amended); and CRIMINAL LAW, EVIDENCE AND PROCEDURE vol 11(1) (2006 Reissue) para 335.

4   See ibid s 31 (as amended); and CRIMINAL LAW, EVIDENCE AND PROCEDURE vol 11(1) (2006 Reissue) para 561.

5   See ibid s 32 (as amended); and CRIMINAL LAW, EVIDENCE AND PROCEDURE vol 11(1) (2006 Reissue) para 156.

6   See CRIMINAL LAW, EVIDENCE AND PROCEDURE vol 11(1) (2006 Reissue) paras 154–156, 335, 561.

7. SEXUAL ORIENTATION DISCRIMINATION

(1) DISCRIMINATION IN THE EMPLOYMENT FIELD

(i) In general

722. Discrimination on grounds of sexual orientation. For the purposes of the Employment Equality (Sexual Orientation) Regulations 2003[1], a person[2] ('A') discriminates against another person ('B') if:

(1) on grounds of sexual orientation[3], A treats B less favourably than he treats or would treat other persons; or

(2) A applies to B a provision, criterion or practice which he applies or would apply equally to persons not of the same sexual orientation as B, but:

    (a) which puts or would put persons of the same sexual orientation as B at a particular disadvantage when compared with other persons;

    (b) which puts B at that disadvantage; and

    (c) which A cannot show to be a proportionate means of achieving a legitimate aim[4].

A comparison of B's case with that of another person under the above provisions must be such that the relevant circumstances in the one case are the same, or not materially different, in the other[5]; and for these purposes, in a comparison of B's case with that of another person the fact that one of the persons, whether or not B, is a civil partner while the other is married is not to be treated as a material difference between their respective circumstances[6].

1 Ie for the purposes of the Employment Equality (Sexual Orientation) Regulations 2003, SI 2003/1661 (as amended). The regulations came into force on 1 December 2003 (reg 1(1)); and do not extend to Northern Ireland (reg 1(2)). They are made by the Secretary of State under the European Communities Act 1972 s 2(2) and implement the relevant provisions of EC Council Directive 2000/78 (OJ L303, 2.12.2000, p 16) establishing a general framework for equal treatment in employment and occupation (the 'EC Framework Employment Directive'): see para 508 ante. As to the regulations that apply in fields other than employment see the Equality Act (Sexual Orientation) Regulations 2007, SI 2007/1263; and para 753 post. As to the Secretary of State and the National Assembly for Wales see para 302 ante.

2 As to the meaning of 'person' see para 344 note 3 ante.

3 For these purposes, 'sexual orientation' means a sexual orientation towards: (1) persons of the same sex; (2) persons of the opposite sex; or (3) persons of the same sex and of the opposite sex: Employment Equality (Sexual Orientation) Regulations 2003, SI 2003/1661, reg 2(1).

4 Ibid reg 3(1). As to direct and indirect discrimination under the Sex Discrimination Act 1975 see paras 344, 351, 355 ante; and as to direct and indirect discrimination under the Race Relations Act 1976 see paras 439–440 ante.

5 Employment Equality (Sexual Orientation) Regulations 2003, SI 2003/1661, reg 3(2).

6 Ibid reg 3(3) (added by SI 2005/2114).

723. Discrimination by way of victimisation. For the purposes of the Employment Equality (Sexual Orientation) Regulations 2003[1], a person[2] ('A') discriminates against another person ('B') if he treats B less favourably than he treats or would treat other persons in the same circumstances, and does so by reason that B has:

(1) brought proceedings against A or any other person under those regulations;

(2) given evidence or information in connection with proceedings brought by any person against A or any other person under those regulations;

(3) otherwise done anything under or by reference to those regulations in relation to A or any other person; or

(4) alleged that A or any other person has committed an act[3] which, whether or not the allegation so states, would amount to a contravention of those regulations,

or by reason that A knows that B intends to do any of those things, or suspects that B has done or intends to do any of them[4]. This does not, however, apply to treatment of B by reason of any allegation made by him, or evidence or information given by him, if the allegation, evidence or information was false and not made or, as the case may be, given in good faith[5].

1   Ie for the purposes of the Employment Equality (Sexual Orientation) Regulations 2003, SI 2003/1661 (as amended).
2   As to the meaning of 'person' see para 344 note 3 ante.
3   For these purposes, 'act' includes a deliberate omission: Employment Equality (Sexual Orientation) Regulations 2003, SI 2003/1661, reg 2(3).
4   Ibid reg 4(1). As to victimisation under the Sex Discrimination Act 1975 see para 358 ante; and as to victimisation under the Race Relations Act 1976 see para 442 ante.
5   Employment Equality (Sexual Orientation) Regulations 2003, SI 2003/1661, reg 4(2).

724.   Harassment on grounds of sexual orientation.   For the purposes of the Employment Equality (Sexual Orientation) Regulations 2003[1], a person[2] ('A') subjects another person ('B') to harassment where, on grounds of sexual orientation[3], A engages in unwanted conduct which has the purpose or effect of:

(1)   violating B's dignity; or
(2)   creating an intimidating, hostile, degrading, humiliating or offensive environment for B[4].

Conduct is to be regarded as having the effect specified in head (1) or head (2) above only if, having regard to all the circumstances, including in particular the perception of B, it should reasonably be considered as having that effect[5].

1   Ie for the purposes of the Employment Equality (Sexual Orientation) Regulations 2003, SI 2003/1661 (as amended).
2   As to the meaning of 'person' see para 344 note 3 ante.
3   For the meaning of 'sexual orientation' see para 722 note 3 ante.
4   Employment Equality (Sexual Orientation) Regulations 2003, SI 2003/1661, reg 5(1). Cf harassment under the Sex Discrimination Act 1975 (see para 347 ante) and under the Race Relations Act 1976 (see para 444 ante).
5   Employment Equality (Sexual Orientation) Regulations 2003, SI 2003/1661, reg 5(2).

(ii)   Discrimination in Employment and Vocational Training

725.   Unlawful discrimination against applicants and employees; exception for genuine occupational requirement.   It is unlawful for an employer[1]:

(1)   in relation to employment[2] by him at an establishment in Great Britain[3], to discriminate[4] against a person:
    (a)   in the arrangements he makes for the purpose of determining to whom he should offer employment;
    (b)   in the terms on which he offers that person employment; or
    (c)   by refusing to offer, or deliberately not offering, him employment[5];
(2)   in relation to a person whom he employs at an establishment in Great Britain, to discriminate against that person:
    (a)   in the terms of employment which he affords him;
    (b)   in the opportunities which he affords him for promotion, transfer, training, or receiving any other benefit[6];
    (c)   by refusing to afford him, or deliberately not affording him, any such opportunity; or
    (d)   by dismissing him[7], or subjecting him to any other detriment[8];
(3)   in relation to employment by him at an establishment in Great Britain, to subject to harassment[9] a person whom he employs or who has applied to him for employment[10].

Head (2) above does not apply to benefits of any description if the employer is concerned with the provision, for payment or not, of benefits of that description to the public, or to a section of the public which includes the employee in question, unless:

(i) that provision differs in a material respect from the provision of the benefits by the employer to his employees; or

(ii) the provision of the benefits to the employee in question is regulated by his contract of employment; or

(iii) the benefits relate to training[11].

In relation to discrimination on grounds of sexual orientation[12], however:

(A) neither head (1)(a) nor head (1)(c) above applies to any employment;

(B) neither head (2)(b) nor head (2)(c) above applies to promotion or transfer to, or training for, any employment; and

(C) head (2)(d) above does not apply to dismissal from any employment,

where either of the specified exceptions[13] applies[14]. The first such exception applies where, having regard to the nature of the employment or the context in which it is carried out, being of a particular sexual orientation is a genuine and determining occupational requirement, it is proportionate to apply that requirement in the particular case, and either the person to whom that requirement is applied does not meet it or the employer is not satisfied, and in all the circumstances it is reasonable for him not to be satisfied, that that person meets it[15]. This exception applies whether or not the employment is for purposes of an organised religion[16]. The second such exception applies where the employment is for purposes of an organised religion, the employer applies a requirement related to sexual orientation so as to comply with the doctrines of the religion, or because of the nature of the employment and the context in which it is carried out, so as to avoid conflicting with the strongly held religious convictions of a significant number of the religion's followers, and either the person to whom that requirement is applied does not meet it or the employer is not satisfied, and in all the circumstances it is reasonable for him not to be satisfied, that that person meets it[17].

1　For these purposes, references to 'employer', in their application to a person at any time seeking to employ another, include a person who has no employees at that time: Employment Equality (Sexual Orientation) Regulations 2003, SI 2003/1661, reg 2(3). As to the meaning of 'person' see para 344 note 3 ante.

2　'Employment' means employment under a contract of service or of apprenticeship or a contract personally to do any work; and related expressions are to be construed accordingly: ibid reg 2(3).

3　For the purposes of ibid Pt II (regs 6–21) (as amended) ('the relevant purposes'), employment is to be regarded as being at an establishment in Great Britain if the employee: (1) does his work wholly or partly in Great Britain; or (2) does his work wholly outside Great Britain and reg 9(2) applies: reg 9(1). Regulation 9(2) applies if: (a) the employer has a place of business at an establishment in Great Britain; (b) the work is for the purposes of the business carried on at that establishment; and (c) the employee is ordinarily resident in Great Britain at the time when he applies for or is offered the employment, or at any time during the course of the employment: reg 9(2). The reference to 'employment' in reg 9(1) includes employment on board a ship only if the ship is registered at a port of registry in Great Britain, and employment on an aircraft or hovercraft only if the aircraft or hovercraft is registered in the United Kingdom and operated by a person who has his principal place of business, or is ordinarily resident, in Great Britain: reg 9(3). Subject to reg 9(5), for the purposes of determining if employment concerned with the exploration of the sea bed or subsoil or the exploitation of their natural resources is outside Great Britain, reg 9 has effect as if references to Great Britain included: (i) any area designated under the Continental Shelf Act 1964 s 1(7) (as amended) (see FUEL AND ENERGY vol 19(2) (Reissue) para 1411) except an area or part of an area in which the law of Northern Ireland applies; and (ii) in relation to employment concerned with the exploration or exploitation of the Frigg Gas Field, the part of the Norwegian sector of the Continental Shelf described in the Employment Equality (Sexual Orientation) Regulations 2003, SI 2003/1661, Sch 1 (reg 9(4)); but this does not apply to employment which is concerned with the exploration or exploitation of the Frigg Gas Field unless the employer is: (A) a company registered under the Companies Act 1985 (see COMPANIES); (B) an oversea company which has established a place of business within Great Britain from which it directs the exploration or exploitation in question; or (C) any other person who has a place of business within Great Britain from which he directs the exploration or exploitation in question (Employment Equality (Sexual Orientation) Regulations 2003, SI 2003/1661, reg 9(5)). For these purposes, 'the Frigg Gas Field' means the naturally occurring gas-bearing sand formations of the lower Eocene age located in the vicinity of the intersection of the line of latitude 59 degrees 53 minutes North and of the dividing line between the sectors of the Continental Shelf of the United Kingdom and the Kingdom of Norway and includes all other gas-bearing strata from which gas at the start of production is capable of flowing into the above-mentioned gas-bearing sand formations; and 'oversea company' has the same meaning as in the Companies Act 1985 s 744 (see COMPANIES vol 7(2) (2004 Reissue) para 1816): Employment Equality (Sexual Orientation) Regulations 2003, SI 2003/1661, reg 9(6).

For the meaning of 'Great Britain' generally see para 325 note 6 ante. For these purposes, 'Great Britain' includes such of the territorial waters of the United Kingdom as are adjacent to Great Britain: reg 2(3). As to the territorial waters of the United Kingdom see WATER vol 49(2) (2004 Reissue) para 15. For the meaning of 'United Kingdom' see para 325 note 6 ante.

4   For the purposes of the Employment Equality (Sexual Orientation) Regulations 2003, SI 2003/1661 (as amended), references to discrimination are references to any discrimination falling within reg 3 (as amended) (discrimination on grounds of sexual orientation: see para 722 ante) or reg 4 (discrimination by way of victimisation: see para 723 ante); and related expressions are to be construed accordingly: reg 2(2).

5   Ibid reg 6(1).

6   'Benefits', except in ibid reg 9A (as added) (trustees and managers of occupational pension schemes: see para 727 post), includes facilities and services: reg 2(3) (definition substituted by SI 2003/2827).

7   In the Employment Equality (Sexual Orientation) Regulations 2003, SI 2003/1661, reg 6(2)(d) (see head (2)(d) in the text), reference to the dismissal of a person from employment includes reference: (1) to the termination of that person's employment by the expiration of any period (including a period expiring by reference to an event or circumstance), not being a termination immediately after which the employment is renewed on the same terms; and (2) to the termination of that person's employment by any act of his (including the giving of notice) in circumstances such that he is entitled to terminate it without notice by reason of the conduct of the employer: reg 6(5). As to the meaning of 'act' see para 723 note 3 ante.

8   Ibid reg 6(2). 'Detriment' does not include harassment within the meaning of reg 5 (see para 724 ante): reg 2(3).

9   For the purposes of the Employment Equality (Sexual Orientation) Regulations 2003, SI 2003/1661 (as amended), references to harassment are to be construed in accordance with reg 5 (harassment on grounds of sexual orientation: see para 724 ante): reg 2(2).

10 Ibid reg 6(3).

11 Ibid reg 6(4).

12 Ie discrimination falling within ibid reg 3 (as amended): see para 722 ante.

13 Ie ibid reg 7(2) or (3): see the text and notes 15–17 infra.

14 Ibid reg 7(1).

15 Ibid reg 7(2)(a)–(c).

16 Ibid reg 7(2).

17 Ibid reg 7(3). The provisions of reg 7(2), (3) have been held to be compatible with EC Council Directive 2000/78 (OJ L303, 2.12.2000, p 16) establishing a general framework for equal treatment in employment and occupation (the 'EC Framework Employment Directive') (see paras 508, 722 ante): *R (on the application of Amicus—MSF section) v Secretary of State for Trade and Industry* [2004] EWHC 860 (Admin), [2004] IRLR 430, [2004] All ER (D) 238 (Apr).

726.   Contract workers. It is unlawful for a principal[1], in relation to contract work[2] at an establishment in Great Britain[3], to discriminate[4] against a contract worker[5]:

(1)   in the terms on which he allows him to do that work;

(2)   by not allowing him to do it or continue to do it;

(3)   in the way he affords him access to any benefits[6] or by refusing or deliberately not affording him access to them; or

(4)   by subjecting him to any other detriment[7].

A principal does not, however, contravene head (2) above by doing any act[8] in relation to a contract worker where, if the work were to be done by a person taken into the principal's employment, that act would be lawful by virtue of the statutory exception[9] for a genuine occupational requirement[10]. Furthermore, heads (1) to (4) above do not apply to benefits of any description if the principal is concerned with the provision, for payment or not, of benefits of that description to the public, or to a section of the public to which the contract worker in question belongs, unless that provision differs in a material respect from the provision of the benefits by the principal to his contract workers[11].

It is also unlawful for a principal, in relation to contract work at an establishment in Great Britain, to subject a contract worker to harassment[12].

1 'Principal' means a person ('A') who makes work available for doing by individuals who are employed by another person who supplies them under a contract made with A: Employment Equality (Sexual Orientation) Regulations 2003, SI 2003/1661, reg 8(5). As to the meaning of 'person' see para 344 note 3 ante.

2 'Contract work' means work made available as described in note 1 supra: ibid reg 8(5).

3 Ibid reg 9 (meaning of employment and contract work at establishment in Great Britain: see para 725 note 3 ante) applies in relation to contract work within the meaning of reg 8 as it applies in relation to employment; and, in its application to contract work, references to 'employee', 'employer' and 'employment' are references to (respectively) 'contract worker', 'principal' and 'contract work' within the meaning of reg 8: reg 9(7). As to the meaning of 'Great Britain' see para 725 note 3 ante.

4 For the meaning of references to discrimination see para 725 note 4 ante.

5 'Contract worker' means any individual who is supplied to the principal under such a contract as is described in note 1 supra: Employment Equality (Sexual Orientation) Regulations 2003, SI 2003/1661, reg 8(5).

6 As to the meaning of 'benefits' see para 725 note 6 ante.

7 Employment Equality (Sexual Orientation) Regulations 2003, SI 2003/1661, reg 8(1). As to the meaning of 'detriment' see para 725 note 8 ante.

8 As to the meaning of 'act' see para 723 note 3 ante.

9 Ie by virtue of the Employment Equality (Sexual Orientation) Regulations 2003, SI 2003/1661, reg 7: see para 725 ante.

10 Ibid reg 8(3).

11 Ibid reg 8(4).

12 Ibid reg 8(2). For the meaning of references to harassment see para 725 note 9 ante.

727. Trustees and managers of occupational pension schemes. It is unlawful, except in relation to rights accrued or benefits payable in respect of periods of service prior to 1 December 2003[1], for the trustees or managers[2] of an occupational pension scheme[3] to discriminate[4] against a member[5] or prospective member[6] of the scheme in carrying out any of their functions in relation to it, including in particular their functions relating to the admission of members to the scheme and the treatment of members of it[7]. It is also unlawful for the trustees or managers of an occupational pension scheme, in relation to the scheme, to subject to harassment[8] a member or prospective member of it[9].

Every occupational pension scheme must be treated as including a provision ('the non-discrimination rule') containing a requirement that the trustees or managers of the scheme refrain from doing any act which is unlawful by virtue of the above provisions[10]; and the other provisions of the scheme are to have effect subject to the non-discrimination rule[11]. The trustees or managers of an occupational pension scheme may:

(1) if they do not otherwise have power to make such alterations to the scheme as may be required to secure conformity with the non-discrimination rule; or

(2) if they have such power but the procedure for doing so is liable to be unduly complex or protracted, or involves the obtaining of consents which cannot be obtained, or can only be obtained with undue delay or difficulty,

by resolution make such alterations to the scheme[12]. Alterations made by such a resolution may have effect in relation to a period before the alterations are made, but may not have effect in relation to any time before 1 December 2003[13].

1 Ie prior to the coming into force of the Employment Equality (Sexual Orientation) Regulations 2003, SI 2003/1661 (as amended): see para 722 note 1 ante.

2   For these purposes, 'trustees or managers' has the meaning given by the Pensions Act 1995 s 124(1) (as amended) (see SOCIAL SECURITY AND PENSIONS vol 44(2) (Reissue) para 612): Employment Equality (Sexual Orientation) Regulations 2003, SI 2003/1661, reg 9A(3)(a), Sch 1A para 1(1), (3) (reg 9A, Sch 1A added by SI 2003/2827).

3   For these purposes, 'occupational pension scheme' has the same meaning as in the Pension Schemes Act 1993 (see SOCIAL SECURITY AND PENSIONS vol 44(2) (Reissue) para 853): Employment Equality (Sexual Orientation) Regulations 2003, SI 2003/1661, Sch 1A para 1(1), (3) (as added (see note 2 supra); definition amended by SI 2006/1031).

4   For the meaning of references to discrimination see para 725 note 4 ante.

5   'Member', in relation to an occupational pension scheme, means any active member, deferred member or pensioner member; and 'active member', 'deferred member' and 'pensioner member' have the meanings given by the Pensions Act 1995 s 124(1) (as amended) (see SOCIAL SECURITY AND PENSIONS vol 44(2) (Reissue) para 612): Employment Equality (Sexual Orientation) Regulations 2003, SI 2003/1661, Sch 1A para 1(1), (3) (as added (see note 2 supra); and amended by SI 2006/1031).

6   'Prospective member', in relation to an occupational pension scheme, means any person who, under the terms of his employment or the rules of the scheme or both: (1) is able, at his own option, to become a member of the scheme; (2) is to become so able if he continues in the same employment for a sufficient period of time; (3) is to be admitted to it automatically unless he makes an election not to become a member; or (4) may be admitted to it subject to the consent of his employer: Employment Equality (Sexual Orientation) Regulations 2003, SI 2003/1661, Sch 1A para 1(1), (3) (as added: see note 2 supra).

7   Ibid reg 9A(1) (as added: see note 2 supra).

8   For the meaning of references to harassment see para 725 note 9 ante.

9   Employment Equality (Sexual Orientation) Regulations 2003, SI 2003/1661, reg 9A(2) (as added: see note 2 supra).

10   Ibid reg 9A(3)(b), Sch 1A para 2 (as added: see note 2 supra).

11   Ibid Sch 1A para 3 (as added: see note 2 supra).

12   Ibid reg 9A(3)(c), Sch 1A para 4 (as added: see note 2 supra).

13   Ibid Sch 1A para 5 (as added: see note 2 supra). See note 1 supra.

728.   Office-holders etc.   The following provisions apply to:

(1)   any office or post to which persons[1] are appointed to discharge functions personally under the direction of another person[2], and in respect of which they are entitled to remuneration[3]; and

(2)   any office or post to which appointments are made by, or on the recommendation of or subject to the approval of, a Minister of the Crown[4], a government department, the National Assembly for Wales[5] or any part of the Scottish Administration[6],

but not to a political office[7] or a case where the provisions relating to applicants and employees[8], contract workers[9], barristers[10] or partnerships[11] apply, or would apply but for the operation of any other provision of the Employment Equality (Sexual Orientation) Regulations 2003[12].

It is unlawful:

(a)   for a relevant person[13], in relation to an appointment to an office or post[14] to which these provisions apply, to discriminate[15] against a person:

(i)   in the arrangements which he makes for the purpose of determining to whom the appointment should be offered;

(ii)   in the terms on which he offers him the appointment; or

(iii)   by refusing[16] to offer him the appointment[17];

(b)   in relation to an appointment to an office or post to which these provisions apply and which is an office or post referred to in head (2) above, for a relevant person on whose recommendation, or subject to whose approval, appointments to the office or post are made to discriminate against a person:

(i)   in the arrangements which he makes for the purpose of determining who should be recommended or approved in relation to the appointment; or

(ii)   in making or refusing to make a recommendation[18], or giving or refusing to give an approval, in relation to the appointment[19];

(c) for a relevant person, in relation to a person who has been appointed to an office or post to which these provisions apply, to discriminate against him:

    (i) in the terms of the appointment;

    (ii) in the opportunities which he affords him for promotion, transfer, training or receiving any other benefit[20], or by refusing to afford him any such opportunity;

    (iii) by terminating the appointment[21]; or

    (iv) by subjecting him to any other detriment[22] in relation to the appointment[23];

(d) for a relevant person, in relation to an office or post to which these provisions apply, to subject to harassment[24] a person:

    (i) who has been appointed to the office or post;

    (ii) who is seeking or being considered for appointment to the office or post; or

    (iii) who is seeking or being considered for a recommendation or approval in relation to an appointment to an office or post referred to in head (2) above[25].

Heads (a) and (c) above do not, however, apply to any act[26] in relation to an office or post where, if the office or post constituted employment[27], that act would be lawful by virtue of the statutory exception for a genuine occupational requirement[28]; and head (b) above does not apply to any act in relation to an office or post where, if the office or post constituted employment, it would be lawful by virtue of that statutory exception to refuse to offer the person such employment[29]. Nor does head (c) above apply to benefits of any description if the relevant person is concerned with the provision, for payment or not, of benefits of that description to the public, or a section of the public to which the person appointed belongs, unless:

(A) that provision differs in a material respect from the provision of the benefits by the relevant person to persons appointed to offices or posts which are the same as, or not materially different from, that which the person appointed holds; or

(B) the provision of the benefits to the person appointed is regulated by the terms and conditions of his appointment; or

(C) the benefits relate to training[30].

1   As to the meaning of 'person' see para 344 note 3 ante.

2   For these purposes, the holder of an office or post is to be regarded as discharging his functions under the direction of another person if that other person is entitled to direct him as to when and where he discharges those functions: Employment Equality (Sexual Orientation) Regulations 2003, SI 2003/1661, reg 10(9)(a).

3   For these purposes, the holder of an office or post is not to be regarded as entitled to remuneration merely because he is entitled to payments: (1) in respect of expenses incurred by him in carrying out the functions of the office or post; or (2) by way of compensation for the loss of income or benefits he would or might have received from any person had he not been carrying out the functions of the office or post: ibid reg 10(9)(b).

4   'Minister of the Crown' includes the Treasury and the Defence Council: ibid reg 2(3). As to the Treasury see CONSTITUTIONAL LAW AND HUMAN RIGHTS vol 8(2) (Reissue) paras 512–517. As to the Defence Council see ARMED FORCES vol 2(2) (Reissue) para 2; CONSTITUTIONAL LAW AND HUMAN RIGHTS vol 8(2) (Reissue) para 443 et seq.

5   As to the National Assembly for Wales see para 302 ante.

6   Matters relating to the composition, procedures and powers of the Scottish Administration are beyond the scope of this work.

7   For these purposes, 'political office' means: (1) any office of the House of Commons held by a member of it; (2) a life peerage within the meaning of the Life Peerages Act 1958 (see CONSTITUTIONAL LAW AND HUMAN RIGHTS vol 8(2) (Reissue) para 212; PARLIAMENT vol 34 (Reissue) para 540; PEERAGES AND DIGNITIES), or any office of the House of Lords held by a member of it; (3) any office mentioned in the House of Commons Disqualification Act 1975 Sch 2 (as amended) (ministerial offices: see PARLIAMENT vol 34 (Reissue) para 611); (4) the offices of Leader of the Opposition, Chief Opposition

Whip or Assistant Opposition Whip within the meaning of the Ministerial and other Salaries Act 1975 (see CONSTITUTIONAL LAW AND HUMAN RIGHTS vol 8(2) (Reissue) para 219); (5) any office of the National Assembly for Wales held by a member of it; (6) in England, any office of a county council, a London borough council, a district council, or a parish council held by a member of it; (7) in Wales, any office of a county council, a county borough council, or a community council held by a member of it; (8) any office of the Greater London Authority held by a member of it; (9) any office of the Common Council of the City of London held by a member of it; (10) any office of the Council of the Isles of Scilly held by a member of it; (11) any office of a political party: Employment Equality (Sexual Orientation) Regulations 2003, SI 2003/1661, reg 10(10)(b). This provision also refers to various Scottish offices, but see note 6 supra. As to local government authorities in England and Wales see LOCAL GOVERNMENT vol 29(1) (Reissue) para 23 et seq; as to London borough councils see LONDON GOVERNMENT vol 29(2) (Reissue) para 35 et seq; as to the Greater London Authority see LONDON GOVERNMENT vol 29(2) (Reissue) para 70 et seq; as to the Common Council of the City of London see LONDON GOVERNMENT vol 29(2) (Reissue) para 51 et seq; and as to the Council of the Isles of Scilly see LOCAL GOVERNMENT vol 29(1) (Reissue) para 40.

8   Ie ibid reg 6: see para 725 ante.

9   Ie ibid reg 8: see para 726 ante.

10 Ie ibid reg 12: see para 730 post. As to advocates see reg 13 (which only applies in relation to Scotland). See note 6 supra.

11 Ie ibid reg 14: see para 731 post.

12 Ibid reg 10(8).

13 For these purposes, 'relevant person', in relation to an office or post, means: (1) any person with power to make or terminate appointments to the office or post, or to determine the terms of appointment; (2) any person with power to determine the working conditions of a person appointed to the office or post in relation to opportunities for promotion, transfer, training or for receiving any other benefit; and (3) any person or body referred to in ibid reg 10(8)(b) (see head (2) in the text) on whose recommendation or subject to whose approval appointments are made to the office or post: reg 10(10)(c).

14 For these purposes, appointment to an office or post does not include election to an office or post: ibid reg 10(10)(a).

15 For the meaning of references to discrimination see para 725 note 4 ante.

16 For these purposes, references to refusal include references to deliberate omission: Employment Equality (Sexual Orientation) Regulations 2003, SI 2003/1661, reg 10(10)(e).

17 Ibid reg 10(1).

18 For these purposes, references to making a recommendation include references to making a negative recommendation: ibid reg 10(10)(d).

19 Ibid reg 10(2).

20 As to the meaning of 'benefits' see para 725 note 6 ante.

21 The reference in head (c)(iii) in the text to the termination of the appointment includes a reference: (1) to the termination of the appointment by the expiration of any period (including a period expiring by reference to an event or circumstance), not being a termination immediately after which the appointment is renewed on the same terms and conditions; and (2) to the termination of the appointment by any act of the person appointed (including the giving of notice) in circumstances such that he is entitled to terminate the appointment without notice by reason of the conduct of the relevant person: Employment Equality (Sexual Orientation) Regulations 2003, SI 2003/1661, reg 10(7).

22 As to the meaning of 'detriment' see para 725 note 8 ante.

23 Employment Equality (Sexual Orientation) Regulations 2003, SI 2003/1661, reg 10(3).

24 For the meaning of references to 'harassment' see para 725 note 9 ante.

25 Employment Equality (Sexual Orientation) Regulations 2003, SI 2003/1661, reg 10(4).

26 As to the meaning of 'act' see para 723 note 3 ante.

27 For the meaning of 'employment' see para 725 note 2 ante.

28 Ie by virtue of the Employment Equality (Sexual Orientation) Regulations 2003, SI 2003/1661, reg 7: see para 725 ante.

29 Ibid reg 10(5).

30 Ibid reg 10(6).

729.   Police and the Serious Organised Crime Agency.   For the purposes of the regulations prohibiting unlawful discrimination in employment and vocational training[1], the holding of the office of constable is to be treated[2] as employment[3]:

    (1)   by the chief officer of police[4] as respects any act[5] done by him in relation to a constable or that office;

(2) by the police authority[6] as respects any act done by it in relation to a constable or that office[7],

and this applies to a police cadet[8] and appointment as a police cadet as it applies to a constable and the office of constable[9].

There must be paid out of the police fund[10]:

(a) any compensation, costs or expenses awarded against a chief officer of police in any proceedings brought against him[11] under the Employment Equality (Sexual Orientation) Regulations 2003[12], and any costs or expenses incurred by him in any such proceedings so far as not recovered by him in the proceedings; and

(b) any sum required by a chief officer of police for the settlement of any claim made against him under those regulations if the settlement is approved by the police authority[13].

A police authority may, in such cases and to such extent as appear to it to be appropriate, pay out of the police fund:

(i) any compensation, costs or expenses awarded in proceedings under the Employment Equality (Sexual Orientation) Regulations 2003 against a person under the direction and control of the chief officer of police;

(ii) any costs or expenses incurred and not recovered by such a person in such proceedings; and

(iii) any sum required in connection with the settlement of a claim that has or might have given rise to such proceedings[14].

For the purposes of the Employment Equality (Sexual Orientation) Regulations 2003[15], any constable or other person who has been seconded to the Serious Organised Crime Agency ('SOCA') to serve as a member of its staff is to be treated as employed by SOCA[16].

1   Ie for the purposes of the Employment Equality (Sexual Orientation) Regulations 2003, SI 2003/1661, Pt II (regs 6–21) (as amended).

2   Ie subject to ibid reg 11A (as added): see the text and notes 15–16 infra.

3   For the meaning of 'employment' see para 725 note 2 ante.

4   For these purposes, and subject to the Employment Equality (Sexual Orientation) Regulations 2003, SI 2003/1661, reg 11(8), 'chief officer of police': (1) in relation to a person appointed or an appointment falling to be made under a specified Act, has the same meaning as in the Police Act 1996 (see POLICE vol 36(1) (Reissue) para 205); (2) in relation to any other person or appointment, means the officer or other person who has the direction and control of the body of constables or cadets in question: reg 11(7) (definition amended by SI 2006/594). In relation to a constable of a force who is not under the direction and control of the chief officer of police for that force, references in the Employment Equality (Sexual Orientation) Regulations 2003, SI 2003/1661, reg 11 (as amended) to the chief officer of police are references to the chief officer of the force under whose direction and control he is: reg 11(8). 'Specified Act' means the Metropolitan Police Act 1829, the City of London Police Act 1839 or the Police Act 1996: Employment Equality (Sexual Orientation) Regulations 2003, SI 2003/1661, reg 11(7).

5   As to the meaning of 'act' see para 723 note 3 ante.

6   For these purposes, and subject to the Employment Equality (Sexual Orientation) Regulations 2003, SI 2003/1661, reg 11(8), 'police authority': (1) in relation to a person appointed or an appointment falling to be made under a specified Act (see note 4 supra), has the same meaning as in the Police Act 1996 (see POLICE vol 36(1) (Reissue) para 202); (2) in relation to any other person or appointment, means the authority by whom the person in question is or on appointment would be paid: reg 11(7) (definition amended by SI 2006/594). In relation to a constable of a force who is not under the direction and control of the chief officer of police for that force, references to the police authority are references to the relevant police authority for the force under whose direction and control he is: Employment Equality (Sexual Orientation) Regulations 2003, SI 2003/1661, reg 11(8). As to the meaning of 'person' see para 344 note 3 ante.

7   Ibid reg 11(1) (amended by SI 2006/594).

8   For these purposes, 'police cadet' means any person appointed to undergo training with a view to becoming a constable: Employment Equality (Sexual Orientation) Regulations 2003, SI 2003/1661, reg 11(7).

9   Ibid reg 11(6).

10   For these purposes, and subject to ibid reg 11(8) (see notes 4, 6 supra), 'police fund': (1) in relation to a chief officer of police within the definition of that term set out in note 4 head (1) supra, has the same meaning as in the Police Act 1996 (see POLICE vol 36(1) (Reissue) para 205); (2) in any other case means money provided by the police authority: Employment Equality (Sexual Orientation) Regulations 2003, SI 2003/1661, reg 11(7).

11   Any proceedings under the Employment Equality (Sexual Orientation) Regulations 2003, SI 2003/1661 (as amended), which, by virtue of reg 11(1) (as amended), would lie against a chief officer of police must be brought against the chief officer of police for the time being or, in the case of a vacancy in that office, against the person for the time being performing the functions of that office; and references in reg 11(3) (see heads (a)–(b) in the text) to the chief officer of police are to be construed accordingly: reg 11(4).

12   Ie under the Employment Equality (Sexual Orientation) Regulations 2003, SI 2003/1661 (as amended).

13   Ibid reg 11(3).

14   Ibid reg 11(5).

15   See note 1 supra.

16   Employment Equality (Sexual Orientation) Regulations 2003, SI 2003/1661, reg 11A(1), (3) (added by SI 2006/594). As to the Serious Organised Crime Agency see POLICE.

730. Barristers. It is unlawful for a barrister or barrister's clerk[1]:

(1)   in relation to any offer of a pupillage[2] or tenancy[3], to discriminate[4] against a person[5]:

     (a)   in the arrangements which are made for the purpose of determining to whom the pupillage or tenancy should be offered;

     (b)   in respect of any terms on which it is offered; or

     (c)   by refusing, or deliberately not offering, it to him[6];

(2)   in relation to a pupil[7] or tenant[8] in the set of chambers[9] in question, to discriminate against him:

     (a)   in respect of any terms applicable to him as a pupil or tenant;

     (b)   in the opportunities for training, or gaining experience, which are afforded or denied to him;

     (c)   in the benefits[10] which are afforded or denied to him; or

     (d)   by terminating his pupillage, or by subjecting him to any pressure to leave the chambers or other detriment[11];

(3)   in relation to a pupillage or tenancy in the set of chambers in question, to subject to harassment[12] a person who is, or has applied to be, a pupil or tenant[13].

It is also unlawful for any person, in relation to the giving, withholding or acceptance of instructions to a barrister, to discriminate against any person by subjecting him to a detriment, or to subject him to harassment[14].

1   'Barrister's clerk' includes any person carrying out any of the functions of a barrister's clerk: Employment Equality (Sexual Orientation) Regulations 2003, SI 2003/1661, reg 12(5). Regulation 12 extends to England and Wales only: reg 12(6).

2   For these purposes, 'pupil' and 'pupillage' have the meanings commonly associated with their use in the context of barristers practising in independent practice: ibid reg 12(5).

3   For these purposes, 'tenancy' and 'tenant' have the meanings commonly associated with their use in the context of barristers practising in independent practice, but also include reference to any barrister permitted to work in a set of chambers who is not a tenant: ibid reg 12(5). See also note 9 infra.

4   For the meaning of references to discrimination see para 725 note 4 ante.

5   As to the meaning of 'person' see para 344 note 3 ante.

6   Employment Equality (Sexual Orientation) Regulations 2003, SI 2003/1661, reg 12(1).

7   See note 2 supra.

8   See note 3 supra.

9   For these purposes, 'set of chambers' has the meaning commonly associated with its use in the context of barristers practising in independent practice: Employment Equality (Sexual Orientation) Regulations 2003, SI 2003/1661, reg 12(5).

10   As to the meaning of 'benefits' see para 725 note 6 ante.

11   Employment Equality (Sexual Orientation) Regulations 2003, SI 2003/1661, reg 12(2). As to the meaning of 'detriment' see para 725 note 8 ante.

12   For the meaning of references to harassment see para 725 note 9 ante.

13 Employment Equality (Sexual Orientation) Regulations 2003, SI 2003/1661, reg 12(3).
14 Ibid reg 12(4).

731. Partnerships. It is unlawful for a firm[1], in relation to a position as partner[2] in the firm:

(1) to discriminate[3] against a person[4]:

  (a) in the arrangements it makes for the purpose of determining to whom it should offer that position;

  (b) in the terms on which it offers him that position;

  (c) by refusing to offer, or deliberately not offering, him that position; or

  (d) in a case where the person already holds that position, in the way it affords him access to any benefits[5] or by refusing to afford, or deliberately not affording, him access to them, or by expelling him from that position[6], or subjecting him to any other detriment[7];

(2) to subject to harassment[8] a person who holds or has applied for that position[9].

Heads (1)(a) to (1)(c) and head (2) above apply in relation to persons proposing to form themselves into a partnership as they apply in relation to a firm[10]. Head (1) above does not, however, apply to any act[11] in relation to a position as partner where, if the position were employment[12], that act would be lawful by virtue of the statutory exception[13] for a genuine occupational requirement[14].

1 For these purposes, 'firm' has the meaning given by the Partnership Act 1890 s 4 (see PARTNERSHIP vol 35 (Reissue) para 1): Employment Equality (Sexual Orientation) Regulations 2003, SI 2003/1661, reg 14(7). Regulation 14 applies to a limited liability partnership as it applies to a firm: reg 14(6).

2 In the case of a limited partnership, references in ibid reg 14 to a partner are to be construed as references to a general partner as defined in the Limited Partnerships Act 1907 s 3 (see PARTNERSHIP vol 35 (Reissue) para 207) (Employment Equality (Sexual Orientation) Regulations 2003, SI 2003/1661, reg 14(5)); and, in the application of reg 14 to a limited liability partnership, references to a partner in a firm are references to a member of the limited liability partnership (reg 14(6)).

3 For the meaning of references to discrimination see para 725 note 4 ante.

4 As to the meaning of 'person' see para 344 note 3 ante.

5 As to the meaning of 'benefits' see para 725 note 6 ante.

6 In the Employment Equality (Sexual Orientation) Regulations 2003, SI 2003/1661, reg 14(1)(d) (see head (1)(d) in the text), reference to the expulsion of a person from a position as partner includes reference: (1) to the termination of that person's partnership by the expiration of any period (including a period expiring by reference to an event or circumstance), not being a termination immediately after which the partnership is renewed on the same terms; and (2) to the termination of that person's partnership by any act of his (including the giving of notice) in circumstances such that he is entitled to terminate it without notice by reason of the conduct of the other partners: reg 14(8).

7 Ibid reg 14(1). As to the meaning of 'detriment' see para 725 note 8 ante.

8 For the meaning of references to harassment see para 725 note 9 ante.

9 Employment Equality (Sexual Orientation) Regulations 2003, SI 2003/1661, reg 14(2).

10 Ibid reg 14(3).

11 As to the meaning of 'act' see para 723 note 3 ante.

12 For the meaning of 'employment' see para 725 note 2 ante.

13 Ie by virtue of the Employment Equality (Sexual Orientation) Regulations 2003, SI 2003/1661, reg 7: see para 725 ante.

14 Ibid reg 14(4).

732. Trade organisations. It is unlawful for a trade organisation[1]:

(1) to discriminate[2] against a person[3]:

  (a) in the terms on which it is prepared to admit him to membership of the organisation; or

  (b) by refusing to accept, or deliberately not accepting, his application for membership[4];

(2) in relation to a member of the organisation, to discriminate against him:

(a) in the way it affords him access to any benefits[5] or by refusing or deliberately omitting to afford him access to them;

(b) by depriving him of membership, or varying the terms on which he is a member; or

(c) by subjecting him to any other detriment[6];

(3) in relation to a person's membership or application for membership of that organisation, to subject that person to harassment[7].

1   For these purposes, 'trade organisation' means an organisation of workers, an organisation of employers, or any other organisation whose members carry on a particular profession or trade for the purposes of which the organisation exists; 'profession' includes any vocation or occupation; and 'trade' includes any business: Employment Equality (Sexual Orientation) Regulations 2003, SI 2003/1661, reg 15(4).
2   For the meaning of references to discrimination see para 725 note 4 ante.
3   As to the meaning of 'person' see para 344 note 3 ante.
4   Employment Equality (Sexual Orientation) Regulations 2003, SI 2003/1661, reg 15(1).
5   As to the meaning of 'benefits' see para 725 note 6 ante.
6   Employment Equality (Sexual Orientation) Regulations 2003, SI 2003/1661, reg 15(2). As to the meaning of 'detriment' see para 725 note 8 ante.
7   Ibid reg 15(3). For the meaning of references to harassment see para 725 note 9 ante.

733.   Qualifications bodies.   It is unlawful for a qualifications body[1]:

(1) to discriminate[2] against a person[3]:

(a) in the terms on which it is prepared to confer a professional or trade qualification on him;

(b) by refusing or deliberately not granting any application by him for such a qualification; or

(c) by withdrawing such a qualification from him or varying the terms on which he holds it[4];

(2) in relation to a professional or trade qualification conferred by it, to subject to harassment[5] a person who holds or applies for such a qualification[6].

1   For these purposes, 'qualifications body' means any authority or body which can confer a professional or trade qualification, but it does not include:
    (1) an educational establishment to which the Employment Equality (Sexual Orientation) Regulations 2003, SI 2003/1661, reg 20 (institutions of further and higher education: see para 737 post) applies, or would apply but for the operation of any other provision of the regulations; or
    (2) a school;
    'confer' includes renew or extend; 'professional or trade qualification' means any authorisation, qualification, recognition, registration, enrolment, approval or certification which is needed for, or facilitates engagement in, a particular profession or trade; and 'profession' and 'trade' have the same meanings as in reg 15 (see para 732 ante): reg 16(3). 'School' has the meaning given by the Education Act 1996 s 4 (as amended) (see EDUCATION vol 15(1) (2006 Reissue) para 81); and references to a school are to an institution in so far as it is engaged in the provision of education under s 4 (as amended): Employment Equality (Sexual Orientation) Regulations 2003, SI 2003/1661, reg 2(3).
2   For the meaning of references to discrimination see para 725 note 4 ante.
3   As to the meaning of 'person' see para 344 note 3 ante.
4   Employment Equality (Sexual Orientation) Regulations 2003, SI 2003/1661, reg 16(1).
5   For the meaning of references to harassment see para 725 note 9 ante.
6   Employment Equality (Sexual Orientation) Regulations 2003, SI 2003/1661, reg 16(2).

734.   Providers of vocational training.   It is unlawful, in relation to a person[1] seeking or undergoing training[2] which would help fit him for any employment[3], for any training provider[4] to discriminate[5] against him:

(1) in the terms on which the training provider affords him access to any training;

(2) by refusing or deliberately not affording him such access;

(3) by terminating his training; or

(4) by subjecting him to any other detriment[6] during his training[7],

but this does not apply if the discrimination only concerns training for employment which, by virtue of the statutory exception for a genuine occupational requirement[8], the employer could lawfully refuse to offer the person seeking training[9].

It is also unlawful for a training provider, in relation to a person seeking or undergoing training which would help fit him for any employment, to subject him to harassment[10].

1   As to the meaning of 'person' see para 344 note 3 ante.
2   For these purposes, 'training' includes: (1) facilities for training; and (2) practical work experience provided by an employer to a person whom he does not employ: Employment Equality (Sexual Orientation) Regulations 2003, SI 2003/1661, reg 17(4). As to the meaning of 'employer' see para 725 note 1 ante.
3   For the meaning of 'employment' see para 725 note 2 ante.
4   For these purposes, 'training provider' means any person who provides, or makes arrangements for the provision of, training which would help fit another person for any employment, but it does not include: (1) an employer in relation to training for persons employed by him; (2) an educational establishment to which the Employment Equality (Sexual Orientation) Regulations 2003, SI 2003/1661, reg 20 (institutions of further and higher education: see para 737 post) applies, or would apply but for the operation of any other provision of the regulations; or (3) a school: reg 17(4). For the meaning of 'school' see para 733 note 1 ante.
5   For the meaning of references to discrimination see para 725 note 4 ante.
6   As to the meaning of 'detriment' see para 725 note 8 ante.
7   Employment Equality (Sexual Orientation) Regulations 2003, SI 2003/1661, reg 17(1).
8   Ie by virtue of ibid reg 7: see para 725 ante.
9   Ibid reg 17(3).
10   Ibid reg 17(2). For the meaning of references to harassment see para 725 note 9 ante.

735. Employment agencies, careers guidance etc. It is unlawful for an employment agency[1] to discriminate[2] against a person:

(1)   in the terms on which the agency offers to provide any of its services;
(2)   by refusing or deliberately not providing any of its services; or
(3)   in the way it provides any of its services[3],

but this does not apply to discrimination if it only concerns employment which, by virtue of the statutory exception for a genuine occupational requirement[4], the employer could lawfully refuse to offer the person in question[5].

It is also unlawful for an employment agency, in relation to a person to whom it provides its services or who has requested it to provide its services, to subject that person to harassment[6].

An employment agency is not subject to any liability under the above provisions if it proves that:

(a)   it acted in reliance on a statement made to it by the employer to the effect that, by reason of the operation of the above-mentioned statutory exception[7], its action would not be unlawful; and
(b)   it was reasonable for it to rely on the statement[8].

A person who knowingly or recklessly makes a statement such as is referred to in head (a) above which in a material respect is false or misleading commits an offence, and is liable on summary conviction to a fine[9].

1   For these purposes: (1) 'employment agency' means a person who, for profit or not, provides services for the purpose of finding employment for workers or supplying employers with workers, but it does not include: (a) an educational establishment to which the Employment Equality (Sexual Orientation) Regulations 2003, SI 2003/1661, reg 20 (institutions of further and higher education: see para 737 post) applies, or would apply but for the operation of any other provision of the regulations; or (b) a school; and (2) references to the services of an employment agency include guidance on careers and any other services related to employment: reg 18(6). For the meanings of 'employer' and 'employment' see para 725 notes 1, 2 ante; and for the meaning of 'school' see para 733 note 1 ante. As to the meaning of 'person' see para 344 note 3 ante.

2   For the meaning of references to discrimination see para 725 note 4 ante.
3   Employment Equality (Sexual Orientation) Regulations 2003, SI 2003/1661, reg 18(1).
4   Ie by virtue of ibid reg 7: see para 725 ante.
5   Ibid reg 18(3).
6   Ibid reg 18(2). For the meaning of references to harassment see para 725 note 9 ante.
7   See note 4 supra.
8   Employment Equality (Sexual Orientation) Regulations 2003, SI 2003/1661, reg 18(4).
9   Ibid reg 18(5). The fine referred to in the text is a fine not exceeding level 5 on the standard scale: see
     reg 18(5). As to the standard scale see para 315 note 15 ante.

736. Assisting persons to obtain employment etc. It is unlawful for the
Secretary of State[1] to discriminate[2] against any person[3] by subjecting him to a
detriment[4], or to subject a person to harassment[5], in the provision of facilities or services
under the statutory arrangements[6] for assisting persons to obtain employment[7].

1   As to the Secretary of State and the National Assembly for Wales see para 302 ante.
2   For the meaning of references to discrimination see para 725 note 4 ante.
3   As to the meaning of 'person' see para 344 note 3 ante.
4   As to the meaning of 'detriment' see para 725 note 8 ante.
5   For the meaning of references to harassment see para 725 note 9 ante.
6   Ie under the Employment and Training Act 1973 s 2 (as substituted and amended): see EMPLOYMENT
     vol 16(1B) (Reissue) para 765.
7   Employment Equality (Sexual Orientation) Regulations 2003, SI 2003/1661, reg 19(1). Regulation 19
     does not apply in a case where: (1) reg 17 (providers of vocational training: see para 734 ante) applies, or
     would apply but for the operation of any other provision of the regulations; or (2) the Secretary of State
     is acting as an employment agency within the meaning of reg 18 (see para 735 ante): reg 19(3).

737. Institutions of further and higher education. The provisions set out
below apply to the following educational establishments in England and Wales, namely:
    (1)   an institution within the further education sector[1];
    (2)   a university[2];
    (3)   an institution[3], other than a university, within the higher education sector[4].
    It is unlawful, in relation to an educational establishment to which these provisions
apply, for the governing body of that establishment to discriminate[5] against a person[6]:
    (a)   in the terms on which it offers to admit him to the establishment as a student[7];
    (b)   by refusing or deliberately not accepting an application for his admission to the
           establishment as a student; or
    (c)   where he is a student of the establishment:
           (i)   in the way it affords him access to any benefits[8];
           (ii)   by refusing or deliberately not affording him access to them; or
           (iii)   by excluding him from the establishment or subjecting him to any other
                   detriment[9],
but this does not apply if the discrimination only concerns training which would help fit
a person for employment[10] which, by virtue of the statutory exception for a genuine
occupational requirement[11], the employer[12] could lawfully refuse to offer the person in
question[13].
    It is also unlawful, in relation to an educational establishment to which these
provisions apply, for the governing body of that establishment to subject to harassment[14]
a person who is a student at the establishment or who has applied for admission to the
establishment as a student[15].

1   Ie within the meaning of the Further and Higher Education Act 1992 s 91(3): see EDUCATION vol 15(2)
     (2006 Reissue) para 579.
2   For these purposes, 'university' includes a university college and a college, school or hall of a university:
     Employment Equality (Sexual Orientation) Regulations 2003, SI 2003/1661, reg 20(6).
3   Ie an institution within the higher education sector within the meaning of the Further and Higher
     Education Act 1992 s 91(5): see EDUCATION vol 15(2) (2006 Reissue) para 646.

4　Employment Equality (Sexual Orientation) Regulations 2003, SI 2003/1661, reg 20(4).
5　For the meaning of references to discrimination see para 725 note 4 ante.
6　As to the meaning of 'person' see para 344 note 3 ante.
7　For these purposes, 'student' means any person who receives education at an educational establishment to which the Employment Equality (Sexual Orientation) Regulations 2003, SI 2003/1661, reg 20 applies: reg 20(6).
8　As to the meaning of 'benefits' see para 725 note 6 ante.
9　Employment Equality (Sexual Orientation) Regulations 2003, SI 2003/1661, reg 20(1). As to the meaning of 'detriment' see para 725 note 8 ante.
10　For the meaning of 'employment' see para 725 note 2 ante.
11　Ie the Employment Equality (Sexual Orientation) Regulations 2003, SI 2003/1661, reg 7: see para 725 ante.
12　As to the meaning of 'employer' see para 725 note 1 ante.
13　Employment Equality (Sexual Orientation) Regulations 2003, SI 2003/1661, reg 20(3). Regulation 20(3) should be construed strictly and, so construed, falls within the ambit of the derogation in EC Council Directive 2000/78 (OJ L303, 2.12.2000, p 16) establishing a general framework for equal treatment in employment and occupation, art 4(1) (see paras 508, 722 ante): see *R (on the application of Amicus—MSF section) v Secretary of State for Trade and Industry* [2004] EWHC 860 (Admin) at [131], [2004] IRLR 430 at [131], [2004] All ER (D) 238 (Apr) at [131] per Richards J.
14　For the meaning of references to harassment see para 725 note 9 ante.
15　Employment Equality (Sexual Orientation) Regulations 2003, SI 2003/1661, reg 20(2).

738.　Relevant relationships which have come to an end. A 'relevant relationship' is a relationship during the course of which an act[1] of discrimination[2] against, or harassment[3] of, one party to the relationship ('B') by the other party to it ('A') is unlawful[4] by virtue of any provisions of the Employment Equality (Sexual Orientation) Regulations 2003[5] regarding discrimination in employment and vocational training[6]. Where a relevant relationship has come to an end, it is unlawful for A:

(1)　to discriminate against B by subjecting him to a detriment[7]; or
(2)　to subject B to harassment,

where the discrimination or harassment arises out of and is closely connected to that relationship[8].

1　As to the meaning of 'act' see para 723 note 3 ante.
2　For the meaning of references to discrimination see para 725 note 4 ante.
3　For the meaning of references to harassment see para 725 note 9 ante.
4　For these purposes, reference to an act of discrimination or harassment which is unlawful includes, in the case of a relationship which has come to an end before 1 December 2003 (i e the date of the coming into force of the Employment Equality (Sexual Orientation) Regulations 2003, SI 2003/1661 (as amended): see para 722 note 1 ante), reference to an act of discrimination or harassment which would, after that date, be unlawful: reg 21(3).
5　Ie ibid Pt II (regs 6–21) (as amended): see para 725 et seq ante.
6　Ibid reg 21(1).
7　As to the meaning of 'detriment' see para 725 note 8 ante.
8　Employment Equality (Sexual Orientation) Regulations 2003, SI 2003/1661, reg 21(2).

(iii)　Other Unlawful Acts

739.　Liability of employers and principals. Anything done by a person[1] in the course of his employment[2] is to be treated for the purposes of the Employment Equality (Sexual Orientation) Regulations 2003[3] as done by his employer[4] as well as by him, whether or not it was done with the employer's knowledge or approval[5].

For these purposes:

(1)　the holding of the office of constable is to be treated[6] as employment by the chief officer of police[7], and as not being employment by any other person, and anything done by a person holding such an office in the performance, or purported performance, of his functions is be treated as done in the course of that employment[8];

(2) the secondment of any constable or other person to the Serious Organised Crime Agency ('SOCA') to serve as a member of its staff is to be treated as employment by SOCA, and not as being employment by any other person, and anything done by a person so seconded in the performance, or purported performance, of his functions is to be treated as done in the course of that employment[9].

Anything done by a person as agent for another person with the authority, whether express or implied, and whether precedent or subsequent, of that other person is to be treated for the purposes of the Employment Equality (Sexual Orientation) Regulations 2003 as done by that other person as well as by him[10].

In proceedings brought under those regulations against any person in respect of an act[11] alleged to have been done by an employee of his, it is, however, a defence for that person to prove that he took such steps as were reasonably practicable to prevent the employee from doing that act or from doing in the course of his employment acts of that description[12].

1   As to the meaning of 'person' see para 344 note 3 ante.
2   For the meaning of 'employment' see para 725 note 2 ante.
3   Ie for the purposes of the Employment Equality (Sexual Orientation) Regulations 2003, SI 2003/1661 (as amended).
4   As to the meaning of 'employer' see para 725 note 1 ante.
5   Employment Equality (Sexual Orientation) Regulations 2003, SI 2003/1661, reg 22(1). See *Jones v Tower Boot Co Ltd* [1997] 2 All ER 406, [1997] IRLR 168, CA (a case under the Race Relations Act 1976); and para 476 ante.
     As to the liability of employers and principals under the Sex Discrimination Act 1975 see para 391 ante; and as to their liability under the Race Relations Act 1976 see para 476 ante.
6   Ie subject to the Employment Equality (Sexual Orientation) Regulations 2003, SI 2003/1661, reg 11A (as added): see head (2) in the text; and para 729 ante.
7   For the meaning of 'chief officer of police' see para 729 note 4 ante.
8   Employment Equality (Sexual Orientation) Regulations 2003, SI 2003/1661, reg 11(2) (amended by SI 2006/594). Head (1) in the text applies to a police cadet and appointment as a police cadet as it applies to a constable and the office of constable: Employment Equality (Sexual Orientation) Regulations 2003, SI 2003/1661, reg 11(6). For the meaning of 'police cadet' see para 729 note 8 ante.
9   Ibid reg 11A(2), (3) (added by SI 2006/594). As to the Serious Organised Crime Agency see POLICE.
10 Employment Equality (Sexual Orientation) Regulations 2003, SI 2003/1661, reg 22(2).
11 As to the meaning of 'act' see para 723 note 3 ante.
12 Employment Equality (Sexual Orientation) Regulations 2003, SI 2003/1661, reg 22(3).

740. Aiding unlawful acts. A person[1] who knowingly aids another person to do an act[2] made unlawful by the Employment Equality (Sexual Orientation) Regulations 2003[3] is to be treated for the purpose of those regulations as himself doing an unlawful act of the like description[4]; and for these purposes, an employee or agent for whose act the employer[5] or principal is liable[6], or would be so liable but for the statutory defence that he took reasonably practicable steps to prevent that act[7], is to be deemed to aid the doing of the act by the employer or principal[8]. A person does not, however, knowingly aid another to do an unlawful act under these provisions if:

(1) he acts in reliance on a statement made to him by that other person that, by reason of any provision of the relevant regulations, the act which he aids would not be unlawful; and

(2) it is reasonable for him to rely on the statement[9].

A person who knowingly or recklessly makes a statement such as is referred to in head (1) above which in a material respect is false or misleading commits an offence, and is liable on summary conviction to a fine[10].

1   As to the meaning of 'person' see para 344 note 3 ante.
2   As to the meaning of 'act' see para 723 note 3 ante.

3   Ie the Employment Equality (Sexual Orientation) Regulations 2003, SI 2003/1661 (as amended).
4   Ibid reg 23(1).
5   As to the meaning of 'employer' see para 725 note 1 ante.
6   Ie under the Employment Equality (Sexual Orientation) Regulations 2003, SI 2003/1661, reg 22: see para 739 ante.
7   Ie but for ibid reg 22(3): see para 739 ante.
8   Ibid reg 23(2). As to aiding discrimination under the Sex Discrimination Act 1975 see para 392 ante; and as to aiding discrimination under the Race Relations Act 1976 see para 477 ante.
9   Employment Equality (Sexual Orientation) Regulations 2003, SI 2003/1661, reg 23(3).
10 Ibid reg 23(4). The fine referred to in the text is a fine not exceeding level 5 on the standard scale: see reg 23(4). As to the standard scale see para 315 note 15 ante.

(iv) General Exceptions

741.   Exception for national security.   Nothing in Part II[1] or Part III[2] of the Employment Equality (Sexual Orientation) Regulations 2003 renders unlawful an act[3] done for the purpose of safeguarding national security, if the doing of the act was justified by that purpose[4].

1   Ie the Employment Equality (Sexual Orientation) Regulations 2003, SI 2003/1661, Pt II (regs 6–21) (as amended): see para 725 et seq ante.
2   Ie ibid Pt III (regs 22–23): see paras 739–740 ante.
3   As to the meaning of 'act' see para 723 note 3 ante.
4   Employment Equality (Sexual Orientation) Regulations 2003, SI 2003/1661, reg 24.
    As to national security under the Sex Discrimination Act 1975 see para 403 ante; as to national security under the Race Relations Act 1976 see para 487 ante; and as to national security under the Disability Discrimination Act 1995 see para 616 ante.

742.   Exception for benefits dependent on a person's status.   Nothing in Part II[1] or Part III[2] of the Employment Equality (Sexual Orientation) Regulations 2003 renders unlawful:

(1)   anything which prevents or restricts access to a benefit[3] by reference to marital status where the right to the benefit accrued or the benefit is payable in respect of periods of service prior to the coming into force of the Civil Partnership Act 2004[4];

(2)   the conferring of a benefit on married persons and civil partners to the exclusion of all other persons[5].

1   Ie the Employment Equality (Sexual Orientation) Regulations 2003, SI 2003/1661, Pt II (regs 6–21) (as amended): see para 725 et seq ante.
2   Ie ibid Pt III (regs 22–23): see paras 739–740 ante.
3   As to the meaning of 'benefits' see para 725 note 6 ante.
4   The majority of the provisions of the Civil Partnership Act 2004 were brought into force on 5 December 2005: see the Civil Partnership Act 2004 (Commencement No 2) Order 2005, SI 2005/3175, arts 2, 3, Schs 1, 2. See further CIVIL PARTNERSHIP.
5   Employment Equality (Sexual Orientation) Regulations 2003, SI 2003/1661, reg 25 (substituted by SI 2005/2114). The Employment Equality (Sexual Orientation) Regulations 2003, SI 2003/1661, reg 25 (as originally enacted) was held to be compatible with EC Council Directive 2000/78 (OJ L303, 2.12.2000, p 16) establishing a general framework for equal treatment in employment and occupation (the 'EC Framework Employment Directive') (see para 508 ante): see *R (on the application of Amicus—MSF section) v Secretary of State for Trade and Industry* [2004] EWHC 860 (Admin), [2004] IRLR 430, [2004] All ER (D) 238 (Apr).

743.   Exceptions for positive action.   Nothing in Part II[1] or Part III[2] of the Employment Equality (Sexual Orientation) Regulations 2003 renders unlawful any act[3]:

(1)   done in or in connection with:

(a)   affording persons[4] of a particular sexual orientation[5] access to facilities for training which would help fit them for particular work; or

(b)   encouraging persons of a particular sexual orientation to take advantage of opportunities for doing particular work,

where it reasonably appears to the person doing the act that it prevents or compensates for disadvantages linked to sexual orientation suffered by persons of that sexual orientation doing that work or likely to take up that work[6];

(2)   done by a trade organisation[7] in or in connection with:

     (a)   affording only members of the organisation who are of a particular sexual orientation access to facilities for training which would help fit them for holding a post of any kind in the organisation; or

     (b)   encouraging only members of the organisation who are of a particular sexual orientation to take advantage of opportunities for holding such posts in the organisation,

where it reasonably appears to the organisation that the act prevents or compensates for disadvantages linked to sexual orientation suffered by those of that sexual orientation holding such posts or likely to hold such posts[8];

(3)   done by a trade organisation[9] in or in connection with encouraging only persons of a particular sexual orientation to become members of the organisation where it reasonably appears to the organisation that the act prevents or compensates for disadvantages linked to sexual orientation suffered by persons of that sexual orientation who are, or are eligible to become, members[10].

1   Ie the Employment Equality (Sexual Orientation) Regulations 2003, SI 2003/1661, Pt II (regs 6–21) (as amended): see para 725 et seq ante.
2   Ie ibid Pt III (regs 22–23): see paras 739–740 ante.
3   As to the meaning of 'act' see para 723 note 3 ante.
4   As to the meaning of 'person' see para 344 note 3 ante.
5   For the meaning of 'sexual orientation' see para 722 note 3 ante.
6   Employment Equality (Sexual Orientation) Regulations 2003, SI 2003/1661, reg 25(1).
7   Ie within the meaning of ibid reg 15: see para 732 ante.
8   Ibid reg 25(2).
9   See note 7 supra.
10   Employment Equality (Sexual Orientation) Regulations 2003, SI 2003/1661, reg 25(3).

(v)   Enforcement

744. Restriction of proceedings for breach of the regulations. Except as provided by the Employment Equality (Sexual Orientation) Regulations 2003[1], no proceedings, whether civil or criminal, lie against any person[2] in respect of an act[3] by reason that the act is unlawful by virtue of a provision of those regulations[4]. This does not, however, prevent the making of an application for judicial review[5] or the investigation or determination of any matter in accordance with Part X of the Pension Schemes Act 1993[6] by the Pensions Ombudsman[7].

1   Ie the Employment Equality (Sexual Orientation) Regulations 2003, SI 2003/1661 (as amended).
2   As to the meaning of 'person' see para 344 note 3 ante.
3   As to the meaning of 'act' see para 723 note 3 ante.
4   Employment Equality (Sexual Orientation) Regulations 2003, SI 2003/1661, reg 27(1).
5   As to judicial review see generally ADMINISTRATIVE LAW vol 1(1) (2001 Reissue) para 59 et seq.
6   Ie in accordance with the Pension Schemes Act 1993 Pt X (ss 145–152) (as amended) (investigations: the Pensions Ombudsman): see SOCIAL SECURITY AND PENSIONS vol 44(2) (Reissue) para 663 et seq.
7   Employment Equality (Sexual Orientation) Regulations 2003, SI 2003/1661, reg 27(2) (amended by SI 2003/2827).

745. Jurisdiction of employment tribunals; time limit and burden of proof.
The following provision applies to any act[1] of discrimination[2] or harassment[3] which is unlawful by virtue of any provision of Part II of the Employment Equality (Sexual Orientation) Regulations 2003[4] other than:

(1) where the act is one in respect of which an appeal or proceedings in the nature of an appeal may be brought under any enactment[5], the provision relating to qualifications bodies[6];

(2) the provision relating to institutions of further and higher education[7]; or

(3) where the act arises out of and is closely connected to a relationship between the complainant and the respondent which has come to an end but during the course of which an act of discrimination against, or harassment of, the complainant by the respondent would have been unlawful by virtue of the provision referred to in head (2) above[8], the provision relating to relevant relationships[9] which have come to an end[10].

A complaint by any person[11] ('the complainant') that another person ('the respondent'): (a) has committed against the complainant an act to which this provision applies; or (b) is to be treated[12] as having committed against the complainant such an act, may be presented to an employment tribunal[13].

Where under the above provision a member[14] or prospective member[15] of an occupational pension scheme[16] presents to an employment tribunal a complaint that the trustees or managers[17] of the scheme:

(i) have committed against him an act which is unlawful by virtue of the provision relating to unlawful discrimination by the trustees and managers of occupational pension schemes[18] or of the provision relating to relevant relationships which have come to an end[19]; or

(ii) are to be treated[20] as having committed against him such an act,

the employer[21] in relation to the scheme is, for the purposes of the rules governing procedure, to be treated as a party and to be entitled to appear and be heard in accordance with those rules[22].

An employment tribunal may not consider a complaint under the above provisions[23] unless it is presented to the tribunal before the end of the period of three months beginning when the act complained of was done[24] or, in a case relating to the armed forces[25], the period of six months so beginning[26]. Where, however, the period within which a complaint must so be presented is extended[27], the period within which the complaint must be presented is the extended period rather than the period mentioned above[28]. A tribunal may nevertheless consider any such complaint which is out of time if, in all the circumstances of the case, it considers that it is just and equitable to do so[29].

Where, on the hearing of any complaint presented under the above provisions[30] to an employment tribunal, the complainant proves facts from which the tribunal could otherwise conclude in the absence of an adequate explanation that the respondent:

(A) has committed against the complainant an act to which the above provisions apply; or

(B) is to be treated[31] as having committed against the complainant such an act,

the tribunal must uphold the complaint unless the respondent proves that he did not commit, or, as the case may be, is not to be treated as having committed, that act[32].

1   As to the meaning of 'act' see para 723 note 3 ante.

2   For the meaning of references to discrimination see para 725 note 4 ante.

3   For the meaning of references to harassment see para 725 note 9 ante.

4   Ie any provision of the Employment Equality (Sexual Orientation) Regulations 2003, SI 2003/1661, Pt II (regs 6–21) (as amended): see para 725 et seq ante.

5   For these purposes, 'enactment' includes an enactment comprised in, or in an instrument made under, an Act of the Scottish Parliament: ibid reg 28(4). Scottish matters generally are beyond the scope of this work.

6   Ie ibid reg 16: see para 733 ante.

7   Ie ibid reg 20 (as amended): see para 737 ante.

8   Ie by virtue of ibid reg 20 (as amended): see para 737 ante. For the purpose of head (3) in the text, reference to an act of discrimination or harassment which would have been unlawful includes, in the case of a relationship which has come to an end before 1 December 2003 (ie the date of the coming into force of the Employment Equality (Sexual Orientation) Regulations 2003, SI 2003/1661 (as amended): see para 722 note 1 ante), reference to an act of discrimination or harassment which would, after that date, have been unlawful: reg 28(3).

9   Ie ibid reg 21: see para 738 ante.

10   Ibid reg 28(2).

11   As to the meaning of 'person' see para 344 note 3 ante.

12   Ie by virtue of the Employment Equality (Sexual Orientation) Regulations 2003, SI 2003/1661, reg 22 or reg 23: see paras 739–740 ante.

13   Ibid reg 28(1). As to employment tribunals and the procedure before them see EMPLOYMENT vol 16(1B) (Reissue) para 816 et seq.

14   For the meaning of 'member' see para 727 note 5 ante.

15   For the meaning of 'prospective member' see para 727 note 6 ante.

16   For the meaning of 'occupational pension scheme' see para 727 note 3 ante.

17   For the meaning of 'trustees or managers' see para 727 note 2 ante.

18   Ie by virtue of the Employment Equality (Sexual Orientation) Regulations 2003, SI 2003/1661, reg 9A (as added): see para 727 ante.

19   See note 9 supra.

20   See note 12 supra.

21   As to the meaning of 'employer' see para 725 note 1 ante.

22   Employment Equality (Sexual Orientation) Regulations 2003, SI 2003/1661, reg 9A(3)(d), Sch 1A para 6 (added by SI 2003/2827).

23   Ie presented under the Employment Equality (Sexual Orientation) Regulations 2003, SI 2003/1661, reg 28: see the text and notes 1–13 supra.

24   For these purposes and the purposes of ibid reg 33 (help for persons in obtaining information etc: see para 748 post): (1) when the making of a contract is, by reason of the inclusion of any term, an unlawful act, that act is to be treated as extending throughout the duration of the contract; and (2) any act extending over a period is to be treated as done at the end of that period; and (3) a deliberate omission is to be treated as done when the person in question decided upon it; and in the absence of evidence establishing the contrary a person is to be taken for these purposes to decide upon an omission when he does an act inconsistent with doing the omitted act or, if he has done no such inconsistent act, when the period expires within which he might reasonably have been expected to do the omitted act if it was to be done: reg 34(4).

25   Ie a case to which ibid reg 36(7) (armed forces) applies: see para 751 post.

26   Ibid reg 34(1). As to time limits under the Sex Discrimination Act 1975 see para 416 ante; and as to time limits under the Race Relations Act 1976 see para 502 ante.

27   Ie by the Employment Act 2002 (Dispute Resolution) Regulations 2004, SI 2004/752, reg 15: see EMPLOYMENT vol 16(1B) Reissue) para 594.

28   Employment Equality (Sexual Orientation) Regulations 2003, SI 2003/1661, reg 34(1A) (added by SI 2004/752).

29   Employment Equality (Sexual Orientation) Regulations 2003, SI 2003/1661, reg 34(3).

30   See note 23 supra.

31   See note 12 supra.

32   Employment Equality (Sexual Orientation) Regulations 2003, SI 2003/1661, reg 29(1), (2). See also *Wong v Igen Ltd (Equal Opportunities Commission and others intervening), Emokpae v Chamberlin Solicitors (Equal Opportunities Commission and others intervening), Webster v Brunel University (Equal Opportunities Commission and others intervening)* [2005] EWCA Civ 142, [2005] 3 All ER 812, [2005] ICR 931, [2005] IRLR 258; and paras 418, 504 ante.

746.   Remedies on complaints in employment tribunals.   Where an employment tribunal finds that a complaint presented to it[1] is well-founded, the tribunal must make such of the following as it considers just and equitable:

(1)   an order declaring the rights of the complainant and the respondent in relation to the act[2] to which the complaint relates;

(2) an order requiring the respondent to pay to the complainant compensation[3] of an amount corresponding to any damages he could have been ordered by a county court to pay to the complainant if the complaint had fallen to be dealt with under the provisions relating to the jurisdiction of county courts[4];

(3) a recommendation that the respondent take within a specified period action appearing to the tribunal to be practicable for the purpose of obviating or reducing the adverse effect on the complainant of any act of discrimination[5] or harassment[6] to which the complaint relates[7].

As respects an unlawful act of discrimination consisting of the application of a provision, criterion or practice[8], if the respondent proves that the provision, criterion or practice was not applied with the intention of treating the complainant unfavourably on grounds of sexual orientation[9], an order may be made under head (2) above only if the employment tribunal:

(a) makes such order under head (1) above, if any, and such recommendation under head (3) above, if any, as it would have made if it had no power to make an order under head (2) above; and

(b) where it makes an order under head (1) above or a recommendation under head (3) above, or both, considers that it is just and equitable to make an order under head (2) above as well[10].

If without reasonable justification the respondent to a complaint fails to comply with a recommendation made by an employment tribunal under head (3) above, then, if it thinks it just and equitable to do so, the tribunal may increase the amount of compensation required to be paid to the complainant in respect of the complaint by an order made under head (2) above or, if an order under that head was not made, the tribunal may make such an order[11].

The above provisions have effect subject to the following provisions relating to occupational pension schemes[12]. Where:

(i) a member[13] or prospective member[14] of an occupational pension scheme[15] ('the complainant') presents to an employment tribunal[16] a complaint against the trustees or managers[17] of the scheme or an employer[18];

(ii) the complainant is not a pensioner member[19] of the scheme;

(iii) the complaint relates to the terms on which persons[20] become members of the scheme, or the terms on which members of the scheme are treated; and

(iv) the tribunal finds the complaint to be well-founded,

then the employment tribunal may, without prejudice to the generality of its power under head (1) above, make an order declaring that the complainant has a right:

(A) where the complaint relates to the terms on which persons become members of the scheme, to be admitted to the scheme;

(B) where the complaint relates to the terms on which members of the scheme are treated, to membership of the scheme without discrimination[21].

Such an order may be made in respect of such period as is specified in the order, but may not be made in respect of any time before 1 December 2003[22]; and it may make such provision as the employment tribunal considers appropriate as to the terms on which, or the capacity in which, the complainant is to enjoy such admission or membership[23]. The employment tribunal may not, however, make an order for compensation under head (2) above, whether in relation to arrears of benefits or otherwise, except for injury to feelings or where without reasonable justification the respondent to a complaint fails to comply with a recommendation[24] made by the tribunal[25].

1 Ie under the Employment Equality (Sexual Orientation) Regulations 2003, SI 2003/1661, reg 28: see para 745 ante.

2   As to the meaning of 'act' see para 723 note 3 ante.

3   Where an amount of compensation falls to be awarded under head (2) in the text, the tribunal may include in the award interest on that amount subject to, and in accordance with, the provisions of the Employment Tribunals (Interest on Awards in Discrimination Cases) Regulations 1996, SI 1996/2803 (amended by virtue of the Employment Rights (Dispute Resolution) Act 1998 s 1(2)): Employment Equality (Sexual Orientation) Regulations 2003, SI 2003/1661, reg 30(4).

       As to guidance on the proper level of damages to be awarded in discrimination cases (of all categories) for injury to feelings and other forms of non-pecuniary damage see *Vento v Chief Constable of West Yorkshire Police* [2002] EWCA Civ 1871, [2003] ICR 318, [2003] IRLR 102, [2002] All ER (D) 363 (Dec); and paras 414, 499 ante.

4   Ie under Employment Equality (Sexual Orientation) Regulations 2003, SI 2003/1661, reg 31: see para 747 post. An award of compensation under head (2) in the text may be made on a joint and several basis so that each respondent is liable to pay the whole of the award of compensation: see *Way v Crouch* [2005] IRLR 603, EAT; and para 414 note 8 ante.

5   For the meaning of references to discrimination see para 725 note 4 ante.

6   For the meaning of references to harassment see para 725 note 9 ante.

7   Employment Equality (Sexual Orientation) Regulations 2003, SI 2003/1661, reg 30(1).

8   Ie an unlawful act of discrimination falling within ibid reg 3(1)(b): see para 722 head (2) ante.

9   For the meaning of 'sexual orientation' see para 722 note 3 ante.

10   Employment Equality (Sexual Orientation) Regulations 2003, SI 2003/1661, reg 30(2).

11   Ibid reg 30(3).

12   Ibid reg 30(5) (added by SI 2003/2828).

13   For the meaning of 'member' see para 727 note 5 ante.

14   For the meaning of 'prospective member' see para 727 note 6 ante.

15   For the meaning of 'occupational pension scheme' see para 727 note 3 ante.

16   See note 1 supra.

17   For the meaning of 'trustees or managers' see para 727 note 2 ante.

18   As to the meaning of 'employer' see para 725 note 1 ante.

19   For the meaning of 'pensioner member' see para 727 note 5 ante.

20   As to the meaning of 'person' see para 344 note 3 ante.

21   Employment Equality (Sexual Orientation) Regulations 2003, SI 2003/1661, reg 9A(3)(d), Sch 1A para 7(1), (2) (reg 9A, Sch 1A added by SI 2003/2827).

22   Ie the date of the coming into force of the Employment Equality (Sexual Orientation) Regulations 2003, SI 2003/1661 (as amended): see para 722 note 1 ante.

23   Ibid Sch 1A para 7(3) (as added: see note 21 supra).

24   Ie by virtue of ibid reg 30(3): see the text and note 11 supra.

25   Ibid Sch 1A para 7(4) (as added: see note 21 supra).

747. Jurisdiction of county courts; time limit, burden of proof and remedies. The following provision applies to any act[1] of discrimination[2] or harassment[3] which is unlawful by virtue of:

(1) the provision relating to institutions of further and higher education[4]; or

(2) where the act arises out of and is closely connected to a relationship between the claimant and the respondent which has come to an end but during the course of which an act of discrimination against, or harassment of, the claimant by the respondent would have been unlawful[5] by virtue of the provision mentioned in head (1) above, the provision relating to relevant relationships[6] which have come to an end[7].

A claim by any person[8] ('the claimant') that another person ('the respondent'):

(a) has committed against the claimant an act to which this provision applies; or

(b) is to be treated[9] as having committed against the claimant such an act,

may be made the subject of civil proceedings in like manner as any other claim in tort for breach of statutory duty[10]. Proceedings so brought may be brought only in a county court[11] and must be instituted before the end of the period of six months beginning when the act complained of was done[12]; but a court may nevertheless consider any such claim which is out of time if, in all the circumstances of the case, it considers that it is just and equitable to do so[13]. Damages in respect of an unlawful act to which this provision applies may include compensation for injury to feelings whether or not they include compensation under any other head[14].

Where, on the hearing of the claim, the claimant proves facts from which the court could otherwise conclude in the absence of an adequate explanation that the respondent:

(i)　has committed against the claimant an act to which the above provision applies; or

(ii)　is to be treated[15] as having committed against the claimant such an act,

the court must uphold the claim unless the respondent proves that he did not commit, or, as the case may be, is not to be treated as having committed, that act[16].

1　As to the meaning of 'act' see para 723 note 3 ante.
2　For the meaning of references to discrimination see para 725 note 4 ante.
3　For the meaning of references to harassment see para 725 note 9 ante.
4　Ie the Employment Equality (Sexual Orientation) Regulations 2003, SI 2003/1661, reg 20: see para 737 ante.
5　For the purposes of head (2) in the text, reference to an act of discrimination or harassment which would have been unlawful includes, in the case of a relationship which has come to an end before 1 December 2003 (ie the date of the coming into force of the Employment Equality (Sexual Orientation) Regulations 2003, SI 2003/1661 (as amended): see para 722 note 1 ante), reference to an act of discrimination or harassment which would, after that date, have been unlawful: reg 31(5).
6　Ie ibid reg 21: see para 738 ante.
7　Ibid reg 31(4).
8　As to the meaning of 'person' see para 344 note 3 ante.
9　Ie by virtue of the Employment Equality (Sexual Orientation) Regulations 2003, SI 2003/1661, reg 22 or reg 23: see paras 739–740 ante.
10　Ibid reg 31(1).
11　Ibid reg 31(2)(a).
12　See ibid reg 34(2). As to when the act was done see reg 34(4); and para 745 note 24 ante.
13　Ibid reg 34(3).
14　See ibid reg 31(3). Cf the position under the Employment Rights Act 1996 s 123(1) (as amended) (compensatory award for unfair dismissal: see EMPLOYMENT vol 16(1B) para 690): see *Dunnachie v Kingston upon Hull City Council* [2004] UKHL 36, [2005] 1 AC 226, [2004] 3 All ER 1011, HL.
　　As to guidance on the proper level of damages to be awarded in discrimination cases (of all categories) for injury to feelings and other forms of non-pecuniary damage see *Vento v Chief Constable of West Yorkshire Police* [2002] EWCA Civ 1871, [2003] ICR 318, [2003] IRLR 102, [2002] All ER (D) 363 (Dec); and paras 414, 499 ante.
15　See note 9 supra.
16　Employment Equality (Sexual Orientation) Regulations 2003, SI 2003/1661, reg 32(1), (2).

748.　Help for persons in obtaining information etc.　In accordance with the following provisions, a person[1] ('the person aggrieved') who considers he may have been discriminated[2] against, or subjected to harassment[3], in contravention of the Employment Equality (Sexual Orientation) Regulations 2003[4], may serve on the respondent[5] to a complaint presented to an employment tribunal[6] or a claim brought in the county court[7] questions in the prescribed form[8] or forms to the like effect with such variation as the circumstances require; and the respondent may if he so wishes reply to such questions by way of the prescribed form[9] or forms to the like effect with such variation as the circumstances require[10].

Where the person aggrieved questions the respondent, whether in accordance with the above provision or not:

(1)　the questions, and any reply by the respondent, whether in accordance with the above provision or not, are, subject to the following provisions, to be admissible as evidence in the proceedings;

(2)　if it appears to the court or tribunal that the respondent deliberately, and without reasonable excuse, omitted to reply within eight weeks of service of the questions or that his reply is evasive or equivocal, the court or tribunal may draw any inference from that fact that it considers it just and equitable to draw, including an inference that he committed an unlawful act[11].

In proceedings before a county court, however, a question is only to be admissible as evidence in pursuance of head (1) above:

(a)   where it was served before those proceedings had been instituted, if it was so served within the period of six months beginning when the act complained of was done[12];

(b)   where it was served when those proceedings had been instituted, if it was served with the leave of, and within a period specified by, the court in question[13],

and in proceedings before an employment tribunal, a question is only to be admissible as evidence in pursuance of head (1) above:

(i)   where it was served before a complaint had been presented to a tribunal, if it was so served within the period of three months beginning when the act complained of was done[14], or, where the period within which a complaint must be presented has been extended[15], within the extended period;

(ii)   where it was served when a complaint had been presented to the tribunal, if it was so served within the period of 21 days beginning with the day on which the complaint was presented, or if it was so served later with leave given, and within a period specified, by a direction of the tribunal[16].

The above provisions are without prejudice to any other enactment or rule of law regulating preliminary matters in proceedings before a county court or employment tribunal, and have effect subject to any enactment or rule of law regulating the admissibility of evidence in such proceedings[17].

Either party may apply to the court to determine whether the question or any reply is admissible under the above provisions[18].

1   As to the meaning of 'person' see para 344 note 3 ante.
2   For the meaning of references to discrimination see para 725 note 4 ante.
3   For the meaning of references to harassment see para 725 note 9 ante.
4   Ie in contravention of the Employment Equality (Sexual Orientation) Regulations 2003, SI 2003/1661 (as amended): see para 722 et seq ante.
5   For these purposes, 'respondent' includes a prospective respondent: ibid reg 33(7). A question and any reply to it may be served on the respondent or, as the case may be, on the person aggrieved: (1) by delivering it to him; (2) by sending it by post to him at his usual or last-known residence or place of business; (3) where the person to be served is a body corporate or is a trade union or employers' association within the meaning of the Trade Union and Labour Relations (Consolidation) Act 1992 (see TRADE, INDUSTRY AND INDUSTRIAL RELATIONS vol 47 (2001 Reissue) para 1201), by delivering it to the secretary or clerk of the body, union or association at its registered or principal office or by sending it by post to the secretary or clerk at that office; (4) where the person to be served is acting by a solicitor, by delivering it at, or by sending it by post to, the solicitor's address for service; or (5) where the person to be served is the person aggrieved, by delivering the reply, or by sending it by post, to him at his address for reply as stated by him in the document containing the questions: Employment Equality (Sexual Orientation) Regulations 2003, SI 2003/1661, reg 33(5).
6   Ie under ibid reg 28: see para 745 ante.
7   Ie under ibid reg 31: see para 747 ante.
8   For the prescribed form see ibid reg 33(1), Sch 2.
9   For the prescribed form see ibid reg 33(1), Sch 3.
10   Ibid reg 33(1).
11   Ibid reg 33(2). As to the meaning of 'act' see para 723 note 3 ante.
12   As to when the act was done see ibid reg 34(4); and para 745 note 24 ante.
13   Ibid reg 33(3).
14   See note 12 supra.
15   Ie where the Employment Equality (Sexual Orientation) Regulations 2003, SI 2003/1661, reg 34(1A) (as added) applies: see para 745 ante.
16   Ibid reg 33(4) (amended by SI 2004/752). See also the Employment Equality (Sexual Orientation) Regulations 2003, SI 2003/1661, reg 34(4); and para 745 note 24 ante.
17   Ibid reg 33(6).

18 See *Practice Direction—Proceedings under Enactments relating to Discrimination* paras 4.1(f), 4.2. The provisions of CPR 3.4 (power to strike out a statement of case: see PRACTICE AND PROCEDURE vol 37 (Reissue) para 917) apply to the question and any answer as they apply to a statement of case: *Practice Direction—Proceedings under Enactments relating to Discrimination* para 4.3.

(vi) Supplemental Provisions

749. Validity and revision of contracts. A term of a contract is void where:

(1) the making of the contract is, by reason of the inclusion of the term, unlawful by virtue of the Employment Equality (Sexual Orientation) Regulations 2003[1];

(2) it is included in furtherance of an act[2] which is unlawful by virtue of those regulations; or

(3) it provides for the doing of an act which is unlawful by virtue of those regulations[3],

but this does not apply to a term the inclusion of which constitutes, or is in furtherance of, or provides for, unlawful discrimination[4] against, or harassment[5] of, a party to the contract, although the term is unenforceable against that party[6].

A term in a contract which purports to exclude or limit any provision of those regulations is unenforceable by any person[7] in whose favour the term would otherwise operate[8]; but this does not apply:

(a) to a contract settling a complaint[9] falling within the jurisdiction of an employment tribunal[10] where the contract is made with the assistance of a conciliation officer[11];

(b) to a contract settling such a complaint if the prescribed conditions regulating compromise contracts[12] are satisfied in relation to the contract; or

(c) to a contract settling a claim falling within the jurisdiction[13] of the county courts[14].

The prescribed conditions regulating compromise contracts are that:

(i) the contract must be in writing;

(ii) the contract must relate to the particular complaint;

(iii) the complainant must have received advice from a relevant independent adviser[15] as to the terms and effect of the proposed contract and in particular its effect on his ability to pursue a complaint before an employment tribunal;

(iv) there must be in force, when the adviser gives the advice, a contract of insurance, or an indemnity provided for members of a profession or professional body, covering the risk of a claim by the complainant in respect of loss arising in consequence of the advice;

(v) the contract must identify the adviser; and

(vi) the contract must state that the prescribed conditions regulating compromise contracts are satisfied[16].

On the application of a person interested in a contract which either contains a void term[17] or a term which is unenforceable[18], a county court may make such order as it thinks fit for removing or modifying any term rendered void[19] or removing or modifying any term made unenforceable[20] by the above provisions, but such an order may not be made unless all persons affected have been given notice in writing of the application, except where under rules of court notice may be dispensed with, and those persons have been afforded an opportunity to make representations to the court[21]. Such an order may include provision as respects any period before the making of the order but after 1 December 2003[22]. A person affected by the proposed variation must be made a respondent to the application unless the court orders otherwise[23].

1 Ie the Employment Equality (Sexual Orientation) Regulations 2003, SI 2003/1661 (as amended).
2 As to the meaning of 'act' see para 723 note 3 ante.

3 Equality (Sexual Orientation) Regulations 2003, SI 2003/1661, reg 35, Sch 4 para 1(1). Schedule 4 para 1(1)–(3) applies whether the contract was entered into before or after 1 December 2003 (ie the date on which the regulations came into force: see para 722 note 1 ante); but, in the case of a contract made before that date, Sch 4 para 1(1)–(3) does not apply in relation to any period before that date: Sch 4 para 1(4).

4 For the meaning of references to discrimination see para 725 note 4 ante.

5 For the meaning of references to harassment see para 725 note 9 ante.

6 Equality (Sexual Orientation) Regulations 2003, SI 2003/1661, Sch 4 para 1(2). See also note 3 supra.

7 As to the meaning of 'person' see para 344 note 3 ante.

8 Equality (Sexual Orientation) Regulations 2003, SI 2003/1661, Sch 4 para 1(3). See also note 3 supra.

9 An agreement under which the parties agree to submit a dispute to arbitration: (1) is to be regarded for the purposes of ibid Sch 4 para 2(1)(a) and (b) (see heads (a)–(b) in the text) as being a contract settling a complaint if: (a) the dispute is covered by a scheme having effect by virtue of an order under the Trade Union and Labour Relations (Consolidation) Act 1992 s 212A (as added and amended) (see EMPLOYMENT vol 16(1B) (Reissue) para 696); and (b) the agreement is to submit it to arbitration in accordance with the scheme; but (2) is to be regarded as neither being nor including such a contract in any other case: Employment Equality (Sexual Orientation) Regulations 2003, SI 2003/1661, Sch 4 para 2(8).

10 Ie a complaint to which ibid reg 28(1) applies: see para 745 ante.

11 Ie within the meaning of the Trade Union and Labour Relations (Consolidation) Act 1992 s 211 (as amended): see TRADE, INDUSTRY AND INDUSTRIAL RELATIONS vol 47 (2001 Reissue) para 1437.

12 Ie the conditions regulating compromise contracts under the Employment Equality (Sexual Orientation) Regulations 2003, SI 2003/1661, Sch 4: see heads (i)–(vi) in the text.

13 Ie a claim to which ibid reg 31 applies: see para 747 ante.

14 Ibid Sch 4 para 2(1).

15 A person is a relevant independent adviser for these purposes: (1) if he is a qualified lawyer; (2) if he is an officer, official, employee or member of an independent trade union who has been certified in writing by the trade union as competent to give advice and as authorised to do so on behalf of the trade union; or (3) if he works at an advice centre (whether as an employee or a volunteer) and has been certified in writing by the centre as competent to give advice and as authorised to do so on behalf of the centre (ibid Sch 4 para 2(3)); but a person is not a relevant independent adviser for these purposes in relation to the complainant: (a) if he is, is employed by or is acting in the matter for the other party or a person who is connected with the other party; (b) in the case of a person within head (2) or head (3) supra, if the trade union or advice centre is the other party or a person who is connected with the other party; or (c) in the case of a person within head (3) supra, if the complainant makes a payment for the advice received from him (Sch 4 para 2(4)). In head (1) supra, 'qualified lawyer' means, as respects England and Wales, a barrister (whether in practice as such or employed to give legal advice), a solicitor who holds a practising certificate, or a person other than a barrister or solicitor who is an authorised advocate or authorised litigator (within the meaning of the Courts and Legal Services Act 1990: see BARRISTERS vol 3(1) (2005 Reissue) para 501; SOLICITORS vol 44(1) (Reissue) paras 78–79) (Employment Equality (Sexual Orientation) Regulations 2003, SI 2003/1661, Sch 4 para 2(5)(a)); and a person is to be treated as being a qualified lawyer if he is a fellow of the Institute of Legal Executives employed by a solicitors' practice (Sch 4 para 2(5A) (added by SI 2004/2519)). In head (2) supra, 'independent trade union' has the same meaning as in the Trade Union and Labour Relations (Consolidation) Act 1992 (see TRADE, INDUSTRY AND INDUSTRIAL RELATIONS vol 47 (2001 Reissue) para 1014): Employment Equality (Sexual Orientation) Regulations 2003, SI 2003/1661, Sch 4 para 2(6). For the purposes of head (a) supra, any two persons are to be treated as connected if one is a company of which the other (directly or indirectly) has control or if both are companies of which a third person (directly or indirectly) has control: Sch 4 para 2(7).

16 Ibid Sch 4 para 2(2).

17 Ie a contract to which ibid Sch 4 para 1(1) applies: see heads (1)–(3) in the text.

18 Ie a contract to which ibid Sch 4 para 1(2) applies: see the text and notes 4–6 supra.

19 Ie by ibid Sch 4 para 1(1): see the text and notes 1–3 supra.

20 Ie by ibid Sch 4 para 1(2): see the text and notes 4–6 supra.

21 Ibid Sch 4 para 3(1).

22 Ibid Sch 4 para 3(2). As to the significance of 1 December 2003 see note 3 supra.

23 See *Practice Direction—Proceedings under Enactments relating to Discrimination* paras 7.1(g), 7.2.

750. Collective agreements and rules of undertakings. The following provisions apply to:

(1) any term of a collective agreement[1], including an agreement which was not intended, or is presumed not to have been intended, to be a legally enforceable contract;

(2) any rule made by an employer[2] for application to all or any of the persons[3] who are employed by him or who apply to be, or are, considered by him for employment[4];

(3) any rule made by a trade organisation[5] or a qualifications body[6] for application to all or any of its members or prospective members, or all or any of the persons on whom it has conferred professional or trade qualifications[7] or who are seeking the professional or trade qualifications which it has power to confer[8].

Any such term or rule is void where:

(a) the making of the collective agreement is, by reason of the inclusion of the term, unlawful by virtue of the Employment Equality (Sexual Orientation) Regulations 2003[9];

(b) the term or rule is included or made in furtherance of an act[10] which is unlawful by virtue of those regulations; or

(c) the term or rule provides for the doing of an act which is unlawful by virtue of those regulations[11],

and this applies whether the agreement was entered into, or the rule made, before or after 1 December 2003[12]; but, in the case of an agreement entered into, or a rule made, before that date, it does not apply in relation to any period before that date[13]. The avoidance by virtue of heads (a) to (c) above of any term or rule which provides for any person to be discriminated[14] against is without prejudice to the following rights, except in so far as they enable any person to require another person to be treated less favourably than himself, namely:

(i) such of the rights of the person to be discriminated against; and

(ii) such of the rights of any person who will be treated more favourably in direct or indirect consequence of the discrimination,

as are conferred by or in respect of a contract made or modified wholly or partly in pursuance of, or by reference to, that term or rule[15].

A person to whom this provision applies[16] may present a complaint to an employment tribunal that a term or rule is void by virtue of the above provisions if he has reason to believe:

(A) that the term or rule may at some future time have effect in relation to him; and

(B) where he alleges that it is void by virtue of head (c) above, that an act for the doing of which it provides may at some such time be done in relation to him, and the act would be unlawful by virtue of the relevant regulations if done in relation to him in present circumstances[17].

When an employment tribunal finds that a complaint so presented to it is well-founded the tribunal must make an order declaring that the term or rule is void[18]; and such an order may include provision as respects any period before the making of the order but after 1 December 2003[19].

1 For these purposes, 'collective agreement' means any agreement relating to one or more of the matters mentioned in the Trade Union and Labour Relations (Consolidation) Act 1992 s 178(2) (meaning of trade dispute: see TRADE, INDUSTRY AND INDUSTRIAL RELATIONS vol 47 (2001 Reissue) para 1301), being an agreement made by or on behalf of one or more employers or one or more organisations of employers or associations of such organisations with one or more organisations of workers or associations of such organisations: Employment Equality (Sexual Orientation) Regulations 2003, SI 2003/1661, reg 35, Sch 4 para 10.

2 As to the meaning of 'employer' see para 725 note 1 ante.

3 As to the meaning of 'person' see para 344 note 3 ante.

4 For the meaning of 'employment' see para 725 note 2 ante.

5   Ie within the meaning of the Employment Equality (Sexual Orientation) Regulations 2003, SI 2003/1661, reg 15: see para 732 ante.
6   Ie within the meaning of ibid reg 16: see para 733 ante.
7   See note 6 supra.
8   Employment Equality (Sexual Orientation) Regulations 2003, SI 2003/1661, Sch 4 para 4(1).
9   Ie by virtue of the Employment Equality (Sexual Orientation) Regulations 2003, SI 2003/1661 (as amended).
10 As to the meaning of 'act' see para 723 note 3 ante.
11 Employment Equality (Sexual Orientation) Regulations 2003, SI 2003/1661, Sch 4 para 4(2).
12 Ie the date when the Employment Equality (Sexual Orientation) Regulations 2003, SI 2003/1661 (as amended) came into force: see para 722 note 1 ante.
13 Ibid Sch 4 para 4(3).
14 For the meaning of references to discrimination see para 725 note 4 ante.
15 Employment Equality (Sexual Orientation) Regulations 2003, SI 2003/1661, Sch 4 para 9.
16 In the case of a complaint about: (1) a term of a collective agreement made by or on behalf of an employer, an organisation of employers of which an employer is a member, or an association of such organisations of one of which an employer is a member; or (2) a rule made by an employer within the meaning of ibid Sch 4 para 4(1)(b) (see head (2) in the text), Sch 4 para 5 (see the text and note 17 infra) applies to any person who is, or is genuinely and actively seeking to become, one of his employees: Sch 4 para 6. In the case of a complaint about a rule made by an organisation or body to which Sch 4 para 4(1)(c) applies (see head (3) in the text), Sch 4 para 5 applies to any person: (a) who is, or is genuinely and actively seeking to become, a member of the organisation or body; (b) on whom the organisation or body has conferred a professional or trade qualification (within the meaning of reg 16: see para 733 note 1 ante); or (c) who is genuinely and actively seeking such a professional or trade qualification which the organisation or body has power to confer: Sch 4 para 7.
17 Ibid Sch 4 para 5.
18 Ibid Sch 4 para 8(1).
19 Ibid Sch 4 para 8(2). As to the significance of 1 December 2003 see note 12 supra.

751.   Application to the Crown etc.   The Employment Equality (Sexual Orientation) Regulations 2003[1] apply:

(1)   to an act[2] done by or for purposes of a Minister of the Crown[3] or government department; or

(2)   to an act done on behalf of the Crown by a statutory body[4], or a person holding a statutory office[5],

as they apply to an act done by a private person[6].

The regulations also apply to:

(a)   service for purposes of a Minister of the Crown or government department[7], other than service of a person holding a statutory office;

(b)   service on behalf of the Crown for purposes of a person holding a statutory office or purposes of a statutory body; or

(c)   service in the armed forces[8],

as they apply to employment[9] by a private person, and so apply as if references to a contract of employment included references to the terms of service[10].

This provision applies to any complaint by a person ('the complainant') that another person:

(i)   has committed an act of discrimination[11] or harassment[12] against the complainant which is unlawful by virtue of the relevant provisions relating to applicants and employees[13]; or

(ii)   is to be treated[14] as having committed such an act of discrimination or harassment against the complainant,

if at the time when the act complained of was done the complainant was serving in the armed forces and the discrimination or harassment in question relates to his service in those forces[15]. A complainant may present a complaint to which the above provision applies to an employment tribunal[16] only if:

(A)　he has made a complaint in respect of the same matter to an officer under the service redress procedures[17] applicable to him; and

(B)　that complaint has not been withdrawn[18],

and for these purposes a complainant is to be treated as having withdrawn his complaint if, having made a complaint to an officer under the service redress procedures applicable to him, he fails to submit that complaint to the Defence Council under those procedures[19]. Where a complaint is so presented to an employment tribunal, the service redress procedures may continue after the complaint is so presented[20].

1　Ie the Employment Equality (Sexual Orientation) Regulations 2003, SI 2003/1661 (as amended).
2　As to the meaning of 'act' see para 723 note 3 ante.
3　As to the meaning of 'Minister of the Crown' see para 728 note 4 ante.
4　For these purposes, 'statutory body' means a body set up by or in pursuance of an enactment: Employment Equality (Sexual Orientation) Regulations 2003, SI 2003/1661, reg 36(11).
5　For these purposes, 'statutory office' means an office set up by or in pursuance of an enactment: see ibid reg 36(11).
6　Ibid reg 36(1). Regulation 36(1), (2) has effect subject to reg 11 (as amended) (police: see paras 729, 739 ante): reg 36(3).
7　For these purposes, 'service for purposes of a Minister of the Crown or government department' does not include service in any office mentioned in the House of Commons Disqualification Act 1975 Sch 2 (as amended) (ministerial offices: see PARLIAMENT vol 34 (Reissue) para 611): Employment Equality (Sexual Orientation) Regulations 2003, SI 2003/1661, reg 36(11).
8　For these purposes, 'armed forces' means any of the naval, military or air forces of the Crown: ibid reg 36(11).
9　For the meaning of 'employment' see para 725 note 2 ante.
10　Employment Equality (Sexual Orientation) Regulations 2003, SI 2003/1661, reg 36(2). See also note 6 supra. Regulation 9(3) (meaning of employment and contract work at establishment in Great Britain: see para 725 note 3 ante) has effect in relation to any ship, aircraft or hovercraft belonging to or possessed by Her Majesty in right of the government of the United Kingdom as it has effect in relation to a ship, aircraft or hovercraft specified in reg 9(3)(a) or (b): reg 36(4). For the meaning of 'United Kingdom' see para 325 note 6 ante.
11　For the meaning of references to discrimination see para 725 note 4 ante.
12　For the meaning of references to harassment see para 725 note 9 ante.
13　Ie by virtue of the Employment Equality (Sexual Orientation) Regulations 2003, SI 2003/1661, reg 6: see para 725 ante.
14　Ie by virtue of ibid reg 22 or reg 23: see paras 739–740 ante.
15　Ibid reg 36(7). The provisions of the Crown Proceedings Act 1947 Pts II–IV (ss 13–40) (as amended) apply to proceedings against the Crown under the Employment Equality (Sexual Orientation) Regulations 2003, SI 2003/1661 (as amended) as they apply to proceedings in England and Wales which by virtue of the Crown Proceedings Act 1947 s 23 (as amended) are treated for the purposes of Pt II (as amended) as civil proceedings by or against the Crown, except that in their application to proceedings under those regulations s 20 (as amended) (removal of proceedings from county court to High Court) does not apply: Employment Equality (Sexual Orientation) Regulations 2003, SI 2003/1661, reg 36(6).
16　Ie under ibid reg 28: see para 745 ante.
17　For these purposes, 'the service redress procedures' means the procedures, excluding those which relate to the making of a report on a complaint to Her Majesty, referred to in the Army Act 1955 s 180 (as substituted and amended), the Air Force Act 1955 s 180 (as substituted and amended) and the Naval Discipline Act 1957 s 130 (as substituted and amended) (see ARMED FORCES vol 2(2) (Reissue) para 314): Employment Equality (Sexual Orientation) Regulations 2003, SI 2003/1661, reg 36(11).
18　Ibid reg 36(8).
19　Ibid reg 36(9). As to the Defence Council see ARMED FORCES vol 2(2) (Reissue) para 2; CONSTITUTIONAL LAW AND HUMAN RIGHTS vol 8(2) (Reissue) para 443 et seq.
20　Ibid reg 36(10).

752.　Application to House of Commons and House of Lords staff.　The Employment Equality (Sexual Orientation) Regulations 2003[1] apply:

(1)　to an act[2] done by an employer[3] of a relevant member of the House of Commons staff[4], and to service as such a member, as they apply to an act done by and to service for purposes of a Minister of the Crown[5] or government department, and accordingly apply as if references to a contract of employment[6] included references to the terms of service of such a member[7];

(2) in relation to employment as a relevant member of the House of Lords staff[8] as they apply in relation to other employment[9].

1 Ie the Employment Equality (Sexual Orientation) Regulations 2003, SI 2003/1661 (as amended): see para 722 et seq ante.
2 As to the meaning of 'act' see para 723 note 3 ante.
3 As to the meaning of 'employer' see para 725 note 1 ante. See also note 4 infra.
4 For these purposes, 'relevant member of the House of Commons staff' means any person:
　　(1) who was appointed by the House of Commons Commission; or
　　(2) who is a member of the Speaker's personal staff,
and the provisions of the Employment Rights Act 1996 s 195(6)–(12) (as amended) (person to be treated as employer of House of Commons staff: see EMPLOYMENT vol 16(1A) (Reissue) para 136) apply, with any necessary modifications, for the purposes of the Employment Equality (Sexual Orientation) Regulations 2003, SI 2003/1661 (as amended): reg 37(2).
5 As to the meaning of 'Minister of the Crown' see para 728 note 4 ante.
6 For the meaning of 'employment' see para 725 note 2 ante.
7 Employment Equality (Sexual Orientation) Regulations 2003, SI 2003/1661, reg 37(1).
8 For these purposes, 'relevant member of the House of Lords staff' means any person who is employed under a contract of employment with the Corporate Officer of the House of Lords; and the Employment Rights Act 1996 s 194(7) (continuity of employment: see EMPLOYMENT vol 16(1A) (Reissue) para 135) applies: Employment Equality (Sexual Orientation) Regulations 2003, SI 2003/1661, reg 38(2).
9 Ibid reg 38(1).

(2) DISCRIMINATION IN OTHER FIELDS

753. Regulations. The Equality Act 2006 enables the Secretary of State[1] to make regulations in relation to discrimination or harassment on grounds of sexual orientation[2]. In exercise of this power he has made the Equality Act (Sexual Orientation) Regulations 2007[3], which have effect from 30 April 2007[4]. The regulations make provision in relation to direct discrimination[5], indirect discrimination[6], and victimisation[7].

For the purposes of the regulations, a person ('A') discriminates against another ('B') if, on grounds of the sexual orientation of B or any other person except A, A treats B less favourably than he treats or would treat others (in cases where there is no material difference in the relevant circumstances)[8]. A person ('A') discriminates against another ('B') if A applies to B a provision, criterion or practice: (1) which he applies or would apply equally to persons not of B's sexual orientation; (2) which puts persons of B's sexual orientation at a disadvantage compared to some or all others (where there is no material difference in the relevant circumstances); (3) which puts B at a disadvantage compared to some or all persons who are not of his sexual orientation (where there is no material difference in the relevant circumstances); and (4) which A cannot reasonably justify by reference to matters other than B's sexual orientation[9]. A person ('A') discriminates against another ('B') if A treats B less favourably than he treats or would treat another and does so by reason of the fact that, or by reason of A's knowledge or suspicion that, B: (a) has brought or intended to bring, or intends to bring, proceedings under the regulations; (b) has given or intended to give, or intends to give, evidence in proceedings under the regulations; (c) has provided or intended to provide, or intends to provide, information in connection with proceedings under the regulations; (d) has done or intended to do, or intends to do, any other thing under or in connection with the regulations; (e) has alleged or intended to allege, or intends to allege, that a person has contravened the regulations[10].

Under the regulations, it is unlawful to discriminate against a person in the provision of goods, facilities and services[11]; in relation to disposal and management of premises[12];

and in relation to education[13]. It is also unlawful for a public authority exercising a function to do any act which constitutes discrimination[14]. Discriminatory practices[15] and discriminatory advertisements[16] are prohibited, as is instructing another to discriminate or causing discrimination[17]. However, nothing in the regulations makes it unlawful to comply with statutory requirements[18].

Special provision is made in relation to organisations relating to religion or belief[19]; adoption and fostering agencies[20]; associations or private clubs[21]; charities[22]; and blood donation services[23].

Provision is made for the enforcement of the regulations[24], and in relation to the liability of employers and principals[25]. It is unlawful to aid a person to do anything which is unlawful under the regulations[26].

1   As to the Secretary of State and the National Assembly for Wales see para 302 ante.

2   Equality Act 2006 s 81(1). For these purposes, 'sexual orientation' has the meaning given by s 35 (see para 305 note 5 ante): s 81(2).
        Section s 81(3) provides that the regulations may, in particular:
      (1)   make provision of a kind similar to Pt 2 (ss 44–80) (discrimination on the ground of religion or belief in the provision of goods, facilities, services and education etc: see para 691 et seq ante);
      (2)   define discrimination;
      (3)   define harassment;
      (4)   make provision for enforcement, which may, in particular, include provision:
         (a)   creating a criminal offence of a kind similar to, and with the same maximum penalties as, an offence created by an enactment relating to discrimination or equality;
         (b)   about validity and revision of contracts;
         (c)   about discriminatory advertisements;
         (d)   about instructing or causing discrimination or harassment;
      (5)   provide for exceptions, whether or not of a kind similar to those provided for by Pt 2 or any other enactment relating to discrimination or equality;
      (6)   make provision which applies generally or only in specified cases or circumstances;
      (7)   make different provision for different cases or circumstances;
      (8)   include incidental or consequential provision, which may include provision amending an enactment;
      (9)   include transitional provision[6].
    For this purpose, 'enactment' includes an enactment in or under an Act of the Scottish Parliament: s 81(5). Scottish matters generally are beyond the scope of this work.
        The regulations: (i) must be made by statutory instrument; and (ii) may not be made unless a draft has been laid before and approved by resolution of each House of Parliament: s 81(4).
        As to the equivalent power to make regulations in relation to Northern Ireland see s 82.

3   Ie the Equality Act (Sexual Orientation) Regulations 2007, SI 2007/1263. As to the application of these regulations to the Crown see reg 33. As to the territorial application of these regulations see reg 34; but note that they do not extend to Northern Ireland (see reg 1(2)).

4   See ibid reg 1(1).

5   See the text and note 8 infra. References in the Equality Act (Sexual Orientation) Regulations 2007, SI 2007/1263, to 'discrimination' are references to any discrimination falling within reg 3 (see the text and notes 8–10 infra); and related expressions are to be construed accordingly: reg 2(1).

6   See the text and note 9 infra.

7   See the text and note 10 infra.

8   Equality Act (Sexual Orientation) Regulations 2007, SI 2007/1263 reg 3(1). In this provision, a reference to a person's sexual orientation includes a reference to a sexual orientation which he is thought to have: reg 3(2).
        For the purposes of reg 3(1) and reg 3(3) (see the text and note 9 infra), the fact that one of the persons (whether or not B) is a civil partner while the other is married is not to be treated as a material difference in the relevant circumstances: reg 3(4).

9   Ibid reg 3(3).

10   Ibid reg 3(5). This provision does not apply where A's treatment of B relates to: (1) B's making or intending to make, not in good faith, a false allegation; or (2) B's giving or intending to give, not in good faith, false information or evidence: reg 3(6).

11   See ibid reg 4. As to exceptions see reg 6. There is also an exception in relation to annuities or life insurance policies, if the less favourable treatment is effected by reference to actuarial or other data from a source on which it is reasonable to rely: see reg 27.

12 See ibid reg 5. As to exceptions see reg 6.
13 See ibid reg 7. As to the responsible bodies to whom this provision applies see reg 7, Sch 3.
      It is not, however, unlawful to do anything by way of meeting special needs for education, training or welfare of persons on grounds of their sexual orientation: see reg 13.
14 See ibid reg 8. This provision binds the Crown: see reg 33(1). Certain bodies, functions and actions are excepted from the provisions of reg 8: see reg 8(3), Sch 1.
15 See ibid reg 9.
16 See ibid reg 10.
17 See ibid reg 11.
18 See ibid reg 12.
19 See ibid reg 14.
20 See ibid reg 15.
21 See ibid reg 16. As to exceptions see reg 17.
22 See ibid reg 18.
23 See ibid reg 28.
24 See ibid regs 19–26. Forms are prescribed for a claimant's questions and for a respondent's reply: see reg 24, Sch 2.
25 See ibid reg 30. Special provision is made in relation to the police: see reg 31.
26 See ibid reg 29.

8. AGE DISCRIMINATION

(1) IN GENERAL

754. Discrimination on grounds of age. For the purposes of the Employment Equality (Age) Regulations 2006[1], a person[2] ('A') discriminates against another person ('B') if:

(1) on grounds of age[3], A treats B less favourably than he treats or would treat other persons; or

(2) A applies to B a provision, criterion or practice which he applies or would apply equally to persons not of the same age group[4] as B, but:

    (a) which puts or would put persons of the same age group as B at a particular disadvantage when compared with other persons; and

    (b) which puts B at that disadvantage,

and A cannot show the treatment or, as the case may be, provision, criterion or practice to be a proportionate means of achieving a legitimate aim[5]. A comparison of B's case with that of another person under the above provisions must be such that the relevant circumstances in the one case are the same, or not materially different, in the other[6].

1   Ie for the purposes of the Employment Equality (Age) Regulations 2006, SI 2006/1031 (as amended).
     These regulations came into force: (1) subject to heads (2) and (3) infra, on 1 October 2006; (2) for the purposes of reg 7 (applicants and employees: see para 758 post) and reg 24 (relationships which have come to an end: see para 782 post), in so far as either regulation relates to arrangements for: (a) the payment of pension contributions; (b) admission to a pension scheme; and (c) the provision of any benefits relating to pensions, on 1 December 2006; and (3) for the purposes of reg 11, Sch 2 (as amended) (pension schemes: see para 760 et seq post), on 1 December 2006: reg 1(1) (substituted by SI 2006/2408).
     Any amendment, repeal or revocation made by the regulations has the same extent as the provision to which it relates (Employment Equality (Age) Regulations 2006, SI 2006/1031, reg 1(2)); but subject to that, the regulations do not extend to Northern Ireland (reg 1(3)).
     The regulations are made by the Secretary of State under the European Communities Act 1972 s 2(2) and implement the relevant provisions of EC Council Directive 2000/78 (OJ L303, 2.12.2000, p 16) establishing a general framework for equal treatment in employment and occupation (the 'EC Framework Employment Directive'): see para 508 ante. As to the Secretary of State and the National Assembly for Wales see para 302 ante.
2   As to the meaning of 'person' see para 344 note 3 ante.
3   The reference in head (2) in the text to B's age includes B's apparent age: Employment Equality (Age) Regulations 2006, SI 2006/1031, reg 3(3)(b).
4   For the purposes of ibid reg 3, 'age group' means a group of persons defined by reference to age, whether by reference to a particular age or a range of ages: reg 3(3)(3)(a).
5   Ibid reg 3(1). As to direct and indirect discrimination under the Sex Discrimination Act 1975 see paras 344, 351, 355 ante; and as to direct and indirect discrimination under the Race Relations Act 1976 see paras 439–440 ante.
6   Employment Equality (Age) Regulations 2006, SI 2006/1031, reg 3(2). See also *Rutherford v Secretary of State for Trade and Industry* [2006] UKHL 19, [2006] IRLR 551, [2006] All ER (D) 30 (May), where it was decided against allowing a form of anticipatory age discrimination under the guise of sex discrimination, the issue in the case being whether the exclusion of employees over 65 from unfair dismissal and redundancy rights indirectly discriminated against men, given that more men than women tend to work past that age; and see para 352 ante.

755. Discrimination by way of victimisation. For the purposes of the Employment Equality (Age) Regulations 2006[1], a person[2] ('A') discriminates against another person ('B') if he treats B less favourably than he treats or would treat other persons in the same circumstances, and does so by reason that B has:

(1) brought proceedings against A or any other person under those regulations;

(2) given evidence or information in connection with proceedings brought by any person against A or any other person under those regulations;

(3)   otherwise done anything under or by reference to those regulations in relation to A or any other person; or

(4)   alleged that A or any other person has committed an act[3] which, whether or not the allegation so states, would amount to a contravention of those regulations,

or by reason that A knows that B intends to do any of those things, or suspects that B has done or intends to do any of them[4]. This does not, however, apply to treatment of B by reason of any allegation made by him, or evidence or information given by him, if the allegation, evidence or information was false and not made or, as the case may be, given, in good faith[5].

1   Ie for the purposes of the Employment Equality (Age) Regulations 2006, SI 2006/1031 (as amended).
2   As to the meaning of 'person' see para 344 note 3 ante.
3   For these purposes, 'act' includes a deliberate omission: Employment Equality (Age) Regulations 2006, SI 2006/1031, reg 2(2).
4   Ibid reg 4(1). As to victimisation under the Sex Discrimination Act 1975 see para 358 ante; and as to victimisation under the Race Relations Act 1976 see para 442 ante.
5   Employment Equality (Age) Regulations 2006, SI 2006/1031, reg 4(2).

756.   Instructions to discriminate.   For the purposes of the Employment Equality (Age) Regulations 2006[1], a person[2] ('A') discriminates against another person ('B') if he treats B less favourably than he treats or would treat other persons in the same circumstances, and does so by reason that:

(1)   B has not carried out, in whole or in part, an instruction to do an act[3] which is unlawful by virtue of those regulations; or

(2)   B, having been given an instruction to do such an act, complains to A or to any other person about that instruction[4].

1   Ie for the purposes of the Employment Equality (Age) Regulations 2006, SI 2006/1031 (as amended).
2   As to the meaning of 'person' see para 344 note 3 ante.
3   As to the meaning of 'act' see para 755 note 3 ante.
4   Employment Equality (Age) Regulations 2006, SI 2006/1031, reg 5.

757.   Harassment on grounds of age.   For the purposes of the Employment Equality (Age) Regulations 2006[1], a person[2] ('A') subjects another person ('B') to harassment where, on grounds of age, A engages in unwanted conduct which has the purpose or effect of:

(1)   violating B's dignity; or

(2)   creating an intimidating, hostile, degrading, humiliating or offensive environment for B[3].

Conduct is to be regarded as having the effect specified in head (1) or head (2) above only if, having regard to all the circumstances, including in particular the perception of B, it should reasonably be considered as having that effect[4].

1   Ie for the purposes of the Employment Equality (Age) Regulations 2006, SI 2006/1031 (as amended).
2   As to the meaning of 'person' see para 344 note 3 ante.
3   Employment Equality (Age) Regulations 2006, SI 2006/1031, reg 6(1). Cf harassment under the Sex Discrimination Act 1975 (see para 347 ante) and under the Race Relations Act 1976 (see para 444 ante).
4   Employment Equality (Age) Regulations 2006, SI 2006/1031, reg 6(2).

(2) DISCRIMINATION IN EMPLOYMENT AND VOCATIONAL TRAINING

(i) Discrimination against Applicants, Employees and Contract Workers; in general

758.   Unlawful discrimination against applicants and employees; exception for genuine occupational requirement.   It is unlawful for an employer[1]:

(1)   in relation to employment[2] by him at an establishment in Great Britain[3], to discriminate[4] against a person:

(a)   in the arrangements he makes for the purpose of determining to whom he should offer employment;

(b)   in the terms on which he offers that person employment; or

(c)   by refusing to offer, or deliberately not offering, him employment[5];

(2)   in relation to a person whom he employs at an establishment in Great Britain, to discriminate against that person:

(a)   in the terms of employment which he affords him;

(b)   in the opportunities which he affords him for promotion, transfer, training, or receiving any other benefit[6];

(c)   by refusing to afford him, or deliberately not affording him, any such opportunity; or

(d)   by dismissing him[7], or subjecting him to any other detriment[8];

(3)   in relation to employment by him at an establishment in Great Britain, to subject to harassment[9] a person whom he employs or who has applied to him for employment[10].

Heads (1)(a) and (1)(c) above do not, however, apply in relation to a person to whom, if he was recruited by the employer, the statutory exception for retirement[11] could apply and either:

(i)   whose age is greater than the employer's normal retirement age[12] or, if the employer does not have a normal retirement age, the age of 65; or

(ii)   who would, within a period of six months from the date of his application to the employer, reach the employer's normal retirement age or, if the employer does not have a normal retirement age, the age of 65[13].

Head (2) above does not apply to benefits of any description if the employer is concerned with the provision, for payment or not, of benefits of that description to the public, or to a section of the public which includes the employee in question, unless:

(A)   that provision differs in a material respect from the provision of the benefits by the employer to his employees; or

(B)   the provision of the benefits to the employee in question is regulated by his contract of employment; or

(C)   the benefits relate to training[14].

In relation to discrimination on grounds of age[15], however, neither head (1)(a) nor head (1)(c) above applies to any employment; neither head (2)(b) or head (2)(c) above applies to promotion or transfer to, or training for, any employment; and head (2)(d) above does not apply to dismissal from any employment, where the specified exception[16] applies[17]. That exception applies where, having regard to the nature of the employment or the context in which it is carried out, possessing a characteristic related to age is a genuine and determining occupational requirement, it is proportionate to apply that requirement in the particular case, and either the person to whom that requirement is applied does not meet it or the employer is not satisfied, and in all the circumstances it is reasonable for him not to be satisfied, that that person meets it[18].

1   For these purposes, references to 'employer', in their application to a person at any time seeking to employ another, include a person who has no employees at that time: Employment Equality (Age) Regulations 2006, SI 2006/1031, reg 2(3). See also note 2 infra. As to the meaning of 'person' see para 344 note 3 ante.

2   'Employment' means employment under a contract of service or of apprenticeship or a contract personally to do any work, and related expressions (such as 'employee' and 'employer') are to be construed accordingly; but this definition does not apply in relation to ibid reg 30 (exception for retirement: see para 785 post), Sch 2 (as amended) (pension schemes: see para 760 et seq post), Sch 6 (as

amended) (duty to consider working beyond retirement: see para 792 et seq post), Sch 7 (transitional provisions relating to retirement) or Sch 8 (amendments, repeals and related transitional provisions): reg 2(2).

3   For the purposes of ibid Pt 2 (regs 7–24) ('the relevant purposes'), employment is to be regarded as being at an establishment in Great Britain if the employee: (1) does his work wholly or partly in Great Britain; or (2) does his work wholly outside Great Britain and reg 10(2) applies: reg 10(1). Regulation 10(2) applies if: (a) the employer has a place of business at an establishment in Great Britain; (b) the work is for the purposes of the business carried on at that establishment; and (c) the employee is ordinarily resident in Great Britain at the time when he applies for or is offered the employment, or at any time during the course of the employment: reg 10(2). The reference to 'employment' in reg 10(1) includes employment on board a ship only if the ship is registered at a port of registry in Great Britain, and employment on an aircraft or hovercraft only if the aircraft or hovercraft is registered in the United Kingdom and operated by a person who has his principal place of business, or is ordinarily resident, in Great Britain: reg 10(3). Subject to reg 10(5), for the purposes of determining if employment concerned with the exploration of the sea bed or subsoil or the exploitation of their natural resources is outside Great Britain, reg 10 has effect as if references to Great Britain included: (i) any area designated under the Continental Shelf Act 1964 s 1(7) (as amended) (see FUEL AND ENERGY vol 19(2) (Reissue) para 1411) except an area or part of an area in which the law of Northern Ireland applies; and (ii) in relation to employment concerned with the exploration or exploitation of the Frigg Gas Field, the part of the Norwegian sector of the Continental Shelf described in the Employment Equality (Age) Regulations 2006, SI 2006/1031, Sch 1 (reg 10(4)); but this does not apply to employment which is concerned with the exploration or exploitation of the Frigg Gas Field unless the employer is: (A) a company registered under the Companies Act 1985 (see COMPANIES); (B) an oversea company which has established a place of business within Great Britain from which it directs the exploration or exploitation in question; or (C) any other person who has a place of business within Great Britain from which he directs the exploration or exploitation in question (Employment Equality (Age) Regulations 2006, SI 2006/1031, reg 10(5)). For these purposes, 'the Frigg Gas Field' means the naturally occurring gas-bearing sand formations of the lower Eocene age located in the vicinity of the intersection of the line of latitude 59 degrees 53 minutes North and of the dividing line between the sectors of the Continental Shelf of the United Kingdom and the Kingdom of Norway and includes all other gas-bearing strata from which gas at the start of production is capable of flowing into the above-mentioned gas-bearing sand formations; and 'oversea company' has the same meaning as in the Companies Act 1985 s 744 (see COMPANIES vol 7(2) (2004 Reissue) para 1816): Employment Equality (Age) Regulations 2006, SI 2006/1031, reg 10(6).
      For the meaning of 'Great Britain' generally see para 325 note 6 ante. For these purposes, 'Great Britain' includes such of the territorial waters of the United Kingdom as are adjacent to Great Britain: reg 2(2). As to the territorial waters of the United Kingdom see WATER vol 49(2) (2004 Reissue) para 15. For the meaning of 'United Kingdom' see para 325 note 6 ante.

4   For the purposes of the Employment Equality (Age) Regulations 2006, SI 2006/1031 (as amended), references to discrimination are references to any discrimination falling within reg 3 (discrimination on grounds of age: see para 754 ante), reg 4 (discrimination by way of victimisation: see para 755 ante) or reg 5 (instructions to discriminate: see para 756 ante); and related expressions are to be construed accordingly: reg 2(2).

5   Ibid reg 7(1).

6   'Benefits', except in ibid reg 11, Sch 2 (as amended) (pension schemes: see para 760 et seq post), includes facilities and services: reg 2(2).

7   In ibid reg 6(2)(d) (see head (2)(d) in the text), reference to the dismissal of a person from employment includes reference: (1) to the termination of that person's employment by the expiration of any period (including a period expiring by reference to an event or circumstance), not being a termination immediately after which the employment is renewed on the same terms; and (2) to the termination of that person's employment by any act of his (including the giving of notice) in circumstances such that he is entitled to terminate it without notice by reason of the conduct of the employer: reg 7(7). As to the meaning of 'act' see para 755 note 3 ante.

8   Ibid reg 7(2). 'Detriment' does not include harassment within the meaning of reg 6 (see para 757 ante): reg 2(2).

9   For the purposes of the Employment Equality (Age) Regulations 2006, SI 2006/1031 (as amended), references to harassment are to be construed in accordance with reg 5 (harassment on grounds of age: see para 757 ante): reg 2(2).

10   Ibid reg 7(3).

11   Ie ibid reg 30: see para 785 post.

12   For these purposes, 'normal retirement age' is an age of 65 or more which meets the requirements of the Employment Rights Act 1996 s 98ZH (as added) (see para 787 note 3 post): Employment Equality (Age) Regulations 2006, SI 2006/1031, reg 7(8).

13   Ibid reg 7(4), (5).

14 Ibid reg 7(6).
15 Ie discrimination falling within ibid reg 3: see para 754 ante.
16 Ie ibid reg 8(2): see the text and note 18 infra.
17 Ibid reg 8(1).
18 Ibid reg 8(2).

759. Contract workers. It is unlawful for a principal[1], in relation to contract work[2] at an establishment in Great Britain[3], to discriminate[4] against a contract worker[5]:

(1)   in the terms on which he allows him to do that work;

(2)   by not allowing him to do it or continue to do it;

(3)   in the way he affords him access to any benefits[6] or by refusing or deliberately not affording him access to them; or

(4)   by subjecting him to any other detriment[7].

A principal does not, however, contravene head (2) above by doing any act[8] in relation to a contract worker where, if the work were to be done by a person taken into the principal's employment, that act would be lawful by virtue of the statutory exception[9] for a genuine occupational requirement[10]. Furthermore, heads (1) to (4) above do not apply to benefits of any description if the principal is concerned with the provision, for payment or not, of benefits of that description to the public, or to a section of the public to which the contract worker in question belongs, unless that provision differs in a material respect from the provision of the benefits by the principal to his contract workers[11].

It is also unlawful for a principal, in relation to contract work at an establishment in Great Britain, to subject a contract worker to harassment[12].

1   'Principal' means a person ('A') who makes work available for doing by individuals who are employed by another person who supplies them under a contract made with A: Employment Equality (Age) Regulations 2006, SI 2006/1031, reg 9(5). As to the meaning of 'person' see para 344 note 3 ante.
2   'Contract work' means work made available as described in note 1 supra: ibid reg 9(5).
3   Ibid reg 10 (meaning of employment and contract work at establishment in Great Britain: see para 758 note 3 ante) applies in relation to contract work within the meaning of reg 9 as it applies in relation to employment; and, in its application to contract work, references to 'employee', 'employer' and 'employment' are references to (respectively) 'contract worker', 'principal' and 'contract work' within the meaning of reg 9: reg 10(7). As to the meaning of 'Great Britain' see para 758 note 3 ante.
4   For the meaning of references to discrimination see para 758 note 4 ante.
5   'Contract worker' means any individual who is supplied to the principal under such a contract as is described in note 1 supra: Employment Equality (Age) Regulations 2006, SI 2006/1031, reg 9(5).
6   As to the meaning of 'benefits' see para 758 note 6 ante.
7   Employment Equality (Age) Regulations 2006, SI 2006/1031, reg 9(1). As to the meaning of 'detriment' see para 758 note 8 ante.
8   As to the meaning of 'act' see para 755 note 3 ante.
9   Ie by virtue of the Employment Equality (Age) Regulations 2006, SI 2006/1031, reg 8: see para 758 ante.
10 Ibid reg 9(3).
11 Ibid reg 9(4).
12 Ibid reg 9(2). For the meaning of references to harassment see para 758 note 9 ante.

(ii)   Discrimination in relation to Pension Schemes

A. IN GENERAL

760. Pension schemes; in general. It is unlawful, except in relation to rights accrued or benefits payable in respect of periods of pensionable service prior to 1 December 2006[1], for the trustees or managers[2] of, or any employer[3] in relation to, an occupational pension scheme[4] to discriminate[5] against a member[6] or prospective member[7] of the scheme in carrying out any of their functions in relation to it, including in particular their functions relating to the admission of members to the scheme and the treatment of members of it[8]. It is also unlawful for the trustees or managers of, or any employer in relation to, an occupational pension scheme, in relation to the scheme, to subject to harassment[9] a member or prospective member of it[10].

Every scheme[11] must be treated as including a provision ('the non-discrimination rule') containing a requirement that the trustees or managers of the scheme refrain from doing any act which is unlawful by virtue of the above provisions[12]; and the other provisions of the scheme are to have effect subject to the non-discrimination rule[13]. The trustees or managers of a scheme may:

(1)   if they do not otherwise have power to make such alterations to the scheme as may be required to secure conformity with the non-discrimination rule; or

(2)   if they have such power but the procedure for doing so is liable to be unduly complex or protracted, or involves the obtaining of consents which cannot be obtained, or can only be obtained with undue delay or difficulty,

by resolution make such alterations to the scheme[14]. Alterations made by such a resolution:

(a)   may have effect in relation to a period before the alterations are made, but may not have effect in relation to any time before 1 December 2006; and

(b)   are subject to the consent of any employer in relation to the scheme whose consent would be required for such a modification if it were to be made under the scheme rules[15].

1   Ie prior to the coming into force of the Employment Equality (Age) Regulations 2006, SI 2006/1031, reg 11 (as amended): see reg 1(1)(c) (substituted by SI 2006/2408).

2   For these purposes, 'managers' has the meaning given by the Pensions Act 1995 s 124(1) (as amended) (see SOCIAL SECURITY AND PENSIONS vol 44(2) (Reissue) para 612): Employment Equality (Age) Regulations 2006, SI 2006/1031, reg 11(3)(a), Sch 2 para 1(5).

3   For these purposes, 'employer' means: (1) in relation to an occupational pension scheme, the employer of persons in the description of employment to which the scheme in question relates; and (2) in relation to a personal pension scheme, where direct payment arrangements exist in respect of one or more members of the scheme who are employees, means an employer with whom those arrangements exist: Pensions Act 2004 s 318(1); definition applied by the Employment Equality (Age) Regulations 2006, SI 2006/1031, Sch 2 para 1(5).

4   For the purposes of ibid reg 11 (as amended), 'occupational pension scheme' means an occupational pension scheme within the meaning of either the Pension Schemes Act 1993 s 1(1) (as amended) (see SOCIAL SECURITY AND PENSIONS vol 44(2) (Reissue) para 853) or the Finance Act 2004 s 150(5) (i e a pension scheme established by an employer or employers and having or capable of having effect so as to provide benefits to or in respect of any or all of the employees of that employer or those employers, or of any other employer, whether or not it also has or is capable of having effect so as to provide benefits to or in respect of other persons: see SOCIAL SECURITY AND PENSIONS): Employment Equality (Age) Regulations 2006, SI 2006/1031, Sch 2 para 1(8) (amended by SI 2006/2931).

       For the purposes of the Employment Equality (Age) Regulations 2006, SI 2006/1031, Sch 2 (as amended), 'occupational pension scheme' generally means an occupational pension scheme within the meaning of the Pension Schemes Act 1993 s 1(1) (as amended) (see SOCIAL SECURITY AND PENSIONS vol 44(2) (Reissue) para 853): Employment Equality (Age) Regulations 2006, SI 2006/1031, Sch 2 para 1(1). However, in relation to rules, practices, actions and decisions identified: (1) in Sch 2 para 7(a) (see para 763 post), 'occupational pension scheme' means an occupational pension scheme within the meaning of the Pension Schemes Act 1993 s 1(1) (as amended) under which only retirement-benefit activities within the meaning of the Pensions Act 2004 s 255(4) (see SOCIAL SECURITY AND PENSIONS) are carried out; and (2) in the Employment Equality (Age) Regulations 2006, SI 2006/1031, Sch 2 paras 3A, 7(b), 9, 15A, 17–21, 23, 24, 25, 25A, 30 (as amended) (see paras 761, 763, 765–768, 770 post), 'occupational pension scheme' means an occupational pension scheme within the meaning of either the Pension Schemes Act 1993 s 1(1) (as amended) (see SOCIAL SECURITY AND PENSIONS vol 44(2) (Reissue) para 853) or the Finance Act 2004 s 150(5) (see SOCIAL SECURITY AND PENSIONS): Employment Equality (Age) Regulations 2006, SI 2006/1031, Sch 2 para 1(2), (3) (amended by SI 2006/2931).

5   For the meaning of references to discrimination see para 758 note 4 ante.

6   'Member', in relation to an occupational pension scheme, means any active member, deferred member or pensioner member (but in the Employment Equality (Age) Regulations 2006, SI 2006/1031, Sch 2

para 12 (as substituted) (see para 766 post) includes any active, deferred or pensioner member within the meaning of the Finance Act 2004 s 151(2)–(4)); and 'active member', 'deferred member' and 'pensioner member' have the meanings given by the Pensions Act 1995 s 124(1) (as amended) (see SOCIAL SECURITY AND PENSIONS vol 44(2) (Reissue) para 612) (but in the Employment Equality (Age) Regulations 2006, SI 2006/1031, Sch 2 para 13 (as substituted) (see para 766 post), 'active member' also includes an active member within the meaning of the Finance Act 2004 s 151(2)): Employment Equality (Age) Regulations 2006, SI 2006/1031, Sch 2 para 1(5).

7 'Prospective member' means any person who, under the terms of his employment or the scheme rules or both: (1) is able, at his own option, to become a member of the scheme; (2) is to become so able if he continues in the same employment for a sufficient period of time; (3) is to be admitted to it automatically unless he makes an election not to become a member; or (4) may be admitted to it subject to the consent of any person: Employment Equality (Age) Regulations 2006, SI 2006/1031, Sch 2 para 1(5).

8 Ibid reg 11(1) (amended by SI 2006/2408; SI 2006/2931).

9 For the meaning of references to harassment see para 758 note 9 ante.

10 Employment Equality (Age) Regulations 2006, SI 2006/1031, reg 11(2) (amended by SI 2006/2931).

11 For the purposes of the Employment Equality (Age) Regulations 2006, SI 2006/1031, Sch 2 (as amended), 'scheme' means an occupational pension scheme, construed in accordance with Sch 2 para 1(1)–(3) (as amended) (see note 4 supra): Sch 2 para 1(4).

12 Ibid reg 11(3)(c), Sch 2 para 2(1).

13 Ibid Sch 2 para 2(2).

14 Ibid reg 11(3)(d), Sch 2 para 2(3).

15 Ibid Sch 2 para 2(4).

761. Length of service exemptions. Nothing in Part 2[1] or Part 3[2] of the Employment Equality (Age) Regulations 2006 renders it unlawful[3] for there to be:

(1) any rule, practice, action or decision of the trustees or managers[4] ('A') of a scheme[5] regarding:

   (a) admission to the scheme ('admission terms'); or

   (b) the accrual of, or eligibility for, any benefit under the scheme ('benefit terms'),

   where the admission terms or the benefit terms put a member[6] ('B') of the scheme at a disadvantage when compared with another member ('C') if and to the extent that the disadvantage suffered by B is because B's length of service with an employer[7] ('D') in relation to the scheme is less than that of C;

(2) any rule, practice, action or decision of an employer ('E') in relation to a scheme regarding the admission terms or benefit terms where it puts a member ('F') of the scheme at a disadvantage when compared with another member ('G') if and to the extent that the disadvantage suffered by F is because F's length of service with E is less than that of G; or

(3) any rule, practice, action or decision of an employer ('H') regarding payment of contributions in respect of a worker[8] ('I') to a personal pension scheme[9] or to a money purchase arrangement[10] ('contribution terms') where it puts I at a disadvantage when compared with another worker ('J') if and to the extent that the disadvantage suffered by I is because I's length of service with H is less than that of J[11].

Where B's, or as the case may be, F's or I's length of service exceeds five years and a length of service criterion in the admission terms or as the case may be, the benefit terms or contribution terms puts B or F or I at a disadvantage, then:

(i) where head (1) above applies, A:

   (A) must ask D to confirm whether the length of service criterion reasonably appears to D to fulfil a business need of D's undertaking, for example by encouraging the loyalty or motivation, or rewarding the experience, of some or all of his workers; and

   (B) may rely on D's confirmation;

(ii) for the purposes of head (i)(B) above, D must:

      (A)   calculate B's length of service[12];

      (B)   provide A with details of B's length of service; and

      (C)   respond to A's request within a reasonable time;

  (iii) where head (1), head (2) or head (3) above applies, it must reasonably appear to D or, as the case may be, E or H that the length of service criterion applies in such a way that it fulfils a business need of his undertaking, for example by encouraging the loyalty or motivation, or rewarding the experience, of some or all of his workers[13].

1   Ie the Employment Equality (Age) Regulations 2006, SI 2006/1031, Pt 2 (regs 7–24) (as amended) (discrimination in employment and vocational training).

2   Ie ibid Pt 3 (regs 25–26) (other unlawful acts): see paras 783–784 post.

3   Ie subject to ibid Sch 2 para 3A(2) (as added): see heads (i)–(iii) in the text.

4   For the meaning of 'managers' see para 760 note 2 ante.

5   For the meaning of 'scheme' see para 760 note 11 ante.

6   For these purposes, a 'member' includes a 'prospective member': Employment Equality (Age) Regulations 2006, SI 2006/1031, reg 11(3)(b), Sch 2 para 3A(5) (Sch 2 para 3A added by SI 2006/2931). For the meanings of 'member' and 'prospective member' see para 760 notes 6, 7 ante.

7   For the meaning of 'employer' for these purposes see para 760 note 3 ante.

8   'Worker' in relation to the Employment Equality (Age) Regulations 2006, SI 2006/1031, reg 32 (see para 803 post), reg 34 (see para 805 post) and Sch 2 (as amended), means, as the case may be: (1) an employee; (2) a person holding an office or post to which reg 12 (office-holders etc: see para 772 post) applies; (3) a person holding the office of constable; (4) a partner within the meaning of reg 17 (partnerships: see para 775 post); (5) a member of a limited liability partnership within the meaning of reg 17 (see para 775 post); (6) a person in Crown employment; (7) a relevant member of the House of Commons staff; (8) a relevant member of the House of Lords staff: reg 2(2). As to the meaning of 'employee' see para 758 note 2 ante; for the meaning of 'Crown employment' see para 785 note 2 post; for the meaning of 'relevant member of the House of Commons staff' see para 785 note 3 post; and for the meaning of 'relevant member of the House of Lords staff' see para 785 note 4 post.

9   For these purposes, 'personal pension scheme' has the meaning given by the Pension Schemes Act 1993 s 1(1) (as amended) (see SOCIAL SECURITY AND PENSIONS vol 44(2) (Reissue) para 710): Employment Equality (Age) Regulations 2006, SI 2006/1031, Sch 2 para 1(7).

10   For these purposes, 'money purchase arrangement' has the meaning given by the Finance Act 2004 s 152(2), but the reference in s 152 to an arrangement is to be read as referring to an arrangement in respect of a member under a scheme as defined in the Pension Schemes Act 1993 s 1(1) (as amended) (see SOCIAL SECURITY AND PENSIONS vol 44(2) (Reissue) para 710) rather than in respect of a member under a pension scheme as defined in the Finance Act 2004 s 150(1) (see SOCIAL SECURITY AND PENSIONS): Employment Equality (Age) Regulations 2006, SI 2006/1031, Sch 2 para 1(5). References to contributions under a money purchase arrangement are to be construed as including amounts credited to a member's account whether or not they reflect payments actually made under the scheme: Sch 2 para 1(7).

11   Ibid Sch 2 para 3A(1) (as added: see note 6 supra).

12   When calculating B's or, as the case may be, F's or I's length of service, D or, as the case may be, E or H must calculate:

     (1) the length of time the member or worker has been working for him doing work which he reasonably considers to be at or above a particular level (assessed by reference to the demands made on the member or worker, eg in terms of effort, skills and decision making); or

     (2) the length of time the member or worker has been working for him in total,

    and it is for D or, as the case may be, E or H to decide which of head (1) or head (2) supra to use: ibid Sch 2 para 3A(3) (as added: see note 6 supra). For the purposes of Sch 2 para 3A(3) (as added), D or, as the case may be, E or H must calculate the length of time a member or worker has been working for him in accordance with reg 32(4)–(7) (exception for provision of certain benefits based on length of service: see para 803 post) and any reference in reg 32(4)–(7) to: (a) 'A' is to be read as if it were a reference to 'D' or, as the case may be, 'E' or 'H'; and (b) 'worker' is, where Sch 2 para 3A(1)(a) or (b) (as added) applies (see heads (1), (2) in the text), to be read as if it were a reference to 'member': Sch 2 para 3A(4) (as so added).

13   Ibid Sch 2 para 3A(2) (as added: see note 6 supra).

B. EXCEPTION FOR RULES ETC RELATING TO OCCUPATIONAL PENSION SCHEMES

762. Exception for rules, practices, actions and decisions relating to occupational pension schemes; in general. Nothing in Part 2[1] or Part 3[2] of the Employment Equality (Age) Regulations 2006 renders it unlawful for an employer[3], or for trustees or managers[4], to maintain or use, in relation to a scheme[5], any of the excepted[6] rules, practices, actions or decisions[7]. The inclusion of a rule, practice, action or decision in the statutory exceptions[8] is not, however, to be taken to mean that, but for that exemption, the use or maintenance by an employer, trustees or managers of a scheme of the rule, practice, action or decision in relation to the scheme would be unlawful[9].

The relevant exceptions relate to:

(1) admission to schemes[10];
(2) the use of age criteria in actuarial calculations[11];
(3) contributions generally[12];
(4) contributions under money purchase arrangements[13];
(5) contributions under defined benefits arrangements[14];
(6) age-related rules, practices, actions and decisions relating to benefit[15];
(7) other rules, practices, actions and decisions relating to benefit[16];
(8) closure of schemes[17];
(9) closure of sections of schemes[18];
(10) other rules, practices, actions and decisions[19]; and
(11) registered pension schemes[20].

1 Ie the Employment Equality (Age) Regulations 2006, SI 2006/1031, Pt 2 (regs 7–24) (as amended) (discrimination in employment and vocational training).
2 Ie ibid Pt 3 (regs 25–26) (other unlawful acts): see paras 783–784 post.
3 For the meaning of 'employer' for these purposes see para 760 note 3 ante.
4 For the meaning of 'managers' see para 760 note 2 ante.
5 For the meaning of 'scheme' see para 760 note 11 ante.
6 Ie any of the rules, practices, actions or decisions set out in the Employment Equality (Age) Regulations 2006, SI 2006/1031, reg 11(3)(b), Sch 2 Pt 2 (as amended).
7 Ibid Sch 2 para 3.
8 Ie inclusion in ibid Sch 2 Pt 2 (as amended).
9 Ibid Sch 2 para 4A(1) (added by SI 2006/2931).
10 See the Employment Equality (Age) Regulations 2006, SI 2006/1031, Sch 2 para 7 (as amended); and para 763 post.
11 See ibid Sch 2 para 8 (as amended); and para 764 post.
12 See ibid Sch 2 para 9 (as amended); and para 765 post.
13 See ibid Sch 2 para 10 (as amended); and 765 post.
14 See ibid Sch 2 paras 11, 11A (Sch 2 para 11A as added); and para 765 post.
15 See ibid Sch 2 paras 12–18 (as amended); and para 766 post.
16 See ibid Sch 2 paras 19–24 (as amended); and para 767 post.
17 See ibid Sch 2 para 25; and para 768 post.
18 See ibid Sch 2 para 25A (as added); and para 768 post.
19 See ibid Sch 2 paras 26–29; and para 769 post.
20 See ibid Sch 2 para 30; and para 770 post.

763. Admission to schemes. The following rules, practices, actions and decisions relating to occupational pension schemes are excepted[1] in relation to admission to a scheme[2]:

(1) a minimum or maximum age for admission, including different ages for admission for different groups or categories of worker[3];
(2) a minimum level of pensionable pay[4] for admission where that minimum:
    (a) does not exceed one and a half times the lower earnings limit[5];

     (b)   does not exceed an amount calculated by reference to the lower earnings limit where the aim is more or less to reflect the amount of the basic state retirement pension[6]; or

     (c)   does not exceed an amount calculated more or less to reflect the amount of the basic state retirement pension plus the additional state retirement pension[7].

1   Ie from the age discrimination provisions by the Employment Equality (Age) Regulations 2006, SI 2006/1031, reg 11(3)(b), Sch 2 para 3: see para 762 ante.

2   For the meaning of 'scheme' see para 760 note 11 ante.

3   For the meaning of 'worker' see para 761 note 8 ante.

4   'Pensionable pay' means that part of a member's pay which counts as pensionable pay under the scheme rules: Employment Equality (Age) Regulations 2006, SI 2006/1031, Sch 2 para 1(5). For the meaning of 'member' see para 760 note 6 ante.

5   'Lower earnings limit' means the amount specified for the tax year in question in regulations made under the Social Security Contributions and Benefits Act 1992 s 5(1)(a)(i) (as substituted) (earnings limits and thresholds for Class 1 contributions: see SOCIAL SECURITY AND PENSIONS vol 44(2) (Reissue) para 34): Employment Equality (Age) Regulations 2006, SI 2006/1031, Sch 2 para 1(5).

6   'Basic state retirement pension' means the basic pension in the Category A retirement pension within the meaning of the Social Security Contributions and Benefits Act 1992 s 44 (as amended) (see SOCIAL SECURITY AND PENSIONS vol 44(2) (Reissue) para 569): Employment Equality (Age) Regulations 2006, SI 2006/1031, Sch 2 para 1(5) (definition added by SI 2006/2931).

7   Employment Equality (Age) Regulations 2006, SI 2006/1031, reg 11(3)(b), Sch 2 para 7 (amended by SI 2006/2931). 'Additional state retirement pension' means the additional pension in the Category A retirement pension within the meaning of the Social Security Contributions and Benefits Act 1992 ss 44, 45 (as amended) (see SOCIAL SECURITY AND PENSIONS vol 44(2) (Reissue) para 569): Employment Equality (Age) Regulations 2006, SI 2006/1031, Sch 2 para 1(5) (definition added by SI 2006/2931).

764.   The use of age criteria in actuarial calculations.   The use of age criteria in actuarial calculations in a scheme[1] is excepted[2], for example in the actuarial calculation of:

     (1)   any age-related benefit[3] commencing before any early retirement pivot age[4] or enhancement of such benefit commencing after any late retirement pivot age[5];

     (2)   member or employer[6] contributions[7] by or in respect of a member to a scheme; or

     (3)   any age-related benefit commuted in exchange for the payment of any lump sum[8].

1   For the meaning of 'scheme' see para 760 note 11 ante.

2   Ie from the age discrimination provisions by the Employment Equality (Age) Regulations 2006, SI 2006/1031, reg 11(3)(b), Sch 2 para 3: see para 762 ante.

3   'Age-related benefit' means benefit provided from a scheme to a member: (1) on or following his retirement (including early retirement on grounds of ill health or otherwise); (2) on his reaching a particular age; or (3) on termination of his service in an employment; and 'employment' includes any trade, business, profession, office or vocation, whether or not a person is employed in it under a contract of employment or is self employed: ibid Sch 2 para 1(5). For the meaning of 'member' see para 760 note 6 ante.

4   'Early retirement pivot age' means, in relation to age-related benefit provided under a scheme, an age specified in the scheme rules (or otherwise determined) as the earliest age at which entitlement arises: (1) without consent (whether of an employer, the trustees or managers of the scheme or otherwise); and (2) without an actuarial reduction, but disregarding any special provision as to early payment on grounds of ill health or otherwise: ibid Sch 2 para 1(5) (definition substituted by SI 2006/2931).

5   'Late retirement pivot age' means an age specified in the scheme rules (or otherwise determined) above which benefit becomes payable with actuarial enhancement: Employment Equality (Age) Regulations 2006, SI 2006/1031, Sch 2 para 1(5) (definition amended by SI 2006/2931).

6   For the meaning of 'employer' for these purposes see para 760 note 3 ante.

7   As to contributions under a money purchase arrangement, and for the meaning of 'money purchase arrangement', see para 761 note 10 ante.

8   Employment Equality (Age) Regulations 2006, SI 2006/1031, reg 11(3)(b), Sch 2 para 8 (amended by SI 2006/2931).

765. Contributions. The following rules, practices, actions and decisions relating to contributions to occupational pension schemes are excepted[1]:

(1) any difference in the rate of member[2] or employer[3] contributions to a scheme[4], by or in respect of different members to the extent that this is attributable to any differences in the pensionable pay[5] or, in the specified circumstances[6], different accrual rates of those members[7];

(2) under a money purchase arrangement[8]:

    (a) different rates of member or employer contributions[9] according to the age of the members by or in respect of whom contributions are made where the aim in setting the different rates is either to equalise the amount of age-related benefit[10] in respect of comparable aggregate periods of pensionable service[11] to which members of different ages who are otherwise in a comparable situation will become entitled under the arrangement, or to make more nearly equal the amount of the age-related benefit, in respect of comparable aggregate periods of pensionable service, to which members of different ages who are otherwise in a comparable situation will become entitled under the arrangement;

    (b) equal rates of member or employer contributions irrespective of the age of the members by or in respect of whom contributions are made;

    (c) any limitation on any employer contributions in respect of a member or member contributions by reference to a maximum level of pensionable pay[12];

(3) under a defined benefits arrangement[13], different rates of member or employer contributions according to the age of the members by or in respect of whom contributions are made, to the extent that:

    (a) each year of pensionable service entitles members in a comparable situation to accrue a right to defined benefits based on the same fraction of pensionable pay; and

    (b) the aim in setting the different rates is to reflect the increasing cost of providing the defined benefits in respect of members as they get older[14];

(4) any limitation on employer contributions in respect of a member or member contributions to a defined benefit arrangement by reference to a maximum level of pensionable pay[15].

1 Ie from the age discrimination provisions by the Employment Equality (Age) Regulations 2006, SI 2006/1031, reg 11(3)(b), Sch 2 para 3: see para 762 ante.
2 For the meaning of 'member' see para 760 note 6 ante.
3 For the meaning of 'employer' for these purposes see para 760 note 3 ante.
4 For the meaning of 'scheme' see para 760 note 11 ante.
5 For the meaning of 'pensionable pay' see para 763 note 3 ante.
6 Ie where the Employment Equality (Age) Regulations 2006, SI 2006/1031, Sch 2 para 19A (as added) applies: see para 767 post.
7 Ibid Sch 2 para 9 (amended by SI 2006/2931).
8 For the meaning of 'money purchase arrangement' see para 761 note 10 ante.
9 As to contributions under a money purchase arrangement see para 761 note 10 ante.
10 For the meaning of 'age-related benefit' see para 764 note 3 ante.
11 For these purposes, 'pensionable service' has the meaning given by the Pensions Act 1995 s 124(1) (as amended) (see SOCIAL SECURITY AND PENSIONS vol 44(2) (Reissue) para 782): Employment Equality (Age) Regulations 2006, SI 2006/1031, Sch 2 para 1(5).
12 Ibid Sch 2 para 10 (amended by SI 2006/2931).
13 For these purposes, 'defined benefits arrangement' has the meaning given by the Finance Act 2004 s 152(6) (see SOCIAL SECURITY AND PENSIONS), but the reference in s 152 to an arrangement is to be read as referring to an arrangement in respect of a member under a scheme as defined in the Pension Schemes Act 1993 s 1(1) (as amended) (see SOCIAL SECURITY AND PENSIONS vol 44(2) (Reissue)

paras 710, 741, 874) rather than in respect of a member under a pension scheme as defined in the Finance Act 2004 s 150(1) (see SOCIAL SECURITY AND PENSIONS): Employment Equality (Age) Regulations 2006, SI 2006/1031, Sch 2 para 1(5).

14 Ibid Sch 2 para 11.

15 Ibid Sch 2 para 11A (added by SI 2006/2931).

766. Age-related rules, practices, actions and decisions relating to benefit.
The following age-related rules, practices, actions and decisions relating to occupational pension schemes are excepted[1]:

(1) a minimum age for any member[2] of a scheme[3] to be entitled to a particular age-related benefit[4] that is paid in accordance with the relevant provision[5] and is paid:

    (a) either with or without consent, whether of an employer[6], the trustees or managers[7] of the scheme or otherwise; and

    (b) before the early retirement pivot age[8] relevant to that age-related benefit[9];

and this also applies to different minimum ages for different groups or categories of members[10] but does not apply to any member who retires on the specified[11] grounds[12];

(2) a minimum age for any active[13] or prospective members[14] of a scheme for payment of or entitlement to a particular age-related benefit before the early retirement pivot age relevant to that age-related benefit where:

    (a) the entitlement to the age-related benefit at a minimum age applies to a member who is an active or prospective member of the scheme on 1 December 2006;

    (b) the age-related benefit may be paid, at a minimum age, to the active or prospective member either with or without consent, whether of an employer, the trustees or managers of the scheme or otherwise; and

    (c) the age-related benefit is enhanced in one or more of the specified[15] ways[16];

and this also applies to different minimum ages for different groups or categories of active or prospective members[17] and continues to apply to any member who after 1 December 2006:

    (i) joins a scheme as a result of a block transfer[18] or relevant transfer[19];

    (ii) joins a scheme as a result of a block transfer or relevant transfer from a scheme to which head (i) above applied; or

    (iii) joins a scheme on the basis that it will provide the same benefits as those provided by the scheme to which heads (a) to (c) above applied[20];

(3) a minimum age for any member of a scheme for payment of or entitlement to a particular age-related benefit on the grounds of redundancy[21] where it is enhanced in accordance with head (4) below and paid either with or without consent, whether of an employer, the trustees or managers of the scheme or otherwise[22]; and this also applies to different minimum ages for different groups or categories of members[23];

(4) the enhancement of any age-related benefit payable to or in respect of a member on the grounds of redundancy where the enhancement is calculated in one or more of the following ways:

    (a) by reference to the years of prospective pensionable service a member would have completed if he had remained in pensionable service until normal pension age[24];

    (b) by reference to a fixed number of years of prospective pensionable service;

    (c) by making an actuarial reduction which is smaller than if early retirement had been on grounds to which head (1) above applied; or (d)　by not making any actuarial reduction for early retirement[25];

(5)　an early retirement pivot age or a late retirement pivot age[26] including:

(a)　different such ages for different groups or categories of member; and

(b)　any early retirement pivot age or late retirement pivot age for deferred members which is different than for active members[27];

(6)　a minimum age for any member of a scheme for payment of or entitlement to a particular age-related benefit on the grounds of ill health where the age-related benefit is enhanced in accordance with head (7) below and paid either with or without consent, whether of an employer, the trustees or managers of the scheme or otherwise[28]; and this also applies to different minimum ages for different groups or categories of members[29];

(7)　the enhancement of any age-related benefit payable to or in respect of a member on the grounds of ill health where the enhancement is calculated in one or more of the following ways:

(a)　by reference to some or all of the years of prospective pensionable service a member would have completed if he had remained in pensionable service until normal pension age;

(b)　by reference to a fixed number of years of prospective pensionable service;

(c)　by making an actuarial reduction which is smaller than if early retirement had been on the grounds to which head (1) above applied; or

(d)　by not making any actuarial reduction for early retirement[30];

(8)　the calculation of any death benefit[31] payable in respect of a member:

(a)　by reference to some or all of the years of prospective pensionable service a member would have completed if he had remained in service until normal pension age; or

(b)　by reference to a fixed number of years of prospective pensionable service[32];

(9)　payment after a member's death of a death benefit calculated by reference to the period remaining in a pension guarantee period[33];

(10)　any difference between the death benefits payable in respect of deferred members who die before normal pension age and the death benefits payable in respect of deferred members who die on or after normal pension age[34];

(11)　any rule, practice, action or decision where:

(a)　the rate of pension to which a pensioner member is entitled is reduced at any time between age 60 and 65 ('the reduction date'), by either an amount not exceeding the relevant state retirement pension rate[35] at the reduction date, or the rate of the pension in payment where on the reduction date the relevant state retirement pension rate is greater than the rate of that pension;

(b)　from the date a member is entitled to present payment of a pension from a scheme, he is entitled to an additional amount of pension which does not exceed the amount of the basic state retirement pension[36] plus the additional state retirement pension[37] that would be payable at state pension age[38]; or

(c)　a member who reaches his state pension age is not entitled to, or no longer entitled to, an additional amount of pension which does not exceed the amount of the basic state retirement pension plus the additional state retirement pension that would be payable at state pension age[39];

(12)　the actuarial reduction of any pension payable from a scheme in consequence of a member's death to any dependant[40] of the member where that dependant is more than a specified number of years younger than the member[41];

(13)   in relation to pensioner members who have retired from a scheme on ill health grounds, discontinuation of any life assurance cover once any such members reach the normal retirement age[42] which applied to them at the time they retired, or in relation to members to whom no such normal retirement age applied, once such members reach the age of 65[43].

1   Ie from the age discrimination provisions by the Employment Equality (Age) Regulations 2006, SI 2006/1031, reg 11(3)(b), Sch 2 para 3: see para 762 ante.

2   For the meaning of 'member' see para 760 note 6 ante.

3   For the meaning of 'scheme' see para 760 note 11 ante.

4   For the meaning of 'age-related benefit' see para 764 note 3 ante.

5   Ie the Employment Equality (Age) Regulations 2006, SI 2006/1031, Sch 2 para 12(2) (as substituted). The age-related benefit must: (1) be actuarially reduced on the basis that the aim is to reflect that it is paid on a date before the applicable early retirement pivot age (see note 8 infra); and (2) not be enhanced by crediting the member with any additional periods of pensionable service or additional benefits: Sch 2 para 12(2) (Sch 2 paras 12–16 substituted, Sch 2 paras 13A, 13B, 15A added, and Sch 2 paras 17, 18 amended, by SI 2006/2931). For the meaning of 'pensionable service' see para 765 note 11 ante.

6   For the meaning of 'employer' for these purposes see para 760 note 3 ante.

7   For the meaning of 'managers' see para 760 note 2 ante.

8   For the meaning of 'early retirement pivot age' see para 764 note 4 ante.

9   Employment Equality (Age) Regulations 2006, SI 2006/1031, Sch 2 para 12(1) (as substituted: see note 5 supra).

10   Ibid Sch 2 para 12(3) (as substituted: see note 5 supra).

11   Ie the grounds to which ibid Sch 2 para 13 (as substituted), Sch 2 para 13A (as added) or Sch 2 para 15 (as substituted) apply: see heads (1), (6), (7) in the text.

12   Ibid Sch 2 para 12(4) (as substituted: see note 5 supra).

13   For the meaning of 'active member' see para 760 note 6 ante.

14   For the meaning of 'prospective member' see para 760 note 7 ante.

15   Ie one or more of the ways specified in the Employment Equality (Age) Regulations 2006, SI 2006/1031, Sch 2 para 13(2) (as substituted). For these purposes, the specified ways are the enhancement of any age-related benefit payable to or in respect of the member calculated in one or more of the following ways: (1) by reference to some or all of the years of prospective pensionable service a member would have completed if he had remained in pensionable service until normal pension age (see note 24 infra); (2) by reference to a fixed number of years of prospective pensionable service; (3) by making an actuarial reduction which is smaller than if early retirement had been on grounds to which Sch 2 para 12 (as substituted) (see head (1) in the text) applies; or (4) by not making any actuarial reduction for early retirement: Sch 2 para 13(2) (as substituted: see note 5 supra).

16   Ibid Sch 2 para 13(1) (as substituted: see note 5 supra).

17   Ibid Sch 2 para 13(3) (as substituted: see note 5 supra).

18   'Block transfer' means a transfer in a single transaction or a series of transactions from a scheme of all the sums and assets held for the purposes of, or representing, or derived from: (1) all accrued rights under a scheme; (2) contracted-out rights; or (3) rights which are not contracted-out rights, relating to a period of continuous pensionable service (or pensionable service which is treated as continuous) or one or more of a number of separate periods of such pensionable service which relate to a member and at least one other member; and 'contracted-out rights' are such rights, under or derived from an occupational pension scheme or an appropriate personal pension scheme as fall within the following categories: (a) entitlement to payment of, or accrued rights to, guaranteed minimum pensions; (b) protected rights; or (c) section 9(2B) rights, but not safeguarded rights (within the meaning of the Pension Schemes Act 1993 s 68A (as added): see SOCIAL SECURITY AND PENSIONS): Employment Equality (Age) Regulations 2006, SI 2006/1031, Sch 2 para 1(5) (definitions added by SI 2006/2931). 'Guaranteed minimum pension' has the meaning given in the Pension Schemes Act 1993 s 8(2) (as amended) (see SOCIAL SECURITY AND PENSIONS vol 44(2) (Reissue) para 878); 'protected rights' has the meaning given in s 10 (as amended) (see SOCIAL SECURITY AND PENSIONS vol 44(2) (Reissue) para 883); and 'section 9(2B) rights' are: (i) rights to the payment of pensions and accrued rights to pensions (other than rights attributable to voluntary contributions) under a scheme contracted-out by virtue of the Pension Schemes Act 1993 s 9(2B) (as added and amended) (see SOCIAL SECURITY AND PENSIONS vol 44(2) (Reissue) para 882), so far as attributable to an earner's service in contracted-out employment on or after 6 April 1997; and (ii) where a transfer payment has been made to such a scheme, any rights arising under the scheme as a consequence of that payment which are derived directly or indirectly from: (A) such rights as are referred to in head (i) supra under another scheme contracted-out by virtue of s 9(2B) (as added and amended); or (B) protected rights under another occupational pension scheme or under a personal pension scheme attributable to payments or contributions in respect of employment on or after 6 April 1997:

Employment Equality (Age) Regulations 2006, SI 2006/1031, Sch 2 para 1(5) (definitions as so added). For the meaning of 'occupational pension scheme' see para 760 note 4 ante; and for the meaning of 'personal pension scheme' see para 761 note 9 ante.

19   'Relevant transfer' has the meaning given in the Transfer of Undertakings (Protection of Employment) Regulations 1981, SI 1981/1794, reg 2(1) (revoked) or, as the case may be, the Transfer of Undertakings (Protection of Employment) Regulations 2006, SI 2006/246, reg 2(1): Employment Equality (Age) Regulations 2006, SI 2006/1031, Sch 2 para 1(5) (definition added by SI 2006/2931). As to the transfer of undertakings see further EMPLOYMENT vol 16(1A) (Reissue) para 110 et seq.

20   Employment Equality (Age) Regulations 2006, SI 2006/1031, Sch 2 para 13A (as added: see note 5 supra).

21   'Redundancy' means being dismissed by reason of redundancy for the purposes of the Employment Rights Act 1996 (see EMPLOYMENT vol 16(1B) (Reissue) para 707 et seq): Employment Equality (Age) Regulations 2006, SI 2006/1031, Sch 2 para 1(5) (definition added by SI 2006/2931).

22   Employment Equality (Age) Regulations 2006, SI 2006/1031, Sch 2 para 13B(1) (as added: see note 5 supra).

23   Ibid Sch 2 para 13B(3) (as added: see note 5 supra).

24   For these purposes, 'normal pension age' has the meaning given by the Pension Schemes Act 1993 s 180 (see SOCIAL SECURITY AND PENSIONS vol 44(2) (Reissue) para 896): Employment Equality (Age) Regulations 2006, SI 2006/1031, Sch 2 para 1(5).

25   Ibid Sch 2 para 13B(2) (as added: see note 5 supra).

26   For the meaning of 'late retirement pivot age' see para 764 note 5 ante.

27   Employment Equality (Age) Regulations 2006, SI 2006/1031, Sch 2 para 14 (as substituted: see note 5 supra). For the meaning of 'deferred member' see para 760 note 6 ante.

28   Ibid Sch 2 para 15(1) (as substituted: see note 5 supra).

29   Ibid Sch 2 para 15(3) (as substituted: see note 5 supra).

30   Ibid Sch 2 para 15(2) (as substituted: see note 5 supra).

31   'Death benefit' means benefit payable from a scheme, in respect of a member, in consequence of his death: ibid Sch 2 para 1(5) (definition amended by SI 2006/2931).

32   Employment Equality (Age) Regulations 2006, SI 2006/1031, Sch 2 para 15A(1) (as added: see note 5 supra).

33   Ibid Sch 2 para 15A(2) (as added: see note 5 supra). For these purposes, a pension guarantee period means a fixed period specified in or permitted by the scheme rules beginning on: (1) the date on which the payment of pension to or in respect of the member began; or (2) if specified in the scheme rules, the date of the member's death on or after normal pension age where payment of pension to or in respect of him had not begun: Sch 2 para 15A(3) (as so added).

34   Ibid Sch 2 para 15A(4) (as added: see note 5 supra).

35   For these purposes, 'relevant state retirement pension rate' has the same meaning as in the Finance Act 2004 Sch 28 para 2(5) (as substituted): Employment Equality (Age) Regulations 2006, SI 2006/1031, Sch 2 para 16(2) (as substituted: see note 5 supra).

36   For the meaning of 'basic state retirement pension' see para 763 note 6 ante.

37   For the meaning of 'additional state retirement pension' see para 763 note 7 ante.

38   For these purposes, 'state pension age' means the pensionable age specified in the rules in the Pensions Act 1995 Sch 4 para 1 (as amended) (see SOCIAL SECURITY AND PENSIONS vol 44(2) (Reissue) para 562): Employment Equality (Age) Regulations 2006, SI 2006/1031, Sch 2 para 16(2) (as substituted: see note 5 supra).

39   Ibid Sch 2 para 16(1) (as substituted: see note 5 supra).

40   'Dependant' means a widow, widower or surviving civil partner or a dependant as defined in the scheme rules: ibid Sch 2 para 1(5) (definition amended by SI 2006/2931).

41   Employment Equality (Age) Regulations 2006, SI 2006/1031, Sch 2 para 17 (as amended: see note 5 supra).

42   'Normal retirement age', in relation to a member, means the age at which workers in the undertaking for which the member worked at the time of his retirement, and who held the same kind of position as the member held at his retirement, were normally required to retire: ibid Sch 2 para 1(5). For the meaning of 'worker' see para 761 note 8 ante.

43   Ibid Sch 2 para 18 (as amended: see note 5 supra).

767.   Other rules, practices, actions and decisions relating to benefit.   The following rules, practices, actions and decisions relating to benefit are excepted[1]:

(1)   any difference in the amount of any age-related benefit[2] or death benefit[3] payable under a scheme[4] to or in respect of members[5] with different lengths of pensionable service[6] to the extent that the difference in amount is attributable to

their differing lengths of service, provided that, for each year of pensionable service, members in a comparable situation are entitled to accrue a right to benefit based upon the same fraction of pensionable pay[7];

(2) any differences in:

(a) the fraction of pensionable pay at which any age-related benefit accrues; or

(b) the amount of death benefit,

to or in respect of active[8] or prospective members[9] of a scheme where the differences are attributable to the specified[10] aim[11];

(3) any differences in age-related benefits which accrue, or entitlement to any death benefits which arises, to or in respect of active or prospective members of a scheme who are in a comparable situation where:

(a) those differences are attributable to the specified aim[12]; and

(b) the member's pensionable service under the arrangement ceases before normal pension age[13];

(4) where head (2) above applies, any limitation on the amount of any age-related benefit or death benefit payable from a scheme where the limitation arises from imposing one or both of the following:

(a) a maximum amount on the age-related benefit or death benefit which is equal to a fraction, proportion or multiple of the member's pensionable pay; or

(b) a minimum period of pensionable service[14];

(5) where heads (2) to (4) above apply, different rates of member or employer[15] contributions[16] according to the age of the members by, or in respect of whom, contributions are made, where for each year of pensionable service members in comparable situations accrue different fractions of pensionable pay[17];

(6) any difference in the amount of any age-related benefit or death benefit payable from a scheme to or in respect of different members to the extent that the difference in amount is attributable to differences over time in the pensionable pay of those members[18];

(7) any limitation on the amount of any age-related benefit or death benefit payable from a scheme where either:

(a) the limitation results from imposing a maximum number of years of pensionable service by reference to which the age-related benefit or death benefit may be calculated[19]; or

(b) the limitation arises from imposing a maximum amount on the age-related benefit or death benefit which is equal to a fraction, proportion or multiple of a member's pensionable pay[20],

or where both head (a) above and head (b) above apply[21];

(8) any rule, practice, action or decision where any age-related benefit or death benefit is only payable from a scheme where a member is entitled[22] to short service benefit[23];

(9) when determining a member's pensionable pay by reference to which any age-related benefit or death benefit payable to or in respect of a member is calculated, to exclude from the member's remuneration an amount which:

(a) does not exceed one and a half times the lower earnings limit[24];

(b) does not exceed an amount calculated by reference to the lower earnings limit where the aim is more or less to reflect the amount of the basic state retirement pension; or

(c) does not exceed an amount calculated more or less to reflect the amount of the basic state retirement pension[25] plus the additional state retirement pension[26];

(10) any difference in the amount of age-related benefit or death benefit payable under a scheme to or in respect of members where the difference is attributable to accrual of age-related benefit at a higher fraction of pensionable pay for pensionable pay over the upper earnings limit[27], and a lower fraction of pensionable pay for pensionable pay under the upper earnings limit, where the aim is to reflect the additional state retirement pension[28];

(11) any limitation on the amount of any age-related benefit or death benefit payable from a scheme where the limitation:

    (a) relates to all members who joined, or who became eligible to join the scheme on, after or before a particular date, or to any group or category of members who joined, or who became eligible to join the scheme on, after or before a particular date; and

    (b) results from imposing a maximum level of pensionable pay by reference to which the age-related benefit or death benefit may be calculated[29].

1   Ie from the age discrimination provisions by the Employment Equality (Age) Regulations 2006, SI 2006/1031, reg 11(3)(b), Sch 2 para 3: see para 762 ante.

2   For the meaning of 'age-related benefit' see para 764 note 3 ante.

3   For the meaning of 'death benefit' see para 766 note 31 ante.

4   For the meaning of 'scheme' see para 760 note 11 ante.

5   For the meaning of 'member' see para 760 note 6 ante.

6   For the meaning of 'pensionable service' see para 765 note 11 ante.

7   Employment Equality (Age) Regulations 2006, SI 2006/1031, Sch 2 para 19 (Sch 2 para 19 amended, Sch 2 paras 19A, 19B, 23A added, and Sch 2 paras 21–24 substituted, by SI 2006/2931). For the meaning of 'pensionable pay' see para 763 note 3 ante.

8   For the meaning of 'active member' see para 760 note 6 ante.

9   For the meaning of 'prospective member' see para 760 note 7 ante.

10 Ie the aim specified in the Employment Equality (Age) Regulations 2006, SI 2006/1031, Sch 2 para 19A(2) (as added). The specified aim is that members in a comparable situation will have the right to age-related benefit or death benefit equal to the same fraction, proportion or multiple of pensionable pay: (1) without regard to each member's length of pensionable service under the scheme; and (2) provided that each member continues in pensionable service under the scheme until normal pension age: Sch 2 para 19A(2) (as added: see note 7 supra). For the meaning of 'normal pension age' see para 766 note 24 ante.

11 Ibid Sch 2 para 19A(1) (as added: see note 7 supra).

12 See note 10 supra.

13 Employment Equality (Age) Regulations 2006, SI 2006/1031, Sch 2 para 19A(3) (as added: see note 7 supra).

14 Ibid Sch 2 para 19A(4) (as added: see note 7 supra).

15 For the meaning of 'employer' for these purposes see para 760 note 3 ante.

16 As to contributions under a money purchase arrangement, and for the meaning of 'money purchase arrangement', see para 761 note 10 ante.

17 Employment Equality (Age) Regulations 2006, SI 2006/1031, Sch 2 para 19B (as added: see note 7 supra).

18 Ibid Sch 2 para 20.

19 See ibid Sch 2 para 21(2) (as substituted: see note 7 supra).

20 See ibid Sch 2 para 21(2) (as substituted: see note 7 supra).

21 Ibid Sch 2 para 21(1) (as substituted: see note 7 supra).

22 Ie under the Pension Schemes Act 1993 s 71 (as amended) (basic principles as to short service benefit): see SOCIAL SECURITY AND PENSIONS vol 44(2) (Reissue) para 932.

23 Employment Equality (Age) Regulations 2006, SI 2006/1031, Sch 2 para 22 (as substituted: see note 7 supra).

24 For the meaning of 'lower earnings limit' see para 763 note 5 ante.

25 For the meaning of 'basic state retirement pension' see para 763 note 6 ante.

26 Employment Equality (Age) Regulations 2006, SI 2006/1031, Sch 2 para 23 (as substituted: see note 7 supra). For the meaning of 'additional state retirement pension' see para 763 note 7 ante.

27 'Upper earnings limit' means the amount specified for the tax year in question in regulations made under the Social Security Contributions and Benefits Act 1992 s 5(1)(a)(iii) (as substituted) (earnings limits and

thresholds for Class 1 contributions: see SOCIAL SECURITY AND PENSIONS vol 44(2) (Reissue) para 34): Employment Equality (Age) Regulations 2006, SI 2006/1031, Sch 2 para 1(5) (definition added by SI 2006/2931).

28   Employment Equality (Age) Regulations 2006, SI 2006/1031, Sch 2 para 23A (as added: see note 7 supra).

29   Ibid Sch 2 para 24 (as substituted: see note 7 supra).

768.   Closure of schemes or sections of schemes.   The closure of a scheme[1] or of any section of a scheme[2], from a particular date, to workers[3] who have not already joined it is excepted[4] for the statutory purposes[5].

1   For the meaning of 'scheme' see para 760 note 11 ante.
2   For these purposes: (1) a scheme may be divided into two or more sections; and (2) a section of a scheme means any of the following groups: (a) any group of members who became eligible to join, or who joined, the scheme on, after or before a particular date on the basis that particular benefits will be provided to or in respect of those members or that a particular level of contributions will be paid in respect of those members; or (b) any group of members who became eligible to join, or who joined, the scheme as a result of a block transfer or relevant transfer: Employment Equality (Age) Regulations 2006, SI 2006/1031, Sch 2 para 25A(2), (3) (Sch 2 para 25A added by SI 2006/2931). For the meaning of 'member' see para 760 note 6 ante; for the meaning of 'block transfer' see para 766 note 18 ante; and for the meaning of 'relevant transfer' see para 766 note 19 ante.
3   For the meaning of 'worker' see para 761 note 8 ante.
4   Ie from the age discrimination provisions by the Employment Equality (Age) Regulations 2006, SI 2006/1031, reg 11(3)(b), Sch 2 para 3: see para 762 ante.
5   Ibid Sch 2 paras 25, 25A(1) (Sch 2 para 25A(1) as added: see note 2 supra).

769.   Other rules, practices, actions and decisions.   The following rules, practices, actions and decisions in relation to occupational pension schemes are excepted[1]:

(1)   increases of pensions in payment which are made to members[2] over 55 but not to members below that age[3];

(2)   any difference in the rate of increase of pensions in payment for members of different ages to the extent that the aim in setting the different rates is to maintain or more nearly maintain the relative value of members' pensions[4];

(3)   any difference in the rate of increase of pensions in payment for members whose pensions have been in payment for different lengths of time to the extent that the aim in setting the different rates is to maintain or more nearly maintain the relative value of members' pensions[5];

(4)   the application of an age limit for transfer of the value of a member's accrued rights into or out of a scheme[6], provided that any such age limit is not more than one year before the member's normal pension age[7].

1   Ie from the age discrimination provisions by the Employment Equality (Age) Regulations 2006, SI 2006/1031, reg 11(3)(b), Sch 2 para 3: see para 762 ante.
2   For the meaning of 'member' see para 760 note 6 ante.
3   Employment Equality (Age) Regulations 2006, SI 2006/1031, Sch 2 para 26.
4   Ibid Sch 2 para 27 (Sch 2 paras 27, 28 amended by SI 2006/2931).
5   Employment Equality (Age) Regulations 2006, SI 2006/1031, Sch 2 para 28 (as amended: see note 4 supra).
6   For the meaning of 'scheme' see para 760 note 11 ante.
7   Employment Equality (Age) Regulations 2006, SI 2006/1031, Sch 2 para 29. For the meaning of 'normal pension age' see para 766 note 24 ante.

770.   Registered pension schemes.   Any rules, practices, actions or decisions relating to entitlement to or payment of benefits under a registered pension scheme[1] are excepted[2] in so far as compliance is necessary to secure any tax relief or exemption available under Part 4 of the Finance Act 2004[3] or to prevent any charge to tax arising under that Part of that Act, whoever is liable in relation to such charge[4]; but this does not apply to any rules, practices, actions or decisions setting a minimum age for entitlement to or payment of any age-related benefit[5].

1 For these purposes, 'registered pension scheme' has the meaning given by the Finance Act 2004 s 150(2) (see SOCIAL SECURITY AND PENSIONS): Employment Equality (Age) Regulations 2006, SI 2006/1031, Sch 2 para 1(7).
2 Ie from the age discrimination provisions by ibid reg 11(3)(b), Sch 2 para 3: see para 762 ante.
3 Ie under the Finance Act 2004 Pt 4 (ss 149–284) (as amended): see SOCIAL SECURITY AND PENSIONS.
4 Employment Equality (Age) Regulations 2006, SI 2006/1031, Sch 2 para 30(1).
5 Ibid Sch 2 para 30(2). For the meaning of 'age-related benefit' see para 764 note 3 ante.

C. EXCEPTED RULES ETC RELATING TO CONTRIBUTIONS BY EMPLOYERS TO PERSONAL PENSION SCHEMES

771. Contributions by employers. Nothing in Part 2[1] or Part 3[2] of the Employment Equality (Age) Regulations 2006 renders it unlawful for an employer[3], in relation to the payment of contributions to any personal pension scheme[4] in respect of a worker[5], to maintain or use any of the excepted[6] rules, practices, actions or decisions[7]. The inclusion of a rule, practice, action or decision in the statutory exceptions[8] is not, however, to be taken to mean that, but for that exemption, the use or maintenance by an employer of the rule, practice, action or decision in relation to the payment of contributions to a personal pension scheme in respect of a worker would be unlawful[9].

The following rules, practices, actions and decisions are excepted for these purposes:
(1) different rates of contributions by an employer according to the age of the workers in respect of whom the contributions are made where the aim in setting the different rates is:
   (a) to equalise the amount of benefit to which workers of different ages who are otherwise in a comparable situation will become entitled under their personal pension schemes; or
   (b) to make the amount of benefit to which such workers will become entitled under their personal pension schemes more nearly equal[10];
(2) any difference in the rate of contributions by an employer in respect of different workers to the extent that this is attributable to any differences in remuneration payable to those workers[11].

1 Ie the Employment Equality (Age) Regulations 2006, SI 2006/1031, Pt 2 (regs 7–24) (as amended) (discrimination in employment and vocational training).
2 Ie ibid Pt 3 (regs 25–26) (other unlawful acts): see paras 783–784 post.
3 For the meaning of 'employer' for these purposes see para 760 note 3 ante.
4 For the meaning of 'personal pension scheme' see para 761 note 9 ante.
5 For the meaning of 'worker' see para 761 note 8 ante.
6 Ie any of the rules, practices, actions or decisions set out in the Employment Equality (Age) Regulations 2006, SI 2006/1031, reg 11(3)(b), Sch 2 Pt 3: see heads (1)–(2) in the text.
7 Ibid Sch 2 para 4.
8 Ie inclusion in ibid Sch 2 Pt 3.
9 Ibid Sch 2 para 4A(2) (added by SI 2006/2931).
10 Employment Equality (Age) Regulations 2006, SI 2006/1031, Sch 2 para 31.
11 Ibid Sch 2 para 32.

(iii) Discrimination by Particular Persons or Bodies

772. Office-holders etc. The following provisions apply to:
(1) any office or post to which persons[1] are appointed to discharge functions personally under the direction of another person[2], and in respect of which they are entitled to remuneration[3]; and
(2) any office or post to which appointments are made by, or on the

recommendation of or subject to the approval of, a Minister of the Crown[4], a government department, the National Assembly for Wales[5] or any part of the Scottish Administration[6],

but not to a political office[7] or a case where the provisions relating to applicants and employees[8], contract workers[9], barristers[10] or partnerships[11] apply, or would apply but for the operation of any other provision of the Employment Equality (Age) Regulations 2006[12].

It is unlawful:

(a) for a relevant person[13], in relation to an appointment to an office or post[14] to which these provisions apply, to discriminate[15] against a person:
   (i) in the arrangements which he makes for the purpose of determining to whom the appointment should be offered;
   (ii) in the terms on which he offers him the appointment; or
   (iii) by refusing[16] to offer him the appointment[17];

(b) in relation to an appointment to an office or post to which these provisions apply and which is an office or post referred to in head (2) above, for a relevant person on whose recommendation, or subject to whose approval, appointments to the office or post are made, to discriminate against a person:
   (i) in the arrangements which he makes for the purpose of determining who should be recommended or approved in relation to the appointment; or
   (ii) in making or refusing to make a recommendation[18], or giving or refusing to give an approval, in relation to the appointment[19];

(c) for a relevant person, in relation to a person who has been appointed to an office or post to which these provisions apply, to discriminate against him:
   (i) in the terms of the appointment;
   (ii) in the opportunities which he affords him for promotion, transfer, training or receiving any other benefit[20], or by refusing to afford him any such opportunity;
   (iii) by terminating the appointment[21]; or
   (iv) by subjecting him to any other detriment[22] in relation to the appointment[23];

(d) for a relevant person, in relation to an office or post to which these provisions apply, to subject to harassment[24] a person:
   (i) who has been appointed to the office or post;
   (ii) who is seeking or being considered for appointment to the office or post; or
   (iii) who is seeking or being considered for a recommendation or approval in relation to an appointment to an office or post referred to in head (2) above[25].

Heads (a) and (c) above do not, however, apply to any act[26] in relation to an office or post where, if the office or post constituted employment[27], that act would be lawful by virtue of the statutory exception for a genuine occupational requirement[28]; and head (b) above does not apply to any act in relation to an office or post where, if the office or post constituted employment, it would be lawful by virtue of that statutory exception to refuse to offer the person such employment[29]. Nor does head (c) above apply to benefits of any description if the relevant person is concerned with the provision, for payment or not, of benefits of that description to the public, or a section of the public to which the person appointed belongs, unless:

(A) that provision differs in a material respect from the provision of the benefits by the relevant person to persons appointed to offices or posts which are the same as, or not materially different from, that which the person appointed holds; or

(B) the provision of the benefits to the person appointed is regulated by the terms and conditions of his appointment; or

(C) the benefits relate to training[30].

1 As to the meaning of 'person' see para 344 note 3 ante.

2 For these purposes, the holder of an office or post is to be regarded as discharging his functions under the direction of another person if that other person is entitled to direct him as to when and where he discharges those functions: Employment Equality (Age) Regulations 2006, SI 2006/1031, reg 12(9)(a).

3 For these purposes, the holder of an office or post is not to be regarded as entitled to remuneration merely because he is entitled to payments: (1) in respect of expenses incurred by him in carrying out the functions of the office or post; or (2) by way of compensation for the loss of income or benefits he would or might have received from any person had he not been carrying out the functions of the office or post: ibid reg 12(9)(b).

4 'Minister of the Crown' includes the Treasury and the Defence Council: ibid reg 2(2). As to the Treasury see CONSTITUTIONAL LAW AND HUMAN RIGHTS vol 8(2) (Reissue) paras 512–517. As to the Defence Council see ARMED FORCES vol 2(2) (Reissue) para 2; CONSTITUTIONAL LAW AND HUMAN RIGHTS vol 8(2) (Reissue) para 443 et seq.

5 As to the National Assembly for Wales see para 302 ante.

6 Matters relating to the composition, procedures and powers of the Scottish Administration fall outside the scope of this work.

7 For these purposes, 'political office' means: (1) any office of the House of Commons held by a member of it; (2) a life peerage within the meaning of the Life Peerages Act 1958 (see CONSTITUTIONAL LAW AND HUMAN RIGHTS vol 8(2) (Reissue) para 212; PARLIAMENT vol 34 (Reissue) para 540; PEERAGES AND DIGNITIES), or any office of the House of Lords held by a member of it; (3) any office mentioned in the House of Commons Disqualification Act 1975 Sch 2 (ministerial offices: see PARLIAMENT vol 34 (Reissue) para 611); (4) the offices of Leader of the Opposition, Chief Opposition Whip or Assistant Opposition Whip within the meaning of the Ministerial and other Salaries Act 1975 (see CONSTITUTIONAL LAW AND HUMAN RIGHTS vol 8(2) (Reissue) para 219); (5) any office of the National Assembly for Wales held by a member of it; (6) in England, any office of a county council, a London borough council, a district council, or a parish council held by a member of it; (7) in Wales, any office of a county council, a county borough council, or a community council held by a member of it; (8) any office of the Greater London Authority held by a member of it; (9) any office of the Common Council of the City of London held by a member of it; (10) any office of the Council of the Isles of Scilly held by a member of it; (11) any office of a political party: Employment Equality (Age) Regulations 2006, SI 2006/1031, reg 12(10)(b). This provision also refers to various Scottish offices, but see note 6 supra. As to local government authorities in England and Wales see LOCAL GOVERNMENT vol 29(1) (Reissue) para 23 et seq; as to London borough councils see LONDON GOVERNMENT vol 29(2) (Reissue) para 35 et seq; as to the Greater London Authority see LONDON GOVERNMENT vol 29(2) (Reissue) para 70 et seq; as to the Common Council of the City of London see LONDON GOVERNMENT vol 29(2) (Reissue) para 51 et seq; and as to the Council of the Isles of Scilly see LOCAL GOVERNMENT vol 29(1) (Reissue) para 40.

8 Ie ibid reg 7: see para 758 ante.

9 Ie ibid reg 9: see para 759 ante.

10 Ie ibid reg 15: see para 774 post. As to advocates see reg 16 (which only applies in relation to Scotland). See note 6 supra.

11 Ie ibid reg 17: see para 775 post.

12 Ibid reg 12(8).

13 For these purposes, 'relevant person', in relation to an office or post, means: (1) any person with power to make or terminate appointments to the office or post, or to determine the terms of appointment; (2) any person with power to determine the working conditions of a person appointed to the office or post in relation to opportunities for promotion, transfer, training or receiving any other benefit; and (3) any person or body referred to in ibid reg 10(8)(b) (see head (2) in the text) on whose recommendation or subject to whose approval appointments are made to the office or post: reg 12(10)(c).

14 For these purposes, appointment to an office or post does not include election to an office or post: ibid reg 12(10)(a).

15 For the meaning of references to discrimination see para 758 note 4 ante.

16 For these purposes, references to refusal include references to deliberate omission: Employment Equality (Age) Regulations 2006, SI 2006/1031, reg 12(10)(e).

17 Ibid reg 12(1).

18 For these purposes, references to making a recommendation include references to making a negative recommendation: ibid reg 12(10)(d).

19 Ibid reg 12(2).

20 As to the meaning of 'benefits' see para 758 note 6 ante.
21 The reference in head (c)(iii) in the text to the termination of the appointment includes a reference: (1) to the termination of the appointment by the expiration of any period (including a period expiring by reference to an event or circumstance), not being a termination immediately after which the appointment is renewed on the same terms and conditions; and (2) to the termination of the appointment by any act of the person appointed (including the giving of notice) in circumstances such that he is entitled to terminate the appointment without notice by reason of the conduct of the relevant person: Employment Equality (Age) Regulations 2006, SI 2006/1031, reg 12(7).
22 As to the meaning of 'detriment' see para 758 note 8 ante.
23 Employment Equality (Age) Regulations 2006, SI 2006/1031, reg 12(3).
24 For the meaning of references to harassment see para 758 note 9 ante.
25 Employment Equality (Age) Regulations 2006, SI 2006/1031, reg 12(4).
26 As to the meaning of 'act' see para 755 note 3 ante.
27 For the meaning of 'employment' see para 758 note 2 ante.
28 Ie by virtue of the Employment Equality (Age) Regulations 2006, SI 2006/1031, reg 8: see para 758 ante.
29 Ibid reg 12(5).
30 Ibid reg 12(6).

773. Police and the Serious Organised Crime Agency. For the purposes of the regulations prohibiting unlawful discrimination in employment and vocational training[1], the holding of the office of constable is to be treated[2] as employment[3]:

(1) by the chief officer of police[4] as respects any act[5] done by him in relation to a constable or that office;

(2) by the police authority[6] as respects any act done by it in relation to a constable or that office[7],

and this applies to a police cadet[8] and appointment as a police cadet as it applies to a constable and the office of constable[9].

There must be paid out of the police fund[10]:

(a) any compensation, costs or expenses awarded against a chief officer of police in any proceedings brought against him[11] under the Employment Equality (Age) Regulations 2006[12], and any costs or expenses incurred by him in any such proceedings so far as not recovered by him in the proceedings; and

(b) any sum required by a chief officer of police for the settlement of any claim made against him under those regulations if the settlement is approved by the police authority[13].

A police authority may, in such cases and to such extent as appear to it to be appropriate, pay out of the police fund:

(i) any compensation, costs or expenses awarded in proceedings under the Employment Equality (Age) Regulations 2006 against a person under the direction and control of the chief officer of police;

(ii) any costs or expenses incurred and not recovered by such a person in such proceedings; and

(iii) any sum required in connection with the settlement of a claim that has or might have given rise to such proceedings[14].

For the purposes of the Employment Equality (Age) Regulations 2006[15], any constable or other person who has been seconded to the Serious Organised Crime Agency ('SOCA') to serve as a member of its staff is to be treated as employed by SOCA[16].

1 Ie for the purposes of the Employment Equality (Age) Regulations 2006, SI 2006/1031, Pt 2 (regs 7–24) (as amended).
2 Ie subject to ibid reg 14: see the text and notes 15–16 infra.
3 For the meaning of 'employment' see para 758 note 2 ante.
4 For these purposes, and subject to the Employment Equality (Age) Regulations 2006, SI 2006/1031, reg 13(8), 'chief officer of police': (1) in relation to a person appointed or an appointment falling to be

made under a specified Act, has the same meaning as in the Police Act 1996 (see POLICE vol 36(1) (Reissue) para 205); (2) in relation to any other person or appointment, means the officer or other person who has the direction and control of the body of constables or cadets in question: reg 13(7). In relation to a constable of a force who is not under the direction and control of the chief officer of police for that force, references in reg 13 to the chief officer of police are references to the chief officer of the force under whose direction and control he is: reg 13(8). 'Specified Act' means the Metropolitan Police Act 1829, the City of London Police Act 1839 or the Police Act 1996: Employment Equality (Age) Regulations 2006, SI 2006/1031, reg 13(7).

5 As to the meaning of 'act' see para 755 note 3 ante.

6 For these purposes, and subject to the Employment Equality (Age) Regulations 2006, SI 2006/1031, reg 13(8), 'police authority': (1) in relation to a person appointed or an appointment falling to be made under a specified Act (see note 4 supra), has the same meaning as in the Police Act 1996 (see POLICE vol 36(1) (Reissue) para 202); (2) in relation to any other person or appointment, means the authority by whom the person in question is or on appointment would be paid: Employment Equality (Age) Regulations 2006, SI 2006/1031, reg 13(7). In relation to a constable of a force who is not under the direction and control of the chief officer of police for that force, references to the police authority are references to the relevant police authority for the force under whose direction and control he is: reg 13(8). As to the meaning of 'person' see para 344 note 3 ante.

7 Ibid reg 13(1).

8 For these purposes, 'police cadet' means any person appointed to undergo training with a view to becoming a constable: ibid reg 13(7).

9 Ibid reg 13(6).

10 For these purposes, and subject to ibid reg 13(8) (see notes 4, 6 supra), 'police fund': (1) in relation to a chief officer of police within the definition of that term set out in note 4 head (1) supra, has the same meaning as in the Police Act 1996 (see POLICE vol 36(1) (Reissue) para 205); (2) in any other case means money provided by the police authority: Employment Equality (Age) Regulations 2006, SI 2006/1031, reg 13(7).

11 Any proceedings under the Employment Equality (Age) Regulations 2006, SI 2006/1031 (as amended), which, by virtue of reg 13(1), would lie against a chief officer of police must be brought against the chief officer of police for the time being or, in the case of a vacancy in that office, against the person for the time being performing the functions of that office; and references in reg 13(3) (see heads (a)–(b) in the text) to the chief officer of police are to be construed accordingly: reg 13(4).

12 Ie under the Employment Equality (Age) Regulations 2006, SI 2006/1031 (as amended).

13 Ibid reg 13(3).

14 Ibid reg 13(5).

15 See note 1 supra.

16 Employment Equality (Age) Regulations 2006, SI 2006/1031, reg 14(1), (3). As to the Serious Organised Crime Agency see POLICE.

774. Barristers. It is unlawful for a barrister or barrister's clerk[1]:

(1) in relation to any offer of a pupillage[2] or tenancy[3], to discriminate[4] against a person[5]:

    (a) in the arrangements which are made for the purpose of determining to whom the pupillage or tenancy should be offered;

    (b) in respect of any terms on which it is offered; or

    (c) by refusing, or deliberately not offering, it to him[6];

(2) in relation to a pupil[7] or tenant[8] in the set of chambers[9] in question, to discriminate against him:

    (a) in respect of any terms applicable to him as a pupil or tenant;

    (b) in the opportunities for training, or gaining experience, which are afforded or denied to him;

    (c) in the benefits[10] which are afforded or denied to him; or

    (d) by terminating his pupillage, or by subjecting him to any pressure to leave the chambers or other detriment[11];

(3) in relation to a pupillage or tenancy in the set of chambers in question, to subject to harassment[12] a person who is, or has applied to be, a pupil or tenant[13].

It is also unlawful for any person, in relation to the giving, withholding or acceptance of instructions to a barrister, to discriminate against any person by subjecting him to a detriment, or to subject him to harassment[14].

1   'Barrister's clerk' includes any person carrying out any of the functions of a barrister's clerk: Employment Equality (Age) Regulations 2006, SI 2006/1031, reg 15(5). Regulation 15 extends to England and Wales only: reg 15(6).
2   For these purposes, 'pupil' and 'pupillage' have the meanings commonly associated with their use in the context of barristers practising in independent practice: ibid reg 15(5).
3   For these purposes, 'tenancy' and 'tenant' have the meanings commonly associated with their use in the context of barristers practising in independent practice, but also include reference to any barrister permitted to work in a set of chambers who is not a tenant: ibid reg 15(5). See also note 9 infra.
4   For the meaning of references to discrimination see para 758 note 4 ante.
5   As to the meaning of 'person' see para 344 note 3 ante.
6   Employment Equality (Age) Regulations 2006, SI 2006/1031, reg 15(1).
7   See note 2 supra.
8   See note 3 supra.
9   For these purposes, 'set of chambers' has the meaning commonly associated with its use in the context of barristers practising in independent practice: Employment Equality (Age) Regulations 2006, SI 2006/1031, reg 15(5).
10 As to the meaning of 'benefits' see para 758 note 6 ante.
11 Employment Equality (Age) Regulations 2006, SI 2006/1031, reg 15(2). As to the meaning of 'detriment' see para 758 note 8 ante.
12 For the meaning of references to harassment see para 758 note 9 ante.
13 Employment Equality (Age) Regulations 2006, SI 2006/1031, reg 15(3).
14 Ibid reg 15(4).

775.   Partnerships.   It is unlawful for a firm[1], in relation to a position as partner[2] in the firm:

(1)   to discriminate[3] against a person[4]:
  (a)   in the arrangements it makes for the purpose of determining to whom it should offer that position;
  (b)   in the terms on which it offers him that position;
  (c)   by refusing to offer, or deliberately not offering, him that position; or
  (d)   in a case where the person already holds that position, in the way it affords him access to any benefits[5] or by refusing to afford, or deliberately not affording, him access to them, or by expelling him from that position[6], or subjecting him to any other detriment[7];

(2)   to subject to harassment[8] a person who holds or has applied for that position[9].

Heads (1)(a) to (1)(c) and head (2) above apply in relation to persons proposing to form themselves into a partnership as they apply in relation to a firm[10]. Head (1) above does not, however, apply to any act[11] in relation to a position as partner where, if the position were employment[12], that act would be lawful by virtue of the statutory exception[13] for a genuine occupational requirement[14].

1   For these purposes, 'firm' has the meaning given by the Partnership Act 1890 s 4 (see PARTNERSHIP vol 35 (Reissue) para 1): Employment Equality (Age) Regulations 2006, SI 2006/1031, reg 17(7). Regulation 17 applies to a limited liability partnership as it applies to a firm: reg 17(6).
2   In the case of a limited partnership, references in ibid reg 17 to a partner are to be construed as references to a general partner as defined in the Limited Partnerships Act 1907 s 3 (see PARTNERSHIP vol 35 (Reissue) para 207) (Employment Equality (Age) Regulations 2006, SI 2006/1031, reg 17(5)); and, in the application of reg 17 to a limited liability partnership, references to a partner in a firm are references to a member of the limited liability partnership (reg 17(6)).
3   For the meaning of references to discrimination see para 758 note 4 ante.
4   As to the meaning of 'person' see para 344 note 3 ante.
5   As to the meaning of 'benefits' see para 758 note 6 ante.
6   In the Employment Equality (Age) Regulations 2006, SI 2006/1031, reg 17(1)(d) (see head (1)(d) in the text), reference to the expulsion of a person from a position as partner includes reference: (1) to the termination of that person's partnership by the expiration of any period (including a period expiring by

reference to an event or circumstance), not being a termination immediately after which the partnership is renewed on the same terms; and (2) to the termination of that person's partnership by any act of his (including the giving of notice) in circumstances such that he is entitled to terminate it without notice by reason of the conduct of the other partners: reg 17(8).

7   Ibid reg 17(1). As to the meaning of 'detriment' see para 758 note 8 ante.

8   For the meaning of references to harassment see para 758 note 9 ante.

9   Employment Equality (Age) Regulations 2006, SI 2006/1031, reg 17(2).

10 Ibid reg 17(3).

11 As to the meaning of 'act' see para 755 note 3 ante.

12 For the meaning of 'employment' see para 758 note 2 ante.

13 Ie by virtue of the Employment Equality (Age) Regulations 2006, SI 2006/1031, reg 8: see para 758 ante.

14 Ibid reg 17(4).

776. Trade organisations. It is unlawful for a trade organisation[1]:

(1)   to discriminate[2] against a person[3]:

    (a)   in the terms on which it is prepared to admit him to membership of the organisation; or

    (b)   by refusing to accept, or deliberately not accepting, his application for membership[4];

(2)   in relation to a member of the organisation, to discriminate against him:

    (a)   in the way it affords him access to any benefits[5] or by refusing or deliberately omitting to afford him access to them;

    (b)   by depriving him of membership or varying the terms on which he is a member; or

    (c)   by subjecting him to any other detriment[6];

(3)   in relation to a person's membership or application for membership of that organisation, to subject that person to harassment[7].

1   For these purposes, 'trade organisation' means an organisation of workers, an organisation of employers, or any other organisation whose members carry on a particular profession or trade for the purposes of which the organisation exists; 'profession' includes any vocation or occupation; and 'trade' includes any business: Employment Equality (Age) Regulations 2006, SI 2006/1031, reg 18(4).

2   For the meaning of references to discrimination see para 758 note 4 ante.

3   As to the meaning of 'person' see para 344 note 3 ante.

4   Employment Equality (Age) Regulations 2006, SI 2006/1031, reg 18(1).

5   As to the meaning of 'benefits' see para 758 note 6 ante.

6   Employment Equality (Age) Regulations 2006, SI 2006/1031, reg 18(2). As to the meaning of 'detriment' see para 758 note 8 ante.

7   Ibid reg 18(3). For the meaning of references to harassment see para 758 note 9 ante.

777. Qualifications bodies. It is unlawful for a qualifications body[1]:

(1)   to discriminate[2] against a person[3]:

    (a)   in the terms on which it is prepared to confer a professional or trade qualification on him;

    (b)   by refusing or deliberately not granting any application by him for such a qualification; or

    (c)   by withdrawing such a qualification from him or varying the terms on which he holds it[4];

(2)   in relation to a professional or trade qualification conferred by it, to subject to harassment[5] a person who holds or applies for such a qualification[6].

1   For these purposes, 'qualifications body' means any authority or body which can confer a professional or trade qualification, but it does not include:

    (1)   an educational establishment to which the Employment Equality (Age) Regulations 2006, SI 2006/1031, reg 23 (institutions of further and higher education: see para 781 post) applies, or would apply but for the operation of any other provision of the regulations; or

    (2)   a proprietor of a school;

'confer' includes renew or extend; 'professional or trade qualification' means any authorisation, qualification, recognition, registration, enrolment, approval or certification which is needed for, or facilitates engagement in, a particular profession or trade; and 'profession' and 'trade' have the same meanings as in reg 18 (see para 776 ante): reg 19(3). 'School' has the meaning given by the Education Act 1996 s 4 (as amended) (see EDUCATION vol 15(1) (2006 Reissue) para 81); and references to a school are references to an institution in so far as it is engaged in the provision of education under s 4 (as amended): Employment Equality (Age) Regulations 2006, SI 2006/1031, reg 2(2). 'Proprietor', in relation to a school, has the meaning given by the Education Act 1996 s 579 (as amended) (see EDUCATION vol 15(1) (2006 Reissue) para 60): Employment Equality (Age) Regulations 2006, SI 2006/1031, reg 2(2).

2   For the meaning of references to discrimination see para 758 note 4 ante.
3   As to the meaning of 'person' see para 344 note 3 ante.
4   Employment Equality (Age) Regulations 2006, SI 2006/1031, reg 19(1).
5   For the meaning of references to harassment see para 758 note 9 ante.
6   Employment Equality (Age) Regulations 2006, SI 2006/1031, reg 19(2).

778.   Providers of vocational training.   It is unlawful, in relation to a person[1] seeking or undergoing training[2] which would help fit him for any employment[3], for any training provider[4] to discriminate[5] against him:

(1)   in the terms on which the training provider affords him access to any training;
(2)   by refusing or deliberately not affording him such access;
(3)   by terminating his training; or
(4)   by subjecting him to any other detriment[6] during his training[7],

but this does not apply if the discrimination only concerns training for employment which, by virtue of the statutory exception for a genuine occupational requirement[8], the employer could lawfully refuse to offer the person seeking training[9].

It is also unlawful for a training provider, in relation to a person seeking or undergoing training which would help fit him for any employment, to subject him to harassment[10].

1   As to the meaning of 'person' see para 344 note 3 ante.
2   For these purposes, 'training' means: (1) all types and all levels of training which would help fit a person for any employment; (2) vocational guidance; (3) facilities for training; (4) practical work experience provided by an employer to a person whom he does not employ; and (5) any assessment related to the award of any professional or trade qualification (within the meaning of the Employment Equality (Age) Regulations 2006, SI 2006/1031, reg 19: see para 777 note 1 ante): reg 20(4). As to the meaning of 'employer' see para 758 note 1 ante.
3   For the meaning of 'employment' see para 758 note 2 ante.
4   For these purposes, 'training provider' means any person who provides, or makes arrangements for the provision of, training which would help fit another person for any employment, but it does not include: (1) an employer in relation to training for persons employed by him; (2) an educational establishment to which the Employment Equality (Age) Regulations 2006, SI 2006/1031, reg 23 (institutions of further and higher education: see para 781 post) applies, or would apply but for the operation of any other provision of the regulations; or (3) a proprietor of a school in relation to any registered pupil: reg 20(4). For these purposes, 'registered pupil' has the meaning given by the Education Act 1996 s 434 (as amended) (see EDUCATION vol 16(1A) (Reissue) para 512): Employment Equality (Age) Regulations 2006, SI 2006/1031, reg 20(4). For the meaning of 'school' see para 777 note 1 ante.
5   For the meaning of references to discrimination see para 758 note 4 ante.
6   As to the meaning of 'detriment' see para 758 note 8 ante.
7   Employment Equality (Age) Regulations 2006, SI 2006/1031, reg 20(1).
8   Ie by virtue of ibid reg 8: see para 758 ante.
9   Ibid reg 20(3).
10   Ibid reg 20(2). For the meaning of references to harassment see para 758 note 9 ante.

779.   Employment agencies, careers guidance etc.   It is unlawful for an employment agency[1] to discriminate[2] against a person:

(1)   in the terms on which the agency offers to provide any of its services;
(2)   by refusing or deliberately not providing any of its services; or
(3)   in the way it provides any of its services[3],

but this does not apply to discrimination if it only concerns employment which, by virtue of the statutory exception for a genuine occupational requirement[4], the employer could lawfully refuse to offer the person in question[5].

It is also unlawful for an employment agency, in relation to a person to whom it provides its services or who has requested it to provide its services, to subject that person to harassment[6].

An employment agency is not subject to any liability under the above provisions if it proves that:

(a)   it acted in reliance on a statement made to it by the employer to the effect that, by reason of the operation of the above-mentioned statutory exception[7], its action would not be unlawful; and

(b)   it was reasonable for it to rely on the statement[8].

A person who knowingly or recklessly makes a statement such as is referred to in head (a) above which in a material respect is false or misleading commits an offence, and is liable on summary conviction to a fine[9].

1   For these purposes: (1) 'employment agency' means a person who, for profit or not, provides services for the purpose of finding employment for workers or supplying employers with workers, but it does not include: (a) an educational establishment to which the Employment Equality (Age) Regulations 2006, SI 2006/1031, reg 23 (institutions of further and higher education: see para 781 post) applies, or would apply but for the operation of any other provision of the regulations; or (b) a proprietor of a school; and (2) references to the services of an employment agency include guidance on careers and any other services related to employment: reg 21(6). For the meanings of 'employer' and 'employment' see para 758 notes 1, 2 ante; and for the meaning of 'school' see para 777 note 1 ante. As to the meaning of 'person' see para 344 note 3 ante.

2   For the meaning of references to discrimination see para 758 note 4 ante.

3   Employment Equality (Age) Regulations 2006, SI 2006/1031, reg 21(1).

4   Ie by virtue of ibid reg 8: see para 758 ante.

5   Ibid reg 21(3).

6   Ibid reg 21(2). For the meaning of references to harassment see para 758 note 9 ante.

7   See note 4 supra.

8   Employment Equality (Age) Regulations 2006, SI 2006/1031, reg 21(4).

9   Ibid reg 21(5). The fine referred to in the text is a fine not exceeding level 5 on the standard scale: see reg 21(5). As to the standard scale see para 315 note 15 ante.

780.   Assisting persons to obtain employment etc.   It is unlawful for the Secretary of State[1] to discriminate[2] against any person[3] by subjecting him to a detriment[4], or to subject a person to harassment[5], in the provision of facilities or services under the statutory arrangements[6] for assisting persons to obtain employment[7].

1   As to the Secretary of State and the National Assembly for Wales see para 302 ante.

2   For the meaning of references to discrimination see para 758 note 4 ante.

3   As to the meaning of 'person' see para 344 note 3 ante.

4   As to the meaning of 'detriment' see para 758 note 8 ante.

5   For the meaning of references to harassment see para 758 note 9 ante.

6   Ie under the Employment and Training Act 1973 s 2 (as substituted and amended): see EMPLOYMENT vol 16(1B) (Reissue) para 765.

7   Employment Equality (Age) Regulations 2006, SI 2006/1031, reg 22(1). Regulation 19 does not apply in a case where: (1) reg 20 (providers of vocational training: see para 778 ante) applies, or would apply but for the operation of any other provision of the regulations; or (2) the Secretary of State is acting as an employment agency within the meaning of reg 21 (see para 779 ante): reg 22(3).

781.   Institutions of further and higher education.   The provisions set out below apply to the following educational establishments in England and Wales, namely:

(1)   an institution within the further education sector[1];

(2)   a university[2];

(3)   an institution[3], other than a university, within the higher education sector[4].

It is unlawful, in relation to an educational establishment to which these provisions apply, for the governing body of that establishment to discriminate[5] against a person[6]:

(a)   in the terms on which it offers to admit him to the establishment as a student[7];

(b)   by refusing or deliberately not accepting an application for his admission to the establishment as a student; or

(c)   where he is a student of the establishment:

(i)   in the way it affords him access to any benefits[8];

(ii)   by refusing or deliberately not affording him access to them; or

(iii)   by excluding him from the establishment or subjecting him to any other detriment[9],

but this does not apply if the discrimination only concerns training which would help fit a person for employment[10] which, by virtue of the statutory exception for a genuine occupational requirement[11], the employer[12] could lawfully refuse to offer the person in question[13].

It is also unlawful, in relation to an educational establishment to which these provisions apply, for the governing body of that establishment to subject to harassment[14] a person who is a student at the establishment or who has applied for admission to the establishment as a student[15].

1   Ie within the meaning of the Further and Higher Education Act 1992 s 91(3): see EDUCATION vol 15(2) (2006 Reissue) para 579.

2   For these purposes, 'university' includes a university college and a college, school or hall of a university: Employment Equality (Age) Regulations 2006, SI 2006/1031, reg 23(6).

3   Ie an institution within the higher education sector within the meaning of the Further and Higher Education Act 1992 s 91(5): see EDUCATION vol 15(2) (2006 Reissue) para 646.

4   Employment Equality (Age) Regulations 2006, SI 2006/1031, reg 23(4).

5   For the meaning of references to discrimination see para 758 note 4 ante.

6   As to the meaning of 'person' see para 344 note 3 ante.

7   For these purposes, 'student' means any person who receives education at an educational establishment to which the Employment Equality (Age) Regulations 2006, SI 2006/1031, reg 23 applies: reg 23(6).

8   As to the meaning of 'benefits' see para 758 note 6 ante.

9   Employment Equality (Age) Regulations 2006, SI 2006/1031, reg 23(1). As to the meaning of 'detriment' see para 758 note 8 ante.

10   For the meaning of 'employment' see para 758 note 2 ante.

11   Ie the Employment Equality (Age) Regulations 2006, SI 2006/1031, reg 8: see para 758 ante.

12   As to the meaning of 'employer' see para 758 note 1 ante.

13   Employment Equality (Age) Regulations 2006, SI 2006/1031, reg 23(3).

14   For the meaning of references to harassment see para 758 note 9 ante.

15   Employment Equality (Age) Regulations 2006, SI 2006/1031, reg 23(2).

782.   Relevant relationships which have come to an end.   A 'relevant relationship' is a relationship during the course of which an act[1] of discrimination[2] against, or harassment[3] of, one party to the relationship ('B') by the other party to it ('A') is unlawful[4] by virtue of provisions of the regulations[5] regarding discrimination in employment and vocational training[6]. Where a relevant relationship has come to an end, it is unlawful for A:

(1)   to discriminate against B by subjecting him to a detriment[7]; or

(2)   to subject B to harassment,

where the discrimination or harassment arises out of and is closely connected to that relationship[8].

1   As to the meaning of 'act' see para 755 note 3 ante.

2   For the meaning of references to discrimination see para 758 note 4 ante.

3   For the meaning of references to harassment see para 758 note 9 ante.

4   For these purposes, reference to an act of discrimination or harassment which is unlawful includes, in the case of a relationship which has come to an end before the date on which the act of discrimination or harassment became unlawful by virtue of the Employment Equality (Age) Regulations 2006,

SI 2006/1031 (as amended), reference to an act of discrimination or harassment which would, after that date, be unlawful: reg 24(3) (amended by SI 2006/2408). The specified date is, for most purposes, 1 October 2006, but for the purposes of certain provisions relating to pensions the specified date is 1 December 2006: see para 754 note 1 ante.

5   Ie the Employment Equality (Age) Regulations 2006, SI 2006/1031, Pt 2 (regs 7–24) (as amended).

6   Ibid reg 24(1).

7   As to the meaning of 'detriment' see para 758 note 8 ante.

8   Employment Equality (Age) Regulations 2006, SI 2006/1031, reg 24(2).

(3) OTHER UNLAWFUL ACTS

783.   Liability of employers and principals. Anything done by a person[1] in the course of his employment[2] is to be treated for the purposes of the Employment Equality (Age) Regulations 2006[3] as done by his employer[4] as well as by him, whether or not it was done with the employer's knowledge or approval[5]. For these purposes:

(1)   the holding of the office of constable is to be treated[6] as employment by the chief officer of police[7], and as not being employment by any other person, and anything done by a person holding such an office in the performance, or purported performance, of his functions is be treated as done in the course of that employment[8];

(2)   the secondment of any constable or other person to the Serious Organised Crime Agency ('SOCA') to serve as a member of its staff is to be treated as employment by SOCA, and not as being employment by any other person, and anything done by a person so seconded in the performance, or purported performance, of his functions is to be treated as done in the course of that employment[9].

Anything done by a person as agent for another person with the authority, whether express or implied, and whether precedent or subsequent, of that other person is to be treated for the purposes of the Employment Equality (Age) Regulations 2006 as done by that other person as well as by him[10].

In proceedings brought under those regulations against any person in respect of an act[11] alleged to have been done by an employee of his, it is, however, a defence for that person to prove that he took such steps as were reasonably practicable to prevent the employee from doing that act or from doing in the course of his employment acts of that description[12].

1   As to the meaning of 'person' see para 344 note 3 ante.

2   For the meaning of 'employment' see para 758 note 2 ante.

3   Ie for the purposes of the Employment Equality (Age) Regulations 2006, SI 2006/1031.

4   As to the meaning of 'employer' see para 758 note 1 ante.

5   Employment Equality (Age) Regulations 2006, SI 2006/1031, reg 25(1). See *Jones v Tower Boot Co Ltd* [1997] 2 All ER 406, [1997] IRLR 168, CA (a case under the Race Relations Act 1976); and para 476 ante.

     As to the liability of employers and principals under the Sex Discrimination Act 1975 see para 391 ante; and as to their liability under the Race Relations Act 1976 see para 476 ante.

6   Ie subject to the Employment Equality (Age) Regulations 2006, SI 2006/1031, reg 14 (as added): see head (2) in the text; and para 773 ante.

7   For the meaning of 'chief officer of police' see para 773 note 4 ante.

8   Employment Equality (Age) Regulations 2006, SI 2006/1031, reg 13(2). Head (1) in the text applies to a police cadet and appointment as a police cadet as it applies to a constable and the office of constable: Employment Equality (Age) Regulations 2006, SI 2006/1031, reg 13(6). For the meaning of 'police cadet' see para 773 note 8 ante.

9   Ibid reg 14(2), (3). As to the Serious Organised Crime Agency see POLICE.

10   Ibid reg 25(2).

11   As to the meaning of 'act' see para 755 note 3 ante.

12   Employment Equality (Age) Regulations 2006, SI 2006/1031, reg 25(3).

784. Aiding unlawful acts. A person[1] who knowingly aids another person to do an act[2] made unlawful by the Employment Equality (Age) Regulations 2006[3] is to be treated for the purpose of those regulations as himself doing an unlawful act of the like description[4]; and for these purposes an employee or agent for whose act the employer[5] or principal is liable[6], or would be so liable but for the statutory defence that he took reasonably practicable steps to prevent that act[7], is to be deemed to aid the doing of the act by the employer or principal[8]. A person does not, however, knowingly aid another to do an unlawful act under these provisions if:

(1) he acts in reliance on a statement made to him by that other person that, by reason of any provision of the relevant regulations, the act which he aids would not be unlawful; and

(2) it is reasonable for him to rely on the statement[9].

A person who knowingly or recklessly makes a statement such as is referred to in head (1) above which in a material respect is false or misleading commits an offence, and is liable on summary conviction to a fine[10].

1   As to the meaning of 'person' see para 344 note 3 ante.
2   As to the meaning of 'act' see para 755 note 3 ante.
3   Ie the Employment Equality (Age) Regulations 2006, SI 2006/1031.
4   Ibid reg 26(1).
5   As to the meaning of 'employer' see para 758 note 1 ante.
6   Ie under the Employment Equality (Age) Regulations 2006, SI 2006/1031, reg 25: see para 783 ante.
7   Ie but for ibid reg 25(3): see para 783 ante.
8   Ibid reg 26(2). As to aiding discrimination under the Sex Discrimination Act 1975 see para 392 ante; and as to aiding discrimination under the Race Relations Act 1976 see para 477 ante.
9   Employment Equality (Sexual Orientation) Regulations 2003, SI 2003/1661, reg 26(3).
10   Ibid reg 26(4). The fine referred to in the text is a fine not exceeding level 5 on the standard scale: see reg 26(4). As to the standard scale see para 315 note 15 ante.

(4) GENERAL EXCEPTION FOR, AND OTHER PROVISIONS RELATING TO, RETIREMENT

(i) General Exception for Retirement

785. Exception for retirement. The following provision applies in relation to an employee[1], a person in Crown employment[2], a relevant member of the House of Commons staff[3] and a relevant member of the House of Lords staff[4]. Nothing in Part 2[5] or Part 3[6] of the Employment Equality (Age) Regulations 2006 renders unlawful the dismissal of a person[7] to whom this provision applies at or over the age of 65 where the reason for the dismissal is retirement[8]. For these purposes, however, whether or not the reason for a dismissal is retirement must be determined in accordance with the relevant provisions[9] of the law relating to unfair dismissal[10].

1   Ie an employee within the meaning of the Employment Rights Act 1996 s 230(1). For those purposes, 'employee' means an individual who has entered into or works under (or, where the employment has ceased, worked under) a contract of employment; and 'contract of employment' means a contract of service or apprenticeship, whether express or implied, and (if it is express) whether oral or in writing: s 230(1), (2).
2   'Crown employment' means: (1) service for purposes of a Minister of the Crown or government department, other than service of a person holding a statutory office; or (2) service on behalf of the Crown for purposes of a person holding a statutory office or purposes of a statutory body: Employment Equality (Age) Regulations 2006, SI 2006/1031, reg 2(2). 'Service for purposes of a Minister of the Crown or government department' does not include service in any office mentioned in the House of Commons Disqualification Act 1975 Sch 2 (as amended) (ministerial offices: see PARLIAMENT vol 34 (Reissue) para 611); 'statutory body' means a body set up by or in pursuance of an enactment, and 'statutory office' means an office so set up: Employment Equality (Age) Regulations 2006, SI 2006/1031, reg 2(2). For the meaning of 'Minister of the Crown' see para 772 note 4 ante.

3   'Relevant member of the House of Commons staff' means any person who was appointed by the House
     of Commons Commission or who is a member of the Speaker's personal staff: ibid reg 2(2).
4   Ibid reg 30(1). 'Relevant member of the House of Lords staff' means any person who is employed under
     a contract of employment with the Corporate Officer of the House of Lords: reg 2(2).
5   Ie ibid Pt 2 (regs 7–24) (as amended): see para 758 et seq ante.
6   Ie ibid Pt 3 (regs 25–26): see paras 783–784 et seq ante.
7   As to the meaning of 'person' see para 344 note 3 ante.
8   Employment Equality (Age) Regulations 2006, SI 2006/1031, reg 30(2).
9   Ie in accordance with the Employment Rights Act 1996 ss 98ZA–98ZF (as added): see para 786 et seq
     post.
10   Employment Equality (Age) Regulations 2006, SI 2006/1031, reg 30(3).

(ii) Retirement and the Law of Unfair Dismissal

A. IN GENERAL

786.   Retirement and the law of unfair dismissal; in general.   For the purposes
of the law relating to unfair dismissal[1], retirement of the employee[2] constitutes a
substantial reason justifying the dismissal of an employee holding the position which he
held[3]. It must be either the sole, or the principal, reason for the dismissal[4]. This is,
however, subject to the particular provisions[5] which provide that retirement is or is not
to be taken as the reason, or a reason, for a dismissal in specified circumstances[6].

In any case where the employer[7] has fulfilled the statutory requirements[8] by showing
that the reason, or the principal reason, for the dismissal is retirement of the employee,
the question whether the dismissal is fair or unfair is to be determined in accordance
with the following provision[9]. If the reason, or principal reason, for a dismissal is
retirement of the employee, the employee is to be regarded as unfairly dismissed if, and
only if, there has been a failure on the part of the employer to comply with an
obligation imposed on him by any of the following provisions of Schedule 6 to the
Employment Equality (Age) Regulations 2006[10]:

(1)   the provision relating to notification of retirement[11], if not already given[12];
(2)   the duty to consider the employee's request not to be retired[13];
(3)   the duty to consider an appeal[14] against a decision to refuse a request not to be
      retired[15].

1   Ie the Employment Rights Act 1996 Pt X (ss 94–134A) (as amended): see EMPLOYMENT vol 16(1B)
     (Reissue) para 631 et seq. As to the modification of Pt X (as amended) in relation to governing bodies of
     schools which are maintained by a local education authority and have a right to a delegated budget see
     EMPLOYMENT vol 16(1A) (Reissue) para 317. For the meaning of 'dismissal' see EMPLOYMENT
     vol 16(1B) (Reissue) para 637.
2   For the meaning of 'employee' see para 785 note 1 ante.
3   See the Employment Rights Act 1996 s 98(1), (2)(ba) (s 98(2)(ba) added by the Employment Equality
     (Age) Regulations 2006, SI 2006/1031, reg 49(1), Sch 8 paras 21, 22(1), (2)).
4   See the Employment Rights Act 1996 s 98(1); and EMPLOYMENT vol 16(1B) (Reissue) para 631.
5   Ie ibid ss 98ZA–98ZF (as added): see para 787 et seq post.
6   See ibid s 98(2A) (added by the Employment Equality (Age) Regulations 2006, SI 2006/1031, Sch 8
     paras 21, 22(1), (3)).
7   For these purposes, 'employer', in relation to an employee, means the person by whom the employee is
     (or, where the employment has ceased, was) employed; 'employment', in relation to an employee, means
     (except for the purposes of the Employment Rights Act 1996 s 171 (employment not under a contract of
     employment: see EMPLOYMENT vol 16(1B) (Reissue) para 710)) employment under a contract of
     employment; and 'employed' is to be construed accordingly: see s 230(4), (5)(a).
8   Ie the requirements of ibid s 98(1): see EMPLOYMENT vol 16(1B) (Reissue) para 631.
9   Ibid s 98(3A) (added by the Employment Equality (Age) Regulations 2006, SI 2006/1031, Sch 8
     paras 21, 22(1), (4)).
10   Ie specified provisions of the Employment Equality (Age) Regulations 2006, SI 2006/1031, reg 47,
     Sch 6: see the text and notes 11–15 infra; and para 792 et seq post.
11   Ie ibid Sch 6 para 4: see para 792 post.

12   Ie under ibid Sch 6 para 2: see para 792 post.
13   Ie ibid Sch 6 paras 6, 7: see para 794 post.
14   Ie ibid Sch 6 para 8: see para 796 post.
15   Employment Rights Act 1996 s 98ZG (added by the Employment Equality (Age) Regulations 2006, SI 2006/1031, Sch 8 paras 21, 23).

B.   WHETHER RETIREMENT IS THE REASON, OR A REASON, FOR DISMISSAL

787.   No normal retirement age; dismissal before 65.   With regard to the dismissal[1] of an employee[2], if:

(1)   the employee has no normal retirement age[3]; and
(2)   the operative date of termination[4] falls before the date when the employee reaches the age of 65,

retirement of the employee is not to be taken to be the reason, or a reason, for the dismissal[5].

1   For the meaning of 'dismissal' see EMPLOYMENT vol 16(1B) (Reissue) para 637.
2   For the meaning of 'employee' see para 785 note 1 ante.
3   'Normal retirement age', in relation to an employee, means the age at which employees in the employer's undertaking who hold, or have held, the same kind of position as the employee are normally required to retire: Employment Rights Act 1996 s 98ZH (ss 98ZA, 98ZH added by the Employment Equality (Age) Regulations 2006, SI 2006/1031, Sch 8 paras 21, 23). For the meaning of 'employer' see para 786 note 7 ante. For a case under the Employment Rights Act 1996 s 109 (repealed) and the Transfer of Undertakings (Protection of Employment) Regulations 1981, SI 1981/1794 (revoked) relating to retirement age see *Cross v British Airways plc* [2006] EWCA Civ 549, [2006] ICR 1239, [2006] IRLR 804.
4   'Operative date of termination' means: (1) where the employer terminates the employee's contract of employment by notice, the date on which the notice expires; or (2) where the employer terminates the contract of employment without notice, the date on which the termination takes effect: Employment Rights Act 1996 s 98ZH (as added: see note 3 supra).
5   Ibid s 98ZA (as added: see note 3 supra). As to retirement and the law of unfair dismissal generally see para 786 ante.

788.   No normal retirement age; dismissal at or after 65.   The following provisions apply to the dismissal[1] of an employee[2] if: (1) the employee has no normal retirement age[3]; and (2) the operative date of termination[4] falls on or after the date when the employee reaches the age of 65[5].

In a case where:

(a)   the employer[6] has notified the employee of his intention to retire him[7] and the contract of employment terminates on the intended date of retirement[8], retirement of the employee is to be taken to be the only reason for the dismissal by the employer and any other reason must be disregarded[9];

(b)   the employer has notified the employee of his intention to retire him[10] but the contract of employment terminates before the intended date of retirement, retirement of the employee is not to be taken to be the reason, or a reason, for dismissal[11];

(c)   the employer has not notified the employee of his intention to retire him[12] and there is an intended date of retirement in relation to the dismissal, but the contract of employment terminates before the intended date of retirement, retirement of the employee is not to be taken to be the reason, or a reason, for dismissal[13].

In all other cases where the employer has not notified the employee of his intention to retire him[14], particular regard must be had to the specified matters[15] when determining the reason, or principal reason, for dismissal[16]. The specified matters are:

(i)   whether or not the employer has notified the employee of his intention to retire him in accordance with his continuing duty to do so[17];

    (ii)   if the employer has notified the employee in accordance with that duty, how long before the notified retirement date[18] the notification was given;

    (iii)   whether or not the employer has followed, or sought to follow, the procedures for holding a meeting[19] to consider the employee's request not to retire[20].

1   For the meaning of 'dismissal' see EMPLOYMENT vol 16(1B) (Reissue) para 637.
2   For the meaning of 'employee' see para 785 note 1 ante.
3   For the meaning of 'normal retirement age' see para 787 note 3 ante.
4   For the meaning of 'operative date of termination' see para 787 note 4 ante.
5   Employment Rights Act 1996 s 98ZB(1) (ss 98ZB, 98ZF, 98ZH added by the Employment Equality (Age) Regulations 2006, SI 2006/1031, reg 49(1), Sch 8 paras 21, 23).
6   For the meaning of 'employer' see para 786 note 7 ante.
7   Ie in accordance with the Employment Equality (Age) Regulations 2006, SI 2006/1031, reg 47, Sch 6 para 2: see para 792 post.
8   'Intended date of retirement' means the date which, by virtue of ibid Sch 6 para 1(2) (see para 792 post), is the intended date of retirement in relation to a particular dismissal: Employment Rights Act 1996 s 98ZH (as added: see note 5 supra).
9   Ibid s 98ZB(2) (as added: see note 5 supra).
10   See note 7 supra.
11   Employment Rights Act 1996 s 98ZB(3) (as added: see note 5 supra).
12   See note 7 supra.
13   Employment Rights Act 1996 s 98ZB(4) (as added: see note 5 supra).
14   See note 7 supra.
15   Ie the matters set out in the Employment Rights Act 1996 s 98ZF (as added): see heads (i)–(iii) in the text.
16   Ibid s 98ZB(5) (as added: see note 5 supra).
17   Ie in accordance with the Employment Equality (Age) Regulations 2006, SI 2006/1031, Sch 6 para 4: see para 792 post.
18   For this purpose, 'notified retirement date' means the date notified to the employee in accordance with ibid Sch 6 para 4 as the date on which the employer intends to retire the employee: Employment Rights Act 1996 s 98ZF(2) (as added: see note 5 supra).
19   Ie the procedures in the Employment Equality (Age) Regulations 2006, SI 2006/1031, Sch 6 para 7: see para 794 post.
20   Employment Rights Act 1996 s 98ZF(1) (as added: see note 5 supra). As to retirement and the law of unfair dismissal generally see para 786 ante.

789. Normal retirement age; dismissal before retirement age. With regard to the dismissal[1] of an employee[2], if:

    (1)   the employee has a normal retirement age[3]; and

    (2)   the operative date of termination[4] falls before the date when the employee reaches the normal retirement age,

retirement of the employee is not to be taken to be the reason, or a reason, for the dismissal[5].

1   For the meaning of 'dismissal' see EMPLOYMENT vol 16(1B) (Reissue) para 637.
2   For the meaning of 'employee' see para 785 note 1 ante.
3   For the meaning of 'normal retirement age' see para 787 note 3 ante.
4   For the meaning of 'operative date of termination' see para 787 note 4 ante.
5   Employment Rights Act 1996 s 98ZC(1), (2) (added by the Employment Equality (Age) Regulations 2006, SI 2006/1031, reg 49(1), Sch 8 paras 21, 23). As to retirement and the law of unfair dismissal generally see para 786 ante.

790. Normal retirement age 65 or higher; dismissal at or after retirement age. The following provisions apply to the dismissal[1] of an employee[2] if: (1) the employee has a normal retirement age[3]; (2) the normal retirement age is 65 or higher; and (3) the operative date of termination[4] falls on or after the date when the employee reaches the normal retirement age[5].

    In a case where:

    (a)   the employer[6] has notified the employee of his intention to retire him[7] and the contract of employment terminates on the intended date of retirement[8], retirement of the employee is to be taken to be the only reason for the dismissal by the employer and any other reason must be disregarded[9];

(b)   the employer has notified the employee of his intention to retire him[10] but the contract of employment terminates before the intended date of retirement, retirement of the employee is not to be taken to be the reason, or a reason, for dismissal[11];

(c)   the employer has not notified the employee of his intention to retire him[12] and there is an intended date of retirement in relation to the dismissal, but the contract of employment terminates before the intended date of retirement, retirement of the employee is not be taken to be the reason, or a reason, for dismissal[13].

In all other cases where the employer has not notified the employee of his intention to retire him[14], particular regard must be had to the specified matters[15] when determining the reason, or principal reason, for dismissal[16].

1   For the meaning of 'dismissal' see EMPLOYMENT vol 16(1B) (Reissue) para 637.
2   For the meaning of 'employee' see para 785 note 1 ante.
3   For the meaning of 'normal retirement age' see para 787 note 3 ante.
4   For the meaning of 'operative date of termination' see para 787 note 4 ante.
5   Employment Rights Act 1996 s 98ZD(1) (s 98ZD added by the Employment Equality (Age) Regulations 2006, SI 2006/1031, reg 49(1), Sch 8 paras 21, 23).
6   For the meaning of 'employer' see para 786 note 7 ante.
7   Ie in accordance with the Employment Equality (Age) Regulations 2006, SI 2006/1031, reg 47, Sch 6 para 2: see para 792 post.
8   For the meaning of 'intended date of retirement' see para 788 note 8 ante.
9   Employment Rights Act 1996 s 98ZD(2) (as added: see note 5 supra).
10   See note 7 supra.
11   Employment Rights Act 1996 s 98ZD(3) (as added: see note 5 supra).
12   See note 7 supra.
13   Employment Rights Act 1996 s 98ZD(4) (as added: see note 5 supra).
14   See note 7 supra.
15   Ie the matters specified in the Employment Rights Act 1996 s 98ZF (as added): see para 788 heads (i)–(iii) ante.
16   Ibid s 98ZD(5) (as added: see note 5 supra). As to retirement and the law of unfair dismissal generally see para 786 ante.

791.   Normal retirement age below 65; dismissal at or after retirement age.
The following provisions apply to the dismissal[1] of an employee[2] if: (1) the employee has a normal retirement age[3]; (2) the normal retirement age is below 65; and (3) the operative date of termination[4] falls on or after the date when the employee reaches the normal retirement age[5].

If it is unlawful discrimination under the Employment Equality (Age) Regulations 2006[6] for the employee to have that normal retirement age, retirement of the employee is not to be taken to be the reason, or a reason, for dismissal[7].

If it is not unlawful discrimination under those regulations for the employee to have that normal retirement age, then in a case where:

(a)   the employer[8] has notified the employee of his intention to retire him[9] and the contract of employment terminates on the intended date of retirement[10], retirement of the employee is to be taken to be the only reason for dismissal by the employer and any other reason must be disregarded[11];

(b)   the employer has notified the employee of his intention to retire him[12] but the contract of employment terminates before the intended date of retirement, retirement of the employee is not to be taken to be the reason, or a reason, for dismissal[13];

(c)	the employer has not notified the employee of his intention to retire him[14] and there is an intended date of retirement in relation to the dismissal, but the contract of employment terminates before the intended date of retirement, retirement of the employee is not to be taken to be the reason, or a reason, for dismissal[15],

and in all other cases where the employer has not notified the employee of his intention to retire him[16], particular regard must be had to the specified matters[17] when determining the reason, or principal reason, for dismissal[18].

1	For the meaning of 'dismissal' see EMPLOYMENT vol 16(1B) (Reissue) para 637.
2	For the meaning of 'employee' see para 785 note 1 ante.
3	For the meaning of 'normal retirement age' see para 787 note 3 ante.
4	For the meaning of 'operative date of termination' see para 787 note 4 ante.
5	Employment Rights Act 1996 s 98ZE(1) (s 98ZE added by the Employment Equality (Age) Regulations 2006, SI 2006/1031, reg 49(1), Sch 8 paras 21, 23).
6	Ie under the Employment Equality (Age) Regulations 2006, SI 2006/1031 (as amended).
7	Employment Rights Act 1996 s 98ZE(2) (as added: see note 5 supra).
8	For the meaning of 'employer' see para 786 note 7 ante.
9	Ie in accordance with the Employment Equality (Age) Regulations 2006, SI 2006/1031, reg 47, Sch 6 para 2: see para 792 post.
10	For the meaning of 'intended date of retirement' see para 788 note 8 ante.
11	Employment Rights Act 1996 s 98ZE(3), (4) (as added: see note 5 supra).
12	See note 9 supra.
13	Employment Rights Act 1996 s 98ZE(3), (5) (as added: see note 5 supra).
14	See note 9 supra.
15	Employment Rights Act 1996 s 98ZE(3), (6) (as added: see note 5 supra).
16	See note 9 supra.
17	Ie the matters specified in the Employment Rights Act 1996 s 98ZF (as added): see para 788 heads (i)–(iii) ante.
18	Ibid s 98ZE(3), (7) (as added: see note 5 supra). As to retirement and the law of unfair dismissal generally see para 786 ante.

### (iii)	Duty to consider Working beyond Retirement

**792.	Duty of employer to inform employee.**	An employer[1] who intends to retire an employee has a duty to notify the employee in writing of the employee's right to make a request not to retire[2], and the date on which he intends the employee to retire, not more than one year and not less than six months before that date[3]. The duty to notify applies regardless of:

(1)	whether there is any term in the employee's contract of employment indicating when his retirement is expected to take place;

(2)	any other notification of, or information about, the employee's date of retirement given to him by the employer at any time; and

(3)	any other information about the employee's right to make a request[4] given to him by the employer at any time[5].

Where the employer has failed to comply with the above provisions, he has a continuing duty to notify the employee in writing as described above until the fourteenth day before the operative date of termination[6].

An employee may present a complaint to an employment tribunal[7] that his employer has failed to comply with the duty[8] to notify him of his right to make a request not to retire[9]. A tribunal may not, however, consider such a complaint unless the complaint is presented:

(a)	before the end of the period of three months beginning with:

(i)	the last day permitted to the employer[10] for complying with the duty to notify; or

(ii)   if the employee did not then know the date that would be the intended date of retirement[11], the first day on which he knew or should have known that date; or

(b)   within such further period as the tribunal considers reasonable in a case where it is satisfied that it was not reasonably practicable for the complaint to be presented before the end of that period of three months[12].

Where a tribunal finds that such a complaint is well-founded it must order the employer to pay compensation to the employee of such amount, not exceeding eight weeks' pay[13], as the tribunal considers just and equitable in all the circumstances[14].

1   For these purposes, 'employee' means a person to whom the Employment Equality (Age) Regulations 2006, SI 2006/1031, reg 30 (exception for retirement: see para 785 ante) applies; and references to 'employer' are to be construed accordingly: reg 47, Sch 6 para 1(1).
2   Ie a request under ibid Sch 6 para 5: see para 793 post.
3   Ibid Sch 6 para 2(1).
4   'Request' means a request made under ibid Sch 6 para 5 (see para 793 post): Sch 6 para 1(1).
5   Ibid Sch 6 para 2(2).
6   Ibid Sch 6 para 4. For these purposes, 'operative date of termination' means (subject to Sch 6 para 10(3): see para 798 post): (1) where the employer terminates the employee's contract of employment by notice, the date on which the notice expires; or (2) where the employer terminates the contract of employment without notice, the date on which the termination takes effect: Sch 6 para 1(1).
    Transitional provisions apply where the date on which notice of dismissal given by an employer expires before 1 April 2007: see reg 48, Sch 7.
7   As to employment tribunals and the procedure before them see EMPLOYMENT vol 16(1B) (Reissue) para 816 et seq.
8   Ie under the Employment Equality (Age) Regulations 2006, SI 2006/1031, Sch 6 para 2: see the text and notes 1–5 supra.
9   Ibid Sch 6 para 11(1).
10 Ie by ibid Sch 6 para 2: see the text to note 3 supra.
11 For these purposes, 'intended date of retirement' means: (1) where the employer notifies a date in accordance with ibid Sch 6 para 2 (see the text and notes 1–5 supra), that date; (2) where the employer notifies a date in accordance with Sch 6 para 4 (see the text and note 6 supra), and either no request is made or a request is made after the notification, that date; (3) where: (a) the employer has not notified a date in accordance with Sch 6 para 2; (b) a request is made before the employer has notified a date in accordance with Sch 6 para 4 (including where no notification in accordance with that provision is given); (c) the request is made by an employee who has reasonable grounds for believing that the employer intends to retire him on a certain date; and (d) the request identifies that date, the date so identified; (4) in a case to which Sch 6 para 3 (see para 797 post) has applied, any earlier or later date that has superseded the date mentioned in head (1), head (2) or head (3) supra as the intended date of retirement by virtue of Sch 6 para 3(3); (5) in a case to which Sch 6 para 10 (see para 798 post) has applied, the later date that has superseded the date mentioned in head (1), head (2) or head (3) supra as the intended date of retirement by virtue of Sch 6 para 10(3)(b): Sch 6 para 1(2), (2).
12 Ibid Sch 6 para 11(2).
13 The Employment Rights Act 1996 Pt XIV Ch II (ss 220–229) (as amended) (calculation of a week's pay: see EMPLOYMENT vol 16(1A) (Reissue) para 116 et seq) applies for these purposes and, in applying Pt XIV Ch II (as amended), the calculation date must be taken to be the date on which the complaint was presented or, if earlier, the operative date of termination; and the limit in s 227(1) (as amended) (maximum amount of a week's pay: see EMPLOYMENT vol 16(1A) (Reissue) para 119) applies for these purposes: Employment Equality (Age) Regulations 2006, SI 2006/1031, Sch 6 para 11(4), (5).
14 Ibid Sch 6 para 11(3).

793.   Statutory right to request not to retire.   An employee[1] may make a request[2] to his employer[3] not to retire on the intended date of retirement[4]. In his request the employee must propose that his employment should continue, following the intended date of retirement:

(1)   indefinitely;

(2)   for a stated period; or

(3)   until a stated date,

and, if the request is made at a time when it is no longer possible for the employer to notify in accordance with his duty to do so not more than one year and not less than six months before the date on which he intends the employee to retire[5], and the employer has not yet notified in accordance with his continuing duty to do so[6], the employee must identify the date on which he believes that the employer intends to retire him[7].

A request must be in writing and state that it is made under these provisions[8]. A request is only a request so made if it is made:

(a)   in a case where the employer has complied with his duty to notify not more than one year and not less than six months before the date on which he intends the employee to retire[9], more than three months but not more than six months before the intended date of retirement; or

(b)   in a case where the employer has not complied with that duty, before, but not more than six months before, the intended date of retirement[10].

An employee may only make one request under these provisions in relation to any one intended date of retirement and may not make a request in relation to a date that supersedes[11] a different date as the intended date of retirement[12].

1   For the meaning of 'employee' see para 792 note 1 ante.
2   For the meaning of 'request' see para 792 note 4 ante.
3   As to the meaning of 'employer' see para 792 note 1 ante.
4   Employment Equality (Age) Regulations 2006, SI 2006/1031, reg 47, Sch 6 para 5(1). For the meaning of 'intended date of retirement' see para 792 note 11 ante.
5   Ie in accordance with ibid Sch 6 para 2: see para 792 ante.
6   Ie in accordance with ibid Sch 6 para 4: see para 792 ante.
7   Ibid Sch 6 para 5(2).
8   Ibid Sch 6 para 5(3).
9   Ie where he has complied with ibid Sch 6 para 2: see para 792 ante.
10   Ibid Sch 6 para 5(5).
11   Ie by virtue of ibid Sch 6 para 3(3) (see para 797 post) or Sch 6 para 10(3)(b) (see para 798 post).
12   Ibid Sch 6 para 5(4). Transitional provisions apply where the date on which notice of dismissal given by an employer expires before 1 April 2007: see reg 48, Sch 7.

794.   Employer's duty to consider a request; meeting to consider a request.
An employer[1] to whom a request[2] is made is under a duty to consider the request in accordance with the prescribed[3] procedure[4].

An employer having such a duty to consider a request must hold a meeting to discuss the request with the employee[5] within a reasonable period after receiving it[6]; and the employer and employee must take all reasonable steps to attend the meeting[7]. The employee has a right to be accompanied at the meeting[8]. The duty to hold a meeting does not, however, apply if:

(1)   before the end of the period that is reasonable:
(a)   the employer and employee agree that the employee's employment will continue indefinitely and the employer gives notice[9] to the employee to that effect; or
(b)   the employer and employee agree that the employee's employment will continue for an agreed period and the employer gives notice to the employee of the length of that period or of the date on which it will end[10];

(2)   it is not practicable to hold a meeting within the period that is reasonable, in which case the employer may consider the request without holding a meeting, provided that he considers any representations made by the employee[11].

The employer must give the employee notice of his decision on the request as soon as is reasonably practicable after the date of the meeting or, if head (2) above applies, his consideration of the request[12]. A notice so given must:

(i)   where the decision is to accept the request, state that it is accepted and:

(A)   where the decision is that the employee's employment will continue indefinitely, state that fact; or

(B)   where the decision is that the employee's employment will continue for a further period, state that fact and specify the length of the period or the date on which it will end[13];

(ii)   where the decision is to refuse the request, confirm that the employer wishes to retire the employee and the date on which the dismissal[14] is to take effect[15],

and, in the case of a notice falling within head (ii) above, and of a notice referred to in head (i) above that specifies a period shorter than the period proposed by the employee in the request, must inform the employee of his right to appeal[16].

1   As to the meaning of 'employer' see para 792 note 1 ante.
2   For the meaning of 'request' see para 792 note 4 ante.
3   As to the prescribed procedure see the Employment Equality (Age) Regulations 2006, SI 2006/1031, reg 47, Sch 6 paras 7–9; the text and notes 4–16 infra; and paras 795–796 post.
4   Ibid Sch 6 para 6.
5   For the meaning of 'employee' see para 792 note 1 ante.
6   Employment Equality (Age) Regulations 2006, SI 2006/1031, reg 47, Sch 6 para 7(1).
7   Ibid Sch 6 para 7(2).
8   See ibid Sch 6 para 9; and para 795 post.
9   All notices given under ibid Sch 6 para 7 must be in writing and must be dated: Sch 6 para 7(8).
10   Ibid Sch 6 para 7(3).
11   See ibid Sch 6 para 7(4), (5).
12   Ibid Sch 6 para 7(6).
13   Ibid Sch 6 para 7(7)(a).
14   For these purposes, 'dismissal' means a dismissal within the meaning of the Employment Rights Act 1996 s 95 (as amended) (see EMPLOYMENT vol 16(1B) (Reissue) para 637): Employment Equality (Age) Regulations 2006, SI 2006/1031, Sch 6 para 1(1).
15   Ibid Sch 6 para 7(7)(b).
16   Ibid Sch 6 para 7(7). Transitional provisions apply where the date on which notice of dismissal given by an employer expires before 1 April 2007: see reg 48, Sch 7.

795. Right to be accompanied at a meeting. Where a meeting is held[1], and the employee[2] reasonably requests to be accompanied at the meeting, the employer[3] must permit the employee to be accompanied at the meeting by one companion who:

(1)   is chosen by the employee;

(2)   is a worker[4] employed by the same employer as the employee;

(3)   is to be permitted to address the meeting, but not to answer questions on behalf of the employee; and

(4)   is to be permitted to confer with the employee during the meeting[5].

An employer must permit a worker to take time off during working hours for the purpose of accompanying an employee in accordance with a request under head (2) above[6].

If an employee has such a right to be accompanied at a meeting, but his chosen companion will not be available at the time proposed for the meeting by the employer, and the employee proposes an alternative time which satisfies the prescribed requirements[7], the employer must postpone the meeting to the time proposed by the employee[8]. An alternative time must:

(a)   be convenient for employer, employee and companion; and

(b)   fall before the end of the period of seven days beginning with the first day after the day proposed by the employer[9].

An employee may present a complaint to an employment tribunal[10] that his employer has failed, or threatened to fail, to comply[11] with heads (1) to (4) above or with the above duty to postpone the meeting[12]. A tribunal may not, however, consider such a complaint in relation to a failure or threat unless the complaint is presented:

(i) before the end of the period of three months beginning with the date of the failure or threat; or

(ii) within such further period as the tribunal considers reasonable in a case where it is satisfied that it was not reasonably practicable for the complaint to be presented before the end of that period of three months[13].

Where a tribunal finds that such a complaint is well-founded it must order the employer to pay compensation to the worker of an amount not exceeding two weeks' pay[14].

An employee has the right not to be subjected to any detriment[15] by any act[16] by his employer done on the ground that he exercised or sought to exercise his right to be accompanied in accordance with the provisions[17] set out above[18]; and a worker[19] has the right not to be subjected to any detriment by any act, or any deliberate failure to act, by his employer done on the ground that he accompanied or sought to accompany an employee pursuant to a request under those provisions[20]. The latter right does not, however, apply where the worker is an employee and the detriment in question amounts to dismissal[21] within the meaning of Part X of the Employment Rights Act 1996[22].

An employee who is dismissed is to be regarded[23] as unfairly dismissed if the reason (or, if more than one, the principal reason) for the dismissal[24] is that he:

(A) exercised or sought to exercise his right to be accompanied in accordance with the provisions set out above; or

(B) accompanied or sought to accompany an employee pursuant to a request under those provisions[25].

1 Ie under the Employment Equality (Age) Regulations 2006, SI 2006/1031, reg 47, Sch 6 para 7 (meeting to consider request: see para 794 ante) or Sch 6 para 8 (appeals: see para 796 post).

2 For the meaning of 'employee' see para 792 note 1 ante.

3 As to the meaning of 'employer' see para 792 note 1 ante.

4 For these purposes, 'worker' means an individual who has entered into or works under (or, where the employment has ceased, worked under): (1) a contract of employment; or (2) any other contract, whether express or implied and (if it is express) whether oral or in writing, whereby the individual undertakes to do or perform personally any work or services for another party to the contract whose status is not by virtue of the contract that of a client or customer of any profession or business undertaking carried on by the individual: Employment Rights Act 1996 s 230(3); definition applied by the Employment Equality (Age) Regulations 2006, SI 2006/1031, Sch 6 para 1(1).

5 Ibid Sch 6 para 9(1).

6 Ibid Sch 6 para 9(5). The Trade Union and Labour Relations (Consolidation) Act 1992 ss 168(3), (4), 169, 171–173 (as amended) (time off for carrying out trade union duties: see EMPLOYMENT vol 16(1A) (Reissue) para 310; TRADE, INDUSTRY AND INDUSTRIAL RELATIONS vol 47 (2001 Reissue) paras 1160, 1163) apply in relation to the Employment Equality (Age) Regulations 2006, SI 2006/1031, Sch 6 para 9(5) as they apply in relation to the Trade Union and Labour Relations (Consolidation) Act 1992 s 168(1) (as amended): Employment Equality (Age) Regulations 2006, SI 2006/1031, Sch 6 para 9(6). Dismissal for exercising, or seeking to exercise, the right to be accompanied, or to accompany another, at a meeting under Sch 6 para 9 is unfair: see the Employment Equality (Age) (Consequential Amendments) Regulations 2007, SI 2007/825, reg 3. See also the Employment Rights Act 1996 s 105(7IA) (as added); and EMPLOYMENT.

7 Ie the requirements of the Employment Equality (Age) Regulations 2006, SI 2006/1031, Sch 6 para 9(4): see heads (a)–(b) in the text.

8 Ibid Sch 6 para 9(3).

9 Ibid Sch 6 para 9(4). Transitional provisions apply where the date on which notice of dismissal given by an employer expires before 1 April 2007: see reg 48, Sch 7.

10 As to employment tribunals and the procedure before them see EMPLOYMENT vol 16(1B) (Reissue) para 816 et seq.

11 Ie where he has failed, or threatened to fail, to comply with the Employment Equality (Age) Regulations 2006, SI 2006/1031, Sch 6 para 9(2) (see the text and notes 3–5 supra) or Sch 6 para 9(3) (see the text and notes 7–8 supra).

12 See ibid Sch 6 para 12(1).

13 Ibid Sch 6 para 12(2).

14 Ibid Sch 6 para 12(3). The Employment Rights Act 1996 Pt XIV Ch II (ss 220–229) (as amended) (calculation of a week's pay: see EMPLOYMENT vol 16(1A) (Reissue) para 116 et seq) applies for these purposes and, in applying Pt XIV Ch II (as amended), the calculation date must be taken to be the date on which the relevant meeting took place (or was to have taken place); and the limit in s 227(1) (as amended) (maximum amount of a week's pay: see EMPLOYMENT vol 16(1A) (Reissue) para 119) applies for these purposes: Employment Equality (Age) Regulations 2006, SI 2006/1031, Sch 6 para 12(4), (5).

15 As to the meaning of 'detriment' see para 758 note 8 ante.

16 As to the meaning of 'act' see para 755 note 3 ante.

17 Ie the Employment Equality (Age) Regulations 2006, SI 2006/1031, Sch 6 para 9: see the text and notes 1–9 supra.

18 Ibid Sch 6 para 13(1). The Employment Rights Act 1996 s 48 (as amended) (complaints to employment tribunals: see EMPLOYMENT vol 16(1A) (Reissue) para 551) applies in relation to contraventions of the Employment Equality (Age) Regulations 2006, SI 2006/1031, Sch 6 para 13(1) or Sch 6 para 13(2) (see the text and notes 19–20 infra) as it applies in relation to contraventions of certain provisions of that Act: Employment Equality (Age) Regulations 2006, SI 2006/1031, Sch 6 para 13(3).

19 For the meaning of 'worker' for these purposes see para 795 note 4 ante.

20 Employment Equality (Age) Regulations 2006, SI 2006/1031, Sch 6 para 13(2). See also note 18 supra.

21 Ie amounts to a dismissal within the meaning of the Employment Rights Act 1996 Pt X (ss 94–134A) (as amended) (unfair dismissal: see EMPLOYMENT vol 16(1B) (Reissue) para 631 et seq).

22 Employment Equality (Age) Regulations 2006, SI 2006/1031, Sch 6 para 13(4).

23 Ie for the purposes of the Employment Rights Act 1996 Pt X (ss 94–134A) (as amended): see EMPLOYMENT vol 16(1B) (Reissue) para 631 et seq.

24 For the meaning of 'dismissal' for these purposes see para 794 note 14 ante.

25 Employment Equality (Age) Regulations 2006, SI 2006/1031, Sch 6 para 13(5). The Employment Rights Act 1996 ss 128–132 (as amended) (interim relief: see EMPLOYMENT vol 16(1B) (Reissue) paras 675–678) apply in relation to dismissal for the reason specified in head (A) or head (B) in the text as they apply in relation to dismissal for a reason specified in s 128(1)(b) (as amended) (see EMPLOYMENT vol 16(1B) (Reissue) para 675): Employment Equality (Age) Regulations 2006, SI 2006/1031, Sch 6 para 13(6).

796. Appeals. An employee[1] is entitled to appeal against:

(1) a decision of his employer[2] to refuse the request[3]; or

(2) a decision of his employer to accept the request where the notice given[4] states that the employee's employment will continue for a further period[5] and specifies a period shorter than the period proposed by the employee in the request,

by giving notice[6] as soon as is reasonably practicable after the date of the notice[7] of the employer's decision[8]. A notice of appeal must set out the grounds of appeal[9].

The employer must hold a meeting with the employee to discuss an appeal within a reasonable period after the date of the notice of appeal[10] and the employer and employee must take all reasonable steps to attend the meeting[11]. The employee has a right to be accompanied at the meeting[12]. The duty to hold a meeting does not, however, apply if:

(a) before the end of the period that is reasonable:

(i) the employer and employee agree that the employee's employment will continue indefinitely and the employer gives notice to the employee to that effect[13]; or

(ii) the employer and employee agree that the employee's employment will continue for an agreed period and the employer gives notice to the employee of the length of that period or of the date on which it will end[14];

(b) it is not practicable to hold a meeting within the period that is reasonable, in which case the employer may consider the appeal without holding a meeting, provided he considers any representations made by the employee[15].

The employer must give the employee notice of his decision on the appeal as soon as is reasonably practicable after the date of the meeting or, if head (b) above applies, his consideration of the appeal[16]. Such a notice must, where the decision is to accept the appeal, state that it is accepted and:

(A) where the decision is that the employee's employment will continue indefinitely, state that fact; or

(B) where the decision is that the employee's employment will continue for a further period, state that fact and specify the length of the period or the date on which it will end[17].

Where, however, the decision is to refuse the appeal, the notice must confirm that the employer wishes to retire the employee and the date on which the dismissal[18] is to take effect[19].

1 For the meaning of 'employee' see para 792 note 1 ante.
2 As to the meaning of 'employer' see para 792 note 1 ante.
3 For the meaning of 'request' see para 792 note 4 ante.
4 Ie the notice given under the Employment Equality (Age) Regulations 2006, SI 2006/1031, reg 47, Sch 6 para 7(6): see para 794 ante.
5 Ie the notice states as mentioned in ibid Sch 6 para 7(7)(a)(ii): see para 794 head (i)(B) ante.
6 Ie in accordance with ibid Sch 6 para 8(2): see the text and note 9 infra. All notices given under Sch 6 para 8 must be in writing and must be dated: Sch 6 para 8(10).
7 See note 4 supra.
8 Employment Equality (Age) Regulations 2006, SI 2006/1031, Sch 6 para 8(1).
9 Ibid Sch 6 para 8(2).
10 Ibid Sch 6 para 8(3).
11 Ibid Sch 6 para 8(4).
12 See ibid Sch 6 para 9; and para 795 ante.
13 Ibid Sch 6 para 8(5)(a).
14 Ibid Sch 6 para 8(5)(b).
15 See ibid Sch 6 para 8(6), (7).
16 Ibid Sch 6 para 8(8).
17 Ibid Sch 6 para 8(9)(a).
18 For the meaning of 'dismissal' see para 794 note 14 ante.
19 Employment Equality (Age) Regulations 2006, SI 2006/1031, Sch 6 para 8(9)(b). Transitional provisions apply where the date on which notice of dismissal given by an employer expires before 1 April 2007: see reg 48, Sch 7.

797. Effect of agreement or notification of new date of dismissal. The following provisions apply if the employer[1] has notified[2] the employee[3] of his right to make a request[4], or the employee has made a request before being notified in accordance with the employer's continuing duty to do so[5], including where no notification in accordance with that continuing duty is given, and:

(1) the employer and employee agree[6] that the dismissal[7] is to take effect on a date later than the relevant date[8];

(2) the employer gives notice to the employee[9] that the dismissal is to take effect on a date later than the relevant date; or

(3) the employer and employee agree that the dismissal is to take effect on a date earlier than the relevant date[10].

The provisions regarding the duty to consider working beyond retirement[11] do not require the employer to give the employee a further notification in respect of dismissal taking effect on a date: (a) agreed as mentioned in head (1) above or notified as mentioned in head (2) above that is later than the relevant date and falls six months or less after the relevant date; or (b) agreed as mentioned in head (3) above that is earlier than the relevant date[12].

If:

(i) a date later than the relevant date is agreed as mentioned in head (1) above or notified as mentioned in head (2) above and falls six months or less after the relevant date; or

(ii) a date earlier than the relevant date is agreed as mentioned in head (3) above, the earlier or later date supersedes the relevant date as the intended date of retirement[13].

1 As to the meaning of 'employer' see para 792 note 1 ante.

2   Ie in accordance with the Employment Equality (Age) Regulations 2006, SI 2006/1031, reg 47, Sch 6 para 2 or Sch 6 para 4: see para 792 ante.

3   For the meaning of 'employee' see para 792 note 1 ante.

4   For the meaning of 'request' see para 792 note 4 ante.

5   Ie in accordance with the Employment Equality (Age) Regulations 2006, SI 2006/1031, Sch 6 para 4: see para 792 ante.

6   Ie in accordance with ibid Sch 6 para 7(3)(b) (see para 794 ante) or Sch 6 para 8(5)(b) (see para 796 ante).

7   For the meaning of 'dismissal' see para 794 note 14 ante.

8   For these purposes, 'the relevant date' means the date that is defined as the intended date of retirement in the Employment Equality (Age) Regulations 2006, SI 2006/1031, Sch 6 para 1(2)(a), (b) or (c) (see para 792 note 11 ante): Sch 6 para 3(4).

9   Ie in accordance with ibid Sch 6 para 7(7)(a)(ii) (see para 794 head (i)(b) ante) or, where the employee appeals, Sch 6 para 8(9)(a)(ii) (see para 796 head (B) ante).

10   Ibid Sch 6 para 3(1).

11   Ie ibid Sch 6 paras 1–13.

12   Ibid Sch 6 para 3(2).

13   Ibid Sch 6 para 3(3). For the meaning of 'intended date of retirement' see para 792 note 11 ante. Transitional provisions apply where the date on which notice of dismissal given by an employer expires before 1 April 2007: see reg 48, Sch 7.

798.   Dismissal before request considered.   The following provisions apply where:

(1)   an employer[1] is under a duty[2] to consider a request[3];

(2)   the employer dismisses the employee[4];

(3)   that dismissal[5] is the contemplated dismissal to which the request relates; and

(4)   the operative date of termination[6] would otherwise[7] fall on or before the day on which the employer gives notice[8] of his decision on the request[9].

The contract of employment continues in force for all purposes[10], including the purpose of determining for any purpose the period for which the employee has been continuously employed, until the day following that on which the notice of decision[11] is given[12]. The day following the day on which that notice is given supersedes:

(a)   the date mentioned in head (4) above as the operative date of termination; and

(b)   the date defined[13] as the intended date of retirement[14].

1   As to the meaning of 'employer' see para 792 note 1 ante.

2   Ie by virtue of the Employment Equality (Age) Regulations 2006, SI 2006/1031, reg 47, Sch 6 para 6: see para 794 ante.

3   For the meaning of 'request' see para 792 note 4 ante.

4   For the meaning of 'employee' see para 792 note 1 ante.

5   For the meaning of 'dismissal' see para 794 note 14 ante.

6   For the meaning of 'operative date of termination' see para 792 note 6 ante.

7   Ie but for the Employment Equality (Age) Regulations 2006, SI 2006/1031, Sch 6 para 10(3): see the text and notes 13–14 infra.

8   Ie in accordance with ibid Sch 6 para 7(6): see para 794 ante.

9   Ibid Sch 6 para 10(1).

10   However, any continuation of the contract of employment under Sch 6 para 10(2) must be disregarded when determining the operative date of termination for the purposes of the Employment Rights Act 1996 ss 98ZA–98ZH (as added) (see para 786 et seq ante): see the Employment Equality (Age) Regulations 2006, SI 2006/1031, Sch 6 para 10(4). For the meaning of 'operative date of termination' for those purposes see para 787 note 4 ante.

11   Ie the notice under ibid Sch 6 para 7(6): see para 794 ante.

12   Ibid Sch 6 para 10(2).

13   Ie defined in ibid Sch 6 para 1(2)(a), (b) or (c) as the intended date of retirement: see para 792 note 11 ante.

14   Ibid Sch 6 para 10(3). Transitional provisions apply where the date on which notice of dismissal given by an employer expires before 1 April 2007: see reg 48, Sch 7.

(5) OTHER GENERAL EXCEPTIONS

799.   Exception for statutory authority.   Nothing in Part 2[1] or Part 3[2] of the Employment Equality (Age) Regulations 2006 renders unlawful any act[3] done in order to comply with a requirement of any statutory provision[4].

1   Ie the Employment Equality (Age) Regulations 2006, SI 2006/1031, Pt 2 (regs 7–24) (as amended): see para 758 et seq ante.
2   Ie ibid Pt 3 (regs 25–26): see paras 783–784 ante.
3   As to the meaning of 'act' see para 755 note 3 ante.
4   Employment Equality (Age) Regulations 2006, SI 2006/1031, reg 27(1). For these purposes, 'statutory provision' means any provision (whenever enacted) of: (1) an Act; or (2) an instrument made by a Minister of the Crown under an Act: reg 27(2)(a), (b). This provision also refers to Scottish provisions, but Scottish matters generally are beyond the scope of this work. For the meaning of 'Minister of the Crown' see para 772 note 4 ante.

800.   Exception for national security.   Nothing in Part 2[1] or Part 3[2] of the Employment Equality (Age) Regulations 2006 renders unlawful an act[3] done for the purpose of safeguarding national security, if the doing of the act was justified by that purpose[4].

1   Ie the Employment Equality (Age) Regulations 2006, SI 2006/1031, Pt 2 (regs 7–24) (as amended): see para 758 et seq ante.
2   Ie ibid Pt 3 (regs 25–26): see paras 783–784 ante.
3   As to the meaning of 'act' see para 755 note 3 ante.
4   Employment Equality (Age) Regulations 2006, SI 2006/1031, reg 28.
    As to national security under the Sex Discrimination Act 1975 see para 403 ante; as to national security under the Race Relations Act 1976 see para 487 ante; and as to national security under the Disability Discrimination Act 1995 see para 616 ante.

801.   Exceptions for positive action.   Nothing in Part 2[1] or Part 3[2] of the Employment Equality (Age) Regulations 2006 renders unlawful any act[3]:
(1)   done in or in connection with:
    (a)   affording persons[4] of a particular age or age group access to facilities for training which would help fit them for particular work; or
    (b)   encouraging persons of a particular age or age group to take advantage of opportunities for doing particular work,
    where it reasonably appears to the person doing the act that it prevents or compensates for disadvantages linked to age suffered by persons of that age or age group doing that work or likely to take up that work[5];
(2)   done by a trade organisation[6] in or in connection with:
    (a)   affording only members of the organisation who are of a particular age or age group access to facilities for training which would help fit them for holding a post of any kind in the organisation; or
    (b)   encouraging only members of the organisation who are of a particular age or age group to take advantage of opportunities for holding such posts in the organisation,
    where it reasonably appears to the organisation that the act prevents or compensates for disadvantages linked to age suffered by those of that age or age group holding such posts or likely to hold such posts[7];
(3)   done by a trade organisation[8] in or in connection with encouraging only persons of a particular age or age group to become members of the organisation where it reasonably appears to the organisation that the act prevents or compensates for disadvantages linked to age suffered by persons of that age or age group who are, or are eligible to become, members[9].

1   Ie the Employment Equality (Age) Regulations 2006, SI 2006/1031, Pt 2 (regs 7–24) (as amended): see para 758 et seq ante.
2   Ie ibid Pt 3 (regs 25–26): see paras 783–784 ante.
3   As to the meaning of 'act' see para 755 note 3 ante.
4   As to the meaning of 'person' see para 344 note 3 ante.
5   Employment Equality (Age) Regulations 2006, SI 2006/1031, reg 29(1).
6   Ie within the meaning of ibid reg 18: see para 776 ante.
7   Ibid reg 29(2).
8   See note 6 supra.
9   Employment Equality (Age) Regulations 2006, SI 2006/1031, reg 29(3).

802. Exception for the national minimum wage. Nothing in Part 2[1] or Part 3[2] of the Employment Equality (Age) Regulations 2006 renders it unlawful:

(1)   for a relevant person[3] ('A') to be remunerated in respect of his work at a rate which is lower than the rate at which another such person ('B') is remunerated for his work where:

    (a)   the hourly rate of the national minimum wage for a person of A's age is lower than that for a person of B's age; and

    (b)   the rate at which A is remunerated is below the single hourly rate for the national minimum wage prescribed[4] by the Secretary of State[5];

(2)   for an apprentice[6] who is not a relevant person to be remunerated in respect of his work at a rate which is lower than the rate at which an apprentice who is a relevant person is remunerated for his work[7].

1   Ie the Employment Equality (Age) Regulations 2006, SI 2006/1031, Pt 2 (regs 7–24) (as amended): see para 758 et seq ante.
2   Ie ibid Pt 3 (regs 25–26): see paras 783–784 ante.
3   For these purposes, 'relevant person' means a person who qualifies for the national minimum wage (whether at the single hourly rate for the national minimum wage prescribed by the Secretary of State under the National Minimum Wage Act 1998 s 1(3) (see EMPLOYMENT vol 16(1A) (Reissue) para 180) or at a different rate): Employment Equality (Age) Regulations 2006, SI 2006/1031, reg 31(3). As to the meaning of 'person' see para 344 note 3 ante.
4   Ie under the National Minimum Wage Act 1998 s 1(3): see EMPLOYMENT vol 16(1A) (Reissue) para 180.
5   Employment Equality (Age) Regulations 2006, SI 2006/1031, reg 31(1).
6   For these purposes, 'apprentice' means a person who is employed under a contract of apprenticeship or, in accordance with the National Minimum Wage Regulations 1999, SI 1999/584, reg 12(3) (as substituted and amended) (see EMPLOYMENT vol 16(1A) (Reissue) para 175), is to be treated as employed under such a contract: Employment Equality (Age) Regulations 2006, SI 2006/1031, reg 31(3).
7   Ibid reg 31(2).

803. Exception for provision of certain benefits based on length of service. Nothing in Part 2[1] or Part 3[2] of the Employment Equality (Age) Regulations 2006 renders it unlawful[3] for a person[4] ('A'), in relation to the award of any benefit[5] by him, to put a worker ('B') at a disadvantage when compared with another worker ('C'), if and to the extent that the disadvantage suffered by B is because B's length of service is less than that of C[6]. Where, however, B's length of service exceeds five years[7], it must reasonably appear to A that the way in which he uses the criterion of length of service, in relation to the award in respect of which B is put at a disadvantage, fulfils a business need of his undertaking, for example, by encouraging the loyalty or motivation, or rewarding the experience, of some or all of his workers[8]. In calculating a worker's length of service for these purposes, A must calculate:

(1)   the length of time the worker has been working for him[9] doing work which he reasonably considers to be at or above a particular level (assessed by reference to the demands made on the worker, for example, in terms of effort, skills and decision making); or

(2)   the length of time the worker has been working for him in total[10],

and on each occasion on which he decides to use the criterion of length of service in relation to the award of a benefit to workers, it is for him to decide which of these definitions to use to calculate their lengths of service[11].

1   Ie the Employment Equality (Age) Regulations 2006, SI 2006/1031, Pt 2 (regs 7–24) (as amended): see para 758 et seq ante.
2   Ie ibid Pt 3 (regs 25–26): see paras 783–784 ante.
3   Ie subject to ibid reg 32(2): see the text and notes 7–8 infra.
4   As to the meaning of 'person' see para 344 note 3 ante.
5   For these purposes, 'benefit' does not include any benefit awarded to a worker by virtue of his ceasing to work for A: Employment Equality (Age) Regulations 2006, SI 2006/1031, reg 32(7). For the meaning of 'worker' see para 761 note 8 ante.
6   Ibid reg 32(1). As a general rule under equal pay law, recourse to the criterion of length of service is appropriate to attain the legitimate objective of rewarding experience acquired which enables a worker better to perform his duties; the employer does not have to justify recourse to this criterion unless the worker provides evidence capable of raising serious doubts: see Case C-17/05 *Cadman v Health and Safety Executive* [2007] All ER (EC) 1, [2006] ICR 1623, ECJ; and paras 420, 422, 430 ante.
7   For these purposes, 'year' means a year of 12 calendar months: Employment Equality (Age) Regulations 2006, SI 2006/1031, reg 32(7).
8   Ibid reg 32(2).
9   For these purposes, in calculating the length of time a worker has been working for him: (1) A must calculate the length of time in terms of the number of weeks during the whole or part of which the worker was working for him; (2) A may discount any period during which the worker was absent from work (including any period of absence which at the time it occurred was thought by A or the worker to be permanent) unless in all the circumstances (including the way in which other workers' absences occurring in similar circumstances are treated by A in calculating their lengths of service) it would not be reasonable for him to do so; (3) A may discount any period of time during which the worker was present at work ('the relevant period') where: (a) the relevant period preceded a period during which the worker was absent from work; and (b) in all the circumstances (including the length of the worker's absence, the reason for his absence, the effect his absence has had on his ability to discharge the duties of his work, and the way in which other workers are treated by A in similar circumstances) it is reasonable for A to discount the relevant period: ibid reg 32(4).
10 For the purposes of head (2) in the text, a worker must be treated as having worked for A during any period during which he worked for another if: (1) that period is treated as a period of employment with A for the purposes of the Employment Rights Act 1996 by virtue of the operation of s 218 (as amended) (see EMPLOYMENT vol 16(1A) (Reissue) para 109); or (2) were the worker to be made redundant by A, that period and the period he has worked for A would amount to 'relevant service' within the meaning of s 155 (see EMPLOYMENT vol 16(1B) (Reissue) paras 708, 727): Employment Equality (Age) Regulations 2006, SI 2006/1031, reg 32(5). In reg 32(5): (a) the reference to being made redundant is a reference to being dismissed by reason of redundancy for the purposes of the Employment Rights Act 1996; (b) the reference to s 155 is a reference to that provision as modified by the Redundancy Payments (Continuity of Employment in Local Government, etc) (Modification) Order 1999, SI 1999/2277 (as amended) (see EMPLOYMENT vol 16(1B) (Reissue) para 727): Employment Equality (Age) Regulations 2006, SI 2006/1031, reg 32(6).
11 Ibid reg 32(3).

804.   Exception for provision of enhanced redundancy payments to employees.   Nothing in Part 2[1] or Part 3[2] of the Employment Equality (Age) Regulations 2006 renders it unlawful for an employer[3]:

(1)   to give a qualifying employee[4] an enhanced redundancy payment[5] which is less in amount than the enhanced redundancy payment which he gives to another such employee if both amounts are calculated in the same way;

(2)   to give enhanced redundancy payments only to those who are qualifying employees by virtue of the specified[6] statutory provisions[7].

1   Ie the Employment Equality (Age) Regulations 2006, SI 2006/1031, Pt 2 (regs 7–24) (as amended): see para 758 et seq ante.
2   Ie ibid Pt 3 (regs 25–26): see paras 783–784 ante.
3   As to the meaning of 'employer' see para 758 note 1 ante.
4   For these purposes, 'qualifying employee' means: (1) an employee who is entitled to a redundancy payment by virtue of the Employment Rights Act 1996 s 135 (see EMPLOYMENT vol 16(1B) (Reissue)

para 708); (2) an employee who would have been so entitled but for the operation of s 155 (see EMPLOYMENT vol 16(1B) (Reissue) paras 708, 727); (3) an employee who agrees to the termination of his employment in circumstances where, had he been dismissed: (a) he would have been a qualifying employee by virtue of head (1) supra; or (b) he would have been a qualifying employee by virtue of head (2) supra: Employment Equality (Age) Regulations 2006, SI 2006/1031, reg 33(2). 'A redundancy payment' has the same meaning as it has in the Employment Rights Act 1996 s 162 (as amended) (see EMPLOYMENT vol 16(1B) (Reissue) para 754): Employment Equality (Age) Regulations 2006, SI 2006/1031, reg 33(2).

5   For these purposes, 'enhanced redundancy payment' means a payment of an amount calculated in accordance with ibid reg 33(3) or (4): reg 33(2). For an amount to be calculated in accordance with reg 33(3), it must be calculated in accordance with the Employment Rights Act 1996 s 162(1)–(3) (see EMPLOYMENT vol 16(1B) (Reissue) para 754): Employment Equality (Age) Regulations 2006, SI 2006/1031, reg 33(3). For an amount to be calculated in accordance with reg 33(4): (1) it must be calculated as in reg 33(3); (2) however, in making that calculation, the employer may do one or both of the following things: (a) he may treat a week's pay as not being subject to a maximum amount or as being subject to a maximum amount above the amount laid down in the Employment Rights Act 1996 s 227 (as amended) (maximum amount of a week's pay: see EMPLOYMENT vol 16(1A) (Reissue) para 119); (b) he may multiply the appropriate amount allowed for each year of employment by a figure of more than one; (3) having made the calculation as in the Employment Equality (Age) Regulations 2006, SI 2006/1031, reg 33(3) (whether or not in making that calculation he has done anything mentioned in head (2) supra), the employer may increase the amount thus calculated by multiplying it by a figure of more than one: reg 33(4). For the purposes of reg 33(3), (4), the reference to 'the relevant date' in the Employment Rights Act 1996 s 162(1)(a) is to be read, in the case of a qualifying employee who agrees to the termination of his employment, as a reference to the date on which that termination takes effect: Employment Equality (Age) Regulations 2006, SI 2006/1031, reg 33(5). 'The appropriate amount' and 'a week's pay' have the same meanings as they have in the Employment Rights Act 1996 s 162 (as amended) (see EMPLOYMENT vol 16(1B) (Reissue) para 754): Employment Equality (Age) Regulations 2006, SI 2006/1031, reg 33(2).

6   Ie by virtue of head (1) or head (3)(a) of the definition of 'qualifying employee' set out in note 4 supra.

7   Employment Equality (Age) Regulations 2006, SI 2006/1031, reg 33(1).

805.   Exception for provision of life assurance cover to retired workers.
Where a person[1] ('A') arranges for workers[2] to be provided with life assurance cover after their early retirement on grounds of ill health, nothing in Part 2[3] or Part 3[4] of the Employment Equality (Age) Regulations 2006 renders it unlawful:

(1)   where a normal retirement age[5] applied in relation to any such workers at the time they took early retirement, for A to arrange for such cover to cease when such workers reach that age;

(2)   in relation to any other workers, for A to arrange for such cover to cease when the workers reach the age of 65[6].

1   As to the meaning of 'person' see para 344 note 3 ante.

2   For the meaning of 'worker' for these purposes see para 761 note 8 ante.

3   Ie the Employment Equality (Age) Regulations 2006, SI 2006/1031, Pt 2 (regs 7–24) (as amended): see para 758 et seq ante.

4   Ie ibid Pt 3 (regs 25–26): see paras 783–784 ante.

5   For these purposes, 'normal retirement age', in relation to a worker who has taken early retirement, means the age at which workers in A's undertaking who held the same kind of position as the worker held at the time of his retirement were normally required to retire: ibid reg 34(2).

6   Ibid reg 34(1).

(6)   ENFORCEMENT

806.   Restriction of proceedings for breach of the regulations.   Except as provided by the Employment Equality (Age) Regulations 2006[1], no proceedings, whether civil or criminal, lie against any person[2] in respect of an act[3] by reason that the act is unlawful by virtue of a provision of those regulations[4]. This does not, however, prevent the making of an application for judicial review[5] or the investigation or determination of any matter in accordance with Part X of the Pension Schemes Act 1993[6] by the Pensions Ombudsman[7].

1 Ie the Employment Equality (Age) Regulations 2006, SI 2006/1031 (as amended).
2 As to the meaning of 'person' see para 344 note 3 ante.
3 As to the meaning of 'act' see para 755 note 3 ante.
4 Employment Equality (Age) Regulations 2006, SI 2006/1031, reg 35(1).
5 As to judicial review see ADMINISTRATIVE LAW vol 1(1) (2001 Reissue) para 59 et seq.
6 Ie in accordance with the Pension Schemes Act 1993 Pt X (ss 145–152) (as amended) (investigations: the Pensions Ombudsman): see SOCIAL SECURITY AND PENSIONS vol 44(2) (Reissue) para 663 et seq.
7 Employment Equality (Age) Regulations 2006, SI 2006/1031, reg 35(2).

807. Jurisdiction of employment tribunals; time limit and burden of proof.
The following provision applies to any act[1] of discrimination[2] or harassment[3] which is unlawful by virtue of any provision of Part 2 of the Employment Equality (Age) Regulations 2006[4] other than:

(1) where the act is one in respect of which an appeal or proceedings in the nature of an appeal may be brought under any enactment[5], the provision relating to qualifications bodies[6];

(2) the provision relating to institutions of further and higher education[7]; or

(3) where the act arises out of and is closely connected to a relationship between the complainant and the respondent which has come to an end but during the course of which an act of discrimination against, or harassment of, the complainant by the respondent would have been unlawful by virtue of the provision referred to in head (2) above[8], the provision relating to relevant relationships[9] which have come to an end[10].

A complaint by any person[11] ('the complainant') that another person ('the respondent'): (a) has committed against the complainant an act to which this provision applies; or (b) is to be treated[12] as having committed against the complainant such an act, may be presented to an employment tribunal[13].

Where under the above provision a member[14] or prospective member[15] of an occupational pension scheme[16] presents to an employment tribunal a complaint that the trustees or managers[17] of the scheme:

(i) have committed against him an act which is unlawful by virtue of the provision relating to unlawful discrimination by the trustees and managers of occupational pension schemes[18] or of the provision relating to relevant relationships which have come to an end[19]; or

(ii) are to be treated[20] as having committed against him such an act,

the employer[21] in relation to the scheme is, for the purposes of the rules governing procedure, to be treated as a party and to be entitled to appear and be heard in accordance with those rules[22].

An employment tribunal may not consider a complaint under the above provisions[23] unless it is presented to the tribunal before the end of the period of three months beginning when the act complained of was done[24]. A tribunal may nevertheless consider any such complaint which is out of time if, in all the circumstances of the case, it considers that it is just and equitable to do so[25].

Where, on the hearing of any complaint presented under the above provisions[26] to an employment tribunal, the complainant proves facts from which the tribunal could otherwise conclude in the absence of an adequate explanation that the respondent:

(A) has committed against the complainant an act to which the above provisions apply; or

(B) is to be treated[27] as having committed against the complainant such an act, the tribunal must uphold the complaint unless the respondent proves that he did not commit, or as the case may be, is not to be treated as having committed, that act[28].

1   As to the meaning of 'act' see para 755 note 3 ante.
2   For the meaning of references to discrimination see para 758 note 4 ante.
3   For the meaning of references to harassment see para 758 note 9 ante.
4   Ie any provision of the Employment Equality (Age) Regulations 2006, SI 2006/1031, Pt 2 (regs 7–24) (as amended): see para 758 et seq ante.
5   For these purposes, 'enactment' includes an enactment comprised in, or in an instrument made under, an Act of the Scottish Parliament: ibid reg 28(4). Scottish matters generally are beyond the scope of this work.
6   Ie ibid reg 19: see para 777 ante.
7   Ie ibid reg 23: see para 781 ante.
8   Ie by virtue of ibid reg 23: see para 781 ante. For the purpose of head (3) in the text, reference to an act of discrimination or harassment which would have been unlawful includes, in the case of a relationship which has come to an end before the date on which the act of discrimination or harassment became unlawful by virtue of the Employment Equality (Age) Regulations 2006, SI 2006/1031 (as amended), reference to an act of discrimination or harassment which would, after that date, have been unlawful: reg 36(3) (amended by SI 2006/2408).
9   Ie the Employment Equality (Age) Regulations 2006, SI 2006/1031, reg 24: see para 782 ante.
10   Ibid reg 36(2).
11   As to the meaning of 'person' see para 344 note 3 ante.
12   Ie by virtue of the Employment Equality (Age) Regulations 2006, SI 2006/1031, reg 25 or reg 26: see paras 783–784 ante.
13   Ibid reg 36(1). As to employment tribunals and the procedure before them see EMPLOYMENT vol 16(1B) (Reissue) para 816 et seq.
14   For the meaning of 'member' see para 760 note 6 ante.
15   For the meaning of 'prospective member' see para 760 note 7 ante.
16   For the meaning of 'occupational pension scheme' see para 760 note 4 ante.
17   For the meaning of 'managers' see para 760 note 2 ante.
18   Ie by virtue of the Employment Equality (Age) Regulations 2006, SI 2006/1031, reg 11: see para 760 ante.
19   See note 9 supra.
20   See note 12 supra.
21   For the meaning of 'employer' see para 760 note 3 ante.
22   Employment Equality (Age) Regulations 2006, SI 2006/1031, reg 11(3)(e), Sch 2 para 5.
23   Ie presented under ibid reg 36: see the text and notes 1–13 supra.
24   Ibid reg 42(1). For these purposes and the purposes of reg 41 (help for persons in obtaining information etc: see para 810 post): (1) when the making of a contract is, by reason of the inclusion of any term, an unlawful act, that act is to be treated as extending throughout the duration of the contract; and (2) any act extending over a period is to be treated as done at the end of that period; and (3) a deliberate omission is to be treated as done when the person in question decided upon it; and in the absence of evidence establishing the contrary a person is to be taken for these purposes to decide upon an omission when he does an act inconsistent with doing the omitted act or, if he has done no such inconsistent act, when the period expires within which he might reasonably have been expected to do the omitted act if it was to be done: reg 42(4).
     As time limits under the Sex Discrimination Act 1975 see para 416 ante; and as to time limits under the Race Relations Act 1976 see para 502 ante.
25   Employment Equality (Age) Regulations 2006, SI 2006/1031, reg 42(3).
26   See note 23 supra.
27   See note 12 supra.
28   Employment Equality (Age) Regulations 2006, SI 2006/1031, reg 37(1), (2). See also *Wong v Igen Ltd (Equal Opportunities Commission and others intervening), Emokpae v Chamberlin Solicitors (Equal Opportunities Commission and others intervening), Webster v Brunel University (Equal Opportunities Commission and others intervening)* [2005] EWCA Civ 142, [2005] 3 All ER 812, [2005] ICR 931; and paras 418, 504 ante.

808. Remedies on complaints in employment tribunals. Where an employment tribunal finds that a complaint presented to it[1] is well-founded, the tribunal must make such of the following as it considers just and equitable:

(1)   an order declaring the rights of the complainant and the respondent in relation to the act[2] to which the complaint relates;

(2) an order requiring the respondent to pay to the complainant compensation[3] of an amount corresponding to any damages he could have been ordered by a county court to pay to the complainant if the complaint had fallen to be dealt with under the provisions relating to the jurisdiction of county courts[4];

(3) a recommendation that the respondent take within a specified period action appearing to the tribunal to be practicable for the purpose of obviating or reducing the adverse effect on the complainant of any act of discrimination[5] or harassment[6] to which the complaint relates[7].

As respects an unlawful act of discrimination consisting of the application of a provision, criterion or practice[8], if the respondent proves that the provision, criterion or practice was not applied with the intention of treating the complainant unfavourably on grounds of age, an order may be made under head (2) above only if the employment tribunal:

(a) makes such order under head (1) above, if any, and such recommendation under head (3) above, if any, as it would have made if it had no power to make an order under head (2) above; and

(b) where it makes an order under head (1) above or a recommendation under head (3) above, or both, considers that it is just and equitable to make an order under head (2) above as well[9].

If without reasonable justification the respondent to a complaint fails to comply with a recommendation made by an employment tribunal under head (3) above, then, if it thinks it just and equitable to do so, the tribunal may increase the amount of compensation required to be paid to the complainant in respect of the complaint by an order made under head (2) above or, if an order under that head was not made, the tribunal may make such an order[10].

The above provisions have effect subject to the following provisions relating to occupational pension schemes[11]. Where:

(i) a member[12] or prospective member[13] of a scheme[14] ('the complainant') presents to an employment tribunal[15] a complaint against the trustees or managers[16] of the scheme or an employer[17];

(ii) the complainant is not a pensioner member[18] of the scheme;

(iii) the complaint relates to the terms on which persons[19] become members of the scheme or the terms on which members of the scheme are treated; and

(iv) the tribunal finds the complaint to be well-founded,

then the employment tribunal may, without prejudice to the generality of its power under head (1) above, make an order declaring that the complainant has a right:

(A) where the complaint relates to the terms on which persons become members of the scheme, to be admitted to the scheme;

(B) where the complaint relates to the terms on which members of the scheme are treated, to membership of the scheme without discrimination[20].

Such an order may be made in respect of such period as is specified in the order, but may not be made in respect of any time before 1 December 2006[21]; and it may make such provision as the employment tribunal considers appropriate as to the terms on which, or the capacity in which, the complainant is to enjoy such admission or membership[22]. The employment tribunal may not, however, make an order for compensation under head (2) above, whether in relation to arrears of benefits or otherwise, except for injury to feelings or where without reasonable justification the respondent to a complaint fails to comply with a recommendation[23] made by the tribunal[24].

1 Ie under the Employment Equality (Age) Regulations 2006, SI 2006/1031, reg 36: see para 807 ante.

2 As to the meaning of 'act' see para 755 note 3 ante.

3   Where an amount of compensation falls to be awarded under head (2) in the text, the tribunal may include in the award interest on that amount subject to, and in accordance with, the provisions of the Employment Tribunals (Interest on Awards in Discrimination Cases) Regulations 1996, SI 1996/2803 (amended by virtue of the Employment Rights (Dispute Resolution) Act 1998 s 1(2)): Employment Equality (Age) Regulations 2006, SI 2006/1031, reg 38(4).
    As to guidance on the proper level of damages to be awarded in discrimination cases (of all categories) for injury to feelings and other forms of non-pecuniary damage see *Vento v Chief Constable of West Yorkshire Police* [2002] EWCA Civ 1871, [2003] ICR 318, [2003] IRLR 102, [2002] All ER (D) 363 (Dec); and paras 414, 499 ante.
4   Ie under the Employment Equality (Age) Regulations 2006, reg 39: see para 809 post. An award of compensation under head (2) in the text may be made on a joint and several basis so that each respondent is liable to pay the whole of the award of compensation: see *Way v Crouch* [2005] ICR 1362, [2005] IRLR 603, EAT; and para 414 note 8 ante.
5   For the meaning of references to discrimination see para 758 note 4 ante.
6   For the meaning of references to harassment see para 758 note 9 ante.
7   Employment Equality (Age) Regulations 2006, SI 2006/1031, reg 38(1).
8   Ie an unlawful act of discrimination falling within ibid reg 3(1)(b): see para 754 head (2) ante.
9   Ibid reg 38(2).
10 Ibid reg 38(3).
11 Ibid reg 38(5).
12 For the meaning of 'member' see para 760 note 6 ante.
13 For the meaning of 'prospective member' see para 760 note 7 ante.
14 For the meaning of 'scheme' see para 760 note 11 ante.
15 See note 1 supra.
16 For the meaning of 'managers' see para 760 note 2 ante.
17 For the meaning of 'employer' see para 760 note 3 ante.
18 For the meaning of 'pensioner member' see para 760 note 6 ante.
19 As to the meaning of 'person' see para 344 note 3 ante.
20 Employment Equality (Age) Regulations 2006, SI 2006/1031, reg 11(3)(e), Sch 2 para 6(1), (2).
21 As to the significance of 1 December 2006 see para 754 note 1 ante.
22 Employment Equality (Age) Regulations 2006, SI 2006/1031, Sch 2 para 6(3) (amended by SI 2006/2408).
23 Ie by virtue of the Employment Equality (Age) Regulations 2006, SI 2006/1031, reg 38(3): see the text and note 10 supra.
24 Ibid Sch 2 para 6(4).

809.   Jurisdiction of county courts; time limit, burden of proof and remedies.   The following provision applies to any act[1] of discrimination[2] or harassment[3] which is unlawful by virtue of:

(1)   the provision relating to institutions of further and higher education[4]; or

(2)   where the act arises out of and is closely connected to a relationship between the claimant and the respondent which has come to an end but during the course of which an act of discrimination against, or harassment of, the claimant by the respondent would have been unlawful[5] by virtue of the provision mentioned in head (1) above, the provision relating to relevant relationships[6] which have come to an end[7].

A claim by any person[8] ('the claimant') that another person ('the respondent'):

(a)   has committed against the claimant an act to which this provision applies; or

(b)   is to be treated[9] as having committed against the claimant such an act,

may be made the subject of civil proceedings in like manner as any other claim in tort for breach of statutory duty[10]. Proceedings so brought may be brought only in a county court[11] and must be instituted before the end of the period of six months beginning when the act complained of was done[12]; but a court may nevertheless consider any such claim which is out of time if, in all the circumstances of the case, it considers that it is just and equitable to do so[13]. Damages in respect of an unlawful act to which this provision applies may include compensation for injury to feelings whether or not they include compensation under any other head[14].

Where, on the hearing of the claim, the claimant proves facts from which the court could otherwise conclude in the absence of an adequate explanation that the respondent:

(i)   has committed against the claimant an act to which the above provision applies; or

(ii)   is to be treated[15] as having committed against the claimant such an act,

the court must uphold the claim unless the respondent proves that he did not commit, or, as the case may be, is not to be treated as having committed, that act[16].

1   As to the meaning of 'act' see para 755 note 3 ante.
2   For the meaning of references to discrimination see para 758 note 4 ante.
3   For the meaning of references to harassment see para 758 note 9 ante.
4   Ie the Employment Equality (Age) Regulations 2006, SI 2006/1031, reg 23: see para 781 ante.
5   For the purposes of head (2) in the text, reference to an act of discrimination or harassment which would have been unlawful includes, in the case of a relationship which has come to an end before the date on which the act of discrimination or harassment became unlawful by virtue of the Employment Equality (Age) Regulations 2006, SI 2006/1031 (as amended), reference to an act of discrimination or harassment which would, after that date, have been unlawful: reg 39(5) (amended by SI 2006/2408)
6   Ie the Employment Equality (Age) Regulations 2006, SI 2006/1031, reg 24: see para 782 ante.
7   Ibid reg 39(4).
8   As to the meaning of 'person' see para 344 note 3 ante.
9   Ie by virtue of the Employment Equality (Age) Regulations 2006, SI 2006/1031, reg 25 or reg 26: see paras 783–784 ante.
10   Ibid reg 39(1).
11   Ibid reg 39(2)(a).
12   See ibid reg 42(2). As to when the act was done see reg 42(4); and para 807 note 24 ante.
13   Ibid reg 42(3).
14   See ibid reg 39(3). Cf the position under the Employment Rights Act 1996 s 123(1) (as amended) (compensatory award for unfair dismissal: see EMPLOYMENT vol 16(1B) para 690): see *Dunnachie v Kingston upon Hull City Council* [2004] UKHL 36, [2005] 1 AC 226, [2004] 3 All ER 1011, HL.
       As to guidance on the proper level of damages to be awarded in discrimination cases (of all categories) for injury to feelings and other forms of non-pecuniary damage see *Vento v Chief Constable of West Yorkshire Police* [2002] EWCA Civ 1871, [2003] ICR 318, [2003] IRLR 102, [2002] All ER (D) 363 (Dec); and paras 414, 499 ante.
15   See note 9 supra.
16   Employment Equality (Age) Regulations 2006, SI 2006/1031, reg 40(1), (2).

810. Help for persons in obtaining information etc. In accordance with the following provisions, a person[1] ('the person aggrieved') who considers he may have been discriminated[2] against, or subjected to harassment[3], in contravention of the Employment Equality (Age) Regulations 2006[4], may serve on the respondent[5] to a complaint presented to an employment tribunal[6] or a claim brought in the county court[7] questions in the prescribed form[8] or forms to the like effect with such variation as the circumstances require; and the respondent may if he so wishes reply to such questions by way of the prescribed form[9] or forms to the like effect with such variation as the circumstances require[10].

Where the person aggrieved questions the respondent, whether in accordance with the above provision or not:

(1)   the questions, and any reply by the respondent, whether in accordance with the above provision or not, are, subject to the following provisions, to be admissible as evidence in the proceedings;

(2)   if it appears to the court or tribunal that the respondent deliberately, and without reasonable excuse, omitted to reply within eight weeks of service of the questions or that his reply is evasive or equivocal, the court or tribunal may draw any inference from that fact that it considers it just and equitable to draw, including an inference that he committed an unlawful act[11].

In proceedings before a county court, however, a question is only to be admissible as evidence in pursuance of head (1) above:

(a)   where it was served before those proceedings had been instituted, if it was so served within the period of six months beginning when the act complained of was done[12];

(b)   where it was served when those proceedings had been instituted, if it was served with the leave of, and within a period specified by, the court in question[13],

and in proceedings before an employment tribunal, a question is only to be admissible as evidence in pursuance of head (1) above:

(i)   where it was served before a complaint had been presented to a tribunal, if it was so served within the period of three months beginning when the act complained of was done[14];

(ii)   where it was served when a complaint had been presented to the tribunal, if it was so served within the period of 21 days beginning with the day on which the complaint was presented or if it was so served later with leave given, and within a period specified, by a direction of the tribunal[15].

The above provisions are without prejudice to any other enactment or rule of law regulating preliminary matters in proceedings before a county court or employment tribunal, and have effect subject to any enactment or rule of law regulating the admissibility of evidence in such proceedings[16].

Either party may apply to the court to determine whether the question or any reply is admissible under the above provisions[17].

1   As to the meaning of 'person' see para 344 note 3 ante.

2   For the meaning of references to discrimination see para 758 note 4 ante.

3   For the meaning of references to harassment see para 758 note 9 ante.

4   Ie in contravention of the Employment Equality (Age) Regulations 2006, SI 2006/1031: see para 754 et seq ante.

5   For these purposes, 'respondent' includes a prospective respondent: ibid reg 41(7). A question and any reply to it may be served on the respondent or, as the case may be, on the person aggrieved: (1) by delivering it to him; (2) by sending it by post to him at his usual or last-known residence or place of business; (3) where the person to be served is a body corporate or is a trade union or employers' association within the meaning of the Trade Union and Labour Relations (Consolidation) Act 1992 (see TRADE, INDUSTRY AND INDUSTRIAL RELATIONS vol 47 (2001 Reissue) para 1201), by delivering it to the secretary or clerk of the body, union or association at its registered or principal office or by sending it by post to the secretary or clerk at that office; (4) where the person to be served is acting by a solicitor, by delivering it at, or by sending it by post to, the solicitor's address for service; or (5) where the person to be served is the person aggrieved, by delivering the reply, or by sending it by post, to him at his address for reply as stated by him in the document containing the questions: Employment Equality (Age) Regulations 2006, SI 2006/1031, reg 41(5).

6   Ie under ibid reg 36: see para 807 ante.

7   Ie under ibid reg 39: see para 809 ante.

8   For the prescribed form see ibid reg 41(1), Sch 3.

9   For the prescribed form see ibid reg 41(1), Sch 4.

10   Ibid reg 41(1).

11   Ibid reg 41(2). As to the meaning of 'act' see para 755 note 3 ante.

12   As to when the act was done see ibid reg 42(4); and para 807 note 24 ante.

13   Ibid reg 41(3).

14   See note 12 supra.

15   Ibid reg 41(4).

16   Ibid reg 41(6).

17   See *Practice Direction—Proceedings under Enactments relating to Discrimination* paras 4.1(d), 4.2. The provisions of CPR 3.4 (power to strike out a statement of case: see PRACTICE AND PROCEDURE vol 37 (Reissue) para 917) apply to the question and any answer as it applies to a statement of case: *Practice Direction—Proceedings under Enactments relating to Discrimination* para 4.3.

(7) SUPPLEMENTAL PROVISIONS

811. Validity and revision of contracts. A term of a contract is void where:

(1) the making of the contract is, by reason of the inclusion of the term, unlawful by virtue of the Employment Equality (Age) Regulations 2006[1];

(2) it is included in furtherance of an act[2] which is unlawful by virtue of those regulations; or

(3) it provides for the doing of an act which is unlawful by virtue of those regulations[3],

but this does not apply to a term the inclusion of which constitutes, or is in furtherance of, or provides for, unlawful discrimination[4] against, or harassment[5] of, a party to the contract, although the term is unenforceable against that party[6].

A term in a contract which purports to exclude or limit any provision of those regulations is unenforceable by any person[7] in whose favour the term would otherwise operate[8]; but this does not apply:

(a) to a contract settling a complaint[9] falling within the jurisdiction of an employment tribunal[10] where the contract is made with the assistance of a conciliation officer[11];

(b) to a contract settling such a complaint if the prescribed conditions regulating compromise contracts[12] are satisfied in relation to the contract; or

(c) to a contract settling a claim falling within the jurisdiction[13] of the county courts[14].

The prescribed conditions regulating compromise contracts are that:

(i) the contract must be in writing;

(ii) the contract must relate to the particular complaint;

(iii) the complainant must have received advice from a relevant independent adviser[15] as to the terms and effect of the proposed contract and in particular its effect on his ability to pursue a complaint before an employment tribunal;

(iv) there must be in force, when the adviser gives the advice, a contract of insurance, or an indemnity provided for members of a profession or professional body, covering the risk of a claim by the complainant in respect of loss arising in consequence of the advice;

(v) the contract must identify the adviser; and

(vi) the contract must state that the prescribed conditions regulating compromise contracts are satisfied[16].

On the application of a person interested in a contract which either contains a void term[17] or a term which is unenforceable[18], a county court may make such order as it thinks fit for removing or modifying any term rendered void[19] or removing or modifying any term made unenforceable[20] by the above provisions, but such an order may not be made unless all persons affected have been given notice in writing of the application, except where under rules of court notice may be dispensed with, and those persons have been afforded an opportunity to make representations to the court[21]. Such an order may include provision as respects any period before the making of the order but after the date on which the inclusion of any term which is the subject of the order becomes unlawful by virtue of the Employment Equality (Age) Regulations 2006[22]. A person affected by the proposed variation must be made a respondent to the application unless the court orders otherwise[23].

1 Ie the Employment Equality (Age) Regulations 2006, SI 2006/1031 (as amended).
2 As to the meaning of 'act' see para 755 note 3 ante.
3 Equality (Age) Regulations 2006, SI 2006/1031, reg 43, Sch 5 para 1(1). Schedule 5 para 1(1)–(3) applies whether the contract was entered into before or after the date on which any term of the contract became

unlawful by virtue of the regulations, but in the case of a contract made before the date on which a term became unlawful, Sch 5 para 1(1)–(3) does not apply to that term in relation to any period before that date: Sch 5 para 1(4) (added by SI 2006/2408).

4　For the meaning of references to discrimination see para 758 note 4 ante.

5　For the meaning of references to harassment see para 758 note 9 ante.

6　Equality (Age) Regulations 2006, SI 2006/1031, Sch 5 para 1(2). See also note 3 supra.

7　As to the meaning of 'person' see para 344 note 3 ante.

8　Equality (Age) Regulations 2006, SI 2006/1031, Sch 5 para 1(3). See also note 3 supra.

9　An agreement under which the parties agree to submit a dispute to arbitration: (1) is to be regarded for the purposes of ibid Sch 5 para 2(1)(a), (b) (see heads (a)–(b) in the text) as being a contract settling a complaint if: (a) the dispute is covered by a scheme having effect by virtue of an order under the Trade Union and Labour Relations (Consolidation) Act 1992 s 212A (as added and amended) (see EMPLOYMENT vol 16(1B) (Reissue) para 696); and (b) the agreement is to submit it to arbitration in accordance with the scheme; but (2) is to be regarded as neither being nor including such a contract in any other case: Employment Equality (Age) Regulations 2006, SI 2006/1031, Sch 5 para 2(9).

10　Ie a complaint to which ibid reg 36(1) applies: see para 807 ante.

11　Ie within the meaning of the Trade Union and Labour Relations (Consolidation) Act 1992 s 211 (as amended): see TRADE, INDUSTRY AND INDUSTRIAL RELATIONS vol 47 (2001 Reissue) para 1437.

12　Ie the conditions regulating compromise contracts under the Employment Equality (Age) Regulations 2006, SI 2006/1031, Sch 5 (as amended): see heads (i)–(vi) in the text.

13　Ie a claim to which ibid reg 39 applies: see para 809 ante.

14　Ibid Sch 5 para 2(1).

15　A person is a relevant independent adviser for these purposes: (1) if he is a qualified lawyer; (2) if he is an officer, official, employee or member of an independent trade union who has been certified in writing by the trade union as competent to give advice and as authorised to do so on behalf of the trade union; or (3) if he works at an advice centre (whether as an employee or a volunteer) and has been certified in writing by the centre as competent to give advice and as authorised to do so on behalf of the centre (ibid Sch 5 para 2(3)); but a person is not a relevant independent adviser for these purposes in relation to the complainant: (a) if he is, is employed by or is acting in the matter for the other party or a person who is connected with the other party; (b) in the case of a person within head (2) or head (3) supra, if the trade union or advice centre is the other party or a person who is connected with the other party; or (c) in the case of a person within head (3) supra, if the complainant makes a payment for the advice received from him (Sch 5 para 2(4)). In head (1) supra, 'qualified lawyer' means, as respects England and Wales, a barrister (whether in practice as such or employed to give legal advice), a solicitor who holds a practising certificate, or a person other than a barrister or solicitor who is an authorised advocate or authorised litigator (within the meaning of the Courts and Legal Services Act 1990: see BARRISTERS vol 3(1) (2005 Reissue) para 501; SOLICITORS vol 44(1) (Reissue) paras 78–79) (Employment Equality (Age) Regulations 2006, SI 2006/1031, Sch 5 para 2(5)(a)); and a person is to be treated as being a qualified lawyer if he is a fellow of the Institute of Legal Executives employed by a solicitors' practice (Sch 5 para 2(6)). In head (2) supra, 'independent trade union' has the same meaning as in the Trade Union and Labour Relations (Consolidation) Act 1992 (see TRADE, INDUSTRY AND INDUSTRIAL RELATIONS vol 47 (2001 Reissue) para 1014): Employment Equality (Age) Regulations 2006, SI 2006/1031, Sch 5 para 2(7). For the purposes of head (a) supra, any two persons are to be treated as connected if one is a company of which the other (directly or indirectly) has control or if both are companies of which a third person (directly or indirectly) has control: Sch 5 para 2(8).

16　Ibid Sch 5 para 2(2).

17　Ie a contract to which ibid Sch 5 para 1(1) applies: see heads (1)–(3) in the text.

18　Ie a contract to which ibid Sch 5 para 1(2) applies: see the text and notes 4–6 supra.

19　Ie by ibid Sch 5 para 1(1): see the text and notes (1)–(3) supra.

20　Ie by ibid Sch 5 para 1(2): see the text and notes 4–6 supra.

21　Ibid Sch 5 para 3(1).

22　Ibid Sch 5 para 3(2) (amended by SI 2006/2408).

23　See *Practice Direction—Proceedings under Enactments relating to Discrimination* paras 7.1(e), 7.2.

812.　Collective agreements and rules of undertakings. The following provisions apply to:

(1)　any term of a collective agreement[1], including an agreement which was not intended, or is presumed not to have been intended, to be a legally enforceable contract;

(2) any rule made by an employer[2] for application to all or any of the persons[3] who are employed by him or who apply to be, or are, considered by him for employment[4];

(3) any rule made by a trade organisation[5] or a qualifications body[6] for application to all or any of its members or prospective members, or all or any of the persons on whom it has conferred professional or trade qualifications[7] or who are seeking the professional or trade qualifications which it has power to confer[8].

Any such term or rule is void where:

(a) the making of the collective agreement is, by reason of the inclusion of the term, unlawful by virtue of the Employment Equality (Age) Regulations 2006[9];

(b) the term or rule is included or made in furtherance of an act[10] which is unlawful by virtue of those regulations; or

(c) the term or rule provides for the doing of an act which is unlawful by virtue of those regulations[11],

and this applies whether the agreement was entered into, or the rule made, before or after the date on which any term of the agreement or rule became unlawful by virtue of those regulations; but in the case of an agreement entered into, or a rule made, before the date on which a term or rule became unlawful, it does not apply in relation to any period before that date[12]. The avoidance by virtue of heads (a) to (c) above of any term or rule which provides for any person to be discriminated[13] against is without prejudice to the following rights, except in so far as they enable any person to require another person to be treated less favourably than himself, namely:

(i) such of the rights of the person to be discriminated against; and

(ii) such of the rights of any person who will be treated more favourably in direct or indirect consequence of the discrimination,

as are conferred by or in respect of a contract made or modified wholly or partly in pursuance of, or by reference to, that term or rule[14].

A person to whom this provision applies[15] may present a complaint to an employment tribunal that a term or rule is void by virtue of the above provisions if he has reason to believe:

(A) that the term or rule may at some future time have effect in relation to him; and

(B) where he alleges that it is void by virtue of head (c) above, that an act for the doing of which it provides may at some such time be done in relation to him, and the act would be unlawful by virtue of the relevant regulations if done in relation to him in present circumstances[16].

When an employment tribunal finds that a complaint so presented to it is well-founded the tribunal must make an order declaring that the term or rule is void[17]; and such an order may include provision as respects any period before the making of the order but after the date on which the inclusion of the term or rule became unlawful by virtue of the Employment Equality (Age) Regulations 2006[18].

1 For these purposes, 'collective agreement' means any agreement relating to one or more of the matters mentioned in the Trade Union and Labour Relations (Consolidation) Act 1992 s 178(2) (meaning of trade dispute: see TRADE, INDUSTRY AND INDUSTRIAL RELATIONS vol 47 (2001 Reissue) para 1301), being an agreement made by or on behalf of one or more employers or one or more organisations of employers or associations of such organisations with one or more organisations of workers or associations of such organisations: Employment Equality (Age) Regulations 2006, SI 2006/1031, reg 43, Sch 5 para 10.

2 As to the meaning of 'employer' see para 758 note 1 ante.

3 As to the meaning of 'person' see para 344 note 3 ante.

4 For the meaning of 'employment' see para 758 note 2 ante.

5 Ie within the meaning of the Employment Equality (Age) Regulations 2006, SI 2006/1031, reg 18: see para 776 ante.

6 Ie within the meaning of ibid reg 19: see para 777 ante.

7   See note 6 supra.
8   Employment Equality (Age) Regulations 2006, SI 2006/1031, Sch 5 para 4(1).
9   Ie by virtue of the Employment Equality (Age) Regulations 2006, SI 2006/1031 (as amended).
10   As to the meaning of 'act' see para 755 note 3 ante.
11   Employment Equality (Age) Regulations 2006, SI 2006/1031, Sch 5 para 4(2).
12   Ibid Sch 4 para 4(3) (substituted by SI 2006/2408).
13   For the meaning of references to discrimination see para 758 note 4 ante.
14   Employment Equality (Age) Regulations 2006, SI 2006/1031, Sch 5 para 9.
15   In the case of a complaint about: (1) a term of a collective agreement made by or on behalf of an employer, an organisation of employers of which an employer is a member, or an association of such organisations of one of which an employer is a member; or (2) a rule made by an employer within the meaning of ibid Sch 5 para 4(1)(b) (see head (2) in the text), Sch 5 para 5 (see the text and note 16 infra) applies to any person who is, or is genuinely and actively seeking to become, one of his employees: Sch 5 para 6. In the case of a complaint about a rule made by an organisation or body to which Sch 5 para 4(1)(c) applies (see head (3) in the text), Sch 5 para 5 applies to any person: (a) who is, or is genuinely and actively seeking to become, a member of the organisation or body; (b) on whom the organisation or body has conferred a professional or trade qualification (within the meaning of reg 19: see para 777 note 1 ante); or (c) who is genuinely and actively seeking such a professional or trade qualification which the organisation or body has power to confer: Sch 5 para 7.
16   Ibid Sch 5 para 5.
17   Ibid Sch 5 para 8(1).
18   Ibid Sch 5 para 8(2) (amended by SI 2006/2408).

813.   Application to the Crown etc.   The Employment Equality (Age) Regulations 2006[1] apply:

(1)   to an act[2] done by or for purposes of a Minister of the Crown[3] or government department; or

(2)   to an act done on behalf of the Crown by a statutory body[4], or a person holding a statutory office[5],

as they apply to an act done by a private person[6].

The regulations also apply to Crown employment[7] as they apply to employment by a private person, and so apply as if references to a contract of employment included references to the terms of service and references to dismissal included references to termination of Crown employment[8].

The regulations do not, however, apply to service in any of the naval, military or air forces of the Crown[9].

1   Ie the Employment Equality (Age) Regulations 2006, SI 2006/1031 (as amended).
2   As to the meaning of 'act' see para 755 note 3 ante.
3   As to the meaning of 'Minister of the Crown' see para 772 note 4 ante.
4   For the meaning of 'statutory body' see para 785 note 2 ante.
5   For the meaning of 'statutory office' see para 785 note 2 ante.
6   Employment Equality (Age) Regulations 2006, SI 2006/1031, reg 44(1). Regulation 44(1), (2) has effect subject to regs 13, 14 (police; Serious Organised Crime Agency: see paras 773, 783 ante): reg 44(3).
7   For the meaning of 'Crown employment' see para 785 note 2 ante.
8   Employment Equality (Age) Regulations 2006, SI 2006/1031, reg 44(2). The provisions of the Crown Proceedings Act 1947 Pts II–IV (ss 13–40) (as amended) apply to proceedings against the Crown under the Employment Equality (Age) Regulations 2006, SI 2006/1031 (as amended) as they apply to proceedings in England and Wales which by virtue of the Crown Proceedings Act 1947 s 23 (as amended) are treated for the purposes of Pt II (as amended) as civil proceedings by or against the Crown, except that in their application to proceedings under those regulations s 20 (as amended) (removal of proceedings from county court to High Court) does not apply: Employment Equality (Age) Regulations 2006, SI 2006/1031, reg 44(6).
     Regulation 10(3) (meaning of employment and contract work at establishment in Great Britain: see para 758 note 3 ante) has effect in relation to any ship, aircraft or hovercraft belonging to or possessed by Her Majesty in right of the government of the United Kingdom as it has effect in relation to a ship, aircraft or hovercraft specified in reg 10(3)(a) or (b): reg 44(5). For the meaning of 'United Kingdom' see para 325 note 6 ante.
9   Ibid reg 44(4).

814–900. Application to House of Commons and House of Lords staff. The Employment Equality (Age) Regulations 2006[1] apply:

(1) in relation to employment[2] as a relevant member of the House of Commons staff[3] as they apply in relation to other employment[4];

(2) to employment as such a member as they apply to employment by a private person[5], and so apply as if references to a contract of employment included references to the terms of employment of such a member and references to dismissal included references to the termination of such employment[6];

(3) in relation to employment as a relevant member of the House of Lords staff[7] as they apply in relation to other employment[8].

1 Ie the Employment Equality (Age) Regulations 2006, SI 2006/1031 (as amended).
2 For the meaning of 'employment' see para 758 note 2 ante.
3 For the meaning of 'relevant member of the House of Commons staff' see para 785 note 3 ante.
4 Employment Equality (Age) Regulations 2006, SI 2006/1031, reg 45(1).
5 As to the meaning of 'person' see para 344 note 3 ante.
6 Employment Equality (Age) Regulations 2006, SI 2006/1031, reg 45(2). In relation to employment as such a member, the Employment Rights Act 1996 s 195(6)–(12) (as amended) (person to be treated as employer of House of Commons staff: see EMPLOYMENT vol 16(1A) (Reissue) para 136) applies, with any necessary modifications, for the purposes of the Employment Equality (Age) Regulations 2006, SI 2006/1031 (as amended): reg 45(3).
7 For the meaning of 'relevant member of the House of Lords staff' see para 785 note 4 ante.
8 Employment Equality (Age) Regulations 2006, SI 2006/1031, reg 46(1). The Employment Rights Act 1996 s 194(7) (continuity of employment: see EMPLOYMENT vol 16(1A) (Reissue) para 135) applies for these purposes: Employment Equality (Age) Regulations 2006, SI 2006/1031, reg 46(2).

DISTRESS

1. NATURE OF THE REMEDY OF DISTRESS

901.   Meaning of distress.   The term 'distress' primarily connotes a summary remedy by which a person is entitled without legal process to take into his possession the personal chattels of another person, to be held as a pledge to compel the performance of a duty, or the satisfaction of a debt or demand[1]. By almost universal sanction the term 'distress' is now used to designate both the process of taking, and the chattels taken[2], though originally it applied only to the taking.

By statute, remedies referred to as distress[3] have been introduced for the recovery of rates[4] and taxes[5] and for the enforcement of certain fines imposed by or orders of magistrates' courts[6]. A statutory right to distrain has also been given to a person for the recovery of tithe rentcharge and for the recovery of annual sums charged on land[7].

Because distress is a remedy to which resort may be made without judicial process (which by its nature involves the taking of property, including that of a third party, and in some instances involves interference with the home) there are doubts whether the law in all instances complies with the Convention for the Protection of Human Rights and Fundamental Freedoms[8].

1   The following definition is given in Bradby *Law of Distresses* (2nd Edn) 1: 'A distress is the taking of a personal chattel, without legal process, from the possession of a wrongdoer, into the hands of the party grieved; as a pledge, for the redress of an injury, the performance of a duty, or the satisfaction of a demand'. As to pledges see generally PLEDGES AND PAWNS.

2   3 Bl Com (14th Edn) 6.

3   For the general distinction between statutory distress which is not for rent or rentcharge and distress for rent see para 904 post.

4   See paras 1104–1126 post.

5   See paras 1127–1133 post.

6   See paras 1134–1147 post.

7   See the Law of Property Act 1925 s 121(2); the Landlord and Tenant Act 1730 s 5 (as amended) (which enabled rents seck to be recovered by distress and sale in the same manner as rent reserved upon a lease); and RENTCHARGES AND ANNUITIES vol 39(2) (Reissue) para 869.

8   Ie the Convention for the Protection of Human Rights and Fundamental Freedoms (Rome, 4 November 1950; TS 71 (1953); Cmd 8969). This is generally beyond the scope of this title but see in particular the Human Rights Act 1998 s 1(3), Sch 1 Pt I arts 6, 8, Pt II art 1; and CONSTITUTIONAL LAW AND HUMAN RIGHTS vol 8(2) (Reissue) para 165. See also *Fuller v Happy Shopper Markets Ltd* [2001] 1 WLR 1681, [2001] 2 Lloyd's Rep 49.

902.   The common law remedy.   The right of the landlord to distrain for arrears of rent arises at common law and need not be expressly reserved[1]. It enables the landlord to secure the payment of rent by seizing goods and chattels found upon the premises in respect of which the rent or obligations are due. Distress has been characterised as an archaic remedy[2].

The common law right of distress was also given in respect of a great number of services in regard to tenure which are now obsolete. Further, the common law right of distress damage feasant which enables a person who has suffered trespass to his land to distrain and impound the thing trespassing has, in relation to trespassing animals, been replaced by statutory provisions[3], but the remedy is also available in respect of inanimate things[4].

When the remedy was exercised, the chattels remained only as a pledge in the hands of the party making the distress, and could not be sold. This continues to be the law with regard to chattels taken by way of distresses where the mode of dealing with the distress has not been altered by Act of Parliament; over such chattels the distrainor has no other power than to retain them until satisfaction is made[5].

The common law remedy has been modified in a number of ways by statutes which have given a power of sale[6] and which regulate the goods which may be distrained[7] and the mode of distress[8].

1 As to distress for rent see para 905 et seq post.

2 See *Abingdon RDC v O'Gorman* [1968] 2 QB 811 at 819, [1968] 3 All ER 79 at 82, CA, per Lord Denning MR.

3 See the Animals Act 1971 s 7; and ANIMALS vol 2(1) (Reissue) paras 630, 633.

4 See *Ambergate, Nottingham and Boston and Eastern Junction Rly Co v Midland Rly Co* (1853) 2 E & B 793; *Easton Estate and Mining Co v Western Waggon and Property Co* (1886) 54 LT 735, DC (railway engine); and RAILWAYS, INLAND WATERWAYS AND PIPELINES vol 39(1) (Reissue) para 295. See also *Arthur v Anker* [1997] QB 564 at 581, [1996] 3 All ER 783 at 796, CA, Hirst LJ (dissenting) (not available to entitle landowner to demand fee for release of car clamped on private land in absence of proof of damage).

5 3 Bl Com (14th Edn) 10.

6 See para 1044 et seq post.

7 See para 928 et seq post.

8 See para 992 et seq post.

903. Express power to distrain. Subject to the provisions by which an instrument giving a power of distress may be void unless registered as a bill of sale[1], a power may be conferred, by express agreement between the parties, to distrain for payments which are not rent, and in cases where the common law requisites are absent[2]. A common example was the right reserved in an instrument creating a rentcharge; but in that case a statutory right is now given to distrain for arrears[3]. Under an express power of distress only the goods of the person giving the power can, as a rule, be taken[4].

An instrument giving a power of distress as security for any present or future debt is, as a rule, deemed to be a bill of sale, and unless registered as regards the chattels seized under the power, is void as regards such chattels[5]. An express power of distress for rent under a lease is not within these provisions[6] nor, it appears, is an express power of distress given to secure the payment of a rentcharge as the instalments of the rentcharge seem not to be debts for this purpose[7].

A power of distress given by way of indemnity against a rent[8] or any part of a rent payable in respect of any land, or against the breach of any covenant or condition relating to land is not a bill of sale[9].

1 See the text to note 5 infra. As to the exception in favour of mining leases and the application of the provisions in other particular cases see note 5 infra. As to the power of distress given by way of indemnity against a rent etc see the text and notes 8–9 infra.

2 See e g *Pollitt v Forrest* (1847) 11 QB 949 at 961. As to what are the common law requisites in the case of rent see paras 907–912 post.

3 See para 901 text and note 7 ante.

4 *Freeman v Edwards* (1848) 2 Exch 732; *Gibbs v Cruikshank* (1873) LR 8 CP 454; *Re Willis, ex p Kennedy* (1888) 21 QBD 384 at 395, CA, per Lindley LJ.

5 See the enactments cited in para 916 note 1 post; and BILLS OF SALE vol 4(1) (2002 Reissue) paras 629, 633, 805. Mining leases are expressly excluded from the instruments affected: see BILLS OF SALE vol 4(1) (2002 Reissue) para 634; and c f para 980 note 2 post. As to distress by agreement on goods or land other than that out of which the rent issues see para 980 post. As to the effect of the provisions stated in the text on attornment clauses or express authority to distrain in mortgages see para 916 post; and BILLS OF SALE vol 4(1) (2002 Reissue) para 636. As to the effect of the provisions on a brewer's lease giving power to distrain for goods supplied see BILLS OF SALE vol 4(1) (2002 Reissue) para 634.

6 See BILLS OF SALE vol 4(1) (2002 Reissue) paras 629, 634.

7 Cf *Re Blackburn and District Benefit Building Society, ex p Graham* (1889) 42 ChD 343 at 346–347, CA, per Lord Esher MR.

8 'Rent' includes a rent service or a rentcharge or other rent, toll duty, royalty, or annual or periodical payment in money or money's worth, reserved or issuing out of or charged upon land but does not include mortgage interest: Law of Property Act 1925 s 205(1)(xxiii).

9 See ibid s 189(1); and BILLS OF SALE vol 4(1) (2002 Reissue) para 635.

904.　　The statutory remedies.　The right to distrain for unpaid rates and council tax[1] or taxes[2] or under the summary jurisdiction of magistrates[3] are more analogous to execution than to the common law right of a landlord to distrain for rent[4]. Statutory rules governing the process of levying distress for rent[5] are not applicable to distress for rates and council tax or for taxes or under the summary jurisdiction. Common law and statutory provisions regarding the things on which distraint for rent may be made[6] do not apply to the other kinds of distress mentioned above[7].

With regard to the right to distrain upon the goods of strangers, different principles apply in relation to the various kinds of distress[8].

1　See para 1104 et seq post.
2　See paras 1127–1133 post.
3　See paras 1134–1147 post.
4　The principle was fully discussed in *Potts v Hickman* [1941] AC 212, [1940] 4 All ER 491, HL. See also *Hutchins v Chambers* (1758) 1 Burr 579; *McCreagh v Cox and Ford* (1923) 92 LJKB 855; *Swaffer v Mulcahy* [1934] 1 KB 608. The statutory remedies by distress are not, however, 'execution' within the Landlord and Tenant Act 1709 s 1 (as amended) (see para 1032 post), so as to entitle a landlord to claim payment in priority for arrears of rent: *Potts v Hickman* supra. As to execution generally see ENFORCEMENT.
5　Ie the Distress for Rent Rules 1988, SI 1988/2050 (as amended): see para 994 et seq post. These rules replace the Distress for Rent Rules 1953, SI 1953/1702 (revoked) which were made under the Law of Distress Amendment Act 1888 s 8 (as amended) and the Law of Distress Amendment Act 1895 s 3: see para 994 post. See also *Walker v Retter* [1911] 1 KB 1103 at 1109 per Lord Alverstone CJ.
6　See para 928 et seq post.
7　*Hutchins v Chambers* (1758) 1 Burr 579 (distress for rates; working tools); *McCreagh v Cox and Ford* (1923) 92 LJKB 855 (distress for rates: animals on land); *MacGregor v Clamp & Son* [1914] 1 KB 288, DC (distress for tax: implements of trade).
8　As to goods of strangers in relation to distress for rent see paras 950–961 post; as to distress for rates and council tax see para 1104 et seq post; as to distress for taxes see paras 1127–1133 post; and as to distress under the Magistrates' Courts Act 1980 see paras 1134–1147 post.

2. DISTRESS FOR RENT

(1) REMEDY BY DISTRESS

905.   Distress in relation to different kinds of rent: historical background.
The distress with which this part of this title is chiefly concerned is distress as between
landlord and tenant for arrears of rent certain in money reserved under a lease, or
payable under a tenancy agreement where the tenant has possession of the land. There
are, however, three kinds of rent: namely rent service, rentcharge and rent seck[1].

A rent service is a rent reserved on a lease or grant of lands as incidental to their
tenure[2] and this was the only kind of rent originally known to the common law. A right
of distress was inseparably incident to it, as long as it was payable to the lord who was
entitled to the fealty of the tenant. It was called rent service because the ancient
retribution was made by the corporal service of the tenant in ploughing his lord's
demesnes, which came afterwards to be changed into gabel or rent; but the service of
fealty remained incident to a rent service[3].

A rentcharge is an annual sum issuing out of land (but not as an incident of the
tenure) the due payment of which is secured by a right of distress[4]. At common law the
right to distrain had normally to be expressly reserved but there is now statutory
provision for distress[5].

A rent seck is a bare rent for which formerly no distress could be made[6]. Such a rent
arose when a rent was granted or reserved out of land otherwise than as an incident of
tenure and no express power of distress was granted or reserved[7]. Moreover a rent
service might be converted into a rent seck if it became separated from the seigniory or
reversion to which it was incident, for example where the lord alienated the rent
without conveying the seigniory or reversion or on a conveyance of the seigniory
reserved to himself the rent[8].

1   Littleton's Tenures s 213; and see para 903 note 8 ante. As to rent see generally LANDLORD AND
    TENANT. As to sums, sometimes called rent, for which distress cannot be levied see para 909 post.
2   Littleton describes a rent service to be where the tenant holds his land by fealty and certain rent, or by
    homage, fealty and certain rent, or by other services and certain rent: see Littleton's Tenures s 213.
3   Bac Abr, Rent (A) 1; Co Litt 87b, 142b; Cru Dig, Rents, c 1, s 5. As to the abolition of fealty on
    enfranchisement under the Law of Property Act 1922 see CUSTOM AND USAGE vol 12(1) (Reissue)
    para 643.
4   See generally RENTCHARGES AND ANNUITIES. As to tithe rentcharges and corn rents see
    ECCLESIASTICAL LAW. As to distress for certain compensation rentcharges payable in respect of
    enfranchised copyholds see CUSTOM AND USAGE vol 12(1) (Reissue) para 723.
5   See para 901 note 7 ante; and see generally RENTCHARGES AND ANNUITIES.
6   Littleton's Tenures s 217–218. A power of distress was later given by statute: see the Landlord and Tenant
    Act 1730 s 5 (as amended); and RENTCHARGES AND ANNUITIES vol 39(2) (Reissue) para 753.
7   Littleton's Tenures ss 217–218. Such a rent seck only differed from a rentcharge in the fact that it was not
    accompanied by a clause of distress: 2 Bl Com (14th Edn) 42. Power of distress was, however, extended
    to rent seck by the Landlord and Tenant Act 1730 s 5 (as amended): see para 901 note 7 ante; and
    RENTCHARGES AND ANNUITIES vol 39(2) (Reissue) para 753.
8   Littleton's Tenures ss 225–228.

906.   Distress as between landlord and tenant.   The common law right of
distress for rent in arrear is a right for the landlord to seize whatever movables he finds
on the premises out of which the rent or service issues, and to hold them until the rent
is paid or the service performed[1].

By statute, in all cases of rent upon any demise, the distrainor may sell the distress
unless replevied within five days[2].

1   *Lyons v Elliott* (1876) 1 QBD 210 at 213 per Blackburn J.

2 See the Distress for Rent Act 1689 s 1 (as amended); and para 1011 post. As to sale of distress see paras 1044–1057 post. As to replevin see para 1081 et seq post.

(2) THE RIGHT TO DISTRAIN

907. Requisites to distress. In order that the right to distrain for rent upon a demise may arise, the relation of landlord and tenant must exist, both when the rent becomes due and when the distress is levied, and the rent must be in arrear[1]. This short proposition involves a number of circumstances (commonly referred to as the essentials to the right of distress) which are dealt with in the following paragraphs[2].

1 *Jolly v Arbuthnot* (1859) 4 De G & J 224 at 242 per Lord Chelmsford.
2 See paras 908–912 post.

908. An existing demise. An actual existing demise is necessary; the common law right to distrain for rent does not arise before the relationship of landlord and tenant is complete[1], nor (apart from the Landlord and Tenant Act 1709[2]) continue after it has determined[3]. A formal instrument of tenancy is not necessary; possession taken by the tenant under an agreement for a tenancy which can be specifically enforced gives the landlord the right to distrain[4]. Further, provided there is a demise, the nature or duration of the tenancy is immaterial, it may be a tenancy at will[5] or a weekly tenancy[6]. The right of distress also exists where, after the expiration of a previous tenancy, a tenant by the consent of both parties continues in possession under such circumstances as to warrant the inference that there is a tacit renewal of the contract of tenancy, but there must be facts to warrant the inference of a renewal of the tenancy[7]. The landlord cannot distrain after treating the tenant as a trespasser by bringing a claim for recovery of land[8]. A tenancy at sufferance, which is not created by demise, does not authorise a distress, the only remedy being by claim for use and occupation[9].

If the relationship between the parties is not that of landlord and tenant but merely that of licensor and licensee, payment made for the use of the premises is not rent and no right to distrain is conferred on the licensor[10].

1 *Dunk v Hunter* (1822) 5 B & Ald 322.
2 See the Landlord and Tenant Act 1709 s 6 (as amended); and para 965 post.
3 *Williams v Stiven* (1846) 9 QB 14.
4 *Walsh v Lonsdale* (1882) 21 ChD 9, CA.
5 *Anderson v Midland Rly Co* (1861) 3 E & E 614; *Morton v Woods* (1869) LR 4 QB 293, Ex Ch.
6 *Yeoman v Ellison* (1867) LR 2 CP 681.
7 See *Right d Flower v Darby and Bristow* (1786) 1 Term Rep 159; *Dougal v McCarthy* [1893] 1 QB 736, CA.
8 *Bridges v Smyth* (1829) 5 Bing 410. As to the loss of the right to distrain see paras 968–978 post.
9 *Alford v Vickery* (1842) Car & M 280; *Jenner v Clegg* (1832) 1 Mood & R 213.
10 *Hancock v Austin* (1863) 14 CBNS 634 (right to 'standings' for machines in factory); *Rendell v Roman* (1893) 9 TLR 192, DC (stall at exhibition to be used between certain hours); and see also *Provincial Bill Posting Co v Low Moor Iron Co* [1909] 2 KB 344, CA. As to the distinction between lease and licence see LANDLORD AND TENANT vol 27(1) (2006 Reissue) para 7 et seq.

909. Rent for which distress may be made. The landlord's right to distrain is founded on the principle that the rent reserved by his demise issues out of the land and he distrains by taking possession, in the nature of a pledge, of goods and chattels found upon such land. In distraining, therefore, the landlord looks to the land demised and to the goods and chattels found on it[1]. Rent for which a distress may be made must be rent reserved out of lands and tenements upon which entry can be made for the purpose of seizing goods found there; and, therefore, rent for which distress may be made cannot be reserved out of any incorporeal hereditament[2].

Sums reserved for the use of chattels confer no right of distress, but when chattels are let with houses or land at one entire rent, the payment issues out of the land and is rent, and may be distrained for[3].

Payments provided for by parol agreement during the currency of a demise by way of increased rent or percentage on the outlay for additions or improvements to be made by the landlord on the premises though expressly called rent, have been held not in fact to be rent, but sums in gross for which a distress cannot be levied[4]. Where, however, the tenancy is one which can be varied by parol, or where the variation is by deed, it is possible to create additional rent in the strict technical sense without a surrender of the old tenancy explicitly or by operation of law and a new lease[5]. A reservation in the demise itself of an increased rent equal to a percentage on the landlord's outlay is good and will support a distress[6].

It has been held that where the lease has been assigned, an assignee of the term will not be liable to distress for rent due prior to the assignment of the term to him and owed by the assignor[7].

1 *British Mutoscope and Biograph Co Ltd v Homer* [1901] 1 Ch 671 at 674 per Farwell J.
2 Co Litt 47a; *Capel v Buszard* (1829) 6 Bing 150 at 161–162, Ex Ch.
3 *Newman v Anderton* (1806) 2 Bos & PNR 224. See also *Selby v Greaves* (1868) LR 3 CP 594 at 602; *Marshall v Schofield* (1882) 52 LJQB 58, CA (premises let with power).
4 *Hoby v Roebuck* (1816) 7 Taunt 157; *Donellan v Read* (1832) 3 B & Ad 899; *Lambert v Norris* (1837) 2 M & W 333. These, however, were pre-Judicature Act cases of parol agreements where it was clearly not the intention of the parties that the benefit of the existing lease should be replaced by an insecure parol holding. See also *Smith v Mapleback* (1786) 1 Term Rep 441 (the lessor agreed with the assignee of the lease that the lessor should lease the demised premises and should pay an annual sum towards the goodwill already paid for by the assignee; it was held that the assignee could not distrain for the annual sum).
5 *Gable Construction Co Ltd v IRC* [1968] 2 All ER 968 at 971–973, [1968] 1 WLR 1426 at 1432–1434 per Goff J (distinguishing *Donellan v Read* (1832) 3 B & Ad 899). Goff J's judgment was approved in *Jenkin R Lewis & Son Ltd v Kerman* [1971] Ch 477 at 497–498, [1970] 3 All ER 414 at 421, CA, per Russell LJ. As to the power to vary a lease under seal by an agreement in writing or an oral agreement see DEEDS AND OTHER INSTRUMENTS para 59 ante.
6 *Re Knight, ex p Voisey* (1882) 21 ChD 442 at 456, CA, per Jessel MR.
7 *Wharfland Ltd v South London Co-operative Building Co Ltd* [1995] 2 EGLR 21; and c f *Whitham v Bullock* [1939] 2 KB 81 at 86, CA, per Clauson LJ. See also *Parry v Robinson-Wyllie Ltd* (1987) 54 P & CR 187, [1987] 2 EGLR 133. See also LANDLORD AND TENANT vol 27(1) (2006 Reissue) paras 108, 278.

910. Rent must be certain. Unless a tenant is to pay a rent certain, the landlord has no right to distrain[1]. To attract the remedy of distress, rent must be certain at the time that it falls due. If that which is agreed upon as the payment is uncertain, it is not rent. A rent is certain, however, if it becomes certain by calculation and upon the happening of certain events, and the mere fact of rent fluctuating from year to year, for example because it is based on the number of acres in crops[2], does not make it uncertain[3]. The necessary certainty may be implied from the acts and dealings of the parties[4]. Rent is sufficiently certain if it can be calculated with certainty at the time when payment comes to be made[5].

1 *Regnart v Porter* (1831) 7 Bing 451 at 454 per Alderson J; and see *Townsend v Charlton* [1922] 1 KB 700, DC. See also *United Scientific Holdings Ltd v Burnley Borough Council* [1978] AC 904 at 935, [1977] 2 All ER 62 at 76, HL, per Lord Diplock; *Concorde Graphics Ltd v Andromeda Investments SA* [1983] 1 EGLR 53, (1982) 265 Estates Gazette 386; *Eren v Tranmac Ltd* [1997] 2 EGLR 211, CA. See para 982 post.
2 *Re Knight, ex p Voisey* (1882) 21 ChD 442, CA (mortgage; attornment clause). See also *Smith v Cardiff Corpn (No 2)* [1955] Ch 159 at 173, [1955] 1 All ER 113 at 120 per Danckwerts J, citing also, as an example of the reservation of a fluctuating rent, *A-G for Ontario v Canadian Niagara Power Co* [1912] AC 852, PC; c f *Re Stockton Iron Furnace Co* (1879) 10 ChD 335, CA (mortgage to secure current account, and including an attornment clause). A stipulation that the rent should be the damage which the landlord

might suffer by certain defaults of the tenant, so that it would have to be ascertained at large or by a tribunal, would be a stipulation for an uncertain payment, which could not be rent: *Re Knight, ex p Voisey* supra at 458 per Brett LJ.

3   Thus a distress may be levied for a rent of so much per cubic yard for marl got and so much per thousand for bricks made (*Daniel v Gracie* (1844) 6 QB 145), or of so much per annum for each loom which the lessee may run (*Walsh v Lonsdale* (1882) 21 ChD 9, CA). See also *Selby v Greaves* (1868) LR 3 CP 594 at 602 per Willes J. As to the amount for which distress may be made see paras 981–991 post.

4   *Knight v Benett* (1826) 3 Bing 364 (rent not stipulated for in agreement but paid for two years).

5   *Greater London Council v Connolly* [1970] 2 QB 100 at 108, [1970] 1 All ER 870 at 874, CA, per Lord Denning MR.

911.   Rent must be in arrear. Distress cannot be made until the rent is in arrear. It is not in arrear until after the last moment of the day on which it is made payable, and therefore there can be no distress until the day after the rent becomes due[1]. If days of grace are given, distress cannot be levied until they have expired[2]; and if payment is postponed by statute the right to distrain is suspended[3].

Rent payable in advance, either by reservation[4] or by custom[5], may be distrained for on the day following that fixed for payment, unless the rent is expressed to be payable in advance if required, in which case a demand for payment must be made before a distress[6]; but in the latter case the demand may be made after the day on which the rent thereby reserved becomes due[7]; and the landlord may distrain immediately after demand, if his rights are in peril[8]. When an express power of distress is given to be exercised after the rent has been 'lawfully demanded', it has been held that it is not necessary to follow the strict common law rules as to demand[9].

Where a tenant has a valid claim against the landlord entitling the tenant to a legal or equitable set-off against the rent, the rent is not due and in arrear. Accordingly, the landlord in such circumstances has no right to distrain[10].

1   *Dibble v Bowater* (1853) 2 E & B 564. As to when distress may be made see paras 962–967 post.

2   *Clun's Case* (1613) 10 Co Rep 127a; and see *Child v Edwards* [1909] 2 KB 753.

3   *Aquis Property Co v Hollebone* as reported in (1914) 59 Sol Jo 102 (a decision under the Postponement of Payments Act 1914 (repealed)); and see *Shottland v Cabins Ltd* (1915) 31 TLR 297 (a case where a distress was levied before the date of proclamation of a moratorium under the Postponement of Payments Act 1914, but the goods had not been sold).

4   *Lee v Smith* (1854) 9 Exch 662; *Harrison v Barry* (1819) 7 Price 690; *Walsh v Lonsdale* (1882) 21 ChD 9, CA.

5   *Buckley v Taylor* (1788) 2 Term Rep 600.

6   *Clarke v Holford* (1848) 2 Car & Kir 540; and see *Mallam v Arden* (1833) 10 Bing 299 (rent payable quarterly or half quarterly if required). For other cases in which a demand is necessary see para 964 post.

7   *Witty v Williams* (1864) 12 WR 755.

8   *London and Westminster Loan and Discount Co v London and North Western Rly Co* [1893] 2 QB 49.

9   *Thorp v Hurt* [1886] WN 96. As to demand in relation to forfeiture for non-payment of rent see e g *Jackson & Co v Northampton Street Tramways Co* (1886) 55 LT 91; and LANDLORD AND TENANT vol 27(1) (2006 Reissue) para 609.

10 See *Eller v Grovecrest Investments Ltd* [1995] QB 272, [1994] 4 All ER 845, CA.

912.   Necessity for existence of a reversion. Unless otherwise provided by statute or by agreement between the parties, the person distraining for rent under a demise must at the time the distress is made possess a reversion to which the rent is incident[1], though it is immaterial how short that reversion may be. Thus a tenant who underlets for the remainder of his term less a day has a sufficient reversion to entitle him to distrain[2]. Apart from statute, the reversion must have been vested in the person distraining at the time the rent distrained for fell due, but it was not necessary that he should have been the reversioner for all the time during which the rent was accruing[3].

A defeasible reversion, until it is defeated, is sufficient to support a distress. So a tenant from year to year, whose estate consists in point of law of a lease for a year certain with a growing interest during every year thereafter springing out of the original contract[4], has a sufficient reversion to support a distress under a demise; and it is immaterial whether he simply underlets from year to year[5] or grants a lease for a long term[6].

A reversion by estoppel will also support a distress[7], though in such a case the goods of a third party cannot be taken[8].

Rent reserved on an assignment cannot be distrained for as there is no reversion[9]. When a leaseholder, whether purporting to assign or underlet, parts with all his interest in a term of years, he cannot distrain for rent due on the underlease, unless he reserves to himself an express power to do so[10]. When he purports to demise for a period coextensive with his own interest or longer, reserving a rent, the transaction is in law an assignment, although purporting to be a demise; for an underlease for the whole of the residue of a term is in law an assignment[11]. It makes no difference that the instrument contains a stipulation that the assignee is to be tenant to the assignor during the term[12], or that the assignee has paid or agreed to pay money as rent[13], but the claim for rent may remain[14]. Since the right to distrain may only be exercised by a person entitled to the reversion, it does not pass to an original tenant or surety who discharges arrears of rent on behalf of an assignee of the lease albeit that the original tenant or surety has a right to bring a claim against the assignee by subrogation[15].

1　Co Litt 47a, 142b. As to a lessor losing his right of distress by parting with the reversion see para 968 post.

2　*Wade v Marsh* (1625) Lat 211.

3　*Thompson v Shaw* (1836) 5 LJCP 234. As to the statutory rights of executors and administrators to levy distress see para 923 post. As to the rights of assignees see para 968 post.

4　*Oxley v James* (1844) 13 M & W 209 at 214 per Parke B; and see LANDLORD AND TENANT vol 27(1) (2006 Reissue) para 208.

5　*Curtis v Wheeler* (1830) Mood & M 493; *Pike v Eyre* (1829) 9 B & C 909.

6　*Oxley v James* (1844) 13 M & W 209. A demise by such a person for a term of years is not an assignment; it is a term for so many years subject to determination by the cessation of the original interest: *Oxley v James* supra. The principle applies to other periodic tenancies: *Peirse v Sharr and Claughton* (1828) 2 Man & Ry KB 418.

7　As to tenancies by estoppel see ESTOPPEL vol 16(2) (Reissue) para 1030 et seq; LANDLORD AND TENANT vol 27(1) (2006 Reissue) para 4. As to estoppel in the case of a mortgage see para 916 text and note 6 post. As to estoppel in the case of a receiver appointed out of court see para 925 note 4 post.

8　*Tadman v Henman* [1893] 2 QB 168.

9　See the text and notes 10–15 infra; and para 968 post.

10　*Preece v Corrie* (1828) 5 Bing 24 (oral tenancy of the last year of a term); *Lewis v Baker* [1905] 1 Ch 46. As to the position when the reversion has been mortgaged see paras 917–918 post.

11　*Lewis v Baker* [1905] 1 Ch 46 at 50 per Swinfen Eady J; *—v Cooper* (1768) 2 Wils 375; *Preece v Corrie* (1828) 5 Bing 24; and see *Beardman v Wilson* (1868) LR 4 CP 57; *Milmo v Carreras* [1946] KB 306, [1946] 1 All ER 288, CA; *Grosvenor Estate Belgravia v Cochran* (1991) 24 HLR 98, [1991] 2 EGLR 83, CA. It would appear that the sum reserved as rent is not an annual sum receivable out of the land or the income thereof so as to enable it to be recovered by distress under the Law of Property Act 1925 s 121(2) (see para 901 note 7 ante; and RENTCHARGES AND ANNUITIES vol 39(2) (Reissue) para 869): see *Lewis v Baker* supra at 52 per Swinfen Eady J.

12　*Parmenter v Webber* (1818) 8 Taunt 593. As to the protection of new leases on termination of existing terms see the Ecclesiastical Leasing Act 1842 ss 16, 17 (both as amended); the Law of Property Act 1925 ss 139, 150; and LANDLORD AND TENANT vol 27(1) (2006 Reissue) para 638.

13　*Hazeldine v Heaton* (1883) Cab & El 40.

14　See *Poultney v Holmes* (1720) 1 Stra 405; *Pollock v Stacy* (1847) 9 QB 1033.

15　*Re Russell, Russell v Shoolbred* (1885) 29 ChD 254, CA.

(3) WHO MAY DISTRAIN

913. Who may distrain for rent. Any person, in whom is vested the reversion incident to a term of years[1], may, by virtue of the common law, distrain for rent due. The right of distress ceases when the reversion or the whole of the estate is parted with[2], but the right has by statute and otherwise been extended to certain persons who may not have a reversionary interest in the ordinary sense of the term[3].

1 See Littleton's Tenures ss 214–215. See also *Manchester Brewery Co v Coombs* [1901] 2 Ch 608 at 617–618 per Farwell J ('distress is a legal remedy and depends on the existence at law of the relation of landlord and tenant'). As to the effect (for purposes of distress, forfeiture etc) of the execution of a transfer and notice to a lessee without actual registration of the transfer see *Scribes West Ltd v Relsa Anstalt* [2004] EWCA Civ 1744, [2005] All ER 690, [2005] 1 WLR 1847.
   As to distress by the Crown see CONSTITUTIONAL LAW AND HUMAN RIGHTS vol 8(2) (Reissue) para 847.
2 See paras 912 ante, 968 post.
3 See paras 924–925 post.

914. Tenants in fee or for years. The only legal estates in land now capable of subsisting are a fee simple absolute in possession and a term of years absolute[1]. Consequently it is to these estates, and to these estates only, that a power of distress for rent service is incident[2]. Tenants for terms of years, who sublet and retain even a day's reversion, can distrain; as also can a tenant from year to year who sublets from year to year or for a term of years[3]. A termor (that is, a tenant for a term of years), whose term has expired, cannot, however, distrain on an undertenant, if the undertenant has declined further to recognise the termor as his landlord[4].

1 Law of Property Act 1925 s 1(1); and see REAL PROPERTY vol 39(2) (Reissue) para 45.
2 Where there are equitable interests, the legal estate will normally be vested in trustees (see REAL PROPERTY vol 39(2) (Reissue) para 46; SETTLEMENTS vol 42 (Reissue) para 609) and by virtue of their legal estate they will be able to distrain.
3 See para 912 text and notes 5–6 ante.
4 *Burne v Richardson* (1813) 4 Taunt 720.

915. Joint tenants. One of several joint tenants[1] may distrain for the whole rent due. No express authority is needed from the others for this purpose, and the discharge given binds all the co-tenants. It is doubtful whether such authority can be actually countermanded by the others; merely declining to authorise the distress does not prevent its legality[2]. If joint tenants make a demise to one of their number the other joint tenants may justify a distress[3].

1 *Pullen v Palmer* (1696) 3 Salk 207.
2 *Robinson v Hofman* (1828) 4 Bing 562; *Leigh v Shepherd* (1821) 2 Brod & Bing 465.
3 *Cowper v Fletcher* (1865) 6 B & S 464. Formerly, where a reversion was held in joint tenancy, severance of the reversion effected by a conveyance by some of the joint tenants deprived the remaining joint tenants of their right to distrain for rent already due (*Stavely v Allcock* (1851) 16 QB 636); but there cannot now be a severance of a joint tenancy of a legal estate (see the Law of Property Act 1925 s 36(2); and REAL PROPERTY vol 39(2) (Reissue) para 198).

916. Mortgagees: attornment in mortgage. Attornment clauses in mortgages are invalid for the purpose of conferring effective powers of distress over personal chattels unless registered as bills of sale, but the invalidity does not extend to cases where the mortgagee has actually entered into possession and has demised the land to the mortgagor at a fair and reasonable rent[1]. The mere relationship of mortgagee and mortgagor gives no right to distrain[2], but the relationship of landlord and tenant involving (subject to the Bills of Sale Acts 1878 and 1882[3]) that right[4] may be created between them by express words of attornment or by conduct[5]; and for this purpose the mortgagor may be estopped from setting up the want of the legal estate in the mortgagee even though that is shown on the face of the mortgage deed[6]. Where the existence of the relationship of landlord and tenant rests on the estoppel of the mortgagor, it seems that any right of the mortgagee to distrain could never have extended to the goods of a third party[7]. A tenancy at will arising from an attornment clause determines on the death of the mortgagor, and subsequent payment of interest by his successor in title will not of itself, in the absence of other evidence that the sums paid were paid as rent, be referred to a new tenancy so as to justify a distress thereunder[8].

1   See the Bills of Sale Act 1878 s 6; the Bills of Sale Act (1878) Amendment Act 1882 s 8; and BILLS OF SALE vol 4(1) (2002 Reissue) paras 636, 735. As to attornment clauses see BUILDING SOCIETIES vol 4(3) (Reissue) para 567; LANDLORD AND TENANT vol 27(1) (2006 Reissue) para 3; MORTGAGE vol 32 (2005 Reissue) paras 428, 543.
2   *Evans v Elliot* (1838) 9 Ad & El 342 at 354; *Rogers v Humphreys* (1835) 4 Ad & El 299.
3   See note 1 supra.
4   Ie the right of a landlord to distrain: see *Pinhorn v Souster* (1853) 8 Exch 763 (distress on goods of person other than the mortgagor); *Re Stockton Iron Furnace Co* (1879) 10 ChD 335, CA (mortgage to bankers; attornment at annual rent; entry by mortgagee and distress for arrears); *Re Threlfall, ex p Queen's Benefit Building Society* (1880) 16 ChD 274, CA (attornment as tenant from year to year; distress for half-year's rent); *Kearsley v Philips* (1883) 11 QBD 621, CA (attornment by mortgagor; distress on goods of stranger). The right to distrain on the goods of a stranger is now subject to the Law of Distress Amendment Act 1908: see para 950 et seq post.
5   *Clowes v Hughes* (1870) LR 5 Exch 160; *Jolly v Arbuthnot* (1859) 4 De G & J 224; *Kearsley v Philips* (1883) 11 QBD 621, CA; *West v Fritche* (1848) 3 Exch 216. A personal licence granted by the mortgagor to the mortgagee to seize goods in default of payment of interest does not involve a tenancy so as to give a right to distrain on the goods of a tenant of the mortgagor: *Gibbs v Cruikshank* (1873) LR 8 CP 454; and see *Kearsley v Philips* (1883) 11 QBD 621 at 624–625, CA, per Brett MR.
6   *Morton v Woods* (1869) LR 4 QB 293, Ex Ch; *Re Kitchin, ex p Punnett* (1880) 16 ChD 226, CA (second mortgage); and see also para 925 note 4 post. A second mortgage by demise, however, would have a legal estate. A legal mortgage of land (whether it is a first or subsequent mortgage) is now effected by demise or by a charge by way of legal mortgage which confers on the mortgagee the same remedies as if it were a mortgage by demise: see the Law of Property Act 1925 ss 39, ss 85–87 (all as amended), Sch 1 Pts I, VII, VIII; and see MORTGAGE vol 32 (2005 Reissue) para 387 et seq. As regards tenancy by estoppel see generally ESTOPPEL.
7   *Tadman v Henman* [1893] 2 QB 168.
8   *Scobie v Collins* [1895] 1 QB 375.

917.   Mortgage subsequent to lease.   In the case of a mortgage of land subsequent to a lease, the mortgagee, where the mortgage is by demise[1], becomes reversioner on the lease[2] and has the same rights against the lessee and those claiming under him as the mortgagor had[3]. In the case of a mortgage created by a charge expressed to be by way of legal mortgage, the mortgagee has the same powers as if he had a term, including the like right to distrain where the land was subject to a lease at the date of the mortgage[4]. The lessee, however, must continue to pay rent to the mortgagor[5] unless he receives notice from the mortgagee of his intention to take possession or to enter into receipt of the rents and profits of the mortgaged land. After receiving the notice the lessee must pay rent to the mortgagee, who can distrain if necessary, even if the lessee after notice has paid the mortgagor[6]. Payment by the lessee before knowledge of the mortgage is protected, but the payment must be strictly in accordance with the terms of the lease, and cannot apply to rent paid in advance of the due date; the rent in such a case would be considered an advance to the landlord[7]. The notice necessary should be by the grantee of the mortgage, but notice by a beneficiary of the trust instead of by trustees is sufficient[8].

1   As to the methods by which a mortgage of a legal estate in land can be effected see para 916 note 6 ante.
2   See e g *Harmer v Bean* (1853) 3 Car & Kir 307; *Re Moore and Hulm's Contract* [1912] 2 Ch 105 at 109. As to the general effect of concurrent leases see LANDLORD AND TENANT vol 27(1) (2006 Reissue) para 104 et seq. See also MORTGAGE vol 32 (2005 Reissue) para 493. The mortgagor while in possession can distrain: see para 921 post. As to the right to recover arrears of rent due when the reversion is assigned see para 968 post.
3   See the Law of Property Act 1925 s 141; and LANDLORD AND TENANT vol 27(1) (2006 Reissue) para 567. No attornment by the tenant to the mortgagee is necessary: s 151(1).
4   See ibid s 87 (as amended); and MORTGAGE vol 32 (2005 Reissue) para 391.
5   See para 921 post.

6   *Moss v Gallimore* (1779) 1 Doug KB 279, confirmed in *Birch v Wright* (1786) 1 Term Rep 378 at 384;
     Rogers v Humphreys (1835) 4 Ad & El 299; *Davies v Law Mutual Building Society* (1971) 219 Estates Gazette
     309, DC.
7   *De Nicholls v Saunders* (1870) LR 5 CP 589.
8   *Lumley v Hodgson* (1812) 16 East 99.

918.   Lease subsequent to mortgage. A lease by a mortgagor subsequent to the
mortgage, unless made under an express power given by the mortgage[1] or under the
statutory power[2], is void as against the mortgagee, who cannot distrain, as there is no
relation of landlord and tenant between him and the lessee[3]. Such a relationship,
however, may arise by express agreement or by conduct[4], but it does not relate back to
notice of the mortgage[5]. An express attornment may relate back[6]. The question whether
a new tenancy between the mortgagee and the tenant has been created is one of fact;
mere failure by the mortgagee to evict the tenant is insufficient[7]; mere notice of the
mortgage deed and of the interest being in arrear accompanied by a demand for rent is
not sufficient, but the fact that rent is paid in accordance with such notice is evidence of
a tenancy[8]. The notice is the offer, and evidence of acceptance of or assent to the offer
is necessary[9].

Even though a lease made after the mortgage by the mortgagor is not made under an
express power or the statutory power there is, as between the mortgagor and the tenant,
a tenancy which will entitle the mortgagor to distrain unless the mortgagee has given
notice of his intention to enter into possession[10].

1   *Rogers v Humphreys* (1835) 4 Ad & El 299.
2   Ie under the Law of Property Act 1925 s 99 (as amended) (see MORTGAGE vol 32 (2005 Reissue)
     paras 545–550): see para 919 post.
3   *Keech v Hall* (1778) 1 Doug KB 21; *Pope v Biggs* (1829) 9 B & C 245; *Rogers v Humphreys* (1835) 4 Ad &
     El 299; *Partington v Woodcock* (1835) 6 Ad & El 690. See also *Dudley and District Benefit Building Society v
     Emerson* [1949] Ch 707, [1949] 2 All ER 252, CA; *Rust v Goodale* [1957] Ch 33, [1956] 3 All ER 373;
     Britannia Building Society v Earl [1990] 2 All ER 469, [1990] 1 WLR 422, CA; and see further BUILDING
     SOCIETIES vol 4(3) (Reissue) para 571; MORTGAGE vol 32 (2005 Reissue) para 496.
4   *Doe d Whitaker v Hales* (1831) 2 Bing 322; *Evans v Elliot* (1838) 9 Ad & El 342 at 355; *Iron Trades Employers
     Insurance Association Ltd v Union Land and House Investors Ltd* as reported in [1937] Ch 313 at 318; *Parker
     v Braithwaite* [1952] 2 All ER 837 at 840–841 per Danckwerts J; *Barclays Bank Ltd v Kiley* [1961] 2 All ER
     849, [1961] 1 WLR 1050.
5   See the comments of Denman CJ in *Evans v Elliot* (1838) 9 Ad & El 342 at 353–354, explaining the dicta
     in *Pope v Biggs* (1829) 9 B & C 245.
6   *Gladman v Plumer* (1845) 15 LJQB 79.
7   *Parker v Braithwaite* [1952] 2 All ER 837.
8   *Evans v Elliot* (1838) 9 Ad & El 342; *Partington v Woodcock* (1835) 6 Ad & El 690; *Towerson v Jackson* [1891]
     2 QB 484, CA.
9   *Towerson v Jackson* [1891] 2 QB 484 at 487, CA, per Bowen LJ (criticising *Brown v Storey* (1840) 1 Man
     & G 117). See also *Corbett v Plowden* (1884) 25 ChD 678 at 681, CA, per Lord Selborne LC (evidence
     might be given of the mortgagees being in substance parties to and authorising the agreement, and that
     it was made by the mortgagor for them as well as for himself). As to tenancies arising by implication see
     LANDLORD AND TENANT vol 27(1) (2006 Reissue) para 199 et seq.
10   See para 921 post. The tenancy in this case is, it seems, a tenancy by estoppel: see e g *Cuthbertson v Irving*
     (1860) 6 H & N 135, Ex Ch; and MORTGAGE vol 32 (2005 Reissue) para 496.

919.   Lease by mortgagor under statute. If a mortgagor makes a lease complying
with the provisions of the Law of Property Act 1925[1], it will be good against the
mortgagee, and is treated as if made with his authority and concurrence. The mortgagor
is entitled to distrain while in possession, and the mortgagee by virtue of his mortgage
term has a reversionary estate expectant on the end of the lease, and he can distrain after
he has given notice that he intends to exercise his rights to act as lessor under the terms
of the lease[2]. Collateral agreements between the mortgagor and the tenant do not bind
the mortgagee[3].

1   See the Law of Property Act 1925 s 99 (as amended) (replacing the Conveyancing Act 1881 s 18); and
     MORTGAGE vol 32 (2005 Reissue) paras 545–550. A mortgagor, if he is in possession and no receiver by
     the mortgagee is acting, may lease the mortgaged property provided that certain provisions as to the
     contents etc of the lease are fulfilled: see the Law of Property Act 1925 s 99 (as amended); and
     MORTGAGE vol 32 (2005 Reissue) para 547. Except where the land to be leased is agricultural land
     subject to the Agricultural Holdings Act 1986 or the Agricultural Tenancies Act 1995 or the lease is under
     an order of the court for the grant of a new business tenancy, the Law of Property Act 1925 s 99 (as
     amended) applies only if and so far as a contrary intention is not expressed in the mortgage deed or
     otherwise in writing: see s 99(13) (as amended), s 99(13A) (as added); the Landlord and Tenant Act 1954
     s 36(4); and MORTGAGE vol 32 (2005 Reissue) para 547.
2   *Municipal Permanent Investment Building Society v Smith* (1888) 22 QBD 70, CA. See also *Wilson v Queen's
     Club* [1891] 3 Ch 522.
3   *Municipal Permanent Investment Building Society v Smith* (1888) 22 QBD 70, CA.

920.   Mortgagee in possession. No obligation lies on a mortgagee in possession to
distrain, nor can he be called upon to do so by the owner of an equity of redemption,
nor is he bound, on a distraint, to continue and defend at law any seizure he may have
made[1].

1   *Cocks v Gray* (1857) 1 Giff 77.

921.   Mortgagor in possession. Where the mortgagee has not given notice of his
intention to take possession or enter into the receipts of the rents and profits of any land,
a mortgagor for the time being entitled to the possession or receipt of the rents and
profits of such land is entitled to distrain for rent accrued due since the date of the
mortgage, whether the lease be prior[1] or subsequent to the mortgage[2]. In these
circumstances, the mortgagor is not liable to account for the rents to the mortgagee[3].
The mortgagor cannot distrain after the mortgagee has appointed a receiver under his
powers in that behalf[4].

1   At common law the mortgagor in receipt of the rents and profits of the land could distrain for them as
     bailiff of the mortgagee: see *Trent v Hunt* (1853) 9 Exch 14; approved in *Snell v Finch* (1863) 13 CBNS
     651. See also *Dean and Chapter of Christchurch, Oxford v Duke of Buckingham and Chandos* (1864) 17 CBNS
     391 at 413 per Willes J; *Reece v Strousberg* (1885) 54 LT 133. See also the Law of Property Act 1925 ss 98,
     141; *Rose v Watson* (1864) 10 HL Cas 672 at 684; *Turner v Walsh* [1909] 2 KB 484, CA; *Re Ind, Coope
     & Co Ltd, Fisher v Ind, Coope & Co Ltd* [1911] 2 Ch 223 at 231–232 per Warrington J; and MORTGAGE
     vol 32 (2005 Reissue) paras 538, 623. See also *Rhodes v Allied Dunbar Pension Services Ltd* [1989] 1 All ER
     1161 at 1166–1167, [1989] 1 WLR 800 at 807, CA, per Nicholls LJ.
2   *Carpenter v Parker* (1857) 3 CBNS 206 at 234, 237; *Trent v Hunt* (1853) 9 Exch 14 at 23.
3   *Ex p Wilson* (1813) 2 Ves & B 252; *Trent v Hunt* (1853) 9 Exch 14.
4   See para 925 post.

922.   Beneficiary of trust. Where the reversion on a demise is held in trust the
beneficiary of the trust is not entitled to distrain for rent in arrear since he is entitled not
to the rent but only to an account from the trustee of the profits received from the trust
property[1]. In order to distrain, one must be entitled to the legal reversion[2]. Although it
has been held that an equitable assignee of the reversion to a lease who has not been
registered as legal owner is entitled to the benefit of a condition in the lease entitling the
landlord to forfeit, it has not been directly decided that a person without a legal estate is
entitled to exercise the legal remedy of distress[3].

1   *Schalit v Joseph Nadler Ltd* [1933] 2 KB 79, construing the Law of Property Act 1925 s 141(2) (see
     LANDLORD AND TENANT vol 27(1) (2006 Reissue) para 567). See also *Scribes West Ltd v Relsa Anstalt
     (No 3)* [2004] EWCA Civ 1744, [2005] 2 All ER 690.
2   See paras 912, 914 ante.
3   See *Scribes West Ltd v Relsa Anstalt (No 3)* [2004] EWCA Civ 1744, [2005] 2 All ER 690.

923.   Executors and administrators. When the reversion incident on the legal
estate is vested in him, a personal representative can distrain for all rent accruing due to

1   See the Sequestration Act 1849 s 1 (as amended); and ECCLESIASTICAL LAW vol 14 para 915. As to the sequestration of benefices generally see ECCLESIASTICAL LAW.

(4) WHAT MAY AND WHAT MAY NOT BE DISTRAINED

(i) General Rule

928. Prima facie all goods may be distrained. Under the common law a landlord can prima facie seize and distrain for rent in arrear all goods and chattels found on the premises out of which the rent issues; the goods and chattels may be the property of the tenant, or of a stranger, the landlord being entitled to have recourse to all chattels actually on his tenant's premises without reference to their ownership[1]. The rule, however, applies only to goods and personal chattels, while chattels of an incorporeal nature and incorporeal hereditaments, such as advowsons, rights of common, fairs, tithes, markets, privileges, franchises, and patent rights, are incapable of physical possession and seizure, and cannot be the subject of distress, although any actual goods the subject of these rights may be taken[2].

Moreover, in the case of personal chattels certain exceptions have been grafted upon the general rule both by the common law and by statute[3]. These exceptions depend in part on the person in whose possession, or the place in which, the goods may be found, and in part on the nature of the goods themselves. Anyone claiming the benefit of one of these exceptions must satisfy the court that his case falls within it. The exceptions are stated in the form of rules and not of principles, and the court will not travel beyond the definitions of the exceptions prescribed[4]. Of these exceptions some are absolute and some are conditional, that is the goods within them can only be taken if there is no other sufficient distress[5]. It does not matter in whose possession the demised land may be[6].

1   3 Bl Com (14th Edn) 8; *Gorton v Falkner* (1792) 4 Term Rep 565; *Gilman v Elton* (1821) 3 Brod & Bing 75; *Muspratt v Gregory* (1838) 3 M & W 677, Ex Ch; *Cramer v Mott* (1870) LR 5 QB 357 at 360 per Blackburn J; *Lyons v Elliott* (1876) 1 QBD 210; *Clarke v Millwall Dock Co* (1886) 17 QBD 494, CA; *Challoner v Robinson* [1908] 1 Ch 49, CA. 'The rule grows out of the relation of landlord and tenant and out of the nature of the thing itself': *Gilman v Elton* supra at 79 per Dallas CJ; and see *Lyons v Elliott* supra at 213 per Blackburn J. As to the goods of strangers see para 950 et seq post; and as to goods comprised in a bill of sale see BILLS OF SALE vol 4(1) (2002 Reissue) para 788.

2   Co Litt 47a; *British Mutoscope and Biograph Co Ltd v Homer* [1901] 1 Ch 671 (chattels subject of patent seized; infringing use restrained); and c f *Horsford v Webster* (1835) 1 Cr M & R 696.

3   As to the goods of strangers see para 930 et seq post.

4   See the authorities cited in note 1 supra. See also *Simpson v Hartopp* (1744) Willes 512 (where the leading common law exceptions are precisely stated). Other exceptions are stated by Alderson B in *Muspratt v Gregory* (1836) 1 M & W 633 at 645; affd (1838) 3 M & W 677, Ex Ch. See also *Clarke v Millwall Dock Co* (1886) 17 QBD 494 at 497, CA, per Lord Herschell LC, and at 601 per Lord Esher MR; *Challoner v Robinson* [1908] 1 Ch 49 at 59, CA, per Cozens-Hardy MR (citing *Clarke v Millwall Dock Co* supra at 899 per Lord Herschell LC, that both the general rule of distraint on strangers' goods and the exception in question were anomalous).

5   For absolute exceptions see paras 930–947 post; and for conditional exceptions see para 948 et seq post.

6   *Humphry v Damion* (1612) Cro Jac 300; *Groom v Bluck* (1841) 2 Man & G 567 (goods of assignor of lease left on premises and seized for rent due by assignee); but see *Re Potter, ex p Parke* (1874) LR 18 Eq 381 (tenants in common attorning as tenants).

929. Crops. At common law growing crops could not be distrained[1], but by statute the landlord may seize, for arrears of rent, all sorts of corn and grass, hops, roots, fruit, pulse or other product whatsoever[2] growing on any part of the land demised[3]. The grantee of a rentcharge is not a landlord for these purposes[4], and it would seem that this statutory power[5] would not authorise a distress of growing crops.

At common law sheaves or cocks of corn were not distrainable[6], but by statute sheaves or cocks of corn, or corn loose or in the straw, or hay lying in any barn or granary or upon any hovel stack or rick, may be seized and may be detained in the place where it is found, until it is replevied, and in default of replevy until it is sold; it must not, however, be removed to the damage of the owner until replevied or sold[7]. In default of replevy it must be sold within five days unless this time is extended[8]. This provision applies to corn thrashed or unthrashed[9]. The owner of a rentcharge may take advantage of the provision[10], even if the goods are those of a stranger[11].

Statutory restrictions on the right to distrain on crops now exist in relation to agricultural holdings[12].

1 1 Roll Abr, Distress (H); Co Litt 47b (note 299 of Hargrave). As to distress for rent of agricultural holdings see AGRICULTURE vol 1(2) (Reissue) paras 333–335.
2 'Other product' does not include trees or shrubs in a nursery ground: *Clark v Gaskarth* (1818) 8 Taunt 431; *Clark v Calvert* (1818) 8 Taunt 742.
3 See the Distress for Rent Act 1737 s 8 (as amended), s 9; and para 1014 post.
4 *Miller v Green* (1831) 8 Bing 92, Ex Ch.
5 Ie under the Law of Property Act 1925 and the Landlord and Tenant Act 1730: see para 901 text and note 7 ante.
6 Co Litt 47a; *Wilson v Ducket* (1675) 2 Mod Rep 61; *Griffin v Scott* (1726) 1 Barn KB 3; *Simpson v Hartopp* (1744) Willes 512 at 515.
7 See the Distress for Rent Act 1689 s 2 (amended by the Statute Law Revision Act 1948). As to impounding see para 1013 et seq post. As to sale see paras 1044, 1050, 1053 post. As to replevin see para 1081 et seq post. As to the effect of payment or tender see para 975 post. As to appraisement see para 1019 post. As to distress after execution see para 1043 post.
8 See paras 1044, 1050 post.
9 *Belasyse v Burbridge* (1696) 1 Lut 213 at 214.
10 *Johnson v Faulkner* (1842) 2 QB 925. See also *Horton v Arnold* (1731) Fortes Rep 361.
11 *Johnson v Faulkner* (1842) 2 QB 925.
12 See the Agricultural Holdings Act 1986 s 17; and AGRICULTURE vol 1(2) (Reissue) para 333.

(ii) Things Absolutely Privileged

930.   Crown property; property of diplomats etc.   The property of the Crown, whether in the possession of the Crown or on premises demised to a subject, cannot be taken in distress[1].

The premises of a diplomatic mission are inviolable, as is the private residence of a diplomatic agent, and such an agent is in general immune from suit and legal process[2]. Provision is made for the granting of corresponding immunities and privileges to international organisations and persons connected with them[3].

1 *Secretary of State for War v Wynne* [1905] 2 KB 845. Nothing in the Law of Property Act 1925 affects this proposition: s 208(1). A postal packet, anything contained in such a packet and a mailbag containing such a packet have, if they are not the property of the Crown but are in the course of transmission by post, the same immunity from seizure under any statutory power or under distress as if they were Crown property: see the Postal Services Act 2000 s 104(1)–(3). As to the inviolability of mails generally see POST OFFICE vol 36(2) (Reissue) para 90.
2 See the Diplomatic Privileges Act 1964 s 2 (as amended), Sch 1 arts 22, 30, 31; and FOREIGN RELATIONS LAW. As to the privileges and immunities of families, members of staffs etc see Sch 1 art 37; the State Immunity Act 1978; the Diplomatic and Consular Premises Act 1987; and FOREIGN RELATIONS LAW.
3 See the International Organisations Act 1968 ss 1, 2, 6, Sch 1 (all as amended); and FOREIGN RELATIONS LAW. As to the immunities and privileges of Commonwealth representatives and organisations see COMMONWEALTH vol 6 (2003 Reissue) para 722 et seq.

931.   Goods in custody of the law.   Goods in custody of the law, when seized by virtue of an execution[1], are immune from distress.

1 See para 1032 post.

932. Trade privilege. Things delivered to a person exercising a public trade, to be carried, wrought, worked up, or managed in the way of his trade, are privileged from distress for rent due from the person in whose custody they are; examples of such things are a horse in a smith's shop, materials sent to a weaver, or cloth sent to a tailor to be made up[1]. There are various statements as to the scope[2] and object[3] of this exception. This branch of privilege has lost most of its former importance owing to the statutory protection given to the goods of strangers[4].

Delivery for the purposes of trade is essential, and the exception stated above does not extend to all cases in which goods happen to be on premises for those purposes, although if an article to be manufactured has been completed, and the person who has the property in it leaves it upon the demised premises to have some alteration made, there may be an equivalent to delivery of the thing manufactured[5].

1   *Simpson v Hartopp* (1744) Willes 512, 1 Smith LC (13th Edn) 494; *Gisbourn v Hurst* (1710) 1 Salk 249. For examples of goods privileged see para 936 post. See also BAILMENT vol 3(1) (2005 Reissue) para 47.
2   See *Clarke v Millwall Dock Co* (1886) 17 QBD 494 at 499–500, CA, cited with approval in *Challoner v Robinson* [1908] 1 Ch 49 at 59, CA. See also *Muspratt v Gregory* (1838) 3 M & W 677, Ex Ch; *Joule v Jackson* (1841) 7 M & W 450 (where it is laid down that this rule ought not to be extended). However, in *Adams v Grane* (1833) 1 Cr & M 380 at 391 per Vaughan B, it was suggested that the rule should not be construed strictly; while in *Findon v M'Laren* (1845) 6 QB 891 at 897 per Patteson J, it was stated that the principles of this exception have been varied according to the state of trade.
3   The exception has been said to be for the sake of 'trade and commerce, which could not be carried on if such things in these circumstances could be distrained for rent': *Simpson v Hartopp* (1744) Willes 512, 1 Smith LC (13th Edn) 494. See *Miles v Furber* (1873) LR 8 QB 77 at 83 per Archibald J, where it is stated that the principle is that 'the trade or business could not be carried on, except the goods were privileged from distress'. According to Dallas CJ in *Gilman v Elton* (1821) 3 Brod & Bing 75, this exception is for the public benefit and convenience; Denman CJ in *Musprat v Gregory* (1838) 3 M & W 677 at 679, Ex Ch, adds 'for public peace'; in *Adams v Grane* (1833) 1 Cr & M 380 at 387, Bayley B says 'interest reipublicae that buyer and seller should be brought together'; and Blackburn J in *Lyons v Elliott* (1876) 1 QBD 210 at 214 states that the ground is 'public policy for the benefit of trade'.
4   See para 950 et seq post.
5   *Clarke v Millwall Dock Co* (1886) 17 QBD 494, CA.

933. Trade privilege: trade must be public. For the goods of a third party in the hands of a trader to be privileged from distress for rent[1] the trade must be a public one, that is a trade or business carried on generally for the benefit of all persons who chose to avail themselves of it, as distinguished from a special employment by particular individuals. The term 'public' is not confined to cases such as those of an innkeeper or common carrier, where all persons have a right to deal with the trader, but includes a trader prima facie open to the dealings of all persons indiscriminately, such as a butcher or trader in corn. The quantity of trade is no criterion, and a workman employed for wages may be carrying on a public trade within the meaning of the exception[2] previously stated[3].

The trade is not public if carried on substantially on behalf of one employer only or in one particular case. Thus an agent who, although entitled to carry on other agency business, holds only one agency beyond that of his regular principals[4], and an artist who has been entrusted with a picture to work up[5] are not carrying on a public trade. Pictures deposited for sale on commission with a restaurant keeper who is not a commission agent are not privileged[6].

1   See para 932 text and note 1 ante.
2   See note 1 supra.
3   See *Challoner v Robinson* [1908] 1 Ch 49 at 56, CA, per Neville J; *Brown v Shevill* (1834) 2 Ad & El 138; *Gibson v Ireson* (1842) 3 QB 39; *Muspratt v Gregory* (1836) 1 M & W 633 at 652 et seq (on appeal (1838) 3 M & W 677, Ex Ch). In pleading the exception as a defence, the publicity of the trade must be pleaded: see *Farrant v Robson* (1834) 3 LJCP 146.
4   *Tapling & Co v Weston* (1883) Cab & El 99.

5   *Von Knoop v Moss and Jameson* (1891) 7 TLR 500.
6   *Edwards v Fox & Son* (1896) 60 JP Jo 404, CA.

934.   Goods must be in trader's possession.   The trade in question, as well as being a public trade[1], must be carried on on premises either regularly or temporarily occupied by the trader, and must not be on premises occupied by the owner of the goods. Goods sent to an auctioneer to be sold on premises temporarily hired for the auction are privileged[2], while those to be sold on the owner's premises are not[3]. The goods may be deposited by the trader in a public warehouse or store kept for depositing goods without losing the privilege[4]. They must, however, be in the trader's possession for the actual purpose of his trade. The privilege was held not to extend to boats brought to salt works (where salt was publicly sold) and left in cuts or canals to be loaded with the salt sold[5]; nor does the privilege extend to machinery delivered with materials for the exercise of the trade (although the tools of trade are conditionally privileged[6]), or to the implements of storage or conveyance[7].

1   See para 933 ante.
2   *Brown v Arundell* (1850) 10 CB 54. See also *Adams v Grane* (1833) 1 Cr & M 380; and *Williams v Holmes* (1853) 8 Exch 861.
3   *Lyons v Elliott* (1876) 1 QBD 210. See also AUCTION vol 2(3) (Reissue) para 231.
4   *Matthias v Mesnard* (1826) 2 C & P 353; *Farrant v Robson* (1834) 3 LJCP 146.
5   *Muspratt v Gregory* (1838) 3 M & W 677, Ex Ch.
6   *Wood v Clarke* (1831) 1 Cr & J 484; and see para 949 post.
7   *Joule v Jackson* (1841) 7 M & W 450 (brewers' casks sent to a publican with beer to remain on the premises until the beer was consumed); *Muspratt v Gregory* (1838) 3 M & W 677, Ex Ch.

935.   Trade privilege: exercise of trade on goods.   The goods must be put into the trader's hands so that he may exercise his trade upon them. Work and skill need not be bestowed upon the goods sent, if the trade in question does not involve such work and skill, and mere storage, whether for sale or otherwise, is enough if the storage or sale constitutes the trade in question, but goods sent to a trader who merely stores them instead of exercising his regular trade upon them are not exempt from distress[1]. The word 'managed' in the exception previously stated[2] must be taken in a wide sense so as to include, if not to be equivalent to, 'disposed of'[3]. Sample articles sent to an agent for exhibition purposes only are not privileged[4].

1   Eg wine in cask or bottle deposited for storage in a wine-warehouseman's cellar is not, whereas wine sent to be bottled is, privileged: *Re Russell, ex p Russell*, (1870) 18 WR 753. The question in these cases is whether the goods are placed in the hands of the tenant merely with the intent that they are to remain upon the premises or with the view of having labour and skill bestowed upon them: *Parsons v Gingell* (1847) 4 CB 545 at 558 per Wilde CJ. However, this dictum is dissented from in *Miles v Furber* (1873) LR 8 QB 77.
2   See para 632 ante.
3   *Challoner v Robinson* [1908] 1 Ch 49, CA.
4   *Simms Manufacturing Co v Whitehead* [1909] WN 95. See also AGENCY vol 2(1) (Reissue) para 176.

936.   Examples of goods subject to trade privilege.   Examples of goods held to be privileged[1] are: cloth left at a clothworker's to be woven and while waiting to be weighed at a neighbouring house[2]; cattle pastured for one night on the way to market[3]; goods in the hands of a carrier for the purpose of carriage[4]; goods sent to a factor for sale[5], or deposited by a factor at a wharfinger's warehouse[6], and goods sent to a wharfinger direct[7]; corn sent to a factor for sale and deposited by him in the warehouse of a granary keeper[8]; goods sent to a commission agent to be exposed for sale or sold[9]; carcasses of beasts which had been sent to a butcher to be slaughtered[10]; goods pledged with a pawnbroker for money advanced[11]; and furniture sent to a depository to be warehoused for hire[12]. Horses and carriages standing at livery have been held distrainable[13].

Where goods are privileged from distress, the instruments or vehicles used for their conveyance are equally privileged[14].

1   Ie privileged from distress for rent: see para 932 ante.
2   *Read v Burley* (1597) Cro Eliz 549, 596.
3   *Tate v Gleed* (1784) 2 Wms Saund 290a, note (q); *Nugent v Kirwan* (1838) 1 Jebb & S 97.
4   *Gisbourn v Hurst* (1710) 1 Salk 249.
5   *Gilman v Elton* (1821) 3 Brod & Bing 75.
6   *Thompson v Mashiter* (1823) 1 Bing 283.
7   *Thompson v Mashiter* (1823) 1 Bing 283 at 285 per Dallas CJ.
8   *Matthias v Mesnard* (1826) 2 C & P 353.
9   *Findon v M'Laren* (1845) 6 QB 891.
10 *Brown v Shevill* (1834) 2 Ad & El 138.
11 *Swire v Leach* (1865) 18 CBNS 479.
12 *Miles v Furber* (1873) LR 8 QB 77.
13 *Francis v Wyatt* (1764) 3 Burr 1498; *Parsons v Gingell* (1847) 4 CB 545. As to this latter case see, however, *Miles v Furber* (1873) LR 8 QB 77. A landlord can distrain horses in a stable let by a tenant to an innkeeper during races: see *Crosier v Tomkinson* (1759) 2 Keny 439.
14 *Muspratt v Gregory* (1836) 1 M & W 633 at 647 (on appeal (1838) 3 M & W 677, Ex Ch); *Wood v Clarke* (1831) 1 Cr & J 484 at 498.

937.   Fixtures. Whatever is part of, or annexed or affixed to, the freehold cannot be distrained, such as kilns, furnaces, cauldrons, windows, shutters, doors, chimney-pieces, anvils in a forge, and the like[1]. No fixtures (so long as they continue such) are distrainable whether those fixtures are irremovable or fixtures severable by a tenant[2]. Whether an article, such as a machine, is a parcel of the freehold, is a question of fact, depending on the circumstances of each case and principally on two considerations: (1) the mode of annexation to the soil or fabric of the house, whether it can easily be removed intact or not, without injury to itself or the fabric of the building; and (2) the purpose of annexation, whether it was for the permanent and substantial improvement of the dwelling or merely for a temporary purpose and the more complete enjoyment of it as a chattel[3]. In any event things cannot be distrained which cannot be restored in the same state in which they were before the distress[4] and if, under a distress, fixtures are wrongfully removed from the freehold so as to be treated as chattels, a claim for conversion will lie at the instance of the tenant[5]. A temporary removal, for example for repair of a fixture, such as an anvil in a smith's shop or a millstone, does not destroy this privilege[6].

1   Co Litt 47b; *Simpson v Hartopp* (1744) Willes 512 at 515, 1 Smith LC (13th Edn) 494; *Pitt v Shew* (1821) 4 B & Ald 206. As to fixtures see LANDLORD AND TENANT vol 27(1) (2006 Reissue) para 172 et seq. See also *Niblet v Smith* (1792) 4 Term Rep 504.
2   *Crossley Bros Ltd v Lee* [1908] 1 KB 86, DC. See also *Provincial Bill Posting Co v Low Moor Iron Co* [1909] 2 KB 344, CA (advertisement hoardings).
3   *Hellawell v Eastwood* (1851) 6 Exch 295 at 312 per Parke B. This statement, as distinct from the decision on the actual facts of the case, has been approved in several subsequent cases: see e g *Holland v Hodgson* (1872) LR 7 CP 328 at 336–337, Ex Ch; *Spyer v Phillipson* [1931] 2 Ch 183 at 194 per Luxmoore J (on appeal [1931] 2 Ch 183 at 209–210, CA, per Romer LJ), where the two considerations stated in *Hellawell v Eastwood* supra were said to be really one, namely what was the object and purpose of the annexation, the mode of annexation and consequences of severance being matters to be considered in determining the object and purpose. The actual decision in *Hellawell v Eastwood* supra was not followed in *Crossley Bros Ltd v Lee* [1908] 1 KB 86, DC; *Walmesley v Milne* (1859) 29 LJCP 97; *Climie v Wood* (1868) LR 3 Exch 257; *Longbottom v Berry* (1869) LR 5 QB 123; *Holland v Hodgson* supra; *Hobson v Gorringe* [1897] 1 Ch 182, CA; *Reynolds v Ashby & Son* [1904] AC 466, HL. A shop counter is not affixed for a 'temporary purpose', but an anchor dropped, or a carpet tacked to a floor, is distrainable: see *Holland v Hodgson* supra at 337. A 'railway' for the better enjoyment of a colliery is not distrainable: see *Turner v Cameron* (1870) LR 5 QB 306.
4   *Darby v Harris* (1841) 1 QB 895 (kitchen ranges, stoves, grates and coppers).
5   *Dalton v Whittem* (1842) 3 QB 961. As to conversion see TORT vol 45(2) (Reissue) para 548 et seq.
6   *Gorton v Falkner* (1792) 4 Term Rep 565 at 567 per Lord Kenyon CJ.

938. Things in use. Whatever is in a man's present use or occupation is for that time privileged from distress, such as a horse when being ridden, or an axe being used for cutting wood, or a net in a man's hand[1]. This privilege extends to a horse drawing a cart and to the harness[2], to wearing apparel actually being worn[3] and to a limited extent to wearing apparel not being worn[4]. In the case of animals, such as a dog, actual manual possession and use is necessary[5].

1   Co Litt 47a; *Read v Burley* (1597) Cro Eliz 549. If this rule did not exist there would be a perpetual liability to a breach of the peace: see *Storey v Robinson* (1795) 6 Term Rep 138. A stocking frame being used by a weaver has been held privileged: *Simpson v Hartopp* (1744) Willes 512 at 517, 1 Smith LC (13th Edn) 494.

2   *Field v Adames* (1840) 12 Ad & El 649.

3   *Bisset v Caldwell* (1791) Peake 50; *Baynes v Smith* (1794) 1 Esp 206. At common law wearing apparel can be distrained, although merely taken off for the purposes of repose.

4   See para 942 post.

5   *Bunch v Kennington* (1841) 1 QB 679.

939. Perishable articles. Things of a perishable nature, or things that cannot be restored in the same state and condition as they were in before being taken or must necessarily be damaged by removal or severance, are exempt from distress[1]. It has been considered that the flesh of animals lately slaughtered cannot, therefore, be distrained[2], nor can milk, fruit or things of a similar nature[3]. However, a cart loaded with corn is not within this rule[4].

1   1 Roll Abr, Distress (H); Bac Abr, Distress (B); Co Litt 47a; *Simpson v Hartopp* (1744) Willes 512, 1 Smith LC (13th Edn) 494. It is on this principle that cocks and sheaves of corn were formerly held not distrainable: see para 929 text and note 6 ante.

2   *Morley v Pincombe* (1848) 2 Exch 101 (carcasses of pigs).

3   3 Bl Com (14th Edn) 9; Bullen *Law of Distress for Rent* (2nd Edn) 103. In Bullen *Law of Distress for Rent* (2nd Edn) 104, grain or flour out of a sack is also instanced.

4   3 Bl Com (14th Edn) 10; Co Litt 47a.

940. Money. Money is not distrainable unless it is in a bag or in such a closed or sealed receptacle that it can be identified[1].

1   Bac Abr, Distress (B). The reason of this rule is to be found in the original law when distress was merely a form of pledge. See also *Wilson v Ducket* (1675) 2 Mod Rep 61.

941. Animals. Animals ferae naturae in which there is no right of property are exempt from distress[1]. Deer, however, may become valuable property by being kept in an inclosed ground or for purposes of profit, so that they can be considered the goods of the tenant[2]. Dogs are now considered to be liable to distress[3], as well as animals kept in cages[4]. Special privilege attaches in certain cases to livestock and farming animals[5].

1   Co Litt 47a; 3 Bl Com (14th Edn) 7–8. For the cases in which there may be a qualified property in animals ferae naturae see ANIMALS vol 2(1) (Reissue) para 510 et seq.

2   *Davies v Powell* (1738) Willes 46; *Morgan v Earl of Abergavenny* (1849) 8 CB 768 (where deer in a park were considered to be reclaimed and to be no longer ferae naturae). See also *Ford v Tynte* (1861) 2 John & H 150.

3   They are included in the exemptions in Co Litt 47a but the modern opinion is that this exemption is no longer the law: see the discussion on this point in the notes to *Simpson v Hartopp* (1744) Willes 512, 1 Smith LC (13th Edn) 494; and see *Bunch v Kennington* (1841) 1 QB 679. As to dogs in actual use see para 938 ante.

4   As to captive animals see ANIMALS vol 2(1) (Reissue) para 512.

5   See AGRICULTURE vol 1(2) (Reissue) paras 334–335. As to agisted animals see para 1042 post; and ANIMALS vol 2(1) (Reissue) paras 521–523, 632.

942. Wearing apparel etc. By statute[1] there are exempted from distress: (1) such tools, books, vehicles and other items of equipment as are necessary to the tenant for use personally by him in his employment, business or vocation; and (2) such clothing, bedding, furniture, household equipment and provisions as are necessary for satisfying the basic domestic needs of the tenant and his family[2]. This does not apply where the lease, term or interest of the tenant has expired and possession of the premises in respect of which the rent is claimed has been demanded, and the distress is made not earlier than seven days after the demand[3]. Where in spite of this statute such goods and chattels have been taken under a distress, a magistrates' court may on complaint direct their restoration and, if they have been sold, may order the person who levied or directed the levy to pay to the complainant such sum as the court may determine to be their value[4].

Bedding includes whatever is used for the purposes of sleeping accommodation, such as a bedstead or a mattress[5].

If an implement of trade, such as a sewing machine, is hired by a husband for the use of his wife, and the wife uses it and devotes her earnings to the support of the household and family, the hirer is held to carry on a trade by the hands of his wife, so as to privilege the implement from distress; the fact that the implement is hired and not the tenant's property is for this purpose immaterial[6]. A cab used by a driver is an implement of trade[7], as is a piano used by a music teacher for teaching[8] and the records, tapes and discs of a presenter of musical programmes[9], but a typewriter used as a sample by a commercial traveller is not[10].

1   At common law wearing apparel, unless in actual use (see *Bisset v Caldwell* (1791) Peake 50; *Baynes v Smith* (1794) 1 Esp 206), and bedding are distrainable. At common law tools are only conditionally privileged: see para 949 post.
2   See the Law of Distress Amendment Act 1888 s 4 (amended by the Statute Law Revision Act 1908); and the County Courts Act 1984 s 89(1)(a) (substituted by the Courts and Legal Services Act 1990 s 15(2)). See also *Boyd Ltd v Bilham* [1909] 1 KB 14.
3   Law of Distress Amendment Act 1888 s 4 proviso. The terms of this proviso are apparently cumulative.
4   See the Law of Distress Amendment Act 1895 s 4; and para 1100 post.
5   *Davis v Harris* [1900] 1 QB 729.
6   *Churchward v Johnson* (1889) 54 JP 326; *Masters v Fraser* (1901) 85 LT 611 at 613 per Lord Alverstone CJ (any lawful possession is sufficient).
7   *Lavell v Richings* [1906] 1 KB 480.
8   *Boyd Ltd v Bilham* [1909] 1 KB 14.
9   *Brookes v Harris* [1995] 1 WLR 918
10   *Addison v Shepherd* [1908] 2 KB 118. Apparently an implement is something to be used for actual work, and not merely to be shown for trade.

943.   Agricultural machinery and breeding stock. Agricultural or other machinery and breeding stock on an agricultural holding are subject to special statutory privilege provided they are the property of a person other than the tenant[1].

1   See AGRICULTURE vol 1(2) (Reissue) paras 334–335. As to other limitations on distress in relation to crops, livestock and farming animals see paras 929 ante, 989, 1042 post; and AGRICULTURE vol 1(2) (Reissue) paras 334–335; ANIMALS vol 2(1) (Reissue) para 632.

944.   Railway rolling stock. Railway rolling stock being in a 'work' is not liable to be distrained for rent payable by a tenant of the work, unless the rolling stock is the tenant's actual property, provided that the ownership of the rolling stock is sufficiently indicated by a metal plate or other distinguishing mark conspicuously affixed[1]. This protection does not, however, extend to a tenant's interest in the stock, which is liable to distress as if the tenant had possessed the whole interest[2]. 'Work' is defined as including any colliery, quarry, mine, manufactory, warehouse, wharf, pier or jetty in or on which is any railway siding, and includes an engine shed on a siding connected with a railway[3]. 'Rolling stock' includes wagons, trucks, carriages of all kinds and locomotive engines used on railways[4].

1 Railway Rolling Stock Protection Act 1872 s 3. A magistrates' court may make against the landlord such summary order for the restoration of rolling stock distrained or for payment of its real value and in respect of costs or otherwise, and may make such an order in the matter, and in respect of costs, against the person distraining, as seems to it just: s 4. If any party thinks himself aggrieved by any order or adjudication of a court of summary jurisdiction under the Railway Rolling Stock Protection Act 1872, or by dismissal of his complaint by any such court, he may appeal to the Crown Court: s 6 (amended by the Courts Act 1971 s 56(2), Sch 9 Pt I). See now also the Supreme Court Act 1981 (prospectively renamed the Senior Courts Act 1981) ss 1(1), 8, 45, 46, 48 (s 1(1) prospectively amended, ss 8, 48 as amended); and COURTS. 'Person' includes a body corporate: Railway Rolling Stock Protection Act 1872 s 2.

2 Ibid s 5. In case of disagreement between the landlord and the parties claiming the rolling stock as to the mode of disposing of the tenant's interest, the disagreement is to be settled by the magistrates' court, and the court may, on the application of either party, make such order as it thinks fit: s 5. There is an appeal to the Crown Court: see s 6 (as amended); and note 1 supra. 'Tenant' includes a lessee, sublessee or other person having an interest in a work under a lease or agreement, or by use and occupation, or being otherwise liable to pay any rent in respect of a work: s 2. 'Rent' includes a royalty or other reservation in the nature of rent: s 2.

3 Ibid s 2; and see *Easton Estate and Mining Co v Western Waggon and Property Co* (1886) 54 LT 735, DC (where the definition clause was held not to be exhaustive of the word 'work').

4 Railway Rolling Stock Protection Act 1872 s 2. In *Easton Estate and Mining Co v Western Waggon and Property Co* (1886) 54 LT 735, DC, the magistrates found as a fact that the engine was in use on a branch line of the railway.

945. Gas fittings. Any gas meter which is connected to a service pipe, and any gas fitting in a consumer's premises which is owned by a gas transporter[1] or gas supplier and is marked or impressed with a sufficient mark or brand indicating its owner is not subject to distress or liable to be taken in execution under process of any court or any proceedings in bankruptcy against the person in whose possession it may be[2]. 'Gas fittings' means gas pipes and meters, and fittings, apparatus and appliances designed for use by consumers of gas for heating, lighting, motive power and other purposes for which gas can be used[3].

1 For the meaning of 'gas transporter' see FUEL AND ENERGY vol 19(1) (Reissue) paras 584–586.

2 Gas Act 1986 s 8B, Sch 2B para 29 (s 8B, Sch 2B both added by the Gas Act 1995 s 9, Sch 2; and the Gas Act 1986 Sch 2B para 29 amended by the Utilities Act 2000 s 108, Sch 6 paras 1, 2(1)). See further FUEL AND ENERGY.

3 Gas Act 1986 s 48(1).

946. Water fittings. Water fittings let for hire by a water undertaker[1] and bearing either a distinguishing metal plate affixed to them or a distinguishing brand or other mark conspicuously impressed or made on them, sufficiently indicating the undertakers as the actual owners of the fittings, are not subject to distress[2]. 'Water fittings' includes pipes (other than water mains), taps, cocks, valves, ferrules, meters, cisterns, baths, water closets, soil pans and other similar apparatus used in connection with the supply and use of water[3].

1 See WATER vol 49(2) (2004 Reissue) para 299 et seq.

2 See the Water Industry Act 1991 s 179(4), (7); and WATER vol 49(3) (2004 Reissue) para 524 et seq.

3 Ibid ss 93(1), 179(7).

947. Electricity fittings. Any electric line, electrical plant or electricity meter belonging to or provided by an electricity distributor[1] or electricity supplier[2] which is marked or impressed with a sufficient mark or brand indicating a supplier or distributor as the owner or provider of it is not, in England and Wales, subject to distress[3].

'Electric line' means any line which is used for carrying electricity for any purpose and includes, unless the context otherwise requires any support for any such line, that is to say, any structure, pole or other thing in, on, by or from which any such line is or may be supported, carried or suspended, any apparatus connected to any such line for the purpose of carrying electricity, and any wire, cable, tube, pipe or other similar thing (including its casing or coating) which surrounds or supports, or is surrounded or supported by, or is installed in close proximity to, or is supported, carried or suspended in association with, any such line[4]. 'Electrical plant' means any plant, equipment, apparatus or appliance used for, or for purposes connected with, the generation, transmission, distribution or supply of electricity, other than an electric line, a meter used for ascertaining the quantity of electricity supplied to any premises, or an electrical appliance under the control of a consumer[5].

1   'Electricity distributor' means any person who is authorised by a distribution licence to distribute electricity except where he is acting otherwise than for purposes connected with the carrying on of activities authorised by the licence; and 'electricity supplier' means any person who is authorised by a supply licence to supply electricity except where he is acting otherwise than for purposes connected with the carrying on of activities authorised by the licence: see the Electricity Act 1989 s 6(9) (substituted by the Utilities Act 2000 s 30); and the Electricity Act 1989 s 64(1) (definitions added by the Utilities Act 2000 s 108, Sch 6 paras 24, 38(1), (4)). See also FUEL AND ENERGY vol 19(2) (Reissue) para 874.
2   See note 1 supra.
3   See the Electricity Act 1989 s 24, Sch 6 para 11 (s 24 amended by the Utilities Act 2000 s 51(1); and the Electricity Act 1989 Sch 6 substituted by the Utilities Act 2000 s 51(2), Sch 4); and FUEL AND ENERGY vol 19(1) (Reissue) para 910.
4   Electricity Act 1989 s 64(1).
5   Ibid s 64(1) (definition amended by the Utilities Act 2000 s 108, Sch 6 paras 24, 38(1), (3)).

(iii)   Things Conditionally Privileged

948.   In general. In certain cases goods can be distrained only if there is no other sufficient distress upon the premises[1]. These include agisted animals[2], beasts of the plough and sheep[3], growing crops which have been seized in execution[4] and instruments of trade[5]. The presence of goods of a third party does not bar distress even if those goods are not protected by privilege[6]. In claims for wrongful distress brought at common law it has been held that the onus of proof that no other sufficient distress can be found lies on the distrainor[7]. Where on a fair estimate of the goods on the premises the distrainor bona fide believed that the distress would not be satisfied without taking goods conditionally privileged, no action will lie against the distrainor for distraining on them, even if ultimately it is shown that the remaining goods would have been sufficient in value to satisfy the landlord's claim, for the circumstances of the distress at the time it is made constitute the test, and no rule exists that if the distrainor in such a case acts bona fide and reasonably the other goods must be disposed of before those conditionally privileged are sold[8]. A landlord can also seize goods conditionally privileged, if there is other sufficient distress on the premises (such as growing crops) which is not immediately available[9]. If insufficient distress is at first seized, the tenant may be subjected to a second seizure[10].

1   *Simpson v Hartopp* (1744) Willes 512, 1 Smith LC (13th Edn) 494; *Muspratt v Gregory* (1838) 3 M & W 677, Ex Ch; *Lyons v Elliott* (1876) 1 QBD 210 at 215 per Lush J.
2   See the Agricultural Holdings Act 1986 s 18(2); para 1042 post; and AGRICULTURE vol 1(2) (Reissue) paras 334–335; ANIMALS vol 2(1) (Reissue) para 632.
3   See AGRICULTURE vol 1(2) (Reissue) paras 334–335. See also *Swaffer v Mulcahy* [1934] 1 KB 608 (privilege not applicable to distress for tithe rentcharge). As to animals generally see para 941 ante. For certain cases in which breeding stock and farming animals are absolutely privileged from distress see para 1042 post; and AGRICULTURE vol 1(2) (Reissue) paras 334–335.
4   See para 1043 post.
5   See para 949 post.
6   *Roberts v Jackson* (1795) Peake Add Cas 36.
7   *Nargett v Nias* (1859) 1 E & E 439. However, compare *Gonsky v Durrell* [1918] 2 KB 71, CA (a case brought under the Law of Distress Amendment Act 1888), in which the Court of Appeal held that where a claim was brought under that Act the onus was on the plaintiff and Scrutton LJ doubted if *Nargett v Nias* supra was correctly decided.

8   See *Jenner v Yolland* (1818) 6 Price 3 (a decision on the statutory privilege of beasts of the plough).
9   *Piggott v Birtles* (1836) 1 M & W 441.
10 *Hutchins v Chambers* (1758) 1 Burr 579. See para 1060 post.

949.   Tools of trade or husbandry.   At common law, the tools and instruments of
a person's trade or profession and instruments of husbandry (if they are not in actual
use)[1] are distrainable only if there are not other goods on the premises sufficient to
countervail the arrears of rent[2]. The axe of a carpenter, the books of a scholar, the
kneading-trough of a baker, the stocking-frame or loom of a weaver and even the cab of
a cabdriver have been held to be within this rule[3]. It is doubtful whether ledgers,
day-books and papers of a business or professional person fall within the exemption[4].

1   See para 938 ante. As to the statutory privilege of agricultural machinery hired by a tenant see
    AGRICULTURE vol 1(2) (Reissue) para 334.
2   Co Litt 47a; 3 Bl Com (14th Edn) 8–9; *Simpson v Hartopp* (1744) Willes 512, 1 Smith LC (13th Edn)
    494; *Gorton v Falkner* (1792) 4 Term Rep 565; *Roberts v Jackson* (1795) Peake Add Cas 36. In addition to
    conditional exemption at common law, protection may also be given by statute under the Law of Distress
    Amendment Act 1888 s 4 (as amended): see para 942 ante. As to other distress on the premises see
    para 948 ante.
3   See Gilbert on Distress and Replevin (4th Edn) 33; *Lavell v Richings* [1906] 1 KB 480; and other
    authorities, relating to the Law of Distress Amendment Act 1888, cited in para 942 ante. See also *Fenton
    v Logan* (1833) 9 Bing 676 (no evidence of other goods); *Nargett v Nias* (1859) 1 E & E 439 (farm
    labourer's spade and fork); *Davies v Aston* (1845) 1 CB 746 at 749 (household goods).
4   *Gauntlett v King* (1857) 3 CBNS 59.

(iv)   Goods of Undertenants, Lodgers and Strangers

950.   Exceptions to common law rule.   The common law rule that a landlord
could distrain for rent on all goods on the demised premises, even though not the
property of the tenant[1], is subject to many qualifications. As already mentioned,
exceptions have been grafted on to the rule in the interests of trade, husbandry and
public convenience[2], and, further, a landlord may by his own act or conduct be estopped
from setting up a right to seize the property of a third person. Thus a landlord cannot
distrain on the goods of a third person brought on the demised premises by the landlord
himself[3] or with his consent[4], and by his conduct he may be held to have waived[5] his
right of distress on a stranger's goods, an agreement not to distrain being implied from
the circumstances where necessary[6].

When a stranger's goods (even those of a lodger or subtenant), which are lawfully on
the premises, are lawfully distrained by the landlord for rent due from someone else, the
owner of the goods is entitled to be reimbursed their value from the person from whom
the rent was due[7].

1   See para 928 ante.
2   See para 930 et seq ante. As to goods bailed to a tenant on hire purchase see para 955 post.
3   *Paton v Carter* (1883) Cab & El 183.
4   *Fowkes v Joyce* (1689) 2 Vern 129.
5   *Welsh v Rose* (1830) 6 Bing 638 (conditional agreement not to distrain). See also para 978 post.
6   *Horsford v Webster* (1835) 1 Cr M & R 696; *Giles v Spencer* (1857) 3 CBNS 244. It was held, in *Cresswell
    v Jeffreys* (1912) 28 TLR 413 (revsd on another point 29 TLR 90, CA), that a statement by the landlord's
    agent, to the effect that in the particular circumstances distraint was not possible, did not constitute an
    estoppel against the landlord; but it is doubtful whether this decision can be relied on as, generally, a
    representation by an authorised agent is as effectual for the purposes of estoppel as if it had been made by
    his principal.
7   3 Bl Com (14th Edn) 8; *Exall v Partridge* (1799) 8 Term Rep 308. See also *Edmunds v Wallingford* (1885)
    14 QBD 811 at 814, CA; *Re Button, ex p Haviside* [1907] 2 KB 180, CA. See also RESTITUTION.

951.   Statutory protection.   By statute[1] an additional measure of protection has
been given to certain undertenants[2], and to lodgers[3], and to any other person not being

a tenant[4] of the premises or of any part of them, and not having any beneficial interest in any tenancy of the premises or of any part of them[5].

1 See the Law of Distress Amendment Act 1908 s 1 (as amended); and paras 952, 956–957 post. See generally *Rhodes v Allied Dunbar Pension Services Ltd, Re Offshore Ventilation Ltd* [1989] 1 All ER 1161 at 1163–1165, [1989] 1 WLR 800 at 803–805, CA, per Nicholls LJ. Provisions similar to those contained in the Law of Distress Amendment Act 1908 ss 1, 2 (as originally enacted) (see para 959 post) were contained in the Lodgers' Goods Protection Act 1871 but restricted to lodgers only. The Lodgers' Goods Protection Act 1871 was repealed, 'wherever and so far as this Act applies' by the Law of Distress Amendment Act 1908 s 8. The exact effect of this repeal is not obvious but, in as much as the provisions of the two Acts in regard to lodgers are almost identical, it is thought unnecessary to state those of the Lodgers' Goods Protection Act 1871, and the cases decided under the earlier Act are treated as authorities for the interpretation of the later Act.
2 See the Law of Distress Amendment Act 1908 s 1(a); and para 952 post. 'Undertenant' does not include a lodger: s 9.
3 Ibid s 1(b). As to lodgers see para 953 post.
4 'Tenant' does not include a lodger: ibid s 9.
5 Ibid s 1(c). See also *Cunliffe Engineering Ltd v English Industrial Estates Corpn* [1994] BCC 972 (bank with charge over tenant's chattels not within the scope of the Law of Distress Amendment Act 1908 s 1 (as amended)).

952.   Undertenants.   For an undertenant[1] to be within the protection of the Law of Distress Amendment Act 1908 he must be liable to pay, by equal instalments not less often than every actual or customary quarter of a year, a rent which would return in any whole year the full annual value of the premises or the part of them comprised in the undertenancy[2]. However, the protection does not extend to an undertenancy created in breach of any covenant or agreement in writing between the landlord and his immediate tenant[3]; nor does it extend to an undertenancy created under a lease existing at the date of the passing of the Act contrary to the landlord's wish in that behalf, where that wish has been expressed in writing and delivered at the premises within a reasonable time after the circumstances have come, or with due diligence would have come, to his knowledge[4]. 'Rent' means a sum of money actually agreed to be paid as between the tenant and undertenant. Thus it does not include the contingent profit or advantage which the tenant may acquire from boarding with the undertenant[5].

1 As to the meaning of 'undertenant' see para 951 note 2 ante.
2 Law of Distress Amendment Act 1908 s 1(a).
3 As to the meaning of 'tenant' see para 951 note 4 ante.
4 Law of Distress Amendment Act 1908 s 5. The date of the passing of the Law of Distress Amendment Act 1908 was 21 December 1908, although it did not come into operation until 1 July 1909.
5 *Parsons v Hambridge* (1916) 33 TLR 117; revsd on appeal (1917) 33 TLR 346, CA, on the ground that there was no evidence that the full annual value was being paid as rent in accordance with the Law of Distress Amendment Act 1908 s 1(a).

953.   Lodgers.   The Law of Distress Amendment Act 1908 does not define the term 'lodger', but it is not included in the terms 'tenant' and 'undertenant'[1], and the word is probably used in its popular meaning. The onus of proving that an individual is within the statute lies on the person claiming protection as a lodger[2]. Whether the claimant is a lodger is a question of fact[3]. A lodger may be an undertenant at the same time[4]. The immediate tenant must retain power and dominion over the house; the lodger may have the exclusive right to the rooms he occupies and uncontrolled right of ingress and egress, but the person letting must have a right to interfere with the general control of the house[5]. The lodger may occupy a very substantial part, but, it seems, not the whole of the house[6]. In general, if the immediate tenant or his agent lives on the premises and manages them himself, or has a servant resident on the premises who manages them on his behalf, the presumption is that the other residents are lodgers, while if he does not so reside, the presumption is that the persons to whom he lets are tenants, but the presumption is not conclusive[7]. The lodger must sleep on the premises to come within the protection of the statute, so that mere occupation of premises for business purposes in the daytime is insufficient[8].

1 As to the meaning of 'tenant' see para 951 note 4 ante; and as to the meaning of 'undertenant' see para 951 note 2 ante.

2 *Morton v Palmer* (1881) 51 LJQB 7, CA. See also *Thwaites v Wilding* (1883) 12 QBD 4 at 7, CA, per Bowen LJ; and see *Bensing v Ramsay* (1898) 62 JP 613. As to the interest and rights of a lodger see LANDLORD AND TENANT vol 27(1) (2006 Reissue) para 16.

3 *Morton v Palmer* (1881) 51 LJQB 7 at 9, CA, per Brett LJ, and at 11 per Lindley LJ. The question of the exact dominion or control of the landlord is one of fact: *Ness v Stephenson* (1882) 9 QBD 245 at 249 per Field J.

4 *Phillips v Henson* (1877) 3 CPD 26.

5 *Toms v Luckett* (1847) 5 CB 23 at 38 per Maule J; *Bradley v Baylis* (1881) 8 QBD 195 at 219, CA, per Jessel MR; *Kent v Fittall* [1906] 1 KB 60 at 70, CA, per Collins MR, and at 76 per Romer LJ (electoral registration cases); *Morton v Palmer* (1881) 51 LJQB 7, CA; *Ness v Stephenson* (1882) 9 QBD 245. See also *Allan v Liverpool Overseers* (1874) LR 9 QB 180 at 191–192; *Noblett and Mansfield v Manley* [1952] SASR 155 at 157–158; and see *Street v Mountford* [1985] AC 809, [1985] 2 All ER 289, HL.

6 *Phillips v Henson* (1877) 3 CPD 26 at 32.

7 See *Honig v Redfern* [1949] 2 All ER 15 at 17, 47 LGR 447 at 449, DC, per Lord Goddard CJ (an aliens' registration case); and see *Bradley v Baylis* (1881) 8 QBD 195 at 220, 241, CA; *Kent v Fittall* [1906] 1 KB 60 at 70, CA, per Collins MR, and at 76 per Romer LJ (both electoral registration cases). See also *Morton v Palmer* (1881) 51 LJQB 7, CA; *Page v Vallis* (1903) 19 TLR 393.

8 *Heawood v Bone* (1884) 13 QBD 179.

954. Goods excluded from protection. The Law of Distress Amendment Act 1908 does not protect goods of the following categories:

(1) goods belonging to the husband or wife or civil partner of the tenant[1] whose rent is in arrear[2];

(2) goods comprised in a settlement made by the tenant[3];

(3) goods in the possession, order or disposition of the tenant by the consent and permission of the true owner under such circumstances that the tenant is the reputed owner of them[4];

(4) any agisted livestock[5] on land comprised in a tenancy to which the Agricultural Holdings Act 1986 applies[6];

(5) goods of a partner of the immediate tenant[7];

(6) goods (not being goods of a lodger[8]) upon premises where any trade or business is carried on in which both the immediate tenant and the undertenant[9] have an interest[10];

(7) goods (not being goods of a lodger) on premises used as offices or warehouses where the owner of the goods neglects for one calendar month after notice which must be given in a like manner as notice to quit to remove the goods and vacate the premises[11];

(8) goods belonging to and in the offices of any company or corporation on premises the immediate tenant whereof is a director or officer or in the employment of such company or corporation[12].

It is competent for two justices, upon hearing the parties, to determine whether any goods are in fact goods included in heads (5) to (8) above[13].

1 As to the meaning of 'tenant' see para 951 note 4 ante.

2 Law of Distress Amendment Act 1908 s 4(1) (amended by the Civil Partnership Act 2004 s 26(1), Sch 27 para 3). Goods let on hire purchase to the husband or wife of the tenant do not 'belong' to such husband or wife: *Shenstone & Co v Freeman* [1910] 2 KB 84, DC; *Rogers, Eungblut & Co v Martin* [1911] 1 KB 19, CA.

3 Law of Distress Amendment Act 1908 s 4(1) (amended by the Consumer Credit Act 1974 s 192(3)(b), Sch 5 Pt I).

4 Law of Distress Amendment Act 1908 s 4(1). See *Re Parker, ex p Turquand* (1885) 14 QBD 636, CA; *Chappell & Co Ltd v Harrison* (1910) 103 LT 594, DC; *Times Furnishings Co Ltd v Hutchings* [1938] 1 KB

775; *North General Wagon and Finance Co Ltd v Graham* [1950] 2 KB 7, [1950] 1 All ER 780, CA; *Moorgate Mercantile Co Ltd v Finch Read* [1962] 1 QB 701, [1962] 2 All ER 467, CA; *Perdana Properties Bhd v United Orient Leasing Co Sdn Bhd* [1982] 1 All ER 193, [1981] 1 WLR 1496, PC; *Cunliffe Engineering Ltd v English Industrial Estates Corpn* [1994] BCC 972; *Salford Van Hire (Contracts) Ltd v Bocholt Developments Ltd* [1996] RTR 103, [1995] 2 EGLR 50, CA. As to goods subject to hire purchase agreements see para 955 post.

    The Law of Distress Amendment Act 1908 s 4(1) (as amended) is not satisfied merely by showing that where a wife hires goods they are found on the premises where she is living with her husband: *Rogers, Eungblut & Co v Martin* [1911] 1 KB 19, CA (hire of piano). Where it is sought to exclude the doctrine of reputed ownership by evidence of usage, that usage must be strictly proved: *Salford Van Hire (Contracts) Ltd v Bocholt Developments Ltd* supra (hired vans not within reputed ownership of tenant); *Chappell & Co Ltd v Harrison* supra (usage alleged of letting pianos to lessees of theatres on hire purchase). Judicial notice will be taken of a usage of hotel keepers to hire the furniture of their hotels: *Re Parker, ex p Turquand* supra; and see CUSTOM AND USAGE vol 12(1) (Reissue) para 684.

5   Ie within the meaning of the Agricultural Holdings Act 1986 s 18(5): see AGRICULTURE vol 1(2) (Reissue) para 334.

6   Law of Distress Amendment Act 1908 s 4(1) (amended by the Agricultural Holdings Act 1986 s 100, Sch 14 para 4; and the Agricultural Tenancies Act 1995 s 40, Schedule para 2).

7   Law of Distress Amendment Act 1908 s 4(2)(a).

8   As to lodgers see para 953 ante.

9   As to the meaning of 'undertenant' see para 951 note 2 ante.

10   Law of Distress Amendment Act 1908 s 4(2)(b).

11   Ibid s 4(2)(c). As to notice to quit see LANDLORD AND TENANT vol 27(1) (2006 Reissue) para 213 et seq.

12   Ibid s 4(2)(d).

13   Ibid s 4(2) proviso (amended by the Access to Justice Act 1999 s 106, Sch 15 Pt V Table (3)). Compare the powers (see para 959 post) of a magistrate or magistrates after service of the declaration and inventory: presumably an ordinary civil claim is necessary to test questions arising under heads (1)–(4) in the text.

955. Hire purchase etc. Goods let to a hirer on hire purchase remain the property of the owner[1] but they are not thereby necessarily protected from distress[2]. Goods bailed under a hire purchase agreement[3] or a consumer hire agreement[4] or agreed to be sold under a conditional sale agreement[5] are, where the relevant agreement has not been terminated[6], excluded from the general protection to the goods of strangers given by the Law of Distress Amendment Act 1908[7], except during the period between the service of a default notice[8] in respect of the goods and the date when the notice expires or is earlier complied with[9]. Goods comprised in an agreement made by the tenant's husband or wife are not excluded from protection[10], but, if such an agreement is made by one of two joint tenants, the goods are excluded from protection[11].

    Goods comprised in a bill of sale are excluded from the general protection of the Law of Distress Amendment Act 1908 except during the period between service of a default notice[12] in respect of goods subject to a regulated agreement[13] under which a bill of sale is given by way of security and the date on which the notice expires or is earlier complied with[14].

    A creditor or owner is not entitled to enforce a term of a regulated agreement by recovering possession of any goods or treating any right conferred on the debtor or hirer as terminated, restricted or deferred except by or after giving the debtor or hirer not less than seven days' notice in a prescribed form of his intention to do so; similar notice is to be required of an intention to terminate a regulated agreement otherwise than on the ground of a breach by the debtor or hirer[15].

    Express provision is frequently made in hire purchase agreements for the automatic termination of the agreement if the landlord of the hirer levies or threatens to levy a distress. It seems that the operation of such a provision may be affected by the statutory restrictions on termination[16]. It has been held that at common law, even where an express provision for termination is made, the goods remain comprised in a hire purchase agreement if any contractual right or agreement still subsists after a purported termination[17]. Even if there is a termination, goods remaining in the possession of the hirer may be within the reputed ownership of the hirer and so liable to distress[18].

Goods let on hire purchase may be exempted from distress by express agreement between the owner and the landlord[19]. Goods let on hire purchase may be protected from distress under provisions relating to goods delivered for the purpose of a public trade[20], fixtures, goods in use[21], wearing apparel, bedding and tools of trade[22], agricultural machinery and breeding stock[23], gas fittings[24], water fittings[25] and electricity fittings[26].

1   See generally CONSUMER CREDIT vol 9(1) (Reissue) para 23 et seq.
2   Cf para 928 ante.
3   'Hire purchase agreement' means an agreement, other than a conditional sale agreement, under which: (1) goods are bailed in return for periodical payments by the person to whom they are bailed; and (2) the property in the goods will pass to that person if the terms of the agreement are complied with and one or more of the following occurs: (a) the exercise of an option to purchase by that person; (b) the doing of any other specified act by any party to the agreement; (c) the happening of any other specified event: Law of Distress Amendment Act 1908 s 4A(3) (s 4A added by the Consumer Credit Act 1974 s 192(3)(a), Sch 4 para 5); and see CONSUMER CREDIT vol 9(1) (Reissue) para 23 et seq.
4   A 'consumer hire agreement' is an agreement made by a person with an individual ('the hirer') for the bailment of goods to the hirer, being an agreement which: (1) is not a hire purchase agreement; (2) is capable of subsisting for more than three months; and (3) does not require the hirer to make payments exceeding £25,000: Consumer Credit Act 1974 s 15(1) (amended by the Consumer Credit (Increase of Monetary Limits) Order 1983, SI 1983/1874, art 4, Schedule Pt II; and the Consumer Credit (Increase of Monetary Limits) (Amendment) Order 1998, SI 1998/996, art 2); definition applied by the Law of Distress Amendment Act 1908 s 4A(3) (as added: see note 3 supra).The Consumer Credit Act 1974 s 15(1)(c) (as amended) (see head (3) supra) and the word 'and' preceding it are repealed by the Consumer Credit Act 2006 ss 2(2), 70, Sch 4 as from a day to be appointed under s 71(2). At the date at which this volume states the law no such day had been appointed. As to consumer hire agreements see CONSUMER CREDIT vol 9(1) (Reissue) para 82.
5   'Conditional sale agreement' means an agreement for the sale of goods under which the purchase price or part of it is payable by instalments, and the property in the goods is to remain in the seller (notwithstanding that the buyer is to be in possession of the goods) until such conditions as to the payment of instalments or otherwise as may be specified in the agreement are fulfilled: Law of Distress Amendment Act 1908 s 4A(3) (as added: see note 3 supra).
6   See the text and notes 15–17 infra.
7   See paras 951 ante, 956 et seq post.
8   See note 15 infra.
9   Law of Distress Amendment Act 1908 s 4A(1) (as added: see note 3 supra).
10   *Shenstone & Co v Freeman* [1910] 2 KB 84, DC; *Rogers, Eungblut & Co v Martin* [1911] 1 KB 19, CA.
11   *AW Gamage Ltd v Payne* (1925) 134 LT 222, DC.
12   Ie under the Consumer Credit Act 1974: see generally CONSUMER CREDIT.
13   'Regulated agreement' means a consumer credit agreement, or consumer hire agreement, other than an exempt agreement: ibid s 189(1); definition applied by the Law of Distress Amendment Act 1908 s 4A(3) (as added: see note 3 supra). See CONSUMER CREDIT vol 9(1) (Reissue) para 2.
14   Ibid s 4A(2) (as added: see note 3 supra). As to bills of sale generally see BILLS OF SALE.
15   See the Consumer Credit Act 1974 ss 76, 98; and CONSUMER CREDIT vol 9(1) (Reissue) paras 234, 262. As to default notices see ss 87–89 (s 88 as amended; prospectively amended); and CONSUMER CREDIT vol 9(1) (Reissue) para 263 et seq.
16   See the text and note 15 supra.
17   See e g *Hackney Furnishing Co v Watts* [1912] 3 KB 225, DC; *Jay's Furnishing Co v Brand & Co* [1915] 1 KB 458, CA; *Smart Bros Ltd v Holt* [1929] 2 KB 303; *Drages Ltd v Owen* (1935) 52 TLR 108; *Times Furnishing Co Ltd v Hutchings* [1938] 1 KB 775, [1938] 1 All ER. 422.
18   *Times Furnishing Co Ltd v Hutchings* [1938] 1 KB 775, [1938] 1 All ER 422; cf para 654 note 4 ante. See further CONSUMER CREDIT vol 9(1) (Reissue) paras 23–44.
19   See note 2 supra.
20   See paras 932–936 ante.
21   See paras 937–938 ante.
22   See para 942 ante.
23   See para 943 ante.
24   See para 945 ante.

25   See para 946 ante.
26   See para 947 ante.

956.   Declaration by person protected.   If any superior landlord[1] levies or authorises the levy of a distress on any furniture, goods or chattels of any person protected by the Law of Distress Amendment Act 1908[2] for arrears of rent due to the superior landlord by his immediate tenant[3], any person so protected may serve the superior landlord, or the bailiff or other agent employed by him to levy such distress, with a declaration in writing[4], setting forth that the immediate tenant has no right of property or beneficial interest in the furniture, goods or chattels so distrained or threatened to be distrained upon, and that the furniture, goods or chattels are the property or in the lawful possession of the person protected, and are not goods or livestock to which the Act is expressed not to apply[5]. If the person serving the declaration is an undertenant or lodger, he must also set forth the amount of rent, if any, then due to his immediate landlord, and the amount of future instalments of rent and times at which those instalments will become due; the declaration must also contain an undertaking to pay to the superior landlord any rent so due or to become due to his immediate landlord until the arrears of rent in respect of which the distress was levied or authorised to be levied have been paid off[6]. The declaration must comply strictly with the Act[7], but it need not, if no rent is due, in terms say so, and if a declaration does not state that any rent is due it will be read as stating that no rent is due[8]. In the case of a partnership it may be made by one partner with the authority of the other partners[9]. In the case of a company the declaration may be signed by a duly authorised agent of the company[10].

1   'Superior landlord' includes a landlord in cases where the goods in question are not those of an undertenant or lodger: Law of Distress Amendment Act 1908 s 9. As to the meaning of 'undertenant' see para 951 note 2 ante. As to lodgers see para 953 ante.
2   See paras 951–955 ante.
3   For the meaning of 'tenant' see para 951 note 4 ante.
4   A statutory declaration is not required: *Rogers, Eungblut & Co v Martin* [1911] 1 KB 19, CA.
5   Law of Distress Amendment Act 1908 s 1. Beneficial interest is not defined in the Act.
6   Ibid s 1.
7   *Druce & Co Ltd v Beaumont Property Trust Ltd* [1935] 2 KB 257.
8   *Ex p Harris* (1885) 16 QBD 130, CA.
9   *Rogers, Eungblut & Co v Martin* [1911] 1 KB 19, CA.
10 *Lawrence Chemical Co Ltd v Rubenstein* [1982] 1 All ER 653, [1982] 1 WLR 284, CA.

957.   Inventory to declaration.   To the declaration[1] must be annexed a correct inventory subscribed by the person so claiming protection of the furniture, goods or chattels referred to in the declaration[2], and if that person knowingly and wilfully makes a statement in such declaration or inventory which is false in a material particular he is guilty of an offence[3].

1   See para 956 ante.
2   Law of Distress Amendment Act 1908 s 1 (amended by the Perjury Act 1911 s 17, Schedule). Where a proper declaration was made and signed with a statement that 'the list of articles hereto annexed is a correct inventory', and the inventory was written on the same piece of paper, but not otherwise signed or subscribed, the inventory was held (under the Lodgers' Goods Protection Act 1871 (repealed) (see para 951 note 1 ante)) sufficiently subscribed within the Act: *Godlonton v Fulham and Hampstead Property Co* [1905] 1 KB 431.
3   See the Perjury Act 1911 s 5 (as amended); and CRIMINAL LAW, EVIDENCE AND PROCEDURE vol 11(2) (2006 Reissue) para 717.

958.   When declaration is to be made.   The declaration[1] must be subsequent to the seizure or threat of seizure, so that a declaration made in consequence of one distress is not available for a second distress, even if the facts in the declaration originally made are still correct at the time of the second distress[2]. The Law of Distress Amendment Act 1908[3] does not specify any time within which the declaration must be served, but if the landlord proceeds to sell within the five days mentioned in the Distress for Rent Act 1689[4], a claim will lie at the suit of the person protected by the Law of Distress Amendment Act 1908, although he has not served any declaration and inventory[5].

1 See para 956 ante.
2 *Thwaites v Wilding* (1883) 12 QBD 4, CA. The rights of the parties must be ascertained at the moment the distress is levied: *Thwaites v Wilding* supra at 7 per Bowen LJ.
3 See the Law of Distress Amendment Act 1908 s 1 (as amended); and paras 956–957 ante.
4 See the Distress for Rent Act 1689 s 1 (as amended); and paras 1044, 1049 post.
5 *Sharpe v Fowle* (1884) 12 QBD 385; and see *Fisher v Algar* (1826) 2 C & P 374.

959. Penalty for disregard of the Law of Distress Amendment Act 1908. If after being served with a declaration and inventory[1], and in the case of an undertenant[2] or lodger[3], after an undertaking has been given[4] and the rent, if any, then due has been paid or tendered in accordance with that undertaking, the superior landlord[5], or any bailiff or other agent levies or proceeds with a distress on the furniture, goods or chattels of any person protected by the Law of Distress Amendment Act 1908, he is deemed guilty of an illegal distress, and any person so protected may apply to a justice of the peace for an order for the restoration to him of the goods[6].

The hearing of the application must be before two justices who inquire into the truth of both the declaration and inventory and make such order for the recovery of the goods, or otherwise, as may be just[7], but the justices cannot award damages for illegal distress[8]. The superior landlord will also be liable in law at the suit of the person so protected[9], and so will the bailiff[10].

1 See paras 956–957 ante.
2 As to the meaning of 'undertenant' see para 951 note 2 ante.
3 As to lodgers see para 953 ante.
4 See para 956 text and note 6 ante.
5 As to the meaning of 'superior landlord' see para 956 note 1 ante.
6 Law of Distress Amendment Act 1908 s 2.
7 Ibid s 2 (amended by the Access to Justice Act 1999 s 78(2), Sch 11 para 11).
8 *Lowe v Dorling & Son* [1905] 2 KB 501 at 504 per Lord Alverstone CJ.
9 Law of Distress Amendment Act 1908 s 2. In the claim the truth of the declaration and inventory may be inquired into: s 2.
10 *Lowe v Dorling & Son* [1906] 2 KB 772, CA (Collins MR dissenting); and see also the judgment of Lord Alverstone CJ in the Divisional Court reported at [1905] 2 KB 501. It seems that *Page v Vallis* (1903) 19 TLR 393 must be regarded as overruled.

960. Procedure to avoid distress. Where the rent of the immediate tenant[1] of the superior landlord[2] is in arrear, the superior landlord may serve upon any undertenant[3] or lodger[4] a notice[5] stating the amount of such arrears of rent, and requiring all future payments of rent, whether already accrued due or not, by the undertenant or lodger to be made direct to the superior landlord, until such arrears have been duly paid[6]. The notice will operate to transfer to the superior landlord the right to recover, receive, and give a discharge for such rent[7]. The appointment of a receiver or manager of tenant's property by the debenture holder of a tenant does not prevent the landlord serving a notice on the subtenant to pay to the landlord rent owing to the tenant[8]. The superior landlord's right takes priority to the right of a rating authority to recover rates from the undertenant or lodger[9].

1 As to the meaning of 'tenant' see para 951 note 4 ante.
2 As to the meaning of 'superior landlord' see para 956 note 1 ante.
3 As to the meaning of 'undertenant' see para 951 note 2 ante.
4 As to lodgers see para 953 ante.

5   Ie by registered post or recorded delivery service addressed to the undertenant or lodger upon the
     premises: Law of Distress Amendment Act 1908 s 6; Recorded Delivery Service Act 1962 ss 1(1), 2(1). As
     the object of the provision is that the notice should come to the notice of the person for whom it was
     intended, personal service of the notice is sufficient: *Jarvis v Hemmings* [1912] 1 Ch 462. The provision for
     service by registered post or recorded delivery service merely enables the landlord to serve the notice
     effectively by that method: *Jarvis v Hemmings* supra.

6   Law of Distress Amendment Act 1908 s 6.

7   Ibid s 6. The marginal note to s 6 is 'to avoid distress', but there is no provision which prevents a landlord
     from distraining upon his immediate tenant after service of the notice; nor is any provision made for an
     undertenant or lodger to take proceedings corresponding to interpleader, if informed by the immediate
     tenant that the superior landlord's notice is in any way wrongful. The service of a notice under s 6 is not
     a 'taking of possession of any property' such as to require the leave of the court under the Reserve and
     Auxiliary Forces (Protection of Civil Interests) Act 1951 s 2(2)(a) (see ARMED FORCES vol 2(2) (Reissue)
     para 85), in a case where the immediate tenant is within the protection of that Act; nor is the actual
     receipt of rent from the subtenant in consequence of a notice such a 'taking of possession of any
     property': see *Wallrock v Equity and Law Life Assurance Society* [1942] 2 KB 82, [1942] 1 All ER 510, CA
     (a decision under the Courts (Emergency Powers) Act 1939 (repealed)). See further ARMED FORCES
     vol 2(2) (Reissue) para 81.

8   See *Rhodes v Allied Dunbar Pension Services Ltd, Re Offshore Ventilation Ltd* [1989] 1 All ER 1161, [1989]
     1 WLR 800, CA.

9   General Rate Act 1967 s 61(2) (saved by the General Rate Act 1967 and Related Provisions (Savings and
     Consequential Provision) Regulations 1990, 1990/777, reg 3(1), Sch 1).

961.   Payment to constitute rent.   For the purposes of the recovery of any sums
payable by an undertenant[1] or lodger[2] to a superior landlord[3] under a notice[4] or under
the undertaking[5], the undertenant or lodger is deemed to be the immediate tenant[6] of
the superior landlord, and the sums payable are deemed to be rent; but, where the
undertenant or lodger has, in pursuance of such a notice or undertaking, paid any sums
to the superior landlord, he may deduct that amount from any rent due, or which may
become due from him to his immediate landlord, and any person (other than the tenant
for whose rent the distress is levied or authorised to be levied) from whose rent a
deduction has been made in respect of such payment may make the like deductions from
any rent due or which may become due from him to his immediate landlord[7].

1   As to the meaning of 'undertenant' see para 951 note 2 ante.
2   As to lodgers see para 953 ante.
3   As to the meaning of 'superior landlord' see para 956 note 1 ante.
4   See para 960 ante.
5   See para 956 ante.
6   As to the meaning of 'tenant' see para 951 note 4 ante.
7   Law of Distress Amendment Act 1908 s 3. The superior landlord, if this notice is not acted upon, is
     apparently entitled to distrain on the undertenant or lodger direct.

(5)   WHEN DISTRESS MAY BE MADE

962.   Earliest time for distress.   A landlord may not distrain until rent is in arrear,
that is, until it is ascertained, due, and unpaid[1]. Rent, although previously demandable,
is not actually due until the last instant of the due day, so that the earliest period at
which a distress for rent may be made is on the day following that on which it falls due[2].
Rent is prima facie not due until the end of each year of a term, but in practice the due
date is generally provided by agreement[3] and by this means, or by custom, rent may be
payable in advance, so that in default of payment distress is legitimate at the beginning of
each quarter or other period[4]. If rent is only payable on a condition precedent, it cannot
be distrained for until the condition is fulfilled[5]. Agreement may also postpone the right
to distress[6], but to negative the common law right express words must be inserted. An
affirmative special right of distress does not oust the common law right[7].

In certain cases the leave of the court must be obtained before the right of distress can be exercised: namely, in the case of a dwelling house let on a protected tenancy or subject to a statutory tenancy[8], or in the case of a dwelling house let on an assured tenancy[9], and in certain cases where the tenant is a serviceman not serving under a regular engagement or is the dependant of such a serviceman[10].

1   3 Bl Com (14th Edn) 6–7.
2   Co Litt 47b; Com Dig, Distress (A2); *Clun's Case* (1613) 10 Co Rep 127a; *Duppa v Mayo* (1669) 1 Wms Saund 275 at 287; *Lord Rockingham v Oxenden* (1711) 2 Salk 578; *Cutting v Derby* (1776) 2 Wm Bl 1075 at 1077 per Blackstone J; *Leftley v Mills* (1791) 4 Term Rep 170 at 174; *Dibble v Bowater* (1853) 2 E & B 564.
3   See LANDLORD AND TENANT vol 27(1) (2006 Reissue) para 242 et seq.
4   *Lee v Smith* (1854) 9 Exch 662; *Buckley v Taylor* (1788) 2 Term Rep 600 (where a custom was proved that a half-year's rent was payable on the day of the tenant's entry into possession). See also *Walsh v Lonsdale* (1882) 21 ChD 9, CA; and para 911 ante.
5   *Mechelen v Wallace* (1836) 7 Ad & El 54n (house to be furnished); *Giles v Spencer* (1857) 3 CBNS 244 (receipts for rent due to superior landlord to be produced); *Fox v Slaughter* (1919) 35 TLR 668 (repairs to be done).
6   *Giles v Spencer* (1857) 3 CBNS 244; *Horsford v Webster* (1835) 1 Cr M & R 696; and see paras 950 text to notes 3–7 ante, 968 text to note 8, 978 post.
7   *Re River Swale Brick and Tile Works Ltd* (1883) 52 LJ Ch 638.
8   See the Rent Act 1977 s 147(1); and LANDLORD AND TENANT vol 27(1) (2006 Reissue) para 282.
9   See the Housing Act 1988 s 19(1); and LANDLORD AND TENANT vol 27(1) (2006 Reissue) para 282.
10 See the Reserve and Auxiliary Forces (Protection of Civil Interests) Act 1951 ss 2(2)(a), 3; and ARMED FORCES vol 2(2) (Reissue) paras 81, 85. As to the procedure on application see ARMED FORCES. If, on an application, the court is of the opinion that the tenant is unable to pay the rent owing to relevant service, the court may refuse leave to distrain or give leave subject to such restrictions and conditions as the court thinks proper: see s 2(4); and ARMED FORCES vol 2(2) (Reissue) para 81. As to the discretion of the court in relation to the order which may be made see *Metropolitan Properties Co Ltd v Purdy* [1940] 1 All ER 188, CA; cf *Blanket v Palmer* [1940] 1 All ER 524, CA (decisions under the Courts (Emergency Powers) Act 1939 (repealed)).

963.   Distress at night or on Sunday.   Distress for rent may not be made at night[1]. Night for this purpose is the interval between sunset and sunrise, and not between dusk and daybreak[2], and, if necessary, the time of sunset and sunrise must be proved as a fact[3]. A landlord who prevents removal by a third party during the night so that he may distrain in the morning is not guilty of conversion[4], though he may be liable in trespass[5]. It was in the past held that a distress may not take place on a Sunday[6], although a distress for rent due on a Sunday may be levied on the Monday following[7].

1   Co Litt 142a; Com Dig, Distress (A 2); *Aldenburgh v Peaple* (1834) 6 C & P 212; *Lamb v Wall* (1859) 1 F & F 503.
2   *Tutton v Darke* (1860) 5 H & N 647; *Nixon v Freeman* (1860) 5 H & N 647, 652. It has been held that the levying of distress after sunset is an irregularity which may be waived by the tenant: *Werth v London and Westminster Loan and Discount Co* (1889) 5 TLR 521 at 522, DC; but see the criticism of this decision in *Perring & Co v Emerson* [1906] 1 KB 1 at 6 per Wills J.
3   *Collier v Nokes* (1849) 2 Car & Kir 1012. As to the power of the court to control evidence see CPR 32.1.
4   *England v Cowley* (1873) LR 8 Exch 126.
5   *England v Cowley* (1873) LR 8 Exch 126 at 132 per Kelly CB.
6   See *Werth v London and Westminster Loan and Discount Co* (1889) 5 TLR 521, DC; and see the Sunday Observance Act 1677 s 6 (repealed).
7   *Child v Edwards* [1909] 2 KB 753.

964.   When a demand is necessary.   The making of a distress in itself constitutes a demand, so that an actual previous demand is generally unnecessary, but by agreement it may be provided that no distraint may be made without a previous demand, or only at a fixed or reasonable time after demand[1]. A demand in fact is also requisite in the case of a penal rent, or where the time for payment is at the election of the landlord, although on the construction of the agreement no interval need necessarily intervene between demand and the levy[2].

1   *Browne v Dunnery* (1618) Hob 208; *Kind v Ammery* (1619) Hut 23; *Witty v Williams* (1864) 12 WR 755; and see para 911 *ante*.
2   *Mallam v Arden* (1833) 10 Bing 299 (prima facie the tenant by his bargain ought to be at hand to pay his rent when due); and see *Clarke v Holford* (1848) 2 Car & Kir 540; *Williams v Holmes* (1853) 8 Exch 861; *London and Westminster Loan and Discount Co v London and North Western Rly Co* [1893] 2 QB 49 (where the effect of a provision that rent was to be paid in advance if required was considered).

965.   Statutory distress after expiration of term.   Distress may be made for any rent in arrear or due upon any lease after the determination of that lease in the same manner as it might have been made but for the determination of the lease whether the lease is for years, or for years determinable on the dropping of a life[1], or at will[2] provided that the distress is made within six calendar months after the determination of the lease, and during the continuance of the landlord's title or interest, and during the possession of the tenant from whom the arrears became due[3].

The possession in question must be that of the tenant, unless an executor or administrator enters on the land as his representative during the term and holds over; mere continuance of occupation by a testator's wife or servant does not constitute a possession by the tenant within the meaning of the statute, even if the wife or other occupier becomes the representative of the late tenant after a distress[4]. In any event the statutory provisions[5] cannot apply to a tenancy at will which has been determined by the tenant's death[6].

The statutory provisions do not apply where a new tenancy is created between the same parties before or at the expiration of the old tenancy, even if the new tenancy relates only in part to the original premises, for there cannot be two concurrent rights of distress; the test is whether the tenant continues in possession under a new right and title or not[7]. A mere holding over after a notice to quit does not imply a new tenancy in the absence of payment of rent or some other overt act[8]. There is no new tenancy where a tenant gives up possession of land but is permitted to occupy the house without paying rent until the landlord requires it[9].

The statutory provisions do not apply where an end has been put to the tenancy by a tenant's own wrongful disclaimer or by forfeiture[10], but do apply where the tenancy has been determined by lapse of time, and, probably, where the tenancy has been determined, by notice to quit[11]. The continuance of the possession of the tenant which is necessary for the enactments to apply need not be tortious[12], and is not confined to a holding over of the whole of the premises, though where the tenant remains in possession of part, distress must be made on the part of which possession is retained[13]. If the landlord treats the occupier as a trespasser he cannot afterwards distrain[14].

Possession by the tenant after determination of the term is evidenced by the keeping of the premises as the party's own, to the exclusion of other people. A small thing, if left on the premises, with a view to maintaining the tenant's retention of possession, will serve, but the mere fact of part or of the whole of the tenant's goods being left on the demised premises does not in itself conclusively indicate that the tenant is continuing in possession[15].

1   See the Law of Property Act 1925 s 149(6) (as amended); and LANDLORD AND TENANT vol 27(1) (2006 Reissue) para 240.
2   See the Landlord and Tenant Act 1709 s 6 (amended by the Statute Law Revision Act 1948). Before the Landlord and Tenant Act 1709 it was usual to provide that the last half-year's rent should be paid on some day before the determination of the lease, so as to enable the landlord to distrain before the removal of the tenant: see Co Litt 47b.
3   Landlord and Tenant Act 1709 s 7; and see *Beavan v Delahay* (1788) 1 Hy Bl 5. The Landlord and Tenant Act 1709 s 6 (as amended) and s 7 are confined to cases between landlord and tenant, and have no application to the case of a claim by an execution creditor: *Lewis v Davies* [1914] 2 KB 469, CA.
4   *Braithwaite v Cooksey* (1790) 1 Hy Bl 465; *Turner v Barnes* (1862) 2 B & S 435.
5   Ie the Landlord and Tenant Act 1709 s 6 (as amended) and s 7: see the text to notes 2–3 *supra*.

6   *Turner v Barnes* (1862) 2 B & S 435; and see *Scobie v Collins* [1895] 1 QB 375 at 377 per Vaughan Williams J.
7   *Wilkinson v Peel* [1895] 1 QB 516.
8   *Jenner v Clegg* (1832) 1 Mood & R 213; *Alford v Vickery* (1842) Car & M 280; but see *Tayleur v Wildin* (1868) LR 3 Exch 303 (where the new tenancy was created in spite of a notice to quit). As to the effect of payment and acceptance of rent after notice to quit see *Clarke v Grant* [1950] 1 KB 104, [1949] 1 All ER 768, CA; and LANDLORD AND TENANT vol 27(1) (2006 Reissue) para 213 et seq.
9   *Lewis v Davies* [1913] 2 KB 37; revsd on other grounds [1914] 2 KB 469, CA.
10 *Doe d David v Williams* (1835) 7 C & P 322; *Grimwood v Moss* (1872) LR 7 CP 360 at 365 per Willes J; *Kirkland v Briancourt* (1890) 6 TLR 441; and cf *Murgatroyd v Silkstone and Dodsworth Coal and Iron Co Ltd, ex p Charlesworth* (1895) 65 LJ Ch 111 (where the landlords had entered into possession of the demised property in pursuance of an order of the court).
11 See *Williams v Stiven* (1846) 9 QB 14.
12 *Nuttall v Staunton* (1825) 4 B & C 51; *Taylerson v Peters* (1837) 7 Ad & El 110 at 114 per Patteson J; *Gray v Stait* (1883) 11 QBD 668 at 673, CA, per Cotton LJ; and see *Lewis v Davies* [1913] 2 KB 37 at 43 per Channell J (on appeal [1914] 2 KB 469, CA).
13 *Nuttall v Staunton* (1825) 4 B & C 51.
14 *Bridges v Smyth* (1829) 5 Bing 410.
15 See *Taylerson v Peters* (1837) 7 Ad & El 110; *Gray v Stait* (1883) 11 QBD 668 at 673, CA, per Bowen LJ; *Aston v Williams* (1910) 45 L Jo 273 (tenant's return to pick apples).

966.   Continuing possession.   Where, by custom or agreement, the interest and connection between the landlord and the tenant is extended beyond the term, and for this purpose the possession of the tenant is allowed to continue, the tenancy is by such custom or agreement so far prolonged during such further possession as to allow the landlord to distrain[1]. When a tenant, under statute[2], holds over in lieu of emblements, the rent may be recovered by distress[3].

Tenancies to which Part II of the Landlord and Tenant Act 1954[4] applies do not come to an end unless terminated in accordance with the provisions of that Part of the Act[5]. It would appear that the landlord retains the right of distress while the tenant remains in possession and the tenancy continues under that Act[6].

1   *Beavan v Delahay* (1788) 1 Hy Bl 5; *Lewis v Harris* (1778) 1 Hy Bl 7n; *Boraston v Green* (1812) 16 East 71; *Knight v Benett* (1826) 3 Bing 364; *Griffiths v Puleston* (1844) 13 M & W 358; and see AGRICULTURE vol 1(2) (Reissue) para 380. For a case as to continuing possession after expiration of the term under a tenant right see *Re Powers, Manisty v Archdale* (1890) 63 LT 626; and para 968 note 7 post.
2   Ie under the Agricultural Holdings Act 1986 s 21: see AGRICULTURE vol 1(2) (Reissue) para 339.
3   *Haines v Welch* (1868) LR 4 CP 91.
4   Ie the Landlord and Tenant Act 1954 ss 23–46 (as amended).
5   See ibid s 24(1) (as amended); and LANDLORD AND TENANT vol 27(2) (2006 Reissue) para 720.
6   The effect of ibid s 24(1) (as amended) is to continue the tenants' common law tenancy with a statutory variation as to the mode of determination: *HL Bolton (Engineering) Co Ltd v TJ Graham & Sons Ltd* [1957] 1 QB 159, [1956] 3 All ER 624, CA. See further LANDLORD AND TENANT.

967.   Exclusion of distress after expiration of tenancy.   Except in the cases already stated[1], a landlord is not entitled to distrain after the expiration of the term or tenancy, even though the tenant continues in occupation after notice to quit has expired[2].

1   See paras 965–966 ante.
2   Co Litt 47b; Com Dig, Distress (A2) ('for he is not in, in privity of the lease'); *Pennant's Case* (1596) 3 Co Rep 64a; *Williams v Stiven* (1846) 9 QB 14; *Turner v Barnes* (1862) 2 B & S 435 at 450. In *Stanfill v Hickes* (1697) 1 Ld Raym 280, a lease for a year and thereafter from year to year was construed as a lease for two years and thereafter a tenancy at will; the landlord was held not to be entitled to distrain after the expiration of two years for rent due for the second year, on the ground that the original tenancy had terminated. In such a case, however, the tenant would now be treated as holding under the original tenancy so long as he remained in possession and his tenancy was not determined by notice: see e g *Legg v Strudwick* (1708) 2 Salk 414 (where it was held that the lessor might distrain in the third year for the rent of the second); *Birch v Wright* (1786) 1 Term Rep 378 at 380; *Cattley v Arnold, Banks v Arnold* (1859) 1 John & H 651 at 660; para 912 note 4 ante; and LANDLORD AND TENANT.

(6) LOSS OF THE RIGHT TO DISTRAIN

968.   Restraint and suspension of right to distrain.   The assignment by the landlord of his reversion (including the assignment for a limited duration by the grant of a concurrent term) destroys the assignor's remedy of distress for arrears of rent due at the date of assignment[1].

In the case of tenancies granted before 1 January 1996, by statute rent reserved by a lease is annexed and incident to and goes with the reversionary estate in the land[2]. By virtue of this statutory provision the assignee of the reversion may sue for rent in arrear at the date of the assignment and may distrain for such rent[3].

In the case of tenancies granted on or after 1 January 1996, the assignee of the reversion becomes entitled to the benefit of the tenant's covenant for rent as from the assignment but does not have any right to sue for rent in relation to any time falling before the assignment[4] (unless the right is expressly assigned) but the benefit of a right of re-entry passes on assignment[5]. Accordingly (at least in the absence of an express assignment of the benefit of rent) the assignee of the reversion has no right to distrain for rent falling due before the assignment.

Further, the right of distress is not taken away by a mere agreement by a person to sell or assign his reversionary interest in the premises[6]; but after a sale and payment of the purchase money, and before a conveyance of the property, the vendor is a trustee for the purchaser, and, although he has the legal estate and therefore the right to distrain, he will be restrained from exercising his legal right in such a way as to prejudice the purchaser[7]. A contract by the landlord to sell the freehold of the premises to the tenant suspends the right of distress pending completion[8].

1   See para 912 ante.
2   See the Law of Property Act 1925 s 141 (re-enacting, with modifications in wording, the Conveyancing Act 1881 s 10); and LANDLORD AND TENANT vol 27(1) (2006 Reissue) para 567.
3   *London and County (A & D) Ltd v Wilfred Sportsman Ltd* [1971] Ch 764, [1970] 2 All ER 600, CA; *Arlesford Trading Co Ltd v Servansingh* [1971] 3 All ER 113, [1971] 1 WLR 1080, CA.
      Before 1881 (i e before the enactment of the Conveyancing Act 1881: see note 2 supra), it had been decided that an assignee had title to the next rent due after the assignment but not to the antecedent rent (see *Flight v Bentley* (1835) 7 Sim 149) but that case was overruled by *London and County (A & D) Ltd v Wilfred Sportsman Ltd* supra at 784 and 606 per Russell LJ. It would also appear that any other pre-1881 decision in so far as it may indicate that a disposition by the landlord of a reversion of a lease destroys the remedy for distress for arrears of rent due at the date of the disposition (see e g *Smith v Day* (1837) 2 M & W 684; *Stavely v Allock* (1851) 16 QB 636) is no longer good law (see *Re King, Robinson v Gray* [1963] Ch 459 at 490, [1963] 1 All ER 781 at 793, CA, per Upjohn LJ).
4   See the Landlord and Tenant (Covenants) Act 1995 s 3(3); and LANDLORD AND TENANT vol 27(1) (2006 Reissue) para 580.
5   See ibid s 23; and LANDLORD AND TENANT vol 27(1) (2006 Reissue) para 580.
6   *Manchester Brewery Co v Coombs* [1901] 2 Ch 608.
7   *Re Powers, Manisty v Archdale* (1890) 63 LT 626.
8   *Ellis v Wright* (1897) 76 LT 522. See also para 978 post.

969.   Effect of grant of future lease.   A future lease takes effect without actual entry, but only from the date of commencement of the term[1]. Hence, if the future lease is granted to a third person, it still does not amount to a parting with the reversion, so as to take away the lessor's right of distress until the term of the future lease commences[2]; while, if it is granted to the first lessee, it operates as an extension of his term[3].

1   See the Law of Property Act 1925 s 149(2); and LANDLORD AND TENANT vol 27(1) (2006 Reissue) para 118. See also s 149(1), which abolished the doctrine of 'interesse termini', i e the rule that a lessee had to perfect his title by entry and until then had no estate in the land: see LANDLORD AND TENANT vol 27(1) (2006 Reissue) para 140. A term, at a rent or granted in consideration of a fine, must be limited to take effect not more than 21 years from the date of the instrument creating it, otherwise it is void: see s 149(3); and LANDLORD AND TENANT vol 27(1) (2006 Reissue) para 106.

2   Not only is the effect of the future term postponed until its commencement (see the text and note 1
    supra), but it is expressly provided that nothing in ibid s 149(1), (2) is prejudicially to affect the right of
    any person to recover any rent: see s 149(4); and LANDLORD AND TENANT vol 27(1) (2006 Reissue)
    para 118. The rule formerly laid down that the grant of a future lease to a third party did not amount to
    a parting with the reversion (see *Smith v Day* (1837) 2 M & W 684) consequently remains in force despite
    the abolition of the doctrine of 'interesse termini'.
3   Cf *Lord Llangattock v Watney, Combe, Reid & Co Ltd* [1910] AC 394, HL; *Knight v City of London
    Brewery Co* [1912] 1 KB 10 (where the addition of a reversionary term to a term in possession was not
    allowed). The effect of these cases is preserved for terms or interests created before 1 January 1926 by the
    Law of Property Act 1925 s 149(4): see LANDLORD AND TENANT vol 27(1) (2006 Reissue) para 118.
        The addition of the future term to the present term prevents the right of distress being lost in
    circumstances such as occurred in *Lewis v Baker* [1905] 1 Ch 46.

970. By determination of lessor's interest. Where the lessor is himself only a
termor[1] his right to distrain ceases with the determination of his interest[2]; and where the
lessor has only some other defeasible interest the expiration of that interest determines
his right to distrain[3].

1   Ie a tenant for a term of years. See also para 914 ante.
2   *Burne v Richardson* (1813) 4 Taunt 720.
3   *Hopcraft v Keys* (1833) 9 Bing 613.

971. By expiration of the tenancy. The common law right to distrain expires
with the tenancy[1]. This right is extended by statute for six months after the
determination of the tenancy provided that the landlord's title continues and the tenant
remains in possession. The statutory provision does not, however, apply where a new
tenancy is created between the same parties before or at the expiration of the old
tenancy[2].

1   See para 967 ante.
2   See para 965 ante.

972. By surrender of the reversion. When the reversion is surrendered or
merges, the rent, so far as regards the person who was entitled to that reversion becomes
extinguished, and his right of distress for arrears due at the date of the surrender or
merger is lost[1]. Where, however, a lease out of which underleases have been derived is
surrendered for the purpose of a renewal, the lessor granting the new lease and any
person deriving title under him is entitled to the same remedy by distress or entry on the
land comprised in any underlease for rent reserved by the new lease (so far as that rent
does not exceed the rent reserved by the original lease) as he would have had if: (1) the
original lease had remained on foot; or (2) a new underlease derived out of the new
lease had been granted to the underlessee or person deriving title under him[2]. In the
case of any other surrender or merger the estate which, as against the underlessee,
confers the next vested right to the land, will become the reversion on the underlease,
with all incidents, including the right of distress[3].

1   *Webb v Russell* (1789) 3 Term Rep 393; *Threr v Barton* (1570) Moore KB 94; *Thorn v Woollcombe* (1832) 3
    B & Ad 586.
2   Law of Property Act 1925 s 150(5) (replacing provisions of the Landlord and Tenant Act 1730 s 6
    (repealed)); and see *Doe d Palk v Marchetti* (1831) 1 B & Ad 715 at 721.
3   See the Law of Property Act 1925 s 139; and *Ecclesiastical Comrs for England v Treemer* [1893] 1 Ch 166.

973. By payment of the rent. Payment of the rent or its equivalent extinguishes
the right to distrain[1]. In certain cases the giving of a bill of exchange or promissory note
for rent has been treated as not affecting the landlord's right to distrain[2]. The giving of a
bill of exchange or promissory note is, however, some evidence of an agreement by the
landlord to suspend his remedy by distress during the currency of the bill or note[3]. An

1   See the Distress for Rent Act 1689 s 1 (as amended); and para 1058 post.
2   *Harding v Hall* (1866) 14 LT 410. See also para 1048 post. As to bailiffs see para 992 et seq post.

(9) LEVYING THE DISTRESS

(i) The Warrant

992.   Authority of bailiff. A landlord may distrain either in person or by an authorised bailiff or agent[1]. The bailiff distrains as agent for the landlord[2].

When a bailiff makes a distress he must have authority to do so from his employer[3]. As the distrainee is entitled to know by what right the bailiff is acting, this authority is generally and should properly be in writing, and is commonly called a distress warrant or warrant of distress; but it is not essential to his authority that a bailiff should be appointed in writing. Even a corporation aggregate may at common law appoint a person to distrain without deed or warrant[4].

A distress made without previous authority may be afterwards recognised and adopted by the landlord, and the adoption relates back to the time of taking the distress and will be as effectual as a previous authority would have been[5].

The authority conferred by a warrant to distrain may be withdrawn at any time before the goods are actually sold[6]. When a warrant to distrain is in fact given to one person, it cannot be executed by another not named in it[7].

In the case of a joint distress, as by joint tenants, the warrant may be signed by all the parties entitled[8] or may be given by one only to authorise a distress for the rent due to all[9].

A distress warrant does not require to be stamped[10].

1   *Symonds v Kurtz* (1889) 61 LT 559, DC. As to who may be a bailiff see para 994 post. As to fees for levying see para 1058 note 1 post.
2   *Re Caidan, ex p Official Receiver v Regis Property Co Ltd* [1942] Ch 90 at 96, [1941] 3 All ER 491 at 496 per Morton J.
3   See note 1 supra.
4   *Cary v Matthews* (1688) 1 Salk 191n; *Randle v Dean and Pope* (1700) 2 Lut 1496 at 1497; *Smith v Birmingham Gas Co* (1834) 1 Ad & El 526. As to statutory powers of corporations to appoint agents see AGENCY vol 2(1) (Reissue) para 35; CORPORATIONS vol 9(2) (2006 Reissue) para 1273.
5   *Trevillian v Pine* (1708) 11 Mod Rep 112; notes to *Potter v North* (1669) 1 Saund 346 at 347; *Haseler v Lemoyne* (1858) 5 CBNS 530; *Duncan v Meikleham* (1827) 3 C & P 172; and see *Whitehead v Taylor* (1839) 10 Ad & El 210 (ratification by executor after probate); *Smith v Birmingham Gas Co* (1834) 1 Ad & El 526; *Church v Imperial Gas Light and Coke Co* (1838) 6 Ad & El 846 at 861 (ratification by corporation).
6   *Harding v Hall* (1866) 14 LT 410.
7   *Symonds v Kurtz* (1889) 61 LT 559, DC.
8   *Buller's Case* (1587) 1 Leon 50.
9   *Leigh v Shepherd* (1821) 2 Brod & Bing 465; *Robinson v Hofman* (1828) 4 Bing 562; *Stedman v Bates* (1695) 1 Ld Raym 64.
10 *Pyle v Partridge* (1846) 15 M & W 20.

993.   Implied indemnity to bailiff. A warrant of distress creates an implied warranty on the part of the landlord that he has the right to distrain and an implied undertaking to indemnify the bailiff against any act properly done in exercise of the authority given to him[1]. It will not, however, indemnify the bailiff against illegal or irregular acts done by him or his employees in the course of the distress, in the absence of an indemnity expressly worded to cover them, unless the conduct of the landlord has been such as to induce the bailiff to believe that he was acting under an indemnity from the landlord covering such acts[2]. Thus a warrant in the ordinary form confers no authority on the bailiff to levy on privileged goods; but where the levy is made by the express direction of the landlord the latter is bound to indemnify the bailiff[3].

1   *Draper v Thompson* (1829) 4 C & P 84. As to authority of bailiff see para 992 ante.
2   *Draper v Thompson* (1829) 4 C & P 84; *Toplis v Grane* (1839) 5 Bing NC 636; *Dugdale v Lovering* (1875) LR 10 CP 196; *Ibbett v De la Salle* (1860) 6 H & N 233.
3   *Toplis v Grane* (1839) 5 Bing NC 636.

(ii) The Bailiff

994. Bailiff must hold certificate. No person may be employed as a bailiff to levy any distress for rent unless he is authorised to act as a bailiff by a certificate in writing under the hand of a judge assigned to a county court district, or acting as a judge so assigned[1]. The certificate may be general or special (that is, applying to a particular distress or distresses)[2]. Every bailiff levying a distress must produce this certificate[3] to the tenant if he is present or, in the absence of the tenant, to such other person present as appears to be in control of the premises[4]. He should also produce his warrant and show the cause of taking the distress if required[5]. Such a certificate may be granted only by a judge[6] and authorises the bailiff named in it to levy at any place in England and Wales[7]. A certificate, unless cancelled, has effect for the period of two years from the date of its grant[8].

No certificate may be granted to any officer of a county court[9]. The judge may not grant a certificate to any applicant[10]: (1) who fails to satisfy the judge, as the case may be, that he is a fit and proper person to hold a certificate, and that he possesses a sufficient knowledge of the law of distress[11]; or (2) who carries on or will be employed in any business which includes buying debts[12]. In applying for a certificate, an applicant must undertake not to levy distress at any premises in respect of which he is regularly employed to collect rent[13]. A minor cannot be appointed bailiff[14].

1   Law of Distress Amendment Act 1888 s 7 (amended by the Courts Act 1971 s 56(1), Sch 8 para 2); *Re Sanders, ex p Sergeant* (1885) 54 LJQB 331.
2   Law of Distress Amendment Act 1888 s 7. As to the issue of certificates see para 995 post; and as to the cancellation of certificates see para 998 post.
3   Ie a certificate to act as a bailiff granted under the Law of Distress Amendment Act 1888, as amended by the Law of Distress Amendment Act 1895 (see the text to notes 1–2 supra): Distress for Rent Rules 1988, SI 1988/2050, r 2(1). These rules are made under the Law of Distress Amendment Act 1888 s 8 (amended by the Statute Law Revision Act 1908), and the Law of Distress Amendment Act 1895 s 3. As to the form of a bailiff's certificate see the Distress for Rent Rules 1988, SI 1988/2050, App 2 Form 1 (amended by SI 1999/2360).
4   Distress for Rent Rules 1988, SI 1988/2050, r 12(1).
5   *Buller's Case* (1587) 1 Leon 50; and see paras 992 ante, 1011 et seq post.
6   'Judge' means a judge of a county court: Distress for Rent Rules 1988, SI 1988/2050, r 2(1).
7   Ibid r 3(1) (amended by SI 1999/2360).
8   Distress for Rent Rules 1988, SI 1988/2050, r 7(1) (amended by SI 1999/2360).
9   Distress for Rent Rules 1988, SI 1988/2050, r 5(3).
10   Ibid r 5(1) (amended by SI 1999/2360). As to complaints regarding fitness to hold a certificate see the Distress for Rent Rules 1988, SI 1988/2050, r 8 (as amended); and para 997 post.
11   Ibid r 5(1)(a) (as amended: see note 10 supra).
12   Ibid r 5(1)(b).
13   Ibid App 2 Form 3 Pt 5 (Form 3 substituted by SI 1999/2360).
14   *Cuckson v Winter* (1828) 2 Man & Ry KB 313. The age of majority is 18: see the Family Law Reform Act 1969 s 1; and CHILDREN AND YOUNG PERSONS vol 5(3) (Reissue) para 1.

995. Application for certificate. The applicant for the grant of a certificate to act as a bailiff[1] is required to lodge in court[2] by way of bond or deposit, or satisfy the judge[3] that there is subsisting by way of bond or deposit, security totalling £10,000[4]. An application for the grant of a certificate must be made in the prescribed form[5]. The applicant must state his address[6] and whether his area of business extends beyond the district of the court at which the application was made, and he must also state whether he has applied for and been refused or had cancelled a certificate[7]. Applications must be filed in the office of the applicant's issuing county court[8], accompanied by the prescribed fee[9], and must be lodged together with certain documents[10]. If so directed, the applicant must lodge such further evidence as the judge may reasonably require in support of his application[11]. The statements in such an application must be verified on oath[12]. The name and address of all applicants for a certificate are to be exhibited in the public area of the court office for the 60 days prior to the hearing of the application[13].

The applicant must cause to be published in an appropriate newspaper[14] a notice in the prescribed form[15] so that the notice appears in three separate editions of that newspaper during the 60 days prior to the hearing of the application[16], and he must, not less than three days before the hearing of the application, file with the court the editions of the appropriate newspaper (or extracts from it) showing such notices[17]. Each issuing county court must compile and maintain a list of appropriate newspapers published within its issuing area[18] and copies of the list are to be exhibited in the public area of the court office of each county court in the issuing area, and given to members of the public on request[19].

An application for a certificate may not be granted except on the personal attendance of the applicant and his examination on oath at the hearing of the application[20].

Each issuing county court must also compile a list of bailiffs carrying on business within that court's issuing area and holding certificates as at 1 February every year, and the list is to be exhibited in the public area of the court office of each county court in the issuing area[21]. When a certificate is cancelled, the list must be amended to include that fact[22].

1   As to the certificate to act as a bailiff see para 994 ante.
2   'Lodge in court' means pay or transfer into court or deposit in court: Court Funds Rules 1987, SI 1987/821, r 2(2); definition applied by the Distress for Rent Rules 1988, SI 1988/2050, r 2(1).
3   For the meaning of 'judge' see para 994 note 6 ante.
4   Distress for Rent Rules 1988, SI 1988/2050, r 6(1) (amended by SI 1999/2360). The security is for the due performance of the bailiff's duties and for any reasonable costs, fees and expenses incurred in the investigation of any complaint lodged against the bailiff, or in the cancellation of his certificate, and is to be applied in accordance with the Distress for Rent Rules 1988, SI 1988/2050, rr 8, 9 (both as amended) (see paras 997–998 post): r 6(2). The bailiff maintains the security throughout the duration of the certificate: r 6(2A) (r 6(2A), (2B) added by SI 1999/2360). If, at any time during the duration of the certificate, for any reason (other than where the Distress for Rent Rules 1988, SI 1988/2050, r 9(2) (see para 998 post) applies), the security no longer exists, or is reduced in value so that it amounts to less than £10,000, the bailiff must provide fresh security under this rule to the satisfaction of the court: r 6(2B) (as so added). Where a deposit is lodged in court, the provisions of the Court Funds Rules 1987, SI 1987/821 (as amended) (see COURTS; PRACTICE AND PROCEDURE) apply: Distress for Rent Rules 1988, SI 1988/2050, rr 2(1), 6(3).
5   Ibid r 4(1) (substituted by SI 1999/2360). For the prescribed form of application for a certificate to levy distress see the Distress for Rent Rules 1988, SI 1988/2050, App 2 Form 3 (substituted by SI 1999/2360; and amended by SI 2000/1481).
6   As to the procedure when a bailiff's details change see para 996 post.
7   Distress for Rent Rules 1988, SI 1988/2050, App 2 Form 3 Pt 1 (as substituted: see note 5 supra). As to cancellation of a certificate see para 998 post.
8   'Issuing county court' means a county court whose name appears in ibid App 3 Table col 2 (App 3 Table added by SI 1999/2360; amended by SI 1999/2564; SI 1999/3186; SI 2000/1481; SI 2000/2737; SI 2001/4026); and 'the applicant's issuing county court' means, in relation to an applicant, the county court whose name appears in the Distress for Rent Rules 1988, SI 1988/2050, App 3 Table col 2 (as added and amended) opposite the name of his home county court: r 2(1) (definitions added by SI 1999/2360). 'Home county court' means, in relation to any person, the county court in whose district that person has his principal place of business or his main residence: Distress for Rent Rules 1988, SI 1988/2050, r 2(1) (definition added by SI 1999/2360).
9   Ie the fee prescribed for the 'commencement of originating proceedings for any other remedy or relief': see the Civil Proceedings Fees Order 2004, SI 2004/3121 (amended by SI 2005/473; SI 2005/3445); and COURTS; PRACTICE AND PROCEDURE.
10 Distress for Rent Rules 1988, SI 1988/2050, r 4(4) (amended by SI 1999/2360). The application and fee must be lodged together with: (1) two references, one of which may be from the applicant's employer or

an approved officer of the Certificated Bailiffs' Association of England and Wales and must deal with the applicant's knowledge of the law of distress and his previous experience of levying distress; (2) a certified copy not more than one month old of the result of a search of the register of county court judgments against the applicant's full name and his home and business addresses for the last six years; (3) two passport sized photographs of the applicant; and (4) copies of the Distress for Rent Rules 1988, SI 1988/2050, App 2 Forms 7, 8 and 9 intended to be used by the applicant when levying distress, which must conform to the design and layout prescribed in App 2 (as amended), must be on paper of durable quality and of the size A4 as specified by the International Standards Organisation, and must be in a clear and legible printed or type-written form: r 4(4) (as so amended).

11 Ibid r 4(6) (amended by SI 1999/2360).
12 Distress for Rent Rules 1988, SI 1988/2050, r 4(5).
13 Ibid r 5(4) (amended by SI 1999/2360).
14 'Appropriate newspaper' means a local newspaper appearing in a list of local newspapers approved by the court officer of the issuing county court for the purpose of publication of notices under the Distress for Rent Rules 1988, SI 1988/2050, r 5(5) (as amended) (see note 16 infra): r 2(1) (definition added by SI 1999/2360). 'Court officer' means a member of the court staff: CPR 2.3(1); definition applied by the Distress for Rent Rules 1988, SI 1988/2050, r 2(1) (definition substituted by SI 1999/2360).
15 Ie the form set out in the Distress for Rent Rules 1988, SI 1988/2050, r 5(7) (added by SI 1999/2360).
16 Distress for Rent Rules 1988, SI 1988/2050, r 5(5) (r 5(5)–(8) added by SI 1999/2360).
17 Distress for Rent Rules 1988, SI 1988/2050, r 5(6) (as added: see note 16 supra).
18 'Issuing area' means, in relation to an issuing county court, the area constituted by the district of that issuing county court and the districts of any other county courts whose names appear in ibid App 3 Table col 1 (as added and amended) (see note 8 supra) opposite the name of that issuing county court: r 2(1) (definition added by SI 1999/2360).
19 Distress for Rent Rules 1988, SI 1988/2050, r 5(8) (as added: see note 16 supra).
20 Ibid r 5(2) (amended by SI 1999/2360).
21 Distress for Rent Rules 1988, SI 1988/2050, r 13(1) (substituted by SI 1999/2360).
22 Distress for Rent Rules 1988, SI 1988/2050, r 13(2). As to the cancellation of a certificate see para 998 post.

996.   Replacement certificates.   Once a certificate[1] has been issued, if there is any change in a bailiff's name, address or other written information appearing on the certificate (the 'relevant details')[2], the bailiff must without delay give written notice of the change to the issuing county court[3] and produce his certificate ('the old certificate') to the court officer of the issuing county court[4]. When a bailiff gives notice and produces the old certificate, the judge[5] of the issuing county court must issue to the bailiff a replacement certificate reflecting the change in the relevant details but in all other respects (including, without limitation, the date of expiry of the certificate[6]) the same as the old certificate[7]. When such a replacement certificate is issued, the court officer must retain and cancel the old certificate[8]. No fee is payable for the issue of such a replacement certificate[9].

1 As to the certificate to act as a bailiff see para 994 ante.
2 Distress for Rent Rules 1988, SI 1988/2050, r 7A(1) (r 7A added by SI 1999/2360).
3 For the meaning of 'issuing county court' see para 995 note 8 ante.
4 Distress for Rent Rules 1988, SI 1988/2050, r 7A(2) (as added: see note 2 supra). For the meaning of 'court officer' see para 995 note 14 ante.
5 For the meaning of 'judge' see para 994 note 6 ante.
6 As to the duration of a certificate see para 994 text to note 8 ante.
7 Distress for Rent Rules 1988, SI 1988/2050, r 7A(3) (as added: see note 2 supra).
8 Ibid r 7A(4) (as added: see note 2 supra).
9 Ibid r 7A(5) (as added: see note 2 supra).

997.   Complaints as to fitness to hold a certificate.   Any complaint as to the conduct or fitness of any bailiff who holds a certificate[1] must be made in the relevant form[2] to the court from which the certificate issued[3]. Upon receipt of any such complaint, the court officer[4] must send written details of the complaint to the bailiff and require him to deliver a written reply to the court office within 14 days thereafter or within such longer time as the court may specify[5].

If the bailiff fails to deliver the reply within the time specified, or if upon reading the reply the judge[6] is unsatisfied as to the bailiff's fitness to hold a certificate, the court officer must issue a notice summoning the bailiff to appear before the judge on a specified date and show cause why his certificate should not be cancelled[7]. If upon reading the reply the judge is satisfied as to the bailiff's fitness to hold a certificate, the court officer must issue a notice to the bailiff to that effect and no further action is to be taken in respect of that complaint[8]. The court officer must send a copy of the appropriate notice to the complainant and any other interested party[9].

If, after a notice has been issued summoning the bailiff to appear before the judge[10], the complainant so applies in writing, and the application is received by the court not later than 14 days before the date set for the hearing, the court officer of the court receiving the complaint must order that the complaint be heard in the issuing county court[11] for the complainant's home county court[12]. In the event of such an order being made, the court officer of the court receiving the complaint must forthwith send: (1) to the court officer of the court hearing the complaint certified copies of any relevant entries in the records of the court receiving the complaint, and copies of all other documents in his custody relating to the bailiff's certificate and to the complaint; and (2) to the bailiff and any other interested party, notice of the order so made[13].

At the hearing the bailiff must attend for examination and may make representations, and the complainant may attend and make representations[14]. The procedure to be followed at the hearing, including the calling of evidence, is such as the judge considers just, and he may proceed with the hearing notwithstanding that the bailiff has failed to attend[15].

If an order is made that the complaint be heard in the issuing county court for the complainant's home county court[16], the court officer of the court hearing the complaint must, following the hearing, send to the court officer of the court which received the complaint certified copies of the order and all other documents in his custody relating to the bailiff's certificate and to the complaint[17].

1 As to the certificate to act as a bailiff see para 994 ante.
2 Ie in the Distress for Rent Rules 1988, SI 1988/2050, App 2 Form 4 (substituted by SI 1999/2360) or, where the complainant has conducted a formal investigation into a complaint by a third party against the bailiff, in the Distress for Rent Rules 1988, SI 1988/2050, App 2 Form 5 (substituted by SI 1999/2360): Distress for Rent Rules 1988, SI 1988/2050, r 8(1) (amended by SI 1999/2360).
3 Distress for Rent Rules 1988, SI 1988/2050, r 8(1).
4 For the meaning of 'court officer' see para 995 note 14 ante.
5 Distress for Rent Rules 1988, SI 1988/2050, r 8(2) (amended by SI 1999/2360).
6 For the meaning of 'judge' see para 994 note 6 ante.
7 Distress for Rent Rules 1988, SI 1988/2050, r 8(3) (amended by SI 1999/2360).
8 Distress for Rent Rules 1988, SI 1988/2050, r 8(3A) (added by SI 1999/2360).
9 Distress for Rent Rules 1988, SI 1988/2050, r 8(4) (amended by SI 1999/2360).
10 Ie under ibid r 8(3) (as amended): see the text to note 7 supra.
11 For the meaning of 'issuing county court' see para 995 note 8 ante.
12 Distress for Rent Rules 1988, SI 1988/2050, r 8(4A) (r 8(4A), (4B) added by SI 1999/2360). The complaint must be heard in the issuing county court whose name appears in the Distress for Rent Rules 1988, SI 1988/2050, App 3 Table col 2 (as added) (see para 995 ante) opposite the name of the complainant's home county court: r 8(4A) (as so added).
13 Ibid r 8(4B) (as added: see note 12 supra).
14 Ibid r 8(5).
15 Ibid r 8(6).
16 Ie under ibid r 8(4A) (as added): see the text to notes 10–12 supra.
17 Ibid r 8(7) (added by SI 1999/2360). This includes the certified copies and copies sent under head (1) in the text: Distress for Rent Rules 1988, SI 1988/2050, r 8(7) (as so added).

998. Cancellation of certificate and forfeiture of security. A certificate[1] granted to a bailiff by a judge[2] of a county court[3] may at any time be cancelled or declared void by a judge of that county court[4]. Following the hearing of any complaint[5] the judge may, whether he cancels the certificate or not, order that the security[6] is to be forfeited either wholly or in part, and that the amount or amounts directed to be forfeited are to be paid to any complainant by way of compensation for failure in due performance of the bailiff's duties, costs or expenses or, where costs, fees and expenses have been incurred by the court, to Her Majesty's Paymaster General[7].

Where an order for the forfeiture of the security, either wholly or in part, is made but the certificate is not cancelled, the judge may direct that fresh security[8] is to be provided[9]. When a certificate is cancelled or expires it nevertheless continues to have effect for the purpose of any distress where the bailiff has entered into possession before the date of cancellation or expiry, unless the judge otherwise directs[10]. When a certificate is cancelled or expires it must be surrendered to the judge, unless he otherwise directs[11]. When a bailiff holding a certificate ceases, for any reason, to carry on business as a bailiff he must forthwith surrender his certificate to the judge at the county court which issued the certificate, unless the judge otherwise directs, and as from the date of the surrender the certificate is to be treated as if it had expired on that date[12].

When a certificate is cancelled the court officer[13] must publish a notice to that effect in an appropriate newspaper[14], and the costs of the notice are deducted from the security[15].

1 As to the certificate to act as a bailiff see para 994 ante.
2 For the meaning of 'judge' see para 994 note 6 ante.
3 Ie under the Law of Distress Amendment Act 1888 s 7 (as amended): see para 994 ante.
4 Law of Distress Amendment Act 1895 s 1 (amended by the Statute Law Revision Act 1908).
5 Ie under the Distress for Rent Rules 1988, SI 1988/2050, r 8 (as amended): see para 997 ante.
6 As to the security see para 995 ante.
7 Distress for Rent Rules 1988, SI 1988/2050, r 9(1). As to Her Majesty's Paymaster General see CONSTITUTIONAL LAW AND HUMAN RIGHTS vol 8(2) (Reissue) para 714. References, in r 9 (as amended), to the cancellation of a certificate do not include the cancellation of a certificate upon the issue of a duplicate certificate, in accordance with r 7A(4) (as added) (see para 995 ante): r 9(7) (added by SI 1999/2360). Where a certificate is cancelled, the order of the judge is to be in a prescribed form and, subject to the provisions of this rule, the security is to be cancelled and the balance of the deposit returned to the bailiff: Distress for Rent Rules 1988, SI 1988/2050, r 9(3). For the form of cancellation of a bailiff's certificate see App 2 Form 6.
8 Ie under ibid r 6 (as amended): see para 995 ante.
9 Ibid r 9(2).
10 Ibid r 9(4).
11 Ibid r 9(5) (amended by SI 1999/2360).
12 Distress for Rent Rules 1988, SI 1988/2050, r 9(5A) (added by SI 1999/2360).
13 For the meaning of 'court officer' see para 995 note 14 ante.
14 For the meaning of 'appropriate newspaper' see para 995 note 14 ante.
15 Distress for Rent Rules 1988, SI 1988/2050, r 9(6) (amended by SI 1999/2360).

999. Consequences of acting without certificate. If any person not holding a certificate[1] levies a distress contrary to the statutory provisions, the person so levying, and any person who has authorised him so to levy, will be deemed to have committed a trespass[2], not only as against the tenant, but also as against a third party whose goods are seized[3]. The effect of this is to make a distress by an uncertificated bailiff an illegal distress, with all the consequences of a trespass ab initio[4]. In addition, an uncertificated bailiff who levies a distress will (without prejudice to any civil liability) be liable on summary conviction to a fine[5].

1 As to the certificate to act as a bailiff see para 994 ante.
2 Law of Distress Amendment Act 1888 s 7. As to trespass see TORT vol 45(2) (Reissue) para 659 et seq.
3 *Perring & Co v Emerson* [1906] 1 KB 1.
4 See para 1076 post.

5   Law of Distress Amendment Act 1895 s 2 (amended by virtue of the Criminal Justice Act 1982 s 46). The
     fine referred to in the text is a fine not exceeding level 1 on the standard scale: see the Law of Distress
     Amendment Act 1895 s 2 (as so amended). 'Standard scale' means the standard scale of maximum fines
     for summary offences as set out in the Criminal Justice Act 1982 s 37 (as amended): see the Interpretation
     Act 1978 s 5, Sch 1 (definition added by the Criminal Justice Act 1988 s 170(1), Sch 15 para 58); and
     CRIMINAL LAW, EVIDENCE AND PROCEDURE vol 11(4) (2006 Reissue) para 1676; MAGISTRATES
     vol 29(2) (Reissue) para 804. At the date at which this volume states the law, the standard scale is as
     follows: level 1, £200; level 2, £500; level 3, £1,000; level 4, £2,500; level 5, £5,000: Criminal Justice
     Act 1982 s 37(2) (substituted by the Criminal Justice Act 1991 s 17(1)). As to the determination of the
     amount of the fine actually imposed, as distinct from the level on the standard scale which it may not
     exceed, see the Criminal Justice Act 2003 s 164; CRIMINAL LAW, EVIDENCE AND PROCEDURE vol 11(4)
     (2006 Reissue) para 1678; MAGISTRATES vol 29(2) (Reissue) para 807.

1000.   Uncertificated landlord may distrain. An uncertificated landlord has the
right to distrain in person, and after a levy he may leave to his uncertificated bailiff the
conduct of the distress from levy to sale; but the managing director of a company is not
in the position of landlord to the tenants of the company, and unless acting under a
certificate as bailiff will be guilty of trespass in distraining[1].

1   *Hogarth v Jennings* [1892] 1 QB 907, CA. In the case, however, only nominal damages were awarded as
     there had been no sale and the goods had only been distrained for a few hours. As to necessity for a bailiff
     to hold a certificate before he can levy a distress see paras 994, 999 ante. As to trespass see TORT vol 45(2)
     (Reissue) para 659 et seq.

1001.   Landlord's liability in respect of bailiff. The bailiff is not an officer of the
court so as to relieve the landlord from liability for the irregular acts of the bailiff. He
remains the agent of the landlord who employs him[1]. The landlord is liable to the tenant
for any irregularities committed by the bailiff in the course of his employment so far as
he is acting within the scope of his employment[2]. For illegal acts outside the scope of
such employment the landlord is not liable without proof that he actually directed them
or ratified and adopted them with knowledge of what had been done, or that he chose
without inquiry to take the risk upon himself and adopted such acts[2].

Thus where, under a warrant in ordinary form authorising him to distrain the goods
and chattels of the tenant, a bailiff seized a fixture which was afterwards sold and the
proceeds paid to the landlord, it was held that the receipt of the proceeds did not make
the landlord liable, it not being shown that he was aware of the illegal seizure[3].
Recognition by the landlord of what has been done may amount to adoption and
ratification[4].

A bailiff is liable to the landlord for damages sustained by the latter by reason of the
former's negligence or misconduct in exceeding his authority[5].

1   *Re Caidan, ex p Official Receiver v Regis Property Co Ltd* [1942] Ch 90 at 96, [1941] 3 All ER 491 at 496
     per Morton J.
2   See *Haseler v Lemoyne* (1858) 5 CBNS 530; *Lewis v Read* (1845) 13 M & W 834; *Hurry v Rickman and
     Sutcliffe* (1831) 1 Mood & R 126. As to vicarious liability see TORT vol 45(2) (Reissue) paras 304, 406,
     815 et seq.
3   *Freeman v Rosher* (1849) 13 QB 780.
4   *Moore v Drinkwater* (1858) 1 F & F 134. See also para 1092 post.
5   *Megson v Mapleton* (1883) 49 LT 744; *White v Heywood* (1888) 5 TLR 115. As to the liability of the
     landlord to indemnify the bailiff see para 993 ante.

1002.   Authority to accept tender. A bailiff holding a warrant to distrain has
implied authority to receive rent and costs when tendered, notwithstanding express
directions to the bailiff by the landlord not to receive them[1].

1   *Hatch v Hale* (1850) 15 QB 10; and see para 976 ante.

(iii) The Entry

1003. Right to enter. The right to distrain necessarily involves the right to enter on the premises where the chattels are for the purpose of taking possession of them, indeed in order to exercise a right of distress it is necessary to enter the premises[1]. The right implies a licence for the distrainor to enter the premises in any way short of breaking into the premises, even though he does that which in the case of any other person would be a trespass[2]. Entering by force would constitute an offence against the Acts prohibiting forcible entry as well as being a trespass[3].

1   *Evans v South Ribble Borough Council* [1992] QB 757, [1992] 2 All ER 695 (service of a notice is not enough). As to the position where the chattels have been fraudulently removed by the tenant see para 1063 et seq post.
2   *Long v Clarke* [1894] 1 QB 119, CA; *American Concentrated Must Corpn v Hendry* (1893) 68 LT 742, CA; *Southam v Smout* [1964] 1 QB 308, [1963] 3 All ER 104, CA; and see *Gould v Bradstock* (1812) 4 Taunt 562 (entry from floor above). As to trespass see TORT vol 45(2) (Reissue) para 659 et seq.
3   Bac Abr, Forcible Entry and Detainer (B); and see *Evans v South Ribble Borough Council* [1992] QB 757, [1992] 2 All ER 695. As to forcible entry see the Criminal Law Act 1977 s 6 (as amended); and CRIMINAL LAW, EVIDENCE AND PROCEDURE vol 11(1) (2006 Reissue) para 602.

1004. Unfastened door. The outer door may be opened in the ordinary way in which persons are accustomed to open it when it is left so as to be accessible to those having occasion to go into the premises[1]. A licence to enter is implied from a door being left unfastened though closed[2]. Thus the latch of the door may be lifted, or a key left outside the door turned, a bolt on the outside drawn back or the door gently pushed open[3]; but the distrainor may not put his hand through a hole and remove a bar which bars an outer door and thus effect an entry[4].

1   *Ryan v Shilcock* (1851) 7 Exch 72 at 75.
2   *Nash v Lucas* (1867) LR 2 QB 590 at 593 per Lush J.
3   *Ryan v Shilcock* (1851) 7 Exch 72; *Eldridge v Stacey* (1863) 15 CBNS 458; *Southam v Smout* [1964] 1 QB 308, [1963] 3 All ER 104, CA.
4   Fitzherbert's Grand Abridgment, Distress, pl 21.

1005. Outer door must not be broken open. An outer door must not be broken open[1]. This immunity from being broken open extends to the outer door of any building whatever, including an outhouse within the curtilage[2], as well as a barn, stable, or outhouse not within the curtilage of the dwelling house[3]. It would seem that entry through an outer door which had been broken open by an independent third party on his own account would not be illegal[4]. An inner door is not, however, part of the wall to a man's 'castle', and once a distrainor has properly obtained admission to a building, he is justified in breaking open an inner door or lock to find goods which are distrainable[5] or to facilitate removal of the goods[6].

A bailiff who lawfully obtains entry through one door may open another door from the inside to permit entry by another bailiff with whom he is conducting a joint operation[7].

1   *Semayne's Case* (1604) 5 Co Rep 91a; *American Concentrated Must Corpn v Hendry* (1893) 62 LJQB 388, CA.
2   *American Concentrated Must Corpn v Hendry* (1893) 62 LJQB 388, CA; and see *Long v Clarke* [1894] 1 QB 119 at 121, CA, per Lord Esher MR.
3   *Brown v Glenn* (1851) 16 QB 254.
4   See *Nash v Lucas* (1867) LR 2 QB 590; *Sandon v Jervis* (1858) EB & E 935.
5   *Browning v Dann* (1735) Bull NP (7th Edn) 81c; *Lee v Gansel* (1774) 1 Cowp 1 at 8.
6   *Pugh v Griffith* (1838) 7 Ad & El 827.
7   *Southam v Smout* [1964] 1 QB 308, [1963] 3 All ER 104, CA.

1006. Entering by window. An open window is a legitimate means of access for the purpose of distraining[1] (as is an open skylight[2]) and when partially open it may be further opened for the purpose of obtaining admission[3]. As a window is not the usual means of obtaining access to a house, a distrainor may not open a closed but unfastened window, for to do so is a breaking into the house[4]. Much less can he obtain admission by breaking open a window[5] or undoing the hasp[6].

1 *Nixon v Freeman* (1860) 5 H & N 647, 652; *Long v Clarke* [1894] 1 QB 119, CA.
2 *Miller v Tebb* (1893) 9 TLR 515, CA.
3 *Crabtree v Robinson* (1885) 15 QBD 312.
4 *Crabtree v Robinson* (1885) 15 QBD 312; *Nash v Lucas* (1867) LR 2 QB 590; *Southam v Smout* [1964] 1 QB 308, [1963] 3 All ER 104, CA.
5 *Attack v Bramwell* (1863) 3 B & S 520.
6 *Hancock v Austin* (1863) 14 CBNS 634.

1007. Gates and fences. Gates may not be broken open or inclosures broken down[1], but the distrainor may climb over a wall or fence from the adjoining premises[2].

1 Co Litt 161a.
2 *Eldridge v Stacey* (1863) 15 CBNS 458; *Long v Clarke* [1894] 1 QB 119, CA, overruling *Scott v Buckley* (1867) 16 LT 573.

1008. Forcible re-entry. After an entry has been made and not abandoned, but the distrainor has been forcibly expelled or driven away by the tenant's violence, he may obtain assistance and break open the outer door, even after a considerable interval[1].

On the same principle a forcible re-entry may be made where the person in possession voluntarily goes away for a short period, and not with the intention of abandoning the distress, and on returning finds the door locked. In such a case he may break open the door[2]. However, a bailiff is not entitled to re-enter a dwelling house by force unless he has been expelled by force or has been deliberately excluded by the tenant[3]. It is a question of fact in each case whether there has been an abandonment[4].

When, after having been evicted, a bailiff re-enters for the purpose of his distress, he should confine himself to the goods originally seized[5].

1 *Eagleton v Gutteridge* (1843) 11 M & W 465; *Eldridge v Stacey* (1863) 15 CBNS 458 (three weeks); but see *Boyd v Profaze* (1867) 16 LT 431 (original entry incomplete).
2 *Bannister v Hyde* (1860) 2 E & E 627.
3 *Khazanchi v Faircharm Investments Ltd* [1998] 2 All ER 901, [1998] 1 WLR 1603, CA.
4 *Eldridge v Stacey* (1863) 15 CBNS 458; *Bagshawes Ltd v Deacon* [1898] 2 QB 173, CA; *Russell v Rider* (1834) 6 C & P 416. Permitting a third person to remove the goods for a temporary purpose is not an abandonment of them: *Kerby v Harding* (1851) 6 Exch 234; and cf *Jones v Biernstein* [1900] 1 QB 100, CA.
    As against the tenant, the necessity for keeping a man in close possession may be avoided by getting the tenant or a responsible person in the house to enter into an agreement for walking possession: see *National Commercial Bank of Scotland Ltd v Arcam Demolition and Construction Ltd* [1966] 2 QB 593, [1966] 3 All ER 113, CA (a case of execution). Walking possession is not, however, sufficient as against a stranger who is not aware of the impounding: *Abingdon RDC v O'Gorman* [1968] 2 QB 811, [1968] 3 All ER 79, CA. See further para 1018 post.
5 *Smith v Torr* (1862) 3 F & F 505.

(iv) Seizure

1009. Seizure of chattels. To complete a distress a seizure of the chattels is necessary. A seizure may be either actual or constructive[1]. It is actual by laying hands on the article, or on one of several articles, and claiming to detain it or them until the rent is satisfied[2]. The most proper manner of making a distress is for the person distraining to go upon any part of the premises out of which the rent issues and take hold of some personal chattel declaring that it is taken as a distress in the name of all the goods, or of so much as will satisfy the rent in arrear, and this will be a good seizure of all[3]. No particular form of words is, however, necessary provided the intention is manifest.

1　*Cramer v Mott* (1870) LR 5 QB 357 at 359 per Cockburn CJ; and see *Central Printing Works Ltd v Walker and Nicholson* (1907) 24 TLR 88. As to constructive seizure see para 1010 post.
2　*Cramer v Mott* (1870) LR 5 QB 357 at 359; *Wood v Nunn* (1828) 5 Bing 10; *Lloyd's and Scottish Finance Ltd v Modern Cars and Caravans (Kingston) Ltd* [1966] 1 QB 764, [1964] 2 All ER 732.
3　*Dod v Monger* (1704) 6 Mod Rep 215.

1010.　Constructive seizure.　A constructive seizure may occur in various ways. It is enough that the landlord or his agent interferes to prevent the removal of the article from off the premises on the ground that rent is in arrear, and he does this when he declares that the article is not to be removed until the rent is paid[1], and it is immaterial that the article is in fact subsequently removed[2].

Any acts indicative of an intention that antecedent steps should be treated as a distress, and assumed by the parties to amount to a distress, will be sufficient evidence of a seizure. Thus if money is paid on the footing that there has been a distress[3], or if the bailiff after intimating his intention to distrain walks round the demised premises and without touching anything gives written notice that he has distrained, that will amount to a seizure[4].

A mere intention to distrain which is obviously abandoned is not sufficient[5]; and as against third parties no action will lie for removal of goods which have not been actually seized[6].

1　*Cramer v Mott* (1870) LR 5 QB 357; *Wood v Nunn* (1828) 5 Bing 10.
2　*Werth v London and Westminster Loan Co* (1889) 5 TLR 320 at 321.
3　*Hutchins v Scott* (1837) 2 M & W 809.
4　*Swann v Earl of Falmouth* (1828) 8 B & C 456.
5　*Spice v Webb and Morris* (1838) 2 Jur 943.
6　*Pool v Crawcour* (1884) 1 TLR 165, CA. As to actual seizure see para 1009 ante.

(v)　Notice of Distress

1011.　Necessity for notice of distress.　No notice of distress was necessary at common law, because at common law all that the distrainor was required to do was to seize the goods and impound them, and, if the impounding was in a private pound, to give notice of the place to which they were taken[1]. By statute, whether the distress is levied by a bailiff or by the landlord in person, notice of the distress is necessary before the goods can be sold[2]; and where a bailiff levies the distress, notice is necessary whether or not a sale is intended[3].

The right of sale to a distress is provided for by the Distress for Rent Act 1689, but before the distrainor can proceed to sale, he must cause notice of the fact of the distress having been made (with the cause of the taking) to be left at the chief mansion-house or other most notorious place on the premises charged with the rent distrained for[4]. It has, however, been held to be sufficient if the notice is delivered personally to the tenant or owner of the goods, as the case may be, even though the delivery is not at 'the chief mansion-house or other most notorious place on the premises', for the intention of the Act[5] is only that the party should have notice, which is more satisfactorily performed in this way than by leaving it at a place[6]. As against a stranger whose goods have been seized, notice to him will satisfy the statute[7]. The notice must be in writing[8], and if the distress is to be levied by a bailiff must be in a prescribed form[9]. An error in the name of the person on whose behalf the distress is made[10], or in the time at which the rent distrained for became due[11], is immaterial, and it is not necessary to specify when the rent became due[12].

1 *Kerby v Harding* (1851) 6 Exch 234 at 240–241 per Parke B. As to impounding see para 1013 et seq post.
2 See the text to notes 4–12 infra.
3 See para 1012 post.
4 See the Distress for Rent Act 1689 s 1 (amended by the Statute Law Revision Act 1948).
5 Ie the Distress for Rent Act 1689 s 1 (as amended): see the text and note 4 supra.
6 *Walter v Rumbal* (1695) 1 Ld Raym 53; and see *Jarvis v Hemmings* [1912] 1 Ch 462.
7 *Walter v Rumbal* (1695) 1 Ld Raym 53.
8 *Wilson v Nightingale* (1846) 8 QB 1034. As to the form of a notice given by a landlord distraining in person see para 1012 post.
9 The requirements of the Distress for Rent Act 1689 s 1 (as amended) as to notice will be satisfied by the memorandum which the bailiff must serve by virtue of the Distress for Rent Rules 1988, SI 1988/2050 (as amended): see para 1012 post.
10 *Wootley v Gregory* (1828) 2 Y & J 536.
11 *Gambrell v Earl of Falmouth* (1835) 4 Ad & El 73.
12 *Moss v Gallimore* (1779) 1 Doug KB 279.

1012. Contents of notice. A bailiff levying distress must deliver to the tenant or leave on the premises where the distress is levied a memorandum in a prescribed form identifying the bailiff and specifying in an inventory the goods distrained on and setting out the amounts for which the distress is levied and the authorised fees, charges and expenses[1]. The prescribed form includes an inventory and, on the back, a statement of the authorised scale of fees, charges and expenses[2].

Where the landlord distrains in person there is no prescribed form of notice[3], but any notice should state the following matters:

(1) The cause of the taking, that is the amount of rent due[4]. At common law no duty is cast on the landlord distraining to inform the tenant what is the arrear of rent for which he distrains, as the tenant is presumed to know what things are in arrear for his land[5]; nor is he bound by an incorrect statement of the amount, since he may distrain at common law for one cause and afterwards in a claim for replevin or other claim he may justify for a different cause[6]; but when it becomes necessary to justify the act of selling the goods it must be shown that the landlord has given a notice showing the cause of the distress[7].

(2) The goods taken[8]. The notice should contain such information as will enable the tenant to know exactly what particular goods have been seized[9]. General words indicating that all goods are distrained may render the notice void[10].

(3) The place of impounding[11], if the goods are impounded off the premises[12].

(4) The time when the goods will be sold unless replevied or the rent and charges paid[13].

1 Distress for Rent Rules 1988, SI 1988/2050, rr 2(2), 10, 12(2), App 1 (as amended), App 2 Form 7; and see para 1058 post. As to the powers under which the rules were made see para 994 note 3 ante. A bailiff or his agent attending to remove goods from the premises or withdrawing from possession prior to sale of the distrained goods must deliver to the tenant or leave on the premises where distress is levied a memorandum in a prescribed form setting out the expenses of removal authorised by and incurred under the Distress for Rent Rules 1988, SI 1988/2050 (as amended): r 12(3). As to the form for removal expenses see App 2 Form 9.
2 Ibid App 2 Form 7. The forms set out in the Distress for Rent Rules 1988, SI 1988/2050 (as amended) may be used with such variations as the circumstances may require: r 2(2).
3 Notice of distress need not be given unless a sale is intended so that the Distress for Rent Act 1689 s 1 (as amended) (see paras 1011 ante, 1044, 1056 post) will apply: see *Trent v Hunt* (1853) 9 Exch 14. See also para 1011 text to notes 4–9 ante.
4 *Kerby v Harding* (1851) 6 Exch 234.
5 *Tancred v Leyland* (1851) 16 QB 669, Ex Ch.
6 *Crowther v Ramsbottom* (1798) 7 Term Rep 654 at 658; *Etherton v Popplewell* (1800) 1 East 139 at 142; *Trent v Hunt* (1853) 9 Exch 14; *Phillips v Whisted* (1860) 29 LJQB 164 at 165 per Cockburn CJ. The mere fact of distraining for more rent than is due is not per se actionable (*Tancred v Leyland* (1851) 16 QB 669, Ex Ch, overruling *Taylor v Henniker* (1840) 12 Ad & El 488) if the goods taken are not more than sufficient to satisfy the rent actually due (*Tancred v Leyland* supra; *French v Phillips* (1856) 1 H & N 564, Ex

      Ch). An allegation that the excessive distress was maliciously made will not render it actionable in the absence of special damage: *Stevenson v Newnham* (1853) 13 CB 285, Ex Ch.

7   See para 1011 ante.

8   This is generally done by furnishing a copy of the inventory of the goods taken. The distress must be restricted to the articles comprised in the inventory (*Sims v Tuffs* (1834) 6 C & P 207), and the fact that goods not comprised in the inventory have been discovered after the notice was given will not justify including them in the distress (*Bishop v Bryant* (1834) 6 C & P 484). The mere fact that articles not distrainable, eg fixtures, are included in the list does not give rise to a cause of action: *Beck v Denbigh* (1860) 29 LJCP 273.

9   *Kerby v Harding* (1851) 6 Exch 234.

10 *Davies v Property and Reversionary Investments Corpn* [1929] 2 KB 222, DC; *Wakeman v Lindsey* (1850) 14 QB 625; *Kerby v Harding* (1851) 6 Exch 234.

11 As to impounding see para 1013 et seq post.

12 Omitting to state that the goods are impounded will not make the impounding void: *Tennant v Field* (1857) 8 E & B 336.

13 The omission to give the requisite notice makes it irregular to sell, but does not render the distress illegal (*Trent v Hunt* (1853) 9 Exch 14); so that if, notwithstanding the want of notice, the landlord sells, the person aggrieved thereby can recover any special damage he may have sustained (see the Distress for Rent Act 1737 s 19; and *Whitworth v Maden* (1847) 2 Car & Kir 517). See also para 1078 post.

(10) PROCEEDINGS BETWEEN SEIZURE AND SALE

(i) Impounding

1013.   Object and manner of impounding. When chattels have been seized, it is necessary to imprison and secure the chattels for safe custody until the cause of distress is satisfied or the statutory period[1] has elapsed at the expiration of which the chattels can be lawfully sold by reason of the tenant failing to replevy them. This imprisonment, called impounding, places the goods in the custody of the law[2]. If before the chattels are impounded the tenant tenders a sufficient amount for rent and costs, it is unlawful to proceed further with the distress[3].

      Chattels may be impounded on the premises[4] unless the tenant otherwise requests, or they may be removed to a pound off the premises[5]. A pound is either overt (open overhead) or covert (covered overhead).

1   See para 1049 post.

2   See eg *Abingdon RDC v O'Gorman* [1968] 2 QB 811, [1968] 3 All ER 79, CA (where the history of impounding was considered); and see *Evans v South Ribble Borough Council* [1992] QB 757 at 765, [1992] 2 All ER 695 at 700–701 per Simon Brown J. A walking possession agreement prevents the tenant from saying that goods are not impounded, but it is not sufficient to constitute impounding against third parties: see paras 1016, 1018 post.

3   *Vertue v Beasley* (1831) 1 Mood & R 21; and see para 975 ante.

4   See the Distress for Rent Act 1737 s 10. Formerly the practice was to remove goods to the public pound as a distress could only be impounded on the premises with the consent of the tenant; public pounds have practically ceased to exist. As to impounding on the premises see para 1016 post.

5   For exceptions to the right to impound off the premises see para 1014 post. As to impounding off the premises see para 1015 post.

1014.   Exceptions to right to impound off the premises. There are two exceptions to the right to impound off the premises: (1) sheaves or cocks of corn, or corn loose or in the straw, or hay cannot be removed from the premises, but must be impounded where found[1]; and (2) growing crops must, after they are cut, be placed in barns or any other proper place on the premises, and cannot be removed except in default of there being a proper place on the premises[2]. In that case notice of the place where the thing distrained is deposited must, within one week after its deposit in such place, be given to the tenant or left at his last place of abode[3].

1   See the Distress for Rent Act 1689 s 2 (amended by the Statute Law Revision Act 1948).

2   See the Distress for Rent Act 1737 s 8 (amended by the Statute Law Revision Act 1988).
3   Distress for Rent Act 1737 s 9.

1015. Impounding off the premises. Goods impounded off the premises are in the custody of the law while on their way to the pound and whilst in the pound. Their removal and retention in the pound are ordinarily plain and obvious to anyone and the impounding is effective against the tenant, or the owner of the goods, or a third party[1]. In impounding off the premises the distrainor must select a suitable pound. Cattle may be impounded in a pound overt, but furniture and goods liable to be damaged by wet weather or to be stolen must be placed in a house or other pound covert[2]. It seems doubtful if chattels can be brought back to the premises for the purpose of impounding after they have once been impounded off the premises[3].

Impounding is for safe custody, and the distrainor is answerable for the condition of the pound at the time the chattels are put in. He must at his peril take care that the place is in a fit and proper state[4], and he is liable for the loss of or injury to the distress if it is not[5]. For instance, if cattle are tied in the pound and strangle themselves the landlord will be liable, but he is not liable if they die by the act of God[6].

1   *Abingdon RDC v O'Gorman* [1868] 2 QB 811 at 819, [1968] 3 All ER 79 at 82, CA, per Lord Denning MR, and at 823 and 84 per Davies LJ.
2   Co Litt 47b. For the meanings of 'pound overt' and 'pound covert' see para 1013 ante.
3   *Smith v Wright* (1861) 30 LJ Ex 313 at 315 per Bramwell B.
4   Ie even in the unlikely event of its being a public pound.
5   *Wilder v Speer* (1838) 8 Ad & El 547; *Bignell v Clarke* (1860) 5 H & N 485.
6   *Vaspor v Edwards* (1702) 12 Mod Rep 658 at 665. As to the feeding of impounded animals see ANIMALS vol 2(1) (Reissue) paras 633, 639.

1016. Impounding on the premises. By statute goods distrained may be impounded or otherwise secured in such place or on such part of the premises as may be fit and convenient for the impounding and securing of the goods[1]. It has been held that the goods should be moved to one or two rooms and locked up[2], but this rule has been mitigated by permitting, with the consent of the tenant, the goods to remain in their ordinary position on the premises[3]. Very slight evidence of such consent is sufficient[4]. The distraint is then good against the tenant[5].

As against strangers, however, goods are impounded or otherwise secured only when there is a distinct act, such as locking them up in a room, making it manifest that the goods are not to be taken away[6].

Cattle may be impounded in an open field[7].

1   See the Distress for Rent Act 1737 s 10.
2   See eg *Washborn v Black* (1774) 11 East 405n; *Abingdon RDC v O'Gorman* [1968] 2 QB 811, [1968] 3 All ER 79, CA. The whole premises should in no case be locked up to the exclusion of the tenant unless the locking up is necessary for the safe keeping of the distress (*Woods v Durrant* (1846) 16 M & W 149; *Cox v Painter* (1837) 7 C & P 767; *Etherton v Popplewell* (1800) 1 East 139; *Walker v Woolcott* (1838) 8 C & P 352 at 353) and it is not practicable to remove the distress to a convenient place off the premises (*Smith v Ashforth* (1860) 29 LJ Ex 259).
3   *Washborn v Black* (1774) 11 East 405n; *Abingdon RDC v O'Gorman* [1968] 2 QB 811, [1968] 3 All ER 79, CA.
4   *Washborn v Black* (1774) 11 East 405n; *Tennant v Field* (1857) 8 E & B 336. As to walking possession agreements see para 1018 post.
5   *Abingdon RDC v O'Gorman* [1968] 2 QB 811, [1968] 3 All ER 79, CA.
6   *Abingdon RDC v O'Gorman* [1968] 2 QB 811 at 821–822, [1968] 3 All ER 79 at 82–83, CA, per Lord Denning MR, and at 824–826 and 84–86 per Davies LJ (not following dicta in *Lavell & Co Ltd v O'Leary* [1933] 2 KB 200, CA).
7   *Castleman v Hicks* (1842) Car & M 266; *Thomas v Harries* (1840) 1 Man & G 695.

1017. Using the distress. Whether impounded on or off the premises, the landlord may not use or work the goods or cattle impounded unless it is necessary to do so for the preservation of the thing distrained and is for the benefit of the owner, for example milch cows may be milked[1]. The distrainor may permit the tenant to use the chattels while impounded, and even license their removal for a temporary purpose[2].

1   *Bagshawe v Goward* (1607) Cro Jac 147; Bac Abr, Distress (D). The dictum of Powis J to the contrary effect in *Vaspor v Edwards* (1702) 12 Mod Rep 658 at 662, would not, it is submitted, be good law now. See ANIMALS vol 2(1) (Reissue) para 630.
2   *Kerby v Harding* (1851) 6 Exch 234.

1018. Nature of possession to be kept.   When the landlord impounds the goods upon the premises[1], leaving them there without anyone in possession, that is sufficient custody, for they are in the custody of the law[2]. If he abandons them, then the possession reverts to the tenant. Whether or not his acts amount to an abandonment is always one of fact when the point arises[3]. If he puts a bailiff in possession it is not necessary that the bailiff should retain continuous physical possession[4].

The modern practice is for the distrainor and the tenant to enter into a walking possession agreement. This permits the tenant to continue to have the use of the goods and to avoid the expense and inconvenience of having a person in possession. The tenant agrees that in consideration of the distrainor not leaving a person in close possession and leaving the goods in their existing positions he will not remove or allow any of the goods to be removed from the premises[5]. Such an agreement may be made by the tenant or a responsible person in the house[6].

Such an agreement prevents the tenant from saying that there has not been an impounding actual or constructive[7]. It does not, however, bind any stranger who is not aware of the impounding[8].

A form of walking possession agreement is prescribed[9] and a charge for walking possession is provided for[10].

1   As to impounding on the premises generally see para 1016 ante.
2   *Swann v Earl of Falmouth* (1828) 8 B & C 456; *Lavell & Co Ltd v O'Leary* [1933] 2 KB 200, CA.
3   *Lumsden v Burnett* [1898] 2 QB 177, CA. As to what amounts to abandonment see para 1061 post.
4   *Bannister v Hyde* (1860) 2 E & E 627; *Jones v Biernstein* [1899] 1 QB 470 (affd [1900] 1 QB 100, CA); and see *Kemp v Christmas* (1898) 79 LT 233, CA. As to the necessity for an impounding to be manifest in order to bind a stranger see the text to note 8 infra; and para 1016 ante. As to the charge of a possession fee see para 1058 notes 1, 7 post.
5   For the prescribed form of walking possession agreement see note 9 infra.
6   *National Commercial Bank of Scotland Ltd v Arcam Demolition and Construction Ltd* [1966] 2 QB 593, [1966] 3 All ER 113, CA (a case of execution). As to walking possession in cases of execution see ENFORCEMENT vol 17(1) (Reissue) para 167.
7   See *Abingdon RDC v O'Gorman* [1968] 2 QB 811, [1968] 3 All ER 79, CA.
8   *Abingdon RDC v O'Gorman* [1968] 2 QB 811, [1968] 3 All ER 79, CA, not following dicta in *Lavell & Co Ltd v O'Leary* [1933] 2 KB 200, CA; and see paras 1016 ante, 1071 post.
9   See the Distress for Rent Rules 1988, SI 1988/2050, App 2 Form 8 (amended by SI 2003/1858). The forms in the Distress for Rent Rules 1988, SI 1988/2050, App 2 (as amended) may be used with such variations as the circumstances may require: r 2(2).
10   See ibid r 10, App 1 para 3(ii) (as amended); and see further para 1058 text and note 8 post. As to the additional charge of a sum equal to value added tax see para 1058 note 1 post.

(ii) Appraisement

1019. Necessity for, and mode of, appraisement.   An appraisement of the chattels distrained is only necessary as a condition precedent to a sale[1], first, when the tenant or owner of the chattels by writing requires such appraisement to be made[2], and, secondly, in the case of growing crops[3]. Where appraisement is necessary, the appraisers must be reasonably competent, though not necessarily professional, appraisers[4], and they must be disinterested persons[5]. Where, however, the broker to save expense has valued the goods at the instance of the person distrained upon, the latter cannot afterwards complain of it[6].

Two appraisers are necessary, whatever the amount of the rent, unless the tenant consents to one acting[7].

1 Under the Distress for Rent Act 1689 s 1 (as amended) (see paras 1011 ante, 1044, 1056 post), before a distress could be sold the distrainor was required with the sheriff or under-sheriff or the constable of the hundred or parish to cause the goods to be appraised by two sworn appraisers. So much of the Act as required the assistance of the sheriff, under-sheriff, and constable was repealed by the Parish Constables Act 1872 s 13 (repealed), and the repeal of the rest of the provisions of the Distress for Rent Act 1689 as to appraisement except upon a requirement was effected by the Law of Distress Amendment Act 1888 s 5.
2 See ibid s 5. As to the fee see the Distress for Rent Rules 1988, SI 1988/2050, App 1 para 4 (amended by SI 2003/1858). As to the addition to the fee of a sum equal to value added tax see para 1058 note 1 post.
3 The reason for appraisement in this case is the Distress for Rent Act 1737 s 8 (amended by the Statute Law Revision Act 1988), which provides that the crops are to be appraised when cut and gathered and not before, and the abolition of appraisement, which was effected by a qualified repeal of the Distress for Rent Act 1689 (see note 1 supra), does not refer to the later statute.
4 *Roden v Eyton* (1848) 6 CB 427.
5 See *Lyon v Weldon* (1824) 2 Bing 334 (landlord should not be appointed); *Westwood v Cowne* (1816) 1 Stark 172; *Rocke v Hills* (1887) 3 TLR 298 (bailiff should not be appointed).
6 *Bishop v Bryant* (1834) 6 C & P 484.
7 *Allen v Flicker* (1839) 10 Ad & El 640.

(11) EFFECT OF INSOLVENCY, RECEIVERSHIP AND EXECUTION

(i) Insolvency

A. IN GENERAL

1020. Legislation. The legislation relating to corporate[1] and individual insolvency[2] affects a landlord's ability to levy distress.

1 See paras 1021–1025 post.
2 See paras 1026–1029 post.

B. CORPORATE INSOLVENCY

1021. Corporate voluntary arrangements and the right to distrain. Where a corporate tenant is subject to a corporate voluntary arrangement[1], the landlord's right to distrain is not affected[2] except to the extent that the corporate voluntary arrangement may have reduced or removed the liability to pay rent to which the right to distrain relates[3].

1 See the Insolvency Act 1986 s 1 (as amended); and COMPANY AND PARTNERSHIP INSOLVENCY vol 7(3) (2004 Reissue) paras 71–72, 108; COMPANY AND PARTNERSHIP INSOLVENCY vol 7(4) (2004 Reissue) paras 1170–1171.
2 See *McMullen & Sons Ltd v Cerrone* (1993) 66 P & CR 351, [1994] 1 BCLC 152.
3 See *Re Naeem (a bankrupt) (No 18 of 1988)* [1990] 1 WLR 48, [1989] 46 LS Gaz R 37; and cf *March Estates plc v Gunmark Ltd* [1996] 2 BCLC 1, [1996] BPIR 439.

1022. Corporate voluntary arrangements and the procedure to avoid distress. The creation of a corporate voluntary arrangement does not in itself prevent the superior landlord[1] of the immediate tenant[2] (where rent of the immediate tenant is in arrear) serving notice pursuant to the Law of Distress Amendment Act 1908 upon any undertenant[3] or lodger[4] stating the amount of rent in arrears and requiring future payments of rent to be made direct to him until the arrears have been duly paid[5].

1 As to the meaning of 'superior landlord' see para 956 note 1 ante.
2 As to the meaning of 'tenant' see para 951 note 4 ante.
3 As to the meaning of 'undertenant' see para 951 note 2 ante.
4 As to lodgers see para 953 ante.
5 See the Law of Distress Amendment Act 1908 s 6; and para 960 ante.

1023. Distress and administration. Administration is a procedure whereby the court orders the appointment of an administrator over a company's affairs[1]. While a company is in administration no legal process (including distress) may be instituted or continued against the company or property of the company except with the consent of the administrator, or with the permission of the court[2]. The company's liability to pay rent is not affected by administration. If the administrator has unreasonably refused to pay rent, the court may give leave to distrain or may refuse leave on terms that rent is paid, and may order the administrator to pay the landlord's costs[4].

1 See the Insolvency Act 1986 s 8 (as substituted), Sch B1 (as added and amended); and COMPANY AND PARTNERSHIP INSOLVENCY vol 7(3) (2004 Reissue) para 145 et seq.
2 See ibid Sch B1 para 43(6) (as added); and COMPANY AND PARTNERSHIP INSOLVENCY vol 7(3) (2004 Reissue) para 263. Where the court gives permission for such a transaction, it may impose a condition on or a requirement in connection with the transaction: see Sch B1 para 43(7) (as added); and COMPANY AND PARTNERSHIP INSOLVENCY vol 7(3) (2004 Reissue) para 263.
4 See *Re Atlantic Computer Systems plc* [1992] Ch 505, [1992] 1 All ER 476, CA.

1024. Staying distress during voluntary liquidation. Where a tenant company is in voluntary liquidation[1], a landlord is not prevented from distraining[2]. However, the liquidator, any contributory or any creditor may apply to the court to determine any question[3] and the court may stay any distress[4]. In the absence of circumstances outside the levying of distress, such as fraud or unfair dealing, the court does not usually stay distress commenced before voluntary liquidation[5]. The court usually stays distress commenced after the commencement of liquidation[6].

1 See the Insolvency Act 1986 Pt I (ss 1–7B) (as amended), Pt IV Chs I–V (ss 73–116) (as amended); and COMPANY AND PARTNERSHIP INSOLVENCY vol 7(4) (2004 Reissue) para 939 et seq.
2 See *Westbury v Twigg & Co Ltd* [1892] 1 QB 77, DC. See also COMPANY AND PARTNERSHIP INSOLVENCY vol 7(4) (2004 Reissue) para 1014.
3 See the Insolvency Act 1986 s 112(1); and COMPANY AND PARTNERSHIP INSOLVENCY vol 7(4) (2004 Reissue) para 1012.
4 *Re Higginshaw Mills and Spinning Co* [1896] 2 Ch 544, CA; *Herbert Berry Associates Ltd v IRC* [1978] 1 All ER 161, [1977] 1 WLR 1437, HL.
5 *Venner's Electrical Cooking and Heating Appliances Ltd v Thorpe* [1915] 2 Ch 404 at 408, CA, per Neville J.
6 *Re Margot Bywaters Ltd* [1942] Ch 121, [1941] 3 All ER 471. See also COMPANY AND PARTNERSHIP INSOLVENCY vol 7(4) (2004 Reissue) para 1014.

1025. Staying distress during compulsory liquidation. Where a petition for the winding-up of a company is presented[1], a distress begun before the presentation of the petition is not affected but the company, any contributory or any creditor may thereafter apply to the court to stay the distress[2]. However, when a winding-up order has been made, distress may not be proceeded with or commenced against the company except with the leave of the court[3]. The court will usually allow distress begun before the commencement of the winding-up of a company to be completed[4]. Distress begun after the commencement of the winding-up is void[5] unless the court gives leave for distress as a claim or proceeding against the company or its property[6]. Leave is not normally given for distress for rent accrued prior to the commencement of winding-up[7]. Leave is usually given for distress for rent falling due during the liquidation, at least where the liquidator is using or retaining the property for the purposes of the liquidation[8]. Leave, however, may be refused if the use of the property by the liquidator benefits the landlord[9]. Further leave is generally not given to distrain for rent due in advance[10].

The landlord's distress is not interfered with if there is no privity between the landlord and the company upon whose goods distress is levied. Thus distress may be levied on the goods of a third party which happen to be on the insolvent tenant's premises[11] or when an insolvent company happens to have chattels on the premises of a tenant against whom its landlord levies distress[12].

1   See the Insolvency Act 1986 Pt IV Ch VI (ss 117–160) (as amended); and see COMPANY AND PARTNERSHIP INSOLVENCY vol 7(3) (2004 Reissue) para 438 et seq.
2   See ibid s 126(1); *Re Memco Engineering Ltd* [1986] Ch 86, [1985] 3 All ER 267; and COMPANY AND PARTNERSHIP INSOLVENCY vol 7(4) (2004 Reissue) para 887.
3   See the Insolvency Act 1986 s 130(2); and *Re Memco Engineering Ltd* [1986] Ch 86, [1985] 3 All ER 267.
4   *Re Roundwood Colliery Co, Lee v Roundwood Colliery Co* [1897] 1 Ch 373, CA; *Re Bellaglade Ltd* [1977] 1 All ER 319.
5   See the Insolvency Act 1986 s 128(1); and COMPANY AND PARTNERSHIP INSOLVENCY vol 7(4) (2004 Reissue) para 888.
6   See ibid s 130(2); *Re Coal Consumers Association* (1876) 4 ChD 625; and COMPANY AND PARTNERSHIP INSOLVENCY vol 7(4) (2004 Reissue) para 893.
7   *Re Traders' North Staffordshire Carrying Co, ex p North Staffordshire Rly Co* (1874) LR 19 Eq 60; *Re Coal Consumers Association* (1876) 4 ChD 625; *Re North Yorkshire Iron Co* (1878) 7 ChD 661; *Re Bridgewater Engineering Co* (1879) 12 ChD 181.
8   *Re Lundy Granite Co, ex p Heavan* (1871) 6 Ch App 462; *Re Silkstone and Dodworth Coal and Iron Co* (1881) 17 ChD 158.
9   *Re Bridgewater Engineering Co* (1879) 12 ChD 181.
10 *Shackell & Co v Chorlton & Sons* [1895] 1 Ch 378.
11 See *Re Traders' North Staffordshire Carrying Co, ex p North Staffordshire Rly Co* (1874) LR 19 Eq 60. See also *Re New City Constitutional Club Co, ex p Pursell* (1887) 34 ChD 646, CA.
12 See *Re Lundy Granite Co, ex p Heavan* (1871) 6 Ch App 462; *Re Carriage Co-Operative Supply Association, ex p Clemence* (1883) 23 ChD 154.

C. INDIVIDUAL INSOLVENCY

1026. Individual voluntary arrangements and the right to distrain. Where an individual tenant is subject to an individual voluntary arrangement[1], the landlord's right to distrain is not affected[2] except to the extent that the individual voluntary arrangement may have reduced or removed the liability to pay rent to which the right to distrain relates[3].

1   See the Insolvency Act 1986 Pt VIII (ss 252–263G) (as amended); and BANKRUPTCY AND INDIVIDUAL INSOLVENCY vol 3(2) (2002 Reissue) para 82 et seq.
2   See *McMullen & Sons Ltd v Cerrone* (1993) 66 P & CR 351.
3   See *Re Naeem (a bankrupt) (No 18 of 1988)* [1990] 1 WLR 48, [1989] 46 LS Gaz R 37.

1027. Individual voluntary arrangements and the procedure to avoid distress. The outcome of an individual voluntary arrangement does not in itself prevent the superior landlord[1] of the immediate tenant[2] (where rent of the immediate tenant is in arrear) serving notice pursuant to the Law of Distress Amendment Act 1908 upon any undertenant[3] or lodger[4] stating the amount of rent in arrears and requiring future payments of rent to be made direct to him until the arrears have been duly paid[5].

1   As to the meaning of 'superior landlord' see para 956 note 1 ante.
2   As to the meaning of 'tenant' see para 951 note 4 ante.
3   As to the meaning of 'undertenant' see para 951 note 2 ante.

4   As to lodgers see para 953 ante.
5   See the Law of Distress Amendment Act 1908 s 6; and para 960 ante.

1028. Distress and administration. The county court has jurisdiction to make an administration order in relation to individual debtors[1]. Where an administration order[2] is in force a creditor may not present a bankruptcy petition[3] without the leave of the court and unless certain conditions are satisfied[4] or have any remedy against the person or property of the debtor in respect of debts notified to the court or included in the court order, without the leave of the court[5]. A landlord may distrain for rent after the date of the order but only in respect of up to six months' rent accrued before that date[6].

1   See the County Courts Act 1984 Pt VI (ss 112–117) (as amended); and BANKRUPTCY AND INDIVIDUAL INSOLVENCY vol 3(2) (2002 Reissue) para 893 et seq. See also COURTS vol 10 (Reissue) para 721.
2   As to administration orders see BANKRUPTCY AND INDIVIDUAL INSOLVENCY vol 3(2) (2002 Reissue) para 863 et seq.
3   As to bankruptcy petitions see BANKRUPTCY AND INDIVIDUAL INSOLVENCY vol 3(2) (2002 Reissue) para 124 et seq.
4   See the County Courts Act 1984 s 112(4) (as amended); and BANKRUPTCY AND INDIVIDUAL INSOLVENCY vol 3(2) (2002 Reissue) para 896. See also s 112(4A), 112A (both prospectively added); and BANKRUPTCY AND INDIVIDUAL INSOLVENCY vol 3(2) (2002 Reissue) para 896.
5   See ibid s 114(1); and BANKRUPTCY AND INDIVIDUAL INSOLVENCY vol 3(2) (2002 Reissue) para 896.
6   See ibid s 116; and BANKRUPTCY AND INDIVIDUAL INSOLVENCY vol 3(2) (2002 Reissue) para 898.

1029. Distress and bankruptcy. The presentation of a bankruptcy petition, the making of a bankruptcy order[1] and the appointment of a trustee in bankruptcy in whom the lease rests[2], do not prevent the landlord exercising his remedy of distress. The landlord, however, is limited to a maximum of six months' rent accrued due before the bankruptcy is commenced[3] and any sum recovered in excess is held for the bankrupt or his estate[4]. This limit does not apply to distress levied upon chattels of third parties found upon the premises[5]. There is no limit on the amount of rent accruing after the commencement of bankruptcy for which distress can be levied[6]. The right to distrain upon the debtor's goods will cease upon his discharge from bankruptcy[7].

1   See *Re Fanshaw & Yorston, ex p Birmingham and Staffordshire Gaslight Co* (1871) LR 11 Eq 615; and cf *Smith v Braintree District Council* [1990] 2 AC 215, [1989] 3 All ER 897, HL.
2   See *Re Binns, ex p Hale* (1875) 1 ChD 285; the Insolvency Act 1986 s 347(9); and BANKRUPTCY AND INDIVIDUAL INSOLVENCY vol 3(2) (2002 Reissue) para 686. As to bankruptcy petitions see BANKRUPTCY AND INDIVIDUAL INSOLVENCY vol 3(2) (2002 Reissue) para 124 et seq.
3   See ibid s 347(1) (as amended); and BANKRUPTCY AND INDIVIDUAL INSOLVENCY vol 3(2) (2002 Reissue) para 686.
4   See ibid s 347(2); and BANKRUPTCY AND INDIVIDUAL INSOLVENCY vol 3(2) (2002 Reissue) para 686.
5   *Brocklehurst and Lowe v Lawe* (1857) 7 E & B 176; *Railton v Wood* (1890) 15 App Cas 363, PC; *Tomlinson v Consolidated Credit and Mortgage Corpn* (1890) 24 QBD 135, CA.
6   *Re Binns, ex p Hale* (1875) 1 ChD 285; *Re Wells* [1929] 2 Ch 269.
7   See the Insolvency Act 1986 s 347(5); and BANKRUPTCY AND INDIVIDUAL INSOLVENCY vol 3(2) (2002 Reissue) para 691.

(ii) Corporate and Individual Receivership

1030. Types of receivership. There are two types of receivership[1] which are applicable in the same manner both to companies and to individuals: (1) receivership of a mortgaged legal estate[2]; and (2) receivers appointed by the court[3].

1   See generally RECEIVERS.
2   See COMPANIES vol 7(2) (2004 Reissue) paras 1600 et seq, 1624 et seq; MORTGAGE vol 32 (2005 Reissue) paras 676–685.
3   See the Supreme Court Act 1981 (prospectively renamed the Senior Courts Act 1981) s 37; and PRACTICE AND PROCEDURE. See also the Landlord and Tenant Act 1987 Pt II (ss 21–24) (as amended) (appointment of managers by a leasehold valuation tribunal); and LANDLORD AND TENANT.

1031. Landlord's entitlement to distrain. The appointment of a receiver over the tenant's property does not affect the tenant's liability for rent[1] and the landlord is entitled to distrain[2]. If the receiver is appointed by the court, it seems that the landlord ought to apply to the court for leave before executing a distress warrant[3]. If distress has been commenced before the receiver is appointed, the landlord need not apply for leave to proceed with the distress[4].

1   *George Barker (Transport) Ltd v Eynon* [1974] 1 All ER 900, [1974] 1 WLR 462, CA; *AMEC Properties Ltd v Planning Research and Systems plc* [1992] BCLC 1149, [1992] 1 EGLR 70, CA.
2   *Re Roundwood Colliery Co, Lee v Roundwood Colliery Co* [1897] 1 Ch 373, CA.
3   *Re Sutton's Estate, Sutton v Rees* (1863) 9 Jur NS 456; *Russell v East Anglian Rly Co* (1850) 3 Mac & G 104 at 118. The application should be made within the claim in which the receiver was appointed: *Searle v Choat* (1884) 25 ChD 723, CA.
4   *Engel v South Metropolitan Brewing and Bottling Co* [1891] WN 31; *Evelyn v Lewis* (1844) 3 Hare 472 at 475.

(iii) Execution

1032. Execution against tenant. The levying of an execution upon the goods of a tenant places them in the custody of the law and protects them from distress by the landlord[1], except in the case of distress by the Crown[2] or when the execution is collusive[3]. The execution creditor may, however, waive his rights[4].

In general, even though the landlord may not distrain on goods seized in execution, goods seized by the sheriff under an execution in the High Court[5] are by statute forbidden to be removed off the premises until any arrears of rent (not exceeding one year's rent) have been paid by the execution creditor[6]. This statutory provision does not apply to executions at the suit of the landlord[7], or so as to enable a ground landlord to claim the benefit of the Landlord and Tenant Act 1709 on an execution against an underlessee[8]. A sequestration has, however, been treated as an execution within the equity of the statute[9], and a landlord's claim for rent will, by order of the court, be paid out of the proceeds of a sequestration if he might have distrained[10]. The provision is not confined to goods and chattels which are distrainable in point of law, but casts the duty upon the sheriff to take care that the goods seized are not removed until the provision is complied with[11]. In as much as the goods of a stranger are not liable to execution, the statute confers on the sheriff no power to seize such goods or to apply the proceeds of their sale in payment of the rent[12]. Should he seize and remove goods belonging to a stranger, he will be liable for a year's arrears of rent, as he has taken off the premises that which the landlord had the right to distrain[13], and he will also be liable to account to the real owner whether he has paid the landlord or not[14]. If two executions are levied the landlord cannot have a year's rent on each[15].

1   *Re Mackenzie, ex p Sheriff of Hertfordshire* [1899] 2 QB 566 at 573, CA; and see Co Litt 47a; *Wharton v Naylor* (1848) 12 QB 673; *Lewis v Davies* [1914] 2 KB 469, CA. The provision forbidding the removal of goods by the sheriff without paying one year's rent (see the text to notes 5–6 infra) does not authorise a distraint on goods in the custody of the law: *Wharton v Naylor* (1848) 12 QB 673 at 679. See also ENFORCEMENT vol 17(1) (Reissue) para 190.
2   *R v Cotton* (1751) Park 112 (confirming *R v Dale* (1719) Bunb 42); *A-G v Leonard* (1888) 38 ChD 622; and see also *R v Hill* (1818) 6 Price 19.
3   *Smith v Russell* (1811) 3 Taunt 400.
4   *Seven v Mihill* (1756) 1 Keny 370.
5   The Landlord and Tenant Act 1709 s 1 (as amended) does not apply to executions in the county court: see the County Courts Act 1984 s 102(1); and ENFORCEMENT vol 17(1) (Reissue) para 191. When goods are seized under county court process the landlord may claim rent in arrear under s 102(2): see para 1041 post; and ENFORCEMENT vol 17(1) (Reissue) para 191. As to the office of sheriff see generally SHERIFFS.
6   See the Landlord and Tenant Act 1709 s 1 (as amended); and ENFORCEMENT vol 17(1) (Reissue) para 190. The levying of a distress for rates, although analogous to execution (see para 904 ante) is not

'execution' within this provision, so as to be subject to the landlord's priority: *Potts v Hickman* [1941] AC 212, [1940] 4 All ER 491, HL. As to weekly and other tenancies for less than a year see para 1040 post. As to the effect of the bankruptcy of the tenant see para 1029 ante. As to the effect of the liquidation of a tenant company on the landlord's right see COMPANY AND PARTNERSHIP INSOLVENCY vol 7(4) (2004 Reissue) para 888. As to the necessity of notice of the landlord's rights to the sheriff see para 1036 post. A receiver may be a landlord within the Landlord and Tenant Act 1709 s 1 (as amended): see *Cox v Harper* [1910] 1 Ch 480, CA.

7   *Taylor v Lanyan* (1830) 6 Bing 536 at 544.
8   *Bennet's Case* (1727) 2 Stra 787; *Re Eastcheap Alimentary Products Ltd* [1936] 3 All ER 276; and c f *Thurgood v Richardson* (1831) 7 Bing 428 (statutory provision applicable between lessees and undertenant).
9   *Dixon v Smith* (1818) 1 Swan 457. A sequestration does not prevent a distress upon the goods of the contemnor by the landlord (*Dixon v Smith* supra) or the removal of his chattels from the premises (*Desbrow v Crommie* (1729) 1 Barn KB 212).
10   *Dixon v Smith* (1818) 1 Swan 457.
11   *Riseley v Ryle* (1843) 11 M & W 16; and see *Smallman v Pollard* (1844) 6 Man & G 1001 at 1009.
12   *Beard v Knight* (1858) 8 E & B 865.
13   *Forster v Cookson* (1841) 1 QB 419.
14   *White v Binstead* (1853) 13 CB 304.
15   *Dod v Saxby* (1735) 2 Stra 1024.

1033.   When restriction upon removal obtains.   Further, it may be taken to be established that the restriction upon removal[1] does not apply except in the case of a subsisting tenancy[2]; but, provided it is subsisting, it may be a tenancy created by an attornment in a mortgage deed[3], or by a stipulation in a purchase agreement under which the purchaser takes possession and pays a fixed yearly rent until completion[4].

The tenancy must be one to which the right of distress is incident, that is to say it must be at a rent certain for which there is a present right to distrain[5].

The rent must be rent actually due at the time of seizure[6], and not that which accrues afterwards, though possession is retained by the sheriff[7]. If it is due it is immaterial that it is reserved payable in advance[8], and the full rent may be claimed though the landlord has been accustomed to remit a portion to the tenant[9]. If the landlord is induced to withdraw a distress on the tenant's false assurance that a particular debt is satisfied, and subsequently execution is levied for the debt, the landlord is entitled to his year's rent[10]. The landlord protected is the person immediately entitled to the rent, or the person who has a title upon which he can bring a claim for recovery of land[11].

1   See the Landlord and Tenant Act 1709 s 1 (as amended); and para 1032 ante.
2   *Cox v Leigh* (1874) LR 9 QB 333; *Hodgson v Gascoigne* (1821) 5 B & Ald 88; *Lewis v Davies* [1914] 2 KB 469, CA. It does not, therefore, apply when the tenancy has determined before the seizure, though within six months of it: *Cox v Leigh* (1874) LR 9 QB 333.
3   *Yates v Ratledge* (1860) 5 H & N 249.
4   *Saunders v Musgrave* (1827) 6 B & C 524.
5   *Riseley v Ryle* (1843) 11 M & W 16 at 25.
6   *Gwilliam v Barker* (1815) 1 Price 274.
7   *Hoskins v Knight* (1813) 1 M & S 245; *Reynolds v Barford* (1844) 7 Man & G 449; *Re Davis, ex p Pollen Trustees* (1885) 55 LJQB 217.
8   *Harrison v Barry* (1819) 7 Price 690.
9   *Williams v Lewsey* (1831) 8 Bing 28.
10   *Wollaston v Stafford* (1854) 15 CB 278.
11   *Colyer v Speer* (1830) 2 Brod & Bing 67 at 69. A claim may be brought by the administrator of the landlord (*Palgrave v Windham* (1719) 1 Stra 212), provided administration has been granted and demand of the rent made before the goods have been removed (*Waring v Dewberry* (1718) 1 Stra 97).

1034.   Removal of goods by sheriff.   The sheriff does not infringe the statutory provision[1] unless he removes or permits the removal of the goods without satisfying the rent[2]. There must be an actual or constructive removal. It is not sufficient that the goods have been seized and sold if there has been no removal[3]. The statutory provision is infringed, however, by the removal of any portion of the goods seized[4]; and, once removed, the wrong cannot be purged by the subsequent return of the goods to the premises[5]. A landlord waives the benefit of the statute by consenting to the removal, even if consent is given upon the faith of an undertaking to pay the rent which is unfulfilled[6].

1   Ie the Landlord and Tenant Act 1709 s 1 (as amended): see para 1032 ante.
2   *Re Davis, ex p Pollen Trustees* (1885) 55 LJQB 217. As to the office of sheriff see generally SHERIFFS.
3   *Smallman v Pollard* (1844) 6 Man & G 1001; *White v Binstead* (1853) 13 CB 304.
4   *Colyer v Speer* (1820) 2 Brod & Bing 67.
5   *Lane v Crockett* (1819) 7 Price 566, Ex Ch; *Wren v Stokes* [1902] 1 IR 167, CA.
6   *Rotherey v Wood* (1811) 3 Camp 24.

1035.   Relinquishing possession.   If the sheriff relinquishes possession of the goods, the possession reverts to the original owner, and they may be distrained[1]. They are likewise distrainable if not removed within a reasonable time after sale by the sheriff[2].

1   *Ackland v Paynter* (1820) 8 Price 95; *Re Mackenzie, ex p Sheriff of Hertfordshire* [1899] 2 QB 566 at 575, CA. See also *Cropper v Warner* (1883) Cab & El 152 (temporary withdrawal pending interpleader proceedings); *Blades v Arundale* (1813) 1 M & S 711; *St John's College, Oxford v Murcott* (1797) 7 Term Rep 259 at 263–264. For a consideration of the meaning of abandonment of possession by the sheriff see *Lloyds and Scottish Finance Ltd v Modern Cars and Caravans (Kingston) Ltd* [1966] 1 QB 764, [1964] 2 All ER 732; and see also *National Commercial Bank of Scotland Ltd v Arcam Demolition and Construction Ltd* [1966] 2 QB 593, [1966] 2 All ER 113, CA; and ENFORCEMENT vol 17(1) (Reissue) para 167. As to abandonment in cases of distress see para 1061 post. As to the office of sheriff see generally SHERIFFS.
2   *Re Davis, ex p Pollen Trustees* (1885) 55 LJQB 217; *Peacock v Purvis* (1820) 2 Brod & Bing 362 at 367; *Wright v Dewes* (1834) 1 Ad & El 641.

1036.   What is sufficient notice to sheriff.   The sheriff is under no obligation to inquire whether any rent is in arrear, and he is under no liability to the landlord for not keeping the goods, unless informed that rent is due[1]. If, however, the sheriff has notice before the goods are removed that rent is due to the landlord, and nevertheless does not keep the goods on the premises, but sells them without paying the landlord, the sheriff becomes liable to the landlord for the wrongful removal[2]. Express notice is not necessary, it is sufficient if the sheriff has knowledge of the claim[3]; and, if he is informed by notice that rent is due, the form of the notice is not material[4]. The notice is in time while the goods or the proceeds of sale remain in the sheriff's hands[5]. When the claim is made by the landlord the sheriff must ascertain that the relationship of landlord and tenant exists, and that rent is really due, and he is entitled to see the lease if there is one[6]. If the relationship is established, slight proof of rent in arrear will generally be accepted, but he is bound as between himself and the execution creditor to ascertain whether the rent is due[7].

1   *Re Mackenzie, ex p Sheriff of Hertfordshire* [1899] 2 QB 566 at 574, CA; *Waring v Dewberry* (1718) 1 Stra 97; *Palgrave v Windham* (1719) 1 Stra 212 at 214; *Arnitt v Garnett* (1820) 3 B & Ald 440. As to the office of sheriff see generally SHERIFFS.
2   *Re Mackenzie, ex p Sheriff of Hertfordshire* [1899] 2 QB 566, CA; *Riseley v Ryle* (1843) 11 M & W 16; *Andrews v Dixon* (1820) 3 B & Ald 645.
3   *Andrews v Dixon* (1820) 3 B & Ald 645.
4   *Colyer v Speer* (1820) 2 Brod & Bing 67.
5   *Arnitt v Garnett* (1820) 3 B & Ald 440.
6   *Augustien v Challis* (1847) 1 Exch 279; *Keightley v Birch* (1814) 3 Camp 521.
7   *Frost v Barclay* (1887) 3 TLR 617 at 618, DC.

1037.   Goods not to be sold after notice, until rent paid.   Where notice has been given to the sheriff by the landlord that rent is due, the sheriff should call upon the execution creditor to pay it[1], and should refuse to sell any of the goods until it is paid; even if there are goods upon the demised premises of a value many times exceeding the amount of rent due, his duty is the same, and he should refuse to sell the smallest part of the goods until the claim of the landlord is satisfied[2]. The landlord's claim must be paid without any deduction for sheriff's fees[3]. The sheriff is not bound to advance the money to pay the rent out of his own pocket. If the execution creditor declines to advance it, the sheriff may refuse to sell[4]; but if the sheriff is willing to do so, he may sell, pay the landlord's rent and apply the surplus, if any, in satisfaction of the debt[5], and if there is no surplus may return nulla bona[6]. If no one will pay the landlord's rent the sheriff can withdraw and return nulla bona[7]. When the goods on the premises are not sufficient to satisfy the rent lawfully demanded the sheriff should withdraw[8]. When he withdraws, the landlord can distrain for his whole rent[9].

1   In Ireland it has been held that the sheriff is not bound to notify the judgment creditor of the landlord's claim: see *Davidson v Allen* (1886) 20 LR Ir 16. As to the office of sheriff see generally SHERIFFS.
2   *Thomas v Mirehouse* (1887) 19 QBD 563 at 566, DC, per Lord Esher MR.
3   *Gore v Gofton* (1725) 1 Stra 643.
4   *Cocker v Musgrove and Moon* (1846) 9 QB 223 at 234; *Thomas v Mirehouse* (1887) 19 QBD 563 at 566, DC.
5   *Cocker v Musgrove and Moon* (1846) 9 QB 223 at 234; *Thomas v Mirehouse* (1887) 19 QBD 563 at 566, DC; *Wintle v Freeman* (1841) 11 Ad & El 539.
6   See ENFORCEMENT.
7   *Wintle v Freeman* (1841) 11 Ad & El 539; *Re Mackenzie, ex p Sheriff of Hertfordshire* [1899] 2 QB 566 at 575, CA.
8   *Foster v Hilton* (1831) 1 Dowl 35.
9   *Re Mackenzie, ex p Sheriff of Hertfordshire* [1899] 2 QB 566 at 575, CA.

1038.   Liability for wrongful removal etc.   If the sheriff infringes the statutory restriction[1] and permits the removal of the goods before the rent is paid, and in consequence the landlord loses any part of his rent, the sheriff is liable at the suit of the landlord for wrongful removal without paying him[2]; and also for a negligent sale of the goods whereby the landlord is damnified[3].

The landlord has no right to require the goods to be sold for his benefit, and if they are sold he cannot maintain a claim against the sheriff for money had and received[4]. No claim will lie against the execution creditor, as he has nothing to do with the removal of the goods[5].

1   Ie under the Landlord and Tenant Act 1709 s 1 (as amended): see para 1032 ante. As to the office of sheriff see generally SHERIFFS.
2   *Re Mackenzie, ex p Sheriff of Hertfordshire* [1899] 2 QB 566 at 575, CA; *Thomas v Mirehouse* (1887) 19 QBD 563, DC; *Calvert v Joliffe* (1831) 2 B & Ad 418. In such a claim the landlord need only prove the fact of occupation; the burden of proving payment of the rent lies upon the sheriff: *Harrison v Barry* (1819) 7 Price 690.
3   *Groombridge v Fletcher* (1834) 2 Dowl 353.
4   *Re Mackenzie, ex p Sheriff of Hertfordshire* [1899] 2 QB 566, CA; *Green v Austin* (1812) 3 Camp 260.
5   *Cocker v Musgrove and Moon* (1846) 9 QB 223.

1039.   Measure of damages.   The measure of damages in a claim against the sheriff at the suit of the landlord is prima facie the amount of rent due[1], but it is competent to the sheriff to prove in mitigation of damages that the real value of the goods removed was not sufficient to pay the rent. All that the landlord has to prove is that the rent is in arrear, that the sheriff has had notice of this, and that he has notwithstanding removed the goods. It then lies on the sheriff to show that the value of the goods removed was less than the rent to reduce his liability[2].

1   Ie not exceeding a year, or six months if the tenant is bankrupt: see paras 1029, 1032 ante. As to the office of sheriff see generally SHERIFFS.
2   *Thomas v Mirehouse* (1887) 19 QBD 563, DC.

1040.   Claims for rent where goods seized in execution: High Court.   In the case of weekly and other tenancies for less than a year the arrears of rent which may be claimed upon an execution[1] are further limited, for no landlord of any tenement let at a weekly rent has a claim or lien upon any goods taken in execution under the process of any court of law for more than four weeks' arrears of rent; and if such tenement is let for any term less than a year other than a weekly term the landlord has no claim or lien on the goods for more than the arrears of rent accruing during four such terms or times of payment[2].

1 See para 1032 ante.
2 Execution Act 1844 s 67 (amended by the Statute Law Revision Act 1891). This provision is repealed, except in so far as it relates to the process of the High Court: see the Supreme Court Act 1981 (prospectively renamed the Senior Courts Act 1981) s 152(4), Sch 7. County court executions are governed by the County Courts Act 1984 s 102 (as amended): see para 1041 post; and ENFORCEMENT vol 17(1) (Reissue) para 191.

1041. Claims for rent where goods seized in execution: county court. Under the county court process the landlord is protected by different provisions[1].

The bailiff must sell under the execution and distress such of the goods as satisfies the claim of the landlord, and the landlord is protected in respect of arrears of rent to the following extent: (1) in a case where the tenement is let by the week, four weeks' rent; (2) in a case where the tenement is let for any other term less than a year, the rent of two terms of payment; (3) in any other case, one year's rent[2].

The landlord of any tenement in which any goods are seized may claim the rent of the tenement in arrear at the date of the seizure, at any time within the five days following that date, or before the removal of the goods, by delivering to the bailiff or officer making the levy a claim in writing, signed by himself or his agent, stating the amount of rent claimed to be in arrear, and the period in respect of which the rent is due[3]. Where such a claim is made, the bailiff or officer making the levy must in addition distrain for the rent so claimed and the cost of the distress, and must not, within five days after the distress, sell any part of the goods seized, unless the goods are of a perishable nature, or the person whose goods have been seized so requests in writing[4]. After the period of five days, the bailiff must sell under execution and distress such of the goods as will satisfy, first, the costs of and incidental to the sale; next, the claim of the landlord not exceeding the amounts set out in heads (1) to (3) above; and lastly, the amount for which the warrant of execution is issued[5].

1 See the County Courts Act 1984 s 102(1); para 1032 ante; and ENFORCEMENT vol 17(1) (Reissue) para 191. As to claims in the High Court see para 1040 ante.
2 See ibid s 102(4)(b).
3 Ibid s 102(2).
4 Ibid s 102(3).
5 Ibid s 102(4).

1042. Agricultural produce and farming animals. Where, under the Sale of Farming Stock Act 1816, a sheriff has sold any crop or produce under an agreement that the purchaser will expend the crop or produce for the benefit of the land, the landlord may not distrain on any corn, hay, straw or other produce which has been severed at the time of such agreement, or on any turnips drawn or growing thus sold, or on any horses, sheep, or other cattle or beasts, or on any wagons or other implements of husbandry kept or used on the land for the purpose of carrying out the agreement[1].

1 See the Sale of Farming Stock Act 1816 ss 3, 6 (both as amended); and ENFORCEMENT vol 17(1) (Reissue) para 158. The restriction applies where the produce has been severed before sale: see *Wright v Dewes* (1834) 1 Ad & El 641 at 652 per Littledale J. As to the interpretation of this statute see *Hutt v Morrell* (1848) 11 QB 425. As to distress on growing crops see para 1043 post. As to distress for rent on agricultural holdings see AGRICULTURE vol 1(2) (Reissue) paras 333–335. As to the office of sheriff see generally SHERIFFS.

1043. Growing crops. Where growing crops are seized and sold by a sheriff or other officer in execution, such crops, as long as they remain on the land, are subject to distress for rent which may accrue due to the landlord after any seizure and sale, but only in default of other sufficient distress[1].

1 See the Landlord and Tenant Act 1851 s 2. As to the office of sheriff see generally SHERIFFS.

(12) SALE OF DISTRESS

(i) In general

1044. Sale of distress. Any goods distrained for rent, which have not been replevied within five days after the distress and notice thereof, may be sold for the best price that can be obtained, towards satisfaction of the rent[1].

Sale is optional and not imperative, and no claim lies against a landlord for not selling[2]; otherwise a landlord could never relinquish a distress by agreement with his tenant. Apparently, however, sheaves or cocks of corn or corn loose or in the straw or hay and growing crops[3] must, in default of replevy, be sold under and subject to the statutory provisions[4].

1 Distress for Rent Act 1689 s 1 (amended by the Statute Law Revision Act 1948); Distress for Rent Act 1737 s 10; Co Litt (Hargrave and Butler Edn) 47b note 305; Com Dig Distress (D8); 3 Bl Com (14th Edn) 14. For the calculation of the five days and as to extension of the time for sale see para 1049 post. As to replevin see para 1081 et seq post. See also para 1046 post.
2 *Philpott v Lehain* (1876) 35 LT 855 (confirming *Lear v Edmonds* (1817) 1 B & Ald 157 and *Hudd v Ravenor* (1821) 2 Brod & Bing 662). The words 'shall' and 'may' in the Distress for Rent Act 1689 s 1 (as amended) are held to be permissive only, and not compulsory; but see para 1049 text to note 6 post.
3 As to the provisions rendering sheaves and cocks of corn etc and growing crops distrainable see para 929 ante.
4 See *Piggott v Birtles* (1836) 1 M & W 441 at 448. As to the time and place of sale see paras 1049–1053 post.

1045. No claim before sale. Until the sale the existence of a distress is an answer to a claim for the rent distrained for, whether the distress is sufficient or not to satisfy the amount for which the distress is levied; for until sale, while the distress is being held, the debt from the tenant is suspended although the property in the goods is not divested[1].

On the sale of the distress, the proceeds of the sale are an instantaneous executed satisfaction of the rent, vesting to that amount in the landlord, and the tenant has only an interest in any surplus[2]. If the proceeds of the sale are insufficient to satisfy the landlord's claim, the landlord can recover the balance due by claim or otherwise[3].

1 *Lehain v Philpott* (1875) LR 10 Exch 242 (in which the earlier authorities are reviewed). The tenant, before sale, if he wishes to avoid sale, must take proceedings in replevin, and by adoption of the principle stated in the text two concurrent claims on the same point are avoided. As to the property not being divested see also *Iredale v Kendall* (1878) 40 LT 362 at 363 per Lopes J. As to replevin see para 1081 et seq post.
2 *Moore v Pyrke* (1809) 11 East 52. For the effect of this on the undertenant's right to be reimbursed see para 1057 post.
3 *Philpott v Lehain* (1876) 35 LT 855; and see *Lehain v Philpott* (1875) LR 10 Exch 242 at 245–246.

1046. Matters prior to sale. Until sale, whether the statutory five days[1] have elapsed or not, and even if the goods have been removed from the premises, the tenant has the right to replevy them, for at common law the goods were at all times repleviable, and the statute did not change this right, until the property passed by sale[2]. A landlord ought not to sell the goods after a tender of the rent and costs has been made at any time within the five days, and if he does so he will be liable in damages to the tenant[3].

An agreement between a tenant and the distrainor relating to the disposition of the goods seized does not debar the tenant from claiming damages for excessive distress[4].

1 See paras 1044 ante, 1049 post. As to extension of the five days see para 1049 post.
2 *Jacob v King* (1814) 5 Taunt 451. As to replevin see para 1081 et seq post.
3 *Johnson v Upham* (1859) 2 E & E 250 (overruling *Ellis v Taylor* (1841) 8 M & W 415). The decision in *Johnson v Upham* supra is based on an equitable construction beneficial to the tenant of the enactments which confer on the landlord a power of sale: see para 1044 note 1 ante. If the decision had been otherwise, the only way for the tenant to seek to prevent a sale of goods seized and impounded would be a claim for replevin in which he would necessarily be defeated: *Johnson v Upham* supra at 264. The decision forms an exception to the general rule (see *Firth v Purvis* (1793) 5 Term Rep 432; *Ladd v Thomas* (1840) 12 Ad & El 117; *Tennant v Field* (1857) 8 E & B 336) that a tender after impounding is bad. As to impounding see para 1013 et seq ante.
4 *Sells v Hoare* (1824) 1 Bing 401; *Willoughby v Backhouse* (1824) 2 B & C 821; and see para 1080 post.

1047. Irregularity in sale. An irregularity in the sale will make the landlord liable to account not merely for the proceeds, but for the value of the goods, and the tenant will be entitled by way of surplus to the full value of the goods less the rent and charges[1]. The value in such a case is a question of fact, and the price reached at an admittedly fair sale is not conclusive[2]; but no damages can be recovered if no actual damage has accrued[3], or if the sale is wholly void[4].

1 *Biggins v Goode* (1832) 2 Cr & J 364 (sale without appraisement); *Whitworth v Maden* (1847) 2 Car & Kir 517 (no notice of distress); *Clark v Holford* (1848) 2 Car & Kir 540 (excessive distress); *Knight v Egerton* (1852) 7 Exch 407 (sale without appraisement). As to notice see paras 1011–1012 ante. As to appraisement see para 1019 ante. As to remedies for irregular distress see para 1095 post.
2 *Smith v Ashforth* (1860) 29 LJ Ex 259 at 260 per Martin B.
3 *Rodgers v Parker* (1856) 18 CB 112; *Lucas v Tarleton* (1858) 3 H & N 116 (where no damage had accrued owing to a sale too soon by one day); and see *Proudlove v Twemlow* (1833) 1 Cr & M 326.
4 *Owen v Legh* (1820) 3 B & Ald 470 (a case of premature sale of standing corn and growing crops); and see para 1050 post. See also *Beck v Denbigh* (1860) 29 LJCP 273.

1048. Bailiff may not sell to cover fees. After a landlord has directed a bailiff to withdraw, the landlord's claim being satisfied, a bailiff may not sell any of the tenant's goods for the payment of his own fees and expenses, and if he does so sell he confers no title on the purchaser[1].

1 *Harding v Hall* (1866) 14 LT 410. See also para 991 ante.

(ii) Time, Place and Price

1049. Time for sale. The sale may not be held until five days have elapsed from the taking of the distress and notice thereof[1]. The five days must be reckoned exclusively of the day of seizure[2], so that the sale cannot take place until the sixth day from the seizure. These five days[3] within which the tenant or owner of the goods distrained is entitled to replevy are extended to a period of not more than 15 days if the tenant or owner of the goods makes a written request to the landlord or other person making the levy and also gives security for any additional cost occasioned by such extension of time[4]. The landlord or such person may, however, with the written request or consent of the tenant or the owner, sell the goods and chattels distrained or part of them at any time before the expiration of the extended period[5]. A landlord may remain in possession for an extended period at the tenant's request; such an arrangement, however, might, as affecting the rights of third parties, be found collusive[6].

1 See the Distress for Rent Act 1689 s 1 (as amended); and para 1044 ante. As to notice of distress see paras 1011–1012 ante.
2 *Robinson v Waddington* (1849) 13 QB 753; and see TIME vol 45(2) (Reissue) para 228.
3 As to replevin see para 1081 et seq post. See also para 1046 ante.

4   Law of Distress Amendment Act 1888 s 6. The security to be given by the replevisor is settled by the county court district judge: see paras 1084–1085 post.

5   Ibid s 6 proviso.

6   *Harrison v Barry* (1819) 7 Price 690. In *Fisher v Algar* (1826) 2 C & P 374, it was held that, if the distrainor did not know which were the tenant's goods and which were a lodger's goods, the tenant's request would justify the distrainor in detaining all the goods beyond what would otherwise have been the proper time limit; but this decision has been criticised. As to the statutory protection of the goods of lodgers see para 951 et seq ante.

1050.   Growing crops and sheaves of corn. Growing crops cannot be sold[1] until they are ripe, and a sale when unripe is wholly void[2]. Sheaves or cocks of corn or corn loose or in the straw or hay[3] must, unless replevied[4], be sold within five days[5] unless the time is extended[6].

1   See the Distress for Rent Act 1737 s 8 (as amended), s 9; and paras 929, 1044 ante.

2   See para 1047 text and note 4 ante.

3   As to the power to distrain corn etc see para 929 ante.

4   As to replevin see para 1081 et seq post.

5   See *Piggott v Birtles* (1836) 1 M & W 441 at 448; and see also para 1044 ante.

6   Ie under the Law of Distress Amendment Act 1888 s 6: see para 1049 ante.

1051.   Premature sale. A premature sale involving no actual damage is in general an irregularity for which no damages can be recovered[1]. A person protected by statute, however, has a right of action against a landlord who sells before the requisite five days[2], although he has not at the time served any declaration[3]. Although the landlord cannot sell until the expiration of the five days, he may remain upon the premises a reasonable time beyond the five days for the purpose of selling the goods distrained; the amount of the reasonable time is a question of fact in each individual case[4]. A continuance in possession or retention of the goods on the premises for an unreasonable time may constitute a trespass[5].

1   See para 1047 note 3 ante. As to a premature sale of growing crops see para 1047 note 4 ante.

2   See paras 1044, 1049 ante.

3   *Sharpe v Fowle* (1884) 12 QBD 385; and see the Law of Distress Amendment Act 1908 s 1 (as amended); and paras 951, 956 ante.

4   *Pitt v Shew* (1821) 4 B & Ald 208; and see *Philpott v Lehain* (1876) 35 LT 855.

5   *Griffin v Scott* (1726) 2 Ld Raym 1424; *Winterbourne v Morgan* (1809) 11 East 395 (where Lord Ellenborough CJ at 400–401 had great doubt whether, on the construction of the Distress for Rent Act 1737 s 19 (see para 1078 post), the mere person of the distrainor remaining on the premises, without any disturbance of the plaintiff's possession would constitute the distrainor a trespasser). As to trespass see TORT vol 45(2) (Reissue) para 659 et seq.

1052.   Place of sale. The sale of distress generally takes place where the goods and chattels are impounded[1], and if the goods are impounded on the premises chargeable with the rent they may be sold on those premises, and any person or persons whatsoever may enter on the premises for the purpose of taking part in the sale and of carrying off or removing goods on account of a purchaser[2]. The tenant or owner of the goods or chattels distrained may by written request, however, require them to be removed to a public auction room or to some other fit and proper place specified in the request and to be sold there[3], the person making the request bearing the costs and expenses attending the removal and any damage to the goods and chattels arising therefrom[4]. A request for removal does not estop the claimant from complaining of an original wrongful seizure of the goods[5].

1   As to impounding see para 1013 et seq ante.

2   Distress for Rent Act 1737 s 10. As to a tenant's licence for any purchaser to enter his premises to fetch away goods sold see *Wood v Manley* (1839) 11 Ad & El 34.

3   The wording of this provision is probably not free from ambiguity, but it seems that it is intended that the tenant or owner should give to the distrainor the option of removing the goods either to any public auction room or to a place specified in the request.

4   Law of Distress Amendment Act 1888 s 5. As to the charging of a fee for removal see para 1058 note 1 post.

5   *Masters v Fraser* (1901) 85 LT 611.

1053. Sale of sheaves of corn etc. Sheaves or cocks of corn or corn loose or in the straw or hay must be locked up or detained and sold on the land where they are found[1], while growing crops must likewise be cut, gathered, and laid up in barns or other proper place on the premises, unless in default of there being such barns or proper place the landlord procures a barn or other place of storage in the neighbourhood, and when these are sold the sale must be at the place of storage[2].

1   See the Distress for Rent Act 1689 s 2 (as amended); and paras 929, 1014 ante.
2   Distress for Rent Act 1737 s 8 (as amended); and see paras 929, 1014 ante.

1054. Best price must be obtained. The goods must be sold at the best price that can be obtained for them[1]. No condition may be imposed at the sale that may restrict the best price from being obtained, even though the tenant himself was bound by the condition in his own user of the goods[2], the landlord by the sale of distress waiving any covenant in the lease restraining such user[3]. In any claim for not selling at the best price, evidence may be given of mismanagement in connection with the handling of the goods at the sale[4].

1   See the Distress for Rent Act 1689 s 1 (as amended); and para 1044 ante.
2   *Hawkins v Walrond* (1876) 1 CPD 280. This case finally decided the point which had previously been the subject of conflicting decisions.
3   *Hawkins v Walrond* (1876) 1 CPD 280 at 285 per Lindley J.
4   *Poynter v Buckley* (1833) 5 C & P 512.

(iii) Mode of Sale

1055. Mode of sale. Although the goods and chattels distrained are generally sold by auction, there is no statutory provision that an auction must be held[1]. An auctioneer purporting to sell under a distress warrant does not give an implied warranty of title in so selling[2].

In order that the property may pass there must be an actual sale to a third person, and the landlord for this purpose cannot take the goods to himself or be the purchaser of them[3]. A landlord who himself purports to purchase does not obtain a valid title, and is liable to be sued for conversion[4]; even if the form of sale by auction is gone through, the goods do not vest in him so as to deprive a third party of their ownership[5]. Apparently, however, the tenant by agreement with the landlord may cede his own goods which have been seized in satisfaction or part satisfaction of the sum distrained for[6]. A true sale, however, although irregular, passes the property in the subject matter of the distress[7]. So long as the party selling acts bona fide there is no rule regulating the order in which the goods must be sold, and apparently all goods not privileged need not be exhausted before goods conditionally privileged are disposed of[8].

1   There is no such provision either in the Distress for Rent Act 1689 s 1 (as amended) (see (see paras 1011, 1044 ante, 1056 post), or in the Law of Distress Amendment Act 1888.
2   *Payne v Elsden* (1900) 17 TLR 161; and see AUCTION vol 2(3) (Reissue) para 252.
3   *King v England* (1864) 4 B & S 782; *Moore, Nettlefold & Co v Singer Manufacturing Co* [1903] 2 KB 168 (affd [1904] 1 KB 820, CA).
4   *Plasycoed Collieries Co Ltd v Partridge, Jones & Co Ltd* [1912] 2 KB 345. In this case, such a sale was held not to be a mere 'irregularity' within the Distress for Rent Act 1737 s 19 (see para 1078 post). As to conversion see TORT vol 45(2) (Reissue) para 548 et seq.

5   *Moore, Nettlefold & Co v Singer Manufacturing Co* [1904] 1 KB 820, CA.

6   *King v England* (1864) 4 B & S 782 at 786 per Blackburn J.

7   *King v England* (1864) 4 B & S 782 at 785–786 per Blackburn J, and at 786 per Mellor J; and see *Lyon v Weldon* (1824) 2 Bing 334 (confirming *Wallace v King* (1788) 1 Hy Bl 13).

8   *Jenner v Yolland* (1818) 6 Price 3 at 13. As to goods conditionally privileged see paras 948–949 ante.

1056.   Overplus. The overplus after the sale, namely the residue after the payment of the rent and of the reasonable charges of distress, appraisement, and sale, if any, should, in strict law, be left in the hands of the sheriff, undersheriff, or constable for the owner's use[1]; but in practice such overplus is generally paid over to the tenant direct[2]. The court, however, may be required to find whether the tenant has or has not received the balance in satisfaction of the real overplus[3].

1   Distress for Rent Act 1689 s 1. As to the office of sheriff see generally SHERIFFS.

2   *Stubbs v May* (1823) 1 LJOSCP 12; *Taylor v Harrison* (1832) 1 LJKB 155; *Lyon v Tomkies* (1836) 1 M & W 603 at 606, where Lord Abinger CB explained that any technical irregularity in the payment without special damage gave no cause of action in accordance with the Distress for Rent Act 1737 s 19 (see para 1078 post). As to the right to recover for irregular distress see para 1078 post.

3   *Lyon v Tomkies* (1836) 1 M & W 603. Charges are now regulated by the Distress for Rent Rules 1988, SI 1988/2050 (as amended): see para 1058 post.

1057.   Tenant's remedy for infringement of statutory provisions. The tenant's remedy, if he suffers damage owing to the provisions of the Distress for Rent Act 1689[1] not being carried out, is by a claim under the statute, and not for money had and received[2]; nor has an undertenant whose goods have been distrained, a claim against the immediate tenant, who owed the rent, to recover the surplus paid over as money paid to his use[3], though he is entitled to be reimbursed the value of the goods by the person from whom the rent was due[4]; nor is a landlord liable to inquire into or act on any notice of claim by a third party either to the surplus proceeds or to the surplus goods. In regard to the latter, although no provision is made by statute, it is proper for the landlord to return unsold goods, which have been removed, to the place from which they were taken[5], or possibly to put them in some convenient place and give the tenant notice of that place[6].

1   Ie the Distress for Rent Act 1689 s 1 (as amended): see paras 1011, 1044, 1056 ante.

2   *Yates v Eastwood* (1851) 6 Exch 805; and see para 1091 post.

3   *Moore v Pyrke* (1809) 11 East 52.

4   See para 950 ante.

5   *Evans v Wright* (1857) 2 H & N 527.

6   *Evans v Wright* (1857) 2 H & N 527 at 533 per Watson B.

(13) EXPENSES OF DISTRESS

1058.   Regulation of expenses. The fees, charges and expenses in and incidental to distress for rent are regulated by the Distress for Rent Rules 1988[1]. No person is entitled to charge, or recover from, a tenant any fees, charges or expenses for levying a distress, or for doing any act or thing in relation thereto, other than those specified in the relevant appendix annexed to the rules[2]. In the case of any difference as to fees, charges and expenses between any of the parties, they are upon application to be assessed, by way of detailed assessment[3], by the district judge of the county court of the district where the distress is levied, and he may make such order as he thinks fit as to the costs of the detailed assessment[4].

 The effect of the provisions set out above is that no charges may be made other than the prescribed charges for any act in the course of the distress or the carrying of the distress into effect or in relation to the levying of the distress and that any agreement to the contrary between the landlord and the tenant or the landlord and the bailiff is invalid[5].

The possession charged for must be real or actual to enable the full charges[6] to be made[7]. A reduced charge is payable for walking possession but only if a walking possession agreement in a prescribed form has been signed[8].

The fee for levying distress is one which the distraining bailiff may retain out of the proceeds of the distress by way of remuneration[9].

1   See the Distress for Rent Rules 1988, SI 1988/2050, App 1 paras 1–9 (as amended). Appendix 1 (as amended) lays down the fees etc for levying distress (App 1 para 1 (substituted by SI 2003/2141)), for attending to levy distress (Distress for Rent Rules 1988, SI 1988/2050, App 1 para 2 (amended by SI 2003/1858)), for taking possession (Distress for Rent Rules 1988, SI 1988/2050, App 1 para 3 (amended by SI 2003/1858)), for appraisement (Distress for Rent Rules 1988, SI 1988/2050, App 1 para 4 (amended by SI 2003/1858)), for attending to remove (Distress for Rent Rules 1988, SI 1988/2050, App 1 para 5 (amended by SI 2003/1858)), and for sale (Distress for Rent Rules 1988, SI 1988/2050, App 1 para 6). Reasonable fees, charges and expenses may be taken where the distress is withdrawn or where no sale takes place, and for negotiations between landlord and tenant respecting the distress, subject to detailed assessment under r 11 (as amended) (see the text and note 4 infra): App 1 para 7 (amended by SI 2003/1858). Provision is made as to the calculation of percentage charges: see the Distress for Rent Rules 1988, SI 1988/2050, App 1 para 8. In addition to any amount authorised by these provisions in respect of the supply of goods or services on which value added tax is chargeable there may be added a sum equivalent to value added tax at the appropriate rate on that amount: App 1 para 9. As to the charge of value added tax on the supply of goods and services see generally VALUE ADDED TAX vol 49(1) (2005 Reissue) para 18 et seq.

        In so far as the Distress for Rent Rules 1988, SI 1988/2050 (as amended) relate to fees, they are made under the power conferred by the Law of Distress Amendment Act 1888 s 8(2): see para 994 note 3 ante.

2   Distress for Rent Rules 1988, SI 1988/2050, r 10, App 1 (as amended: see note 1 supra).
3   Ie under CPR Pt 47.
4   Distress for Rent Rules 1988, SI 1988/2050, r 11(1) (r 11 amended by SI 1999/2360; and by virtue of the Courts and Legal Services Act 1990 s 74). Where the court in which the detailed assessment is conducted is not the court in which the bailiff was granted his certificate (see para 995 ante) and the district judge is of opinion on the detailed assessment that there has been overcharging of such magnitude as to call into question the fitness of a bailiff to hold a certificate, the court officer must send to the court in which the bailiff was granted his certificate a copy of the completed bill indorsed with a note of the district judge's opinion: Distress for Rent Rules 1988, SI 1988/2050, r 11(2) (as so amended). The receipt of a bill under r 11(2) (as amended) is to be treated as a complaint under r 8(1) (as amended) (see para 997 ante): r 11(3).
5   *Day v Davies* [1938] 2 KB 74, [1938] 1 All ER 686, CA. The actual type of agreement in question in *Day v Davies* supra, namely an agreement for walking possession, is now, however, permitted in distress for rent subject to a limitation on charges: see the text and note 8 infra.
6   Ie under the Distress for Rent Rules 1988, SI 1988/2050, App 1 para 3(i) (amended by SI 2003/1858).
7   *Ex p Arnison* (1868) LR 3 Exch 56, where an attempt failed to charge full possession fees for the technical possession of growing crops.
8   Distress for Rent Rules 1988, SI 1988/2050, App 1 para 3(ii) (amended by SI 2003/1858). For the prescribed form see the Distress for Rent Rules 1988, SI 1988/2050, App 2 Form 8 (amended by SI 2003/1858). As to walking possession see para 1018 ante.
9   *Philipps v Rees* (1889) 24 QBD 17, CA. Although this decision was actually under the Agricultural Holdings (England) Act 1883 Sch 2 (repealed), the reasoning applies equally to fees under the Distress for Rent Rules 1988, SI 1988/2050 (as amended): see *Philipps v Rees* supra at 23 per Lopes LJ.

(14) SECOND DISTRESS

1059.   No second distress for same rent.   The remedy by distress must not be used in an oppressive manner, and the general rule is that a landlord may not split one entire demand and distrain twice for the same rent when he might have taken enough on the first occasion.

If he levies for too small a sum or seizes goods of inadequate value when he had a fair opportunity to seize more it is his own fault, and he cannot repair it by a second levy[1].

The rule is limited to a second distress made for the same rent. Separate rents may be reserved under one lease in respect of separate parcels and separately distrained for[2]; and where the rent in arrear consists of several instalments of rent falling due on different days, there may be a separate distress for each[3]. It is immaterial that the first distress is taken for the rent which last became due[4]. The same goods, after being replevied, may be distrained upon a second time for another instalment of rent[5].

1   *Dawson v Cropp* (1845) 1 CB 961; *Wallis v Savill* (1701) 2 Lut 1532 at 1536; *Hutchins v Chambers* (1758) 1 Burr 579 at 589; *Owens v Wynne* (1855) 4 E & B 579; *Bagge v Mawby* (1853) 8 Exch 641; *Grunnell v Welch* [1905] 2 KB 650 at 653 per Kennedy J (on appeal [1906] 2 KB 555, CA).
2   Shep Touch 81. See paras 979, 983 ante.
3   *Gambrell v Earl of Falmouth* (1835) 4 Ad & El 73.
4   *Palmer v Stanage* (1661) 1 Lev 43.
5   *Hefford v Alger* (1808) 1 Taunt 218; and see *Wilton v Wiffen* (1830) 8 LJOSKB 303. As to replevin see para 1081 et seq post.

1060.   Exceptions.   In the following cases the general rule against a second distress[1] does not apply and a second distress may be taken:

(1)   if there are not sufficient goods on the premises on the first occasion[2];

(2)   if the person seizing the goods on the first occasion has reasonably mistaken their value, for example where the goods were pictures, jewels· or racehorses or other objects of uncertain value[3] or, owing to circumstances not anticipated at the time of the distress, the goods failed to realise their market value[4];

(3)   if the conduct of the tenant has prevented the landlord realising the fruits of the distress[5];

(4)   if cattle die in the pound by the act of God[6].

1   See para 1059 ante.
2   *Wallis v Savill* (1701) 2 Lut 1532.
3   *Hutchins v Chambers* (1758) 1 Burr 579 at 589.
4   *Rawlence and Squarey v Spicer* [1935] 1 KB 412, CA (distress for tithe rentcharge; only two tenders on sale owing to anti-tithe agitation, the higher being by the person on whom the distress had been levied).
5   *Bagge v Mawby* (1853) 8 Exch 641; *Lee v Cooke* (1858) 3 H & N 203, Ex Ch. So also if a combination of the person on whom the distress was levied and other persons prevents the sale from being effective: *R v Judge Clements, ex p Ferridge* [1932] 2 KB 535; *Rawlence and Squarey v Spicer* [1935] 1 KB 412, CA (cases of distress for title rentcharge).
6   *Anon* (1568) 3 Dyer 280a pl 14; *Anon* (1700) 12 Mod Rep 397.

1061.   Voluntary abandonment.   The rule against a second distress[1] applies where the landlord having distrained enough voluntarily abandons the distress, that is to say where he surrenders or forbears to exercise his power of making the distress fruitful[2]. Abandonment is a question of fact[3]. Merely quitting possession of goods after the distress is not necessarily an abandonment[4]; nor is failure to resume immediate possession upon being forcibly expelled[5]; nor is allowing the goods of a stranger which have been distrained to be removed for a temporary purpose[6]. Further, a distrainor does not abandon if he enters into a walking possession agreement with a tenant[7] or with a responsible person in the tenant's house[8].

An exception to the application of the rule in the case of voluntary abandonment is where the landlord is induced in good faith to withdraw the distress at the request of or by the procurement of the tenant[9]; but the procurement must have been that of the tenant, and not of a stranger[10].

1   See para 1059 ante.
2   *Bagge v Mawby* (1853) 8 Exch 641; *Dawson v Cropp* (1845) 1 CB 961; *Smith v Goodwin* (1833) 4 B & Ad 413.
3   *Eldridge v Stacey* (1863) 15 CBNS 458; *Lumsden v Burnett* [1898] 2 QB 177, CA.
4   *Bannister v Hyde* (1860) 2 E & E 627; *Jones v Biernstein* [1899] 1 QB 470 (affd [1900] 1 QB 100, CA).

5   *Eldridge v Stacey* (1863) 15 CBNS 458.
6   *Kerby v Harding* (1851) 6 Exch 234.
7   *Lumsden v Burnett* [1898] 2 QB 177, CA; *Lloyds and Scottish Finance Ltd v Modern Cars and Caravans (Kingston) Ltd* [1966] 1 QB 764, [1964] 2 All ER 732 (a case of execution). See also *Abingdon RDC v O' Gorman* [1968] 2 QB 811, [1968] 3 All ER 79, CA.
8   As to walking possession see para 1018 ante.
9   *Bagge v Mawby* (1853) 8 Exch 641 at 649–650 per Parke B; *Crosse v Welch* (1892) 8 TLR 709 at 710, CA; and see also *Wollaston v Stafford* (1854) 15 CB 278 (false representation); *Thwaites v Wilding* (1883) 12 QBD 4, CA (arrangement not carried out).
10 Where a landlord withdrew his distress in consequence of a creditor stating that he was proceeding against a tenant in bankruptcy and warning the landlord not to sell, a second distress was illegal, as he should have disregarded the warning: *Bagge v Mawby* (1853) 8 Exch 641.

1062.   When first distress unlawful.   For the rule against a second distress[1] to apply, the proceedings in the first distress must have been such that if they had been carried out they would have resulted in the landlord getting what he got in the second proceedings; and where a purported first distress was a mere trespass and void ab initio as a distress, so that the landlord could not satisfy his claim for rent by means of that proceeding, he may lawfully distrain again for the same rent[2].

1   See para 1059 ante.
2   *Grunnell v Welch* [1906] 2 KB 555, CA (where the first distress was a trespass, and upon the authority of *Attack v Bramwell* (1863) 3 B & S 520, was void ab initio).

(15)   FRAUDULENT REMOVAL

1063.   Landlord's powers on fraudulent removal by tenant.   When the tenant fraudulently or clandestinely removes his goods or chattels from the demised premises to prevent the landlord from distraining them, the landlord, or any person empowered by him, may within 30 days after such removal seize the goods and chattels from wherever they are to be found[1] and sell them as if they had actually been distrained upon the demised premises[2]; provided that the goods and chattels have not been sold in good faith and for a valuable consideration before such seizure to any person not privy to the fraud[3].

1   See *Southam v Smout* [1964] 1 QB 308 at 326, [1963] 3 All ER 104 at 109, CA, per Lord Denning. This case concerned the arrest of a debtor at a stranger's house but the authorities as to right of entry by bailiffs were reviewed. As to right of entry on the premises of a third party for the purposes of execution see generally ENFORCEMENT.
2   Distress for Rent Act 1737 s 1 (amended by the Statute Law Revision Act 1948). At common law there was nothing to prevent a tenant from clandestinely and fraudulently removing his goods to avoid their being distrained.
3   Distress for Rent Act 1737 s 2. See also para 980 ante.

1064.   When powers exist.   The statutory provision relating to the landlord's powers on the fraudulent removal of goods by the tenant[1] only applies in the following cases.

(1)   The removal must be shown to be fraudulent or clandestine. A removal may be fraudulent even if not made clandestinely and even if it is made openly with the landlord's knowledge[2]. It is not fraudulent if made in the honest belief that the landlord had no legal right to distrain[3]; but the mere fact of removing goods without leaving sufficient to satisfy the rent may be some evidence of fraud[4]. The burden of proving that the removal is fraudulent or clandestine is on the landlord[5].

(2)   The removal must have been to avoid a distress[6]. The tenant's participation in the removal need not be shown and it is sufficient if done with his privity[7].

(3)   The landlord must show that no sufficient distress remains on the premises after the removal[8].

(4)   The removal must have taken place after the rent has fallen due (though not necessarily in arrear), that is on or after the day fixed for payment[9], though it is not necessary to show that the landlord contemplated a distress at the time of removal[10].

(5)   The goods must have been those of the tenant and not of a stranger or lodger[11].

(6)   The goods must have been distrainable by the landlord either at common law or under the Landlord and Tenant Act 1709[12], if they had remained on the premises[13]; so that if the landlord had parted with his reversion[14], or if the tenancy had determined and the tenant had given up possession[15], or if there was no demise at an ascertained rent[16], the landlord could not follow them, nor can he follow and distrain the goods until after the rent is actually in arrear[17].

(7)   The removal must have been on behalf of the tenant; if a mortgagee, creditor or other person having a charge on the goods removes the goods in assertion of his title to them, with the privity and sanction of the tenant, the statute[18] does not apply[19].

(8)   Where the removed goods are claimed by a purchaser in good faith he must prove his title to them[20].

1   See para 1063 ante.
2   *Opperman v Smith* (1824) 4 Dow & Ry KB 33.
3   *John v Jenkins* (1832) 1 Cr & M 227.
4   *Opperman v Smith* (1824) 4 Dow & Ry KB 33.
5   *Inkop v Morchurch* (1861) 2 F & F 501.
6   *Parry v Duncan* (1831) 7 Bing 243.
7   *Lister v Brown* (1823) 3 Dow & Ry KB 501.
8   *Parry v Duncan* (1831) 7 Bing 243. This has, however, been questioned: see *Gillam v Arkwright* (1850) 16 LTOS 88; *Gegg v Perrin* (1845) 9 JP 619.
9   *Rand v Vaughan* (1835) 1 Bing NC 767; *Dibble v Bowater* (1853) 2 E & B 564; *Watson v Main* (1799) 3 Esp 15. In *Dibble v Bowater* supra, the tenant removed the goods on the morning of the day on which rent was due, and the landlord, after the rent had become in arrear and within 30 days of the removal, followed and seized the goods as a distress; the seizure was held justified, the rent being due and payable, though not in arrear at the time of the removal. This case was considered in *Re Aspinall, Aspinall v Aspinall* [1961] Ch 526, [1961] 2 All ER 751, where the lessor died on the morning of the day on which rents were due and the question arose whether the rents were capital or income of his estate.
10 *Stanley v Wharton* (1822) 10 Price 138.
11 *Thornton v Adams* (1816) 5 M & S 38; *Fletcher v Marillier* (1839) 9 Ad & El 457; *Postman v Harrell* (1833) 6 C & P 225; *Foulger v Taylor* (1860) 5 H & N 202.
12 See the Landlord and Tenant Act 1709 s 6 (as amended), s 7; and para 965 ante.
13 *Gray v Stait* (1883) 11 QBD 668, CA.
14 *Ashmore v Hardy* (1836) 7 C & P 501; *Angell v Harrison* (1847) 17 LJQB 25.
15 *Gray v Stait* (1883) 11 QBD 668, CA.
16 *Anderson v Midland Rly Co* (1861) 3 E & E 614.
17 *Stanley v Wharton* (1822) 10 Price 138; *Norman v Wescombe* (1837) 2 M & W 349.
18 Ie the Distress for Rent Act 1737: see paras 1063 ante, 1065 post.
19 *Bach v Meats* (1816) 5 M & S 200; *Tomlinson v Consolidated Credit and Mortgage Corpn* (1889) 24 QBD 135, CA.
20 *Williams v Roberts* (1852) 7 Exch 618.

1065.   Penalty.   To deter the tenant from making a fraudulent removal, as well as others from aiding him, it is provided that if a tenant fraudulently removes and conveys away[1] his goods or chattels to prevent the landlord from distraining them, or if any person wilfully and knowingly aids or assists[2] him in such fraudulent conveying away or carrying off of any part of his goods or chattels or in concealing the same, every person so offending must forfeit to the landlord double the value of the goods or chattels carried off or concealed by him as aforesaid; the penalty to be recovered by action[3].

It is not necessary to show that a distress was in progress or even contemplated[4], or to prove the amount of rent as alleged in the claim[5]. In a claim against a third person the acts and orders of the tenant are admissible evidence of the fraud of the defendant if by other evidence he is proved to have contributed to the proceeding, and circumstances of suspicion may be adduced to prove a fraudulent co-operation between them[6]. A claim under the statute is a penal one, so that the claimant is not entitled to obtain disclosure by delivering requests for information to the defendant[7], and must prove his case strictly[8].

1 The tenant's actual participation in the removal is not necessary if such removal is effected by a third person with his privity: *Lister v Brown* (1823) 3 Dow & Ry KB 501.
2 In the case of a third person he must be shown to have actually assisted the tenant and to have been privy to his fraudulent intent: *Brooke v Noakes* (1828) 8 B & C 537. The removal must have been on behalf of the tenant: see paras 1064 text and notes 18–19 ante.
3 See the Distress for Rent Act 1737 s 3 (amended by the Statute Law Revision Act 1948). For an alternative remedy when the goods do not exceed £50 see para 1066 post. The relevant court is now the High Court by virtue of the Supreme Court Act 1981 (prospectively renamed the Senior Courts Act 1981) s 1(1) (prospectively amended), ss 19(1), (2), 151(5), Sch 4 para 1: see COURTS.
4 *Stanley v Wharton* (1822) 10 Price 138.
5 *Gwinnet v Philips* (1790) 3 Term Rep 643.
6 *Stanley v Wharton* (1822) 10 Price 138.
7 *Hobbs & Co v Hudson* (1890) 25 QBD 232, CA.
8 *Brooke v Noakes* (1828) 8 B & C 537.

1066. Criminal proceedings where value does not exceed £50. To deter the tenant from making a fraudulent removal, as well as others from aiding him, there is a remedy where the goods fraudulently carried off or concealed do not exceed the value of £50[1]. In that case the landlord or his agent may exhibit an information[2] against the offender before two or more justices of the peace, not being interested in the lands whence the goods were removed, who may determine in a summary way whether the parties are guilty, inquire as to the value of the goods fraudulently removed, and order the offender to forfeit double their value[3]. Even when the goods are under the value of £50 the landlord may elect to proceed by claim instead of before the magistrates[4].

1 As to an alternative remedy under the Distress for Rent Act 1737 s 3 (as amended) see para 1065 ante.
2 See the Magistrates' Courts Act 1980 s 50.
3 Distress for Rent Act 1737 s 4 (amended by the Summary Jurisdiction Act 1884 s 4, Schedule; the Statute Law Repeals Act 1888; the Statute Law Revision Act 1948; the Justices of the Peace Act 1949 s 46(2), Sch 7; the Access to Justice Act 1999 s 76(2), Sch 10 para 2; and the Courts Act 2003 s 109(1), (3), Sch 8 para 2, Sch 10). For the enforcement of payment see para 1134 post; and MAGISTRATES. See also *Coster v Wilson* (1838) 3 M & W 411.
4 *Stanley v Wharton* (1822) 10 Price 138; *Bromley v Holden* (1828) Mood & M 175; and see *Horsefall v Davy* (1816) 1 Stark 169.

1067. Appeal. Any person aggrieved by the order of the justices may appeal to the Crown Court[1]. If the appellant enters into a recognisance with one or two sufficient surety or sureties in double the sum ordered to be paid, with condition to appear at the Crown Court, the order will not be executed against him in the meantime[2].

1 Distress for Rent Act 1737 s 5 (s 5 amended by the Summary Jurisdiction Act 1884 s 4, Schedule; and the Distress for Rent Act 1737 ss 5, 6 amended by the Courts Act 1971 s 56(1), Sch 8 para 2). See also *R v Cheshire Justices* (1833) 5 B & Ad 439. The notice of appeal must be given within 21 days after the decision: see the Crown Court Rules 1982, SI 1982/1109, r 7(3); and COURTS.
2 Distress for Rent Act 1737 s 6 (as amended: see note 1 supra).

1068. Forcible entry to remove goods. Where any goods fraudulently or clandestinely removed by the tenant or his servant or agent or other person aiding or assisting are put in any house, barn, stable, outhouse, yard, close, or place locked up or otherwise secured, so as to prevent the goods from being seized as a distress for arrears of rent, the landlord or his steward, bailiff, receiver or other person empowered may (after first summoning a constable, who is required to assist, and, in the case of a dwelling house, after making oath before a justice of the peace of a reasonable ground to suspect that the goods are therein) in the daytime break open and enter the premises and seize the goods as a distress[1].

A previous request is unnecessary in order to give the landlord the right to break into the premises for the purpose of seizing the goods[2].

There must be a constable present at the breaking in[3], but he may be a special constable appointed by a warrant for the particular occasion[4].

1   Distress for Rent Act 1737 s 7 (amended by the Statute Law Revision Act 1888).
2   *Williams v Roberts* (1852) 7 Exch 618.
3   *Rich v Woolley* (1831) 7 Bing 651.
4   *Cartwright v Smith and Batty* (1833) 1 Mood & R 284.

(16) RESCUE AND POUND-BREACH

(i) Nature of Offences

1069.   Rescue and pound-breach.   In as much as a distress does not until sale divest the tenant of the property in the chattels, or, in point of law, vest the possession of such chattels in the landlord, the latter, where the goods are removed or otherwise interfered with, cannot maintain a claim against the tenant or a stranger for conversion[1] (or, apparently, detinue[2]). His remedy is in respect of the rescue or pound-breach, as the case may be. Both are offences at common law, for which a claim for rescue or pound-breach will lie[3], and for which an additional and more satisfactory remedy has been provided by statute[4].

1   *R v Cotton* (1751) 2 Ves Sen 288 at 294 per Parker CB (distrainor cannot maintain conversion or trespass); *Moneux v Goreham* (1741) 2 Selwyn's NP (11th Edn) 1335; *Wilbraham v Snow* (1670) 2 Wms Saund 47; and see *Turner v Ford* (1846) 15 M & W 212. As to conversion see TORT vol 45(2) (Reissue) para 548 et seq.
2   Detinue was not maintainable without a right of possession and a right of property: see *Jarvis v Williams* [1955] 1 All ER 108 at 111, [1955] 1 WLR 71 at 75, CA, per Sir Raymond Evershed MR. As to the abolition of detinue see TORT vol 45(2) (Reissue) para 544.
3   3 Bl Com (14th Edn) 146. As to rescue see para 1070 post; and as to pound-breach see para 1071 post.
·4   See the Distress for Rent Act 1689 s 3 (as amended); and para 1073 post.

1070.   Rescue.   Goods distrained are regarded from the seizure as being taken by a process of law, and not merely by an assertion of a private right of the distrainor, and the taking of them out of the custody of the distrainor before they are impounded is regarded in the light of a resistance of lawful authority, and is termed a rescue or rescous[1]. To prevent a distress being made is not a rescue, but to prevent it being impounded is[2]. There may be a rescue without any act of the owner in bringing about the escape of cattle, if he resists their recapture; for example, when a distress has been taken and the cattle distrained, as they are being driven to the pound, go into the house of the owner who refuses to deliver them to the distrainor when he demands them, there is a rescue in law[3]. There can be no rescue until the thing is actually distrained, and in any case in which the distrainor abandons or quits possession of the chattels, the retaking by the owner is not a rescue[4].

1   Com Dig Distress (D3). Rescous is a taking away and setting at liberty against law a distress taken or a person arrested by the process or course of law: Co Litt 160b.
2   *Iredale v Kendall* (1878) 40 LT 362 (sale by auctioneer after seizure).

3   Co Litt 161a.
4   *Dod v Monger* (1704) 6 Mod Rep 215 at 216; *Knowles v Blake* (1829) 5 Bing 499.

1071.   Pound-breach.   Pound-breach is the retaking from the custody of the law of a chattel which has been impounded[1]. A person cannot be guilty of pound-breach unless he knows that the goods have been impounded or otherwise secured[2]. Where the goods have been impounded on the premises[3] and left in their existing position under a walking possession agreement[4] between the tenant and the distrainor, the tenant will be guilty of pound-breach if he removes the goods, but not so a stranger if he removes the goods in ignorance of the impounding[5]. Furniture removers who, in the ordinary course of their business, remove goods which have already been brought outside the premises where they were impounded are not guilty of pound-breach[6]. A person who removes impounded goods may be guilty of pound-breach even though the tenant has been given permission to use the goods temporarily[7]. Where goods are impounded or otherwise secured, and either the tenant or a stranger knowing of the impounding does that which, if the goods were the property of or in the possession of the landlord, would as against him amount to conversion, then, it seems, the offender is guilty of pound-breach[8]. The sheriff may be liable if execution is levied on goods in the possession of a bailiff under a distress[9].

1   As to impounding see para 1013 et seq ante. As to pound-breach in respect of cattle and other animals see
    ANIMALS vol 2(1) (Reissue) para 633.
2   *Abingdon RDC v O'Gorman* [1968] 2 QB 811, [1968] 3 All ER 79, CA.
3   For the general principle that goods may be impounded either on or off the premises see para 1013 ante.
    As to impounding on the premises see para 1016 ante.
4   As to walking possession agreements see para 1018 ante.
5   *Abingdon RDC v O'Gorman* [1968] 2 QB 811, [1968] 3 All ER 79, CA (disapproving dicta as to the
    effectiveness of walking possession against third parties which were expressed in *Lavell & Co Ltd v
    O'Leary* [1933] 2 KB 200, CA). As to the necessity for an impounding on the premises to be manifest if
    it is to be effective against a stranger see para 1016 ante.
        Where goods are impounded off the premises, the impounding will ordinarily be plain and obvious
    to anyone so that a stranger who removes them will be guilty of pound-breach: see para 1015 ante.
6   *Lavell & Co Ltd v O'Leary* [1933] 2 KB 200, CA.
7   *Bevir v British Wagon Co Ltd* (1935) 80 L Jo 162.
8   Thus granting a replevin without authority may constitute pound-breach: *Trevannian's Case* (1704) 11
    Mod Rep 32. As to replevin see para 1081 et seq post.
9   *Reddell v Stowey* (1841) 2 Mood & R 358; *Turner v Ford* (1846) 15 M & W 212; but see *Story v Finnis*
    (1851) 6 Exch 123 (where the sheriff's officer merely prevented the removal of the goods from the
    premises).

1072.   Justifying rescue etc.   Rescue[1] may be justified in certain cases where the distress is unlawful[2]. Pound-breach[3] is an offence against the dignity of the law, and can never be justified[4]. If the distrainor himself takes the distress out of the pound for the unlawful purpose of using it, the owner may retake possession of it from him without being guilty of either rescue or pound-breach[5].

1   As to rescue see para 1070 ante.
2   See para 1102 post.
3   As to pound-breach see para 1071 ante.
4   *Cotsworth v Betison* (1696) 1 Ld Raym 104; *Parrett Navigation Co v Stower* (1840) 6 M & W 564; *Firth v
    Purvis* (1793) 5 Term Rep 432; Co Litt 47a.
5   *Smith v Wright* (1861) 6 H & N 821.

(ii)   The Remedies

1073.   Remedies for rescue and pound-breach.   The remedies in the case of both rescue[1] and pound-breach[2] are either by recaption or action, and in the case of pound-breach also by indictment.

The right of recaption, that is to pursue and retake the goods wherever the landlord may happen to find them, obtains in each case[3], but in exercising the right the landlord must not commit a breach of the peace; and in the case of a rescue the recaption must be 'upon a fresh pursuit', that is without delay[4], and there is authority for saying that the same limitation applies in the case of pound-breach[5].

The landlord has a common law right of action in the case of rescue and pound-breach[6]. The claim commonly brought is, however, under the Distress for Rent Act 1689[7], to recover treble damages against the offender, or, where they have come into his possession, against the owner of the goods distrained[8]. The claim is maintainable by the landlord without proof of any actual damage[9], and it is not necessary that notice of the distress has been given[8]. Tender of the rent and costs after the goods have been impounded is no defence[10]. The claim is a penal one, and the claimant is not entitled to disclosure of documents[11]. The claim lies at the instance of the landlord and not the bailiff[12].

1   As to rescue see para 1070 ante.
2   As to pound-breach see para 1071 ante.
3   *Rich v Woolley* (1831) 7 Bing 651.
4   *Rich v Woolley* (1831) 7 Bing 651 at 661.
5   See *Turner v Ford* (1846) 15 M & W 212.
6   See para 1069 ante.
7   See the Distress for Rent Act 1689 s 3 (amended by the Statute Law Revision Act 1888; and the Administration of Justice Act 1965 s 34(1), Sch 2).
8   See *Berry v Huckstable* (1850) 14 Jur 718.
9   *Kemp v Christmas* (1898) 79 LT 233, CA.
10 *Belasyse v Burbridge* (1696) 1 Lut 213.
11 *Firth v Purvis* (1793) 5 Term Rep 432.
12 *Jones v Jones* (1889) 22 QBD 425.
13 *Always v Broome* (1695) 2 Lut 1259. In that case, it was held that if the bailiff sustained injury the landlord can recover in respect of that injury but it is doubtful if that decision is still good law.

1074.   Goods on premises of third person. The landlord has the same remedy for rescue and pound-breach whether the chattels are to be or are impounded on or off the premises[1]. It is, however, doubtful whether a claim can be maintained under the Distress for Rent Act 1737[2] in the case of goods fraudulently removed by the tenant and followed and distrained on the premises of a third person and afterwards rescued by such third person[3]. The fact that the goods are found in the possession of a person who has previously claimed to be owner of them is not sufficient to render him liable without proof that the pound was broken by him[4].

1   Distress for Rent Act 1737 s 10; *Firth v Purvis* (1793) 5 Term Rep 432. As to impounding see para 1013 et seq ante. As to rescue see para 1070 ante; and as to pound-breach see para 1071 ante.
2   Ie the Distress for Rent Act 1689 s 3 (as amended): see para 1073 ante.
3   *Harris v Thirkell* (1852) 20 LTOS 98.
4   *Castleman v Hicks* (1842) Car & M 266.

1075.   Indictment. Pound-breach is an indictable offence at common law[1]. The indictment lies where goods have been taken out of the custody of the law[2].

1   Co Litt 47b; 2 Hawk PC c 10, s 56; *R v Butterfield* (1893) 17 Cox CC 598; *R v Nicholson and King* (1901) 65 JP 298 (a case of rescue). The punishments are fine and imprisonment: see CRIMINAL LAW, EVIDENCE AND PROCEDURE vol 11(2) (2006 Reissue) para 746. As to pound-breach see para 1071 ante.
2   *R v Bradshaw* (1835) 7 C & P 233. It is doubtful whether an indictment lies in such a case, if a person retakes his own goods which have been unlawfully seized: *R v Walshe* (1876) IR 10 CL 511; *R v Knight* (1908) 73 JP 15, CCA.

(17) ILLEGAL, IRREGULAR OR EXCESSIVE DISTRESS, AND THE ASSOCIATED REMEDIES

(i) Illegal Distress

1076. Circumstances in which distress is illegal. An illegal distress is one which is wrongful at the very outset, that is to say either where there was no right to distrain or where a wrongful act was committed at the beginning of the levy invalidating all subsequent proceedings. In such a case the distrainor is a trespasser ab initio, and it is no defence that the goods have been applied in discharge of the rent[1]. As the distrainor has in himself no right to seize the particular chattels, he can confer no title to them upon a person to whom, under colour of the distress, they may purport to have been sold.

The following are instances of illegal distress: a distress by a landlord after he has parted with his reversion[2]; a distress by a person in whom the reversion is not vested[3]; a distress when no rent is in arrear[4]; or for a claim or debt which is not rent, as a payment for the hire of chattels[5]; a distress made after a valid tender of rent has been made[6]; a second distress for the same rent[7]; a distress off the premises or on the highway[8]; a distress in the night, that is between sunset and sunrise[9]; a distress made in an unlawful manner, as by breaking open an outer door or opening a closed window[10]; distraining things privileged from distress[11]; distraining goods contrary to an agreement with the tenant[12] or with a stranger[13]; a distress levied or proceeded with contrary to the Law of Distress Amendment Act 1908[14]; selling goods not distrained, or not included in the inventory[15].

Where the act done is wrongful, but is wrongful merely as to part of the goods, no wrong being done as to the residue, the wrongdoer is a trespasser as to that part of the goods only in respect of which the wrongful act is done[16].

The remedies for an illegal distress are rescue, replevin, or damages[17].

1   *Attack v Bramwell* (1863) 3 B & S 520.
2   See paras 968–969, 972 ante.
3   See para 912 ante.
4   Co Litt 160b; and see para 911 ante. As to claims for double value see para 1098 post.
5   See para 909 ante.
6   Co Litt 160b; *Bennett v Bayes* (1860) 5 H & N 391; and see para 975 ante.
7   See paras 1059–1062 ante.
8   See para 979 ante. When a distress is illegal because it is taken in the highway, the proper remedy is rescue (see para 1102 post); and if the injured party seeks relief by action he should rely on 52 Hen 3 (Statute of Marlborough) (1267) c 15 (see para 979 note 1 ante).
9   Co Litt 142a; and see para 963 ante.
10   *Attack v Bramwell* (1863) 3 B & S 520; and see paras 1005–1006 ante.
11   *Keen v Priest* (1859) 4 H & N 236; *Swire v Leach* (1865) 18 CBNS 479; and see para 930 et seq ante.
12   *Giles v Spencer* (1857) 3 CBNS 244; and see *Sier v Bullen* (1915) 84 LJKB 1288.
13   *Horsford v Webster* (1835) 1 Cr M & R 696; and see para 978 ante.
14   See the Law of Distress Amendment Act 1908 s 2 (as amended); *Interoven Stove Co Ltd v Hibbard and Painter and Shepherd* [1936] 1 All ER 263; and para 959 ante.
15   See para 1012 ante. If things are removed or sold which were not seized under the distress in the first instance, nor included in the inventory, the distrainor is as to such things an absolute trespasser: *Sims v Tuffs* (1834) 6 C & P 207; *Bishop v Bryant* (1834) 6 C & P 484.
16   *Harvey v Pocock* (1843) 11 M & W 740.
17   As to rescue see para 1102 post; as to replevin see para 1081 et seq post; and as to claims for damages see para 1090 et seq post.

(ii) Irregular Distress

1077. Circumstances in which distress is irregular. A distress is irregular when, although the levy was legal and in order, the subsequent proceedings have been conducted in an unlawful manner. The following are instances of irregular distress: selling without having served notice of the distress with copy of inventory on the tenant[1]; selling within the five or 15 days allowed to replevy[2]; selling growing crops before they are gathered[3]; selling without appraisement when it is still requisite[4]; selling for otherwise than the best price[5]; improper dealing with any overplus[6]; detaining[7] or removing[8] the chattels distrained when a tender of rent and costs is made after distress and before impounding; selling the distress when a tender of rent and costs is made after impounding but within the time allowed for replevin[9].

1 See paras 1011–1012 ante.
2 See para 1049 ante. As to replevin see para 1081 et seq post.
3 *Proudlove v Twemlow* (1833) 1 Cr & M 326; *Rodgers v Parker* (1856) 18 CB 112. See also para 1050 ante.
4 As to appraisement see para 1019 ante.
5 *Poynter v Buckley* (1833) 5 C & P 512; *Walter v Rumbal* (1695) 1 Ld Raym 53; *Clarke v Holford* (1848) 2 Car & Kir 540; *Rapley v Taylor and Smith* (1883) Cab & El 150. As to the requirement to sell for the best price see para 1054 ante.
6 As to overplus see paras 1056–1057 ante.
7 *Loring v Warburton* (1858) EB & E 507.
8 *Vertue v Beasley* (1831) 1 Mood & R 21; and see para 975 ante.
9 *Johnson v Upham* (1859) 2 E & E 250. As to impounding see para 1013 et seq ante.

1078. Distrainor not a trespasser. For a distress that is only irregular, and not illegal at the outset[1], the distrainor is not treated as a trespasser ab initio, and the tenant can only recover the actual damage he has suffered[2].

1 Where the distress is illegal at the outset, e g where the landlord gains entry to the premises by breaking in, the Distress for Rent Act 1737 s 19 does not apply: see *Attack v Bramwell* (1863) 3 B & S 520; and paras 1006 note 5, 1076 note 10 ante.
2 Distress for Rent Act 1737 s 19; *Rodgers v Parker* (1856) 18 CB 112; and see para 1095 post.
    At common law there was no distinction between an illegal and an irregular distress, and any irregularity in the conduct of the distress rendered the entire proceedings void and the party distraining a trespasser ab initio: *Six Carpenters' Case* (1610) 8 Co Rep 146a, 1 Smith LC (13th Edn) 134. This was found to occasion hardships to landlords and was remedied by the Distress for Rent Act 1737.

1079. Purchaser's title to goods. A person who purchases goods under a distress which is merely irregular acquires a good title to the goods, for in such a case conversion would not lie against the landlord, and the remedy of the tenant is in damages as against his landlord[1].

A sale to the landlord himself is not a mere irregularity; he does not obtain a valid title and may be sued for conversion[2].

1 *Wallace v King* (1788) 1 Hy Bl 13; *Whitworth v Smith* (1832) 1 Mood & R 193; c f the effect of sale under an illegal distress; and see paras 1076, 1078 ante.
2 *Plasycoed Collieries Co Ltd v Partridge, Jones & Co Ltd* [1912] 2 KB 345; and see para 1055 ante. As to conversion see TORT vol 45(2) (Reissue) para 548 et seq.

(iii) Excessive Distress

1080. What is excessive distress. The distrainor must be careful not to seize more goods than are reasonably sufficient to satisfy the rent in arrear and the costs of the distress[1]. An excessive distress is wrongful both at common law[2] and by statute[3].

To be proved excessive the value of the goods seized must be clearly disproportionate to the rent and costs, taking into consideration the conditions under which a forced sale of the effects must take place[4]. To avoid an excess all that is required is that the distrainor should exercise a reasonable and honest discretion in estimating what the goods will realise at a broker's sale by auction without considering what value the tenant himself could have obtained for them or what an incoming tenant in the same line of business would pay for them. The landlord is authorised to protect himself by seizing what any reasonable man would think adequate to the satisfaction of the claim[5]. Where the goods have been appraised before sale, that is not conclusive against the tenant as to their real value[6], for the best means may not have been taken to ascertain their value[7]; and though the price realised at an auction is prima facie evidence of value as regards excess[8], it is not conclusive[9]. The question of excess is one of fact, and a claim will lie for an excessive distress although the sale, less the expenses, did not equal the arrears of rent[10]. The mere fact that the chattels were sold at an undervalue does not necessarily show that the distress was an excessive one[11]. A claim will lie for an excessive distress of growing crops when the probable produce is capable of being estimated at the time of seizure[12].

The distrainor is not bound to calculate precisely the value of the property seized. He must take care that a reasonable proportion is kept between the value of the property and the sum for which he is entitled to take it[13].

Taking a single chattel, though of considerably greater value than the rent, is not excessive if there is no other distress on the land which can be taken, or even if there are other articles, but of an aggregate value less than sufficient to satisfy the distress[14]. If the distrainor had the opportunity of taking goods of smaller value than those which he actually took and the goods of smaller value would have been sufficient to cover the rent, he may be liable for taking an excessive distress[15].

Claiming and distraining for a greater amount of rent than is actually due does not give a right of action if the distress is not excessive for the rent really due[16]. If, however, more goods are seized than are necessary to satisfy the actual arrears, the right of action arises[17]. A claim will not lie for merely distraining for more rent than is in arrear, even though it is alleged that the distress was made maliciously[18].

In cases of excessive distress the tenant cannot sue the person into whose possession the goods have come; his remedy is against his landlord[19].

1   *Carter v Carter* (1829) 5 Bing 406 (rent reduced by land tax and outgoings; landlord distraining for full rent).
2   See 2 Co Inst 107; *Bayliss v Fisher* (1830) 7 Bing 153; *Piggott v Birtles* (1836) 1 M & W 441 at 447 per Parke B. Blackstone, however, comments: 'An action of trespass is not maintainable on this account, it being no injury at common law' (3 Bl Com (14th Edn) 12); and see *Lynne v Moody* (1729) 2 Stra 851.
3   See 52 Hen 3 (Statute of Marlborough) (1267) c 4 (which enacts that distress is to be reasonable and not too great and that he that takes great and unreasonable distress is to be grievously amerced for the excess of such distresses); and para 979 note 1 ante.
4   *Field v Mitchell* (1806) 6 Esp 71; *Rapley v Taylor and Smith* (1883) Cab & El 150.
5   *Roden v Eyton* (1848) 6 CB 427; *Wells v Moody* (1835) 7 C & P 59.
6   *Cook v Corbett* (1875) 24 WR 181, CA; and see para 1019 ante.
7   *Clarke v Holford* (1848) 2 Car & Kir 540.
8   *Rapley v Taylor and Smith* (1883) Cab & El 150.
9   *Smith v Ashforth* (1860) 29 LJ Ex 259. If it were conclusive, probably no distress could be deemed excessive (*Smith v Ashforth* supra at 260 per Martin J), for the goods may have been improperly lotted or allowed to stand in the rain, or otherwise sold under unfair conditions, so that they have not been sold at the best price *(Poynter v Buckley* (1833) 5 C & P 512).
10 *Smith v Ashforth* (1860) 29 LJ Ex 259.
11 *Thompson v Wood* (1843) 4 QB 493.
12 *Piggott v Birtles* (1836) 1 M & W 441.
13 *Willoughby v Backhouse* (1824) 2 B & C 821 at 823; *Roden v Eyton* (1848) 6 CB 427. Thus it is an excessive distress to distrain two or three oxen for a small sum, or a horse or an ox for a small sum when a beast of less value might have been taken (2 Co Inst 107); but it is not for every trifling excess that an action for excessive distress is maintainable *(Field v Mitchell* (1806) 6 Esp 71 at 72 per Lord Ellenborough).
14 2 Co Inst 107; *Avenell v Croker* (1828) Mood & M 172; *Field v Mitchell* (1806) 6 Esp 71.
15 *Roden v Eyton* (1848) 6 CB 427.
16 *Tancred v Leyland* (1851) 16 QB 669, Ex Ch; *French v Phillips* (1856) 1 H & N 564, Ex Ch; *Glynn v Thomas* (1856) 11 Exch 870; *Phillips v Whitsed* (1860) 2 E & E 804.
17 *Crowder v Self* (1839) 2 Mood & R 190.

18 *Stevenson v Newnham* (1853) 13 CB 285, Ex Ch. If, however, the tenant pays the excess, he may recover it back in a claim for excessive distress (*Fell v Whittaker* (1871) LR 7 QB 120); but not in a claim for money had and received (*Glynn v Thomas* (1856) 11 Exch 870). The rule may be contrasted with that in cases of execution where an officer of the court may be liable even in the absence of malice: *Moore v Lambeth County Court Registrar (No 2)* [1970] 1 QB 560, [1970] 1 All ER 980, CA.

19 *Whitworth v Smith* (1832) 5 C & P 250.

(iv) Replevin

1081. Meaning of replevin. Replevin is a process to obtain a redelivery to the owner of chattels which have been wrongfully distrained or taken from him, upon his finding sufficient security for the rent and costs of the claim and undertaking that he will pursue a claim against the distrainor to determine the right to distrain. The term 'replevin' is applied both to the redelivery of the goods[1] and the claim in which the right is tried[2]. Wherever the object of proceedings is to procure the restitution of the specific chattels taken instead of compensation in damages, the proper course is an action of replevin; as an alternative, damages can be recovered in trespass[3].

1 This is also known as the 'replevy'.
2 Co Litt 145b; Bac Abr, Replevin and Avowry (A).
3 *Gibbs v Cruikshank* (1873) LR 8 CP 454 at 459; *Mennie v Blake* (1856) 6 E & B 842.

1082. When replevin is available. Replevin is not available where the distress was originally lawful[1]; but whenever there has been a distress which is wholly illegal, and not merely irregular or excessive, the tenant has his remedy by replevin[2]. Thus it lies where the relationship of landlord and tenant did not exist[3]; where there was occupation but no demise at a fixed rent[4]; where no rent was in fact due, or where rent due was released before distress, or where the tenant has satisfied the rent by payments on behalf of the landlord necessary to protect his own possession[5]; or where the rent distrained for is not due though other rent is due[6]; where the title of the person distraining has expired and he is not entitled to the rent[7]; where the entry was illegal[8]; where the goods have been detained after tender of rent and costs before the impounding[9]; or where the things distrained are privileged[10]. It may be resorted to in order to obtain the return of all goods and cattle which may be lawfully distrained, but not of fixtures[11], animals ferae naturae in a wild state, and other things which from their nature cannot be the subject of distress[12].

1 *Johnson v Upham* (1859) 28 LJQB 252 at 256 per Lord Campbell. Thus it will not lie if any part of the rent claimed was due, for in such a case the distress is not illegal: *White v Greenish* (1861) 11 CBNS 209 (a case in which a person who was entitled only to a half of the rent has distrained for the whole).
2 As to illegal distress see para 1076 ante; and as to irregular distress see para 1077 ante.
3 *Walker v Giles* (1849) 6 CB 662; and see para 908 ante.
4 *Hegan v Johnson* (1809) 2 Taunt 148; *Dunk v Hunter* (1822) 5 B & Ald 322; *Regnart v Porter* (1831) 7 Bing 451; and see paras 908–909 ante.
5 *Sapsford v Fletcher* (1792) 4 Term Rep 511; *Taylor v Zamira* (1816) 6 Taunt 524; *Davis v Gyde* (1835) 2 Ad & El 623; *Cooper v Robinson* (1842) 10 M & W 694 (release).
6 *Roskruge v Caddy* (1852) 7 Exch 840 at 842–843; and see para 911 ante.
7 *Downs v Cooper* (1841) 2 QB 256; and see para 913 et seq ante.
8 *Tunnicliffe v Wilmot* (1847) 2 Car & Kir 626; and see para 1003 et seq ante.
9 *Evans v Elliott* (1836) 5 Ad & El 142; and see para 1013 et seq ante.
10 *Eaton v Southby* (1738) Willes 131; and see para 930 et seq ante.
11 *Gibbs v Cruikshank* (1873) LR 8 CP 454.
12 *Niblet v Smith* (1792) 4 Term Rep 504; *Darby v Harris* (1841) 10 LJQB 294 at 295 per Patteson J.

1083. Who may proceed and against whom. Proceedings in replevin consist of two independent parts: (1) the replevy, which is the tenant giving security that he will prosecute an action for replevin, whereupon the goods are restored; and (2) the claim so undertaken to be brought, in which the right to the goods is tried. The tenant may replevy so long as the goods remain unsold[1], but only within six years[2].

The proceedings must be brought by the owner of the goods, that is the person who has the property, absolute or qualified, in the goods[3]. A special property in them, such as that of a bailee or pledgee, is sufficient[4]. An executor may sue in replevin to recover his testator's goods[5].

The claim will lie either against the person actually making the distress, or the person who has authorised the distress, or both of them[6].

1   *Jacob v King* (1814) 5 Taunt 451.
2   Limitation Act 1980 s 2; and see LIMITATION OF ACTIONS vol 28 (Reissue) para 885.
3   Co Litt 145b; *Peacock v Purvis* (1820) 2 Brod & Bing 362; *Fenton v Logan* (1833) 9 Bing 676.
4   Co Litt 145b; *Swaffer v Mulcahy* [1934] 1 KB 608.
5   *Arundell v Trevill* (1662) 1 Sid 81 at 82.
6   Bullen *Law of Distress for Rent* (2nd Edn) 279.

1084.   Commencement of replevin proceedings.   Proceedings in replevin are commenced in the county court of the district in which the goods subject to replevin have been seized[1], irrespective of the value of the goods seized. The district judge is empowered to approve of replevin bonds, to grant replevins, and to issue all necessary process in relation thereto; any such process is executed by a bailiff of the court[2]. The district judge, at the instance of the party whose goods are seized, must cause the same goods to be replevied to that party upon his giving security[3] to prosecute a claim against the distrainor, either in the High Court or in the county court[4].

1   See the County Courts Act 1984 s 144, Sch 1 para 1(2), (3) (as amended); notes 2–3 infra; and COURTS.
2   Ibid Sch 1 para 1(2) (Sch 1 para 1 amended by virtue of the Courts and Legal Services Act 1990 s 74).
3   County Courts Act 1984 Sch 1 para 1(3) (as amended: see note 2 supra).
4   See ibid Sch 1 para 2(1); and para 1085 post.

1085.   Security.   It must be made a condition of the security that the replevisor will commence a claim against the seizor in the High Court within one week from the date when the security is given or in a county court within one month from the date[1].

In either case the replevisor must give security, to be approved by the district judge having power in the matter, for such amount as the district judge thinks sufficient to cover both the probable cost of the claim and the alleged rent or damage in respect of which the distress has been made[2]. In either case the security is conditioned to prosecute the claim with effect[3] and without delay[4] and to make return of the goods if their return is ordered in the claim[5].

Upon delivery of the goods to the replevisor the goods become liable to distress for subsequent rent; and will pass to the tenant's trustee in bankruptcy[6]. When the goods have been replevied the lien of the distrainor is determined[7].

1   County Courts Act 1984 s 144, Sch 1 para 2(1).
2   Ibid Sch 1 para 2(2)(a)(i) (amended by virtue of the Courts and Legal Services Act 1990 s 74). In a case where the goods replevied have been seized otherwise than under colour of distress, the value of the goods is to be covered instead of the alleged rent or damage in respect of which the distress was made: County Courts Act 1984 Sch 1 para 2(2)(a)(ii).
3   This means to a successful termination: *Tummons v Ogle* (1856) 6 E & B 571; *Morgan v Griffith* (1740) 7 Mod Rep 380; *Perreau v Bevan* (1826) 5 B & C 284; *Jackson v Hanson* (1841) 8 M & W 477; *Tunnicliffe v Wilmot* (1847) 2 Car & Kir 626.
4   This means with due diligence, for though the condition is satisfied if a suit is commenced and carried on according to the ordinary practice of the court, want of due diligence may constitute a breach of the condition: *Gent v Cutts* (1847) 11 QB 288; *Morris v Matthews* (1841) 2 QB 293; *Harrison v Wardle* (1833) 5 B & Ad 146; and see *Axford v Perrett* (1828) 4 Bing 586. If the claimant in replevin is hindered from prosecuting his suit by the default of the defendant the latter will be restrained from proceeding on the claimant's bond: *Evans v Bowen* (1849) 7 Dow & L 320.

5   County Courts Act 1984 Sch 1 para 2(2)(b).
6   *Bradyll v Ball* (1785) 1 Bro CC 427 at 432–433; *Wilton v Wiffen* (1830) 8 LJOSKB 303.
7   Formerly the sheriff was liable if he accepted insufficient sureties (see *Scott v Waithman* (1822) 3 Stark 168; and *Plumer v Brisco* (1847) 11 QB 46), but it is understood that the district judge (who now has responsibility for replevin to the exclusion of the sheriff: see the County Courts Act 1984 Sch 1 para 1 (as amended); and para 1084 ante) is not so liable. As to the office of sheriff see generally SHERIFFS.

1086.   Proceedings.   In the claim for replevin the replevisor is claimant and the distrainor is defendant[1], and after the issue of the claim form[2] the claim proceeds in the same way as any other[3]. Unless the proceedings are removed to the High Court the county court has full jurisdiction whatever the amount of the rent, and though title comes into question[4].

If any party to any proceedings in a county court is dissatisfied with the determination of the judge or jury, he may appeal from it to the Court of Appeal in such manner and subject to such conditions as may be provided by the Civil Procedure Rules[5].

1   See para 1083 text to note 6 ante.
2   See CPR Pt 7.
3   See *Bradyll v Ball* (1785) 1 Bro CC 427.
4   *Fordham v Akers* (1863) 4 B & S 578; *R v Raines* (1853) 1 E & B 855.
5   County Courts Act 1984 s 77(1) (amended by the Civil Procedure Act 1997 s 10, Sch 2 para 2(7)); *Smith v Enright* (1893) 63 LJQB 220; and COURTS; PRACTICE AND PROCEDURE vol 37 (Reissue) para 1518. Appeals are regulated by CPR Pt 52.

1087.   Damages.   If the claimant succeeds, as the goods are restored on the replevin, he is generally awarded the expenses of the replevy and no other damages. He is, however, entitled to recover any actual damage suffered by reason of the wrongful taking or detention of the goods[1], including annoyance and injury to reputation if alleged and proved[2]. After judgment for the claimant in replevin he is precluded from bringing any other claim for damages for taking the same goods in respect of which the replevin was brought[3], but the bar does not extend to other causes of action arising out of the same distress, such as trespass to the land[4]. A new trial will only be granted under special circumstances[5].

1   *Gibbs v Cruikshank* (1873) LR 8 CP 454.
2   *Smith v Enright* (1893) 63 LJQB 220; and cf *Dixon v Calcraft* [1892] 1 QB 458, CA.
3   *Gibbs v Cruikshank* (1873) LR 8 CP 454.
4   *Gibbs v Cruikshank* (1873) LR 8 CP 454; and see generally ESTOPPEL.
5   *Parry v Duncan* (1831) 7 Bing 243; and see *Edgson v Cardwell* (1873) LR 8 CP 647.

1088.   If defendant succeeds.   If the defendant succeeds he is entitled, when suing in the High Court, to a return of the goods distrained and his costs (not including the costs of distress)[1], for which he will have a writ of fieri facias[2].

1   *Jamieson v Trevelyan* (1855) 10 Exch 748. If the goods were not returned the defendant could formerly obtain a 'capias in withernam' requiring the sheriff to take other equal distress of the plaintiff and deliver it to the defendant to keep until the original distress is restored. The process has never been abolished, but is, perhaps, to be regarded as obsolete.
2   As to writs of fieri facias see ENFORCEMENT vol 17(1) (Reissue) para 102.

1089.   Breach of security bond.   If the replevisor breaks the condition of the bond, as by non-prosecution of the claim, the distrainor may recover damages in respect of the loss which he has suffered by virtue of the breach[1]. The claim may be brought in the county court in a case falling within its jurisdiction[2]. The sureties are liable only for rent actually in arrear at the date of the distress and the costs of the replevin claim[3], and in no case can their liability exceed the amount of the penalty and the costs of the claim on the bond[4]. The fact that, in the replevin claim, the distrainor has obtained a judgment for the amount of the rent which is unsatisfied is no defence to the claim on the bond[5].

When goods of an undertenant, lodger or stranger are taken, an order can be obtained for their restoration in certain cases[6].

1   The damages recoverable will ordinarily be the arrears of rent and the expenses of the distrainor. In *Dix v Groom* (1880) 5 Ex D 91, it was held that the plaintiff had the option of claiming either the sum secured by the replevin bond or damages, and that, if he claimed the sum secured, and the judgment went by default, he might sign final judgment subject to the defendant's right to obtain a stay on payment of the amount actually due and costs; on the other hand, if he claimed damages, any judgment by default would be interlocutory only pending the ascertainment of damages; cf CPR 12.3(2), 12.5(1), (2), (3), 15.3. It seems that now the usual and proper course is to claim the actual sum recoverable: see DEEDS AND OTHER INSTRUMENTS para 130.
2   As to the jurisdiction of county courts of contract claims see COURTS vol 10 (Reissue) para 712.
3   *Ward v Henley* (1827) 1 Y & J 285; *Dix v Groom* (1880) 5 Ex D 91.
4   *Hefford v Alger* (1808) 1 Taunt 218; *Branscombe v Scarborough* (1844) 6 QB 13.
5   *Turnor v Turner* (1820) 2 Brod & Bing 107.
6   See para 959 ante.

(v) Claim for Damages

1090.   Right of claim for wrongful distress. A claim for damages lies for any wrongful distress whether it is illegal, irregular, or excessive[1].

1   As to proceedings under the Law of Distress Amendment Act 1908 s 2 (as amended) see para 959 ante. As to claims for double value see para 1098 post. As to illegal distress see para 1076 ante; as to irregular distress see para 1077 et seq ante; and as to excessive distress see para 1080 ante. As to damages generally see DAMAGES.

1091.   Who may sue. For any form of wrongful distress a claim will lie at the suit of the tenant, or the owner of the goods, or of a person having the mere enjoyment and use of the chattels[1].

Where the cause of action is that the landlord has retained the overplus[2], the tenant must not sue for money had and received for his use, but in tort for the breach of the statutory obligation to pay over the surplus to the sheriff or the under-sheriff[3].

1   *Swire v Leach* (1865) 18 CBNS 479 (illegal distress: see para 1076 ante); *Kerby v Harding* (1851) 6 Exch 234 (irregular distress: see para 1077 et seq ante); *Fell v Whittaker* (1871) LR 7 QB 120; *Fisher v Algar* (1826) 2 C & P 374; *Wilkinson v Ibbett* (1860) 2 F & F 300 (excessive distress: see para 1080 ante).
2   As to overplus see para 1056 ante.
3   *Yates v Eastwood* (1851) 6 Exch 805; *Evans v Wright* (1857) 2 H & N 527.

1092.   Illegal distress; who may be sued. A claim for illegal distress may be brought against the landlord if he distrained personally. In the case of distraint by a bailiff, a claim for illegal distress may be brought against the bailiff; but a claim will also lie against the landlord if he authorised the illegal act[1] or ratified it after it came to his knowledge[2]. Thus the landlord will be liable where he has authorised a distress when he has no right to distrain; but it must be shown that he has in fact authorised it[3].

If the landlord detains goods privileged from distress, and therefore must have knowledge of the illegality, he will be deemed to have ratified the bailiff's act[4], and his presence on the demised premises at or immediately after the commission of the illegal act is some evidence that he assented to it[5]. Similarly, the landlord is deemed to have ratified if he retains the proceeds of sale of distrained goods knowing that it is alleged that his bailiff has made an illegal distress[6]. The mere receipt of the proceeds of sale, however, without inquiry and without knowledge of anything illegal done by the bailiff is not sufficient to make the landlord liable; for if the landlord had no knowledge that a trespass had been committed and received the money in the belief that his warrant had been lawfully executed, the receipt is no evidence of assent[7]; and if, when he knows the circumstances, he repudiates the act he will not be liable[8].

An agent of the landlord who authorises an illegal distress will be liable personally if he is the person actually ordering the thing to be done, but not where he is a mere transmitter of authority from the landlord to the bailiff and does not interfere further[9].

1   See the text and note 3 infra.
2   See *Lewis v Read* (1845) 13 M & W 834, where it was said that the landlord was not liable unless he ratified the wrongful act after it came to his knowledge or unless he meant to take upon himself, without inquiry, the risk of any wrongful acts which the bailiff might have committed and to adopt all his acts. See also the text and notes 4–8 infra.
3   *Jones v Buckley* (1838) 2 Jur 204; and see *Botteley v Rogers* (1847) 8 LTOS 559; *Crabb v Killick* (1834) 6 C & P 216 (a case of irregular and excessive distress).
4   *Gauntlett v King* (1857) 3 CBNS 59.
5   *Moore v Drinkwater* (1858) 1 F & F 134; and see para 1001 ante.
6   *Carter v St Mary Abbots, Kensington Vestry* (1900) 64 JP 548, CA; *Becker v Riebold* (1913) 30 TLR 142.
7   *Lewis v Read* (1845) 13 M & W 834; *Freeman v Rosher* (1849) 13 QB 780; *Green v Wroe* [1877] WN 130.
8   *Hurry v Rickman and Sutcliffe* (1831) 1 Mood & R 126.
9   *Bennett v Bayes* (1860) 5 H & N 391.

1093.   Irregular and excessive distress; who may be sued.   In the case of an irregular distress a claim is against the landlord if he personally committed the act constituting the irregularity. Where the irregular act was committed by a bailiff, the claim lies at the election of the claimant either against the bailiff or his employer provided that the employer authorised or ratified the distress[1] and it makes no difference that the irregular act was done without the employer's knowledge or subsequent sanction[2]. If thought fit the employer and bailiff may be made co-defendants[3].

In like manner a claim for an excessive distress may be brought either against the bailiff or the landlord; but where an excessive distress has been made, the landlord may compensate the tenant and recover the amount against the bailiff[4].

1   For the rule that the employer is liable for any irregularities committed by the bailiff in the course of his employment see para 1001 ante. For the rule that a distress may be retrospectively adopted see para 992 ante. As to irregular distress see para 1077 et seq ante.
2   *Haseler v Lemoyne* (1858) 5 CBNS 530. 'Where I send a man to distrain and he distrains something else than I authorised him to distrain I am not liable; but if he does distrain on the things I authorised him to distrain it is then my business to see that he does what is requisite to make it a good distress of such things; and if I do not see to it myself I am answerable for any irregularity he may commit': *Haseler v Lemoyne* supra as reported in 28 LJCP 103 at 104 per Cockburn CJ.
3   *Child v Chamberlain* (1834) 6 C & P 213.
4   *Megson v Mapleton* (1883) 49 LT 744. As to excessive distress see para 1080 ante.

1094.   Damages recoverable for illegal distress.   In the case of an illegal distress the distrainor is a trespasser ab initio, and the full value of the goods which have been lost to the claimant, without any deduction for rent, is recoverable as damages[1], unless there are circumstances of mitigation which the court ought to take into consideration[2]. If after proceedings are commenced, the landlord returns the goods, the tenant may still give evidence of their damaged condition[3]. The fact that the claimant has only a limited property in the goods is irrelevant[4]. Where the landlord has placed a man in possession, the claimant is entitled to damages, although he has had the use of the goods all the time[5]; and it has been held that substantial damages may be awarded even if no actual damage can be proved[6]. Where the wrong complained of is the removal of fixtures, the measure of damages is not the amount of the proceeds of their sale after being severed, but may be their value to an incoming tenant, or may be their cost to the tenant[7]. If the distress is lawful as to part and illegal as to part (as where privileged goods are included in the seizure), the claimant is only entitled to damages in respect of the illegal part[8]. In the case of goods privileged from distress and improperly seized and sold, an action for conversion lies, and the claimant is entitled to recover the full value of the goods, though he may be only a bailee of them[9].

1   *Attack v Bramwell* (1863) 3 B & S 520; *Keen v Priest* (1859) 4 H & N 236; *Grunnell v Welch* [1906] 2 KB 555, CA. As to illegal distress see para 1076 ante.
2   *Edmondson v Nuttall* (1864) 17 CBNS 280 at 294–296 per Willes J; and see *Smith v Enright* (1893) 63 LJQB 220; *Harvey v Pocock* (1843) 11 M & W 740.
3   *M'Grath v Bourne* (1876) IR 10 CL 160; and see *Lamb v Wall* (1859) 1 F & F 503; *Hogarth v Jennings* [1892] 1 QB 907, CA.
4   See *Swire v Leach* (1865) 18 CBNS 479; and see para 1091 text and note 1 ante.
5   *Bayliss v Fisher* (1830) 7 Bing 153.
6   *Interoven Stove Co Ltd v Hibbard and Painter and Shepherd* [1936] 1 All ER 263; and cf *Rookes v Barnard* [1964] AC 1129, [1964] 1 All ER 367, HL.
7   *Moore v Drinkwater* (1858) 1 F & F 134.
8   *Harvey v Pocock* (1843) 11 M & W 740; and see *Bail v Mellor* (1850) 19 LJ Ex 279.
9   *Swire v Leach* (1865) 18 CBNS 479.

1095. Damages for irregular distress. In a claim for damages for irregular distress[1] a claimant can only recover such special damage as he may prove[2], though in appropriate cases this may be the full value of the goods seized less the rent in arrear and the proper charges of the distress[3]. In the absence of proof of special damage the claimant cannot recover even nominal damages and the defendant is entitled to the verdict[4].

1   As to irregular distress see para 1077 et seq ante.
2   See the Distress for Rent Act 1737 s 19.
3   *Knotts v Curtis* (1832) 5 C & P 322.
4   *Lucas v Tarleton* (1858) 3 H & N 116; *Rodgers v Parker* (1856) 18 CB 112; *Rocke v Hills* (1887) 3 TLR 298.

1096. Damages for excessive distress. For an excessive distress, the damages, in case of a sale of the goods, are the fair value of the goods after deducting rent and costs[1]. The tenant does not waive his right of action by entering into an agreement with the distrainor respecting the sale of the goods seized[2]. If no sale has taken place the claimant is entitled to nominal damages, even though he does not prove any actual damage, since the law will presume damage from a man being prevented from dealing with his property[3]. If the distress is made for more rent than is in arrear, and the tenant pays the sum to get rid of the distress, he may recover the excess he was obliged to pay and damages for the annoyance he may have suffered[4]. Whether the goods are impounded on the premises or off the premises, the tenant is entitled to recover such actual damage as he has sustained through loss of the use and enjoyment of the excess taken, or of the power of disposing freely thereof, or through the inconvenience and expense in procuring sureties to a larger amount than he otherwise would have required on replevying[5]. It has been held that exemplary damages may not be awarded where the seizure has taken place by mistake[6]; although it remains open for consideration whether on proof of malice a claimant may be able in appropriate cases to recover exemplary damages[7].

1   *Wells v Moody* (1835) 7 C & P 59; *Clarke v Holford* (1848) 2 Car & Kir 540; *Smith v Ashforth* (1860) 29 LJ Ex 259. As to excessive distress see para 1080 ante.
2   *Willoughby v Backhouse* (1824) 2 B & C 821; *Sells v Hoare* (1824) 1 Bing 401.
3   *Chandler v Doulton* (1865) 3 H & C 553; *Mudhun Mohun Doss v Gokul Doss* (1866) 10 Moo Ind App 563, PC. As to the position in an illegal distress see para 1094 ante.
4   *Fell v Whittaker* (1871) LR 7 QB 120.
5   *Piggott v Birtles* (1836) 1 M & W 441. There were not allowed, as damages for excessive distress, the extra costs of a replevin action beyond those allowed on taxation in that action: *Grace v Morgan* (1836) 2 Bing NC 534. As to replevin see para 1081 et seq ante.
6   *Moore v Lambeth County Court Registrar (No 2)* [1970] 1 QB 560, [1970] 1 All ER 980, CA.

7   *Moore v Lambeth County Court Registrar (No 2)* [1970] 1 QB 560 at 572, [1970] 1 All ER 980 at 986, CA,
    per Sachs LJ. As to exemplary damages see DAMAGES vol 12(1) (Reissue) paras 811, 1115–1116.

1097.   Jurisdiction of county court.   A claim for irregular, excessive, or illegal
distress may be brought in the county court[1].

1   See the County Courts Act 1984 s 15(1) (as amended); and COURTS vol 10 (Reissue) para 712. As to
    irregular distress see para 1077 et seq ante; as to illegal distress see para 1076 ante; and as to excessive
    distress see para 1080 ante.

(vi)   Other Remedies

1098.   Double value.   As well as the remedy provided by the common law for an
illegal distress[1] in the particular instance of a distress for rent when no rent is in arrear
followed by a sale of the goods, the owner of the goods is entitled by statute to recover
in a claim against the distrainor double the value of the goods taken and sold[2].

The offence is not complete unless a sale of the chattels actually takes place[3].

The provision is absolute, so that less damages than double value cannot be awarded
to a successful claimant[4].

1   See paras 1090, 1092, 1094, 1097 ante. As to illegal distress see para 1076 ante.
2   Distress for Rent Act 1689 s 4 (amended by the Statute Law Revision Act 1888; and the Administration
    of Justice Act 1965 s 34(1), Sch 2). The provision in the Distress for Rent Act 1689 s 4 (as amended) that
    the owner could recover 'with full costs' was repealed by the Administration of Justice Act 1965 s 34(1),
    Sch 2. A tenant who is not the owner of the goods distrained cannot recover the double value: see
    Chancellor v Webster (1893) 9 TLR 568.
3   See *Masters v Farris* (1845) 1 CB 715, but the statute was held to apply where the goods were distrained
    after judgment had been obtained for the rent, though the judgment had not been satisfied: *Potter v
    Bradley & Co* (1894) 10 TLR 445 at 446.
4   *Masters v Farris* (1845) 1 CB 715.

1099.   Injunction to restrain distress.   An injunction may be granted in
proceedings commenced by the tenant[1] where he complains either that a distress made is
wrongful[2] or that a wrongful distress is threatened[3]. However, in as much as the right of
a landlord to distrain for rent is a legal right enabling him if the rent is in arrear to obtain
security for its payment, the court will not generally interfere by injunction (unless it is
a flagrant case) except upon the condition of the applicant paying the amount claimed
for rent into court[4].

1   The High Court may by order (whether interim or final) grant an injunction or appoint a receiver in all
    cases in which it appears to the court to be just and convenient to do so: Supreme Court Act 1981
    (prospectively renamed the Senior Courts Act 1981) s 37(1).
2   *Walsh v Lonsdale* (1882) 21 ChD 9, CA.
3   *Shaw v Earl of Jersey* (1879) 4 CPD 120; on appeal 4 CPD 359, CA.
4   *Shaw v Earl of Jersey* (1879) 4 CPD 359, CA; *Carter v Salmon* (1880) 43 LT 490, CA; and see *Sanxter v
    Foster* (1841) Cr & Ph 302 at 303. See also *Steel Linings Ltd v Bibby & Co (a firm)* [1993] RA 27, [1993]
    NLJR 511, CA (distress for rates); and para 111 post.

1100.   Wearing apparel etc.   The wearing apparel and bedding of the tenant or his
family and the tools and implements of his trade, are exempt from distress[1]. On
complaint that goods or chattels so exempt from distress for rent have been taken under
a distress, a magistrates' court may by summary order direct that the goods and chattels
so taken, if not sold, be restored, or if they have been sold, that such sum as the court
may determine to be their value is to be paid to the complainant by the person who
levied the distress or directed it to be levied[2].

1   See the Law of Distress Amendment Act 1888 s 4 (as amended); the County Courts Act 1984 s 89(1)(a) (as substituted); and para 942 ante.
2   Law of Distress Amendment Act 1895 s 4.

1101. Agricultural holdings. In the case of agricultural holdings there are special provisions for settling any dispute arising in respect of any distress having been levied contrary to statutory restriction[1].

1   See the Agricultural Holdings Act 1986 s 19; and AGRICULTURE vol 1(2) (Reissue) para 335.

1102. Rescue. Although it is generally a breach of the law, a rescue[1] is a legal remedy of an aggrieved person when a distress is wholly wrongful and not merely irregular or excessive, for example, if the distress has been made for a payment which is not rent or if privileged goods are taken[2]. The rescue must take place before the goods are impounded, for after the impounding, whether the distress was lawful or not, the goods cannot be retaken[3], unless after impounding the distrainor abuses the distress by working it[4].

In these cases, rescue can only be legally made by the tenant or the owner of the chattels or his employee or agent, and not by a stranger[5], so that if the goods of two persons are wrongfully taken in one distress each can rescue only his own goods, in as much as he is a stranger as regards the other goods[6].

1   See paras 1070, 1072 ante.
2   *Keen v Priest* (1859) 4 H & N 236 at 241. As to illegal distress see para 1076 ante; as to irregular distress see para 1077 et seq ante; and as to excessive distress see para 1080 ante.
3   *Cotsworth v Betison* (1696) 1 Ld Raym 104. As to impounding see para 1013 et seq ante.
4   *Smith v Wright* (1861) 6 H & N 821.
5   1 Roll Abr, Distress (Q).
6   Fitz Nat Brev 102.

1103. Fines. An early statute, passed to discourage the use of self-help for redressing wrongs, forbids the levying by any person of any revenge or unlawful[1] distress upon his neighbour or any other person of his own authority without an award of the court, even though he may have received damage or injury for which he seeks amends[2]. If any person takes any such revenge of his own authority without award of the court and is convicted thereof, he is punishable by fine, according to the trespass; if one neighbour takes a distress of another person without award of the court as a result of which the other person suffers damage, the offender is to be punished in the same way according to the quantity of the trespass; full and sufficient amends are nevertheless to be made to persons who have sustained loss by such distresses[3].

1   The enactment applies only to distresses levied for purposes which are not according to law: 2 Co Inst 104.
2   See the Distress Act (1267). As far as can be ascertained, there have been no cases under this Act for at least the last 100 years. As to remedies for illegal distress see para 1076 ante.
3   See note 2 supra.

3. DISTRESS FOR NON-DOMESTIC RATES AND DRAINAGE RATES

(1) NON-DOMESTIC RATES

1104. Enforcement of payment of non-domestic rates by distress.
Non-domestic rates are a form of taxation leviable by local authorities[1]. The authorities responsible for levying non-domestic rates are known as billing authorities[2]. Non-domestic rates are leviable only in respect of non-domestic properties[3].

The payment of non-domestic rates may be enforceable by distress[4], or as an alternative, may be recovered in a court of competent jurisdiction[5].

The power of distress for rates is purely statutory; in its nature it is somewhat analogous to an execution levied to enforce a legal money liability[6]. The statutory rules relating to distress for rent[7] do not apply to distress for rates.

1   As to non-domestic rates generally see RATING AND COUNCIL TAX vol 39(1) (Reissue) para 602 et seq.
2   As to billing authorities for the purposes of non-domestic rates see RATING AND COUNCIL TAX vol 39(1) (Reissue) para 606. As to billing authorities for the purposes of council tax rating see para 816 post; and RATING AND COUNCIL TAX vol 39(1) (Reissue) para 821.
    The functions of a billing authority in relation to the administration and enforcement of non-domestic rates may, to the prescribed extent, be exercised by, or by the employees of, such person as may be authorised to exercise them by the authority whose functions they are: see the Local Authorities (Contracting Out of Tax Billing, Collection and Enforcement Functions) Order 1996, SI 1996/1880; and RATING AND COUNCIL TAX vol 39(1) (Reissue) para 606.
3   See RATING AND COUNCIL TAX vol 39(1) (Reissue) para 608 et seq. As to the council tax which is levied in relation to domestic properties see para 1116 et seq post; and RATING AND COUNCIL TAX vol 39(1) (Reissue) para 817 et seq.
4   See the Non-Domestic Rating (Collection and Enforcement) (Local Lists) Regulations 1989, SI 1989/1058, reg 14 (as amended); and RATING AND COUNCIL TAX vol 39(1) (Reissue) paras 788, 790.
5   See ibid reg 20 (as amended); and RATING AND COUNCIL TAX vol 39(1) (Reissue) paras 788, 795.
6   See *Potts v Hickman* [1941] AC 212, [1940] 4 All ER 491, HL (where, however, it was held that a distraint for rates was not 'execution' within the Landlord and Tenant Act 1709 s 1 (as amended) (see para 1032 ante), so as to entitle a landlord to claim payment of arrears of rent in priority).
7   Ie the Distress for Rent Rules 1988, SI 1988/2050 (as amended): see para 994 et seq ante. See also para 904 ante; and cf para 1108 post.

1105. Pre-requisites of distress for non-domestic rates. No distress proceedings may be taken unless a liability order[1] has been made[2]. Before a liability order can be made the billing authority[3] must serve a reminder notice[4].

1   For the meaning of 'liability order' see RATING AND COUNCIL TAX vol 39(1) (Reissue) para 788.
2   See the Non-Domestic Rating (Collection and Enforcement) (Local Lists) Regulations 1989, SI 1989/1058, reg 14(1); and RATING AND COUNCIL TAX vol 39(1) (Reissue) para 790. Under the General Rate Act 1967, distress for rates was levied after the issue of a distress warrant by the justices: see s 97 (repealed).
3   As to billing authorities for the purposes of non-domestic rates see para 1104 ante; and RATING AND COUNCIL TAX vol 39(1) (Reissue) para 606.
4   See RATING AND COUNCIL TAX vol 39(1) (Reissue) paras 788–790. For the meaning of 'reminder notice' see RATING AND COUNCIL TAX vol 39(1) (Reissue) para 788.

1106. Power of the authority to levy the appropriate amount by distress.
Where a liability order[1] has been made, the billing authority[2] which applied for the order may levy the 'appropriate amount'[3] by distress and sale of the goods of the debtor[4] against whom the order was made[5]. A distress may be made anywhere in England and Wales[6].

The person levying distress on behalf of a billing authority must carry with him the written authorisation of the authority which he must show to the debtor if so requested[7].

1   For the meaning of 'liability order' see RATING AND COUNCIL TAX vol 39(1) (Reissue) para 788. As to pre-requisites of distress for non-domestic rates see para 1105 ante.
2   As to billing authorities for the purposes of non-domestic rates see para 1104 ante; and RATING AND COUNCIL TAX vol 39(1) (Reissue) para 606.
3   The appropriate amount for the purposes of the Non-Domestic Rating (Collection and Enforcement) (Local Lists) Regulations 1989, SI 1989/1058, reg 14(1) is the aggregate of: (1) an amount equal to any outstanding sum which is or forms part of the amount in respect of which the liability order was made (reg 14(2)(a)); and (2) a sum determined in accordance with reg 14(2)(b), Sch 3 (as substituted and amended) in respect of charges connected with the distress (reg 14(2)(b)). See further RATING AND COUNCIL TAX vol 39(1) (Reissue) para 790.
4   For the meaning of 'debtor' see RATING AND COUNCIL TAX vol 39(1) (Reissue) para 790.
5   Non-Domestic Rating (Collection and Enforcement) (Local Lists) Regulations 1989, SI 1989/1058, reg 14(1); and see RATING AND COUNCIL TAX vol 39(1) (Reissue) para 790.
6   Ibid reg 14(6); and see RATING AND COUNCIL TAX vol 39(1) (Reissue) para 790. See also *Quinlan v Hammersmith and Fulham London Borough Council* [1989] RA 43, 153 JP 180, CA (distress on a public highway is lawful).
7   See the Non-Domestic Rating (Collection and Enforcement) (Local Lists) Regulations 1989, SI 1989/1058, reg 14(5); and RATING AND COUNCIL TAX vol 39(1) (Reissue) para 790. The person levying the distress must hand to the debtor, or leave at the premises where the distress is levied, a copy of reg 14 (as amended) and Sch 3 (as substituted and amended) and a memorandum setting out the appropriate amount, and must hand to the debtor a copy of any close or walking possession agreement entered into: reg 14(5). A failure to comply with reg 14(5) does not render the distraint process itself unlawful and the debtor is only entitled to recover special damage which has resulted from the irregularity: *Wilson v South Kesteven District Council* [2000] 4 All ER 577, [2001] 1 WLR 387, CA; and see para 1110 below.

1107.   Goods on which distress may be levied.   Distress for non-domestic rates may be levied on the goods of the debtor[1]. Enactments which protect goods of any class from distress are not affected by the provision authorising distress for rates[2]. It is expressly provided in relation to distress for non-domestic rates that no person making a distress may seize any goods of the debtor which comprise such clothing, bedding, furniture, household equipment and provisions as are necessary for satisfying the basic domestic needs of the debtor and his family[3].

1   See the Non-Domestic Rating (Collection and Enforcement) (Local Lists) Regulations 1989, SI 1989/1058, reg 14(1); para 1106 ante; and RATING AND COUNCIL TAX vol 39(1) (Reissue) para 790. For the meaning of 'debtor' see RATING AND COUNCIL TAX vol 39(1) (Reissue) para 790. Permission of the court is usually required for the taking of proceedings in execution of a judgment against a national serviceman or certain reservists or auxiliaries, including distress for rates: see the Reserve and Auxiliary Forces (Protection of Civil Interests) Act 1951 s 6(2); and ARMED FORCES vol 2(2) (Reissue) para 85.
2   Non-Domestic Rating (Collection and Enforcement) (Local Lists) Regulations 1989, SI 1989/1058, reg 14(8); and see RATING AND COUNCIL TAX vol 39(1) (Reissue) para 790. The provision authorising distress for rates is reg 14 (as amended) (see RATING AND COUNCIL TAX vol 39(1) (Reissue) para 790): see reg 14(8).
3   See ibid reg 14(1A) (added by SI 1993/774); and RATING AND COUNCIL TAX vol 39(1) (Reissue) para 790.

1108.   Who may levy distress.   No distress for non-domestic rates[1] may be made other than by a person who is authorised to act as a bailiff by a general certificate granted under the Law of Distress Amendment Act 1888[2].

1   Ie under the Non-Domestic Rating (Collection and Enforcement) (Local Lists) Regulations 1989, SI 1989/1058, reg 14 (as amended): see RATING AND COUNCIL TAX vol 39(1) (Reissue) para 790.
2   Ibid reg 14(6A) (added by SI 1998/3089). For a general certificate granted under the Law of Distress Amendment Act 1888 see s 7 (as amended); and paras 994, 999 ante. As to certification of bailiffs see para 994 ante.

1109. Tender and payment before sale. If, before any goods are seized, the appropriate amount[1] (including charges arising up to the time of the payment or tender) is paid or tendered to the billing authority[2], the authority must accept the amount and the levy must not be proceeded with[3]. Where the authority has seized goods of the debtor[4] in pursuance of the distress, but before the sale of those goods the appropriate amount (including charges arising up to the time of the payment or tender) is paid or tendered to the authority, the authority must accept the amount, the sale must not be proceeded with and the goods must be made available for collection by the debtor[5].

1 For the meaning of 'appropriate amount' see para 1106 note 3 ante.

2 As to billing authorities for the purposes of non-domestic rates see para 1104 ante; and RATING AND COUNCIL TAX vol 39(1) (Reissue) para 606.

3 Non-Domestic Rating (Collection and Enforcement) (Local Lists) Regulations 1989, SI 1989/1058, reg 14(3); and see RATING AND COUNCIL TAX vol 39(1) (Reissue) para 790. As to the power of the billing authority to levy the appropriate amount by distress see para 1106 ante; and RATING AND COUNCIL TAX vol 39(1) (Reissue) para 790.

   A debtor cannot halt the distraint process by tendering payment while seizure of goods is in progress: *Wilson v South Kesteven District Council* [2000] 4 All ER 577, [2001] 1 WLR 387, CA.

4 For the meaning of 'debtor' see RATING AND COUNCIL TAX vol 39(1) (Reissue) para 790.

5 Non-Domestic Rating (Collection and Enforcement) (Local Lists) Regulations 1989, SI 1989/1058, reg 14(4); and see RATING AND COUNCIL TAX vol 39(1) (Reissue) para 790. See *Wilson v South Kesteven District Council* [2000] 4 All ER 577, [2001] 1 WLR 387, CA; and note 3 supra.

1110. Irregularities. A distress is not to be deemed unlawful on account of any defect or want of form in the liability order[1], and no person making a distress is to be deemed a trespasser on that account[2]. No person making a distress is to be deemed a trespasser from the beginning on account of any subsequent irregularity in making the distress, but a person sustaining special damage by reason of the subsequent irregularity may recover full satisfaction for the special damage (and no more) by proceeding in trespass or otherwise[3].

1 For the meaning of 'liability order' see RATING AND COUNCIL TAX vol 39(1) (Reissue) para 788. As to the pre-requisites of distress for non-domestic rates see para 1105 ante.

2 Non-Domestic Rating (Collection and Enforcement) (Local Lists) Regulations 1989, SI 1989/1058, reg 14(7); and see RATING AND COUNCIL TAX vol 39(1) (Reissue) para 790.

3 Ibid reg 14(7); and see RATING AND COUNCIL TAX vol 39(1) (Reissue) para 790. See also *Quinlan v Hammersmith and Fulham London Borough Council* [1989] RA 43, 153 JP 180, CA; *Wilson v South Kesteven District Council* [2000] 4 All ER 577, [2001] 1 WLR 387, CA.

1111. Excessive distress. Distress in excess of the appropriate amount is a wrongful interference with goods since the power of the billing authority[1] is limited to levying distress for the appropriate amount[2]. A person whose goods have been unlawfully seized may bring proceedings for their recovery and for damages[3]. An injunction may be granted restraining bailiffs from disposing of goods seized in the course of an excessive distress, and ordering the goods to be made available for return[4].

1 As to billing authorities for the purposes of non-domestic rates see para 1104 ante; and RATING AND COUNCIL TAX vol 39(1) (Reissue) para 606.

2 *Steel Linings Ltd v Bibby & Co (a firm)* [1993] RA 27, [1993] NLJR 511, CA. See also *Quinlan v Hammersmith and Fulham London Borough Council* [1989] RA 43, 153 JP 180, CA (no excessive or illegal distress; distress on a public highway is lawful); *Evans v South Ribble Borough Council* [1992] QB 757, [1991] RA 191 (no effective distress where no entry to debtor's premises). For the meaning of 'appropriate amount' see para 1106 note 3 ante. As to wrongful interference with goods see TORT vol 45(2) (Reissue) para 542 et seq.

3 See TORT vol 45(2) (Reissue) paras 612 et seq, 670 et seq.

4 *Steel Linings Ltd v Bibby & Co (a firm)* [1993] RA 27, [1993] NLJR 511, CA. As to injunctions see generally INJUNCTIONS.

1112.   Appeal against distress.   A person aggrieved by the levy of, or an attempt to levy, a distress may appeal to a magistrates' court[1]. The appeal may be instituted by making a complaint to a justice of the peace[2], and requesting the issue of a summons directed to the billing authority which levied or attempted to levy the distress to appear before the court to answer to the matter by which he is aggrieved[3].

If the court is satisfied that a levy was irregular, it may order the goods distrained to be discharged if they are in the possession of the authority[4]. The court may also by order award compensation in respect of any goods distrained and sold of an amount equal to the amount which, in the opinion of the court, would be awarded by way of special damages in respect of the goods if proceedings were brought in trespass or otherwise in connection with the irregularity[5]. If the court is satisfied that an attempted levy was irregular, it may by order require the authority to desist from levying in the manner giving rise to the irregularity[6]. In any proceedings upon an appeal in connection with distress, a statement contained in a document constituting or forming part of a record compiled by the applicant authority or an authorised person[7] is admissible as evidence of any fact stated in it of which direct oral evidence would be admissible[8].

1   Non-Domestic Rating (Collection and Enforcement) (Local Lists) Regulations 1989, SI 1989/1058, reg 15(1); and see RATING AND COUNCIL TAX vol 39(1) (Reissue) para 791. As to persons aggrieved see ADMINISTRATIVE LAW vol 1(1) (Reissue) para 56.
2   See RATING AND COUNCIL TAX vol 39(1) (Reissue) para 791. The magistrates' are under no duty to hear a complaint where alternative civil proceedings are more appropriate because of the factual and legal complexity of the matter: *R v Basildon Justices, ex p Holding & Barnes plc* [1994] RA 157, 158 JP 980.
3   Non-Domestic Rating (Collection and Enforcement) (Local Lists) Regulations 1989, SI 1989/1058, reg 15(2); and see RATING AND COUNCIL TAX vol 39(1) (Reissue) para 791.
4   Ibid reg 15(3); and see RATING AND COUNCIL TAX vol 39(1) (Reissue) para 791.
5   Ibid reg 15(3); and see RATING AND COUNCIL TAX vol 39(1) (Reissue) para 791. Proceedings could be brought under reg 14(7) (see para 1110 ante; and RATING AND COUNCIL TAX vol 39(1) (Reissue) para 790): see reg 15(3). If, following irregular distress, the goods are still in the possession of the authority, the magistrates' court can only order discharge and may not award compensation: see *R v Epping Magistrates, ex p Howard and Leach* [1997] RA 258.
6   Non-Domestic Rating (Collection and Enforcement) (Local Lists) Regulations 1989, SI 1989/1058, reg 15(4); and see RATING AND COUNCIL TAX vol 39(1) (Reissue) para 791.
7   For the meaning of 'authorised person' see RATING AND COUNCIL TAX vol 39(1) (Reissue) para 796.
8   Non-Domestic Rating (Collection and Enforcement) (Local Lists) Regulations 1989, SI 1989/1058, reg 21(4) (added by SI 1992/474; and amended by SI 1996/1880); and see RATING AND COUNCIL TAX vol 39(1) (Reissue) para 796.

1113.   Committal to prison where distress is insufficient.   Where a billing authority[1] has sought to levy an amount by distress[2], the debtor[3] is an individual, and the person making the distress reports to the authority that he was unable (for whatever reason) to find any or sufficient goods of the debtor on which to levy the amount, the authority may apply to a magistrates' court for the issue of a warrant committing the debtor to prison[4].

1   As to billing authorities for the purposes of non-domestic rates see para 1104 ante; and RATING AND COUNCIL TAX vol 39(1) (Reissue) para 606.
2   Ie under the Non-Domestic Rating (Collection and Enforcement) (Local Lists) Regulations 1989, SI 1989/1058, reg 14 (as amended) (see RATING AND COUNCIL TAX vol 39(1) (Reissue) para 790).
3   For the meaning of 'debtor' see RATING AND COUNCIL TAX vol 39(1) (Reissue) para 790.
4   Non-Domestic Rating (Collection and Enforcement) (Local Lists) Regulations 1989, SI 1989/1058, reg 16(1) (amended by SI 1992/474; and SI 1993/616); and see RATING AND COUNCIL TAX vol 39(1) (Reissue) para 792.

1114.   Further steps.   Where a warrant of commitment[1] is issued against (or a term of imprisonment is fixed in the case of) a person[2] because of the insufficiency of goods on which to levy distress[3], no steps, or no further steps, may be taken[4] by way of distress or bankruptcy in relation to the relevant amount[5]. The 'relevant amount' is the aggregate of: (1) the appropriate amount[6], or, as the case may be, so much of it as remains outstanding; and (2) a sum of an amount equal to the costs reasonably incurred by the applicant in respect of the application for committal[7].

Steps by way of distress, commitment, bankruptcy, or winding up may not be taken against a person under a liability order[8] while steps by way of another of those methods are being taken against him under it[9]. Subject to this, distress may be resorted to more than once[10]. Where a step is taken by way of distress for the recovery of an outstanding sum which is, or forms part of, an amount in respect of which a liability order has been made, any sum recovered thereby which is less than the aggregate of the amount outstanding and any charges arising from the statutory provisions[11] is to be treated as discharging first the charges, the balance (if any) being applied towards the discharge of the outstanding sum[12].

1   See para 1113 ante; and RATING AND COUNCIL TAX vol 39(1) (Reissue) para 792.
2   Ie under the Non-Domestic Rating (Collection and Enforcement) (Local Lists) Regulations 1989, SI 1989/1058, reg 16(3): see RATING AND COUNCIL TAX vol 39(1) (Reissue) para 792.
3   As to insufficient distress see para 1113 ante.
4   Ie under the Non-Domestic Rating (Collection and Enforcement) (Local Lists) Regulations 1989, SI 1989/1058, Pt III (regs 10–23) (as amended).
5   See ibid reg 19(1); and RATING AND COUNCIL TAX vol 39(1) (Reissue) para 794. As to the power of the billing authority to levy the appropriate amount by distress see para 1106; and RATING AND COUNCIL TAX vol 39(1) (Reissue) para 790. See also RATING AND COUNCIL TAX vol 39(1) (Reissue) para 792.
6   For the meaning of 'appropriate amount' see para 1106 note 3 ante.
7   See the Non-Domestic Rating (Collection and Enforcement) (Local Lists) Regulations 1989, SI 1989/1058, regs 16(4), 19(1); and RATING AND COUNCIL TAX vol 39(1) (Reissue) paras 792, 794.
8   For the meaning of 'liability order' see RATING AND COUNCIL TAX vol 39(1) (Reissue) para 788.
9   See the Non-Domestic Rating (Collection and Enforcement) (Local Lists) Regulations 1989, SI 1989/1058, reg 19(2); and RATING AND COUNCIL TAX vol 39(1) (Reissue) para 794.
10 Ibid reg 19(3); and see RATING AND COUNCIL TAX vol 39(1) (Reissue) para 794.
11 Ie under ibid reg 14(2)(b), Sch 3 (as substituted and amended): see RATING AND COUNCIL TAX vol 39(1) (Reissue) para 794.
12 See ibid reg 19(4); and RATING AND COUNCIL TAX vol 39(1) (Reissue) para 794.

(2) DRAINAGE RATES

1115.   Drainage rates.   Arrears of drainage rates may be recovered by the drainage board for an internal drainage district in the same manner in which arrears of a non-domestic rate may be recovered by a billing authority[1].

1   Land Drainage Act 1991 s 54(1) (amended by virtue of the Local Government Finance Act 1992 s 1). See further WATER vol 49(2) (2004 Reissue) para 229. As to distress for non-domestic rates see paras 1104–1114 ante. As to billing authorities for the purposes of non-domestic rates see para 1104 ante; and RATING AND COUNCIL TAX vol 39(1) (Reissue) para 606.

4. DISTRESS FOR COUNCIL TAX

1116.   Enforcement of payment of council tax by distress.   Council tax is a form of taxation leviable by local authorities[1]. The authorities responsible for levying council tax are known as billing authorities[2]. Council tax is leviable in respect of dwellings[3].

The payment of council tax is enforceable by distress[4] as well as by other prescribed methods[5].

The power of distress for council tax is purely statutory; in its nature it is somewhat analogous to an execution levied to enforce a legal money liability[6]. The statutory rules relating to distress for rent[7] do not apply to distress for council tax.

1   As to council tax generally see RATING AND COUNCIL TAX vol 39(1) (Reissue) para 817 et seq.
2   As to billing authorities for the purposes of council tax see RATING AND COUNCIL TAX vol 39(1) (Reissue) para 821. As to billing authorities for the purposes of non-domestic rating see para 1104 ante; and RATING AND COUNCIL TAX vol 39(1) (Reissue) para 606.
3   See RATING AND COUNCIL TAX vol 39(1) (Reissue) para 823 et seq. As to the non-domestic rate which is levied in relation to non-domestic properties see para 1104 ante; and RATING AND COUNCIL TAX vol 39(1) (Reissue) para 602 et seq.
4   See the Local Government Finance Act 1992 s 14(3), Sch 4 (as amended); the Council Tax (Administration and Enforcement) Regulations 1992, SI 1992/613, reg 45 (as amended); and RATING AND COUNCIL TAX vol 39(1) (Reissue) paras 902 et seq, 921 et seq.
5   As to provision for distress see the Council Tax (Administration and Enforcement) Regulations 1992, SI 1992/613 (as amended); and RATING AND COUNCIL TAX vol 39(1) (Reissue) para 922.
6   See *Potts v Hickman* [1941] AC 212, [1940] 4 All ER 491, HL (where, however, it was held that a distraint for rates was not 'execution' within the Landlord and Tenant Act 1709 s 1 (as amended) (see para 1032 ante), so as to entitle a landlord to claim payment of arrears of rent in priority). See also para 1104 ante.
7   Ie the Distress for Rent Rules 1988, SI 1988/2050 (as amended): see para 994 et seq ante. See also para 904 ante.

1117.   Pre-requisites of distress for council tax.   No distress proceedings may be taken unless a liability order[1] has been made[2]. Further, no distress may be made[3] unless, no less than 14 days before a visit in connection with the distress is first made to the premises where it is to be levied, the billing authority[5] has sent to the debtor[4] written notice of the following matters[6]:

(1)   the fact that a liability order has been made against the debtor[7];
(2)   the amount in respect of which the liability order was made and, where this is a different amount, the amount which remains outstanding[8];
(3)   a warning that unless the amount specified has been paid before the expiry of 14 days beginning on the date of the sending of the notice, distress may be levied[9];
(4)   notice that if distress is levied further costs will be incurred by the debtor[10];
(5)   the fees prescribed[11];
(6)   the address and telephone number at which the debtor can communicate with the authority[12].

1   For the meaning of 'liability order' see RATING AND COUNCIL TAX vol 39(1) (Reissue) para 903.
2   See the Council Tax (Administration and Enforcement) Regulations 1992, SI 1992/613, reg 45(1) (as amended); para 1118 post; and RATING AND COUNCIL TAX vol 39(1) (Reissue) para 922.
3   Ie under the Council Tax (Administration and Enforcement) Regulations 1992 SI 1992/613 (as amended).
4   For the meaning of 'debtor' see RATING AND COUNCIL TAX vol 39(1) (Reissue) para 906.
5   As to billing authorities for the purposes of council tax see para 1116 ante; and RATING AND COUNCIL TAX vol 39(1) (Reissue) para 821.
6   Council Tax (Administration and Enforcement) Regulations 1992, SI 1992/613, reg 45A(1) (reg 45A added by SI 1998/295); and see RATING AND COUNCIL TAX vol 39(1) (Reissue) para 923.
7   Council Tax (Administration and Enforcement) Regulations 1992, SI 1992/613, reg 45A(2)(a) (as added: see note 6 supra); and see RATING AND COUNCIL TAX vol 39(1) (Reissue) para 923.

8 Ibid reg 45A(2)(b) (as added: see note 6 supra); and see RATING AND COUNCIL TAX vol 39(1) (Reissue) para 923.
9 Ibid reg 45A(2)(c) (as added: see note 6 supra); and see RATING AND COUNCIL TAX vol 39(1) (Reissue) para 923.
10 Ibid reg 45A(2)(d) (as added: see note 6 supra); and see RATING AND COUNCIL TAX vol 39(1) (Reissue) para 923.
11 Ibid reg 45A(2)(e) (as added: see note 6 supra); and see RATING AND COUNCIL TAX vol 39(1) (Reissue) para 923. See para 1118 post.
12 Ibid reg 45A(2)(f) (as added: see note 6 supra); and see RATING AND COUNCIL TAX vol 39(1) (Reissue) para 923.

1118.   Powers of the authority to levy the appropriate amount by distress.
Where a liability order[1] has been made, the billing authority[2] which applied for the order may[3] levy the appropriate amount[4] by distress and sale of the goods of the debtor[5] against whom the order was made[6]. Distress may be made anywhere in England and Wales[7].

The person levying distress on behalf of an authority must carry with him the written authorisation of the authority, which he must show to the debtor if so requested[8].

1 For the meaning of 'liability order' see RATING AND COUNCIL TAX vol 39(1) (Reissue) para 903.
2 As to billing authorities for the purposes of council tax see para 1116 ante; and RATING AND COUNCIL TAX vol 39(1) (Reissue) para 821.
3 Ie subject to the Council Tax (Administration and Enforcement) Regulations 1992, SI 1992/613, reg 45A (as added): see para 1117 ante; and RATING AND COUNCIL TAX vol 39(1) (Reissue) para 923.
4 The 'appropriate amount' is the aggregate of: (1) an amount equal to any outstanding sum which is or forms part of the amount in respect of which the liability order was made (ibid reg 45(2)(a)); and (2) a sum determined in accordance with reg 45(2)(b), Sch 5 (as substituted and amended) in respect of charges connected with the distress (reg 45(2)(b)).
5 For the meaning of 'debtor' see RATING AND COUNCIL TAX vol 39(1) (Reissue) para 906.
6 Council Tax (Administration and Enforcement) Regulations 1992, SI 1992/613, reg 45(1) (amended by SI 1989/295); and see RATING AND COUNCIL TAX vol 39(1) (Reissue) para 922.
7 Council Tax (Administration and Enforcement) Regulations 1992, SI 1992/613, reg 45(6); and see RATING AND COUNCIL TAX vol 39(1) (Reissue) para 922. See also *Quinlan v Hammersmith and Fulham London Borough Council* [1989] RA 43, 153 JP 180, CA (distress on a public highway is lawful).
8 See the Council Tax (Administration and Enforcement) Regulations 1992, SI 1992/613, reg 45(5); and RATING AND COUNCIL TAX vol 39(1) (Reissue) para 922. The person levying the distress must hand to the debtor or leave at the premises where the distress is levied a copy of reg 45 (as amended) and Sch 5 (as substituted and amended) and a memorandum setting out the appropriate amount, and must hand to the debtor a copy of any close or walking possession agreement entered into: reg 45(5).

1119.   Goods on which distress may be levied and protection from distress.
Distress for council tax may be levied on the goods of the debtor[1]. Enactments which protect goods of any class from distress are not affected by the provision authorising distress for council tax[2]. It is expressly provided in relation to distress for council tax that no person making a distress may seize any goods of the debtor which comprise such tools, books, vehicles and other items of equipment as are necessary to the debtor for use personally by him in his employment, business or vocation, and such clothing, bedding, furniture, household equipment and provisions as are necessary for satisfying the basic domestic needs of the debtor and his family[3].

1 See the Council Tax (Administration and Enforcement) Regulations 1992, SI 1992/613, reg 45(1) (as amended); para 1118 ante; and RATING AND COUNCIL TAX vol 39(1) (Reissue) para 922. For the meaning of 'debtor' see RATING AND COUNCIL TAX vol 39(1) (Reissue) para 906. Permission of the court is usually required for the taking of proceedings in execution of a judgment against a national serviceman or certain reservists or auxiliaries, including distress for rates: see the Reserve and Auxiliary Forces (Protection of Civil Interests) Act 1951 s 6(2); and ARMED FORCES vol 2(2) (Reissue) para 85.
2 See the Council Tax (Administration and Enforcement) Regulations 1992, SI 1992/613, reg 45(8); and RATING AND COUNCIL TAX vol 39(1) (Reissue) para 922. The provision authorising distress for rates is reg 45 (as amended): see RATING AND COUNCIL TAX vol 39(1) (Reissue) para 922.

3　　See ibid reg 45(1A) (added by SI 1993/773); and RATING AND COUNCIL TAX vol 39(1) (Reissue) para 922.

1120. Who may levy distress. No distress for council tax[1] may be made other than by a person who is authorised to act as a bailiff by a general certificate granted under the Law of Distress Amendment Act 1888[2].

1　　Ie under the Council Tax (Administration and Enforcement) Regulations 1992, SI 1992/613, reg 45 (as amended).
2　　Ibid reg 45(6A) (added by SI 1998/295). For a general certificate granted under the Law of Distress Amendment Act 1888 see s 7 (as amended); and paras 994, 999 ante. As to certification of bailiffs see para 994 ante. As to the requirement that the person levying the distress must carry written authorisation see para 1118 ante.

1121. Tender and payment before sale. If, before any goods are seized, the appropriate amount[1] (including charges arising up to the time of the payment or tender) is paid or tendered to the billing authority[2], the authority must accept the amount and the levy must not be proceeded with[3]. Where the authority has seized goods of the debtor[4] in pursuance of the distress, but before the sale of those goods the appropriate amount (including charges arising up to the time of the payment or tender) is paid or tendered to the authority, the authority must accept the amount, the sale must not be proceeded with and the goods must be made available for collection by the debtor[5].

1　　For the meaning of 'appropriate amount' see para 1118 note 4 ante.
2　　As to billing authorities for the purposes of council tax see para 1116 ante; and RATING AND COUNCIL TAX vol 39(1) (Reissue) para 821.
3　　Council Tax (Administration and Enforcement) Regulations 1992, SI 1992/613, reg 45(3); and see RATING AND COUNCIL TAX vol 39(1) (Reissue) para 922. As to the power of the authority to levy the appropriate amount by distress see para 1118 ante; and RATING AND COUNCIL TAX vol 39(1) (Reissue) para 922.
4　　For the meaning of 'debtor' see RATING AND COUNCIL TAX vol 39(1) (Reissue) para 906.
5　　Council Tax (Administration and Enforcement) Regulations 1992, SI 1992/613, reg 45(4); and see RATING AND COUNCIL TAX vol 39(1) (Reissue) para 922.

1122. Irregularities. A distress is not to be deemed unlawful on account of any defect or want of form in the liability order[1], and no person making a distress is to be deemed a trespasser on that account[2]. No person making a distress is to be deemed a trespasser from the beginning on account of any subsequent irregularity in making the distress, but a person sustaining special damage by reason of the subsequent irregularity may recover full satisfaction for the special damage (and no more) by proceeding in trespass or otherwise[3].

1　　For the meaning of 'liability order' see RATING AND COUNCIL TAX vol 39(1) (Reissue) para 903. As to the pre-requisites of distress for council tax see para 1117 ante.
2　　Council Tax (Administration and Enforcement) Regulations 1992, SI 1992/613, reg 45(7); and see RATING AND COUNCIL TAX vol 39(1) (Reissue) para 922.
3　　Ibid reg 45(7); and see RATING AND COUNCIL TAX vol 39(1) (Reissue) para 922. See also *Quinlan v Hammersmith and Fulham London Borough Council* [1989] RA 43, 153 JP 180, CA.

1123. Excessive distress. Distress in excess of the appropriate amount is a wrongful interference with goods since the power of the billing authority[1] is limited to levying distress for the appropriate amount[2]. A person whose goods have been unlawfully seized may bring proceedings for their recovery and for damages[3]. An injunction may be granted restraining bailiffs from disposing of goods seized in the course of an excessive distress, and ordering the goods to be made available for return[4].

1　　As to billing authorities for the purposes of council tax see para 1116 ante; and RATING AND COUNCIL TAX vol 39(1) (Reissue) para 821.

2   *Steel Linings Ltd v Bibby & Co (a firm)* [1993] RA 27, [1993] NLJR 511, CA. See *Quinlan v Hammersmith and Fulham London Borough Council* [1989] RA 43, 153 JP 180, CA (no excessive or illegal distress; distress on a public highway is lawful); *Evans v South Ribble Borough Council* [1992] QB 757, [1991] RA 191 (no effective distress where no entry to debtor's premises). For the meaning of 'appropriate amount' see para 1118 note 4 ante. As to wrongful interference with goods see TORT vol 45(2) (Reissue) para 542 et seq.

3   See TORT vol 45(2) (Reissue) paras 612 et seq, 670 et seq.

4   *Steel Linings Ltd v Bibby & Co (a firm)* [1993] RA 27, [1993] NLJR 511, CA. As to injunctions generally see INJUNCTIONS.

1124.   Appeal against distress.   A person aggrieved by the levy of, or an attempt to levy, a distress may appeal to a magistrates' court[1]. The appeal may be instituted by making a complaint to a justice of the peace[2], and requesting the issue of a summons directed to the billing authority[3] which levied or attempted to levy the distress to appear before the court to answer to the matter by which he is aggrieved[4].

If the court is satisfied that a levy was irregular, it may order the goods distrained to be discharged if they are in the possession of the authority[5]. The court may also by order award compensation in respect of any goods distrained and sold of an amount equal to the amount which, in the opinion of the court, would be awarded by way of special damages in respect of the goods if proceedings were brought in trespass or otherwise in connection with the irregularity[6]. If the court is satisfied that an attempted levy was irregular, it may by order require the authority to desist from levying in the manner giving rise to the irregularity[7]. In any proceedings upon an appeal in connection with distress, a statement contained in a document constituting or forming part of a record compiled by the applicant authority or an authorised person[8] is admissible as evidence of any fact stated in it of which direct oral evidence would be admissible[9].

1   Council Tax (Administration and Enforcement) Regulations 1992, SI 1992/613, reg 46(1); and see RATING AND COUNCIL TAX vol 39(1) (Reissue) para 924. As to persons aggrieved see ADMINISTRATIVE LAW vol 1(1) (2001 Reissue) para 66.

2   The magistrates are under no duty to hear a complaint where alternative civil proceedings are more appropriate because of the factual and legal complexity of the matter: *R v Basildon Justices, ex p Holding & Barnes plc* [1994] RA 157, 158 JP 980.

3   As to billing authorities for the purposes of council tax see para 1116 ante; and RATING AND COUNCIL TAX vol 39(1) (Reissue) para 821.

4   Council Tax (Administration and Enforcement) Regulations 1992, SI 1992/613, reg 46(2); and see RATING AND COUNCIL TAX vol 39(1) (Reissue) para 924.

5   Ibid reg 46(3); and see RATING AND COUNCIL TAX vol 39(1) (Reissue) para 924.

6   Ibid reg 46(3); and see RATING AND COUNCIL TAX vol 39(1) (Reissue) para 924. Proceedings may be brought under reg 45(7) (see para 1122 ante; and RATING AND COUNCIL TAX vol 39(1) (Reissue) para 922): see reg 46(3). If, following irregular distress, the goods are still in the possession of the authority, the magistrates' court can only order discharge and may not award compensation: see *R v Epping Magistrates, ex p Howard and Leach* [1997] RA 258.

7   Council Tax (Administration and Enforcement) Regulations 1992, SI 1992/613, reg 46(4); and see RATING AND COUNCIL TAX vol 39(1) (Reissue) para 924.

8   For the meaning of 'authorised person' see RATING AND COUNCIL TAX vol 39(1) (Reissue) para 930.

9   Council Tax (Administration and Enforcement) Regulations 1992, SI 1992/613, reg 53(4) (amended by SI 1996/1880); and see RATING AND COUNCIL TAX vol 39(1) (Reissue) para 930.

1125.   Committal to prison where distress is insufficient.   Where a billing authority[1] has sought to levy an amount by distress[2], the debtor[3] is an individual who has attained the age of 18 years, and the person making the distress reports to the authority that he was unable (for whatever reason) to find any or sufficient goods of the debtor on which to levy the amount, the authority may apply to a magistrates' court for the issue of a warrant committing the debtor to prison[4].

1   As to billing authorities for the purposes of council tax see para 1116 ante; and RATING AND COUNCIL TAX vol 39(1) (Reissue) para 821.

2   Ie under the Council Tax (Administration and Enforcement) Regulations 1992, SI 1992/613, reg 45 (as amended) (see RATING AND COUNCIL TAX vol 39(1) (Reissue) para 922): see reg 47(1).
3   For the meaning of 'debtor' see RATING AND COUNCIL TAX vol 39(1) (Reissue) para 906.
4   Council Tax (Administration and Enforcement) Regulations 1992, SI 1992/613, reg 47(1); and see RATING AND COUNCIL TAX vol 39(1) (Reissue) para 926.

1126.   Further steps.   Where a warrant of commitment[1] is issued against (or a term of imprisonment is fixed in the case of) a person[2] (because of the insufficiency of goods on which to levy distress[3]), no steps, or no further steps, may be taken[4] by way of distress in relation to the relevant amount[5]. The 'relevant amount' is the aggregate of: (1) an amount equal to the appropriate amount[6] or (as the case may be) so much of it as remains outstanding; and (2) a sum of an amount equal to the costs reasonably incurred by the applicant in respect of the application for committal[7].

Steps by way of attachment of allowances, attachment of earnings, distress, commitment, bankruptcy, winding up or charging may not be taken against a person under a liability order[8] while steps by way of another of those methods are being taken against him under it[9]. Subject to this, distress may be resorted to more than once[10], and attachment of allowances, attachment of earnings, deductions under the Income Support Regulations[11] or distress may be resorted to in any order or alternately (or both)[12]. Where a step is taken by way of distress for the recovery of an outstanding sum which is or forms part of an amount in respect of which a liability order has been made, any sum recovered thereby which is less than the aggregate of the amount outstanding and any charges arising[13] is to be treated as discharging first the charges, the balance (if any) being applied towards the discharge of the outstanding sum[14].

1   See para 1125 ante; and RATING AND COUNCIL TAX vol 39(1) (Reissue) para 926.
2   Ie under the Council Tax (Administration and Enforcement) Regulations 1992, SI 1992/613, reg 47(3): see RATING AND COUNCIL TAX vol 39(1) (Reissue) para 926.
3   As to insufficient distress see para 1125 ante.
4   Ie under the Council Tax (Administration and Enforcement) Regulations 1992, SI 1992/613, Pt VI (regs 32–57) (as amended).
5   Ibid reg 52(1) (amended by SI 1993/773); and see RATING AND COUNCIL TAX vol 39(1) (Reissue) para 928.
6   For the meaning of 'appropriate amount' see para 1118 note 4 ante.
7   See the Council Tax (Administration and Enforcement) Regulations 1992, SI 1992/613, regs 47(4), 52(1) (as amended: see note 5 supra); and RATING AND COUNCIL TAX vol 39(1) (Reissue) para 926.
8   For the meaning of 'liability order' see RATING AND COUNCIL TAX vol 39(1) (Reissue) para 903.
9   See the Council Tax (Administration and Enforcement) Regulations 1992, SI 1992/613, reg 52(2)(a) (as amended); and RATING AND COUNCIL TAX vol 39(1) (Reissue) para 928.
10   See ibid reg 52(3)(a) (as amended); and RATING AND COUNCIL TAX vol 39(1) (Reissue) para 928.
11   The 'Income Support Regulations' means the Council Tax (Deductions from Income Support) Regulations 1993, SI 1993/494 (as amended) (see RATING AND COUNCIL TAX vol 39(1) (Reissue) para 899): Council Tax (Administration and Enforcement) Regulations 1992, SI 1992/613, reg 32(1) (added by SI 1993/733). See also RATING AND COUNCIL TAX vol 39(1) (Reissue) para 928.
12   See the Council Tax (Administration and Enforcement) Regulations 1992, SI 1992/613, reg 52(3)(b); and RATING AND COUNCIL TAX vol 39(1) (Reissue) para 928.
13   Ie under ibid reg 45(2)(b), Sch 5 (as substituted and amended): see RATING AND COUNCIL TAX vol 39(1) (Reissue) para 901.
14   See ibid reg 52(4); and RATING AND COUNCIL TAX vol 39(1) (Reissue) para 928.

5. DISTRESS FOR TAXES

1127. Taxes recoverable by distress. Income tax[1], corporation tax[2] and capital gains tax[3] which are assessed taxes under the care and management of the Commissioners for Her Majesty's Revenue and Customs[4], are by statute made recoverable by distress[5]. Distress for this purpose is a statutory remedy more analogous to execution than to distress for rent, much of the law concerning which, accordingly, does not apply[6]. There are no statutory provisions allowing for the recovery by distress of stamp duties[7] which are similarly under the care and management of the Commissioners[8].

The Commissioners may by regulations[9] make provision for: (1) authorising distress to be levied on the goods and chattels of any person refusing or neglecting to pay any amount of relevant tax[10] due from him, or any amount recoverable as if it were relevant tax due from him[11]; (2) the disposal of any goods or chattels on which distress is levied in pursuance of the regulations[12]; and (3) the imposition and recovery of costs, charges, expenses and fees in connection with anything done under the regulations[13].

1 Ie tax under the Income and Corporation Taxes Act 1988: see INCOME TAXATION. Remedies for recovery of this tax other than the remedy of distress are discussed in INCOME TAXATION.
2 See the Income and Corporation Taxes Act 1988; and INCOME TAXATION. Remedies for recovery of this tax other than the remedy of distress are discussed in INCOME TAXATION.
3 See the Taxation of Chargeable Gains Act 1992; and CAPITAL GAINS TAXATION. Remedies for the recovery of this tax other than the remedy of distress are discussed in CAPITAL GAINS TAXATION.

4 See the Taxes Management Act 1970 s 1(1) (substituted by the Commissioners for Revenue and Customs Act 2005 s 50(6), Sch 4 paras 11, 12); and INCOME TAXATION vol 23(1) (Reissue) para 31.
   The Commissioners for Her Majesty's Revenue and Customs are appointed under the Commissioners for Revenue and Customs Act 2005 s 1 and have taken over the functions of the former Inland Revenue and Her Majesty's Customs and Excise: see CUSTOMS AND EXCISE; INCOME TAXATION. References in any enactment, instrument or other document to the Commissioners of Customs and Excise or to the Commissioners of Inland Revenue must now be taken to be references to the Commissioners for Her Majesty's Revenue and Customs, and references to the officers and other persons specified in s 6(2) or s 7(3) must now be taken to be references to an officer of Revenue and Customs: see the Commissioners for Revenue and Customs Act 2005 s 50(1), (2), (3), (7).
5 See the Taxes Management Act 1970 s 61 (as amended); and INCOME TAXATION vol 23(1) (Reissue) para 1815.

6 See para 904 ante. Thus the Distress for Rent Rules 1988, SI 1988/2050 (as amended) (see para 994 et seq ante), made under the Law of Distress Amendment Act 1888 (see para 994 ante), do not apply; but apart from exceptions relating to the classes of goods privileged from distress and express statutory modification, the common law rules will, in general, apply. As to the common law and statutory rules under which certain goods are privileged from distress see para 930 et seq ante. See also *MacGregor v Clamp & Son* [1914] 1 KB 288, DC (implements of trade not privileged from distress for taxes).
7 As to stamp duties see generally STAMP DUTIES AND STAMP DUTY RESERVE TAX.
8 See the Stamp Duties Management Act 1891 ss 1, 27 (amended by virtue of the Commissioners for Revenue and Customs Act 2005 s 50(1), (7)); and STAMP DUTIES AND STAMP DUTY RESERVE TAX vol 44(1) (Reissue) para 1001.

9 See the Distress for Customs and Excise Duties and Other Indirect Taxes Regulations 1997, SI 1997/1431; and CUSTOMS AND EXCISE vol 12(3) (2007 Reissue) para 1140 et seq.

10 'Relevant taxes', for these purposes, are any duty of customs or excise (other than vehicle excise duty), value added tax, insurance premium tax, landfill tax, aggregates levy, any agricultural levy of the European Community, and climate change levy: Finance Act 1997 s 51(5) (amended by the Finance Act 2001 s 27, Sch 5 paras 7, 14). As to distress in respect of amounts due relating to unlicensed vehicles see para 1134 note 6 post.
11 Finance Act 1997 s 51(1)(a). See further CUSTOMS AND EXCISE vol 12(3) (2007 Reissue) para 1139; VALUE ADDED TAX vol 49(1) (2005 Reissue) para 330.
12 Ibid s 51(1)(b).
13 Ibid s 51(1)(c).

1128.   Distraint in respect of income tax.   If a person neglects or refuses to pay[1] the sum charged upon him in respect of tax on demand[2] made by the collector of taxes[3], the collector may distrain upon the goods and chattels[4] of the person charged[5].

A reasonable time must elapse between the delivery of the demand for payment and the distraint[6], but no special provision is made by the Taxes Management Act 1970 as to the time within which the distraint must be made. The power may, however, be lawfully exercised after the expiration of the year in respect of which the tax is payable[7]; but it seems that after the collector's account for the year has been closed, the collector may not distrain without a special authorisation from the Commissioners for Her Majesty's Revenue and Customs[8].

1   Non-payment after service of the demand note is evidence of refusal to pay: *Lumsden v Burnett* [1898] 2 QB 177 at 181–182, 185, CA.

2   For these purposes, 'tax', where neither income tax nor capital gains tax nor corporation tax nor development land tax (now abolished) is specified, means any of those taxes: Taxes Management Act 1970 s 118(1) (definition amended by the Development Land Tax Act 1976 s 41, Sch 8 para 32; and the Finance Act 1976 s 57(2)). As to the issue of demand notes see the Taxes Management Act 1970 s 60; and INCOME TAXATION vol 23 (Reissue) para 1710. As to delivery and service of documents see s 115 (as amended); and INCOME TAXATION vol 23(2) (Reissue) para 1797. Distraint following irregular service of a demand is unlawful and an action for wrongful distress will lie: see *Berry v Farrow* [1914] 1 KB 632. But issues as to the merits of an assessment must be determined on appeal to the Commissioners for Her Majesty's Revenue and Customs (formerly the Commissioners of Inland Revenue) and cannot be raised on proceedings for recovery: *IRC v Pearlberg* [1953] 1 All ER 388, [1953] 1 WLR 331, CA. As to the Commissioners for Her Majesty's Revenue and Customs see para 1127 note 4 ante.

3   In *R v Ford* (1835) 4 Nev & MKB 451, it was held that to justify a distress for taxes under 43 Geo 3 c 99 (Taxes) (1803) (repealed) the demand could be made by a person duly authorised by the collector; and that the amount due need not be specified in the demand note if it is understood by the taxpayer and not objected to by him.

4   As to the extent of distraint see para 1129 post.

5   Taxes Management Act 1970 s 61(1) (amended by Finance Act 1989 s 152(2)). This provision is applied with modifications to petroleum revenue tax: see the Oil Taxation Act 1975 s 1(5), Sch 2 para 1.

     Generally the obligation to appoint collectors of taxes has been imposed on the Commissioners for Her Majesty's Revenue and Customs (formerly the Commissioners for Inland Revenue). Thus where a person has removed to another division or district leaving tax in arrear or unpaid, the collector for the division or district to which the person has removed may distrain as if the tax had been charged in that division or district: see *Rutherford v Lord Advocate* (1931) 16 TC 145 (recovery of tax in Scotland in respect of an assessment made in England).

     In the event of insolvency following distraint under the Taxes Management Act 1970 s 61 (as amended), the distrained goods are not assets available for distribution to the taxpayer's creditors: *Re Modern Jet Support Centre Ltd* [2005] EWHC 1611 (Ch), [2005] 1 WLR 3880.

6   See *Gibbs v Stead* (1828) 8 B & C 528 (distraint held to be unlawful, where a collector distrained immediately after the demand and in the absence of the occupier of the premises).

7   See *Elliot v Yates* [1900] 2 QB 370, CA.

8   See *Elliot v Yates* [1900] 2 QB 370 at 375, CA, per Vaughan Williams LJ.

1129.   Extent of distraint.   As regards assessments in respect of lands and premises[1], the collector of taxes can distrain any goods found thereon, including the goods of a third party[2]. In effect the tax is charged on the premises[3]. As regards other assessments made upon persons, the collector can only distrain the goods of the person charged[4].

1   Ie income tax and corporation tax chargeable under the Income and Corporation Taxes Act 1988 Schedule A (as substituted and amended): see s 15 (as amended), Pt II (ss 21A–42A) (as amended); and INCOME TAXATION vol 23(1) (Reissue) para 45 et seq. Although tax under Schedule A (as substituted and amended) is charged on annual profits or gains arising in respect of rents and like receipts and not on or in respect of the land itself, it is considered that for the purposes of the Taxes Management Act 1970 s 61 (as amended) (see INCOME TAXATION vol 23(2) (Reissue) para 1815), such tax should probably be treated for these purposes as being charged in respect of lands, tenements and premises.

2   *Juson v Dixon* (1813) 1 M & S 601 (house and window tax collector; goods of a third party available for distress); *MacGregor v Clamp & Son* [1914] 1 KB 288, DC (if the tax is not purely personal but is charged

upon premises, it does not matter that the goods seized belong to a third person); *Reading v Chew* (1898) 78 LT 681 (an occupier took up occupation in April 1897, and his goods were distrained for tax due in respect of the previous year).

3   *Tennant v Smith* [1892] AC 150 at 154, 3 TC 158 at 163, HL, per Lord Halsbury LC; and see *Eastwood v McNab* [1914] 2 KB 361, CA (a lessee contracted to pay all taxes 'charged upon the premises'; the lessor had been assessed to and had paid inhabited house duty; it was held that he could recover the amount paid from the lessee).

4   *Earl of Shaftesbury v Russell* (1823) 1 B & C 666 (where tax is charged on a person, and not on premises, only the goods of a person charged can be seized by distraint); *Dolan v Joyce and Kirwan* [1928] IR 559 (arrears of tax due from a former occupier under Schedule B cannot be recovered from a subsequent occupier; the tax under Schedule B is imposed on the occupier).

1130.   Levying the distress.   For the purpose of levying a distress a justice of the peace, on being satisfied by information on oath that there is reasonable ground for believing that a person is neglecting or refusing to pay a sum charged, may issue a warrant[1] in writing authorising a collector of taxes to break open, in the daytime, any house or premises, calling to his assistance any constable[2], who must, when so required, aid and assist the collector in the execution of the warrant and in levying the distress in the house or premises[3].

A levy or warrant to break open must be executed by, or under the direction of, and in the presence of, the collector[4].

1   The warrant must be in accordance with the form prescribed from time to time by the Commissioners for Her Majesty's Revenue and Customs (see the Taxes Management Act 1970 ss 113(3), 118(1) (amended by virtue of the Commissioners for Revenue and Customs Act 2005 s 50(1), (7))), but if purporting to be made in pursuance of any provision of the Taxes Acts is not to be quashed or deemed to be void or voidable for want of form, or to be affected by reason of a mistake, defect or omission in it, provided it is in substance and effect in conformity with and according to the intent and meaning of the Taxes Acts, and if the person charged or property charged or intended to be charged or affected is designated in the warrant according to common intent and understanding (s 114(1)). As to the Commissioners for Her Majesty's Revenue and Customs see para 1127 note 4 ante. For the meaning of 'the Taxes Acts' see the Taxes Management Act 1970 s 118(1) (as amended); and INCOME TAXATION vol 23(1) (Reissue) para 21.

2   This means any person holding the office of constable, not a member of a police force holding the rank of constable: see POLICE vol 36(1) (Reissue) paras 201–205. As to the attestation of constables see POLICE vol 36(1) (Reissue) para 203.

3   Taxes Management Act 1970 s 61(2) (amended by the Finance Act 1989 s 152(3)). See also *R v Clark* (1835) 4 Nev & MKB 671 (a collector may distrain without having his warrant with him and should only take the constable into a house where there is reason to fear a breach of the peace); cf *Foss v Racine* (1838) 4 M & W 419 (under the Land Tax Act 1797 s 17 (repealed), it was held that a collector could not break open unless a constable was present).

4   Taxes Management Act 1970 s 61(3).

1131.   Impounding, appraisement and sale.   A distress levied by a collector of taxes must be kept for five days at the costs and charges of the person in default[1]. If that person does not pay the sum due, together with the costs and charges then the distress must be appraised by one or more independent persons appointed by the collector, and sold by public auction by the collector for payment of the sum due and all costs and charges[2]. Any overplus coming by the distress, after the deduction of the costs and charges and of the sum due, is to be restored to the owner of the goods distrained[3].

1   Taxes Management Act 1970 s 61(4) (amended by the Finance Act 1989 s 152(4)). As to impounding see para 1013 et seq ante.

2   Taxes Management Act 1970 s 61(5) (amended by the Finance Act 1989 ss 152(5), 187, Sch 17 Pt VIII). As to the appropriate scale of costs and charges see para 832 post.

3   Taxes Management Act 1970 s 61(5) (as amended: see note 2 supra). As to overplus see paras 1056–1057 ante.

1132.   Scale of costs and charges. The Treasury[1] may by regulations[2] make provision with respect to: (1) the fees chargeable on or in connection with the levying of distress; and (2) the costs and charges recoverable where distress has been levied[3].

1   'The Treasury' means the Commissioners of Her Majesty's Treasury: Interpretation Act 1978 s 5, Sch 1. As to the Treasury see CONSTITUTIONAL LAW AND HUMAN RIGHTS vol 8(2) (Reissue) paras 512–517.
2   Any such regulation must be made by statutory instrument which is subject to annulment in pursuance of a resolution of the House of Commons: Taxes Management Act 1970 s 61(6) (added by the Finance Act 1989 s 152(6)). As to the regulations made see the Distraint by Collectors (Fees, Costs and Charges) Regulations 1994, SI 1994/236 (amended by SI 1995/2151); and the Distraint by Collectors (Fees, Costs and Charges) (Stamp Duty Penalties) Regulations 1999, SI 1999/3263.
3   Taxes Management Act 1970 s 61(6) (as added: see note 2 supra).

1133.   Priority of claim for tax. If at any time at which goods or chattels belonging to any person in default[1] are liable to be taken by virtue of any execution or other process, warrant, or authority whatever, or by virtue of any assignment, on any account or pretence whatever (except at the suit of the landlord for rent), the person in default is in arrears in respect of[2]:

(1)   sums due from the person in default on account of deductions of income tax from taxable earnings[3] paid during the period of 12 months next before the date of seizure being deductions which the person in default was liable to make under PAYE regulations[4] less the amount of the repayments of income tax which he was liable to make during that period[5]; and

(2)   sums due from the person in default in respect of deductions required to be made by him for that period[6],

the goods or chattels may not be so taken unless, on demand made by the collector of taxes, the person at whose suit the execution or seizure is made, or to whom the assignment was made, pays or causes to be paid to the collector, before the sale or removal of the goods or chattels, all such sums as have fallen due at or before the date of the seizure[7]. Nevertheless where tax is claimed for more than one year, the person at whose instance the seizure has been made, may, on paying to the collector the tax which is due for one whole year, proceed in his seizure as if no tax had been claimed[8]. If these sums are not paid within 10 days of the date of the demand, the collector may distrain the goods and chattels notwithstanding the seizure or assignment, and may proceed to the sale thereof for the purpose of obtaining payment of the whole of those sums, and the reasonable costs and charges attending such distress and sale[9]. Every collector distraining in this manner is to be indemnified[10].

A bill of sale is no protection in respect of personal chattels included in the bill of sale which, but for that bill of sale, would have been liable to distress under a warrant for the recovery of taxes and poor and other parochial rates[11].

1   See para 1128 text and note 5 ante.
2   Taxes Management Act 1970 s 62(1) (amended by the Finance Act 1989 s 153(2)).
3   Ie as defined by the Income Tax (Earnings and Pensions) Act 2003 s 10: see INCOME TAXATION.
4   Ie regulations made under the Income Tax (Earnings and Pensions) Act 2003 ss 684, 685 (as amended): see INCOME TAXATION vol 23(1) (Reissue) paras 755–759.
5   Taxes Management Act 1970 s 62(1A)(a) (s 62(1A) added by the Finance Act 1989 s 153(3); and the Taxes Management Act 1970 s 62(1A)(a) amended by the Income Tax (Earnings and Pensions) Act 2003 s 722, Sch 6 paras 123, 132).
6   Taxes Management Act 1970 s 62(1A)(b) (s 62(1A) as added (see note 5 supra); and s 62(1A)(b) amended by the Finance Act 2004 s 76, Sch 12 para 4). The text refers to sums due under the Finance Act 2004 s 61 (deductions on account of tax for contract payments to sub-contractors in the construction industry): see INCOME TAXATION vol 23(1) (Reissue) para 810.
7   Taxes Management Act 1970 s 62(1) (as amended: see note 2 supra).
8   Ibid s 62(1) proviso.
9   Ibid s 62(2) (amended by the Finance Act 1989 s 153(4)).

10 Taxes Management Act 1970 s 62(2) (as amended: see note 9 supra).
11 Bills of Sale Act (1878) Amendment Act 1882 s 14; and see BILLS OF SALE vol 4(1) (2002 Reissue) para 789.

6. DISTRESS UNDER THE MAGISTRATES' COURTS ACT 1980

1134.   Jurisdiction.   Where default is made in paying a sum adjudged to be paid by a conviction or order of a magistrates court[1], the court may issue[2] a warrant of distress for the purpose of levying the sum or issue a warrant committing the defaulter to prison[3]. The expression 'sum adjudged to be paid by a conviction or order of a magistrates' court' includes a reference to any costs, damages or compensation adjudged to be paid by the conviction or order of which the amount is ascertained by the conviction or order[4].

Payment of a sum adjudged to be paid to a magistrates' court on the forfeiture of a recognisance may be enforced as if the sum were a fine[5]. By statute certain further sums are to be treated for purposes of enforcement as if they were fines enforced by, or recognisances forfeited by, magistrates' courts[6].

Where a magistrates' court is required to enforce payment of a fine imposed or a recognisance forfeited by a Crown Court or by a coroner[7] or where a magistrates' court allows time for payment of a sum adjudged to be paid by a summary conviction, or directs that the sum be paid by instalments, or where the offender is absent[8] when a sum is adjudged to be paid by a summary conviction, a warrant of distress or commitment is not to be issued until the designated officer for the court has served[9] on the offender notice in writing stating the amount of the sum and, if it is to be paid by instalments, the amount of the instalments, the date on which the sum, or each of the instalments, is to be paid and the places and times at which payment may be made[10].

A warrant of distress may not be issued for failure to pay a sum enforceable as a civil debt unless the defendant has been previously served[11] with a copy of the minute of the order, or the order was made in his presence and the warrant issued on that occasion[12]. A 'sum enforceable as a civil debt' is any sum recoverable summarily as a civil debt[13] which is adjudged to be paid by the order of a magistrates' court[14] or any other sum expressed by any Act to be so enforceable[15].

The restrictions upon the issue of a warrant of commitment in default of payment of a sum adjudged to be paid on conviction[16] do not affect the power to enforce payment by distress, nor do the restrictions upon the issue of a warrant of commitment where default is made in paying a sum ordered to be paid by a magistrates' court maintenance order[17] apply to the issue of a distress warrant. Where a magistrates' court has power to issue a warrant of distress[18], the court, if it thinks it expedient to do so, may postpone the issue of the warrant until such time and on such conditions, if any, as the court thinks just[19].

1   'Magistrates' court' means any justice or justices of the peace acting under any enactment or by virtue of his or their commission or under the common law: Magistrates' Courts Act 1980 s 148(1); and see generally MAGISTRATES. Except where the contrary is expressed, anything authorised or required by the Magistrates' Courts Act 1980 to be done by, to or before the magistrates' court by, to or before which any other thing was done, or is to be done, may be done by, to or before any magistrates' court acting in the same local justice area as that court: s 148(2) (amended by the Courts Act 2003 s 109(1), Sch 8 para 248).

2   As to the power to postpone issuing a warrant see the text to note 19 infra.

3   Magistrates' Courts Act 1980 s 76(1) (amended by the Criminal Justice Act 1982 s 78, Sch 16). This is expressed to be subject to the provisions of the Magistrates' Courts Act 1980 Pt III (ss 75–96A) (as amended; prospectively amended), and s 132 (see MAGISTRATES). As to the enforcement, otherwise than by distress, of judgments for payment of money made by magistrates' courts and committal see generally MAGISTRATES.

4   Ibid s 150(3). The expression does not include non-domestic rates or council tax: see paras 1104–1114, 1116–1126 ante. In the case of a fine imposed in respect of certain fishery offences a distress may be

levied against a fishing boat and its gear and catch and any property of the person convicted for the purpose of levying the fine: see the Sea Fisheries Act 1968 s 12(1)(a) (as amended); note 19 infra; and para 1140 note 1 post. See further FISHERIES.

5   See the Magistrates' Courts Act 1980 s 120 (as amended); and MAGISTRATES.

6   Such sums include: (1) fines imposed, or recognisances forfeited, by the Crown Court or by the criminal division of the Court of Appeal or by the House of Lords on appeal from that division (see the Powers of Criminal Courts (Sentencing) Act 2000 s 140 (as amended; prospectively amended); and CRIMINAL LAW, EVIDENCE AND PROCEDURE vol 11(4) (2006 Reissue) para 1684); (2) fines imposed by coroners on jurors or witnesses and recognisances forfeited at inquests (see the Coroners Act 1988 s 10(1), (2) (as amended); the Criminal Justice Act 1988 s 67 (as amended); and CORONERS vol 9(2) (Reissue) paras 886, 915); (3) certain amounts payable by keepers of unlicensed vehicles (see the Vehicle Excise and Registration Act 1994 ss 30, 32(2), (3)(a); and CUSTOMS AND EXCISE vol 12(3) (2007 Reissue) para 778); (4) and, upon the order of the judge, any fine imposed by a county court (see the County Courts Act 1984 s 129; and COURTS vol 10 (Reissue) para 704). As to the enforcement of decisions on appeals from magistrates' courts see para 1139 post.

7   As to the enforcement by magistrates' courts of fines imposed and recognisances forfeited by the Crown Court or by coroners see note 6 supra.

8   A party represented before a magistrates' court by a legal representative is deemed not to be absent: Magistrates' Courts Act 1980 s 122(1), (2) (s 122(1) amended by the Courts and Legal Services Act 1990 s 125(3), Sch 18 para 25). 'Legal representative' means an authorised advocate or authorised litigator, as defined by the Courts and Legal Services Act 1990 s 119(1) (see BARRISTERS vol 3(1) (2005 Reissue) para 501; SOLICITORS vol 44(1) (Reissue) paras 78–79): Magistrates' Courts Act 1980 s 150(1) (definition added by the Courts and Legal Services Act 1990 s 125(3), Sch 18 para 25).

9   A notice under this rule is to be served by delivering it to the offender or by sending it to him by post in a letter addressed to him at his last known or usual place of abode: Magistrates' Courts Rules 1981, SI 1981/552, r 46(2).

10   Ibid r 46(1) (amended by SI 2001/610; SI 2003/1236; SI 2005/617).

11   A copy of the minute of the order is to be served by delivering it to the defendant or by sending it to him by post in a letter addressed to him at his last known or usual place of abode: see the Criminal Procedure Rules 2005, SI 2005/384, r 52.7(1).

12   See ibid r 52.7(2).

13   In addition to any sum expressed by or under a statute to be recoverable summarily as a civil debt, any sum, the payment of which may be ordered by a magistrates' court, is so recoverable, except a sum recoverable on complaint for a magistrates' court maintenance order, or a sum that may be adjudged to be paid by a summary conviction or by an order enforceable as if it were a summary conviction: Magistrates' Courts Act 1980 s 58(2) (amended by the Family Law Reform Act 1987 s 33(1), Sch 2 para 80). 'Magistrates' court maintenance order' means a maintenance order enforceable by a magistrates' court: Magistrates' Courts Act 1980 s 150(1) (definition added by the Family Law Reform Act 1987 Sch 2 para 88). 'Maintenance order' means any order specified in the Administration of Justice Act 1970 s 28(1), Sch 8 (as amended) and includes such an order which has been discharged, if any arrears are recoverable thereunder: Magistrates' Courts Act 1980 s 150(1) (definition added by the Family Law Reform Act 1987 Sch 2 para 88).

14   A magistrates' court has power to make an order on complaint for the payment of any money recoverable summarily as a civil debt: Magistrates' Courts Act 1980 s 58(1).

15   Ibid s 150(1). For an instance where an order of the Crown Court is enforceable summarily as a civil debt see the Administration of Justice Act 1970 s 41(2), Sch 9 para 16 (as substituted); and MAGISTRATES.

16   See the Magistrates Court Act 1980 s 82 (as amended; prospectively amended); and MAGISTRATES.

17   See ibid s 93(6) (as amended); and MAGISTRATES.

18   Ie under ibid Pt III (ss 75–96A) (as amended): see MAGISTRATES.

19   Ibid s 77(1). This provision applies to a warrant of distress issued under the Sea Fisheries Act 1968 s 12 (as amended): see s 12(3) (as amended); and FISHERIES. See note 4 supra.

    There is no specific statutory power to suspend a warrant once it has been issued and old authorities on earlier statutes are inconclusive: see eg *Barons v Luscombe* (1835) 3 Ad & El 589; *Kendall v Wilkinson* (1855) 24 LJMC 89; *R v Paget* (1881) 8 QBD 151, DC. It is thought that the court has power to suspend in an appropriate case: cf the following custody cases *Re S (an infant)* [1958] 1 All ER 783, [1958] 1 WLR 391; *B (BPM) v B (MM)* [1969] P 103, sub nom *B (B) v B (M)* [1969] 1 All ER 891, DC; *Smith v Smith* (1971) 115 Sol Jo 444, DC (power of justices to grant stay of execution of orders as to custody pending appeal).

1135.   Exercise of discretion. The exercise of the jurisdiction to issue a warrant for distress[1] must be exercised judicially[2]. There is no requirement to hold an inquiry into the defaulter's means before issuing a warrant for distress[3], but if an inquiry is made as to the defaulter's means, the justices may require affirmative evidence that the defendant has goods before issuing a warrant for distress[4]. If there is a reasonable likelihood that the defaulter has assets available to satisfy the sum he owes, the justices should proceed by way of warrant for distress rather than by way of a warrant for commitment[5]. Where justices do conduct a means inquiry and the defaulter is unrepresented, and the court has in mind the issue of a distress warrant, sufficient notice should be given to the defaulter that such a course is being considered so that the defaulter has a sufficient opportunity of making representations[6].

1   See para 1134 ante; and MAGISTRATES.
2   *R v Hereford Magistrates' Court, ex p MacRae* (1998) 163 JP 433, DC.
3   *R v Hereford Magistrates' Court, ex p MacRae* (1998) 163 JP 433, DC.
4   *R v German* (1891) 56 JP 358, DC; *R v Mortimer* (1906) 70 JP 542, DC.
5   *R v Birmingham Justices, ex p Bennett* [1983] 1 WLR 114, (1982) 147 JP 279, DC.
6   *R v Guildford Justices, ex p Rich* [1997] 1 Cr App Rep (S) 49, (1996) 160 JP 645, DC.

1136.   Commitment and distress.   Subject to certain restrictions[1], the magistrates' court[2] has power to issue a warrant committing the defaulter to prison either instead of issuing a warrant of distress or where it appears on the return to the warrant of distress that the money and goods of the defaulter are insufficient to satisfy the sum with the costs and charges of levying the sum[3]. In the case of a sum adjudged to be paid by an order, as distinct from a sum adjudged to be paid by a conviction or treated by any enactment as so adjudged to be paid, the power of committal is exercisable only in respect of default under a magistrates' court maintenance order[4], an order for the payment of any one of certain taxes, contributions, premiums or liabilities[5], or an order relating to the provision of funded services[6]. In certain cases the court may make an attachment of earnings order instead of issuing a warrant for distress or commitment[7].

1   As to the restrictions see para 1134 note 3 ante.
2   For the meaning of 'magistrates' court' see para 1134 note 1 ante.
3   Magistrates Court Act 1980 s 76(2).
4   For the meaning of 'magistrates' court maintenance order' see para 1134 note 13 ante.
5   Ie specified in the Administration of Justice Act 1970 Sch 4 (as amended): see EXECUTION; MAGISTRATES.
6   See the Magistrates Court Act 1980 s 92(1) (amended by the Access to Justice Act 1999 s 24, Sch 4 paras 15, 17). As to the provision of funded services see the Access to Justice Act 1999 s 17 (as amended); and LEGAL AID. A person may not be committed to prison in default of payment of a sum enforceable as a civil debt or for want of sufficient distress to satisfy such a sum except by an order made on complaint and on proof of means: see the Magistrates' Courts Act 1980 s 96(1); the Magistrates' Courts Rules 1981, SI 1981/552, r 58 (amended by SI 2005/617); and MAGISTRATES. As to restrictions on the power to impose imprisonment in default of payment of fines see the Magistrates' Courts Act 1980 s 82 (as amended; prospectively amended); and MAGISTRATES.
7   See the Attachment of Earnings Act 1971 ss 1(3), 3(4) (both as amended); and CRIMINAL LAW, EVIDENCE AND PROCEDURE vol 11(4) (2006 Reissue) para 2100; MAGISTRATES.

1137.   Issue of warrant.   A distress warrant[1] may be issued by the magistrates' court[2] which convicted or made the order or in any magistrates' court acting in the same local justice area as the court which convicted or made the order[3]. The warrant must be signed by the justice issuing it or by the clerk of a magistrates' court where this is permitted[4]. A warrant issued by a justice of the peace does not cease to have effect by reason of his death or his ceasing to be a justice[5].

Where a warrant is issued by a justice of the peace for any local justice area at a time when the office of the designated officer of that area is closed, the applicant for the warrant must within 72 hours serve upon the designated officer any information on which the warrant was issued[6].

1   As to the general power to issue a warrant of distress where default is made in paying a sum adjudged to
    be paid by a magistrates' court see para 1134 ante.
2   For the meaning of 'magistrates' court' see para 1134 note 1 ante.
3   See the Magistrates' Courts Act 1980 s 148(2) (amended by the Courts Act 2003 s 109(1), Sch 8
    para 248). For circumstances where a distress warrant may issue in respect of a conviction of another
    court see para 1134 note 6 ante. As to transfer of fine order see the Magistrates' Courts Act 1980 s 89 (as
    amended); and MAGISTRATES vol 29(2) (Reissue) para 856. As to transfer of fine orders from Scotland or
    Northern Ireland see s 91 (as amended); and MAGISTRATES vol 29(2) (Reissue) para 858. As to
    enforcement of magistrates' court maintenance orders see the Magistrates' Courts Rules 1981,
    SI 1981/552, r 59 (amended by SI 2001/610; SI 2005/617).
4   See the Criminal Procedure Rules 2005, SI 2005/384, r 5.3.
5   Magistrates' Courts Act 1980 s 124.
6   See the Magistrates' Courts Rules 1981, SI 1981/552, r 95A (added by SI 1993/1183; and amended by
    SI 2005/617).

1138.   Form of warrant.   A warrant of distress[1] issued for the purpose of levying a
sum adjudged to be paid by a summary conviction or order[2] must be directed to the
constables of the police area[3] in which the warrant is issued or to the civilian
enforcement officers for the area in which they are employed, or to a person named in
the warrant and must, subject to and in accordance with the provisions relating to the
execution of distress warrants[4], require them to levy the said sum by distress and sale of
the goods[5] belonging to the said person[6].

The warrant must require the person charged with the execution to pay the sum to
be levied to the designated officer for the court that issued the warrant[7].

1   As to forms of distress warrant see the Magistrates' Courts (Forms) Rules 1981, SI 1981/553, r 2(1).
2   As to the power to issue a warrant for this purpose see para 1134 ante.
3   As to police areas see POLICE vol 36(1) (Reissue) paras 313–315. The warrant, if directed to the
    constables of a police area, may, instead of being executed by any of those constables, be executed by any
    person under the direction of a constable: see the Magistrates' Courts Rules 1981, SI 1981/552,
    r 54(1)(c); and para 1141 post.
4   Ie in accordance with the provisions of ibid r 54 (as amended): see the text and note 6 infra.
5   For descriptions of goods which are exempt see para 1144 post.
6   Magistrates' Courts Rules 1981, SI 1981/552, r 54(1)(b) (amended by SI 1990/1190). As to who may
    execute the warrant see para 1141 post.
7   Magistrates' Courts Rules 1981, SI 1981/552, r 54(3) (amended by SI 2005/617).

1139.   Distress after appeal.   After the determination by the High Court of an
appeal by case stated, or by the Crown Court of an appeal against a conviction or order
of a magistrates' court, the decision of the appeal court is enforceable as if it were the
decision of the magistrates' court against whose decision the appeal had been brought,
and, accordingly, that magistrates' court may issue a distress warrant[1] to enforce the
decision of the High Court[2] or of the Crown Court[3].

1   As to the power to issue a distress warrant to enforce the decision of a magistrates' court see para 1134
    ante.
2   Magistrates' Courts Act 1980 s 112.
3   Ibid s 110. The decision of the Crown Court has effect as if it had been made by the magistrates' court
    against whose decision the appeal was brought: s 110.

1140.   Effect of defect in warrant.   A warrant of distress issued for the purpose of
levying a sum adjudged to be paid by the conviction[1] or order of a magistrates' court[2],
if it states that the sum has been so adjudged to be paid, will not be held void by reason
of any defect in the warrant[3]; nor will a person acting under such a warrant be deemed
to be a trespasser from the beginning by reason only of any irregularity in the execution
of the warrant[4]. Special damages in respect of any loss caused by such a defect or
irregularity are, however, recoverable[5].

1   The provisions stated in the text apply to warrants of distress issued against fishing boats, their gear and catch and the property of persons convicted of certain fishery offences: see the Sea Fisheries Act 1968 s 12(3) (as amended); and FISHERIES vol 18 (Reissue) para 803. As to distress against fishing boats etc see para 1134 note 4 ante; and FISHERIES.
2   As to the power to issue a distress warrant for such a purpose see para 1134 ante.
3   Magistrates' Courts Act 1980 s 78(1).
4   Ibid s 78(2). In connection with trespass ab initio see *Six Carpenters' Case* (1610) 8 Co Rep 146a; and see para 1076 et seq ante. As to trespass see TORT vol 45(2) (Reissue) para 659 et seq.
5   Magistrates' Courts Act 1980 s 78(3).

1141.   Execution of warrant.   A warrant of distress issued for the purpose of levying a sum adjudged to be paid by a summary conviction or order[1] which is directed to the constables of a police area[2] may be executed by any of the constables to whom it is directed, or by any person under the direction of a constable[3]. A warrant of distress issued by a justice of the peace for such a purpose may be executed anywhere in England and Wales by any person to whom it is directed[4] or by any constable acting within his police area[5].

A warrant of distress issued in England or Wales and indorsed in pursuance of the Summary Jurisdiction (Process) Act 1881 will be executed in Scotland as if it were a Scottish warrant of poinding and sale; and a Scottish warrant of poinding and sale similarly indorsed will be executed in England or Wales as if it were a warrant of distress issued in England or Wales[6].

1   As to the power to issue a distress warrant for such a purpose see para 1134 ante.
2   As to police areas see POLICE vol 36(1) (Reissue) paras 313–315.
3   Magistrates' Courts Rules 1981, SI 1981/552, r 54(1)(c).
4   As to the persons to whom a warrant may be directed see para 1138 ante.
5   See the Magistrates' Courts Act 1980 s 125(2).
6   Summary Jurisdiction (Process) Act 1881 s 5. The operation of this Act is extended so that its provisions apply as between England and the Isle of Man: see the Summary Jurisdiction Process (Isle of Man) Order 1928, SI 1928/377, art 1. Poinding is the taking of a debtor's moveables by way of execution.

1142.   Time and manner of execution.   The distress levied under any warrant issued for the purpose of levying a sum adjudged to be paid by a summary conviction or order[1] must be sold within such period beginning not earlier than the sixth day after the making of the distress as may be specified in the warrant, or, if no period is specified in the warrant, within a period beginning on the sixth day and ending on the fourteenth day after the making of the distress[2]. The sale must be by public auction[3] or in such other manner as the person against whom the distress is levied may in writing allow[4].

Subject to any direction to the contrary in the warrant, where the distress is levied on household goods, the goods may not, without the consent in writing of the person against whom the distress is levied, be removed from the house until the day of sale; and so much of the goods are to be impounded as is in the opinion of the person executing the warrant sufficient to satisfy the distress, by affixing to the articles impounded a conspicuous mark[5]. The removal of goods so marked, or the removal or defacing of the mark, is punishable on summary conviction by a fine[6]. The person charged with the execution of the warrant is required to cause the distress to be sold[7], and may deduct out of the amount realised all costs and charges incurred in effecting the sale[8]. If any person charged with the execution of the warrant wilfully retains from the proceeds of sale, or otherwise exacts, any greater costs and charges than those properly payable, or makes any improper charge, he is liable on summary conviction to a fine[9].

1   As to the power to issue a distress warrant for this purpose see para 1134 ante. As to the persons who may be charged with the execution of a warrant see para 1138 ante.
2   Magistrates' Courts Rules 1981, SI 1981/552, r 54(5). With the consent in writing of the person against whom the distress is levied, the distress may be sold before the beginning of this period: r 54(5).

3   As to sale by auction see para 1055 ante; and AUCTION.
4   Magistrates' Courts Rules 1981 r 54(6). The distress must not be sold if the sum mentioned in the warrant and the charges of taking and keeping the distress have been paid: r 54(7).
5   Ibid r 54(8). As to impounding generally see para 1013 et seq ante. The expression 'household goods' is not defined; but wearing apparel and bedding of a person and his family are exempt: see para 1144 post. Goods seized by a constable under a distress warrant are in legal custody, and a landlord has no right to distrain or make a claim upon them; goods seized under a distress warrant issued by a magistrates' court may be removed without regard to any claim by the landlord for arrears of rent such as may be made under the Landlord and Tenant Act 1709 s 1 (as amended) (see para 1032 ante), in the case of goods seized in execution: see *Potts v Hickman* [1941] AC 212, [1940] 4 All ER 491, HL (a case of goods seized for rates); and para 1032 ante.
6   Magistrates' Courts Act 1980 s 78(4) (amended by virtue of the Criminal Justice Act 1982 ss 37, 46; and by the Courts Act 2003 s 109(1), Sch 8 para 219(a)). The text refers to a fine not exceeding level 1 on the standard scale: see the Magistrates' Courts Act 1980 s 78(4) (as so amended). As to the standard scale see para 999 note 5 ante.
7   Where the distress warrant was issued to enforce a sum due under a forfeited recognisance, the magistrates' court that issued the warrant may, at any time before the actual sale, remit the whole or any part of the sum absolutely or on such conditions as the court thinks just: see ibid s 120(4). A magistrates' court must not, under this power, remit the whole or any part of a fine imposed, or sum due under a recognisance forfeited, by the Crown Court, the criminal division of the Court of Appeal, or the House of Lords on appeal from that division, without the consent of the Crown Court: Powers of Criminal Courts (Sentencing) Act 2000 s 140(5). As from a day to be appointed, the reference to the House of Lords is replaced by a reference to the Supreme Court: s 140(5) (prospectively amended by the Constitutional Reform Act s 40(4), Sch 9 para 69). At the date at which this volumes states the law no such day had been appointed.
8   Magistrates' Courts Rules 1981, SI 1981/552, r 54(9) (amended by SI 2001/167). He must return to the owner the balance, if any, after retaining the amount of the sum for which the warrant was issued and the proper costs and charges of the execution of the warrant: r 54(9).
9   Magistrates' Courts Act 1980 s 78(5) (amended by virtue of the Criminal Justice Act 1982 ss 37, 46). The text refers to a fine not exceeding level 1 on the standard scale: see the Magistrates' Courts Act 1980 s 78(5) (as so amended).

1143.   Payment or tender to avoid distress.   If any person pays or tenders to the person charged with its execution the sum mentioned in the distress warrant, or produces a receipt for that sum given by the designated officer for the court that issued the warrant, and also pays the amount of the costs and charges of the distress up to the time of the payment or tender or the production of the receipt, the person must not execute the warrant, or must cease to execute it[1].

1   Magistrates' Courts Rules 1981, SI 1981/552, r 54(11) (amended by SI 2001/167; SI 2005/617). As to the persons who may be charged with the execution of a distress warrant issued for the purpose of levying a sum adjudged to be paid by a summary conviction or order see para 1138 ante.

1144.   Items exempt from distress.   There must not be taken under the warrant of distress[1] the clothing or bedding of any person or his family or the tools, books, vehicles or other equipment which he personally needs to use in his employment, business or vocation[2].

Water fittings let for hire by a water undertaker and suitably marked as to indicate ownership[3], gas meters connected to a service pipe and gas fittings in a consumer's premises which are owned by a gas transporter or gas supplier and marked or impressed with a sufficient mark or brand indicating the owner[4], and electric lines, electrical plants lines or electricity meters belonging to or provided by an electricity distributor or electricity supplier which is marked or impressed with a sufficient mark or brand indicating an electricity supplier or electricity distributor as the owner or provider[5], may not be subject to distress or be liable to be taken in execution under any process of any court or in any proceedings in bankruptcy against a person in whose possession they may be[6].

1   As to the power to levy such a distress see para 1134 ante.

2   Magistrates' Courts Rules 1981, SI 1981/552, r 54(4) (substituted by SI 1999/2765). The reference to
     'person' does not, for these purposes, include a corporation: see the Magistrates' Courts Rules 1981,
     SI 1981/552, r 54(4) (as so substituted).
3   Water Industry Act 1991 s 179(4)(b). See further WATER vol 49(2) (2004 Reissue) para 364.
4   See the Gas Act 1986 s 8B, Sch 2B para 29(1)(a) (s 8B, Sch 2B both added by the Gas Act 1995 s 9,
     Sch 2; and the Gas Act 1986 Sch 2B para 29(1)(a) amended by the Utilities Act 2000 s 108, Sch 6 paras 1,
     2(1)); and FUEL AND ENERGY.
5   See the Electricity Act 1989 s 24, Sch 6 para 11 (s 24 amended by the Utilities Act 2000 s 51(1); and the
     Electricity Act 1989 Sch 6 substituted by the Utilities Act 2000 s 51(2), Sch 4); and FUEL AND ENERGY.
6   See the text and notes 3–5 supra.

1145.   Seizure of money. A distress warrant issued for the purpose of levying a sum
adjudged to be paid by a summary conviction or order[1] authorises the person charged
with its execution to take the money as well as the goods of the person against whom
the distress is levied[2]. Any money so taken is to be treated as if it were the proceeds of
the sale of goods taken under the warrant[3].

1   As to the power to issue such a warrant see para 1134 ante. As to the form of warrant and the persons to
     whom it may be directed see para 1138 ante.
2   Magistrates' Courts Rules 1981, SI 1981/552, r 54(2).
3   Ibid r 54(2).

1146.   Account of costs and charges. The person charged with the execution of
a warrant of distress issued for the purpose of levying a sum adjudged to be paid by a
summary conviction or order[1] must as soon as practicable send to the designated officer
for the court which issued the warrant a written account of the costs and charges
incurred in executing it[2]. The designated officer must allow the person against whom
the distress was levied to inspect the account within one month after the levy of the
distress at any reasonable time to be appointed by the court[3].

1   As to the power to issue such a warrant see para 1134 ante. As to the persons to whom it may be directed
     see para 1138 ante.
2   Magistrates' Courts Rules 1980, SI 1980/552, r 54(10) (amended by SI 2001/167; SI 2005/617).
3   Magistrates' Courts Rules 1980, SI 1980/552, r 54(10) (as amended: see note 2 supra).

1147.   Return of insufficient distress. Where the person to whom the duty of
executing a distress warrant[1] is entrusted is unable, after diligent search, to find sufficient
money and goods to satisfy the sum mentioned in the warrant, together with the costs
and charges of levying that sum, he is required by a direction in the warrant to certify
the same to the court that issued the warrant[2]. The powers of a magistrates' court to
enforce, otherwise than by means of distress, the payment of sums adjudged to be paid
are dealt with elsewhere in this work[3].

1   Ie a distress warrant issued for the purpose of levying a sum adjudged to be paid by a summary
     conviction or order. As to the power to issue such a warrant see para 1134 ante. As to the persons to
     whom it may be directed see para 1138 ante.
2   See also para 1138 note 1 ante.
3   See para 1136 ante; and MAGISTRATES.

INDEX

Deeds and Other Instruments

References are to paragraph numbers; superior figures refer to notes

References are to paragraph numbers; superior figures refer to notes

References are to paragraph numbers; superior figures refer to notes

References are to paragraph numbers; superior figures refer to notes

Discrimination

References are to paragraph numbers; superior figures refer to notes

References are to paragraph numbers; superior figures refer to notes

References are to paragraph numbers; superior figures refer to notes

References are to paragraph numbers; superior figures refer to notes

References are to paragraph numbers; superior figures refer to notes

DISABILITY
    DISCRIMINATION—*continued*
  trade organisation—
    meaning, 541n[1]
    adjustments, duty to make, 542
    unlawful discrimination or harassment,
      541
    void rule, 614
  vicarious liability, 527
  victimisation, by way of, 526
  work placement—
    adjustments, duty to make, 552
    unlawful discrimination or harassment,
      551

DISABILITY RIGHTS COMMISSION. *See
    also* COMMISSION FOR EQUALITY AND
    HUMAN RIGHTS
  accounts, 647
  action plan, 653
  additional commissioners, 648n[7]
  agreement in lieu of enforcement action,
    652
  annual report, 647
  assistance in proceedings, 656
  chairman, 646
  chief executive, 646
  codes of practice, 655
  commissioners, 646
  compliance notice, 592
  conciliation of disputes, 657
  constitution, 646
  corporate status, 646
  disclosure of information, restrictions, 658
  dissolution, 306
  duties, 647
  establishment, 507, 646
  formal investigation—
    additional commissioners, 648n[7]
    agreement in lieu of, 652
    conduct of, 649
    disclosure of information, restrictions,
      658
    notice requirements, 649
    power to conduct, 648
    recommendations and report, 649
    terms of reference, 649
  functions and powers, 647
  injunction, power to apply for, 575, 654
  investigation by. *See* formal investigation
    above
  list of organisations consulted, 647
  non-discrimination notice—
    agreement in lieu of, 652
    appeal against, 651
    contents, 650
    enforcement, 651

DISABILITY RIGHTS
    COMMISSION—*continued*
  non-discrimination notice—*continued*
    offences, 659
    power to issue, 650
    procedure, 651
    register of final notices, 651
  offences as to enforcement action, 659
  proceedings, 646
  quorum, 646
  Scottish commissioner, 646n[4]
  status, 646
  validity of proceedings, 646

DISABLED PERSON
  meaning, 511
  certificate of registration, 521
  Disability Rights Commission. *See*
    DISABILITY RIGHTS COMMISSION
  discrimination against. *See* DISABILITY
    DISCRIMINATION
  guidance as to disability, 512
  harassment, 533

DISCRIMINATION
  age discrimination. *See* AGE
    DISCRIMINATION
  categories, 301
  Commission for Equality and Human
    Rights. *See* COMMISSION FOR
    EQUALITY AND HUMAN RIGHTS
  Convention rights, 303, 304
  disability discrimination. *See* DISABILITY
    DISCRIMINATION
  Equal Opportunities Commission. *See*
    EQUAL OPPORTUNITIES COMMISSION
  equal pay. *See* EQUAL PAY
  Human Rights Act 1998 . . . 303
  legal assistance, 334
  public sector duties, assessment and
    compliance notices, 336
  racial discrimination. *See* RACIAL
    DISCRIMINATION
  religious discrimination. *See* RELIGIOUS
    DISCRIMINATION
  scope of title, 301
  Secretary of State's functions, 302
  sex discrimination. *See* SEX
    DISCRIMINATION
  sexual orientation discrimination. *See*
    SEXUAL ORIENTATION
    DISCRIMINATION
  unlawful act—
    meaning, 316n[10]
    Commission's powers. *See* COMMISSION
      FOR EQUALITY AND HUMAN
      RIGHTS (enforcement powers)
  Welsh Assembly functions, 302

References are to paragraph numbers; superior figures refer to notes

References are to paragraph numbers; superior figures refer to notes

References are to paragraph numbers; superior figures refer to notes

References are to paragraph numbers; superior figures refer to notes

Distress

References are to paragraph numbers; superior figures refer to notes

References are to paragraph numbers; superior figures refer to notes

References are to paragraph numbers; superior figures refer to notes

References are to paragraph numbers; superior figures refer to notes

References are to paragraph numbers; superior figures refer to notes

Words and Phrases

Words in parentheses indicate the context in which the word or phrase is used

accessibility certificate (disability
　discrimination), 639n[7]
action plan (Equality Act 2006), 329
act—
　(age discrimination), 755n[3]
　(disability discrimination), 510n[3]
　(race relations), 442n[7]
　(religious discrimination), 661n[3]
　(sex discrimination), 359n[1]
　(sexual orientation discrimination), 723n[3]
action (Equality Act 2006), 697n[4]
activity (sex discrimination), 339n[2]
addiction, 523n[5]
additional maternity leave, 350n[5]
additional retirement pension, 763n[7]
administration bond, 100
advertisement—
　(race relations), 473n[1]
　(sex discrimination), 388n[1]
advisory committee (Commission for Equality
　and Human Rights), 308
age, 754n[3]
age group, 754n[4]
age-related benefit, 764n[3]
agricultural wages order (equal pay), 433n[1]
ambiguous instrument, 208
ancient instrument, 206
annual report (Commission for Equality and
　Human Rights), 309
applicant's issuing county court (distress),
　995n[8]
apprentice (age discrimination), 802n[6]
appropriate amount—
　(distress for council rates), 1118n[4]
　(distress for rates), 1106n[3]
appropriate newspaper (bailiff's certificate)
　(distress), 995n[14]
approval certificate (disability discrimination),
　639n[8]
arrangements (sex discrimination), 348n[10]
armed forces—
　(equal pay), 432n[4]
　(race relations), 457n[7]
　(religious discrimination), 689n[8]
　(sex discrimination), 375n[1]
　(sexual orientation discrimination), 751n[8]
arrears date (equal pay), 432n[14], 435n[21]
assistance dog (disability discrimination),
　633n[5]
associate (disability discrimination), 596n[11]

associated employer (disability
　discrimination), 360n[4]
authorised person (PSV), 637n[6]
authority (disability discrimination), 558n[1]
basic state retirement pension (age
　discrimination), 763n[6]
belief—
　(Equality Act 2006), 691
　(religious discrimination), 660n[3]
benefits—
　(age discrimination), 758n[6]
　(disability discrimination), 534n[9]
　(religious discrimination), 663n[6]
　(sex discrimination), 377n[10]
　(sexual orientation discrimination), 725n[6]
billing authority (non-domestic rates), 1104
binding obligation, 560n[17], 532n[34]
block transfer (age discrimination), 766n[18]
body (race relations), 457n[11]
bond, 89
capital redemption business, 95
charitable instrument—
　(disability discrimination), 615n[2]
　(race relations), 481n[2]
　(religious discrimination), 703n[6]
　(sex discrimination), 395n[2]
charitable purposes (disability
　discrimination), 615n[2]
charity—
　(disability discrimination), 615n[6]
　(Equality Act 2006), 703n[6]
chief officer of police—
　(age discrimination), 773n[4]
　(disability discrimination), 554n[5]
　(sex discrimination), 371n[4]
　(sexual orientation discrimination), 729n[4]
　(religious discrimination), 667n[4]
child—
　(sex discrimination), 384n[15]
　(race relations), 463n[20]
code of practice (disability discrimination),
　655n[2]
collective agreement—
　(age discrimination), 812n[1]
　(disability discrimination), 614n[1]
　(race relations), 479n[1]
　(religious discrimination),
　(sex discrimination), 393n[18]
　(sexual orientation discrimination), 750n[1]
Commission for Equality and Human
　Rights, 305

Commissioner—
  (race relations), 488n[2]
  (sex discrimination), 404n[2]
Commissioners (Commission for Equality and Human Rights), 305
common money bond, 93, 96
communications (disability discrimination), 556n[13]
competence standard (disability discrimination), 549n[2], 570n[9], 579n[9], 580n[3]
conciliation officer (disability discrimination), 613n[17]
conciliation services (Equality Act 2006), 333n[3]
conditional bond, 91
conditional covenant, 91, 257
conditional sale agreement, 955n[5]
confidentiality request (disability discrimination), 563n[13], 571n[28]
construction site, 480n[3], 681n[4]
consumer hire agreement, 955n[4]
contract work—
  (age discrimination), 759n[2]
  (disability discrimination), 540n[1]
  (sexual orientation discrimination), 726n[2]
  (religious discrimination), 664n[2]
contract worker—
  (age discrimination), 759n[5]
  (disability discrimination), 540n[1]
  (race relations), 448n[4]
  (religious discrimination), 664n[5]
  (sexual orientation discrimination), 726n[5]
contracted-out rights (age discrimination), 766n[18]
controller of let premises (disability discrimination), 604n[2], 607n[7]
Convention rights, 303n[3]
conveyance, convey, 14n[1]
court officer (distress for rent), 995n[14]
covenant, 247
criminal investigation—
  (disability discrimination), 644n[22]
  (race relations), 500n[26]
  (sex discrimination), 394n[6]
criminal proceedings—
  (disability discrimination), 593n[17]
  (race relations), 470n[14]
Crown employment (age discrimination), 785n[2]
death benefit (age discrimination), 766n[31]
debenture (Companies Act 1985), 93n[10]
decision-making committee (Commission for Equality and Human Rights), 308, 312
deed—
  (common law), 1

deed—continued
  (Law of Property (Miscellaneous Provisions) Act 1989), 8
deed inter partes, 3
deed not inter partes, 3
deed poll, 3
deferred member (disability discrimination), 556n[4]
defined benefits arrangement (age discrimination), 765n[13]
dependant (age discrimination), 766n[40]
detriment—
  (age discrimination), 758n[8]
  (disability discrimination), 534n[14]
  (race relations), 446n[17]
  (religious discrimination), 663n[8]
  (sex discrimination), 353
  (sexual orientation discrimination) 725n[8]
direct discrimination—
  (Directive 76/207), 338n[3]
  (disability discrimination), 531
  (race relations), 439
  (sex discrimination), 344
disabled person—
  (disability discrimination), 511
  (Equality Act 2006), 305n[9]
disabled pupil, 561n[6], 564 n[4]
disabled student, 569 n[6]
Disability Committee (Commission for Equality and Human Rights), 312
disability matters (Equality Act 2006), 312n[14]
discrimination—
  (age discrimination), 758n[4]
  (disability discrimination), 647n[2]
  (Equality Act 2006), 692
  (religious discrimination), 663n[4]
  (sex discrimination), 344n[4]
  (sexual orientation discrimination), 725n[4]
discrimination on racial grounds, 439n[3], 471n[3]
discriminatory practice—
  (race relations), 471n[3]
  (sex discrimination), 386n[3]
dismissal—
  (age discrimination), 794n[14]
  (race relations), 446n[16]
dispose—
  (race relations), 463n[5]
  (sex discrimination), 384n[4]
disposition (deeds), 34n[6]
distress warrant, 992
diversity (Equality Act 2006), 316n[5]
double or conditional bond, 91
duty to make reasonable adjustments (disability discrimination), 530n[7]
early retirement pivot age, 764n[4]

References are to paragraph numbers; superior figures refer to notes

References are to paragraph numbers; superior figures refer to notes

References are to paragraph numbers; superior figures refer to notes